ASSESSMENT OF CHILDHOOD DISORDERS

Third Edition

ASSESSMENT OF CHILDHOOD DISORDERS

Third Edition

Edited by
ERIC J. MASH
University of Calgary

LEIF G. TERDAL
Oregon Health Sciences University

THE GUILFORD PRESS
New York London

© 1997 The Guilford Press
A Division of Guilford Publications, Inc.
72 Spring Street, New York, NY 10012
www.guilford.com

Printed in the United States of America

This book is printed on acid-free paper.

Last digit is print number: 9 8 7 6 5 4

Library of Congress Cataloging-in-Publication Data

Assessment of childhood disorders / edited by Eric J. Mash
  and Leif G. Terdal. — 3rd ed.
      p. cm.
    Updated and expanded version of: Behavioral assessment of
childhood disorders. 2nd ed. c1988.
    Includes bibliographical references and indexes.
    ISBN 1-57230-194-5 (hc.)   ISBN 1-57230-587-8 (pbk.)
    1. Mental illness—Diagnosis. 2. Behavioral assessment of
children. 3. Psychodiagnostics. 1. Mash, Eric J.
II. Terdal, Leif G., 1937–   . III. Behavioral assessment of
childhood disorders.
    [DNLM: 1. Child Behavior Disorders—diagnosis.
2. Developmental Disabilities—diagnosis. 3. Mental
Disorders—in infancy & childhood.   WS 350.6 A845 1997]
RJ503.5.B43 1997
618.92′89075—DC21
DNLM/DLC
for Library of Congress   97-5159
                                                      CIP

To Heather and Marjorie

CONTRIBUTORS

Russell A. Barkley, PhD, Department of Psychiatry, University of Massachusetts Medical Center, Worcester, Massachusetts

Billy A. Barrios, PhD, Department of Psychology, University of Mississippi, Oxford, Mississippi

Karen L. Bierman, PhD, Department of Psychology, Pennsylvania State University, University Park, Pennsylvania

Jo-Ann Birt, PhD, Department of Psychology, Children's Hospital of Western Ontario, London, Ontario, Canada

Sandra A. Brown, PhD, Department of Psychiatry, University of California at San Diego, La Jolla, California; Psychology Service, Department of Veterans Affairs Medical Center, San Diego, California

Bruce E. Compas, PhD, Department of Psychology, University of Vermont, Burlington, Vermont

Annette K. Estes, MS, Department of Psychology, University of Washington, Seattle, Washington

Jack M. Fletcher, PhD, Department of Pediatrics, University of Texas–Houston Medical School, Houston, Texas

John P. Foreyt, PhD, Nutrition Research Clinic, Baylor College of Medicine, Houston, Texas

Sharon L. Foster, PhD, California School of Professional Psychology, San Diego, California

Benjamin L. Handen, PhD, Child Development Unit, Children's Hospital of Pittsburgh, Pittsburgh, Pennsylvania

Donald P. Hartman, PhD, Department of Psychology, University of Utah, Salt Lake City, Utah

Christine A. Hovanitz, PhD, Department of Psychology, University of Cincinnati, Cincinnati, Ohio

Suzanne Bennett Johnson, PhD, Center for Pediatric Psychology and Family Studies, J Hillis Miller Health Center, Gainesville, Florida

Eric J. Mash, PhD, Department of Psychology, University of Calgary, Calgary, Alberta, Canada

Andrea McEachran, BA, Department of Psychology, University of Western Ontario, London, Ontario, Canada

Robert J. McMahon, PhD, Department of Psychology, University of Washington, Seattle, Washington

Carmen Mikhail, PhD, Department of Pediatrics, Baylor College of Medicine, Houston, Texas

Mark G. Myers, PhD, Department of Psychiatry, University of California at San Diego, La Jolla, California; Psychology Service, Department of Veterans Affairs Medical Center, San Diego, California

Crighton Newsom, PhD, Southwest Ohio Developmental Center, Batavia, Ohio

Arthur L. Robin, PhD, Department of Pediatrics, Wayne State University School of Medicine, Detroit, Michigan

James R. Rodrigue, PhD, Center for Pediatrics Psychology and Family Studies, University of Florida Health Science Center, Gainesville, Florida

H. Gerry Taylor, PhD, Department of Pediatrics, Rainbow Babies and Children's Hospital, Cleveland, Ohio

Leif G. Terdal, PhD, Child Development and Rehabilitation Center, Oregan Health Sciences University, Portland, Oregon

Peter W. Vik, PhD, Department of Psychology, Idaho State University, Pocatello, Idaho

Janet A. Welsh, PhD, Department of Psychology, Pennsylvania State University, University Park, Pennsylvania

David A. Wolfe, PhD, Department of Psychology, University of Western Ontario, London, Ontario, Canada

Vicky Veitch Wolfe, PhD, Division of Child and Adolescent Psychology, London Health Sciences Centre, London, Ontario, Canada

PREFACE

This is a book about assessment and diagnosis, clinical decision making, child and family development, developmental psychopathology, clinical child psychology, measurement and psychometrics, social values, ethics, and cognitive-behavioral therapy. Although this overview may sound more like an institute than a book, we make this statement only to sensitize the reader to our view that all assessments of children experiencing problems are embedded in a complex network of overlapping disciplines and bodies of knowledge. The complexities of developing children and their social systems are a fact that renders any narrow approach to child and family assessment inadequate. Over the past decade, new empirical findings and conceptualizations in the areas of developmental psychopathology and child and family development have served to further deepen the complexity and richness surrounding the assessment of childhood disorders. In this volume, we have attempted to capture the dramatic changes that have taken place in the field, and to cover the most recent advances in the principles and procedures for assessing disturbed children and their families.

Updating and expanding upon the first two editions of *Behavioral Assessment of Childhood Disorders* (Mash & Terdal, 1981, 1988), this volume considers the assessment of disturbed children and families from a behavioral systems perspective. In its simplest formulation, behavioral systems assessment (BSA) emphasizes that assessment should proceed as an empirically grounded enterprise that is sensitive to the ongoing and reciprocal interactions among behaviors, cognitions, and affects as they unfold within the child's social network. A major focus of the book is on the family and the broader social environment as a con-

text for understanding the child's strengths and weaknesses and as a focus for assessment and intervention.

As described in this volume, BSA represents a set of general problem-solving strategies for understanding disturbed children and families. It is believed that the effectiveness of these strategies can be enhanced through knowledge pertaining to specific childhood disorders, such that the methods used in assessment are directed at understanding the parameters that research and clinical practice have identified as important for particular classes of problems. The emphasis in BSA is on individualized assessment, the importance of situational influences, the utilization of multimethod assessment strategies, and the need to formulate assessment information in a way that is meaningful for clinical decision making about individual children and their families.

Each chapter author, who is a recognized expert in the assessment and treatment of children and families, provides an empirically grounded conceptual framework to guide assessment practice and research for the specific disorder under discussion. Each chapter presents exciting new developments and new data in our conceptualization of childhood disorders and current social issues that affect assessment. The emphasis throughout is on assessment practices that can be used to inform clinical interventions. Also reflected in the chapters are contemporary themes such as the need for developmental and cultural sensitivity in assessment, combining categorical diagnosis with dimensional classification, assessment as a decision-making process, accountability in assessment, and prevention-oriented assessments.

We have attempted to survey the widest possible range of childhood disorders including behavioral disorders, emotional and social disorders, developmental disorders, health-related disorders, children at risk, and adolescent problems. Contemporary concerns related to the assessment of child physical abuse and neglect, child sexual abuse, and substance use in adolescents receive extensive coverage in separate chapters. We hope that the wealth of information concerning the definition, prevalence, course, and etiology of childhood disorders, combined with practical illustrations, and numerous examples of assessment methods for children and families, will make this volume a valuable reference for all professionals who work with children and their families and for students who are planning to do so. The volume should also be useful in applied settings and training programs for clinicians who wish to introduce new assessment procedures into their work. The work also serves as a compendium of empirically supported outcome measures for clinicians who wish to evaluate treatment outcomes for specific childhood disorders.

We are indebted to our chapter authors for the consistently high quality of their scholarship and for their generosity in taking time from their busy schedules to contribute to this volume. We would like to also express our gratitude to many individuals who assisted with the preparation of this volume. At the Guilford Press, we are most ap-

preciative of the expert production editing by Jodi Creditor, the marketing talents of Marian Robinson and her staff, and the unwavering support of this and other projects over the past 16 years by Seymour Weingarten, Editor-in-Chief, and Robert Matloff, President. The secretarial magic, enthusiasm, and organizational skills of Alison Wiigs at the University of Calgary also contributed greatly to the completion of this project. During the preparation of this book, Eric Mash was supported by a sabbatical fellowship and a grant from the Vice-President (Research) at the University of Calgary. This support is gratefully acknowledged.

ERIC J. MASH, PHD
University of Calgary

LEIF G. TERDAL, PHD
Oregon Health Sciences University

REFERENCES

Mash, E. J., & Terdal, L. G. (Eds.). (1981). *Behavioral assessment of childhood disorders.* New York: Guilford Press.

Mash, E. J., & Terdal, L. G. (Eds.). (1988). *Behavioral assessment of childhood disorders* (2nd ed.). New York: Guilford Press.

CONTENTS

Part I. INTRODUCTION

1. Assessment of Child and Family Disturbance:
   A Behavioral–Systems Approach   3
   Eric J. Mash and Leif G. Terdal

Part II. BEHAVIOR DISORDERS

2. Attention-Deficit/Hyperactivity Disorder   71
   Russell A. Barkley

3. Conduct Problems   130
   Robert J. McMahon and Annette M. Estes

Part III. EMOTIONAL AND SOCIAL DISORDERS

4. Depression in Children and Adolescents   197
   Bruce E. Compas

5. Fears and Anxieties   230
   Billy A. Barrios and Donald P. Hartmann

6. Social Relationship Deficits   328
   Karen L. Bierman and Janet A. Welsh

Part IV. DEVELOPMENTAL AND HEALTH-RELATED DISORDERS

7. Mental Retardation   369
   Benjamin L. Handen

8. Autistic Disorder   408
   Crighton Newsom and Christine A. Hovanitz

9. **Children with Brain Injury**   453
   Jack M. Fletcher and H. Gerry Taylor

10. **Health-Related Disorders**   481
    Suzanne Bennett Johnson and James R. Rodrigue

Part V. CHILDREN AT RISK

11. **Child Physical Abuse and Neglect**   523
    David A. Wolfe and Andrea McEachran

12. **Child Sexual Abuse**   569
    Vicky Veitch Wolfe and Jo-Ann Birt

Part VI. PROBLEMS OF ADOLESCENCE

13. **Family Conflict and Communication in Adolescence**   627
    Sharon L. Foster and Arthur L. Robin

14. **Anorexia Nervosa and Bulimia Nervosa**   683
    John P. Foreyt and Carmen Mikhail

15. **Adolescent Substance Use Problems**   717
    Peter W. Vik, Sandra A. Brown, and Mark G. Myers

Author Index   749

Subject Index   781

ASSESSMENT OF CHILDHOOD DISORDERS

Third Edition

Part I

INTRODUCTION

Chapter One

ASSESSMENT OF CHILD AND FAMILY DISTURBANCE: A BEHAVIORAL–SYSTEMS APPROACH

Eric J. Mash
Leif G. Terdal

Almost from the time of their conception, children in North American society are assessed, evaluated, and labeled with respect to their physical condition, behavior, cognitive status, educational achievement, social competence, mood, and personality. These assessments are guided by the implicit assumptions about child development and behavior held by significant others and by society. Parents, teachers, physicians, siblings, peers, and community members all participate in this ongoing process, as do the children themselves. For most children, these evaluations occur during everyday social transactions and, to a lesser degree, during periodic formal evaluations best characterized as "routine" (e.g., regular medical checkups). As a result of these assessments, some children are identified as deviating from a normal course of development with regard to their behavior, physical condition, or violation of social norms and expectations (Kagan, 1983; Mash & Dozois, 1996). When a negative valence is assigned to these deviations, a child is likely to be informally labeled as belonging to a group of children who display similar characteristics (e.g., "difficult," "shy," "overactive"). Such children and their families then come to the attention of society's professional assessors, who utilize special strategies to build upon the informal assessments that led to the referrals (Kamphaus, 1993; Kamphaus & Frick, 1996; Mash & Terdal, 1988a; Messick, 1983; Ollendick & Hersen, 1993b; Reynolds & Kamphaus, 1990a, 1990b; Sattler, 1992, 1997).

Although there is much agreement concerning the need for systematic assessments of children—particularly children exhibiting problems, or at risk for later problems—there has been and continues to be considerable disagreement regarding how childhood disorders should be defined; what child characteristics, adaptations, and contexts should be assessed; by whom and in what situations children should be assessed; what methods should be employed; and how the outcomes of assessments should be integrated, interpreted, and utilized. Despite such disagreement, there exists a general consensus on the need for the development of assessment strategies not as an endpoint, but rather as a prerequisite for designing and evaluating effective and efficient services for children (Mash & Terdal, 1988b). Such a functional/utilitarian approach to the assessment of children and families is a major theme underlying this volume—one that transcends many of the conceptual and methodological differences and preferences that emerge in the current discussion.

This volume describes current approaches to the behavioral–systems assessment (BSA) of child and family disorders. BSA evolved from the concepts and methods of child behavioral assessment (Bornstein, Bornstein, & Dawson, 1984; Cone, 1987; Cone & Hoier, 1986; Evans & Nelson, 1977; Nay, 1979; Nelson & Hayes, 1979; Ollendick & Hersen, 1984), and continues to embrace many of its fundamental ideas, principles, and methods (Cone, 1993; Hayes & Follette, 1993; Mash & Hunsley, 1990; Mash & Terdal, 1988b; Ollendick & Hersen, 1993a). Among these are the importance of context in assessment; the view of assessment as an ongoing process; the use of multimethod strategies, including direct observations of behavior; the use of multiple informants; an emphasis on assessment information that will lead to the design of effective interventions; the use of empirically justifiable assessment methods; and the ongoing evaluation of treatment outcomes as an integral part of the assessment process. The purpose of this introductory chapter is to present the current concepts and practices of BSA with disturbed children and families, and to discuss some of the broader issues and implications surrounding their development and use.

RECENT DEVELOPMENTS

In the introductory chapter to the first edition of *Behavioral Assessment of Childhood Disorders*, we stated (Mash & Terdal, 1981b): "Recognizing the likelihood of ongoing and future changes in assessment strategies related to new empirical findings, emergent ideas, practical concerns, and shifts in the broader sociocultural milieu in which assessments are carried out, this chapter—indeed, this book—should be viewed as a working framework for understanding current behavioral approaches to the assessment of children" (p. 4).

As reflected throughout the present volume, behavioral approaches to the assessment of child and family disorders have changed dramatically over the last two decades. Some of the more notable developments are as follows:

1. An increased emphasis on incorporating developmental considerations into the design, conduct, and interpretation of assessments (Peterson, Burbach, & Chaney, 1989; Yule, 1993); into the implementation of treatments (Kendall, Lerner, & Craighead, 1984; McMahon & Peters, 1985); and into the study of child and family psychopathology more generally (e.g., Cicchetti & Cohen, 1995a, 1995b; Hersen & Ammerman, 1995; Lewis & Miller, 1990; Mash & Barkley, 1996).

2. A heightened interest in issues related to diagnosis and classification, with concomitant efforts to integrate extant diagnostic practices with BSA strategies (Barlow, 1986; Harris & Powers, 1984; Kazdin, 1983; Last & Hersen, 1989; Mash & Terdal, 1988a).

3. An elaborated view of BSA as an ongoing decision-making process (Adelman & Taylor, 1988; Evans & Meyer, 1985; Kanfer & Schefft, 1988; La Greca & Lemanek, 1996). This view has generated interest in the judgmental heuristics that influence this complex information-processing

task (Evans, 1985; Kanfer, 1985: Kanfer & Busemeyer, 1982; Tabachnik & Alloy, 1988), and has spawned efforts to develop both clinically and empirically derived decision-making models for specific clinical problems and populations (Herbert, 1981; Loeber, Dishion, & Patterson, 1984; Nezu & Nezu, 1993; Sanders & Lawton, 1993).

4. A growing attention to prevention-oriented and socially relevant assessments for high-risk populations. Such attention has emanated from current social issues and concerns, such as divorce (Emery, 1982; Hetherington, Law, & O'Connor, 1993), single-parent families and stepfamilies (Santrock & Sitterle, 1987; Santrock, Sitterle, & Warshak, 1988; Stevenson, Colbert, & Roach, 1986), working mothers (Cotterell, 1986), unemployment (Kates, 1986), children in day care (Molnar, 1985), poverty (Duncan, Brooks-Gunn, & Klebanov, 1994), accidental injuries (Peterson & Brown, 1994), child abductions (Flanagan, 1986), sexual abuse (Finkelhor & Associates, 1986; Wolfe & Birt, Chapter 12, this volume), family violence (Azar, 1986; Goldstein, Keller, & Erne, 1985; Kelly, 1983; Neidig & Friedman, 1984), teen delinquency and violence (Hinshaw & Anderson, 1996), substance use problems (Vik, Brown, & Myers, Chapter 15, this volume), and adolescent suicide (Petersen & Compas, 1993).

5. An increasing emphasis on understanding the interrelated influences of child and family cognitions (Crick & Dodge, 1994), affects (Dix, 1991; Gottman & Levenson, 1986), and behavior, as assessed within the context of ongoing social interactions (e.g., Bradbury & Fincham, 1987; Gottman, Katz, & Hooven, 1996; Gottman & Levenson, 1985; Hops et al., 1987).

6. The extension and assimilation of BSA concepts and practices into health care settings (Karoly, 1985; Strosahl, 1996) within the general frameworks of behavioral–developmental pediatrics (Gross & Drabman, 1990), pediatric behavioral medicine (Hobbs, Beck, & Wansley, 1984), and pediatric psychology (La Greca, 1994; Roberts, 1995).

7. A growing recognition of the need for empirically driven theoretical models as the basis for organizing and implementing assessment strategies with children and families (Mash & Barkley, 1996; McFall, 1986; Patterson, 1986; Patterson & Bank, 1986).

8. The introduction of technological advances, including the use of computers, the Internet, and the World Wide Web (WWW) during both the data-gathering and decision-making phases of assessment (Ager, 1991; Ancill, Carr,

& Rogers, 1985; Carr & Ghosh, 1983; Farrell, 1991; Romanczyk, 1986). Suggested computer and WWW applications have included collecting interview, self-monitoring, and observational data; psychophysiological recording; training; organizing, synthesizing, and analyzing behavioral assessment data; utilization review; monitoring treatment appropriateness; and supporting decision making (Dow, Kearns, & Thornton, 1996; Farrell, 1991). Technological advances have led to a heightened interest in the utility and feasibility of using actuarial models in clinical decision making (Achenbach, 1985; Dow et al., 1996; Mash, 1985; Rachman, 1983; Wiggins, 1981).

9. Conceptual and methodological convergence on an ecologically oriented systems model (Belsky, Lerner, & Spanier, 1984; Bronfenbrenner, 1986; Hartup, 1986) as the appropriate framework for organizing and understanding assessment information derived from children and families (Evans, 1985; Wasik, 1984). This has led to a heightened interest in the assessment of whole-family variables (Forman & Hagan, 1984; Holman, 1983; Mash & Johnston, 1996a; Rodick, Henggeler, & Hanson, 1986) and the relationships between family systems and the broader sociocultural milieu (Barling, 1986; Dunst & Trivette, 1985, 1986; Parke, MacDonald, Beital, & Bhavnagri, 1988).

10. Increased recognition of the growing cultural diversity in North America and the need to consider culture, ethnicity, and religious beliefs in the assessment and treatment of children and families (Forehand & Kotchick, 1996; Foster & Martinez, 1995; Rowan, 1996; Tharp, 1991).

11. Further attention to accountability in assessment and to the development of cost-effective assessment strategies (Hayes, 1996; Hayes, Follette, Dawes, & Grady, 1995). Such attention has been fueled by the growing concern for reducing costs within changing health care systems (Mash & Hunsley, 1993a; Strosahl, 1994).

12. Increased emphasis on the evaluation functions of behavioral assessment in light of a growing concern for empirically validated treatments (Hibbs & Jensen, 1996). This concern has focused attention on the need to develop meaningful and practical outcome measures for use in clinical practice (Clement, 1996; Mash & Hunsley, 1993b; Nelson-Gray, 1996; Ogles, Lambert, & Masters, 1996), and to develop methods for the analysis of change (Gottman, 1995; Gottman & Rush, 1993).

It is apparent from this brief and selective overview of recent developments that current be-havioral–systems approaches to child and family assessment are complex and varied. These approaches are best conceptualized within a broad assessment framework that examines a child's functioning in the context of the social systems and decisional processes in which the child and family are typically embedded. The current view of BSA extends well beyond earlier views of child behavior assessment as being synonymous with the direct observation of target behaviors.

SOME GENERAL COMMENTS ABOUT BEHAVIORAL ASSESSMENT

Several writers have described the meteoric rise of behavioral assessment during the 1960s and 1970s, as reflected in numerous books, book chapters, conference papers, symposia, and journal articles on the topic (e.g., Mash & Terdal, 1981b; Nelson, 1983). This rapid increase continued unabated into the 1980s, with the appearance of new books devoted exclusively to behavioral assessment (Ciminero, Calhoun, & Adams, 1986; Nelson & Hayes, 1986; Mash & Terdal, 1981a, 1988a; Ollendick & Hersen, 1984). The 1990s have witnessed a decline in behavioral assessment as a distinct field, but a growing assimilation of its principles and methods into mainstream assessment practices with disturbed children and families, which now routinely include contextually and empirically grounded assessment information. As we consider current approaches to BSA, several observations concerning the development of behavioral assessment are germane to the current discussion:

1. Although the growth of the field was rapid, it was not without "growing pains" (Hartmann, 1983). Expressions of dissatisfaction were directed both at the techniques of behavioral assessment and at its conceptual adequacy. For example, Nelson (1983) noted the lack of convergence across both differing and similar measures of the same behavior; the impracticality of many recommended behavioral assessment techniques, especially direct observation; and the inability of the field to generate a set of well-standardized and psychometrically sound procedures. Dissatisfaction with the conceptual foundations of behavioral assessment centered on such issues as how information concerning a specific child could be related to knowledge concerning similar children obtained in other situations at other times, difficulties surrounding the assessment of covert and/or infre-

quently occurring events, and the potential limitations of molecular analysis for the detection of larger patterns of behavior (Achenbach, 1985).

2. A disproportionate emphasis on the behavioral assessment of adults relative to children was righted to a degree with the appearance of several books whose primary focus was on child behavior analysis and assessment (e.g., Gelfand & Hartmann, 1984; Mash & Terdal, 1981a, 1988a; Ollendick & Hersen, 1984). In addition, general texts on assessment, child behavior therapy, and clinical child psychology now provide greater coverage of behavioral assessment concepts and methods (e.g., Hersen & Van Hasselt, 1987; Kratochwill & Morris, 1993; Ollendick & Cerny, 1981; Ollendick & Hersen, 1993b; Sattler, 1992; Walker & Roberts, 1992). Increased attention to the behavioral assessment of children and families relative to adults has also been stimulated by recent conceptual and methodological advances in developmental psychology and developmental psychopathology, and by the growing acceptance of systems-oriented, family-focused approaches to treatment. Conceptualizations that view children and adults as partners in an interacting network of systems and subsystems create a context in which child and adult assessments are viewed as equally important for understanding system functioning.

3. The structure and content of child behavioral assessment strategies and methods, although maintaining an idiographic focus, have shown increasingly greater sensitivity to the unique characteristics and needs of the childhood disorder being assessed. In this regard, observational coding systems for families of children with Attention-Deficit/Hyperactivity Disorder (ADHD) (Barkley, Chapter 2, this volume) or conduct problems (McMahon & Estes, Chapter 3, this volume) are quite different from those used with families in which a child has a developmental delay (Dunst, 1984), or a family member is clinically depressed (Hops et al., 1986). The elaboration of a problem-specific approach to child and family assessment is predicated on the availability of conceptual models for specific disorders that indicate what variables are important to assess, and the empirical specification of the controlling variables, parameters, and regulatory processes most relevant to the description and modification of particular childhood disorders (Cicchetti, 1996; Kazdin & Kagan, 1994; Mash & Barkley, 1996).

4. Along with the need for disorder-specific assessments, research also supports the presence of a number of nonspecific assessment parameters that cut across different types of child and family problems. For example, McKinney and Peterson (1987) found that within a population of developmentally delayed children, the children's diagnosis did not contribute significantly to the parents' reported stress, relative to such factors as spouse support, perceived control, and other child characteristics. Also, the disturbances exhibited by children in families experiencing marital discord, divorce, or parental psychopathology (e.g., substance use problems, depression) are often quite similar. Lee and Gotlib (1991) suggest that common to these types of family disruptions are parental distress, an increased self-focus, and the consequent unavailability of parents to meet the emotional needs of their children. Similarly, Cummings and Davies (1995) have proposed that different sources of stress (e.g., maternal depression or marital conflict) may lead to children's emotional insecurity and difficulties in self-regulation, to efforts to overregulate others, and to poor relationships in general. To the extent that different child problems are associated with common sources of stress (e.g., reduction in parents' time for themselves, marital strain), the use of standardized measures of common effects across different problem populations complements the idiographic and disorder-specific information needed in assessments of children and families.

5. It was commonplace for writers on behavioral assessment to cite surveys that called attention to (a) the discrepancy between idealized recommendations as to how behavioral assessments should be carried out, and how such assessments are actually conducted in clinical practice; and (b) the fact that many behaviorally oriented clinicians continued to use personality tests, intellectual tests, neuropsychological assessments, and projective techniques (Ford & Kendall, 1979; Piotrowski & Keller, 1984; Swan & MacDonald, 1978; Wade, Baker, & Hartmann, 1979). However, many of these "we don't do that in real life" surveys did not focus specifically on assessment practices with children and families. There is evidence to indicate that child behavioral assessment is viewed as an integral component in the training of clinical child psychologists (Elbert, 1985a, 1985b) and in the assessment of many specific child problems, such as ADHD (Rosenberg & Beck, 1986) and conduct problems (McMahon & Estes, Chapter 3, this volume). Components of BSA—for example, functional analysis—have been successfully integrated into outpatient clinical services for children and families (Harding & Wacker, 1994; Wacker & Berg, 1994), inpatient units, and spe-

cial education classrooms (e.g., Derby & Wacker, 1994).

Implicit in criticisms concerning the failure to translate behavioral assessment principles into clinical practice has been the tendency to equate behavioral assessment with direct observation, and then to note the impracticality of carrying out such observations in the clinical context. Although such a narrow perspective on behavioral assessment may exist in the abstract, it does not reflect current clinical practices or research. Recent surveys indicate that cognitive-behavioral practitioners continue to use a wide variety of assessment procedures, *and* that the use of direct observation and behavior rating scales has increased over the past 15 years (Elliott, Miltenberger, Kaster-Bundgaard, & Lumley, 1996; Watkins, Campbell, & McGregor, 1990). BSA has evolved into a problem-solving strategy that utilizes a wide range of methods. The exclusion of direct observation from an assessment is not synonymous with the exclusion of a behavioral–systems approach. Even so, about 80% of cognitive-behavioral practitioners report using direct observation with about half their clients (Elliott et al., 1996). The richness of observational assessments and their potentially large clinical yield compel us to continue to seek effective ways to incorporate observational assessments into clinical practice (Mash, 1984; Mash & Barkley, 1986; Mash & Hunsley, 1993a).

6. Advances in child behavioral assessment have been seriously hampered by a failure to develop well-standardized and widely used measures of child and family characteristics. Agreement on how certain child and family behaviors are best described and measured for particular purposes is a prerequisite for the advancement of knowledge in the field, and yet the proliferation of idiosyncratic child and family assessment instruments has continued. It would seem that an agreed-upon set of procedures for measuring activity in an overactive child, or patterns of interaction in an abusive family situation, would not be that difficult to achieve; however, this goal has eluded behavioral assessors. Some have argued against standardization, espousing the view that the use of preferred, well-standardized, reliable, and well-validated assessment devices may conflict with the idiographic, problem-oriented focus in behavioral assessment (e.g., Nelson, 1983). However, we believe that psychometrically sound and well-standardized assessment procedures can be effectively used in a flexible problem-solving framework that is sensitive to the individual needs of specific families and situations.

DEFINING BEHAVIORAL–SYSTEMS ASSESSMENT

The continuing development of strategies for BSA of disturbed children and families is linked, although not exclusively, to concomitant and parallel changes in the theoretical models and clinical practices of child and family behavior therapy (Hersen & Van Hasselt, 1987; Ross, 1981; Mash & Barkley, in press), behavior modification (Martin & Pear, 1996), applied behavior analysis (Sulzer-Azaroff & Mayer, 1991), behavioral pediatrics (Gross & Drabman, 1990), cognitive-behavioral therapy (Kendall, 1991; Meichenbaum, 1977), and cognitive-behavioral family therapy (Schwebel & Fine, 1994). The link between BSA and child and family intervention is integral to understanding this approach, since one of its cardinal features is to generate information that will inform the design and evaluation of treatment and prevention programs (Haynes, 1988; Haynes & Uchigakiuchi, 1993a). Part of the difficulty in precisely defining BSA relates to the fact that concepts and practices in the aforementioned approaches to intervention have been continually evolving; the constructs and procedures that may be admissible by some as targets for assessment are not accepted by others.

In addition to the heterogeneity within these intervention approaches that are presumed to have certain shared assumptions, recent efforts have also attempted to integrate cognitive-behavioral therapies with other approaches, which are themselves diverse (Kendall, 1982). Therapy integration, which in the child and family areas is typified by recent efforts to integrate behavioral, cognitive-behavioral, and family systems approaches, further obscures the boundaries between what constitutes behavioral and cognitive-behavioral intervention and what does not (e.g., Alexander & Parsons, 1982; Harris, 1984; Foster & Robin, Chapter 13, this volume; Fauber & Kendall, 1992; Robin & Foster, 1989; Schwebel & Fine, 1992, 1994). Therapy integration has also prompted integration at the level of assessment from the standpoint of what is to be assessed (e.g., behavior, cognition, affect) and the methods used (e.g., interview, self-report, direct observation).

Although current BSA practices are by no means restricted to situations in which cognitive-behavioral treatments are used, it is believed that BSA can best be understood in relation to the development of these interventions. Early behavioral approaches to the treatment of child and family disorders involved the specification of target behaviors and their alteration through the arrangement or rearrangement of both antecedent and consequent stimulus events in a manner loosely conforming to learning principles encompassed under the operant, classical, and observational learning paradigms (Ullmann & Krasner, 1965). The central features of these applications included a focus on easily defined and observable events, current behaviors, situational determinants, and the child as the primary target for assessment and treatment (Bijou & Peterson, 1971). Early behavioral assessments consisted primarily of obtaining frequency, rate, and duration measures describing the behaviors of interest, and the pinpointing, recording, and consequating of target behaviors, which provided a direct and often highly effective method for producing behavioral change.

The significance of systematic assessments of target behaviors during the early development of child and family behavior therapy cannot be overstated. The early work stimulated a broadly empirical approach to problems in clinical child psychology—one that has been carried forward in a current emphasis on empirically validated treatments (Hibbs & Jensen, 1996). It established continuity between assessment and intervention by emphasizing the need to evaluate treatment outcomes via objective behavioral measures; reinforced the need for individualized assessments; sensitized assessors to the importance of evaluating behavior in context; and led to the development of assessment methods with high face validity (Kanfer, 1979; Nelson, 1983; O'Leary, 1979).

As behavior therapy with children and families evolved, a much greater emphasis was placed on evaluating ongoing *patterns* of child behavior, and on viewing the child as part of a larger network of interacting social systems and subsystems (Patterson, 1976, 1982; Wahler, 1976). This emphasis was consistent with parallel developments in the fields of developmental psychology (Belsky, 1981; Bronfenbrenner, 1986) and developmental psychopathology (Sroufe & Rutter, 1984). Although assessments continued to be viewed as individualized in relation to the system under consideration (e.g., the child–parent subsystem), they did not necessarily occur at the level of the individual. A much wider range of variables, encompassing the marital relationship, sibling relationships, peer relationships, family stress, parental psychopathology, social isolation and support, and community resources, as well as the relationships among these variables and the parent–child interaction, were often targeted for assessment and treatment (e.g., Brody, Pellegrini, & Sigel, 1986; Miller & Prinz, 1990; Pannaccione & Wahler, 1986). Within the various subsystems designated, increasing recognition was given to the important role of cognition and affect in mediating child and family change, to reciprocal influences, and to the role of more distal events in the neighborhood and community (Wahler & Graves, 1983). These developments changed the nature of a behavioral approach from target behavior measurement to a more general set of problem-solving strategies encompassing a wider range of system variables and a greater variety of methods than were characteristic of earlier work (Evans, 1985; Evans & Nelson, 1977, 1986; Kanfer & Busemeyer, 1982; Kanfer & Nay, 1982; Mash & Terdal, 1988b).

In this chapter, we use the term "BSA" to describe a range of deliberate problem-solving strategies for understanding both disturbed and nondisturbed children and their social systems, including families and peer groups. These strategies employ a flexible and ongoing process of hypothesis testing regarding the nature of the problem, its causes, likely outcomes in the absence of intervention, and the anticipated effects of various treatments. Such hypothesis testing proceeds from a particular assumptive base and is carried out in relation to existing data, for certain purposes, using specific methods. The nature of this assumptive base, the relevant data sets, the relevant methods, and the particular purposes for which assessments are carried out are elaborated upon in this and subsequent chapters of this volume. We also believe that the use of BSA with children and families should not preclude the complementary use of alternative conceptual frameworks and methods, when such methods can be shown to assist in our understanding of the problem and our efforts to bring about change. It is our view that the generation of better hypotheses to test at the idiographic level can best proceed from an understanding of the general theories and principles of psychological assessment (e.g., Anastasi & Urbina, 1997; Cronbach, 1990; Nunnally, 1994); from information concerning normal and abnormal child and family development (e.g., Cicchetti & Cohen, 1995a, 1995b; Mussen, 1983); and from knowledge about groups of children and families showing similar types of problems, including information about incidence, prevalence, developmental characteristics, biological influences, and system parameters (Achenbach, 1982; Mash & Barkley, 1996). This general viewpoint is reflected throughout the chapters in this volume.

A COMMENT ON BEHAVIORAL VERSUS TRADITIONAL ASSESSMENT

A number of writers have noted that much of the early impetus for the development of behavioral assessment strategies during the 1960s was derived from a dissatisfaction with the conceptual foundations and techniques of the assessment models prevailing at that time (Mash & Terdal, 1981b, 1988a; Nelson, 1983). The "offending" paradigms, which included the medical, psychodynamic, and psychometric traditions, were lumped together under the general rubric of "traditional" assessment approaches. Early definitions of behavioral assessment were based on contrasts with a potpourri of assumptions and techniques characteristic of these traditional approaches (e.g., Bornstein et al., 1984; Cone & Hawkins, 1977; Goldfried & Kent, 1972; Hartmann, Roper, & Bradford, 1979; Mash & Terdal, 1981b, 1988b; Mischel, 1968). These contrasts often reflected statements regarding what behavioral assessment was not, rather than what it was. As behavioral assessment has become less and less insular and provincial, the contrasts between behavioral and traditional approaches to assessment have become less distinct (Hartmann, 1983; Haynes, 1983).

We believe that the depiction of behavioral assessment in contrast with traditional approaches was useful and perhaps necessary during the formative stages of the field. However, an overemphasis on this distinction at present may have a number of potentially negative effects. First, the categories "behavioral" and "traditional" have each been shown to encompass a heterogeneous range of conceptual and methodological approaches to assessment, and global comparisons between the two categories inevitably obscure a host of important and subtle distinctions that exist within each approach (Mash & Terdal, 1988b). Second, the behavioral–traditional contrast tends to perpetuate a view of the field as predominantly reactionary, when there are many strengths of the behavioral assessment approach that stand on their own merits. Third, definitions based on contrasts with traditional views tend to foster the blanket acceptance or rejection of certain ideas (e.g., stable traits) or procedures (e.g., personality tests, psychiatric diagnosis), when such categorical decisions are often unnecessary or undesirable within the problem-solving model being advocated here. Finally, it would appear that the practices of clinicians and researchers concerned with child and family assessment do not readily conform to these global designations. In practice, the use of concepts and procedures characterized as traditional or behavioral is often based on a variety of pragmatic considerations reflecting administrative requirements (e.g., billing practices, journal criteria for defining specific disorders), normative assessment practices in a particular clinical or research setting, resources for assessment, and individual preferences and priorities. We believe that a radical definition of behavioral assessment—one that requires the presence of certain essential ingredients, such as a focus on observable behavior, a natural-scientific perspective, idiographic analysis, and criterion-referenced performance (see Cone & Hoier, 1986, for a lucid description of this position)—could result in the abandonment of a "behavioral identity" by many individuals who feel that their practices do not strictly adhere to such a narrow and constraining definition, and who see no need to exclude concepts and techniques that they have found to be both clinically and empirically useful.

BEHAVIORAL–SYSTEMS ASSESSMENT OF CHILD AND FAMILY DISORDERS: A PROTOTYPE-BASED VIEW

Rather than attempting to define BSA in terms of its necessary or defining features, we believe that a prototype-based view (e.g., Cantor, Smith, French, & Mezzich, 1980) best depicts the current state of the field. Within such a framework, the general category of BSA is based on sets of imperfectly correlated features, referred to as "prototypes" (Rosch, 1978). Assessment cases having the largest number of general-category features would be considered the most typical examples of BSA. The prototypical view also recognizes that within the more general category of BSA there can exist a hierarchically but imperfectly nested set of subcategories, such as "BSA of young children" or "BSA of adolescents." BSA may take many different forms, depending on the specific parameters associated with different child and family problems. For example, the prototype for BSA with a 4-year-old child with Oppositional Defiant Disorder is likely to be very different from that for BSA with a depressed and suicidal adolescent. This view is consistent with the relativistic, contextually based, and idiographic nature of BSA strategies, and with the organization of the present volume around categories of commonly occurring childhood disorders.

Since judgments concerning whether or not a particular assessment protocol fits the category of BSA appear to be of little consequence in and of themselves, we have not attempted to rigorously derive either a conceptually or an empirically based prototype for BSA. Rather, in the points that follow, we use the prototype-based view to represent some of the more commonly occurring conceptual, strategic, and procedural characteristics of BSA (Mash & Terdal, 1988b):

1. BSA is based on conceptualizations of personality and abnormal behavior that give greater relative emphasis to a child's thoughts, feelings, and behaviors, as these occur in specific situations, than to global underlying traits or dispositions.

2. BSA is predominantly idiographic and individualized (Wolpe, 1986). Greater relative emphasis is given to understanding the individual child and family than to making nomothetic comparisons that describe individuals primarily in relation to group norms.

3. BSA emphasizes the role of situational influences on behavior. It is recognized that the patterning and organization of an individual's behavior across situations are highly idiographic (Mischel, 1968, 1973), and it is therefore important to describe both behaviors *and* situations. The theoretical debates surrounding the issue of situational specificity have been extensive and are not discussed here (e.g., Bem & Funder, 1978; Endler & Magnusson, 1976). However, the pragmatic outcomes of the emphasis on situational specificity in BSA have been a greater sensitivity to the measurement of situational dimensions, and a corresponding increase in the range of environments sampled. For example, home, school, playground, and neighborhood observations have been added to samples of a child's and parent's behavior previously obtained under highly controlled and non-interactive testing conditions in the clinic.

4. BSA emphasizes both the instability and stability of child and family behaviors over time. This is in contrast to approaches that emphasize the consistency of behavior over time as a reflection of stable and enduring underlying causes. Conceptually, BSA would predict either consistency or variability in behavior over time as a function of the degree of stability or variation in context. However, because externally and internally induced situational changes appear to be the norm rather than the exception throughout childhood and adolescence, the predominant BSA view has emphasized change.

This view of change, however, fails to capture the complexity of the question in a number of ways. First, consistency can be assessed in relation to many levels of behavior, and, depending on the specificity of the behavior under consideration, different results may be obtained. If a child's behavior is described in terms of a highly idiographic response topography (e.g., whining), then we may find little consistency over time. In contrast, definitions based on broader response classes that encompass a wide range and pattern of behaviors (e.g., aggression), both within and across age levels, may have more enduring qualities. Furthermore, if we look at response functions rather than specific topographies, we may find that phenotypically different responses reflect a dynamic stability in which certain patterns of adjustment are repeated over time. As stated by Garber (1984), "although there is little evidence of homotypic continuity—symptomatic isomorphism from early childhood—there is some evidence that children may show consistency in their general adaptive or maladaptive pattern of organizing their experiences and interacting with their environment" (p. 34). This organizational–developmental viewpoint has been supported by findings from longitudinal studies of development, which have suggested that patterns expressed in early relationships may repeat themselves over time (Kaye, 1985; Sroufe & Fleeson, 1986). The type of child or family characteristic being assessed also has implications for the question of temporal stability. For example, some characteristics may show stability over time (e.g., achievement motivation, dependence and passivity in females, serious aggressive behavior, and intellectual mastery), whereas others may not (Garber, 1984).

5. BSA is systems-oriented. It is directed at describing and understanding (a) characteristics of the child and family; (b) the contexts in which such characteristics are expressed; and (c) the structural organizations and functional relationships that exist among situations, behaviors, thoughts, and emotions.

6. BSA emphasizes contemporaneous controlling variables relative to historical ones. However, when information about temporally remote events (e.g., age at onset) can facilitate an understanding of current influences, such information will be sought and used in assessment. For example, knowing that a mother was physically abused as a child may help an assessor to understand her current attitudes and behavior toward her own child (Cicchetti & Rizley, 1981). Simi-

larly, knowledge of early attachment patterns may assist in understanding a child's current pattern of social disturbance (Crick & Dodge, 1994).

7. BSA is more often concerned with behaviors, cognitions, and affects as direct samples of the domains of interest than as signs of some underlying or remote causes. For example, assessments focusing on a child's cognitive deficiencies or cognitive distortions (i.e., misattributions) consider these events as functional components of the problem to be modified, rather than as symptoms of some other problem. Nevertheless, an increasing emphasis in BSA on response–system covariations suggests that the assessment of some behaviors may be of interest primarily because of their relationship to some other, more central aspect of the problem (Kazdin, 1982b; Voeltz & Evans, 1982).

8. BSA focuses on obtaining assessment information that is directly relevant to treatment. "Relevance for treatment" usually refers to the usefulness of information in identifying treatment goals, selecting targets for intervention, designing and implementing interventions, and evaluating the outcomes of therapy (Carr, 1994; Mace, 1994).

9. BSA relies on a multimethod assessment strategy, which emphasizes the importance of using different informants and a variety of procedures, including interviews, questionnaires, and observations. The inherent superiority of one method over another is not assumed; the methods chosen should be based on the purposes and needs associated with specific assessments (McFall, 1986). Direct observations of behavior in naturalistic contexts are more commonly used in BSA than in other assessment approaches (Foster & Cone, 1986; Reid, Patterson, Baldwin, & Dishion, 1988).

10. BSA is an ongoing and self-evaluating process. Instead of assessments' being conducted on one or two occasions prior to treatment, the need for further assessment is dictated by the efficacy of the methods in facilitating desired treatment outcomes.

11. BSA is empirically anchored. The assessment strategy—in particular, the decision regarding which variables to assess—should be guided by (a) knowledge concerning the characteristics of the child and family being assessed, and (b) the research literature on specific disorders (Mash & Barkley, 1996). Where assessments are theoretically driven, theories should be closely tied to the data.

COMMON ASSESSMENT PURPOSES

Inherent in the view of BSA as an ongoing problem-solving strategy is the recognition that assessments of children and families are always carried out in relation to one or more purposes. Along with the assessor's working assumptions and conceptualizations about child and family behavior, these purposes will determine which individuals, behaviors, and settings are evaluated; the choice of assessment methods; the way in which findings are interpreted; the specification of assessment and treatment goals; and the manner in which these goals are evaluated. Questions surrounding the assessment of child and family disturbances can be considered only within the context of the intended assessment purpose(s). Therefore, decisions regarding the appropriateness or usefulness of particular assessment methods and procedures are always made in relation to the needs of the situation. Discussions concerning the relative merits of information obtained via self-report versus direct observation methods have little meaning outside of the assessment context and purposes. A multicategory observational coding system may be appropriate for assessments designed to identify potential controlling variables to be altered with treatment, but inappropriate for evaluating the outcome of a highly focused intervention to reduce a child's bedwetting.

Many writers have outlined the more common purposes for which child and family assessments are conducted (e.g., Bornstein et al., 1984; Hawkins, 1979; Kanfer & Nay, 1982; Mash & Terdal, 1980, 1988b). Broadly conceived, these include (1) diagnosis, or assessment activities focusing on determining the nature or cause of the problem; (2) prognosis, or the generation of predictions concerning future behavior under specified conditions; (3) treatment design, or the gathering of information that will assist in the development and implementation of effective interventions; and (4) evaluation, or assessments intended to assess treatment efficacy, effectiveness, efficiency, acceptability, and satisfaction. Although these purposes characterize BSA with children and families, they are not specific to any one theoretical, methodological, or therapy approach. Because these purposes have been discussed previously and are addressed in relation to each of the specific disorders in the chapters following, we comment on them only briefly here.

Diagnosis

The four purposes of assessment mentioned above often occur in phases for individual cases. Early diagnostic assessments are concerned with questions relating to general screening and administrative decision making (e.g., can the child be appropriately served by a particular agency or educational program?), to determining whether or not there is a problem (e.g., does the child's behavior deviate from an appropriate behavioral or social norm?), and to defining the nature and extent of the problem (e.g., what is it that the child is doing or not doing that results in a distressed family or school situation?).

The term "diagnosis" has acquired two meanings (Achenbach, 1985). The first, "taxonomic diagnosis," views diagnosis and classification as equivalent, and focuses on the formal assignment of cases to specific categories drawn either from a system of disease classification such as the *Diagnostic and Statistical Manual of Mental Disorders* (DSM-IV; American Psychiatric Association, 1994), or from empirically derived taxometric categories, prototypes, or typologies (Achenbach, 1993). The second and much broader meaning given to the term "diagnosis," "problem-solving analysis," considers diagnosis to be an analytic information-gathering process directed at understanding the nature of a problem, its possible causes, treatment options, and outcomes. This broader view of diagnosis is more consistent with the concepts and practices of BSA, although BSA recognizes the utility of taxonomic diagnosis as a useful (albeit insufficient) organizational framework for guiding assessments with children and families (Harris & Powers, 1984; Kazdin, 1983; Mash & Terdal, 1988b; Powers, 1984).

The diagnostic phase within BSA is conducted with the expectation that assessment will lead directly to recommendations for treatment. Questions often asked during the diagnostic phase of BSA include these: (1) What is the child doing, thinking, or feeling that causes distress or that brings them into conflict with the environment? and (2) What are the potential controlling variables for these problems? Behavioral diagnoses are often highly individualized and based on direct empirical support. The methods employed during the early diagnostic phase of BSA tend to be global and extensive—they have been described as having broad bandwidth but low fidelity—and the use of unstructured interviews, global self-report instruments, and observational narratives is common.

Prognosis

Every child and family assessment carries with it some projection regarding short- and long-term outcomes for the child under varying conditions. Knowledge of risk and protective factors, and of the likely outcomes for certain behaviors during later periods of development, is required for making judgments concerning deviance. Since many childhood problems are not intrinsically pathological and are exhibited to some extent by most children, decisions regarding whether or not to treat often depend on prognostic implications. Implicit in any decision to initiate intervention is a projection that things will remain the same, improve, or deteriorate in the absence of treatment, or that outcomes will vary as a function of differing treatments. With children, treatments are often directed at enhancing developmental processes rather than at removing symptoms or restoring a previous level of functioning. Information concerning developmental processes may also provide the basis for anticipatory interventions in high-risk situations where the prognosis is known to be poor. There are also numerous decisions related to children's mental health and the legal system for which information concerning prognosis is required—for example, assessments of a parent's ability to provide an adequate caregiving environment for a child (Reppucci, Weithorn, Mulvey, & Monahan, 1984).

Questions concerning prognosis are often considered in relation to longitudinal information, as derived, for example, from studies of risk or resilience in high-risk children. For example, findings reported by Masten (1986) indicate that children with more resources (e.g., intellectual ability, stable and supportive families) are generally more competent and show more adaptive patterns of dealing with stress. Although data such as these can provide a basis for making general predictions, their direct applicability to decision making for individual children and their families is not always clear. Studies of individual children at risk who do well may provide suggestions as to the types of interventions that could be appropriate in high-risk situations. For example, Masten (1986) describes a child who coped extremely well with stress by creating a more positive environment for himself through drawing on adults outside the home, maintaining a positive outlook and disposition, and consciously using humor in his interactions.

Longitudinal studies of long-term outcomes for children with different types of disorders also provide information about prognosis. For example, the most persistent and pernicious types of Conduct Disorder are associated with a family history of antisocial behavior, early neuropsychological deficits, comorbid ADHD, early onset and variety of antisocial and aggressive symptoms, and poor family functioning (Hinshaw & Anderson, 1996).

Questions concerning prognosis are frequently raised early in the assessment process. However, such questions are also important following treatment in assessing the likelihood that treatment gains will be maintained, especially when long-term maintenance for certain problems (e.g., aggression) is known to be poor. The systematic assessment of treatment maintenance in the child and family areas has received limited attention to date.

Design

The design phase of BSA focuses on obtaining information that is directly relevant to devising effective treatment strategies. This gathering of information includes further specification and measurement of potential controlling variables (e.g., patterns of social rewards and punishments, cognitive distortions or misattributions) (Horner, 1994); determination of the child's and family's resources for change (e.g., behavioral assets, self-regulatory skills); assessment of potential social and physical resources that can be used in carrying out treatment; assessment of the motivation for treatment of both the child and significant others; indication of potential reinforcers; specification of specific and realistic treatment objectives; and recommendations for types of treatments that are likely to be most acceptable and effective for the child and family.

Hypothesis testing during this phase is the norm, and determining the effectiveness of prior assessments and the need for further information gathering is an iterative process based on whether specified goals are achieved. The assessment procedures that characterize this phase are more problem-focused than during the diagnostic phase, and specific types of problem checklists (e.g., fear survey schedules, measures of impulsivity, depression inventories), observational assessments (e.g., command–compliance analogues), and specific behav-ior codes (e.g., on-task behavior, self-stimulation, aggression) are more likely to be used than during earlier stages of assessment.

Evaluation

The evaluation phase of BSA is a continuing one. It commonly involves the use of procedures designed to determine whether treatment objectives are being met, whether changes that have occurred are attributable to specific interventions, whether the changes are long-lasting and generalizable across behaviors and situations, whether the treatment is economically viable, and whether treatments and treatment outcomes are acceptable to the participants. Assessments for determining whether treatment goals are being met require the measurement of targeted objectives over time. Such measurement will indicate the presence or absence of change, which in many cases may be sufficient. However, to determine whether changes are a function of the treatments introduced for individual children and families, it is necessary to collect observations in a controlled fashion—for example, by using single-case experimental designs (Barlow & Hersen, 1984). Although such designs have been an integral component of behavior therapy and assessment, a key question at present concerns the adequacy of single-case designs for representing the often complex system parameters and relationships that characterize treatment goals in current cognitive-behavioral therapy approaches with children and families (Mash & Barkley, in press).

Evaluations relative to the acceptability of treatments and treatment changes have been discussed under the headings of social validity (Kazdin, 1977; Wolf, 1978), treatment acceptability (Kazdin, 1981, 1984), and consumer satisfaction (Kiesler, 1983; LeBow, 1982; McMahon & Forehand, 1983). Such issues are especially pertinent to interventions for children, which must be gauged against ongoing or projected developmental changes. BSA has also become increasingly sensitive to measurement issues surrounding long-term follow-up (Mash & Terdal, 1980). The methods used during the evaluation phase of assessment tend to be highly focused and specific in comparison to earlier assessment phases. The need for reliable, valid, and cost-efficient measures of treatment outcome is becoming increasingly important in the current health care context in which services for children and families are being delivered.

The purposes described thus far relate to clinical decision making for individual children, since this is characteristically the focus of BSA. There is also a need to recognize that broader societal and institutional purposes often underlie assessment practices with children. These include classification for administrative record keeping, program development and evaluation, policy planning, and the advancement of scientific knowledge (Hawkins, 1979; Hobbs, 1975). The types of assessments required to meet these purposes may differ substantially from those required for the assessment of individual children and families.

CHILDREN'S FUNCTIONING AND ITS DETERMINANTS

Childhood Disorders versus Target Behaviors

Although early behavioral approaches to child and family disorders were explicit in their rejection of classification systems characteristic of medical and psychodynamic models of psychopathology, it has been noted that many books written from this perspective organized their subject matter according to chapters roughly corresponding to traditional diagnostic categories (e.g., Barlow, 1981; Hersen & Van Hasselt, 1987; Mash & Barkley, 1989; Mash & Terdal, 1988a; Morris & Kratochwill, 1983). Such an organization is also characteristic of this volume, and reflects the view that children and families present themselves for assessment showing characteristic patterns, clusters, or constellations of problems, rather than isolated target symptoms. There is both clinical and empirical evidence to suggest that broad patterns of child disturbance labeled "externalizing" (e.g., aggression, delinquency, impulsivity) and "internalizing" (e.g., fears, anxiety, depression, somatic complaints) are relatively stable over time and across raters (Achenbach & Edelbrock, 1978). We believe that assessment can best proceed from an empirically based understanding of characteristic patterns of behavior (Kazdin & Kagan, 1994). As noted by Barlow (1986), "the identification of behaviors and cognitions that seem to cluster together is not an insidious influence but rather something that all behavior therapists engage in formally or informally as a first step preceding a thorough behavioral analysis" (p. 100).

We concur with Kanfer's (1979) view that "different problem areas require development of separate methods and conceptualizations that take into account the particular parameters of that area," and that "it may turn out that in some domains progress in behavioral assessment will be blocked until conceptual models or data are available to permit a functional analysis on which target selection for assessment and rules for generalization of observations can be based" (p. 39). Empirically derived conceptual models of child and family disorders to guide assessments in both clinical and research contexts are emerging at a rapid rate (see Mash & Barkley, 1996). One of the best-articulated, theory-driven, empirically based models for assessment is represented by Gerald Patterson's (1982) work with children and families exhibiting antisocial problems. Through the use of multiple methodologies, and complex statistical methods such as structural equation modeling (Connell & Tanaka, 1987; Joreskog & Sorbom, 1983), a number of important constructs and their relationships have been implicated in the development of children's antisocial behavior (Patterson, 1986; Patterson & Bank, 1986). Although this work evolved in a research context, it suggests several molar and molecular variables that are important to assess when working with antisocial children and their families (e.g., whether the children are rejected or perceived as antisocial by others; the likelihood of the children's unprovoked negative behavior toward parents and siblings, and its duration; the extent to which parents monitor their children and spend time with them; and the parents' inept discipline, as reflected in their use of explosive forms of punishment, negative actions and reactions, and inconsistent/erratic behavior). Each chapter in this volume provides one or more conceptual models and an empirical base for the specific disorder under discussion, and the assessment strategies that are presented follow from this framework.

The specification of particular childhood disorders as a basis for discussing assessment strategies is suggestive of the syndrome and trait views that behavioral assessors previously avoided. However, as described by Achenbach and Edelbrock (1978, p. 1294), there are different ways of viewing the role of syndromes in the classification of children:

1. The syndrome may be viewed as representing a personality or character type that endures beyond the immediate precipitating events requiring professional attention.

2. The syndrome may be viewed as reflecting dimensions or traits, so that children are best described individually in terms of their scores on all syndromes, rather than by categorization according to their resemblance to a particular syndrome.

3. The syndrome may be viewed as a reaction type, whose form is as much a function of specific precipitating stresses as of individual characteristics.

4. The syndrome may be viewed as a collection of behaviors that happen to be statistically associated because the environmental contingencies supporting them are statistically associated.

The latter two views of syndromes as reflecting either reaction types or classes of correlated behaviors are consistent with many of the assumptions underlying BSA. Nevertheless, the different views of syndromes are not necessarily independent of one another. It may be that reaction types that become well established early in development eventually emerge as enduring, but not necessarily irreversible, character types. For example, research has suggested that preferential orientations toward others, self, and the object world when confronted with interactive stress may be exhibited by infants as young as 6 months of age (Tronick & Gianino, 1986).

The concept of syndromes in BSA with children and families is represented in work that has examined the notions of "response class" and "response covariation" (e.g., Kazdin, 1982b, 1983; Voeltz & Evans, 1982; Wahler, 1975). These notions imply that (1) certain behaviors tend to co-occur, or to be correlated with one another; and/or (2) that certain behaviors tend to covary, such that changes in one are associated with changes in the other. In both cases, the behaviors that co-occur or covary may be topographically similar or dissimilar. Research into response covariation has suggested indirect paths of clinical intervention—for example, when decreases in a child's noncompliant behavior lead to a reduction in bedwetting (Nordquist, 1971) or stuttering (Wahler, Sperling, Thomas, Teeter, & Luper, 1970). The existence of such response clusters has important implications for assessment, in that mapping out these relationships and covariations is likely to suggest courses of intervention that are maximally effective (i.e., ones in which the least intrusive and most cost-efficient procedures may be used to bring about the most widespread changes).

Although an extensive discussion of the many issues surrounding the concepts of response class and response covariation is beyond the scope of the current chapter, several important questions will need to be addressed before these concepts can have widespread applicability in child and family BSA:

1. There is currently little information as to how one goes about identifying response classes. Potential response classes have been derived via serendipitous discovery, from clinically described syndromes, from conceptual models or theories about child and family disorders, from statistical methods for grouping data, and through systematic functional analysis. In light of the potentially infinite number of topographically dissimilar responses that could be related, guidelines are needed for limiting the number and range of responses to be assessed.

2. Response-class representations are miniature systems (e.g., Minuchin, 1985), and guidelines are needed for mapping out the structural organizations and functional relationships that describe a particular response class, as well as for describing its relationships to other systems. Recent discussions of the comorbidity of childhood disorders are relevant to understanding relationships among different response classes (e.g., Achenbach, 1995; Caron & Rutter, 1991).

3. Although the focus in child and family BSA has been on response classes, we are more often talking about constellations of responses, cognitions, emotions, and physiological reactions. The more varied and complex response classes become, the more they seem to approximate classical descriptions of clinical disorders.

4. Are response classes to be defined idiographically, or can we expect them to have some generality across individuals?

5. The relationship between response classes and situations has received little attention (Wahler & Graves, 1983). Can we expect that response classes will be situation-specific, as some research has suggested (Patterson & Bechtel, 1977), or will some response clusters show generality across situations?

6. Most discussions of response classes have focused on the individual. However, it would be equally feasible to identify response clusters for more complex social units—for example, sibling dyads, the marital relationship, or the family.

Although these issues are in need of further investigation, research on response covariation has sensitized assessors to the fact that consideration of only a narrow range of target behaviors fails to adequately represent the more general network of behaviors of which the target behaviors may be a part, or the fact that these behaviors may be functionally embedded in a larger social system.

The BSA view of child and family disorders presented in this volume focuses on common patterns of behavior and behavior–context disturbances. Rather than emphasizing assessment techniques, such as the interview, self-report, and direct observation, this volume considers these techniques only in relation to the specific problems and contexts in which they are to be used. As noted by Ross (1978), "the emphasis in behavior therapy should be on the conceptualization of problems and not on specific techniques" (p. 592). This statement is equally applicable to BSA. Although there are general principles associated with the development and use of particular assessment techniques, the nature and specifics of an interview with the parent of a depressed child should be different from one with the parent of a child with Autistic Disorder. It is believed that an understanding of the specific parameters associated with Autistic Disorder (Newsom & Hovanitz, Chapter 8, this volume) or childhood depression (Compas, Chapter 4, this volume), in coordination with the general principles of interviewing (e.g., Sattler, 1997) or behavioral interviewing (e.g., Turkat, 1986), will serve to generate more specialized and ultimately more useful assessments in each of these problem areas.

Classification and Diagnosis

One of the most controversial areas in the assessment and treatment of disturbed children and families has been the use of diagnostic labels based upon global classification systems. In commenting on the high proportion (estimates of 40%) of clinic-referred children whose problems were (and sometimes still are) labeled in global and nondescript terms such as "adjustment reaction" (Cerreto & Tuma, 1977), Dreger et al. (1964) stated: "Looked at realistically, what this means is that after the elaborate procedures used in most clinics are completed, the child is placed in a category, which says exactly what we knew about him in the first place, that he has a problem" (p. 1). In some studies, as many as 30% of parents surveyed who had been in contact with professionals indicated that their children had been described with three or more labels (Gorham, DesJardins, Page, Pettis, & Scheiber, 1975). Over time the same labels may be used to describe different sets of clinical phenomena (Zachary, Levin, Hargreaves, & Greene, 1981), and different labels may be used to describe the same clinical disorder (e.g., hyperactivity, hyperkinesis, Attention Deficit Disorder, ADHD). Systems for the classification of childhood disorders have received extensive discussion, and these discussions have increased since the

appearance of DSM-III, which included an increased number of child categories (American Psychiatric Association, 1980), and its most recent revision, DSM-IV (American Psychiatric Association, 1994).

There is some agreement regarding the general neglect of meaningful taxonomic frameworks for describing children and families, and the need for classification systems for guiding theory, research, and practice. For example, Achenbach and Edelbrock (1978) have stated that "the study of psychopathology in children has long lacked a coherent taxonomic framework within which training, treatment, epidemiology, and research could be integrated" (p. 1275). Despite their increased use, all classification systems to emerge thus far have been met with criticism. For example, as Nathan (1986) states, "For the most part, when more effective treatments have been developed or more light has been shed on etiology, it has not been by virtue of one or another classification scheme that this has come about" (p. 201).

Although BSA recognizes the need for a classification system of child and family disorders, including widely accepted systems such as the DSM (Harris & Powers, 1984; Powers, 1984; Taylor, 1983), there continues to be dissatisfaction with the currently available approaches, especially those based on the Kraepelinian tradition (Evans & Nelson, 1986; Mash & Terdal, 1988a). These dissatisfactions with existing classification systems center around empirical inadequacy; the implicit etiological assumptions that underlie the categories; the subjective-impressionistic criteria used to derive individual categories; the failure to provide empirically derived operational criteria for assignment to categories; the static nature of the categories when applied to a developing child; the use of diagnostic criteria that are unadjusted for the child's age or sex; the lack of demonstrated relevance for treatment; the potentially undesirable consequences of labeling; and a general insensitivity of diagnostic criteria to contextual influences, including the role of culture, and to relational problems (see Kaslow, 1996).

Despite these criticisms, an alternative to current classification schemes has yet to emerge, in spite of the long-standing recognition of the need (Adams, Doster, & Calhoun, 1977; Adelman, 1995; Arkowitz, 1979; Ferster, 1965; Follette & Hayes, 1992; Hayes & Follette, 1992; Haynes & O'Brien, 1988). The lack of development in this area probably reflects the priority in BSA for idiographic and treatment-oriented goals. It is not clear that the development of global classification systems for childhood disorders will do much to facilitate these goals, although they have the potential to improve communication, the combining of data from diverse sources, epidemiological study, comparison of treatments, and understanding of causes (Kessler, 1971).

Classification efforts for childhood disorders have followed three traditions: categorical diagnosis, dimensional classification, and developmental diagnosis.

Categorical Diagnosis

The first tradition has involved the development of clinically derived categories for classification based mostly upon subjective consensus, as exemplified by the systems developed by the Group for the Advancement of Psychiatry (1974), the World Health Organization (1992), the Zero to Three/National Center for Clinical Infant Programs (1994), and the American Psychiatric Association (1980, 1987, 1994). Although it is beyond the scope of this chapter to review these systems in detail (see Achenbach, 1985, for an excellent review of classification paradigms), commonly occurring categories are exemplified by those provided in DSM-IV. The DSM-IV disorders of infancy, childhood, and adolescence include the following: attention-deficit and disruptive behavior disorders, including ADHD, Oppositional Defiant Disorder, and Conduct Disorder; feeding and eating disorders, such as Pica, Rumination Disorder, and Feeding Disorder of Infancy or Early Childhood; tic disorders, such as Tourette's Disorder and Chronic Motor or Vocal Tic Disorder; elimination disorders, such as Enuresis and Encopresis; Separation Anxiety Disorder; Selective Mutism; Reactive Attachment Disorder of Infancy or Early Childhood; and Stereotypic Movement Disorder. Also included among the juvenile disorders in DSM-IV are Mental Retardation; learning disorders, such as Reading Disorder, Mathematics Disorder, and Disorder of Written Expression; Developmental Coordination Disorder; communication disorders, such as Expressive Language Disorder, Mixed Receptive–Expressive Language Disorder, Phonological Disorder, and Stuttering; and pervasive developmental disorders, such as Autistic Disorder, Rett's Disorder, Childhood Disintegrative Disorder, and Asperger's Disorder. In addition, many other diagnostic categories for anxiety, mood, and relational disturbances used for diagnosis with adults are also used with chil-

dren. DSM-IV criteria for assignment to specific categories are presented throughout the chapters of this volume. Generally, these criteria include the presence of a specified number of symptoms, a minimum time period during which the specified symptoms must be present, age criteria, and exclusionary criteria if the problem is secondary to other disorders.

In recognizing that a simple enumeration of symptoms may not be sufficient for treatment planning or predicting individual outcomes, DSM-IV also provides a multiaxial classification scheme. This includes the following: clinical disorders and other conditions that may be a focus of clinic attention (Axis I); personality disorders and Mental Retardation (Axis II); general medical conditions (Axis III); psychosocial and environmental problems (Axis IV); and a global assessment of functioning (Axis V). However, only the first three axes constitute an official diagnostic evaluation; the amount of differentiation for Axes I and II is disproportionately large when compared with that for Axes IV and V; and Axes IV and V are of limited or undetermined reliability or validity (Goldman & Skodal, 1992; Van Goor-Lambo, 1987).

Efforts to increase the accuracy and reliability of psychiatric diagnoses have resulted in the development of a number of structured and semistructured interview protocols for obtaining information to assist in making a diagnosis. The use of these procedures for the identification of groups of children in assessment and treatment outcome studies has increased, and DSM-IV terminology is increasingly finding its way into BSA work with children and families. It has been suggested that the DSM-IV criteria could provide direction regarding the range of behaviors that might then be assessed in a more intensive idiographic fashion (Powers, 1984). It is likely that until assessors are willing and able to invest the time and resources to develop and to promote an empirically based classification alternative to DSM-IV, administrative requirements, the need to communicate with other professionals, and the need for a taxonomy to direct and organize research and clinical activities will all contribute to increased acceptance and use of the DSM-IV in BSA with children and families.

Dimensional Classification

A second major approach to the classification of childhood disorders is an empirical one, involving the utilization of multivariate statistical methods, such as factor analysis and cluster analysis

(Achenbach, 1991a, 1993; McDermott & Weiss, 1995; Naglieri, LeBuffe, & Pfeiffer, 1994; Reynolds & Kamphaus, 1992). This approach assumes that there are a number of independent dimensions of behavior, and that all children possess these sets of behavior to varying degrees. In contrast to classification approaches that use clinically derived categories of childhood disorder, the dimensional approach focuses on empirically derived categories of behavioral covariation. Although empirically derived classifications are more objective and potentially more reliable, they also possess associated problems. No classification system can be better than the items that constitute it, and, as noted by Achenbach (1985), "subjective judgment is involved in selecting the samples and attributes to be analyzed, the analytic methods, and the mathematical criteria" (p. 90). Other concerns include possible interactions between the methods of data collection (e.g., ratings, direct observations, questionnaires) or the informants (e.g., parents vs. teachers) and the dimensions that emerge, and the lack of sensitivity of global trait dimensions to situational influences (e.g., age of child, duration of disorder, setting in which behavior is rated, time when ratings are made).

As noted earlier, multivariate studies are consistent in identifying two broad dimensions of child behavior labeled "externalizing" and "internalizing." The best-known group of assessment instruments based on multivariate analysis—the Child Behavior Checklist/4–18 (CBCL/4–18; Achenbach, 1991b) and its companions, the Teacher's Report Form (Achenbach, 1991c) and the Youth Self-Report (Achenbach, 1991d)—accordingly includes Externalizing and Internalizing broadband domains. More specific syndromes that have been verified via confirmatory factor analysis, and that constitute "cross-informant" constructs on the CBCL family of instruments, include Aggressive Behavior and Delinquent Behavior (Externalizing syndromes), Anxious/Depressed, Somatic Complaints, and Withdrawn (Internalizing syndromes), and Attention Problems, Thought Problems, and Social Problems (Achenbach, 1993).

Much of the recent impetus for the development of multivariate classification approaches in child and family assessment comes from the extensive work of Thomas Achenbach and his colleagues with the CBCL group of instruments and their associated Profiles (Achenbach, 1991b, 1991c, 1991d, 1992). It is not possible to do justice to the scope and magnitude of this work in this brief discussion, and the interested reader is referred to eloquent expositions on the "merits of multivariates" by Achenbach (1985, 1993). Briefly, Achenbach describes a number of advantages associated with utilizing a taxometric integration of prototypical syndromes, in which an individual child may be classified on the basis of the similarity of his or her profile of syndrome scores with the centroid of each previously derived profile type. Beginning with the rationale that child syndromes consist of imperfectly correlated features, the argument is made that a prototype-based view of classification is preferable to one that employs the assignment of individuals to categories based on the presence of a small number of essential or cardinal features. Although it has been recognized that the conceptual derivation of prototypes for syndromes is possible (e.g., Horowitz, Post, French, Wallis, & Siegelman, 1981; Horowitz, Wright, Lowenstein, & Parad, 1981), operational definitions of prototypical syndromes can be generated via multivariate analyses. It is argued that the use of quantitative indices, standardized assessment data, and computerized data processing will permit the integration of large and complex data sets, reduce the likelihood that information-processing biases will influence clinical judgments, and enable the clinician to focus on other aspects of assessment and treatment that are not easily standardized.

In light of current views of BSA as a problem-solving strategy that employs a variety of methods to assess multiple child and family characteristics, the use of actuarial approaches in BSA seems most appropriate (Mash, 1985; Rachman, 1983). The multivariate emphasis on empirical decision making is quite consistent with many of the assumptions of BSA. In addition, multivariate approaches are becoming increasingly multidimensional and sensitive to contextual influences in defining dimensions of psychopathology (e.g., McDermott, 1993). Achenbach (1985), for example, has proposed a multiaxial approach to assessment that describes children of different ages on five axes: (I) Parent Perceptions, (II) Teacher's Perceptions, (III) Cognitive Assessment, (IV) Physical Conditions, and (V) Clinician's Assessment. These axes are intended to reflect different settings, different informants, and different assessment methods. Although this approach is promising, and clearly offers more than the current multiaxial elaborations of DSM-IV, the approach as presented is limited in its focus on context and development. For example, for the first 2 years of life, the primary emphasis is on information about developmental milestones and on clinical impressions; a rich data base describing interactive developmental processes, such as attachment quality, emotional regulation, purposeful communication, and cognitive development, receives little attention. The specific axes that are proposed also tend to confound settings, informants, methods, and the dimension being assessed. Nevertheless, this approach is consistent with the multitrait–multimethod emphasis in BSA; it reflects the emergence of multivariate assessment strategies that rely on a wider range of methods, informants, and settings than was previously the case.

As reflected throughout this volume, the use of multivariate assessment procedures in the BSA of children and families has increased considerably. This increased use is a reflection of the relationships that have been found between verbal report measures and direct observations of behavior (e.g., Mash & Johnston, 1983a; Patterson & Bank, 1986); the availability and relative ease of use of these procedures; and a growing interest in child and parent perceptions as mediators of behavior and behavior change (e.g., Mash & Johnston, 1983b, 1990). Many of the criticisms of the multivariate approach from a BSA perspective have been based on dissatisfaction with the often global and ambiguous content being assessed, the fact that information is heavily based on subjective reports, and the general lack of sensitivity to situational influences. However, these criticisms are not inherent to the approach per se, since it would be quite possible to derive "syndromes" that were based on other theories, had different contents, employed other methods (e.g., direct observation), and sampled a broader range of settings than is currently the case. Conceivably, syndromes of reaction types could also be derived that were specific to particular situations (e.g., profiles of reaction types to stressful family events, social confrontation, medical procedures, or academic tasks).

More serious criticisms of the multivariate strategy within a BSA framework are its nomothetic emphasis on comparisons between an individual child and some group norm, and the limited relevance of this approach for treatment (Peterson, 1968). Despite these criticisms, current BSA has integrated standardized multivariate assessments into clinical practice in formulating treatment goals—for example, in cases where a parent's perceptions indicate that a child is deviant, but observations of the child's behavior suggest otherwise (e.g., Mash, Johnston, & Kovitz, 1983)—and as one outcome measure for assessing the impact of treatment on parent and teacher perceptions of the child's behavior.

Developmental Diagnosis

A third approach to classification follows from a developmental perspective on child psychopathology. Although this perspective is often adopted (albeit unsystematically) in clinical practice, it has not had a significant impact on institutionalized diagnostic practices with children. For example, many of the DSM-IV categories for children are simple extensions of those used to categorize adults, and the focus of the multivariate approaches has been on the categorization of isolated behaviors and traits rather than on the patterns of adaptation characteristic of developmental change. The recently introduced classification system for children from birth to 3 years has a strong developmental emphasis, but has yet to be systematically evaluated in research or clinical practice (Zero to Three, 1994).

Garber (1984) has presented an insightful developmental perspective on classification, and has outlined many of the complexities and challenges that underlie this approach. Central to this view is the need to assess children's levels of functioning within different developmental domains (e.g., emotional, cognitive, social, physical) and their patterns of coping in relation to major developmental tasks (e.g., regulation of biological functions, attachment, dependence, autonomy, self-control, conformity to rules). Children are diagnosed in relation to their successes or failures in negotiating normative developmental expectations and demands, and it is believed that diagnostic models should emphasize adaptations and organizations of behavior at various developmental levels, rather than static traits, signs, or symptoms.

A developmental perspective is quite consistent with the emphasis in BSA on describing children's reactions in relation to situational demands, but it presents some formidable challenges in practice; not the least of these are mapping out and defining "normative" developmental sequences and creating a relevant taxonomy of developmental tasks. Current longitudinal studies in child development and developmental psychopathology are beginning to provide a rich data base from which developmental adaptations can be assessed and classified during the first few years of life (e.g., Greenspan & Lourie, 1981), and, more recently, during middle childhood and adolescence. This data base increases the promise of a developmentally anchored classification system, although this promise is still a long way from being realized. Nevertheless, a developmental perspective on classification, and developmental models more generally, are an integral part of BSA with children and families.

The classification systems that we have discussed thus far, especially DSM-IV and the multivariate approaches, have tended to focus on the individual child. They are derived from models that view childhood disorders as residing in the child, rather than in the ongoing and reciprocal interactions between the child and the larger social system in which he or she functions. Classification models for describing larger social systems, such as the parent–child dyad (Egeland & Sroufe, 1981; Oldershaw, 1986), sibling relationships (Ellis & DeKeseredy, 1994), the marital relationship (Weiss & Margolin, 1986), and the family (Mash & Johnston, 1996b; Mink, Meyers, & Nihara, 1984; Mink, Nihara, & Meyers, 1983; Moos & Moos, 1978), are only beginning to emerge. It is believed that these types of classification approaches have the potential for incorporating the BSA emphasis on contextual influences into our diagnostic practices. Similarly, there continues to be an enormous need in assessments with children and families for the development of taxonomies that describe situations (Mischel, 1977; Schlundt & McFall, 1987). Most assessment procedures continue to focus on individuals, and the degree of measurement sophistication that has been achieved in describing the situations in which children and families function is still quite primitive—often reflecting global topographical features of the setting, such as home versus school. Elaborated classification schemes reflecting the differentiation that occurs within settings are needed, and previous work on the ecological assessment of environments should provide some direction in this regard (e.g., Vincent & Trickett, 1983). For example, the Classroom Environment Scale (Moos & Trickett, 1974) looks at classroom environments in terms of Relationship (e.g., Involvement, Affiliation, Teacher Support), Personal (e.g., Task Orientation, Competition), System Maintenance (e.g., Order and Organizations, Rule Clarity, Teacher Control), and System Change (e.g., Innovation) dimensions.

Outcomes of Labeling Children

Much has been written about the positive and negative aspects of assigning diagnostic labels to children. On the positive side, it is argued that labels help to summarize and order observations; facilitate communication among professionals with different backgrounds; guide treatment strategies in a global fashion; put therapists in touch with a preexisting relevant body of more detailed research and clinical data; and facilitate etiological, epidemiological, and treatment outcome studies (Rains, Kitsuse, Duster, & Friedson, 1975). On the negative side are criticisms regarding how effective currently available diagnostic labels are in achieving any of the aforementioned purposes, and a concern about negative effects associated with the assignment of labels to children. Possible negative effects include how others perceive and react to the children (Bromfield, Weisz, & Messer, 1986), and how the labels influence children's perceptions of themselves and their behavior (Guskin, Bartel, & MacMillan, 1975).

The use of labels can bias professionals toward seeing psychopathology in children, although there is some evidence to suggest that behavior therapists may be less easily biased by labels (Langer & Abelson, 1974). Studies have shown that a particular behavior, if believed to be exhibited by a child who is "disturbed" or "handicapped," leads to different reactions than when the same behavior occurs in a child who is not believed to be disturbed or handicapped (Stevens-Long, 1973). Labeling children as "behaviorally disturbed" or as "normal" has also been shown to result in distortions in recall on the part of trained observers for negative behaviors in children labeled "disturbed" (Yates, Klein, & Haven, 1978), and positive behaviors in children labeled "normal" (Yates & Hoage, 1979). Other studies have shown that labels may produce negatively stereotypical expectations on the part of teachers (Foster, Ysseldyke, & Reese, 1975). These illustrative studies, and many others, provide indirect support for the potentially negative effects of diagnostic labeling by professionals. Furthermore, research on clinical information processing suggests that many sources of bias surround human judgment, including those involved in the assignment of labels (Achenbach, 1985; Mischel, 1979).

On the positive side, some investigators have suggested that the use of labels can serve as a convenient reference point for tolerance toward and acceptance of particular sets of child behaviors (Algozzine, Mercer, & Countermine, 1977), may provide parents with closure and understanding regarding their children's problems (Fernald & Gettys, 1978), and is consistent with the natural tendencies of humans to think in terms of categories. If parents believe that a label explains why their child is the way he or she is, then attention may be directed at coping with the problem that is believed to exist, rather than at searching for the *real* cause through repeated contacts with agencies and professionals. Whether such suggested benefits outweigh the negative effects of labeling has yet to be demonstrated.

The most important outcomes associated with the labeling of disturbed children may not be the ones associated with labeling or diagnosis by professionals. Rather, the informal labeling processes surrounding child and family behavior, and the interpretations of formal labels by parents, teachers, and children themselves, are likely to have the greatest impact (e.g., Coie & Pennington, 1976; Compas, Friedland-Bandes, Bastien, & Adelman, 1981; Dollinger, Thelan, & Walsh, 1980). Further study and assessment of the general beliefs and everyday cognitions of parents and teachers, the ways parents and teachers use labels to organize their experiences with both normal and disturbed children, and the ways such labeling influences their responses to and feelings about children are likely to increase our understanding of child and family disturbances (Sigel, McGillicuddy-DeLisi, & Goodnow, 1992). Several lines of research that appear promising in this regard include studies that have examined labeling and attribution processes in parents of disturbed (Bugental, 1993; Dix & Lochman, 1990; Larrance & Twentyman, 1983) and nondisturbed (Dix, 1993; Dix, Ruble, Grusec, & Nixon, 1986) children, and those that have looked at "parents as problem solvers" in common but demanding child-rearing situations (e.g., crying, refusal, noncompliance, trips to the supermarket) (Holden, 1985a, 1985b, 1985c). Labeling is a prepotent human response, and there is a need to find methods to assess the usual ways in which child behaviors are organized by those interacting with children. In identifying the types of labels that are used, the conditions under which they are used, and the effects associated with their use, it is likely that we will need to consider the unique characteristics of the interactants, as well as the universal processes characterizing humans as information processors (Kanfer, 1985).

Etiological Assumptions Regarding Childhood Disorders

A prevalent misconception associated with behavioral views of child and family disorders has been that deviant behaviors are the exclusive results of children's interactions with their physical and social environments. Implicit in this view is that both child and family deviance represent faulty learning, and therefore that in assessing the problem one should look for causes in the external environment, giving minimal attention to intraorganismic events or to internal cognitions and affects.

To be sure, early behavioral views of child and family disorders emphasized the significant role of environmental events as controlling variables, but even then they did not do so to the exclusion of other important variables. If anything, the behavioral and social learning viewpoints that emerged in the 1960s provided a more balanced approach to the study of child and family psychopathology, which had previously emphasized physical causes such as brain dysfunction, or internal events such as unconscious impulses and drives (e.g., Bandura, 1969; Kanfer & Phillips, 1970). It was unfortunate that the attempt to give greater emphasis to important and observable environmental influences was inaccurately perceived by many as the total rejection of all intraorganismic controlling variables. Current strategies for BSA with children and families examine a broad range of internal and external controlling conditions and their interactions.

Several important points can be made concerning the relationship between BSA and etiological assumptions about childhood disorders:

1. The first concerns multiple causality. Given that a child is embedded in a complex and changing system, it is likely that many potentially relevant controlling variables contribute to the problem, including physical and social environmental events, and intraorganismic variables of both a physiological and a cognitive nature.

2. No *a priori* assumptions are made regarding the primacy of controlling variables that contribute to child and family disorders. This view rejects particular sets of controlling variables as being more important than others (e.g., physical vs. social causes), either contemporaneously or historically; it is intended to counteract the popular belief in many child assessment and treatment settings that the identification of malfunctioning physical systems through medical examination, neuropsychological testing, or historical information somehow provides a more fundamental explanation for a child's problems. Such an analysis is both incomplete and inaccurate, because it gives excessive weight to physical

causes in explaining child behavior and ignores potential environmental influences of equal or greater importance.

3. Although no assumptions are made in BSA about the primacy of etiological influences, primacy may be given to certain variables when such variables are suggested by data, or for the sake of methodological or practical expediency. Variables that are observable, easily measured, and readily modified may become the focus for assessment when such an approach facilitates remediation of the problem.

4. It is assumed that there is an ongoing and reciprocal interaction among relevant controlling variables, so that attempts to identify *original* causes in assessment are not likely to be fruitful. Causes that occur earlier in development (e.g., birth injury or social deprivation) cannot be assumed to be more significant contributors to the child and family's difficulties than current physical conditions and social processes.

5. The processes by which relevant controlling variables for most deviant child and family behaviors exert their influence are assumed to be similar and often continuous with those for nondeviant behavior. Principles related to basic biological and social processes are equally applicable in understanding both deviant and nondeviant behavior.

6. Although controlling variables that are contemporaneous and situationally present are frequently emphasized as important influences in behavioral views of child and family disorders, there is also the need to consider both extra-situational and temporally more remote events. For example, external stressors such as marital discord may have a direct impact on a mother's immediate reaction to her child's behavior. Passman and Mulhern (1977) have shown that a mother's punitiveness toward her child increases with the amount of external stress to which she is exposed, and Wahler (1980) has reported an inverse relationship between contacts with people outside the family and child behavior problems. There is increasing evidence that children's behaviors *in situ* represent only one contributor to parental reactions (e.g., Mash & Johnston, 1983a), which may be influenced by external factors of the types just mentioned (Dunst & Trivette, 1986), as well as by the general rules, strategies, and propositions that parents apply in interacting with their children (Dix & Ruble, 1989; Geller & Johnston, 1995; Lytton, 1979). Therefore, it is not surprising when treatment-induced changes in children's behavior do not necessarily lead to changes in parents' perceptions of or reactions to their children.

DIMENSIONS OF CHILD AND FAMILY BEHAVIORAL–SYSTEMS ASSESSMENT

One of the most salient characteristics of developing children is the active dialogue that takes place between each child and his or her biological makeup, physical and social environments, and cultural milieu (D'Antonio & Aldous, 1983; Lamb, 1982). Guided by genetic endowment and neuromuscular maturation, relentlessly working at understanding the surrounding physical realities and social expectations, the child is nurtured, shaped, and socialized. No passive partner in this dialogue, the child in return shapes the social world, and sets his or her own expectations and demands (Bell & Harper, 1977; Emery, Binkoff, Houts, & Carr, 1983). This developmental engagement is characterized by conflict and equilibrium in the cognitive, emotional, and social domains, and almost always by quantitative and qualitative movement and change. It begins at the time of conception and continues thereafter. Any consideration of the assessment of children and families must begin with a recognition of the ebb and flow of this developmental dialogue, because it has critical implications for the manner in which child behaviors are conceptualized, measured, classified, diagnosed, changed, and evaluated. The recognition that child and family behaviors are embedded within normative developmental sequences guided by organizational principles, and that they occur within a nested hierarchical context of interacting micro- and macrosocial influences (Bronfenbrenner, 1979, 1986), necessitates a view of BSA that reflects both the uniqueness and the multidimensionality of children. This view leads to a number of important generalizations about child assessment:

1. Developing children represent a unique population for which there are special assessment considerations of a conceptual, methodological, and practical nature.

2. The assessment of childhood disorders necessarily involves normative judgments as to what constitutes (a) developmental deviation, (b) performance variation in relation to an appropriate reference group, (c) developmentally appropriate adaptation to a range of situational demands, and (d) unexpected deviation from a projected course of individual development. Of necessity, judgments will usually include comparisons of a child with both group and individual norms.

3. Assessment of children and their families invariably involves multiple targets, including

somatic and physiological states, behaviors, cognitions, and affects.

4. Given the large number and variety of factors at the individual and systems levels that are implicated in most child and family disorders, decision rules are needed for the selection of meaningful targets for assessment and intervention (Evans, 1985; Kanfer, 1985; Mash, 1985).

5. Similarly, when one considers the potentially infinite number of variables and their interactions that *could* be assessed in disturbed family systems, empirically validated decision rules are needed to determine what factors *should* be assessed via what methods, and what factors should not.

6. The situations in which children function are varied and include family, day care, school, and formal and informal peer groups. Embedded within each of these global settings are numerous subsettings. In light of this, multisituational analysis is the rule in BSA, and one of the tasks of assessment is to determine which aspects of a child's functioning are unique to specific contexts and which are cross-situational.

7. The pervasiveness of developmental change and situational variation in children suggests the need to assess patterns of behavior over time, as well as more global situational consistencies in the family, neighborhood, community, and culture.

Special Considerations in Assessing Children

Although the assessment of children has much in common with the assessment of adults, many characteristic conditions and constraints associated with assessing children are not ordinarily encountered when assessing adults, including many unique ethical and legal concerns (e.g., Koocher, 1993; Melton & Ehrenreich, 1993). The uniqueness of child assessment follows from generalizations about children as a group, characteristics of children and their contexts at different ages that may interact with the types of assessments being carried out, and common features of situations in which children ordinarily function and in which they are assessed.

Rapid and Uneven Developmental Change

With respect to generalizations about children as a group, a most noteworthy characteristic is their rapid and uneven developmental change (Evans & Nelson, 1977). Such change has implications both for judgments concerning child deviance and for the selection of appropriate methods of assessment. Studies have described both the age trends

for many child behaviors and ways in which the social significance and meaning of a problem may vary with the age of the child (e.g., Achenbach, Howell, Quay, & Conners, 1991; Achenbach & Edelbrock, 1981; MacFarlane, Allen, & Honzik, 1954; Prugh, Engel, & Morse, 1975). Many behaviors that are common at an earlier age are considered inappropriate in an older child (e.g., tantrums). In fact, some childhood disorders (e.g., Conduct Disorder) suggest a pattern of "arrested socialization" (Patterson, 1982).

Developmental deviation has been defined empirically in relation to a variation from observed behavioral norms for children of a similar age and gender (Achenbach & Edelbrock, 1981; Achenbach et al., 1991), and theoretically either in terms of a deviation from some expected behavioral pattern characteristic of particular stages of cognitive or psychosexual development (Santostefano, 1978), or in terms of the child's failure to reorganize his or her behavior over time in relation to age-appropriate developmental adaptations (Greenspan & Porges, 1984). BSA places greater emphasis on developmental norms based upon observed behavior or observed patterns of behavior in context than on norms derived from inferred theoretical constructs.

Cross-sectional and longitudinal data describing age trends for a range of normal and problem child behaviors are beginning to accumulate, and much of this information comes from the developmental literature. Prior data based exclusively on global parent reports are being buttressed by direct observations of ongoing social interactions. Information concerning proportions of children at different ages exhibiting various problems is also being reinforced with more specific information concerning children's success or failure in making age-related adaptations, such as the formation of a secure attachment, the development of purposeful communication, and the regulation of emotions. Much of this research has been conducted in the area of developmental psychopathology and is just beginning to find its way into clinical assessments with children and families (Cicchetti & Cohen, 1995a, 1995b). Making normative judgments in the context of adaptations over time is quite compatible with the assumptions of BSA, since an organizational approach requires careful specification of situational demands (e.g., developmental tasks).

Normative information describing *qualitative* changes across age is needed. Although qualitative change is difficult to assess, it would appear that many childhood problems, such as fears (Barrios & Hartmann, Chapter 5, this volume), ADHD (Barkley, Chapter 2, this volume), and conduct problems (McMahon & Estes, Chapter 3, this volume), change both qualitatively and quantitatively with age. Judgments regarding deviance must be made in relation to both types of change.

Rapid and uneven developmental change also carries implications for the stability or instability of assessment information over time. Assessment of behavior at one age may not be predictive of behavior at a later time, especially for assessments with very young children. For example, in examining aggressive behavior in males, Olweus (1979) reported that the degree of stability tended to decrease linearly as the interval between the two times of measurement increased, and that stability in aggressive behavior could be broadly described as a positive linear function of the interval covered and the subject's age at the time of the initial measurement.

Plasticity and Modifiability

A second characteristic of children as a group that has implications for assessment and treatment relates to the plasticity and modifiability of infants and young children in relation to environmental influences. Experience can shape not only behavior, but neural structure and function (Dawson & Hessl, 1994). Since children's behavior is under the strong and immediate social control of parents and other children, the need for assessment of these environmental influences is usually greater than in assessments with adults.

Age and Gender

Several writers have emphasized the need for an integration of behavioral and developmental approaches to assessment and treatment (Edelbrock, 1984; Harris & Ferrari, 1983; Mash & Terdal, 1988b; Yule, 1993). Developmental characteristics such as a child's age and gender have implications not only for judgments about deviance, but also for the assessment methods that are most appropriate. One obvious difference relates to the constraints placed on the use of child self-report measures as a function of age-related language and cognitive abilities. The nature of children's reaction to being observed and their understanding of the purposes of assessment will also vary with age. Assessments of young children may be affected by the children's wariness of strangers, whereas adolescents may also be wary of being assessed by adults, but for quite different reasons.

A child's gender also plays an important role in judgments of deviance, with concomitant implications for the interpretations of assessment information. Studies have shown that the norms used to make judgments about child behavior and the overt behavioral reactions of parents and teachers will vary as a function of whether a child is male or female. Other studies have found differences in the rates and expression of childhood disorders for boys versus girls (Eme, 1979; Kavanagh & Hops, 1994; Zahn-Waxler, 1993; Zoccolillo, 1993). The dimensions that emerge from multivariate studies of child behavior problems differ for boys versus girls after the age of 3 (Achenbach, 1993), and recent work suggests that the same disorder (e.g., depression, Conduct Disorder) may manifest itself in different ways, depending on the sex of the child.

Common Features of Assessment Situations

Several common features in the types of situations in which children are typically evaluated have implications for assessment (Evans & Nelson, 1977; Mash & Terdal, 1988b). Childhood distress is typically framed in terms of its impact on others. Children are referred by adults, which means that some children may not be experiencing subjective distress and may not understand the reasons why they are being assessed (Reid et al., 1988). Adult referral suggests the need to consider those factors that have been shown to influence the referral process, including the type and severity of problem, parent and teacher characteristics, social class, and culture.

There is a strong relationship between learning and behavior problems in childhood, and BSA is often carried out in the context of cognitive or intellectual evaluations (Kaufman & Reynolds, 1984; Reynolds & Kamphaus, 1990a; Sattler, 1992). The co-occurrence of learning and behavior problems in children reflects the more general observation that problem child behaviors rarely occur in isolation. This means that child assessment is typically multidisciplinary, involving such professionals as educators, psychologists, and a variety of health care personnel.

It is also the norm that children who are referred for assessment will undergo repeated evaluations. This is especially the case for children with chronic disabilities or conditions, for whom repeated evaluation and planning are often dictated by legislative requirements. Repeated evaluations also occur with children displaying less severe or acute problems, reflecting both the fragmentation that is characteristic of mental health delivery systems for children and families, and, more positively, the need to reevaluate children following remedial behavioral or educational programs. Repeated evaluations necessitate that assessment methods with children be robust across ages and relatively insensitive to the effects of practice.

Normative Comparisons

The emphasis in BSA on the functioning of individual children and families has resulted in minimal attention to the development of normative information, which attempts to establish an individual child's position on some dimension relative to the performance of other members of a suitable reference group (Furman & Drabman, 1981). In emphasizing the role of assessment in evaluating changes associated with treatment, practitioners have focused on the establishment of intraindividual as opposed to group norms. For example, intraindividual normative comparisons are implicit in any assessment that examines a child's current performance in relation to his or her behavior under baseline conditions. Although intraindividual comparisons of this type will identify the child as improving, not improving, or getting worse, they provide little guidance as to whether the child's level of performance is meaningful with respect to generally accepted performance criteria as derived from significant others or cultural informants (Kazdin, 1977).

Assessment approaches that emphasize the child's accomplishments in relation to specific performance criteria, rather than in relation to some reference group's average, are consistent with the treatment emphasis in BSA (Hartmann et al., 1979; Kendall et al., 1984). Such "edumetric" or "criterion-referenced" testing approaches (Carver, 1974) seem especially applicable in areas such as academic performance, athletic skill, or task completion, or areas where easily identifiable and sometimes absolute performance goals are specifiable. On the other hand, the current unavailability of accepted standards of performance related to social behavior and adjustment makes a criterion-referenced approach more difficult to apply in these areas. Efforts to identify the types of child social behaviors that lead to popularity and are reinforced by peers (Cone & Hoier, 1986; Hops & Greenwood, 1988), or the types of child responses that are likely to be either approved of or viewed as disturbing by adults (Mooney & Algozzine, 1978), may provide the basis for generally accepted criterion standards in some of the more subjective areas of social behavior. Models of social performance that distinguish between social skills (e.g., behavioral components) and social competence (e.g., components based on social judgments) have the potential for delineating the specific behavioral components that may lead to judgments of skilled performance under specific conditions (e.g., Hops, 1983; McFall, 1982).

In considering the applicability of group norms in BSA, it is important to examine issues related to the utility of normative comparisons generally and to the kinds of normative information that are likely to be most useful. Hartmann et al. (1979) have outlined a number of potential uses for normative comparisons in assessment. These include the following:

1. Normative comparisons are frequently useful in the identification of deficient or excessive performance. For example, if a child engages in excessively high rates of aggressive behavior, normative information about comparable children's rates of aggression in comparable situations may serve as a basis for identifying the child as potentially problematic, depending on social judgments and environmental reactions to the behavior.

2. When presenting complaints about children reflect parental expectations that differ markedly from existing norms, as may be the case in some abusive family situations (Mash et al., 1983), the focus and type of intervention may be quite different than in the absence of such normative information.

3. When norms exist to suggest that childhood problems are common or transient at particular ages (e.g., early reactions to separation, certain fears, bedwetting), such information may be used to guide decisions regarding the need for intervention. This is not to argue that normative difficulties are not a real concern for a child and family, or that educative or coping strategies would not be helpful in dealing with these problems. Normative disruptive behavior should not be considered to be "normal" without careful consideration of the context in which it occurs and of its relationship to other responses and other individuals. Most normative behaviors, especially those derived from multivariate studies, are typically presented in terms of their frequency of occurrence for the general population. For example, Edelbrock (1984) noted that "arguing" was reported as a problem by more than half of the parents of nonreferred children, and "the fact that it is such a common complaint about normal children sug-

gests that it should not receive high priority as a target for clinical treatment" (p. 29). However, it is possible that the "functions" of arguing in a population of children referred for treatment may be qualitatively different than in a nonreferred population, so that in one group arguing functions as a cue for further escalation of coercive behavior, whereas in another group it may not (Patterson, 1982). Under these circumstances, frequent reports of arguing in nonclinic samples would not provide a sound basis for giving this response a low priority in treatment for clinic-referred children. Nevertheless, in many instances, knowledge that a problem is common and transient will suggest that extensive clinical intervention is not required.

4. When norms exist for skilled versus inept performances, such information may be used for establishing both intermediate treatment targets and long-term treatment goals.

5. Norms may be useful for grouping children into relatively homogeneous treatment groups, which subsequently may produce greater precision with respect to the types of treatment that are most effective for children with particular difficulties.

6. Normative information for specific assessment measures may enhance the comparability of findings obtained through different data sources. For example, parent report measures and direct observation may yield equivalent information when the scores on each reflect a similar degree of deviation, as in the case of a child who is rated one standard deviation above the mean on the two different measures.

7. Normative information may be useful in evaluating the clinical significance or social validity of treatment outcomes—for example, to determine whether a treated child's behavior is comparable to that of nonproblem children following treatment. Research has found improvement in the behavior of children with ADHD and Conduct Disorder with treatment, but a significant number of these children continue to function well outside the normative range (Barkley & Guevremont, 1992; Kazdin & Esveldt-Dawson, 1987).

Although the above-described uses of norms refer primarily to norms for behavior, normative information about situational determinants may also help to identify some situations as being high-risk settings for the development of particular problems. For example, normative information regarding the quality of the child's school environment (high expectations, good group management, ef-

fective feedback and praise, good models of behavior presented by teachers, pleasant working conditions, and placement of students in positions of trust and responsibility) may serve as a basis for the detection of early problems when such conditions are deficient, with a subsequent focus on prevention (Rutter, 1979). Similarly, norms regarding the presence or absence of certain family background variables for particular childhood disorders—for example, those related to a parental history of alcoholism (Lee & Gotlib, 1991), parental Antisocial Personality Disorder (Frick et al., 1992), or child abuse (Wolfe, 1985)—may also serve to identify high-risk situations. In general, norms for contextual factors have not received as much attention as those for individual child behaviors.

Multiple Targets

BSA with children is typically directed at behavior and potential controlling variables. Although early work emphasized overt motor behaviors, current BSA adopts a much broader view of child behavior that encompasses intraorganism activities, including physiological reactions, cognitions, and affects. Controlling variables are those interacting antecedent and consequent events in the child's internal and external environment that influence the child's behavior. The heuristic "S-O-R-K-C" serves as a convenient way of organizing relevant classes of assessment information into broad categories of antecedent and consequent events, any one of which may be designated as a potential target for treatment (Kanfer & Phillips, 1970; Kanfer & Schefft, 1988).

"S" refers to prior events, or the stimuli or environments that have some functional relationship to the behavior. Given that the functional properties of environments for many child behaviors have not been empirically established, assessment often involves the designation of S variables that are *hypothesized* to be important.

"O" refers to the biological status of the organism (i.e., the child) and to internal events that reflect representations of past experience, schematic propositions, standards, values, information-processing mechanisms, and affect. The numerous studies supporting the interaction between biological and social variables in determining child behavior and development require that information regarding the child's biological status be brought to bear in any assessment (Strayhorn, 1987). Information regarding physical status is especially important with children, given the frequent and rapid physical changes that occur throughout childhood and adolescence. The blending of assessment information related to biological and social variables has increased dramatically, concomitant with the increased use of behavioral procedures in child health settings (e.g., Johnson & Rodrigue, Chapter 10, this volume) and the growing recognition of the potential importance of biological factors in understanding normal variations in child temperament (Rubin & Stewart, 1996) and childhood disorders more generally (Mash & Barkley, 1996).

There has been an increasing emphasis in BSA on the definition and measurement of cognitions and emotions, including construction abilities, encoding strategies, expectancies, values, plans, self-statements, metacognitive processes, mood, and emotion regulation (e.g., Karoly, 1981; Kendall & Hollon, 1981; Mash & Dozois, 1996; Mischel, 1973). The assessment of internal events has evolved from an exclusive focus on individuals to a focus on cognitions and affects that are operative in a variety of social systems and subsystems (e.g. marital relationships, mother–child relationships, etc.) (Bradbury & Fincham, 1987).

"R" refers to the response, which is taken in BSA to encompass motor behavior, cognitive/verbal behavior, and physiological/emotional behavior (Cone, 1979). Following from both theory and practical concerns, early developments in BSA focused primarily on the measurement of motor behavior, and to a lesser extent on physiological and cognitive responses; however, there is currently an emphasis on all three response systems.

Although treatment efforts have focused mostly on behavioral content, there is also much to suggest that the structural and qualitative elements of behavior may be as important as the content of the response per se, if not more so. For example, Wahler and Dumas (1986) and others have identified patterns of responses in which mothers adopt an indiscriminate response style; that is, their responses are independent of the immediately preceding child behavior. Mischel (1977) has discussed how such indiscriminate responding involving nonconformance to changes in the situation may be maladaptive. Yet, to date, there has been little systematic effort to target and modify these types of structural response features.

"K" refers to the contingency relationships between behavior and its consequences, including the frequency and timing of response outcomes. Schedules of reinforcement clearly influence the form and topography of behavior, and constitute an important category of assessment information (Ferster & Skinner, 1953). It has been suggested, for example, that under continuous-reward conditions the performance of ADHD and normal children may not differ, whereas children with ADHD may display response decrements under conditions of partial reward (Douglas & Parry, 1994).

"C" refers to the consequences of behavior and may include a wide variety of social and nonsocial events that vary in their valence. Consequences are typically embedded within naturalistic social exchanges and have accompanying affective components that have not, until recently, received much attention. As is the case with prior stimulation, it is important to distinguish between events following behavior that are functionally related to altering future probabilities, and consequences that are contiguous but that have not been demonstrated to have response-controlling properties.

It should be evident from this brief overview that the S-O-R-K-C designations, although useful for organizing assessment information, are arbitrary and reflect a somewhat static and linear view of the relationship between child behavior and its surrounding context. The categories are foci of convenience, and responses may serve as antecedents or consequences, depending on one's perspective and purpose. Moreover, intrapersonal, biological, and behavioral events may occur within each of these categories. With the view that child–behavior–environment relationships are continuous, ongoing, interactive, and embedded in many different systems, it becomes apparent that behavior may be a controlling variable for environmental events and for itself, as emphasized in much of the work on behavioral self-regulation (Karoly, 1981). Many studies have shown that a child's behavior may alter the contingency systems to which he or she is exposed. For example, children's reactions immediately prior to adult-administered consequences such as punishment influence the amount of punishment they receive (Parke & Sawin, 1977). Children who seek to make reparations for their misdeeds receive less punishment from adults than those who act defiantly. These points highlight some of the complexities of S-O-R-K-C definitions and their interactions. With an increasingly systemic emphasis, there is a need in BSA to elaborate the structural and functional S-O-R-K-C relationships between individuals and between systems of individuals (Kanfer & Schefft, 1988).

Selection of Treatment Goals

The identification of behaviors that are targeted for change has been a hallmark of BSA with children and families. However, many reports begin with a designation of the problem to be treated, without much information regarding the decisional processes utilized in this selection (Hawkins, 1975; Mash, 1985). A number of important points concerning the selection of target behaviors in cognitive-behavioral therapy have been made (Evans, 1985; Kanfer, 1985; Kazdin, 1985; Kratochwill, 1985; Mash, 1985; Mash & Terdal, 1988b):

1. Models of therapy and assessment that focus on a single target behavior as being synonymous with the goals of treatment provide incomplete representations of both the assessment and change process.

2. A more appropriate representation of the problem space for BSA is provided by a systems framework encompassing a wide range of potentially important responses, individuals, and contexts that may be contributing to the problem.

3. Such system representations of the child's and family's problems require decision rules for determining how best to conceptualize the system of interest, and what aspects of the system should be modified in order to bring about the most widespread, meaningful, and lasting changes.

4. In practice, the decision rules that are often employed reflect the theoretical preferences and subjective judgments of practicing clinicians. Such clinical decision making is subject to a variety of information-processing errors, many of which stem from the basic limitations (e.g., limited attention and memory) of human information processors in dealing with complex data sets under conditions that often involve time pressures and high levels of uncertainty (Achenbach, 1985; Cantor, 1982).

5. An actuarial approach to the selection of treatment goals and the ways these goals might be most effectively achieved offers promise as an adjunct to clinical decision making (Achenbach, 1985; Cattell, 1983; Meehl, 1954; Rachman, 1983). The increasing availability of high-speed computers is likely to facilitate such an approach (Farrell, 1991; Dow et al., 1996; Romanczyk, 1986).

6. If treatment goals are conceptualized in a systems framework, then the derivation of empirically based decision rules for intervention requires that the structural and functional interrelationships between different aspects of the system be documented and described. The identification of constellations of target behaviors and response covariations becomes important (Kazdin, 1982b, 1985; Voeltz & Evans, 1982).

7. Target behavior selection is conceptualized as a dynamic and ongoing process in which information derived from assessment and the impact of various interventions may be utilized in reformulating treatment goals. Such an approach is consistent with the emphasis in BSA on the important relationship between assessment and treatment. Not only does assessment information lead to treatment recommendations, but treatment outcomes are used to determine the need for additional assessment and reformulation of the problem.

The points made above call attention to the fact that the specification of target behaviors for an individual child is, *by itself*, not likely to provide a complete representation of a family's difficulties or the range of desired treatment goals. Nevertheless, information concerning the types of child behaviors that are often the focus of intervention can be useful within the context of a broader decision-making framework (Mash & Terdal, 1988b). Such information reflects both conceptual and empirical guidelines that commonly underlie target behavior selection.

Some of the more commonly mentioned *conceptual* guidelines for selecting target behaviors for treatment include the following:

1. The behavior is considered to be physically dangerous to the child and/or to others in the child's environment.

2. The behavior should provide an entry point into the natural reinforcement community of the child.

3. The target behaviors selected should be positive, in order to avoid a problem focus in treatment.

4. Behaviors that are viewed as essentials for development should be given high priority. For example, language, cognitive development and school performance, motor skills, rule-governed behavior, problem-solving skills, and peer relationships are common treatment targets. Implicit in this emphasis is the notion that many of these behaviors are embedded in normal developmental sequences, such that the failure to take corrective action early will result in cumulative deficits, with the child falling even further behind.

5. Behaviors that are viewed as essential early elements for more complex response chains have also received priority. Classes of general imitative

behavior, compliance, and cognitive styles have been viewed as requisite behaviors that enable a range of other responses.

6. Behaviors that maximize the flexibility of the child in adapting to changing new environments are viewed as important treatment targets. The current emphasis on teaching children general coping skills and self-regulatory strategies is consistent with this notion.

7. Behaviors that dramatically alter the existing contingency system for the child, such that maladaptive environmental reactions to the child are altered, are viewed as likely to contribute to long-term benefit (Stokes, Fowler, & Baer, 1978).

Some of the more commonly cited *empirical* criteria for selecting particular child behaviors for treatment are as follows:

1. The behaviors are consistent with some developmental or local norms for performance.

2. The behaviors have been shown, as a result of careful task analysis, to be critical components for successful performance; teaching classroom survival skills such as attending or peer discussion about class work is an example of this approach (Hops & Cobb, 1973).

3. The behaviors are subjectively rated as positive by recognized community standards (Wolf, 1978).

4. The behaviors effectively discriminate between "skilled" and "nonskilled" performers.

5. The behavior's natural history is known to have a poor long-term prognosis.

The preceding conceptual and empirical criteria represent decision-making guidelines for the selection of treatment targets, and need to be considered in relation to the unique characteristics of the child and family being assessed and the broader context in which assessments are carried out.

Multisituational Analysis

Information regarding the context in which the child's behavior, cognitions, and affects occur is an essential ingredient for any BSA concerned with the identification of relevant controlling variables to be utilized in the design of effective treatments. Contextual information is crucial, since children function in many different settings. The criteria for "competent" performance are likely to vary with the parameters of the situation, suggesting the need for situation-specific measures of behavior (e.g., Dodge, McClaskey, & Feldman,

1985) and ecological assessments (Willems, 1973, 1974). Identification of the functional properties of specific setting events permits behavioral alterations based on the utilization of stimulus control procedures (Wahler & Fox, 1981). Despite its acknowledged importance in BSA with children and families, the assessment of situations continues to be an area of relative neglect. It is believed that greater within-situation differentiation, which recognizes both differences and potential functional similarities in dissimilar environments, will be needed if the potential of situational analysis for the development of effective interventions is to be realized.

One type of molecular situational analysis has examined children's differential responses to varying antecedent social stimuli—for example, parents' use of different types of commands or language constructions to direct their children's behavior (Forehand, 1977). Other studies have attempted to identify different types of home, classroom, or institutional situations or task structures that predict particular child responses. For example, situations involving the mother's being occupied, situations with time constraints (e.g., dinnertime, bedtime, getting dressed, or going to school), or situations involving social evaluation (e.g., visits to others' homes, going to the store, or visits to restaurants) increase the likelihood of problem behaviors in both normal and disturbed children (Barkley, Chapter 2, this volume; Barkley & Edelbrock, 1987).

Other studies have examined classroom activity structures that predict different types of child social and academic behavior; examples include instructional arrangements (Greenwood, Delquadri, Stanley, Terry, & Hall, 1985), group versus individual activities (Patterson & Bechtel, 1977), quiet versus noisy conditions (Whalen, Henker, Collins, Finck, & Dotemoto, 1979), self-paced versus other-paced activities (Whalen et al., 1979), room size, seating arrangements, groupings of children based on different levels of ability, and formal versus informal task requirements (Jacob, O'Leary, & Rosenblad, 1978). Similar variables have been examined in institutional and day care environments. In addition, general environmental conditions related to space, noise, and temperature are variables of potential importance. For example, systematic variations in the rates of desirable and undesirable child behavior in the home, associated with temporal and climatic variables (e.g., time of day, day of the week, precipitation, and temperature), have been reported (Russell & Bernal, 1977).

It is likely that situational variation will mediate not only behaviors, but cognitions and affects in family members as well. For example, in examining cognitions relating to perceptions of equity within the marital relationship, Skitka (1986) found that such perceptions differed, depending on the context that was being assessed (e.g., sex, finances, etc.). There is a need to develop a taxonomy of situations to guide both research and applied work in child and family BSA (e.g., Schlundt & McFall, 1987). Are there groups of situations that can be specified on the basis of classification principles paralleling those relating to the classification of behavior? In attempts to build such situational taxonomies, the following remarks by Mischel (1977) are of importance:

> Depending on one's purpose many different classifications are possible and useful. To seek any single "basic" taxonomy of situations may be as futile as searching for a final or ultimate taxonomy of traits; we can label situations in as many different ways as we can label people. It is important to avoid emerging simply with a trait psychology of situations, in which events and settings, rather than people, are merely given different labels. The task of naming situations cannot substitute for the job of analyzing how conditions and environments interact with people in them. (pp. 337–338)

Expanded Temporal and Contextual Base

Early approaches to the behavioral assessment of children focused on contemporaneous behavior and controlling conditions. Current influences were seen as those that were proximal to the behavior in time and to the situation in which the behavior was assessed. For example, an observational assessment of parent–child interaction looked for the causes of child behavior in terms of the parent's responses to the child in that situation (e.g., cues and consequences). Information about the child's developmental history was not given a particularly important role, and the parent's response was viewed as a direct reaction to the child's immediate behavior in the situation rather than as the result of the cumulative effects of many prior experiences with the child, or of the parent's belief system. However, numerous findings suggest that parents' responses are based on more than the immediate behaviors of their children. For example, parents of children who are aggressive may respond harshly even when their children are behaving appropriately (Patterson, Reid, & Dishion, 1992).

Similarly, early BSA placed minimal emphasis on the broader contextual variables that were related to ongoing child behaviors. However, such factors as parental personality, family climate, peer group relations, marital relationships, family support, and community conditions have been shown to be potent sources of influence for a child's behavior—indeed, as important as or more important than the reactions of significant others to the child's behavior at the time of its occurrence (Mash & Dozois, 1996). Some studies have shown the warmth and permissiveness of the home to be a significant factor in the effectiveness of social reinforcement by parents (Patterson, Littman, & Hinsey, 1964). Others have demonstrated that maternal punitiveness to the child can be influenced by the amount of external stress placed on the mother in the situation (Passman & Mulhern, 1977). Friedrich (1979) reported that marital satisfaction was the best overall predictor of the coping behaviors of mothers of handicapped children, and Wahler (1980) has reported a direct relationship between the degree of "insularity" of the family and problem child behavior.

Given the multitude of situationally and temporally remote distal events that have been shown to be important determinants of the child and family behavior (e.g., Dumas, 1986; Patterson & Bank, 1986) and of treatment outcomes (Dumas & Wahler, 1983), the early behavioral emphasis on contemporaneous information in assessment is no longer tenable. Although it is important, current information needs to be considered within a broader developmental, temporal, and social context.

METHODS OF ASSESSMENT

The methods used in BSA cannot in and of themselves be considered unique (Evans & Nelson, 1986). For the most part, these methods are the same as those used in assessments with children and families more generally (e.g., Goldstein & Hersen, 1990; Ollendick & Hersen, 1993b; Sattler, 1992; Rutter, Tuma, & Lann, 1988). The use of structured and unstructured interviews (Bierman, 1983; Edelbrock & Costello, 1990; Gross, 1984; Sattler, 1997; Turkat, 1986), behavioral checklists and questionnaires (Barkley, 1988; Jensen & Haynes, 1986; Reynolds, 1993), self-monitoring procedures (Bornstein, Hamilton, & Bornstein, 1986; Shapiro & Cole, 1993), analogue methods (Hughes & Haynes, 1978; Nay, 1986), psychophysiological recordings (Kallman & Feuerstein, 1986; King, 1993), and direct observations of behavior (Barrios, 1993; Foster & Cone, 1986) obviously predates the emergence of BSA as a distinct approach. At the present time, BSA methods are characterized by (1) the use of multimethod strategies; (2) the flexible use of such methods within a decision-making model based on the BSA prototype; (3) a relative emphasis on the use of assessment instruments whose content represents a sample of the behaviors, cognitions, and affects of interest, rather than indirect signs of some underlying trait; (4) an emphasis on the use of assessment instruments designed to sample relevant situational content; and (5) the use of assessment instruments and measures that can be employed repeatedly over time in an evaluation framework directed at assessing whether or not the goals of treatment are being met.

There are now many comprehensive reviews of the methods that have been used in behavioral approaches to child and family assessment (e.g., Bellack & Hersen, 1988; Ciminero et al., 1986; Ciminero & Drabman, 1977; Evans & Nelson, 1977, 1986; Filsinger & Lewis, 1981; Ollendick & Hersen, 1984). In the discussion that follows, we highlight prevalent concerns and issues associated with the use of particular methods, as well as methodological developments in child and family BSA. We emphasize again that the major underlying theme of this volume is that methods are best used in relation to specific types of child and family difficulties. Nevertheless, since part of the assessment task is to initially identify the problem category that best describes the individual child and his or her family, it is also the case that some methods (e.g., screening instruments, diagnostic interviews, general behavioral checklists) are not problem-specific. In addition, some assessment methods have applicability across different problems.

Selection of Methods

In our efforts to study and help children and families who are experiencing problems, it would seem that much of the relevant content of interest has been identified. If we consider the literature on the clinical assessment of children and families, along with writings in child development, abnormal child psychology, developmental psychology, developmental psychpathology, education, behavioral therapy, cognitive-behavioral therapy, and family therapy, there is clearly no shortage of available instruments with which to assess children and families. Hundreds of different coding systems have been used to describe child compliance, and even more to describe parent–child and family interaction. In other areas of assessment, such as social support or family stress, the number of available measures is also large (Dunst & Trivette, 1985). What is lacking at this time seems to be an agreed-upon set of decisional criteria and rules concerning which of the available measures are best suited for particular purposes, and when and how these measures are to be used (Hartmann, 1984; Mash & Terdal, 1988b).

In practice, the most frequently used decision criteria often equate the quantity of assessment information with its quality. The rather crude heuristic here is that the best assessments are those that sample as many domains as possible, using the widest variety of methods. Traditional test batteries, in which a child receives a standardized evaluation that includes an interview with the parent and child, an IQ test, a projective personality test, and a test for organicity or perceptual dysfunction, illustrate this approach. Criticisms of these procedures as being insufficient for diagnosis and treatment have come from both behaviorally and nonbehaviorally oriented clinicians (e.g., Santostefano, 1978).

Although there is much empirical support for the notion that different methods of assessment may and often do yield different kinds of information about a child, the view that using as many different methods as possible will result in a truer or more useful description of the child and family has not been tested. In some instances, the accumulation of greater amounts of information in the clinical context may actually serve to reduce accuracy while increasing judgmental confidence (Nisbett, Zukier, & Lemley, 1981). With large amounts of information, the influence of relevant diagnostic data may be diluted by the presence of an increased number of nondiagnostic features. It is important that attention be given to the incremental validity associated with using multiple methods, in order to avoid the perpetuation of potentially unnecessary and costly procedures. Presumably, such incremental validity can be assessed by examining the relationship between amount and types of assessment information obtained as it relates to the effectiveness of treatment (Hayes, 1988; Hayes & Nelson, 1987, 1989; Mash, 1979; Nelson, 1983).

The multiple purposes for which assessments with children and families are carried out suggest that not all children should be assessed in all possible ways. What are some of the factors that contribute to decision making regarding the selection of methods? Although it is not possible to discuss all factors in detail, the choice of assessment methods in a particular case is based on such considerations as the purpose of the assessment (e.g., screening vs. treatment evaluation); the nature of the problem behavior (e.g., overt vs. covert, chronic vs. acute); characteristics of the child (e.g., age, sex, cognitive, and language skills) and of the family (e.g., social class, education, single parent vs. intact marriage); the assessment setting (e.g., clinic, home, classroom); characteristics of the assessor (e.g., conceptual preferences, level of training, available time); and characteristics of the method (e.g., reliability, validity, complexity, and amount of technical resources or training required for use, sensitivity to particular interventions). Common considerations in the selection of particular methods for specific childhood disorders are discussed in each of the chapters of this volume.

Standardization, Reliability, and Validity

The need for standardized measures in child psychopathology, family assessment, and child development generally, and in child and family BSA in particular, has been recognized for some time (Kanfer, 1972; Mash, 1985; Mash & Terdal, 1988b). Despite this recognition, there has been a proliferation of methods for assessing children and families that are idiosyncratic to the situation in which they are used, unstandardized, and of unknown reliability and validity (Strosahl & Linehan, 1986). The early rejection of many traditionally used psychological tests by behavioral assessors, concomitant with their emphasis on individually focused and prescriptive assessments, created a void that was filled by instruments with high face validity but unknown psychometric properties (e.g., Cautela, Cautela, & Esonis, 1983).

Since many instruments for the assessment of children and families have not been used repeatedly by different assessors, the accumulation of meaningful reliability and validity information has been limited. With the exception of a small number of verbal report measures of children's fears, anxieties, and social skills, and a slightly larger number of observational coding schemes that were originally developed as research instruments for studying children in the home and classroom but have since been applied in the clinical context (e.g., Forehand & McMahon, 1981; Mash, Terdal, & Anderson, 1973; O'Leary, Roman-

czyk, Kass, Dietz, & Santogrossi, 1971; Reid, 1978; Wahler, House, & Stambaugh, 1976), there are few standardized BSA measures for children and families. In fact, the more standardized measures of child and family behavior that are being used with increasing frequency in cognitive-behavioral research and practice have developed out of other traditions. These include, for example, parent report instruments of child behavior (e.g., Achenbach, 1991b), measures of children's depression or anxiety (e.g., Kovacs, 1981; Spielberger, 1973), and reports of marital satisfaction or distress (e.g., Johnson & O'Leary, 1996; Spanier, 1976), parental depression (Piotrowski, 1996), and family environment (Moos & Moos, 1986).

If BSA with children and families is to have scientific or clinical merit, the proliferation of idiosyncratic assessment methods must be replaced by the development and utilization of more standardized and population-specific assessments. There has been some movement in this direction, with the availability of observational codes describing specific problems such as family aggression (Reid, 1978), depression (Hops et al., 1986), ADHD (Abikoff, Gittelman, & Klein, 1980), and autism (Freeman & Schroth, 1984), and of analogue measures designed to assess specific problems such as ADHD (Milich, Loney, & Landau, 1982) and noncompliance (Roberts & Powers, 1988).

Some have argued against the development of a standardized set of behavioral assessment techniques (Cone & Hoier, 1986; Nelson, 1983). These arguments appear to be based on (1) the notion that the individuality and contextual specificity of child and family behavior would require an inordinately large number of techniques to sample all situations and behaviors of interest, which would render a standardized approach impractical; and (2) the inappropriateness of using psychometric criteria as the basis for development and selection of particular standardized measures. In regard to the latter reason, it is presumed that BSA conceptualizations based upon response instability over time and situational specificity of behavior are incompatible with the trait-oriented assumptions underlying psychometric concepts such as reliability and validity. For example, if one rejects the view that stable traits manifest themselves in similar ways over time, then viewing variability of scores over time as reflecting unreliability of the measuring instrument rather than inherent behavioral inconsistency would be inappropriate. Similarly, concurrent validity has little meaning if one accepts cross-situational variability as the norm, because a lack of situational consistency reflects things as they are, rather than invalidity of the measurement procedure (Kazdin, 1979).

Several writers have noted the ways in which psychometric considerations might be applied to BSA, even with its differing assumptions (Cone, 1977). Others have advocated the use of "other than psychometric" criteria (e.g., accuracy) for assessing the adequacy of behavioral assessment procedures (Cone & Hoier, 1986). The myriad of issues surrounding the relevance of psychometric concepts for BSA has been discussed extensively (Cone, 1978, 1981; Hartmann et al., 1979; Strosahl & Linehan, 1986), and the interested reader is referred to the sources cited for further discussion. However, a few brief comments are in order.

First, in spite of ongoing debate, there has been little resolution of these issues—perhaps because the arguments reflect fundamental differences in views regarding the utility of differing models of human functioning in the context of clinical assessment. The key issue centers around the compatibility or lack of compatibility of the idiographic and nomothetic approaches to assessment. Arguments for and against the integration of nomothetically derived trait measures of personality with idiographically derived behavioral assessments have been presented (Collins & Thompson, 1993; Haynes & Uchigakiuchi, 1993b). We would concur with the view that these approaches are complementary, and that both are necessary to our understanding, assessment, and treatment of child and family disorders. This view is expressed in the following statement by Strosahl and Linehan (1986):

> By using nomothetic principles, the behavioral assessor starts with a framework within which the idiographic elements of the individual case can be developed and refined. Nomothetic principles deliver hypotheses that can be tested idiographically. Conversely, idiographic data can sometimes point the way for nomothetic research, which in turn can be used to guide further idiographic testing. (p. 36)

As illustrated throughout the chapters of this volume, current approaches to the BSA of child and family disturbance reflect an integration of the nomothetic and idiographic approaches. This is suggested by increasing attention to diagnostic issues and normative information, the use of multivariate procedures for the assessment of traits, and efforts to aggregate information about individuals into broader patterns of responding.

Interviews with Parents and Others

Regardless of therapeutic orientation, and despite numerous criticisms concerning reliability and validity, the clinical interview continues to be the most universally used assessment procedure (Matarazzo, 1983; Sattler, 1997). However, the interviewer's behaviors and expectations, the kinds of information obtained in the interview, the meaning assigned to that information, and the degree of standardization will vary across theoretical orientations (Sattler & Mash, 1997). Consequently, the interviews used in the BSA of children and families are often different in purpose and format from those conducted by clinicians with other orientations (Turkat & Meyer, 1982). As information-gathering procedures, clinical interviews are used flexibly on repeated occasions and are frequently integrated with other assessment methods, such as observations of family interaction to assess such things as family problem-solving skills, compliance to treatment, and nonverbal patterns of communication.

Given that a social learning conceptualization of child and family disorders requires an understanding of reciprocal social relationships, and because children are typically referred by adults, it is almost always necessary to obtain descriptions from adults about the nature of the children's difficulties, social circumstances, physical status, and general development. Most typically a child's parent(s), usually the mother, will be the primary informant(s). However, other adults (e.g., teachers, relatives, and neighbors) and other children (e.g., siblings and peers) can provide potentially useful assessment information as well, although they are less frequently called upon (La Greca, 1990).

An interview with a parent will provide information about the child, about the parent, about the parent–child relationship, and about family relationships and characteristics more generally. The relative focus given to each of these areas will vary with the nature of the presenting problem and the purposes for which the interview is carried out. Research has identified relationships between parental characteristics and children's functioning in both the family and school settings (e.g., Forehand, Long, Brody, & Fauber, 1986), and between parental affects such as depression and child behavior. These findings suggest that the base for information gathering in the interview needs to include a focus on the child, the parent(s), sibling relationships, and the marriage (if there is one), as well as on the relationships between these various systems and subsystems.

The purposes of the interview in BSA have been summarized by Haynes and Jensen (1979). These purposes, adapted to the interview with a parent, include the following:

1. Gathering information about parental concerns, expectations, and goals.
2. Assessing parental perceptions and feelings about the child's problems, concerns, and goals.
3. Identifying possible factors that may be maintaining or eliciting problem behaviors.
4. Obtaining historical information about problem and nonproblem behaviors and about prior treatment efforts.
5. Identifying potentially reinforcing events for both child and parent.
6. Educating the parent with respect to the nature of the childhood problem, its prevalence, its prognosis, and its possible etiologies.
7. Providing the parent with an adequate rationale for proposed interventions.
8. Assessing the parent's affective state, motivation for changing the situation, and resources for taking an active role in helping to mediate behavior change.
9. Obtaining informed consent.
10. Providing data for the assessment of treatment outcomes.
11. Communicating with the parent about procedures, and setting realistic goals for assessment and intervention.

The many interview purposes described means that the degree of structure, the content, and the style of parental interviews will vary greatly, and that lack of uniformity may be the rule rather than the exception. Several general points related to interviews with parents require discussion.

Generality and Flexibility

The first point involves the level of generality and flexibility of the interview. Typically, interviews with parents have been used either as diagnostic or screening instruments to determine treatment eligibility, or as methods of gaining information that will facilitate the design of effective treatments. These purposes necessarily define such interviews as being general, and also require the interviewer to adapt his or her behavior to the various concerns being raised by parents. The degree of structure and standardization in interviews with parents is usually low, but it can be increased for other interview purposes—for example, when interview information is to be used as an outcome measure, or when the interview is being used to make a formal diagnosis. Alternatively, if pretreatment questionnaires include life history information and/or reinforcement surveys, then initial interviews can be structured around the information obtained from these questionnaires.

A number of guidelines and standardized formats have been suggested for interviews with parents from a BSA perspective (e.g., Bersoff & Grieger, 1971; Holland, 1970; Kanfer & Grimm, 1977; Kanfer & Saslow, 1969; Wahler & Cormier, 1970). These formats are useful, although they are also quite general and make no *a priori* assumptions regarding the specific interview content that is likely to be most meaningful. In effect, these nonspecific interview formats do not include information that is available from informal assessments that may have already taken place, or from research on the specific disorder under consideration. Clinical experience and training are presumed to lead the interviewer into asking the right questions within some of the general areas suggested by the formats that have been presented (Kanfer, 1985). Consistent with the theme of this book, we believe that problem-specific interview formats are the most appropriate. For instance, interviews with children with anxiety should focus on anxiety-related symptoms (e.g., Silverman, 1987), and those with parents of children with autism should systematically obtain information regarding commonly identified problems, situations, and controlling variables associated with autism (e.g., language, social interaction, and possible negative reinforcement). Rather than assuming that interviewers will have the specific information needed to guide interview content and process, we believe that interview schedules that include disorder- and context-specific information will lead to more systematic, standardized, efficient, and useful interviews possessing greater reliability and validity. Such problem-specific interview schedules are described in the chapters of this volume, and many are presented in the comprehensive volume on interviewing by Sattler (1997).

Reliability and Validity

It should be emphasized that questions concerning reliability and validity are meaningful only in relation to the interview purpose. So, for example, if the purpose of the interview is to gain information about a mother's perception of her child as a possible controlling variable for her reactions to her child, a lack of correspondence between maternal report and that of other informants is of less concern than it would be if the mother's report were being used to assess rates of child behavior over time in order to assess the impact of treatment.

With respect to reliability, primary concerns relate to such issues as these: (1) whether information obtained on one occasion is comparable to information obtained on other occasions from the same parent (e.g., stability); (2) whether information obtained from the parent is comparable to information obtained from another informant—for example, mother versus father (i.e., interobserver agreement; Edelbrock, Costello, Dulcan, Conover, & Kalas, 1986; Schwarz, Barton-Henry, & Pruzinsky, 1985); (3) whether the information reported by the parent is consistent with other information given by the parent in the same interview (i.e., internal consistency); and (4) whether the information obtained by one interviewer is comparable to that obtained by another interviewer with the same parent (i.e., method error).

The first reliability concern is especially relevant in interviews that require parents to report retrospectively on their children's developmental/social history—one of the more common elements of most child assessments (Yarrow, Campbell, & Burton, 1970). In reviewing the reliability of such recall by parents, Evans and Nelson (1977) concluded that retrospective reports are likely to be unreliable and frequently distorted in the direction of socially desirable responses and dominant cultural themes. Interestingly, the degree of reliability appears related to the nature of the events that parents are reporting and to the level of specificity of behavior being described (Lapouse & Monk, 1958).

It should be recognized, however, that although parental reports may conform to the demand characteristics of the interview situation, such characteristics may not always predict socially desirable responses. For example, there may be a parental bias toward reporting more negative behaviors and greater distress when eligibility for treatment is a concern, whereas posttreatment interviews may be associated with an implicit demand to report improvements in child behavior and reductions in distress. This latter point is especially important when interview information is used as a measure of treatment outcome. Mothers of problem children may also be realistic about their children's

behavior, in contrast to mothers of nonproblem children, who may describe their children in an overly positive fashion. Interobserver agreement in relation to mother–father and teacher report is difficult to evaluate, because disagreement may reflect differences in the situation in which each of these informants observes the child. In general, mothers may be more reliable informants than fathers and may provide descriptions of their children's behavior that are much more differentiated and situation-specific (McGillicuddy-DeLisi, 1985).

Interviews with other significant adults or with the child's friends, peers, or siblings may be potentially useful but have received little attention in assessment, in part because of ethical concerns associated with obtaining such information. For example, interviews with peers may further stigmatize the child as having a problem, with subsequent changes in how the peers and others interact with the child. At the same time, data suggest that peer evaluations may be particularly sensitive in identifying children with problems (Bierman & Welsh, Chapter 6, this volume; Cowen, Pederson, Babigian, Izzo, & Trost, 1973), although it is not known whether peer judgments regarding the precise nature of these problems are likely to be accurate. The general problems associated with obtaining verbal reports from children, particularly younger children, suggest that structured tasks or game-like assessment procedures involving child and peer interactions may be more sensitive measures than unstructured interviews with peers. Information obtained from siblings may also be important, in that many problem families are characterized by high rates of sibling conflict (Dunn & Munn, 1986). Studies with nonproblem families have suggested that children's views of their siblings are represented by patterns of positive and negative behaviors mixed with positive and negative feelings (Pepler, Corter, & Abramovitch, 1982). However, it may be that both perceptions and behaviors for siblings in problem families are more negatively toned (Patterson, 1982).

Structured Parental Reports about Child Behavior

In addition to unstructured interviews with parents, reports concerning child behavior and adjustment have also been obtained via other, more structured methods (Barkley, 1988; Humphreys & Ciminero, 1979; Piacentini, 1993). The most widely used methods have been global behavior checklists requiring either binary judgments concerning the presence or absence of particular child behaviors (e.g., the Louisville Behavior Checklist—Miller, Hampe, Barrett, & Noble, 1971; Miller & Roid, 1988; the Missouri Children's Behavior Checklist—Sines, 1986) or ratings concerning the degree to which the behavior is present or perceived as a problem (e.g., the CBCL/4–18 and 1991 Profile—Achenbach, 1991b; the BASC Parent Rating Scale—Reynolds & Kamphaus, 1992; the Conners Parent Rating Scale—Conners, 1990; the Parent Attitudes Test—Cowen, Huser, Beach, & Rappaport, 1970; the Behavior Problem Checklist—Hinshaw, Morrison, Carte, & Cornsweet, 1987; Quay & Peterson, 1975; the Yale Children's Inventory—Shaywitz, Schnell, Shaywitz, & Towle, 1986). These checklists cover a wide range of presenting complaints and, to a lesser extent, areas of child competence; offer a degree of standardization that is uncharacteristic of clinical interviews; permit normative comparisons between children; are economical to administer and score; may be readily used as treatment outcome measures; and provide a rich source of information about parents' perceptions of their children's behavior, including possible discrepancies in the perceptions of parents in the same family, and the discrepancies between parental perceptions and data derived through other sources, such as reports by teachers (e.g., McDermott, 1993).

In the clinical context, these checklists can serve as comprehensive but general screening instruments, most typically during the diagnostic phase of assessment. They provide a reasonable estimate of parental perceptions of a child's overall behavior and adjustment as aggregated across a wide variety of situations. They fail to provide situation-specific information about behavior, or information that can be easily incorporated into a program of intervention. Most of the checklists noted above have been used with children of at least school age, but, consistent with an emphasis on prevention-oriented assessments, several measures have now been developed for use with younger children and toddlers (e.g., the CBCL/2–3 and 1992 Profile—Achenbach, 1992; the Behavior Checklist for Infants and Toddlers—Bullock, MacPhee, & Benson, 1984; the Toddler Behavior Checklist—Larzelere, Martin, & Amberson, 1985). For children younger than 2, the most commonly used parent report measures have been subsumed under the general heading of temperament (e.g., Goldsmith & Campos, 1986; Rothbart, 1981).

As we have noted, extensive multivariate analyses of parent-completed checklists have yielded consistent factors; not surprisingly, these factors vary with the age and sex of the child and with the setting and informant (e.g., Gdowski, Lachar, & Kline, 1985). Within a BSA framework, such variations are consistent with the view that behaviors will vary in degree and type across situations, and that different informants will structure their views of the child in different ways. Although there is a need for more measures with situational norms, the likelihood that the most frequently used checklists will be modified in this direction seems quite low, in light of the large-scale empirical efforts that often go into establishing a psychometrically sound normative data base for checklists.

One concern surrounding the use of parent checklists has been the degree of correspondence between mothers' and fathers' reports (e.g., Achenbach, McConaughy, & Howell, 1987). Some researchers have reported high agreement (correlation of .69) between parents on global checklists for both narrow- and broad-band syndromes (Achenbach, 1985, p. 104). However, the degree of agreement or disagreement between parents will probably depend on the type of measure being compared (e.g., narrow-band syndromes vs. profiles) and the type of agreement index that is used. Reports by mothers versus fathers can lead to different profile interpretations and judgments of clinical significance (Hulbert, Gdowski, & Lachar, 1986). Furthermore, when different raters seeing children in different contexts have been compared, interrater agreement tends to be quite low (Achenbach et al., 1987).

In addition to global checklists and structured interviews, several parent-completed measures that focus on specific content areas or problems have also been developed. These include, for example, parental ratings of a child's overall development (e.g., the Minnesota Child Development Inventory—Ireton & Thwing, 1974), ADHD (e.g., Barkley, Chapter 2, this volume; Werry & Sprague, 1970), autism (Gilliam, 1995), personality (e.g., the Minnesota Multiphasic Personality Inventory—Adolescent—Butcher et al., 1992; the Personality Inventory for Children—Lachar, 1982; Wirt, Lachar, Klinedinst, & Seat, 1990; the Personality Inventory for Youth—Lachar & Gruber, 1994), self-control (Kendall & Wilcox, 1979; Reynolds & Stark, 1986), child psychopathy (Frick & Hare, in press), and preferred reinforcers (Clement & Richard, 1976).

Another type of parent report, often used to monitor changes during treatment, has been parent recording of targeted child behaviors. Typically, parents collect baseline data on one or two general (e.g., compliance) or specific (e.g., swearing) behaviors that may subsequently be targeted for modification. Less frequently, parents also collect systematic data about antecedent and consequent events in order to identify potentially important controlling variables to be utilized in treatment. Many different forms have been presented to assist parents in recording their children's behavior (e.g., Madsen & Madsen, 1972). Such forms are common fare in almost all manuals that have been used in parent management training programs (see Bernal & North, 1978, for a review of 26 commonly used parent training manuals). Records kept by parents have the advantage of providing ongoing, *in situ* information about behaviors of interest that might not otherwise be accessible to observation, and may also provide secondary benefits that are not directly related to assessment. These include teaching parents better observation, tracking, and monitoring skills; assessing parental motivation; and providing parents with more realistic estimates of their children's rate of responding and feedback on the effects of treatment. On the negative side, there are many practical problems in getting parents to keep accurate records, and parental recordings of behavior may be reactive in the home situation, producing unrepresentative data. In addition, although parent recordings have been used extensively, there is little information available concerning their reliability or validity.

In most cases, parents are the primary informants in assessments of their children, because it is parental perceptions that often determine what (if anything) will be done about their children's problems. Furthermore, professionals' judgments regarding childhood disorders may be influenced more by what parents say about their children than by observed child behavior. Because parent-completed checklists can provide more information more quickly than could otherwise be obtained through interviews, and since they are also more economical with respect to cost, effort, and therapists' time, they are likely to receive continued use in child and family BSA. We believe that the utility of such checklists for assessment and treatment of individual children can be enhanced through the inclusion of more situational content.

Parent Self-Ratings

Recent approaches to BSA have increasingly emphasized the importance of assessing parents' self-reported perceptions, cognitions, and feelings (Mash & Terdal, 1988b). Earlier work tended to utilize parents' reports about themselves primarily in areas directly related to the children's problems (e.g., "How does it make you feel when he does not listen to you?"). Parents' feelings, attitudes, and cognitions were considered as important variables, but usually in relation to their influences on how parents reacted to their children or as predictors of the likelihood that parents would involve themselves in treatment. Although these considerations continue, parents' reports about themselves have increasingly been viewed as important to assess in understanding the nature of the families' problems and as potential targets for intervention. The importance of obtaining self-report information from both mothers and fathers is recognized; in practice, however, mothers more frequently provide information than fathers.

Parent self-ratings have included a variety of procedures designed to assess parental behavior and disciplinary practices, parental cognitions, and parental affects. One type of self-rating has been concerned with reported parenting practices. These are assessed via questionnaires that ask parents about their use of discipline (Arnold & O'Leary, 1993) or rewards and punishments (e.g., Gordon, Jones, & Nowicki, 1979), or questionnaires that provide the parents with brief written scenarios of child behavior or situations and ask the parents to specify what they would do in those situations (e.g., Patterson & Colleagues, 1984). Similar assessments have presented either audiotaped (e.g., Grusec & Kuczynski, 1980; Martin, Johnson, Johansson, & Wahl, 1976) or videotaped (e.g., Disbrow & Doerr, 1983; Miller & Clarke, 1978; Wolfe & LaRose, 1986) samples of children's behavior, and the parents' verbal and/or physiological responses are recorded. Such analogue measures are reflections of how parents think they would respond, and the degree of correspondence between expressed intent and actual parent behavior in these situations has received little empirical investigation.

The increasing focus on cognitive variables in BSA and cognitive-behavioral treatment, and in the study of parent–child relationships more generally (e.g., Sigel, 1985; Sigel et al., 1992), has led to the development of a host of self-report measures for describing different types of parental cognitions. Such measures have been used to assess the following:

1. General attitudes about children and child rearing (e.g., the Parent Attitude Research Instrument—Schaefer & Bell, 1958; the Belief Scale—Bristol, 1983a) and implicit

theories about discipline (Dix & Ruble, 1989).

2. Satisfaction in areas concerned with spouse support, the child–parent relationship, parent performance, family discipline, and control (e.g., the Parent Satisfaction Scale—Guidubaldi & Cleminshaw, 1985; the Satisfaction with Parenting Scale—Crnic & Greenberg, 1983).

3. Parenting self-esteem, as reflected in degree of comfort in the parenting role and perceived effectiveness as a parent (e.g., the Parenting Sense of Competence Scale—Gibaud-Wallston & Wandersman, 1978; Johnston & Mash, 1989; Self-Perceptions of the Parental Role—MacPhee, Benson, & Bullock, 1984).

4. Expectations for development and developmentally appropriate behavior (e.g., the Parent Opinion Survey—Azar, Robinson, Hekemian, & Twentyman, 1984; the Child Development Questionnaire—Mash & Johnston, 1980).

5. Attributional processes related to the causes of child behavior (e.g., Dix & Grusec, 1985; Larrance & Twentyman, 1983; Miller, 1995), child-rearing outcomes (the Parent Attribution Test—Bugental, 1993), or specific problems such as enuresis (Butler, Brewin, & Forsythe, 1986).

6. Problem-solving skills in regard to commonly occurring child behaviors and child-rearing situations (e.g., Holden, 1985a, 1985b, 1985c; the Parent Problem Solving Instrument—Wasik, Bryant, & Fishbein, 1980).

7. Empathy in general (e.g., Chlopan, McBain, Carbonell, & Hagen, 1985) and empathy in the parenting domain (e.g., Feshbach, 1989; Newberger, 1978).

8. Emotion recognition (e.g., Kropp & Haynes, 1987).

Studies into the cognitive and affective processes of parents have provided information concerning relationships between parental cognitions and behavior; possible differences in the cognitions of parents in disturbed versus nondisturbed families; and the ways in which parents process information about demanding child-rearing situations, including their use of anticipatory or proactive strategies (Holden, 1985d), the influence of anger on thinking (Dix & Reinhold, 1990), and the effects of maternal mood on child evaluation

and parent–child interaction (Jouriles, Murphy, & O'Leary, 1989; Jouriles & Thompson, 1993). Information concerning the decisional processes of parents seems especially relevant to formulating treatment goals, since parents' problem-solving styles may be directly targeted for treatment (e.g., Blechman, 1985). Many of the measures described have been used in a research context, and their potential utility in clinical assessment needs to be demonstrated. Furthermore, a number of different cognitive dimensions have been assessed, and more work is needed to determine whether or not these are in fact independent dimensions (Sigel et al., 1992).

An interest in how parents of problem (Mash & Johnston, 1983b), handicapped (Zeitlin, Williamson, & Rosenblatt, 1985), and nonproblem children cope with the stresses involved in child rearing has led to the development of measures designed to assess the stresses associated with being a parent (e.g., the Parenting Stress Index—Abidin, 1983, 1995); the degree to which specific types of child behavior may be perceived as disturbing (e.g., Mooney & Algozzine, 1978); and the impact on parents of specific handicapping child conditions, such as hearing loss (Meadow-Orlans, 1986). Similarly, growing interest in the social networks surrounding disturbed families has led to the development of measures of perceived social support and/or social isolation (e.g., Bristol, 1983b; Dunst, Jenkins, & Trivette, 1984; Dunst & Trivette, 1985; Salzinger, Kaplan, & Artemyeff, 1983; Wahler, Leske, & Rogers, 1979).

Much recent work has also been directed at parents' reports of their own mood states, particularly maternal depression (e.g., Billings & Moos, 1986; Forehand, Fauber, Long, Brody, & Slotkin, 1986), and more recently maternal anxiety. The most frequently utilized measure of mood has been the Beck Depression Inventory (BDI; Beck, Ward, Mendelson, Mock, & Erbaugh, 1961; Piotrowski, 1996). There is a rapidly growing literature documenting the profound impact that maternal depression can have on child functioning and family relationships, beginning in early infancy (Hammen, 1991). Although the prevalence of self-reported depression in mothers of problem children is high, whether this mood state is a determinant or an outcome of disturbed family interactions has not yet been established (Patterson, 1982).

It is also the case that mothers' feelings of depression may negatively color their views of their children. Friedlander, Weiss, and Traylor (1986) reported a .71 correlation between maternal BDI scores and the Depression subscale of the CBCL. Edelbrock (1984) notes that parental endorsement of the CBCL item "unhappy, sad, or depressed" discriminated between clinically referred and non-referred children more strongly than any other item. However, in light of the high correlation between mothers' self-reports of depression and ratings of their children, it is not clear whether the sensitivity of this item related to the mothers' or to the children's depression. The fact that the same item best discriminated between referred and non-referred children even when teacher ratings were used (Edelbrock & Achenbach, 1985) suggests that the item's sensitivity may not be the result of a negative response bias per se. Additional support for this view comes from a study (Billings & Moos, 1986) showing that independent ratings of child functioning made by depressed parents and their nondepressed spouses were highly correlated, and from a comprehensive review paper that did not find evidence for depression-related distortions (Richters, 1992). Nevertheless, even with non-depressed teachers or spouses, ratings of a child as unhappy could reflect an attribution that follows from a negative view of the child and his or her behavior, rather than being indicative of the child's actual distress.

In summary, parent self-ratings represent a variety of important characteristics that may contribute to how parents react to, and are affected by, their disturbed children. In addition, many of the cognitions and affects being assessed are likely to suggest fruitful areas for needed interventions. In consideration of the future use and development of such self-ratings, a number of evaluative criteria for selecting a self-report inventory have been suggested: whether it can be administered repeatedly as an outcome measure; whether it provides sufficient specificity; whether it is sensitive to treatment changes; whether it guards against common self-report biases, such as social desirability, acquiescence, demand characteristics, faking, or lying; and whether it possesses adequate reliability, validity, and norms (Hartmann, 1984). Many of the parent self-ratings that have been used thus far in child and family BSA do not meet these criteria.

Child Self-Report

Concerns regarding the reliability, validity, and practical difficulties associated with obtaining self-report information from children, especially young children, resulted in a minimal reliance on such measures in early work in child and family BSA.

More recently, there has been an increase in the use of interviews and child-completed checklists and questionnaires (Bierman, 1983; Bierman & Schwartz, 1986; Reynolds, 1993) throughout the various phases of assessment and treatment. This increase is related to a number of factors:

1. The growing recognition of children's unique position as observers of themselves and their social environment.
2. An accumulation of data in support of the notion that cognitions and emotions directly influence children's behavior and often mediate the effects of intervention.
3. An increased emphasis on children's thoughts and feelings as potential targets for treatment, with a concomitant increase in the use of cognitively based therapy procedures.
4. A growing concern about such childhood disorders as depression (Compas, Chapter 4, this volume) and anxiety (Barrios & Hartmann, Chapter 5, this volume; Klein & Last, 1989)—disorders that require the direct assessment of children's self-reported feelings.
5. A greater sensitivity to developmental issues in assessment, which has reinforced the idea that methods need to be adapted to the qualitatively different information-processing and interpersonal styles characteristic of children at different ages. Although interviews and checklists of the types administered to adults may not be very informative with children of preschool or grade school age, flexible interview formats that are consistent with a child's developmental level can provide important information about the child's behavior, thought processes, affect, self-perceptions, and views of the environment.
6. The development and widespread availability of a number of well-standardized and psychometrically sound structured and semistructured interview and questionnaire procedures.

Unstructured Interviews

The format and content of assessment interviews with children should vary in relation to the children's developmental status, the nature of their problems, and the interview purposes. Purposes will vary, but typically include attempts to elicit information regarding children's perceptions of themselves and their problems, and to obtain samples of how children handle themselves in a social situation with an adult (Greenspan, 1981; Gross, 1984; Sattler, 1997). Children's views of the circumstances that have brought them to the clinic, expectations for improvement, and comprehension of the assessment situation are all important to assess, as is the manner in which the children interpret significant events in their lives, such as divorce (Kurdek, 1986) or family violence (Wolfe & McEachran, Chapter 11, and Wolfe & Birt, Chapter 12, this volume). In addition, children's perceptions of their parents, siblings, teachers, and peers (Bierman & Welsh, Chapter 6, this volume; Furman & Buhrmester, 1985a, 1985b; Hymel, 1986) will probably influence their reactions to these people; evaluating these perceptions is therefore especially important for understanding the children's problems, designing interventions, and assessing the suitability of employing such individuals as mediators in behavioral intervention programs. Interviews may also focus on obtaining more specific types of information that children are in a unique position to report, such as their preferred reinforcers or preferences for immediate versus delayed rewards.

Semistructured and Structured Interviews

Unstructured clinical interviews can be extremely unreliable for purposes of diagnosis when such diagnosis is concerned with assignment to diagnostic categories. Sources of unreliability stem from a variety of factors, including a lack of clarity concerning decision rules, and the operation of confirmatory biases and other types of judgmental errors (Achenbach, 1985; Costello, 1986). Although the use of structured interviews in clinical practice with children has not been widespread, such procedures have received increased use in research studies where the primary focus has been on identifying homogeneous populations of children conforming to particular diagnostic criteria. Such interviews may also receive increased use in clinical practice, in light of their easy adaptability to computerized administration and scoring, and the continuing administrative demands for assigning children to institutionalized diagnostic categories.

A number of structured and semistructured diagnostic interviews for children and adolescents were first developed in the late 1970s and early 1980s, each having different degrees of structure. Recent versions of these include the Diagnostic Interview for Children and Adolescents (Herjanic & Reich, 1982); the Schedule for Affective Disorders and Schizophrenia for School-Age Children (Ambrosini, Metz, Prabucki, & Lee, 1989; Chambers et al., 1985); the Diag-

nostic Interview Schedule for Children—Revised (Shaffer et al., 1993); the Interview Schedule for Children (Kovacs, 1985); the Child Assessment Schedule (Hodges, 1985); the Mental Health Assessment Form for School-Age Children (Kestenbaum & Bird, 1978); and the Psychological Screening Inventory (Langner et al., 1976). These interview schedules have undergone changes to accommodate revisions in DSM criteria, and the reader is referred to Edelbrock and Costello (1990) and Hodges and Zeman (1993) for comprehensive reviews of these developments.

Numerous empirical investigations with these interviews have produced interesting findings that have implications for the assessment of children more generally. For example, the reliability of the interview may interact with the particular dimension (e.g., affective, cognitive, behavioral) being evaluated. Edelbrock, Costello, Dulcan, Kalas, and Conover (1985) found that in descriptions of internal states, the reliability of an interview was related to a child's age; children under age 10 showed little consistency in their interview reports, even over periods as brief as 1 or 2 weeks. Young children showed a particular tendency to change their responses from affirmative during an initial interview to negative in a second interview several days later.

The potential utility of structured psychiatric interviews for BSA is not clear at this time. Certainly, the increased standardization and gains in reliability associated with using these procedures provide some advantage in both applied and basic research with children and families. However, most of the structured interview formats tend to produce global indices concerning the presence or absence of a disorder, rather than the more specific information needed to formulate a picture of a particular child, family, and peer group for the purposes of intervention.

Few structured child interviews have been developed specifically for use in BSA. Bierman (1983) has presented some extremely useful guidelines in this regard, showing how empirical information about developmental processes (e.g., person perception as related to age) may be used to guide the types of questions asked in an interview. The few structured formats that have been presented have been developed primarily as research instruments (Patterson & Colleagues, 1984). The growing interest in children's perceptions and feelings in BSA suggests that greater standardization in interview procedures with children may be warranted. Presumably, such standardized instruments should look at children's reports in relation to a variety of commonly occurring situations in the home and classroom.

Child-Completed Checklists and Questionnaires

The use of child-completed checklists and questionnaires in child assessment has also increased (Reynolds, 1993). Although the content and response format for child-completed measures have varied with children's developmental status, for the most part these instruments have been used with older children and often as one type of treatment outcome measure. Many different self-report instruments have been developed for describing the cognitive, affective, and behavioral domains. Although many of the early self-report measures were downward extensions of instruments initially developed for adults, currently used measures have followed more closely from work with children. Some of the more frequently used instruments and the areas they assess are as follows:

1. General personality dimensions such as introversion–extroversion (e.g., Eysenck & Rachman, 1965).
2. Perceived locus of control (e.g., Bugental, Whalen, & Henker, 1977; Nowicki & Duke, 1974; Nowicki & Strickland, 1973).
3. Social relationships and assertion (e.g., Deluty, 1979; Hops & Lewin, 1984; Michelson & Wood, 1982; Ollendick, 1984; Scanlon & Ollendick, 1985).
4. Self-esteem and self-concept in general, and in specific domains such as academic or social functioning (e.g., Coopersmith, 1967; Harter, 1982, 1983; Harter & Pike, 1984; Piers & Harris, 1963; Williams & Workman, 1978).
5. Reinforcer preferences (e.g., Clement & Richard, 1976; Tharp & Wetzel, 1969).
6. Anger (e.g., Nelson & Finch, 1978).
7. Depression (e.g., Compas, Chapter 4, this volume; Kovacs, 1981; Reynolds, 1989; Smucker, Craighead, Craighead, & Green, 1986).
8. Anxiety (e.g., Barrios & Hartmann, Chapter 5, this volume; Castenada, McCandless, & Palermo, 1956; Reynolds & Richmond, 1985; Silverman & Nelles, 1986; Ronan, 1996; Spielberger, 1973).
9. Irrational cognitions such as catastrophizing, overgeneralizing, personalizing, and selective abstraction, as expressed in the social, academic, and athletic domains

(e.g., Leitenberg, Yost, & Carroll-Wilson, 1986).
10. Perceptions of family members (e.g., Furman & Buhrmester, 1985b; Hazzard, Christensen, & Margolin, 1983).
11. Perceptions of peers and peer relationships (e.g., Asher, Hymel, & Renshaw, 1984; Bierman & McCauley, 1987).
12. Perceived behavior problems and areas of competence (e.g., Achenbach & McConaughy, 1985).

Specific examples of the items constituting many of these checklists for specific problems are provided in the chapters that follow.

Self-Monitoring Procedures

Several discussions of the types of self-monitoring procedures that have been used in assessments with children, as well as of related methodological issues, are available (e.g., Bornstein et al., 1986; Shapiro & Cole, 1993). Children have used self-monitoring for such behaviors as classroom attending (Broden, Hall, & Mitts, 1971), academic responses (Lovitt, 1973), class attendance (McKenzie & Rushall, 1974), talking out in class (Broden et al., 1971), aggression (Lovitt, 1973), room cleaning (Layne, Rickard, Jones, & Lyman, 1976), and appropriate verbalizations (Nelson, Lipinski, & Boykin, 1978). In most instances, the use of self-monitoring procedures with children has been undertaken as part of a larger set of self-assessment procedures, including recording and evaluation, that are intended to modify the behavior being monitored. There are few descriptions of children monitoring their own behavior and life situations in order to provide diagnostic information for developing treatments or measuring treatment outcomes. Consequently, the assessment functions of self-monitoring procedures with children have not received much elaboration.

Direct Observations of Behavior: Some Comments and Cautions

We have previously described a direct observational procedure as a method for obtaining samples of behaviors and settings determined to be clinically important (in relation to diagnosis, design, prognosis, and evaluation), in a naturalistic situation or in an analogue situation that is structured in such a way as to provide information about behaviors and settings comparable to what would have been obtained *in situ* (Mash & Terdal, 1976).

Direct observational methods usually involve the recording of behavior when it occurs; the use of trained and impartial observers who follow clearly specified rules and procedures regarding the timing of observations and their context; the use of previously designated categories that require a minimal degree of inference; and some procedure for assessing reliability (Barrios, 1993; Cone & Foster, 1982; Hartmann, 1982; Reid et al., 1988).

The role ascribed to direct observations of ongoing child behavior as the *sine qua non* of early work in behavioral assessment (Johnson & Bolstad, 1973) was so great that the use of observational procedures became synonymous with the practice of behavioral assessment. Many reports, for example, presented only direct observations of target behavior as a measure of change. The strong and sometimes overzealous emphasis on direct observations as the primary data source in behavioral assessment was probably related to an increased recognition of the need for greater objectivity in clinical child assessment, and to the compatibility of direct and less inferential data sources with the nonmediational focus characterizing earlier behavior therapy approaches. There has, however, been a lessening emphasis on the exclusive use of direct observational procedures, concomitant with the increasing systems orientation in child and family BSA and with the growing recognition of the importance of evaluating cognition and affect in both cognitive-behavioral therapy and assessment (Jacobson, 1985; Kendall, 1991; Wasik, 1984).

The early emphasis in behavioral assessment on direct observational procedures was part of the general reaction against the indirect and often highly inferential assessments characterizing traditional forms of child assessment (Goldfried & Kent, 1972). Parent ratings, personality inventories, children's self-reports, and responses to projective test stimuli or doll play situations, as they were traditionally used to generate inferences regarding emotional conflict and intrapsychic processes, often seemed far removed from the major presenting problems of children and their families.

It has been argued that direct observation is less subject to bias and distortion than are verbal reports from either children or parents and teachers. However, this question cannot really be addressed without considering the informant, the child or family behavior being described, and the context and purposes for assessment. Furthermore, support for this argument comes more from studies demonstrating poor reliability and validity associated with verbal report than from studies directly demonstrating observational data to be accurate and unbiased. In fact, many studies have shown that observed behavior can be readily distorted by biases on the part of both observers and those being observed. For example, Johnson and Lobitz (1974) demonstrated that parents of nonproblem children could make their children look either good or bad when instructed to do so. However, it is possible that some types of problem families may find it difficult to make themselves look good to outside observers. For example, it has been reported that abusive mothers continue to behave in ways considered to be socially undesirable, even when they are being observed (Mash et al., 1983; Reid, Taplin, & Lorber, 1981). Nevertheless, in light of the demand characteristics of most observation situations (e.g., relating to diagnosis of the problem, eligibility for treatment, educational placement, legal adjudication, and evaluation of treatment change), it seems likely that most families will attempt to systematically influence what is being observed.

Although there have been a host of methodological investigations concerned with the issues surrounding the use of observational procedures (Barrios, 1993; Hops & Davis, 1995; Kazdin, 1982a), these studies, taken together, have not been as informative as one would hope. One reason for this is that many of the studies have explored questions concerning bias and reactivity in general, and questions of this nature do not readily address the issues of bias and reactivity under highly specific conditions. Bias and reactivity are likely to vary as a function of the answers to the question "What is being assessed, who is being assessed, by whom, using what methods, for what purposes, and in what situations?"

The preceding comments are not intended to diminish the potential importance of direct observational procedures for the BSA of children and families. Rather, our remarks are intended to caution against the steadfast adherence to direct observation as the preferred method of assessment under all circumstances, in the face of an increasing conceptual emphasis on cognitive and affective variables, contradictory empirical findings related to possible biases and reactivity, the potential unrepresentativeness of observational data, the relativity of assessment purposes, and the many practical concerns and demands associated with the use of observational procedures.

Observational Procedures with Children and Families

Many types of observational procedures have been used to assess children and families. These range from simple single-behavior or single-purpose recording schemes that can be conducted with a minimal amount of observer training, to complex and exhaustive multibehavior–multicontext interaction code systems (e.g., Conger, 1982; Dishion et al., 1984; Hops et al., 1986; Mash et al., 1973; Reid, 1978; Toobert, Patterson, Moore, & Halper, 1982; Wahler et al., 1976) requiring substantial initial and ongoing observer training (Reid, 1982). The factors involved in selecting an appropriate observational procedure are numerous and include the stage of the assessment process, the characteristics of the behaviors of interest, the situation in which observation is to occur, observer characteristics, and technical resources (Mash & Terdal, 1981b).

There are currently several detailed discussions of direct observational procedures and of the methodological and practical issues surrounding their use (e.g., Barrios, 1993; Foster & Cone, 1986; Hartmann, 1982). These issues are concerned with factors influencing the objectivity and reliability of observations, such as code system characteristics (e.g., number, complexity, and molecularity of categories); characteristics of the behaviors being observed (rate and complexity); methods of assessing reliability (e.g., awareness of reliability checks); observer characteristics (e.g., age, sex); methods of calculating reliability; sources of observer and observee bias under a range of conditions; reactivity to being observed; and ways in which observational data should be summarized and interpreted. An extensive discussion of these issues is beyond the scope of this chapter, but a sensitivity to these methodological concerns is a necessary part of any observational assessment of children, because they have a direct bearing on the validity of the findings. A minimally acceptable set of criteria for any observational code would be that it is objective (e.g., two observers will classify behavior in the same way), that it has mutually exclusive subcategories, and that it provides data that are amenable to objective analysis. Given these minimal requirements, a wide range of goals and purposes is possible.

Selecting Code Categories

The use of observational codes requires decisions relating to both the content (e.g., types of catego-ries to include) and the structure (e.g., number of categories, temporal base, mechanics for observing and recording) of the code system (Hawkins, 1982). With regard to content, the selection of particular categories of child and family behavior to observe—either in the construction of one's own code system or in the selection of an already existing code system—presupposes an existing set of hypotheses. Many such implicit hypotheses underlie the existing observational code systems that have been used most often in behavioral assessment. For example, the greater prevalence and range of codes for categorizing child compliance and parental directiveness, relative to codes for children's and parents' affectional responses (e.g., Twardosz & Nordquist, 1983), have followed from and contributed to the development of hypotheses of disturbed family behavior centering around command–compliance sequences (e.g., Patterson, 1982). This is not to say that such hypotheses lack validity and/or utility, but rather that the nature of the existing code systems may favor some assessment outcomes over others. Most of the earlier observational codes for children focused on family interactions to a greater extent than interactions with peers, and for some time this limited our understanding of the importance of peer interactions and the relationships between family and peer group behavior.

For the most part, code selection and observational system construction have been carried out on a rational basis. Consistent with the view of maintaining low levels of inference, the family behaviors observed are often those directly reported as problematic by parents and teachers, or those that fit with the theories or experiences of the assessor. Established code systems, because of their procedural development, availability, and ease of application, may often be utilized inappropriately with particular populations or in situations that differ from those set forth in the initial rationale for construction. We believe that category and code system selection can be improved with greater attention to the parameters associated with the specific populations of families being observed and the settings in which they function. Specialized codes of this nature are provided in the chapters of this volume related to conduct problems, fears and anxieties, autism, and social relationship deficits. The categories included reflect behaviors and setting variables that have been empirically shown to be relevant for the populations under study.

It may also be useful to examine existing code systems in order to identify base rates at which particular categories are used in assessment, and the reasons given for their inclusion or exclusion. Such data are available in the literature but have not, with few exceptions (McIntyre et al., 1983), been systematically examined. In addition, the ways in which similar categories have been defined need further specification. It is not uncommon for similarly labeled behavior categories to be defined in quite different ways (Mash & Dalby, 1979), reflecting the lack of standardization mentioned previously. Such idiosyncratic code construction seems unnecessary and can only contribute to poor communication among assessors. Perhaps a behavior and setting code dictionary that provides standardized categories and definitions relevant to specific child populations and settings will lead to greater consistency in the use of observational procedures (Mash & Barkley, 1986).

Recently there has been greater attention to observations that focus not only on molecular responses, but also on larger, more global units for describing family interaction. Implicit in this trend are the notions (1) that larger response chains have qualitative features of their own, and although molecular codes may not reveal these dimensions, subjective impressions by trained or "culturally sensitive" human observers may; and (2) that global ratings can provide a more efficiently obtained and equivalent integrative summary of the molecular responses. Weiss and Chaffin (1986) compared two marital code systems that were based either on global ratings of communication or on many specific categories, and found that the degree of overlap was moderate. It was pointed out that the two systems might be useful for different purposes, and that in light of the high costs of using complex category systems, the use of more global ratings might be explored. Several researchers have supplemented molecular observations with more global judgments and have found that experienced raters whose global judgments are averaged and composited can often provide reliable and valid indices of psychologically complex behaviors (Moskowitz & Schwarz, 1982; Weinrott, Reid, Bauske, & Brummett, 1981). It would appear that there are both assets and liabilities associated with the use of molar and molecular ratings, and that some combination of the two may be useful (Cairns & Green, 1979). If future empirical work can establish the utility, reliability, and validity of more global ratings for specific purposes, there will clearly be some practical advantage in using these procedures in the clinical context.

Early observational assessments focused both on molecular response units and on frequency, rate, and duration measures. Consistent with the recent interest in more global ratings, there is currently an interest not only in how much and for how long a behavior is seen, but also in the "qualitative" manner in which the behavior is expressed. For example, adult disciplinary reactions seem to be based not simply on the type of child misbehavior, but also on how it is expressed. When noncompliance is accompanied by expressions of overt opposition, such as anger and verbal refusal, stronger parental reactions may occur (Trickett & Kuczynski, 1986). There is currently a need to better define the qualitative features of responding that may influence both judgments and subsequent reactions. Recent work has suggested that the coding of nonverbal cues, such as facial expressions (Gottman & Levenson, 1986); proxemic features, such as how slowly or quickly the response is performed; the prosodic features of language; or the intensity of the behavior (Henker, Astor-Dubin, & Varni, 1986) may all reveal features of the interaction that are not evident from molecular response codes. Other structural aspects of performance, such as latency and duration, may also provide important information. For example, Kotsopoulos and Mellor (1986) examined speech breath and speech latency variables with anxiety-disordered and conduct-disordered children. Children with anxiety disorders showed increased breath rate and lower output of speech per breath, whereas Conduct Disorder was associated with short initial hesitation before speaking, which could reflect an absence of specific cognitive processes such as planning.

There has also been an increased interest in coding the affective qualities of interactions, in part as a result of the many studies that have found relationships between depression and behavior problems in families. Some code systems have superimposed a more subjectively based valence code over the behavioral dimension. It is possible, for example, to code compliant behavior that has either positive or negative accompanying affect (Dishion et al., 1984). Other observational systems code specific affects (e.g., anger, contempt, whining, sadness, or fear) directly (Gottmann & Levenson, 1986), or code *categories* of affect (e.g., aversive, dysphoric, happy, or caring; Hops et al., 1986). The work on affective coding in child and family behavioral assessment is relatively recent, and the empirical findings are sparse. In addition, most of this work has been conducted in a research context, and its direct applicability to clinical assessment and intervention is just being explored. Nevertheless, it would appear that this is a promising trend in the observational assessment of children and families, and one that will probably continue.

Settings for Observation

Following from a situation-specific view of behavior, observational assessments with children have been carried out in a wide range of settings, the most common of which are the clinic, the home, and the classroom (Harris & Reid, 1981; Zangwill & Kniskern, 1982). Other examples of observational settings have included institutional environments, such as group homes for delinquent adolescents, living environments for retarded or autistic children, playgrounds, supermarkets, and children's groups. More specific situations within each of these global settings have also provided structure for observation—for example, free play versus command–compliance instructions in the clinic, or observation at mealtime versus bedtime in the home.

A major concern associated with the choice of observational settings has been the degree of control imposed on the situation by the assessor. Behavioral assessors have previously emphasized the importance of observing in the child and family's natural environment, imposing the least amount of structure as possible, in order to see things "as they typically occur." This emphasis has reflected a reaction against the nonrepresentative and exclusive clinic observations characteristic of many clinical child assessments. Although *in situ* assessment is still recognized as an important part of BSA with children, there has also been an increased recognition that unstructured observations—in the home or preschool, for example—may not always be the most efficient or practical method for obtaining samples of the behaviors of interest.

Observation in natural environments may be especially unrevealing with behaviors that occur at a low rate or that are especially reactive to observation. Many nonstructured family and peer interactions consist of no interactions or low-rate "chatty" exchanges (Mash & Barkley, 1986). For example, in one study of nonproblem families, over one-third of the observations were characterized by mutual noninvolvement of family members (Baskett, 1985). In another study in which dominance and dependent behaviors were observed in the preschool, almost 8 weeks of observation were required in order to obtain generalizable data (Moskowitz & Schwarz, 1982). Such findings would suggest that in some circumstances the use of "evocative" situations, in order to high-

light infrequently occurring response systems, may prove to be a more efficient and reliable assessment strategy than the use of unstructured naturalistic observations.

To make a further point about naturalistic versus structured observations, the assumption that home observations are "natural" and that observations in the clinic or laboratory are "artificial" is an oversimplification. Home observations may at times provide us with artificial reactions to natural conditions, whereas clinic observations may provide us with natural reactions to artificial conditions. Which information is more meaningful depends a great deal on the purpose of the assessment. When cross-setting comparisons of behavior (e.g., home vs. clinic) do not agree, this cannot be assumed to be a function of the unrepresentativeness of behavior in the clinic unless there is some independent verification of the representativeness of the home observation. In most instances there is no such verification, and it is therefore inaccurate to equate representativeness with the naturalness of the physical setting, as is often done.

When home or classroom observations have been neither feasible nor appropriate, a variety of structured laboratory or clinic observation settings for sampling the behaviors of interest can be utilized (Hughes & Haynes, 1978). Such analogue situations have provided a wide range of structures for assessing parent–child behaviors, including free-play interactions between mother and child; various command–compliance situations, such as the mother's having the child clean up or put away play materials, or occupy himself or herself while the mother is busy reading or talking on the telephone; academic task situations; problem-solving situations, such as figuring out how to play a game together; and highly structured observations of the social reinforcement properties or punishment styles of parents. The range of potentially relevant analogue situations to be used in assessment is restricted only by the ingenuity and physical resources of the assessor. The challenge, however, is for systematic assessments of reliability and validity that would permit the use of more standardized and psychometrically well-developed analogues than has been the case to date.

Using and Interpreting Observational Data

Direct observational data are utilized for a number of purposes: They can serve as treatment outcome measures, provide a data base for the construction of theories about childhood disorders, and serve as a basis for making recommendations for treatment. In practice, the last-mentioned use is perhaps the most common but the least understood, because the processes by which direct observations have been translated into clinical recommendations are often poorly defined, unspecified, or oversimplified. For example, the observation of a positive adult response to a negative child behavior (e.g., teacher attention for misbehavior) or of a negative adult response to a positive child behavior (e.g., parental scolding following a child's use of age-appropriate grammatical constructions) may lead to treatment recommendations centering around better contingency management. Alternatively, adult presentation of ambiguous antecedent cues for behavior (e.g., overly complex or vague parental commands) may result in treatments centering around the alteration of stimulus control functions. However, in practice, these types of observation-based treatment recommendations represent informal hypothesis testing rather than systematically or empirically derived outcomes. It is also not clear whether such recommendations represent the fitting of observations to preferred and/or common hypotheses regarding contingencies, or the derivation of hypotheses that are genuinely based upon what has been observed.

Interpretations of observational data have typically followed from summarizations of "child behavior, adult response" sequences over relatively brief time intervals. The pattern of behavior based upon interactional responses in immediately adjacent time intervals is often the focus of interpretations, with the assumption that immediate cues and reactions serve as major controlling events. A mother's reaction to her child's behavior is assumed to follow from the child's response that preceded it. However, the causes for both child and adult behavior may emanate from more remote points in observational sequences than those immediately adjacent in time; there is a need for empirical and conceptual criteria that can be utilized to formulate interpretations of observational data based on stylistic patterns of responding and in relation to more distal controlling events.

A recurrent issue in the use of observational procedures has been that of the costs involved. This has been noted as one factor in the lack of use of observational procedures by behavioral clinicians. However the cost (including "dry runs," observer time, travel costs, and data summarization) of a comprehensive observational assessment can amount to less than the cost of a comprehensive personality assessment (Reid et al., 1988).

Family Assessment Methods

Concomitant with a growing trend toward conceptualizing (Sroufe & Fleeson, 1986) and treating (Alexander & Parsons, 1982; Szykula, 1986) childhood disorders in the context of the family, measures designed to tap family functioning have proliferated. Many of these "family measures" are being incorporated into BSA with children and families (Foster & Robin, Chapter 13, this volume). A myriad of tools have been created for assessing relational problems in the family (Mash & Johnston, 1996a, 1996b). For example, in the *Handbook of Family Measurement Techniques* (Touliatos, Perlmutter, & Straus, 1990), nearly 1,000 instruments are reviewed, and this handbook is currently being revised to include even more measures. For more specific information related to family assessment methods, the reader is referred to (1) the comprehensive volumes on family assessment by Touliatos et al. (1990), Grotevant and Carlson (1989), Jacob and Tennenbaum (1988), McCubbin and Thompson (1987), and Straus and Brown (1978); (2) a review of family rating scales by Carlson and Grotevant (1987); and (3) chapters by Markman and Notarius (1987), Margolin (1987), and Skinner (1987) on direct observations, participant/observer methods, and self-report methods, respectively.

Available family assessment instruments run the gamut of interviews, individual and family-completed self-report questionnaires, projective tasks, and codes for observing family interactions either in naturalistic contexts (e.g., the home) or in structured situations involving family discussions or problem-solving tasks. Many of these measures possess solid psychometric properties and normative information; however, many others have little demonstrated reliability, validity, or utility. One important question is this: What aspect of an assessment method makes it a "family" measure? Family assessment occurs at two levels. At one level, family assessment is a strategy in which information is obtained in order to understand the manner in which different family members relate to themselves and to one another. Information derived from the assessment of an individual family member's behaviors or feelings may be conceptually or empirically aggregated into a statement regarding how the family functions as a whole. This approach reflects the type of orientation that has characterized most BSA applications of family assessment with children and families.

At the second level, family assessment encompasses measures describing the functional or structural organization of the family at a level that is usually higher than that of the individual or dyad. Such views conceptualize families as systems, and attempt to describe the interdependencies, rules, relationships, and interactional processes that serve to regulate the system in the face of ongoing internal and external stressors. Although many assessment procedures have included the word "family" in their title, most have not systematically tapped the kinds of functions characteristic of this view.

Measures designed to assess family dimensions have evolved from several traditions. Without question, the family therapy approaches have provided the richest conceptual base for describing families (Gurman & Kniskern, 1991). A discussion of these approaches is beyond the scope of this chapter; however, many family therapy constructs (e.g., enmeshment, adaptability, cohesion, triangulation, alliances, executive behavior, power locus, etc.) all seem to capture larger units of family functioning than do the molecular recordings that have characterized much of the previous work in child and family behavioral assessment. Nevertheless, these constructs have not been well operationalized, and the methods for assessing them that have been devised by family therapists (see Forman & Hagan, 1984, for a review; Szapocznik, 1984) have not been widely used in BSA.

BSA with families initially focused on specific dyads or observation of interactions when all family members were present. However, few of these studies attempted to describe family interactions in terms that went "beyond the dyad." When family dimensions emerged, these were derived empirically through the use of statistical transformations that tended to support a higher-order process (e.g., coercion). However, these constructs have tended to be more theoretical than practical. For example, although the coercive interchanges of aggressive families have been well described, there is no single measure that can be used to describe the level of coercive process characterizing an entire family.

Another approach to describing family dimensions has evolved out of the developmental literature, with its emphasis on developmental systems and the emergence of early relationships (Hartup, 1986; Kaye, 1984). Much of this work has been with infants and preschoolers, and has focused on such things as communication patterns and the quality of early attachments. Illustrative of the systems approach are those studies that have identified "higher-order" effects—for example, the way in which the behavior of family members may vary with the interpersonal structure

of the interaction setting (e.g., which family members are present). For example, Gjerde (1986) found that the presence of the father enhanced the quality of mother–son relations, whereas the presence of the mother reduced the quality of father–son relations. Also, mothers tended to show more differentiation between boys and girls when their husbands were present, whereas fathers did so when their wives were absent. This study and others like it point up the need to examine family interactions under a wide range of interpersonal contexts, and offer a rich conceptual and empirical base for carrying BSA with families of young children. To date, however, few of the family measures that have been used in developmental investigations have been used extensively to assess children and families in a clinical context.

One of the positive outcomes resulting from the increased interest in family assessment has been a much wider sampling of family subsystems than was previously the case in child and family behavioral assessment. This is especially true of measures designed to describe the marital (e.g., Margolin, 1983; Weiss & Margolin, 1986) and sibling (e.g., Brody & Stoneman, 1983; Mash & Johnston, 1983c) subsystems.

There is a trend toward the integration of some of the more global concepts and measures of families that have evolved from family systems views, and the operational specificity characteristic of BSA (see Foster & Robin, Chapter 13, this volume). For example, Rodick et al. (1986) found that in families with balanced degrees of cohesion and adaptability, the mothers' communication was more supportive and explicit, and the mother–child dyads evidenced significantly greater warmth and affection, than in families with extremes of cohesion and adaptability. This study provides a good example of efforts to operationalize subjectively defined global dimensions of family functioning by relating them to more directly observed empirical referents.

As the assessment focus has shifted toward understanding the dynamic systems in which children and families function, there has also been an increased interest in statistical methods that can be used to adequately describe the complexity of these systems. For example, in describing reciprocal social interaction over time, much recent attention has been given to sequential analysis as a primary data-analytic strategy (e.g., Bakeman & Gottman, 1986; Gottman, 1982; Gottman & Ringland, 1981; Gottman & Roy, 1990; Whitehurst, Fischel, DeBaryshe, Caulfield, & Falco, 1986). Wampold (1986) has described some of the developments in this area as well as some of the difficulties, one of the primary ones being the way in which observations of sequential events can be integrated with more distal occurrences.

Formal Testing with Children

Regardless of whether BSA represents a break from traditional psychometric test approaches or a logical extension of such approaches, as some have suggested (Evans & Nelson, 1977), the fact remains that the use of developmental scales, intelligence and achievement tests (Kaufman & Kaufman, 1983; Nelson, 1980), perceptual–motor tests, and neuropsychological assessments (Fletcher & Taylor, Chapter 9, this volume) with children is common practice among clinicians from a wide range of orientations who work with children and families. The reader is referred to individual chapters in this volume for discussions of the utility of tests in BSA with specific populations of children, and to general resources describing the use of more traditional tests (e.g., Reynolds & Kamphaus, 1990a, 1990b; Sattler, 1992).

SUMMARY

In this introductory chapter, we have described some of the more general issues characterizing the BSA of disturbed children and families. In doing so, we have tried to set the stage for the detailed discussions of the assessment of specific types of childhood disturbances in the chapters that follow. We have presented the view that BSA with children and families is best depicted as a general problem-solving strategy for understanding children's behavior and its determinants. It is a highly empirical approach to clinical child assessment that is based on an understanding of child development, developmental psychopathology, and psychological testing. This problem-solving strategy is carried out in relation to common purposes, follows from a particular set of assumptions about children's behavior and its causes, designates particular behaviors and controlling variables as important, and employs multiple methods and informants.

Recent work in the area has become increasingly systems-oriented and sensitive to developmental parameters. A general theme that has been emphasized in this introduction is that BSA of children and families will be most meaningful when strategies are derived in relation to specific childhood disorders. This theme underlies the chapters that follow.

ACKNOWLEDGMENT

During the writing of this chapter, Eric Mash was supported by a grant from the University of Calgary Research Grants Committee.

REFERENCES

Abidin, R. R. (1983). *Parenting Stress Index*. Charlottesville, VA: Pediatric Psychology Press.
Abidin, R. R. (1995). *Parenting Stress Index: Professional manual* (3rd ed.). Odessa, FL: Psychological Assessment Resources.
Abikoff, H., Gittelman, R., & Klein, D. F. (1980). Classroom observation code for hyperactive children: A replication of validity. *Journal of Consulting and Clinical Psychology*, 555–565.
Achenbach, T. M. (1982). *Developmental psychopathology* (2nd ed.). New York: Wiley.
Achenbach, T. M. (1985). *Assessment and taxonomy of child and adolescent psychopathology*. Beverly Hills, CA: Sage.
Achenbach, T. M. (1991a). *Integrative guide for the 1991 CBCL/4–18, YSR and TRF profiles*. Burlington: University of Vermont, Department of Psychiatry.
Achenbach, T. M. (1991b). *Manual for the Child Behavior Checklist/4–18 and 1991 Profile*. Burlington: University of Vermont, Department of Psychiatry.
Achenbach, T. M. (1991c). *Manual for the Teacher's Report Form and 1991 Profile*. Burlington: University of Vermont, Department of Psychiatry.
Achenbach, T. M. (1991d). *Manual for the Youth Self-Report and 1991 Profile*. Burlington: University of Vermont, Department of Psychiatry.
Achenbach, T. M. (1992). *Manual for the Child Behavior Checklist/2–3 and 1992 Profile*. Burlington: University of Vermont, Department of Psychiatry.
Achenbach, T. M. (1993). *Empirically based taxonomy: How to use syndromes and profile types derived from the CBCL/4–18, TRF, and YSF*. Burlington: University of Vermont, Department of Psychiatry.
Achenbach, T. M. (1995). Diagnosis, assessment, and comorbidity in psychosocial treatment research. *Journal of Abnormal Psychology*, 23, 45–65.
Achenbach, T. M., & Edelbrock, C. S. (1978). The classification of child psychology: A review and analysis of empirical efforts. *Psychological Bulletin*, 85, 1275–1301.
Achenbach, T. M., & Edelbrock, C. S. (1981). Behavioral problems and competencies reported by parents of normal and disturbed children aged four through sixteen. *Monographs of the Society for Research in Child Development*, 46(1, Serial No. 188).
Achenbach, T. M., Howell, C. T., Quay, H. C., & Conners, C. K. (1991). National survey of problems and competencies among four- to sixteen-year-olds. *Monographs of the Society for Research in Child Development*, 56(3, Serial No. 225).

Achenbach, T. M., & McConaughy, S. H. (1985). *Child Interview Checklist—Self-Report Form; Child Interview Checklist—Observation Form.* Burlington: University of Vermont, Department of Psychiatry.

Achenbach, T. M., McConaughy, S. H., & Howell, C. T. (1987). Child/adolescent behavioral and emotional problems: Implications of cross-informant correlations for situational specificity. *Psychological Bulletin, 101,* 213–232.

Adams, H. E., Doster, J. A., & Calhoun, K. S. (1977). A psychologically based system of response classification. In A. R. Ciminero, K. S. Calhoun, & H. E. Adams (Eds.), *Handbook of behavioral assessment* (pp. 47–78). New York: Wiley.

Adelman, H. S. (1995). Clinical psychology: Beyond psychopathology and clinical interventions. *Clinical Psychology: Science and Practice, 2,* 28–44.

Adelman, H. S., & Taylor, L. (1988). Clinical child psychology: Fundamental intervention questions and problems. *Clinical Psychology Review, 8,* 637–665.

Ager, A. (Ed.). (1991). *Microcomputers and clinical psychology: Issues, applications, and further developments.* Chichester: Wiley.

Alexander, J. G., & Parsons, B. V. (1982). *Functional family therapy.* Monterey, CA: Brooks/Cole.

Algozzine, B., Mercer, C. D., & Countermine, T. (1977). The effects of labels and behavior on teacher expectations. *Exceptional Children, 44,* 131–132.

Ambrosini, P. J., Metz, C., Prabucki, K., & Lee, J. (1989). Videotape reliability of the third revised edition of the K-SADS. *Journal of the American Academy of Child and Adolescent Psychiatry, 28,* 723–728.

American Psychiatric Association. (1980). *Diagnostic and statistical manual of mental disorders* (3rd ed.). Washington, DC: Author.

American Psychiatric Association. (1987). *Diagnostic and statistical manual of mental disorders* (3rd ed., rev.). Washington, DC: Author.

American Psychiatric Association. (1994). *Diagnostic and statistical manual of mental disorders* (4th ed.). Washington, DC: Author.

Anastasi, A., & Urbina, S. (1997). *Psychological testing* (7th ed.). Upper Saddle River, NJ : Prentice-Hall.

Ancill, R. J., Carr, A. C., & Rogers, D. (1985). Comparing computerized self-rating scales for depression with conventional observer ratings. *Acta Psychiatrica Scandinavica, 71,* 315–317.

Arkowitz, H. (1979). Behavioral assessment comes of age. *Contemporary Psychology, 24,* 296–297.

Arnold, D. S., & O'Leary, S. G. (1993). The Parenting Scale: A measure of dysfunctional parenting in discipline situations. *Psychological Assessment, 5,* 137–144.

Asher, S. R., Hymel, S., & Renshaw, P. D. (1984). Loneliness in children. *Child Development, 55,* 1456–1464.

Azar, S. T. (1986). A framework for understanding child maltreatment: An integration of cognitive behavioural and developmental perspectives. *Canadian Journal of Behavioural Science, 18,* 340–355.

Azar, S. T., Robinson, D. R., Hekimian, E., & Twentyman, C. T. (1984). Unrealistic expectations and problem-solving ability in maltreating and comparison mothers. *Journal of Consulting and Clinical Psychology, 52,* 687–691.

Bakeman, R., & Gottman, J. M. (1986). *Observing interaction: An introduction to sequential analysis.* New York: Cambridge University Press.

Bandura, A. (1969). *Principles of behavior modification.* New York: Holt, Rinehart & Winston.

Barkley, R. A. (1988). A review of child behavior rating scales and checklists for research in child psychopathology. In M. Rutter, H. Tuma, & I. Lann (Eds.), *Assessment and diagnosis in child psychopathology* (pp. 113–155). New York: Guilford Press.

Barkley, R. A., & Edelbrock, C. (1987). Assessing situational variation in children's behavior problems: The Home and School Situations Questionnaires. In R. Prinz (Ed.), *Advances in behavioral assessment of children and families* (Vol. 3, pp. 157–174). Greenwich, CT: JAI Press.

Barkley, R. A., & Guevremont, D. C. (1992). A comparison of three family therapy programs for treating family conflicts in adolescents with Attention-Deficit Hyperactivity Disorder. *Journal of Consulting and Clinical Psychology, 60,* 450–462.

Barling, J. (1986). Fathers' work experiences, the father–child relationship and children's behaviour. *Journal of Occupational Behaviour, 7,* 61–66.

Barlow, D. H. (Ed.). (1981). *Behavioral assessment of adult disorders.* New York: Guilford Press.

Barlow, D. H. (1986). In defense of Panic Disorder with Agoraphobia and the behavioral treatment of panic: A comment on Kleiner. *The Behavior Therapist, 9,* 99–100.

Barlow, D. H., & Hersen, M. (1984). *Single case experimental designs: Strategies for studying behavior change* (2nd ed.). Elmsford, NY: Pergamon Press.

Barrios, B. A. (1993). Direct observation. In T. H. Ollendick & M. Hersen (Eds.), *Handbook of child and adolescent assessment* (pp. 140–164). Needham Heights, MA: Allyn & Bacon.

Baskett, L. M. (1985). Understanding family interactions: Most probable reactions by parents and siblings. *Child and Family Behavior Therapy, 7,* 41–50.

Beck, A. T., Ward, C. H., Mendelson, M., Mock, J., & Erbaugh, J. (1961). An inventory for measuring depression. *Archives of General Psychiatry, 4,* 53–63.

Bell, R. Q., & Harper, L. V. (1977). *Child effects on adults.* Hillsdale, NJ: Erlbaum.

Bellack, A. S., & Hersen, M. (1988). *Behavioral assessment: A practical handbook* (3rd ed.). Elmsford, NY: Pergamon Press.

Belsky, J. (1981). Early human experience: A family perspective. *Developmental Psychology, 17*, 3–23.

Belsky, J., Lerner, R. M., & Spanier, G. B. (1984). *The child in the family.* New York: Random House.

Bem, D. M., & Funder, D. C. (1978). Predicting more of the people more of the time: Assessing the personality of situations. *Psychological Review, 85*, 485–501.

Bernal, M. E., & North, J. (1978). A survey of parent training manuals. *Journal of Applied Behavior Analysis, 11*, 533–544.

Bersoff, D. N., & Grieger, R. M. (1971). An interview model for the psychosituational assessment of children's behavior. *American Journal of Orthopsychiatry, 41*, 483–493.

Bierman, K. L. (1983). Cognitive development and clinical interviews with children. In B. B. Lahey & A. E. Kazdin (Eds.), *Advances in clinical child psychology* (Vol. 6, pp. 217–250). New York: Plenum Press.

Bierman, K. L., & McCauley, E. (1987). Children's descriptions of their peer interactions: Useful information for clinical child assessment. *Journal of Clinical Child Psychology, 16*, 9–18.

Bierman, K. L., & Schwartz, L. A. (1986). Clinical child interviews: Approaches and developmental considerations. *Journal of Child and Adolescent Psychotherapy, 3*, 267–278.

Bijou, S. W., & Peterson, R. F. (1971). Functional analysis in the assessment of children. In P. McReynolds (Ed.), *Advances in psychological assessment* (Vol. 2). Palo Alto, CA: Science & Behavior Books.

Billings, A. G., & Moos, R. H. (1986). Children of parents with unipolar depression: A controlled l-year follow-up. *Journal of Abnormal Child Psychology, 14*, 149–166.

Blechman, E. A. (1985). *Solving child behavior problems at home and school.* Champaign, IL: Research Press.

Bornstein, P. H., Bornstein, M. T., & Dawson, B. (1984). Integrated assessment and treatment. In T. H. Ollendick & M. Hersen (Eds.), *Child behavioral assessment: Principles and procedures* (pp. 223–243). Elmsford, NY: Pergamon Press.

Bornstein, P. H., Hamilton, S. B., & Bornstein, M. (1986). Self-monitoring procedures. In A. R. Ciminero, K. S. Calhoun, & H. E. Adams (Eds.), *Handbook of behavioral assessment* (2nd ed., pp. 176–222). New York: Wiley.

Bradbury, T. N., & Fincham, F. D. (1987). Affect and cognition in close relationships: Towards an integrative model. *Cognition and Emotion, 1*, 59–87.

Bristol, M. M. (1983a). The Belief Scale. In M. Bristol, A. Donovan, & A. Harding (Eds.), *The broader impact of intervention: A workshop on measuring stress and support.* Chapel Hill, NC: Frank Porter Graham Child Development Center.

Bristol, M. M. (1983b). Carolina Parent Support Scale. In M. Bristol, A. Donovan, & A. Harding (Eds.), *The broader impact of intervention: A workshop on measuring stress and support.* Chapel Hill, NC: Frank Porter Graham Child Development Center.

Broden, M., Hall, R. V., & Mitts, B. (1971). The effect of self-recording on the classroom behavior of two eighth grade students. *Journal of Applied Behavior Analysis, 4*, 191–199.

Brody, G. H., Pellegrini, A. D., & Sigel, I. E. (1986). Marital quality and mother–child and father–child interactions with school aged children. *Developmental Psychology, 22*, 291–296.

Brody, G. H., & Stoneman, Z. (1983). Children with atypical siblings: Socialization outcomes and clinical participation. In B. B. Lahey & A. E. Kazdin (Eds.), *Advances in clinical child psychology* (Vol. 6, pp. 285–325). New York: Plenum Press.

Bromfield, R., Weisz, J. R., & Messer, I. (1986). Children's judgments and attributions in response to the "mentally retarded" label: A developmental approach. *Journal of Abnormal Psychology, 95*, 81–87.

Bronfenbrenner, U. (1979). *The ecology of human development: Experiments by nature and design.* Cambridge, CA: Harvard University Press.

Bronfenbrenner, U. (1986). Ecology of the family as a context for human development: Research perspectives. *Developmental Psychology, 22*, 723–742.

Bugental, D. B. (1993). Communication in abusive relationships: Cognitive constructions of interpersonal power. *American Behavioral Scientist, 36*, 288–308.

Bugental, D. B., Whalen, C. K., & Henker, B. (1977). Causal attributions of hyperactive children and motivational assumptions of two behavior-change approaches: Evidence for an interactionist position. *Child Development, 48*, 874–884.

Bullock, D., MacPhee, C., & Benson, J. B. (1984). *Behavior Checklist for Infants and Toddlers.* Unpublished manuscript, University of Denver.

Butcher, J. N., Williams, C. L., Graham, J. R., Archer, R. P., Tellegen, A., Ben-Porath, Y. S., & Kaemmer, B. (1992). *MMPI-A, Minnesota Multiphasic Personality Inventory—Adolescent: Manual for administration, scoring, and interpretation.* Minneapolis: University of Minnesota Press.

Butler, R. J., Brewin, C. R., & Forsythe, W. I. (1986). Maternal attributions and tolerance for nocturnal enuresis. *Behaviour Research and Therapy, 24*, 307–312.

Cairns, R. B., & Green, J. A. (1979). How to assess personality and social patterns: Observations or ratings? In R. B. Cairns (Ed.), *The analysis of social interactions: Methods, issues and illustrations* (pp. 209–226). Hillsdale, NJ: Erlbaum.

Cantor, N. (1982). "Everyday" versus normative models of clinical and social judgment. In G. Weary & H. L. Mirels (Eds.), *Integrations of clinical and social psychology* (pp. 27–47). New York: Oxford University Press.

Cantor, N., Smith, E. E., French, R. deS., & Mezzich, J. (1980). Psychiatric diagnosis as prototype categorization. *Journal of Abnormal Psychology, 89,* 181–193.

Carlson, C. I., & Grotevant, H. D. (1987). A comparative review of family rating scales: Guidelines for clinicians and researchers. *Journal of Family Psychology, 1,* 23–47.

Caron, C., & Rutter, M. (1991). Comorbidity in child psychopathology: Concepts, issues, and research strategies. *Journal of Child Psychology and Psychiatry, 32,* 1063–1080.

Carr, A. C., & Ghosh, A. (1983). Accuracy of behavioural assessment by computer. *British Journal of Psychiatry, 142,* 66–70.

Carr, E. G. (1994). Emerging themes in the functional analysis of problem behavior. *Journal of Applied Behavior Analysis, 27,* 393–399.

Carver, R. P. (1974). Two dimensions of tests: Psychometric and edumetric. *American Psychologist, 29,* 512–518.

Castenada, A., McCandless, B., & Palermo, D. (1956). The children's form of the Manifest Anxiety Scale. *Child Development, 27,* 317–326.

Cattell, R. B. (1983). Let's end the duel. *American Psychologist, 38,* 769–776.

Cautela, J. R., Cautela, J., & Esonis, S. (1983). *Forms for behavior analysis with children.* Champaign, IL: Research Press.

Cerreto, M. C., & Tuma, J. M. (1977). Distribution of DSM-II diagnoses in a child psychiatric setting. *Journal of Abnormal Child Psychology, 5,* 147–153.

Chambers, W. J., Puig-Antich, J., Hirsch, M., Paez, P., Ambrosini, P. J., Tabrizi, M. A., & Davies, M. (1985). The assessment of affective disorders in children and adolescents by semi-structured interview: Test–retest reliability of the Schedule for Affective Disorders and Schiophrenia for School-Age Children, Present Episode Version. *Archives of General Psychiatry, 42,* 696–702.

Chlopan, B. E., McBain, M. L., Carbonell, J. L., & Hagen, R. L. (1985). Empathy: Review of available measures. *Journal of Personality and Social Psychology, 48,* 635–653.

Cicchetti, D. (1996). Editorial: Regulatory processes in development and psychopathology. *Development and Psychopathology, 8,* 1–2.

Cicchetti, D., & Cohen, D. J. (1995a). *Developmental psychopathology: Vol. 1. Theory and methods.* New York: Wiley–Interscience.

Cicchetti, D., & Cohen, D. J. (1995b). *Developmental psychopathology: Vol. 2. Risk, disorder, and adaptation.* New York: Wiley–Interscience.

Cicchetti, D., & Rizley, R. (1981). Developmental perspectives on the etiology, intergenerational transmission, and sequelae of child maltreatment. In D. Cicchetti & R. Rizley (Eds.), *New Directions for Child Development: No. 11. Developmental perspectives on child maltreatment* (pp. 31–55). San Francisco: Jossey-Bass.

Ciminero, A. R., Calhoun, K. S., & Adams, H. E. (Eds.). (1986). *Handbook of behavioral assessment* (2nd ed.). New York: Wiley.

Ciminero, A. R., & Drabman, R. S. (1977). Current developments in the behavioral assessment of children. In B. B. Lahey & A. E. Kazdin (Eds.), *Advances in clinical child psychology* (Vol. 1, pp. 47–82). New York: Plenum Press.

Clement, P. W. (1996). Evaluation in private practice. *Clinical Psychology: Science and Practice, 3,* 146–159.

Clement, P. W., & Richard, R. C. (1976). Identifying reinforces for children: A Children's Reinforcement Survey. In E. J. Mash & L. G. Terdal (Eds.), *Behavior therapy assessment; Diagnosis, design, and evaluation* (pp. 207–216). New York: Springer.

Coie, J. D., & Pennington, B. F. (1976). Children's perceptions of deviance and disorder. *Child Development, 47,* 407–413.

Collins, F. L., & Thompson, J. K. (1993). The integration of empirically derived personality assessment data into a behavioral conceptualization and treatment plan: Rationale, guidelines, and caveats. *Behavior Modification, 17,* 58–71.

Compas, B. E., Friedland-Bandes, R., Bastien, R., & Adelman, H. S. (1981). Parent and child causal attributions related to the child's clinical problem. *Journal of Abnormal Child Psychology, 9,* 389–397.

Cone, J. D. (1977). The relevance of reliability and validity for behavioral assessment. *Behavior Therapy, 8,* 411–426.

Cone, J. D. (1978). The Behavioral Assessment Grid (BAG): A conceptual framework and a taxonomy. *Behavior Therapy, 9,* 882–888.

Cone, J. D. (1979). Confounded comparisons in triple response mode assessment research. *Behavioral Assessment, 1,* 85–95.

Cone, J. D. (1981). Psychometric considerations. In M. Hersen & A. S. Bellack (Eds.), *Behavioral assessment: A practical handbook* (2nd ed., pp. 38–68). Elmsford, NY: Pergamon Press.

Cone, J. D. (1987). Behavioral assessment with children and adolescents. In M. Hersen & V. B. Van Hasselt (Eds.), *Behavior therapy with children and adolescents: A clinical approach* (pp. 29–49). New York: Wiley.

Cone, J. D. (1993). The current state of behavioral assessment. *European Journal of Psychological Assessment, 9,* 175–181.

Cone, J. D., & Foster, S. L. (1982). Direct observation in clinical psychology. In P. C. Kendall & J. N. Butcher (Eds.), *Handbook of research methods in clinical psychology* (pp. 311–354). New York: Wiley.

Cone, J. D., & Hawkins, R. P. (Eds.). (1977). *Behavior assessment: New directions in clinical psychology.* New York: Brunner/Mazel.

Cone, J. D., & Hoier, T. S. (1986). Assessing children: The radical behavioral perspective. In R. J. Prinz

(Ed.), *Advances in behavioral assessment of children and families* (Vol. 2, pp. 1–27). Greenwich, CT: JAI Press.

Conger, R. D. (1982). *Social interactional scoring system: Observer training manual.* Unpublished manuscript, University of Illinois.

Connell, J. P., & Tanaka, J. S. (Eds.). (1987). Special section on structural equation modeling. *Child Development, 58,* 1–175.

Conners, C. K. (1990). *Conners Rating Scales.* North Tonawanda, NY: Multi-Health Systems.

Coopersmith, S. (1967). *The antecedents of self-esteem.* San Francisco: W. H. Freeman.

Costello, A. J. (1986). Assessment and diagnosis of affective disorders in children. *Journal of Child Psychology and Psychiatry, 27,* 565–574.

Cotterell, J. L. (1986). Work and community influences on the quality of child rearing. *Child Development, 57,* 362–371.

Cowen, E. L., Huser, J., Beach, D. R., & Rappaport, J. (1970). Parental perceptions of young children and their relation to indexes of adjustment. *Journal of Consulting and Clinical Psychology, 34,* 97–103.

Cowen, E. L., Pederson, A., Babigian, H., Izzo, L. D., & Trost, M. A. (1973). Long-term follow-up of early detected vulnerable children. *Journal of Consulting and Clinical Psychology, 41,* 438–445.

Crick, N. R., & Dodge, K. A. (1994). A review and reformation of social information-processing mechanisms in children's social adjustment. *Psychological Bulletin, 115,* 73–101.

Crnic, K. A., & Greenberg, K. (1983). *Inventory of Parent Experiences: Manual.* Unpublished manuscript, University of Washington.

Cronbach, L. J. (1990). *Essentials of psychological testing* (5th ed.). New York: Harper & Row.

Cummings, E. M., & Davies, P. T. (1995). The impact of parents on their children: An emotional security perspective. *Annals of Child Development, 10,* 167–208.

D'Antonio, W. V., & Aldous, J. (Eds.). (1983). *Families and religions: Conflict and change in modern society.* Beverly Hills, CA: Sage.

Dawson, G., & Hessl, D. (1994). Social influences of early developing biological and behavioral systems related to risk for affective disorder. *Development and Psychopathology, 6,* 759–779.

Deluty, R. H. (1979). Children's Action Tendency Scale: A self-report measure of aggressiveness, assertiveness, and submissiveness in children. *Journal of Consulting and Clinical Psychology, 47,* 1061–1071.

Derby, K. M., & Wacker, D. P. (1994). Functional analysis of separate topographies of aberrant behavior. *Journal of Applied Behavior Analysis, 27,* 267–278.

Disbrow, M., & Doerr, H. (1983). *Parent–child interaction videotapes.* Unpublished material, University of Washington.

Dishion, T., Gardner, K., Patterson, G. R., Reid, J., Spyrou, S., & Thibodeaux, S. (1984). *The Family Process Code: A multidimensional system for observing family interactions.* Unpublished manual, Oregon Social Learning Center, Eugene.

Dix, T. (1991). The affective organization of parenting: Adaptive and maladaptive processes. *Psychological Bulletin, 110,* 3–25.

Dix, T. (1993). Attributing dispositions to children: An interactional analysis of attribution in socialization. *Personality and Social Psychology Bulletin, 19,* 633–643.

Dix, T., & Grusec, J. E. (1985). Parent attribution processes in the socialization of children. In I. Sigel (Ed.), *Parental belief systems: The psychological consequences for children* (pp. 201–233). Hillsdale, NJ: Erlbaum.

Dix, T., & Lochman, J. E. (1990). Social cognition and negative reactions to children: A comparison of mothers of aggressive and nonaggressive boys. *Journal of Social and Clinical Psychology, 9,* 418–438.

Dix, T., & Reinhold, D. P. (1990). Mothers' judgment in moments of anger. *Merrill–Palmer Quarterly, 36,* 465–486.

Dix, T., & Ruble, D. N. (1989). Mothers' implicit theories of discipline: Child effects, parent effects, and the attribution process. *Child Development, 60,* 1373–1391.

Dix, T., Ruble, D. N., Grusec, J. E., & Nixon, S. (1986). Social cognition in parents: Inferential and affective reactions to children of three age levels. *Child Development, 57,* 879–894.

Dodge, K. A., McClaskey, C. L., & Feldman, E. (1985). Situational approach to the assessment of social competence in children. *Journal of Consulting and Clinical Psychology, 53,* 344–353.

Dollinger, S. J., Thelan, M. H., & Walsh, M. L. (1980). Children's conceptions of psychological problems. *Journal of Clinical Child Psychology, 9,* 191–194.

Douglas, V. I., & Parry, P. A. (1994). Effects of reward and nonreward on frustration and attention in Attention Deficit Disorder. *Journal of Abnormal Child Psychology, 22,* 281–302.

Dow, M. G., Kearns, W., & Thornton, D. H. (1996). The Internet II: Future effects on cognitive behavioral practice. *Cognitive and Behavioral Practice, 3,* 137–157.

Dreger, R. M., Lewis, P. M., Rich, T. A., Miller, K. S., Reid, M. P., Overlade, D. C., Taffel, C., & Flemming, E. L. (1964). Behavioral classification project. *Journal of Consulting Psychology, 28,* 1–13.

Dumas, J. E. (1986). Indirect influence of maternal social contacts on mother–child interactions. *Journal of Abnormal Child Psychology, 14,* 205–216.

Dumas, J. E., & Wahler, R. G. (1983). Predictors of treatment outcome in parent training: Mother insularity and socioeconomic disadvantage. *Behavioral Assessment, 5,* 301–313.

Duncan, G. J., Brooks-Gunn, J., & Klebanov, P. K. (1994). Economic deprivation and early-childhood development. *Child Development, 65*, 296–318.

Dunn, J., & Munn, P. (1986). Sibling quarrels and maternal intervention: Individual differences in understanding and aggression. *Journal of Child Psychology and Psychiatry, 27*, 583–597.

Dunst, C. J. (1984). *Parent–Child Interaction Rating Scale.* Unpublished manuscript, Western Carolina Center, Morganton, NC.

Dunst, C. J., Jenkins, V., & Trivette, C. M. (1984). The Family Support Scale: Reliability and validity. *Journal of Individual, Family, and Community Wellness, 1*, 45–52.

Dunst, C. J., & Trivette, C. M. (1985). *A guide to measures of social support and family behavior* (Monograph of the Technical Assistance Development System, No. 1). Chapel Hill: University of North Carolina, Technical Assistance Development System.

Dunst, C. J., & Trivette, C. M. (1986). Looking beyond the parent–child dyad for the determinants of maternal styles of interaction. *Infant Mental Health Journal, 7*, 69–80.

Edelbrock, C. (1984). Developmental considerations. In T. H. Ollendick & M. Hersen (Eds.), *Child behavioral assessment: Principles and procedures* (pp. 20–37). Elmsford, NY: Pergamon Press.

Edelbrock, C., & Achenbach, T. M. (1985). *Manual for the Teacher's Report Form and Teacher Version of the Child Behavior Profile.* Burlington: University of Vermont, Department of Psychiatry.

Edelbrock, C., & Costello, A. J. (1990). Structured inteviews for children and adolescents. In G. Goldstein & M. Hersen (Eds.), *Handbook of psychological assessment* (2nd ed., pp. 308–323). Elmsford, NY: Pergamon Press.

Edelbrock, C., Costello, A. J., Dulcan, M. J., Conover, N. C., & Kalas, R. (1986). Parent–child agreement of child psychiatric symptoms assessed via structured interview. *Journal of Child Psychology and Psychiatry, 27*, 181–190.

Edelbrock, C., Costello, A. J., Dulcan, M. J., Kalas, R., & Conover, N. C. (1985). Age differences in the reliability of the psychiatric interview of the child. *Child Development, 56*, 265–275.

Egeland, B., & Sroufe, L. A. (1981). Attachment and early maltreatment. *Child Development, 52*, 44–52.

Elbert, J. C. (1985a). Current trends and future needs in the training of child diagnostic assessment. In J. M. Tuma (Ed.), *Proceedings: Conference on training clinical child psychologists* (pp. 82–87). Baton Rouge: Louisiana State University, Department of Psychology.

Elbert, J. C. (1985b). Training in child diagnostic assessment. A survey of clinical psychology graduate programs. *Journal of Clinical Child Psychology, 13*, 122–133.

Ellis, D., & DeKeseredy, W. (1994, March). *Pre-test report on the frequency, severity, and patterning of sibling violence in Canadian families: Causes and consequences.* Report to Family Violence Prevention Division, Health Canada, LaMarsh Centre on Violence & Conflict Resolution, North York, Ontario, Canada.

Elliott, A. J., Miltenberger, R. G., Kaster-Bundgaard, J., & Lumley, V. (1996). A national survey of assessment and therapy techniques used by behavior therapists. *Cognitive and Behavioral Practice, 3*, 107–125.

Eme, R. F. (1979). Sex differences in childhood psychopathology: A review. *Psychological Bulletin, 86*, 574–595.

Emery, R. E. (1982). Interparental conflict and the children of discord and divorce. *Psychological Bulletin, 92*, 310–330.

Emery, R. E., Binkoff, J. A., Houts, A. C., & Carr, E. G. (1983). Children as independent variables: Some clinical implications of child effects. *Behavior Therapy, 14*, 398–412.

Endler, N. S., & Magnusson, D. (Eds.). (1976). *Interactional psychology and personality.* Washington, DC: Hemisphere.

Evans, I. M. (1985). Building systems models as a strategy for target behavior selection in clinical assessment. *Behavioral Assessment, 7*, 21–32.

Evans, I. M., & Meyer, L. H. (1985). *An educative approach to behavior problems: A practical decision model for interventions with severely handicapped learners.* Baltimore: Paul H. Brookes.

Evans, I. M., & Nelson, R. O. (1977). Assessment of child behavior problems. In A. R. Ciminero, K. S. Calhoun, & H. E. Adams (Eds.), *Handbook of behavioral assessment* (pp. 603–681). New York: Wiley.

Evans, I. M., & Nelson, R. O. (1986). Assessment of children. In A. R. Ciminero, K. S. Calhoun, & H. E. Adams (Eds.), *Handbook of behavioral assessment* (2nd ed., pp. 601–630). New York: Wiley.

Eysenck, H. J., & Rachman, S. (1965). *The causes and cures of neurosis.* London: Routledge & Kegan Paul.

Farrell, A. D. (1991). Computers and behavioral assessment: Current applications, future possibilities, and obstacles to routine use. *Behavioral Assessment, 13*, 159–179.

Fauber, R. L., & Kendall, P.C. (1992). Children and families: Integrating the focus of interventions. *Journal of Psychotherapy Integration, 2*, 107–123.

Fernald, C. D., & Gettys, L. (1978, August). *Effects of diagnostic labels or perceptions of children's behavior disorders.* Paper presented at the annual meeting of the American Psychological Association, Toronto.

Ferster, C. B. (1965). Classification of behavioral pathology. In L. Krasner & L. P. Ullmann (Eds.), *Research in behavior modification: New developments and implications* (pp. 6–26). New York: Holt, Rinehart & Winston.

Ferster, C. B., & Skinner, B. F. (1953). *Schedules of reinforcement.* New York: Appleton-Century-Crofts.

Feshbach, N. (1989). *The construct of empathy and the phenomenon of physical maltreatment of children.* In D. Cicchetti & V. Carlson (Eds.), *Child maltreatment: Theory and research on the causes and consequences of child abuse and neglect* (pp. 349–373). Cambridge: Cambridge University Press.

Filsinger, E. E., & Lewis, R. A. (Eds.). (1981). *Assessing marriage: New behavioral approaches.* Beverly Hills, CA: Sage.

Finkelhor, D., & Associates. (1986). *A sourcebook on child sexual abuse.* Beverly Hills, CA: Sage.

Flanagan, R. (1986). Teaching young children responses to inappropriate approaches by strangers in public places. *Child and Family Behavior Therapy, 8,* 27–43.

Follette, W. C., & Hayes, S. C. (1992). Behavioral assessment in the DSM era. *Behavioral Assessment, 14,* 293–295.

Ford, J. D., & Kendall, P. C. (1979). Behavior therapists' professional behaviors: Converging evidence for a gap between theory and practice. *The Behavior Therapist, 2,* 37–38.

Forehand, R. (1977). Child noncompliance to parental requests: Behavioral analysis and treatment. In M. Hersen, R. M. Eisler, & P. M. Miller (Eds.), *Progress in behavior modification* (Vol. 5, pp. 111–147). New York: Academic Press.

Forehand, R., Fauber, R., Long, N., Brody, G. H., & Slotkin, J. (1986). *Maternal depressive mood following divorce: An examination of predictors and adolescent adjustment from a stress model perspective.* Unpublished manuscript, University of Georgia.

Forehand, R., & Kotchick, B. A. (1996). Cultural diversity: A wake-up call for parent training. *Behavior Therapy, 27,* 171–186.

Forehand, R., Long, N., Brody, G. H., & Fauber, R. (1986). Home predictors of young adolescents' school behavior and academic performance. *Child Development, 57,* 1528–1533.

Forehand, R., & McMahon, R. J. (1981). *Helping the noncompliant child: A clinician's guide to parent training.* New York: Guilford Press.

Forman, B. D., & Hagan, B. J. (1984). Measures for evaluating total family functioning. *Family Therapy, 11,* 1–36.

Foster, G. G., Ysseldyke, J. E., & Reese, J. H. (1975). I wouldn't have seen it, if I hadn't believed it. *Exceptional Children, 41,* 469–473.

Foster, S. L., & Cone, J. D. (1986). Design and use of direct observation procedures. In A. R. Ciminero, K. S. Calhoun, & H. E. Adams (Eds.), *Handbook of behavioral assessment* (2nd ed., pp. 253–324). New York: Wiley.

Foster, S. L., & Martinez, C. R., Jr. (1995). Ethnicity: Conceptual and methodological issues in child clinical research. *Journal of Clinical Child Psychology, 24,* 214–226.

Freeman, B. J., & Schroth, P. C. (1984). The development of the Behavioral Observation System (BOS) for autism. *Behavioral Assessment, 6,* 177–187.

Frick, P. J., & Hare, R. (in press). *The Psychopathy Screening Device—PSD.* Toronto: Multi-health Systems.

Frick, P. J., Lahey, B. B., Loeber, R., Stouthamer-Loeber, M., Christ, M. A. G., & Hanson, K. (1992). Familial risk factors to Oppositional Defiant Disorder and Conduct Disorder: Parental psychopathology and maternal parenting. *Journal of Consulting and Clinical Psychology, 60,* 49–55.

Friedlander, S., Weiss, D. S., & Traylor, J. (1986). Assessing the influence of maternal depression on the validity of the Child Behavior Checklist. *Journal of Abnormal Child Psychology, 14,* 123–133.

Friedrich, W. N. (1979). Predictors of the coping behavior of mothers of handicapped children. *Journal of Consulting and Clinical Psychology, 57,* 1140–1141.

Furman, W., & Buhrmester, D. (1985a). Children's perceptions of the personal relationships in their social networks. *Developmental Psychology, 21,* 1016–1024.

Furman, W., & Buhrmester, D. (1985b). Children's perceptions of the qualities of sibling relationships. *Child Development, 56,* 448–461.

Furman, W., & Drabman, R. (1981). Methodological issues in child behavior therapy. In M. Hersen, R. M. Eisler, & P.M. Miller (Eds.), *Progress in behavior modification* (Vol. 11, pp. 31–64). New York: Academic Press.

Garber, J. (1984). Classification of child psychopathology: A developmental perspective. *Child Development, 55,* 30–48.

Gdowski, C. L., Lachar, D., & Kline, R. B. (1985). A PIC profile typology of children and adolescents: I. Empirically derived alternative to traditional diagnosis. *Journal of Abnormal Psychology, 91,* 346–361.

Gelfand, D. M., & Hartmann, D. P. (1984). *Child behavior analysis and therapy* (2nd ed.). Elmsford, NY: Pergamon Press.

Geller, J., & Johnston, C. (1995). Predictors of mothers' responses to child noncompliance: Attributions and attitudes. *Journal of Clinical Child Psychology, 24,* 272–278.

Gibaud-Wallston, J., & Wandersman, L. P. (1978, August). *Development and utility of the Parenting Sense of Competence Scale.* Paper presented at the meeting of the American Psychological Association, Toronto.

Gilliam, J. E. (1995). *Gilliam Autism Rating Scale examiner's manual.* Austin, TX: Pro-Ed.

Gjerde, P. F. (1986). The interpersonal structure of family interaction settings: Parent–adolescent relations in dyads versus triads. *Developmental Psychology, 22,* 297–304.

Goldfried, M. R., & Kent, R. N. (1972). Traditional versus behavioral assessment: A comparison of methodological and theoretical assumptions. *Psychological Bulletin, 77,* 409–420.

Goldman, H. H., & Skodal, A. E. (1992). Revising Axis V for DSM-IV: A review of measures of social functioning. *American Journal of Psychiatry, 149,* 1148–1156.

Goldsmith, H. H., & Campos, J. J. (1986). Fundamental issues in the study of early temperament: The Denver Twin Temperament Study. In M. E. Lamb, A. L. Brown, & B. Rogoff (Eds.), *Advances in developmental psychology* (Vol. 4, pp. 231–283). Hillsdale, NJ: Erlbaum.

Goldstein, A. P., Keller, H., & Erne, D. (1985). *Changing the abusive parent.* Champaign, IL: Research Press.

Goldstein, G., & Hersen, M. (1990). *Handbook of psychological assessment* (2nd ed.). Elmsford, NY: Pergamon Press.

Gordon, D. A., Jones, R. H., & Nowicki, S. (1979). A measure of intensity of parental punishment. *Journal of Personality Assessment, 43,* 485–496.

Gorham, K. A., DesJardins, C., Page, R., Pettis, E., & Scheiber, B. (1975). Effect on parents. In N. Hobbs (Ed.), *Issues in the classification of children* (Vol. 2, pp. 154–188). San Francisco: Jossey-Bass.

Gottman, J. M. (Ed.). (1995). *The analysis of change.* Hillsdale, NJ: Erlbaum.

Gottman, J. M. (1982). *Time-series analysis: A comprehensive introduction for social scientists.* New York: Cambridge University Press.

Gottman, J. M., Katz, L. F., & Hooven, C. (1996). Parental meta-emotion philosophy and the emotional life of families: Theoretical models and preliminary data. *Journal of Family Psychology, 10,* 243–268.

Gottman, J. M., & Levenson, R. W. (1985). A valid procedure for obtaining self-report of affect in marital interaction. *Journal of Consulting and Clinical Psychology, 53,* 151–160.

Gottman, J. M., & Levenson, R. W. (1986). Assessing the role of emotion in marriage. *Behavioral Assessment, 8,* 31–48.

Gottman, J. M., & Ringland, J. T. (1981). The analysis of dominance and bidirectionality in social development. *Child Development, 52,* 393–412.

Gottman, J., & Roy, A. (1990). *Sequential analysis: A guide for behavioral researchers.* New York: Cambridge University Press.

Gottman, J., & Rush, R. H. (1993). The analysis of change: Issues, fallacies, and new ideas. *Journal of Consulting and Clinical Psychology, 61,* 907–910.

Greenspan, S. I. (1981). *The clinical interview of the child.* New York: McGraw-Hill.

Greenspan, S. I., & Lourie, R. S. (1981). Developmental structuralist approach to the classification of adaptive and pathologic personality organizations: Infancy and early childhood. *American Journal of Psychiatry, 138,* 725–735.

Greenspan, S. I., & Porges, S. W. (1984). Psychopathology in infancy and early childhood: Clinical perspectives on the organization of sensory and affective thematic experience. *Child Development, 55,* 49–70.

Greenwood, C. R., Delquadri, J. C., Stanley, S. O., Terry, B., & Hall, R. V. (1985). Assessment of ecobehavioral interaction in school settings. *Behavioral Assessment, 7,* 331–348.

Gross, A. M. (1984). Behavioral interviewing. In T. H. Ollendick & M. Hersen (Eds.), *Child behavioral assessment: Principles and procedures* (pp. 61–79). Elmsford, NY: Pergamon Press.

Gross, A. M., & Drabman, R. S. (1990). *Handbook of clinical behavioral pediatrics.* New York: Plenum Press.

Grotevant, H. D., & Carlson, C. I. (1989). *Family assessment: A guide to methods and measures.* New York: Guilford Press.

Group for the Advancement of Psychiatry. (1974). *Psychopathological disorders in childhood: Theoretical considerations and a proposed classification.* New York: Jason Aronson.

Grusec, J. E., & Kuczynski, L. (1980). Direction of effect in socialization: A comparison of the parent's versus the child's behavior as determinants of disciplinary techniques. *Developmental Psychology, 16,* 1–9.

Guidubaldi, J., & Cleminshaw, H. K. (1985). The development of the Cleminshaw–Guidubaldi Parent Satisfaction Scale. *Journal of Clinical Child Psychology, 14,* 293–298.

Gurman, A. S., & Kniskern, D. P. (Eds.). (1991). *Handbook of family therapy* (Vol. 2). New York: Brunner/Mazel.

Guskin, S. L., Bartel, N. R., & MacMillan, D. L. (1975). Perspective of the labeled child. In N. Hobbs (Ed.), *Issues in the classification of children* (Vol. 2, pp. 185–212). San Francisco: Jossey-Bass.

Hammen, C. L. (1991). *Depression runs in families: The social context of risk and resilience in children of depressed mothers.* New York: Springer-Verlag.

Harding, J., & Wacker, D. P. (1994). Brief hierarchical assessment of potential treatment components with children in an outpatient clinic. *Journal of Applied Behavior Analysis, 27,* 291–300.

Harris, A. M., & Reid, J. B. (1981). The consistency of a class of coercive child behavior across school settings for individual subjects. *Journal of Abnormal Child Psychology, 9,* 219–227.

Harris, S. L. (1984). The family of the autistic child: A behavioral systems view. *Clinical Psychology Review, 4,* 227–239.

Harris, S. L., & Ferrari, M. (1983). Developmental factors in child behavior therapy. *Behavior Therapy, 14,* 54–72.

Harris, S. L., & Powers, M. D. (1984). Diagnostic issues. In T. H. Ollendick & M. Hersen (Eds.), *Child behavioral assessment: Principles and procedures* (pp. 38–57). Elmsford, NY: Pergamon Press.

Harter, S. (1982). The Perceived Competence Scale for Children. *Child Development, 53,* 87–97.

Harter, S. (1983). Developmental perspectives on the self-system. In E. M. Hetherington (Vol. Ed.), *Handbook of child psychology* (4th ed.): Vol. 4. *Socialization, personality, and social development* (pp. 275–386). New York: Wiley.

Harter, S., & Pike, R. (1984). The Pictorial Scale of Perceived Competence and Social Acceptance for Young Children. *Child Development, 55,* 1969–1982.

Hartmann, D. P. (1982). *Using observers to study behavior.* San Francisco: Jossey-Bass.

Hartmann, D. P. (1983). Editorial. *Behavioral Assessment, 5,* 1–3.

Hartmann, D. P. (1984). Assessment strategies. In D. H. Barlow & M. Hersen (Eds.), *Single case experimental designs: Strategies for studying behavior change* (2nd ed., pp. 107–139). Elmsford, NY: Pergamon Press.

Hartmann, D. P., Roper, B. L., & Bradford, D. C. (1979). Some relationships between behavioral and traditional assessment. *Journal of Behavioral Assessment, 1,* 3–21.

Hartup, W. W. (1986). On relationships and development. In W. W. Hartup & Z. Rubin (Eds.), *Relationships and development* (pp. 1–26). Hillsdale, NJ: Erlbaum.

Hawkins, R. P. (1975). Who decided that was the problem? Two stages of responsibility for applied behavior analysis. In W. S. Wood (Ed.), *Issues in evaluating behavior modification* (pp. 195–214). Champaign, IL: Research Press.

Hawkins, R. P. (1979). The functions of assessment: Implications for selection and development of devices for assessing repertoires in clinical, educational, and other settings. *Journal of Applied Behavior Analysis, 12,* 501-516.

Hawkins, R. P. (1982). Developing a behavior code. In D. P. Hartmann (Ed.), *Using observers to study behavior* (pp. 21–35). San Francisco: Jossey-Bass.

Hayes, S. C. (1988). *Treatment validity: An approach to evaluating the quality of assessment* (National Institute on Drug Abuse: Research Monograph No. 77, pp. 113–127). Washington, DC: U.S. Government Printing Office.

Hayes, S. C. (1996). Creating the empirical clinician. *Clinical Psychology: Science and Practice, 3,* 179–181.

Hayes, S. C., & Follette, W. C. (1992). Can functional analysis provide a substitute for syndromal classification? *Behavioral Assessment, 14,* 345–365.

Hayes, S. C., & Follette, W. C. (1993). The challenge faced by behavioral assessment. *European Journal of Psychological Assessment, 9,* 182–188.

Hayes, S. C., Follette, W. C., Dawes, R. D., & Grady, K. (Eds.). (1995). *Scientific standards of psychological practice: Issues and recommendations.* Reno, NV: Context Press.

Hayes, S. C., & Nelson, R. O. (1987). The treatment utility of assessment: A functional approach to evaluating assessment quality. *American Psychologist, 42,* 963–974.

Hayes, S. C., & Nelson, R. O. (1989). The applicability of treatment utility. *American Psychologist, 44,* 1242–1243.

Haynes, S. N. (1983). Behavioral assessment. In M. Hersen, A. E. Kazdin, & A. S. Bellack (Eds.), *Clinical psychology handbook* (pp. 397–426). Elmsford, NY: Pergamon Press.

Haynes, S. N. (1988). Causal models and the assessment–treatment relationship in behavior therapy. *Journal of Psychopathology and Behavioral Assessment, 10,* 171–183.

Haynes, S. N., & Jensen, B. J. (1979). The interview as a behavioral assessment instrument. *Behavioral Assessment, 1,* 97–106.

Haynes, S. N., & O'Brien, W. H. (1988). The Gordian knot of DSM-III-R use: Integrating principles of behavior classification and complex causal models. *Behavioral Assessment, 10,* 95–105.

Haynes, S. N., & Uchigakiuchi, P. (1993a). Functional analytic causal models and the design of treatment programs: Concepts and clinical applications with childhood behavior problems. *European Journal of Psychological Assessment, 9,* 189–205.

Haynes, S. N., & Uchigakiuchi, P. (1993b). Incorporating personality trait measures in behavioral assessment: Nuts in a fruitcake or raisins in a Mai Tai? *Behavior Modification, 17,* 72–92.

Hazzard, A., Christensen, A., & Margolin, G. (1983). Children's perceptions of parental behaviors. *Journal of Abnormal Child Psychology, 11,* 49–60.

Henker, B., Astor-Dubin, L., & Varni, J. W. (1986). Psychostimulant medication and perceived intensity in hyperactive children. *Journal of Abnormal Child Psychology, 14,* 105–114.

Herbert, M. (1981). *Behavioural treatment of problem children: A practice manual.* London: Academic Press.

Herjanic, B., & Reich, W. (1982). Development of a structured psychiatric interview for children. *Journal of Abnormal Child Psychology, 10,* 307–324.

Hersen, M., & Ammerman, R. T. (1995). *Advanced abnormal child psychology.* Hillsdale, NJ: Erlbaum.

Hersen, M., & Van Hasselt, V. B. (Eds.). (1987). *Behavior therapy with children and adolescents: A clinical approach.* New York: Wiley.

Hetherington, E. M., Law, T. C., & O'Connor, T. G. (1993). Divorce: Challenges, changes, and new chances. In F. Walsh (Ed.), *Normal family processes* (2nd ed., pp. 208–234). New York: Guilford Press.

Hibbs, E. D., & Jensen, P. S. (Eds.). (1996). *Psychosocial treatments for child and adolescent disorders: Empirically based strategies for clinical practice.* Washington, DC: American Psychological Association.

Hinshaw, S. P., & Anderson, C. A. (1996). Conduct and Oppositional Defiant Disorders. In E. J. Mash & R. A. Barkley (Eds.), *Child psychopathology* (pp. 113–149). New York: Guilford Press.

Hinshaw, S. P., Morrison, D. C., Carte, E. T., & Cornsweet, C. (1987). Factorial dimensions of the Revised Behavior Problem Checklist: Replication and validation within a kindergarten sample. *Journal of Abnormal Child Psychology, 15*, 309–327.

Hobbs, N. (Ed.). (1975). *Issues in the classification of children* (Vols. 1 & 2). San Francisco: Jossey-Bass.

Hobbs, S. A, Beck, S. I., & Wansley, R. A. (1984). Pediatric behavioral medicine: Directions in treatment and intervention. In M. Hersen, R. M. Eisler, & P. M. Miller (Eds.), *Progress in behavior modification* (Vol. 16, pp. 1–29). New York: Academic Press.

Hodges, K. (1985). *Manual for the Child Assessment Schedule* (CAS). Durham, NC: Duke University Medical Center.

Hodges, K., & Zeman, J. (1993). Interviewing. In T. H. Ollendick & M. Hersen (Eds.), *Handbook of child and adolescent assessment* (pp. 65–81). Needham Heights, MA: Allyn & Bacon.

Holden, G. W. (1985a). Analyzing parental reasoning with microcomputer-presented problems. *Simulation and Games, 16*, 203–210.

Holden, G. W. (1985b, July). *Caregiving experience and adults' cognitive responses to a problematic parent–child setting.* Paper presented at the biennial meeting of the International Society for the Study of Behavioural Development, Tours, France.

Holden, G. W. (1985c, April). *Diagnosing why a baby is crying: The effect of caregiving experience.* Paper presented at the biennial meeting of the Society for Research in Child Development, Toronto.

Holden, G. W. (1985d). How parents create a social environment via proactive behavior. In T. Garling & J. Valsiner (Eds.), *Children within environments* (pp. 193–215). New York: Plenum Press.

Holland, C. J. (1970). An interview guide for behavioral counseling with parents. *Behavior Therapy, 1*, 70–79.

Holman, A. M. (1983). *Family assessment: Tools for understanding and intervention.* Beverly Hills, CA: Sage.

Hops, H. (1983). Children's social competence and skill: Current research practices and future directions. *Behavior Therapy, 14*, 3–18.

Hops, H., Biglan, A., Sherman, L., Arthur, J., Friedman, L., & Osteen, V. (1987). Home observations of family interactions of depressed women. *Journal of Consulting and Clinical Psychology, 55*, 341–346.

Hops, H., Biglan, A., Sherman, L., Arthur, J., Warner, P., Holcomb, C., Oosternink, N., & Osteen, V. (1986). *Revised LIFE (Living in Familiar Environments) system.* Unpublished manuscript, Oregon Research Institute, Eugene.

Hops, H., & Cobb, I. A. (1973). Survival behaviors in the educational setting: Their implications for research and intervention. In L. A. Hamerlynck, L. C. Handy, & E. J. Mash (Eds.), *Behavior change: Methodology. concepts and practice* (pp. 193–208). Champaign, IL: Research Press.

Hops, H., & Davis, B. (1995). Methodological issues in direct observation: Illustrations with the Living in Familial Environments (LIFE) coding system. *Journal of Clinical Child Psychology, 24*, 193–203.

Hops, H., & Greenwood, C. (1988). Social skills deficits. In E. J. Mash & L. G. Terdal (Eds.), *Behavioral assessment of childhood disorders* (2nd ed., pp. 263–316). New York: Guilford Press.

Hops, H., & Lewin, L. (1984). Peer sociometric forms. In T. H. Ollendick & M. Hersen (Eds.), *Child behavioral assessment: Principles and procedures* (pp. 124–147). Elmsford, NY: Pergamon Press.

Horner, R. H. (1994). Functional assessment: Contributions and future directions. *Journal of Applied Behavior Analysis, 27*, 401–404.

Horowitz, L. M., Post, D. L., French, R. deS., Wallis, K. D., & Siegelman, E. Y. (1981). The prototype as a construct in abnormal psychology: 2. Clarifying disagreement in psychiatric judgments. *Journal of Abnormal Psychology, 90*, 575–585.

Horowitz, L. M., Wright, J. C., Lowenstein, E., & Parad, H. W. (1981). The prototype as a construct in abnormal psychology: 1. A method for deriving prototypes. *Journal of Abnormal Psychology, 90*, 568–574.

Hughes, H. M., & Haynes, S. N. (1978). Structured laboratory observation in the behavioral assessment of parent–child interactions: A methodological critique. *Behavior Therapy, 9*, 428–447.

Hulbert, T. A., Gdowski, C. L., & Lachar, D. (1986). Interparent agreement on the Personality Inventory for Children: Are substantial correlations sufficient? *Journal of Abnormal Child Psychology, 14*, 115–122.

Humphreys, L. E., & Ciminero, A. R. (1979). Parent report measures of child behavior: A review. *Journal of Clinical Child Psychology, 5*, 56–63.

Hymel, S. (1986). Interpretations of peer behavior: Affective bias in childhood and adolescence. *Child Development, 57*, 431–445.

Ireton, H., & Thwing, E. J. (1974). *Minnesota Child Development Inventory.* Minneapolis: Behavior Science Systems.

Jacob, R. G., O'Leary, K. D., & Rosenblad, C. (1978). Formal and informal classroom settings: Effects on hyperactivity. *Journal of Abnormal Child Psychology, 6*, 47–59.

Jacob, T., & Tennenbaum, D. L. (1988). *Family assessment: Rationale, methods, and future directions.* New York: Plenum Press.

Jacobson, N. S. (1985). The role of observational measures in behavior therapy outcome research. *Behavioral Assessment, 7*, 297–308.

Jensen, B. I., & Haynes, S. N. (1986). Self-report questionnaires and inventories. In A. R. Ciminero, K. S. Calhoun, & H. E. Adams (Eds.), *Handbook of behavioral assessment* (2nd ed., pp. 150–179). New York: Wiley.

Johnson, P. L., & O'Leary, K. D. (1996). Behavioral components of marital satisfaction: An individualized assessment approach. *Journal of Consulting and Clinical Psychology, 64,* 417–423.

Johnson, S. M., & Bolstad, O. D. (1973). Methodological issues in naturalistic observation: Some problems and solutions for field research. In L. A. Hamerlynck, L. C. Handy, & E. J. Mash (Eds.), *Behavior change: Methodology, concepts, and practice* (pp. 7–67). Champaign, IL: Research Press.

Johnson, S. M., & Lobitz, G. K. (1974). Parental manipulation of child behavior in home observations. *Journal of Applied Behavior Analysis, 7,* 23–32.

Johnston, C., & Mash, E. J. (1989). A measure of parenting satisfaction and efficacy. *Journal of Clinical Child Psychology, 18,* 167–175.

Joreskog, K. G., & Sorbom, D. (1983). *LISREL VI: Analysis of linear structure of relationships by maximum likelihood and least squares methods* (2nd ed.). Chicago: Natural Education Resources.

Jouriles, E. N., Murphy, C. M., & O'Leary, K. D. (1989). Effects of maternal mood on mother–son interaction patterns. *Journal of Abnormal Child Psychology, 17,* 513–525.

Jouriles, E. N., & Thompson, S. M. (1993). Effects of mood on mothers' evaluations of children's behavior. *Journal of Family Psychology, 6,* 300–307.

Kagan, J. (1983). Classifications of the child. In W. Kessen (Vol. Ed.), *Handbook of child psychology* (4th ed.): *Vol. 1. History, theory, and methods* (pp. 527–560). New York: Wiley.

Kallman, W. M., & Feuerstein, M J. (1986). Psychophysiological procedures. In A. R. Ciminero, K. S. Calhoun, & H. E. Adams (Eds.), *Handbook of behavioral assessment* (2nd ed., pp. 325–352). New York: Wiley.

Kamphaus, R. W. (1993). *Clinical assessment of children's intelligence.* Needham Heights, MA: Allyn & Bacon.

Kamphaus, R. W., & Frick, P. J. (1996). *Clinical assessment of child and adolescent personality and behavior.* Needham Heights, MA: Allyn & Bacon.

Kanfer, F. H. (1972). Assessment for behavior modification. *Journal of Personality Assessment, 36,* 418–423.

Kanfer, F. H. (1979). A few comments on the current status of behavioral assessment. *Behavioral Assessment, 1,* 37–39.

Kanfer, F. H. (1985). Target selection for clinical change programs. *Behavioral Assessment, 7,* 7–20.

Kanfer, F. H., & Busemeyer, J. R. (1982). The use of problem-solving and decision-making in behavior therapy. *Clinical Psychology Review, 2,* 239–266.

Kanfer, F. H., & Grimm, L. G. (1977). Behavioral analysis: Selecting target behaviors in the interview. *Behavior Modification, 1,* 7–28.

Kanfer, F. H., & Nay, W. R. (1982). Behavioral assessment. In G. T. Wilson & C. M. Franks (Eds.), *Contemporary behavior therapy: Conceptual and empirical foundations* (pp. 367–402). New York: Guilford Press.

Kanfer, F. H., & Phillips, J. S. (1970). *Learning foundations of behavior therapy.* New York: Wiley.

Kanfer, F. H., & Saslow, G. (1969). Behavioral diagnosis. In C. M. Franks (Ed.), *Behavior therapy: Appraisal and status* (pp. 417–444). New York: McGraw-Hill.

Kanfer, F. H., & Schefft, B. K. (1988). *Guiding the process of therapeutic change.* Champaign, IL: Research Press.

Karoly, P. (1981). Self-management problems in children. In E. J. Mash & L. G. Terdal (Eds.), *Behavioral assessment of childhood disorders* (pp. 79–126). New York: Guilford Press.

Karoly, P. (1985). *Measurement strategies in health psychology.* New York: Wiley–Interscience.

Kaslow, F. W. (Ed.). (1996). *Handbook of relational diagnosis and dysfunctional family patterns.* New York: Wiley.

Kates, N. (1986). *The psychological impact of unemployment.* Unpublished manuscript, East Region Mental Health Services, Hamilton, Ontario, Canada.

Kaufman, A. S., & Kaufman, N. L. (1983). *Kaufman Assessment battery for Children.* Circle Pines, MN: American Guidance Service.

Kaufman, A. S., & Reynolds, C. R. (1984). Intellectual and academic achievement tests. In T. H. Ollendick & M. Hersen (Eds.), *Child behavioral assessment: Principles and procedures* (pp. 195–222). Elmsford, NY: Pergamon Press.

Kavanagh, K., & Hops, H. (1994). Good girls? Bad boys? Gender and development as contexts for diagnosis and treatment. *Advances in Clinical Child Psychology, 16,* 45–79.

Kaye, K. (1985). Toward a developmental psychology of the family. In L. L'Abate (Ed.), *Handbook of family psychology and therapy.* Homewood, IL: Dorsey Press.

Kazdin, A. E. (1977). Assessing the clinical or applied importance of behavior change through social validation. *Behavior Modification, 1,* 427–452.

Kazdin, A. E. (1979). Situational specificity: The two-edged sword of behavioral assessment. *Behavioral Assessment, 1,* 57–75.

Kazdin, A. E. (1981). Acceptability of child treatment techniques: The influence of treatment efficacy and adverse side effects. *Behavior Therapy, 12,* 493–506.

Kazdin, A. E. (1982a). Observer effects: Reactivity of direct observation. In D. P. Hartmann (Ed.), *Using observers to study behavior* (pp. 5–19). San Francisco: Jossey-Bass.

Kazdin, A. E. (1982b). Symptom substitution, generalization, and response covariation: Implications for psychotherapy outcome. *Psychological Bulletin, 91,* 349–365.

Kazdin, A. E. (1983). Psychiatric diagnosis, dimensions of dysfunction and child behavior therapy. *Behavior Therapy, 14,* 73–99.

Kazdin, A. E. (1984). Acceptability of aversive procedures and medication as treatment alternatives for deviant child behavior. *Journal of Abnormal Child Psychology, 12,* 289–302.

Kazdin, A. E. (1985). Selection of target behaviors: The relationship of the treatment focus to clinical dysfunction. *Behavioral Assessment, 7,* 33–47.

Kazdin, A. E., & Esveldt-Dawson, K. (1987). Problem-solving skills training and relationship therapy in the treatment of antisocial child behavior. *Journal of Consulting and Clinical Psychology, 55,* 76–85.

Kazdin, A. E., & Kagan, J. (1994). Models of dysfunction in developmental psychopathology. *Clinical Psychology: Science and Practice, 1,* 35–52.

Kelly, J. A. (1983). *Treating child-abusive families: Intervention based on skills training.* New York: Plenum Press.

Kendall, P. C. (1982). Integration: Behavior therapy and other schools of thought. *Behavior Therapy, 13,* 550–571.

Kendall, P. C. (Ed.). (1991). *Child and adolescent therapy: Cognitive–behavioral procedures.* New York: Guilford Press.

Kendall, P. C., & Hollon, S . D. (Eds.). (1981). *Cognitive–behavioral interventions: Assessment methods.* New York: Academic Press.

Kendall, P. C., Lerner, R. M., & Craighead, W. E. (1984). Human development and intervention in child psychopathology. *Child Development, 55,* 71–82.

Kendall, P. C., & Wilcox, L. E. (1979). Self-control in children: Development of a rating scale. *Journal of Consulting and Clinical Psychology, 47,* 1020–1029.

Kessler, J. W. (1971). Nosology in child psychopathology. In H. E. Rie (Ed.), *Perspectives in child psychopathology* (pp. 85–129). Chicago: Aldine–Atherton.

Kestenbaum, C. J., & Bird, H. R. (1978). A reliability study of the Mental Health Assessment Form for School-Age Children. *Journal of the American Academy of Child Psychiatry, 7,* 338–347.

Kiesler, C. A. (1983). Social psychological issues in studying consumer satisfaction with behavior therapy. *Behavior Therapy, 14,* 226–236.

King, N. J. (1993). Physiological assessment. In T. H. Ollendick & M. Hersen (Eds.), *Handbook of child and adolescent assessment* (pp. 180–191). Needham Heights, MA: Allyn & Bacon.

Klein, R. G., & Last, C. G. (1989). *Anxiety disorders in children.* Newbury Park, CA: Sage.

Koocher, G. P. (1993). Ethical issues in the psychological assessment of children. In T. H. Ollendick & M. Hersen (Eds.), *Handbook of child and adolescent assessment* (pp. 51–64). Needham Heights, MA: Allyn & Bacon.

Kotsopoulos, S., & Mellor, C. (1986). Extralinguistic speech characteristics of children with conduct and anxiety disorders. *Journal of Child Psychology and Psychiatry, 27,* 99–108.

Kovacs, M. (1981). Rating scales to assess depression in school-aged children. *Acta Paedopsychiatrica, 46,* 305–315.

Kovacs, M. (1985). ISC (The Interview Schedule for Children). *Psychopharmacology Bulletin, 21,* 991–994.

Kratochwill, T. R. (1985). Selection of target behaviors in behavioral consultation. *Behavioral Assessment, 7,* 49–62.

Kratochwill, T. R., & Morris, R. J. (Eds.). (1993). *Handbook of psychotherapy with children and adolescents.* Needham Heights, MA: Allyn & Bacon.

Kropp, J. P., & Haynes, O. M. (1987). Abusive and nonabusive mothers' ability to identify general and specific emotion signals of infants. *Child Development, 58,* 187–190.

Kurdek, L. A. (1986). Children's reasoning about parental divorce. In R. D. Ashmore & D. M. Brodzinsky (Eds.), *Thinking about the family: Views of parents and children* (pp. 233–276). Hillsdale, NJ: Erlbaum.

Lachar, D. (1982). *Personality Inventory for Children—Revised (PIC-R).* Los Angeles: Western Psychological Services.

Lachar, D., & Gruber, C. P. (1994). *The Personality Inventory for Youth.* Los Angeles: Western Psychological Services.

La Greca, A. M. (Ed.). (1990). *Through the eyes of the child: Obtaining self-reports from children and adolescents.* Boston: Allyn & Bacon.

La Greca, A. M. (1994). Assessment in pediatric psychology: What's a researcher to do? *Journal of Pediatric Psychology, 19,* 283–290.

La Greca, A. M., & Lemanek, K. L. (1996). Editorial: Assessment as a process in pediatric psychology. *Journal of Pediatric Psychology, 21,* 137–151.

Lamb, M. E. (Ed.). (1982). *Nontraditional families: Parenting and child development.* Hillsdale, NJ: Erlbaum.

Langer, E. J., & Abelson, R. P. (1974). A patient by any other name: Clinician group difference in labeling bias. *Journal of Consulting and Clinical Psychology, 42,* 4–9.

Langner, T. S., Gersten, J. C., McCarthy, E. D., Eisenberg, G., Greene, E. L., Hersen, J. H., & Jameson, J. D. (1976). A screening inventory for assessing psychiatric impairment in children six to eight. *Journal of Consulting and Clinical Psychology, 44,* 286–296.

Lapouse, R., & Monk, M. A. (1958). An epidemiologic study of behavior characteristic in children. *American Journal of Public Health, 48,* 1134–1144.

Larrance, D. T., & Twentyman, C. T. (1983). Maternal attributions and child abuse. *Journal of Abnormal Psychology, 9,* 449–457.

Larzelere, R. E., Martin, J. A., & Amberson, T. G. (1985). *Toddler Behavior Checklist, Form B.* Unpublished manuscript, Biola University, La Mirada, CA.

Last, C. G., & Hersen, M. (Eds.). (1989). *Handbook of child psychiatric diagnosis*. New York: Wiley–Interscience.

Layne, C. C., Rickard, H. C., Jones, M. T., & Lyman, R. D. (1976). Accuracy of self-monitoring on a variable ratio schedule of observer verification. *Behavior Therapy, 7*, 481–488.

LeBow, J. (1982). Consumer satisfaction with mental health treatment. *Psychological Bulletin, 91*, 244–259.

Lee, C. M., & Gotlib, I. H. (1991). Family disruption, parental availability, and child adjustment. In R. J. Prinz (Ed.), *Advances in behavioral assessment of children and families* (Vol. 5, pp. 171–199). London: Jessica Kingsley.

Leitenberg, H., Yost, L. W., & Carroll-Wilson, M. (1986). Negative cognitive errors in children: Questionnaire development, normative data, and comparisons between children with and without self reported symptoms of depression, low self-esteem, and evaluation anxiety. *Journal of Consulting and Clinical Psychology, 54*, 528–536.

Lewis, M., & Miller, S. M. (Eds.). (1990). *Handbook of developmental psychopathology*. New York: Plenum Press.

Loeber, R., Dishion, T. J., & Patterson, G. R. (1984). Multiple gating: A multistage assessment procedure for identifying youths at risk for delinquency. *Journal of Research in Crime and Delinquency, 21*, 7–37.

Lovitt, T. C. (1973). Self-management projects with children with learning disabilities. *Journal of Learning Disabilities, 6*, 15–28.

Lytton, H. (1979). Disciplinary encounters between young boys and their mothers and fathers: Is there a contingency system? *Developmental Psychology, 15*, 256–268.

Mace, F. C. (1994). The significance and future of functional analysis methodologies. *Journal of Applied Behavior Analysis, 27*, 385–392.

MacFarlane, J. W., Allen, L., & Honzik, M. P. (1954). *A developmental study of the behavior problems of normal children between twenty-one months and fourteen years*. Berkeley: University of California Press.

MacPhee, D., Benson, J. B., & Bullock, D. (1984). *Self-Perceptions of the Parental Role*. Unpublished manuscript, University of Denver.

Madsen, C. K., & Madsen, C. H. (1972). *Parents, children, discipline: A positive approach*. Boston: Allyn & Bacon.

Margolin, G. (1983). An interactional model for the behavioral assessment of marital relationships. *Behavioral Assessment, 5*, 103–127.

Margolin, G. (1987). Participant observation procedures in marital and family assessment. In T. Jacob (Ed.), *Family interaction and psychopathology* (pp. 391–426). New York: Plenum Press.

Markman, H. J., & Notarius, C. I. (1987). Coding marital and family interaction: Current status. In T. Jacob (Ed.), *Family interaction and psychopathology* (pp. 329–390). New York: Plenum Press.

Martin, G., & Pear, J. (1996). *Behavior modification: What it is and how to do it* (5th ed.). Upper Saddle River, NJ: Prentice-Hall.

Martin, S., Johnson, S., Johansson, S., & Wahl, G. (1976). The comparability of behavioral data in laboratory and natural settings. In E. J. Mash, L. A. Hamerlynck, & L. C. Handy (Eds.), *Behavior modification and families* (pp. 189–203). New York: Brunner/Mazel .

Mash, E. J. (1979). What is behavioral assessment? *Behavioral Assessment, 1*, 23–29.

Mash, E. J. (1984). Families with problem children. In A. Doyle, D. Gold, & D. Moskowitz (Eds.), *Children in families under stress* (pp. 65–84). San Francisco: Jossey-Bass.

Mash, E. J. (1985). Some comments on target selection in behavior therapy. *Behavioral Assessment, 7*, 63–78.

Mash, E. J., & Barkley, R. A. (1986). Assessment of family interaction with the Response-Class Matrix. In R. J. Prinz (Ed.), *Advances in the behavioral assessment of children and families* (pp. 29–67). Greenwich, CT: JAI Press.

Mash, E. J., & Barkley, R. A. (Eds.). (1989). *Treatment of childhood disorders*. New York: Guilford Press.

Mash, E. J., & Barkley, R. A. (Eds.). (1996). *Child psychopathology*. New York: Guilford Press.

Mash, E. J., & Barkley, R. A. (Eds.). (in press). *Treatment of childhood disorders* (2nd ed.). New York: Guilford Press.

Mash, E. J., & Dalby, J. T. (1979). Behavioral interventions for hyperactivity. In R. L. Trites (Ed.), *Hyperactivity in children: Etiology, measurement, and treatment implications* (pp. 161–216). Baltimore: University Park Press.

Mash, E. J., & Dozois, D. J. A. (1996). Child psychopathology: A developmental–systems perspective. In E. J. Mash & R. A. Barkley (Eds.), *Child psychopathology* (pp. 3–60). New York: Guilford Press.

Mash, E. J., & Hunsley, J. (1990). Behavioral assessment: A contemporary approach. In A. S. Bellack, M. Hersen, & A. E. Kazdin (Eds.), *International handbook of behavior modification and therapy* (2nd ed., pp. 87–106). New York: Plenum Press.

Mash, E. J., & Hunsley, J. (1993a). Assessment considerations in the assessment of failing psychotherapy: Bringing the negatives out of the darkroom. *Psychological Assessment: A Journal of Consulting and Clinical Psychology, 5*, 292–301.

Mash, E. J., & Hunsley, J. (1993b). Behavior therapy and managed mental health care: Integrating effectiveness and economics in managed mental health care. *Behavior Therapy, 24*, 67–90.

Mash, E. J., & Johnston, C. (1980). *Child Development Questionnaire*. Unpublished manuscript, University of Calgary.

Mash, E. J., & Johnston, C. (1983a). A note on the prediction of mothers' behavior with their hyperactive children during play and task situations. *Child and Family Behavior Therapy, 5,* 1–14.

Mash, E. J., & Johnston, C. (1983b). Parental perceptions of child behavior problems, parenting self-esteem and mothers' reported stress in younger and older hyperactive and normal children. *Journal of Consulting and Clinical Psychology, 51,* 86–99.

Mash, E. J., & Johnston, C. (1983c). Sibling interactions of hyperactive and normal children and their relationship to reports of maternal stress and self-esteem. *Journal of Clinical Child Psychology, 12,* 91–99.

Mash, E. J., & Johnston, C. (1990). Determinants of parenting stress: Illustrations from families of hyperactive children and families of physically abused children. *Journal of Clinical Child Psychology, 19,* 313–328.

Mash, E. J., & Johnston, C. (1996a). Family relational problems. In V. E. Caballo, J. A. Carrobles, & G. Buela-Casal (Eds.), *Handbook of psychopathology and psychiatric disorders* (pp. 589–621). Madrid: Siglo XXI.

Mash, E. J., & Johnston, C. (1996b). Family relationship problems: Their place in the study of psychopathology. *Journal of Emotional and Behavioral Disorders, 4,* 240–254.

Mash, E. J., Johnston, C., & Kovitz, K. (1983). A comparison of the mother–child interactions of physically abused and non-abused children during play and task situations. *Journal of Clinical Child Psychology, 12,* 337–346.

Mash, E. J., & Terdal, L. G. (Eds.). (1976). *Behavior therapy assessment: Diagnosis, design, and evaluation.* New York: Springer.

Mash, E. J., & Terdal, L. G. (1980). Follow-up assessments in behavior therapy. In P. Karoly & J. J. Steffen (Eds.), *The long-range effects of psychotherapy: Models of durable outcome* (pp. 99–147). New York: Gardner Press.

Mash, E. J., & Terdal, L. G. (Eds.). (1981a). *Behavioral assessment of childhood disorders.* New York: Guilford Press.

Mash, E. J., & Terdal, L. G. (1981b). Behavioral assessment of childhood disturbance. In E. J. Mash & L. G. Terdal (Eds.), *Behavioral assessment of childhood disorders* (pp. 3–76). New York: Guilford Press.

Mash, E. J., & Terdal, L. G. (Eds.). (1988a). *Behavioral assessment of childhood disorders* (2nd ed.). New York: Guilford Press.

Mash, E. J., & Terdal, L. G. (1988b). Behavioral assessment of childhood disturbance. In E. J. Mash & L. G. Terdal (Eds.), *Behavioral assessment*

of childhood disorders (2nd ed., pp. 3–65). New York: Guilford Press.

Mash, E. J., Terdal, L. G., & Anderson, K. (1973). The Response-Class Matrix: A procedure for recording parent–child interactions. *Journal of Consulting and Clinical Psychology, 40,* 163–164.

Masten, A. S. (1986, August). *Patterns of adaptation to stress in middle childhood.* Paper presented at the meeting of the American Psychological Association, Washington, DC.

Matarazzo, J. D. (1983). Computerized psychological testing. *Science, 221,* 323–328.

McCubbin, H. I., & Thompson, A. I. (Eds.). (1987). *Family assessment inventories for research and practice.* Madison: University of Wisconsin, Family Stress Coping and Health Project.

McDermott, P. A. (1993). National standardization of uniform multisituational measures of child and adolescent behavior pathology. *Psychological Assessment, 5,* 413–424.

McDermott, P. A., & Weiss, R. V. (1995). A normative typology of healthy, subclinical, and clinical behavior styles among American children and adolescents. *Psychological Assessment, 7,* 162–170.

McFall, R. M. (1982). A review and reformulation of the concept of social skills. *Behavioral Assessment, 4,* 1–33.

McFall, R. M. (1986). Theory and method in assessment: The vital link. *Behavioral Assessment, 8,* 3–10.

McGillicuddy-DeLisi, A. V. (1985). The relationship between parental beliefs and children's cognitive level. In I. Sigel (Ed.), *Parental belief systems: The psychological consequences for children* (pp. 7–24). Hillsdale, NJ: Erlbaum.

McIntyre, T. J., Bornstein, P. H., Isaacs, C. D., Woody, D. J., Bornstein, M. T., Clucas, T. J., & Long, G. (1983). Naturalistic observation of conduct disordered children: An archival analysis. *Behavior Therapy, 14,* 375–385 .

McKenzie, T. L., & Rushall, B. S. (1974). Effects of self-recording on attendance and performance in a competitive swimming training environment. *Journal of Applied Behavior Analysis, 7,* 199–206.

McKinney, B., & Peterson, R. A. (1987). Predictors of stress in parents of developmentally disabled children. *Journal of Pediatric Psychology, 12,* 133–150.

McMahon, R. J., & Forehand, R. (1983). Consumer satisfaction in behavioral treatment of children: Types, issues, and recommendations. *Behavior Therapy, 14,* 209–225.

McMahon, R. J., & Peters, R. DeV. (Eds.). (1985). *Childhood disorders: Behavioral–developmental approaches.* New York: Brunner/Mazel.

Meadow-Orlans, K. P. (1986). *Impact of a child's hearing loss: A questionnaire for parents.* Unpublished manuscript, Gallaudet College Research Institute, Washington, DC.

Meehl, P. H. (1954). *Clinical versus statistical prediction: A theoretical analysis and review of the evidence.* Minneapolis: University of Minnesota Press.

Meichenbaum, D. (1977). *Cognitive-behavior modification: An integrative approach.* New York: Plenum Press.

Melton, G. B., & Ehrenreich, N. S. (1993). Ethical and legal issues in mental health services for children. In C. E. Walker & M. C. Roberts (Eds.), *Handbook of clinical child psychology* (2nd ed., pp. 1035–1055). New York: Wiley.

Messick, S. (1983). Assessment of children. In W. Kessen (Vol. Ed.), *Handbook of child psychology* (4th ed.): *Vol. 1. History, theory, and methods* (pp. 477–526). New York: Wiley.

Michelson, L., & Wood, R. (1982). Development and psychometric properties of the Children's Assertive Behavior Inventory. *Journal of Behavioral Assessment, 4,* 3–13.

Milich, R., Loney, J., & Landau, S. (1982). The independent dimensions of hyperactivity and aggression: A validation with playroom observation data. *Journal of Abnormal Psychology, 91,* 183–198.

Miller, G. E., & Prinz, R. J. (1990). Enhancement of social learning family interventions for childhood Conduct Disorder. *Psychological Bulletin, 108,* 291–307.

Miller, H., & Clarke, D. (1978). *Effective parental attention* [Videotape]. Los Angeles: University of California at Los Angeles.

Miller, L. C., Hampe, E., Barrett, C., & Noble, H. (1971). Children's deviant behavior within the general population. *Journal of Consulting and Clinical Psychology, 37,* 16–22.

Miller, L. C., & Roid, G. H. (1988). Factor-analytically derived scales for the Louisville Behavior Checklist. *Journal of Consulting and Clinical Psychology, 56,* 302–304.

Miller, S. A. (1995). Parents' attributions for their children's behavior. *Child Development, 66,* 1557–1584.

Mink, I. T., Meyers, C. E.. & Nihara, K. (1984). Taxonomy of family life styles: II. Homes with slow-learning children. *American Journal of Mental Deficiency, 89,* 111–123.

Mink, I. T., Nihira, K., & Meyers, C. E. (1983). Taxonomy of family life styles: I. Homes with TMR children. *American Journal of Mental Deficiency, 87,* 484–497.

Minuchin, P. (1985). Families and individual development: Provocations from the field of family therapy. *Child Development, 56,* 289–302.

Mischel, W. (1968). *Personality and assessment.* New York: Wiley.

Mischel, W. (1973). Toward a cognitive social learning reconceptualization of personality. *Psychological Review, 80,* 252–283.

Mischel, W. (1977). The interaction of person and situation. In D. Magnusson & N. S. Endler (Eds.), *Personality at the crossroads: Current issues in interactional psychology* (pp. 333–352). Hillsdale, NJ: Erlbaum.

Mischel, W. (1979). On the interface of cognition and personality: Beyond the person–situation debate. *American Psychologist, 34,* 740–754.

Molnar, J. M. (1985, August). *Home and day care contexts: Interactive influences on children's behavior.* Paper presented at the meeting of the American Psychological Association, Los Angeles.

Mooney, C., & Algozzine, B. (1978). A comparison of the disturbingness of behaviors related to learning disability and emotional disturbance. *Journal of Abnormal Child Psychology, 6,* 401–406.

Moos, R. H., & Moos, B. S. (1978). A typology of family social environments. *Family Process, 17,* 357–371.

Moos, R. H., & Moos, B. S. (1986). *Family Environment Scale manual* (2nd ed.). Palo Alto, CA: Consulting Psychologists Press.

Moos, R. H., & Trickett, E. J. (1974). *Classroom Environment Scale manual.* Palo Alto, CA: Consulting Psychologists Press.

Morris, R. J., & Kratochwill, T. R. (1983). *Treating children's fears and phobias: A behavioral approach.* Elmsford, NY: Pergamon Press.

Moskowitz, D. S., & Schwarz, J. C. (1982). Validity comparisons of behavior counts and ratings by knowledgeable informants. *Journal of Personality and Social Psychology, 42,* 518–528.

Mussen, P. H. (General Ed.). (1983). *Handbook of child psychology* (4th ed., 4 vols.). New York: Wiley.

Naglieri, J. A., LeBuffe, P. A., & Pfeiffer, S. I. (1994). *Devereux Scales of Mental Disorders.* New York: Psychological Corporation.

Nathan, P. E. (1986). [Review of R. K. Blashfield, *The classification of psychopathology*]. *Behavioral Assessment, 8,* 199–201.

Nay, W. R. (1979). *Multimethod clinical assessment.* New York: Gardner Press.

Nay, W. R. (1986). Analogue measures. In A. R. Ciminero, K. S. Calhoun, & H. E. Adams (Eds.), *Handbook of behavioral assessment* (2nd ed., pp. 223–252). New York: Wiley.

Neidig, P. H., & Friedman, D. H. (1984). *Spouse abuse: A treatment program for couples.* Champaign, IL: Research Press.

Nelson, R. O. (1980). The use of intelligence tests in behavioral assessment. *Behavioral Assessment, 2,* 417–423.

Nelson, R. O. (1983). Behavioral assessment: Past, present, future. *Behavioral Assessment, 5,* 195–206.

Nelson, R. O., & Hayes, S. C. (1979). Some current dimensions of behavioral assessment. *Behavioral Assessment, 1,* 1–16.

Nelson, R. O., & Hayes, S. C. (Eds.). (1986). *Conceptual foundations of behavioral assessment.* New York: Guilford Press.

Nelson, R. O., Lipinski, D. P., & Boykin, R. A. (1978). The effects of self-recorders' training and the obtrusiveness of the self-recording device on the accuracy and reactivity of self-monitoring. *Behavior Therapy, 9,* 200–208.

Nelson-Gray, R. O. (1996). Treatment outcome measures: Nomothetic or idiographic? *Clinical Psychology: Science and Practice, 3,* 164–167.

Nelson, W. M., & Finch, A. J. (1978). *The Children's Inventory of Anger.* Unpublished manuscript, Xavier University, Cincinnati, OH.

Newberger, C. M. (1978). *Parental conceptions of children and child rearing: A structural developmental analysis.* Unpublished doctoral dissertation, Harvard University.

Nezu, A. M., & Nezu, C. M. (1993). Identifying and selecting target problems for clinical interventions: A problem-solving model. *Psychological Assessment, 5,* 254–263.

Nisbett, R. E., Zukier, H., & Lemley, R. E. (1981). The dilution effect: Nondiagnostic information weakens the implications of diagnostic information. *Cognitive Psychology, 13,* 248–277.

Nordquist, V. M. (1971). The modification of a child's enuresis: Some response–response relationships. *Journal of Applied Behavior Analysis, 4,* 241–247.

Nowicki, S., & Duke, M. P. (1974). A preschool and preliminary internal–external control scale. *Developmental Psychology, 6,* 874–880.

Nowicki, S., & Strickland, B. R. (1973). A locus of control scale for children. *Journal of Consulting and Clinical Psychology, 40,* 148–154.

Nunnally, J. C. (1994). *Psychometric theory* (3rd ed.). New York: McGraw-Hill.

Ogles, B. M., Lambert, M. J., & Masters, K. S. (1996). *Assessing outcome in clinical practice.* Needham Heights, MA: Allyn & Bacon.

Oldershaw, L. (1986). *A behavioral approach to the classification of different types of physically abusive mothers.* Unpublished manuscript, University of Toronto.

O'Leary, K. D. (1979). Behavioral assessment. *Behavioral Assessment, 1,* 31–36.

O'Leary, K. D., Romanczyk, R. G., Kass, R. E., Dietz. A., & Santogrossi, D. (1971). *Procedures for classroom observations of teachers and children.* Unpublished manuscript, State University of New York at Stony Brook.

Ollendick, T. H. (1984). Development and validation of the Children's Assertiveness Inventory. *Child and Family Behavior Therapy, 5,* 1–15.

Ollendick, T. H., & Cerny, J. A. (1981). *Clinical behavior therapy with children.* New York: Plenum Press.

Ollendick, T. H., & Hersen, M. (Eds.). (1984). *Child behavioral assessment: Principles and procedures.* Elmsford, NY: Pergamon Press.

Ollendick, T. H., & Hersen, M. (1993a). Child and adolescent behavioral assessment. In T. H. Ollendick & M. Hersen (Eds.), *Handbook of child and adolescent assessment* (pp. 3–14). Needham Heights, MA: Allyn & Bacon.

Ollendick, T. H., & Hersen, M. (Eds.). (1993b). *Handbook of child and adolescent assessment.* Needham Heights, MA: Allyn & Bacon.

Olweus, D. (1979). Stability of aggressive reaction patterns in males. *Psychological Bulletin, 86,* 852–875.

Pannaccione, V. F., & Wahler, R. G. (1986). Child behavior, maternal depression, and social coercion as factors in the quality of child care. *Journal of Abnormal Child Psychology, 14,* 263–278.

Parke, R. D., MacDonald, K. B., Beital, A., & Bhavnagri, N. (1988). The role of the family in the development of peer relationships. In R. DeV. Peters & R. J. McMahon (Eds.), *Social learning and systems approaches to marriage and family* (pp. 17–44). New York: Brunner/Mazel.

Parke, R. D., & Sawin, D. B. (1977). *The child's role in sparing the rod.* Unpublished manuscript, University of Illinois.

Passman, R. H., & Mulhern, R. K. (1977). Maternal punitiveness as affected by situational stress: An experimental analogue of child abuse. *Journal of Abnormal Psychology, 86,* 565–569.

Patterson, G. R. (1976). The aggressive child: Victim and architect of a coercive system. In E. J. Mash, L. A. Hamerlynck, & L. C. Handy (Eds.), *Behavior modification and families* (pp. 267–316). New York: Brunner/Mazel.

Patterson, G. R. (1982). *Coercive family process.* Eugene, OR: Castalia.

Patterson, G. R. (1986). Performance models for antisocial boys. *American Psychologist, 41,* 432–444.

Patterson, G. R., & Bank, L. (1986). Bootstrapping your way in the nomological thicket. *Behavioral Assessment, 8,* 49–73.

Patterson, G. R., & Bechtel, G. C. (1977). Formulating situational environment in relation to states and traits. In R. B. Cattell & R. M. Greger (Eds.), *Handbook of modern personality theory* (pp. 254–268). Washington, DC: Halstead.

Patterson, G. R., & Colleagues. (1984). *Assessment protocol from the Oregon Social Learning Center Longitudinal Study.* Unpublished manuscript, Oregon Social Learning Center, Eugene.

Patterson, G. R., Littman, R. A., & Hinsey, W. C. (1964). Parental effectiveness as reinforcer in the laboratory and its relation to child-rearing practices and child adjustment in the classroom. *Journal of Personality, 32,* 180–199.

Patterson, G. R., Reid, J. B., & Dishion, T. J. (1992). *Antisocial boys.* Eugene, OR: Castalia.

Pepler, D. J., Corter, C., & Abramovitch, R. (1982). *Am I my brother's brother? Sibling perceptions.* Paper presented at the Waterloo Conference on Child Development, Waterloo, Ontario, Canada.

Petersen, A. C., & Compas, B. E. (1993). Depression in adolescence. *American Psychologist, 48,* 155–168.

Peterson, D. R. (1968). *The clinical study of social behavior.* New York: Appleton-Century-Crofts.

Peterson, L., & Brown, D. (1994). Integrating child injury and abuse–neglect research: Common histories, etiologies, and solutions. *Psychological Bulletin, 116,* 293–315.

Peterson, L., Burbach, D. J., & Chaney, J. (1989). Developmental issues. In C. G. Last & M. Hersen (Eds.), *Handbook of child psychiatric diagnosis* (pp. 463–482). New York: Wiley–Interscience.

Piacentini, J. (1993). Checklists and rating scales. In T. H. Ollendick & M. Hersen (Eds.), *Handbook of child and adolescent assessment* (pp. 82–97). Needham Heights, MA: Allyn & Bacon.

Piers, E. V., & Harris, D. B. (1963). *The Piers–Harris Self-Concept Scale.* Unpublished manuscript, Pennsylvania State University.

Piotrowski, C. (1996). Use of the Beck Depression Inventory in clinical practice. *Psychological Reports, 79,* 873–874.

Piotrowski, C., & Keller, J. W. (1984). Attitudes toward clinical assessment by members of the AABT. *Psychological Reports, 55,* 831–838.

Powers, M. D. (1984). Syndromal diagnosis and the behavioral assessment of childhood disorders. *Child and Family Behavior Therapy, 6*(3), 1–15.

Prugh, D. G., Engel, M., & Morse, W. C. (1975). Emotional disturbance in children. In N. Hobbs (Ed.), *Issues in the classification of children* (Vol. 1, pp. 261–299). San Francisco: Jossey-Bass.

Quay, H. C., & Peterson, D. R. (1975). *Manual for the Behavior Problem Checklist.* Unpublished manuscript.

Rachman, S. (1983). Behavioural medicine, clinical reasoning, and technical advances. *Canadian Journal of Behavioural Science, 15,* 318–333.

Rains, P. M., Kitsuse, J. I., Duster, T., & Friedson, E. (1975). The labeling approach to deviance. In N. Hobbs (Ed.), *Issues in the classification of children* (Vol. 1, pp. 88–100). San Francisco: Jossey-Bass.

Reid, J. B. (Ed.). (1978). *A social learning approach to family intervention: Vol. 2. Observation in home settings.* Eugene, OR: Castalia.

Reid, J. B. (1982). Observer training in naturalistic research. In D. P. Hartmann (Ed.), *Using observers to study behavior* (pp. 37–50). San Francisco: Jossey-Bass.

Reid, J. B., Patterson, G. R., Baldwin, D. V., & Dishion, T. J. (1988). Observations in the assessment of childhood disorders. In M. Rutter, A. H. Tuma, & I. Lann (Eds.), *Assessment and diagnosis in child psychopathology* (pp. 156–195). New York: Guilford Press.

Reid, J. B., Taplin, P. S., & Lorber, R. (1981). A social interactional approach to the treatment of abusive families. In R. B. Stuart (Ed.), *Violent behavior: Social learning approaches to prediction management and treatment* (pp. 83–101). New York: Brunner/Mazel.

Reppucci, N. D., Weithorn, L. A., Mulvey, E. P., & Monahan, J. (Eds.). (1984). *Children, mental health, and the law.* Beverly Hills, CA: Sage.

Reynolds, C. R., & Kamphaus, R. W. (Eds.). (1990a). *Handbook of psychological and educational assessment of children: Intelligence and achievement.* New York: Guilford Press.

Reynolds, C. R., & Kamphaus, R. W. (Eds.). (1990b). *Handbook of psychological and educational assessment of children: Personality, behavior, and context.* New York: Guilford Press.

Reynolds, C. R., & Kamphaus, R. W. (1992). *Behavior Assessment System for Children (BASC).* Circle Pines, MN: American Guidance Service.

Reynolds, C. R., & Richmond, B. O. (1985). *Revised Children's Manifest Anxiety Scale (RCMAS).* Los Angeles: Western Psychological Services.

Reynolds, W. M. (1989). *Reynolds Child Depression Scale.* Odessa, FL: Psychological Assessment Resources.

Reynolds, W. M. (1993). Self-report methodology. In T. H. Ollendick & M. Hersen (Eds.), *Handbook of child and adolescent assessment* (pp. 98–123). Needham Heights, MA: Allyn & Bacon.

Reynolds, W. M., & Stark, K. D. (1986). Self-control in children: A multimethod examination of treatment outcome measures. *Journal of Abnormal Child Psychology, 14,* 13–23.

Richters, J. E. (1992). Depressed mothers as informants about their children: A critical review of the evidence for distortion. *Psychological Bulletin, 112,* 485–499.

Roberts, M. C. (Ed.). (1995). *Handbook of pediatric psychology* (2nd ed.). New York: Guilford Press.

Roberts, M. W., & Powers, S. W. (1988). The compliance test. *Behavioral Assessment, 10,* 375–398.

Robin, S. L., & Foster, A. L. (1989). *Negotiating parent–adolescent conflict.* New York: Guilford Press.

Rodick, J. D., Henggeler, S. W., & Hanson, C. L. (1986). An evaluation of the Family Adaptability and Cohesion Evaluation Scales and the Circumplex Model. *Journal of Abnormal Child Psychology, 14,* 77–87.

Romanczyk, R. G. (1986). *Clinical utilization of microcomputer technology.* Elmsford, NY: Pergamon Press.

Ronan, K. R. (1996). Building a reasonable bridge in childhood anxiety assessment: A practitioner's resource guide. *Cognitive and Behavioral Practice, 3,* 63–90.

Rosch, E. (1978). Principles of categorization. In E. Rosch & B. B. Lloyd (Eds.), *Cognition and categorization* (pp. 27–48). Hillsdale, NJ: Erlbaum.

Rosenberg, R. P., & Beck, S. (1986). Preferred assessment methods and treatment modalities for hyperactive children among clinical child and school psychologists. *Journal of Clinical Child Psychology, 15,* 142–147.

Ross, A. O. (1978). Behavior therapy with children. In S. L. Garfield & A. E. Bergin (Eds.), *Handbook of psychotherapy and behavior change: An empirical analysis* (2nd ed., pp. 592–620). New York: Wiley.

Ross, A. O. (1981). *Child behavior therapy: Principles procedures and empirical basis.* New York: Wiley.

Rothbart, M. K. (1981). Measurement of temperament in infancy. *Child Development, 52,* 569–578.

Rowan, A. B. (1996). The relevance of religious issues in behavioral assessment. *The Behavior Therapist, 19,* 55–57.

Rubin, K. H., & Stewart, S. L. (1996). Social withdrawal. In E. J. Mash & R. A. Berkley (Eds.), *Child psychopathology* (pp. 277–307). New York: Guilford Press.

Russell, M. B., & Bernal, M. E. (1977). Temporal and climatic variables in naturalistic observation. *Journal of Applied Behavior Analysis, 10,* 399–405.

Rutter, M. (1979). Maternal deprivation, 1972–1978: New findings, new concepts, new approaches. *Child Development, 50,* 283–305.

Rutter, M., Tuma, A. H., & Lann, I. (Eds.). (1988). *Assessment and diagnosis in child psychopathology.* New York: Guilford Press.

Salzinger, S., Kaplan, S., & Artemyeff, C. (1983). Mothers' personal social networks and child maltreatment. *Journal of Abnormal Psychology, 92,* 68–76.

Sanders, M. R., & Lawton, J. M. (1993). Discussing assessment findings with families: A guided participation model of information transfer. *Child and Family Behavior Therapy, 15,* 5–35.

Santostefano, S. (1978). *A biodevelopmental approach to clinical child psychology: Cognitive controls and cognitive control therapy.* New York: Wiley.

Santrock, J. W., & Sitterle, K. A. (1987). Parent–child relationships in stepmother families. In K. Pasley & M. Ihinger-Tallman (Eds.), *Remarriage and stepfamilies today: Research and theory* (pp. 273–299). New York: Guilford Press.

Santrock, J. W., Sitterle, K. A., & Warshak, R. A. (1988). Parent–child relationships in stepfather families. In P. Bronstein & C. P. Cowan (Eds.), *Fatherhood today: Men's changing role in the family* (pp. 144–165). New York: Wiley.

Sattler, J. M. (1992). *Assessment of children: Revised and updated third edition.* San Diego, CA: Jerome M. Sattler, Publisher.

Sattler, J. M. (1997). *Interviewing children and families: Guidelines for the mental health, education, pediatric, and child maltreatment fields.* San Diego, CA: Jerome M. Sattler, Publisher.

Sattler, J. M., & Mash, E. J. (1997). Introduction to clinical assessment interviewing. In J. M. Sattler, *Interviewing children and families: Guidelines for the mental health, education, pediatric, and child maltreatment fields.* San Diego, CA: Jerome M. Sattler, Publisher.

Scanlon, E. M., & Ollendick, T. H. (1985). Children's assertive behavior: The reliability and validity of three self-report measures. *Child and Family Behavior Therapy, 7,* 9–21.

Schaefer, E. S., & Bell, R. Q. (1958). Development of a Parent Attitude Research Instrument. *Child Development, 9,* 339–361.

Schlundt, D. G., & McFall, R. M. (1987). Classifying social situations: A comparison of five methods. *Behavioral Assessment, 9,* 21–42.

Schwarz, J. C., Barton-Henry, M. L., & Pruzinsky, T. (1985). Assessing child rearing behaviors: A comparison of ratings made by mother, father and sibling on the CRPBI. *Child Development, 56,* 462–479.

Schwebel, A. L., & Fine, M. A. (1992). Cognitive-behavioral family therapy. *Journal of Family Psychotherapy, 3,* 73–91.

Schwebel, A. L., & Fine, M. A. (1994). *Understanding and helping families: A cognitive-behavioral approach.* Hillsdale, NJ: Erlbaum.

Shaffer, D., Schwab-Stone, M., Fisher, P., Cohen, P., Piacentini, J., Davies, M., Conners, C. K., & Regiers, D. (1993). The Diagnostic Interview Schedule for Children—Revised Version (DISC-R): I. Preparation, field testing, interrater reliability, and acceptability. *Journal of the American Academy for Child and Adolescent Psyciatry, 32,* 643–650.

Shapiro, E. S., & Cole, C. L. (1993). Self-monitoring. In T. H. Ollendick & M. Hersen (Eds.), *Handbook of child and adolescent assessment* (pp. 124–139). Needham Heights, MA: Allyn & Bacon.

Shaywitz, S. E., Schnell, C., Shaywitz, B. A., & Towle, V. R. (1986). Yale Children's Inventory: An instrument to assess children with attentional deficits and learning disabilities. I. Scale development and psychometric properties. *Journal of Abnormal Child Psychology, 14,* 347–364.

Sigel, I. (Ed.). (1985). *Parental belief systems: The psychological consequences for children.* Hillsdale, NJ: Erlbaum.

Sigel, I., McGillicuddy-DeLisi, A. V., & Goodnow, J. J. (Eds.). (1992). *Parental belief systems: The psychological consequences for children* (2nd ed.). Hillsdale, NJ: Erlbaum.

Silverman, W. K. (1987). *Anxiety Disorders Interview Schedule (ADIS) for children.* Albany, NY: Graywind.

Silverman, W. K., & Nelles, W. B. (1986, November). *Further considerations in the assessment of childhood anxiety: Mothers and children's reports.* Paper presented at the meeting of the Association for Advancement of Behavior Therapy, Chicago.

Sines, J. O. (1986). Normative data for the Revised Missouri Children's Behavior Checklist—Parent Form (MCBC-P). *Journal of Abnormal Child Psychology, 14,* 89–94.

Skinner, H. A. (1987). Self-report instruments for family assessment. In T. Jacob (Ed.), *Family inter-*

action and psychopathology (pp. 427–452). New York: Plenum Press.

Skitka, L. J. (1986, April). *The role of gender and resources in equity considerations of interpersonal relationships.* Paper presented at the annual meeting of the Western Psychological Association, Seattle, WA.

Smucker, M. R., Craighead, W. E., Craighead, L. W., & Green, B. (1986). Normative and reliability data for the Children's Depression Inventory. *Journal of Abnormal Child Psychology, 14,* 25–39.

Spanier, G. B. (1976). Measuring dyadic adjustment: New scales for assessing marriage and similar dyads. *Journal of Marriage and the Family, 38,* 15–28.

Spielberger, C. D. (1973). *State–Trait Anxiety Inventory for Children.* Palo Alto, CA: Consulting Psychologists Press.

Sroufe, L. A., & Fleeson, J. (1986). Attachment and the construction of relationships. In W. Hartup & Z. Rubin (Eds.), *Relationships and development.* Hillsdale, NJ: Erlbaum.

Sroufe, L. A., & Rutter, M. (1984). The domain of developmental psychopathology. *Child Development, 55,* 17–29.

Stevens-Long, J. (1973). The effect of behavioral context on some aspects of adult disciplinary practice and affect. *Child Development, 44,* 476–484.

Stevenson, M. B., Colbert, K. K., & Roach, M. A. (1986, October). *Transition to parenthood in adolescent and adult single mothers.* Unpublished manuscript, University of Wisconsin–Madison.

Stokes, T. F., Fowler, S. A., & Baer, D. M. (1978). Training preschool children to recruit natural communities of reinforcement. *Journal of Applied Behavior Analysis, 11,* 285–303.

Straus, M. A., & Brown, B. W. (1978). *Family measurement techniques: Abstracts of published instruments, 1935–1974.* Minneapolis: University of Minnesota Press.

Strayhorn, J. M., Jr. (1987). Medical assessment of children with behavioral problems. In M. Hersen & V. B. Van Hasselt (Eds.), *Behavior therapy with children and adolescents: A clinical approach* (pp. 50–74). New York: Wiley–Interscience.

Strosahl, K. D. (1994). Entering the new frontier of managed mental health care: Gold mines and land mines. *Cognitive and Behavioral Practice, 1,* 5–23.

Strosahl, K.D. (1996). Confessions of a behavior therapist in primary care: The odyssey and the ecstasy. *Cognitive and Behavioral Practice, 3,* 1–28.

Strosahl, K. D., & Linehan, M. M. (1986). Basic issues in behavioral assessment. In A. R. Ciminero, K. S. Calhoun, & H. E. Adams (Eds.), *Handbook of behavioral assessment* (2nd ed., pp. 12–46). New York: Wiley.

Sulzer-Azaroff, B., & Mayer, G. R. (1991). *Behavior analysis for lasting change.* Fort Worth, TX: Holt, Rinehart & Winston.

Swan, G. E., & MacDonald, M. L. (1978). Behavior therapy in practice: A national survey of behavior therapists. *Behavior Therapy, 9,* 799–807.

Szapocznik, J. (1984). *Manual for family task rating.* Unpublished manuscript, University of Miami, Coral Gables, FL.

Szykula, S. (1986). *Child focused strategies and behavioral family therapy processes: Hypothetical case study comparisons.* Unpublished manuscript, University of Utah School of Medicine.

Tabachnik, N., & Alloy, L. B. (1988). Clinician and patient as aberrant actuaries: Expectation-based distortions in assessment of covariation. In L. Y. Abramson (Ed.), *Social cognition and clinical psychology: A synthesis* (pp. 295–365). New York: Guilford Press.

Taylor, C. B. (1983). DSM-III and behavioral assessment. *Behavioral Assessment, 5,* 5–14.

Tharp, R. G. (1991). Cultural diversity and treatment of children. *Journal of Consulting and Clinical Psychology, 59,* 799–812.

Tharp, R. G., & Wetzel, R. J. (1969). *Behavior modification in the natural environment.* New York: Academic Press.

Toobert, D., Patterson, G. R., Moore, D., & Halper, V. (1982). *MOSAIC: A multidimensional description of family interaction.* Unpublished technical report, Oregon Social Learning Center, Eugene.

Touliatos, J., Perlmutter, B. F., & Straus, M. A. (Eds.). (1990). *Handbook of family measurement techniques.* Newbury Park, CA: Sage.

Trickett, P. K., & Kuczynski, L. (1986). Children's misbehaviors and parental disciplinary strategies in abusive and nonabusive families. *Developmental Psychology, 22,* 115–123.

Tronick, E. O., & Gianino, A. (1986). Interactive mismatch and repair: Challenges to the coping infant. *Zero to Three, 6,* 1–6.

Turkat, I. D. (1986). The behavioral interview. In A. R. Ciminero, K. S. Calhoun, & H. E. Adams (Eds.), *Handbook of behavioral assessment* (2nd ed., pp. 109–149). New York: Wiley.

Turkat, I. D., & Meyer, V. (1982). The behavior-analytic approach. In P. Wachtel (Ed.), *Resistance: Psychodynamic and behavioral approaches* (pp. 157–184). New York: Plenum Press.

Twardosz, S., & Nordquist, V. N. (1983). The development and importance of affection. In B. B. Lahey & A. E. Kazdin (Eds.), *Advances in clinical child psychology* (Vol. 6, pp. 129–168). New York: Plenum Press.

Ullmann, L. P., & Krasner, L. (Eds.). (1965). *Case studies in behavior modification.* New York: Holt, Rinehart & Winston.

Van Goor-Lambo, G. (1987). The reliability of Axis V of the multiaxial classification scheme. *Journal of Child Psychology and Psychiatry, 28,* 597–612.

Vincent, T. A., & Trickett, E. J. (1983). Preventive interventions and the human context: Ecological approaches to environmental assessment and change. In R. D. Felner, L. A. Jason, J. N.

Moritsugu, & S. S. Farber (Eds.), *Preventive psychology: Theory, research and practice* (pp. 67–86). Elmsford, NY: Pergamon Press.

Voeltz, L. M., & Evans, I. M. (1982). The assessment of behavioral interrelationships in child behavior therapy. *Behavioral Assessment, 4,* 131–165.

Wacker, D. P., & Berg, W. K. (1994). The impact of functional analysis methodology on outpatient clinic services. *Journal of Applied Behavior Analysis, 27,* 405–407.

Wade, T. C., Baker, T. B., & Hartmann, D. P. (1979). Behavior therapists' self-reported views and practices. *The Behavior Therapist, 2,* 3–6.

Wahler, R. G. (1975). Some structural aspects of deviant child behavior. *Journal of Applied Behavior Analysis, 8,* 27–42.

Wahler, R. G. (1976). Deviant child behavior within the family: Developmental speculations and behavior change strategies. In H. Leitenberg (Ed.), *Handbook of behavior modification and behavior therapy* (pp. 516–543). Englewood Cliffs, NJ: Prentice-Hall.

Wahler, R. G. (1980). The insular mother: Her problems in parent–child treatment. *Journal of Applied Behavior Analysis, 13,* 207–219.

Wahler, R. G., & Cormier, W. H. (1970). The ecological interview: A first step in outpatient child behavior therapy. *Journal of Behavior Therapy and Experimental Psychiatry, 1,* 279–289.

Wahler, R. G., & Dumas, J. E. (1986). Maintenance factors in coercive mother–child interactions: The compliance and predictability hypotheses. *Journal of Applied Behavior Analysis, 19,* 13–22.

Wahler, R. G., & Fox, J. J. (1981). Setting events in applied behavior analysis: Toward a conceptual and methodological expansion. *Journal of Applied Behavior Analysis, 14,* 327–338.

Wahler, R. G., & Graves, M. G. (1983). Setting events in social networks: Ally or enemy in child behavior therapy? *Behavior Therapy, 14,* 19–36.

Wahler, R. G., House, A. E., & Stambaugh, E. E. (1976). *Ecological assessment of child problem behavior: A clinical package for home, school, and institutional settings.* Elmsford, NY: Pergamon Press.

Wahler, R. G., Leske, G., & Rogers, E. D. (1979). The insular family: A deviance support system for oppositional children. In L. A. Hamerlynck (Ed.), *Behavioral systems for the developmentally disabled: Vol. 1. School and family environments* (pp. 102–127). New York: Brunner/Mazel.

Wahler, R. G., Sperling, K. A., Thomas, M. R., Teeter, N. C., & Luper, H. L. (1970). The modification of childhood stuttering: Some response-response relationships. *Journal of Experimental Child Psychology, 9,* 411–428.

Walker, C., & Roberts, M. C. (Eds.). (1992). *Handbook of clinical child psychology* (2nd ed.). New York: Wiley.

Wampold, B. E. (1986). State of the art in sequential analysis: Comment on Lichtenberg and Heck. *Journal of Counseling Psychology, 33,* 182–185.

Wasik, B. H. (1984). Clinical applications of direct behavioral observation: A look at the past and the future. In B. B. Lahey & A. E. Kazdin (Eds.), *Advances in clinical child psychology* (Vol. 8, pp. 156–193). New York: Plenum Press.

Wasik, B. H., Bryant, D. M., & Fishbein, J. (1980, November). *Assessing parent problem solving skills.* Paper presented at the meeting of the Association for Advancement of Behavior Therapy, Toronto.

Watkins, C. E., Campbell, V. L., & McGregor, P. (1990). What types of psychological tests do behavioral (and other) counseling psychologists use? *The Behavior Therapist, 13,* 115–117.

Weinrott, M. R., Reid, J. B., Bauske, B. W., & Brummett, B. (1981). Supplementing naturalistic observations with observer impressions. *Behavioral Assessment, 3,* 151–159.

Weiss, R. L., & Chaffin, L. (1986, May). *Micro- and macro-coding of marital interactions.* Paper presented at the meeting of the Western Psychological Association, Seattle, WA.

Weiss, R. L., & Margolin, G. (1986). Assessment of marital conflict and accord. In A. R. Ciminero, K. S. Calhoun, & H. E. Adams (Eds.), *Handbook of behavioral assessment* (2nd ed., pp. 561–600). New York: Wiley.

Werry, J. S., & Sprague, R. L. (1970). Hyperactivity. In C. G. Costello (Ed.), *Symptoms of psychopathology: A handbook* (pp. 397–417). New York: Wiley.

Whalen, C. K., Henker, B., Collins, B. E., Finck, D., & Dotemoto, S. (1979). A social ecology of hyperactive boys: Medication effects in structured classroom environments. *Journal of Applied Behavior Analysis, 12,* 65–81.

Whitehurst, G. J., Fischel, J. E., DeBaryshe, B., Caulfield, M. B., & Falco, F. L. (1986). Analyzing sequential relations in observational data: A practical guide. *Journal of Psychopathology and Behavioral Assessment, 8,* 129–148.

Wiggins, J. S. (1981). Clinical and statistical prediction: Where are we and where do we go from here? *Clinical Psychology Review, 1,* 3–18.

Willems, E. P. (1973). Go ye into all the world and modify behavior: An ecologist's view. *Representative Research in Social Psychology, 4,* 93–105.

Willems, E. P. (1974). Behavioral technology and behavioral ecology. *Journal of Applied Behavior Analysis, 7,* 151–165.

Williams, R. L., & Workman, E. A. (1978). The development of a behavioral self-concept scale. *Behavior Therapy, 9,* 680–681.

Wirt, R. D., Lachar, D., Klinedinst, J. K., & Seat, P. S. (1990). *Personality Inventory for Children—1990 edition.* Los Angeles: Western Psychological Services.

Wolf, M. M. (1978). Social validity: The case for subjective measurement, or how applied behavior analysis is finding its heart. *Journal of Applied Behavior Analysis, 11,* 203–214.

Wolfe, D. A. (1985). Child abusive parents: An empirical review and analysis. *Psychological Bulletin, 97,* 462–482.

Wolfe, D. A., & LaRose, L. (1986). *Child videotape series* [Videotape]. London, Ontario, Canada: University of Western Ontario.

Wolpe, I. (1986). Individualization: The categorical imperative of behavior therapy practice. *Journal of Behavior Therapy and Experimental Psychiatry, 17,* 145–153.

World Health Organization. (1992). *The ICD-10 classification of mental and behavioral disorders: Clinical descriptions and diagnostic guidelines.* Geneva: Author.

Yarrow, M. R., Campbell, J. D., & Burton, R. V. (1970). Recollections of childhood: A study of the retrospective method. *Monographs of the Society for Research in Child Development, 35* (Serial No. 138).

Yates, B. T., & Hoage, C. M. (1979, December). *Mnemonic stigma in behavior observation: An interaction of diagnostic label, relative frequency of positive versus negative behavior, and type of behavior recalled.* Paper presented at the meeting of the Association for Advancement of Behavior Therapy, San Francisco.

Yates, B. T., Klein, S. B., & Haven, W. G. (1978). Psychological nosology and mnemonic reconstruction: Effects of diagnostic labels on observ-

ers' recall of positive and negative behavior frequencies. *Cognitive Therapy and Research, 2,* 377–387.

Yule, W. (1993). Developmental consideration in child assessment. In T. H. Ollendick & M. Hersen (Eds.), *Handbook of child and adolescent assessment* (pp. 15–25). Needham Heights, MA: Allyn & Bacon.

Zachary, R. A., Levin, B., Hargreaves, W. A., & Greene, J. A. (1981). *Trends in the use of psychiatric diagnoses for children: 1960–1979.* Unpublished manuscript, University of California at San Francisco.

Zahn-Waxler, C. (1993). Warriors and worriers: Gender and psychopathology. *Development and Psychopathology, 5,* 79–89.

Zangwill, W. M., & Kniskern, J. R. (1982). Comparison of problem families in the clinic and at home. *Behavior Therapy, 13,* 145–152.

Zeitlin, S., Williamson, G. G., & Rosenblatt, W. (1985). *Coping with stress model as used with families in an early intervention program.* Unpublished manuscript, John F. Kennedy Medical Center, Edison, NJ.

Zero to Three/National Center for Clinical Infant Programs. (1994). *Diagnostic classification of mental health and developmental disorders of infancy and early childhood* (*Diagnostic Classification: 0–3*). Washington, DC: Author.

Zoccolillo, M. (1993). Gender and the development of Conduct Disorder. *Development and Psychopathology, 5,* 65–78.

Part II

BEHAVIOR DISORDERS

Chapter Two

ATTENTION-DEFICIT/ HYPERACTIVITY DISORDER

Russell A. Barkley

Since the first edition of this chapter appeared more than 15 years ago (Barkley, 1981b), much has occurred in research on hyperactivity in children, or what has now come to be known as Attention-Deficit/Hyperactivity Disorder (ADHD; American Psychiatric Association, 1994). It remains one of the most frequently studied childhood disorders, probably reflecting its status as one of the problems most commonly referred to child guidance centers in the United States. Greater information now exists on the disorder's nature, prevalence, developmental course, prognosis, and etiology (for reviews, see Barkley, 1990; Hinshaw, 1994; Ross & Ross, 1982; Weiss, 1992; Weiss & Hechtman, 1993). Advances also continue to occur in its theoretical conceptualization (Barkley, 1994, 1997a; Quay, 1989; Sergeant, 1988). Happily for those faced with the clinical demands of assessing and treating these children, more useful assessment techniques and treatment programs are now available than was previously the case. This chapter highlights information culled from the vast body of literature on this disorder, and briefly summarizes its current status in the field of child psychopathology. Guidelines are then suggested for the clinical assessment of ADHD in children.

OVERVIEW

History

One of the earliest papers to appear on the subject of ADHD in children was a three-part article by Still (1902), in which children described in terms closely resembling modern-day ADHD and Conduct Disorder were concluded to be suffer-ing from defects in "moral control" and "volitional inhibition." Little additional research was published on ADHD until the late 1940s. Scientific writers at that time were struck by the similarity of behavioral problems between ADHD children and those with documented brain injury. As a result, overactivity, distractibility, inattention, and poor impulse control were believed to signify brain injury, despite the absence of hard neurological evidence (Strauss & Lehtinen, 1947). Distractibility and excessive activity were believed to be the chief difficulties of such children. From these notions would later spring the terms "minimal brain damage" and eventually "minimal brain dysfunction" (MBD; Clements & Peters, 1962). These terms were used to imply an underlying brain impairment (Wender, 1971), despite the dearth of medical evidence supporting the brain injury hypothesis (Rutter, 1977; Taylor, 1983).

By the late 1970s, the concept of MBD was on the wane (Rie & Rie, 1980), mainly because of the lack of evidence for any interrelationships among its symptoms (Routh & Roberts, 1972; Ullman, Barkley, & Brown, 1978; Werry, Weiss, & Douglas, 1964). The emphasis on overactivity as the hallmark of this disorder increased into the 1960s (Chess, 1960; Clements, 1966). But as more measures of other constructs were included in research, it became apparent that overactivity was not the only problem experienced by such children, nor was it necessarily the primary one. In a series of studies by Douglas and her colleagues, a persuasive case was made for attentional deficits and impulse control problems as the primary symptoms of this disorder (Douglas, 1972). Substantial evidence has since accumulated in support of this notion (Douglas, 1980, 1983; Douglas & Peters, 1979). So convincing was this body of research that when the second edition of the *Diagnostic and Statistical Manual of Mental Disorders* (DSM-II; American Psychiatric Association, 1968), was revised, the diagnosis Hyperkinetic Reaction of Childhood was replaced with Attention Deficit Disorder (ADD) with or without Hyperactivity, and three primary symptoms were now described: inattention, impulsivity, and overactivity (American Psychiatric Association, 1980). The DSM-III also provided a list of items describing the behaviors characteristic of each symptom. Children who were inattentive and impulsive but not overactive were to be diagnosed as having ADD without Hyperactivity, whereas those with all three symptoms were to be described as having ADD with Hyperactivity.

In 1987 the DSM-III underwent a subsequent revision, becoming the DSM-III-R. The name of the disorder was now changed to Attention-Deficit Hyperactivity Disorder, and the status of hyperactivity as a symptom was elevated in its importance to the disorder (American Psychiatric Association, 1987). A single list of behavioral items was provided that described all three of the primary symptoms of the disorder. Children who only had difficulties with attention were now to be diagnosed as Undifferentiated ADHD; this diagnosis was relegated to a minor status within the taxonomy because of limited research to guide the developers in its differentiation from ADHD, and hence in the construction of diagnostic criteria for it.

Most recently, the DSM-IV has been published (American Psychiatric Association, 1994), and the name Attention-Deficit/Hyperactivity Disorder has been retained (with a slight punctuation change). However, instead of a single list of symptom descriptions as in the DSM-III-R, two separate lists are now provided—one for inattention and the other for hyperactive–impulsive behavior, considered jointly. Presently, a child can be diagnosed as having ADHD if he or she has *only* problems with inattention, which are described as ADHD, Predominantly Inattentive Type. Although research supporting this latter subclassification was almost nonexistent at the time of its creation, the very creation of the subtype prompted further research into its possible existence (see Barkley, Grodzinsky, & DuPaul, 1992; Goodyear & Hynd, 1992; Lahey & Carlson, 1992, for reviews). Ironically, it is becoming increasingly evident that this subtype of ADHD may not be a subtype at all, but an entirely distinct disorder having a qualitatively different form

of inattention from that seen in ADHD, and a different pattern of comorbid psychiatric disorders and psychological impairments associated with it (Barkley, 1990; Barkley, DuPaul, & McMurray, 1990). Perhaps in future editions of the DSM, it may be granted a separate diagnostic label and its own symptom list, along with other diagnostic criteria.

Children who are chiefly hyperactive–impulsive but not inattentive are diagnosed as having ADHD, Predominantly Hyperactive–Impulsive Type; those with both sets of symptoms (inattention and hyperactivity–impulsivity) are described as having ADHD, Combined Type. Current evidence suggests that these may simply be separate developmental stages for the same disorder, given that the hyperactive–impulsive behavior appears to arise first in development (typically at about ages 2–4, to be followed within a few years by the symptoms of inattention (Hart et al., 1996; Loeber, Green, Lahey, Christ, & Frick, 1992). If so, then the diagnosis of ADHD, Predominantly Hyperactive–Impulsive Type will probably be given primarily to preschool-age children, many of whom will then move into the Combined Type by their elementary school years.

Not only have diagnostic labels and criteria evolved over this century, particularly within the past 30 years, but so have conceptualizations of ADHD. During the 1980s, for example, reports began to challenge the notion that ADHD is primarily a disturbance in attention; these reports instead focused upon problems with motivation generally, and an insensitivity to response consequences specifically (Barkley, 1989; Haenlein & Caul, 1987; Glow & Glow, 1979). Research was demonstrating that children with ADHD did not respond to alterations in contingencies of reinforcement or punishment in the same way as normal children. Under conditions of continuous reward, the performances of ADHD children were often indistinguishable from those of normal children on various laboratory tasks, but when reinforcement patterns shifted to partial-reward or to extinction (no-reward) conditions, the children with ADHD showed significant declines in their performance (Douglas & Parry, 1983, 1994; Parry & Douglas, 1983). More recently, however, several studies have not found ADHD children to respond abnormally to schedules of partial reinforcement (Barber, Milich, & Welsh, 1996); these findings raise questions about the existence of an insensitivity to consequences.

It was also becoming evident to some that deficits in the manner in which rules and instructions govern behavior characterizes these children

(Barkley, 1981a, 1989, 1990). When rules specifying behavior were given that competed with the prevailing immediate consequences in the setting for other forms of action, the rules did not control behavior in ADHD children as well as in normal children. Thus, it was hypothesized that the class of human behavior initiated and sustained by rules (and language), called "rule-governed behavior" by behaviorists (Skinner, 1953; Hayes, 1989), may be impaired in those with ADHD.

Moreover, researchers employing information-processing paradigms to study children with ADHD were having a difficult time demonstrating that these children's problems in attending to tasks were actually attentional in nature. Problems in response inhibition and motor system control were more reliably demonstrated instead (Barkley, Grodzinsky, & DuPaul, 1992; Schachar & Logan, 1990; Sergeant, 1988; Sergeant & Scholten, 1985a, 1985b; Sergeant & van der Meere, 1989). Researchers were also finding that the problems with hyperactivity and impulsivity were not separate symptoms, but formed a single dimension of behavior (Achenbach, 1991b; Goyette, Conners, & Ulrich, 1978; Lahey, Pelham, et al., 1988), which I have previously described as "disinhibition" (Barkley, 1990). In other words, the symptoms of hyperactivity and impulsivity seem to be both a single problem and a signal problem for the disorder.

Debate continues over the core deficit(s) in ADHD, with increasing weight being given to the central problem of behavioral inhibition. The field seems to be returning, in a general sense, to the early notion of Still (1902) that defects in "volitional inhibition" (i.e., impulse control) and the "moral control" of behavior (i.e., the regulation of behavior by rules) are part of this disorder.

Definition, Diagnosis, and Primary Symptoms

A number of commonalities can be distilled from prior efforts at describing and defining ADHD. These appear to be (1) an emphasis on *age-inappropriate* levels of inattention, impulsivity, and overactivity; (2) the inability of these children, relative to same-age normal children, to restrict their behavior to situational demands (self-regulation); (3) the emergence of these problems by early childhood; (4) the pervasiveness of these problems across several settings and/or caregivers; (5) the chronicity of these symptoms throughout development; and (6) the inability of obvious developmental disabilities (i.e., mental retardation, severe language delay, etc.), neurological diseases

(i.e., gross brain damage, epilepsy, etc.), or severe psychopathology (i.e., autism, schizophrenia, etc.) to account for these behavioral deficits.

Definition and Diagnostic Criteria

Many different definitions for ADHD have been proposed throughout the history of this disorder. Few, however, have been particularly operational (Barkley, 1982). A great improvement in this state of affairs occurred in the DSM-III, where guidelines for the types and number of behavioral descriptors, the age of onset, and the duration of these symptoms were specified. These criteria have evolved to become the DSM-IV criteria for ADHD, as noted above; the DSM-IV criteria are presented in Table 2.1. A more detailed examination and critique of these criteria can be found elsewhere (Barkley, 1996b).

It is possible for children to exhibit symptoms of ADHD after the age of 6 years as a result of central nervous system trauma or disease. In such cases, I suggest that all DSM-IV criteria other than B (age of onset) must be met, and that the disorder should be referred to as "Acquired ADHD Secondary to _____." The known etiology should be specified in the blank space, so as to distinguish these children from those with the more common, developmental, idiopathic form of the disorder described in the vast majority of research on the subject. It should be noted that these criteria do not preclude the children's receiving additional diagnoses of Oppositional Defiant Disorder or Conduct Disorder. As mentioned later, these disorders overlap substantially with ADHD and would be expected to occur in the majority of such children.

I am in agreement with other experienced researchers in this field (Hinshaw, 1994) in viewing ADHD as probably being a trait that exists on a dimension or continuum with normal child behavior. Deficits in attention, impulsivity, and activity may be to ADHD what delays in intelligence are to mental retardation: Both conditions lie on a continuum with normal development, and their presence is established by using a somewhat arbitrary cutoff point along this continuum. Yet one must recognize the existence of borderline conditions lying close to but not beyond this cutoff point. The condition is not necessarily static, in that once so diagnosed a child always remains within the boundaries for this category. Although ADHD is generally chronic, with a high degree of stability over development for most children (see Barkley, Fischer, Edelbrock, & Smallish, 1990; Campbell, Schleifer, & Weiss,

TABLE 2.1. DSM-IV Criteria for ADHD

A. Either (1) or (2):

   (1) six (or more) of the following symptoms of **inattention** have persisted for at least 6 months to a degree that is maladaptive and inconsistent with developmental level:

   Inattention
   (a) often fails to give close attention to details or makes careless mistakes in schoolwork, work, or other activities
   (b) often has difficulty sustaining attention in tasks or play activities
   (c) often does not seem to listen when spoken to directly
   (d) often does not follow through on instructions and fails to finish schoolwork, chores, or duties in the workplace (not due to oppositional behavior or failure to understand instructions)
   (e) often has difficulty organizing tasks and activities
   (f) often avoids, dislikes, or is reluctant to engage in tasks that require sustained mental effort (such as schoolwork or homework)
   (g) often loses things necessary for tasks or activities (e.g., toys, school assignments, pencils, books, or tools)
   (h) is often easily distracted by extraneous stimuli
   (i) is often forgetful in daily activities

   (2) six (or more) of the following symptoms of **hyperactivity–impulsivity** have persisted for at least 6 months to a degree that is maladaptive and inconsistent with developmental level:

   Hyperactivity
   (a) often fidgets with hands or feet or squirms in seat
   (b) often leaves seat in classroom or in other situations in which remaining seated is expected
   (c) often runs about or climbs excessively in situations in which it is inappropriate (in adolescents or adults, may be limited to subjective feelings of restlessness)
   (d) often has difficulty playing or engaging in leisure activities quietly
   (e) is often "on the go" or often acts as if "driven by a motor"
   (f) often talks excessively

   Impulsivity
   (g) often blurts out answers before the questions have been completed
   (h) often has difficulty awaiting turn
   (i) often interrupts or intrudes on others (e.g., butts into conversations or games)

B. Some hyperactive–impulsive or inattentive symptoms that caused impairment were present before age 7 years.

C. Some impairment from the symptoms is present in two or more settings (e.g., at school [or work] and at home).

D. There must be clear evidence of clinically significant impairment in social, academic, or occupational functioning.

E. The symptoms do not occur exclusively during the course of a Pervasive Developmental Disorder, Schizophrenia, or other Psychotic Disorder, and are not better accounted for by another mental disorder (e.g., Mood Disorder, Anxiety Disorder, Dissociative Disorder, or a Personality Disorder).

Code based on type:
314.01   **Attention-Deficit/Hyperactivity Disorder, Combined Type:** if both Criteria A1 and A2 are met for the past 6 months
314.00   **Attention-Deficit/Hyperactivity Disorder, Predominantly Inattentive Type:** if Criterion A1 is met but Criterion A2 is not met for the past 6 months
314.01   **Attention-Deficit/Hyperactivity Disorder, Predominantly Hyperactive–Impulsive Type:** if Criterion A2 is met but Criterion A1 is not met for the past 6 months
Coding note: For individuals (especially adolescents and adults) who currently have symptoms that no longer meet full criteria, "In Partial Remission" should be specified).

Note. From American Psychiatric Association (1994, p. 85). Copyright 1994 by the American Psychiatric Association. Reprinted by permission.

1978; Fischer, Barkley, Fletcher, & Smallish, 1993a), those lying nearest to the cutoff point may move into or out of the condition over the course of their development as their individual scores fluctuate.

From this viewpoint, ADHD might be defined by consensus as follows: *ADHD is a developmental disorder of attention span and/or overactivity– impulsivity in which these deficits are significantly inappropriate for the child's mental age; have an onset in early childhood; are significantly pervasive or cross-situational in nature; are generally chronic or persistent over time; and are not the direct result of severe language delay, deafness, blindness, autism, or childhood psychosis.*

Primary Symptoms

Substantial evidence exists that ADHD children are significantly different from normal children on measures of attention span, activity level, and impulse control (for reviews, see Barkley, 1990; Hinshaw, 1987, 1994; Luk, 1985; Ross & Ross, 1982; Whalen & Henker, 1980). However, many of these studies have shown substantial disparities in the types of measures on which such differences occurred, the kinds of settings in which the measures were taken, and the definitions used to select the ADHD children; these factors have led to many failures to replicate the findings on these constructs (Barkley, 1982). Although space precludes a full elucidation of the issue here, it is clear that the constructs of inattention, overactivity, and impulsivity are not unitary, but are multidimensional (Barkley, 1991; Douglas & Peters, 1979; Milich & Kramer, 1984). There are many different types of inattention, overactivity, and impulsivity, and numerous ways to measure them, not all of which have consistently revealed differences between ADHD and normal children. Moreover, research has not always been successful in demonstrating the more important distinction between ADHD and other psychiatric disorders on measures of these primary symptoms (Firestone & Martin, 1979; Sandberg, Rutter, & Taylor, 1978). And so, although this chapter may frequently refer to such constructs as if they were unitary and as if they consistently differentiated ADHD children from other groups of children, the complexity inherent in these terms and the disparity among studies should not be ignored.

Inattention

The problem with attention is seen in the ADHD child's inability to sustain attention or responding to tasks or play activities as long as others of the same age can, and to follow through on rules and instructions as well as others do. It is also seen in the child's being more disorganized, distracted, and forgetful than others of the same age. Parents and teachers frequently complain that ADHD children do not seem to listen as well as they should for their age, cannot concentrate, are easily distracted, fail to finish assignments, daydream, and change activities more often than others (Barkley, DuPaul, & McMurray, 1990). Research employing objective measures of these attributes corroborates their presence in ADHD children, who, when compared to normal children, are often recorded as being more "off-task," as less likely to complete as much work, as looking away more from the activities they are requested to do (including television), as persisting less in correctly performing boring activities (e.g., in continuous-performance tests [CPTs], and as being slower and less likely to return to an activity once interrupted (Corkum & Siegel, 1993; Luk, 1985; Milich & Lorch, 1994; Schachar, Tannock, & Logan, 1993). These behaviors have also been noted to distinguish them from children with learning disabilities (Barkley, DuPaul, & McMurray, 1990) or with other psychiatric disorders (Werry, Elkind, & Reeves, 1987). Yet objective research does not find children with ADHD to be generally more distracted by extraneous events occurring during their task performance, although they may be so distracted if the irrelevant stimuli are embedded within the task itself (Campbell, Douglas, & Morgenstern, 1971; Cohen, Weiss, & Minde, 1972; Rosenthal & Allen, 1980; Steinkamp, 1980).

Hyperactive–Impulsive Behavior (Disinhibition)

The problems with disinhibition noted in children with ADHD are manifested in difficulties with fidgetiness; staying seated when required; moving about, running, and climbing more than other children; playing noisily; talking excessively; interrupting others activities; and being less able than others to wait in line or take turns in games (American Psychiatric Association, 1994). Parents and teachers describe them as incessantly in motion and unable to wait for events to occur. Research has objectively documented them to be more active than other children (Barkley & Cunningham, 1979; Luk, 1985; Porrino et al., 1983; Teicher, Ito, Glod, & Barber, 1996; Zentall, 1985), to be less mature in controlling motor overflow movements (Denckla & Rudel, 1978), and to have considerable difficulties with stopping an ongoing behavior (Schachar et al., 1993; Milich, Hartung,

Matrin, & Haigler, 1994). Children with ADHD have also been shown to talk more than others (Barkley, Cunningham, & Karlsson, 1983); to interrupt others' conversations (Malone & Swanson, 1993); to be less able to resist immediate temptations and delay gratification (Anderson, Hinshaw, & Simmel, 1994; Campbell, Szumowski, Ewing, Gluck, & Breaux, 1982; Rapport, Tucker, DuPaul, Merlo, & Stoner, 1986); and to respond too quickly and too often when they are required to wait and watch for events to happen, as is often seen in impulsive errors on CPTs (Corkum & Siegel, 1993). Although less frequently examined, differences in activity and impulsiveness have been found between children with ADHD and those with learning disabilities (Barkley, DuPaul, & McMurray, 1990) or with other psychiatric disorders (Halperin, Matier, Bedi, Sharma, & Newcorn, 1992; Roberts, 1990; Werry et al., 1987).

As mentioned earlier, the problems with disinhibition arise first (at about 2–4 years of age), with those related to inattention emerging in the developmental course of ADHD (at about 5–7 years), or by entry into formal schooling; the problems with inattention may emerge even later, by the early to middle elementary school grades, if only these problems are the principal difficulties (Hart et al., 1996; Loeber et al., 1992). And whereas the symptoms of disinhibition in the DSM item lists seem to decline with age, those of inattention remain relatively stable during the elementary grades (Hart et al., 1996). Yet even they decline by adolescence (Fischer et al., 1993a). Why the inattention arises later than the disinhibitory symptoms and does not decline when the latter do over development remains an enigma. One explanation of this is advanced below in connection with a theoretical model of ADHD that I have recently advanced (Barkley, 1994, 1996, 1997a).

Situational and Contextual Factors

As I have noted elsewhere (Barkley, 1990), the symptoms that constitute ADHD are greatly affected in their level of severity by a variety of situational and contextual factors (indeed, this is true for most forms of childhood psychopathology). Douglas (1972) commented on the greater variability in task performances by ADHD children as compared to control children. Many others since then have found that when ADHD children must perform multiple trials within a task assessing attention and impulse control, the range of scores around their own mean performance is frequently greater than in normal children (see Douglas, 1983). The finding is sufficiently common in measures of reaction time (Chee, Logan, Schachar, Lindsay, & Wachsmuth, 1989; Zahn, Krusei, & Rapoport, 1991) to have led several developers of CPTs marketed for commercial use in diagnosing ADHD to recommend that the variability in this measure should serve as an indicator for the disorder (Conners, 1995; Greenberg & Waldman, 1992).

A number of other factors have been noted to influence the ability of children with ADHD to sustain their attention to task performance, control their impulses to act, regulate their activity level, and produce work consistently. These include (1) time of day or fatigue (Porrino et al., 1983; Zagar & Bowers, 1983); (2) increasing task complexity, such that organizational strategies are required (Douglas, 1983); (3) extent of restraint demanded for the context (Barkley & Ullman, 1975; Luk, 1985); (4) level of stimulation within the setting (Zentall, 1985); (5) the schedule of immediate consequences associated with the task (Douglas & Parry, 1983, 1994); and (6) the absence of adult supervision during task performance (Draeger, Prior, & Sanson, 1986; Gomez & Sanson, 1994).

The aforementioned factors chiefly apply to task performance, but variability in ADHD children's behavior has also been documented across more macroscopic settings. For instance, researchers using a rating scale of various contexts within the home have shown that children with ADHD are most problematic in their behavior when persistence in work-related tasks is required (e.g., chores, homework, etc.) or where behavioral restraint is necessary, especially in settings involving public scrutiny (e.g., in church, in restaurants, when a parent is on the phone, etc.) (Altepeter & Breen, 1992; Barkley & Edelbrock, 1987; DuPaul & Barkley, 1992). Such children are least likely to pose behavioral management problems during free play, when little self-control is required. Although they will be more disruptive when their fathers are at home than during free play, children with ADHD are still rated as much less problematic when their fathers are at home than in most other contexts. Fluctuations in the severity of ADHD symptoms have also been documented across a variety of school contexts (Barkley & Edelbrock, 1987; DuPaul & Barkley, 1992). In this case, contexts involving task-directed persistence are the most problematic, with significantly less severe problems posed by contexts involving an absence of supervision (e.g., at lunch, in hallways, at recess, etc.), and even less severe problems being posed during special events (e.g., field trips, assemblies, etc.) (Altepeter & Breen, 1992).

Associated Cognitive Impairments

Although ADHD is defined by the presence of the two major symptom dimensions noted above (inattention and disinhibition), research finds that children with ADHD often demonstrate deficiencies in many other abilities. As noted elsewhere (Barkley, 1997a), the most reliably demonstrated among these are difficulties with the following: (1) motor coordination and sequencing (Barkley, 1997a; Barkley, DuPaul, & McMurray, 1990; Breen, 1989; Denckla & Rudel, 1978; Mariani & Barkley, 1997a); (2) working memory and mental computation (Barkley, 1997a; Mariani & Barkley, 1997a; Zentall & Smith, 1993); (3) planning and anticipation (Barkley, Grodzinsky, & DuPaul, 1992; Douglas, 1983; Grodzinsky & Diamond, 1992); (4) verbal fluency and confrontational communication (Grodzinsky & Diamond, 1992; Zentall, 1988); (5) effort allocation (Douglas, 1983; Voelker, Carter, Sprague, Gdowski, & Lachar, 1989); (6) application of organizational strategies (Hamlett, Pellegrini, & Conners, 1987; Voelker et al., 1989; Zentall, 1988); (7) internalization of self-directed speech (Berk & Potts, 1991; Copeland, 1979); (8) adherence to restrictive instructions (Barkley, 1985; Danforth, Barkley, & Stokes, 1991; Roberts, 1990; Routh & Schroeder, 1976); and (9) self-regulation of emotional arousal (Barkley, 1997a; Cole, Zahn-Waxler, & Smith, 1994; Douglas, 1983; Hinshaw, Buhrmeister, & Heller, 1989). Several studies have also demonstrated what both Still (1902) and Douglas (1972) noted anecdotally years ago—namely, that ADHD may be associated with less mature or diminished moral reasoning (Hinshaw, Herbsman, Melnick, Nigg, & Simmel, 1993; Nucci & Herman, 1982; & Simmel & Hinshaw, 1993).

The commonality among most or all of these seemingly disparate abilities is that all have been considered to fall within the domain of "executive functions" in the field of neuropsychology (Denckla, 1994; Torgesen, 1994) or "metacognition" in developmental psychology (Torgesen, 1994; Welsh & Pennington, 1988), or to be affected by these functions. And all have been considered to be mediated by the frontal cortex, particularly the prefrontal lobes (Fuster, 1989; Stuss & Benson, 1986).

"Executive functions" have been defined as those neuropsychological processes that permit or assist with human self-regulation (Barkley, 1997a). "Self-regulation" itself has been defined as any private behavior by a person that modifies the probability of a subsequent behavior by that person so as to alter the probability of a later consequence (Kanfer & Karoly, 1972; Skinner, 1953). When thoughts or cognitive actions are conceived of as private behavior, one can understand how these actions fall within the definition of human self-regulation: They are private behaviors that modify other behaviors so as to alter the likelihood of later consequences for the individual. And because the frontal lobes generally, and the prefrontal cortex particularly, play an important role in these executive abilities, it is easy to see why researchers have repeatedly speculated that ADHD probably arises out of some disturbance or dysfunction of this brain region (Benton, 1991; Heilman, Voeller, & Nadeau, 1991; Mattes, 1980).

Related Characteristics

ADHD children have been found to experience a number of cognitive, academic, emotional, social, and physical problems in addition to their primary problems. Such children seem more likely to have deficits in general intelligence (see Barkley, 1997a, for a discussion); problems with academic achievement (Barkley, 1990; Cantwell & Satterfield, 1978) and language development (Hartsough & Lambert, 1985; Cantwell & Baker, 1992); depression and anxiety (Biederman, Faraone, & Lapey, 1992; Tannock, in press); and poor peer acceptance (Johnston, Pelham, & Murphy, 1985; Pelham & Bender, 1982). ADHD children also appear to have more minor physical anomalies (Quinn & Rapoport, 1974), although the reliability, specificity for ADHD, and meaning of such differences remain obscure (Krouse & Kauffman, 1982). Accidental poisonings and injuries (Hartsough & Lambert, 1985; Stewart, Thach, & Friedin, 1970), allergies (Trites, Tryphonas, & Ferguson, 1980), motor incoordination (Denckla & Rudel, 1978), enuresis and encopresis (Safer & Allen, 1976), and vision and chronic general health problems (Hartsough & Lambert, 1985) have been observed to be more common in ADHD than in normal or non-ADHD children. Studies comparing ADHD and normal children on various psychophysiological measures have produced conflicting results, but what little agreement there is suggests greater variability in responding and underreactivity of responding in ADHD children (Ferguson & Pappas, 1979; Hastings & Barkley, 1978; Rosenthal & Allen, 1978). Nevertheless, it is unclear what relationship such findings have to the behavioral problems of these children or their differential response to treatment; the specificity of these findings for ADHD as compared to other psychiatric disorders in children is likewise unclear.

Prevalence

The occurrence of ADHD in the population has been somewhat difficult to estimate as a result of the considerable variation in definitions. Prevalence estimates range from as low as 1% to as much as 20% of the school-age population. A generally cited figure is 3–5% (American Psychiatric Association, 1994). This figure is similar to that reached by Szatmari (1992), who found a range from 4% to 6.4% to be typical of most studies of the prevalence of ADHD, especially those using clinical diagnostic criteria.

If only cutoff scores on teacher rating scales are used, prevalence rates of 9–20% for boys and 2–9% for girls may be found (if a score greater than 1.5 standard deviations above the mean is used; O'Leary, Vivian, & Nisi, 1985; Trites, Dugas, Lynch, & Ferguson, 1979). More stringent scores, such as the criterion of 2 standard deviations above the mean recommended earlier, yield 5–7% for boys and 2–4% for girls. When different social definers (parents, teachers, and physicians) are used, the incidence varies from 1.15% when agreement among all three definers is required to 4.92% when at least one definer reports a child to have ADHD (Lambert, Sandoval, & Sassone, 1978). Boys are reported as having the disorder more often than girls, with ratios ranging from 2:1 to 9:1 across studies (Szatmari, 1992). Generally accepted boy–girl ratios are 6:1 within clinic samples and 3:1 in community samples (Trites et al., 1979; Szatmari, 1992). The prevalence also appears to vary somewhat with socioeconomic status (Lambert et al., 1978), although the differences across socioeconomic levels are not especially impressive.

The rate of occurrence of ADHD fluctuates to some extent across countries and cultures. The following rates have been noted for specific countries, with much of the range within each country attributable to gender and age differences: Italy, 3–20% (O'Leary et al., 1985); United States, 2–9% (Szatmari, 1992; Trites et al., 1979); Japan, 2–13% (Kanbayashi, Nakata, Fujii, Kita, & Wada, 1994); Germany, 3.9–9% (Baumgartel, 1994); and India, 5–29% (Bhatia, Nigam, Bohra, & Malik, 1991). Some of the extraordinarily high rates are the re-

sult of using merely cutoff scores on rating scales or samples biased toward children highly likely to have behavior problems (e.g., pediatric clinic referrals in the study by Bhatia et al., 1991). Ross and Ross (1982) noted that among Chinese-Americans in New York City and children residing in Salt Lake City, Utah, the prevalence of ADHD was low to nonexistent. The reasons for this are not clear.

Subtyping

As noted earlier, ADHD is a heterogeneous disorder. Over the past 20 years, efforts have been made to classify children with ADHD into more homogeneous subtypes. One promising approach has been to subdivide ADHD according to the presence and degree of aggressiveness (Loney & Milich, 1982; Milich & Loney, 1979). "Aggression" in these studies is not usually defined as physical attacks against others; rather, it is viewed as a constellation of negative temperament (e.g., temper outbursts) and oppositional and defiant behavior (e.g., being quarrelsome, not cooperating, acting "smart"). ADHD children who are also significantly aggressive tend to have more severe primary symptoms, greater academic performance problems, greater peer relationship problems, poorer outcome in adolescence and young adulthood, and a greater incidence of psychopathology in their parents than do ADHD children not considered aggressive (Barkley, 1990; Hinshaw, 1987, 1994). The latter subgroup tends to have problems primarily in academic performance.

A second approach to subtyping has been to define ADHD as either "situational" or "pervasive." Situational ADHD is ADHD defined as such by either parents or teachers, whereas pervasive ADHD is the disorder defined as such by both. Children with pervasive ADHD have been found to have greater behavioral disturbance, greater persistence of their disturbance over time, and greater cognitive and learning impairments (Schachar, Rutter, & Smith, 1981). However, these findings have not been replicated by others (Cohen & Minde, 1983; McGee, Williams, & Silva, 1984a, 1984b). It appears that the aforementioned subtyping approach based on degree of aggression may account for these results. Children with pervasive ADHD are more likely to fall into the subtype of ADHD with aggression, and as a result may have greater problems with deviance, chronicity, and cognitive impairments than children with situational ADHD.

A third subtyping distinction was that set forth

in the DSM-III: ADD with or without Hyperactivity. The results of studies on this classification have been conflicting. Several have not found important differences between ADD with and without Hyperactivity (Maurer & Stewart, 1980; Rubinstein & Brown, 1984). However, others have found that children classified as having ADD with Hyperactivity have greater conduct problems and oppositional behavior, greater peer relationship difficulties, and more academic performance problems than those classified as having ADD without Hyperactivity (Lahey & Carlson, 1992). Children in the former group also have difficulties with persistence of behavior, or the sustained element of attention, whereas children in the latter group seem to have more difficulties with focused or selective attention (Barkley, DuPaul, & McMurray, 1990; Barkley, Grodzinsky, & DuPaul, 1992; Goodyear & Hynd, 1992; Lahey & Carlson, 1992). Despite the fact that many of these studies have serious methodological flaws, I believe the evidence to suggest the conclusion that ADD without Hyperactivity (or its current equivalent, ADHD, Predominantly Inattentive Type) is a qualitatively different disorder from ADD with Hyperactivity (or ADHD, Predominantly Hyperactive–Impulsive Type and Combined Type), rather than a subtype of it.

THEORETICAL FRAMEWORK

Many different theories of ADHD have been proposed over the past century to account for the diversity of findings so evident in this disorder. Yet there is little doubt that current theorists are focusing on poor behavioral inhibition as playing a central role in ADHD (for reviews, see Barkley, 1990, 1994, 1996, 1997a; Quay, 1989; Schachar & Logan, 1990). Although this conclusion is important in the progress of our understanding about ADHD, it still leaves at least two important questions on the nature of ADHD unresolved. First, how does this account for the numerous other associated symptoms found in ADHD (described above) and apparently subsumed under the concept of "executive functions"? And, second, how does this account for the involvement of the separate problem with inattention (poor sustained attention) in the disorder? A recently proposed theoretical model of ADHD not only encompasses many of these earlier explanations but may hold the answers to these questions, as well as some unexpected directions that future researchers on ADHD may wish to pursue (Barkley, 1994, 1996, 1997a).

Inhibition, Executive Functions, and Time

The model of ADHD set forth below and in Figure 2.1 has also been discussed in more detail in a recent paper on ADHD (Barkley, 1997a). This model places behavioral inhibition at a central point in its relation to four other executive functions, which are dependent upon it for their own effective execution. These four executive functions, as suggested above, permit and subserve human self-regulation, bringing behavior progressively more under the control of internally represented information (including sense of time, as well as the influence of the future over immediate consequences). The end result is a greater capacity for predicting and controlling one's environment (and one's own behavior within it), so as to maximize the probability of future positive consequences for the individual. More generally, the interaction of these executive functions permits far more effective adaptive functioning.

Several assumptions are important in understanding the model as it is applied to ADHD: (1) The capacity for behavioral inhibition begins to emerge first in development, ahead of these four executive functions; (2) these executive functions emerge at different times in development, may have different developmental trajectories, and are interactive; (3) the impairment that ADHD creates in these executive functions is *secondary* to the primary deficit it creates in behavioral inhibition (if the capacity for inhibition is improved, these executive functions should likewise improve); (4) the deficit in behavioral inhibition arises principally from genetic and neurodevelopmental origins, rather than purely social ones, although its expression is certainly influenced by social factors over development; (5) the secondary deficits in self-regulation created by the primary deficiency in inhibition feed back to contribute further to poor behavioral inhibition, given that self-regulation contributes to the enhancement of self-restraint (inhibition); and, finally, (6) the model does not apply to those having ADD without Hyperactivity, or what is now called ADHD, Predominantly Inattentive Type. The model has been derived from earlier theories on the evolution of human language (Bronowski, 1977) and the functions of the prefrontal cortex (Fuster, 1989). The evidence for the model as applied to ADHD and for the assertions above is reviewed elsewhere (Barkley, 1994, 1997a).

"Behavioral inhibition" is viewed as consisting

of two related processes: (1) the capacity to inhibit prepotent responses either prior to their initiation or once they are initiated, and thus to create a delay in the response to an event ("response inhibition"); and (2) the protection of this delay, the self-directed actions occurring within it, and the resulting goal-directed behaviors from interference by competing events and their prepotent responses ("interference control"). Through the postponement of the prepotent response and the creation of this protected period of delay, the occasion is set for four other executive functions to act effectively in modifying the individual's eventual response(s) to the event. The chain of goal-directed, future-oriented behaviors set in motion by these acts of self-regulation is then also protected from interference during its performance by this same process of inhibition (interference control). And even if the chain is disrupted, the individual retains the capacity or intention (via

working memory) to return to the goal-directed actions until the outcome is successfully achieved or judged to be no longer necessary. The four executive functions are now briefly described, as is motor control/fluency/syntax (see Figure 2.1).

Working Memory

The capacity to inhibit an initial prepotent response to an event creates a delay in responding. During this delay, information can be held in mind that will prove useful to planning and executing the eventual response. This capacity for "prolongation" of mental representations of events is dependent upon inhibition and has been noted to arise as early as infancy (Diamond, 1990; Diamond, Cruttenden, & Niederman, 1994). As this capacity increases developmentally, it forms the basis for "working memory," which has been defined as the ability to maintain mental informa-

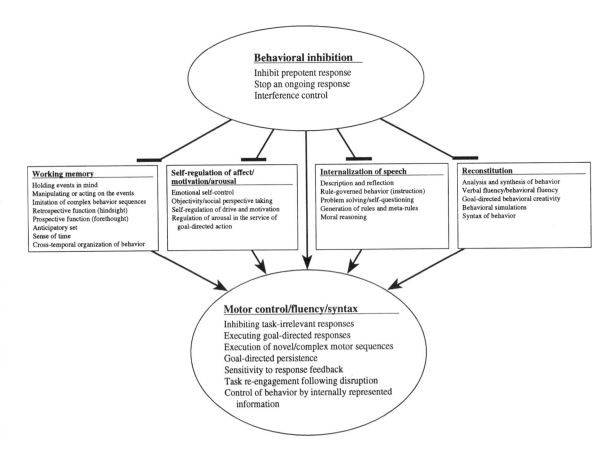

FIGURE 2.1. A schematic configuration of the model linking behavioral inhibition with four executive functions, which then influence the performance of motor behavior. From Barkley (1997a, p. 73). Copyright 1997 by the American Psychological Association. Reprinted by permission.

tion on-line while acting upon it. These prolonged mental representations of events can also be stored in long-term memory for later retrieval back into working memory, as their information may be pertinent to considering a response to a current event. This recall of past events for the sake of preparing a current response has been called "hindsight" (Bronowski, 1977; Fuster, 1989). For an individual to carry out such a process, events must be held in their proper sequence or temporal order. And this retention of events in a temporal sequence has been shown to contribute to the subjective estimation of time (Michon, 1985). Analysis of temporal sequences of events for recurring patterns can then be used to predict hypothetical future events—the individual's best guess as to what may happen next or later in time, based upon the detection of recurring patterns in past event sequences. This permits the individual to create a preparation or intention to act, sometimes called an "anticipatory set" (Fuster, 1989). This extension of hindsight forward into time also creates "forethought," forming a temporally symmetrical counterpart to the retrospective function of hindsight (Bronowski, 1977; Fuster, 1989). And from this sense of future events likely emerges the progressively greater valuation of future consequences over immediate ones, which develops throughout not only childhood but adult life as well (Green, Fry, & Meyerson, 1994). Extrapolated to ADHD, the model predicts that deficits in behavioral inhibition lead to deficiencies in all of these subfunctions related to working memory.

Self-Regulation of Affect

According to the model shown in Figure 2.1, behavioral inhibition sets the occasion for the development of self-regulation of affect in a child. The delay in responding this creates allows the child time to engage in self-directed behaviors, which will modify both the eventual response to the event and the emotional reaction that may accompany it. This is believed to permit greater objectivity on the part of the child in determining an eventual response to an event. However, it is not just affect that is being managed by the development of self-regulation, but drive and motivation as well (Fuster, 1989). That is, self-regulation permits the child actually to learn to modify or induce drive or motivational states that may be required for the initiation and maintenance of goal-directed behavior. Extending this model to ADHD leads to the following predictions: Those with ADHD should display (1) greater emotional expression in their reactions to events; (2) less objectivity in the selection of a response to an event; (3) diminished social perspective taking, because they do not delay their initial emotional reactions long enough to take the views of others and their own needs into account; and (4) diminished ability to regulate and induce drive and motivational states in themselves, in the service of goal-directed behavior.

Internalization of Speech

One of the more fascinating developmental processes in children is the progressive internalization or privatization of speech. During the early preschool years, speech, once developed, is initially employed for communication with others. As behavioral inhibition progresses, the delays in responding it permits allow language to be turned on the self. Language now becomes not just a means of influencing the behavior of others, but a means of reflection (self-directed description), as well as a means for controlling one's own behavior (Berk & Potts, 1991; Bronowski, 1977). Self-directed speech progresses from being public to being subvocal to finally being private, all over the course of perhaps 6–10 years (Berk & Potts, 1991). With this progressive privatization of speech comes the increasing control it permits over one's own behavior (Berk & Potts, 1991; Kopp, 1982). Language in general, and rules (behavior-specifying stimuli) in particular, gain an increasing degree of control over motor behavior; this results in a tremendously increased capacity for self-control, planfulness, and goal-directed behavior. It has even been conjectured (Barkley, 1997a) that this internalization of speech represents a larger process that may encompass the internalization of action or responding. Thus, not only does speech become private, creating the means for verbal thought (Berk & Potts, 1991); other forms of self-directed behavior also become private, permitting other modes of thinking as well (e.g., inner seeing, or imagination).

For those with ADHD, the model stipulates that the privatization of speech should be less mature or advanced than it is in others of the same age. This should result in greater public speech (excessive talking), less reflection before acting, less organized and rule-oriented self-speech, and a diminished influence of self-directed speech in controlling one's own behavior. The self-control and rule-governed behavior permitted by the internalization of speech should therefore be diminished in those with ADHD as well (Barkley, 1997a).

Reconstitution

Language is used to represent the objects of the world, actions, and their properties. This provides a means by which the world, through internalized speech, can be taken apart and recombined, just as is done with the parts of speech that represent the world. The delay in responding that behavioral inhibition permits allows time for events to be mentally prolonged and then disassembled, so as to extract more information about the event before preparing a response to it. Internal speech permits analysis, and out of this process comes its complement—synthesis. Just as the parts of speech can be recombined to form new sentences, the parts of the world represented in speech are likewise recombined to create entirely new ideas about the world (Bronowski, 1977) and entirely new responses to that world. The world is seen as having parts rather than consisting of inviolate wholes, and these parts are seen as capable of multiple and novel recombinations. As Bronowski (1977) has stated, this permits humans a far greater capacity for creativity and problem solving than is evident in our closest relatives, the primates. The process of reconstitution, he asserts, is as evident as everyday speech in its fluency. It becomes even more obvious when speech is task- or goal-directed, as the rapid, efficient, and often novel combination of the parts of speech into entire messages that represent the ideas of the individual is now evident.

As applied to ADHD, such a model predicts that those with the disorder will demonstrate a diminished use of analysis and synthesis in the formation of responses to events. The capacity to generate multiple plans of action (options) in the service of goal-directed behavior should therefore be diminished in those with ADHD, as should goal-directed creativity more generally. And this impairment in reconstitution will be most evident in everyday verbal fluency, when the person with ADHD is required by a task or situation to assemble the parts of speech rapidly, accurately, and efficiently into messages (sentences) in order to accomplish the goal or requirements of the task. It should also be evident in other forms of behavior, where those with ADHD should have difficulties in constructing lengthy, novel, complex sequences of goal-directed actions.

Motor Control / Fluency / Syntax

The four executive functions displayed in the middle tier of the model in Figure 2.1 influence the motor system by bringing motor behavior under the control of internally represented (self-directed) events. Over development, these functions come to permit the construction and execution of lengthy, complex, and novel chains of goal-directed behavior under the control of internally represented information. Such behaviors are protected from disruption by interference until they have been completed. As applied to ADHD, the model stipulates that those with the disorder should display greater difficulties with the development of motor coordination, and especially in the planning and execution of complex, lengthy, and novel chains of goal-directed responses.

Clarifying the Nature of Inattention in ADHD

To return to the second question raised earlier, how is the problem with inattention—and, more specifically, with poor sustained attention—accounted for in this model? First, it is critical to distinguish between two forms of sustained attention that are traditionally confused in the research literature on ADHD. I have called the first of these "contingency-shaped attention" (Barkley, 1997a); this refers to continued responding in a situation or to a task as a function of the motivational or reinforcement properties of that context, and specifically a function of the contingencies of reinforcement provided by the task or activity. Responding that is maintained under these conditions is directly dependent on the immediate environmental contingencies, and so is described as shaped by these contingencies. Therefore, it is not surprising that many factors can be found to affect this form of sustained attention or responding: (1) the novelty of the task, (2) the intrinsic interest the activity may hold for the individual, (3) the immediate reinforcement contingencies it provides for responding in the task, (4) the state of fatigue of the individual, and (5) the presence or absence of an adult supervisor (or other stimuli signaling other consequences for performance that are outside the task itself). These and other factors are all important to determining the extent to which the individual, or any animal, will sustain its responding within that context. This type of sustained attention is not affected by ADHD, according to this model.

But as children mature, a second form of sustained attention emerges—one that is better termed "goal-directed persistence." It arises as a direct consequence of the development of self-regulation. This form of persistence derives from the child's development of a progressively greater capacity to hold events, goals, and plans in mind (working memory); to adhere to rules governing behavior, and to formulate and follow such rules as are needed; and to self-induce motivational or drive states supportive of the plans and goals formulated by the child, so as to maintain goal-directed behavior. In short, the interaction of the components of the model that give rise to self-regulation permits substantially longer, more complex, and even novel chains of behavior to be constructed and sustained despite interruptions, until the goal is attained. "Persistence of effort" (Douglas, 1983), "volition" (Still, 1902), or "will" (James, 1890/1950) may be other terms used to describe this capacity to initiate and sustain chains of goal-directed behavior in spite of the absence of immediate environmental contingencies for their performance. Such behavior is clearly less dependent upon the current context and its immediate contingencies for its performance. And, more significantly, it may often be associated with a state of self-imposed deprivation of reinforcement (or, less often, even infliction of immediate aversive or punitive states) if this maximizes the probability of later consequences that are more important than immediate ones. These acts of self-deprivation are often called "deferred gratification," "self-discipline," "will power," or "resistance to temptation," and result directly from acts of self-regulation. And it is this type of sustained attention—goal-directed persistence arising out of self-regulation—that is disrupted by ADHD. This explanation may help to account for why tasks assessing resistance to temptation have often been successful in distinguishing children with ADHD from normal children (Barkley, 1997a; Campbell et al., 1982; Hinshaw, Heller, & McHale, 1992). Distinguishing between contingency-shaped (context-dependent) and goal-directed (self-dependent) sustained attention may also explain why parents report that their children with ADHD are able to play video games for hours, but cannot sustain their efforts at doing school homework or boring chores for more than a few minutes at a time.

As will become evident later in the discussion of assessment of ADHD, this distinction between forms of sustained attention is important in guiding the clinician's interviewing of parents and teachers about potentially problematic areas and contexts of behavior for children being evaluated for ADHD. It is also important in the selection of any tests or measures that may have some value in the evaluation of these children; for instance, it may explain why CPTs or vigilance tests may have

some sensitivity to ADHD (as noted later in the discussion of laboratory tests and measures). Finally, this distinction may be of further value in explaining to parents, teachers, and social critics why children with ADHD are able to attend to some activities (those that interest the children or offer immediate rewards) for far longer periods than they can to other activities (those that involve little or no reward or interest for the children).

Implications of the Model for Assessment

Several implications for assessment arise from this model of ADHD. First, a complete picture of ADHD and its impact on a child's functioning will be difficult to capture in office evaluations. Some degree of inhibitory difficulties may be impressive in an office setting, but not always and not in most children presenting for evaluation of ADHD. The disruption in the four executive functions will prove even harder to pin down, given that few psychological tests assessing these functions exist for clinical purposes, and that few rating scales contain items focusing explicitly upon them. This leads to a second implication of this model, which is that the opinions of parents and teachers about a child's behavior and self-regulation in natural settings will prove far more instructive concerning the presence of ADHD in the child. Caregivers will have had far longer spans of time over which to evaluate the child's deficiencies in self-regulation, disorganization in regard to time, ineffective cross-temporal organization of goal-directed behaviors, impersistence in task- or goal-directed behavior (inattention), and failure to defer gratification and maximize longer-term consequences over short-term or immediate ones. A third implication of the model, then, is that multiple observations of the child's behavior and task performance in natural settings may prove more informative about the presence and degree of ADHD in the child than will a brief office evaluation or psychological testing.

Fourth, the complexity of ADHD is likely to increase over development, given that the four executive functions being disrupted by the child's poor behavioral inhibition emerge in a staggered fashion across development. The older the child is at the time of evaluation, the more likely the clinician is to find that caregivers are complaining not only about the child's poor inhibition, but also about deficits in those executive functions that normal children have recently developed. For instance, parents of 3- to 5-year-old ADHD children are unlikely to complain about the children's poor sense of time, planning, and forethought, but parents of 10- to 16-year-olds are far more likely to note such problems in their ADHD children. Thus, the scope and complexity of impairments broaden in children with ADHD as their development proceeds. This makes it essential for the clinician to ask the parents of an older child about deficiencies in these executive functions and their impact on the child's adaptive functioning at home and in school. And, finally, this model suggests that the full impact of ADHD on the child's adaptive functioning will require longer spans of time to appreciate than is likely to be evident in an initial evaluation of only a few hours. Using measures of adaptive functioning besides the usual methods of interviewing and obtaining behavior ratings will probably prove useful to some degree in capturing this impact of ADHD on the child's daily life.

Once the evaluation of children with ADHD comes to document the deficiencies in behavioral inhibition, executive functions, and self-control, it is likely to lead to a number of suggestions for treatment, as discussed elsewhere (Barkley, 1994). These include ways to bridge time delays in tasks. Such delays often exist between the points when assignments are given and the points when the responses to them are required, as well as between the times when the responses occur and the times when their consequences come to pass. For instance, a book report often involves periods of weeks between the original assignment and the day the final report is due, as well as between the day the report is turned in and the day the child finally receives the grade for it. Teachers or clinicians who know that tasks involving time and the future (planning) are the nemesis of those with ADHD will be able to suggest ways of "bridging time" that may prove helpful to such children. Breaking tasks down into smaller units, which are done more frequently and for which immediate token rewards are given, is but one means of "bridging time." Because time and rules are ineffectively internalized in children with ADHD, these must be externalized again (as if returning to an earlier stage in normal child development) in order to make these domains of information more likely to control the children's behavior. For instance, placing cooking timers, "countdown" audiotapes, clocks, metronomes, or other concrete timing devices in front of the children during task performance may help the children regulate their behavior relative to time and deadlines for task performance better than they would if no such concrete "externalized" cues were utilized. And in view of the problems with self-motivation likely to be uncovered during the evaluation of an ADHD child, the use of artificial, "prosthetic" reward programs will be an indispensable and long-term part of the total treatment plan to be developed for such a child.

In summary, the present model provides for a theory-driven rationale behind the areas of development that must be assessed in children with ADHD. Just as important, the model also provides a similar rationale for the types of interventions that will be required to assist these children in coping with or even compensating for their various deficiencies in executive functioning and self-control.

DEVELOPMENTAL COURSE AND PREDICTORS OF OUTCOME

It is commonly accepted that ADHD arises early in childhood, and that precursors of the disorder may in fact be identified in infancy. Infants of difficult temperament who are excessively active, have poor sleeping and eating habits, and are negative in their moods are at greater risk for later ADHD than are children with more normal temperaments (Barkley, 1990; Ross & Ross, 1982). However, not all children who are eventually diagnosed as having ADHD have a history of difficult temperament in infancy, and even those children who do are not necessarily destined to develop ADHD (Chamberlin, 1977).

By 3 years of age, more than half of all ADHD children have begun to manifest behavioral problems, particularly overactivity, impulsiveness, and noncompliant behavior. "Childproofing" the home is often necessary, given the greater risk noted earlier of accidental injuries and poisonings (Hartsough & Lambert, 1985; Mitchell, Aman, Turbott, & Manku, 1987; Stewart et al., 1970; Taylor, Sandberg, Thorley, & Giles, 1991), particularly if problems with defiant or aggressive behavior are associated with the children's ADHD symptoms (Bijur, Golding, Haslum, & Kurzon, 1988; Davidson, Taylor, Sandberg, & Thorley, 1992). As a result of noncompliance, toilet training at this age may be difficult and may occur later than normal (Hartsough & Lambert, 1985). For those ADHD children who begin attendance at nursery or preschool programs, complaints from teachers about their restlessness, inattention, and oppositional behavior appear to be common (Campbell, 1990).

Research suggests that once children are noted to be excessive in those areas of behavior characteristic of ADHD, their problems remain relatively stable over time from their preschool years into their early formal schooling (Campbell et al., 1978; Campbell, March, Pierce, Ewing, & Szumowski, 1991). By 6 years of age, over 90% of ADHD children will have been identified as problematic by their parents or teachers. Continuing problems with attention span, on-task behavior, compliance with classroom rules and directions, and restlessness are noted. Many ADHD children will have problems in their relationships with peers because of their selfishness, immaturity, heightened emotionality, conduct problems, and general lack of age-appropriate social skills (Cunningham & Siegel, 1987; Pelham & Bender, 1982). With exposure to broader social situations (school, community, public places), ADHD children pose even greater management difficulties for their parents, particularly in unsupervised situations (Altepeter & Breen, 1992). At an age when children often come to be trusted to follow appropriate social rules when they are not under parental supervision, ADHD children are often described by their parents as incapable of being trusted when alone. Parents may now have difficulty getting babysitters to sit with the children because of the history of chronic behavioral problems under such conditions. Parents often find themselves spending most of the children's waking day supervising their activities. They may even come to spend less time with the children in recreational pursuits because of the frequent management problems posed by the children under such conditions (Cunningham, Benness, & Siegel, 1988). Stress in the parental role, as well as reports of parental depression, may arise or increase at this time (Anastopoulos, Guevremont, Shelton, & DuPaul, 1992; Breen & Barkley, 1988; Fischer, 1990; Mash & Johnston, 1983a, 1990; Murphy & Barkley, 1996c).

During middle to late childhood (6 to 11 years of age), complaints about ADHD children at school may focus not only upon underachievement and failure to complete assignments, but upon disruptive classroom conduct, continuing poor social skills, and difficulties with self-control in unsupervised situations (hallways, riding the bus, recess, lunchtime, etc.; Altepeter & Breen, 1992; Barkley & Edelbrock, 1987). Learning disabilities may now be observed in 25% or more of children with ADHD (Barkley, 1990; Cantwell & Baker, 1992). Whether or not they are formally noted, learning disabilities may emerge in many ADHD children. Some children are eventually placed for part of their school day within programs described with the unfortunate label of "emotionally disturbed." Nevertheless, smaller classroom environments allowing for greater teacher attention, more individualized instruction, and more frequent use of contingency management methods may be needed for elementary-age ADHD children (Barkley, DuPaul, & McMurray, 1990).

In the home, parents may now complain that these children are unable to take responsibility for routine chores and activities, such as dressing for school on time, cleaning their rooms, doing homework, assisting with other household jobs, or other forms of adaptive functioning (Barkley, DuPaul, & McMurray, 1990; Roizen, Blondis, Irwin, & Stein, 1994). Neighborhood children may already have labeled the ADHD children as undersirable because of their prior reputations for aggressiveness and immature conduct, as well as their often poor athletic abilities (stemming from delayed motor development). Parents of ADHD children bemoan the children's lack of friends and may find their children gravitating toward associations with other problematic children. Within the community, lying, stealing, and destructiveness of others' property may appear in those children with prior histories of aggressive and oppositional behavior.

Several factors appear to play a role in the outcome of childern with ADHD as they reach adolescence. Those children with "pure" ADHD (i.e., ADHD that is not associated with significant aggressiveness, comorbid mood disorders, family adversity, or peer relationship problems) are likely to have problems primarily in school performance (Paternite & Loney, 1980); they are typically described as "underachieving." They may also have a higher chance of early remission of the disorder, however (Biederman et al., 1996). Those with associated aggression and conduct problems apparently fare much worse (Barkley, Fischer, et al., 1990; Weiss & Hechtman, 1993). Not only are school performance problems significant, but difficulties with predelinquent or delinquent behavior in the community may emerge, and peer relationship problems remain significant or increase in severity (Barkley, Fischer, et al., 1990; Fischer, Barkley, Edelbrock, & Smallish, 1990). Such ADHD children are also more likely to have a form of ADHD that persists into later adolescence (Biederman et al., 1996). Although ADHD children are less active, inattentive, and noncompliant at this age than in their childhood years, significant problems with rebelliousness, defiance of authority, violation of family rules, and immature or irresponsible conduct are often described by parents (Barkley, Anastopoulos, Guevremont, &

Fletcher, 1991; Barkley, Fischer, et al., 1990; Barkley, Fischer, Edelbrock, & Smallish, 1991). Some evidence suggests that ADHD children may be more likely to abuse alcohol (Barkley, Fischer, et al., 1990; Blouin, Bornstein, & Trites, 1978), while other research suggests not (Weiss, Hechtman, Perlman, Hopkins, & Wener, 1979). Yet the research by Weiss et al. (1979) suggests that ADHD children are more likely than control children to use hallucinogens. ADHD children also appear more likely than other teenagers to have car accidents (Barkley, Guevremont, Anastopoulos, DuPaul, & Shelton, 1993; Barkley, Murphy, & Kwasnik, 1996; Weiss et al., 1979). Many continue to have feelings of low self-esteem, poor social acceptance, and depression (Hechtman, Weiss, & Perlman, 1980). Approximately 30% or more will fail to complete high school; of those who do, most will fail to pursue any university degree programs (Weiss, Hechtman, Milroy, & Perlman, 1985).

As young adults, ADHD children appear to make a more adequate adjustment to their employment setting than they did to school (Weiss, Hechtman, & Perlman, 1978). Still, between 30% and 66% are reported to have continuing problems with restlessness, inattention, impulsivity, low self-esteem, and feelings of sadness and depression, compared to same-age control subjects followed over time (Hechtman et al., 1980; Mannuzza, Gittelman-Klein, Bessler, Malloy, & LaPadula, 1993; Weiss et al., 1985). Over 75% complain of interpersonal problems or significant psychological difficulties, and more ADHD young adults will make suicide attempts than will normal or control subjects (Weiss & Hechtman, 1993; Weiss et al., 1985). Between 23% and 45% may eventually receive a diagnosis of adult Antisocial Personality Disorder (Loney, Whaley-Klahn, Kosier, & Conboy, 1983; Weiss et al., 1985). Approximately 27% may be diagnosed as alcoholic by adulthood; although this rate is greater than that expected for normal adults, it is not different from the rate of alcoholism among their siblings. Common genetic disposition or family environments, then, rather than ADHD itself, may be related to alcoholism in these children (Hechtman, Weiss, Perlman, & Amsel, 1984; Loney et al., 1983). In general, follow-up studies find ADHD children as young adults to be doing less well socially, psychologically, academically, and occupationally than control children or even their siblings (Loney et al., 1983; Thorley, 1984; Weiss & Hechtman, 1993). Such findings clearly indicate that adult disorders exist that are equivalent to ADHD or are residual conditions of childhood ADHD (Barkley & Murphy, 1996; Murphy & Barkley, 1996a; Wender, Reimherr, & Wood, 1981; Wood, Reimherr, Wender, & Johnson, 1976).

Studies examining predictors of outcome in ADHD children typically find few predictors of significance, and even these account for only a small percentage of the variance in outcome (Mannuzza & Klein, 1992). Some studies have identified low intelligence in childhood, aggressiveness and oppositional behavior, poor peer acceptance, emotional instability, and extent of parental psychopathology as predictors of poorer outcomes (Fischer, Barkley, Fletcher, & Smallish, 1993b; Hechtman et al., 1984; Loney et al., 1983; Paternite & Loney, 1980). Although extensive, long-term treatment during adolescence may make some improvement in outcome (Satterfield, Satterfield, & Cantwell, 1981), lesser degrees of treatment, including stimulant drug therapy, provide only marginal benefit to the adult outcome of this group; in the case of stimulant drugs, this is probably because the medication is typically no longer continued into this age group in most cases (Barkley, Anastopoulos, et al., 1991; Barkley, Fischer, et al., 1990; Hechtman et al., 1984; Paternite & Loney, 1980; Weiss & Hechtman, 1993).

ETIOLOGY

Various causes of ADHD have been proposed, and many now view the disorder as arising from multiple etiologies, much as other developmental disabilities (e.g., mental retardation) do. The evidence discussed below, however, applies only to ADHD, Predominantly Hyperactive–Impulsive Type and Combined Type. Little research exists that might shed some light on the etiologies of ADHD, Predominantly Inattentive Type, and so conclusions about this subtype must await future research.

Neurological Factors

Brain damage was initially believed to be a primary cause of this disorder (Strauss & Lehtinen, 1947), but more recent research suggests that fewer than 5% of ADHD children have hard evidence of neurological damage (Rutter, 1977). And although it is possible for brain injury to lead to the development of attention deficits and hyperactivity, most brain-injured children do not develop such difficulties (Rutter, Chadwick, & Shaffer, 1983). Some research suggests potential neurotransmitter abnormalities in ADHD children (Shaywitz, Cohen, & Shaywitz, 1978; Shaywitz, Shaywitz, Cohen, & Young, 1983), but such studies often produce conflicting results and rely on models of central neurotransmitter functioning based upon samples from peripheral systems (blood serotonin, urinary metabolites of neurotransmitters, etc.) that may or may not reliably reflect central biochemical activities. Research using computed tomographic (CT) scan techniques to evaluate ADHD children has not found any significant structural abnormalities (Shaywitz, Shaywitz, Byrne, Cohen, & Rothman, 1983). However, later studies using more sensitive magnetic resonance imaging (MRI) methods have documented reduced brain size and density in the frontal lobes and striatum (Castellanos et al., 1994; Hynd et al., 1993; Rapoport, 1996). Decreased levels of cerebral blood flow within these regions, suggesting decreased activity or stimulation, have also been documented in ADHD children as compared to dysphasic children or other control groups (Lou, Henriksen, & Bruhn, 1984; Lou, Henriksen, Bruhn, Borner, & Nielsen, 1989). Likewise, decreased brain metabolic activity has been demonstrated in adults with ADHD (Zametkin et al., 1990) but has been less consistently found in ADHD adolescents (Ernst et al., 1994; Zametkin et al., 1993). Such findings may explain the observations of decreased electrical reactivity to stimulation often, though not always, found in psychophysiological research with ADHD children (Hastings & Barkley, 1978; Klorman, 1992). Finally, some investigators (Kinsbourne, 1977) have proposed that neurological immaturity may be a cause of ADHD. Although there is suggestive evidence from the behavioral symptoms and psychophysiological research for such a hypothesis, the notion remains both vague and difficult to test directly with current neurological evaluative methods.

Diet

Various dietary substances have been proposed as causes of ADHD in children. Some authors (e.g., Feingold, 1975) have proposed that toxic or allergic reactions to such food additives as artificial colorings cause over 60% of ADHD in children. Placement on a diet relatively free of the offending additives is proposed as the most effective treatment. However, a substantial body of research suggesting that this is hardly the case has accrued (for reviews, see Conners, 1980; Mattes & Gittelman, 1981). This research can be summarized as indicating that the vast majority of ADHD children show no changes in behavior when placed on such diets; among the 5% who do, the changes noted are quite small, are usually limited to changes in parent or teacher rating scales, and can hardly be considered clinically therapeutic effects. Other authors (e.g., Taylor, 1980) have proposed that much of ADHD behavior is a reaction to allergens in the environment. ADHD children may have more allergies than other children (Trites et al., 1980), but there is no evidence that the removal of the suspected allergens or other treatment of the allergic children results in clinically significant improvements in the children, although minor improvements in behavior may be noted (Trites et al., 1980).

Sugar in children's diets has also been proposed as a cause of ADHD, among other childhood disorders (Smith, 1976). However, researchers who have challenged ADHD children with sucrose, and have used aspartame as the placebo control condition, have found no increases in ADHD symptoms following the sucrose challenges (M. D. Gross, 1984; Milich, Wolraich, & Lindgren, 1986; Wolraich, Milich, Stumbo, & Schultz, 1985). A recent meta-analysis of the 16 experimental studies concluded that sugar does not affect children's behavior or cognitive performance (Wolraich, Wilson, & White, 1995).

Neurotoxins

Elevated blood lead levels have been implicated as a cause of ADHD symptoms in children (David, 1974), with some studies finding as many as 25–35% of lead-exposed children to have such symptoms (Baloh, Sturm, Green, & Gleser, 1975; de la Burde & Choate, 1972, 1974). However, other studies have obtained conflicting results (Milar, Schroeder, Mushak, & Boone, 1981; Needleman et al., 1979) or have found the association to be weak at best (Fergusson, Fergusson, Horwood, & Kinzett, 1988; Gittelman & Eskinazi, 1983; Silva, Hughes, Williams, & Faed, 1988). Even at relatively high levels of body lead, fewer than 38% of children are rated as displaying hyperactivity on a teacher rating scale (Needleman et al., 1979); the rates of children with a clinical diagnosis of ADHD would be much lower than this.

Some research exists to show an association between maternal alcohol consumption and smoking during pregnancy, and symptoms of ADHD in the children born of such pregnancies (Bennett, Wolin, & Reiss, 1988; Denson, Nanson, & McWatters, 1975; Nichols & Chen, 1981;

Shaywitz, Cohen, & Shaywitz, 1980; Streissguth et al., 1984). However, the causal link here is unclear. Although ingestion of such substances during pregnancy may well result in toxic effects on the fetus that make ADHD symptoms more likely, women who are more likely to have ADHD children may also be more likely to smoke or consume alcohol during pregnancy, by virtue of their own increased risk of psychiatric disturbance (Cunningham et al., 1988; Murphy & Barkley, 1996a; Pelham & Lang, 1993). The indication of a greater frequency of psychiatric disturbance and alcohol use among parents and relatives of ADHD children, and the fact that fathers and stepfathers of ADHD children were also found to smoke more heavily than fathers and stepfathers of normal children (Denson et al., 1975), at least call into question the causal direction proposed among these variables.

Genetic Factors

A hereditary contribution for ADHD has become the focus of increased research. Investigators have long recognized the increased incidence of various psychiatric disorders, particularly psychopathy, Antisocial Personality Disorder, depression, Conduct Disorder, alcoholism, and ADHD among biological relatives of ADHD children (Biederman, Faraone, Keenan, & Tsuang, 1991; Cantwell, 1975; Faraone et al., 1992; Morrison & Stewart, 1971, 1973). The relatively high concordance for activity level among monozygotic twins (Lopez, 1965; Willerman, 1973), and the increased incidence of ADHD among the biological parents and siblings of ADHD children (Biederman et al., 1992; Welner, Welner, Stewart, Palkes, & Wish, 1977), are all suggestive of some as yet unspecified mode of inheritance for these characteristics. Large-scale studies of twins have been able to estimate the contribution of heredity to the behavioral pattern underlying ADHD (inattention, hyperactivity, etc.) and have found it to be of a moderate to large degree, with heritabilities ranging from .50 to .90 and averaging .80 (out of a possible 1.00) (Edelbrock, Rende, Plomin, & Thompson, 1995; Gilger, Pennington, & DeFries, 1992; Levy & Hay, 1996; Stevenson, 1994). A study examining the pattern of ADHD among biological relatives concluded that a single gene might well be able to account for the pattern of apparent genetic association (Faraone et al., 1992). More recently, an association was found between ADHD and the dopamine transporter gene; if this

is replicated, it may provide some of the first clues as to the precise nature of the genetic contribution to the disorder (Cook et al., 1995). Although the evidence for a genetic contribution to ADHD is quite reliable and strong, it does not mean that the environment is of no importance. Evidence indicates that the environment plays some role in determining the expression and severity of the symptoms of ADHD, its comorbid conditions, and even its persistence over development (Biederman et al., 1995, 1996; Goodman & Stevenson, 1989).

Social Factors

There have been few efforts to articulate a purely environmental cause for ADHD in children. Block (1977) proposed that an increase in the incidence of hyperactivity over time, coupled with a corresponding increase in the "cultural tempo" of our times, may have resulted in greater stimulation of children and hence a greater likelihood of hyperactivity in those children already predisposed to such characteristics. Ross and Ross (1982) found little evidence for such a view. Willis and Lovaas (1977) have proposed that ADHD is a deficit in the stimulus control of behavior by parental commands, and that it derives from poor child management techniques employed by the parents. Although mothers of ADHD children do provide more commands and supervision to their children, this appears to be partly a function of the type of task required of the children (Luk, 1985; Tallmadge & Barkley, 1983) and the age of the children (Barkley, Karlsson, & Pollard, 1985; Mash & Johnston, 1982), and is substantially diminished when the children are treated with stimulant medication (Barkley & Cunningham, 1980; Barkley, Karlsson, Strzelecki, & Murphy, 1984; Humphries, Kinsbourne, & Swanson, 1978). Such results suggest that the behavior of the mothers is more likely a reaction to than a chief cause of the behavioral difficulties in ADHD children (Fischer, 1990; Mash & Johnston, 1990).

Despite the absence of any well-articulated or substantiated psychosocial theory of ADHD, this should not be taken to mean that psychological and social factors have no importance to the disorder. As discussed earlier, Oppositional Defiant Disorder and Conduct Disorder are frequently associated with ADHD and constitute some of the best-substantiated predictors of later risks for school suspensions and expulsions, delinquency, antisocial behavior, driving accidents and speeding violations, and substance experimentation/

abuse. Family dysfunction, parent–child conflict, poor child management and monitoring, parental psychopathology, and socioeconomic disadvantage have a significant association with Oppositional Defiant Disorder and Conduct Disorder (Barkley, Anastopoulos, Guevremont, & Fletcher, 1992; Hinshaw, 1987; Lahey, Piacentini, et al., 1988; Loeber, 1990); such factors may also play some role in the severity of expression of a child's ADHD symptoms (Biederman et al., 1995; Murphy & Barkley, 1996c). Given this relationship, it could be argued that such family and social factors have a significant influence on the course and outcome of ADHD children as well. Further evidence for environmental influences on the expression of ADHD comes from the earlier-cited findings regarding situational and contextual factors that affect symptom expression and fluctuation. Thus, although genetic and neurodevelopmental factors may well be the chief variables that predispose children toward ADHD, family and other social factors undoubtedly influence the ultimate degree of these symptoms, some of the disorders likely to coexist with them, and the developmental course and outcome of the disorder for any particular child.

Summary

In summary, ADHD is a disorder with potentially numerous etiologies, among which the neurobiological factors, and particularly genetic mechanisms, appear to have the greatest support. Most likely, the causes of the disorder should be viewed much as those of mental retardation are viewed: Multiple causes have an impact upon a final common pathway that inevitably affects the development of particular abilities (in the case of ADHD, inhibition, persistence, and self-regulation). As with other developmental disorders, the symptom severity, comorbidities, courses, and outcomes for those with ADHD are likely to be affected by a number of environmental factors.

IMPLICATIONS FOR ASSESSMENT

The material reviewed to this point has a number of important implications for the clinical assessment of children with ADHD:

1. The primary problems of these children appear to be in the areas of behavioral inhibition, persistence, and overactivity specifically, and self-regulation more generally. This necessitates that these areas be the major targets of assessment and, of course, intervention. Given the considerable incidence of other disorders coexisting with ADHD, such as learning disabilities, Oppositional Defiant Disorder, Conduct Disorder, mood and anxiety disorders, and elimination disorders (enuresis and encopresis), a comprehensive assessment must also include methods to address these areas. This chapter does not discuss the assessment of these latter problems, as their evaluation is the subject of other chapters in this text to which the reader should refer. Assessment methods must be chosen for their ability to evaluate these major domains of difficulty.

2. Given that current diagnostic criteria require that a child's behavioral problems be developmentally inappropriate for his or her mental age, the use of assessment techniques with adequate normative data is necessary.

3. The cross-situational or pervasive nature of ADHD dictates that an evaluation collect information on a child's functioning in different settings and with different caregivers.

4. The chronic nature of ADHD throughout childhood and adolescence makes it critical to take time to assess a child's developmental history, so as to establish not only the age of onset of various behavioral problems and impairments, but also their chronicity (both of which are part of the diagnostic criteria for the disorder). Chronicity also means that it will be extremely useful to have assessment methods that are appropriate across wide age ranges, with adequate normative data at each age. The need for periodic reassessments of a child over time, to evaluate maturational changes in behavior as well as to determine whether that behavior remains problematic or statistically atypical, should encourage the clinician to use such developmentally referenced techniques.

5. The prevalence of parenting stress, family adversity, and frank psychiatric disorders is greater among the parents of ADHD children than among those of non-ADHD children. Given the likelihood that such difficulties may interfere with the delivery of treatment for a child, it will prove important to expand the scope of the evaluation to include some measures of these domains of parental functioning and the parents' own needs for treatment.

6. Research is also beginning to demonstrate that teachers experience increased stress in their teaching roles when ADHD children must be educated within their classes, and that such stress

can affect the behavioral adjustment and academic success of ADHD children under those teachers' care (Greene, 1996). The evaluation of teacher stress and plans for its management may also be of importance if major behavioral interventions are planned for implementation in a particular teacher's classroom on behalf of an ADHD student.

7. Finally, as with all childhood disorders, methods must be chosen for the convenient monitoring of the effects and side effects of treatments that are to be implemented if treatment efficacy is to be properly evaluated.

ASSESSMENT

The evaluation of ADHD children incorporates multiple assessment methods, relies upon several informants, and examines the nature of the children's difficulties (and strengths!) across multiple situations. Thus, parent, child, and teacher interviews; parent and teacher rating scales of child behavior; parent self-report measures of relevant psychiatric conditions; laboratory measures of ADHD symptoms; direct observational techniques; and measures of parent and family functioning must all be part of the clinical protocol.

There are several goals to bear in mind in the evaluation of children for ADHD. A major goal of such an assessment is not only the determination of the presence or absence of ADHD, but also the differential diagnosis of ADHD as opposed to other childhood psychiatric disorders. This requires extensive clinical knowledge of these other psychiatric disorders (see Mash & Barkley, 1996). Suggestions for making such a differential diagnosis are discussed in more detail in an earlier comprehensive textbook on ADHD (Barkley, 1990). In doing so, it may be necessary to draw upon measures that are normed for the individual's ethnic background (if such instruments are available), so as to preclude the overdiagnosis of minority children when diagnostic criteria developed with white children are extrapolated to them (Bauermeister, 1996; Bauermeister, Berrios, Jimenez, Acevedo, & Gordon, 1990).

A second purpose of the evaluation is to begin delineating the types of interventions that will be needed to address the psychiatric disorder(s) and psychological, academic, and social impairments identified in the course of assessment. As noted later, these may include individual counseling, parent training in behavior management, family therapy, classroom behavior modification, stimu-

lant or antidepressant medications, and formal special educational services, to name just a few (Mash & Barkley, 1989).

Another important purpose of the evaluation is the determination of comorbid conditions and whether or not these may affect prognosis or decisions about treatment. For instance, the presence of high levels of anxiety specifically, and of internalizing symptoms more generally, has been shown to be a predictor of poorer responses to stimulant medication (DuPaul & Barkley, 1990). Similarly, the presence of high levels of hostile, defiant behavior or Oppositional Defiant Disorder has been shown to be a marker for greater family conflict (Barkley, Anastopoulos, et al., 1992; Barkley, Fischer, et al., 1991), which may interfere with successful parent training or family therapy. As noted earlier, it has also been shown to be a predictor of risk for later Conduct Disorder, antisocial behavior, and substance misuse (Barkley, Fischer, et al., 1990; Fischer et al., 1993b; Mannuzza et al., 1993).

A further objective of the evaluation is to identify the pattern of the child's psychological strengths and weaknesses and to consider how these may affect treatment planning. This may also include gaining some impression of the parents' own abilities to carry out the treatment program, as well as the parents' social and economic circumstances and the treatment resources that may (or may not) be available within their community and cultural group. The evaluation will usually also need to determine the child's eligibility for special educational services within the school district. Such eligibility has been granted to ADHD children under federal legislation over the past 20 years (i.e., the Individuals with Disabilities in Education Act and Section 504 of the Rehabilitation Act; see DuPaul & Stoner, 1994; Latham & Latham, 1992), but the particular state regulations that institute these federal policies in a child's home school district may vary.

As this discussion illustrates, the identification of ADHD in a child is itself but one of many purposes of the clinical evaluation of children with ADHD. As I and others have previously noted (Atkins & Pelham, 1992; Barkley, 1990; Barkley, Grodzinsky, & DuPaul, 1992; DuPaul & Stoner, 1994; Grodzinsky & Barkley, 1996; Hinshaw, 1994), the pursuit of this multipurpose evaluation requires some appreciation of the concepts of reliability, validity, and predictive power as they apply to the instruments selected for use in the evaluation, as well as of the assumptions inherent in the use of those instruments. A brief discussion of different methods of assessment as they pertain to ADHD follows. More thorough discussions can be found elsewhere (Barkley, 1990; DuPaul & Stoner, 1994).

Parental Interview

Although often criticized for its unreliability and subjectivity, the parental (often maternal) interview remains an indispensable part of the clinical assessment of children. In fact, as Hinshaw (1994) rightly notes, if clinicians were limited to a single method to evaluate a child with ADHD, most would unhesitatingly choose the parental (maternal) interview. Whether parental reports are wholly accurate or not, they provide the most ecologically valid and important source of information concerning the children's difficulties (Barkley, 1991). It is the parents' complaints that have often led to the referral of the children, will affect the parents' perceptions of and reactions to the children, and will influence the parents' adherence to the treatment recommendations.

Moreover, the reliability and accuracy of the parental interview have much to do with the manner in which it is conducted and the specificity of the questions offered by the examiner. Interviewing that includes highly specific questions about psychopathological symptoms empirically demonstrated to have a high degree of association with particular disorders greatly enhances diagnostic reliability. The interview must also, however, focus upon the specific complaints about the child's psychological adjustment and any functional parameters (eliciting and consequating events) associated with those problems, if psychosocial and educational treatment planning is to be based upon the evaluation.

After the examiner obtains the routine demographic data concerning the child and family (e.g., ages of child and family members; child's date of birth; parents' names, addresses, employers, occupations, and religion[s]; and the child's school, teacher[s], and physician), the interview proceeds to the major referral concerns of the parents (and of the professional referring the child, where appropriate). General descriptions by parents must be followed with specific questions by the examiner to elucidate the details of the problems and their functional relationships. For general guidelines on clinical interviewing, readers may wish to consult A. M. Gross (1984).

A behavioral interview probes not only for the specific nature, frequency, age of onset, and chronicity of the problematic behaviors, but also for the situational and temporal variation in the behaviors and their consequences. If the problems are chronic (which they often are), determining what prompted the referral at this time reveals much about parental perceptions of the child's problems, current family circumstances related to the problems' severity, and parental motivation for treatment.

Following this, the examiner should review with the parents problems that may exist in the developmental domains of motor, language, intellectual, thinking, academic, emotional, and social functioning. Such information greatly aids in the differential diagnosis of the child's problems. Accomplishing this requires that the examiner have an adequate knowledge of the diagnostic features of other childhood disorders, some of which may present superficially as ADHD. For instance, many children with pervasive developmental disorders or early Bipolar I Disorder may be viewed by their parents as having ADHD, because the parents are more likely to have heard about the latter disorder than the former ones and will recognize some of ADHD's qualities in their children. Questioning about inappropriate thinking, affect, social relations, and motor peculiarities may reveal a more seriously and pervasively disturbed child. Inquiry must be made as to the presence or history of tics in the child or the immediate biological family members. When these are noted, they should result in a recommendation for the cautious use of low doses of such medicine so as not to bring on or exacerbate a tic disorder (DuPaul & Barkley, 1990). A sample interview used with the parents of ADHD children can be found elsewhere (Barkley, 1990).

Developmental, medical, school, and family histories are then obtained. The family history includes a discussion of potential psychiatric difficulties in the parents and siblings; marital difficulties; and any family problems centered around chronic medical conditions, employment problems, or other actually or potentially stressful events within the family. Of course, the examiner will want to obtain some information about prior treatments received by the child and other family members for these presenting problems. Where the history suggests potentially treatable medical or neurological conditions (allergies, seizures, Tourette syndrome, etc.), a referral to a physician is essential. Without evidence of such problems, however, referral to a physician for examination usually fails to reveal any further information of use in the treatment of the child. An exception to this is a case in which the use of stimulant medications is contemplated; for this, a referral to a physician is clearly indicated.

As part of the general interview of the parents, the examiner will need to cover the symptoms of the major child psychiatric and developmental disorders. Highly structured interviews have become increasingly common in clinical research studies for this purpose (see Hodges, 1993, for a review) and have been adopted by some clinicians. Others (e.g., Barkley, 1997b) have created structured interviews for the clinical evaluation of children with ADHD that may be less detailed and cumbersome than the ones used for research purposes, such as the Diagnostic Interview Schedule for Children (DISC), but that still provide coverage of the symptoms of other DSM childhood disorders besides ADHD. Regardless of the particular method chosen, some review of the major childhood disorders in the DSM-IV (American Psychiatric Association, 1994) in some semistructured or structured way is imperative if any semblance of a reliable and differential approach to diagnosis and the documentation of comorbid disorders is to occur.

In applying the diagnostic criteria for ADHD (see Table 2.1) to any given case, the examiner should keep several problems with the criteria in mind and make adjustments for these as needed. These are discussed in more detail (see Barkley, 1990, for DSM-III-R, and Barkley, 1996, 1997b, for DSM-IV) and are only briefly noted here.

1. The cutoff scores on both DSM-IV symptom lists (six of nine symptoms on each list) were primarily developed on children aged 4–16 years. The extrapolation of these thresholds to age ranges outside of those in the field trial is questionable. Studies of large populations of children (Achenbach, 1991b, 1991c; DuPaul, 1991) indicate that the behaviors associated with ADHD tend to decline in frequency within the population over development. A recent study of a central Massachusetts community sample of adults aged 17–84 (Murphy & Barkley, 1996b) showed the same trends continuing across the life span. Thus, somewhat higher thresholds may be needed for preschool children (ages 2–4), whereas increasingly lower thresholds will most likely be needed across the age groups of 17–29, 30–49, and 50–84 years (Murphy & Barkley, 1996b) if the same developmentally relative level of deviance (93rd percentile) is to be used to define the disorder. The Murphy and Barkley (1996b) study suggests that adjusted thresholds (four inattention symptoms

and five hyperactivity–impulsivity symptoms for the 17–29 age group; three and four, respectively, for the 30–49 group; and two and three, respectively, for the 50–84 group) may be more appropriate if the 93rd percentile is to be the cutoff point for ADHD.

2. The children used in the DSM-IV field trial were predominantly males. Studies of large samples of children reliably demonstrate that parents and teachers report lower levels of those behaviors associated with ADHD in girls than in boys (Achenbach, 1991b, 1991c; DuPaul, 1991). It is thus possible that the cutoff points on the DSM-IV symptom lists, because they are based mainly on males, are unfairly high for females. In other words, a girl must meet a higher standard of deviance relative to girls than a boy must do relative to boys in order to be diagnosed as having ADHD. The argument hinges on the critical point of whether such a girl demonstrates impairment, despite having a lower level of symptoms than a boy does; this point has not yet been adequately studied. Nevertheless, the issue has led some to recommend that gender-adjusted thresholds be evaluated in the field trial for the next version of the DSM and be given more serious consideration for inclusion in the final criteria (Barkley, 1996b; McGee & Feehan, 1991).

3. The specific age of onset of 7 years is not particularly critical for identifying ADHD children. The field trial for the DSM-IV found that ADHD children with various ages of onset were essentially similar in their nature and severity of impairments, as long as their symptoms had developed prior to ages 10–12 years (Applegate et al., 1996). Therefore, stipulating an onset of symptoms in childhood is probably sufficient for purposes of clinical diagnosis.

4. The criterion that duration of symptoms be at least 6 months was not specifically studied in the field trial and was held over from earlier DSMs primarily because of tradition. Some research on preschool children suggests that a large number of 2- to 3-year-olds may manifest the symptoms of ADHD as part of that developmental period, and that these symptoms may remain present for periods of 3–6 months or longer (Campbell, 1990; Palfrey, Levine, Walker, & Sullivan, 1985). Children whose symptoms persisted for at least a year or more, however, were likely to remain deviant in their behavior pattern into the elementary school years (Campbell & Ewing, 1990; Palfrey et al., 1985). Adjusting the duration criterion to 12 months would seem to make good clinical sense.

5. The criterion that symptoms must be evident in two or more settings (e.g., home and school or work) essentially requires that children have sufficient symptoms of ADHD by both parent and teacher report before they can qualify for the diagnosis. This requirement bumps up against a methodological problem inherent in comparing parent and teacher reports. On average, the relationship of behavior ratings from these two sources tends to be fairly modest, averaging about .30 (Achenbach, McConaughy, & Howell, 1987). If parent and teacher ratings are unlikely to agree across various behavioral domains being rated, the requirement that such ratings must agree sets limits unnecessarily on the number of children qualifying for the diagnosis of ADHD. Fortunately, some evidence demonstrates that children who meet DSM criteria (in this case, DSM-III-R) by parent reports have a high probability of meeting the criteria by teacher reports (Biederman, Keenan, & Faraone, 1990). Even so, stipulating that parents and teachers *must* agree on the diagnostic criteria before a diagnosis can be rendered is probably unwise and unnecessarily restrictive.

An examiner should keep the foregoing issues in mind when applying the DSM criteria to particular clinical cases, as they will help him or her to appreciate the fact that the DSM represents guidelines for diagnosis, not rules of law or dogmatic religious proscriptions. Some clinical judgment is always going to be needed in the application of such guidelines to individual cases in clinical practice. For instance, if a child meets all criteria for ADHD (including parent and teacher agreement on symptoms), except that the age of onset for the symptoms and impairment is 9 years, should the diagnosis be withheld? Given the discussion above concerning the lack of specificity for an age of onset of 7 years, the wise clinician would grant the ADHD diagnosis anyway. Likewise, if an 8-year-old girl shows six of the inattention symptoms but only five of the hyperactivity–impulsivity symptoms, and all other conditions are met for ADHD, the diagnosis should probably be granted, given the comments above about gender bias within these criteria. Some flexibility (and common sense!) must be incorporated into the clinical application of any DSM criteria.

For years, some clinicians have entirely eschewed diagnosing children, viewing it as a mechanistic and dehumanizing practice that merely results in unnecessary labeling of children. Moreover, they may have felt that diagnosing gets in the way of appreciating the clinical uniqueness of each case—in other words, that it unnecessarily homogenizes the heterogeneity of clinical cases. Some may even have believed that labeling a child's condition with a diagnosis is unnecessary, as it is far more important to articulate the child's pattern of behavioral and developmental excesses and deficits in planning behavioral treatments than to give a diagnosis. Although there may have been some justification for these views in the past, particularly prior to the development of more empirically based diagnostic criteria, this is no longer the case in view of the wealth of research that went into creating the DSM-IV childhood disorders and their criteria. This is not to say that clinicians should not proceed to document patterns of behavioral deficits and excesses (indeed, such documentation is important for treatment planning)—only that this should not be used as an excuse not to diagnose at all. Furthermore, given that the protection of children's rights and access to educational and other services may actually hinge on the awarding or withholding of the diagnosis of ADHD, dispensing with diagnosis altogether could well be considered professional negligence. For these reasons and others, clinicians must review in some systematic way with the parents of all children referred to them the symptom lists and other diagnostic criteria for various childhood mental disorders.

Following the generic interview, the examiner can pursue more details about the nature of the parent–child interactions pertaining to the child's following of rules. All ADHD children have problems complying or sustaining compliance with certain types of commands, directions, and assigned tasks. Such problems usually consist of failures to finish assigned activities, particularly when these are boring, effortful, and have few or no immediate consequences. Up to 60% of ADHD children, however, have also acquired a repertoire of oppositional, defiant, and coercive behaviors—a repertoire that contributes further to conflictual interactions with their parents over rules. Therefore, the parents of each child should be questioned about the child's ability to accomplish commands and requests in a satisfactory manner in various settings, to adhere to rules of conduct governing behavior in various situations, and to demonstrate self-control (rule following) appropriate to the child's age in the absence of adult supervision. To accomplish this, I have found it useful to follow the format set forth in Table 2.2, in which parents are questioned about their interactions with their child in a variety of home and public situations. Where problems are said to occur, the examiner follows up with the list of questions in the right-hand column of Table 2.2.

TABLE 2.2. Parental Interview Format

Situations to be discussed with parents	Follow-up questions for each problematic situation
General — overall interactions Playing alone Playing with other children Mealtimes Getting dressed in morning During washing and bathing While parent is on telephone While watching television While visitors are at home While visiting others' homes In public places (supermarkets, shopping centers, etc.) While mother is occupied with chores or activities When father is at home When child is asked to do a chore At bedtime Other situations (in car, in church, etc.)	1. Is this a problem area? If so, then proceed with questions 2 to 9. 2. What does the child do in this situation that bothers you? 3. What is your response? 4. What will the child do next? 5. If the problem continues, what will you do next? 6. What is usually the outcome of this interaction? 7. How often do these problems occur in this situation? 8. How do you feel about these problems? 9. On a scale of 0 to 10 (0 = no problem; 10 = severe problem), how severe is this problem to you?

Note. Adapted from interview used by C. Hanf (1976), University of Oregon Health Sciences Center. Reprinted from Barkley (1981b, p. 148). Copyright 1981 by The Guilford Press. Reprinted by permission.

Such an approach yields a wealth of information on the nature of parent–child interactions across settings; the type of noncompliance shown by the child (e.g., stalling, starting the task but failing to finish it, outright opposition and defiance, etc.); the particular management style employed by parents to deal with noncompliance; and the particular types of coercive behaviors used by the child as part of the noncompliance. This may add an additional 30–40 minutes to the parental interview, but it is well worth the time invested when it is possible to do so, especially if parent training in child behavior management is likely to be subsequently recommended for this family. When time constraints are problematic, a rating scale can be used that was developed to provide similar types of information. This scale is called the Home Situations Questionnaire (HSQ) and is presented in Table 2.3. After parents complete the scale, they can be questioned about one or two of the problem situations, using the same follow-up questions as in Table 2.2. A limited set of norms for the HSQ on samples of children (mainly from Wisconsin) is available as well (Barkley, 1990).

This interview may also reveal that one parent, usually the mother, has more difficulty managing the ADHD child than the other. Care should be taken to discuss differences in the parents' approaches to management and any marital problems this may have spawned. Such difficulties in child management can often lead to reduced leisure and recreational time for the parents, to increased conflict within the marriage, and often to conflict within the extended family if relatives live nearby. It is often helpful to inquire as to the parents' beliefs about the causes or origins of their child's behavioral difficulties, as this may unveil areas of ignorance or misinformation that will require attention later during the initial counseling of the family about the child's disorder (or disorders) and its likely causes. The examiner also should briefly inquire about the nature of parental and family social activities to determine how isolated, or "insular," the parents are from the usual social support networks in which many parents are involved. Research by Wahler (1980) has shown that the degree of maternal insularity is significantly associated with failure in subsequent parent training programs. When parental insularity is present to a significant degree, the clinician may want to consider addressing the isolation as an initial goal of treatment, rather than progressing directly to child behavior management training with the family.

The parental interview can then conclude with a discussion of the child's positive characteristics and attributes, as well as potential rewards and reinforcers — that is, things the child desires that

TABLE 2.3. Home Situations Questionnaires (HSQ)

Child's name _____ Date _____

Name of person completing this form _____

Instructions: Does your child present any problems with compliance to instructions, commands, or rules for you in any of these situations? If so, please circle the word Yes and then circle a number beside that situation that describes how severe the problem is for you. If your child is not a problem in a situation, circle No and go on to the next situation on the form.

Situations	Yes/No		Mild			*If yes, how severe?*					Severe
While playing alone	Yes	No	1	2	3	4	5	6	7	8	9
While playing with other children	Yes	No	1	2	3	4	5	6	7	8	9
At mealtimes	Yes	No	1	2	3	4	5	6	7	8	9
Getting dressed	Yes	No	1	2	3	4	5	6	7	8	9
Washing and bathing	Yes	No	1	2	3	4	5	6	7	8	9
While you are on the telephone	Yes	No	1	2	3	4	5	6	7	8	9
While watching television	Yes	No	1	2	3	4	5	6	7	8	9
When visitors are in your home	Yes	No	1	2	3	4	5	6	7	8	9
When you are visiting someone's home	Yes	No	1	2	3	4	5	6	7	8	9
In public places (restaurants, stores, church, etc.)	Yes	No	1	2	3	4	5	6	7	8	9
When father is home	Yes	No	1	2	3	4	5	6	7	8	9
When asked to do chores	Yes	No	1	2	3	4	5	6	7	8	9
When asked to do homework	Yes	No	1	2	3	4	5	6	7	8	9
At bedtime	Yes	No	1	2	3	4	5	6	7	8	9
While in the car	Yes	No	1	2	3	4	5	6	7	8	9
When with a babysitter	Yes	No	1	2	3	4	5	6	7	8	9

-- For Office Use Only ---

Total number of problem settings _____ Mean severity score_____

Note. From Barkley (1997b, p. 177). Copyright 1997 by The Guilford Press. Reprinted by permission.

will prove useful later as the parents are trained in contingency management methods. Some parents of ADHD children have had such chronic and pervasive management problems that, upon initial questioning, they may find it hard to report anything positive about their children. Getting them to begin thinking of such attributes is actually an initial step toward treatment, as the early phases of parent training will teach parents to focus on and attend to desirable child behaviors (Forehand & McMahon, 1981).

Child Interview

Some time should always be spent interacting directly with an ADHD child. The length of this interview depends upon the child's age, intellectual level, and language abilities. For a preschool child, the interview may serve merely as a time to become acquainted with the child, noting his or her appearance, behavior, developmental characteristics, and general demeanor. For an older child or adolescent, this time can be fruitfully spent inquiring about the child's views of the reasons for

the referral and evaluation, perceptions of the family's functioning, additional problems the child feels he or she may have, school performance, degree of acceptance by peers and classmates, and possible changes in the family that might make life for the child happier at home. Like the parents, the child can also be asked about potential rewards and reinforcers for use in later contingency management programs.

Children below the age of 9–12 years are not especially reliable in their reports of their own problems or those of other family members, and the problem is compounded by the frequently diminished self-awareness and impulse control of typical ADHD children (Hinshaw, 1994). ADHD children often show little reflection about the examiner's questions and may lie or distort information in a more socially pleasing direction. Some will report that they have many friends, have no interaction problems at home with their parents, and are doing well at school, in direct contrast with the extensive parental and teacher complaints of inappropriate behavior by these children. Because of this tendency of ADHD children and adolescents to underreport the seriousness of their behavior, particularly in the realm of disruptive or externalizing behaviors (Barkley, Fischer, et al., 1991; Fischer et al., 1993b), the diagnosis of ADHD is never based solely upon child self-reports. Nevertheless, children's reports of their internalizing symptoms (e.g., anxiety and depression) are more reliable, and so these should play some role in the diagnosis of comorbid anxiety or mood disorders in children with ADHD (Hinshaw, 1994). Some structured psychiatric interviews, such as the DISC, are available for the purposes of clinically interviewing children, although they were originally intended for use in epidemiological studies of the prevalence of mental disorders in the population.

Although notation of ADHD children's behavior, compliance, attention span, activity level, and impulse control within the clinic is useful, clinicians must guard against drawing any diagnostic conclusions from cases where such children are not problematic in the clinic or office. Many ADHD children do not misbehave in clinicians' offices, and so heavy reliance upon such observations would clearly lead to false negatives in the diagnosis (Sleator & Ullmann, 1981). In some instances, a child's behavior with the parents in the waiting area prior to the appointment may be a better indication of the child's management problems at home than is the child's behavior toward the clinician, particularly when this involves a one-to-one interaction between the child and the examiner.

This is not to say that a child's office behavior is entirely useless. When it is grossly inappropriate or extreme, it may well signal the likelihood of problems in the child's natural settings, particularly school. It is the presence of relatively normal conduct by the child that may be an unreliable indicator of the child's behavior elsewhere. For instance, in an ongoing study of 205 children aged 4–6 years, my colleagues and I have examined the relationship of office behavior to parent and teacher ratings. Of these children, 158 were identified at kindergarten registration as being 1.5 standard deviations above the mean (93rd percentile) on parent ratings of ADHD and aggressive symptoms (Oppositional Defiant Disorder). These children were subsequently evaluated for nearly 4 hours in a clinic setting, after which the examiner completed a rating scale of each child's behavior in the clinic. We then classified the children as falling below or above the 93rd percentile on these clinic ratings, using data from a normal control group being tested as part of this project. The children were also classified as falling above

or below this threshold on parent ratings of home behavior and teacher ratings of school behavior. We have found to date that there is no significant relationship between children's clinic behavior (normal or abnormal) and the ratings by their parents. However, there is a significant relationship between abnormal ratings in the clinic and abnormal ratings by teachers, in that 70% of the children classified as abnormal in their clinic behavior were also classified as such in the teacher ratings of class behavior, particularly on the externalizing behavior dimension. Normal behavior, however, was not necessarily predictive of normal behavior in either parent or teacher ratings. This suggests that abnormal or significantly disruptive behavior during a lengthy clinical evaluation may be a marker for similar behavioral difficulties in a school setting. Nevertheless, the wise clinician will contact the child's teacher directly to learn about the child's school adjustment, rather than relying entirely on clinic office behavior for inferences about school behavior.

Teacher Interview

At some point during or soon after the initial evaluative session with the family, contact with a child's teacher(s) is essential to further clarifying the nature of the child's problems. This will most likely be done by telephone unless the clinician works within the child's school system. Interviews with teachers have all of the same merits as do interviews with parents; they provide a second ecologically valid source of indispensable information about the child's psychological adjustment (in this case, in the school setting). Like parent reports, teacher reports are also subject to bias, and the integrity of any reporter of information must always be weighed in addition to the information itself.

Teacher versions of some structured interviews, such as the DISC, are available for purposes of reviewing the symptoms of the major childhood psychiatric disorders with teachers. However, they are cumbersome, detailed, and time-consuming. Time might profitably be spent in reviewing the results of the teacher rating scales (see below) before interviewing a teacher; this will help the clinician to focus the discussion on the symptoms of the disorders most likely to be present, in view of the scale results.

The vast majority of ADHD children have problems with academic performance and classroom behavior, and the details of these difficulties need to be obtained. Although this may initially be done by telephone, a visit to the classroom and direct observation and recording of an ADHD child's behavior can prove quite useful in further documenting the child's behaviors and in planning later contingency management programs for the classroom. Granted, such visits are unlikely to prove feasible for clinicians working outside of school systems — particularly in the new climate of managed health care, in which the evaluation time that will be compensated is severely restricted. But for those professionals working within school systems, direct behavioral observations can prove very fruitful for diagnosis and especially for treatment planning (Atkins & Pelham, 1992; DuPaul & Stoner, 1994).

As noted above, teachers should also be sent the rating scales discussed in the next section. These should be sent as a packet prior to the actual evaluation so that the results are available for discussion with the parents during the interview with them, as well as with the teacher during the subsequent telephone contact or school visit.

The teacher interview should focus upon the specific nature of a child's problems in the school environment, again following a behavioral format. The settings, nature, frequency, consequating events, and eliciting events for the major behavioral problems should also be explored. The follow-up questions used in the parental interview on parent–child interactions and shown in Table 2.2 may prove useful here as well. In addition, the teacher should be questioned about potential learning disabilities in the ODD or ADHD child, given the greater likelihood of such disabilities in this population. When evidence suggests their existence, the evaluation of the child should be expanded to explore the nature and degree of such deficits as viewed by the teacher. Even when learning disabilities do not exist, ADHD children are more likely to have problems with sloppy handwriting, careless approaches to tasks, poor organization of their work materials, and academic underachievement relative to their tested abilities. Time should be taken with the teacher to explore the possibility of these problems.

Child Behavior Rating Scales for Parent and Teacher Reports

Child behavior checklists and rating scales have become an essential element in the evaluation and diagnosis of ADHD in children. The availability of several scales with excellent normative data across a wide age range of children, and with ac-

ceptable reliability and validity, makes their incorporation into the assessment protocol quite convenient and extremely useful. Such information is invaluable in determining the statistical deviance of the children's problem behaviors, the extent to which the children meet the diagnostic criteria for ADHD, and the degree to which other problems may be present. As a result, it is useful to mail a packet of these scales out to a child's parents prior to the initial appointment, and to ask that these be returned on or before the day of the evaluation. This permits the examiner to review and score them before interviewing the parents, allows for vague or significant answers to be elucidated in the interview, and serves to focus the subsequent interview on those areas of abnormality that may be highlighted in the responses to scale items. As noted earlier, a packet should be mailed in advance to the child's teacher as well.

Numerous child behavior rating scales exist, and the reader is referred to other reviews (Barkley, 1988, 1990; Hinshaw & Nigg, in press) for additional details on the more commonly used scales and for discussions of the requirements and underlying assumptions of behavior rating scales — assumptions that are all too easily overlooked in the clinical use of these instruments. Despite their limitations, behavior rating scales offer a means of gathering information from informants who may have spent months or years with the child. Apart from interviews, there is no other means of obtaining such a wealth of information for so little investment of time. The fact that such scales provide a means of quantifying the opinions of others (often along qualitative dimensions), and of comparing these scores to norms collected on large groups of children, are further merits of these instruments. Nevertheless, behavior rating scales are opinions and are subject to the oversights, prejudices, and limitations on reliability and validity such opinions may have.

Initially, it is advisable to utilize a "broad-band" rating scale that provides coverage of the major dimensions of child psychopathology known to exist, such as depression, anxiety, withdrawal, aggression, delinquent conduct, and (of course) inattentive and hyperactive–impulsive behavior. These scales should be completed by parents and teachers. Such scales include the Behavioral Assessment System for Children (BASC; Reynolds & Kamphaus, 1994) and the Child Behavior Checklist (CBCL; Achenbach, 1991a), both of which have versions for parents and teachers and satisfactory normative information. The Personality Inventory for Children (Lachar, 1982) may also serve this purpose, provided that one of the shortened versions is employed for convenience and the more contemporary norms are used for scoring purposes. It is, however, only a scale for parents to complete precluding the informative comparison that can (and should) be made between parent and teacher reports on the same scale. The Conners Parent and Teacher Rating Scales (Conners, 1990) can also be used for this initial screening for psychopathology, but they do not provide the same breadth of coverage across all of these dimensions of psychopathology as do the aforementioned scales; this is particularly so for the revised versions of the Conners scales. The normative samples used for these scales have been more limited than those for the CBCL and BASC, although this may be corrected by a new normative study now underway.

More narrow-band scales that focus more specifically on the assessment of ADHD symptoms should also be employed in the initial screening of children. Such scales include the ADHD Rating Scale (DuPaul, 1991), the Swanson-Nolan-and-Pelham (SNAP) Checklist (Swanson & Pelham, 1988), the Child Attention Problems Scale (see Barkley, 1990), the ADD-H Comprehensive Teacher Rating Scale (ACTeRS; Ullmann, Sleator, & Sprague, 1984), and the Attention Deficit Disorders Evaluation Scale (ADDES; McCarney, 1989). Each of these scales assesses inattention and hyperactive–impulsive behavior separately, to permit some assistance with distinguishing the subtypes of ADHD set forth in the DSM-III and DSM-IV. The ADHD Rating Scale and the SNAP Checklist have the advantage of employing the symptom lists taken directly from the DSM-III-R, and both have recently been updated to the DSM-IV item lists, although norms for the DSM-IV versions are not yet published. To illustrate such scales, the ADHD Rating Scale—Home Version, using DSM-IV symptoms as items, is presented in Table 2.4.

TABLE 2.4. ADHD Rating Scale—Home Version

Child's name _____ Age _____ Grade _____ Completed by_____

Circle the number that *best describes* your child's home behavior over the past 6 months.

	Never or Rarely	Sometimes	Often	Very Often
1. Fails to give close attention to details or makes careless mistakes in schoolwork.	0	1	2	3
2. Fidgets with hands or feet or squirms in seat.	0	1	2	3
3. Has difficulty sustaining attention in tasks or play activities.	0	1	2	3
4. Leaves seat in classroom or in other situations in which remaining seated is expected.	0	1	2	3
5. Does not seem to listen when spoken to directly.	0	1	2	3
6. Runs about or climbs excessively in situations in which it is inappropriate.	0	1	2	3
7. Does not follow through on instructions and fails to finish work.	0	1	2	3
8. Has difficulty playing or engaging in leisure activities quietly.	0	1	2	3
9. Has difficulty organizing tasks and activities.	0	1	2	3
10. Is "on the go" or acts as if "driven by a motor."	0	1	2	3
11. Avoids tasks (e.g., schoolwork, homework) that require mental effort.	0	1	2	3
12. Talks excessively.	0	1	2	3
13. Loses things necessary for tasks or activities.	0	1	2	3
14. Blurts out answers before questions have been completed.	0	1	2	3
15. Is easily distracted.	0	1	2	3
16. Has difficulty awaiting turn.	0	1	2	3
17. Is forgetful in daily activities.	0	1	2	3
18. Interrupts or intrudes on others.	0	1	2	3

Note. Developed by G. J. DuPaul, A. Anastopoulos, R. A. Barkley, and K. Murphy (1994). Reprinted by permission of the developers.

Another narrow-band scale specific to ADHD is the Child Attention Problems scale (Barkley, 1990). This has the advantage of being drawn directly from the Teacher Report Form of the CBCL, and thus benefits from the rigor of standardization and norming that went into the CBCL's development (Achenbach, 1991c). Its disadvantage is that, unlike several of the specialized scales noted above, it does not employ the precise symptom lists for inattention and hyperactivity–impulsivity from the DSM-IV. Therefore, the results of this scale alone would not automatically support a diagnosis of ADHD.

The pervasiveness of the child's behavior problems within the home and school settings should also be examined, as such measures of situational pervasiveness appear to have as much stability over time as the aforementioned scales do, if not more (Fischer et al., 1993a). The HSQ (see Table 2.3) and the School Situations Questionnaire (SSQ; Barkley, 1987, 1990) provide a means for doing so, and normative information for these scales is now available (Altepeter & Breen, 1992; Barkley, 1990; Barkley & Edelbrock, 1987; DuPaul & Barkley, 1992). The HSQ, as shown in Table 2.3, requires parents to rate their child's behavior problems across 16 different home and public situations. The SSQ is presented in Table 2.5; it obtains teacher reports of problems in 12 different school situations. Such information may be of assistance in

planning behavioral interventions for ADHD children within the home or school settings.

The more specialized or narrow-band scales focusing on symptoms of ADHD, as well as the HSQ and SSQ, can be used to monitor treatment response when given prior to, throughout, and at the end of active treatment programs. For instance, the revised Conners Parent and Teacher Rating Scales, the ADHD Rating Scale, the SNAP, and the HSQ and SSQ have all been used to monitor the behavioral effects of stimulant medication on children with ADHD (Barkley, 1990; Barkley, DuPaul, & McMurray, 1991; Barkley, Fischer, Newby, & Breen, 1988; Pelham & Milich, 1991). Likewise, the HSQ and SSQ have been employed in the measurement of treatment effects in behavioral parent training programs (Barkley, 1987; Pollard, Ward, & Barkley, 1983), as has the ADHD Rating Scale (Anastopoulos, Shelton, DuPaul, & Guevremont, 1993).

Another type of specialized rating scale that may be of some use in the evaluation of children with ADHD is the Self-Control Rating Scale (SCRS; Kendall & Wilcox, 1979). As discussed earlier, ADHD children have substantial difficulties with self-control. To evaluate these deficits, Kendall and Wilcox (1979) developed the 33-item SCRS, which contains specific questions about children's ability to inhibit behavior, follow rules, and con-

---

TABLE 2.5. School Situations Questionnaires (SSQ)

Child's name _____ **Date** _____

Name of person completing this form _____

Instructions: Does this child present any . . . problems . . . for you in any of these situations? If so, [indicate how severe they are].

Situations	Yes/No		Mild				If yes, how severe?				Severe
When arriving at school	Yes	No	1	2	3	4	5	6	7	8	9
During individual desk work	Yes	No	1	2	3	4	5	6	7	8	9
During small group activities	Yes	No	1	2	3	4	5	6	7	8	9
During free playtime in class	Yes	No	1	2	3	4	5	6	7	8	9
During lectures to the class	Yes	No	1	2	3	4	5	6	7	8	9
At recess	Yes	No	1	2	3	4	5	6	7	8	9
At lunch	Yes	No	1	2	3	4	5	6	7	8	9
In the hallways	Yes	No	1	2	3	4	5	6	7	8	9
In the bathroom	Yes	No	1	2	3	4	5	6	7	8	9
On field trips	Yes	No	1	2	3	4	5	6	7	8	9
During special assemblies	Yes	No	1	2	3	4	5	6	7	8	9
On the bus	Yes	No	1	2	3	4	5	6	7	8	9

-- For Office Use Only---

Total number of problem settings _____ Mean severity score_____

Note. From Barkley (1997b, p. 178). Copyright 1997 by The Guilford Press. Reprinted by permission.

trol impulsive reactions. The scale yields a single summary score and has been shown to measure a relatively homogeneous construct, which the developers call "self-control." The nature and specificity of the items makes this scale quite useful with teachers (or parents) in evaluating self-control deficits in ADHD children. However, normative data are available only for a small Minneapolis sample ($n = 110$) of children in grades 3 to 6 (Kendall & Wilcox, 1979). Test–retest coefficients are satisfactory, but no interteacher reliability estimates are available. The scale correlates significantly with direct classroom observations of off-task behavior and "bugging others"; it discriminates ADHD children from normal children and those with other psychiatric disorders; and it is sensitive to treatment effects in self-control training programs (Barkley, 1988).

One of the most common problem areas for children with ADHD is in their academic productivity. The amount of work typically accomplished by ADHD children at school is often substantially less than that done by their peers within the same period of time. Demonstrating such an impact of ADHD on school functioning is often critical for ADHD children to be eligible for special educational services (DuPaul & Stoner, 1994). The Academic Performance Rating Scale (see Barkley, 1990) was developed to provide a means of quickly screening for this domain of school functioning; it is a teacher rating scale of academic productivity and accuracy in major subject areas, with norms based on a sample of children from central Massachusetts (DuPaul, Rapport, & Perriello, 1991). The scale is presented in Table 2.6.

Self-Report Behavior Rating Scales for Children

Achenbach and Edelbrock (1991d) have developed a form of the CBCL that can be completed by children aged 11 to 18 years (Youth Self-Report Form). Most items are similar to those on the parent form and the Teacher Report Form of the CBCL, except that they are worded in the first person. A later revision of this scale (Cross-Informant Version; Achenbach, 1991a) now permits direct comparisons of results among the parent, teacher, and youth versions of this popular rating scale. Research suggests that although the self-reports of ADHD children and teens are more deviant than the self-reports of youths without ADHD, the ADHD youths' self-reports (whether by interview or by the CBCL Youth Self-Report Form) are often less severe than the reports provided by par-

ents and teachers (Fischer et al., 1993a; Loeber, Green, Lahey, & Stouthamer-Loeber, 1991). Specialized scales for child self-reports of ADHD symptoms are not yet available with normative data, and so the clinical utility of such self-ratings for the purpose of clinical diagnosis remains uncertain.

As noted earlier, the reports of children about internalizing symptoms, such as anxiety and depression, are more reliable and likely to be more valid than the reports of parents and teachers about these symptoms in their children (Achenbach et al., 1987; Hinshaw, Han, Erhardt, & Huber, 1992). For this reason, the self-reports of ADHD children and youths should still be collected, as they may have more pertinence to the diagnosis of comorbid disorders in ADHD children than to their ADHD itself.

Adaptive Behavior Scales and Inventories

Research has begun to show that a major area of life functioning affected by ADHD is the realm of general adaptive behavior (Barkley, DuPaul, & McMurray, 1990; Roizen et al., 1994). "Adaptive behavior" refers to children's development of skills and abilities that will assist them in becoming more independent, responsible, and self-caring individuals. This domain generally includes (1) self-help skills, such as dressing, bathing, feeding, and toileting requirements, as well as telling and using time and understanding and using money; (2) interpersonal skills, such as sharing, cooperation, and trust; (3) motor skills, such as fine motor skills (zipping, buttoning, drawing, printing, use of scissors, etc.) and gross motor abilities (walking, hopping, negotiating stairs, bike riding, etc.); (4) communication skills; and (5) social responsibility, such as degree of freedom permitted within and outside the home, running errands, performing chores, and so on. So substantial and prevalent is this area of impairment among children with ADHD that Roizen et al. (1994) have even argued that a significant discrepancy between IQ and adaptive behavior scores (expressed as standard scores) may be a hallmark of ADHD.

Several instruments are available for the assessment of this domain of functioning, and these are dealt with in more detail in the chapter on mental retardation in this text (see Handen, Chapter 7). The Vineland Adaptive Behavior Inventory (Sparrow, Balla, & Cicchetti, 1984) is probably the most commonly used measure for assessing adaptive functioning and was the instrument used in the aforementioned studies of ADHD

TABLE 2.6. Academic Performance Rating Scale

Student _____   Date _____

Age _____   Grade _____   Teacher _____

For each of the below items, please estimate the above student's performance over the *past week*. For each item, please circle *one* choice only.

1. Estimate the percentage of written math work *completed* (regardless of accuracy) relative to classmates.	0–49%	50–69%	70–79%	80–89%	90–100%
	1	2	3	4	5
2. Estimate the percentage of written language arts work *completed* (regardless of accuracy) relative to classmates.	0–49%	50–69%	70–79%	80–89%	90–100%
	1	2	3	4	5
3. Estimate the *accuracy* of completed written math work (i.e., percent correct of work done).	0–64%	65–69%	70–79%	80–89%	90–100%
	1	2	3	4	5
4. Estimate the *accuracy* of completed written language arts work (i.e., percent correct of work done).	0–64%	65–69%	70–79%	80–89%	90–100%
	1	2	3	4	5
5. How consistent has the quality of this child's academic work been over the past week?	Consistently poor	More poor than successful	Variable	More successful than poor	Consistently successful
	1	2	3	4	5
6. How frequently does the student accurately follow teacher instructions and/or class discussion during *large-group* (e.g., whole-class) instruction?	Never	Rarely	Sometimes	Often	Very often
	1	2	3	4	5
7. How frequently does the student accurately follow teacher instructions and/or class discussion during *small-group* (e.g., reading group) instruction?	Never	Rarely	Sometimes	Often	Very often
	1	2	3	4	5
8. How quickly does this child learn new material (i.e., pick up novel concepts)?	Very slowly	Slowly	Average	Quickly	Very quickly
	1	2	3	4	5
9. What is the quality or neatness of this child's handwriting?	Poor	Fair	Average	Above average	Excellent
	1	2	3	4	5
10. What is the quality of this child's reading skills?	Poor	Fair	Average	Above average	Excellent
	1	2	3	4	5
11. What is the quality of this child's speaking skills?	Poor	Fair	Average	Above average	Excellent
	1	2	3	4	5
12. How often does the child complete written work in a careless, hasty fashion?	Never	Rarely	Sometimes	Often	Very often
	1	2	3	4	5

(continued)

TABLE 2.6. (*continued*)

13. How frequently does the child take more time to complete work than his/her classmates?	Never 1	Rarely 2	Sometimes 3	Often 4	Very often 5
14. How often is the child able to pay attention without you prompting him/her?	Never 1	Rarely 2	Sometimes 3	Often 4	Very often 5
15. How frequently does this child require you assistance to accurately complete his/her academic work?	Never 1	Rarely 2	Sometimes 3	Often 4	Very often 5
16. How often does the child begin written work prior to understanding the directions?	Never 1	Rarely 2	Sometimes 3	Often 4	Very often 5
17. How frequently does this child have difficulty recalling material from a previous day's lessons?	Never 1	Rarely 2	Sometimes 3	Often 4	Very often 5
18. How often does the child appear to be staring excessively or "spaced out"?	Never 1	Rarely 2	Sometimes 3	Often 4	Very often 5
19. How often does the child appear withdrawn or tend to lack an emotional response in a social situation?	Never 1	Rarely 2	Sometimes 3	Often 4	Very often 5

Note. From Barkley (1990, pp. 307–308). Copyright 1990 by The Guilford Press. Reprinted by permission.

that identified this area of impairment in ADHD children. More recently, I have been using the Normative Adaptive Behavior Checklist (NABC; Adams, 1984) for assessing this domain because of its greater ease of administration. The CBCL completed by parents and teachers (see above) also contains several short scales that provide a cursory screening of several areas of adaptive functioning (activities, social, and school) in children, but it is no substitute for the more in-depth coverage provided by the Vineland and the NABC.

Laboratory Tests and Measures

In the first edition of this chapter (Barkley, 1981b), I decried the unavailability of objective laboratory tests and instruments for evaluating attention span, activity level, and impulse control in ADHD children. What measures were available had no normative data and therefore were of little clinical utility in establishing deviance of the children from

same-age normal peers on these constructs. There have been several promising developments since then in the standardization of a number of instruments, although much remains to be done before these devices can be recommended for widespread clinical use. These measures are reviewed in connection with the constructs they appear to assess.

Vigilance and Sustained Attention

Probably among the most widely used measures of attention span or vigilance in the research literature on ADHD children are CPTs. Variations of the continuous-performance method abound, but the most common type of CPT requires a child to observe a screen while individual letters or numbers are projected onto it at a rapid pace, usually one item per second. The child is required to press a button when a certain stimulus or sequence of stimuli appears (say, a 1 followed by a 9). The measures derived from the method are usually the number correct, the number of stimuli missed (omissions), and the number of incorrect stimuli to which the child responded (commissions). The number correct and number of omissions are believed to assess vigilance or sustained attention, whereas the number of commissions may reflect both sustained attention and impulse control. Several CPTs are now available commercially to clinicians and have norms that permit the clinical interpretation of their scores: the Conners Continuous Performance Test (Conners, 1995), the Gordon Diagnostic System (Gordon, 1983), and the Test of Variables of Attention (Greenberg & Waldman, 1992).

CPTs have been shown to be among the most reliable measures for discriminating groups of ADHD from normal children (Barkley, 1991; Barkley, Grodzinsky, & DuPaul, 1992; Corkum & Siegel, 1993), and the measures are sensitive to stimulant drug effects (Barkley, 1977a; Rapport & Kelly, 1993). CPT measures also correlate significantly with teacher ratings of inattention and hyperactivity, as well as with other laboratory measures of attention and impulse control. However, the magnitude of these associations is low to moderate (typically .25–.35), suggesting limited ecological and construct validity for such instruments (Barkley, 1991).

Most important for considering the clinical application of CPTs for the diagnosis of ADHD are the positive and negative predictive powers of these tests for accurately classifying children as having ADHD or not. "Positive predictive power" is the probability that a child has ADHD, given an abnormal score on the test; "negative predictive power" is the probability that the child does not have the disorder, given a normal score on the test. Until recently, such critical information was not available for the CPTs. Three separate studies have now examined this issue, and their results are quite important for those wishing to use CPTs as part of a diagnostic assessment battery for ADHD (Barkley & Grodzinsky, 1994; Grodzinsky & Barkley, 1996; Matier-Sharma, Perachio, Newcorn, Sharma, & Halperin, 1995). These studies show that clinic-referred children receiving abnormal scores have a high probability of having ADHD (about a 90% chance). However, clinic-referred children receiving normal scores also have an unacceptably high likelihood of having ADHD (a 35–50% chance or more), and so the negative predictive power of the CPTs is poor. In other words, the tests have an unsatisfactory level of false-negative diagnoses, so that normal scores should not be interpreted as ruling out

the diagnosis of ADHD. It is also well known that other diagnostic groups of children (such as schizophrenic and autistic children, as well as those at risk for schizophrenia) perform poorly on CPTs. Such groups of children were not included in these studies of CPT "hit rates." Had such groups also been included, it is most unlikely that the CPTs would have fared as well as they did in their positive predictive power. In view of these sobering statistics, caution should be exercised in the clinical use of these measures for diagnostic purposes. Such measures should never be the sole basis for making a diagnostic decision. And, although these measures may be sensitive to the effects of stimulant medication on groups of ADHD children, the fact that they are less sensitive to low doses of medication than are parent and teacher ratings (Barkley et al., 1988; Barkley, McMurray, Edelbrock, & Robbins, 1989) means that CPT results alone should never be the basis for determining medication response.

Impulse Control

Other methods of assessing impulsivity have been used in research with groups of ADHD children, but they have not fared well in evaluations of their ability to discriminate ADHD from non-ADHD children correctly. The Matching Familiar Figures Test (MFFT; Kagan, 1966) has an extensive history of use in research assessing impulse control in normal and disturbed children. Its scores have been found to discriminate groups of ADHD from normal children (Campbell et al., 1971) and aggressive from nonaggressive ADHD children (Milich, Landau, & Loney, 1981). The measure also correlates with clinic playroom measures of activity level and attention (Milich et al., 1981) and is somewhat sensitive to stimulant drug effects (Barkley, 1977a). A longer version of the MFFT with 20 stimulus sets (MFFT20) has been developed (Cairns & Cammock, 1978); it is believed to be more stable and reliable than the shorter version, particularly for children in the older age range (Messer & Brodzinsky, 1981).

Despite these positive findings, the MFFT does not appear to classify ADHD and non-ADHD children with a sufficient degree of accuracy to warrant its clinical adoption for diagnostic purposes (Barkley & Grodzinsky, 1994; Grodzinsky & Barkley, 1996). The test fared much worse than the scores from the CPTs, discussed above; that is, it showed low levels of both positive and negative predictive power. Studies over the past decade have also found that the test does not always discriminate groups of ADHD from normal children (Barkley, DuPaul, & McMurray, 1990; Milich & Kramer, 1984) and is not always sensitive to dose effects of stimulant medication (Barkley, DuPaul, & McMurray, 1991).

Another commercially available test of impulsivity is the Delay Task from the Gordon Diagnostic System, described above as a CPT. In this task, the child sits before the device and is told to wait, then press a blue button on the device; if the child has waited long enough, he or she earns a point. The child is not told how long to wait before pushing the button—merely to wait, press the button, then wait again, then press the button again. The task is comparable to a direct-reinforcement-of-latency procedure and may assess a different form of impulsivity than tasks such as the MFFT do. The task produces three measures: the number of rewards (correct responses), the number of button presses (total responses), and the ratio of rewards to button presses (efficiency ratio). All three measures were found to significantly discriminate ADHD from non-ADHD clinic-referred children and to correlate significantly with ratings from the original Conners Teacher and Parent Rating Scales (Gordon, 1979; Gordon & McClure, 1983; McClure & Gordon, 1984). However, subsequent research did not find the measure to be sensitive to the effects of stimulant medication (Barkley et al., 1988). Its correlations with parent and teacher ratings of inattention and hyperactive–impulsive behavior are quite modest (Barkley, 1991). Such findings would argue for cautious use of this measure in clinical assessments and would weigh against its use for monitoring of stimulant drug treatment.

The Stroop Color–Word Association Test (Stroop, 1935) has been used frequently in neuropsychological research as a measure of inhibition, particularly that element known as "interference control." In the most difficult portion of the test, children are required to say the color of ink in which a word is printed. The word is the name of a color, which can differ from the color of the ink the child is to report. Consequently, children must inhibit the prepotent response of reading the word in order to focus on and correctly report the color of the ink in which the word is printed. The test has been found to distinguish groups of ADHD from normal children (Barkley, Grodzinsky, & DuPaul, 1992; Grodzinsky & Diamond, 1992). It has also been shown to be as accurate in its positive predictive power as the CPTs (Barkley & Grodzinsky, 1994; Grodzinsky & Barkley, 1996), but it suffers from the same

problem of mediocre negative predictive power (unsatisfactory level of false negatives) as do the CPTs.

Milich and Kramer (1984) have provided an excellent review and critique of other measures of impulsivity; their review is worth reading prior to undertaking the clinical interpretation of these laboratory tests. Another measure of impulse control being employed increasingly in research with ADHD children is the stop-signal paradigm (Schachar & Logan, 1990). However, the administration procedures are relatively complex and require a personal computer as well as additional peripheral components, making it unwieldy for clinical purposes. Moreover, many of the laboratory tasks used in research on ADHD are not normed and so should not be employed in clinical evaluations of children suspected of having the disorder.

Activity Level

Like the constructs of attention span and impulsivity, activity level is a multidimensional construct having a multiplicity of definitions and measures. "Activity level" can refer to a wide range of phenomena, from cellular functions and electrophysiological measures to movement of a small muscle group or appendage to total body motion or locomotor movements. Which of these is meant in references to the "hyperactivity" of the ADHD child is not often made clear. In general, most prior research has focused on movement of the appendages, locomotor motion, or more vague and global concepts of "fidgetiness" and "out-of-seat behaviors." The two latter concepts are discussed below under "Direct Observational Procedures," as they are often assessed with such procedures. Mechanical devices are often employed in evaluating movement of the appendages, and so these devices are briefly discussed here as laboratory measures.

Numerous devices for measuring appendage activity level have been used to study ADHD children. Modified self-winding wrist watches, called "actometers," have been used to measure wrist and ankle activity (see Tryon, 1984), as have pedometers attached to a waist belt, wrist, or ankle (Barkley, 1977b). Motion transducers using small mercury switches and attached to various locations on a child's trunk have also been used to measure hyperactivity (see Tryon, 1984). A solid-state acceleration monitor was also developed for 24-hour monitoring of activity (Porrino et al., 1983).

Montagu and Swarbrick (1975) employed pneumatic pads on a playroom floor for mechanical recording of locomotor activity, whereas others have used grid-marked floors of playrooms to measure locomotion (Routh & Schroeder, 1976). Seat restlessness has been measured by means of stabilimetric cushions attached to a chair seat (Barkley, 1977b; Tryon, 1984).

Such instruments have not been widely used by clinicians, chiefly because of a lack of normative data, concerns about reliability, and issues of validity in obtaining representative samples of the type of "hyperactivity" that is the chief clinical complaint. Studies are conflicting as to whether such measures correlate significantly with direct observations of children's behavior and activity level in the home or classroom (Barkley, 1991; Kendall & Brophy, 1981; Rapoport & Benoit, 1975). They have also not been reliably found to relate significantly to parent, teacher, or clinician ratings of hyperactivity (Barkley, 1991; Barkley & Ullman, 1975; Kendall & Brophy, 1981; Milich, Loney, & Landau, 1982; Routh & Schroeder, 1976).

Summary

In summary, although adequate normative studies for these instruments may eventually make them more appealing for establishing the statistical deviance of a child's attention span, impulse control, or activity level, such quantitative scores collected in isolation from the natural social environment have several limitations. Many of these measures are taken in laboratory playroom or analogue settings, rather than in those natural settings most problematic to these children; this places the representativeness of the scores in question. The reliability of scores over time is also not well established. Moreover, the measures are highly influenced by situational factors (Porrino et al., 1983) and have only low-order correlations with other measures of the construct, even when they are taken in the same settings at the same time (Barkley & Ullman, 1975; Ullman et al., 1978). Such measures also correlate to a low degree, if at all, with measures of the same construct taken in other settings (e.g., clinic vs. home, clinic vs. classroom, testing room vs. classroom, etc.) (Kendall & Brophy, 1981; Milich et al., 1981; Rapoport & Benoit, 1975). More troublesome for treatment planning is the fact that laboratory measures often reveal little information about the possible controlling variables for activity level, attention, or impulse control. An understanding of such controlling variables is often essential to planning behavioral interventions. Furthermore, though these tests and measures have shown some use in monitoring drug treatment effects, they have not yet shown that they are sensitive to other types of interventions for ADHD children. Finally, there is little indication that these measures correlate significantly with the behaviors that parents and teachers find most objectionable in ADHD children (Barkley, 1991; Barkley & Cunningham, 1980).

Direct Observational Procedures

New developments have also taken place in the area of direct observational procedures for evaluating ADHD children. Many of these remain useful only in research programs, as normative data are not available for making clinical decisions about children. Nevertheless, several of them are sufficiently promising to warrant mention here. They vary in the focus of the target behaviors being assessed, the degree of training necessary for their reliable use, and the facilities and resources required for their implementation. And although the yield from such direct observations is usually quite rich, the training requirements and limited cost-effectiveness of the procedures raise doubts about their feasibility for clinical practice. Such observations, when taken in clinics, often have only low to moderate ecological validity in predicting behavior in more natural settings, such as home and school (Barkley, 1991); this limits their clinical utility further. Thus, such direct observational procedures may be most useful when employed by school personnel in the assessment of children in their natural classroom settings.

Classroom and Playroom Behaviors

Various behavioral observation and recording methods have been developed specifically to capture the symptoms of ADHD in research programs. Jacob, O'Leary, and Rosenblad (1978) describe a procedure known as the Hyperactive Behavior Code, for recording ADHD behaviors in the natural classroom setting. An interval-sampling procedure is used to record the following categories: Solicitation (seeks interaction with teacher), Aggression, Refusal, Change of Position, Daydreaming, and Weird Sounds (nonspeech vocalizations or noises). These measures are collapsed into a single score representing hyperactive behavior. The developers have found the system to discriminate ADHD from normal children, chiefly in formal or highly structured as opposed to informal classroom settings. The measure also correlates well with teacher ratings of hyperactivity, conduct problems, and inattention on the Conners Teacher Rating Scale.

Another observational system developed for recording classroom ADHD behavior is that by Abikoff, Gittelman-Klein, and Klein (1977). The system contains 14 behavioral categories scored on an interval-sampling basis. These categories pertain to off-task behavior, movement about the classroom, and other behaviors that occur more often in ADHD than in normal children. Of the 14 categories, 12 significantly differentiated ADHD and normal children. The system, however, may be cumbersome for clinical practice because of the large number of categories and the training time needed to score them reliably. Nonetheless, the system, like that of Jacob et al. (1978), would seem useful for clinicians wishing to make direct observations of ADHD behaviors in the natural environment.

Several observation codes have been developed for use in coding the symptoms of ADHD in children observed in clinic playroom analogue settings (Barkley et al., 1988; Routh & Schroeder, 1976; Roberts, 1990). These observation codes could just as easily be used in classroom observations by school personnel. The coding systems have been found to discriminate ADHD children from those who are purely aggressive, from those with both ADHD and aggression, and from a group of psychiatric control children (Milich et al., 1982). The measures derived from the coding procedure also show significant stability over a 2-year period in normal children (Milich, 1984).

For instance, in the playroom observation system developed by Roberts (1990) and used in the study by Milich (1984), two situations are employed in the clinic playroom: free play and a restricted academic period. In the free-play procedure, the child is placed alone in the room and told to play freely with the toys. Toys are available for play; four tables are in the room; and the floor of the playroom is divided into 16 squares with black tape placed on the tile floors. During the restricted academic setting, the child is requested to remain seated, to complete a series of worksheets (the task on these worksheets is similar to the Coding subtest from the Wechsler Intelligence Scale for Children—Revised), and not to play with any of the toys in the room. Each situation lasts for 15 minutes. Throughout this time, observers are continuously recording six behavioral categories: grid crossings, out-of-seat behavior, fidgeting, vocalization, on-task behavior, and attention shifts.

In the restricted academic setting, two additional measures are taken; time spent touching forbidden toys and the number of worksheet items completed by the child.

The method seems to be promising for objectively recording ADHD behaviors in a clinic analogue setting, particularly given its ability to discriminate between ADHD children with and without aggression and between children with these ADHD subtypes and purely aggressive as well as clinical control groups. The stability of the measure over time, and its significant correlation with clinician ratings of hyperactivity as well as measures of impulsivity, are particularly impressive for such brief samples of clinic playroom behavior. The measures have also been shown to be sensitive to stimulant medication effects (Barkley et al., 1988, 1989).

Achenbach (1991b) has also developed a Direct Observation Form (DOF) of the CBCL. The observer visits the child's classroom and observes the child for a period of time—typically at least 10 minutes, and preferably an hour or more. The observer then completes the DOF items, which are similar to the items on other forms of the CBCL. There is little published research on this method of observation. My use of it in an ongoing study of elementary-age ADHD children, however, suggests that it is easier to learn, is more convenient to use, and results in better interrater reliability than more discrete direct observations like those described above (Jacob et al., 1978; Roberts, 1990; Barkley, 1990).

Adult–Child Interactions

Because ADHD children display significant problems with noncompliance, difficulties in completing assigned tasks, and (in many cases) defiant and oppositional behavior, it may be useful to take some measures of the interactions of ADHD children with adults. Most procedures developed for recording such interactions have concentrated on parent–child as compared to teacher–child dyads. These systems focus primarily upon recording noncompliant and negative behaviors by the children, and commands and other controlling behaviors used by the parents.

A relatively easy-to-use coding system for recording noncompliance in parent–child interactions in a clinic playroom has been developed by Forehand and McMahon (see McMahon & Estes, Chapter 3, this volume). For those interested in obtaining a more detailed assessment of parent–child interactions, more complicated observational systems have been developed. The Response-Class Matrix (Mash, Terdal, & Anderson, 1973) has been used extensively in research on ADHD, as well as other childhood disorders (see Mash & Barkley, 1986, for a review). The manual and coding forms are described in the text by Barkley (1981a). The system requires two coders, one of whom records parent behaviors and subsequent child behaviors, while the other codes the child behaviors as antecedents and the parent behaviors as consequences. The parent behaviors recorded include commands, questions, interactions, praise, negatives, and others; the child behaviors include compliance, play, questions, interactions, and negatives.

Recording systems have also been developed by Patterson (1982), Wahler, House, and Stambaugh (1976), and Robinson and Eyberg (1981) for coding parent–child interactions, particularly in conduct problem children. Like the Response-Class Matrix, these systems require extended time for training and may be cumbersome to utilize in the typical clinical setting, where such time and resources are limited.

The aforementioned recording systems have been used chiefly for recording interactions between parents and preadolescent children. Such observation systems and their analogue settings may not be especially useful for evaluating the issues that bring families with ADHD adolescents to child guidance centers. In these cases, it would seem more useful to evaluate the areas of conflict existing between parents and adolescents, since an understanding of these is more likely to lead to useful treatment planning within a behavioral family therapy approach. Robin and Foster (1989) have developed a direct observational recording procedure for assessing conflicts in communication patterns between parents and adolescents. The system is an excellent substitute for these other coding systems when the subject of an evaluation is an ADHD teenager (see Foster & Robin, Chapter 13, this volume).

Advantages and Limitations

Direct observational methods can overcome some of the limitations described above for laboratory measures, in that they are capable of recording behaviors in a child's natural environment or in analogue settings structured to elicit behaviors representative of those problems occurring outside the clinic. In so doing, they offer more ecologically valid measures of the actual behaviors of ADHD children about which parents and teach-

ers are most concerned. The parent–child interaction coding systems in particular can record the antecedents and consequences of these behaviors, which are essential to understanding the social context in which the behaviors are occurring and to suggesting potential changes in the interactions as part of behavioral treatment. These procedures can also be used to monitor the changes in behavior brought about by both drug and behavioral interventions — particularly the latter, as the procedures frequently focus upon the targets of such behavioral training programs (parental management of the children).

However, normative data are lacking on such observational systems; this makes them less useful for determining the statistical deviance of child behaviors, which is necessary for rendering a diagnosis. Such normative data, if collected, would be problematic because of the sensitivity of these observational systems to changes in environmental parameters (e.g., room size, lighting, furniture, toys, presence or absence of the examiner, and even examiner characteristics). These problems would apply to both clinic analogue and natural classroom or playroom observations. As a result, any norms might not prove useful in geographically separate clinics, where such conditions would certainly differ from those under which the norms were collected.

There are several methods for partially overcoming this dilemma. First, clinics can collect local normative data, using their own standard observational system and playroom procedures. Local university students can assist with this process in return for stipends, course credit, or even completion of student research projects, while helping to build up a data base on normal children to be used for clinical purposes.

Second, in situations where exact quantitative measures of deviation from the norm are not essential, using a method of yoked controls may help to provide an approximate indication of deviance. For classroom observations, this is easily achieved by asking the teacher to point out a child representative of the typical children in the class and taking observations on this child during the same school visit used to record the ADHD child's behavior. As long as the child's name is not disclosed to the observer, such observations should not violate ethical guidelines. For clinic analogue observations, having a normal sibling of the ADHD child come in for the observations provides useful contrasting information, particularly when the siblings are close in age and parent–child interactions are being recorded. Such a procedure has been used (Tarver-Behring, Barkley, & Karlsson, 1985) to show that ADHD children are less compliant with parental commands than their normal siblings.

Third, it may be time to consider establishing central clinical/research centers for various geographic regions. Such centers could develop the resources, facilities, and personnel necessary to conduct more comprehensive behavioral assessments according to standardized protocols for specialized disorders. Professionals in the surrounding communities could then refer cases for these specific protocols (Mash & Barkley, 1986). Such a procedure would be similar to the establishment of regional MRI laboratories at large hospital/medical school complexes to which patients with neurological diseases can be referred for complicated evaluations, the equipment for which is often far too expensive for typical clinicians to purchase themselves. These regional behavioral assessment centers would certainly have the resources necessary to develop normative data banks on the local population for addressing the question of statistical deviance of child behaviors. Done properly, such specialized assessment centers could be well received within the regions; cost-effective, given the large volume of service likely to result; and useful for large-scale research programs drawing upon the unique patient population.

Peer Relationship Measures

As noted earlier, children with ADHD often demonstrate significant difficulties in their interactions with peers (Cunningham & Siegel, 1987; Pelham & Bender, 1982), and such difficulties are associated with an increased likelihood that their disorder will persist (Biederman et al., 1996). A number of different methods for assessing peer relations have been employed in research with ADHD children, such as direct observation and recording of social interactions, peer- and subject-completed sociometric ratings, and parent and teacher rating scales of children's social behavior. Most of these assessment methods have no norms and so would not be appropriate for use in the clinical evaluation of children with ADHD. Reviews of the methods for obtaining peer sociometric ratings can be found elsewhere (Asher & Coie, 1990; Newcomb, Bukowski, & Pattee, 1993). For clinical purposes, rating scales may offer the most convenient and cost-effective means of evaluating this important domain of childhood functioning. The CBCL and BASC, described earlier, contain scales that evaluate children's social behavior. As discussed above, norms are available for these scales, permitting their use in clinical settings. Three other scales that focus specifically on social skills are the Matson Evaluation of Social Skills with Youngsters (Matson, Rotatori, & Helsel, 1983), the Taxonomy of Problem Social Situations for Children (Dodge, McClaskey, & Feldman, 1985), and the Social Skills Rating System (Gresham & Elliott, 1990). The last of these also has norms, making it appropriate for use in clinical contexts.

Parent Self-Report Measures

It has become increasingly apparent that child behavioral disorders, their level of severity, and their response to intervention are in part functions of factors affecting parents and the family at large. As noted earlier, several types of psychiatric disorders, and especially ADHD, are likely to occur more often among family members of children with ADHD than among relatives of matched groups of control children. That these problems may further influence the frequency and severity of behavioral problems in ADHD children has been demonstrated in studies over the past 15 years. We (Murphy & Barkley, 1996c) recently demonstrated that the severity of parent ratings of children's ADHD symptoms was associated with significantly younger parental age, lower socioeconomic status, less marital satisfaction, and greater psychological distress. Mash and Johnston (1983a, 1983b, 1990) have studied the role of parent stress, perceived competence, and self-esteem in parent–child interactions and ratings of child deviance in ADHD families, as have others (Breen & Barkley, 1988; Fischer, 1990). Research by Wahler (1980) has also shown that social isolation in mothers of behaviorally disturbed children influences the severity of the children's behavioral disorders, as well as the outcomes of parent training. Others have also shown separate and interactive contributions of maternal depression and marital discord to decisions to refer children for clinical assistance, conflict in parent–child interactions, and parent ratings of child deviance (see McMahon & Estes, Chapter 3, this volume). And Patterson (1982) has shown how coercive family interaction processes affect parent–child conflict and child aggression. Assessing the psychological integrity of parents is therefore essential for the clinical assessment of ADHD children, the differential diagnosis of their prevailing disorders, and the planning of treatments stemming from such assessments. Thus, evaluating a child for ADHD often involves assessing the family rather than the child alone. Although space does not permit a thorough discussion of the clinical assessment of adults and their disorders, brief mention is made here of some assessment methods that may be of value in at least providing a preliminary screening for certain variables of importance to the treatment of ADHD children.

Parental ADHD

Family studies of the aggregation of psychiatric disorders among the biological relatives of children with ADHD have clearly demonstrated an increased prevalence of ADHD among the parents of these children (Biederman et al., 1991; Faraone et al., 1993). In general, there seems to be at least a 40–50% chance that one of the two parents of a child with ADHD will have adult ADHD (15–20% of mothers and 25–30% of fathers). The manner in which ADHD in a parent may influence the behavior of an ADHD child specifically and the family environment more generally has not been well studied. Adults with ADHD have been shown to be more likely to have problems with anxiety, depression, alcohol use/abuse, and marital difficulties; to change their employment and residence more often; and to have less education and lower socioeconomic status than adults without ADHD (Barkley & Murphy, 1996; Biederman et al., 1995; Murphy & Barkley, 1996a; Shekim, Asarnow, Hess, Zaucha, & Wheeler, 1990). Greater diversity and severity of psychopathology are particularly apparent among the subgroup of ADHD children with Oppositional Defiant Disorder or Conduct Disorder (Barkley, Anastopoulos, et al., 1992; Lahey, Piacentini, et al., 1988). More severe ADHD also seems to be associated with younger age of parents (Murphy & Barkley, 1996c), suggesting that pregnancy during their own teenage or young adult years is more characteristic of parents of ADHD children than those of non-ADHD children. It is not difficult to see that these factors, as well as the primary symptoms of ADHD, may influence not only the manner in which the ADHD child's behavior is managed within the family but the quality of home life for such a child more generally. Ongoing research in our clinic suggests that when a parent has ADHD, the probability that the child with ADHD will also have Oppositional Defiant Disorder increases markedly. A recent clinical case (Evans, Vallano, & Pelham, 1994) suggests that ADHD in a parent may interfere with the ability to benefit from a typical behavioral parent training program. Treatment of the parent's ADHD (with medication) resulted in greater success in subsequent retraining of the parent. These preliminary findings are suggestive of the importance of determining the presence of ADHD in the parents of children undergoing evaluation for the disorder.

Recently, the DSM-IV symptom list for ADHD has been cast in the form of a behavior rating scale, and some limited regional norms on more than 700 adults aged 17–84 years have been collected (Murphy & Barkley, 1996b). Adults complete the rating scale twice—once for their current behavioral adjustment, and a second time for their recall of their childhood behavior between the ages of 5 and 12 years. Norms for both current symptoms and childhood recall were obtained in this study. As noted earlier, results of this study found that the cutoff scores for each of the two symptom lists need not reach six of nine symptoms in order to be statistically deviant for adults (>93rd percentile). Thresholds identifying the 93rd percentile declined with increasing age in that study.

The use of such scales in the screening of parents of ADHD children should be a useful first step in determining whether the parents also have ADHD. If the screening instruments prove positive, then referral of the parents for a more thorough evaluation and differential diagnosis might be in order. At the very least, positive findings from the screening would suggest the need to take them into account in treatment planning and parent training.

Marital Discord

Many instruments exist for evaluating marital discord in parents. The one most often used in research on childhood disorders has been the Locke–Wallace Marital Adjustment Scale (Locke & Wallace, 1959). Research has found parents of ADHD children, regardless of child gender, to have higher ratings of discord than parents of normal children (Breen & Barkley, 1988; Murphy & Barkley, 1996c), especially in the subgroup of ADHD children with Oppositional Defiant Disorder or Conduct Disorder (Barkley, Anastopoulos, et al., 1992; Barkley, Fischer, et al., 1991; Befera & Barkley, 1985).

Parental Depression and General Psychological Distress

Parents of ADHD children are frequently more depressed than those of normal children (Befera & Barkley, 1985; Mash & Johnston, 1983a; Murphy & Barkley, 1996c), and this may affect their responsiveness to behavioral parent training programs (Forehand & McMahon, 1981). A scale often used to provide a quick assessment of parental depression is the Beck Depression Inventory

(Beck, Steer, & Garbin, 1988). Greater levels of psychopathology generally and psychiatric disorders specifically have also been found in parents of children with ADHD (Breen & Barkley, 1988; Lahey, Piacentini, et al., 1988). One measure for assessing this area of parental difficulties is the Symptom Checklist 90—Revised (SCL-90-R; Derogatis, 1986). This instrument has not only a scale assessing depression in adults, but also scales measuring other dimensions of adult psychopathology and psychological distress. Research using the SCL-90-R with parents of ADHD children has shown that such parents obtain higher scores on the Depression, Hostility, Anxiety, and Interpersonal Difficulties subscales (Barkley, Anastopoulos, et al., 1992; Barkley, Fischer, et al., 1991; Murphy & Barkley, 1996c). However, such findings are also characteristic of parents of clinic-referred children with other psychiatric disorders (Breen & Barkley, 1988). Nevertheless, the assessment of parental psychological distress in general and psychiatric disorders in particular makes sense, in view of their likely impact on the course of a child's ADHD and the implementation of the child's treatments (typically delivered by the parents).

Parental Stress

Research over the past 15 years suggests that parents of ADHD children report more stress in their families and their parental role than do those of normal or clinic-referred non-ADHD children (Anastopoulos et al., 1992; Breen & Barkley, 1988; Fischer, 1990; Mash & Johnston, 1990). One measure frequently used in such research to evaluate this construct has been the Parenting Stress Index (PSI; Abidin, 1986). The original PSI is a 150-item multiple-choice questionnaire that yields six scores pertaining to child behavioral characteristics (e.g., distractibility, mood, etc.), eight scores pertaining to maternal characteristics (e.g., depression, sense of competence as a parent, etc.), and two scores pertaining to situational and life stress events. These scores can be summed to yield three domain or summary scores, these being Child Domain, Mother Domain, and Total Stress. A shorter version of the PSI is now available (Abidin, 1986).

Summary

It should be clear from the lengthy foregoing discussion that the assessment of ADHD children is a complex and serious endeavor requiring adequate time (3 or more hours); knowledge of the relevant research and clinical literature, as well as of differential diagnosis; skillful clinical judgment in sorting out the pertinent issues; and sufficient resources to obtain multiple types of information from multiple sources (parents, children, teachers) with a variety of assessment methods. When time and resources permit, direct observations of ADHD behaviors in the classroom can also be made by school personnel. At the very least, telephone contact with an ADHD child's teacher should be made, to follow up on his or her responses to the child behavior rating scales and to obtain more details about the child's classroom behavior problems. To this list of assessment methods should be added any others necessary to address the specific problems often occurring in conjunction with ADHD but discussed in other chapters of this text (e.g., learning disabilities, Oppositional Defiant Disorder and Conduct Disorders, anxiety and depression, social skills deficits, etc.).

TREATMENT IMPLICATIONS

A multimethod assessment protocol for ADHD in children will usually reveal various areas of deficits, excesses, and impairments requiring clinical intervention, and perhaps even more detailed behavioral assessment than has been described here. The subsequent treatments will undoubtedly be based upon those deficit areas found to be the most salient, the most significant to the concerns of the referral agent(s) (e.g., parent, physician, teacher, etc.), or the most important for present and future adjustment. Such treatment recommendations may range from just parent counseling about the disorder in those cases found to have few or no impairments, to residential treatment for those ADHD children with severe, chronic, or even dangerous forms of conduct problems or depression. Between these extremes, treatment recommendations may focus on improving the primary ADHD symptoms through stimulant medication or classroom behavioral interventions; improving the oppositional behavior of ADHD children through parent training in effective child management procedures; or addressing the conflicts of ADHD teenagers and their parents through a behavioral problem-solving approach to family therapy. Many ADHD children have peer relationship problems that may benefit from individual or group social skills training, provided that such training is implemented within the school or neighborhood settings in which such skills should be used. In most cases, the evaluation will reveal the need for multiple interventions for the child, or even the other family members, to fully address the issues raised therein. Regardless of the treatments suggested by the initial evaluation, ongoing, periodic reassessment using many of the methods described above will be necessary to document change (or the lack thereof) throughout treatment, maintenance of treatment gains over time after treatment termination, and generalization (or the lack of it) of treatment effects to other problematic behaviors and environments.

Treatments abound for ADHD children (see Barkley, 1990; Hinshaw, 1994), only some of which have demonstrated their efficacy. A brief survey of those that have shown the greatest promise for dealing with the primary problems in ADHD children follows, along with suggestions for methods to evaluate the outcomes of these particular therapies.

Stimulant Medication

There is overwhelming evidence for the efficacy of stimulant drugs in the treatment of ADHD children (Barkley, 1977a; DuPaul & Barkley, 1990; Rapport & Kelly, 1993; Swanson, McBurnett, Christian, & Wigal, 1995). Used alone, these drugs are not able to address all of the myriad difficulties of these children; however, in conjunction with other treatments for children over 4 years of age with moderate to severe ADHD, they can be an indispensable part of a total treatment program and often its most effective component. The primary effects of the stimulants (Ritalin, Dexedrine, and Cylert) are improved attention span, decreased impulsivity, diminished task-irrelevant activity (especially in structured situations), and generally decreased disruptive behavior in social situations. Secondary effects of these changes appear to include increased compliance to commands and instructions (Barkley, 1985; Danforth et al., 1991); increased productivity on academic assignments (Rapport, Stoner, DuPaul, Birmingham, & Tucker, 1985); improved peer interactions and increased peer acceptance (Cunningham, Siegel, & Offord, 1985; Pelham, Vodde-Hamilton, Murphy, Greenstein, & Vallano, 1991; Whalen et al., 1989); and decreased parent and teacher reprimands, supervision, and punishment (Whalen, Henker, & Dotemoto, 1980).

Approximately 75% of ADHD children over 5 years of age respond positively to medication (Barkley, 1977a; Barkley, DuPaul, & McMurray, 1991; Rapport, DuPaul, & Denny, 1993). The behavioral action of stimulant medications is short-lived (3–8 hours), and thus they must be given several times each day for adequate behavioral control. The drugs can be used throughout childhood and adolescence if necessary. Most side effects are not serious, are dose-related, and dissipate within several days of treatment onset (DuPaul & Barkley, 1990). In 1–5%, tic reactions may develop. Some research suggests that children with higher pretreatment levels of anxiety are less likely to respond well to the stimulants (DuPaul, Barkley, & McMurray, 1994). Although the stimulant medications have been shown to be the most effective medications for ADHD, tricyclic antidepressants have also shown some effectiveness relative to placebo treatments (Biederman, Baldessarini, Wright, Knee, & Harmatz, 1989; Ryan, 1990).

The decision to refer an ADHD child for a medication trial will be based upon the following information from the evaluation: (1) the age of the child and the duration and severity of the presenting problems; (2) the history and success of prior treatment efforts; (3) the absence of a personal or family history of tics or Tourette syndrome; (4) a normal level of anxiety in the child (rating scales may help here); (5) parental motivation for such treatment; (6) an absence of stimulant abuse in the parents or other siblings living within the home; and (7) the likelihood that the parents will employ the medication responsibly and in compliance with the physician's directions.

One protocol for evaluating stimulant drug and dose responding over a 4-week interval involves three doses of medication and a placebo (a 1-week trial per condition), with the child evaluated at the end of each week. A more complete description of these procedures can be found elsewhere (Barkley, 1990; Barkley, DuPaul, & McMurray, 1991; Barkley et al., 1988). This protocol assumes that the more comprehensive initial evaluation discussed earlier has been conducted. The methods used to assess responding may include the ADHD Rating Scale, the HSQ and SSQ, and the Side Effects Questionnaire. (See Table 2.3 and 2.5 for the HSQ and SSQ, respectively, and Table 2.4 for the ADHD Rating Scale; Barkley, 1990, for the Side Effects Questionnaire). These can be supplemented with the revised Conners Parent and Teacher Rating Scales (Conners, 1990) when ratings of conduct problems are of interest, in addition to ratings of ADHD symptoms. When more objective information on drug response is desired, laboratory tests of vigilance and impulse control (e.g., a CPT) and clinic playroom observations of ADHD behaviors during performance of academic work (see Milich, 1984; Roberts, 1990; Barkley, 1990) can also be employed. However, as noted earlier, the decision about drug response and dose should never be based solely on such clinic tests or observations. If these clinic tests and observations are not feasible, the parent and teacher rating scales should be sufficient.

Parent Training in Contingency Management

Many parent training programs exist for teaching parents to manage their behavior problem children (Forehand & McMahon, 1981; Schaefer & Briesmeister, 1989). Such parent training can be effective in improving parental interactions with ADHD children (Dubey, O'Leary, & Kaufman, 1983; Pisterman et al., 1989; Pollard et al., 1983). I have elsewhere described a program designed specifically for parents of ADHD children (Barkley, 1990, 1997b). The program is based upon the skills taught in the program by Forehand and McMahon (1981), but it includes additional sessions to provide information to families about ADHD, to train them in establishing home token reinforcement systems, and to teach them to deal with misbehavior in public places. Briefly, the program covers the following: (1) an overview of ADHD; (2) the causes of child misbehavior; (3) developing and enhancing parental attending skills; (4) attending to child compliance; (5) implementing the home chip/point system; (6) time out from reinforcement; (7) managing children in public places; (8) coping with future behavior problems; and (9) a 1-month review and booster session.

The decision to employ parent training procedures should be based upon the information obtained in the initial evaluation with respect to the child's level of noncompliant, oppositional, or defiant behaviors at home, in addition to the primary ADHD symptoms; the parents' educational and intellectual level, as well as degree of motivation for training; and the absence of a degree of parental (or maternal) insularity, depression, stress, personal psychopathology, and marital discord sufficient to interfere with training. The age of the child will of course determine the appropriateness of this approach. In general, the program described above seems useful for children 2 to 11 years of age. After that time, the problem-solving training for families of ADHD adolescents developed by Robin (see below) seems most appropriate. At least once throughout training and at posttreatment, the following assessment protocol can be used to

evaluate treatment effects: the Conners Parent Rating Scale—Revised, the HSQ, and clinic analogue observations of parent–child interactions during task performance. The CBCL or BASC and several of the parent self-report measures can also be used when longer time spans between pre- and posttreatment are involved.

Self-Control Training

Kendall and Braswell (1985) have developed an approach for training impulsive children in self-control strategies. The program utilizes a variety of problem tasks as vehicles to teach children to (1) inhibit responding; (2) repeat the problem or instruction; (3) describe the nature of the problem; (4) describe possible alternative approaches to the problem; (5) evaluate the possible consequences/outcomes of each; (6) undertake the problem solution while engaging in self-instructed guidance; and (7) evaluate their own performance. This encapsulation of the program does not do justice to its complexity, and the reader is referred to Kendall and Braswell (1982, 1985) and to Douglas (1980) for more detailed descriptions of this approach. Contingency management methods are often incorporated into the training sessions to enhance motivation and sustain performance, while parents and/or teachers use similar contingency management methods and prompting of the skills to insure generalization of the skills to their settings.

The program seemed initially to have some promise for improving the self-control deficits evident in ADHD children, as suggested in some early research (Douglas, Parry, Marton, & Garson, 1976; Kendall & Braswell, 1985; Whalen, Henker, & Hinshaw, 1985). Later studies, however, were far less supportive, leading some reviewers of this literature to conclude eventually that self-control training had not demonstrated its utility for ADHD children (Abikoff, 1985, 1987).

Parent–Adolescent Intervention

Robin and Foster (1989; Robin, 1990) have designed a useful approach to resolving parent–adolescent conflicts in families with ADHD teenagers. The approach is often combined with advice to parents on contingency management methods appropriate to this age group (e.g., point systems, behavioral contracts, etc.). Forgatch and Patterson (1990) have designed a similar approach for addressing parent–teen conflicts. In my experience, by the time ADHD children reach this age range (13–18 years), the most significant issues in the family center around the acceptance of responsibility (chores, homework, school performance, etc.) by the teenagers; disagreements over the teenagers' rights and privileges; and the social activities in which the teenagers may be engaged. Although attention span, impulsivity, and emotional control are often better in this age group than in the earlier childhood years, they remain problematic and appear to express themselves through these conflictual issues when combined with the normal striving for independence typical of this developmental stage. And when conduct problems and oppositional behavior persist into this stage, as they often do, the level of family conflict is greatly exacerbated. Robin and Foster's approach directs itself at resolving these conflicts, and it is recommended when ADHD youths are too old for child management programs, such as the Barkley (1997b) and Forehand and McMahon (1981) programs.

Briefly, the Robin and Foster approach involves (1) training the parents and adolescent in a set of problem-solving steps to be used with each conflict area; (2) teaching the parents and adolescent a behavioral style for approaching the use of these steps; and (3) addressing irrational beliefs that may be held by the parents or adolescent, which may govern their evaluations of and subsequent demands upon each other. The decision to use this treatment program should be based upon various findings from the evaluation, not the least of which are the age of the ADHD adolescent, the severity of conduct problems and oppositional behavior (the approach is not especially helpful with severe Conduct Disorder), the adolescent's and parents' motivation for family therapy, and the level of verbal intelligence of the family members who are to participate.

This approach was compared to a more traditional behavioral parent training program, and to Minuchin's form of family therapy, in the treatment of conflicts between adolescents with ADHD and their parents; many of the adolescents were also oppositional (Barkley, Guevremont, Anastopoulos, & Fletcher, 1992). Results indicated that though all three groups improved significantly over time, only 35% or fewer of the families showed reliable change as a result of treatment, with the Robin and Foster program having the highest percentage of positive responders.

Classroom Management

Given that the majority of ADHD children exhibit behavior problems in their classrooms, classroom interventions are likely to be employed with most such children. These may include training teachers in contingency management methods (see Pfiffner & Barkley, 1990), transferring the ADHD children to special education classes for behavioral disorders, or both. Token reinforcement programs, home-based evaluation/reinforcement programs, increased attending by teachers to child compliance, in-class time-out procedures, and behavioral contracts may all be employed in the reduction of ADHD behaviors in the classroom.

Certainly, whether such interventions are undertaken will be based upon a number of findings from the evaluation, including the level of the child's school behavior and performance problems, the degree of parent and teacher commitment to complying with these methods, the extent of previous school interventions, the degree to which stimulant medication may address these difficulties, and the eligibility of the child for special educational programs under federal and state statutes. An assessment protocol for evaluating treatment effects may involve the Conners Teacher Rating Scale—Revised, the SSQ, the SCRS, a daily or weekly school report card (see Barkley, 1990), and possibly direct classroom observations of ADHD behaviors by school personnel. The Teacher Report Form of the CBCL or the Teacher Form of the BASC can also be included when longer time spans between pre- and posttreatment assessments are involved.

Much evidence exists for the effectiveness of behavior modification techniques in reducing the classroom behavior problems and improving the productivity of children with ADHD (Pelham et al., 1993; Pelham & Hinshaw, 1992; Pfiffner & Barkley, 1990; Pfiffner & O'Leary, 1993). Less clear, however, is the extent to which these methods may normalize the behavior of ADHD children, and to what extent treatment gains persist once the behavioral techniques are withdrawn or the children move on to another grade, classroom, or teacher. Some evidence suggests that behavior, although improved, is not brought into the normal range for ADHD children as a group (Abikoff & Gittelman, 1984).

Residential Treatment

A few ADHD children and adolescents with severe degrees of oppositional behavior or conduct problems will require placement in residential treatment centers before intervention can be attempted with them and their families. The need for such placement becomes clear from the evaluation when severe levels of aggression, delinquency, and misconduct are noted on the rating scales; when parents admit during the interview that they no longer exert control over the behavior of the ADHD child, out of fear of physical retaliation; when the child has a history of running away from home; or when family functioning is so chaotic or disorganized as to make outpatient intervention unlikely.

Summary

In the majority of instances, multiple interventions are involved in treating the plethora of difficulties of ADHD children and their families; these often include parent training in child management skills, classroom management programs, home-based reinforcement systems, and stimulant medication. In the case of ADHD adolescents, parent–adolescent problem-solving training is substituted for the child management training program. Although initial interventions are often short-term, periodic reintervention is often necessary as the children develop. New problems frequently arise in connection with the parental and societal demands of later developmental stages and the children's inabilities to meet these demands adequately. Assessment and intervention, therefore, are closely intertwined; the process becomes one of assessing, intervening, reassessing, reintervening, and so on.

LEGAL AND ETHICAL ISSUES

Of the various legal and ethical issues involved in the general practice of providing mental health services to children, several may be more likely than usual to occur in the evaluation of children with ADHD. The first of these involves the issue of custody or guardianship of a child who may have ADHD, as it pertains to who can request an evaluation of the child. Children with ADHD are more likely than those without the disorder to come from families where the parents have separated or divorced, or where significant marital discord may exist between the biological parents. As a result, the clinician must take care at the point of first contact with such a family to determine who has legal custody of the child, and particularly who has the right to request mental health services on behalf of the minor. It must also be determined in cases of joint custody (an increasingly common status in divorce/custody situations) whether the nonresident parent has the right to dispute the referral for the evaluation, to consent to the evaluation, to attend on the day of appointment, and/or to have access to the final report. This right to

review or dispute mental health services may also extend to the provision of treatment to the ADHD child. Failing to attend to these issues before the evaluation can lead to great contentiousness, frustration, and even legal action among the parties to the evaluation, much or all of which could have been avoided had greater care been taken to resolve these issues beforehand.

A second issue that also commonly arises in evaluations of children but may be more likely in cases involving ADHD is a clinician's duty to report to state agencies any suspicion of physical or sexual abuse or neglect of a child that arises or is reported during an evaluation. *Before* starting formal evaluation procedures, clinicians should routinely forewarn parents of this duty to report as it applies in a particular state. In view of the greater stress that ADHD children appear to pose for their parents, as well as the greater psychological distress their parents are likely to report, the risk for abuse of ADHD children may be higher than average. The greater likelihood of parental ADHD or other psychiatric disorders may contribute further toward this risk, resulting in a greater likelihood that evaluations of children with ADHD may involve suspicions of abuse. Understanding this legal duty as it applies in a given state or region, and taking care to exercise it properly yet with sensitivity to the larger clinical issues likely to be involved, are the responsibilities of any clinician involved in providing mental health services to children.

Increasingly over the past decade, ADHD children have been gaining access to government entitlements—sometimes thought of as legal rights—that make it necessary for clinicians to be well informed about these legal issues if they are to properly and correctly advise the parents and school staff involved in each case. For instance, children with ADHD are now entitled to formal special educational services in the United States under the "Other Health Impaired" category of the Individuals with Disabilities in Education Act, if their ADHD is sufficiently serious to interfere significantly with their school performance. This is becoming commonly known throughout the United States. Less commonly understood is that such children also have legal protections and entitlements under Section 504 of the Rehabilitation Act of 1973 as it applies to the provision of an appropriate education to disabled children. And should children have sufficiently severe ADHD and reside in low-income families, they may also be eligible for financial assistance under the Social Security Act. Space precludes a more complete explication of these legal entitlements here;

the reader is referred to the excellent texts by DuPaul and Stoner (1994) and Latham and Latham (1992) for fuller accounts of these matters. Suffice it to say here that clinicians working with ADHD children need to familiarize themselves with these various rights and entitlements if they are to be effective advocates for the children they serve.

A final legal issue related to children with ADHD pertains to their legal accountability for their own actions, in view of the argument made earlier that ADHD is a developmental disorder of self-control. Should children with ADHD be held legally responsible for the damage they may cause to property, the injury they may inflict on others, or the crimes they may commit? In short, is ADHD an excuse to behave irresponsibly without being held accountable for the consequences of one's actions? The answer is unclear, and the question deserves the attention of sharper legal minds than mine. It has been my opinion, however, that ADHD provides an explanation for why certain impulsive acts may have been committed, but does not constitute sufficient disturbance of mental faculties to serve as an excuse from legal accountability (as might occur under the insanity defense, for example). Nor should it be permitted to serve as an extenuating factor in the determination of guilt or the sentencing of an individual involved in criminal activities, particularly violent crimes. This opinion is predicated on the fact that the vast majority of children with ADHD do not become involved in violent crimes as they grow up. Moreover, studies attempting to predict criminal conduct within samples of ADHD children followed to adulthood have either not been able to find adequate predictors of such outcomes or have found them to be so weak as to account for a paltry amount of variance in such outcomes. And those variables that may make a significant contribution to the prediction of criminal or delinquent behavior much more often involve parental and family dysfunction, as well as social disadvantage; they involve ADHD symptoms much less often, if at all. Until this matter receives greater legal scrutiny, it seems wise to view ADHD as one of several explanations for impulsive conduct, but not as a direct, primary, or immediate cause of criminal conduct for which the individual should not be held accountable.

CONCLUSION

In this chapter, ADHD has been viewed as a category made up of two distinct developmental disorders. One form is a developmental disorder of behavioral inhibition that results in hyperactivity and poor self-regulation. This interferes with the control of behavior by internally represented information, so that the child with ADHD has great difficulty engaging in age-appropriate goal-directed persistence and the cross-temporal organization of behavior. Consequently, the child is less able to direct behavior away from the moment and immediate context, and toward the future and the maximization of long-term positive consequences. The difficulties in behavioral inhibition have an onset in early childhood; are relatively pervasive in nature; are frequently chronic throughout development; and are not the result of mental retardation, serious language delay, sensory deficits, or severe psychopathology. The disorder occurs more in males than in females. It has multiple etiologies, chief among which are biological contributions; yet it displays substantial situational variation and responsiveness to environmental influences.

The second type of ADHD is predominantly characterized by problems with inattention, not with impulsivity or hyperactivity. This predominantly inattentive type is probably a qualitatively distinct disorder from the impulsive–hyperactive type. It appears to represent a true disorder of attention, most likely in the realm of focused or selective attention, and should probably be removed from the category of ADHD and the larger realm of the disruptive behavior disorders.

The numerous additional problems coexisting with both types of ADHD make the assessment of the disorders a complex and challenging affair. The comprehensive assessment of ADHD in children includes parent, teacher, and child interviews; parent and teacher rating scales; and parent self-report measures. Laboratory measures of attention span and impulse control, and direct observations of ADHD behaviors and parent–child interactions, may be of some additional benefit when they are feasible. The persistent nature of ADHD means that periodic assessment and intervention will be needed throughout the development of children with the disorder.

REFERENCES

Abidin, R. R. (1986). *The Parenting Stress Index*. Charlottesville, VA: Pediatric Psychology Press.

Abikoff, H. (1985). Efficacy of cognitive training intervention in hyperactive children: A critical review. *Clinical Psychology Review, 5,* 479–512.

Abikoff, H. (1987). An evaluation of cognitive behavior therapy for hyperactive children. In B. Lahey

& A. Kazdin (Eds.), *Advances in clinical child psychology* (Vol. 10, pp. 171–216). New York: Plenum Press.

Abikoff, H., & Gittelman, R. (1984). Does behavior therapy normalize the classroom behavior of hyperactive children? *Archives of General Psychiatry, 41,* 449–454.

Abikoff, H., Gittelman–Klein, R., & Klein, D. (1977). Validation of a classroom observation code for hyperactive children. *Journal of Consulting and Clinical Psychology, 45,* 772–783.

Achenbach, T. M. (1991a). *Integrative Guide for the 1991 CBCL/4–18, YSR, and TRF Profiles.* Burlington: University of Vermont, Department of Psychiatry.

Achenbach, T. M. (1991b). *Manual for the Child Behavior Checklist/4–18 and 1991 Profile.* Burlington: University of Vermont, Department of Psychiatry.

Achenbach, T. M., (1991c). *Manual for the Teacher's Report Form and 1991 Profile.* Burlington: University of Vermont, Department of Psychiatry.

Achenbach, T. M. (1991d). *Manual for the Youth Self-Report and 1991 Profile.* Burlington: University of Vermont, Department of Psychiatry.

Achenbach, T. M., McConaughy, S. H., & Howell, C. T. (1987). Child/adolescent behavioral and emotional problems: Implications of cross–informant correlations for situational specificity. *Psychological Bulletin, 101,* 213–232.

Adams, G. L. (1984). *Normative Adaptive Behavior Checklist.* San Antonio, TX: Psychological Corporation.

Altepeter, T. S., & Breen, M. J. (1992). Situational variation in problem behavior at home and school in Attention Deficit Disorder with Hyperactivity: A factor analytic study. *Journal of Child Psychology and Psychiatry, 33,* 741–748.

American Psychiatric Association. (1968). *Diagnostic and statistical manual of mental disorders* (2nd ed.). Washington, DC: Author.

American Psychiatric Association. (1980). *Diagnostic and statistical manual of mental disorders* (3rd ed.). Washington, DC: Author.

American Psychiatric Association. (1987). *Diagnostic and statistical manual of mental disorders* (3rd ed., rev.). Washington, DC: Author.

American Psychiatric Association. (1994). *Diagnostic and statistical manual of mental disorders* (4th ed.). Washington, DC: Author.

Anastopoulos, A. D., Guevremont, D. C., Shelton, T. L., & DuPaul, G. J. (1992). Parenting stress among families of children with Attention Deficit Hyperactivity Disorder. *Journal of Abnormal Child Psychology, 20,* 503–520.

Anastopoulos, A. D., Shelton, T. L., DuPaul, G. J., & Guevremont, D. C. (1993). Parent training for Attention-Deficit Hyperactivity Disorder: Its impact on parent functioning. *Journal of Abnormal Child Psychology, 21,* 581–596.

Anderson, C. A., Hinshaw, S. P., & Simmel, C. (1994). Mother–child interactions in ADHD and comparison boys: Relationships with overt and covert externalizing behavior. *Journal of Abnormal Child Psychology, 22,* 247–265.

Applegate, B., Lahey, B. B., Hart, E. L., Waldman, I., Biederman, J., Hynd, G. W., Barkley, R. A., Ollendick, T., Frick, P. J., Greenhill, L., McBurnett, K., Newcorn, J., Kerdyk, L., Garfinkel, B., & Shaffer, D. (1996). *The age of onset for DSM-IV Attention-Deficit Hyperactivity Disorder: A report of the DSM-IV field trials.* Submitted for publication.

Asher, S. R., & Coie, J. D. (1990). *Peer rejection in childhood.* New York: Cambridge University Press.

Atkins, M. S., & Pelham, W. E. (1992). School-based assessment of Attention Deficit-Hyperactivity Disorder. In S. E. Shaywitz & B. A. Shaywitz (Eds.), *Attention Deficit Disorder comes of age: Toward the twenty-first century* (pp. 69–88). Austin, TX: Pro-Ed.

Baloh, R., Sturm, R., Green, B., & Gleser, G. (1975). Neuropsychological effects of chronic asymptomatic increased lead absorption. *Archives of Neurology, 32,* 326–330.

Barber, M. A., Milich, R., & Welsh, R. (1996). Effects of reinforcement schedule and task difficulty on the performance of Attention Deficit Hyperactivity Disordered and control boys. *Journal of Clinical Child Psychology, 25,* 66–76.

Barkley, R. A. (1977a). A review of stimulant drug research with hyperactive children. *Journal of Child Psychology and Psychiatry, 18,* 137–165.

Barkley, R. A. (1977b). The effects of methylphenidate on various measures of activity level and attention in hyperkinetic children. *Journal of Abnormal Child Psychology, 5,* 351–369.

Barkley, R. A. (1981a). *Hyperactive children: A handbook for diagnosis and treatment.* New York: Guilford Press.

Barkley, R. A. (1981b). Hyperactivity. In E. J. Mash & L. G. Terdal (Eds.), *Behavioral assessment of childhood disorders* (pp. 127–184). New York: Guilford Press.

Barkley, R. A. (1982). Specific guidelines for defining hyperactivity in children (Attention Deficit Disorder with Hyperactivity). In B. Lahey & A. Kazdin (Eds.), *Advances in clinical child psychology* (Vol. 5, pp. 137–180). New York: Plenum Press.

Barkley, R. A. (1985). The social interactions of hyperactive children: Developmental changes, drug effects, and situational variation. In R. McMahon & R. Peters (Eds.), *Childhood disorders: Behavioral–developmental approaches* (pp. 218–243). New York: Brunner/Mazel.

Barkley, R. A. (1988). Child behavior rating scales and checklists. In M. Rutter, H. Tuma, & I. Lann (Eds.), *Assessment and diagnosis in child psychopathology* (pp. 113–155). New York: Guilford Press.

Barkley, R. A. (1989). The problem of stimulus control and rule–governed behavior in children with

Attention Deficit Disorder with Hyperactivity. In J. Swanson & L. Bloomingdale (Eds.), *Attention Deficit Disorders* (pp. 203–234). Elmsford, NY: Pergamon Press.

Barkley, R. A. (1990). *Attention-Deficit Hyperactivity Disorder: A handbook for diagnosis and treatment.* New York: Guilford Press.

Barkley, R. A. (1991). The ecological validity of laboratory and analogue assessment methods of ADHD symptoms. *Journal of Abnormal Child Psychology, 19,* 149–178.

Barkley, R. A. (1994). Impaired delayed responding: A unified theory of Attention Deficit Hyperactivity Disorder. In D. K. Routh (Ed.), *Disruptive behavior disorders: Essays in honor of Herbert Quay* (pp. 11–57). New York: Plenum Press.

Barkley, R. A. (1996). Attention-Deficit/Hyperactivity Disorder. In E. J. Mash & R. A. Barkley (Eds.), *Child psychopathology* (pp. 63–112). New York: Guilford Press.

Barkley, R. A. (1997a). Behavioral inhibition, sustained attention, and executive functions: Constructing a unifying theory of ADHD. *Psychological Bulletin, 121,* 65–94.

Barkley, R. A. (1997b). *Defiant children* (2nd ed.): A clinician's manual for assessment and parent training.* New York: Guilford Press.

Barkley, R. A., Anastopoulos, A. D., Guevremont, D. G., & Fletcher, K. F. (1991). Adolescents with Attention Deficit Hyperactivity Disorder: Patterns of behavioral adjustment, academic functioning, and treatment utilization. *Journal of the American Academy of Child and Adolescent Psychiatry, 30,* 752–761.

Barkley, R. A., Anastopoulos, A. D., Guevremont, D. G., & Fletcher, K. F. (1992). Adolescents with Attention Deficit Hyperactivity Disorder: Mother–adolescent interactions, family beliefs and conflicts, and maternal psychopathology. *Journal of Abnormal Child Psychology, 20,* 263–288.

Barkley, R. A., & Cunningham, C. E. (1979). Stimulant drugs and activity level in hyperactive children. *American Journal of Orthopsychiatry, 49,* 491–499.

Barkley, R. A., & Cunningham, C. E. (1980). The parent–child interactions of hyperactive children and their modification by stimulant drugs. In R. Knights & D. Bakker (Eds.), *Treatment of hyperactive and learning disordered children* (pp. 219–236). Baltimore: University Park Press.

Barkley, R., Cunningham, C., & Karlsson, J. (1983). The speech of hyperactive children and their mothers: Comparisons with normal children and stimulant drug effects. *Journal of Learning Disabilities, 16,* 105–110.

Barkley, R. A., DuPaul, G. J., & McMurray, M.B. (1990). A comprehensive evaluation of Attention Deficit Disorder with and without Hyperactivity. *Journal of Consulting and Clinical Psychology, 58,* 775–789.

Barkley, R. A., DuPaul, D. G., & McMurray, M. B. (1991). Attention Deficit Disorder with and without Hyperactivity: Clinical response to three dose levels of methylphenidate. *Pediatrics, 87,* 519–531.

Barkley, R. A., & Edelbrock, C. S. (1987). Assessing situational variation in children's behavior problems: The Home and School Situations Questionnaires. In R. Prinz (Ed.), *Advances in behavioral assessment of children and families* (Vol. 3, pp. 157–176). Greenwich, CT: JAI Press.

Barkley, R. A., Fischer, M., Edelbrock, C. S., & Smallish, L. (1990). The adolescent outcome of hyperactive children diagnosed by research criteria: I. An 8 year prospective follow–up study. *Journal of the American Academy of Child and Adolescent Psychiatry, 29,* 546–557.

Barkley, R. A., Fischer, M., Edelbrock, C. S., & Smallish, L. (1991). The adolescent outcome of hyperactive children diagnosed by research criteria: III. Mother–child interactions, family conflicts, and maternal psychopathology. *Journal of Child Psychology and Psychiatry, 32,* 233–256.

Barkley, R. A., Fischer, M., Newby, R., & Breen, M. (1988). Development of a multi–method clinical protocol for assessing stimulant drug responses in ADHD children. *Journal of Clinical Child Psychology, 17,* 14–24.

Barkley, R. A., & Grodzinsky, G. M. (1994). Are tests of frontal lobe functions useful in the diagnosis of attention deficit disorders? *The Clinical Neuropsychologist, 8,* 121–139.

Barkley, R. A., Grodzinsky, G., & DuPaul, G. (1992). Frontal lobe functions in Attention Deficit Disorder with and without Hyperactivity: A review and research report. *Journal of Abnormal Child Psychology, 20,* 163–188.

Barkley, R. A., Guevremont, D. G., Anastopoulos, A. D., DuPaul, G. J., & Shelton, T. L. (1993). Driving–related risks and outcomes of Attention Deficit Hyperactivity Disorder in adolescents and young adults: A 3–5 year follow–up survey. *Pediatrics, 92,* 212–218.

Barkley, R. A., Guevremont, D. G., Anastopoulos, A. D., & Fletcher, K. (1992). A comparison of three family therapy programs for treating family conflicts in adolescents with Attention-Deficit Hyperactivity Disorder. *Journal of Consulting and Clinical Psychology, 60,* 450–462.

Barkley, R. A., Karlsson, J., & Pollard, S. (1985). Effects of age on the mother–child interactions of hyperactive children. *Journal of Abnormal Child Psychology, 13,* 631–638.

Barkley, R. A., Karlsson, J., Strzelecki, E., & Murphy, J. (1984). Effects of age and Ritalin dosage on the mother–child interactions of hyperactive children. *Journal of Consulting and Clinical Psychology, 52,* 750–758.

Barkley, R. A., McMurray, M. B., Edelbrock, C. S., & Robbins, K. (1989). The response of aggressive and non–aggressive ADHD children to two doses of methylphenidate. *Journal of the American Academy of Child and Adolescent Psychiatry, 28,* 873–881.

Barkley, R. A., & Murphy, K. R. (1996). Psychological adjustment and adaptive impairments in young adults with ADHD. *Journal of Attention Disorders, 1,* 41–54.

Barkley, R. A., Murphy, K. R., & Kwasnik, D. (1996). Motor vehicle driving competencies and risks in teens and young adults with ADHD. *Pediatrics, 98,* 1089–1095.

Barkley, R. A., & Ullman, D. G. (1975). A comparison of objective measures of activity level and distractibility in hyperactive and nonhyperactive children. *Journal of Abnormal Child Psychology, 3,* 213–244.

Bauermeister, J. J. (1996). Teacher rating scales for the assessment of ADD and ADHD in Hispanic (Puerto Rican) children. *The ADHD Report, 3*(6), 9–10.

Bauermeister, J. J., Berrios, V., Jimenez, A. L., Acevedo, L., & Gordon, M. (1990). Some issues and instruments for the assessment of Attention-Deficit Hyperactivity Disorder in Puerto Rican children. *Journal of Clinical Child Psychology, 19,* 9–16.

Baumgaertel, A. (1994, June). *Assessment of German school children using DSM criteria based on teacher report.* Paper presented at the annual meeting of the International Society for Research in Child and Adolescent Psychopathology, London.

Beck, A. T., Steer, R. A., & Garbin, M. G. (1988). Psychometric properties of the Beck Depression Inventory: Twenty-five years of evaluation. *Clinical Psychology Review, 8,* 77–100.

Befera, M., & Barkley, R. A. (1985). Hyperactive and normal girls and boys: Mother–child interactions, parent psychiatric status, and child psychopathology. *Journal of Child Psychology and Psychiatry, 26,* 439–452.

Bennett, L. A., Wolin, S. J., & Reiss, D. (1988). Cognitive, behavioral, and emotional problems among school-age children of alcoholic parents. *American Journal of Psychiatry, 145,* 185–190.

Benton, A. (1991). Prefrontal injury and behavior in children. *Developmental Neuropsychology, 7,* 275–282.

Berk, L. E., & Potts, M. K. (1991). Development and functional significance of private speech among Attention–Deficit Hyperactivity Disorder and normal boys. *Journal of Abnormal Child Psychology, 19,* 357–377.

Bhatia, M. S., Nigam, V. R., Bohra, N., & Malik, S. C. (1991). Attention Deficit Disorder with Hyperactivity among paediatric outpatients. *Journal of Child Psychology and Psychiatry, 32,* 297–306.

Biederman, J., Baldessarini, R. J., Wright, V., Knee, D., & Harmatz, J. S. (1989). A double-blind placebo controlled study of desipramine in the treatment of ADD: I. Efficacy. *Journal of the American Academy of Child and Adolescent Psychiatry, 28,* 777–784.

Biederman, J., Faraone, S. V., Keenan, K., & Tsuang, M. T. (1991). Evidence of a familial association between Attention Deficit Disorder and major affective disorders. *Archives of General Psychiatry, 48,* 633–642.

Biederman, J., Faraone, S. V., & Lapey, K. (1992, October). Comorbidity of diagnosis in Attention-Deficit Hyperactivity Disorder. *Child and Adolescent Psychiatric Clinics of North America, 1*(2), 335–360.

Biederman, J., Faraone, S. V., Millberger, S., Curtis, S., Chen, L., Marrs, A., Ouellette, C., Moore, P., & Spencer, T. (1996). Predictors of persistence and remission of ADHD into adolescence: Results from a four-year prospective follow-up study. *Journal of the American Academy of Child and Adolescent Psychiatry, 35,* 343–351.

Biederman, J., Keenan, K., & Faraone, S. V. (1990). Parent-based diagnosis of Attention Deficit Disorder predicts a diagnosis based on teacher report. *Journal of the American Academy of Child and Adolescent Psychiatry, 29,* 698–701.

Biederman, J., Milberger, S., Faraone, S. V., Kiely, K., Guite, J., Mick, E., Ablon, J. S., Warbutron, R., Reed, E., & Davis, S. G. (1995). Impact of adversity on functioning and comorbidity in children with Attention-Deficit Hyperactivity Disorder. *Journal of the American Academy of Child and Adolescent Psychiatry, 34,* 1495–1503.

Bijur, P., Golding, J., Haslum, M., & Kurzon, M. (1988). Behavioral predictors of injury in school-age children. *American Journal of Diseases of Children, 142,* 1307–1312.

Block, G. H. (1977). Hyperactivity: A cultural perspective. *Journal of Learning Disabilities, 110,* 236–240.

Blouin, A. G., Bornstein, M. A., & Trites, R. L. (1978). Teenage alcohol abuse among hyperactive children: A five year follow-up study. *Journal of Pediatric Psychology, 3,* 188–194.

Breen, M. J. (1989). Cognitive and behavioral differences in ADHD boys and girls. *Journal of Child Psychology and Psychiatry, 30,* 711–716.

Breen, M. J., & Barkley, R. A. (1988). Child psychopathology and parenting stress in girls and boys having Attention Deficit Disorder with Hyperactivity. *Journal of Pediatric Psychology, 13,* 265–280.

Bronowski, J. (1977). Human and animal languages. In J. Bronowski (Ed.), *A sense of the future* (pp. 104–131). Cambridge, MA: MIT Press.

Cairns, E., & Cammock, T. (1978). Development of a more reliable version of the Matching Familiar Figures Test. *Developmental Psychology, 11,* 244–248.

Campbell, S. B. (1990). *Behavior problems in preschool children.* New York: Guilford Press.

Campbell, S. B., Douglas, V. I., & Morganstern, G. (1971). Cognitive styles in hyperactive children and the effect of methylphenidate. *Journal of Child Psychology and Psychiatry, 12,* 55–67.

Campbell, S. B., & Ewing, L. J. (1990). Follow-up of hard to manage preschoolers: Adjustment at age

9 and predictors of continuing symptoms. *Journal of Child Psychology and Psychiatry*, 31, 871–889.

Campbell, S. B., March, C. L., Pierce, E. W., Ewing, L. J., & Szumowski, E. K. (1991). Hard-to-manage preschool boys: Family context and the stability of externalizing behavior. *Journal of Abnormal Child Psychology*, 19, 301–318.

Campbell, S. B., Schleifer, M., & Weiss, G. (1978). Continuities in maternal reports and child behaviors over time in hyperactive and comparison groups. *Journal of Abnormal Child Psychology*, 6, 33–45.

Campbell, S. B., Szumowski, E. K., Ewing, L. J., Gluck, D. S., & Breaux, A. M. (1982). A multidimensional assessment of parent-identified behavior problem toddlers. *Journal of Abnormal Child Psychology*, 10, 569–592.

Cantwell, D. P. (1975). *The hyperactive child*. New York: Spectrum.

Cantwell, D. P., & Baker, L. (1992). Association between Attention Deficit-Hyperactivity Disorder and learning disorders. In S. E. Shaywitz & B. A. Shaywitz (Eds), *Attention Deficit Disorder comes of age: Toward the twenty-first century* (pp. 145–164). Austin, TX: Pro-Ed.

Cantwell, D. P., & Satterfield, J. H. (1978). The prevalence of academic underachievement in hyperactive children. *Journal of Pediatric Psychology*, 3, 168–171.

Castellanos, F. X., Giedd, J. N., Eckburg, P., Marsh, W. L., Vaituzis, C., Kaysen, D., Hamburger, S. D., & Rapoport, J. L. (1994). Quantitative morphology of the caudate nucleus in Attention Deficit Hyperactivity Disorder. *American Journal of Psychiatry*, 151, 1791–1796.

Chamberlin, R. W. (1977). Can we identify a group of children at age two who are at risk for the development of behavioral or emotional problems in kindergarten or first grade? *Pediatrics*, 59(Suppl.), 971–981.

Chee, P., Logan, G., Schachar, R., Lindsay, P., & Wachsmuth, R. (1989). Effects of event rate and display time on sustained attention in hyperactive, normal, and control children. *Journal of Abnormal Child Psychology*, 17, 371–391.

Chess, S. (1960). Diagnosis and treatment of the hyperactive child. *New York State Journal of Medicine*, 60, 2379–2385.

Clements, S. D. (1966). *Task force one: Minimal brain dysfunction in children* (National Institute of Neurological Diseases and Blindness, Monograph No. 3). Washington, DC: U.S. Department of Health, Education and Welfare.

Clements, S. D., & Peters, J. E. (1962). Minimal brain dysfunction in the school-age child. *Archives of General Psychiatry*, 6, 185–197.

Cohen, N. J., & Minde, K. (1983). The "hyperactive syndrome" in kindergarten children: Comparison of children with pervasive and situational symptoms. *Journal of Child Psychology and Psychiatry*, 24, 443–455.

Cohen, N. J., Weiss, G., & Minde, K. (1972). Cognitive styles in adolescents previously diagnosed as hyperactive. *Journal of Child Psychology and Psychiatry*, 13, 203–209.

Cole, P. M., Zahn-Waxler, C., & Smith, D. (1994). Expressive control during a disappointment: Variations related to preschoolers' behavior problems. *Developmental Psychology*, 30, 835–846.

Conners, C. K. (1980). *Food additives and hyperactive children*. New York: Plenum Press.

Conners, C. K. (1990). *The Conners Rating Scales*. North Tonawanda, NY: Multi-Health Systems.

Conners, C. K. (1995). *The Conners Continuous Performance Test*. North Tonawanda, NY: Multi-Health Systems.

Cook, E. H., Stein, M. A., Krasowski, M. D., Cox, N. J., Olkon, D. M., Kieffer, J. E., & Leventhal, B. L. (1995). Association of Attention Deficit Disorder and the dopamine transporter gene. *American Journal of Human Genetics*, 56, 993–998.

Copeland, A. P. (1979). Types of private speech produced by hyperactive and nonhyperactive boys. *Journal of Abnormal Child Psychology*, 7, 169–177.

Corkum, P. V., & Siegel, L. S. (1993). Is the continuous performance task a valuable research tool for use with children with Attention-Deficit-Hyperactivity Disorder? *Journal of Child Psychology and Psychiatry*, 34, 1217–1239.

Cunningham, C. E., Benness, B. B., & Siegel, L. S. (1988). Family functioning, time allocation, and parental depression in the families of normal and ADDH children. *Journal of Clinical Child Psychology*, 17, 169–177.

Cunningham, C. E., & Siegel, L. S. (1987). Peer interactions of normal and Attention-Deficit Disordered boys during free-play, cooperative task, and simulated classroom situations. *Journal of Abnormal Child Psychology*, 15, 247–268.

Cunningham, C. E., Siegel, L. S., & Offord, D. R. (1985). A developmental dose response analysis of the effects of methylphenidate on the peer interactions of Attention Deficit Disordered boys. *Journal of Child Psychology and Psychiatry*, 26, 955–971.

Danforth, J. S., Barkley, R. A., & Stokes, T. F. (1991). Observations of parent–child interactions with hyperactive children: Research and clinical implications. *Clinical Psychology Review*, 11, 703–727.

David, O. J. (1974). Association between lower level lead concentrations and hyperactivity. *Environmental Health Perspective*, 7, 17–25.

Davidson, L. L., Taylor, E. A., Sandberg, S. T., & Thorley, G. (1992). Hyperactivity in school-age boys and subsequent risk of injury. *Pediatrics*, 90, 697–702.

de la Burde, B., & Choate, M. (1972). Does asymptomatic lead exposure in children have latent sequelae? *Journal of Pediatrics, 81,* 1088–1091.

de la Burde, B., & Choate, M. (1974). Early asymptomatic lead exposure and development at school age. *Journal of Pediatrics, 8,* 638–642.

Denckla, M. B. (1994). Measurement of executive function. In G. R. Lyon (Ed.), *Frames of reference for the assessment of learning disabilities: New views on measurement issues* (pp. 117–142). Baltimore, MD: Paul H. Brookes.

Denckla, M. B., & Rudel, R. G. (1978). Anomalies of motor development in hyperactive boys. *Annals of Neurology, 3,* 231–233.

Denson, R., Nanson, J. L., & McWatters, M. A. (1975). Hyperkinesis and maternal smoking. *Canadian Psychiatric Association Journal, 20,* 183–187.

Derogatis, L. (1986). *Manual for the Symptom Checklist 90 — Revised (SCL-90-R).* Baltimore: Author.

Diamond, A. (1990). The development and neural bases of memory functions as indexed by the AB and delayed response task in human infants and infant monkeys. *Annals of the New York Academy of Sciences, 608,* 276–317.

Diamond, A., Cruttenden, L., & Niederman, D. (1994). AB with multiple wells: 1. Why are multiple wells sometimes easier than two wells? 2. Memory or memory + inhibition? *Developmental Psychology, 30,* 192–205.

Dodge, K. A., McClaskey, C. L., & Feldman, E. (1985). A situational approach to the assessment of social competence in children. *Journal of Consulting and Clinical Psychology, 53,* 344–353.

Douglas, V. I. (1972). Stop, look, and listen: The problem of sustained attention and impulse control in hyperactive and normal children. *Canadian Journal of Behavioural Science, 4,* 259–282.

Douglas, V. I. (1980). Higher mental processes in hyperactive children: Implications for training. In R. Knights & D. Bakker (Eds.), *Treatment of hyperactive and learning disordered children* (pp. 65–92). Baltimore: University Park Press.

Douglas, V. I. (1983). Attention and cognitive problems. In M. Rutter (Ed.), Developmental neuropsychiatry (pp. 280–329). New York: Guilford Press.

Douglas, V. I., & Parry, P. A. (1983). Effects of reward on delayed reaction time task performance of hyperactive children. *Journal of Abnormal Child Psychology, 11,* 313–326.

Douglas, V. I., & Parry, P. A. (1994). Effects of reward and non-reward on attention and frustration in Attention Deficit Disorder. *Journal of Abnormal Child Psychology, 22,* 281–302.

Douglas, V. I., Parry, P., Marton, P., & Garson, C. (1976). Assessment of a cognitive training program for hyperactive children. *Journal of Abnormal Child Psychology, 4,* 389–410.

Douglas, V. I., & Peters, K. G. (1979). Toward a clearer definition of the attentional deficit of hyperactive children. In G. A. Hale & M. Lewis (Eds.), *Attention and the development of cognitive skills* (pp. 173–248). New York: Plenum Press.

Draeger, S., Prior, M., & Sanson, A. (1986). Visual and auditory attention performance in hyperactive children: Competence or compliance. *Journal of Abnormal Child Psychology, 14,* 411–424.

Dubey, D. R., O'Leary, S. G., & Kaufman, K. F. (1983). Training parents of hyperactive children in child management: A comparative outcome study. *Journal of Abnormal Child Psychology, 11,* 229–246.

DuPaul, G. R. (1991). Parent and teacher ratings of ADHD symptoms: Psychometric properties in a community-based sample. *Journal of Clinical Child Psychology, 20,* 245–253.

DuPaul, G. J., & Barkley, R. A. (1990). Medication therapy. In R. A. Barkley, *Attention-Deficit Hyperactivity disorder: A handbook for diagnosis and treatment* (pp. 573–611). New York: Guilford Press.

DuPaul, G. J., & Barkley, R. A. (1992). Situational variability of attention problems: Psychometric properties of the Revised Home and School Situations Questionnaires. *Journal of Clinical Child Psychology, 21,* 178–188.

DuPaul, G. J., Barkley, R. A., & McMurray, M. B. (1994). Response of children with ADHD to methylphenidate: Interaction with internalizing symptoms. *Journal of the American Academy of Child and Adolescent Psychiatry, 33,* 894–903.

DuPaul, G. J., Rapport, M. D., & Periello, L. M. (1991). Teacher ratings of academic skills: The development of the Academic Performance Rating Scale. *School Psychology Review, 20,* 284–300.

DuPaul, G. J., & Stoner, G. (1994). *ADHD in the schools.* New York: Guilford Press.

Edelbrock, C. S., Rende, R., Plomin, R., & Thompson, L. A. (1995). A twin study of competence and problem behavior in childhood and early adolescence. *Journal of Child Psychology and Psychiatry, 36,* 775–786.

Ernst, M., Liebenauer, L. L., King, A. C., Fitzgerald, G. A., Cohen, R. M., & Zametkin, A. J. (1994). Reduced brain metabolism in hyperactive girls. *Journal of the American Academy of Child and Adolescent Psychiatry, 33,* 858–868.

Evans, S. W., Vallano, G., & Pelham, W. (1994). Treatment of parenting behavior with a psychostimulant: A case study of an adult with Attention-Deficit Hyperactivity Disorder. *Journal of Child and Adolescent Psychopharmacology, 4,* 63–69.

Faraone, S. V., Biederman, J., Chen, W. J., Krifcher, B., Keenan, K., Moore, C., Sprich, S., & Tsuang, M. T. (1992). Segregation analysis of Attention Deficit Hyperactivity Disorder. *Psychiatric Genetics, 2,* 257–275.

Faraone, S. V., Biederman, J., Lehman, B., Keenan, K., Norman, D., Seidman, L. J., Kolodny, R., Kraus, I., Perrin, J., & Chen, W. (1993). Evidence for the independent familial transmission of Attention Deficit Hyperactivity Disorder and learning disabilities: Results from a family genetic study. *American Journal of Psychiatry, 150,* 891–895.

Feingold, B. (1975). *Why your child is hyperactive.* New York: Random House.

Ferguson, H. B., & Pappas, B. A. (1979). Evaluation of psychophysiological, neurochemical, and animal models of hyperactivity. In R. L. Trites (Ed.), *Hyperactivity in children* (pp. 61–92). Baltimore: University Park Press.

Fergusson, D. M., Fergusson, I. E., Howrood, L. J., & Kinzett, N. G. (1988). A longitudinal study of dentine lead levels, intelligence, school performance, and behaviour. *Journal of Child Psychology and Psychiatry, 29,* 811–824.

Firestone, P., & Martin, J. E. (1979). An analysis of the hyperactive syndrome: A comparison of hyperactive, behavior problem, asthmatic, and normal children. *Journal of Abnormal Child Psychology, 7,* 261–273.

Fischer, M. (1990). Parenting stress and the child with Attention Deficit Hyperactivity Disorder. *Journal of Clinical Child Psychology, 19,* 337–346.

Fischer, M., Barkley, R. A., Edelbrock, C. S., & Smallish, L. (1990). The adolescent outcome of hyperactive children diagnosed by research criteria: II. Academic, attentional, and neuropsychological status. *Journal of Consulting and Clinical Psychology, 58,* 580–588.

Fischer, M., Barkley, R. A., Fletcher, K., & Smallish, L. (1993a). The stability of dimensions of behavior in ADHD and normal children over an 8 year period. *Journal of Abnormal Child Psychology, 21,* 315–337.

Fischer, M., Barkley, R. A., Fletcher, K., & Smallish, L. (1993b). The adolescent outcome of hyperactive children diagnosed by research criteria: V. Predictors of outcome. *Journal of the American Academy of Child and Adolescent Psychiatry, 32,* 324–332.

Forehand, R., & McMahon, R. (1981). *Helping the noncompliant child: A clinician's guide to parent training.* New York: Guilford Press.

Forgatch, M., & Patterson, G. R. (1990). *Parents and adolescents living together.* Eugene, OR: Castalia.

Fuster, J. M. (1989). *The prefrontal cortex.* New York: Raven Press.

Gilger, J. W., Pennington, B. F., & DeFries, J. C. (1992). A twin study of the etiology of comorbidity: Attention-Deficit Hyperactivity Disorder and dyslexia. *Journal of the American Academy of Child and Adolescent Psychiatry, 31,* 343–348.

Gittelman, R., & Eskinazi, B. (1983). Lead and hyperactivity revisited. *Archives of General Psychiatry, 40,* 827–833.

Glow, P. H., & Glow, R. A. (1979). Hyperkinetic impulse disorder: A developmental defect of motivation. *Genetic Psychological Monographs, 100,* 159–231.

Gomez, R. & Sanson, A. V. (1994). Mother–child interactions and noncompliance in hyperactive boys with and without conduct problems. *Journal of Child Psychology and Psychiatry, 35,* 477–490.

Goodman, J. R., & Stevenson, J. (1989). A twin study of hyperactivity: II. The aetiological role of genes, family relationships, and perinatal adversity. *Journal of Child Psychology and Psychiatry, 30,* 691–709.

Goodyear, P., & Hynd, G. (1992). Attention Deficit Disorder with (ADD/H) and without (ADD/WO) Hyperactivity: Behavioral and neuropsychological differentiation. *Journal of Clinical Child Psychology, 21,* 273–304.

Gordon, M. (1979). The assessment of impulsivity and mediating behaviors in hyperactive and nonhyperactive children. *Journal of Abnormal Child Psychology, 7,* 317–326.

Gordon, M. (1983). *The Gordon Diagnostic System.* DeWitt, NY: Gordon Systems.

Gordon, M., & McClure, F. D. (1983, August). *The objective assessment of Attention Deficit Disorders.* Paper presented at the 91st Annual Convention of the American Psychological Association, Anaheim, CA.

Goyette, C. H., Conners, C. K., & Ulrich, R. F. (1978). Normative data on revised Conners Parent and Teacher Rating Scales. *Journal of Abnormal Child Psychology, 6,* 221–236.

Green, L., Fry, A. F., & Meyerson, J. (1994). Discounting of delayed rewards: A life-span comparison. *Psychological Science, 5,* 33–36.

Greenberg, L. M., & Waldman, I. D. (1992). *Developmental normative data on the Test of Variables of Attention (T.O.V.A.).* Minneapolis: University of Minnesota Medical School, Department of Psychiatry.

Greene, R. W. (1996). Students with Attention-Deficit Hyperactivity Disorder and their teachers: Implications of a goodness-of-fit perspective. In T. Ollendick & R. J. Prinz (Eds.), *Advances in clinical child psychology* (Vol. 18, pp. 205–230). New York: Plenum Press.

Gresham, F., & Elliott, S. (1990). *Social Skills Rating System.* Circle Pines, MN: American Guidance Service.

Grodzinsky, G. M., & Barkley, R. A. (1996, February). *The predictive power of frontal lobe tests in the Diagnosis of Attention Deficit Hyperactivity Disorder.* Paper presented at the annual meeting of the International Neuropsychological Society, Chicago.

Grodzinsky, G. M., & Diamond, R. (1992). Frontal lobe functioning in boys with Attention-Deficit Hyperactivity Disorder. *Developmental Neuropsychology, 8,* 427–445.

Gross, A. M. (1984). Behavioral interviewing. In T. H. Ollendick & M. Hersen (Eds.), *Child behavioral assessment* (pp. 61–79). Elmsford, NY: Pergamon Press.

Gross, M. D. (1984). Effects of sucrose on hyperkinetic children. *Pediatrics, 74,* 876–878.

Haenlein, M., & Caul, W. F. (1987). Attention Deficit Disorder with Hyperactivity: A specific hypothesis of reward dysfunction. *Journal of the American Academy of Child and Adolescent Psychiatry, 26,* 356–362.

Halperin, J. M., Matier, K., Bedi, G., Sharma, V., & Newcorn, J. H. (1992). Specificity of inattention, impulsivity, and hyperactivity to the diagnosis of Attention-Deficit Hyperactivity Disorder. *Journal of the American Academy of Child and Adolescent Psychiatry, 31,* 190–196.

Hamlett, K. W., Pellegrini, D. S., & Conners, C. K. (1987). An investigation of executive processes in the problem-solving of Attention Deficit Disorder-Hyperactive children. *Journal of Pediatric Psychology, 12,* 227–240.

Hart, E. L., Lahey, B. B., Loeber, R., Applegate, B., Green, S., & Frick, P. J. (1996). Developmental change in Attention-Deficit Hyperactivity Disorder in boys: A four-year longitudinal study. *Journal of Abnormal Child Psychology, 23,* 729–750.

Hartsough, C. S., & Lambert, N. M. (1985). Medical factors in hyperactive and normal children: Prenatal, developmental, and health history findings. *American Journal of Orthopsychiatry, 55,* 190–210.

Hastings, J., & Barkley, R. A. (1978). A review of psychophysiological research with hyperactive children. *Journal of Abnormal Child Psychology, 7,* 413–437.

Hayes, S. (1989). *Rule-governed behavior.* New York: Plenum Press.

Hechtman, L., Weiss, G., & Perlman, T. (1980). Hyperactives as young adults: Self-esteem and social skills. *Canadian Journal of Psychiatry, 25,* 478–483.

Hechtman, L., Weiss, G., Perlman, T., & Amsel, R. (1984). Hyperactives as young adults: Initial predictors of outcome. *Journal of the American Academy of Child Psychiatry, 23,* 250–260.

Heilman, K. M., Voeller, K. K. S., & Nadeau, S. E. (1991). A possible pathophysiological substrate of Attention Deficit Hyperactivity Disorder. *Journal of Child Neurology, 6,* 74–79.

Hinshaw, S. P. (1987). On the distinction between attentional deficits/hyperactivity and conduct problems/aggression in child psychopathology. *Psychological Bulletin, 101,* 443–463.

Hinshaw, S. P. (1994). *Attention deficits and hyperactivity in children.* Thousand Oaks, CA: Sage.

Hinshaw, S. P., Buhrmeister, D., & Heller, T. (1989). Anger control in response to verbal provocation: Effects of stimulant medication for boys with ADHD. *Journal of Abnormal Child Psychology, 17,* 393–408.

Hinshaw, S. P., Han, S. S., Erhardt, D., & Huber, A. (1992). Internalizing and externalizing behavior problems in preschool children: Correspondence among parent and teacher ratings and behavior observations. *Journal of Clinical Child Psychology, 21,* 143–150.

Hinshaw, S. P., Heller, T., & McHale, J. P. (1992). Covert antisocial behavior in boys with Attention-Deficit Hyperactivity Disorder: External validation and effects of methylphenidate. *Journal of Consulting and Clinical Psychology, 60,* 274–281.

Hinshaw, S. P., Herbsman, C., Melnick, S., Nigg, J., & Simmel, C. (1993, February). *Psychological and familial processes in ADHD: Continuous or discontinuous with those in normal comparison children?* Paper presented at the annual meeting of the International Society for Research in Child and Adolescent Psychopathology, Santa Fe, NM.

Hinshaw, S. P., & Nigg, J. (in press). Behavioral rating scales in the assessment of disruptive behavior disorders in childhood. In D. Shaffer & J. Richters (Eds.), *Assessment in child psychopathology.* New York: Plenum Press.

Hodges, K. (1993). Structured interviews for assessing children. *Journal of Child Psychology and Psychiatry, 34,* 49–68.

Humphries, T., Kinsbourne, M., & Swanson, J. (1978). Stimulant effects on cooperation and social interaction between hyperactive children and their mothers. *Journal of Child Psychology and Psychiatry, 19,* 13–22.

Hynd, G. W., Hern, K. L., Novey, E. S., Eliopulos, D., Marshall, R., Conzalez, J. J., & Voeller, K. K. (1993). Attention-Deficit Hyperactivity Disorder and asymmetry of the caudate nucleus. *Journal of Child Neurology, 8,* 339–347.

Jacob, R. G., O'Leary, K. D., & Rosenblad, C. (1978). Formal and informal classroom settings: Effects on hyperactivity. *Journal of Abnormal Child Psychology, 6,* 47–59.

James, W. (1950). *The principles of psychology* (2 vols.). New York: Dover. (Original work published 1890)

Johnston, C., Pelham, W. E., & Murphy, H. A. (1985). Peer relationships in ADDH and normal children: A developmental analysis of peer and teacher ratings. *Journal of Abnormal Child Psychology, 13,* 89–100.

Kagan, J. (1966). Reflection–impulsivity: The generality and dynamics of conceptual tempo. *Journal of Abnormal Psychology, 71,* 17–24.

Kanbayashi, Y., Nakata, Y., Fujii, K., Kita, M., & Wada, K. (1994). ADHD-related behavior among non-referred children: Parents' ratings of DSM-III-R symptoms. *Child Psychiatry and Human Development, 25,* 13–29.

Kanfer, F. H., & Karoly, P. (1972). Self-control: A behavioristic excursion into the lion's den. *Behavior Therapy, 3,* 398–416.

Kendall, P. C., & Braswell, L. (1982). Cognitive-behavioral self-control therapy for children: A component analysis. *Journal of Consulting and Clinical Psychology, 50,* 672–689.

Kendall, P. C., & Braswell, L. (1985). *Cognitive-behavioral therapy for impulsive children*. New York: Guilford Press.

Kendall, P. C., & Brophy, C. (1981). Activity and attentional correlates of teacher ratings of hyperactivity. *Journal of Pediatric Psychology, 6*, 451–458.

Kendall, P. C., & Wilcox, L. E. (1979). Self-control in children: Development of a rating scale. *Journal of Consulting and Clinical Psychology, 47*, 1020–1029.

Kinsbourne, M. (1977). The mechanism of hyperactivity. In M. Blau, I. Rapin, & M. Kinsbourne (Eds.), *Topics in child neurology* (pp. 289–306). New York: Spectrum.

Klorman, R. (1992). Cognitive event-related potentials in Attention Deficit Disorder. In S. E. Shaywitz & B. A. Shaywitz (Eds.), *Attention Deficit Disorder comes of age: Toward the twenty-first century* (pp. 221–244). Austin, TX: Pro-Ed.

Kopp, C. B. (1982). Antecedents of self-regulation: A developmental perspective. *Developmental Psychology, 18*, 199–214.

Krouse, J. P., & Kauffman, J. M. (1982). Minor physical anomalies in exceptional children: A review and critique of research. *Journal of Abnormal Child Psychology, 10*, 247–264.

Lachar, D. (1982). *Personality Inventory for Children (PIC): Revised format manual supplement*. Los Angeles: Western Psychological Services.

Lahey, B. B., & Carlson, C. L. (1992). Validity of the diagnostic category of Attention Deficit Disorder without Hyperactivity: A review of the literature. In S. E. Shaywitz & B. A. Shaywitz (Eds.), *Attention Deficit Disorder comes of age: Toward the twenty-first century* (pp. 119–144). Austin, TX: Pro-Ed.

Lahey, B. B., Pelham, W. E., Schaughency, E. A., Atkins, M. S., Murphy, H. A., Hynd, G. W., Russo, M., Hartdagen, S., & Lorys-Vernon, A. (1988). Dimensions and types of Attention Deficit Disorder with Hyperactivity in children: A factor and cluster-analytic approach. *Journal of the American Academy of Child and Adolescent Psychiatry, 27*, 330–335.

Lahey, B. B., Piacentini, J. C., McBurnett, K., Stone, P., Hartdagen, S., & Hynd, G. W. (1988). Psychopathology in the parents of children with Conduct Disorder and hyperactivity. *Journal of the American Academy of Child and Adolescent Psychiatry, 27*, 163–170.

Lambert, N. M., Sandoval, J., & Sassone, D. (1978). Prevalence of hyperactivity in elementary school children as a function of social system definers. *American Journal of Orthopsychiatry, 48*, 446–463.

Latham, P., & Latham, R. (1992). *ADD and the law*. Washington, DC: JKL Communications.

Levy, F., & Hay, D. (1996, January). *ADHD in twins and their siblings*. Paper presented at the annual meeting of the International Society for Research in Child and Adolescent Psychopathology, Santa Monica, CA.

Locke, H. J., & Wallace, K. M. (1959). Short marital adjustment and prediction tests: Their reliability and validity. *Journal of Marriage and Family Living, 21*, 251–255.

Loeber, R. (1990). Development and risk factors of juvenile antisocial behavior and delinquency. *Clinical Psychology Review, 10*, 1–41.

Loeber, R., Green, S. M., Lahey, B. B., & Stouthamer-Loeber, M. (1991). Differences and similarities between children, mothers, and teachers as informants on disruptive behavior disorders. *Journal of Abnormal Child Psychology, 19*, 75–95.

Loeber, R., Green, S. M., Lahey, B. B., Christ, M. A. G., & Frick, P. J. (1992). Developmental sequences in the age of onset of disruptive child behaviors. *Journal of Child and Family Studies, 1*, 21–41.

Loney, J., & Milich, R. (1982). Hyperactivity, inattention, and aggression in clinical practice. In D. Routh & M. Wolraich (Eds.), *Advances in developmental and behavioral pediatrics* (Vol. 3, pp. 113–147). Greenwich, CT: JAI Press.

Loney, J., Whaley-Klahn, M. A., Kosier, T., & Conboy, J. (1983). Hyperactive boys and their brothers at 21: Predictors of aggressive and antisocial outcomes. In K. T. van Dusen & S. A. Mednick (Eds.), *Prospective studies of crime and delinquency* (pp. 181–206). Boston: Kluwer–Nijhoff.

Lopez, R. (1965). Hyperactivity in twins. *Canadian Psychiatric Association Journal, 10*, 421–426.

Lou, H. C., Henriksen, L., & Bruhn, P. (1984). Focal cerebral hypoperfusion in children with dysphasia and/or Attention Deficit Disorder. *Archives of Neurology, 41*, 825–829.

Lou, H. C., Henriksen, L., Bruhn, P., Borner, H., & Nielsen, J. B. (1989). Striatal dysfunction in attention deficit and hyperkinetic disorder. *Archives of Neurology, 46*, 48–52.

Luk, S. (1985). Direct observations studies of hyperactive behaviors. *Journal of the American Academy of Child and Adolescent Psychiatry, 24*, 338–344.

Malone, M. A., & Swanson, J. M. (1993). Effects of methylphenidate on impulsive responding in children with Attention Deficit Hyperactivity Disorder. *Journal of Child Neurology, 8*, 157–163.

Mannuzza, S., & Klein, R. (1992, October). Predictors of outcome of children with Attention-Deficit Hyperactivity Disorder. *Child and Adolescent Psychiatric Clinics of North America, 1*(2), 567–578.

Mannuzza, S., Gittelman-Klein, R., Bessler, A., Malloy, P., & LaPadula, M. (1993). Adult outcome of hyperactive boys: Educational achievement, occupational rank, and psychiatric status. *Archives of General Psychiatry, 50*, 565–576.

Mariani, M., & Barkley, R. A. (1997). Neuropsychological and academic functioning in preschool children with Attention Deficit Hyperactivity Disorder. *Developmental Neuropsychology, 13,* 111–129.

Mash, E. J., & Barkley, R. A. (1986). Assessment of family interaction with the Response Class Matrix. In R. Prinz (Ed.), *Advances in behavioral assessment of children and families* (Vol. 2, pp. 29–67). Greenwich, CT: JAI Press.

Mash, E. J., & Barkley, R. A. (Eds.). (1989). *Treatment of childhood disorders.* New York: Guilford Press.

Mash, E. J., & Barkley, R. A. (Eds.). (1996). *Child psychopathology.* New York: Guilford Press.

Mash, E. J., & Johnston, C. (1982). A comparison of mother–child interactions of younger and older hyperactive and normal children. *Child Development, 53,* 1371–1381.

Mash, E. J., & Johnston, C. (1983a). Sibling interactions of hyperactive and normal children and their relationship to reports of maternal stress and self-esteem. *Journal of Clinical Child Psychology, 12,* 91–99.

Mash, E. J., & Johnston, C. (1983b). The prediction of mothers' behavior with their hyperactive children during play and task situations. *Child and Family Behavior Therapy, 5,* 1–14.

Mash, E. J., & Johnston, C. (1990). Determinants of parenting stress: Illustrations from families of hyperactive children and families of physically abused children. *Journal of Clinical Child Psychology, 19,* 313–328.

Mash, E. J., Terdal, L., & Anderson, K. (1973). The Response Class Matrix: A procedure for recording parent–child interactions. *Journal of Consulting and Clinical Psychology, 40,* 163–164.

Matier-Sharma, K., Perachio, N., Newcorn, J. H., Sharma, V., & Halperin, J. M. (1995). Differential diagnosis of ADHD: Are objective measures of attention, impulsivity, and activity level helpful? *Child Neuropsychology, 1,* 118–127.

Matson, J. L., Rotatori, A. F., & Helsel, W. J. (1983). Development of a rating scale to measure social skills in children: The Matson Evaluation of Social Skills with Youngsters (MESSY). *Behaviour Research and Therapy, 21,* 335–340.

Mattes, J. A. (1980). The role of frontal lobe dysfunction in childhood hyperkinesis. *Comprehensive Psychiatry, 21,* 358–369.

Mattes, J. A., & Gittelman, R. (1981). Effects of artificial food colorings in children with hyperactive symptoms. *Archives of General Psychiatry, 38,* 714–718.

Maurer, R. G., & Stewart, M. (1980). Attention Deficit Disorder without Hyperactivity in a child psychiatry clinic. *Journal of Clinical Psychiatry, 41,* 232–233.

McCarney, S. B. (1989). *Attention Deficit Disorders Evaluation Scale* (ADDES). Columbia, MO: Hawthorne Educational Services.

McClure, F. D., & Gordon, M. (1984). Performance of disturbed hyperactive and nonhyperactive children on an objective measure of hyperactivity. *Journal of Abnormal Child Psychology, 12,* 561– 572.

McGee, R., & Feehan, M. (1991). Are girls with problems of attention under-recognized? *Journal of Psychopathology and Behavioral Assessment, 13,* 187–198.

McGee, R., Williams, S., & Silva, P. A. (1984a). Behavioral and developmental characteristics of aggressive, hyperactive, and aggressive–hyperactive boys. *Journal of the American Academy of Child Psychiatry, 23,* 270–279.

McGee, R., Williams, S., & Silva, P. A. (1984b). Background characteristics of aggressive, hyperactive, and aggressive–hyperactive boys. *Journal of the American Academy of Child and Adolescent Psychiatry, 23,* 280–284.

Messer, S., & Brodzinsky, D. M. (1981). Three year stability of reflection–impulsivity in young adolescents. *Developmental Psychology, 17,* 848–850.

Michon, J. (1985). Introduction. In J. Michon & T. Jackson (Eds.), *Time, mind, and behavior* (pp. 27–37). Berlin: Springer-Verlag.

Milar, C. R., Schroeder, S. R., Mushak, P., & Boone, L. (1981). Failure to find hyperactivity in preschool children with moderately elevated lead burden. *Journal of Pediatric Psychology, 6,* 85–95.

Milich, R. (1984). Cross-sectional and longitudinal observations of activity level and sustained attention in a normative sample. *Journal of Abnormal Child Psychology, 12,* 261–276.

Milich, R., Hartung, C. M., Matrin, C. A., & Haigler, E. D. (1994). Behavioral disinhibition and underlying processes in adolescents with disruptive behavior disorders. In D. K. Routh (Ed.), *Disruptive behavior disorders in childhood* (pp. 109–138). New York: Plenum Press.

Milich, R., & Kramer, J. (1984). Reflections on impulsivity: An empirical investigation of impulsivity as a construct. In K. Gadow & I. Bialer (Eds.), *Advances in learning and behavioral disabilities* (Vol. 3, pp. 57–94). Greenwich, CT: JAI Press.

Milich, R., Landau, S., & Loney, J. (1981, August). *The inter-relationships among hyperactivity, aggression, and impulsivity.* Paper presented at the annual meeting of the American Psychological Association, Los Angeles.

Milich, R., & Loney, J. (1979). The role of hyperactive and aggressive symptomatology in predicting adolescent outcome among hyperactive children. *Journal of Pediatric Psychology, 4,* 93–112.

Milich, R., Loney, J., & Landau, S. (1982). The independent dimensions of hyperactivity and aggression: A validation with playroom observation data. *Journal of Abnormal Psychology, 91,* 183–198.

Milich, R., & Lorch, E. P. (1994). Television viewing methodology to understand cognitive processing of ADHD children. In T. H. Ollendick & R. J. Prinz (Eds.), *Advances in clinical child psychology* (Vol. 16, pp. 177–202). New York: Plenum Press.

Milich, R., Wolraich, M., & Lindgren, S. (1986). Sugar and hyperactivity: A critical review of empirical findings. *Clinical Psychology Review, 6,* 493–513.

Mitchell, E. A., Aman, M. G., Turbott, S. H., & Manku, M. (1987). Clinical characteristics and serum essential fatty acid levels in hyperactive children. *Clinical Pediatrics, 26*, 406–411.

Montagu, J., & Swarbrick, L. (1975). Effect of amphetamines in hyperkinetic children: Stimulant or sedative? *Developmental Medicine and Child Neurology, 17*, 293–298.

Morrison, J., & Stewart, M. (1971). A family study of the hyperactive child syndrome. *Biological Psychiatry, 3*, 189–195.

Morrison, J., & Stewart, M. (1973). The psychiatric status of the legal families of adopted hyperactive children. *Archives of General Psychiatry, 28*, 888–891.

Murphy, K. R., & Barkley, R. A. (1996a). ADHD adults: Comorbidities and adaptive impairment. *Comprehensive Psychiatry, 37*, 393–401.

Murphy, K., & Barkley, R. A. (1996b). Prevalence of DSM-IV ADHD symptoms in adult licensed drivers. *Journal of Attention Disorders, 1*, 147–161.

Murphy, K. R., & Barkley, R. A. (1996c). Parents of children with Attention-Deficit/Hyperactivity Disorder: Psychological and attentional impairment. *American Journal of Orthopsychiatry, 66*, 93–102.

Needleman, H. L., Gunnoe, C., Leviton, A., Reed, R., Peresie, H., Maher, C., & Barrett, P. (1979). Deficits in psychologic and classroom performance of children with elevated dentine lead levels. *New England Journal of Medicine, 300*, 689–695.

Newcomb, A. F., Bukowski, W. M., & Pattee, L. (1993). Children's peer relations: A meta-analytic review of popular, rejected, neglected, controversial, and average sociometric status. *Psychological Bulletin, 113*, 99–128.

Nichols, P. L., & Chen, T. C. (1981). *Minimal brain dysfunction: A prospective study.* Hillsdale, NJ: Erlbaum.

Nucci, L. P., & Herman, S. (1982). Behavioral disordered children's conceptions of moral, conventional, and personal issues. *Journal of Abnormal Child Psychology, 10*, 411–426.

O'Leary, K. D., Vivian, D., & Nisi, A. (1985). Hyperactivity in Italy. *Journal of Abnormal Child Psychology, 13*, 485–500.

Palfrey, J. S., Levine, M. D., Walker, D. K., & Sullivan, M. (1985). The emergence of attention deficits in early childhood: A prospective study. *Journal of Developmental and Behavioral Pediatrics, 6*, 339–348.

Parry, P. A., & Douglas, V. I. (1983). Effects of reinforcement on concept identification in hyperactive children. *Journal of Abnormal Child Psychology, 11*, 327–340.

Paternite, C., & Loney, J. (1980). Childhood hyperkinesis: Relationships between symptomatology and home environment. In C. K. Whalen & B. Henker (Eds.), *Hyperactive children: The social ecology of identification and treatment* (pp. 105–141). New York: Academic Press.

Patterson, G. R. (1982). *Coercive family process.* Eugene, OR: Castalia.

Pelham, W. E., & Bender, M. E. (1982). Peer relationships in hyperactive children: Description and treatment. In K. D. Gadow & I. Bialer (Eds.), *Advances in learning and behavioral disabilities* (Vol. 1, pp. 365–436). Greenwich, CT: JAI Press.

Pelham, W. E., Carlson, C., Sams, S. E., Vallano, G., Dixon, M. J., & Hoza, B. (1993). Separate and combined effects of methylphenidate and behavior modification on the classroom behavior and academic performance of ADHD boys: Group effects and individual differences. *Journal of Consulting and Clinical Psychology, 61*, 506–515.

Pelham, W. E., & Hinshaw, S. P. (1992). Behavioral intervention for ADHD. In S. M. Turner, K. S. Calhoun, & H. E. Adams (Eds.), *Handbook of clinical behavior therapy* (2nd ed., pp. 259–283). New York: Wiley.

Pelham, W. E., & Lang, A. R. (1993). Parental alcohol consumption and deviant child behavior: Laboratory studies of reciprocal effects. *Clinical Psychology Review, 13*, 763–784.

Pelham, W. E., & Milich, R. (1991). Measuring ADHD children's response to psychostimulant medication: Prediction and individual differences. In L. L. Greenhill & B. P. Osmon (Eds.), *Ritalin: Theory and patient management* (pp. 203–221). New York: Mary Ann Liebert.

Pelham, W. E., Vodde-Hamilton, M., Murphy, D. A., Greenstein, J., & Vallano, G. (1991). The effects of methylphenidate on ADHD adolescents in recreational, peer group, and classroom settings. *Journal of Clinical Child Psychology, 20*, 301–312.

Pfiffner, L. J., & Barkley, R. A. (1990). Educational placement and classroom management. In R. A. Barkley, *Attention-Deficit Hyperactivity Disorder: A handbook for diagnosis and treatment* (pp. 498–538). New York: Guilford Press.

Pfiffner, L. J., & O'Leary, S. G. (1993). Psychological treatments: School–based. In J. L. Matson (Ed.), *Hyperactivity in children: A handbook* (pp. 234–255). Elmsford, NY: Pergamon Press.

Pisterman, S. McGrath, P., Firestone, P., Goodman, J.T., Mallory, I., & Webster, R. (1989). Parent-mediated treatment of hyperactive preschoolers. *Journal of Consulting and Clinical Psychology, 57*, 628–635.

Pollard, S., Ward, E. M., & Barkley, R. A. (1983). The effects of parent training and Ritalin on the parent–child interactions of hyperactive boys. *Child and Family Therapy, 5*, 51–69.

Porrino, L. J., Rapoport, J. L., Behar, D., Sceery, W., Ismond, D. R., & Bunney, W. E., Jr. (1983). A naturalistic assessment of the motor activity of hyperactive boys. *Archives of General Psychiatry, 40*, 681–687.

Quay, H. C. (1989). The behavioral reward and inhibition systems in childhood behavior disorder. In L. M. Bloomingdale (Ed.), *Attention Deficit Dis-*

order III: New research in treatment, psychophar-macology, and attention (pp. 176–186). Elmsford, NY: Pergamon Press.

Quinn, P. O., & Rapoport, J. L. (1974). Minor physical anomalies and neurological status in hyperactive boys. *Pediatrics, 53,* 742–747.

Rapoport, J. L. (1996, January). *Anatomic magnetic resonance imaging in Attention Deficit Hyperactivity Disorder.* Paper presented at the annual meeting of the International Society for Research in Child and Adolescent Psychopathology, Santa Monica, CA.

Rapoport, J. L., & Benoit, M. (1975). The relation of direct home observations to the clinic evaluation of hyperactive school age boys. *Journal of Child Psychology and Psychiatry, 16,* 141–147.

Rapport, M. D., DuPaul, G. J., & Denny, C. (1993, February). *Methylphenidate effects on behavior and academic functioning in children with ADDH: An empirical examination of dosage effects, outcome probabilities, and normalization rates in 76 children.* Paper presented at the annual meeting of the International Society for Research in Child and Adolescent Psychopathology, Santa Fe, NM.

Rapport, M. D., & Kelly, K. L. (1993). Psychostimulant effects on learning and cognitive function in children with Attention Deficit Hyperactivity Disorder: Findings and implications. In J. L. Matson (Ed.), *Hyperactivity in children: A handbook* (pp. 97–136). Elmsford, NY: Pergamon Press.

Rapport, M. D., Stoner, G., DuPaul, G. J., Birmingham, B. K., & Tucker, S. (1985). Attention Deficit Disorder and methylphenidate: A multilevel analysis of dose–response effects on children's impulsivity across settings. *Journal of the American Academy of Child and Adolescent Psychiatry, 27,* 60–69.

Rapport, M. D., Tucker, S. B., DuPaul, G. J., Merlo, M., & Stoner, G. (1986). Hyperactivity and frustration: The influence of control over and size of rewards in delaying gratification. *Journal of Abnormal Child Psychology, 14,* 181–204.

Reynolds, C., & Kamphaus, R. (1994). *Behavioral Assessment System for Children.* Circle Pines, MN: American Guidance Service.

Rie, H. E., & Rie, E. D. (1980). *Handbook of minimal brain dysfunction.* New York: Wiley.

Roberts, M. A. (1990). A behavioral observation method for differentiating hyperactive and aggressive boys. *Journal of Abnormal Child Psychology, 18,* 131–142.

Robin, A. R. (1990). Training families with ADHD adolescents. In R. A. Barkley, *Attention-Deficit Hyperactivity Disorder: A handbook for diagnosis and treatment* (pp. 462–497). New York: Guilford Press.

Robin, A. R., & Foster, S. (1989). *Negotiating parent–adolescent conflict.* New York: Guilford Press.

Robinson, E. A., & Eyberg, S. M. (1981). The Dyadic Parent–Child Interaction Coding System: Stan-dardization and validation. *Journal of Consulting and Clinical Psychology, 49,* 245–250.

Roizen, N. J., Blondis, T. A., Irwin, M., & Stein, M. (1994). Adaptive functioning in children with Attention-Deficit Hyperactivity Disorder. *Archives of Pediatric and Adolescent Medicine, 148,* 1137–1142.

Rosenthal, R. H., & Allen, T. W. (1978). An examination of attention, arousal, and learning dysfunctions of hyperkinetic children. *Psychological Bulletin, 85,* 689–715.

Rosenthal, R. H., & Allen, T. W. (1980). Intratask distractibility in hyperkinetic and nonhyperkinetic children. *Journal of Abnormal Child Psychology, 8,* 175–187.

Ross, D. M., & Ross, S. A. (1982). *Hyperactivity: Research, theory and action.* New York: Wiley.

Routh, D. K., & Roberts, R. D. (1972). Minimal brain dysfunction in children: Failure to find evidence for a behavioral syndrome. *Psychological Reports, 31,* 307–314.

Routh, D. K., & Schroeder, C. S. (1976). Standardized playroom measures as indices of hyperactivity. *Journal of Abnormal Child Psychology, 4,* 199–207.

Rubinstein, R. A., & Brown, R. T. (1984). An evaluation of the validity of the diagnostic category of Attention Deficit Disorder. *American Journal of Orthopsychiatry, 54,* 398–414.

Rutter, M. (1977). Brain damage syndromes in childhood: Concepts and findings. *Journal of Child Psychology and Psychiatry, 18,* 1–21.

Rutter, M., Chadwick, O., & Shaffer, D. (1983). Head injury. In M. Rutter (Ed.), *Developmental neuropsychiatry* (pp. 83–111). New York: Guilford Press.

Ryan, N. D. (1990). Heterocyclic antidepressants in children and adolescents. *Journal of Child and Adolescent Psychopharmacology, 1,* 21–32.

Safer, D. J., & Allen, R. (1976). *Hyperactive children.* Baltimore: University Park Press.

Sandberg, S. T., Rutter, M., & Taylor, E. (1978). Hyperkinetic disorder in psychiatric clinic attenders. *Developmental Medicine and Child Neurology, 20,* 279–299.

Satterfield, J. H., Satterfield, B. T., & Cantwell, D. P. (1981). Three-year multimodality treatment study of 100 hyperactive boys. *Journal of Pediatrics, 98,* 650–655.

Schachar, R. J., & Logan, G. D. (1990). Impulsivity and inhibitory control in normal development and childhood psychopathology. *Developmental Psychology, 26,* 710–720.

Schachar, R. J., Rutter, M., & Smith, A. (1981). The characteristics of situationally and pervasively hyperactive children: Implications for syndrome definition. *Journal of Child Psychology and Psychiatry, 22,* 375–392.

Schachar, R. J., Tannock, R., & Logan, G. (1993). Inhibitory control, impulsiveness, and Attention Deficit Hyperactivity Disorder. *Clinical Psychology Review, 13,* 721–740.

Schaefer, C. E., & Briesmeister, J. M. (1989). *Handbook of parent training*. New York: Wiley.

Sergeant, J. (1988). From DSM–III Attention Deficit Disorder to functional defects. In L. Bloomingdale & J. Sergeant (Eds.), *Attention Deficit Disorder: Criteria, cognition, and intervention* (pp. 183–198). Elmsford, NY: Pergamon Press.

Sergeant, J., & Scholten, C. A. (1985a). On data limitations in hyperactivity. *Journal of Child Psychology and Psychiatry, 26,* 111–124.

Sergeant, J., & Scholten, C. A. (1985b). On resource strategy limitations in hyperactivity: Cognitive impulsivity reconsidered. *Journal of Child Psychology and Psychiatry, 26,* 97–109.

Sergeant, J., & van der Meere, J. J. (1989). The diagnostic significance of attentional processing: Its significance for ADDH classification in a future DSM. In T. Sagvolden & T. Archer (Eds.), *Attention Deficit Disorder: Clinical and basic research* (pp. 151–166). Hillsdale, NJ: Erlbaum.

Shaywitz, B. A., Shaywitz, S. E., Byrne, T., Cohen, D. J., & Rothman, S. (1983). Attention Deficit Disorder: Quantitative analysis of CT. *Neurology, 33,* 1500–1503.

Shaywitz, S. E., Cohen, D. J., & Shaywitz, B. A. (1978). The biochemical basis of minimal brain dysfunction. *Journal of Pediatrics, 92,* 179–187.

Shaywitz, S. E., Cohen, D. J., & Shaywitz, B. E. (1980). Behavior and learning difficulties in children of normal intelligence born to alcoholic mothers. *Journal of Pediatrics, 96,* 978–982.

Shaywitz, S. E., Shaywitz, B. A., Cohen, D. J., & Young, J. G. (1983). Monoaminergic mechanisms in hyperactivity. In M. Rutter (Ed.), *Developmental neuropsychiatry* (pp. 330–347). New York: Guilford Press.

Silva, P. A., Hughes, P., Williams, S., & Faed, J. M. (1988). Blood lead, intelligence, reading attainment, and behaviour in eleven year old children in Dunedin, New Zealand. *Journal of Child Psychology and Psychiatry, 29,* 43–52.

Simmel, C., & Hinshaw, S. P. (1993, March). *Moral reasoning and antisocial behavior in boys with ADHD.* Poster presented at the biennial meeting of the Society for Research in Child Development, New Orleans.

Skinner, B. F. (1953). *Science and human behavior.* New York: Macmillan.

Sleator, E. K., & Ullmann, R. K. (1981). Can the physician diagnose hyperactivity in the office? *Pediatrics, 67,* 13–17.

Smith, L. (1976). *Your child's behavior chemistry.* New York: Random House.

Shekim, W., Asarnow, R. F., Hess, E., Zaucha, K., & Wheeler, N. (1990). An evaluation of attention deficit disorder—residual type. *Comprehensive Psychiatry, 31,* 416–425.

Sparrow, S. S., Balla, D. A., & Cicchetti, D. V. (1984). *Vineland Adaptive Behavior Scales.* Circle Pines, MN: American Guidance Service.

Steinkamp, M. W. (1980). Relationships between environmental distractions and task performance of hyperactive and normal children. *Journal of Learning Disabilities, 13,* 40–45.

Stevenson, J. (1994, June). *Genetics of ADHD.* Paper presented at the meeting of the Professional Group for ADD and Related Disorders, London.

Stewart, M. A., Thach, B. T., & Friedin, M. R. (1970). Accidental poisoning and the hyperactive child syndrome. *Diseases of the Nervous System, 31,* 403–407.

Still, G. F. (1902). Some abnormal psychical conditions in children. *Lancet, i,* 1008–1012, 1077–1082, 1163–1168.

Strauss, A. A., & Lehtinen, L. E. (1947). *Psychopathology and education of the brain-injured child.* New York: Grune & Stratton.

Streissguth, A. P., Martin, D. C., Barr, H. M., Sandman, B. M., Kirchner, G. L., & Darby, B. L. (1984). Intrauterine alcohol and nicotine exposure: Attention and reaction time in 4-year-old children. *Developmental Psychology, 20,* 533–541.

Stroop, J. P. (1935). Studies of interference in serial verbal reactions. *Journal of Experimental Psychology, 18,* 643–662.

Stuss, D. T., & Benson, D. F. (1986). *The frontal lobes.* New York: Raven Press.

Swanson, J. M., McBurnett, K., Christian, D. L., & Wigal, T. (1995). Stimulant medications and the treatment of children with ADHD. In T. H. Ollendick & R. J. Prinz (Eds.), *Advances in clinical child psychology* (Vol. 17, pp. 265–321). New York: Plenum Press.

Swanson, J., & Pelham, W. E. (1988). *A rating scale for the diagnosis of Attention Deficit Disorders: Teacher norms and reliability.* Unpublished manuscript, University of Pittsburgh, Western Psychiatric Institute and Clinics.

Szatmari, P. (1992, October). The epidemiology of Attention-Deficit Hyperactivity Disorders. *Child and Adolescent Psychiatric Clinics of North America, 1*(2), 361–372.

Tallmadge, J., & Barkley, R. A. (1983). The interactions of hyperactive and normal boys with their mothers and fathers. *Journal of Abnormal Child Psychology, 11,* 565–579.

Tannock, R. (in press). Attention Deficit Disorders with anxiety disorders. In T. E. Brown (Ed.), *Subtypes of Attention Deficit Disorders in children, adolescents, and adults.* Washington, DC: American Psychiatric Press.

Tarver-Behring, S., Barkley, R. A., & Karlsson, J. (1985). The mother–child interactions of hyperactive boys and their normal siblings. *American Journal of Orthopsychiatry, 55,* 202–209.

Taylor, E. A. (1983). Drug response and diagnostic validation. In M. Rutter (Ed.), *Developmental neuropsychiatry* (pp. 348–368). New York: Guilford Press.

Taylor, E. A., Sandberg, S., Thorley, G., & Giles, S. (1991). *The epidemiology of childhood hyperactivity.* London: Oxford University Press.

Taylor, J. F. (1980). *The hyperactive child and the family.* New York: Random House.

Teicher, M. H., Ito, Y., Glod, C. A., & Barber, N. I. (1996). Objective measurement of hyperactivity and attentional problems in ADHD. *Journal of the American Academy of Child and Adolescent Psychiatry, 35,* 334–342.

Thorley, G. (1984). Review of follow-up and follow-back studies of childhood hyperactivity. *Psychological Bulletin, 96,* 116–132.

Torgesen, J. K. (1994). Issues in the assessment of of executive function: An information-processing perspective. In G. R. Lyon (Ed.), *Frames of reference for the assessment of learning disabilities: New views on measurement issues* (pp. 143–162). Baltimore: Paul H. Brookes.

Trites, R. L., Dugas, F., Lynch, G., & Ferguson, B. (1979). Incidence of hyperactivity. *Journal of Pediatric Psychology, 4,* 179–188.

Trites, R. L., Tryphonas, H., & Ferguson, H. B. (1980). Diet treatment for hyperactive children with food allergies. In R. Knight & D. Bakker (Eds.), *Treatment of hyperactive and learning disordered children* (pp. 151–166). Baltimore: University Park Press.

Tryon, W. W. (1984). Principles and methods of mechanically measuring motor activity. *Behavioral Assessment, 6,* 129–140.

Ullman, D. G., Barkley, R. A., & Brown, H. W. (1978). The behavioral symptoms of hyperkinetic children who successfully responded to stimulant drug treatment. *American Journal of Orthopsychiatry, 48,* 425–437.

Ullmann, R., Sleator, E., & Sprague, R. (1984). A new rating scale for diagnosis and monitoring of ADD children. *Psychopharmacology Bulletin, 20,* 160–164.

Voelker, S. L., Carter, R. A., Sprague, D. J., Gdowski, C. L., & Lachar, D. (1989). Developmental trends in memory and metamemory in children with Attention Deficit Disorder. *Journal of Pediatric Psychology, 14,* 75–88.

Wahler, R. G. (1980). The insular mother: Her problems in parent–child treatment. *Journal of Applied Behavior Analysis, 13,* 207–219.

Wahler, R. G., House, A. E., & Stambaugh, E. E. (1976). *Ecological assessment of child problem behavior.* Elmsford, NY: Pergamon Press.

Weiss, G. (Ed.). (1992, October). Attention-Deficit Hyperactivity Disorder [Special issue]. *Child and Adolescent Psychiatry Clinics of North America, 1*(2).

Weiss, G., & Hechtman, L. T. (1993). *Hyperactive children grown up* (2nd ed.): *ADHD in children, adolescents, and adults.* New York: Guilford Press.

Weiss, G., Hechtman, L., Milroy, T., & Perlman, T. (1985). Psychiatric status of hyperactives as adults: A controlled prospective 15 year follow up of 63 hyperactive children. *Journal of the American Academy of Child Psychiatry, 23,* 211–220.

Weiss, G., Hechtman, L., & Perlman, T. (1978). Hyperactives as young adults: School, employer, and self-rating scales obtained during ten-year follow-up evaluation. *American Journal of Orthopsychiatry, 48,* 438–445.

Weiss, G., Hechtman, L., Perlman, T., Hopkins, J., & Wener, A. (1979). Hyperactives as young adults: A controlled prospective ten-year follow-up of 75 children. *Archives of General Psychiatry, 36,* 675–681.

Welner, Z., Welner, A., Stewart, M., Palkes, H., & Wish, E. (1977). A controlled study of siblings of hyperactive children. *Journal of Nervous and Mental Disease, 165,* 110–117.

Welsh, M. C., & Pennington, B. F. (1988). Assessing frontal lobe functioning in children: Views from developmental psychology. *Developmental Neuropsychology, 4,* 199–230.

Wender, P. H. (1971). *Minimal brain dysfunction in children.* New York: Wiley.

Wender, P. H., Reimherr, F. W., & Wood, D. R. (1981). Attention Deficit Disorder ("minimal brain dysfunction") in adults: A replication study of diagnosis and drug treatment. *Archives of General Psychiatry, 38,* 449–456.

Werry, J. S., Elkind, G. S., & Reeves, J. S. (1987). Attention deficit, conduct, oppositional, and anxiety disorders in children: III. Laboratory differences. *Journal of Abnormal Child Psychology, 15,* 409–428.

Werry, J. S., Weiss, G., & Douglas, V. (1964). Studies on the hyperactive child: I. Some preliminary findings. *Canadian Psychiatric Association Journal, 9,* 120–130.

Whalen, C. K., & Henker, B. (1980). *Hyperactive children: The social ecology of identification and treatment.* New York: Academic Press.

Whalen, C. K., Henker, B., Buhrmester, D., Hinshaw, S. P., Huber, A., & Laski, K. (1989). Does stimulant medication improve the peer status of hyperactive children? *Journal of Consulting and Clinical Psychology, 57,* 535–549.

Whalen, C. K., Henker, B., & Dotemoto, S. (1980). Methylphenidate and hyperactivity: Effects on teacher behaviors. *Science, 208,* 1280–1282.

Whalen, C. K., Henker, B., & Hinshaw, S. P. (1985). Cognitive-behavioral therapies for hyperactive children: Premises, problems, and prospects. *Journal of Abnormal Child Psychology, 13,* 391–410.

Willerman, L. (1973). Activity level and hyperactivity in twins. *Child Development, 44,* 288–293.

Willis, T. J., & Lovaas, I. (1977). A behavioral approach to treating hyperactive children: The parent's role. In J. B. Millichap (Ed.), *Learning disabilities and related disorders* (pp. 119–140). Chicago: Year Book Medical.

Wolraich, M., Milich, R., Stumbo, P., & Schultz, F. (1985). The effects of sucrose ingestion on the behavior of hyperactive boys. *Pediatrics, 106,* 675–682.

Wolraich, M., Wilson, D. B., & White, J. W. (1995). The effect of sugar on behavior or cognition in children. *Journal of the American Medical Association, 274,* 1617–1621.

Wood, D. R., Reimherr, F. W., Wender, P. H., & Johnson, G. E. (1976). Diagnosis and treatment of minimal brain dysfunction in adults. *Archives of General Psychiatry, 33,* 1453–1460.

Zagar, R., & Bowers, N. D. (1983). The effect of time of day on problem–solving and classroom behavior. *Psychology in the Schools, 20,* 337–345.

Zahn, T. P., Krusei, M. J. P., & Rapoport, J. L. (1991). Reaction time indices of attention deficits in boys with disruptive behavior disorders. *Journal of Abnormal Child Psychology, 19,* 233–252.

Zametkin, A. J., Liebenauer, L. L., Fitzgerald, G. A., King, A. C., Minkunas, D. V., Herscovitch, P., Yamada, E. M., & Cohen, R. M. (1993). Brain metabolism in teenagers with Attention-Deficit Hyperactivity Disorder. *Archives of General Psychiatry, 50,* 333–340.

Zametkin, A. J., Nordahl, T. E., Gross, M., King, A. C., Semple, W. E., Rumsey, J., Hamburger, S., & Cohen, R. (1990). Cerebral glucose metabolism in adults with hyperactivity of childhood onset. *New England Journal of Medicine, 323,* 1361–1366.

Zentall, S. S. (1985). A context for hyperactivity. In K. Gadow & I. Bialer (Eds.), *Advances in learning and behavioral disabilities* (Vol. 4, pp. 273–343). Greenwich, CT: JAI Press.

Zentall, S. S. (1988). Production deficiencies in elicited language but not in the spontaneous verbalizations of hyperactive children. *Journal of Abnormal Child Psychology, 16,* 657–673.

Zentall, S. S., & Smith, Y. S. (1993). Mathematical performance and behaviour of children with hyperactivity with and without coexisting aggression. *Behaviour Research and Therapy, 31,* 701–710.

Chapter Three

CONDUCT PROBLEMS

Robert J. McMahon
Annette M. Estes

Conduct problems in children constitute a broad range of "acting-out" behaviors, ranging from annoying but relatively minor behaviors such as yelling, whining, and temper tantrums to aggression, physical destructiveness, and stealing. Typically, these behaviors do not occur in isolation but as a complex or syndrome, and there is strong evidence to suggest that oppositional behaviors (e.g., noncompliance, argumentativeness) are developmental precursors to more serious forms of antisocial behavior. When displayed as a cluster, these behaviors have been referred to as "oppositional," "antisocial," and "conduct-disordered" (see Hinshaw & Anderson, 1996, for a thorough discussion of terminology). In this chapter, we use the term "conduct problems" (CP) to refer to this constellation of behaviors. Terminology from the *Diagnostic and Statistical Manual of Mental Disorders* (DSM; American Psychiatric Association, 1980, 1987, 1994) is used only in those instances in which a formal DSM diagnosis is being discussed or referred to (e.g., Conduct Disorder [CD] or Oppositional Defiant Disorder [ODD]).

The primary purpose of this chapter is to present and critically evaluate the procedures currently used to assess CP in children. We first present brief descriptions of CP, associated characteristics, and developmental pathways. We also discuss various associated child characteristics, familial and peer influences, and broader contextual influences. Careful assessment of these factors is essential in dealing with children with CP.

CONDUCT PROBLEMS IN CHILDREN AND ADOLESCENTS

Epidemiology

The prevalence of CP in both the general population and clinic-referred samples suggests the importance of developing and evaluating effective methods and approaches for the assessment of children with these problems. CP is among the most frequently occurring child behavior disorders, with prevalence rates ranging from 2% to 9% for CD and 6% to 10% for ODD in various nonclinic samples (as summarized in Costello, 1990). Children with CP also make up the largest single source of referrals to outpatient and inpatient child mental health settings, accounting for one-third to one-half of referrals (Kazdin, 1995b; Sholevar & Sholevar, 1995). Prevalence rates have been shown to vary as a function of age and sex of the child, as well as the type of CP behavior. For example, younger children are more likely to engage in oppositional behaviors, whereas older children and adolescents are more likely to engage in more covert CP behaviors (e.g., stealing). In general, boys are more likely to begin engaging in overt CP behaviors earlier and at higher rates than girls throughout the developmental period. During adolescence, gender differences in prevalence decrease dramatically; this seems to be largely accounted for by an increase in the number of girls engaging in covert CP behaviors.

With respect to the course of CP, it is important to differentiate between single behaviors engaged in by large numbers of nonreferred children (e.g., temper tantrums) and the constellation of behaviors that constitute the CP syndrome. Studies of nonreferred children indicate that many children exhibit individual CP behaviors at some point in their childhood and adolescence (e.g., Achenbach, 1991b; Campbell, 1995).

The stability of CP has been well established over both short- and long-term intervals, and in epidemiological community samples and clinic-referred samples in the United States and in other countries. There is a high degree of continuity in CP behaviors from early childhood to later childhood (e.g., Campbell, 1995), from childhood to adolescence (e.g., Lahey et al., 1995; Offord et al., 1992), and from adolescence to adulthood (e.g., Farrington, 1995; Rutter, Harrington, Quinton, & Pickles, 1994). There is also evidence for cross-generational consistency (Huesmann, Eron, Lefkowitz, & Walder, 1984). Stability also appears comparable for boys and girls (Coie & Dodge, in press).

Classification

There are a number of current approaches to the description and classification of CP behavior. In the DSM-IV (American Psychiatric Association, 1994), the two diagnostic categories that are most relevant to CP (ODD and CD) are described as Disruptive Behavior Disorders in the manual. The essential feature of ODD is a "recurrent pattern of negativistic, defiant, disobedient, and hostile behavior toward authority figures" (p. 91). The pattern of behavior must have a duration of at least 6 months, and at least four of the following eight behaviors must be present: losing temper, arguing with grownups, actively defying or not complying with grownups' rules or requests, deliberately doing things that annoy other people, blaming others for own mistakes, being touchy or easily becoming annoyed by others, exhibiting anger and resentment, and showing spite or vindictiveness. The behaviors must have a higher frequency than is generally seen in other children of similar developmental level and age. Furthermore, the behaviors must lead to meaningful impairment in academic and social functioning.

The essential feature of CD is a "repetitive and persistent pattern of behavior in which the basic rights of others or major age-appropriate societal norms or rules are violated" (American Psychiatric Association, 1994, p. 85). At least 3 of the 15 behaviors listed below must have been present in the past 12 months, with at least one of the behav-

iors present in the past 6 months. The behaviors are categorized into four groups: aggressiveness to people and animals (bullying, fighting, using a weapon, physical cruelty to people, physical cruelty to animals, stealing with confrontation of victim, forced sexual activity); property destruction (fire setting, other destruction of property); deceptiveness or theft (breaking and entering, lying for personal gain, stealing without confronting victim); and serious rule violations (staying out at night [before age 13], running away from home, being truant [before age 13]).

Two subtypes of CD are described in the DSM-IV; these are differentiated on the basis of the child's age at the appearance of the first symptom of CD. The Childhood-Onset Type is defined by the onset of at least 1 of the 15 behaviors prior to 10 years of age, whereas CD behavior does not appear until age 10 or older in the Adolescent-Onset Type. The severity of CD (Mild, Moderate, or Severe) may also be noted, based on the number of behaviors and their relative seriousness. Although ODD includes behaviors (e.g., noncompliance) that are also included in CD, it does not involve the more serious behaviors that represent violations of either the basic rights of others or age-appropriate societal norms or rules. Thus, if a child meets the diagnostic criteria for both disorders, only the diagnosis of CD is made.

The diagnosis of Disruptive Behavior Disorder Not Otherwise Specified may be used in situations in which a child presents with a number of oppositional or conduct-disordered behaviors, but these behaviors do not meet the frequency criteria specified in the DSM-IV for ODD or CD. Similarly, a coding of Child or Adolescent Antisocial Behavior may be employed in situations in which a child has engaged in more isolated acts of antisocial behavior, rather than the pattern of such activities specified for CD.

Field trials for assessing the psychometric properties of the DSM-IV diagnoses of ODD and CD have demonstrated that the internal-consistency and test–retest reliabilities of the DSM-IV versions are higher than those of their DSM-III-R counterparts (Lahey et al., 1994). Furthermore, agreement with clinicians' validating diagnoses is slightly improved for DSM-IV ODD and CD. The validity of the Childhood-Onset and Adolescent-Onset Types of CD has also been supported, in that children with the Childhood-Onset Type were more likely to display more aggressive symptoms, to be boys, and to receive additional diagnoses of ODD and Attention-Deficit/Hyperactivity Disorder (ADHD) (Waldman & Lahey, 1994). This is consistent with other data supporting this distinction (see below).

Multivariate statistical approaches to classification have identified other dimensions on which CP behaviors can be subtyped, in addition to age of onset. Loeber and Schmaling (1985a) have proposed a bipolar unidimensional typology of "overt" and "covert" CP behaviors. Overt CP behaviors include those that involve direct confrontation with or disruption of the environment (e.g., aggression, temper tantrums, argumentativeness), whereas covert CP behaviors include those that usually occur without the awareness of adult caretakers (e.g., lying, stealing, fire setting). In a recent extension of this investigation, Frick et al. (1993) conducted a meta-analysis of 60 factor analyses with more than 28,000 children. They identified a similar "overt–covert" dimension, but also extracted a second bipolar dimension of "destructive–nondestructive." When individual CP behaviors were plotted, four subtypes were obtained: "property violations," "aggression," "status violations," and "oppositional" (see Figure 3.1). Symptoms of CD fall into the first three quadrants, whereas symptoms of ODD fall into the fourth quadrant. Cluster analyses of an independent sample of clinic-referred boys aged 7–12 indicated one group of boys who displayed high elevations on the oppositional quadrant score and moderate elevations on the aggression quadrant score, and another group of boys who showed high elevations on the property violations, oppositional, and aggression quadrant scores. These clusters approximated those groups of boys who received diagnoses of ODD and CD, respectively.

There is evidence that various family-related risk factors vary as a function of the extent to which CP behavior is overt, covert, or a combination of the two (Forehand, Long, & Hedrick, 1987; Kazdin, 1992; Loeber & Schmaling, 1985b). For example, Loeber and Schmaling found that families with boys who engaged either primarily in overt CP or both overt and covert CP were more likely to demonstrate poorer monitoring skills and to have rejecting mothers than families in which the boys engaged in neither overt nor covert CP.

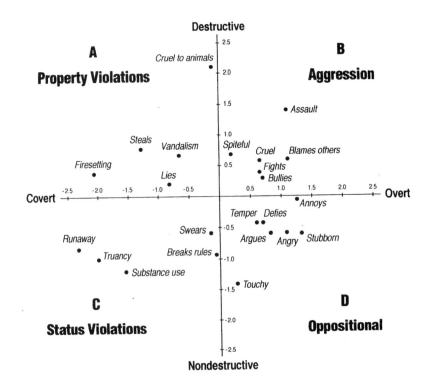

FIGURE 3.1. Meta-analysis of parent and teacher ratings of child conduct problems using multidimensional scaling. From Frick et al. (1993, p. 327). Copyright 1993 by Elsevier Science Ltd. Reprinted by permission.

Focusing specifically on aggressive behavior, Dodge (1991; Dodge & Coie, 1987) has distinguished between "reactive" and "proactive" forms of aggression. The former is a response to perceived provocation, whereas the latter occurs as a means of obtaining some self-serving outcome. Differential responses from teachers and peers have been noted as a function of these subtypes (e.g., Day, Bream, & Pal, 1992), although many aggressive children display both types of aggression (Dodge & Coie, 1987).

Noncompliance (i.e., excessive disobedience to adults) appears to be a keystone behavior in the development of both overt and covert CP. Loeber and Schmaling (1985a) found that noncompliance is positioned near the zero point of their unidimensional overt–covert scale of CP behaviors. Patterson and colleagues (e.g., Chamberlain & Patterson, 1995; Patterson, Reid, & Dishion, 1992) have developed a comprehensive theoretical model for the development and maintenance of CP; in their model, early child noncompliance not only is the precursor of severe manifestations of CP behaviors later in childhood and adolescence, but plays a role in these children's subsequent academic and peer relationship problems as well. There is also empirical support for the premise that noncompliance appears early in the progression of CP, and continues to be manifested in subsequent developmental periods (e.g., Edelbrock, 1985; Loeber et al., 1993; Patterson et al., 1992). Low levels of compliance are also associated with referral for services in children with CP (Dumas, 1996). Furthermore, intervention research has shown that when child noncompliance is targeted, there is often concomitant improvement in other CP behaviors as well (Russo, Cataldo, & Cushing, 1981; Wells, Forehand, & Griest, 1980).

Associated/Comorbid Conditions

Children with CP are at increased risk for manifesting a variety of other behavior disorders and adjustment problems as well. These include ADHD; various internalizing disorders, such as anxiety and depressive disorders and Somatization Disorder (e.g., Loeber & Keenan, 1994); substance use disorders; psychopathy (Frick, O'Brien, Wootton, & McBurnett, 1994); and academic underachievement (Hinshaw, 1992). In their review of the relationship of CP to various comorbid conditions, Loeber and Keenan (1994) have stressed the importance of considering the temporal ordering of comorbid conditions, as well as the different pat-

terns and influences of these comorbid disorders for boys versus girls. Although girls are less likely to display CP than are boys, when girls do display CP, they may be more likely than boys to develop one or more of these comorbid disorders.

ADHD is the comorbid condition most commonly associated with CP, and is thought to precede the development of CP in the majority of cases. In fact, some investigators consider ADHD (or, more specifically, the impulsivity or hyperactivity components of ADHD) to be the "motor" that drives the development of early-onset CP, especially for boys (e.g., Coie & Dodge, in press; Loeber & Keenan, 1994; White et al., 1994). Coexisting ADHD also predicts a more negative life outcome than does CP alone (see Abikoff & Klein, 1992, and Hinshaw, Lahey, & Hart, 1993, for reviews).

Internalizing disorders, such as the depressive and anxiety disorders and Somatization Disorder, also co-occur with CP at rates higher than expected by chance (see Zoccolillo, 1992). In most cases, CP precedes the onset of depressive symptoms (Loeber & Keenan, 1994), although in some cases depression may precipitate CP behavior (e.g., Kovacs, Paulauskas, Gatsonis, & Richards, 1988). Risk for suicidality has also been shown to increase as a function of preexisting CP (e.g., Capaldi, 1991, 1992), and this risk appears to be higher for girls than for boys (Loeber & Keenan, 1994).

The picture for anxiety disorders and Somatization Disorder is somewhat less clear. Loeber and Keenan (1994) indicate that anxiety disorders do co-occur with CP at a greater than chance level, especially for girls. In some studies, boys with CP and a comorbid anxiety disorder are less seriously impaired than are children with CP alone (e.g., J. L. Walker et al., 1991); in other studies, the presence of a comorbid anxiety disorder has not been shown to have a differential effect (e.g., Campbell & Ewing, 1990). A separate but related body of research on shy/withdrawn children who also display CP behaviors suggests that they may be at increased risk for negative life outcomes than children who display only CP (e.g., McCord, 1988; Serbin, Moskowitz, Schwartzman, & Ledingham, 1991). Somatization Disorder has been shown to co-occur in some adolescents with CP (Lilienfeld, 1992). Although the base rate of this disorder alone is much higher in girls than in boys, its comorbid occurrence with CP may actually be higher in boys (Offord, Alder, & Boyle, 1986). To date, there is very little information concerning the role of Somatization Disorder in the development and maintenance of CP.

As noted above, substance use has been associated with a history of CP. Although not all youth who use substances have a history of CP, both longitudinal and cross-sectional studies have documented that preexisting CP constitutes a significant risk factor for substance use (e.g., Hawkins, Catalano, & Miller, 1992; Loeber, 1988). This may be particularly true for girls (Loeber & Keenan, 1994). In addition, concurrent substance use may increase the risk of more serious delinquent behavior (Loeber & Keenan, 1994).

Psychopathy, which is characterized by superficial charm, lack of concern for others, lack of guilt, and absence of anxiety, has recently been investigated in samples of school-age children by Frick and his colleagues (Frick et al., 1994; O'Brien & Frick, 1996). CP and psychopathy were moderately correlated, but they displayed differential associations on a number of variables. Psychopathy was positively associated with sensation seeking and negatively correlated with anxiety, whereas CP was not associated with sensation seeking and was positively correlated with anxiety. O'Brien and Frick (1996) demonstrated that a "reward-dominant" response style (in which behavior is more dependent on rewards than on avoidance of punishment) was associated with psychopathy, regardless of CP status. Children with ODD or CD who also displayed psychopathic characteristics were more likely to have a positive paternal arrest history than were either children with ODD or CD alone or children without ODD or CD who displayed psychopathic characteristics (67% vs. 21% and 11%, respectively) (Frick et al., 1994).

An association between CP and academic underachievement has long been noted. In a comprehensive review, Hinshaw (1992) concluded that during preadolescence, this relationship is actually a function of comorbid ADHD, rather than of CP per se. In adolescence, the relationship is more complex, with preexisting ADHD (and perhaps other neuropsychological deficits), a history of academic difficulty and failure, and long-standing socialization difficulties with family and peers all playing interacting roles.

Developmental Progressions

The preceding description of CP and various comorbid conditions fails to convey three different but related considerations that must guide assessment and intervention procedures for children with CP: the developmental, contextual, and transactional aspects of CP. With respect to developmental considerations, it is clear that the behavioral manifestation of CP (as well as the base rates of various comorbid disorders) changes over time. With respect to context, the development and maintenance of CP are influenced by genetic/constitutional characteristics of the child (e.g., temperament), family (parent–child interaction, parenting practices and social cognition, parental personal and marital adjustment), peers (the "deviant peer group"), and broader ecologies (the school, neighborhood, and community). Ethnicity and cultural considerations may also apply to these contexts. By "transactional," we mean that these developmental and contextual processes unfold over time and continuously influence one another.

Space considerations preclude an extensive description of the roles these various developmental, contextual, and transactional influences play in the development and maintenance of CP. Instead, we present summary descriptions of two developmental progressions of CP as a means of illustrating many of these influences.[1] The reader is referred to several recent excellent reviews on CP for more extensive treatment of these issues (Coie & Dodge, in press; Dishion, French, & Patterson, 1995; Hinshaw & Anderson, 1996; Kazdin, 1995b; Moffitt, 1993).

Numerous longitudinal studies have now examined the developmental course of CP (see McMahon, 1994, for a review). These investigations have been conducted with various types of samples (e.g., community-based epidemiological, high-risk, clinic-referred) and for varying lengths of follow-up (i.e., 1 to 30 years or more). It is becoming increasingly accepted that multiple pathways lead to the display of CP behaviors during childhood and adolescence (and, in many cases, into adulthood). However, current thinking is that there are at least two different primary pathways for the development of serious CP in childhood and adolescence: the "early-starter" and "late-starter" pathways.

Early-Starter Pathway

The most thoroughly delineated pathway, and the one that seems to have the most negative long-term prognosis, has been variously referred to as the "early-starter" (Patterson, Capaldi, & Bank, 1991), "childhood-onset" (Hinshaw et al., 1993), "life-course-persistent" (Moffitt, 1993), or "aggressive-versatile" (Loeber, 1988) pathway. The Childhood-Onset Type of CD in DSM-IV would seem to be a likely diagnostic outcome of this pathway.

The early-starter pathway is characterized by the onset of CP in the preschool and early school-age years, and by a high degree of continuity throughout childhood and into adolescence and adulthood. It is thought that these children progress from relatively less serious (e.g., noncompliance, temper tantrums) to more serious (e.g., aggression, stealing, substance abuse) CP behaviors over time; that overt behaviors (e.g., defiance, fighting) appear earlier than covert behaviors (e.g., lying, stealing); and that later CP behaviors expand the children's behavioral repertoire rather than replacing earlier behaviors (Edelbrock, 1985; Frick et al., 1993; Lahey & Loeber, 1994). Furthermore, there is an expansion of the settings in which the CP behaviors occur over time, from the home to other settings such as the school and the broader community. Thus, although there is a high degree of continuity across the developmental period, the specific behaviors manifested will change as a function of a child's developmental stage and of particular opportunities presented in the child's environment (Moffitt, 1993).

There is a growing body of evidence concerning the many individual, familial, and broader contextual factors that may increase the likelihood of a child's entering and progressing along the early-starter pathway. As noted above, a number of researchers have proposed that early hyperactivity is a significant (and perhaps necessary) risk factor for the early-starter pathway (e.g., Loeber & Keenan, 1994; Moffitt, 1993). Certainly, there is ample evidence that children who display both CP and hyperactivity display more serious and higher levels of CP, and that they have a poorer prognosis than do children with CP or hyperactivity only (see reviews by Abikoff & Klein, 1992, and Hinshaw et al., 1993). Moffitt (1993) has described a process by which hyperactivity may develop. She posits that subtle neuropsychological variations in the infant's central nervous system increase the likelihood that the infant will be "temperamentally difficult," displaying characteristics such as irritability, hyperactivity, impulsivity, and the like.

Although the definitions of the constructs of "temperament" and "temperamental difficulty" appear to be in a state of flux among developmentalists (e.g., Goldsmith et al., 1987), child temperament (usually viewed as involving "constitutionally based individual difference in reactivity and self-regulation"; Rothbart, Posner, & Hershey, 1995, p. 315) has received increased attention from clinicians as a possible contributing factor to CP. Of particular interest is the "temperamentally difficult" child, who is intense, irregular, negative, and nonadaptable from very early in life (Thomas, Chess, & Birch, 1968). Such a child is thought to be predisposed to the development of subsequent behavior problems, because of the increased likelihood of maladaptive parent–child interactions.

Temperament has often been found to have a low to moderate relation to subsequent CP in early and middle childhood (e.g., Bates, Bayles, Bennett, Ridge, & Brown, 1991; Webster-Stratton & Eyberg, 1982) and in late childhood and adolescence (Caspi, Henry, McGee, Moffitt, & Silva, 1995; Olweus, 1980). Olweus found that temperament contributed substantially to the prediction of aggressive behavior in adolescent boys. However, temperament variables did not contribute to the explanatory variance as much as did family variables, such as maternal negativism and permissiveness of aggression. Other investigators have shown that the combination of difficult temperament in infancy with other concurrently measured risk factors, such as maternal perception of difficulty, male gender, prematurity, and low socioeconomic status (SES) (Sanson, Oberklaid, Pedlow, & Prior, 1991) or inappropriate parenting (Bates et al., 1991), is what best predicts subsequent CP.

The development of the child's social-cognitive skills may also be affected by the neuropsychological deficits noted above. Dodge and colleagues (see Coie & Dodge, in press, and Crick & Dodge, 1994, for reviews) have demonstrated that children with CP display a variety of deficits in the processing of social information. For example, children with CP have been shown to have deficits in encoding (e.g., lack of attention to relevant social cues, hypervigilant biases), to make more hostile attributional biases and errors in the interpretation of social cues, to have deficient quantity and quality of generated solutions to social situations, to evaluate aggressive solutions more positively, and to be more likely to decide to engage in aggressive behavior. These deficiencies and biases in social-cognitive skills have been shown to predict the subsequent development of CP in kindergarten, and are associated with parental report of earlier harsh disciplinary practices (Weiss, Dodge, Bates, & Pettit, 1992).

These child characteristics (i.e., difficult temperamental style and deficits in social information processing) may then predispose the child to both the development of an insecure attachment to the parent (Greenberg, Speltz, & DeKlyen, 1993) and a coercive style of parent–child interaction (Patterson et al., 1992). Both of these interaction patterns have been implicated in the development of CP. However, the relationship between insecure (avoidant or ambivalent) patterns of attachment in infancy and later CP has been inconsistent, with high-risk families (e.g., low-SES families, single parents) more likely to exhibit such an association than low-risk families (Greenberg et al., 1993). More recently, Lyons-Ruth (1996) has noted the stronger association between "disorganized" (Main & Solomon, 1990) patterns of infant attachment and subsequent CP. In addition, cross-sectional studies with clinic-referred oppositional children (primarily boys) demonstrated that they were much more likely than nonreferred children to display the preschool analogue of disorganized attachment ("controlling–disorganized" attachment) (Greenberg, Speltz, DeKlyen, & Endriga, 1991; Speltz, Greenberg, & DeKlyen, 1990). Furthermore, ratings of attachment security and separation were powerful discriminators of clinic–nonclinic status (Speltz, DeKlyen, Greenberg, & Dryden, 1995). Attachment researchers (e.g., Greenberg et al., 1993; Lyons-Ruth, 1996) have noted the necessity of adopting a transactional perspective, in that attachment security is probably mediated by other risk or protective factors (e.g., parenting practices, maternal depression, family adversity) over time.

The critical role of parenting practices in the development and maintenance of CP has been well established (see Loeber & Stouthamer-Loeber, 1986; Patterson et al., 1992; and Kendziora & O'Leary, 1992, for reviews). The most comprehensive family-based formulation for the early-starter pathway has been the coercion model developed by Patterson and his colleagues (Patterson, 1982; Patterson et al., 1992; Snyder, 1995). The model describes a process of "basic training" in CP behaviors, which occurs in the context of an escalating cycle of coercive parent–child interactions in the home that begins prior to school entry. The proximal cause for entry into the coercive cycle is thought to be ineffective parental management strategies, particularly in regard to child compliance with parental directives during the preschool period. Child noncompliance is coupled with negative, resistant verbalizations and behavior, which often result in parental withdrawal or failure to follow through with a command. This pattern of negative reinforcement then sets into motion an escalating cycle of reciprocal coercion between parent and child, in which each person is reinforced for increasingly negativistic and/or aggressive behaviors. As this "training" continues over long periods, significant increases in the rate and intensity of these coercive behaviors occur as

family members are reinforced by engaging in aggressive behaviors. Furthermore, the child also observes his or her parents engaging in coercive responses, and this provides the opportunity for modeling of aggression to occur (Patterson, 1982).

The findings from several longitudinal studies are consistent with the coercion model (e.g., Bates et al., 1991; Campbell, 1991, 1995). For example, several studies conducted by Campbell (1991) and her colleagues have shown that high levels of externalizing behavior problems during the preschool period, in conjunction with high levels of negative maternal control in observed parent–child interactions and maternal personal and/or familial distress, predict subsequent externalizing problems several years later.

Various other risk factors that may have an impact on the family and serve to precipitate or maintain child CP have been identified. These include familial factors such as parental social cognitions (e.g., adult attachment style, perceptions of the child), parental personal and marital adjustment, other familial stressors, and certain extrafamilial factors. Less clear are the mechanisms by which these factors exert their effects on CP and on one another, the extent to which child CP may reciprocally influence them, and the role of timing and duration (Kazdin, 1995b). For example, these risk factors may have a direct effect on child CP, or they may exert their effects by disrupting parenting practices (Patterson et al., 1992). In some cases, the "risk" factor may be a *result* of CP, rather than a potential cause. With these caveats in mind, we note some of the relationships of these factors to CP.

Parents of children with CP display more maladaptive social cognitions, and they experience more personal (e.g., depression, antisocial behavior), interparental (marital problems), and extrafamilial (e.g., isolation) distress, than do parents of nonreferred children. It has been suggested that these stressors may interact to impede parental tracking of child behavior and lead to perceptual biases (Wahler & Dumas, 1989). With respect to social cognitions, Johnston (1996a) has proposed a model that places parental cognitions (expectancies, perceptions, and attributions concerning child behavior and sense of parenting efficacy) in a mediational role vis-à-vis parenting behavior. Parents of clinic-referred children with CP are more likely to misperceive child behaviors (Holleran, Littman, Freund, & Schmaling, 1982; Middlebrook & Forehand, 1985; Wahler & Sansbury, 1990), to have fewer positive and more negative family-referent cognitions (Sanders & Dadds,

1992), and to perceive CP behaviors as intentional and to attribute them to stable and global causes (Baden & Howe, 1992). In a nonclinic sample, a similar attributional style has been shown to predict more intense parenting responses (Geller & Johnston, 1995). Sense of parenting efficacy has been shown to relate negatively to child CP in both clinic-referred and nonreferred samples (e.g., Johnston, 1996b; Johnston & Mash, 1989; Roberts, Joe, & Rowe-Hallbert, 1992). In addition, the parents' own insecure adult attachment style has been shown to be related to child CP in both clinic-referred and nonreferred samples (Cowan, Cohn, Cowan, & Pearson, 1996; DeKlyen, 1996).

Maternal depression is related to a broad spectrum of child behavior disorders, including CP (e.g., Cummings & Davies, 1994b; Forehand, Furey, & McMahon, 1984). Some evidence suggests not only that maternal depression may adversely affect the mothers' parenting behavior, but that it may also negatively bias maternal perceptions of children with CP (e.g., Dumas & Serketich, 1994; Fergusson, Lynskey, & Horwood, 1993; Forehand, Lautenschlager, Faust, & Graziano, 1986). However, others have presented evidence suggesting that depressed mothers do not possess a negative perceptual bias in their reports of their children's CP behaviors and that they may be accurate reporters (Richters, 1992). Recent investigators have suggested that chronicity of maternal depression may be particularly related to child CP (Alpern & Lyons-Ruth, 1993; Fergusson & Lynskey, 1993).

Parental antisocial behavior has received increasing attention as both a direct and an indirect influence on the development and maintenance of CP. Links between parental criminality, aggressive behavior, and a diagnosis of Antisocial Personality Disorder (APD) and childhood delinquency, aggression, and CD/ODD diagnoses have been reported by a number of investigators (see Frick & Jackson, 1993, for a review). This association appears specific to CP, occurs more frequently in parents whose children are diagnosed with CD rather than ODD (but see Frick et al., 1993), and is not associated with increased occurrence of ADHD or other child disorders (Frick et al., 1992). Parental APD (in combination with children's lower verbal intelligence) also predicted the persistence of CD over a 4-year period (Lahey et al., 1995). There is some evidence to suggest that parental antisocial behavior may play a more central role than other risk factors in its effect on parenting practices and child CP (e.g., Frick et al., 1992; Patterson & Capaldi, 1991; Patterson et al.,

1992). For example, parenting and marital status were not associated with child CP independently of parental APD (Frick et al., 1992). In a sample of boys at high risk for CP, Patterson et al. (1992) reported that both paternal and maternal (in married and single-parent families) antisocial behavior was negatively correlated with parenting practices; furthermore, parental antisocial behavior mediated the effect of social disadvantage and divorce/remarriage transitions in predicting parenting practices.

Similarly, parental substance abuse has been associated with child CP and substance use, at least partly because of its association with disrupted parenting practices (Dishion, Reid, & Patterson, 1988; Patterson et al., 1992; Wills, Schreibman, Benson, & Vaccaro, 1994). Observations of parent–child interactions in families with parental alcohol problems suggest that the parents are less able to engage their children and are less congenial (Jacob, Krahn, & Leonard, 1991; Whipple, Fitzgerald, & Zucker, 1995). In a review of laboratory studies examining the effects of alcohol consumption on parent–child interaction, Pelham and Lang (1993) concluded not only that alcohol consumption had a deleterious effect on parenting practices, but that the children's inappropriate behavior increased parental alcohol consumption (for parents with a positive family history of alcohol problems) and distress (for all parents).

Marital distress and conflict have been shown to be associated with child CP, negative parenting behavior, and parental perceptions of child maladjustment (Amato & Keith, 1991; Cummings & Davies, 1994a). Several constructs have been identified as potential contributors to CP, including general marital satisfaction (e.g., Bond & McMahon, 1984), marital conflict (Cummings & Davies, 1994a; Katz & Gottman, 1993), and marital distress related to parenting issues (Jouriles et al., 1991). The most commonly offered hypothesis for the relationship has been that marital distress or conflict interferes with the parents' ability to engage in appropriate parenting practices, which then leads to child CP; however, other explanations are possible (see Rutter, 1994). These include direct modeling of aggressive and coercive behavior, and the cumulative stressful effects of such conflict, including maternal depression. It has been suggested that both child CP and parental marital distress/conflict may be the result of parental antisocial behavior (Frick, 1994). Child characteristics such as age and gender appear to moderate the relationship between specific aspects of marital adjustment and CP (Dadds & Powell,

1991; Katz & Gottman, 1993). Some investigators (e.g., Abidin & Brunner, 1995; Jouriles et al., 1991; Porter & O'Leary, 1980) have focused more narrowly on specific aspects of marital conflict that relate directly to parenting, such as disagreement over child-rearing practices, marital conflict in a child's presence, or the strength of the parenting alliance. There is some indication that these more narrowly focused constructs may demonstrate stronger relationships to CP than may broader constructs such as marital distress.

Parents of children with CP also appear to experience higher frequencies of stressful events, both minor ones (e.g., daily hassles) and more significant ones (e.g., unemployment, major transitions) (see Patterson, 1983, and Webster-Stratton, 1990, for reviews). The effects of stress on child CP may be mediated through parenting practices such as disrupted parental discipline (e.g., Forgatch, Patterson, & Skinner, 1988; Snyder, 1991) and maladaptive parental social cognitions (Johnston, 1996a; Middlebrook & Forehand, 1985; Wahler & Dumas, 1989).

CP has been associated with a number of extrafamilial factors, such as low SES (Dodge, Pettit, & Bates, 1994), neighborhood risk (Attar, Guerra, & Tolan, 1994; Duncan, Brooks-Gunn, & Klebanov, 1994), and parental insularity/low social support (Jennings, Stagg, & Connors, 1991; Wahler, Leske, & Rogers, 1979). Some parents of children with CP may be quite isolated from friends, neighbors, and the community. Wahler and his colleagues have developed a construct called "insularity," which is defined as a "specific pattern of social contacts within the community that is characterized by a high level of negatively perceived coercive interchanges with relatives and/or helping agency representatives and by a low level of positively perceived supportive interchanges with friends" (Wahler & Dumas, 1984, p. 387). Insularity is positively related to negative parent behavior directed toward children and oppositional child behavior directed toward parents (Dumas & Wahler, 1985; Wahler, 1980). It has also been associated with poor maintenance of treatment effects (e.g., Dumas & Wahler, 1983). Thus, when a mother has a large proportion of aversive interactions outside the home, the interactions between the mother and her child in the home are likely to be negative as well.

Upon school entry, this child's coercive style of interaction is likely to extend to interactions with teachers and peers, resulting in frequent disciplinary confrontations with school personnel, rejection by peers, and continued coercive interchanges with parents (some of which now center around school-related problems) (e.g., Patterson et al., 1992). Difficulties in the acquisition of basic academic skills are most likely consequences of the preexisting neuropsychological deficits noted above (which now may be manifested as verbal deficits, self-control difficulties, social-cognitive deficits and biases, and/or ADHD), as well as the child's coercive interactional style. Moffitt (1990) has documented early motor skills deficits, IQ deficits by age 5, and reading difficulties soon after school entry in boys with CP and hyperactivity at age 13. The CP behaviors may become more serious, more frequent, and more covert (e.g., stealing) during the elementary school years.

By age 10 or 11, this recurrent constellation of negative events places the child at increased risk for association with a deviant peer group in middle school and high school (with a likely escalation in the CP behaviors) and/or for depression. The role of the peer group in the maintenance and escalation of CP behaviors during middle and late childhood and early adolescence has been documented in several longitudinal investigations, in terms of both peer rejection (e.g., Coie, Lochman, Terry, & Hyman, 1992) and subsequent involvement with antisocial peers (e.g., Dishion, Patterson, Stoolmiller, & Skinner, 1991). Children with CP (particularly boys) are also at increased risk for depression by the time they reach adolescence (see Ollendick & King, 1994). For example, Capaldi (1991, 1992) found co-occurrence of CP and depressive symptoms in an at-risk community sample of early adolescent boys in sixth grade. The boys with both CP and depressive symptoms displayed higher levels of suicidal ideation than boys with depressive symptoms only over the next 2 years, and they also had a 65% arrest level and poor academic achievement. The boys with CP who were depressed also appeared to initiate substance use at an earlier age than boys with CP only.

It is not surprising that adolescents who have progressed along the early-starter pathway are at significant risk for continuing to engage in more serious CP behaviors throughout adolescence and into adulthood (e.g., Farrington, 1995; Moffitt, 1993; Rutter et al., 1994). As adults, not only are such individuals at high risk for subsequent diagnosis of APD; they are also at increased risk for other psychiatric diagnoses and a variety of negative life outcomes (e.g., lower occupational adjustment and educational attainment, poorer physical health). Prediction studies of adolescent and adult outcome have consistently found that factors related to a child's CP behaviors (e.g., age of onset, frequency, variety of CP behaviors), and, to a somewhat lesser extent, the family (e.g., poor supervision and discipline, parental rejection, parental antisocial behavior) are stronger predictors of subsequent outcome than are broader contextual factors such as SES (see Kazdin, 1995b, and Loeber & Stouthamer-Loeber, 1986, for reviews).

Late-Starter Pathway

A second major pathway for the development of CP has been proposed, but there has been less consistency in how it has been described. In general, this second pathway begins in adolescence rather than early childhood; it is also thought to result in less serious forms of CP (e.g., property offenses rather than violent offenses) and to have a higher rate of desistance. However, more children are involved in this pathway than in the early-starter pathway (e.g., 24% vs. 7%, respectively, in the Dunedin Multidisciplinary Health Study; Moffitt, Caspi, Dickson, Silva, & Stanton, 1996). It has been referred to as the "late-starter" (Patterson et al., 1991), "adolescent-onset" (Hinshaw et al., 1993), "adolescence-limited" (Moffitt, 1993), or "nonaggressive-antisocial" (Loeber, 1988) pathway. The Adolescent-Onset Type of CD in DSM-IV would seem to be a likely diagnostic outcome of this pathway.

Empirical support for the late-starter pathway has been recently provided in both epidemiological (e.g., McGee, Feehan, Williams, & Anderson, 1992; Moffitt, 1990; Moffitt et al., 1996) and high-risk (Loeber et al., 1993) samples. In the Dunedin sample, a large increase in nonaggressive (but not aggressive) CP behaviors has been noted between ages 11 and 15 for both boys and girls (McGee et al., 1992). Moffitt (1990) found that the late starters made up 73% of her delinquent sample of boys at age 13, and had levels of CP behaviors at age 13 comparable to those displayed by the early-starter boys. However, in contrast to the early-starter boys, the late-starter boys had engaged in very low levels of CP in childhood, and there was no evidence of verbal IQ deficits, reading difficulties, preexisting family adversity, temperamental difficulty (Moffitt et al., 1996), or perinatal or motor skills difficulties. Furthermore, they were less likely to have been convicted of violent criminal offenses than were the early-starter boys (Moffitt et al., 1996). These findings illustrate the power of longitudinal (rather than cross-sectional) research designs for distinguishing groups of individuals with different developmental histories who appear similar in their behavioral presentation at a single assessment; they also underscore the importance of appropriate history taking during clinical assessments. Similarly, Capaldi and Patterson (1994) presented data on a high-risk sample indicating that late-starter boys were less likely than early-starter boys to live in families characterized by inappropriate parental discipline practices, unemployment, divorce, parental antisocial behavior, and low SES.

Patterson et al. (1991) have hypothesized that the process leading to the late-starter pathway begins in families that have marginally effective family management skills as a result either of significant stressors (e.g., divorce, unemployment) or of the typical strains placed on families as children become adolescents. Inadequate parental supervision and the relative lack of supervision in middle and high school increase the likelihood of significant involvement in a deviant peer group. However, because these adolescents have a higher level of social skills and a longer learning history of employing such skills successfully than do early starters, they are far less likely to continue to engage in CP behaviors than are early starters. Moffitt (1993) has conjectured that participation in CP behaviors by late starters is a form of social mimicry of early starters that is one way of asserting independence from the family. The basis for desistance among the late starters is thought to be the gradual increase in opportunities to engage in more legitimate adult roles and activities as these adolescents grow older. Whether these suppositions about desistance will prove to be valid is yet to be determined; Hämäläinen and Pulkkinen (1996) found that late starters constituted nearly one-third of their group of young adult (age 27) criminal offenders. However, it is the case that there is a dramatic decline in CP behaviors by early adulthood (e.g., Farrington, 1986).

Girls and CP

Gender is the most consistently documented risk factor for CP (Robins, 1991). However, much of the research on CP has focused exclusively on boys, or, when girls have been included, has failed to consider possible gender effects. Space considerations preclude discussion of possible factors and processes that may be responsible for these sex differences. Instead, the reader is referred to Eme and Kavanaugh (1995), Zahn-Waxler (1993), and Zoccolillo (1993).

The relatively few studies that have examined the developmental course of CP with girls have reported contradictory findings concerning whether there is a differential prognosis for boys and girls with respect to later display of CP behaviors, with various studies reporting outcome to be better, the same, or worse for girls (see Robins, 1986, for a review). Some investigators that have reported findings supporting components of the early-starter pathway for boys have failed to find similar support with girls (e.g., Tremblay et al., 1992), although other investigators have reported both early-starter and late-starter pathways for girls (e.g., Caspi, Lynam, Moffitt, & Silva, 1993). Early menarche, in conjunction with exposure to deviant peers, may be a significant risk factor for girls' entry into the late-starter pathway.

There is also some evidence from both cross-sectional and longitudinal research that whereas girls may be somewhat less likely to engage in serious and persistent CP behaviors in adolescence or adulthood than boys, they may be more at risk for a broad array of other adverse outcomes, including various internalizing behavior problems (e.g., Loeber & Keenan, 1994; Robins, 1986; Zoccolillo, 1993). Particularly disturbing are the findings that girls with CP or a combination of CP and withdrawal are at later risk for teen parenthood and an unresponsive parenting style with their own children, and that their children display early developmental lags, perhaps setting the stage for another generation of children with significant CP (Serbin, Peters, McAffer, & Schwartzman, 1991).

Although the pathways described above are certainly not fully developed at this time, they do provide a conceptual framework for the assessment of children with CP. We now turn to a discussion of the assessment process itself.

ASSESSMENT

In this section of the chapter, we discuss the assessment of children with CP and their families. Three major areas for assessment are discussed separately: child behavior per se and in an interactional context; other child characteristics and disorders, such as temperament and ADHD; and familial and extrafamilial factors, such as parenting practices, parents' (and teachers') social cognitions, personal and marital adjustment of the parents, parental stress, maternal insularity, and parental satisfaction with treatment. In each section, the particular methods (e.g., interviews, questionnaires, observations) that are most appropriate for assessing the questions of interest are discussed.

We focus our discussion of methods on assessment procedures that have been employed specifically with populations of children with CP. In some instances (e.g., where the choice of assessment procedures is limited), other assessment procedures are mentioned, but these are not described in detail. Although the emphasis is on preintervention assessment and a functional analysis of CP in children, many of these procedures can also be used to evaluate treatment as it progresses and treatment outcome at termination and follow-up.

Child Behavior per se and in an Interactional Context

The primary focus of an assessment of a child with CP is on the referred child's behavior per se, and, because of the interactional nature of CP, on the behavior of relevant individuals in the child's environment. In virtually every case this means the parents, but the behavior of other relevant adults (e.g., teacher[s], babysitter, grandparents), siblings, and peers may also need to be assessed.

With respect to child behavior, the clinician should keep a number of points in mind during the assessment. First and foremost, it should be determined whether the child is in fact engaging in CP behaviors. If so, then the next step is to determine whether the child's behavior is consistent with either the early-starter or late-starter pathway (McMahon, 1994). In some cases, it may be important to determine whether the child meets DSM-IV diagnostic criteria for ODD or CD. In addition, given the importance of child noncompliance as a keystone behavior for both overt and covert types of CP (Loeber & Schmaling, 1985a; Chamberlain & Patterson, 1995), the fact that it occurs very early in the progression of CP (Edelbrock, 1985), and the demonstrated utility of targeting this behavior in treatment (e.g., McMahon & Forehand, 1984; Russo et al., 1981), it is essential to assess child noncompliance thoroughly. Given that the developmental pathways of CP and ADHD may often be closely intertwined, and that ADHD may exert its influence upon CP in different ways at different developmental periods, it is especially important to screen for ADHD in children referred for CP (see Barkley, Chapter 2, this volume). Because children who display high levels of both CP and internalizing behavior problems may be at particularly high risk for negative outcomes, it is also important to screen for comorbid internalizing problems as well (see Compas, Chapter 4, and Barrios & Hartmann, Chapter 5, this volume).

Given the central theoretical role accorded to parenting skill deficits in the development and maintenance of child CP and the interactional nature of CP, it is essential to assess parental behavior in the context of interactions with the referred child. This is particularly true for mothers, but it is important for fathers as well. Although fathers often play a secondary role in child management compared to mothers (Patterson, 1982), it is important to assess the extent to which a father is involved in child management, the quality of his interactions with the child, and the degree of consistency and support between the parents.

Finally, it is critical to use methods, informants, and settings that are relevant for the developmental level and clinical presentation of the child being assessed (McMahon, 1994). In the context of the early-starter and late-starter pathways described above, information concerning the child's behavior can be used to provide some hypotheses as to how far the child has progressed in his or her development of these CP behaviors and the extent to which these behaviors are being manifested in multiple settings. For example, more serious and covert behaviors (e.g., stealing) displayed by a young school-age child would suggest a more advanced progression of CP, poorer prognosis, and a different treatment approach than if that child engaged only in mild overt behaviors (e.g., arguing). Assessment in both the home and school settings, with attention to the peer group, would be essential to determine the pervasiveness of the child's CP behaviors.

In order to obtain a representative and meaningful account of the referred child's CP behaviors, particularly with regard to their interactional aspects, the clinician must rely on multiple methods of assessment (e.g., Achenbach, 1993b; Chamberlain & Bank, 1989; Kamphaus & Frick, 1996). Interviews with the parents, the child, and other relevant parties (e.g., teachers); behavioral rating scales; and behavioral observations in clinic, home, and/or school settings can all be employed. Measures of these types that are particularly applicable to the assessment of children with CP are described below.

Interviews

Interviews conducted with children with CP, their families, and other important adults can be divided into two general categories: clinical interviews and structured diagnostic interviews.

Clinical Interviews

In this subsection, we review parent, child, and teacher interviews. The clinical interview is usually the first contact the clinician has with the identified client (i.e., the child) and with the significant adults in the child's life (i.e., parents, teachers). The primary function of the clinical interview is to set the stage for effective therapeutic intervention. The interview accomplishes this task by providing the clinician with reports about the behaviors to be targeted for treatment and the conditions maintaining the CP behaviors, and it helps identify treatment goals. Because interactional processes with parents, other adults, and peers have been shown to play significant roles in the development and maintenance of CP, the interview focuses on the pattern of interaction between the child and others. The interview is also a time to establish rapport with the family, clarify the assessment process, and obtain child self-reports. Information about external factors that may affect parent–child interactions or the implementation of the treatment plan is also obtained during the interview. Such factors include family background (e.g., family structure, child care, finances); familial and extrafamilial relationships; the child's developmental, medical, and educational history, history of exposure to violence or conflict, and previous mental health services received; neighborhood safety; and expectations for treatment. Detailed information on conducting clinical interviews with children, parents, and teachers may be found in Breen and Altepeter (1990), Kamphaus and Frick (1996), and Sanders and Dadds (1993).

Interview with Parents. Two preliminary issues must be considered prior to the parent interview (Forehand & McMahon, 1981). First, it is strongly recommended that in a two-parent family, both parents be involved in the initial interview if possible. This permits the clinician to obtain a more complete picture of interaction patterns between each parent and the child, the degree of consistency between parents in their child-rearing philosophy and behavior, and a behavioral sample of the marital interaction. It also sends a message to the family that both parents are valuable sources of information and necessary for optimal child treatment. However, assessment in cases of divorce, separation, and domestic violence can raise a variety of additional considerations. The level of conflict between some parents may preclude inviting both to the same meeting. For example, in custody disputes, assessment can be undermined if there is a threat that information obtained about family life will be subpoenaed. In cases of suspected domestic violence, the primary assessment concern is the physical safety of all family members, and frank discussion may be impossible because of the covert threat of violence. The reader is referred to Holtzworth-Munroe, Beatty, and Anglin (1995) and La Taillade and Jacobson (in press) for more detailed information concerning the assessment of marital violence.

The second preliminary issue is whether the child should be present during the parent interview. We prefer to interview the parents alone, since this allows the parents to discuss their relationship with their child more freely, and it avoids the situation in which the child's CP behaviors disrupt the interview. Behavioral samples of the parent–child interaction can be gathered more systematically through clinic or home observations. Sanders and Dadds (1993) suggest asking parents in advance about whether the child has difficulties with separation. If the parents report separation difficulties, then either having the parents come alone to the first session or providing alternate child care is an option.

The major purpose of the initial behaviorally oriented interview with the parents is to determine the nature of the typical parent–child interactions that are problematic, the antecedent stimulus conditions under which CP behaviors occur, and the consequences that accompany such behaviors. The interview typically begins with a general question, such as "Tell me what types of problems you have been having with your child," or "What brings you to the clinic?" In our experience, most parents, not surprisingly, respond globally to such a global question.

We have found the interview format developed by Hanf (1970) and presented elsewhere (Forehand & McMahon, 1981) to be extremely useful in structuring the interview to obtain specific information on current parent–child interactions. Although this format is designed specifically for use with parents of 3- to 8-year-old children, many of the areas are relevant to children of all ages. The Problem Guidesheet presented in Figure 3.2 may be employed with these families. Following the parents' statements of the primary concerns about their child, the clinician presents situations that may or may not be problem areas for the particular family. Parents are asked whether their child is disruptive in situations such as the following: getting dressed in the morning, mealtimes, visiting in a friend's home, riding in the car, shopping, adult–adult conversations, parental telephone con-

versations, bathtime, and bedtime. Information is also elicited as to whether the child experiences academic or behavioral difficulties in school, and about the child's relationship with other family members as well as peers. If the parents report that a particular behavior or setting is not problematic, the clinician moves to the next situation. If the parents report that a particular situation is a problem area for them, then the clinician examines the antecedent conditions of the situation ("What happens just before [the problem interaction]?"), the child's behavior ("What does the child do?"), the parents' response ("What do you do?"), and the child's reaction to the parents' intervention ("What does the child do then?").

The analysis of both the parents' and the child's behavior in the problem situation should be continued until the clinician has a clear understanding of the nature and extent of the parent–child interaction. Other relevant information, such as the frequency ("How often . . . ?") and duration ("How long . . . ?") of the problem behavior, should also be obtained. At this point, it is also appropriate to ask historical/developmental questions specific to the problem interaction. Examples of specific interviewing techniques are presented in Forehand and McMahon (1981). Barkley (1987) has developed the Home Situations Questionnaire, which is a parent rating scale based on this type of interview. (An adaptation of the Home Situations Questionnaire for adolescents has also been developed; see Adams, McCarthy, & Kelley, 1995). If this questionnaire is completed by the parents prior to the first assessment session, it may serve to structure this part of the interview.

Wahler and Cormier (1970) have described an interview format in which the parent completes preinterview checklists that list various home and community situations and inappropriate child behaviors. The clinician then has the parents elaborate on the problem behaviors in each setting, including the parental consequences that follow the child behaviors. Patterson and his colleagues have developed several structures for the initial interview, which also focus on various child CP behaviors and parental responses to those behaviors (Patterson & Bank, 1986; Patterson, Reid, Jones, & Conger, 1975).

The interview as an assessment tool does not end with the first contact, but continues throughout treatment formulation and implementation. The interview is used to obtain information necessary for the development of interventions, to assess the effectiveness of the intervention and its implementation, and to alter the intervention if necessary (Breen & Altepeter, 1990).

Child: Interviewer(s):
Interviewee(s):   Date:

Setting	*Description*	*Frequency*	*Duration*	*Parent Response*	*Child Response*
Bedtime (A.M. and P.M.)					
Mealtime					
Bath time					
On phone					
Visitors — at home					
Visiting others					
Car					
Public places (stores, etc.)					
School					
Siblings					
Peers					
Other parent/ relative					
Discipli- nary pro- cedures					
Other					

FIGURE 3.2. Problem guidesheet. From Forehand and McMahon (1981, p. 19). Copyright 1981 by The Guilford Press. Reprinted by permission.

Interview with the Child. With very young children (5 years and younger), an individual interview is usually not beneficial, at least with respect to content. Children below the age of 10 are not usually reliable reporters of their own behavioral symptoms (Edelbrock, Costello, Dulcan, Kalas, & Conover, 1985). However, even a few minutes spent privately with a younger child in play, or in a walk to the soda machine, can provide the clinician with a subjective evaluation of the child's cognitive, affective, and behavioral characteristics (e.g., verbal and social skills) (Bierman, 1983). It also provides the clinician with an opportunity to assess the child's perception of why he or she has been brought to the clinic, and to begin to enlist the child's participation in the assessment process. With an older child, an individual interview can provide the clinician with additional pertinent information.

The interview in the clinic typically begins with setting the child at ease. This might include introductions and asking the child his or her teacher's name or grade in school. It should also include assessing the child's understanding of the purpose of the meeting. This can be done with the statement "Tell me why you are here today." After the child has responded, the clinician should explain his or her own view of why the child is at the clinic. The explanation might be this: "Your parents are concerned because you and they don't seem to be getting along very well. They came to see us to get some help so things will be more pleasant for you all at home." If the problems are largely school-centered, this might be the explanation: "Your parents are concerned because you and Mr./Ms. [teacher's name] aren't getting along very well. They came to the clinic with you to see if we could help so things would be more pleasant for you and your teacher at school."

The clinician then proceeds to ask the child about various situations at home and/or at school, in an attempt to obtain the child's perception about what is happening in these problem situations. Sometimes such questioning is fruitless; at other times the child's understanding of the situation and the role he or she plays is quite accurate. Other questions to ask a child include those in the following areas:

- Family: "What kinds of things do you do with your father/mother/brothers/sisters? What can you do to make your father/mother happy/mad?"
- School: "Tell me about school. What do you like best at school? What do you dislike most at school?"
- Social: "Tell me about your friends. What kinds of things do you do with [friend's name]?"
- Personal: "What are your favorite things? What do you like to do most?"

As part of the interview process, the child and clinician together can fill in a reinforcement survey (e.g., Cautela, Cautela, & Esonis, 1983) for use later in the development of treatment programs. This type of structured activity can be helpful in building rapport.

Interview with Teacher(s). If the presenting problem concerns classroom behavior, an interview with the child's teacher or teachers is necessary. Teachers are also often in a better position than parents to comment on children's academic achievement and social skills, and are better able to make social and developmental comparisons of child behavior (Walker, 1995). Furthermore, academic underachievement is of particular interest because of its high incidence in children with CP (see above). Before contacting a teacher, the clinician must obtain parental consent to do so. Breen and Altepeter (1990) have provided the following outline for a brief interview with the teacher, which can be conducted at the school or by telephone: (1) introduction (e.g., rationale for assessment, teacher's main concerns); (2) medical background/implications (e.g., attendance, tardiness, appearance and health, medications and compliance with medication); (3) cognitive issues (e.g., academic skills, grades, language skills, attention, discrepancies between grades and ability); (4) social interactions (e.g., relations with peers, relations with teacher, compliance, anger, aggression); (5) general emotional issues (e.g., self-esteem, affect, temperament, frustration); and (6) interventions (e.g., type of interventions tried, how long).

The interview with the teacher can follow a format similar to the format for parent interviews, described above. The situations to be covered can be based on Barkley's (1987) School Situations Questionnaire (or the adolescent version; Adams et al., 1995) and on Wahler and Cormier's (1970) preinterview checklist. Areas of interest include school arrival, individual deskwork, small-group activities, recess, lunch, field trips, assemblies, free time in class, and particular academic topics (e.g., math, social studies). If the teacher indicates that a particular situation is a problem, then the clinician obtains a description of the situation ("What is the class doing?"), the child's behavior ("What does the child do?"), the teacher's responses to the child ("What do you do?"), and the child's responses to the teacher's interventions ("What does the child do then?"). The frequency and duration of the problem, and the role of other children in escalating or inhibiting the problem, should also be assessed.

In addition, a focus on behaviors that create challenges to classroom management can provide useful information. Typical questions include "Does the child leave his or her desk inappropriately?", "Does the child bother classmates while they are working?", Does the child talk out of turn?", "Does the child demand excessive teacher attention?", and so forth. Once a particular rule violation has been identified, then questions concerning antecedent events (e.g., "In what situation is the child more likely to hit another student?"), the exact behavior of the child, the teacher's responses, and the child's responses to the teacher's interventions are asked.

In talking with the teacher, the clinician is also interested in understanding exactly what the teacher considers appropriate student behavior in each of the problem situations. For example, what does he or she think the best-behaved child would do, and what would most children do? This information is necessary to specify intervention goals. The clinician also explores with the teacher potential positive reinforcers and consequences available in the classroom. If the teacher is to execute the treatment program, the reinforcers and consequences used must be acceptable to the teacher (see Witt & Elliott, 1985). To help structure the interview and maximize efficiency, Walker (1995) and Breen and Altepeter (1990) suggest collecting teacher ratings of child behavior (see below) prior to the interview. Throughout the interview, the clinician is evaluating the willingness, motivation, and ability of the teacher to work with the clinician in carrying out the treatment program.

Structured Interviews

In this subsection, we describe structured diagnostic interviews as well as some examples of other types of structured interviews. Increasingly, structured interviews have been used in efforts to improve the reliability and validity of diagnostic interviewing, particularly for research purposes (Edelbrock & Costello, 1988b). Structured diagnostic interviews are also used in clinical settings, usually in conjunction with other assessment techniques (Kamphaus & Frick, 1996). The structured diagnostic interviews most commonly employed to assess children with CP are the Diagnostic Interview Schedule for Children (DISC; Shaffer, Fisher, Piacentini, Schwab-Stone, & Wicks, 1991; Shaffer et al., 1993) and the Diagnostic Interview for Children and Adolescents (DICA; Boyle et al., 1993; Herjanic & Reich, 1982; Reich & Welner, 1988). For reviews of these and other structured diagnostic interviews, readers are referred to Bird and Gould (1995), Edelbrock and Costello (1988b), and Hodges and Zeman (1993).

These structured interviews share a number of characteristics. They can be employed with multiple informants, such as parents, children, and sometimes teachers. They are designed to broadly assess symptoms and behaviors associated with child psychopathology and to provide diagnoses for disorders as defined by the DSM (American Psychiatric Association, 1980, 1987, 1994) classification system. Although they vary in the degree of structure, these interviews all have explicit guidelines for administration, wording of questions, and scoring.

The National Institute of Mental Health's DISC is a highly structured interview with 231 core questions and 1,186 potential follow-up questions. It has been frequently updated to reflect changes in the DSM. The child version (DISC-C) is for children aged 9–17, and the parent version (DISC-P) is for children aged 6–17. An experimental teacher version (DISC-T) was used in the DSM-IV field trials (Lahey et al., 1994). In addition to specific diagnoses, one can also group specific diagnoses into larger categories or use individual items to form scale scores (Rubio-Stipec et al., 1996). The interview can be administered in 40–60 minutes by paraprofessionals with only 3–4 days of training because of the highly structured administration format and computer scoring algorithm.

Psychometric data on the DISC-C showed acceptable reliability in a sample of children and adolescents aged 11–17 (Edelbrock, Costello, et al., 1985). However, younger children (6 to 9 years old) were likely to report fewer symptoms at the retest than at the initial interview. On the basis of these findings, Edelbrock and colleagues concluded that children below the age of 10 are not reliable in reporting their own behavioral symptoms. Schwab-Stone et al. (1993) reported acceptable test–retest reliability (1–3 weeks) on the parent version of the DISC 2.3 for ODD and CD, respectively (kappa = .88, .87). On the child version, however, test–retest reliability (1–3 weeks) was lower for ODD and CD (kappa = .16, .55). Internal consistency was acceptable for ODD and CD on both the DISC-P (alpha = .75, .56) and the DISC-C (alpha = .67, .59).

The parent version of the revised DISC showed moderate agreement with a criterion interview by clinicians for ODD (kappa = .51) and CD (kappa = .60), although the child version had low agreement for ODD (kappa = .28) and CD (kappa = .21) (Piacentini et al., 1993). The authors reported, however, that most cases of disagreement were close to the diagnostic threshold. In addition, false-positive diagnoses were a problem on the DISC-P for ODD and on the DISC-C for ODD and CD. Validity studies of the DISC indicated a strong and consistent relationship between the DISC and statistically derived syndromes on the Child Behavior Checklist (CBCL) and Youth Self Report rating scales (YSR) (Edelbrock & Costello, 1988a;

Jensen et al., 1996). (The various versions of the CBCL are described later.)

Rubio-Stipec et al. (1996) derived ODD and CD scales, using factor analysis from items on the DISC 2.3. On parent, child, and combined scores, the nine items on the ODD scale and the seven items on the CD scale showed acceptable internal-consistency reliability (alpha = .57–.79) and test–retest (2-week) reliability (kappa = .68–.84). Initial validity data indicated that each scale was related to the corresponding diagnostic category as measured by a clinician, although the symptoms on the two scales were also related to each other. The authors noted that scaled scores may allow researchers several statistical advantages over categorical classification and are shorter and less costly to administer.

A second structured, DSM-based diagnostic interview is the DICA (Boyle et al., 1993; Herjanic & Reich, 1982; Reich & Welner, 1988). Like the DISC, the DICA has been repeatedly revised to reflect revisions of the DSM classification system. The DICA has three versions: for children aged 6–12, for adolescents aged 13–17, and for parents. It yields information about onset, duration, and severity of 185 symptoms, as well as summary scores in six areas: Relationship Problems, School Behavior, School Learning, Neurotic Symptoms, Somatic Symptoms, and Psychotic Symptoms (Herjanic & Reich, 1982). The DICA was originally designed for use in epidemiological research and can be administered by paraprofessional interviewers. Parent reports showed low to moderate test–retest reliability (1–3 weeks) for 6- to 11-year-olds and 12- to 17-year-olds, respectively (ODD kappas = .32, .67; CD kappas = –.01, .87). The test–retest reliability of child and adolescent self-reports was fair for ODD (kappas = .33, .28) and fair to good for CD (kappas = .37, .92). Boyle and colleagues (1993) concluded that parent assessment of CD, ODD, and ADHD was more reliable in the older than in the younger age group. Parent–child agreement levels were generally low (90% of kappas were below .40, and only one exceeded .60).

Boyle et al. (1993) reported that concordance between paraprofessional interviewers and child psychiatrists administering the revised DICA was substantial (kappa = .84 for parent and child reports of CD/ODD). In a community sample, Boyle et al. (1993) found that the parent version of the DICA may misclassify what is normal child behavior as mild to moderate ODD. Parent-identified cases of ODD in this sample were 15.4% for 6- to 11-year-olds and 10.4% for 12- to 16-year-olds, significantly higher than would be expected in the general population. Psychometric properties of the symptom scores are unknown at this time (Hodges & Zeman, 1993).

An alternative approach to interviewing children has been developed by McConaughy and Achenbach (1994). The Semistructured Clinical Interview for Children and Adolescents (SCICA) is a broad interview administered to children (ages 6–18) that employs a protocol of open-ended questions to assess a variety of areas of child functioning. Achenbach (1993b) has suggested that this approach is more developmentally sensitive to children than the more structured approach taken by the DISC and DICA. Following the conclusion of the interview, the interviewer scores the child's responses to 107 self-report items, as well as 117 items based on the interviewer's observations during the interview. Dimensional scores similar to those obtained from various versions of the CBCL family of instruments (Achenbach, 1993b; see below) can also be derived from these items, but only for children aged 6–12. Psychometric data on the SCICA are presented in McConaughy and Achenbach (1994). Because of its recent appearance and relatively limited use to date, the extent to which the SCICA may present a useful alternative to more structured diagnostic instruments such as the DISC and the DICA is unknown at this time.

Kolko and Kazdin have developed several semistructured interviews for parents and children that have been used to assess various aspects of fire setting and playing with matches in inpatient, outpatient, and community samples of children. The Firesetting History Screen (Kolko & Kazdin, 1988), the Firesetting Risk Interview (Kolko & Kazdin, 1989a), and the Children's Firesetting Interview (Kolko & Kazdin, 1989b) are completed by parents and children, and tap into a variety of areas related to fire-setting behavior and domains of risk. The Fire Incident Analysis (Kolko & Kazdin, 1991b), which is administered to parents, is designed to classify children's motivation for fire setting (i.e., curiosity vs. anger). Finally, the Fire Safety/Prevention Knowledge Interview (Kolko, Watson, & Faust, 1991) is administered to children to assess their knowledge about various fire-related stimuli, situations, and consequences. Evidence for the reliability and validity of these interviews is encouraging.

Summary

The behaviorally oriented clinical interview is, and will certainly continue to be, an indispensable part of the assessment. For the clinician, the interview is a necessary but not a sufficient assessment procedure. Interviews must be used in conjunction with other assessment procedures in developing a valid functional analysis of the referral problem. The clinical utility of structured diagnostic interviews is somewhat less clear at this point, because of their length and relative lack of attention to contextual factors. In addition, sole reliance on categorical scoring criteria may lead to a situation in which children who display borderline levels of CP are incorrectly diagnosed. Therefore, structured diagnostic interviews should also be employed in conjunction with other assessment methods. For research purposes, these interviews may provide a psychometrically sound addition to the developing picture of child CP. Kolko and Kazdin's efforts to develop semistructured interviews to assess various aspects of fire setting represent potentially important advances in the assessment of covert types of CP.

Behavioral Rating Scales

Behavioral rating scales are assessment instruments that are completed by adults or the child in reference to the child's behavior or characteristics. Advantages of these instruments are that they permit the assessment of a broad range of behaviors and behavioral dimensions, including low-frequency behaviors; require relatively little time to administer, score, and interpret; facilitate the gathering of normative data; are readily quantifiable; and can incorporate the perceptions of significant individuals in the child's life, such as parents or teachers (Kamphaus & Frick, 1996; McConaughy, 1992; Piacentini, 1993). Some of the rating scales can provide data relevant to diagnostic decisions. Behavioral rating scales have been extensively employed as treatment outcome measures with children with CP (Atkeson & Forehand, 1978), and they have also been a primary source of data concerning social validation (Kazdin, 1977) of treatment effects with children with CP and their families (e.g., Forehand, Wells, & Griest, 1980). (However, see Hoge & Andrews, 1992, for a caution about using teacher-completed behavioral rating scales for treatment selection and outcome.) Parents' and teachers' perceptions of the child are important treatment goals in their own right, and behavioral rating scales provide ready access to such data (see below). Completion of behavioral rating scales by parents, teachers, and children prior to initial interviews may help structure the interview and provide for more efficient use of time (Elliott, Busse, & Gresham, 1993).

There are literally hundreds of behavioral rating scales, and most of these include CP behaviors along with other child behavior problems. We first present brief reviews of several broad-band behavioral rating scales that have been frequently employed with samples of children with CP. Our discussion of these rating scales focuses on aspects specific to the assessment of CP. Several other behavioral rating scales are then described that are more focused on CP behaviors. For more extensive reviews of behavioral rating scales, see Kamphaus and Frick (1996), McConaughy (1992), and Piacentini (1993).

Broad-Band Rating Scales

Three broad-band rating scales are discussed in this subsection: the CBCL family of instruments (Achenbach, 1993b), the Revised Behavior Problem Checklist (RBPC; Quay & Peterson, 1983), and the Conners Parent and Teacher Rating Scales (Conners, 1990). The CBCL family of instruments is designed for use with children between the ages of 2 and 18. The goal of its developer is to provide a comprehensive behavioral assessment battery for behaviorally disordered children, with parallel versions of the CBCL for parents, teachers, youths, observers, and clinicians (Achenbach, 1993a). The parent (CBCL/2–3, CBCL/4–18), teacher (Teacher Report Form or TRF), and youth (YSR) versions are described here. The interview (SCICA) and observational (Direct Observation Form or DOF) versions are described elsewhere in the chapter.

The CBCL, TRF, and YSR are highly similar in terms of structure, items, scoring, and interpretation. They are designed to be self-administered, and each can usually be completed in 15–20 minutes. The CBCL currently consists of two different rating scales: one completed by parents of children aged 4–18 (CBCL/4–18; Achenbach, 1991b) and another rating scale completed by parents of children aged 2–3 (CBCL/2–3; Achenbach, 1992). The TRF is completed by teachers of children between the ages of 5 and 18, and the YSR is completed by children from 11 to 18 years of age. The instruments include sections concerning Competence and Problem items (the CBCL/2–3 includes only Problem items). There are 89 items that are common to the CBCL/4–18, TRF, and YSR, as well as several additional items that are present on a given instrument. Each item is rated for its applicability to the child on a 3-point scale. The time basis for the ratings varies somewhat for each instrument—6 months for the CBCL/4–18 and the

YSR, and 2 months for the CBCL/2–3 and the TRF.

The Problem items are scored and presented as a profile that indicates the child's standing on two broad-band (Internalizing, Externalizing) and eight narrow-band syndromes (there are six narrow-band syndromes on the CBCL/2–3). A Total Problem score can be obtained as well. The 1991 Profiles have separate norms for boys and girls at two age levels (4–11 [5–11 on the TRF] and 12–18). The Externalizing dimension on the CBCL/4–18, TRF, and YSR includes CP behaviors on two of the narrow-band scales (Aggressive Behavior, Delinquent Behavior). On the CBCL/2–3, the Aggressive and Destructive narrow-band scales include CP behaviors. The items defining the narrow-band scales that make up the Externalizing broad-band scale on the CBCL/4–18, TRF, and YSR are presented in Table 3.1 (Achenbach, 1991a). As can be seen, the Aggressive Behavior syndrome maps more closely onto the DSM-IV category of ODD, whereas the Delinquent Behavior syndrome more closely resembles the DSM-IV category of CD (see Biederman et al., 1993; Edelbrock & Costello, 1988a; Jensen, Salzberg, Richters, Watanabe, & Roper, 1993). The Competence scales on the 1991 Profiles include items related to various activities, social relationships, and success in school.

The psychometric properties of the various forms of the CBCL, the TRF, and the YSR are described thoroughly in their respective manuals (Achenbach, 1991b, 1991c, 1991d, 1992). A few examples that relate specifically to populations of children with CP follow. The CP-related scales of the CBCL correlate highly with their counterparts on the Conners Parent Rating Scale (Conners, 1973) (r's = .76–.88) and the RBPC (Quay & Peterson, 1983) (r's = .52–.88). Interparental agreement is higher on items from the Externalizing scale than on items from the Internalizing scale (Christensen, Margolin, & Sullaway, 1992). The CBCL/4–18 is also sensitive to treatment changes resulting from parent training (e.g., Eisenstadt, Eyberg, McNeil, Newcomb, & Funderburk, 1993; Webster-Stratton, 1994; Webster-Stratton & Hammond, 1997) and child cognitive-behavioral therapy (e.g., Kazdin, Bass, Siegel, & Thomas, 1989) for the treatment of CP.

Within inpatient groups, the CBCL was shown to differentiate boys with DSM-III diagnoses of CD or Major Depression from children with other diagnoses (Kazdin & Heidish, 1984). With respect to the children with CD (6- to 11-year-old boys), their parents reported significantly

TABLE 3.1. Items Defining the Externalizing, Delinquent Behavior and Aggressive Behavior Syndromes on the CBCL/4–18, TRF, and YSR

Externalizing Syndromes	
Delinquent Behavior	Aggressive Behavior
Lacks guilt	Argues
Bad companions	Brags
Lies	Mean to others
Prefers older kids	Demands attention
Runs away from home[c]	Destroys own things
Sets fires[c]	Destroys others' things
Steals at home[c]	Disobedient at school
Steals outside home	Jealous
Swearing, obscenity	Fights
Truancy	Attacks people
Alcohol, drugs	Screams
	Shows off
Specific to CBCL/4–18	Stubborn, irritable
Thinks about sex too much	Sudden mood changes
Vandalism[a,c]	Talks too much
	Teases
Specific to TRF	Temper tantrums
Tardy[a,b]	Threatens
	Loud
	Specific to CBCL/4–18
	Disobedient at home[c]
	Specific to TRF
	Defiant[a,b]
	Disturbs others[a,b]
	Talks out of turn[a,b]
	Disrupts class[a,b]
	Explosive[a,b]
	Easily frustrated[a,b]

Note. Adapted from Achenbach (1991a, p. 50). Copyright 1991 by T. M. Achenbach. Adapted by permission.
[a]Not on YSR.
[b]Not on CBCL/4–18.
[c]Not on TRF.

greater problems on the Aggressive and Delinquent narrow-band scales and on the Externalizing broad-band scale, but they did not differ on the other scales. The CBCL has also been shown to differentiate children who set fires and/or play with matches from those who do not set fires in nonpatient, outpatient, and inpatient samples (Kolko & Kazdin, 1991a; Kolko, Kazdin, & Meyer, 1985), and to a certain extent in a sample of incarcerated delinquents (Forehand, Wierson, Frame, Kemptom, & Armistead, 1991). In general, these findings indicate that children with CP who set fires are more extreme in their behavior than children with CP who do not engage in fire setting.

The Problem items on the TRF (Achenbach, 1991c) have been adapted from the parent version of the CBCL, with several items being replaced by ones that are more appropriate to classroom situations. There are six scale scores related to school performance and adaptive functioning on the Adaptive Functioning scales. Scores on the Externalizing scales (especially Aggressive) of the TRF correlate quite highly with the various scales of the revised Conners Teacher Rating Scale (Edelbrock, Greenbaum, & Conover, 1985). The TRF has also been shown to discriminate clinic-referred from nonreferred children (Edelbrock & Achenbach, 1984). Total Problem scores are correlated with classroom observational measures as obtained on the DOF (Reed & Edelbrock, 1983). Pretreatment scores on the Internalizing, Externalizing, and Total Problem scores on the TRF (but not the CBCL) have been shown to discriminate dropouts from treatment completers in an outpatient sample of children with CP and their families (Kazdin, Mazurick, & Siegel, 1994). The TRF is also sensitive to the effects of cognitive-behavioral therapy and parent training for children with CP and their families (e.g., Kazdin et al., 1994; Kazdin, Siegel, & Bass, 1992; Kendall, Reber, McLeer, Epps, & Ronan, 1990).

Much of the research on the YSR has been conducted with inpatient samples of adolescents. The broad-band factor structure of the YSR has been replicated in such samples; however, additional factors were identified on the narrow-band Aggressive Behavior (active, affect, and attention-focusing aggressive behavior) and Delinquent Behavior (general and serious delinquent behavior) scales (Song, Singh, & Singer, 1994). In addition, the Attention Problems scale loaded on the Externalizing broad-band scale for boys but not for girls. Thurber and colleagues have provided support for the construct validity of the broad-band scales in a similar inpatient sample. However, they also suggest that the Externalizing scale, as well as the Aggressive Behavior and Delinquent Behavior narrow-band scales, may be influenced by the response sets of social desirability and denial of symptoms, especially for girls (Thurber & Hollingsworth, 1992; Thurber & Snow, 1990). The Delinquent Behavior scale is associated with a diagnosis of CD as derived from the DISC-C (Weinstein, Noam, Grimes, Stone, & Schwab-Stone, 1990). Children who set fires had higher Externalizing scores than those who did not, but they did not differ significantly from children who played with matches (Kolko & Kazdin, 1991a). Finally, in a community sample of 13-year-olds,

Externalizing scores on the YSR were significantly higher than those on the CBCL (mothers and fathers) or the TRF (Stanger & Lewis, 1993).

The various CBCL measures offer a number of compelling advantages. First, they represent the culmination of extensive empirical analyses of data gathered from a variety of informants concerning both child behavior problems and areas of competence. In fact, they are among the few behavioral rating scales to assess prosocial behaviors. Second, their psychometric qualities are adequate, and extensive normative data are provided for children of different ages and sexes. Third, the development of equivalent forms for different informants should maximize the amount of information that can be gathered about the child, and should permit comparisons across informants and situations. Fourth, the provision of both broad-band and narrow-band syndromes (including broad coverage of CP behaviors) means that the CBCL instruments can be used for both general and more specific purposes, including classification, screening, diagnosis, and treatment evaluation. With children with CP, the comprehensive coverage can be useful in screening for some of the disorders that are often comorbid with CP, such as ADHD and depression. However, it is important to note some of the limitations of the CBCL family of instruments as well (see Drotar, Stein, & Perrin, 1995, and Kamphaus & Frick, 1996, for more details). These include a limited assessment of social competence; use of a normative sample that excluded children who had recently received mental health services; and limited sensitivity to behaviors occurring in the subclinical range. In addition, it is essential to note that the interpretations of both broad- and narrow-band scale scores from the 1991 revision of the CBCL family of instruments are not necessarily comparable to those obtained from previous versions. For example, earlier versions of the Externalizing scale included the equivalent of the Attention Problems narrow-band scale, which is not included on the 1991 version of the Externalizing scale. Song et al. (1994) have noted that the item composition of the Aggressive Behavior scale on the 1991 YSR is quite different from that of the previous version.

Other broad-band rating scales that have been widely used in the past are the RBPC (Quay & Peterson, 1983) and the Conners scales (Conners, 1990). The RBPC, which consists of 89 items and can be completed by parents or teachers, yields six factors, two of which are relevant to CP: Conduct Disorder and Socialized Aggression. Limited norms are available for teacher ratings from kindergarten through 12th grade and for maternal ratings for children aged 5 to 16 years. Reliability estimates are adequate, and support for various types of validity is promising. For example, teacher ratings on the Conduct Disorder scale have been shown to correlate highly with peer nominations of aggression ($r = .72$) and with observed levels of initiated aggression ($r = .60$) and cooperation ($r = -.45$) in peer interactions (Quay & Peterson, 1983). Caspi et al. (1995) reported that, consistent with the early-starter pathway, childhood temperament predicted scores on the Conduct Disorder scale, but not the Socialized Aggression scale, in adolescence. In a clinical setting, the RBPC can be considered for use as a general screening device, as an instrument for identifying dimensions of deviant behavior, and as a measure of treatment outcome. However, the limited normative data base, the lack of clinical cutoffs, and the omission of positive behaviors or areas of competence from the scale make it less useful than the CBCL (Kamphaus & Frick, 1996; McConaughy, 1992).

The Conners scales are another set of instruments that assess a broad range of child behavior. However, they have been used primarily to discriminate hyperactive from nonhyperactive children and to assess the effects of various drug treatments with these children. Several recent reviewers have failed to recommend the Conners scales as broad-band rating scales, given the confusion concerning multiple versions of both the parent and teacher forms, spotty psychometric data, the lack of social competence items, and the availability of other rating scales without these problems (e.g., the CBCL) (Kamphaus & Frick, 1996; McConaughy, 1992). However, one scale derived from a subset of items on the Conners Teacher Rating Scale is particularly relevant to the assessment of children with CP. The IOWA Conners Teacher Rating Scale (Loney & Milich, 1982) attempts to discriminate children with CP from children with hyperactivity. Half of the 10 items load highly on the Conduct Problem factor, and the remaining items load highly on the Hyperactivity factor. Separate norms and cutoff scores for boys and girls at each of three grade levels (kindergarten to first grade, second to third grades, and fourth to fifth grades) have been presented (Pelham, Milich, Murphy, & Murphy, 1989), and the differential validity of this version of the Conners Teacher Rating Scale has been demonstrated (Milich & Fitzgerald, 1985; Milich & Landau, 1988).

CP-Specific Behavioral Rating Scales

Various other behavioral rating scales, completed by parents, teachers, or children, focus on specific aspects of CP. Examples of parent or teacher report measures include the Eyberg Child Behavior Inventory and Sutter–Eyberg Student Behavior Inventory (ECBI and SESBI; Eyberg, 1992), the Interview for Antisocial Behavior (IAB; Kazdin & Esveldt-Dawson, 1986), and the Children's Hostility Inventory (CHI; Kazdin, Rodgers, Colbus, & Siegel, 1987).

The ECBI (see Eyberg, 1992, for the instrument and a review) is a parent-completed behavioral rating scale that has been explicitly developed to assess disruptive behaviors in children. There is now also a parallel instrument that is designed to be completed by teachers, the SESBI (Eyberg, 1992). The ECBI is intended for use with children from ages 2 through 16, and takes less than 10 minutes to complete. Parents rate each item on both a 7-point frequency of occurrence (Intensity) scale and a yes–no problem identification (Problem) scale. The use of these two scales permits a fine-grained analysis of the presenting problems and may provide useful information concerning the role of parental perceptions of a child in the rating process (Robinson, Eyberg, & Ross, 1980). Although the two scores are moderately correlated (e.g., $r = .72$ in a nonreferred sample, Burns & Patterson, 1990; $r = .87$ in a clinic-referred sample, Eisenstadt, McElreath, Eyberg, & McNeil, 1994), they may provide unique information. Eyberg (1992) has suggested that a low Intensity score in conjunction with a high Problem score may indicate that the parent (or teacher) is intolerant or personally distressed. On the other hand, a high Intensity score and a low Problem score may occur when a parent (or teacher) has a very high tolerance level or is reluctant to admit that the child's behavior is a problem.

Normative data for children aged 2–12 (Robinson et al., 1980) and adolescents aged 13–16 (Eyberg & Robinson, 1983a) have been presented. Based on these data, Eyberg and Ross (1978) recommended clinical cutoff points of 127 or higher for the Intensity score and 11 or higher for the Problem score. In nonreferred populations, approximately 8–10% of the children fall in the clinical range when these cutoff points are employed (Burns & Patterson, 1990; Burns, Patterson, Nussbaum, & Parker, 1991). Despite sex differences on both dimensions of the ECBI (with boys scoring higher than girls) in the original standardization sample, Robinson et al. (1980) chose to report normative data for children aged 2–12 by age only. Analyses with a normative sample of adolescents (Eyberg & Robinson, 1983a) and with larger and more rigorously selected standardization samples (Burns & Patterson, 1990; Burns et al., 1991; Eyberg & Colvin, 1994) have not found meaningful gender or ethnic differences. However, Burns and Patterson (1990; Burns et al., 1991) have reported that scores tended to decrease with children's ages, especially the Intensity score.

With respect to other psychometric considerations, adequate test–retest, split-half, and internal-consistency reliabilities have been reported (Burns & Patterson, 1990; Burns et al., 1991; Eyberg, 1992; Eyberg & Colvin, 1994). Eyberg (1992) reports that mean levels of scores are stable across time as well. Interparent agreement on the ECBI is moderate to strong for both the Intensity ($r =$ .69) and Problem ($r = .61$) scales (e.g., Eisenstadt et al., 1994); mothers give higher scores than fathers on both scales in clinic-referred samples (e.g., Eisenstadt et al., 1994; Webster-Stratton, 1988), but not most nonreferred samples (e.g., Burns & Patterson, 1990; Burns et al., 1991; Eyberg & Ross, 1978). Scores on both ECBI scales and on individual items have been shown to discriminate children with CP from other clinic-referred children (e.g., children with learning disabilities) and from nonreferred children (e.g., Burns & Patterson, 1990; Burns et al., 1991; Eyberg, 1992; Eyberg & Colvin, 1994). The ECBI is significantly correlated with both the Externalizing and Internalizing broad-band scales of the original CBCL, although the correlations are stronger with the Externalizing scale, especially for children of elementary school age (Boggs, Eyberg, & Reynolds, 1990). The ECBI has been found to correlate significantly with various clinic-based observational coding systems, but only modestly with a maternal report measure of child temperament (Robinson & Eyberg, 1981; Webster-Stratton, 1985; Webster-Stratton & Eyberg, 1982). Responses on the ECBI have been shown to be independent of social desirability factors (Robinson & Anderson, 1983). The ECBI is also sensitive to treatment effects from parent training interventions with young children (e.g., Eisenstadt et al., 1993; Eyberg, Boggs, & Algina, 1995; McNeil, Eyberg, Eisenstadt, Newcomb, & Funderburk, 1991; Webster-Stratton, 1994; Webster-Stratton & Hammond, 1997).

The SESBI is identical in format to the ECBI, with 36 items that are rated on both Intensity and Problem scales. Items on the ECBI that are not relevant to the school setting are replaced by 13 new items. Standardization studies have been done on the SESBI with preschoolers (Burns, Sosna, & Ladish, 1992; Funderburk & Eyberg, 1989) and with children in kindergarten through sixth grade (Burns & Owen, 1990; Burns, Walsh, & Owen, 1995). Correlations between the Intensity and Problem scales are comparable to those reported for the ECBI. High levels of internal-consistency, interrater, and test–retest reliabilities have been reported in these investigations. There is minimal or no decrease in scores as a function of repeated administration after intervals ranging from 1 week (Funderburk & Eyberg, 1989) to 1 year (Burns et al., 1995) (but see Burns et al., 1992, for different findings). Recommended cut-off scores have not yet been proposed.

With respect to validity, the SESBI scales have been shown to correlate with other teacher rating scales and to be more highly correlated with subscales related to disruptive behavior problems than with subscales for other types of problems (Burns et al., 1992; Funderburk & Eyberg, 1989). Nonreferred preschoolers and school-age children can be distinguished from children referred for disruptive behavior problems (but not from those children referred for learning or developmental problems) on the basis of their scores on the SESBI (Burns & Owen, 1990; Funderburk & Eyberg, 1989). Teegarden and Burns (1993) found that children with high SESBI scores could be distinguished from their classmates who scored in the normal range on the SESBI on the basis of disruptive and off-task behavior in the classroom (as assessed by the DOF) 7 months later. No systematic age effects were reported in the standardization studies, but Burns and Owen (1990) did find that teachers rated boys more highly than girls. Interestingly, scores on the ECBI and SESBI are not correlated, at least in preschool-age samples (Funderburk & Eyberg, 1989; McNeil et al., 1991). However, McNeil et al. (1991) reported that there was significantly greater improvement in SESBI scores for children whose parents had received a parent training intervention than for either an untreated comparison group or a normal classroom control group; in addition, *change* scores on the Intensity scale of the SESBI were highly correlated with change scores on the ECBI ($r = .78$).

Although the ECBI and SESBI have been described previously by their developers (Eyberg, 1992) and others (e.g., McMahon & Forehand, 1988) as measures of CP per se, they have been more recently and correctly referred to as measures of "disruptive behaviors." This distinction in terminology is important, because the items that make up the ECBI and SESBI contain items that are consistent with the DSM-IV diagnostic categories of ODD, CD, *and* ADHD (Burns & Patterson, 1991). (However, it should be noted that most of the items in both measures relate to CP behaviors rather than ADHD.) Interpretations of factor analyses of the ECBI have differed as to whether the instrument is a unidimensional or multidimensional measure of disruptive behaviors. Both earlier (Eyberg & Robinson, 1983a; Robinson et al., 1980) and more recent (Eyberg & Colvin, 1994) factor analyses conducted by Eyberg and her associates, as well as independent work by Burns and Patterson (1990; Burns et al., 1991), were interpreted as indicating that a single-factor solution best accounted for the structure of the measure. However, Burns and Patterson (1991) also suggested that a three-factor solution is more appropriate, with factors similar to ODD (32–33% of the variance), CD (6–7% of the variance), and ADHD (5–7% of the variance). Similarly, factor analyses of the SESBI (Burns & Owen, 1990; Burns et al., 1995) have suggested the presence of three or four factors: overt aggressive behavior, which includes behaviors consistent with CD, ODD, and ADHD (51–53% of the variance); oppositional behavior (7–8%); attentional difficulties (4–5%); and perhaps covert CP (4%).

Thus, children whose scores exceed the cutoff points on the ECBI or the SESBI are probably a heterogeneous group who may present with ADHD as well as ODD or CD. Given the increasing attention paid to comorbidity of ADHD and CP, this represents a potentially serious limitation of the ECBI. When it is important to identify children who are presenting with "pure" CP, one potential solution might be to score only those items related to either ODD (or ODD and CD), which would facilitate the selection of more homogeneous samples of children (but would preclude the use of existing normative data and cutoff scores).

Despite this potential limitation, the ECBI and SESBI show promise as useful rating scales in clinical settings, where they can be employed as screening instruments and as treatment outcome measures for disruptive behaviors (broadly defined) as rated by parents and teachers. However, their unidimensional assessment of disruptive behaviors limits their utility as broad-band screening instruments. In situations in which a broader screening is desired or when information pertinent to differential diagnosis is sought, use of the CBCL and TRF is recommended.

The IAB (Kazdin & Esveldt-Dawson, 1986) is a 30-item rating scale that is completed by parents and that lists a variety of CP behaviors. Two factors (Arguing/Fighting, Covert Antisocial Behavior) that parallel the overt–covert distinction of CP can be obtained. It discriminates between children with CD and other diagnoses, is associated with higher scores on the CHI (Kazdin, 1992; Kazdin et al., 1987), and is sensitive to intervention effects (Kazdin et al., 1994). The CHI consists of 38 items that load on two factors: Aggression and Hostility. The Hostility scale discriminates children with and without CD, as well as those classified as aggressive versus nonaggressive (Kazdin et al., 1987). Elevations on the Hostility scale are associated with overt, rather than covert, CP (Kazdin, 1992). Both the IAB and the CHI distinguish fire setters from other children; they also distinguish recidivistic from nonrecidivistic children who have engaged in fire-setting behavior (Kolko & Kazdin, 1991a, 1992).

Examples of child self-report measures that focus specifically on CP include the Self-Report Delinquency Scale (SRD; Elliott, Huizinga, & Ageton, 1985) and the Self-Reported Antisocial Behavior Scale (SRA; Loeber, Stouthamer-Loeber, Van Kammen, & Farrington, 1989). The SRD is probably the most widely used youth self-report measure of CP behaviors. It consists of 47 items that are derived from offenses listed in the Uniform Crime Reports and covers index offenses (e.g., stole motor vehicle, aggravated assault), other delinquent behaviors (e.g., hit parent, panhandled), and drug use. The SRD is intended for use by 11- to 19-year-olds, who report on the frequency of engagement in each behavior over the past year. It has been employed primarily in epidemiological and community samples to assess prevalence of CP (e.g., Elliott et al., 1985; Loeber et al., 1989), but it has also been employed as a measure of intervention outcome in clinic-referred samples (e.g., Kazdin et al., 1992, 1994; Scherer, Brondino, Henggeler, Melton, & Hanley, 1994). Pretreatment levels of CP behaviors as assessed by the SRD were predictive of teacher ratings of child behavior problems following a cognitive-behavioral therapy intervention (Kazdin, 1995a).

Because of concerns as to whether elementary school-age children can understand and accurately estimate their engagement in CP behaviors, this type of self-report rating scale is much less common for younger children. The SRA (Loeber et al., 1989) is a self-report measure that has been employed successfully with children as early as first and fourth grades. The SRA consists of 33 items, many of which were adapted from the SRD. Analyses indicated that first- and fourth-grade boys understood the meaning of nearly all of the items; the least understood were those related to smoking marijuana and sniffing glue. In comparisons with parent reports, a tendency for boys to underreport was evident at first and fourth grades on the SRA and at seventh grade on the SRD. Both of these measures have been employed to document the occurrence of substance use in elementary and middle school children, as well as the relationship of substance use to other forms of CP (Van Kammen, Loeber, & Stouthamer-Loeber, 1991).

Summary

There are numerous behavioral rating scales available for use in the assessment of children with CP. Depending upon the specific purposes of the assessment, the clinician has a wide range of instruments from which to choose. These include a comprehensive set of instruments that are designed to assess both broad- and narrow-band dimensions of child disorders and that can be completed by parents, teachers, the children themselves, independent observers, or clinicians (the CBCL family of instruments); and rating scales designed to focus solely on disruptive behaviors as rated by parents and teachers (the ECBI and SESBI). In addition, several rating scales assess specific aspects of CP. On the basis of the available data, we feel that the CBCL family of instruments and the ECBI/SESBI are most likely to meet the general needs of clinicians and researchers dealing with CP. The SRD is a good choice when self-reports of CP behaviors from adolescents are required. The other rating scales described here may be selected to supplement the information provided by these measures.

Behavioral Observation

Direct behavioral observation has been widely employed to assess parent–child, teacher–child, or peer interactions. Given the possibility of perceptual biases among adults intimately involved with a child on a day-to-day basis (e.g., parents, teachers), sole reliance on their reports, whether by interview or questionnaire methods, is unwise (see Patterson & Forgatch, 1995; Reid, Baldwin, Patterson, & Dishion, 1988). Observational methods also have weaknesses, however, such as expense, time investment, reactivity of the observed, and the difficulty of observing infrequent behav-

iors (Breen & Altepeter, 1990; Kamphaus & Frick, 1996). For reviews of direct observation methods, see Barrios (1993), Gottman and Roy (1990), and Reid et al. (1988).

Through the appropriate use of behavioral observation, one is able to obtain information about the frequency and duration of child CP and about events in the environment that maintain or exacerbate CP. This information may provide target behaviors for treatment. Comparisons of observational data with those gathered via other means can assist the clinician in determining whether the focus of intervention should be on the adult–child interaction or on adult perceptual and/or personal adjustment issues. In this section, we describe several observational systems developed for independent observers and significant adults (such as parents and teachers) to measure CP behaviors in an interactional context. Each setting has unique properties that exert some influence on the information obtained during the observation (Dadds & Sanders, 1992). Thus, this section is organized by the settings in which the observation can take place: clinic, home, and school.

Observation by Independent Observers

Observation in the Clinic. Use of a structured clinic observation has several advantages: It efficiently elicits problem interactions; observation can occur unobtrusively through one-way windows; and the standard situation allows within- and between-client comparisons (Hughes & Haynes, 1978). Compared to home or school observations, clinic observations are more efficient for the observer: They can conserve travel time and lower assessment expenses.

Observations in the clinic generally focus on parent–child interactions, but peer interactions (e.g., Dishion, Andrews, & Crosby, 1995) and children's covert CP (e.g., Hinshaw, Heller, & McHale, 1992) have been observed in this setting as well. We review three widely used, structured, microanalytic observation procedures available for assessing parent–child interactions in the clinic: the system developed by Forehand and his colleagues (Forehand & McMahon, 1981); the Dyadic Parent–Child Interaction Coding System II (DPICS II; Eyberg, Bessmer, Newcomb, Edwards, & Robinson, 1994); and the Interpersonal Process Code (IPC; Rusby, Estes, & Dishion, 1991). The Forehand system and the DPICS II are modifications of the assessment procedure developed by Hanf (1970) for the observation of parent–child interactions in the clinic. All three of these systems have also been employed in home observations. Space considerations preclude discussion of observation procedures and coding systems for the assessment of parent–adolescent problem solving and communication; the reader is referred to Foster and Robin (Chapter 13, this volume) for a review of these methods.

In the Forehand observation system, each parent–child pair is observed in a clinic playroom equipped with a one-way window and wired for sound. The playroom contains various age-appropriate toys, such as building blocks, toy trucks and cars, dolls, puzzles, crayons, and paper. An observer codes the parent–child interaction from an adjoining observation room. Prior to the clinic observation, each parent is instructed to interact with his or her child in two different contexts, referred to as the "Child's Game" and the "Parent's Game." In the Child's Game, the parent is instructed to engage in any activity that the child chooses, and to allow the child to determine the nature and rules of the interaction. Thus, the Child's Game is essentially a free-play situation. In the Parent's Game, the parent is instructed to engage the child in activities whose rules and nature are determined by the parent. The Parent's Game is therefore essentially a command situation.

The clinic observation consists of coding the parent–child interaction in both the Child's Game and the Parent's Game (5 minutes each). Six parent behaviors and three child behaviors are recorded during the observation. The parent behaviors include rewards (praise or positive physical attention); attends (description of the child's behavior, activity, or appearance); questions; commands (including both alpha commands, which are directives to which a motoric response is appropriate and feasible, and beta commands, which are commands to which the child has no opportunity to demonstrate compliance); warnings; and time out. The child behaviors are compliance, noncompliance, and inappropriate behavior (whine–cry–yell–tantrum, aggression, deviant talk).

Following the clinic observation, the data are summarized for both the Child's Game and the Parent's Game. Parent behaviors are expressed as rate per minute of attends, rewards, questions, commands (alpha, beta, and total), warnings, and time outs. In addition, the percentage of parental attention contingent upon child compliance (i.e., rewards plus attends emitted within 5 seconds after child compliance) and the ratio of alpha commands to total commands are computed. Child behaviors are expressed in percentages: percentage of child compliance to alpha commands, percentage of child compliance to total commands, and percentage of inappropriate child behavior. Because the time spent in assessing the parent–child interactions is relatively short (10 minutes), this clinic observation procedure can be repeated at each clinic visit, thus providing the clinician with continuing assessment of treatment effects.

Figure 3.3 shows a sample score sheet for the observation of parent–child interactions during the Parent's Game in the clinic. Data are recorded in 30-second intervals. With one exception, the frequency of occurrence of each behavior is scored in each interval. Inappropriate behavior is recorded on an occurrence–nonoccurrence basis for each 30-second interval. The data from the sample observation are summarized at the bottom of the figure. As can be seen, the observed child engaged in inappropriate behavior (e.g., whining, crying, hitting) in 40% of the 10 observation intervals. His compliance to the total number of commands given by the parent was 19%. However, his compliance to clear, direct commands (alpha commands) was much higher (75%). The parent provided positive consequences to only 17% of the child's compliances. Differentiating child compliance to alpha and to beta commands provides the clinician with information about the antecedent events that are maintaining child noncompliance. In this example, the large difference between the percentage of compliance to alpha commands and that to total commands indicated that modification of the parent's command behavior would be essential to treatment success. Based on this observation, the treatment goals would be to (1) teach the parent to give a greater proportion of alpha commands, (2) teach the parent to give fewer beta commands, (3) increase the parent's positive consequation of child compliance, and (4) decrease the child's inappropriate behavior by teaching the parent a time-out procedure.

Using this coding system, Forehand and Peed (1979) have reported an average interobserver agreement of 75%. The coding system possesses adequate test–retest reliability as well. Data from repeated observations of nonintervention parent–child interactions are stable and consistent with this coding system (Peed, Roberts, & Forehand, 1977). With respect to validity, Forehand, King, Peed, and Yoder (1975) found significant differences in rate of parental commands and percentage of child compliance between clinic-referred

Page____1____

SCORE SHEET

Child's Name __*Begood,*_____ *Jack*_____
                    Last   First
Date __*9/17/81*_____ Time __*5:30*_____
Coder's Name ___*JKL*_____
Session ___*1*_____ Place ___*Clinic*_____

ROW 1
C command
W warning
Q question
A attend
R reward

ROW 2
C compliance
N noncompliance

ROW 3
A attend
R reward

CIRCLE
✓ inappropriate child beh.
O appropriate child beh.

OTHER
TO time-out

32/5	=	6.4	Total commands/min.
8/5	=	1.6	Alpha commands/min.
24/5	=	4.8	Beta commands/min.
1/5	=	.2	Warnings/min.

11/5	=	2.2	Quest./min.
7/5	=	1.4	Attends/min.
3/5	=	.6	Rewards/min.

6/8	=	75%	Compliance to alpha commands
6/32	=	19%	Compliance to total commands
1/6	=	17%	Contingent attention
4/10	=	40%	Inappropriate child behavior

FIGURE 3.3. Sample score sheet from observation of parent–child interaction during the Parent's Game in the clinic. From Forehand and McMahon (1981, p. 37). Copyright 1981 by The Guilford Press. Reprinted by permission.

and nonreferred children's interactions with their parents, observed in a clinic. Griest, Forehand, Wells, and McMahon (1980) reported significant differences in compliance in the home setting between clinic-referred and nonreferred children. In other studies, parent–child interactions in the clinic have been shown to be similar to those observed in the home (Peed et al., 1977) and to predict child behavior in the home (Forehand, Wells, & Sturgis, 1978). The observation procedure is also sensitive enough to measure significant treatment effects in the clinic and home (see McMahon & Forehand, 1984, for a review). More specifically, treatment effects observed in the clinic coincide with treatment effects observed in the home (Peed et al., 1977).

The second observational system for coding parent–child interaction in the clinic is the DPICS II (Eyberg et al., 1994). Because of its common roots in the work of Hanf (1970), the DPICS II is quite similar to the Forehand system. The suggested setting for observing with the DPICS II in the clinic is much the same as the setting suggested for the Forehand system, although Eyberg et al. include a third structured task, called "Clean-Up." Another difference is that the "Child-Directed Interaction" (Child's Game in the Forehand system) and the "Parent-Directed Interaction" (Parent's Game in the Forehand system) are separated into two 10-minute segments, with the first 5 minutes of each interaction deemed a "warm-up" (Eyberg et al., 1994).

The DPICS II is a revised version of the DPICS (Eyberg & Robinson, 1983b); although similar in purpose and structure, it has undergone substantial expansion from the original version. The DPICS II includes 26 behavioral categories that were selected because of their theoretical relevance to children with CP. It is designed for use with children whose verbal skills are at least at the 2-year-old level (Eyberg et al., 1994). There are five categories of behavior: verbalizations (e.g., behavioral description, labeled praise, direct command, criticism), vocalizations (e.g., laugh, whine), physical behaviors (e.g., physical positive, destructive), responses following commands (e.g., compliance, noncompliance), and responses following information questions (e.g., answer, no answer). Each behavior may be coded for both parents and children.

The DPICS II is flexible in the specific behavioral categories used. The full 26 categories are used for comprehensive assessment of parent–child interaction, usually for research purposes. Fewer categories may be used for clinical purposes

and focused research questions. The shorter, clinical version includes parent verbalizations, all inappropriate child behavior, and child responses to commands and information questions. Eyberg et al. (1994) also encourage researchers and clinicians to define their own category ("other" behavior) for specific behaviors of interest not specified in the DPICS II (e.g., somatic complaints).

The coding categories may be reported as individual frequencies or combined into summary variables, such as total praise (labeled praise + unlabeled praise), command ratio (direct commands/total commands), or inappropriate behavior (whine + physical negative + yell + destructive). The DPICS II also offers flexibility in the methods for recording data. Observations can be coded via a paper-and-pencil system that yields frequency counts; a paper-and-pencil system in which behaviors are recorded sequentially in 10-second intervals; or a computer software program that records data in real time, yielding frequencies, sequences, and reliability estimates (Celebi & Eyberg, 1994). The choice depends on the type of data needed and the resources available to the clinician or researcher.

The original DPICS standardization study (Robinson & Eyberg, 1981) reported adequate interobserver reliability, with the means for parent and child categories being .91 and .92, respectively. The clinical version of the DPICS II has been examined for reliability during the Child-Directed Interaction and Parent-Directed Interaction tasks (Bessmer, 1993, cited in Eyberg et al., 1994) with a sample of 20 nonproblem families. The authors reported acceptable reliability estimates for nearly all parent and child categories.

Initial investigations into the validity of the DPICS II suggest that differences between referred and nonreferred children (Bessmer & Eyberg, 1993) are detectable, indicating that the DPICS II may have similar discriminant validity to the DPICS. The DPICS was successful in describing the parent–child interactions of children with CP (Wruble, Sheeber, Sorensen, Boggs, & Eyberg, 1991); was a sensitive measure of treatment outcome for these children in both the clinic (e.g., Eisenstadt et al., 1993) and the home (Webster-Stratton, 1994); and was used in conjunction with attachment variables to discriminate clinic-referred boys with CP from control boys (Speltz et al., 1995). A recent investigation using the DPICS II indicates that it may perform similarly in the clinic setting (Eyberg et al., 1995).

The IPC (Rusby et al., 1991) is based on observational research at the Oregon Social Learning

Center. Its origins can be traced to the Family Interaction Coding System, developed by Patterson and his colleagues (Patterson, Ray, Shaw, & Cobb, 1969; Reid, 1978). Although this system was a successful measure of treatment outcome and coercive family processes, it did not provide sequential or durational measures of behavior. Several revisions resulted in the Family Process Code (Dishion et al., 1984), which was developed for a longitudinal study of the development and maintenance of CP behaviors. It included prosocial as well as deviant behaviors, provided ratings of affect for each coded behavior, and recorded interactions in real time (see McMahon & Forehand, 1988, for a description).

Eventually, the Oregon Social Learning Center's program of research led to the study of peer contributions to the development of CP behaviors (Dishion, 1990; Patterson & Dishion, 1985). The basic structure of the Family Process Code was used to develop the Peer Process Code, which assessed the interactions of adolescent boys and their friends in a structured task in the clinic. The Peer Process Code was then simplified into the Playground Code to assess peer interaction on the playground. The proliferation of coding systems with similar structures and content gave rise to the desire for an omnibus system that could be used across multiple contexts and participants; thus, the IPC was developed.

The IPC provides a sequential account of the subject's interactions, so that the relationship of particular antecedent and consequent behaviors can be examined. It has been used in a number of different interactional contexts, such as teaching and free-play situations in the clinic with young school-age children and their families; problem solving in the clinic with preadolescents and their families; live playground observations; and family therapy process. These different settings require flexibility regarding the placement of the observer, instructions to the participants, and the length of the observation. However, unlike the DPICS II, the IPC itself (i.e., the number and description of each code) and the data-recording method do not vary among settings.

The observation session is broken into 5- to 10-minute segments. Each segment has a designated focal person determined at random. Codes are recorded for behavior emitted by that person or directed to that person. The child's behavior may be summarized by computing the frequency of each aversive behavior and the frequency of total aversive behavior (TAB; Patterson et al., 1992; Reid, 1978). The TAB score is a composite of code categories deemed aversive by the investigator or clinician, and is designed to measure general coerciveness. The TAB score from the Oregon Social Learning Center's earlier coding systems correlates highly with parent, teacher, and child self-reports (.73, .58, and .54, respectively) when it is included as an indicator of the "child antisocial" construct (Patterson et al., 1992), and it predicts arrests 2 years later (Patterson & Forgatch, 1995).

The IPC consists of three behavioral dimensions: activity, content, and affect, which are recorded concurrently. The activity codes refer to the global context of the interaction. Up to nine activity codes can be used, depending on the specific purpose of the research and the setting in which the observation occurs. For example, suggested activity codes for adolescent peer interactions in the clinic are "antisocial" (e.g., the content of the conversation is antisocial) and "neutral" (the conversation is not antisocial); for family problem-solving interactions suggested codes are "on-task" and "off-task."

The content codes are mutually exclusive and exhaustive. The codes are divided among three relatively independent categories: verbal, nonverbal, or physical. Within each category, behaviors are defined as positive, neutral, or negative with regard to their interpersonal impact (see Table 3.2). Affect codes, adapted from the categories developed in the Living in Familial Environments coding system (Hops et al., 1990), are coded independently of the content codes. They are on a nominal scale that includes "happy," "caring," "neutral," "distress," "aversive," and "sad."

Data for the IPC are entered in real time on a hand-held event recorder. After the observation session, the data are downloaded to a computer where reliability, frequency, duration, and sequential analysis of codes may be calculated. Interobserver agreement of the IPC has been found to be satisfactory on the playground (average kappas = .69 content, .50 affect; average percentages of agreement = 80% content, 95% affect) and on clinic problem-solving tasks (average kappas = .72 content, .64 affect; average percentages of agreement = 87% content, 90% affect) (M. Eddy, personal communication, May 11, 1996). Preliminary data from a prevention program for children with CP and their families show that the IPC is sensitive to treatment effects (Reid, Eddy, Bank, & Fetrow, 1994).

The Oregon Social Learning Center has also developed several versions of the Observer Impressions Inventory (Weinrott, Reid, Bauske, & Brummett, 1981) to supplement microanalytic obser-

TABLE 3.2. Content Codes of the Interpersonal Process Code (IPC)

Category	Positive	Neutral	Negative
Verbal	Positive talk Positive interpersonal	Talk Advise Directive	Negative talk Negative interpersonal
Nonverbal	Cooperative	Social involvement	Noncooperative
Physical	Positive physical	Physical interact	Negative physical

Note. From Rusby et al. (1991). Adapted by permission.

vations. The original version consists of 25 items (most of which are rated on Likert-type scales) and is completed by the observer immediately following an observation. A cluster analysis of the items revealed four dimensions: Hostility, Disorganization, Child Aggression, and Parental Reactivity to Being Observed. The inventory showed adequate internal consistency (alphas = .73 to .88) and discriminated between families with and without children with CP. Two of the four dimensions (Disorganization, Child Aggression) were significantly correlated with baseline TAB scores from the Family Interaction Coding System (r's = .55 and .38, respectively), and predicted posttreatment TAB scores as well. Combining the Observer Impressions Inventory data with the baseline TAB scores resulted in the strongest predictor of deviant behavior at posttreatment. A revised version of the Observer Impressions Inventory consisting of 46 items has been shown to contribute significantly to the "parental inept discipline" construct described by Patterson and Bank (1986).

Each of the coding systems described above was developed for use in clinical research to provide a rigorous assessment of interactions between children with CP and their parents. The use of these systems in general clinical practice is desirable but rare. To obtain data on CP behaviors and antecedent and consequent events, the coding systems are necessarily complex. Partially as a result of their complexity, the time needed to train and maintain adequate levels of reliability by independent observers is lengthy. For example, most investigators (e.g., Forehand & McMahon, 1981; Reid, 1978) report a minimum of 20 hours of training prior to the start of observations and weekly 1-hour training sessions during the collection of observations. In current training on the IPC, an average of 12 weeks is needed to obtain reliability.

Coding systems such as the clinical version of the DPICS II (Eyberg et al., 1994) and a simplified version of the Forehand system (McMahon & Estes, 1993; see below) are designed to reduce

the demands of these systems on their users and may prove more useful to clinicians. Even with these simplified coding systems, however, few clinical settings have the resources to provide such extensive assessment. An example of a more narrowly focused coding system is the Compliance Test (CT; Roberts & Powers, 1988). The CT is a standardized measure of child compliance to parental commands. The suggested setting is a clinic playroom with a standardized set of toys, a one-way window for observation, and a "bug-in-the-ear" device for communication between the parent and the clinician. A cassette tape signals 5-second intervals for observation of compliance after each parental command is issued. The parent is instructed to give a series of 30 standard commands, without helping or following up on the commands with other verbalizations or nonverbal cues. In the first version of the CT (CT-1), two-part commands are given (e.g., "[Child's name], put the [toy] in the [container]"). In the second version (CT-2), the commands are separated into two codeable units (e.g., "[Child's name], pick up the [toy]. Put it in the [container]"). Thus, in CT-1 the child has the opportunity to comply 30 times, and in CT-2 the child has 60 opportunities for compliance. Roberts and Powers report that the CT takes between 5 and 15 minutes to complete.

Roberts and Powers (1988) present evidence for the interobserver agreement of the CT-1 and CT-2 (97.3% and 97.4%, respectively). The CT-1 showed adequate test–retest reliability (r = .73; mean interval = 11.8 days), although a significant decline in compliance was detected at retest. The CT was related to other home and clinic observational measures, although it did not converge with parent questionnaire data. However, in a subsequent study (Roberts et al., 1992), parental locus of control (see below) was associated with child performance on the CT. The CT appears to be a useful measure in identifying noncompliant children in research and clinical settings (Roberts & Powers, 1990). Because the CT does not measure parental instruction giving, Roberts and Powers (1988) recommend that it be used in conjunction with a less structured task that allows coding of parental behavior (e.g., Parent's Game from Forehand & McMahon, 1981, or Clean-Up from Eyberg et al., 1994).

Another example of a more narrowly focused clinic-based assessment is one developed by Hinshaw et al. (1992) to assess the covert CP behaviors of stealing, property destruction, and cheating in samples of boys aged 6–12 with ADHD (most of them also had ODD or CD) and a comparison group. Each child was asked to complete an academic worksheet alone in a room that contained a completed answer sheet, money, and toys. Stealing was measured by conducting a count of objects in the room immediately following the work session, whereas property destruction and cheating were assessed by observing the child's behavior during the session. Each of these observational measures of covert CP was correlated with parental ratings on the Delinquency scale of the CBCL. Stealing and property destruction were also associated with staff ratings of potential for covert CP behaviors; when the boys with ADHD were being treated with methylphenidate, they decreased to a level similar to that displayed by boys in the comparison condition. None of the three measures of covert CP were significantly correlated with each other.

Kolko et al. (1991) employed a very brief (1-minute) observation to assess children's preference for fire-related stimuli (e.g., a simulated book of matches) over toys in a play setting. Interobserver agreement for percentage of time in contact with fire-related stimuli, picking up the matchbook, or attempting to strike a match ranged from 93% to 100%. All three indices demonstrated significant decreases from pretreatment to posttreatment in an inpatient sample of children with ODD, CD, and/or ADHD, who also engaged in match play or fire setting.

In general, we recommend the use of structured clinic observations such as those described here to assess parent–child interactions. If there is a discrepancy between the clinic observations and the parent reports of interactions at home, home observation may be necessary.

Observation in the Home. Home observation is often referred to as "naturalistic observation" because families and children are observed in familiar environments (Reid et al., 1988). In general, the use of a coding system in the home setting instead of the clinic requires changes primarily in the structure of the observation. In addition to training time, home observations require transportation time and scheduling flexibility. If home observations are planned to coincide with the times when the problem child behaviors are more likely to occur, they require more flexibility in the observers' schedules. Drotar and Crawford (1987) discuss many of the issues involved in conducting home observations.

The Forehand system, the DPICS, and the IPC, discussed above, are all designed for use in the home as well as the clinic. Although these coding systems are designed to record social interactions among family members in their "natural" environment (the home), home observation sessions are not completely unstructured. For example, prior to the observation, members of the family are typically given instructions such as the following: (1) Everyone in the family must be present; (2) no guests should be present during observations; (3) the family is limited to two rooms; (4) no telephone calls are to be made, and incoming calls must be answered briefly; (5) no television viewing is permitted; (6) no conversations may be held with observers while they are coding; and (7) therapy-related issues are not to be discussed with the observer (Reid, 1978).

When employed in the home setting, the Forehand coding system (Forehand & McMahon, 1981) is used to collect data in blocks of four 40-minute observations. The observations are conducted on different days and may be done at different times of the day. The Forehand coding system only permits the behavior of a single adult and a single child to be recorded at a given time. If more than one parent is being observed, then separate observation sessions may occur with each parent and child, or the observer can code the behavior of each parent with the child in alternating 5-minute periods (Forehand & McMahon, 1981).

We (McMahon & Estes, 1993) have developed a simplified version of Forehand and McMahon's (1981) original coding system that has been employed in structured observations in the home. It has fewer codes, in order to maximize reliability and minimize training time while retaining important treatment outcome information about parent–child interactions. Observers use a standardized set of toys and give standardized instructions to the parents before the interaction begins. The structure of the session includes the Child's Game (5 minutes), the Parent's Game (5 minutes), a Lego Task (in which the child is told to construct a developmentally challenging Lego figure and the parent is instructed to give only verbal aid) (5 minutes), and Clean-Up (3 minutes).

Throughout each task, three parent behaviors (commands, positive attention, negative attention) and two child behaviors (compliance and noncompliance) are recorded sequentially during 30-second intervals. In addition, there is an interval-sampling measure of child disruptive behavior. Observers use an audio recorder with standardized 30-second interval prompts and a paper-and-pencil-data-recording sheet.

Although the original DPICS was developed as a clinic-based observation system, it has been employed in home observations on a number of occasions as well. Some of these investigations have assessed the relationship between parent–child interactions as observed in the clinic and in the home. For example, Zangwill and Kniskern (1982) found that in a clinic-referred sample, mother and child behaviors observed in the clinic were correlated to a moderate degree with the same behaviors observed in the home. However, the rates of the behaviors tended to be higher in the clinic than in the home. Webster-Stratton (1985) concluded that the similarity of the structure of the observations, rather than setting per se, was the key to clinic–home comparability. She found that the strongest correlations between clinic and home observations occurred when the clinic observations were relatively unstructured, thus making them similar in format to the home observations. However, she recommended that the Parent-Directed Interaction (analogous to the Parent's Game in Forehand's coding system) be employed as a "challenge test" in the clinic, since it elicited higher rates of deviant mother and child behaviors in her clinic-referred sample than either the Child-Directed Interaction (analogous to the Child's Game in Forehand's coding system) or the unstructured clinic observation. On the basis of our own clinical experience with the Parent's Game and Child's Game observational formats, we feel that the Child-Directed Interaction format also provides useful data concerning the parent's reinforcement of appropriate child behavior and possible difficulties with parental directives (i.e., high rates of commands).

As noted above, the IPC is designed for use in various settings, including the home, with the same constellation of codes. The home observation session typically lasts 50 minutes. Six activity codes are suggested for use in the home: work (e.g., household maintenance, homework), play, read, eat, attend (e.g., watching others), and unspecified (e.g., inactivity, between activities). Following three or more observation sessions in the home, the child's behavior may be summarized by computing the frequency of each aversive behavior and the frequency of TAB.

Observation in the School. Direct observations in the school have the same practical problems as those mentioned above for home observations. The necessity of training reliable observers and the lengthy observation time are similar. Unfortunately, the clinician does not have the option of observing teacher–child interactions in the clinic. Therefore, if the presenting problems concern behavior at school (whether in the classroom or on the playground), observation in that setting may be necessary.

The clinician must first obtain the permission of the parents, the principal, and the teacher(s) before scheduling the observations. As with home observations, behavior observations in the classroom should be timed to occur when the problem interactions are most frequent. For example, if the teacher reports that the child is particularly disruptive during seatwork in the morning, the observation should take place during that period, not during reading class in the afternoon.

Several of the coding systems described above have been employed in the school (e.g., Breiner & Forehand, 1981; Rusby et al., 1991). Breiner and Forehand (1981) modified the Forehand and McMahon (1981) coding system for use in the classroom setting. Interobserver agreement figures were 80% or higher for each teacher and child behavior. Adoption of these coding systems has the advantage of facilitating cross-situational (home–school) comparisons during assessment of treatment outcome. McNeil et al. (1991) used a combination of the Breiner and Forehand system and "academic engaged time" (see below) to provide evidence for parent training treatment generalization from home to school for children with CP.

Cobb and Hops (1972) designed a system specifically for the acting-out child in the classroom. With this coding system, the behaviors of teachers and peers that precede and follow the child's acting-out behavior are recorded, thus providing a sequential pattern identifying the antecedent and consequent events of the child's behavior. There are 37 different behavioral categories, which can be grouped under eight headings: approvals and disapprovals, attention and looking at, management questions, academic talk, commands, disruption and inappropriate locale, physical negative and punishment, and miscellaneous. Using a modified form of the coding system that included 19 categories, Walker and Hops (1976) reported interobserver agreement reliabilities above 95%.

Furthermore, the system discriminated between teacher-referred children with CP and their classroom peers in terms of appropriate behavior, and was sensitive to classroom intervention procedures.

The Fast Track School Observation Program (Wehby, 1993; Wehby, Dodge, Valente, & the Conduct Problems Prevention Research Group, 1993) measures children's positive and negative interactions with teachers and peers. It consists of nine mutually exclusive event codes and eight durational measures of activities. The event codes include teacher positive and negative commands, child initiation/peer positive response, child initiation/peer negative response, peer initiation/child positive response, peer initiation/child negative response, child-to-peer aggression, peer-to-child aggression, and child disruptive behavior. The durational measures indicate the type of activity in which the child is engaged (teacher engaged/disengaged, peer engaged/disengaged, solitary engaged/disengaged, transition engaged/disengaged). These codes are recorded in real time via a computer system called the Multiple Option Observation System for Experimental Studies (Tapp, Wehby, & Ellis, 1995). At the end of each observation session, global ratings are made with an adaptation of the Teacher Observation of Classroom Adaptation—Revised rating scale (Werthamer-Larsson, Kellam, & Wheeler, 1991) and a postobservation inventory.

School observations were conducted on a community sample of first-graders, including children at risk for CP. Each child was observed for 2 hours across four 30-minute segments on different days. At least 45 minutes of the 2 hours occurred during unstructured time, such as recess or lunch. Event codes averaged 88% agreement with a mean kappa of .74, and durational codes averaged 75% agreement. Wehby et al. (1993) reported preliminary evidence for the discriminant validity of this coding system. Children categorized as high-risk received more negative commands from teachers, and showed a trend toward more disruptive behavior and more solitary/disengaged time, than their non-high-risk peers.

The DOF of the CBCL (Achenbach, 1991b) is intended for use with children aged 5–14. It may be used as part of a multimodal assessment with the other versions of the CBCL described in this chapter. There is a high degree of overlap between the 96 Problem items on the DOF and the teacher (85 common items) and parent (72 common items) forms of the CBCL. Three to six 10-minute observations of the child on different days and at different times of the day are collected. The child is observed for 10 minutes, during which the observer writes a narrative description of the child's behavior. At the end of each minute, the child is observed for 5 seconds, and the presence or absence of on-task behavior is recorded. At the end of the observation, the observer then completes the DOF. Each item is rated on a 4-point scale, with higher ratings indicative of greater intensity and/or duration. Achenbach recommends that observations of two same-sex control children in the classroom be conducted as well—one prior to observation of the target child, and the other immediately afterward.

The DOF yields a Total Problem score, a measure of on-task behavior, and two broad-band scales (Internalizing and Externalizing) and six narrow-band scales (Withdrawn–Inattentive, Nervous–Obsessive, Depressed, Hyperactive, Attention-Demanding, Aggressive). Clinical cutoff points are presented in Achenbach (1991b). Acceptable levels of interobserver reliability for the Total Problem and on-task scores, as well as for individual items on the DOF, have been reported (McConaughy, Achenbach, & Gent, 1988; Reed & Edelbrock, 1983). The DOF scores are also correlated with corresponding teacher ratings on the TRF (Reed & Edelbrock, 1983) and the SESBI (Teegarden & Burns, 1993), and they discriminate between referred and nonreferred children in the classroom (e.g., Reed & Edelbrock, 1983). The broad-band Externalizing scale and the Hyperactive, Attention-Demanding, and Aggressive narrow-band scales differentiate children with externalizing behavior problems from children with other behavior problems (McConaughy et al., 1988).

Academic engaged time is the amount of time a child spends appropriately engaged in on-task behavior during classtime. It may be measured by stopwatch (Walker, Colvin, & Ramsey, 1995) or by a specially programmed computer (Wehby et al., 1993). Walker et al. (1995) recommend observing children during two 15-minute periods. Observers start a stopwatch and allow it to run when the child is academically engaged (as defined by Walker et al., 1995). Academic engaged time has been shown to correlate positively with academic performance (Walker, 1995) and to discriminate boys at risk for CP from boys not at risk (e.g., Walker, Shinn, O'Neill, & Ramsey, 1987).

Observation by Significant Adults

An alternative to observations by independent observers in the natural setting is to train significant adults in the child's environment to observe and record certain types of child behavior. For example, Patterson (Patterson et al., 1975), Forehand (Forehand & McMahon, 1981; Furey & Forehand, 1983), and others (Walker, 1995) report the use of parents and/or teachers as observers in addition to, or instead of, independent observers in the natural setting.

The Parent Daily Report (PDR; Chamberlain & Reid, 1987) is probably the most widely used measure of this type. The PDR is typically administered during a series of brief (5- to 10-minute) telephone interviews. Originally developed in 1969, it exists in multiple forms. Current versions consist of 22–34 negative overt and covert behaviors common to children (Chamberlain & Reid, 1987; Patterson & Bank, 1986; Webster-Stratton & Spitzer, 1991). Parents are asked whether any of the targeted behaviors have occurred in the past 24 hours. Two scores are derived from the PDR: Targeted Behavior, which is the sum of all occurrences of behaviors targeted as problematic by parents at the initial interview; and Total Behavior, which is the sum of all occurrences of the total list of behaviors (Chamberlain & Reid, 1987). Parent behaviors, ranging from a single item indicating whether the parent has spanked the child in the past 24 hours to parental monitoring of the child, positive reinforcement directed to the child, and the occurrence of crises and social support, are included in some versions of the PDR (Chamberlain & Reid, 1987; Patterson & Bank, 1986). Some versions also record the setting in which the problem behavior is occurring (home, school, community, other). In a parallel form of the PDR for children (Patterson & Bank, 1986), the child is asked whether he or she has engaged in any of various overt and covert CP behaviors, what the state of his or her mood is, and whether the parents have engaged in any of several monitoring behaviors (e.g., talk about the child's activities).

Normative data on both PDR scores are presented in Chamberlain and Reid (1987) for parents of children aged 4–10. The mean daily numbers of problem behaviors reported for the PDR Targeted Behavior and Total Behavior scores were 2.29 and 5.33, respectively. The Targeted Behavior score is a more useful measure than the Total Behavior score, since only the former score has adequate interparent reliability and concurrent validity (Chamberlain & Reid, 1987).

The PDR can be employed on a pretreatment basis to assess the magnitude of behavior problems and to check the information presented by the parents in the initial interview. It can also be used during intervention to monitor the progress of the family. Finally, the PDR has been employed extensively as a measure of treatment outcome (e.g., Chamberlain & Reid, 1994; Patterson, Chamberlain, & Reid, 1982; Sheeber & Johnson, 1994; Webster-Stratton & Hammond, 1997). Reviews of the psychometric characteristics of the PDR are presented by Patterson (1982) and Chamberlain and Reid (1987). The PDR possesses adequate intercaller and interparent reliability, as well as internal consistency and temporal stability. With respect to stability, Chamberlain and Reid (1987) have noted that PDR scores tend to be inflated on the first day but stable thereafter, at least with nonreferred families. It may thus be advisable to discard data from the first telephone interview with the PDR.

The PDR has been shown to correlate significantly with direct observation measures in populations of socially aggressive, stealing, and normal children (Patterson, 1982; Webster-Stratton & Spitzer, 1991). Although the PDR has proven quite sensitive to treatment effects, Patterson (1982) has suggested that it is highly reactive in this regard, at least when compared to observational data gathered by independent observers. The PDR has shown moderate convergent validity with other parent report measures of child behavior and parental adjustment (Chamberlain & Reid, 1987; Webster-Stratton & Spitzer, 1991). Chamberlain and Reid (1987) reported that social desirability factors seem to exert minimal influence on PDR scores, at least with nonreferred families.

The Daily Telephone Discipline Interview (DDI; Webster-Stratton & Spitzer, 1991) was developed as an addendum to the PDR to provide more detailed information about parental interventions subsequent to child misbehavior reported on the PDR. For each behavior endorsed on the PDR, the interviewer asks, "How did you handle this problem?" Answers are recorded verbatim and coded for 43 behaviors that are included in one of six broader categories: physical force (e.g., spank, restrain); critical verbal force (yell, argue); limit setting (time out, logical consequences); teaching (reasoning, rewards); empathy (identifying warmly with child's feelings); and guilt induction (humiliation, reminding child of mistake). Two additional scores are possible with the DDI: flexibility and inappropriateness of disciplinary strategy. Interrater agreement was adequate (80%), ranging from 60% to 88% for individual categories. Test–retest reliability (1 week) was adequate (r's = .45 to .75), especially given that the behaviors reported upon changed between the two interviews. Internal consistency was moderate (alphas = .59 to .86). DDI variables were significantly related to the Total Problem score on the CBCL; to parent self-reports of depression, marital adjustment, anxiety, parenting stress, spouse abuse, and child abuse; and to observed parent and child behavior (Webster-Stratton & Spitzer, 1991). The inappropriateness of discipline strategy score predicted long-term parent training intervention outcome (1–2 years posttreatment) for girls' (but not boys') teacher-rated CP (Webster-Stratton, 1996).

Another example of a parent-reported observation procedure is the Child Conflict Index (CCI; Frankel & Weiner, 1990). The CCI measures common child behaviors associated with CP, such as interpersonal conflict, misbehavior, noncompliance, arguing, "bad mood," and teasing. It is administered over the telephone to parents of children aged 2–12 years, and refers only to behaviors that have occurred during the previous day. Slightly different versions of the CCI are employed with parents of boys (10 items) and girls (8 items). Internal consistency and interobserver agreement were acceptable. Scores on the CCI were negatively correlated with observed child compliance in a clinic analogue setting. The CCI also successfully discriminated referred and nonreferred boys and girls.

In Forehand's parent observation procedure (Forehand & McMahon, 1981), parents select 3 problem behaviors from a list of 11 at the initial interview (whine, physical negative, humiliate, destructiveness, tease, smart talk, noncompliance, ignore, yell, demand attention, and temper tantrum). Parents are required to record the frequency of each of the selected problem behaviors during the 24 hours preceding four home observations both before and after treatment. The independent observers collect the parent-recorded data at the end of each 24-hour period when they visit the home for observations. No reliability data have been reported. Furthermore, Forehand, Griest, and Wells (1979) reported that the parent-recorded data during the 24-hour period did not correlate significantly with observer measures of child compliance and child deviant behavior during a subsequent 40-minute observation, suggesting that the two methods of data collection may yield different conclusions.

Walker (1995) presents guidelines and examples of simple observation procedures appropriate for use by teachers in the classroom. He suggests that the stopwatch method of assessing academic engaged time (described above) may be employed by teachers not only to assess such time in the classroom, but also to assess the amount of prosocial behavior directed by a child with CP to his or her peers on the playground. Kubany and Sloggett (1973) developed a simple but reliable procedure for classroom teachers to estimate the amount of on-task, passive, and disruptive behaviors in which particular students are engaging. Recordings are made on either a 4-, 8-, or 16-minute variable-interval schedule. A kitchen timer is used to signal recording times.

With certain low-rate behaviors, such as stealing, fire setting, and truancy, parent- and/or teacher-collected data may be the only sources of information on the occurrence of these behaviors. The coding procedure for teachers developed by Kubany and Sloggett (1973) and described above can also be modified to record low-rate behaviors in the classroom. The teacher simply notes whether the behavior occurred at any time during the interval. Patterson and his colleagues (e.g., Patterson et al., 1975) have developed specific techniques for the assessment and treatment of children who steal. Because behaviors such as stealing are rarely observed, the target behavior is redefined as "the child's taking, or being in possession of, anything that does not clearly belong to him" or the parent's "receiving a report or complaint by a reliable informant" (Patterson et al., 1975, p. 137). Jones (1974) reports the development of a brief daily interview similar to the PDR for collecting data on the occurrence–nonoccurrence of stealing by children between the ages of 5 and 15. The parent is queried as to whether stealing took place, and, if so, the item(s) stolen and their value, the location and social context of the theft, the way the parent learned of the theft, and the parent's response to the theft. This Telephone Interview Report on Stealing and Social Aggression has adequate test–retest reliability and is sensitive to the effects of treatment procedures designed to reduce stealing (Reid, Hinojosa-Rivera, & Lorber, 1980).

Summary

Behavioral observation is probably the most important and useful assessment procedure for obtaining a functional analysis of CP in children. Unfortunately, it is also the most costly in terms of time. As a result, efforts are being made to develop alternative observational procedures that are more efficient but that maintain or enhance the quality of the information obtained. It is unclear whether such technological innovations as the use of computers to enter data in real time (e.g., Rusby et al., 1991; Wehby et al., 1993) or the use of audiotape recording equipment in the home to record family observations more unobtrusively (e.g., Christensen, 1979) are cost-effective, especially for use in clinical settings. Perhaps brief structured tasks that elicit interactional behaviors of interest in the clinic setting and that employ simple coding systems will prove to be useful alternatives. Examples presented in this chapter are the CT (Roberts & Powers, 1988), the procedures for assessing covert CP behaviors developed by Hinshaw et al. (1992) and Kolko et al. (1991), and the stopwatch measure of academic engaged time in the classroom (Walker et al., 1995).

Associated Child Characteristics

In earlier sections of this chapter, we have discussed various child attributes that in at least some cases are associated with CP. These include developmental and medical difficulties; temperamental variables; and specific disorders or conditions, such as ADHD, depression, psychopathy, and peer relationship and academic problems. In this section, we briefly discuss the assessment of these factors.

Developmental and Medical History

Usually as part of the initial behavioral interview with the parents, a brief developmental and medical history of the child should be obtained. The purpose of this line of questioning is to determine whether any medical factors may be associated with either the development or maintenance of the child's CP behaviors (e.g., past or current evidence of neurological injury or disease, hearing difficulties, extended or frequent hospitalizations). The interview should cover difficulties during pregnancy, birth, and early childhood; ages at which developmental milestones such as sitting, standing, walking, and talking were reached; medical (especially neurological), speech, and hearing problems; and the presence or absence of various toileting problems. If the clinician suspects any of these problems, an appropriate referral (e.g., physician, audiologist) may need to be made prior to, or concomitant with, intervention. Examples of interview questions of this type are presented in

Breen and Altepeter (1990), Kamphaus and Frick (1996), and Sanders and Dadds (1993).

Temperament

The most widely recognized classification of temperament comes from the New York Longitudinal Survey (e.g., Thomas & Chess, 1977; Thomas et al., 1968), which identified nine dimensions of temperament: activity level; rhythmicity (regularity of sleeping, eating, etc.); approach to or withdrawal from new stimuli; adaptability to new situations; intensity of reaction; threshold of responsiveness; quality of mood; distractibility; and attention span. The clinician may choose to query the parents on these dimensions in the context of the developmental interview mentioned above, or temperament may be assessed in a more formal manner. However, factor-analytic studies of various temperament questionnaires have often failed to duplicate this model (Slabach, Morrow, & Wachs, 1991). Instead, a smaller number of factors have tended to emerge, including distress to novelty, other distress-proneness or irritability, positive affect/approach, activity level, and persistence (Rothbart et al., 1995).

A number of standardized parent interviews (e.g., Thomas & Chess, 1977) and questionnaires exist for assessing temperament; however, they present difficulties in terms of lengthy administration and scoring procedures, and/or problems with respect to the adequacy of their psychometric properties (see Slabach et al., 1991, for a review). One questionnaire with adequate psychometric properties that has been shown to relate early temperament to subsequent CP is the Infant Characteristics Questionnaire, which is suitable for parents of children from 4 to 24 months of age (Bates, Freeland, & Lounsbury, 1979). It provides scores on three dimensions of temperament: difficultness, unadaptability, and unmanageability.

Although measures of infant temperament are of interest for the prediction of CP in longitudinal research, their use in clinical work is less likely to be useful. Temperament measures for preschoolers, older children, and adolescents are less common (see Capaldi & Rothbart, 1992, for an example of an instrument for assessing temperament in early adolescence). In addition, it is important to be aware of the potential overlap between items on temperament questionnaires and behavioral rating scales, which can contaminate the interpretation of both predictive and concurrent relationships (e.g., Sanson, Prior, & Kyrios, 1990; Slabach et al., 1991). However, others have presented data suggesting that this may not be a problem (Bates, 1990; Sheeber, 1995).

Associated/Comorbid Disorders and Conditions

As noted earlier, children with CP may also present with a variety of other behavior disorders, including ADHD, internalizing disorders (especially depressive disorders, and to a lesser extent anxiety disorders and Somatization Disorder), and substance use disorders. Awareness of the various potential developmental pathways for CP should assist the clinician in determining the breadth and direction of his or her assessment of other disorders. Behavioral rating scales that provide information about a wide range of narrow-band behavior disorders, such as the CBCL family of instruments (Achenbach, 1993b), can serve as a useful screening device. If there are significant elevations on the relevant scales of the CBCL, then a more thorough assessment of these disorders is warranted. For example, the Attention Problems scale of the CBCL has been shown to be an accurate screen for possible ADHD (Chen, Faraone, Biederman, & Tsuang, 1994), although it does not permit subtyping. More detailed information on the assessment of these comorbid disorders may be found in the relevant chapters in this volume, as well as in Kamphaus and Frick (1996).

Instruments to assess psychopathy and the related construct of sensation seeking in children have recently been developed. The Psychopathy Screening Device (Frick & Hare, in press), which is completed by parents or teachers, consists of 20 items, 16 of which have been shown to load on one of two factors: Impulsivity/Conduct Problems and Callous/Unemotional (Frick et al., 1994). The former factor seems to tap into typical CP behaviors, whereas the latter factor is analogous to the construct of psychopathy as it has been measured in adults, and includes items concerning a lack of guilt, insincerity, and lack of concern for the feelings of others. The two scales were moderately correlated ($r = .50$). Internal consistency was adequate for each scale (alphas > .70). The Callous/Unemotional scale was correlated with other measures of CP, but to a lesser extent than the Impulsivity/Conduct Problem scale. However, it was positively associated with measures of sensation seeking (see below) and a "reward-dominant" response style (O'Brien & Frick, 1996), and negatively correlated with measures of anxiety. As noted earlier in the chapter, children with ODD or CD

and a high score on the Callous/Unemotional scale were much more likely to have a positive paternal arrest history than children with ODD or CD alone or children with elevated scores on the Callous/Unemotional scale only (Frick et al., 1994).

The Sensation-Seeking Scale for Children (SSSC; Russo et al., 1991, 1993) is an adaptation of Zuckerman's Sensation-Seeking Scale for adults. The child responds to 26 items in a forced-choice format. Internal-consistency and test–retest reliabilities are adequate. The SSSC is scored on three factor-analytically derived scales (Thrill and Adventure Seeking, Drug and Alcohol Attitudes, and Social Disinhibition) and a Total Sensation Seeking score. It discriminated boys with and without CD in a clinic-referred sample (Russo et al., 1991, 1993); however, it did not discriminate between boys with CP and boys in a community sample (Russo et al., 1991). An earlier version of the SSSC was positively correlated with maternal, but not paternal, scores on the adult version of the scale (Russo et al., 1991). Frick et al. (1994) reported that scores on the Callous/Unemotional scale of the Psychopathy Screening Device, but not ODD/CD status, predicted to scores on the SSSC.

As noted above, children with CP frequently have problems with peer interactions. If the information from behavioral interviews, behavioral rating scales (e.g., the Competence scales of the CBCL; Achenbach, 1991b), and observations indicate that peer relationships are problematic for a particular child, additional assessment of the child's social skills is necessary. The assessment should examine not only the behavioral aspects of the social skills difficulties, but cognitive and affective dimensions as well. Traditionally, assessment of social skills has involved behavioral observations, sociometric measures, and questionnaires. A more recent development is the assessment of social-cognitive processes through standardized written or videotaped vignettes of social situations (e.g., Dodge, McClaskey, & Feldman, 1985). Bierman and Welsh (Chapter 6, this volume) provide strategies for the assessment of social relationship problems, and Demaray et al. (1995) review several behavioral rating scales for the assessment of social competence.

If the presenting problem concerns classroom behavior, a functional analysis of the problem behaviors should also include an assessment of the child's academic behavior. Although interviews, observations, and rating scales can provide information concerning the child's academic behavior, additional evaluation in the form of intelligence and achievement tests is necessary to determine whether the child may have learning difficulties in addition to CP. Walker (1995) discusses the use of a standardized method for retrieving and using school records (the School Archival Records System; H. M. Walker, Block-Pedego, Todis, & Severson, 1991) with children with CP. This system is a reliable (interobserver agreement = 96%) method of collecting such information, and has been shown to discriminate children with CP from children with internalizing problems and normal control children (H. M. Walker et al., 1991). It includes information such as standardized achievement test scores, report card grades, grade placement for the upcoming year, academic and behavioral referrals, individualized education plans, attendance, and disciplinary contacts. Lyon (1994) provides a complete review of assessment strategies with which to evaluate learning problems.

Familial and Extrafamilial Factors

In this section, we discuss the assessment of six familial and extrafamilial areas that are relevant to CP in children: parenting practices; parents' (and teachers') social cognitions; parents' perceptions of their own personal and marital adjustment; parental stress; parental functioning in extrafamilial social contexts; and parental satisfaction with treatment.

Parenting Practices

As noted above, parenting practices have typically been assessed via direct observation of parent–child interaction. Although this has been, and will continue to be, an important and useful means of assessing parental behavior, several questionnaires that have been specifically designed to assess parenting practices have been developed over the past several years. (Measures that are designed to measure global child-rearing attitudes as opposed to specific parenting practices are not discussed here; see Holden & Edwards, 1989). These questionnaires may be potentially quite useful as adjuncts to behavioral observations and/or as ways to assess parental behaviors that either occur infrequently or are otherwise difficult to observe (e.g., physical discipline, parental monitoring practices). They may also prove useful as screening instruments in a multiple-gating procedure to determine when more expensive observational procedures may be indicated, and to measure the effects of parent training interventions.

Several broad self-report measures of parenting practices have been developed recently. The Parenting Scale (PS; Arnold, O'Leary, Wolff, & Acker, 1993) consists of 30 items that describe parental discipline practices in response to misbehavior by young children (i.e., 2- to 3-year-olds). Each of the items consists of a 7-point rating scale that is anchored by statements of the effective and ineffective forms of a particular parenting behavior (e.g., "I coax or beg my child to stop" and "I firmly tell my child to stop"). Items are worded at a sixth-grade level or below, and the measure takes 5–10 minutes to complete.

Factor analyses of the PS have indicated that there are three factors, accounting for 37% of the variance: Laxness, Overreactivity, and Verbosity (Arnold et al., 1993). The PS may be scored on each of the factors, as well as a Total score that includes an additional four items addressing conceptually important practices (e.g., monitoring). The factor scales and the Total score have adequate internal-consistency (.63–.84) and 2-week test–retest (r's = .79–.84) reliabilities, and they have been shown to relate to similar ratings obtained by independent observers in a structured observation of parent–child interaction (r's = .53–.73). With the exception of Verbosity, the scales and Total score have also been shown to differentiate clinic-referred and nonreferred groups and to be significantly correlated with observed child behavior in a structured parent–child interaction task (r's = .62–.69). All of the scales and the Total score were positively correlated with the maternal report on the CBCL Externalizing scale (r's = .22–.54) and negatively correlated with the Short Marital Adjustment Test measure of marital satisfaction (r's = -.35–.53).

The Parent Practices Scale (PPS; Strayhorn & Weidman, 1988) consists of 34 items relating to parenting behaviors and cognitions that are based on parent training goals with preschool-age children. Most of the items employ a 5- to 7-point Likert-type scale to assess frequency of use of the parenting behavior, but some items have parents select from a list of parenting strategies they would be most likely to employ in a particular situation with their child. The PPS has been employed with a sample of lower-SES mothers, primarily African-American, and their 3- to 4-year-old children. It possesses adequate internal-consistency (alpha = .78–.79) and test–retest (r = .79 at 6 months) reliabilities. The PPS was correlated with parental behaviors observed in videotaped parent–child interactions, and negatively correlated with a measure of unreasonable commands. More appropriate parenting on the PPS was associated with lower parental depression scores on the Beck Depression Inventory ($r = .40$). The PPS has also been used to assess the immediate and 1-year follow-up effects of a parent training intervention for preschool-age children with mixed behavior problems (Strayhorn & Weidman, 1989, 1991).

The Alabama Parenting Questionnaire (APQ; Frick, 1991) has been developed for use with parents of children aged 6–13. It consists of 42 items that have been divided into five *a priori* constructs—Involvement, Positive Parenting, Poor Monitoring/Supervision, Inconsistent Discipline, and Corporal Punishment—and a set of "other discipline practices." The items are presented in both global report (i.e., questionnaire) and telephone interview formats, and there are separate versions of each format for parents and children. Thus, there are currently four different versions of the APQ. The questionnaire format employs a 5-point Likert-type frequency scale and asks the informant how frequently each of the various parenting practices typically occurs. Four telephone interviews are conducted, and the informant is asked to report the frequency with which each parenting practice has occurred over the previous 3 days.

Preliminary data concerning the psychometric properties of the APQ suggest that the two child versions may not be acceptable, at least with children of elementary school age (Shelton, Frick, & Wootton, 1996). There was evidence of a response set bias on the telephone interview format; also, neither version differentiated the parenting practices of parents of children with ODD, CD, and/or ADHD, from those of parents of children without these disorders. In contrast, both the parent-completed questionnaire and the parent telephone interview versions of the APQ did differentiate these two groups of parents, primarily because of differential elevations on the three scales measuring negative parenting practices. The diagnosis of DBD was based on teacher report for the analyses of the parent versions of the APQ, so the findings were not attributable to shared method variance. Most of the scales of the parent-completed questionnaire and the parent telephone interview demonstrated adequate internal consistency (with the exception of the Corporal Punishment scale, which only consists of three items, and the Poor Monitoring/Supervision scale on the parent telephone interview). Several scales showed expected correlations with child age (e.g., poorer monitoring and decreased positive parenting with older children). In general, a social desirability response

set did not appear to influence parental responses, with the exception of Inconsistent Discipline (both parent versions) and Corporal Punishment (parent telephone interview only). Thus, although additional information is clearly needed concerning the APQ (e.g., its relationship with observed parent behavior, confirmatory factor analyses, normative data), the parent questionnaire version is promising.

One self-report measure of parenting practices that has been employed primarily in studies of family violence, rather than in populations of children with CP, is the parent-to-child version of the Conflict Tactics Scales (CTS-Parent; Straus, 1979, 1990). The CTS-Parent requires parents to report on the frequency in which they have engaged in 18 different behaviors with their children over the past 12 months. Factor-analytically derived scales include Reasoning, Verbal Aggression, and Physical Aggression. Psychometric properties of the various forms of the CTS are presented in Straus (1979, 1990). Although the CTS-Parent has been employed primarily in studies of family violence, Strassberg, Dodge, Pettit, and Bates (1994) demonstrated a predictive relationship between parental reports of spanking and more serious forms of physical punishment (derived from a modified version of the CTS-Parent) with subsequent peer-related aggression during kindergarten. Thus, further examination of the CTS-Parent in families of children with CP may be warranted. A revised version of the CTS-Parent (the Parent–Child CTS; Straus, Hamby, Finkelhor, & Runyan, 1996) is under development.

A brief (20-minute) videotape analogue procedure for assessing parental coercive discipline has been developed by Fagot (1992). Parents respond to each of 14 videotaped vignettes of toddlers engaging in annoying (e.g., pulling tissues out of a box) or risky (e.g., starting to walk down a long flight of stairs) behaviors by indicating one of five responses: do nothing, warning, verbal redirection, verbal reprimand, or physical punishment. The measure demonstrated moderate internal-consistency reliability and high test–retest reliability over a 1-month period ($r = .72$). Of most interest, it was the only one of several measures to predict both parental report of aggressive behavior (on the Aggressive scale of the CBCL/2–3) and observed aggression in a play group 1 year later.

In summary, most of the self-report measures appear suited to the broad assessment of parenting practices. The PS is appropriate for parents of younger preschool-age children (2–3 years old), whereas the PPS has been employed with somewhat older preschoolers (3–4 years old). Their applicability to older children is unknown at this time. The APQ has been designed for parents of children aged 6–13. Preliminary data concerning the psychometric properties of these instruments are encouraging, but additional work in this area with larger and more representative samples is clearly necessary. Establishment of normative data would be particularly useful. Finally, development of a similar instrument that is appropriate for parents of adolescents is needed, so that parenting practices can be assessed throughout the developmental period by at least one of these instruments. Of course, the ideal would be a well-validated measure of parenting practices that can be employed with parents of preschoolers, preadolescents, and adolescents; to our knowledge, however, such a measure does not exist. None of the measures has yet been employed to assess treatment outcome for parents of children with CP, although the PPS was used in this way with a sample of children with mixed behavior problems. Use of the CTS-Parent may warrant further study, especially when investigation of family violence in samples of children with CP and their families is of interest.

The videotaped analogue measure described by Fagot (1992) may perhaps be an alternative, and potentially more valid, approach to self-report measures of parenting practices. However, Fagot cautions that before this type of measure is extensively employed in clinical settings, it needs to include examples of positive child behaviors; furthermore, tapes for children of different ages are needed. Despite these cautions, Fagot has demonstrated the potential utility of this approach to assessing parenting practices.

Parents' (and Teachers') Social Cognitions

In a comprehensive review of instruments designed to assess parental attitudes toward child rearing, Holden and Edwards (1989) cited the need for instruments focusing on distinct domains of parental social cognition. In this section of the chapter, we first discuss the assessment of parents' (and teachers') perceptions of child adjustment. We then review measures that have been employed to assess aspects of parenting self-esteem: satisfaction, self-efficacy, and locus of control with the parenting role.

Perceptions of Child Adjustment

Parental perception of a child is a strong predictor of referral for CP, perhaps even more so than the child's actual behavior (e.g., Griest et al., 1980). A similar situation may hold true in the classroom situation with teachers (see Hoge & Andrews, 1992), although it has been suggested that teachers may be less susceptible to bias than parents because they have a more extensive normative base for their ratings (Walker, 1995). Analogue studies have shown that both nonreferred parents and teachers perceive children who display aggressive behavior as having less control over their behavior than they see children who display inattentive/overactive behavior as having; they also report more negative affective responses to the aggressive children (Johnston & Patenaude, 1994; Lovejoy, 1996). As noted above, studies with parents of clinic-referred children have shown that these parents are more likely to misperceive child behaviors than are parents of nonreferred children (Holleran et al., 1982; Middlebrook & Forehand, 1985; Wahler & Sansbury, 1990).

These findings suggest that some measure of significant adults' perceptions of the child is an essential component of the assessment process. The behavioral rating scales described above are the most readily available sources of such data. When examined in the context of behavioral observation data and the clinician's own impressions, these behavioral rating scales can be important indicators as to whether the informants (parents, teachers) appear to have a perceptual bias in their assessment of the referred child's behavior.

An alternative methodology for assessing potential perceptual biases in the parents of children with CP is the use of brief written (e.g., Holleran et al., 1982; Middlebrook & Forehand, 1985), audiotaped, or videotaped scenarios or vignettes describing parent–child interactions in which a child displays a variety of inappropriate, neutral, and positive behaviors. Wahler and Sansbury (1990) employed previously recorded videotaped interactions of the mother–child dyad in the home as stimulus materials. Although such methods have been employed on a limited basis in the research literature, their validity and utility in clinical settings has yet to be examined. A more clinically relevant method for assessing parents' and children's perceptions of themselves and each other has been developed by Sanders and Dadds (1992). In their video-mediated recall procedure, the parent views a videotape of a previously recorded problem-solving discussion with his or her child. The videotape is stopped every 20 seconds, and the parent describes what he or she was thinking at that point in the interaction. Sanders and Dadds demonstrated that this procedure discriminated clinic-referred families with children with CP from nonreferred families. The clinic-referred parents stated fewer self- and family-referent positive cognitions and more family-referent negative cognitions than did the nonreferred parents. Furthermore, the video-mediated recall procedure was superior to an alternative thought-listing procedure.[2]

Parenting Self-Esteem

Several measures that assess aspects of parental self-esteem are the Parenting Sense of Competence Scale (PSOC; as adapted by Johnston & Mash, 1989, from Gibaud-Wallston & Wandersman, 1978), the Cleminshaw–Guidubaldi Parent Satisfaction Scale (CGPSS; Guidubaldi & Cleminshaw, 1985), and the Parental Locus of Control Scale (PLOC; Campis, Lyman, & Prentice-Dunn, 1986).

The PSOC consists of 16 items that make up two factors: Satisfaction, which refers to the extent to which the parent reports satisfaction with the parenting role, and Efficacy, which reflects the parent's self-report of skill and familiarity with the parenting role. In a small normative sample of parents of 4- to 9-year-olds, Johnston and Mash (1989) reported adequate internal-consistency reliabilities for the Total, Satisfaction, and Efficacy scales (r's = .79, .75, and .76, respectively). These scores were negatively correlated with the CBCL Externalizing score, although Efficacy was not correlated with the CBCL for mothers. There were no effects of child age or gender on the PSOC scores.

The PSOC has been employed with several clinic-referred populations, including physically abused children (Mash, Johnston, & Kovitz, 1983) and children with ADHD (e.g., Mash & Johnston, 1983) and ADHD plus CP (Johnston, 1996b). Johnston (1996b) reported that the total PSOC score distinguished among parents (mothers and fathers) of nonreferred children, children with ADHD plus low levels of oppositional behavior, and children with ADHD plus high levels of oppositional behavior. However, in another clinic-referred sample of children with externalizing behavior problems (mostly children with ADDH plus ODD/CD), the PSOC was not correlated with mother or child behavior observed in a structured laboratory observation (Johnston & Pelham, 1990). The PSOC has been shown to be sensitive to the effects of parent training in a sample of children with ADHD (Pisterman et al., 1992); to our knowledge, it has not been employed in interventions with children with CP.

The CGPSS consists of 50 items that load on five factor-analytically derived scales: Spouse Support, Child–Parent Relationship, Parent Performance, Family Discipline and Control, and General Satisfaction. A total score can be derived as well. Internal-consistency coefficients range from .76 to .93 (Guidubaldi & Cleminshaw, 1985). The scale and total scores are positively correlated with the Dyadic Adjustment Scale (r's = .17–.56). In a clinic-referred sample, Mouton and Tuma (1988) found that mothers of clinic-referred children with CP were significantly less satisfied on the first three scales of the CGPSS than were mothers of nonreferred children. In addition, scores on the CGPSS were positively correlated with the PLOC (see below) (r = .69) and negatively correlated with the Parenting Stress Index (r = –.87). The Child–Parent Relationship scale (but not the Family Discipline and Control scale) has been shown to be sensitive to the effects of a parent training intervention focused on child temperament (Sheeber & Johnson, 1994). Improvements on this scale were related to completion of homework assignments during the intervention.

The PLOC consists of 47 items that load on five factors: Parental Efficacy, Parental Responsibility, Child Control of Parent's Life, Parental Belief in Fate/Chance, and Parental Control of Child's Behavior. Adequate internal-consistency and test–retest reliabilities have been demonstrated (Campis et al., 1986; Roberts et al., 1992). Parents of clinic-referred children have a more external locus of control than do parents of nonreferred children (Campis et al., 1986; Mouton & Tuma, 1988; Roberts et al., 1992). Scores on the PLOC have been shown to be affected by social desirability (Campis et al., 1986). The total score on the PLOC is correlated with the Parenting Stress Index (Mouton & Tuma, 1988), but not with observed parent behavior (Roberts et al., 1992). It is associated with observed severity of child oppositional behavior on the CT (Roberts et al., 1992). Parents who completed a parent training program had a more internal locus of control by the end of treatment (Eyberg et al., 1995; Roberts et al., 1992). Roberts et al. also reported that locus of control was not associated with treatment dropout.

Parental Personal and Marital Adjustment

Exposition and discussion of the various parental personal (e.g., depression, antisocial behavior, substance abuse) and marital adjustment problems that may occur in parents of children with CP is beyond the scope of this chapter. Instead, a set of brief screening procedures is needed to ascertain whether a more complete and thorough assessment for a particular problem or group of problems is required. Questions related to these issues can best be incorporated into the initial interview with the parents. In some cases, the child can also be asked for his or her perceptions as well (e.g., "Does your dad or mom ever seem to have too much to drink?" or "How do your mom and dad get along with each other?"). In conjunction with the judicious use of the various self-report measures described below, the clinician should be able to make a decision about the necessity of pursuing any of these areas in greater detail. Should that be the case, then guidelines for conducting behavioral assessments for these types of problems are presented in Bellack (1993) and Ciminero, Adams, and Calhoun (1986). Additional sources are cited in the relevant subsections below.

Depression

The Beck Depression Inventory (BDI; Beck, Rush, Shaw, & Emery, 1979) has been the most frequently employed measure for the assessment of depression in parents (especially mothers of children with CP) (see Dumas & Serketich, 1994). The BDI consists of 21 items, each of which is scored on a 4-point scale, with higher scores indicating greater depression. It is typically self-administered, is written at a fifth- to sixth-grade reading level, and can be completed in 5–10 minutes. The following cutoff points have been recommended: 0–9, no depression or minimal depression; 10–20, mild depression; 21–30, moderate to severe depression; 31–63, severe depression (Kendall, Hollon, Beck, Hammen, & Ingram, 1987). (Note that slightly different cutoff scores are offered by Beck, Steer, & Garbin, 1988.)

Psychometric data on the BDI with various populations are quite extensive and are not reviewed here; suffice it to say that adequate reliability and validity have been established (see review by Beck et al., 1988). For example, mean coefficient alphas for psychiatric and nonpsychiatric samples are .86 and .81, respectively, and test–retest correlations are greater than .60. Scores on the BDI correlate significantly with clinicians' ratings of depression and with other self-report measures of depression.

With respect to its use with parents of children with CP, the BDI differentiates mothers of nonreferred children and clinic-referred children with CP (e.g., Griest et al., 1980); relative to other types of measures (e.g., behavioral observations of child behavior), it has been found to be the best predictor of maternal perceptions of clinic-referred children with CP (Forehand, Wells, McMahon, Griest, & Rogers, 1982; Webster-Stratton, 1988). It has also been shown to change in a positive direction following completion of a parent training program and/or child cognitive-behavioral therapy (e.g., Forehand et al., 1980; Kazdin et al., 1992; Webster-Stratton, 1994), and to predict dropout and response to treatment (e.g., Kazdin, 1995a; McMahon, Forehand, Griest, & Wells, 1981).

It should be noted that the BDI is not intended as an instrument for diagnosing depression; rather, it is a measure of the severity of various depressive symptoms (particularly cognitive symptoms). It has been recommended that distressed individuals identified solely on the basis of BDI scores, especially with scores of 20 or below, be referred to as "dysphoric" rather than "depressed" (Haaga & Solomon, 1993; Kendall et al., 1987). Thus, when employed with parents of children with CP, the BDI is probably best regarded as an indicator of parental personal distress rather than of depression per se. Patterson's (1982) data indicating that mothers of children with CP demonstrate elevations on most of the clinical scales of the Minnesota Multiphasic Personality Inventory (MMPI), compared to mothers of nonreferred children, is consistent with this idea. Given the high intercorrelations of depression with measures of anxiety, marital adjustment, and insularity, a similar conclusion might be drawn concerning these other measures as well (Forehand et al., 1984).

It is also important to note that extremely low scores (i.e., 0 or 1) on the BDI may be indicative of other forms of psychopathology (e.g., psychopathy, hypomania) or even depression (Field et al., 1991; Kendall et al., 1987). For example, Field et al. reported that mothers who scored 0 on the BDI received lower scores on activity level, expressiveness, and vocalization in observed interactions with their young infants (i.e., they acted more "depressed") than did mothers with low scores on the BDI or mothers who scored above 12. Furthermore, the infants of the mothers who scored 0 on the BDI were less responsive than the infants of "depressed" mothers. Whether a similar phenomenon occurs in samples of older children awaits investigation.

Antisocial Behavior

Although several studies have demonstrated the association between parental antisocial behavior and child CP, such behavior has been assessed in a variety of ways. Perhaps the two most frequently used types of instruments have been structured diagnostic interviews and the MMPI. With respect to the former, the Schedule for Affective Disorders and Schizophrenia (Spitzer & Endicott, 1978) has been used to obtain a DSM diagnosis of APD (e.g., Frick et al., 1992; Lahey et al., 1995). Other investigators have relied upon self-report personality instruments such as the MMPI. For example, Frick, Lahey, Hartdagen, and Hynd (1989) employed a composite score of the *F*, Psychopathic Deviate, and Manic scales as their indicator of antisocial behavior. Patterson and colleagues (Bank, Forgatch, Patterson, & Fetrow, 1993; Patterson & Capaldi, 1991; Patterson et al., 1992) included this MMPI score along with other indicators of antisocial behavior (e.g., suspension of driving license, arrest records, self-reported drug use) to develop risk index measures. Finally, some investigators have simply relied upon information gleaned from archival records (e.g., police, court, or prison records).

Use of structured diagnostic interviews or the MMPI to obtain information about parental antisocial behavior does not seem warranted, given the time and expense involved in their administration, scoring, and interpretation, unless they are being administered to obtain other information as well. Zucker and Fitzgerald (1992) have recently developed a more specific self-report instrument, the Antisocial Behavior Checklist (ASB Checklist); this consists of 46 items describing a variety of overt and covert antisocial activities that may have occurred from childhood through adulthood. Each item is rated on a 4-point scale for frequency of occurrence over the life span. A cutoff score of 24 is considered indicative of antisocial behavior and is consistent with DSM-III-R criteria for APD (with a sensitivity of .85 and specificity of .83). Ham, Zucker, and Fitzgerald (1993) have presented encouraging data concerning the psychometric properties of the instrument. Internal-consistency coefficients ranging from .77 to .97 were obtained in samples from prison populations, court offenders, community-based alcoholics, court-referred alcoholics, university students, and the community. Four-week test–retest reliability was .94 with the university sample. As expected, prisoners scored more highly than court-referred alcoholics, who scored more highly than community controls. Men generally scored higher than women within each sample, except for those samples recruited from within the legal system. Scores on the ASB Checklist were negatively correlated with SES and education, and positively correlated with measures of hostility, depression, and alcohol-related problems.

In a sample of families with alcoholic fathers, scores on the ASB Checklist were significantly higher for both the alcoholic fathers and their spouses than for fathers and mothers in comparison families (Fitzgerald et al., 1993). However, neither paternal nor maternal ASB Checklist scores were significant predictors of child behavior problems (externalizing or internalizing) in 3-year-old sons. In a subsequent report, both the alcoholic fathers and the mothers of 3- to 5-year-old boys who scored above the clinical cutoff on the CBCL Total Problem score had higher scores on the ASB Checklist than the parents of boys who scored below the CBCL cutoff (Jansen, Fitzgerald, Ham, & Zucker, 1995). Both maternal and paternal scores on the ASB Checklist contributed to the prediction of CBCL scores for the total sample.

To our knowledge, this measure has not been employed with samples of parents of children with CP. However, given the findings with alcoholic families described above, its use as a measure of parental antisocial behavior appears promising.

Substance Abuse

There are dozens of instruments for screening and in-depth assessment of substance use in adults. The reader is referred to recent reviews of these instruments for assessing alcohol (Allen & Columbus, 1995) and drug (National Institute on Drug Abuse, 1994) use problems (see also Vik, Brown, & Myers, Chapter 15, this volume). Some of the more frequently employed screening instruments that may prove useful in working with parents of children with CP include the short version of the Michigan Alcoholism Screening Test (SMAST; Selzer, Vinokur, & van Rooijen, 1975), the Drug Abuse Screening Test (DAST; Skinner, 1982), and the recently developed Alcohol Use Disorders Identification Test (AUDIT; Saunders, Aasland, Babor, de la Fuente, & Grant, 1993).

Marital Adjustment

There are several excellent discussions of the assessment of general marital adjustment (e.g., Burnett, 1987; Harrison & Westhuis, 1989) and marital violence (Holtzworth-Munroe et al., 1995; La Taillade & Jacobson, in press), as well as of observational methods for assessing marital interaction (e.g., Jacob & Tennenbaum, 1988; Markman & Notarius, 1987). We review two widely used measures of general marital adjustment, and several measures of marital conflict that have been used with parents of children with CP or are potentially useful with this population.

The Marital Adjustment Test (MAT; Locke & Wallace, 1959) and the Dyadic Adjustment Scale (DAS; Spanier, 1976) are measures of marital adjustment. The MAT has been shown to discriminate between distressed and nondistressed couples (Locke & Wallace, 1959) and to correlate with child CP (Frick et al., 1989; also see below). Although the MAT has been criticized for applying only to traditional couples and for its system of differentially weighting items to score the instrument, it has been widely used. The MAT has shown high levels of reliability, stability (i.e., 2 years; Kimmel & van der Veen, 1974), and validity (Burgess, Locke, & Thomes, 1971). It has also shown convergent validity with independent observations of marital interaction (Julien, Markman, & Lindahl, 1989) and with scores on the DAS (Busby, Christensen, Crane, & Larson, 1995). In families in which a child has been referred for treatment of noncompliant behavior, marital distress as measured by the MAT was found to be associated with deviant child behavior and parental behavior (Forehand & Brody, 1985). Webster-Stratton (1988) found that marital distress as measured by the MAT contributed to negative perceptions of child behavior and to increased negative maternal behavior.

A factor analysis of the MAT by Kimmel and van der Veen (1974) yielded two factors, which they labeled Sexual Congeniality and Compatibility. The Compatibility factor was negatively correlated with a measure of child aggressive behavior in nonreferred families (Kimmel, 1970, cited in Kimmel & van der Veen, 1974). However, an investigation with clinic-referred families failed to find any relationship between two measures of child behavior (compliance, deviant behavior) and the Compatibility factor of the MAT (Schaughency, Middlebrook, Forehand, & Lahey, 1984). Schaughency et al. did find that child compliance was inversely related to the Sexual Congeniality factor of the MAT. The authors concluded that low sexual congeniality may be an aspect of parental distress that contributes to inappropriate parent referrals for child treatment.

The DAS (Spanier, 1976) is a 32-item self-report inventory that contains four subscales of marital adjustment: Dyadic Consensus (spouses' agreement regarding various marital issues), Dyadic Cohesion (extent to which the partners involve themselves in joint activities), Dyadic Satisfaction (overall evaluation of the marital relationship and level of commitment to the relationship), and Affectional Expression (degree of affection and sexual involvement in the relationship). It has been found to discriminate distressed from nondistressed couples reliably (Crane, Allgood, Larson, & Griffin, 1990). Adequate internal-consistency reliability for the total scale and for each of the subscales has been found by several investigators (alphas =.73–.96; Carey, Spector, Lantinga, & Krauss, 1993; Spanier, 1976).

In collecting normative data for this scale, Spanier (1976) reported a mean score of 114.8 and a standard deviation of 17.8 for a sample of 218 married couples. On the basis of these data, Jacobson and Anderson (1980) suggested that a cutoff score of 97 (i.e., 1 standard deviation below the mean) be used to classify individuals as maritally distressed. Others (Bond & McMahon, 1984; Crane et al., 1990) have suggested a cutoff score of 107. Marital dissatisfaction, as measured by the DAS, has been shown to relate to greater oppositional behavior in elementary school-age boys through the indirect pathway of rejection by fathers (Mann & MacKenzie, 1996).

Two questionnaires are often used to assess general marital conflict: the O'Leary–Porter Scale (OPS; Porter & O'Leary, 1980), and the Conflict Tactics Scales—Partner (CTS-Partner; Straus, 1979, 1990). The OPS is a 10-item parent-completed questionnaire designed to assess the frequency of various forms of overt marital hostility (e.g., quarrels, sarcasm, and physical abuse) witnessed by the child. There is some evidence that this scale is more strongly associated with various scales of Quay's (1977) original Behavior Problem Checklist (including Conduct Problem and Socialized Delinquency) than is the MAT, at least for clinic-referred boys (Porter & O'Leary, 1980). Mann and MacKenzie (1996) found that conflict as measured by the OPS was related to increased oppositional behavior in boys through disruptions in maternal discipline. Forehand et al. (1987) reported that young adolescents who engaged in either overt CP or both overt and covert CP had parents who reported significantly higher conflict as measured by the OPS, compared with adolescents not exhibiting CP.

The CTS-Partner is a 38-item parent report questionnaire that assesses the strategies couples use to resolve conflict. Like the CTS-Parent, it includes a range of strategies from discussion to yelling, pushing, threatening or beating up the partner. Straus (1979, 1990) reported adequate reliability, validity, and norms to use in interpreting scores on the CTS-Partner. O'Leary, Vivian, and Malone (1992) suggest that the CTS-Partner may be a particularly accurate method for obtaining reports of physical aggression, as wives tend to underreport such aggression in written self-reports and interviews. Marital physical and nonphysical aggression as measured by the CTS-Partner has been shown to be positively correlated with child CP, thus lending support to the validity of the use of this form of the CTS in this population (Jouriles, Norwood, McDonald, Vincent, & Mahoney, 1996). The CTS-Partner has been extensively revised. Preliminary evidence of the psychometric properties of this latest revision are presented in Straus, Hamby, Boney-McCoy, and Sugarman (1996).

Three examples of instruments designed to measure parenting-related conflict are described. The Parenting Alliance Inventory (PAI; Abidin, 1988) is a 20-item parent report instrument designed to measure this specific aspect of marital adjustment, which Abidin and Brunner (1995) define as the degree of parental collaboration in child rearing. Parents are asked to rate their agreement on a 5-point scale with statements such as "I feel good about my child's other parent's judgment about what is right for our child." Reading level has been assessed at grade 5.6. No data on the reliability of the instrument are currently available, although initial psychometric data were reported by Abidin and Brunner (1995). They found a significant difference between mothers' and fathers' responses on the PAI, although factor analysis showed that the factor structure was the same for mothers and fathers. Scores on the PAI distinguished married, separated, single, and divorced mothers from one another and correlated in the expected direction with reports of marital satisfaction on the MAT and with the Parenting domain score on Abidin's Parenting Stress Index (see below).

Jouriles et al. (1991) reported the use of a 21-item measure of Child Rearing Disagreements with parents of 3- to 5-year-old boys. The items rate the frequency of disagreements over the past 6 months regarding such issues as "not taking an equal hand in disciplining our son," "not keeping a close enough eye on our son's whereabouts," and "not sticking to agreements we made about child care or rearing." Jouriles et al. (1991) report adequate internal consistency (alpha = .86) and preliminary evidence for the validity of this instrument (e.g., correlations with the MAT and CBCL in expected directions). They found that the measure significantly predicted CP even after general marital dissatisfaction as measured by the MAT was controlled.

Dadds and Powell (1991) developed a 16-item measure of interparental parenting conflict, the Parent Problem Checklist. The checklist measures disagreements over rules and discipline, open conflict regarding parenting, and alienation of the child's affection. Principal component analysis revealed a single factor (alpha = .70) and high test–retest (8-week) reliability ($r = .90$). Regarding validity, the checklist correlates moderately with the DAS (r's = .40–.70) and with the BDI (r's = .40–.50). Dadds and Powell (1991) reported that higher levels of parenting conflict on this checklist were associated with higher levels of aggression in 3- to 8-year-old children.

Parental Stress

Two types of measures that assess stress have been employed with parents of children with CP: general measures of stress (e.g., life event scales) and specific measures of parenting-related stress. Life event scales survey a range of potential stressors and can be used to rate the intensity or disruption caused by a stressor. The scales can usually be adapted for use as either questionnaires or structured interviews. Although the life events approach to assessing stress has been criticized for obscuring the idiosyncratic impact of events on individuals, sampling low-base-rate events, and confounding the causes and consequences of stress, this approach has nevertheless become common in the study of family functioning (e.g., Crnic & Greenberg, 1990; Pianta & Egeland, 1990; Whipple & Webster-Stratton, 1991).

The Life Experiences Survey (LES; Sarason, Johnson, & Siegel, 1978) is a frequently used scale that is also representative of life event scales in general. The LES is a 47-item self-report measure. The items survey a variety of negative and positive life events, such as death of a relative, engagement, outstanding achievement, sexual difficulties, minor law violations, borrowing money, or moving. Respondents indicate whether each stressor has occurred, note the recency of the stressor (0–6 months or 7–12 months), and separately rate the degree of impact of the stressor on a 7-point scale from "extremely negative" to "extremely positive." A total Life Change score is computed, based on the frequency of events occurring in the past year. Events experienced as negative are summed for a Negative Change score; this score is most closely related to stress. The LES has been shown to be a moderately reliable instrument.

Parents of children with CP have been shown to have higher scores on the LES (Johnston, 1996b). In families with children with CP, the LES has discriminated abusive from nonabusive parents (Whipple & Webster-Stratton, 1991).

Pianta and Egeland (1990) reported the use of a semistructured, 39-item life event scale with a sample of at-risk families. Mothers indicated whether an event had occurred, their feelings about the event, and their assessment of the impact of that event on family functioning. Independent coders rated the disruptiveness of the event on a 3-point scale. If an event occurred frequently and affected or involved a close relationship, it was given the highest rating. A factor-analytically derived Personal Stress scale accounted for significant variance in maternal parenting (particularly for girls) at 6 and 42 months.

The Family Events List (FEL; Patterson, 1982) is a self-report measure with 46 minor but "hassling" events that may occur in daily living (e.g., child care problems, car problems, work-related problems). The respondent circles the events that occurred in the previous 48 hours and indicates their impact on a Likert scale (−3, "very aversive"; 0, "neutral"; +3, "very positive"). A Recent Hassles scale constructed from the FEL contains 12 items with adequate internal consistency (alpha = .75) (Forgatch et al., 1988). In one analysis, items from the FEL that could not be attributed to interpersonal skills or maladjustment were used as indicators on a "stress" construct (Capaldi & Patterson, 1989). Subsequent analyses indicated that stress disrupts parenting practices in single-parent families and in families in which the parent becomes depressed (Patterson et al., 1992). Similarly, Snyder (1991) found that when mothers of children with CP experienced frequent hassles (as assessed by the FEL) and negative mood, they tended to respond to their children's negative behavior in a more coercive manner.

Although the FEL and the Pianta and Egeland (1990) measures have not received extensive psychometric evaluation, they may prove useful as screening instruments to assist the clinician in noting parental perceptions of the frequency, intensity, and valence of various family-related stressors. The types of stressors on the life event scales reported above vary, in that some scales include day-to-day hassles as well as (or instead of) larger life events. The time frame for reporting the stressors also varies: The FEL includes only the past 48 hours, whereas the LES encompasses the past year. This is important because proximal stressors, such as those on the FEL, may have a different relationship to family functioning, parenting behavior, and CP than the distal stressors on the LES.

Several measures specific to parenting-related stress have been developed. Parenting Daily Hassles is a 20-item self-report questionnaire measuring events in parenting and parent–child interactions (Crnic & Greenberg, 1990). The parents rate the frequency, the degree of hassle, and the intensity of each hassle. The Frequency and Intensity scales show adequate internal consistency (alphas = .81–.90) and are highly correlated (r = .78). More hassles are reported in families with children 2–3 years of age and in families with more than one child (O'Brien, 1996). In a nonreferred sample, Crnic and Greenberg (1990) found that the cumulative effects of relatively minor stresses related to parenting were important predictors of parent and child behaviors. Daily hassles were more predictive of child CP than were scores on the LES. Belsky, Woodworth, and Crnic (1996) found that greater mother-reported daily hassles (as measured by a factor-analytically derived scale composed of items from the Parenting Daily Hassles and a similar measure by Kanner, Coyne, Schaeffer, & Lazarus, 1981), was related to greater trouble managing toddler behavior.

The Parenting Stress Index (PSI; Abidin, 1995), is designed as a screening instrument for assessing relative levels of stress in the early parent–child system (0–3 years), although it has been used with children up to 12 years of age. Its design was theoretically driven and includes domains that are related to stress and coping in parents and child temperament. The PSI consists of 120 items and requires approximately 20 minutes to complete. The Child domain of the PSI includes six subscales concerning the child's adaptability, reinforcing qualities, demandingness, activity level, mood, and acceptability to the parent. The Parent domain includes scales related to depression, attachment to the child, spousal and social system support, parental health, perceived restrictions of role, and the parent's sense of competence. High total scores (above 260) may indicate risk for problems in development. Low scores (below 175) may also be a reason for concern, either because of a "fake good" response set or because of indication of lack of parental involvement with the child. A high score in the Parent domain may indicate difficulty with parental functioning. High scores in the Child domain may indicate a child with difficult characteristics (i.e., "temperamentally difficult"). Webster-Stratton (1990) reported that the mean Child domain score in a sample of 120 children with CP was 136 (*SD* = 16), above the 95th percentile.

The PSI's construction was based on a conceptual rather than an empirical approach. Therefore, not surprisingly, factor analysis of the PSI reveals low loadings of many items on each scale (over half of the items in the Parent domain and two-thirds of the items in the Child domain have loadings of less than .40 on the theoretically derived scales). The short form of the PSI (Abidin, 1995) uses factor-analytically derived subscales (Total Stress, Parental Distress, Parent–Child Dysfunctional Interaction, Difficult Child) that differ from those of the PSI. Thirty-six items from the original PSI are retained on this version. The short form's subscales do correlate with those of the full-length PSI in the expected pattern. The subscales have shown adequate internal-consistency reliability (alphas = .80–.91) and test–retest (6-month) reliability (*r*'s = .68–.85).

Recent studies with CP samples provide evidence for the PSI's validity. Scores on the PSI obtained in infancy have been used to predict child CP 4½ years later in nonclinical samples (Abidin, Jenkins, & McGaughey, 1992). Higher PSI scores have been related to CP in several samples (e.g., Cuccaro, Holmes, & Wright, 1993; Eyberg, Boggs, & Rodriguez, 1992; Webster-Stratton, 1990). Webster-Stratton and Hammond (1988) found that the Parent domain score on the PSI, in combination with the LES Negative Change score, discriminated depressed from nondepressed mothers in families of children with CP. Treatment outcome in families of children with CP has also been evaluated with the PSI (e.g., Acton & During, 1992; Eisenstadt et al., 1993; Webster-Stratton, 1994), and higher scores on the Child and Parent domains of the PSI have been linked with premature termination of treatment for CP (Kazdin, 1990).

Parental Functioning in Extrafamilial Contexts

There is increasing recognition of the importance of assessing the extrafamilial functioning of parents of children with CP. The assessment of social support in families is beyond the scope of this chapter (see Pierce, Sarason, & Sarason, 1996). Most of the research on the extrafamilial functioning of parents of children with CP has focused on maternal insularity. The Community Interaction Checklist (CIC; Wahler et al., 1979), which is a brief interview designed to assess maternal insularity, has been extensively employed in this re-search. The mother is asked to recall extrafamily contacts over the previous 24 hours. The number of contacts is recorded, as are the identity of the person (e.g., friend, relative, helping agency representative) who initiated the contact, the duration of the contact, its distance from home, and its perceived valence (positive, negative, neutral). The CIC is administered by an observer after each home observation; thus, multiple administrations of the CIC are the norm. Mothers are categorized as insular if they report at least twice as many daily contacts with relatives and/or helping agency representatives as with friends, and if at least one-third of the daily contacts are reported as neutral or aversive (Dumas & Wahler, 1983, 1985).

Internal-consistency reliabilities of .79 or higher have been reported (e.g., Dumas & Wahler, 1983, 1985). Mothers characterized as insular on the CIC are more aversive and indiscriminate in the use of aversive consequences with their children than are noninsular mothers, and the children of insular mothers are also more aversive (Dumas & Wahler, 1985). Coercive exchanges between insular mothers and their children are of longer duration than those involving noninsular mother–child dyads (Wahler, Hughey, & Gordon, 1981). Aversive maternal contacts with adults as measured on the CIC are associated with aversive maternal behavior directed toward the children on the same day (Wahler, 1980; Wahler & Graves, 1983). Finally, classification as insular on the CIC has been found to be a strong predictor of poor maintenance of the effects of parent training interventions for children with CP (e.g., Dumas & Wahler, 1983; Wahler, 1980). None of the mothers who were both insular and socioeconomically disadvantaged had a favorable outcome over the 1-year period.

Parental Satisfaction with Treatment

Behavior therapists have long recognized the importance of "social validity"—that is, the necessity of demonstrating that therapeutic changes are "clinically or socially important to the client" (Kazdin, 1977, p. 429). One type of social validity is consumer satisfaction with the outcome of treatment (Wolf, 1978). It has been suggested that consumer satisfaction with a particular treatment strategy or an entire treatment approach is likely to be a factor in the ultimate effectiveness of the intervention (Yates, 1978). In a review of consumer satisfaction with child behavior therapy, McMahon and Forehand (1983) delineated four areas in which consumer satisfaction should be assessed: treatment outcome, therapists, treatment procedures, and teaching format. They found that the majority of studies have focused on adult participants in treatment (usually parents involved in parent training interventions for the treatment of children with CP, although teachers have occasionally been assessed). However, the children themselves have rarely been asked to evaluate their satisfaction with treatment, probably because of the difficulty in developing appropriate measures for children of various ages.

At present, no single consumer satisfaction measure is appropriate for use in all types of interventions for children with CP and their families. However, two measures have been developed to assess parental satisfaction with parent training programs designed to modify child noncompliance and other CP behaviors (Eyberg & Boggs, 1989; Forehand & McMahon, 1981). The Therapy Attitude Inventory (TAI; Eyberg, 1974) consists of 10 items concerning parental satisfaction with the outcome of treatment. Each item is rated on a 5-point Likert-type scale. The TAI and a modified version for use in parent training workshops are presented in Eyberg (1993). Eisenstadt et al. (1993) reported data supporting the internal consistency (alpha = .88) and discriminant validity of the TAI.

The Parents' Consumer Satisfaction Questionnaire (PCSQ; presented in Forehand & McMahon, 1981) assesses parental satisfaction with the overall program (including some items from the TAI), the teaching format, the specific parenting techniques that are taught, and the therapists. Items examining both the usefulness and difficulty of the teaching format and specific parenting techniques are also included. In all of these areas, parents respond to items on a 7-point Likert-type scale. Parents also have the opportunity to reply to several open-ended questions concerning their reactions to the parenting program.

The PCSQ has been used extensively by its developers, and adapted by others (e.g., Webster-Stratton, 1989). Webster-Stratton reported internal-consistency figures ranging from .71 to .90 for the overall satisfaction with the overall program, teaching format, and parenting technique sections of the PCSQ. There is evidence for its discriminant validity, in that the PCSQ has revealed differential levels of parental satisfaction as a function of different variations of these parent training programs (e.g., McMahon, Forehand, & Griest, 1981; McMahon, Tiedemann, Forehand, & Griest, 1984; Webster-Stratton, 1989; Webster-Stratton & Hammond, 1997). Using a modified version of the PCSQ, Baum and Forehand (1981) found that

parental satisfaction was maintained 1 to 4 years after treatment termination.

CONCLUSIONS

In this chapter, we have described characteristics of children with CP and their families; summarized current formulations of developmental pathways of CP; and detailed a variety of methods for assessing three important areas (child behavior per se and in an interactional context, other child characteristics, and familial and extrafamilial factors). The methods described include interviews with parents, teachers, and children; behavioral rating scales pertaining to the child's behavior or characteristics; behavioral observations in the clinic, home, and school settings; and questionnaires of various types to assess parenting practices and social cognitions, parental personal and marital adjustment, stress, parental functioning outside the family, and satisfaction with treatment.

The assessment of children with CP has advanced considerably since the second edition of *Behavioral Assessment of Childhood Disorders* (Mash & Terdal, 1988). The delineation of different developmental pathways is a major advance that provides structure and suggests a framework for designing and conducting assessments of children with CP. Although these efforts are continuing, they have a number of important implications for the assessment of children with CP. First, the assessment must be developmentally sensitive, not only with respect to the child's age and sex, but also in terms of the child's status and progression on a particular developmental pathway of CP. The possibility of comorbid conditions such as ADHD and internalizing disorders should also be investigated. In addition, the assessment must be contextually sensitive; that is, it should cover not only child CP behaviors and other behavior problems, but also other child characteristics, as well as familial and peer influences. Furthermore, this assessment must examine the broader ecologies of home, school, neighborhood, and community to the extent that each is warranted. Cultural sensitivity in the development, administration, and interpretation of assessment instruments requires increased attention as well (Prinz & Miller, 1991). Finally, the clinician needs to recognize the transactional nature of these developmental and contextual processes, and to conduct the assessment accordingly.

As we have emphasized throughout this chapter, a proper assessment of a child with CP must make use of multiple methods (e.g., behavioral rating scales, observation) completed by multiple informants (parents, teacher, child) concerning the child's behavior in multiple settings (e.g., home, school) (Achenbach, 1993b; Chamberlain & Bank, 1989; Kamphaus & Frick, 1996; Reid et al., 1988). Considerable attention has been paid to how best to interpret and maximize these different sources of information. It has been suggested that simple "either–or" approaches to combining information from multiple informants (e.g., considering a behavior as "true" if it is reported by parent, teacher, or child) work as well as or better than more complex weighting approaches (Piacentini, Cohen, & Cohen, 1992). However, Kamphaus and Frick (1996) caution that this approach should also be tempered by data generally suggesting that adults are better informants than children about overt CP, but that children may be better sources about covert CP, particularly as they get older (e.g., Loeber, Green, Lahey, & Stouthamer-Loeber, 1991).

"Multiple-gating" approaches to screening are an example of one strategy for employing multiple assessment measures that may prove to be cost-effective (e.g., Reid et al., 1988). In this approach, less costly assessment procedures (e.g., interviews, behavioral rating scales) can be employed as screening instruments with all children who are clinic-referred for the treatment of CP. More expensive assessment methods, such as observations in the home or school, can be used to assess only that subgroup of children for whom the less expensive methods have indicated the desirability of further assessment. An analogous procedure could be applied in the assessment of other child characteristics and familial and extrafamilial factors, in that low-cost methods such as interview questions (e.g., concerning the child's early temperament) and/or brief questionnaires (e.g., the BDI) could be employed as screening measures. Should additional assessment in these various areas be indicated, then a more thorough (and expensive) assessment (e.g., one employing observational procedures and/or structured interviews) could be conducted.

Walker and his colleagues have developed the Early Screening Project (Walker, Severson, & Feil, 1995) and the Systematic Screening for Behavior Disorders (Walker & Severson, 1990) for identifying children of preschool age and elementary school age, respectively, with CP and other behavior problems in the school setting. This approach consists of three gates, made up of teacher ratings, behavioral observations, and parent rat-

ings. Other multiple-gating approaches have been used to identify samples of children who are at high risk for the development of CP (August, Realmuto, Crosby, & MacDonald, 1995; Lochman & the Conduct Problems Prevention Research Group, 1995). Both of these investigations employed teacher and parent ratings of child behavior, as well as self-report measures of parenting practices.

More clinically oriented strategies for integrating and interpreting information from comprehensive assessments, such as the ones described in this chapter for children with CP are presented in Breen and Altepeter (1990), Kamphaus and Frick (1996), and Sanders and Lawton (1993). Sanders and Lawton describe a detailed model for discussing assessment findings with families, which they have employed with families of children with CP. The continued development and refinement of the CBCL family of instruments have been particularly noteworthy. Achenbach (1993b) has proposed a Multiaxial Empirically Based Assessment system for integrating and interpreting data obtained from parents, teachers, children, direct observations, and clinical interviews via the CBCL family of instruments. The compatibility and complementarity of these dimensional approaches to assessment with the more categorical approaches employed by structured diagnostic interviews have been demonstrated on a number of occasions. However, the clinical utility of structured diagnostic interviews is still open to question. In addition, the development of these interviews for teachers is still in the early stages.

Progress toward the development of brief, clinically useful assessment methods has also occurred, but in a limited way. On one front have been attempts to simplify well-validated but complex observational systems, such as the DPICS II and the Forehand system. On another front has been the development of new structured clinic analogue methods (e.g., the CT; Roberts & Powers, 1988). Especially encouraging have been the strides made in developing methods for assessing covert CP. The brief observational analogue methods and structured interviews developed to assess stealing, cheating, and property destruction (Hinshaw et al., 1992), and fire setting/match play (e.g., Kolko & Kazdin, 1989a; Kolko et al., 1991) represent very exciting developments. In addition, prototype methods using videotape technologies for assessing parental coercive discipline (Fagot, 1992) and parental social cognitions (e.g., video-mediated recall; Sanders & Dadds, 1992) have also appeared. Although the ultimate clinical utility of these methods has yet to be demonstrated, clinicians now at least have a number of brief assessment methods with some empirical support from which to choose.

ACKNOWLEDGMENTS

We would like to thank Katie Weaver and Jeff Munson for their assistance in the preparation of the manuscript.

NOTES

1. Portions of this section are based on McMahon (1994).
2. The video-mediated recall procedure was also successfully employed with a clinic-referred sample of children with CP aged 7–14 years.

REFERENCES

Abidin, R. R. (1988). *Parenting Alliance Inventory*. Unpublished manuscript, University of Virginia.

Abidin, R. R. (1995). *Parenting Stress Index—professional manual* (3rd ed.). Odessa, FL: Psychological Assessment Resources.

Abidin, R. R., & Brunner, J. F. (1995). Development of a Parenting Alliance Inventory. *Journal of Clinical Child Psychology, 24*, 31–40.

Abidin, R. R., Jenkins, C. L., & McGaughey, M. C. (1992). The relationship of early family variables to children's subsequent behavioral adjustment. *Journal of Clinical Child Psychology, 21*, 60–69.

Abikoff, H., & Klein, R. G. (1992). Attention-Deficit Hyperactivity and Conduct Disorder: Comorbidity and implications for treatment. *Journal of Consulting and Clinical Psychology, 60*, 881–892.

Achenbach, T. M. (1991a). *Integrative Guide for the 1991 CBCL/4–18, YSR, and TRF Profiles*. Burlington: University of Vermont, Department of Psychiatry.

Achenbach, T. M. (1991b). *Manual for the Child Behavior Checklist/4–18 and 1991 Profile*. Burlington: University of Vermont, Department of Psychiatry.

Achenbach, T. M. (1991c). *Manual for the Teacher's Report Form and 1991 Profile*. Burlington: University of Vermont, Department of Psychiatry.

Achenbach, T. M. (1991d). *Manual for the Youth Self-Report and 1991 Profile*. Burlington: University of Vermont, Department of Psychiatry.

Achenbach, T. M. (1992). *Manual for the Child Behavior Checklist/2–3 and 1992 Profile*. Burlington: University of Vermont, Department of Psychiatry.

Achenbach, T. M. (1993a). *Empirically based taxonomy: How to use syndromes and profile types derived from the CBCL/4–18, TRF, and YSR*. Burlington: University of Vermont, Department of Psychiatry.

Achenbach, T. M. (1993b). Implications of multiaxial empirically based assessment for behavior therapy with children. *Behavior Therapy, 24*, 91–116.

Acton, R. G., & During, S. M. (1992). Preliminary results of aggression management training for aggressive parents. *Journal of Interpersonal Violence, 7*, 410–417.

Adams, C. D., McCarthy, M., & Kelley, M. L. (1995). Adolescent versions of the Home and School Situations Questionnaires: Initial psychometric properties. *Journal of Clinical Child Psychology, 24*, 377–385.

Allen, J. P., & Columbus, M. (Eds.). (1995). *Assessing alcohol problems: A guide for clinicians and researchers* (NIAAA Treatment Handbook No. 4, DHHS Publication No. NIH 95-3745). Washington, DC: U.S. Government Printing Office.

Alpern, L., & Lyons-Ruth, K. (1993). Preschool children at social risk: Chronicity and timing of maternal depressive symptoms and child behavior problems at school and at home. *Development and Psychopathology, 5*, 371–387.

Amato, P. R., & Keith, B. (1991). Parental divorce and the well-being of children: A meta analysis. *Psychological Bulletin, 110*, 26–46.

American Psychiatric Association. (1980). *Diagnostic and statistical manual of mental disorders* (3rd ed.). Washington, DC: Author.

American Psychiatric Association. (1987). *Diagnostic and statistical manual of mental disorders* (3rd ed., rev.). Washington, DC: Author.

American Psychiatric Association. (1994). *Diagnostic and statistical manual of mental disorders* (4th ed.). Washington, DC: Author.

Arnold, D. S., O'Leary, S. G., Wolff, L. S., & Acker, M. M. (1993). The Parenting Scale: A measure of dysfunctional parenting in discipline situations. *Psychological Assessment, 5*, 137–144.

Atkeson, B. M., & Forehand, R. (1978). Parent behavioral training for problem children: An examination of studies using multiple outcome measures. *Journal of Abnormal Child Psychology, 6*, 449–460.

Attar, B. K., Guerra, N. G., & Tolan, P. H. (1994). Neighborhood disadvantage, stressful life events, and adjustment in urban elementary-school children. *Journal of Clinical Child Psychology, 23*, 391–400.

August, G. J., Realmuto, G. M., Crosby, R. D., & MacDonald, A. W. (1995). Community-based multiple-gate screening of children at risk for Conduct Disorder. *Journal of Abnormal Child Psychology, 23*, 521–544.

Baden, A. D., & Howe, G. W. (1992). Mothers' attributions and expectancies regarding their conduct-disordered children. *Journal of Abnormal Child Psychology, 20*, 467–485.

Bank, L., Forgatch, M. S., Patterson, G. R., & Fetrow,

R. A. (1993). Parenting practices of single mothers: Mediators of negative contextual factors. *Journal of Marriage and the Family, 55,* 371–384.

Barkley, R. A. (1987). *Defiant children: A clinician's manual for parent training.* New York: Guilford Press.

Barrios, B. A. (1993). Direct observation. In T. H. Ollendick & M. Hersen (Eds.), *Handbook of child and adolescent assessment* (pp. 140–164). Needham Heights, MA: Allyn & Bacon.

Bates, J. E. (1990). Conceptual and empirical linkages between temperament and behavior problems: A commentary on the Sanson, Prior, and Kyrios study. *Merrill–Palmer Quarterly, 36,* 193–199.

Bates, J. E., Bayles, K., Bennett, D. S., Ridge, B., & Brown, M. M. (1991). Origins of externalizing behavior problems at eight years of age. In D. J. Pepler & K. H. Rubin (Eds.), *The development and treatment of childhood aggression* (pp. 93–120). Hillsdale, NJ: Erlbaum.

Bates, J. E., Freeland, C. A. B., & Lounsbury, M. L. (1979). Measurement of infant difficultness. *Child Development, 50,* 794–803.

Baum, C. G., & Forehand, R. (1981). Long-term follow-up assessment of parent training by use of multiple-outcome measures. *Behavior Therapy, 12,* 643–652.

Beck, A. T., Rush, A. J., Shaw, B. F., & Emery, G. (1979). *Cognitive therapy of depression.* New York: Guilford Press.

Beck, A. T., Steer, R. A., & Garbin, M. G. (1988). Psychometric properties of the Beck Depression Inventory: Twenty-five years of evaluation. *Clinical Psychology Review, 8,* 77–100.

Bellack, A. S. (Ed.). (1993). *Behavioral assessment* (3rd ed.). Needham Heights, MA: Allyn & Bacon.

Belsky, J., Woodworth, S., & Crnic, K. (1996). Trouble in the second year: Three questions about family interaction. *Child Development, 67,* 556–578.

Bessmer, J. L., & Eyberg, S. (1993). *Dyadic Parent–Child Interaction Coding System II (DPICS II): Initial reliability and validity of the clinical version.* Unpublished manuscript, University of Florida.

Biederman, J., Faraone, S. V., Doyle, A., Krifcher-Lehman, B., Kraus, I., Perrin, J., & Tsuang, M. T. (1993). Convergence of the Child Behavior Checklist with structured interview-based psychiatric diagnoses of ADHD children with and without comorbidity. *Journal of Child Psychology and Psychiatry, 34,* 1241–1251.

Bierman, K. L. (1983). Cognitive development and clinical interviews with children. In B. B. Lahey & A. E. Kazdin (Eds.), *Advances in clinical child psychology* (Vol. 6, pp. 217–250). New York: Plenum Press.

Bird, H. R., & Gould, M. S. (1995). The use of diagnostic instruments and global measures of functioning in child psychiatry epidemiological studies. In F. C. Verhulst & H. M. Koot (Eds.), *The epidemiology of child and adolescent psychopathology* (pp. 86–103). New York: Oxford University Press.

Boggs, S. R., Eyberg, S., & Reynolds, L. A. (1990). Concurrent validity of the Eyberg Child Behavior Inventory. *Journal of Clinical Child Psychology, 19,* 75–78.

Bond, C. R., & McMahon, R. J. (1984). Relationships between marital distress and child behavioral problems, maternal personal adjustment, maternal personality, and maternal parenting behavior. *Journal of Abnormal Psychology, 93,* 348–351.

Boyle, M. H., Offord, D. R., Racine, Y., Sanford, M., Szatmari, P., Fleming, J. E., & Price-Munn, N. (1993). Evaluation of the Diagnostic Interview for Children and Adolescents for use in general population samples. *Journal of Abnormal Child Psychology, 21,* 663–681.

Breen, M. J., & Altepeter, T. S. (1990). *Disruptive behavior disorders in children: Treatment-focused assessment.* New York: Guilford Press.

Breiner, J. L., & Forehand, R. (1981). An assessment of the effects of parent training on clinic-referred children's school behavior. *Behavioral Assessment, 3,* 31–42.

Burgess, E. W., Locke, H. J., & Thomes, M. M. (1971). *The family.* New York: Van Nostrand Reinhold.

Burnett, P. (1987). Assessing marital adjustment and satisfaction: A review. *Measurement and Evaluation in Counseling and Development, 20,* 113–121.

Burns, G. L., & Owen, S. M. (1990). Disruptive behaviors in the classroom: Initial standardization data on a new teacher rating scale. *Journal of Abnormal Child Psychology, 18,* 515–525.

Burns, G. L., & Patterson, D. R. (1990). Conduct problem behaviors in a stratified random sample of children and adolescents: New standardization data on the Eyberg Child Behavior Inventory. *Psychological Assessment, 2,* 391–397.

Burns, G. L., & Patterson, D. R. (1991). Factor structure of the Eyberg Child Behavior Inventory: Unidimensional or multidimensional measure of disruptive behavior? *Journal of Clinical Child Psychology, 20,* 439–444.

Burns, G. L., Patterson, D. R., Nussbaum, B. R., & Parker, C. M. (1991). Disruptive behaviors in an outpatient pediatric population: Additional standardization data on the Eyberg Child Behavior Inventory. *Psychological Assessment, 3,* 202–207.

Burns, G. L., Sosna, T. D., & Ladish, C. (1992). Distinction between well-standardized norms and the psychometric properties of a measure: Measurement of disruptive behaviors with the Sutter–Eyberg Student Behavior Inventory. *Child and Family Behavior Therapy, 14,* 43–54.

Burns, G. L., Walsh, J. A., & Owen, S. M. (1995). Twelve-month stability of disruptive classroom behavior as measured by the Sutter–Eyberg Student Behavior Inventory. *Journal of Clinical Child Psychology, 24,* 453–462.

Busby, D. M., Christensen, C., Crane, D. R., & Larson, J. H. (1995). A revision of the Dyadic Adjustment Scale for use with distressed and nondistressed couples: Construct hierarchy and multidimensional scales. *Journal of Marital and Family Therapy, 21,* 289–308.

Campbell, S. B. (1991). Longitudinal studies of active and aggressive preschoolers: Individual differences in early behavior and in outcome. In D. Cicchetti & S. L. Toth (Eds.), *Rochester Symposium on Developmental Psychopathology: Vol. 2. Internalizing and externalizing expressions of dysfunction* (pp. 57–90). Hillsdale, NJ: Erlbaum.

Campbell, S. B. (1995). Behavior problems in preschool children: A review of recent research. *Journal of Child Psychology and Psychiatry, 36,* 113–149.

Campbell, S. B., & Ewing, L. J. (1990). Follow up of hard to manage preschoolers: Adjustment at age 9 and predictors of continuing symptoms. *Journal of Child Psychology and Psychiatry, 31,* 871–889.

Campis, L. K., Lyman, R. D., & Prentice-Dunn, S. (1986). The Parental Locus of Control Scale: Development and validation. *Journal of Clinical Child Psychology, 15,* 260–267.

Capaldi, D. M. (1991). Co-occurrence of conduct problems and depressive symptoms in early adolescent boys: I. Familial factors and general adjustment at age 6. *Development and Psychopathology, 3,* 277–300.

Capaldi, D. M. (1992). Co-occurrence of conduct problems and depressive symptoms in early adolescent boys: II. A 2-year follow-up at grade 8. *Development and Psychopathology, 4,* 125–144.

Capaldi, D. M., & Patterson, G. R. (1989). *Psychometric properties of fourteen latent constructs from the Oregon Youth Study.* New York: Springer-Verlag.

Capaldi, D. M., & Patterson, G. R. (1994). Interrelated influences of contextual factors on antisocial behavior in childhood and adolescence for males. In D. C. Fowles, P. Sutker, & S. H. Goodman (Eds.), *Progress in experimental personality and psychopathology research* (pp. 165–198). New York: Springer.

Capaldi, D. M., & Rothbart, M. K. (1992). Development and validation of an early adolescent temperament measure. *Journal of Early Adolescence, 12,* 153–173.

Carey, M. P., Spector, I. P., Lantinga, L. J., & Krauss, D. J. (1993). Reliability of the Dyadic Adjustment Scale. *Psychological Assessment, 5,* 238–240.

Caspi, A., Henry, B., McGee, R. O., Moffitt, T. E., & Silva, P. A. (1995). Temperamental origins of child and adolescent behavior problems: From age three to fifteen. *Child Development, 66,* 55–68.

Caspi, A., Lynam, D., Moffit, T. E., & Silva, P. A. (1993). Unraveling girls' delinquency: Biological, dispositional, and contextual contributions to adolescent misbehavior. *Developmental Psychology, 29,* 19–30.

Cautela, J. R., Cautela, J., & Esonis, S. (1983). *Forms for behavior analysis with children.* Champaign, IL: Research Press.

Celebi, S., & Eyberg, S. (1994). *Dyadic Parent–Child Interaction Coding System II: User manual for the coding and analysis software.* Unpublished manuscript, University of Florida.

Chamberlain, P., & Bank, L. (1989). Toward an integration of macro and micro measurement systems for the researcher and the clinician. *Journal of Family Psychology, 3,* 199–205.

Chamberlain, P., & Patterson, G. R. (1995). Discipline and child compliance in parenting. In M. H. Bornstein (Ed.), *Handbook of parenting: Vol. 4. Applied and practical parenting* (pp. 205–225). Hillsdale, NJ: Erlbaum.

Chamberlain, P., & Reid, J. B. (1987). Parent observation and report of child symptoms. *Behavioral Assessment, 9,* 97–109.

Chamberlain, P., & Reid, J. B. (1994). Differences in risk factors and adjustment for male and female delinquents in treatment foster care. *Journal of Child and Family Studies, 3,* 23–39.

Chen, W. J., Faraone, S. V., Biederman, J., & Tsuang, M. T. (1994). Diagnostic accuracy of the Child Behavior Checklist scales for Attention-Deficit Hyperactivity Disorder: A receiver-operating characteristic analysis. *Journal of Consulting and Clinical Psychology, 62,* 1017–1025.

Christensen, A. (1979). Naturalistic observation of families: A system for random audio recordings in the home. *Behavior Therapy, 10,* 418–422.

Christensen, A., Margolin, G., & Sullaway, M. (1992). Interparental agreement on child behavior problems. *Psychological Assessment, 4,* 419–425.

Ciminero, A. R., Adams, H. E., & Calhoun, K. S. (Eds.). (1986). *Handbook of behavioral assessment* (2nd ed.). New York: Wiley.

Cobb, J. A., & Hops, H. (1972). *Coding manual for continuous observation of interactions by single subjects in an academic setting* (Report No. 9). Eugene: University of Oregon, Center at Oregon for Research in the Behavioral Education of the Handicapped.

Coie, J. D., & Dodge, K. A. (in press). Aggression and antisocial behavior. In W. Damon & N. Eisenberg (Vol. Eds.), *Handbook of child psychology* (5th ed.): *Vol. 3. Social, emotional, and personality development.* New York: Wiley.

Coie, J. D., Lochman, J. E., Terry, R., & Hyman, C. (1992). Predicting early adolescent disorder from childhood aggression and peer rejection. *Journal of Consulting and Clinical Psychology, 60,* 783–792.

Conners, C. K. (1973). Rating scales for use in drug studies with children. *Psychopharmacology Bulletin, 9,* 24–84.

Conners, C. K. (1990). *Conners Rating Scales manual*. North Tonawanda, NY: Multi-Health Systems.

Costello, E. J. (1990). Child psychiatric epidemiology: Implications for clinical research and practice. In B. B. Lahey & A. E. Kazdin (Eds.), *Advances in clinical child psychology* (Vol. 13, pp. 53–90). New York: Plenum Press.

Cowan, P. A., Cohn, D. A., Cowan, C. P., & Pearson, J. L. (1996). Parents' attachment histories and children's externalizing and internalizing behaviors: Exploring family systems models of linkage. *Journal of Consulting and Clinical Psychology, 64*, 53–63.

Crane, D. R., Allgood, S. M., Larson, J. H., & Griffin, W. (1990). Assessing marital quality with distressed and nondistressed couples: A comparison and equivalency table for three frequently used measures. *Journal of Marriage and the Family, 52*, 87–93.

Crick, N. R., & Dodge, K. A. (1994). A review and reformulation of social information-processing mechanisms in children's social adjustment. *Psychological Bulletin, 115*, 74–101.

Crnic, K. A., & Greenberg, M. T. (1990). Minor parenting stresses with young children. *Child Development, 61*, 1628–1637.

Cuccaro, M. L., Holmes, G. R., & Wright, H. H. (1993). Behavior problems in preschool children: A pilot study. *Psychological Reports, 72*, 121–122.

Cummings, E. M., & Davies, P. (1994a). *Children and marital conflict: The impact of family dispute resolution*. New York: Guilford Press.

Cummings, E. M., & Davies, P. T. (1994b). Maternal depression and child development. *Journal of Child Psychology and Psychiatry, 35*, 73–112.

Dadds, M. R., & Powell, M. B. (1991). The relationship of interparental conflict and global marital adjustment to aggression, anxiety, and immaturity in aggressive and nonclinic children. *Journal of Abnormal Child Psychology, 19*, 553–567.

Dadds, M. R., & Sanders, M. R. (1992). Family interaction and child psychopathology: A comparison of two observation strategies. *Journal of Child and Family Studies, 1*, 371–391.

Day, D. M., Bream, L. A., & Pal, A. (1992). Proactive and reactive aggression: An analysis of subtypes based on teacher perceptions. *Journal of Clinical Child Psychology, 21*, 210–217.

DeKlyen, M. (1996). Disruptive behavior disorder and intergenerational attachment patterns: A comparison of clinic-referred and normally functioning preschoolers and their mothers. *Journal of Consulting and Clinical Psychology, 64*, 357–365.

Demaray, M. K., Ruffalo, S. L., Carlson, J., Busse, R. T., Olson, A. E., McManus, S. M., & Leventhal, A. (1995). Social skills assessment: A comparative evaluation of six published rating scales. *School Psychology Review, 24*, 648–671.

Dishion, T. J. (1990). The family ecology of boys' peer relations in middle childhood. *Child Development, 61*, 874–892.

Dishion, T. J., Andrews, D. W., & Crosby, L. (1995). Antisocial boys and their friends in early adolescence: Relationship characteristics, quality, and interactional process. *Child Development, 66*, 139–151.

Dishion, T. J., French, D. C., & Patterson, G. R. (1995). The development and ecology of antisocial behavior. In D. Cicchetti & D. J. Cohen (Eds.), *Developmental psychopathology: Vol. 2. Risk, disorder, and adaptation* (pp. 421–471). New York: Wiley.

Dishion, T., Gardner, K., Patterson, G., Reid, J., Spyrou, S., & Thibodeaux, S. (1984). *The Family Process Code: A multidimensional system for observing family interactions* (Oregon Social Learning Center Technical Report). (Available from Oregon Social Learning Center, 207 E. 5th Avenue, Suite 202, Eugene, OR 97401)

Dishion, T. J., Patterson, G. R., Stoolmiller, M., & Skinner, M. L. (1991). Family, school, and behavioral antecedents to early adolescent involvement with antisocial peers. *Developmental Psychology, 27*, 172–180.

Dishion, T. J., Reid, J. B., & Patterson, G. R. (1988). Empirical guidelines for a family intervention for adolescent drug use. *Journal of Chemical Dependency Treatment, 1*, 189–224.

Dodge, K. A. (1991). The structure and function of reactive and proactive aggression. In D. J. Pepler & K. H. Rubin (Eds.), *The development and treatment of childhood aggression* (pp. 201–218). Hillsdale, NJ: Erlbaum.

Dodge, K. A., & Coie, J. D. (1987). Social-information processing factors in reactive and proactive aggression in children's peer groups. *Journal of Personality and Social Psychology, 53*, 1146–1158.

Dodge, K. A., McClaskey, C. L., & Feldman, E. (1985). Situational approach to the assessment of social competence in children. *Journal of Consulting and Clinical Psychology, 53*, 344–353.

Dodge, K. A., Pettit, G. S., & Bates, J. E. (1994). Socialization mediators of the relation between socioeconomic status and child conduct problems. *Child Development, 65*, 649–665.

Drotar, D., & Crawford, P. (1987). Using home observation in the clinical assessment of children. *Journal of Clinical Child Psychology, 16*, 342–349.

Drotar, D., Stein, R. E. K., & Perrin, E. C. (1995). Methodological issues in using the Child Behavior Checklist and its related instruments in clinical child psychology research. *Journal of Clinical Child Psychology, 24*, 184–192.

Dumas, J. E. (1996). Why was this child referred? Interactional correlates of referral status in families of children with disruptive behavior problems. *Journal of Clinical Child Psychology, 25*, 106–115.

Dumas, J. E., & Serketich, W. J. (1994). Maternal depressive symptomatology and child maladjustment: A comparison of three process models. *Behavior Therapy*, 25, 161–181.

Dumas, J. E., & Wahler, R. G. (1983). Predictors of treatment outcome in parent training: Mother insularity and socioeconomic disadvantage. *Behavioral Assessment*, 5, 301–313.

Dumas, J. E., & Wahler, R. G. (1985). Indiscriminate mothering as a contextual factor in aggressive–oppositional child behavior: "Damned if you do and damned if you don't." *Journal of Abnormal Child Psychology*, 13, 1–17.

Duncan, G. J., Brooks-Gunn, J., & Klebanov, P. K. (1994). Economic deprivation and early childhood development. *Child Development*, 65, 296–318.

Edelbrock, C. S. (1985). *Conduct problems in childhood and adolescence: Developmental patterns and progressions.* Unpublished manuscript.

Edelbrock, C. S., & Achenbach, T. M. (1984). The teacher version of the Child Behavior Profile: 1. Boys aged 6–11. *Journal of Consulting and Clinical Psychology*, 52, 207–217.

Edelbrock, C. S., & Costello, A. J. (1988a). Convergence between statistically derived behavior problem syndromes and child psychiatric diagnoses. *Journal of Abnormal Child Psychology*, 16, 219–231.

Edelbrock, C. S., & Costello, A. J. (1988b). Structured psychiatric interviews for children. In M. Rutter, A. H. Tuma, & I. S. Lann (Eds.), *Assessment and diagnosis in child psychopathology* (pp. 87–112). New York: Guilford Press.

Edelbrock, C. S., Costello, A. J., Dulcan, M. K., Kalas, R., & Conover, N. C. (1985). Age differences in the reliability of the psychiatric interview of the child. *Child Development*, 56, 265–275.

Edelbrock, C. S., Greenbaum, R., & Conover, N. C. (1985). Reliability and concurrent relations between the teacher version of the Child Behavior Profile and the Conners Revised Teacher Rating Scale. *Journal of Abnormal Child Psychology*, 13, 295–303.

Eisenstadt, T. H., Eyberg, S., McNeil, C. B., Newcomb, K., & Funderburk, B. (1993). Parent–child interaction therapy with behavior problem children: Relative effectiveness of two stages and overall treatment outcome. *Journal of Clinical Child Psychology*, 22, 42–51.

Eisenstadt, T. H., McElreath, L. H., Eyberg, S. M., & McNeil, C. B. (1994). Interparent agreement on the Eyberg Child Behavior Inventory. *Child and Family Behavior Therapy*, 16, 21–27.

Elliott, D. S., Huizinga, D., & Ageton, S. S. (1985). *Explaining delinquency and drug use.* Beverly Hills, CA: Sage.

Elliott, S. N., Busse, R. T., & Gresham, F. M. (1993). Behavior rating scales: Issues of use and development. *School Psychology Review*, 22, 313–321.

Eme, R. F., & Kavanaugh, L. (1995). Sex differences in conduct disorder. *Journal of Clinical Child Psychology*, 24, 406–426.

Eyberg, S. M. (1974). *Therapy Attitude Inventory.* (Available from Sheila M. Eyberg, PhD, Department of Clinical and Health Psychology, Box 100165, Health Science Center, University of Florida, Gainesville, FL 32610-0165)

Eyberg, S. M. (1992). Parent and teacher behavior inventories for the assessment of conduct problem behaviors in children. In L. VandeCreek, S. Knapp, & T. L. Jackson (Eds.), *Innovations in clinical practice: A source book* (Vol. 11, pp. 261–270). Sarasota, FL: Professional Resource Exchange.

Eyberg, S. M. (1993). Consumer satisfaction measures for assessing parent training programs. In L. VandeCreek, S. Knapp, & T. L. Jackson (Eds.), *Innovations in clinical practice: A source book* (Vol. 12, pp. 377–382). Sarasota, FL: Professional Resource Exchange.

Eyberg, S. M., Bessmer, J., Newcomb, K., Edwards, D., & Robinson, E. (1994). *Dyadic Parent–Child Interaction Coding System II: A manual.* Unpublished manuscript, University of Florida.

Eyberg, S. M., & Boggs, S. R. (1989). Parent training for oppositional-defiant preschoolers. In C. E. Schaefer & J. M. Briesmeister (Eds.), *Handbook of parent training: Parents as co-therapists for children's behavior problems* (pp. 105–132). New York: Wiley.

Eyberg, S. M., Boggs, S. R., & Algina, J. (1995). Parent–child interaction therapy: A psychosocial model for the treatment of young children with conduct problem behavior and their families. *Psychopharmacology Bulletin*, 31, 83–91.

Eyberg, S. M., Boggs, S. R., & Rodriguez, C. M. (1992). Relationships between maternal parenting stress and child disruptive behavior. *Child and Family Behavior Therapy*, 14, 1–9.

Eyberg, S. M., & Colvin, A. (1994, August). *Restandardization of the Eyberg Child Behavior Inventory.* Paper presented at the annual meeting of the American Psychological Association, Los Angeles.

Eyberg, S. M., & Robinson, E. A. (1983a). Conduct problem behavior: Standardization of a behavioral rating scale with adolescents. *Journal of Clinical Child Psychology*, 12, 347–357.

Eyberg, S. M., & Robinson, E. A. (1983b). Dyadic Parent–Child Interaction Coding System: A manual. *Psychological Documents*, 13 (Ms. No. 2582).

Eyberg, S. M., & Ross, A. W. (1978). Assessment of child behavior problems: The validation of a new inventory. *Journal of Clinical Child Psychology*, 7, 113–116.

Fagot, B. I. (1992). Assessment of coercive parent discipline. *Behavioral Assessment*, 14, 387–406.

Farrington, D. P. (1986). Age and crime. In M. Tonry & N. Morris (Eds.), *Crime and justice: An annual review of research* (pp. 189–250). Chicago: University of Chicago Press.

Farrington, D. P. (1995). The development of offending and antisocial behaviour from childhood: Key findings from the Cambridge study in delinquent development. *Journal of Child Psychology and Psychiatry, 36,* 929–964.

Fergusson, D. M., & Lynskey, M. T. (1993). The effects of maternal depression on child conduct disorder and attention deficit behaviours. *Social Psychiatry and Psychiatric Epidemiology, 28,* 116–123.

Fergusson, D. M., Lynskey, M. T., & Horwood, L. J. (1993). The effect of maternal depression on maternal ratings of child behavior. *Journal of Abnormal Child Psychology, 21,* 245–269.

Field, T., Morrow, C., Healy, B., Foster, T., Adlestein, D., & Goldstein, S. (1991). Mothers with zero Beck depression scores act more "depressed" with their infants. *Development and Psychopathology, 3,* 253–262.

Fitzgerald, H. E., Sullivan, L. A., Ham, H. P., Zucker, R. A., Bruckel, S., Schneider, A. M., & Noll, R. B. (1993). Predictors of behavior problems in three-year-old sons of alcoholics: Early evidence for the onset of risk. *Child Development, 64,* 110–123.

Forehand, R., & Brody, G. (1985). The association between parental personal/marital adjustment and parent–child interactions in a clinic sample. *Behaviour Research and Therapy, 23,* 211–212.

Forehand, R., Furey, W. M., & McMahon, R. J. (1984). The role of maternal distress in a parent training program to modify child non-compliance. *Behavioural Psychotherapy, 12,* 93–108.

Forehand, R., Griest, D., & Wells, K. C. (1979). Parent behavioral training: An analysis of the relationship among multiple outcome measures. *Journal of Abnormal Child Psychology, 7,* 229–242.

Forehand, R., King, H. E., Peed, S., & Yoder, P. (1975). Mother–child interactions: Comparison of a non-compliant clinic group and a nonclinic group. *Behaviour Research and Therapy, 13,* 79–84.

Forehand, R., Lautenschlager, G. J., Faust, J., & Graziano, W. G. (1986). Parent perceptions and parent–child interactions in clinic-referred children: A preliminary investigation of the effects of maternal depressive moods. *Behaviour Research and Therapy, 24,* 73–75.

Forehand, R., Long, N., & Hedrick, M. (1987). Family characteristics of adolescents who display overt and covert behavior problems. *Journal of Behavior Therapy and Experimental Psychiatry, 18,* 325–328.

Forehand, R., & McMahon, R. J. (1981). *Helping the noncompliant child: A clinician's guide to parent training.* New York: Guilford Press.

Forehand, R., & Peed, S. (1979). Training parents to modify noncompliant behavior of their children.

In A. J. Finch, Jr., & P. C. Kendall (Eds.), *Treatment and research in child psychopathology* (pp. 159–184). New York: Spectrum.

Forehand, R., Wells, K. C., & Griest, D. L. (1980). An examination of the social validity of a parent training program. *Behavior Therapy, 11,* 488–502.

Forehand, R., Wells, K. C., McMahon, R. J., Griest, D. L., & Rogers, T. (1982). Maternal perceptions of maladjustment in clinic-referred children: An extension of earlier research. *Journal of Behavioral Assessment, 4,* 145–151.

Forehand, R., Wells, K. C., & Sturgis, E. T. (1978). Predictors of child noncompliant behavior in the home. *Journal of Consulting and Clinical Psychology, 46,* 179.

Forehand, R., Wierson, M., Frame, C. L., Kemptom, T., & Armistead, L. (1991). Juvenile firesetting: A unique syndome or an advanced level of antisocial behaviour? *Behaviour Research and Therapy, 29,* 125–128.

Forgatch, M. S., Patterson, G. R., & Skinner, M.L. (1988). A mediational model for the effect of divorce on antisocial behavior in boys. In E. M. Hetherington & J. D. Arasteh (Eds.), *Impact of divorce, single parenting, and stepparenting on children* (pp. 135–154). Hillsdale, NJ: Erlbaum.

Frankel, F., & Weiner, H. (1990). The Child Conflict Index: Factor analysis, reliability and validity for clinic-referred and nonreferred children. *Journal of Clinical Child Psychology, 3,* 239–248.

Frick, P. J. (1991). *The Alabama Parenting Questionnaire.* Unpublished manuscript, University of Alabama.

Frick, P. J. (1994). Family dysfunction and the disruptive behavior disorders: A review of recent empirical findings. In T. H. Ollendick & R. J. Prinz (Eds.), *Advances in clinical child psychology* (Vol. 16, pp. 203–226). New York: Plenum Press.

Frick, P. J., & Hare, R. D. (in press). *The Psychopathy Screening Device.* North Tonawanda: Multi-Health Systems.

Frick, P. J., & Jackson, Y. K. (1993). Family functioning and childhood antisocial behavior: Yet another reinterpretation. *Journal of Clinical Child Psychology, 22,* 410–419.

Frick, P. J., Lahey, B. B., Hartdagen, S., & Hynd, G. W. (1989). Conduct problems in boys: Relations to maternal personality, marital satisfaction, and socioeconomic status. *Journal of Clinical Child Psychology, 18,* 114–120.

Frick, P. J., Lahey, B. B., Loeber, R., Stouthamer-Loeber, M., Christ, M. A. G., & Hanson, K. (1992). Familial risk factors to Oppositional Defiant Disorder and Conduct Disorder: Parental psychopathology and maternal parenting. *Journal of Consulting and Clinical Psychology, 60,* 49–55.

Frick, P. J., O'Brien, B. S., Wootton, J. M., & McBurnett, K. (1994). Psychopathy and conduct problems in children. *Journal of Abnormal Psychology, 103,* 700–707.

Frick, P. J., Van Horn, Y., Lahey, B. B., Christ, M. A. G., Loeber, R., Hart, E. A., Tannenbaum, L., & Hanson, K. (1993). Oppositional Defiant Disorder and Conduct Disorder: A meta-analytic review of factor analyses and cross-validation in a clinic sample. *Clinical Psychology Review, 13,* 319–340.

Funderburk, B. W., & Eyberg, S. M. (1989). Psychometric characteristics of the Sutter–Eyberg Student Behavior Inventory: A school behavior rating scale for use with preschool children. *Behavioral Assessment, 11,* 297–313.

Furey, W., & Forehand, R. (1983). The Daily Child Behavior Checklist. *Journal of Behavioral Assessment, 5,* 83–95.

Geller, J., & Johnston, C. (1995). Predictors of mothers' responses to child noncompliance: Attributions and attitudes. *Journal of Clinical Child Psychology, 24,* 272–278.

Gibaud-Wallston, J., & Wandersman, L. P. (1978, August). *Development and utility of the Parenting Sense of Competence Scale.* Paper presented at the meeting of the American Psychological Association, Toronto.

Goldsmith, H. H., Buss, A. H., Plomin, R., Rothbart, M. K., Thomas, A., Chess, S., Hinde, R. A., & McCall, R. B. (1987). Roundtable: What is temperament? Four approaches. *Child Development, 58,* 505–529.

Gottman, J. M., & Roy, A. K. (1990). *Sequential analysis: A guide for behavioral researchers.* New York: Cambridge University Press.

Greenberg, M. T., Speltz, M. L., & DeKlyen, M. (1993). The role of attachment in the early development of disruptive behavior problems. *Development and Psychopathology, 5,* 191–213.

Greenberg, M. T., Speltz, M. L., DeKlyen, M., & Endriga, M. C. (1991). Attachment security in preschoolers with and without externalizing behavior problems: A replication. *Development and Psychopathology, 3,* 413–430.

Griest, D. L., Forehand, R., Wells, K. C., & McMahon, R. J. (1980). An examination of differences between nonclinic and behavior-problem clinic-referred children and their mothers. *Journal of Abnormal Psychology, 89,* 497–500.

Guidubaldi, J., & Cleminshaw, H. K. (1985). The development of the Cleminshaw–Guidubaldi Parent Satisfaction Scale. *Journal of Clinical Child Psychology, 14,* 293–298.

Haaga, D. A., & Solomon, A. (1993). Impact of Kendall, Hollon, Beck, Hammen, and Ingram (1987) on treatment of the continuity issue in "depression" research. *Cognitive Therapy and Research, 17,* 313–324.

Ham, H. P., Zucker, R. A., & Fitzgerald, H. E. (1993, June). *Assessing antisocial behavior with the Antisocial Behavior Checklist: Reliability and validity studies.* Paper presented at the annual meeting of the American Psychological Society, Chicago.

Hämäläinen, M., & Pulkkinen, L. (1996). Problem behavior as a precursor of male criminality. *Development and Psychopathology, 8,* 443–455.

Hanf, C. (1970). *Shaping mothers to shape their children's behavior.* Unpublished manuscript, University of Oregon Medical School.

Harrison, D. F., & Westhuis, D. J. (1989). Rating scales for marital adjustment. *Journal of Social Service Research, 13,* 87–105.

Hawkins, J. D., Catalano, R. F., & Miller, J. Y. (1992). Risk and protective factors for alcohol and other drug problems in adolescence and early adulthood: Implications for substance abuse prevention. *Psychological Bulletin, 112,* 64–105.

Herjanic, B., & Reich, W. (1982). Development of a structured psychiatric interview for children: Agreement between child and parent on individual symptoms. *Journal of Abnormal Child Psychology, 10,* 307–324.

Hinshaw, S. P. (1992). Externalizing behavior problems and academic underachievement in childhood and adolescence: Causal relationships and underlying mechanisms. *Psychological Bulletin, 111,* 127–155.

Hinshaw, S. P., & Anderson, C. A. (1996). Conduct and Oppositional Defiant Disorders. In E. J. Mash & R. A. Barkley (Eds.), *Child psychopathology* (pp. 113–149). New York: Guilford Press.

Hinshaw, S. P., Heller, T., & McHale, J. P. (1992). Covert antisocial behavior in boys with Attention-Deficit Hyperactivity Disorder: External validation and effects of methylphenidate. *Journal of Consulting and Clinical Psychology, 60,* 274–281.

Hinshaw, S. P., Lahey, B. B., & Hart, E. L. (1993). Issues of taxonomy and comorbidity in the development of Conduct Disorder. *Development and Psychopathology, 5,* 31–49.

Hodges, K., & Zeman, J. (1993). Interviewing. In T. H. Ollendick & M. Hersen (Eds.), *Handbook of child and adolescent assessment* (pp. 65–81). Needham, MA: Allyn & Bacon.

Hoge, R. D., & Andrews, D. A. (1992). Assessing conduct problems in the classroom. *Clinical Psychology Review, 12,* 1–20.

Holden, G. W., & Edwards, L. A. (1989). Parental attitudes toward child rearing: Instruments, issues, and implications. *Psychological Bulletin, 106,* 29–58.

Holleran, P. A., Littman, D. C., Freund, R. D., & Schmaling, K. B. (1982). A signal detection approach to social perception: Identification of negative and positive behaviors by parents of normal and problem children. *Journal of Abnormal Child Psychology, 10,* 547–558.

Holtzworth-Munroe, A., Beatty, S. B., & Anglin, K. (1995). The assessment and treatment of marital violence. In N. S. Jacobson & A. S. Gurman (Eds.), *Clinical handbook of couple therapy* (2nd ed., pp. 317–339). New York: Guilford Press.

Hops, H., Biglan, A., Tolman, A., Sherman, L., Arthur, J., Warner, P., Romano, J., Turner, J., Friedman, L., Bulcroft, R., Holcomb, C., Oosternink, N., & Osteen, V. (1990). *Living in Familial Environments (LIFE) coding system: Training/procedures and reference manual for coders* (rev. ed.). Eugene: Oregon Research Institute.

Huesmann, L. R., Eron, L. D., Lefkowitz, M. M., & Walder, L. O. (1984). Stability of aggression over time and generations. *Developmental Psychology*, 20, 1120–1134.

Hughes, H. M., & Haynes, S. N. (1978). Structured laboratory observation in the behavioral assessment of parent–child interactions: A methodological critique. *Behavior Therapy*, 9, 428–447.

Jacob, T., Krahn, G. L., & Leonard, K. (1991). Parent–child interactions in families with alcoholic fathers. *Journal of Consulting and Clinical Psychology*, 59, 176–181.

Jacob, T., & Tennenbaum, D. L. (1988). *Family assessment: Rationale, methods, and future direction.* New York: Plenum Press.

Jacobson, N. S., & Anderson, E. A. (1980). The effects of behaviour rehearsal and feedback on the acquisition of problem-solving skills in distressed and non-distressed couples. *Behaviour Research and Therapy*, 18, 25–36.

Jansen, R. E., Fitzgerald, H. E., Ham, H. P., & Zucker, R. A. (1995). Pathways into risk: Temperament and behavior problems in three- to five-year-old sons of alcoholics. *Alcoholism: Clinical and Experimental Research*, 19, 501–509.

Jennings, K. D., Stagg, V., & Connors, R. E. (1991). Social networks and mothers' interactions with their preschool children. *Child Development*, 62, 966–978.

Jensen, P. S., Salzberg, A. D., Richters, J. E., Watanabe, H. K., & Roper, M. (1993). Scales, diagnoses, and child psychopathology: I. CBCL and DISC relationships. *Journal of the American Academy of Child and Adolescent Psychiatry*, 32, 397–406.

Jensen, P. S., Watanabe, H. K., Richters, J. E., Roper, M., Hibbs, E. D., Salzberg, A. D., & Liu, S. (1996). Scales, diagnoses, and child psychopathology: II. Comparing the CBCL and the DISC against external validators. *Journal of Abnormal Child Psychology*, 24, 151–168.

Johnston, C. (1996a). Addressing parent cognitions in interventions with families of disruptive children. In K. S. Dobson & K. D. Craig (Eds.), *Advances in cognitive–behavioral therapy* (pp. 193–209). Thousand Oaks, CA: Sage.

Johnston, C. (1996b). Parent characteristics and parent–child interactions in families of nonproblem children and ADHD children with higher and lower levels of oppositional-defiant behavior. *Journal of Abnormal Child Psychology*, 24, 85–104.

Johnston, C., & Mash, E. J. (1989). A measure of parenting satisfaction and efficacy. *Journal of Clinical Child Psychology*, 18, 167–175.

Johnston, C., & Patenaude, R. (1994). Parent attributions of inattentive–overactive and oppositional-defiant child behaviors. *Cognitive Therapy and Research*, 18, 261–275.

Johnston, C., & Pelham, W. E. (1990). Maternal characteristics, ratings of child behavior, and mother–child interactions in families of children with externalizing disorders. *Journal of Abnormal Child Psychology*, 18, 407–417.

Jones, R. R. (1974). *"Observation" by telephone: An economical behavior sampling technique* (Oregon Research Institute Technical Report No. 1411). Eugene: Oregon Research Institute.

Jouriles, E. N., Murphy, C. M., Farris, A. M., Smith, D. A., Richters, J. E., & Waters, E. (1991). Marital adjustment, parental disagreements about child rearing, and behavior problems in boys: Increasing the specificity of the marital assessment. *Child Development*, 62, 1424–1433.

Jouriles, E. N., Norwood, W. D., McDonald, R., Vincent, J. P., & Mahoney, A. (1996). Physical violence and other forms of marital aggression: Links with children's behavior problems. *Journal of Family Psychology*, 10, 223–234.

Julien, D., Markman, H. J., & Lindahl, K. M. (1989). A comparison of a global and a microanalytic coding system: Implications for future trends in studying interactions. *Behavioral Assessment*, 11, 81–100.

Kamphaus, R. W., & Frick, P. J. (1996). *Clinical assessment of child and adolescent personality and behavior.* Needham Heights, MA: Allyn & Bacon.

Kanner, A., Coyne, J., Schaeffer, C., & Lazarus, R. (1981). Comparisons of two models of stress measurement: Daily hassles and uplifts versus major life events. *Journal of Behavioral Medicine*, 4, 1–39.

Katz, L. F., & Gottman, J. M. (1993). Patterns of marital conflict predict children's internalizing and externalizing behavior. *Developmental Psychology*, 29, 940–950.

Kazdin, A. E. (1977). Assessing the clinical or applied importance of behavior change through social validation. *Behavior Modification*, 1, 427–452.

Kazdin, A. E. (1990). Premature termination from treatment among children referred for antisocial behavior. *Journal of Child Psychology and Psychiatry*, 31, 415–425.

Kazdin, A. E. (1992). Overt and covert antisocial behavior: Child and family characteristics among psychiatric inpatient children. *Journal of Child and Family Studies*, 1, 3–20.

Kazdin, A. E. (1995a). Child, parent and family dysfunction as predictors of outcome in cognitive-behavioural treatment of antisocial children. *Behaviour Research and Therapy*, 33, 271–281.

Kazdin, A. E. (1995b). *Conduct disorders in childhood and adolescence* (2nd ed.). Thousand Oaks, CA: Sage.

Kazdin, A. E., Bass, D., Siegel, T., & Thomas, C. (1989). Cognitive-behavioral therapy and relationship therapy in the treatment of children referred for antisocial behavior. *Journal of Consulting and Clinical Psychology, 57,* 522–535.

Kazdin, A. E., & Esveldt-Dawson, K. (1986). The Interview for Antisocial Behavior: Psychometric characteristics and concurrent validity with child psychiatric inpatients. *Journal of Psychopathology and Behavioral Assessment, 8,* 289–303.

Kazdin, A. E., & Heidish, I. E. (1984). Convergence of clinically derived diagnoses, and parent checklists among inpatient children. *Journal of Abnormal Child Psychology, 12,* 421–436.

Kazdin, A. E., Mazurick, J. L., & Siegel, T. C. (1994). Treatment outcome among children with externalizing disorder who terminate prematurely versus those who complete psychotherapy. *Journal of the American Academy of Child and Adolescent Psychiatry, 33,* 549–557.

Kazdin, A. E., Rodgers, A., Colbus, D., & Siegel, T. (1987). Children's Hostility Inventory: Measurement of aggression and hostility in psychiatric inpatient children. *Journal of Clinical Child Psychology, 16,* 320–328.

Kazdin, A. E., Siegel, T. C., & Bass, D. (1992). Cognitive problem-solving skills training and parent management training in the treatment of antisocial behavior in children. *Journal of Consulting and Clinical Psychology, 60,* 733–747.

Kendall, P. C., Hollon, S. D., Beck, A. T., Hammen, C. L., & Ingram, R. E. (1987). Issues and recommendations regarding use of the Beck Depression Inventory. *Cognitive Therapy and Research, 11,* 289–299.

Kendall, P. C., Reber, M., McLeer, S., Epps, J., & Ronan, K. R. (1990). Cognitive-behavioral treatment of conduct-disordered children. *Cognitive Therapy and Research, 14,* 279–297.

Kendziora, K. T., & O'Leary, S. G. (1992). Dysfunctional parenting as a focus for prevention and treatment of child behavior problems. In T. H. Ollendick & R. J. Prinz (Eds.), *Advances in clinical child psychology* (Vol. 15, pp. 175–206). New York: Plenum Press.

Kimmel, D. C., & van der Veen, F. (1974). Factors of marital adjustment in Locke's Marital Adjustment Test. *Journal of Marriage and the Family, 36,* 57–63.

Kolko, D. J., & Kazdin, A. E. (1988). Parent–child correspondence in identification of firesetting among child psychiatric patients. *Journal of Child Psychology and Psychiatry, 29,* 175–184.

Kolko, D. J., & Kazdin, A. E. (1989a). Assessment of dimensions of childhood firesetting among patients and nonpatients: The Firesetting Risk Interview. *Journal of Abnormal Child Psychology, 17,* 157–176.

Kolko, D. J., & Kazdin, A. E. (1989b). The Children's Firesetting Interview with psychiatrically referred and nonreferred children. *Journal of Abnormal Child Psychology, 17,* 609–624.

Kolko, D. J., & Kazdin, A. E. (1991a). Aggression and psychopathology in matchplaying and firesetting children: A replication and extension. *Journal of Clinical Child Psychology, 20,* 191–201.

Kolko, D. J., & Kazdin, A. E. (1991b). Motives of childhood firesetters: Firesetting characteristics and psychological correlates. *Journal of Child Psychology and Psychiatry, 32,* 535–550.

Kolko, D. J., & Kazdin, A. E. (1992). The emergence and recurrence of child firesetting: A one-year prospective study. *Journal of Abnormal Child Psychology, 20,* 17–37.

Kolko, D. J., Kazdin, A. E., & Meyer, E. C. (1985). Aggression and psychopathology in childhood firesetters: Parent and child reports. *Journal of Consulting and Clinical Psychology, 53,* 377–385.

Kolko, D. J., Watson, S., & Faust, J. (1991). Fire safety/prevention skills training to reduce involvement with fire in young psychiatric inpatients: Preliminary findings. *Behavior Therapy, 22,* 269–284.

Kovacs, M., Paulauskas, S., Gatsonis, C., & Richards, C. (1988). Depressive disorders in childhood. *Journal of Affective Disorders, 15,* 205–217.

Kubany, E. S., & Sloggett, B. B. (1973). Coding procedure for teachers. *Journal of Applied Behavior Analysis, 6,* 339–344.

Lahey, B. B., Applegate, B., Barkley, R. A., Garfinkel, B., McBurnett, K., Kerdyck, L., Greenhill, L., Hynd, G. W., Frick, P. J., Newcorn, J., Biederman, J., Ollendick, T., Hart, E. L., Perez, D., Waldman, I., & Shaffer, D. (1994). DSM-IV field trials for Oppositional Defiant Disorder and Conduct Disorder in children and adolescents. *American Journal of Psychiatry, 151,* 1163–1171.

Lahey, B. B., & Loeber, R. (1994). Framework for a developmental model of Oppositional Defiant Disorder and Conduct Disorder. In D. K. Routh (Ed.), *Disruptive behavior disorders in childhood* (pp. 139–180). New York: Plenum Press.

Lahey, B. B., Loeber, R., Hart, E. L., Frick, P. J., Applegate, B., Zhang, Q., Green, S. M., & Russo, M. F. (1995). Four-year longitudinal study of Conduct Disorder in boys: Patterns and predictors of persistence. *Journal of Abnormal Psychology, 104,* 83–93.

La Taillade, J. J., & Jacobson, N. S. (in press). Domestic violence: Antisocial behavior in the family. In J. Breiling, J. D. Maser, & D. M. Stoff (Eds.), *Handbook of antisocial behavior.* New York: Wiley.

Lilienfeld, S. O. (1992). The association between Antisocial Personality and Somatization Disorders: A review and integration of theoretical models. *Clinical Psychology Review, 12,* 641–662.

Lochman, J. E., & the Conduct Problems Prevention Research Group. (1995). Screening of child behavior problems for prevention programs at school entry. *Journal of Consulting and Clinical Psychology, 63,* 549–559.

Locke, H. J., & Wallace, K. M. (1959). Short marital adjustment and prediction tests: Their reliability and validity. *Marriage and Family Living, 21,* 251–255.

Loeber, R. (1988). Natural histories of conduct problems, delinquency, and associated substance use: Evidence for developmental progressions. In B. B. Lahey & A. E. Kazdin (Eds.), *Advances in clinical child psychology* (Vol. 11, pp. 73–124). New York: Plenum Press.

Loeber, R., Green, S. M., Lahey, B. B., & Stouthamer-Loeber, M. (1991). Differences and similarities between children, mothers, and teachers as informants on disruptive child behavior. *Journal of Abnormal Child Psychology, 19,* 75–95.

Loeber, R., & Keenan, K. (1994). Interaction between Conduct Disorder and its comorbid conditions: Effects of age and gender. *Clinical Psychology Review, 14,* 497–523.

Loeber, R., & Schmaling, K. B. (1985a). Empirical evidence for overt and covert patterns of antisocial conduct problems: A meta-analysis. *Journal of Abnormal Child Psychology, 13,* 337–352.

Loeber, R., & Schmaling, K. B. (1985b). The utility of differentiating between mixed and pure forms of antisocial child behavior. *Journal of Abnormal Child Psychology, 13,* 315–336.

Loeber, R., & Stouthamer-Loeber, M. (1986). Family factors as correlates and predictors of juvenile conduct problems and delinquency. In M. Tonry & N. Morris (Eds.), *Crime and justice* (Vol. 7, pp. 29–149). Chicago: University of Chicago Press.

Loeber, R., Stouthamer-Loeber, M., Van Kammen, W. B., & Farrington, D. P. (1989). Development of a new measure of self-reported antisocial behavior for young children: Prevalence and reliability. In M. W. Klein (Ed.), *Cross national research and self-reported crime and delinquency* (pp. 203–225). Dordrecht, The Netherlands: Kluwer–Nijhoff.

Loeber, R., Wung, P., Keenan, K., Giroux, B., Stouthamer-Loeber, M., Van Kammen, W. B., & Maughan, B. (1993). Developmental pathways in disruptive child behavior. *Development and Psychopathology, 5,* 101–131.

Loney, J., & Milich, R. S. (1982). Hyperactivity, inattention, and aggression in clinical practice. In M. Wolraich & D. K. Routh (Eds.), *Advances in developmental and behavioral pediatrics* (Vol. 2, pp. 113–147). Greenwich, CT: JAI Press.

Lovejoy, M. C. (1996). Social inferences regarding inattentive–overactive and aggressive child behavior and their effects on teacher reports of discipline. *Journal of Clinical Child Psychology, 25,* 33–42.

Lyon, G. R. (Ed.). (1994). *Frames of reference for the assessment of learning disabilities: New views on measurement issues.* Baltimore, MD: Paul H. Brookes.

Lyons-Ruth, K. (1996). Attachment relationships among children with aggressive behavior problems: The role of disorganized early attachment patterns. *Journal of Consulting and Clinical Psychology, 64,* 64–73.

Main, M., & Solomon, J. (1990). Procedures for identifying infants as disorganized/disoriented during the Ainsworth Strange Situation. In M. Greenberg, D. Cicchetti, & E. M. Cummings (Eds.), *Attachment in the preschool years: Theory, research and intervention* (pp. 121–160). Chicago: University of Chicago Press.

Mann, B. J., & MacKenzie, E. P. (1996). Pathways among marital functioning, parental behaviors, and child behavior problems in school-age boys. *Journal of Clinical Child Psychology, 25,* 183–191.

Markman, H. J., & Notarius, C. I. (1987). Coding marital and family interaction. In T. Jacob (Ed.), *Family interaction and psychopathology: Theories, methods, and findings* (pp. 329–390). New York: Plenum Press.

Mash, E. J., & Johnston, C. (1983). Sibling interactions of hyperactive and normal children and their relationship to reports of maternal stress and self-esteem. *Journal of Clinical Child Psychology, 12,* 91–99.

Mash, E. J., Johnston, C., & Kovitz, K. (1983). A comparison of the mother–child interactions of physically abused and non-abused children during play and task situations. *Journal of Clinical Child Psychology, 12,* 337–346.

Mash, E. J., & Terdal, L. G. (Eds.). (1988). *Behavioral assessment of childhood disorders* (2nd ed.). New York: Guilford Press.

McConaughy, S. H. (1992). Objective assessment of children's behavioral and emotional problems. In C. E. Walker & M. C. Roberts (Eds.), *Handbook of clinical child psychology* (2nd ed., pp. 163–180). New York: Wiley.

McConaughy, S. H., & Achenbach, T. M. (1994). *Manual for the Semistructured Clinical Interview for Children and Adolescents.* Burlington: University of Vermont, Department of Psychiatry.

McConaughy, S. H., Achenbach, T. M., & Gent, C. L. (1988). Multiaxial empirically based assessment: Parent, teacher, observational, cognitive, and personality correlates of Child Behavior Profile types for 6- to 11-year-old boys. *Journal of Abnormal Child Psychology, 16,* 485–509.

McCord, J. (1988). Identifying developmental paradigms leading to alcoholism. *Journal of Studies on Alcohol, 49,* 357–362.

McGee, R., Feehan, M., Williams, S., & Anderson, J. (1992). DSM-III disorders from age 11 to age 15 years. *Journal of the American Academy of Child and Adolescent Psychiatry, 31,* 50–59.

McMahon, R. J. (1994). Diagnosis, assessment, and treatment of externalizing problems in children: The role of longitudinal data. *Journal of Consulting and Clinical Psychology, 62,* 901–917.

McMahon, R. J., & Estes, A. (1993). *Fast Track parent–child interaction task: Observational data collection manuals.* Unpublished manuscript, University of Washington.

McMahon, R. J., & Forehand, R. (1983). Consumer satisfaction in behavioral treatment of children: Types, issues, and recommendations. *Behavior Therapy, 14,* 209–225.

McMahon, R. J., & Forehand, R. (1984). Parent training for the noncompliant child: Treatment outcome, generalization, and adjunctive therapy procedures. In R. F. Dangel & R. A. Polster (Eds.), *Parent training: Foundations of research and practice* (pp. 298–328). New York: Guilford Press.

McMahon, R. J., & Forehand, R. (1988). Conduct disorders. In E. J. Mash & L. G. Terdal (Eds.), *Behavioral assessment of childhood disorders* (2nd ed., pp. 105–153). New York: Guilford Press.

McMahon, R. J., Forehand, R., & Griest, D. L. (1981). Effects of knowledge of social learning principles on enhancing treatment outcome and generalization in a parent training program. *Journal of Consulting and Clinical Psychology, 49,* 526–532.

McMahon, R. J., Forehand, R., Griest, D. L., & Wells, K. C. (1981). Who drops out of treatment during parent behavioral training? *Behavioral Counseling Quarterly, 1,* 79–85.

McMahon, R. J., Tiedemann, G. L., Forehand, R., & Griest, D. L. (1984). Parental satisfaction with parent training to modify child noncompliance. *Behavior Therapy, 15,* 295–303.

McNeil, C. B., Eyberg, S., Eisenstadt, T. H., Newcomb, K., & Funderburk, B. (1991). Parent–child interaction therapy with behavior problem children: Generalization of treatment effects to the school setting. *Journal of Clinical Child Psychology, 20,* 140–151.

Middlebrook, J. L., & Forehand, R. (1985). Maternal perceptions of deviance in child behavior as a function of stress and clinic versus non-clinic status of the child: An analogue study. *Behavior Therapy, 16,* 494–502.

Milich, R., & Fitzgerald, G. (1985). Validation of inattention/overactivity and aggression ratings with classroom observations. *Journal of Consulting and Clinical Psychology, 53,* 139–140.

Milich, R., & Landau, S. (1988). Teacher ratings of inattention/overactivity and aggression: Cross-validation with classroom observations. *Journal of Clinical Child Psychology, 17,* 92–97.

Moffitt, T. E. (1990). Juvenile delinquency and Attention Deficit Disorder: Boys' developmental trajectories from age 3 to age 15. *Child Development, 61,* 893–910.

Moffitt, T. E. (1993). "Adolescence-limited" and "life-course-persistent" antisocial behavior: A developmental taxonomy. *Psychological Review, 100,* 674–701.

Moffitt, T. E., Caspi, A., Dickson, N., Silva, P., & Stanton, W. (1996). Childhood-onset versus adolescent-onset antisocial conduct problems in males: Natural history from ages 3 to 18 years. *Development and Psychopathology, 8,* 399–424.

Mouton, P. Y., & Tuma, J. M. (1988). Stress, locus of control, and role satisfaction in clinic and control mothers. *Journal of Clinical Child Psychology, 17,* 217–224.

National Institute on Drug Abuse. (1994). *Assessing drug abuse among adolescents and adults: Standardized instruments* (DHHS Publication No. NIH 94-3757). Washington, DC: U.S. Government Printing Office.

O'Brien, B. S., & Frick, P. J. (1996). Reward dominance: Associations with anxiety, conduct problems, and psychopathy in children. *Journal of Abnormal Child Psychology, 24,* 223–240.

O'Brien, M. (1996). Child rearing difficulties reported by parents of infants and toddlers. *Journal of Pediatric Psychology, 21,* 433–446.

O'Leary, K. D., Vivian, D., & Malone, J. (1992). Assessment of physical aggression against women in marriage: The need for multimodal assessment. *Behavioral Assessment, 14,* 5–14.

Offord, D. R., Alder, R. J., & Boyle, M. H. (1986). Prevalence and sociodemographic correlates of Conduct Disorder. *American Journal of Social Psychiatry, 6,* 272–278.

Offord, D. R., Boyle, M. H., Racine, Y. A., Fleming, J. E., Cadman, D. T., Blum, H. M., Byrne, C., Links, P. S., Lipman, E. L., MacMillan, H. L., Grant, N. I. R., Sanford, M. N., Szatmari, P., Thomas, H., & Woodward, C. A. (1992). Outcome, prognosis, and risk in a longitudinal follow-up study. *Journal of the American Academy of Child and Adolescent Psychiatry, 31,* 916–923.

Ollendick, T. H., & King, N. J. (1994). Diagnosis, assessment, and treatment of internalizing problems in children: The role of longitudinal data. *Journal of Consulting and Clinical Psychology, 62,* 918–927.

Olweus, D. (1980). Familial and temperamental determinants of aggressive behavior in adolescent boys: A causal analysis. *Developmental Psychology, 16,* 644–660.

Patterson, G. R. (1982). *Coercive family process.* Eugene, OR: Castalia.

Patterson, G. R. (1983). Stress: A change agent for family process. In N. Garmezy & M. Rutter (Eds.), *Stress, coping and development in children* (pp. 235–264). New York: McGraw-Hill.

Patterson, G. R., & Bank, L. (1986). Bootstrapping your way in the nomological thicket. *Behavioral Assessment, 8,* 49–73.

Patterson, G. R., & Capaldi, D. M. (1991). Antisocial parents: Unskilled and vulnerable. In P. A. Cowan & E. M. Hetherington (Eds.), *Family transitions* (pp. 195–218). Hillsdale, NJ: Erlbaum.

Patterson, G. R., Capaldi, D., & Bank, L. (1991). An early starter model for predicting delinquency. In D. J. Pepler & K. H. Rubin (Eds.), *The develop-*

ment and treatment of childhood aggression (pp. 139–168). Hillsdale, NJ: Erlbaum.

Patterson, G. R., Chamberlain, P., & Reid, J. B. (1982). A comparative evaluation of a parent training program. *Behavior Therapy, 13*, 638–650.

Patterson, G. R., & Dishion, T. J. (1985). Contributions of family and peers to delinquency. *Criminology, 23*, 63–79.

Patterson, G. R., & Forgatch, M. S. (1995). Predicting future clinical adjustment from treatment outcome and process variables. *Psychological Assessment, 7*, 275–285.

Patterson, G. R., Ray, R. S., Shaw, D. A., & Cobb, J. A. (1969). *Manual for coding of family interactions* (rev. ed.). New York: Microfiche.

Patterson, G. R., Reid, J. B., & Dishion, T. J. (1992). *Antisocial boys*. Eugene, OR: Castalia.

Patterson, G. R., Reid, J. B., Jones, R. R., & Conger, R. E. (1975). *A social learning approach to family intervention: Vol. 1. Families with aggressive children*. Eugene, OR: Castalia.

Peed, S., Roberts, M., & Forehand, R. (1977). Evaluation of the effectiveness of a standardized parent training program in altering the interaction of mothers and their noncompliant children. *Behavior Modification, 1*, 323–350.

Pelham, W. E., & Lang, A. R. (1993). Parental alcohol consumption and deviant child behavior: Laboratory studies of reciprocal effects. *Clinical Psychology Review, 13*, 763–784.

Pelham, W. E., Milich, R., Murphy, D. A., & Murphy, H. A. (1989). Normative data on the IOWA Conners Teacher Rating Scale. *Journal of Clinical Child Psychology, 18*, 259–262.

Piacentini, J. C. (1993). Checklists and rating scales. In T. H. Ollendick & M. Hersen (Eds.), *Handbook of child and adolescent assessment* (pp. 82–97). Needham Heights, MA: Allyn & Bacon.

Piacentini, J. C., Cohen, P., & Cohen, J. (1992). Combining discrepant diagnostic information from multiple sources: Are complex algorithms better than simple ones? *Journal of Abnormal Child Psychology, 20*, 51–63.

Piacentini, J. C., Shaffer, D., Fisher, P. W., Schwab-Stone, M., Davies, M., & Gioia, P. (1993). The Diagnostic Interview Schedule for Children—Revised Version (DISC-R): III. Concurrent criterion validity. *Journal of the American Academy of Child and Adolescent Psychiatry, 32*, 658–665.

Pianta, R. C., & Egeland, B. (1990). Life stress and parenting outcomes in a disadvantaged sample: Results of the mother–child interaction project. *Journal of Clinical Child Psychology, 19*, 329–336.

Pierce, G. R., Sarason, B. R., & Sarason, I. G. (Eds.). (1996). *Handbook of social support and the family*. New York: Plenum Press.

Pisterman, S., Firestone, P., McGrath, P., Goodman, J. T., Webster, I., Mallory, R., & Goffin, B. (1992). The effects of parent training on parenting stress

and sense of competence. *Canadian Journal of Behavioural Science, 24*, 41–58.

Porter, B., & O'Leary, K. D. (1980). Marital discord and childhood behavior problems. *Journal of Abnormal Child Psychology, 8*, 287–295.

Prinz, R. J., & Miller, G. E. (1991). Issues in understanding and treating childhood conduct problems in disadvantaged populations. *Journal of Clinical Child Psychology, 20*, 379–385.

Quay, H. C. (1977). Measuring dimensions of deviant behavior: The Behavior Problem Checklist. *Journal of Abnormal Child Psychology, 5*, 277–287.

Quay, H. C., & Peterson, D. R. (1983). *Interim manual for the Revised Behavior Problem Checklist*. Unpublished manuscript, University of Miami.

Reed, M. L., & Edelbrock, C. (1983). Reliability and validity of the Direct Observation Form of the Child Behavior Checklist. *Journal of Abnormal Child Psychology, 11*, 521–530.

Reich, W., & Welner, Z. (1988). *Revised version of the Diagnostic Interview for Children and Adolescents (DICA-R)*. St. Louis, MO: Washington University School of Medicine, Department of Psychiatry.

Reid, J. B. (Ed.). (1978). *A social learning approach to family intervention: Vol. 2. Observation in home settings*. Eugene, OR: Castalia.

Reid, J. B., Baldwin, D. V., Patterson, G. R., & Dishion, T. J. (1988). Observations in the assessment of childhood disorders. In M. Rutter, A. H. Tuma, & I. S. Lann (Eds.), *Assessment and diagnosis in child psychpathology* (pp. 156–195). New York: Guilford Press.

Reid, J. B., Eddy, J. M., Bank, L., & Fetrow, R. (1994, November). *Some preliminary findings from a universal prevention program for Conduct Disorder*. Paper presented at the Fourth National Institute of Mental Health National Conference on Prevention Research, Washington, DC.

Reid, J. B., Hinojosa-Rivera, G., & Lorber, R. (1980). *A social learning approach to the outpatient treatment of children who steal*. Unpublished manuscript, Oregon Social Learning Center, Eugene.

Richters, J. E. (1992). Depressed mothers as informants about their children: A critical review of the evidence for distortion. *Psychological Bulletin, 112*, 485–499.

Roberts, M. W., Joe, V. C., & Rowe-Hallbert, A. (1992). Oppositional child behavior and parental locus of control. *Journal of Clinical Child Psychology, 21*, 170–177.

Roberts, M. W., & Powers, S. W. (1988). The Compliance Test. *Behavioral Assessment, 10*, 375–398.

Roberts, M. W., & Powers, S. W. (1990). Adjusting chair timeout enforcement procedures for oppositional children. *Behavior Therapy, 21*, 257–271.

Robins, L. N. (1986). The consequences of Conduct Disorder in girls. In D. Olweus, J. Block, & M. Radke-Yarrow (Eds.), *Development of antisocial and prosocial behavior* (pp. 385–414). Orlando, FL: Academic Press.

Robins, L. N. (1991). Conduct Disorder. *Journal of Child Psychology and Psychiatry, 32*, 193–209.

Robinson, E. A., & Anderson, L. L. (1983). Family adjustment, parental attitudes, and social desirability. *Journal of Abnormal Child Psychology, 11*, 247–256.

Robinson, E. A., & Eyberg, S. M. (1981). The Dyadic Parent–Child Interaction Coding System: Standardization and validation. *Journal of Consulting and Clinical Psychology, 49*, 245–250.

Robinson, E. A., Eyberg, S. M., & Ross, A. W. (1980). The standardization of an inventory of child conduct problem behaviors. *Journal of Clinical Child Psychology, 9*, 22–29.

Rothbart, M. K., Posner, M. I., & Hershey, K. L. (1995). Temperament, attention, and developmental psychopathology. In D. Cicchetti & D. J. Cohen (Eds.), *Developmental psychopathology: Vol. 1. Theory and methods* (pp. 315–340). New York: Wiley.

Rubio-Stipec, M., Shrout, P. E., Canino, G., Bird, H. R., Jensen, P., Dulcan, M., & Schwab-Stone, M. (1996). Empirically defined symptom scales using the DISC 2.3. *Journal of Abnormal Child Psychology, 24*, 67–83.

Rusby, J. C., Estes, A., & Dishion, T. (1991). *The Interpersonal Process Code (IPC)*. Unpublished manuscript, Oregon Social Learning Center, Eugene.

Russo, D. C., Cataldo, M. F., & Cushing, P. J. (1981). Compliance training and behavioral covariation in the treatment of multiple behavior problems. *Journal of Applied Behavior Analysis, 14*, 209–222.

Russo, M.F., Lahey, B.B., Christ, M.A., Frick, P.J., McBurnett, K., Walker, J.L., Loeber, R., Stouthamer-Loeber, M., & Green, S. (1991). Preliminary development of a Sensation Seeking Scale for Children. *Personality and Individual Differences, 12*, 399–405.

Russo, M. F., Stokes, G. S., Lahey, B. B., Christ, M. A. G., McBurnett, K., Loeber, R., Stouthamer-Loeber, M., & Green, S. M. (1993). A Sensation Seeking Scale for Children: Further refinement and psychometric development. *Journal of Psychopathology and Behavioral Assessment, 15*, 69–86.

Rutter, M. (1994). Family discord and Conduct Disorder: Cause, consequence, or correlate? *Journal of Family Psychology, 8*, 170–186.

Rutter, R., Harrington, R., Quinton, D., & Pickles, A. (1994). Adult outcome of Conduct Disorder in childhood: Implications for concepts and definitions of patterns of psychopathology. In R. D. Ketterlinus & M. E. Lamb (Eds.), *Adolescent problem behaviors: Issues and research* (pp. 57–80). Hillsdale, NJ: Erlbaum.

Sanders, M. R., & Dadds, M. R. (1992). Children's and parents' cognitions about family interaction: An evaluation of video-mediated recall and thought listing procedures in the assessment of conduct-disordered children. *Journal of Clinical Child Psychology, 21*, 371–379.

Sanders, M. R., & Dadds, M. R. (1993). *Behavioral family intervention*. Needham Heights, MA: Allyn & Bacon.

Sanders, M. R., & Lawton, J. M. (1993). Discussing assessment findings with families: A guided participation model of information transfer. *Child and Family Behavior Therapy, 15*, 5–35.

Sanson, A., Oberklaid, F., Pedlow, R., & Prior, M. (1991). Risk indicators: Assessment of infancy predictors of pre-school behavioural maladjustment. *Journal of Child Psychology and Psychiatry, 32*, 609–626.

Sanson, A., Prior, M., & Kyrios, M. (1990). Contamination of measures in temperament research. *Merrill–Palmer Quarterly, 36*, 179–192.

Sarason, I. G., Johnson, J. H., & Siegel, J. M. (1978). Assessing the impact of life changes: Development of the Life Experiences Survey. *Journal of Consulting and Clinical Psychology, 46*, 932–946.

Saunders, J. D., Aasland, O. G., Babor, T. F., de la Fuente, J. R., & Grant, M. (1993). Development of the Alcohol Use Disorders Identification Test (AUDIT): WHO collaborative project on early detection of persons with harmful alcohol consumption—II. *Addiction, 88*, 791–804.

Schaughency, E. A., Middlebrook, J. L., Forehand, R., & Lahey, B. B. (1984, November). *The relationship of separate facets of marital adjustment to child behavior problems.* Paper presented at the meeting of the Association for Advancement of Behavior Therapy, Philadelphia.

Scherer, D. G., Brondino, M. J., Henggeler, S. W., Melton, G. B., & Hanley, J. H. (1994). Multisystemic family preservation therapy: Preliminary findings from a study of rural and minority serious adolescent offenders. *Journal of Emotional and Behavioral Disorders, 2*, 198–206.

Schwab-Stone, M., Fisher, P. W., Piacentini, J., Shaffer, D., Davies, M., & Briggs, M. (1993). The Diagnostic Interview Schedule for Children—Revised Version (DISC-R): II. Test–retest reliability. *Journal of the American Academy of Child and Adolescent Psychiatry, 32*, 651–657.

Selzer, M. L., Vinokur, A., & van Rooijen, L. (1975). A self-administered short Michigan Alcoholism Screening Test. *Journal of Studies on Alcohol, 36*, 117–126.

Serbin, L. A., Moskowitz, D. S., Schwartzman, A. E., & Ledingham, J. E. (1991). Aggressive, withdrawn, and aggressive/withdrawn children in adolescence: Into the next generation. In D. J. Pepler & K. H. Rubin (Eds.), *The development and treatment of childhood aggression* (pp. 55–70). Hillsdale, NJ: Erlbaum.

Serbin, L. A., Peters, P. L., McAffer, V. J., & Schwartzman, A. E. (1991). Childhood aggression and withdrawal as predictors of adolescent pregnancy, early parenthood, and environmental risk for the next generation. *Canadian Journal of Behavioural Science, 23*, 318–331.

Shaffer, D., Fisher, P., Piacentini, J., Schwab-Stone, M., & Wicks, J. (1991). *NIMH Diagnostic Interview Schedule for Children—Version 2.3.* New York: New York State Psychiatric Institute.

Shaffer, D., Schwab-Stone, M., Fisher, P., Cohen, P., Piacentini, J., Davies, M., Conners, C. K., & Regier, D. (1993). The Diagnostic Interview Schedule for Children—Revised Version (DISC-R): I. Preparation, field testing, interrater reliability, and acceptability. *Journal of the American Academy of Child and Adolescent Psychiatry, 32,* 643–650.

Sheeber, L. B. (1995). Empirical dissociations between temperament and behavior problems: A response to the Sanson, Prior, and Kyrios study. *Merrill–Palmer Quarterly, 41,* 554–561.

Sheeber, L. B., & Johnson, J. H. (1994). Evaluation of a temperament-focused, parent-training program. *Journal of Clinical Child Psychology, 23,* 249–259.

Shelton, K. K., Frick, P. J., & Wootton, J. (1996). Assessment of parenting practices in families of elementary school-age children. *Journal of Clinical Child Psychology, 25,* 317–329.

Sholevar, G. P., & Sholevar, E. H. (1995). Overview. In G. P. Sholevar (Ed.), *Conduct disorders in children and adolescents* (pp. 3–26). Washington, DC: American Psychiatric Press.

Skinner, H. A. (1982). The Drug Abuse Screening Test. *Addictive Behaviors, 7,* 363–371.

Slabach, E. H., Morrow, J., & Wachs, T. D. (1991). Questionnaire measurement of infant and child temperament: Current status and future directions. In J. Strelau & A. Angleitner (Eds.), *Explorations in temperament: International perspectives on theory and measurement* (pp. 205–234). New York: Plenum Press.

Snyder, J. J. (1991). Discipline as a mediator of the impact of maternal stress and mood on child conduct problems. *Development and Psychopathology, 3,* 263–276.

Snyder, J. J. (1995). Coercion: A two-level theory of antisocial behavior. In W. O'Donohue & L. Krasner (Eds.), *Theories of behavior therapy: Exploring behavior change* (pp. 313–348). Washington, DC: American Psychological Association.

Song, L. Y., Singh, J., & Singer, M. (1994). The Youth Self-Report inventory: A study of its measurement fidelity. *Psychological Assessment, 6,* 236–245.

Spanier, G. B. (1976). Measuring dyadic adjustment: New scales for assessing the quality of marriage and similar dyads. *Journal of Marriage and the Family, 38,* 15–28.

Speltz, M. L., DeKlyen, M., Greenberg, M. T., & Dryden, M. (1995). Clinic referral for Oppositional Defiant Disorder: Relative significance of attachment and behavioral variables. *Journal of Abnormal Child Psychology, 23,* 487–507.

Speltz, M. L., Greenberg, M. T., & DeKlyen, M. (1990). Attachment in preschoolers with disruptive behavior: A comparison of clinic-referred and nonproblem children. *Development and Psychopathology, 2,* 31–46.

Spitzer, R. L., & Endicott, J. (1978). *Schedule for Affective Disorders and Schizophrenia.* New York: New York State Psychiatric Institute.

Stanger, C., & Lewis, M. (1993). Agreement among parents, teachers, and children on internalizing and externalizing behavior problems. *Journal of Clinical Child Psychology, 22,* 107–115.

Strassberg, Z., Dodge, K. A., Pettit, G. S., & Bates, J. E. (1994). Spanking in the home and children's subsequent aggression toward kindergarten peers. *Development and Psychopathology, 6,* 445–461.

Straus, M. A. (1979). Measuring intrafamily conflict and violence: The Conflict Tactics (CT) Scales. *Journal of Marriage and the Family, 41,* 75–88.

Straus, M. A. (1990). The Conflict Tactics Scales and its critics: An evaluation and new data on validity and reliability. In M. A. Straus & R. J. Gelles (Eds.), *Physical violence in American families: Risk factors and adaptations to violence in 8,145 families* (pp. 49–73). New Brunswick, NJ: Transaction.

Straus, M. A., Hamby, S. L., Boney-McCoy, S., & Sugarman, D. B. (1996). The Revised Conflict Tactics Scales (CTS2): Development and preliminary psychometric data. *Journal of Family Issues, 17,* 283–316.

Straus, M. A., Hamby, S. L., Finkelhor, D., & Runyan, D. (1996). *The Parent–Child Conflict Tactics Scales (PCCTS): Development and psychometric data for a national sample of parents.* Manuscript in preparation.

Strayhorn, J. M., & Weidman, C. S. (1988). A Parent Practices Scale and its relation to parent and child mental health. *Journal of the American Academy of Child and Adolescent Psychiatry, 27,* 613–618.

Strayhorn, J. M., & Weidman, C. S. (1989). Reduction of attention deficit and internalizing symptoms in preschoolers through parent–child interaction training. *Journal of the American Academy of Child and Adolescent Psychiatry, 28,* 888–896.

Strayhorn, J. M., & Weidman, C. S. (1991). Follow-up one year after parent–child interaction training: Effects on behavior of preschool children. *Journal of the American Academy of Child and Adolescent Psychiatry, 30,* 138–143.

Tapp, J., Wehby, J., & Ellis, D. (1995). A Multiple Option Observation System for Experimental Studies: MOOSES. *Behavior Research Methods, Instruments and Computers, 27,* 25–31.

Teegarden, L. A., & Burns, G. L. (1993). Construct validity of the Sutter–Eyberg Student Behavior Inventory: Relation between teacher perception of disruptive behavior and direct observation of problem classroom behavior over a seven month period. *Child and Family Behavior Therapy, 15,* 43–58.

Thomas, A., & Chess, S. (1977). *Temperament and development.* New York: Brunner/Mazel.

Thomas, A., Chess, S., & Birch, H. G. (1968). *Temperament and behavior disorders in children*. New York: New York University Press.

Thurber, S., & Hollingsworth, D. K. (1992). Validity of the Achenbach and Edelbrock Youth Self-Report with hospitalized adolescents. *Journal of Clinical Child Psychology, 21,* 249–254.

Thurber, S., & Snow, M. (1990). Assessment of adolescent psychopathology: Comparison of mother and daughter perspectives. *Journal of Clinical Child Psychology, 19,* 249–253.

Tremblay, R. E., Masse, B., Perron, D., Leblanc, M., Schwartzman, A. E., & Ledingham, J. E. (1992). Early disruptive behavior, poor school achievement, delinquent behavior, and delinquent personality: Longitudinal analyses. *Journal of Consulting and Clinical Psychology, 60,* 64–72.

Van Kammen, W. B., Loeber, R., & Stouthamer-Loeber, M. (1991). Substance use and its relationship to conduct problems and delinquency in young boys. *Journal of Youth and Adolescence, 20,* 399–413.

Wahler, R. G. (1980). The insular mother: Her problems in parent–child treatment. *Journal of Applied Behavior Analysis, 13,* 207–219.

Wahler, R. G., & Cormier, W. H. (1970). The ecological interview: A first step in outpatient child behavior therapy. *Journal of Behavior Therapy and Experimental Psychiatry, 1,* 279–289.

Wahler, R. G., & Dumas, J. E. (1984). Changing the observational coding styles of insular and noninsular mothers: A step toward maintenance of parent training effects. In R. F. Dangel & R. A. Polster (Eds.), *Parent training: Foundations of research and practice* (pp. 379–416). New York: Guilford Press.

Wahler, R. G., & Dumas, J. E. (1989). Attentional problems in dysfunctional mother–child interactions: An interbehavioral model. *Psychological Bulletin, 105,* 116–130.

Wahler, R. G., & Graves, M. G. (1983). Setting events in social networks: Ally or enemy in child behavior therapy? *Behavior Therapy, 14,* 19–36.

Wahler, R. G., Hughey, J. B., & Gordon, J. S. (1981). Chronic patterns of mother–child coercion: Some differences between insular and noninsular families. *Analysis and Intervention in Developmental Disabilities, 1,* 145–156.

Wahler, R. G., Leske, G., & Rogers, E. S. (1979). The insular family: A deviance support system for oppositional children. In L.A. Hamerlynck (Ed.), *Behavioral systems for the developmentally disabled: Vol. 1. School and family environments* (pp. 102–127). New York: Brunner/Mazel.

Wahler, R. G., & Sansbury, L. E. (1990). The monitoring skills of troubled mothers: Their problems in defining child deviance. *Journal of Abnormal Child Psychology, 18,* 577–589.

Waldman, I. D., & Lahey, B. B. (1994). Design of the DSM-IV Disruptive Behavior Disorder field trials.

Child and Adolescent Psychiatric Clinics of North America, 3, 195–208.

Walker, H. M. (1995). *The acting-out child: Coping with classroom disruption* (2nd ed.). Longmont, CO: Sopris West.

Walker, H. M., Block-Pedego, A., Todis, B., & Severson, H. (1991). *School Archival Records Search (SARS): User's guide and technical manual.* Longmont, CO: Sopris West.

Walker, H. M., Colvin, G., & Ramsey, E. (1995). *Antisocial behavior in school: Strategies and best practices.* Pacific Grove, CA: Brooks/Cole.

Walker, H. M., & Hops, H. (1976). Use of normative peer data as a standard for evaluating classroom treatment effects. *Journal of Applied Behavior Analysis, 9,* 159–168.

Walker, H. M., & Severson, H. H. (1990). *Systematic Screening for Behavior Disorders (SSBD): User's guide and technical manual.* Longmont, CO: Sopris West.

Walker, H. M., Severson, H. H., & Feil, E. G. (1995). *The Early Screening Project: A proven child-find process.* Longmont, CO: Sopris West.

Walker, H. M., Shinn, M. R., O'Neill, R. E., & Ramsey, E. (1987). A longitudinal assessment of the development of antisocial behavior in boys: Rationale, methodology, and first-year results. *RASE: Remedial and Special Education, 8,* 7–16, 27.

Walker, J. L., Lahey, B. B., Russo, M. F., Frick, P. J., Christ, M. A., McBurnett, K., Loeber, R., Stouthamer-Loeber, M., & Green, S. M. (1991). Anxiety, inhibition, and Conduct Disorder in children: I. Relations to social impairment. *Journal of the American Academy of Child and Adolescent Psychiatry, 30,* 187–191.

Webster-Stratton, C. (1985). Comparisons of behavior transactions between conduct-disordered children and their mothers in the clinic and at home. *Journal of Abnormal Child Psychology, 13,* 169–184.

Webster-Stratton, C. (1988). Mothers' and fathers' perceptions of child deviance: Roles of parent and child behaviors and parent adjustment. *Journal of Consulting and Clinical Psychology, 56,* 909–915.

Webster-Stratton, C. (1989). Systematic comparison of consumer satisfaction of three cost-effective parent training programs for conduct problem children. *Behavior Therapy, 20,* 103–115.

Webster-Stratton, C. (1990). Stress: A potential disruptor of parent perceptions and family interactions. *Journal of Clinical Child Psychology, 19,* 302–312.

Webster-Stratton, C. (1994). Advancing videotape parent training: A comparison study. *Journal of Consulting and Clinical Psychology, 62,* 583–593.

Webster-Stratton, C. (1996). Early-onset conduct problems: Does gender make a difference? *Journal of Consulting and Clinical Psychology, 64,* 540–551.

Webster-Stratton, C., & Eyberg, S. M. (1982). Child

temperament: Relationship with child behavior problems and parent–child interactions. *Journal of Clinical Child Psychology, 11*, 123–129.

Webster-Stratton, C., & Hammond, M. (1988). Maternal depression and its relationship to life stress, perceptions of child behavior problems, parenting behaviors, and child conduct problems. *Journal of Abnormal Child Psychology, 16*, 299–315.

Webster-Stratton, C., & Hammond, M. (1997). Treating children with early-onset conduct problems: A comparison of child and parent training interventions. *Journal of Consulting and Clinical Psychology, 65*, 93–109.

Webster-Stratton, C., & Spitzer, A. (1991). Development, reliability, and validity of the Daily Telephone Discipline Interview. *Behavioral Assessment, 13*, 221–239.

Wehby, J. (1993). *Fast Track School Observation Program*. Unpublished manuscript, Vanderbilt University.

Wehby, J., Dodge, K. A., Valente, E., & the Conduct Problems Prevention Research Group. (1993). School behavior of first grade children identified as at-risk for development of conduct problems. *Behavioral Disorders, 19*, 67–78.

Weinrott, M. R., Reid, J. B., Bauske, B. W., & Brummett, B. (1981). Supplementing naturalistic observations with observer impressions. *Behavioral Assessment, 3*, 151–159.

Weinstein, S. R., Noam, G. G., Grimes, K., Stone, K., & Schwab-Stone, M. (1990). Convergence of DSM-III diagnoses and self-reported symptoms in child and adolescent inpatients. *Journal of the American Academy of Child and Adolescent Psychiatry, 29*, 627–634.

Weiss, B., Dodge, K. A., Bates, J. E., & Pettit, G. S. (1992). Some consequences of early harsh discipline: Child aggression and a maladaptive social information processing style. *Child Development, 63*, 1321–1335.

Wells, K. C., Forehand, R., & Griest, D. L. (1980). Generality of treatment effects from treated to untreated behaviors resulting from a parent training program. *Journal of Clinical Child Psychology, 9*, 217–219.

Werthamer-Larsson, L., Kellam, S., & Wheeler L. (1991). Effect of first-grade classroom environment on shy behavior, aggressive behavior, and concentration problems. *American Journal of Community Psychology, 19*, 585–602.

Whipple, E. E., Fitzgerald, H. E., & Zucker, R. A. (1995). Parent–child interactions in alcoholic and nonalcoholic families. *American Journal of Orthopsychiatry, 65*, 153–159.

Whipple, E. E., & Webster-Stratton, C. (1991). The role of parental stress in physically abusive families. *Child Abuse and Neglect, 15*, 279–291.

White, J. L., Moffitt, T. E., Caspi, A., Bartusch, D. J., Needles, D., & Stouthamer-Loeber, M. (1994). Measuring impulsivity and examining its relationship to delinquency. *Journal of Abnormal Psychology, 103*, 1922–1205.

Wills, T. A., Schreibman, D., Benson, G., & Vaccaro, D. (1994). Impact of parental substance use on adolescents: A test of a mediational model. *Journal of Pediatric Psychology, 19*, 537–555.

Witt, J. C., & Elliott, S. N. (1985). Acceptability of classroom intervention strategies. In T. R. Kratochwill (Ed.), *Advances in school psychology* (Vol. 4, pp. 251–288). Hillsdale, NJ: Erlbaum.

Wolf, M. M. (1978). Social validity: The case for subjective measurement, or how applied behavior analysis is finding its heart. *Journal of Applied Behavior Analysis, 11*, 203–214.

Wruble, M. K., Sheeber, L. B., Sorensen, E. D., Boggs, S. R., & Eyberg, S. (1991). Empirical derivation of child compliance times. *Child and Family Behavior Therapy, 13*, 57–68.

Yates, B. T. (1978). Improving the cost-effectiveness of obesity programs: Three basic strategies for reducing the cost per pound. *International Journal of Obesity, 2*, 249–266.

Zahn-Waxler, C. (1993). Warriors and worriers: Gender and psychopathology. *Development and Psychopathology, 5*, 79–89.

Zangwill, W. M., & Kniskern, J. R. (1982). Comparison of problem families in the clinic and at home. *Behavior Therapy, 13*, 145–152.

Zoccolillo, M. (1992). Co-occurrence of Conduct Disorder and its adult outcomes with depressive and anxiety disorders: A review. *Journal of the American Academy of Child and Adolescent Psychiatry, 31*, 547–556.

Zoccolillo, M. (1993). Gender and the development of Conduct Disorder. *Development and Psychopathology, 5*, 65–78.

Zucker, R. A., & Fitzgerald, H. E. (1992). *The Antisocial Behavior Checklist*. (Available from Michigan State University Family Study, Michigan State University, Department of Psychology, East Lansing, MI 48824–1117)

Part III

EMOTIONAL AND SOCIAL DISORDERS

Chapter Four

DEPRESSION IN CHILDREN AND ADOLESCENTS

Bruce E. Compas

Depression represents a significant mental health concern for children and adolescents. Research with both community and clinical populations has established that depressive symptoms and disorders occur with increasing prevalence over the course of childhood and adolescence (e.g., Fleming & Offord, 1990; Petersen et al., 1993). Moreover, depressive problems are associated with significant impairment in the lives of children and adolescents—including disruption in academic achievement, peer relations, family functioning, and sense of self—and are strong predictors of referral for mental health services (Hammen & Rudolph, 1996). The tendency for depression to co-occur with other problems and disorders further underscores the importance of careful consideration of depressive problems in children and youths. Patterns of comorbidity suggest that a thorough understanding of depression in young people may facilitate knowledge of other problems and disorders as well (Compas & Hammen, 1994).

This chapter provides an overview of concepts and methods for behavioral assessment of depression in young people. First, the nature of depression in young people is described with respect to three levels of depressive phenomena—depressed mood, depressive syndromes, and depressive disorders. This includes a brief discussion of current conceptual models of depression during childhood and adolescence, with emphasis on the need for a broad, integrative perspective, and consideration of developmental and normative processes. Second, the methods for the assessment of depression are critically reviewed, including self-report questionnaires, behavior checklists, and diagnostic interviews. Third, the measurement of related constructs is reviewed, to provide guidance for the

assessment of depression in a broader context. Finally, the implications of this material for clinical assessment of and intervention for depression in young people are outlined.

NATURE OF DEPRESSION IN YOUNG PEOPLE

Nick is 15 years old and lives with his mother at the time that she brings him to the psychology clinic (his father left his mother before Nick was born). Prior to this visit, Nick was arrested for shoplifting at a local store. The store owner, a long-time friend of Nick and his mother, chose not to press formal charges, but expressed his concerns about Nick's behavior to his mother. She reports that the shoplifting incident was merely the "straw that broke the camel's back"—she has been very concerned about Nick for the past year. She reports that they are constantly arguing and fighting, and that the slightest problem seems to send Nick into a fit of anger. He is irritable and sullen much of the time, and his angry outbursts have escalated recently, including several incidents in which he has thrown things and punched holes in the walls or doors at home. Nick's mother also reports that he seems to be unhappy and withdrawn, spending more and more time at home alone. Her work schedule requires her to leave the house early in the morning, and Nick is expected to get himself up and off to school after she leaves. Nick has not been following through on this plan, however, and he is now absent from school more days than not.

An initial interview with Nick corroborates much of what his mother has reported. Nick is sullen and aloof during the interview, and shows little emotion. He describes a typical day as beginning in this manner: He wakes up early in the morning, after having stayed up late the night before watching television, but he lies in bed until 9:00 or 10:00 A.M. He then spends much of the day at home alone playing video games or watching television. He reports that he is having trouble controlling his appetite; he eats junk food and snacks all day long, and has gained considerable weight as a result. His mother returns home from work late in the afternoon, and they typically get into an argument about his having missed another day of school. They eat dinner together silently while watching television, and then spend much of the evening arguing about his homework, his school attendance problems, and his refusal to go to bed before midnight. Over the course of the interview, Nick reports that he is very unhappy, has very few sources of pleasure in his life, and feels hopeless that things could improve for him. Nick was born with a curvature of his spine; as a result, he walks awkwardly and is limited in his physical abilities. He reports that he is self-conscious about his appearance, feels that he is disliked and teased by his peers, and hates himself. Nick thus exemplifies many of the features that we associate with depression in young people —sad or dysphoric affect, irritability, disruption of sleep and appetite, social withdrawal, low self-worth, and a sense of hopelessness or pessimism about the future.

One of the major challenges facing researchers and clinicians concerned with depression during childhood and adolescence involves operationally defining and measuring this construct. Several factors have impeded the development of methods to measure and understand depression in young people (Poznanski & Mokros, 1994). The first was the theoretical position, derived from the psychoanalytic perspective, that depression is not possible in children because of inadequate development of the superego. The second impediment was the belief that depression can occur but that it is masked by other characteristics or problem behaviors. For example, depression was often assumed to be masked by the presentation of disruptive behaviors. Both of these beliefs have now been thoroughly disproven by research verifying that children and adolescents do indeed experience and clinically present with depression (Carlson & Cantwell, 1980; Hammen & Compas, 1994). Controversy continues, however, regarding the ways that depression is conceptualized in young people.

Taxonomy and Assessment

Current research and clinical practice concerning depression in children and adolescents have been hindered by two factors. First, researchers and clinicians have drawn upon different definitions of depression and different taxonomic systems, including a focus on (1) depressed mood, (2) empirically derived syndromes that include depressive symptoms, and (3) a constellation of symptoms meeting diagnostic criteria for a categorical disorder. These three approaches to depressive phenomena during childhood and adolescence have all been included under the general label of "depression," and this has led to confusion and miscommunication. Second, many different types of assessment and diagnostic tools have been used in the measurement of child/adolescent depression. These measures have varied in the breadth versus specificity of the symptoms that are assessed; in their sources of information (children/adolescents, parents, teachers, clinicians); and in their psychometric quality. This heterogeneity in the conceptualization and measurement of depression during childhood and adolescence has resulted in a fragmentation of research efforts and has impeded determination of the prevalence of depressive phenomena, understanding of the developmental course of depression, and identification of etiological factors. Therefore, clarifying the relations among the three approaches is the first step toward understanding the nature of depression in childhood and adolescence.

Defining and understanding child/adolescent depression are dependent on the paradigms one uses for the assessment and taxonomy of psychopathology. Broadly defined, "assessment" is concerned with the identification of distinguishing features of individual cases, whereas "taxonomy" is concerned with the grouping of cases according to their distinguishing features (Achenbach, 1985, 1993). Assessment and taxonomy are linked to each other, in that the grouping of cases in a taxonomic system should be based on clearly defined criteria and procedures for identifying the central features that distinguish among cases. Similarly, assessment procedures should reflect certain basic assumptions of the underlying system for classifying the phenomena of interest.

Three approaches to the assessment and taxonomy of child/adolescent psychopathology have been reflected in the literature (Angold, 1988; Cantwell & Baker, 1991; Compas, Ey, & Grant, 1993; Kovacs, 1989). The first approach does not involve a full taxonomic or assessment paradigm;

it is concerned with depressed mood or affect, as represented by the work of Petersen (e.g., Petersen, Sarigiani, & Kennedy, 1991), Kandel (e.g., Kandel & Davies, 1982), and others. The study of depressed mood during childhood and adolescence has emerged from developmental research in which depressive emotions are studied along with other features of biological, cognitive, and social development. The second approach is concerned with syndromes of behaviors and emotions that reflect depression; depressive syndromes are identified empirically through the reports of children/adolescents and other informants (e.g., parents, teachers). This strategy involves the use of multivariate statistical methods in the assessment and taxonomy of child and adolescent psychopathology, represented by the empirically based taxonomy of Achenbach (1985, 1993). The third approach is based on assumptions of a disease or disorder model of psychopathology; it is currently reflected in the categorical diagnostic system of the *Diagnostic and Statistical Manual of Mental Disorders*, fourth edition (DSM-IV; American Psychiatric Association, 1994) and the *International Classification of Diseases and Health-Related Problems*, 10th revision (ICD-10; World Health Organization, 1992).

In addition to reflecting different paradigms of assessment and taxonomy, these three approaches to depression are concerned with different levels of analysis. The "depressed mood" approach is concerned with depression as a symptom or emotional state; the term "depression" refers to the presence of sadness, unhappiness, or blue feelings for an unspecified period of time. No assumptions are made regarding the presence or absence of other symptoms (e.g., poor appetite, insomnia).

The "depressive syndrome" approach is concerned with depression as a constellation of behaviors and emotions. "Depression" refers to a set of emotions and behaviors that have been found statistically to occur together in an identifiable pattern at a rate that exceeds chance, without implying any particular model for the nature or causes of these associated symptoms. Differences between individuals are viewed in terms of quantitative deviations in levels of symptoms. An empirically deprived syndrome of depressive symptoms is best represented in the research of Achenbach and colleagues (e.g., Achenbach, 1993). Most pertinent here is the syndrome labeled Anxious/Depressed, composed of symptoms reflecting a mixture of anxiety and depression (see Table 4.1). The syndrome has been replicated in large samples in both the United States and The Netherlands (Achenbach, Conners, Quay, Verhulst, & Howell, 1989; De Groot, Koot, & Verhulst, 1994).

TABLE 4.1. Symptoms of the Anxious/Depressed Syndrome, Based on Parent (Child Behavior Checklist) and Adolescent (Youth Self-Report) Reports

Parent report[a]	Adolescent report[b]
Complains of loneliness	I feel lonely
Cries a lot	I cry a lot
Fears s/he might do something bad	I am afraid I might think or do something bad
Feels s/he has to be perfect	I feel that I have to be perfect
Feels or complains that no one loves him/her	I feel that no one loves me
Feels others are out to get him/her	I feel that others are out to get me
Feels worthless or inferior	I feel worthless or inferior
Nervous, highstrung, or tense	I am nervous or tense
Too fearful or anxious	I am too fearful or anxious
Feels too guilty	I feel too guilty
Self-conscious or easily embarrassed	I am self-conscious or easily embarrassed
Suspicious	I am suspicious
Unhappy, sad, or depressed	I am unhappy, sad, or depressed
Worrying	I worry a lot
	I deliberately try to hurt or kill myself
	I think about killing myself

[a]The items in this column are from Achenbach (1991b, p. 45). Copyright 1991 by Thomas M. Achenbach. Reprinted by permission.

[b]The items in this column are from Achenbach (1991d, p. 37). Copyright 1991 by Thomas M. Achenbach. Reprinted by permission.

A more "pure" depressive syndrome did not emerge in the reports of parents, teachers, and adolescents.

The "categorical diagnostic" approach views depression as a psychiatric disorder. This approach not only assumes that "depression" includes the presence of an identifiable syndrome of associated symptoms; it also assumes that these symptoms are associated with significant levels of current distress or disability and with increased risk for impairment in the individual's current functioning (American Psychiatric Association, 1994). Differences among individuals are considered in terms of quantitative and qualitative differences in the pattern, severity, and duration of symptoms. With only a few exceptions, child/adolescent depression is diagnosed according to the same DSM-IV criteria as adult depression. Depressive disorders are classified under the broad category of mood disorders and, to a lesser extent, under adjustment disorders. Key exclusionary criteria are that a diagnosis of mood disorder is not to be made if the symptoms are caused by an established organic factor or occur in conjunction with psychotic disorders (e.g., Schizophrenia, Delusional Disorder, Schizophreniform Disorder). Within the mood disorders, depression is divided into two categories: bipolar disorders and depressive disorders. In distinguishing between bipolar and depressive disorders, bipolar disorders are defined by the presence of manic or hypomanic symptoms that may alternate with depression. As this section emphasizes depressive disorders without manic or hypomanic symptoms, the reader is referred to the DSM-IV for more information regarding bipolar disorders (see also Carlson, 1994).

To meet the criteria for a Major Depressive Episode (MDE), the child or adolescent must have experienced five (or more) of the specified symptoms for *at least a 2-week period* at a level that differs from prior functioning, and at least one of the symptoms must be either (1) depressed or irritable mood, or (2) anhedonia (see Table 4.2). Irritable mood may be observed in lieu of depressed mood in children/adolescents and is believed to be more common in this age group than in adults. A diagnosis of Major Depressive Disorder (MDD) is made when a child/adolescent has experienced one or more MDEs and no Manic, Hypomanic, or Mixed Episodes. Diagnosis of MDD in children and adolescents is further differentiated by severity and nature of the symptoms; a range of specifiers may be applied (see Table 4.2).

The criteria for a diagnosis of Dysthymic Disorder (DD) in childhood and adolescence are that for at least a period of 1 year (as compared to 2 years for adults), a young person must display depressed or irritable mood daily without more than 2 months symptom-free, along with additional symptoms as specified in Table 4.3. There must be no evidence of an MDE during the first year of DD. DD is further classified by age of onset; occurrence of the disorder prior to 21 years of age is designated as Early Onset.

Although a diagnosis of MDD takes precedence over a diagnosis of DD, children/adolescents may be diagnosed with DD for 1 year and subsequent MDD if the more severe depression follows. These cases of MDD juxtaposed with the history of more chronic and less severe DD are often referred to as "double depression." An additional diagnostic category of Depressive Disorder Not Otherwise Specified may be used to classify children/adolescents with symptoms of MDD, DD, Adjustment Disorder With Depressed Mood, or Adjustment Disorder With Mixed Anxiety and Depressed Mood. The DSM-IV cites examples such as recurrent mild depression that is not severe enough to meet the MDD criteria.

Developmental and Normative Considerations

Interpretation of data obtained from these three approaches to conceptualizing depression are best considered in light of normative developmental data on the base rates of symptoms and disorders. In analyses of a single item reflecting unhappy, sad, or depressed mood, Achenbach (1991b) found that parents reported 10–20% of nonreferred boys and 15–20% of nonreferred girls as experiencing this symptom at least somewhat or sometimes during the previous 6 months. Adolescents' self-reports (Achenbach, 1991d) indicated that 20–35% of nonreferred boys and 25–40% of non-referred girls reported feeling sad or depressed during the prior 6 months. Gender differences were small in both parental and adolescent reports of this symptom, with girls scoring slightly higher than boys. Petersen et al. (1991) examined self-reports of depressed mood in a longitudinal study of 335 individuals from early adolescence through young adulthood. Depressed mood increased during adolescence for girls, but remained relatively stable for boys throughout adolescence. These same authors also found that reports of significant episodes of depressed mood (lasting 2 weeks or longer) increased from early adolescence (i.e., episodes occurring between sixth and eighth grades) to late adolescence (i.e., episodes occur-

TABLE 4.2. DSM-IV Criteria for Major Depressive Episode (MDE)

A. Five (or more) of the following symptoms have been present during the same 2-week period and represent a change from previous functioning; at least one of the symptoms is either (1) depressed mood or (2) loss of interest or pleasure. **Note:** Do not include symptoms that are clearly due to a general medical condition, or mood-incongruent delusions or hallucinations.

   (1) depressed mood most of the day, nearly every day, as indicated by subjective report (e.g., feels sad or empty) or observation made by others (e.g., appears tearful). **Note:** In children and adolescents, can be irritable mood.

   (2) markedly diminished interest or pleasure in all, or almost all, activities most of the day, nearly every day (as indicated by either subjective account or observation made by others).

   (3) significant weight loss when not dieting or weight gain (e.g., a change of more than 5% of body weight in a month), or decrease or increase in appetite nearly every day. **Note:** In children, consider failure to make expected weight gains.

   (4) insomnia or hypersomnia nearly every day

   (5) psychomotor agitation or retardation nearly every day (observable by others, not merely subjective feelings of restlessness or being slowed down)

   (6) fatigue or loss of energy nearly every day

   (7) feelings of worthlessness or excessive or inappropriate guilt (which may be delusional) nearly every day (not merely self-reproach or guilt about being sick)

   (8) diminished ability to think or concentrate, or indecisiveness, nearly every day (either by subjective account or as observed by others)

   (9) recurrent thoughts of death (not just fear of dying), recurrent suicidal ideation without a specific plan, or a suicide attempt or a specific plan for committing suicide

B. The symptoms do not meet criteria for a Mixed Episode.

C. The symptoms cause clinically significant distress or impairment in social, occupational, or other important areas of functioning.

D. The symptoms are not due to the direct physiological effects of a substance (e.g., a drug of abuse, a medication) or a general medical condition (e.g., hypothyroidism).

E. The symptoms are not better accounted for by Bereavement, i.e., after the loss of a loved one, the symptoms persist for longer than 2 months or are characterized by marked functional impairment, morbid preoccupation with worthlessness, suicidal ideation, psychotic symptoms, or psychomotor retardation.

Note. From American Psychiatric Association (1994, p. 327). Copyright 1994 by the American Psychiatric Association. Reprinted by permission.

When the criteria for MDE are used to make a diagnosis of Major Depressive Disorder (MDD), these specifiers can be used to describe the current MDE: Mild, Moderate, Severe Without Psychotic Features, Severe With Psychotic Features, In Partial Remission, In Full Remission, Chronic, With Catatonic Features, With Melancholic Features, With Atypical Features. (The remaining specifier, With Postpartum Onset, would not apply to children.) If the MDD is recurrent, these additional specifiers can be used: With and Without Interepisode Recovery, With Seasonal Pattern.

ring between 9th and 12th grades) for both boys and girls, with a more pronounced effect for girls. Girls reported more episodes of depressed mood than boys at all age levels, with this gender difference increasing from early to late adolescence.

There is now substantial documentation that children and adolescents who meet DSM-III-R or DSM-IV criteria for MDD and DD can be reliably identified in community samples (e.g., Fleming & Offord, 1990). Ten studies of MDD in community samples of children and adolescents reported *lifetime* prevalence rates ranging from 0% to 31%, with a mean of 11% (Petersen et al., 1993). Prevalence is greater among high-risk groups, most notably children and adolescents whose parents

are depressed (e.g., Weissman et al., 1987). *Point* prevalence estimates have been provided by Lewinsohn and colleagues from a large community sample of adolescents (Lewinsohn, Rohde, Seeley, & Hops, 1991; Rohde, Lewinsohn, & Seeley, 1991). On the basis of structured diagnostic interviews, 2.9% of a sample of 1,710 adolescents received a current diagnosis of either MDD, DD, or comorbid MDD and DD (Lewinsohn et al., 1991). Lifetime prevalence of depressive disorders was 20% in this sample—a finding within the range of lifetime prevalence rates in the earlier studies reviewed by Fleming and Offord (1990). In further analyses with this sample, Lewinsohn, Hops, Roberts, Seeley, and Andrews (1993) found

TABLE 4.3. Criteria for Dysthymic Disorder (DD)

A. Depressed mood for most of the day, for more days than not, as indicated either by subjective account or observation by others, for at least 2 years. **Note:** In children and adolescents, mood can be irritable and duration must be at least 1 year.

B. Presence, while depressed, of two (or more) of the following:
   (1) poor appetite or overeating
   (2) insomnia or hypersomnia
   (3) low energy or fatigue
   (4) low self-esteem
   (5) poor concentration or difficulty making decisions
   (6) feelings of hopelessness

C. During the 2-year period (1 year for children or adolescents) of the disturbance, the person has never been without the symptoms in Criteria A and B for more than 2 months at a time.

D. No Major Depressive Episode (see [Table 4.2]) has been present during the first 2 years of the disturbance (1 year for children and adolescents); i.e., the disturbance is not better accounted for by chronic Major Depressive Disorder, or Major Depressive Disorder, In Partial Remission.

Note: There may have been a previous Major Depressive Episode provided there was a full remission (no significant signs or symptoms for 2 months) before the development of the Dysthymic Disorder. In addition, after the initial 2 years (1 year in children or adolescents) of Dysthymic Disorder, there may be superimposed episodes of Major Depressive Disorder, in which case both diagnoses may be given when the criteria are met for a Major Depressive Episode.

E. There has never been a Manic Episode . . . , a Mixed Episode . . . , or a Hypomanic Episode . . . , and criteria have never been met for Cyclothymic Disorder.

F. The disturbance does not occur exclusively during the course of a chronic Psychotic Disorder, such as Schizophrenia or Delusional Disorder.

G. The symptoms are not due to the direct physiological effects of a substance (e.g., a drug of abuse, a medication) or a general medical condition (e.g., hypothyroidism).

H. The symptoms cause clinically significant distress or impairment in social, occupational, or other important areas of functioning.

Specify if:
   Early Onset: if onset is before age 21 years
   Late Onset: if onset is age 21 years or older

Specify (for most recent 2 years of Dysthymic Disorder):
   With Atypical Features . . .

Note. From American Psychiatric Association (1994, p. 349). Copyright 1994 by the American Psychiatric Association. Reprinted by permission.

significant sex differences in point prevalence at the initial data collection, with girls qualifying for diagnosis more often than boys. However, at follow-up 1 year later, sex differences were nonsignificant. Sex differences for lifetime prevalence rates were significant, with girls showing higher rates than boys. Age effects and the interaction of age and sex were nonsignificant, although older adolescents were more likely to be diagnosed with DD.

Early to middle adolescence is widely believed to be the developmental period when significant increases occur in depression and when girls begin to experience significantly more depression than boys (e.g., Angold & Rutter, 1992; Nolen-Hoeksema & Girgus, 1994; Petersen et al., 1991). However, documentation of the *emergence* of gender differences in depression during adolescence is most strongly supported by a significant interaction of age and sex—that is, evidence that girls become more depressed relative to boys as they grow older. Two reviews of the research on adolescent depression have revealed that despite the increasing theoretical and empirical work devoted to explaining age and sex differences in depression during adolescence, these differences are not as robust as is widely assumed (Petersen, Compas, & Brooks-Gunn, 1992; Leadbeater, Blatt, & Quinlan, 1995). Specifically, many studies of depression during adolescence have not examined age and sex differences. Among studies that have examined such differences, findings have been inconsistent with respect to the main effects of age and sex, and, most importantly, the interaction of age and sex. For example, we (Petersen et al., 1992) reviewed 30 studies of "depressed affect" published between 1975 and 1991. Of the eight studies that tested age effects, six reported no main effects for age. Of the 13 studies that tested sex effects, 11 reported higher rates for girls, while 2 found no sex differences. Leadbeater et al. (1995) reported that 14 out of 21 studies found more depressive symptoms among girls than boys; 6 studies found no sex differences; and the remaining study found higher rates for boys than girls in a working-class sample. Neither we (Petersen et al., 1992) nor Leadbeater et al. (1995) reported findings with respect to age × sex interactions.

Four recent community studies provide some clarification of the relation between age and sex in depression during adolescence. In a longitudinal community-based study, Ge, Lorenz, Conger, Elder, and Simons (1994) found a significant age × sex interaction for cross-sectional analyses of depressed mood, with the rate for girls increasing relative to that for boys between the ages of 13 and 16, and decreasing thereafter. Consecutive reports from analyses of the Dunedin, New Zealand longitudinal sample also showed an emergence of gender differences during adolescence. Girls were found to be four times *less* likely than boys to have an MDE at age 13 (Kashani et al., 1987); however, when examined 2 years later at age 15, girls were 1.8 times *more* likely to have an MDE than boys (McGee et al., 1990). Similarly, using retrospective reports of 18-year-old high school students, Giaconia et al. (1993) found that MDE was most likely to occur between the ages of 14 and 17 (age effect), and that girls were at much greater risk for an MDE during this high-risk period than were boys (age × sex interaction). Most recently, we (Hinden et al., 1996) examined age and sex differences in a nationally representative sample of children and adolescents with respect to depressed mood versus the Anxious/Depressed syndrome, parent report versus youth self-report, and cross-sectional versus longitudinal research designs. Overall analyses revealed expected sex differences, with girls showing higher levels of depression than boys across operational definitions, informants, and designs. Age differences and the

interaction of age and sex were less consistent, however, and differences overall were of small magnitude. In a complementary study, we (Compas et al., in press) found that gender differences in depressed mood, the Anxious/Depressed syndrome, and an analogue of MDD were more consistent and significantly larger in magnitude in a sample of adolescents who had been referred for mental health services than in a nonreferred sample. These findings suggest that the emergence of gender differences in depressive symptoms in adolescence may be limited to a subgroup of adolescent girls, who represent an extreme of the distribution of depressive symptoms among the adolescent population.

Conceptual Models of Depression in Young People

The nature, etiology, correlates, and developmental course of depression in children and adolescents have been viewed from a wide range of theoretical perspectives. These include psychodynamic, behavioral, cognitive, interpersonal, family, biological, and environmental models that vary in their comprehensiveness and in their level of empirical support. A review of these various models is beyond the scope of this chapter (see Hammen & Rudolph, 1996, for a discussion of these models). The implication of these models for the assessment of depression in young people is clear: Each model has led to the development of measures of constructs that are hypothesized to be related to depression (these measures are reviewed below). On the other hand, these various conceptual models have not influenced the assessment of depression per se, as the assessment of depression is guided by the taxonomic approaches described above.

It has been argued that a broad integrative approach will prove more fruitful than will viewing these various conceptual models as competing explanations of depression in children and adolescents. As Hammen and Rudolph (1996) state, "These models share many common features: the contributions of early family socialization to subsequent functioning, the emergence of internal representations or working models of relationships, the interplay between individual vulnerabilities and external experience, and the role of depression as both a consequence of prior psychological disturbances and as a risk factor for future difficulties" (pp. 184–185). Integration of these various perspectives has led to a developmental–biopsychosocial perspective on depression during childhood and adolescence (e.g., Cicchetti, Rogosch, & Toth, 1994; Gotlib & Hammen, 1992; Hammen & Rudolph, 1996; Petersen et al., 1993). Integrative models have important implications for the assessment of depression in young people. First, they emphasize that developmental processes and a young person's developmental level must be taken into account in the assessment process. Second, they highlight the need to assess a range of factors that may be associated with depression in children and adolescents; these include internal characteristics of the child or adolescent, as well as features of his or her social context. Third, integrative models take into account that the interplay among these factors and their salience may change with development. These issues are considered in more detail below.

ASSESSMENT OF DEPRESSION

The assessment of depression in children and adolescents has drawn on three primary methodologies—self-report questionnaires, behavior checklists, and structured diagnostic interviews. Each of these methods is reviewed, along with its relationship to the taxonomic perspectives (mood, syndrome, disorder) described above. The integration of these methods is also considered.

Self-Report Questionnaires

All individuals experience periods of sadness, unhappiness, or dysphoric mood at various points in their lives. These periods of depressed mood may occur in response to a variety of environmental and internal stimuli, may last for varying lengths of time, and may be associated with either few or many emotional and behavioral correlates. One approach to research on depression during childhood and adolescence takes depressed mood and associated symptoms as its central focus. From this perspective, no attempt is made to catalogue the features of a depressive disorder, nor are any assumptions made about the underlying etiology of depressed mood. Because depressed affect is an internalizing problem that may not be readily observable to others, several different measures have been developed to obtain children's and adolescents' reports of their negative mood.

Self-report measures have included single items, scales designed specifically to assess depressed mood, and subscales of existing measures. Numer-

ous measures of child/adolescent psychological distress and psychopathology contain single-item indices of depressed mood. For example, the measures developed by Achenbach and colleagues (see "Behavior Checklists," below) all contain an item for "unhappy, sad, or depressed" affect. Numerous self-report scales and subscales have been used to assess self-reports of symptoms of depression, including the Children's Depression Inventory (CDI; Kovacs, 1980); the Beck Depression Inventory (BDI; Beck, Ward, Mendelson, Mock, & Erbaugh, 1961); the Reynolds Child Depression Scale (RCDS; Reynolds, 1989) and the Reynolds Adolescent Depression Scale (RADS; Reynolds, 1986); the Children's Depression Scale (CDS; Tisher & Lang, 1983); the Center for Epidemiologic Studies Depression Scale (CES-D; Radloff, 1977); the Emotional Tone scale of the Self-Image Questionnaire for Young Adolescents (SIQYA; Petersen, Schulenberg, Abramowitz, Offer, & Jarcho, 1984); and the Kandel Depression Scale (KDS; Kandel & Davies, 1982). The BDI and CES-D were developed for adults and have been applied without adaptation to adolescents; the other scales were all designed specifically for use with children or adolescents.

Scales used to measure depressed mood share several common features (see Reynolds, 1994, for a review of self-report scales of child/adolescent depression). They all include lists of emotions and symptoms that reflect the central features of depressive disorders. For most of the measures, these symptoms are at least loosely based on the Research Diagnostic Criteria (RDC) for depression (Spitzer, Endicott, & Robins, 1978a, 1978b), the DSM, or measures of adult depression (e.g., the BDI; Beck et al., 1961). An exception is the Emotional Tone scale, which is part of a measure of adolescent self-image (the SIQYA; Petersen et al., 1984). The measures use either a Likert-type scale for respondents to rate the degree to which each symptom applies to them, or choices from a series of responses for each item reflecting varying levels of the severity of that symptom.

The CDI is noteworthy because of its wide usage in studies of clinically referred and non-referred children and adolescents, and because the full scale includes a wide range of symptoms other than depressed mood (see Table 4.4 for sample items and format of the CDI). A comprehensive factor-analytic study (Weiss et al., 1991) identified a subset of items reflective of depressed affect through reanalysis of data collected from five previous studies on samples of clinically referred

TABLE 4.4. Sample Items from the Children's Depression Inventory (CDI)

Pick out the sentences that describe your feelings and ideas in the past two weeks.

1. ___ I am sad once in a while
   ___ I am sad many times
   ___ I am sad all the time
2. ___ Nothing will ever work out for me
   ___ I am not sure if things will work out for me
   ___ Things will work out for me okay
3. ___ I do most things okay
   ___ I do many things wrong
   ___ I do everything wrong
4. ___ I have fun in many things
   ___ I have fun in some things
   ___ Nothing is fun at all
5. ___ I am bad all the time
   ___ I am bad many times
   ___ I am bad once in a while
6. ___ I think about bad things happening to me
        once in a while
   ___ I worry that bad things will happen to me
   ___ I am sure that terrible things will happen to
        me
7. ___ I hate myself
   ___ I do not like myself
   ___ I like myself

Note. From Kovacs (1980). Copyright 1980 by Scandinavian University Press. Reprinted by permission.

children (*n* = 515, ages 8–12 years) and adolescents (*n* = 768, ages 13–16 years). Five factors were identified in separate factor analyses of children's and adolescents' responses; the first of these was labeled Negative Affect With Somatic Concerns for both age groups (the remaining factors differed somewhat for the two groups). This factor included the items "I feel like crying every day," "I am sad all the time," and "Things bother me all the time" for adolescents, whereas for children only the sadness item loaded on this factor. Somatic items also loaded on this factor, including "I worry about aches and pains all the time," "Most days I do not feel like eating," "I have trouble sleeping at night," and "I am tired all the time." Although a Negative Affect With Somatic Concerns factor was identified in both children's and adolescents' responses, only items concerning frequent sadness, fatigue, and aches and pains were common to both age groups. Frequent crying, being bothered by things, trouble sleeping, and poor appetite were unique to adolescents' responses, whereas not having friends was the only item unique to children's reports. Thus, the responses of children and adolescents on the CDI contain a relatively distinct factor that reflects depressed mood along with somatic symptoms. The structure of the Negative Affect factor, however, appears to differ somewhat for children and adolescents.

With regard to psychometric properties, all of the scales meet at least minimal criteria for internal-consistency reliability, test–retest reliability, and stability over moderate periods of time. For example, the Emotional Tone scale has shown adequate internal consistency for boys (alpha = .81) and girls (alpha = .85) (Petersen et al., 1984), and the KDS has a similar level of internal consistency (alpha = .79; Kandel & Davies, 1982). Internal-consistency data have not been reported on the Negative Affect With Somatic Concerns scale of the CDI; however, internal consistency of the overall scale has been found to be adequate (e.g., alpha = .80; Smucker, Craighead, Craighead, & Green, 1986). Test–retest reliability also tends to be adequate for these measures (e.g., r = .79 over 5–6 months on the KDS; Kandel & Davies, 1982). However, some research with the CDI suggests that depressed mood may be much less stable in nonreferred samples than in referred samples. For example, Saylor, Finch, Spirito, and Bennett (1984) found lower stability in the responses of a nonclinical sample (r = .38) than in those of an "emotionally disturbed" sample (r = .87).

Establishing the validity of self-report measures has been more challenging, as external criteria for validation have been difficult to identify. For example, the KDS has been shown to correlate significantly with depressive items from the Symptom Checklist 90 (r = .92; Kandel & Davies, 1984). Although this provides a minimal check of the criterion validity of the measure, the meaning of this correlation is difficult to interpret, in light of the high degree of overlap in the items on the two scales and the fact that both measures were completed by adolescents at a single administration.

Correlations between self-reports of depressed mood/symptoms and measures of constructs that are hypothesized to be related to depression represents another step in the validation of the former scales. Important correlates of self-reports of depressed mood and symptoms have included low self-esteem (e.g., Petersen et al., 1984), hopelessness (e.g., Kazdin, Rogers, & Colbus, 1986), negative cognitions and cognitive errors (e.g., Leitenberg, Yost, & Carroll-Wilson, 1986), low levels of perceived control (e.g., Weisz, Sweeney, Proffitt, & Carr, 1993), and stressful life events (e.g., Compas, Grant, & Ey, 1994). Correlations of these other variables with depressed mood have typically been moderate, most often ranging from .30 to .50.

The discriminant validity of self-report scales has proven much more difficult to establish (Kendall, Cantwell, & Kazdin, 1989). Measures of depressed mood are highly correlated with measures of other negative emotions, most notably anxiety (Brady & Kendall, 1992). This is not surprising, in light of the tendency of depressed emotions to load strongly on a broader factor of negative affect that includes sad, dysphoric, anxious, and angry affect (Finch, Lipovsky, & Casat, 1989; King, Ollendick, & Gallone, 1991; Watson & Clark, 1992). It appears that the most appropriate conclusion that can be reached about scales of depressed mood during childhood and adolescence is that they are reliable and valid measures of one component of negative affect, along with additional, heterogeneous symptoms.

Behavior Checklists

A second approach to the assessment of child and adolescent psychopathology is concerned with depressive phenomena as they relate to a wider range of other child/adolescent problem behaviors and emotions (e.g., social withdrawal, attentional problems, aggression). This approach does not *a priori* assume the presence of an underlying structure of psychological disorders in childhood and adolescence. Rather, it is assumed that the structure and pattern of symptoms and disorders is best understood from data obtained from the most relevant informants about child/adolescent behavior. In this sense, the identification of depressive syndromes is based on a deductive method, moving from the general (data on large samples) to the specific (the defining characteristics of an individual case). The three primary sources of information on child/adolescent behavior that have been used most frequently are parents, teachers, and children/adolescents themselves.

Researchers taking this approach are faced with the task of aggregating and organizing the responses of large samples of respondents concerning the frequency and intensity of a range of child/adolescent behaviors and emotions. It is assumed that if a disorder involves a syndrome of behaviors and emotions, it will be reflected in the statistical associations (intercorrelations) among problems that are reported as occurring together in samples of individuals. Specifically, if there is a syndrome of depression in childhood and adolescence, it will

appear as a set of recognizable problems that co-occur in reports by parents, teachers, and/or children/adolescents.

Various broadly focused parent, teacher, and self-report measures have been used to obtain reports of behaviors and emotions that are pertinent to the construct of child/adolescent depression. Parent report measures have included the Revised Behavior Problem Checklist (Quay & Peterson, 1983), the Conners Parent Rating Scale (Conners, 1973), and the Child Behavior Checklist (CBCL; Achenbach, 1991b). Teacher checklists include the Conners Teacher Rating Scale (Conners, 1973); the Louisville Behavior Checklist (Miller, 1984); and the Teacher Report Form (TRF), a variation of the CBCL (Achenbach, 1991c). Multivariate measures of a wide range of behavioral and emotional problems that obtain adolescents' self-reports have been more limited. The only extensive analyses of adolescent self-reports have involved the Youth Self-Report (YSR), which is another variation of the CBCL (Achenbach, 1991d), and the Minnesota Multiphasic Personality Inventory (MMPI; e.g., Archer, Pancoast, & Klinefelter, 1989; Williams & Butcher, 1989a, 1989b). These instruments differ from scales of depressed mood, in that they are designed to assess a wide range of internalizing and externalizing problems in addition to depression. Self-report behavior checklists have not been used with preadolescent children, as it is assumed that limits in young children's cognitive abilities and reading skills preclude the use of such measures with this age group (Achenbach, 1991d). Thus, the use of self-report measures of depressive syndromes applies only to adolescence.

Depressive syndromes have been derived from factor analyses or principal-component analyses of the responses of large samples of clinically referred children and adolescents. The most extensive empirically based multivariate approach to the classification of child and adolescent psychopathology is represented by the ongoing work of Achenbach and colleagues. This system serves as the basis for discussion here, because (1) it is the only approach to date that involves the empirical integration of data from parents, teachers, and adolescents; (2) it is the only attempt to generate an empirically based taxonomy of adolescent (and child) psychopathology; and (3) one of the measures (the CBCL) has been examined in a larger study of the Achenbach, Conners, and Quay Behavior Checklist (ACQ), in which items from other multivariate measures were also included (Achenbach, Howell, Quay, & Conners, 1991).

The use of the CBCL (Achenbach, 1991b), TRF (Achenbach, 1991c), and YSR (Achenbach, 1991d) to generate a taxonomy of child and adolescent psychopathology is now in its second iteration. In both phases of the development of this taxonomy, principal-component analyses of checklist responses by parents, teachers, and adolescents have been used to identify sets of behaviors and emotions that co-occur in the reports of these informants. The question most pertinent here is whether a syndrome of behaviors and emotions has been identified that reflects depression.

In the first stage of work on this taxonomy, data were analyzed separately as a function of the age and sex of the target children or adolescents and as a function of the source of information (Achenbach & Edelbrock, 1981). However, the use of different syndromes for different age groups, for boys and girls, and for different measures proved to be cumbersome in both research and practice. In the second generation of research on this system, steps were taken to integrate data from multiple sources and to identify core syndromes and cross-informant syndromes across ages, sexes, and sources of information (Achenbach, 1991a, 1993). In principal-component analyses of CBCL, TRF, and YSR responses with samples of clinically referred children and adolescents, eight syndromes were found to be common across ages, sexes, and informants (these were labeled "cross-informant constructs"): Anxious/Depressed, Withdrawn, Somatic Complaints, Social Problems, Thought Problems, Attention Problems, Delinquent Behavior, and Aggressive Behavior. Most pertinent to depression, a syndrome of mixed anxiety and depressive symptoms emerged in these analyses (see Table 4.1 for the symptoms constituting this syndrome). A similar syndrome was identified in parents' reports from the larger item pool used in the ACQ (Achenbach et al., 1991). Thus, the characteristics of this syndrome are not limited to the items included only on the CBCL, YSR, and TRF; that is, the syndrome is not an artifact of the use of these scales.

Correlations among different informants have been low in previous research, typically in the range of .20–.30 (Achenbach, McConaughy, & Howell, 1987). More recent research examining parent, teacher, and adolescent reports on the Anxious/Depressed syndrome has shown somewhat stronger correspondence among these reports than has been found on earlier syndrome scores (Achenbach, 1991a). Based on correlational analyses with referred and nonreferred adolescents, the mean of the cross-informant correlations (mother × father, parent × teacher, parent × adolescent, teacher × adolescent) was .42 for both boys and girls. These correlations ranged from a low of .22 between reports of boys on the YSR and teachers on the TRF, to highs of .66 between mothers and fathers of girls and .70 between mothers and fathers of boys on the CBCL. Girls' reports on the Anxious/Depressed syndrome were correlated with their parents' reports ($r = .44$) at a significantly higher level than were boys' reports with their parents' reports ($r = .32$). Thus, moderate agreement was found across different informants. Although the scores generated from the most recent versions of the profiles for the CBCL, YSR, and TRF are moderately related to one another, they remain relatively distinct measures of anxious and depressed symptoms in adolescents. It appears best to continue to consider these as distinct perspectives on depressive syndromes in childhood and adolescence.

The CBCL, TRF, and YSR all meet the necessary standards for acceptable internal-consistency reliability and test–retest reliability, and all are based on adequate norms from a nationally representative sample of nonreferred children and adolescents (Achenbach, 1991b, 1991c, 1991d). Internal-consistency reliabilities (as reflected by the alpha statistic) for the Anxious/Depressed scale on the CBCL, YSR, and CBCL were all above .85. One-week test–retest reliabilities were also strong, ranging from .74 for boys on the YSR to .87 for girls on the YSR and parents' reports of boys' symptoms on the CBCL.

The validity of the CBCL, YSR, and TRF has been established by comparing scores of referred and nonreferred youths. Referred youths scored significantly higher than nonreferred adolescents on the Anxious/Depressed scale on all three scales. Referral status accounted for 20% of the variance in Anxious/Depressed scores for adolescent boys and 22% for adolescent girls on the CBCL. Rates were lower on the YSR, with referral status accounting for 8% and 13% of the variance in Anxious/Depressed scores for boys and girls, respectively. Clinical cutoffs have been established that discriminate between referred and nonreferred youths. For example, 34% of referred adolescents scored above the cutoff for the Anxious/Depressed scale, as compared with only 5% of the nonreferred sample above this cutoff. This translates into a relative odds ratio of 10:1 (i.e., the odds of being above the cutoff were 10 times greater for referred than for nonreferred youths).

Other researchers have used items from these checklists to develop depression scales that are distinct from the Anxious/Depressed syndrome (e.g., Clarke, Lewinsohn, Hops, & Seeley, 1992; Connor et al., 1996; Gerhardt, Compas, Connor, Hinden, & Achenbach, 1996; Nurcombe et al., 1989; Seifer, Nurcombe, Scioli, & Grapentine, 1989). These scales have been derived both empirically (Nurcombe et al., 1989) and rationally (Gerhardt et al., 1996). For example, Gerhardt et al. (1996) identified a set of symptoms on the CBCL and YSR corresponding to the DSM-IV criteria for MDE, with matching items identified for all items except the one pertaining to anhedonia. The percentages (2.3% based on adolescents' self-reports, 1% based on parents' reports) of children and adolescents in a nationally representative sample who exceeded a cutoff for MDE (Gerhardt et al., 1996) were roughly comparable to the rate reported for community studies in which a diagnostic interview was used to derive diagnoses (e.g., Lewinsohn et al., 1993). These findings suggest that checklists can be used to generate a representative analogue of DSM symptoms of MDE, with the caveat that they do not reflect DSM criteria for duration and level of impairment.

In summary, the multivariate scales developed by Achenbach and colleagues meet the necessary psychometric criteria for use in the assessment of a depression-related syndrome labeled Anxious/Depressed. Although the scores generated from the most recent versions of the profiles for the CBCL, YSR, and TRF are moderately related to one another, they remain relatively distinct measures of anxious and depressed symptoms in adolescents. It appears best to continue to consider these distinct perspectives on the Anxious/Depressed syndrome in childhood and adolescence.

Structured Diagnostic Interviews

The categorical diagnostic approach to assessment of child/adolescent depression is represented in the use of structured or semistructured diagnostic interviews based on various versions of the DSM. The DSM-IV is based more upon the clinical literature of the symptomatology of disorders than on the empirical literature of the covariation of symptoms and syndromes. As such, it reflects an inductive approach, in which clinical information on specific cases is used to develop diagnostic decision rules that can be generalized to the larger population. The most extensively researched and widely used of these interviews are the Schedule for Affective Disorders and Schizophrenia for School-Age Children (K-SADS; Puig-Antich & Chambers, 1978), the Child Assessment Schedule (CAS; Hodges, Kline, Stern, Cytryn, & McKnew, 1982), the Diagnostic Interview Schedule for Children (DISC; Costello, Edelbrock, Dulcan, Kalas, & Klaric, 1984), the Interview Schedule for Children (Kovacs, 1985), and the Diagnostic Interview for Children and Adolescents (Herjanic, Herjanic, Brown, & Wheatt, 1975). The present discussion focuses on the K-SADS, CAS, and DISC as representative examples of different types of diagnostic interviews for depression.

The K-SADS was developed for youths 6–17 years old and was based on the adult Schedule for Affective Disorders and Schizophrenia (SADS). Although the SADS and K-SADS used the RDC for depressive disorders as a foundation, DSM-IV criteria may also be applied. The K-SADS is designed to be administered by a trained clinician to determine the onset, duration, and severity of current and past episodes of mood and anxiety disorders, Conduct Disorder, and psychotic disorders. Two versions of the K-SADS are available: one to assess a present episode (K-SADS-P), and an epidemiological version (K-SADS-E) to assess prior history. (See Table 4.5 for sample items from the K-SADS-P.)

The semistructured assessment format consists of separate interviews with the youth's parents and the youth for approximately 1 hour each. Once the presence of a symptom has been established, the interviewer may use further questions to determine the severity and chronicity of the symptom. If responses to initial questions are negative, the interviewer skips to the next section and thereby reduces the interview time for asymptomatic youths. Upon completion of the interview, the interviewer uses his or her clinical judgment to determine a summary diagnosis from the two sources of data (Chambers et al., 1985). Twelve summary scales, including four Depression scales, are generated and may be translated into diagnoses by the interviewer. Specifically, MDD, minor depressive disorder (currently a criteria set provided for further study), anxiety disorders, and Conduct Disorder may be diagnosed. More recently, the K-SADS has been used to generate diagnoses of DD and Adjustment Disorder with Depressed Mood. The decision to convert scales and individual items into a diagnostic category is based upon the clinician's judgment rather than a computer algorithm (Edelbrock & Costello, 1988b). In addition, when the parent's and the child/adolescent's accounts differ, the interviewer may meet with both parties to attempt to resolve the differences or make a judgment about which information to use in making a diagnosis (Chambers et al, 1985).

TABLE 4.5. Sample Items from the Schedule for Affective Disorders and Schizophrenia for School-Age Children, Present Version (K-SADS-P)

Note—If a mood disorder is present, the examiner should inquire if manic or hypomanic periods have or have not occurred. If a manic or hypomanic episode is suspected, the examiner should proceed . . . to establish presence or absence and the exact time periods. Items [here] refer only to a depressive episode, not to a manic episode.

Depressed Mood

This refers to subjective feelings of depression based on verbal complaints of feeling depressed, sad, blue, gloomy, down, empty, bad feelings, feels like crying. Do not include ideational items (like discourage-ment, pessimism, worthlessness), suicide attempts or depressed appearance. Some children will deny feeling "sad" and report only feeling "bad," so it is important to inquire specifically about each dysphoric affect.

How have you been feeling?
Have you felt sad, blue, moody, down, empty, like crying? (ASK EACH ONE)
Is this a good feeling or a bad feeling?
Have you had any other bad feelings?
Have you cried or been tearful?
Do you feel (_____) all the time, most of the time, some of the time . . . ?
Does it come and go? How often? Every day?
How long does it last? All day?
How bad is the feeling?
Can you stand it?
What do you think brings it on?
Do you feel sad when mother is away?

IF SEPARATION FROM MOTHER IS GIVEN AS A CAUSE:

Do you feel (_____) when mother is with you?
Do you feel a little better or is the feeling totally gone?
Can other people tell when you are sad?
How can they tell? Do you look different?

0	No information.
1	Not at all or less than once a week.
2	Slight, e.g., occasionally has dysphoric mood (at least once [a] week), or more frequent but it is completely relieved by the presence of a parent.
3	Mild, e.g., often experiences dysphoric mood. It is not completely relieved by the presence of a parent.
4	Moderate, e.g., most of the time feels "depressed."
5	Severe, e.g., most of the time feels "wretched."
6	Extreme, e.g., most of the time feels extreme depression which "I can't stand."
7	Very extreme, e.g., constant unrelieved, extremely painful feelings of depression.

▼ SKIP TO BROODING, WORRYING

WHAT ABOUT DURING THE LAST WEEK?   LAST WEEK: 0   1   2   3   4   5   6   7

If the child has frequent dysphoric mood which is *completely* and *totally* relieved by the presence of the parent(s) (surrogate), check here   ☐

Note—Sometimes the child will initially give a negative answer at the start of the interview but will become obviously sad as the interview goes on. Then these questions should be repeated, eliciting the present mood and using it as an example to determine its frequency. Similarly, if the mother's report is that the child is sad most of the time and the child denies it, he/she should be confronted with the mother's opinion and he/she should be asked why does he/she think his/her mother believes he/she feels sad so often.

Note. From Puig-Antich and Chambers (1978, p. 7).

The reliability of the K-SADS has been dem-onstrated more easily than the validity. Over a 72-hour period, test–retest reliability of the K-SADS (as reflected by the kappa statistic) with 52 psychi-atrically referred 6- to 17-year-olds was established as on average .55 for individual items, .68 for sum-mary scales, and .24–.70 for diagnoses (Chambers et al., 1985). Specifically, the four depression sum-mary scales (Depressed Mood and Ideation, En-dogenous Features, Depression-Associated Fea-tures, and Suicidal Ideation and Behavior) showed test–retest reliability above .67 and internal-consistency reliability above .68 (Chambers et al., 1985). Clinical syndromes and diagnoses are based upon the summary scores for particular symptoms found to be present. Agreement between parents and children/adolescents was on average .53 for symptoms (range = –.08 to .96).

The validity of the K-SADS is based on its ability to detect the prespecified diagnostic criteria and treatment effects (Edelbrock & Costello, 1988b). The K-SADS, for example, was sensitive to pharmacological treatment of affective disorders in preadolescent children (Puig-Antich, Perel, et al., 1979). In addition, Puig-Antich, Chambers, et al. (1979) found that diagnoses from the RDC correlated with four case studies of biological correlates of depression. Finally, the K-SADS-P version was found to be correlated with the K-SADS-E administered 6 months to 2 years later about lifetime symptoms. Out of 17 children between the ages of 6 and 17, 16 received the same diagnoses with both versions (Orvaschel, Puig-Antich, Chambers, Tabrizi, & Johnson, 1982). No information is yet available on the instrument's discriminant validity, although Edelbrock and Costello (1988b) have suggested that the K-SADS may be able to differentiate between disorders through questioning about anxiety disorders, Conduct Disorder, and psychotic disorders in addition to depressive disorders. Finally, no epidemiological data have been provided for the purpose of normative comparisons.

Unlike the K-SADS, the CAS was developed from a traditional child clinical interview (Hodges & Cools, 1990). It is thematically organized around 11 topic areas: school; friends; activities; family; fears; worries and anxieties; self-image; mood (especially sadness); physical complaints; anger; and reality testing. (See Table 4.6 for sample CAS items.) Responses are scored on symptom scales and can be used to generate DSM-IV diagnoses according to detailed scoring instructions. Originally developed for use with children, the CAS has been successfully extended to adolescents (e.g., Kashani, Reid, & Rosenberg, 1989). Most pertinent to the present discussion are the Mood Content scale and the diagnostic scales for MDD and DD.

The reliability of the CAS has been well established. Test–retest reliabilities of psychiatric inpatients over 9 days for the MDD scale ($r = .89$) and the DD scale ($r = .86$) were adequate (Hodges, Cools, & McKnew, 1989). Internal-consistency reliabilities of child/adolescent and parent scores on the MDD and DD scales were also adequate. Internal consistency was higher for a psychiatric sample (.83 for MDD and .86 for DD for child/adolescent interviews; .85 for MDD and .88 for DD for parent interviews) than for a community sample (.68 for MDD and .75 for child/adolescent interviews; .55 for MDD and .67 for DD for parent interviews) (Hodges, Saunders, Kashani, Hamlett, & Thompson, 1990).

TABLE 4.6. Sample Items from the Child Assessment Schedule (CAS)

H. Mood and Behavior
   Most children have a number of different moods or feelings. What kind of mood are you usually in?

What is the worst you have felt lately?

(*If desired*, ask about each response item as follows:)
Would you say that you have been feeling:
   Mark "yes" if it applies:
142. sad? (or gloomy, blue, or down in the dumps)?
143. crabby, irritable, things get on your nerves easily?
144. feeling "empty" inside?
145. feel like you don't care about things anymore?
146. as if nothing is fun anymore?
(If child responds "yes" to any of the feelings in #142–146 above, or indicates nontransient sadness, ask:) I have been asking you about your feelings.
  • How much (often) have you been feeling this way?
    Feels sad nearly every day (or irritable, empty, hopeless, or has loss of pleasure).
  • When you feel this way, do you feel this way while doing most everything you do, or just some things?
  • Experiences sadness (or equivalents mentioned above) when doing all or almost all usual activities.

Note. From Hodges, Kline, Stern, Cytryn, and McKnew (1982, p. 186). Copyright 1982 by Plenum Publishing Corporation. Reprinted by permission.

The validity of the CAS has been examined through the comparison of child/adolescent and parent responses, the association of the CAS with other clinical interviews, and the association of the CAS with self-report questionnaires. Parent and child responses were moderately correlated on the MDD scale ($r = .46$) and the DD scale ($r = .47$) (Hodges, Gordon, & Lennon, 1990). Children and adolescents who received a diagnosis of MDD on the basis of the CAS differed from nondepressed youths on the CDI (Hodges, 1990) and, more specifically, on subscales of the CDI related to dysphoric mood, loss of personal and social interest, and self-deprecation (Hodges & Craighead, 1990).

In contrast to the K-SADS and the CAS, the DISC may be administered by clinicians or lay interviewers because of its structured format. The DISC was developed as a youth version of the Diagnostic Interview Schedule for adults. Several revisions (DISC-R, DISC 2, DISC 2.1, DISC 2.25, DISC 2.3, DISC 3) have been reported in the literature (e.g., Bidaut-Russell et al., 1995; Fisher et al., 1993; Jensen et al., 1995; Shaffer et al., 1988, 1992, 1993; Schwab-Stone et al., 1993), and the DISC is likely to continue to undergo revision. Intended as a research tool for use in epidemiological studies of psychopathology, the DISC is a comprehensive approach to detecting the presence, severity, onset, and duration of a broad range of symptoms in 6- to 18-year-olds. The results may be presented in two ways: (1) as the number and severity of symptoms or (2) as scored DSM-IV diagnoses. DSM-IV diagnoses are developed from a set of operational rules on the level of symptoms needed to meet stringent criteria. The criteria are considered stringent, because more than the minimum number of symptoms required to meet DSM-IV criteria must be present in order for the child to be assigned a diagnosis from the DISC (Costello, Edelbrock, & Costello, 1985). Diagnoses are generated from computer algorithms of the DISC items, and computer profiles are usually interpreted by trained clinicians. Hence the instrument has the capability to present symptoms and clinical disorders and syndromes based upon a set of stringent diagnostic rules. The DISC consists of separate interviews with a parent and a child/adolescent for approximately 60–70 minutes and 40–60 minutes, respectively. (See Table 4.7 for sample items from the DISC 2.3 for a child informant.)

Reliability of the DISC has been shown through interrater reliability of lay interviewers (.98 on symptom scores) and 2-week period test–retest reliability of the symptom scores (.76 on average for parents) (Edelbrock, Costello, Dulcan, Kalas, & Conover, 1985). A sample of 316 psychiatrically referred youths varied in terms of the reliability of their symptom scores over the 2-week period. On average, adolescents (14–18 years old) were found to have higher test–retest reliability scores (.71) than younger children (.43). Interestingly, parental reports on adolescents were less reliable than those of preadolescent children. More recent reports suggest increased reliability with revised versions of the DISC (Schwab-Stone et al., 1993; Shaffer et al., 1992, 1993).

Symptom scores from parent interviews detected DSM-III criteria moderately reliably (average kappa = .56, range = .35–.81). Less reliable diagnoses were derived from adolescent interviews (average kappa = .36, range = .12–.71). Interinformant agreement was higher for the 14-

TABLE 4.7. Sample Questions from the Diagnostic Interview Schedule for Children (DISC), Child Informant, Version 2.3

MDD/DD
Now I'm going to change the subject a bit and ask about some other feelings kids sometimes have. I'm going to start off with asking you about depression and feeling sad.

1. In the past 6 months, were there times when you were very sad?

| | IF YES | A. When you feel sad this way, does it last most of the day? |

    IF YES   A. When you feel sad this way, does it last most of the day?
                B. Would you say you have been very sad a lot of the time for as long as a year?
    IF YES, C. Would you say most of the time?
    IF YES, D. Were you very sad most of the time for as long as 2 years?
                E. Now thinking about just the last 6 months . . . Was there a time when you were sad almost every day?
    IF YES, F. Did this go on for 2 weeks or more?

Note. From Shaffer et al. (1992).

to 18-year-old group (r's = .29–.35) than for children, and higher for externalizing (behavior/conduct) problems than for internalizing problems. The average correlations between separate parent and youth interviews was .27 (Edelbrock et al., 1985). Parent and child data are scored separately to yield diagnoses. Moderate diagnostic agreement has been reported for revisions of the DISC (Piacentini et al., 1993).

The question of the DISC's validity has been addressed by examining the instrument's ability to discriminate between youths referred for pediatric and psychiatric problems, as well as the DISC's correlation with parent and teacher ratings of Total Behavior Problems on the CBCL and TRF, respectively. Using the parent version of the DISC, Costello et al. (1985) found that 40 children (aged 7–11 years) referred for psychiatric problems scored significantly higher on all the symptom areas and the total symptom score than did 40 same-age children referred for pediatric problems.

Significant correlations with the CBCL and TRF provide some support for the concurrent validity of the DISC (Costello et al., 1984). For example, the Total Behavior Problems score of the parent CBCL correlated .70 with the total symptom score of the DISC-R. Considering the evidence that there is often substantial parent–child disagreement on measures (Achenbach et al., 1987), it is not surprising that the child version of the DISC was correlated only .30 with the CBCL. Nonetheless, the internalizing disorders identified by the parent report on the DISC did not correlate more strongly with the TRF and CBCL Internalizing scale than with the Externalizing scale (Costello et al., 1985), suggesting that the DISC may not be as able to detect the internalizing (e.g., depressive) disorders. An alternative explanation is that there is a strong relationship between internalizing and externalizing disorders. Costello et al. (1985) found that the specificity of the DISC's parent version decreased from 95% to 30% when more than one disorder was present in their sample of psychiatrically referred children (40 children aged 7–11).

Overall, structured interviews have several benefits. The foremost strength of structured interviews is that they constitute the only accepted method for deriving a DSM diagnosis of MDD or DD. In addition, Hodges (1990) and others argue that self-report questionnaires are often unable to differentiate between different disorders within a clinical sample. For example, the CDI failed to differentiate between adolescents with and without depressive disorders in a psychiatric sample

(Lipovsky, Finch, & Belter, 1989). Of course, the diagnoses of the adolescents being compared to the CDI results are drawn from diagnostic interviews. Finally, diagnostic interviews have shown sensitivity to change brought about by treatment.

Nonetheless, there are some issues of concern with all the diagnostic interviews. As described by Hodges and Cools (1990), the use of clinical judgment to make diagnoses when a parent and a youth provide discrepant information can be problematic. They cited the description by Poznanski, Mokros, Grossman, and Freeman (1985) of how diagnostic decisions in clinical research meetings represent more of a "battle of the wills" than a "meeting of the minds." Established guidelines for making these decisions are needed to improve the validity of these instruments, and such guidelines are currently being prepared for the DISC and other interviews (e.g., Piacentini et al., 1993).

Integration of Assessment Methods for Depressed Mood, Syndromes, and Disorders

The research and assessment methods reviewed above present a fragmented picture of research and clinical practice pertaining to depression in young people. Given this rather disorganized state of affairs, can research and practice concerning depressed mood, depressive syndromes, and diagnostic categories of MDD and DD be integrated? These three approaches appear to be at odds with one another, as depression is conceptualized and measured differently within each approach. The differences between self-report measures and diagnostic interviews for adult depression have been examined in detail. One perspective is represented by Coyne and colleagues, who argue that self-report measures of depressive symptoms reflect generalized psychological distress and not clinical depression (e.g., Coyne & Downey, 1991; Fechner-Bates, Coyne, & Schwenk, 1994). Self-report measures for adults have only moderate to poor correspondence with diagnostic interviews for depression, as reflected in moderate rates of specificity (true positives) but poor sensitivity (true negatives). For example, in a study of 425 primary medical care patients who completed the CES-D and a structured interview for the DSM-III-R, most subjects who scored high on the CES-D did not meet diagnostic criteria for MDD; a fifth of the patients with MDD had low scores on the CES-D; and the CES-D performed as well in detecting anxiety as in detecting depression (Fechner-Bates et al., 1994). Furthermore, the psychosocial factors that correlate with self-report measures differ from the correlates of MDD (Coyne & Downey, 1991). Whether these same patterns are evident with children and adolescents is addressed below.

Comparison of Features of Depressed Mood, Syndromes, and Disorders

As a first step in comparing the core features of these three approaches to child/adolescent depression, abbreviated versions of the items from a self-report questionnaire (CDI); items from the Anxious/Depressed syndrome derived from the CBCL, YSR, and TRF (Achenbach, 1991a); and the symptom criteria for MDE from DSM-IV are presented in Table 4.8. Asterisked items (*) are those that are common to at least two of the three approaches. Comparison of these items indicates only moderate overlap in the central features of these approaches. Only three symptoms—sad or depressed mood, feelings of worthlessness, and feelings of guilt—are common to all three approaches. Five items are common to the CDI and the Anxious/Depressed syndrome but are not included in the DSM criteria; six items are common to the CDI and the DSM but are not part of the Anxious/Depressed syndrome; and no items are included in both the syndrome and the DSM that do not also appear on the CDI. Finally, 13 items appear only on the CDI; six items in the Anxious/Depressed syndrome have no corresponding items on the CDI or the DSM; and one item appears on the DSM criteria but not on the CDI or in the syndrome.

The CDI offers good coverage of the DSM-IV criteria for MDE, with the exception of an item reflecting psychomotor agitation or retardation. In addition, the CDI oversamples some of the DSM criteria and includes several items that are not part of the criteria for MDE. For example, feelings of worthlessness are oversampled, as they are represented by five items. Items assessing noncompliance and fighting with peers are included on the CDI but are not part of the DSM criteria.

The Anxious/Depressed syndrome differs from both the CDI and the DSM criteria for MDE by its inclusion of anxiety symptoms and by the exclusion of items representing the neurovegetative symptoms of depression (e.g., sleep disturbance, appetite problems, fatigue). The absence of these items is not the result of their absence from the measures used to derive the Anxious/Depressed syndrome, however, as the CBCL, YSR, and TRF include items representing all of these symptoms. It is noteworthy that these symptoms did not load

with the other core DSM symptoms (sadness, worthlessness, guilt) in the principal-component analyses used to derive the syndrome (Achenbach, 1991a). On the other hand, symptoms characteristic of both depression and anxiety did form a reliable syndrome in the reports of parents, teachers, and youths. In this way, the Anxious/Depressed syndrome is similar to the broad construct of "negative affect" or "mixed anxiety–depression" (Watson & Clark, 1984, 1992; Watson & Kendall, 1989).

From the limited overlap among depressive symptoms in these various approaches, one would expect only low to moderate correspondence in the identification of depressive problems when these approaches are applied to individual cases. Empirical studies of the correspondence among some of these approaches are now reviewed.

Empirical Studies of Self-Report Questionnaires, Behavior Checklists, and Diagnostic Interviews

Correspondence among the three approaches to measuring child/adolescent depression has been examined by using diagnostic interviews to assign DSM-III-R or DSM-IV diagnoses and collecting questionnaire or behavior checklist data on the same sample of individuals. This method has been applied in four studies examining self-report inventories of depressive symptoms and diagnostic interviews (Garrison, Addy, Jackson, McKeown, & Waller, 1991; Gotlib, Lewinsohn, & Seeley, 1995; Kazdin, Esveldt-Dawson, Unis, & Rancurello, 1983; Roberts, Lewinsohn, & Seeley, 1991), and in three studies examining behavior checklists and diagnostic interviews (Edelbrock & Costello, 1988a; Rey & Morris-Yates, 1991, 1992; Weinstein, Noam, Grimes, Stone, & Schwab-Stone, 1990). Each study provides some evidence for the convergence of these different approaches to assessment of child/adolescent depression.

Both Roberts et al. (1991) and Garrison et al. (1991) examined the relation between self-report inventories of depressive symptoms and diagnoses of depressive disorders based on clinical interviews in large community samples of children or adolescents. Garrison et al. examined the CES-D and the K-SADS; Roberts et al. examined both the CES-D and the BDI, along with the K-SADS. Both studies found that these scales served as useful screening instruments for diagnoses of MDD and DD, but that both the BDI and the CES-D produced substantial rates of false positives. That is, most adolescents who received a diagnosis of

TABLE 4.8. Comparison of Abbreviated Items from CDI; Core Anxious/Depressed Syndrome on CBCL, YSR, and TRF; and DSM-IV Criteria for MDE

CDI	CBCL, YSR, and TRF Anxious/Depressed	DSM-IV MDE
*Frequent sadness	*Unhappy, sad, depressed	*Depressed or irritable mood
*Feels self is not as good as most people	*Feels worthless	*Feelings of worthlessness [or guilt]
*Guilt	*Feels too guilty	*Feelings of [worthlessness or] guilt
*Feels lonely	*Lonely	—
*Bothered by things	*Hurt when criticized (TRF only)	—
*Frequent crying	Cries a lot	—
*Worries bad things are going to happen	Worries	—
*Feels unloved	*Feels unloved	—
*Anhedonia	—	*Diminished interest or pleasure
*Poor appetite	—	*Weight loss or gain
*Trouble sleeping	—	*Insomnia or hypersomnia
*Thinks about suicide	—	*Recurrent thoughts about death, suicidal ideation
*Fatigue	—	*Fatigue or loss of energy
*Indecisive	—	*Diminished ability to think or concentrate
School failure and poor motivation	—	—
Feels ugly	—	—
Concerned about aches and pains	—	—
Doesn't have fun at school	—	—
Doesn't have friends	—	—
Feels inferior to others	—	—
Noncompliant	—	—
Frequently gets into fights	—	—
Hopelessness	—	—
Incompetent	—	—
Sees self as "bad"	—	—
Self-hatred	—	—
Doesn't want to be with people	—	—
—	Fears own impulses	—
—	Needs to be perfect	—
—	Feels persecuted	—
—	Fearful, anxious	—
—	Self-conscious	—
—	Suspicious	—
—	—	Psychomotor retardation or agitation

Note. Asterisked items (*) are included in two or more measures. Dashes (—) indicate that a corresponding item was not found.

MDD or DD also reported elevated scores on the CES-D or BDI, but large numbers of individuals with elevated scores on the symptom measures were not judged to be clinically depressed on the basis of interview data. In a study of inpatient children, Kazdin et al. (1983) examined the correspondence of child and parent reports on the CDI with interviews to assess depression. Within-informant responses on the CDI and the interview were moderately correlated (r's = .62 for children, .71 for mothers, and .54 for fathers). Correspondence of the CDI and the interview across informants was low, however, with mother–child and father–child correlations (r's = .16 and .33, respectively) lower than mother–father correspondence (r = .65).

A recent study by Gotlib et al. (1995) provides the most comprehensive information on the association of self-report questionnaires and diagnostic interviews. In addition to examining the sensitivity and specificity of the CES-D and the K-SADS in a large community sample of adolescents, they carefully examined the characteristics of the false positives within the sample (i.e., those with high CES-D scores who did not meet diagnostic criteria for MDD). Adolescents classified as false positives manifested higher levels of current and future psychopathology than did the true negatives (those who scored low on both the CES-D and did not meet criteria for MDD). More importantly, the false-positive individuals did not differ significantly from the true-positive participants on a wide range of measures of psychosocial dysfunction. The authors concluded that individuals who score high on a self-report measure of depressive symptoms but do not meet diagnostic criteria for MDD are far from a "normal" group; rather, these individuals are experiencing significant distress and impairment in psychosocial functioning (Gotlib et al., 1995). The false positives differed from the true negatives on the number of DSM diagnoses they received, suggesting that the CES-D is a measure of general distress rather than depression specifically. However, the only specific diagnoses other than depression that distinguished the two groups were anxiety disorders. This elevation on diagnoses of depression and anxiety is consistent with the high rates of comorbidity of these two groups of disorders that have been reported in previous work (Compas & Hammen, 1994). Furthermore, those who met criteria for MDD also demonstrated a high rate of comorbidity of depression and anxiety. It appears, therefore, that the CES-D may be related more strongly to symptoms of depression and anxiety than to symptoms associated with other forms of psychopathology. Finally, the false-positive participants were at least twice as likely as the true-negative participants to develop a psychiatric disorder over the course of the study. The authors conclude that being identified as a false-positive participant is clearly not benign (Gotlib et al., 1995).

Two studies including diagnostic interviews with parents and parent reports on the CBCL have found considerable correspondence between the two approaches. Edelbrock and Costello (1988a), in a study of clinically referred children and adolescents (ages 6 through 16 years), found that scores on the Depressed Withdrawal scale of the CBCL (derived from the initial version of the CBCL profile) for girls aged 12–16 correlated significantly with diagnoses of MDD and DD, and that scores on the Uncommunicative scale of the CBCL for boys ages 6–16 correlated with DSM-III diagnoses of Overanxious Disorder of Childhood, MDD, and DD. The broad-band Internalizing scale and Externalizing scale were also correlated with diagnoses of MDD (.31, $p < .001$, and .14, $p < .01$, respectively) and DD (.43, $p < .001$, and .22, $p < .001$, respectively). They also found that scores on the Depression scale for children aged 6–11 were linearly related to the probability of receiving a diagnosis of either MDD or DD. This finding suggests that there was not a specific threshold score of symptoms on this scale above which children received a depressive diagnosis and below which they did not. It will be important to determine whether a similar pattern is found for adolescents.

In a study of 667 clinically referred Australian adolescents, Rey and Morris-Yates (1991) generated DSM-III diagnoses on the basis of clinical interviews and calculated scores on a Depression scale of the CBCL (identified by Nurcombe et al., 1989). To examine the correspondence between diagnoses and CBCL scale scores, these authors used receiver operating characteristic (ROC) techniques developed in signal detection theory as an overall index of diagnostic accuracy (in terms of sensitivity and specificity) in analyses of continuous scores. Individuals with a diagnosis of MDD ($n = 23$) were compared in separate analyses with individuals with all other diagnoses ($n = 634$), individuals with a diagnosis of DD ($n = 62$), and individuals with a diagnosis of Separation Anxiety Disorder ($n = 57$). Those with a diagnosis of MDD scored significantly higher on the CBCL Depression scale than those in any of the other diagnostic groups. Furthermore, ROC analyses indicated that the CBCL scale functioned at a level better than chance in discriminating the MDD group from each of the other three diagnostic groups. Rates of sensitivity (83%) and specificity (55%) were better in distinguishing MDD from all other diagnoses than in distinguishing MDD from DD or Separation Anxiety Disorder. Additional analyses with this sample compared the sensitivity and specificity of six depression scales extracted from the CBCL and the YSR (Rey & Morris-Yates, 1992). All of the scales performed at a level better than chance in ROC analyses discriminating adolescents with MDD diagnoses from those without.

Using adolescents' self-reports on the YSR and the child version of the DISC, Weinstein et al. (1990) also found evidence for a significant positive association between DSM-III diagnoses of affective disorders and scores on the YSR Depressed scale (derived from the initial version of the YSR profile). However, adolescents who were diagnosed with MDD and/or DD scored higher than those without the diagnosis of an affective disorder on all narrow-band scales on the YSR (Depressed, Unpopular, Somatic Complaints, Aggressive, Delinquent, Thought Disorder) and on the broader scales of Internalizing and Externalizing problems.

Finally, Gerhardt et al. (1996) examined the correspondence among depressed mood, the Anxious/Depressed syndrome, and an analogue measure of MDD in parent and adolescent reports on the CBCL and YSR. Adolescents' self-reports on the YSR indicated that of those who met the DSM analogue criteria for MDD, 59% were also in the clinical range on the Anxious/Depressed syndrome; of those who were in the clinical range on the Anxious/Depressed syndrome, 17% met the criteria for the analogue of MDD. The pattern was similar for parents' reports on the CBCL: 71% of adolescents who met the DSM analogue criteria also were in the clinical range on the Anxious/Depressed syndrome; 12% of those who were in the clinical range on the syndrome also met the criteria for the analogue of MDD. Relative-risk odds ratios indicated that youths who met criteria for the Anxious/Depressed syndrome at one assessment were 9.3 times more likely based on parent reports and 15.5 times more likely based on self-reports to meet criteria on the analogue of MDD 3 years later (Gerhardt et al., 1996). Thus, the Anxious/Depressed syndrome identified a larger group of children and youths, a subset of whom also met criteria associated with clinical depression. A substantial portion of those who met criteria for MDD, however, were not in the clinical range on the Anxious/Depressed syndrome. Those children and adolescents who exceeded criteria on both indices were significantly more impaired on a number of measures than those who only exceeded either the syndrome cutoff or the MDD cutoff (Gerhardt et al., 1996).

These studies indicate that diagnoses of MDD and DD derived from clinical interviews are related, albeit imperfectly, both to scores on self-report inventories of depressive symptoms (including depressed mood) and to depressive syndrome scores from multivariate checklists. We (Compas et al., 1993) have proposed a hierarchical and sequential model to describe the association among depressed mood (as measured by self-report questionnaires), depressive syndromes (as measured by behavior checklists), and depressive disorders (as measured by diagnostic interviews). These three levels of depressive phenomena are hypothesized to reflect progressively severe manifestations of depressive problems, with depressed mood functioning as a risk for the development of the syndrome, and the syndrome functioning as a risk factor for the disorder. The data described above are generally consistent with this model, although the overlap of the three levels of depressive problems is imperfect. Moreover, it is important to be aware that children/adolescents who obtain high depressive symptom scores on self-report questionnaires, who score in the clinical range on the Anxious/Depressed syndrome, or who meet DSM-IV criteria for MDD or DD all represent significant clinical problems. That is, youths in all of these groups are experiencing significant levels of emotional distress and substantial levels of impairment in social functioning (Gerhardt et al., 1996; Gotlib et al., 1995).

ASSESSMENT OF CONSTRUCTS RELATED TO DEPRESSION

The biopsychosocial perspective on depression in young people (Petersen et al., 1993) emphasizes the need to consider a range of important correlates of depression. Assessment of only the core symptoms of a depressive syndrome or disorder will offer an inadequate understanding of a child's or adolescent's functioning, the potential causes of the problem, co-occurring or comorbid problems, and associated factors that could serve as the target for interventions. The number of associated factors is vast, however, and a thorough review of the assessment of these factors is beyond the scope of this chapter. An overview of these factors and their measurement, although limited, is instructive to guide a more comprehensive approach to the assessment of depression.

Biological Factors

Current evidence points to the central role of neuroendocrine functioning in depression (Brooks-Gunn, Petersen, & Compas, 1995; Shelton, Hollon, Purdon, & Loosen, 1991). The vegetative symptoms of depression (e.g., sleep and appetite disturbances), as well as mood disturbances, are believed to be related to dysregulation of the limbic system. The limbic system, involved in the regulation of drive, instinct, and emotions, has been studied through two key pathways: the hypothalamic–pituitary–adrenal (HPA) axis and the hypothalamic–pituitary–thyroid (HPT) axis.

In spite of significant advances in research on the biological correlates of depression in children and adolescents, there are no standardized biological measures that have proven useful in identifying depression in young people. Much of the adult and child/adolescent research on biological correlates of depression has focused on the study of the HPA axis. The functioning of the HPA axis is monitored by measurement of the level of cortisol released in response to a known suppressor, dexamethasone. Cortisol, a substance released by the adrenal glands in response to hormones released by the hypothalamus and pituitary, is described as preparing the organs for physical action. Through the dexamethasone suppression test (DST), depressed adults have been identified as having abnormally high levels of cortisol in the presence of dexamethasone (for a review, see Arana, Baldessarini, & Ornstein, 1985). The DST has been found to have an overall sensitivity of 45% and specificity of 96% with depressed adults. However, these rates are lower in children and adolescents (Kutcher et al., 1991; Hughes & Preskorn, 1989). For example, in one study of adolescents, only 40% of the depressed subjects and 69% of the normal subjects were identified correctly with the DST (Kutcher et al., 1991). Researchers of child/adolescent depression have concluded that the DST has not yet been shown to be a reliable or valid diagnostic tool for children or adolescents. The difference between child/adolescent depressives' and adult depressives' cortisol responses on the DST is thought to be a result of possible maturational differences of the neuroendocrine systems (Dahl et al., 1989, as cited in Kutcher et al., 1991). Additional explanations of the age difference in DST results offered by Dahl and associates (1989, as cited in Kutcher et al., 1991) include the following: (1) There may be age differences in the effects of chronic stress responses on cortisol patterns in children and adolescents; (2) adult depression may have had longer to affect the central nervous system; and (3) a history of adult antidepressive medication may affect adult neuroendocrine responsivity.

The other neuroendocrine pathway studied in relation to depression, the HPT axis, involves measurement of the level of thyrotropin-releasing hormone (TRH). TRH, believed to be associated with an increased sense of relaxation, activity, and positive mood (Garcia et al., 1991), stimulates the production of thyroid-stimulating hormone (TSH) in the pituitary gland. In depressed adults, administration of TRH causes "blunted or decreased" production and release of TSH (Garcia et al., 1991). Studies with depressed children/adolescents and controls matched for age and sex have failed to find consistent significant differences in the TSH levels in response to TRH (Garcia et al., 1991; Kutcher et al., 1991).

The neuroendocrine system's functioning in depressed children and adolescents has been further examined through levels of growth hormone. Whereas the evidence for hypersecretion of growth hormone in depressed adults remains conflicting, nocturnal secretions of growth hormone were found to be significantly higher in depressed adolescents (Kutcher et al., 1991). The measurement of nocturnal growth hormone showed 99% sensitivity and 93% specificity with respect to the identification of depressed adolescents. Nonetheless, the researchers suggested that more study of 24-hour differences in growth hormone levels in depressed adolescents is required, because of the complexity of growth hormone secretion. It is, however, the only neuroendocrine marker that reliably distinguished depressed adolescents from their normal peers.

Finally, disruptions of biological rhythms have been studied through the monitoring of sleep patterns. Research on adult depressives indicated that there are sleep continuity disturbances, reduced delta (slow-wave) sleep, high rapid-eye-movement (REM) density, and shortened REM latency (onset of REM after sleep begins) (see Emslie, Rush, Weinberg, Rintelmann, & Roffwarg, 1990). Although Emslie et al. (1990) cited evidence of some sleep disruptions among depressed adolescents (e.g., shortened REM latency, REM density and sleep continuity problems), they concluded that the findings are still too conflicting to use polysomnographic measures as a diagnostic tool of child/adolescent depression.

In sum, neuroendocrine dysfunction and biological rhythm disruptions appear to be related to child/adolescent depression, but at this time they cannot be reliably used as diagnostic measures of the presence, severity, and type of depressive symptoms. Differences in growth hormone levels and sleep patterns show some promise in terms of being able to distinguish depressed children or adolescents from their peers. It is unclear whether these biological processes also distinguish between depressed children/adolescents and other psychiatric groups (e.g., those with Conduct Disorder vs. those with MDD). Furthermore, all of the neuroendocrine assessment procedures require insertion of a catheter or needle to make frequent blood withdrawals over a 24-hour period. The invasive nature of these procedures raises serious questions about their use in outpatient settings.

Social-Cognitive Factors

Extensive empirical evidence now links a number of social-cognitive factors to levels of depressive symptoms in children and adolescents. These factors include self-schemas, cognitive errors or distortions, views of the self, hopelessness, perceived control, and attributional or explanatory style (see Kaslow, Brown, & Mee, 1994, for a review). With regard to each of these constructs, evidence suggests that depressive symptoms in children and adolescents are associated with more negative views of the self, the social world, and the future. The quality and level of standardization of measures of each of these domains vary considerably, however. As a result, some of these aspects of social-cognitive functioning are better suited than others for assessment in clinical contexts.

Several studies have indicated that higher levels of depressive symptoms are associated with more negative self-schemas. In both incidental recall of self-descriptive traits (Hammen & Zupan, 1984; Prieto, Cole, & Tageson, 1992) and recall of words from a word association task (Prieto et al., 1992; Whitman & Leitenberg, 1990), children with higher levels of depressive symptoms recalled more negative words. This suggests that depressive symptoms are associated with more negative cognitive structures, especially those that reflect representations of the self. Standardized measures of cognitive schemas that can be used in clinical contexts are not available, however.

Drawing on Beck's cognitive model of depression in adults, several investigators have examined cognitive errors and distortions that may be associated with depressive symptoms in children and adolescents. Measures of children's cognitive errors include the Cognitive Bias Questionnaire for Children (Haley, Fine, Marriage, Moretti, & Freeman, 1985), the Children's Negative Cognitive Error Questionnaire (Leitenberg et al., 1986), and the Automatic Thoughts Questionnaire for children (Kazdin, 1990). These measures are all self-report questionnaires that present respondents with either hypothetical situations (Leitenberg et al., 1986) or a list of statements (Kazdin, 1990) reflecting negative cognitive distortions about the self, the world, or the future. The reliability and validity of these scales have been established, and

they have been constructed specifically for use with children and adolescents (i.e., they are not simply downward extensions of adult measures).

Negative views of the self are central to cognitive models of depression in young people, and several measures are available to assess various aspects of children's self-concept, self-esteem, or perceptions of personal competence. The most comprehensive and widely used of these scales is the Self-Perception Profile for Children (SPPC; Harter, 1985) and the parallel form for adolescents (Harter, 1988). The SPPC is noteworthy in several regards. First, it was designed to assess multiple dimensions of the self, including perceptions of academic competence, social relations, physical appearance, athletic competence, behavioral conduct, and global self-worth. This yields a more detailed and differentiated profile of children's self-perceptions than can be obtained from other measures of self-esteem or self-concept. Second, the format of the scale is designed to reduce social desirability in responding. Third, the psychometric properties of the scale have been well established. And fourth, the SPPC has been used in a number of studies and has been shown to be related to depressive symptoms in children and adolescents (e.g., Harter & Marold, 1992; Robinson, Garber, & Hilsman, 1995).

Perceptions of personal control play an important role in several models of depression, and have been examined in studies of depressive symptoms in children. This research suggests that simple, unidimensional conceptualizations of control along an internal–external dimension are inadequate; more complete models indicate that control beliefs are the result of judgments of contingencies and personal competence (Skinner, 1995; Weisz, 1986). For example, Weisz and colleagues have shown that depressive symptoms are predicted more strongly by beliefs about competence and control than by beliefs about contingencies (Weisz, Weiss, Wasserman, & Rintoul, 1987), although a recent study found associations of depressive symptoms with both competence and contingency beliefs (Weisz et al., 1993). Contingency and competence beliefs were measured most successfully by a set of simple probes to assess each of these constructs—probes that can be used easily in both clinical and research contexts (Weisz et al., 1987).

Finally, the most extensive research on social-cognitive processes in child and adolescent depression has been based on the model of learned helplessness. This has involved measurement of what has been variously labeled "attributional style," "explanatory style," or "pessimism." Regardless of which label is applied, measures have focused on the ways in which children and adolescents perceive the causes of success and failure in their lives. The most widely used measure of attributional style is the Children's Attributional Style Questionnaire (CASQ; Seligman et al., 1984). The CASQ consists of a series of hypothetical success and failure situations; the respondent is asked to choose between two attributions for the cause of each event. The responses are forced choices that vary the dimensions of internal–external, stable—unstable, and global–specific causes. The psychometric properties of the CASQ are established.

A number of cross-sectional and prospective studies have used the CASQ and found a relationship between a maladaptive attributional style and depressive symptoms. Moreover, attributions interact with other factors, including stressful life events and self-perceptions of competence, in predicting depressive symptoms (e.g., Hilsman & Garber, 1995; Robinson et al., 1995; Turner & Cole, 1994). Furthermore, the findings of Nolen-Hoeksema, Girgus, and Seligman (1992) indicate that the association between attributions and depressive symptoms may change with development.

Behavioral and Interpersonal Factors

Deficits in interpersonal skills, problem-solving skills, and coping strategies are all implicated in depression in children and adolescents. Higher depressive symptoms are associated with poorer interpersonal competence (Cole, 1990, 1991; Cole & White, 1993), inadequate problem-solving skills (Rudolph, Hammen, & Burge, 1994), and a coping style associated with poor regulation or management of emotions (Garber, Braafladt, & Weiss, 1995). Unfortunately, many of the measures of these constructs are not easily adapted for use in current clinical practice, as they either involve peer nominations (which are difficult to obtain in clinical settings) or are measures with unknown or inadequate psychometric qualities.

Family Factors

The primary family characteristics that have been implicated in depression in young people are the presence of depressive symptoms or a depressive disorder in a mother or father (Hammen, 1991; Phares & Compas, 1992). Specifically, a history of depressive disorder in parents is a well-established risk factor for emotional and behavioral problems in children and adolescents, including

(but not limited to) increased risk for depressive symptoms and disorders (Hammen, 1991). In addition to a prior history of mood disorder, current levels of depressive symptoms in mothers have been shown to constitute a powerful predictor of depressive symptoms in children (e.g., Hammen et al., 1987; Hammen, Burge, & Adrian, 1991). These findings indicate that comprehensive assessment of depression in children and adolescents will be informed by the assessment of current depressive symptoms and prior history of depressive disorder in parents. This can be accomplished through the use of symptom inventories such as the BDI or the CES-D, and the use of structured diagnostic inventories designed for adults.

Other aspects of family functioning have been implicated in childhood depression, but the evidence and measures are not sufficiently well established to warrant use in clinical practice at this time. For example, childhood depression is associated with negative parent–child interactions; family environments that are perceived as less cohesive, less open to emotional expressiveness, and more hostile and rejecting; and more stressful family environments (see Hammen & Rudolph, 1996). Although these factors remain high priorities for future research, their application in clinical contexts appears to be premature at this time.

Environmental Factors

In addition to the family, other aspects of the social environment have been implicated as correlates of depressive symptoms in children and adolescents. Foremost among these is the occurrence of stressful major life events, as well as exposure to ongoing stresses and strains (sometimes referred to as "minor events," "daily hassles," or "recurrent strains"). Several prospective longitudinal studies have shown that stressors, particularly minor events or hassles, are predictive of subsequent depressive symptoms even after initial depressive symptoms are controlled for (e.g., Compas, Howell, Phares, Williams, & Giunta, 1989; DuBois, Felner, Brand, Adan, & Evans, 1992; Nolen-Hoeksema et al., 1992). That is, stress predicts increased depressive symptoms over time, but depressive symptoms also predict increased minor or chronic stress (Adrian & Hammen, 1993; Compas et al., 1989).

The measurement of major and minor stressful events in the lives of children and adolescents has been accomplished through questionnaires completed by parents (e.g., Coddington, 1972), questionnaires completed by children or adolescents (e.g., Compas, Davis, Forsythe, & Wagner, 1987), and structured interviews with parents and/or children and adolescents (e.g., Hammen, 1988). Although these procedures are useful in generating detailed information about current sources of stress in the lives of children and adolescents, most are quite long and thus too cumbersome to be used in clinical practice.

Comorbid Disorders and Co-Occurring Problems

Symptoms, syndromes, or disorders rarely occur alone during childhood and adolescence. Nowhere is this phenomenon, referred to as the "covariation" or "co-occurrence" of symptoms and the "comorbidity" of disorders, more evident than for depressive problems in children and youths (Angold & Costello, 1993; Compas & Hammen, 1994).

Several studies have shown that during childhood and adolescence, as in adulthood, depressed mood is closely related to other negative emotions. First, monomethod studies (i.e., studies relying on a single method, such as child/adolescent self-reports) have failed to distinguish depressed mood (and other symptoms of depression) from other negative emotions, including anxiety, anger, and hostility. For example, Saylor et al. (1984) found that children and adolescents classified as high and low in depressive symptoms on the CDI also differed significantly on self-reported anxiety. Furthermore, multitrait–multimethod validity studies examining reports from different informants (e.g., children/adolescents, teachers, parents) of various negative emotions (depression, anxiety, anger) have found that strong associations between youths' depressed mood and other negative emotions, especially anxiety, are not limited to youths' self-reports of emotions. That is, reports of youths' depressed mood by one group of informants are correlated more highly with reports of other negative emotions by those same informants than they are correlated with reports of depressed mood obtained by other groups of informants (e.g., Wolfe et al., 1987). These findings are consistent with the results of principal-component analyses of the CBCL, YSR, and TRF, which revealed the syndrome of mixed anxiety and depression symptoms discussed earlier.

It is noteworthy that parent and teacher reports of youths' emotions and behaviors also show considerable covariance in levels of depressed and anxious mood (Finch et al., 1989). Thus, the association of depressed mood with other elements of the broader construct of negative affect (see below) is not the result of a simple bias in young people's reports about their internal emotional states. Finch et al. (1989) suggest that anxiety and depression are not separable in children and adolescents, and that the distinction between these two forms of negative affect should be put to rest. These findings must be interpreted with a level of caution, however, as there is some degree of item contamination between measures of depressed and anxious mood. For example, Brady and Kendall (1992) have identified several items that are included on both the CDI and standard self-report scales of anxiety. The extent to which item similarity on these measures accounts for the degree of association between the scales has not been clarified.

Concerns about confounding of measures notwithstanding, these findings can be understood by considering them within the broader framework of theories of emotion (e.g., Watson & Tellegen, 1985). Extensive evidence from studies of the structure of emotions in children, adolescents, college students, and adults indicates that self-rated mood is dominated by two broad factors: "negative affect," which is composed of negative emotions and distress, and "positive affect," which is made up of positive emotions (King et al., 1991; Watson, 1988; Watson & Tellegen, 1985). Depressed mood is one component of the broader construct of negative affect, whereas positive emotions are important in distinguishing among subtypes of negative emotion (Watson & Clark, 1984).

Research with adults indicates that although depressed mood is strongly intercorrelated with other negative emotions, it appears to be distinguishable from anxiety, if not other forms of negative affect, on the basis of its association with positive emotions (e.g., happiness, excitement, pride, contentment). Specifically, whereas anxiety is uncorrelated with positive affect, depressed mood shows a consistent inverse relationship with positive affect (Watson & Kendall, 1989). Thus, highly anxious individuals may be low, moderate, or high in positive affect, as anxiety and positive emotions can co-occur. In contrast, highly depressed individuals are likely to experience low levels of positive emotions (i.e., anhedonia). The relation between positive affect and depressed mood during adolescence warrants further research. In general, research suggests that sad or depressed mood is a phenomenologically distinct emotional state that, although closely related to the experience of other forms of negative affect, is distinguished by its relation to positive affect (Watson & Clark, 1992).

The intercorrelations of the Anxious/Depressed core syndrome with the other core syndromes indicate substantial covariation. These correlations have been reported separately for the CBCL, TRF, and YSR for clinically referred and nonreferred adolescent boys and girls (Achenbach, 1991a). Although these correlations vary substantially, ranging from .27 (with Delinquent for referred boys on the YSR) to .80 (with Self-Destructive for referred boys on the YSR), the overall mean correlation of the Anxious/Depressed syndrome with the other core syndromes is .51, indicating substantial covariance. Furthermore, the Anxious/Depressed syndrome correlated highly with both internalizing syndromes (Withdrawn, Somatic Complaints) and externalizing syndromes (Aggressive Behavior, Attention Problems). Thus, the degree of covariation of the Anxious/Depressed syndrome with other syndromes is substantial. The covariation of the Anxious/Depressed syndrome with other syndromes remains high after measurement factors are controlled for (Hinden, Compas, Achenbach, & Howell, in press). Further research is needed to understand the implications of this high degree of covariation for the etiology, course, treatment, and prevention of depressive syndromes (Compas & Hammen, 1994).

The comorbidity of MDD with other psychiatric diagnoses has been examined in epidemiological studies of nonreferred samples of children/ adolescents in the community. Community samples rather than clinical samples are necessary to determine true rates of comorbidity, as rates of comorbidity in clinical samples will be disproportionately high because of a number of factors (Caron & Rutter, 1991). Comorbidity appears to be the rule for child/adolescent depression (for reviews, see Brady & Kendall, 1992; Compas & Hammen, 1994; Angold & Costello, 1993). The recent community studies by Lewinsohn and colleagues described above are illustrative in this regard (Lewinsohn et al., 1991; Rohde et al., 1991). The current comorbidity rate for MDD and DD was 20 times greater than that expected by chance, and the lifetime comorbidity rate was three times greater than chance (Lewinsohn et al., 1991). Levels of comorbidity with disorders other than mood disorders were also high, as 43% of adolescents with a depressive disorder received at least one additional diagnosis—a rate that was 9.5 times greater than chance (Rohde et al., 1991). Current comorbidity was highest for anxiety disorders (18%), substance use disorders (14%), and disruptive behavior disorders (8%).

IMPLICATIONS FOR ASSESSMENT AND INTERVENTION

Given the possible relations, as well as differences, among levels of depressive phenomena, how can researchers and clinicians select from among the myriad of methods for assessing child and adolescent depression? More specifically, how is one to decide among self-report questionnaires, behavior checklists, and diagnostic interviews? The following criteria are offered to guide the choice of measures of depression in children and adolescents.

1. *The measure must reflect a specific diagnostic or classification scheme.* That is, the researcher or practitioner must readily acknowledge the taxonomic paradigm that is guiding his or her work and select a measure commensurate with that paradigm. For example, it is widely recognized that self-report measures such as the CDI are adequate measures of depressive symptoms, but do not provide adequate information on the severity and duration of the full complement of depressive symptoms to enable the clinician to make a diagnostic judgment. As indicated above, the various assessment methods are linked to specific taxonomic systems.

2. *The measure must be psychometrically sound.* Most of the measures that have been reviewed meet the minimal criteria with regard to internal-consistency reliability and test–retest reliability. However, test–retest reliability of measures of depressed affect may differ substantially for clinically referred and nonreferred populations (e.g., Saylor et al., 1984). As indicated above, validity has proven a more difficult issue to address. Some measures have also established construct validity through factor analysis or principal-component analysis of their underlying structure. Establishing criterion validity has proven much more difficult for each of the types of measures that we have reviewed, in part because of the low rates of agreement across different informants. In spite of these limitations, the majority of the instruments described in this chapter meet the minimum criteria for use in research and practice.

3. *The measure must be developmentally appropriate for use with children and adolescents.* The content and wording of the items must have been generated for use with this age group. If this is not the case, the measure may reflect the error of making either a downward extension of an adult measure or an upward extension of a child measure. Unfortunately, most of the assessment

procedures for child/adolescent depression fail to meet this criterion. For example, the BDI has been extended to research with adolescents without any changes in the content or wording of the items to make them suitable for this age group. Further refinement of some measures may be needed to insure that they are developmentally appropriate for adolescents.

4. *The measure must provide sufficient epidemiological data to developmental and normative data comparisons.* This is especially important if a cutoff or criterion score is to be used to distinguish between clinical and nonclinical groups. Behavior checklists have been used to generate extensive, nationally representative normative data bases. As one might expect, norms for scales of depressed mood are much more limited, since these measures were not designed for use in making categorical decisions. Diagnostic judgments using clinical interviews are made independently of normative data on children/adolescents and rely instead on clinical criteria. However, interpretation of these criteria will be strengthened as larger normative data sets are generated through clinical interviews with community samples.

5. *If one adheres to a categorical diagnostic model, the measure must provide criteria for making distinctions between clinical disorders and subclinical phenomena.* Furthermore, it is important that these criteria not be solely a function of the judgment of the individual clinician. DSM-IV criteria and the RDC have been used as the basis for most diagnostic decisions with the K-SADS, CAS, DISC, and other structured interviews. These criteria appear to be adequate, as acceptable levels of interrater agreement have been generated for these interviews.

6. *The measure must be sufficiently sensitive to change for use in the assess of prevention and treatment effects.* The first step in determining sensitivity to change is establishing relatively high test–retest reliability over very short periods of time, to rule out effects of random error in responses or large fluctuations in scores as a result of highly state-dependent factors. In addition, data must be provided to indicate that scores tend to be highly stable over longer periods of time in the absence of any intervention or other major perturbation. The field could benefit from more longitudinal data obtained on all of the measures described above.

7. *The measure must be sufficiently broad in focus to allow for determination of co-occurrence of other symptoms or comorbidity of other disorders.* This is a limitation of many measures that are designed to assess only specified symptoms of depression. Although these measures may be sensitive to depressive symptoms, they may lead the researcher or clinician to the mistaken conclusion that symptomatic elevations are limited to a particular depressive syndrome or disorder. Possible covariation with other symptoms or comorbidity with other disorders will be overlooked.

8. *Measures of depressive symptoms or disorders need to be complemented by measures of related domains of functioning, including social-cognitive processes, parental depressive symptoms, and interpersonal competence.* Data obtained from these measures will play an important role in the planning, implementation, and evaluation of interventions to address depressive problems in children and adolescents. The selection of measures of other constructs should be guided by one's conceptual framework and by data that support the utility of these constructs in understanding the nature and course of depressive problems in young people. As noted above, measures of a number of these constructs (e.g., stressful life events) are not currently well suited for use in clinical practice, but are likely to continue to play an important role in research.

With these criteria in mind, it is useful to consider a "multiple-gating" procedure in clinical practice and research, as suggested by several investigators (e.g., Roberts et al., 1991). However, because of the need to attend to the high rates of covariance of depressive symptoms with other symptoms and comorbidity of depressive syndromes and disorders with other disorders, the procedures recommended here are slightly different from those outlined by others. As a first step, broad-band checklists should be used to assess a wide range of symptoms and problems, including (but not limited to) depressive symptoms. These checklists should include the perspectives of children/adolescents, parents, and teachers as the primary interested parties in identifying child/adolescent depression. The integrative package of the YSR, CBCL, and TRF offers the most integrated set of measures to accomplish this goal (Achenbach, 1991a). Along with these broad-band measures, a more focused measure of depressive symptoms should be used to target the emotions associated with depressive disorders. Of the many measures that are available, the CDI has shown the greatest strengths for assessing recent depressive symptoms. The CDI should be administered on at least two occasions over a 2-week period to determine the persistent versus transient nature of these symptoms. These four measures (the YSR, CBCL, TRF, and CDI) can be used to identify individuals who exceed clinical criteria on the Anxious/Depressed syndrome on the multivariate scales and on the total score on the CDI. In addition to examining scores on the Anxious/Depressed syndrome, the clinician can accomplish an initial screening for the presence of clinical elevations on other problems by examining scores on the other seven core syndromes on the YSR, CBCL, and TRF. In summary, the CDI, YSR, CBCL, and TRF should be used to screen for clinically significant elevations in negative affect, the core Anxious/Depressed syndrome, and other clinical syndromes that could indicate the presence of other internalizing and/or externalizing problems.

Individuals who exceed the clinical cutoff on the CDI or the Anxious/Depressed syndrome on one or more of the checklists should then be designated for further assessment through a diagnostic interview to determine the presence of diagnosable depressive disorders. Through this sequence of assessment procedures, several distinct subgroups of individuals could be identified who warrant different intervention procedures.

REFERENCES

Achenbach, T. M. (1985). *Assessment and taxonomy of child and adolescent psychopathology.* Beverly Hills, CA: Sage.

Achenbach, T. M. (1991a). *Integrative guide for the 1991 CBCL/4–18, YSR, and TRF Profiles.* Burlington: University of Vermont, Department of Psychiatry.

Achenbach, T. M. (1991b). *Manual for the Child Behavior Checklist and 1991 Profile.* Burlington: University of Vermont, Department of Psychiatry.

Achenbach, T. M. (1991c). *Manual for the Teacher's Report Form and 1991 Profile.* Burlington: University of Vermont, Department of Psychiatry.

Achenbach, T. M. (1991d). *Manual for the Youth Self-Report and 1991 Profile.* Burlington: University of Vermont, Department of Psychiatry.

Achenbach, T. M. (1993). *Empirically based taxonomy.* Burlington: University of Vermont, Department of Psychiatry.

Achenbach, T. M., Conners, C. K., Quay, H. C., Verhulst, F. C., & Howell, C. T. (1989). Replication of empirically derived syndromes as a basis for a taxonomy of child/adolescent psychopathology. *Journal of Abnormal Child Psychology, 17,* 299–323.

Achenbach, T. M., & Edelbrock, C. (1981). Behavioral problems and competencies reported by parents of normal and disturbed children aged four to sixteen. *Monographs of the Society for Research in Child Development, 46*(1, Serial No. 188).

Achenbach, T. M., Howell, C. T., Quay, H. C., & Conners, C. K. (1991). National survey of problems and competencies among four- to sixteen-year-olds: Parents' reports for normative and clinical samples. *Monographs of the Society for Research in Child Development, 56*(Whole No. 3).

Achenbach, T. M., McConaughy, S. H., & Howell, C. T. (1987). Child/adolescent behavioral and emotional problems: Implications of cross-informant correlations for situational specificity. *Psychological Bulletin, 101,* 213–232.

Adrian, C., & Hammen, C. (1993). Stress exposure and stress generation in children of depressed mothers. *Journal of Consulting and Clinical Psychology, 61,* 354–359.

American Psychiatric Association (1994). *Diagnostic and statistical manual of mental disorders* (4th ed.). Washington, DC: Author.

Angold, A. (1988). Childhood and adolescent depression: I. Epidemiological and aetiological aspects. *British Journal of Psychiatry, 152,* 601–617.

Angold, A., & Costello, E. J. (1993). Depressive comorbidity in children and adolescents: Empirical, theoretical, and methodological issues. *American Journal of Psychiatry, 150,* 1779–1791.

Angold, A., & Rutter, M. (1992). Effects of age and pubertal status on depression in a large clinical sample. *Development and Psychopathology, 4,* 5–28.

Arana, G. W., Baldessarini, R. J., & Ornstein, M. (1985). The dexamethasone suppression test for diagnosis and prognosis in psychiatry. *Archives of General Psychiatry, 42,* 1193–1204.

Archer, R. P., Pancoast, D. L., & Klinefelter, D. (1989). A comparison of MMPI code types produced by traditional and recent adolescent norms. *Psychological Assessment: A Journal of Consulting and Clinical Psychology, 1,* 23–29.

Beck, A. T., Ward, C. H., Mendelson, M., Mock, J. E., & Erbaugh, J. K. (1961). An inventory for measuring depression. *Archives of General Psychiatry, 4,* 561–571.

Bidaut-Russell, M., Reich, W., Cottler, L. B., Robins, L. N., Compton, W. M., & Mattison, R. E. (1995). The Diagnostic Interview Schedule for Children (PC-DISC v. 3.0): Parents and adolescents suggest reasons for expecting discrepant results. *Journal of Abnormal Child Psychology, 23,* 641–659.

Brady, E. U., & Kendall, P. C. (1992). Comorbidity of anxiety and depression in children and adolescents. *Psychological Bulletin, 111,* 244–255.

Brooks-Gunn, J., Petersen, A. C., & Compas, B. E. (1995). Physiological processes and the development of childhood and adolescent depression. In I. M. Goodyer (Ed.), *The depressed child and adolescent: Developmental and clinical perspectives* (pp. 81–109). New York: Cambridge University Press.

Cantwell, D. P., & Baker, L. (1991). Manifestations of depressive affect in adolescence. *Journal of Youth and Adolescence, 20,* 121–133.

Carlson, G. A. (1994). Adolescent bipolar disorder: Phenomenology and treatment implications. In W. M. Reynolds & H. F. Johnston (Eds.), *Handbook of depression in children and adolescents* (pp. 41–60). New York: Plenum Press.

Carlson, G. A., & Cantwell, D. P. (1980). Unmasking masked depression in children and adolescents. *American Journal of Psychiatry, 137,* 445–449.

Caron, C., & Rutter, M. (1991). Comorbidity in child psychopathology: Concepts, issues and research strategies. *Journal of Child Psychology and Psychiatry, 32,* 1063–1080.

Chambers, W. J., Puig-Antich, J., Hirsch, M., Paez, P., Ambrosini, P. J., Tabrizi, M., & Davies, M. (1985). The assessment of affective disorders in children and adolescents by semistructured interview. *Archives of General Psychiatry, 42,* 696–702.

Cicchetti, D., Rogosch, F. A., & Toth, S. L. (1994). A developmental psychopathology perspective on depression in children. In W. M. Reynolds & H. F. Johnston (Eds.), *Handbook of depression in children and adolescents* (pp. 97–122). New York: Plenum Press.

Clarke, G. N., Lewinsohn, P. M., Hops, H., & Seeley, J. R. (1992). A self- and parent-report measure of adolescent depression: The Child Behavior Checklist Depression scale. *Behavioral Assessment, 14,* 443–463.

Coddington, R. D. (1972). The significance of life events as etiologic factors in the diseases of children—I. *Journal of Psychosomatic Research, 16,* 205–213.

Cole, D. A. (1990). Relation of social and academic competence to depressive symptoms in childhood. *Journal of Abnormal Psychology, 99,* 422–429.

Cole, D. A. (1991). Preliminary support for a competency-based model of depression in children. *Journal of Abnormal Psychology, 100,* 181–190.

Cole, D. A., & Turner, J. E. (1993). Models of cognitive mediation and moderation in child depression. *Journal of Abnormal Psychology, 102,* 271–281.

Cole, D. A., & White, K. (1993). Structure of peer impressions of children's competence: Validation of the peer nomination of multiple competencies. *Psychological Assessment, 5,* 449–456.

Compas, B. E., Davis, G. E., Forsythe, C. J., & Wagner, B. M. (1987). Assessment of major and daily stressful events during adolescence: The Adolescent Perceived Events Scale. *Journal of Consulting and Clinical Psychology, 55,* 534–541.

Compas, B. E., Ey, S., & Grant, K. E. (1993). Taxonomy, assessment, and diagnosis of depression during adolescence. *Psychological Bulletin, 114,* 323–344.

Compas, B. E., Grant, K., & Ey, S. (1994). Psychosocial stress and child/adolescent depression: Can we be more specific? In W. M. Reynolds & H. F. Johnston (Eds.), *Handbook of depression in children and adolescents* (pp. 509–523). New York: Plenum Press.

Compas, B. E., & Hammen, C. L. (1994). Depression in childhood and adolescence: Covariation and comorbidity in development. In R. J. Haggerty, N. Garmezy, M. Rutter, & L. Sherrod (Eds.), *Risk and resilience in children: Developmental approaches* (pp. 223–267). New York: Cambridge University Press.

Compas, B. E., Howell, D. C., Phares, V., Williams, R. A., & Giunta, C. T. (1989). Risk factors for emotional–behavioral problems in young adolescents: A prospective analysis of adolescent and parent stress. *Journal of Consulting and Clinical Psychology, 57,* 732–740.

Compas, B. E., Oppedisano, G., Connor, J. K., Gerhardt, C. A., Hinden, B. R., Achenbach, T. M., & Hammen, C. (in press). Gender differences in depressive symptoms in adolescence: Comparison of national samples of clinically-referred and non-referred youth. *Journal of Consulting and Clinical Psychology.*

Connor, J. K., Compas, B. E., Gerhardt, C. A., Oppedisano, G., Hinden, B. R., & Achenbach, T. M. (1996). *Analogue measures of DSM mood and anxiety disorders.* Manuscript submitted for publication.

Conners, C. K. (1973). Rating scales for use in drug studies with children. *Psychopharmacology Bulletin: Special Issue, Pharmacotherapy with Children,* 24–84.

Costello, E. J., Edelbrock, C. S., & Costello, A. J. (1985). Validity of the NIMH Diagnostic Interview Schedule for Children: A comparison between psychiatric & pediatric referrals. *Journal of Abnormal and Child Psychology, 13*(4), 579–595.

Costello, A. J., Edelbrock, C., Dulcan, M. K., Kalas, R., & Klaric, S. H. (1984). *Development and testing of the NIMH Diagnostic Interview Schedule for Children in a clinic population.* (Final report, Contract No. RFP-DB-81-0027). Rockville, MD: Center for Epidemiologic Studies, National Institute of Mental Health.

Coyne, J. C., & Downey, G. (1991). Social factors and psychopathology: Stress, social support, and coping processes. *Annual Review of Psychology, 42,* 401–425.

DeGroot, A., Koot, H. M., & Verhulst, F. C. (1994). Cross-cultural generalizability of the Child Behavior Checklist cross-informant syndromes. *Psychological Assessment, 7,* 299–323.

DuBois, D. L., Felner, R. D., Brand, S., Adan, A. M., & Evans, E. G. (1992). A prospective study of life stress, social support, and adaptation in early adolescence. *Child Development, 63,* 542–557.

Edelbrock, C., & Costello, A. J. (1988a). Convergence between statistically derived behavior problem syndromes and child psychiatric diagnoses. *Journal of Abnormal Child Psychology, 16,* 219–231.

Edelbrock, C., & Costello, A. J. (1988b). Structured psychiatric interviews for children. In M. Rutter, A. H. Tuma, & I. S. Lann (Eds.) *Assessment and diagnosis in child psychopathology* (pp. 87–112). New York: Guilford Press.

Edelbrock, C., Costello, A. J., Dulcan, M. K., Kalas, R., & Conover, N. C. (1985). Age differences in the reliability of the psychiatric interview of the child. *Child Development, 56,* 265–275.

Emslie, G. J., Rush, J., Weinberg, W. A., Rintelmann, J. W., & Roffwarg, H. P. (1990). Children with major depression show reduced rapid eye movement latencies. *Archives of General Psychiatry, 47,* 119–124.

Fechner-Bates, S., Coyne, J. C., & Schwenk, T. L. (1994). The relationship of self-reported distress to depressive disorders and other psychopathology. *Journal of Consulting and Clinical Psychology, 62,* 550–559.

Finch, A. J., Lipovsky, J. A., & Casat, C. D. (1989). Anxiety and depression in children & adolescents: Negative affectivity or separate constructs? In P. C. Kendall & D. Watson (Eds.), *Anxiety and depression: Distinctive and overlapping features.* New York: Academic Press.

Fisher, P. W., Shaffer, D., Piacentini, J., Lapkin, J., Kafantaris, V., Leonard, H., & Herzog, D. B. (1993). Sensitivity of the Diagnostic Interview Schedule for Children, 2nd edition (DISC-2.1) for specific diagnoses of children and adolescents. *Journal of the American Academy of Child and Adolescent Psychiatry, 32,* 666–673.

Fleming, J. E., & Offord, D. R. (1990). Epidemiology of childhood depressive disorders: A critical review. *Journal of the American Academy of Child and Adolescent Psychiatry, 29,* 571–580.

Garber, J., Braafladt, N., & Weiss, B. (1995). Affect regulation in children and young adolescents. *Development and Psychopathology, 7,* 93–115.

Garcia, M. R., et al. (1991). Thyroid stimulating hormone response to thyrotropin in prepubertal depression. *Journal of the American Academy of Child and Adolescent Psychiatry, 30,* 398–406.

Garrison, C. Z., Addy, C. L., Jackson, K. L., McKeown, R. E., & Waller, J. L. (1991). The CES-D as a screen for depression and other psychiatric disorders in adolescents. *Journal of the American Academy of Child and Adolescent Psychiatry, 30,* 636–641.

Ge, X., Lorenz, F. O., Conger, R. D., Elder, G. H., & Simons, R. L., (1994). Trajectories of stressful life events and depressive symptoms during adolescence. *Developmental Psychology, 30,* 467–483.

Gerhardt, C., Compas, B. E., Connor, J. K., Hinden, B. R., & Achenbach, T. M. (1996). *Understanding the nature of adolescent depression: Relations among mood, syndrome, and diagnosis.* Manuscript submitted for publication.

Giaconia, R. M., Reinherz, H. Z., Silverman, A. B., Pakiz, B., Frost, A. K., & Cohen, E. (1993). Ages of onset of psychiatric disorders in a community population of older adolescents. *Journal of the American Academy of Child and Adolescent Psychiatry, 33,* 706–717.

Gotlib, I. H., & Hammen, C. L. (1992). *Psychological aspects of depression: Toward a cognitive-interpersonal integration.* London: Wiley.

Gotlib, I. H., Lewinsohn, P. M., & Seeley, J. R. (1995). Symptoms versus a diagnosis of depression: Differences in psychosocial functioning. *Journal of Consulting and Clinical Psychology, 63,* 90–100.

Haley, G. M. T., Fine, S., Marriage, K., Moretti, M. M., & Freeman, R. J. (1985). Cognitive bias and depression in psychiatrically disturbed children and adolescents. *Journal of Consulting and Clinical Psychology, 53,* 535–537.

Hammen, C. (1988). Self-cognitions, stressful events, and the prediction of depression in children of depressed mothers. *Journal of Abnormal Child Psychology, 16,* 347–360.

Hammen, C. (1991). *Depression runs in families: The social context of risk and resilience in children of depressed mothers.* New York: Springer-Verlag.

Hammen, C., Adrian, C., Gordon, D., Burge, D., Jaenicke, C., & Hiroto, D. (1987). Children of depressed mothers: Maternal strain and symptoms predictors of dysfunction. *Journal of Abnormal Psychology, 96,* 190–198.

Hammen, C., Burge, D., & Adrian, C. (1991). Timing of mother and child depression in a longitudinal study of children at risk. *Journal of Consulting and Clinical Psychology, 59,* 341–345.

Hammen, C. & Compas, B. E. (1994). Unmasking unmasked depression in children and adolescents: The problem of comorbidity. *Clinical Psychology Review, 14,* 585–603.

Hammen, C., & Rudolph, K. D. (1996). Childhood depression. In E. J. Mash & R. A. Barkley (Eds.), *Child psychopathology* (pp. 153–195). New York: Guilford Press.

Hammen, C., & Zupan, B. A. (1984). Self-schemas, depression, and processing of personal information in children. *Journal of Experimental Child Psychology, 37,* 598–608.

Harter, S. (1985). *The Self-Perception Profile for Children.* Denver, CO: University of Denver, Department of Psychology.

Harter, S. (1988). *The Self-Perception Profile for Adolescents.* Denver, CO: University of Denver, Department of Psychology.

Harter, S., & Marold, D. B. (1992). The directionality of the link between self-esteem and affect: Beyond causal modeling. In D. Cicchetti & S. L. Toth (Eds.), *Rochester Symposium on Developmental Psychopathology: Vol. 5. The self and its disorders* (pp. 333–369). Rochester, NY: University of Rochester Press.

Herjanic, B., Herjanic, M., Brown, F., & Wheatt, T. (1975). Are children reliable reporters? *Journal of Abnormal Child Psychology, 3,* 41–48.

Hilsman, R., & Garber, J. (1995). A test of the cognitive diathesis–stress model of depression in children: Academic stressors, attributional style, perceived competence, and control. *Journal of Personality and Social Psychology, 69,* 370–380.

Hinden, B. R., Compas, B. E., Achenbach, T. M., Hammen, C., Oppedisano, G., Connor, J. K., & Gerhardt, C. A. (1996). *Charting the course of depressive symptoms during adolescence: Do we have the right map?* Manuscript submitted for publication.

Hinden, B. R., Compas, B. E., Achenbach, T. M., & Howell, D. C. (1997). Comorbidity of depression during adolescence: Separating fact from artifact. *Journal of Consulting and Clinical Psychology, 65,* 6–14.

Hodges, K. H. (1990). Depression and anxiety in children: A comparison of self-report questionnaires to clinical interview. *Psychological Assessment: A Journal of Consulting and Clinical Psychology, 2,* 376–381.

Hodges, K. H., & Cools, J. N. (1990). Structured diagnostic interviews. In A. M. La Greca (Ed.), *Through the eyes of the child* (pp. 109–149). Boston: Allyn & Bacon.

Hodges, K. H., Cools, J. N., & McKnew, D. (1989). Test–retest reliability of a clinical research interview for children: The Child Assessment Schedule (CAS). *Psychological Assessment: A Journal of Consulting and Clinical Psychology, 1,* 317–322.

Hodges, K. H., & Craighead, W. E. (1990). Relationship of Children's Depression Inventory factors to diagnosed depression. *Psychological Assessment: A Journal of Consulting and Clinical Psychology, 2,* 489–492.

Hodges, K. H., Gordon, Y., & Lennon, M. (1990). Parent–child agreement on symptoms assessed via a clinical research interview for children: The Child Assessment Schedule (CAS). *Journal of Child Psychology and Psychiatry, 31,* 427–431.

Hodges, K. H., Kline, J., Stern, L., Cytryn, L., & McKnew, D. (1982). The development of a Child Assessment Schedule for research and clinical use. *Journal of Abnormal Child Psychology, 10,* 173–189.

Hodges, K. H., Saunders, W., Kashani, J., Hamlett, K., & Thompson, R. (1990). Internal consistency of DSM-III diagnoses using the symptom scales of the Child Assessment Schedule (CAS). *Journal of the American Academy of Child and Adolescent Psychiatry, 29,* 635–641.

Hughes, C. W., & Preskorn, S. H. (1989). Depressive syndromes in children and adolescents: Diagnosis and treatment. *Annals of Clinical Psychiatry, 1,* 109–118.

Jensen, P., Roper, M., Fisher, P. W., Piacentini, J., Canino, G., Richters, J., Rubio-Stipec, M., Dulcan, M., Goodman, S., Davies, McRae, D., Shaffer, D., Bird, H., Lahey, B., & Schwab-Stone, M. (1995). Test–retest reliability of the Diagnostic Interview Schedule for Children (DISC 2.1): Parent, child, and combined algorithms. *Archives of General Psychiatry, 52,* 61–71.

Kandel, D. B., & Davies, M. (1982) Epidemiology of depressive mood in adolescents. *Archives of General Psychiatry, 39,* 1205–1212.

Kashani, J. H., Carlson, G. A., Beck, N. C., Hoeper, E. W., Corcoran, C. M., McAllister, J. A., Fallahi, C., Rosenberg, T. K., & Reid, J. C. (1987). Depression, depressive symptoms, and depressed mood among a community sample of adolescents. *American Journal of Psychiatry, 144,* 931–934.

Kashani, J. H., Reid, J. C., & Rosenberg, T. K. (1989). Levels of hopelessness in children and adolescents: A developmental perspective. *Journal of Consulting and Clinical Psychology, 57,* 496–499.

Kaslow, N. J., Brown, R. T., & Mee, L. L. (1994). Cognitive and behavioral correlates of childhood depression: A developmental perspective. In W. M. Reynolds & H. F. Johnston (Eds.), *Handbook of depression in children and adolescents* (pp. 97–122). New York: Plenum Press.

Kazdin, A. E. (1990). Evaluation of the Automatic Thoughts Questionnaire: Negative cognitive processes and depression among children. *Psychological Assessment, 2,* 73–79.

Kazdin, A. E., Esveldt-Dawson, K., Unis, A. S., & Rancurello, M. D. (1983). Child and parent evaluations of depression and aggression in psychiatric inpatient children. *Journal of Abnormal Child Psychology, 11,* 401–413.

Kazdin, A. E., Rogers, A., & Colbus, D. (1986). The Hopelessness Scale for Children: Psychometric characteristics and concurrent validity. *Journal of Consulting and Clinical Psychology, 54,* 241–245.

Kendall, P. C., Cantwell, D. P., & Kazdin, A. E. (1989). Depression in children and adolescents: Assessment issues and recommendations. *Cognitive Therapy and Research, 13,* 109–146.

King, N. J., Ollendick, T. H., & Gallone, E. (1991). Negative affectivity in children and adolescents: Relations between anxiety and depression. *Clinical Psychology Review, 11,* 441–460.

Kovacs, M. (1980). Rating scales to assess depression in school-aged children. *Acta Paediatrica, 46,* 305–315.

Kovacs, M. (1985). The Interview Schedule for Children. *Psychopharmacology Bulletin, 21,* 991–994.

Kovacs, M. (1989). Affective disorders in children and adolescents. *American Psychologist, 44,* 209–215.

Kutcher, S., Malkin, D., Silverberg, J., Marton, P., Williamson, P., Malkin, A., Szalai, J., & Katic, M. (1991). Nocturnal cortisol, thyroid stimulating hormone, and growth hormone secretory profiles in depressed adolescents. *Journal of the American Academy of Child and Adolescent Psychiatry, 30*(3), 407–414.

Leadbeater, B. J., Blatt, S. J., & Quinlan, D. M. (1995). Gender-linked vulnerabilities to depressive symptoms, stress, and problem behaviors in adolescents. *Journal of Research on Adolescence, 5*, 1–29.

Leitenberg, H., Yost, L. W., & Carroll-Wilson, M. (1986). Negative cognitive errors in children: Questionnaire development, normative data, and comparisons between children with and without self-reported symptoms of depression, low self-esteem, and evaluation anxiety. *Journal of Consulting and Clinical Psychology, 54*, 528–536.

Lewinsohn, P. M., Hops, H., Roberts, R. E., Seeley, J. R., & Andrews, J. A. (1993). Adolescent psychopathology: I. Prevalence and incidence of depression and other DSM-III-R disorders in high school students. *Journal of Abnormal Psychology, 102*, 133–144.

Lewinsohn, P. M., Rohde, P., Seeley, J. R., & Hops, H. (1991). Comorbidity of unipolar depression: I. Major depression with dysthymia. *Journal of Abnormal Psychology, 100*, 205–213.

Lipovsky, J. A., Finch, A. J., & Belter, R. W. (1989). Assessment of depression in adolescents: Objective and projective measures. *Journal of Personality Assessment, 53*, 449–458.

McGee, R., Feehan, M., Williams, S., Partridge, F., Silva, P., & Kelly, J. (1990). DSM-III disorders in a large sample of adolescents. *Journal of the American Academy of Child and Adolescent Psychiatry, 29*, 611–619.

Miller, L. C. (1984). *Louisville Behavior Checklist manual.* Los Angeles: Western Psychological Services.

Nolen-Hoeksema, S., & Girgus, J. S. (1994). The emergence of gender differences in depression during adolescence. *Psychological Bulletin, 115*, 424–443.

Nolen-Hoeksema, S., Girgus, J. S., & Seligman, M. E. P. (1992). Predictors and consequences of childhood depressive symptoms: A 5-year longitudinal study. *Journal of Abnormal Psychology, 101*, 405–422.

Nurcombe, B., Seifer, R., Scioli, A., Tramontana, M. G., Grapentine, W. L., & Beauchesne, H. C. (1989). Is Major Depressive Disorder in adolescence a distinct entity? *Journal of the American Academy of Child and Adolescent Psychiatry, 28*, 333–342.

Orvaschel, H., Puig-Antich, J., Chambers, W., Tabrizi, M. A., & Johnson, R. (1982). Retrospective assessment of prepubertal major depression with the Kiddie-SADS-E. *Journal of the American Academy of Child Psychiatry, 21*, 392–397.

Petersen, A. C., Compas, B. E., & Brooks-Gunn, J. (1992). *Depression in adolescence: Current knowledge, research directions, and implications for programs and policy.* Washington DC: Carnegie Council on Adolescent Development.

Petersen, A. C., Compas, B. E., Brooks-Gunn, J., Stemmler, M., Ey, S., & Grant, K. E. (1993). Depression in adolescence. *American Psychologist, 48*, 155–168.

Petersen, A. C., Sarigiani, P. A., & Kennedy, R. E. (1991). Adolescent depression: Why more girls? *Journal of Youth and Adolescence, 20*, 247–271.

Petersen, A. C., Schulenberg, J. E., Abramowitz, R. H., Offer, D., & Jarcho, H. D. (1984). A Self-Image Questionnaire for Young Adolescents (SIQYA): Reliability and validity studies. *Journal of Youth and Adolescence, 13*, 93–111.

Phares, V., & Compas, B. E. (1992). The role of fathers in child and adolescent psychopathology: Make room for daddy. *Psychological Bulletin, 111*, 387–412.

Piacentini, J., Shaffer, D., Fisher, P. W., Schwab-Stone, M., Davies, M., & Gioia, P. (1993). The Diagnostic Interview Schedule for Children—Revised Version (DISC-R): III. Concurrent criterion validity. *Journal of the American Academy of Child and Adolescent Psychiatry, 32*, 658–665.

Poznanski, E. O., & Mokros, H. B. (1994). Phenomenology and epidemiology of mood disorders in children and adolescents. In W. M. Reynolds & H. F. Johnston (Eds.), *Handbook of depression in children and adolescents* (pp. 19–40). New York: Plenum Press.

Poznanski, E., Mokros, H., Grossman, J., & Freeman, L. (1985). Diagnostic criteria in childhood depression. *American Journal of Psychiatry, 142*, 1168–1173.

Prieto, S. L., Cole, D. A., & Tageson, C. W. (1992). Depressive self-schemas in clinic and nonclinic children. *Cognitive Therapy and Research, 16*, 521–534.

Puig-Antich, J., & Chambers, W. (1978). *The Schedule for Affective Disorders and Schizophrenia for School-Age Children (Kiddie-SADS).* New York: New York State Psychiatric Institute.

Puig-Antich, J., Chambers, W., Halpern, F., Hanlon, C., & Sacher, E. J. (1979). Cortisol hypersecretion in prepubertal depressive illness: A preliminary study. *Psychoneuroendocrinology, 4*, 191–197.

Puig-Antich, J., Perel, J. M., Lupatkin, W., Chambers, W. J., Shea, C., Tabrizi, M. D., & Stiller, B. (1979). Plasma levels of imipramine (IMI) and desmethylimipramine (DMI) and clinical response in prepubertal major depressive disorder: A preliminary report. *Journal of American Academy of Child Psychiatry, 18*, 616–627.

Quay, H. C., & Peterson, L. C. (1983). *Interim manual for the Revised Behavior Problem Checklist.* Unpublished manuscript, University of Miami.

Radloff, L. S. (1977). The CES-D Scale: A self-report depression scale for research in the general population. *Applied Psychological Measurement, 1*, 385–401.

Rey, J. M., & Morris-Yates, A. (1991). Adolescent depression and the Child Behavior Checklist. *Journal of the American Academy of Child and Adolescent Psychiatry, 30*, 423–427.

Rey, J. M., & Morris-Yates, A. (1992). Diagnostic accuracy in adolescents of several depression rating scales extracted from a general purpose behavior checklist. *Journal of Affective Disorders*, 26, 7–16.

Reynolds, W. M. (1986). *Reynolds Adolescent Depression Scale*. Odessa, FL: Psychological Assessment Resources.

Reynolds, W. M. (1989). *Reynolds Child Depression Scale*. Odessa, FL: Psychological Assessment Resources.

Reynolds, W. M. (1994). Assessment of depression in children and adolescents by self-report questionnaires. In W. M. Reynolds & H. F. Johnston (Eds.), *Handbook of depression in children and adolescents* (pp. 209–234). New York: Plenum Press.

Roberts, R. E., Lewinsohn, P. M., & Seeley, J. R. (1991). Screening for adolescent depression: A comparison of depression scales. *Journal of the American Academy of Child and Adolescent Psychiatry, 30*, 58–66.

Robinson, N. S., Garber, J., & Hilsman, R. (1995). Cognitions and stress: Direct and moderating effects on depressive versus externalizing symptoms during the junior high school transition. *Journal of Abnormal Psychology, 104*, 453–463.

Rohde, P., Lewinsohn, P. M., & Seeley, J. R. (1991). Comorbidity of unipolar depression: II. Comorbidity with other mental disorders in adolescents and adults. *Journal of Abnormal Psychology, 54*, 653–660.

Rudolph, K. D., Hammen, C., & Burge, D. (1994). Interpersonal functioning and depressive symptoms in childhood: Addressing the issues of specificity and comorbidity. *Journal of Abnormal Child Psychology, 22*, 355–371.

Saylor, C. F., Finch, A. J., Spirito, A., & Bennett, B. (1984). The Children's Depression Inventory: A systematic evaluation of psychometric properties. *Journal of Consulting and Clinical Psychology, 52*, 955–967.

Schwab-Stone, M., Fisher, P. W., Piacentini, J., Shaffer, D., Davies, M., & Briggs, M. (1993). The Diagnostic Interview Schedule for Children—Revised Version (DISC-R): II. Test–retest reliability. *Journal of the American Academy of Child and Adolescent Psychiatry, 32*, 651–657.

Seifer, R., Nurcombe, B., Scioli, A., & Grapentine, W. L. (1989). Is Major Depressive Disorder in childhood a distinct diagnostic entity? *Journal of the American Academy of Child and Adolescent Psychiatry, 28*, 935–941.

Seligman, M. E. P., Peterson, C., Kaslow, N. J., Tanenbaum, R. L., Alloy, L. B., & Abramson, L. Y. (1984). Attributional styles and depressive symptoms among children. *Journal of Abnormal Psychology, 93*, 235–238.

Shaffer, D., Fisher, P., Dulcan, D., Davies, M., Piacentini, J., Schwab-Stone, M., Lahey, B., Bordon, K., Jensen, P., Bird, H., Canino, B., & Rejier, D. (1992). *National Institute of Mental Health Diagnostic Interview Schedule for Children version 2.3 (DISC 2.3)*. Unpublished manuscript, New York State Psychiatric Institute, New York.

Shaffer, D., Schwab-Stone, M., Fisher, P. W., Cohen, P., Piacentini, J., Davies, M., Conners, C. K., & Regier, D. (1993). The Diagnostic Interview Schedule for Children—Revised Version (DISC-R): I. Preparation, field testing, interrater reliability, and acceptability. *Journal of the American Academy of Child and Adolescent Psychiatry, 32*, 643–650.

Shaffer, D., Schwab-Stone, M., Fisher, P., Davies, M., Piacentini, J., & Gioia, P. (1988). *Results of a field trial and proposals for a new instrument (DISC-R)* (Grant Nos. MH 36971 & MH CRC 30906-10). Bethesda, MD: National Institute of Mental Health.

Shelton, R. C., Hollon, S. D., Purdon, S. E., & Loosen, P. T. (1991). Biological and psychological aspects of depression. *Behavior Therapy, 22*, 201–228.

Skinner, E. (1995). *Motivation, coping and control*. Newbury, CA: Sage.

Smucker, M. R., Craighead, W. E., Craighead, L. W., & Green, B. J. (1986). Normative and reliability data for the Children's Depression Inventory. *Journal of Abnormal Child Psychology, 14*, 25–39.

Spitzer, R. L., Endicott, J., & Robins, E. (1978a). Research Diagnostic Criteria: Rationale and reliability. *Archives of General Psychiatry, 35*, 773–782.

Spitzer, R. L., Endicott, J., & Robins, E. (1978b). *Research Diagnostic Criteria for a selected group of functional disorders* (3rd ed.). New York: New York State Psychiatric Institute.

Tisher, M., & Lang. M. (1983). The Children's Depression Scale: Review and further developments. In D. P. Cantwell & G. A. Carlson (Eds.), *Affective disorders in childhood and adolescence: An update* (pp. 181–202). New York: Spectrum.

Watson, D., & Clark, L. A. (1984). Negative affectivity: The disposition to experience aversive emotional states. *Psychological Bulletin, 96*, 465–490.

Watson, D., & Clark, L. A. (1992). Affects separable and inseparable: On the hierarchical arrangement of the negative affects. *Journal of Personality and Social Psychology, 62*, 489–505.

Watson, D., & Kendall, P. C. (1989). Common and differentiating features of anxiety and depression: Current findings and future directions. In P. C. Kendall & D. Watson (Eds.), *Anxiety and depression: Distinctive and overlapping features* (pp. 493–508). New York: Academic Press.

Watson, D., & Tellegen, A. (1985). Toward a consensual structure of mood. *Psychological Bulletin, 98*, 219–235.

Weinstein, S. R., Noam, G. G., Grimes, K., Stone, K., & Schwab-Stone, M. (1990). Convergence of DSM-III diagnoses and self-reported symptoms in child and adolescent inpatients. *Journal of the American Academy of Child and Adolescent Psychiatry, 29*, 627–634.

Weiss, B., Weisz, J. R., Politano, M., Carey, M., Nelson, W. M., & Finch, A. J. (1991). Developmental differences in the factor structure of the

Children's Depression Inventory. *Psychological Assessment: A Journal of Consulting and Clinical Psychology, 3,* 38–45.

Weissman, M. M., Gammon, G. D., John, K., Merikangas, K. R., Warner, V., Prusoff, B. A., & Sholomskas, D. (1987). Children of depressed parents: Increased psychopathology and early onset of major depression. *Archives of General Psychiatry, 44,* 847–853.

Weisz, J. R. (1986). Understanding the developing understanding of control. In M. Perlmutter (Ed.), *Minnesota Symposium on Child Psychology: Vol. 18. Social cognition* (pp. 219–278). Hillsdale, NJ: Erlbaum.

Weisz, J. R., Sweeney, L., Proffitt, V., & Carr, T. (1993). Control-related beliefs and self-reported depressive symptoms in late childhood. *Journal of Abnormal Psychology, 102,* 411–418.

Weisz, J. R., Weiss, B., Wasserman, A. A., & Rintoul, B. (1987). Control-related beliefs and depression among clinic-referred children and adolescents. *Journal of Abnormal Psychology, 96,* 149–158.

Whitman, P. B., & Leitenberg, H. (1990). Negatively biased recall in children with self-reported symptoms of depression. *Journal of Abnormal Child Psychology, 18,* 15–27.

Williams, C. L., & Butcher, J. N. (1989a). An MMPI study of adolescents: I. Empirical validity of the standard scales. *Psychological Assessment: A Journal of Consulting and Clinical Psychology, 1,* 251–259.

Williams, C. L., & Butcher, J. N. (1989b). An MMPI study of adolescents: II. Verification and limitations of code type classifications. *Psychological Assessment: A Journal of Consulting and Clinical Psychology, 1,* 260–265.

Wolfe, V. V., Finch, A. J., Saylor, C. F., Blount, R. L., Pallmeyer, T. P., & Carek, D. J. (1987). Negative affectivity in children: A multitrait-multimethod investigation. *Journal of Consulting and Clinical Psychology, 55*(2), 245–250.

World Health Organization. (1992). *International classification of diseases and health-related problems* (10th revision). Geneva: Author.

Chapter Five

FEARS AND ANXIETIES

Billy A. Barrios
Donald P. Hartmann

One cannot be a serious student of behavior therapy and not have some passing knowledge of children's fears and anxieties. These conditions have had too conspicuous a hand in shaping the discipline of behavior therapy—its theories, its treatments, and its boundaries—for them to go unnoticed. Consider the three cases of Albert, Peter, and Hans. Watson and Rayner's (1920) attempt to condition fear of a white rat in 1-year-old Albert was seen as early crucial support for the nascent school of behaviorism, and continues to be cited as evidence for a classical conditioning account of anxiety (Harris, 1979; Öst, 1985, 1991). Offering additional early support for the school of behaviorism was Mary Cover Jones's (1924) desensitization and modeling treatments of 3-year-old Peter's fear of rabbits—treatments that to this day continue to be used to alleviate the fears and anxieties of children. And then there is the classic case of young Hans's morbid fear of horses—a case whose original formulation by Freud (1909/1955) did little to promote behaviorism, but whose reinterpretation by Wolpe and Rachman (1960) most certainly did.

Though these cases attest to the influence of the study of children's fears and anxieties on the development of the discipline of behavior therapy, behavior therapists have for the most part ignored the fears and anxieties of children. Instead, they have devoted most of their attention and efforts to the study of adults' fears and anxieties—attempting to delineate the response elements of these fears and anxieties (e.g., Barlow, Cohen, et al., 1984; Kolb & Keane, 1988), to draw definite distinctions among them (e.g., Brown, Moras, Zinbarg, & Barlow, 1993; Turner & Beidel, 1985; Turner, Beidel, & Larkin, 1986), and to identify possible mechanisms behind their expression (e.g.,

Bandura, 1986; Beck & Emery, 1985; Borkovec, Metzger, & Pruzinsky, 1986; Lang, 1984). In recent years, though, more and more behavior therapists have come to see the fears and anxieties of children as subjects worthy of concern and concerted study. And as a consequence, more and more behavior therapists have begun turning their attention and efforts to understanding and treating the fears and anxieties of children (e.g., Beidel, 1991; Bernstein & Borchardt, 1991; Strauss, 1990).

This view of children's fears and anxieties as subjects worthy of study in their own right is one that we wholeheartedly share. And in the present chapter we address one aspect of the systematic study of children's fears and anxieties: their behavioral assessment. The reader should be forewarned, though, that the present chapter is intended to serve not as a "cookbook," but as a source book for practitioners and researchers interested in the sound and sensitive assessment of children's fears and anxieties. In the pages that follow, we discuss the various terms, definitions, and categories pertaining to children's fears and anxieties. We also review the available epidemiological and developmental findings about patterns of fears and anxieties, as well as the instruments available for their assessment. And finally, we describe the major parameters involved in a comprehensive clinical assessment and the major matters recommended for future examination.

DEFINITIONAL CONSIDERATIONS

Many, many terms have been coined and definitions proposed in attempts to specify and classify children's fears and anxieties. Among these terms are "fear," "anxiety," "wariness," "apprehension," "worry," "concern," "phobia," "phobic reaction," "phobic disorder," "clinical fear," "subclinical fear," "anxiety state," "anxiety reaction," and "anxiety disorder." Most of the early attempts at delineation and classification were founded on differentiating three of these terms: "fears," "anxieties," and "phobias." "Fears" were defined as reactions to perceived threats, with these reactions taking the form of escape from or avoidance of the threatening stimuli; subjective feelings of distress in anticipation of or upon presentation to the stimuli; and physiological changes of discomfort in anticipation of or upon actual exposure to the stimuli. "Anxieties" were distinguished from fears largely on the basis of the specificity of the threatening stimuli and the unity of the accompanying responses (Jersild, 1954). Fears were thought of as highly cohesive reactions to specific stimuli such as natural events (e.g., lightning, darkness) or abstract concepts (e.g., war, rejection), whereas anxieties were thought of as more diffused reactions to nonspecific stimuli or, to borrow Johnson and Melamed's (1979) expression, as "apprehension without apparent cause" (p. 107). Clinical fears, or "phobias," were distinguished from nonclinical fears primarily on the bases of their persistence, maladaptiveness, and magnitude; similar bases were used to distinguish clinical anxieties from nonclinical anxieties (e.g., Berecz, 1968; Crider, 1949; Marks, 1969; Miller, Barrett, & Hampe, 1974; Morris & Kratochwill, 1983b).

More recent attempts at delineation and classification have been founded on differentiating a similar set of three terms: "anxiety," "fear," and "anxiety disorder." "Anxiety" has been defined as a broad collection of distressing subjective, motoric, and somatic responses; "fear" has been conceptualized as a narrow subset of these responses that is of considerable intensity and is associated with a discrete stimulus context. A broader subset of these anxiety responses that is of comparable intensity, but is associated with a larger stimulus context, has been termed "anxiety disorder" (e.g., American Psychiatric Association, 1980, 1987, 1994; Bell-Dolan, Last, & Strauss, 1990; Kashani & Orvaschel, 1988, 1990).

Symptoms

Many different responses or symptoms have been ascribed to children's fears and anxieties. Consider, for example, the following four case accounts: Rachman's (1978) description of a 7-year-old child's reaction to a bee; Bankart and Bankart's (1983) description of a 9-year-old child's reaction to a new school; Peterson's (1987) narrative of an 8-year-old girl's reaction to being home alone; and Garland and Smith's (1990) depiction of an 8-year-old boy's reaction to the sight of a bear in the wild. When confronted with a bee, Rachman's 7-year-old became "white, sweaty, cold and trembly, and his legs were like jelly" (p. 4). When faced with attending a new school, Bankart and Bankart's 9-year-old showed "intense feelings of fear and dread, uncontrollable crying, nausea, bowel disturbance, headache, fever, and insomnia" (p. 81). Asked to portray through a child doll her reaction to being home alone, Peterson's 8-year-old reported that "her thoughts raced so fast that logical thought was impossible. . . . she forgot all the right things to do, her heart pounded, and she experienced muscle tightness, difficulty in breathing, and uncontrollable tears" (p. 383). Having encountered a bear at a safe distance in the wild, Garland and Smith's 8-year-old recounted "feelings of unreality, a sense that sounds were louder than usual while his vision was blurring, feeling that his hands were 'fat' and numb, palpitations, nausea, and chest tightness" (p. 786).

Other descriptions of fears and anxieties have children voicing feelings of terror, helplessness, impending doom, and imminent death; children exhibiting physiological changes of rapid respiration, dizziness, abdominal pain, and breathlessness; and children displaying motor acts of urgent pleas for assistance, exaggerated flight, and complete immobility (e.g., Ballenger, Carek, Steele, & Cornish-McTighe, 1989; Hatcher, 1989; McNamara, 1988; Singer, Ambuel, Wade, & Jaffe, 1992).

Classification Schemes

Numerous schemes have been proposed for the classification of children's fears and anxieties. At one time it was fashionable to provide long lists of exotic-sounding phobias, such as "paraliphobia" (fear of precipitating disaster by having omitted or forgotten something), "pantophobia" (fear of practically everything), and "phobophobia" (fear of phobias). More sensible attempts at grouping children's fears and anxieties into broader categories have been of three types: theoretically derived, statistically derived, or clinically derived classification schemes.[1]

Two examples of theoretically derived taxonomies are the ones put forth by Hebb (1946) and by Seligman (1971). In Hebb's (1946) system, fear and anxiety reactions are classified according to their presumed etiology, with those purportedly produced by conflicts or sensory deficits forming one class of reactions, and those purportedly produced by constitutional disturbances or maturational forces forming a different class of reactions. In Seligman's (1971) system, stimuli of evolutionary significance in the phylogenetic history of the organism are referred to as "prepared," and stimuli of evolutionary insignificance are referred to as "unprepared." Fears and anxieties to prepared stimuli are thought to be easier to acquire and harder to overcome than fears and anxieties to unprepared stimuli. Among those stimuli identified as prepared are snakes, spiders, heights, and darkness; among those identified as unprepared are flowers, mushrooms, and chocolates (Öhman, 1979; Rachman & Seligman, 1976).

Several of the classification systems have as the basis for their groupings the results from multivariate statistical analyses. The earliest of these factor-analytically derived systems is that of Scherer and Nakamura (1968), in which the fears of children fall into eight categories: Failure and Criticism; Social Events; Small Animals; Medical Procedures; Death; Darkness; Home and School; and Miscellaneous Events. Subsequent analyses have produced similar but shorter lists of categories. Miller, Barrett, Hampe, and Noble (1972) classify the fears of children into three categories: Physical Injury, Natural Events, and Psychic Stress. Ollendick and associates (Ollendick, 1983, 1987; Ollendick, King, & Frary, 1989; Ollendick, Matson, & Helsel, 1985) classify the fears of children into five categories: Failure and Criticism; the Unknown; Minor Injury and Small Animals; Danger and Death; and Medical Procedures.

Two other statistically derived classification systems have fears and anxieties as features of larger, supraordinate classes of problem behaviors. In Quay's (1979) system, the problem behaviors of children cluster into four patterns: Conduct Disorder, Anxiety–Withdrawal, Immaturity, and Socialized Aggression. Fears and anxieties are located within the general pattern of Anxiety–Withdrawal, a pattern that has among its elements the following: anxiousness, fearfulness, tension, shyness, timidity, bashfulness, withdrawal, social isolation, seclusiveness, depression, aloofness, and secretiveness. In Achenbach's (1991a, 1991b, 1991c) system, over 100 different problem behaviors are reduced to eight distinct syndromes: a set of Internalizing disorders, consisting of the Withdrawn, Somatic Complaints, Anxious/Depressed, Social Problems, and Thought Problems syndromes; and a set of Externalizing disorders, con-

sisting of the Attention Problems, Delinquent Behavior, and Aggressive Behavior syndromes. A central shared feature of the Internalizing disorders is an excess of anxious behaviors, whereas a central shared feature of the Externalizing disorders is an absence of socially prescribed anxious behaviors.

Still another set of classification schemes has as the basis for its groupings the insights and observations of clinical practitioners and researchers. Perhaps the earliest of such schemes is that put forth by Angelino, Dollins, and Mech (1956). From the reports of over 1,000 children, they reduced the fears and anxieties of children to nine stimulus categories: animals, personal appearance, personal conduct, personal health, physical safety, school, world events, natural events, and supernatural events. A little over a decade later, Bandura and Menlove (1968) collapsed parents' ratings of their preschoolers' fears and anxieties into three groups: those related to small animals, those related to interpersonal events, and those related to events of nature.

Much more influential and controversial than the two aforementioned classification systems have been the diagnostic categories proposed by the American Psychiatric Association (1980, 1987, 1994). Founded on clinical observation, developed by committee consensus, and refined by field research, the Association's current system devotes 14 categories to human fears and anxieties. Of these 14 categories, 12 are applicable to the fears and anxieties of children: Separation Anxiety Disorder, Agoraphobia Without History of Panic Disorder, Social Phobia, Specific Phobia, Panic Disorder with Agoraphobia, Panic Disorder without Agoraphobia, Obsessive–Compulsive Disorder, Posttraumatic Stress Disorder, Acute Stress Disorder, Generalized Anxiety Disorder, Substance-Induced Anxiety Disorder, and Anxiety Disorder Not Otherwise Specified.

The first four of these disorders are all similar, in that the child's anxiety is linked to one or more fairly discernible situations. They differ from one another primarily in terms of the nature of the various situations. For Separation Anxiety Disorder, the display of age-inappropriate, excessive anxiety is a reaction to separation from home or a significant attachment figure. The excessive anxiety is of at least 4 weeks' duration and is evidenced by at least three of the following: recurrent distress in anticipation of or upon separation; unrealistic worry about harm to attachment figure; unrealistic worry about harm to self; persistent opposition to school attendance; persistent opposition to being home alone; persistent opposition to sleeping alone or to sleeping away from home; recurrent nightmares involving separation; and recurrent physical complaints in anticipation or upon separation.

For Agoraphobia Without History of Panic Disorder, the feared situations are ones in which assistance might not be forthcoming if incapacitating symptoms were to arise. Examples of such feared situations, which are avoided or endured with marked distress or approached only with the accompaniment of a companion, are crowded stores, elevators, bridges, and buses. And examples of such incapacitating or embarrassing symptoms are dizziness, fainting, heart palpitations, loss of bladder control, and loss of bowel control.

For Social Phobia, the feared stimuli are social or performance situations involving unfamiliar others or potential scrutiny by others. The fear of appearing foolish is of at least 6 months' duration, and it is evidenced when in the presence of unfamiliar peers and not just unfamiliar adults. Examples of such social situations, which are avoided or endured with marked distress, are writing, speaking, and eating in public. And examples of such fear and anxiety symptoms are crying, "freezing," and "shrinking" from others. This fear of social or performance situations is distressing or disruptive, and may or may not be recognized by the child as being excessive and unreasonable.

For Specific Phobia, the feared stimulus is any circumscribed object or situation other than those mentioned above (e.g., separation from a significant other, speaking in the presence of others) or below (e.g., obsessions, trauma). Examples of such stimuli, which again are avoided or endured with marked distress, are animals, darkness, heights, and hypodermic needles. And examples of such fear and anxiety symptoms are tantrums, trembling, crying, and clinging. Fear of these stimuli is disturbing to the child or interfering with the development of the child, and may or may not be recognized as excessive or unreasonable by the child.

At the heart of the two types of Panic Disorder is the unexpected occurrence of discrete periods of intense anxiety, referred to as Panic Attacks. Panic Attacks are made up of a constellation of four or more somatic and cognitive symptoms (e.g., sweating, speeded-up heartbeat, tingling sensations, ruminations over losing control). Because the attacks occur unexpectedly, they are not linked to any given situation. In Panic Disorder with Agoraphobia, recurring Panic Attacks are accompanied by persistent concern or significant changes related to the attacks, and by intense fear of situations in which escape might be difficult or embarrassing or in which help might not be forthcoming if incapacitating symptoms were to arise. In Panic Disorder without Agoraphobia, the recurring Panic Attacks are accompanied by persistent concern or significant behavioral changes related to the attacks, but there is no such fear of situations in which escape or help might not be available.

Distressing or debilitating fear and anxiety are also not situationally bound in Generalized Anxiety Disorder. Instead, excessive anxiety and pervasive worry cover a wide range of events and activities, from school-related tasks to natural disasters. This excessive anxiety and pervasive worry have been characteristic of the child's life for the past 6 months and are evidenced by at least one of six symptoms (e.g., restlessness, fatigue, inability to concentrate, disrupted sleep).

Fear and anxiety are linked to varying degrees to specific stimuli in the five remaining psychiatric categories. In Obsessive–Compulsive Disorder, fear and anxiety are tied to the presence of obsessions (i.e., recurring repugnant thoughts, images, or impulses) or compulsions (i.e., repetitive, ineffectual behaviors or mental acts). Common themes of such thoughts, which exceed the boundaries of ordinary worry and resist suppression, are contamination, doubts, and orderliness. Common examples of such repetitive behaviors or mental acts, which are unrealistically aimed at reducing distress or preventing dread, are washing of hands, checking, counting, and ordering. The fear and anxiety associated with these obsessions and compulsions are distressing, time-consuming, or interfering with normal development, yet may not be recognized by the child as excessive or unreasonable.

In Posttraumatic Stress Disorder and Acute Stress Disorder, anxiety is tied to a catastrophic event that was experienced directly or vicariously and that involved serious actual or threatened harm to self or others. Examples of such terrifying or horrific events are physical attack, sexual assault, natural disaster, torture, and violent automobile accident. The catastrophic event is repeatedly relived through play, dreams, or flashbacks, and is accompanied by intense psychological distress or physiological upset. Stimuli associated with the catastrophic event are actively avoided, and general emotional responsiveness is greatly diminished. Marked anxiety associated with the event is also manifested through a heightened state of general arousal (e.g., poor circulation, exaggerated startle response, hypervigilance, sleep disturbances, anger outbursts). This distressing and/or debilitating state of anxiety is of at *least* 1 month's duration for Posttraumatic Stress Disorder and no *greater* than 4 weeks' duration for Acute Stress Disorder.

Substance-Induced Anxiety Disorder differs from all previously described disorders, in that the anxiety symptoms are attributed to the direct physiological effects of a substance (e.g., cannabis, hallucinogens, inhalants). The anxiety symptoms exceed those typically associated with intoxication or withdrawal from the substance and constitute a significant source of distress or impediment to functioning. The final diagnostic category, Anxiety Disorder Not Otherwise Specified, includes those fear and anxiety reactions that do not fall neatly into any of the aforementioned diagnostic categories. Examples of such reactions are a mixture of significant but not severe anxiety and depression symptoms, and a pattern of avoidance of social and performance situations stemming from the eating disorder of Anorexia Nervosa.

Summary

At present, we find no compelling reason for adopting any of the distinctions that have been raised regarding the terms "fear" and "anxiety." The distinctions have not produced any significant advances in theory or treatment to date, and it does not appear that they will ever do so. Instead, we favor collapsing the various distinctions and definitions, and viewing fear and anxiety as a complex pattern of three types of reactions to a perceived threat: subjective reactions such as reports of distress, discomfort, and terror; motor reactions, such as avoidance, escape, and tentative approach; and physiological reactions, such as heart palpitations, profuse sweating, and rapid breathing (e.g., Lang, 1968; Marks, 1969; Morris & Kratochwill, 1983a, 1983b).[2] Thus, we favor the view and the use of the terms "fear" and "anxiety" as interchangeable.

Implicit in this definition of fear and anxiety is potential variation in responding. Within each of the three categories of reactions, responding may take many different forms. For example, escape, avoidance, trembling, flailing, crying, clinging, stuttering, swaying, rocking, and nail biting have all been cited as referents or symptoms of the motor component of children's fears and anxieties (Esveldt-Dawson, Wisner, Unis, Matson, & Kazdin, 1982; Fox & Houston, 1981; Glennon & Weisz, 1978; Katz, Kellerman, & Siegel, 1980; Melamed & Siegel, 1975). Reports of terror, doom, discomfort, impending harm, sadness, monsters, and helplessness have all served as referents or symptoms of the subjective component

(Giebenhain & Barrios, 1986; LaGreca, Dandes, Wick, Shaw, & Stone, 1988; Laurent & Stark, 1993; Prins, 1985). And increases in heart rate, pulse volume, respiration, skin conductance, and muscular tension have all served as referents for the physiological component (Beidel, 1988; Beidel, Christ, & Long, 1991; Jay, Ozolins, Elliott, & Caldwell, 1983; Melamed, Yurcheson, Fleece, Hutcherson, & Hawes, 1978; Van Hasselt, Hersen, Bellack, Rosenblum, & Lamparski, 1979). A long but still partial list of the many motor, subjective, and physiological referents or symptoms of children's fears and anxieties is provided in Table 5.1.

Variation in responding may also occur among children who are frightened of the same stimulus situation. For example, the fear of attending school may take the form for one child of tantrums and clinging to parents, whereas it may take the form for another child of entering the school but refusing to participate in social and evaluative activities (Kearney & Silverman, 1993). Given the varying task demands of different contexts, a given child's responses to different feared situations are also likely to vary. For example, a given child may react to being placed in the dentist's chair by screaming, kicking, and gasping for air, and to being called upon in the classroom by trembling, stuttering, and tearing of eyes.

This view of children's fears and anxieties accords well with current theorizing on emotions, as well as with current behavioral conceptualizations of adult emotional disorders. Contemporary theories conceive of emotions as having three sets of components—subjective, motor, and physiological—that merge with one another to form a complex, organized state of activity (see Ekman & Davidson, 1994; Izard, Kagan, & Zajonc, 1984; Plutchik & Kellerman, 1980, 1983). Emotions are not seen as verbal reports or overt behavioral acts or somatovisceral responses, but as combinations of the three (e.g., Lang, 1984; Lang, Rice, & Sternbach, 1972). As particular types of emotions, "fear" and "anxiety" are defined in a similar fashion (e.g., Lang, 1984). Contemporary behavioral theories of adult fears and anxieties put forth very similar views (Barlow, 1988; Borkovec et al., 1986; Delprato & McGlynn, 1984).

With the limited data currently available, it is not clear that any of the aforementioned classification schemes has "carved nature at its joints"; nor is it clear that any of the proposed schemes has been or will be of great use to therapists (see Morris & Kratochwill, 1983b, for a detailed review of these classification systems). At this time, it seems to us that the most prudent approach both empirically and theoretically is to categorize chil-

TABLE 5.1. A Partial Listing of the Motoric, Physiological, and Subjective Responses of Children's Fears and Anxieties

Motoric responses	Physiological responses	Subjective responses
Avoidance	Heart rate	Thoughts of being scared
Gratuitous arm, hand, and leg movements	Basal skin response	Thoughts of monsters
	Palmar sweat index	Thoughts of being hurt
Trembling voice	Galvanic skin response	Images of monsters
Crying	Muscle tension	Images of wild animals
Feet shuffling	Skin temperature	Thoughts of danger
Screaming	Respiration	Self-deprecatory thoughts
Nail biting	Palpitation	Self-critical thoughts
Thumb sucking	Breathlessness	Thoughts of inadequacy
Rigid posture	Nausea	Thoughts of incompetence
Eyes shut	Pulse volume	Thoughts of bodily injury
Avoidance of eye contact	Headache	Images of bodily injury
Clenched jaw	Stomach upset	Thoughts racing
Stuttering	Stomachache	Thoughts of imminent death
Physical proximity	Urination	Thoughts of appearing foolish
White knuckles	Defecation	Blanking out
Trembling lip	Vomiting	Thoughts of going crazy
Certain verbalizations[a]	Labored breathing	Difficulty concentrating
Immobility	Blurred vision	Forgetfulness
Swallowing	Numbness	Thoughts of contamination
Twitching	Dizziness	Images of harm to loved ones
Walking rituals	Flushes/chills	Depersonalization

Note. The responses listed have been documented in the following studies: Ballenger, Carek, Steele, and Cornish-McTighe (1989); Beidel, Christ, and Long (1991); Esveldt-Dawson, Wisner, Unis, Matson, and Kazdin (1982); Garland and Smith (1990); Glennon and Weisz (1978); Hatcher (1989); Hoehn-Saric, Maisami, and Wiegand (1987); Katz, Kellerman, and Siegel (1980); Laurent and Stark (1993); LeBaron and Zeltzer (1984); Lewis and Law (1958); McNamara (1988); Melamed, Hawes, Heiby, and Glick (1975); Melamed and Siegel (1975); Milos & Reiss (1982); Peterson (1987); Rettew, Swedo, Leonard, Lenane, and Rapoport (1992); Ross, Ross, and Evans (1971); Siegel and Peterson (1980); Simpson, Ruzicka, and Thomas (1974); Singer, Ambuel, Wade, and Jaffe (1992); Sonnenberg and Venham (1977); Van Hasselt, Hersen, Bellack, Rosenblum, and Lamparski (1979); Zatz and Chassin (1983).
[a]In some cases the distinction between motor and subjective responses may be difficult to draw. For example, the shouted statement "I am scared!" in response to a large, barking dog is similar to a scream (a motor response), and is of course the expression of a thought (a subjective response).

dren's fears and anxieties by the stimuli to which they appear to be linked. Doing so implies that children's fears and anxieties are context-bound and that they may be inferred in part from a knowledge of each situation's unique task demands—two assumptions shared by most developmental, behavioral, and emotional theorists (e.g., Campos & Barrett, 1984; Cicchetti, 1993; Delprato & McGlynn, 1984; Fischer, Shaver, & Carnochan, 1989; Lang, Levin, Miller, & Kozak, 1983; Lewis & Michalson, 1983). For these reasons, it is the approach we employ in the material that follows.

DEVELOPMENTAL CONSIDERATIONS

The incidence and course of children's fears and anxieties have been explored in a number of epidemiological and related investigations (see reviews by Berecz, 1968; Campbell, 1986; Ferrari, 1986; Graziano, DeGiovanni, & Garcia, 1979; Jersild, 1954; Marks, 1969; Miller et al., 1974; Morris & Kratochwill, 1983b; Orvaschel & Weissman, 1986). Differing procedures and methodological problems make these studies difficult to compare, but a few generalizations can be advanced with reasonable confidence.

Incidence

The fears and anxieties of children of all ages are numerous; research spanning over 60 years attests to this. In the classic work by Jersild and Holmes (1935), mothers reported an average of four to five fears for their 2- through 6-year-old children, with one of these fears being displayed on the average of every 4–5 days. Seventy percent of the 540 fifth- and sixth-graders in Pinter and Lev's (1940) study identified themselves as having 10 or more worries. And in two separate studies by Pratt (1945), several hundred 4- through 16-year-olds reported an average of five to eight fears.

Other studies carried out in subsequent decades have obtained similar numbers of fears and anxieties for children of similar ages. In their investigation of a large sample of 6- through 12-year-old children, Lapouse and Monk (1959) found 43% of the mothers reporting seven or more fears for their children.[3] Maurer's (1965) interviews with over 100 children aged 5 through 14 revealed an average of four to five fears. And in a replication of the Pinter and Lev (1940) investigation, Orton (1982) obtained numbers of worries among his sample of 645 fifth- and sixth-graders comparable to those obtained in the original study. Concurring with the findings from these three large-scale studies are the estimates gathered from a host of smaller-scale investigations (e.g., Angelino et al., 1956; Bamber, 1974; Croake & Knox, 1973; Eme & Schmidt, 1978; Nalven, 1970; Ollendick, 1983).

Many recent researchers have sought to include adolescents in their studies of the incidence of fears and anxieties. In Kirkpatrick's (1984) sample, 30 children and adolescents between 7 and 18 years of age averaged between 11 and 14 intense fears; in Slee and Cross's (1989) sample, 1,243 children and adolescents between 4 and 19 years of age averaged between 8 and 10 intense fears. Additional studies by Ollendick and associates (Ollendick & King, 1994; Ollendick et al., 1989) employed samples of 1,185 and 648 youths, who ranged in age from 7 to 16 and from 12 to 17 years, and who averaged from 12 to 17 and 7 to 10 severe fears, respectively.

Several of the most recent investigations have also sought to estimate the occurrence of certain types and clusters of anxiety symptoms among children at large. Beidel, Christ, and Long (1991) interviewed 76 children ranging in age from 8 to 13 years for the presence or absence of 16 different somatic fear responses (e.g., difficulty catching breath, chest pains, dizziness, sweating, headache). The percentage of children endorsing the presence of any given somatic symptom ranged from 10% to 70%, and the average number of somatic symptoms endorsed as present ranged from three to seven. Bell-Dolan et al. (1990) interviewed a sample of 62 "never psychiatrically ill" youths ranging in age from 5 to 18 years for the presence and severity of 90 anxiety symptoms. Seventeen of these symptoms were reported present by at least 10%; for these 17 symptoms, 11.3% to 35.4% of the youths judged the severity to be moderate to severe. In two community stud-ies of the prevalence of anxiety symptoms and clusters of anxiety symptoms, Kashani and Orvaschel (1988, 1990) interviewed over 350 children/adolescents and their parents. In the first of these studies, over 17% of the sample of 14-, 15-, and 16-year-olds were judged to have sufficient numbers of anxiety symptoms to warrant concern, and over 8% to warrant designation as "cases." And in the second study, 21% of the sample of 8-, 12-, and 17-year-olds were judged on the basis of their self-reports to have sufficient numbers of anxiety symptoms to warrant concern, and over 13% were concluded on the basis of their parents' reports to warrant concern.

Age Trends

With increasing age, there are changes in the frequency, foci, and form of children's fears and anxieties. Though there are conflicting data, the majority of the studies show a general decline in the number of fears with increasing age. For example, Holmes (1935) observed the reactions of 2- through 5-year-olds to strangers, darkness, and the like, and found that the younger the child, the greater the number of fears displayed. Similar age trends have been reported by MacFarlane, Allen, and Honzik (1954) for 2- through 14-year-olds; by Bauer (1976) for 4- through 12-year-olds; by Maurer (1965) for 5- through 14-year-olds; by Barrios, Replogle, and Anderson-Tisdelle (1983) for 5- through 16-year-olds; by Lapouse and Monk (1959) for 6- through 12-year-olds; and by Bamber (1974) for 12- through 18-year-old boys. More recent studies surveying greater numbers of children and age groups have likewise noted fewer fears for older children and adolescents (e.g., Dong, Yang, & Ollendick, 1994; Gullone & King, 1992; Ollendick & King, 1994; Ollendick et al., 1985, 1989; Slee & Cross, 1989). As noted above, some studies have found no such decline in the numbers of fears and anxieties with age (e.g., Angelino et al., 1956; Angelino & Shedd, 1953; Croake & Knox, 1973; Dunlop, 1952; Maurer, 1965; Morgan, 1959; Ollendick, 1983; Ollendick, Yule, & Ollier, 1991; Ryall & Dietiker, 1979). These studies have tended to survey a narrower range of age groups than have the studies detecting a decline in the number of fears with age.

Accompanying this overall drop in the number of children's fears and anxieties with age is a shift in the nature of the fears that are prominent. Young infants are frightened by the loss of support; by height; and by sudden, intense, and unexpected stimuli, such as loud noises (Ball & Tronick, 1971; Bronson, 1972; Jersild, 1954). As children mature and face new developmental challenges, the foci of their fears also change. Children aged 1 and 2 are afraid of strangers, of toileting activities, and of being injured (Jersild & Holmes, 1935; Miller et al., 1974), but are as yet unafraid of snakes (Jones & Jones, 1928). Imaginary creatures are common sources of fear for preschool children, as are animals and the dark (e.g., Bauer, 1976; Jersild & Holmes, 1935; Slee & Cross, 1989). Young children in elementary school continue to be frightened by small animals and darkness, concerned with their physical safety, and fearful of such natural events as lightning and thunder (e.g., Croake & Knox, 1973; Maurer, 1965; Poznanski, 1973; Pratt, 1945). As children enter the middle school years, academic, social, and health-related fears become prominent (e.g., Bauer, 1976; Mauer, 1965; Nalven, 1970; Ollendick, 1983; Scherer & Nakamura, 1968). For example, Kennedy (1965) estimated the incidence of serious fear reactions to school to be 17 per 1,000; Strickler and Howitt (1965) estimated as many as 16% of all school-age children as having serious fear and anxiety related to dental treatment; and both Scherer and Nakamura (1968) and Ollendick et al. (1985) identified terror of being sent to the principal and having one's parents arguing as the primary fears of children in middle school. Older children and adolescents become increasingly frightened of physical illness and medical procedures; public speaking; test taking; sexual matters; and economic and political catastrophes, such as war (e.g., Allan & Hodgson, 1968; Angelino et al., 1956; Herbertt & Innes, 1979; Kirkpatrick, 1984; Ollendick & King, 1994; Slee & Cross, 1989).[4]

With increasing age may also come changes in the exact form of a fear reaction to a particular stimulus situation. In their investigation of the various ways in which children express fear and anxiety over separation from an attachment figure, Francis, Last, and Strauss (1987) observed several differences among young (5 to 8 years), middle-age (9 to 12 years), and old (13 to 16 years) children. Most young children reported nightmares involving separation, whereas few middle-age and old children did so; most young and middle-age children displayed extreme distress upon separation, whereas few old children did so; and all old children complained of physical ailments on school/separation days, whereas only slightly over half of the young and middle-age children did so. In a subsequent investigation of generalized anxiety, these same researchers noted greater worry over the appropriateness of past behavior on the part of older children than younger children, and greater numbers of anxiety symptoms among older children than younger children (Strauss, Lease, Last, & Francis, 1988). Other researchers have detected age-related trends with respect to the exact expression of other specific fears and anxieties (e.g., Honjo, Hirano, & Murase, 1989; Minichiello, Baer, Jenike, & Holland, 1990).

Individual Differences

The fears and anxieties of children vary not only according to age, but also according to gender, ethnicity, and socioeconomic status. Regardless of age, girls tend to report greater numbers of fears and anxieties than boys do (e.g., Bamber, 1974; Croake, 1969; Croake & Knox, 1974; Gullone & King, 1992; King, Ollier, et al., 1989; Kirkpatrick, 1984; Ollendick, 1983; Ollendick et al., 1985; Spence & McCathie, 1993). In addition, girls tend to report greater numbers of anxiety symptoms than boys do (e.g., Kashani & Orvaschel, 1988, 1990). Data has also accumulated suggesting that girls differ from boys in terms of the types of fears and anxieties they experience: Fears of animals and of physical illness and injury are more common among girls than boys, and fears of economic and academic failure are more common among boys than girls (e.g., Bamber, 1974; Kirkpatrick, 1984; Ollendick, 1983; Orton, 1982; Pinter & Lev, 1940; Pratt, 1945; Scherer & Nakamura, 1968; Winker, 1949).[5]

The far fewer studies examining ethnic differences point to greater numbers of fears and anxieties and of anxiety symptoms among African-American children than among European-American children (Kashani & Orvaschel, 1988; Lapouse & Monk, 1959; Last & Perrin, 1993). No differences, however, have yet to emerge between the two groups of children in terms of the types of fears and anxieties experienced and the form of their expression (Kashani & Orvaschel, 1988, 1990; Last & Perrin, 1993; Last et al., 1992). Such differences have been noted between Chinese children and Western children (Dong et al., 1994), with Chinese children reporting more pronounced social-evaluative fears (e.g., failing a test, getting poor grades) than Western children.

With respect to socioeconomic status, children from lower-income families tend to be similar to children from middle-income families in the number of fears and anxieties, but dissimilar in the targets of these fears and anxieties (Richman, Stevenson, & Graham, 1982). Though both groups are fearful of animals, lower-income children tend to be frightened of rats and roaches, whereas middle-income children tend to be frightened of poisonous insects. The same appears to be true for the two groups' fears of economic misfortune: Lower-income children tend to be anxious and worried about the necessities of life, whereas middle-income children tend to be anxious and worried about luxury and status items (e.g., Angelino et al., 1956; Nalven, 1970; Pinter & Lev, 1940; Pratt, 1945; Simon & Ward, 1974). We should note that apart from these common-sense differences, investigators have found no strong and reliable association between socioeconomic status and the number of anxiety symptoms or the severity of anxiety reactions to such common stimulus situations as separation from an attachment figure and school attendance (Kashani & Orvaschel, 1988, 1990).

Co-Occurrence

Several studies employing diverse samples and diverse methodologies have found that with the appearance of one severe fear reaction comes an increased likelihood of the occurrence of another severe fear reaction. For example, in the two community studies of nonreferred children and adolescents conducted by Kashani and Orvaschel (1988, 1990), approximately 40% of the respondents who met criteria for an extreme anxiety reaction to one type of situation also met criteria for such a reaction to another type of situation. The numerous surveys described in the earlier section on the incidence of children's fears and anxieties also found a sizable proportion of their samples to be troubled by extreme reactions to two or more stimulus situations (e.g., Kirkpatrick, 1984; Lapouse & Monk, 1959; Slee & Cross, 1989). Even higher percentages of concurrent anxiety reactions have been observed among samples of clinic-referred children. For example, of the 188 children referred to the clinic of Last et al. (1992) for a specific anxiety condition, 62–96% met the criteria for an additional anxiety condition. To repeat, this diverse collection of studies has revealed a heightened tendency for the appearance of a marked fear reaction to one stimulus situation to be accompanied by a marked fear reaction to another stimulus situation. Yet to be revealed, though, is a pattern depicting which types of anxiety reactions are likely to be associated with one another.

A similar body of research has linked the occurrence of fears and anxieties with the mood disturbance of depression (see Brady & Kendall, 1992). As part of their two community-wide studies of fears and anxieties, Kashani and Orvaschel (1988, 1990) also assessed for depression and assorted behavioral difficulties. Anxious children of all ages reported significantly greater depression than did their nonanxious peers, and one-third of the anxious children who met criteria for designation as "clinical cases" also met criteria for designation as "cases" of depression. In another investigation of a nonreferred sample, Anderson, Williams, McGee, and Silva (1987) noted a somewhat lower percentage (16%) of depression among those children who were identified as anxious. Studies of clinic-referred children have tended to report higher estimates of an accompanying condition of depression. Eighty-one percent of Bernstein and Garfinkel's (1986) school refusers who were classified as anxious were also classified as depressed; 45% of Kolvin, Berney, and Bhate's (1984) school-avoidant children were also diagnosed as depressed; 28% of Strauss, Last, Hersen, and Kazdin's (1988) fearful and anxious children and adolescents also met criteria for depression; and 25–56% of Last et al.'s (1992) children with various anxiety conditions also displayed a depressive condition. These children evidencing coexisting anxiety and depressive reactions were found to be older in years and higher in the severity of their anxiety than children evidencing an anxiety reaction with no coexisting depressive reaction (Bernstein, 1991; Strauss, Last, et al., 1988).

A small body of research has uncovered ties, albeit tentative and modest ones, between the appearance of an anxiety reaction and the appearance of certain behavioral difficulties. For example, Kashani and Orvaschel's (1990) anxious 8-year-olds reported significantly more problems in concentration, more symptoms of acting out, and more complaints of physiological distress than did their nonanxious 8-year-olds. Approximately 8–28% of the anxious children referred to the clinic of Last et al. (1992) were also identified as exhibiting one or more classes of severe disruptive behaviors.

Prognosis

Available research paints a mixed picture regarding the persistence of most childhood fears and anxieties. Findings from the early studies tend to suggest that most children's fears are short-lived, whereas later studies tend to imply that these fears may be more enduring. Slater (1939), for example, reported that frequent displays of fearful and anxious behaviors (e.g., tics, requests for mother, postural tensions) on the part of 2- and 3-year-old nursery children had almost entirely abated after 4 weeks. Cummings (1944, 1946) reported that fears, though not generalized anxiety reactions, were quite transitory in 2- through 7-year-olds. And Hagman (1932) found that 54% of childhood fears had disappeared after 3 months, and that even the most recalcitrant fears were gone after 3 years.

Other early studies support this sanguine view of the natural course of children's fears and anxieties. In a 5-year follow-up of an earlier epidemiological study, Agras, Chapin, and Oliveau (1972) noted that all 10 of the children who had been initially identified as phobic were improved or had recovered. In their 2-year follow-up of treated and untreated phobic children, Hampe, Noble, Miller, and Barrett (1973) found 80% of the children to be "symptom-free" and only 7% of the children to continue to have a serious fear reaction. These findings led the researchers to conclude that "the lifespan of phobias in children appears to be somewhere between two weeks and two years, with most phobias dissipating within one year of onset" (Hampe et al., 1973, p. 452).

More recent investigations have found the fears and anxieties of children to be much more persistent. For example, 2 months after a lightning disaster, Dollinger, O'Donnell, and Staley (1984) questioned the child victims and their parents about fear and anxiety symptoms (e.g., trembling and crying during storms, refusal to sleep alone, and tearfulness upon separation from parents). Of the 38 children, 40% continued to show mild upset, 18% to show moderate upset, and 21% to show severe upset, with half of this last group requiring some form of professional counseling for their fear and anxiety symptoms. One year after a major hurricane, Garrison, Weinrich, Hardin, Weinrich, and Wang (1993) questioned over 1,000 youths aged 11 to 17 for signs of trauma. Of these youths, 20% reported repeated reexperiencing of the catastrophic event, 9% reported active avoidance of stimuli associated with the event, and 18% reported heightened general arousal. And of the various groups surveyed, 1.5% to 6.2% of the youths complained of all three types of symptoms and merited diagnosis as having severe anxiety reactions.

Several other studies employing slightly different methodologies have found the self-reported fears and anxieties of children and adolescents to be markedly to moderately stable over time periods ranging from 1 week to 2 years. For example, for a 1-week interval, Gullone and King (1992)

obtained stability coefficients ranging from .85 to .94 for their sample of 918 youths aged 7 through 18. For a 1-month interval, Barrios et al. (1983) obtained an average stability coefficient of .82 for their sample of 74 adolescents aged 14 through 16; and for a 1½-month interval, McCathie and Spence (1991) obtained stability coefficients ranging from .79 to .83 for their sample of 45 children aged 7 through 12. Estimates for longer intervals have been somewhat lower, as one would expect. For example, for a 3-month period, Ollendick (1983) obtained stability coefficients ranging from .55 to .60 for his sample of 60 children aged 8 through 11; for a 6-month period, Dong et al. (1994) obtained stability coefficients ranging from .60 to .70 for their sample of 825 youths aged 7 through 17; and for a 2-year period, Spence and McCathie (1993) obtained stability coefficients ranging from .39 to .56 for their sample of 94 children aged 7 to 10. Additional investigations have reported remarkably similar estimates for these time periods (e.g., Eme & Schmidt, 1978; Giebenhain & Barrios, 1986; Ollendick, 1983; Ryall & Dietiker, 1979).

Recent studies of the age of acquisition of the fears and anxieties of adults also point to the fears and anxieties of children as being far more enduring than was once thought (e.g., Burke, Burke, Regier, & Rae, 1990; Öst, 1987, 1991; Reich, 1986; Thyer, Parrish, Curtis, Neese, & Camerson, 1985). For example, in a large epidemiological study of dental fear, Milgrom, Fiset, Melnick, and Weinstein (1988) identified 67% of their adult respondents as having acquired their fear reaction in early childhood and an additional 18% as having acquired their fear reaction during adolescence. And in a series of longitudinal studies, Berg and associates (Berg, 1976; Berg, Marks, McGuire, & Lipsedge, 1974) noted strong links between school phobia in childhood and agoraphobia in adulthood.

Seriousness

Though numerous, the fears and anxieties of children have long been thought of as not very serious. The aforementioned early studies on the persistence of children's fears and anxieties painted a picture of them as short-lived; this was also suggested by the results of the early Isle of Wight epidemiology study and the few clinic surveys of treatment referrals. In the Isle of Wight epidemiology study, Rutter, Tizard, and Whitmore (1970) screened the total population of 10- and 11-year-olds and found a prevalence rate for serious fears of only 7 per 1,000, with animal, darkness, school, and disease phobias the most common. Prevalence data of this kind prompted Miller et al. (1974) to suggest that the intensity of children's fears is best described by a J-shaped distribution curve, with numerous reports of mild fears and infrequent reports of severe fear reactions. The data reported by MacFarlane et al. (1954), for example, provide a good fit with this description. Other investigators, though, have reported data that are not consistent with this description (e.g., Croake & Knox, 1973; Kirkpatrick, 1984; Ollendick, 1983; Ollendick et al., 1985; Ollendick & King, 1994).

Reports based on referrals to treatment agencies suggest that most fears are not sufficiently indisposing to children or troubling to parents or teachers as to require professional assistance. For example, Graham (1964) noted 10 specific phobias in 239 consecutive cases referred to the Children's Department of the Maudsley Hospital in London. In their review of mental health literature, Johnson and Melamed (1979) found phobic disorders accounting for only 3–4% of all child cases presented for treatment. And in a small survey of child behavior therapists conducted by Graziano and DeGiovanni (1979), repondents identified few children (7–8%) as having been referred for fear-related problems.

Recent data by Ollendick and King (1994) challenge this long-standing and prevailing view of children's fears and anxieties as not very serious. Asking 648 youths aged 12 to 17 to rate the degree to which their fears prevented them from engaging in desired or required activities, the researchers found over 60% of the youths reporting high levels of daily interference and distress, and an additional 26% of the youths reporting moderate levels. These data point to the need for a more inductive, less inferential approach to determining the seriousness of children's fears and anxieties.

Summary

The bulk of epidemiological and related evidence suggests that we would do well to maintain a developmental perspective when evaluating children's fears and anxieties. According to this perspective, the seriousness of a fear response is partly a function of the extent to which that response is common to children of a similar age. Thus, a fear of ghosts under the bed might be of minor concern if displayed by a 5-year-old, but might be a more serious matter if reported by a 13-year-old. A developmental perspective also might help restrain those of us who are inclined to overinterpret

children's fearful reactions. Kanner (1960) provides an amusing example of the salutary effects of developmental norms in evaluation of children's fearful and anxious behavior. In the early years of child psychopathology, the seemingly innocent response of nail biting was variously viewed as "a stigma of degeneration," "an exquisite psychopathic symptom," and "a sign of an unresolved Oedipus complex." A survey disclosing that 66% of school children had been nail-biters at one time or another prompted Kanner to remark that it was "hardly realistic to assume that two-thirds of our youth are degenerate, exquisitely psychopathic, or walking around with a unresolved Oedipus complex" (p. 18).

OTHER CONSIDERATIONS IN DECIDING WHETHER TO TREAT

Although developmental and prognostic factors are important in deciding whether or not to accept a fearful or anxious child for treatment, many other factors will contribute to the overall decision. In particular, a clinician may want to consider the child's and concerned adults' views of the problem; the relationship the fear or anxiety bears to other problem behaviors; the anticipated costs and benefits associated with available treatments; and other practical and ethical matters. The following questions highlight these issues.

1. *Who is complaining?* Children are rarely self-referred for treatment; instead, they are referred by parents, teachers, or physicians (Evans & Nelson, 1977). The perceptions of one or more of these adults, not the child's fearful or anxious behavior, may be more important in determining whether the child is brought to the attention of a therapist (Lobitz & Johnson, 1975). Thus, even though the child is fearful or anxious, he or she may be unmotivated or otherwise unwilling to participate in treatment. In other cases, a child's behavior may be appropriate, but an adult's demands or expectations for fearless behavior may be unreasonable. When this occurs, the adult rather than the child may be the appropriate recipient of treatment.

2. *How is the behavior a problem?* According to Karoly (1975), a problem exists when a behavior reliably disrupts one's pursuit of personal goals; one's ability to adjust to the environment; or one's sense of comfort, satisfaction, and freedom. With a child client, a clinician would want to examine the impact of the fear or the anxiety on individual,

family, and classroom functioning; its interference with normal development and learning experiences; and the resulting curtailment of behavior choices and creation of subjective discomfort.

3. *How are fears related to other areas of the child's behavior?* The fearful or anxious behavior identified by an adult may not be the problem that needs modifying. Enuresis, tantrums, and sleep disturbances may occur in conjunction with anxiety reactions (Kanner, 1957). Anxiety may also be a reaction to other problems, such as learning difficulties, faulty parenting techniques, or physical illnesses, and an acute anxiety attack or phobia may precede or accompany a psychotic reaction (Chess & Hassibi, 1978). The child's fear may be linked to a parent's problems or may be indicative of maladaptive family functioning (Eisenberg, 1958; Gambrill, 1977; Singer, 1965). The presence of associated difficulties may mean that a problem other than the child's fear or anxiety should be treated, or that both the fear or anxiety and another problem should be treated.

4. *What are the costs of treatment, if there are effective interventions for the problem?* A child may be embarrassed about or resentful of treatment, despite the promise of improved behavior and increased attractiveness to others. For parents and other adults, treatment involves expending time, money, and effort and disrupting regular activities in return for a fearless child (Barrios & O'Dell, 1989).

5. *What would be different for the child and others in his or her natural environment without the problem?* The clinician must examine alternatives to the current situation and determine whether changes would be positive events for all the persons involved. The clinician must also consider the implications of not treating a child's fear or anxiety. Although epidemiological data suggest that some childhood fears may be transient, failure to provide the best available intervention may result in ethical or legal problems, as well as certain deleterious short- and long-term consequences for the child. For example, a child's fear of dentists, injections, and other medical procedures may be short-lived, but the fear's interference with adequate care may lead to permanent physical damage, serious disease, and general poor health.

Answers to questions such as these will assist a clinician in deciding whether treatment is warranted. If the decision is made to treat a child, then the clinician must consider other issues in selecting an appropriate procedure to implement (Barrios & O'Dell, 1989).

INSTRUMENTS FOR ASSESSING FEARS AND ANXIETIES

Classification and Review

In this section, we review the available instruments for assessing children's fears and anxieties. For the purposes of presentation and analysis, the instruments have been classified along three dimensions: the nature of the threatening stimulus, the response system assessed, and the method of assessment. For each stimulus category, the instruments have been separated according to the type of fearful and anxious responding they assess. As stated earlier, fear and anxiety reactions are conceptualized as complex, organized patterns of activity within three response systems—subjective, motor, and physiological. As such, any instrument concerned with the assessment of children's fears and anxieties must focus on activity in one or more of these response systems. Also noted earlier, and illustrated by the listing of specific symptoms in Table 5.1, are the varied forms that activity from each of these response systems may take. Though we have made no attempt to classify the instruments in terms of the specific symptoms they assess, we do offer such information in our descriptions of the instruments.

Classified by stimulus category and by response system, the instruments have been further subdivided in terms of their method of assessment, as measurement of most aspects of children's fears and anxiety reactions can be carried out through multiple means (e.g., Cone, 1979; Morris & Kratochwill, 1983b). For our purposes, the instruments have been identified as employing one of three basic methods of measurement: self-report, observational, or mechanical (e.g., bioelectronic recording).

The Appendix provides a brief description and appraisal of the available instruments for assessing the fears and anxieties of children. This brief description of each instrument includes information on its administration and scoring. With respect to administration, information is given on the nature and number of assessment stimuli and on the obtrusiveness and immediacy of data collection. With respect to scoring, information is given on the scaling properties of individual test items and on the aggregation of responses to individual items into composite values.

The Appendix lists over 160 instruments for assessment of children's fear and anxiety reactions to some 13 stimulus categories. Inspection of the Appendix reveals more instruments available for the assessment of fearful reactions to medical procedures than for the assessment of reactions to any other stimulus condition. In fact, there are nearly twice as many instruments for medical procedures than for the next-ranking stimulus category—a finding that we suspect reflects behavior therapy's burgeoning interest in behavioral medicine (e.g., Blanchard, 1982; Gross & Drabman, 1990; Karoly & Jensen, 1987; Melamed & Siegel, 1980; Peterson & Harbeck, 1988; Russo, 1984; Varni, 1983). Of the 160-odd instruments, approximately one-half are concerned with the assessment of the motor (or behavioral) aspects of children's fear and anxiety reactions; approximately one-third with the assessment of the subjective aspects; and the remaining one-sixth with the assessment of the physiological aspects.

Most of the instruments for assessing the motor aspects of children's fears and anxieties are observational in nature; those for assessing the subjective aspects are primarily self-report in nature; and those for assessing the physiological aspects are mainly mechanical in nature. Though activity from a response system is assessed primarily through one method of measurement, the exact form that this method of measurement takes does vary from instrument to instrument. In what follows, we review the major forms of each of the three methods for measuring children's fears and anxieties: observational, self-report, and mechanical.

Observational Methods

As stated above, the vast majority of the instruments for assessing the motor aspects of children's fears and anxieties employ direct observations as their method of measurement. That is, an independent person or persons observe and report on the children's display of certain motor behaviors. Those instruments that assess motor responses through other means have the children themselves observe, recall, and report on these referents of fears and anxieties.[6] As the method of measurement for 77 of the instruments, direct observations take one of five general forms: behavioral avoidance tests (BATs), observational rating systems, checklists, global ratings, or interviews.

Behavioral Avoidance Tests

BATs have been used to assess children's motor reactions to blood, darkness, heights, medical procedures, school-related events, strangers, and water. Although some BATs have been in use since the early 1900s (Jersild & Holmes, 1935; Jones, 1924),

those developed in the last 30 years have been patterned after the procedure described by Lang and Lazovik (1963). Generally, this entails placing the child in a setting that contains the feared stimulus, then having the child perform a series of graduated tasks that call for approach to and interaction with the feared stimulus. Some passive variants of the procedure have the child remain stationary and bring the feared stimulus in a graduated fashion closer to the child (e.g., Giebenhain & Barrios, 1986; Kelley, 1976; Murphy & Bootzin, 1973; Van Hasselt et al., 1979). Whatever the variant, BATs have as their hallmark tight control over all aspects of the assessment situation.

At present, BATs have a number of characteristics that limit their usefulness. Principal among these is the absence of a standardized BAT, both within and across stimulus categories. Assessors appear inclined to design their own BATs, with unique sets of steps and instructions, rather than to employ an existing BAT. Such a practice may be consistent with an idiographic bent toward assessment (e.g., Cone, 1981, 1988; Nelson & Hayes, 1979, 1981), but it makes cross-study comparisons highly problematic. For example, the number of steps in BATs for small animals ranges from 1 (Evans & Harmon, 1981) to 29 (Ritter, 1968); in those for darkness, from 1 (e.g., Leitenberg & Callahan, 1973; Sheslow, Bondy, & Nelson, 1982) to 10 (Giebenhain & Barrios, 1986); and in those for the stimulus categories as a whole, from 1 to 85 (Ultee, Griffioen, & Schellekens, 1982). If there is any generality to the adult finding of greater approach with BATs including more gradations (Nawas, 1971), then comparing performances on BATs that differ in number of steps may be very risky.

The BATs also vary widely in the instructions that are given to the child, and this variability further handicaps attempts to integrate findings from different studies. Some BATs provide factual information about the feared stimulus (e.g., Bandura, Grusec, & Menlove, 1967; Murphy & Bootzin, 1973), while others do not (e.g., Davis, Rosenthal, & Kelley, 1981; Evans & Harmon, 1981). Having factual information may reduce ignorance of the feared stimulus, which in turn may lead to greater approach (Bernstein & Paul, 1971). The instructions for some BATs try to allay apprehension over possible danger and harm (e.g., Kornhaber & Schroeder, 1975), while the instructions for others make no attempt to do so (e.g., Giebenhain & Barrios, 1986). With adults, reducing uncertainty about threat has been shown to lead to greater approach and less physiological upset (Lick, Unger, & Condiotte, 1978). We think it reasonable to assume that similar reductions in children's uncertainty would result in comparable changes in responding.

Aside from information on the attributes of the feared stimulus, the BATs differ in their instructions for task performance. Some BATs describe all of the steps only at the outset of testing (e.g., Giebenhain & Barrios, 1986), while others stagger their description of the steps throughout the course of testing (e.g., Kornhaber & Schroeder, 1975). Some of the descriptions of the tasks are delivered live (e.g., Murphy & Bootzin, 1973; Van Hasselt et al., 1979), while others are delivered through recordings (e.g., Kornhaber & Schroeder, 1975). The instructions may ask the child "to perform as many of the steps as you can," "to perform as many of the steps as you can without feeling scared," or "to try as hard as you can to perform all of the steps." With adults, all of these variations have been found to influence BAT performance (see Bernstein & Nietzel, 1974). For example, there is greater approach when the instructions for each step are presented live and upon execution of the preceding step than when the instructions for all steps are recorded and presented at the onset of testing (Bernstein & Nietzel, 1973). With children, only the influence of instructional "demand" on BAT performance has been investigated. And even for this variable the degree of influence is not known, as the findings to date have been conflicting (Kelley, 1976; Sheslow et al., 1982).

The tight control that is a hallmark of the BATs may also be a serious drawback, because performance in the laboratory may not generalize to the naturalistic setting. The BATs expose children to a safe form of the feared stimulus within the context of a safe environment. With adults, the approach exhibited within the safety of the laboratory has not always transferred to the possibly more dangerous confines of the naturalistic setting (Lick & Unger, 1975, 1977). We think it is fair to assume that the BAT performance of children will likewise not always generalize beyond the laboratory.

Despite these shortcomings, the BATs have a number of points in their favor. First, the BATs are very straightforward procedures; they lend themselves well to reliable administration, and thus to standardization. Second, the BATs allow for the assessment of multiple motor responses. Some of the motor responses that have been measured in conjunction with approach are grimacing, stiffness, eye contact, nervous giggling, hesitation, crying, scanning, and nail biting (Esveldt-Dawson

et al., 1982; Evans & Harmon, 1981; Giebenhain & Barrios, 1986). And third, the BATs allow for the concurrent monitoring of activity from the subjective and physiological response systems. Thus, they are suitable vehicles for carrying out triple-response-system assessments of children's fears and anxieties (Barrios & Shigetomi, 1985). With their BATs for blood and heights, Van Hasselt et al. (1979) collected measures of approach, as well as measures of heart rate, finger pulse volume, and subjective distress. With their BAT for darkness, Giebenhain and Barrios (1986) collected measures of approach along with ones of heart rate, articulated thoughts, subjective distress, and self-statements. These two studies are good examples of the potential of BATs.

Observational Rating Systems

Although the BATs have as their hallmark the strict control of stimulus conditions, the observational rating systems have as their hallmark the lack of such control. The rating systems are used to assess children's motor reactions to events in the natural environment—events over which the assessor typically has little or no control. Children's reactions are observed directly, and the observations are recorded with some immediacy.

Observational rating systems have been developed for the assessment of children's motor reactions to darkness, medical procedures, public speaking, separation, social contact, and test taking. The rating systems vary in the number and type of motor responses they monitor. For example, Milos and Reiss's (1982) Observation of Separation-Relevant Play monitors the frequency of the single molar behavior of anxiety-relevant play, whereas Glennon and Weisz's (1978) Preschool Observational Scale of Anxiety monitors the frequency of 30 molecular behaviors.

Several of the rating systems used to monitor fear and anxiety reactions to medical procedures are sophisticated in their development, design, and scoring. The oldest of these is Melamed and Siegel's (1975) Observer Rating Scale of Anxiety. Developed for use with children undergoing surgery, the Observer Rating Scale of Anxiety consists of 28 response categories such as "crying," "stutters," and "trembling hands." Monitored for their frequency, the behaviors for all of the categories are combined to form a single (motor response) anxiety score for the entire observation period.

Melamed and her colleagues (Melamed, Hawes, Heiby, & Glick, 1975; Melamed, Weinstein, Hawes, & Katin-Borland, 1975; Melamed et al., 1978) have developed a similar instrument for assessing the motor responses of children to dental treatment. The Behavior Profile Rating Scale has 27 response categories (e.g., "crying," "kicking," "refusal to open mouth," "rigid posture," "verbal complaints," "white knuckles"), which are recorded for their frequency of occurrence throughout the observation period. The frequency scores for the various categories are combined to form a single, weighted composite score, with the weights representing how disruptive the behaviors are to the efficient treatment of the child as determined by the dentist.

Four other impressive observational rating systems for use in medical settings are the Procedure Behavioral Rating Scale (Katz et al., 1980), the Procedure Behavior Checklist (LeBaron & Zeltzer, 1984), the Observational Scale of Behavioral Distress (Jay & Elliott, 1984; Jay et al., 1983), and the Child–Adult Medical Procedure Interaction Scale—Revised (Blount et al., 1989; Blount, Sturges, & Powers, 1990). All four of these rating systems were developed for assessment of children's reactions to the same medical procedure—bone marrow aspiration. The first three systems are very similar to one another; in fact, the latter two can be viewed as modified versions of the former. In constructing the Procedure Behavioral Rating Scale, Katz et al. (1980) first compiled what they believed to be an exhaustive list of anxiety responses to bone marrow aspiration. For response items, they drew upon their own extensive clinical experience with children with cancer, as well as upon the experience of medical personnel who routinely performed bone marrow aspirations. Of the original 25 items generated, 12 were eliminated because of infrequency of occurrence or lack of correlation with other measures of anxiety.[7] The remaining 13 items serve as the scale. Each of the 13 behaviors is monitored for its occurrence–nonoccurrence across an observation session, with the total number of behaviors occurring standing as the response score for the session. Examples of the scale's response items and their operational definitions are "cry" (tears in eyes or running down face); "cling" (physically holds on to parent, significant other, or nurse); "scream" (no tears, raises voice, verbal or nonverbal); "flail" (random gross movements of arms or legs, without intention to make aggressive contact); and "muscular rigidity" (any of the following behaviors: clenched fists, white knuckles, gritted teeth, clenched jaw, wrinkled brow, eyes clenched shut, contracted limbs, body stiffness) (Katz et al., 1980, p. 359).

The Procedure Behavior Checklist (LeBaron & Zeltzer, 1984) differs from the Procedure Behavioral Rating Scale in number of items and format of scoring. Each of the system's eight behaviors is observed for its occurrence and is rated for its intensity of occurrence on a 1- to 5-point scale. The ratings are summed across behaviors to yield a total response score for the observation period.

The Observational Scale of Behavioral Distress (Jay & Elliott, 1984; Jay et al., 1983) differs from the Procedure Behavioral Rating Scale in its number, recording, and scoring of items. Each of the 11 items of this scale is recorded for occurrence–nonoccurrence every 15 seconds throughout the observation period. Each of the items is weighted for intensity of distress; the weights have been determined by medical personnel experienced in the bone marrow aspiration procedure. Occurrences for individual items are tallied, adjusted for their intensity of distress, and then summed.

In the Child–Adult Medical Procedure Interaction Scale—Revised (Blount et al., 1989, 1990), the verbal behaviors of the child and the parent are assigned to one of six categories: "child coping" (e.g., audible deep breathing, humor, nonprocedural talk), "child distress" (e.g., cry, scream, request emotional support), "child neutral" (e.g., request relief from nonprocedural discomfort), "adult coping-promoting" (e.g., humor to child, command to use coping strategy), "adult distress-promoting" (e.g., criticism, reassuring comments, empathy), and "adult neutral" (e.g., humor to adults, procedural talk to adults, checking child's status). The six categories encompass a total of 35 specific response codes. A proportion score for each of the six categories is computed for each of nine phases of the bone marrow aspiration/lumbar puncture procedure by dividing the number of occurrences for a category by the total number of occurrences for the combined child or adult categories.

Among the other noteworthy observational rating systems are the Preschool Observational Scale of Anxiety (Glennon & Weisz, 1978); the Observation of Classroom Behavior (Wine, 1979); and two versions of Paul's (1966) Timed Behavior Checklist—the Revised Timed Behavior Checklist (Fox & Houston, 1981) and the Modified Timed Behavior Checklist (Giebenhain & Barrios, 1986). Though it is most often used to assess children's behavioral responses to separation, the Preschool Observational Scale of Anxiety was designed for use across a broad range of stimulus situations. The scale is made up of 30 overt behaviors, all of which appeared in the literature as observable indicators of children's anxiety, were screened by clinical child psychologists for their appropriateness, and were tested for their ability to be reliably and accurately observed. The individual behaviors are observed for their occurrence–nonoccurrence every 30 seconds; the occurrences are summed across 30-second intervals and behaviors to form a motor behavior score for the entire assessment period. Examples of the scale's 30 responses are "gratuitous leg movement," "trunk contortions," "lip-licking," "whisper," and "fingers touching mouth area."

The Observation of Classroom Behavior (Wine, 1979) is a detailed scheme for observing children's anticipatory reactions to an academic examination. Though originally used in conjunction with video recordings of the children's classroom behavior, the system appears quite amenable for live use. A 15-minute sample of each child's behavior is divided into 30-second intervals; for each interval, the occurence–nonoccurrence of 22 discrete observable behaviors is recorded. The behaviors are grouped into five categories: Attending Behaviors (e.g., child orients head and eyes toward the teacher when he or she is addressing the class), Task-Related Behaviors (e.g., child works quietly on assignment), Activity (e.g., child leaves desk), Communication (e.g., child initiates communication with a classmate), and Interactional Behaviors (e.g., child aggresses against another child). Occurrences for each of the 22 behaviors are summed across the 30-second intervals to yield 22 response scores for the observational period.

Paul's (1966) Timed Behavior Checklist has been used in the assessment of older children's reactions to public speaking (Cradock, Cotler, & Jason, 1978; Gilbert, Johnson, Silverstein, & Malone, 1989) and has been modified for use in the assessment of younger children's reactions to public speaking (Fox & Houston, 1981) and to darkness (Giebenhain & Barrios, 1986). Based on a factor-analytic study of anxiety signs in speech research (Clevanger & King, 1961), the Timed Behavior Checklist was designed to measure overt anxiety in situations involving public speaking. The checklist consists of 20 behaviors (e.g., stammering, hand tremors, foot shuffling) that are monitored every 30 seconds for their occurrence–nonoccurrence. Occurrences are summed across behaviors and intervals to yield a single anxiety response score for the entire period. The Fox and Houston (1981) and the Giebenhain and Barrios (1986) versions of the rating system differ from the original only in terms of the number of response items: The Fox and Houston (1981) adap-

tation has 12 items, whereas the Giebenhain and Barrios (1986) adaptation has 9 items.

Checklists

A third type of observational instrument for the assessment of the motor component of children's fears and anxieties is the checklist. Like an observational rating system, a checklist is composed of multiple responses that are monitored for their occurrence in the naturalistic setting. Unlike the observational rating system, the checklist provides retrospective data, as there may be a considerable delay between the monitoring of the checklist items and the recording of those observations.

Checklists exist for the assessment of children's motor reactions to specific situations (e.g., darkness, separation, test taking), as well as to multiple situations (i.e., generalized anxiety). The checklists vary not only in their stimulus situations, but also in the number and nature of their response items and the timetable for their observations and recordings. This variation is illustrated in the two checklists available for the assessment of children's responses to darkness—the Fear Strength Questionnaire and the Direct Home Observation (Graziano & Mooney, 1980). It can also be seen in the three available for the assessment of children's responses to separation: the Parent Anxiety Rating Scale—Separation (Doris, McIntyre, Kelsey, & Lehman, 1971), the Teachers' Separation Anxiety Scale (Doris et al., 1971), and the Teacher Rating of Separation Anxiety (Hall, 1967).

The Fear Strength Questionnaire has nine response items that are observed and reported on for an indeterminate time period. These are the frequency, duration, and intensity of nighttime fear episodes; the episodes' disruption of the child's, the siblings', and the parents' behavior; the seriousness of the fear episodes; the degree of school disruption; and the impairment in the child's social adjustment. The Direct Home Observation has a shorter list of response items, a shorter period of observation, and a shorter interval between observation and recording than the Fear Strength Questionnaire. The five items (e.g., number of minutes required to fall asleep, avoidance and delay behaviors displayed) are monitored and marked on a nightly basis.

The three checklists for separation anxiety show similar variation in number and nature of response items, span of observation period, and delay between observation and measurement. The Parent Anxiety Rating Scale—Separation has six response items that cover an extended, indeterminate period of observation of the child. The Teachers' Separation Anxiety Scale has 11 response items covering a much more circumscribed period of monitoring (i.e., the interval following the parent's placement of the child in school and the parent's departure), but the observations are not recorded until the end of the school day. And the Teacher Rating of Separation Anxiety has three items asking for reports of both recent and past reactions to separation from the parent (i.e., reports of the child's reaction to separation from the parent at the onset of the school year, for the last 2 weeks, and for the entire time that school has been in session).

Global Ratings

The fourth type of observational instrument for the assessment of the motor component of children's fears and anxieties is the global rating. The simplest (and surely the most suspect) of all the observational instruments, the global rating calls for a single, overall evaluation of the child's response to the problematic situation. Some form of global rating has been used to assess children's reactions to the medical procedures of bone marrow aspiration (Hubert, Jay, Saltoun, & Hayes, 1988; LeBaron & Zeltzer, 1984), cardiac catheterization (Bradlyn, Christoff, Sikora, O'Dell, & Harris, 1986), dental treatment (Melamed, Hawes, et al., 1975; Melamed, Weinstein, et al., 1975; Venham, Gaulin-Kremer, Munster, Bengston-Audia, & Cohan, 1980), insulin injection (Gilbert et al., 1982), and surgery (Peterson & Shigetomi, 1981; Vernon, Foley, & Schulman, 1967). These global ratings, though, differ from one another in terms of number of scale points and descriptions of those scale points. The global ratings range from ones having a 5-point scale (Hubert et al., 1988; LeBaron & Zeltzer, 1984; Peterson & Shigetomi, 1981; Venham et al., 1980) to ones employing a 10-point scale (Gilbert et al., 1982 Melamed, Hawes, et al., 1975; Melamed, Weinstein, et al., 1975), with few of them providing response definitions for each of the scale points. Four that do provide descriptive anchors are the Approach–Avoidance scale of the Nurse Rating (Hubert et al., 1988), the Global Mood Scale (Vernon et al., 1967), the Venham Anxiety-Rating Scale (Venham et al., 1980), and the Venham Behavior-Rating Scale (Venham et al., 1980). Even these four, though, allow for considerable inference in the assignment of ratings. For example, the descriptive anchors for the two endpoints of the Nurse Ratings' Approach–Avoidance scale are "child actively avoids nurse/consistently refuses to look at, talk to, or interact/does not indicate yes–no response" and "child actively approaches nurses by consistently initiating interactions such as asking questions, beginning conversation, requesting participation." The descriptive anchors for the two endpoints of the Global Mood Scale are "attentive and active in happy or contented way" and "scream full blast, intense and constant crying." For the midpoint of the Venham Behavior-Rating Scale, the descriptive anchor is "protest presents real problems to dentist, complies reluctantly, body movement"; for the midpoint of the Venham Anxiety-Rating Scale, the descriptive anchor is "shows reluctance to enter situation, difficulty in correctly assessing situational threat, pronounced verbal protest, crying, using hands to stop procedure, protest out of proportion, copes with great reluctance."

Interviews

Two of the instruments gather information on the motor component of children's fears and anxieties through use of the traditional avenue of the clinical interview: the Children's Anxiety Evaluation Form (Hoehn-Saric et al., 1987) and the Anxiety Disorders Interview Schedule for Children—Parent Version (Silverman & Nelles, 1988; Silverman & Eisen, 1992). The two instruments differ dramatically in terms of who serves as the observer/informant regarding the child's fear behavior and how the observations are quantified and utilized. In the Children's Anxiety Evaluation Form, the interviewer notes the appearance and rates the severity of 18 overt signs of anxiety over the course of an approximately 30-minute interview with the child. The ratings of the 18 behavioral signs (e.g., nail biting, stuttering, and swallowing) are then drawn upon to render an overall global rating of overt anxiety, which is combined with ratings of other self-report and archival data to form a total anxiety score. In the Anxiety Disorders Interview Schedule for Children—Parent Version, the interviewer questions the parent about the anxious child's symptomatology, symptom history, symptom severity, precipitating events, and anticipatory cues. Drawing upon the observations of the parent, the interviewer then assigns a psychiatric diagnosis to the child's fear reaction. A more detailed discussion of the interview as a data collection strategy appears in the following section on self-report methods.

Summary

By definition, all five types of observational instruments—BATs, observational ratings, checklists, global ratings, and interviews—employ human observers. As such, they must all contend with the host of measurement issues that surround (but are not confined to) the collection of observational data. These issues include the accuracy and reactivity of observational assessment and the intrusion of bias, drift, and expectancies into observers' recordings (Barrios, 1993; Foster, Bell-Dolan, & Burge, 1988; Foster & Cone, 1980; Harris & Lahey, 1982a, 1982b; Hartmann & Wood, 1982; Haynes & Horn, 1982; Kazdin, 1981; Kent & Foster, 1977). These issues of construct and external validity (e.g., Cook & Campbell, 1979) have yet to be addressed in earnest by developers and users of observational instruments for the assessment of children's fears and anxieties. In the section on the evaluation and selection of assessment instruments, this concern for the validity of the measures is taken up more fully.

Self-Report Methods

Of the 160-plus instruments listed in the Appendix, 66 are self-report in nature. Though the measurement method of self-report lends itself to the assessment of all three components of children's fears and anxieties, most of these 66 self-report instruments have as their sole focus the subjective component.[8] From these numbers, it is obvious that behavior therapists have not overlooked children's inner worlds—their experiences, thoughts, and expectations—in their assessment of children's fears and anxieties. Such was not the case at the time of the first edition of *Behavioral Assessment of Childhood Disorders* (Mash & Terdal, 1981), as few instruments existed then for the measurement of a child's subjective reactions (see Barrios, Hartmann, & Shigetomi, 1981). The many instruments now available may indicate just how widely accepted the three-system conceptualization of fear and anxiety is among behavior therapists (e.g., Morris & Kratochwill, 1983b; Silverman, 1987), and also just how widely emphasized the cognitive component is in the assessment and treatment practices of behavior therapists (e.g., Kendall et al., 1992). These self-report instruments for assessing children's fears and anxieties can be separated into six types: interviews, global ratings, self-monitoring, questionnaires, think-aloud procedures, and thought-listing procedures.

Interviews

In recent years, we have witnessed a return to favor of the interview in the behavioral assessment of childhood disorders. Encouraged by such wise and sensitive commentators as the editors of this volume (Mash & Terdal, 1988), behavior therapists have begun making use of the structured interview in their comprehensive assessment of childhood disorders. Among the problem conditions that are now being routinely assessed through use of the structured interview are children's fears and anxieties (e.g., Ollendick & Francis, 1988).

Essentially, there are two major classes of interview schedules for the assessment of children's fears and anxieties: those that address a wide range of problem conditions, in which fears and anxieties are included, and those that address only the specific problem conditions of fears and anxieties. Among the former are the Child Assessment Schedule (Hodges, Kline, Stern, Cytryn, & McKnew, 1982), the Diagnostic Interview for Children and Adolescents (Herjanic & Reich, 1982), the Diagnostic Interview Schedule for Children (Costello, Edelbrock, Dulcan, Kalas, & Klaric, 1984), the Interview Schedule for Children (Kovacs, 1983), and the Schedule for Affective Disorders and Schizophrenia for School-Age Children (Puig-Antich & Chambers, 1978). And among the latter are the Children's Anxiety Evaluation Form (Hoehn-Saric et al., 1987), the Children's Post-Traumatic Stress Disorder Inventory (Saigh, 1987, 1989a), and the Anxiety Disorders Interview Schedule for Children—Child Version (Silverman & Eisen, 1992; Silverman & Nelles, 1988). Because the focus of this chapter is condition-specific, we limit our discussion to the interview schedules of the latter class.

The three interview schedules for the assessment of children's fears and anxieties vary greatly in the scope of their questioning and the scoring of the interviewees' replies. In the Children's Anxiety Evaluation Form, a child is questioned as to the nature, frequency, severity, and situational specificity of several classes of anxiety symptoms (e.g., tension, sleep difficulty, anxious mood, somatic, cardiovascular, respiratory, gastrointestinal). The interviewer rates the frequency and severity of the symptoms for each of the classes, and then draws upon these multiple ratings to render a single, global rating of symptom frequency and severity. This global rating is subsequently combined with global ratings derived from archival data and observational data to produce a total anxiety score. Thus, the interview yields a continuous measure of anxiety spanning a wide range of responses and a wide range of situations. In the Children's Post-Traumatic Stress Disorder Inventory, the child is questioned in four areas: the experience of a traumatic event, the experience of unwanted trauma-related ideation, the experience of general affective changes, and the experience of diverse postevent disturbances. The interviewer notes the presence or absence of various symptoms addressed in the various lines of questioning, and renders a diagnosis on the basis of these notations. Thus, the interview yields a dichotomous measure of the presence–absence of the specific anxiety reaction of Posttraumatic Stress Disorder. In the Anxiety Disorders Interview Schedule for Children—Child Version, the child is questioned at length about anxious symptoms, symptom history, symptom severity, precipitating events, and anticipatory cues. From the child's reports of symptom occurrence and the interviewer's ratings of symptom severity, the interviewer arrives at a diagnosis with respect to several specific anxiety reactions. Thus, the interview yields dichotomous measures of the presence–absence of each of these specific reactions.

Global Self-Ratings

Global self-ratings differ from global observer ratings solely in terms of who serves as the evaluator. In the former, the child serves as both the evaluator and the evaluated; in the latter, a person other than the child serves as the evaluator. A global self-rating consists of a multipoint scale on which the child rates his or her overall reaction to a troublesome stimulus situation. The stimulus conditions for which global ratings have been obtained are blood (Van Hasselt et al., 1979), darkness (Giebenhain & Barrios, 1986; Kelley, 1976), cardiac catheterization (Bradlyn et al., 1986), bone marrow aspiration (LeBaron & Zeltzer, 1984), dental treatment (Melamed, Hawes, et al., 1975; Melamed, Weinstein, et al., 1975), test taking (Van Hasselt et al., 1979), and separation (Glennon & Weisz, 1978).

Despite the simplicity of this assessment approach, there is no uniformly accepted format for global self-rating scales. Instead, there are many different scales differing in length and in detail. For example, the Target Complaint Scales of Van Hasselt et al. (1979) has the child rate his or her level of fear on a 12-point scale that includes a descriptive term at every third point (e.g., "none," "pretty much," "couldn't be worse"). Others,

such as the fear thermometers of Kelley (1976) and Melamed (Melamed, Hawes, et al., 1975; Melamed et al., 1978) employ a 5-point scale with a denotative color at each point. And still other global rating scales employ drawings of figures or facial expressions as their descriptive anchors, such as the Faces—Subjective Units of Disturbance (Bradlyn et al., 1986), the Faces Test of Anxiety (LeBaron & Zeltzer, 1984), the fear thermometer of Giebenhain and Barrios (1986), and the Global Self-Rating (Glennon & Weisz, 1978).

Self-Monitoring

In self-monitoring, the child tracks certain aspects of his or her performance and provides an ongoing record of them (Shapiro, 1984). In essence, self-monitoring constitutes a measurement procedure calling for the self-initiation of repeated assessments of one's own performance. Seemingly convenient and inexpensive, self-monitoring has been used in the assessment of children's fears and anxieties on only two occasions to date. And on these two occasions, the two self-monitoring procedures have differed greatly in their focus and form.

The Self-Monitoring Log developed by McNamara (1988) consists of a recording sheet on which the child notes school attendance and number of subject lessons attended. Beside the recording of each lesson attended, the child provides a rating of self-confidence on a 0- to 100-point scale, with 0 denoting being "dreadfully upset" and 100 denoting being "completely at ease." With the Daily Diary developed by Beidel, Neal, and Lederer (1991), the child completes a checklist upon the occurrence of an anxiety-provoking situation. The checklist calls for the recording of the date, time, location, and nature of the anxiety-provoking event (e.g., test, being called upon to perform in front of others, return of an exam), as well as the nature of the responses emitted to this situation (e.g., cried, closed eyes, feigned sickness, avoided). The checklist also calls for a rating of arousal experienced to the situation through use of a 5-point pictorial scale.

Questionnaires

A fourth type of self-report instrument for assessing the subjective dimension of children's fears and anxieties is the questionnaire. Unlike the global rating, which has a single response item, the questionnaire has multiple response items that are either categorical or continuous in nature. The

Appendix lists 43 questionnaires, 23 of which have as their focus the child's reactions to a specific stimulus situation and 20 of which have no such stimulus restrictions. The former are referred to collectively as "specific fear questionnaires," the latter as "general anxiety questionnaires."

Specific fear questionnaires are available for the following stimuli: darkness (Giebenhain & Barrios, 1986), fire (Jones, Ollendick, McLaughlin, & Williams, 1989), medical and dental procedures (Bradlyn et al., 1986; Melamed, Hawes, et al., 1975; Peterson, Schultheis, Ridley-Johnson, Miller, & Tracy, 1984; Venham, Bengston, & Cipes, 1977), school attendance (Kearney & Silverman, 1990, 1993), small animals (Kornhaber & Schroeder, 1975), social interaction (Barlow & Seidner, 1983; Clark et al., 1994; Glass, Merluzzi, Biever, & Larsen, 1982; LaGreca & Stone, 1993), solitariness (Peterson, 1987), test taking (Harnisch, Hill, & Fyans, 1980; Houston, Fox, & Forbes, 1984; Meece, 1981; Sarason, Davidson, Lighthall, Waite, & Ruebush, 1960; Zatz & Chassin, 1983, 1985), and water (Menzies & Clarke, 1993).

As might be expected, there is little consistency in the format of these questionnaires, either within or across stimulus situations. The questionnaires vary in their number of response items from 7 (i.e., Cognitive Behavior Questionnaire, Test Comfort Index, and Water Phobia Survey Schedule) to 50 (i.e., Children's Cognitive Assessment Questionnaire). They also vary in the nature and number of subjective responses assessed. Many of the questionnaires ask for repeated ratings of overall fear and anxiety to a number of related aspects of the same troublesome situation. For example, the Fear Inventory for Fire Safety (Jones et al., 1989) has the child estimate how afraid he or she is of 33 fire-related events; the Hospital Fears Rating Scale (Melamed & Siegel, 1975), how afraid he or she is of 16 hospital events; the Children's Fear Survey Schedule—Dental (Melamed, Hawes, et al., 1975; Melamed, Weinstein, et al., 1975), how afraid he or she is of 15 dental events; and the Fear and Avoidance Hierarchy Ratings (Barlow & Seidner, 1983), how afraid he or she is of 10 social events. Other questionnaires ask for ratings of different subjective responses to the same stimulus situation. For example, the Children's Cognitive Assessment Questionnaire (Zatz & Chassin, 1985) has the child estimate the occurrence of 50 different thoughts related to test taking; the Social Interaction Self-Statement Test (Glass et al., 1982), the occurrence of 30 different thoughts related to a social encounter; and the Self-Statement Checklist (Giebenhain & Barrios, 1986), the occurrence of 10 different thoughts related to darkness.

The 20 general fear questionnaires can be separated into two groups: those instruments that assess the child's subjective reactions to a wide range of life situations, and those that assess a wide range of the child's subjective reactions to his or her overall life situation. The former group consists of the eight fear survey schedules; the latter group consists of the 12 more trait-oriented instruments (e.g., the Children's Manifest Anxiety Scale, the Negative Affect Self-Statement Questionnaire, the State–Trait Anxiety Inventory for Children).

Among the eight fear survey schedules, the oldest is the 80-item Fear Survey Schedule for Children, developed by Scherer and Nakamura (1968). Appropriate for use with children between the ages of 9 and 12, the schedule has the child rate on a 5-point scale his or her level of fear to each of the 80 stimulus items. In order to render the schedule suitable for use with younger or less intelligent children, Ollendick (1978, 1983) replaced the instrument's 5-point rating scale with a 3-point rating scale. And in order to insure the continued content relevance and coverage of the schedule, Gullone and King (1992) replaced the instrument's dated stimulus items with more current ones and reduced the length of the survey by 5 items. Very similar to the Fear Survey Schedule for Children and its revisions is the Louisville Fear Survey Schedule (Miller et al., 1972), which contains 81 items, employs a 3-point rating scale, and is appropriate for use with children between the ages of 4 and 18. Of the remaining fear survey schedules, two of them (i.e., the Children's Fear Survey Schedule and its revision) employ a 3-point rating scale with 50 stimulus items, and one of them (i.e., the Fear Survey for Children With and Without Mental Retardation) employs a 2-point rating scale with 60 stimulus items.

The group of general fear questionnaires that assess a wide range of children's subjective responses to their overall life situation contains two of the most frequently employed instruments in all of child psychology: the Children's Manifest Anxiety Scale (Castaneda, McCandless, & Palermo, 1956) and the State–Trait Anxiety Inventory for Children (Spielberger, 1973). The original version of the Children's Manifest Anxiety Scale contains 53 items—42 that assess the child's general anxiety state and 9 that assess the child's tendency to falsify reports. Reynolds and Richmond (1978) revised the scale in order to decrease administration time, to lower the required reading level, and to increase item clarity and conformity with test standards. Their revision of the scale contains 37 items—29 that assess the child's general anxiety state (e.g., "I have trouble making up my mind," "I am afraid of a lot of things") and 8 that assess the child's tendency to falsify reports (e.g., "I am always good," "I never lie").

Patterned after the adult form of the instrument (Spielberger, Gorsuch, & Lushene, 1970), the State–Trait Anxiety Inventory for Children consists of two 20-item scales: a State scale, which measures transitory anxiety reactions to particular situations; and a Trait scale, which measures a stable predisposition to act anxiously, regardless of the situation. From this inventory, Fox and Houston (1983) have constructed two other instruments: the Cognitive and Somatic State Anxiety Inventory, and the Cognitive and Somatic Trait Anxiety Inventory. The two instruments differ from the original in that they divide the State and Trait scales into subscales for the subjective and for the physiological dimensions of anxiety.

Think-Aloud Procedures

A fifth type of self-report instrument for the assessment of the subjective component is the think-aloud procedure. First, the child is asked to verbalize his or her thoughts in anticipation of and/or exposure to a distressing stimulus. Recordings of the verbalized thoughts are then scored for certain categories of responses—a not-so-simple task, for it involves the generation and delineation of classes of verbalized thoughts.

To date, we know of only two attempts to assess the subjective aspects of children's fears and anxieties by means of the think-aloud procedure (i.e., Giebenhain & Barrios, 1986; Houston et al., 1984). The two procedures both have the child voice his or her thoughts into a tape recorder, but differ in their systems for scoring the spoken thoughts. Houston and his colleagues rate the child's verbalizations in terms of seven categories of thoughts, including analytic attitude (e.g., "I think the game is very colorful"), derogation of other (e.g., "I don't even see why I'm doing this"), justification of positive attitude (e.g., "I just think it's really fun to do things like this because a lot of kids don't get to do this"), performance denigration (e.g., "I'm feeling sort of scared about this"), and situation-irrelevant thoughts (e.g., "Wonder what I'm going to do when school's out"). Giebenhain and Barrios (1986) score the child's verbalizations for three classes of thoughts: fearful (e.g., "I'm getting scared"), coping (e.g., "I know nothing bad is going to happen to me"),

and other (e.g., "I hope Mom makes me hamburgers tonight"). In addition to these three response scores, the child's entire think-aloud performance is rated for overall level of fear.

Thought-Listing Procedures

A final type of self-report instrument for the assessment of children's fears and anxieties is the thought-listing procedure. In this approach, the child is asked to recall and to report all thoughts experienced during the course of a recent anxiety-provoking situation.[9] The four thought-listing procedures that have been developed to date differ in the prompts they provide to the child and in the scores they derive from the child's recollections.

Beidel and Turner (1988) have the child write down all thoughts that appeared during a just-completed 10-minute vocabulary test or a just-completed 10-minute oral reading. The written responses are then rated as positive, negative, or neutral, according to a scoring scheme developed by Last, Barlow, and O'Brien (1984). Prins (1985, 1986) has the child participate in a semistructured interview consisting of questions pertaining to fearfulness (e.g., "How scared were you?"), self-speech (e.g., "What did you think/say to yourself while you were standing on the high board?"), self-regulation (e.g., "Did you have a trick/strategy to be less fearful?"), knowledge of self-regulation (e.g., "Can you think of another trick you could use?"), and perception of personal control (e.g., "You were scared, but it went all right. Why was that?"). Responses to the questions addressing self-speech are categorized as positive, negative, or neutral; responses to the questions addressing self-regulation are categorized as cognitive or behavioral self-regulation. Johnson and Glass (1989) have the youth listen to an audiotape recording of a social interaction in which he or she has just participated. The youth stops the tape at every juncture in the interaction in which a thought experienced at that point in the interaction is recalled. The recollected thoughts are rated for focus (i.e., self-evaluative, nonevaluative, partner, conversation, irrelevant) and valence (i.e., positive, negative, neutral). For each of the eight response categories, the cumulative ratings are converted to a proportion of the total number of thoughts recalled.

Summary

All of the questions that have historically surrounded self-report measures can be raised about all of the instruments in this section. Chief among these are the questionable validity of the measures and the susceptibility of the measures to response bias, demand, and social desirability (e.g., Haynes, 1978; Haynes & Wilson, 1979; Jayaratne & Levy, 1979). The various types of self-report instruments described in this section are also subject to many implementation and measurement questions that are peculiar to each of them. For the interview schedules, these include issues of interviewer training, interviewer expectancies, and interviewer consistency (Hughes, 1989; Saigh, 1992); for the self-monitoring procedures, these include issues of compliance, reactivity, and accuracy (Barlow, Hayes, & Nelson, 1984; Nelson, 1977). In general, these fundamental and individual matters of method and measurement have yet to be examined in depth by the developers and users of self-report devices for the assessment of children's fears and anxieties. In the section on the evaluation and selection of assessment instruments, these concerns for the applicability, reliability, and validity of the measures are discussed at greater length.

Mechanical Methods

Few of the instruments listed in the Appendix employ direct mechanical recording in their assessment of children's fears and anxieties. Of the mere 16 that do, all but 1 have as their focus the physiological component of children's fears and anxieties. Their small numbers attest to the difficulties and complexities involved in directly assessing the activity of the physiological component. Chief among these complicating factors is the absence of a simple response or combination of responses that reliably denotes physiological upset across persons and stimuli (Johnson & Lubin, 1972). The classic work of the Laceys (Lacey, 1956; Lacey & Lacey, 1967) clearly demonstrates that life's stressors are numerous, and that for any given stressor there are individual differences in the exact expression of physiological upset. For the assessor of children's fear and anxieties, the implication is that adequate measurement of the physiological component will entail the measurement of multiple physiological responses.

Adequate measurement of the physiological component also entails the proper selection and operation of equipment across the appropriate parameters of assessment (e.g., Averill & Opton, 1968; Martin & Venables, 1980). Moreover, adequate recording and quantification of physio-

logical activity call for sensitivity to such phenomena as adaptation (see Barlow, Leitenberg, & Agras, 1969; Montague & Coles, 1966) and initial values (Benjamin, 1963; Lacey, 1956; Ray & Raczynski, 1981; Wilder, 1950), as well as to such measurement contaminants as room temperature and extraneous movement (e.g., Fehr, 1970; Martin & Venables, 1980; Shapiro, 1975).

Despite the complexity of physiological assessment, measures of heart rate, finger pulse volume, respiration, skin conductance, and blood pressure have been collected. In some instances, elaborate electronic equipment (e.g., a physiograph) has been used to obtain the measures (e.g., Faust & Melamed, 1984; Klingman, Melamed, Cuthbert, & Hermecz, 1984; Melamed et al., 1978; Van Hasselt et al., 1979); in other instances, less expensive and technical equipment has been employed (e.g., Giebenhain & Barrios, 1986; Melamed & Siegel, 1975). The latter type of equipment warrants description, for it circumvents the major obstacle to assessment of the physiological component of children's fears and anxieties: its infeasibility.

One of these feasible instruments is the palmar sweat index (Johnson & Dabbs, 1967; Thomson & Sutarman, 1953). The technique calls for brushing a plastic solution onto either the child's fingertips or palm—two sites that contain a high concentration of sweat glands. When active, a sweat gland leaves a distinct impression on the plastic coating. A measure of the child's electrodermal response is thus provided by simply counting the number of impressions that appear on the coating's surface.

Other practical and relatively inexpensive instruments are the many portable devices for recording physiological activity. One such device—a digital pulse monitor (Lafayette Instruments, Model 77065)—was used by Giebenhain and Barrios (1986) to assess the heart rates of children in response to various shades of darkness. The instrument's finger clip, in which the sensing element resides, was decorated to look like a Band-Aid and was referred to as one in order to assuage the children's apprehension about the device. Through use of the digital pulse monitor, Giebenhain and Barrios (1986) were able to assess the children's physiological responses (i.e., heart rate) as they assessed their motor and subjective responses. Thus, in addition to being economical, the portable recording devices can be employed in concert with instruments assessing other components of children's fears and anxieties.

EVALUATION AND SELECTION OF ASSESSMENT INSTRUMENTS

With over 160 instruments for the assessment of children's fears and anxieties to choose from, the task facing clinicians is to select for use those that best meet the needs and constraints of their unique working situations. The judicious selection of assessment instruments hinges upon a host of clinical and practical considerations. In the practice of behavior therapy, clinicians look to assessment data for assistance in rendering a series of critical decisions (e.g., Barrios, 1988; Barrios & Hartmann, 1986). Initially, they determine from each presenting complaint the likelihood of the existence of a particular problem condition; given a reasonable likelihood of its existence, they next determine whether or not the condition constitutes a problem. Should a problem condition be identified or diagnosed, clinicians then decide whether or not treatment is warranted; and given a decision that treatment is called for, they subsequently select or develop a procedure to carry out. Finally, upon implementation of the treatment, they determine whether or not the intervention is having the desired effects.

As stated above, clinicians draw upon assessment data for guidance in rendering each one of these critical decisions. How helpful the assessment data are with respect to any given decision is largely a function of their fidelity, generality, and interpretability. The fidelity of the assessment data is reflected in the three traditional measurement properties of "item reliability," "interscorer reliability," and "occasion reliability" (i.e., the extent to which response scores are consistent across the items of the instrument, the extent to which the scores are consistent across independent evaluators, and the extent to which the scores are stable across time periods of no treatment). The generality of the assessment data is reflected in the three traditional measurement properties of "convergent validity," "diagnostic validity," and "nomological validity" (i.e., the degree to which response scores correspond with other measures of the same problem condition, the degree to which the scores discriminate individuals with varying levels of the problem condition, and the degree to which the scores fluctuate in accord with treatments for the problem condition). And the interpretability of the assessment data is reflected in the availability of a backdrop (e.g., a body of normative estimates, a standard for criterion performance). From this listing, it follows

that judicious selection of assessment instruments calls for careful examination of these measurement properties.[10]

As stated earlier, all of the assessment instruments prescribe certain types of situational controls and data collection strategies. Achieving the prescribed situational arrangement and collecting the response data in the prescribed fashion mean that clinicians must have certain types of resources, assistance, and authority. It follows, then, that judicious selection of assessment instruments includes close inspection of these practical requirements.

In the Appendix, under the heading of "Appraisal," we summarize the available data on the aforementioned properties (i.e., reliability, validity, and interpretive framework) for each of the 160-plus instruments. We also comment on the major uses to which each of the instruments can be put (i.e., screening, problem identification, treatment selection, and treatment evaluation) and the major settings in which each can be employed (i.e., the clinic and the laboratory). The ideal is for an instrument to be suitable for use in both the clinic and the laboratory, because information from both settings is critical to our understanding of children's fears; however, the practical requirements for the implementation of an instrument and the exigencies of the clinical situation are often at odds. We trust that our recommendations reflect sensitivity and solutions to this tension.

Direct Observations

Of the three methods of measurement—direct observation, self-report, and mechanical—more is known about the psychometric properties of direct observation instruments than about the properties of the other two methods. This is not altogether surprising, given that the observational instruments have as their focus the motor component of children's fears, which has been the principal component of interest among behavior therapists. Of the nearly 80 observational instruments listed in the Appendix, approximately one-half have estimates attesting to their interscorer reliability, their convergent validity (i.e., convergence with other measures of motor activity), and their treatment sensitivity (i.e., fluctuations in scores as a function of theoretically active interventions). Approximately one-third of the instruments have estimates testifying to their stability over time and their convergence with measures of the subjective and physiological components of children's fears.[11] Few of the instruments have information on their internal consistency, their ability to discriminate children known to differ in level of fearfulness, and their generality across relevant settings. And only one of the instruments has data on norms or base rates.

Of the five types of observational instruments—BATs, observational rating systems, checklists, global ratings, and interview observations and ratings—the observational rating systems tend to have the strongest psychometric properties. This superiority may be attributable to their frequency of use as well as to their format. Observational rating systems have been used more frequently than the other observational methods; with this more frequent use, more information about their psychometric properties has accrued. This information has provided feedback as to the adequacy of the instruments and has thus led to improvements. The makeup of the rating systems and the way in which the observations are recorded and scored are especially conducive to reliable assessment. Rating systems are composed of multiple response items, each of which is specifically defined and immediately recorded, and the recordings from these items are summed to yield a composite score. Such features help reduce errors in measurement that might result from the inattentiveness of observers or the instability of single response items.

Both BATs and checklists have been used sporadically; as a consequence, a sizable body of information on their properties has yet to accrue. With more regular use, individual BATs may prove to be valuable instruments for assessing children's fears and anxieties. Their straightforwardness and their suitability for standardization and for the measurement of multiple responses would certainly suggest as much.[12] In their current form, checklists do not appear to have this potential. For many of the checklists, the response items are vague, and the delay between observing and recording may be substantial. The checklists are, however, easy to implement—a feature that makes them very attractive to practitioners. In order for the checklists to be both useful and easy to use, they will need to undergo some alterations to remedy their obvious defects.

It is doubtful that any amount of alteration will make the global ratings sound instruments for assessing children's fears and anxieties. In addition to being notoriously unreliable and conceptually barren (e.g., Nunnally, 1978), single-item measures such as the global ratings listed in the Appendix lack clarity of content. In this case, they fail to specify what aspects of children's performance are to be observed; in doing so, they fail to specify what it is they measure. This ambiguity of meaning is the global ratings' most serious drawback and argues against their continued use.[13] Despite these misgivings, behavior therapists in unison are unlikely to abandon the global ratings; the ease with which the ratings can be collected all but guarantees their continued use in some cases.

Self-Reports

Though the numbers of self-report instruments for the assessment of children's fears and anxieties are fast approaching the numbers of observational instruments, much less is known about the measurement properties of the former than about those of the latter. Of the 60-plus self-report instruments listed in the Appendix, information on reliability and validity is available for only a third of them. And information on all-important norms is available for but a handful of them. This lack of psychometric data can be attributed in large part to the recency with which many of the instruments have been developed, employed and examined. In the first and second editions of *Behavioral Assessment of Childhood Disorders*, we noted the scarcity of techniques for assessing the subjective reactions of children and the incompatibility of the few existing techniques with the prevailing behavioral conceptualizations of fear and anxiety (Barrios & Hartmann, 1988; Barrios et al., 1981). Now, however, we are pleased to note that there are several self-report techniques for the assessment of children's fears and anxieties (e.g., interviews, questionnaires, self-monitoring procedures, think-aloud procedures), and that these appear completely in accord with current behavioral accounts of fear and anxiety.

The self-report instruments listed in the Appendix vary greatly in their merits as tools for the assessment of children's fears and anxieties. Least promising are the global self-ratings, such as the fear thermometers and the faces tests.[14] Like the global observer ratings, the global self-ratings are single-item measures; thus, they suffer from the same limitations as all single-item measures (i.e., instability, poor discrimination, and ambiguous meaning). And, as with the global observer ratings, it is doubtful that these limitations will completely override their attractive but less critical features (i.e., their face validity and ease of administration).

Much more promising for the assessment of children's fears and anxieties are the questionnaires, the thought-listing procedures, the think-aloud procedures, the self-monitoring procedures, and the interviews. We should note, though, that these types of self-report instruments are also not without their problems. For example, the fear survey schedules resemble the global self-ratings in design, and as a consequence are similarly lacking in clarity of content. Both sets of instruments ask for an overall self-evaluation of fear or anxiety that is felt in either a single situation (global ratings) or each of several situations (fear survey schedules). Both sets of instruments leave undefined what it is they measure. Two fear survey schedules that do not suffer from this short coming are the Children's Fear Survey Schedule—Revised (Barrios et al., 1983) and the Fear Frequency and Avoidance Survey Schedule for Children (McCathie & Spence, 1991). The former makes use of rating scales for three specific responses: the self-statement "I am afraid," heart rate, and avoidance. Each of the three rating scales is applied to each of the schedule's 50 stimulus situations, yielding three measures of specified content. The latter consists of two rating scales: one pertaining to the frequency with which the child worries, and one pertaining to the extent to which the child avoids. Both of the rating scales are applied to each of the schedule's 80 stimulus situations and are summed to form total frequency and avoidance scores. For the other fear survey schedules to be of similar assistance in elucidating the nature of children's fears and anxieties, rating scales of similar detail may need to be incorporated.

Ambiguity of a similar sort pervades the questionnaires that ask for self-ratings of several specific responses to either a discrete situation or situations in general (i.e., which response component of fear and anxiety is being assessed?). Many of the traditional questionnaires—such as the Children's Manifest Anxiety Scale and the State–Trait Anxiety Inventory for Children—contain items that address the subjective component of fear and anxiety, as well as items that address other components. Problems in meaning (and in interpretation) arise when the items are combined to form a single response score. This ambiguity can be avoided by grouping items by response component, and then summing across items for each grouping. This method was used in developing instruments for assessing cognitive and somatic anxiety from the items of the State–Trait Anxiety Inventory for Children (Fox & Houston, 1983).

By virtue of the explicitness of their instructions, the thought-listing and think-aloud procedures are very clear as to what response component of fear and anxiety they assess. The procedures are much less clear, though, as to how well the responses gathered from one format or the measures derived from one scoring scheme generalize to other formats or to other scoring schemes. For example, the two applications of the think-aloud procedure (i.e., Giebenhain & Barrios, 1986; Houston et al., 1984) differ in the dimensions along which the children's verbalizations are examined and the responses that are subsumed by each of those dimensions. The comparability of the measures derived from the two scoring systems awaits determination.

Questions of generality also surround the three interview schedules for the assessment of children's fears and anxieties. All three appear to call for considerable skill and experience in soliciting information from children and in organizing this information. The extent to which information of comparable quality and quantity can be gathered by interviewers of varying skill and experience has yet to be investigated. Also yet to be systematically examined is the generality of the various categorical and numerical indices derived from the three schedules (e.g., the correspondence between a diagnostic designation and detailed measures of discrete fear responses).

The principal concern facing self-monitoring procedures for the assessment of children's fears and anxieties is their feasibility, for the few data available at this time suggest that large numbers of children will not comply fully with instructions to track and record small numbers of fairly discrete responses. For example, Beidel, Neal, and Lederer (1991) found fewer than 40% of their well-trained child subjects completing their brief Daily Diaries for the entire 14-day recording period. Such poor compliance with instructions to record renders highly suspect the fidelity of the information that was recorded; in turn, this calls into question the feasibility and utility of the self-monitoring assessment procedure. Strategies that have been successful in enhancing the compliance and the accuracy of self-monitoring among adults may be tested with children (Barlow, Hayes, & Nelson, 1984; Nelson, 1981). And should such strategies prove to be effective, self-monitoring may prove to be a viable and useful approach for the assessment of children's fears and anxieties.

Mechanical Methods

In general, the direct recordings of physiological responses have not fared well in the measurement of children's fears and anxieties. Little correspondence has been found between the different responses of the physiological component and those of the subjective and motor components. Moreover, the physiological measures have not been particularly sensitive to treatment manipulations, to which they presumably should be sensitive. This is not a problem unique to mechanical methods for assessing children's fears and anxieties, as assessors of adults' fears and anxieties have reported similar problems in their efforts to locate reliable and valid physiological measures (e.g., Arena, Blanchard, Andrasik, Cotch, & Myers, 1983; Holden & Barlow, 1986). The situation is one, then, in which many mechanical devices are available for assessing the physiological component of children's fears and anxieties, but none have yet demonstrated the required validity. Some readers may view this situation as grounds for deemphasizing or even discontinuing the assessment of the physiological responses of children's fears and anxieties. We, however, see it as indicating the need for greater sensitivity to the mechanics of psychophysiological assessment and to the quantification of those data.

ADDITIONAL ASSESSMENT CONSIDERATIONS

Several factors determine the scope as well as the form of an assessment of a child's fears and anxieties. Our previous discussion has emphasized three principal factors: the conceptualization of the disorder, the available instruments for measuring the disorder, and the developmental considerations involved in whether or not to treat the disorder. This section focuses on the roles of three other influential factors: treatment prerequisites, dispositional variables, and familial variables.

Treatment Considerations

Optimum use of any of the available treatments for a child's fears and anxieties calls for certain skills on the child's part, and in some cases certain skills on the parents' part as well. To assist a clinician in selecting the most appropriate treatment for a given anxious child, the assessment should include an evaluation of these prerequisite skills. In the paragraphs that follow, we describe the major steps and prerequisites for each of the major behavioral procedures for the treatment of children's fears and anxieties.

Systematic Desensitization and Its Variants

Systematic desensitization consists of the following sequence of activities: training a child in deep muscle relaxation; having the child rank-order from least to most distressing, a series of scenes depicting the feared stimulus; and having the child imagine each of the scenes in this series while in a relaxed state. This pairing of the relaxed state with images of the feared stimulus begins with the least distressing scene and ends with the most distressing one, with progression through the series being contingent upon imagining a scene without undue discomfort (see Hatzenbuehler & Schroeder, 1978; Morris & Kratochwill, 1983a, 1983b).

For faithful application of the treatment, the child must be able to arrange the stimulus scenes in the order of the distress they cause, generate vivid images of those scenes, and detect subtle bodily changes in response to them. At present, several instruments are available for the assessment of the first two abilities. Among the many simple and reliable tests for the concept of ordinality are those developed by Inhelder and Piaget (1969) and by Giebenhain and Barrios (1986). And among the numerous simple and reliable tests for imagery capacity are the Memory for Objects (Radaker, 1961), the Tri-Model Imagery Scale (Bergan & Macchiavello, 1966), the Visual Imagery Index (Radaker, 1961), and the Image Clarity Scale (Hermecz & Melamed, 1984). Though we know of no instruments at this time for the assessment of children's ability to detect bodily changes (e.g., gross and subtle fluctuations in heart rate, muscle tension, respiration, and sweating), several of the tests developed for adults appear to be adaptable for use with children. Among these are the Autonomic Perception Questionnaire (Mandler, Mandler, & Uviller, 1958), the heart-tracking task (Brener, 1977), and the visceral perception test (Pennebaker, Gonder-Frederick, Stewart, Elfman, & Skelton, 1982).

We should note that systematic desensitization does not provide the child with detailed instruction in the proper way to interact with the feared stimulus. On the contrary, the procedure assumes that the child already has this pattern in his or her repertoire. Assessment of whether or not this is the case (and thus of whether or not systematic desensitization is an appropriate treatment) might be patterned along the lines of LaGreca and Santogrossi's (1980) assessment of children's problem-solving skills. In their procedure, children view videotapes of other children in social predicaments, then offer recommendations as to how these problem situations might best be resolved. The responses are audiotaped and scored with respect to effective problem-solving behaviors. In assessing knowledge of adaptive responding, the fearful child would view or listen to taped depictions of other children facing the feared stimulus, and would be asked to describe how best to behave in these situations.

Variations of this basic desensitization procedure have taken the form of group adminstration (e.g., Barabasz, 1973) and utilization of the actual feared stimulus as opposed to an imaginal representation of it (e.g., Miller, 1972). For the former treatment, a child must have the same set of prerequisite abilities as those for the basic procedure; for the latter treatment, the ability to generate vivid images is no longer needed.

Prolonged Exposure and Its Variants

Prolonged exposure calls for a child to confront the feared stimulus immediately and remain in its presence indefinitely (see Barrios & O'Dell, 1989). In the variant known as "flooding," the child faces an intense, extended presentation of the actual feared stimulus or an imaginal representation of it (e.g., Kandel, Ayllon, & Rosenbaum, 1977); in the variant known as "implosion," the child imagines an unrealistic yet nevertheless horrific scenario involving the feared stimulus (e.g., Ollendick & Gruen, 1972); and in the variant known as "reinforced practice," the child is rewarded for remaining in the prescence of the feared stimulus for progressively longer periods of time (e.g., Leitenberg & Callahan, 1973). None of the three procedures instruct the child in how to interact adaptively with the feared stimulus; thus, all three of the procedures require the child to be in possession of such knowledge prior to treatment. Imaginal flooding and implosion carry with them the additional requirement of imagery ability. Assessment of these two prerequisites can take the form of the methods described above.

Modeling and Its Variants

Modeling treatments for fears and anxieties consist of having a frightened child observe another child interacting adaptively with the feared stimulus (see Melamed & Siegel, 1980; Morris & Kratochwill, 1983a, 1983b). This demonstration of effective responding may be either live (e.g., Bandura et al., 1967) or filmed (e.g., Melamed et al., 1978), with observation followed by either little or considerable practice and coaching in the modeled behaviors (e.g., Esveldt-Dawson et al., 1982). In contrast to the desensitization and exposure treatments, the modeling therapies call for no skills and abilities other than the capacity to attend to and retain sensory information.

Contingency Management

Interventions that manipulate the external consequences of a frightened child's movement away or toward the feared stimulus are generally referred to as "contingency management procedures" (see Morris & Kratochwill, 1983a; Richards & Siegel, 1978). In some instances a reward is administered for approach (e.g., Vaal, 1973), taken away for avoidance behavior (e.g., Waye, 1979), or both (e.g., Ayllon, Smith, & Rogers, 1970; Boer & Sipprelle, 1970). In other instances, rewards are delivered for venturing progressively closer to the feared stimulus (e.g., Luiselli, 1978), or penalties are imposed for failing to do so (e.g., Tobey & Thoresen, 1976). All of the various procedures carry with them but one prerequisite—that of having the physical makeup to act appropriately.

Though designed by a therapist, a contingency management program is usually entrusted to a child's parents to implement (see Barrios & O'Dell, 1989). That is, the parents monitor the child's performance and dole out the consequences accordingly. The consistency and thoroughness with which the parents carry out these duties appear to be a function of a host of variables, the most important of which are their mood state and their causal attributions regarding the child's maladaptive behavior (see O'Dell, 1986). Parents who are depressed and who view their child's behavior in trait-like terms typically fail to carry out their treatment duties. A clinician who is considering a contingency management procedure for the treatment of a child's fear would be wise to assess the child's parents for these two variables. Numerous instruments are available for the assessment of adult depression (see Lewinsohn & Lee, 1981; Rehm, 1976, 1981, 1988). No instruments are available at this time for the assessment of parents' causal attributions regarding their child's fears and anxieties. There do exist, however, instruments for addressing parents' perceptions of other child problem behaviors; simple alterations of these instruments should render them suitable for the present purpose. Examples of such instruments are the questionnaires developed by Forehand (Forehand, Wells, McMahon, Griest, & Rogers, 1982; McMahon, Forehand, Griest, & Wells, 1981) and by O'Dell (1982, 1986) for their studies of parent training and child noncompliance.

Self-Management

In self-management treatments, the focus is on changing a frightened child's subjective and physiological reactions to the feared stimulus (see Melamed, Klingman, & Siegel, 1984; Morris & Kratochwill, 1983a). Typically this is done by training the child in deep muscle relaxation, in distracting imagery, and in brave and comforting self-talk. To benefit from this type of training, the child is presumed to be sensitive to differing bodily states, adept at imagery, and knowledgeable in adaptive ways of overtly responding to the feared stimulus. Methods of assessing each of these skills have been described above.

In some self-management programs, the parents are instrumental in training the child in each of the techniques and in instructing the child as to when and where he or she might best exercise each of them (e.g., Peterson & Shigetomi, 1981; Peterson & Toler, 1984). We suspect that parents' ability to carry out their part in these programs may be a function of the same variables as those moderating parents' ability to carry out their part in contingency management programs (i.e., mood state and causal attributions). When considering the use of such a self-management program, a clinician should therefore include an assessment of these two parental variables. Such an assessment might be conducted along the lines suggested above.

Compound Interventions

Various treatment combinations have been fashioned from the five interventions previously described. These compound interventions represent combinations not only of the operations of the individual treatments, but also of the prerequisites. Two illustrative programs and their prerequisites are described below.

Graziano and his associates (Graziano & Mooney, 1980; Graziano, Mooney, Huber, & Ignasiak, 1979) have developed a home-based treatment for children's nighttime fears that combines elements of contingency and self-management training; the treatment, therefore, has the prerequisites associated with both of these procedures. In their program, a child receives instruction in deep muscle relaxation, pleasant imagery, and courageous self-talk. Each night the child practices the techniques and is rewarded by a parent for his or her behavior during practice and for the remainder of the evening.

In Peterson's (Peterson & Shigetomi, 1981; Siegel & Peterson, 1980) combination of modeling and self-management treatment for children's hospital-related fears, a child and parent are coached together in the three coping techniques of cue-controlled relaxation, distracting imagery, and comforting self-talk. And, together, the parent and child watch a film depicting the hospital facilities, the medical procedure the child is to undergo, and the appropriate reactions to these procedures. The parent is responsible for seeing that the child rehearses the techniques and for prompting the child when to perform the techniques. Preequisites for the program are the same as those for self-management and modeling, with the exception of knowledge of adaptive responding, which is provided by the treatment's modeling component.

Dispositional Variables

Of the many dispositional variables that have been examined to date, two have emerged as consistent predictors of children's fear responses and fearful children's responses to treatment. These are "temperament" and "defensiveness"; the former is a broad and stable collection of tendencies that underlie and moderate emotional reactions and expressions (e.g., Goldsmith et al., 1987; Thomas, Chess, & Birch, 1968), and the latter is a more discrete and selective strategy for coping with stressful situations (e.g., Peterson, 1989; Peterson, Harbeck, Chaney, Farmer, & Thomas, 1990).

Of the many different tendencies that coalesce to form the temperament construct, the specific tendency of "behavioral inhibition to the unfamiliar" has been the one most often linked to the development of childhood anxiety disorders (Biederman et al., 1990). This general tendency to fear and withdraw from novel situations has also been found to run counter to the common treatment practice of information provision, in that the providing of factual information about a stressful stimulus tends to exacerbate rather than reduce the distress inhibited children experience in regard to this stimulus (Lumley, Abeles, Melamed, Pistone, & Johnson, 1990).

Given that this temperament characteristic of behavioral inhibition contraindicates certain intervention strategies and suggests the need for certain aggressive strategies, an assessment of this characteristic appears warranted. Such an assessment might take the form of the laboratory-based procedure developed by Kagan and colleagues (Garcia-Coll, Kagan, & Reznick, 1984; Kagan, Reznick, Clarke, Snidman, & Garcia-Coll, 1984), the Parent Temperament Questionnaire (Thomas & Chess, 1977), or the Emotionality, Activity, and Shyness (EAS) Temperament Survey for Children (Buss & Plomin, 1984).

The dispositional variable of defensiveness or information avoidance has been found to be a reliable correlate of children's distress to a wide range of stressful situations (see Peterson et al., 1990). Furthermore, defensiveness has consistently been found to mitigate the beneficial effects of modeling-based treatments (Faust & Melamed, 1984; Klingman et al., 1984; Melamed et al., 1978). Thus, like the temperament charatristic of behavioral inhibition, the dispositional characteristic of defensiveness appears to contraindicate the application of certain information-based treatments and to suggest the implementation of more distraction-based interventions (e.g., Lumley et al., 1990; Peterson et al., 1990). As such, it too warrants assessment. Available for the assessment of this tendency toward denial on the part of children are the Defensive Questionnaire (Wallach & Kogan, 1965), the Children's Version of the Repression–Sensitization Scale (Peterson & Toler, 1984), and the Lie scales from the Children's Manifest Anxiety Scale (Castaneda et al., 1965) and its revision (Reynolds & Richmond, 1978).

Familial Variables

Because much of children's behavior is thought to be instigated and supported by the immediate social environment, numerous familial variables have been linked to children's fears and anxieties. Among the most frequently cited and assiduously investigated of these variables are maternal anxiety, sibling anxiety, and parenting strategies. Despite the considerable attention afforded to these three variables, the exact relationship of each of them to children's fears has yet to be fully elucidated.

Studies of the relationship between maternal anxiety and child anxiety have tended to take one of four forms. One is to compare the incidence of anxiety among mothers and children through the use of structured diagnostic interviews (e.g.,

Bernstein & Garfinkel, 1988; Frick, Silverthorn, & Evans, 1944; Last, Hersen, Kazdin, Francis, & Grubb, 1987). Because companion structured interview schedules do not exist, such interview schedules as the Family History Research Diagnostic Criteria (Endicott, Andreasen, & Spitzer, 1975) and the Diagnostic Interview Schedule—Version IIIA (Robins & Helzer, 1985) are used to assess for maternal anxiety, and such interview schedules as the Diagnostic Interview for Children and Adolescents (Herjanic & Campbell, 1977) and the National Institute of Mental Health Diagnostic Interview Schedule for Children—Version 2.3 (Shaffer, Fisher, Piacentini, Schwab-Stone, & Wicks, 1992) are used to assess for child anxiety. Another approach is to correlate measures of mothers' general or trait anxiety with measures of children's anxiety reactions to a particular situation (e.g., Dolgin, Phipps, Harow, & Zeltzer, 1990; Klorman, Michael, Hilpert, & Sveen, 1979; Klorman, Ratner, Arata, King, & Sveen, 1978; Wright, Alpern, & Leake, 1973). Instruments such as the Taylor Manifest Anxiety Scale (Taylor, 1953), the Trait scale of the State–Trait Anxiety Inventory (Spielberger et al., 1970), and the Symptom Checklist 90—Revised (Derogatis, 1983) are used to assess the general anxiety of the mothers. Still another approach is to correlate the anxiety reactions of mothers and children to the same stimulus situation (e.g., Johnson & Baldwin, 1968, 1969; Klorman et al., 1978, 1979; Melamed & Siegel, 1975; Melamed et al., 1978). Either the State scale of the State–Trait Anxiety Inventory (Spielberger et al, 1970) or a specific fear inventory such as the Maternal Anxiety Questionnaire (Melamed et al., 1978) is employed in the assessment of the mothers' responses to the specific stimulus situation. And a final strategy is to compare the responsiveness of children to treatment with their mothers' impressions of that treatment (e.g., Bradlyn et al., 1986; Peterson & Shigetomi, 1981). Specially developed scales such as the Parent Self-Report (Peterson & Shigetomi, 1981) are used to assess maternal reactions to the intervention.

Findings from the four types of studies clearly show the relationship between child anxiety and maternal anxiety to be a reliable one; they also generally show the correspondence between maternal anxiety and child anxiety to be stronger for younger children than for older children (see Winer, 1982). For a young child, then, assessment and treatment of the mother's anxiety may be necessary. We should note that some recent data suggest just the opposite—stronger correspondence between maternal anxiety and child anxiety for older children than for younger children (Frick et al., 1994). Such a relationship is suggested by the epidemiological findings summarized earlier. The preponderance of intense fears among young children may not allow for the variation needed for a significant relationship with maternal anxiety to emerge, whereas the diminishment and refinement of these intense fears with age may do so. With these recent data, then, have come questions as to the exact way in which age may moderate the relationship between maternal anxiety and child anxiety. And with these questions has come the possibility that for both younger and older children, the assessment and treatment of mothers' anxiety may be necessary.

Sibling anxiety has been investigated far less than maternal anxiety, but the findings have been far more consistent. In general, the fears and anxieties of siblings have been found to parallel those of target children, with the correspondence being stronger for specific fears than for general anxiety (e.g., Bailey, Talbot, & Taylor, 1973; Bernstein & Garfinkel, 1988; DeFee & Himmelstein, 1969; Ghose, Giddon, Shiere, & Fogels, 1969). The direction of influence between the specific fears of children in a family, though, remains unclear. Some data suggest that the line of influence is from an older sibling to a younger sibling (e.g., Ghose et al., 1969), whereas other data suggest the opposite (e.g., Hawley, McCorkle, Witteman, & Van Ostenberg, 1974). Given this uncertainty over the direction of influence, it would seem prudent to assess the siblings of fearful children for their fear reactions, and to treat those reactions if they should be judged problematic. Assessment of the siblings' responses could, of course, be carried out along the same lines as assessment of the target children's responses.

Parenting or child-rearing practices have been examined from a number of different perspectives and through a number of different methods. One tack has been to assess general family functioning, interrelationships, and interactions, and to infer from these global assessments specific relationships between parent behaviors and child fears (e.g., Bernstein & Garfinkel, 1988; Dumas & LaFrenière, 1993; Kashani et al., 1990; LaFrenière & Dumas, 1992). Assessment of general family dynamics has taken the form of such inventories as the Family Assessment Measure—3R (Skinner, Steinhauer, & Santa Barbara, 1983), the Child Rearing Practice Questionnaire (Venham, Murray, & Gaulin-Kremer, 1979), and the Family Relations scale of the Personality Inventory for Chil-

dren (Wirt, Lachar, Klinedinst, & Seat, 1977), as well as such observational systems as the INTER-ACT (Dumas, 1987). Another strategy has been to assess parents's management of children's fearful responses to specific stimulus situations (e.g., Bush, Melamed, Sheras, & Greenbaum, 1986; Dolgin et al., 1990; Lumley, Melamed, & Abeles, 1993). Among the specific stimulus situations assessed have been medical procedures and thunderstorms. And among the assessment instruments employed have been the Child Development Questionnaire (Zabin & Melamed, 1980), the Dyadic Prestressor Interaction Scale (Bush et al., 1986), and the Child–Adult Medical Procedure Interaction Scale—Revised (Blount et al., 1989).

From these studies of varying levels of analysis and varying methods of measurement a fairly definite list of parent behavior correlates has emerged. For young children, permissive child-rearing practices appear to be associated with the presence of anxiety reactions (Allan & Hodgson, 1968; Sarnat, Peri, Nitzan, & Perlberg, 1972; Venham et al., 1979), whereas for older children, intrusive and restrictive ones appear to be so (Bernstein & Garfinkel, 1988; LaFreniere & Dumas, 1992). For both frightening situations and situations in general, parental use of punishment, force, and criticism appears to be deleterious (Blount et al., 1990; Bush & Cockrell, 1987; Dolgin et al., 1990; Kashani et al., 1990). All of this suggests that for successful treatment of an anxious child, the assessment and possible alteration of the parents' child management behaviors may be necessary. Instruments for carrying out such an assessment include those cited above, as well as all those available from the area of parent training (see O'Dell, 1986).

SUMMARY AND RECOMMENDATIONS

A major theme in clinical behavior therapy is the intimate interplay between assessment and intervention (e.g., Barrios, 1988; Barrios & Hartmann, 1986; Kanfer & Phillips, 1970; Kanfer & Saslow, 1969; Masters, Burish, Hollon, & Rimm, 1987). Assessment data are enlisted in the selection of the target behavior, the selection of treatment, and the evaluation of treatment effectiveness. Information about the child, the problem condition, the circumstances under which the problem occurs, the prognosis of the condition, the reactions of peers, and other variables all presumably aids the clinician in determining whether or not treatment is warranted. If treatment is judged to be warranted, then all such information also presumably helps in identifying the specific target, the optimal treatment, and the primary and collateral dependent variables. Unfortunately, reality falls far short of this ideal. At present, there continues to be no generally accepted model for selecting target and treatment; consequently, decisions are based primarily on clinical impressions or on the availability of techniques (Barrios & O'Dell, 1989; Last, 1988; Ollendick & Francis, 1988). Only in developing a technology for measuring dependent variables and evaluating treatment effectiveness have behavior assessors achieved reasonable success (Barrios & Shigetomi, 1985; Barrios et al., 1982).

Several conditions contribute to the continuing inability of assessment data to assist in identifying problem reactions, treatment foci, and treatment strategies. First and foremost among these conditions is the nonspecific topography of children's fears and anxieties. Assessors have defined children's fears and anxieties as complex patterns of subjective, motor, and physiological responses, but they have yet to pinpoint the specific subjective, motor, and physiological responses that constitute the patterns. Most attempts to delineate the response profiles of children's fears and anxieties have assumed some degree of response invariance across stimulus situations, developmental periods, or both. Many of the current data and theories on emotional expression, however, suggest otherwise. That is, they suggest that the exact expression of fear and anxiety will vary as a function of the task demands of the stimulus context and the developmental stage of the child (e.g., Campos & Barrett, 1984; Campos, Barrett, Lamb, Goldsmith, & Stenberg, 1983; Lang, 1984; Lang et al., 1983; Melamed, 1993; Vasey, 1993). It would appear productive, then, to begin tracing the response profiles of children's fears and anxieties with these two factors in mind.

A second condition is the absence of an objective criterion for fear and anxiety. Global parental reports have long served as the ultimate indicators of the fearful and anxious responding of children. Such reports, though, are fraught with difficulties. They are highly suspect from a psychometric standpoint (e.g., Nunnally, 1978) and are highly susceptible to bias and distortion (e.g., Christensen, Phillips, Glasgow, & Johnson, 1983; Forehand et al., 1982). Moreover, they have been found to relate only tenuously to accepted subjective, motor, and physiological measures of fear and

anxiety (e.g., Barrios et al., 1983; Bradlyn et al., 1986; Giebenhain & Barrios, 1986; Jay & Elliott, 1984; Peterson & Shigetomi, 1981). Two possible solutions to the lingering criterion problem come to mind. One is the establishment of cutoff scores on accepted, standardized measures of children's fears and anxieties. Such a proposal has been put forth for certain adult anxiety disorders (e.g., Himadi, Boice, & Barlow, 1985), and child behavior assessors may wish to do likewise. Putting forth such guidelines is, of course, predicated on there being several sets of widely endorsed, well-standardized measures for the several types of children's fears and anxieties. The fact that there are no such sets of measures at this time is discussed and bemoaned below. The other possible solution to the criterion problem is the determination of level of interference associated with level of responding. As stated in an earlier section, responding tends to be seen as problematic when it disrupts one's pursuit of personal goals; one's ability to adjust to the environment; or one's sense of comfort, satisfaction, and freedom. For a child, such disruption translates into interference with normal development and learning, and curtailment of behavioral choices and pursuits. Attempts to ascertain the levels of interference that correspond with levels of fear responses have already been initiated (Ollendick & King, 1994). Continuation and expansion of these efforts may yield a satisfactory resolution to the long-standing criterion problem.

Third is the absence of a well-proven system for classifying children's fears and anxieties. Of the many systems that have been proposed, the categories put forth by the American Psychiatric Association (1994) dominate the current scene. Such domination is odd in that the dependability and utility of these categories have yet to be determined. Such categories may not be the ones that best advance the understanding, assessment, and treatment of children's fears and anxieties. Epidemiological data clearly show that the objects of children's fears and anxieties vary with age. A classification system that reflects these age-related variations, and thus is organized along developmental lines, may be one that better serves our needs (Cicchetti, 1993). Epidemiological data also clearly show considerable heterogeneity among children frightened of the same stimulus situation. A classification system that includes theoretically —and/or empirically—derived subtypes may also be one that better serves the needs of behavior assessors (Kearney & Silverman, 1990, 1993).

Fourth, the 20-year old contention by Marks (1977) continues to stand—namely, that no existing theoretical account of the acquisition and maintenance of fears and anxieties is sufficiently broad to explain the many cultural, interpersonal, and constitutional factors involved in these disorders. Marks (1977) discusses seven aspects of naturally occurring fears and anxieties that are not well explained by most current models. These are (1) selection of the feared stimulus, (2) individual differences in susceptibility, (3) maturational changes, (4) physiological controlling variables, (5) social influences, (6) the role of trauma, and (7) the association of fears with other psychological disturbances. Although more work is clearly needed in the development of theoretical models, consideration of currently prominent though incomplete models may enhance the assessment process.

For example, the prepotency or preparedness model put forth by Marks (1969) and Seligman (1971) may provide insights into the selective nature of children's fears and anxieties. According to this theory, some stimuli, such as snakes, spiders, dogs, and heights may "act as a magnet for phobias" (Marks, 1977, p. 194); other stimuli, such as wooden ducks, macaroni, and shoelaces, may not have this capacity to elicit fear and anxiety. Initial laboratory tests of the theory tended to bear out these predictions; they showed reliable differences in the rates of conditioning and extinguishing emotional responses to different stimuli (cf. Öhman, 1979; Öhman, Dimberg, & Öst, 1985). More recent investigations have clarified the phenomena associated with prepared stimuli and have identified contemporary as opposed to evolutionary mechanisms for the preparedness effects (e.g., Davey, 1992a, 1992b; Hamm, Vaitl, & Lang, 1989; Honeybourne, Matchett, & Davey, 1993; McNally, 1987).

The social referencing theory of emotional development (e.g., Campos & Barrett, 1984; Klinnert, Campos, Sorce, Emde, & Svejda, 1983) may offer clues into the shifting targets of children's fears and anxieties. As a general explanatory framework of emotions, its main tenets apply to all emotions, including fear and anxiety. The theory's cornerstone proposition—that persons seek out information on emotional expression from significant others in their environment whenever they are confronted with a situation that is ambiguous or that exceeds their appraisal capacities (see Klinnert et al., 1983)—implies for the developing child that fears arise (and are associated with) the

change from a safe, certain environment to an uncertain, unfamiliar environment. For example, fears should develop when the child is removed from the arms of the mother and placed in those of a strange caretaker, when the child is removed from the home and placed in a school setting, and when the child moves from one school setting to another.

Transactional models of emotional disorders (e.g., Blount, Davis, Powers, & Roberts, 1991; LaFrenière & Dumas, 1992; Melamed, 1993) may uncover the social forces and child factors involved in the acquisition and perpetuation of children's fears and anxieties. Fundamental to the models are multiple interactions and multiple etiologies— multiple interactions among changing environmental demands, caregiving strategies, and child responses; multiple etiologies because of varying risk factors across developmental periods, as well as varying child and caregiver responses to these risk factors and to each other (e.g., Cicchetti, 1990; Rubin & Mills, 1991). The models have already had some success in isolating influential child characteristics, caregiver characteristics, and child–caregiver interactions related to children's fears and anxieties (e.g., Blount et al., 1991; LaFrenière & Dumas, 1992; Lumley et al., 1990; Peterson et al., 1990). We are hopeful that more success awaits them.

Finally, for a target and treatment selection model to be useful, it must be founded upon sound, standardized assessment (Mash, 1985)—a situation that does not currently exist for the assessment of children's fears and anxieties. As the present review testifies, there is no shortage of measures of children's fears and anxieties. However, there is a shortage of standardized, content-valid assessments of children's fears and anxieties. Protocols that measure the subjective, motor, and physiological responses of children's fears and anxieties are needed. Although such protocols have been developed by Melamed and colleagues and by Peterson and colleagues, many more are needed. Along with more content-valid assessment protocols is the need for more data on the psychometric properties of the measures obtained from such protocols, including data on the measures' reliability (i.e., interscorer consistency, internal consistency, and temporal stability across intervals of varying length and for children of different ages), validity (i.e., convergence with measures within and across response components, divergence with measures of presumably distinctive disorders, sensitivity to experimental manipulations, and generality across relevant settings), and norms (i.e., scores of age-appropriate reference groups). Information of this sort is likely to be of greatest assistance in selecting targets and treatments for children's fears and anxieties.

Each of the aforementioned recommendations represents a life's work—a life's work whose correctness and usefulness will in all likelihood not be determined in our lifetimes. We trust that child behavior therapists will not be daunted by this situation. We trust that such therapists will not only continue but intensify their efforts "to respond more humanely and adequately to the profound fears and anxiety of young children so as to further the latter's healthy development" (Dibrell & Yamamoto, 1988, p. 24).

NOTES

1. The designation of a given classification system as theoretically, statistically, or clinically derived is of course a matter of degree, as more than one of these processes are always involved in the creation of any taxonomy.
2. Even this view is not without its problems. For example, we can conceive of a number of the classic fear responses' being developed and maintained independently of a threatening stimulus. For example, school avoidance can be acquired and maintained through parent-mediated consequences, regardless of the fear-eliciting qualities of the school.
3. The Lapouse and Monk (1959) investigation is also noteworthy, in that findings from a smaller validation sample suggested that maternal reports may underestimate the prevalence of children's fears and anxieties. Since then, many investigations have echoed this suggestion (e.g., Earls, Smith, Reich, & Jung, 1988; Herjanic & Reich, 1982; Kashani & Orvaschel, 1990; Saylor, Swenson, & Powell, 1992).
4. Data have accrued to suggest that the major types of fears may be fairly constant across the various ages of childhood. For example, Ollendick et al. (1985) found considerable overlap in the 10 most common fears reported by 7- to 9-year-olds, 10- to 12-year-olds, 13- to 15-year-olds, and 16- to 18-year-olds. The eight fears cited by all four age groups were fears of not being able to breathe, a burglar breaking into the house, fire, getting hit by a vehicle, death or dead people, bomb attacks or being invaded, looking foolish, and getting poor grades. Gullone and King (1992) likewise found good agreement in the 10 most common fears indicated by their three age groups of 7- to 10-year-olds, 11- to 14-year-olds, and 15- to 18-year-olds. The 10 shared fears pertained to the following: AIDS, someone in the family dying, not being able to breathe, being threatened with a gun, taking dangerous drugs, being kidnapped, dying, nuclear war, murderers, and sharks.

5. We should note that some studies have failed to find these differences between girls and boys in the number of fears and anxieties (Angelino et al., 1956; Eme & Schmidt, 1978; Maurer, 1965; Nalven, 1970), the number of anxiety symptoms (Last, Perrin, Hersen, & Kazdin, 1992; Zohar, et al., 1992), and the types of fears and anxieties (Gullone & King, 1992; King, Ollier, et al., 1989; Ollendick et al., 1985, 1989). At present, though, these studies appear to be in the minority.
6. Fifteen of the instruments assess the motor component through children's self-reports: the Children's Fear Survey Schedule—Revised (Barrios et al., 1983), the Nightime Coping Response Inventory (Mooney, 1985), the School Refusal Assessment Scale—Child Version (Kearney & Silverman, 1990, 1993), the Self-Monitoring Log (McNamara, 1988), the Daily Diary (Beidel, Neal, & Lederer, 1991), the Social Phobia and Anxiety Inventory for Adolescents (Clark et al., 1994), the Social Anxiety Scale for Children—Revised (LaGreca et al., 1988; LaGreca & Stone, 1993), the Leyton Obessional Inventory—Child Version (Berg, Rapoport, & Flament, 1986), the Maudsley Obessional–Compulsive Inventory (Clark & Bolton, 1985; Hodgson & Rachman, 1977), the Fear Frequency and Avoidance Schedule for Children (McCathie & Spence, 1991), the Beck Anxiety Inventory (Beck, Brown, Epstein, & Steer, 1988; Jolly, Aruffo, Wherry, & Livingston, 1993), the Children's Anxiety Evaluation Form (Hoehn-Saric, Maisami, & Wiegand, 1987), the Anxiety Disorders Interview Schedule for Children (Silverman & Nelles, 1988), and the Children's Posttraumatic Stress Disorder Inventory (Saigh, 1987, 1989a). Because these instruments are primarily concerned with the assessment of the subjective component of children's fears and anxieties, they are discussed in the section on self-report methods.
7. These item selection procedures may impose an unsubstantiated (and faulty) theory of anxiety and fear—one assuming that all anxiety indicators are common and substantially correlated for all individuals. In doing so, they may impair an idiographically oriented assessment, as items excluded because of low occurrence or low correlations with other items may be highly relevant to some anxious children.
8. We should note that 22 of the instruments focus upon one or more components in addition to the subjective, and that 3 of the instruments focus upon one or more components in the absence of the subjective.
9. This recollecting of thoughts thus makes the thought-listing procedure more retrospective than the think-aloud procedure in its assessment of the subjective component of children's fears and anxieties.
10. For a detailed discussion of the pertinent measurement properties associated with each of these key clinical decisions, see Barrios and Hartmann (1986).
11. We shold note that ordinary stability coefficients completely confound two sources of inconsistency: actual changes in the targeted behavior that occur over

repeated assessments, and inaccuracies (i.e., measurement error) in the assessment device.

12. For over 15 years, we have been encouraging behavior therapists to be systematic and consistent in their use of BATs (Barrios & Hartmann, 1988; Barrios et al., 1981; Barrios & Shigetomi, 1985; Barrios, Shigetomi, & Giebenhain, 1982). But as our most recent review reveals, few have heeded our words. It is unlikely, then, that the promise we see in the BATs will soon (if ever) be realized.

13. There is one clear use for global ratings: their use in social validation—that is, the assessment of social significance and acceptability of treatment (e.g., Kazdin, 1977; Wolf, 1978).

14. In fact, it could be argued that the major justifiable role for global self-ratings is as therapeutic tools rather than as assessment tools. The worth of global ratings may lie in the facilitation of rapport, motivation, and compliance, and not in their provision of information for clinical decision making.

REFERENCES

Achenbach, T. M. (1991a). *Manual for the Child Behavior Checklist/4–18 and 1991 Profile.*Burlington: University of Vermont, Department of Psychiatry.

Achenbach, T. M. (1991b). *Manual for the Teacher's Report Form and 1991 Profile.* Burlington: University of Vermont, Department of Psychiatry.

Achenbach, T. M. (1991c). *Manual for the Youth Self-Report and 1991 Profile.* Burlington: University of Vermont, Department of Psychiatry.

Agras, W. S., Chapin, H. N., & Oliveau, D. C. (1972). The natural history of phobia. *Archives of General Psychiatry, 26,* 315–317.

Allan, T. K., & Hodgson, E. W. (1968). The use of personality measurements as a determinant of patient cooperation in an orthodontic practice. *American Journal of Orthodontics, 54,* 433–440.

Ambuel, B., Hamlett, K. W., Marx, C. M., & Blumer, J. L. (1992). Assessing distress in pediatric intensive care environments: The COMFORT Scale. *Journal of Pediatric Psychology, 17,* 95–109.

American Psychiatric Association. (1980). *Diagnostic and statistical manual of mental disorders* (3rd ed.). Washington, DC: Author.

American Psychiatric Association. (1987). *Diagnostic and statistical manual of mental disorders* (3rd ed., rev.). Washington, DC: Author.

American Psychiatric Association. (1994). *Diagnostic and statistical manual of mental disorders* (4th ed.). Washington, DC: Author.

Anderson, J. C., Williams, S., McGee, R., & Silva, P. A. (1987). DSM-III disorders in preadolescent children. *Archives of General Psychiatry, 44,* 69–76.

Angelino, H., Dollins, J., & Mech, E. V. (1956). Trends in the "fears and worries" of school children as related to socio-economic status and age. *Journal of Genetic Psychology, 89,* 263–276.

Angelino, H., & Shedd, C. (1953). Shifts in the content of fears and worries relative to chronological age. *Proceedings of the Oklahoma Academy of Science, 34,* 180–186.

Arena, J. G., Blanchard, E. B., Andrasik, F., Cotch, P. A., & Myers, P. E. (1983). Reliability of psychophysiological assessment. *Behaviour Research and Therapy, 21,* 447–460.

Averill, J. R., & Opton, E. M. (1968). Psychophysiological assessment: Rationale and problems. In P. R. McReynolds (Ed.), *Advances in psychological assessment* (Vol. 1, pp. 265–288). Palo Alto, CA: Science & Behavior Books.

Ayllon, T., Smith, D., & Rogers, M. (1970). Behavioral management of school phobia. *Journal of Behavior Therapy and Experimental Psychiatry, 1,* 125–138.

Bailey, P. M., Talbot, A., & Taylor, P. P. (1973). A comparison of maternal anxiety levels with anxiety levels manifested in child dental patients. *Journal of Dentistry for Children, 40,* 277–284.

Ball, W., & Tronick, E. (1971). Infant responses to impending collision: Optical and real. *Science, 171,* 818–820.

Ballenger, J. C., Carek, D. J., Steele, J. J., & Cornish-McTighe, D. (1989). Three cases of Panic Disorder with Agoraphobia in children. *American Journal of Psychiatry, 146,* 922–924.

Bamber, J. H. (1974). The fears of adolescents. *Journal of Genetic Psychology, 125,* 127–140.

Bandura, A. (1986). *Social foundations of thought and action: A social cognitive theory.* Englewood Cliffs, NJ: Prentice-Hall.

Bandura, A., Grusec, E., & Menlove, F. L. (1967). Vicarious extinction of avoidance behavior. *Journal of Personality and Social Psychology, 5,* 16–23.

Bankart, C. P., & Bankart, B. B. (1983). The use of song lyrics to alleviate a child's fears. *Child and Family Behavior Therapy, 5,* 81–83.

Barabasz, A. (1973). Group desensitization of test anxiety in elementary schools. *Journal of psychology, 83,* 295–301.

Barlow, D. H. (1988). *Anxiety and its disorders: The nature and treatment of anxiety and panic.* New York: Guilford Press.

Barlow, D. H., Cohen, A. S., Waddell, M., Vermilyea, B. B., Klosko, J. S., Blanchard, E. B., & DiNardo, P. A. (1984). Panic and Generalized Anxiety Disorders: Nature and treatment. *Behavior Therapy, 15,* 431–449.

Barlow, D. H., Hayes, S. C., & Nelson, R. O. (1984). *The scientist practitioner: Research and accountability in clinical and educational settings.* Elmsford, NY: Pergamon Press.

Barlow, D. H., Leitenberg, H., & Agras, W. S. (1969). Experimental control of sexual deviation through manipulation of the noxious scene in covert sensitization. *Journal of Abnormal Psychology, 74,* 596–601.

Barlow, D. H., & Seidner, A. L. (1983). Treatment of adolescent agoraphobics: Effects on parent–adolescent relations. *Behaviour Research and Therapy, 21,* 519–526.

Barrios, B. A. (1988). On the changing nature of behavioral assessment. In A. S. Bellack & M. Hersen (Eds.), *Behavioral assessment: A practical handbook* (3rd ed., pp. 3–41). Elmsford, NY: Pergamon Press.

Barrios, B. A., (1993). Direct observation. In T. H. Ollendick & M. Hersen (Eds.), *Handbook of child and adolescent assessment* (pp. 140–164). Needham Heights, MA: Allyn & Bacon.

Barrios, B. A., & Hartmann, D. P. (1986). The contributions of traditional assessment: Concepts, issues, and methodologies. In R. O. Nelson & S. C. Hayes (Eds.), *Conceptual foundations of behavioral assessment* (pp. 81–110). New York: Guilford Press.

Barrios, B. A., & Hartmann, D. P. (1988). Fears and anxieties. In E. J. Mash & L. G. Terdal (Eds.), *Behavioral assessment of childhood disorders* (2nd ed., pp. 196–264). New York: Guilford Press.

Barrios, B. A., Hartmann, D. P., & Shigetomi, C. (1981). Fears and anxieties in children. In E. J. Mash & L. G. Terdal (Eds.), *Behavioral assessment of childhood disorders* (pp. 259–304). New York: Guilford Press.

Barrios, B. A., & O'Dell, S. L. (1989). Fears and anxieties. In E. J. Mash & R. A. Barkley (Eds.), *Treatment of childhood disorders* (pp. 167–221). New York: Guilford Press.

Barrios, B. A., Replogle, W., & Anderson-Tisdelle, D. (1983, December). *Multisystem–unimethod analysis of children's fears.* Paper presented at the meeting of the Association for Advancement of Behavior Therapy, Washington, DC.

Barrios, B. A., & Shigetomi, C. C. (1985). Assessment of children's fears: A critical review. In T. R. Kratochwill (Ed.), *Advances in school psychology* (Vol. 4, pp. 89–132). Hillsdale, NJ: Erlbaum.

Barrios, B. A., Shigetomi, C., & Giebenhain, J. (1982, November). Advances in the assessment of children's fears. In T. R. Kratochwill (Chair), *Assessment and treatment of children's fears.* Symposium at the meeting of the Association for Advancement of Behavior Therapy, Los Angeles.

Bauer, D. H. (1976). An exploratory study of developmental changes in children's fears. *Journal of Child Psychology and Psychiatry, 17,* 69–74.

Beck, A. T., Brown, G., Epstein, N., & Steer, R. A. (1988). An inventory for measuring clinical anxiety: Psychometric properties. *Journal of Consulting and Clinical Psychology, 56,* 893–897.

Beck, A. T., Brown, B., Steer, R. A., Eidelson, J. I., & Riskind, J. H. (1987). Differentiating anxiety and depression utilizing the Cognition Checklist. *Journal of Abnormal Psychology, 96,* 179–183.

Beck, A. T., & Emery, G. (1985). *Anxiety disorders and phobias: A cognitive perspective.* New York: Basic Books.

Beck, A. T., & Steer, R. A. (1991). Relationship between the Beck Anxiety Inventory and the Hamilton Anxiety Rating Scale with anxious outpatients. *Journal of Anxiety Disorders, 5,* 213–223.

Beidel, D. C. (1988). Psychophysiological assessment of anxious emotional states in children. *Journal of Abnormal Psychology, 97,* 80–82.

Beidel, D. C. (1991). Social Phobia and Overanxious Disorder in school-age children. *Journal of the American Academy of Child and Adolescent Psychiatry, 30,* 545–552.

Beidel, D. C., Christ, M. A. G., & Long, P. J. (1991). Somatic complaints in anxious children. *Journal of Abnormal Child Psychology, 19,* 659–670.

Beidel, D. C., Neal, A. M., & Lederer, A. S. (1991). The feasibility and validity of a daily diary for the assessment of anxiety in children. *Behavior Therapy, 22,* 505–517.

Beidel, D. C., & Turner, S. M. (1988). Comorbidity of test anxiety and other anxiety disorders in children. *Journal of Abnormal Child Psychology, 16,* 275–287.

Bell-Dolan, D. J., Last, C. G., & Strauss, C. C. (1990). Symptoms of anxiety disorders in normal children. *Journal of the American Academy of Child and Adolescent Psychiatry, 29,* 759–765.

Benjamin, L. S. (1963). Statistical treatment of the law of initial values (LIV) in autonomic research: A review and recommendation. *Psychosomatic Medicine, 25,* 556–566.

Berecz, J. M. (1968). Phobias of childhood: Etiology and treatment. *Psychological Bulletin, 70,* 694–720.

Berg, C. J., Rapoport, J. L., & Flament, M. (1986). The Leyton Obsessional Inventory—Child Version. *Journal of the American Academy of Child Psychiatry, 25,* 84–91.

Berg, I. (1976). School phobia in the children of agoraphobic women. *British Journal of Psychiatry, 128,* 86–89.

Berg, I., Marks, I., McGuire, R., & Lipsedge, M. (1974). School phobia and agoraphobia. *Psychological Medicine, 4,* 428–434.

Bergan, J. R., & Macchiavello, A. (1966). *Visual imagery and reading achievement.* Paper presented at the meeting of the American Education Research Association, Chicago.

Bernstein, D. A., & Nietzel, M. T. (1973). Procedural variation in behavioral avoidance tests. *Journal of Consulting and Clinical Psychology, 41,* 165–174.

Bernstein, D. A., & Nietzel, M. T. (1974). Behavioral avoidance tests: The effects of demand characteristics and repeated measures on two types of subjects. *Behavior Therapy, 5,* 183–192.

Bernstein, D. A., & Paul, G. L. (1971). Some comments on therapy analogue research with small animal "phobias." *Journal of Behavior Therapy and Experimental Psychiatry, 2,* 225–237.

Bernstein, G. A., (1991). Comorbidigy and severity of anxiety and depressive disorders in a clinic sample. *Journal of the American Academy of Child and Adolescent Psychiatry, 30,* 43–50.

Bernstein, G. A., & Borchardt, C. M. (1991). Anxiety disorders of childhood and adolescence: A critical review. *Journal of the American Academy of Child and Adolescent Psychiatry, 30,* 519–532.

Bernstein, G. A., & Garfinkel, B. D. (1986). School phobia: The overlap of affective and anxiety disorders. *Journal of the American Academy of Child Psychiatry, 2,* 235–241.

Bernstein, G. A., & Garfinkel, B. D. (1988). Pedigrees, functioning, and psychopathology in families of school phobic children. *American Journal of Psychiatry, 145,* 70–74.

Biederman, J., Rosenbaum, J. F., Hirshfeld, D. R., Faraone, S. V., Bolduc, E. A., Gersten, M., Meminger, S. R., Kagan, J., Snidman, N., & Reznick, J. S. (1990). Psychiatric correlates of behavioral inhibition in young children of parents with and without psychiatric disorders. *Archives of General Psychiatry, 47,* 21–26.

Blanchard, E. B. (Ed.). (1982). Behavioral medicine [Special issue]. *Journal of Consulting and Clinical Psychology, 50*(6).

Blount, R. L., Corbin, S. M., Sturges, J. W., Wolfe, V. V., Prater, J. M., & James, L. D. (1989). The relationship between adults' behavior and child coping and distress during BMA/LP procedures: A sequential analysis. *Behavior Therapy, 20,* 585–601.

Blount, R. L., Davis, N., Powers, S. W., & Roberts, M. C. (1991). The influence of environmental factors and coping style on children's coping and distress. *Clinical Psychology Review, 11,* 93–116.

Blount, R. L., Sturges, J. W., & Powers, S. W. (1990). Analysis of child and adult behavioral variations by phase of medical procedure. *Behavior Therapy, 21,* 33–48.

Boer, A. P., & Sipprelle, C. N. (1970). Elimination of avoidance behavior in the clinic and its transfer to the normal environment. *Journal of Behavior Therapy and Experimental Psychiatry, 1,* 169–174.

Borkovec, T. D., Metzger, R., & Pruzinsky, T. (1986). Anxiety, worry, and the self. In L. Hartmann & K. R. Blankenstein (Eds.), *Perceptions of self in emotional disorders and psychopathology* (pp. 219–260). New York: Plenum Press.

Bornstein, P. H., & Knapp, M. (1981). Self-control desensitization with a multi-phobic boy: A multiple baseline design. *Journal of Behavioral therapy and Experimental Psychiatry, 12,* 281–285.

Bradlyn, A. S., Christoff, K., Sikora, T., O'Dell, S. L., & Harris, C. V. (1986). The effects of a videotape preparation package in reducing children's arousal and increasing cooperation during cardiac catherization. *Behaviour Research and Therapy, 24,* 453–459.

Brady, E. V., & Kendall, P. C. (1992). Comorbidity of anxiety and depression in children and adolescents. *Psychological Bulletin, 111,* 244–255.

Brener, J. (1977). Visceral perception. In J. Beatty & H. Legewie (Eds.), *Biofeedback and behavior* (pp. 235–259). New York: Plenum Press.

Bronson, G. W. (1972). Infants' reactions to unfamiliar persons and novel objects. *Monographs of the Society for Research in Child Development, 37*(3, Serial No. 148).

Brown, T. A., Moras, K. Zinbarg, R. E., & Barlow, D. H. (1993). Diagnostic and symptom distinguishability of Generalized Anxiety Disorder and Obsessive–Compulsive Disorder. *Behavior Therapy, 24,* 227–240.

Burke, K. C., Burke, J. D., Regier, D. A., & Rae, D. S. (1990). Age at onset of selected mental disorders in five community populations. *Archives of General Psychiatry, 47,* 511–518.

Bush, J. P., & Cockrell, C. S. (1987). Maternal factors predicting parenting behaviors in the pediatric clinic. *Journal of Pediatric Psychology, 12,* 505–518.

Bush, J. P., Melamed, B. G., Sheras, P. L., & Greenbaum, P. E. (1986). Mother–child patterns of coping with anticipatory medical stress. *Health Psychology, 5,* 137–157.

Buss, A. H., & Plomin, R. (1984). *Temperament: Early developing personality traits.* Hillsdale, NJ: Erlbaum.

Campbell, S. B. (1986). Developmental issues. In R. Gittelman (Ed.), *Anxiety disorders of childhood* (pp. 24–57). New York: Guilford Press.

Campos, J. J., & Barrett, K. C. (1984). Toward a new understanding of emotions and their development. In C. E. Izard, J. Kagan, & R. B. Zajonc (Eds.), *Emotions, cognition, and behavior* (pp. 229–263). New York: Cambridge University Press.

Campos, J., Barrett, K., Lamb, M., Goldsmith, H., & Stenberg, C. (1983). Socioemotional development. In M. Haith & J. Campos (Vol. Eds.), *Handbook of child psychology* (4th ed.): *Vol. 2. Infancy and developmental psychobiology.* New York: Wiley.

Castaneda, A., McCandless, B. R., & Palermo, D. S. (1956). The children's form of the Manifest Anxiety Scale. *Child Development, 27,* 317–236.

Chess, S., & Hassibi, M. (1978). *Principles and practice of child psychiatry.* New York: Plenum Press.

Christensen, A., Phillips, S., Glasgow, R. E., & Johnson, S. M. (1983). Parental chracteristics and interactional dysfunction families with child behavior problems: A preliminary investigation. *Journal of Abnormal Child Psychology, 11,* 153–166.

Cicchetti, D. (1990). The organization and coherence of socioemotional, cognitive, and representational development: Illustrations through a developmental psychopathology perspective on Down syndrome and child maltreatment. In R. Thompson (Ed.), *Nebraska Symposium on Motivation* (Vol.

36, pp. 259–366). Lincoln: University of Nebraska Press.

Cicchetti, D. (1993). Developmental psychopathology: Reactions, reflections, projections. *Developmental Review, 13*, 471–502.

Clark, D. A., & Bolton, D. (1985). An investigation of two self-report measures of obsessional phenomena in obsessive–compulsive adolescents: Research note. *Journal of Child Psychology and Psychiatry, 26*, 429–437.

Clark, D. B., Turner, S. M., Beidel, D. C., Donovan, J. E., Kirisci, L., & Jacob, R. G. (1994). Reliability and validity of the Social Phobia and Anxiety Inventory for Adolescents. *Psychological Assessment, 6*, 135–140.

Clevanger, T., & King, T. R. (1961). A factor analysis of the visible symptoms of stage fright. *Speech Monographs, 28*, 296–298.

Cone, J. D. (1979). Confounded comparisons in triple response mode assessment research. *Behavioral Assessment, 1*, 85–95.

Cone, J. D. (1981). Psychometric considerations. In M. Hersen & A. S. Bellack (Eds.), *Behavior assessment: A practical handbook* (2nd ed., pp. 38–70). Elmsford, NY: Pergamon Press.

Cone, J. D. (1988). Psychometric considerations and the multiple models of behavioral assessment. In A. S. Bellack & M. Hersen (Eds.), *Behavioral assessment: A practical handbook* (3rd ed., pp. 42–66). Elmsford, NY: Pergamon Press.

Cook, T. D., & Campbell, D. T. (Eds.). (1979). *Quasi-experimentation: Design and analysis issues for field settings*. Chicago: Rand McNally.

Cooper, J. (1970). The Leyton Obsessional Inventory. *Psychological Medicine, 1*, 48–64.

Costello, A. J., Edelbrock, C. S., Dulcan, M. K., Kalas, R., & Klaric, S. H. (1984). *Report on the NIMH Diagnostic Interview Schedule for Children (DISC)*, Rockville, MD: National Institute of Mental Health.

Cradock, C., Cotler, S., & Jason, L. A. (1978). Primary prevention: Immunization of children for speech anxiety. *Cognitive Therapy and Research, 2*, 389–396.

Crider, B. (1949). Phobias: Their nature and treatment. *Journal of Psychology, 27*, 217–229.

Croake, J. W. (1969). Fears of children. *Human Development, 12*, 239–247.

Croake, J. W., & Knox, F. H. (1973). The changing nature of children's fears. *Child Study Journal 3*, 91–105.

Cummings, J. D. (1944). The incidence of emotional symptoms in school children. *British Journal of Educational Psychology, 14*, 151–161.

Cummings, J. D. (1946). A follow-up study of emotional symptoms in school children. *British Journal of Educational Psychology, 16*, 163–177.

Davey, G. C. L. (1992a). An expectancy model of laboratory preparedness effects. *Journal of Experimental Psychology: General, 121*, 24–40.

Davey, G. C. L. (1992b). Classical conditioning and acquisition of human fears and phobias: A review and synthesis of the literature. *Advances in Behaviour Research and Therapy, 14*, 29–66.

Davis, A. F., Rosenthal, T. L., & Kelley, J. E. (1981). Actual fear cues, prompt therapy, and rationale enhance participant modeling with adolescents. *Behavior Therapy, 12*, 536–542.

DeFee, J. F., Jr., & Himmelstein, P. (1969). Children's fear in a dental situation as a function of birth order. *Journal of Genetic Psychology, 115*, 253–255.

Delprato, D. J., & McGlynn, F. D. (1984). Behavioral theories of anxiety disorders. In S. M. Turner (Ed.), *Behavioral treatment of anxiety disorders* (pp. 63–122). New York: Plenum Press.

Derogatis, L. R. (1983). *SCL-90-R: Administration, scoring, and procedures manual II*. Towson, MD: Clinical Psychometric Research.

Dibrell, L. L., & Yamamoto, K. (1988). In their own words: Concerns of young children. *Child Psychiatry and Human Development, 19*, 14–25.

Dolgin, M. J., Phipps, S., Harow, E., & Zeltzer, L. K. (1990). Parental management of fear in chronically ill and healthy children. *Journal of Pediatric Psychology, 15*, 733–744.

Dollinger, S. J., O'Donnell, J. P., & Staley, A. A. (1984). Lightning-strike disaster: Effects on children's fears and worries. *Journal of Consulting and Clinical Psychology, 52*, 1023–1038.

Dong, Q., Yang, B., & Ollendick, T. H. (1994). Fears in Chinese children and adolescents and their relations to anxiety and depression. *Journal of Child Psychology and Psychiatry, 35*, 351–363.

Doris, J., McIntyre, A., Kelsey, C., & Lehman, E. (1971). Separation anxiety in nursery school children. *Proceedings of the 79th Annual Convention of the American Psychological Association, 79*, 145–146. (Summary)

Dorkey, M., & Amen, E. W. (1947). A continuation study of anxiety reactions in young children by means of a projective technique. *Genetic Psychology Monographs, 35*, 139–183.

Dumas, J. E. (1987). INTERACT—a computer-based coding and data management system to assess family interactions. In R. J. Prinz (Ed.), *Advances in behavioral assessment of children and families* (Vol. 3, pp. 177–202). Greenwich, CT: JAI Press.

Dumas, J. E., & LaFrenière, P. J. (1993). Mother–child relationships as sources of support or stress: A comparison of competent, average, aggressive, and anxious dyads. *Child Development, 64*, 1732–1754.

Dunlop, G. (1952). *Certain aspects of children's fears*. Unpublished master's thesis, University of North Carolina–Raleigh.

Earls, F., Smith, E., Reich, W., & Jung, K. G. (1988). Investigating psychopathological consequences of a disaster in children: A pilot study incorporating a structured diagnostic interview. *Journal of the American Academy of Child and Adolescent Psychiatry, 27*, 90–95.

Eisen, A. R., & Silverman, W. K. (1991). Treatment of an adolescent with bowel movement phobia using self-control therapy. *Journal of Behavior Therapy and Experimental Psychiatry, 22,* 45–51.

Eisenberg, L. (1958). School phobia: A study in the communication of anxiety. *American Journal of Psychiatry, 114,* 712–718.

Ekman, P., & Davidson, R. J. (Eds.). (1994). *Emotions.* Hillsdale, NJ: Erlbaum.

Eme, R., & Schmidt, D. (1978). The stability of children's fears. *Child Development, 49,* 1277–1279.

Endicott, J., Andreasen, N., & Spitzer, R. L. (1975). *Family History Research Diagnostic Criteria.* New York: New York State Psychiatric Institute, Biometrics Research.

Epkins, C. C. (1993). A preliminary comparison of teacher ratings and child self-report of depression, anxiety, and aggression in inpatient and elementary school samples. *Journal of Abnormal Child Psychology, 21,* 649–661.

Esveldt-Dawson, K., Wisner, K. L., Unis, A. S., Matson, J. L., & Kazdin, A. E. (1982). Treatment of phobias in a hospitalized child. *Journal of Behavior Therapy and Experimental Psychiatry, 13,* 77–83.

Evans, I. M., & Nelson, R. O. (1977). Assessment of child behavior problems. In A. R. Ciminero, K. S. Calhoun, & H. E. Adams (Eds.), *Handbook of behavioral assessment* (pp. 603–682). New York: Wiley.

Evans, P. D., Harmon, G. (1981). Children's self-initiated approach to spiders. *Behaviour Research and Therapy, 19,* 543–546.

Faust, J., & Melamed, B. G. (1984). Influence of arousal, previous experience, and age on surgery preparation of same day of surgery and in-hospital pediatric patients. *Journal of Consulting and Clinical Psychology, 52,* 359–365.

Faust, J., Olson, R., & Rodriguez, H. (1991). Same-day surgery preparation. Reduction of pediatric patient arousal and distress through particpant modeling. *Journal of Consulting and Clinical Psychology, 59,* 475–478.

Fehr, F. S. (1970). A simple method for assessing body movement and potential artifacts in the physiological recording of young children. *Psychophysiology, 7,* 787–789.

Feld, S. C., & Lewis, J. (1969). The assessment of achievement anxieties in children. In C. P. Smith (Ed.), *Achievement related motives in children* (pp. 79–93). New York: Sage.

Ferrari, M. (1986). Fears and phobias in childhood: Some clinical and developmental considerations. *Child Psychiatry and Human Development, 17,* 75–87.

Fincham, F. D., Hokoda, A., & Sanders, R., Jr. (1989). Learned helplessness, test anxiety, and academic achievement: A longitudinal analysis. *Child Development, 60,* 138–145.

Fischer, K. W., Shaver, P. R., & Carnochan, P. (1989). A skill approach to emotional development: From basic — to subordinate — category emotions. In W. Damon (Ed.), *Child development today and tomorrow* (pp. 107–136). San Francisco: Jossey-Bass.

Forehand, R., Wells, K. C., McMahon, R. J., Griest, D. L., & Rogers, T. (1982). Maternal perception of maladjustment in clinic-referred children: An extension of earlier research. *Journal of Behavioral Assessment, 4,* 145–151.

Foster, S. L., Bell-Dolan, D. J., & Burge, D. A. (1988). Behavioral observation. In A. S. Bellack & M. Hersen (Eds.), *Behavioral assessment: A practical handbook* (3rd ed., pp. 119–160). Elmsford, NY: Pergamon Press.

Foster, S. L., & Cone, J. D. (1980). Current issues in direct observation. *Behavioral Assessment, 2,* 313–338.

Fox, J. E., & Houston, B. K. (1981). Efficacy of self-instructional training for reducing children's anxiety in evaluative situation. *Behaviour Research and Therapy, 19,* 509–515.

Fox, J. E., & Houston, B. K. (1983). Distinguishing between cognitive and somatic trait and state anxiety in children. *Journal of Personality and Social Psychology, 45,* 862–870.

Francis, G., Last, C. G., & Strauss, C. C. (1987). Expression of Separation Anxiety Disorder: The roles of age and gender. *Child Psychiatry and Human Development, 18,* 82–89.

Freeman, B. J., Roy, R. R., & Hemmick, S. (1976). Extinction of a phobia of physical examination in a seven-year-old mentally retarded boy — a case study. *Behaviour Research and Therapy, 14,* 63–64.

Freud, S. (1955). Analysis of a phobia in a five-year-old boy. In J. Strachey (Ed. and Trans.), *The standard edition of the complete psychological works of Sigmund Freud* (Vol. 10, pp. 3–149). London: Hogarth Press. (Original work published 1909)

Frick, P. J., Silverthorn, P., & Evans, C. (1994). Assessment of childhood anxiety using structured interviews: Patterns of agreement among informants and association with maternal anxiety. *Psychological Assessment, 6,* 372–379.

Friedman, A. G., & Ollendick, T. H. (1989). Treatment programs for severe night-time fears: A methodological note. *Journal of Behavior Therapy and Experimental Psychiatry, 20,* 171–178.

Gambrill, E. D. (1977). *Behavior modification: Handbook of assessment, intervention, and evaluation.* San Francisco: Jossey-Bass.

Garcia-Coll, C., Kagan, J., & Reznick, J. S. (1984). Behavioral inhibition in young children. *Child Development, 55,* 1005–1019.

Garland, E. J., & Smith, D. H. (1990). Panic Disorder on a child psychiatric consultation service. *Journal of the American Academy of Child and Adolescent Psychiatry, 29,* 785–788.

Garrison, C. Z., Weinrich, M. W., Hardin, S. B., Weinrich, S., & Wang, L. (1993). Post-Traumatic

Stress Disorder in adolescents after a hurricane. *American Journal of Epidemiology, 138,* 522–530.

Ghose, L. J., Giddon, D. B., Shiere, F. R., & Fogels, H. R. (1969). Evaluation of sibling support. *Journal of Dentistry for Children, 36,* 35–40.

Giebenhain, J., & Barrios, B. A. (1986, November). *Multichannel assessment of children's fears.* Paper presented at the meeting of the Association for Advancement of Behavior Therapy, Chicago.

Giebenhain, J. E., & O'Dell, S. L. (1984). Evaluation of a parent-training manual for reducing children's fear of the dark. *Journal of Applied Behavior Analysis, 17,* 121–125.

Gilbert, B. O., Johnson, S. B., Silverstein, J., & Malone, J. (1989). Psychological and physiological responses to acute laboratory stressors in insulin-dependent diabetes mellitus adolescents and nondiabetic controls. *Journal of Pediatric Psychology, 14,* 577–591.

Gilbert, B. O., Johnson, S. B., Spillar, R., McCallum, M., Silverstein, J. H., & Rosenbloom, A. (1982). The effects of a peer-modeling film on children learning to self-inject insulin. *Behavior Therapy, 13,* 186–193.

Glass, C. R., Merluzzi, T. V., Biever, J. L., & Larsen, K. H. (1982). Cognitive assesment of social anxiety: Development and validation of a self-statement questionnaire. *Cognitive Therapy and Research, 6,* 37–55.

Glennon, B., & Weisz, J. R. (1978). An observational approach to the assessment of anxiety in young children. *Journal of Consulting and Clinical Psychology, 46,* 1246–1257.

Goldsmith, H. H., Buss, A. H., Plomin, R., Rothbart, M. K., Thomas, A., Chess, S., Hinde, R. A., & McCall, R. B. (1987). Roundtable: What is temperament? Four approaches. *Child Development, 58,* 505–529.

Gonzales, J. C., Routh, D. K., Saab, P. G., Armstrong, F. D., Shifman, L., Guerra, E., & Fawcett, N. (1989). Effects of parent presence on children's reactions to injections: Behavioral, physiological, and subjective aspects. *Journal of Pediatric Psychology, 14,* 449–462.

Graham, P. (1964). *Controlled trial of behavior therapy vs. conventional therapy: A pilot study.* Unpublished doctoral dissertation, University of London.

Graziano, A. M., & DeGiovanni, I. S. (1979). The clinical significance of childhood phobias: A note on the proportion of child-clinical referrals for the treatment of children's fears. *Behaviour Research and Therapy, 17,* 161–162.

Graziano, A. M., DeGiovanni, I. S., & Garcia, K. A. (1979). Behavioral treatment of children's fears: A review. *Psychological Bulletin, 86,* 804–830.

Graziano, A. M., & Mooney, K. C. (1980). Family self-control instruction for children's nighttime fear reduction. *Journal of Consulting and Clinical Psychology, 48,* 206–213.

Graziano, A. M., & Mooney, K. C., Huber, C., & Ignasiak, K. D. (1979). Self-control instructions for children's fear-reduction. *Journal of Behavior Therapy and Experimental Psychiatry, 10,* 221–227.

Grindler, M. (1988). Effects of cognitive monitoring strategies on the test anxieties of elementary students. *Psychology in the Schools, 25,* 428–436.

Gross, A. M., & Drabman, R. S. (Eds.). (1990). *Handbook of clinical behavioral pediatrics.* New York: Plenum Press.

Gullone, E., & King, N. J. (1992). Psychometric evaluation of a revised Fear Survey Schedule for Children and Adolescents. *Journal of Child Psychology and Psychiatry, 33,* 987–998.

Hagman, E. R. (1932). A study of fears of children of preschool age. *Journal of Experimental Education, 1,* 110–130.

Hall, T. W. (1967). *Some effects of anxiety on the fantasy play of school children.* Unpublished doctoral dissertation, Yale University.

Hamm, A. O., Vaitl, D., & Lang, P. J. (1989). Fear conditioning, meaning, and belongingness: A selective analysis. *Journal of Abnormal Psychology, 98,* 395–406.

Hampe, E., Noble, H., Miller, L. C., & Barrett, C. L. (1973). Phobic children one and two years posttreatment. *Journal of Abnormal Psychology, 82,* 446–453.

Harnisch, D. L., Hill, K. T., & Fyans, L. J. (1980, April). *Development of a shorter, more reliable and valid measure of test motivation.* Paper presented at the annual meeting of the National Council on Measurement in Education, Boston.

Harris, B. (1979). Whatever happened to Little Albert? *American Psychologist, 34,* 151–160.

Harris, F. C., & Lahey, B. B. (1982a). Recording system bias in direct observational methodology: A review and critical analysis of factors causing inaccurate coding behavior. *Clinical Psychology Review, 2,* 539–556.

Harris, F. C., & Lahey, B. B. (1982b). Subject reactivity in direct observational assessment: A review and critical analysis. *Clinical Psychology Review, 2,* 523–538.

Hartmann, D. P., & Wood, D. D. (1982). Observational methods. In A. S. Bellack, M. Hersen, & A. E. Kazdin (Eds.), *International handbook of behavior modification and therapy* (pp. 109–138). New York: Plenum Press.

Hatcher, S. (1989). A case of doll phobia. *British Journal of Psychiatry, 155,* 255–257.

Hatzenbuehler, L. C., & Schroeder, H. E. (1978). Desensitization procedures in the treatment of childhood disorders. *Psychological Bulletin, 85,* 831–844.

Hawley, B. P., McCorkle, A. D., Witteman, J. K., & Van Ostenberg, P. (1974). The first dental visit for children from low socioeconomic families. *Journal of Dentistry for Children, 41,* 376–331.

Haynes, S. N. (1978). *Principles of behavioral assessment*. New York: Gardner Press.

Haynes, S. N., & Horn, W. F. (1982). Reactivity in behavioral observation: A review. *Behavioral Assessment, 4*, 369–385.

Haynes, S. N., & Wilson, C. C. (1979). *Behavioral assessment*. San Francisco: Jossey-Bass.

Hebb, D. O. (1946). On the nature of fear. *Psychological Review, 53*, 259–276.

Herbertt, R. M., & Innes, J. M. (1979). Familiarization and preparatory information in the reduction of anxiety in child dental patients. *Journal of Dentistry for Children, 46*, 319–323.

Herjanic, B., & Campbell, W. (1977). Differentiating psychiatrically disturbed children on the basis of a structured interview. *Journal of Abnormal Child Psychology, 5*, 127–134.

Herjanic, B., & Reich, W. (1982). Development of a structured psychiatric interview for children: Agreement between child and parent on individual symptoms. *Journal of Abnormal Child Psychology, 10*, 307–324.

Hermecz, D. A., & Melamed, B. G. (1984). The assessment of emotional imagery training in fearful children. *Behavior Therapy, 15*, 156–172.

Hill, J. H., Liebert, R. M., & Mott, D. E. W. (1968). Vicarious extinction of avoidance behavior through films: An initial test. *Psychological Reports, 22*, 192.

Hill, K. T., & Wigfield, A. (1984). Test anxiety: A major educational problem and what can be done about it. *Elementary School Journal, 85*, 105–126.

Himadi, W. G., Boice, R., & Barlow, D. H. (1985). *Assessment of agoraphobia: Measurement of clinical change*. Unpublished manuscript, Center for Stress and Anxiety Disorders, Albany, NY.

Hodges, K. (1990). Depression and anxiety in children: A comparison of self-report questionnaires to clinical interview. *Psychological Assessment, 2*, 376–381.

Hodges, K., Kline, J., Stern, L., Cytryn, L., & McKnew, D. (1982). The development of a child assessment interview for research and clinical use. *Journal of Abnormal Child Psychology, 10*, 173–189.

Hodgson, R., & Rachman, S. (1977). Obsessional–compulsive complaints. *Behaviour Research and Therapy, 15*, 389–395.

Hoehn-Saric, E., Maisami, M., & Wiegand, D. (1987). Measurement of anxiety in children and adolescents using semistructured interviews. *Journal of the American Academy of Child and Adolescent Psychiatry, 26*, 541–545.

Holden, A. E., Jr., & Barlow, D. H. (1986). Heart rate and heart rate variability recorded *in vivo* in agoraphobics and nonphobics. *Behavior Therapy, 17*, 26–42.

Holmes, F. B. (1935). An experimental study of the fears of young children. In A. T. Jersild & F. B. Holmes (Eds.), *Children's fears* (Child Development Monograph No. 20, pp. 167–296). New York: Columbia University Press.

Honeybourne, C., Matchett, G., & Davey, G. C. L. (1993). Expectancy models of laboratory preparedness effects: A UCS-expectancy bias in phylogenetic and ontogenetic fear-relevant stimuli. *Behavior Therapy, 24*, 253–264.

Honjo, S., Hirano, C., & Murase, S. (1989). Obsessive–compulsive symptoms in childhood and adolescence. *Acta Psychiatria Scandinavica, 80*, 83–91.

Houston, B. K., Fox, J. E., & Forbes, L. (1984). Trait anxiety and children's state anxiety, cognitive behaviors, and performance under stress. *Cognitive Therapy and Research, 8*, 631–641.

Hubert, N. C., Jay, S. M., Saltoun, M., & Hayes, M. (1988). Approach–avoidance and distress in children undergoing preparation for painful medical procedures. *Journal of Clinical Child Psychology, 17*, 194–202.

Huffington, C. M., & Sevitt, M. A. (1989). Family interaction in adolescent school phobia. *Journal of Family Therapy, 11*, 353–275.

Hughes, J. N. (1989). The child interview. *School Psychology Review, 18*, 247–259.

Inhelder, B., & Piaget, J. (1969). *The early growth of logic in the child*. New York: Norton.

Izard, C. E., Kagan, J., & Zajonc, R. B. (1984). Introduction. In C. E. Izard, J. Kagan, & R. B. Zajonc (Eds.), *Emotions, cognition, and behavior* (pp. 1–14). New York: Cambridge University Press.

Jay, S. M., & Elliott, C. H. (1984). Behavioral observation scales for measuring children's distress: The effects of increased methodological rigor. *Journal of Consulting and Clinical Psychology, 52*, 1106–1107.

Jay, S. M., Elliott, C. H., Ozolins, M., Olson, R. A., & Pruitt, S. D. (1985). Behavioral management of children's distress during painful medical procedures. *Behaviour Research and Therapy, 23*, 523–520.

Jay, S. M., Ozolins, M., Elliott, C. H., & Caldwell, S. (1983). Assessment of children's distress during painful medical procedures. *Journal of Health Psychology, 2*, 133–147.

Jayaratne, S., & Levy, R. L. (1979). *Empirical clinical practice*. New York: Columbia University Press.

Jersild, A. T. (1954). Emotional development. In L. Carmichael (Ed.), *Manual of child psychology* (2nd ed., pp. 833–917). New York: Wiley.

Jersild, A. T., & Holmes, F. (Eds.). (1935). *Children's fears* (Child Development Monograph No. 20). New York: Columbia University Press.

Johnson, L. C., & Lubin, A. (1972). On planning psychophysiological experiments: Design, measurement, and analysis. In N. S. Greenfield & R. A. Sternbach (Eds.), *Handbook of psychophysiology* (pp. 125–158). New York: Holt, Rinehart & Wilson.

Johnson, R., & Baldwin, D. C., Jr. (1968). Relationship of maternal anxiety to the behavior of young children undergoing dental extraction. *Journal of Dental Research, 47*, 801–805.

Johnson, R., & Baldwin, D. C., Jr. (1969). Maternal anxiety and child behavior. *Journal of Dentistry for Children, 36*, 87–92.

Johnson, R., & Dabbs, J. M. (1967). Enumeration of active sweat glands: A simple physiological indicator of psychological changes. *Nursing Research, 16*, 273–276.

Johnson, R. L., & Glass, C. R. (1989). Heterosocial anxiety and direction of attention in high school boys. *Cognitive Therapy and Research, 13*, 509–526.

Johnson, S. B., & Melamed, B. G. (1979). The assessment and treatment of children's fears. In B. B. Lahey & A. E. Kazdin (Eds.), *Advances in clinical child psychology* (Vol. 2, pp. 107–139). New York: Plenum Press.

Johnson, T., Tyler, V., Thompson, R., & Jones, E. (1971). Systematic desensitization and assertive training in the treatment of speech anxiety in middle-school students. *Psychology in the Schools, 8*, 263–267.

Jolly, J. B., Aruffo, J., Wherry, J. N., & Livingston, R. L. (1993). The utility of the Beck Anxiety Inventory with inpatient adolescents. *Journal of Anxiety Disorders, 7*, 95–106.

Jolly, J. B., & Dykman, R. A. (1994). Using self-report data to differentiate anxious and depressive symptoms in adolescents: Cognitive content specificity and global distress? *Cognitive Therapy and Research, 18*, 25–37.

Jones, H. E., & Jones, M. C. (1928). Fear. *Childhood Education, 5*, 136–143.

Jones, M. C. (1924). A laboratory study of fear: The case of Peter. *Pedagogical Seminar, 31*, 308–315.

Jones, R. T., Ollendick, T. H., McLaughlin, K. J., & Williams, C. E. (1989). Elaborative and behavioral rehearsal in the acquisition of fire emergency skills and the reduction of fear of fire. *Behavior Therapy, 20*, 93–101.

Kagan, J., Reznick, J. S., Clarke, C., Snidman, N., & Garcia-Coll, C. (1984). Behavioral inhibition to the unfamiliar. *Child Development, 55*, 2212–2225.

Kandel, H. J., Ayllon, T., & Rosenbaum, M. S. (1977). Flooding or systematic exposure in the treatment of extreme social withdrawal in children. *Journal of Behavior Therapy and Experimental Psychiatry, 8*, 75–81.

Kanfer, F. H., Karoly, P., & Newman, A. (1975). Reduction of children's fear of the dark by confidence-related and situational threat-related verbal cues. *Journal of Consulting and Clinical Psychology, 43*, 251–258.

Kanfer, F. H., & Phillips, J. S. (1970). *Learning foundations of behavior therapy.* New York: Wiley.

Kanfer, F. H., & Saslow, G. (1969). Behavioral diagnosis. In C. M. Franks (Ed.), *Behavior therapy:*

Appraisal and status (pp. 417–444). New York: McGraw-Hill.

Kanner, L. (1957). *Child psychiatry.* Springfield, IL: Charles C Thomas.

Kanner, L. (1960). Do behavior symptoms always indicate psychopathology? *Journal of Child Psychology and Psychiatry, 1*, 17–25.

Kane, M. T., & Kendall, P. C. (1989). Anxiety disorders in children: A multiple-baseline evaluation of a cognitive-behavioral treatment. *Behavior Therapy, 20*, 499–508.

Karoly, P. (1975). Operant methods. In F. H. Kanfer & A. P. Goldstein (Eds.), *Helping people change* (pp. 195–228). Elmsford, NY: Pergamon Press.

Karoly, P., & Jensen, M. P. (1987). *Multimethod assessment of chronic pain.* Elmsford, NY: Pergamon Press.

Kashani, J. H., & Orvaschel, H. (1988). Anxiety disorders in mid-adolescence: A community sample: *American Journal of Psychiatry, 145*, 960–964.

Kashani, J. H., & Orvaschel, H. (1990). A community study of anxiety in children and adolescents. *American Journal of Psychiatry, 147*, 313–318.

Kashani, J. H., & Vaidya, A. F., Soltys, S. M., Dandoy, A. C., Katz, L. M., & Reid, J. C. (1990). Correlates of anxiety in psychiatrically hospitalized children and their parents. *American Journal of Psychiatry, 147*, 319–323.

Katz, E. R., Kellerman, J., & Siegel, S. E. (1980). Behavioral distress in children with cancer undergoing medical procedures: Developmental consideration. *Journal of Consulting and Clinical Psychology, 48*, 356–365.

Kazdin, A. E. (1977). Assessing the clinical or applied importance of behavior change through social validation. *Behavior Modificiation, 1*, 427–452.

Kazdin, A. E. (1981). Behavioral observation. In M. Hersen & A. S. Bellack (Eds.), *Behavioral assessment: A practical handbook* (2nd ed., pp. 101–124). Elmsford, NY: Pergamon Press.

Kearney, C. A., & Silverman, W. K. (1990). A preliminary analysis of a functional model of assessment and treatment for school refusal behavior. *Behavior Modification, 14*, 340–366.

Kelley, C. K. (1976). Play desensitization of fear of darkness in preschool children. *Behaviour Research and Therapy, 14*, 79–81.

Kendall, P. C., Chansky, T. E., Kane, M. T., Kim, R., Kortlander, E., Ronan, K. R., Sessa, F. M., & Siqueland, L. (1992). *Anxiety disorders in youth: Cognitive-behavioral interventions.* Needham, MA: Allyn & Bacon.

Kennedy, W. A. (1965). School phobia: Rapid treatment of fifty cases. *Journal of Abnormal Psychology, 70*, 285–289.

Kent, R. N., & Foster, S. L. (1977). Direct observational procedures: Methodological issues in naturalistic settings. In A. R. Ciminero, K. S. Calhoun,

& H. E. Adams (Eds.), *Handbook of behavioral assessment* (pp. 279–328). New York: Wiley.

King, N. J., Cranstoun, F., & Josephs, A. (1989). Emotive imagery and children's nighttime fears: A multiple baseline design evaluation. *Journal of Behavior Therapy and Experimental Psychiatry, 20,* 125–135.

King, N. J., Ollier, K., Iacuone, R., Schuster, S., Bays, K., Gullone, E., & Ollendick, T. H. (1989). Fears of children and adolescents: A cross-sectional Australian study using the Revised Fear Survey Schedule for Children. *Journal of Child Psychology and Psychiatry, 30,* 775–784.

Kirkpatrick, D. R. (1984). Age, gender and patterns of common intense fears among adults. *Behaviour Research and Therapy, 22,* 141–150.

Klingman, A., Melamed, B. G., Cuthbert, M. I., & Hermecz, D. A. (1984). Effects of participant modeling on information acquisition and skill utilization. *Journal of Consulting and Clinical Psychology, 52,* 414–422.

Klinnert, M. D., Campos, J. J., Sorce, J. F., Emde, R. N., & Svejda, M. (1983). Emotions as behavior regulators: Social referencing in infancy. In R. Plutchik & H. Kellerman (Eds.), *Emotion: Theory, research, and experience* (Vol. 2, pp. 57–86). New York: Academic Press.

Klorman, R., Michael, R., Hilpert, P. L., & Sveen, O. B. (1979). A further assessment of predictors of child behavior in dental treatment. *Journal of Dental Research, 58,* 2338–2343.

Klorman, R., Ratner, J., Arata, C. L., King, J. B., & Sveen, O. B. (1978). Predicting the child's uncooperativeness in dental treatment from maternal trait, state, and dental anxiety. *Journal of Dentistry for Children, 45,* 62–67.

Kolb, L. C., & Keane, T. (1988). *Physiology study of chronic Post-Traumatic Stress Disorder* (Cooperative Studies Program No. 334). Washington, DC: Veterans Administration.

Kolvin, I., Berney, P., & Bhate, S. R. (1984). Classification and diagnosis of depression in school phobia. *British Journal of Psychiatry, 145,* 347–357.

Kornhaber, R. C., & Schroeder, H. E. (1975). Importance of model similarity on extinction of avoidance behavior in children. *Journal of Consulting and Clinical Psychology, 43,* 601–607.

Kovacs, M. (1983). *The Interview Schedule for Children (ISC): Interrater and parent–child agreement.* Unpublished manuscript.

Kuroda, J. (1969). Elimination of children's fears of animals by the method of experimental desensitization: An application of learning theory to child psychology. *Psychologia: An International Journal of Psychology in the Orient, 12,* 161–165.

Lacey, J. L. (1956). The evaluation of autonomic responses: Toward a general solution. *Annals of the New York Academy of Sciences, 67,* 123–164.

Lacey, J. I., & Lacey, B. C. (1967). The law of initial value in the longitudinal study of autonomic constitution: Reproductivity of autonomic responses and response patterns over a four year interval. *Annals of the New York Academy of Sciences, 38,* 1257–1290.

LaFrenière, P. J., & Dumas, J. E. (1992). A transactional analysis of early childhood anxiety and social withdrawal. *Development and Psychopathology, 4,* 385–402.

LaFrenière, P. J., Dumas, J. E., Capuano, F., & Dubeau, D. (1992). The development and validation of the Preschool Socioaffective Profile. *Psychological Assessment, 4,* 442–450.

LaGreca, A. M., Dandes, S. K., Wick, P., Shaw, K., & Stone, W. L. (1988). Development of the Social Anxiety Scale for Children: Reliability and concurrent validity. *Journal of Clinical Child Psychology, 17,* 84–91.

LaGreca, A. M., & Santogrossi, D. A. (1980). Social skills training with elementary school students: A behavioral group approach. *Journal of Consulting and Clinical Psychology, 48,* 220–227.

LaGreca, A. M., & Stone, W. L. (1993). Social Anxiety Scale for Children—Revised: Factor structure and concurrent validity. *Journal of Clinical Child Psychology, 22,* 17–27.

Lang, P. J. (1968). Fear reduction and fear behaviors: Problems in treating a construct. In J. M. Shlien (Ed.), *Research in psychotherapy* (Vol. 3, pp. 90–103). Washington, DC: American Psychological Association.

Lang, P. J. (1984). Cognition in emotion: Concept and action. In C. E. Izard, J. Kagan, & R. B. Zajonc (Eds.), *Emotions, cognition, and behavior* (pp. 192–226). New York: Cambridge University Press.

Lang, P. J., & Lazovik, A. D. (1963). Experimental desensitization of a phobia. *Journal of Abnormal and Social Psychology, 66,* 519–525.

Lang, P. J., Levin, D. N., Miller, G. A., & Kozak, M. J. (1983). Fear behavior, fear imagery, and the psychophysiology of emotion: The problem of affective response integration. *Journal of Abnormal Psychology, 92,* 276–306.

Lang, P. J., Rice, D. G., & Sternbach, R. A. (1972). The psychophysiology of emotion. In N. Greenfield & R. A. Sternbach (Eds.), *Handbook of psychophysiology* (pp. 623–644). New York: Holt, Rinehart & Winston.

Lapouse, R., & Monk, M. A. (1959). Fears and worries in a representative sample of children. *American Journal of Orthopsychiatry, 29,* 223–248.

Last, C. G. (Ed.). (1988). Child anxiety disorders [Special issue]. *Behavior Modification, 12*(2).

Last, C. G. (1991). Somatic complaints in anxiety disordered children. *Journal of Anxiety Disorders, 5,* 125–138.

Last, C. G., Barlow, D. H., & O'Brien, G. T. (1984). Cognitive changes during *in vivo* exposure in an agoraphobic. *Behavior Modification, 8*, 93–119.

Last, C. G., Hersen, M., Kazdin, A. E., Francis, G., & Grubb, H. J. (1987). Psychiatric illness in the mothers of anxious children. *American Journal of Psychiatry, 144*, 1580–1583.

Last, C. G., & Perrin, S. (1993). Anxiety disorders in African-American and white children. *Journal of Abnormal Child Psychology, 21*, 153–164.

Last, C. G., Perrin, S., Hersen, M., & Kazdin, A. E. (1992). DSM-III-R anxiety disorders in children: Sociodemographic and clinical characteristics. *Journal of the American Academy of Child and Adolescent Psychiatry, 31*, 1070–1076.

Laurent, J., & Stark, K. D. (1993). Testing the cognitive content-specificity hypothesis with anxious and depressed youngsters. *Journal of Abnormal Psychology, 102*, 226–267.

LeBaron, S., & Zeltzer, L. (1984). Assessment of acute pain and anxiety in children and adolescents by self-reports, observer reports, and a behavior checklist. *Journal of Consulting and Clinical Psychology, 52*, 729–738.

Leitenberg, H., & Callahan, E. J. (1973). Reinforced practice and education of different kinds of fears in adults and children. *Behaviour Research and Therapy, 11*, 19–30.

Lewinsohn, P. M., & Lee, W. M. L. (1981). Assessment of affective disorders. In D. H. Barlow (Ed.), *Behavioral assessment of adult disorders* (pp. 129–179). New York: Guilford Press.

Lewis, M., & Michalson, L. (1983). *Children's emotions and moods: Developmental theory and measurement.* New York: Plenum Press.

Lewis, S. (1974). A comparison of behavior therapy techniques in the reduction of fearful avoidant behavior. *Behavior Therapy, 5*, 648–655.

Lewis, T. M., & Law, D. B. (1958). Investigation of certain autonomic responses of children to a specific dental stress. *Journal of the American Dental Association, 57*, 769–777.

Lick, J. R., & Unger, T. E. (1975). External validity of laboratory fear assessment: Implications from two case studies. *Journal of Consulting and Clinical Psychology, 43*, 864–866.

Lick, J. R., & Unger, T. E. (1977). The external validity of behavioral fear assessment. *Behavior Modification, 1*, 283–306.

Lick, J. R., Unger, T. E., & Condiotte, M. (1978). Effects of uncertainty about the behavior of a phobic stimulus on subject's fear reactions. *Journal of Consulting and Clinical Psychology, 46*, 1559–1560.

Lobitz, G. K., & Johnson, S. M. (1975). Normal versus deviant children: A multimethod comparison. *Journal of Abnormal Child Psychology, 3*, 353–374.

Luiselli, J. K. (1978). Treatment of an autistic child's fear of riding a school bus through exposure and reinforcement. *Journal of Behavior Therapy and Experimental Psychiatry, 9*, 169–172.

Lumley, M. A., Abeles, L. A., Melamed, B. G., Pistone, L. M., & Johnson, J. H. (1990). Coping outcomes in children undergoing stressful medical procedures: The role of child–environment variables. *Behavioral Assessment, 12*, 233–238.

Lumley, M. A., Melamed, B. G., & Abeles, L. A. (1993). Predicting children's presurgical anxiety and subsequent behavior changes. *Journal of Pediatric Psychology, 18*, 481–497.

MacFarlane, J., Allen, L., & Honzik, M. (1954). *A developmental study of the behavior problems of normal children between twenty-one months and fourteen years.* Berkeley: University of California Press.

Mandler, G., Mandler, J. M., & Uviller, E. T. (1958). Autonomic feedback: The perception of autonomic activity. *Journal of Abnormal and Social Psychology, 56*, 367–373.

Marks, I. M. (1969). *Fears and phobias.* New York: Academic Press.

Marks, I. M. (1977). Phobias and obsessions: Clinical phenomena in search of laboratory models. In J. D. Maser & M. E. P. Seligman (Eds.), *Psychopathology: Experimental methods* (pp. 174–213). San Francisco: W. H. Freeman.

Martin, I., & Venables, P. H. (Eds.). (1980). *Techniques in psychophysiology.* New York: Wiley.

Mash, E. J. (1985). Some comments on target selection in behavior therapy. *Behavioral Assessment, 7*, 63–78.

Mash, E. J., & Terdal, L. G. (Eds.). (1981). *Behavioral assessment of childhood disorders.* New York: The Guilford Press.

Mash, E. J., & Terdal, L. G. (1988). Behavioral assessment of child and family disturbance. In E. J. Mash & L. G. Terdal (Eds.), *Behavioral assessment of childhood disorders* (2nd ed., pp. 3–65). New York: Guilford Press.

Masters, J. C., Burish, T., Hollon, S. D., & Rimm, D. C. (1987). *Behavior therapy: Techniques and empirical findings* (3rd ed.). New York: Academic Press.

Matson, J. L. (1981). Assessment and treatment of clinical fears in mentally retarded children. *Journal of Applied Behavior Analysis, 14*, 287–294.

Mattison, R. E., & Bagnato, S. J. (1987). Empirical measurement of Overanxious Disorder in boys 8 to 12 years old. *Journal of the American Academy of Child and Adolescent Psychiatry, 26*, 536–540.

Mattison, R. E., Bagnato, S. J., & Brubaker, B. H. (1988). Diagnostic utility of the Revised Children's Manifest Anxiety Scale in children with DSM-III anxiety disorders. *Journal of Anxiety Disorders, 2*, 147–155.

Maurer, A. (1965). What children fear. *Journal of Genetic Psychology, 106*, 265–277.

McCathie, H., & Spence, S. H. (1991). What is the Revised Fear Survey Schedule for Children measuring? *Behaviour Research and Therapy, 29*, 495–502.

McMahon, R. J., Forehand, R., Griest, D. L., & Wells, K. C. (1981). Who drops out of treatment during behavioral training? *Behavioral Counseling Quarterly*, *1*, 79–85.

McNally, R. J. (1987). Preparedness and phobias: A review. *Psychological Bulletin*, *101*, 283–303.

McNamara, E. (1988). The self-management of school phobia: A case study. *Behavioral Psychotherapy*, *16*, 217–229.

Meece, J. (1981). *Individual differences in the affective reactions of middle and high school students to mathematics: A social cognitive perspective*. Unpublished doctoral dissertation, University of Michigan.

Meece, J. L., Wigfield, A., & Eccles, J. S. (1990). Predictors of math anxiety and its influence on young adolescent course enrollment intentions and performance in mathematics. *Journal of Educational Psychology*, *82*, 60–70.

Melamed, B. G. (1993). Putting the family back in the child. *Behaviour Research and Therapy*, *31*, 239–248.

Melamed, B. G., Hawes, R. R., Heiby, E., & Glick, J. (1975). Use of filmed modeling to reduce uncooperative behavior of children during dental treatment. *Journal of Dental Research*, *54*, 757–801.

Melamed, B. G., Klingman, A., & Siegel, L. J. (1984). Childhood stress and anxiety: Individualizing cognitive behavioral strategies in the reduction of medical and dental stress. In A. W. Meyers & W. E. Craighead (Eds.), *Cognitive behavior therapy with children* (pp. 289–314.) New York: Plenum Press.

Melamed, B. G., & Siegel, L. J. (1975). Reduction of anxiety in children facing hospitalization by use of filmed modeling. *Journal of Consulting and Clinical Psychology*, *43*, 511–521.

Melamed, B. G., & Siegel, L. J. (1980). *Behavioral medicine*. New York: Springer.

Melamed, B. G., Weinstein, D., Hawes, R., & Katin-Borland, M. (1975). Reduction of fear-related dental management using filmed modeling. *Journal of the American Dental Association*, *90*, 822–826.

Melamed, B. G., Yurcheson, R., Fleece, E. L., Hutcherson, S., & Hawes, R. (1978). Effects of film modeling on the reduction of anxiety-related behaviors in individuals varying in level or previous experience in the stress situation. *Journal of Consulting and Clinical Psychology*, *46*, 1357–1367.

Menzies, R. G., & Clarke, J. C. (1993). A comparison of *in vivo* and vicarious exposure in the treatment of childhood water phobia. *Behaviour Research and Therapy*, *31*, 9–15.

Milgrom, P., Fiset, L., Melnick, S., & Weinstein, P. (1988). The prevalence and practice management consequences of dental fear in a major US city. *Journal of the American Dental Association*, *116*, 641–647.

Milgrom, P., Jie, Z., Yang, Z., & Tay, K. M. (1994). Cross-cultural validity of a parent's version of the Dental Fear Survey Schedule for Children in Chinese. *Behaviour Research and Therapy*, *32*, 131–135.

Miller, L. C., Barrett, C. L., & Hampe, E. (1974). Phobias of childhood in a prescientific era. In S. Davids (Ed.), *Child personality and psychopathology* (pp. 89–134). New York: Wiley.

Miller, L. C., Barrett, C. L., Hampe, E., & Noble, H. (1972). Factor structure of childhood fears. *Journal of Consulting and Clinical Psychology*, *39*, 264–268.

Miller, P. M. (1972). The use of visual imagery and muscle relaxation in the counterconditioning of a phobic child: A case study. *Journal of Nervous and Mental Disease*, *154*, 457–460.

Milos, M. E., & Reiss, S. (1982). Effects of three play conditions on separation anxiety in young children. *Journal of Consulting and Clinical Psychology*, *50*, 339–395.

Minichiello, W. E., Baer, L., Jenike, M. A., & Holland, A. (1990). Age of onset of major subtypes of Obsessive–Compulsive Disorder. *Journal of Anxiety Disorders*, *4*, 147–150.

Montague, J. D., & Coles, E. M. (1966). Mechanism and measurement of the galvanic skin response. *Psychological Bulletin*, *65*, 261–279.

Mooney, K. D. (1985). Children's nighttime fears: Ratings of content and coping behaviors. *Cognitive Therapy and Research*, *9*, 309–319.

Morgan, G. A. V. (1959). Children who refuse to go to school. *Medical Officer*, *102*, 221–224.

Morris, R. J., & Kratochwill, T. R. (1983a). Childhood fears and phobias. In R. J. Morris & T. R. Kratochwill (Eds.), *The practice of child therapy* (pp. 53–85). Elmsford, NY: Pergamon Press.

Morris, R. J., & Kratochwill, T. R. (1983b). *Treating children's fears and phobias: A behavioral approach*. Elmsford, NY: Pergamon Press.

Murphy, C. M., & Bootzin, R. R. (1973). Active and passive participation in the contact desensitization of snake fear in children. *Behavior Therapy*, *4*, 203–211.

Nalven, F. B. (1970). Manifest fears and worries of ghetto vs. middle-class suburban children. *Psychological Reports*, *27*, 285–286.

Nawas, M. M. (1971). Standardized schedules desensitization. Some unstable results and an improved program. *Behaviour Research and Therapy*, *9*, 35–38.

Neisworth, J. T., Madle, R. A., & Goeke, I. K. E., (1975). "Errorless" elimination of separation anxiety: A case study. *Journal of Behavior Therapy and Experimental Psychiatry*, *6*, 79–82.

Nelson, R. O. (1977). Assessment and therapeutic functions of self-monitoring. In M. Hersen, R. M. Eisler, & P. M. Miller (Eds.), *Progress in behavior modification* (Vol. 5, pp. 264–309). New York: Academic Press.

Nelson, R. O. (1981). Realistic dependent measures for clinical use. *Journal of Consulting and Clinical Psychology, 49,* 168–182.

Nelson, R. O., & Hayes, S. C. (1979). The nature of behavioral assessment: A commentary. *Journal of Applied Behavior Analysis, 12,* 491–500.

Nelson, R. O., & Hayes, S. C. (1981). Nature of behavioral assessment. In M. Hersen & A. S. Bellack (Eds.), *Behavioral assessment: A practical handbook* (2nd ed., pp. 3–37). Elmsford, NY: Pergamon Press.

Nunnally, J. (1978). *Psychometric theory* (2nd ed.). New York: McGraw-Hill.

O'Connor, R. D. (1969). Modification of social withdrawal through symbolic modeling. *Journal of Applied Behavior Analysis, 2,* 15–22.

O'Dell, S. L. (1982). Enhancing parent involvement in training: A discussion. *The Behavior Therapist, 5,* 9–13.

O'Dell, S. L. (1986). Progress in parent training. In M. Hersen, R. M. Eisler, & P. M. Miller (Eds.), *Progress in behavior modification* (Vol. 17, pp. 57–108). New York: Academic Press.

Öhman, A. (1979). Fear relevance, autonomic conditioning, and phobias. A laboratory model. In P. O. Sjödén, S. Bates, & W. S. Dockens III (Eds.), *Trends in behavior therapy* (pp. 107–133). New York: Academic Press.

Öhman, A., Dimberg, U., & Öst, L. G. (1985). Animal and social phobias: Biological constraints in learned fear responses. In S. Reiss & R. R. Bootzin (Eds.), *Theoretical issues in behavior therapy* (pp. 123–175). San Diego, CA: Academic Press.

Ollendick, T. H. (1978). *The Fear Survey Schedule for Children—Revised.* Unpublished manuscript, Indiana State University.

Ollendick, T. H. (1983). Reliability and validity of the Revised Fear survey Schedule for Children (FSSC-R). *Behaviour Research and Therapy, 21,* 685–692.

Ollendick, T. H. (1987). The Fear Survey Schedule for Children—Revised. In M. Hersen & A. S. Bellack (Eds.), *Dictionary of behavioral assessment techniques* (pp. 218–220). Elmsford, NY: Pergamon Press.

Ollendick, T. H., & Francis, G. (1988). Behavioral assessment and treatment of childhood phobias. *Behaviour Modification, 12,* 165–204.

Ollendick, T. H., & Gruen, G. E. (1972). Treatment of a bodily injury phobia with implosive therapy. *Journal of Consulting and Clinical Psychology, 38,* 389–393.

Ollendick, T. H., & King, N. J. (1994). Fears and their level of interference in adolescents. *Behaviour Research and Therapy, 32,* 635–638.

Ollendick, T. H., King, N. J., & Frary, R. B. (1989). Fears in children and adolescents: Normative data. *Behaviour Research and Therapy, 23,* 465–467.

Ollendick, T. H., Yule, W., & Ollier, K. (1991). Fears in British children and their relationship to manifest anxiety and depression. *Journal of Child Psychology and Psychiatry, 32,* 321–331.

Orton, G. L. (1982). A comparative study of children's worries. *Journal of Psychology, 110,* 153–162.

Orvaschel, H., & Weissman, M. M. (1986). Epidemiology of anxiety disorders in children: A review. In R. Gittelman (Ed.), *Anxiety disorders of childhood* (pp. 58–72). New York: Guilford Press.

Öst, L. G. (1985). Ways of acquiring phobias and outcome of behavioural treatments. *Behaviour Research and Therapy, 23,* 683–689.

Öst, L. G. (1987). Age of onset in different phobias. *Journal of Abnormal Psychology, 46,* 223–229.

Öst, L. G. (1991). Acquisition of blood and injection phobia and anxiety response patterns in clinical patients. *Behaviour Research and Therapy, 29,* 323–332.

Paul, G. L. (1966). *Insight vs. desensitization in psychotherapy.* Stanford, CA: Stanford University Press.

Pennebaker, J. W., Gonder-Frederick, L., Stewart, H., Elfman, M. L., & Skelton, J. A. (1982). Physical symptoms associated with blood pressure. *Psychophysiology, 19,* 201–210.

Perrin, S., & Last, C. G. (1992). Do children anxiety measures measure anxiety? *Journal of Abnormal Child Psychology, 20,* 567–578.

Peterson, L. (1987). Not safe at home: Behavioral treatment of a child's fear of being at home alone. *Journal of Behavior Therapy and Experimental Psychiatry, 18,* 381–385.

Peterson, L. (1989). Coping by children undergoing stressful medical procedures: Some conceptual, methodological, and therapeutic issues. *Journal of Consulting and Clinical Psychology, 57,* 380–387.

Peterson, L., & Harbeck, C. (1988). *The pediatric psychologist: Issues in professional development and practice.* Champaign, IL: Research Press.

Peterson, L., Harbeck, C., Chaney, J., Farmer, J., & Thomas, A. M. (1990). Children's coping with medical procedures: A conceptual overview and integration. *Behavioral Assessment, 12,* 197–212.

Peterson, L., Schultheis, K., Ridley-Johnson, R., Miller, D. J., & Tracy, K. (1984). Comparison of three modeling procedures on the presurgical and postsurgical reactions of children. *Behavior Therapy, 15,* 197–203.

Peterson, L., & Shigetomi, C. (1981). The use of coping techniques in minimizing anxiety in hospitalized children. *Behavior Therapy, 12,* 1–14.

Peterson, L., & Toler, S. M. (1984). Self-reported presurgical preparation for children. In B. Stabler (Chair), *Behavioral management of illness in children.* Symposium conducted at the annual meeting of the American Psychological Association, Toronto.

Pinter, R., & Lev, J. (1940). Worries of school children. *Journal of Genetic Psychology, 56,* 67–76.

Plutchik, R., & Kellerman, H. (Eds.). (1980). *Emotion: Theory, research, and experience* (Vol. 1). New York: Academic Press.

Plutchik, R., & Kellerman, H. (Eds.). (1983). *Emotion: Theory, research, and experience* (Vol. 2). New York: Academic Press.

Poznanski, E. (1973). Children with excessive fears. *American Journal of Orthopsychiatry, 43,* 438–439.

Pratt, K. C. (1945). A study of the "fears" of rural children. *Journal of Genetic Psychology, 67,* 179–194.

Prins, P. J. M. (1985). Self-speech and self-regulation of high and low-anxious children in the dental situation. An interview study. *Behaviour Research and Therapy, 23,* 641–650.

Prins, P. J. M. (1986). Children's self-speech and self-regulation during a fear-provoking behavioral test. *Behaviour Research and Therapy, 24,* 181–191.

Puig-Antich, J., & Chambers, W. (1978). *The Schedule for Affective Disorders and Schizophrenia for School-Age Children (Kiddie-SADS).* New York: New York State Psychiatric Institute.

Quay, H. C. (1979). Classification. In H. C. Quay & J. S. Werry (Eds.), *Psychopathological disorders of childhood* (2nd ed., pp. 1–42). New York: Wiley.

Rachman, S. J. (1978). *Fear and courage.* San Francisco: W. H. Freeman.

Rachman, S. J., & Hodgson, R. (1980). *Obsessions and compulsions.* Englewood Cliffs, NJ: Prentice-Hall.

Rachman, S. J., & Seligman, M. E. P. (1976). Unprepared phobias: "Be prepared." *Behaviour Research and Therapy, 14,* 333–338.

Radaker, L. D. (1961). The visual imagery of retarded children and the relationship to memory for word forms. *Exceptional Children, 27,* 524–530.

Ramirez, S. Z., & Kratochwill, T. R. (1990). Development of the Fear Survey for Children With and without Mental Retardation. *Behavioral Assessment, 12,* 457–470.

Ray, W. J., & Raczynski, J. M. (1981). Psychophysiological assessment. In M. Hersen & A. S. Bellack (Eds.), *Behavioral assessment: A practical handbook* (2nd ed., pp. 175–211). Elmsford, NY: Pergamon Press.

Rehm, L. P. (1976). Assessment of depression. In M. Hersen & A. S. Bellack (Eds.), *Behavioral assessment: A practical handbook* (pp. 233–260). Elmsford, NY: Pergamon Press.

Rehm, L. P. (1981). Assessment of depression. In M. Hersen & A. S. Bellack (Eds.), *Behavioral assessment: A practical handbook* (2nd ed., pp. 246–295). Elmsford, NY: Pergamon Press.

Rehm, L. P. (1988). Assessment of depression. In A. S. Bellack & M. Hersen (Eds.), *Behavioral assessment: A practical handbook* (3rd ed., pp. 313–364). Elmsford, NY: Pergamon Press.

Reich, J. (1986). The epidemiology of anxiety. *Journal of Nervous and Mental Disease, 174,* 129–135.

Rettew, D. C., Swedo, S. E., Leonard, H. L., Lenane, M. C., & Rapoport, J. L. (1992). Obsessions and compulsions across time in 79 children and adolescents with obsessive–compulsive disorder. *Journal of the American Academy of Child and Adolescent Psychiatry, 31,* 1050–1056.

Reynolds, C. R., & Richmond, B. O. (1978). What I think and feel: A revised measure of children's manifest anxiety. *Journal of Abnormal Child Psychology, 6,* 271–280.

Richards, C. S., & Siegel, L. J. (1978). Behavioral treatment of anxiety states and avoidance behaviors in children. In D. Marholin II (Ed.), *Child behavior therapy* (pp. 274–338). New York: Gardner Press.

Richman, N., Stevenson, J., & Graham, P. (1982). Prevalence of behavior problems in 3-year-old children: An epidemiological study in a London borough. *Journal of Child Psychology and Psychiatry, 16,* 272–287.

Ritter, B. (1968). The group treatment of children's snake phobias using vicarious and contact desensitization procedures. *Behaviour Research and Therapy, 6,* 1–6.

Robins, L. N., & Helzer, J. E. (1985). *Diagnostic Interview Schedule—Version IIIA.* St. Louis, MO: Washington University School of Medicine.

Ronan, K. R., Kendall, P. C., & Rowe, M. (1994). Negative affectivity in children: Development and validation of a self-statement questionnaire. *Cognitive Therapy and Research, 18,* 509–528.

Ross, D. M., Ross, S. A., & Evans, T. A. (1971). The modification of extreme social withdrawal by modeling with guided participation. *Journal of Behavior Therapy and Experimental Psychiatry, 2,* 273–279.

Rubin, K. H., & Mills, R. S. L. (1991). Conceptualizing developmental pathways to internalizing disorders in childhood. *Canadian Journal of Behavioral Science, 23,* 300–317.

Russo, D. C. (Ed.). (1984). Pediatric health psychology [Special issue]. *Clinical Psychology Review, 4*(5).

Rutter, M., Tizard, J., & Whitmore, K. (1970). *Education, health, and behavior.* New York: Wiley.

Ryall, M. R., & Dietiker, K. E. (1979). Reliability and clinical validity of the Children's Fear Survey Schedule. *Journal of Behavior Therapy and Experimental Psychiatry, 10,* 303–310.

Saigh, P. A. (1986). *In vitro* flooding in the treatment of a six-year-old boy's Posttraumatic Stress Disorder. *Behaviour Research and Therapy, 24,* 685–688.

Saigh, P. A. (1987, November). *The development and validation of the Children's Posttraumatic Stress Disorder Inventory.* Paper presented at the meeting of the Association for Advancement of Behavior Therapy, Boston.

Saigh, P. A. (1989a). A comparative analysis of the affective and behavioral symptomatology of traumatized and nontraumatized children. *Journal of School Psychology, 27,* 247–255.

Saigh, P. A. (1989b). The validity of the DSM-III Post-traumatic Stress Disorder classification as applied to children. *Journal of Abnormal Psychology, 98,* 189–192.

Saigh, P. A. (1992). Structured clinical interviews and the inferential process. *Journal of School Psychology, 36,* 141–149.

Sarason, S. B., Davidson, K. S., Lighthall, F. F., Waite, R. R., & Ruebush, B. K. (1960). *Anxiety and elementary school children.* New York: Wiley.

Sarnat, H., Peri, J. N., Nitzan, E., & Perlberg, A. (1972). Factors which influence cooperation between dentist and child. *Journal of Dental Education, 36,* 9–15.

Saylor, C. F., Swenson, C. C., & Powell, P. (1992). Hurricane Hugo blows down the broccoli: Preschoolers' post-disaster play and adjustment. *Child Psychiatry and Human Development, 22,* 139–149.

Scherer, M. W., & Nakamura, C. Y. (1968). A Fear Survey Schedule for Children (FSS-FC): A factor analytic comparison with manifest anxiety (CMAS). *Behaviour Research and Therapy, 6,* 173–182.

Seligman, M. E. P. (1971). Phobias and preparedness. *Behavior Therapy, 2,* 307–320.

Shaffer, D., Fisher, P., Piacentini, J. C., Schwab-Stone, M., & Wicks, J. (1992). *The NIMH Diagnostic Interview Schedule for Children—Version 2.3.* New York: Columbia University.

Shapiro, A. H. (1975). Behavior of kibbutz and urban children receiving an injection. *Psychophysiology, 12,* 79–82.

Shapiro, E. S. (1984). Self-monitoring procedures. In T. H. Ollendick & M. Hersen (Eds.), *Child behavioral assessment: Principles and procedures* (pp. 148–165). Elmsford, NY: Pergamon Press.

Sheslow, D. V., Bondy, A. S., & Nelson, R. O. (1982). A comparison of graduated exposure, verbal coping skills, and their combination in the treatment of children's fear of the dark. *Child and Family Behavior Therapy, 4,* 33–45.

Siegel, L. J., & Peterson, L. (1980). Stress reduction in young dental patients through coping skills and sensory information. *Journal of Consulting and Clinical Psychology, 48,* 785–787.

Silverman, W. K. (1987). Childhood anxiety disorders: Diagnostic issues, empirical support, and future research. *Journal of Child and Adolescent Psychotherapy, 4,* 121–126.

Silverman, W. K., & Eisen, A. R. (1992). Age differences in the reliability of parent and child reports of child anxious symptomatology using a structured interview. *Journal of American Academy of Child and Adolescent Psychiatry, 31,* 117–124.

Silverman, W. K., & Nelles, W. B. (1988). The Anxiety Disorders Interview Schedule for Children. *Journal of American Academy of Child and Adolescent Psychiatry, 27,* 772–778.

Simon, A., & Ward, L. (1974). Variables influencing the sources, frequency, and intensity of worry in secondary school pupils. *British Journal of Social and Clinical Psychology, 13,* 391–396.

Simpson, W. J., Ruzicka, R. L., & Thomas, N. R. (1974). Physiologic responses of children to initial dental experience. *Journal of Dentistry for Children, 41,* 465–470.

Singer, E. (1965). *Key concepts in psychotherapy.* New York: Random House.

Singer, L. T., Ambuel, B., Wade, S., & Jaffe, A. C. (1992). Cognitive-behavioral treatment of health-impairing food phobias in children. *Journal of the American Academy of Child and Adolescent Psychiatry, 31,* 847–852.

Skinner, H. A., Steinhauer, P. D., & Santa Barbara, J. (1983). The Family Assessment Measure. *Canadian Journal of Community Mental Health, 2,* 91–105.

Slater, E. (1939). Responses to a nursery school situation of 40 children. *Monographs of the Society for Research in Child Development, 2*(No. 4).

Slee, P. T., & Cross, D. G. (1989). Living in the nuclear age: An Australian study of children's and adolescent's fears. *Child Psychiatry and Human Development, 19,* 270–278.

Sonnenberg, E., & Venham, L. (1977). Human figure drawing as a measure of the child's response to dental visits. *Journal of Dentistry for Children, 44,* 438–442.

Spence, S. H., & McCathie, H. (1993). The stability of fears in children: A two-year prospective study. *Journal of Child Psychology and Psychiatry, 34,* 579–585.

Spielberger, C. D. (1973). *Manual for the State–Trait Anxiety Inventory for Children.* Palo Alto, CA: Consulting Psychologists Press.

Spielberger, C. D., Gorsuch, R. L., & Lushene, R. E. (1970). *Manual for the State–Trait Anxiety Inventory.* Palo Alto, CA: Consulting Psychologists Press.

Strahan, R. F., Todd, J. B., & Inglis, G. B. (1974). A palmar sweat measure particularly suited for naturalistic research. *Psychophysiology, 11,* 715–720.

Strauss, C. C. (1987). *Modification of Trait portion of State–Trait Anxiety Inventory for Children—Parent Form.* Unpublished manuscript, Western Psychiatric Institute and Clinic, Pittsburgh.

Strauss, C. C. (1990). Anxiety disorders of childhood and adolescence. *School Psychology Review, 19,* 142–157.

Strauss, C. C., Last, C. G., Hersen, M., & Kazdin, A. E. (1988). Association between anxiety and depression in children and adolescents with anxiety disorders. *Journal of Abnormal Child Psychology, 16,* 57–68.

Strauss, C. C., Lease, C. A., Last, C. G., & Francis, G. (1988). Overanxious Disorder: An examination of developmental differences. *Journal of Abnormal Child Psychology, 16,* 433–443.

Strickler, G., & Howitt, J. W. (1965). Physiological recording during simulated dental appointments. *New York State Dental Journal, 51,* 204–206.

Taylor, J. A. (1953). A personality scale of manifest anxiety. *Journal of Abnormal and Social Psychology, 48,* 285–290.

Thomas, A., & Chess, S. (1977). *Temperament and development.* New York: Brunner/Mazel.

Thomas, A., Chess, S., & Birch, H. G. (1968). *Temperament and behavior disorders in children.* New York: New York University Press.

Thomson, M. L., & Sutarman, M. (1953). The identification and enumeration of active sweat glands in man from plastic impressions of the skin. *Transactions of the Royal Society of Tropical Medicine and Hygiene, 47,* 412–417.

Thyer, B. A., Parrish, R. T., Curtis, G. C., Neese, R. M., & Camerson, O. G. (1985). Ages of onset of DSM-III anxiety disorders. *Comprehensive Psychiatry, 26,* 113–122.

Tobey, T. S., & Thoresen, C. E. (1976). Helping Bill reduce aggressive behaviors: A nine-year-old makes good. In J. D. Krumboltz & C. E. Thoresen (Eds.), *Counseling methods* (pp. 163–173). New York: Holt, Rinehart & Winston.

Turner, S. M., & Beidel, D. C. (1985). Empirically derived subtypes of social anxiety. *Behavior Therapy, 16,* 384–392.

Turner, S. M., Beidel, D. C., & Larkin, K. T. (1986). Situational determinants of social anxiety in clinic and non-clinic samples: Physiological and cognitive correlates. *Journal of Consulting and Clinical Psychology, 54,* 523–527.

Ultee, C. A., Griffioen, D., & Schellekens, J. (1982). The reduction of anxiety in children: A comparison of the effects of 'systematic desensitization *in vitro*' and 'systematic desensitization *in vivo.*' *Behaviour Research and Therapy, 20,* 61–67.

Vaal, J. J. (1973). Applying contingency contracting to a school phobic: A case study. *Journal of Behavior therapy and Experimental Psychiatry, 4,* 371–373.

Van Hasselt, V. B., Hersen, M., Bellack, A. S., Rosenblum, N. D., & Lamparski, D. (1979). Tripartite assessment of the effects of systematic desensitization in a multi-phobic child: An experimental analysis. *Journal of Behavior Therapy and Experimental Psychiatry, 10,* 15–55.

Varni, J. W. (1983). *Clinical behavioral pediatrics: An interdisciplinary biobehavioral approach.* Elmsford, NY: Pergamon Press.

Vasey, M. W. (1993). Development and cognition in childhood anxiety: The example of worry. In T. H. Ollendick & R. J. Prinz (Eds.), *Advances in clinical child psychology* (Vol. 15, pp. 1–39). New York: Plenum Press.

Venham, L. L., Bengston, D., & Cipes, M. (1977). Children's responses to sequential dental visits. *Journal of Dental Research, 56,* 454–459.

Venham, L. L., Gaulin-Kremer, E., Munster, E., Bengston-Audia, D., & Cohan, J. (1980). Interval rating scales for children's dental anxiety and uncooperative behavior. *Pediatric Dentistry, 2,* 195–202.

Venham, L. L., Murray, P., & Gaulin-Kremer, E. (1979). Child-rearing variables affecting the preschool child's response to dental stress. *Journal of Dental Research, 58,* 2042–2045.

Vernon, D. T. A. (1973). Use of modeling to modify children's responses to a natural, potentially stressful situation. *Journal of Applied Psychology, 58,* 351–356.

Vernon, D. T. A., Foley, J. M., & Schulman, J. L. (1967). Effect of mother–child separation and birth order on young children's responses to two potentially stressful experiences. *Journal of Personality and Social Psychology, 5,* 162–174.

Vernon, D. T. A., Schulman, J. L., & Foley, J. M. (1966). Changes in children's behavior after hospitalization. *American Journal of Diseases of Children, 3,* 581–593.

Wallach, M. A., & Kogan, N. (1965). *Models of thinking in young children.* New York: Holt, Rinehart & Winston.

Watson, J. B., & Rayner, P. (1920). Conditioned emotional reactions. *Journal of Experimental Psychology, 3,* 1–14.

Waye, M. F. (1979). Behavioral treatment of a child displaying comic-book mediated fear of hand shrinking: A case study. *Journal of Pediatric Psychology, 4,* 43–47.

Wigfield, A., & Meece, J. (1988). Math anxiety in elementary school students. *Journal of Educational Psychology, 80,* 210–216.

Wilder, J. (1950). The law of initial values. *Psychosomatic Medicine, 12,* 392–401.

Williams, C. E., & Jones, R. T. (1989). Impact of self-instructions on response maintenance and children's fear of fire. *Journal of Clinical Child Psychology, 18,* 84–89.

Wine, J. D. (1979). Test anxiety and evaluation threat: Children's behavior in the classroom. *Journal of Abnormal Child Psychology, 7,* 45–59.

Winer, G. A. (1982). A review and analysis of children's fearful behavior in dental settings. *Child Development, 53,* 1111–1133.

Winker, J. B. (1949). Age trends and sex differences in the wishes, identifications, activities and fears of children. *Child Development, 20,* 191–196.

Wirt, R. D., Lacher, D., Klinedinst, J. H., & Seat, P. D. (1977). *Multidimensional description of child personality: A manual for the Personality Inventory for Children.* Los Angeles: Western Psychological Services.

Wolf, M. (1978). Social validity: the case for subjective measurement, or how applied behavior analysis is finding its heart. *Journal of Applied Behavior Analysis, 11,* 203–214.

Wolpe, J., & Rachman, S. (1960). Psychoanalytic "evidence": A critique based on Freud's case of Little Hans. *Journal of Nervous and Mental Disease, 130*, 135–148.

Wright, G. Z., Alpern, G. D., & Leake, J. L. (1973). The modifiability of maternal anxiety as it relates to children's cooperative behavior. *Journal of Dentistry for Children, 40*, 265–271.

Zabin, M. A., & Melamed, B. G. (1980). Relationship between parental discipline and children's ability to cope with stress. *Journal of Behavioral Assessment, 2*, 17–38.

Zatz, S., & Chassin, L. (1983). Cognitions of test-anxious children. *Journal of Consulting and Clinical Psychology, 51*, 526–534.

Zatz, S., & Chassin, L. (1985). Cognitions of test-anxious children under naturalistic test-taking conditions. *Journal of Consulting and Clinical Psychology, 53*, 393–401.

Zohar, A. H., Ratzoni, G., Pauls, D. L., Apter, A., Bleich, A., Kron, S., Rappaport, M., Weizman, A., & Cohen, D. J. (1992). An epidemiological study of Obsessive–Compulsive Disorder and related disorders in Israeli adolescents. *Journal of the American Academy of Child and Adolescent Psychiatry, 31*, 1057–1061.

APPENDIX. Description and Appraisal of Instruments for Assessing Children's Fears and Anxieties

Instrument/author(s)	Response system	Method of measurement	Description	Appraisal
			Blood	
Behavioral avoidance test Van Hasselt, Hersen, Bellack, Rosenblum, & Lamparski (1979)	Motor	Observational	A blood-soaked pillowcase 15 feet away is brought 1 foot closer every 15 seconds until the child motions to stop.	Excellent temporal stability across 3 weeks. Scores fluctuate in accord with treatment, but bear no systematic relationship to physiological and subjective measures. Easy to administer and score; suitable for both the laboratory and the clinic for problem identification and treatment evaluation.
Target Complaint Scale Van Hasselt et al. (1979)	Subjective	Self-report	Subjective fear experienced during the behavioral avoidance test is rated on a 12-point scale, with descriptive anchors (e.g., "none," "pretty much," "couldn't be worse") at every third point.	Excellent temporal stability across 3 weeks. Scores fluctuate in accord with treatment, but bear no systematic relationship to physiological and motor measures. A global rating of ambiguous meaning and suspect soundness and utility. Addition of more response items of distinct content may make the instrument useful to the researcher and clinician in identifying problematic fear and evaluating treatments.
Heart rate Van Hasselt et al. (1979)	Physiological	Mechanical	Monitored throughout the behavioral avoidance test. Heart rate response score is calculated by subtracting the rate for the last 15 seconds of baseline from the rate for the last 15 seconds of final approach item.	Good temporal stability across 3 weeks. No evidence of validity (e.g., fluctuations with treatment, convergence with other measures); thus, no data to support the usefulness of this method of recording and quantifying heart rate activity.
Finger pulse volume Van Hasselt et al. (1979)	Physiological	Mechanical	Monitored throughout the behavioral avoidance test. Response score is calculated by subtracting amplitude for last 15 seconds of baseline from the amplitude for last 15 seconds of final approach item.	Good temporal stability across 3 weeks. No evidence of validity (e.g., fluctuations with treatment, convergence with other measures); thus, no data to support the usefulness of this method of recording and quantifying cardiovascular activity.

(continued)

APPENDIX. (*continued*)

Instrument/author(s)	Response system	Method of measurement	Description	Appraisal
			Darkness	
Behavioral avoidance test Giebenhain & Barrios (1986)	Motor	Observational	Room illumination is progressively dimmed in 10 steps, with 30-second intervals between steps, until the child tolerates 30 seconds of total darkness or motions to stop.	Excellent temporal stability over 3 weeks. Convergence with other motor and subjective measures of fear. Discriminates between groups known to differ in fearfulness toward darkness. Easy to administer and score; suitable for use in both the laboratory and clinic for problem and treatment evaluation.
Fear thermometer Giebenhain & Barrios (1986)	Physiological	Self-report	Level of physiological upset during the behavioral avoidance test is rated on a 5-point scale with animated figures as descriptive anchors at each point.	Poor temporal stability over 3 weeks. Convergence with other subjective measures of fear. A global rating of ambiguous meaning and questionable utility. Addition of more response items of distinct content may make scores more stable and useful in problem identification and treatment evaluation.
Heart rate Giebenhain & Barrios (1986)	Physiological	Mechanical	Monitored throughout the behavioral avoidance test. Response score is calculated by subtracting mean baseline rate from mean rate for the final approach item.	Poor temporal stability over 3 weeks and no evidence of validity (e.g., convergence with other fear measures, discrimination of known groups); therefore, no support for the usefulness of this method of monitoring and quantifying heart rate activity.
Modified Timed Behavior Checklist Giebenhain & Barrios (1986)	Motor	Observational	During the behavioral avoidance test, the occurrence–nonoccurrence of nine responses (e.g., rocking, shuffling feet, clenching fists, nail biting, facial grimacing) is recorded for each gradation. Response score is calculated by dividing the number of gradations tolerated into the total number of occurrences.	Excellent interrater reliability, acceptable temporal stability over 3 weeks. Convergence with other motor and subjective measures of fear. Discriminates between groups known to differ in their fearfulness toward darkness. Need for trained raters probably restricts its use to research for purposes of problem identification and treatment evaluation.

Measure			Description	Evaluation
Self-Statement Checklist Giebenhain & Barrios (1986)	Subjective	Self-report	Child rates, on a 4-point scale from "never" to "a lot," the frequency of five fearful thoughts (e.g., "I kept thinking about how scared I was") and five coping or mastery thoughts (e.g., "I kept thinking that I am brave") experienced during the behavioral avoidance test. A response score for each type of thinking is obtained by summing across the five items.	Poor Temporal stability over 3 weeks. Convergence with other subjective, motor, and physiological measures of fear. Discriminates groups known to differ in fearfulness toward darkness. Addition of more response items may render scores more stable. Easy to administer and score; suitable for use in both the laboratory and clinic for purpose of problem identification and treatment evaluation.
Think-aloud statements Giebenhain & Barrios (1986)	Subjective	Self-report	Audiotaped recordings of "thinking aloud" during the behavioral avoidance test are scored for the percentage of fearful, coping, and irrelevant statements. Entire transcript is rated for affect on a 7-point scale (e.g., "not at all afraid," "extremely afraid").	Excellent interrater reliability; good temporal stability over 3 weeks. Convergente with other subjective, motor, and physiological measures of fear. Discriminates groups known to differ in fearfulness toward darkness. Scoring of think-aloud audiotapes is tedious and time-consuming; therefore, the procedure appears to be restricted to use by researchers for the purposes of problem identification and treatment evaluation.
Bedtime Illumination Test Giebenhain & O'Dell (1984)	Motor	Observational	Child selects from 1 of 11 levels (total darkness to total brightness) the nighttime illumination for the bedroom.	Excellent temporal stability over 1 month. Scores fluctuate in accord with treatment. Easy to administer and score. Suitable for both the laboratory and clinic for purposes of treatment evaluation.
Direct Home Observation Graziano & Mooney (1980)	Motor	Observational	Parents record nightly the number of minutes after request the child requires to go to bed, the number of minutes to fall asleep, the occurrence of avoidance and delay behaviors (e.g., requesting a glass of water, telling of a story), a rating of willingness to go to bed, and a judgment of whether or not the child is afraid.	Good interrater reliability. Some evidence of stability for some of the measures through aggregation (Friedman & Ollendick, 1989). Scores discriminate between groups known to differ in fearfulness toward darkness; scores also fluctuate in accord with treatment. Appears suitable for both researchers and clinicians for the purposes of problem identification and treatment evaluation.

(continued)

APPENDIX. (*continued*)

Darkness

Instrument/author(s)	Response system	Method of measurement	Description	Appraisal
Fear Strength Questionnaire Graziano & Mooney (1980)	Motor	Observational	Child's fear reaction is rated along nine dimensions (e.g., frequency, intensity, duration per incident, level of disruption, seriousness, degree of school interference).	Good temporal stability over 4 weeks. Scores fluctuate in accord with treatment. Ease of administration and scoring makes it suitable for both the laboratory and the clinic, but lack of data on interrater reliability and convergence with other fear measures restrict its use to treatment evaluation.
Darkness Tolerance Test Kanfer, Karoly, & Newman (1975)	Motor	Mechanical	Two variants: one has the child in total darkness for 180 seconds before adjusting the illumination to a comfortable level; the other has the child in total illumination, dimming the light to complete darkness or some intermediate point.	Excellent temporal stability across 35 days of repeated assessment (King, Cranstoun, & Josephs, 1989). Scores on the two forms correlate with each other, fluctuate in accord with treatment, and generalize to other relevant settings. Mixed findings in terms of convergence with subjective measures of fear. Simple to administer and score; appropriate for both the laboratory and the clinic for the purposes of problem identification and treatment evaluation.
Behavioral avoidance test Kelley (1976)	Motor	Observational	Room illumination is decreased from full brightness in five steps until child tolerates 60 seconds of total darkness or motions to stop. Response score is number of seconds of the steps tolerated.	No estimates of reliability. Modest relationship to subjective measure of fear. Test performance sensitive to instructional demand for approach behavior. Lack of reliability and validity data argues against its use.
Fear thermometer Kelley (1976)	Subjective	Self-report	Level of fear experienced during the behavioral avoidance test is rated on a scale of 1–5 by moving a lever up a multicolored board.	No estimates of reliability. Modest relationship to motor measure of fear. A global rating of ambiguous meaning and suspect soundness. Not recommended for use at present.

Instrument	Component	Method	Description	Evaluation
Behavioral avoidance test Leitenberg & Callahan (1973)	Motor	Observational	Number of seconds of total darkness tolerated is recorded.	Excellent temporal stability over 4 weeks. Scores fluctuate in accord with treatment. Simple to administer and score; suitable for use in the laboratory and the clinic for purposes of treatment evaluation.
Nighttime Coping Response Inventory Mooney (1985)	Subjective, motor	Self-report	Retrospective 5-point ratings are made of the frequencies of 20 nighttime coping responses from five categories: Self-Control (e.g., "think happy or pleasant thought"), Social Support (e.g., "go into bed with Mom or Dad"), Clinging to Inanimate Objects, Control over Inanimate Environment, and Control over Others. A composite score for each response category is obtained by summing across the four appropriate items.	No estimates of reliability. Scores discriminate groups known to differ in fearfulness toward the dark. Easy to administer and score, but difficult to interpret because items addressing the subjective component are lumped with ones addressing the motor component. Separate scales may be developed for the two components. With these modifications and additional reliability and validity data, the inventory may be useful in problem identification, treatment selection, and treatment evaluation.
Nighttime Fear Inventory Mooney (1985)	Subjective	Self-report	Child completes 5-point ratings of the level of worry or fear experienced to 28 images from seven stimulus categories: Personal Security (e.g., "dying or thinking I am going to die"), Separation from Others (e.g., "wonder if Mom or Dad are hurt or not"), Imaginal (e.g., "ghosts or spooks"), Inherent Characteristics, Dreams, Dark, and Neutral. A composite score for each stimulus category is obtained by summing across the four relevant items.	No estimates of reliability. Scores discriminate groups known to differ in fearfulness toward the dark. Ease of administration and scoring makes it appropriate for use in both the laboratory and the clinic. Lack of reliability and validity data argues for cautious use.
Darkness Tolerance Test Sheslow, Bondy, & Nelson (1982)	Motor	Observational	The number of seconds of total darkness tolerated is recorded.	Excellent interrater reliability. Scores fluctuate in accord with treatment. Ease of administration and scoring makes it suitable for use in both the laboratory and the clinic. Lack of temporal stability data calls for cautious use of the instrument to evaluate treatment effectiveness.

(continued)

APPENDIX. (*continued*)

Instrument/author(s)	Response system	Method of measurement	Description	Appraisal
			Fire	
Fear Inventory for Fire Safety Jones, Ollendick, McLaughlin, & Williams (1989); Williams & Jones (1989)	Subjective	Self-report	Child rates level of fear ("none," "some," or "a lot") to 33 items addressing various fire-related situations (e.g., "smelling smoke in your room"). Ratings are summed across items to form a total fear score.	Poor temporal stability over an unspecified time period. No other estimates of reliability reported. Some evidence of fluctuations in scores in accordance with treatment. Given the increasing numbers of latchkey children and the likelihood that increasing numbers of them suffer from fears of such emergencies as fires, this scale may be drawn upon by researchers and practitioners. Efforts should therefore be made to examine and enhance its reliability via item analyses.
			Heights	
Ladder climb Van Hasselt et al. (1979)	Motor	Observational	Number of feet the child goes up a 12-foot ladder is recorded.	Excellent temporal stability over 3 weeks. Convergence with physiological measure of fear and fluctuation in accord with treatment. Suitable for use in laboratory and clinic for purposes of treatment evaluation.
Target Complaint Scale Van Hasselt et al. (1979)	Subjective	Self-report	Subjective fear experienced during the ladder climb is rated on a 12-point scale, with descriptive anchors at every third point (e.g., "none," "pretty much," "couldn't be worse").	Excellent temporal stability over 3 weeks. Fluctuations in accord with treatment. A global rating of ambiguous meaning and suspect utility. Addition of response items of distinct content may yield a reliable instrument for use in problem identification and treatment evaluation.
Heart rate Van Hasselt et al. (1979)	Physiological	Mechanical	Heart rate is recorded upon arrival to the laboratory and immediately prior to the ladder climb. Former is subtracted from latter to yield a heart rate response score.	Excellent temporal stability over 3 weeks. Convergence with motor measure of fear and fluctuation in accord with treatment. Expensive recording apparatus may

restrict this measurement of heart rate to the laboratory, where it might be used for the purposes of problem identification and treatment evaluation.

Illness

Instrument			Description	Evaluation
Fear-related verbalizations Bornstein & Knapp (1981)	Subjective	Self-report	Parents record on an hourly basis the frequency of fear-related verbal remarks.	Excellent interrater reliability; poor temporal stability. Scores fluctuate in accord with treatment. Ease of data collection makes it suited for both the researcher and clinician for assessing outcome. Stability may be improved through aggregation.

Medical procedures

Instrument			Description	Evaluation
Maternal Anxiety Rating Bradlyn, Christoff, Sikora, O'Dell, & Harris (1986)	Motor	Observational	Mother rates her child's current level of anxiety on a 7-point scale.	No estimates of reliability; scores fluctuate with treatment. A global rating of ambiguous meaning and suspect utility. Addition of more items of definite content may render it useful.
Faces—Subjective Units of Disturbance Bradlyn et al. (1986)	Subjective	Self-report	Child indicates present level of anxiety by pointing to one of five faces, each depicting a level of fear.	No evidence of reliability or validity. A global rating of uncertain meaning and utility. Addition of response items of distinct content may transform the instrument into a useful one. In its present form, though, it is of little worth.
Hospital Fears Schedule Bradlyn et al. (1986)	Subjective	Self-report	Using the 5-point Faces scale, child rates degree of anxiety to 10 hospital-related situations. Ratings are summed across items to yield a total fear score.	No evidence of reliability or validity. Test score is actually a composite of 10 global ratings; thus, suffers from the same limitations as the global rating (e.g., instability, ambiguous content). Increasing the clarity of the rating scale may improve its reliability and validity.
Observational Behavior Scale Bradlyn et al. (1986); Klorman, Ratner, King, & Sveen (1978)	Motor	Observational	Occurrence–nonoccurrence of seven motor responses (e.g., kicking, hand to face, crying) is recorded every 15 seconds and summed across responses and intervals to yield a total motor score.	Excellent interrater reliability. Scores are relatively stable across successive exposures to medical procedures. Scores correlate with parental ratings and self-ratings of anxiety. Small number of response categories makes it feasible for both clinical and research use.

(continued)

Medical procedures

Instrument/author(s)	Response system	Method of measurement	Description	Appraisal
Ratings of Anxiety and Cooperation Bradlyn et al. (1986)	Motor	Observational	Physician and nurse or technician rate on a 7-point scale the child's level of anxiety and level of cooperation during the procedure.	No estimates of reliability. Scores fluctuate in accord with treatment. A single-item measure of uncertain meaning and questionable utility. Introduction of more items of specified content may enhance the usefulness of the instrument.
Self-Statements Inventory—Revised Bradlyn et al. (1986)	Subjective	Self-report	Child rates on a 7-point scale the frequency of 18 thoughts of two types (coping, disruptive) experienced during the medical procedure. The nine coping thoughts (e.g., "How much were you thinking that the test didn't hurt, and how easy it was to get through it?") and the nine disruptive thoughts (e.g., "How much were you worrying that the test might kill you?") are summed to yield a composite score for each type.	No estimates of reliability of validity. May have too few items on each scale for adequate reliability. Addition of more items may enhance reliability, which in turn may enhance the usefulness of the inventory.
Behavioral avoidance test Freeman, Roy, & Hemmick (1976)	Motor	Observational	Number of steps completed in an 11-step physical examination is recorded.	No estimates of reliability. Scores fluctuate in accord with treatment. Ease of administration and scoring makes the procedure well suited for both the laboratory and the clinic. Lack of data on temporal stability calls for caution in using the measure as an index of treatment outcome.
Behavioral Profile Rating Scale—Revised Gilbert et al. (1982); Gilbert, Johnson, Silverstein, & Malone (1989)	Motor	Observational	Frequency of several anxiety-related behaviors is recorded during self-injection of insulin. Frequencies are summed to yield a single motor fear score.	Good interrater reliability. No evidence of validity (e.g., convergence with other fear measures, fluctuations with treatment). Employing a weighted as opposed to an unweighted scoring system may enhance the usefulness of the instrument. The need for trained observers restricts its use to research.

Measure	Type	Domain	Description	Comments
Global Anxiety Rating Gilbert et al. (1982)	Observational	Motor	The child's level of anxiety during insulin self-injection is rated on a scale of 1–10.	Good interrater reliability. No evidence of validity. A single-item measure of unknown meaning and questionable worth. The addition of response items of definite content may improve the instrument's usefulness.
Observational Scale of Behavioral Distress Jay & Elliott (1984); Jay, Ozolins, Elliott, & Caldwell (1983); Jay, Elliott, Ozolins, Olson, & Pruitt (1985); Gonzales et al. (1989)	Observational	Motor	Occurrence–nonoccurrence of 11 behaviors (e.g., cry, scream, physical restraint, muscular rigidity) is recorded in 15-second intervals. The behaviors are differentially weighted according to intensity of distress, and summed to yield a weighted composite score.	Excellent interrater reliability. Convergence with other motor, subjective, and physiological measures of fear. Fluctuations in scores as a function of treatment. Need for trained observers may restrict its use to research for the purposes of problem identification.
Procedure Behavioral Rating Scale Katz, Kellerman, & Seigel (1980)	Observational	Motor	Occurrence–nonoccurrence of 13 behaviors (e.g., cling, flail, stall, scream) is recorded during entire procedure. Recordings are summed across behaviors to yield a single motor score.	Excellent interrater reliability, good temporal stability over 1½ years. Convergence with other measures of fear. Need for trained observers may restrict its employment to research for the purposes of problem identification and treatment evaluation.
Procedure Behavior Checklist LeBaron & Zeltzer (1984)	Observational	Motor	Occurrence–nonoccurrence and intensity of eight behaviors (e.g., muscle tension, crying, restraint used, physical resistance) are recorded during the entire medical procedure. Intensity is rated on a scale of 1–5. Recordings are summed across behaviors to yield a single occurrence score and a single intensity score.	Acceptable interrater reliability. Convergence with other motor and subjective measures of fear. Need for trained observers may restrict its use to research for purposes of treatment evaluation.
Observer Rating of Anxiety LeBaron & Zeltzer (1984)	Observational	Motor	The child's level of anxiety during a portion of the medical procedure is rated on a 5-point scale.	No estimate of reliability. Convergence with other motor and subjective measures of anxiety. Single-item measure of ambiguous meaning. Addition of items of stated content may enhance the usefulness of the measure.

(continued)

APPENDIX. (*continued*)

Instrument/author(s)	Response system	Method of measurement	Description	Appraisal
			Medical procedures	
Faces Test of Anxiety LeBaron & Zeltzer (1984)	Subjective	Self-report	Child rates degree of anxiety experienced during the procedure by pointing to one of five faces, each depicting a level of fear.	No estimate of reliability. Convergence with motor measures of anxiety. Global rating of undetermined content and limited utility. Addition of items of known content may increase the reliability and validity of the test.
Behavior Profile Rating Scale Klingman, Melamed, Cuthbert, & Hermecz (1984); Melamed, Hawes, Heiby, & Glick (1975); Melamed, Weinstein, Hawes, & Katin-Borland (1975); Melamed, Yurcheson, Fleece, Hutcherson, & Hawes (1978)	Motor	Observational	The frequencies of 27 behaviors (e.g., crying, refusal to open mouth, rigid posture, kicking) are recorded during the dental treatment procedure. Each behavior is weighted according to its degree of disruption, and a total score is obtained by summing across the weighted values.	Excellent interrater reliability. Convergence with other observational and self-report measures of dental anxiety; scores fluctuate in accord with treatment. Large number of response categories and need for trained observers confine its use to research. May be of assistance in problem identification and treatment evaluation.
Children's Fear Survey Schedule—Dental Melamed, Hawes, et al. (1975); Melamed, Weinstein, et al. (1975); Melamed et al. (1978)	Subjective	Self-report	Children rate on a scale of 1–5 their level of fear of 15 dental-related situations. Ratings on the items are summed to yield a single fears score.	Good temporal stability over 7 days. Convergence with other subjective, motor, and physiological measures of dental anxiety; scores fluctuate in accord with treatment. Global nature of the rating scale makes interpretation problematic. Having a more descriptive scale may circumvent this problem.
Dental Ratings of Anxiety and Cooperation Melamed, Hawes, et al. (1975); Melamed, Weinstein, et al. (1975); Melamed et al.(1978)	Motor	Observational	Dentist rates children on a 10-point scale for their level of anxiety and level of cooperation during dental procedures.	Excellent interrater reliability; acceptable temporal stability over 1 day. Convergence with other observational measures of dental anxiety and self-report of general anxiety. A single global rating of undefined content and questionable utility. Addition of more response items of specified content would facilitate interpretation of scores.

Measure			Description	Comments
Fear thermometer Melamed, Hawes, et al. (1975); Melamed, Weinstein, et al. (1975); Melamed et al. (1978)	Subjective	Self-report	Children rate on a 5-point scale their current degree of fear.	Acceptable test-retest reliability. Correspondence with observational measures of dental anxiety and self-report of general anxiety. A single, global rating of undefined content and questionable utility. Addition of more response items of specified content would facilitate interpretation of scores.
Heart rate Klingman et al. (1984); Melamed et al. (1978)	Physiological	Mechanical	Heart rate is monitored throughout and sampled at 10- to 30-second intervals. Baseline rate is subtracted from phase rates to yield response scores.	No estimates of reliability. Scores fluctuate in accord with treatment. Expensive recording equipment limits its use to research. May serve as a measure of treatment outcome.
Observer Ratings of Anxiety and Cooperation Melamed, Hawes et al. (1975); Melamed, Weinstein, et al. (1975); Melamed et al. (1978)	Motor	Observational	Independent observer rates on a 10-point scale the child's level of anxiety and level of cooperation during a dental procedure.	Excellent interrater reliability; acceptable same-day temporal stability. Convergence with other observational and self-report measures of dental anxiety. Global nature of rating makes interpretation of scores problematic. More response items of known content needed to overcome limitations of single-item, global ratings.
Respiration Klingman et al. (1984)	Physiological	Mechanical	Respiration is monitored throughout. Baseline rate is subtracted from phase rates to yield response scores.	No evidence of reliability or validity; thus, no support for its employment. Different system of sampling and quantification may yield more encouraging statistics.
Hospital Fears Rating Scale Faust & Melamed (1984); Melamed & Siegel (1975); Peterson & Shigetomi (1981)	Subjective	Self-report	Children rate on a scale of 1–5 their level of anxiety regarding 16 hospital-related situations and 9 non-hospital-related situations. The ratings for the 16 hospital items are summed to form a single subjective score.	Good internal consistency. No evidence of validity. The measure is a composite of global ratings, and as such suffers from the limitations inherent to all global ratings (e.g., instability, obscure meaning). Adding greater specificity to the rating scale may yield stable and useful measures.

(continued)

289

Medical procedures

Instrument/author(s)	Response system	Method of measurement	Description	Appraisal
Observer Rating Scale of Anxiety Melamed & Siegel (1975)	Motor	Observational	Occurrence–nonoccurrence of 29 verbal and skeletal–motor behaviors (e.g., crying, trembling hands, stuttering) is recorded for a 3-minute interval. Recordings are summed across behaviors and intervals to form a single motor response score.	Excellent interrater reliability and immediate test–retest reliability. Scores fluctuate in accord with treatment. Large number of response categories and the need for trained observers limit it to research use, where it may serve as a measure of treatment outcome.
Palmar sweat index Faust & Melamed (1984); Gilbert et al. (1982); Melamed & Siegel (1975)	Physiological	Mechanical	A plastic impression on the child's index finger that registers active sweat glands, the number of which serves as the response score.	Excellent interrater reliability. Correspondence with other physiological and motor measures of anxiety; scores fluctuate in accordance with treatment. One of the more practical methods for measuring physiological responses; lends itself to use in both the laboratory and clinic.
Child Behavior Checklist Peterson, Schultheis, Ridley-Johnson, Miller, & Tracy (1984); Peterson & Shigetomi (1981)	Motor	Observational	Occurrence–nonoccurrence, magnitude, and duration of 16 behaviors (e.g., crying, hair twisting) are recorded per phase of the medical procedure. Magnitude and duration are rated on a scale of 1–3, and behaviors are weighted for degree of disruption. Magnitude rating, duration rating, and weight are combined multiplicatively for each behavior, then summed across behaviors.	Good interrater reliability; poor internal consistency. Scores fluctuate in accord with treatment. Addition of a few more response items may increase internal consistency to acceptable level. Number of response categories and need for trained observers make the instrument practical only for research use as a measure of treatment outcome.
Child Behavior Observational Rating Peterson et al. (1984); Peterson & Shigetomi (1981)	Motor	Observational	Children are rated on a 5-point scale for their level of anxiety, cooperation, and tolerance during the medical procedure.	Excellent interrater reliability; good internal consistency. Scores fluctuate in accord with treatment. Measure is a composite of three global ratings, and therefore is of indeterminate content and meaning. Increased detail in the three scales may circumvent these problems.

Measure	Type	Format	Description	Comments
Child Self-Report Peterson et al. (1984)	Subjective	Self-report	Children use a five-piece thermometer to rate the attractiveness of three hospital-related pictures (e.g., coming to the nurse's desk, getting a blood test) and three non-hospital-related pictures (e.g., playing with favorite toys). A score for each scene category is obtained by summing across the appropriate three pictures.	No evidence of reliability or validity. Having only three items per category may preclude obtainment of reliable measurement. Additional items may lead to improved reliability, which would allow for investigation of validity.
Faces Affect Scale Venham, Bengston, & Cipes (1977)	Subjective	Self-report	Children select from eight pairs of calm–upset faces the one that best matches current mood state. A total upset score is obtained by summing across the eight pairs.	Acceptable internal consistency. Low to modest correlations with other subjective, motor, and physiological measures of anxiety. Molar nature of the response items may preclude scores from being sensitive indicators of treatment effects or correlating with other fear measures. Items of greater specificity may prove to be more useful.
Venham Anxiety-Rating Scale Venham, Gaulin-Kremer, Munster, Bengston-Audia, & Cohan (1980)	Motor	Observational	Child's level of anxiety is rated on a descriptive scale of 0 (e.g., "relaxed, smiling") to 5 (e.g., "loud crying, physical restraint required") for each of three periods. The ratings are averaged to yield a score for the entire procedure.	Excellent interrater reliability. Convergence with other motor, subjective, and physiological measures of anxiety. The multiple descriptive anchors pose interpretive problems. Rating the child on each one of the descriptors would avoid these problems.
Venham Behavior-Rating Scale Venham et al. (1980)	Motor	Observational	Child's disruptive behavior is rated on a descriptive scale of 0 (e.g., "no crying or protest") to 5 (e.g., "no compliance, physical restraint required") for each of three periods. The ratings are averaged to yield a score for the entire period.	Excellent interrater reliability. Convergence with other motor, subjective, and physiological measures of anxiety. Multiple descriptive anchors create problems in interpretation of scores. It would be preferable to rate the child on each of these descriptors, thus avoiding confusion as to the scores' meaning.
Global Mood Scale Vernon, Foley, & Schulman (1967)	Motor	Self-report	Child's overall mood is rated on a descriptive scale of 1 (e.g., "attentive, contented") to 7 (e.g., "intense crying, loud screaming") for each of four periods. The ratings are averaged across the periods to yield a score for the entire procedure.	Excellent interrater reliability. Convergence with motor and physiological measures of anxiety. Scale points have multiple, vague descriptive anchors, which make interpretation of scores problematic. Interpretive problems could be avoided by rating the child on each response descriptor.

(continued)

APPENDIX. (*continued*)

Instrument/author(s)	Response system	Method of measurement	Description	Appraisal
			Medical procedures	
Hospital Scenes Dorkey & Amen (1947); Vernon (1973)	Subjective	Self-report	Child is presented with 14 hospital scenes in which the face of the central child figure is left blank, and is asked to select either a happy or a sad face for the scenes. Total number of sad faces selected serves as measure of subjective response.	Excellent internal consistency; poor test–retest reliability. Convergence with observational measures of anxiety. Global nature of the two scale points produces scores of ambiguous meaning.
Posthospital Behavior Questionnaire Vernon (1973); Vernon, Schulman, & Foley (1966)	Motor	Observational	Mother rates on a scale of 1 ("much less than before") to 5 ("much more than before") the frequency of 27 child behaviors (e.g., fear of leaving the house, refusal to enter the dark, trailing parents). Ratings are summed across response items to yield a composite motor score.	Good test–retest reliability. Convergence with interview data from mothers. Large number of response categories and retrospective nature of ratings cast doubt on the utility of the instrument. May have some usefulness in the assessment of generalization or social validity.
COMFORT Scale Ambuel, Hamlett, Marx, & Blumer (1992)	Motor, physiological	Observational, mechanical	Observer rates the child's level of distress to a pediatric intensive care unit according to eight response categories: alertness, calmness, respiratory response, movement, mean arterial pressure, heart rate, muscle tone, and facial expression. Ratings are made upon completion of a 2-minute observation period, according to separate 5-point behaviorally anchored scales. Assignment of ratings for the physiological responses calls for the reading of charts and monitors. A total COMFORT score is arrived at by summing the ratings for all eight response categories.	Moderate to excellent estimates of interrater reliability for individual category and total scores. High estimate of internal consistency for total score. Convergence among the various response categories and convergence between total scores and another observational measure of distress (nurse's global rating). Authors suggest more repeated readings of monitors and systematic review of the readings in order to enhance the interrater reliability of the physiological response categories. Estimates of the temporal stability of the category and total ratings are needed, as are estimates of the correspondence with subjective measures. Ease with which the ratings can be collected and the amount of useful information obtained make the scale suitable for both clinical and research use.

Child–Adult Medical Procedure Interaction Scale–Revised Blount et al. (1989); Blount, Sturges, & Powers (1990)	Motor	Observational	Audiotapes of bone marrow aspiration/lumbar puncture procedures are made, transcribed, and coded according to the following six child and adult vocalization categories: child coping (e.g., audible deep breathing, humor, nonprocedural talk), child distress (e.g., cry, scream, request emotional support), child neutral (e.g., request relief from nonprocedural discomfort), adult coping-promoting (e.g., humor to child, command to use coping strategy), adult distress-promoting (e.g., criticism, reassuring comments, empathy), and adult neutral (e.g., humor to adults, procedural talk to adults, checking child's status). The six categories encompass a total of 35 specific response codes. A proportion score for each of the six categories is computed for each of the nine phases of the bone marrow aspiration/lumbar puncture procedures; this is done by dividing the number of occurrences for the category by the total number of occurrences for the child or adult categories for a given phase.	Acceptable estimates of interrater reliability for 32 of the 35 response codes. Adult and child behaviors covary both within and across phases as hypothesized. Estimates of correspondence with other motor behaviors are needed, as are estimates of correspondence with subjective and physiological responses. Extensive training required for raters and elaborateness of coding scheme restrict the use of the scale to research purposes.
Pediatric Recovery Room Rating Scale Faust, Olson, & Rodriguez (1991)	Motor	Observational	Observer records the display of five negative/distress response categories: moaning/whimpering, crying, kicking/hitting, verbal/physical resistance to medical procedures, and utterances of fear and pain. Recordings are carried out during the first four 15-minute intervals during recovery, and may be summed across categories and intervals to yield a single behavioral distress score.	Excellent estimates of interrater reliability. Scores fluctuate in accordance with treatment. Estimates of correspondence with subjective and physiological measures are needed. Brevity of the observation period and of the list of behaviors observed makes the scale suitable for both clinical and research use.

(continued)

APPENDIX. (*continued*)

Instrument/author(s)	Response system	Method of measurement	Description	Appraisal
Medical procedures				
Heart rate Faust et al. (1991)	Physiological	Mechanical	Photoplethysmograph attached to earlobe monitors provides a digital readout of heart rate. After 1 minute is allowed for habituation, three consecutive readings are obtained for the baseline and surgery-entry phases. The three readings for the respective phases are averaged to form a mean heart rate score.	Prior research attests to the internal reliability of the readings. Scores fluctuate in accordance with treatment. Precise estimates of temporal stability, as well as correspondence with motor, subjective, and physiological measures, are needed. Compact, convenient, and reliable nature of the instrument makes it suitable for both clinical and research use.
Sweat bottle Strahan, Todd, & Inglis (1974); Faust et al. (1991)	Physiological	Mechanical	Sweat levels are obtained for baseline and surgery-entry phases by means of the sweat bottle method, which calls for collecting sweat ions by inverting a small bottle of distilled water onto the child's hand. The ions increase the conductivity of the bottle's content; thus, conductivity measurements serve as sweat level scores for the two phases.	Prior research provides support for the temporal stability of the scores. There is mixed support for fluctuations in the scores as a function of treatment. Because the method lends itself so well to use in both controlled and naturalistic settings, continued examination of its merits is recommended. Estimates of reliability based upon child samples are needed, as are estimates of convergence with subjective, motor, and other physiological measures.
Behavioral Approach–Avoidance and Distress Scale Hubert, Jay, Saltoun, & Hayes (1988)	Motor	Observational	Independent observer rates the child's approach-avoidance and distress at five stages in the preparation for bone marrow aspiration procedure. Ratings are provided on 5-point behaviorally anchored scales. For the Approach–Avoidance scale, descriptive anchors for the low point are "turns away/tries to escape or change situation"; for the midpoint, "watches but does not participate verbally or nonverbally"; and for the high	Excellent estimates of internal consistency for the total Approach–Avoidance and Distress scores. Strong inverse relationship between the two scales. Convergence between Approach–Avoidance scores and other observational measures of the same subset of motor behaviors (Activity Specialist Ratings, Observational Scale of Behavioral Distress). Convergence between distress scores and other motor

Measure	Response system	Type	Description	Evaluation
			point, "looks/touches/questions/initiates involvement." For the Distress scale, descriptive anchors for the low point are "no distress/calm appearance/no crying"; for the midpoint, "moderate distress/some crying/moderate tension"; and for the high point, "extreme distress/agitation/screaming/extreme muscle tension." Ratings are summed across the five measurement phases to yield a total Approach–Avoidance and a total Distress score.	and subjective response measures (Activity Specialist Ratings, Observational Scale of Behavioral Distress, Nurse Ratings, Faces Test). Estimates of interobserver reliability are needed. The vague nature of the behavioral anchors for the intermediate points of the scales may attenuate the reliability and sensitivity of the instrument. Substituting more concrete descriptors may circumvent these problems and enhance the instrument's usefulness as a problem identification, treatment selection, and treatment evaluation device.
Nurse Ratings Hubert et al. (1988)	Motor	Observational	Nurse provides ratings on 5-point scales of the child's approach–avoidance and distress over the first 2 days of hospitalization. A single Approach–Avoidance rating is provided through use of a behaviorally anchored scale, with the endpoint of 1 (withdrawal) having the descriptors "child actively avoids nurse/consistently refuses to look at, talk to, or interact/does not indicate yes/no response" and the endpoint of 5 (approach) having the descriptors "child actively approaches nurses by consistently initiating interactions such as asking questions, beginning conversation, requesting participation." Ratings of the child's distress to four routine medical procedures (i.e., taking vital signs, taking temperature, venipunctures, other blood tests) are summed to form a total Distress score.	No estimates of reliability reported. Strong inverse relationship between the two scores. Convergence with other observational measures of approach–avoidance and distress (Behavioral Approach–Avoidance and Distress Scale, Observational Scale of Behavioral Distress). Global nature of the ratings may limit their reliability and sensitivity as response measures. Best suited for use as social validation measures.
Activity Specialist Ratings Hubert et al. (1988)	Motor	Observational	Medical specialist rates on 5-point scales the child's approach–avoidance and distress during preparation for bone marrow aspiration.	No estimates of reliability are reported. Approach–Avoidance and Distress scores converge with other observational measures (Behavioral Approach–Avoidance and Distress Scale). Global nature of the ratings limits their use to social validation.

(continued)

Instrument/author(s)	Response system	Method of measurement	Description	Appraisal
			Medical procedures	
Heart rate Hubert et al. (1988)	Physiological	Manual	Heart rate is recorded manually at three time periods: prior to preparation procedure, after preparation procedure, and after bone marrow aspiration. Heart rate for the first period is subtracted from heart rate for each of the latter two periods to form two change scores.	No reliability estimates reported. No correspondence with observational measures of approach–avoidance and distress. Through more frequent measurement and aggregation, a reliable and valid physiological measure may be obtained.
Dental Fear Survey Schedule—Parent Version Milgrom, Jie, Yang, & Tay (1994)	Motor	Observational	Parent rates on a 5-point scale the child's level of fear to 15 dental procedure items (e.g., "the dentist drilling"). Ratings to the items are summed to yield a composite index of child dental fear.	Excellent internal consistency for summary score. Convergence with observational measures of child's motor behavior during dental treatment. Global nature of the rating scale makes interpretation problematic. Introduction of more descriptive anchors may circumvent this problem.
Child Dental Behavior Milgrom et al. (1994)	Motor	Observational	Independent observer rates child's behavior during dental treatment according to one of four categories: no movement or verbalizations, minor movement or verbalizations not interfering with treatment, considerable movement or verbalizations delaying treatment, or major movement and verbalizations precluding treatment.	No estimates of interrater reliability and temporal stability are reported. Convergence with parental report of child's fear of dental procedures. Summary ratings may not be representative of responding at various points across the assessment session. Intermittent ratings that are summed may yield a more representative and reliable measure.
Interview Prins (1985)	Subjective	Self-report	A semistructured interview of 12 questions addressing dental fear (e.g., "What makes you frightened at the dentist?"), self-speech (e.g., "What do you think/say to yourself when you're on your way to the dentist?"), self-regulation (e.g., "Can you think of another trick you could use?"), and perception of	Excellent interrater reliability for all response categories. Scores for negative self-speech correlated with dentist's rating of fear level. Estimates of temporal stability are needed, as are estimates of convergence with measures of motor and physiological responses. Tediousness of

Measure	Category	Type	Description	Comments
			personal control (e.g., "If children try to be brave at the dentist, if they try to control themselves and it doesn't work, why is that?"). Responses to questions addressing self-speech are categorized as positive (e.g., "I have to be brave if it's difficult"), neutral (e.g., "What will the dentist do?"), or negative (e.g., "I keep thinking about the pain and drilling"). Responses to questions about self-regulation are categorized as cognitive self-regulation (e.g., "thinking about something funny or pleasant") or behavioral self-regulation (e.g., "I don't look at the instruments").	transcribing and scoring interview responses limit the use of the instrument to research activities.

Separation

Measure	Category	Type	Description	Comments
Fear-related verbalizations Bornstein & Knapp (1981)	Subjective	Self-report	Parents record hourly the frequency of the child's fear-related verbal remarks.	Excellent interrater reliability; poor temporal stability across 19 days. Scores fluctuate in accord with treatment. Ease with which data are collected makes it attractive for both clinical and research use. Stability of scores may be increased through aggregation.
Preschool Observational Scale of Anxiety Glennon & Weisz (1978)	Motor	Observational	Occurrence–nonoccurrence of 30 behavioral categories (e.g., trembling voice, lip locking, trunk contortions, avoidance of eye contact) is recorded for 30-second intervals. Scores are summed across categories and 20 intervals to give a single anxiety score.	Good interrater reliability; acceptable internal consistency. Convergence with other motor measures of anxiety; scores fluctuate with stimuli differing in threat. The large number of response categories and need for trained observers may restrict the system's use to research.
Parent Anxiety Rating Scale— Separation Doris, McIntyre, Kelsey, & Lehman (1971); Glennon & Weisz (1978)	Motor	Observational	Parents rate the child on 6 items dealing with separation anxiety and 19 items dealing with general anxiety. Ratings are summed across respective items to form total separation anxiety and general anxiety scores.	No estimates of reliability. Convergence with other observational measures of separation anxiety. May not have sufficient number of items for reliable measurement; reliability could be improved by adding several more items to the scale.

(continued)

APPENDIX. (*continued*)

Instrument/author(s)	Method of measurement	Description	Response system	Appraisal
		Separation		
Teachers' Separation Anxiety Scale Doris et al. (1971); Glennon & Weisz (1978)	Observational	Teacher rates the child at the end of the school day on 11 items related to separation anxiety.	Motor	No estimates of reliability. Convergence with other observational measures of separation anxiety. Retrospective nature of the ratings casts doubt on their accuracy and usefulness. May be of some use as a social validation measure.
Global Anxiety Rating Glennon & Weisz (1978)	Observational	Child is rated on a scale of 1–6 for level of anxiety during testing session.	Motor	No evidence of reliability or validity. Suffers from the same limitations of all global, single-item measures (e.g., instability, ambiguous meaning). Additional items of distinct content may improve its worth.
Global Self-Rating Glennon & Weisz (1978)	Self-report	Child rates level of anxiety experienced during session by selecting one face from among six depicting progressive levels of anxiety.	Subjective	No evidence of reliability or validity. A single, overall self-rating of ambiguous meaning and worth. Addition of detailed response items may render it useful.
Teacher Rating of Separation Anxiety Hall (1967); Milos & Reiss (1982)	Observational	Teacher rates on a descriptive scale of 1–5 the child's level of separation anxiety at the onset of the school year, level of separation anxiety for the past 2 weeks, and overall level of separation anxiety. An average of the three ratings is computed.	Motor	Acceptable interrater reliability. No evidence of validity. Small number of items spanning different time periods may preclude the measure from being stable and useful.
Observation of Separation-Relevant Play Milos & Reiss (1982)	Observational	Frequency of anxiety-relevant play (e.g., desire to be with mother, ambivalence in the use of the mother doll) is recorded for 30-second intervals. Frequencies are summed across intervals to produce a total anxiety play score.	Motor	Excellent interrater reliability. Scores fluctuate with treatment. Small number of response categories makes it suitable for use by both researchers and clinicians. Limited validity data suggests that its use be confined to treatment evaluation.

298

Measure		Description	Comments
Quality of Play Rating Milos & Reiss (1982)	Motor Observational	Child's play is rated for degree of expression of separation themes and willingness to master anxiety. A descriptive scale of 1 (e.g., avoidance of separation themes) to 5 (e.g., child doll plays with peers after mother doll leaves) is used.	Acceptable interrater reliability. Correspondence with other observational measure of separation anxiety. Highly global in nature, the rating is of ambiguous meaning, suspect soundness, and suspect worth. The addition of more well-defined response items may increase the utility of the measure.
Separation Anxiety Neisworth, Madle, & Goeke (1975)	Motor Observational	Duration of child's crying, screaming, and sobbing for a 3-hour period is recorded.	Excellent interscorer reliability. Congruence with mothers' reports of child behavior; generality across relevant settings. Length of observation period and need for raters may restrict its use to research.
Speech Disturbance Milos & Reiss (1982)	Motor Observational	Child responds to six separation-relevant questions (e.g., "What happens when Mommy and/or Daddy leaves?") and four separation-irrelevant questions (e.g., "What do you do on your birthday?"). The number of each of seven types of speech disturbances (e.g., sentence corrections, word repetitions, sentence incompletions) is recorded. For each category of questions, the total number of speech disturbances is divided by the total number of words spoken. The ratio for the separation-irrelevant questions is subtracted from that for the separation-relevant questions to yield a single response score.	Acceptable interscorer reliability. Corresponds with other motor measure of separation anxiety; responsive to treatment; discriminates between groups known to differ in fearfulness toward separation. Tedious and time-consuming nature of the ratings may restrict the instrument's use to research.

Small animals

Measure		Description	Comments
Behavioral avoidance test Bandura, Grusec, & Menlove (1967)	Motor Observational	Approach to a live dog is performed in 17 steps. Number of steps performed and degree of fearfulness, vacillation, and reluctance preceding and accompanying each approach response are recorded. The recordings are summed to form a single fear score.	Excellent interrater reliability; acceptable temporal stability over 5 days. Scores fluctuate in accord with treatment and generalize to other relevant settings. Appropriate for use in both the laboratory and clinic for the purposes of problem identification and treatment evaluation.

(continued)

299

APPENDIX. (*continued*)

Instrument/author(s)	Response system	Method of measurement	Description	Appraisal
Small animals				
Behavioral avoidance test Davis, Rosenthal, & Kelley (1981)	Motor	Observational	Approach to a live spider is performed in 27 steps. Number of steps performed and duration of performance are recorded.	Excellent temporal stability over 3 weeks. Measures of approach correlate with self-reports of fear, and fluctuate as a function of treatment. Suitable for use in both the laboratory and clinic for purposes of problem identification and treatment outcome.
Behavioral avoidance test Evans & Harmon (1981)	Motor	Observational	Latency to approach, number of contacts, and cumulative time of contacts with a live spider are recorded.	Good temporal stability over an unspecified time period. Scores correspond to self-reports of fear and discriminate groups known to differ in fearfulness toward spiders. Practical for use by both researchers and clinicians for the purpose of problem identification.
Behavioral avoidance test Hill, Liebert, & Mott (1968)	Motor	Observational	Approach to a live dog is performed in three steps.	No estimates of reliability. Scores fluctuate in accord with treatment. Small number of steps allows for only gross discriminations in fear level.
Behavioral avoidance test Kornhaber & Schroeder (1975)	Motor	Observational	Approach to a live snake is performed in 14 steps.	Acceptable temporal stability over 30 minutes. Convergence with subjective measure of snake fear; fluctuations in accord with treatment. Appropriate for use in the laboratory and the clinic for the purposes of problem identification and treatment evaluation.
Snake Attitude Measure Kornhaber & Schroeder (1975)	Subjective	Self-report	Children select from 10 sets of three animal pictures which one they like and which one they don't like. Nine of the sets contain one picture of a snake; one set contains two pictures of snakes. A response score is	Acceptable temporal stability over 30 minutes. Convergence with motor measure of snake fear; fluctuations in accord with treatment. Administration and scoring of responses are relatively simple.

			computed by subtracting the number of snake pictures disliked from the number of snake pictures liked.	Scores, however, yield little information in regard to the subjective component. The addition of more specific rating scales may enhance the usefulness of the instrument.
Behavioral avoidance test Kuroda (1969)	Motor	Observational	Approaches to live frogs, earthworms, and cats are performed in three steps.	No estimates of reliability. Scores fluctuate in accord with treatment. Having only three graduations, it is capable of making only gross discriminations in fear level.
Active behavioral avoidance test Murphy & Bootzin (1973)	Motor	Observational	Approach to a live snake is performed in 8–18 steps.	Poor temporal stability over 10 days. Correspondence with passive variant of test; fluctuations in accord with treatment. Instability of scores argues against its use.
Passive behavioral avoidance test Murphy & Bootzin (1973)	Motor	Observational	A live snake is brought progressively closer to the child in 8–18 steps.	Poor temporal stability over 10 days. Correspondence with active variant of test; fluctuations in accord with treatment. Instability of scores argues against its employment.
Behavioral avoidance test Ritter (1968)	Motor	Observational	Approach to a live dog is performed in 29 steps.	Good temporal stability over 1 week. Scores converge with self-reports of fear and vary with exposure to treatment. Appropriate for use in both the laboratory and clinic for purposes of problem identification and treatment evaluation.

Social and stranger interaction

Fear and Avoidance Hierarchy Ratings Barlow & Seidner (1983)	Subjective, motor	Self-report	Child rates on a scale of 0–8 the degree of anxiety and avoidance to a 10-item individualized hierarchy of social situations. Ratings are summed across anxiety and avoidance and across items to yield a single fear score.	No estimates of reliability. Converges with mothers' reports of behavior, changes as function of exposure to treatment. Multidimensional nature of response score makes interpretation problematic. Such difficulties could be circumvented by computing separate subjective and motor response scores.

(continued)

Instrument/author(s)	Response system	Method of measurement	Description	Appraisal
			Social and stranger interaction	
Role-Play Test Esveldt-Dawson, Wisner, Unis, Matson, & Kazdin (1982)	Motor	Observational	Child role-plays five situations involving an unfamiliar male (e.g., "asking a man for a donation to a children's hospital"). For each role play, ratings are made of six behaviors (e.g., stiffness, nervous mannerisms) on a scale of either 1–3 or 1–5. Ratings are summed across role plays.	Excellent interrater reliability and temporal stability over 14 days. Some correspondence among the six response measures; scores fluctuate in accord with treatment. Ease with which the role plays can be administered and the performance can be scored makes it suitable for both the laboratory and the clinic. Best used for the evaluation of treatment.
Behavioral approach test Matson (1981)	Motor	Observational	Approach (in feet) and number of words spoken to a stranger are recorded.	Acceptable interrater reliability; excellent temporal stability over 9 days. Concordance between the two measures and with self-rating of fear. Changes in scores as a function of treatment. Lends itself to use in both the laboratory and clinic for the purposes of problem identification and treatment evaluation.
Social Interaction Scale O'Connor (1969)	Motor	Observational	Occurrence–nonoccurrence of five response categories (e.g., physical proximity, verbal interaction with other) is recorded for 15-second intervals. Response occurrences are summed across intervals.	Excellent interrater reliability. Scores fluctuate with exposure to treatment. Schedule of observations may be too demanding for clinical use. Information is needed on how well the individual response categories correlate with one another, and thus can be interpreted as a collective measure. May be best used by researchers as a measure of treatment outcome.
Peer Interaction and Avoidance Ross, Ross, & Evans (1971)	Motor	Observational	Occurrence–nonoccurrence of five social interaction behaviors (e.g., physical proximity, physical contact) is recorded for 15-second intervals. An interval receives a score	Excellent interrater reliability. Scores fluctuate in accordance with treatment. Schedule of data collection may be too strenuous for clinical use. Information is

Instrument	Response	Method	Description	Comments
			of 1 if any of the five behaviors occurs. Frequencies of eight avoidance behaviors (e.g., lowering of eyes to avoid visual contact, turning away when a peer initiates contact) during 15-minute periods are recorded and combined.	needed on the interrelationships among and between the individual behaviors of the two response composites. Scores appear best suited as measures of treatment outcome.
Social Phobia and Anxiety Inventory for Adolescents Clark et al. (1994)	Subjective, motor, physiological	Self-report	Adolescent rates on a 7-point scale the frequency of various subjective, motor (e.g., avoidance), and somatic (e.g., sweating, heart palpitations) responses to 45 items depicting various social situations (e.g., strangers, opposite sex). Scores are derived for two subscales: Social Phobia and Agoraphobia. The latter is subtracted from the former to yield a total score, which controls for social anxiety attributable to agoraphobia.	Excellent internal consistency for total and subscale scores. Convergence among the three scale scores and with other self-report measures of subjective, motoric, and somatic responses (Fear Survey Schedule for Children—Revised State–Trait Anxiety Inventory for Children, Schedule for Affective Disorders and Schizophrenia for School-Age Children). Estimates of temporal stability and convergence with other measurement methods are needed in order to fully explore the inventory's potential as a diagnostic, treatment selection, and treatment evaluation tool in clinical and research settings.
Behavioral avoidance test Eisen & Silverman (1991)	Motor	Observational	Child is asked to be a passenger on a 10-minute automobile ride, and whether or not the child does so is noted.	No estimates of reliability are reported. Correspondence with physiological (heart rate) and subjective (fear thermometer) measures. Fluctuations in scores in accordance with treatment. The monitoring of motor responses in addition to approach–avoidance would enhance the informativeness and usefulness of the test.
Heart rate Eisen & Silverman (1991)	Physiological	Mechanical	Heart rate is monitored during four periods associated with the behavioral avoidance test: 10-minute adaptation, 5-minute pretest baseline, 10-minute behavioral avoidance test, and 5-minute posttest baseline. Average heart rate for each period is calculated by noting the number of heartbeats for the first	No reliability estimates are reported. Correspondence with motor (behavioral avoidance test) and subjective (fear thermometer) measures. Some evidence of fluctuations in scores in accord with treatment. Estimates of consistency in response scores across the recording intervals for

(continued)

Instrument/author(s)	Response system	Method of measurement	Description	Appraisal
				the various periods are needed, as are estimates of the temporal stability of the scores.
Social and stranger interaction				
Social Interaction Self-Statement Test Glass, Merluzzi, Biever, & Larsen (1982); Johnson & Glass (1989)	Subjective	Self-report	Upon completion of the Behavioral Assessment (see below), the adolescent rates the frequency with which 30 different self-statements (e.g., "I wish I could leave and avoid the whole situation," "If I mess up this conversation I'll really lose my confidence," "This will be a good opportunity") were evidenced before, during, and immediately after the interaction. Ratings are provided on a 5-point scale, with 1 = "hardly" and 5 = "very often." Ratings to the 15 positive self-statements are summed to yield a total Positive Thoughts score, and ratings to the 15 negative self-statements are summed to yield a total Negative Thoughts score.	Although acceptable estimates of item and alternative-form reliability based on adult samples have been reported, no estimates of reliability based on an adolescent sample are available. Both scores have been found to differentiate groups of boys known to differ in fear of social situations, with anxious boys reporting significantly more negative thoughts and significantly fewer positive thoughts than nonanxious boys. Estimates of reliability are needed, as are estimates of correspondence with motor and physiological measures. Ease with which the instrument can be administered across a range of performance situations and tasks makes it attractive for use in both the laboratory and the clinic.
Behavioral Assessment Johnson & Glass (1989)	Motor	Observational	Adolescent male participates in a 5-minute unstructured conversation with a female confederate who is pleasant but only moderately responsive. Observers record speech behavior (i.e., speech dysfluencies, pauses, total talk time) and conversational content (i.e., unelaborated response to confederate question, initiation of new topic, on-topic statement, on-topic question, minimal encouragement of confederate's	Excellent estimates of interrater reliability for all measures. All speech behaviors and two of the conversational contents (i.e., unelaborated response and on-topic statement) discriminate groups known to differ in level of anxiety toward social interactions. Convergence between anxiety rating and measure of subjective responding (Audiotape-Aided Thought Recall's self-evaluative score). Estimates of

Measure			Description	Evaluation
			speech) and rate on 7-point scale the overall anxiety level. A continuous measure for each of the speech behaviors is derived, whereas a proportion of the adolescent's total utterances is derived for each of the different conversational contents.	temporal stability and responsiveness to treatment are needed. Complexity of recording and scoring limits use of the observational scheme to the research setting.
Audiotape-Aided Thought Recall Johnson & Glass (1989)	Self-report	Subjective	Upon completion of the Behavioral Assessment, an audiotape of the interaction is played, and the adolescent is instructed to stop the tape whenever he recalls a thought experienced at a given point in the interaction. Recollected thoughts are rated for focus (i.e., self-evaluative, nonevaluative, confederate, conversation, irrelevant) and valence (i.e., positive, negative, neutral). For each of these eight response categories, the ratings are converted to a proportion of the total number of thoughts recalled.	Excellent estimates of interrater reliability for all response categories. None of the scores discriminate groups known to differ in level of anxiety toward social situations. Convergence between scores for self-evaluative thoughts and observer's ratings of anxiety. Lack of powers of discrimination, and of evidence of convergence with other fear measures, argues against its use.
Preschool Socioaffective Profile LaFrenière, Dumas, Capuano, & Dubeau (1992); LaFrenière & Dumas (1992); Dumas & LaFrenière (1993)	Observational	Motor	Teacher rates the child on 30 items addressing social competence (e.g., "cooperates with other children"), angry–aggressive behaviors (e.g., "hits, bites, or kicks other children"), and anxious–withdrawal behaviors (e.g., "remains apart, isolated from the group"). Factor-analytically derived subscale scores are computed for the aforementioned categories.	Acceptable estimates of interrater reliability, internal consistency, and temporal stability across a 2-week period for all factor scores. Negative relationship between Social Competence scores and Anxious–Withdrawn and Angry–Aggressive scores; with no relationship between the latter two. Convergence with another observational measure (Child Behavior Checklist—Teacher Report Form), and discriminative efficiency in differentiating groups of children known to differ in level of anxiety. As is, may be useful as a screening device or as an aid to problem identification.
Social Anxiety Scale for Children—Revised LaGreca, Dandes, Wick, Shaw, & Stone (1988); LaGreca & Stone (1993)	Mechanical	Subjective	Child rates on a 5-point scale the self-descriptiveness of 22 items (e.g., "I worry about being teased," "I am quiet when I'm with a group of kids"). Three factor-analytically derived subscales are com-	Acceptable internal consistency for each of the subscales. Convergence among the subscale scores and fluctuations as a function of treatment. Scores differentiate children of various peer status groups.

(continued)

Instrument/author(s)	Response system	Method of measurement	Description	Appraisal
			Social and stranger interaction	
			puted: Fear of Negative Evaluation, Social Avoidance and Distress—New, and Social Avoidance and Distress—General.	Although acceptable temporal stability over a 2-week period has been obtained for the original version of the scale, temporal stability has yet to be examined for the revised version. This is important, as the scale has been used and will probably continue to be used in problem identification and treatment evaluation in both laboratory and clinical settings.
Home-Related Anxiety Peterson (1987)	Subjective	Self-report	Child rates on a 5-point scale the level of fear to 12 items addressing various events while at home alone (e.g., experience a cut, occurrence of a fire). Ratings are summed across items to yield a total fear score.	No estimates of reliability reported. Fluctuations in scores as a function of treatment. Given the increasing numbers of latchkey children and the likelihood that increasing numbers of them suffer from a fear of being alone, this scale may be drawn upon by many. Further investigation of its fundamental properties is therefore recommended.
			School-related events	
Revised Timed Behavior Checklist Fox & Houston (1981)	Motor	Observational	Occurrence–nonoccurrence of 12 behavioral signs of public-speaking anxiety (e.g., sways, foot movements, face muscles tense) is recorded. The recordings are summed across behaviors and intervals to yield a composite score.	Excellent interrater reliability. Scores correlate with other motor and subjective (State scale of the State–Trait Anxiety Inventory for Children) measures of performance anxiety. Scores do not vary as a function of treatment. Need for trained raters restricts its use to research; insensitivity to presumably active treatments restricts its use to the task of problem identification.

Measure			Description	Comments
Cognitive Behavior Questionnaire Houston, Fox, & Forbes (1984)	Subjective	Self-report	Children rate on a 5-point scale the frequencies of seven types of thoughts (e.g., "Were you thinking that this is kind of an interesting situation?" "Were you thinking that you have a reason not to worry about the game/test?") for a given time period.	No estimates of reliability. Convergence with the other subjective measure (Think Aloud) of test anxiety; scores vary as a function of stimuli differing in threat. Ease with which it can be administered and scored makes it practical for both research and clinical use. More data are needed on the measure's motor and physiological correlates and on its sensitivity as an index of treatment outcome.
Think Aloud Houston et al. (1984)	Subjective	Self-report	Transcripts of child "thinking aloud" are rated on a 5-point scale for the prominence of seven categories of thoughts (e.g., analytic attitude, performance denigration, preoccupation).	Excellent interrater reliability. Correlates with the other subjective measure (Cognitive Behavior Questionnaire) of test anxiety; scores vary with stimulus conditions differing in threat. Tedious, time-consuming nature of the ratings probably precludes the measure's clinical use. More information is needed on the scores' motor and physiological correlates and responsiveness to treatment.
Teacher Rating Scale Sarason, Davidson, Lighthall, Waite, & Ruebush (1960)	Motor	Observational	Teacher rates on a 5-point scale the level of 17 child behaviors (e.g., voice trembles when asked to speak); the ratings are summed across behaviors.	No evidence of reliability. Scores correlate with the other subjective measure (Test Anxiety Scale for Children) of test anxiety and with measures of academic performance and intelligence. Though practical for both clinical and research use, lack of reliability data calls for caution in its employment.
Test Anxiety Scale for Children Sarason et al. (1960)	Subjective, physiological	Self-report	Children rate on a scale of 0–1 their anxiety to 30 test-related situations. Ratings are summed across items.	Good internal consistency and temporal stability over 4 weeks. Correspondence with observational measures of test anxiety (Teacher Rating Scale, Observation of Classroom Behavior) and with self-report measure of general anxiety (General Anxiety Scale for Children). Interpreta-

(continued)

Instrument/author(s)	Response system	Method of measurement	Description	Appraisal
				tion is problematic because items addressing subjective responses are combined with those addressing physiological ones. This difficulty could be avoided by having separate subjective and physiological subscales.
		School-related events		
Analogue Test Taking Van Hasselt et al. (1979)	Motor	Observational	Seven letters are presented sequentially on a memory drum. After initial presentation, child is asked to anticipate each letter in the series. The number of trials required for errorless anticipation of the letters is recorded.	Good temporal stability over 1 week. Scores fluctuate in accord with treatment. Practical for both research and clinical use for the purposes of treatment evaluation.
Finger pulse volume Van Hasselt et al. (1979)	Physiological	Mechanical	Monitored throughout the Analogue Test Taking. Volume for last 15 seconds of baseline is subtracted from volume for 15-second sample of each trial, then summed across trials for sessions.	Good temporal stability over 1 week. No evidence of validity (e.g., convergence with other fear measures, sensitivity to treatments); thus, no support for this method of monitoring and quantifying cardiovascular reactivity.
Heart rate Van Hasselt et al. (1979)	Physiological	Mechanical	Monitored throughout the Analogue Test Taking. Average baseline heart rate is subtracted from heart rate for last 15 seconds of each trial, then summed across trials.	Good temporal stability over 1 week. No evidence of validity; thus, no support for this specific method of sampling and quantifying heart rate responses to test taking.
Target Complaint Scale Van Hasselt et al. (1979)	Subjective	Self-report	Child rates level of fear for each session by means of a 12-point scale with descriptive anchors at every third point (e.g., "none," "pretty much," "couldn't be worse").	Excellent temporal stability over 3 weeks. Scores fluctuate in accord with treatment. A global rating of ambiguous meaning and questionable utility. Addition of response items of definite content may enhance the scale's worth.

308

Instrument	Type	Description	Comments
Observation of Classroom Behavior Wine (1979)	Motor Observational	Occurrence–nonoccurrence of 22 behaviors (e.g., works quietly, stands, initiates communication with teacher) is recorded in 30-second intervals. The behaviors are grouped into five categories (i.e., Attending Behaviors, Task-Related Behaviors, Activity, Communication, and Interactional Behaviors). Occurrences for each behavior are summed across intervals.	Excellent interrater reliability. Scores correlate with subjective measure of test anxiety (Test Anxiety Scale for Children), discriminate groups known to differ in anxiety toward test taking, and vary as a function of stimulus conditions varying in threat. Large number of behaviors observed and need for trained observers probably limit the instrument to research use.
Children's Cognitive Assessment Questionnaire Zatz & Chassin (1983, 1985)	Subjective Self-report	Children rate on a 4-point scale (i.e., "never" to "all the time") the frequency with which they experienced 50 different thoughts during an exam. The thoughts are grouped into five categories: On-Task Thoughts (e.g., "Read each question carefully"), Off-Task Thoughts (e.g., "I wish this were over"), Positive Self-Statements (e.g., "I do well on tests like this"), Negative Self-Statements (e.g., "I am doing poorly."), and Coping Self-Statements (e.g., "Try to calm down"). Ratings are summed across each category's respective items.	Good internal consistency and temporal stability over 6 weeks. Correspondence with motor, subjective, and physiological measures of test anxiety (anagrams, Test Anxiety Scale for Children); discrimination of groups known to differ in anxiety toward test taking. Easy to administer and score; appropriate for both research and clinical use. At present, best used for the purposes of problem identification.
Personal Report of Confidence as a Speaker Cradock, Cotler, & Jason (1978); Johnson, Tyler, Thompson, & Jones (1971); Paul (1966)	Subjective, motor, physiological Self-report	Child rates "true" or "false" 30 statements describing his or her actions to speaking before a group (e.g., "My hands tremble when I try to handle objects on the platform," "I am terrified at the thought of speaking before a group of people," "I perspire and tremble just before getting up to speak"). Responses are summed across items to produce a single self-report measure of anxiety.	Excellent internal consistency and temporal stability over 6 weeks. Scores converge with motor measure of public-speaking anxiety (i.e., Timed Behavior Checklist) and fluctuate in accord with treatment. Multidimensional nature of the test score makes interpretation problematic. This could be rectified by developing three subscales (one for each response component); additional items may, however, be needed in order for subscale scores to be sufficiently reliable. The instrument's sophisticated wording restricts its use to teenagers.

(continued)

Instrument/author(s)	Response system	Method of measurement	Description	Appraisal
School-related events				
Role-Play Assessment Esveldt-Dawson et al. (1982)	Motor	Observational	Child role-plays five school-related situations (e.g., speaking in front of a class, being accused of cheating by the teacher) and is rated on a 3- or 5-point scale for level of six behaviors (e.g., stiffness, eye contact, nervous mannerisms). Ratings for each behavior are summed across scenes.	Excellent interrater reliability and temporal stability over 15 days. Good correspondence among the behaviors and with a self-rating of fear; scores fluctuate as a function of exposure to treatment. Ease of administration and small number of behaviors to observe make it practical for both clinical and research use.
Timed Behavior Checklist Cradock et al. (1978); Paul (1966)	Motor	Observational	Child is observed every 30 seconds for the occurrence–nonoccurrence of 20 response categories (e.g., pacing, swaying, hand tremors, quivering voice, speech blocking). Occurrences are summed across categories and intervals to produce a composite motor response score.	Excellent interrater reliability. Scores correlate with subjective (Personal Report of Confidence as a Speaker) and physiological measures of public-speaking anxiety, and fluctuate in accord with treatment. Schedule of observations and number of behaviors observed appear too demanding for routine clinical use.
Heart rate, blood pressure Beidel (1988)	Physiological	Mechanical	Heart rate and blood pressure monitored at 2-minute intervals throughout the performance of 10-minute vocabulary and oral reading tasks. Baseline values are subtracted from interval to yield response change scores.	Good consistency in response measures across the intervals of the tasks. Heart rate discriminates groups known to differ in anxiety toward test taking, but blood pressure does not. Estimates of convergence with subjective, motor, and other physiological response measures are needed. Compact recording equipment lends itself well to use in both the laboratory and the clinic.
Daily Diary Beidel, Neal, & Lederer (1991)	Motor, physiological, subjective	Self-report	Child completes a daily checklist, indicating the time and nature of the anxiety-provoking situation (e.g., test, perform in front of others) and responses emitted (e.g., cried, stomachache). Child also provides a rating of arousal through use of a pictorial 5-point scale.	Moderate compliance in recording over a 2-week period, and modest correspondence in recordings separated by a 6-month period. Test-anxious children tend to report greater numbers of anxiety-provoking events and greater distress than

Measure	Response class	Method	Description	Evaluation
				do nonanxious children. Slight alterations in the format, such as offering incentive and expanding the checklist categories, may enhance the consistency, diagnostic utility, and treatment utility of the recordings.
Cognitive Assessment Beidel & Turner (1988)	Subjective	Self-report	Upon completion of each of two behavioral tasks (i.e., a 10-minute vocabulary task and a 10-minute oral reading task), the child writes down any thoughts experienced during the course of performing the tasks. The written responses are rated as positive, negative, or neutral, according to a scoring scheme developed by Last, Barlow, and O'Brien (1984).	Excellent estimates of interrater reliability. Number of negative thoughts discriminate test-anxious children from non-test-anxious children. Good convergence between scores for the two tasks, but little convergence with other self-report measures of anxiety. The lack of convergence with other measures could be attributable to the low number of negative thoughts (i.e., restriction in range). The inclusion of prompts or alterations in the format might increase the range of scores, and thus increase correspondence with other anxiety measures.
School Refusal Assessment Scale Kearney & Silverman (1990, 1993)	Motor	Self-report, observational	Child and parent versions call for rating on a 7-point scale the frequency of 16 behaviors grouped into four classes: avoidance of school-related events, escape from social situations, attention-seeking, and tangible reward-seeking. Ratings to the four items for each of the four classes are summed, averaged, and then averaged across child and parent to yield a mean score for each of the classes. A teacher version of the scale is also available.	Acceptable temporal stability across 1- to 2-week period for both child and parent ratings. Moderate interrater reliability for mother and father parent ratings. Convergence among the scores for the four classes of behavior. Correspondence with other self-report and observational measures of subjective, physiological, and motoric fear responses (Fear Survey Schedule for Children—Revised, Children's Manifest Anxiety Scale—Revised, State–Trait Anxiety Inventory for Children, Social Anxiety Scale for Children, Child Behavior Checklist—Teacher Report Form). Ease of administering and scoring makes it suitable for use in both the laboratory and the clinic for the purposes of problem identification, treatment selection, and treatment evaluation.

(continued)

311

Instrument/author(s)	Response system	Method of measurement	Description	Appraisal
			School-related events	
School Absence Questionnaire Huffington & Sevitt (1989)	Motor	Observational	Parents respond "yes" or "no" to seven questions regarding the child's school attendance (e.g., "Does your child get emotionally upset at the prospect of going to school?") and whereabouts during nonattendance (e.g., "When your child is not at school, do you know where he/she is?"). High scores are interpreted as school phobia, low scores as truancy.	No estimates of reliability are reported. Convergence with other observational measure of motor responses (Rutter Behaviour Scale B for Teachers). Its brevity suggests that it might be best used as a screening device for identifying school phobics and for distinguishing school refusers from truants.
Math Anxiety Questionnaire Meece (1981); Meece, Wigfield, & Eccles (1990); Wigfield & Meece (1988)	Subjective, physiological	Self-report	Children and adolescents provide ratings to 11 items addressing the intensity of their physiological reactions (e.g., "When in math, I usually feel not at all at ease and relaxed") and their subjective concerns (e.g., "In general, how much do you worry about how well you are doing in math?") to school math activities. Ratings are made on a 7-point scale, with 1 = "not at all" and 7 = "very much." Two factor-analytically derived subscale scores are computed by summing ratings across appropriate subsets of items: a Negative Affective Reactions score and a Worry score.	Acceptable estimates of internal consistency. High factorial validity across younger and older school children. Convergence between the two subscale scores, and convergence between each of the subscales and math grades. Normative estimates available. Estimates of temporal stability are needed, as are estimates of correspondence with other measures of math anxiety. Highly suitable for use in both the clinic and the laboratory for the purposes of problem identification, treatment selection, and treatment evaluation.
Test Comfort Index Harnisch, Hill, & Fyans (1980); Hill & Wigfield (1984); Fincham, Hokoda, & Sanders (1989)	Physiological	Self-report	Child indicates the presence or absence of physiological upset to test taking by endorsing either "yes" or "no" to seven items (e.g., "Do you feel relaxed while you are taking a test?"). All of the items are drawn from Feld and Lewis's (1969) positively worded, modified version of the Test Anxiety Scale for Children. Endorsements are summed across the seven items to yield a total comfort score.	Acceptable estimates of internal consistency. Correspondence with academic achievement across various grade levels. Norms available. Estimates of temporal stability are needed, along with estimates of convergence with other measures of test anxiety. Ease of administration and availability of norms make the scale suitable for use for both clinical and research purposes; however, questions exist as to its sensitivity as an outcome measure (Grindler, 1988).

Measure	Type	Construct	Description	Evaluation
Self-Monitoring Log McNamara (1988)	Self-report	Motor, physiological	Through use of self-recording sheet, the child notes school attendance and the number of subject lessons attended, and rates self-confidence level for each lesson on a 0- to 100-point scale, with 0 = "dreadfully upset, felt sick, tummy ache" and 100 = "completely at ease."	No estimates of reliability or validity are reported. High compliance, though, has been reported, as have fluctuations in scores in accordance with treatment. Given the promise of self-monitoring for integrating assessment and treatment activities, continued investigation of this form of measurement is recommended.

Travel

Fear-related verbalizations Bornstein & Knapp (1981)	Self-report	Subjective	Parents record hourly the frequency of fear-related verbal remarks.	Excellent interrater reliability; poor temporal stability over 29 days. Scores fluctuate with exposure to treatment. Ease with which data can be collected and scored makes it appropriate for both research and clinical use. Stability of scores may be improved through aggregation.

Water

Behavior Rating Scale Lewis (1974)	Observational	Motor	Child's performance of 16 swimming-related behaviors rated on a scale of 1 ("did not try behavior") to 4 ("completed behavior quickly and spontaneously"). Ratings are summed across behaviors to yield a single approach score.	Excellent interrater reliability and temporal stability over 5 days. Scores correlate significantly with observer ratings of skill, fear, and avoidance, and fluctuate in accordance with treatment. Administered under naturalistic conditions; therefore, probably best suited for research purposes.
Behavioural Rating Scale Menzies & Clarke (1993)	Observational	Motor	Performance of a series of 17 water-related activities, beginning with "enters pool" and ending with "jumps in and dog-paddles unaided in the deep." Independent observers rate the performance of each step according to a 4-point scale, with 0 = "child did not attempt the item" and 3 = "child completed the item easily and spontaneously." Ratings are summed across items to yield a total performance score.	Excellent estimates of interrater reliability. Mixed evidence in terms of fluctuation in accordance with treatment. Estimates of temporal stability are needed, as are estimates of convergence with other response measures. Until clear estimates are available along all these fronts, cautious use of the scale is advised.

(continued)

313

APPENDIX. (*continued*)

Instrument/author(s)	Response system	Method of measurement	Description	Appraisal
			Water	
Water Phobia Survey Schedule Menzies & Clarke (1993)	Subjective	Self-report, observational	Seven water-related activities are described orally to the child, who then rates each according to a 7-point scale, with 1 = "very bad, terrible" and 7 = "really great." Cartoon faces serve as descriptive anchors for the various points of the scale. In the parent version of the instrument, the parent rates the child's reaction to the seven items through use of the same 7-point scale.	Acceptable temporal stability over a 4-week period for scores on the child version; moderate temporal stability for scores on the parent version over the same time period. Acceptable convergence between the two versions across all measurement occasions. Mixed evidence in terms of fluctuations in scores in accordance with treatment. Used in conjunction with the Behavioural Rating Scale; thus, might be expanded to include all 17 activities addressed in the scale. Such expansion may enhance the correspondence between the two versions and the correspondence between each of the versions and the Behavioural Rating Scale.
Overall Reaction Menzies & Clarke (1993)	Motor	Observational	Observer rates the child's overall response to the Behavioural Rating Scale through use of the same 7-point gradient employed in the Water Phobia Survey Schedule.	Excellent interrater reliability; nevertheless, is a global rating of ambiguous meaning. Best used as a social validation measure.
Behavior Test Prins (1986)	Motor	Observational	Child is asked to perform three tasks of varying levels of fearfulness: jumping off the high board of a swimming pool, jumping off the low board, and again jumping off the high board.	Fluctuations in test performance over an unspecified period of time raise questions as to the temporal stability of the measure. Convergence with other observational measures of performance (Behavior Observation Scale, teacher's rating, interviewer's rating) and with measures of self-speech (Behavioral Interview). Small number of tasks limits the discriminative powers of the measure. Increasing the

			Description	Comments
				number of tasks while not compromising the collection of concurrent measures may increase the meaningfulness and usefulness of the test.
Behavior Observation Scale Prins (1986)	Motor	Observational	Independent observer rates, on a scale of 1 (not anxious) to 3 (extremely anxious), seven motor features of the child's performance on each of the tasks of the Behavior Test.	Excellent interrater reliability. Scores discriminate groups known to vary in level of fearfulness. Scores converge with other observational measures of performance (teacher's ratings, interviewer's ratings) and with measures of self-speech (Behavioral Interview). Estimates of temporal stability and the interrelationships among the scale's seven motor categories are needed, so that the precise pattern of subjective and motor fear responses can be better traced.
Behavioral Interview Prins (1986)	Subjective	Self-report	After each task of the Behavior Test, the child participates in a semistructured interview consisting of six to nine questions addressing fearfulness and difficulty of task (e.g., "How scared were you?"), self-speech (e.g., "What did you think/say to yourself while you were standing on top of the high board?"), self-regulation (e.g., "Did you have a trick/strategy to be less fearful?"), knowledge of self-regulation (e.g., "Can you think of a trick/strategy you could use?"), and perception of personal control (e.g., "You were scared, but it went all right. Why was that?"). Responses to questions addressing self-speech are categorized as positive (e.g., "This time I can do it"), neutral (e.g., "It's high"), or negative (e.g., "Will it hurt again?"). Responses to questions addressing self-regulation are categorized as behavioral self-regulation (e.g., "I don't look down") or cognitive self-regulation (e.g., "I don't think about the height").	Excellent interrater reliability. Scores for negative self-speech vary with level of fearfulness (as determined by Behavior Test and Behavior Observation Scale). Decreases in responding to repeated questioning, and reports of boredom and irritation on the part of the children, suggest the need to streamline the interview's format. This may be accomplished by retaining only the questions addressing fearfulness and difficulty of task and self-speech.

(continued)

315

Instrument/author(s)	Response system	Method of measurement	Description	Appraisal
			General	
Children's Fear Survey Schedule—Revised Barrios, Replogle, & Anderson-Tisdelle (1983)	Subjective, motor, physiological	Self-report	Children rate on a 3-point scale 50 situations for level of subjective, motor, and physiological responses. Ratings are summed across items to yield General Subjective Anxiety, General Motor Anxiety, and General Physiological Anxiety scores.	Good temporal stability over 1 month. Good convergence among the instrument's three scales; moderate correspondence with parental ratings. Ease of administration and scoring makes it practical for both clinical and research use. Aside from the assessment of generalized anxiety, the instrument may serve as a screening device or a measure of treatment generalization effects.
Children's Manifest Anxiety Scale Castaneda, McCandless, & Palermo (1956)	Subjective, motor, physiological	Self-report	Children indicate which of 53 statements (e.g., "I worry most of the time," "Often I feel sick to my stomach") apply to them. Those endorsed are summed.	Good test–retest reliability and internal consistency. Over 100 pieces of research attesting to its validity. Significant relationships with other subjective measures (e.g., State–Trait Anxiety Inventory for Children, global self-ratings) and motor measures (e.g., errors on learning tasks) of anxiety, and with behavioral problems. Normative estimates available for a variety of child groups. Interpretation, though, is problematic because of the multidimensional nature of the score. This could be rectified by creating three subscales—one for each of anxiety's three response components.
Cognitive and Somatic Trait Anxiety Inventory Fox & Houston (1983)	Subjective, physiological	Self-report	Children respond to 24 items, 15 of which pertain to cognitive trait anxiety and 9 of which pertain to somatic trait anxiety. Total scores for the Cognitive and Somatic scales are obtained by summing across their respective items.	Acceptable internal consistency. The Cognitive and Somatic scales correlate highly with each other. Scores on the Cognitive scale are related to scores on subjective (i.e., the Cognitive scale of the Cognitive and Somatic State Anxiety

Instrument	Response modes	Description	Comments
			Inventory, the Think Aloud, the Cognitive Behavior Questionnaire), motor (i.e., performance errors), and physiological (i.e., the Somatic scale of the Cognitive and Somatic State Anxiety Inventory) measures of situational anxiety (i.e., test taking). Appropriate for both research and clinical use. May be helpful in problem identification and treatment planning for generalized anxiety and in evaluation of treatments' generalized effects. Information is needed on scores' temporal stability.
Cognitive and Somatic State Anxiety Inventory Fox & Houston (1983)	Subjective, physiological	Children respond to 27 items, 18 of which pertain to cognitive state anxiety and 9 of which pertain to somatic state anxiety. Total scores for the Cognitive and Somatic scales are obtained by summing across their respective items.	Good internal consistency. The two scales correlate well with each other and with subjective measures of test anxiety (i.e., Think Aloud, Cognitive Behavior Questionnaire). The Cognitive subscale also correlates well with the Cognitive subscale of, and the Somatic subscale with the Somatic subscale of, the Cognitive and Somatic Trait Anxiety Inventory. Considerable evidence in support of its diagnostic utility (Bell-Dolan, Last, & Strauss, 1990; Last, 1991; Perrin & Last, 1992; Strauss, Last, Hersen, & Kazdin, 1988). Appropriate for both the clinical and research assessment of any situation-specific fear or anxiety. May be most helpful in treatment planning and selection.
Parent Anxiety Rating Scale—General Doris et al. (1971); Glennon & Weisz (1978)	Motor	Parents answer 19 items pertaining to the child's general anxiety; responses are summed across items.	No estimates of reliability. Scores vary in accord with stimulus conditions purported to differ in anxiety-eliciting properties. Lack of reliability and validity data suggests that the instrument be used cautiously.

(continued)

Instrument/author(s)	Response system	Method of measurement	Description	Appraisal
			General	
Louisville Fear Survey Schedule Miller, Barrett, Hampe, & Noble (1972)	Subjective, motor	Self-report, observational	Children rate on a 5-point scale their level of fear in 104 situations, or parents rate their children's level of fear in the situations using the same scale. Ratings are summed across items.	Excellent internal consistency. Moderate correspondence of children's ratings with parental ratings. Scores are of ambiguous meaning because of the global nature of the rating scale. Addition of scales of explicit content may improve interpretation and utility. In its current form, the instrument may be of some use as a quick screening device or measure of treatment generalization effects.
Fear Survey Schedule for Children—Revised Ollendick (1978, 1983)	Subjective	Self-report	Children rate on a 3-point scale their level of fear in 80 situations. Ratings are summed across items to give an overall fear score. Factor-analytically derived subscale scores are computed for the following: Failure and Criticism; the Unknown; Minor Injury and Small Animals; Danger and Death; and Medical Procedures.	Excellent internal consistency; good temporal stability over 7-day and 6-week (McCathie & Spence, 1991) periods; acceptable temporal stability over 3-month period. Scores converge with another self-report measure of general anxiety (i.e., State–Trait Anxiety Inventory for Children) and discriminates groups known to differ in anxiety. Factor structure has been replicated across various age groups and cultures. Norms available. Mixed evidence in support of the instrument's diagnostic utility (Bell-Dolan et al., 1990; Ollendick, 1983; Perrin & Last, 1992, Strauss, Last, et al., 1988). Mixed findings of fluctuations in scores as a function of treatment (Friedman & Ollendick, 1989; King, Cranstoun, & Josephs, 1989). Global nature of the rating scale makes interpretation problematic. Addition of scales of specific content may enhance its useful-

ness (e.g., McCathie & Spence, 1991). As is, the instrument may be of use as a screening device or a measure of treatment generalization effects.

Instrument	Response components	Format	Description	Comments
Children's Manifest Anxiety Scale—Revised Reynolds & Richmond (1978)	Subjective, physiological, motor	Self-report	Children respond to 37 items, 28 of which pertain to anxiety. The responses to these 28 items are summed to form a general anxiety score.	Good internal consistency. Correlations with another subjective and physiological measure of generalized anxiety (i.e., State–Trait Anxiety Inventory for Children). Norms available for preschoolers. Mixed evidence in support of its diagnostic utility (Hodges, 1990; Hoehn-Saric, Maismi, & Weigand, 1987; Kashani et al., 1990; Mattison & Bagnato, 1987; Mattison, Bagnato, & Brubaker, 1988; Perrin & Last, 1992; Saigh, 1987, 1989a, 1989b; Strauss, Last, et al., 1988). Interpretation of scores is problematic because of their multidimensional nature. Establishment of subscales, one for each of anxiety's three components, would facilitate interpretation and use as a measure of generalized anxiety or treatment generalization effects.
Children's Fear Survey Schedule Ryall & Dietiker (1979)	Subjective	Self-report	Children rate on a 3-point scale their level of anxiety in 48 situations. Ratings are summed to form a general anxiety score.	Good test–retest reliability. Scores discriminate groups known to differ in anxiety. Global nature of the rating scale makes interpretation of scores problematic. Introduction of rating scales of specific content would allow for more ready interpretation and use as a measure of generalized anxiety. As is, may be helpful in screening or assessing treatment generalization.
General Anxiety Scale Sarason et al. (1960)	Subjective, physiological	Self-report	Children indicate which of 45 statements (34 pertaining to anxiety) are typical of them. Number of the 34 anxiety-related items endorsed serves as general anxiety score.	No estimates of reliability. Scores correlate with self-report of test anxiety (i.e., Test Anxiety Scale for Children), intelligence, and school achievement. Interpretation of scores is problematic

(continued)

General

Instrument/author(s)	Response system	Method of measurement	Description	Appraisal
				because items addressing the subjective component of anxiety are combined with those addressing the physiological component. Construction of subscales would rectify this problem and enhance the potential usefulness of the instrument. As is, may be helpful in assessing treatment generalization effects. Lack of reliability data calls for cautious use.
Fear Survey Schedule for Children Scherer & Nakamura (1968)	Subjective	Self-report	Children rate on a 5-point scale their level of fear in 80 situations. The ratings are summed across items to form a general anxiety score.	Excellent internal consistency. Scores correlate with another subjective and physiological measure of generalized anxiety (i.e., Children's Manifest Anxiety Scale), and with measures of dental anxiety (i.e., Behavior Profile Rating Scale, Dental and Observer Ratings of Anxiety and Cooperation, fear thermometer, palmar sweat index). Scores are of ambiguous meaning because of the global nature of the rating scale. Addition of rating scales of specific content would allow for more straightforward interpretation. As is, the instrument may be helpful in screening or assessing treatment generalization.
State–Trait Anxiety Inventory for Children Spielberger (1973)	Subjective, physiological	Self-report	Children respond to two 20-item inventories, one pertaining to situationally linked anxiety and the other pertaining to cross-situational anxiety. Responses are summed across the appropriate items to yield a State anxiety score and a Trait anxiety score.	Good internal consistency; acceptable temporal stability over same day and 3 months. Scores correlate with another subjective and physiological measure of generalized anxiety (i.e., Children's Manifest Anxiety Scale) and with measures of intelligence and school performance.

Measure	Type	Response components	Description	Comments
				Scores vary with exposure to stimuli varying in threat. Norms are available for different child groups. Some evidence of fluctuations in scores as a function of treatment (Kane & Kendall, 1989). Mixed evidence in support of its diagnostic utility (Hodges, 1990; Hoehn-Saric et al., 1987). A parent version of the inventory has been developed (Strauss, 1987), but little is known of its soundness. Interpretation of scores is problematic because subjective component items are combined with physiological component items. Items could be segregated as in the Cognitive and Somatic State and Trait Anxiety Inventories. In its current form, the inventory may be useful as a screening device or as a treatment generalization measure.
Beck Anxiety Inventory Beck, Brown, Epstein, & Steer (1988); Beck & Steer (1991); Jolly, Aruffo, Wherry, & Livingston (1993); Jolly & Dykman (1994)	Self-report	Subjective, motor, physiological	A 21-item inventory in which the adolescent rates the severity of various subjective, motor, and physiological responses on a 4-point scale.	Excellent estimates of internal consistency. Convergence with other measures of symptom severity (clinical ratings, Modified Cognition Checklist) and discrimination between adolescent groups known to differ in anxiety. Estimates of temporal stability are needed, along with estimates of correspondence with other methods of measurement. The formation of subjective, motor, and physiological subscales would facilitate the precise delineation of the pattern of responding, which would in turn aid in treatment selection and evaluation.
Leyton Obsessional Inventory—Child Version Berg, Rapoport, & Flament (1986)	Self-report	Subjective, motor	A modified version of the adult Leyton Obsessional Inventory (Cooper, 1970). The child responds "yes" or "no" to 44 items addressing such obsessive–compulsive symptom categories as "persistent thoughts," "checking," "order," "repeti-	Excellent temporal stability over a 5-week period. High intercorrelations among the three scores. Scores differentiate psychiatrically diagnosed obsessive children from normal controls, and scores fluctuate in accord with treatment. Lack of correspon-

(continued)

Instrument/author(s)	Response system	Method of measurement	Description	Appraisal
			General	
			tion," and "indecision." For those items endorsed, the child indicates the degree of resistance by selecting one of five cards onto which are printed the following descriptors: "sensible," "habit," "not necessary," "try to stop," and "try very hard to stop." The child indicates the degree of interference associated with each of the endorsed items by selecting one of four cards reading as follows: "no interference," "interferes a little," "interferes moderately," and "interferes a lot." Three scores are derived: a "yes" score by summing the items endorsed, a "resistance" score by summing the weighted ratings to the items (with "sensible" = 0, "habit" = 1, "not necessary" = 1, "try to stop" = 2, and "try very hard to stop" = 3), and an "interference" score by summing the weighted ratings to the items (with "no interference" = 0, "interferes a little" = 1, "interferes moderately" = 2, and "interferes a lot" = 3).	dence with staff global ratings of symptom severity. "Card-sorting" format of the inventory lends itself well to use with children and allows for the collection of observational measures. Further investigation of instrument's fundamental properties is recommended (e.g., insensitivity to slight procedural alterations, stability over varying time periods, aid in treatment selection, convergence with other response measures).
Teacher Rating Form Epkins (1993)	Motor, subjective, physiological	Observational	Teacher rates on a 7-point scale how descriptive 61 anxiety, depression, and aggression response items are of the child, with 1 = "does not describe at all" and 7 = "describes perfectly." The 24 items addressing anxiety are patterned after those of the Children's Manifest Anxiety Scale—Revised; thus, they call for ratings of not only the child's motor responses, but also the child's subjective and physiological ones.	Excellent estimates of internal consistency. Moderate convergence with self-reports of a community sample of children, but no convergence with self-reports of an inpatient sample of children. Estimates of interrater reliability and temporal stability are needed, as are estimates of correspondence with response measures of other methods of measurement. At this time, best limited to use as a screening device.

Instrument	Response modes	Method	Description	Comments
Fear Survey Schedule for Children—II Gullone & King (1992)	Subjective	Self-report	Child rates on a 3-point scale ("not scared," "scared," "very scared") level of fear to 75 items addressing a wide range of stimuli. A total fear score, along with five factor-analytically derived subscale scores (i.e., Fear of Death and Danger, Fear of the Unknown, Fear of Failure and Criticism, Animal Fear, Psychic Stress and Medical Fears), can be computed.	Excellent internal consistency and temporal stability over a 1-week period. Convergence with other self-report measures (Children's Manifest Anxiety Scale—Revised, State–Trait Anxiety Inventory for Children Trait subscale). Generality of factor structure across children (7- to 12-year-olds) and adolescents (13- to 18-year-olds). Because of the recency with which the schedule's items were generated, the instrument's content relevance and coverage may be superior to those of the other fear survey schedules. Suitable for use in problem identification and assessment of treatment generalization effects.
Maudsley Obsessional–Compulsive Inventory Hodgson & Rachman (1977); Rachman & Hodgson (1980); Clark & Bolton (1985)	Subjective, motor	Self-report	Adolescent responds to 30 items addressing a wide range of obsessive–compulsive symptoms. Ratings to items are summed to yield a total score and four factor scores (i.e., Checking, Cleaning, Slowness, and Doubting).	Though reliability and validity estimates based upon adult samples have been reported, none based upon adolescent samples are available. Modest evidence in support of the diagnostic utility of the inventory. At present, the instrument appears highly suspect as a diagnostic and treatment evaluation tool.
Children's Anxiety Evaluation Form Hoehn-Saric et al. (1987)	Subjective, motor, physiological	Self-report, observational	Form is made up of three parts. Part I consists of review of hospital admission records for the presence or absence of six categories of anxiety symptoms, and assignment of a global rating of symptom severity on a 5-point scale (0 = "mild," 4 = "very severe"). Part II consists of a semistructured interview addressing the nature, frequency, and severity of individual anxiety symptoms (e.g., fearful anticipation, pain in chest, nausea). Upon completion of the interview, a global rating of distress is assigned on the same 5-point scale. In conjunction with the interview, Part III	Acceptable interrater reliability for total score and part ratings. Convergence with the self-report measures of the Children's Manifest Anxiety Scale—Revised and the State–Trait Anxiety Inventory for Children Trait subscale. Estimates of temporal stability and diagnostic utility are needed, as are estimates of convergence with more direct measures of motor and physiological responses. A more sophisticated scoring scheme may enhance the diagnostic and treatment utility of this interview schedule.

(continued)

323

Instrument/author(s)	Response system	Method of measurement	Description	Appraisal
			General	
			consists of noting the appearance and rating the severity of 18 overt signs of anxiety (e.g., nail biting, stuttering, swallowing), then assigning a global rating of overt anxiety on the aforementioned 5-point scale. The three global ratings for the three parts are summed to produce a total anxiety score. The interview requires approximately 30 minutes to complete.	
Modified Cognition Checklist Jolly & Dykman (1994)	Subjective	Self-report	A modified version of the adult Cognition Checklist (Beck, Brown, Steer, Eidelson, & Riskind, 1987), in which the adolescent rates the frequency of 26 anxious and depressive thoughts. Ratings to 14 of the items are summed to form a Depression subscale score, and ratings to 12 items (e.g., "Something awful is going to happen") are summed to form an Anxiety subscale score.	Acceptable estimates of internal consistency for both subscales. Convergence between Anxiety subscale scores and another self-report measure of motor, physiological, and subjective responses (Beck Anxiety Inventory). Estimates of temporal stability are needed, as are estimates of convergence with other methods of measurement. Suitable for both clinical and research use for the purposes of problem identification, treatment selection, and treatment evaluation.
Thought Checklist for Children Laurent & Stark (1993)	Subjective	Self-report	Patterned after the Cognition Checklist for adults (Beck et al., 1987), the instrument consists of two 18-item scales: one addressing anxious thoughts and one addressing depressive thoughts. Ratings of the frequency with which various thoughts occur in the context of one of four situations (i.e., attending a party, with a friend, experiencing pain/discomfort, taking a test) or occur in	Acceptable estimates of internal consistency for both subscales. High correspondence between subscale scores. Anxiety subscale discriminates known anxious children from normal control children. Estimates of temporal stability are needed, along with estimates of convergence with motor, physiological, and other subjective measures of anxiety. May be useful in

Measure	Response system	Format	Description	Comments
			general are made on a 4-point scale, with 0 = "never" and 3 = "all the time." Each context and its items are presented in the form of a scenario (e.g., "Imagine that this Saturday one of your classmates is having a party. Everyone at school has been talking all week about the party. Everybody in your class is going to be there. Please rate how often you have the following thought: 'I will do something that will make me look foolish.'").	treatment selection and treatment evaluation.
Fear Frequency and Avoidance Survey Schedule for Children McCathie & Spence (1991)	Subjective, motor	Self-report	Child provides two ratings to each of the 80 stimulus items of the Fear Survey Schedule for Children—Revised: one rating of the frequency ("never," "sometimes," "every day") with which the child worries about the stimulus item, and one rating of the extent to which the child avoids situations ("not at all," "a little," "a lot") because of the stimulus item. Ratings are summed across items to form total Frequency and Avoidance scores.	Excellent internal consistency and temporal stability over a 6-week period for both scores. The two scales correlate highly with one another and with scores on the Fear Survey Schedule for Children—Revised and the Trait subscale of the State–Trait Anxiety Inventory for Children. Both scales discriminate groups known to differ in level of fearfulness. Best suited for use as a screening device and/or in the assessment of treatment generalization effects.
Fear Survey for Children With and Without Mental Retardation Ramirez & Kratochwill (1990)	Subjective	Self-report	Child indicates the presence or absence of fear to 60 stimulus items by responding orally "yes" or "no." For items answered in the affirmative, child indicates level of fear by responding "a little" or "very." Administration includes a procedure for assessing comprehension of the rating task and a fear word preference procedure (i.e., "afraid, scared, or nervous"). Ten of the 60 items assess for acquiescence, and two of the items allow for idiosyncratic stimuli.	Good stability in the number of fears reported and in the total fear score across a 2-week period. Convergence with self-report measures of motoric and physiological responses (Fear Verification Questions). Ease of administration and linkage with other clinical activities make it highly suitable as a screening device and as an aid in problem identification. Wide range of stimuli addressed may aid in the assessment of treatment generalization effects.
Negative Affect Self-Statement Questionnaire Ronan, Kendall, & Rowe (1994)	Subjective, physiological	Self-report	Child rates on a scale of 1–5 the frequency of various anxious and depressive self-statements, with 1 = "not at all" and 5 = "all	Excellent estimates of internal consistency and temporal stability over a 2-week period. Anxious-Specific scores

(continued)

Instrument/author(s)	Response system	Method of measurement	Description	Appraisal
			General	
			the time." The version of the questionnaire for 7- to 10-year-olds consists of 11 anxiety items (e.g., "I thought I would fail," "I felt weak like I was going to faint"), whereas the version of the questionnaire for 11- to 15-year-olds consists of 21 anxiety items (e.g., "I get confused," "I feel like my heart is in my throat"). For the former, two subscale scores are derived by summing across the appropriate subsets of items: an Anxious-Specific score and a Depression-Specific score. for the latter version, three subscale scores are derived by summing across the appropriate subsets of items: Anxious-Specific score, a Depression-Specific score, and a Negative Affect score.	discriminate groups known to differ in their level of anxiety. Convergence between Anxious-Specific subscale scores and other self-report measures of subjective, physiological, and motor responses (Children's Manifest Anxiety Scale—Revised, State–Trait Anxiety Inventory for Children Trait subscale). Fluctuations in Anxious-Specific subscale scores as a function of treatment. Estimates of temporal stability over longer time periods are needed, as are estimates of correspondence with response scores from other methods of measurement. Appears highly suitable for use in both research and clinical settings for the purposes of problem identification, treatment selection, and treatment evaluation.
Behavioral avoidance test Saigh (1986)	Motor	Observational	Approach to the scene of a traumatic event is performed in 10 steps. Instructions to perform the behavioral sequence is accompanied by the request to remain at the site of the last step for 20 minutes. Independent observers unobtrusively record the number of steps performed.	Acceptable estimates of interrater reliability. No estimates of temporal stability reported. Fluctuations in performance in accord with treatment. Convergence with self-report ratings of distress (Children's Manifest Anxiety Scale—Revised, subjective units of disturbance). Use of telemetric devices in conjunction with more detailed observations by unobtrusive raters may expand the usefulness of the test for both clinical and research purposes.

| Children's Posttraumatic Stress Disorder Inventory Saigh (1987, 1989a) | Subjective, motor, physiological | Self-report | A structured interview consisting of four subsets of questions addressing Posttraumatic Stress Disorder symptomatology: experience of a traumatic event (e.g., "Have you had a very bad experience?"), unwanted trauma-related ideation (e.g., "Do you sometimes feel as if this experience is about to happen again?"), general affect (e.g., "Have you become less interested in seeing friends or doing things that you used to enjoy?"), and diverse postevent disturbances (e.g., "Have you not been able to sleep well?"). Responses are scored for the presence or absence of each of the symptoms. | Excellent agreement between experienced clinicians in the assignment of diagnoses. Excellent agreement with another self-report method (i.e., unstructured interview) in the assignment of diagnoses. Convergence with another self-report measure of subjective, motor, and physiological responses (Children's Manifest Anxiety Scale—Revised). Estimates of temporal stability are needed, as well as estimates of correspondence with other methods of measurement. Experience and skill needed to solicit and score interview responses may limit use of the inventory to specialty clinics. |
| Anxiety Disorders Interview Schedule for Children Silverman & Nelles (1988); Silverman & Eisen (1992) | Subjective, motor, physiological | Self-report, observational | A semistructured interview addressing the DSM-III-R listing of anxiety disorders. Questions are posed regarding anxious symptomatology, symptom history, and precipitating cues, with most questions requiring more than a simple "yes" or "no" response. The child version of the interview includes more detailed coverage of symptomatology and phenomenology than does the parent version, whereas the parent version includes more detailed coverage of history, environmental events, and other childhood disorders than does the child version. Administration requires approximately 1 hour. | Excellent agreement between clinicians on diagnoses arrived at through review of child interview, parent interview, and their composite. Acceptable stability of anxiety diagnoses and anxiety symptom ratings across a 10- to 14-day period, with higher stability estimates of the former obtained for younger children than older children, and higher stability estimates of the latter obtained for older children than younger children. Estimates of correspondence with response measures gathered from other methods of measurement are needed. Experience and skill needed to solicit and score responses may limit the generality with which the schedule can be used. |

Note. Portions of this table have appeared in Barrios and Shigetomi (1985, pp. 99–119). Copyright 1985 by Lawrence Erlbaum Associates. Adapted by permission.

Chapter Six

SOCIAL RELATIONSHIP DEFICITS

Karen L. Bierman
Janet A. Welsh

Few would question the significant role that parent–child relations play in the process of socialization and social-emotional development, or the need to include assessment of parent–child relations in comprehensive evaluations of child psychosocial functioning. Since the late 1970s, research has been accumulating to suggest that, in addition to parent–child relations, peer relations play a critical and influential role in the process of child social-emotional development. Social experiences with peers affect the development of children's social behavior, social cognitions, and affect (Parker, Rubin, Price, & DeRosier, 1995). Although parent–child interactions may "set the stage" for a child's entry into the peer system (Parke & Ladd, 1992), the experiences a child has within that peer system influence development in a way that is distinct from and complementary to the developmental influence exerted by parents (Hartup, 1983). Clinical and developmental research document the critical role that peer relations play in child social-emotional development, and suggest that peer relations warrant attention in clinical assessments and intervention plans.

Clinical research, for example, has established a definitive link between poor peer relations and concurrent and future maladaptation. For example, retrospective studies have revealed that adults with serious psychiatric disturbances (especially Antisocial Personality Disorder) often had childhood histories of problematic social behavior and poor peer relations (see Parker et al., 1995). Prospective studies have confirmed predictive links between childhood peer rejection and a variety of difficulties in later life, including school difficulties, mental health problems, and antisocial behavior (Parker & Asher, 1987; Parker et al., 1995). In fact, in one study, peer ratings proved to be a more sensitive predictor of later mental health

problems than school records, teacher ratings, or achievement and IQ scores (Cowen, Pederson, Babigian, Izzo, & Trost, 1973). In addition, poor peer relations are prevalent in samples of emotionally disturbed and behaviorally disordered children (Dodge, 1989). Impaired peer relations constitute a primary diagnostic criterion for a number of major *Diagnostic and Statistical Manual of Mental Disorders*, fourth edition (DSM-IV) child and adolescent disorders (American Psychiatric Association, 1994), including the pervasive developmental disorders, Attention-Deficit/Hyperactivity Disorder, Conduct Disorder, Oppositional Defiant Disorder, and Selective Mutism. Poor peer relations are also listed as an associated feature of DSM-IV Mental Retardation, learning disorders, communication disorders, and Separation Anxiety Disorder, and have been implicated in Major Depressive Disorder (American Psychiatric Association, 1994).

Complementing clinical research linking poor peer relations with maladjustment, developmental research has revealed several critical roles played by positive peer relations in promoting adaptive social development. For example, peers rather than parents become children's preferred companions as they grow older, providing important sources of entertainment and support (Furman & Robbins, 1985). In the context of peer interactions, shared fantasy and role-taking activities take place. These promote the development of perspective-taking skills; foster an understanding of social norms and social conventions; and provide an arena for the development of reciprocal, give-and-take social abilities, such as cooperation and negotiation skills (Parker et al., 1995). During adolescence, peer relations take on a particularly influential role as young people struggle with the process of identity formation. In adolescence, peer relations may provide a critical source of emotional support, facilitating autonomy striving; alternatively, they may become a source of stress, contributing to feelings of loneliness and self-derogation (O'Brien & Bierman, 1988). Hence, peer relations appear to play important roles in adaptive social-emotional development, and opportunities for positive peer interaction appear critical for the development of social competence.

During the last two decades, research on peer relations has proliferated. Notable advances have been made in our understanding of how to conceptualize and assess the various facets of problematic social relations. Initial studies of peer relations in the 1930s and 1940s first employed sociometric techniques to identify liked and disliked children. Methodological variations characterized different studies, and questions about liking versus disliking and positive versus negative social behaviors were used somewhat interchangeably to assess social adjustment (see Parker et al., 1995, for a historical overview). After a hiatus during the 1950s and 1960s, when most social-developmental research focused on parent–child interactions, studies on peer relations reemerged in the late 1970s (Hartup, 1983). Whereas early studies tended to use single measures of peer relations interchangeably, the research that accumulated quickly during the next decade made it clear that more careful and more comprehensive assessments were needed to characterize the true quality of a child's peer relations and social adjustment (Kupersmidt, Coie, & Dodge, 1990). For example, peer relations are multifaceted; social group status, mutual friendships, and peer affiliation networks are distinct aspects of peer relations. These different dimensions of peer experience are linked differentially to adjustment, with different correlates and consequences (Cicchetti & Bukowski, 1995; Parker et al., 1995). Therefore, assessments of children's social relations need to be multifaceted, taking into account the various dimensions of peer relations that have proven to have a differential impact on the developmental process. It has become clear that the variables involved in peer liking are different from those involved in peer disliking; hence, an assessment of a child's status within the peer group must include measures of both liking and disliking (Coie, Dodge, & Coppotelli, 1982). In addition, although a child's behavior is often linked with his or her group status, children who are rejected by peers constitute a behaviorally heterogeneous group. Hence, assessments must focus on the child's social behavior as well as the child's social status (French, 1988;

Bierman, 1986). The quantity and quality of a child's mutual friendships must be assessed separately from the child's status within the peer group, as friendship quality plays a distinct role in the developmental process (Furman & Robbins, 1985). Finally, the characteristics of the peers with whom a child is affiliated may affect the child's developmental trajectory, particularly if those peers engage in antisocial activities (Dishion & Skinner, 1989).

In addition to providing more complex models to guide the conceptualization and assessment of social relationship problems, recent research has also begun to explore theoretical models delineating the potential mechanisms and processes through which various negative peer experiences may affect development and adjustment. That is, although clinical and developmental studies leave little doubt that childhood peer rejection is an important "marker" of maladaptive social-emotional development and risk for later adjustment, it has not been clear whether poor peer relations are simply the effects of other disorders or whether they play an active role in exacerbating negative developmental trajectories. In many cases, poor peer relations may be the consequences (more than the causes) of child social-emotional maladjustment, and may serve as indicators of the severity of the developmental disorder (Parker & Asher, 1987). For example, children who are aggressive and rejected by peers are more likely to show more severe difficulties in the areas of attention deficits, emotional dysregulation, and internalizing problems than are aggressive children who are not rejected by their peers (Bierman, Smoot, & Aumiller, 1993).

In addition, recent research suggests that poor peer relations may play a more active role in the developmental process. The experience of peer rejection may limit or distort a child's developmental opportunities. For example, being deprived of positive peer interactions and positive peer socialization influences may inhibit the development of prosocial skills and empathy (Coie, 1990). Rejected children may also be exposed to hostile overtures, ostracism, or even victimization by peers (Perry, Kusel, & Perry, 1988), which can promote the development of depressed mood and psychological distress (Boivin, Hymel, & Bukowski, 1995).

Developmental models have also been articulated to describe factors that may contribute to the development of social competence, or, conversely, factors that may impede a child's ability to maintain positive peer relations. In particular, the influence of parent–child interactions and of family experiences on children's developing social behavior and social competence has been examined (Parke & Ladd, 1992). In addition, considerable research has focused on social-cognitive processing and the child's developing sense of self as potential mediators linking past social experiences with future social behavior (Crick & Dodge, 1994).

It has become clear, then, that positive peer relations play an important role supporting the process of adaptive social and emotional development, and that problematic peer relations are associated with both current and future maladjustment of children. Hence, social relationship problems warrant the attention of developmental and clinical investigators. Understanding, assessing, and treating peer relationship problems require a multifaceted approach in which the various dimensions of peer relationships are considered and the potential contributions of child characteristics and socialization contexts are evaluated. In this chapter, issues relevant to the conceptualization of children's social relations, and methodology for assessing problems in these relations, are reviewed. First, because it is difficult to understand the nature of peer-related deficits without an adequate appreciation of normal developmental processes, a brief outline of normative social development and gender differences is provided. Second, the characteristics of children with peer problems are discussed. Studies of peer problems in the areas of group status, close friendships, and peer network affiliations are reviewed in separate sections. Third, three factors that may mediate children's peer difficulties are considered: family influences, social-cognitive information-processing skills, and social self-perceptions. Finally, methods and instruments useful for the assessment of these various aspects of social relationships are reviewed.

A CONCEPTUAL FRAMEWORK FOR ASSESSING SOCIAL RELATIONS

Normative Trends in Social Development

Peer relations appear to play an important role in facilitating social-emotional adjustment across the life span; however, the correlates of peer acceptance and rejection change with development, as do the nature and impact of group acceptance, close friendships, and peer networks (Parker et al., 1995). Developmental differences in the quantity and quality of children's peer relations emerge over time as children advance in their capacity for complex social-cognitive reasoning, as their preferences for various types of social activities and entertainment change, and as the characteristics of the peer group context are affected by differences in school structure and organization (Hartup, 1983). It is therefore critically important when one is assessing social competence to consider the child's age, gender, and developmental status, as well as the peer-related tasks and challenges associated with different stages of childhood and adolescence (Bierman & Montminy, 1993). In addition, because different cultural and subcultural groups vary widely in their attitudes toward such social behaviors as aggression and reticence, a thorough assessment of social skills includes consideration of the values and customs of the child's culture.

During the preschool years, most peer interactions revolve around shared play activities, particularly fantasy play. Children who do well with peers in this type of play are those who can sustain their attention to the play task, who exhibit positive affect and an agreeable disposition toward their play partners, and who willingly engage in reciprocal play sequences. The abilities to communicate clearly with a play partner and to regulate behavior in the face of intense emotional arousal enhance peer acceptance and may be fostered by frequent opportunities to practice these skills in the context of naturalistic peer interactions (Hymel & Rubin, 1985). Because preschool children are just learning to coordinate their social behavior, their interactions are often short in duration and marked by frequent squabbles, and friendships are often unstable (Hartup, 1983). Children's social behavior is also less "cohesive" during the preschool years than in later years. For example, rates of positive and negative behavior are not consistently correlated, and although negative behaviors such as aggression are correlated significantly with peer dislike, they are typically less strongly related than they are during the middle childhood years (Coie, Dodge, & Kupersmidt, 1990; Hartup, 1983).

During middle childhood, structured board games and group games with complex sets of rules become more common contexts for peer interactions. The ability to attend to, understand, and comply with game rules becomes important for peer acceptance, along with the ability to regulate affect appropriately in competitive peer interactions (Hartup, 1983). Children who display friendly, helpful, and supportive behaviors are well liked (Coie et al., 1990; Hymel & Rubin, 1985).

Normative rates of rough-and-tumble play and interpersonal aggression decline markedly during the early grade school years, and children who continue to display disruptive and aggressive behaviors are increasingly likely to suffer peer rejection. Norm-breaking behaviors, such as poor sportsmanship, excessive dependence, and immaturity, also become more frequent bases for peer rejection (Coie et al., 1990; Pope, Bierman, & Mumma, 1989).

In addition, during the middle years of grade school, stable best friendships or chumships begin to emerge. At this age, children form friendships almost exclusively with same-sex peers, and their relationships are more temporally stable and less contextually bound than those of preschoolers. Although friends continue to spend much of their time together playing, the relative importance of play declines, and children develop expectations for certain types of behaviors and allegiance from friends that do not apply to more casual acquaintances. Studies have revealed that grade school children expect their friends to be not only accepting but trustworthy, helpful, dependable, and loyal (Bukowski & Hoza, 1989; Furman & Bierman, 1984).

During the preadolescent and early adolescent years, communication (including sending notes, calling on the phone, "hanging out," and talking) becomes a major focus for peer interactions. Intimate self-disclosure becomes a central feature of friendship, and reciprocity in relationships is indexed by the degree to which friends share thoughts and feelings with one another, especially for girls (Laursen, 1993). When adolescent friends squabble, their conflicts typically center around relationship issues, such as gossiping, disclosing secrets, or loyalty issues (Hartup & Laursen, 1989). It is at this stage that friends and romantic partners consistently rival parents as the primary source of intimacy and social support (Furman & Buhrmester, 1992).

Adolescents also become more aware of peer group norms, and they increasingly seek to associate with peers and use peer standards to evaluate their own and others' social behavior (O'Brien & Bierman, 1988). Whereas in grade school "peer status" refers to one's state of acceptance or rejection by the classroom group, by adolescence one's peer status is complicated by the nature of the various groups in which one may seek and attain (or be refused) membership status. As in grade school, adolescents who are cooperative, helpful, and competent are typically well regarded by the majority group of their peers, and those who engage in high rates of aggressive and antisocial behavior are rejected by the majority group (Parkhurst & Asher, 1992). However, a number of shifts in social dynamics occur during adolescence. First, the increased levels of social awareness and self-consciousness that accompany the advanced social reasoning of adolescence, as well as the increased importance that adolescents place on peer acceptance, may strengthen the impact of perceived peer rejection on emotional adjustment and self-concept (O'Brien & Bierman, 1988). Second, persistent withdrawal from interactions with peers, and the social ostracism that accompanies such withdrawal, may also become more important determinants of peer rejection during adolescence than at younger ages (Coie et al., 1990). Finally, as coherent "deviant" peer groups begin to emerge during the preadolescent and early adolescent years, some aggressive and antisocial children may forge friendships with other deviant peers, where their negative behaviors may be supported and reinforced (Dishion & Skinner, 1989).

In addition to developmental changes, normative patterns of social relationships and friendships are affected by gender differences, which are evident in early childhood and continue throughout life. Perhaps encouraged by parents' toy selections and teachers' reinforcement, young boys tend to prefer movable toys and active games, whereas girls tend to engage in more dramatic play and fine motor activities (e.g., drawing and painting). Across ages, children tend to seek out the company of their own gender and to avoid mixed-sex interactions (Hartup, 1983). Boys often choose to interact with peers in large groups that emphasize competition, whereas girls tend toward more exclusive dyadic or triadic relationships (Eder & Hallinan, 1978). It is therefore not surprising that school-age boys report having more friends than girls, whereas females of all ages report higher levels of intimacy, validation, support, help, and companionship in their same-sex friendships than do males (Bukowski, Hoza, & Boivin, 1994; Parker & Asher, 1993). In adolescence and adulthood, both males and females report greater intimacy in relationships with women than with men (Furman & Buhrmester, 1992; Parker & Asher, 1993).

The developmental and gender differences that characterize peer relations across the preschool, middle childhood, and adolescent years provide an important backdrop for the assessment of deficient peer relations. In the following sections, research is reviewed that describes the child characteristics associated with adaptive and problematic peer relations in the domains of group status, close friendships, and peer networks. The developmental role of, and importance of assessment of, a child's functioning in these three domains of peer relations change with development. For example, learning to get along within a peer group context is an important developmental task that begins in the preschool years; close friendships begin to take on special importance later in grade school; and the characteristics of the peers who make up the child's social network become particularly influential during the preadolescent and adolescent years.

Social Relations in Peer Group Contexts

Definitions of Social Competence

"Social competence" has been defined in a variety of ways, and no one definition has received universal approval (Dodge, 1985). In general, however, it has been defined as the capability to elicit positive social responses (and avoid negative responses) from others in a variety of different social contexts (Dodge & Murphy, 1984). To be socially competent, individuals must posses repertoires of socially appropriate behaviors, as well as the social-cognitive capabilities that allow them to select and enact these behaviors in a way that is sensitive and responsive to the situation and the social cues of other individuals involved in the interaction. Specific abilities, such as prosocial behaviors, adaptive social problem-solving skills, and well-modulated emotional displays, are often identified as social skills that increase the likelihood of a child's receiving positive evaluations and responses from others. Sociometric assessments are often used to assess the general evaluation of a child by his or her peer group, which provides an indication of the child's social competence. Additional assessment methods, including observations, teacher and peer ratings, and child interviews, may be used to assess problem behaviors and social skill deficits that may be contributing to low levels of social competence and problematic social relationships. The sociometric method and sociometric classification systems are described below in more detail, as are the behavioral correlates of sociometric status. Then we review the literature concerning the contributions that social-cognitive skills and emotion regulation skills make to the child's ability to display socially skillful behaviors and to attain social competence.

The Sociometric Method

Most recent research on children's peer relations dates from the late 1970s, when investigators began to employ the sociometric method widely in studies to identify the characteristics of children who were or were not able to gain acceptance or avoid rejection within the peer group (see Hartup, 1983, and Parker et al., 1995, for historical reviews of the area). Although several variations exist, the basic sociometric method involves eliciting positive ("like most") or negative ("like least") nominations from children about their classmates. One of the first findings to emerge from this research was evidence suggesting that the determinants of peer liking were different from the determinants of peer disliking. Hence, instead of being a unidimensional construct, group relations were apparently characterized by two dimensions—the extent to which children were liked or accepted by peers, and the extent to which they were disliked or rejected by peers.

Data compiled from studies using child interviews, direct observations, and teacher ratings all suggested that the primary determinants of peer liking in these studies were positive social behaviors. Well-liked children were friendly and engaged readily in conversation, cooperative interaction, and conforming behaviors (Hymel & Rubin, 1985). They were described by their peers as helpful, friendly, understanding, supportive, cooperative, physically attractive, good leaders, and good at games (Coie et al., 1982). In contrast, peer dislike was associated with behavior problems, especially noncompliance, interference with others, derogation, attacks, and threats (Bierman, 1986). Correspondingly, children described disliked classmates as disruptive, short-tempered, and unattractive, and as likely to brag, to start fights, and to get in trouble with the teacher (Coie et al., 1982).

In order to describe peer relations in a way that would take into account the degree of both peers' liking and peers' disliking for a child, categorical models of social status were developed, including one by Coie and Dodge (1983). In this system, which has become widely used, children who receive many positive nominations and few negative nominations are classified as "popular"; those who receive few positive and few negative nominations are designated "neglected"; those who receive many positive and many negative nominations are labeled "controversial"; and those who receive few positive and many negative nominations are classified as "rejected." Children are designated "average" if they receive an average number of positive and negative nominations. The usefulness of these categories was soon established by studies showing strong correlations between sociometric status and other indices of social-emotional adaptation, including school problems, delinquency, and mental health disorders (Coie et al., 1990). In particular, critical differences became evident in the concurrent and predictive correlates of the two types of friendless children identified within the sociometric classification systems — neglected children, who were not liked but not disliked, and rejected children, who were not liked and actively disliked.

Peer Neglect versus Peer Rejection

Across studies, accumulating evidence suggested that rejected children tended to have more behavioral problems, to exhibit more psychological distress, and to have more cross-situational and temporally stable adjustment difficulties than did neglected children (Coie & Kupersmidt, 1983). For example, whereas the behavior problems exhibited by neglected children were typically limited to social isolation and withdrawal, many rejected children showed high rates of disruptive and aggressive behaviors (Coie & Kupersmidt, 1983; Foster & Ritchey, 1985; Ladd, 1983). Academic problems and elevated anxiety emerged as correlates of both neglected and rejected status, but high classroom rates of behavior problems, off-task behaviors, and hostile isolation characterized only the rejected children (French & Waas, 1985). Rejected children were more likely than neglected children to express loneliness and social dissatisfaction (Asher & Wheeler, 1985).

As longitudinal studies comparing the developmental trajectories of neglected and rejected children accrued, it became evident that neglected status was less stable over time than was rejected status, as neglected children often improved their social status when they moved into new peer groups (Coie & Kupersmidt, 1983). Coie and Kupersmidt (1983) suggested that the lower levels of social involvement displayed by some neglected children might reflect their reaction to a particular peer group, rather than any actual child deficits or maladjustment. Other investigators, such as Hymel and Rubin (1985) and Parker and Asher (1987), suggested that more empirical evidence was needed before the potential risk associated with peer neglect could be dismissed. In addition, researchers warned against assuming that all socially withdrawn children are simply neglected and not rejected by peers. Indeed, they suggested that social withdrawal may indicate more serious consequences for children's development when it leads to or is accompanied by peer rejection.

More recent research on rejected children supports the hypothesis that they are a heterogeneous group with regard to their behavioral characteristics. Given the evidence for the stability and negative predictability of rejected status, recent investigations have focused on understanding the child characteristics and peer group dynamics associated with peer rejection, and in particular on understanding the relations between aggressive and withdrawn behavior problems and peer rejection. It has become clear that rejected children who show high rates of either aggressive or withdrawn behavior (or both) may be at high risk for stable adjustment difficulties (Coie, 1990; Rubin & Stewart, 1996). It has also become clear that assessments of the social adjustment difficulties of either aggressive–rejected or withdrawn–rejected children requires a careful evaluation of the nature of the children's behavior as well as their peer status, as described further below.

Peer Rejection and Aggression

One of the strongest findings to emerge in research on children's peer relations has been the relation between aggressive behavior and rejection. Across ages (i.e., preschool, grade school, and adolescent samples), aggressive and disruptive behaviors are the primary correlates of rejected status in the classroom (Coie et al., 1990; French, Conrad, & Turner, 1995). Despite this strong correlation, recent research has shown that not all aggressive children are rejected and not all rejected children are aggressive. Three groups have emerged in the developmental literature: aggressive–rejected children, aggressive–nonrejected children, and children who are rejected but do not display aggressive behavior (Bierman, 1986; French, 1988). When compared to aggressive children who are accepted by peers, aggressive–rejected children are likely to have more severe behavioral problems and are more likely to suffer from stable and long-term social adjustment difficulties.

A number of studies have been undertaken to explore the factors that may explain why some aggressive children are rejected by peers whereas other aggressive children are not. Among the factors that appear to differentiate rejected from nonrejected aggressive children are the severity and the range of disruptive behavior problems exhibited. That is, aggressive boys who become rejected typically show a wide range of conduct problems (including disruptive, hyperactive, and disagreeable behaviors, as well as physical aggression), whereas the problem behaviors of aggressive boys who are accepted by peers are more likely to include primarily elevations of physical and direct aggression (Bierman et al., 1993). The physical aggression (particularly instrumental aggression) that characterizes the peer-accepted aggressive boys appears to be more acceptable to peers than are the additional forms of aggressive behavior that characterize aggressive–rejected boys, which include tantrums, verbal insults, cheating, or tattling (Dodge & Coie, 1987). Several investigators have suggested that the broad spectrum of undercontrolled behaviors displayed by aggressive–rejected children reflects core difficulties with emotion regulation, which impair their ability to form effective alliances with other children (Bierman & Wargo, 1995; Coie & Lenox, 1994).

A second set of factors distinguishing aggressive children who are rejected from those who are accepted by their peers involves prosocial behavior and adaptive social skills. Aggressive children are more likely to be rejected if they display elevated rates of inattentive and immature behaviors, and low levels of prosocial skills (Bierman et al., 1993; French, 1988; Pope et al., 1989).

Thus, aggressive children who become rejected by peers are likely to display high rates of aggression, along with a broad spectrum of dysregulated, undercontrolled behaviors. Aggressive–rejected children are also likely to be socially insensitive and deficient in prosocial skills. In addition to the behavioral excesses and deficits that increase the developmental risks of future maladjustment for aggressive–rejected children, the experience of being rejected (and the increased risk for experiencing victimization by peers) may create a developmental context of social stress; this may exacerbate the long-term risks faced by aggressive–rejected children, compared to the risks faced by aggressive children who are not rejected by their peers (Coie, 1990).

Investigators are just beginning to explore the longitudinal outcomes associated with the different profiles of aggressive–rejected, aggressive–nonrejected, and nonaggressive–rejected status. Initial investigations suggest that children who show elevated rates of both aggressive behavior and peer rejection may have more stable negative outcomes than children who show either problem alone (Bierman & Wargo, 1995; Cillessen, van Ijzendoorn, van Lieshout, & Hartup, 1992; Dodge,

1993). For example, studies have revealed that aggressive–rejected boys are more likely than nonaggressive–rejected boys to maintain their rejected status over time (Cillessen et al., 1992; Dodge, 1993), and peer ratings of aggression contribute significant amounts of variance to the prediction of later social status beyond that accounted for by initial social preference scores alone (Coie & Dodge, 1983; Coie, Terry, Lenox, Lochman, & Hyman, 1996). Conversely, early measures of rejection also boost the prediction of later aggressive behavior (Coie et al., 1996; Dodge, 1993).

These findings have several implications for assessment. In order to evaluate the key risk factors associated with aggressive–rejected status, it appears important to evaluate the child's social status; the extent to which the child exhibits a broad range of conduct problems (including disruptive, hyperactive, and inattentive behaviors, as well as direct aggressive behaviors); the extent to which the child exhibits deficits in positive interaction skills; the opportunities available to the child for positive peer interaction; and the extent to which the child may be experiencing ostracism and negative peer treatment. All of these factors appear to be critical features determining the negative developmental trajectory associated with aggressive–rejected status (Bierman & Wargo, 1995), and hence they warrant assessment as potential treatment targets.

Peer Rejection and Social Withdrawal

Although aggressive behaviors constitute a prominent correlate of peer rejection, approximately one-half of all rejected children do not exhibit elevated rates of aggressive behaviors. Children who are rejected for reasons other than aggressive behavior appear to be a heterogeneous group. Some nonaggressive-rejected children show few or no behavior problems; these "nonsymptomatic" children are considerably less likely than aggressive–rejected children to show stable social adjustment difficulties (Bierman & Wargo, 1995; Cillessen et al., 1992). Other nonaggressive rejected children appear to be ostracized for such factors as odd appearance, handicaps, or "atypical" social behavior (Bierman et al., 1993). A key subgroup of nonaggressive–rejected children exhibit low rates of prosocial and cooperative behavior, and high levels of social anxiety, withdrawal, and hostile isolation (French, 1988; Ladd, 1983); these children do warrant clinical attention, as they may well be at increased risk for stable social adjustment difficulties (Rubin & Stewart, 1996).

A careful assessment of the nature of the behavioral problems accompanying peer rejection is as important for withdrawn children as it is for aggressive children. Some forms of social withdrawal (like some forms of aggression) are more predictive of social maladjustment than others are, and confusion associated with the definition and assessment of "social withdrawal" has led to mixed findings regarding the stability and clinical significance of shy and withdrawn behavior (Rubin & Stewart, 1996). From a developmental perspective, one might expect to find social isolation and withdrawal correlated with delays or deficits in social-emotional development, as withdrawn children may be deprived of the positive peer interactions that are critical to healthy socialization. In addition, withdrawal is a prominent feature of several adult psychiatric disorders, including several of the anxiety disorders as well as Schizoid and Avoidant Personality Disorders; thus, withdrawal is implicated as a marker of maladaptive social adjustment (American Psychiatric Association, 1994). However, definitional and methodological issues, including the lack of clear distinction among such frequently interchanged terms as "neglect," "withdrawal," "shyness," and "inhibition," have contributed to a lack of clarity about the type of social withdrawal that has negative implications for development.

Shy children are sometimes neglected by peers, receiving few nominations (either positive or negative) in sociometric assessments. Unlike peer rejection, this type of neglect is typically not stable or predictive of psychological disorder (Parker & Asher, 1987). However, when shy and withdrawn behaviors occur in the context of peer rejection, they may indicate significant risk for continuing social maladjustment (Rubin & Stewart, 1996).

Behavioral withdrawal, which is usually assessed with direct behavioral observation, peer description, or parent or teacher report, can occur for a number of reasons; hence, a careful assessment of the nature of the social behavior is needed, in order to determine the degree to which it may indicate social maladjustment (Rubin, 1993). Children who engage in high rates of solitary play, for example, often have a marked preference for constructive and manipulative play, and show correspondingly lower rates of social play (Coplan, Rubin, Fox, Calkins, & Stewart, 1994). In contrast, some children, often termed "reticent," show high rates of "hovering"—that is, unoccupied observation of other children's play (Rubin, 1993). Coplan et al. (1994) found that reticent behavior was associated with indices of anxiety, whereas solitary passive behavior was unrelated to any indicators of social maladjusment. Similarly, reticent behavior, but not solitary active or solitary passive play, proved to be stable from early to middle childhood (Calkins, Fox, Rubin, Coplan, & Stewart, 1994). These findings suggest that the accurate assessment of peer problems requires an awareness of the typology of social withdrawal, particularly for young children. Children who frequently play alone because they prefer constructive, object-oriented play do not appear to be at high risk for social maladjustment (Asendorpf, 1991; Rubin, 1993). In contrast, children who are fearful or anxious around others and who spend time alone because they seem unable to enter the play of others are more likely to experience peer rejection, stable social isolation, and psychological distress.

Reticent or withdrawn–rejected children may be caught in a negative socialization cycle, in which their social anxiety and social skill deficits contribute to deprive them of those positive peer experiences that might be corrective. For these children, Rubin and Stewart (1996) hypothesize a stable, negative trajectory that begins with an interaction between inhibited dispositional characteristics and insecure attachment in infancy, and proceeds through childhood with high levels of social anxiety and strong tendencies to avoid peer interaction—all at high cost to normal social development. Indeed, social anxiety is correlated with poor peer relations (Hymel & Franke, 1985; LaGreca, Dandes, Wick, Shaw, & Stone, 1988; Boivin, Thomassin, & Alain, 1989), and children who are withdrawn and rejected often report elevated levels of depression, loneliness, and low self-esteem (Asher & Wheeler, 1985; Boivin, Poulin, & Vitaro, 1994; Rubin & Asendorpf, 1993). At younger ages, reticent children are likely to be adult-dependent and unassertive; by adolescence, they become increasingly likely to show depressive attributions and to express feelings of loneliness and depressed mood (Rubin & Krasnor, 1986; Asendorpf, 1993).

It is also important to note that rejected children may show elevated rates of both aggressive and withdrawn behaviors. Some research suggests that the comorbidity of aggressive and withdrawn behavior may indicate particularly high risk for stable social maladjustment (Ledingham, 1981; Schwartzman, Ledingham, & Serbin, 1985). Aggressive–withdrawn–rejected children may face the negative consequences associated with aggressive behavior problems (emotional dysregulation, disruptive and inattentive behaviors), as well as the risk of peer victimization and psychological distress associated with withdrawal (Boivin et al., 1994).

In assessments of social relationship problems, it is thus important to evaluate the degree to which a child exhibits socially reticent behavior. Social reticence is not well indexed by simple rate-of-interaction measures, as they provide no discrimination between children who prefer solitary play and those who are anxious, afraid, and avoidant of social interaction. Instead, techniques for assessing social withdrawal (direct observations, teacher ratings, and peer ratings) must be designed to differentiate children who are rejected by their peers, are anxious and avoidant in their social interactions, and show low levels of positive skills from those children who show low rates of social interaction because they prefer solitary, constructive play. The degree to which children may be experiencing loneliness, depressed mood, and negative perceptions of their own social competence is also an important component in a comprehensive assessment of social relationship problems, and is discussed further in a later section.

Age, Gender, and Cultural Differences

Recent research suggests that important gender and age differences may exist in the patterns of behavior problems typically associated with peer rejection. For example, whereas physical aggression, verbal aggression, and hyperactive, disruptive behaviors are primary characteristics of many rejected boys, such behaviors are much less common among girls. A cluster analysis of peer-rejected girls conducted by French (1990) revealed two clusters—one characterized by high levels of withdrawal, anxiety, and academic difficulties, and the other characterized by moderate levels of withdrawal and low levels of self-control. It may be that learning difficulties, withdrawal, and anxiety, rather than aggression, are prominent behaviors associated with rejection in girls. Alternatively, recent work by Crick and Grotpeter (1995) suggests that research linking aggressive behavior to peer difficulties for girls may have underestimated the importance of aggression by focusing primarily on acts of physical and verbal aggression. Their research suggests that girls may express interpersonal hostility by threatening exclusion or starting gossip ("relational aggression"), rather than by committing overtly aggressive acts. Clearly, more research is needed for a fuller understanding of gender differences in peer relation prob-

lems, as well as an understanding of the problematic behaviors linked with stable peer rejection for girls.

In addition, developmental research has indicated changes in the frequency and nature of aggression as children grow older. For example, instrumental physical aggression is common in preschoolers and not necessarily predictive of peer rejection (Hartup, 1983). In middle childhood, however, physical aggression becomes less normative and more highly correlated with rejection. Hostile aggression (e.g., verbal aggression, including name calling, taunts, and threats) constitutes a greater proportion of the aggressive acts exhibited by older grade school children than does direct physical aggression, and these additional forms of aggression become important predictors of peer rejection (Bierman et al., 1993). By adolescence, more covert forms of antisocial behavior, such as vandalism and stealing, become more common and more predictive of poor peer relations (French et al., 1995).

Similarly, age and gender differences are apparent in the relations between withdrawal and peer rejection. Whereas isolate behavior in preschool is not necessarily related to internalizing problems or peer rejection, the associations among social withdrawal, internalizing problems, and peer rejection become stronger during middle childhood and adolescence. As they get older, socially withdrawn children are increasingly less socially effective, and their social bids are more likely to be ignored by their peers (Stewart & Rubin, 1995). In addition, negative self-perceptions begin to be associated with withdrawal during middle childhood. For example, withdrawn behavior at age 7 (assessed via peer assessments and teacher ratings) emerged as a significant predictor of low self-esteem and loneliness at age 14 (Rubin & Stewart, 1996). Particularly in adolescence, withdrawn children come to be viewed as deviant and are frequently rejected by peers (Hymel & Rubin, 1985; Rubin, Hymel, LeMare, & Rowden, 1989); not coincidentally, they also report significant loneliness and alienation from their peer group (Rubin, 1993; Rubin, Coplan, Fox, & Calkins, 1995).

Gender also appears to moderate the effects of social withdrawal on development. Studies suggest that withdrawal is more normative for girls, and may more often indicate maladjustment for boys. For example, in a study of toddlers and preschoolers, Engfer (1993) found that shyness and inhibition were correlated with parental ratings of negative behaviors and characteristics (e.g., low social and cognitive competence, moodiness, temperamental difficulty) for boys, but were associated with positive traits (e.g., greater compliance) for girls. In addition, inhibition has been found to be more stable for boys (Engfer, 1993), and it is more strongly correlated with low self-esteem and peer problems for boys than for girls (Morrison & Masten, 1991). Finally, in a study of life course adaptations of people identified as shy in childhood, males were found to experience delayed entry into marriage and careers, and were more likely than their nonshy peers to experience vocational and marital instability. No such patterns were discovered for shy females, who differed from nonshy women only in their tendency to be more traditional with regard to gender stereotypes (Caspi, Elder, & Bem, 1988). It seems likely that these gender differences are related to the cultural norms of Western societies, which regard socially withdrawn, nonassertive behavior as normative for females. Withdrawn males, by contrast, may be viewed by peers as "sissified" or unmasculine, and thus subjected to disapproval and rejection, which may further exacerbate their low self-esteem and social problems.

In addition to age and gender, cultural norms may affect the determinants of peer rejection. That is, the acceptability of some social behaviors may depend upon the extent to which they are compatible with group norms—a hypothesis termed the "similarity model of social judgment" by Tversky (1977). A few studies have found support for the similarity model in children's peer relations. For example, Wright, Giammarino, and Parad (1986) examined the social judgments made by boys at a summer camp for children with behavioral problems. Some groups at this camp included a number of boys with elevated levels of aggressive behavior problems. In these groups, aggressive behavior was not related to peer status; instead, withdrawn behavior predicted peer rejection in groups that included many aggressive boys. Conversely, aggression (but not withdrawal) was associated with peer rejection in groups of boys who exhibited low rates of aggression. Wright et al. (1986) concluded that the extent to which aggressive and withdrawn behaviors predict peer rejection varies as a function of the extent to which these behaviors are normative (or non-normative) in particular groups.

Boivin, Dodge, and Coie (1995) replicated and extended these findings in a more representative population—play groups drawn from a normative sample of African-American boys. Like Wright et al. (1986), Boivin, Dodge, and Coie (1995) found that reactive aggression was negatively re-lated to peer status in low-reactive-aggression play groups, but unrelated to peer status in high-aggression play groups. Similarly, in the later study solitary play was negatively related to peer status in groups where solitary play was non-normative, but was unrelated to status in groups where it was normative. Other social behaviors appear to have more "absolute" value in terms of their social impact, and may emerge as more "universal" predictors of positive (or problematic) social relations. For example, both Wright et al. (1986) and Stormshak et al. (1995) found that prosocial behavior predicted positive peer status across a variety of peer groups. Stormshak et al. (1995) also found that disruptive, hyperactive behaviors impeded the establishment of positive peer relations, even when these behaviors occurred at high levels within the peer group.

Apparently, then, cultural differences in the normativeness of various social behaviors (particularly aggressive and withdrawn behaviors) may determine the extent to which these behaviors contribute to negative peer evaluations. Other social behaviors (e.g., prosocial behaviors; inattentive, disruptive, hyperactive behaviors) may have more "absolute" value across various cultural groups: They may serve either to promote (in the case of prosocial behaviors) or to impede (in the case of inattentive, hyperactive behaviors) positive peer relations.

One other aspect of cultural status that requires attention in the assessment of social relations involves the impact of minority status on social judgments. Children who have minority status in the classroom (most often assessed in terms of racial minority status) may receive fewer positive nominations and more negative nominations than children of majority status (Coie et al., 1982; Kistner, Metzler, Gatlin, & Risi, 1993). There is some evidence suggesting that girls in particular suffer when they have minority status in the classroom, perhaps because minority girls are more likely to be shut out of the small, exclusive groups of friends that grade school girls often form (Kistner et al., 1993). Boys, who are more likely to play in larger groups, may experience less group exclusion because of their minority status (Kistner et al., 1993); however, minority status may still contribute to peer rejection in ways that reduce the predictive significance of rejection as a marker of individual maladjustment. For example, Kupersmidt and Coie (1990) found that rejection contributed to the prediction of later disorder only for European-American children who were part of their majority sample, and not for their African-American minority sample. They postulated that racial bias may have inflated the rejection scores of the minority children, so that rejection provided a less valid indicator of these children's behavioral adjustment or social skills. Certainly, the effects of cultural norms and majority–minority status must be considered in assessments of children's social relationships.

Implications

The findings reviewed above have three important implications for the assessment of children's peer relations. First, they suggest that an assessment must include both an evaluation of the extent to which a child is rejected by peers, and an evaluation of the sorts of behaviors the child is exhibiting that may be contributing to the rejection. Reflecting this issue, Parker et al. (1995) refer to the importance of differentially assessing *whether* the child is liked by peers (i.e., peer status) and *what* the child is like when he or she is with peers (i.e., behavioral description). A second implication of the research reviewed in this section is that the assessment of the child's social behavior should include a broad representation of behavior types— including not only aggressive behaviors, but also a range of other disruptive behaviors (including hyperactive, inattentive, emotionally reactive, and immature/insensitive behaviors), withdrawn and socially anxious behaviors, and any prosocial behaviors displayed. Finally, it is important in evaluating a child's social behavior to have an awareness of the cultural norms of the particular social contexts within which the child functions. The degree to which particular social behaviors should be considered problematic is at least partially dependent upon the values and dynamics of the child's cultural group (Osterweil & Nagano-Nakamura, 1992).

In general, the research conducted in the past two decades has provided extensive information about the factors that affect children's ability to get along in a structured peer group setting, such as the classroom or play group. More recently, researchers have also struggled to move beyond the classroom-based assessment of peer relations; they have examined other aspects of peer relations that may affect development and reflect adjustment, such as the nature of children's close friendships.

Friendships

Unlike group status, a friendship is a mutual, dyadic relationship. There are a number of reasons to believe that the close personal relationships reflected in friendships are distinct from (although not unrelated to) group acceptance. First, empirical studies have revealed that although sociometrically popular and average children are much more likely to report having friends than rejected children are, some popular children do not have close friends, whereas some rejected children do (Parker & Asher, 1993). In addition, although the positive characteristics that promote popularity (such as cooperativeness, friendliness, and consideration for others) also assist children in developing and maintaining friends, additional factors are associated with friendships. Friendships emerge when children share similar activities and interests, and also when they develop a positive and mutual affective bond in the context of these shared activities (Asher, Parker, & Walker, 1993).

One of the earliest theorists to suggest that group acceptance and close friendships had different implications for development was H. S. Sullivan (1953), who believed that both were important for healthy adaptation, but that they served different functions and followed different developmental timetables. Sullivan believed that the need to be accepted by a peer group emerged in middle childhood, and that group affiliation helped children to negotiate issues involving competition, conformity, and achievement. In contrast, Sullivan felt that the need for intimate, dyadic relationships did not develop until preadolescence, and that it was within the context of these friendships that the development of empathy and perspective-taking skills occurred. Furthermore, he argued that these first dyadic friendships served as prototypes for intimate and romantic relationships later in life. More recent ideas regarding the different developmental functions of friendships and group acceptance have been similar to Sullivan's. For example, Furman and Robbins (1985) have suggested that close friendships meet social needs of children in a way that is unique and complementary to positive group relations. Three particular social needs—the needs for affection, intimacy, and reliable alliance—are met exclusively in close friendships, whereas group acceptance fulfills a need for a sense of inclusion. In addition, both close friendships and group acceptance fulfill needs for companionship and nurturance, and cultivate a sense of self-worth.

A number of qualities are involved in friendship that may or may not be relevant to group social status. Similarity is an important factor in friendship throughout life, as friends tend to be similar in age, gender, race, and social class (Hartup,

1983). In addition, for adolescents, similarity in orientation toward school and various aspects of peer culture becomes highly salient to friendship. Reciprocity is another characteristic of friendship, although the nature of reciprocity in friendships changes with age. For young children, reciprocity involves concrete behaviors (e.g., sharing toys and taking turns); older children and adolescents, in contrast, expect psychological reciprocity from friends in the form of mutual intimacy and social support (Laursen, 1993). A third feature of friendship, commitment, becomes particularly salient in adolescence, when young people begin to expect their friends to be loyal, trustworthy, and sincere (Berndt, 1982).

Several investigators have also suggested that when children are rejected from the peer group, the negative impact of that rejection may be mediated by having a best friend (Furman & Robbins, 1985; Parker & Asher, 1993). That is, peer rejection may be less damaging to a child if that child has a best friend with whom to spend time and from whom to receive support. However, the extent to which a close friend may provide a buffer against the negative impact of peer rejection may depend on both the characteristics of that friend and the quality of the relationship (Berndt, 1992). If the friend models and supports antisocial behavior, and if the friendship is conflictual, the friendship may add to the risk of group rejection: It may provide an additional source of stress and a context in which an aggressive, coercive interactional style and an antisocial orientation are modeled and reinforced (Berndt, 1992; Dishion, Andrews, & Crosby, 1995).

Hoza, Molina, Bukowski, and Sippola (1995) have suggested that close friendships may serve an important preventive function, reducing the likelihood that children will develop behavioral problems; however, they argue that close friendships may not provide a buffer against the negative impact of group rejection. For example, in their study, children who were high on passive isolation or were rejected and withdrawn were not protected from the development of internalizing problems when they had a mutual friend. Mutual friends also failed to reduce the risk that these children would develop externalizing problems, probably because these passive, isolated children were not at high risk for developing acting-out difficulties. By contrast, the children who benefited from mutual friendships in terms of reduced risk for internalizing and externalizing problems were those children who showed low levels of passive isolation and were not actively rejected by the peer group. Apparently, mutual friendships can play an important protective role in development, but cannot typically counteract the negative effects of group rejection.

In part, the failure to find a positive buffering effect for close friendships on rejected children's risk for internalizing problems may reflect the fact that the mutual friendships of rejected children are often qualitatively inferior to the friendships of nonrejected children. Friends of rejected children are often also of low sociometric status, and these relationships tend to involve more conflict and less stability than friendships among higher-status children do (Hartup, 1989; Parker & Asher, 1993). In addition, low-status children report less caring, instrumental aid, and intimacy, and more conflict and betrayal, in their reciprocated best friendships than do higher-status peers (Parker & Asher, 1993). Furthermore, the finding that close friendships do not reduce the risk for externalizing problems of rejected children may reflect a more negative influence. For example, Kupersmidt, Burchinal, and Patterson (1995) found that a reciprocated best friend actually *increased* a rejected child's risk of developing externalizing behavior problems. Children with aggressive and antisocial behavior problems often select mutual friends who have similar behavior problems; such friendships do not reduce the likelihood of continued difficulties, but instead may increase them (Dishion et al., 1995; Dobkin, Tremblay, Masse, & Vitaro, 1995).

Apparently, group status and friendships are distinct aspects of children's social relationships, and children can have problems in both domains of peer relations. Children who are rejected by the group are likely to have fewer friends than their popular and average counterparts, and these friendships are likely to be qualitatively inferior. The relationship options for children who are chronically rejected by peers are often limited and grim. These youngsters may wind up forming friendships with each other and risk the consolidation and reinforcement of maladaptive social behaviors, or they may struggle through childhood and adolescence largely without friends. Although longitudinal data have highlighted the developmental risks associated with chronic peer rejection and association with deviant peers, virtually nothing is known about the long-term effects of friendlessness per se on child development. Studies of adults have revealed that friendship is a critical source of social support and protects against the negative effects of life stress. People with few friends are at elevated risk for depression, anxiety, and other forms of psychopathology (Parker et al., 1995). When one is assessing a child's social relationships, it may therefore be important to include an assessment of the child's close friendships as well as his or her group status. One assessment question involves the extent to which the child has been able to establish reciprocal and mutual close friendships. A second question involves the nature and the quality of those friendships, and the extent to which the child's interpersonal skills enable him or her to sustain a positive, mutual friendship over time.

In addition to group status and close friendships, a third dimension of children's peer relations—one that may become particularly influential as children move into adolescence—involves the treatment they receive from peers and the characteristics of the peers who make up their affiliative networks.

Peer Group Dynamics and Network Characteristics

Even during the preschool and grade school years, the treatment a child receives from peers may influence the child's social behavior and adjustment. Once rejected by peers, disliked children may find themselves excluded from peer activities and exposed to ostracism or even victimization by peers (Perry et al., 1988). Peers may develop negatively biased attitudes and expectations for rejected children, and may treat these children differently (with more counteraggression and hostility) than they treat their well-accepted peers (Asarnow, 1983; Hymel, Wagner, & Butler, 1990).

Peer responses may serve to elicit and reinforce aggressive social behavior in some children. For example, Patterson, Littman, and Bricker (1967) found that preschool children who were able to use aggression effectively to gain instrumental rewards (e.g., possession of toys) or to terminate aversive peer behavior exhibited increased rates of aggression over the course of the year. Negative peer responses can lead to escalations in aggressive interactions, as aggressive children often believe that counteraggression will terminate aversive peer treatment (Asarnow, 1983; Perry, Perry, & Rasmussen, 1986).

Negative peer responses may include victimizing behaviors directed toward rejected children, such as hostile overtures, teasing, and bullying (Perry et al., 1988). Children who are inhibited, anxious, awkward, and passive in their social interactions are at particularly high risk for peer

victimization (Boivin, Hymel, & Bukowski, 1995; Olweus, 1993). The experience of victimization may increase social anxiety and withdrawal, which paradoxically may increase the likelihood of further victimization and create a cycle of persistent victimization and damage to self-esteem (Boivin, Hymel, & Bukowski, 1995). In addition, children who are reactively aggressive and who exhibit emotionally dysregulated externalizing behaviors (hyperactive, disruptive, and inattentive behaviors; emotional outbursts) may also be victimized by peers (Dodge & Coie, 1987). These children, termed "provocative victims" by Olweus (1993), may aggravate peers with their intrusive and aggressive social behavior. Perhaps because of their emotional dysregulation or lack of social competence, they are unsuccessful at using their aggression to defend themselves and may become caught in escalating cycles of victimization by peers; thus, they may suffer negative consequences similar to those experienced by "passive victims" (Olweus, 1993). Victimization by peers is likely to have serious consequences for the child's developing sense of self, and has been linked with elevated levels of anxiety, loneliness, and depression (Boivin, Hymel, & Bukowski, 1995; Olweus, 1993).

Children who are particularly stressed cognitively and behaviorally by the academic demands of school, such as those aggressive–rejected children with attentional deficits or hyperactive behaviors, may also be at increased risk for negative interactions with teachers. Over time, teachers tend to become less positive and less contingent in their reactions to these problematic students; this decreases their effectiveness as behavior managers or social skills instructors (Strain, Lambert, Kerr, Stagg, & Lenkner, 1983). In addition, the likelihood that peer influences will contribute to the negative escalation of behavior problems in school is increased in classrooms that contain a high proportion of children with aggressive propensities (Kellam et al., 1991). Unfortunately, children at high risk for behavioral problems and Conduct Disorder often attend schools in which there is a high density of other high-risk children. The results may be a difficult teaching environment and an increased exposure to peer influences that model and contribute to the escalation of conduct problems.

One of the consequences of peer rejection is that children typically have fewer options in terms of play partners and peer affiliations. For example, when Ladd (1983) compared the play patterns of children from different social status groups, he found that rejected children (as compared to popular or average children) more often played in smaller groups with younger and/or more unpopular companions. As a result of negative peer treatment and active ostracism, some rejected children may feel pushed out of conventional peer groups within the classroom, and/or find themselves attracted to nonconventional peers who display social behaviors and social preferences similar to their own. Whether because of exclusion from conventional groups or attraction to similar groups, research suggests that many aggressive children choose to associate with other aggressive children, forming networks of affiliation with peers who share their aggressive orientations (Cairns, Neckerman, & Cairns, 1989).

During the preadolescent and adolescent years, affiliations with deviant peers may begin to exert a strong influence on children, shaping their attitudes and social behaviors and increasing the likelihood of future antisocial and deviant behavior (Cairns et al., 1989). Particularly in adolescence, youths turn to their peer groups for guidance in matters of dress, social behavior, social attitudes, and identity formation. In peer networks containing many members who exhibit high rates of aggression, group norms are likely to be accepting of aggression (Wright et al., 1986). Hence, although affiliations with deviant peers may provide companionship and support, the "cost" of such affiliations may be great in terms of their exacerbation of antisocial behavior and attitudes. Preadolescent children who form friendships with antisocial peers appear to be at heightened risk for later antisocial behavior, including delinquency, drug use, and school dropout (Dishion & Skinner, 1989).

Research on the influence of peer group dynamics and network affiliations has two major implications for the assessment of children's social relations. First, in addition to attempts to characterize the social behavior of the child targeted for assessment, it may be important to evaluate the behaviors and attitudes that peers are directing toward this child. The extent to which the child has a negative reputation among peers, and the extent to which peers may hold negative expectations and hostile attributions about the child, may affect the design of remedial interventions. If peer or teacher behaviors are functioning to elicit and/ or inadvertently to reinforce inappropriate child behaviors, these attitudes and behaviors may need to be addressed if intervention is to be effective.

Second, assessment of older children should address the characteristics of their peer network affiliations, with particular attention to the identification of potential alliances with deviant peers that may be serving to exacerbate antisocial behavior.

An assessment of a child's social relations should thus take into account the child's status and behavior in the context of the peer group, the extent and quality of the child's close friendships, and the extent to which negative responses or deviant affiliations characterize the child's peer interactions. When the child's interactions in each of these areas of social relations are considered, a comprehensive picture of the child's social adjustment can be attained. However, to guide broader intervention efforts for children with disordered social relations, three more factors may warrant attention in the assessment process: family interaction patterns; the child's social-cognitive information-processing skills; and the child's perceptions of and feelings about his or her peer relations. Although these three factors are not dimensions of peer relations per se, each may play an important role in mediating or influencing the child's social behavior in peer relation contexts. Each of these factors is now discussed in more detail.

Models of Family Contributions

Historically, the role of the family in social development has been studied by developmental researchers quite separately from the world of peer relations. However, recent conceptualizations have illustrated ways in which interactions within the primary social context of the family may influence the development and maintenance of peer relations. Three core models have emerged: Family interactions may affect peer relations through (1) discipline styles that promote various types of behaviors in the child; (2) parent–child relationship quality, which affects the development of emotion regulation processes and representational models of relationships; and (3) parental behaviors that teach (or fail to teach) children aspects of social competence. Each of these models of influence is reviewed briefly here; for more details on this topic, see the reviews by Parke and Ladd (1992), Pettit and Mize (1993), and Putallaz and Heflin (1990).

Discipline Strategies

As described previously, disruptive behavior problems are often associated with problematic peer relationships. Previous research suggests that parental discipline practices and family interaction patterns may play a primary role in the development or exacerbation of noncompliant and aggressive child behaviors. Parental discipline strategies may also contribute to the development of socially withdrawn and anxious behaviors, although this is less well documented.

An extensive body of research has linked parental discipline practices conclusively with the development of elevated levels of child aggressive behavior (Patterson, 1986). In particular, high rates of parental commands, combined with inconsistent, harsh, and punitive discipline strategies, have been linked with escalating cycles of negative transactions in families and elevated levels of child aversive behaviors (Patterson, 1982). If children generalize the aggressive and oppositional behavior they have learned at home to their peer interactions, peer alienation and counteraggression may result. Indeed, research has documented associations between punitive parental discipline and peer rejection, via the mediating link of elevated levels of child aggressive behavior (Bierman & Smoot, 1991; Dishion, 1990; Dodge, Bates, & Pettit, 1990). Coercive discipline strategies may also contribute to elevated levels of conflict among siblings, which in turn can foster child aggression (Stormshak, Bellanti, Bierman, & the Conduct Problems Prevention Research Group, 1996). By adolescence, children who are rejected by mainstream peers and who begin to associate with deviant peer groups become increasingly difficult for parents to monitor or control. Low levels of parental monitoring, in turn, are associated with deviant peer involvement and elevated risk for serious Conduct Disorder (Patterson & Stouthamer-Loeber, 1984).

Research data linking socially anxious and withdrawn behaviors to parental discipline strategies are less conclusive than the data linking discipline practices to aggression, but they suggest that there may be some linkages (Rubin & Stewart, 1996). Specifically, some investigators have postulated that overprotective and overcontrolling discipline strategies may facilitate the development of social anxiety and withdrawal, particularly in children who are temperamentally inclined toward social inhibition (Rubin & Stewart, 1996). Although direct evidence to support the link between overprotective and controlling parenting practices and social reticence in the peer setting is lacking, research suggests that high levels of control without warmth (Baumrind, 1967) and high levels of anxious parental overprotection (Olweus, 1993) may play a role in fostering child social anxiety and withdrawal.

Parent–Child Relationships

Children with poor peer relations, whether they exhibit aggressive or withdrawn behavior, often show deficits in social competence and emotion regulation capabilities that have been linked with dysfunctions in parent–child relationships. For example, aggressive–rejected children are often disruptive, impulsive, and poorly regulated emotionally; withdrawn–rejected children are often socially anxious and avoidant. Several investigators have postulated that a child's capacity to regulate emotions in the context of interpersonal relationships derives largely from early experiences with his or her parents, which serve as a prototypes for the child's later interpersonal expectancies and affect (Greenberg, Kusche, & Speltz, 1991). Poor emotion regulation, which may contribute either to oppositional and angry reactions or to avoidant and anxious reactions to social interactions, may result from poor-quality interactions with primary caregivers during the formative first years of life. Research with infants and toddlers suggests that when caregivers respond to children's distress with consistency and sensitivity, children are less irritable, less anxious, and better emotionally regulated (Ainsworth, Blehar, Waters, & Wall, 1978)—possibly as a result of greater feelings of security, as well as of modeling and internalization of calming behaviors. In addition, such caregivers may help children develop the cognitive and verbal skills to recognize and discuss their feelings, and thereby help them develop greater flexibility in coping adaptively and regulating their emotional arousal (Greenberg et al., 1991). In contrast, children whose caregivers show high rates of inconsistency, insensitivity to the children's signals, or emotional unavailability often demonstrate elevated rates of anxiety and negative emotionality, and can only be soothed with difficulty once they are aroused (Rubin et al., 1995). Children in these situations may directly model their parents' unresponsiveness and negativity, becoming avoidant and anxious in social interactions. Alternatively, they may react to parental insensitivity with feelings of anger and frustration, and may learn to elicit responses from others with intrusive, demanding behaviors that are not easily ignored (Jacobvitz & Sroufe, 1987). In either case, generalization

of these socially aversive behaviors to peer interaction contexts may result in rejection by peers,
difficulty in forming friendships, and vulnerability to peer victimization.

Teaching Social Competence

In addition to the effects of discipline and the
parent–child relationship on the development of
social behavior and emotion regulation, several
investigators have identified parental practices that
may contribute to the development of social competence or, alternatively, may lead to social skill
deficits. First, parents may serve as "gatekeepers,"
arranging opportunities for and monitoring the
positive peer interactions of their children (Ladd
& Hart, 1992). Second, in addition to arranging
peer contacts, parents may foster children's social
competence by providing sensitive supervision of
peer interactions and by participating in discussions with their children about strategies for handling peer problems (Parker et al., 1995). Finally,
parents may promote the development of social
competence by modeling positive social interaction styles and engaging in play interactions that
foster the development of perspective taking and
play skills (Putallaz & Heflin, 1990).

Thus, there are a number of ways in which family interaction patterns may foster positive peer
relations, or, alternatively, may contribute to peer
relation difficulties. When attention is paid to the
possible role that family interaction patterns may
be playing in the peer problems of a child undergoing assessment, the need for family-focused
interventions as a collateral treatment to child- or
peer-group-focused intervention for improving the
child's social relations can be evaluated.

Neighborhood and Family Context Contributions

Beyond the immediate environment of the family is the neighborhood context in which family
interactions take place. Neighborhood and cultural influences may affect family interactions, and
may also make direct contributions to child development that interact with or add to familial
influences. Different cultural groups vary widely
in their beliefs and attitudes regarding aggression,
withdrawal, and other social behaviors, and assessment of peer relations should consider the degree
to which a child's behavior is regarded as normal
within his or her culture. Significant differences
in patterns of peer-related verbal aggression, physi-

cal aggression, and victimization have been found
across several European cultures and U.S. subcultural groups. For example, in a study of 8-year-olds,
Ostermann, Bjorkvist, Lagerspetz, and Kaukianen
(1994) found that U.S. children in general were
more verbally and physically aggressive than were
Polish or Finnish children, and that inner-city
African-American children (the most economically deprived group in the sample) had the highest rates of aggression. Although boys as a group
were more aggressive than girls in all of the groups
studied, culture was a stronger determinant of both
peer-nominated and self-reported aggression than
gender was. To some extent, elevated levels of
child aggressive behavior may reflect parental strategies that are designed to help children develop
the capacity to act definitively and assertively, protecting themselves from victimization in dangerous and violent communities.

Similarly, studies have revealed significant cultural differences in reticent, withdrawn behavior.
For example, Native American preschoolers have
been rated by teachers as less socially skilled and
less assertive than European-American children
(Powless & Elliott, 1987)—a difference that is
probably related to the emphasis on deference and
verbal restraint in Native American cultures. As
mentioned previously, parents in Western societies regard withdrawn, nonassertive behavior as
problematic, especially for males (Morrison &
Masten, 1991). By contrast, some Asian cultures
value and reinforce inhibited, cautious behavior
in children, which they regard as indicative of
maturity and self-restraint; in these contexts, withdrawal has been found to correlate with indices
of social competence (Ho & Kang, 1984; King &
Bond, 1985).

Although social behaviors and traits should be
interpreted within a cultural context, it is also
important to consider situations in which a behavior shaped by one cultural context may be problematic in another setting. For example, aggressive behavior may be an important self-protective
capability in a dangerous community; yet it is still
linked with negative school adjustment and Conduct Disorder (Ostermann et al., 1994). Similarly,
reticence may be valued in a Chinese elementary
school, but may prove problematic for a Chinese
child in a U.S. peer group.

Cultural and contextual influences on family
interactions and child socialization have implications for the assessment of, and design of interventions for, children with social relationship problems. Specifically, it is important to consider the

contexts in which a child's social behavior is being shaped, and to evaluate the functional significance of the child's social behavior for his or her adaptation in these various contexts. The appropriate goal for intervention may not be simply increasing or reducing specific social behaviors across settings, but rather facilitating the child's ability to adjust his or her social behavior flexibly to match the demands and expectations of various contexts. Social-cognitive processes, including sensitive social perceptions, flexible interpretive capabilities, and multifaceted response generation and evaluation skills, may be particularly important factors in the development of social responding that is sensitive and responsive to the characteristics and demands of varied social settings.

Social Cognitions

Researchers have postulated that rejected, aggressive, and withdrawn children may have deficiencies or distortions in social information processing. For example, aggressive children often make impulsive, incomplete, and inaccurate social judgments, and show deficits in social problem-solving skills (Dodge, Pettit, McClaskey, & Brown, 1986; Lochman, 1987). Rejected children also often exhibit high rates of inattentive and hyperactive behaviors; these reflect deficits in the development of cognitive control systems, such as the ability to inhibit impulsive responding, focus and sustain attention, and regulate behavior according to internalized rules (Barkley, 1990; Hinshaw, 1994). Deficiencies or delays in cognitive control functions, particularly impulse and attentional control systems, may contribute not only to high rates of impulsive social behavior, but also to insensitive and unresponsive behavior and to a failure to benefit from corrective social feedback, because of the reduced accuracy of social perception and interpretation skills (Hinshaw, 1994).

Crick and Dodge (1994) have developed a model that describes the ways in which errors may occur at various stages in social information processing and lead to social difficulties and behavioral problems. In their model, the first two steps of social information processing are encoding and interpreting social information. Across a number of studies, aggressive children have demonstrated encoding and interpretation distortions: They are more likely than nonaggressive children to attend to aggressive cues and to make impulsive judgments based upon incomplete information. In addition, aggressive children are more likely to interpret the ambiguous behavior of peers as hostile.

Crick and Dodge hypothesize that in addition to difficulties with social perception and interpretation, children with poor peer relations may identify social goals that are self-protective or self-serving rather than prosocial. For example, aggressive–rejected children often select goals that focus on instrumental gains or retribution rather than on the maintenance of positive peer relations (Dodge, Asher, & Parkhurst, 1989). In turn, the selection of asocial goals may increase the likelihood of difficulties in the next two steps of social information processing—the generation and evaluation of response options. Compared to nonaggressive peers, aggressive children generate fewer prosocial and more aggressive responses to social situations (Dodge et al., 1986). Aggressive children also show biased response evaluations; that is, they often expect that aggressive behavior will lead to desired outcomes (Crick & Ladd, 1990; Perry et al., 1986). There is less information on the social-cognitive processes of withdrawn—rejected children, but a few studies suggest that these children generate more submissive strategies for resolving social conflicts than do other children, and are more likely to expect negative outcomes for assertive responses (Crick & Ladd, 1990; Deluty, 1981; Rubin, 1982).

In addition to outlining the pitfalls encountered by socially maladjusted children at each stage of the social-cognitive process, Crick and Dodge (1994) also consider more global ways in which social cognition may be related to poor peer relations. For example, children with peer difficulties often display patterns of social behavior and social cognitive understanding similar to those of younger, nonproblematic children, which may be an indication of a general delay in social-cognitive development. In addition, Crick and Dodge hypothesize that many impulsive, undercontrolled children may be engaging in "preemptive processing," which involves skipping several steps in the social-cognitive process and proceeding directly to an insufficiently analyzed behavioral response.

Social information processing may be affected by past social experiences with family members and peers. For example, Crick and Dodge (1994) postulate that attachment-related experiences and mental representations of relationships are stored in the form of an affect-laden informational data base that influences social perceptions, interpretations, and decision making about social responding. Children who have experienced insensitive or hostile social interactions in family or peer interactions may be "primed" cognitively to respond to ambiguous social situations in self-protective ways. That is, children who have experienced rejection in the past may become particularly vigilant to signs of potential rejection in the future. In order to protect themselves from harm, they may become biased to select self-protective rather than other-oriented social goals, to attribute hostile intentions, and to respond preemptively with aggression or avoidant withdrawal. These types of responses further decrease the likelihood of positive responses from others. Hence, stored memories of negative interpersonal experiences may contribute to biases in social information processes that promote a "self-fulfilling prophecy," in which children who fear rejection or hostile interpersonal treatment behave in ways that increase the likelihood of rejection and victimization (Crick & Dodge, 1994).

Past interpersonal experiences and social information processing may contribute to another aspect of children's social cognitions about their peer relations, which involves the way they think and feel about their social relations.

Self-Perceptions and Feelings of Social Distress

In recent reviews, researchers have suggested that more attention should be paid to the nature and implications of children's own views of their peer relations. These include their perceptions of the extensiveness and nature of their peer contacts; their self-perceptions of social competence and sense of self-efficacy with peers; their social concerns and anxiety; and their feelings of loneliness and depression (Hymel & Franke, 1985; Parker et al., 1995).

Group status has been linked to feelings of belonging (Bukowski et al., 1994), and rejected children report greater loneliness and social dissatisfaction than do nonrejected children (Asher, Parkhurst, Hymel, & Williams, 1990). Both rejected and neglected groups are likely to view themselves as less socially competent than higher-status children, and low levels of perceived self-competence may lead to socially avoidant behaviors (Bukowski & Hoza, 1989). Interestingly, however, studies have found significant heterogeneity among the social appraisals of rejected children, revealing that only some express considerable distress about their social problems and report below-average levels of self-esteem (Boivin & Begin, 1989; Williams & Asher, 1987). In general, rejected children who express no distress about their low status are more likely to be aggressive youngsters who attribute their social failures to external causes, whereas rejected children who express distress are more likely to be socially withdrawn and to attribute their problems to internal factors.

To some extent, supportive friendships may protect children from feelings of loneliness (Asher et al., 1993). However, as noted earlier, the quality of a friendship may have a greater effect than the simple availability of the friendship on the extent to which the friendship provides a source of social support. Students' tendencies to perceive their friendships as high-quality are related to higher academic attainment and fewer behavior problems in school, while a lack of perceived support is associated with loneliness, depression, and adjustment problems (Bukowski et al., 1994; Laursen, 1993). In general, rejected children report feeling less support, trust, and validation in their friendships than do nonrejected children (Parker & Asher, 1993); low-quality and conflictual friendships, in turn, do not appear to protect rejected children from the development of internalizing problems such as anxiety and depression (Hoza et al., 1995).

Given the variability among rejected children in terms of the extent to which they may have negative self-perceptions and feelings of social distress, an important goal in the assessment of a child's social relations may be to determine the degree to which the child is experiencing negative self-appraisals and anxious or depressed affect, as well as the role that these negative affective states may be playing in the exacerbation of the child's peer problems.

ASSESSMENT METHODS

Initial Considerations

It follows from the preceding review that the assessment of a child's social relationships need to be multifaceted. It needs to include an assessment of the adequacy of the child's relations within the peer group at school, the availability of close friendships, and the nature of the child's affiliative network. An initial issue to be addressed in assessment is the extent to which a child's peer relations are deficient—in particular, the extent to which the child is rejected by the group. Further issues to be addressed are the quality of the child's social behavior (both in the group and in the context of close relationships), and an identification of any factors in addition to the child's social behavior that may be contributing to the child's social difficulties. Developmental considerations are important in the assessment process; normative patterns of peer relations and peer influence, as well as the contributions of particular social behaviors or peer attitudes to peer rejection, may depend to a significant extent upon the age, gender, and developmental status of the child. In addition to determining whether a child displays problematic social relations and maladaptive social behavior, an assessment may provide more useful guides for intervention when it also includes an evaluation of proximal mediators that may contribute to the child's social behavioral deficits or excesses, such as deviant family interaction patterns, child social cognitions, and child self-perceptions.

In general, as in all areas of assessment, multiple methods of evaluation are preferable; these should include peer and teacher ratings, parent reports, self-reports, and direct observations (Coie & Dodge, 1988). Multimethod assessment is particularly important in the description of children's social relationships, because previous research suggests that although each type of measure has particular strengths, each also has limitations (Coie & Dodge, 1988). For example, peers may have the best opportunities to observe and comment on the aspects of social behavior they find aversive, but their perceptions may be biased (Hymel et al., 1990) and, in the case of younger children, relatively undifferentiated (Younger, Schwartzman, & Ledingham, 1986). Conversely, teachers may provide more differentiated ratings, but may not have access to the variety of social contexts in which important peer interactions occur, and may be influenced heavily by the impressions children make in classroom settings (Coie & Dodge, 1988). Parents may be able to describe aspects of the child's social behavior and peer contacts outside of school, but often have little information about group peer relations in the classroom setting (Graham & Rutter, 1968). Direct observation provides a more objective measure of children's peer interactions; however, some behaviors that may be "critical events" in terms of their social impact (e.g., fighting or stealing) may be covert or occur with relatively low frequency, and thus are difficult to assess in the restricted times and settings sampled by observations (Foster & Ritchey, 1985). Given the strengths and limitations of each measurement technique, the use of multiple measures (peer ratings, teacher ratings, parent ratings, self-ratings and behavioral observations) provides a more reliable basis for interpretation than does the use of any one method alone (Coie & Dodge, 1988).

In the following sections, specific assessment strategies and measures are identified for the evaluation of the core domains and major mediators of social relationships described earlier in the chapter: (1) group status, (2) social behavior, (3) close friendships, (4) peer group dynamics and network affiliations, (5) familial contributions, (6) social cognitions, and (7) self-perceptions.

Group Status

Sociometric Nominations to Assess Peer Rejection

The basic sociometric method used to assess peer rejection involves the use of positive (or "like most") nominations and negative (or "like least") nominations. For positive nominations, children are asked to name the classmates they most like. For negative nominations, children are asked to name the classmates they least like. Sometimes children are asked to limit their nominations to the top three; in other cases, unlimited nominations are accepted. Sociometrics are often collected in classroom-based group assessments, although individual interviews with children are not uncommon, particularly at the younger ages (preschool and grades 1–2). Nominations are then summed across classmates and divided by the number of raters, in order to compute a score representing either the proportion of peers who particularly like or dislike that child. Scores are then standardized within class or group, and these standardized scores are used for classification purposes. These measures are quite reliable when used with grade school children. For example, 1-year test–retest correlations for both positive and negative nominations are usually in the range of .50–.70 and remain significant (range of .30–.40) even after 3–4 years (Coie & Dodge, 1983). Simplified nomination and rating procedures have also proven to be reliable with preschool children (Asher, Singleton, Tinsley, & Hymel, 1979; Ladd & Mars, 1986). Investigators must decide whether to use same-sex or both-sex nominations, depending upon the goals and purpose of the assessment and the characteristics of the peer group (for a review of these issues, see Foster, Bell-Dolan, & Berler, 1986).

In order to assess a child's social status within a group, classification systems use both positive and negative nominations. The Coie and Dodge

(1983) method is the most widely used for this classification purpose. It involves calculations of "social preference" (positive nominations – negative nominations) and "social impact" (positive nominations + negative nominations) to identify five status groups: "popular," "average," "controversial," "neglected," and "rejected." Rejected status (standardized social preference scores less than a standard deviation below the class mean, positive nomination scores below the class mean, negative nomination scores above the class mean) has proven to be a valid predictor of current and future maladjustment, particularly when combined with evidence of elevated aggressive/disruptive behavior problems or anxious withdrawal (Parker & Asher, 1987; Rubin & Stewart, 1996). Although the base rates for number of positive and negative nominations may vary as a function of age and group size, the standardization of these scores within a classroom (or within a peer group) provides a valid index of group peer relations across the preschool, grade school, and adolescent years.

Alternatives to Negative Nomination Procedures

Despite their value in identifying children at risk, the collection of sociometric nominations (particularly negative nominations) is sometimes difficult because of the concerns raised about the potential negative impact of these assessment procedures. Specifically, parents, school personnel, and researchers have expressed concern that asking children to nominate disliked peers might inadvertently sanction negative talk about others, increase the social ostracism of unpopular children, and cause peers to behave even more negatively toward them (Asher & Hymel, 1981; Bell-Dolan, Foster, & Sikora, 1989). A number of studies were conducted to investigate this issue, but none documented any increases in feelings of rejection or heightened peer negativity toward rejected children as a result of sociometric assessment (Bell-Dolan, Foster, & Sikora, 1989; Hayvren & Hymel, 1984). In one in-depth study conducted by Bell-Dolan, Foster, and Christopher (1992), the vast majority of third- through fifth-grade girls involved in a sociometric interview enjoyed their participation and were unaffected by it, according to their own, parents', and teachers' reports. There were no perceived differences in the experiences of rejected versus nonrejected children, although 25% of the sample did report dislike of the negative nomination procedure and nearly 50% violated the confidentiality agreement.

Although negative sociometric interviews have not been found to have negative effects for the children involved, researchers have explored alternatives to negative nomination procedures that might be more palatable to parents or school personnel with concerns about negative nominations. One alternative is a procedure of repeated positive nominations, in which children repeatedly identify two classmates with whom they like to play until the entire class has been rank-ordered. In one study comparing this technique with the standard positive–negative nomination technique, classification results were quite similar across assessment methods (Bell-Dolan, Foster, & Tishelman, 1989). The repeated positive nominations identified 82% of the rejected, 66% of the popular, and 50% of the neglected children classified by standard positive–negative nominations; these findings suggest that the former technique might be a valid alternative method in attempts to identify rejected children (although it provides a less valid assessment of neglected children).

In another study, Asher and Dodge (1986) explored the possibility of using positive nominations and a rating scale to accurately identify rejected children. For the rating scale, children were presented with a roster of their classmates and asked to rate on a 5-point scale how much they liked to play and how much they liked to work with each of them (from 1 = "not at all" to 5 = "very much") (Roistacher, 1974). Each child then received an average rating score, consisting of the average of the ratings he or she received from all of his or her classmates. This rating scale technique provides a score that is highly correlated with social preference scores based upon nominations, and has the advantage of providing data on how each group member feels about all others. Used alone, this rating scale does not distinguish well between rejected and neglected children (Asher & Hymel, 1981). However, Asher and Dodge (1986) found that the frequency of "1" ratings on the rating scale could be used as a proxy for negative nominations and combined with positive nominations to identify rejected children. The proportion of "1" ratings received by children correlated .80 with traditional negative nominations, and, when used with traditional positive nominations, identified 91% of the rejected children accurately. Hence, the combination of positive nominations and a rating scale may be a good substitute for traditional positive and negative nominations, and may reduce the concerns parents and school personnel sometimes raise about negative nominations.

Teacher Estimates of Group Status

In clinical settings, it may be difficult to collect sociometric nominations for a particular child. Asking children in a classroom to rate one classmate cannot be done without drawing undue attention to that child; on the other hand, schools often will not allow the collection of sociometric data on an entire classroom in order to facilitate the assessment of a single child. In such cases, clinicians may need to consider alternative informants (teachers, parents, or the children themselves) in order to assess potential rejection. Of these informants, teachers are by far the superior raters, providing descriptions of peer interactions and ratings of group acceptance that are closest to those provided by peers themselves (Glow & Glow, 1980). For example, Connelly and Doyle (1981) found teacher and peer ratings of popularity to correlate .55 for preschool children, and Landau, Milich, and Whitten (1984) reported correlations between teacher ratings and peer positive and negative nominations of .50 and −.59, respectively, for grade school children. Although teacher ratings are not as effective as peer ratings in predicting children's social behavior with peers (Landau et al., 1984), they may provide a "second-best" estimate of peer relations when direct sociometric evaluations are unavailable. In contrast, neither parent ratings nor children's self-ratings are likely to estimate group acceptance or rejection accurately (Graham & Rutter, 1968; Ledingham, Younger, Schwartzman, & Bergeron, 1982).

As described earlier, group status is an important variable to assess because it provides an index of the extent to which a child's peer relations and social competence are impaired. However, although problematic group status (e.g., peer rejection) indicates a significant level of risk, the factors that may be contributing to this risky status must be evaluated before appropriate interventions can be designed. That is, children may be rejected for a variety of reasons, and different factors may contribute to the social difficulties being experienced by various children. Evidence of peer rejection indicates that there is a problem with social relations; further assessment is needed to determine the nature of that problem.

Social Behavior

Given the amount of behavioral heterogeneity that exists among peer-rejected children, it is important to assess positive as well as negative aspects of social behavior, in order to identify not only potential behavioral bases for peer aversion to a particular child but potential bases for intervention. In addition, the diversity of behavior problems that may contribute to poor peer relations should be evaluated—not just aggression, but inattentive, hyperactive, and disruptive behaviors, as well as withdrawal, hostile avoidance, and low levels of prosocial behavior. Commonly used assessment methods include behavioral observation, teacher ratings, and peer ratings of social behavior. Parent ratings may also be useful in the description of social behavior outside of the school setting, and with adolescents, self-ratings may provide information about covert problem behaviors that are not easily assessed in other ways.

Observational Strategies

Naturalistic school settings or arranged analogue situations can be used as contexts for the observation of a child's social behavior. Within the school setting, unstructured situations (e.g., recess, lunch, or transition periods in the classroom) provide a better opportunity to observe the quality of peer interactions than do structured classroom situations, although in the classroom one can assess inattentive and disruptive behavior (Foster & Ritchey, 1985). Key behaviors to look for include (1) aggressive, disruptive, and intrusive behaviors; (2) insensitive, immature, or awkward behavior; (3) isolative and unoccupied behavior; (4) positive and prosocial behavior; and (5) responsiveness to other children (Bierman et al., 1993).

Across studies, investigators have varied somewhat in the specific ways in which they have set up naturalistic observations of children's peer interactions, and in the specific content of their coding categories. The observational method used in the study by Bierman et al. (1993) is described in detail here as one example of how naturalistic observation can be done. In this study, children were observed for 16 minutes at lunch and 16 minutes at recess during at least 2 (nonconsecutive) days. Trained observers used a time-sampling technique (observing for 6 seconds and recording for 6 seconds) and recorded the occurrence of six types of social behaviors (see Table 6.1 for coding category examples). Both child initiations and peer responses were coded. That is, coders recorded the number of intervals in which the target child exhibited any of the six types of social behavior, and, separately, recorded the number of times peers directed any of the six types of social behavior toward the target child. This procedure provided

TABLE 6.1. Coding Categories (with Definitions and Examples) for Assessing Naturalistic Peer Interactions

Physical aggression

Definition: This category is coded whenever a child physically attacks or attempts to attack another person. The attack must be of sufficient intensity or intended to potentially inflict pain.

Examples: Hitting, kicking, slapping, taking an object roughly, swinging fists, throwing objects, destroying another's property.

Verbal aggression

Definition: This category includes verbal behavior that is intended to punitively control another person's actions, to express negative feelings toward another person, or to cause harm to the other person's feelings or reputation.

Examples: Negatively toned commands, yelling derisively, insults, taunting, cussing or swearing, mimicking another sarcastically, threatening, making negative insinuations.

Rough and tumble play

Definition: This category includes interactions which involve non-negative rigorous physical contact with others, or attempted rigorous contact. In contrast to physical aggression, the intent is to play rather than to harm.

Examples: Wrestling, playful restraint, carrying others, jumping on others in a playful manner, tackling or chasing others.

Prosocial/agreeable

Definition: This category includes verbal and non-verbal behaviors which are other directed and prosocial in orientation, designed to help or please the other. Also included here are verbal and non-verbal behaviors that signal agreement with or acknowledgement of another's idea, suggestion or command.

Examples: Helping behaviors, sharing, taking turns, compliance to suggestions, praise, invitations to play, affectionate physical contact, agreements.

Neutral interaction

Definition: This category includes other forms of verbal or play interactions that are neither clearly aggressive, rough play, or prosocial in nature.

Examples: Conversation, play behaviors, simple (non-negative) commands.

Solitary/unoccupied

Definition: This category refers to behavior which is solitary and unengaged. It does not include constructive solitary play, but refers to non-interactive and unengaged behavior.

Examples: Hovering onlooker behavior, unoccupied wandering, sitting on the sidelines and observing play.

---

information about how the child was behaving toward others, and also provided information about how peers were behaving toward the child (which, as described earlier, is an important factor to assess and perhaps to include in intervention).

With proper observer training techniques, it is possible to collect reliable observations even of fast-paced naturalistic interactions. In the Bierman et al. (1993) study, for example, interrater reliability (kappa) averaged .75 across categories. When compared with other assessment devices (e.g., teacher and peer ratings), these observational coding categories demonstrated concurrent and discriminant validity. High rates of verbal and physical aggression provided significant estimates of conduct problem ratings; high rates of solitary behavior, along with low rates of neutral interaction and low rates of prosocial interaction, provided significant estimates of naturalistic rates of peer interaction (Bierman et al., 1993).

Because of the differences that may exist in the normativeness of these behaviors for children of various age levels, culture groups, and genders, an evaluation of the target child relative to comparison children within the peer group is advisable. In addition, observing in school settings allows one to evaluate the behaviors and responses directed by teachers and peers to the target child—again, information that may be useful in formulating hypotheses about the extent to which noncontingent responding, hostile treatment, or negative reinforcement processes may be operating to elicit and/or maintain deviant social behavior in the target child.

Although naturalistic observations of children in school settings can be quite valuable, it is sometimes difficult to collect sufficient data in naturalistic settings on which to base clear judgments about the social behavioral repertoire and social skill abilities of particular children. Classroom behavior is often structured, routine, and tightly controlled by teachers, and hence often provides few opportunities to observe the sorts of poorly controlled social behaviors that can interfere with peer relations (Foster & Ritchey, 1985). Even in less structured recess or lunch settings, aggressive children may engage in only a few negative behaviors in any given 30-minute period. Although such behaviors may be "critical events" that have a strong negative impact on peer relations, the low base rates can make such behaviors difficult to observe naturalistically (Foster & Ritchey, 1985). A number of studies have supplemented or replaced naturalistic observations with arranged play group observations (Bierman & Furman, 1984; Coie & Kupersmidt, 1983; Dodge, 1983). The advantage of the play group observation setting is that tasks can be given to children in order to elicit communication, cooperation, negotiation, emotion regulation, and problem-solving skills. For example, children may be asked to work on a cooperative art project, negotiate play with a limited number of toy choices, play with affectively arousing toys (e.g., toy soldiers), solve a group problem, or make a group decision. Play group observations thus often permit closer examination of the more subtle aspects of children's interaction skills — including their group entry skills, conflict management and problem-solving skills, and skills at sustaining mutually rewarding interactions — than do observations in school classrooms. Play groups also offer the opportunity to evaluate behaviors that might be aversive to peers, including bossy, self-centered, intrusive, insensitive, or irritating behaviors.

Regardless of the observational strategy selected, observations are by nature time-limited and may not include a complete or reliable sample of the child's everyday behavior within the peer group. Teacher and peer ratings of social behavior, though potentially biased, have the advantage of providing an evaluation of the target child's social behavior that is based upon multiple observations across a sustained period of time.

Teacher Ratings

Numerous standardized instruments have been developed for teachers to rate children's positive and negative social and school behavior. Given the plethora of teacher rating scales available, the selection of a particular scale should be made with careful consideration. For example, the similarity of the sample used for the development of each scale to the child or children being assessed, and the characteristics of other rating scales already included in the assessment battery, are two important points to consider. For example, if a teacher rating of behavior problems at school is already included in the assessment battery, it may be redundant to include a teacher rating of social adjustment that includes scales focused on behavior problems as well as social competence. On the other hand, if no concurrent teacher rating measures are planned, it may be especially important to select a teacher rating scale that includes behavior problems as well as social competence, given the important role of behavior problems in the establishment of peer relation problems. In addition to these considerations, the availability of validated parallel forms for ratings by peers, parents, or children themselves may be important for some assessment purposes, and the length of the measure may be an additional consideration.

A number of teacher rating forms are available to assess problem behaviors in the classroom (see McMahon & Estes, Chapter 3, this volume), and these measures may play an important role in identifying problem behaviors that may be contributing to poor peer relations. The Walker Problem Behavior Identification Checklist (WPBIC; Walker, 1983) is one such measure. It includes 50 items reflecting five subscales: Acting Out, Distractibility, Disturbed Peer Relations, Withdrawal, and Immaturity. Reliability and validity studies are available for the WPBIC, and a parallel form is available for parent report (Strain, Steele, Ellis, & Timm, 1982). Similarly, the Teacher Report Form (TRF) of the Child Behavior Checklist (CBCL; Achenbach, 1991b) provides teacher ratings on a range of behavior problems, including both externalizing and internalizing problems. Attention and learning problems, which may contribute to poor peer relations, are rated on the TRF; and the form also provides a scale assessing social problems and several items describing aspects of the child's social competence at school. The Social Problems scale and Social Competence ratings on the TRF do not provide enough detail to characterize the child's social adjustment difficulties, but do provide a screen that may help identify social adjustment as a potential area of difficulty for a child. The comprehensive Behavior Problems scale of the TRF (and other similar measures) can provide important information about behavior problems in the school setting that may be contributing to peer difficulties.

In addition to teacher reports of school behavior problems, a number of teacher rating scales have been developed specifically to assess children's social competence with more precision. For example, the Teacher Rating of Social Skills—Children (TROSS-C; Clark, Gresham, & Elliott, 1985; Gresham, Elliott, & Black, 1987) is a 52-item teacher checklist whose subscales reflect four specific areas of social skill: Social Initiation, Cooperation, Peer Reinforcement, and Academic Performance. Validity studies suggest that scores on this measure are moderately correlated with academic achievement scores and (inversely) with school behavior problems. Parallel forms have been developed for parents and children themselves. Similarly, the Walker–McConnell Scale of Social Competence and School Adjustment (Walker & McConnell, 1988) has 43 items and these subscales: Teacher Preferred Social Behavior, Peer Preferred Social Behavior, and School Adjustment. The Walker–McConnell instrument is psychometrically sound with regard to both test–retest reliability and internal consistency.

There are also teacher rating scales that include assessments of both behavior problems and social competence, such as the 36-item Teacher–Child Rating Scale (T-CRS; Hightower et al., 1986). The T-CRS includes six scales (three 6-item problem scales and three 6-item competence scales): Act-

ing Out, Shy Anxious, Learning Problems, Frustration Tolerance, Assertive Social Skills, and Task Orientation. It has proven to be an effective screening device to identify children with social adjustment difficulties in the classroom.

There are also several teacher rating scales available for use with preschool populations. The Preschool Behavior Questionnaire (Behar & Stringfield, 1974) is a 30-item checklist evaluating problem behaviors. Teachers rate behaviors on a 3-point scale ("doesn't apply," "sometimes applies," "always applies"). This checklist was standardized on an ethnically diverse sample of preschoolers both with and without behavior problems, and yields three factors of behavior problems: Hostile/Aggressive, Anxious/Fearful, and Hyperactive/Distractible. It has been widely used as a screening instrument with young children, and provides useful information about social behaviors that may contribute to peer relation difficulties.

Designed to assess social competence in younger children, as well as grade school children and adolescents, the Matson Evaluation of Social Skills with Youngsters (MESSY; Matson, Rotatori, & Helsel, 1983) is a 64-item teacher report scale. Teachers use a 5-point, likert-type response format to rate children on each of the items, and the scale provides summary scores for both behavior problems and social competence. A parallel 62-item self-report form is also available for the MESSY. Table 6.2 provides sample items from some of the more commonly used teacher rating scales.

TABLE 6.2. Sample Items from Teacher Ratings of Children's Social Behavior

Instrument name	Population	Sample items
Teacher–Child Rating Scale (T-CRS; Hightower et al., 1986)	Grades K–6	Is disruptive in class. Is shy and timid. Has many friends. Has a good sense of humor.
Walker–McConnell Scale of Social Competence and School Adjustment (Walker & McConnell, 1988)	Grades K–6	Uses free time appropriately. Controls temper. Displays independent study skills.
Teacher Rating of Social Skills—Children (TROSS-C; Clark, Gresham, & Elliott, 1985)	Grades K–6	Follows teachers' verbal instructions. Appropriately joins activity. Shares materials with others.
Preschool Behavior Questionnaire (Behar & Stringfield, 1974)	Ages 3–6	Squirmy and fidgety. Bullies other children. Has stutter or stammer.
Matson Evaluation of Social Skills with Youngsters (MESSY; Matson, Rotatori & Helsel, 1983)	Ages 4–18	Always wants to be first. Makes fun of others. Plays by rules of game. Sticks up for friends.

Peer Ratings

Although teacher ratings of children's social behavior are often moderately and sometimes highly correlated with peer ratings, peer ratings of children's social behavior typically provide the best predictions of sociometric status and social behavior observations (Landau et al., 1984). Three common approaches to the collection of peer ratings of social behavior are (1) peer ratings based on multi-item scales, (2) peer nominations for behavior patterns, and (3) peer interviews.

One commonly used peer behavioral rating form is the Pupil Evaluation Inventory (PEI; Pekarik, Prinz, Liebert, Weintraub, & Neale, 1976). Presented with 35 items describing social behaviors and a roster containing the names of classmates, students indicate with a check mark any classmates who fit each behavioral description. Each child in the classroom then receives a score indicating the proportion of classmates who nominated him or her for each item. Item scores are summed into three scales: Aggression, Withdrawal–Ostracism, and Likability. The items on the Aggression scale cover verbally/physically aggressive and disruptive behaviors, and include "Those who start fights," "Those who bother others when they are trying to work," and "Those who are mean and cruel to other children." Items on the Withdrawal scale cover shyness ("Those who are too shy to make friends easily"), emotional sensitivity and sad mood ("Those who are unhappy and sad," "Those whose feelings are too easily hurt"), and social isolation ("Those who don't want to play," "Those who have few friends"). Likability scale items cover prosocial behaviors ("Those who help others") and friendship inclusion ("Those who are your best friend"). A similar approach to peer ratings is taken with the Revised Class Play (Masten, Morrison, & Pellegrini, 1985), in which children identify classmates who they feel "fit" various behavioral roles. Children in the classroom each receive summed scores for three behavioral dimensions: Sociability–Leadership (e.g., "Good leader," "Plays fair"), Aggressive–Disruptive (e.g., "Picks on other kids"), and Sensitive–Isolated (e.g., "Very shy").

A second method of attaining behavioral descriptions from classmates involves a nomination method in which children respond to more complex single-item descriptive statements. For example, students may be asked to name the children in their classroom who fit descriptions such as "Some kids start fights or say mean things or hit others," or "Some kids cooperate a lot—they help others and share." Although this nomination method relies on scales made up of only a few items or even a single item, the availability of multiple peer informants provides a broad base for measurement. Indeed, this peer nomination method has proven effective in producing stable and predictive descriptions of children's social behavior (Coie & Dodge, 1988).

Finally, a third method of gathering information about children's social behavior from their classmates involves the use of a semistructured interview. For example, Bierman et al. (1993) conducted individual interviews with peers, asking them five open-ended questions about target children:

1. Describe the child; tell me what he/she is like.
2. What might some children like about that child?
3. What might some children not like about that child?
4. Why might some children not want to be friends with that child?
5. Why might some children want to be friends with that child?

In addition to descriptions of aggressive, disruptive, and withdrawn behaviors, this interview elicited comments about nonbehavioral characteristics and about insensitive or atypical behaviors that were affecting children's peer relations but were not well assessed by standardized teacher and peer ratings or by observations. For example, in the Bierman et al. (1993) study, open-ended interview responses describing the reasons that children were liked or disliked were classified into the following main categories:

1. Physical Aggression—comments that referred to a child's tendency to initiate (or refrain from initiating) behaviors such as fighting, kicking, hitting, or damaging things.
2. Verbal Aggression—descriptors that focused on the child's propensity to engage in (or refrain from) behaviors such as threatening, teasing, arguing, or bossing.
3. Rule Violation—comments describing cheating, disruptiveness, or stealing.
4. Play Partner—statements that referred to the child's suitability as a partner in play, such as his or her inclusion in games and athletic skills.
5. Solitary–Shy—comments that referred to solitary behaviors or shy dispositional orientation.

6. Prosocial—descriptors referring to prosocial behaviors and positive interpersonal orientations, such as nurturant behaviors, or positive traits, such as being kind or nice.
7. Atypical Characteristics—descriptions that focused on characteristics of a child that differentiated him or her from the norm, such as handicapping conditions or odd appearance.
8. Insensitive Behaviors—descriptions of behaviors indicating an insensitivity to peer norms, such as peculiar habits, poor hygiene, and egocentric or immature behaviors (e.g., "shows off," "acts like a baby").

Of these categories, the last two (Atypical Characteristics and Insensitive Behavior) proved to be important distinguishing characteristics of rejected children that were not well assessed by other measurement methods (e.g., observations, standard peer or teacher ratings).

Developmental considerations are important when one is choosing a peer rating method for eliciting behavioral descriptions. Although even preschool children can give reliable behavioral descriptions of their classmates (Ladd & Mars, 1986), the behavioral perceptions of young children tend to be polarized and not well differentiated (Younger et al., 1986). Hence, at the preschool level, teacher ratings may provide more valid and predictive behavioral descriptions of rejected children than do peer ratings (Connelly & Doyle, 1981). In particular, behaviors that are more subtle indicators of potential social difficulties, such as anxious withdrawal, are difficult to assess well with peer ratings at the preschool or early grade school level (Younger et al., 1986). At older ages, however, peers are preferred raters, as their descriptions of child behaviors are more predictive of observed child social behavior than are teacher ratings (Landau et al., 1984).

Parent Ratings

In addition to teachers and peers, parents can be asked to provide ratings of children's social behavior. Although parents often have trouble estimating the overall quality of their children's peer relations (Graham & Rutter, 1968), they can provide useful information in several other areas relevant to child social adjustment. First, parent ratings can provide information about behavior problems in the home setting that may be interfering with social adjustment, including aggressive and noncompliant behaviors and anxious withdrawal.

Standard parent rating measures of behavior problems, such as the CBCL (Achenbach, 1991a), provide estimates of externalizing and internalizing behavior problems that can be compared to well-established gender-based and age-based norms. Other measurement options for assessing behavior problems that may interfere with social relations are discussed by McMahon and Estes (Chapter 3, this volume). Second, parents may provide useful information about their children's extracurricular social activities and interpersonal behavior. Several teacher rating forms have parallel versions designed for parents to report on their children's social competence; these include the WPBIC (Strain et al., 1982; Walker, 1983) and the TROSS-C (Clark, Gresham, & Elliott, 1985). In addition, the CBCL (Achenbach, 1991a) includes questions about a child's activities and level of social involvement, with age and gender norms available for comparison. Parents may also provide information about the number of peer contacts their child has outside of the school context and the characteristics of the neighborhood peers with whom their child interacts.

Assessments of social status and of social behavior focus primarily on the ways in which children function in the context of the peer group, and with the exception of the parent ratings, they focus on the peer group defined by the classroom. As described in the preceding review, however, the nature of children's friendships and close relationships is not well captured by these group-focused assessments and requires additional assessment methods.

Friendships and Close Relationships

The assessment of children's friendships and close relationships involves a consideration of both the number and quality of these relationships. In addition, because one of the core functions of close friendships is the provision of emotional and social support, it is important to consider both the child's subjective perceptions of his or her close friendships and more objective indices of these relationships.

Typically, the sociometric method of positive nominations, described above, has been used to assess the number and identity of a child's friends. The peers named by a child reflect the child's perceptions of who his or her friends are; a consideration of those peers who, in return, name the child as one of their friends provides an assessment of reciprocated friendships. The major drawback to this method is that it becomes difficult to identify the reciprocal friendships of children who are not in the same school (Parker & Asher, 1993).

Although sociometric data may answer the "who" and "how many" questions regarding children's friendships, they provide no information about the nature of specific relationships or the roles that friends play for particular children. A few instruments assessing qualitative aspects of children's friendships have recently been developed; most of these are intended for preadolescents and adolescents rather than younger children. The Friendship Qualities Scale (Bukowski et al., 1994) is a 10-item questionnaire that assesses two domains of friendship—security and closeness. Children identify a particular "best friendship" and rate that relationship on a 5-point scale (1 = "not true at all about the friendship," 5 = "really true") for each item. Similarly, the Intimate Friendship Scale (Sharabany, 1994) uses 32 items to assess eight dimensions of friendship: frankness/spontaneity, sensitivity/knowing, attachment, exclusiveness, giving/sharing, imposition, common activities, and trust/loyalty. This instrument also asks children to identify one particular friendship and rate it on a 6-point scale (1 = "strongly disagree," 6 = "strongly agree"). Both of these instruments measure children's perceptions about the nature of their relationships with specific people. In the original research studies using these scales, mutuality (or lack thereof) of the friendships assessed was first determined by means of a modified sociometric procedure, and was found to be significantly related to friendship quality.

A similar approach to the assessment of friendships has been taken by Furman and Buhrmester (1992), who utilized a structured interview approach to assess children's perceptions of relationship quality in domains such as conflict, intimacy,

affection, and support. These authors then developed the Network of Relationships Inventory (Furman & Buhrmester, 1992), which can be used with grade school children as well as adolescents, and which focuses on multiple close relationships (e.g., siblings, parents, and romantic partners) as well as same-sex friends. The inventory was designed to evaluate the functions and subjective importance of relationships by asking young people about the quality of their interpersonal interactions. Sample items from the Friendship Qualities Scale, the Intimate Friendship Scale, and the Network of Relationships Inventory are presented in Table 6.3.

In addition to group status, social behavior, and close relationships, the treatment that a child receives from his or her peers and the characteristics of these peers may have an impact on the child's social development and adaptation. As mentioned above, observational strategies can offer some information about how a child is treated by peers. In addition, teacher ratings and peer ratings can be used to evaluate important aspects of peer group dynamics and networks affecting various children.

Peer Group Dynamics and Network Affiliations

Although rejected children are not liked by their classmates, they may or may not be the recipients of hostile treatment (Perry et al., 1988). To determine the extent to which children might be the recipients of hostile treatment from peers, Perry et al. (1988) developed a peer nomination inventory. This measure includes seven items reflecting victimization (e.g., "Kids make fun of him/her," "He/she gets hit and pushed by other kids"),

TABLE 6.3. Sample Items from Assessments of Friendship and Close Relationships

Instrument name	Sample items
Network of Relationships Inventory (Furman & Buhrmester, 1992)	How much free time do you spend with this person? How much do you share your secrets and private feelings with this person?
Friendship Qualities Scale (Bukowski, Hoza, & Boivin, 1994)	My friend and I spend all our free time together. My friend and I can argue a lot. My friend would help me if I needed it. If my friend had to move away, I would miss him/her.
Intimate Friendship Scale (Sharabany, 1994)	I feel close to him/her. I know which kinds of books, games, activities he/she likes. I can use his/her things without permission. I will not go along with others to do anything against him/her.

as well as aggressive and neutral "filler" items, and has demonstrated high levels of internal consistency and stability (3-month stability $r = .93$).

Some children who are rejected by the majority group may find companions among other outcasts. When aggressive children affiliate with one another, the risk for the escalation of their aggressive and antisocial behavior over time is increased (Dishion & Skinner, 1989). Hence, in addition to establishing the extent to which a child may be ostracized by the majority peer group, it may be important to determine the extent to which he or she may be affiliating with deviant peers. One method for determining the network affiliations of children is to look at the "map" of mutual relationships defined by positive sociometric nominations. A second method involves asking peer informants to indicate "who hangs around with whom" in the classroom (Cairns et al., 1989).

In some cases, it is not possible to gain access to the peers with whom a child associates for an assessment of the characteristics of those peers. Older children or adolescents can sometimes be interviewed directly about the behaviors and characteristics of their friends in such cases (Dishion et al., 1995; Elliot, Huizinga, & Menard, 1989). For example, the National Youth Survey is sometimes used to assess the degree to which youths report the frequency of their own antisocial behavior and the frequency with which their friends engage in antisocial behavior (Elliot et al., 1989).

An assessment focused on group status, child social behavior, close friendships, and peer group treatment/affiliation will provide a comprehensive description of the child's peer relations. In addition, intervention planning may be facilitated by an assessment of factors that may mediate behavioral and relational deficits, such as family interaction processes.

Family Interaction Patterns

An assessment of family interaction patterns may be important for two reasons. First, it is possible that some of the maladaptive behavioral responses that may be contributing to a child's difficulties with peers, such as aggressive behavior, may be supported in the home setting—either by coercive treatment and punitive punishment, or by parental support for self-protective aggressive behavior. To the extent that family interactions may be fostering aggressive or destructive social behavior with peers (or supporting anxious and withdrawn behavior), it may be important to include family members in intervention efforts. Second, given evidence that parents serve as important gatekeepers, monitors, and advice givers shaping the peer interaction opportunities of their children (Parke & Ladd, 1992), an evaluation of their abilities and willingness to become involved in intervention efforts can help guide intervention design. Other chapters in this volume discuss assessment methods to evaluate the quality of parental discipline practices and parent–child interaction patterns. In addition, observations of parents' social interaction style with their children, and assessment of parents' attitudes, intentions, and childrearing practices with regard to the support of their children's peer relations, may also warrant consideration (Putallaz, Costanzo, & Smith, 1991).

Yet another important area for assessment is that of children's social-cognitive processes, because these may also serve as mediators of children's social difficulties and may provide potential targets for intervention.

Social-Cognitive Processes

Social behavior is multiply determined; hence, a child who does not behave in a socially skillful manner may be experiencing problems for a number of reasons. One contributing factor may be deficits or distortions in the child's social-cognitive processing, including difficulties in perceiving or interpreting social information accurately, avoiding negatively biased expectations, choosing appropriate social goals, or generating and selecting adaptive response options. One common method of assessing children's perceptions and attributional styles is to present them with written or videotaped vignettes of social situations and ask them to interpret the situation and/or generate possible response options. For example, Dodge and his colleagues (Dodge, Murphy, & Buchsbaum, 1984; Dodge & Coie, 1987) have developed videotapes to assess intention cue detection skills, hostile attributional biases, and response tendencies. They use a set of twelve 30-second vignettes, each of which shows a situation involving some form of peer provocation or conflict (e.g., a peer knocks down another's block tower, a peer takes a child's toy). Vignettes display a variety of affect and intentions on the part of the provocateur; in various scenes, the intent displayed is hostile, ambiguous, or positive. Children watch each videotaped segment, and are then asked to give their interpretation of the intentions displayed by the provocateur and to state how they themselves would respond in the situation.

Measures that use stories to present hypothetical situations to children have also proven valid in the assessment of attributional biases and response generation. The Taxonomy of Problem Situations (Dodge, McClaskey, & Feldman, 1985) and the Social Knowledge Interview (Geraci & Asher, 1980) are two published examples of standardized methods used to assess children's social perceptions and attributions. Focusing specifically on young adolescents' ability to generate adaptive responses to social problems, the Alternative Solutions Test (Caplan, Weissberg, Bersoff, Ezekowitz, & Wells, 1986) was developed to assess the quantity and quality of problem-solving responses. In this test, children generate solutions for three hypothetical peer conflict situations, and receive scores for (1) the number of alternative solutions generated, (2) the number of non-redundant responses generated, and (3) the effectiveness of the solutions generated. The effectiveness of each response is rated on a 4-point scale, and these scores are averaged to compute a total effectiveness score. Social goals and outcome expectancies can also be assessed as social-cognitive processes that may contribute to aggressive behaviors, and thereby to poor peer relations (Perry et al., 1986).

In addition to the use of hypothetical situations, children's social cognitive processing can be assessed in actual situations. For example, Putallaz (1983) first videotaped children as they attempted to enter a new group situation. She then reviewed the tape with the target children, stopping the tape periodically to question the children about their social perceptions, their goals, and the cues to which they were attending. This method, although more time-consuming than techniques employing analogues, may be valuable because it assesses a child's cognitions in the context of his or her own behavior.

Self-Perceptions and Feelings of Social Distress

Despite the findings that children's self-appraisals and ratings of their social relations are only moderately correlated with peer and teacher ratings (Ledingham et al., 1982), these perceptions may be important to assess, as they may contribute to a child's relational difficulties and may be important to address in intervention. Several standardized questionnaires have been developed to assess various aspects of children's own perceptions of their peer relations.

In the domain of perceived competence and efficacy, two commonly used scales are the Perceived Competence Scale for Children (Harter, 1982) and its adapted version for preschoolers (Harter & Pike, 1984), which assess children's awareness of their social skill and the ways in which they are viewed by others. As mentioned previously, perceived competence is correlated with peer status and behavioral style, and can provide a useful index of the way in which children view their social situations. The Perceived Competence Scale for Children has 28 items that make up four subscales: Cognitive, Social, Physical, and General competence. A two-step answer format is used, so that a child first chooses between two statements, identifying the statement that is accurate for him or her (e.g., "Some kids find it hard to make friends, but for other kids it's pretty easy to make friends"). Once the child has indicated the statement that is most like him or her, the child is asked whether the statement is "sort of" true or "really true" for him or her. Items are scored along a 4-point response scale (from 1 = "really true, negative" to 4 = "really true, positive"). The Perceived Competence Scale has been widely used, and has a parallel form for teachers.

Whereas the Perceived Competence Scale for Children (Harter, 1982) focuses on how children feel about their efficacy and competence, another approach to assessing self-perceptions has focused on children's descriptions of their activities and behaviors. For example, self-ratings have been collected using the PEI, in order to assess the extent to which children perceive themselves as engaging in various aggressive, withdrawn, or prosocial behaviors (Ledingham et al., 1982). In a similar vein, the Friendship Questionnaire (Bierman & McCauley, 1987) asks children to describe the extensiveness of their peer network, and to rate the extent to which they regularly experience a list of positive and negative interactions with peers in school and in home settings (see examples in Table 6.4).

Investigators have postulated that self-perceptions of peer relations may be particularly important in the prediction of psychological distress and internalizing problems, as children who feel that they are without peer support or who feel victimized by peers may be at high risk for loneliness and depression (Boivin, Hymel, & Bukowski, 1995). Correspondingly, some measures have been developed to assess children's perceptions of their peer relations in terms of the quality of support offered by these relationships. For example, My

Family and Friends (Reid, Landesman, Treder, & Jaccard, 1989) is a qualitative, individualized interview, in which children are asked to indicate specific roles filled by specific relationships in their lives. The interviewer describes a particular social situation in one of five domains (emotional support, informational support, instrumental support, companionship, and conflict), and children name an individual who helps them in this manner and indicate how successful they are at eliciting the desired aid. This measure does not focus on friendships alone, but allows the evaluator to assess the extent to which friends are listed as sources of various types of support.

Focusing more specifically on children's affective reactions to their peer relations, the Loneliness Scale was developed by Asher, Hymel, and Renshaw (1984). This brief measure can be ad-

ministered orally or completed in written form; it provides information regarding the degree to which children experience loneliness and feel they have no friends and do not belong to a group. Sample items from the Perceived Competence Scale for Children, the Loneliness Scale, the Friendship Questionnaire, and the My Family and Friends assessment are provided in Table 6.4.

ASSESSMENT-TO-TREATMENT CONNECTIONS

A comprehensive assessment of a child's social relationships provides information that is critical for treatment planning. Various interventions have been designed to improve peer relations (Bierman, 1989; Coie & Koeppl, 1990); determining the in-

TABLE 6.4. Sample Items from Self-Report Assessments of Children's Social Behavior

Instrument name	Population	Sample items
Loneliness Scale (Asher, Hymel, & Renshaw, 1984)	Elementary (modifications for adolescents possible)	It's hard for me to make friends. I'm lonely. I don't have anyone to play with. I'm well liked by the kids in my class.
Friendship Questionnaire (Bierman & McCauley, 1987)	Elementary	Is there someone who saves you a seat at lunch? (How often?) Is there someone you get mad at? (How often?) Is there someone you tease and make fun of? (How often?) Is there someone you have sleep overnight at your house? (How often?)
Perceived Competence Scale for Children (Harter, 1982)	Elementary	Some kids feel that they are really good at school work, but other kids worry about whether they can do the work assigned to them. Some kids find it hard to make friends, but for other kids it's pretty easy to make friends.
My Family and Friends (Reid, Landesman, Treder, & Jacard, 1989)	Ages 5–14	Who do you go to when you want to share your feelings? Who do you go to when there is something that you don't know too much about or when you need more information? Who do you go to when you want to hang out or do fun things?

tervention components that are appropriate for a particular child or group of children requires assessment. The assessment should provide answers to several key questions relevant to intervention design. The first of these is the question of whether intervention should target the child's social relationships. As reviewed in this chapter, intervention for social relationships is indicated if a child is rejected by the peer group, particularly if the child shows high rates of aggressive/disruptive and/or anxious/avoidant behavior, either of which indicates high risk for stable rejection and negative outcomes.

Second, the assessment should identify the child behaviors and skills that require attention in intervention. Several training techniques have been developed to increase positive social-cognitive skills and behavioral skills, with the ultimate goal of supporting positive peer relations (Bierman, 1989; Coie & Koeppl, 1990). Such training is likely to be particularly effective when it addresses social skills that are deficient for a particular child. In addition, behavioral management and cognitive-behavioral intervention strategies have been developed to improve self-control skills and to decrease aggression. Such intervention strategies are particularly relevant for children whose high rates of aggression disturb peer relations, but may be irrelevant for children whose social problems do not stem from elevated rates of aggression (Coie & Koeppl, 1990). Given the behavioral heterogeneity among children who have social relationship problems, a comprehensive assessment is needed in order to identify the deficient skills and problem behaviors that are contributing to the peer difficulties of a particular child or subgroup of children; these can then be targeted in treatment.

Third, assessment can provide information about available friends and friendship affiliations, which may also require attention in intervention. As described earlier, friendships appear to play unique roles in development, which are complementary to the roles played by group acceptance. Interventions that are designed to improve behavior and improve peer status may not be effective in altering friendships (Parker et al., 1995). Assessments that provide information about the quantity and quality of a child's friendships can address questions about the extent to which interventions need to focus on building friendships as well as group status. Conversely, in some cases, assessments will reveal the existance of deviant friendships—friendships that may be contributing to increasing social difficulties and may be encouraging antisocial attitudes and

coercive interpersonal behaviors (Dishion et al., 1995). Separation from and replacement of these deviant partnerships may then become important intervention goals.

A fourth and related issue addressed by a comprehensive assessment is the extent to which the peer group is playing a role in a child's social relationship difficulties. A negative reputation among peers, as well as ostracism and/or victimization by peers, may have a negative impact on the rejected child. Intervention strategies that focus on the peer group (rather than the target child) may be needed in order to reduce victimization and create opportunities for positive peer interaction for a rejected child (Bierman & Furman, 1984). A comprehensive assessment can provide information about the network affiliations of a child and about the way in which that child is being treated by peers, and thus can indicate whether interventions focused on the peer group treatment of the child are needed.

A fifth goal of the comprehensive assessment is the examination of factors that may be mediating the child's social relationship problems. For example, family interaction patterns, social-cognitive variables, and self-perceptions may all serve as mediators of peer problems in some cases. Such variables may require attention in intervention. For example, if a child is rejected at school because of aggressive behavior, and that aggressive behavior is supported at home by punitive discipline practices, treatment may be most effective when it includes components that target the rejection, the aggressive behavior, *and* the punitive discipline practices (Bierman, 1989).

Social relationship problems rarely exist in isolation from other child adjustment difficulties. The goal of the assessment is thus to describe "the whole child"—that is, to provide an overview of all relevant target areas (child skills/behaviors as well as school and home contextual factors) so that multicomponent, developmentally informed interventions can be designed.

SUMMARY

In summary, assessing a child's social relationships requires attention to multiple relational dimensions, including group status and behavior, close friendships, peer group treatment, and peer network affiliations. Factors that may mediate the quality of a child's social behavior and relations, such as family relationships, social-cognitive processes, and self-perceptions, also warrant attention; these factors may play important roles in remedial intervention plans. Multiple methods of assessment are encouraged, including direct observations, as well as a consideration of teacher, peer, parent, and child viewpoints.

Because problematic peer relations are associated with a number of childhood disorders and behavioral difficulties, it is particularly important to take a broad perspective in assessment—that is, to consider both how behavior problems and other difficulties may be negatively affecting peer relations, and, conversely, how problematic peer relations may be exacerbating behavioral maladjustment. Recent longitudinal studies suggest that poor peer relations are not simply a "side effect" of behavior problems. Rather, they indicate that peer relations provide an important context for socialization and emotional development, and exert an active influence on the direction of a child's developmental trajectory. Recent research has contributed to an increasingly rich conceptual framework to guide our understanding of how peer relations function in the process of child development. Future research may help us to refine our developmental models further, and may improve our ability both to assess and to remediate deficits in children's social relationships.

REFERENCES

Achenbach, T. (1991a). *Manual for the Child Behavior Checklist and 1991 Profile*. Burlington: University of Vermont, Department of Psychiatry.

Achenbach, T. (1991b). *Manual for the Teacher's Report Form and 1991 Profile*. Burlington: University of Vermont, Department of Psychiatry.

Ainsworth, M. D. S., Blehar, M. C., Waters, E., & Wall, S. (1978). *Patterns of attachment*. Hillsdale, NJ: Erlbaum.

American Psychiatric Association. (1994). *Diagnostic and statistical manual of mental disorders* (4th ed.). Washington, DC: Author.

Asarnow, J. R. (1983). Children with peer adjustment problems: Sequential and non-sequential analyses of school behaviors. *Journal of Consulting and Clinical Psychology, 51*, 709–717.

Asendorpf, J. B. (1991). Development of inhibited children's coping with unfamiliarity. *Child Development, 62*, 1460–1474.

Asendorpf, J. B. (1993). Beyond temperament: A two-factorial coping model of the development of inhibition during childhood. In K. H. Rubin & J. B. Asendorpf (Eds.), *Social withdrawal, inhibition and shyness in childhood* (pp. 265–289). Hillsdale, NJ: Erlbaum.

Asher, S. R., & Dodge, K. A. (1986). Identifying children who are rejected by their peers. *Developmental Psychology, 22*, 444–449.

Asher, S. R., & Hymel, S. (1981). Children's social competence in peer relations: Sociometric and behavioral assessment. In J. D. Wine & M. D. Smye (Eds.), *Social competence* (pp. 122–157). New York: Guilford Press.

Asher, S. R., Hymel, S. & Renshaw, P. D. (1984). Loneliness in children. *Child Development, 55*, 1456–1464.

Asher, S. R., Parker, J. G., & Walker, D. L. (1993). Distinguishing friendship from acceptance: Implications for intervention and assessment. In W. M. Bukowski, A. F. Newcomb, & W. W. Hartup (Eds.), *The company they keep: Friendship during childhood and adolescence* (pp. 366–405). New York: Cambridge University Press.

Asher, S. R., Parkhurst, J. T., Hymel, S., & Williams, G. A. (1990). Peer rejection and loneliness in childhood. In S. R. Asher & J. D. Coie (Eds.), *Peer rejection in childhood*, (pp. 253–273). Cambridge, England: Cambridge University Press.

Asher, S. R., Singleton, L. C., Tinsley, B. R., & Hymel, S. (1979). A reliable sociometric measure for preschool children. *Developmental Psychology, 15*, 443–444.

Asher, S. R., & Wheeler, V. A. (1985). Children's loneliness: A comparison of rejected and neglected peer status. *Journal of Consulting and Clinical Psychology, 53*, 500–505.

Barkley, R. A. (1990). *Attention-Deficit Hyperactivity Disorder: A handbook for diagnosis and treatment*. New York: Guilford Press.

Baumrind, D. (1967). Child care practices anteceding three patterns of preschool behavior. *Genetic Psychology Monographs, 76*, 43–88.

Behar, L. B., & Stringfield, S. (1974). A behavior rating scale for the preschool child. *Developmental Psychology, 10*, 601–610.

Bell-Dolan, D. J., Foster, S. L., & Christopher, J. S. (1992). Children's reactions to participating in a peer relations study: An example of cost-effective assessment. *Child Study Journal, 22*(2), 137–155.

Bell-Dolan, D. J., Foster, S. L., & Sikora, D. M. (1989). Effects of sociometric testing on children's behavior and loneliness in school. *Developmental Psychology, 25*, 306–311.

Bell-Dolan, D. J., Foster, S. L., & Tishelman, A. (1989). An alternative to negative nomination sociometric measures. *Journal of Clinical Child Psychology, 18*(2), 153–157.

Berndt, T. J. (1982). The features and effects of friendship in early adolescence. *Child Development, 53*, 1447–1460.

Bierman, K. L. (1986). The relationship between social aggression and peer rejection in middle childhood. In R. Prinz (Ed.), *Advances in behav-*

ioral assessment of children and families (Vol. 2, pp. 151–178). Greenwich, CT: JAI Press.

Bierman, K. L. (1989). Improving the peer relationships of rejected children. In B. Lahey & A. Kazdin (Eds.), *Advances in clinical child psychology* (Vol. 6, pp. 53–84). New York: Plenum Press.

Bierman, K. L., & Furman, W. (1984). The effects of social skills training and peer involvement on the social adjustment of preadolescents. *Child Development*, 55, 151–162.

Bierman, K. L., & McCauley, E. (1987). Children's descriptions of their peer interactions: Useful information for clinical child assessment. *Journal of Clinical Child Psychology*, 16, 9–18.

Bierman, K. L., & Montminy, H. P. (1993). Developmental issues in social skills assessment and intervention with children and adolescents. *Behavior Modification*, 17, 229–254.

Bierman, K. L., & Smoot, D. L. (1991). Linking family characteristics with poor peer relations: The mediating role of conduct problems. *Journal of Abnormal Child Psychology*, 19, 341–356.

Bierman, K. L., Smoot, D. L., & Aumiller, K. (1993). Characteristics of aggressive–rejected, aggressive (nonrejected), and rejected (non-aggressive) boys. *Child Development*, 64, 139–151.

Bierman, K. L., & Wargo, J. (1995). Predicting the longitudinal course associated with aggressive–rejected, aggressive (non-rejected) and rejected (non-aggressive) status. *Development and Psychopathology*, 7, 669–682.

Boivin, M., & Begin, G. (1989). Peer status and self-perception among early elementary school children: The case of rejected children. *Child Development*, 60, 591–596.

Boivin, M., Dodge, K. A., & Coie, J. D. (1995). Individual–group behavioral similarity and peer status in experimental playgroups of boys: The social misfit revisited. *Journal of Personality and Social Psychology*, 69(2), 269–279.

Boivin, M., Hymel, S., & Bukowski, W. M. (1995). The roles of social withdrawal, peer rejection, and victimization by peers in predicting loneliness and depressed mood in childhood. *Development and Psychopathology*, 7, 765–785.

Boivin, M., Poulin, J., & Vitaro, F. (1994). Depressed mood and peer rejection in childhood. *Development and Psychopathology*, 6, 483–498.

Boivin, M., Thomassin, L., & Alain, M. (1989). Peer rejection and self-perceptions among early elementary school children: Aggressive-rejectees vs. withdrawn-rejectees. In B. H. Schneider, G. Attili, J. Nadel, & R. P. Weissberg (Eds.), *Social competence in developmental perspective* (pp. 392–394). Dordrecht, The Netherlands: Kluwer.

Bukowski, W., & Hoza, B. (1989). Popularity and friendship: Issues in theory, measurement and outcome. In T. J. Berndt & G. W. Ladd (Eds.), *Peer relationships in child development* (pp. 15–45). New York: Wiley.

Bukowski, W., Hoza, B., & Boivin, M. (1994). Measuring friendship quality during pre- and early adolescence: The development and psychometric properties of the Friendship Qualities Scale. *Journal of Social and Personal Relationships*, 11, 471–484.

Cairns, R. B., Neckerman, H. J., & Cairns, B. D. (1989). Social networks and the shadows of synchrony. In G. R. Adams, T. P. Gulotta, & R. Montemayor (Eds.), *Advances in adolescent development* (Vol. 1, pp. 275–305). Beverly Hills, CA: Sage.

Calkins, S. D., Fox, N. A., Rubin, K. H., Coplan, R. J., & Stewart, S. (1994). *Longitudinal outcomes of behavioral inhibition: Implications for behavior in a peer setting.* Unpublished manuscript, University of Maryland.

Caplan, M., Weissberg, R. P., Bersoff, D. M., Ezekowitz, W., & Wells, M. L. (1986). *The middle school Alternative Solutions Test (AST) scoring manual.* Unpublished manuscript.

Caspi, A., Elder, G. H., & Bem, D. J. (1988). Moving away from the world: Life-course patterns of shy children. *Developmental Psychology*, 24, 824–831.

Cicchetti, D., & Bukowski, W. M. (1995). Developmental processes in peer relations and psychopathology. *Development and Psychopathology*, 7, 587–589.

Cillessen, A. H. N., van Ijzendoorn, H. W., van Lieshout, C. F. M., & Hartup, W. W. (1992). Heterogeneity of peer rejected boys. *Child Development*, 63, 893–905.

Clark, L., Gresham, F. M., & Elliott, S. N. (1985). Development and validation of a social skills assessment measure: The TROSS-C. *Journal of Psychoeducational Assessment*, 3, 347–356.

Coie, J. D. (1990). Toward a theory of peer rejection. In S. R. Asher & J. D. Coie (Eds.), *Peer rejection in childhood* (pp. 365–401). Cambridge, England: Cambridge University Press.

Coie, J. D., & Dodge, K. A. (1983). Continuities and changes in children's social status: A five-year longitudinal study. *Merrill–Palmer Quarterly*, 29, 261–282.

Coie, J. D., & Dodge, K. A. (1988). Multiple sources of data on social behavior and social status in the school: A cross-age comparison. *Child Development*, 59, 815–829.

Coie, J. D., Dodge, K. A., & Coppotelli, H. (1982). Dimensions and types of status: A cross-age perspective. *Developmental Psychology*, 18, 557–570.

Coie, J. D., Dodge, K. A., & Kupersmidt, J. B. (1990). Peer group behavior and social status. In S. R. Asher & J. D. Coie (Eds.), *Peer rejection in childhood* (pp. 17–59). Cambridge, England: Cambridge University Press.

Coie, J. D., & Koeppl, G. K. (1990). Adapting intervention to the problems of aggressive and disruptive children. In S. R. Asher & J. D. Coie (Eds.),

Peer rejection in childhood (pp. 275–308). Cambridge, England: Cambridge University Press.

Coie, J. D., & Kupersmidt, J. B. (1983). A behavior analysis of emerging social status in boys' groups. *Child Development, 54,* 1400–1416.

Coie, J. D., & Lenox, K. F. (1994). The development of antisocial individuals. In D. Fowles, P. Sutker, & S. Goodman (Eds.), *Psychopathy and antisocial personality: A developmental perspective* (pp. 45–72). New York: Springer.

Coie, J. D., Terry, R., Lenox, K., Lochman, J., & Hyman, C. (1996). Childhood peer rejection and aggression as predictors of stable patterns of adolescent disorder. *Development and Psychopathology, 7,* 697–713.

Connelly, J., & Doyle, A. (1981). Assessment of social competence in preschoolers: Teachers versus peers. *Developmental Psychology, 17,* 454–462.

Coplan, R. J., Rubin, K. H., Fox, N. A., Calkins, S. D., & Stewart, S. L. (1994). Being alone, playing alone, and acting alone: Distinguishing among reticence and passive and active solitude in young children. *Child Development, 65,* 129–137.

Cowen, E. L., Pederson, A., Babigian, H., Izzo, L. D., & Trost, M. A. (1973). Long-term follow up of early detected vulnerable children. *Journal of Consulting and Clinical Psychology, 41,* 438–446.

Crick, N. R., & Dodge, K. A. (1994). A review and reformulation of social information-processing mechanisms in children's social adjustment. *Psychological Bulletin, 115,* 74–101.

Crick, N. R., & Grotpeter, J. K. (1995). Relational aggression, gender, and social-psychological aggression. *Child Development, 66,* 710–722.

Crick, N. R., & Ladd, G. W. (1990). Children's perceptions of the outcomes of aggressive strategies: Do the ends justify being mean? *Developmental Psychology, 26,* 612–620.

Deluty, R. H. (1981). Alternative thinking ability of aggressive, assertive and submissive children. *Cognitive Therapy and Research, 5,* 309–312.

Dishion, T. J. (1990). The family ecology of boys' peer relations in middle childhood. *Child Development, 61,* 874–892.

Dishion, T. J., Andrews, D. W., & Crosby, L. (1995). Antisocial boys and their friends in early adolescence: Relationship characteristics, quality and interactional process. *Child Development, 66,* 139–151.

Dishion, T. J., & Skinner, M. (1989, April). *A process model for the role of peer relations in adolescent social adjustment.* Paper presented at the biennial meeting of the Society for Research in Child Development, Kansas City, MO.

Dobkin, P. L., Tremblay, R. E., Masse, L. C., & Vitaro, F. (1995). Individual and peer characteristics in predicting boys' early onset of substance abuse: A seven year longitudinal study. *Child Development, 66,* 1198–1214.

Dodge, K. A. (1983). Behavioral antecedents of peer status. *Child Development, 51,* 162–170.

Dodge, K. A. (1985). Attributional bias in aggressive children. In P. C. Kendall (Ed.), *Advances in cognitive and behavioral research and therapy* (Vol. 4, pp. 73–110). San Diego, CA: Academic Press.

Dodge, K. A. (1989). Problems in social relationships. In E. Mash & R. Barkley (Eds.), *Treatment of childhood disorders* (pp. 222–244). New York: Guilford Press.

Dodge, K. A. (1993, March). *Social information processing and peer rejection factors in the development of behavior problems in children.* Paper presented at the biennial meeting of the Society for Research in Child Development, New Orleans.

Dodge, K. A., Asher, S. R., & Parkhurst, J. T. (1989). Social life as a goal coordination task. In C. Ames & R. Ames (Eds.), *Research on motivation in education* (Vol. 3, pp. 107–135). San Diego, CA: Academic Press.

Dodge, K. A., Bates, J. E., & Pettit, G. S. (1990). Mechanisms in the cycle of violence. *Science, 250,* 1678–1683.

Dodge, K. A., & Coie, J. D. (1987). Social information-processing factors in reactive and proactive aggression in children's playgroups. *Journal of Personality and Social Psychology, 53,* 1146–1158.

Dodge, K. A., McClaskey, C. L., & Feldman, E. (1985). A situational approach to assessment of social competence in children. *Journal of Consulting and Clinical Psychology, 53,* 344–353.

Dodge, K. A., & Murphy, R. R. (1984). The assessment of social competence in adolescents. *Advances in Child Behavior Analysis and Therapy, 3,* 61–96.

Dodge, K. A., Murphy, R. R., & Buchsbaum, K. (1984). The assessment of intention-cue detection skills in children: Implications for developmental psychopathology. *Child Development, 55,* 163–173.

Dodge, K. A., Pettit, G. S., McClaskey, C. L., & Brown, M. M. (1986). Social competence in children. *Monographs of the Society for Research in Child Development, 51*(2, Serial No. 213).

Eder, D., & Hallinan, M. T. (1978). Sex differences in children's friendships. *American Sociological Review, 43,* 237–250.

Elliot, S., Huizinga, D., & Menard, S. (1989). *Multiple problem youth.* New York: Springer-Verlag.

Engfer, A. (1993). Antecedents and consequences of shyness in boys and girls: A 6-year longitudinal study. In K. H. Rubin & J. Asendorpf (Eds.), *Social withdrawal, inhibition and shyness in childhood* (pp. 49–80). Hillsdale, NJ: Erlbaum.

Foster, S. L., Bell-Dolan, D., & Berler, E. S. (1986). Methodological issues in the use of sociometrics for selecting children for social skills research training. *Advances in Behavioral Assessment of Children and Families, 2,* 227–248.

Foster, S. L., & Ritchey, W. L. (1985). Behavioral correlates of sociometric status of fourth, fifth and sixth grade children in two classroom situations. *Behavioral Assessment, 7,* 79–93.

French, D. C. (1988). Heterogeneity of peer rejected boys: Aggressive and nonaggressive subtypes. *Child Development, 59,* 976–985.

French, D. C. (1990). Heterogeneity of peer rejected girls. *Child Development, 61,* 2028–2031.

French, D. C., Conrad, J., & Turner, T. M. (1995). Adjustment of antisocial and nonantisocial adolescents. *Development and Psychopathology, 7,* 857–874.

French, D. C., & Waas, G. A. (1985). Behavior problems of peer-neglected and peer-rejected elementary-age children: Parent and teacher perspectives. *Child Development, 56,* 246–252.

Furman, W., & Bierman, K. L. (1984). Perceived determinants of friendship: A multidimensional study of developmental changes. *Developmental Psychology, 20,* 925–931.

Furman, W., & Buhrmester, D. (1992). Age and sex differences in perceptions of networks of personal relationships. *Child Development, 63,* 103–115.

Furman, W., & Robbins, P. (1985). What's the point?: Selection of treatment objectives. In B. Schneider, K. H. Rubin, & J. E. Ledingham (Eds.), *Children's peer relations: Issues in assessment and intervention* (pp. 41–54). New York: Springer-Verlag.

Geraci, R. L., & Asher, S. R. (1980). *Social knowledge interview materials for elementary school children.* Champaign: Bureau of Educational Research, University of Illinois.

Glow, R. A., & Glow, P. H. (1980). Peer and self-rating: Children's perception of behavior relevant to hyperkinetic impulse disorder. *Journal of Abnormal Child Psychology, 8,* 397–404.

Graham, P., & Rutter, M. (1968). The reliability and validity of the psychiatric assessment of the child: II. Interview with the parent. *British Journal of Psychiatry, 114,* 581–592.

Greenberg, M. T., Kusche, C. A., & Speltz, M. (1991). Emotional regulation, self-control, and psychopathology: The role of relationships in early childhood. In D. Cicchetti & S. L. Toth (Eds.), *Rochester Symposium on Developmental Psychopathology: Vol. 2. Internalizing and externalizing expressions of dysfunction* (pp. 21–55). Hillsdale, NJ: Erlbaum.

Gresham, F. M., Elliott, S. N., & Black, F. L. (1987). Factor structure replication and bias in the investigation of the Teacher Rating of Social Skills. *Journal of School Psychology, 25,* 81–92.

Harter, S. (1982). The Perceived Competence Scale for Children. *Child Development, 53,* 87–97.

Harter, S., & Pike, R. (1984). The Pictorial Scale of Perceived Competence and Social Acceptance for Young Children. *Child Development, 55,* 1969–1982.

Hartup, W. W. (1983). The peer system. In E. M. Hetherington (Vol. Ed.), *Handbook of child psychology* (4th ed.): *Vol. 4. Socialization, personality and social development* (pp. 103–196). New York: Wiley.

Hartup, W. W. (1989). Social relationships and their developmental significance. *American Psychologist, 44*(2), 120–126.

Hartup, W. W., & Laursen, B. (1989, March). *Contextual constraints and children's friendship relations.* Paper presented at the biennial meeting of the Society for Research in Child Development, Kansas City, MO.

Hayvren, M., & Hymel, S. (1984). Ethical issues in sociometric testing: The impact of sociometric measures on interaction behavior. *Developmental Psychology, 20,* 844–849.

Hightower, A. D., Work, W. C., Cowen, E. L., Lotyczewski, B. S., Spinell, A. P., Guare, J. C., & Rohrbeck, C. A. (1986). The Teacher–Child Rating Scale: A brief objective measure of elementary school children's school problem behaviors and competencies. *School Psychology Review, 15,* 393–409.

Hinshaw, S. P. (1994). *Attention deficits and hyperactivity in children.* Thousand Oaks, CA: Sage.

Ho, D. V., & Kang, T. K. (1984). Intergenerational comparisons of child rearing attitudes and practices in Hong Kong. *Developmental Psychology, 20,* 1004–1016.

Hoza, B., Molina, B. S. G., Bukowski, W. M., & Sippola, L. R. (1995). Peer variables as predictors of later childhood adjustment. *Development and Psychopathology, 7,* 782–802.

Hymel, S., & Franke, S. (1985). Children's peer relations: Assessing self-perceptions. In B. H. Schneider, K. H. Rubin, & J. E. Ledingham (Eds.), *Children's peer relations: Issues in assessment and intervention* (pp. 75–91). New York: Springer-Verlag.

Hymel, S., & Rubin, K. (1985). Children with peer relationship and social skills problems: Conceptual, methodological and developmental issues. In G. J. Whitehurst (Ed.), *Annals of child development* (Vol. 2, pp. 251–297). Greenwich, CT: JAI Press.

Hymel, S., Wagner, E., & Butler, E. J. (1990). Reputational bias: View from the peer group. In S. R. Asher & J. D. Coie (Eds.), *Peer rejection in childhood* (pp. 156–186). Cambridge, England: Cambridge University Press.

Jacobvitz, D., & Sroufe, L. A. (1987). The early caregiver–child relationship and Attention Deficit Disorder with Hyperactivity in kindergarten: A prospective study. *Child Development, 58,* 1496–1504.

Kellam, S. G., Werthamer-Larsson, L., Dolan, L. J., Brown, C. H., Mayer, L. S., Rebok, G. W., Anthony, J. C., Laudolff, J., Edelsohn, G., & Wheeler, L. (1991). Developmental epidemiologically based prevention trials: Baseline modeling of early target behaviors and depressive symptoms. *American Journal of Community Psychology, 19,* 563–584.

King, A. Y. C., & Bond, M. H. (1985). The confucian paradigm of man: A sociological review. In W. S. Tseng & D. Y. H. Wu (Eds.), *Chinese culture and mental health* (pp. 29–45). New York: Academic Press.

Kistner, J., Metzler, A., Gatlin, D., & Risi, S. (1993). Classroom racial proportions and children's peer relations: Race and gender effects. *Journal of Educational Psychology, 85,* 446–452.

Kupersmidt, J. B., Burchinal, M., & Patterson, C. J. (1995). Developmental patterns of childhood peer relations as predictors of externalizing behavior problems. *Development and Psychopathology, 7,* 825–843.

Kupersmidt, J. B., & Coie, J. D. (1990). Preadolescent peer status, aggression, and school adjustment as predictors of externalizing problems in adolescence. *Child Development, 61,* 1350–1362.

Kupersmidt, J. B., Coie, J. D., & Dodge, K. A. (1990). The role of poor peer relationships in the development of disorder. In S. R. Asher & J. D. Coie (Eds.), *Peer rejection in childhood* (pp. 274–305). Cambridge, England: Cambridge University Press.

Ladd, G. W. (1983). Social networks of popular, average and rejected children in school settings. *Merrill–Palmer Quarterly, 29,* 282–307.

Ladd, G. W., & Hart, C. H. (1992). Creating informal play opportunities: Are parents' and preschoolers' initiations related to children's competence with peers? *Developmental Psychology, 28,* 1179–1187.

Ladd, G. W., & Mars, K. T. (1986). Reliability and validity of preschoolers' perceptions of peer behavior. *Journal of Clinical Psychology, 15,* 16–25.

LaGreca, A. M., Dandes, S. K., Wick, P., Shaw, K., & Stone, W. L. (1988). Development of the Social Anxiety Scale for Children: Reliability and concurrent validity. *Journal of Clinical Child Psychology, 17,* 84–91.

Landau, S., Milich, R., & Whitten, P. (1984). A comparison of teacher and peer assessment of social status. *Journal of Clinical Child Psychology, 13,* 44–49.

Laursen, B. (1993). Conflict management among close peers. In B. Laursen (Ed.), *Close friendships in adolescence* (pp. 39–54). San Francisco: Jossey-Bass.

Ledingham, J. E. (1981). Developmental patterns of aggressive and withdrawn behavior in childhood: A possible method for identifying preschizophrenics. *Journal of Abnormal Child Psychology, 9,* 1–22.

Ledingham, J. E., Younger, A. S., Schwartzman, A. E., & Bergeron, G. (1982). Agreement among teacher, peer, and self ratings of children's aggression, withdrawal, and likability. *Journal of Abnormal Child Psychology, 10,* 363–372.

Lochman, J. E. (1987). Self and peer perceptions and attributional biases of aggressive and nonaggressive boys in dyadic interactions. *Journal of Consulting and Clinical Psychology, 55,* 404–410.

Masten, A. S., Morrison, P., & Pelligrini, D. (1985). A Revised Class Play method of peer assessment. *Developmental Psychology, 21,* 523–533.

Matson, J. L., Rotatori, A. F., & Helsel, W. J. (1983). Development of a rating scale to measure social skills in children: The Matson Evaluation of Social Skills with Youngsters (MESSY). *Behaviour Research and Therapy, 21,* 335–340.

Morrison, P., & Masten, A. S. (1991). Peer reputation in middle childhood as a predictor of adaptation in adolescence: A seven-year follow up. *Child Development, 62,* 991–1007.

O'Brien, S. F., & Bierman, K. L. (1988). Conceptions and perceived influence of peer groups: Interviews with preadolescents and adolescents. *Child Development, 59,* 1360–1365.

Olweus, D. (1993). Victimization by peers: Antecedents and long-term outcomes. In K. H. Rubin & J. B. Asendorpf (Eds.), *Social withdrawal, inhibition and shyness in childhood* (pp. 315–344). Hillsdale, NJ: Erlbaum.

Ostermann, K., Bjorkvist, K., Lagerspetz, K. M., & Kaukianen, A. (1994). Peer and self estimated aggression and victimization from five ethnic groups. *Aggressive Behavior, 20,* 411–428.

Osterweil, Z., & Nagano-Nakamura, K. (1992). Maternal views on aggression: Japan and Israel. *Aggressive Behavior, 18,* 263–270.

Parke, R. D., & Ladd, G. W. (1992). *Family–peer relationships: Modes of linkage.* Hillsdale, NJ: Erlbaum.

Parker, J. G., & Asher, S. R. (1987). Peer acceptance and later personal adjustment: Are low-accepted children at risk? *Psychological Bulletin, 102,* 357–389.

Parker, J. G., & Asher, S. R. (1993). Beyond group acceptance: Friendship adjustment and friendship quality as distinct dimensions of children's peer adjustment. In D. Perlman & W. H. Jones (Eds.), *Advances in personal relationships* (Vol. 4, pp. 261–294). London: Kingsley.

Parker, J. G., Rubin, K. H., Price, J. M., & DeRosier, M. E. (1995). Peer relationships, child development, and adjustment: A developmental psychopathology perspective. In D. Cicchetti & D. Cohen (Eds.), *Developmental psychopathology: Vol. 2. Risk, disorder and adaptation* (pp. 96–161). New York: Wiley.

Parkhurst, J. T., & Asher, S. R. (1992). Peer rejection in middle school: Subgroup differences in behavior, loneliness, and interpersonal concerns. *Developmental Psychology, 28,* 231–241.

Patterson, G. R. (1982). *Coercive family process.* Eugene, OR: Castalia.

Patterson, G. R. (1986). Performance models for antisocial boys. *American Psychologist, 41*(4), 432–444.

Patterson, G. R., Littman, R. A., & Bricker, W. (1967). Assertive behavior in children: A step toward a theory of aggression. *Monographs of the Society for Research in Child Development, 32*(5, Serial No. 18b).

Patterson, G. R., & Stouthamer-Loeber, M. (1984). The correlation of family management practices and delinquency. *Child Development, 55,* 1299–1307.

Pekarik, E. G., Prinz, R. J., Liebert, D. E., Weintraub, S., & Neale, J. M. (1976). The Pupil Evaluation Inventory: A sociometric technique for assessing children's social behavior. *Journal of Abnormal Child Psychology, 14,* 83–97.

Perry, D. G., Kusel, S. J., & Perry, L. C. (1988). Victims of peer aggression. *Developmental Psychology, 24,* 807–814.

Perry, D. G., Perry, L. C., & Rasmussen, P. (1986). Cognitive social learning mediators of aggression. *Child Development, 57,* 700–711.

Pettit, G. S., & Mize, J. (1993). Substance and style: Understanding the ways in which parents teach children about social relationships. In S. Duck (Ed.), *Learning about relationships* (pp. 118–151). Newbury Park, CA: Sage.

Pope, A. W., Bierman, K. L., & Mumma, G. H. (1989). Relations between hyperactive and aggressive behavior and peer relations at three elementary grade levels. *Journal of Abnormal Child Psychology, 3,* 253–267.

Powless, D. L., & Elliott, S. N. (1987). Assessment of social skills of Native American preschoolers: Teachers' and parents' ratings. *Journal of School Psychology, 31,* 293–307.

Putallaz, M. (1983). Predicting children's sociometric status from their behavior. *Child Development, 54,* 1417–1426.

Putallaz, M., Costanzo, P. R., & Smith, R. B. (1991). Maternal recollections of childhood peer relationships: Implications for their children's social competence. *Journal of Social and Personal Relationships, 8,* 403–422.

Putallaz, M., & Heflin, A. H. (1990). Parent–child interaction. In S. R. Asher & J. D. Coie (Eds.), *Peer rejection in childhood* (pp. 189–216). Cambridge, England: Cambridge University Press.

Reid, M., Landesman, S., Treder, R., & Jaccard, J. (1989). "My family and friends": Six- to twelve-year-old children's perceptions of social support. *Child Development, 60,* 896–910.

Roistacher, R. C. (1974). A microeconomic model of sociometric choice. *Sociometry, 37,* 219–238.

Rubin, K. H. (1982). Social and social-cognitive developmental characteristics of young isolate, normal, and sociable children. In K. H. Rubin & H. S. Ross (Eds.), *Peer relationships and social skills in childhood* (pp. 353–374). New York: Springer-Verlag.

Rubin, K. H. (1993). The Waterloo Longitudinal Project: Correlates and consequences of social withdrawal from childhood to adolescence. In K. H. Rubin & J. Asendorpf (Eds.), *Social with-* *drawal, inhibition and shyness in childhood* (pp. 291–314). Hillsdale, NJ: Erlbaum.

Rubin, K. H., & Asendorpf, J. (Eds.). (1993). *Social withdrawal, inhibition, and shyness in childhood.* Hillsdale, NJ: Erlbaum.

Rubin, K. H., Coplan, R. J., Fox, N. A., & Calkins, S. D. (1995). Emotionality, emotion regulation, and preschoolers' social adaptation. *Development and Psychopathology, 7,* 49–62.

Rubin, K. H., Hymel, S., LeMare, L., & Rowden, L. (1989). Children experiencing social difficulties: Sociometric neglect reconsidered. *Canadian Journal of Behavioural Science, 21,* 94–111.

Rubin, K. H., & Krasnor, L. R. (1986). Social cognitive and social behavioral perspectives on problem solving. In M. Perlmutter (Ed.), *Minnesota Symposia on Child Psychopathology* (Vol. 18, pp. 1–68). Hillsdale, NJ: Erlbaum.

Rubin, K. H., & Stewart, S. L. (1996). Social withdrawal. In E. J. Mash & R. A. Barkley (Eds.), *Child psychopathology* (pp. 277–310). New York: Guilford Press.

Schwartzman, A. E., Ledingham, J. E., & Serbin, L. (1985). Identification of children at risk for adult schizophrenia: A longitudinal study. *International Review of Applied Psychology, 34,* 363–380.

Sharabany, R. (1994). Intimate Friendship Scale: Conceptual underpinnings, psychometric properties and construct validity. *Journal of Social and Personal Relationships, 11,* 449–469.

Stewart, S. L., & Rubin, K. H. (1995). The social problem solving of anxious–withdrawn children. *Development and Psychopathology, 7,* 323–336.

Stormshak, E. A., Bellanti, C. J., Bierman, K. L., & the Conduct Problems Prevention Research Group. (1996). The quality of sibling relationships and the development of social competence and behavioral control in aggressive children. *Developmental Psychology, 32,* 1–11.

Stormshak, E. A., Bierman, K. L., Bruschi, C., Dodge, K. A., Coie, J. D. & the Conduct Problems Prevention Research Group. (1995). *The relation between behavior problems and peer preference in different classroom contexts.* Unpublished manuscript.

Strain, P. S., Lambert, D. L., Kerr, M. M., Stagg, V., & Lenkner, D. A. (1983). Naturalistic assessment of children's compliance to teachers' requests and consequences for compliance. *Journal of Applied Behavior Analysis, 16,* 243–249.

Strain, P. S., Steele, P., Ellis, R., & Timm, M. A. (1982). Long term effects of oppositional child treatment with mothers as therapists and therapist trainers. *Journal of Applied Behavior Analysis, 15,* 163–169.

Sullivan, H. S. (1953). *The interpersonal theory of psychiatry.* New York: Norton.

Tremblay, R. E., Masse, L. C., Vitaro, F., & Dobkin, P. L. (1995). The impact of friends' deviant behavior on early onset of delinquency: Longitudinal data from 6 to 13 years of age. *Development and Psychopathology, 7,* 649–688.

Tversky, A. (1977). Features of similarity. *Psychological Review, 84,* 327–352.

Walker, H. M. (1983). *Walker Problem Behavior Identification Checklist: Test and manual* (2nd ed.). Los Angeles: Western Psychological Services.

Walker, H. M., & McConnell, S. (1988). *Scale of Social Competence and School Adjustment.* Austin, TX: Pro-Ed.

Williams, G. A., & Asher, S. R. (1987, April). *Peer and self perceptions of peer rejected children: Issues in classification and subgrouping.* Paper presented at the biennial meeting of the Society for Research in Child Development, Baltimore.

Wright, J. C., Giammarino, M., & Parad, H. W. (1986). Social status in small groups: Individual–group similarity and the social misfit. *Journal of Personality and Social Psychology, 50,* 523–536.

Younger, A. J., Schwartzman, A. E., & Ledingham, J. E. (1986). Age-related differences in children's perceptions of social deviance: Changes in behavior or in perspective? *Developmental Psychology, 22,* 531–542.

Part IV

DEVELOPMENTAL AND HEALTH-RELATED DISORDERS

Chapter Seven

MENTAL RETARDATION

Benjamin L. Handen

The field of mental retardation has gone through a number of significant changes during the latter half of the 20th century. For example, there has been a major movement over the last 30 years to deinstitutionalize residents of state schools for individuals with mental retardation. Today, a significant number of such institutions have closed, and it is the exception rather than the rule that a child or adult with mental retardation is referred to such a setting. In addition, an important group of laws guaranteeing education for children with mental retardation has been enacted. These began with the Education for All Handicapped Children Act of 1975 (Public Law 94-142) in which the concepts of "normalization" and "least restrictive environment" were stressed. Other laws, such as Public Law 99-457 (Education of the Handicapped Act Amendments) in 1986, recognized the need for comprehensive early intervention services and enhanced educational services for infants and young children with disabilities (including mental retardation). And most recently, there has been a growing movement to include children with mental retardation in U.S. schools and communities, as called for by the Individuals with Disabilities Education Act of 1990 (formerly known as the Education for All Handicapped Children Act). This is exemplified by the full-time inclusion of children with mental retardation in classrooms with typically developing peers.

With such significant changes in the field, assessing children with mental retardation has become ever more challenging. It requires a knowledge of the service delivery system; familiarity with etiological and developmental issues; the ability to work with families; experience in using and adapting standardized assessment tools; an understanding of the legal rights of children and their families; a knowledge of the best clinical practices

for intervention; and an appreciation of the history of treatment of children with mental retardation. The purpose of the present chapter is to present guidelines for the assessment of children with mental retardation—guidelines that take into account the rapidly changing service delivery system.

HISTORY

The lot of individuals with mental retardation and other disabilities has changed considerably during the past 200 years (Wolfensberger, 1969; Zigler & Hodapp, 1986). Perhaps the most significant changes in the field of mental retardation in the United States began in the middle of the 19th century. Motivated in part by the work of Edouard Seguin in France, some U.S. educators came to believe that individuals with a variety of handicapping conditions could be taught if provided appropriate training. As a result, a number of schools for children and adults with mental retardation (as well as training centers for individuals who were deaf, blind, or mentally ill) were established. These early institutions were based on the principle of "moral education"—that is, the assumption that through education, individuals with mental retardation could be elevated to a level of normal human existence. However, within a few decades it became apparent that this experiment had been a failure, and that only a small percentage of individuals with mental retardation had been successfully returned to society and independent living situations. Gradually, institutions began to change in character, serving less of an educational and more of a custodial purpose as a means of protecting individuals with mental retardation from society (Wolfensberger, 1969).

With the publication of Galton's (1952) work on genius across British families, Dugdale's (1910) study of the Juke family, and Goddard's (1913) study of the Kallikaks, the role of genetic heredity in intelligence became generally accepted. Related studies reported that adults with mental retardation had higher-than-expected rates of illegitimacy, criminality, and poverty (see Baumeister, 1970). At about this same time, intelligence testing was introduced to the United States by Henry Goddard (whose work was based upon that of Alfred Binet in France); it quickly gained popularity. Repeated testing by Goddard of individuals with mental retardation who resided at the Training School in Vineland, New Jersey, found little improvement in intellectual functioning over time (see Zigler & Hodapp, 1986). Institutions gradually became larger and greater in number and were placed further from urban areas. The role of the institution changed as well, to that of protecting society from individuals with mental retardation. As public fears grew, the first eugenics laws were passed in the early part of the 20th century, requiring the forced sterilizations of men and women with mental retardation. By 1936, 25 states had passed such laws (see Zigler & Hodapp, 1986). With the exception of a few experiments in the provision of community services, the numbers of institutions and of individuals residing in them grew steadily until the 1960s. In fact, as recently as 30 years ago, pediatricians commonly suggested to parents of newborn infants with Down syndrome or other developmental disabilities that they place their children in institutions as soon as possible.

The deinstitutionalization movement began in earnest in the 1960s; it stemmed in large part from four events or trends, according to Zigler and Hodapp (1986). First, a number of individuals made public the deplorable conditions in some U.S. institutions. For example, the book *Christmas in Purgatory* (Blatt & Kaplan, 1966) provided pictorial evidence of how residents were treated at several of these institutions; the subject also received increased attention from the news media (e.g., a television exposé of the Willowbrook facility in Staten Island, New York, by Geraldo Rivera). Second, the National Association for Retarded Citizens began to mount political pressure to change institutions. Third was the development of the principle of "normalization"—that is, the idea that individuals with mental retardation have the right to as normal a life style as possible. Finally, the Education for All Handicapped Children Act of 1975 was enacted. In addition to stressing the doctrine of the "least restrictive environment," it mandated "a free appropriate public education" as a right for all children, regardless of level of impairment or disability. All children were to be placed in the "least restrictive" school environment and provided with an individualized education program (IEP).

Like any other social reform movement, the deinstitutionalization movement began with grand hopes and plans. However, the shifting of funds to community programming did not always follow the closing of large institutions. Yet, despite such funding difficulties, a strong continuum of services for children with developmental disabilities and/or mental retardation exists today—from early intervention programs for infants, to developmental preschool programs, to special education programs in regular public schools, to full-inclusion programs. The goal of today's service providers is to include all children within the community in the least restrictive setting.

The enactment of laws affecting individuals with disabilities has significantly influenced assessment practices, as have changes in the service provision model. For example, with the enactment of Public Laws 94-142 and 99-457, families have been given a more central role in the assessment and decision-making process. In addition, with the advent of IEPs, children and adolescents with disabilities must receive programming designed to meet their individual needs, instead of simply being fitted into existing programs or services. Consequently, an assessment must focus upon identifying a child's or adolescent's strengths and deficits so that appropriate services can be recommended. As will be discussed below, the most recent definition of mental retardation (American Association on Mental Retardation [AAMR], 1992) is more functionally based. This new model for assessment not only addresses diagnostic issues, but focuses upon identifying needs in up to 10 adaptive areas, examining psychological/emotional concerns, and considering physical/health/etiological issues that may influence the types of services required. The assessment product is a profile of specific supports needed to address each area of weakness.

DEFINITIONS

"Mental retardation" refers to a particular state of functioning beginning prior to age 18, in which limitations in intelligence coexist with deficits in adaptive skills (AAMR, 1992). Although deficits in intellectual functioning may be related to a specific etiology (e.g., Down syndrome, fragile-X syndrome), mental retardation is not always synonymous with that etiology. In other words, every individual with a condition commonly associated with mental retardation does not necessarily have a diagnosis of mental retardation.

The definition of mental retardation has been revised a number of times during the past few decades, in response to advances in our understanding of the disorder as well as to various consumer, professional, political, and social forces. Even now, there is some controversy over the definition and diagnosis of mental retardation (MacMillan, Gresham, & Siperstein, 1995). Yet, without an agreed-upon definition of mental retardation, it is difficult for professionals to fully understand the nature of this disorder or for significant gains to be made in improving the lives of children and adults with the disorder (Zigler & Hodapp, 1986). The confusion in this area can be illustrated by examining the changes in the definition of mental retardation that have been adopted by the AAMR (previously known as the American Association on Mental Deficiency, or AAMD) during the past 35 years.

In 1959, the AAMD definition of mental retardation specified that individuals with IQ scores 1 standard deviation or more below the mean of 100 were to be considered to have mental retardation (Heber, 1959). With most IQ tests having a mean of 100 and a standard deviation of 15–16 points, this placed a significant portion of the population (up to 16%, or 32 million people) in this group. The cutoff was amended in 1973 to 2 standard deviations below the mean (i.e., IQ below 70), thereby lowering the incidence of mental retardation to about 3%, or 6 million individuals. The subsequent 1983 revision of the AAMD definition reads as follows: "Mental retardation refers to significantly subaverage intellectual functioning resulting in or associated with impairments in adaptive behavior and manifested during the developmental period" (Grossman, 1983, p. 11). This definition involved three specific factors: (1) an IQ below 70, (2) associated adaptive deficits, and (3) deficits occurring prior to age 18. Although this revision represented an improvement over earlier attempts to define mental retardation, it also placed greater emphasis than did prior definitions on associated deficits in adaptive functioning. This created some difficulties, because few if any reliable and valid measures of adaptive functioning were available at the time, and there was little agreement on either how to define or

how to assess adaptive behavior (Zigler & Hodapp, 1986).

However, basing a diagnosis of mental retardation on an IQ score alone was not without its problems. For example, the past two decades have seen much criticism of the use of intelligence tests for school placement purposes, because of concerns that such tests are biased against certain minorities (e.g., Hawkins & Cooper, 1990). Therefore, using a score on an IQ test as the sole factor in defining mental retardation may have resulted in a greater number of children from minority groups being diagnosed with mental retardation and placed in special education classes. Such concerns were reflected in a 1974 court decision in California (*Larry P. v. Riles*, 1974), in which the use of IQ tests for purposes of special education placement by California school districts was eliminated.

In 1992, the AAMR proposed and adopted a new definition, which reads as follows:

> Mental retardation refers to substantial limitations in present functioning. It is characterized by significantly subaverage intellectual functioning, existing concurrently with related limitations in two or more of the following applicable adaptive skills areas: communication, self-care, home living, social skills, community use, self-direction, health and safety, functional academics, leisure, and work. Mental retardation manifests before age 18. (p. 5)

The following four assumptions are considered essential to the application of the definition:

1. Valid assessment considers cultural and linguistic diversity as well as differences in communication and behavioral factors;
2. The existence of limitations in adaptive skills occurs within the context of community environments typical of the individual's age peers and is indexed to the person's individualized needs for supports;
3. Specific adaptive limitations often coexist with strengths in other adaptive skills or other personal capabilities; and
4. With appropriate supports over a sustained period, the life functioning of the person with mental retardation will generally improve. (AAMR, 1992, p. 5)

This newest definition stresses the importance of functioning, as well as the interaction between the person, the environment, and the level of needed support. In addition to the revised definition, the AAMR has proposed a three-step process for the assessment of mental retardation: (1) diagnosis of mental retardation, to determine the eligibility for supports; (2) classification and description, to identify strengths and weaknesses and the need for supports; and (3) identification of the profile and intensities of needed supports. Therefore, in addition to diagnosis, a thorough assessment should include a description of the level of support an individual requires.

Two aspects of the AAMR's new definition remain controversial. First, the IQ range has once again been changed, this time to "an IQ standard score of approximately 70 to 75 or below" (AAMR, 1992, p. 5). The second concern about this new definition is the requirement that up to 10 areas of adaptive functioning be assessed. Unfortunately, the availability of valid and reliable tests of adaptive behavior has changed little since the early 1980s. In fact, there are no agreed-upon parameters for assessing adaptive behavior in a number of the areas mentioned in the AAMR definition (MacMillan et al., 1995). Finally, the AAMR has eliminated the previously used classification system, which divides individuals with mental retardation into four categories based upon the level of cognitive functioning—a change that is discussed in the following section.

CLASSIFICATION

A number of ways to classify children with mental retardation have been developed during the past few decades. Such systems are clearly required because of the heterogeneous makeup of this group of individuals, and they serve a number of purposes. Most importantly, they serve as a means of determining the level and intensity of services required by different individuals, as well as of examining long-term prognosis and treatment outcome. The two most common means of classification are categorization by functional ability and by etiology. In some respects, these two systems overlap considerably.

Different professional groups have tended to develop their own classification systems. For example, the AAMR has recently adopted a system based upon the level of support needed ("intermittent," "limited," "extensive," or "pervasive"). Conversely, the profession of psychiatry has retained levels of cognitive functioning to describe individuals with mental retardation (i.e., "mild," "moderate," "severe," or "profound" mental retardation), although it has accepted the 1992 AAMR definition of the disorder in the most recent revision of the *Diagnostic and Statistical Manual of Mental Disorders* (DSM-IV; American Psychiatric Association [APA], 1994). Educators have a separate system of classification, based upon IQ level with associated deficits in adaptive functioning (see, e.g., Special Education Services and Programs, 1990; West Virginia Department of Education, 1985). Consequently, it is important that clinicians who assess children with mental retardation both understand the different classification systems and be able to move comfortably among them, depending upon the agencies with which they are communicating.

The 1973 and 1983 AAMD definitions of mental retardation divided severity of disability into four categories (mild, moderate, severe, and profound); this classification system is still widely accepted and used (e.g., by the APA; see Table 7.1). Children who function within the mild range of mental retardation account for approximately 89% of children diagnosed with the disorder. This group of children has also been classified within many educational systems as "educable mentally retarded" (EMR). Most children with mild mental retardation can be expected to succeed within an academic curriculum, although most will remain below their typically developing peers in terms of reading and arithmetic levels. Many of these children can participate in vocational training, succeed in competitive employment, and live independent and self-supporting lives. Children with moderate mental retardation make up approximately 6% of children with the disorder; this group has been labeled as "trainable mentally retarded" (TMR) within many educational systems. Curriculum for these individuals often focuses on life skills and functional academics. With proper vocational training and community support, individuals with moderate mental retardation may be able to function in competitive or semi-competitive employment situations. Children with severe mental retardation make up approximately 3.5% of the population of children with the disorder. This group of individuals typically has less extensive communicative and social skills. A more basic, functional curriculum is often provided, with emphasis on life and self-help skills. Finally, fewer than 1.5% of children with mental retardation fall into the category of profound mental retardation. These children tend to develop very limited communicative and self-help skills.

The descriptions above of the levels of academic and social development that might be expected on the basis of cognitive level are provided with some hesitation. The limits placed on individuals with mental retardation and other handicapping conditions are constantly being pushed. In

TABLE 7.1. Classification of Mental Retardation

Level of mental retardation (APA, 1994)	Educational classification	Support required (AAMR, 1992)[a]	IQ range	Percentage of persons with mental retardation
Mild	Educable	Intermittent	55–69	89.0
Moderate	Trainable	Limited	40–55	6.0
Severe	Severe or trainable (dependent)	Extensive	25–39	3.5
Profound	Profound or custodial	Pervasive	<25	1.5

Note. Adapted from Sattler (1988, p. 648). Copyright 1988 by Jerome M. Sattler, Publisher. Adapted by permission.
[a]Intensities of support do not necessarily correlate directly with other classification systems. For example, an individual with mild mental retardation is likely to require intermittent support in many areas, but specific areas of strength may require no support and specific areas of weakness may require limited or extensive support.

some school districts, children with severe disabilities are instructed in regular classrooms; some sections of the United States have entirely eliminated sheltered workshops, and young adults with disabilities are in competitive or supported employment situations; in other areas, adults with significant cognitive deficits are residing in independent living situations with minimal support. Consequently, rather than focusing upon these individuals' cognitive and adaptive skills *deficits*, educators and clinicians should focus upon the creative and proper use of supports for children so that their *successes* can be maximized.

As noted above and in Table 7.1, the 1992 AAMR classification system places individuals along just such a continuum of needed levels of support (i.e., intermittent, limited, extensive, or pervasive). Consequently, an individual with mental retardation is described in terms of his or her needs—for example, "an 8-year-old male with mental retardation who requires limited supports in communication and extensive supports in self-care." Although one might assume that most children previously diagnosed with mild mental retardation will require intermittent supports in most areas, this is not necessarily true. For example, a child with an IQ of 65 may require no assistance in self-care and intermittent supports in social skills, but may require extensive supports in communication because of a severe expressive language disorder. Such descriptions are designed to be helpful to educators in planning for a child's service needs following an assessment.

Schools have tended to develop their own classification systems for purposes of educational placement. Terms such as "EMR classrooms" (for children functioning in the mild range of mental retardation) or "TMR classrooms" (for children functioning in the moderate range of mental retardation) have been used for some time. However, with the growing trend toward inclusion practices, such educational labels may be of little use. Instead, districts may gradually move toward more functional descriptors for children's needs, since placement is less and less likely to be based upon level of cognitive functioning. Appropriate services will need to be provided for children in any number of settings, including regular education classrooms.

An alternative classification system divides individuals on the basis of etiology. It has been generally accepted that between 25% and 50% of individuals with mental retardation have an organic etiology for their cognitive and adaptive skills deficits (see Zigler & Hodapp, 1986). Mental retardation in the remaining group of individuals is assumed to be the result of psychosocial or familial factors. However, the new AAMR (1992) standards suggest that this two-factor classification system is no longer appropriate. First, as Masland (1988) argues, the fact that there is no known cause in many cases for the presence of mental retardation does not necessarily mean that organic etiological explanations do not exist. It may be that our knowledge and technology are not yet advanced enough to detect many of the causes of mental retardation. For example, it was not until 1969 that fragile-X syndrome was discovered (Lubbs, 1969). This syndrome, which may account for a considerable number of males with mental retardation, is caused by what appears to be a pinching of the tips of the long arm of the X chromosome. There has also been a greater appreciation in recent years of the potential adverse effects of lead poisoning, even at subclinical levels. Raloff (1982) has estimated that as many as 20% of inner-city minority preschoolers may have cognitive or learning deficits because of lead intake. Second, McLaren and Bryson (1987) conducted a review of 13 epidemiological studies and found that in approximately 50% of cases of mental retardation, there were multiple possible causal factors; some of these might be considered familial and others organic. The AAMR (1992) proposes a multifactorial approach to etiology involving the following four categories:

1. Biomedical: factors that relate to biologic processes, such as genetic disorders or nutrition
2. Social: factors that relate to social and family interaction, such as stimulation and adult responsiveness
3. Behavioral: factors that relate to potentially causal behaviors, such as dangerous (injurious) activities or maternal substance abuse
4. Educational: factors that relate to the availability of educational supports that promote mental development and the development of adaptive skills (p. 71)

PREVALENCE

Mental retardation occurs in approximately 3–5% of the U.S. population, depending upon the IQ cutoff used. Based upon the expected normal distribution of intelligence, approximately 2.3% of the population falls 2 standard deviations below the mean IQ of 100 (i.e., IQ below 70). Yet this fails to take into account those individuals whose mental retardation results from organic factors that would not reflect normal variations in intelligence. This would raise the prevalence rate well above 3%. Another issue making it difficult to determine prevalence rates for mental retardation is that of differences in reported rates across age groups. For example, infants, toddlers, and preschoolers are generally not diagnosed with mental retardation (except in cases in which children evidence severe developmental delays). Individual children develop at such different rates that parents tend not to identify delays until the onset of spoken language; moreover, tests of cognitive functioning for infants and young children are poor at predicting later intellectual functioning. Consequently, there is a tendency to defer diagnosis until a child approaches or reaches school age (Zigler & Hodapp, 1986). This practice, although clinically responsible, tends to decrease estimates of the rate of mental retardation in the newborn to 5-year age group.

Conversely, the prevalence of mental retardation seems to be greatest at school age, when children having learning difficulties are typically assessed and diagnosed. Even with the recent emphasis on adaptive functioning, inability to function within a school environment increases the probability of a child's meeting diagnostic criteria for mental retardation. Yet, once individuals reach adulthood, the reported rate of mental retardation decreases. One possible explanation for this finding is that the mortality rate for individuals with mild cognitive deficits is 1.7 times that of the general population, and the death rate for individuals with more severe disabilities is 4.1 times that of the general population (Forssman & Akesson, 1970). However, the decrease in reported rates of mental retardation among adults can also be attributed in part to the fact that with an end to the academic demands of school, some adults with previous diagnoses of mental retardation obtain jobs, evidence only minimal adaptive skills deficits, and need few if any supportive services. According to the 1992 AAMR definition of mental retardation, such individuals may no longer meet criteria for a diagnosis of mental retardation. Conversely, Zigler and Hodapp (1986) attribute much of the variability in the reported incidence of mental retardation across the age range simply to differences in detection rates.

An additional problem in determining the prevalence of mental retardation involves the use of a two-factor definition of mental retardation (i.e., significant deficits in both cognitive and adaptive skills). According to Silverstein (1973), the prevalence of mental retardation can range from as few as 120,000 to as many as 5.5 million, depending upon the correlation between the cognitive and adaptive measures used for diagnosis. In other words, if these two measures are poorly correlated, fewer individuals will meet diagnostic criteria for mental retardation. In a study by Mastenbrook (1978), 300 children with IQ scores between 50 and 70 were also assessed on adaptive behavior measures. Fewer than 35% of these children were found to meet diagnostic criteria for mental retardation, based upon a two-factor definition.

CAUSES

As indicated earlier, approximately 25–50% of individuals with mental retardation have an organic or biological basis for their disorder (Zigler & Hodapp, 1986). In any attempt to determine possible biological causes of mental retardation in an individual, three possible time spans for onset should be examined: the prenatal, perinatal, and postnatal periods. Table 7.2 outlines the general

TABLE 7.2. Hypotheses and Strategies for Determining Etiology

Hypothesis	Possible strategies
I. Prenatal onset	
A. Chromosomal disorder	Extended physical examination
	Referral to geneticist
	Chromosomal analysis, including fragile-X study and high-resolution banding
B. Syndrome disorder	Extended family history and examination of relatives
	Extended physical examination
	Referral to clinical geneticist or neurologist
C. Inborn error of metabolism	Screening for amino acids and organic acids
	Quantification of amino acids in blood, urine, and/or cerebrospinal fluid
	Analysis of organic acids by gas chromotography-mass spectroscopy or other methods
	Blood levels of lactate, pyruvate, carnitine, and long-chain fatty acids
	Arterial ammonia and gases
	Assays of specific enzymes
	Biopsies of specific tissue for light and electron microscopic study and biochemical analysis
D. Developmental disorder of brain formation	Computed tomographic (CT) scan of brain
	Magnetic resonance imaging (MRI) scan of the brain
E. Environmental influence	Growth charts
	Placental pathology
	Maternal history and physical examination of mother
	Toxicological screening of mother at prenatal visits and of child at birth
	Referral to clinical geneticist
II. Perinatal onset	Review maternal records (prenatal care, labor, and delivery)
	Review birth and neonatal records
III. Postnatal onset	
A. Head injury	Detailed medical history
	Skull X-rays, CT or MRI scan (for evidence of sequelae)
B. Infection	Detailed medical history
C. Demyelinating disorder	CT or MRI scan
D. Degenerative disorder	CT or MRI scan
	Evoked potential studies
	Assays of specific enzymes
	Biopsy of specific tissue for light and electron microscopy and biochemical analysis
E. Seizure disorder	Electroencephalography
F. Toxic–metabolic disorder	See "Inborn error of metabolism" (IC)
	Toxicological studies, heavy metal assays
G. Malnutrition	Body measurements
	Detailed nutritional history
	Family history of nutrition
H. Environmental deprivation	Detailed social history
	Psychological evaluation
	Observation in new environment
I. Hypoconnection syndrome	Detailed morphological study of tissue (Huttenlocher, 1991)

Note. From AAMR (1992, pp. 76–77). Copyright 1992 by the American Association on Mental Retardation. Reprinted by permission.

hypotheses and strategies for determining possible causes of mental retardation in each of these time spans. It should be noted that the presence of a particular etiology does not indicate in and of itself that an individual will have mental retardation. For example, approximately 50% of individuals with cerebral palsy have mental retardation. Other disorders, such as neurofibromatosis, involve a gradual regression in skills and cognitive functioning over time. Consequently, a child with this disorder may exhibit age-appropriate functioning during early assessments, but will probably be diagnosed with mental retardation at some later point.

Five major types of predisposing factors may explain the presence of mental retardation (APA, 1994). Heredity accounts for about 5% of cases of mental retardation; inherited factors include metabolic errors present at conception (e.g., Tay–Sachs disease), single-gene anomalies with Mendelian inheritance patterns and varying expression (e.g., tuberous sclerosis), and chromosomal abnormalities (e.g., translocation Down syndrome). Early alterations of embryonic development account for approximately 30% of mental retardation cases and include chromosomal aberrations (e.g., trisomy 21 Down syndrome) or toxin-induced prenatal injury (e.g., maternal alcohol consumption). Later pregnancy and perinatal problems account for about 10% of cases; these include fetal malnutrition, hypoxia, prematurity, various infections, and traumas. General medical conditions acquired in infancy or childhood account for approximately 5% of cases and include traumas, infections, and poisoning. Finally, environmental influences (e.g., deprivation) and other mental disorders (e.g., autism) account for approximately 15–20% of cases.

Biological causes of mental retardation are identified more often in children with significant cognitive delays. For example, McLaren and Bryson (1987) found approximately 70% of individuals with severe mental retardation, but only 50% of individuals with mild mental retardation, to have a known organic cause for their cognitive and adaptive skills deficits. Some children's cognitive deficits may simply reflect the lower end of the normal IQ distribution (Achenbach, 1982); in such cases, functioning represents an interaction of genetic and environmental factors. Factors such as poverty, neglect, abuse, limited stimulation, and poor parent–child interactions are only a few of the psychosocial factors that have been found to be related to intellectual functioning (Robinson & Robinson, 1976).

Determining etiology may be helpful for a number of reasons. First, family members often have a desire to understand why a child has cognitive and adaptive skills deficits. This may help them with the process of coming to accept the child's difficulties, and may allow them to move ahead to insure that his or her needs are appropriately met. Second, if a genetic basis for a child's disability is identified, there may be a need for parents or siblings to pursue genetics counseling for future planning. Third, with a clear etiology, a clinician may be able to provide information on long-term course and the types of supports a child will be likely to need. Fourth, there may be clear treatment implications if certain etiologies are determined (e.g., phenylketonuria, hydrocephalus, lead intoxication, seizure disorders). Finally, determining the etiological basis for mental retardation in general allows individuals to be placed in more homogeneous groupings and results in improved research in the field.

COMORBID PSYCHIATRIC DISORDERS

Although the majority of individuals with mental retardation are free of significant behavior problems (Menolascino, 1977), it is estimated that between 20% and 35% of noninstitutionalized children and adults with mental retardation have comorbid psychiatric diagnoses or behavior disorders (Parsons, May, & Menolascino, 1984). Estimates are even greater for individuals residing in residential settings, with behavioral concerns reported in up to 59% of this population (Hill & Bruininks, 1984). Prevalence estimates may also vary because of such factors as gender (Koller, Richardson, Katz, & McLaren, 1983), age (Jacobson, 1982), level of mental retardation (Koller et al., 1983), and psychiatric diagnostic criteria (Fraser, Leudar, Gray, & Campbell, 1986). The rates of behavioral and/ or psychiatric disorders in children and adolescents with mental retardation have been found to be four to five times those of children and adolescents without mental retardation (Rutter, Graham, & Yule, 1970; Koller et al., 1983). The most common maladaptive behaviors have been reported to include disruptive behavior, injury to self, injury to others, damage to property, and breaking of rules (Hill & Bruininks, 1984). Perhaps some of the best data documenting the extent of behavior problems in this population were obtained by Jacobson (1982), who surveyed over 30,000 individuals with mental retardation residing in New York State. Of these, 8,784 were under the age of 21. Table 7.3 summarizes the overall rates of behavior problems noted in the Jacobson survey, according to age and cognitive functioning level. The percentages of children and adolescents with mental retardation and behavior problems appeared to increase with age and degree of cognitive impairment (i.e., those with lower IQs had a greater percentage of behavior problems), with the exception of children and adolescents with profound mental retardation.

TABLE 7.3. Percentages of Behavior Problems by Age and Level of Functioning

Cognitive level	Age	*n* (cases)	Percentage with behavior problems
Mild mental retardation	0–12	708	40
Mild mental retardation	13–21	818	55
Moderate mental retardation	0–12	640	47
Moderate mental retardation	13–21	1,163	60
Severe mental retardation	0–12	652	54
Severe mental retardation	13–21	1,208	65
Profound mental retardation	0–12	1,056	38
Profound mental retardation	13–21	2,539	57

Note. From Jacobson (1982, p. 129). Copyright 1982 by Elsevier Science Ltd. Reprinted by permission.

Studies of children with mental retardation indicate that the full range of psychiatric disorders is represented among them (Eaton & Menolascino, 1982). For example, estimates of the prevalence of Attention-Deficit/Hyperactivity Disorder (ADHD) in children with mental retardation range from 9% to 18% (Ando & Yoshimura, 1978; Epstein, Cullinan, & Gadow, 1986; Jacobson, 1982) —three to four times the rates found among typically developing children. By contrast, much less is known about the rate of depression in children and adolescents with mental retardation. For example, in a 1971 study of all persons with mental retardation in a South London district, none of the 140 children (15 years of age or less) with IQs less than 50 were diagnosed with an affective disorder (Corbett, 1979). A study conducted in a Swedish city of all adolescents with IQs between 50 and 70 (*n* = 83) found only a single case of an affective disorder (Gillberg, 1987). Yet up to 8% of children with mental retardation admitted to inpatient psychiatric settings have been found to meet diagnostic criteria for a depressive disorder (Matson, Barrett, & Helsel, 1988). In diagnosing psychiatric disorders in children and adolescents with mental retardation, the clinician must often rely on observable behavior rather than self-report (MacLean, 1993). It is generally accepted that standard diagnostic criteria for psychiatric disorders, such as the DSM-IV criteria (APA, 1994), can be reasonably applied to children and adolescents functioning at IQs above 50. However, such criteria appear to be less appropriate for individuals functioning below that level (MacLean, 1993).

A number of conditions are often associated with specific maladaptive behavior disorders. For example, children with fragile-X syndrome typically function in the mild to moderate range of mental retardation and often exhibit attentional deficits, hyperactivity, hand flapping, hand biting, perseverative speech, preoccupation with inanimate objects, shyness, and poor social interaction (Hagerman & Sobesky, 1989). Lesch–Nyhan syndrome is often associated with severe self-injury (Nyhan, 1976). Rett syndrome is typically characterized by regression in skills following a normal early course of development and the subsequent appearance of stereotyped hand movements (APA, 1994). Children with autism often engage in a range of maladaptive behaviors, such as repetitive and stereotyped motor behaviors (e.g., hand or finger flapping), impaired social interactions, and deficits in communication (e.g., delayed development of expressive language, repetitive/stereotyped use of language)(APA, 1994). The presence of specific maladaptive behaviors during an assessment may suggest that a particular disorder or syndrome be considered. This will further determine the conduct of the assessment, including the types of questions to be asked, the possible need for more extended observation of the child or adolescent, and the need for evaluation by other professionals (e.g., specialists in genetics or endocrinology). Similarly, when a child or adolescent with a specific disorder or syndrome is referred for evaluation, knowledge of the associated behavioral indices will be necessary to guide the evaluation.

LEGAL ISSUES AND STATE POLICIES

Several laws enacted since the mid-1970s have significantly affected both the assessment and delivery of services to children and adolescents with mental retardation. As noted earlier, the Education for All Handicapped Children Act of 1975 (Public Law 94-142), mandated that children be educated within the least restrictive environment, that those identified with special needs have IEPs designed for them, and that parents be granted access to their children's records and allowed to participate in the development of educational objectives. The law included a number of additional provisions, such as the right of parents to obtain an independent evaluation of their child if they disagreed with the assessment conducted by the local school district, the right of parents to due process if they chose to reject the placement decision, and a requirement that a child be reevaluated at least every 3 years.

In 1986, Public Law 99-457 was enacted, which involved amendments to Public Law 94–142. This law extended the rights and protections of Public Law 94–142 to children ages 3 through 5 with developmental disabilities. In addition, early intervention services for infants and toddlers (birth to 2 years of age) with developmental disabilities and their families were authorized. Infants and toddlers defined as being in need of early intervention services were those diagnosed with a physical or mental condition with a high probability of resulting developmental delay, or those exhibiting developmental delays in one or more of the following areas (as measured by an appropriate diagnostic instrument): cognitive development, physical development, language and speech development, psychosocial development, or self-help skills. Individualized family service plans were to be developed for identified infants and toddlers.

Public Law 94-142 was most recently reauthorized in 1990 as the Individuals with Disabilities Education Act (Public Law 101-476). During the summer of 1995, the first substantial revisions of the law since it was enacted in 1975 were introduced to Congress. These revisions are intended to strengthen the IEP process and to facilitate greater involvement by parents (Heumann, 1995).

The clinician not only must be well versed in the provisions of certain federal laws, but must have a working knowledge of state legal decisions affecting the assessment and placement of children in special education programs. For example, two court cases in the early 1970s (*Pennsylvania Association of Retarded Children* [PARC] *v. Pennsylvania*, 1971; *Mills v. Board of Education*, 1972) were "class actions" that established the legal rights of children with mental retardation to a free public education and as normalized an educational placement as possible. Such cases set the stage for the enactment of laws such as Public Law 94-142. In 1974, a California court decision (*Larry P. v. Riles*) disallowed the use of IQ tests for purposes of classroom placement in that state, because standardized intelligence tests were found to be racially and culturally biased by the court. A number of other states have been affected by similar court decisions regarding the assessment and placement of minority children in special education.

Other court cases, such as *Bales v. Clark* (1981) and *Battle v. Pennsylvania* (1981), focused on a school district's responsibilities in meeting a child's educational needs. In the *Bales* case, the family of a 13-year-old girl who had sustained a head injury following an accident requested that the district provide funding for the girl to attend a specialized private school located outside the district. The U.S. Circuit Court of Appeals for the Eighth Circuit sided with the school district by ruling that costs may be considered in placement decisions. The court also ruled that the family need not be reimbursed for the cost of a tutor over the summer. Only in cases where irreparable loss of progress during the summer months could be documented would districts be required to provide year-round schooling. Conversely, in the *Battle* case, the U.S. Court of Appeals for the Third Circuit recognized that some children who are severely or profoundly impaired tend to acquire skills more slowly and to forget what has been learned more quickly than their typically developing peers. Consequently, a school year limited to 180 days may not meet the requirement of "a free appropriate public education" for such individuals. Cases such as these will have an impact upon a family's ability to obtain year-round services for a child, and may require that a clinician carefully document the effects of summer breaks upon a child's or adolescent's progress.

In addition to delineating the types of services school districts must provide for children with mental retardation, the courts have had an impact upon districts' ability to manage disruptive students. For example, in *Honig v. Doe* (1988), the U.S. Supreme Court held that school systems could not unilaterally exclude a child from the classroom for dangerous or disruptive behavior resulting from his or her disability. For additional information on litigation involving children with mental retardation, the reader is referred to Beyer (1991).

Each state also uses different terminology to describe the continuum of special education services. For example, in Pennsylvania, children with mild mental retardation are often placed in learning support classrooms. However, in the neighboring state of West Virginia, the same children would be placed in EMR classrooms. States also use different cutoff scores for determining eligibility for special education services. In Pennsylvania, a child with an IQ of 77 and significant deficits in adaptive functioning may be labeled as having mental retardation and placed in a learning support program (Special Education Services and Programs, 1990). If the child's family were to move across the state line to West Virginia, this same child might not be identified as needing special services and could be placed in a regular classroom (West Virginia Department of Education, 1985). It is incumbent upon clinicians to become well versed in their state's terminology, regulations, and relevant court decisions affecting the assessment of and provision of services for children and adolescents with mental retardation.

APPROACH TO ASSESSMENT

Parents or other caregivers may request an evaluation of a child for a number of reasons. Some may be referred by the school or another agency to determine why the child is progressing poorly; some may require an assessment as part of the requirements for obtaining services (e.g., Supplemental Security Income); others may want a second opinion about a previous diagnosis; and still others may have accepted the diagnosis of mental retardation, but are seeking assistance with specific behavior problems (e.g., aggression, self-injury) or skills deficits (e.g., toilet training, social skills problems). Employing a standard battery of assessment tools and procedures for all individuals with mental retardation will clearly "miss the mark" for a large number of cases.

For many clinicians, the most common reason for assessment is to determine whether a child is in need of special education services. Bagnato, Neisworth, and Munson (1989) describe a comprehensive developmental assessment model for use in early childhood special education, which illustrates one approach to evaluation. Their diagnostic–prescriptive model is based upon the premise that assessment and treatment are inseparable components of the same larger process. Figure 7.1 illustrates the four-phase sequence as a series of wide- to narrow-angle sighting lenses. The clinician would choose to use a wide-angle lens for screening purposes to obtain a broad overview of a child's skills and deficits. A more narrow-angle lens would be reserved for other tasks, such as developing a comprehensive prescriptive assessment (Neisworth & Bagnato, 1987).

The first phase of Neisworth and Bagnato's (1987) assessment model involves screening for

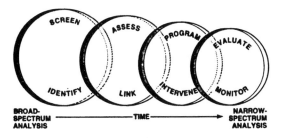

FIGURE 7.1. Linking assessment–intervention goals. From Neisworth and Bagnato (1987, p. 183). Copyright 1987 by Plenum Publishing Corporation. Reprinted by permission.

general capabilities (using global norm-based or judgment-based developmental measures) across multiple domains (e.g., cognitive, language, motor, personal–social, sensory) to determine whether a child is at risk. The second phase involves comprehensive developmental assessment across multiple domains, using curriculum-based, norm-based, and judgment-based scales. Norm-based instruments may be useful for diagnostic purposes (i.e., does the child have mental retardation?), whereas curriculum-based instruments provide a precise description of the child's range of functioning. In the third phase, curriculum-based instruments are used to develop sequential objectives for the child. The final phase encompasses elements of the previous phases, including documentation of child progress and program effectiveness. Recent trends in service delivery have made program evaluation and accountability essential to the assessment process (Bagnato et al., 1989).

In addition to general assessment models, some guiding principles apply specifically to the assessment of children with mental retardation:

1. *Understanding the referral question.* The clinician should create an oral "contract" with the family members regarding what specific questions they hope will be answered at the conclusion of the evaluation. Even the most thorough assessment will be of little value if it fails to answer a family's questions. In cases where the family members pose unrealistic questions, establishing the ground rules early (e.g., "It is unlikely that we will be able to tell you exactly why your child has mental retardation") will facilitate discussion and the framing of more appropriate questions.

2. *Using multiple sources.* The clinician should obtain information from as many sources as possible (e.g., schools, residences, agencies, other clinicians), as children may behave differently

across environments. There is some research evidence that parents and teachers describe the behaviors and skills of children with mental retardation in different ways. For example, we (Handen, Feldman, & Honigman, 1987) examined parent–teacher agreement on a questionnaire assessing self-help skills, speech and language, play skills, and behavior problems in a group of 98 children with developmental disabilities. Although significant levels of parent–teacher agreement were noted for 77% of items assessed, the mean level of agreement was only 68.1%. In addition, when a specific behavior problem (e.g., temper tantrums, hits others) was endorsed by either a parent or a teacher, the probability that the same problem would be endorsed by the other respondent was at or below chance levels. In a study of the reliability of parent and child reports of symptoms, parents were found to be more reliable informants (r's of .73 to .76) than their typically developing children (r's of .43 to .71) (Edelbrock, Costello, Dulcan, Kalas, & Conover, 1985). This same study found typically developing children under the age of 10 to be extremely unreliable informants (with the exception of reporting simple fears). Such findings cast suspicion upon the clinical utility of information provided by parents, children, or teachers alone, and suggest that additional information be gathered whenever conflicting reports are obtained from two or more informants.

3. *Using disorder-specific knowledge.* Whenever possible, a clinician should use disorder-specific knowledge as a framework for organizing his or her approach to assessment. For example, if a child with fragile-X syndrome is being assessed, the focus may be on such behaviors as echolalia, social nonresponsiveness, and self-stimulation. Therefore, a behavioral assessment conducted as part of the evaluation will need to be designed to elicit such behaviors. By contrast, if a child with Williams syndrome is being assessed, feeding problems may be expected if the child is an infant or toddler. Therefore, the assessment will need to include observation of mealtime behavior. Other disorders often present with specific strengths and/ or deficits, which may influence the choice of assessment tools or the interpretation of results. For example, children with Down syndrome have a unique pattern of language development. Miller (1992) has found that such children have smaller vocabularies and construct sentences of lower grammatical complexity than do other children of the same mental age. Conversely, their receptive language skills develop as expected for their cognitive abilities. Therefore, the clinician may want

to assess their receptive and expressive language skills independently (i.e., to use an instrument to assess receptive language skills that does not require an expressive language response).

4. *Using appropriate assessment strategies.* The clinician should use tools that are appropriate with respect to such areas as functioning level, language skills, and motor skills. For example, a test such as the third edition of the Wechsler Intelligence Scale for Children (WISC-III), which is standardized for children aged 6 years, 0 months to 16 years, 11 months, may be inappropriate for a 7-year-old with suspected mental retardation; even the easiest test items may be below the child's ability level. A standardized IQ test such as the fourth edition of the Stanford–Binet, which requires a high level of language skills, may be inappropriate for a child with significant expressive language deficits. A test of visual–motor skills, such as the Bender Visual Motor Gestalt Test, will be of limited value if a child has significant motor or visual impairments.

5. *Using a multiple assessment approach.* Sattler (1988) outlines "four pillars of assessment": norm-referenced tests (standardized tools); interviews (with parents, teachers, the child, and other individuals familiar with the child); observations (both in the clinic and in settings such as the home or school); and informal assessments (nonstandardized tools, such as language samples or assessments of a child's ability to benefit from systematic cues). Significant discrepancies among assessment findings will require further investigation before a diagnosis and recommendations can be offered. For example, Sattler (1988) cites a case in which a child scored within the mentally retarded range on a test of cognitive functioning, but interviews and assessment of adaptive functioning suggested age-appropriate skills. Clearly, a diagnosis of mental retardation would not be made and additional assessment would be necessary.

6. *Collaborating with other professionals.* The clinician should include professionals from other disciplines (e.g., communication disorders, psychiatry, education, developmental pediatrics, genetics, occupational therapy) in the assessment or refer the child to such professionals, depending upon the question being asked and the need to determine potential causes for a particular deficit or behavior problem. For example, a child's inattention may indicate a possible hearing loss (suggesting the need for an audiology evaluation), or the presence of a number of dysmorphic features may suggest the need for a genetics consultation. In a child with Down syndrome, receptive lan-

guage skills that fall below expected levels may suggest the need for an audiology evaluation, as about 50% of children with Down syndrome have some hearing loss because of ear infections or neurological impairment (Miller, 1992).

7. *Providing appropriate feedback.* The clinician should provide feedback at a level that is appropriate to the family's language, education, and culture. Using overly professional language, or simply stating numbers from various tests, should be kept to a minimum. Shea (1984) recommends that a feedback session about a diagnosis of mental retardation should have these three goals: (a) to provide specific information about the child's developmental functioning, and to answer all of the parents' questions about these findings; (b) to support and help the parents as they begin to cope emotionally with the knowledge of their child's disability; and (c) to assist the parents in making plans to carry out specific recommendations and interventions.

ASSESSMENT OF
COGNITIVE FUNCTIONING

Despite the aforementioned issues regarding the role of adaptive behavior in children with mental retardation, evaluation of cognitive functioning remains the first and primary step in assessing mental retardation. Most school districts continue to overemphasize IQ testing for purposes of determining a child's eligibility for special needs services (Furlong & LeDrew, 1985; Reschly & Ward, 1991). Even among researchers in the field, the majority of published papers in the area of mental retardation use IQ alone as the inclusionary or exclusionary criterion for entry into studies (Hawkins & Cooper, 1990). Numerous cognitive assessment tools are available to evaluate a child for the presence of mental retardation. These tools are called "norm-based" or "norm-referenced" scales, in that they compare a child's test performance to that of others of similar age and gender. The normative sample may also be similar on other dimensions, such as socioeconomic status or race.) As a result, such tests must be standardized across a large group of individuals. Norm-referenced tests are able to assess relative performance across a wide range of developmental domains. (Indeed, many of the measures discussed in later sections of the chapter are also norm-referenced.) These tests are almost exclusively individually administered and, according to Morgenstern and Klass (1991), meet a number of underlying conditions:

1. The examiner must be skilled in test administration and have experience with a wide range of available tests.

2. The examiner must be knowledgeable about normal and abnormal development, and about the particular needs of children with mental retardation, in order to interpret test results most accurately.

3. The tests given must be reliable and valid.

4. Tests are not valid for every purpose. Therefore, tests must be chosen that are appropriate for their purpose, particularly if they enhance the prediction of nontest behavior.

5. It is assumed that a child is giving his or her best performance. Problems with poor concentration, anxiety, or poor motivation will compromise the reliability and validity of a test score.

Scales for Infants
and Preschool-Age Children

Table 7.4 provides a summary of the most frequently used standardized cognitive and language assessment tools for infants, preschool-age, and school-age children. In general, infant and preschool scales do not correlate well with later levels of cognitive functioning. For example, McCall (1976) found essentially no correlation between performance among infants 0–6 months of age and IQ scores after age 5. Correlations remained only in the .20s when measures taken between 7 and 18 months of age were used to predict IQ scores at ages 5–18 years. Correlations ranged from .40 to .55 when performance was assessed between 19 and 30 months of age and compared to later IQ. It is not until the age of 5 years or more that one begins to observe stability in intelligence test performance over time. Correlations between performance at age 5 and later IQ fall around .60 (Bayley, 1949), whereas correlations of .80 have been found between children assessed at age 7 and subsequently at age 18 (McCall, Appelbaum, & Hogarty, 1973). Only in the case of infants and preschoolers with significant developmental delays are early test results predictive of future functioning (DuBose, 1981).

The two most commonly used tests for infants and toddlers are the Bayley Scales of Infant Development, second edition (Bayley, 1993), and the Gesell Developmental Schedules (Ames, Gillespie, Haines, & Ilig, 1979). The Bayley was standardized on 1,700 infants, toddlers, and preschoolers between 1 and 42 months of age. Three rating scales are provided: a Mental scale, a Motor scale, and a Behavior Rating scale. Performance results can be expressed as a developmental age or developmen-

TABLE 7.4. Frequently Used Standardized Tests for Cognitive and Language Assessment

Test	Age range	Description/comments
Bayley Scales of Infant Development, second edition (Bayley, 1993)	1–42 months	Provides indices of early cognitive and motor development. For children above 42 months, can use age-equivalents.
Gesell Developmental Schedules (Ames et al., 1979)	0–72 months	Tests language, fine and gross motor, cognitive, and personal–social domains. For children above 72 months, can use age equivalents.
Infant Mullen Scales of Early Learning (Mullen, 1989)	0–42 months	Assesses motor, visual, and language skills. Results can be expressed in terms of age scores, T-scores, or developmental stages.
Stanford–Binet, fourth edition (Thorndike et al., 1986)	2 years, 0 months–23 years, 11 months	Provides a Composite Index score and 15 subscales involving verbal, visual, and quantitative reasoning and memory.
Wechsler Preschool and Primary Scale of Intelligence—Revised (Wechsler, 1989)	3 years, 0 months–7 years, 3 months	Provides Full Scale, Verbal, and Performance IQs, along with 12 subtests. Performance subtests may be useful for assessing children with language disorders.
McCarthy Scales of Children's Abilities (McCarthy, 1972)	2 years, 6 months–8 years, 6 months	Provides 18 subtests and five global scales (Verbal, Perceptual–Performance, Quantitative, Memory, Motor, and General Cognitive Index). Data suggest that results may be lower for children with mental retardation than on other tests (Sattler, 1988).
Kaufman Assessment Battery for Children (Kaufman & Kaufman, 1983)	2 years, 6 months–12 years, 5 months	Four global scores (Simultaneous Processing, Sequential Processing, Achievement, and Non-verbal). Also provides 16 subtests and a Composite score. The Nonverbal scale is useful for assessing children with hearing impairments or language disorders.
Wechsler Intelligence Test for Children, third edition (Wechsler, 1991)	6 years, 0 months–16 years, 11 months	Provides Full Scale, Verbal, and Performance IQs, along with 13 subtests. Performance subtests may be useful for assessing children with language disorders.
Peabody Picture Vocabulary Test—Revised (Dunn & Dunn, 1981)	2 years, 6 months–adult	Provides a measure of receptive language, but should not be used as a measure of cognitive functioning. The use of a pointing response makes it useful for children with expressive language deficits.
Test of Auditory Comprehension of Language—Revised (Carrow-Woolfolk, 1985)	3 years, 0 months–9 years, 11 months	A pictorial multiple-choice test with three sections: Word Classes and Relations, Grammatical Morphemes, and Elaborated Sentences. Requires pointing response by child.
Clinical Evaluation of Language Fundamentals—Preschool (Wiig et al., 1992)	3 years, 0 months–6 years, 11 months	Assesses wide range of expressive and receptive language skills. Manual assists in developing individualized treatment program based upon assessment results.
Clinical Evaluation of Language Fundamentals—Revised (Semel et al., 1987)	5 years, 0 months–16 years, 11 months	Assesses wide range of expressive and receptive language skills. Manual assists in developing individualized treatment program based upon assessment results.
Pictorial Test of Intelligence (French, 1964)	3–8 years	Subtests include Picture Vocabulary, Form Discrimination, Information and Comprehension, Similarities, Size and Number, and Immediate Recall. Is a supplemental measure of learning aptitude for children with motor or language deficits.

(continued)

TABLE 7.4. (*continued*)

Test	Age range	Description/comments
Leiter International Performance Scale (Leiter, 1969)	2–18 years	Assessing intelligence with nonverbal items. Can serve as a supplementary test of intelligence for children with significant expressive language deficits. However, norms are outdated and standardization is poor.
Hiskey–Nebraska Test of Learning Aptitude (Hiskey, 1966)	3–17 years	Provides a nonverbal measure of intelligence. Subtests assess verbal labeling, categorization, concept formation, and rehearsal. Out-of-date norms, but useful tool to assess children with hearing impairments.
Blind Learning Aptitude Test (Newland, 1971)	6–16 years	Assesses recognition of differences and similarities, identification of progressions and missing elements, and ability to complete a figure. Uses a format of dots and lines, similar to Braille. Best used as supplement to test of verbal skills.

tal quotient (DQ). The Gesell has a normative reference group and assesses 350–400 behaviors from birth to 72 months of age. The test examines language, fine motor, gross motor, cognitive, and personal–social domains. Like results on the Bayley, results on the Gesell can be expressed as a developmental age or DQ. A more recently developed infant assessment tool is the Infant Mullen Scales of Early Learning (Mullen, 1989). The Mullen was standardized on a sample of 1,231 children from birth to 42 months of age, and has five scales (including ones of motor, visual, and language areas).

As children approach preschool age, tests tend to emphasize more language-mediated tasks. The Stanford–Binet, fourth edition (Thorndike, Hagan, & Sattler, 1986), and the Wechsler Preschool and Primary Scale of Intelligence — Revised (WPPSI-R; Wechsler, 1989), are the most commonly used cognitive tests for this age group. The Binet was revised in 1986 and standardized on 10,000 children and adults. Appropriate for use for individuals between 2 years, 0 months and 23 years, 11 months of age, it assesses functioning across four domains: Verbal Reasoning, Abstract–Visual Reasoning, Short-term Memory, and Test Composite. Scores are expressed as a deviation IQ, with a mean of 100 and a standard deviation of 16. The test is not appropriate for individuals functioning in the severe to profound range of mental retardation, because the test is highly unreliable for IQ scores below 45 (with 36 being the lowest IQ score given). The WPPSI-R (Wechsler, 1989) is appropriate for preschoolers between 3 years, 0 months and 7 years, 3 months of age. It includes 12 subtests (2 of which are supplemental) and expresses its results in terms of Verbal IQ, Performance IQ, and Full Scale IQ. The test was standardized on a sample of 10,000 preschoolers, with mean score of 100 and a standard deviation of 15. Like the Binet, this test is also inappropriate for children functioning within the severe to profound ranges of mental retardation, as the lowest possible Full Scale score is 41.

A third alternative test for preschoolers is the McCarthy Scales of Children's Abilities (McCarthy, 1972). The test consists of 18 subtests and five global scales: Verbal, Perceptual–Performance, Quantitative, Memory, and Motor scales, and a General Cognitive Index. The McCarthy was standardized on 1,032 children between 2 years, 6 months and 8 years, 6 months of age, and was stratified on multiple variables. It has excellent validity and reliability. Neisworth and Bagnato (1987) caution that although this tool was conceptualized as a measure of cognitive functioning, it may be better viewed as an effective measure of developmental and learning readiness. The test is inappropriate for children functioning at or below the moderate range of mental retardation (its General Cognitive Index floor is 50).

A final alternative for assessing children under the age of 6 years is the Kaufman Assessment Battery for Children (K-ABC; Kaufman & Kaufman, 1983). This instrument assesses a child's capabilities in four areas: (1) Simultaneous Processing, which taps an individual's ability to integrate inputs from multiple sources at the same time; (2) Sequential Processing, which taps an individual's ability to solve problems based on the arrangement of arrays of information; (3) Achievement; and (4) Nonverbal. The K-ABC is made up of 16 subtests spanning the age range of 2 years, 6 months to 12 years, 5 months, and was standardized on a sample of 2,000 children based upon 1980 census data. Reliability and validity are satisfactory. The Nonverbal scale of the K-ABC is particularly useful in assessing children with hearing impairments or language disorders. However, the K-ABC should not be used to classify mental retardation across the entire age range of the scale. For example, the Mental Processing Composite score has a floor of 79 for children aged 2 years, 6 months; 70 for 3-year-olds; and 60 for 4-year-olds.

Tests for School-Age Children

The fourth edition of the Stanford–Binet, the school-age version of the Wechsler tests (the WISC-III), and the K-ABC are the most commonly used tools for assessing cognitive functioning in school-age children. The Stanford–Binet and the K-ABC have been discussed above. The WISC-III (Wechsler, 1991) is structurally similar to the WPPSI-R, but spans the age range of 6 through 16 years. It consists of 10 primary and 3 supplementary subtests, which are divided into two major scales: Verbal (Information, Similarities, Arithmetic, Vocabulary, Comprehension, Digit Span) and Performance (Picture Completion, Picture Arrangement, Block Design, Object Assembly, Coding, Symbol Search, Mazes). The most recent revision was standardized on 2,200 children. The test has excellent reliability and validity. However, the Full Scale IQ range of 40–160 does not meet the needs for assessing children who may function within the severe to profound range of mental retardation.

Alternative Measures

It is often difficult to use measures such as the Stanford–Binet and the Wechsler tests to assess children with significant neuromotor or language-based disorders. Because of the limited IQ ranges covered by the tests, these tools are also inappropriate for evaluating children functioning from the low end of the moderate to the profound range of mental retardation. Moreover, tests such as the Stanford–Binet, WISC-III, and K-ABC require the evaluator to present items in a highly standardized manner; deviations from this may significantly affect the validity of the test results. The option of making alterations in response modalities (e.g., using yes–no responses or gestures), or excluding those items that require responses a particular child is unable to provide (e.g., eliminating all verbal items or all items requiring motor responses), does not allow for comparison with

the standardization group. Therefore, alternative measures—measures that are normed for children with specific handicaps (e.g., visual or motor impairments), or that have standardized adaptations for children with mental retardation (Neisworth & Bagnato, 1987)—will often need to be used to provide valid estimates of cognitive functioning for this group of children.

One option, according to Morgenstern and Klass (1991), is to use tools such as the Bayley or Gesell in order to provide information on the course of growth and development across a range of skill areas (e.g., social, adaptive, language, and motor). For children who are nonverbal or have significant language-based deficits, a number of alternative assessment tools are available for assessing receptive language skills. One such tool, the Peabody Picture Vocabulary Test–Revised (PPVT-R; Dunn & Dunn, 1981), requires a child to point to one of four pictorial plates in response to a question from the evaluator (e.g., "Point to the ball"). The PPVT-R is normed on 5,028 children and adults and has good reliability and validity. However, the PPVT-R has not been normed on a population with special needs. It should be considered a screening device for identifying language comprehension difficulties.

The Test of Auditory Comprehension of Language—Revised (Carrow-Woolfolk, 1985) is an individually administered test of auditory comprehension (receptive language functioning) that requires only a pointing response. It contains three sections: Word Classes and Relations, Grammatical Morphemes, and Elaborated Sentences. Sattler (1988) notes that children who are inattentive/distractible or who speak in dialects that differ from standard English may perform poorly on this test. The Clinical Evaluation of Language Fundamentals—Preschool (CELF-Preschool) (Wiig, Secord, & Semel, 1992) and the Clinical Evaluation of Language Fundamentals—Revised (CELF-Revised; Semel, Wiig, & Secord, 1987) can be used to assess a wide range of receptive and expressive language functions in preschool-age and school-age children. Both of the CELF manuals include a section on developing individualized treatment goals based upon the test results.

Two purely nonverbal assessment tools are also frequently used to obtain estimates of cognitive functioning in children with severe language deficits. The Pictorial Test of Intelligence (French, 1964) was designed to assess intellectual functioning in both typically developing children and children with physical handicaps from 3 to 8 years of age. The test uses oversized picture cards, so that a range of response modalities can be used (e.g., eye localization, head localization). The standardization sample of 1,830, including children with handicaps, makes this one of the best norm-referenced adaptive measures available for assessing children with special needs (Neisworth & Bagnato, 1987).

The Leiter International Performance Scale (Leiter, 1969) was designed to assess general cognitive functioning in children with language and/ or hearing impairments, as well as those for whom English is not a primary language. The test involves no verbal instructions, but depends upon the use of visual demonstration to elicit responses that involve matching-to-sample behaviors on the part of the child. Various stimulus cards are placed in a wooden frame, and the child is required to match blocks with pictures corresponding to those on the stimulus cards. Although the standardization sample provides normative data for individuals between 2 and 18 years of age, the norms are based on only 289 children. Despite these drawbacks, the Leiter remains a frequently used tool for assessing children with special needs and significant language deficits. It is presently being revised.

The Hiskey–Nebraska Test of Learning Aptitude (Hiskey, 1966) remains the most reliable tool for assessing children with hearing impairments. With a standardization sample of 1,079 deaf and 1,074 non-hearing-impaired children, this tool provides normative data for children from 3 to 17 years of age. There are 12 subtests, and directions can be given in pantomime. Reliability and validity data are adequate. Finally, the Blind Learning Aptitude Test (Newland, 1971) was specifically developed to assess children with visual impairments. With a standardization sample of 961 visually impaired children, this tool provides normative data for individuals 6 to 16 years of age. Items use a raised-dot Braille-like format; directions are given orally and require a pointing response. The test, which assesses nonverbal skills, should be used in conjunction with a verbal test. It is most useful for children of elementary school age, as it appears to lose some of its discriminating power with children over 12 years of age (Sattler, 1988).

ASSESSMENT OF ACADEMIC ACHIEVEMENT

Table 7.5 includes a summary of the tests most frequently used to assess academic achievement

skills. The assessment of academic achievement is the primary means of determining how a child with mental retardation is faring in school. Such data also allow for the comparison of a child's abilities (as estimated with a test of cognitive functioning) with actual school performance. A child whose school achievement is significantly below what would be expected from his or her IQ score may have other problems that will need to be investigated as part of the overall assessment. These may range from psychiatric disorders (e.g., ADHD, depression), which may adversely affect the child's ability to concentrate and perform in school, to significant family stressors or inappropriate classroom placement and instruction. Numerous norm-referenced academic assessment tools are available; these typically measure abilities in reading, spelling, and mathematics.

Perhaps the most popularly used measure to assess school achievement is the Wide Range Achievement Test—3 (WRAT-3; Wilkinson, 1993), which takes only 15–25 minutes and should be considered as a screening measure. The WRAT-3 is a paper-and-pencil test that provides a measure of a child's skills in the areas of reading, spelling, and arithmetic. The test was recently revised and standardized on a national sample of 5,600 individuals ranging in age from 5 through 74 years. Results are transformed into standard scores ($\bar{X} = 100$, $SD = 15$) and also provide grade equivalents and percentiles. A second achievement measure is the Woodcock–Johnson Psycho-Educational Battery—Revised (Woodcock & Johnson, 1989). It assesses a range of skills, including cognitive and academic areas; however, the academic subtests can be given alone. The test was standardized on a sample of 4,252 children ranging in age from 5 to 18 years (preschool, college, and adult samples were also used to standardize the test from ages 2 to 90+). Results can be presented as standard scores ($\bar{X} = 100$, $SD = 15$), grade equivalents, or percentile ranks.

A recently developed test of achievement is the Wechsler Individual Achievement Test (Wechsler, 1992). This test was normed with a sample of 4,252 children aged 5–19 years and consists of eight subtests and five factors, including Reading, Mathematics, Language, Writing, and a Composite score. The Peabody Individual Achievement Test—Revised (PIAT-R; Markwardt, 1989) has a somewhat different format from those of the tools discussed previously. Rather than providing paper-and-pencil tasks, the PIAT-R requires that a child respond by pointing to the correct picture from an array of four items. Consequently, the PIAT-R

TABLE 7.5. Tests Frequently Used to Assess Achievement Skills, Perceptual–Motor Skills, and Neuropsychological Functioning

Test	Age range	Description/comments
	Achievement tests	
Wide Range Achievement Test–3 (Wilkinson, 1993)	5 years, 0 months– 74 years, 11 months	Assesses skills in reading, spelling, and arithmetic. Serves as a brief screening device.
Woodcock–Johnson Psycho-Educational Battery—Revised (Woodcock & Johnson, 1989)	2–90+ years	Contains 35 subtests that assess both intelligence and academic achievement. Academic subtests can be given alone and include Spelling, Reading, and Arithmetic.
Wechsler Individual Achievement Test (Wechsler, 1992)	5–19 years	Contains eight subtests and five factors: Reading, Mathematics, Language, Writing, and a Composite score.
Peabody Individual Achievement Test— Revised (Markwardt, 1989)	Kindergarten– 12th grade	Contains five subtests areas: General Information, Reading Recognition, Reading Comprehension, Mathematics, Spelling, and General Information. Multiple-choice format makes it a good choice for children with learning deficits.
KeyMath Revised: A Diagnostic Inventory of Essential Mathematics (Connolly, 1988)	1st–9th grades	Contains 13 subtests in four areas: Basic Concepts, Operations, Applications, and Total Test score. Useful for obtaining more in-depth information on arithmetic skills.
	Perceptual–motor tests	
Bender Visual Motor Gestalt Test (Bender, 1938)	5 years, 0 months– 11 years, 11 months	Contains nine geometric figures child must copy. Koppitz (1975) norms are used for children.
Developmental Test of Visual–Motor Integration, third edition (Beery & Buktenica, 1989)	4 years, 0 months– 17 years, 11 months	Contains 24 geometric forms arranged in order of difficulty.
Motor-Free Visual Perception Test (Colarusso & Hammill, 1972)	4–8 years	Useful for assessing children with significant motor impairments. Requires a pointing response.
Bruininks–Oseretsky Test of Motor Proficiency (Bruininks, 1978)	4 years, 6 months– 14 years, 6 months	Useful measure of fine and gross motor skills, with eight subtests.
	Neuropsychological assessment (process analysis)	
Neuropsychological Evaluation of Older Children (Reitan & Wolfson, 1992)	9–14 years	Battery consists of cognitive and perceptual–motor tests for assessment of brain damage. Requires 4–6 hours to complete.
Reitan–Indiana Neuro-psychological Test Battery for Children (Reitan, 1993)	5–8 years	Battery consists of cognitive and perceptual–motor tests for assessment of brain damage. Requires 4–6 hours to complete.
Luria–Nebraska Neuro-psychological Battery: Children's Revision (Golden, 1987)	8–12 years	Battery consists of cognitive, perceptual, and sensorimotor tests for assessment of brain damage. Requires 2½ hours to complete.
Wide Range Assessment of Memory and Learning (Sheslow & Adams, 1990)	5 years, 0 months– 17 years, 11 months	Consists of nine subtests and three indices: Verbal Memory, Visual Memory, and Learning.

(continued)

TABLE 7.5. (*continued*)

Test	Age range	Description/comments
Neuropsychological assessment (interactive analysis)		
Brazelton Neonatal Behavioral Assessment Scale—Revised (Brazelton, 1984)	Infants and young children with severe handicaps	Surveys primitive reflexes and interactive neurophysiological abilities. Can be used to derive developmental ages for children with profound mental retardation.
Carolina Record of Individual Behavior (Simeonsson et al., 1982)	Young children with severe handicaps	Assesses developmental and behavioral capabilities.
Home Observation for Measurement of the Environment (Caldwell & Bradley, 1978)	36–72 months	Rates interactional style of mother with child, as well as organization of environment and opportunities for daily stimulation.

is a good choice for assessing a child with motor impairment or language deficits. The test was standardized on approximately 200 students at each grade level (kindergarten through 12th).

Finally, the KeyMath Revised: A Diagnostic Inventory of Essential Mathematics (Connolly, 1988) is an individually administered test of arithmetic skills. It provides considerably more depth than most other available tools, with 13 subtest areas. The test was standardized on 1,798 children from kindergarten through ninth grade. The absence of reading and writing requirements makes this a good assessment tool for children with mental retardation.

ASSESSMENT OF PERCEPTUAL–MOTOR SKILLS

Evaluation of visual–motor perception and integration is particularly useful in assessing children with possible learning and neurological deficits (see Table 7.5). Children with mental retardation also often have deficits in perceptual–motor skills. However, one must be cautious when interpreting test results for children with accompanying visual impairments or motor delays.

The most widely used visual–motor test is the Bender Visual Motor Gestalt Test (Bender, 1938). This is an individually administered paper-and-pencil test in which the child is asked to copy nine geometric figures drawn in black and printed on 4" × 6" white cards. Koppitz (1975) has developed the most commonly used scoring system, which provides both a developmental score and guidelines for scoring emotional indicators. The Koppitz

norms are based on a group of 975 children from 5 years, 0 months to 11 years, 11 months of age. Reliability and validity are adequate when the Bender is used as a test of perceptual–motor development.

The third edition of the Developmental Test of Visual–Motor Integration (VMI; Beery & Buktenica, 1989) is a paper-and-pencil test in which the child is required to copy up to 24 geometric forms. Forms are arranged in order of increasing difficulty, and testing is discontinued following three consecutive incorrect responses. The VMI provides somewhat greater structure than the Bender, in that forms are copied in clearly outlined spaces. The test was normed on a sample of 3,000 children from 4 years, 0 months to 17 years, 11 months of age. Results can be presented as percentiles, standard scores ($\bar{X} = 10, SD = 3$), or age equivalents.

The Motor-Free Visual Perception Test (Colarusso & Hammill, 1972) is a useful tool for assessing children who have significant motor impairments. The child is asked to point to the one of four figures on a page that matches a target figure. The test was standardized on a sample of 881 children between the ages of 4 and 8 years. Results can be presented as percentiles, standard scores ($\bar{X} = 10$, $SD = 3$), or age equivalents. Finally, the Bruininks–Oseretsky Test of Motor Proficiency (Bruininks, 1978) assesses both gross and fine motor skills. The test contains 46 items arranged into eight subtest areas. Three scores—Gross Motor, Fine Motor, and Battery Composite scores—are obtained ($\bar{X} = 15$, $SD = 5$). The test was standardized on a sample of 765 children from 4 years, 6 months to 14 years, 6 months of age.

ASSESSMENT OF NEUROPSYCHOLOGICAL FUNCTIONING

Several measures are designed to assess specific neuropsychological processes, such as attention, memory, and perception (see Table 7.5). Neisworth and Bagnato (1987) provide a number of reasons why neuropsychological tests may be helpful in assessing children with mental retardation: (1) to define a particular child's strongest individual modality for learning; (2) to monitor medication efficacy; (3) to assess progress or deterioration in children with traumatic brain injuries; and (4) to learn more about how the brain mediates control of behavior (e.g., verbal mediation and emotional self-control). Neisworth and Bagnato divide the available neuropsychological assessment tools into those involving "process analysis" and those involving "interactive analysis."

Tests Involving Process Analysis

Three extensive batteries are available to evaluate neuropsychological processes in children: (1) the Neuropsychological Evaluation of Older Children (Reitan & Wolfson, 1992), which is designed for children aged 9 to 14 years; (2) the Reitan–Indiana Neuropsychological Test Battery for Children (Reitan, 1993), which is designed for children aged 5 to 8 years; and (3) the Luria–Nebraska Neuropsychological Battery: Children's Revision (Golden, 1987), which is designed for children aged 8 to 12 years. All three batteries involve process analysis; the Halstead–Reitan and Reitan–Indiana are made up of cognitive and perceptual–motor tests, whereas the Luria–Nebraska consists of tests that assess sensory–motor, perceptual, and cognitive abilities. An assessment involving the full version of any of these three batteries requires several hours to complete and typically includes at least a separate assessment of cognitive functioning (e.g., the WISC-III). Data on reliability and validity for the Halstead–Reitan and Reitan–Indiana are limited, and the Luria–Nebraska manual provides less than adequate information on standardization and reliability (Sattler, 1988). Therefore, some caution must accompany the use of these tools, especially in children with mental retardation.

Numerous other options remain for assessing processes that reflect specific brain functions. Tools discussed previously, such as the K-ABC and the McCarthy Scales of Children's Abilities, can assess functions such as attention, memory, and processing. The study of patterns of subtest performance on the WISC-III, or tools such as the Bender Gestalt, can also provide information on brain functions. Various assessment tools are also available to evaluate more specific functions. For example, the Wide Range Assessment of Memory and Learning (Sheslow & Adams, 1990) provides a means of examining memory process in depth for children from 5 years, 0 months to 17 years, 11 months of age. Obtaining more specific data on verbal and auditory memory can be extremely helpful in making treatment or instructional recommendations.

Tests Involving Interactive Analysis

Tests that involve interactive analysis have been increasingly used to assess children with significant delays. Such scales make greater use of clinical judgment in their scoring. One scale, the Brazelton Neonatal Behavioral Assessment Scale—Revised (Brazelton, 1984), was originally designed to assess newborn and premature infants. The scale surveys primitive reflexes and examines interactive and neurophysiological capabilities. The Brazelton has six factors or clusters (Habituation, Orientation, Motor, State Variation, State Regulation, and Autonomic Stability). It has been normed so that one can derive functioning levels in terms of gestational and postterm developmental ages.

Other scales that examine how a child interacts with the environment have been developed specifically for children with developmental disabilities. For example, the Carolina Record of Individual Behavior (Simeonsson, Huntingdon, Short, & Ware, 1982) assesses young children with significant delays in such areas as social communication, participation, object orientation, activity level, reactivity, and goal-setting skills.

The Home Observation for Measurement of the Environment (Caldwell & Bradley, 1978) assesses child qualities, parent behavior, and the home environment in areas such as emotional and verbal responsiveness of the mother, avoidance of restriction and punishment, organization of the environment, provision of appropriate play materials, interaction with the child, and opportunities for daily stimulation. The scale is useful for children who function in the 36-month to 72-month age range.

ASSESSMENT OF ADAPTIVE BEHAVIOR

Table 7.6 summarizes the most frequently used adaptive behavior scales. Adaptive behavior reflects an individual's ability to meet the independent needs

TABLE 7.6. Tests Frequently Used to Assess Adaptive Functioning

Test	Age range	Description/comments
Vineland Adaptive Behavior Scales (Sparrow et al., 1984)	Newborn to adult	Assesses Communication, Daily Living Skills, Socialization, and Motor Skills domains.
Adaptive Behavior Scale—School (Lambert et al., 1993)	3–21 years	Useful informal measures, with norms for children with and without mental retardation. Teacher is respondent.
Developmental Profile II (Alpern et al., 1989)	Birth–12 years, 6 months	Well-standardized tool that covers a number of dimensions and contains 186 items.
Adaptive Behavior Inventory for Children (Mercer & Lewis, 1978)	5 years, 0 months–18 years, 11 months	Measures six areas of adaptive behavior with parent as respondent
Adaptive Behavior Inventory (Brown & Leigh, 1986)	5 years, 0 months–18 years, 11 months	Standardized on both a normal-IQ sample and a sample of children with mental retardation.
T.M.R. School Competency Scales (Levine et al., 1976)	5–21 years	Measures adaptive behavior in children with moderate mental retardation. Validity data not available. Teacher is respondent.
Balthazar Scales of Adaptive Behavior (Balthazar, 1976)	5–57 years	Assesses adaptive behavior in individuals with severe and profound mental retardation. Respondent can be any adult who knows the individual child well.
Wisconsin Behavior Rating Scale (Song et al., 1984)	Any age	Primarily used to assess adaptive behavior in individuals functioning below a 3-year developmental level.

and social demands of the environment. Although the identification of deficits in adaptive functioning is a prerequisite for making a diagnosis of mental retardation (AAMR, 1992), the definition of adaptive behavior tends to be imprecise, and measurement of adaptive skills is extremely difficult (Zigler & Hodapp, 1986). Many of the available tools for measuring adaptive behavior are poorly standardized and lack clarity regarding the construct of adaptive behavior (Evans, 1990; Kamphaus, 1987). Most have focused on such areas as language skills, daily living skills, and social skills. Yet no single scale has been devised to measure all 10 adaptive areas suggested by the AAMR (1992), and there remains an absence of guidelines for determining adaptive skill limitations (MacMillan et al., 1995). Consequently, the determination that a child or adolescent has limitations in two or more adaptive skills (one of the requirements for a diagnosis of mental retardation) tends to be more subjective and often requires clinical judgment (AAMR, 1992).

Two scales in particular have had a history of extended use, and other, less well-known scales remain as additional options. On the Vineland Adaptive Behavior Scales (Sparrow, Balla, & Cicchetti, 1984), perhaps the best-known tool, a respondent (either a parent, a teacher, or another professional) who knows the individual well answers behavior-oriented questions about the individual's adaptive skills. The examiner needs some level of supervised training, as the Vineland involves an open-ended question format. Three forms are available: the Interview Edition Survey, the Expanded Form, and the Classroom Edition. The Vineland covers the domains of Communication, Daily Living Skills, Socialization, and Motor Skills. Results can be expressed as a standard score ($\overline{X}= 100, SD = 15$), percentiles, or age equivalents in each domain, as well as in the form of an Adaptive Behavior Composite. The Interview Edition Survey and Expanded Form were standardized on 3,000 individuals from birth to 18 years, 11 months of age; separate norms are available for children with mental retardation, emotional disorders, and physical handicaps. An additional 3,000 children ranging in age from 3 to 12 years served as the normative group for the Classroom Edition. Reliability and validity appear adequate, although there is some concern about the norming procedures, in that means and standard deviations differ across age groups (Silverstein, 1986).

A second frequently used scale is the AAMR Adaptive Behavior Scale—School, which was revised in 1993 (Lambert, Nihira, & Leland, 1993). The scale was normed on two groups aged 3 to 21 years: a sample of 2,000 students with mental retardation, and a sample of 1,000 typically developing students. The scale should be completed by someone who knows the child or adolescent well; results are expressed as either standard scores ($\bar{X}$ = 10, SD = 3), percentiles, or age equivalents. There are nine skill domains and seven maladaptive behavior domains.

Several other adaptive behavior scales remain available for use, although most have only limited data on reliability and validity. One that is exceptionally well standardized is the Developmental Profile II (Alpern, Boll, & Shearer, 1989), a 186-item inventory for children from birth to 12 years, 6 months of age. Other options include the Adaptive Behavior Inventory for Children (Mercer & Lewis, 1978), normed with children from 5 years, 0 months to 11 years, 11 months of age; the Adaptive Behavior Inventory (Brown & Leigh, 1986), standardized on a normal-IQ sample as well as a sample of children with mental retardation (both samples aged 5 years, 0 months to 18 years, 11 months); the T.M.R. School Competency Scales (Levine, Elzey, Thormahlen, & Cain, 1976), designed for children functioning in the moderate range of mental retardation; the Balthazar Scales of Adaptive Behavior (Balthazar, 1976), developed for individuals 5 to 57 years of age who are functioning within the severe to profound range of mental retardation; and the Wisconsin Behavior Rating Scale (Song et al., 1984), which is designed for individuals functioning within the profound range of mental retardation whose skills fall below the 3-year level.

CRITERION-BASED ASSESSMENT

Table 7.7 provides a summary of a number of criterion-based assessment tools and specialized curricula. Whereas norm-referenced assessment tools are used primarily for diagnostic purposes, criterion- or curriculum-based assessment tools allow for the merging of test results, teaching, and progress evaluation within a single process (Neisworth & Bagnato, 1987). Criterion-based tools also allow for the comparison of a child to himself or herself (once baseline levels are established), rather than to a normative group of peers. Consequently, these tools are used to monitor progress via performance on a range of task analyses of basic developmental skills. Depending upon a child's progress, a specific treatment or teaching plan can be devised. Neisworth and Bagnato (1987) divide criterion-based assessment tools into "develop-

mental measures" (in which the content and objectives are developmentally sequenced) and "specialized curriculum measures" (in which content and objectives have been designed and field-tested for distinct groups of children with developmental disabilities).

Criterion-based assessment measures are increasingly being used with children functioning within the severe to profound range of mental retardation, as standardized, norm-referenced tests are of limited use with this population. White and Haring (1978) note that norm-referenced tests are relatively insensitive to developmental changes in children with IQs below 35. Even assessment measures that employ normal developmental scales may be inappropriate for this population, because the development of children with severe or profound mental retardation does not necessarily proceed like that of typically developing children (White & Haring, 1978).

A number of curricula have been developed and field-tested specifically for preschool programs serving children with developmental disabilities. For example, the HICOMP Preschool Curriculum (Willoughby-Herb & Neisworth, 1982) covers over 700 objectives for preschoolers from birth to 60 months of age across four domains: communication, own care, motor, and problem solving. The Hawaii Early Learning Profile (Parks, 1992) covers 685 skills and behaviors within six domains for children with developmental disabilities from birth to 36 months of age. The Carolina Curriculum for Infants and Toddlers with Special Needs (Johnson-Martin, Jens, Attermeier, & Hacker, 1991) provides 25 curriculum sequences for children under the age of 24 months. The Carolina Curriculum for Preschoolers with Special Needs (Johnson-Martin, Attermeier, & Hacker, 1990) offers 25 curriculum sequences for children aged 2 to 5 years. Finally, the Brigance Diagnostic Inventory of Early Development (Brigance, 1991) provides criterion-referenced task analyses across 11 domains for children from birth to 84 months of age. However, unlike the previously discussed tools, the Brigance is not a curriculum, in that it does not provide specific teaching strategies or activities based upon the test results.

Specialized measures have also been developed to assess and provide curricula for specific subgroups of children. For example, the Oregon Project Curriculum for Visually Impaired and Blind Preschool Children (Brown, Simmons, & Methvin, 1986) assesses children with both visual and other impairments from birth to 72 months of age. The Uniform Performance Assessment

TABLE 7.7. Criterion-Based Assessment Tools and Specialized Curricula

Test	Age range	Description/comments
HICOMP Preschool Curriculum (Willoughby-Herb & Neisworth, 1982)	Birth–60 months	Covers over 700 objectives in four domains (communication, own care, motor, and problem solving).
Hawaii Early Learning Profile (Parks, 1992)	Birth–36 months	Covers 685 skills and behaviors within six domains.
Carolina Curriculum for Infants and Toddlers with Special Needs (Johnson-Martin et al., 1991)	Birth–24 months	Provides 25 curriculum sequences.
Carolina Curriculum for Preschoolers with Special Needs (Johnson-Martin et al., 1990)	2–5 years	Provides 25 curriculum sequences.
Brigance Diagnostic Inventory of Early Development (Brigance, 1991)	Birth–84 months	Provides criterion-referenced task analyses for 11 domains. However, the Brigance is not a curriculum.
Oregon Project Curriculum for Visually Impaired and Blind Preschool Children (Brown et al., 1986)	Birth–72 months	Assesses children with visual and other impairments.
Uniform Performance Assessment System (Haring et al., 1981)	Birth–72 months	Assesses children with moderate to severe mental retardation.
Programmed Environments Curriculum (Tawney et al., 1979)	Birth–36 months	Evaluates functional living skills in children with moderate to profound mental retardation.
Pyramid Scales (Cone, 1984)	Birth–8 years	Evaluates sensory, primary, and secondary skills in children with severe handicaps.
Community Living Assessment and Teaching System (Slentz et al., 1982)	School age	All three tools assess self-help skills, social-emotional functioning, motor skills, and language skills in school-age children and adolescents with significant cognitive deficits.
Early Independence: A Developmental Curriculum (Cooke et al., 1981)	School age	
Prescriptive Behavioral Checklist of the Severely and Profoundly Retarded (Popovich, 1981)	School age	All provide curriculum recommendations based upon the assessment results.

System (Haring, White, Edgar, Affleck, & Hayden, 1981) assesses children with moderate to severe mental retardation from birth to 72 months of age across five areas: preacademic/fine motor, communication, social/self-help, gross motor, and behavior management. The Programmed Environments Curriculum (Tawney, Knapp, O'Reilly, & Pratt, 1979) evaluates functional living skills in children from birth to 36 months of age who have moderate to profound mental retardation. The Pyramid Scales (Cone, 1984) constitute a criterion-referenced tool for children with severe handicaps from birth to 8 years of age. These scales assess three general areas: sensory skills (e.g., auditory and visual responsiveness), primary skills (e.g., motor skills, social skills, activities of daily living), and secondary skills (recreation and leisure skills). Still other specialized curricula are available for older children with significant cognitive deficits, to assess such areas as self-help skills, social-emotional

functioning, motor skills, and language skills. Examples include the Community Living Assessment and Teaching System (Slentz, Close, Benz, & Taylor, 1982); Early Independence: A Developmental Curriculum (Cooke, Apollini, & Sundberg, 1981); and A Prescriptive Behavioral Checklist for the Severely and Profoundly Retarded (Popovich, 1981). Again, these tools provide both means of assessing present skill levels and guidelines for teaching subsequent steps and skills.

ASSESSMENT OF PSYCHOSOCIAL FACTORS

As discussed previously, various psychosocial factors have been found to be associated with mental retardation (Robinson & Robinson, 1976). It is important to assess such factors, both to gain an understanding of potential contributions to a child's intellectual dysfunction and develop recommendations for treatment. There is a considerable literature indicating that families of children with mental retardation experience significantly more life stress than other families (Crnic, Friedrich, & Greenberg, 1983). The level of stress perceived by a family can be influenced by a number of factors, such as a child's diagnosis (Crnic et al., 1983), the severity of the handicapping condition (Donovan, 1988), the severity of the child's behavior problems (Margalit, Shulman, & Stuchiner, 1989), the child's age (Bristol, 1979), race (Flynt & Wood, 1989), the mother's age (Flynt & Wood, 1989), the family's socioeconomic status (Rabkin & Streuning, 1976), and whether the parents are married or unmarried (Salisbury, 1987). The additional caregiving requirements for children with developmental disabilities are often a significant source of stress to families, with level of stress positively associated with caregiving demands for mothers (Beckman, 1991). The availability of informal supports has also been found to be negatively associated with mothers' stress levels (Beckman, 1991).

Interestingly, siblings of children with mental retardation appear to experience fewer adjustment problems than their parents. For example, Dyson (1989) compared 55 older siblings of young children with handicaps to 55 matched siblings of nonhandicapped children. Results indicated similar levels of self-concept, behavior problems, and social competence in the two groups. In a further examination of sibling functioning based on type of handicap, siblings of children with mental retardation evidenced the best adjustment levels. These findings are consistent with other reports (e.g., Breslau, Weitzman, & Messenger, 1981; Lobato, Barbour, Hall, & Miller, 1987).

Numerous structured questionnaires are available to assess family functioning. For example, the Parenting Stress Index (PSI; Abidin, 1990) is a 120-item questionnaire that assesses family stress related to child characteristics, parent characteristics, and life stressors. The tool was normed with 2,633 parents (3.6% of the sample included parents of clinically referred children) of children 1 through 12 years of age. Referenced group profiles are provided for families of children with autism as well as with other developmental disabilities. The PSI has been used frequently by researchers examining stress in families of children with developmental disabilities. For example, McKinney and Peterson (1987) documented significant differences in the level of stress experienced by parents of children with development disabilities, in contrast to the PSI standardization sample. Beck-

man (1991) also used the PSI to examine stress in mothers and fathers of young children with and without developmental disabilities. Mothers were found to report more stress than fathers did, and parents of children with developmental disabilities reported greater levels of stress across all domains than parents of typically developing children did.

Another assessment tool, the short form of the Questionnaire on Resources and Stress (Friedrich, Greenberg, & Crnic, 1983), is a 52-item self-report questionnaire developed primarily for assessing stress in families who care for children with developmental disabilities or mental retardation. It is a psychometrically derived version of the 285-item Questionnaire on Resources and Stress (Holroyd, 1974) and uses a true–false format. This tool was used by Dyson, Edgar, and Crnic (1989) to examine adjustment in siblings of children with developmental disabilities. Greater parental stress (as measured by the Friedrich et al. instrument) and some dimensions of the family social environment (e.g., fewer family social supports, poor family relationships) were found to be most significant in predicting problems with self-concept, behavior, and social competence in siblings.

ASSESSMENT OF PSYCHIATRIC PROBLEMS

As discussed earlier, the rate of psychiatric problems in children and adolescents with mental retardation is four to five times that of typically developing peers (Rutter et al., 1970; Koller et al., 1983). Moreover, children and adolescents with mental retardation experience the entire range of psychiatric disorders (Eaton & Menolascino, 1982). For the majority of children and adolescents with mental retardation, a psychiatric diagnosis can be made with some confidence. However, for those functioning within the severe to profound range of mental retardation, psychiatric diagnosis can be an ambiguous task (Reiss, 1993). Reiss suggests that a psychiatric diagnosis be based on recognizable patterns of symptomatology; a single behavior problem (e.g., aggression) is not sufficient for such a diagnosis. Reiss also recommends that the clinician look for changes in behavior to discriminate between behavior problems that are expressions of mental retardation and ones that indicate psychopathology. For example, an adolescent who develops eating problems and is described as frequently tearful may be exhibiting signs of depression.

One well-documented problem in making a psychiatric diagnosis in individuals with mental retardation is a phenomenon called "diagnostic overshadowing" (Reiss & Szyszko, 1983). This refers to situations in which the presence of mental retardation decreases the diagnostic significance of a psychiatric disorder. In other words, behaviors that might be seen as evidence of psychopathology in typically developing children and adolescents are attributed to cognitive deficits in individuals with mental retardation.

In assessing children and adolescents with mental retardation, the clinician must be aware of certain symptom clusters that may indicate the presence of a specific disorder often associated with mental retardation. For example, such behaviors as echolalia, self-stimulation, and social unresponsiveness may suggest a diagnosis of autism or some other pervasive developmental disorder (APA, 1994). A child who has exhibited some regression in skills (e.g., a loss of previously acquired language skills) along with unusual behaviors (e.g., stereotyped hand movements) may be displaying symptoms consistent with Rett syndrome (APA, 1994).

Similarly, when a child or adolescent with a previously diagnosed disorder is being evaluated, it is important that the clinician be aware of any associated behavioral sequelae, as such behaviors are often the reason for referral. For example, when a child has mental retardation secondary to lead poisoning, questions regarding pica (the persistent eating of non-nutritive substances) should be asked (APA, 1994). A child seen for evaluation with a diagnosis of Prader–Willi syndrome will probably be exhibiting behaviors related to compulsive eating (Pueschel & Thuline, 1991).

Structured Diagnostic Interviews

To improve the reliability of open-ended psychiatric interviews, a number of more structured psychiatric interview tools have been developed. Such interviews involve groups of questions that are asked in a standard manner and order. The rater indicates the presence or absence of each symptom; the ratings are then tallied at the conclusion of the interview, and a diagnosis is determined. Matson and Frame (1983) note a number of advantages to structured psychiatric interviews: (1) Both interviewer and interviewee bias are reduced; (2) with the use of standardized questions and explicit definitions of terms, there is improved clarity of communication between the interviewer and interviewee; and (3) assignment of a particular diagnosis is easier and more reliable.

Three structured interview tools have received the most attention in the literature. Each has a parent and a child version, but none have been normed with children or adolescents with mental retardation. The Schedule for Affective Disorders and Schizophrenia for School-Age Children (K-SADS; Orvaschel & Puig-Antich, 1987) is a semistructured diagnostic interview to assess past and present psychopathology in children and adolescents aged 6 to 17. It covers all major DSM-III-R diagnoses applicable to this age group. The Diagnostic Interview for Children and Adolescents—Revised (DICA-R; Reich & Welner, 1989) was developed for children and adolescents aged 6 to 17, and has a more structured format than the K-SADS. It too assesses all major DSM-III-R diagnoses for children and adolescents. Finally, the Diagnostic Interview Schedule for Children Version 2.3 (DISC 2.3; Shaffer et al., 1992) is a highly structured, standardized interview schedule with versions for both children and parents. Again it is based upon DSM-III-R criteria and covers young people aged 6 to 17 years (for the parent version). A revised version of the DISC 2.3 based upon DSM-IV diagnostic criteria is near completion.

One recently developed self-report interview may be of particular interest to clinicians who assess children with mental retardation. Valla, Bergerson, Berube, Gaudet, and St.-Georges (1994) have published validity and reliability data on a structured pictorial questionnaire to assess DSM-III-R-based diagnoses in children aged 6 to 11 years. A child is shown a number of drawings of a peer in situations associated with various childhood psychiatric disorders, and is simply asked whether the same kind of thing has happened to him or her. This tool may be potentially useful for assessing children with mental retardation because of its pictorial format and the fact that it requires only a yes or no response.

A few structured psychiatric interview schedules which have been developed specifically for children and adolescents with mental retardation. For example, the Structured Clinical Interview (Spragg, 1988) is designed to be given to individuals with mental retardation. It uses simple language, relying on open-ended questions and items with choice formats. Twelve areas are assessed: behavioral observations and mental status; presenting problem/chief complaint; cognitive–affective–behavioral relationships; evaluation of coping skills; perception of self; interpersonal functioning; relationships with authority; anxiety screening; depression screening; psychiatric screening;

evaluation of psychosocial supports; and summary and feedback. This instrument would appear best suited for individuals with borderline intelligence, mild mental retardation, and possibly moderate mental retardation (Aman, 1991). The Structured Clinical Interview is in the early stages of development, and there are few psychometric data available.

The Schedule of Handicaps, Behaviour, and Skills—Revised (Wing, 1982; Wing & Gould, 1978) was originally developed for children with mental retardation or autism. The present revised schedule is appropriate for children and adults functioning within the mild to profound range of mental retardation. Information is obtained from a caregiver by means of a semistructured interview. The instrument contains both a Developmental Skills component and a Behavioural Abnormalities component. An appendix addresses psychiatric disorders and behavior problems, including depression, mania, obsessions, schizophrenia, and personality disorders. Total interview time ranges from 45 minutes to 2½ hours (Aman, 1991). There are relatively few available data on the psychometric properties of the schedule (Aman, 1991).

Finally, Lord et al. (1989) have developed a highly sophisticated instrument called the Autism Diagnostic Observation Schedule. This is a standardized instrument for the observation of social and communicative behavior associated with autism; it has been shown to discriminate among children with autism, matched typically developing children and matched children with mental retardation (all between 6 and 18 years of age). It consists of eight tasks presented by an examiner (e.g., asking the child to tell a story, requiring that the child take turns with the examiner during a drawing game). The evaluation is intended to be videotaped and requires 20–30 minutes to administer. Behaviors targeted for each task (e.g., asking for help, telling a sequential story) are coded by raters during the evaluation, and general ratings of a variety of behaviors (e.g., facial expression, immediate echolalia, unusual preoccupations) are made at the completion of the assessment on a 3-point ordinal scale (0 = "within normal limits," 1 = "infrequent or possible abnormality," 2 = "definite abnormality").

Behavior Problem Checklists and Self-Report Scales

Behavior problem checklists have been used extensively to augment the diagnosis of psychiatric disorders in children with mental retardation.

Such tools have also provided documentation of changes in behavior following a range of interventions, especially pharmacological treatment (e.g., Aman, Kern, McGhee, & Arnold, 1993; Handen, Breaux, Gosling, Ploof, & Feldman, 1990). Checklists can be completed by primary informants, such as teachers or parents, as well as by a child or adolescent. From an assessment standpoint, these tools allow one to obtain information from informants (e.g., teachers) who would otherwise not be available during the assessment. These tools also provide structure for informants and permit the behavior of the child being evaluated to be compared with that of same-age and same-gender peers.

Table 7.8 summarizes the most commonly used behavior problem checklists and self-report scales for children and adolescents with mental retardation. Among the best-known checklists are the Conners Rating Scales (Conners, 1990), which have been used extensively as supplemental data sources for assessing ADHD. They have also been used to assess the efficacy of a wide range of psychotropic medications (e.g., methylphenidate, thioridazine, clonidine) in children with mental retardation and/or autism (Aman, Marks, Turbott, Wilsher, & Merry, 1991; Handen et al., 1992; Jaselskis, Cook, Fletcher, & Leventhal, 1992). The most frequently used forms of the Conners Rating Scales consist of a list of 28 behavioral items on the teacher version and 48 items on the parent version. Each item is rated on a 4-point scale for frequency of occurrence (from "not at all" to "very often"). The parent version has six subscales (Conduct Problems, Anxiety, Impulsivity–Hyperactivity, Learning Problems, Psychosomatic, and Hyperactivity Index) and the teacher version has four subscales (Conduct Problems, Hyperactivity Inattention–Passivity, and Hyperactivity Index).

Although the Conners Rating Scales have been normed on typically developing children, they continue to be used as tools for both establishing research criteria for ADHD in children with mental retardation and documenting medication efficacy (e.g., Handen et al., 1992; Aman et al., 1993). A recent study by Pearson and Aman (1994) compared the results of using mental age versus chronological age in applying the Conners norms to children with mental retardation. The study was prompted by the recommendation of some researchers and clinicians that mental age rather than chronological age be used when the scores of a child with mental retardation are compared with those of the norm group (Barkley, 1990). However, Pearson and Aman found significant

TABLE 7.8. Behavior Problem Checklists and Self-Report Questionnaires

Test	Age range	Description/comments
Conners Rating Scales (Conners, 1990)	3–17 years	Provides profile for five school and eight home factors. Sensitive to stimulant drug effects in children with ADHD. Parent and teacher versions.
Aberrant Behavior Checklist (Aman & Singh, 1986)	6 years–adult	Provides profile for five factors. Normed on children and adults with mental retardation. Teachers and residential staff members are respondents.
Preschool Behavior Questionnaire (Behar & Stringfield, 1974)	3–5 years	Recently normed on preschoolder with developmental disbilities. Provides three factors and total score. Teachers are respondents.
Behavior Evaluation Rating Scale (Sprague, 1982)	12 years–adult	Scale for adolescents and adults with mild to severe mental retardation; 15 items.
Emotional Problems Scales: Behavior Rating Scales (Strohmer & Prout, 1991)	12 years–adult	Scale for adolescents with mild mental retardation; 135 items.
Emotional Disorders Rating Scale (Feinstein et al., 1988)	Children and adolescents	Sale for individuals with mild and moderate mental retardation; 59 items. Child care workers are respondents.
Adolescent Behavior Checklist (Demb et al., 1993)	12–21 years	Scale for adolescents with borderline to mild mental retardation; 86 items.
Developmental Behavior Checklist (Einfeld & Tonge, 1990)	6 years–adult	Adaptation of the Child Behavior Checklist; 98 items. Normed on individuals with mild to profound mental retardation.
Fear Survey for Children With and Without Mental Retardation (Ramirez & Kratochwill, 1990)	10–13 years	Simplified 60-item version of the Children's Fear Survey Schedule. Appropriate for children with mild mental retardation. A self-report scale.

correlations in only 4 of 27 comparisons between scale ratings and mental age; thus, their study provides little support for guidelines stating that mental age be used to determine which norms should be applied when children with mental retardation are evaluated.

Several additional behavior problem checklists have been developed and specifically normed for children and adolescents with mental retardation. The reader is also referred to a 1991 monograph and a 1994 paper by Aman, which review many of the published and nonpublished behavior problem checklists available for use with this population.

The most extensively validated tool is the Aberrant Behavior Checklist (ABC; Aman & Singh, 1986). A Community Version of the ABC was validated in 1992 (Marshburn & Aman, 1992). The ABC consists of a list of 58 behavioral items, rated on a 3-point scale. The Community Version has been normed on a group of 666 children (ages 6 to 15) and 1,024 adults. A factor analysis resulted in five subscales: Irritability, Agitation/Crying, Lethargy/Social withdrawal, Stereotypic Behavior, and Hyperactivity. There are separate norms for children of different ages and genders. The Community Version is completed by teachers or other staff members who work with individuals with mental retardation.

The Preschool Behavior Questionnaire (Behar & Stringfield, 1974), one of the few available preschool rating scales, has some potential utility for preschoolers with developmental disabilities. One unpublished study by Rheinscheld (1989) found Behar and Stringfield's original factor structure to be largely validated in ratings of a group of 203 preschoolers with developmental disabilities. Other scales that have been normed for children and adolescents include the Behavior Evaluation Rating Scale (Sprague, 1982), a 15-item scale for adolescents and adults with mild to severe mental retardation; the Emotional Problems Scales: Behavior Rating Scales (Strohmer & Prout, 1991), a 135-item instrument for adolescents and adults with mild mental retardation; the Emotional Disorders Rating Scale (Feinstein, Kaminer, Barrett, & Tylenda, 1988), a 59-item tool for assessing children and adolescents with developmental delays;

the Adolescent Behavior Checklist (Demb, Brier, & Huron, 1989), an 86-item scale for adolescents 12 to 21 years of age with borderline intelligence or mild mental retardation; and the Developmental Behaviour Checklist (Einfeld & Tonge, 1990), an adaptation of the Child Behavior Checklist (Achenbach, 1991) specifically for children and adults with mental retardation. The last-mentioned scale seems to be particularly useful for individuals functioning within the moderate to severe range of mental retardation (Aman, 1991).

Few self-report scales have been normed with individuals with mental retardation. One of the obvious problems with such scales is the validity of the responses. The Fear Survey for Children With and Without Mental Retardation (Ramirez & Kratochwill, 1990) is a simplified 60-item revision of the Children's Fear Survey Schedule (Ryan & Dietiker, 1979). The test involves asking the child to indicate whether an item makes him or her scared, afraid, or nervous. Although it appears to be appropriate for children with mild mental retardation, the study sample included children with mental retardation in the age range of 10–13 years only. The Self-Report Depression Questionnaire (Reynolds, 1989) is an orally administered scale for assessing depression in adolescents and adults with mild to moderate mental retardation who are capable of responding orally.

In summary, for children and adolescents functioning within the moderate to mild range of mental retardation, scales such as the Conners Rating Scales and the Preschool Behavior Questionnaire can be useful, but should be interpreted cautiously. Supplementing these scales with one normed and developed specifically for individuals with mental retardation may be the best practice. However, with only a few exceptions (e.g., the ABC), most of these scales are not well known and have not had extensive use in the literature. Finally, one should be particularly cautious in using a self-report scale as the sole or primary source of information during an assessment.

BEHAVIORAL OBSERVATION

Direct behavioral observation is an important component in a multimethod assessment of a child's strengths and weaknesses. When the referral question relates to specific behavior problems (e.g., self-injury, inattention), direct observation becomes paramount. Unfortunately, the clinic is not necessarily the best setting in which to observe a child. There is considerable reactivity when a child is first seen in a new and strange place. Therefore, when possible, home or school visits are effective (although not necessarily efficient) means of obtaining valid information regarding a child's behavior. Because such visits are not always possible, researchers and clinicians have developed a number of different analogue in-clinic situations that attempt to replicate home and school settings as closely as possible. It is hoped that such situations can elicit behaviors similar to those observed outside the clinic.

Once the target behaviors have been identified (e.g., noncompliance, out-of-seat behavior, aggression), a child can be observed in a variety of different situations within the clinic. However, it may require some ingenuity on the part of the clinician to provide a specific setting in which the target behaviors can be elicited and observed. For the child who is noncompliant, having the parent work with the child on easy and demanding task (e.g., simulating a homework session) may provide an opportunity both to see the behavior and to observe how it is handled by the parent. Sometimes the assessment situation itself can elicit the behavior of concern. Such might be the case for a child who uses aggression or other disruptive behaviors to obtain attention. The youngster may attempt to interrupt or disrupt the parent when talking with the clinician. Observing such interactions between parent and child provides a rich data base for understanding the problem and recommending solutions.

Various methods are available for quantifying direct observations of children alone or interacting with their parents. The most commonly used strategy is frequency recording, or counting the number of occurrences of an event. For example, Kern, Mauk, Marder, and Mace (1995) examined the functional relationship between breath holding and various situations (e.g., being placed alone in a room, playing, being provided with adult attention) in a child with severe mental retardation and Cornelia de Lange syndrome. The dependent measure was simply the number of breath-holding episodes observed during each 10-minute observation. A second strategy involves recording the duration of an event. This may be useful for behaviors such as remaining in seat or playing appropriately; the clinician can simply record the total time a child engages in the target behaviors during the observation period.

More complex observation strategies have involved the use of event sequences—that is, the recording of social interactions by scoring ongoing sequences of behavioral events (e.g., those that occur during a mother–child interaction). Such data provide information on interactional patterns of behavior that can be used in treatment. For example, Breiner and Forehand (1982) examined mother–child interactions in oppositional preschoolers with and without developmental disabilities. They found that the mothers of the children with delays used significantly more commands than the mothers of the nondelayed children, and that the delayed children exhibited greater noncompliance than the typically developing children. Similarly, we (Caro-Martinez, Lurier, & Handen, 1994) observed mothers and their developmentally delayed preschoolers (a group with behaviors suggestive of ADHD and a group of controls) during a clinic task in which each mother asked her child to comply with 10 requests. Delayed preschoolers in the control group were significantly more compliant than those in the ADHD group; as a result, mothers in the control group used significantly more praise and less physical assistance.

Particular emphasis has been placed by behavior analysts on conducting a functional assessment of the target behaviors. Such an assessment can be done in a variety of ways. One strategy involves the taking of data over a period of a few days or weeks (depending upon the rate of the behavior of interest) by caregivers. When the target behavior occurs, information on possible antecedents (e.g., date, time, who was involved, what was occurring at the time), the actual behavior, and the consequences (i.e., how the behavior was managed) is gathered. With this information, the clinician can begin to develop hypotheses as to the function of the behavior, as well as appropriate treatment interventions. Behavior analysts have typically divided the function of behavior into four categories: task avoidance, attention seeking, self-stimulation, and a combination of functions.

In one example of the use of this model, Iwata, Dorsey, Slifer, Bauman, and Richman (1994) conducted a functional assessment to clarify the variables that either produced or maintained self-injury in nine children with developmental disabilities. Over a number of weeks, children were repeatedly observed for 15-minute periods in one of four experimental conditions: social disapproval for self-injury; academic demands, in which the clinician turned away for 30 seconds following self-injury (with praise given for task completion); a no-demand play situation (with self-injury ignored); and a solitary condition. Six of the nine subjects consistently evidenced higher levels of self-injury in specific stimulus conditions, suggest-

ing that within-subject variability was a function of features of the environment. Figure 7.2 shows the percentages of 10-second intervals in which self-injury was observed for four children. These findings have implications for the selection of appropriate treatment intervention.

A number of other researchers have also used this model to assess children in a variety of outpatient clinic settings. For example, Cooper et al. (1992) conducted a functional assessment of 10 children with behavior problems during single outpatient visits. Each child was observed in five different situations: free play; a difficult academic task, which was not preferred by the child; an easy academic task, which was highly preferred by the child; parent attention during the best previous condition; and a therapist attention condition. For 8 of the 10 children, distinct patterns of performance occurred, leading to specific treatment recommendations based upon assessment results.

Several clinicians and researchers have also developed highly complex observation systems to code behavior in the home or school. Such systems typically involve an interval-recording strategy. This method divides time into small intervals (e.g., 10–15 seconds); observers record the presence or absence of as many as 25 possible behaviors during each interval. For example, McGee, Almeida, Sulzer-Azaroff, and Feldman (1992) used such a system to code social interactions between preschoolers with autism and typically developing peers. Daily 5-minute sessions between two peers were videotaped and coded in 10-second intervals. Coded behaviors included giving and/or receiving interactions and type of response (e.g., positive vs. negative, verbal vs. gestural). Breiner and Forehand (1982) observed mother–child interactions by coding both parent and child behaviors as they occurred in a sequential manner. A 30-second interval-recording system was used and involved the coding of behaviors such as rewards (parental praise or attention), parental commands, child compliance, and inappropriate behavior (e.g., crying, destruction of materials).

ASSESSMENT OF COMMUNITY RESOURCES

There has been growing recognition of the role community resources play in serving children with special needs and their families. This approach is one aspect of a model based upon family-centered assessment and intervention (see Dunst, Trivette, & Deal, 1994). The goals of this model include

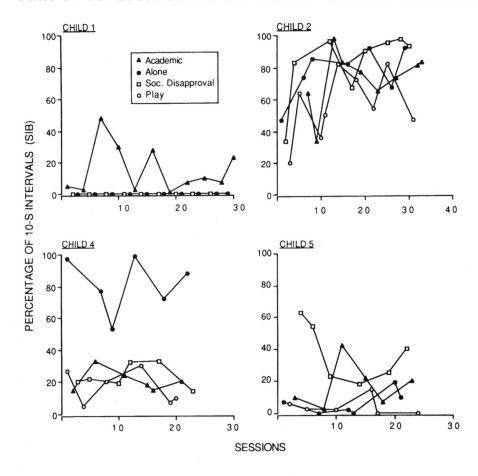

FIGURE 7.2. Percentages of intervals of self-injury for subjects 1, 2, 4, and 5 across sessions and experimental conditions. From Iwata, Dorsey, Slifer, Bauman, and Richman (1994, p. 205). Copyright 1994 by the *Journal of Applied Behavior Analysis*. Reprinted by permission.

(1) identifying families' needs, priorities, or concerns; (2) locating both formal and informal resources for meeting the needs; and (3) helping families identify and use their strengths and capabilities to procure resources in ways that strengthen family functioning (Hobbs et al., 1984). Community resources are in direct contrast to the services typically provided by agencies and school systems. These services have been defined as "specific or particular activit[ies] employed by a professional or professional agency for rendering help or assistance to an individual or group, such as occupational therapy or special instruction" (Trivette, Dunst, & Deal, 1996, p. 75). Conversely, community resources are defined as "the full range of possible types of community help or assistance . . . that might be mobilized and used to meet the needs of an individual or group" (Trivette et al.,

1996, p. 76). Dunst, Trivette, and their colleagues emphasize the utilization of multiple informal and formal community resources to address the needs of a child and his or her family, rather than sole reliance on professional assistance.

The professional service model has a number of inherent weaknesses, according to Trivette et al. (1996). First, it tends to be limited because it is defined by what professionals do and is professionally centered. Second, the professional service model is based upon scarcity of resources; the limited available services are provided only to the most needy, and the extent of a family's need is determined by professionals. Finally, formal professional services often limit the use of richer, more diverse, informal service and support networks in the community.

There is growing empirical evidence supporting a community resources model. Three recent studies conducted by Dunst and his colleagues seem to suggest that community-resource-based practices have significantly greater beneficial impacts on families than service-based interventions do. The first study, involving 22 families, was an extensive case study of the characteristics and effects of various types of practices employed by human service agencies (Dunst, Trivette, Starnes, Hamby, & Gordon, 1993). The families were asked to rate their reactions or feelings to service-based versus resource-based practices, as well as to rate the treatment outcome for each type of intervention (both sets of ratings were made on a 5-point scale). Practices defined as resource-based were associated with significantly more positive outcomes than were service-based practices. A second study compared 30 families randomly assigned to either service-based (formal respite care) or resource-based (collaborative effort to identify a range of community-based child care options) early intervention programming. Telephone follow-up found that the families assigned to the resource-based approaches demonstrated significantly greater change than did those assigned to the service-based models on the following measures: number of individuals who provided child care, successful attempts to obtain child care, perceived control over obtaining child care, and overall satisfaction with child care (Dunst, 1991). Finally, Trivette and her colleagues (Trivette et al., 1996) surveyed 1,300 parents of children participating in early intervention programs, requesting that they rate the extent to which the programs' practices emphasized community resources, the level of progress their children made, and the extent to which parents felt they had control over the kinds or services and activities provided. Results indicated significantly higher ratings of child progress and parental control when practices were resource-based rather than service-based.

Dunst, Trivette, and Deal (1988, pp. 18–19) describe 12 specific categories of community resources:

- Economic resources
- Physical and environmental resources
- Food and clothing resources
- Medical and dental care resources
- Employment and vocational resources
- Transportation and communication resources
- Adult education and enrichment resources
- Child education and intervention resources
- Child care resources
- Recreational resources
- Emotional resources
- Cultural and social resources

Specific examples of community resources include story times at a local library, classes at the YMCA/YWCA or community center, play groups, and children's programs offered at churches.

According to Trivette et al. (1996), the first step in assessing community resources is to identify a family's needs, concerns, and priorities, as noted earlier. The next step is to identify specific resources for meeting each of these needs. This is accomplished via the development of a community network map. Such a map identifies individuals and institutions who come in contact with the family, as well as other resources that might be tapped to address family concerns. Trivette et al. (1996) recommend that resources available to address each concern be mapped separately, so as to insure that this process will remain focused.

INTEGRATING ASSESSMENT RESULTS

With data and information gathered from a wide array of sources, it may initially seem a formidable task to integrate the assessment results, let alone to make treatment recommendations. Morgenstern and Klass (1991) suggest that the primary referral question should serve as the frame of reference for determining the answers to be provided during feedback to the family and in any subsequent report. Sattler (1988) recommends that several questions guide the integration of information gathered during the assessment. The most important of these are how the assessment results will help to answer the referral question, and what questions still remain to be answered. Once these issues have been addressed, the clinician must decide upon which major findings to interpret, which trends to develop in the feedback or report (e.g., do the results suggest developmental delays across all areas? Do the results indicate consistent patterns of errors or relative weaknesses?), and what recommendations to make. Crnic (1988) provides a list of six questions that may be useful in integrating assessment results. Briefly, they are as follows:

1. Is there significant test scatter across skills areas?
2. How do the results compare with the results of any previous assessments?
3. Did changes in the structure of testing (e.g.,

testing limits or allowing the use of alternative strategies) affect performance?

4. What behavioral factors were problems, and what factors were strengths? Did they affect the assessment outcome?

5. Did performance or behavior vary across settings?

6. Are historical variables (e.g., developmental, medical, behavioral) relevant to the child's performance?

When one is formulating specific recommendations following the assessment of a child with mental retardation, Sattler (1988) suggests that a number of questions be considered. They are as follows:

1. Do the results indicate a diagnosis of mental retardation?

2. Is the child eligible for special services?

3. What are the least restrictive options for programming?

4. If mainstreaming or inclusion is possible, what additional supports will be needed?

5. What are the child's social skills strengths and weaknesses?

6. What skills will be needed for productive employment (for adolescents)?

7. As the individual reaches adulthood, what types of supports will he or she require to live independently? If this is not possible, what type of living arrangement will be needed?

PROVIDING FEEDBACK

The success of the feedback session depends in large part on how the initial interview was conducted and on the extent to which the clinician and family have developed a shared referral question. Assisting the family to frame the proper question early in the assessment process sets the stage for a productive and useful feedback. The clinician should be careful not to focus the feedback solely on a child's or adolescent's deficits. Instead, it is important to stress strengths, as well as areas on which interventions will be focused. Perhaps the most difficult feedback to offer a family is the actual diagnosis of mental retardation. It is not unusual to find that others have already evaluated the child and found identical results, but have never used the term "mental retardation" when talking with the family. This places the clinician in an awkward and in some ways unfair position. Yet it is important that this information be shared with the family.

The clinician should also offer to meet again with the family members, to help them process the information and to insure that the recommendations have been followed. Specific recommendations should be provided in writing at the time of feedback whenever possible. These should include the names and phone numbers of individuals and agencies to contact for appropriate services; names and numbers for parent support groups; and local and state resources for services such as respite care, summer camps, and so on. Providing reading materials at the time can also be helpful. In addition, the family members should receive a copy of the clinician's report as soon as possible. Assessment results should not simply be exchanged among professionals and agencies, but should be shared with families. In fact, reports should be written with families in mind; they should be clear and understandable, with as little jargon as possible. Often, when the members of a family hear stressful news, it is difficult for them to hear the remainder of the findings and recommendations. Written reports provide another chance for family members to react to the results and recommendations.

Preator and McAllister (1995) provide some useful guidelines for providing feedback to parents of children and adolescents with developmental disabilities. These are presented in adapted form in Table 7.9.

SUMMARY

Behavioral assessment of a child or adolescent with mental retardation is a considerable challenge and requires a number of important skills on the part of the clinician. These include the ability to work with families; knowledge of developmental and etiological issues; experience in using a range of standardized and criterion-based assessment tools; understanding of the service delivery system; knowledge of the law as it pertains to developmental disabilities; and experience in providing clinical interventions with this population. The heterogeneity of this group of children makes assessment a particularly daunting task. Consequently, the clinician will need to gather data from as many sources as possible; to assess a wide range of areas of functioning; and to work closely with the family, as well as with professionals from other disciplines. Finally, the clinician should work with family members to push the limits often placed upon individuals with mental retardation. This means suggesting the creative use of supports to maximize the involvement of children and ado-

TABLE 7.9. Suggestions for Providing Feedback to Parents

Both parents, and/or other supporting family members, should be present if possible.

If the client is an adolescent, he or she should either be present or be given feedback by the clinician at a separate time. Having a younger child present may be preferable, but should be left up to the family.

The clinician should provide information about the child's strengths and positive characteristics, along with information on developmental functioning.

Jargon, including relatively common professional terms, should be avoided.

The limits of prognostication and the range of possible outcomes should be explained.

The family members should have as much time as they need to ask questions.

Parents should be provided with the opportunity to express their feelings, but should not be required to do so.

Parents should be assisted in making plans to carry out specific recommendations and interventions. Additional sources of information should be provided.

The opportunity to contact other parents should be facilitated.

A follow-up session should be offered.

Consideration should be given to providing the family with private time at the conclusion of the discussion.

Note. Adapted from Preator and McAllister (1995, p. 783). Copyright 1995 by the National Association of School Psychologists. Adapted by permission.

lescents with mental retardation in their schools, communities, and families.

REFERENCES

Abidin, R. R. (1990). *Manual for the Parenting Stress Index* (3rd ed.). Charlottesville, VA: Pediatric Psychology Press.

Achenbach, T. M. (1982). *Developmental psychopathology* (2nd ed.). New York: Ronald Press.

Achenbach, T. M. (1991). *Manual for the Child Behavior Checklist/4–18 and 1991 Profile.* Burlington: University of Vermont, Department of Psychiatry.

Alpern, G., Boll, T. J., & Shearer, M. (1989). *Developmental Profile II.* Aspen, CO: Psychological Development.

Aman, M. G. (1991). *Assessing psychopathology and behavior problems in persons with mental retardation: A review of available instruments.* Rockville, MD: U.S. Department of Health and Human Services.

Aman, M. G. (1994). Instruments for assessing treatment effects in developmentally disabled populations. *Assessment in Rehabilitation and Exceptionality, 1,* 1–20.

Aman, M. G., Kern, R. A., McGhee, D. E., & Arnold, E. (1993). Fenfluramine and methylphenidate in children with mental retardation and ADHD: Clinical and side effects. *Journal of the American Academy of Child and Adolescent Psychiatry, 32,* 851–859.

Aman, M. G., Marks, R., Turbott, S., Wilsher, C., & Merry, S. (1991). The clinical effects of methylphenidate and thioridazine in intellectually subaverage children. *Journal of the American Academy of Child and Adolescent Psychiatry, 30,* 246–256.

Aman, M. G., & Singh, N. N. (1986). *Manual for the Aberrant Behavior Checklist.* East Aurora, NY: Slosson Educational.

American Association on Mental Retardation (AAMR). (1992). *Mental retardation: Definition, classification, and systems of supports* (9th ed.). Washington, DC: Author.

American Psychiatric Association (APA). (1994). *Diagnostic and statistical manual of mental disorders* (4th ed.). Washington, DC: Author.

Ames, L. B., Gillespie, C., Haines, J., & Ilig, F. (1979). *The Gesell Institute's child from 1 to 6: Evaluating the behavior of the preschool child.* New York: Harper & Row.

Ando, H., & Yoshimura, I. (1978). Prevalence of maladaptive behavior in retarded children as a function of IQ and age. *Journal of Abnormal Child Psychology, 6,* 345–349.

Bagnato, S. J., Neisworth, J. T., & Munson, S. M. (1989). *Linking developmental assessment and early intervention: Curriculum-based prescriptions* (2nd ed.). Rockville, MD: Aspen.

Bales v. Clark, 523 F. Supp. 1366 (8th Cir. 1981).

Balthazar, E. E. (1976). *Balthazar Scales of Adaptive Behavior.* Palo Alto, CA: Consulting Psychologists Press.

Barkley, R. A. (1990). *Attention-Deficit Hyperactivity Disorder: A handbook for diagnosis and treatment.* New York: Guilford Press.

Battle v. Pennsylvania, 629 F.2d 269 (3d Cir. 1980), cert. denied 452 U.S. 968 (1981).

Baumeister, A. (1970). American residential institution: Its history and character. In A. Baumeister & E. Butterfield (Eds.), *Residential facilities for the mentally retarded* (pp. 1–28) Chicago: Aldine.

Bayley, N. (1949). Consistency and variability in the growth of intelligence from birth to eighteen years. *Journal of Genetic Psychology, 75,* 165–196.

Bayley, N. (1993). *Manual for the Bayley Scales of Infant Development* (2nd ed.). San Antonio, TX: Psychological Corporation.

Beckman, P. J. (1991). Comparison of mothers' and fathers' perceptions of the effect of young children with and without disabilities. *American Journal of Mental Retardation, 95*, 585–595.

Beery, K. E., & Buktenica, N. A. (1989). *Manual for the Developmental Test of Visual–Motor Integration* (3rd ed.). Cleveland, OH: Modern Curriculum Press.

Behar, L. B., & Stringfield, S. A. (1974). A behavior rating scale for the preschool child. *Developmental Psychology, 10*, 601–610.

Bender, L. (1938). A *Visual Motor Gestalt Test and its clinical use* (American Orthopsychiatric Association Research Monograph No. 3). New York: American Orthopsychiatric Association.

Beyer, H. A. (1991). Litigation involving people with mental retardation. In J. L. Matson & J. A. Mulick (Eds.), *Handbook of mental retardation* (2nd ed., pp. 74–96). Elmsford, NY: Pergamon Press.

Blatt, B., & Kaplan, F. (1966). *Christmas in purgatory*. Boston: Allyn & Bacon.

Brazelton, B. (1984). *Brazelton Neonatal Behavioral Assessment Scale—Revised*. Philadelphia: Lippincott.

Breiner, J., & Forehand, R. (1982). Mother–child interactions: A comparison of a clinic-referred developmentally delayed group and two non-delayed groups. *Applied Research in Mental Retardation, 3*, 175–183.

Breslau, N., Weitzman, M., & Messenger, K. (1981). Psychologic functioning of siblings of disabled children. *Pediatrics, 67*, 344–353.

Brigance, A. (1991). *Brigance Diagnostic Inventory of Early Development*. North Billerica, MA: Curriculum Associates.

Bristol, M. M. (1979). *Maternal coping with autistic children: Adequacy of interpersonal support and effect of child's characteristics*. Unpublished doctoral dissertation, University of North Carolina.

Brown, D., Simmons, V., & Methvin, J. (1986). *Oregon Project Curriculum for Visually Impaired and Blind Preschool Children*. Eugene, OR: Jackson County Education Service District.

Brown, L., & Leigh, J. (1986). *Manual for the Adaptive Behavior Inventory*. Austin, TX: Pro-Ed.

Bruininks, R. H. (1978). *Bruininks–Oseretsky Test of Motor Proficiency*. Circle Pines, MN: American Guidance Service.

Caldwell, B., & Bradley, R. (1978). *Home Observation for Measurement of the Environment*. Little Rock: University of Arkansas.

Caro-Martinez, L., Lurier, A., & Handen, B. L. (1994, October). *Developmentally disabled preschoolers with and without Attention Deficit Hyperactivity Disorder: A comparison study*. Paper presented at the Conference on Children and Adolescents with Emotional or Behavioral Disorders, Virginia Beach, VA.

Carrow-Woolfolk, E. (1985). *Test of Auditory Comprehension of Language* (rev. ed.). Allen, TX: DLM Teaching Resources.

Colarusso, R., & Hammill, D. (1972). *Manual for the Motor-Free Visual Perception Test*. Novato, CA: Academic Therapy.

Cone, J. D. (1984). *The Pyramid Scales: Criterion-referenced measures of adaptive behavior in severely handicapped persons*. Austin, TX: Pro-Ed.

Conners, C. K. (1990). *Conners Rating Scales manual*. North Tonawanda, NY: Multi-Health Systems.

Connolly, A. J. (1988). *Manual for the KeyMath Revised: A diagnostic inventory of essential mathematics*. Circle Pines, MN: American Guidance Service.

Cooke, T., Apollini, T., & Sundberg, D. (1981). *Early Independence: A Developmental Curriculum*. Bellevue, WA: Edmark.

Cooper, L., Wacker, D., Thursby, E., Plagmann, L., Harding, J., Millard, T., & Derby, M. (1992). Analysis of the effects of task preferences, task demands, and adult attention on child behavior in outpatient and classroom settings. *Journal of Applied Behavior Analysis, 25*, 823–840.

Corbett, J. A. (1979). Psychiatric morbidity and mental retardation. In F. E. James & R. P. Snaith (Eds.), *Psychiatric illness and mental handicap* (pp. 11–25). London: Gaskell.

Crnic, K. A. (1988). Mental retardation. In E. J. Mash & G. Terdal (Eds.), *Behavioral assessment of childhood disorders* (2nd ed., pp. 317–354). New York: Guilford Press.

Crnic, K. A., Friedrich, W., & Greenberg, M. (1983). Adaptation of families with mentally retarded children: A model of stress, coping, and family ecology. *American Journal of Mental Deficiency, 88*, 125–138.

Demb, H. B., Brier, N., & Huron, R. (1989). *The Adolescent Behavior Checklist (ABC)*. Unpublished manuscript, Rose F. Kennedy Center, Albert Einstein College of Medicine.

Donovan, A. (1988). Family stress and ways of coping with adolescents who have handicaps: Maternal perceptions. *American Journal on Mental Retardation, 92*, 502–509.

DuBose, R. (1981). Assessment of severely impaired young children: Problems and recommendations. *Topics in Early Childhood Special Education, 1*(2), 9–22.

Dugdale, R. L. (1910). *The Jukes: A study in crime, pauperism, disease and heredity*. New York: Putnam.

Dunn, L. M., & Dunn, L. M. (1981). *Peabody Picture Vocabulary Test—Revised*. Circle Pines, MN: American Guidance Service.

Dunst, C. J. (1991, February). *Empowering families: Principles and outcomes*. Paper presented at the 4th Annual Research Conference, "A System of Care of Children's Mental Health: Expanding the Research Base," Tampa, FL.

Dunst, C. J., Trivette, C. M., & Deal, A. G. (1988).

Enabling and empowering families: Principles and guidelines for practice. Cambridge, MA: Brookline Books.

Dunst, C. J., Trivette, C. M., & Deal, A. G. (1994). *Supporting and strengthening families: Methods, strategies and practices* (Vol. 1). Cambridge, MA: Brookline Books.

Dunst, C. J., Trivette, C. M., Starnes, A. L., Hamby, D. W., & Gordon, N. J. (1993). *Building and evaluating family support initiatives: A national study of programs for persons with developmental disabilities.* Baltimore: Paul H. Brookes.

Dyson, L. L. (1989). Adjustment of siblings of handicapped children: A comparison. *Journal of Pediatric Psychology, 14,* 215–229.

Dyson, L. L., Edgar, E., & Crnic, K. (1989). Psychological predictors of adjustment by siblings of developmentally disabled children. *American Journal on Mental Retardation, 94,* 292–302.

Eaton, I., & Menolascino, F. (1982). Psychiatric disorder in the mentally retarded: Types, problems, and challenges. *American Journal of Mental Deficiency, 139,* 1297–1303.

Edelbrock, C. S., Costello, A. J., Dulcan, M. K., Kalas, R., & Conover, N. C. (1985). Age differences in the reliability of the psychiatric interview of the child. *Child Development, 56,* 265–275.

Education of the Handicapped Act Amendment, Pub. L. No. 99-457, 20, U.S.C. §1471 (1986).

Education for All Handicapped Children Act, Pub. L. No. 94-142, 20 U.S.C. §1401 (1975).

Einfeld, S. L., & Tonge, B. J. (1990). *Development of an instrument to measure psychopathology in mentally retarded children and adolescents.* Unpublished manuscript, University of New South Wales, Sydney, Australia.

Epstein, M. H., Cullinan, D., & Gadow, K. (1986). Teacher ratings of hyperactivity in learning-disabled, emotionally disturbed, and mentally retarded children. *Journal of Special Education, 22,* 219–229.

Evans, I. M. (1990). Testing and diagnosis: A review and evaluation. In L. H. Meyer, C. A. Peck, & L. Brown (Eds.), *Critical issues in the lives of people with severe disabilities* (pp. 25–44). Baltimore: Paul H. Brookes.

Feinstein, C., Kaminer, Y., Barrett, R., & Tylenda, B. (1988). The assessment of mood and affect in developmentally disabled children and adolescents: The Emotional Disorders Rating Scale. *Research in Developmental Disabilities, 9,* 109–121.

Flynt, S. W., & Wood, T. A. (1989). Stress and coping of mothers of children with moderate mental retardation. *American Journal on Mental Retardation, 94,* 278–283.

Forssman, H., & Akesson, H. (1970). Mortality in the mentally deficient: A study of 12,903 institutionalized subjects. *Journal of Mental Deficiency Research, 14,* 276–294.

Fraser, W., Leudar, I., Gray, J., & Campbell, I. (1986).

Psychiatric and behaviour disturbance in mental handicap. *Journal of Mental Deficiency Research, 30,* 49–57.

Friedrich, W., Greenberg, M., & Crnic, K. (1983). A short-form of the Questionnaire on Resources and Stress. *American Journal on Mental Deficiency, 88,* 41–48.

French, J. L. (1964). *Manual: Pictorial Test of Intelligence.* Chicago: Riverside.

Furlong, J. M., & LeDrew, L. (1985). IQ = 68 = mildly retarded? Factors influencing multidisciplinary team recommendations on children with FS IQs between 63 and 75. *Psychology in the Schools, 22,* 5–9.

Galton, F. (1952). *Heredity genius: An inquiry into its laws and consequences.* New York: Horizon Press.

Gillberg, C. (1987). Associated neuropsychiatric problems in Swedish school children with mild mental retardation. *Uppsala Journal of Medical Science* (Suppl. 44), 111–114.

Goddard, H. H. (1913). *The Kallikak family: A study in heredity of feeble-mindedness.* New York: Macmillan.

Golden, C. J. (1987). *Luria–Nebraska Neuropsychological Battery: Children's Revision.* Los Angeles: Western Psychological Services.

Grossman, J. J. (Ed.). (1983). *Classification in mental retardation.* Washington, DC: American Association on Mental Deficiency.

Hagerman, R. J., & Sobesky, W. E. (1989). Psychopathology in fragile X syndrome. *American Journal of Orthopsychiatry, 59,* 142–152.

Handen, B. L., Breaux, A. M., Gosling, A., Ploof, D., & Feldman, H. (1990). Efficacy of methylphenidate among mentally retarded children with Attention Deficit Hyperactivity Disorder. *Pediatrics, 86,* 922–930.

Handen, B. L., Breaux, A. M., Janosky, J., McAuliffe, S., Feldman, & Gosling, A. (1992). Effects and non-effects of methylphenidate in children with mental retardation and ADHD. *Journal of the American Academy of Child and Adolescent Psychiatry, 31,* 455–461.

Handen, B. L., Feldman, R. S., & Honigman, A. (1987). Comparison of parent and teacher assessments of developmentally delayed children's behavior. *Exceptional Children, 54,* 137–144.

Haring, N., White, O., Edgar, E., Affleck, J., & Hayden, A. (1981). *Uniform Performance Assessment System.* Columbus, OH: Charles E. Merrill.

Hawkins, G. D., & Cooper, D. H. (1990). Adaptive behavior measures in mental retardation research: Subject description in AJMD/AJMR articles (1979–1987). *American Journal on Mental Retardation, 94,* 654–660.

Heber, R. (1959). A manual on terminology and classification in mental retardation. *American Journal of Mental Deficiency, 56* (Monograph Supplement, rev.).

Heumann, J. E. (1995, September). Making a good law better: IDEA proposal stresses greater parental involvement and student inclusion. *Exceptional Parent*, pp. 44–46.

Hill, B., & Bruininks, R. (1984). Maladaptive behavior of mentally retarded individuals in residential facilities. *American Journal of Mental Deficiency*, 88, 380–387.

Hiskey, M. S. (1966). *Manual for the Hiskey–Nebraska Test of Learning Aptitude*. Lincoln, NE: Union College Press.

Hobbs, N., Dokecki, P., Hoover-Dempsey, K., Moroney, R., Shayne, M., & Weeks, K. (1984). *Strengthening families*. San Francisco: Jossey-Bass.

Holroyd, J. (1974). The Questionnaire on Resources and Stress: An instrument to measure family response to a handicapped family member. *Journal of Community Psychology*, 2, 92–94.

Honig v. Doe, 108 S. Ct. 592 (1988).

Huttenlocher, P. R. (1991). Dendritic and synaptic pathology in mental retardation. *Pediatric Neurology*, 7, 79–85.

Individuals with Disabilities Education Act, Pub. L. No. 101-476, 20, U.S.C. §1400. (1990).

Iwata, B., Dorsey, M., Slifer, K., Bauman, K., & Richman, G. (1994). Toward a functional analysis of self-injury. *Journal of Applied Behavior Analysis*, 27, 197–210.

Jacobson, J. W. (1982). Problem behavior and psychiatric impairment within a developmentally disabled population: I. Behavior frequency. *Applied Research in Mental Retardation*, 3, 369–381.

Jaselskis, C. A., Cook, E. H., Jr., Fletcher, K. E., & Leventhal, B. L. (1992). Clonidine treatment of hyperactive and impulsive children with Autistic Disorder. *Journal of Clinical Psychopharmacology*, 12, 322–327.

Johnson-Martin, N., Attermeier, S., & Hacker, B. (1990). *The Carolina Curriculum for Preschoolers with Special Needs*. Baltimore: Paul H, Brookes.

Johnson-Martin, N., Jens, K., Attermeier, S., & Hacker, B. (1991). *The Carolina Curriculum for Infant and Toddlers with Special Needs*. Baltimore: Paul H. Brookes.

Kamphaus, R. W. (1987). Conceptual and psychometric issues in the assessment of adaptive behavior. *Journal of Special Education*, 21, 27–35.

Kaufman, A. S., & Kaufman, N. L. (1983). *The Kaufman Assessment Battery for Children*. Circle Pines, MN: American Guidance Service.

Kern, L., Mauk, J., Marder, T., & Mace, F. C. (1995). Functional analysis and intervention for breath holding. *Journal of Applied Behavior Analysis*, 28, 339–340.

Koller, H., Richardson, S., Katz, M., & McLaren, J. (1983). Behavior disturbance since childhood among 5-year birth cohort of all mentally retarded young adults in a city. *American Journal of Mental Deficiency*, 87, 386–395.

Koppitz, E. M. (1975). *The Bender Gestalt Test for young children: Vol. 2. Research and application, 1963–1973*. New York: Grune & Stratton.

Lambert, N., Nihira, K., & Leland, H. (1993). *Manual for the Adaptive Behavior Scale—School* (2nd ed.). Austin, TX: Pro-Ed.

Larry P. v. Riles, 343 F. Supp. 1306 (9th Cir. 1974).

Leiter, R. G. (1969). *General instructions for the Leiter International Performance Scale*. Chicago: Stoelting.

Levine, S., Elzey, R., Thormahlen, P., & Cain, L. (1976). *Manual for the T.M.R. School Competency Scales*. Palo Alto, CA: Consulting Psychologists Press.

Lobato, D., Barbour, L., Hall, L. J., & Miller, C. T. (1987). Psychosocial characteristics of preschool siblings of handicapped and nonhandicapped children. *Journal of Abnormal Child Psychology*, 15, 329–338.

Lord, K., Rutter, M., Goode, S., Heemsbergen, J., Jordan, H., Mawhood, J., & Schopler, D. (1989). Autism Diagnostic Observation Schedule: A standardized observation of communicative and social behavior. *Journal of Autism and Developmental Disorders*, 19, 185–212.

Lubbs, H. A. (1969). A marker-X chromosome. *American Journal of Human Genetics*, 21, 231–244.

MacLean, W. E., Jr. (1993). Overview. In J. L. Matson & R. P. Barrett (Eds.), *Psychopathology in the mentally retarded* (2nd ed., pp. 1–14). Needham Heights, MA: Allyn & Bacon.

MacMillan, D. L., Gresham, F. M., & Siperstein, G. N. (1995). Heightened concerns over the 1992 AAMR definition: Advocacy versus precision. *American Journal of Mental Retardation*, 100, 87–97.

Margalit, M., Shulman, S., & Stuchiner, N. (1989). Behavior disorders and mental retardation: The family system perspective. *Research in Developmental Disabilities*, 10, 315–326.

Markwardt, F. C., Jr. (1989). *Manual for the Peabody Individual Achievement Test—Revised*. Circle Pines, MN: American Guidance Service.

Marshburn, E., & Aman, M. (1992). Factor validity and norms for the Aberrant Behavior Checklist in a community sample of children with mental retardation. *Journal of Autism and Developmental Disorders*, 22, 357–373.

Masland, R. H. (1988). *Career research award address*. Paper presented at the annual meeting of the American Academy of Mental Retardation, Washington, DC.

Mastenbrook, J. (1978, September). Future directions in adaptive behavior assessment: Environmental adaptation measures. In A. T. Fisher (Chair), *Impact of adaptive behavior: ABIC and the environmental adaptation measure*. Symposium presented at the meeting of the American Psychological Association, Toronto.

Matson, J. L., Barrett, R. P., & Helsel, W. J. (1988). Depression in mentally retarded children. *Research in Developmental Disabilities*, 9, 39–46.

Matson, J. L., & Frame, C. (1983). Psychopathology. In J. L. Matson & S. E. Breuning (Eds.), *Assess-

ing the mentally retarded (pp. 115–142). New York: Grune & Stratton.

McCall, R. B. (1976). Toward an epigenetic conception of mental development in the first three years of life. In M. Lewis (Ed.), *Origins of intelligence: Infancy and early childhood* (pp. 97–122). New York: Plenum Press.

McCall, R. B., Appelbaum, M. I., & Hogarty, P. S. (1973). Developmental changes in mental performance. *Monographs of the Society for Research in Child Development, 38*(3, Serial No. 150), 1–83.

McCarthy, D. (1972). *Manual for the McCarthy Scales of Children's Abilities.* New York: Psychological Corporation.

McGee, G. C., Almeida, M. C., Sulzer-Azaroff, B., & Feldman, R. (1992). Promoting reciprocal interactions via peer incidental teaching. *Journal of Applied Behavior Analysis, 25,* 117–126.

McKinney, B., & Peterson, R. A. (1987). Predictors of stress in parents of developmentally disabled children. *Journal of Pediatric Psychology, 12,* 133–150.

McLaren, J., & Bryson, S. E. (1987). Review of recent epidemiological studies of mental retardation: Prevalence, associated disorders, and etiology. *American Journal of Mental Retardation, 92,* 243–254.

Menolascino, F. (1977). *Challenges in mental retardation: Progressive ideology and services.* New York: Human Sciences Press.

Mercer, J., R., & Lewis, J. F. (1978). *System of Multicultural Pluralistic Assessment.* San Antonio, TX: Psychological Corporation.

Miller, J. F. (1992). Development of speech and language in children with Down syndrome. In I. T. Lott & E. E. McCoy (Eds.), *Down syndrome: Advances in medical care* (pp. 39–50). New York: Wiley.

Mills v. Board of Education, 348 F. Supp. 866 (1972).

Morgenstern, M., & Klass, E. (1991). Standard intelligence tests and related assessment techniques. In J. L. Matson & J. A. Mulick (Eds.), *Handbook of mental retardation* (2nd ed., pp. 195–210). Elmsford, NY: Pergamon Press.

Mullen, E. M. (1989). *Infant Mullen Scales of Early Learning.* Cranston, RI: T.O.T.A.L. Child.

Neisworth, J. T., & Bagnato, S. J. (1987). Developmental retardation. In V. Van Hasselt & M. Hersen (Eds.), *Psychological evaluation of the developmentally and physically disabled* (pp. 179–211). New York: Plenum Press.

Newland, T. E. (1971). *Blind Learning Aptitude Test.* Champaign: University of Illinois Press.

Nyhan, W. L. (1976). Behavior in the Lesch–Nyhan Syndrome. *Journal of Autism and Childhood Schizophrenia, 6,* 235–252.

Orvaschel, H., & Puig-Antich, J. (1987). *Schedule for Affective Disorders and Schizophrenia for School-Age Children* (4th ed.). Unpublished manuscript, University of Pittsburgh, Western Psychiatric Institute and Clinic.

Parks, S. (1992). *Hawaii Early Learning Profile (HELP).* Palo Alto, CA: VORT.

Parsons, J. A., May, J. G., & Menolascino, F. J. (1984). The nature and incidence of mental illness in mentally retarded individuals. In F. J. Menolascino & J. A. Stark (Eds.), *Handbook of mental illness in the mentally retarded* (pp. 3–44). New York: Plenum Press.

Pearson, D., & Aman, M. G. (1994). Ratings of hyperactivity and developmental indices: Should clinicians correct for developmental level? *Journal of Autism and Developmental Disorders, 24,* 395–404.

Pennsylvania Association of Retarded Children (PARC) v. Pennsylvania, 334 F. Supp. 1257 (E.D. Pa. 1971).

Popovich, D. (1981). *A Prescriptive Behavioral Checklist for the Severely and Profoundly Retarded* (Vol. 3). Baltimore: University Park Press.

Preator, K., & McAllister, J. (1995). Best practices assessing infants and toddlers. In A. Thomas & J. Grimes (Eds.), *Best practices in school psychology* (pp. 775–788). Washington, DC: National Association of School Psychologists.

Pueschel, S. M., & Thuline, H. C. (1991). Chromosome disorders. In J. L. Matson & J. A. Mulick (Eds.), *Handbook of mental retardation* (2nd ed., pp. 115–138). Elmsford, NY: Pergamon Press.

Rabkin, J. G., & Streuning, E. L. (1976). Life events, stress and illness. *Science, 194,* 1013–1020.

Raloff, J. (1982). Childhood lead: Worrisome national levels. *Science News, 121,* 88.

Ramirez, S. A., & Kratochwill, T. R. (1990). Development of the Fear Survey for Children With and Without Mental Retardation. *Behavioral Assessment, 12,* 457–470.

Reich, W., & Welner, Z. (1989). *Diagnostic Interview for Children and Adolescents—Revised.* St. Louis: Washington University, Division of Child Psychiatry.

Reiss, S. (1993). Assessment of psychopathology in persons with mental retardation. In J. L. Matson & R. P. Barrett (Eds.), *Psychopathology in the mentally retarded* (2nd ed., pp. 17–38). Needham Heights, MA: Allyn & Bacon.

Reiss, S., & Szyszko, J. (1983). Diagnostic overshadowing and professional experience with mentally retarded persons. *American Journal of Mental Deficiency, 86,* 567–574.

Reitan, R. M. (1993). *Manual for the Reitan–Indiana Neuropsychological Test Battery for Children.* S. Tucson, AZ: Reitan Neuropsychological Laboratory.

Reitan, R. M., & Wolfson, D. (1992). *Neuropsychological evaluation of older children.* S. Tucson, AZ: Neuropsychology Press.

Reschly, D. J., & Ward, S. M. (1991). Use of adaptive behavior and overrepresentation of black students in programs for students with mild mental retardation. *American Journal of Mental Retardation, 96,* 257–268.

Reynolds, W. M. (1989). *Self-Report Depression Questionnaire (SRDA) administration booklet*. Odessa, FL: Psychological Assessment Resources.

Rheinscheld, T. L. (1989). *A factor analytic study of the Preschool Behavior Questionnaire with developmentally delayed children ages 3–6*. Unpublished master's thesis, Ohio State University.

Robinson, N. M., & Robinson, H. B. (1976). *The mentally retarded child* (2nd ed.). New York: McGraw-Hill.

Rutter, M., Graham, P., & Yule, W. (1970). *A neuropsychiatric study in childhood*. London: Spastics International.

Ryan, M. R., & Dietiker, K. E. (1979). Reliability and clinical validity of the Children's Fear Survey Schedule. *Journal of Behavior Therapy and Experimental Psychiatry, 9*, 303–309.

Salisbury, C. (1987). Stressors of parents with young handicapped and nonhandicapped children. *Journal of the Division for Early Childhood, 11*, 154–160.

Sattler, J. M. (1988). *Assessment of children*. San Diego, CA: Jerome M. Sattler, Publisher.

Semel, E., Wiig, E., & Secord, W. (1987). *Manual for the Clinical Evaluation of Language Fundamentals–Revised*. San Antonio, TX: Psychological Corporation.

Shaffer, D., Fisher, P., Dulcan, D., Davies, M., Piacentini, J., Schwab-Stone, M., Lahey, B., Bordon, K., Jensen, P., Bird, H., Canino, G., & Rejier, D. (1992). *National Institute of Mental Health Diagnostic Interview Schedule for Children, Version 2.3 (DISC 2.3)*. Unpublished manuscript, New York State Psychiatric Institute.

Shea, V. (1984). Explaining mental retardation and autism to parents. In E. Schopler & G. B. Mesibov (Eds.), *The effects of autism on the family* (pp. 265–288). New York: Plenum Press.

Sheslow, D., & Adams, W. (1990). *Manual for the Wide Range Assessment of Memory and Learning*. Wilmington, DE: Jastak.

Silverstein, A. B. (1973). Note on prevalence. *American Journal of Mental Deficiency, 77*, 380–382.

Silverstein, A. B. (1986). Nonstandard standard scores on the Vineland Adaptive Behavior Scales: A cautionary note. *American Journal of Mental Deficiency, 91*, 1–4.

Simeonsson, R. J., Huntingdon, G. S., Short, R. J., & Ware, W. B. (1982). The Carolina Record of Individual Behavior. *Characteristics of Handicapped Infants and Children, 2*, 43–55.

Slentz, K., Close, D., Benz, M., & Taylor, V. (1982). *Community Living Assessment and Teaching System (CLATS): Self-care curriculum*. Omro, WI: Conover.

Song, A., Jones, S., Lippert, J., Metzgen, K., Miller, J., & Borreca, C. (1984). Wisconsin Behavior Rating Scale: Measure of adaptive behavior for the developmental levels of 0 to 3 years. *American Journal of Mental Deficiency, 88*, 401–410.

Sparrow, S. S., Balla, D. A., & Cicchetti, D. V. (1984). *Vineland Adaptive Behavior Scales*. Circle Pines, MN: American Guidance Service.

Special Education Services and Programs under General Provisions §342.1, 20 Pa. Bull. (1990).

Spragg, P. A. (1988). *Structured Clinical Interview*. Unpublished instrument, University of Colorado Health Sciences Center, Denver.

Sprague, R. L. (1982). *BeERS (Behavior Evaluation Rating Scale)*. Unpublished manuscript, University of Illinois.

Strohmer, D. & Prout, H. (1991). *Emotional Problems Scales: Behavior Rating Scales*. Schenectady, NY: Genium.

Tawney, J, Knapp, D., O'Reilly, C., & Pratt, S. (1979). *Programmed Environments Curriculum*. Columbus, OH: Charles E. Merrill.

Thorndike, R. L., Hagan, E. P., & Sattler, J. M. (1986). *Guide for administering and scoring the Stanford–Binet Intelligence Scale* (4th ed.). Chicago: Riverside.

Trivette, C. M., Dunst, C. J., & Deal, A. G. (1996). Resource-based early intervention practices. In S. K. Thuran, J. R. Cornwell, & S. R. Gottwald (Eds.), *The contexts of early intervention: Systems and settings* (pp. 73–92). Baltimore: Paul H. Brookes.

Valla, J., Bergeron, L., Berube, H., Gaudet, N., & St.-Georges, M. (1994). A structured pictorial questionnaire to assess DSM-III-R-based diagnoses in children (6–11 years): Development, validity, and reliability. *Journal of Abnormal Child Psychology, 22*, 403–423.

Wechsler, D. (1989). *Manual for the Wechsler Preschool and Primary Scale of Intelligence—Revised*. San Antonio, TX: Psychological Corporation.

Wechsler, D. (1991). *Wechsler Intelligence Scale for Children* (3rd. ed.). San Antonio, TX: Psychological Corporation.

Wechsler, D. (1992). *Manual for the Wechsler Individual Achievement Test*. San Antonio, TX: Psychological Corporation.

West Virginia Department of Education. (1985). *Regulations for the education of exceptional students* (Office of Special Education, Policy #2419). Charleston: Author.

White, O. R., & Haring, N. G. (1978). Evaluating educational programs serving the severely and profoundly handicapped. In N. G. Haring & D. D. Bricker (Eds.), *Teaching the severely handicapped* (Vol. 3, pp. 153–200). Seattle: American Association for the Education of the Severely/Profoundly Handicapped.

Wiig, E., Secord, W., & Semel, E. (1992). *Manual for the Clinical Evaluation of Language Fundamentals—Preschool*. San Antonio, TX: Psychological Corporation.

Wilkinson, G. S. (1993). *Manual for the Wide Range Achievement Test—3*. Wilmington, DE: Jastak.

Willoughby-Herb, S. J., & Neisworth, J. T. (1982).

HICOMP Preschool Curriculum. Columbus, OH: Charles E. Merrill.

Wing, L. (1982). *Schedule of Handicaps, Behaviour and Skills*. Unpublished manuscript, MRC Social Psychiatry Unit, Institute of Psychiatry, London.

Wing, L., & Gould, J. (1978). Systematic recording of behaviors and skills of retarded and psychotic children. *Journal of Autism and Childhood Schizophrenia, 8*, 79–97.

Wolfensberger, W. (1969). The origin and nature of our institutional models. In R. B. Kugel & W. Wolfensberger (Eds.), *Changing patterns in residential services for the mentally retarded* (pp. 59–171). Washington, DC: U.S. Government Printing Office.

Woodcock, R., & Johnson, W. B. (1989). *Manual for the Woodcock–Johnson Psycho-Eucational Battery—Revised*. Allen, TX: DLM Teaching Resources.

Zigler, E., & Hodapp, R. (1986). *Understanding mental retardation*. Cambridge, England: Cambridge University Press.

Chapter Eight

AUTISTIC DISORDER

Crighton Newsom
Christine A. Hovanitz

Autism has attracted considerable interest since the disorder was first named and described by the psychiatrist Leo Kanner at Johns Hopkins University Hospital in 1943. Much of the professional, scientific, and even lay fascination with autistic children undoubtedly springs from their severe deficits in socialization, communication, and imagination, in combination with relatively spared motor functioning and (in some autistic children) islets of special or extraordinary abilities.

This chapter selectively reviews contemporary assessment practices, emphasizing diagnostic considerations, treatment planning, work with families, and methods for the functional analysis of problem behaviors. First, a discussion of diagnostic issues addresses (1) Kanner syndrome and (2) the pervasive developmental disorders of the *Diagnostic and Statistical Manual of Mental Disorders*, fourth edition (DSM-IV; American Psychiatric Association, 1994), with Autistic Disorder receiving most of the attention. Next, a critical review of diagnostic checklists/interviews, diagnostic observational procedures, and rating scales is undertaken, to indicate the current state of the art in efforts to make the diagnosis of autism more objective. Then assessment for treatment planning and evaluation is considered, addressing intelligence tests, adaptive behavior scales, and ecological assessment methods. Some approaches to the assessment of families are presented next, followed by methods developed specifically for behavior management efforts.

DIAGNOSIS

The classification of severely behavior-disordered children has long posed significant problems and generated controversy. In what is the oldest surviving detailed description of a child who was probably autistic, Itard (1801/1962) noted that he and his mentor Pinel disagreed on the diagnosis and prognosis of the Wild Boy of Aveyron. During the rest of the 19th and early 20th centuries, scattered case reports of markedly atypical children appeared, believed to be cases of very-early-onset schizophrenia or neurological deterioration (Rutter & Schopler, 1988). From the 1930s through the 1950s, many psychiatrists—including Potter (1933), Bender (1947), Despert (1938), Kanner (1943), and Mahler (1952)—described and attempted to classify the severely disturbed children they saw. Most of the syndromes that they identified as subclasses of "childhood psychosis" or "childhood schizophrenia" have not survived in formal nosologies, because research by Kolvin and others (Kolvin, 1971; Kolvin, Ounsted, Humphrey, & McNay, 1971; Makita, 1974) showed that severe disorders with early childhood onsets can be differentiated from disorders resembling adult schizophrenia. The latter are virtually never seen before age 7 and typically do not begin until puberty. In more recent decades, various international committees, conferences, and task forces with access to a large, constantly expanding research literature have worked on the problems in this area (e.g., Rutter et al., 1969; Schopler & Mesibov, 1988; Spitzer, 1980; Volkmar et al., 1994). Some progress has been made, as seen in DSM-IV. The Schizophrenia, Childhood Type of DSM-II has been superseded by four categories in DSM-IV: Autistic Disorder, Rett's Disorder, Childhood Disintegrative Disorder, and Asperger's Disorder. The presentation of these four syndromes is an advance over previous diagnostic schemes, but may create the impression of greater specificity and distinctiveness among these groups of children than is actually the case. In reality, there is considerable overlap among these categories, as well as between these categories and other conditions (such as mental retardation and learning disabilities). Factors contributing to diagnostic difficulties in this area (Stone & Hogan, 1993) are the low prevalence rate (Zahner & Pauls, 1987), individual differences in symptom expression (Lord, 1991), and changing concepts of pervasive developmental disorders over the years (Rutter & Schopler, 1988).

Kanner Syndrome

The "early infantile autism" identified by Kanner in 1943 is a narrower concept than the Autistic Disorder of DSM-IV. Over time, the former has become known simply as "Kanner syndrome" or "classical autism," to distinguish it from the more generic syndrome described in DSM and most of the literature. The point of mentioning Kanner syndrome here, however, is not simply to note its historical significance (valuable as that is in understanding the earlier literature and continuing controversies), but to emphasize that this disorder is distinguishable from other autistic syndromes and may differ in etiology (Lotter, 1966; Wing, Yeates, Brierley, & Gould, 1976).

Table 8.1 lists Kanner's criteria as abstracted from his original paper (1943). The language and cognitive criteria (points 2 and 4) indicate that Kanner initially saw what would now be considered a fairly high-functioning subgroup of autistic children (i.e., children with intelligence in the moderately retarded range or higher). Later, after seeing many more children, he relegated these two criteria to secondary status and changed the physical development criterion (point 5) to emphasize fascination for objects. "Extreme self-isolation" and "insistence on the preservation of sameness" continued as the primary criteria, the *sine qua non* for the diagnosis (Eisenberg & Kanner, 1956). Unfortunately, the main effect of emphasizing only two essential features that are difficult to operationalize was to create the opening wedge for subsequent confusion and misapplication of the diagnosis (Newsom & Rincover, 1981; Rutter, 1978). In current clinical practice, children with Kanner syndrome are diagnosed as cases of Autistic Disorder, but in research the more specific designation of Kanner syndrome is preferred when it is warranted (i.e., a child meets all the criteria in Table 8.1). Children with Kanner syndrome can be discriminated from other autistic children primarily by a history of not being cuddly at ages 2–5 years and the presence of ritualistic routines, distress over changes in the environment, "splinter" skills, good fine-motor coordination, and fascination with mechanical objects or appliances (Prior, Perry, & Gajzago, 1975; Rimland, 1971).

TABLE 8.1. Diagnostic Criteria for Kanner Syndrome

1. Extreme autistic aloneness from birth that ignores or shuts out all outside stimuli, as indicated by a failure to assume the normal anticipatory posture prior to being picked up in infancy, feeding problems, fear of loud noises and moving objects, unresponsiveness to other people's verbalizations, failure to look at others' faces, failure to play with other children, and failure to notice the comings and goings of the parents.
2. Language abnormalities, including mutism (which appears to be elective) in a minority of children, and noncommunicative speech in the majority. The speaking children learn to name objects easily and repeat nursery rhymes, prayers, songs, and lists requiring an excellent rote memory but no comprehension. They also exhibit lack of spontaneous sentence formation and immediate or delayed echolalia, resulting in the reversal of personal pronouns in requests. There is extreme literalness in the use of prepositions and "affirmation by repetition" ("yes" is indicated by simply echoing the question).
3. An anxiously obsessive desire for the maintenance of sameness that nobody but the child may disrupt. Changes in daily routine, furniture arrangement, an arrangement of objects, or the wording of requests, or the sight of anything broken or incomplete, will produce tantrums or despair. There is a limitation in the variety of spontaneous activity, including rhythmic movements and a preoccupation with objects that do not change their appearance or position except when manipulated by the child.
4. Good cognitive potential, as indicated by intelligent and serious-minded, yet "anxiously tense," facial expressions; excellent memory for previous events, poems, names, and complex patterns and sequences; and good performance on nonverbal tests.
5. Essentially normal physical development, with better fine motor than gross motor skills.

Note. Abstracted from Kanner (1943, pp. 217–250).

Pervasive Developmental Disorders

The term "pervasive" is used to distinguish Autistic Disorder and the three related disorders in DSM-IV from the "specific" developmental disorders (learning, communication, motor, etc.) described elsewhere in DSM-IV. "Pervasive" also highlights the fact that severe impairments across multiple areas of functioning are present. The use of "developmental" connotes two important ideas: first, that biological rather than social or psychogenic factors are believed to be paramount in the etiologies of these disorders; and, second, that they are related to other developmental disorders (e.g., mental retardation and learning disabilities), and are not simply childhood versions of adult disorders.

Autistic Disorder is the category that applies to most cases of severe behavior disorders first evident in infancy. Rett's Disorder characterizes children who begin to exhibit several specific deficits after a period of normal development. Childhood Disintegrative Disorder describes children who show a marked regression in many areas following a period of normal development. Asperger's Disorder applies to children who show the same kinds of social impairments and restricted, stereotyped interests as autistic children, but not the language impairments. Pervasive Developmental Disorder Not Otherwise Specified is a residual category for children who show pervasive impairments but do not fully meet the criteria for one of the other categories. Autistic Disorder is now discussed in detail.

Autistic Disorder

The DSM-IV criteria for Autistic Disorder appear in Table 8.2. This criterion set is not, strictly speaking, a revision of the DSM-III-R criteria, but a somewhat shortened version of the criteria in the *International Classification of Diseases*, 10th revision (ICD-10; World Health Organization, 1992). This approach was taken because the DSM-III-R

TABLE 8.2. DSM-IV Diagnostic Criteria for Autistic Disorder

A. A total of six (or more) items from (1), (2), and (3), with at least two from (1), and one each from (2) and (3):
   (1) qualitative impairment in social interaction, as manifested by at least two of the following:
      (a) marked impairment in the use of multiple nonverbal behaviors such as eye-to-eye gaze, facial expression, body postures, and gestures to regulate social interaction
      (b) failure to develop peer relationships appropriate to developmental level
      (c) a lack of spontaneous seeking to share enjoyment, interests, or achievements with other people (e.g., by a lack of showing, bringing, or pointing out objects of interest)
      (d) lack of social or emotional reciprocity
   (2) qualitative impairments in communication as manifested by at least one of the following:
      (a) delay in, or total lack of, the development of spoken language (not accompanied by an attempt to compensate through alternative modes of communication such as gesture or mime)
      (b) in individuals with adequate speech, marked impairment in the ability to initiate or sustain a conversation with others
      (c) stereotyped and repetitive use of language or idiosyncratic language
      (d) lack of varied, spontaneous make-believe play or social imitative play appropriate to developmental level
   (3) restricted repetitive and stereotyped patterns of behavior, interests, and activities, as manifested by at least one of the following:
      (a) encompassing preoccupation with one or more stereotyped and restricted patterns of interest that is abnormal either in intensity or focus
      (b) apparently inflexible adherence to specific, nonfunctional routines or rituals
      (c) stereotyped and repetitive motor mannerisms (e.g., hand or finger flapping or twisting, or complex whole-body movements)
      (d) persistent preoccupation with parts of objects

B. Delays or abnormal functioning in at least one of the following areas, with onset prior to age 3 years: (1) social interaction, (2) language as used in social communication, or (3) symbolic or imaginative play.

C. The disturbance is not better accounted for by Rett's Disorder or Childhood Disintegrative Disorder.

Note. From American Psychiatric Association (1994, pp. 70–71). Copyright 1994 by the American Psychiatric Association. Reprinted by permission.

criteria were found to be overly broad, resulting in too many false positives, especially among individuals with severe mental retardation (Volkmar, Bregman, Cohen, & Cicchetti, 1988). The ICD-10 criteria had the best combination of sensitivity (the proportion of true cases meeting the criteria) and specificity (the proportion of true noncases failing to meet the criteria), as well as the highest level of agreement with clinicians' diagnoses, in comparison with DSM-III and DSM-III-R (Volkmar et al., 1994).

The Autistic Disorder diagnosis requires that there be least two identifiable deficits in social interaction (A1), one each in communication (A2) and stereotyped behavior (A3), and two more in any of these three areas. These criteria are discussed further below. Criterion B requires that the delays or abnormalities in these three areas be present by 3 years of age, thus reinstating the age-of-onset criterion that was lacking in DSM-III-R. Criterion C excludes children with Rett's Disorder or Childhood Disintegrative Disorder.

Areas of Deficit: The DSM-IV A Criteria

A1. Qualitative Impairment in Social Interaction

The identification of impaired social interaction requires that the child's level of social development be significantly below his or her level of intelligence, so that social deficits attributable solely to mental retardation can be ruled out. Rutter and Schopler (1988) have summarized the basic social deficits in autistic children as an inadequate appreciation of social and affective cues, lack of response to others' emotions, lack of modulation of behavior according to social context, and lack of social and emotional reciprocity.

Examples of the kinds of social abnormalities seen in autistic children at different ages are as follows. In early infancy, there may be no response to a human voice, as well as failure to develop social smiling. The baby may not adopt an anticipatory posture of the arms or shoulders when about to be picked up. Autistic infants tend not to be cuddly when held; instead of adjusting to a parent's body, they remain either limp or stiff. The curiosity and visual exploratory behaviors characteristic of normal infants are absent or grossly deficient (Wing, 1976).

Between 1 and 5 years of age, signs of social aloofness become more obvious. Autistic toddlers generally ignore parents and siblings except to get their immediate needs met. They show no significant preference for interacting with their mothers instead of a stranger in a play setting, but they may show some degree of attachment by staying in close proximity to the mother when she returns from a brief absence (Sigman & Ungerer, 1984). Observed among peers in a classroom during unstructured time, they will usually be physically distant from other children, never initiating and only rarely responding to social interactions. They may respond positively to an adult's tickling or rough-and-tumble play, but not to questions or conversations. Cooperative and symbolic play with toys is lacking (Black, Freeman, & Montgomery, 1975). Play instead consists of repetitive, unimaginative manipulations of objects (e.g., spinning the wheels on a toy truck) or appropriate but limited and stereotyped routines (e.g., repeatedly loading and unloading a toy truck) rather than imaginative activities (Wing, Gould, Yeates, & Brierley, 1977). Lack of imitation is common (Smith & Bryson, 1994), although autistic children who do imitate tend to be better at tasks requiring manipulation of objects than at tasks requiring reproduction of actions (DeMyer et al., 1972).

Lack of eye contact, or gaze avoidance, is usually considered particularly characteristic of autistic children. Rutter (1978), however, has suggested that their eye contact is not so much lacking as it is deviant. Unlike normal children, they fail to look directly at others' eyes when they want to get the others' attention or when they are being spoken to (Mirenda, Donnellan, & Yoder, 1983). Instead, they may look at others only out of the corners of their eyes, or use an indirect, off-center gaze that creates in a recipient the impression of being stared through.

In later childhood, improvements in social behavior usually occur, especially if language and social skills have been directly taught. A certain superficial quality often remains in an autistic child's social interactions, however. Studies by Schreibman and Lovaas (1973), Hobson (1983, 1987), and Baron-Cohen, Leslie, and Frith (1986) indicate that autistic children differ from both normal and retarded children of the same mental age in discriminating age- and gender-related cues and in appreciating what other people are thinking. Even higher-functioning autistic adolescents and adults tend to show a lack of cooperative group play, failure to make close friendships, and inability to recognize feelings in others or to show deep affection. They are usually described as "loners" who may desire social contact but do not know how to establish or sustain it, and may feel inadequate and isolated (Volkmar & Cohen, 1985).

A2. *Qualitative Impairments in Communication*

As many as 80% of autistic children are mute when first diagnosed in early childhood (Ornitz, Guthrie, & Farley, 1977), and about 50% remain mute for life in the absence of intensive treatment (Rutter, Greenfeld, & Lockyer, 1967). Most of these individuals are not completely silent, but are what is termed "functionally mute." They are able to produce vocal noises, phonemes, and word approximations, but not to articulate words and phrases. As a result, the parent or pediatrician may suspect a hearing impairment or Selective Mutism, but these hypotheses are rarely substantiated in audiological and language evaluations. However, evaluation of auditory perceptual functioning may reveal overselective attention to certain sounds and ignoring of others (Reynolds, Newsom, & Lovaas, 1974), or severe deficits in attending to the multiple acoustic features of speech stimuli (Schreibman, Kohlenberg, & Britten, 1986). Unlike children with hearing impairment or specific language disorders, autistic children typically do not develop gestural or other nonverbal means of communicating complex messages (Paul, 1987).

Both retarded and nonretarded autistic children show severe speech delays. Bartak and Rutter (1976) studied autistic children with IQs above and below 70. For the lower group, the mean age of the first use of single words was 4.7 years; for the higher group, it was 2.6 years. Frequently mentioned in association with language deficits are abnormalities or deficits in prelinguistic skills, including babbling, pointing, showing, and turn taking (Bartak, Rutter, & Cox, 1975; Ricks, 1975). Curcio (1978) noted that autistic children fail to engage in behaviors to direct an adult's attention to an object as normal toddlers do, unless they want the item. Then they either look and wait or take the adult's hand and guide it to the item. Thus, they lack the joint attention strategies of "protodeclarative" pointing (i.e., pointing to something to draw someone else's attention to it simply for the purpose of sharing an observation), although they often do have "proto-imperative" pointing (pointing at something to request it) (Baron-Cohen, 1989).

Comprehension is somewhat less delayed than expressive language. Parents of autistic children recall the understanding of simple nouns occurring at a median age of 24 months, or 12 months later than reported by parents of normal children (Ornitz et al., 1977). Frequently, comprehension remains limited to concrete nouns associated with strong reinforcers and punishers, familiar aspects of the daily routine, and requests accompanied by gestures, indicating dependence on visual cues. In speaking children, problems persist with understanding abstract concepts, feelings, humor, idiomatic expressions, and words varying with speaker and context, such as pronouns and prepositions (Ricks & Wing, 1976). Intonation may be flat, singsong, or hypernasal, and volume may be poorly controlled (Fay, 1980).

The area of greatest deficit among speaking autistic children is "pragmatics"—that is, the appropriate use of language to accomplish social objectives. They make poor use of prosodic cues in others' speech when conversing (Frankel, Simmons, & Richey, 1987); they are also less able than normals to respond correctly to speech or gestures used to direct their attention, or to use attention-directing cues themselves when making requests (Landry & Loveland, 1988). They often fail to listen, interpret words too literally, make irrelevant comments, and persist in peculiar uses of speech (Rumsey, Rapoport, & Sceery, 1985). In response to requests for clarification, they are less likely than matched retarded controls to be specific or to add useful information to help the listener (Paul & Cohen, 1984).

Children with minimal speech typically exhibit both "immediate" and "delayed" echolalia. Immediate echolalia is the repetition of an utterance of another person within a few seconds. The voicing, intonation, and articulation are usually faithful to the original utterance and better than in the child's own spontaneous speech. Echoes of whole sentences may preserve only the latter part of the sentence, apparently because of auditory memory span limitations. Immediate echolalia may be "exact" or "mitigated"—that is, may include alterations in content or structure. Unlike the more common exact echolalia, mitigated echolalia occurs infrequently in autistic children, but when it does, it indicates some processing of verbal input and thus a somewhat higher level of language development (Fay, 1980). One major determinant of immediate echolalia is the child's failure to comprehend the utterance just heard (Carr, Schreibman, & Lovaas, 1975; Fay, 1969). Some immediate echolalia appears to serve communicative functions, such as affirmation, turn taking, requests, rehearsal, and self-regulation (Prizant & Duchan, 1981). The presence of either immediate or delayed echolalia is significant for language prognosis. Echolalic children invariably progress faster and farther in language acquisition than initially mute children (Lovaas, 1977), particularly if remediation begins when they are young (Howlin, 1981; Lovaas, 1987).

Delayed echolalia may occur hours, days, or weeks after the original verbal input. The content is often either melodic (TV commercial jingles or snatches of songs) or emotional (commands, reprimands, or fragments of arguments between others). Delayed echolalia may be intrinsically reinforcing (Lovaas, Varni, Koegel, & Lorsch, 1977), and it can function as an attempt to avoid demands (Durand & Crimmins, 1987), as well as sometimes having other communicative functions (Charlop & Haymes, 1994; Prizant & Rydell, 1984).

Echolalic children often show "pronominal reversal"—that is, echoing the second- or third-person pronoun in sentences heard, instead of substituting "I" as is required when shifting from listener to speaker. When asked, "Do you want a cookie?," the child responds, "You want a cookie?" Fay (1980) has noted that the term "pronominal reversal" is possibly misleading, because the child is not deliberately exchanging pronouns but is simply repeating what is heard. Evidence that the phenomenon is attributable to echolalia and memory deficits rather than to deficiencies in self-concept, as once thought, has been provided by Bartak and Rutter (1974).

Finally, a few speaking autistic children exhibit "metaphorical language," Kanner's (1946) term for a variety of rare and little-studied idiosyncratic usages. In some cases, delayed echolalic utterances become functional responses after participation in contingencies of reinforcement. For example, Furneaux (1966) described an autistic girl who asked, "Do you want to go in the garden?" whenever she wanted to go outside. In other cases, the child uses names that are tangential to their referents. Kanner (1946) describes cases in which a 55-year-old grandmother was called "Fifty-Five" and the number 6 became "Hexagon."

A3. *Restricted Repetitive and Stereotyped Patterns of Behavior, Interests, and Activities*

An autistic child may resist changes in the environment, such as the rearrangement of furniture, a new place at the dinner table, or the relocation of toys, any of which may evoke distress or tantrums. The child may also resist changes in his or her own rigidified behavior patterns, including bedtime routines, lining up objects, or other repetitive, stereotyped behaviors.

The child may collect and hoard simple objects (e.g., pieces of string or glass), or become strongly attached to a favorite doll or blanket at an older age than occurs in normal toddlers (Marchant, Howlin, Yule, & Rutter, 1974). Interest in or attachments to moving objects may be shown by fascination with spinning tops or fans, washing machines, or windshield wipers. Music, flashing lights, or other kinds of sensory stimulation may also be strongly reinforcing (Rincover, Newsom, Lovaas, & Koegel, 1977). There is some limited evidence that profiles of specific topographies may differentiate retarded autistic children from retarded nonautistic children. Repetitive vocalizations, rubbing surfaces, hand flapping, whirling, and posturing were found to be significantly higher in a sample of young autistic children than in retarded controls (Freeman et al., 1979). Wing et al. (1977) found that retarded autistic children were much more likely than nonautistic retarded children to engage in stereotyped and repetitive routines with toys and objects instead of symbolic play. Higher-functioning children may have obsessions with numbers, letters, timetables, or expressway signs, showing excellent long-term memory for items related to their idiosyncratic interests (Epstein, Taubman, & Lovaas, 1985). The stereotypies of autistic children apparently develop out of the normal repetitive behaviors of infancy (Thelen, 1979) or neurochemical abnormalities (Lewis & Baumeister, 1982), and constitute an internally regulated behavior state in very young or profoundly retarded autistic children (Guess & Carr, 1991). Later, they often come to be maintained by their arousal-regulating function (Zentall & Zentall, 1983), by operant escape/avoidance contingencies (Durand & Carr, 1987), and/or by the sensory reinforcement they automatically produce for the child (Lovaas, Newsom, & Hickman, 1987).

Age of Onset

Criterion B (Table 8.2) requires that the delays or abnormal functioning in social interaction, social communication, or imaginative play be apparent prior to 3 years of age. In the DSM-IV field trials, the mean age of onset for a large sample of autistic children was found to be 12.7 months, with a large standard deviation of 10.7 months (Volkmar et al., 1994). Further empirical support for the age criterion comes primarily from a group of studies on the age distribution of severe childhood disorders. Rutter (1978) observed that studies in England, Japan, and the (former) Soviet Union agreed in showing a bimodal distribution in age of onset, with one peak in infancy and another at about puberty.

Determining age of onset requires professional observation of the child by 3 years of age, or, if the child is older, an interview with a parent or other good informant who can at least roughly date the emergence of abnormal behaviors. The child is most likely to be brought for evaluation and diagnosis between 2½ and 5 years of age (Ornitz et al., 1977). The parents will have been worried for 2 or 3 years that the child might be retarded, neurologically impaired, or deaf. Their chief complaint will usually center on the child's failure to develop language. Other specific problems noticed during the first 2 years often include social unresponsiveness, slow or unusual motor development, excessive quietness or irritability, excessive rocking or bouncing, cessation of speech, and hypersensitivity to sounds (DeMyer, 1979). About 20–30% of cases have a period of apparently normal development before a setback or a failure to keep up with developmental milestones (DeMyer, 1979; Lotter, 1966). In such cases it is necessary to rule out Rett's Disorder and Childhood Disintegrative Disorder, in both of which there is also an early period of normal development. It may be helpful to question the informant comprehensively about very early social, language, and play behaviors, to try to establish whether or not abnormal signs were present but overlooked. Sometimes parents will simply say that the child often seemed "odd" or "strange" as an infant; probes for the specific incidents and behaviors producing this impression may be very informative.

Associated Features

Mental Retardation

The most frequent comorbid condition is mental retardation, affecting about 85% of autistic children. The largest sample for which IQ scores have been reported consisted of 623 cases from a 10-year period in North Carolina (Lord & Schopler, 1985). In this sample various tests were used, and it was found that 85% were in the retarded range (IQ < 70). IQs obtained in middle and later childhood remain relatively stable in retarded autistic children receiving conventional special education (DeMyer et al., 1974; Freeman, Ritvo, Needleman, & Yokota, 1985; Lord & Schopler, 1988) but increase significantly in most children receiving intensive behavior therapy (Lovaas, Koegel, Simmons, & Long, 1973; Lovaas, 1987).

Sensory/Perceptual Abnormalities

Another associated feature—abnormal responses to sensory stimuli—is so common that in some

investigators' views, sensory and perceptual disturbances are cardinal symptoms of autism even though they are not recognized as such in DSM-IV (Lovaas, Koegel, & Schreibman, 1979; Ornitz & Ritvo, 1968; Schopler, Reichler, DeVellis, & Daly, 1980). Both under- and overresponding, especially to sounds, may occur at different times in the same child, so that the problem is best characterized as inconsistent responding. The child may cover his or her ears when a vacuum cleaner is turned on, yet may fail to blink when a car backfires nearby. He or she may fail to look when called by name, yet orient to the sound of a crinkling candy wrapper or cry at the sound of a distant siren. About 60% of autistic children show such behaviors (Kolvin et al., 1971; Prior et al., 1975). Perception and attention deficits have been implicated to a greater degree than any basic sensory impairments (Lovaas et al., 1979; Newsom & Simon, 1977).

Self-Injury

One of the more distressing features commonly associated with autism is self-injurious behavior. Self-injurious behavior includes head banging; hitting, slapping, scratching, or biting oneself; and other topographies. In one study, self-injury was reported by the parents of 71% of retarded autistic children and 32% of nonretarded autistic children (Bartak & Rutter, 1976). Like repetitive, stereotyped behavior, it fails to distinguish autistic children because it is also seen in retarded children, but it occurs significantly more often in autistic children (Ando & Yoshimura, 1979; Lord, Rutter, & Le Couteur, 1994). A number of variables have been implicated in the motivation of self-injurious behavior, including neurochemical abnormalities (Harris, 1992), medical problems (Gunsett, Mulick, Fernald, & Martin, 1989), positive reinforcement in the form of adult attention (Lovaas & Simmons, 1969), negative reinforcement through escape from demands (Carr, Newsom, & Binkoff, 1976), and the sensory stimulation provided by the behavior (Rincover & Devany, 1982).

Emotional Abnormalities

Mood lability and fears are more frequent in autistic than in normal children (Matson & Love, 1991). An autistic child may suddenly begin to laugh or cry for no apparent reason, and then just as quickly may shift to the opposite emotion. Sometimes a child may stare into space while giggling, suggesting the possibility of hallucinations, but their occurrence has never been confirmed. It is likely that some impairment in hormone regulation or neurochemical homeostasis is involved (see Coleman & Gillberg, 1985). Another aspect of the lack of emotional control exhibited by autistic children is their tendency toward extreme overreaction to slight frustrations or unexpected changes. Prolonged bouts of crying or screaming occur; these may lead to severe tantrums that include self-injurious, aggressive, or destructive behaviors. Social phobias, fear of loud noises, and anxiety over changes in routines are common, but autistic children also show common childhood fears, such as those related to dogs, snakes, storms, or the dark (Matson & Love, 1991).

Prevalence

The best studies of the prevalence of autistic disorder were conducted in England by Lotter (1966) and Wing et al. (1976). They used similar methods, including actual observation and testing of the most likely children, and obtained very similar prevalence rates of 4.5 per 10,000 aged 8–10 years (Lotter) and 4.8 per 10,000 aged 5–14 years (Wing et al.). When the Wing et al. rate is applied to U.S. Census projections (*World Almanac*, 1994, p. 382), it can be predicted that there will be about 34,500 autistic children and adolescents 0–17 years of age in the United States in the year 2000.

Etiology

Autistic Disorder can result from any of a number of different possible etiologies. Unfortunately, in the majority of cases the etiology is impossible to establish with any degree of certainty; only in 5–10% of cases are medical conditions that are likely to be causal actually found (Rutter, Bailey, Bolton, & Le Couteur, 1994). It seems very likely that a predisposition to autism is inherited, and in some cases, neurological abnormalities can be identified that seem to have etiological significance. The evidence for the heritability of autism comes from twin and family studies. In twin studies, unusually high rates of concordance for autism are found in identical pairs, and very low rates are found in fraternal pairs (Folstein & Rutter, 1977; Ritvo, Ritvo, & Brothers, 1982). Studies of families have indicated that 2–6% of the siblings of autistic children are also autistic, and that 8% of the extended families will include another member who is autistic (Baird & August, 1985; Coleman & Rimland, 1976; Gillberg, 1984).

These percentages are low; however, when compared with the base rate of autism (0.048%), they represent a significant increase in risk for developing autism (Rutter & Bartak, 1971; Coleman & Gillberg, 1985). Family studies also reveal an increased prevalence of mental retardation and specific cognitive disabilities in the siblings of autistic children, particularly those who are themselves severely retarded. This suggests that what might be inherited is not an "autism gene," but rather a nonspecific factor that increases the liability for all cognitive impairments, including autism (August, Stewart, & Tsai, 1981; Baird & August, 1985; Folstein & Rutter, 1977). The mode of transmission is unclear, but most cases seem to fit an autosomal recessive model (Coleman & Gillberg, 1985; Coleman & Rimland, 1976), with the high ratio of males to females of about 4.5:1 (Volkmar et al., 1994) implicating a sex-linked pattern.

Evidence of neurological abnormalities comes from the existence of autistic subgroups among children with genetic, infectious, or metabolic disorders known to affect the central nervous system. These include tuberous sclerosis (Valente, 1971; Riikonen & Amnell, 1981), prenatal rubella (Chess, Fernandez, & Korn, 1978), and phenylketonuria (Knobloch & Pasamanick, 1975; Lowe, Tanaka, Seashore, Young, & Cohen, 1980). Structural, electrophysiological, and biochemical abnormalities that are sometimes associated with autism and may be pathogenic include brainstem dysfunction (Ornitz, 1983; Student & Sohmer, 1978); epilepsy and various other electroencephalographic (EEG) abnormalities (Deykin & MacMahon, 1979; Riikonen & Amnell, 1981; Tsai, Tsai, & August, 1985); ventricle enlargement (Damasio, Maurer, Damasio, & Chui, 1980; Campbell et al., 1982); hydrocephalus (Damasio et al., 1980); and abnormal levels of serotonin or dopamine (Goldstein, Mahanand, Lee, & Coleman, 1976; Campbell, Friedman, DeVito, Greenspan, & Collins, 1974). The most consistent autopsy and magnetic resonance imaging findings are brainstem and cerebellum abnormalities (Courchesne, 1995). Comprehensive recent reviews of the biological factors associated with autism appear in Bailey (1993), Cooke (1990), and Rutter et al. (1994).

The contemporary clinician still occasionally encounters parents who mistakenly believe that they caused their child's condition through faulty child-rearing practices. Such parents should be reassured that there is now considerable evidence that parental personality and child-rearing practices are not responsible for the development of autism (Cantwell & Baker, 1984). It is important to be alert to the possibility that interpretations of well-intended but deleterious social contingencies as developing and maintaining problem behaviors may be misunderstood by parents as blame for the child's autism. The sensitive clinician will make sure that the parents understand that autism is a neurological condition, but that the child's behavioral excesses may be understood and treated in terms of social learning variables, just as they often are in normal children.

Subclassification

The autistic disorder diagnosis provides only one broad term for a very heterogeneous population. Under this one label are subsumed children who are profoundly retarded, mute, and totally absorbed in self-stimulation, as well as children whose intelligence is in the normal range, who have considerable communicative language, and who engage in elaborate, highly organized rituals. The DSM system is an example of a single classification method, a typological system (Siegel, Anders, Ciaranello, Bienenstock, & Kraemer, 1986). Its criteria do not include possible dimensions (variables with specified distance relations, such as relations established by correlation or the lack of it) or hierarchies (e.g., range of severity).

Subclassification by etiologies is not yet possible, given the difficulty in establishing the etiology with any degree of certainty in most cases. Therefore, some investigators have suggested that the most realistic subclassification approach is to use IQ as an index of overall severity (Rutter & Garmezy, 1983; Volkmar, 1987). Measured intelligence is a good predictor of general outcome, verbal communication, and likelihood of brain dysfunction (DeMyer, Hingtgen, & Jackson, 1981; Rutter & Garmezy, 1983), as well as practical to obtain and capable of contributing to distinctions based on cognitive strengths and weaknesses (Fein, Waterhouse, Lucci, & Snyder, 1985). Other investigators, while granting the importance of cognitive variation among autistic children, have sought to make distinctions based on social, linguistic, and behavioral variables that are more clinically meaningful for research and educational efforts. Several such subclassification schemes have been presented—some based on clinical judgment (e.g., DeMyer, Churchill, Pontius, & Gilkey, 1971; Lotter, 1974; Wing, 1981a), some on multivariate discriminant analysis (e.g., Eaves, Ho, & Eaves, 1994; Prior et al., 1975; Rescorla, 1988; Siegel et al., 1986), and even one based on

a nonlinear pattern recognition system (Cohen, Sudhalter, Landon-Jimenez, & Keogh, 1993).

The most influential scheme, and the only one that has been replicated so far, is one based on quality of social functioning (Wing, 1981a; Wing & Attwood, 1987; Wing & Gould, 1979). On the basis of extensive developmental and behavioral data from an epidemiological study of a district of London, Wing and her associates subdivided 132 pervasively disordered and mentally retarded children on the basis of quality of social interaction. The autistic children in the sample fell into one of three groups. The first group was termed "aloof"; it contained children who were socially aloof and indifferent in all situations, or who would make approaches only to obtain things they wanted. Some liked simple physical contact with adults, such as cuddling, tickling, or games of chase, but had no interest in the purely social aspects of the contact. The second group was termed "passive." These children did not make contact spontaneously, but accepted social approaches and did not resist if other children dragged them into their games. The third group was called "active but odd." These children did make social approaches, but mostly to adults rather than other children, in order to indulge some repetitive, idiosyncratic preoccupation. They had no interest in and no feeling for the needs of others. They tended to pester others and were sometimes rejected by their peers because of their peculiar behavior. Wing and Gould (1979) found that their system resulted in more statistically significant relationships with language, play, and medical variables than did a simple autistic–nonautistic classification.

Volkmar, Cohen, Bregman, Hooks, and Stevenson (1989) found that independent raters could assign autistic children to Wing's categories with good reliability (kappa = .73). Borden and Ollendick (1994) found that raters agreed in 72% of 32 cases, yielding a kappa of .56—a fair level of chance-corrected agreement. Most of the disagreements concerned assignment to the passive group. Castelloe and Dawson (1993) found that clinicians' assignments agreed with each other ($r = .71$) and with parents' assignments ($r = .73$). In an examination of validity, Borden and Ollendick (1994) found significant group differences on several measures, including the Vineland Adaptive Behavior Scales age equivalent (Sparrow, Balla, & Cicchetti, 1984), the total score on the Childhood Autism Rating Scale (CARS; Schopler, Reichler, & Renner, 1986), and scores on three areas of the Autism Diagnostic Observation Schedule (Lord et al., 1989). Castelloe and Dawson (1993) also found significant group differences for the Vineland Communication domain age equivalent, sex, mental age, and total CARS score. These studies indicate that Wing's approach is a valid way of subclassifying autistic and other pervasively disordered children.

Differential Diagnosis

The difficulties in differential diagnosis lie at the extremes of intelligence. At the lower end of the continuum, autism often overlaps with severe and profound mental retardation, Childhood Disintegrative Disorder, and Rett's Disorder. At the higher end, it shades into Asperger's Disorder, schizophrenia, and learning disabilities (Shea & Mesibov, 1985; Wing, 1981a, 1981b). The following considerations may help in distinguishing autistic from other severely impaired children.

Mental Retardation

Mental retardation usually coexists with Autistic Disorder and is diagnosed in addition to autism when warranted by measures of intelligence and adaptive behavior. Retardation is diagnosed *instead* of Autistic Disorder when the deficits in cognitive, language, social, and motor functioning are all at a fairly uniform level, rather than showing peaks and valleys. Autistic children exhibit greater deficits in social and language development, but better motor skills, than would be expected on the basis of their overall level of mental retardation. The fact that autistic children tend to show a higher level of motor development than comparable retarded children is an aspect that is especially useful in distinguishing autistic from profoundly retarded nonautistic children. The most difficult cases involve severely retarded nonautistic children (Wing, 1981b), because they often exhibit immediate echolalia and high levels of stereotypy. Unlike autistic children, severely retarded children are usually responsive to simple social interactions. In doubtful cases, it is best to be conservative and defer an Autistic Disorder diagnosis until it is clear whether or not a child meets all the criteria.

Childhood Disintegrative Disorder

Childhood Disintegrative Disorder is the DSM-IV term for children who were formerly diagnosed with Heller disease. There is apparently normal development for at least the first 2 years after birth, and sometimes 3 or 4 years, as indicated by the attainment of developmental milestones in motor skills, communication, social relationships, play, and adaptive behavior. Then there is a significant regression in multiple areas. There may be a premorbid period of vague illness with restlessness, irritability, and anxiety. Over the course of a few months, the child may lose all speech, regress in toilet training, become withdrawn, and engage in stereotypies (Rutter, 1985). Various nonspecific neurological signs may be present, such as EEG abnormalities or seizures. Sometimes the condition may be traced to some type of encephalitis, but in other cases the etiology is never discovered (Evans-Jones & Rosenbloom, 1978).

Rett's Disorder

Rett's Disorder also begins after a period of apparently normal development, but in this case the period is shorter than in Childhood Disintegrative Disorder—typically, about 9–12 months (Kerr, 1995). It occurs only in girls in its classic form, but some boys having a close variant have been reported (Christen & Hanefeld, 1995). Pregnancy and birth are usually normal, but the infant may show subtle motor and attention deviations in infancy (Kerr, 1995). Between ages 5 and 48 months, head growth decelerates, and there is a loss of purposeful hand movements. Between 6 and 30 months, the child develops highly characteristic stereotyped hand movements resembling hand washing or hand wringing, accompanied by social withdrawal and deterioration of any language that may have developed. Jerky ataxia of the trunk, gait apraxia, and general gross motor deterioration are seen (Hagberg, Aicardi, Dias, & Ramos, 1983). After the regression, there is a stage of some recovery of social and communicative skills, along with continued slow neuromotor decline into adolescence (Hagberg, 1995). Standardized test results usually show profound mental retardation and adaptive behaviors below the 3-year-old level (Perry, Sarlo-McGarvey, & Haddad, 1991). The child often shows intermittent hyperventilation, and may also show EEG abnormalities, seizures, and spasticity (Hagberg & Witt-Engerstrom, 1986).

Asperger's Disorder

Asperger's Disorder closely resembles Autistic Disorder in normally intelligent children; indeed, there is controversy over whether it constitutes a separate entity (DeLong & Dwyer, 1988; Frith, 1991; Tantam, 1988). In DSM-IV, two of the criteria for Asperger's Disorder—impaired social interaction, and restricted and stereotyped behaviors and interests—are identical with the corresponding criteria for Autistic Disorder. Children with Asperger's Disorder differ from autistic children in not showing significant language delay or mutism. They often speak quite fluently by age 5 years, although their language is noticeably odd, with abnormalities in comprehension and pragmatics. They typically have large vocabularies, but tend to ramble on about things of interest only to themselves (Frith, 1991). Also unlike autistic children, they usually show clumsiness, a lack of motor coordination, and a stiff, awkward gait (Gillberg, 1991). As they grow older, they become interested in other people, but remain inept in social encounters. They are highly egocentric and have great difficulty understanding other people's feelings. They become preoccupied with some abstract subject having no practical value, which they pursue strenuously (Asperger, 1944/1991; Frith, 1991). Complicating the differential diagnosis are occasional cases in which the child is clearly autistic in early childhood, but begins to acquire language rapidly at about 4–5 years of age and clearly has Asperger's Disorder in adolescence (Wing, 1991; Gillberg, 1991). In cases like this, of course, one makes the diagnosis that fits at the time the child or adolescent is seen.

Schizophrenia

Children with schizophrenia can usually be distinguished from children with autism or Asperger's Disorder by their much later age of onset (usually after age 6 and typically at about puberty), as well as some differences in symptomatology. Schizophrenic children exhibit a progressive narrowing of interests; negativism and interpersonal difficulties; irrational and paranoid fears; bizarre somatic complaints; delusions; and identification with other persons, animals, or objects (Eggers, 1978). Auditory hallucinations are common, but the echolalia, pronoun reversal, and inconsistent responses to sounds seen in autistic children are absent (Kolvin et al., 1971).

Developmental Language Disorders

Higher-functioning autistic children differ from children with receptive and expressive dysphasia in the following ways: (1) Autistic children show more echolalia, pronoun reversal, and noncontextual utterances; (2) their comprehension deficits are more severe than those of children with

receptive dysphasia; (3) they fail to use gestures and facial expressions as alternative means of communication; and (4) they often fail to use the speech they have for communicative purposes, seldom initiating or maintaining a conversation (Bartak et al., 1975).

DIAGNOSTIC CHECKLISTS AND INTERVIEWS

In an effort to put the diagnosis of autism on a more objective footing, several checklists and interview protocols have been developed. At present, none of the available instruments is sufficiently sound to serve as the sole diagnostic tool, for reasons identified by Volkmar, Cicchetti et al. (1988). First, any diagnostic instrument must span a wide range of intelligence and language ability. Second, considerable change can occur during the course of development, requiring an instrument to discriminate psychopathology from developmentally appropriate behaviors at different ages and developmental levels. Third, diagnostic instruments have typically followed a deviance model (Zigler, 1969); this raises the question of appropriate comparison groups. Fourth, some instruments rely on parental report, which may be unreliable (particularly for past events). The better-known instruments are reviewed below in terms of three properties important to their practical application: interrater reliability, concurrent validity, and discriminant validity.

Childhood Autism Rating Scale

The CARS (Schopler et al., 1980, 1986) is the most widely employed diagnostic instrument. It is used to rate developmentally disabled children on 15 subscales: Relationships with People, Imitation, Affect, Use of Body, Relation to Nonhuman Objects, Adaptation to Environmental Change, Visual Responsiveness, Auditory Responsiveness, Near Receptor Responsiveness, Anxiety Reaction, Verbal Communication, Nonverbal Communication, Activity Level, Intellectual Functioning, and General Impressions. The child is observed and the items are scored during or immediately after a testing session or an observation in a classroom or home. For each subscale, there are instructions on how to create opportunities to observe the behaviors of interest. For example, for the Relationships with People subscale, an adult should engage the child in such activities as playing with toys and following instructions, varying the amount of direction from "persistent, intensive intrusion" to "complete nonintrusion." The rater is instructed to consider the amount and intensity of intrusion required on the part of the adult to elicit a response, how much interaction the child initiates, and the child's reactions to physical affection. Each subscale includes definitions for rating the child from 1 ("within normal limits for age") to 4 ("severely abnormal"). Children who obtain a total score of less than 30 are designated "not autistic"; children who obtain a total score of 37 or higher and who are rated 3 or higher on any five subscales are designated "severely autistic"; children who obtain a score of 30 or higher but fail to be rated 3 or higher on five subscales are designated "mildly–moderately autistic."

A principal-component factor analysis of the CARS yielded a three-factor solution (DiLalla & Rogers, 1994). Most of the variance (52%) was accounted for by 10 of the 15 subscales, consisting primarily of those covering social and communicative behaviors; this factor was labeled Social Impairment. The other two factors, termed Negative Emotionality and Distorted Sensory Response, consisted of three subscales each and accounted for 9% and 8% of the variance, respectively. The autistic children in the study had significantly higher (more deviant) mean scores on Social Impairment than did children with other pervasive developmental disorders, who in turn had higher scores than children with mental retardation or behavior disorders.

Interrater reliability with the CARS has been assessed by correlating the scores on individual subscales administered by two independent trained observers, who rated 280 children (Schopler et al., 1980). Correlation coefficients averaged .71 and ranged from .55 (Intellectual Functioning) to .93 (Relationships with People). Kurita, Miyake, and Katsuno (1989) correlated the scores on a Japanese translation of the CARS given by a psychologist and a psychiatrist to 128 children of various diagnoses, including 36 autistic children. Pearson r's ranged from .46 (Anxiety Reaction) to .75 (Relationships with People), with a mean of .62. Sevin, Matson, Coe, Fee, and Sevin (1991) examined interrater reliability between pairs of psychology graduate students rating 24 autistic children and adolescents. Significant Pearson r's ranging from .43 to .85 were found for 11 of the 15 subscales and for the total score, whose coefficient was .68. Practice with the CARS is essential to obtaining good reliability on all subscales. When pairs of graduate students familiar with the scale but lacking extensive practice with it rated 19 autistic and psychotic children, intraclass correlation coefficients ranged from .10 (Activity Level) to .87 (Relationships with People), with a mean of .56 across subscales. Five of the 15 subscales had coefficients below the minimally acceptable level of .50 (Matese, Matson, & Sevin, 1994).

Concurrent validity has been addressed by correlating total CARS scores with ratings of degree of autism by clinicians (type, number, and experience unspecified) and with judgments made by a child psychologist and a child psychiatrist. The reported coefficients were .84 and .80 (Schopler et al., 1980). Kurita et al. (1989) also correlated total CARS scores with ratings of degree of autism by a psychologist and a psychiatrist, obtaining correlations of .76 and .77. Sevin et al. (1991) examined the total CARS scores of 21 children and adolescents previously diagnosed as autistic by an experienced psychologist using DSM-III-R criteria. Nineteen of the 21 met the CARS cutoff criterion of a total score of 30 or greater.

Schopler et al. (1980) also analyzed their results in terms of other sets of diagnostic criteria. The Diagnostic Checklist (Form E-2) was completed for 450 cases and scored by Rimland. Only 8 of the 450 met the criteria for Kanner syndrome. Of these eight, three were classified as not autistic on the CARS. When 125 severely autistic cases were compared with Rutter's (1978) criteria, which are similar to the DSM-IV criteria, only 49 (39%) were found to meet them. Clearly, the CARS definition of autism is a broad one.

There is evidence for discriminant validity of the CARS. Garfin, McCallon, and Cox (1988) compared CARS scores in a group of 20 autistic adolescents and a group of 20 nonautistic handicapped adolescents matched on age, IQ, sex, and ethnicity. The CARS total scores were significantly different for the autistic and nonautistic subjects, averaging 36.1 for the autistic adolescents and 20.5 for the nonautistic adolescents. Kurita et al. (1989) compared CARS total scores in groups of children previously diagnosed with autism, other pervasive developmental disorders, mental retardation, specific developmental disorders, or Attention Deficit Disorder. The CARS scores for the autistic group and the group with other pervasive developmental disorders were not significantly different from each other, but were both significantly higher than the scores for the other groups. DiLalla and Rogers (1994) used the Social Impairment factor mean score for autistic children as a cutoff criterion for assignment to autistic versus nonautistic groups. This produced an overall accuracy rate of 78% of 69 children correctly classified. It showed moderate sensitivity of 64% (21 of 33 autistic children correctly classified) and high specificity of 92% (33 of 36 nonautistic children correctly classified).

In summary, the CARS has adequate reliability and allows the user to quantify the severity of a number of behavioral dimensions in pervasively developmentally disordered children. Its conception of autism is quite broad; note that a child scoring an average of 2 ("mildly abnormal") on all 15 items will be designated as mildly—moderately autistic. It should also be noted that several of its subscales (Affect, Near Receptor Responsiveness, Activity Level) are only tangentially relevant to current conceptions of autism, yet are weighted equally with the other, more relevant subscales.

Autism Behavior Checklist

The Autism Behavior Checklist (ABC; Krug, Arick, & Almond, 1980) is part of a package of five assessment procedures included in the Autism Screening Instrument for Educational Planning (ASIEP; Krug, Arick, & Almond, 1978). Here we discuss only the ABC; the other four components are described later. The ABC was developed as a screening instrument for use by teachers in identifying children with high levels of autistic behavior in severely handicapped samples. It consists of 57 items divided into five categories: Sensory, Relating, Body and Object Use, Language, and Social and Self-Help. Each item is scored as present or absent and is weighted from 1 to 4, with items weighted 4 considered to be the best predictors of autism. Thus, the higher a child's total score, the more autistic he or she is considered to be. Profiles of category scores for autistic and other severely handicapped children (retarded, severely emotionally disturbed, deaf–blind) at different age levels are provided in the ABC manual to assist in making the diagnosis.

Interrater reliability for the ABC was examined by having 14 groups of three independent raters complete checklists for each of 14 children (Krug et al., 1980). Agreement averaged 95% across the 42 raters, but descriptions of the children and the raters were not reported. Volkmar, Cicchetti, et al. (1988) examined agreement between two teachers completing the ABC independently on 32 autistic adolescents and adults. Only 17 of the 57 items showed at least 70% agreement and kappa values of .40 or greater. Although the ABC is worded in jargon-free language that permits it to

be completed easily by parents, Szatmari, Archer, Fisman, and Streiner (1994) found virtually no correlation (.08) between teachers' and parents' ratings of 75 children with Autistic Disorder, Asperger's Disorder, and other pervasive developmental disorders. Volkmar, Cicchetti, et al. (1988) found that parents' scores tended to be significantly higher than teachers' scores.

Concurrent validity was examined by Krug et al. (1980) by administering the ABC to a new sample of 62 children previously diagnosed as autistic. Eighty-six percent of this sample received scores within 1 standard deviation of the mean of the autistic group in the standardization sample. The other 14% had scores within 1.5 standard deviations. Details about the sources of the diagnoses and the checklist administration procedure are lacking. However, Sevin et al. (1991) obtained ABC scores for a group of 21 autistic children and adolescents who had previously been diagnosed by an experienced psychologist according to DSM-III-R criteria. Only 10 of the 21 met or exceeded the ABC criteria for designation as autistic.

Discriminant validity for the ABC was investigated by comparing the mean scores for each of the ABC categories (Sensory, Relating, etc.) and the mean total scores for the autistic group with those for each of the other groups studied (retarded, deaf–blind, emotionally disturbed, normal). The category scores and the total scores were significantly higher for the autistic group than for each of the other four groups. Krug et al. (1980) recommended the following interpretation of total scores: 67 or above, "highly probable autism"; 53–67, "questionable autism"; and below 53, "unlikely autism." However, Volkmar, Cicchetti, et al. (1988) obtained results suggesting that the cutoff score of 67 may be set too high, at least for older subjects. They obtained ABC scores for 94 autistic adolescents and adults and 63 nonautistic developmentally disabled adolescents and adults, all of whom had been previously diagnosed in accordance with DSM-III criteria. Although the autistic sample scored significantly higher on each of the categories and total score, the suggested criterion of 67 identified only 57% of the autistic subjects as probably autistic, and it misclassified 14% of the nonautistic subjects as probably autistic.

Wadden, Bryson, and Rodger (1991) investigated alternative scoring procedures for the ABC with a group of 57 autistic children and a group of 56 mentally retarded and learning-disabled children matched on chronological age and nonverbal IQ. They found that a cutoff score of 44 predicted group membership for the autistic children with 87% accuracy and for the nonautistic children with 96% accuracy. The classification rates were virtually unchanged (85% and 93%, respectively) when only the more highly weighted items (i.e., those weighted 3 and 4) were used. This suggests that a shorter checklist consisting of only the 34 higher-weighted items would work as well as the full checklist in distinguishing children with and without autism. When the criteria recommended by Krug et al. (1980) were used, only 76% of the autistic children were identified as either probably or questionably autistic. Wadden et al. (1991) noted that differences in diagnostic criteria and IQ between the samples may account for the differences. For example, 9 of 16 children rated as unlikely to be autistic were functioning at a relatively high intellectual level.

Yirmiya, Sigman, and Freeman (1994) obtained additional evidence indicating that the ABC may not yield valid results with higher-functioning, older autistic children. They studied 18 children and adolescents 9–16 years old with IQs in the normal range, who were diagnosed as having either autism or autism, residual state, by clinicians using observations, interactions, and parental interviews. Parents completed the ABC twice—once for the child's current behaviors, and once for the child's behaviors at 3–5 years of age. Only 4 of the 18 children fell into the questionable or highly probable ranges of scores for autism on the ABC for current behaviors, but all 18 scored in these ranges on the ABC for behaviors at 3–5 years.

Oswald and Volkmar (1991) used signal detection analysis to examine the ability of the ABC to discriminate autistic from nonautistic samples previously diagnosed by experienced clinicians. Three scoring procedures were found to correctly classify 67% of the cases: the standard cutoff score of 67; a cutoff score of 58; and a cutoff score of 20 in a procedure in which the item weights were ignored and each item was simply scored dichotomously (yes = 1, no = 0). Interestingly, a single item (item 47, "Looks through people") was as robust a discriminator of diagnostic group as any of these cutoff scores; it correctly classified 68% of cases. The authors noted that this finding should not be interpreted to suggest that a single behavior is diagnostic of autism. Rather, it suggests that many behaviors commonly included in diagnostic schemes possess relatively less capacity to discriminate autistic from nonautistic individuals.

In sum, the ABC would appear to have its greatest usefulness as originally intended (i.e., as

a screening tool to help identify young children who may be autistic and should be referred for further evaluation). It is easy to administer and relatively brief, but its recommended cutoff scores may be set too high, as autism is currently broadly diagnosed. This is especially likely with older and higher-functioning individuals.

Diagnostic Checklist for Behavior-Disturbed Children

The most frequently studied version of Rimland's (1964) Diagnostic Checklist, Form E-2, contains 80 items regarding development and behavior from birth to age 5 to be completed by a parent. The first 17 questions concern the child's age, sex, birth order, age of onset, possible perinatal complications, sensory–perceptual functioning, self-stimulatory behaviors, motor skills, and intelligence. The next 41 questions address behaviors mentioned by Kanner as part of the classical autism syndrome, such as imitative ability, ritualistic behaviors, visual and auditory responsiveness, social interactions, splinter skills, and physical appearance. Another 17 questions concern language, including its presence or absence, initial and subsequent utterances, echolalia, use of pronouns, use of "yes" and "no," and comprehension. Three questions ask about the parents' educational levels and the occurrence of psychiatric disorders in the extended family. The final question asks the parents to read over all the items and indicate which 10 best describe their child.

The stated purpose of the Diagnostic Checklist is to discriminate classically autistic children, or those with Kanner syndrome, from other autistic and schizophrenic children. A total "classical autism" (Kanner syndrome) score is derived by subtracting "nonautistic" points from "autistic" points, with +20 being the cutoff score for identifying Kanner syndrome. The diagnosis corresponding to scores between +20 and +10 is "uncertain," and children with scores below +10 are definitely excluded from a diagnosis of Kanner syndrome (Rimland, 1971).

Only limited data on interrater reliability of the Diagnostic Checklist exist. Albert and Davis (1971) administered Form E-1 (an early version of the checklist appearing in the first printing of Rimland, 1964) to 62 parents of normal preschoolers and found a significant correlation ($r = .72$) between mothers' and fathers' ratings. Prior and Bence (1975) compared parents' responses on Form E-2 for nine children with those of treatment staff members. The parents reported fewer abnormal behaviors than the staff members, but in only one case were the differences in total scores sufficient to change the diagnosis. Davids (1975) and a student completed Form E-1 from the files of 66 children, 41 of who were diagnosed with some form of childhood psychosis. The parents of 21 of these children also completed Form E-1 retrospectively. The correlation between the E-1 scores from the case histories and from the parents was a statistically significant but moderate .54.

In a unique but informal approach to concurrent validity, Rimland (1971) analyzed the scores of 22 cases reportedly diagnosed as autistic by Kanner himself. The mean score was +13.2, well below Rimland's conservative criterion of +20. Possible reasons for the discrepancy include the unknown reliability of parental reports of Kanner's diagnosis, and the intentionally high setting of the criterion to reject false positives at the expense of some true cases (Rimland, 1971).

In the first study of the discriminant validity of Form E-2, Douglas and Sanders (1968) found that it was highly effective in distinguishing autistic from mentally retarded children. Rimland (1971) compared E-2 results for 118 "especially high-scoring" (Kanner syndrome) children with results for 230 "autistic-like" children who had scored in the –10 to +5 range. Six items discriminated children with Kanner syndrome from autistic-like children: suspected deafness, not cuddly at ages 2–5 years, exceptional fine motor skills, fascination with mechanical objects or appliances, gets upset when certain things are changed, and indicating "yes" by echoing the question.

DeMyer et al. (1971) studied the discriminant validity of both Forms E-1 and E-2 with four small groups (n's = 8–15) of children independently diagnosed by two psychiatrists as higher-functioning autistic, lower-functioning autistic, early schizophrenic, and nonpsychotic brain-damaged or retarded children. The E-1 scale, with a criterion of +30 points, discriminated the higher-functioning autistic group from the others at a significant level. However, DeMyer et al. (1971) noted that group means were misleading. Only 5 of the 10 higher-functioning autistic children scored above or close to +30, and 9 children from other diagnostic groups achieved borderline scores. The revised scale, Form E-2, failed to discriminate the four groups or any combinations of groups. The failure of either Form E-1 or Form E-2 to make better discriminations can probably be attributed to different definitions of autism. Rimland's Diagnostic Checklist defines autism strictly in terms of the characteristics originally

described by Kanner (1943), whereas DeMyer et al. used broader criteria.

When Prior et al. (1975) defined Kanner syndrome cases as those scoring +17 or higher on a modified Form E-2, a computer program was able to distinguish the 37 Kanner syndrome cases from 105 other cases of pervasive developmental disorder of either early or late onset. Moreover, the Kanner syndrome cases could be distinguished from 43 other autistic children by items indicating preservation of sameness, islets of special ability, and fine motor skill.

Leddet et al. (1986) compared Form E-2 scores with diagnoses made by experienced clinicians who used the DSM-III criteria and had access to each child's developmental history, neurological findings, and psychological and language assessment data. Form E-2 scores discriminated autistic children with and without neurological signs from nonautistic retarded and nonautistic psychiatrically disordered children. Furthermore, a group of 16 children clinically diagnosed as cases of infantile autism without neurological signs could be discriminated from a group of 37 diagnosed as autistic with neurological conditions, as well as from the group of 21 cases of nonautistic retarded and psychiatrically disordered children. However, none of the autistic children achieved an E-2 score greater than +11; thus, they scored well below Rimland's (1971) recommended cutoff point of +20 for identifying cases of Kanner syndrome.

The general conclusion to be drawn from the studies just reviewed is that both Forms E-1 and E-2 of the Diagnostic Checklist identify children with Kanner syndrome but reject many individuals who today would be diagnosed as having Autistic Disorder. Therefore, the Diagnostic Checklist is most useful in situations where there is an interest specifically in identifying children with Kanner syndrome. A continuing difficulty in using this checklist is knowing where to set the cutoff score. Most investigators, including Rimland himself (1971), have noted that +20 for Form E-2 is extremely conservative, with many children who seem clinically to fit Kanner's (1943) criteria failing to achieve it. Only 9.7% of a sample of 2,218 completed forms yielded scores at or above +20 in an early study (Rimland, 1971). This small percentage is the basis for Rimland's (1971) and Kanner's (reported by Rimland, 1964) conclusion that only about 1 in 10 autistic children has Kanner syndrome, but Rimland (1971) has noted that the optimal cutoff score may actually lie somewhere in the range from +13 to +20. Satisfactory results have been obtained with +17 (Prior et al., 1975) and +15 (Prior, Gajzago, & Knox, 1976) in subclassification and epidemiological studies.

One study has directly compared the CARS, the ASIEP, and Form E-2. Teal and Wiebe (1986) administered each scale to 20 autistic and 20 mentally retarded children and conducted discriminant analyses of the results. The CARS fared best in this study. A combination of total scores and number of subscales rated 3 or greater predicted group membership for each child perfectly, for a pooled group accuracy of 100%. Among the five subtests of the ASIEP, the ABC, the Interaction Assessment, and the Educational Assessment were significant variables for the discriminant analysis procedures. Autistic group membership was correctly predicted for 100% of the autistic children, and mentally retarded group membership was correctly predicted for 95% of the retarded children, for a pooled group accuracy of 97.5%. Form E-2 correctly predicted group membership for 85% of the autistic group and 95% of the retarded group, with a pooled group accuracy of 90%.

Autism Diagnostic Interview

The Autism Diagnostic Interview (ADI; Le Couteur et al., 1989) is a structured interview protocol used with the child's principal caregiver. Its 129 items focus on the three areas emphasized in current conceptions of autism—reciprocal social interaction, communication and language, and repetitive, stereotyped behaviors. In addition, the ADI covers problem behaviors and early development. Many items focus on the 4- to 5-year age period and probe for qualities of behaviors indicating developmental deviance instead of developmental delay. Each item is scored from 0 to 2 on the basis of its frequency and severity.

Reliability was asessed by having four trained raters at two sites score videotaped interviews with the mothers of 16 previously diagnosed autistic children and 16 mentally retarded children. A subset of 36 items was selected that most closely matched the specific abnormalities noted in the autism criteria in the ICD-10 (which closely parallel the DSM-IV criteria). For these items, interrater reliability was good, with kappa statistics ranging from .69 to .89 within pairs of raters. A scoring algorithm based on these items discriminated perfectly between the autistic and the mentally retarded groups, locating each child in the correct group. The algorithm was slightly less successful with a group of normal-IQ autistic children and

adolescents studied by Yirmiya et al. (1994); in this study, 3 of the 15 subjects were misclassified as not autistic. It was also less successful with a group of high-functioning children studied by Szatmari et al. (1994). An experienced clinician used information from the ADI and diagnosed 57% of a sample of 83 pervasively disordered children as autistic, whereas the algorithm diagnosed 80% as autistic.

The ADI is time-consuming to administer and was intended primarily for use in research. However, a revised version of the ADI has recently been developed for clinical use. The Autism Diagnostic Interview—Revised (ADI-R; Lord et al., 1994) has been shortened, and many items have been revised to reflect more recent research on the characteristics of autism and to increase their discriminating power. An algorithm comparable to that in the original ADI was created by selecting items depicting specific abnormalities described in the ICD-10 and DSM-IV diagnostic guidelines in the areas of social interaction, communication, and repetitive, stereotyped behaviors, with abnormalities in at least one of these areas occurring before 36 months of age. The algorithm items are shown in Table 8.3.

Reliability was assessed with videotaped interviews of the mothers of 10 autistic children and 10 mentally retarded or language-impaired children 3–5 years of age (Lord et al., 1994). Each taped interview was independently scored by four trained medical or graduate students who were unaware of the children's diagnoses. Percentages of agreement for the algorithm items ranged from 88% to 96%; weighted kappas ranged from .64 to .89. Validity was studied with the 20 children in the reliability sample plus another 30 children (15 autistic, 15 nonautistic). All but 1 of the 25 clinically diagnosed autistic children met the ADI-R algorithm criteria for a diagnosis of autism. Only 2 of the 25 mentally retarded/language-impaired children were misclassified as autistic by the ADI-R.

The ADI-R was developed with careful attention to psychometric issues, and it may well become the instrument of choice for diagnosing young autistic children. Further research is needed with larger samples, with older children and adults, and with individuals who have other pervasive developmental disorders.

Checklist for Autism in Toddlers

The Checklist for Autism in Toddlers (CHAT; Baron-Cohen, Allen, & Gillberg, 1992) is a very brief screening instrument designed specifically for

TABLE 8.3. Algorithm Items from Autism Diagnostic Interview—Revised

Qualitative abnormalities in reciprocal social interaction
  B1. Failure to use eye-to-eye gaze, facial expression, body posture, and gesture to regulate social interaction
  B2. Failure to develop peer relationships
  B3. Lack of social-emotional reciprocity and modulation to context
  B4. Lack of sharing own enjoyment

Qualitative impairments in communication and language
  C1. Delay or total lack of spoken language, not compensated by gesture
  C2. Relative failure to initiate or sustain conversational interchange
  C3. Stereotyped and repetitive use of language
  C4. Lack of varied spontaneous make-believe or social imitative play

Restricted, repetitive behaviors and interests
  D1. Encompassing preoccupations
  D2. Apparently compulsive adherence to nonfunctional rituals
  D3. Stereotyped and repetitive motor mannerisms
  D4. Preoccupation with part-objects or nonfunctional elements of materials

Note. From Lord, Rutter, and Le Couteur (1994, pp. 668–669). Copyright 1994 by Plenum Publishing Corporation. Reprinted by permission.

the early detection of autism in children of about 18 months of age. It consists of nine questions for a parent and five brief interactions for an examiner and a child. The questions for the parent address the presence versus absence of social play, social interest in other children, pretend play, joint attention, protodeclarative pointing, rough-and-tumble play, motor development, protoimperative pointing, and functional play. The first five of these items are usually exhibited by normal 18-month-olds but are usually lacking in autistic toddlers. The authors recommend that toddlers who fail any combination of two or more of these items be referred for further evaluation. The activities for the examiner to administer include simple tests for pretend play, protodeclarative pointing, eye contact, social interaction, and general level of intelligence. The first two of these items are intended as a reliability check on the parent's response to the similar items in the checklist. In a study of 50 normal toddlers, the parents' reports and the examiners' observations were in agreement for 92% of the children. Validity was addressed by administering the CHAT to 50 normal toddlers and 41 toddlers considered to be at risk for autism because they were the younger siblings of autistic children. Only four children, all in the sibling group, failed two or more of the five "autism" items. All of these children and none of the others in either group were diagnosed 2½ years later as autistic at ages 24–30 months by independent professionals.

The CHAT is brief—perhaps too brief to be consistently accurate—and needs further study and replication by independent investigators. If further work supports its ability to identify toddlers likely to be confirmed as autistic, it will deserve serious consideration as a screening tool for at-risk young children.

Parent Interview for Autism

Another recently introduced instrument for use in the diagnosis of young autistic children is the Parent Interview for Autism (PIA; Stone & Hogan, 1993), intended for children under 6 years old. It consists of 118 items organized into the following 11 dimensions: Social Relating, Affective Responses, Motor Imitation, Peer Interactions, Object Play, Imaginative Play, Language Understanding, Nonverbal Communication, Motoric Behaviors, Sensory Responses, and Need for Sameness. Items reflecting normal as well as abnormal development are included. The parent is asked to rate the frequency of each behavior on a scale from 1 ("almost never") to 5 ("almost always").

No interrater reliability has been reported. However, Stone and Hogan (1993) looked at test–retest reliability across 2 weeks with the parents of 29 developmentally disabled children, of whom half were autistic; they found Pearson correlations of .70 or greater for 7 of the 11 dimensions and .93 for the total scores. Concurrent validity was assessed by correlating total PIA scores with total scores on the CARS and total number of DSM-III-R criteria met. Significant but moderate correlations in the –.40s were obtained (lower PIA scores indicate greater likelihood of autism). Discriminant validity was assessed with a group of 58 autistic children and a group of mentally retarded, nonautistic children matched on chronological age, mental age, race, sex, and level of maternal education. Significant group differences were obtained for the total PIA score as well as 6 of the 11 dimension scores. In a stepwise discriminant analysis, four dimensions (Social Relating, Peer Interactions, Motor Imitation, and Nonverbal Communication) correctly classified 78% of the children—86% of the autistic children and 63% of the retarded children.

The PIA does not provide cutoff scores for diagnostic classification, but appears to fulfill its purpose of eliciting clinically relevant information during a parental interview. It deserves consideration in programs serving young developmentally disabled children.

STANDARDIZED DIAGNOSTIC OBSERVATIONAL PROCEDURES

Two groups of investigators have attempted the difficult task of translating the informal clinical observations that contribute to the diagnosis of autism into formal observational procedures. The challenges in creating a standardized obervational diagnostic procedure include (1) selecting tasks that can be standardized across examiners yet will evoke diagnostically significant behaviors, and (2) selecting behavior measures and data analyses that will maximize the sensitivity and specificity of the procedure.

Autism Diagnostic Observation Schedule

The Autism Diagnostic Observation Schedule (ADOS; Lord et al., 1989) was designed primarily for higher-functioning, verbal autistic children and adolescents, and focuses on social interactions and language. It consists of eight tasks presented by a trained examiner in a 20- to 30-minute session. Four tasks focus on social behaviors and four on communicative behaviors, as shown in Table 8.4. There are two sets of materials for most tasks, so that children of various ages and developmental levels can be tested. The child's responses to each task are scored, along with a notation of exactly how the child responded. For example, in the first task, a construction activity (puzzle or pegboard) is presented in a way that requires the child to request additional pieces from the examiner to complete the task. A highly trained examiner presents a hierarchy of prompts ranging from an opportunity for spontaneous behavior to directing the child in quite specific ways if no response occurs earlier in the hierarchy. The child is scored not only on whether or not he or she indicates the need for more pieces, but also on how this is indicated. In addition, overall "general" ratings are made at the end of the session in four areas: reciprocal social interaction, communication, stereotyped behaviors, and mood and nonspecific abnormal behaviors (e.g., overactivity, negativism, anxiety). The general ratings are made on a 3-point scale, with 0 = "within normal limits" and 2 = "definite abnormality." Finally, a global "autism" rating is included.

Interrater reliability was assessed with 20 autistic children and adolescents and 20 mentally retarded and borderline retarded children and adolescents matched for age, sex, and Verbal IQ. Five

TABLE 8.4. Autism Diagnostic Observation Schedule: Tasks and Target Behaviors

Task	Target behavior(s)
Construction task	Asking for help
Unstructured presentation of toys	Symbolic play
	Reciprocal play
	Giving help to interviewer
Drawing game	Taking turns in a structured task
Demonstration task	Descriptive gesture and mime
Poster task	Description of agents and actions
Book task	Telling a sequential story
Conversation	Reciprocal communication
Socioemotional questions	Ability to use language to discuss socioemotional topics

Note. From Lord et al. (1989, p. 189). Copyright 1989 by Plenum Publishing Corporation. Reprinted by permission.

trained raters scored videotaped and live sessions. Weighted kappas ranged from .61 to .92 for task items and from .58 to .87 for general items. Discriminant validity was measured with four groups of 20 children, classified as nonretarded autistic, mildly retarded autistic, mentally retarded, and normal. Twenty-five of the 41 items were significantly higher (more abnormal) in the two autistic groups combined than in the two nonautistic groups. There were also significant differences between the nonretarded autistic and the retarded autistic groups on most of the same items. Very few items discriminated between nonretarded autistic and normal children or between retarded autistic and retarded children.

An algorithm based on items judged to exemplify ICD-10/DSM-IV criteria for autism was used to examine discriminant validity. Although the algorithm correctly excluded all the mentally retarded and normal children from a diagnosis of autism, it also excluded 8 of the 20 retarded autistic children and 15 of the 20 nonretarded autistic children. The problem lay in the items representing restricted, stereotyped behaviors, which were too infrequent during the ADOS sessions to exceed the algorithm cutoff score, even though all the parents of the autistic children reported such behaviors as common in other contexts.

A downward extension of the ADOS for young children of developmental ages less than 3 years has recently been published as the Pre-Linguistic Autism Diagnostic Observation Schedule (PL-ADOS; DiLavore, Lord, & Rutter, 1995). It consists of 12 brief play activities addressing such areas as joint attention, play, imitation, separation/reunion with the mother, requesting strategies, and turn taking. It is scored in a similar manner to the ADOS. In a reliability study with 20 children of various diagnoses, well-trained raters scoring videotaped test sessions achieved weighted kappas of .63 to .95 for the task items and the general items. A diagnostic algorithm based on social/communicative scores and restricted/repetitive behaviors scores correctly classified 16 of 21 autistic children and 40 of 42 children with developmental disorders other than autism.

The ADOS and the PL-ADOS are promising but still experimental procedures for standardizing clinical observations of autistic individuals. Details of administration and scoring remain to be published, and this has hampered evaluation of these tools. However, the comprehensive attention paid to psychometric soundness by the developers indicates that the final products may contribute greatly to accurate diagnosis in this field.

Behavior Observation System

The Behavior Observation System (BOS; Freeman, Ritvo, & Schroth, 1984) is a free-play observation procedure. The BOS originally covered a list of 74 behaviors, but subsequent analyses of the reliability, stability, and discriminating power of individual items have resulted in 25 surviving items in four categories: Solitary Behaviors, Relation to Objects/Toys, Relation to Examiner, and Language. The procedure is conducted by videotaping a child through a one-way mirror in a room containing an adult observer and a number of toys, chairs, and a table. The child is brought in and told to "do whatever you want." Each BOS item is scored in 10-second intervals from 0 to 3, depending on its frequency of occurrence. Each child is typically observed in three sessions on 3 different days.

Factor analyses of BOS results with autistic, retarded, and normal children have been carried out (Freeman, Schroth, Ritvo, Guthrie, & Wake, 1980). The autistic group could best be characterized by behaviors indicating inappropriate interaction with people and objects (i.e., preoccupation with objects, visual detail scrutiny, rubbing surfaces, undifferentiated holding of objects, ignoring the examiner, resisting being held, and deviant ball play). The mentally retarded group was characterized by solitary behaviors, whereas the normal group was characterized by appropriate interactions with people and objects.

Interrater reliability, in terms of correlation coefficients between trained observers, has been reported (Freeman et al., 1984). Observers were trained to a criterion of 80% or better agreement on each behavior with a pilot group, and were unaware of the diagnoses of the 63 autistic, 34 retarded, and 40 normal children who were scored in the study. Agreement was .70 or better on all but eight behaviors.

In several studies, the BOS has identified behaviors that are significantly different in frequency or in the number of children exhibiting them between groups of autistic children and groups of retarded and normal controls (Adrien, Ornitz, Barthelemy, Sauvage, & Lelord, 1987; Freeman, Guthrie, Frankel, Ornitz, & Ritvo, 1977; Freeman et al., 1979; Freeman et al., 1981; Freeman & Schroth, 1984). For example, Adrien et al. (1987) studied autistic, retarded, and normal children matched for developmental age, and found that nine behaviors occurred more often in the autistic children than in the other two groups: lack of eye contact, lack of social smile, using objects ritualistically, ignoring objects, rubbing surfaces, finger flicking, body rocking, repetitive jumping, and absent response to stimuli. Some of these behaviors (lack of eye contact, lack of social smile, rubbing surfaces) have been found in other studies to occur more often in autistic children than in controls (Freeman et al., 1979, 1981; Freeman & Schroth, 1984).

The discriminant validity of the BOS has been assessed in several studies. Freeman, Ritvo, Guthrie, Schroth, and Ball (1978) compared 30 autistic, 30 mentally retarded, and 23 normal children, all 2–5 years old. The discriminant function yielded an overall correct classification rate of 63%. When the autistic and mentally retarded children were compared without the normal children, the overall classification rate improved somewhat, to 72% (80% of the autistic and 63% of the retarded children). The authors noted that the most likely reason for the moderate discrimination between the groups was the fact that some of the behaviors varied with chronological or mental age. In a subsequent study, Freeman et al. (1984) compared 21 normal-IQ autistic children with 40 normal children, and 42 retarded autistic children with 34 retarded controls. In the former comparison, 87.7% of the children were correctly classified (71.4% of the normal-IQ autistics and 95.5% of the normal children). In the latter comparison, 75% of the children were correctly classified (69% of the retarded autistics and 82.4% of the retarded nonautistic children). The authors speculated that better discrimination of the groups would require adding qualitative measures of social interaction to the procedure.

Although the BOS is able to detect differences between groups in the frequencies of various behaviors and in the percentages of children exhibiting certain behaviors, no uniform set of behaviors has been identified across studies that reliably distinguishes autistic from retarded and normal children. The lack of a scoring algorithm for the diagnostic interpretation of the results renders the BOS more suitable for tracking behaviors over time and across treatments than for diagnosing individual children.

Limitations of the Observational Procedures

The ADOS and the BOS are important milestones in the continuing effort to standardize the diagnosis of Autistic Disorder. Both procedures began with the admirable but elusive goal of putting diagnosis on a sound quantitative basis by measuring operationally defined behaviors in a standardized manner. Because autism is a behaviorally defined syndrome, this question arises: Why don't these behavioral diagnostic procedures result in better discrimination between autistic and retarded groups? First, part of the problem lies in the content of the procedures. By emphasizing free play with toys, the BOS is well suited for capturing repetitive, stereotyped behaviors and nonfunctional object use, but fails to elicit social and language behaviors that might be observed if it included relevant interactions between the adult and the child. The ADOS, on the other hand, emphasizes social and communicative interactions, with a relative neglect of stereotyped behaviors and sensory abnormalities. These limitations make both the BOS and the ADOS relatively weak in discriminating between autistic children and age- and IQ-matched retarded and normal children. Perhaps the ideal procedure would include both standardized interaction and unstructured play components. Second, the fact that the BOS and the ADOS procedures are laboratory-based and relatively brief renders them unable to sample the range of behaviors necessary to make more reliable diagnostic distinctions. Information from parents and teachers about a child's behaviors in other settings is essential. Lord et al. (1989) noted the value of including information from parent interviews in applying the ADOS diagnostic algorithm. When parents' reports of restricted, repetitive behaviors were used instead of observational data for this category, the algorithm successfully classified all of the children in the four groups studied, with the exception of only 3 of the 20 nonretarded autistic children.

BEHAVIOR RATING SCALES

Behavior rating scales can be a better alternative than informal impressions in situations in which it is desirable to measure a broad range of behaviors repeatedly and efficiently, but more accurate direct observation procedures are impractical. Three such scales have been developed for use with autistic children—the Real Life Rating Scale (RLRS; Freeman, Ritvo, Yokota, & Ritvo, 1986), the Behavioral Summarized Evaluation (BSE; Barthelemy et al., 1990), and the Behavior Rating Instrument for Autistic and Other Atypical Children (Ruttenberg, Kalish, Wenar, & Wolf, 1977). The first two are reviewed here; a review of the third appears in Newsom, Hovanitz, and Rincover (1988).

Real Life Rating Scale

The RLRS (Freeman et al., 1986) is a rating scale based on BOS items. It is designed to be used in naturalistic settings to measure changes in behavior over time and across treatments. It consists of 47 behaviors in five categories: Sensory Motor, Social Relationship to People, Affectual Responses, Sensory Responses, and Language. At the end of a 30-minute observation period, each behavior is rated 0–3 for frequency of occurrence.

Freeman et al. (1986) found that interrater reliability was good for raters who had considerable previous experience with the BOS; their overall average Pearson r was .90 across the 47 behaviors in 50 pairs of observations. However, it was poor for novice raters, who had only three training sessions prior to rating; their average Pearson r was .40, and it was a nonsignificant .20 for the Sensory Motor subscale. Sevin et al. (1991) examined the reliability of the RLRS between pairs of minimally trained psychology graduate students rating 24 autistic children and adolescents. The mean kappa coefficient across items was significantly greater than chance, but was only a modest .31. Pearson correlation coefficients were calculated for each of the five scale scores and for the overall score of the RLRS. The scale score Pearson r's ranged from .70 to .89, except that the r for Social Relationship was only .32, apparently because its items were infrequently observed. The correlation for the total score was .82. In another study with relatively inexperienced graduate students as raters, intraclass correlation coefficients ranged from –.18 to .97, with a mean of .59; 14 of 47 items had coefficients below the acceptable minimum of .50 (Matese et al., 1994). Clearly, experience is needed before one can use the RLRS with confidence in its results.

Behavioral Summarized Evaluation

The BSE (Barthelemy et al., 1990) is a 20-item rating scale intended to measure changes in behaviors in autistic children and adolescents. Every item is scored on a scale from 0 ("never observed") to 4 ("always observed"). Typically, the BSE is scored once a week by someone having daily contact with the child. A total score (Global score) is obtained by summing the item scores. To date, the BSE has been used by its developers as a weekly or biweekly measure of the clinical status of autistic children in research on drug effects, neurophysiology, and educational interventions (e.g., Barthelemy, Bruneau, et al., 1989; Barthel-

emy, Hameury, & Lelord, 1989; Bruneau, Garreau, Roux, & Lelord, 1987).

Very limited information is currently available on the reliability and validity of the BSE. The interrater reliability of the BSE was investigated by having two sets of trained raters score 31 autistic children (Barthelemy et al., 1990). The intraclass correlation coefficient for the Global scores was .96. Fourteen of the individual items had good reliability, as indicated by kappa statistics of .60 or greater.

The validity of the BSE was studied by correlating the Global scores and the sum of the scores of the Autism factor items with ratings of severity of autism of 90 autistic children by two psychiatrists. These scores were weighted by the factor loading of each item. Significant Spearman rank-order correlation coefficients were found for the Autism factor items, for the Global score, and for the severity ratings.

Although not initially designed to serve as a diagnostic tool, the BSE has been analyzed for its ability to discriminate autistic from retarded children. Barthelemy et al. (1992) matched 58 autistic children with 58 mentally retarded children on age and IQ. The BSE was completed on all children by nurses who saw them daily in a hospital day care program. A discriminant analysis correctly classified 49 (85%) of the autistic children and 56 (97%) of the retarded children. However, studies to determine scoring criteria suitable for clinical use remain to be done.

ASSESSMENT FOR TREATMENT PLANNING AND EVALUATION

This section first describes the most frequently used standardized intelligence scales, as well as some specialized scales for autistic children that resemble more familiar tests in format and purpose. Adaptive behavior scales are considered next, followed by a discussion of methods representative of "ecological" (Brown et al., 1979) or "ecobehavioral" (Rogers-Warren, 1984) approaches to assessment.

Standardized Intelligence Tests

There are several important uses for intelligence tests with this population. First, in diagnosis, it is important to know the child's general intelligence level in order to judge whether or not the social and language impairments are below what would be expected as a function of cognitive level. Second, in the assessment of higher-functioning autistic children for classroom placement purposes, IQ scores (along with the results of other tests) can serve their traditional function of roughly predicting academic achievement. Third, in research concerned with differences between autistic children and those of other diagnostic groups, or between samples of autistic children at different levels of functioning, intelligence scores can be used as one variable for matching or distinguishing the groups, respectively. Finally, in studies concerned with treatment outcome and follow-up, pre–post test scores are commonly obtained and reported. This section provides some information on findings with the use of familiar instruments; later, some instruments that resemble conventional intelligence tests but were designed specifically for autistic children are described.

The Stanford–Binet and the Wechsler scales can be used with autistic children and adolescents who have some communicative language. An obvious advantage of using one of these established scales whenever possible is their high degree of familiarity to other professionals. Studies with the fourth edition of the Stanford–Binet (Thorndike, Hagan, & Sattler, 1986) have found that autistic children tend to score lowest on the Absurdities subtest and highest on the Pattern Analysis subtest (Harris, Handleman, & Burton, 1990). Carpentieri and Morgan (1994) compared autistic and retarded children matched on age, sex, and IQ (mean Stanford–Binet composite of 48). The Verbal Reasoning area was significantly lower for the autistic group than the retarded group, as were the Comprehension and Absurdities subtests. Within the autistic group, Quantitative Reasoning was the highest area, but there were no significant differences among subtest scores. Autistic children who were excluded from the study because they failed to earn scores on all subtests were most likely to have failed Absurdities and Sentence Memory.

The Wechsler Intelligence Scale for Children—Revised (WISC-R; Wechsler, 1974) and the Wechsler Adult Intelligence Scale—Revised (Wechsler, 1981) require considerable receptive language ability, with the possible exception of the Block Design and Object Assembly subtests, on which autistic children and adults often achieve their highest scores (Lincoln, Courchesne, Kilman, Elmasian, & Allen, 1988; Rumsey & Hamburger, 1988; Venter, Lord, & Schopler, 1992). Autistic individuals tend to show their poorest performance on the Comprehension and Vocabulary subtests (Asarnow, Tanguay, Bott, & Freeman, 1987; Lincoln et al., 1988; Rumsey & Hamburger,

1988; Venter et al., 1992), and to score higher on Performance than on Verbal scales (Lincoln et al., 1988; Ohta, 1987; Ozonoff, Rogers, & Pennington, 1991). Unfortunately, the WISC-R does not provide IQs below 40, and this severely limits its usefulness with most autistic children. There are currently no published reports on the use of the WISC-III (Wechsler, 1991) with autistic children, but it seems safe to assume that when such reports are available, they will show similar patterns of results.

For autistic children who are mute, minimally verbal, or deaf, the Leiter International Performance Scale (Leiter, 1969), the Pictorial Test of Intelligence (French, 1964), and Raven's Coloured Progressive Matrices (Raven, Court, & Raven, 1977) are popular alternatives to the Stanford–Binet and Wechsler scales (Clark & Rutter, 1979; Maltz, 1981; Shah & Holmes, 1985; Szatmari et al., 1994). The main advantage of the Leiter is that it can be administered completely without verbal instructions. It does, however, require that the child be able to imitate and to match to sample in an unusual task format (placing blocks in the slots of a wooden bar). The Leiter IQ is correlated with but significantly greater than the WISC-R Full Scale IQ in autistic children (Shah & Holmes, 1985).

In testing young and very low-functioning children, an examiner can choose between one of the developmental scales (e.g., Bayley Scales of Infant Development, Merrill–Palmer Scale, Cattell Infant Intelligence Scale) or Alpern and Kimberlin's (1970) Cattell–Binet Short Form. The Cattell–Binet is a combination of the Cattell Scale (Cattell, 1960) and the Stanford–Binet, in which two items from each age level are used. It has a wide range of applicability with retarded autistic examinees, because it extends down to the 2-month age level. Additional advantages include its high correlation (.97) with the full 1972 Stanford–Binet, its brief administration time (less than 20 minutes), and its yield of mental ages and IQs that are calculated in a similar way to those obtained from the Stanford–Binet. Disadvantages include the high degree of judgment involved in scoring many of the infant items; the paucity of reliability and validity data beyond those provided in the original article on a small sample of retarded autistic children; and, of course, the outdated norms of the two tests it uses. In one study of children with various developmental disabilities, the obtained scores differed by 6 points or more from those obtained with the full Stanford–Binet for about a third of the sample (Bloom, Klee, & Raskin, 1977).

Several neuropsychological researchers have adapted certain standardized tests for use with autistic individuals, including the Halstead–Reitan battery for adolescents and adults (Dawson, 1983) and the McCarthy and Peabody tests for higher-functioning children (Fein et al., 1985). Adaptations of Piagetian tasks have been used successfully with autistic children by several investigators (Curcio, 1978; Lancy & Goldstein, 1982; Sigman & Ungerer, 1981; Wetherby & Gaines, 1982). Two of these studies cast doubt on the notion that most autistic children are permanently arrested at Piaget's sensorimotor stage of development. When properly assessed, some are capable of functioning at a stage appropriate for their chronological age (Lancy & Goldstein, 1982; Wetherby & Gaines, 1982).

Specialized Scales

There are two published instruments that have been specifically designed to provide assessments of autistic children, and at least one designed specifically for autistic adolescents and adults. They emphasize content areas and items more suitable for lower-functioning autistic individuals than those found in conventional intelligence tests; they also focus on patterns of strengths and weaknesses rather than composite summary scores. They are intended primarily for individual program planning and for within-subject comparisons over time.

The Psychoeducational Profile (PEP; Schopler & Reichler, 1979) is intended for children 1 to 12 years of age who are functioning at a preschool level. It consists, first, of tasks similar to those found in infant scales, which are organized into six developmental areas: Imitation, Perception, Motor, Eye–Hand Integration, Cognitive–Performance, and Cognitive–Verbal. In addition, there are a number of specified informal observations to be made in five "pathology" areas: Affect, Relating/Cooperating/Human Interest, Play and Interest in Materials, Sensory Modes, and Language. Each item is scored "pass," "emerge," or "fail," with the "emerge" scores indicating partial success and considered most relevant for educational planning. The developmental scale yields a profile of raw scores, which is keyed to a hierarchy of chronological age norms obtained from a sample of normal children 1 to 7 years of age. A companion scale, the Adolescent and Adult Psychoeducational Profile (AAPEP; Mesibov, Schopler, Schaffer, & Landrus, 1988), consists of two checklists covering behaviors in the home and school/work settings in six areas: Vocational Skills, Independent

Functioning, Leisure Skills, Vocational Behavior, Functional Communication, and Interpersonal Behavior. The AAPEP also includes a series of tests, including vocational tasks, administered directly to the individual. Information on reliability and validity is sparse, but indicates good interrater reliability for a small sample of autistic adults and validity in producing useful training recommendations (Mesibov, 1988). For moderately to profoundly retarded autistic children, PEP scores are highly correlated with AAPEP scores obtained 5 years later (Perez & Fortea Sevilla, 1993).

The ASIEP (Krug et al., 1978), mentioned earlier in the chapter, consists of five instruments that can be used in combination or separately. Its components include (1) the ABC, discussed previously; (2) a Sample of Vocal Behavior, a procedure for recording 50 representative vocalizations and analyzing them for repetitiveness, communicative function, vocal complexity, syntactic complexity, and language age; (3) an Interaction Assessment, which involves time-sampling several categories of behavior (Interaction, Constructive Independent Play, No Response, and Aggressive/Negative) in a standard play setting; (4) an Educational Assessment, with tasks in the areas of In-Seat Behavior, Receptive Language, Expressive Language, Body Concept, and Speech Imitation; and (5) a Prognosis of Learning Rate, based on performance on a series of shape- and color-sequencing tasks. For each component, profiles of normative data from autistic and nonautistic severely handicapped children are provided. Statistical analyses indicate that the performance of autistic children is significantly different from that of other severely handicapped children on each component (Krug, Arick, & Almond, 1981).

Adaptive Behavior Scales

Although adaptive behavior scales are more useful than intelligence tests in defining important strengths and weaknesses for program planning, there are no scales which have been normed on autistic children. However, Kozloff (1974) has presented a scale for parents and teachers designed primarily for younger autistic children. The Behavior Evaluation Scale organizes 99 behaviors into seven areas: (1) Learning Readiness Skills; (2) Looking, Listening, and Moving Skills; (3) Motor Imitation Skills; (4) Verbal Imitation Skills; (5) Functional Speech; (6) Chores and Self-Help Skills; and (7) Problem Behaviors. The behaviors in each area (except Problem Behaviors) are arranged in an easy-to-difficult sequence, and the most important behaviors are indicated by asterisks and capital letters. The scale also includes questions concerned with the degree and frequency of prompting needed to evoke the behaviors and the child's reactions to attempts to teach the behaviors. The Behavior Evaluation Scale is most useful in parent training programs and in developing classroom programs for young autistic children and severely/profoundly retarded older autistic children.

In most clinical and educational settings, adaptive behavior scales developed for retarded and normal populations are used most often with older autistic children and adolescents. The two most widely used instruments are the American Association on Mental Retardation (AAMR) Adaptive Behavior Scale (Lambert, Nihira, & Leland, 1993) and the Vineland Adaptive Behavior Scales (Sparrow et al., 1984). The AAMR Adaptive Behavior Scale is probably most useful as a criterion-referenced scale in identifying important deficits in a large number of practical domains and in evaluating educational progress (Ando, Yoshimura, & Wakabayashi, 1980; Sloan & Marcus, 1981). The Vineland, on the other hand, is probably the instrument of choice in situations where a norm-referenced assessment is desired in the areas of Communication, Daily Living Skills, Socialization, and Motor Skills (Szatmari et al., 1994; Volkmar, Cicchetti, et al., 1988; Volkmar et al., 1987). Standard scores on all domains of the Vineland tend to be significantly lower than scores on intelligence tests (Venter et al., 1992). Several studies have found that higher-functioning autistic children show lower scores on the Socialization domain than on other domains (as might be expected, given the autism diagnosis), and that their Socialization scores are lower than those of matched retarded children (Loveland & Kelley, 1991; Rodrigue, Morgan, & Geffken, 1991; Volkmar et al., 1987). This suggests that for higher-functioning children, the Vineland Socialization score can serve as one way of operationalizing the social deficit criterion when making the diagnosis. However, autistic children with Performance IQs below about 30 tend to have Socialization scores similar to those of matched retarded children (Schatz & Hamdan-Allen, 1995). The choice of the informant can be important with the Vineland. Szatmari et al. (1994) found that although parents' and teachers' responses for 75 children with autism and other pervasive developmental disorders correlated highly (.74), teachers' Adaptive Behavior Composite scores averaged 11 points higher than those of parents.

Those working with very young or severely/profoundly retarded older autistic children might also consider the Balthazar Scales of Adaptive Behavior (Balthazar, 1972, 1973). The Balthazar Scales focus on toileting, feeding, dressing, and some social, communicative, play, and maladaptive behaviors. Instead of relying on an informant's report, an examiner scores most areas through direct observation. This makes these scales particularly suitable for objective evaluations of daily living skills training programs.

Ecobehavioral Assessment

Conventional evaluations based on interviews, standardized tests and checklists, and observations in one or two contrived settings are increasingly being viewed as insufficient to generate treatment plans that adequately address an autistic child's problems in generalizing learning across settings (Rincover & Koegel, 1975) and the child's need to acquire skills that are functional in everyday environments. Johnson and Koegel (1982), for example, have argued that when educational objectives are based solely on normal developmental sequences, autistic children often receive instruction on tasks or skills that are inappropriate for their chronological age, that are not functional in natural environments, and that are taught and exhibited only in highly artificial settings. Consequently, despite years of special education, autistic adults may remain incapable of living independent and productive lives. Others concerned with the education of autistic and other severely handicapped children have made the same argument (e.g., Brown et al., 1979; Sailor & Guess, 1983; Snell & Browder, 1986). They advocate that the evaluation process include "ecological" assessments of a child's behaviors in the context of the natural environments and social situations that the child currently experiences, as well as those he or she is likely to experience in the future. Such an approach can be subsumed under the general concept of "ecobehavioral analysis" (Rogers-Warren, 1984), because it is concerned with ecology–behavior interactions—that is, with interactions between settings, activities, and persons on the one hand and the child's behaviors on the other. Rogers-Warren (1984) has noted that the utility of an ecobehavioral analysis lies in its implications for expanding the range of possible interventions by identifying a larger set of environmental variables influencing a child's behavior than is normally considered.

The ecobehavioral approach is relevant to assessment and treatment development with autistic children in at least three major ways. First, it suggests that the primary assessment question is this: "In what specific ways does this child's behavioral repertoire fail to meet the demands and expectations of his or her environment?" This is a rather different question from the more usual one: "How do this child's cognitions and behaviors differ from those of normal children of the same age?" The latter question is concerned with the mismatch between the child and his or her normal peers, and relates to diagnostic and placement issues; the former is concerned with the mismatch between the child and everyday settings, and focuses attention on the child's individual treatment and educational needs. Although adaptive behavior scales can provide some answers to the former question, examiners will also find it useful to conduct supplementary observations in relevant settings to develop valid treatment plans. A possible strategy, based on the suggestions of Brown et al. (1979), begins with an "ecological inventory" consisting of the following steps:

1. Determine the most important environments in which the child is currently functioning or will function in the near future (e.g., natural home, group home, school, workshop, restaurant, supermarket, etc.).
2. Divide the environments into subenvironments (e.g., kitchen, living room, bathroom, etc.).
3. Delineate the most important activities that occur in each subenvironment (e.g., cooking food, washing dishes, etc.).
4. Delineate the specific skills needed in order for the child to participate fully or partially in the activities.

The delineation of the specific skills needed is based on a "repertoire inventory" for each activity (Brown et al., 1979). The steps are as follows:

1. Analyze and record the skill sequences demonstrated by normal persons in performing the activity.
2. Determine which of the steps in the skill sequence the handicapped child can do by observing his or her performance in either the actual environment or a simulated environment.
3. Compare the child's performance with that of a normal individual to find which skills are missing from the child's repertoire.
4. If necessary, consider possible adaptations of skills, materials, rules, or devices that would allow or enhance participation in the activity. For ex-

ample, a mute child can be taught to use pictures instead of speech to order food in a fast-food restaurant, or a child who cannot make change can be taught to make purchases by handing over the number of dollars indicated on the cash register plus one and waiting for the change.

Many of the steps just described are evident in educational efforts with autistic children. Bailey, Prystalski, Kozlowski, Mielke, and Owen (1984) have developed a useful form for evaluating the performance of autistic children in natural environments, as shown in Figure 8.1, where the performance of an autistic child is compared with that of a normal individual in a fast-food restaurant. Blew, Schwartz, and Luce (1985) assessed the performances of autistic children in reference to task analyses of customary behaviors in several community locations, and then employed a normal peer as a tutor to teach them functional skills (e.g., making purchases at a convenience store, crossing a public street, and checking a book out of a library). On a larger scale, Lovaas (1987) focused the treatment of young autistic children on the actual behaviors required successively in home, neighborhood, nursery school, and kindergarten or first-grade environments. At each step, informal observations of normal children in the relevant settings determined each child's "curriculum" of individualized training and treatment objectives (Lovaas, 1987; Lovaas et al., 1981). The success of this model, which helped 47% of the children to succeed in regular first-grade classrooms, strongly recommends attention to ecological variables.

A second way in which ecobehavioral methods have been used with autistic children has been in the assessment of relationships between certain settings or activities and a range of typical behaviors. For example, Charlop, Schreibman, Mason, and Vesey (1983) observed five settings in each of three classrooms of autistic children: group work, individual work with the teacher, independent work, free play, and time out. The children's behaviors were recorded in eight categories: Out-of-Seat, Self-Stimulation, Echolalia, Tantrum, Appropriate Verbal, Work, Play, and Social. After "mapping" mean levels of the behaviors by settings, the investigators were able to make some data-based recommendations for program redesign. For example, it was found that the highest levels of work-related behaviors and appropriate verbalizations occurred during individual work with the teacher, as expected; however, contrary to the teachers' assumptions, more work and ap-

PERFORMANCE FORM

1. Dom. Voc. R/L (C-at-L) (circle one domain) Date of N/H person inventory __7-6-83__
2. Environment __McDonald's (Stratford Square)__ Inventoried by __V. Owen__
3. Sub-environment ____ Date of student inventory __1-7-83__
4. Sub-sub environment ____ Inventoried by __D. Peel__
5. Activity or activities __ordering, finding a table, eating, clean-up__

Natural S^D	Performance steps for nonhandicapped person	Criterion for nonhandicapped person	Student Performance + or -	Communication Requirements	Additional Comments
hunger/lunch hour	walk to counter		-	RESPOND TO ANY NEEDED PROMPTS	
	wait in line		-		
Clerk says "MAY I help you?"	Place order—coke fries hamburger	respond in 3 seconds	-	look at clerk, comprehend "may I take order"	
Clerk says "IS that to go or..."	Reply "It's for here"	respond in 3 seconds	-	Indicate "for here"	
Clerk says "that will be $2.07"	get money out & pay clerk	respond with $2.07 or more	-	Comprehend "pay for order" will give clerk	If given money will give clerk
Clerk returns change	receive change and return change to wallet		+	Comprehend "wait for change"	
Clerk gives food on tray	pick up tray of food		+		
Clerk says "thank you come again"	carry tray to clean empty table	without dropping/spilling food	+	possible communicative	
	sit down		+	interacted with companions	
	unwrap food				
	eat food	in an appropriate amount of time depending on conversation	-		needs some assistance—eats sandwich quick
food consumed no longer hungry	Clean-up, putting paper and leftover food on tray		-		
	carry tray to garbage can and empty contents	disposable contents only	-		drops entire tray into garbage can
	walk to door		-		

FIGURE 8.1. Form for comparing the performance of an autistic child with that of a nonhandicapped person in a natural setting. Item 1 refers to the following curricular domains: Domestic, Vocational, Recreation/Leisure, and Community-at-Large. From Bailey, Prystalski, Kozlowski, Mielke, and Owen (1984, p. 44). Copyright 1984 by Northern Illinois University.

propriate speech occurred during independent work at desks than during group work at a table. This finding suggested that the group arrangement be replaced by more time in individual sessions with the teacher, alternating with independent tasks at desks.

Finally, ecological considerations influence process measures in evaluations of treatment and educational programs for autistic children. For example, Dyer, Schwartz, and Luce (1984) assessed the quality of the activities provided by staff members for autistic children in a residential setting. During random daily observation sessions, each child in a residence was observed briefly in turn; the observer scored the activity in which the child was engaged according to three attributes (Functional Tasks, Functional Materials, and Age-Appropriateness), and judged whether or not the activity could be categorized into one of four functional curricular domains (Recreation/Leisure, Domestic, Self-Care, or Vocational). If a child happened to be receiving a prescribed behavioral treatment for an inappropriate behavior, the "activity" was scored as Reducing Socially Inappropriate Behavior. The definitions of the attributes and curricular domains are listed in Table 8.5. A total score for each child was based on the assignment of 1 point for each activity attribute and 1 point for the curricular domain, or a total of only 1 point if Reducing Socially Inappropriate Behavior was scored. For each residence of seven to nine children, an average score was calculated. This measure proved to be sensitive to a supervisory intervention that included posting the definitions of the attributes and domains, and providing corrective feedback and praise to staff members. A very similar approach was used by Green et al. (1986) to evaluate and establish norms for classroom programs for autistic and other developmentally disabled children.

ASSESSMENT OF FAMILIES

Early studies involving the assessment of families with autistic children were primarily attempts to identify variables etiologically involved in the disorder. This interest stemmed from Kanner's statement that the parents of autistic children seemed emotionally cold and perfectionistic (Kanner, 1943). Subsequent theorists considered the possibility that early psychological trauma, severe parental psychopathology, or deviant parent–child communication patterns played a causal role. At this time, empirical research does not support these early hypotheses (Cantwell & Baker, 1984), but the effects of the initial orientation toward parents and the family have been slow to dissipate

---

TABLE 8.5. Definitions of Functional Attributes and Domains

A. Functional activity attributes
1. *Functional materials*: Materials that would be encountered in the student's own community when engaged in similar activities there. Examples include clothing, roller skates, vending machines, and record players. Nonfunctional materials include pegboards, inch cubes, and buttoning boards.
2. *Functional tasks*: Tasks that would have to be performed by someone else if the student did not perform the task. Examples include toileting and dressing oneself. Nonfunctional tasks include walking a balance beam and stacking rings.
3. *Age-appropriateness*: Activities usually performed by nonhandicapped, age-matched peers, without regard for the child's tested mental age. Examples include doing homework and emptying the trash. Non-age-appropriate activities include assembling a wooden inlay puzzle and having an adult tie shoelaces by children over 6 years.

B. Curricular domains
1. *Recreation/leisure activities*: Those that teach the student how to spend leisure time appropriately. Examples include using playground equipment, card games, and roller skating.
2. *Domestic activities*: Those that teach skills normally required for home living. Examples include washing clothes and setting tables.
3. *Self-care activities*: Those that are necessary to exhibit and maintain good grooming, health, and personal safety. Examples include toothbrushing, hair care, and toileting.
4. *Vocational activities*: Those that contribute directly to the ability of the student to assume a vocation that would enable some degree of economic independence. Examples include tasks performed in sheltered workshops or community jobs.

Note. From Dyer, Schwartz, and Luce (1984, pp. 250–251). Copyright 1984 by the Society for the Experimental Analysis of Behavior, Inc.

(Smith, Chung, & Vostanis, 1994). Parents, once regarded as the primary cause of their child's disorder, are now regarded as "cotherapists, advocates, developmental agents, and the primary cure" (Schopler & Mesibov, 1984, p. 3) for the problems of a child suffering a severe neurological impairment.

The following discussion on assessment of families with autistic children is undertaken from the perspective of intervention. Family assessment can be undertaken with the intent to improve the functioning or well-being of the other family members, who are perhaps adversely affected by the stresses associated with having an autistic child or sibling. Family assessment can also aid choice of intervention and timing to optimize success for the handicapped child. Finally, because parent training is now recognized as a crucial intervention by most therapists, the need exists for assessment of the parents and the family environment. An understanding of the key factors influencing the effectiveness of parents as teachers should help identify those parents who can profit from parent training, should help identify obstacles to parent training, and may increase the maintenance of gains made through parent training.

Assessing the Effects of an Autistic Child on the Family

Nearly 20 years ago, McAdoo and DeMyer (1978) suggested that the most productive approach to research in the area of family factors in autism would be to focus on the autistic individual as a source of chronic stress on the family. Time has borne out that prediction; most published research on families with autistic children is in this area. Sources of stress in the family of an autistic child have been assessed by a variety of objective means. Several studies have used the CARS (Schopler et al., 1986) in an attempt to determine the degree of stress associated with various symptoms of autism as reported by the parents. In one study (Factor, Perry, & Freeman, 1990), a 14-item adaptation of the CARS was completed by both the fathers and the mothers of autistic children. The parents rated their children on the degree of severity for each symptom, using a 4-point scale; parents also rated how stressful they found that symptom, using a similar 4-point scale. Fathers and mothers agreed on both symptom severity and stress ratings. Linguistic and cognitive impairments of the children were identified as the most severe sources of stress, with social impairment and emotional inappropriateness the next

most stressful. Interestingly, professionals judged families to be more stressed by the children's behavior than the families judged themselves as being. A very similar study using the CARS (Freeman, Perry, & Factor, 1991) on a sample that was apparently independent of the one studied by Factor et al. (1990) reported much the same pattern of relationships. In the latter report, however, professionals appeared to agree with parents regarding the stressfulness of the children's behavior. Konstantareas and Homatidis (1989) also assessed child symptom severity and stress with the CARS. They found that the best predictor of stress for both parents was a child's self-injury. Mothers also reported hyperirritability and older age of a child as factors.

Two measures of stress related to problems in families demonstrate some utility for treatment. Holroyd's (1974, 1987) Questionnaire on Resources and Stress (QRS) appears in several forms. Bristol (1987) used a portion of an early form (Holroyd, 1974) to assess the extent to which family members had to pass up educational, vocational, or other self-development opportunities because of an autistic child. Factor et al. (1990), using Form F of the QRS (Friedrich, Greenberg, & Crnic, 1983), found that parents who described their children as having significantly more difficult characteristics and more physical incapacitation were more likely to use respite care. Koegel et al. (1992) compared the stress profiles of the QRS obtained from mothers who lived in different cultural and geographic environments with children of different ages and different levels of functioning. They found major differences in these mothers of autistic children, relative to the normative sample, on scales measuring stress associated with dependence and management, cognitive impairment, limits on family opportunity, and life span care. Finally, Konstantareas, Homatidis, and Plowright (1992) described a 78-item modification of the QRS, which was designed to address the concern that the QRS may be too inclusive and not necessarily relevant to families of severely dysfunctional individuals.

Another measure, the Parenting Stress Index (Form 6; Loyd & Abidin, 1985), is used to assess stress in the parent–child system as well as to identify the sources of stress. Wolf, Noh, Fisman, and Speechley (1989) found that increased parenting stress, measured in this manner, was related to maternal depression. Szatmari et al. (1994) compared parent and teacher ratings of stress, and found that parents reported higher levels of stress associated with autistic behaviors than did teachers.

Also potentially useful is the Coping Health Inventory for Parents (McCubbin & Patterson, 1981). This 45-item instrument is intended to measure the perceived helpfulness of three major types of coping patterns used in dealing with the stress of a handicapped or chronically ill child: (1) maintaining family integration and an optimistic definition of the situation; (2) maintaining self-esteem and reaching out for informed social support; and (3) maintaining contact with professionals and other experts in seeking information and services for the child. Bristol (1987) used this measure to obtain information about the specific coping responses parents used in dealing with the stress of having a handicapped child. Two important aspects of coping identified by Gill and Harris (1991) are hardiness—that is, the presence of feelings of control, commitment, and challenge, as measured by a questionnaire developed by Maddi, Kobasa, and Hoover (1979)—and perceived (not actual) availability of social support. Mothers of autistic children high in hardiness and perceived social support showed less depression and fewer somatic complaints than mothers low on both variables.

The effects of an autistic child on the general family environment are frequently evaluated with the Moos Family Environment Scale (Moos & Moos, 1981). Previous researchers note that families with autistic children tend to report spending significantly less time participating in leisure and recreational activities (Koegel, Schreibman, O'Neill, & Burke, 1983). Because some data indicate that the prognosis for autistic children is better in families whose members maintain a high frequency of outdoor recreational activities, assessment of this factor may be particularly important. A concept somewhat related to family environment, family adaptation, can be measured in a structured interview with the parent. The Home Quality Rating Scale (Meyers, Mink, & Nihira, 1977) is completed by an in-home observer after a 1½- to 2-hour structured interview with the parent. Factor 1, Harmony of Home and Quality of Parenting, consists of ratings on seven behaviorally anchored items measuring growth promotion as a policy in child rearing, acceptance of the child, rejection of the child, observed ability of the parent to cope with the child, and adjustment and harmony in the home. Bristol (1987) found that family adaptation was positively predicted by social support and active coping in 45 families of autistic and communication-impaired children.

Sibling relationships were studied by McHale, Simeonsson, and Sloan (1984) and McHale, Sloan, and Simeonsson (1986) with a 24-item rating scale that assessed four dimensions of behavior: the degree of acceptance, hostility, support, and embarrassment displayed by siblings toward each other. The behaviors that constitute each of these dimensions are rated by their mothers. McHale et al. (1984) found that mean ratings for "normal–normal" sibling dyads were very similar to those for "normal–autistic" sibling dyads. Mothers, surprisingly, indicated on average that the relationship between a normal child and an autistic child was more positive than the relationship between two normal children. However, the mean ratings masked another pattern: A much broader range of sibling behaviors (i.e., much more negative as well as more positive behaviors) was found in the normal–autistic child dyads. This pattern suggests that assessment of sibling relationships in a clinical setting might reveal significant issues worthy of intervention.

The presence of an autistic child in a family is likely to be stressful. Clinical observations, interviews with the mothers of autistic children, and the results of objective testing all suggest that stress is almost invariably present (Harris, 1983). Several justifications exist for the routine assessment of family stress and adjustment. First, the well-being of the family as a unit is of concern in its own right. Moreover, only by attending to the needs of each individual, including their own needs, can the parents hope to have the resources necessary to care for their autistic child (Bristol, 1984). Finally, stress is known to interfere with the proper utilization of existing skills and areas of competence (Marcus, 1984); thus, a failure to recognize the stress experienced by a family is likely to result in less than optimal results of interventions with an autistic child (Harris & Powers, 1984; Kozloff, 1984).

Treatment Issues and Family Assessment

Parent training is presently one of the most widely accepted intervention methods for autistic children. This fact makes the assessment of families centrally relevant to the treatment of these children. Many reasons exist for the popularity of parent training. One advantage is superiority to other methods, as assessed by prognosis and by improvement across settings (Koegel, Schreibman, Britten, Burke, & O'Neill, 1982; Lovaas, 1987). Another reason is that parents may require special skills in managing their daily lives with an autistic child (Berk & Berk, 1979; Schreibman, Koegel,

Mills, & Burke, 1984). Finally, parents are simply around their autistic child more than anyone else and have the opportunity to provide an around-the-clock treatment environment (Schreibman et al., 1984).

Parent training is a particularly labor-intensive undertaking. All health care providers, across disciplines and pathologies, are necessarily interested in prescriptive interventions, and the time required by parent training makes identification of those families who will profit all the more important. Yet the recent development of parent training has not yet permitted prescriptive intervention based on objective measurement. Only some suggestive information is available.

McHale et al. (1984) suggest that a family's level of functioning prior to a handicapped child's birth may be an extremely important factor in the family's ultimate level of adjustment, independent of intervention. Bristol (1984) evaluated whether certain characteristics of the family environment were related to successful adaptation of an autistic child. Using the Moos Family Environment Scale (Moos & Moos, 1981), she found that degree of cohesion, expressiveness, and an active recreational orientation were predictive of successful adjustment. On the Coping Health Inventory (described earlier), higher scores on all three coping factors were significantly related to interview ratings of acceptance and quality of parenting.

Some clinicians observe that the major problem of parent training is that although teaching parents the behavioral skills they need is relatively easy, insuring that parents will continue to use these skills once training ends is much more problematic (Harris & Powers, 1984). For example, Kozloff (1984) found that about one-third of families had changed little, if at all, after an entire year of a program designed to teach parents to interact productively with their autistic children. Failures to benefit from parent training are generally attributed to a failure to understand aspects of family life that interfere with the family members' ability to produce beneficial change. Certain conditions and attitudes must be present to motivate members to make the effort to participate.

Kozloff (1984) describes assessment of the following factors as relevant to a parent's or other family member's "readiness to change," prior to the initiation of a treatment program:

1. Trust in the consultant.
2. Confidence in what the consultant has to offer.
3. A recognition of the need to conduct a home education program.

4. A recognition that each person in the family mutually affects and is affected by the behavior of the others.
5. A recognition that for beneficial change to take place in the child, one needs to change some of one's own behavior.
6. An expectation of success at changing one's own and the child's behavior.
7. The willingness and ability to temporarily shelve some time and outside interests so that one can participate in meetings and conduct a home educational program.
8. Energy, or the belief that one has energy, sufficient to participate in the program and to conduct a home educational program.
9. A tentative acceptance of the behavioral-educational approach (i.e., some of its basic assumptions and methods). (pp. 173–174)

At the present time, the evaluation of treatment readiness is quite subjective. Most of the concerns assessed have to do with the degree and quality of motivation of the parents, as well as the degree and strength of competing contingencies. An alternative approach taken by some clinicians is to create the necessary motivation "artificially," by requiring parents to sign contracts prior to the initiation of treatment.

The effects of parent training on parents and family functioning may also be a relevant concern in many situations. Schreibman, Kaneko, and Koegel (1991) compared the emotional state of parents while implementing two types of parent training procedures. They found more positive affect, as rated by observers of parents, when the parents were implementing a naturalistic procedure than when they were using highly structured, discrete-trial procedures. In a study evaluating the effects of parent training on family functioning, Schreibman et al. (1984) described the use of a 24-hour diary (or Time Activity Budget) that determines how parents spend their time during the day. These activities are evaluated during one weekday and one weekend. When the amount of time parents spent was tabulated in the categories of teaching activities and direct custodial care activities, the investigators found that parents undergoing training spent twice as much time in teaching activities as parents whose children were being treated in a clinic setting only. In addition, the parents undergoing training spent significantly less time in direct custodial care activities. These two studies suggest techniques and strategies that may be useful during the implementation of a parent training program to optimize program effectiveness.

The importance of family assessment has increased with the growing evidence of the utility of parent training. Objective assessment for the purpose of prescriptive intervention is in its infancy, but this area should expand greatly in the near future as alternative interventions are developed. Assessment of factors likely to influence the success and course of intervention is also in the early stages of development. Objective assessment of family functioning after intervention indicates positive gains rather than losses (Schreibman et al., 1984), but some have noted that treatment itself may be a stressor and may lead to deterioration in the overall functioning of the family (Harris & Powers, 1984). This observation suggests that formal assessment of the effects of treatment on the family may be required not only to demonstrate treatment gains, but also to verify the absence of significant new difficulties.

ASSESSMENT FOR BEHAVIOR MANAGEMENT

Clinicians working in settings that serve autistic children spend a significant proportion of their time addressing such problem behaviors as tantrums, aggression, self-injury, stereotypies, property destruction, and noncompliance. Until fairly recently, the technology for assessing and treating such problems was straightforward and conceptually simple. Baseline data were obtained for 1 or 2 weeks; then an appropriate behavior reduction plan was implemented and subsequently modified on the basis of ongoing data. More recently, there has been an increased emphasis on conducting a thorough analysis of the variables that are functionally related to the problem behavior, prior to the implementation of treatment procedures (Axelrod, 1987; Donnellan, Mirenda, Mesaros, & Fassbender, 1984; Iwata, Vollmer, & Zarcone, 1990; Pyles & Bailey, 1990). When such a "functional analysis" is successful in identifying the setting events, antecedents, and motivating consequences of a behavior, a treatment derived logically from the analysis can often be implemented with considerable gains in timeliness, effectiveness, and accountability (Carr, Robinson, & Palumbo, 1990).

Some methods for analyzing the problem behaviors of autistic children are described in this final section. We restrict our focus to examples of procedures most useful to practitioners in clinical and educational settings. Procedures for conducting functional analyses in highly structured

analogue situations are reviewed in Newsom et al. (1988).

The first step in a behavior management consultation is to obtain some basic information from parents, teachers, or direct care staff members about the nature of the problem behavior and the situations and events that appear to be related to occurrences of it. A questionnaire that is intended to identify some functionally relevant consequences of problem behaviors is the Motivation Assessment Scale (MAS; Durand & Crimmins, 1992). The MAS is a list of 16 questions about a child's most frequent disruptive behavior. The 16 questions are composed of four questions in four categories, each category related to one of the following possible motivators: Attention, Escape (from demands or other aversive stimuli), Self-Stimulation, and Tangible Reward (e.g., food or toys). Examples of the questions related to each source of motivation are shown in Table 8.6. The sources of motivation shown in Table 8.6 were selected because they have been found in experimental studies to be functionally related to severe behavior disorders in autistic and retarded children (see reviews by Carr & Durand, 1985, and Iwata et al., 1990). The informant answers each question by circling the appropriate rating on a 7-point scale ranging from "never" (0) to "always" (6). A mean score is obtained for each of the four categories of consequences. The relative standing of the resulting mean scores indicates the relative contribution of each of the types of motivation to the problem behavior. Factor analyses of the MAS have yielded four-factor solutions that correspond closely with the four MAS categories, unless very low-frequency behaviors are rated (Bihm, Kienlen, Ness, & Poindexter, 1991; Singh et al., 1993).

In an interrater reliability study by Durand and Crimmins (1988), 20 pairs of teachers rated a total of 50 autistic and retarded children. Pearson correlations between the ratings on individual items ranged from .66 to .92, and those for mean scores ranged from .80 to .95. Rank-order correlation coefficients for the category mean scores were also highly significant, indicating that different raters tended to rank the sources of motivation for a given child similarly. However, other studies have failed to replicate the high reliability found by Durand and Crimmins (Kearney, 1994; Newton & Sturmey, 1991; Zarcone, Rodgers, Iwata, Rourke, & Dorsey, 1991). For example, interrater agreement on the primary motivation for self-injury occurred for only 16 of 55 subjects in the Zarcone et al. (1991) study.

TABLE 8.6. Motivation Assessment Scale: Categories and Sample Questions

Attention
    3. Does this behavior occur when you are talking to other persons in the room?
    7. Does this behavior occur whenever you stop attending to him or her?
Escape
    2. Does this behavior occur following a command to perform a difficult task?
    6. Does this behavior occur when *any* request is made of your child?
Self-stimulation
    1. Would this behavior occur continuously if the child was left alone for long periods of time?
    5. Does this behavior occur repeatedly, over and over, in the same way?
Tangible reward
    8. Does this behavior occur when you take away a favorite toy or food?
    12. Does this behavior *stop* occurring shortly after you give the child the toy or food he or she has requested?

Note. Adapted from Durand and Crimmins (1992). Copyright 1992 by Monaco & Associates. Adapted by permission.

Validity data with a small sample demonstrated that the primary category of motivation identified by the MAS predicted the subsequent occurrence of problem behaviors in a corresponding analogue condition (Durand & Crimmins, 1988). For example, children whose disruptive behaviors were rated on the MAS as most likely to occur when demands were made later demonstrated those behaviors much more frequently in the Escape analogue condition, which included difficult tasks, than in the other conditions. In fact, ranks of the categories of motivation derived from the MAS ratings correlated .99 with ranked data from the four analogue conditions, indicating almost perfect prediction of the children's performance in the analogue conditions by the teachers' ratings. Additional validation of the MAS was obtained by Durand, Crimmins, Caulfield, and Taylor (1989). They found that the reinforcers identified by the MAS for several problem behaviors could be used to reinforce appropriate behaviors in skill training programs. The MAS did not fare as well in a study by Crawford, Brockel, Schauss, and Miltenberger (1992) on stereotyped behaviors in four adults. The MAS identified sensory consequences as the motivation for all subjects, but analogue assessments identified different patterns of motivators across subjects.

In summary, the MAS is brief and convenient to use when one needs information quickly about the possible motivating consequences of a problem behavior. However, it appears to be less reliable and valid in institutional or other settings where the staff members may be less trained or experienced than the special education teachers and aides studied by its authors (Kearney, 1994; Sturmey, 1994).

A more comprehensive instrument for record-ing such information is the Functional Analysis Interview Form (FAIF) developed by O'Neill, Horner, Albin, Storey, and Sprague (1990). It is part of a package of procedures and forms designed to assist in interviewing relevant caregivers, conducting direct observations of clients, testing hypotheses through analogue assessment procedures, and writing behavior intervention programs. The FAIF has nine major sections: (1) description of the behavior, (2) ecological events, (3) situations normally predictive of occurrences of the behavior, (4) the typical consequences of the behavior, (5) the efficiency of the behavior in achieving its typical consequences, (6) the individual's communication abilities, (7) potential positive reinforcers for skill training, (8) potential alternative behaviors, and (9) a history of previous intervention efforts. Most of the items in the form are open-ended instead of including checklists or rating scales, because the FAIF is not intended to be a psychometric instrument. It is best considered as a useful tool for identifying and recording possibly relevant causal variables in an organized way.

Interviews are followed by direct observation of an individual in the settings in which the problem behaviors are most likely to occur. A comprehensive method for recording and analyzing the observations has been presented by Carr et al. (1994). They present a model based on three steps: Describe, Categorize, and Verify. The Describe step addresses *in vivo* observations. Each time an episode of the behavior occurs, the observer fills out a card like that shown in the upper panel of Figure 8.2, recording the antecedent interpersonal context and the staff's social reaction as well as the behavior. After a large number of cards are collected, a panel of three people who are involved in the client's treatment and are also knowledgeable about common sources of motivation in developmentally disabled individuals examine each card separately, paying particular attention to the "social reaction" section, and make a hypothesis about the likely purpose of the behavior. The categories of purposes are Attention, Escape, Tangible, and Other (for nonsocial purposes not fitting one of the first three categories). This is recorded on the back of the card, as shown in the bottom panel of Figure 8.2 if at least two out of three of the panel members agree on the purpose. If all three disagree, the card is eliminated. Carr et al. (1994) noted that poor reliability of this nature is rare, occurring for only 2 or 3 cards out of the 100 or so typically collected in each case. If it occurs at a higher rate, further observations need to be made.

Next, the cards are grouped by category on a large bulletin board under the headings of the categories (Attention, Escape, Tangibles, Other). To reduce the selection of potential interventions, the panel members try to find common themes among groups of cards. This task is facilitated by focusing on the "interpersonal context" section of the cards. For the largely escape-motivated child in Figure 8.2, the panel found that most of the situations in which Gary displayed problem behavior to escape involved three themes: completing a task (10 cards), response to negative feedback (48 cards), and request to perform a nonpreferred task (14 cards). The themes that emerge within a category provide guides to tailoring a manageable number of interventions to different situations.

The final step is to verify the hypothesized purposes by carrying out sessions in which the relevant interpersonal contexts and social reactions are manipulated in the client's environment. This is typically done for 10% or four cards within a theme, whichever is greater. For example, for the 48 cards with the theme of negative feedback, the panel conducted sessions replicating the contexts and reactions for five of the cards selected at random. Four verification sessions are conducted—two in which the client's desired social reactions

```
NAME:    Gary          OBSERVER:  Rob          DATE:    3/10/95

GENERAL CONTEXT:   Gathering work materials   TIME:    9:30 AM

INTERPERSONAL CONTEXT:   Cal asked Gary to bring over a
    wheelbarrow full of potting soil to the workbench.

BEHAVIOR PROBLEM:   Gary punched Cal in the chest and tried
    to punch him a second time in the face but Cal ducked.

SOCIAL REACTION:   Cal told Gary to "keep cool" and moved
    away from him.  After a few minutes, Cal got the
    wheelbarrow himself.
```

```
HYPOTHESIS (PURPOSE):  Gary punches in this situation in
    order to avoid having to do heavy physical labor.
    (ESCAPE)

PANEL MEMBERS:   Rob, Bob, and Ms. Ibsen
```

FIGURE 8.2. Example of cards filled out during observations of problem behavior in natural environment. Top: Front of card, describing behavior in one situation. Bottom: Back of card, showing categorization of purpose of behavior by three-member panel. From Carr, et al. (1994, p. 66). Copyright 1994 by Paul H. Brookes Publishing Company. Reprinted by permission.

are made contingent on the problem behavior (which should produce high levels of the problem behavior), and two in which the desired reactions are provided in response to socially appropriate behavior (which should result in low levels of the problem behavior).

Carr et al. (1994) reported a field test in which four supervisors rated the degree of implementation of their assessment procedures by 450 teachers, parents, and group home staff members over a 1-year period after training. A scale from 1 ("never") to 7 ("often") was used to rate skill clusters in various areas. For the Describe, Categorize, and Verify clusters, the mean ratings were 6.3, 6.9, and 6.3, indicating a high degree of acceptance of the procedures by trained caregivers. Additional ratings indicated that the use of the assessment procedures and communication-based interventions recommended by the authors were successful in changing behaviors of the clients. Thus, although the Carr et al. (1994) approach to functional analysis requires independent study, it shows considerable promise as a comprehensive approach that addresses the frequent concern about what to do with assessment information once it is obtained.

In most settings, data on problem behaviors are customarily reduced to line graphs of the daily frequency, rate, or percentage of time samples the behavior was observed. Although useful for determining the effectiveness of treatment interventions, such graphs contribute little to the analysis of behaviors, because they ordinarily provide no information about the situations that are differentially associated with high, low, and zero probabilities of the behavior. An alternative method of data presentation that does capture relationships between behaviors and situations is the scatter plot suggested by Touchette, MacDonald, and Langer (1985). One of the investigators' examples, which shows the data of an aggressive autistic adolescent, appears in Figure 8.3. The ordinate is divided into time periods appropriate to the length of most of the elements of the client's daily schedule; here, they are half hours. The abscissa shows successive days. Within the grid, blank areas indicate nonoccurrence of the problem behavior, and filled areas indicate that the behavior occurred during that interval. Filled circles represent two or more assaults on peers or staff members, and open squares represent one assault.

The scatter plot indicates that aggression was

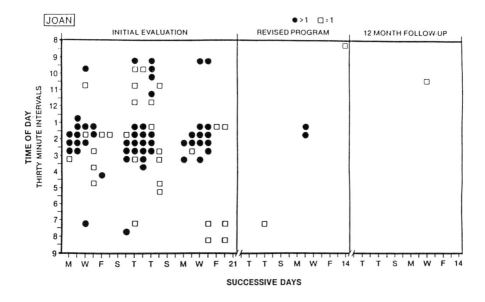

FIGURE 8.3. Scatter plot of assaultive behaviors by an autistic adolescent. Filled circles indicate 30-minute intervals during which more than one assault occurred; open squares indicate intervals with only one assault. From Touchette, MacDonald, and Langer (1985, p. 347). Copyright 1985 by the Society for the Experimental Analysis of Behavior, Inc.

most likely to occur during weekdays from 1:00 to 4:00 P.M., when the client was in group prevocational and community living classes. Aggression was least likely to occur during morning one-to-one instruction, Friday afternoon field trips, and evening and weekend activities. Consequently, intervention began with the elimination of afternoon class participation and the scheduling of activities like those available during evenings and weekends (e.g., listening to stories, trying on cosmetics, playing with stickers). The first 2 weeks of treatment are shown in the "Revised Program" panel of Figure 8.3. Over the following 12 months, the client was exposed to classroom activities for gradually increasing periods of time; she was eventually able to spend most of the afternoon in class with minimal aggression, as shown in the third panel of Figure 8.3.

The usefulness of a scatter plot depends primarily on the use of a code that is easily understood. Touchette et al. (1985) caution that using more than two or three symbols (representing presence–absence of the behavior or high, low, and zero rates) tends to make the grid difficult to interpret. In applied settings, all that is usually needed for treatment decisions is a code that discriminates "major" or "significant" episodes of a particular problem behavior from "minor" or "negligible" episodes. Although the same information provided by a scatter plot could in principle be obtained from a multiple-baseline graph, a graph equivalent to the grid in Figure 8.3 would require at least five or six curves (one for each major portion of the day), and thus would be far more troublesome to plot and to read. A scatter plot is also useful even if no patterns in the behavior emerge, because the lack of patterning should eliminate some initial hypotheses and suggest consideration of the following possibilities: (1) An unstable, poorly structured environment exists (see Touchette et al., 1985, Case 3); (2) the behavior is not under external stimulus control, but instead is a "pure" operant (Skinner, 1938) maintained by intermittent social or sensory reinforcers; or (3) the behavior results from randomly occurring environmental factors (e.g., the presence of substitute staff members) or physical conditions (e.g., ear infections, toothaches, gastrointestinal upsets).

CONCLUDING COMMENTS

As this review demonstrates, the assessment of autistic children is a multifaceted enterprise that frequently crosses the traditional boundaries between clinical psychology, psychiatry, applied behavior analysis, and special education. Some familiarity with the relevant contributions of each of these disciplines is necessary to understand the issues bearing on the evaluation of autistic children. Equally important is the need to maintain a pragmatic, functional perspective at the level of the individual child. Of the many available assessment procedures, only a few are needed at a given point in time. The selection of the specific procedures to be used should depend on the major current needs of the child and on the specific questions raised by parents, teachers, or other referral sources. Selecting among possible procedures is in any event inevitable with children so pervasively impaired, because their problems are so numerous as to preclude a truly comprehensive assessment in a limited period of time. Assessment activities must therefore be ongoing, flexible, and individualized to be beneficial to all concerned.

REFERENCES

Adrien, J. L., Ornitz, E., Barthelemy, C., Sauvage, D., & Lelord, G. (1987). The presence or absence of certain behaviors associated with infantile autism in severely retarded autistic and nonautistic retarded children and very young normal children. *Journal of Autism and Developmental Disorders*, 17, 407–416.

Albert, R., & Davis, A. (1971). A reliability study of interparental agreement on the Rimland Diagnostic Check List. *Journal of Clinical Psychology*, 27, 499–502.

Alpern, G. D., & Kimberlin, C. C. (1970). Short intelligence test ranging from infancy levels through childhood levels for use with the retarded. *American Journal of Mental Deficiency*, 75, 65–71.

American Psychiatric Association. (1994). *Diagnostic and statistical manual of mental disorders* (4th ed.). Washington, DC: Author.

Ando, H., & Yoshimura, I. (1979). Effects of age on communication skill levels and prevalence of maladaptive behaviors in autistic and mentally retarded children. *Journal of Autism and Developmental Disorders*, 9, 83–93.

Ando, H., Yoshimura, I., & Wakabayashi, S. (1980). Effects of age on adaptive behavior levels and academic skill levels in autistic and mentally retarded children. *Journal of Autism and Developmental Disorders*, 10, 173–184.

Asarnow, R. F., Tanguay, P. E., Bott, L., & Freeman, B. J. (1987). Patterns of intellectual functioning in non-retarded autistic and schizophrenic children. *Journal of Child Psychology and Psychiatry*, 28, 273–280.

Asperger, H. (1991). "Autistic psychopathy" in childhood. In U. Frith (Ed.), *Autism and Asperger syndrome* (pp. 37–92). New York: Cambridge University Press. (Original work published 1944)

August, G. J., Stewart, M. A., & Tsai, L. (1981). The incidence of cognitive disabilities in the siblings of autistic children. *British Journal of Psychiatry, 138,* 416–422.

Axelrod, S. (1987). Functional and structural analyses of behavior: Approaches leading to reduced use of punishment procedures? *Research in Developmental Disabilities, 8,* 165–178.

Bailey, A. (1993). The biology of autism. *Psychological Medicine, 23,* 7–11.

Bailey, S. L., Prystalski, P., Kozlowski, S., Mielke, C., & Owen, V. (1984). The curriculum. In S. L. Bailey, V. E. Owen, D. S. Hurd, & C. A. Conley (Eds.), *Instructional procedures for educating students with autism in the Communication Disorders Program* (pp. 13–44). DeKalb: Northern Illinois University Autism Program.

Baird, T. D., & August, G. J. (1985). Familial heterogeneity in infantile autism. *Journal of Autism and Developmental Disorders, 15,* 315–321.

Balthazar, E. E. (1972). *Balthazar Scales of Adaptive Behavior: Vol. 1. Scales of functional independence.* Palo Alto, CA: Consulting Psychologists Press.

Balthazar, E. E. (1973). *Balthazar Scales of Adaptive Behavior: Vol. 2. Scales of social adaptation.* Palo Alto, CA: Consulting Psychologists Press.

Baron-Cohen, S. (1989). Perceptual role-taking and protodeclarative pointing in autism. *British Journal of Developmental Psychology, 7,* 113–127.

Baron-Cohen, S., Allen, J., & Gillberg, C. (1992). Can autism be detected at 18 months? The needle, the haystack, and the CHAT. *British Journal of Psychiatry, 161,* 839–843.

Baron-Cohen, S., Leslie, A. M., & Frith, U. (1986). Mechanical, behavioural and intentional understanding of picture stories in autistic children. *British Journal of Developmental Psychology, 4,* 113–125.

Bartak, L., & Rutter, M. (1974). The use of personal pronouns by autistic children. *Journal of Autism and Childhood Schizophrenia, 4,* 217–222.

Bartak, L., & Rutter, M. (1976). Differences between mentally retarded and normally intelligent autistic children. *Journal of Autism and Childhood Schizophrenia, 6,* 109–120.

Bartak, L., Rutter, M., & Cox, A. (1975). A comparative study of infantile autism and specific developmental receptive language disorder. I: The children. *British Journal of Psychiatry, 126,* 127–145.

Barthelemy, C., Adrien, J. L., Roux, S., Garreau, B., Perrot, A., & Lelord, G. (1992). Sensitivity and specificity of the Behavioral Summarized Evaluation (BSE) for the assessment of autistic behaviors. *Journal of Autism and Developmental Disorders, 22,* 23–31.

Barthelemy, C., Adrien, J. L., Tanguay, P., Garreau, B., Fermanian, J., Roux, S., Sauvage, D., & Lelord, G. (1990). The Behavioral Summarized Evaluation: Validity and reliability of a scale for the assessment of autistic behaviors. *Journal of Autism and Developmental Disorders, 20,* 189–204.

Barthelemy, C., Bruneau, N., Jouve, J., Martineau, J., Muh, J., & Lelord, G. (1989). Urinary dopamine metabolites as indicators of the responsiveness to fenfluramine treatment in children with autistic behavior. *Journal of Autism and Developmental Disorders, 19,* 241–254.

Barthelemy, C., Hameury, I., & Lelord, G. (1989). Exchange and development therapies (EDT) for children with autism: A treatment program from Tours, France. In C. Gillberg (Ed.), *Autism: The state of the art* (pp. 263–284). New York: Elsevier.

Bender, L. (1947). Childhood schizophrenia: Clinical study of one hundred schizophrenic children. *American Journal of Orthopsychiatry, 17,* 40–56.

Berk, R. A., & Berk, S. F. (1979). *Labor and leisure at home: Content and organization of the household day.* Beverly Hills, CA: Sage.

Bihm, E. M., Kienlen, T. L., Ness, M. E., & Poindexter, A. R. (1991). Factor structure of the Motivation Assessment Scale for persons with mental retardation. *Psychological Reports, 68,* 1235–1238.

Black, M., Freeman, B. J., & Montgomery, J. (1975). Systematic observations of play behavior in autistic children. *Journal of Autism and Childhood Schizophrenia, 5,* 363–371.

Blew, P. A., Schwartz, I. S., & Luce, S. C. (1985). Teaching functional community skills to autistic children using nonhandicapped peer tutors. *Journal of Applied Behavior Analysis, 18,* 337–342.

Bloom, A. S., Klee, S. H., & Raskin, L. M. (1977). A comparison of the Stanford–Binet abbreviated and complete forms for developmentally disabled children. *Journal of Clinical Psychology, 33,* 477–480.

Borden, M. C., & Ollendick, T. H. (1994). An examination of the validity of social subtypes in autism. *Journal of Autism and Developmental Disorders, 24,* 23–37.

Bristol, M. M. (1984). Family resources and successful adaptation to autistic children. In E. Schopler & G. Mesibov (Eds.), *The effects of autism on the family* (pp. 289–310). New York: Plenum Press.

Bristol, M. M. (1987). Mothers of children with autism or communication disorders: Successful adaptation and the double ABCX model. *Journal of Autism and Developmental Disorders, 17,* 469–486.

Brown, L., Branston, M., Hamre-Nietupski, S., Pumpian, I., Certo, N., & Gruenewald, L. (1979). A strategy for developing chronological age-appropriate and functional curricular content for severely handicapped adolescents and young adults. *Journal of Special Education, 13,* 81–90.

Bruneau, N., Garreau, B., Roux, S., & Lelord, G. (1987). Modulation of auditory evoked potentials with increasing stimulus intensity in autistic children. *Electroencephalography and Clinical Neurophysiology, 40,* 584–589.

Campbell, M., Friedman, E., DeVito, E., Greenspan, L., & Collins, P. (1974). Blood serotonin in psychotic and brain damaged children. *Journal of Autism and Childhood Schizophrenia, 4,* 33–41.

Campbell, M., Rosenbloom, S., Perry, R., George, A. E., Kricheff, I. I., Anderson, L., Small, A. M., & Jennings, S. J. (1982). Computerized axial tomography in young autistic children. *American Journal of Psychiatry, 139,* 510–512.

Cantwell, D. P., & Baker, L. (1984). Research concerning families of children with autism. In E. Schopler & G. B. Mesibov (Eds.), *The effects of autism on the family* (pp. 41–63). New York: Plenum Press.

Carpentieri, S. C., & Morgan, S. B. (1994). Brief report: A comparison of patterns of cognitive functioning of autistic and nonautistic retarded children on the Stanford–Binet—Fourth Edition. *Journal of Autism and Developmental Disorders, 24,* 215–223.

Carr, E. G., & Durand, V. M. (1985). The social-communicative basis of severe behavior problems in children. In S. Reiss & R. Bootzin (Eds.), *Theoretical issues in behavior therapy* (pp. 219–254). New York: Academic Press.

Carr, E. G., Levin, L., McConnachie, G., Carlson, J. I., Kemp, D. C., & Smith, C. E. (1994). *Communication-based intervention for problem behavior: A user's guide for producing positive change.* Baltimore: Paul H. Brookes.

Carr, E. G., Newsom, C. D., & Binkoff, J. A. (1976). Stimulus control of self-destructive behavior in a psychotic child. *Journal of Abnormal Child Psychology, 4,* 139–153.

Carr, E. G., Robinson, S., & Palumbo, L. W. (1990). The wrong issue: Aversive vs. nonaversive treatment. The right issue: Functional vs. nonfunctional treatment. In A. C. Repp & N. N. Singh (Eds.), *Perspectives on the use of nonaversive and aversive interventions for persons with developmental disabilities* (pp. 361–379). Sycamore, IL: Sycamore.

Carr, E. G., Schreibman, L., & Lovaas, O. I. (1975). Control of echolalic speech in psychotic children. *Journal of Abnormal Child Psychology, 3,* 331–351.

Castelloe, P., & Dawson, G. (1993). Subclassification of children with autism and pervasive developmental disorder: A questionnaire based on Wing's subgrouping scheme. *Journal of Autism and Developmental Disorders, 23,* 229–241.

Cattell, P. (1960). *Cattell Infant Intelligence Scale.* New York: Psychological Corporation.

Charlop, M. H., & Haymes, L. K. (1994). Speech and language acquisition and intervention: Behavioral approaches. In J. L. Matson (Ed.), *Autism in children and adults: Etiology, assessment, and intervention* (pp. 213–240). Pacific Grove, CA: Brooks/Cole.

Charlop, M. H., Schreibman, L., Mason, J., & Vesey, W. (1983). Behavior–setting interactions of autistic children: A behavioral mapping approach to assessing classroom behaviors. *Analysis and Intervention in Developmental Disabilities, 3,* 359–373.

Chess, S., Fernandez, P., & Korn, S. (1978). Behavioral consequences of congenital rubella. *Journal of Pediatrics, 93,* 699–703.

Christen, H. J., & Hanefeld, F. (1995). Male Rett variant. *Neuropediatrics, 26,* 81–82.

Clark, P., & Rutter, M. (1979). Task difficulty and task performance in autistic children. *Journal of Child Psychology and Psychiatry, 20,* 271–285.

Cohen, I. L., Sudhalter, V., Landon-Jimenez, & Keogh, M. (1993). A neural network approach to the classification of autism. *Journal of Autism and Developmental Disorders, 23,* 443–466.

Coleman, M., & Gillberg, C. (1985). *The biology of the autistic syndromes.* New York: Praeger.

Coleman, M., & Rimland, B. (1976). Familial autism. In M. Coleman (Ed.), *The autistic syndromes* (pp. 175–182). Amsterdam: North-Holland.

Cooke, E. H. (1990). Autism: Review of neurochemical investigation. *Synapse, 6,* 292–308.

Courchesne, E. (1995). New evidence of cerebellar and brainstem hypoplasia in autistic infants, children, and adolescents: The MR imaging study by Hashimoto and colleagues. *Journal of Autism and Developmental Disorders, 25,* 19–22.

Crawford, J., Brockel, B., Schauss, S., & Miltenberger, R. G. (1992). A comparison of methods for the functional assessment of stereotyped behavior in persons with mental retardation. *Journal of the Association for Persons with Severe Handicaps, 17,* 77–86.

Curcio, F. (1978). Sensorimotor functioning and communication in mute autistic children. *Journal of Autism and Childhood Schizophrenia, 8,* 281–292.

Damasio, H., Maurer, R. G., Damasio, A. R., & Chui, H. C. (1980). Computerized tomographic scan findings in patients with autistic behavior. *Archives of Neurology, 37,* 504–510.

Davids, A. (1975). Childhood psychosis: The problem of differential diagnosis. *Journal of Autism and Childhood Schizophrenia, 5,* 129–138.

Dawson, G. (1983). Lateralized brain dysfunction in autism: Evidence from the Halstead–Reitan Neuropsychological Battery. *Journal of Autism and Developmental Disorders, 13,* 269–288.

DeLong, G. R., & Dwyer, J. T. (1988). Correlation of family history with specific autistic subgroups: Asperger's syndrome and bipolar affective disease. *Journal of Autism and Developmental Disorders, 18,* 593–600.

DeMyer, M. K. (1979). *Parents and children in autism.* Washington, DC: Winston.

DeMyer, M. K., Alpern, G. D., Barton, S., DeMyer, W. E., Churchill, D. W., Hingtgen, J. N., Bryson, C. Q., Pontius, W., & Kimberlin, C. (1972). Imitation in autistic, early schizophrenic, and non-psychotic subnormal children. *Journal of Autism and Childhood Schizophrenia, 2,* 263–287.

DeMyer, M. K., Barton, S., Alpern, G. D., Kimberlin, C., Allen, J., Yang, E., & Steele, R. (1974). The measured intelligence of autistic children. *Journal of Autism and Childhood Schizophrenia, 4,* 42–60.

DeMyer, M. K., Churchill, D., Pontius, W., & Gilkey, K. (1971). A comparison of five diagnostic systems for childhood schizophrenia and infantile autism. *Journal of Autism and Childhood Schizophrenia, 1,* 175–189.

DeMyer, M. K., Hingtgen, J. N., & Jackson, R. K. (1981). Infantile autism reviewed: A decade of research. *Schizophrenia Bulletin, 7,* 388–451.

Despert, J. C. (1938). Schizophrenia in children. *Psychiatric Quarterly, 12,* 366–371.

Deykin, E. Y., & MacMahon, B. (1979). The incidence of seizures among children with autistic symptoms. *American Journal of Psychiatry, 136,* 1310–1312.

DiLalla, D. L., & Rogers, S. J. (1994). Domains of the Childhood Autism Rating Scale: Relevance for diagnosis and treatment. *Journal of Autism and Developmental Disorders, 24,* 115–128.

DiLavore, P. C., Lord, C., & Rutter, M. (1995). The Pre-Linguistic Autism Diagnostic Observation Schedule. *Journal of Autism and Developmental Disorders, 25,* 355–379.

Donnellan, A. M., Mirenda, P. L., Mesaros, R. A., & Fassbender, L. L. (1984). Analyzing the communicative functions of aberrant behavior. *Journal of the Association for the Severely Handicapped, 9,* 201–212.

Douglas, V. I., & Sanders, F. A. (1968). A pilot study of Rimland's Diagnostic Check List with autistic and mentally retarded children. *Journal of Child Psychology and Psychiatry, 9,* 105–109.

Durand, V. M., & Carr, E. G. (1987). Social influences on "self-stimulatory" behavior: Analysis and treatment application. *Journal of Applied Behavior Analysis, 20,* 119–132.

Durand, V. M., & Crimmins, D. B. (1987). Assessment and treatment of psychotic speech in an autistic child. *Journal of Autism and Developmental Disorders, 17,* 17–28.

Durand, V. M., & Crimmins, D. B. (1988). Identifying the variables maintaining self-injurious behavior. *Journal of Autism and Developmental Disorders, 18,* 99–117.

Durand, V. M., & Crimmins, D. B. (1992). *The Motivation Assessment Scale.* Topeka, KS: Monaco.

Durand, V. M., Crimmins, D. B., Caulfield, M., & Taylor, J. (1989). Reinforcer assessment: I. Using problem behaviors to select reinforcers. *Journal of the Association of Persons with Severe Handicaps, 14,* 113–126.

Dyer, K., Schwartz, I. S., & Luce, S. C. (1984). A supervision program for increasing functional activities for severely handicapped students in a residential setting. *Journal of Applied Behavior Analysis, 17,* 249–259.

Eggers, C. (1978). Course and prognosis of childhood schizophrenia. *Journal of Autism and Childhood Schizophrenia, 8,* 21–36.

Eaves, L. C., Ho, H. H., & Eaves, D. M. (1994). Subtypes of autism by cluster analysis. *Journal of Autism and Developmental Disorders, 24,* 3–22.

Eisenberg, L., & Kanner, L. (1956). Early infantile autism, 1943–1955. *American Journal of Orthopsychiatry, 26,* 556–566.

Epstein, L. J., Taubman, M. T., & Lovaas, O. I. (1985). Changes in self-stimulatory behaviors with treatment. *Journal of Abnormal Child Psychology, 13,* 281–294.

Evans-Jones, L. G., & Rosenbloom, L. (1978). Disintegrative psychosis in childhood. *Developmental Medicine and Child Neurology, 20,* 462–470.

Factor, D. C., Perry, A., & Freeman, N. (1990). Brief report: Stress, social support, and respite care use in families with autistic children. *Journal of Autism and Developmental Disorders, 20,* 139–146.

Fay, W. H. (1969). On the basis of autistic echolalia. *Journal of Communication Disorders, 2,* 38–47.

Fay, W. H. (1980). Aspects of language. In W. H. Fay & A. L. Schuler (Eds.), *Emerging language in autistic children* (pp. 51–85). Baltimore: University Park Press.

Fein, D., Waterhouse, L., Lucci, D., & Snyder, D. (1985). Cognitive subtypes in developmentally disabled children: A pilot study. *Journal of Autism and Developmental Disorders, 15,* 77–95.

Folstein, S., & Rutter, M. (1977). Genetic influences and infantile autism. *Nature, 265,* 726–728.

Frankel, F., Simmons, J. Q., & Richey, V. E. (1987). Reward value of prosodic features of language for autistic, mentally retarded, and normal children. *Journal of Autism and Developmental Disorders, 17,* 103–113.

Freeman, B. J., Guthrie, D., Frankel, F., Ornitz, E., & Ritvo, E. (1977, August). *Behavior correlates of the syndrome of autism.* Paper presented at the annual convention of the American Psychological Association, San Francisco.

Freeman, B. J., Guthrie, D., Ritvo, E., Schroth, P., Glass, R., & Frankel, F. (1979). Behavior Observation Scale: Preliminary analysis of the similarities and differences between autistic and mentally retarded children. *Psychological Reports, 44,* 519–524.

Freeman, N. L., Perry, A., & Factor, D. C. (1991). Child behaviours as stressors: Replicating and extending the use of the CARS as a measure of stress. *Journal of Child Psychology and Psychiatry, 32,* 1025–1030.

Freeman, B. J., Ritvo, E. R., Guthrie, D., Schroth, P., & Ball, J. (1978). The Behavior Observation Scale for Autism. *Journal of the American Academy of Child Psychiatry, 17,* 576–588.

Freeman, B. J., Ritvo, E. R., Needleman, R., & Yokota, A. (1985). The stability of cognitive and linguistic parameters in autism: A 5 year study. *Journal of the American Academy of Child Psychiatry, 24,* 290–311.

Freeman, B. J., Ritvo, E. R., & Schroth, P. C. (1984). Behavior assessment of the syndrome of autism: Behavior Observation System. *Journal of the American Academy of Child Psychiatry, 23,* 588–594.

Freeman, B. J., Ritvo, E. R., Schroth, P. C., Tonick, I., Guthrie, D., & Wake, L. (1981). Behavioral characteristics of high- and low-IQ autistic children. *American Journal of Psychiatry, 138,* 25–29.

Freeman, B. J., Ritvo, E. R., Yokota, A., & Ritvo, A. (1986). A scale for rating symptoms of patients with the syndrome of autism in real life settings. *Journal of the American Academy of Child Psychiatry, 25,* 130–136.

Freeman, B. J., & Schroth, P. C. (1984). The development of the Behavioral Observation System (BOS) for autism. *Behavioral Assessment, 6,* 177–187.

Freeman, B. J., Schroth, P., Ritvo, E., Guthrie, D., & Wake, L. (1980). The Behavior Observation Scale for Autism (BOS): Initial results of factor analyses. *Journal of Autism and Developmental Disorders, 10,* 343–346.

French, J. (1964). *Pictorial Test of Intelligence.* Boston: Houghton Mifflin.

Friedrich, W. N., Greenberg, M. T., & Crnic, K. (1983). A short form of the Questionnaire on Resources and Stress. *American Journal of Mental Deficiency, 88,* 41–48.

Frith, U. (1991). Asperger and his syndrome. In U. Frith (Ed.), *Autism and Asperger syndrome* (pp. 1–36). New York: Cambridge University Press.

Furneaux, B. (1966). The autistic child. *British Journal of Disorders of Communication, 1,* 85–90.

Garfin, D. G., McCallon, D., & Cox, R. (1988). Validity and reliability of the Childhood Autism Rating Scale with autistic adolescents. *Journal of Autism and Developmental Disorders, 18,* 367–378.

Gill, M. J., & Harris, S. L. (1991). Hardiness and social support as predictors of psychological discomfort in mothers of children with autism. *Journal of Autism and Developmental Disorders, 21,* 407–416.

Gillberg, C. (1984). Infantile autism and other childhood psychoses in a Swedish urban region: Epidemiological aspects. *Journal of Child Psychology and Psychiatry, 25,* 35–43.

Gillberg, C. (1991). Clinical and neurobiological aspects of Asperger syndrome in six family studies. In U. Frith (Ed.), *Autism and Asperger syndrome* (pp. 122–146). New York: Cambridge University Press.

Goldstein, M., Mahanand, D., Lee, J., & Coleman, M. (1976). Dopamine-beta-hydroxylase and endogenous total 5-hydroxyindole levels in autistic patients and controls. In M. Coleman (Ed.), *The autistic syndromes* (pp. 57–63). Amsterdam: North-Holland.

Green, C. W., Reid, D. H., McCarn, J. E., Schepis, M. M., Phillips, J. F., & Parsons, M. B. (1986). Naturalistic observations of classrooms serving severely handicapped persons: Establishing evaluative norms. *Applied Research in Mental Retardation, 7,* 37–50.

Guess, D., & Carr, E. (1991). Emergence and maintenance of stereotypy and self-injury. *American Journal on Mental Retardation, 96,* 299–319.

Gunsett, R. P., Mulick, J. A., Fernald, W. B., & Martin, J. L. (1989). Brief report: Indications for medical screening prior to behavioral programming for severely and profoundly mentally retarded clients. *Journal of Autism and Developmental Disorders, 19,* 167–172.

Hagberg, B. (1995). Clinical delineation of Rett syndrome variants. *Neuropediatrics, 26,* 62.

Hagberg, B., Aicardi, J., Dias, K., & Ramos, O. (1983). A progressive syndrome of autism, dementia, ataxia, and loss of purposeful hand use in girls: Rett's syndrome. Report of 35 cases. *Annals of Neurology, 14,* 471–479.

Hagberg, B., & Witt-Engerstrom, I. (1986). Rett syndrome: A suggested staging system for describing impairment profile with increasing age towards adolescence. *American Journal of Medical Genetics, 24,* 47–60.

Harris, J. C. (1992). Neurobiological factors in self-injurious behavior. In J. K. Luiselli, J. L. Matson, & N. N. Singh (Eds.), *Self-injurious behavior: Analysis, assessment, and treatment* (pp. 59–92). New York: Springer-Verlag.

Harris, S. L. (1983). *Families of the developmentally disabled: A guide to behavioral intervention.* Elmsford, NY: Pergamon Press.

Harris, S. L., Handleman, J., & Burton, J. (1990). The Stanford–Binet profiles of young children with autism. *Special Services in the Schools, 6,* 135–143.

Harris, S. L., & Powers, M. D. (1984). Behavior therapists look at the impact of an autistic child on the family system. In E. Schopler & G. Mesibov (Eds.), *The effects of autism on the family* (pp. 207–224). New York: Plenum Press.

Hobson, R. P. (1983). The autistic child's recognition of age-related features of people, animals and things. *British Journal of Developmental Psychology, 4,* 343–352.

Hobson, R. P. (1987). The autistic child's recognition of age- and sex-related characteristics of people. *Journal of Autism and Developmental Disorders, 17,* 63–80.

Holroyd, J. (1974). The Questionnaire on Resources and Stress: An instrument to measure family response to a handicapped member. *Journal of Community Psychology, 2,* 92–94.

Holroyd, J. (1987). *Manual for the Questionnaire on Resources and Stress.* Brandon, VT: Clinical Psychology Press.

Howlin, P. A. (1981). The effectiveness of operant language training with autistic children. *Journal of Autism and Developmental Disorders, 11,* 89–105.

Itard, J. M. G. (1962). *The wild boy of Aveyron* (G. Humphrey & M. Humphrey, Trans.). New York: Appleton-Century-Crofts. (Original work published 1801)

Iwata, B. A., Vollmer, T. R., & Zarcone, J. R. (1990). The experimental (functional) analysis of behavior disorders: Methodology, applications, and limitations. In A. C. Repp & N. N. Singh (Eds.), *Perspectives on the use of nonaversive and aversive interventions for persons with developmental disabilities* (pp. 301–330). Sycamore, IL: Sycamore.

Johnson, J., & Koegel, R. L. (1982). Behavioral assessment and curriculum development. In R. L. Koegel, A. Rincover, & A. L. Egel (Eds.), *Educating and understanding autistic children* (pp. 1–32). San Diego, CA: College-Hill Press.

Kanner, L. (1943). Autistic disturbances of affective contact. *The Nervous Child, 2,* 181–197.

Kanner, L. (1946). Irrelevant and metaphorical language in early infantile autism. *American Journal of Psychiatry, 103,* 242–246.

Kearney, C. A. (1994). Interrater reliability of the Motivation Assessment Scale: Another, closer look. *Journal of the Association of Persons with Severe Handicaps, 19,* 139–142.

Kerr, A. M. (1995). Early clinical signs in the Rett disorder. *Neuropediatrics, 26,* 67–71.

Knobloch, H., & Pasamanick, B. (1975). Some etiologic and prognostic factors in early infantile autism and psychosis. *Journal of Pediatrics, 55,* 182–191.

Koegel, R. L., Schreibman, L., Britten, K. R., Burke, J. C., & O'Neill, R. E. (1982). A comparison of parent training to direct child treatment. In R. L. Koegel, A. Rincover, & A. L. Egel (Eds.), *Educating and understanding autistic children* (pp. 260–279). San Diego, CA: College-Hill Press.

Koegel, R. L., Schreibman, L., Loos, L. M., Dirlich-Wilhelm, H., Dunlop, G., Robbins, F. R., & Plienis, A. J. (1992). Consistent stress profiles in mothers of children with autism. *Journal of Autism and Developmental Disorders, 22,* 205–216.

Koegel, R. L., Schreibman, L., O'Neill, R. E., & Burke, J. C. (1983). Personality and family interaction characteristics of families with autistic children. *Journal of Consulting and Clinical Psychology, 51,* 683–692.

Kolvin, I. (1971). Studies in the childhood psychoses: I. Diagnostic criteria and classification. *British Journal of Psychiatry, 118,* 381–384.

Kolvin, I., Ounsted, C., Humphrey, M., & McNay, A. (1971). Studies in the childhood psychoses: II. The phenomenology of childhood psychoses. *British Journal of Psychiatry, 118,* 385–395.

Konstantareas, M. M., & Homatidis, S. (1989). Assessing child symptom severity and stress in parents of autistic children. *Journal of Child Psychology and Psychiatry, 30,* 459–470.

Konstantareas, M. M., Homatidis, S., & Plowright, C. M. S. (1992). Assessing resources and stress in parents of severely dysfunctional children through the Clarke modification of Holroyd's Questionnaire on Resources and Stress. *Journal of Autism and Developmental Disorders, 22,* 217–234.

Kozloff, M. A. (1974). *Educating children with learning and behavior problems.* New York: Wiley.

Kozloff, M. A. (1984). A training program for families of children with autism. In E. Schopler & G. Mesibov (Eds.), *The effects of autism on the family* (pp. 163–186). New York: Plenum Press.

Krug, D. A., Arick, J., & Almond, P. (1978). *Autism Screening Instrument for Educational Planning.* Portland, OR: ASIEP Education.

Krug, D. A., Arick, J., & Almond, P. (1980). Behavior checklist for identifying severely handicapped individuals with high levels of autistic behavior. *Journal of Child Psychology and Psychiatry, 21,* 221–229.

Krug, D. A., Arick, J. R., & Almond, P. J. (1981). The Autism Screening Instrument for Educational Planning: Background and development. In J. E. Gilliam (Ed.), *Autism: Diagnosis, instruction, management, and research* (pp. 64–78). Springfield, IL: Charles C Thomas.

Kurita, H., Miyake, Y., & Katsuno, K. (1989). Reliability and validity of the Childhood Autism Rating Scale—Tokyo Version (CARS-TV). *Journal of Autism and Developmental Disorders, 19,* 389–396.

Lambert, N., Nihira, K., & Leland, H. (1993). *AAMR Adaptive Behavior Scale—School* (2nd ed.). Austin, TX: Pro-Ed.

Lancy, D., & Goldstein, G. (1982). The use of nonverbal Piagetian tasks to assess the cognitive development of autistic children. *Child Development, 53,* 1233–1241.

Landry, S. H., & Loveland, K. A. (1988). Communication behaviors in autism and developmental language delay. *Journal of Child Psychology and Psychiatry, 29,* 621–634.

Le Couteur, A., Rutter, M., Lord, C., Rios, P., Robertson, S., Holdgrafter, M., & McLennan, J. (1989). Autism Diagnostic Interview: A standardized investigator-based instrument. *Journal of Autism and Developmental Disorders, 19,* 363–387.

Leddet, I., Larmande, C., Barthelemy, C., Chalons, F., Sauvage, D., & LeLord, G. (1986). Comparison of clinical diagnoses and Rimland E-2 scores in severely disturbed children. *Journal of Autism and Developmental Disorders, 16,* 215–225.

Leiter, R. G. (1969). *Leiter International Performance Scale.* Los Angeles: Western Psychological Services.

Lewis, M. H., & Baumeister, A. A. (1982). Stereotyped mannerisms in mentally retarded persons: Animal models and theoretical analyses. In N. R. Ellis (Ed.), *International review of research in mental retardation* (Vol. 11, pp. 123–161). New York: Academic Press.

Lincoln, A. J., Courchesne, E., Kilman, B. A., Elmasian, R., & Allen, M. (1988). A study of intellectual abilities in high-functioning people with autism. *Journal of Autism and Developmental Disorders, 18,* 505–524.

Lord, C. (1991). Methods and measures of behavior in the diagnosis of autism and related disorders. *Psychiatric Clinics of North America, 14,* 69–80.

Lord, C., Rutter, M., Goode, S., Heembsbergen, J., Jordan, H., Mawhood, L., & Schopler, E. (1989). Autism Diagnostic Observation Schedule: A standardized observation of communicative and social behavior. *Journal of Autism and Developmental Disorders, 19,* 185–212.

Lord, C., Rutter, M., & Le Couteur, A. (1994). Autism Diagnostic Interview—Revised: A revised version of a diagnostic interview for caregivers of individuals with possible pervasive developmental disorders. *Journal of Autism and Developmental Disorders, 24,* 659–685.

Lord, C., & Schopler, E. (1985). Differences in sex ratios in autism as a function of measured intelligence. *Journal of Autism and Developmental Disorders, 15,* 185–193.

Lord, C., & Schopler, E. (1988). Intellectual and developmental assessment of autistic children from preschool to schoolage: Clinical implications of two follow-up studies. In E. Schopler & G. B. Mesibov (Ed.), *Diagnosis and assessment in autism* (pp. 167–181). New York: Plenum Press.

Lotter, V. (1966). Epidemiology of autistic conditions in young children: I. Prevalence. *Social Psychiatry, 1,* 124–137.

Lotter, V. (1974). Factors related to outcome in autistic children. *Journal of Autism and Childhood Schizophrenia, 4,* 263–277.

Lovaas, O. I. (1977). *The autistic child: Language development through behavior modification.* New York: Irvington.

Lovaas, O. I. (1987). Behavioral treatment and normal educational and intellectual functioning in young autistic children. *Journal of Consulting and Clinical Psychology, 55,* 3–9.

Lovaas, O. I., Ackerman, A., Alexander, D., Firestone, P., Perkins, M., & Young, D. B. (1981). *Teaching developmentally disabled children.* Baltimore: University Park Press.

Lovaas, O. I., Koegel, R. L., & Schreibman, L. (1979). Stimulus overselectivity in autism: A review of research. *Psychological Bulletin, 86,* 1236–1254.

Lovaas, O. I., Koegel, R. L., Simmons, J. Q., & Long, J. S. (1973). Some generalization and follow-up measures on autistic children in behavior therapy. *Journal of Applied Behavior Analysis, 6,* 131–166.

Lovaas, O. I., Newsom, C., & Hickman, C. (1987). Self-stimulatory behavior and perceptual reinforcement. *Journal of Applied Behavior Analysis, 20,* 45–68.

Lovaas, O. I., & Simmons, J. Q. (1969). Manipulation of self-destruction in three retarded children. *Journal of Applied Behavior Analysis, 2,* 143–157.

Lovaas, O. I., Varni, J. W., Koegel, R. L., & Lorsch, N. (1977). Some observations on the non-extinguishability of children's speech. *Child Development, 48,* 1121–1127.

Loveland, K. A., & Kelley, M. L. (1991). Development of adaptive behavior in adolescents and young adults with autism or Down syndrome. *American Journal on Mental Retardation, 96,* 13–20.

Lowe, T. L., Tanaka, K., Seashore, M. R., Young, J. G., & Cohen, D. J. (1980). Detection of phenylketonuria in autistic and psychotic children. *Journal of the American Medical Association, 243,* 126–128.

Loyd, B. H., & Abidin, R. R. (1985). Revision of the Parenting Stress Index. *Journal of Pediatric Psychology, 10,* 169–177.

Maddi, S. R., Kobasa, S. C., & Hoover, M. (1979). An alienation test. *Journal of Humanistic Psychology, 19,* 73–76.

Mahler, M. S. (1952). On child psychosis and schizophrenia: Autistic and symbiotic infantile psychoses. *Psychoanalytic Studies of the Child, 7,* 286–305.

Makita, K. (1974). What is this thing called childhood schizophrenia? *International Journal of Mental Health, 2,* 179–193.

Maltz, A. (1981). Comparison of cognitive deficits among autistic and retarded children on the Arthur Adaptation of the Leiter International Performance Scales. *Journal of Autism and Developmental Disorders, 11,* 413–426.

Marchant, R., Howlin, P., Yule, W., & Rutter, M. (1974). Graded change in the treatment of the behavior of autistic children. *Journal of Child Psychology and Psychiatry, 15,* 221–227.

Marcus, L. M. (1984). Coping with burnout. In E. Schopler & G. B. Mesibov (Eds.), *The effects of autism on the family* (pp. 311–326). New York: Plenum Press.

Matese, M., Matson, J. L., & Sevin, J. (1994). Comparison of psychotic and autistic children using behavioral observation. *Journal of Autism and Developmental Disorders, 24,* 83–94.

Matson, J. L., & Love, S. R. (1991). A comparison of parent-report fear for autistic and normal age-matched children and youth. *Australian and New Zealand Journal of Developmental Disabilities, 16,* 349–358.

McAdoo, W. G., & DeMyer, M. K. (1978). Personality characteristics of parents. In M. Rutter & E. Schopler (Eds.), *Autism: A reappraisal of concepts and treatment* (pp. 251–267). New York: Plenum Press.

McCubbin, H. I., & Patterson, J. M. (1981). *Systematic assessment of family stress, resources, and coping.* St. Paul, MN: Family Stress Project, University of Minnesota.

McHale, S. M., Simeonsson, R. J., & Sloan, J. L. (1984). Children with handicapped brothers and sisters. In E. Schopler & G. B. Mesibov (Eds.), *The effects of autism on the family* (pp. 327–342). New York: Plenum Press.

McHale, S. M., Sloan, J., & Simeonsson, R. J. (1986). Sibling relationships of children with autistic, mentally retarded, and nonhandicapped brothers and sisters. *Journal of Autism and Developmental Disorders, 16,* 399–413.

Mesibov, G. B. (1988). Diagnosis and assessment of autistic adolescents and adults. In E. Schopler & G. B. Mesibov (Eds.), *Diagnosis and assessment in autism* (pp. 227–238). New York: Plenum Press.

Mesibov, G. B., Schopler, E., Schaffer, B., & Landrus, R. (1988). *Adolescent and Adult Psychoeducational Profile.* Austin, TX: Pro-Ed.

Meyers, E., Mink, I., & Nihira, K. (1977). *Home Quality Rating Scale.* Pomona, CA: NPI–Lanterman State Hospital.

Mirenda, P. L., Donnellan, A. M., & Yoder, D. E. (1983). Gaze behavior: A new look at an old problem. *Journal of Autism and Developmental Disorders, 13,* 397–409.

Moos, R. J., & Moos, B. S. (1981). *Family Environment Scale.* Palo Alto, CA: Consulting Psychologists Press.

Newsom, C., Hovanitz, C., & Rincover, A. (1988). Autism. In E. J. Mash & L. G. Terdal (Eds.), *Behavioral assessment of childhood disorders* (2nd ed., pp. 355–401). New York: Guilford Press.

Newsom, C., & Rincover, A. (1981). Autism. In E. J. Mash & L. G. Terdal (Eds.), *Behavioral assessment of childhood disorders* (pp. 397–439). New York: Guilford Press.

Newsom, C., & Simon, K. M. (1977). A simultaneous discrimination procedure for the measurement of vision in nonverbal children. *Journal of Applied Behavior Analysis, 10,* 633–644.

Newton, T., & Sturmey, P. (1991). The Motivation Assessment Scale: Inter-rater reliability and internal consistency in a British sample. *Journal of Intellectual Disabilities Research, 35,* 372–374.

Ohta, M. (1987). Cognitive disorders of infantile autism: A study employing the WISC, spatial relationship conceptualization, and gesture imitations. *Journal of Autism and Developmental Disorders, 17,* 45–62.

O'Neill, R. E., Horner, R. H., Albin, R. W., Storey, K., & Sprague, J. R. (1990). *Functional analysis of problem behavior.* Sycamore, IL: Sycamore.

Ornitz, E. M. (1983). The functional neuroanatomy of infantile autism. *International Journal of Neuroscience, 19,* 85–124.

Ornitz, E. M., Guthrie, D., & Farley, A. J. (1977). The early development of autistic children. *Journal of Autism and Childhood Schizophrenia, 7,* 207–229.

Ornitz, E. M., & Ritvo, E. R. (1968). Perceptual inconstancy in early infantile autism. *Archives of General Psychiatry, 18,* 76–98.

Oswald, D. P., & Volkmar, F. R. (1991). Brief report: Signal detection analysis of items from the Autism Behavior Checklist. *Journal of Autism and Developmental Disorders, 21,* 543–549.

Ozonoff, S., Rogers, S. J., & Pennington, B. F. (1991). Asperger's syndrome: Evidence of an empirical distinction from highly functioning autism. *Journal of Child Psychology and Psychiatry, 32,* 1107–1122.

Paul, R. (1987). Communication. In D. J. Cohen & A. M. Donnellan (Eds.), *Handbook of autism and pervasive developmental disorders* (pp. 61–84). Silver Spring, MD: Winston.

Paul, R., & Cohen, D. J. (1984). Responses to contingent queries in adults with mental retardation and pervasive developmental disorders. *Applied Psycholinguistics, 5,* 349–357.

Perez, J. M., & Fortea Sevilla, M. D. (1993). Psychological assessment of adolescents and adults with autism. *Journal of Autism and Developmental Disorders, 23,* 653–664.

Perry, A., Sarlo-McGarvey, N., & Haddad, C. (1991). Brief report: Cognitive and adaptive functioning in 28 girls with Rett syndrome. *Journal of Autism and Developmental Disorders, 21,* 551–556.

Potter, H. W. (1933). Schizophrenia in children. *American Journal of Psychiatry, 12,* 1253–1270.

Prior, M., & Bence, R. (1975). A note on the validity of the Rimland Diagnostic Checklist. *Journal of Clinical Psychology, 31,* 510–513.

Prior, M. R., Gajzago, C. C., & Knox, D. T. (1976). An epidemiological study of autistic and psychotic children in the four eastern states of Australia. *Australian and New Zealand Journal of Psychiatry, 10,* 173–184.

Prior, M., Perry, D., & Gajzago, C. (1975). Kanner's syndrome or early-onset psychosis: A taxonomic analysis of 142 cases. *Journal of Autism and Childhood Schizophrenia, 5,* 71–80.

Prizant, B., & Duchan, J. (1981). The functions of immediate echolalia in autistic children. *Journal of Speech and Hearing Disorders, 46,* 241–249.

Prizant, B., & Rydell, P. J. (1984). Analysis of functions of delayed echolalia in autistic children. *Journal of Speech and Hearing Research, 27,* 183–192.

Pyles, D. A. M., & Bailey, J. S. (1990). Diagnosing severe behavior problems. In A. C. Repp & N. N. Singh (Eds.), *Perspectives on the use of nonaversive and aversive interventions for persons with developmental disabilities* (pp. 381–401). Sycamore, IL: Sycamore.

Raven, J. C., Court, J. H., & Raven, J. (1977). *The Coloured Progressive Matrices*. London: H. K. Lewis.

Rescorla, L. (1988). Cluster analytic identification of autistic preschoolers. *Journal of Autism and Developmental Disorders, 18*, 475–492.

Reynolds, B. S., Newsom, C. D., & Lovaas, O. I. (1974). Auditory overselectivity in autistic children. *Journal of Abnormal Child Psychology, 2*, 253–263.

Ricks, D. M. (1975). Vocal communication in preverbal normal and autistic children. In N. O'Connor (Ed.), *Language, cognitive deficits and retardation* (pp. 75–83). London: Butterworths.

Ricks, D. M., & Wing. L. (1976). Language, communication, and the use of symbols. In L. Wing (Ed.), *Early childhood autism* (2nd ed., pp. 93–134). Elmsford, NY: Pergamon Press.

Riikonen, R., & Amnell, G. (1981). Psychiatric disorders in children with earlier infantile spasms. *Developmental Medicine and Child Neurology, 23*, 747–760.

Rimland, B. (1964). *Infantile autism*. New York: Appleton-Century-Crofts.

Rimland, B. (1971). The differentiation of childhood psychoses: An analysis of checklists for 2,218 psychotic children. *Journal of Autism and Childhood Schizophrenia, 1*, 161–174.

Rincover, A., & Devany, J. (1982). The application of sensory extinction procedures to self-injury. *Analysis and Intervention in Developmental Disabilities, 2*, 67–81.

Rincover, A., & Koegel, R. L. (1975). Setting generality and stimulus control in autistic children. *Journal of Applied Behavior Analysis, 8*, 235–246.

Rincover, A., Newsom, C. D., Lovaas, O. I., & Koegel, R. L. (1977). Some motivational properties of sensory stimulation in psychotic children. *Journal of Experimental Child Psychology, 24*, 312–323.

Ritvo, E. R., Ritvo, E. C., & Brothers, A. M. (1982). Genetic and immunohematologic factors in autism. *Journal of Autism and Developmental Disorders, 12*, 109–114.

Rodrigue, J. R., Morgan, S. B., & Geffken, G. R. (1991). A comparative evaluation of adaptive behavior in children and adolescents with autism, Down Syndrome, and normal development. *Journal of Autism and Developmental Disorders, 21*, 187–197.

Rogers-Warren, A. K. (1984). Ecobehavioral analysis. *Education and Treatment of Children, 7*, 283–303.

Rumsey, J., & Hamburger, A. D. (1988). Neuropsychological findings in high-functioning men with infantile autism, residual state. *Journal of Clinical and Experimental Neuropsychology, 10*, 201–221.

Rumsey, J., Rapoport, J. L., & Sceery, W. R. (1985). Autistic children as adults: Psychiatric, social, and behavioral outcomes. *Journal of the American Academy of Child Psychiatry, 24*, 465–473.

Ruttenberg, B. A., Kalish, B. I., Wenar, C., & Wolf, E. G. (1977). *BRIAAC: Behavior-Rating Instrument for Autistic and Other Atypical Children*. Chicago: Stoelting.

Rutter, M. (1978). Diagnosis and definition of childhood autism. *Journal of Autism and Childhood Schizophrenia, 8*, 139–161.

Rutter, M. (1985). Infantile autism and other pervasive developmental disorders. In M. Rutter & L. Hersov (Eds.), *Child and adolescent psychiatry* (2nd ed., pp. 545–566). Oxford: Blackwell.

Rutter, M., Bailey, A., Bolton, P., & LeCouteur, A. (1994). Autism and known medical conditions: Myth and substance. *Journal of Child Psychology and Psychiatry, 35*, 311–322.

Rutter, M., & Bartak, L. (1971). Causes of infantile autism: Some considerations from recent research. *Journal of Autism and Childhood Schizophrenia, 1*, 20–32.

Rutter, M., & Garmezy, N. (1983). Developmental psychopathology. In E. M. Hetherington (Vol. Ed.), *Handbook of child psychology* (4th ed.): *Vol. 4. Socialization, personality, and social development* (pp. 775–912). New York: Wiley.

Rutter, M., Greenfeld, D., & Lockyer, L. (1967). A five to fifteen year follow-up study of infantile psychosis. *British Journal of Psychiatry, 113*, 1183–1199.

Rutter, M., Lebovici, S., Eisenberg, L., Sneznevskij, A. V., Sadoun, R., Brooke, E., & Lin, T. Y. (1969). A tri-axial classification of mental disorders in childhood. *Journal of Child Psychology and Psychiatry, 10*, 41–61.

Rutter, M., & Schopler, E. (1988). Autism and pervasive developmental disorders: Concepts and diagnostic issues. In E. Schopler & G. B. Mesibov (Eds.), *Diagnosis and assessment in autism* (pp. 15–36). New York: Plenum Press.

Sailor, W., & Guess, D. (1983). *Severely handicapped students: An instructional design*. Boston: Houghton Mifflin.

Schatz, J., & Hamdan-Allen, G. (1995). Effects of age and IQ on adaptive behavior domains for children with autism. *Journal of Autism and Developmental Disorders, 25*, 51–60.

Schopler, E., & Mesibov, G. B. (1984). Professional attitudes toward parents: A forty-year progress report. In E. Schopler & G. B. Mesibov (Eds.), *The effects of autism on the family* (pp. 3–17). New York: Plenum Press.

Schopler, E., & Mesibov, G. B. (Eds.). (1988). *Diagnosis and assessment in autism*. New York: Plenum Press.

Schopler, E., & Reichler, R. J. (1979). *Individualized assessment and treatment for autistic and developmentally delayed children: Vol. 1: Psychoeducational Profile*. Baltimore: University Park Press.

Schopler, E., Reichler, R. J., DeVellis, R. F., & Daly, K. (1980). Toward objective classification of childhood autism: Childhood Autism Rating

Scale (CARS). *Journal of Autism and Developmental Disorders, 10,* 91–103.

Schopler, E., Reichler, R. J., & Renner, B. R. (1986). *The Childhood Autism Rating Scale.* Los Angeles: Western Psychological Services.

Schreibman, L., Kaneko, W. M., & Koegel, R. L. (1991). Positive affect of parents of autistic children: A comparison across two teaching techniques. *Behavior Therapy, 22,* 479–490.

Schreibman, L., Koegel, R. L. , Mills, D. L., & Burke, J. C. (1984). Training parent–child interactions. In E. Schopler & G. Mesibov (Eds.), *The effects of autism on the family* (pp. 187–205). New York: Plenum Press.

Schreibman, L., Kohlenberg, B. S., & Britten, K. R. (1986). Differential responding to content and intonation components of a complex auditory stimulus by nonverbal and echolalic autistic children. *Analysis and Intervention in Developmental Disabilities, 6,* 109–125.

Schreibman, L., & Lovaas, O. I. (1973). Overselective response to social stimuli by autistic children. *Journal of Abnormal Child Psychology, 1,* 152–168.

Sevin, J. A., Matson, J. L., Coe, D. A., Fee, V. E., & Sevin, B. A. (1991). A comparison and evaluation of three commonly used autism scales. *Journal of Autism and Developmental Disorders, 21,* 417–432.

Shah, A., & Holmes, N. (1985). The use of the Leiter International Performance Scale with autistic children. *Journal of Autism and Developmental Disorders, 15,* 195–203.

Shea, V., & Mesibov, G. B. (1985). The relationship of learning disabilities and higher-level autism. *Journal of Autism and Developmental Disorders, 15,* 425–435.

Siegel, B., Anders, T. F., Ciaranello, R. D., Bienenstock, B., & Kraemer, H. C. (1986). Empirically derived subclassification of the autistic syndrome. *Journal of Autism and Developmental Disorders, 16,* 275–293.

Sigman, M., & Ungerer, J. A. (1981). Sensorimotor skills and language comprehension in autistic children. *Journal of Abnormal Child Psychology, 9,* 149–165.

Sigman, M., & Ungerer, J. A. (1984). Attachment behaviors in autistic children. *Journal of Autism and Developmental Disorders, 14,* 231–244.

Singh, N. N., Donatelli, L. S., Best, A., Williams, E. E., Barrera, F. J., Lenz, M. W., Landrum, T. J., Ellis, C. R., & Moe, T. L. (1993). Factor structure of the Motivation Assessment Scale. *Journal of Intellectual Disabilities Research, 37,* 65–73.

Skinner, B. F. (1938). *The behavior of organisms.* New York: Appleton-Century.

Sloan, J. L., & Marcus, L. (1981). Some findings on the use of the Adaptive Behavior Scale with autistic children. *Journal of Autism and Developmental Disorders, 11,* 191–199.

Smith, B., Chung, M. C., & Vostanis, P. (1994). The path to care in autism: Is it better now? *Journal of Autism and Developmental Disorders, 24,* 551–563.

Smith, I. M., & Bryson, S. E. (1994). Imitation and action in autism: A critical review. *Psychological Bulletin, 116,* 259–273.

Snell, M. E., & Browder, D. M. (1986). Community-referenced instruction: Research and issues. *Journal of the Association for Persons with Severe Handicaps, 11,* 1–11.

Sparrow, S. S., Balla, D. A., & Cicchetti, D. V. (1984). *Vineland Adaptive Behavior Scales.* Circle Pines, MN: American Guidance Service.

Spitzer, R. L. (1980). Introduction. In American Psychiatric Association, *Diagnostic and statistical manual of mental disorders* (3rd ed., pp. 1–12). Washington, DC: American Psychiatric Association.

Stone, W. L., & Hogan, K. L. (1993). A structured parent interview for identifying young children with autism. *Journal of Autism and Developmental Disorders, 23,* 639–652.

Student, M., & Sohmer, H. (1978). Evidence from auditory nerve and brainstem evoked responses for an organic brain lesion in children with autistic traits. *Journal of Autism and Childhood Schizophrenia, 8,* 13–20.

Sturmey, P. (1994). Assessing the functions of aberrant behaviors: A review of psychometric instruments. *Journal of Autism and Developmental Disorders, 24,* 293–304.

Szatmari, P., Archer, L., Fisman, S., & Streiner, D. L. (1994). Parent and teacher agreement in the assessment of pervasive developmental disorders. *Journal of Autism and Developmental Disorders, 24,* 703–717.

Tantam, D. (1988). Lifelong eccentricity and social isolation: II. Asperger's syndrome or Schizoid Personality Disorder? *British Journal of Psychiatry, 153,* 783–791.

Teal, M. B., & Wiebe, M. J. (1986). A validity analysis of selected instruments used to assess autism. *Journal of Autism and Developmental Disorders, 16,* 485–494.

Thelen, E. (1979). Rhythmical stereotypies in normal human infants. *Animal Behaviour, 27,* 699–715.

Thorndike, R. L., Hagan, E. P., & Sattler, J. M. (1986). *Stanford–Binet Intelligence Scale* (4th ed.). Chicago: Riverside.

Touchette, P. E., MacDonald, R. F., & Langer, S. N. (1985). A scatter plot for identifying stimulus control of problem behavior. *Journal of Applied Behavior Analysis, 18,* 343–351.

Tsai, L. Y., Tsai, M. C., & August, G. J. (1985). Implications of EEG diagnoses in the subclassification of infantile autism. *Journal of Autism and Developmental Disorders, 15,* 339–344.

Valente, M. (1971). Autism: Symptomatic and idiopathic—and mental retardation. *Pediatrics, 48,* 495–496.

Venter, A., Lord, C., & Schopler, E. (1992). A follow-up study of high-functioning autistic children. *Journal of Child Psychology and Psychiatry, 33*, 489–507.

Volkmar, F. R. (1987). Diagnostic issues in the pervasive developmental disorders. *Journal of Child Psychology and Psychiatry, 28*, 365–369.

Volkmar, F. R., Bregman, J., Cohen, D. J., & Cichetti, D. V. (1988). DSM-III and DSM-III-R diagnosis of autism. *American Journal of Psychiatry, 145*, 1404–1408.

Volkmar, F.R., Cicchetti, D. V., Dykens, E., Sparrow, S. S., Leckman, J. F., & Cohen, D. J. (1988). An evaluation of the Autism Behavior Checklist. *Journal of Autism and Developmental Disorders, 18*, 81–97.

Volkmar, F. R., & Cohen, D. J. (1985). A first person account of the experience of infantile autism by Tony W. *Journal of Autism and Developmental Disorders, 15*, 47–54.

Volkmar, F. R., Cohen, D. J., Bregman, J. D., Hooks, M. Y., & Stevenson, J. M. (1989). An examination of social typologies in autism. *Journal of the American Academy of Child and Adolescent Psychiatry, 28*, 82–86.

Volkmar, F. R., Klin, A., Siegel, B., Szatmari, P., Lord, C., Campbell, M., Freeman, B. J., Cicchetti, D. V., Rutter, M., Kline, W., Buitelaar, J., Hattab, Y., Fombonne, E., Fuentes, J., Werry, J., Stone, W., Kerbeshian, J., Hoshino, Y., Bregman, J., Loveland, K., Szymanski, L., & Towbin, K. (1994). Field trial for Autistic Disorder in DSM-IV. *American Journal of Psychiatry, 151*, 1361–1367.

Volkmar, F. R., Sparrow, S. A., Goudreau, D., Cicchetti, D. V., Paul, R., & Cohen, D. J. (1987). Social deficits in autism: An operational approach using the Vineland Adaptive Behavior Scales. *Journal of the American Academy of Child Psychiatry, 26*, 156–161.

Wadden, N. P. K., Bryson, S. E., & Rodger, R. S. (1991). A closer look at the Autism Behavior Checklist: Discriminant validity and factor structure. *Journal of Autism and Developmental Disorders, 21*, 529–541.

Wechsler, D. (1974). *Wechsler Intelligence Scale for Children—Revised.* New York: Psychological Corporation.

Wechsler, D. (1981). *Wechsler Adult Intelligence Scale—Revised.* New York: Psychological Corporation.

Wechsler, D. (1991). *Wechsler Intelligence Scale for Children* (3rd ed.). San Antonio, TX: Psychological Corporation.

Wetherby, A. M., & Gaines, B. (1982). Cognition and language development in autism. *Journal of Speech and Hearing Disorders, 47*, 63–70.

Wing, L. (1976). Diagnosis, clinical description, and prognosis. In L. Wing (Ed.), *Early childhood autism* (2nd ed., pp. 15–64). Elmsford, NY: Pergamon Press.

Wing, L. (1981a). Language, social, and cognitive impairments in autism and severe mental retardation. *Journal of Autism and Developmental Disorders, 11*, 31–44.

Wing, L. (1981b). Asperger's syndrome: A clinical account. *Psychological Medicine, 11*, 115–129.

Wing, L. (1991). The relationship between Asperger's syndrome and Kanner's autism. In U. Frith (Ed.), *Autism and Asperger syndrome* (pp. 93–121). New York: Cambridge University Press.

Wing, L., & Attwood, A. (1987). Syndromes of autism and atypical development. In D. J. Cohen & A. M. Donnellan (Eds.), *Handbook of autism and pervasive developmental disorders* (pp. 3–19). New York: Wiley.

Wing, L., & Gould, J. (1979). Severe impairments of social interaction and associated abnormalities in children: Epidemiology and classification. *Journal of Autism and Developmental Disorders, 9*, 11–29.

Wing, L., Gould, J., Yeates, S. R., & Brierley, L. M. (1977). Symbolic play in severely mentally retarded and in autistic children. *Journal of Child Psychology and Psychiatry, 18*, 167–178.

Wing, L., Yeates, S. R., Brierley, L. M., & Gould, J. (1976). The prevalence of early childhood autism: Comparison of administrative and epidemiological studies. *Psychological Medicine, 6*, 89–100.

Wolf, L. C., Noh, S., Fisman, S. N., & Speechley, M. (1989). Brief report: Psychological effects of parenting stress on parents of autistic children. *Journal of Autism and Developmental Disorders, 19*, 157–166.

World almanac and book of facts. (1994). Mahwah, NJ: Funk & Wagnalls.

World Health Organization. (1992). *International classification of diseases* (10th rev.). Geneva: Author.

Yirmiya, N., Sigman, M., & Freeman, B. J. (1994). Comparison between diagnostic instruments for identifying high-functioning children with autism. *Journal of Autism and Developmental Disorders, 24*, 281–291.

Zahner, G. E. P., & Pauls, D. L. (1987). Epidemiological surveys of infantile autism. In D. J. Cohen & A. M. Donnellan (Eds.), *Handbook of autism and pervasive developmental disorders* (pp. 199–207). Silver Spring, MD: Winston.

Zarcone, J. R., Rodgers, T. A., Iwata, B. A., Rourke, D. A., & Dorsey, M. F. (1991). Reliability analysis of the Motivation Assessment Scale. *Research in Developmental Disabilities, 12*, 349–360.

Zentall, S. S., & Zentall, T. R. (1983). Optimal stimulation: A model of disordered activity and performance in normal and deviant children. *Psychological Bulletin, 94*, 446–471.

Zigler, E. (1969). Developmental versus difference theories of mental retardation and the problem of motivation. *American Journal of Mental Deficiency, 73*, 536–549.

Chapter Nine

CHILDREN WITH BRAIN INJURY

Jack M. Fletcher
H. Gerry Taylor

When an earlier version of this chapter (Fletcher, 1988) was published in the second edition of *Behavioral Assessment of Childhood Disorders* (Mash & Terdal, 1988), it opened with a standard, perfunctory paragraph describing how brain injury in children had received little scrutiny from psychologists and how neuropsychological approaches to assessment were in the beginning phases of development. Given developments since that time, such statements are no longer necessary. Research on children with brain injury is flourishing, with enormous implications for the assessment of such children. To illustrate, many disorders have been the subject of recent books and/or literature reviews, including a variety of diffuse, multifocal injuries: traumatic brain injury (Broman & Michel, 1995); spina bifida and hydrocephalus (Dennis, 1995; Fletcher, Levin, & Butler, 1995; Wills, 1993); hypoxic–ischemic encephalopathy (Shaywitz & Fletcher, 1993); meningitis (Taylor, Schatschneider, & Rich, 1991) and other viral and infectious diseases (Palumbo, Davidson, Peloquin, & Gigliotti, 1995); epilepsy (Klein, 1991); and cerebral palsy (Fletcher, Levin, & Butler, 1995; Nelson, Swaiman, & Russman, 1993). In addition, there are new studies of children with well-documented focal lesions (Aram, 1990). Disorders that influence brain development because of genetic and/or metabolic factors have also been reviewed, including phenylketonuria (Pennington, 1991); Williams syndrome, Turner syndrome, and neurofibromatosis (Broman & Grafman, 1994); and a variety of central nervous system (CNS) disorders in children (Rourke, 1995; Spreen, Risser, & Edgell, 1995). Several authoritative chapters and texts on the neuropsychological assessment of children have also appeared (Baron, Fennell, & Voeller,

1995; Bernstein & Waber, 1990; Fletcher, Taylor, Levin, & Satz, 1995; Pennington, 1991; Reitan & Wolfson, 1992; Rourke, Fisk, & Strang, 1986; Taylor & Fletcher, 1990).

The advances in research clearly drive the advances in the clinical assessment of children with brain injury. Two major factors in the research advances involve (1) the routine use of neuroimaging—particularly magnetic resonance imaging (MRI)—with children who have sustained brain injury; and (2) the major developments in the cognitive sciences that have enhanced understanding of language, memory, and other cognitive processes (Pennington, 1991). The joint application of these two advances through research has led to the emergence of a cognitive neuroscience of children and a greater understanding of how cognitive processes are mediated by the brain.

Additional factors underlying research advances for children with brain injury have included the clear adoption of developmental approaches and the attempt to address research questions driven by an interest in children and their disabilities—not by models of adult brain injury (Dennis, 1987, 1988; Fletcher & Taylor, 1984). For example, it is increasingly rare to find in the literature concerns about differences in the expression and outcome of aphasia in children and adults; this change reflects the greater recognition that the causes of language disturbance are different in children and adults, and that the manifestations reflect the maturity of the language system and the brain (Dennis, 1987, 1988). Approaches to assessment are clearly more child-oriented and place greater emphasis on the context in which the child develops.

For clinical assessment, most approaches continue to rely on psychometric tests. However, the emphasis on cognitive processes has led to continued refinement of tests and a much greater ability to fractionate and measure children's discrete abilities. At the same time, approaches to assessment other than those relying strictly on psychometric tests are becoming more fully developed.

It is apparent that many cognitive processes can be conceptualized and measured by means of behavioral paradigms, particularly ones utilizing stimulus control procedures. For example, attention processes (i.e., attending) can be articulated as examples of stimulus control that are developed and maintained by antecedents and consequences for attending behaviors. These behaviors can be changed by manipulating the antecedents and consequences through reinforcement and punishment (Barkley, 1996; McIlvane, Dube, & Callahan, 1996). Similarly behavioral conceptions of the constructs subsumed under "executive functions" have been advanced (Hayes, Gifford, & Ruckstuhl, 1996). Such formulations are directly related to intervention approaches that might be used to address a problem with attention in a child with brain injury.

Another recent development is the use of observational paradigms that directly sample the behaviors of interest. These approaches are most apparent in the area of language, where studies of discourse can be conducted based on the application of models of language and cognition to actual language samples and narratives of brain-injured children (Chapman, 1995; Dennis, Jacennik, & Barnes, 1994). Observational approaches have also been used to evaluate goal-directed adaptive behavior and motivation in children with spina bifida or with HIV infection and AIDS (Landry, Jordan, & Fletcher, 1994; Moss et al., 1994). Such approaches could be used to evaluate social competence in children with brain injury. Although observational paradigms are common in studies of infants and of difficult-to-assess populations (e.g., children with autism), it is becoming apparent that such approaches may have broader applications to neuropsychological assessment of children with brain injury, particularly for behaviors that involve novelty or interactions with other people.

The purpose of this chapter is to describe neuropsychological approaches to children with brain injury. Consequently, its major focus is on the use of psychometric tests for assessment. Approaches using behavioral and observational methodologies are addressed, but primarily to illustrate how such approaches can be used to expand contemporary neuropsychological approaches. These approaches are in the early stages of application, and more work remains before they can be fully evaluated and appreciated as assessment tools for children with brain injury. Prior to discussing assessment procedures, we provide an overview of the nature of brain disorders in children, along with an indication of some of the advances in the knowledge base that are critical to assessment practices.

NATURE OF ACQUIRED BRAIN DISORDERS AND INJURY IN CHILDREN

There are many types of brain disorders and injury in children, including trauma, infection, congenital malformations, genetic/metabolic/degenerative disorders, tumors, vascular disorders, and paroxysmal disorders (epilepsy). The purpose of this section is not to review these disorders in detail (see Menkes, 1995; Spreen et al., 1995), but to describe some of them in order to illustrate the nature and heterogeneity of brain injury in children. Table 9.1 provides an overview of the disorders to be reviewed here. It is important to rec-

TABLE 9.1. Major Forms and Manifestations of Acquired Brain Disorders in Children

1. Traumatic brain injury
   a. Head injury
   b. Perinatal trauma

2. Congenital malformations
   a. Neural tube defects
      1. Spina bifida
      2. Midline defects
   b. Other malformations
      1. Dandy–Walker syndrome
      2. Aqueductal stenosis
   c. Hydrocephalus

3. Genetic/metabolic/degenerative disorders
   a. Williams syndrome
   b. Turner syndrome

4. Tumors
   a. Neoplasms
   b. Neurofibromatosis

5. Infectious disorders
   a. Prenatal
   b. Postnatal

6. Cerebrovascular disease

7. Epilepsy

ognize that the cause of brain injury (etiology) and the effects on the brain (pathophysiology) are not directly linked, but are related to a variety of other factors, such as the severity of the injury and how it is treated. This is illustrated by the reviews of traumatic brain injury and congenital malformations, which are more detailed than the reviews of other disorders. The greater emphasis on these disorders is also consistent with their higher prevalence as causes of brain injury in children. Epidemiological data are generally organized by etiology, whereas this review is organized from a more pathophysiological viewpoint. Consequently, prevalence figures are not consistently provided (see Menkes, 1995, and Spreen et al., 1995, for available prevalence data).

Traumatic Brain Injury

The most common cause of brain injury in children is trauma. This trauma can occur because of the exertion of external physical force on the head. It can also occur because the brain is deprived of a critically needed substance, such as oxygen.

Head Injury

The term "traumatic brain injury" (hereafter abbreviated as TBI) is usually reserved for cerebral trauma that occurs in the postnatal period. This type of injury represents the leading cause of death in children and a major cause of disability and handicap. Prevalence studies show that approximately 10 per 100,000 children die of TBI yearly, with an overall rate of about 180 cases per 100,000 children (Kraus, 1995). Most cases are mild in severity, and the bulk (over 90%) are caused by closed head injuries, in which the skull is not penetrated. The most common causes of closed head injuries are accidents and child abuse. Penetrating injuries result from gunshot wounds and accidents involving sharp objects (Ewing-Cobbs, DuHaime, & Fletcher, 1995). Males are approximately twice as likely to be victims of TBI (Kraus, 1995).

Mechanisms of Injury

The primary mechanisms of injury involve the effects on the brain of acceleration–deceleration forces and the compressive effects of the blow. When the head comes in contact with physical forces, the brain shifts inside the skull. This leads to stretching of axonal fibers and tearing of the brain tissue on bony parts of the skull, particularly

in the frontal, temporal, and occipital poles. Injury also occurs because of changes in the brain at the site of impact ("coup injury") and compression factors at sites away from the site of injury ("contrecoup injury"). There are secondary sources of injury that involve the response of the brain to primary injury, including edema, hypoxic injury, and increased intracranial pressure (Bruce, 1995).

Pathophysiology

Given these factors, it is not surprising that the pathological effects on the brain vary considerably across individual children. Recent MRI studies continue to show that diffuse axonal injury is the most common type of lesion, represented by multiple focal areas of abnormal signal in the white matter (Levin et al., 1992). However, cortical contusions (hemorrhages) are also common, with MRI studies currently reporting a higher frequency of contusional injuries than previously reported in studies based on cerebral computed tomography. For example, Levin et al. (1992) showed that 75% of TBI children had evidence of contusional injury, particularly in the frontal lobes (40% of cases). The brain can also be diffusely injured because of swelling, increased intracranial pressure, and hypoxia (Bruce, 1995).

Assessing Injury Severity

The assessment of severity is still critically important and directly related to prognosis. The most common measure of severity is the Glasgow Coma Scale (GCS; Teasdale & Jennett, 1974). On this scale, which is administered at the time of resuscitation, severe head injury is typically indicated by GCS scores of ≤ 8; moderate injury is represented by GCS scores of 9–12; and mild injury is represented by GCS scores in the 13–15 range.

The GCS has three scales representing the best motor, verbal, and eye responses. It can be used with individuals from the ages of 3 years through adulthood, but must be modified for use in children under 3 years of age (Ewing-Cobbs, DuHaime, &Fletcher, 1995). (See Fletcher, 1988, for a more thorough description of the GCS.)

In children, a more useful index is the duration of unconsciousness. This can be operationalized as the amount of time required for a child to respond to commands. It is practically measured from the Motor scale of the GCS and can be represented as the number of days the Motor scale score is <6. Severe injury is represented by an inability to follow commands within 24 hours. The duration of unconsciousness is particularly useful for a case in which GCS scores are initially in the severe range, but the child emerges from unconsciousness very quickly, indicating a less severe injury and better prognosis.

The most recent development in the assessment of injury severity involves the measurement of posttraumatic amnesia (PTA—that is, the period during which the child is unable to store and recall ongoing events; Russell & Smith, 1961). Length of PTA can be assessed with the Children's Orientation and Amnesia Test (COAT; Ewing-Cobbs, Levin, Fletcher, Miner, & Eisenberg, 1990). The COAT consists of 16 items assessing three domains: (1) General orientation (orientation to person and place, recall of biographical information; (2) Temporal Orientation (administered to children 8 years and older); and (3) Memory (immediate, short-term, and remote, which are summed to obtain a total score). Using data collected on normal children ranging in age from 3 to 15 years, Ewing-Cobbs et al. (1990) defined PTA as the interval during which a child's total score falls two or more standard deviations below the mean for his or her age. This study and that of Jaffe et al. (1992) showed that duration of PTA, as measured by the COAT, was more predictive of later memory functioning at 6 and 12 months than was the GCS score.

Assessment and Outcome Issues

Survivors who sustain *severe* TBI, particularly as designated by an inability to follow commands within 24 hours of injury, are at high risk for a range of sequelae; these include problems with cognitive and motor skills, as well as academic and behavioral difficulties (Levin, Ewing-Cobb, & Eisenberg, 1995). The nature of these sequelae reflects the pathophysiological changes of the brain in response to the injury and its treatment, the child's environment before and after the injury, and preexisting conditions. Assessing injury severity does not provide a complete picture of the injury; also needed are neuroimaging studies, a review of the circumstances surrounding the injury, and a knowledge of the child's subsequent recovery during the subacute phase of the injury (Bruce, 1995; Taylor, Drotar, et al., 1995). In less severe cases, the role of contusional injury becomes more critical, since the location of the contusions may have a direct effect on outcomes.

In a case where a child is actually hospitalized, assessment by a neuropsychologist is a part of routine care in major trauma centers. Assessment begins with the monitoring of consciousness until resolution of PTA. At that point, a more formal assessment is completed to help plan for rehabilitation and return to school and home. The child is usually followed semiannually for the first year, and then yearly to establish sequelae, evaluate recovery, and revise treatment plans.

The sequelae of *mild* TBI caused by closed head injury have been more controversial, but they illustrate the importance of assessing preinjury functioning of the child and family. In children under 2 years of age, it is clear that even relatively mild injuries are associated with poor outcomes (Ewing-Cobbs, DuHaime, & Fletcher, 1995). However, in older children, serious sequelae less frequently occur. If mild injury is prospectively defined as GCS scores of 13–15, normal neuroimaging studies, normal neurological exam, and no evidence of subsequent deterioration, it is clear that sequelae 3–6 months postinjury are infrequent (Asarnow et al., 1995; Fay et al., 1993). When sequelae are apparent in such cases, they can usually be associated with preexisting conditions and postinjury factors, such as the psychological stress of the injury and litigation.

Examining preexisting conditions is critical. For example, Bijur, Haslum, and Golding (1990) found in a prospective epidemiological survey that 49% of children who had sustained a mild TBI at 10 years of age were described as hyperactive when examined prior to injury at 5 years of age. Much of the confusion over outcomes reflects the failure to screen and evaluate antecedent neurobehavioral disorders. In reporting the results of a recent large-scale study of mild TBI, Asarnow et al. (1995) concluded that children admitted to emergency rooms with mild TBI "do not show clinically significant neuropsychological impairments at either 1, 6, or 12 months postinjury. . . . Fundamentally different conclusions would have been reached had we not controlled for preinjury level of functioning" (pp. 141–142).

Perinatal Trauma

At the time of birth, the brain can be subjected to a variety of stresses. These can include mechanical trauma, perinatal asphyxia, infarcts, and intracranial hemorrhage. Children with these injuries are commonly evaluated by infant specialists. It is not unusual for a neuropsychologist to evaluate an older child with a history of perinatal trauma. However, such evaluations rarely occur because of perinatal trauma, but in the context of a disorder associated with birth defects, such as cerebral palsy and hydrocephalus. As with postnatal TBI, the causes are variable and the pathophysiological effects on the brain vary across cases.

Causes of Injury

"Mechanical trauma" usually refers to an injury to the head sustained during the birth process. The infant's head is relatively soft and can be shaped or molded during birth. At times, mechanical trauma is induced by obstetrical techniques used to facilitate the delivery. Lesions involving the CNS are actually quite rare in relation to labor and delivery.

More common is brain injury caused by oxygen deprivation. Damage to the brain occurs not only because of hypoxia, but also because of ischemia and excessive levels of carbon dioxide (Shaywitz & Fletcher, 1993). These pathophysiological events can lead to brain swelling and alterations of blood flow (Volpe, 1989). A variety of pathological lesions can result, including encephalomalacia and porencephalic cysts, periventricular leukomalacia, and infarcts. Such lesions are often observed in children subsequently identified as having cerebral palsy (Nelson et al., 1993). There has been a tendency to view such a lesion as a focal, unilateral event when the lesion is apparent in only one hemisphere. However, though lateralizing signs may be apparent (e.g., hemiplegia), it is important to understand that such a lesion emerges as a product of a diffuse insult to the brain. Because of the differences in pathophysiology, these lesions are by no means comparable to the unilateral, focal lesions produced by vascular disorders in adults who are victims of strokes. Strokes that involve the middle cerebral artery can occur during the prenatal period, but these are rare.

Although perinatal asphyxia occurs in about 5–6 of every 1,000 full-term births, it is a common factor in the survival of premature, low-birthweight infants. At one time, intraventricular hemorrhage (IVH) was also common during the first 30 hours after birth in premature children with birthweights below 1,500 grams. However, the incidence of IVH is clearly declining (Volpe, 1989). The severity of IVH varies, but it can cause ventricular dilation and progressive hydrocephalus. When the progression cannot be checked, it is sometimes necessary to employ neurosurgical interventions (usually a shunt to direct the flow of cerebrospinal fluid [CSF]).

Assessment and Outcome Issues

It is common to provide "developmental" assessments of high-risk infants; these are usually conducted by developmental psychologists or neuropsychologists trained to work with infants and young children (Wilson, 1986). The evaluations address the degree to which these infants are at risk for problems in their development, and are designed to help develop treatment plans.

Outcomes after perinatal trauma are variable. Many children show normal development and never require evaluation. Other children are referred for assessment of learning and behavioral problems. Although epidemiological studies show that such problems seem more common in children with a history of perinatal trauma (Breslau et al., 1996), it is not possible to establish the degree to which such trauma is related to later developmental disorders in an individual case, particularly when neuroimaging studies are normal. However, children who sustain encephalomalacia, periventricular leukomalacia, infarcts, and progressive hydrocephalus often present at older ages with significant developmental problems. Even here, the relationship of outcome and perinatal trauma can be difficult to assess because of social and cultural factors as well as other factors associated with the birth, particularly in premature infants. For example, premature, low-birthweight infants are more likely to come from lower socioeconomic classes with poorer prenatal care. These children can also develop problems with other organ systems (e.g., the eyes) or chronic lung diseases (e.g., bronchopulmonary dysplasia), either of which can clearly impair development. In children where these processes do not develop, the prognosis is much better. It is more difficult to establish relationships of outcome and these early events, but evidence is mounting for a relationship of degree of low birthweight and problems with learning and behavior (Breslau et al., 1996; Hack et al., 1994; Shaywitz & Fletcher, 1993; Taylor, Hack, Klein, & Schatschneider, 1995). Outcomes are quite variable, and the assessment is usually oriented toward identification of strengths and weaknesses in a variety of basic skill areas relative to psychosocial and environmental factors.

Congenital Malformations

The most common forms of congenital malformation of the CNS occur in association with neural tube defects. These defects, which occur during the first month of gestation, lead to brain and spine malformations such as anencephaly, spina bifida, a variety of midline defects (holoprosencephaly, septo-optic dysplasia), Dandy–Walker syndrome, and possibly aqueductal stenosis.

Neural Tube Defects

Approximately 2–6 per 1,000 births are associated with a neural tube defect, usually during the first month of gestation (Mathers & Field, 1983). Anencephaly, which is basically the absence of a brain, is always fatal, but is also the most common congenital malformation of the brain. Most common in survivors is the group of spinal dysraphisms known collectively as "spina bifida." In children with spina bifida meningomyelocele, characterized by an open sac in which the spinal cord protrudes, the Arnold–Chiari II brain malformation is common (Barkovich, 1995). This malformation reflects changes in the hindbrain and cerebellum that usually block the flow of CSF, leading to hydrocephalus that usually requires shunting. Children with spina bifida meningomyelocele often have problems with ambulation and bladder control. Other spinal dysraphisms are less frequent (e.g., meningocele, in which the spinal cord bulges but is not herniated) and typically do not occur in association with other brain malformations or result in hydrocephalus. Children with spina bifida meningomyelocele also have other brain malformations, particularly partial agenesis of the corpus callosum. Many studies of children with spina bifida have not separated cases according to type of spinal lesion, presence of hydrocephalus, or presence of other CNS anomalies (Brookshire et al., 1995; Fletcher, Brookshire, Bohan, Brandt, & Davidson, 1995; Wills, 1993). In general, children with meningomyelocele account for many of the problems with development commonly ascribed to children with spina bifida.

Midline defects include holoprosencephaly, or failure to develop a forebrain. In contrast to anencephaly, which involves the spine and the caudal end of the neural tube, holoprosencephaly and other midline defects involve the brain and the rostral end of the neural tube, with no spinal involvement (Menkes, 1995). Holoprosencephaly is rare and occurs at different levels of severity, but is usually associated with generalized mental deficiency. A common variant is septo-optic dysplasia, characterized by agenesis of the septum pellucidum and problems with the optic system that result in vision defects. Mental deficiency and neuroendocrinological disorders are common in these children.

The Dandy–Walker syndrome involves agenesis of the cerebellar vermis with extension of the fourth ventricle and an enlarged posterior fossa. Shunted hydrocephalus is common. Outcomes vary, but mental deficiency is common, and few children with Dandy–Walker syndrome have normal learning skills (Dennis, 1996).

Aqueductal stenosis is a congenital narrowing of the aqueduct of Sylvius that commonly leads to hydrocephalus. Although the exact cause is not understood, it has been hypothesized that aqueductal stenosis is a form of neural tube defect. Children with aqueductal stenosis are usually not identified unless they develop symptoms, usually in association with hydrocephalus (Menkes, 1995).

Common to all these congenital brain malformations is hydrocephalus, which frequently requires shunting (see below). Cerebellar abnormalities are also common, along with partial agenesis of the corpus callosum. The cerebellum and corpus callosum abnormalities are part of the broader spectrum of deficits in neural immigrations associated with the antenatal development of children with neural tube defects (Barkovich, 1995).

Hydrocephalus

A major variable influencing the outcome of children who survive congenital CNS malformations is hydrocephalus, a condition in which the ventricular system expands because the flow of cerebrospinal fluid is obstructed. This leads to increased intracranial pressure and ventricular dilation. Raimondi (1994) has recently proposed that the effects of increased intracranial pressure and changes in flow and accumulation of CSF represent different stages in the development of hydrocephalus. In this view, hydrocephalus is classified as (1) intraparenchymal, representing increases in the intracranial volume of CSF that produces accumulation inside the parenchyma of the brain; or (2) extraparenchymal, reflecting CSF accumulation in the subarachnoid spaces, cisterns, or ventricles.

Hydrocephalus is not a single disease entity or syndrome. Rather, hydrocephalus is the common endpoint of a series of pathological events that involve a variety of etiological factors—including traumatic brain injury, congenital malformations, tumors, infectious diseases, and other disorders. It is always secondary to some other pathological event.

When significant hydrocephalus occurs, there are major consequences for brain development (Del Bigio, 1993). Hydrocephalus can stretch and destroy the corpus callosum, leading to hypoplasia, in which all corpus callosum structures are thinned but present. Other white matter tracts can be stretched, including projection fibers near the midline that connect the hemispheres to the diencephalon and other anterior brain regions. Vision problems can result from optic tract damage. Longer-term consequences of hydrocephalus included disrupted myelination. The thickness of the cortical mantle is reduced, as is overall brain mass. Children who develop hydrocephalus often have associated motor problems, exhibit ocular–motor disturbances such as strabismus, and may develop seizures. Parents of a child with hydrocephalus must monitor the child's condition, with recurrent concerns about possible shunt dysfunction and the need for additional surgeries.

Outcome and Assessment Issues

Children with congenital malformations vary considerably according to etiology and the nature, extent, and treatment of any resultant hydrocephalus. Congenital malformations, particularly those involving the cerebellum or midline structures (especially the corpus callosum), are clearly correlated with poorer outcomes in motor and perceptual skills (Fletcher, Brookshire, Bohan, et al., 1995). Hydrocephalus and its treatment also directly influence outcomes in nonverbal skill domains (Wills, 1993). In general, children who develop hydrocephalus commonly experience problems with a variety of nonverbal skills. Motor, perceptual–motor, and visual–spatial skills are commonly impaired. Comparisons of psychometric intelligence test scores tend to show significantly lower scores on performance-based measures than on verbal measures (Dennis, 1995; Fletcher, Brookshire, Bohan, et al., 1995; Wills, 1993). Some aspects of language ability may be relatively preserved (e.g., semantic language), but children with hydrocephalus have significant problems with discourse (Dennis et al., 1994). Studies of memory, attention, and executive functions suggest an uneven pattern of functioning in children with hydrocephalus (Fletcher et al., 1996; Wills, 1993). Achievement tests show that decoding skills are intact, but problems with writing, math computation, and reading comprehension and verbal learning have been described (Barnes & Dennis, 1992; Wills, 1993; Yeates, Enrile, Blumenstein, & Delis, 1995). Studies of behavioral adjustment have shown a higher rate of both internalizing and externalizing disorders in children with hydrocephalus (Donders, Rourke, &

Canady, 1992; Fletcher, Brookshire, Landry, et al., 1995). Fletcher, Brookshire, Landry, et al. (1995) were able to relate the presence of behavior problems to the presence of hydrocephalus.

Assessment issues involve the evaluation of various basic areas of competence in relation to social and environmental issues. Particularly important is the assessment of cognitive skills in relation to the motor deficits common in these children. For example, when assessing spatial skills, an evaluator must be careful to determine whether the observed deficit is simply a product of task requirements for motor output or a more general spatial processing deficit. Tasks that involve either copying or recognition of geometric figures, or both, can be used to make this assessment (Fletcher et al., 1992). In children with spinal dysraphisms, assessment must incorporate an evaluation of problems with ambulation, neurogenic bladder, and other problems related to the spinal lesions. Because these disorders are chronic, effects on a child's social development and influences of the family and school environment are very important.

Genetic/Metabolic/Degenerative Disorders

The broad category of genetic/metabolic/degenerative disorders includes a variety of disorders that have recently become the subjects of neuropsychological investigation. Broman and Grafman (1994) reviewed studies of Williams syndrome, Down syndrome, Turner syndrome, and neurofibromatosis, all of which involve combinations of problems with brain and other organ systems, metabolic deficiencies, and physical dysmorphology. Genetic factors are clearly prominent in all these syndromes. Rourke (1995) has reviewed velocardiofacial syndrome, Williams syndrome, de Lange syndrome, Sotos syndrome, and Turner syndrome, along with endocrinological disorders and multiple sclerosis. Reviewing each of these disorders is beyond the scope of this chapter, so the texts cited above should be consulted. What is important is the emerging development of a knowledge base on the neurobehavioral correlates of these disorders. This is most apparent in studies of Williams syndrome. Although most children with Williams syndrome are mentally deficient, many children show preservation of some language skills. Their speech is often fluent and well formed, with good expressive vocabulary. However, their understanding of vocabulary is quite deficient. Although face perception is intact, children with Williams syndrome show profound difficulties with spatial and constructional abilities (Bellugi, Wang, & Jernigan, 1994).

Other disorders, such as Turner syndrome, do not necessarily involve mental deficiency. Turner syndrome occurs in girls and is usually caused by loss of a single X chromosome or other abnormality involving the X chromosome (White, 1994). Individuals with Turner syndrome have a variety of physical and somatic problems, including growth deficiencies, ovarian failure, and skeletal/facial abnormalities. Although no specific cognitive phenotype has been established, problems with visual–spatial and math skills relative to intact language and reading abilities are commonly observed (Rovet, 1995).

To take Williams syndrome and Turner syndrome as examples, the assessment issues relevant to these disorders parallel those relevant for the assessment of children with mental deficiency and common developmental disorders, such as dyslexia and Attention-Deficit/Hyperactivity Disorder (ADHD). Children with Williams syndrome have brain abnormalities as part of their phenotype, but are not "brain-injured" in the sense that some external agent (trauma, disease) has caused brain damage. Assessment involves the full range of basic areas of competence—not just IQ testing—modified as necessary for the age and overall mental capabilities of the child. Particularly critical is the assessment of adaptive behavior, including socialization and everyday living skills, since these skills may need to be directly trained.

Children with Turner syndrome do not present with obvious brain abnormalities, and neuroimaging studies are often normal. The most critical issues often involve how a child functions in school, particularly given the high frequency of learning disabilities in this population (Rovet, 1995). In addition, questions about ADHD often arise, along with problems with social adjustment secondary to the problems with sexual maturation in girls with Turner syndrome.

Tumors

Tumors are common sources of brain injury. In children, tumors can occur throughout the brain, but are particularly common in the posterior fossa and brainstem. In contrast to adults, cortical tumors occur much less frequently. It is also common to separate midline tumors, such as craniopharyngioma and pinealomas, because of commonalities in presentation and clinical course (Spreen et al., 1995).

For treatment purposes, pathology classifications are very important. Astrocytomas, gliomas, and medulloblastomas grow at different rates and respond differently to chemotherapy and radiation. Neurobehavioral deficiencies are related not only to the location and size of a tumor, but to the effects of the tumor on endocrinological and metabolic functions, cerebral blood flow and CSF flow, and a host of other factors. In addition to surgical excision, treatments can have adverse effects on the brain. High-dose chemotherapy is often associated with anomalies of the peripheral nervous system (e.g., peripheral neuropathy). CNS radiation at very high levels is sometimes necessary and can have effects on the cerebral white matter, particularly in younger children (Fletcher & Copeland, 1988).

Because of these factors, neurobehavioral studies of children with brain tumors are difficult. The children tend to be quite heterogeneous and often cannot be studied prior to treatment. All studies show a very high rate of deficiencies in multiple areas of adaptive functioning, but outcomes vary considerably, depending on the type of tumor and its treatment as well as on environmental factors (Carlson-Green, Morris, & Krawiecki, 1995). Factors that seem particularly relevant are younger age at diagnosis, tumor size, location, stage, surgical interventions, and treatment with cranial radiation (Carlson-Green et al., 1995; Dennis, Spiegler, Fitz, et al., 1991; Dennis, Spiegler, Hoffman, et al., 1991; Dennis, Spiegler, Obonsawin, et al., 1991).

In addition to neoplastic tumors, studies of children with neurofibromatosis are emerging. Menkes (1995) identifies neurofibromatosis as one of several neurocutaneous syndromes, which also include Sturge–Weber syndrome, tuberous sclerosis, and other rarer disorders. The most common example is neurofibromatosis. This disorder, which appears to be genetically transmitted, involves the development of tumors in the CNS, the peripheral nervous system, and the skin. These tumors can evolve to lumps in the skin, bone deformities, and (less frequently) CNS tumors. Neuroimaging studies (especially MRI) commonly reveal neural migration abnormalities, hamartomas, and "unidentified bright objects," which are areas of increased signal on MRI. These areas of increased signal can occur across the brain and cerebellum, but have questionable neuropathological significance.

Outcomes in children with neurofibromatosis vary considerably. Academic deficits are common, but it is not clear whether these problems should be described as "learning disabilities" (Hofman, Harris, Bryan, & Denckla, 1994). Problems with spatial and motor skills are commonly reported, but few studies to date have provided particularly comprehensive assessments. Regardless of the nature of the problem, children with neurofibromatosis frequently have cognitive problems. In general, unless a child develops a CNS tumor, assessment issues are similar to those described for children with Turner syndrome.

Infectious Disorders

A variety of infectious disorders can affect a child's CNS. These disorders can occur prenatally or postnatally. Prenatal disorders include cytomegalovirus, rubella, and HIV infection/AIDS. Postnatal disorders include encephalitis, meningitis, and Reye syndrome (Palumbo et al., 1995; Spreen et al., 1995).

Prenatal infectious disorders affect the fetus and have wide-ranging effects on development. These effects can include growth retardation, sensory disorders (deafness, blindness), and a range of cognitive sequelae. The degree to which the brain is affected varies, and the underlying pathophysiology is not well understood. Most studies of sequelae focus on neonates, since these infections are identified early in development. Studies of school-age children with cytomegalovirus have suggested subtle learning and attention problems, but these sequelae are not well documented in the absence of clear evidence for CNS involvement. Similar statements can be made about children who suffer other prenatal infectious disorders (Palumbo et al., 1995).

Postnatal infectious disorders can involve the meninges of the brain (viral and bacterial meningitis) or the entire brain (encephalitis, Reye syndrome). A major issue in any of these disorders is the development of secondary pathophysiological CNS effects, particularly brain swelling and edema, ventricular dilation and hydrocephalus, and seizures.

Neuropsychological aspects of bacterial meningitis have been extensively studied by research groups in the United States and Australia (Grimwood et al., 1995; Taylor et al., 1991). In a study by Taylor et al. (1990), comparisons of children who had recovered from *Haemophilus influenzae* meningitis relative to their siblings revealed disease effects on both neuropsychological performances and academic skills. Similar results have been obtained in comparing children with men-

ingitis to classmate controls (Grimwood et al., 1995). In a recent factor-analytic study, Taylor, Schatschneider, Petrill, Barry, and Owens (1996) demonstrated specific impairments in perceptual–motor abilities and executive functions. Outcomes of meningitis are related to social factors, illness complications in the acute phase, and residual CNS deficits (Grimwood et al., 1995; Taylor et al., 1991; Taylor & Schatschneider, 1992b).

There are various types of encephalitis, which have been studied since epidemics of measles encephalitis earlier this century. A major issue in many cases in the extent to which the temporal lobes and limbic system are involved. Herpes simplex encephalitis has a particular predilection for the temporal lobes and has been associated with the development of frank amnestic syndromes in adolescents and adults (Squire, 1987). True amnestic syndromes are rare in children, but problems with memory, attention, and behavior are commonly reported sequelae of all children with encephalitis.

Like treatment for other infectious disorders, treatment for Reye syndrome has resulted in dramatically improved outcomes. Reye syndrome was commonly associated with death or severe neurological sequelae. More recent studies of survivors show that the most severe sequelae are transitory, but continue to raise the issue of more subtle deficits (Palumbo et al., 1995).

The assessment of children with prenatal infectious disorders usually begins early in development and follows paradigms developed for other high-risk infant populations. Such children are dealt with along the lines described in this chapter for children with perinatal trauma.

For children with postnatal infections, the assessment issues are similar to those described for children with severe TBI. Such a child is often developing normally and becomes ill, resulting in hospitalization with alterations of consciousness and issues of survival. The child needs early monitoring of levels of consciousness and amnesia, with serial evaluations to document treatment needs and recovery. Careful evaluation of preinjury factors and the postinjury environment is critical.

Cerebrovascular Disease

Actual strokes in children are rare. When they do occur, the children often suffer from another disorder or a disorder that represents congenital abnormalities of the vascular system of the brain. For example, children with infections and perinatal trauma can develop infarcts, or ischemic strokes. These infarcts can lead to hemiplegia. At one time, children undergoing cardiac catherization suffered strokes because of embolic obstruction. Many of the children with unilateral focal lesions studied by Aram (1990) had strokes after cardiac catherization.

Children can also have congenital aneurysms and arteriovenous malformations that lead to hemorrhagic strokes. Even more common are cerebrovascular accidents in children with Moya Moya syndrome or sickle cell anemia, in both of which congenital abnormalities of the vascular system are part of the disorder (Menkes, 1995).

What is important to recognize is the low frequency of cerebrovascular disorders in children; again, this highlights the difficulties of comparative studies of outcome in adults and children. With the exception of TBI, diseases in adults and children are generally different. Children are most likely to suffer from diseases and injuries that have widespread effects on the brain. Even when a focal lesion is present, it is usually superimposed on a diffuse pathological process. When assessing a child with cerebrovascular disease, an evaluator must pay careful attention to the pathophysiological effects on the brain, as well as the systemic effects of the underlying disease. In general, assessment issues are like those described for children with neoplastic tumors.

Epilepsy

Although epilepsy is not an actual form of brain injury, it is reviewed separately here because it is a common problem in children, with an overall prevalence rate of about 10.5 per 1,000 cases of active epilepsy (Baron et al., 1995). The term "epilepsy" refers to the presence of seizures resulting from abnormal electrical discharges in the brain. Epilepsy commonly occurs in association with another neurological disorder; thus, such seizures are often *secondary* to any of the disorders reviewed above. Epilepsy can also occur as the *primary* disorder in the absence of another neurological disorder. When epilepsy is primary, the cause is often unknown, and such cases are often not complicated by other problems. It is widely believed that primary or idiopathic epilepsy is genetically transmitted and is more responsive to treatment (Menkes, 1995). In contrast, secondary epilepsy occurs in association with many neurological disorders. Seizures can also occur on a transient basis in reaction to a nonrecurrent event, such as fever.

Classifications of epilepsy vary, but are usually based on descriptions of seizure types. For example, Spreen et al.'s (1995) discussion of epilepsy is based on the International Classification of Epilepsies of Childhood, whereas the discussion by Baron et al.(1995) is based on the Revised Classification of Epilepsies and Epileptic Syndromes developed by the International League Against Epilepsy. The former classification subdivides seizures into primary generalized epilepsies (e.g., petit mal, myoloclonic), secondary generalized epilepsies (e.g., seizures occurring in association with diffuse brain disease), primary partial epilepsies (nongeneralized seizures with motor, affective, or visual symptoms), and secondary partial epilepsies (i.e., seizures with a lesional basis). The latter classification subdivides seizures into two major types: localization-related epilepsies (i.e., focal or partial complex seizures) and generalized epilepsies (i.e., seizures involving diffuse brain areas). Within each major type, seizures are further subdivided into idiopathic (no known cause), symptomatic (secondary to some disease), and cryptogenic (symptomatic, often as part of a syndrome).

Epilepsy classifications are driven primarily by an interest in treatment. To the extent that treatment reflects causation, such variables are important. However, secondary epilepsies are treated primarily according to seizure type, particularly in the choice of anticonvulsants.

Most treatments of epilepsy include anticonvulsants, which are usually effective. When anticonvulsants are not effective, a child may receive polypharmacy (i.e., may be subjected to a variety of pharmacological agents). When the seizures persist, they are called "intractable." Children with intractable seizures are commonly evaluated in hospital-based epilepsy units that permit extensive evaluations, including 24-hour electrophysiological monitoring. This is particularly helpful in establishing whether the seizures are truly neurological or whether they are non-neurological or "pseudoseizures." The latter require psychosocial interventions. In the former, identification of a true lesional basis sometimes makes a child a candidate for surgical excision of the epileptogenic brain tissue, which is often an effective cure.

In cases of primary epilepsy, the most common reason for evaluating a child is the presence of a learning or attention problem. Such problems occur at a higher rate in children with idiopathic epilepsy, but are not always caused by the epilepsy (Aldenkamp, Alpherts, Dekker, & Overweg, 1990). In many cases, the learning or attention disorder is comorbid and requires the type of evaluation necessary for any other developmental disorder. The relationship of learning and attention problems to all forms of epilepsy is an area clearly requiring further research. Secondary epilepsy usually requires evaluation because of the brain disease or injury associated with the disorder (e.g., TBI, spina bifida, tumor, etc.). As such, the evaluation should include the methods and procedures necessary to evaluate the underlying disorder.

Epilepsy per se rarely results in a need for neuropsychological evaluation except when the seizures are intractable or where there are accompanying learning or behavior problems. In epilepsy-monitoring units designed for children (and adults) with intractable seizures, a neuropsychological evaluation is a common component of the overall evaluation. The goal is to identify the nature of the epilepsy and the factors that make it intractable. In some cases surgery is a viable option, as noted above, and a major goal is to try to identify a lesion that is the true origin of the seizures. It is common to use neuropsychological tests as one component of the search for a lesion. In cases where pseudoseizures are involved, the neuropsychologist must incorporate a thorough evaluation of family and emotional factors that influence the intractability of the seizures, and must provide a treatment plan addressing these factors.

Another issue is whether anticonvulsants have deleterious effects on cognitive skills—a question often put to neuropsychologists by parents. In an excellent review, Cull and Trimble (1989) have concluded that "no anticonvulsant is free of potentially disruptive effects on cognitive functions in some individuals" (p. 95). However, they also point out that the evidence linking specific drugs with specific cognitive side effects is weak and involves consideration of a child's cognitive functioning and brain status, the efficacy of the drug in controlling seizure frequency, and possible toxicity. The question is not simple and requires consideration of a host of factors.

Conclusions

The nature of CNS disorders in children has major implications for assessment. The notion that the primary purpose of a neuropsychological evaluation is to identify an underlying lesion or process is not widely accepted by child neuropsychologists (Fletcher & Taylor, 1984). Even in children with well-described unilateral lesions, such as those studied by Aram (1990), substantial reorganization of mental processes and behavior occurs; thus,

there may not be a direct relationship between test performance and lesion location. Issues of plasticity and recovery of function, reviewed in Fletcher (1988), remain complex and are far from fully understood in children with brain injury. Equally relevant are depictions of the number and extent of basic competencies impaired (Rourke et al., 1986), as well as evaluation of the integrity of control processes, such as executive functions (Bernstein & Waber, 1990; Pennington, 1991). Although it is certainly possible to relate the results of a neuropsychological assessment to an evaluation of CNS integrity, particularly when neuroimaging studies are obtained, evaluation of the severity of the disorder and how it was treated is equally relevant. In the next sections, general approaches to neuropsychological assessment are described, along with a discussion of a general approach to child neuropsychological assessment.

APPROACHES TO NEUROPSYCHOLOGICAL ASSESSMENT OF CHILDREN

Neuropsychological assessment of children is often identified on the basis of the particular battery of tests selected for administration. In fact, test batteries vary widely across practitioners. In some settings, the practitioner administers a fixed test battery to each child. In other settings, tests are selected according to the presenting problems, and there may be little commonality across evaluations of individual children. Still other practitioners use a core of fixed tests that are administered to each child, but add additional tests depending on the results of the assessment and purposes underlying the referral. From this perspective, at least five examples of the neuropsychological assessment of children can be described that have been systematically depicted in the literature.

An Approach to Evaluating Infants and Preschoolers

One approach, described by Wilson (1986), is designed primarily for infants and preschoolers. Wilson uses a variety of standardized instruments appropriate for the age range of the children evaluated. In this respect, measures such as the McCarthy Scales of Children's Abilities (McCarthy, 1972), the fourth edition of the Stanford–Binet Intelligence Scale (Thorndike, Hagen, & Sattler, 1988), and the second edition of the Bayley Scales of Infant Development (Bayley, 1993) are commonly employed. However, Wilson (1986) often selects specific subtests from these scales to evaluate a particular core skill. The nature of the tests used varies across individual children. As in any other approach to neuropsychological assessment, the underlying premises are that the tests measure certain discrete skills and that there is a need to measure a broad range of skills and abilities, resulting in the use of a multitest battery. Wilson (1986) places great weight on observations of the child during the testing, as well as observations in less structured situations. Whenever possible, multiple tests are used to measure the same underlying skill in an effort to improve the reliability of the assessment. Younger children can be difficult to assess. The measures have less inherent reliability and may be more subject to factors that are not under the examiner's control.

Variations of the Halstead–Reitan Approach

One of the best-known approaches to neuropsychological assessment of children with brain injury involves the use of a fixed battery of tests, commonly known as the Halstead–Reitan Neuropsychological Test Battery. Examples of this approach have been described by Reitan and Wolfson (1992), and a well-known variant described by Rourke and colleagues (Rourke et al., 1986).

The approach of Rourke et al. (1986) is based on considerations of the relationship between the child's neuropsychological ability structure and variables related to the lesion. The evaluation of the latter factors represents the first step in the assessment process; they are evaluated in relationship to the immediate and long-term demands of the environment. A remediation plan is then developed, implemented, and reevaluated. Testing includes the standard Halstead–Reitan Neuropsychological Test Battery (see Table 9.2), usually supplemented by additional measures of language skills, attention, and problem-solving abilities.

Pennington (1991) also uses a variation on this test battery for some cases, with an even greater emphasis on measures of problem-solving skills, memory, and executive functions (see Table 9.3). Pennington's (1991) approach is largely oriented toward the assessment of children with learning and attention disorders, but there are also special considerations for children with brain injury. The focus is on differential diagnosis in the cognitive domain, with additional emphasis on distinguishing cognitive and emotional functions.

A Flexible Approach

A well-developed example of a more flexible approach to assessment has been described by Bernstein and Waber (1990). Their method, which is heavily influenced by the "process approach" to adult neuropsychological assessment, emphasizes the relationship of the neuropsychological and psychological aspects of assessment. Guiding the assessment is a hypothetical model of the CNS, conceptualized along three primary axes: anterior–posterior, left–right, and cortical–subcortical. The psychological component addresses a variety of cognitive substructures, developmental timetables, and the context in which the child develops. Behavior is represented as a product of the dynamic interaction of the behavioral, neurological, and psychological axes in the context of the child's environment. A major emphasis of this approach is on the qualitative assessment of behavior displayed by the child during testing. In this approach, specific procedures are often designed to assess the child's ability to flexibly use and develop alternative cognitive strategies. This ability has particular implications for the development of a remedial plan, with an emphasis on problem-solving skills that the child might use in a compensatory model. As in Pennington's (1991) approach, test procedures can be flexible and involve many of the tests described in Table 9.2. However, there is also a significant emphasis on problem-solving measures, as well as on more qualitative evaluations of a child's performance. Tests are often chosen to address issues apparent during the evaluation. As in Wilson's (1986) approach, test administration is often modified to identify approaches that the child might use to successfully complete a task.

Common Assumptions

Despite the diversity of tests and of approaches to test interpretations, many practitioners combine different features from these approaches in assessing a child. Common to all approaches is the use of psychometric tests to help define the nature of the presenting problem and to measure cognitive skills that are presumably correlated with the presenting disorder. A second common factor is an emphasis on environmental variables that might impinge on the child's performance. The third factor is the attempt to interpret test findings in the context of the environment in which the child is developing. The fourth common factor is an

TABLE 9.2. Modified Version of the Halstead–Reitan Neuropsychological Test Battery for Children Used by Rourke and Colleagues

I. Tactile-perceptual skills
   A. Reitan–Kløve Tactile-Perceptual and Tactile-Forms Recognition Tests
      1. Tactile Imperception and Suppression
      2. Finger Agnosia
      3. Fingertip Number-Writing Perception (9–15 years), Fingertip Symbol-Writing Recognition (5–8 years)
      4. Coin Recognition (9–15 years), Tactile-Forms Recognition (5–8 years)

II. Visual-perceptual skills
   A. Reitan–Kløve Visual-Perceptual Tests
   B. Target Test
   C. Constructional Dyspraxia Items, Halstead–Wepman Aphasia Screening Test
   D. Wechsler Intelligence Scale for Children (WISC) Picture Completion, Picture Arrangement, Block Design, Object Assembly subtests
   E. Trail Making Test for Children, Part A (9–15 years)
   F. Color Form Test (5–8 years)
   G. Progressive Figures
   H. Individual Performance Test (5–8 years)
      1. Matching Figures
      2. Star Drawing
      3. Matching V's
      4. Concentric Squares Drawing

III. Auditory-perceptual and language-related
   A. Reitan–Kløve Auditory-Perceptual Test
   B. Seashore Rhythm Test (9–15 years)
   C. Auditory Closure Test
   D. Auditory Analysis Test
   E. Peabody Picture Vocabulary Test
   F. Speech-Sounds Perception Test
   G. Sentence Memory Test
   H. Verbal Fluency Test
   I. WISC Information, Comprehension, Similarities, Vocabulary, Digit Span subtests
   J. Aphasoid Items, Aphasia Screening Test

IV. Problem solving, concept formation, reasoning
   A. Halstead Category Test
   B. Children's Word-Finding Test
   C. WISC Arithmetic subtest
   D. Matching Pictures Test (5–8 years)

V. Motor and psychomotor skills
   A. Reitan–Kløve Lateral Dominance Examination
   B. Dynamometer
   C. Finger Tapping Test
   D. Foot Tapping Test
   E. Kløve–Matthews Motor Steadiness Battery
      1. Maze Coordination Test
      2. Static Steadiness Test
      3. Grooved Pegboard Test

VI. Other
   A. Underlining Test
   B. WISC Coding subtest
   C. Tactual Performance Test
   D. Trail Making Test for Children, Part B (9–15 years)

TABLE 9.3. Neuropsychological Assessment
Procedures for Evaluation of Cognitive Skills
Used by Pennington

I. Language
   1. Boston Naming Test
   2. Goldman–Friscoe–Woodcock Auditory
      Discrimination
   3. Pig Latin (Phoneme Segmentation)
   4. Speech-Sounds Perception Test
   5. Aphasia Screening Test
   6. Word Fluency

II. Spatial cognition
   1. Beery Developmental Test of Visual–Motor
      Integration
   2. Children's Embedded Figures Test
   3. Constructional Dyspraxia Items, Aphasia
      Screening Test
   4. Tactual Performance Test

III. Motor skills
   1. Finger Tapping Test
   2. Grooved Pegboard Test
   3. Hand Dynamometer

IV. Sensory-perceptual skills
    Modified Reitan–Kløve Tactile-Perceptual Test

V. Memory
   1. Story Recall
   2. Figure Recall
   3. Verbal Selective Reminding

VI. Social cognition
   1. Childhood Autism Rating Scale
   2. Theory of Other Minds
   3. Imitation
   4. Emotional Perception

VII. Executive functions
   1. Wisconsin Card Sorting Test
   2. Tower of Hanoi
   3. Matching Familiar Figures Test
   4. Continuous-performance test
   5. Contingency Naming Test
   6. Halstead Category Test
   7. Trail Making Test

emphasis on the use of the assessment as a guide in developing remedial plans.

Although there are certainly situations in which a primary purpose of testing is to identify a lesion, most evaluations have as an eventual outcome the development of a treatment plan. One example of the former "lesion identification" strategy is the use of testing to help pinpoint lesions in cases of intractable epilepsy, where correct identification is essential to surgical interventions. The neuropsychological evaluation is one of many tools used for this determination. There are also situations

in which the cause of a child's disorder is truly unknown, in which case neuropsychological tests can be used to shed light on the possibility of brain-based impairments. However, the more common scenario is to know that the child has sustained a brain injury and to have access to a significant amount of material that describes the child's injury. Hence, what many neuropsychologists commonly do either before or after the evaluation is to evaluate the child's test performance in light of medical, historical, and environmental data, and to establish relationships between the child's ability structure and factors that may represent compromised CNS integrity. The goal is not so much to specify the exact nature of neuropathology as to develop a remedial plan that highlights areas for intervention, methods for remediation, and potential modes of intervention. However, even this assessment occurs in the broader context of the child's environment.

In the next section, a biobehavioral systems approach to the neuropsychological assessment of brain-injured children is presented. This approach places the different levels of inference underlying neuropsychological assessment into a coherent framework, and integrates the various sources of information essential to neuropsychological assessment of a child.

A BIOBEHAVIORAL SYSTEMS APPROACH: APPLICATIONS TO BRAIN INJURY

Overview

Figure 9.1 depicts the framework underlying a biobehavioral approach to neuropsychological assessment of children with brain injury. As this figure shows, a neuropsychological evaluation involves the assessment of four different types of variables: manifest disability, child traits (cognitive and psychosocial), biological factors, and environmental factors.

The first set of variables represents the child's manifest disability. The manifest disability is the presenting problem—that is, the child's inability to fulfill the expectations of the family, culture, or school. This inability to meet expectations leads to the referral for the evaluation.

The second set of variables consists of child traits, which can be either cognitive or psychosocial. The cognitive traits are the basic areas of competence that are assessed with psychometric tests. These basic areas of competence include motor, perceptual–motor, visual–spatial, language, memory, attention, and problem-solving skills. In

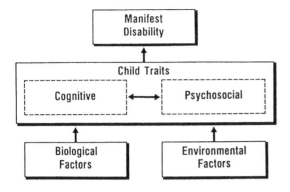

FIGURE 9.1. Schematic representation of the bio-behavioral systems approach to child neuropsychological assessment. From Taylor and Fletcher (1990, p. 233).

contrast, psychosocial traits are behaviors that are not considered to be strictly cognitive. These traits include factors such as the child's behavioral adjustment, personality, self-esteem, and other aspects of the child's development that are generally considered to be more the products of environmental events or learning history. In contrast, the cognitive traits are presumed to have more of a constitutional origin (Taylor & Schatschneider, 1992b). Together, the cognitive and psychosocial factors that represent the child's traits represent the behavioral underpinnings of the manifest disability. As Figure 9.1 shows, these two domains influence each other to produce the manifest disability.

Whereas the child traits are presumed to influence the manifest disability directly, biological and environmental factors are presumed to have more indirect effects on the manifest disability (see Figure 9.1). The third set of variables (biological factors) includes actual CNS lesions and other neuroimaging findings; the nature and severity of the disease or disorder that resulted in the brain injury; the way the brain injury was treated; and a variety of other factors. In contrast, the fourth set of variables (environmental factors) involves the child's family and cultural background; parental practices in regard to child management and discipline; the school environment; and the child's learning history.

Assumptions

Underlying these four levels of analysis are four fundamental assumptions. First, it is presumed that a thorough neuropsychological evaluation of

a brain-injured child involves the assessment of all four types of variables: the manifest disability, the child's cognitive and psychosocial traits, biological variables, and environmental/sociocultural variables. Second (see Bernstein & Waber, 1990), it is assumed that although the manifest disability is partly a product of the child's patterns of strengths and weaknesses in basic cognitive skills, the impact of the cognitive profile on the child's everyday functioning is dependent on other child characteristics and the environmental context in which the child develops. These factors moderate the relationship of the manifest disability and different cognitive skills.

Third, it is expected that there will be covariation among cognitive skills, as well as between the cognitive skills, and the manifest disability. However, particularly relevant to assessment is the emergence of skill dissociations related to either congenital or postnatal neurological disorder. Examples of such skill dissociations include the significantly poorer development of motor and spatial skills relative to verbal abilities seen in children with early hydrocephalus, or the interesting contrast of spatial and verbal abilities observed in children with Williams syndrome. The skill dissociations will be apparent in studies that average the results obtained by individual children, but they will also be present in individual children and will form a primary basis for understanding the impact of constitutional factors on outcome. A child's cognitive profile is also the key to development of an intervention plan.

Fourth, it is assumed that child traits vary in the extent to which they reflect neurological versus environmental variability, and that an evaluation of all four types of variables in a biobehavioral systems approach will help elucidate the extent to which the manifest disability reflects biological and environmental influences. Because both environmental and biological factors are involved in the development of child traits, the role of the CNS can be best understood by incorporating environmental factors into the assessment. A major goal of a neuropsychological assessment is to establish the extent to which the manifest disability actually is consistent with the biological factors representing the effects of the disease or injury that led to the assessment.

Implications for Assessment

It is clear that this approach to assessment identifies the CNS as one of many influences on learning and behavior. A general conceptualization that is particularly relevant for assessment of the child with brain injury views the manifest disability as a set of outcomes and asks about the different factors that would result in this particular set of outcomes. These factors include the status of the CNS, but also a host of other factors, such as the child's environment, prior learning history, availability of remedial resources, and related factors. The goal of an assessment is to account for the different sources of variability that explain individual differences in outcome; this is a *sine que non* of any study of a brain-injured child (Taylor & Schatschneider, 1992b).

Another implication of this approach to assessment is the need to systematically evaluate and relate both cognitive and psychosocial traits that underlie the disability. The model emphasizes the study of relationships among different levels of analysis, again in an attempt to understand variations and outcomes across classes of disorders and within a particular disorder.

Finally, the approach does not necessarily wed the examiner to a particular test battery. There is an emphasis on a broad range of behavioral characteristics and areas of adaptation. A major emphasis is on how other areas of psychology can contribute to the knowledge base underlying outcomes for children with brain injury. In particular, this approach is consistent with what is now called "cognitive neuroscience" because of the emphasis on assessment of cognitive skills and a systematic attempt to relate these assessments to the biological factors representing the integrity of the CNS.

This framework is flexible and is typically implemented with a core set of tests; these tests are supplemented with other tests, depending on the nature of the disorder, the referral question, and the results of the core assessment. Another emphasis is on the longitudinal follow-up of children with any form of brain injury, consistent with Rourke et al. (1986). In particular, children who are acutely ill (e.g., those with TBI or infectious diseases) are followed from the inception of their illness for several years. In children who have congenital disorders (e.g., hydrocephalus), the follow-ups are less frequent, but longitudinal evaluation is still emphasized because the children's needs will change. In particular, follow-up evaluations are essential to evaluating the success of any remedial plan. As recommended by Pennington (1991), careful feedback and interpretations to the parents in the form of personal conferences as well as written reports are provided. Case management is critical, and parents, schools, and other potential intervention agents should have easy access to the neuropsychologist. In cases of brain injury, other practitioners and school personnel often have little understanding of the nature of these disorders and are often uncomfortable talking with medical providers. The evaluation is used to provide an interface between the biological component of a child's treatment and the psychosocial component of intervention. Evaluation findings can be particularly helpful for establishing appropriate expectations for the child at home and at school. Emphasis is placed on proactive approaches in identifying problems and preventing secondary morbidity, which can occur as a consequence of placement in an inappropriate school setting or a parent's not truly understanding the extent to which a child may be impaired by a brain injury or disease.

Even relatively common disorders such as spina bifida meningomyelocele are not always well understood from a neuropsychological viewpoint. In many public schools, these children with these disorders are frequently identified as orthopedically handicapped, despite shunting for hydrocephalus and abnormalities of the corpus callosum and other brain structures that have a significant impact on learning and memory. On a practical level, children with spina bifida are often viewed as unmotivated and passive, when in fact they have cognitive problems secondary to brain injury. Assessment results and interpretations can change the eligibility rubric used by the public school from one involving orthopedic handicaps to one that includes provisions for neurological impairments. The neuropsychologist also evaluates individualized education plans (IEPs), and attempts to provide a full range of alternative resources to the parents of a child with a brain injury. The assessment is important, but it is only the beginning of the child's habilitation. It is often necessary to provide continuing consultation to parents and schools, to help parents gain access to services, and to modify recommendations according to the availability of resources and services. An assessment that is limited to one report and one conference is not likely to have great impact on the development of the brain-injured child; guiding parents through subsequent interventions is essential.

IMPLEMENTATION OF THE BIOBEHAVIORAL SYSTEMS APPROACH

Assessment of the Manifest Disability

The first step in implementing a biobehavioral systems approach is to evaluate the manifest disability. In general, this involves an intake evaluation and assessment of a particular referral question. Referral questions can come from inpatient or outpatient services. Inpatient referrals usually reflect concerns about the relationship of an illness to cognitive function, or the identification of a possible problem not necessarily related to the brain injury, such as a learning disability. Outpatient referrals usually reflect concerns about the child's failure to meet expectations at school or home. Such failure is often represented by academic problems or by behavioral difficulties. It is important to recognize that in many of these latter referrals, the nature of the injury is often known prior to the assessment. The goal of assessment is not to establish direct links between the academic or behavioral problems and the brain injury, but instead to characterize the actual disability and determine the degree to which biological and environmental factors contribute to the disability. This is important in part because in many children with brain injury, academic or behavioral problems do not have the same correlates in terms of child traits that are expected for common developmental problems, such as dyslexia and ADHD (Taylor & Schatschneider, 1992a; Taylor, Drotar, et al., 1995). For example, many children with a brain injury may show intact reading skills, but cannot demonstrate their reading proficiency in school because of other problems, such as difficulties with memory, attention, or problem-solving skills (Barnes & Dennis, 1992). Difficulties with paper-and-pencil tasks are more common in children with brain insults than in children with other developmental disabilities. These problems may obscure a child's actual capabilities, particularly when the child's motor functions are impaired because of a brain injury. Similarly, children with frank brain damage are more likely to exhibit attentional deficits in the absence of other behavioral problems; again, this pattern represents a contrast to the presenting problems that instigate referrals for more common developmental disorders, particularly ADHD. Although achievement tests and questionnaires are used to assess manifest disability for both acquired and developmental disorders, the child's traits are likely to differ substantially, depending on the nature of the brain injury.

The assessment of the manifest disability involves a thorough review of the factors that resulted in the referral, and an analysis of the child's difficulties as they actually occur at home or school. This information is obtained from three sources: (1) parent and teacher questionnaires, school/ medical records, and previous evaluations; (2) parent and teacher interviews; and (3) testing of potential problem areas, such as achievement and/ or problem-solving skills. In this third instance, tests of cognitive functions can be used, but they are employed to evaluate the manifest disability and establish the nature of the problems to be accounted for in the assessment.

Table 9.4 provides a list of questionnaires and interviews that are commonly used to evaluate the manifest disability. This list includes standard parent and teacher behavior rating scales, such as the Child Behavior Checklist (CBCL; Achenbach, 1991) and the Personality Inventory for Children—Revised (PIC-R; Wirt, Lachar, Klinedinst, & Seat, 1990). Standardized measures of adaptive behavior, such as the Vineland Adaptive Behavior Scales (Sparrow, Balla, & Cichetti, 1984), and of academic achievement are also included. It is important that the achievement tests entail assessment of real-word and pseudoword decoding skills, written spelling, computational arithmetic, reading rate and accuracy, and reading comprehension. In the child with brain injury, some of these assessments have to be carefully evaluated in light of other information concerning the child's difficulties. For example, it is common to receive a teacher form indicating concerns about reading comprehension, but to find that the child's ability on tests of reading comprehension is in the average range. This does not mean that the child has normal reading comprehension;

TABLE 9.4. Procedures for Assessing Manifest Disability

I. Parent-based questionnaires and rating scales
  1. Child history form
  2. Child Behavior Checklist and Teacher Report Form (Achenbach, 1991)
  3. Vineland Adaptive Behavior Scales (Sparrow et al., 1984)
  4. Personality Inventory for Children—Revised (Wirt et al., 1990)
  5. Conners Parent and Teacher Rating Scales (Conners, 1990)

II. Academic achievement
  1. Wide Range Achievement Test—3 (Wilkinson, 1993)
  2. Peabody Individual Achievement Test— Revised (Dunn & Markwardt, 1989)
  3. Woodcock–Johnson Psycho-Educational Test Battery—Revised (Woodcock, 1988)
  4. Kaufman Test of Educational Achievement (Kaufman, 1992)

instead, it raises questions as to why the child is unable to comprehend text under some circumstances but not others. In these situations, the goal of the assessment is to identify deficits that would explain why the child's test performance is not paralleled by his or her actual performance in the school.

Parent interviews are also critical. However, as Rourke et al. (1986) note, parents can be interviewed *after* other sources of information are obtained. Parent and teacher questionnaires are commonly sent out prior to the initial evaluation session. When the child arrives for the evaluation, the examiner solicits parents' concerns and their reasons for seeking an evaluation. It is not necessary, however, to obtain complete histories or to evaluate parental reactions at the first encounter. Approaching the evaluation in this stepwise manner often enhances the credibility of the evaluation with parents and provides some guidelines for a more detailed interview at later points in the assessment process.

Semistructured interviews such as the Vineland scales are also extremely helpful, particularly in terms of clarifying the extent to which the child is handicapped in his or her everyday environment. The Vineland scales yield age-adjusted scores in several important areas of everyday functioning, including Communication Skills, Daily Living Skills, and Socialization. The interview procedure can also be enlightening with regard to the approach taken by the child and parent in dealing with any disabilities.

Achievement testing is a critical component of any child neuropsychological evaluation, including brain injury. In addition to providing important information concerning the child's actual skill development in a variety of critical areas, such assessments enhance the credibility of the report with the public schools. When an evaluation incorporates the types of tests that particular school districts are likely to use, the results will often be more readily acted on by the school in arranging for placements and accommodations. Use of these tests can also reduce the time required to develop an IEP for the child, as well as build rapport between the neuropsychologist and the school.

To summarize, evaluation of manifest disability involves both formal and informal assessment practices. The end result of the assessment should be a clear understanding of exactly how the child is failing to meet expectations at home and at school. Description and analysis of the manifest disability are best presented at the beginning of the neuropsychological report.

Assessment of Cognitive Traits

Table 9.5 presents a number of cognitive domains and tests that are commonly used to assess the child's cognitive functions. Children with brain injury more often require systematic domain-by-domain assessment than do children with developmental disorders. The child with a learning disability may be well served by a more focused assessment. For example, a child with a learning problem who has excellent decoding skills may not require a detailed assessment of phonological processing skills. However, in a child with brain injury, such an assessment may be impor-

TABLE 9.5. Neuropsychological Assessment Procedures for Evaluation of Basic Areas of Competence in the Biobehavioral Systems Approach

I. Language
   A. Word Fluency
   B. Rapid Automatized Naming
   C. Auditory Analysis Test
   D. Token Test
   E. Peabody Picture Vocabulary Test—Revised
   F. Boston Naming Test

II. Visual–spatial and constructional skills
   A. Beery Developmental Test of Visual–Motor Integration
   B. Judgment of Line Orientation
   C. Test of Visual-Perceptual Skills

III. Somatosensory abilities
   Tactile Figure Test

IV. Motor skills
   A. Finger Tapping Test
   B. Grooved Pegboard Test
   C. Purdue Pegboard
   D. Bruininks–Oseretsky Test of Motor Proficiency

V. Memory and learning
   A. Wide Range Assessment of Memory—Story Recall, Design Recall subtests
   B. Continuous Recognition Memory Test
   C. Verbal Selective Reminding
   D. Nonverbal Selective Reminding

VI. Attention
   A. Continuous-performance test
   B. Verbal Cancellation Test

VII. Executive functions
   A. Wisconsin Card Sorting Test
   B. Tower of London
   C. Contingency Naming Test

tant because skills necessary for future development of reading may be impaired after injury. Well-automated decoding abilities prior to injury may be in large part preserved immediately post-injury, thereby obscuring a more insidious disorder in skill acquisition.

Intelligence Tests

As in any approach to neuropsychological assessment, measures of motor, perceptual–motor, and visual–spatial skills; language abilities; memory; attention; and executive functions are included. Formal intelligence testing is not considered paramount in the assessment process. Although intelligence tests are often utilized, they are frequently used to obtain data on specific abilities. Composite scores, although sometimes useful, must be interpreted with caution. Many schools require an intelligence test, so the results of intelligence testing will often be presented separately in order to facilitate acceptance of the report by the school. However, *intellectual assessment is not a necessary or sufficient condition of the assessment.*

It is certainly true that intelligence tests can be sensitive to the behavioral effects of brain injury. However, such measures provide only a limited assessment of various skills that are critical to the adaptation of children with brain injuries. In particular, memory, attentional, and problem-solving skills are not directly assessed by most IQ tests. A related issue is that an emphasis on IQ tests for brain-injured children can lead to misinterpretations of their ability structure. For example, recovery of IQ scores in children with severe TBI is fairly rapid, but problems with memory, attention, and problem-solving skills are much more persistent (Levin et al., 1995). Correlations between neuropsychological tests and measures of academic achievement are robust even when the relationship with IQ is partialed out of the correlations (Taylor, 1989). In general, IQ tests are predictive of general learning and achievement skills, but do not measure a full range of distinct processing abilities. It is often difficult, moreover, to draw conclusions concerning specific cognitive strengths and weaknesses from performance on intelligence tests.

The measures listed in Table 9.5 are generally well known and widely accepted at this time, and thus are not described in detail. These measures have some form of age norming, but the norms are often based on small, poorly defined samples and may be restricted to a particular geographic area. Consequently, it is common to emphasize the *pattern* of strengths and weaknesses across tests, as opposed to the level at which the child performs on any particular test (Rourke et al., 1986). More generally, a major goal of the assessment of cognitive traits is to identify skill dissociations. Areas of strength represent a potential avenue for intervention, and areas of weakness may provide important clues regarding injury consequences and potential cognitive mechanisms underlying the manifest disability. The *pattern* of test results and dissociations is always most critical to neuropsychologists, as opposed to the absolute level of performance on any particular test (Reitan & Wolfson, 1992; Rourke et al., 1986). Most neuropsychologists also assume that there will be some relationship between particular patterns of cognitive function and a given disorder (Morris, Francis, & Fletcher, 1993). These patterns may emerge as subtypes that are differentially related to biological and environmental factors.

Nonverbal Perceptual and Motor Skills

Impairments in motor, visual–spatial, and constructional abilities (II, III, and IV in Table 9.5) are common with many forms of congenital brain injury (e.g., spina bifida meningomyelocele). There is a very broad trend in these children toward relative preservation of language skills and compromise of nonverbal skills (Taylor et al., 1991). Rourke (1989) has noted that problems with nonverbal skill development are associated with a variety of forms of brain injury in children, representing what he terms the "nonverbal learning disability syndrome" (see Rourke, 1995). Equally important, however, is the assessment of memory and learning (V), attention (VI), and abilities commonly conceptualized as "executive functions" (VII). Individual children often vary in their profiles across these domains.

Memory and Learning Skills

A major emphasis is placed on the assessment of memory and learning skills in our work with brain-injured children. These measures have been derived from contemporary models of information processing that emphasize constructs of encoding, storage, and retrieval in the development of memory functions in children. Consequently, Table 9.5 includes verbal and nonverbal versions of selective reminding procedures (Buschke, 1974) to evaluate storage and retrieval skills in children. More recently, the California Verbal Learning Test—Children's Version has been developed and nationally standardized (Delis, Kramer, Kaplan, & Ober, 1994). This test provides a good basis for the assessment of encoding and retrieval skills in children with brain injury and has documented sensitivity to brain injury (Yeates et al., 1995). We also use measures of prose recall, and immediate and delayed conditions to evaluate contextual recall. In addition, recognition memory can be assessed by measures such as the Continuous Recognition Memory Test (Hannay, Levin, & Grossman, 1979).

The assessment of memory and learning is important because of the high frequency of memory problems in children in the brain disease. Careful assessment is imperative in analysis of the nature of the memory impairment. In many instances, the problem is not one involving memory systems; instead, it reflects poor attention on the part of the child. Memory disorders are also diverse. Deficits in this area can be distinguished according to the type of encoding (e.g., phonological vs. semantic), modality of preservation (e.g., verbal vs. nonverbal), type of storage (e.g., immediate vs. long-term, declarative vs. procedural), and even rehearsal strategies required (Lyon & Krasnegor, 1996).

Attentional Skills

In assessing children with brain injury, we also place special emphasis on assessment of attentional skills. In contrast to such problems in children with ADHD (Barkley, 1996), the attention problems in brain-injured children are less readily documented by history and rating scales and are often less overtly evident in general. Cognitive assessment is therefore needed to appreciate attentional deficits. As Table 9.5 shows, measures of focused attention, such as cancellation tests, are employed for this purpose. In general, when such tests are used it is important to rule out alternative explanations for poor performance, including weaknesses in motor skills or language impairment (Denckla, 1996). Computer-based measures, such as a continuous-performance test (see Mirsky, 1996), are also used. This is an area that needs more development. Mirsky (1996) has developed a general neuropsychological model of attention in children that separates five aspects of attentional functions: focus/execution, encoding, shifting, sustaining, and response stability. Each of these components can be operationalized with neuropsychological tests. Future research will help establish the possibility of subtypes of attention disorders in children with brain injury.

Executive Functions

Executive functions constitute a more inclusive category of skills. They subsume attention, but they also encompass planning, problem solving, task maintenance, generalization, strategy control and monitoring, self-regulation, and other metacognitive functions. Research on executive functions is having increasing influence on the neuropsychological assessment of children with brain injury. Deficits in executive skills have long been recognized as common sequelae of brain injury in adults and children, particularly frontal lobe injury (Fletcher, Levin, & Butler, 1995; Levin et al., 1993, 1995).

The construct of executive functions is also under investigation in several different areas of cognitive research. For example, in the area of memory, there has been an intense focus on metacognitive aspects of memory performance. Relevant research includes studies of factors such as the application and maintenance of strategies for learning and remembering, and subjects' awareness of their own role in remembering (Borkowski & Burke, 1996). More recent models of memory commonly emphasize the construct of "working memory." Pennington (1994) has defined working memory as "a computational area, in which information relevant to a current task is both maintained on-line and subjected to further processing" (p. 246). According to this conception, working memory is a type of "mental scratch pad" in which internal representations are made and resources can be allocated to other modules making up the cognitive system. Both animal and human studies support the prominent role of working memory as an executive component of cognition. Findings from animal studies suggest that working memory is mediated in part by the prefrontal cortex (Goldman-Rakic, 1994). Pennington (1994) has suggested that many brain injury syndromes produce cognitive deficits because of impairments in working memory, caused either by prefrontal brain damage or by insults to pathways connected to the prefrontal areas. Findings from studies of children with TBI involving damage to the frontal lobes are consistent with this hypothesis (Ewing-Cobbs, Fletcher, & Levin, 1995).

Emphasis has also been placed on assessment of executive functions as distinct ability constructs. Denckla (1996), for example, has described executive functions as control processes that are organized in a different manner than the more modular domains of cognition, such as language and visual–spatial functions. She lists a number of tests that are likely to be sensitive to executive functions, but stresses that these tests also measure other skills. Evaluation of performance may therefore require the type of qualitative analysis described by Bernstein and Waber (1990). Placing the measurement of executive functions into the broader context advocated as part of the biobehavioral systems approach also facilitates the subdivision of test performance into skill components that include executive functions (Taylor, 1996).

All the approaches to neuropsychological assessment described in this chapter emphasize the assessment of executive functions. In the various modifications of the Halstead–Reitan approach, these skills are measured with tests such as the Categories Test and the Trail Making Test (Part B). Pennington (1991) and Taylor and Fletcher (1990) list a number of measures of executive functions, including the Wisconsin Card Sorting Test, the Tower of Hanoi, and the Contingency Naming Test. Wilson (1986) and Bernstein and Waber (1990) emphasize behavioral observation and on-the-spot experimental assessments to evaluate executive functions. Bernstein and Waber (1990) also evaluate performance on measures such as the Rey–Osterrieth Complex Figure Test, which has significant perceptual, motor, and organizational components. Consistent with Denckla's (1996) recommendations, scoring systems have been developed to isolate each of these three components underlying test performance (Waber & Holmes, 1986).

Assessment of Psychosocial Traits

It is common when one is completing a neuropsychological evaluation to identify a number of behavioral, social, and motivational traits that influence not only test performance, but also the manifest disability (see Table 9.4). For example, children with spina bifida and hydrocephalus are often described as lacking in initiative, passive, and unmotivated (Wills, 1993). It is important to determine whether these characteristics are manifestations of the cognitive problems that such a child experiences, factors reflecting the child's adjustment to the handicap and family situation, or both. It is common to assess these factors with parent and teacher rating scales, such as the PIC-R (Wirt et al., 1990) and the CBCL (Achenbach, 1991). However, it is also apparent that these more generic scales are sometimes insensitive to the psychosocial traits or behavior deviations of greatest

relevance to the manifest disability. Scales such as the PIC-R and CBCL were designed to identify psychopathological factors influencing child adjustment more generally, and may be less applicable to children with brain injury. Measures that address adaptive behavior, such as the Vineland Adaptive Behavior Scales (Sparrow et al., 1984); measures of self-perception, such as the Self-Perception Profile for Children (Harter, 1985); or neurobehavioral manifestations of brain disease, such as the Pediatric Inventory of Neurobehavioral Symptoms (Roberts, 1992), may be more useful in brain-injured populations. Research on outcomes of TBI in children suggests that measures such as the CBCL and the PIC-R are insensitive to the effects of injury severity, whereas measures of adaptive behavior are more discriminating (Fletcher, Ewing-Cobbs, Miner, Levin, & Eisenberg, 1990). More recent research also demonstrates that parents of children with severe TBI are more aware of cognitive dysfunction than of behaviors associated with psychopathology (Fletcher et al., 1996). This does not mean that psychosocial traits are not relevant for the assessment of children with brain injury, but only that assessment procedures developed for mental health populations may be less relevant in evaluating children with brain injury.

Supplementing any attempt to obtain parent-based rating scales should be a similar attempt to obtain information from the teacher and other professionals working with a child, as well as a careful interview of the child and observations of the child during the evaluation and in an interview.

Assessment of Biological Variables

In evaluating a child with brain injury, it is critical to obtain as much information concerning the child's neurological condition as possible. Good starting points are an interview with the parent and completion of a detailed medical and developmental history. The results of neuroimaging studies and neurological evaluations should be reviewed. It may also be helpful to obtain information regarding pre- and perinatal complications, as well as the child's clinical condition during any periods of illness. In cases of hospitalization for TBI, a careful review of medical records is indicated. Moreover, review of serial GCS scores, the duration of impaired consciousness, intensive care unit notes concerning levels of intracranial pressure, neurosurgical procedures that may have been used, and the results of any neurological evaluations are all critical for appreciating the seriousness of TBI, establishing risks for injury sequelae, and deciding on follow-up procedures. The amount of time required by the child to move through the acute and subacute phases of injury also provides important information on injury severity and prognosis.

Table 9.6 provides a brief summary of relevant medical variables. It is important to keep in mind that direct evidence for neuropathology is sometimes absent, even in instances of obviously severe trauma with accompanying neurobehavioral consequences. This is why it is important to compare, for example, neuroimaging studies with a careful evaluation of the child's condition during the immediate postinjury period. Careful evaluation of location and extent of CNS lesions, including systemic and metabolic effects, is also important. Secondary complications involving hypoxia, hydrocephalus, edema, and other factors that produce superimposed diffuse effects on any specific injury must be considered as well. Table 9.6 also notes the need to evaluate the child's clinical condition acutely and over time, as well as late-emerging effects, such as atrophy and seizures. A recent review of studies of children with a variety of CNS disorders reveals that biological variables are clearly related to both cognitive and psychosocial traits (Fletcher, Levin, & Butler, 1995). Evaluating biological variables also sheds light on the extent to which child traits are affected by brain disease or injury, as opposed to postinjury psychosocial factors (Taylor, Drotar, et al., 1995). Finally, brain insults alter cognitive function, and in so doing permit analysis of how variations in cognitive skills affect ecologically relevant behavior and learning traits.

Assessment of Environmental Variables

The environmental influences on a child's development are multiple and clearly have a direct bearing on the child's psychosocial functioning. Table 9.7 summarizes some of the relevant variables, including family, school, and community factors. Cultural values, language background, social and educational opportunities, and parental attitudes are important environmental influences. Identifying sources of the child's manifest disability requires an understanding of the types of demands the environment places on the child. Identifying family factors, particularly those that produce stress in relationship to caretaking, is critically important. Caretaking stresses can arise from burdens imposed by everyday management of the child; related financial problems; or marital, other interpersonal, or intrapsychic problems of family members (Taylor, Drotar, et al., 1995). Understanding the child's placement in school is also important, particularly since the placement may not be appropriate and may induce feelings of failure and poor self-esteem. Actually reviewing the child's educational plan is a critical part of the evaluation of environmental influences.

Evaluating these sources is accomplished by interviewing the parent, obtaining teacher reports, and reviewing school records. More formal measures can also be used, such as assessments of life events, family environment, parental attitudes toward education, and child-rearing practices (Taylor, Drotar, et al., 1995). In general, scales of this type may be more useful for research, since it is not yet clear that these measures provide information beyond what can be obtained in a thorough clinical interview.

Interpretation and Management

When the assessment and analysis of the four sets of variables that constitute a biobehavioral systems

TABLE 9.6. Variables to Consider for Evaluation of Biological Factors

1. Etiology of the disorder
2. Underlying pathophysiological process
3. Location and extent of CNS lesion
4. Secondary complications
5. Treatment factors
6. The child's clinical condition acutely and over time
7. Late-emerging effects

TABLE 9.7. Environmental Factors That Influence the Relationship of the Manifest Disability and Basic Areas of Competence

I. Family
   1. Marital adjustment
   2. Familial stability
   3. Cultural background
   4. Financial resources

II. School
   1. Availability of resources
   2. Receptiveness to outside professionals
   3. Curriculum
   4. Eligibility guidelines

III. Community
   1. Availability of resources for child
   2. Parent support groups and advocacy associations

approach are completed, it is important to summarize information for the parents in language that they can understand (Pennington, 1991). It is usually helpful to inform the parents of general impressions of the child, including strengths and weaknesses; to obtain parental feedback to confirm these impressions and hypotheses; and to assist parents in reframing their perspective of the child. The feedback session also permits a dialogue with the family and helps reduce any resistance the parents may have to interpretations they may not have previously considered. It is usually helpful to review potential environmental and biological factors at this point, and to allow the family time to acknowledge these factors.

An emphasis on recommendations and programming possibilities is critically important. The eventual result should be a written report that incorporates a detailed treatment plan for the child (see Rourke et al., 1986). It is often necessary to make contact with the school, to have periodical consultations with the parents, and to monitor the child's response to the treatment plan over time. Recommendations must reflect an awareness of the availability of resources at the level of the school and community, and must provide a thorough assessment of all aspects of the manifest disability. In general, the results of assessment are best utilized to advocate for constructive action on behalf of the child.

CONCLUSIONS

The present chapter provides a comprehensive overview of the nature and assessment of brain injury in children. One of the primary purposes of providing this information is to highlight the differences between the types of cases seen by specialists in child versus adult neuropsychology. The causes of brain injury are clearly different in children and adults, and there are several major problems in extrapolating adult-based methods to children (Fletcher & Taylor, 1984). The five approaches to neuropsychological assessment in current use are also outlined. Although a major emphasis is placed on the biobehavioral systems approach, it is important to recognize that the five approaches overlap significantly and that variations in test selection are based primarily on personal preferences and training. There is little evidence that would support the use of one test battery over another. Nevertheless, the reliability and validity of testing have come under increasing scrutiny in recent years, and results provide information that is useful in test selection and interpretation (Brown, Rourke, & Cicchetti, 1989; Leckliter, Forster, Klonoff, & Knights, 1992; Taylor & Schatschneider, 1992a; Taylor et al., 1996).

The most important component of a neuropsychological assessment is not any part of the assessment itself, but the child neuropsychologist's knowledge of developmental and neurological disorders and of the types of cognitive, educational, and behavior problems that can accompany these disorders. This knowledge base provides a foundation for an understanding of the nature of the disorder, and for summarizing for parents and other professionals information related to the outcome and treatment of the disorder. There is a considerable literature that describes the cognitive and psychosocial functioning of children with various different types of brain insults. The clinical neuropsychologist must be able to summarize this information and integrate the results of the assessment with what is known about the disorder and with factors related to variability in outcomes. This information, when combined with the actual results of the evaluation, leads to a treatment plan that is reasonable and helpful to the child.

In order to accomplish these goals, assessment must place a major emphasis on evaluations of the child's behavior and cognitive development within a broad biopsychosocial context (Taylor & Schatschneider, 1992a). The biobehavioral systems framework emphasizes the need to evaluate presenting behavioral or learning problems as the first step in a more comprehensive analysis of the child traits and the biological and environmental factors that account for these problems. Children are developing organisms. Any attempt to understand a brain-injured child must consider a range of influences on development. Some of these influences are biological, but environmental factors are also critically important.

In the future, it is likely that assessment of children with brain injury will expand beyond an emphasis on psychometric approaches alone. Such expansion reflects increasing recognition of the contribution of the environmental context to outcomes, as well as some of the limitations of formal psychometric assessments. Procedures for examining the overt behavioral manifestations of brain insults, such as expressions of attentional or executive dysfunction, maladaptive behaviors, and problems in social cognition, are also likely to occupy a more prominent position in research and clinical work with children. Such approaches are not likely to replace psychometric assessments, but they will offer valuable new insights into the nature of the clinical disorders, with direct implications for intervention. A further trend is the emerging emphasis on observational paradigms, including discourse processing and observations of children in interpersonal situations. Performance on psychometric tests frequently fails to capture impairments in these areas. The use of observational paradigms is also likely to become more popular, as these methods are increasingly utilized in research on children with brain injury. More generally, the expanding data base on brain injury in children suggests that practitioners are likely to continue to work within the scientist/practitioner model. A continued focus on research will enhance our understanding of brain-related disabilities and will also improve clinical evaluation and treatment of the individual child.

ACKNOWLEDGMENTS

The writing of this chapter was supported in part by National Institutes of Health Grant Nos. NS25368, Neurobehavioral Development of Hydrocephalus Children; HD 27597, Neuropsychological Sequelae of Pediatric Head Injury; and NS21889, Neurobehavioral Outcomes of Head Injury in Children. It was also supported in part by Grant No. MCJ-390611 from the Maternal and Child Health Research Bureau (Title V, Social Security Act), Health Resources and Services Administration, U.S. Department of Health and Human Services, and M01-RR02558, the University Clinical Research Center at Hermann Hospital.

REFERENCES

Achenbach, T. M. (1991). *Manual for the Child Behavior Checklist/4–18 and 1991 Profile.* Burlington: University of Vermont, Department of Psychiatry.

Aldenkamp, A. P., Alpherts, W.C.J., Dekker, M.J.A., & Overweg, J. (1990). Neuropsychological aspects of learning disabilities in epilepsy. *Epilepsia, 31* (Suppl. 4), 509–520.

Aram, D. M. (1990). Brain lesions in children: Implications for developmental language disorders. In J. F. Miller (Ed.), *Research on child language disorders: A decade of progress,* (pp. 309–320). San Diego: College Hill Press.

Asarnow, R. F., Satz, P., Light, R., Zaucha, K., Lewis, R., & McClearly, C. (1995). The UCLA study of mild closed head injury in children and adolescents. In S. H. Broman & M. E. Michel (Eds.), *Traumatic head injury in children* (pp. 117–146). New York: Oxford University Press.

Barkley, R. A. (1996). Linkages between attention and executive functions. In G. R. Lyon & N. A. Krasnegor (Eds.), *Attention, memory, and executive function* (pp. 307–326). Baltimore: Paul H. Brookes.

Barkovich, A. J. (1995). *Pediatric neuroimaging* (2nd ed.). New York: Raven Press.

Baron, I.S., Fennell, E., & Voeller, K. (1995). *Pediatric neuropsychology in the medical setting.* New York: Oxford University Press.

Barnes, M. A., & Dennis, M. (1992). Reading in children and adolescents after early onset hydrocephalus and in normally developing age peers: Phonological analysis, word recognition, word comprehension, and passage comprehension skills. *Journal of Pediatric Psychology, 17,* 445–465.

Bayley, N. (1993). *Bayley Scales of Infant Development* (2nd ed.). San Antonio, TX: Psychological Corporation.

Bellugi, V., Wang, P.O., & Jernigan, T. L. (1994). Williams syndrome: An unusual neuropsychological profile. In S.H. Broman & J. Grafman (Eds.), *Atypical cognitive deficits in developmental disorders* (pp. 23–56). Hillsdale, NJ: Erlbaum.

Bernstein, J. H, & Waber, D. P. (1990). Developmental neuropsychological assessment: The systemic approach. In A. A. Boulton, G. B. Baker, & M. Hiscock (Eds.), *Neuropsychology: Vol. 17. Neuromethods* (pp. 311–371). Clifton, NJ: Humana Press.

Bijur, P. E., Haslum, M., & Golding, J. (1990). Cognitive and behavioral sequelae of mild head injury in children. *Pediatrics, 86,* 337–344.

Borkowski, J. G., & Burke, J. E. (1996). Theories, models, and measurements of executive functioning: An information processing perspective. In G. R. Lyon & N. A. Krasnegor (Eds.), *Attention, memory, and executive function* (pp. 235–263). Baltimore: Paul H. Brookes.

Breslau, N., Brown, G. G., Del Dotto, J. E., Kumar, S., Ezhuthachan, S., Andreski, P., & Hufnagle, K. G. (1996). Psychiatric sequelae of low birth weight at six years of age. *Journal of Abnormal Child Psychology, 24,* 385–400.

Broman, S. H., & Grafman, J. (Eds.). (1994). *Atypical cognitive deficits in developmental disorders: Implications for brain function.* Hillsdale, NJ: Erlbaum.

Broman, S.H., & Michel, M. E. (Eds.) (1995). *Traumatic head injury in children.* New York: Oxford University Press.

Brookshire, B. L., Fletcher, J. M., Bohan, T. P., Landry, S. H., Davidson, K. C., & Francis, D. J. (1995). Verbal and nonverbal skill discrepancies in children with hydrocephalus: A five-year longitudinal follow-up. *Journal of Pediatric Psychology, 20,* 785–800.

Brown, S. J., Rourke, B. P., & Cicchetti, D. V. (1989). Reliability of tests and measures used in the neuropsychological assessment of children. *The Clinical Neuropsychologist, 3,* 353–368.

Bruce, D. A. (1995). Pathophysiological responses of the child's brain following trauma. In S. H.

Broman & M. E. Michel (Eds.), *Traumatic head injury in children* (pp. 40–54). New York: Oxford University Press.

Buschke, H. (1974). Components of verbal learning in children: Analysis by selective reminding. *Journal of Experimental Child Psychology, 18,* 488–496.

Carlson-Green, B., Morris, R. D., & Krawiecki, N. (1995). Family and illness predictors of outcome in pediatric brain tumors. *Journal of Pediatric Psychology, 20,* 769–784.

Chapman, S. B. (1995). Discourse as an outcome measure in pediatric head injured populations. In S. H. Broman & M. E. Michel (Eds.), *Traumatic head injury in children* (pp. 95–116). New York: Oxford University Press.

Conners, C. K. (1990). *Conners Rating Scales.* North Tonawanda, NY: Multi-Health Systems.

Cull, C. A., & Trimble, M. R. (1989). Effects of anticonvulsant medications on cognitive functioning in children with epilepsy. In B. P. Hermann & M. Seidenberg (Eds.), *Childhood epilepsies: Neuropsychological, psychosocial, and intervention aspects* (pp. 83–104). New York: Wiley.

Del Bigio, M. R. (1993). Neuropathological changes caused by hydrocephalus. *Acta Neuropathologica, 85,* 573–585.

Delis, D. C., Kramer, J. H., Kaplan, E., & Ober, B. A. (1994). *California Verbal Learning Test—Children's Version.* San Antonio, TX: Psychological Corporation.

Denckla, M. B. (1996). A theory and model of executive function: A neuropsychological perspective. In G. R. Lyon & N. A. Krasnegor (Eds.), *Attention, memory, and executive function* (pp. 263–278). Baltimore: Paul H. Brookes.

Dennis, M. (1987). Using language to parse the young damaged brain. *Journal of Clinical and Experimental Neuropsychology, 9,* 723–753.

Dennis, M. (1988). Language in the young damaged brain. In T. Boll & B. K. Bryant (Eds.), *Clinical neuropsychology and brain function: Research measurement and practice* (pp. 85–123). Washington, DC: American Psychological Association.

Dennis, M. (1996). Hydrocephalus. In M. J. G. Beaumont, P. M. Kenealy, & J. C. Rogers (Eds.), *The Blackwell dictionary of neuropsychology* (pp. 406–411). Oxford: Blackwell.

Dennis, M., Jacennik, B., & Barnes, M. A. (1994). The content of narrative discourse in children and adolescents after early-onset hydrocephalus and in normally-developing age peers. *Brain and Language, 46,* 129–165.

Dennis, M., Spiegler, B. J., Fitz, C. R., Hoffman, H. J., Hendrick, E. B., Humphreys, R. P., & Chuang, S. (1991). Brain tumors in children and adolescents: II. The neuroanatomy of deficits in working, associative and serial-order memory. *Neuropsychologia, 29,* 829–841.

Dennis, M., Spiegler, B. J., Hoffman, H. J., Hendrick, E. B., Humphreys, R. P., & Becker, L. E. (1991).

Brain tumors in children and adolescents: I. Effects on working, associative and serial-order memory, IQ, age at tumor onset, and age of tumor. *Neuropsychologia, 29,* 813–828.

Dennis, M., Spiegler, B. J., Obonsawin, M. C., Maria, B. L., Cowell, C., Hoffman, H. J., Hendrick, E. B., Humphreys, R. P., Bailey, J. D., & Ehrlich, R. M. (1991). Brain tumors in children and adolescents: III. Effects of radiation and hormone status on intelligence and on working, associative and serial-order memory. *Neuropsychologia, 30,* 257–268.

Donders, J., Rourke, B. P., & Canady, A. I. (1992). Behavioral adjustment of children with hydrocephalus and of their parents. *Journal of Child Neurology, 7,* 375–380.

Dunn, R. M., & Markwardt, F. C. (1989). *Peabody Individual Achievement Test—Revised.* Circle Pines, MN: American Guidance Service.

Ewing-Cobbs, L., DuHaime, A. C., & Fletcher, J. M. (1995). Inflicted and noninflicted traumatic brain injury in infants and preschoolers. *Journal of Head Trauma Rehabilitation, 10,* 13–24.

Ewing-Cobbs, L., Fletcher, J. M., & Levin, H. S. (1995). Traumatic brain injury. In B. P. Rourke (Ed.), *Syndrome of nonverbal learning disabilities: Neurodevelopmental manifestations* (pp. 433–459). New York: Guilford Press.

Ewing-Cobbs, L., Levin, H. S., Fletcher, J. M., Miner, M. E., & Eisenberg, H. M. (1990). The Children's Orientation and Amnesia Test: Relationship to severity of acute head injury and to recovery of memory. *Neurosurgery, 27,* 683–691.

Fay, G. C., Jaffe, K. M., Polissar, N. L., Liao, S., Martin, K. M., Shurtleff, H. A., Rivara, J. B., & Winn, H. R. (1993). Mild pediatric traumatic brain injury: A cohort study. *Archives of Physical Medicine and Rehabilitation, 74,* 895–901.

Fletcher, J. M. (1988). Brain-injured children. In E. J. Mash & L. G. Terdal (Eds.), *Behavioral assessment of childhood disorders* (2nd ed., pp. 451–489). New York: Guilford Press.

Fletcher, J. M., Brookshire, B. L., Bohan, T. P., Brandt, M., & Davidson, K. C. (1995). Early hydrocephalus. In B.P. Rourke (Ed.), *Syndrome of nonverbal learning disabilities: Neurodevelopmental manifestations* (pp. 206–238). New York: Guilford Press.

Fletcher, J. M., Brookshire, B. L., Bohan, T. P., Davidson, K. C., Brandt, M., Landry, S. H., & Francis, D. J. (1996). Executive functions in children with early hydrocephalus. *Developmental Neuropsychology, 12,* 53–76.

Fletcher, J. M., Brookshire, B. L., Landry, S. H., Bohan, T. P., Davidson, K. C., Francis, D. J., Thompson, N. M., & Miner, M. E. (1995). Behavioral adjustment of children with hydrocephalus: Relationships with etiology, neurological, and family status. *Journal of Pediatric Psychology, 20,* 765–781.

Fletcher, J. M., & Copeland, D. R. (1988). Neuro-behavioral effects of central nervous system pro-phylactic treatment for childhood cancer. *Journal of Clinical and Experimental Neuropsychology, 10*, 495–537.

Fletcher, J. M., Ewing-Cobbs, L., Miner, M. E., Levin, H. S., & Eisenberg, H. M. (1990). Behavioral changes after closed head injury in children. *Journal of Consulting and Clinical Psychology, 58*, 93–98.

Fletcher, J. M., Francis, D. J., Thompson, N. M., Brookshire, B. L., Bohan, T. P., Landry, S. H., Davidson, K., & Miner, M. E. (1992). Verbal and nonverbal skill discrepancies in hydrocephalic children. *Journal of Clinical and Experimental Neuropsychology, 14*, 593–609.

Fletcher, J. M., Levin, H. S., Lachar, D., Kusnerik, L., Harward, H., Mendelssohn, D., & Lilly, M. A. (1996). Behavioral adjustment after pediatric closed head injury: Relationships with age, sever-ity, and lesion size. *Journal of Child Neurology, 11*, 283–290.

Fletcher, J. M., Levin, H. S., & Butler, I. J. (1995). Neurobehavioral effects of brain injury in chil-dren: Hydrocephalus, traumatic brain injury, and cerebral palsy. In M. Roberts (Ed.), *Handbook of pediatric psychology* (2nd ed., pp. 362–383). New York: Guilford Press.

Fletcher, J. M., & Taylor, H. G. (1984). Neuropsycho-logical approaches to children: Towards a devel-opmental neuropsychology. *Journal of Clinical Neuropsychology, 6*, 39–56.

Fletcher, J. M., Taylor, H. G., Levin, H. S., & Satz, P. (1995). Neuropsychological assessment of chil-dren. In H. I. Kaplan & B. J. Sadock (Eds.), *Com-prehensive textbook of psychiatry* (6th ed., pp. 581–601). Baltimore: Williams & Wilkins.

Goldman-Rakic, P. S. (1994). Specification of higher cortical functions. In S. H. Broman & J. Grafman (Eds.), *Atypical cognitive deficits in developmen-tal disorders* (pp. 3–17). Hillsdale, NJ: Erlbaum.

Grimwood, K., Anderson, V. A., Bond, L., Catroppa, C., Hre, R. L., Keir, E. H., Nolan, T., & Robert-son, D. M. (1995). Adverse outcomes of bacterial meningitis in school-age survivors. *Pediatrics, 95*, 646–656.

Hack, M., Taylor, H. G., Klein, N., Eiben, R., Schat-schneider, C., & Mercuri-Minich, N. (1994). School-age outcomes in children with birth-weights under 740 g. *New England Journal of Medicine, 331*, 753–759.

Harter, S. (1985). *Self-Perception Profile for Children.* Denver, CO: University of Denver.

Hannay, H. J., Levin, H. S., & Grossman, R. G. (1979). Impaired recognition memory after head injury. *Cortex, 15*, 269–283.

Hayes, S. C., Gifford, E. V., & Ruckstuhl, Jr., L. E. (1996). Relational frame theory and executive function: A behavioral approach. In G. R. Lyon & N. A. Krasnegor (Eds.), *Attention, memory, and*

executive function (pp. 279–306). Baltimore: Paul H. Brookes.

Hofman, K. J., Harris, E. L., Bryan, N., & Denckla, M. B. (1994). Neurofibromatosis type 1: The cog-nitive phenotype. *Journal of Pediatrics, 124*, 51–58.

Jaffe, K. M., Fay, G. C., Polissar, N. L., Martin, K. M., Shurtleff, H., Rivara, J. B., & Winn, H. R. (1992). Severity of pediatric traumatic brain injury and early neurobehavioral outcome: A cohort study. *Archives of Physical Medicine and Rehabilitation, 73*, 540–547.

Kaufman, A. F. (1992). *Kaufman Test of Educational Achievement.* Circle Pines, MN: American Guid-ance Service.

Klein, S. K. (1991). Cognitive factors and learning disabilities in children with epilepsy. In O. Devin-sky & W. H. Theodore (Eds.), *Epilepsy and be-havior* (pp. 171–179). New York: Wiley–Liss.

Kraus, J. F. (1995). Epidemiological features of brain injury in children: Occurrence, children at risk, causes and manner of injury, severity, and out-comes. In S. H. Broman & M. E. Michel (Eds.), *Traumatic head injury in children* (pp. 22–39). New York: Oxford University Press.

Landry, S. H., Jordan, T. J., & Fletcher, J. M. (1994). Developmental outcomes for children with spina bifida and hydrocephalus. In M. B. Tramontana & S. R. Hooper (Eds.), *Advances in child neuro-psychology* (Vol. 2, pp. 85–117). New York: Springer-Verlag.

Leckliter, I. N., Forster, A. A., Klonoff, H., & Knights, R. M. (1992). A review of reference group data from normal children for the Halstead–Reitan Neuropsychological Test Battery for Older Chil-dren. *The Clinical Neuropsychologist, 6*, 201–229.

Levin, H. S., Aldrich, E. F., Saydjari, C., Eisenberg, H. M., Foulkes, M. A., Bellefleur, M., Luerssen, T. G., Jane, J. A., Marmarou, A., Marshall, L. F., & Young, H. F. (1992). Severe head injury in children: Experience of the Traumatic Coma Data Bank. *Neurosurgery, 31*, 435–444.

Levin, H. S., Culhane, K. A., Mendelssohn, D., Lilly, M. A., Bruce, D., Fletcher, J. M., Chapman, S. B., Harward, H., & Eisenberg, H. M. (1993). Cognition in relation to magnetic resonance im-aging in head-injured children and adolescents. *Archives of Neurology, 50*, 897–905.

Levin, H. S., Ewing-Cobbs, L., & Eisenberg, H. M. (1995). Neurobehavioral outcome of pediatric closed head injury. In S.H. Broman & M.E. Michel (Eds.), *Traumatic head injury in children* (pp. 70–94). New York: Oxford University Press.

Lyon, G. R., & Krasnegor, N. A. (Eds.). (1996). *Atten-tion, memory, and executive function.* Baltimore: Paul H. Brookes.

Mash, E., & Terdal, L. (Eds.). (1988). *Behavioral as-sessment of childhood disorders* (2nd ed.). New York: Guilford Press.

Mathers, C. D., & Field, B. (1983). Some international

trends in the incidence of neural tube defects. *Community Health Studies, 7,* 60–66.

McCarthy, D. (1972). *McCarthy Scales of Children's Abilities.* New York: Psychological Corporation.

McIlvane, W. J., Dube, W. V., & Callahan, T. D. (1996). Attention: A behavior analysis perspective. In G.R. Lyon & N.A. Krasnegor (Eds.), *Attention, memory, and executive function* (pp. 97–118). Baltimore: Paul H. Brookes.

Menkes, J. (1995). *Textbook of child neurology* (5th ed.). Philadelphia: Lea & Febiger.

Mirsky, A. F. (1996). Disorders of attention: A neuropsychological perspective. In G. R. Lyon & N. A. Krasnegor (Eds.), *Attention, memory, and executive function* (pp. 71–96). Baltimore: Paul H. Brookes.

Morris, R. D., Francis, D. J., & Fletcher, J. M. (1993). Conceptual and psychometric issues in the neuropsychological assessment of children: Measurement of ability discrepancy and change. In I. Rapin & S. Segalovitz (Eds.), *Handbook of neuropsychology* (Vol. 7, pp. 341–352). Amsterdam: Elsevier.

Moss, H. A., Brouwers, P., Wolters, P. L., Wiener, L., Hersh, S., & Pizzo, P. A. (1994). The development of a Q-sort behavioral rating procedure for pediatric HIV patients. *Journal of Pediatric Psychology, 19,* 27–46.

Nelson, K. B., Swaiman, K. F., & Russman, B. S. (1993). Cerebral palsy. In K. Swaiman (Ed.), *Principles of pediatric neurology* (pp. 471–488). St. Louis, MO: C. V. Mosby.

Palumbo, D. R., Davidson, P. W., Peloquin, L. J., & Gigliotti, F. (1995). Neuropsychological aspects of pediatric infectious diseases. In M. Roberts (Ed.), *Handbook of pediatric psychology* (2nd ed., pp. 342–361). New York: Guilford Press.

Pennington, B. F. (1991). *Diagnosing learning disorders: A neuropsychological framework.* New York: Guilford Press.

Pennington, B. F. (1994). The working memory function of the prefrontal cortices: Implications for developmental and individual differences in cognition. In M. M. Haith, J. Benson, R. Roberts, & B. F. Pennington (Eds.), *Future oriented processes in development* (pp. 243–289). Chicago: University of Chicago Press.

Raimondi, A. J. (1994). A unifying theory for the definition and classification of hydrocephalus. *Child's Nervous System, 10,* 2–12.

Reitan, R. M., & Wolfson, D. (1992). *Neuropsychological evaluation of older children.* Tucson, AZ: Neuropsychology Press.

Roberts, M. A. (1992). *Pediatric Inventory of Neurobehavioral Symptoms.* Iowa City: University of Iowa, Department of Pediatrics.

Rourke, B. P. (1989). *Nonverbal learning disabilities: The syndrome and the model.* New York: Guilford Press.

Rourke, B. P. (Ed.). (1995). *Syndrome of nonverbal learning disabilities: Neurodevelopmental manifestations.* New York: Guilford Press.

Rourke, B. P., Fisk, J., & Strang, J. (1986). *Neuropsychological assessment of children.* New York: Guilford Press.

Rovet, J. (1995). Turner syndrome. In B. P. Rourke (Ed.), *Syndrome of nonverbal learning disabilities: Neurodevelopmental manifestations* (pp. 351–371). New York: Guilford Press.

Russell, W. R., & Smith, A. (1961). Post-traumatic amnesia and closed head injury. *Archives of Neurology, 5,* 4–17.

Shaywitz, B. A., & Fletcher, J. M. (1993). Neurologic, cognitive, and behavioral sequelae of hypoxic–ischemic encephalopathy. *Seminars in Perinatology, 17,* 357–366.

Sparrow, S., Balla, D., & Cicchetti, D. (1984). *Vineland Adaptive Behavior Scales.* Circle Pines, MN: American Guidance Service.

Spreen, O., Risser, A. H., & Edgell, D. (1995). *Developmental neuropsychology* (rev. ed.). New York: Oxford University Press.

Squire, L. R. (1987). *Memory and brain.* New York: Oxford University Press.

Taylor, H. G. (1989). Neuropsychological testing: Relevance for assessing children's learning disabilities. *Journal of Consulting and Clinical Psychology, 56,* 795–800.

Taylor, H. G. (1996). Critical issues and future directions in the development of theories, models, and measurements for attention, memory, and executive functions. In G. R. Lyon & N. A. Krasnegor (Eds.), *Attention, memory, and executive function* (pp. 399–412). Baltimore: Paul H. Brookes.

Taylor, H. G., Drotar, D., Wade, S., Yeates, K., Stancin, T., & Klein, S. (1995). Recovery from traumatic brain injury in children: The importance of the family. In S. H. Broman & M. E. Michel (Eds.), *Traumatic head injury in children* (pp. 188–218). New York: Oxford University Press.

Taylor, H. G., & Fletcher, J. M. (1990). Neuropsychological assessment of children. In G. Goldstein & M. Hersen (Eds.), *Handbook of psychological assessment* (2nd ed., pp. 228–255). New York: Pergamon Press.

Taylor, H. G., Hack, M., Klein, N., & Schatschneider, C. (1995). Achievement in children with birthweights less than 750 grams with normal cognitive abilities: Evidence for specific learning disabilities. *Journal of Pediatric Psychology, 20,* 703–719.

Taylor, H. G., Mills, E. L., Ciampi, A., duBerger, R., Watters, G. V., Gold, R., MacDonald, N., & Michaels, R. H. (1990). The sequelae of *Haemophilus influenzae* meningitis in school-age children. *New England Journal of Medicine, 323,* 1657–1663.

Taylor, H. G., & Schatschneider, C. (1992a). Academic achievement following childhood brain disease: Implications for the concept of learning disabilities. *Journal of Learning Disabilities, 25,* 630–638.

Taylor, H. G., & Schatschneider, C. (1992b). Child neuropsychological assessment: A test of basic assumptions. *The Clinical Neuropsychologist, 3,* 259.

Taylor, H. G., Schatschneider, C., Petrill, S., Barry, C. T., & Owens, C. (1996). Executive dysfunction in children with early brain disease: Outcomes post *Haemophilus influenzae* meningitis. *Developmental Neuropsychology, 12,* 35–51.

Taylor, H. G., Schatschneider, C., & Rich, D. (1991). Sequelae of *Haemophilus influenzae* meningitis: Implications for the study of brain disease and development. In M. Tramontana & S. Hooper (Eds.), *Advances in child neuropsychology* (Vol. 1, pp. 50–108). New York: Springer-Verlag.

Teasdale, G., & Jennett, B. (1974). Assessment of coma and impaired consciousness: A practical scale. *Lancet, ii,* 81–84.

Thorndike, R. L., Hagen, E. P., & Sattler, J. M. (1988). *The Stanford–Binet Intelligence Scale* (4th ed.). Chicago: Riverside.

Volpe, J. L. (1989). Intraventricular hemorrhage in the premature infant–current concepts: Part I. *Annals of Neurology, 25,* 3–11.

Waber, D. P., & Holmes, J. M. (1986). Assessing children's memory productions of the Rey–Osterrieth Complex Figure. *Journal of Clinical and Experimental Neuropsychology, 8,* 264–280.

White, B. J. (1994). The Turner syndrome: Origin, cytogenetic variants, and factors influencing the phenotypes. In S. H. Broman & J. Grafman (Eds.), *Atypical cognitive deficits in developmental disorders: Implications for brain function* (pp. 183–196). Hillsdale, NJ: Erlbaum.

Wilkinson, G. S. (1993). *Wide Range Achievement Test—3.* Wilmington, DE: Jastak.

Wills, K. E. (1993). Neuropsychological functioning in children with spina bifida and/or hydrocephalus. *Journal of Clinical Child Psychology, 22,* 247–265.

Wilson, B. (1986). Neuropsychological assessment of preschool children. In S. Filskov & T. J. Boll (Eds.), *Handbook of clinical neuropsychology* (Vol. 2, pp. 121–171). New York: Wiley.

Wirt, R. D., Lachar, D., Klinedinst, J. K., & Seat, P. D. (1990). *Multidimensional description of child personality: A manual for the Personality Inventory for Children.* Los Angeles: Western Psychological Services.

Woodcock, R. W. (1988). *Woodcock–Johnson Psycho-Educational Test Battery.* Allen, TX: DLM Teaching Resources.

Yeates, K. O., Enrile, B. G., Loss, N., Blumenstein, E., & Delis, D. (1995). Verbal learning and memory in children with myelomeningocele. *Journal of Pediatric Psychology, 20,* 801–816.

Chapter Ten

HEALTH-RELATED DISORDERS

Suzanne Bennett Johnson
James R. Rodrigue

For many centuries, the drugs or remedies prescribed by the medical profession were worthless or even harmful; the physician's effectiveness was dependent upon psychological factors (i.e., the placebo effect), as well as the body's remarkable ability to heal itself (Shapiro, 1978). In the 17th century, van Leeuwenhoek improved his microscopes and discovered creatures too small to be seen by the naked eye. It was two more centuries before Pasteur and Koch developed the germ theory of disease. The notion of germs causing disease had several important consequences. The development by Lister of aseptic techniques resulted in drastic reductions in fatalities from operations. The development of vaccines and sanitation to prevent certain diseases, and the production of effective antibiotic and antiviral agents, substantially reduced morbidity from acute infectious diseases (Miller, 1983; O'Dougherty, 1983). At the beginning of this century, the leading causes of death were influenza, pneumonia, diphtheria, tuberculosis, and gastrointestinal infections; today few people die of these disorders. Medicine's conquest of infectious disease has produced a major change in the health problems facing industrialized societies. Table 10.1 shows that the most frequently cited causes of death in the United States in 1990 were chronic diseases and injuries. However, McGinnis and Foege (1993) have made a convincing argument that *actual* causes of death are not diseases but behaviors: smoking, poor diet and exercise habits, alcohol and other substance use, accidents associated with firearms or motor vehicles, and unsafe sexual behavior (see Table 10.1). Many of these high-risk behaviors begin in childhood or adolescence.

This changing pattern of health and illness characterizes child as well as adult populations. For centuries, children were the common victims of infectious disease. With acute illness more successfully controlled, chronic diseases have become more evident. Improvements in the management of chronic conditions have further prolonged life, making chronic illness a larger part of pediatric practice (Haggerty, 1984). Insulin, for example, was discovered in 1922. Before then, children with diabetes typically lived less than a year; now they have a life expectancy approximately 75% of normal (Travis, Brouhard, & Schreiner, 1987). Strides

TABLE 10.1. Leading Causes of Death in the United States in 1990

Cited	Actual
1. Heart disease	1. Tobacco
2. Cancer	2. Diet/activity
3. Cerebrovascular disease	3. Alcohol
4. Accidents	4. Microbial agents
5. Chronic obstructive pulmonary disease	5. Toxic agents
6. Pneumonia/influenza	6. Firearms
7. Diabetes mellitus	7. Sexual behavior
8. Suicide	8. Motor vehicles
9. Chronic liver disease/ cirrhosis	9. Illicit use of drugs

Note. From J. McGinnis and W. Foege (1993, p. 2208). Copyright 1993 by the American Medical Association. Reprinted by permission.

have also been made in the treatment of childhood cancer; cure rates have increased from 20% in the early 1950s to 50% in the late 1980s (Cecalupo, 1994). Cystic fibrosis remains a fatal disease, but longevity has improved steadily over the years: 50% of these youngsters are now surviving into adulthood (McCoy, 1994).

Chronically ill children are now accounting for larger portions of pediatric practice; the overall rate of children with any chronic condition is usually estimated at 10–30% (Cadman, Boyle, Szatmari, & Offord, 1987; Gortmaker & Sappenfield, 1984; Newacheck, 1994). Table 10.2 provides prevalence rates for childhood chronic disease or chronic conditions for youngsters under 18 years of age living in the United States in 1988 (Newacheck, 1994). An estimated 31% had one or more chronic conditions. Most had mild conditions resulting in no limitations in childhood activities, but approximately 10% of children had serious conditions resulting in more than occasional distress and/or limitations in daily functioning. In the United States, poverty is associated with a higher prevalence of severe chronic conditions (Newacheck, 1994).

It is no surprise that physically ill children use disproportionate amounts of health care services. An interesting study by Smyth-Staruch, Breslau, Weitzman, and Gortmaker (1984) compared hospitalization and the use of outpatient services during a 1-year period by 369 children with cystic fibrosis, cerebral palsy, myelodysplasia, or multiple physical handicaps. A random sample of 456 children without congenital conditions served as controls. The average chronically ill or disabled child used 10 times more services than the average comparison child. However, great heterogeneity was noted within the ill or disabled group. All hospital care was accounted for by one-third of the children. Three-quarters of all outpatient care was accounted for by one-quarter of the sample. The small subset of ill youngsters who utilized most of the health care services were not confined to one diagnostic group. In other words, health service utilization varied dramatically within each diagnostic category.

In the United States, health care utilization also varies by socioeconomic status. Children with chronic conditions living in poverty are twice as likely to be uninsured and 18 times more likely to have Medicaid coverage, whereas children living in more affluent homes are three times more likely to be privately insured. Insurance translates into access to outpatient care; sick children with insurance receive more outpatient care than sick children without insurance. However, factors other than insurance availability also seem to be involved. Poor children with insurance use outpatient health care services less than their more affluent peers (Newacheck, 1994). Some of these factors may be economic (e.g., transportation problems), but some may be ethnic or cultural (e.g., distrust of, or lack of comfort with, the established health care system). Although poor children use outpatient health care services less, they are hospitalized more (Newacheck, 1994). This could be a result of the fact that poor children experience more serious disorders, or it may be the result of their reduced use of outpatient services, which are often designed to prevent hospitalizations.

The current U.S. health care debate often centers around cost and access; those in greatest need are often denied access because of the increased cost. Although poor children may receive health care under Medicaid and more affluent children may have private insurance through a parent's family coverage, chronically ill youngsters are often denied health insurance once they become adults, because they are deemed to have "preexisting" conditions. Providers and families who care for chronically ill youngsters are often frustrated by the barriers within the current health care system that serve to deny these children access to a lifetime of adequate health care.

TABLE 10.2. 1988 Prevalence of Chronic Conditions among U.S. Children under 18 Years of Age

Condition	Cases per 1,000
Musculoskeletal impairments	15.2
Deafness and hearing loss	15.3
Blindness and vision impairment	12.7
Speech defects	26.2
Cerebral palsy	1.8
Diabetes	1.0
Sickle cell disease	1.2
Anemia	8.8
Asthma	42.5
Respiratory allergies	96.8
Eczema and skin allergies	32.9
Epilepsy and seizures	2.4
Arthritis	4.6
Heart disease	15.2
Frequent or repeated ear infections	83.4
Frequent diarrhea/bowel trouble	17.1
Digestive allergies	22.3
Frequent or severe headaches	25.3
Other	19.8

Note. From Newacheck (1994, p. 1146).

PSYCHOLOGICAL ASPECTS
OF CHRONIC ILLNESS:
A HISTORICAL PERSPECTIVE

The current interest in psychological aspects of physical conditions is nothing new. Hippocrates, for example, believed in a strong association between personality types (melancholic, phlegmatic, sanguine, and choleric) and physical symptoms (Hawkins, 1982). Galen claimed that 60% of his patients had symptoms that were emotionally rather than organically induced (Shapiro, 1978). Although the interplay between the psychological and the physical has long been a topic of discussion, theories concerning this interplay have changed. In the 17th century, René Descartes argued that the mind and body are distinct entities with different laws of causality. This mind–body dualism strongly influenced Western thinking. The terms "psychosomatic" or "psychophysiological" began to be used to describe physical disorders caused by psychological factors. Attempts were made to classify illness as psychosomatic, somatoform, or organic (Bakal, 1979).

From the 1930s to the 1950s, influenced by psychoanalytic theory, various personality types were specified as etiologically involved with certain diseases (Dunbar, 1955). Investigators compared ill populations to healthy controls, using measures of personality, psychopathology, or adjustment. However, the empirical data generated did not support the theory; specific personality types were not consistently associated with specific diseases (Latimer, 1979).

Today, there is a greater interest in psychological factors that influence health status and adjustment *within* an illness population. Patients with a specific illness are now seen as heterogeneous rather than homogeneous (i.e., some do better than others). As a consequence, research is now directed at psychological factors that may be related to health and functioning in patients suffering from a particular illness. The psychological factors studied have changed as well. Instead of focusing only on general measures of psychological functioning and adjustment, researchers are paying greater attention to disease-specific behavior. Disease-related pain and discomfort, patients' knowledge about the disease, and adherence behaviors are becoming primary concerns for many psychologists working in health care settings. Furthermore, the interplay between the psychological and the physical is presumed to be determined by a number of interacting variables. Influenced by both behavioral and systems theories, investigators now view a patient as functioning within a social context. Disease variables, patient variables, and environmental variables (most notably the family and the health care setting) all interact. The patient is no longer studied in isolation. This is particularly true for pediatric practices, since children are so strongly influenced by their family environment.

CURRENT ASSESSMENT MODELS

Changing theories mean changing conceptualizations underlying psychological assessments. Psychoanalytic models resulted in patient-oriented assessments; behavioral and systems models mean that the patient must be assessed within a social context. Assessments are often made of multiple persons (e.g., patient, parents, peers, health care providers), as well as of multiple variables. Usually the role of the disease itself, the characteristics of the child, and the family's functioning are considered. Peer relationships, cultural factors, and health care providers' behavior are other social context variables sometimes assessed. Both general functioning and disease-specific functioning are usually evaluated. Always, the complex, bidirectional interaction of the variables involved must be kept in mind (see Figure 10.1).

Although this multivariate complexity is generally accepted, there is a tendency to simplify the conceptual model underlying an assessment, depending upon the identified reason for the patient's or family's referral. Many chronically ill children receive psychological evaluations because of poor health or suspected noncompliance. In such a case, the patient's poor health is often presumed to be a product of the patient's behavior (e.g., noncompliance), which in turn is presumed to be a product of the social environment. Assessment in this case is directed at the patient's behavior and environmental factors that may be supporting inappropriate behavior or interfering with appropriate behavior (unidirectional model 1, Figure 10.1). With young children, parents are presumed to play a primary role in the management of the disease. An alternative conceptual model places the social context (in this case, the parents' behavior) in direct rather than indirect association with the patient's health status (unidirectional model 2, Figure 10.1), changing the conceptual assumptions underlying the assessment.

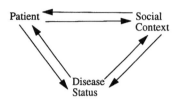

Bidirectional Model

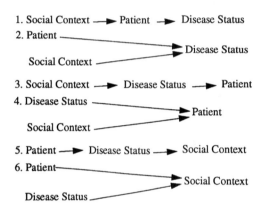

FIGURE 10.1. Bidirectional and various unidirectional models of assessment.

In other cases, the patient's low self-esteem, depression, or poor acceptance of the disease may be the primary reason for referral. In this case, unidirectional models 3 and 4 (Figure 10.1) are often considered. The child's poor health may result in inadequate psychological adjustment in the child, and the youngster's health may be primarily a product of inadequate parental management of the disease (unidirectional model 3). More commonly, the effects of both disease status and social context on the patient's adjustment are considered (unidirectional model 4).

Occasionally, some aspect of the patient's social environment is the reason for the assessment. A parent may feel depressed and helpless over a teenager's poor health, which is presumed to be the direct result of noncompliant behavior on the part of the patient. A health care provider may feel equally helpless and frustrated (unidirectional model 5). Or a parent may be having trouble adjusting to the possibility of a child's death and may feel overwhelmed by the patient's manipulative,

demanding, or regressive behaviors (unidirectional model 6).

The unidirectional models depicted in Figure 10.1 are, of course, components of the larger bidirectional model. From both clinical and research standpoints, it is often useful to consider these simpler unidirectional models, so long as their place in the larger context is not forgotten. Often a model used initially in assessment is discarded and replaced with other models. For example, an adolescent may be referred for evaluation for poor diabetes control. The evaluation may initially be conceptualized in terms of unidirectional models 1 or 2. Perhaps it is determined that the youngster is so severely depressed that the depression should be the initial focus of treatment. In this case, the assessment focus changes, and the model or models underlying the assessment change as well.

DIAGNOSTIC CLASSIFICATION

Children with medical conditions, like physically healthy children, may meet the criteria for any one of a number of disorders in the *Diagnostic and Statistical Manual of Mental Disorders*, fourth edition (DSM-IV; American Psychiatric Association, 1994). However, certain DSM-IV categories and diagnoses are especially relevant to physically ill youngsters. The group of mental disorders due to a general medical condition is one such DSM-IV category. However, for a child to receive a diagnosis in this category (e.g., Personality Change Due to a General Medical Condition, Anxiety Disorder Due to a General Medical Condition), the presenting symptoms must be the direct *physiological* consequence of the medical condition. Although mental and physical disorders can and do co-occur, this diagnostic category should not be used unless there is an etiological link via a known *physiological* mechanism between the medical condition and the psychological or behavioral symptoms (e.g., when hypothyroidism is the direct cause of depressive symptoms). The group of substance-related disorders (e.g., Substance-Induced Mood Disorder, Substance-Induced Anxiety Disorder) is a similar diagnostic category, relevant to symptom presentation that is a direct result of medication administration or its withdrawal. Factitious disorders (e.g., Factitious Disorder with Predominantly Physical Signs and Symptoms), in which physical or psychological symptoms are feigned, are rarely diagnosed in children. However, physically ill youngsters are very familiar with the sick role and may learn to mimic symptoms they have experienced as part of their medical condition (e.g., a child with epilepsy may feign a seizure; a child with diabetes may fake an insulin reaction). If a child's physical complaints do not appear to be intentionally produced and cannot be fully explained by the child's medical condition, the child may meet the diagnostic criteria for one of the somatoform disorders. For example, if pain complaints predominate, a subtype of Pain Disorder should be considered. Nevertheless, pain associated with a medical condition is *not* considered a mental disorder. Only when psychological factors are deemed to be a significant component in the onset, severity, exacerbation, or maintenance of the pain should a Pain Disorder diagnosis be considered (e.g., Pain Disorder Associated with Both Psychological Factors and a General Medical Condition). Subtypes of Adjustment Disorder (e.g., Adjustment Disorder with Depressed Mood, Adjustment Disorder with Anxiety) are far more common. The disorder may be acute (e.g., in response to the diagnosis of an illness) or chronic (e.g., in response to the multiple repeated stresses associated with an illness). However, an Adjustment Disorder diagnosis should not be made if the youngster's symptoms represent a normal reaction to the stress of learning to live with a serious medical illness. Only when symptoms or distress are in excess of what would be normally expected should an Adjustment Disorder diagnosis be given. One of the most prevalent DSM-IV diagnoses seen in medically ill youngsters referred for psychological assistance is Psychological Factors Affecting Medical Conditions; the diagnostic criteria for this are presented in Table 10.3. The diagnostician chooses the name from the following options, based on the nature of the psychological factors affecting the medical condition: Mental Disorder Affecting . . . [Indicate the General Medical Condition] (e.g., a child's Oppositional Defiant Disorder interferes with the medical management of the child's cystic fibrosis); Psychological Symptoms Affecting . . . [Indicate the General Medical Condition] (e.g., an adolescent's depressed mood interferes with adequate diabetes self-care); Personality Traits or Coping Style Affecting . . . [Indicate the General Medical Condition] (e.g., a youngster who denies the seriousness of an illness may skip medications for the treatment of the youngster's cancer); Maladaptive Health Behaviors Affecting . . . [Indicate the General Medical Condition] (e.g., a child with diabetes who eats sweets and high-fat foods will be in poor metabolic control); or Stress-Related

---

TABLE 10.3. DSM-IV Diagnostic Criteria for Psychological Factors Affecting Medical Condition

A. A general medical condition is present.

B. Psychological factors adversely affect the general medical condition in one of the following ways:
   (1) the factors have influenced the course of the general medical condition as shown by a close temporal association between the psychological factors and the development or exacerbation of, or delayed recovery from, the general medical condition
   (2) the factors interfere with the treatment of the general medical condition
   (3) the factors constitute additional health risks for the individual
   (4) stress-related physiological responses precipitate or exacerbate symptoms of the general medical condition

Note. From American Psychiatric Association (1994, p. 678). Copyright 1994 by the American Psychiatric Association. Reprinted by permission.

Physiological Response Affecting . . . [Indicate the General Medical Condition] (e.g., stress-related airway restriction may precipitate an attack in an asthmatic child).

The DSM-IV's multiaxial system can provide a useful way to capture the complexity of a medically ill youngster's condition. On Axis I, the clinical disorders just discussed are coded. Personality disorders and Mental Retardation are coded on Axis II. Axis II codes are important because they too may interfere with the medical management of the child (e.g., a mentally retarded adolescent will require far more parental supervision of medical care than an intellectually normal youngster). The youngster's medical condition is coded on Axis III, while Axis IV highlights the psychosocial or environmental issues (e.g., family conflict; poor school performance; inadequate access to appropriate health care) that may interfere with or complicate the child's care. Axis V provides a global assessment of the youngster's functioning. However, only the youngster's psychosocial functioning is to be rated; physical limitations associated with the medical illness are excluded.

Although many physically ill youngsters may meet criteria for an Axis I diagnosis, many will not. Most young people living with chronic medical conditions cope remarkably well—a testament to the resilience of these youths (Johnson, 1994a). Behavioral assessment and intervention should not be limited to those with an Axis I diagnosis; both can prove useful to all children with physical disorders. Furthermore, psychological assessments of childhood chronically ill populations differ from more traditional mental health assessments, in that sophistication is required about diseases, medical management (e.g., medications used and their side effects), and disease-related behaviors (e.g., dietary constraints, exercise prescriptions, disease-monitoring behaviors). Consequently, this chapter addresses disease-specific assessment methods, as well as issues relevant to the more traditional assessment of a patient's and family's general functioning.

GENERAL FUNCTIONING

In addition to assessing how the child and his or her family cope with the patient's disease, the clinician typically assesses the patient's general psychological and social adjustment and may conduct similar assessments of other family members.

Patient Functioning

Although most studies have focused on the child's general psychological adaptation, there has been recent increased interest in school performance and peer relationships as well.

Psychological Adjustment

As mentioned previously, there is a relatively large literature comparing chronically ill and physically healthy children on traditional measures of psychological adjustment. Reviews of these studies offer little support for a "disease-specific personality," nor do they suggest that psychopathology is characteristic of most children facing chronic disease. Nevertheless, there is good evidence that a minority (e.g., 20–30%) of chronically ill children do have adjustment problems, and that the number of such children is larger than would be expected among physically healthy youngsters (Bennett, 1994; Gortmaker, Walker, Weitzman, & Sobol, 1990; Lavigne & Faler-Routman, 1992; Pless, 1984). In a population-based survey study, Cadman et al. (1987) estimated that 14% of healthy youngsters had one or more psychiatric disorders, compared to 23% of chronically ill youngsters. Ill youngsters who were disabled (i.e., who had limitations in physical functioning or activities of daily living) were particularly likely to have a psychiatric disorder, with a prevalence estimate of 33%. Although 67% of the ill children had seen a physician in the previous 6 months,

only 28% of those with a co-occurring psychiatric disorder had received specialized mental health services during this interval. However, mental health service utilization among physically ill youngsters with psychiatric difficulties was higher than among physically healthy youngsters experiencing similar psychiatric problems; only 11% of healthy children who needed mental health services had received them.

Studies designed to assess the psychological adjustment of physically ill youngsters often rely on standard measures of child adjustment, such as the Child Behavior Checklist (Achenbach, 1991). However, since standard measures of adjustment were developed and validated with physically healthy youngsters, questions have been raised concerning their appropriateness for physically ill children (e.g., Perrin, Stein, & Drotar, 1991). Some items on these measures involve somatic complaints (e.g., fatigue, dizziness, vomiting, stomachaches) that are indicative of psychological difficulties in healthy children but could be the consequence of a disease process in ill children. Hence, in some cases, physically ill youngsters may obtain inflated scores (suggesting greater psychological maladjustment) purely as a function of their medical condition. Consequently, caution should be exercised when psychological assessment instruments developed with healthy populations are applied to youngsters with chronic medical disorders.

Although it appears that children whose health is compromised face an increased risk of psychological difficulties, there exists considerable variability in adaptation both within and between diseases. Disease status and family context appear to be the variables most consistently related to psychological adjustment (Lavigne & Faler-Routman, 1993).

Disease Status

Disease type, illness severity, appearance, and functional impairment have all been linked to youngsters' psychological adjustment. A recent meta-analysis of the literature indicates that more serious illnesses, ones with a poorer prognosis, and ones involving greater functional impairment are associated with poorer psychological adaptation; physical appearance per se has not been consistently associated with behavioral or emotional adjustment (Lavigne & Faler-Routman, 1993). Children with sensory or neurological disorders appear to be particularly at risk (Lavigne & Faler-Routman, 1992), possibly because many of these children have significant functional impairment. Walker and Greene (1991) developed the Functional Disability Inventory for school-age children and adolescents. The 15-item child form is provided in Table 10.4. A parent form, which includes the same items but in reference to the parent's child, is available as well. The instrument has been used with both acutely and chronically ill youngsters, appears reliable when used with both young patients and their parents, discriminates between physically ill and well children, appears sensitive to changes in health status, and exhibits expected associations to measures of psychological adjustment (e.g., somatization, depression, and anxiety).

Most studies of patient adjustment and disease status are predicated on the assumption that disease status plays a causal role in patient adjustment (similar to unidirectional models 3 and 4 in Figure 10.1). As mentioned previously, for purposes of hypothesis testing, it sometimes makes sense to specify such unidirectional causal models. Nevertheless, most available studies are correlational, making interpretation of findings sometimes difficult. Although it seems likely that conditions associated with brain abnormalities "cause" learning and behavior problems, an association between anxiety, depression, or low self-esteem on the one hand and the frequency of asthma attacks on the other may be more difficult to explain. Poor health may lead to poor patient adjustment, but poor adjustment may as easily lead to poor health. Longitudinal studies in which change is induced in one variable (e.g., health status), and concomitant change is observed in a second variable (e.g., adjustment), can sometimes help delineate the causal nature of a documented association between variables. Staudenmayer (1982), for example, evaluated 63 asthmatic children's anxiety in three areas (despair over social debilitation, quality of life, and dread of illness) before and after treatment at a specialty hospital. After treatment, the patients had fewer asthma attacks, experienced less interference with physical activities, and missed fewer school days. Both before and after treatment, measures associated with poor health (i.e., number of days spent in a hospital, school days missed, emergency room visits) were significantly related to patient anxiety: Those youngsters in poorer health were more anxious. However, high anxiety before treatment was *not* associated with poorer treatment outcome; in fact, quite the opposite occurred. On some measures of illness-related debilitation (i.e., number of asthma attacks, emergency room visits, days hospitalized), higher pretreatment anxiety was associated with greater

pre- to posttreatment improvement. For other measures (i.e., number of school days missed, parental ratings of interference with strenuous physical activities), treatment was equally effective for low- and high-anxiety patients. The authors interpreted their findings as supporting the causal role of medical management in patient adjustment. Anxiety, rather than causing poor health, appeared to be the consequence of poor medical control of the disease.

Since the Staudenmayer (1982) study attempted to change health status while measuring concomitant change in the patients' psychological functioning, it offers a more convincing demonstration of the causal role health status may play in patients' adjustment than do correlational studies conducted at a single point in time. Nevertheless, it remains possible that the treatments employed, although primarily medical, had psychological sequelae (e.g., the patients had confidence in the new treatment, which led to reductions in anxiety and depression and to a more optimistic outlook on life), which in turn led to improvements in health status. Interpretation of studies linking health status to patient adjustment will always be difficult, because of our inability to experimentally manipulate all relevant variables while continually monitoring patients under controlled conditions. Ethically, we cannot randomly assign patients to diseases; we cannot deliberately make patients worse; and we cannot repeatedly monitor patients' psychological and physical status in a noninvasive manner. However, the consistency of the available literature does suggest that poor health can lead to adjustment problems in some patients. This possibility is certainly deserving of attention during any psychological assessment of a chronically ill child.

Family Context

Since family context is an important determinant of psychological adjustment in healthy youngsters, it is not surprising that it is an important predictor of psychological status in physically ill children as well. In a now classic study, Pless, Roghmann, and Haggerty (1972) documented the relationship among child adjustment, family functioning, and chronic illness in a large sample of youngsters living in upstate New York; 209 chronically ill children were compared to 113 healthy controls. Using semistructured household interviews, parent and teacher ratings, and the child's responses to a self-esteem inventory, the investigators rated each youngster on a mental health adjustment

TABLE 10.4. Functional Disability Inventory—Child Form

When people are sick or not feeling well, it is sometimes difficult for them to do their regular activities. In the last few days, would you have had any physical trouble or difficulty doing these activities?

	No Trouble	A Little Trouble	Some Trouble	A Lot of Trouble	Impossible
1. Walking to the bathroom.	No Trouble	A Little Trouble	Some Trouble	A Lot of Trouble	Impossible
2. Walking up stairs.	No Trouble	A Little Trouble	Some Trouble	A Lot of Trouble	Impossible
3. Doing something with a friend (for example, playing a game).	No Trouble	A Little Trouble	Some Trouble	A Lot of Trouble	Impossible
4. Doing chores at home.	No Trouble	A Little Trouble	Some Trouble	A Lot of Trouble	Impossible
5. Eating regular meals.	No Trouble	A Little Trouble	Some Trouble	A Lot of Trouble	Impossible
6. Being up all day without a nap or rest.	No Trouble	A Little Trouble	Some Trouble	A Lot of Trouble	Impossible
7. Riding the school bus or traveling in the car.	No Trouble	A Little Trouble	Some Trouble	A Lot of Trouble	Impossible
8. Being at school all day.	No Trouble	A Little Trouble	Some Trouble	A Lot of Trouble	Impossible
9. Doing the activities in gym class (or playing sports).	No Trouble	A Little Trouble	Some Trouble	A Lot of Trouble	Impossible
10. Reading or doing homework.	No Trouble	A Little Trouble	Some Trouble	A Lot of Trouble	Impossible
11. Watching TV.	No Trouble	A Little Trouble	Some Trouble	A Lot of Trouble	Impossible
12. Walking the length of a football field.	No Trouble	A Little Trouble	Some Trouble	A Lot of Trouble	Impossible
13. Running the length of a football field.	No Trouble	A Little Trouble	Some Trouble	A Lot of Trouble	Impossible
14. Going shopping.	No Trouble	A Little Trouble	Some Trouble	A Lot of Trouble	Impossible
15. Getting to sleep at night and staying asleep.	No Trouble	A Little Trouble	Some Trouble	A Lot of Trouble	Impossible

Note. From Walker and Greene (1991, pp. 54–56). Copyright 1991 by Plenum Publishing Corporation. Reprinted by permission.

index and each family on a family functioning index. Both family functioning and health status appeared to contribute to a child's adjustment. Chronically ill youngsters and those from more dysfunctional families showed more adjustment problems. However, youngsters who were victims of a chronic illness and who lived in poorly functioning families had the highest incidence of psychological disturbance. This was particularly true for older youngsters, suggesting that there may be a cumulative effect over time of poor health and an unfavorable family situation. A recent meta-analysis of the available literature has provided important confirmation of these early findings: Poor maternal adjustment, marital discord, and family conflict are all associated with poorer psychological adjustment in physically ill children (Lavigne & Faler-Routman, 1993). Family stress can make management of a child's chronic illness more difficult, and it can exacerbate the course of chronic illness for the child by affecting adherence behaviors and/or physiological and biochemical functioning (Brand, Johnson, & Johnson, 1986; Kager & Holden, 1992; Patterson, 1985; Patterson & Garwick, 1994; Patterson, McCubbin, & Warwick, 1990; Wysocki, 1993).

Nevertheless, it is often difficult to ascertain whether dysfunctional family patterns existed prior to a child's illness or emerged as a consequence of the illness. Similarly, it may be that certain family patterns characteristic of "normal" or healthy populations can have more dysfunctional consequences in chronically ill populations. Simonds (1977), for example, compared 40 youths in good diabetes control to 40 patients in poor control and 40 nondiabetic youngsters. The youths in good diabetes control appeared to be in the best mental health, living in families with fewer interpersonal conflicts and lower rates of divorce. The youngsters in poor control were similar to the nondiabetic controls. These results suggest the interesting hypothesis that a family may need to be unusually psychologically healthy to manage the demands of a child with a chronic illness.

School Adjustment

There is increasing evidence that children with chronic medical conditions experience an increased prevalence of school-related problems. They miss more days of school than their healthy counterparts (Fowler, Johnson, & Atkinson, 1985; Weitzman, 1986; Weitzman, Walker, & Gortmaker, 1986) and are more likely to have repeated a grade or received remedial services (Cadman

et al., 1987). However, there is considerable within- and between-disease variability (Fowler et al., 1985; Gortmaker et al., 1990). As would be expected, children with conditions associated with brain abnormalities such as epilepsy and spina bifida frequently perform poorly on achievement tests (Fowler et al., 1985; Wills, Holmbeck, Dillon, & McLone, 1990). However, academic problems (including sometimes subtle neuropsychological impairments) have been documented in a variety of other diseases and conditions, including recurrent otitis media (Feagans, Sanyal, Henderson, Collier, & Appelbaum, 1987; Roberts, Burchinal, & Campbell, 1994), leukemia (Williams, Ochs, Williams, & Mulhern, 1991), hemophilia (Colegrove & Huntzinger, 1994; Loveland et al., 1994), liver disease (Stewart, Campbell, McCallon, Waller, & Andrews, 1992; Stewart et al., 1991), Turner syndrome (McCauley, Ross, Kushner, & Cutler, 1995), short stature (Stabler et al., 1994), and diabetes (Ryan, 1990). There are multiple possible etiologies for these academic difficulties, including missed instruction because of school absences, insults to the brain as a consequence of the disease process or its treatment, and differential parental and teacher expectations of ill children compared to their healthy counterparts.

Although many school districts did not offer services to physically handicapped or medically ill children before the 1970s, the Education for All Handicapped Children Act of 1975 guarantees educational services to these youngsters. Today, even those afflicted with acquired immune deficiency syndrome (AIDS) must be provided educational services (Kermani, 1988; Spencer, Zanga, Passo, & Walker, 1986). By law, children must be educated in the least restrictive environment and with healthy peers, if possible. The school is required to administer necessary medications in order for an ill youngster to remain in school. However, there is sometimes conflict between the school's and parents' or health care providers' preferences for educating a child. The school may prefer a more restrictive approach, such as providing home-bound instruction, and may be reluctant to provide necessary care (e.g., insulin injections or blood glucose testing in a youngster with diabetes); by contrast, the parents and health care providers may consider it important for the child to be educated within the context of a normal classroom environment. Often a health care provider must become involved in educating school personnel so that they become sufficiently comfortable caring for a child while the youngster attends school.

Peer Relationships

As might be expected, some children with chronic medical conditions experience peer relationship difficulties, but most do not (Cadman et al., 1987; Colegrove & Huntzinger, 1994; Graetz & Shute, 1995; Lemanek, Horwitz, & Ohene-Frempong, 1993; Nassau & Drotar, 1995; Noll, Bukowski, Davies, Koontz, & Kulkarni, 1993; Perrin, Ramsey, & Sandler, 1987; Stabler et al., 1994). Peer sociometric ratings may be more sensitive to differences between ill and healthy children than self-, parent, or teacher ratings may be (Armstrong, Rosenbaum, & King, 1992).

Studies of healthy children's attitudes toward disabled peers suggest that type of disability, prior experience with children who have a particular disability, the social context, the disabled children's age and gender, and views about the children's role or responsibility in acquiring their disability are all influential (Harper, Wacker, & Cobb, 1986; Newberry & Parrish, 1986; Royal & Roberts, 1987; Santilli & Roberts, 1993; Sigelman & Begleym, 1987). Older female children, who have had prior experiences with youngsters who have a particular disability, have more positive attitudes. Situations that do not place an ill child at a disadvantage result in more favorable peer attitudes. Similarly, if peers perceive a child as having no responsibility or role in the acquisition of the condition, more positive peer attitudes result. However, children with AIDS may experience less peer acceptance than youngsters with other types of chronic conditions (Santilli & Roberts, 1993).

Developmental Issues

As a child grows older, social and cognitive as well as physical changes occur. These changes interact with the changing nature of the disease itself. Consequently, when evaluating a child's psychological, social, and school adjustment, both the child's development and the development of the disease must be considered. For example, longitudinal work by Kovacs, Brent, Steinberg, Paulauskas, and Reid (1986) suggests that anxiety and depression may be heightened at the time of disease diagnosis but may dissipate thereafter. The impact of certain disease processes may be particularly powerful at certain developmental periods. For example, neuropsychological impairment may be more likely if a disease is present at times of critical brain development (Ryan, 1990; Stewart et al., 1991, 1992). Similarly, disease-related interference with normal processes of social and cognitive development may place a youngster at increased risk for social, emotional, or behavioral problems.

Family Functioning

In addition to assessing a child's general psychological functioning, the clinician is also concerned with the impact of the child's illness on the family. Childhood chronic illness may affect families by increasing financial and caregiving burdens, disrupting daily routines and activities, and/or reducing social opportunities outside of the family. Measures are now available to assess illness impact on the family, although traditional psychological tests are often used. Specific instruments that may prove useful include the Impact on Family Scale (Stein & Riessman, 1980), the Parenting Sense of Competence Scale (Gibaud-Wallston & Wandersman, 1978; Johnston & Mash, 1989), the Coping Health Inventory for Parents (McCubbin, 1987), and the Family Inventory of Resources for Management (McCubbin & Comeau, 1987), among others. In addition, family interaction tasks developed for use with families of healthy youngsters experiencing parent–adolescent conflict (e.g., the Unrevealed Differences Task; Henggeler & Tavormina, 1980) can be adapted for use in families with childhood chronic disease. In this task, each individual family member is asked to respond independently to eight items (see Table 10.5 for sample items) by rank-ordering the available options in order of preference. Upon completion, individual responses are collected, and family members are instructed to respond to the same items as a family and to resolve any conflicts as they occur. Interactions are then scored for warmth, control, and conflict (Henggeler et al., 1986).

Financial Burden

The financial impact of childhood chronic illness, though clearly relevant in the context of any clinical evaluation, has not been the focus of much research. Socioeconomic status has been used as a covariate or correlate in numerous child health studies, but this construct does not adequately capture the financial burden experienced in families with a chronically ill child. Furthermore, research has suggested that the perceived financial burden may vary both across illness types and within families. For instance, Rodrigue and his colleagues have shown that fathers perceive more financial burden than do mothers, and that this

TABLE 10.5. The Unrevealed Differences Task: Sample Items for Families with a Chronically Ill Adolescent

The best thing about our family is how we:
_____ talk about our personal feelings
_____ support and encourage each other
_____ take care of ourselves
_____ help each other out when needed
_____ have strong ties with other relatives

The teenager was supposed to be at home by 6:00 P.M. to take daily medication. It is now 8:30 P.M. when the teenager comes home. How should this problem be handled?
_____ the parents and teenager should sit down and discuss the teenager's reasons for staying out later than s/he was supposed to
_____ the teenager should be told to come home and take medications on time in the future
_____ the teenager should keep the medication with her/him at all times
_____ the teenager should be warned that if s/he is late in taking medication again, s/he will be grounded for four weeks
_____ the parents should tell the teenager that they are very angry and disappointed with him

In our family we need more:
_____ giving up things for each other
_____ closeness and loyalty
_____ love
_____ individual freedom
_____ discipline

The teenager is doing things that the doctor has said would make her/his illness worse. How should this situation be handled?
_____ the parents and the teenager should sit down and explain to the teenager how not following the doctor's recommendations could affect her/his health and future
_____ the teenager should be told to stop disobeying the doctor's recommendations
_____ the teenager should lose television, stereo, and computer privileges for a week
_____ the parents should take the teenager back to the doctor and have the doctor discuss these issues with the teenager
_____ the parents should tell the teenager that they are very angry and disappointed with her/him

Note. Adapted from S. W. Henggeler (personal communication, June 1996). Adapted by permission of the author.

discrepancy persists over time (Rodrigue et al., 1996; Rodrigue, Morgan, & Geffken, 1992).

In survey studies, approximately 60% of parents with severely disabled children feel they have financial problems (Satterwhite, 1978). One or both parents often take on supplemental employment, leaving less time for the children and for each other (McCollum, 1971). How well a child's illness is controlled has a direct bearing on the family's finances, as more seriously ill children require more frequent and more expensive medical intervention (McCollum, 1971; Vance & Taylor, 1971). In addition to costs of medicines, special equipment, and hospitalizations, there are less obvious expenses associated with prescribed diets, custom-made clothing, special living arrangements, travel to see the doctor, time off work for medical visits, and increased insurance premiums. For some children, health insurance is unavailable; insurance companies refuse coverage, citing the youngsters' "preexisting" condition. Furthermore, costs may persist even after successful medical treatment of a serious chronic disease. For instance, families of children who have successfully undergone transplantation for liver or kidney disease face medications costs up to $3,000 per month for life, and must pay enormously high insurance premiums; monthly installments on medical and hospital bills become lifetime obligations.

Family and Social Impact

A youngster's illness may affect relationships both within and outside of the family (e.g., Hamlett, Pellegrini, & Katz, 1992; Kazak, Segal-Andrews, & Johnson, 1995; Roberts & Wallander, 1992; Shapiro, 1983; Thompson, 1985). In survey studies, a substantial minority of parents report increased friction between parents (9–20%) and reductions in social activities for the parents outside the family context (12–35%; Satterwhite, 1978). Divorce rates are not higher than those found in the general population (Begleiter, Burry, & Harris, 1976; Lansky, Cairns, Hassanein, Wehr, & Lowman, 1978; Lavigne, Traisman, Marr, & Chasnoff, 1982; Sabbeth & Leventhal, 1984). However, the effects of a child's chronic illness on marital relationships may be too subtle to be indexed by divorce rates. Some studies suggest that marital stress may be more common among parents of chronically ill children and may be influenced by the severity and longevity of the illness (Ferrari, 1984; Lansky et al., 1978; Sabbeth & Leventhal, 1984), although not all studies have found deleterious effects (e.g., Sabbeth & Leventhal, 1984; Spaulding & Morgan, 1986). Measures that can more sensitively assess the influence of a child's illness on spouse communication, support, and time spent together need to be developed.

Family interactions, as well as marital relationships, may be influenced by a child's illness. Parents report feeling that their child's illness has affected family satisfaction and family adjustment (e.g., Ferrari, Matthews, & Barabas, 1983; Gayton, Friedman, Tavormina, & Tucker, 1977), and that the stressors within the family (e.g., role definitions and expectations, finances, child rearing) increase during the child's hospitalization (Rodrigue et al., 1996). However, more recent well-controlled investigations have found few relationship differences between chronically ill and healthy families (e.g., Wysocki, 1993). It is possible that chronic illness per se may not interfere with family interactions, but that certain types of chronic conditions may have a more negative impact than others.

Many parents struggle with disciplinary issues in regard to their youngsters. These can be particularly salient with a chronically ill child, and may lead to feelings of inadequacy in the parenting role (Rodrigue, Geffken, Clark, & Fishel, 1994). Although a few studies point toward the resilience of parents in managing the behavior of an ill child (Boll, Dimino, & Mattsson, 1978; Davies, Noll, DeStefano, Bukowski, & Kulkarni, 1991; Ievers, Drotar, Dahms, Doershuk, & Stern, 1994), others provide evidence that parenting styles differ in families of chronically ill versus healthy children. Parents may view themselves as more dominant and strict when dealing with a sick son or daughter (Long & Moore, 1979), whereas siblings may see parents as overindulgent and overprotective of the ill child (Cairns, Clark, Smith, & Lansky, 1979). Indeed, sick role theory posits that expectations of responsibility and behavior change when a child is ill; consequently, the sick child may not be held responsible for normal role behavior (Parsons, 1951; Whitt, 1984). Consistent with this theory, Walker, Garber, and Greene (1993) found that children with recurrent pain perceived their parents as giving them relief from usual responsibilities and granting them special privileges. These perceptions existed even when there was no identifiable organic basis for a child's pain symptoms. In a subsequent investigation, Walker, Garber, and Van Slyke (1995) found that the misbehavior of children with medically explained pain was viewed as less intentional and more excusable than the misbehavior of children with medically unexplained pain, depression, or no physical illness. Ill children were held less responsible for their misbehavior, and parents were less likely to respond to such misbehavior with anger, disappointment, or punishment. These findings are consistent with earlier research by Peterson (1972), who found that overtly sick youths perceived both their parents and siblings

as treating them better because of their illness, although parents were also perceived as more controlling. Furthermore, these youngsters admitted to pretending to be ill more often than did their healthy peers. Clearly, parents' attributions and reactions to a child's misbehavior may vary with illness type and symptomatology; some patients may use their illness to get things they want or to avoid experiences or responsibilities they dislike.

Personal Strain

Childhood chronic illness may cause personal distress not only for the patient, but for family members who must react daily to the youngster's disease. Although the patient has been the primary focus of most adjustment-to-illness studies, there is a small literature assessing the impact of childhood chronic illness on mothers, fathers, and siblings.

Mothers, in particular, appear to experience increased distress associated with parenting a chronically ill child (Patterson, Leonard, & Titus, 1992; Speltz, Armsden, & Clarren, 1990; Tarnowski, Rasnake, Gavaghan-Jones, & Smith, 1991; Wysocki, Huxtable, Linscheid, & Wayne, 1989). Depression, anxiety, and somatic complaints have been noted (Fielding et al., 1985; Forgays, Hasazi, & Wasserman, 1992; Hodges, Kline, Barbero, & Flannery, 1985; Miller, Gordon, Daniele, & Diller, 1992; Walker & Greene, 1989; Wallander, Varni, Babani, Banis, et al., 1989). Perhaps this is not surprising, since mothers are the primary caretakers of chronically ill children (Hauenstein, 1990). However, a number of factors appear to influence maternal adaptation: the severity of a child's illness; the extent of the burden placed on the mother for the child's daily care; family context (e.g., family support or conflict); and maternal coping style (Berenbaum & Hatcher, 1992; Breslau, Staruch, & Mortimer, 1982; Kronenberger & Thompson, 1992; McKinney & Peterson, 1987; Mullins et al., 1991; Thompson et al., 1994; Thompson, Gustafson, Hamlett, & Spock, 1992; Walker, Van Slyke, & Newbrough, 1992; Wallander, Varni, Babani, DeHaan, et al., 1989). Mothers caring for more seriously ill or more functionally impaired youngsters; mothers experiencing greater daily stress, more family conflict, and less family support; and mothers who use more avoidant coping styles appear to be more poorly adjusted.

Fewer data are available on the impact of childhood chronic illness on fathers, possibly because fathers are less involved in their children's daily care (Hauenstein, 1990). Some studies report more emotional disturbance among fathers than among mothers (Gayton et al., 1977); others report similar levels of distress for mothers and fathers (Fielding et al., 1985); and still others report greater distress in mothers (Borner & Steinhausen, 1977; Patterson et al., 1992; Tavormina, Boll, Dunn, Luscomb, & Taylor, 1981). Studies of fathers with ill children compared to fathers of healthy youngsters provide similar inconsistencies (Borner & Steinhausen, 1977; Cummings, 1976).

There is a somewhat larger literature on sibling adjustment. Reviews suggest that the presence of a chronically ill child within a family is not consistently associated with emotional or behavioral problems in healthy siblings (Drotar & Crawford, 1985; Lobato, Faust, & Spirito, 1988). However, recent data from a population survey (Cadman, Boyle, & Offord, 1988) and a multisite collaborative study (Sahler et al., 1994) suggest that although most physically healthy siblings are well adjusted, there is an increased prevalence of behavioral and emotional problems in siblings of chronically ill youngsters compared to siblings of well children.

Several investigators have suggested variables that may moderate the effect of a child's illness on a sibling's adjustment. Lavigne and Ryan (1979) provide evidence that the more visible the disease, the more likely it is that a sibling will develop emotional or behavioral problems. Hoare (1984) found that siblings of newly diagnosed epileptics were no more disturbed than children from the general population. However, siblings who had lived with an epileptic brother or sister for some time did show more adjustment problems, suggesting that the impact of the illness may take its toll over time. Ferrari (1984) found that same-sex siblings had more emotional and behavioral difficulties than did opposite-sex siblings. However, since siblings of male ill children only were studied, it is difficult to interpret these findings, since male children typically obtain scores indicating a greater prevalence of psychological difficulties. Lobato (1983) has pointed out that firstborn female children assume greater responsibility for care of siblings than either firstborn male children or later-born children of either sex. Consequently, a female child older than an ill child may be particularly vulnerable. Lobato presents supporting evidence for this hypothesis from studies of older female siblings of retarded children. Breslau, Weitzman, and Messenger (1981) reported similar results in their analysis of the impact on siblings of cystic fibrosis, cerebral palsy, myelodysplasia, and other multiple handicaps.

When one considers the literature on patient, parent, and sibling adjustment, it becomes apparent that there is no simple association between childhood chronic illness and psychological dysfunction in the patient or in family members. Several different variables have been postulated as moderators of illness impact. These include the visibility, severity, and disabling nature of the disease, as well as whether or not the central nervous system is involved. Disease duration, sibling sex, and birth order have also been implicated, as have family context and coping style. No doubt there are other moderator variables worthy of consideration. Of course, different variables may moderate illness impact for different members of the family.

Developmental Issues

Since many chronic conditions exhibit a changing course over time, the personal strain experienced by all family members may change as a function of disease processes. For example, the time of disease diagnosis is associated with heightened anxiety that dissipates over time. However, maternal adjustment at the time of diagnosis appears to predict long-term adjustment up to 6 years later: Mothers who cope poorly with the news of a child's illness may continue to have difficulty managing the disease on a daily basis (Kovacs et al., 1985, 1990). Similarly, certain periods during the child's growth and development may be associated with increased parental strain. For example, the preschool period may be particularly difficult because of the child's limited verbal ability (Speltz et al., 1990; Walker, Ford, & Donald, 1987; Wysocki et al., 1989). Adolescence always presents a number of challenges; the presence of a chronic disease or condition may add further strain to an already difficult developmental period (Walker et al., 1987).

Mastery

Although studies typically presume that a child's illness will have a negative influence on marital relationships, it is possible that there are positive effects as well. In fact, in a study involving 158 couples of children with chronic illness, Walker, Manion, Cloutier, and Johnson (1992) found that marital adjustment was significantly higher in this group than in a standardization sample consisting of couples with healthy youngsters.

Stein and Riessman (1980) suggested that there may be positive as well as negative consequences of childhood chronic illness on the family. They termed the positive consequences "mastery." Few studies have addressed this issue, as the impact of the illness has generally been presumed to be negative. Sargent et al. (1995) found that siblings of children with cancer identified positive as well as negative effects of the cancer diagnosis. Positive outcomes were more often identified by older siblings. Ferrari (1984) reported that mothers of patients with diabetes and mothers of pervasively developmentally delayed youngsters rated their ill children's siblings as more socially competent, compared to similar ratings made by mothers of healthy children. Siblings of the patients with diabetes were also viewed by their teachers as more prosocial. These results may be interpreted in a number of ways. Siblings of ill children may learn to be more empathetic and helpful. Or mothers of ill or disabled children may rate siblings differently than mothers of healthy youngsters do, because an ill child provides a different basis for comparison. Clearly, more empirical research is needed on the potentially positive effects of living in a home with a chronically ill child.

DISEASE-SPECIFIC FUNCTIONING

Most of the studies reviewed above under "General Functioning" can be characterized by unidirectional models 3 through 6 in Figure 10.1; they focus on how the disease (in conjunction with other factors) affects the psychological functioning of a patient, a parent, a sibling, or the family as a whole. Although some knowledge about the patient's illness is required, assessments of this type often use methods and measures typically employed in traditional mental health care settings. These include self-report questionnaires, checklists, and interviews. The better studies use standardized measures with some documented reliability and normative data. Rarely have observational procedures been employed.

Historically, studies of psychological functioning in relationship to health and illness have focused on the patient's general psychological adjustment. Given their training, many mental health professionals have retained this focus. The pediatrician, however, is often more interested in patient and family behavior that is directly relevant to the patient's health status.

Both chronic and acute illness usually require a variety of health-related behaviors. Nevertheless, chronic and acute illness differ in several important respects. Not only is acute illness short-lived,

but the goal of treatment is often to cure the illness. There is typically no cure for a chronic disease; the goal is to manage the illness appropriately and to minimize functional disability. Because the disease management process often lasts the patient's lifetime, the patient or parent becomes the primary health care provider. Although the physician remains involved, it is the patient and family who must manage the patient's illness on a daily basis.

The remainder of this chapter focuses on patient and parent behaviors that are directly relevant to managing and coping with childhood chronic illness (unidirectional models 1 and 2 in Figure 10.1). Assessment procedures relevant to the pain and discomfort associated with the illness, knowledge of the disease, and adherence behaviors will be discussed. Factors that may interfere with adherence are considered as well.

Pain and Discomfort

Pain or discomfort can be an acute, relatively short-lived experience or a continuous, chronic state. It may be predictably associated with a particular event (e.g., receiving an injection), or it may be an unpredictable symptom of underlying physical pathology (e.g., a brain tumor). The pain experience itself can differ in severity (e.g., excruciating vs. uncomfortable) and quality (e.g., piercing, throbbing, aching).

Varni, Katz, and Dash (1982) have offered a four-category description of pediatric pain: (1) pain associated with an observable physical injury (e.g., a cut); (2) pain associated with a disease state; (3) pain associated with a medical or dental procedure; and (4) pain not associated with a well-defined disease or physical injury. Since this chapter addresses medical illness, the acute pain associated with the first category is not discussed further here. However, all three remaining categories have relevance to assessment issues in childhood chronic disease.

Pain Associated with Chronic Disease

A number of childhood chronic illnesses have painful symptomatology. Juvenile rheumatoid arthritis, for example, is a disease of the connective tissues that results in joint stiffness and pain. Chronic joint pain also occurs in patients with hemophilia, because of internal hemorrhaging. Children with cancer may suffer pain associated with tumor growth. Sickle cell anemia can produce severe pain when a patient's sickle-shaped cells block the flow of oxygen into the capillaries.

Disease-related pain, though often persistent in nature, is not always predictable and may be either recurrent or continuous.

The presence or absence of disease-related pain may be used as a sign of disease process or deterioration. In cases where the pain is an inherent aspect of the disease, helping the patient manage or cope with pain may be a primary goal of psychological intervention.

Pain Associated with Medical Treatment Procedures

Treatment of a child's condition can also be pain-inducing. Children with diabetes must take daily insulin injections in order to survive. Daily glucose testing in these patients requires a finger stick in order to obtain a sample of blood. Pediatric cancer patients must experience routine bone marrow aspirations and lumbar punctures, which can be excruciatingly painful. Nausea and vomiting are common responses to anticancer medications. Internal hemorrhaging in children with hemophilia is treated by intravenous infusion of blood products to replace the children's missing clotting factor.

Pain associated with a medical procedure may interfere with correct, efficient administration of the procedure. For example, bone marrow aspiration and lumbar punctures are difficult to accomplish on a screaming, thrashing child. Pain management in such cases is primarily designed to increase patient cooperation and compliance.

Since medications are often used to treat childhood pain and discomfort, it is important to be aware of the cognitive, behavioral, and affective changes that may accompany medication for disease management as well as for pain management (Waters & Milch, 1993). However, only a small body of literature exists in this area; consequently, we know very little about the deleterious effect of pediatric medicines. Nevertheless, pediatric psychologists are often in an excellent position to assess and monitor the side effects of medications. To do so requires a comprehensive knowledge of child development, clinical child psychology, and pediatric pharmacology (DuPaul & Kyle, 1995).

Chronic Pain Not Associated with a Well-Specified Disease or Injury

For many children, the organic basis of their pain is not very clear. Headache, abdominal pain, and limb (growing) pain, for instance, are some of the most common complaints of childhood.

Schechter (1984) estimated that only 5–7% of children with these pain complaints have any identifiable organic etiology. Headaches occur in approximately 5–10% of children and tend to be either migraine or tension headaches (Vieyra, Hoag, & Masek, 1991; Williamson, Baker, & Cubic, 1993). Research has shown that, relative to healthy children, those with chronic headaches have more somatic complaints, depression, and anxiety (e.g., Andrasik et al., 1988). Approximately 10–15% of children report experiencing recurrent abdominal pain (Hodges & Burbach, 1991). Prevalence rates are higher for girls than for boys, particularly between the ages of 9 and 12. Although recurrent abdominal pain of this type can be a symptom of serious organic pathology, most cases cannot be traced to any specific disease or physical abnormality; indeed, as many as one-fifth of those with recurrent abdominal pain undergo unnecessary medical or surgical intervention (Dolgin & Jay, 1989). Like children with chronic headaches, children with recurrent abdominal pain may experience more depressive symptoms (Walker & Greene, 1989) and anxiety (Garber, Zeman, & Walker, 1990; Wasserman, Whitington, & Rivara, 1988). Unfortunately, research on limb pain is virtually nonexistent, and little is known about its etiology, clinical course, or psychological concomitants.

In years past, chronic pain was classified as organic or psychogenic; if no organic etiology was discovered, the pain was assumed to be psychogenic. Various factors were presumed to "cause" psychogenic pain, including stressful events, modeling of pain behavior by other family members, and reinforcing consequences of a child's pain reaction. More recently, however, health professionals have moved away from viewing children's pain as necessarily an "either–or" phenomenon (i.e., as either organic or psychogenic). For instance, many somatic predispositions or dysfunctions cannot be classified as true organic illness. These somatic conditions, in combination with life style habits, environmental factors, and learned response patterns, may result in chronic pain. This position typifies the biobehavioral view of childhood chronic pain, in which pain is understood in terms of an interaction among biological, behavioral, and socioenvironmental factors (Katz, Varni, & Jay, 1984; Peterson, Harbeck, Farmer, & Zink, 1991; Walker, Greene, et al., 1993). In addition to traditional medical examination and laboratory assessment procedures, childhood chronic pain assessment typically involves a search for antecedent events that are consistently associated with pain (e.g., particular foods, stressful events), as well as for consequating events that may be maintaining pain behavior (e.g., avoiding chores and school, obtaining increased parental support and attention). Environmental factors that may influence the expression of pain are also considered. Identified factors associated with pain are modified if possible (e.g., dietary changes), or the patient is taught alternative ways to prevent or cope with the pain (Masek, Russo, & Varni, 1984). Indeed, successful treatment of childhood pain and its associated symptomatology may reduce the risk of long-term pain difficulties, including chronic pain syndrome in adulthood (Ross & Ross, 1988; Routh, Ernst, & Harper, 1988).

Pain Assessment Methods

Coleman, Friedman, and Gates (1994) have identified several principal goals of chronic pain assessment: obtaining a baseline measure of the child's pain, in order to evaluate improvement during intervention; identifying those factors that may be contributing to and maintaining pain behaviors; and determining the degree to which the child's pain is interfering with daily activities and family functioning. The assessment of pain should be global or systems-based, rather than focused narrowly or exclusively on the pain behavior itself. Communication with the child's physician, and thorough examination of the systems in which the child is embedded (e.g., family, school, peers), are essential components of any pain assessment.

Because pain is a subjective experience, interview and self-report methods are most commonly used. Information usually obtained during pain assessment interviews includes a detailed medical history and assessment of medication usage; factors related to the onset of the pain condition; the advantages and disadvantages of the pain; changes in family dynamics; child and family coping resources; antecedent factors; consequences of pain expression; cognitive mediators of pain; family mental and physical health; parental attitudes and beliefs about health and illness; and the child's perception of pain (Karoly, 1991, 1995). To supplement interview information, children and/or their parents may be asked to complete one of several available questionnaires. These include the Varni–Thompson Pediatric Pain Questionnaire (Varni, Thompson, & Hanson, 1987), the Children's Comprehensive Pain Questionnaire (McGrath, 1987), and the Pediatric Pain Questionnaire (Savedra, Gibbons, Tesler, Ward, & Wegner, 1982).

Children are sometimes asked to rate their pain experience on visual analogue scales, "pain thermometers," or similar visual instruments (e.g., Beyer & Aradine, 1986, 1987; Rodrigue, Graham-Pole, Kury, Kubar, & Hoffman, in press; Varni et al., 1987). Varni et al. (1987) and Walco and Dampier (1990) reported good to excellent agreement between children's visual analogue pain responses and parents' and physicians' ratings of the children's pain. Good agreement was also observed between the parents' and physicians' ratings. Visual analogue scales appear to offer reliable and valid measurement of the pain experience in children as young as 5 years old (McGrath & deVeber, 1986; Rodrigue et al., in press). Other investigators have employed Likert-type scales, in which numerical scores are anchored by verbal descriptors (e.g., 1 = "no pain" to 5 = "severe pain"; Kolko & Rickard-Figueroa, 1985; Labbe & Williamson, 1984; Zeltzer & LeBaron, 1982). Sometimes faces depicting emotional states are used to help children rate the degree of distress or pain (LeBaron & Zeltzer, 1984; Manne et al., 1990; McGrath, deVeber, & Hearn, 1985). Correlations between this type of self-report and an observer's estimate of a child's distress have been moderately strong (LeBaron & Zeltzer, 1984; Zeltzer & LeBaron, 1982).

Occasionally, symptom checklists are used in which a child selects distress symptoms experienced (e.g., nausea, nail biting, insomnia; Kolko & Rickard-Figueroa, 1985). This may be particularly helpful when the distress experience is of long duration (e.g., the 24-hour period *before* a routine bone marrow aspiration). Since "pain" and "discomfort" are abstract terms, symptom checklists, if presented in concrete terms, may be particularly useful for younger children. Lollar, Smits, and Patterson (1982) used pictures of pain experiences and had children sort them into color-coded pain categories. This approach seems to offer another method of assessing children's pain, in a manner less abstract than that offered by visual analogue scales or Likert-type scales. However, its utility with young, chronically ill youngsters remains to be determined.

When the purpose of an assessment is to learn more about a child's pain within a social context, diaries are often used. They are particularly helpful in chronic pain cases, where the goal of the assessment is to learn more about the nature of the pain (e.g., duration and intensity), factors associated with its onset, and events that occur in response to the pain. Diaries also are quite helpful in monitoring a child's daily pain-related activities and may prove useful in evaluating the effectiveness of treatment (Coleman et al., 1994). Typically recorded in diaries are time of pain symptoms; severity of the pain; events that occurred prior to and subsequent to the pain event; and any salient events that may have occurred during the day. With younger children, parents can be asked to record this information.

Observational methods have also been used to assess childhood distress behaviors presumed to be associated with pain or anxiety. The more sophisticated approaches use multiple-behavior observation scales, in which observers record the presence or absence of behaviors during specified time intervals. As noted by Ross and Ross (1988), the unobtrusive nature of observation methods not only permits the psychologist to augment interview and self-report data, but permits the assessment of neonates and infants and allows for the evaluation of important nonverbal expressive behavior. Several researchers have developed very reliable observation methods to assess the pain or distress reactions of infants and children undergoing circumcision (Gunnar, Fisch, & Malone, 1984), heel lancing (Craig, Hadjistavropoulos, Grunau, & Whitfield, 1994), bone marrow aspiration (Blount et al., 1989; Elliott, Jay, & Woody, 1987; Katz, Kellerman, & Ellenberg, 1987), lumbar punctures (Blount et al., 1989; Jay, Ozolins, Elliott, & Caldwell, 1983), chemotherapy (Kolko & Rickard-Figueroa, 1985), insulin injections (Gilbert et al., 1982), and burn debridement (Elliott & Olson, 1983). Several sophisticated observational measures have proven very useful in documenting children's pain reactions. These include the Observation Scale of Behavioral Distress (Elliott et al., 1987; Jay & Elliott, 1981; Jay et al., 1983), the Procedural Behavior Rating Scale (Katz, Kellerman, & Siegel, 1980; Katz et al., 1987), the Neonatal Facial Coding System (Craig et al., 1994), the Pain Behavior Checklist (LeBaron & Zeltzer, 1984), the Parent Observation Record (Sanders, Shepherd, Cleghorn, & Woolford, 1994), and the Children's Hospital of Eastern Ontario Pain Scale (McGrath, Johnson et al., 1985).

More recently, Blount and his colleagues (Blount, Corbin, Powers, Sturges, & Maieron, 1988; Blount et al., 1989; Blount, Corbin, & Wolfe, 1987) have advanced the pain observation field by developing the Child–Adult Medical Procedure Interaction Scale (CAMPIS) and its recent revision, the CAMPIS-R (Blount, Landolf-Fritsche, Powers, & Sturges, 1991; Blount, Sturges, & Powers, 1990). These measures assess the interplay among children's pain experience, their specific coping responses (both adaptive and maladaptive), and the reactions of adults to the children's pain. Interobserver reliability for the CAMPIS and CAMPIS-R has been consistently high (Blount et al., 1990, 1991). Assessment of the dynamic child–adult interactions in the context of procedural pain allows the clinician to formulate systems-level intervention strategies.

Although formal behavioral observation of children's distress is a highly reliable methodology, it can be both expensive and time-consuming. Consequently, global ratings of children's pain, anxiety, or distress on a simple numerical scale are frequently used. Global ratings have proven to be reliable (Gilbert et al., 1982; LeBaron & Zeltzer, 1984), and both parents' and nurses' global ratings of anxiety have been found to correlate significantly with children's observed distress (Jay et al., 1983; Katz et al., 1980).

Physiochemical assessment of children's pain or distress is relatively uncommon, although some investigators have used such measures in well-controlled settings where acute pain occurs (e.g., dentists' offices). Muscle tension, cardiac rate, palmar sweating, blood pressure, respiration rate, endorphin concentrations, blood plasma cortisol levels, and electrical activity in the brain have all been employed (Karoly, 1991; Karoly & Jensen, 1987). However, it is noteworthy that attempts to delineate the relationship between physiochemical measures and fluctuations in pain have yielded equivocal findings (Ross & Ross, 1988). The physiological measures selected for investigation vary from study to study, depending upon the purpose of the assessment and the presumed linkages between psychological/emotional stimuli and physiological responses of particular relevance to a specific illness or chronic condition.

Developmental Issues

A child's level of cognitive development has important implications for the youngster's experience of pain, conceptions of pain, and selection of pain coping strategies (Brown, O'Keeffe, Sanders, & Baker, 1986; Bush, 1987; Craig & Gruneau, 1991; Gedaly-Duff, 1991; McGrath & Pisterman, 1991; Peterson et al., 1991). Some researchers have found that younger children tend to focus more on physical causes of pain, whereas older children consider both physical and psychological factors in etiology (Gaffney & Dunne, 1986; Savedra et al., 1982). More recently, however, Harbeck and Peterson (1992) found that although age was a strong predictor of more cognitively mature pain perceptions, very few children or adolescents were knowledgeable about the actual physiological or psychological causes of pain.

Observational data on children's distress behaviors also suggest strong developmental effects. Children younger than 7 years of age exhibit more distress behaviors than their older counterparts, and differ in types of distress behaviors as well (e.g., they are more likely to cry, scream, and require physical restraint; Jay et al., 1983; Katz et al., 1980; LeBaron & Zeltzer, 1984). In fact, younger children, who are cognitively more concrete, may exhibit much greater distress when presented with an obvious but insignificant injury (e.g., a small cut) than when experiencing internal pain indicative of more serious pathology (e.g., joint pain). When pain is a signal to take some sort of therapeutic action, younger children may be more likely to ignore their pain instead of engaging in the suggested treatment procedure (e.g., restriction of activity). This may be particularly true when the pain is internal (e.g., joint pain). Clearly, children's changing conceptualizations of and reactions to illness and its associated pain or discomfort have important implications for both research and intervention efforts.

Knowledge about the Illness

Chronic illness places numerous demands upon a patient and family. Because the illness requires home management on a daily basis, the patient and family must have adequate knowledge of the disease and its treatment if they are to provide successful home care. Although patients and families are invariably educated about the disorder, learning may not be adequate; studies suggest that serious learning deficiencies exist in patients and parents alike. For example, errors in insulin administration and glucose testing are common in both children and adults with diabetes (Epstein, Coburn, Becker, Drash, & Siminerio, 1980; Johnson et al., 1982; Watkins, Roberts, Williams, Martin, & Coyle, 1967). Parents treating children with hemophilia by factor replacement frequently use incorrect techniques (Sergis-Deavenport & Varni, 1983). Children with asthma often demonstrate poor knowledge of how to prevent or control attacks (Eiser, Town, & Tripp, 1988; Fritz, Klein, & Overholser, 1990). Poor understanding of one's own disease has been documented in populations with childhood epilepsy (Sanger, Perrin, & Sandler, 1993) and juvenile rheumatoid arthritis (Berry, Hayford, Ross, Pachman, & Lavigne, 1993).

Studies of mothers', fathers', and patients' knowledge about the children's illness suggest that mothers are typically the most knowledgeable family members. However, adolescents are often as knowledgeable as their mothers and more knowledgeable than their fathers (Etzwiler & Sines, 1962; Garner, Thompson, & Partridge, 1969; Johnson et al., 1982; Karp, Manor, & Laron, 1970; Partridge, Garner, Thompson, & Cherry, 1972). These findings are consistent with the fact that mothers are usually the primary caretakers of chronically ill children (Etzwiler & Sines, 1962; Hauenstein, 1990; Tavormina et al., 1981).

Learning about a chronic disease can be an exceedingly complex task. Managing the illness on a daily basis usually means more than knowing the "facts" about its etiology and treatment. Usually the patient must learn to problem solve, or apply the facts about the illness in a variety of situations. More than cognitive knowledge is often required. Patients or parents must give injections, conduct tests, administer intravenous medications, or carry out physical therapies at home. All of these tasks require considerable skill. Furthermore, there may be little relationship between different aspects of disease knowledge, even within a particular disease. For example, a patient may know the facts about diabetes, but may be unable to apply those facts in a variety of situations, or may be administering insulin or testing glucose inaccurately (Harkavy et al., 1983; Johnson et al., 1982). This suggests that knowledge of *all* important aspects of a disease's management must be assessed; for most chronic illnesses, patients' or parents' answers to brief questionnaires will probably not accurately reflect knowledge in all relevant areas.

Knowledge about an illness has not been consistently associated with adherence or health status (Mazzuca, 1982; Johnson, 1992, 1995). However, it would be inappropriate to conclude that disease knowledge is unimportant. Rather, it is best to view it as a necessary but not sufficient condition for good adherence and good health to occur.

Knowledge Assessment Methods

Assessment of knowledge about the child's illness requires the development of assessment methods for specific diseases and for specific tasks within specific diseases. This has been accomplished through the use of observational methods and questionnaires.

Behavioral observational methods are particularly useful for the assessment of skills. Such methods have been developed for assessing patients' with diabetes skili at insulin injection (Johnson, 1985; see Table 10.6) and home glucose monitoring (Epstein et al., 1980; Gilbert et al., 1982; Harkavy et al., 1983; Johnson, Lewis-Meert, & Alexander, 1981; Johnson et al., 1982), and have been employed for assessing factor replacement therapy performance with hemophiliac pediatric patients in the home care setting (Sergis-Deavenport & Varni, 1983). Excellent interobserver agreement is usually obtained.

Cognitive knowledge of the disease and the application of this knowledge to different situations can be reliably measured by interview or questionnaire (Berry et al., 1993; Bluebond-Langer, Perkel, Goertzel, Nelson, & McGeary, 1990; Harkavy et al., 1983; Johnson et al., 1982; Hess & Davis, 1983; Dunn et al., 1984; Sanger et al., 1993). For example, the Test of Diabetes Knowledge: General Information and Problem Solving (Johnson, 1984) is a multiple-choice test designed to test child and parent knowledge about diabetes. Sample items are provided in Table 10.7. The General Information component focuses on facts about diabetes, whereas the Problem Solving section attempts to assess the respondent's understanding of diabetes management in different situations. The instrument has proved to be reliable (Harkavy et al., 1983; Johnson, 1995; Johnson et al., 1982), sensitive to cognitive-developmental differences in children (Johnson, 1995), predictive of diabetes regimen adherence (Johnson, 1995), and sensitive to the acquisition of new knowledge over the course of a 2-week diabetes summer camp (Harkavy et al., 1983).

The successful assessment of disease knowledge requires disease-specific measurement development, since each disease differs in etiology, course, and treatment. Although not all diseases of childhood have psychometrically adequate measures of disease knowledge, the assessment methodologies developed in diabetes, for example, could be readily applied to other chronic illness conditions.

Developmental Issues

The importance of children's cognitive-developmental level to their understanding of disease and its management is one of the most robust findings in the literature. Older children are generally more knowledgeable and more skilled at carrying out disease management tasks than younger children (Berry et al., 1993; Harkavy et al., 1983; Johnson, 1995; Johnson et al., 1982; Sanger et al., 1993; Weist, Finney, Barnard, Davis, & Ollendick, 1993). These findings are consistent with the literature

on healthy children's concepts of illness (DeLoye, Henggeler, & Daniels, 1993; Osborne, Kistner, & Helgemo, 1993; Sigelman, Mukai, Woods, & Alfeld, 1995; Walsh & Bibace, 1991).

Adherence to Recommended Treatment

"Adherence" and "compliance" are the terms typically used to describe how well a patient or a parent follows the recommended treatment for the youngster's illness. Treatment cannot be effective if the patient or parent does not engage in the necessary treatment behaviors. At a more basic level, the evaluation of any medical treatment conducted in the home care setting depends on adherence to the treatment protocol. Only when adherence is good can a valid test of the medical prescriptions be undertaken. Consequently, the assessment of the patient's or family's adherence behaviors is a critical component of patient health care management. Studies of pediatric chronically ill populations repeatedly document high rates of nonadherence to recommended treatment (Creer, 1993; DiRaimondo & Green, 1988; Greene & Strickler, 1983; Johnson, 1992; Litt & Cuskey, 1981; Phipps & DeCuir-Whalley, 1990; Smith, Rosen, Trueworthy, & Lowman, 1979; Varni & Jay, 1984).

Adherence has been traditionally conceptualized as a trait-like characteristic of the patient. Some patients are viewed as adherent and others as nonadherent, suggesting that if a patient is adherent (or nonadherent) to one component of the treatment regimen, the patient will be adherent (or nonadherent) to the remaining components. Recent research has rejected this view. Complex medical regimens require multiple behaviors that appear unrelated to one another; adherence to one treatment component is not predictive of adherence to the remaining treatment components (Gross, Samson, Sanders, & Smith, 1988; Johnson, Silverstein, Rosenbloom, Carter, & Cunningham, 1986; Johnson, Tomer, Cunningham, & Henretta, 1990). Consequently, for many chronic diseases, adherence assessment methods must be selected or developed that adequately capture the complex array of behaviors required.

Adherence Assessment Methods

Most health care providers rely on patients or parents to tell them what they usually do to manage the child's illness. Unfortunately, what patients or parents say they usually do may bear little resemblance to what they actually do. The poor

TABLE 10.6. The Skills Test for Insulin Injection

EXAMINER: Establish rapport with the child and create an atmosphere of assurance that he/she will do well, trying to alleviate any performance anxiety. Ask the child what type and how much insulin the doctor has prescribed for him/her.

*1. States prescribed amount and type of insulin. (Score after checking dose in medical record.) Child's response: A.M.: ___ P.M.: ___	P	F

EXAMINER: Tell the youngster you would like him/her to demonstrate how to self-inject (EXCEPT—"If this isn't a regular injection time for you, DON'T INJECT YOURSELF; inject the fruit or cup").

2. Mixes insulin appropriately (rolls, does not shake)	P	F
3. Cleans top of insulin bottle with alcohol pad	P	F
4. Pulls plunger back so syringe fills with air and the top of the plunger is within ±5 unit marks of the previously stated amount of insulin (see #1)	P	F
5. Takes top off needle properly	P	F
6. Inserts needle into rubber top of insulin bottle	P	F
7. Injects air into the bottle, but not into the insulin	P	F
8. Turns bottle upside down with syringe in place	P	F
9. Looks for air bubbles. (Inquire about what the youngster is doing.)	P	F
10. Flicks syringe with finger or uses some other method to remove air bubbles. (Inquire about what the youngster is doing.)	P	F
*11. No air bubbles are visible	P	F
*12. Amount of insulin in syringe is at the unit mark previously stated by the youngster after syringe is removed from bottle	P	F
13. Needle cover is placed back on	P	F

EXAMINER: Say to the child, "Point to where you injected the last time."

14. Points to abdomen, thigh, buttock, or arm (or other appropriate injection site)	P	F

EXAMINER: Say to the child, "If you were going to give a shot now, point to where you would do it."

15. Indicates a different injection site	P	F

EXAMINER: Say to the child, "Show me what you would do next, as if you were giving a shot there."

16. Cleans area with alcohol	P	F
17. Makes skin taut or pinches skin up	P	F

EXAMINER: Say to the child, "Instead of pushing the needle into your skin, pretend this is you (indicate Styrofoam or paper cup, fruit, or doll), and show me how you would give the shot."

18. Inserts needle vertically (not less than 45-degree angle)	P	F
19. Inserts needle completely	P	F
*20. Pushes plunger down all the way	P	F
21. Wipes injection site with alcohol	P	F
22. Breaks needle, and destroys syringe	P	F
23. Throws away syringe in the proper receptacle	P	F

*IMPORTANT ITEMS: Failures may result in administration of improper insulin dose. Indicate to the child the correct method for these failed items.

Note. From Johnson (1985). Copyright 1985 by S. B. Johnson. A scoring manual is available from the author.

TABLE 10.7. Test of Diabetes Knowledge: General Information and Problem Solving (Sample Items)

General Information

1. When giving insulin injections, you should:
   a. Inject into the same area.
   b. Inject into a different area every time.
   c. Inject only in the leg.
   d. I don't know.

2. Insulin is normally produced in the:
   a. Kidneys.
   b. Pancreas.
   c. Liver.
   d. I don't know.

3. Insulin:
   a. Lowers the blood sugar level.
   b. Raises the blood sugar level.
   c. Increases sugar in the urine.
   d. I don't know.

4. Ketones in the urine of a person with diabetes are:
   a. A warning sign of an insulin reaction.
   b. A warning sign of acidosis.
   c. A warning sign of hypoglycemia.
   d. I don't know.

Problem Solving

1. You are at a school football game and begin to feel dizzy, shaky, and faint. You should:
   a. Leave the game right away and go straight home.
   b. Buy a Coke and hot dog and eat them.
   c. Lie down, until you feel better.
   d. I don't know.

2. You are trying out for your school's swimming team and practice is midafternoon. Your blood sugar is usually 80–180. You should:
   a. Not take your insulin the days you practice.
   b. Eat a big lunch that day and keep a snack handy.
   c. Increase your insulin to give you more energy that day.
   d. I don't know.

3. You have a big test coming up next period in your hardest subject. You are worried about it, because you feel unprepared. Thirty minutes before the test you begin to feel weak, shaky, and sweaty, and your heart begins to beat fast. You should:
   a. Go to the school nurse so you won't have to take the test.
   b. Eat something.
   c. Take extra regular insulin so you'll be ready for the test.
   d. I don't know.

4. You have the flu, with a high fever, and you don't feel like eating. Your blood sugar is 400. Your urine has large ketones. You should:
   a. Hold your morning insulin because you are not eating as much.
   b. Add regular insulin to your usual morning dose and call your doctor.
   c. Do nothing different because everybody gets the flu.
   d. I don't know.

Note. From Johnson (1984). Copyright 1984 by S. B. Johnson. Scoring directions are available from the author.

quality of such data has led many behavioral psychologists to be highly critical of self-report data in general.

In our experience, however, good-quality self-report data may be obtained if the information requested is highly specific and time-limited. We have successfully used 24-hour recall interviews with patients and their mothers to obtain information about daily diabetes management behaviors. Each respondent is asked to recall the day's events in temporal sequence, beginning with the time the patient woke up in the morning and ending with the time the patient retired to bed. The interviewer records all diabetes-relevant activities on the Diabetes Daily Record (see Figure 10.2). The record provides space for recording details concerning insulin injection (i.e., frequency, type, timing, who injected, whether the parent observed the injection), glucose testing (i.e., frequency, type of test, timing, results, who tested, whether the parent observed the test), food intake (i.e., frequency, timing, description/quantity of food consumed, whether the parent observed the meal or snack consumed), and exercise (i.e., type, timing, duration, and whether the parent observed the exercise), as well as any comments concerning unusual aspects of the child's day (e.g., illness, stress). A similar interview is independently conducted with the patient's mother (or primary caretaker) concerning the child's behavior. Patients and parents are interviewed on at least three separate occasions (two interviews concern weekday behavior, and one concerns weekend behavior) in order to obtain a more representative behavioral sample. Interviews are usually conducted by telephone and take approximately 20 minutes. Data obtained can then be used to quantify a wide variety of diabetes care behaviors. In a series of studies using this methodology, we were able to demonstrate adequate parent–child agreement for most behaviors; good agreement between child 24-hour recall data and independent observations of the child's behaviors; stability of the measures across time; sensitivity to different environmental contexts (e.g.,

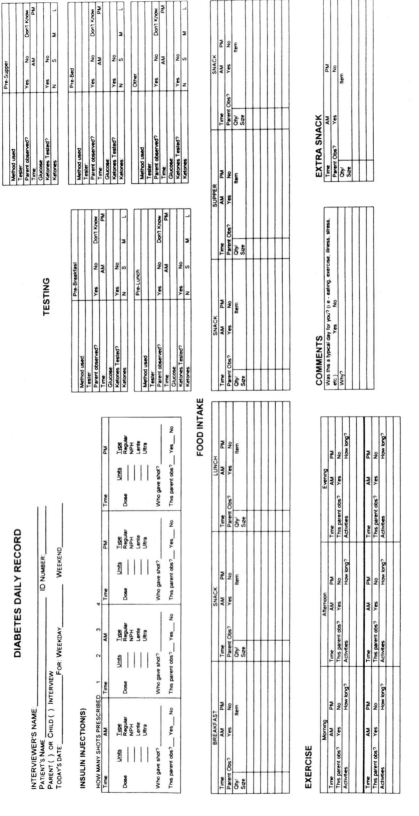

FIGURE 10.2. The Diabetes Daily Record.

502

youngsters were more adherent at diabetes summer camp than at home); procedural nonreactivity (i.e., youngsters did not appear to change their behavior as a function of participating in the 24-hour recall procedure); and a reliable factor structure consisting of six relatively independent constructs (insulin injection behaviors; exercise; testing/eating frequency; total calories ingested; relative contribution of fat, protein, and carbohydrates to total diet; and amount of concentrated sweets consumed) (Freund, Johnson, Silverstein, & Thomas, 1991; Johnson, 1995; Johnson, Freund, Silverstein, Hansen, & Malone, 1990; Johnson et al., 1986, 1992; Johnson, Tomer, et al., 1990; Reynolds, Johnson, & Silverstein, 1990; Spevack, Johnson, & Riley, 1991). This research is corroborated by earlier work in which 24-hour recall interviews were used to collect dietary intake data from children. Interview data of this type compared favorably to dietary intake data collected by observation, weighing, or chemical analysis (Emmons & Hayes, 1973; Greger & Etnyre, 1978; Samuelson, 1970; Stunkard & Waxman, 1981). Although 24-hour recall interviews are not devoid of methodological problems, the available literature suggests that they can provide useful information in a relatively noninvasive manner.

Occasionally, patients are asked to monitor their own behavior and to keep daily written records. Although self-monitoring has long been of interest to behavioral psychologists, this method of measuring adherence behaviors among chronically ill childhood populations has not been extensively tested. In our experience, such data are reliable if the patient keeps complete records. Unfortunately, we find that only half of our patients keep complete records when asked to do so. Diabetes is an extremely complex disease to manage on a daily basis. Other diseases, with fewer daily demands, may yield better-quality data from patients' written records. Another alternative is to ask patients with complex treatment demands to keep written records of a limited number of adherence behaviors, instead of all behaviors relevant to their disease management. Schafer, Glasgow, and McCaul (1982), for example, asked three 16- to 18-year-old youths with diabetes to self-monitor three target behaviors (e.g., wearing diabetes identification, exercise frequency, glucose-testing frequency). Crist et al. (1994) asked parents of 4- to 7-year-olds with cystic fibrosis to record all foods consumed by the child for 3 days. Limiting the target behaviors to be monitored by the patient or parent also requires astute selection of which of all possible behaviors should be self-monitored. Of

course, the usual concern for the potential reactivity of self-recorded data must be kept in mind.

Health care providers are sometimes asked to rate their patients' adherence to recommended treatment. However, reliability and validity data are rarely provided. Earlier studies that addressed this issue found physician estimates of patient adherence to be extremely poor (Caron & Roth, 1968; Charney et al., 1967; Davis, 1968), although none of these studies were conducted with childhood chronically ill populations. A more recent study of physician estimates of adherence in adolescents with diabetes yielded more favorable results (Bobrow, AvRuskin, & Siller, 1985). A variety of parameters may influence health care provider ratings (e.g., how well the physician knows the patients; whether the physician is asked to rate specific behaviors or is asked to provide a more global adherence rating; how skilled the physician is in obtaining information from patients and families). Under certain conditions, health care providers may be able to provide useful information concerning patient adherence. However, these conditions have not been clearly delineated. Of particular concern are possible biases introduced by a physician's knowledge of a patient's health status. Many physicians believe that poor patient health is a product of poor patient compliance; thus, they may automatically rate a patient in poor health as noncompliant, and may collect no independent behavioral data confirming such a judgment. As a consequence, unless data on reliability and validity are provided, health care providers' ratings of patients' adherence should be viewed with caution.

Behavioral observation of targeted adherence behaviors has been successfully used in a number of studies (e.g., Epstein et al., 1981; Sergis-Deavenport & Varni, 1982). Lowe and Lutzker (1979), for example, had a mother observe her daughter's diabetes foot care, glucose testing, and dietary behavior. Observational methods are particularly useful with individual patients who present obvious adherence problems. The behaviors observed vary, depending upon the problems presented. The quality of the data is determined by parents' or other family members' willingness to carefully monitor and record the behaviors targeted. With motivated patients and families, this approach may be useful as both an assessment strategy and an intervention strategy.

Counting tangible products associated with adherence behaviors is another available adherence assessment technique. For example, a patient is given a bottle of medication and is asked to return the medication bottle to the physician in 1 month. At that time, the remaining pills are counted and subtracted from the number originally prescribed as an estimate of medication adherence. With most diseases, some type of tangible product associated with illness management can be identified and counted. Zora, Lutz, and Tinkelman (1989), for example, assessed compliance in asthmatic children using inhalers by weighing the medication canisters before and after a 2-week period. These indirect measures of patients' compliance behavior are not entirely foolproof. A patient may lose medications, let others take medications, or purposely dispose of medications in order to avoid detection as a noncomplier. Nevertheless, tangible products can be creatively used to corroborate self-reports or other types of adherence data.

Some types of adherence behaviors (e.g., medication ingestion) can be assessed via assays of bodily fluids, such as blood, urine, or saliva (Christiaanse, Lavigne, & Lerner, 1989; Friedman et al., 1986; Tebbi et al., 1986). However, the results of such assays may vary according to individual absorption and metabolism rates, as well as timing of the test in relationship to medication ingestion. Moreover, assay procedures for all drugs are not available. Those that exist may be time-consuming and expensive, and they certainly require the cooperation of the patient for the bodily fluid sample to be obtained (Epstein & Cluss, 1982). Biochemical assays are not practical methods of measuring most adherence behaviors, but in some instances they can provide important information to supplement patients' self-reports.

Perhaps more common is the use of health status measures as a method of assessing adherence; healthier patients are presumed to be more compliant (e.g., Clarke, Snyder, & Nowacek, 1985). However, this approach confuses adherence with therapeutic outcome and may lead to erroneous conclusions with relatively serious consequences. Patients who are adherent to an ineffective treatment cannot be distinguished from patients who are nonadherent to an effective treatment. Unless adherence behavior is assessed independently of health status, a health care provider will be unable to ascertain whether a patient's health problems are the results of a faulty treatment plan or are the consequences of the patient's failure to follow the provider's prescription. Very different intervention strategies would follow, depending on whether the source of the problem was the health care provider's disease management recommendations or the patient's response to those recommendations (Johnson, 1994b).

Barriers to Adherence

Since poor adherence is so common in chronically ill populations, an assessment of barriers to good adherence is often required. Common barriers include knowledge or skill deficits, parent–child interactions, social interactions, and health care provider behavior.

Knowledge or Skill Deficits

Inadvertent noncompliance occurs when the patient believes he or she is adhering to recommended treatment but, through errors in knowledge or skill, is actually noncompliant. This is probably more common than most health care providers realize. Johnson et al. (1982) found that 40% of youngsters studied made errors of this type when self-injecting insulin, and that 80% made significant errors when testing glucose. Tebbi et al. (1986) reported that many pediatric cancer patients who were noncompliant with medications did not understand instructions concerning how to take their medication.

Parent–Child Interactions

It is obvious that the quality of parent–child interactions may either promote or impede adherence behaviors. As discussed previously, family disturbance has been linked to poorer psychological adjustment in chronically ill children. However, the relationship between family interaction patterns and adherence to a medical regimen has not been studied as extensively.

Parent–child conflict and communication difficulties appear to be associated with poorer adherence across a wide variety of chronic diseases: asthma (Christiaanse et al., 1989), epilepsy (Friedman et al., 1986), juvenile rheumatoid arthritis (Chaney & Peterson, 1989), and diabetes (Bobrow et al., 1985; Hauser et al., 1990). Heightened parental anxiety has also been linked to increased patient distress in youngsters facing painful medical procedures (Jay et al., 1983). A more supportive parenting style has been linked to better treatment adherence in youngsters with cancer (Manne, Jacobsen, Gorfinkle, Gerstein, & Redd, 1993). Of course, all of these studies are correlational in nature. Parental anxiety or parent–child communication problems could be either the cause or the result of the patients' nonadherence. Further research is needed to delineate the nature of these relationships.

There is increasing evidence that such research

will be most useful if it is specific to the disease and its management requirements. An interesting study by Schafer, Glasgow, McCaul, and Dreher (1983) illustrates this point. Both a general measure of family functioning (the Moos Family Environment Scale; Moos & Moos, 1981) and a measure of family interaction patterns specific to diabetes care (the Diabetes Family Behavior Checklist) were employed. The authors reported a stronger relationship between adherence and the diabetes-specific measure than between adherence and the general measure of family interaction. Johnson (1995) also reported that a disease-specific measure—supervision of a child's daily medical care tasks—was a significant predictor of adherence in youngsters with diabetes. These findings highlight the importance of using disease-specific measures when one is studying family and other environmental correlates of adherence in chronically ill childhood populations.

Social Interactions

Social interactions outside the family may also support or impede adherence behaviors. Adolescents' desire for peer acceptance has often been linked to adherence problems. Tattersall and Lowe (1981) have speculated that diabetes interferes with most of the goals of normal adolescence. Peer conformity is important; yet youngsters with the disease may feel "different" because of delayed sexual maturation, daily regimens of injections and glucose testing, and dietary constraints. Under the increased social pressure, it becomes more difficult to refuse "junk" food or to eat when others are not eating. Similar speculations could be made about potential social interference variables relevant to other chronic illnesses. Of course, there may be social interaction variables that facilitate adherence as well. Neither interfering nor facilitating variables have received much empirical attention, although social skills training has been used to assist youngsters handling difficult social situations (Follansbee, LaGreca, & Citrin, 1983; Gross, Johnson, Wildman, & Mullett, 1981; Kaplan, Chadwick, & Schimmel, 1985).

Health Care Provider Behavior

A health care provider educates a patient and family about disease management, monitors the youngster's health status on a regular basis, and attempts to intervene when problems develop. Although a number of adherence-enhancing strategies have been documented (Kulik & Carlino,

1987; Maiman, Becker, Liptak, Nazarian, & Rounds, 1988), providers rarely use these strategies (Thompson, Dahlquist, Koenning, & Bartholomew, 1995). Furthermore, a number of studies suggest that provider–family communication is poor. For example, Page, Verstraete, Robb, and Etzwiler (1981) compared recommendations given by the health care providers in a childhood diabetes clinic with patients' and parents' recall of these recommendations. On the average, providers gave seven recommendations per patient. Patients (and parents of younger children) recalled an average of two recommendations. However, 40% of the patient- or parent-recalled recommendations were *not* recorded by the providers! Patients or parents who do not accurately recall provider recommendations can hardly be expected to adhere to those recommendations.

There appear to be a number of factors contributing to poor provider–family communication. Korsch and her colleagues have documented the extensive use of medical jargon in pediatric practice, which is often seriously misunderstood by patients or parents (Korsch, Gozzi, & Francis, 1968). Children's cognitive or conceptual capabilities may be ignored or inaccurately estimated. Perrin and Perrin (1983), for example, gave clinicians children's responses to five questions regarding illness mechanisms, and asked them to estimate the children's ages from the quality of the responses. The health care provider participants in the study (who had experience working with children) typically overestimated the age of younger children and underestimated the age of older children. They seemed to have difficulty detecting age-related differences in youngsters' conceptual understanding of illness.

The affective quality of the provider–patient interaction may be as important as the information provided. Both parents' and children's satisfaction with medical care has been linked to regimen adherence in chronically ill (Hazzard, Hutchinson, & Krawiecki, 1990) and acutely ill (Francis, Korsch, & Morris, 1969; Freemon, Negrete, Davis, & Korsch, 1971; Korsch et al., 1968) child populations; greater satisfaction is associated with better adherence. A number of instruments are now available to measure parent and patient satisfaction with a clinic visit (see Tables 10.8 and 10.9) (Krahn, Eisert, & Fifield, 1990; Simonian, Tarnowski, Park, & Bekeny, 1993).

Provider–family communication and rapport may be further undermined by negative stereotypes about ill children often held by providers (Stern, Ross, & Bielass, 1991). In addition, par-

TABLE 10.8. Final Metro Assessment of Child Satisfaction (MACS) Items

1. Did the doctor talk to you *before* he/she did something?
2. Did the doctor listen to what you said?
3. Do you want to see *this* doctor again?
4. Would you tell your friends to see *this* doctor?
5. Did the doctor talk too much?
6. Did you understand what the doctor said to you?
7. Did the doctor like you?
8. Did the doctor ask you how you felt?

Note. From Simonian, Tarnowski, Park, and Bekeny (1993, p. 9). Copyright 1993 by Williams & Wilkins. Reprinted by permission.

ents and providers may have different goals or expectations for children's medical care, which may impede adherence to the providers' recommendations. Marteau, Johnston, Baum, and Bloch (1985) compared physicians' goals with those of parents of children with diabetes. Parents' goals focused primarily on avoiding hypoglycemia, while physicians' goals emphasized avoidance of the long-term complications of diabetes. The youngsters' health status was more strongly associated with the parents' than with the physicians' goals— a finding that highlights the importance of developing an alliance between providers and parents. Wysocki et al. (1992) also reported large discrepancies between parents and providers as to the ages at which children should be expected to master various diabetes care skills. Such disagreements could potentially interfere with a family's willingness to carry out a provider's recommendations.

Developmental Issues

Although adolescents have a more sophisticated understanding of their illness than younger patients, they are also wrestling with issues of identity, independence, and peer acceptance. Both clinical impressions and empirical investigations suggest that adolescence is associated with poorer adherence across a variety of diseases, including asthma (Christiaanse et al., 1989), cancer (Dolgin, Katz, Doctors, & Siegel, 1986; Tebbi et al., 1986), and childhood diabetes (see Johnson, 1992). During this developmental period, adolescents become less rule-oriented in their approach to disease care (Johnson, 1995) and begin to question the effectiveness of health care providers and medical procedures (Hackworth & McMahon, 1991). At the same time, parental supervision of the youngsters decreases, often leaving the ill ado-

lescents primarily responsible for the management of the disease (Drotar & Evans, 1994; Ingersoll, Orr, Herrold, & Golden, 1986; Johnson, 1995).

In contrast, skill or knowledge deficits may be more likely to undermine adherence in younger patients, since very young children rarely have the cognitive capability to carry out complex treatment tasks. Research with childhood diabetes populations suggests that education programs addressing different adherence behaviors should be emphasized at different ages (Gilbert et al., 1982; Harkavy et al., 1983; Johnson et al., 1982; Wysocki, Meinhold, Cox, & Clarke, 1990; Wysocki et al., 1992). This does not preclude children from participating in health care activities at a younger age than suggested. However, parental monitoring and supervision of these activities will be necessary until the youngsters show competence.

Younger children are also sometimes less reliable reporters about their own adherence behaviors. Early studies of healthy youngsters found that 6- to 8-year-olds provided poorer-quality dietary recall data than older youngsters (Emmons & Hayes, 1973; Samuelson, 1970). More recent research has examined the quality of 24-hour recall data in 6- to 18-year-old patients with diabetes; younger children had more difficulty accurately recalling information about time (e.g., time of insulin injections, time of meals, duration of an exercise activity), but this difficulty could be successfully addressed by giving younger children more practice with the recall method (Freund et al., 1991; Johnson et al., 1986). However, this adherence assessment strategy has not been successfully employed with children younger than 6 years of age.

Developmental issues are also important to provider–family communication. Providers do not always change their vocabulary and communication style to match the needs of children of different ages (Perrin & Perrin, 1983). They may expect children to take on disease management tasks before the youngsters are sufficiently mature (Wysocki et al., 1990), or their expectations of the children may differ from those of the youngsters' parents (Wysocki et al., 1992).

CONCLUDING COMMENTS

Behavioral assessment methodology has a number of advantages. It is empirical, emphasizes behavioral specificity, and has an underlying theoretical rationale. Clearly, the principles of behavioral assessment can be used to enhance our

TABLE 10.9. Assessment of Parent Satisfaction

Please help us improve our program by answering some questions about the services you have received. We are interested in your honest opinions, whether they are positive or negative. *Please answer all of the questions.* We welcome your comments and suggestions, and we appreciate your help.

1. How long did you wait to get an appointment after initial request?
   1 _____ 0–4 weeks
   2 _____ 4–6 weeks
   3 _____ 6–8 weeks
   4 _____ more than 8 weeks
   5 _____ don't know

2. Did this waiting time seem
   1 _____ short
   2 _____ acceptable
   3 _____ somewhat long
   4 _____ very long

3. What did you think about the total length of the visit?
   4 _____ too short
   1 _____ all right
   4 _____ too long

4. The staff was
   a) 1 _____ very helpful   b) 4 _____ late   c) 1 _____ very easy to understand
      2 _____ somewhat helpful   3 _____ somewhat late   2 _____ somewhat easy to understand
      3 _____ not very helpful   2 _____ mostly on time   3 _____ somewhat hard to understand
      4 _____ not helpful at all   1 _____ on time   4 _____ very hard to understand

Parental Perceptions of Quality

5. The information you received was
   4 _____ confusing
   3 _____ not very clear
   2 _____ somewhat unclear
   1 _____ clear

6. The recommendations you received were
   1 _____ useful
   2 _____ somewhat useful
   3 _____ not very useful
   4 _____ useless

7. To what extent has our program met your needs?
   4 _____ none met
   3 _____ only a few met
   2 _____ most met
   1 _____ almost all met

8. In an overall sense, how satisfied are you with the service you received?
   1 _____ very satisfied
   2 _____ mostly satisfied
   3 _____ indifferent/mildly dissatisfied
   4 _____ quite dissatisfied

9. If you were to seek help again, would you return to our program?
   4 _____ no, definitely not
   3 _____ no, I think not
   2 _____ yes, I think so
   1 _____ yes, definitely

10. a. What did you like best about the clinic?

_____

_____

_____

   b. What would you like us to change about the clinic?

_____

_____

_____

_____

Note. From Krahn, Eisert, and Fifield (1990, pp. 772–773). Copyright 1990 by Plenum Publishing Corporation. Reprinted by permission.

understanding of childhood health and illness. Furthermore, the empiricism of behavioral assessment and treatment is consistent with the current health care climate's emphasis on cost-effectiveness and accountability. Nevertheless, it remains to be seen whether an increased focus on cost containment will result in poorer health outcomes (Belar, 1995; Friedman, Sobel, Myers, Caudill, & Benson, 1995). Unless health and well-being remain the primary outcomes of health care systems, the empiricism of behavioral approaches will have no particular advantage over cheaper, less scientifically based procedures.

We assume that investigators and clinicians will continue to use and develop behavioral assessment methods. However, several issues should be kept in mind. All of these have been mentioned previously, but are highlighted again here.

Disease Specificity versus Generality

Chronic illnesses differ in etiology, prognosis, disability, discomfort, visibility, and management. All these differences mean that the health or pediatric psychologist must learn a great deal about a particular illness and its treatment in order to develop assessment methods that will be relevant to a specific disease. At the same time, investigators are often interested in searching for relationships between behavior and health status that appear consistent across diseases. Although disease-specific measures are often most useful in assessments of such relationships within a disease, they lack generality across diseases. Similarly, health systems analysts are often interested in the cost-effectiveness of care both within and across diseases. More general measures are often favored because they permit large-scale, across-system comparisons. However, general measures may prove insensitive when one is conducting a cost–benefit comparison of two or more treatments for a particular disease. There will continue to be a tension between the development and selection of disease-specific versus more general assessment strategies. The purpose of the assessment must guide the investigator or clinician as to which strategy is more appropriate.

Disease Complexity

The management of a particular illness can be quite complex, and the assessment methods selected or developed must match the complexity of the disease. For a disease like childhood diabetes, assessment methods must successfully tap different kinds of disease-related knowledge and skills, as well as the numerous and distinct treatment demands imposed on a child on a daily basis.

Developmental Issues

Throughout this chapter, developmental issues have repeatedly surfaced. Younger and older children describe and respond to disease-related pain and discomfort differently. They vary in their understanding of their illness and in disease management skills. They differ in their attitudes toward health care providers and are given different amounts of responsibility for illness care by their parents. They describe adherence behaviors with varying degrees of accuracy. Disease management compliance rates and primary barriers to adherence often change in relationship to a child's cognitive and social-emotional development. Health care providers need to become more sensitive to developmental issues when communicating with their young patients and designing educational programs. Similarly, any psychologist who plans to treat or study this population must acknowledge not only that children are different from adults, but that children themselves change fundamentally during the course of childhood and adolescence. Many diseases change and develop as well. The behaviors and reactions of newly diagnosed patients may be different from those who have lived with the disease for some time. The psychological sequelae of diseases that are dynamic or associated with progressive deterioration may differ from those of chronic conditions that are more static. The growing child often lives within the context of a changing disease. Thus, issues of both child development and disease development must be addressed.

Construct Independence

It is important that the variables selected for assessment be defined clearly and measured independently. Often the same individual (e.g., a child's physician) rates the child's and family's adherence to recommended treatment, as well as the child's current health status. This introduces the possibility of spurious relationships between variables. In this example, the physician may be measuring what the physician believes is the relationship between adherence and health, rather than an actual association between behavior and health status. Even more serious is the lack of clear differentiation between constructs. This occurs when health status measures are used to assess treatment adherence behaviors. Although disease management behaviors are presumed to be related to a child's health, these two constructs must be defined and assessed separately if their relationship is to be understood.

Among chronically ill children, health status measures are also commonly used as a measure of treatment outcome. However, when the target of the intervention is a behavior, health status measures may or may not change in response to modifications made in the target behavior. This is entirely dependent upon how closely the target behavior is linked to a youngster's health. Relationships between behavior and health status are not always as clear and consistent as many health care providers would like to believe. It is important to make a conceptual distinction between behavior and health status, to measure both, and to use the information obtained to more clearly delineate actual relationships between the two in individual patients.

Theory Building and Hypothesis Testing

The literature on childhood chronic illness has often been characterized by the study of general associations between variables. The investigation of specific mechanisms by which two variables might be related is typically lacking. Family conflict or dysfunction, for example, is commonly studied for its association with health status in chronically ill children. However, the mechanisms by which family dysfunction might affect a child's health (e.g., inadequate disease knowledge, poor adherence, lack of parental supervision) are typically left unspecified. Theoretical models need to be developed in which environment–behavior–health linkages are hypothesized and tested.

ACKNOWLEDGMENT

The writing of this chapter was supported by Grant No. R01 HD13820 from the National Institute of Child Health and Human Development.

REFERENCES

Achenbach, T. M. (1991). *Manual for the Child Behavior Checklist/4–18 and 1991 Profile*. Burlington: University of Vermont, Department of Psychiatry.

American Psychiatric Association. (1994). *Diagnostic and statistical manual of mental disorders* (4th ed.). Washington, DC: Author.

Andrasik, F., Kabela, E., Quinn, S., Attanasio, V., Blanchard, E. B., & Rosenbloom, E. L. (1988). Psychological functioning of children who have recurrent migraine. *Pain, 34,* 43–52.

Armstrong, R., Rosenbaum, P., & King, S. (1992). Self-perceived social function among disabled children in regular classrooms. *Journal of Developmental and Behavioral Pediatrics, 13,* 11–16.

Bakal, D. A. (1979). *Psychology and medicine: Psychobiological dimensions of health and illness.* New York: Springer.

Belar, C. D. (1995). Collaboration in capitated care: Challenges for psychology. *Professional Psychology: Research and Practice, 26,* 139–146.

Begleiter, M. L., Burry, V. F., & Harris, D. J. (1976). Prevalence of divorce among parents of children with cystic fibrosis and other chronic diseases. *Social Biology, 23,* 260–264.

Bennett, D. (1994). Depression among children with chronic medical problems: A meta-analysis. *Journal of Pediatric Psychology, 19,* 149–169.

Berenbaum, J., & Hatcher, J. (1992). Emotional distress of mothers of hospitalized children. *Journal of Pediatric Psychology, 17,* 359–372.

Berry, S., Hayford, J., Ross, C., Pachman, L., & Lavigne, J. (1993). Conceptions of illness by children with juvenile rheumatoid arthritis: A cognitive developmental approach. *Journal of Pediatric Psychology, 18,* 83–97.

Beyer, J. E. & Aradine, C. R. (1986). Content validity of an instrument to measure young children's perceptions of the intensity of their pain. *Journal of Pediatric Nursing, 1,* 386–395.

Beyer, J. E., & Aradine, C. R. (1987). Patterns of pediatric pain intensity: A methodological investigation of a self-report scale. *Clinical Journal of Pain, 3,* 130–141.

Blount, R. L., Corbin, S. M., Powers, S. W., Sturges, J. W., & Maieron, M. J. (1988). Toward a more comprehensive conceptualization of pediatric pain and distress. *Newsletter of the Society of Pediatric Psychology, 12,* 14–20.

Blount, R. L., Corbin, S. M., Sturges, J. W., Wolfe, V. V., Prater, J. M., & James, L. D. (1989). The relationship between adults' behavior and child coping and distress during BMA/LP procedures: A sequential analysis. *Behavior Therapy, 20,* 585–601.

Blount, R. L., Corbin, S. M., & Wolfe, V. V. (1987, April). *The Child–Adult Medical Procedure Interaction Scale (CAMPIS).* Paper presented at the meeting of the Southeastern Psychological Association, Atlanta.

Blount, R. L., Landolf-Fritsche, B., Powers, S. W., & Sturges, J. W. (1991). Differences between high and low coping children and between parent and staff behaviors during painful medical procedures. *Journal of Pediatric Psychology, 16,* 795–809.

Blount, R. L., Sturges, J. W., & Powers, S. W. (1990). Analysis of child and adult behavioral variations by phase of medical procedure. *Behavior Therapy*, *21*, 33–48.

Bluebond-Langner, M., Perkel, D., Goertzel, T., Nelson, K., & McGeary, J. (1990). Children's knowledge of cancer and its treatment: Impact of an oncology camp experience. *Journal of Pediatrics, 116*, 207–213.

Bobrow, E. S., AvRuskin, T. W., & Siller, J. (1985). Mother–daughter interaction and adherence to diabetes regimen. *Diabetes Care, 8*, 146–151.

Boll, T. J., Dimino, E., & Mattsson, A. E. (1978). Parenting attitudes: The role of personality style and childhood long-term illness. *Journal of Psychosomatic Research, 22*, 209–213.

Borner, S., & Steinhausen, H. C. (1977). A psychological study of family characteristics in juvenile diabetes. *Pediatric and Adolescent Endocrinology, 3*, 46–51.

Brand, A., Johnson, J., & Johnson, S. (1986). Life stress and diabetic control in children and adolescents with insulin-dependent diabetes. *Journal of Pediatric Psychology, 11*, 481–495.

Breslau, N., Staruch, K. S., & Mortimer, E. A. (1982). Psychological distress in mothers of disabled children. *American Journal of Diseases of Children, 136*, 682–686.

Breslau, N., Weitzman, M., & Messenger, K. (1981). Psychologic functioning of siblings of disabled children. *Pediatrics, 67*, 344–353.

Brown, J. M., O'Keeffe, J., Sanders, S. H., & Baker, B. (1986). Developmental changes in children's cognition to stressful and painful situations. *Journal of Pediatric Psychology, 11*, 343–357.

Bush, J. P. (1987). Pain in children: A review of the literature from a developmental perspective. *Psychology and Health, 1*, 215–236.

Cadman, D., Boyle, M., & Offord, D. (1988). The Ontario Child Health Study: Social adjustment and mental health of siblings of children with chronic health problems. *Journal of Developmental and Behavioral Pediatrics, 13*, 11–16.

Cadman, D., Boyle, M., Szatmari, P., & Offord, D. (1987). Chronic illness, disability, and mental and social well-being: Findings of the Ontario Child Health Study. *Pediatrics, 79*, 805–813.

Cairns, N. U., Clark, G. M., Smith, S. D., & Lansky, S. B. (1979). Adaptation of siblings to childhood malignancy. *Journal of Pediatrics, 95*, 484–487.

Caron, H. S., & Roth, H. P. (1968). Patients' cooperation with a medical regimen. *Journal of American Medical Association, 203*, 120–124.

Cecalupo, A. (1994). Childhood cancers. In R. Olson, L. Mullins, J. Gillman, & J. Chaney (Eds.), *The sourcebook of pediatric psychology* (pp. 90–97). Boston: Allyn & Bacon.

Charney, E., Bynum, R., Eldredge, D., Frank, D., MacWhinney, J. B., McNabb, N., Scheiner, A., Sumpter, E. A., & Iker, H. (1967). How well do patients take oral penicillin? A collaborative study in private practice. *Pediatrics, 40*, 188–195.

Chaney, J., & Peterson, L. (1989). Family variables and disease management in juvenile rheumatoid arthritis. *Journal of Pediatric Psychology, 14*, 389–403.

Christiaanse, M., Lavigne, J., & Lerner, C. (1989). Psychosocial aspects of compliance in children and adolescents with asthma. *Journal of Developmental and Behavioral Pediatrics, 10*, 75–80.

Clarke, W. L., Snyder, A. L., & Nowacek, G. (1985). Outpatient pediatric diabetes: I. Current practices. *Journal of Chronic Diseases, 38*, 85–90.

Coleman, C. A., Friedman, A. G., & Gates, D. (1994). Behavioral assessment and treatment of chronic pain in children. In L. Vandecreek, S. Knapp, & T. L. Jackson (Eds.), *Innovations in clinical practice: A source book* (Vol. 13, pp. 55–72). Sarasota, FL: Professional Resource Exchange.

Colegrove, R., & Huntzinger, R. (1994). Academic, behavioral, and social adaptation of boys with hemophilia/HIV disease. *Journal of Pediatric Psychology, 19*, 457–473.

Craig, K. D., & Gruneau, R.V.E. (1991). Developmental issues: Infants and toddlers. In J. P. Bush & S. W. Harkins (Eds.), *Children in pain: Clinical and research issues from a developmental perspective* (pp. 171–193). New York: Springer–Verlag.

Craig, K. D., Hadjistavropoulos, H. D., Grunau, R.V.E., & Whitfield, M. F. (1994). A comparison of two measures of facial activity during pain in the newborn child. *Journal of Pediatric Psychology, 19*, 305–318.

Creer, T. (1993). Medication compliance and childhood asthma. In N. Krasnegor, L. Epstein, S. B. Johnson, & S. Yaffe (Eds.), *Developmental aspects of health compliance behavior* (pp. 303–333). Hillsdale, NJ: Erlbaum,.

Crist, W., McDonnell, P., Beck, M., Gillespie, C., Barrett, P., & Mathews, J. (1994). Behavior at mealtimes and the young child with cystic fibrosis. *Journal of Developmental and Behavioral Pediatrics, 15*, 157–161.

Cummings, S. T. (1976). The impact of the child's deficiency on the father: A study of fathers of mentally retarded and of chronically ill children. *American Journal of Orthopsychiatry, 46*, 246–255.

Davies, W. H., Noll, R. B., DeStefano, L., Bukowski, W. M., & Kulkarni, R. (1991). Differences in the child-rearing practices of parents of children with cancer and controls: The perspectives of parents and professionals. *Journal of Pediatric Psychology, 16*, 295–306.

Davis, M. S. (1968). Physiologic, psychological and demographic factors in patient compliance with doctor's orders. *Medical Care, 6*, 115–122.

DeLoye, G., Henggeler, S., & Daniels, C. (1993). Developmental and family correlates of children's knowledge and attitudes regarding AIDS. *Journal of Pediatric Psychology, 18*, 209–219.

DiRaimondo, C., & Green, N. (1988). Brace-wear compliance in patients with adolescent idiopathic scoliosis. *Journal of Pediatric Orthopedics*, 8, 143–146.

Dolgin, M. J., Katz, E., Doctors, S., & Siegel, S. (1986). Caregivers' perceptions of medical compliance in adolescents with cancer. *Journal of Adolescent Health Care*, 7, 22–27.

Dolgin, M. J., & Jay, S. M. (1989). Pain management in children. In E. J. Mash & R. A. Barkley (Eds.), *Treatment of childhood disorders* (pp. 383–404). New York: Guilford Press.

Drotar, D., & Crawford, P. (1985). Psychological adaptation of siblings of chronically ill children: Research and practice implications. *Journal of Developmental and Behavioral Pediatrics*, 6, 355–362.

Drotar, D., & Evans, C. (1994). Age differences in parent and child responsibilities for management of cystic fibrosis and insulin-dependent diabetes mellitus. *Journal of Developmental and Behavioral Pediatrics*, 4, 265–272.

Dunbar, F. (1955). *Emotions and bodily changes*. New York: Columbia University Press.

Dunn, S. M., Bryson, J. M., Hoskins, P. L., Alford, J. B., Handelsman, D. J., & Turtle, J. R. (1984). Development of the Diabetes Knowledge (DKN) Scales: Forms DKNA, DKNB, and DKNC. *Diabetes Care*, 7, 36–41.

DuPaul, G. J., & Kyle, K. E. (1995). Pediatric pharmacology and psychopharmacology. In M. C. Roberts (Ed.), *Handbook of pediatric psychology* (2nd ed., pp. 741–758). New York: Guilford Press.

Eiser, C., Town, C., & Tripp, J. (1988). Illness experience and related knowledge amongst children with asthma. *Child: Care, Health and Development*, 14, 11–24.

Elliott, C. H., Jay, S. M., & Woody, P. (1987). An observation scale for measuring children's distress during medical procedures. *Journal of Pediatric Psychology*, 12, 543–551.

Elliott, C. H., & Olson, R. A. (1983). The management of children's distress in response to painful medical treatment for burn injuries. *Behaviour Research and Therapy*, 21, 675–683.

Emmons, L., & Hayes, M. (1973). Accuracy of 24-hour recalls of young children. *Journal of the American Dietetic Association*, 62, 409–415.

Epstein, L. H., Beck, S., Figuero, J., Farkas, G., Kazdin, A. E., Daneman, D., & Becker, D. (1981). The effects of targeting improvements in urine glucose on metabolic control in children with insulin-dependent diabetes. *Journal of Applied Behavior Analysis*, 14, 365–375.

Epstein, L. H., & Cluss, P. A. (1982). A behavioral medicine perspective on adherence to long-term medical regimens. *Journal of Consulting and Clinical Psychology*, 50, 950–971.

Epstein, L. H., Coburn, P. C., Becker, D., Drash, A., & Siminerio, L. (1980). Measurement and modification of the accuracy of the determinants of urine glucose concentration. *Diabetes Care*, 3, 535–536.

Etzwiler, D. D., & Sines, L. K. (1962). Juvenile diabetes and its management: Family, social, and academic implications. *Journal of the American Medical Association*, 181, 94–98.

Feagans, L., Sanyal, M., Henderson, F., Collier, A., & Appelbaum, M. (1987). Relationship of middle ear disease in early childhood to later narrative and attention skills. *Journal of Pediatric Psychology*, 12, 581–594.

Ferrari, M. (1984). Chronic illness: Psychosocial effects on siblings: I. Chronically ill boys. *Journal of Child Psychology and Psychiatry*, 25, 459–476.

Ferrari, M., Matthews, W. S., & Barabas, G. (1983). The family and the child with epilepsy. *Family Process*, 22, 53–59.

Fielding, D., Moore, B., Dewey, M., Ashley, P., McKendrick, T., & Pinderton, P. (1985). Children with end-stage renal failure: Psychological effects on patients, siblings, and parents. *Journal of Psychosomatic Research*, 29, 457–465.

Follansbee, D. J., LaGreca, A. M., & Citrin, W. C. (1983, June). *Coping skills training for adolescents with diabetes*. Paper presented at the annual meeting of the American Diabetes Association, San Antonio, TX.

Forgays, D., Hasazi, J., & Wasserman, R. (1992). Recurrent otitis media and parenting stress in mothers of two-year-old children. *Journal of Developmental and Behavioral Pediatrics*, 13, 321–325.

Fowler, M. G., Johnson, M. P., & Atkinson, S. S. (1985). School achievement and absence in children with chronic health conditions. *Journal of Pediatrics*, 106, 683–687.

Francis, V., Korsch, B. M., & Morris, M. J. (1969). Gaps in doctor–patient communication: Patients' response to medical advice. *New England Journal of Medicine*, 280, 535–540.

Freemon, B., Negrete, V. F., Davis, M., & Korsch, B. M. (1971). Gaps in doctor–patient communication: Doctor–patient interaction analysis. *Pediatric Research*, 5, 298–311.

Freund, A., Johnson, S. B., Silverstein, J., & Thomas, J. (1991). Assessing daily management of childhood diabetes using 24-hour recall interviews: Reliability and stability. *Health Psychology*, 10, 200–208.

Friedman, I., Litt, I., King, D., Henson, R., Holtzman, D., Halverson, D., & Kraemer, H. (1986). Compliance with anticonvulsant therapy by epileptic youth. *Journal of Adolescent Health Care*, 7, 12–17.

Friedman, R., Sobel, D., Myers, P., Caudill, M., & Benson, H. (1995). Behavioral medicine, clinical health psychology, and cost offset. *Health Psychology*, 14, 509–518.

Fritz, G., Klein, R., & Overholser, J. (1990). Accuracy of symptom perception in childhood asthma. *Journal of Developmental and Behavioral Pediatrics*, 11, 69–72.

Gaffney, A., & Dunne, E.A. (1986). Developmental

aspects of children's definitions of pain. *Pain, 26,* 105–117.

Garber, J., Zeman, J. L., & Walker, L. S. (1990). Recurrent abdominal pain in children: Psychiatric diagnoses and maternal psychopathology. *Journal of the American Academy of Child and Adolescent Psychiatry, 29,* 648–656.

Garner, A., Thompson, C., & Partridge, J. (1969). Who knows best? *Diabetes Bulletin, 45,* 3–4.

Gayton, W. F., Friedman, S. B., Tavormina, J. F., & Tucker, F. (1977). Children with cystic fibrosis: I. Psychological test findings of patients, siblings, and parents. *Pediatrics, 59,* 888–894.

Gedaly-Duff, V. (1991). Developmental issues: Preschool and school-age children. In J. P. Bush & S. W. Harkins (Eds.), *Children in pain: Clinical and research issues from a developmental perspective* (pp. 195–229). New York: Springer-Verlag.

Gibaud-Wallston, J., & Wandersman, L. P. (1978, September). *Development and utility of the Parenting Sense of Competence Scale.* Paper presented at the annual meeting of the American Psychological Association, Toronto.

Gilbert, B. O., Johnson, S. B., Spillar, R., McCallum, M., Silverstein, J. H., & Rosenbloom, A. (1982). The effects of a peer-modeling film on children learning to self-inject insulin. *Behavior Therapy, 13,* 186–193.

Gortmaker, S. L., & Sappenfield, W. (1984). Chronic childhood disorders: Prevalence and impact. *Pediatric Clinics of North America, 31,* 3–18.

Gortmaker, S., Walker, D., Weitzman, M., & Sobol, A. (1990). Chronic conditions, socioeconomic risks, and behavioral problems in children and adolescents. *Pediatrics, 85,* 267–276.

Graetz, B., & Shute, R. (1995). Assessment of peer relationships in children with asthma. *Journal of Pediatric Psychology, 20,* 205–216.

Greene, W. B., & Strickler, E. M. (1983). A modified isokinetic strengthening program for patients with severe hemophilia. *Developmental Medicine and Child Neurology, 25,* 189–196.

Greger, J., & Etnyre, G. (1978). Validity of 24-hour dietary recalls by adolescent females. *American Journal of Public Health, 68,* 70–72.

Gross, A. M., Johnson, W. G., Wildman, H. E., & Mullett, M. (1981). Coping skills training with insulin-dependent preadolescent diabetics. *Child Behavior Therapy, 3,* 141–153.

Gross, A. M., Samson, G., Sanders, S., & Smith, C. (1988). Patient noncompliance: Are children consistent? *American Journal of Orthodontics and Dentofacial Orthopedics, 93,* 518–519.

Gunnar, M. R., Fisch, R. O., & Malone, S. (1984). The effects of a pacifying stimulus on behavioral and adrenocortical responses to circumcision in the newborn. *Journal of the American Academy of Child Psychiatry, 23,* 34–38.

Hackworth, S. R., & McMahon, R. J. (1991). Factors mediating children's health care attitudes. *Journal of Pediatric Psychology, 16,* 69–85.

Haggerty, R. J. (1984). Foreword: Symposium on chronic disease in children. *Pediatric Clinics of North America, 31,* 1–2.

Hamlett, K. W., Pellegrini, D. S., & Katz, K. S. (1992). Childhood chronic illness as a family stress. *Journal of Pediatric Psychology, 17,* 33–47.

Harbeck, C., & Peterson, L. (1992). "Elephants dancing in my head": A developmental approach to children's concepts of specific pains. *Child Development, 63,* 138–149.

Harkavy, J., Johnson, S. B., Silverstein, J., Spillar, R., McCallum, M., & Rosenbloom, A. (1983). Who learns what at diabetes summer camp. *Journal of Pediatric Psychology, 8,* 143–153.

Harper, D., Wacker, D., & Cobb, L. (1986). Children's social preferences toward peers with visible physical differences. *Journal of Pediatric Psychology, 11,* 323–342.

Hauenstein, J. (1990). The experience of distress in parents of chronically ill children: Potential or likely outcome? *Journal of Clinical Child Psychology, 19,* 356–364.

Hauser, S., Jacobson, A., Lavori, P., Wolfsdort, J., Herskowitz, R., Milley, J., & Bliss, R. (1990). Adherence among children and adolescents with insulin-dependent diabetes mellitus over a 4 year longitudinal follow-up: II. Immediate and long-term linkages with family milieu. *Journal of Pediatric Psychology, 15,* 527–542.

Hawkins, D. R. (1982). Specificity revisited: Personality profiles and behavioral issues. *Psychotherapy and Psychosomatics, 38,* 54–63.

Hazzard, A., Hutchinson, S., & Krawiecki, N. (1990). Factors related to adherence to medication regimens in pediatric seizure patients. *Journal of Pediatric Psychology, 15,* 543–555.

Henggeler, S. W., Rodick, J. D., Borduin, C. M., Hanson, C. L., Watson, S. M., & Urey, J. R. (1986). Multisystemic treatment of juvenile offenders: Effects on adolescent behavior and family interaction. *Developmental Psychology, 22,* 132–141.

Henggeler, S. W., & Tavormina, J. R. (1980). Social class and race differences in family interaction: Pathological, normative, or confounding methodological factors? *Journal of Genetic Psychology, 137,* 211–222.

Hess, G. E., & Davis, W. K. (1983). The validation of a diabetes patient knowledge test. *Diabetes Care, 6,* 591–596.

Hoare, P. (1984). Psychiatric disturbance in the families of epileptic children. *Developmental Medicine and Child Neurology, 26,* 14–19.

Hodges, K., & Burbach, D. J. (1991). Recurrent abdominal pain. In J. P. Bush & S. W. Harkins (Eds.), *Children in pain: Clinical and research issues from a developmental perspective* (pp. 251–273). New York: Springer-Verlag.

Hodges, K., Kline, J., Barbero, G., & Flannery, R. (1985). Depressive symptoms in children with recurrent abdominal pain and their families. *Journal of Pediatrics*, 107, 622–626.

Ievers, C. E., Drotar, D., Dahms, W. T., Doershuk, C. F., & Stern, R. C. (1994). Maternal child-rearing behavior in three groups: Cystic fibrosis, insulin-dependent diabetes mellitus, and healthy children. *Journal of Pediatric Psychology*, 19, 681–687.

Ingersoll, G., Orr, D., Herrold, A., & Golden, M. (1986). Cognitive maturity and self-management among adolescents with insulin-dependent diabetes mellitus. *Journal of Pediatrics*, 108, 620–623.

Jay, S. M., & Elliott, C. H. (1981). *Observation Scale of Behavioral Distress*. Los Angeles: Division of Hematology–Oncology, Children's Hospital of Los Angeles.

Jay, S. M., Ozolins, M., Elliott, C. H., & Caldwell, S. (1983). Assessment of children's distress during painful medical procedures. *Health Psychology*, 2, 133–147.

Johnson, S. B. (1984). *Test of Diabetes Knowledge Revised—3*. Gainesville: University of Florida, Department of Psychiatry.

Johnson, S. B. (1985). *The Skills Test for Insulin Injection*. Gainesville: University of Florida, Department of Psychiatry.

Johnson, S. B. (1992). Methodological issues in diabetes research: Measuring adherence. *Diabetes Care*, 15, 1658–1667.

Johnson, S. B. (1994a). Chronic illness in children. In G. Penny, B. Bennett, & M. Herbert (Eds.), *Health psychology: A lifespan perspective* (pp. 31–50). Chur, Switzerland: Harwood Academic.

Johnson, S. B. (1994b). Health behavior and health status: Concepts, methods, and applications. *Journal of Pediatric Psychology*, 19, 129–141.

Johnson, S. B. (1995). Managing insulin-dependent diabetes mellitus in adolescence: A developmental perspective. In J. Wallander & L. Siegel (Eds.), *Adolescent health problems: Behavioral perspectives* (pp. 265–288). New York: Guilford Press.

Johnson, S. B., Freund, A., Silverstein, J., Hansen, C., & Malone, J. (1990). Adherence/health status relationships in childhood diabetes. *Health Psychology*, 9, 606–631.

Johnson, S. B., Kelly, M., Henretta, J., Cunningham, W., Tomer, A., & Silverstein, J. (1992). A longitudinal analysis of adherence and health status in childhood diabetes. *Journal of Pediatric Psychology*, 17, 537–553.

Johnson, S. B., Lewis-Meert, C., & Alexander B. (1981). *Administration and scoring manual for Chemstrip Skill Demonstration Test*. Gainesville: University of Florida, Department of Psychiatry.

Johnson, S. B., Pollak, T., Silverstein, J. H., Rosenbloom, A. L., Spillar, R., McCallum, M., & Harkavy, J. (1982). Cognitive and behavioral knowledge about insulin dependent diabetes among children and parents. *Pediatrics*, 69, 708–713.

Johnson, S. B., Silverstein, J., Rosenbloom, A., Carter, R., & Cunningham, W. (1986). Assessing daily management of childhood diabetes. *Health Psychology*, 5, 545–564.

Johnson, S. B., Tomer, A., Cunningham, W., & Henretta, J. (1990). Adherence in childhood diabetes: Results of a confirmatory factor analysis. *Health Psychology*, 9, 493–501.

Johnston, C., & Mash, E. J. (1989). A measure of parenting satisfaction and efficacy. *Journal of Clinical Child Psychology*, 18, 167–175.

Kager, V., & Holden, E. (1992). Preliminary investigation of the direct and moderating effects of family and individual variables on the adjustment of children and adolescents with diabetes. *Journal of Pediatric Psychology*, 17, 491–502.

Kaplan, R. M., Chadwick, M. W., & Schimmel, L. E. (1985). Social learning intervention to promote metabolic control in type I diabetes mellitus: Pilot experiment results. *Diabetes Care*, 8, 152–155.

Karoly, P. (1991). Assessment of pediatric pain. In J. P. Bush & S. W. Harkins (Eds.), *Children in pain: Clinical and research issues from a developmental perspective* (pp. 59–82). New York: Springer-Verlag.

Karoly, P. (1995). The assessment of pain: Concepts and issues. In P. Karoly (Ed.), *Measurement strategies in health psychology* (pp. 461–515). New York: Wiley.

Karoly, P., & Jensen, M. P. (1987). *Multimethod assessment of chronic pain*. Oxford: Pergamon Press.

Karp, M., Manor, M., & Laron, Z. (1970). What do juvenile diabetics and their families know about diabetes? In Z. Laron (Ed.), *Habilitation and rehabilitation of juvenile diabetics* (pp. 83–89). Leiden, The Netherlands: H. E. Stenfert Kroese.

Katz, E. R., Kellerman, J., & Ellenberg, L. (1987). Hypnosis in the reduction of acute pain and distress with cancer. *Journal of Pediatric Psychology*, 12, 379–394.

Katz, E. R., Kellerman, J., & Siegel, S. E. (1980). Behavioral distress in children with cancer undergoing medical procedures: Developmental considerations. *Journal of Consulting and Clinical Psychology*, 48, 356–365.

Katz, E. R., Varni, J. W., & Jay, S. M. (1984). Behavioral assessment and management of pediatric pain. *Progress in Behavior Modification*, 18, 163–193.

Kazak, A., Segal-Andrews, A., & Johnson, K. (1995). Pediatric psychology research and practice: A family/systems approach. In M. Roberts (Ed.), *Handbook of pediatric psychology* (2nd ed., pp. 84–104). New York: Guilford Press.

Kermani, E. (1988). Handicapped children and the law: Children afflicted with AIDS. *Journal of the American Academy of Child and Adolescent Psychiatry*, 27, 152–154.

Kolko, D. J., & Rickard-Figueroa, J. L. (1985). Effects of video games on the adverse corollaries of chemotherapy in pediatric oncology patients: A single-case analysis. *Journal of Consulting and Clinical Psychology, 53,* 223–228.

Korsch, B. M., Gozzi, E. K., & Francis, V. (1968). Gaps in doctor–patient communication: I. Doctor–patient interaction and patient satisfaction. *Pediatrics, 42,* 855–871.

Kovacs, M., Brent, D., Steinberg, T., Paulauskas, S., & Reid, J. (1986). Children's self-reports of psychological adjustment and coping strategies during the first year of insulin-dependent diabetes mellitus. *Diabetes Care, 9,* 568–575.

Kovacs, M., Finkelstein, R., Feinberg, R., Crouse-Novak, M., Paulauskas, S., & Pollock, M. (1985). Initial psychological responses of parents to the diagnosis of insulin-dependent diabetes mellitus in their children. *Diabetes Care, 8,* 568–575.

Kovacs, M., Iyengar, S., Goldston, D., Obrosky, D., Stewart, J., & Marsh, J. (1990). Psychological functioning among mothers of children with insulin-dependent diabetes mellitus: A longitudinal study. *Journal of Consulting and Clinical Psychology, 58,* 189–195.

Krahn, G., Eisert, D., & Fifield, B. (1990). Obtaining parental perceptions of the quality of services for children with special health needs. *Journal of Pediatric Psychology, 15,* 761–774.

Kronenberger, W., & Thompson, R. (1992). Psychological adaptation of mothers of children with spina bifida: Association with dimensions of social relationships. *Journal of Pediatric Psychology, 17,* 1–14.

Kulik, J., & Carlino, C. (1987). The effect of verbal commitment and treatment choice on medication compliance in a pediatric setting. *Journal of Behavioral Medicine, 10,* 367–376.

Labbe, E. L., & Williamson, D. A. (1984). Treatment of childhood migraine using autogenic feedback training. *Journal of Consulting and Clinical Psychology, 52,* 968–976.

Lansky, S. B., Cairns, N. U., Hassanein, R., Wehr, J., & Lowman, J. T. (1978). Childhood cancer: Parental discord and divorce. *Pediatrics, 62,* 184–188.

Latimer, P. (1979). Psychophysiologic disorders: A critical appraisal of concept and theory illustrated with reference to the irritable bowel syndrome (IBS). *Psychological Medicine, 9,* 71–80.

Lavigne, J. V., & Faler-Routman, J. (1992). Psychological adjustment to pediatric physical disorders: A meta-analytic review. *Journal of Pediatric Psychology, 17,* 133–157.

Lavigne, J. V., & Faler-Routman, J. (1993). Correlates of psychological adjustment to pediatric physical disorders: A meta-analytic review and comparison with existing models. *Journal of Developmental and Behavioral Pediatrics, 14,* 117–123.

Lavigne, J. V., & Ryan, M. (1979). Psychologic adjustment to siblings of children with chronic illness. *Pediatrics, 63,* 616–627.

Lavigne, J. V., Traisman, H. S., Marr, T. J., & Chasnoff, I. J. (1982). Parental perceptions of the psychological adjustment of children with diabetes and their siblings. *Diabetes Care, 5,* 420–426.

LeBaron, S., & Zeltzer, L. (1984). Assessment of acute pain and anxiety in children and adolescents by self-reports, observer reports, and a behavior checklist. *Journal of Consulting and Clinical Psychology, 52,* 729–738.

Lemanek, K., Horwitz, W., & Ohene-Frempong, K. (1994). A multiperspective investigation of social competence in children with sickle cell disease. *Journal of Pediatric Psychology, 19,* 443–456.

Litt, I. F., & Cuskey, W. R. (1981). Compliance with salicylate therapy in adolescents with juvenile rheumatoid arthritis. *American Journal of Diseases of Children, 135,* 434–436.

Lobato, D. (1983). Siblings of handicapped children: A review. *Journal of Autism and Developmental Disorders, 13,* 347–363.

Lobato, D., Faust, D., & Spirito, A. (1988). Examining the effects of chronic disease and disability on children's sibling relationships. *Journal of Pediatric Psychology, 13,* 389–407.

Lollar, D. J., Smits, S. J., & Patterson, D. L. (1982). Assessment of pediatric pain: An empirical perspective. *Journal of Pediatric Psychology, 7,* 267–277.

Long, C. G., & Moore, J. R. (1979). Parental expectations for their epileptic children. *Journal of Child Psychology and Psychiatry, 20,* 299–312.

Loveland, K., Stehbens, J., Contant, C., Bordeaux, J., Sirois, P., & Bell, T. (1994). Hemophilia growth and development study: Baseline neurodevelopmental findings. *Journal of Pediatric Psychology, 19,* 223–239.

Lowe, K., & Lutzker, J. R. (1979). Increasing compliance to a medical regimen with a juvenile diabetic. *Behavior Therapy, 10,* 57–64.

Maiman, L., Becker, M., Liptak, G., Nazarian, L., & Rounds, K. (1988). Improving pediatricians' compliance-enhancing practices: A randomized trial. *American Journal of Diseases of Children, 142,* 773–779.

Manne, S., Jacobsen, P., Gorfinkle, K., Gerstein, F., & Redd, W. H. (1993). Treatment adherence difficulties among children with cancer: The role of parenting style. *Journal of Pediatric Psychology, 8,* 47–62.

Manne, S., Redd, W. H., Jacobsen, P., Gorfinkle, K., Schorr, O., & Rapkin, B. (1990). Behavioral intervention to reduce child and parent distress during venipuncture. *Journal of Consulting and Clinical Psychology, 58,* 565–572.

Marteau, T., Johnston, M., Baum, J., & Bloch, S. (1985). Goals of treatment in diabetes: A comparison of doctors and parents of children with diabetes. *Journal of Behavioral Medicine, 10,* 33–48.

Masek, B. J., Russo, D. C., & Varni, J. W. (1984). Behavioral approaches to the management of chronic pain in children. *Pediatric Clinics of North America, 31,* 1113–1131.

Mazzuca, S. (1982). Does patient education in chronic disease have therapeutic value? *Journal of Chronic Diseases, 35,* 521–529.

McCauley, E., Ross, J., Kushner, H., & Cutler, G. (1995). Self-esteem and behavior in girls with Turner syndrome. *Journal of Developmental and Behavioral Pediatrics, 16,* 82–88.

McCollum, A. T. (1971). Cystic fibrosis: Economic impact upon the family. *American Journal of Pediatric Health, 61,* 1335–1340.

McCoy, K. (1994). Cystic fibrosis. In R. Olson, L. Mullins, J. Gillman, & J. Chaney (Eds.), *The sourcebook of pediatric psychology* (pp. 199–203). Boston: Allyn & Bacon.

McCubbin, M. A. (1987). Coping Health Inventory for Parents. In H. I. McCubbin & A. I. Thompson (Eds.), *Family assessment inventories for research and practice* (pp. 175–192). Madison: University of Wisconsin, Family Stress Coping and Health Project.

McCubbin, H. I., & Comeau, J. (1987). FIRM: Family Inventory of Resources for Management. In H. I. McCubbin & A. I. Thompson (Eds.), *Family assessment inventories for research and practice* (pp. 145–160). Madison: University of Wisconsin, Family Stress Coping and Health Project.

McGinnis, J., & Foege, W. (1993). Actual causes of death in the United States. *Journal of the American Medical Association, 270,* 2207–2212.

McGrath, P. A. (1987). The multidimensional assessment and management of recurrent pain syndromes in children. *Behaviour Research and Therapy, 25,* 251–262.

McGrath, P. A., & deVeber, L. L. (1986). The management of acute pain evoked by medical procedures in children with cancer. *Journal of Pain and Symptom Management, 1,* 145–150.

McGrath, P. A., deVeber, L. L., & Hearn, M. T. (1985). Multidimensional pain assessment in children. In H. L. Fields, R. Dubner, & F. Cervero (Eds.), *Advances in pain research and therapy: Proceedings of the Fourth World Congress on Pain* (Vol. 9, pp. 387–393). New York: Raven Press.

McGrath, P. J., & Pisterman, S. (1991). Developmental issues: Adolescent pain. In J. P. Bush & S. W. Harkins (Eds.), *Children in pain: Clinical and research issues from a developmental perspective* (pp. 231–248). New York: Springer-Verlag.

McGrath, P. J., Johnson, G., Goodman, J. T., Schillinger, J., Dunn, J., & Chapman, J. (1985). CHEOPS: A behavioral scale for rating post-operative pain in children. In H. L. Fields, R. Dubner, & F. Cervero (Eds.), *Advances in pain research and therapy* (Vol. 9, pp. 395–402). New York: Raven Press.

McKinney, B., & Peterson, R. (1987). Predictors of stress in parents of developmentally disabled children. *Journal of Pediatric Psychology Research, 12,* 133–150.

Miller, A., Gordon, R., Daniele, R., & Diller, L. (1992). Stress, appraisal, and coping in mothers of disabled and nondisabled children. *Journal of Pediatric Psychology, 17,* 587–605.

Miller, N. E. (1983). Behavioral medicine: Symbiosis between laboratory and clinic. *Annual Review of Psychology, 34,* 1–34.

Moos, R., & Moos, B. (1981). *Family Environment Scale manual.* Palo Alto, CA: Consulting Psychologists Press.

Mullins, L., Olson, R., Reyes, S., Bernardy, N., Huszti, H., & Volk, R. (1991). Risk and resistance factors in the adaptation of mothers of children with cystic fibrosis. *Journal of Pediatric Psychology, 16,* 701–715.

Nassau, J., & Drotar, D. (1995). Social competence in children with IDDM and asthma: Child, teacher, and parent reports of children's social adjustment, social performance, and social skills. *Journal of Pediatric Psychology, 20,* 187–204.

Newacheck, P. (1994). Poverty and childhood chronic illness. *Archives of Pediatric and Adolescent Medicine, 148,* 1143–1149.

Newberry, M., & Parrish, T. (1986). Enhancement of attitudes toward handicapped children through social interactions. *Journal of Social Psychology, 127,* 59–62.

Noll, R., Bukowski, W., Davies, W., Koontz, K., & Kulkarni, R. (1993). Adjustment to the peer system in adolescents with cancer: A two-year study. *Journal of Pediatric Psychology, 18,* 351–364.

O'Dougherty, M. M. (1983). *Counseling the chronically ill child: Psychological impact and intervention.* Lexington, MA: Lewis.

Osborne, M., Kistner, J., & Helgemo, B. (1993). Developmental progression in children's knowledge of AIDS: Implications for education and attitudinal change. *Journal of Pediatric Psychology, 18,* 177–192.

Page, P., Verstraete, D. G., Robb, J. R., & Etzwiler, D. D. (1981). Patient recall of self-care recommendations in diabetes. *Diabetes Care, 4,* 96–98.

Parsons, T. (1951). *The social system.* New York: Free Press.

Partridge, J. W., Garner, A. M., Thompson, C. W., & Cherry, T. (1972). Attitudes of adolescents toward their diabetes. *American Journal of Diseases of Children, 124,* 226–229.

Patterson, J. M. (1985). Critical factors affecting family compliance with cystic fibrosis. *Family Relations, 34,* 79–89.

Patterson, J. M., & Garwick, A. W. (1994). The impact of chronic illness on families: A family systems perspective. *Annals of Behavioral Medicine, 16,* 131–142.

Patterson, J. M., Leonard, B., & Titus, J. (1992). Home care for medically fragile children: Impact on family health and well-being. *Journal of Developmental and Behavioral Pediatrics, 13,* 248–255.

Patterson, J. M., McCubbin, H. I., & Warwick, W. J. (1990). The impact of family functioning on health changes in children with cystic fibrosis. *Social Science and Medicine, 31,* 159–164.

Perrin, E. C., & Perrin, J. M. (1983). Clinician's assessments of children's understanding of illness. *American Journal of Diseases of Children, 137,* 874–878.

Perrin, E. C., Ramsey, B., & Sandler, H. (1987). Competent kids: Children and adolescents with a chronic illness. *Child: Care, Health and Development, 13,* 13–32.

Perrin, E. C., Stein, E., & Drotar, D. (1991). Cautions in using the Child Behavior Checklist: Observations based on research about children with a chronic illness. *Journal of Pediatric Psychology, 16,* 411–421.

Peterson, E. T. (1972). The impact of adolescent illness on parental relationships. *Journal of Health and Social Behavior, 13,* 429–437.

Peterson, L., Harbeck, C., Farmer, J., & Zink, M. (1991). Developmental contributions to the assessment of children's pain: Conceptual and methodological implications. In J. P. Bush & S. W. Harkins (Eds.), *Children in pain: Clinical and research issues from a developmental perspective* (pp. 33–58). New York: Springer-Verlag.

Phipps, S., & DeCuir-Whalley, S. (1990). Adherence issues in pediatric bone marrow transplantation. *Journal of Pediatric Psychology, 15,* 459–475.

Pless, I. B. (1984). Clinical assessment: Physical and psychological functioning. *Pediatric Clinics of North America, 31,* 33–45.

Pless, I. B., Roghmann, K., & Haggerty, R. J. (1972). Chronic illness, family functioning, and psychological adjustment: A model for the allocation of preventive mental health services. *International Journal of Epidemiology, 1,* 271–277.

Reynolds, L., Johnson, S. B., & Silverstein, J. (1990). Assessing daily diabetes management by 24-hr recall interview: The validity of children's reports. *Journal of Pediatric Psychology, 15,* 493–509.

Roberts, J., Burchinal, M., & Campbell, F. (1994). Otitis media in early childhood and patterns of intellectual development and later academic performance. *Journal of Pediatric Psychology, 19,* 347–367.

Roberts, M. C., & Wallander, J. L. (Eds.). (1992). *Family issues in pediatric psychology.* Hillsdale, NJ: Erlbaum.

Rodrigue, J. R., Geffken, G. R., Clark, J. E., & Fishel, P. (1994). Parenting satisfaction and efficacy among caregivers of children with diabetes. *Children's Health Care, 23,* 181–191.

Rodrigue, J. R., Graham-Pole, J., Kury, S. P., Kubar, W., & Hoffman, R. G. (in press). Behavioral distress, fear, and pain among children hospitalized for bone marrow transplantation. *Clinical Transplantation.*

Rodrigue, J. R., MacNaughton, K., Hoffmann, R. G., Graham-Pole, J., Andres, J., Novak, D., & Fennell, R. (1996). *Transplantation in children: A longitudinal assessment of mothers' stress, coping and perceptions of family functioning.* Manuscript submitted for publication.

Rodrigue, J. R., Morgan, S. B., & Geffken, G. R. (1992). Psychosocial adaptation of fathers of children with autism, Down syndrome, and normal development. *Journal of Autism and Developmental Disorders, 22,* 249–263.

Ross, D. M., & Ross, S. M. (1988). *Childhood pain: Current issues, research, and management.* Baltimore: Urban & Schwarzenberg.

Routh, D. K., Ernst, A. R., & Harper, D. C. (1988). Recurrent abdominal pain in children and Somatization Disorder. In D. K. Routh (Ed.), *Handbook of pediatric psychology* (pp. 492–504). New York: Guilford Press.

Royal, G., & Roberts, M. (1987). Students' perceptions of and attitudes toward disabilities: A comparison of twenty conditions. *Journal of Clinical Child Psychology, 16,* 122–132.

Ryan, C. (1990). Neuropsychological consequences and correlates of diabetes in childhood. In C. Holmes (Ed.), *Neuropsychological and behavioral aspects of diabetes* (pp. 58–84). New York: Springer-Verlag.

Sabbeth, B. F., & Leventhal, J. M. (1984). Marital adjustment to chronic childhood illness: A critique of the literature. *Pediatrics, 73,* 762–768.

Sahler, O., Roghmann, K., Carpenter, P., Mulhern, R., Dolgin, M., Sargent, J., Barbarin, O., Copeland, D., & Zeltzer, L. (1994). Sibling adaptation to childhood cancer collaborative study: Prevalence of sibling distress and definition of adaptation levels. *Journal of Developmental and Behavioral Pediatrics, 15,* 353–366.

Samuelson, G. (1970). An epidemiological study of child health and nutrition in a northern Swedish county: II. Methodological study of the recall technique. *Nutrition and Metabolism, 12,* 321–340.

Sanders, M. R., Shepherd, R. W., Cleghorn, G., & Woolford, H. (1994). The treatment of recurrent abdominal pain in children: A controlled comparison of cognitive–behavioral family intervention and standard pediatric care. *Journal of Consulting and Clinical Psychology, 62,* 306–314.

Sanger, M., Perrin, E., & Sandler, H. (1993). Development of children's causal theories of their seizure disorders. *Journal of Developmental and Behavioral Pediatrics, 14,* 88–93.

Santilli, L., & Roberts, M. (1993). Children's perceptions of ill peers as a function of illness conceptualization and attributions of responsibility: AIDS as a paradigm. *Journal of Pediatric Psychology, 18,* 193–207.

Sargent, J., Sahler, O., Roghman, K., Mulhern, R., Barbarian, O., Carpenter, P., Copeland, D., Dolgin, M., & Zeltzer, L. (1995). Sibling adaptation to childhood cancer collaborative study: Siblings' perceptions of the cancer experience. *Journal of Pediatric Psychology, 20,* 151–164.

Satterwhite, B. B. (1978). Impact of chronic illness on child and family: An overview based on five surveys with implications for management. *International Journal of Rehabilitation Research, 1,* 7–17.

Savedra, M., Gibbons, P., Tesler, M., Ward, J., & Wegner, C. (1982). How do children describe pain? A tentative assessment. *Pain, 14,* 95–104.

Schafer, L. C., Glasgow, R. E., & McCaul, K. D. (1982). Increasing adherence of diabetic adolescents. *Journal of Behavioral Medicine, 5,* 353–363.

Schafer, L. C., Glasgow, R. E., McCaul, K. D., & Dreher, M. (1983). Adherence to IDDM regimens: Relationship to psychosocial variables and metabolic control. *Diabetes Care, 6,* 493–498.

Schechter, N. L. (1984). Recurrent pains in children: An overview and an approach. *Pediatric Clinics of North America, 31,* 949–968.

Sergis-Deavenport, E., & Varni, J. W. (1983). Behavioral assessment and management of adherence to factor replacement therapy in hemophilia. *Journal of Pediatric Psychology, 8,* 367–377.

Shapiro, A. K. (1978). Placebo effects in medical and psychological therapies. In S. L. Garfield & A. E. Bergin (Eds.) *Handbook of psychotherapy and behavior change: An empirical analysis* (2nd ed., pp. 369–410). New York: Wiley.

Shapiro, J. (1983). Family reactions and coping strategies in response to the physically ill or handicapped child: A review. *Social Science and Medicine, 17,* 913–931.

Sigelman, C., & Begleym, N. (1987). The early development of reactions to peers with controllable and uncontrollable problems. *Journal of Pediatric Psychology, 12,* 99–115.

Sigelman, C., Mukai, T., Woods, T., & Alfeld, C. (1995). Parents' contributions to children's knowledge and attitudes regarding AIDS: Another look. *Journal of Pediatric Psychology, 20,* 61–77.

Simonian, S., Tarnowski, K., Park, A. & Bekeny, P. (1993). Child, parent, and physician perceived satisfaction with pediatric outpatient visits. *Journal of Developmental and Behavioral Pediatrics, 14,* 8–12.

Simonds, J. F. (1977). Psychiatric status of diabetic youth matched with a control group. *Journal of the American Diabetes Association, 26,* 921–925.

Smith, S. D., Rosen, D., Trueworthy, R. C., & Lowman, J. T. (1979). A reliable method for evaluating drug compliance in children with cancer. *Cancer, 43,* 169–173.

Smyth-Staruch, K., Breslau, N., Weitzman, M., & Gortmaker, S. (1984). Use of health services by chronically ill and disabled children. *Medical Care, 22,* 310–328.

Spaulding, B. R., & Morgan, S. B. (1986). Spina bifida children and their parents: A population prone to family dysfunction? *Journal of Pediatric Psychology, 11,* 359–374.

Speltz, M., Armsden, G., & Clarren, S. (1990). Effects of craniofacial birth defects on maternal functioning. *Journal of Pediatric Psychology, 15,* 177–196.

Spencer, C., Zanga, J., Passo, M., & Walker, D. (1986). The child with arthritis in the school setting. *Pediatric Clinics of North America, 33,* 1251–1264.

Spevack, M., Johnson, S. B., & Riley, W. (1991). The effect of diabetes summer camp on adherence behaviors and glycemic control. In J. Johnson & S. B. Johnson (Eds.), *Advances in child health psychology* (pp. 285–292). Gainesville: University of Florida Presses.

Stabler, B., Clopper, R., Siegel, P., Stoppani, C., Compton, P., & Underwood, L. (1994). Academic achievement and psychological adjustment in short children. *Journal of Developmental and Behavioral Pediatrics, 15,* 1–6.

Staudenmayer, H. (1982). Medical manageability and psychosocial factors in childhood asthma. *Journal of Chronic Diseases, 35,* 183–192.

Stein, R. E., & Riessman, C. K. (1980). The development of an impact-on-family scale: Preliminary findings. *Medical Care, 18,* 465–472.

Stern, M., Ross, S., & Bielass, M. (1991). Medical students' perceptions of children: Modifying a childhood cancer stereotype. *Journal of Pediatric Psychology, 16,* 27–38.

Stewart, S., Campbell, R., McCallon, D., Waller, D., & Andrews, W. (1992). Cognitive patterns in school-age children with end-stage liver disease. *Journal of Developmental and Behavioral Pediatrics, 13,* 331–338.

Stewart, S., Silver, C., Nici, J., Waller, D., Campbell, R., Uauy, R., & Andrews, W. (1991). Neuropsychological function in young children who have undergone liver transplantation. *Journal of Pediatric Psychology, 16,* 569–583.

Stunkard, A., & Waxman, M. (1981). Accuracy of self-reports of food intake. *Journal of the American Dietetic Association, 79,* 547–551.

Tarnowski, K., Rasnake, L., Gavaghan-Jones, M., & Smith, M. (1991). Psychosocial sequelae of pediatric burn injuries: A review. *Clinical Psychology Review, 11,* 371–398.

Tattersall, R. B., & Lowe, J. (1981). Diabetes in adolescence. *Diabetologia, 20,* 517–523.

Tavormina, J., Boll, R., Dunn, N., Luscomb, R., & Taylor, J. (1981). Psychosocial effects on parents of raising a physically handicapped child. *Journal of Abnormal Child Psychology, 9,* 121–131.

Tebbi, C., Cummings, M., Zevon, M., Smith, L., Richards, M., & Mallon, J. (1986). Compliance of pediatric and adolescent cancer patients. *Cancer, 58,* 1179–1184.

Thompson, R. I. (1985). Coping with the stress of chronic childhood illness. In A. N. O'Quinn (Ed.), *Management of chronic disorders of childhood* (pp. 11–41). Boston: G. K. Hall.

Thompson, R. I., Gil, K., Burbach, D., Keith, B., & Kinney, T. (1993). Psychological adjustment of mothers of children and adolescents with sickle cell disease: The role of stress, coping methods, and family functioning. *Journal of Pediatric Psychology, 18,* 549–559.

Thompson, R. I., Gil, K., Gustafson, K., George, B., Keith, B., Spock, A., & Kinney, T. (1994). Stability and change in the psychological adjustment of mothers of children and adolescents with cystic fibrosis and sickle cell disease. *Journal of Pediatric Psychology, 19,* 171–188.

Thompson, R. I., Gustafson, K., Hamlett, K., & Spock, A. (1992). Stress, coping, and family functioning in the psychological adjustment of mothers of children and adolescents with cystic fibrosis. *Journal of Pediatric Psychology, 17,* 573–586.

Thompson, S., Dahlquist, L., Koenning, G., & Bartholomew, K. (1995). Brief report: Adherence-facilitating behaviors of a multidisciplinary pediatric rheumatology staff. *Journal of Pediatric Psychology, 20,* 291–297.

Travis, L., Brouhard, B., & Schreiner, B. (1987). *Diabetes mellitus in children and adolescents.* Philadelphia: W. B. Saunders.

Vance, V. J., & Taylor, W. F. (1971). The financial cost of chronic childhood asthma. *Annals of Allergy, 29,* 455–460.

Varni, J. W., & Jay, S. M. (1984). Biobehavioral factors in juvenile rheumatoid arthritis: Implications for research and practice. *Clinical Psychology Review, 4,* 543–560.

Varni, J. W., Katz, E. R., & Dash, J. (1982). Behavioral and neurochemical aspects of pediatric pain. In D. C. Russo & J. W. Varni (Eds.), *Behavioral pediatrics: Research and practice* (pp. 117–224). New York: Plenum Press.

Varni, J. W., Thompson, K. L., & Hanson, V. (1987). The Varni–Thompson Pediatric Pain Questionnaire: I. Chronic musculoskeletal pain in juvenile rheumatoid arthritis. *Pain, 28,* 27–38.

Vieyra, M. B., Hoag, N. L., & Masek, B. J. (1991). Migraine in childhood: Developmental aspects of biobehavioral treatment. In J. P. Bush & S. W. Harkins (Eds.), *Children in pain: Clinical and research issues from a developmental perspective* (pp. 373–395). New York: Springer-Verlag.

Walco, G. A., & Dampier, C. D. (1990). Pain in children and adolescents with sickle cell disease: A descriptive study. *Journal of Pediatric Psychology, 15,* 643–658.

Walker, J. G., Manion, I. G., Cloutier, P. F., & Johnson, S. M. (1992). Measuring marital distress in couples with chronically ill children: The Dyadic Adjustment Scale. *Journal of Pediatric Psychology, 17,* 345–357.

Walker, L. S., Ford, M., & Donald, W. (1987). Cystic fibrosis and family stress: Effects of age and severity of illness. *Pediatrics, 79,* 239–246.

Walker, L. S., Garber, J., & Greene, J. W. (1993). Psychosocial characteristics of recurrent childhood pain: A comparison of children with recurrent abdominal pain, organic illness, and psychiatric disorders. *Journal of Abnormal Psychology, 102,* 248–258.

Walker, L. S., Garber, J., & Van Slyke, D. A. (1995). Do parents excuse the misbehavior of children with physical or emotional symptoms? An investigation of the pediatric sick role. *Journal of Pediatric Psychology, 20,* 329–345.

Walker, L. S., & Greene, J. W. (1989). Children with recurrent abdominal pain and their parents: More somatic complaints, anxiety, and depression than other patient families. *Journal of Pediatric Psychology, 14,* 231–243.

Walker, L. S., & Greene, J. W. (1991). The Functional Disability Inventory: measuring a neglected dimension of child health status. *Journal of Pediatric Psychology, 16,* 39–58.

Walker, L. S., Greene, J. W., Garber, J., Horndasch, R. L., Barnard, J., & Ghishan, F. (1993). Psychosocial factors in pediatric abdominal pain: Implications for assessment and treatment. *The Clinical Psychologist, 46,* 206–213.

Walker, L. S., Van Slyke, D., & Newbrough, J. (1992). Family resources and stress: A comparison of families of children with cystic fibrosis, diabetes, and mental retardation. *Journal of Pediatric Psychology, 17,* 327–343.

Wallander, J., Varni, J., Babani, L., Banis, H., DeHaan, C., & Wilcox, K. (1989). Disability parameters, chronic strain, and adaptation of physically handicapped children and their mothers. *Journal of Pediatric Psychology, 14,* 23–42.

Wallander, J., Varni, J., Babani, L., DeHaan, C., Wilcox, K., & Banis, H. (1989). The social environment and the adaptation of mothers of physically handicapped children. *Journal of Pediatric Psychology, 14,* 371–387.

Walsh, M., & Bibace, R. (1991). Children's conceptions of AIDS: A developmental analysis. *Journal of Pediatric Psychology, 16,* 273–285.

Wasserman, A., Whitington, P., & Rivara, J. B. (1988). Psychogenic basis for abdominal pain in children and adolescents. *Journal of the American Academy of Child and Adolescent Psychiatry, 27,* 179–184.

Waters, B., & Milch, A. (1993). Psychoactive effects of medical drugs. In J. S. Werry & M. G. Aman (Eds.), *Practitioner's guide to psychoactive drugs for children and adolescents* (pp. 347–371). New York: Plenum Press.

Watkins, J. D., Roberts, D. E., Williams, T. F., Martin, D. A., & Coyle, V. (1967). Observations of medication errors made by diabetic patients in the home. *Diabetes, 16,* 882–885.

Weist, M., Finney, J., Barnard, M., Davis, C., & Ollendick, T. (1993). Empirical selection of psychosocial treatment targets for children and adolescents with diabetes. *Journal of Pediatric Psychology, 18,* 11–28.

Weitzman, M. (1986). School absence rates as outcome measures in studies of children with chronic illness. *Journal of Chronic Diseases, 39,* 799–808.

Weitzman, M., Walker, D., & Gortmaker, S. (1986). Chronic illness, psychosocial problems, and school absences: Results of a survey of one county. *Clinical Pediatrics, 25*, 137–141.

Whitt, J. K. (1984). Children's adaptation to chronic illness and handicapping conditions. In M. G. Eisenberg, L. C. Sutkin, & M. A. Jansen (Eds.), *Chronic illness and disability through the life span: Effects on self and family* (pp. 69–102). New York: Springer.

Williams, K., Ochs, J., Williams, J., & Mulhern, R. (1991). Parental report of everyday cognitive abilities among children treated for acute lymphoblastic leukemia. *Journal of Pediatric Psychology, 16*, 13–26.

Williamson, D. A., Baker, J. D., & Cubic, B. A. (1993). Advances in pediatric headache research. In T. H. Ollendick & R. J. Prinz (Eds.), *Advances in clinical child psychology* (Vol. 16, pp. 275–304). New York: Plenum Press.

Wills, K., Holmbeck, G., Dillon, D., & McLone, D. (1990). Intelligence and achievement in children with myelomeningocele. *Journal of Pediatric Psychology, 15*, 161–177.

Wysocki, T. (1993). Associations among teen–parent relationships, metabolic control, and adjustment to diabetes in adolescents. *Journal of Pediatric Psychology, 18*, 441–452.

Wysocki, T., Huxtable, K., Linscheid, T., & Wayne, W. (1989). Adjustment to diabetes mellitus in preschoolers and their mothers. *Diabetes Care, 12*, 524–529.

Wysocki, T., Meinhold, P., Abrams, K., Barnard, M., Clarke, W., Bellando, B., & Bourgeois, M. (1992). Parental and professional estimates of self-care independence of children and adolescents with IDDM. *Diabetes Care, 15*, 43–52.

Wysocki, T., Meinhold, P., Cox, D. & Clarke, W. (1990). Survey of diabetes professionals regarding developmental changes in diabetes self-care. *Diabetes Care, 13*, 65–67.

Zeltzer, L., & LeBaron, S. (1982). Hypnosis and non-hypnotic techniques for reduction of pain and anxiety during painful procedures in children and adolescents with cancer. *Journal of Pediatrics, 101*, 1032–1035.

Zora, J., Lutz, C., & Tinkelman, D. (1989). Assessment of compliance in children using inhaled beta adrenergic agonists. *Annals of Allergy, 62*, 406–409.

Part V

CHILDREN AT RISK

Chapter Eleven

CHILD PHYSICAL ABUSE AND NEGLECT

David A. Wolfe
Andrea McEachran

Over the past decade we have seen an explosion of reports, studies, committees, and panels commissioned to highlight our existing knowledge of child maltreatment, and to advance efforts at discovering effective prevention and intervention services (e.g., American Psychological Association, 1994; National Research Council [NRC], 1993; U.S. Advisory Board on Child Abuse and Neglect [USABCAN], 1990, 1993). In its first report to the nation, the USABCAN (1990) emphasized that extraordinary changes have occurred in the structure of U.S. families since 1960 (e.g., a 50% decline in the fertility rate; a fourfold increase in births outside marriage; a fourfold increase in the divorce rate; and a nearly threefold increase in the proportion of working mothers with small children), all of which have contributed to increasing stress on families and their access to resources. Not surprisingly, the board went on to announce that the scope of the problem of child maltreatment was so enormous and serious, and the failure of the system designed to deal with the problem was so catastrophic, that the crisis had reached the level of a national emergency. Three years later, in its proposal to develop a new national strategy for child protection and family assistance, the board continued its lament: "Tragically, the state of emergency remains in effect and may in fact be even more dire today than it was in 1990" (USABCAN, 1993, p. 3).

It is striking to consider that when Kempe and his colleagues first identified the "battered child syndrome" in the early 1960s (Kempe, Silverman, Steele, Droegemueller, & Silver, 1962), they esti-

mated that this phenomenon applied to only about 300 U.S. children. By the time of the USABCAN's first report in 1990, the number of official reports of suspected maltreatment had reached 2.4 million, and it climbed again to almost 3 million by the release of the 1993 report (Melton & Barry, 1994). In parallel, social science research has burgeoned over the past decade and a half, and has been at the forefront of recent efforts to curtail the rising incidence of child maltreatment.

In this chapter we present a comprehensive update and review of the major findings on child maltreatment, in order to formulate a multilevel framework for psychological assessment. Our emphasis here is on physical abuse and neglect (child sexual abuse is considered separately in Chapter 12 of this volume, though it and emotional abuse are mentioned from time to time here). Because of the advances in theory and research that have occurred since the last edition of this chapter (Wolfe, 1988), considerable new information has led to many changes and refinements in our assessment strategy. Most notably, assessment of the child is much more detailed because of the sizable number of new instruments and approaches that have been investigated; previously, assessment of the parent received the lion's share of attention, and little information was available as to either the effects on or the needs of the child. Although physical abuse again receives more coverage than child neglect, many recent studies have added more specificity to their procedures, and this allows for a better discrimination among factors relevant to assessment.

The scope of the chapter includes definitional issues, a developmental perspective on the abused/neglected child, a theoretical analysis of child maltreatment, and specific approaches for assessing parents and children where physical abuse and/or neglect are at issue. Research studies involving members of maltreating families are presented to facilitate an understanding of the complex interrelationships among social and psychological variables affecting the occurrence of child maltreatment (e.g., parental history, child-rearing skills, stressful events, etc.). Overall, the approach to assessment that is derived from this organization of the research and clinical literature is a multi-stage process—one that profits from recent advances in observational and self-report assessment strategies.

CHILD MALTREATMENT AND THE RISK OF IMPAIRED DEVELOPMENT

Children who lack the basic social and psychological necessities of life—food, affection, medical care, education, and intellectual and social stimulation—are considered to be at risk for impaired development, relative to children who do not lack such opportunities (Crouch & Milner, 1993). For example, a stressful or disadvantaged environment is associated with pronounced developmental impairments in intellectual, social, and affective functioning (Egeland, 1991). Epidemiological studies suggest that although a child may be able to tolerate a single chronic stressor or risk factor (e.g., poor housing, parental separation, school disruption, etc.) with little or no apparent harm, additional stressors may geometrically increase the risk of such adjustment problems as delinquency and school failure (Rutter, 1979). Similarly, abuse, neglect, emotional deprivation, and related forms of maltreatment do not appear to affect children in a predictable, characteristic fashion. Rather, the effects of these events upon children vary as a function of their frequency, intensity, and duration, coupled with the children's own resources and compensating experiences (Zahn-Waxler, Cole, Welsh, & Fox, 1995). Therefore, to understand the degree of potential risk of impaired development in a case of child maltreatment, we must evaluate the nature and severity of the maltreatment in relation to the child's personal and family resources. This calls for a developmental, systems-oriented approach to assessment—one that focuses on the characteristics of the parent, the child, and the circumstances surrounding the incident(s).

Definitions of Child Abuse and Neglect

The existence of adequate definitions of "abuse" and "neglect" is central to the entire system of service delivery to problem families. Communities must distinguish between families that need help and those that do not, and they also must educate all community members in the currently acceptable and unacceptable forms of child rearing (right or wrong, this is typically accomplished by defining or identifying the "failures" of the system). Although most communities have legal definitions to justify social intervention in cases of child maltreatment, the laws do not clearly specify what is or is not acceptable in operational terms. Legal definitions fall short of practical requirements because, as a function of cultural values, history, and community standards, one person's "abuse" may be another person's "discipline" (Korbin, 1994). Furthermore, standards used to determine whether a type of maltreatment has occurred or might occur tend to vary across different agencies within the same community. For example, hospital staff members may define "abuse" very conservatively (e.g., scratches or bruises on a child that are greater in number than those on other children attending a clinic), and may become frustrated or angered at the apparent unresponsiveness of the child protection agency in a particular case. *Ipso facto*, the protection agency may feel constrained by the requirements of the juvenile court for physical evidence to justify its involvement in a family's affairs.

The Child Abuse Prevention and Treatment Act of 1974 defines child abuse and neglect as follows:

> The physical or mental injury, sexual abuse or exploitation, negligent treatment, or maltreatment of a child under the age of eighteen, or the age specified by the child protection law of the State in question, by a person (including any employee of a residential facility or any staff person providing out-of-home care) who is responsible for the child's welfare under circumstances which indicate that the child's health or welfare is harmed or threatened thereby, as determined in regulations prescribed by the Secretary.

This definition was expanded in the Child Abuse, Prevention, Adoption and Family Services Act of 1988 to indicate that the behavior had to be avoidable and nonaccidental. This general definition, moreover, separates abuse into two categories: (1) moderate injury or impairment not requiring professional treatment but remaining observable for a minimum of 48 hours; and (2) serious injury or impairment involving a life-threatening condition, long-term impairment of physical capacities, or treatment to avoid such impairments. Based on these general criteria, acts considered to define physical abuse usually include scalding, beatings with an object, severe physical punishment, slapping, punching, and kicking; acts defining neglect include deficiencies in caretaker obligations (such as failure to meet the educational, supervisory, shelter, safety, medical, physical, or emotional needs of a child), as well as physical abandonment. For both types of maltreatment, the determination of occurrence is a judgment that must take into consideration such intangible factors as intensity, frequency, and duration of purported incidents, as well as the potential or real harm to the child.

For purposes of assessment and intervention, the definition of child abuse and neglect often includes cases of high-risk parenting practices that may fall short of documented injuries. Instead of employing a dichotomous definition (abusive vs. not abusive), such a view considers the full continuum of child-rearing acts, which may range from appropriate and developmentally sensitive behaviors to physically and verbally abusive ones (Wolfe, 1991). Accordingly, examples of family problems that are addressed by this assessment strategy include reliance upon high-intensity physical punishment; excessive criticism and verbal harassment of a child (i.e., "emotional abuse"); use of unorthodox disciplinary techniques (e.g., pressure points, shaking, public ridicule); lack of physical or verbal affection toward the child; failure to provide developmentally appropriate stimulation or opportunities to the child; extreme adult inconsistencies and "mood swings" that restrict the child's ability to adapt to his or her family environment; and similar episodes of parental inadequacy or ineffectiveness that warrant professional involvement. Because the determination of such events involves the judgment of professionals (rather than "evidence" per se), the definition of child abuse and neglect will vary somewhat in accordance with the purpose of the assessment and intervention concerns. This limited ambiguity is considered to be necessary and acceptable, in view of the current state of knowledge and the presumed advantage to a child and family in seeking assistance for wide-ranging problems (as opposed to labeling or punishing family members).

Incidence and Profile

Compared to all U.S. children, maltreated children are twice as likely to live in a single-parent, female-headed household; they are four times as likely to be supported by public assistance; and they experience numerous family stress factors, such as health problems, alcohol abuse/dependence, and partner abuse (Russell & Trainor, 1984). Based on yearly samples of over 1 million *confirmed* cases of maltreatment, child neglect/deprivation of necessities (e.g., inadequate clothing, nutrition or medical care, exposure to hazards, or being left unattended) continues to account for the sizable majority of cases, followed by physical abuse, sexual abuse, and emotional maltreatment. Notably, comparative analyses of data across time between 1983 and 1986 show that the percentage of neglect cases has been decreasing (45.7% to 36.1%), while the overall percentage of abuse reports (i.e., physical and sexual abuse) has been increasing (27.9% to 35.0%). This relative decline in neglect reports appears to be due to the dramatic increase in child sexual abuse reports—from 0.86 per 10,000 children in 1976 to 20.89 per 10,000 children in 1986 (NRC, 1993).

The number of *substantiated* victims of maltreatment (i.e., all forms of abuse and neglect) reported by 51 jurisdictions across the United States in 1993 was over 1 million (1,018,692), which represents an overall increase of 331% in the rate of substantiated reports since 1976. The majority of this increase is accounted for by rising reports of both physical abuse (up 58%) and sexual abuse (up 300%; National Center on Child Abuse and Neglect [NCCAN], 1995). This incidence figure results in a national child maltreatment reporting rate of 43 per 1,000 children in the under-18 population of the United States (NCCAN, 1995). Disturbingly, fatalities attributed to reports of abuse have also risen, from 899 in 1986 to 1,237 in 1989 (Daro, Casey, & Abrahams, 1990).

With these considerations in mind, several findings stand out in the analyses of trends in child maltreatment reporting statistics over the past two decades (NCCAN, 1995):

1. Earlier concerns about a possible reporting bias because of race have not been substantiated (i.e., blacks were not more likely to be reported than whites).

2. The strong relationship that has consistently emerged between abuse/neglect reports and pov-

erty is considered to be a reliable finding, rather than a bias in reporting. In other words, there is a consensus that child maltreatment is related to economic inequality, and that it occurs disproportionately more often among economically and socially disadvantaged families.

3. The only major reporting bias seems to be related to a child's age: Younger children are much more likely to be reported than adolescents.

4. Recent research on child death rates suggests that child abuse and neglect death rates did not change significantly during the period 1979 through 1988; however, 85% of child abuse and neglect deaths have been systematically misidentified as resulting from other causes (Ewigman, Kivlahan, & Land, 1993; McClain, Sacks, & Frohlke, 1993; NRC, 1993). Of the cases studied, 38% were listed as accidents; 15% were listed as cases of sudden infant death syndrome; 9% were listed as natural deaths; and 7% were listed as deaths of undetermined intentionality (NRC, 1993). Proposed reasons for these misclassifications include poor medical diagnoses, incomplete police and child protection investigations, inaccurate or incomplete crime reports, and flaws in the way the cause of death is recorded on death certificates (Ewigman et al., 1993; McClain et al., 1993). A more realistic estimate of annual child deaths from abuse and neglect, known and unknown, appears to be approximately 2,000, or approximately five children every day (USABCAN, 1995). Furthermore, according to data from the state of Illinois, most child fatality victims (70%) are under 2 years old (Illinois Department of Children and Family Services, 1993).

Although the official incidence rates provide a useful year-to-year comparison of *reported* rates of child maltreatment, they have been criticized as being significant underestimates of the actual prevalence of severe abuse by parents throughout the country (Gelles, 1992; Straus, 1994). Evidence to support this conclusion was shown in a recent Gallup Poll Report (1995) involving 1,000 U.S. parents nationwide. Parents were asked "how they treated one of their children (randomly selected) when that child did something that was wrong" (p. 1). A total of 23 possible actions were included in the telephone survey, ranging from nonviolent to severely violent. Notably, the number of physical abuse victims estimated by this Gallup survey was about 16 times the official number of reported victims for 1993 (the official rate of severe abuse was 3 children per 1,000, vs. 49 per 1,000 from the survey of par-

ents). These results make clear that many parents do admit to taking severe actions toward their children; they bring us closer to recognizing the full scope of the problem of child physical abuse in particular. Therefore, interpretation of incidence figures should take into account the fact that reporting rates are influenced by the allocation of federal money, the strengthening of state laws, education of community members, and similar circumstances.

Comparing the overall incidence of maltreatment in the United States to that of Canada indicates that the former country has about double the rate of maltreatment (43 per 1,000 persons in the United States vs. 21 per 1,000 in Canada; Trocme, McPhee, Kwan Tam, & Hay, 1994); this can be accounted for mainly by the number of neglect investigations' being twice as high in the United States. The greater number of neglect investigations may reflect the higher rates of poverty in the United States, in addition to the more limited social services, medical care, and educational programs available to many U.S. families (Trocme et al., 1994).

Demographic Characteristics of Maltreated Children and Their Families

Certain child characteristics have been identified through incidence studies that help to identify the overall probability and type of maltreatment. The sex of victims has not shown a discriminatory pattern over the years in reports of various forms of maltreatment (with the exception of sexual abuse): Males account for 45% of the victims, and females account for 51% (with 4% not recorded; NCCAN, 1995). In terms of child age, physical abuse affects a sizable proportion of all age groups, although the highest rate of physical injury is found among the oldest children. Approximately half (51%) of physically abused children are 7 years of age or younger, and over a quarter (26%) are 3 years of age or younger; adolescents account for the third largest age group (20%; NCCAN, 1995). In contrast to physical abuse, it appears that age is relevant to the incidence of child neglect. As children grow older, the chances of neglect decrease notably for both males and females.

One of the more detailed breakdowns on racial characteristics of child victims by type of maltreatment was provided by the state of New Jersey. These data showed that Caucasian child victims were involved in 38% of physical abuse cases, 50% of sexual abuse cases, and 29% of neglect cases; African-American victims were involved in 38%

of physical abuse cases, 28% of sexual abuse cases, and 54% of neglect cases. In contrast, the proportion of Hispanic children verified as maltreated in the state was more evenly distributed across each type of maltreatment (NCCAN, 1994).

The majority of perpetrators of all forms of child maltreatment (i.e., physical and sexual abuse, neglect, and emotional abuse) are either parents or other close relatives of the victims (nearly 9 out of every 10 perpetrators), according to data from 40 reporting states (NCCAN, 1995). Parents account for 77% of perpetrators, while other relatives account for another 12% and persons who are not in a caretaking relationship account for an additional 5% (these percentages have remained relatively stable since 1990). With respect to specific categories of child maltreatment, 69% of the perpetrators of neglect were female, and 82% of the perpetrators of sexual abuse were male. Relatively equal proportions of males and females were reported as the offenders in cases of physical abuse (NCCAN, 1994).

Several recent studies have demonstrated that the "typical" maltreating parent is in his or her mid-20s, lives near or below the poverty level and/or is unemployed, often has not finished high school, is depressed and unable to cope with stress, and has experienced violence firsthand (Holden, Willis, & Corcoran, 1992). It is important to keep in mind, however, that there are many exceptions to the "average" profile (USABCAN, 1995). In addition, abusive and neglectful parents are more likely than nonmaltreating parents to be single (Holden et al., 1992; Zuravin, 1988), to have a large number of closely spaced children (Belsky, 1992; Holden et al., 1992), to have a larger family size (Belsky, 1992), and to be less educated but not less intelligent (U.S. Congress, 1988).

Single-parent, particularly female-headed, families are inextricably linked with poverty (Coulton, Chow, & Pandey, 1990; Coulton, Pandey, & Chow, 1990). Because of this link, the contribution of family structure to abuse and neglect is difficult to separate from conditions of poverty, as reflected in the finding that families with incomes under $15,000 were seven times more likely than families with incomes over $15,000 to be reported for child neglect (NCCAN, 1994). Although persons from all social strata engage in violence against children, the more severe forms of violence occur more often among poor families. Poor, young, single mothers with young children are at greatest risk of engaging in violent behaviors toward their children (Connelly & Straus, 1992; Gelles, 1992). In a major review, Peterson and Brown (1994) found poverty, family chaos and unpredictability, household crowding, and frequent residence changes as being characteristic of both accidental and nonaccidental (i.e., abuse and neglect) child injuries. They also argued that the risk of multiple forms of maltreatment is amplified as the number of such stressors increases.

A recent discovery that most physical abuse *fatalities* are caused by enraged or extremely stressed fathers and other male caretakers raises important new issues (Levine, Compaan, & Freeman, 1995). The most common forms of assault these men inflict upon infants and small children include beating their heads and bodies, shaking them violently, intentionally suffocating them, immersing them in scalding water, and performing other brutal acts. These findings stand in contrast to the commonly held belief that mothers are the offenders in most abuse and neglect deaths. Birth fathers, stepfathers, boyfriends, and other male caretakers appear to be much greater risks to small children than previously recognized or reported. (Parenthetically, these findings also clearly demonstrate the need to rethink the design of the majority of prevention and treatment strategies, which now target a primarily female population.)

Another common assumption that has been called into question by recent data is that fatal abuse and neglect are largely caused by teenage parents or young single parents living alone. In fact, several studies undertaken since 1988 have concluded that the typical offender is in his or her mid-20s, although many of them first became parents as teenagers (Connelly & Straus, 1992). Moreover, the majority of serious perpetrators are not raising their children alone. For example, Alfaro (1988) found that most child abuse and neglect deaths occurred in two-adult families where a male was present, and Ewigman et al. (1993) showed that married individuals represented half of the perpetrators of abuse and neglect deaths.

CHILD MALTREATMENT AND DEVELOPMENTAL PSYCHOPATHOLOGY

The development of the abused or neglected child seldom follows a predictable course, because child maltreatment is characterized by many other negative socialization forces, such as family instability, parental inconsistency, and socioeconomic disadvantage. Research on the developmental sequelae of maltreatment has gradually grown from its early beginnings (i.e., case histories, clinical interventions, comparative studies of abused and nonabused children) to include longitudinal investigations (e.g., Egeland, 1991) as well. These studies, however, continue to suggest that maltreated children as a group do not reveal characteristic adjustment patterns or long-term developmental problems that clearly distinguish them from nonmaltreated children (Wolfe, 1987). On the other hand, the range and extent of problems in this population implicate abuse and neglect as contributory factors in a wide range of child (e.g., delinquency, school problems, speech and language delays) and adult (e.g., criminal behavior, marital conflict, child-rearing problems) developmental impairments (Wekerle & Wolfe, 1996; Widom, 1989).

A developmental psychopathology perspective on abuse and neglect views the emergence of maladaptive behaviors, such as peer aggression, school failure, and delinquency, within a longitudinal and multidimensional framework (Cicchetti & Rizley, 1981; Starr, MacLean, & Keating, 1991). This perspective does not attempt to relate maltreatment in a causal manner to specific developmental outcomes, since the interactive nature of the problem usually limits predictive and linear relationships between maltreatment (the suspected "cause") and particular adjustment problems (the putative "effect"). Rather, this perspective facilitates an ongoing investigation of the *changes over time* that are observed among samples of maltreated children, and attempts to account for these changes on the basis of both global (e.g., socioeconomic and normative factors affecting all children) and more specific (e.g., type of maltreatment, child and family resources) intervening variables.

The origins of such a framework can be attributed to early clinical and research studies of abused children, which reported a high frequency of conduct problems and developmental delays (e.g., Elmer & Gregg, 1967; Johnson & Morse, 1968; Kempe & Kempe, 1978). These initial reports led to controlled studies of abused and nonabused infants' characteristics, parent–child interactions, and parent and teacher descriptions to determine whether the behavior of abused children (i.e., academic, social, affective, or cognitive aspects of behavior) was distinguishable from that of their nonabused counterparts. One of the biggest challenges to such research, however, continues to be the difficulty in separating the effects of child maltreatment from the more generic effects on

child development of abnormal child care (e.g., social isolation, poor prenatal and infant care, and insufficient sensory stimulation), which often accompanies abuse and neglect (Cicchetti, Toth, & Bush, 1988). Thus, at the present time it is uncertain that child maltreatment per se is responsible for developmental impairments. A more cautious statement would be this: Maltreatment is associated with a wide range of developmental deviations (to be discussed below) to such an extent as to warrant assessment and intervention services that curtail both the maltreatment *and* the concomitant environmental/family factors (e.g., insufficient stimulation, economic stability, marital conflict) that are suspected to impair child development.

Infancy

The quality of infant–caregiver attachment is believed to be the product of characteristic styles of mutual interaction over the first year of life (Ainsworth, 1980), involving such parental characteristics as sensitivity and responsiveness to the infant's needs and signals in relation to infant temperament and self-regulation (i.e., sleep, feeding, and arousal patterns; Sroufe, 1985). At a general level, the emerging parent–child relationship serves a number of different but interrelated functions: It provides a context for many different areas of socialization (e.g., communication, emotion regulation, self-development); it constitutes a resource that enables the child to function more independently in the world at large; and it serves as a model for future relationships (Hartup, 1986). Because maltreating family environments are often characterized by physical and emotional rejection, harsh treatment, insensitivity, and verbal assaults, researchers have been very interested in how the developing parent–child interactions may be affected under such adverse circumstances (Aber & Cicchetti, 1984).

The results of recent comparative and prospective studies indicate that child maltreatment during infancy is associated with insecure child–caregiver attachment relationships (see Crittenden & Ainsworth, 1989, and Spieker & Booth, 1988, for reviews). In fact, the vast majority of maltreated infants form insecure attachments with their caregivers (from 70% to 100% across studies; Cicchetti et al., 1988), which suggests the lack of confidence and security such a child feels toward the mother as an available, caring, and responsive caregiver. Infants in these studies who had been abused or neglected by their mothers were significantly more likely than controls to cling to the mothers and/or to display negative affect (e.g., screaming, fearfulness, muscle rigidity). For example, Drotar (1992) demonstrated dysfunctional development in neglected children's expectations of caregiver availability, affect regulation, ability to solve problems, social relationships, and effective coping abilities in new or stressful situations; these effects were attributed to insecure attachment, maternal detachment, and maternal lack of availability.

Insecurely attached children are also at risk for future struggles with low self-esteem, since they view themselves more negatively than comparison children (Allen & Tarnowski, 1989). These researchers have speculated that maltreatment during infancy produces an insecure attachment over a period of time that adversely affects a child's later intellectual and socioemotional development. These conclusions are supported by several well-designed prospective investigations that have begun to link early problems in attachment to patterns of declining developmental abilities over the first 2 years of life (e.g., Egeland, 1991). These suggestive findings emphasize the importance of the early parent–child relationship; they also indicate possible beginnings of parent–child conflict, such as parental avoidance or lack of contingent responding to infant demands, parental failure to provide stimulation and comfort to the infant, and infant characteristics that interact with parental ability.

Physical abuse and neglect may affect a young infant in vastly different ways. Whereas physically abused infants may present a wide variety of external signs of physical injury, ranging from bruises, lacerations, scars, and abrasions to burns, sprains, or broken bones, one of the physical effects of neglect is failure-to-thrive (FTT) syndrome. FTT is manifested by a significant growth delay, which results from inadequate caloric intake linked to poor caregiving (Benoit, 1993). If a child gains weight with hospitalization or after the age of 2, when children are able to obtain food for themselves, FTT is considered to be an issue (Mrazek, 1993). Moreover, over 90% of FTT children are considered to show insecure attachment to their mothers, compared to fewer than 50% of control children. This finding suggests that fear, anger, and anxiety may characterize these infants' relationship to their mothers (Crittenden, 1987; Valenzuela, 1990). FTT, which is closely linked to child neglect, thus results in children who have low confidence in their mothers' availability and responsiveness to their needs, and mothers who show more aversive, less positive, and less contingent responsiveness to their children.

Early Childhood

Early childhood (ages 2–5) is a period of child development that is commonly considered to be very demanding of caretakers' time, energy, and patience. Preschool children are generally described by their parents as difficult to control, overly active, and attention-seeking (Achenbach, 1966), all of which can place them in jeopardy of harsh parental treatment or physical abuse. Related to risk of physical harm are concerns about the possible long-range impairments that may result from maltreatment during this period of rapid development. A preschooler's optimal cognitive, emotional, and behavioral development requires a nurturant, supportive environment (e.g., limits on the range of permissible behavior; verbal and physical responsiveness; predictable adult behavior). For this reason, child maltreatment researchers have focused attention upon maltreated preschoolers' development across a wide range of cognitive and behavioral indicators.

Behavioral Dimension

Heightened aggressiveness and hostility toward others (especially authority figures), as well as angry outbursts with little or no provocation, are prominent behavioral characteristics of younger abused children in particular (Kolko, 1992). Such children are more likely to engage in power struggles and to counteract peer aggression with aggression or resistance, whereas nonmaltreated children tend to respond to aggression with distress (Howes & Eldredge, 1985). In contrast, neglected preschoolers have been observed as being more socially avoidant (Hoffman-Plotkin & Twentyman, 1984), and seem to have more difficulty dealing with challenging tasks or interpersonal situations, than either abused or normal children (Egeland, Sroufe, & Erickson, 1983). Although it would be premature to draw firm conclusions, these findings suggest that neglected preschoolers are relatively inactive and deficient in social skills (i.e., low rates of verbal and physical interactions with peers and adults) as compared to normal peers, whereas abused preschoolers are more overactive and disruptive.

A behavioral pattern labeled "compulsive compliance" has also been described among samples of younger physically abused children (Crittenden & DiLalla, 1988). This term refers to a child's ready and quick compliance to significant adults, which occurs in the context of the child's general state of vigilance or watchfulness for adult cues.

Such compliant behavior may be accompanied by masked facial expressions, ambiguous affect, an incongruence between verbal and nonverbal behavior, and/or rote verbal responses. The emergence of this pattern of behavior coincides with the emergence of a child's abstraction abilities (i.e., at about 12 months of age), in which the child develops the ability to form a stable mental representation of the caregiver.

Compulsive compliance may have an important adaptive function: Abused infants learn to inhibit behaviors that have been associated with maternal anger (e.g., requests for attention, protests against intrusions), and by toddlerhood they may actively behave in a manner designed to please their mothers. Crittenden and DiLalla (1988) found compulsive compliance to predominate in physically abused and abused/neglected children, in response to a controlling, hostile, and punitive parenting style. Such increases in compulsive compliance, as well as in cooperative behavior, are most evident from the ages of 1 year through 2½ years among maltreated children; their behavior contrasts with that of adequate-care children, who usually display the normative independence-striving behaviors ("testing limits") expected of toddlers. Although compulsive compliance may be adaptive in terms of reducing the risk of violence and increasing the possibility of positive mother–child interactions during early childhood, this pattern may lead to inflexible strategies of behavior over time, with the consequence of reduced reciprocity in interactions (Crittenden, 1992).

Cognitive and Social-Cognitive Dimension

Early studies found that maltreated preschool children were significantly more likely than peers to show developmental delays, especially in areas related to cognitive development, language acquisition, and the ability to discriminate emotions in others (Barahal, Waterman, & Martin, 1981; Friedrich, Einbender, & Luecke, 1983; Frodi & Smetana, 1984; Hoffman-Plotkin & Twentyman, 1984; Main & George, 1985; Sandgrund, Gaines, & Green, 1974). Cicchetti and Beeghly (1987) found that maltreated toddlers used fewer "internal-state" words (e.g., talk about their own and others' feelings and emotions) in interactions with their mothers than their nonmaltreated peers did; the maltreated children also spoke less often about their negative internal states (i.e., negative affect and physiological states). Cicchetti and Beeghly

(1987) suggest that inhibition of emotional language may be adaptive for maltreated children, because expressing feelings may serve to trigger further maltreatment. Beeghly and Cicchetti (1994) found that toddlers at greatest risk for delayed internal-state language were maltreated children with insecure attachments, as compared to maltreated toddlers with secure attachments and comparison toddlers with insecure attachments.

A recent study by Harrington, Dubowitz, Black, and Binder (1995) raises some questions about the impact of a neglectful environment on the development of younger children. These researchers examined the relations among maternal substance use, neglectful parenting, and early childhood cognitive development among 51 women with a history of substance use and a comparison sample of 67 women. Contrary to expectations, maternal substance use was not found to affect the developmental status of children, and the substance use and comparison groups were not found to differ in the adequacy of their maternal caregiving. As for the effect of neglectful caregiving and home environment on children's cognitive, motor, or language development, only receptive language development was shown to suffer somewhat; neglectful parenting was not related to the cognitive, motor, or expressive language development of children. This finding opposes earlier findings concerning negative effects of neglectful parenting on children's cognitive and language development (e.g., Allen & Oliver, 1982; Egeland, 1991; Erickson, Egeland, & Pianta, 1989). Harrington et al. (1995) explain that their study defined neglect along a continuum of parenting behavior rather than by the involvement of protective services; therefore, it is possible that previous studies contained more severe cases of neglectful caregiving. As for the effect of home environment on receptive language development, Harrington et al. (1995) speculate that cognitive and motor development may be less vulnerable to inadequate parenting and poor home environments than is language development at a young age.

In addition to cognitive delays, various aspects of a child's development of social awareness may be compromised by maltreatment (e.g., social behavior, social relationships). Dodge, Bates, and Pettit (1990) found deviant patterns of processing social information in physically abused 4-year-old children, with the children demonstrating more aggressive behavior at age 5. The physically abused children were significantly less attentive to social cues, were more likely to attribute hostile intent to others' actions, and demonstrated greater difficulty in successfully managing personal problems.

Socioemotional Dimension

Whereas social behavior and interpersonal relationships constitute one aspect of the socioemotional arena, the ability to empathize and the development of appropriate affect and emotion regulation are other important variables that appear to suffer in the course of maltreatment. For example, Zahn-Waxler et al. (1995) hypothesized that child characteristics may interact with an adverse environment (e.g., exposure to violence, physical abuse, or neglect) to delay or arrest the development of interpersonal sensitivity. However, even among some preschool children who possessed difficult temperaments (e.g., aggressive, oppositional), several were nonetheless able to empathize with, comfort, and help others in distress. These latter "resilient" children came from families where such early child difficulties were recognized and identified by parents, who then sought both information and help.

Regardless of the adverse environment, this concern demonstrated by the parents for their children was evidence for the presence and maintenance of emotional investment and bonds. In other words, a child's ability to empathize may be kept intact, despite personality or environmental difficulties, if parents maintain some sense of emotional investment. Based on these findings, Zahn-Waxler et al. (1995) suggest that children from more impoverished backgrounds with less involved and less caring parents may not forever lose the ability to empathize and remain sensitive to others' emotions, although maltreatment and exploitation both within the family and in society may retard the development of empathy, and therefore the capacity for healthy interpersonal relationships.

The development of self-esteem among maltreated preschoolers has also been investigated. Because early attachment relationships help children form a "working model" of their interpersonal relationships (Sroufe & Fleeson, 1986), such experiences are considered to be crucial to the ongoing development of a child's self-concept. Consistent with this view are findings that maltreated children possess poor self-images and a distorted view of themselves in comparison with others (Cicchetti et al., 1988); these characteristics are building blocks for low self-esteem and poor self-control (Schneider-Rosen & Cicchetti, 1991).

Middle Childhood

Behavioral Dimension

As maltreated children grow older, they are faced with a second important period of relationship development, this time with peers and adults other than their caregivers. Peer acceptance and reciprocity play a critical role in providing children with the social experiences and social support they require in order to learn to adapt successfully to a wide range of situations—not only in the behavioral domain, but in the areas of socioemotional and cognitive development as well. Not surprisingly, the social competence of children who have been maltreated also shows impairment as the children enter unfamiliar peer and school situations (Feldman et al., 1995).

Early studies using observational coding systems and comparison groups found that abused children exhibited high rates of aggressive and aversive behaviors, such as yelling, hitting, and destructiveness, when interacting in the home with their parents (Bousha & Twentyman, 1984; Lorber, Felton, & Reid, 1984; Reid, Taplin, & Lorber, 1981). Similarly, parent, teacher, and child report measures of behavior problems (e.g., destructiveness, fighting with siblings) have consistently indicated that the abused school-age child is perceived as more difficult to manage, less socially mature, and less capable of developing trust with others (Herrenkohl, Herrenkohl, Toedter, & Yanushefski, 1984; Kinard, 1980; Salzinger, Kaplan, Pelcovitz, Samit, & Kreiger, 1984; Wolfe & Mosk, 1983). Based on these findings, a consensus has emerged that physically abused children in particular exhibit high rates of aversive and aggressive behavior across different settings (Ammerman, 1991).

Neglected children, on the other hand, are reported to adopt notably different styles of social interaction with peers. For example, Crittenden (1992) found that neglected preschool and school-age children tended to remain isolated during opportunities for free play with other children. In addition, neglected school-age children, compared to nonmaltreated children, have been found to be more passive (Crittenden, 1992), to display fewer overtures of affection, and to produce less frequent initiations of play behavior in interactions with their mothers (Bousha & Twentyman, 1984).

Prino and Peyrot (1994) examined the differential effects of physical abuse and neglect on the social behavior of children. Comparing three groups of children (i.e., physically abused, *n* = 21;

nonabused/neglected, $n = 26$; and nonmaltreated, $n = 21$), these investigators found physically abused children to display significantly more aggressive behavior than either the neglected or the nonmaltreated children. The neglected children, in comparison, were significantly more withdrawn than either the physically abused or the nonmaltreated children, while the nonmaltreated children displayed significantly more prosocial behavior than either the abused or the neglected children. Similarly, Downey and Walker (1992) reported increased aggression among their sample of physically abused children, and noted that abuse was associated with both child aggression and depression.

A recent study of the social relationships of physically abused 8- to 12-year-olds documents many of the prevailing findings pertaining to the behavioral adjustment of abused children (Salzinger, Feldman, Hammer, & Rosario, 1993): (1) They are at increased risk for lower social status, especially peer rejection, in the classroom; (2) they receive fewer positive and more negative nominations as friends by classmates, indicating less positive reciprocity in their relationships with peers; and (3) they are perceived by their classmates as demonstrating more negative and fewer positive social behaviors. These data further suggest that friends appear to give less social support to abused children than to their nonabused peers. Peer rejection is a major concern in the development of an abused child, because peer rejection is the strongest predictor of school dropout and delinquency in adolescence. When peer rejection occurs, it tends to remain stable throughout the years and is often found to correlate with aggression, possibly making rejection an even better predictor of poor outcome than aggression itself (Salzinger et al., 1993).

Cognitive and Social-Cognitive Dimension

Neglected children are at particularly increased risk for displaying deficits on measures of language ability and intelligence (Crouch & Milner, 1993). For example, Fox, Long, and Langlois (1988) found significant differences in language comprehension skills between groups of preschool and school-age children who were either physically abused, generally neglected (no physical injury to a child occurred as a result of the neglect), or severely neglected (a child's person or health was endangered or damaged as a result of the neglect). In particular, they found that nonmaltreated children demonstrated the highest language comprehension ability, followed by the generally neglected and physically abused groups, respectively; the severely neglected children scored lowest in language comprehension ability.

There have also been suggestions that neglected children, like other groups of maltreated children, demonstrate differences in school performance and adjustment. In general, the school adjustment of physically abused children is poor, with many exhibiting problems completing the work required of them in school, and often creating havoc in the classroom (Erickson et al., 1989). For example, Wodarski, Kurtz, Gaudin, and Howing (1990) found that in comparison to nonmaltreated counterparts, neglected school-age and adolescent children performed at lower levels on several measures of overall school performance, including tests of language, reading, and math skills. Similarly, Salzinger et al. (1984) found that both abused children ($n = 30$) and neglected children ($n = 26$) performed at 2 years below grade level in verbal and math abilities compared to nonmaltreated children ($n = 480$), with approximately one-third of the maltreated children failing one or more subjects and/or being placed in a special classroom.

Attempts at separating the effects of maltreatment on child cognitive development from the effects of low socioeconomic status (SES) suggest that maltreatment does have a significant impact above and beyond the influence of low SES. For example, Egeland and Erickson (1987) found maltreated children to perform worse in the cognitive and socioemotional areas of development from infancy through the early school years, compared to nonmaltreated children with similar SES backgrounds. Similarly, Kurtz, Gaudin, Wodarski, and Howing (1993) and Trickett, Aber, Carlson, and Cicchetti (1991) have found maltreated school-age children and adolescents to display extensive and severe academic and socioemotional problems, even when the effects of SES are covaried out. Rather than improving, school performance and behavior problems tended to keep worsening as the children approached adolescence. Nightingale and Walker (1991), however, offer opposing findings. These investigators compared the cognitive functioning of maltreated children with that of two groups of nonmaltreated children: those matched for age and SES, and those matched only for age. Maltreated children from low-SES backgrounds were found to demonstrate deficits in cognitive functioning; however, these deficits were no more problematic than those found in nonmaltreated children from the same low-SES backgrounds. In the aggregate, these findings from several studies on the influence of maltreatment in relation to SES suggest that maltreatment may be "less noticeable" as an etiological factor when other considerable risk factors (i.e., impoverished environments) are evident, although its role is still evident in a significant proportion of children.

Kurtz et al. (1993) found severe academic delays to be the most consistent risk factor for neglected children, who regularly scored well below their nonmaltreated peers on standardized tests of reading, language, and math. Like that of the physically abused children, the adaptive functioning of the neglected children was developmentally normal, and they were no different from the nonmaltreated children on any of the socioemotional measures. It is not surprising that school performance suffers most dramatically in neglect cases, because cognitive development relies upon ongoing parent–child interaction and stimulating environments. The cognitive development of a child, therefore, is directly threatened by unavailable/neglectful parents. Low educational aspirations, lack of language stimulation, little encouragement for learning, and the absence of acknowledgments for a child's achievements all serve to undermine academic success. Notably, this effect on academic ability may be mediated by the high mobility rate among maltreating families. Using a LISREL model to predict the academic performance of 360 maltreated and 366 nonmaltreated children, Eckenrode, Rowe, Laird, and Brathwaite (1995) determined that frequent moves (i.e., twice as many moves as nonmaltreated children during their school years) accounted significantly for the maltreated children's academic problems.

Moral development/reasoning is another important social-cognitive function that has been studied in relation to maltreatment. A child's emerging view of the world, and his or her development of moral reasoning and social judgments, are encouraged through parental guidance. In a case of maltreatment, however, judgments are actively constructed from prior social experiences that may reflect the child's victimization experiences (Wolfe, 1987). Maltreating parents generally fail to instill empathy in their children, particularly in a way that their children will internalize and mimic (Maccoby & Martin, 1983). Moral reasoning is a covert cognitive process that is difficult to examine empirically; this difficulty has led researchers to infer the presence or absence of moral reasoning from aspects of children's behavior, judgments, and/or affect. As an example, researchers may define moral reasoning in terms of a child's use of aggression or force to get something

or to hurt someone; the child's judgment of such behavior as acceptable; and/or the child's lack of remorse (Astor, 1994). Kelly (1983) further suggested that the social behavior of maltreated children is associated with their interpretation of hostile, aggressive, and unfair situations and events.

An an illustration, Cerezo and Frias (1994) examined 10-year-old children with case histories of at least 2 years of physical and emotional parental abuse for their attributional styles and symptoms of depression. In comparison with nonabused controls, the abused children perceived the negative events in their lives as unpredictable, which in turn generated feelings of helplessness; furthermore, they possessed lower levels of self-esteem and self-worth, and they tended to exhibit stronger feelings of sadness. In addition to the obvious help abused children need with respect to their adverse environments and their poor caregiver relationships, this study demonstrates that such children are in need of assistance in reworking their dysfunctional views and feelings concerning themselves, others, and the world. Efforts to increase their sense of control over positive outcomes (e.g., rewards, praise, self-guidance), therefore, are suggested by these findings.

Socioemotional Dimension

In addition to behavioral, social, and cognitive deficits, increasing evidence points to the association between maltreatment (especially physical abuse) and depressed symptomatology, even when SES is controlled for (Allen & Tarnowski, 1989; Downey & Walker, 1992; Kaufman, 1991; Kinard, 1995; Toth, Manly, & Cicchetti, 1992). In one of the most complete studies of this issue, Toth et al. (1992) compared physically abused ($n = 46$), neglected ($n = 35$), and nonmaltreated ($n = 72$) children, using several measures of depression and social adjustment (e.g., the Children's Depression Inventory, the Child Behavior Checklist). After controlling for age and cognitive functioning, they found that the presence of depressive symptomatology was the only dimension that differentiated children from physically abusive homes and children from neglectful homes. More specifically, 22% of the children in the physically abused group demonstrated "clinical" criteria for depression, compared to 6% of the nonmaltreated group and 3% of the neglected group. The findings serve to emphasize the damaging effects of maltreatment—specifically, physical abuse—on the child's growing sense of self, and the contribution this dysfunctional development of self makes in the emergence of depression. Consistent with this conclusion is evidence that physically abused children demonstrate lower levels of self-esteem on self-report measures (Allen & Tarnowski, 1989; Kinard, 1982) as well as parent report measures (Kaufman & Cicchetti, 1989).

Kinard (1995) found that perceptions of social support from mothers and peers on the part of abused children were important for improving global self-worth and alleviating depression. For example, competence levels were evaluated more positively by the children if they perceived greater social support. These results reinforce common findings from other studies linking support from within and outside the family, as well as individual characteristics (e.g., high self-esteem), to successful adaptation. Moreover, they stress the importance of receiving sufficient social support from family, peers, and teachers if abused children are to be able to construct positive images and feelings of themselves, as well as to be at lower risk for depression.

The ability to recognize and understand others' emotions is a valuable skill acquired in middle childhood, and is used to initiate and maintain social behavior and interpersonal relationships. Not surprisingly, abused children have been found to perform at a lower level than nonabused controls on measures of affective and cognitive role taking, social sensitivity, and the ability to discriminate emotions in others (Barahal et al., 1981; Frodi & Smetana, 1984; Straker & Jacobson, 1981). Similarly, "affect regulation" refers to a child's ability to modulate, modify, redirect, and otherwise control emotions (particularly intense emotions), thus facilitating adaptive functioning (Cicchetti, Ganiban, & Barnett, 1990). Difficulties with affect regulation appear particular to be problems for abused children, resulting in affective extremes and in lack of awareness and/or control over body states and physiological responses (e.g., extreme depressive symptomatology and angry outbursts; Herman, 1992). Self-injurious behaviors are examples of manifestations of both affect regulation difficulties and lack of awareness of feelings.

A recent investigation aptly summarizes the primary cognitive, behavioral, and socioemotional effects of maltreatment discussed to this point. In a sample of 56 children from 34 families involved with child protective services because of maltreatment (i.e., physical abuse, sexual abuse, neglect, and/or emotional abuse), Kaufman, Jones, Stieglitz, Vitulano, and Mannarino (1994) found that neglect was significantly associated with variation in intellectual functioning and ability, whereas physi-

cal abuse explained the greatest amount of variance in externalizing symptoms (e.g., aggression). Moreover, ratings of emotional maltreatment were related to the presence of depressive symptoms in the children. This study suggests why some maltreated children develop particular types of problems while others do not; it also stresses the significance of examining the effects of combined maltreatment as well as the individual types of maltreatment on child adjustment (see also Wolfe & McGee, 1994).

Adolescence and Adulthood

Until recently, most controlled studies on the consequences of abuse and neglect were limited to short-term effects (e.g., the children were assessed within a year of the discovery of maltreatment). However, several retrospective and longitudinal studies of these child populations have begun to document a moderately strong association between childhood maltreatment and the emergence of adjustment problems and criminal behavior during adolescence. For example, Williamson, Borduin, and Howe (1991) found that maltreated youths obtained higher global scores on a checklist of psychiatric symptoms, and involvement in drug use and criminality has been documented among abused adolescents (Burgess, Hartman, & McCormack, 1987; Cohen & Densen-Gerber, 1982). Not surprisingly, the relationship between childhood abuse and adjustment problems appearing during adolescence is strongest among samples drawn from delinquent populations; several authors have noted that the most striking factor distinguishing violent from nonviolent delinquents is the amount of violence in the children's past (Lewis, Pincus, & Glaser, 1979; Lorber, Weissman, & Reid, 1983; Tarter, Hegedus, Winsten, & Alterman, 1984).

Although data indicate that childhood abuse is clearly implicated in later antisocial behavior, the mechanisms underlying this relationship have not been clarified empirically. One explanation for the suspected relationship between abuse during early and middle childhood and subsequent adjustment was offered in an early study by Herzberger, Potts, and Dillon (1981), who posited that abused children may develop distorted or maladaptive perceptions of parental characteristics, discipline techniques, and emotional acceptance–rejection that affect their subsequent behavior. Interviews were conducted with 14 boys (aged 8–14 years) who had been abused previously and were living in a residential group home. These children had been removed from their parents (and abusive treatment) for an average of 2½ years, and they were compared to 10 males living in the same group home who had not been abused (this sample was matched on IQ, age, months of residence in group home, and months since residence with principal caretakers). The study found that, relative to the controls, the abused children described their abusive parents in more negative terms and generally believed that their treatment was more emotionally rejecting (i.e., when asked whether or not their parents cared about them, gave them a lot of love, and liked having them around). There was also wide variability in the children's perceptions of their parents and treatment, further indicating that children's interpretations of abusive incidents are important to consider. The authors postulate that seeing abuse as an indicant of parental rejection may have more harmful effects on children's development than perceiving abuse as being caused by parents' externally imposed frustrations (e.g., difficult child behavior), because children actively construct a view of their social environment and then respond according to this construction (Herzberger et al., 1981).

Recent studies have also looked at the effects of maltreatment in terms of deficits in social information processing and/or depression. For example, Gross and Keller (1992) assessed whether some of the correlates of learned helplessness (i.e., depression, low self-esteem, and a maladaptive attributional style) are long-term consequences of child maltreatment. Although psychological abuse was found to be a critical variable in predicting levels of depression, self-esteem, and attributional style, physical abuse did not significantly contribute to the variance in these variables. Adolescents reporting both psychological abuse and physical abuse reported a greater tendency toward depression than nonmaltreated adolescents, or adolescents experiencing only psychological abuse or physical abuse.

Steinberg, Lamborn, Darling, Mounts, and Dornbusch (1994) studied the development of 14- to 18-year-olds from families with different parenting styles (i.e., authoritative, authoritarian, indulgent, and neglectful) over a 1-year period, and found clear disadvantages for adolescents who had been raised in homes in which parents neglected the needs of the children. The most pronounced effect of dysfunctional parenting on the adjustment of these neglected adolescents occurred during the high school years. At the time of first assessment, these adolescents already displayed both psychological and behavioral problems, compared to their nonmaltreated peers. Over the

1-year period, however, neglected adolescents demonstrated continuing deterioration in functioning, with marked drops in work orientation and school orientation, and definite increases in delinquency and substance use. The scores of these neglected adolescents in both school orientation and work orientation declined by about one-third of a standard deviation over the course of a year. In addition, delinquency and substance use increased by about one-fourth of a standard deviation.

Moran and Eckenrode (1992) examined whether internal locus of control and high self-esteem protected female adolescent victims of maltreatment from depression. As predicted, external locus of control for good events and lower self-esteem were found to be the strongest indicators of depression among the maltreated girls in particular; *ipso facto*, maltreated adolescent females who possessed higher self-esteem and internal locus of control for good events were no more depressed than their nonmaltreated peers. Importantly, lower self-esteem, external (rather than internal) locus of control for good events, and greater depression were more evident if abuse or neglect commenced before a child was 11 years old. One explanation proposed by the researchers is that long-term maltreatment is related to lower levels of protective personality characteristics during adolescence, because these characteristics develop most rapidly during childhood and are dependent on positive parent–child relationships. Internal locus of control develops gradually, especially during preadolescence; moreover, external locus of control is related to parental rejection and inconsistent caretaking. Thus, maltreatment that begins during childhood (i.e., the time of increasing internality) may prevent this personal resource from developing, leading to external locus of control in adolescence. On the other hand, if maltreatment does not begin until adolescence, the victim is more likely to have already established internal locus of control.

Posttraumatic Stress Disorder (PTSD) has also been examined as a possible outcome of child physical abuse, because of the emotional trauma experienced by these children. Although PTSD-related symptoms and disorders are reported commonly for sexually abused children (see Wekerle & Wolfe, 1996) and children who witnessed domestic violence (see Wolfe & Jaffe, 1991), little evidence currently exists to indicate such problems among physically abused children. In one of the few controlled studies, Pelcovitz et al. (1994) compared 27 physically abused adolescents with 27 matched, nonabused controls on measures of

PTSD and social and behavioral difficulties. Their findings indicated significantly higher rates of depression, Conduct Disorder, internalizing and externalizing behavior problems, and social deficits in the abused adolescents than in the nonabused controls, leading these researchers to conclude that physically abused adolescents may be more at risk for behavioral and social difficulties than for PTSD. Further studies may help to clarify this issue, particularly by clarifiying the nature of the trauma in sexual abuse versus physical abuse that leads to the development of PTSD-related symptoms.

Summary

The perspective on physically abused and neglected children presented herein has focused on the wide range of developmental changes and deviations documented among this diverse population. This developmental viewpoint embraces the subtly interacting conditions that work in combination either to attenuate the effects of powerful traumatic events or to turn a minor developmental crisis into a major impairment (Lipsett, 1983). Accordingly, the evidence related to infant–caregiver attachment has revealed that maltreatment during infancy is strongly associated with characteristics of both anxious and disorganized attachments (e.g., clinging, rigidity, withdrawal), which may adversely affect the child's intellectual and socioemotional development over time. Similarly, preschool-age abused children have been shown in studies to be more difficult to manage and to have more marked developmental delays in language, self-control, and peer interactions than nonclinic samples of children. Studies of abused school-age children concur with those of younger children, finding that such children often have significant learning and motivational problems at school, and a higher rate of aggressive and destructive behavior. Finally, studies of chronically abused children who have reached adolescence have confirmed a correlational relationship between abuse and juvenile crime that exceeds the variance accounted for by family socioeconomic factors alone.

A CONCEPTUAL MODEL FOR ASSESSMENT OF CHILD ABUSE AND NEGLECT

A well-established consensus indicates that child maltreatment does not result from any single risk factor or etiological process that provides a necessary or sufficient basis for such behavior (NRC, 1993). Current approaches to understanding these phenomena emphasize the combination of individual, family, environmental, and social/cultural risk factors that can result in increased risk of maltreatment, as well as the possible protective mechanisms that disrupt this etiological process. Accordingly, most models seeking to explain physical abuse and neglect in particular have focused their attention on the nature of the parent–child relationship and the factors that influence the normal formation of a healthy, child-focused relationship. The assessment of such abuse and neglect, therefore, may actually reflect a combination of methods for analyzing elements within a comprehensive systems model, with assumptions about how the elements interact and their relative importance in regard to changing the system. Important concerns underlie a multifactorial, systems-based approach to understanding child maltreatment (Wolfe, 1988):

1. Maltreating parents often lack the skills and resources necessary to cope effectively with child rearing and other stressful life demands (such as unemployment, crowded housing, and constant child attention). Ineffective parenting may in turn lead to a greater number of child behavior problems, which progressively serve to increase parental stress and poor coping.

2. In recognition of the range and intensity of identified problems among maltreated children, this approach is concerned with the characteristics of a child that may be contributing to and/or maintaining a parent's maladaptive and/or abusive behavior.

3. Maltreating behavior is private and illegal behavior that occurs at a relatively low frequency, making it difficult to observe and study directly. Therefore, less extreme, routine interactions are to be studied (e.g., parental commands, criticisms, and types of punishers; child demands, aversive behavior, and prosocial behavior). An important assumption arising from this approach to low-frequency behavior is that there is continuity between everyday interactions and extreme maltreatment.

4. Although maltreatment (especially abuse) would appear to be a specific action between a parent and a single child, it is actually embedded within a network of family events. Therefore, it is necessary to study the entire family.

5. An etiological model of child physical abuse and neglect must include conceptually distinct

levels of individual, family, and environmental factors. This involves investigation of critical antecedents; significant historical or developmental characteristics of the parent and child; the nature of the maltreatment and its impact on the child; the consequences that maintain such behavior; the nature of the family context; and the larger social system in which maltreatment occurs.

6. This paradigm is based upon evidence that child maltreatment, like other forms of intrafamilial violence, is seldom attributable to some extremely abnormal or pathological influence. On the contrary, child maltreatment is viewed as the culmination of interrelated events both within and outside of the family. This argument provides the major basis for studying maltreating behavior within a multilevel context of individual, family, and societal events. These events may be extreme forms of things that all families may experience to some degree.

A major implication of this conceptual model is that child maltreatment is seldom related to any particular event or any particular parent or child attribute. Rather, it is viewed as the product of multiple factors that potentiate one another in the absence of compensatory, protective factors or buffers (Cicchetti & Rizley, 1981). As an illustration of this social interaction model, consider such common problems shown by a young child as crying, whining, screaming, and noncompliance. When faced with these annoying behaviors, a parent may not be capable of dealing with them other than through the use of physical punishment or verbal threats (the methods most familiar to him or her). Under normal circumstances, the parent may be able to deal with the situation without becoming overly irritated or violent. However, hostile aggression (i.e., abuse) is more likely to occur if the parent is emotionally "aroused" (Baron, 1977; Berkowitz, 1983), such as when the parent has had an encounter with an angry neighbor earlier in the day that has left him or her feeling tense and upset (feelings that the parent may not necessarily recognize or admit). At this point, the risk of overreacting or abusing the child increases, especially if the parent is unaware of the source of extraneous arousal and misattributes it to the provocation—that is, the child's crying or noncompliance (Averill, 1983). As discussed by Patterson and Cobb (1973), physical punishment may "work," or it may lead over time to a standoff between the parent and child, forcing the parent to increase the severity of his or her punishment and the child to escalate his or her aversiveness.

The following discussion reviews the data regarding several key components in the etiology of child maltreatment that are relevant to assessment, including precursors, parent and child characteristics, response topography, and major consequences.

Specific Circumstances Related to Child Maltreatment

The specific circumstances surrounding the occurrence of child physical abuse have received considerable attention (Herrenkohl, Herrenkohl, & Egolf, 1983; Kadushin & Martin, 1981). These circumstances can be clustered into two conceptually important categories of antecedents: proximal events that may have precipitated an abusive incident, and distal events that are associated indirectly with abuse. Neglect has also been studied in this regard, but less frequently.

Proximal Events

Child behavior has been implicated as a major factor in triggering abusive episodes. Existing evidence suggests that abusive incidents occur most often during difficult, but not uncommon, episodes of child behavior. In such contexts, aversive child behavior (e.g., crying) may produce anger and tension in some adults, which contribute to aggressive responding (Frodi & Lamb, 1980; Vasta, 1982; Wolfe, Fairbank, Kelly, & Bradlyn, 1983). A study of 825 official case records of physical abuse incidents revealed that abuse was most often associated with oppositional child behaviors, such as refusal, fighting/arguing, accidental occurrences, immoral behavior, dangerous behavior, a child's sexual behavior, and inconveniences caused by the child (Herrenkohl et al., 1983). Interestingly, this latter study also revealed that circumstances preceding incidents of neglect were characterized more by chronic adult inadequacy (i.e., a parent's refusing to meet family needs, inadequate adult supervision, the parent's lack of knowledge, inappropriate use of medical facilities, unsafe home environment, and a child's dangerous behavior), in contrast to child behavior. These findings on the physically abused child, in particular, are consistent with an interactive model of abuse that stresses the child's contribution to his or her own maltreatment through misbehavior. However, it should be emphasized that the child is not *responsible* for the assault in a legalistic or moralistic sense. Child abuse remains primarily a parental act in which the child is the major victim.

Adult conflict, another suspected powerful antecedent to abuse, has received considerable attention in recent studies. In their first nationwide study of familial violence, Straus, Gelles, and Steinmetz (1980) noted that marital disharmony and violence were significantly associated with higher rates of severe violence toward children (the authors estimated that in approximately 40% of the families where the adults were violent toward each other, there was also violence toward a child at some point during a 12-month period). Concurrently, recent findings in the marital and child clinical literature have documented the relationship between adult conflict and increased child behavior problems (Cummings, in press). This is not surprising, because the escalation of emotional arousal and/or physical aggression that accompanies conflicts between adults (e.g., Jacobson et al., 1994) can easily carry over to interactions with a child. The child may be caught in the "crossfire" between the parents (or other adults in the home), or the child may precipitate a marital conflict by creating a stress on either or both parents (e.g., disobeying the mother by claiming that the father gave permission). Subsequently, child injuries may occur during attempts to interrupt the fighting, escape from the situation, or continue with routine activities (e.g., finishing dinner, watching television).

Distal Events

Although child- and adult-related conflicts are common antecedents to reported cases of child physical abuse, it is clear that such events account for only a small, albeit significant, percentage of the total variance associated with child abuse and neglect (on the order of 6%; Herrenkohl et al., 1983). In addition to proximal events that are directly linked to a particular abusive incident, an understanding of maltreatment must take into account many contextual factors that are suspected to be indirect precursors to abusive/neglectful situations. Research has pointed to socioeconomic stress—that is, factors associated with poverty and inadequate physical resources and social support systems—as the single most influential aggregated variable contributing to child abuse and neglect (Gil, 1970; Pelton, 1978). For example, socioeconomic factors accounted for 36% of the variance in rates of child abuse in Pennsylvania (Garbarino, 1976). Unemployment (Light, 1973), restricted educational and occupational opportunities (Gil, 1970), unstable and/or violent family situations (Straus et al., 1980), and similar disadvantages

(e.g., poor housing, lack of privacy, and high noise and pollution levels) often associated with lower SES have all emerged as major sociocultural factors influencing rates of child abuse and neglect in North America.

The perspective that emerges from a consideration of proximal and distal setting events is that physical child abuse in particular may be understood as a special case of aggression, in which child behavior often represents an immediate aversive stimulus that precipitates adult aggression (Averill, 1983). This perspective also recognizes the significance of contextual factors, such as crowded housing, ambient noise level, and socioeconomic disadvantages, as contributors to both physical abuse and neglect. Although such precursors are highly relevant to our understanding of the problem, the question remains as to why only a relatively small percentage of adults exhibit such behavior in the presence of these common aversive events. To answer this question, a consideration of parent, child, and situational characteristics that may serve to accent or buffer the impact of such events is required.

Characteristics of Maltreating Parents

Child maltreatment is best described as a pattern of behavior rather than a psychiatric or personality disturbance. That is, problematic behavior patterns that are specific to child rearing—such as difficulties in managing difficult child behavior, in problem solving with other family members, or in handling chronic or acute episodes of stress—appear to define this population more accurately than psychopathology per se (Wolfe, 1985). Although personality features alone cannot adequately explain these complicated phenomena, the psychopathology viewpoint is essentially an attempt to understand individual characteristics of maltreating parents in relation to prior experience and current demands. Major adult factors associated with abuse and neglect have been the subject of considerable research, such as a parent's own childhood experiences, personality attributes and behaviors, knowledge and perceptions of children, and perceived social supports. A synopsis of these findings is presented below (see also Milner, in press; Wolfe, 1987).

Childhood Experiences

There has been considerable interest in physically abusive parents' early family experiences, since prior abuse and family violence are presumed to perpetuate a cycle of violence across generations. Retrospective studies of abusers and violent delinquents provide the most consistent empirical support for the conclusion that abusive parents have themselves often been exposed to violence as children (Widom, 1989). It must be noted, however, that only a small minority (fewer than 15%) of adults who were abused as children were themselves found to be abusive toward their own children (as defined by parental methods used to discipline or resolve conflicts) in one nationwide study that involved interviews with hundreds of randomly selected U.S. families (Straus et al., 1980). A number of positive influences, such as supportive adults within and outside of the family, siblings, and successful school achievement, may serve over time to moderate the effect of abuse or other stressors in childhood (see Rutter, 1979); therefore, we should exercise caution in weighing the significance of this factor in isolation. Also, the long-term effects of physical abuse and neglect must be considered in relation to concomitant psychological injuries to the child that can be most damaging, such as rejection, lack of affection, and exposure to dangerous situations (e.g., strangers in the home, poor supervision; Herrenkohl et al., 1984), as well as events outside of the family (e.g., aggressive and delinquent peers; Martin, 1990).

Personality Attributes and Behavior

An alternative explanation (to the psychopathology viewpoint) of the relationship between parental adjustment and child maltreatment focuses upon those parental characteristics that are related both specifically and globally to the child-rearing role (Wolfe, 1985). Psychological and physical symptoms noted among maltreating parents may reflect the parents' inability to tolerate or cope with the amount of stress impinging upon them from many child- and non-child-related sources. This possibility is reflected in the finding that abusive and neglectful parents report similar *levels* of stress as do nonabusive parents, but that they rate the *impact* of these stressors more severely than controls do (Wolfe, 1985). A systems perspective on the interaction among contextual factors, child situations, and parental symptomatology provides guidance for assessing maltreating behavior from multiple sources and for avoiding an overreliance upon psychopathology as the "cause" of such aberrant behavior. Moreover, instruments designed to detect psychiatric symptomatology, though important in the clinical assessment of some maltreating parents, may be inadequate or inappropriate for assessing more situation-specific disturbances in the parent–child relationship, such as those encountered during disciplinary or instructional situations.

Because abuse and neglect most often occur in the context of *child rearing* (i.e., they are not premeditated and do not occur in isolation), studies of the everyday interactions between maltreating parents and their children have afforded a useful understanding of the nature of these processes. Findings from observations in the home and clinic (reviewed in Wolfe, 1985) support the overall conclusion that both neglectful and abusive parents show infrequent positive behavior during interactions with their children and other family members, leading to negatively imbalanced interactions. Neglectful parents, furthermore, actively *avoid* interacting with their children (e.g., they avoid the children's appropriate bids for attention and escape from difficult situations), whereas abusers tend to administer excessive forms of verbal and physical control that exceed the demands of the situation. Therefore, it is helpful both to observe a parent's behavior with a child (e.g., rates of praise, criticism, and physical negatives) and to observe and/or inquire about the parent's level of arousal and distress during age-representative types of family situations, such as infant care, feeding, and stimulation (with a very young child) or compliance tasks, teaching, and disciplinary situations (with an older child).

Knowledge and Perceptions of Children

Inaccurate perceptions and judgments of their children's behavior have also been identified as possible reasons why some parents justify their coercive behavior or their avoidance of parental responsibilities (Kravitz & Driscoll, 1983). For example, a parent may believe that there is "nothing wrong with punishing a nine-month-old for crying too much" (an item from the Parent Opinion Questionnaire; Azar, Robinson, Hekimian, & Twentyman, 1984), and may act accordingly. Such distorted or negative perceptions that relate specifically to the parent's own experience and/or perceptions of the child-rearing role may reflect the developmental immaturity that has been reported among samples of abusive parents (e.g., Kempe & Kempe, 1978) and the extent to which they accurately recognize the demands and responsibilities that accompany child rearing. Furthermore, in accounting for abusive rather than aversive parental behavior, Milner (1993) places special emphasis on a parent's estimation of "wrongness." That is, an abusive parent not only perceives a child's problem behavior and attributes responsibility and negative intent to the child, but also evaluates the behavior as "very wrong" in order to justify severe disciplinary actions. From an assessment standpoint, therefore, it is critical that a parent's knowledge of child development be distinguished from the more significant concern of the parent's application of his or her knowledge, experience, and expectations to judgments and decisions affecting the parent's actions toward the child. These cognitive abilities and resultant behavior toward the child can best be revealed during naturalistic observations, discussions of actual situations that have recently occurred with the child, and structured questionnaires that are designed to assess parental opinion in the context of common child-rearing situations.

Social Supports

Because the availability of adequate social supports has been linked to enhanced parental functioning (Cutrona, 1984), the absence of such supports (i.e., social isolation) has been viewed as an important etiological or risk factor in child maltreatment (Garbarino, 1976). Despite considerable clinical interest and support for this notion, however, the role of social isolation as a consequence or cause of maltreatment remains uncertain. In reviewing this literature, Seagull (1987) concludes that there is little scientific evidence demonstrating the significant role that larger social networks or lack of social support may play in the etiology of physical abuse. However, an individual's perception of the adequacy of "intimacy" in his or her social network may be a mechanism that serves as a barrier to stress (Cohen & Adler, 1986; Henderson & Moran, 1983). On the other hand, the evidence is clearer regarding the social isolation of neglectful parents: Lack of social support is regarded as one manifestation of the characterological problems of these parents (Polansky, Gaudin, & Kilpatrick, 1992). That is, rather than being a causal factor in the etiology of child neglect, social isolation may be another indicator of the degree of a parent's or family's social incompetence (i.e., a capacity for interpersonal positiveness; the social skills to interact with another person in ways that are rewarding to both interactants; an ability to recognize demands of a situation and respond accordingly—see Burgess & Youngblade, 1988). The degree or pervasiveness of such a pattern of social incompetence may reflect the extent

and severity of parent–child problems that warrant assessment.

In sum, both abusive and neglectful parents can be characterized as coming from multiproblem families of origin, where they were exposed to traumatic or negative childhood experiences such as family violence and instability. As adults, they are often incapable of managing the levels of stress found in their environment, and tend to avoid social contacts that could be perceived as additional sources of stress. Inadequate or inappropriate exposure to positive parental models and supports (in both the present and past), coupled with limited intellectual and problem-solving skills (i.e., the ability to make appropriate judgments during child-rearing situations), may serve to make child rearing a difficult and aversive event. Consequently (or concomitantly), such parents may report symptoms indicative of health and coping problems, which further impair their ability to function effectively as parents. Although it is true that maltreating parents are often multiply handicapped individuals, differences in situationally defined parental competence (i.e., interpersonal positiveness, social skills, and accurate observation and judgment in the parental role) may be a useful framework for investigating failures and successes among diverse child-rearing populations.

Maintaining the Coercive Process

Drawing upon related research with problem families (Patterson, 1982), we believe that parental aggression toward a child is shaped and maintained by its reinforcing consequences and the reciprocation of aversive behavior between the parent and child that escalates in intensity and frequency over time. Whether the initial stimulus was child behavior or not, a parent's use of coercive methods (e.g., verbally and physically threatening gestures) to control aversive events (e.g., loud children, bothersome neighbors) may be negatively reinforced by the termination of the event or a reduction in his or her unpleasant mood state, or it may be positively reinforced by approval from significant others (Friedman, Sandler, Hernandez, & Wolfe, 1981). The child (and perhaps other family members as well) may also be learning to be more coercive and aggressive in his or her manner of dealing with the parent, because this shaping process involves the reciprocation of behavior between the parties.

In time, the abusive parent may maintain that the use of excessive punishment and force is absolutely necessary to control the child's behavior, or the neglectful parent may rely on inappropriate avoidance of responsibility. Provocative stimuli, such as child behavior problems, frustration, and emotional arousal, can become more commonplace, and the parent's response to such events (such as abusive interchanges or neglectful avoidance) correspondingly escalates in intensity, duration, and frequency. By this point, parents often perceive that they are trapped into continuing to use harsh or extreme methods to control their children. Although this perception is somewhat accurate (because children can habituate to harsher approaches and thus may not respond as well to them), this belief justifies their use of even more extreme methods. Parents are now caught in the vicious cycle of using coercive or avoidant methods to diminish tension and irritation, and they may receive some short-term gain through such methods by the reduction of the children's aversive behavior (Wolfe, 1991). Thus, one must consider how a parent perceives the "value" or consequences of coercive or avoidant behavior, in conjunction with the parent's overall style of child rearing and problem solving.

Implications for Assessment of Child Abuse and Neglect

The preceding overview has emphasized the interplay of a constellation of factors involving the entire family, which is known to include the parent's childhood and early adult history; the parent's child-rearing skills, recent stressful events, and social relationships; and features of the child, among other things. We have also seen that the causes and outcomes of abuse and neglect are entwined with general background factors that may impair child development, such as low income level, birth status, health status, and family instability. In view of the complexity of this problem, several implications for the assessment of maltreating families emerge. Although home and clinic observations of behavior have demonstrated their value for pinpointing specific problem areas, such observations may be insufficient by themselves to reveal the range and significance of contextual events that may be dramatically influencing parent and child behavior (Wolfe, 1985). Therefore, indirect assessment methods (e.g., self-report and collateral report instruments, interviews, and standardized psychological tests) that assess such things as parental attitudes, perceived

social supports, and physical and emotional health are important methods for examining low-frequency behaviors and qualitative factors that relate to parental competence and possible marital, social, or financial problems.

Another assessment issue that deserves emphasis relates to the extremely wide range of behaviors that may be shown by maltreated children. Typically, functional components of the maltreatment process, such as marital conflict, family instability, and elevated expressions of anger, are associated with an unusual pattern of child behavior. However, it is not uncommon to find maltreated children who either lack any signs of overt problems or distress, or who exhibit very self-defeating behavior with no obvious function. Rather than assuming that an apparent absence of distress is indicative of the benign effects of maltreatment, an assessor must carefully consider other alternatives. Therefore, the ongoing assessment of maltreated children's development and behavior over an extended time period may be necessary to understand the relationship of their behavior to previous and current experiences, as well as to determine the (possible) adaptive nature of their coping and adjustment patterns at different developmental periods.

ASSESSMENT METHODS

The assessment of abusive or neglectful families is a multistage process, often beginning with impressionistic data from reporting and referral sources, and narrowing toward the evaluation of more specific intervention needs. The psychologist's role should be coordinated with the role of the child protective services agency to promote an interdisciplinary approach to working with multi-problem families. Consultation with the family social worker can enable the psychologist to review the allegations, evidence, proceedings, and decisions that affect the evaluation, and to formulate appropriate assessment questions. The social worker's perspective on the family should be carefully outlined, as well as preliminary goals that the worker has prepared with the family.

Although the assessment of maltreating families overlaps considerably with assessment of families with conduct problem children (see McMahon & Estes, Chapter 3, this volume) and parent–adolescent conflict (see Foster & Robin, Chapter 13, this volume), several unique aspects deserve attention:

1. A maltreating family has often been referred for psychological services involuntarily or under duress. This has implications for eliciting the necessary accurate information from the parents, as well as for establishing credibility and rapport that will increase the parents' motivation to change their parenting style. In general, such clients are more reserved and defensive than self-referred clients in terms of their need for mental health services and their willingness to establish and meet therapeutic goals.

2. Physical abuse in particular represents an extreme form of parent–child conflict in which the target behavior cannot be readily observed. However, once an abusive parent has "lost control" of his or her response to the child, the possibility of recurrence becomes an ongoing concern. This may necessitate more careful monitoring and detailed assessment than would typically be the case with nonabusive parent–child problems.

3. The task of learning unfamiliar child management procedures may appear overwhelming to maltreating parents, and may strengthen their desire to adhere to more familiar, aversive control methods. This "resistance to change" is also embedded in sociodemographic factors (e.g., proclivity toward physical punishment and rigid control) that may conflict with a therapist's style of assistance and intended goals for a family.

4. Maltreating families are a very heterogeneous group of multiproblem families that possess unique combinations of assets and liabilities. Thus, each family often requires a uniquely tailored, ongoing assessment strategy that is sensitive to the family's particular needs.

These added concerns require a management strategy that prioritizes assessment and treatment needs for each family in order to maximize the probability of benefit.

Common Assessment Purposes

The psychological assessment of abuse and neglect must meet several intermediate goals prior to case management decisions or initiating recommendations for intervention. An overview of an assessment strategy for child abuse and neglect is presented in Table 11.1, which includes several decisions and precautionary statements that may be associated with each assessment purpose. The first two assessment purposes are directed at general concerns requiring initial screening and attention, which are then followed by more specific details where indicated (i.e., identifying parental and child needs).

A very common and salient issue that arises in the assessment of abuse and neglect is the detection of possible maltreatment among clinical child populations, and the overriding concern of potential risk to a child of further maltreatment. The examiner may be asked to assist in the pending decision to place a child in foster care, and must carefully weigh the risks and benefits of this shared decision. Situations in which physical abuse may be suspected include those in which (1) the history of the child's injury given by the parent is incompatible with the present injury; (2) the parent's account of the "accident" changes during the course of questioning; (3) repeated episodes of trauma or accidents are known to the agency or setting, or are documented in interagency records; and/or (4) there is an unexplicable delay in seeking treatment for the child's injury or illness. Typically, such assessment or screening is done by emergency care staffs in hospitals and child protection agencies, although any professional who comes into contact with families may be called upon to offer his or her opinion about the nature and probable cause of an atypical pattern of child injuries, developmental delays, or behavior. Although the decision to take a child into protective custody ultimately rests with child welfare department officials, mental health professionals may have significant input at this stage in terms of treatment directions.

After the initial detection of maltreatment, the examiner must begin to identify the major strengths and problem areas of the family system (see Table 11.1) in preparation for involvement of additional community resources, directions for protective services, and specific treatment needs. An interview with the parent(s) may facilitate a preliminary screening to identify possible major psychopathology (e.g., thought disorder, homicidal/suicidal ideation, etc.) and the most probable and significant etiological factors. The interviewer should pay particular attention to defining the family's present situation in terms of specific current problems that may be correlates of maltreatment (e.g., financial, housing, or legal difficulties), as well as the course and nature of these problems (i.e., historical origins, any attempts to modify the situation, any attenuating and accentuating circumstances that have been identified). Precautionary considerations during this stage of assessment include recognizing that involvement of too many professionals or resources may be counterproductive, and avoiding premature decisions based upon a parent's report of transient crises.

TABLE 11.1. Child Abuse and Neglect Assessment Strategy: An Overview

Purpose	Pending decisions	Precautions
A. Determining dangerousness and risk to the child in cases of detected or undetected maltreatment	Taking child into protective custody Alternative placement of child	Removing and returning child to family is highly stressful Initial impression of family may be distorted
B. Identifying general strengths and problem areas of the family system Family background Marital relationship Perceived areas of stress and support Symptomatology (preliminary screening)	Identification of major factors (antecedents, consequences, and individual characteristics) suspected to be operative within the family Directions for protective services, supports, additional community services	Involvement of too many professionals may overwhelm family "Crises" that family members report may change dramatically Parent–child problems may be embedded in chronic family problems (e.g., financial, marital) that resist change
C. Identification of parental needs Symptomatology (in more detail) Child-rearing methods and skills Anger and arousal toward child Perceptions and expectations of children	Behavioral intervention planning and establishing priority of needs	Parental behavior toward child may be a function of both proximal (e.g., child behavior) and distal (e.g., job stress) events Numerous factors that can interfere with treatment must be identified (e.g., resistance, SES, marital problems)
D. Identification of child needs Child behavior problems with family members Child adaptive abilities and cognitive and emotional development	Referral to school-based intervention Behavioral interventions (e.g., parent training) Returning child to family	Expression of symptoms/impairments may be unclear or delayed Child's behavior may be partially a function of recent family separation and change

The second major focus in assessing maltreating families is the identification of parental and child needs (see Table 11.1). At this point the examiner is concerned with identification or development of possible treatment alternatives for the family; this requires more specialized assessment instruments and skills. A detailed analysis of a parent's response patterns and a child's behavior can be completed (as detailed below), allowing for the establishment of priorities for the family and a timetable for meeting the agency's, court's, or practitioner's objectives. The following sections describe specific assessment methods that have been developed for the assessment of abusive family systems, with an emphasis on parent and child focal areas. These methods are largely applicable in the assessment of neglecting families, with specific modifications noted.

Issues in Assessing Maltreating Adults

The assessment of maltreating parents must be tailored to the needs of the referral source as well as the particular family. Because of the complex array of factors that contribute toward abuse and neglect, the assessment approach must be organized in a manner that attends to the major problem areas in a progressive fashion, without becoming overburdened by the number of potential concerns.

Because the possible consequences associated with the family's participation during assessment and issues of confidentiality are often unclear, parents may initially behave in a cautious or defensive manner. It is important that the interviewer explain his or her professional role (i.e., to assess areas in need of change) and the standards concerning client confidentiality; however, it is equally important to clarify for the parents the interviewer's legal obligation to report any suspicions of child maltreatment to protective services. Usually this can be done in a matter-of-fact manner during the beginning of the session, by stating:

> I'll be asking you to tell me a lot of details about your child's behavior and your feelings and actions related to your child. My role is to find out whether the problems you are having can be lessened in any way. Please understand that I'm not here to make any judgments about your parenting ability without your agreement and understanding. I am under no obligation to report what we discuss to anyone outside of this room, unless it has to do with the harm of your child. This means that if you tell me that you hurt your child or may hurt him or her, I must notify your caseworker [or protective services]. Beyond the immediate safety of your child, I will not discuss anything with your caseworker unless we have both agreed to this beforehand (such as your efforts to work on your problems). If you have any other concerns about your situation and my role, let's discuss them now before proceeding with the interview.

A mental health professional who has been asked by the court to prepare a written report on parental competence and risk will have to modify this statement to clarify for the parent exactly what the court is asking and what the professional does and does not have to report.

Issues in Assessing Maltreated Children

Methods relevant to assessing the abused or neglected child have increased at a geometric rate in recent years, in relation to the expansive knowledge of the developmental consequences of these acts. The previous edition of this chapter (Wolfe, 1988) for example, described only a handful of measures that had been either specifically developed for this population or adequately explored in relation to child maltreatment. Today there are several well-developed instruments to choose from, although most techniques rely on child self-report and/or interview procedures alone, with little corresponding advance in the development of alternative strategies. If the assessment purpose is primarily to document the nature and extent of developmental impairment and/or deviation (as is often the case when a child is placed in foster care), many of these methods are quite suitable for determining a child's response relative to appropriate comparison groups (e.g., other maltreated children, a normal population). However, if the assessment purpose includes determining inter-

vention needs and priorities as well, the clinician will need to observe the child in his or her natural environment on several occasions prior to treatment recommendations. As noted elsewhere (Mash & Terdal, Chapter 1, this volume), such observational procedures need not necessarily be accompanied by formal coding of behavior, but are intended to provide the clinician with additional firsthand knowledge of a particular child's behavior across significant settings (school, home, peer groups, etc.).

Because of the sheer number of measures and objectives involved, the remainder of this chapter is organized into a discussion of clinical procedures (i.e., the bulk of the text), as well as resource tables (which contain different possible measures in cross-reference to each psychological dimension, principal assessment needs, and reporting sources). Moreover, because the majority of cases involve assessment of both the child and the parent, the strategy presented here considers both parties (including the family context if appropriate) throughout each step of the assessment. A case example depicting a typical referral for assessment of abused children and their parents illustrates several of the issues involved here. The assessment strategy is presented in a step-by-step, problem-solving manner, including (I) identifying general problem areas; (II) assessing individual strengths and problem areas; and (III) assessing the parent–child relationship. The emphasis here is on assessment of parents and of younger maltreated children (through school age); however, issues that pertain to older children and adolescents are noted for each of these steps as well, with reference to instruments that might serve this age group more appropriately.

Case Example: Referral Information and Background

The following case overview is intended to illustrate some of the interview and initial assessment issues detailed in the following sections. This example does not represent a full and complete assessment; rather, it offers some clinical application of the decision-making assessment processes being considered. The background of the case is presented briefly here; a subsequent section (i.e., "Clinical Illustration: Parent and Child Initial Interviews") describes the initial interview and assessment stage with this family.

Two children (Tammy, age 8, and Dan, age 6) and their biological parents were referred by child protective services for a psychological assessment.

The primary purpose of the assessment was to offer an opinion about the protection needs of these children if they were to be returned to either or both parents, as well as about their immediate placement and treatment needs. The family had been seen by a psychologist some years previously, because allegations of child sexual abuse had been made against the father by an older (out-of-the-home) adult daughter from a previous marriage. An assessment of each parent's risk of maltreatment and parenting abilities was also requested.

Child protective services had recently become reinvolved with this family because both parents were alleged to have physically abused the children. Mrs. W. was charged with three counts of assault, based on reports that she had grabbed Tammy by the hair on the back of her head, lifted her daughter off her tricycle, and dragged her home while pulling her daughter's hair. Mrs. W. was also charged with assault with a weapon against both children, after reports that she was making a swinging motion toward the children with a garden shovel and chasing them around the kitchen table with the shovel. Mr. W. was charged with assault after being seen grabbing Dan's arm and pulling him over the back of a chair; slapping him across the side of his head, causing the child to drop to the floor; hitting Dan on the head and kicking him in the back; and grabbing Dan's arm and swinging him into a wall.

Following these charges, Mr. and Mrs. W. separated from each other, and both children were placed in a foster home. Mrs. W. lived in a women's shelter for a period of time immediately following the separation, and was now in a second-stage housing program. Although she did not report him as being violent toward her prior to the separation, Mrs. W. feared that her husband might become abusive toward her, now that they had separated. Each parent had regular supervised access to the children, arranged separately.

Step I: Identifying General Problem Areas

Parent: Clinical Interview and Initial Assessment

Initial information concerning both parent and child functioning is typically obtained through a semistructured interview with the parent, as well as through reports from others. To assist in organizing the material in a comprehensive fashion, Table 11.2 is a "parent interview and assessment guide" that provides an overview of the major issues to be addressed here and in later sections. In conjunction with adult interview procedures and topics, relevant psychometric instruments for assessing general problems encountered in the family context are presented in Table 11.3. These measures are described throughout the following subsections in regard to their use in conjunction with the interview to obtain a comprehensive and normative picture of a parent's functioning in areas associated with maltreatment (i.e., marital issues, family experiences, etc.). Segments of an interview are then presented as an illustration.

Family Background

The importance of careful investigation of previous childhood experiences that may affect current behavior cannot be overstated. Maltreating parents can often relate to the examiner several significant events (e.g., early rejection or abuse during childhood) or strong cultural values (e.g., adherence to corporal punishment and disavowal of "bribery methods") that have influenced or guided their behavior within the family. Although these events and perceptions may have little to do with changing current behaviors per se, they may suggest to the examiner the type of treatment approach that might be most effective (i.e., emphasis on cognitive and attitudinal change, modeling, problem solving, etc.). Most importantly, knowledge of a parent's history will enable the therapist to develop an intervention plan that is most likely to succeed in relation to the parent's expectations, abilities, and needs.

The interview should trace the origins and development of significant areas of stress within the family system, beginning with family planning and the effects of children on the marital relationship. This discussion includes, for example, whether the maltreated child was planned, the effect of the pregnancy on parental attitudes and life style, support of the biological father, the mother's/father's preparedness and sense of competence in child rearing (i.e., emotional maturity, family support, peer influences), and early problems of the child (e.g., illnesses, trauma, temperament). It is often useful to allow for general discussion of the child throughout the interview, because the parent may have justified or rationalized his or her actions on the basis of the child's "difficult behavior." The parent can be encouraged to describe the child's desirable and undesirable behaviors, and to discuss how he or she would like to see the latter changed. In addition, Table 11.3 lists several instruments that have been developed to aid the interview process, primarily by addressing early

TABLE 11.2. Parent Interview and Assessment Guide

The following is a selected summary of the major factors associated with child abuse and neglect, requiring further interviewing and assessment of the parent, as indicated. The framing and emphasis of each question are left up to the discretion of the interviewer.

   I. Identifying general problem areas
      A. Family background
         1. Early rejection or abuse during own childhood; relationship with biological and/or psychological parents
         2. Methods of punishment and reward during own childhood
         3. Family planning and effect of children on the marital relationship
         4. Preparedness for and sense of competence in child rearing
         5. Early physical, emotional, behavioral problems of child (i.e., illnesses, trauma, temperament)
      B. Marital relationship
         1. Length, stability, and quality of present relationship
         2. Examples of conflict of physical violence
         3. Support from partner in family responsibilities
         4. Substance abuse/dependence
      C. Areas of perceived stress and support
         1. Employment history and satisfaction
         2. Family income and expenses; chronic economic problems
         3. Stability of occupation, income, and living arrangements
         4. Perceived support from within or outside of the family
         5. Daily/weekly contacts with others (e.g., neighbors, social workers)
         6. Quality of social contacts and major life events (i.e., positive vs. negative influence on the parent)

  II. Assessing individual strengths and problem areas
      A. Symptomatology
         1. Recent or chronic health problems; treatment; drug and alcohol use
         2. Identifiable mood and affect changes; anxiety; social dysfunction
         3. Previous psychiatric evaluations of treatment
      B. Emotional reactivity
         1. Perception of how particular child differs from siblings or other children known to the parent
         2. Feelings of anger and "loss of control" when interacting with child (describe circumstances, how the parent felt, how the parent reacted)
         3. Typical ways of coping with arousal during/following stressful episodes

 III. Assessing the parent–child relationship
         1. Parental expectations of child (i.e., accuracy of expectations for child behavior and development, in reference to child's actual developmental status)
         2. Examples of recent efforts to teach new or desirable behavior to child
         3. "Preferred" and "typical" manner of controlling/disciplining child
         4. Attitudes toward learning "different" or unfamiliar child-rearing methods
         5. Perceived effectiveness of parent's teaching and discipline approach
         6. Pattern of child behavior in response to typical discipline methods (i.e., accelerating, decelerating, manipulative, responsive)

experiences of the parent and his or her feelings of support from family members. Although these measures are useful clinical adjunct devices, they have not been widely studied.

Marital and Family Adjustment

Because a parent's child-rearing effectiveness and appropriateness are often related to his or her interactions and experiences with other significant adults (Griest & Wells, 1983), the interviewer

should be careful to assess areas of non-child-related stress within the family. In many instances of child maltreatment, the marital (or common-law) relationship is a primary source of added conflict and stress that interferes with childrearing. A discussion of the length, stability, and quality of the present relationship may provide insight into the manner in which adult conflict may influence parent–child interactions, such as tolerance for child misbehavior, noise, and interruptions. In addition, the interviewer should be sensitive to

TABLE 11.3. Assessment of Abusive/Neglectful Parents: Relevant Psychometric Instruments for Identifying General Problem Areas

Assessment needs	Instruments used in studies of abusive/neglectful parents
Family of origin/Family background	1. Parental Acceptance and Rejection Questionnaire (Rohner, 1991) 2. Childhood History Questionnaire (Milner et al., 1990)
Marital and family adjustment	1. Family Environment Scale (Moos & Moos, 1981) 2. Dyadic Adjustment Scale (DAS; Spanier, 1976) 3. Conflict Tactics Scales (CTS; Straus, 1979b) 4. Abusive Behavior Inventory (Shepard & Campbell, 1992)
Areas of perceived stress and supports	1. Child Abuse Potential Inventory (CAPI; Milner, 1986) 2. Childhood Level of Living Scale (CLLS; Polansky et al., 1981) 3. Parenting Stress Index (PSI; Abidin, 1986). 4. Perceived Social Support Questionnaire (Procidano & Heller, 1983) 5. Home Observation for Measurement of the Environment (HOME; Bradley & Caldwell, 1979; Bradley et al., 1994)

other signs of major distress or conflict in the family system that may be the primary source of child maltreatment, especially physical violence between partners, extramarital relationships, substance abuse or dependence, interference from relatives, and lack of assistance from a partner in handling family affairs. These topics may need to be addressed during private individual sessions with each partner as circumstances require. Instruments that offer assistance in assessing problems associated with adult relationships are discussed below.

Marital conflict and satisfaction can be assessed through several methods, including interviews, standardized instruments, and observations of interactions during conflict resolution tasks. In cases where the partners have not requested marital counseling and are often hesitant to discuss other issues, it is often useful to follow the interview procedure (above) with a brief satisfaction measure, such as the Dyadic Adjustment Scale (DAS; Spanier, 1976). Because of the strong association between child physical abuse and marital conflict in particular, the interviewer should also address the possibility of physical violence between partners. An instrument called the Conflict Tactics Scales (CTS; Straus, 1979b) has been specifically designed to elicit information concerning conflict resolution tactics between adults and/or between parents and child in a sensitive and revealing fashion that makes its use with abusive families especially pertinent. The CTS is administered in an interview fashion, whereby each partner is separately asked to rate the frequency of occurrence (on a 7-point scale ranging from "never" to "more than 20 times") of tactics that he or she has used toward their partner during disputes over the past 12 months. These tactics include, for example, "discussed the issue calmly," "insulted or swore at the other one," "threatened to hit or throw something at the other one," "kicked, bit, or hit with a fist." This instrument has been widely used in clinical and research studies to assess verbal and physical aggression in the family (e.g., Straus, 1979a; Straus et al., 1980; Wolfe, Jaffe, Wilson, & Zak, 1985). However, information obtained from this approach should be combined with other sources (e.g., interview, direct observation) to provide the best estimate of marital conflict resolution tactics (Jouriles & O'Leary, 1985; see Dutton, 1995, and Jacobson et al., 1994, for additional procedures for assessing marital violence).

Areas of Perceived Stress and Support

The major purposes of assessing the family's or individual parent's degree of perceived stress and support are to locate areas that are perceived as highly stressful and to determine what resources family members use to manage these areas of stress, either effectively or ineffectively. Assessment of socioeconomic factors that may be highly stressful can be accomplished during the interview by discussing employment history and satisfaction, family income and expenses, housing and living arrangements, and similar circumstances that may be contributing to family problems.

The indirect manner in which such socioeconomic factors and life events influence child development and child-rearing practices can also be determined by means of instruments designed to assess aspects of the child's environment, parental stress, and social supports. Polansky, Chalmers, Buttenweiser, and Williams (1981) developed the Childhood Level of Living Scale (CLLS) to assess the extent of positive and negative influences present in the child's home environment. This instrument is particularly well suited for assessing neglectful families, in that it lists the major areas of concern to children's minimal health, safety, and stimulation requirements. The CLLS has two main scales: Physical Care, containing items that make up five subscales labeled General Positive Care, State of Repair of House, Negligence, Quality of Household Maintenance, and Quality of Health Care and Grooming; and Emotional/ Cognitive Care, with subscales labeled Encouraging Competence, Inconsistency of Discipline and Coldness, Encouraging Superego Development, and Material Giving. The 99 items are rated "yes" or "no" by home visitors. The authors provide preliminary normative data for this instrument, with cutoff scores indicating neglectful care, adequate care, and good care, although reliability and validity data are limited (with the exception of one report indicating discriminative validity between neglect and control families; Polansky et al., 1981).

Two similar instruments have been developed to assess the adequacy of the environment for the child (again, these are especially useful for neglect): the Child Well-Being Scales (CWBS; Magura & Moses, 1986), and the Home Observation for Measurement of the Environment (HOME; Bradley & Caldwell, 1979; Bradley, Mundfrom, Whiteside, Casey, & Barrett, 1994). Each requires only an unstructured home visit to complete. For example, the HOME is a well-researched criterion checklist that reflects the quality of the child's environment more precisely than do social class or SES designations alone. This inventory was designed to sample certain aspects of the quantity and quality of social, emotional, and cognitive support available to a young child (different forms are available for children from birth to 3 years and from 3 to 5 years of age). The

HOME is completed following visits to the family's residence, and items not obtained via direct observation (e.g., "takes child out of home more than twice per week") are based on parental report. The rater's "yes" or "no" responses to the 45-item checklist result in six subscales reflecting emotional and verbal responsiveness of the mother, avoidance of restriction and punishment, organization of the physical and temporal environment, provision of appropriate play materials, maternal involvement with the child, and opportunities for variety in daily stimulation. As mentioned previously, Harrington et al. (1995) recently used both instruments to study the relationship among maternal substance use, neglectful parenting, and child development; they found that although maternal substance use was not related to neglectful parenting in their sample, children's receptive language development was predicted by (combined) scores on these two instruments.

Child: Clinical Interview and Initial Assessment

An individual assessment of the infant, preschooler, or school-age child can assist the examiner in understanding the child's overall functioning and can provide insight as to current fears or anxieties, which may be quite debilitating. The possibility that an older child (age 6 or older) has developed a distorted perspective of family life in which violence is commonplace or acceptable should be investigated by discussing attitudes about interpersonal aggression, sex roles, and responsibility for aggressive behavior. The child may also respond to the examiner in a very guarded manner that is not a valid reflection of his or her typical behavior, out of possible fear of reprisal or confusion over the events that have occurred. For this reason, the examiner should enable the child to establish a sense of trust and comfort prior to discussing the family's problems (see Hughes & Baker, 1990, for further detail regarding developmentally sensitive interviewing).

A good beginning point is a discussion of the child's comprehension of and reaction to family problems, using a semistructured interview format. The interview begins with a general discussion of activities and events that the child enjoys; this leads into a more specific discussion of recent crisis events. The child's "crisis adjustment" is assessed in reference to (1) his or her feelings about changes in the family (e.g., foster care, parental separation); and (2) a discussion of major life events (aided by, e.g., the Life Events Checklist for Children; Johnson & McCutcheon, 1980). Safety skills (e.g., "What do you do if Mom and Dad are arguing?" "How can you tell when Mom or Dad is angry?"; "Who do you call in an emergency?") are also important areas to consider during the child interview. The child's comprehension of personal safety and knowledge of appropriate actions to take provides useful information for planning for the child's immediate needs (e.g., out-of-home placement, alternative actions to avoid high-conflict situations).

Discussion can then turn to the child's attitudes and responses to interpersonal conflict and expression of anger, by encouraging the child to discuss events that "make you really mad," followed by identification of his or her actions, feelings, and attitudes about such "anger situations." We find it useful to describe attitudes and reactions to anger provocation in reference to favorite television characters, in order to determine the child's ability to recognize the artificiality and inappropriateness of aggressive behavior. For example, some abused children reveal the influence of aggressive modeling in the family or on TV through their inability to recognize nonviolent means for resolving interpersonal conflicts. Although this is by no means unique to abused children, the presence of such rigid adherence to coercive problem solving signals a need for exposure to alternative strategies.

Clinical Illustration: Parent and Child Initial Interviews

Mother

Mrs. W. (age 42) appeared well dressed and comfortable throughout the interview, which began with a discussion of limits to confidentiality and the necessity of a court report following this assessment. The examiner also clarified that this was not a custody-and-access assessment, but rather was directed at the welfare of the children, due to the fact that Mrs. W. had recently separated from her husband. Mrs. W. expressed anger in response to 2 years of child protective services involvement, suggesting that the agency did not follow through, in her opinion, with a psychologist's previous recommendations. Notably, she denied any suggestion of her husband's physically assaulting herself, although she did express fear that she might now be at some risk of physical abuse by her husband because of their separation. She also expressed

concerns that her children's needs were not being properly addressed by the agency at the present time, and she was willing to cooperate fully with this assessment in the children's best interests.

Father

Mr. W., who stated his age as 49 years, was seen for an initial intake by the examiner (a previous history was made available by the referral source). Mr. W. indicated that he was not able to read the items on the test questionnaires, and throughout this initial interview the examiner found him to be extremely difficult to keep on topic. He preferred to review his early childhood and early adulthood, and to emphasize his business ventures and his contributions to the community. He was obviously very proud of his success at "rising above" his own negative childhood background, and saw himself as a "self-made man." Mr. W. denied hurting his wife in any fashion. He stated that he believed that his wife was "running around on me," and that this upset him greatly, but that he had not harmed her in any way. Overall, the interview with Mr. W. was not productive. There were many tangents and "war stories," and he denied any physical, sexual, or verbal mistreatment of his adult daughters by his first marriage, his children by his current marriage, or his estranged wife.

Children

The following information was obtained during initial interviews with each child, to determine the presence of any current major developmental or psychological problems and to direct future assessment, placement, and treatment decisions.

Tammy, who was 8 years old, was very quiet and seemed uncomfortable during the private interview. She indicated that she enjoyed her current living arrangement, especially the school and her teachers. She expressed a number of favorite activities, and expressed sadness regarding the breakup of her family. She also indicated that she felt scared "when people yell at me." She denied being physically or sexually mistreated by any members of her family. Notably, when asked the question "Where do you go in the house if Mom and Dad are fighting?", she indicated, "I hide in my room" (this is a common response of children who witness adult conflict). She indicated feeling scared when this happened, but she did not know why her parents fought or what they fought about.

Tammy expressed a considerable amount of positive feelings about her parents, with significantly fewer negative perceptions. She indicated being slapped or spanked only once by each parent.

Dan, age 6, was willing to talk to the examiner and seemed comfortable throughout the interview. He seemed to understand that the purpose of the interview was to determine whether he could go back with his parents. He said that he enjoyed his present placement, because they "treat me good and they have good food." He had no complaints about the foster placement. When asked about things that might make him feel sad, Dan indicated that this happened "when no one is paying any attention to me and I'm all alone." He also expressed concerns about being teased about being in a foster home; he claimed that kids had occasionally beaten him up at school last year because of his family circumstances. Dan seemed to have an understanding of the events leading up to his parental separation, stating, "My parents were arrested for beating up on me—that didn't really happen, though." When asked what happened, he related a story of how his mom had chased him around with a plastic shovel, and was angry because he had broken his sister's toy. He added that "Dad was charged for spanking us," and stated that he had been hit with his father's hand (not a belt, as alleged).

Dan did not express attitudes consistent with a belief in violence, and he seemed to understand that hitting others is wrong. He also seemed to know whom he could talk to if someone was mistreating him, such as the police, his mother, or a teacher. When asked how he felt when he heard Mom and Dad arguing, he answered, "Sad," and indicated that he would go and hide under these circumstances. When asked, "Do you think Mom and Dad ever fight about you or your brothers and sisters?", he replied, "No, 'cause we usually hide because we're scared that they will take it out on us; it never happens because we hide." Finally, Dan stated that they had been a happy family until his older half-sister had "told on" his parents. In closing the interview, the examiner asked Dan how he hoped everything would turn out. He indicated that he would like to be back with his parents and sister as a family, but if they did not all get back together, he hoped he could live with his dad because his father needed him to work on the farm. Then he added that he hoped he could go to his mom's because they could go to the park whenever they wanted. Like his sister, Dan expressed more positive than negative perceptions of both parents.

Step II: Assessing Individual Strengths and Problem Areas

Parent: Assessment of Emotional Regulation and Symptomatology

During the interview, the parent's clinical symptomatology may be addressed by discussing mood and affect changes, anxiety, recent or chronic health problems, and medical treatments. This interview procedure may be assisted by the administration of a standardized psychiatric symptom checklist or inventory to rule out particular forms of psychopathology and/or to determine the extent of psychopathology, as listed in the top portion of Table 11.4. The Symptom Checklist 90—Revised (SCL-90-R; Derogatis, 1983) is a self-report symptom inventory designed to reflect the respondent's psychological and health-related symptoms over the past 7 days; it has been shown to have strong psychometric properties. Two subscales of this 90-item questionnaire are particularly useful indicators of adult interpersonal sensitivity: (1) Interpersonal Sensitivity, which measures personal inadequacy and inferiority (e.g., self-deprecation, feelings of uneasiness); and (2) Hostility, which reflects thoughts, feelings, or actions that are characteristic of the negative affect state of anger. These subscales have been shown to discriminate young adults with histories of abuse from those without (Wolfe, Wekerle, Reitzel-Jaffe, & Lefebvre, in press), and the full instrument is useful as a descriptive and screening measure of overall stress and symptomatology (e.g., MacMillan, Olson, & Hanson, 1991).

The parent's reactivity to unpleasant or aversive environmental events is an important factor believed to mediate anger and aggression (Berkowitz, 1983). Because emotional reactivity involves involuntary somatic responses (e.g., changes in cardiovascular function, temperature of peripheral organs, muscle tension) that are very difficult to observe or measure under realistic conditions, self-report ratings of annoyance, anger, or unpleasant changes in affect have been the most commonly used measures. Abusive parents are often willing to describe their feelings of anger and "loss of control" when provided with distinctive cues or examples, such as interacting with their children in a high-conflict situation or discussing a recent conflict (e.g., Koverola, Elliot-Faust, & Wolfe, 1984). That is, feelings of anger, tension, and frustration can be identified by asking a parent to provide recent examples of irritating child behaviors, the circumstances in which these behaviors occurred, and how the parent felt and reacted. At

TABLE 11.4. Assessment of Abusive/Neglectful Parents: Relevant Psychometric Instruments for Assessing Individual Strengths/Problem Areas and the Parent–Child Relationship

Assessment needs	Instruments used
Individual strengths and weaknesses: Emotional regulation and symptomatology	1. CAPI (Milner, 1986) 2. Beck Depression Inventory (BDI; Beck et al., 1961) 3. Symptom Checklist 90—Revised (SCL-90-R; Derogatis, 1983)
The parent–child relationship: Child-rearing beliefs and methods	Self-report methods 1. CAPI (Milner, 1986) 2. Adult–Adolescent Parenting Inventory (Bavolek, 1984) 3. Parental Problem-Solving Measure (PPSM; Hanson et al., 1995) 4. PSI (Abidin, 1986) 5. Parent Opinion Questionnaire (Azar & Rohrbeck, 1986) Observational methods 1. Maternal Observation Matrix (MOM; Tuteur et al., 1995) 2. Mother–Child Interaction Scale (MCIS; Tuteur et al., 1995) 3. HOME (Bradley & Caldwell, 1979) 4. Parenting Behavior Rating Scales (King et al., 1994) 5. Child Well-Being Scales (CWBS; Magura & Moses, 1986)

the same time, the clinician can ask the parent to identify fluctuations in mood (especially depression, anxiety, and agitation) that precede or follow incidences of parent–child conflict (MacMillan et al., 1991).

Self-monitoring of annoyance, anger, or similar feelings that precede aggressive responding toward the child in actual situations can be obtained by means of a simple Anger Diary (Wolfe, Sandler, & Kaufman, 1981) that the parent completes in the home or clinic. The parent is instructed to record a description of each incident in which the child did something that led the parent to feel anger, frustration, or tension. The parent also indicates how he or she dealt with the problem, how it finally was resolved or ended, and how he or she felt afterward about the entire incident. Parental compliance with this self-monitoring task is often forthcoming if the procedure is described as one in which the parent can inform the therapist more precisely about "the problems you have to face every day with your child's behavior," rather than the manner in which the parent reacts to the child. Although the connection between the child's problem behavior and the parent's inappropriate actions is a two-way street,

it is often more fruitful to focus the parent's efforts initially on his or her "problems with the child," followed by increasing recognition of the parent's responsibility during subsequent treatment sessions.

Child: Assessment of Behavioral, Cognitive, and Emotional Development

In formulating an assessment strategy for an individual child, the clinician must be concerned about achieving some balance among child self-report (both interview and questionnaires), parental report (especially if a parent is suspected of maltreatment), and observation of the child with peers and/or caregivers (Achenbach, McConaughy, & Howell, 1987). The assessment usually begins with reports from significant sources in the child's life (including the referral source), because, generally speaking, such information from corollary sources (e.g., teachers, parents, social workers) provides a global understanding of the child that can then be used to narrow down the choices for additional self-report, interview, or observational procedures. Following a clinical interview, self-report and observational methods yield considerable information concerning the child's strengths and deficits, especially in terms of his or her views of self and others (social-cognitive characteristics) and feeling states (socio-emotional qualities).

Again, the task of assessing all potentially relevant dimensions of child psychopathology can become unmanageable unless a systematic, problem-solving approach is used. Tables 11.5, 11.6, and 11.7 describe the more prominent instruments that have been used in reported studies involving maltreated children. These tables have been organized to reflect assessment methods that pertain to each of three psychological dimensions (i.e., behavioral, cognitive, and socioemotional development), as well as principal assessment issues summarized from the previous review. As well, the tables indicate those measures that are more suitable for younger children or older children/adolescents, and whether the instruments rely on self-report, report from others, or observation. Examples and highlights of how one might use these tools to conduct a child assessment are discussed in the following text.

Interpersonal Behavior

The child's primary caregiver, usually the parent, is a critical source of information concerning the child's development and behavior. Parental report of child behavior is a useful starting point for assessment and intervention planning, because it permits the clinician to obtain a broad spectrum of information as to the parent's perception of problem areas in the parent–child relationship. Most parents who have been accused of abuse or who have admitted to their fear of harming their children share a willingness to discuss the children's misdeeds and to complete a checklist of behavioral strengths and weaknessess that best describe their children. Although the degree of parental distortion or exaggeration of problems is not known, at least one study (Wolfe & Mosk, 1983) has demonstrated interparent agreement (internalizing problems, $r = .61$; externalizing problems, $r = .84$) in a sample of abusing parents who completed the Child Behavior Checklist (CBCL; Achenbach, 1991a). The CBCL requires only a sixth-grade reading level and takes about 20 minutes to complete, and the results can be easily discussed with the respondent to clarify the nature and specific circumstances surrounding their report of child behavior problems. For example, when examining the social relationships of physically abused 8- to 12-year-olds, Sal-zinger et al. (1993) found that the behavioral effect best documented by both direct observation and parent and teacher ratings was that physically abused children were more aggressive and hostile than nonabused children. On these other-report measures, abused children were described as meaner, as more likely to engage in arguments and fights, and as showing less cooperation and fewer leadership skills than their nonabused classmates.

For older children and adolescents, several new self-report instruments may be useful in assessing their behavior with peers and dating partners. These dimensions are of particular importance for this age group, because maltreated children are at an increased risk of becoming victims or victimizers during the formation of intimate relationships in early to middle adolescence (Wolfe, Wekerle, & Scott, 1997). We developed the Conflicts in Relationships Questionnaire (CIRQ; Wolfe, Reitzel-Jaffe, Gough, & Wekerle, 1994) specifically to serve as a measure of positive and negative conflict resolution in reference to dating situations. The CIRQ is a 60-item instrument that uses a 4-point scale (0 = "never," 1 = "rarely," 2 = "sometimes," 3 = "often") to measure the frequency of physically, sexually, and emotionally abusive and nonabusive behaviors experienced by the respondent. The self-report measure is identical for males and females, except for pronoun changes and the elimination of two items concerning sexual coercion that would not apply to females. To separate victimization experiences from offending behaviors, items are repeated in two sections: Part A reflects behaviors the respondent has shown toward a dating partner (i.e., offending behaviors, such as "did something to make her feel jealous"), whereas Part B reflects behaviors a dating partner has shown toward the respondent (i.e., victimization experiences). The measure was constructed to reflect aspects of physical and sexual coercion, psychological abuse, and positive communication strategies. A factor analysis of the scale resulted in three factors (i.e., Positive Communication, Coercion, and Emotional Abuse), and each factor discriminated youths with histories of maltreatment from nonmaltreated youths (Wolfe et al., in press).

The 25-item Peer Relations Inventory (PRI; Wolfe, Grasley, & Wekerle, 1994) was also developed by our research team to assess a youth's typical behavior with peers. Responding on a scale from 1 ("not at all") to 5 ("very much"),

TABLE 11.5. Assessment of Abused/Neglected Children: Methods for Assessing Interpersonal Behavior

Principal assessment issues	Child measures	Adolescent measures

Peer relations
    Aggression
    Withdrawal
    Lack of prosocial behavior
    Delinquency/antisocial
        behavior
Child–caregiver relations
    Difficult temperament
    Attachment
    Noncompliance
    Compulsive compliance
Self-regulation
    Impulse control
    Lack of creative initiative
    Frustration and anger
	Interview and self-report methods
	1. Child Self-Control Rating Scale (Rohrbeck et al., 1991)[4]
	2. Woodcock–Johnson Scales of Independent Behavior (Bruininks et al., 1984)[1,2,4]
	
	Other-report methods
	1. Child Behavior Checklist (CBCL; Achenbach, 1991a)[1]
	2. Teacher Report Form (Achenbach, 1991b)[1]
	3. Infant Characteristics Questionnaire (Bates et al., 1991)[3,4]
	
	Observational methods[a]
	1. Parent–child dyadic interactions (maternal attention, reciprocity, affective tone; Alessandri, 1991)[3,4]
	2. Children's play (social initiation, reciprocation, physical and verbal aggression, rough play; Haskett & Kistner, 1991)[2,4]
	
	Children's play (functional, constructive, dramatic; games; Alessandri, 1992)[2,4]
		Self-report methods
		1. Conflicts in Relationships Questionnaire (CIRQ; Wolfe, Reitzel-Jaffe, et al., 1994)[2,4]
		2. Peer Relations Inventory (PRI; Wolfe, Grasley, & Wekerle, 1994)[2]
		3. Measure of Adolescent Social Performance (Cavell & Kelley, 1992)[2]
		4. Youth Self-Report (Achenbach, 1991c)[1]
		5. Adolescent Interpersonal Competence Questionnaire (AICQ; Buhrmester, 1990)[2,3]
		
		Other-report methods
		1. PRI—Teacher report (Wolfe, Grasley, & Wekerle, 1994)[2]

Note. Superscripts refer to the global or specific purposes of each method: [1]Global measure. [2]Peer relations. [3]Child–caregiver relations. [4]Self-regulation.
[a]Additional observational methods are described in Tables 11.4 and 11.7.

teachers (or other familiar adults) and youths separately rate perceptions of the youths' peer relations in reference to positive interactions (e.g., "Do you stand up for your rights?"), offensive jokes (e.g., "Do you laugh at or make sexist jokes or remarks?"), and physical coercion (e.g., "Do you annoy or tease girls to get what you want?"). The PRI was inspired by previous research aimed at assessing change in prosocial and antisocial behavior among delinquent youths (i.e., the Missouri Peer Relations Inventory; Borduin, Blaske, Treloar, Mann, & Hazelrigg, 1989), although items for the PRI were written to reflect aspects of harassment, gender-based aggression, and prosocial communication that have been theoreti-

cally linked to the cycle of violence (Wolfe et al., in press). Separate subscale scores are available for both versions of this measure, corresponding to three factors labeled Positive Peer Behavior (14 items; alphas = .86 and .93 for the youth and teacher versions, respectively); Aggression (7 items; alphas = .81 and .90); and Jokes (3 items; alpha = .77 and .94).

Cognitive and Social-Cognitive Development

Research with both child and adult victims of violence points to the importance of a victim's assessment of the conflict, because this may in turn influence the victim's emotional reaction to it. For

TABLE 11.6. Assessment of Abused/Neglected Children: Methods for Assessing Cognitive and Social-Cognitive Functioning

Principal assessment issues	Child measures	Adolescent measures

Peer relations
    Hostile attributional bias/style
    Perspective taking
    Social support
Child–caregiver relations
    Perception of caregiver
    Attributions of blame, trust,
      etc.
Self-regulation
    Self-efficacy/problem solving
    Effective coping ability
    Self-esteem
    Moral reasoning and
      development
Learning abilities
    Intellectual impairments
    Language/communication
      skills
    Problem-solving ability
    Problematic school
      performance
	Interview and self-report methods
	1. Harter Self-Perception Profile for Children (Harter, 1985a)[1,2,4]
	2. Harter Social Support Scale for Children (Harter, 1985b)[2,3]
	3. Narrative story stem technique (Buchsbaum et al., 1992)[3,4,5]
	4. Children's Moral Reasoning Interview (Astor, 1994)[4,5]
	5. Children's Attributional Style Questionnaire (Kaslow et al., 1978)[2,3,4]
	6. Attributions Questionnaire (Dodge et al., 1990)[2,3,4]
	7. Attribution for Maltreatment Interview (AFMI; McGee, 1990)[2,3,4]
	
	Other-report methods
	1. CBCL (Achenbach, 1991a)[1]
		Self-report methods
		1. AICQ (Buhrmester, 1990)[2,3]
		2. Adolescent Self-Perception Profile (Harter, 1982)[2,4]
		
		Other-report methods
		1. AICQ (Buhrmester, 1990)[2,3]

Note. Superscripts refer to the global or specific purposes of each method: [1]Global measure. [2]Peer relations. [3]Child–caregiver relations. [4]Self-regulation. [5]Learning abilities.

example, the child who attributes physical maltreatment to his or her parent's "mean" character would be expected to fare worse than the child who sees the same behavior as caused by the parent's external circumstances (e.g., job stress). Moreover, as the severity of the maltreatment increases, attributions of blame to the perpetrator increase (Wolfe & McGee, 1991). If attributions of blame (either to self or the perpetrator) result from the maltreatment, then emotional reactions of sadness or anger will be more likely to result. This finding is congruent with studies involving adult victims of wife assault (Holtzworth-Munroe, 1988); furthermore, it suggests the importance of carefully assessing the dimensions of maltreatment (severity, chronicity, frequency, etc.), in order to determine their impact on the attributional process (e.g., see Kaufman et al., 1994; Wolfe & McGee, 1994).

Attributional assessment can often be done through an interview procedure, such as the Attribution for Maltreatment Interview (AFMI; McGee, 1990). The AFMI consists of four structured interviews, corresponding to hostile maltreatment (i.e., physical and emotional abuse), exposure to family violence, sexual abuse, and neglect (respondents are only administered those interviews that pertain to their experiences). After generating a list of all possible causes for their maltreatment, they are asked to make agreement ratings (from 1 = "do not agree" to 4 = "strongly agree") in relation to 26 statements read aloud by the interviewer. For each of the maltreatment types, the AFMI yields five subscales (derived from theory and factor analysis): Self-Blaming Cognition, Self-Blaming Affect, Self-Excusing, Perpetrator Blame, and Perpetrator Excusing. In a study involving 160 maltreated youths, McGee, Wolfe, and Olson (1995) found that the majority viewed the offenders as the major cause for their maltreatment; however, for physical and emotional abuse, one-third of the sample identified their own misbehavior as the major cause for what happened. This finding underscores the importance of assessing a child's attributions for maltreatment, so that therapy can (if necessary) target self-blame statements, as well as the child's underlying beliefs that he or she could have pre-

TABLE 11.7. Assessment of Abused/Neglected Children: Methods for Assessing Socioemotional Adjustment

Principal assessment issues	Child measures	Adolescent measures

Peer relations
   Social sensitivity/empathy
Child–caregiver relations
   Perceived parental support
   Attachment
Self-regulation
   Emotion regulation (affect
     regulation)
   Depression
   Anxiety
   PTSD (extreme physical abuse)
	Interview and self-report methods
	1. Children's Depression Inventory (Kovacs, 1994)[4]
	2. Present Episode version of the Schedule for Affective Disorder and Schizophrenia for School-Age Children (K-SADS-P; Chambers et al., 1985)[4]
	3. Harter Dimensions of Depression Profile for Children and Adolescents (Harter & Nowakowski, 1987)[4]
	4. State–Trait Anxiety Inventory for Children (Spielberger, 1973)[4]
	5. Narrative story stem technique (Buchsbaum et al., 1992)[4]
	6. PTSD section of the Diagnostic Interview for Children and Adolescents—Revised (DICA-R; Reich & Welner, 1988)[4]
	
	Observational methods[a]
	1. Strange Situation (Ainsworth et al., 1978)[3,4]
	2. MOM (Tuteur et al., 1995)[3,4]
		Self-report methods
		1. BDI (Beck et al., 1961)[4]
		2. SCL-90-R (Derogatis, 1983)[1]
		3. DICA-R (Reich & Welner, 1988)[4]
		4. Hilson Adolescent Personality Questionnaire (Inwald, 1986)[1]

Note. Superscripts refer to the global or specific purposes of each method: [1]Global measure. [2]Peer relations. [3]Child–caregiver relations. [4]Self-regulation.
[a]Additional observational methods are described in Tables 11.4 and 11.5.

vented such acts and was therefore somewhat at fault.

Cicchetti et al. (1988) contend that maltreatment interferes with children's development of a "success-based orientation"—that is, the degree of control they perceive having over the impact of their actions. For this reason, these authors suggest an assessment strategy that documents both children's school performance and their level of social competence (i.e., social problem solving and coping skills; see Table 11.6). For example, Aber, Allen, Carlson, and Cicchetti (1989) measured children's "effectance motivation," defined as the children's tendency to perceive some control over the effect of their actions, by having them interact with an unfamiliar adult. Effectance motivation was measured on the basis of a child's pictorial curiosity, variability seeking, and level of aspiration while engaging in games with the adult. Maltreated children differed significantly from a

matched sample of nonmaltreated children in terms of displaying less "secure readiness to learn" and less "outer-directedness," two factors derived from the researchers' theoretical domains of social-cognitive and emotional development.

In addition to interview techniques to assess attributions and beliefs, older children and adolescents can also provide relevant data concerning their self-perceived competence with peers. The Adolescent Interpersonal Competence Questionnaire (AICQ; Buhrmester, 1990) is a 32-item measure assessing domains of competence that are important in adolescents' close relationships: self-disclosure, providing emotional support to friends, management of conflicts, and negative assertion. This measure can also be completed by another respondent (a dating partner, a parent, etc.) who knows the person well. The adolescent or other respondent rates the adolescent's competence on a 5-point scale (1 = "poor at this; would be so uncomfortable and unable to handle this situation that it would be avoided if possible"; 5 = "extremely good at this; would feel very comfortable and could handle this situation very well"). Reliability for the factor scores has been high, and the scales correlate with adjustment and friendship intimacy measures (Buhrmester, 1990). This instrument has not been used specifically with maltreated children or youths, although in a preliminary study our research laboratory has shown it to be sensitive to the issues pertaining to this population (Wolfe et al., in press).

Because a child's moral reasoning and development subsequent to a history of maltreatment often reflect poor self-regulation and aggressive themes (e.g., Smetana, Kelly, & Twentyman, 1984), innovative procedures that prompt such a child's thinking process merit recognition. One prominent example was reported by Buchsbaum, Toth, Clyman, Cicchetti, and Emde (1992), in which a play narrative "stem technique" was used to elicit a child's internal representations of relationships and emotion regulation. The interviewer begins a story (the "stem"), using doll play, and the child is asked to complete it. In addition to recording verbal and behavioral responses, standard probes are used to challenge the child to resolve the dilemma posed by the stem and to pursue his or her reasons for completing the story a particular way. The stories were developed to elicit certain themes of moral reasoning—for example, empathic or prosocial responses; ways to adhere to a rule in the face of temptation; maternal responses to stealing; parental responses to a transgression in which the transgression results in potential harm to the child; or conflict between members of the family/parents. In their study involving a sample of over 100 maltreated preschool-age children and a matched comparison sample, Buchsbaum et al. (1992) found that the narratives of the maltreated children tended to have more themes involving inappropriate aggression, neglect, and sexualized behaviors. Their self-statements also reflected their views of themselves as "bad," as well as more punitive and abusive language. This standard form of administration of story stems serves to avoid the problem of leading questions (which often plagues interviews with maltreated children), and it offers considerable promise for assessing younger children's belief systems and moral reasoning.

Socioemotional Adjustment

Researchers have been very interested in how the developing parent–child relationship may be af-

fected by the adverse conditions of emotional rejection, harsh treatment, insensitivity, and verbal and physical assaults (Aber & Cicchetti, 1984). The two predominant approaches to understanding the socioemotional development of maltreated children have focused on assessment of (1) attachment formation in infants and toddlers, and (2) preschool and school-age maltreated children's ability to empathize with their peers and form positive peer relationships.

Often, a child's current anxieties and fears may be assessed via observation (during the interview) and self-report instruments. The interviewer should be sensitive to the child's verbal and somatic indications of anxiety or negative affect (e.g., poor eye contact, twitching movements, long silences, sadness), and should make every attempt to determine the origins or reference for such emotion (which is often linked to foster care placement, uncertainty over family reunion, and/or fear of further maltreatment).

A common strategy for assessing children's expression and recognition of emotions, as well as their interpersonal behavior, involves parent–child or peer interactions (Feshbach, 1989). The assessment of this developmental ability, moreover, can be conducted by relying on known strategies of naturalistic observations with children and adults (see also procedures used by Cummings, 1987; Hinchey & Gavelek, 1982). A study by Haskett and Kistner (1991), for example, illustrates a useful peer observational procedure. Peer interactions were observed among a sample of 14 preschool-age children with a history of physical abuse and a matched sample of 14 nonabused children. In addition to teacher report data, peer sociometric ratings were obtained. Children were observed during three 10-minute free-play sessions across three different mornings. Quality of the children's social behaviors was indexed by the number of initiations of positive interaction (i.e., social initiation and peer reciprocation) and the occurrence of aggression (both instrumental and hostile), negative verbalization, and rough play. The findings confirmed that abused children initiated fewer positive interactions with peers and exhibited a higher proportion of negative behaviors than the comparison children; moreover, peers were less likely to reciprocate the initiations of the abused children, although they approached these children just as often as they did other peers. Thus, despite the alternative peer and adult role models available in an out-of-home day care setting, some abused children experience disturbed social interactions that warrant assessment and early intervention.

Step III: Assessing the Parent–Child Relationship

Parental Child-Rearing Beliefs and Methods (Self-Report)

Despite the formidable influence of parental background, psychological functioning, and situational and life stressors upon child maltreatment, such maltreatment is strongly linked to events that involve the child in some manner (Wolfe, 1985). Therefore, a comprehensive assessment of a parent's typical daily behavior with his or her child includes self-report and observational data in reference to situations that lead to anger and that may be precursors to abusive episodes in particular. This requires an analysis of idiosyncratic arousal patterns, fluctuations in mood and affect, and characteristic response styles during commonly occurring child-rearing situations. During the interview, the parent should be encouraged to discuss his or her expectations of the child (e.g., at dinnertime, while getting dressed, when going to bed, etc.), and to discuss his or her preferred or typical manner of controlling the child. These interview topics can then be followed up by more formal assessment of child-rearing beliefs and methods, as presented below and summarized in the bottom portion of Table 11.4.

The Child Abuse Potential Inventory (CAPI; Milner, 1986) has become a standard self-report instrument for assessing abusive adults. The CAPI was specifically designed to measure problem areas related to parental and family background (such as those identified above) that are associated with an increased probability of abuse. Since its development in the late 1970s, this instrument has undergone considerable psychometric investigations by its author and others (see Milner, 1989) that have produced norms for general and abusive populations, as well as reliability and validity information. The major Abuse scale consists of six factor subscales: Distress, Rigidity, Unhappiness, Problems with Child and Self, Problems with Family, and Problems with Others. In addition, there is a Lie scale that indicates the degree of deceptive responding (e.g., "I love all children"). The 160 items on the scale are written at the third-grade reading level and require only an "agree" or "disagree" response (e.g., "I am often mixed up," "A child should never talk back," "My parents did not understand me"). The CAPI appears to be measuring a parent's general psychological functioning and child-rearing attitudes, and as such may be an alternative to standardized psychological tests (e.g., the Minnesota Multi-phasic Personality Inventory, the Beck Depression Inventory).

Data on the classification rates of the CAPI Abuse scale have been in the mid-80% to the low 90% range (reported in Caliso & Milner, 1994). However, in most studies using equal numbers of abusers and nonabusers, more false-negative than false-positive classifications have been reported. As shown in a recent study, caution should be used when subjects with a history of abuse are screened with the CAPI because of problems with false-positive classifications, although the Rigidity and Unhappiness factors remain robust in their ability to discriminate abusers and nonabusers (Caliso & Milner, 1994). Finally, the predictive validity data show a significant relationship between elevated Abuse scores and subsequent child physical abuse (Milner, Gold, Ayoub, & Jacewitz, 1984). As suggested by its author, the CAPI offers considerable information regarding an adult's beliefs and child-rearing methods, and as such is often a very valuable clinical and research tool. However, as with other psychometric devices developed for low-frequency, illegal behavior, considerable caution must be used in drawing conclusions about the propensity to harm a child; moreover, because of false positives, the CAPI should *not* be used as a means of detecting child abuse or labeling an individual.

The Parental Problem-Solving Measure (PPSM; Hanson, Pallotta, Christopher, Conaway, & Lundquist, 1995), a procedure for measuring parental skill at resolving common child-rearing issues, fills a much-needed gap in the assessment protocol with maltreating parents. In the development of this measure, 50 problematic situations were classified into one of five problem areas: child behavior and child management problems, anger and stress control problems, financial problems, child care resource problems, and interpersonal problems. A final list of 25 randomly chosen "problematic situations" was then developed. An example of a situation pertaining to child behavior problems is offered by Hanson et al. (1995): "Your child's teacher calls you and says that your child is misbehaving at school. Your child teases other children, is disruptive in the classroom, and gets in fights on the playground. The teacher is very upset and says that you must do something." The parent is asked to imagine being in that situation and to "(a) tell me *all* of the ways in which you *could* solve the problem; (b) tell me which solution you *would* try if you were in that situation; and (c) tell me *exactly how* you would carry out that solution" (Hanson et al., 1995, p. 323; emphasis in original). Parental responses are audio-recorded and then rated for the number of solutions and effectiveness of the best solution. In a study involving 27 maltreating parents, 12 non-maltreating parents seeking clinical services, and 21 nonmaltreating, non-help-seeking parents, Hanson et al. (1995) demonstrated good convergent and discriminant validity for the PPSM.

Observational Procedures

The consensus among child maltreatment researchers appears to support the validity and feasibility of direct observations with this population (Wolfe, 1985). There are several ways to approach this task, each with advantages and disadvantages. For example, observing families in the home may provide the most naturalistic setting; yet the family's typical pattern of interaction may be so disrupted that little information is gained (this is especially problematic with abusive parents who have not requested service). In terms of setting, structured clinic observations have gained wide acceptability and support as a valid means of assessing parent–child interactions (Hughes & Haynes, 1978), and they have the potential advantage of videotaping the observed interactions. In addition to coding behavior from the tape, the observer can play back the scenes in order to have the parent retrospectively indicate his or her emotional reactions, level of arousal, and thoughts during the interaction. Another consideration in using structured clinic observations is that observations of low-frequency behaviors (such as yelling, grabbing, etc.) yield more relevant data in a more efficient manner when structured tasks are presented (e.g., Burgess & Conger, 1978; Friedman et al., 1981; Herrenkohl et al., 1984; Mash, Johnston, & Kovitz, 1983; Oldershaw, Walters, & Hall, 1986; Wolfe et al., 1981).

Observations of child behavior conducted in the home or clinic serve two assessment functions: They provide a measure of the child's "typical" behavior with his or her parent, and they also allow the examiner to view the child's range of behavior under controlled conditions. By observing the parent and child from behind an observational mirror, the examiner may record selected target behaviors during contrived situations and free interaction. For very young children and infants, these situations are limited primarily to basic caregiving, such as feeding, holding, verbal and physical forms of communication, and simple compliance or instructional tasks (e.g., attending to a parent's voice commands). Preschool and older children may be given more specific instructions by the parent to engage in activities that resemble common areas of conflict at home (e.g., to complete one activity and then switch to another).

During parent–child interactions, the observer should be watchful for child "avoidant" behaviors (e.g., dodging, flinching, staring at the parent, or similar hypervigilance), which suggest that the child is fearful of the parent. Similarly, the observer should determine the manner in which the child approaches both parents. Often a preschool-age abused child will seek to gain the parent's attention by highly aversive means, such as grabbing, pinching, tugging, or whining, despite the parent's attempts to punish such behavior. The child's use of eye contact, appropriate speech, attention span, compliance, and positive and negative physical contact with the parent are additional examples of behavior categories that may be recorded during structured observations by means of standardized coding systems (such as those mentioned below). To gain an understanding of the child's range of developmentally appropriate behavior, the examiner may wish to interact with the child while the parent observes from behind the mirror or another part of the room. This enables the examiner to elicit the child's responses to adult praise and attention, unfamiliar learning tasks (such as a puzzle or matching-figures game), compliance tasks (e.g., cleaning up and putting toys away), and (if necessary) time out or similar punishment procedures—responses that the parent may not be capable of eliciting during the assessment period. The examiner may also instruct the child to play alone with a desirable and/or a less desirable toy, in order to assess the child's attention span and distractability. Following this procedure, the parent can share his or her impressions of the child's recent behavior; this serves as a method for eliciting more objective descriptions from the parent of recent child behavior (without the bias or influence of being part of the same interaction).

Quantitative assessment of family interactions is best approached by using an existing or modified structured procedure for coding family interactions. Since no particular behavior categories are unique to maltreating families, the investigator can choose from among an expanding variety of family observation systems, and base his or her choice upon such considerations as diversity of definitional codes, ability to conduct sequential interactions, and field experience. Systems that seem especially suited for aggressive families and are based on considerable field research and development include the Behavioral Observation Scoring

System (Conger, McCarty, Yang, Lahey, & Kropp, 1984), the Family Process Code (Patterson, 1982), the Response-Class Matrix (Mash et al., 1983), the Interact coding system (Dumas, 1989), the Behavioral Coding System (Forehand & McMahon, 1981), and the more recent Maternal Observation Matrix (Tuteur, Ewigman, Peterson, & Hosokawa, 1995). These observational systems all contain definitional codes for the major dimensions of parenting discussed previously (e.g., verbal and physical positive behaviors; criticism; commands; verbal and physical negative behavior, etc.), which allow for a comprehensive appraisal of the parent's and child's aversive and prosocial behaviors. The availability of computer entry and scoring systems accompanying these methods will markedly enhance data collection and analysis.

Clinical rating scales designed to obtain impressionistic ratings of both positive and negative parent–child interactions have also been investigated. For clinical assessment, these methods have advantages over standard observational coding procedures: They are less expensive and time-consuming, and they tend to look at qualitative (as well as quantitative) aspects of the parent–child relationship (however, they may not be as suitable for research purposes if discrete counts of behavior are of interest). For example, the Mother–Child Interaction Scale (MCIS; Tuteur et al., 1995) consists of items in eight qualitative categories: degrees of positive or negative parental direction of the child, names mother called child, maternal touch, maternal observation of the child, maternal expression, manner in which child approached mother, quality of control, and manner in which mother physically moved child. Ratings are made on a 3-point scale ranging from "negative" to "positive," and are summed to yield a total MCIS score. In a study of 12 abusers and 20 nonabusers, the researchers found that 84% of the 32 parent–child dyads were correctly classified when a total cutoff score of 19 or less for abusive mothers was used.

Similarly, King, Rogers, Walters, and Oldershaw (1994) defined seven (7-point) rating scales on the basis of an established behavioral coding scheme: approval–approving, disapproval–disapproving, commands–commanding, ignore–ignoring, humiliation–humiliating, threat–threatening, and cooperation–cooperative. Raters (32 male and 32 female) viewed one of four videotapes depicting either an abusive mother or a matched nonabusive control to determine the discriminative validity of the ratings. Results supported the reliability and validity of these rating scales for assessing abusive mothers: The scales correlated significantly with behavioral frequency data, and discriminated between the abusive and nonabusive mothers on each of two tapes.

Integrating Assessment Information

What should emerge from an assessment of the child's current adaptive abilities and cognitive and emotional development is an understanding of the child's resources for coping with the level of family problems that may exist, as well as his or her current attitudes, beliefs, and emotional and behavioral expression concerning his or her role in the family. Children who have been removed from the home (or who have had their parents separate or leave the home), as well as older children who have experienced prolonged family conflict and abuse, often display the more extreme signs of adjustment difficulties (e.g., aggression, withdrawal, peer problems, anger at family members). This finding presumably reflects the relationship between child behavior and critical situational variables that must be considered throughout the interpretation of a child's needs. Information provided by the parent, child, and caseworker, and information obtained through interview procedures, should be integrated in a fashion that permits a comparison of how the parent views the child with how the child views his or her own situation, behavior, and affect; this follows from the assessment procedures described herein. Furthermore, objective information on the child's cognitive development and behavioral adjustment, obtained through observational or normative assessment devices, can provide a framework for establishing treatment priorities that are consistent with the child's abilities and needs.

SUMMARY

This chapter has described a multifaceted approach to assessment of child maltreatment and family dysfunction. Research in recent years has improved our understanding of the functional relationships among diverse etiological variables, and these advances are reflected in the availability of a variety of assessment strategies and methods for abused/neglected children and their families. The emphasis throughout this chapter has been on examining child physical abuse and neglect within the context of family and other situational variables, rather than limiting the focus primarily to deficits of the parent and/or child.

Consideration of the developmental consequences of child maltreatment indicates increasing support for the position that family violence and other environmental stressors interfere with the child's development of adaptive and prosocial behavior. Characteristics of the parent and child have also been discussed in terms of how they interact with significant environmental events to affect the likelihood of abusive or neglectful behavior. This has resulted in the identification of major antecedents to maltreatment (such as difficult child behavior and marital conflict), and of several variables that mediate the expression of maltreating behavior (such as the parent's emotional responsivity, perceived social supports, and child management skills).

Because of the nature of child maltreatment, the scope of assessment is often limited by restrictions on observing low-frequency, private behaviors occurring between family members. This challenge has been met by investigators who have attempted to define higher-profile behaviors that can be observed during parent–child interactions. In addition, this chapter has argued that in order to assess crucial aspects of parent and child behavior, assessment procedures can be expanded and integrated with other approaches to yield complementary information. Accordingly, a wide variety of assessment procedures has been presented, including direct observation in structured and naturalistic settings, parent self-reports of problem situations and emotional reactivity, standardized tests, interviews, and self-monitoring techniques. This comprehensive approach to the assessment of maltreating families is intended to enable practitioners to select those methods that are most suitable for different assessment purposes. In parallel, methods for assessing the psychological needs of maltreated children, which have expanded tremendously over the past decade, have been reviewed. In addition to standardized self-report measures for assessing internal states, we now have several innovative interviewing procedures for eliciting sensitive information from younger children; notably, assessment methods (self-report and other-report) for adolescents have also been developed, permitting an expansion of research and services to this overlooked age group.

REFERENCES

Aber, J. L., Allen, J. P., Carlson, V., & Cicchetti, D. (1989). The effects of maltreatment on development during early childhood: Recent studies and their theoretical, clinical and policy implications. In D. Cicchetti & V. Carlson (Eds.), *Child maltreatment: Theory and research on causes and consequences* (pp. 579–619). New York: Cambridge University Press.

Aber, J. L., & Cicchetti, D. (1984). The socio-emotional development of maltreated children: An empirical and theoretical analysis. In H. Fitzgerald, B. Lester, & M. Yogman (Eds.), *Theory and research in behavioral pediatrics* (Vol. 2, pp. 147–205). New York: Plenum Press.

Abidin, R. (1986). *Parenting Stress Index (PSI) manual* (2nd ed.). Charlottesville, VA: Pediatric Psychology Press.

Achenbach, T. M. (1966). The classification of children's psychiatric symptoms: A factor-analytic study. *Psychological Monographs, 80* (Whole No. 615).

Achenbach, T. M. (1991a). *Manual for the Child Behavior Checklist/4–18 and 1991 Profile.* Burlington: University of Vermont, Department of Psychiatry.

Achenbach, T. M. (1991b). *Manual for the Teacher's Report Form and 1991 Profile.* Burlington: University of Vermont, Department of Psychiatry.

Achenbach, T. M. (1991c). *Manual for the Youth Self-Report and 1991 Profile.* Burlington: University of Vermont, Department of Psychiatry.

Achenbach, T. M., McConaughy, S. H., & Howell, C. T. (1987). Child/adolescent behavioral and emotional problems: Implications of cross-informant correlations for situational specificity. *Psychological Bulletin, 101*, 213–232.

Ainsworth, M. D. S. (1980). Attachment and child abuse. In G. Gerbner, C. J. Ross, & E. Zigler (Eds.), *Child abuse: An agenda for action* (pp. 35–47). New York: Oxford University Press.

Ainsworth, M. D. S., Blehar, M. C., Waters, E., & Wall, S. (1978). *Patterns of attachment: A psychological study of the Strange Situation.* Hillsdale, NJ: Erlbaum.

Alessandri, S. M. (1991). Play and social behavior in maltreated preschoolers. *Development and Psychopathology, 3*, 191–205.

Alessandri, S. M. (1992). Mother–child interactional correlates of maltreated and nonmaltreated children's play behavior. *Development and Psychopathology, 4*, 257–270.

Alfaro, J. (1988). What can we learn from child abuse fatalities? In D. Besharov (Ed.), *Protecting children from abuse and neglect: Policy and practice.* Springfield, IL: Charles C Thomas.

Allen, D. M., & Tarnowski, K. J. (1989). Depressive characteristics of physically abused children. *Journal of Abnormal Child Psychology, 17*, 1–11.

Allen, R. E., & Oliver, J. M. (1982). The effects of child maltreatment on language development. *Child Abuse and Neglect, 6*, 299–305.

American Psychological Association. (1994). *Task Force on Child Abuse and Neglect: Committee report.* Washington, DC: Author.

Ammerman, R. T. (1991). The role of the child in physical abuse: A reappraisal. *Violence and Victims, 6,* 87–101.

Astor, R. A. (1994). Children's moral reasoning about family and peer violence: The role of provocation and retribution. *Child Development, 65,* 1054–1067.

Averill, J. R. (1983). Studies on anger and aggression: Implications for theories of emotion. *American Psychologist, 38,* 1145–1160.

Azar, S. T., Robinson, D. R., Hekimian, E., & Twentyman, C. T. (1984). Unrealistic expectations and problem-solving ability in maltreating and comparison mothers. *Journal of Consulting and Clinical Psychology, 52,* 687–691.

Azar, S. T., & Rohrbeck, C. A. (1986). Child abuse and unrealistic expectations: Further validation of the Parent Opinion Questionnaire. *Journal of Consulting and Clinical Psychology, 54,* 867–868.

Barahal, R. M., Waterman, J., & Martin, H. P. (1981). The social cognitive development of abused children. *Journal of Consulting and Clinical Psychology, 49,* 508–516.

Baron, R. A. (1977). *Human aggression.* New York: Plenum Press.

Bates, J. E., Ridge, B., Marvinney, D., & Shroff, J. M. (1991). *Validation of a retrospective version of the Infant Characteristics Questionnaire measure of temperament.* Unpublished manuscript.

Bavolek, S. J. (1984). *Adult–Adolescent Parenting Inventory (AAPI).* Eau Claire, WI: Family Development Resources.

Beck, A. T., Ward, C., Mendelson, M., Mock, J., & Erbaugh, J. (1961). An inventory for measuring depression. *Archives of General Psychiatry, 4,* 53–63.

Beeghly, M., & Cicchetti, D. (1994). Child maltreatment, attachment, and the self system: Emergence of an internal state lexicon in toddlers at high social risk. *Development and Psychopathology, 6,* 5–30.

Belsky, J. (1992). *The etiology of child maltreatment: An ecological–contextual analysis.* Paper prepared for the Panel on Research on Child Abuse and Neglect, National Research Council, Washington, DC.

Benoit, D. (1993). Failure to thrive and feeding disorders. In C. H. Zeanah, Jr. (Ed.), *Handbook of infant mental health* (pp. 317–331). New York: Guilford Press.

Berkowitz, L. (1983). Aversively stimulated aggression: Some parallels and differences in research with animals and humans. *American Psychologist, 38,* 1135–1134.

Borduin, C. M., Blaske, D. M., Treloar, L., Mann, B. J., & Hazelrigg, M. (1989). *Development and validation of a measure of adolescent peer relations: The Missouri Peer Relations Inventory.* Unpublished manuscript, University of Missouri.

Bousha, D. M., & Twentyman, C. T. (1984). Mother–child interactional style in abuse, neglect, and control groups: Naturalistic observations in the home. *Journal of Abnormal Psychology, 93,* 106–114.

Bradley, R. H., & Caldwell, B. M. (1979). Home Observation for Measurement of the Environment: A revision of the Preschool scale. *American Journal of Mental Deficiency, 84,* 235–244.

Bradley, R. H., Mundfrom, D. J., Whiteside, L., Casey, P. H., & Barrett, K. (1994). A factor analytic study of the infant–toddler and early childhood versions of the HOME inventory administered to white, black, and Hispanic American parents of children born preterm. *Child Development, 65,* 880–888.

Bruininks, R. H., Woodcock, R. W., Weatherman, R. F., & Hill, B. K. (1984). *Scales of Independent Behavior: Woodcock–Johnson Psycho-Educational Test Battery, Part IV.* Allen, TX: DLM Teaching Resources.

Buchsbaum, H. K., Toth, S. L., Clyman, R. B., Cicchetti, D., & Emde, R. N. (1992). The use of narrative story stem technique with maltreated children: Implications for theory and practice. *Development and Psychopathology, 4,* 603–625.

Buhrmester, D. (1990). Intimacy of friendship, interpersonal competence, and adjustment during preadolescence and adolescence. *Child Development, 61,* 1101–1111.

Burgess, R. L., & Conger, R. (1978). Family interactions in abusive, neglectful, and normal families. *Child Development, 49,* 1163–1173.

Burgess, A. W., Hartman, C. R., & McCormack, A. (1987). Abused to abuser: Antecedents of socially deviant behaviors. *American Journal of Psychiatry, 144,* 1431–1436.

Burgess, R. L., & Youngblade, L. M. (1988). Social incompetence and the intergenerational transmission of abusive parental practices. In G. T. Hotaling, D. Finkelhor, J. T. Kirkpatrick, & M. A. Straus (Eds.), *Family abuse and its consequences: New directions in research* (pp. 38–60). Beverly Hills, CA: Sage.

Caliso, J. A., & Milner, J. S. (1994). Childhood physical abuse, childhood social support, and adult child abuse potential. *Journal of Interpersonal Violence, 9,* 27–44.

Cavell, T. A., & Kelley, M. L. (1992). The Measure of Adolescent Social Performance: Development and initial validation. *Journal of Clinical Child Psychology, 21,* 107–114.

Cerezo, M. A., & Frias, D. (1994). Emotional and cognitive adjustment in abused children. *Child Abuse and Neglect, 18,* 923–932.

Chambers, W. J., Puig-Antich, J., Hirsch, M., Paez, P., Ambrosini, P. J., Tabrizi, M. A., & Davies, M. (1985). The assessment of affective disorders in children and adolescents by semistructured interview: Test–retest reliability of the Schedule for Affective Disorder and Schizophrenia for School-Age Children, Present Episode version. *Archives of General Psychiatry, 42,* 696–702.

Child Abuse Prevention and Treatment Act of 1974, Pub. L. No. 93-247.

Child Abuse Prevention, Adoption and Family Services Act of 1988, Pub. L. 100-294.

Cicchetti, D., & Beeghly, M. (1987). Symbolic development in maltreated youngsters: An organizational perspective. In D. Cicchetti & M. Beeghly (Eds.), *New directions for child development: No. 36. Symbolic development in atypical children* (pp. 5–29). San Francisco: Jossey-Bass.

Cicchetti, D., Ganiban, J., & Barnett, D. (1990). Contributions from the study of high risk populations to understanding the development of emotion regulation. In K. Dodge & J. Garber (Eds.), *The development of emotion regulation* (pp. 1–54). New York: Cambridge University Press.

Cicchetti, D., & Rizley, R. (1981). Developmental perspectives on the etiology, intergenerational transmission, and sequelae of child maltreatment. In D. Cicchetti & R. Rizley (Eds.), *New directions for child development: No. 11. Developmental perspectives on child maltreatment* (pp. 31–55). San Francisco: Jossey-Bass.

Cicchetti, D., Toth, S., & Bush, M. (1988). Developmental psychopathology and incompetence in childhood: Suggestions for intervention. In B. B. Lahey & A. E. Kazdin (Eds.), *Advances in clinical child psychology* (Vol. 11, pp. 1–77). New York: Plenum Press.

Cohen, C. I., & Adler, A. (1986). Assessing the role of social network interventions with an inner-city population. *American Journal of Orthopsychiatry, 56*, 278–288.

Cohen, F. S., & Densen-Gerber, J. (1982). A study of the relationship between child abuse and drug addiction in 178 patients: Preliminary results. *Child Abuse and Neglect, 6*, 383–387.

Conger, R., McCarty, J. A., Yang, R. K., Lahey, B. B., & Kropp, J. P. (1984). Perception of child, child-rearing values, and emotional distress as mediating links between environmental stressors and observed maternal behavior. *Child Development, 55*, 2234–2247.

Connelly, C. D., & Straus, M. A. (1992). Mothers' age and risk for physical abuse. *Child Abuse and Neglect, 16*, 709–718.

Coulton, C., Chow, J., & Pandey, S. (1990). *An analysis of poverty and related conditions in Cleveland area neighborhoods.* Unpublished manuscript, Case Western Reserve University.

Coulton, C., Pandey, S., & Chow, J. (1990). Concentration of poverty and the changing ecology of low-income urban neighborhoods: An analysis of the Cleveland area. *Social Work Research and Abstracts, 26*, 5–16.

Crittenden, P. M. (1987). Non-organic failure-to-thrive: Deprivation or distortion? *Infant Mental Health Journal, 8*, 51–64.

Crittenden, P. M. (1992). Children's strategies for coping with adverse home environments: An interpretation using attachment theory. *Child Abuse and Neglect, 16*, 329–343.

Crittenden, P. M., & Ainsworth, M. D. S. (1989). Child maltreatment and attachment theory. In D. Cicchetti & V. Carlson (Eds.), *Child maltreatment: Theory and research on the causes and consequences of child abuse and neglect* (pp. 432–463). New York: Cambridge University Press.

Crittenden, P. M., & DiLalla, D. L. (1988). Compulsive compliance: The development of an inhibitory coping strategy in infancy. *Journal of Abnormal Child Psychology, 16*, 585–599.

Crouch, J. L., & Milner, J. S. (1993). Effects of child neglect on children. *Criminal Justice and Behavior, 20*, 49–65.

Cummings, E. M. (1987). Coping with background anger in early childhood. *Child Development, 58*, 976–984.

Cummings, E. M. (in press). Marital conflict, abuse, and adversity in the family and child adjustment: A developmental psychopathology perspective. In D. A. Wolfe, R. McMahon, & R. D. Peters (Eds.), *Child abuse: New directions in prevention and treatment across the lifespan.* Thousand Oaks, CA: Sage.

Cutrona, C. E. (1984). Social support and stress in the transition to parenthood. *Journal of Abnormal Psychology, 93*, 378–390.

Daro, D. K., Casey, K., & Abrahams, N. (1990). *Reducing child abuse 20% by 1990: Preliminary assessment* (Working Paper No. 843). Chicago: National Committee for Prevention of Child Abuse.

Derogatis, L. R. (1983). *SCL-90-R administration, scoring, and procedures manual—II.* Towson, MD: Clinical Psychometric Research.

Dodge, K. A., Bates, J. E., & Pettit, G. S. (1990). Mechanisms in the cycle of violence. *Science, 250*, 1678–1683.

Downey, G., & Walker, E. (1992). Distinguishing family-level and child-level influences on the development of depression and aggression in children at risk. *Development and Psychopathology, 4*, 81–95.

Drotar, D. (1992). Prevention of neglect and non-organic failure to thrive. In D. J. Willis, E. W. Holden, & M. Rosenberg (Eds), *Prevention of child maltreatment: Developmental and ecological perspectives* (pp. 115–149). New York: Wiley.

Dumas, J. E. (1988). *Interact-Data collection and analysis software manual.* Unpublished manuscript, Purdue University. Available from author.

Dutton, D. G. (1995). *The domestic assault of women: Psychological and criminal justice perspectives.* Vancouver: University of British Columbia Press.

Eckenrode, J., Rowe, E., Laird, M., & Brathwaite, J. (1995). Mobility as a mediator of the effects of child maltreatment on academic performance. *Child Development, 66*, 1130–1142.

Egeland, B. (1991). A longitudinal study of high-risk families: Issues and findings. In R. H. Starr, Jr., & D. A. Wolfe (Eds.), *The effects of child abuse and neglect: Issues and research* (pp. 33–56). New York: Guilford Press.

Egeland, B., & Erickson, M. F. (1987). Psychologically unavailable caregiving. In M. Brassard, B. Germain, & S. Hart (Eds.), *Psychological maltreatment of children and youth* (pp. 110–120). Elmsford, NY: Pergamon Press.

Egeland, B., Sroufe, A., & Erickson, M. (1983). The developmental consequence of different patterns of maltreatment. *Child Abuse and Neglect, 7,* 459–469.

Elmer, E., & Gregg, G. S. (1967). Developmental characteristics of abused children. *Pediatrics, 40,* 596–602.

Erickson, M. F., Egeland, B., & Pianta, R. (1989). The effects of maltreatment on the development of young children. In D. Cicchetti & V. Carlson (Eds.), *Child maltreatment: Theory and research on the causes and consequences of child abuse and neglect* (pp. 647–684). New York: Cambridge University Press.

Ewigman, B., Kivlahan, C., & Land, G. (1993). The Missouri child fatality study: Underreporting of maltreatment fatalities among children younger than five years of age, 1983 through 1986. *Pediatrics, 91,* 330–337.

Feldman, R. S., Salzinger, S., Rosario, M., Alvarado, L., Caraballo, L., & Hammer, M. (1995). Parent, teacher, and peer ratings of physically abused and nonmaltreated children's behavior. *Journal of Abnormal Child Psychology, 23,* 317–334.

Feshbach, N. D. (1989). The construct of empathy and the phenomenon of physical maltreatment of children. In D. Cicchetti & V. Carlson (Eds.), *Child maltreatment: Theory and research on the causes and consequences of child abuse and neglect* (pp. 349–373). New York: Cambridge University Press.

Forehand, R., & McMahon, R. (1981). *Helping the noncompliant child: A clinician's guide to parent training.* New York: Guilford Press.

Fox, L., Long, S. H., & Langlois, A. (1988). Patterns of language comprehension deficit in abused and neglected children. *Journal of Speech and Hearing Disorders, 53,* 239–244.

Friedman, R., Sandler, J., Hernandez, M., & Wolfe, D. (1981). Child abuse. In E. J. Mash & L. G. Terdal (Eds.), *Behavioral assessment of childhood disorders* (pp. 221–255). New York: Guilford Press.

Friedrich, W. N., Einbender, A. J., & Luecke, W. J. (1983). Cognitive and behavioral characteristics of physically abused children. *Journal of Consulting and Clinical Psychology, 51,* 313–314.

Frodi, A. M., & Lamb, M. E. (1980). Child abusers' responses to infant smiles and cries. *Child Development, 51,* 238–241.

Frodi, A. M., & Smetana, J. (1984). Abused, neglected, and nonmaltreated preschoolers' ability to discriminate emotions in others: The effects of IQ. *Child Abuse and Neglect, 8,* 459–465.

The Gallup Organization. (1995, December). *Disciplining children in America.* Princeton, NJ: Author.

Garbarino, J. (1976). A preliminary study of some ecological correlates of child abuse: The impact of socioeconomic stress on mothers. *Child Development, 47,* 178–185.

Gelles, R. J. (1992). Poverty and violence toward children. *American Behavioral Scientist, 35,* 258–274.

Gil, D. G. (1970). *Violence against children: Physical child abuse in the United States.* Cambridge, MA: Harvard University Press.

Griest, D. L., & Wells, K. C. (1983). Behavioral family therapy with conduct disorders in children. *Behavior Therapy, 13,* 37–53.

Gross, A., & Keller, H. (1992). Long-term consequences of childhood physical and psychological maltreatment. *Aggressive Behavior, 18,* 171–185.

Hanson, D. J., Pallotta, G. M., Christopher, J. S., Conaway, R. L., & Lundquist, L. M. (1995). The Parental Problem-Solving Measure: Further evaluation with maltreating and non-maltreating parents. *Journal of Family Violence, 10,* 319–336.

Harrington, D., Dubowitz, H., Black, M. M., & Binder, A. (1995). Maternal substance use and neglectful parenting: Relations with children's development. *Journal of Clinical Child Psychology, 24,* 258–263.

Harter, S. (1982). The Perceived Competence Scale for Children. *Child Development, 53,* 87–97.

Harter, S. (1985a). *Manual for the Self-Perception Profile for Children.* (Available from Susan Harter, PhD, Department of Psychology, University of Denver, Denver, CO 80210)

Harter, S. (1985b). *Manual for the Social Support Scale for Children.* (Available from Susan Harter, PhD, Department of Psychology, University of Denver, Denver, CO 80210)

Harter, S., & Nowakowski, M. (1987). *Manual for the Dimensions of Depression Profile for Children and Adolescents.* (Available from Susan Harter, PhD, Department of Psychology, University of Denver, Denver, CO 80210)

Hartup, W. W. (1986). On relationships and development. In W. W. Hartup & Z. Rubin (Eds.), *Relationships and development* (pp. 1–26). Hillsdale, NJ: Erlbaum.

Haskett, M. E., & Kistner, J. A. (1991). Social interactions and peer perceptions of young physically abused children. *Child Development, 62,* 979–990.

Herman, J. L. (1992). *Trauma and recovery: The aftermath of violence—from domestic abuse to political terror.* New York: Basic Books.

Henderson, A. S., & Moran, P. A. P. (1983). Social relationships during the onset and remission of neurotic symptoms: A prospective community study. *British Journal of Psychiatry, 143,* 467–472.

Herrenkohl, R. C., Herrenkohl, E. C., & Egolf, B. P. (1983). Circumstances surrounding the occurrence of child maltreatment. *Journal of Consulting and Clinical Psychology, 51,* 424–431.

Herrenkohl, E. C., Herrenkohl, R. C., Toedter, L., & Yanushefski, A. M. (1984). Parent–child interactions in abusive and non-abusive families. *Journal of the American Academy of Child Psychiatry, 23,* 641–648.

Herzberger, S. D., Potts, D. A., & Dillon, M. (1981). Abusive and nonabusive parental treatment from the child's perspective. *Journal of Consulting and Clinical Psychology, 49,* 81–90.

Hinchey, F. S., & Gavelek, J. R. (1982). Empathic responding in children of battered mothers. *Child Abuse and Neglect, 6,* 395–401.

Hoffman-Plotkin, D., & Twentyman, C. T. (1984). A multimodal assessment of behavioral and cognitive deficits in abused and neglected preschoolers. *Child Development, 55,* 794–802.

Holden, E. W., Willis, D. J., & Corcoran, M. (1992). Preventing child maltreatment during the prenatal/perinatal period. In D. J. Willis, E. W. Holden, & M. Rosenberg (Eds.), *Prevention of child maltreatment: Developmental and ecological perspectives* (pp. 17–46). New York: Wiley.

Holtzworth-Munroe, A. (1988). Causal attributions in marital violence: Theoretical and methodological issues. *Clinical Psychology Review, 8,* 331–344.

Howes, C., & Eldredge, R. (1985). Responses of abused, neglected, and non-maltreated children to the behaviors of their peers. *Journal of Applied Developmental Psychology, 6,* 261–270.

Hughes, J. N., & Baker, D. B. (1990). *The clinical child interview.* New York: Guilford Press.

Hughes, H. M., & Haynes, S. N. (1978). Structured laboratory observation in the behavioral assessment of parent–child interactions: A methodological critique. *Behavior Therapy, 9,* 428–447.

Illinois Department of Children and Family Services. (1993). *Child abuse and neglect fatality overview.* Springfield: Author.

Inwald, R. E. (1986). *The Hilson Adolescent Profile.* Kew Gardens, NY: Hilson Research.

Jacobson, N. S., Gottman, J. M., Waltz, J., Rushe, R., Babcock, J., & Holtzworth-Munroe, A. (1994). Affect, verbal content, and psychophysiology in the arguments of couples with a violent husband. *Journal of Consulting and Clinical Psychology, 62,* 982–988.

Johnson, B., & Morse, H. A. (1968). Injured children and their parents. *Children, 15,* 147–152.

Johnson, J. H., & McCutcheon, S. M. (1980). Assessing life stress in older children and adolescents: Preliminary findings with the Life Events Checklist. In I. G. Sarason & C. D. Spielberger (Eds.), *Stress and anxiety* (Vol. 7, pp. 111–125). Washington, DC: Hemisphere.

Jouriles, E. N., & O'Leary, K. D. (1985). Interspousal reliability of reports of marital violence. *Journal of Consulting and Clinical Psychology, 53,* 419–421.

Kadushin, A., & Martin, J. A. (1981). *Child abuse: An interactional event.* New York: Columbia University Press.

Kaslow, N. J., Tanenbaum, R. L., & Seligman, M. E. P. (1978). *The KASTAN-R: A Children's Attributional Style Questionnaire (KASTAN-R, CASQ).* Unpublished manuscript, University of Pennsylvania.

Kaufman, J. (1991). Depressive disorders in maltreated children. *Journal of the American Academy of Child and Adolescent Psychiatry, 30,* 257–265.

Kaufman, J., & Cicchetti, D. (1989). The effects of maltreatment on school-aged children's socioemotional development: Assessments in a day-camp setting. *Developmental Psychology, 25,* 516–524.

Kaufman, J., Jones, B., Stieglitz, E., Vitulano, L., & Mannarino, A. P. (1994). The use of multiple informants to assess children's maltreatment experiences. *Journal of Family Violence, 9,* 227–247.

Kelly, J. A. (1983). *Treating abusive families: Intervention based on skills training principles.* New York: Plenum Press.

Kempe, C. H., Silverman, F., Steele, B., Droegemueller, W., & Silver, H. (1962). The battered child syndrome. *Journal of the American Medical Association, 181,* 17–24.

Kempe, R. S., & Kempe, C. H. (1978). *Child abuse.* Cambridge, MA: Harvard University Press.

Kinard, E. M. (1980). Emotional development in physically abused children. *American Journal of Orthopsychiatry, 50,* 686–696.

Kinard, E. M. (1982). Experiencing child abuse: Effects on emotional adjustment. *American Journal of Orthopsychiatry, 52,* 82–91.

Kinard, E. M. (1995). Perceived social support and competence in abused children: A longitudinal perspective. *Journal of Family Violence, 10,* 73–98.

King, G. A., Rogers, C., Walters, G. C., & Oldershaw, L. (1994). Parenting Behavior Rating Scales: Preliminary validation with intrusive, abusive mothers. *Child Abuse and Neglect, 18,* 247–259.

Korbin, J. (1994). Sociocultural factors in child maltreatment. In G. B. Melton & F. D. Barry (Eds.), *Protecting children from abuse and neglect: Foundations for a new national strategy* (pp. 182–223). New York: Guilford Press.

Kolko, D. J. (1992). Characteristics of child victims of physical violence: Research findings and clinical implications. *Journal of Interpersonal Violence, 7,* 244–276.

Kovacs, M. (1994). *Children's Depression Inventory manual.* Toronto: Mental Health Systems.

Koverola, C., Elliot-Faust, D., & Wolfe, D. A. (1984). Clinical issues in the behavioral treatment of a child abusive mother experiencing multiple life stresses. *Journal of Clinical Child Psychology, 13,* 187–191.

Kravitz, R. I., & Driscoll, J. M. (1983). Expectations for childhood development among child-abusing and non-abusing parents. *American Journal of Orthopsychiatry, 53,* 336–344.

Kurtz, P. D., Gaudin, J. M., Jr., Wodarski, J. S., & Howing, P. T. (1993). Maltreatment and the school-aged child: School performance consequences. *Child Abuse and Neglect, 17,* 581–589.

Levine, M., Compaan, C., & Freeman, J. (1995). Maltreatment-related fatalities: Issues of policy and prevention. *Law & Policy, 16,* 449–471.

Lewis, D. O., Pincus, J. H., & Glaser, G. H. (1979). Violent juvenile delinquents: Psychiatric, neurological, psychological, and abuse factors. *Journal of the American Academy of Child Psychiatry, 18,* 307–319.

Light, R. (1973). Abused and neglected children in America: A study of alternative policies. *Harvard Educational Review, 43,* 556–598.

Lipsett, L. (1983). Stress in infancy: Toward understanding the origins of coping behavior. In N. Garmezy & M. Rutter (Eds.), *Stress, coping, and development in children* (pp. 161–190). New York: McGraw-Hill.

Lorber, R., Felton, D. K., & Reid, J. (1984). A social learning approach to the reduction of coercive processes in child abusive families: A molecular analysis. *Advances in Behavior Research and Therapy, 6,* 29–45.

Lorber, R., Weissman, W., & Reid, J. (1983). Family interactions of assaultive adolescents, stealers, and nondelinquents. *Journal of Abnormal Child Psychology, 11,* 1–14.

Maccoby, E. E., & Martin, J. A. (1983). Socialization in the context of the family: Parent–child interaction. In E. M. Hetherington (Vol. Ed.), *Handbook of child psychology* (4th ed.): Vol. 4. *Socialization, personality, and social development* (pp. 1–101). New York: Wiley.

MacMillan, V. M., Olson, R. L., & Hanson, D. J. (1991). Low and high deviance analogue assessment of parent-training with physically abusive parents. *Journal of Family Violence, 6,* 279–301.

Main, M., & George, C. (1985). Responses of abused and disadvantaged toddlers to distress in agemates: A study in the day care setting. *Developmental Psychology, 21,* 407–412.

Magura, S., & Moses, B. S. (1986). *Outcome measures for child welfare services: Theory and applications.* Washington, DC: Child Welfare League of America.

Martin, B. (1990). The transmission of relationship difficulties from one generation to the next. *Journal of Youth and Adolescence, 19,* 181–199.

Mash, E. J., Johnston, C., & Kovitz, K. (1983). A comparison of the mother–child interactions of physically abused and non-abused children during play and task situations. *Journal of Clinical Child Psychology, 12,* 337–346.

McClain, P., Sacks, J., & Frohlke, R. (1993). Estimates of fatal child abuse and neglect, United States, 1979 through 1988. *Pediatrics, 91,* 338–343.

McGee, R. (1990). *Multiple maltreatment, attribution of blame, and adjustment among adolescents.* Unpublished doctoral dissertation, University of Western Ontario.

McGee, R., Wolfe, D. A., & Olson, J. (1995, June). *Why me? A content analysis of adolescents' causal attributions for their maltreatment experiences.* Paper presented at the convention of the Canadian Psychological Association, Charlottetown, Prince Edward Island.

Melton, G. B., & Barry, F. D. (1994). Neighbors helping neighbors: The vision of the U.S. Advisory Board on Child Abuse and Neglect. In G. B. Melton & F. D. Barry (Eds.), *Protecting children from abuse and neglect: Foundations for a new national strategy* (pp. 1–13). New York: Guilford Press.

Milner, J. S. (1986). *The Child Abuse Potential Inventory: Manual* (2nd ed.). Webster, NC: Psytec.

Milner, J. S. (1989). Additional cross-validation of the Child Abuse Potential Inventory. *Psychological Assessment: A Journal of Consulting and Clinical Psychology, 1,* 219–233.

Milner, J. S. (1993). Social information processing and physical child abuse. *Clinical Psychology Review, 13,* 275–294.

Milner, J. S. (in press). Characteristics of abusive parents. In D. A. Wolfe, R. McMahon, & R. D. Peters (Eds.), *Child abuse: New directions in prevention and treatment across the lifespan.* Thousand Oaks, CA: Sage.

Milner, J. S., Gold, R. G., Ayoub, C., & Jacewitz, M. M. (1984). Predictive validity of the Child Abuse Potential Inventory. *Journal of Consulting and Clinical Psychology, 52,* 879–884.

Milner, J. S., Robertson, K. R., & Rogers, D. L. (1990). Childhood history of abuse and adult child abuse potential. *Journal of Family Violence, 5,* 15–34.

Moos, R. H., & Moos, B. S. (1981). *Manual for the Family Environment Scale.* Palo Alto, CA: Consulting Psychologists Press.

Moran, P. B., & Eckenrode, J. (1992). Protective personality characteristics among adolescent victims of maltreatment. *Child Abuse and Neglect, 16,* 743–754.

Mrazek, P. J. (1993). Maltreatment and infant development. In C. H. Zeanah, Jr. (Ed.), *Handbook of infant mental health* (pp. 159–170). New York: Guilford Press.

National Center on Child Abuse and Neglect (NCCAN). (1994). *Child maltreatment 1992: Reports from the states to the National Center on Child Abuse and Neglect.* Washington, DC: U.S. Government Printing Office.

National Center on Child Abuse and Neglect (NCCAN). (1995). *Child maltreatment 1993: Reports from the states to the National Center on Child Abuse and Neglect* (Contract Number ACF-105-91-1802). Washington, DC: U.S. Government Printing Office.

National Research Council. (1993). *Understanding child abuse and neglect*. Washington, DC: National Academy Press.

Nightingale, N. N., & Walker, E. F. (1991). The impact of social class and parental maltreatment on the cognitive functioning of children. *Journal of Family Violence, 6*, 115–129.

Oldershaw, L., Walters, G. C., & Hall, D. K. (1986). Control strategies and noncompliance in abusive mother–child dyads: An observational study. *Child Development, 57*, 722–732.

Patterson, G. R. (1982). *Coercive family process*. Eugene, OR: Castalia.

Patterson, G. R., & Cobb, J. A. (1973). Stimulus control for classes of noxious behaviors. In J. Knutson (Ed.), *The control of aggression: Implications from basic research* (pp. 145–199). Chicago: Aldine.

Pelcovitz, D., Kaplan, S., Goldenberg, B., Mandel, F., et al. (1994). Post-Traumatic Stress Disorder in physically abused adolescents. *Journal of the American Academy of Child and Adolescent Psychiatry, 33*, 305–312.

Pelton, L. H. (1978). Child abuse and neglect: The myth of classlessness. *American Journal of Orthopsychiatry, 48*, 608–617.

Peterson, L., & Brown, D. (1994). Integrating child injury and abuse–neglect research: Common histories, etiologies, and solutions. *Psychological Bulletin, 116*, 293–315.

Polansky, N. A., Chalmers, M., Buttenwieser, E., & Williams, D. (1981). *Damaged parents: An anatomy of child neglect*. Chicago: University of Chicago Press.

Polansky, N. A., Gaudin, J. M., & Kilpatrick, A. C. (1992). Family radicals. *Children and Youth Services Review, 14*, 19–26.

Prino, C. T., & Peyrot, M. (1994). The effect of child physical abuse and neglect on aggressive, withdrawn, and prosocial behavior. *Child Abuse and Neglect, 18*, 871–884.

Procidano, M. E., & Heller, K. (1983). Measures of perceived social support from friends and from family: Three validation studies. *American Journal of Community Psychology, 11*(1), 1–24.

Reich, W., & Welner, Z. (1988). *Revised version of the Diagnostic Interview for Children and Adolescents* (DICA-R). St. Louis, MO: Department of Psychiatry, Washington University School of Medicine.

Reid, J. B., Taplin, P., & Lorber, R. (1981). A social interactional approach to the treatment of abusive families. In R. B. Stuart (Ed.), *Violent behavior: Social learning approaches to prediction, management, and treatment* (pp. 83–101). New York: Brunner/Mazel.

Rohner, R. P. (1991). *Handbook for the study of parental acceptance and rejection* (rev. ed.). Storrs: University of Connecticut, Center for the Study of Parental Acceptance and Rejection.

Rohrbeck, C. A., Azar, S. T., & Wagner, P. E. (1991). Child Self-Control Rating Scale: Validation of a child self-report measure. *Journal of Clinical Child Psychology, 20*, 179–183.

Russell, A. B., & Trainor, C. M. (1984). *Trends in child abuse and neglect: A national perspective*. Denver, CO: American Humane Association.

Rutter, M. (1979). Protective factors in children's responses to stress and disadvantage. In M. W. Kent & J. E. Rolf (Eds.), *Primary prevention of psychopathology: Social competence in children* (pp. 49–74). Hanover, NH: University Press of New England.

Salzinger, S., Feldman, R. S., Hammer, M., & Rosario, M. (1993). The effects of physical abuse on children's social relationships. *Child Development, 64*, 169–187.

Salzinger, S., Kaplan, S., Pelcovitz, D., Samit, C., & Kreiger, R. (1984). Parent and teacher assessment of children's behavior in child maltreating families. *Journal of the American Academy of Child Psychiatry, 23*, 458–464.

Sandgrund, A., Gaines, R. W., & Green, A. H. (1974). Child abuse and mental retardation: A problem of cause and effect. *Journal of Mental Deficiency, 79*, 327–330.

Schneider-Rosen, K., & Cicchetti, D. (1991). Early self-knowledge and emotional development: Visual self-recognition and affective reactions to mirror self-image in maltreated and non-maltreated toddlers. *Developmental Psychology, 27*, 471–478.

Seagull, E. A. W. (1987). Social support and child maltreatment: A review of the evidence. *Child Abuse and Neglect, 11*, 41–52.

Shepard, M. F., & Campbell, J. A. (1992). The Abusive Behavior Inventory: A measure of psychological and physical abuse. *Journal of Interpersonal Violence, 7*, 291–305.

Smetana, J., Kelly, M., & Twentyman, C. (1984). Abused, neglected, and nonmaltreated children's judgments of moral and social transgressions. *Child Development, 55*, 277–287.

Spanier, G. B. (1976). Measuring dyadic adjustment: New scales for measuring the quality of marriage and similar dyads. *Journal of Marriage and the Family, 38*, 15–28.

Spieker, S. J., & Booth, C. (1988). Family risk typologies and patterns of insecure attachment. In J. Belsky & T. Nezworski (Eds.), *Clinical implications of attachment* (pp. 95–135). Hillsdale, NJ: Erlbaum.

Spielberger, C. D. (1973). *Manual for the State–Trait Anxiety Inventory for Children*. Palo Alto, CA: Consulting Psychologists Press.

Sroufe, L. A. (1985). Attachment classification from the perspective of infant–caregiver relationships and infant temperament. *Child Development, 56*, 1–14.

Sroufe, L. A., & Fleeson, J. (1986). Attachment and the construction of relationships. In W. W. Hartup & Z. Rubin (Eds.), *Relationships and development* (pp. 51–71). Hillsdale, NJ: Erlbaum.

Starr, R. H., Jr., MacLean, D. J., & Keating, D. P. (1991). Life-span developmental outcomes of child maltreatment. In R. H. Starr, Jr., & D. A. Wolfe (Eds.), *The effects of child abuse and neglect: Issues and research* (pp. 1–32). New York: Guilford Press.

Steinberg, L., Lamborn, S. D., Darling, N., Mounts, N. S., & Dornbusch, S. M. (1994). Over-time changes in adjustment and competence among adolescents from authoritative, authoritarian, indulgent, and neglectful families. *Child Development, 65,* 754–770.

Straker, G., & Jacobson, R. S. (1981). Aggression, emotional maladjustment, and empathy in the abused child. *Developmental Psychology, 17,* 762–765.

Straus, M. A. (1979a). Family patterns and child abuse in a nationally representative American sample. *Child Abuse and Neglect, 3,* 213–225.

Straus, M. A. (1979b). Measuring intrafamily conflict and violence: The Conflict Tactics (CT) Scales. *Journal of Marriage and the Family, 41,* 75–88.

Straus, M. A. (1994). *Beating the devil out of them: Corporal punishment by parents and its effects on children.* Lexington, MA: Lexington Books.

Straus, M. A., Gelles, R. J., & Steinmetz, S. (1980). *Behind closed doors: Violence in the American family.* Garden City, NY: Doubleday/Anchor.

Tarter, R. E., Hegedus, A. E., Winsten, N. E., & Alterman, A. I. (1984). Neuropsychological, personality, and familial characteristics of physically abused delinquents. *Journal of the American Academy of Child Psychiatry, 23,* 668–674.

Toth, S. L., Manly, J. T., & Cicchetti, D. (1992). Child maltreatment and vulnerability to depression. *Development and Psychopathology, 14,* 97–112.

Trickett, P. K., Aber, J. L., Carlson, V., & Cicchetti, D. (1991). Relationship of socioeconomic status to the etiology and developmental sequelae of physical child abuse. *Developmental Psychology, 27,* 148–158.

Trocme, N., McPhee, D., Kwan Tam, K., & Hay, T. (1994). *Ontario incidence study of reported child abuse and neglect.* (Available from the Ontario Ministry of Community and Social Services, Queen's Park, Toronto, Ontario)

Tuteur, J. M., Ewigman, B. E., Peterson, L., & Hosokawa, M. C. (1995). The Maternal Observation Matrix and the Mother–Child Interaction Scale: Brief observational screening instruments for physically abusive mothers. *Journal of Clinical Child Psychology, 24,* 55–62.

U.S. Advisory Board on Child Abuse and Neglect (USABCAN). (1990). *Child abuse and neglect: Critical first steps in response to a national emergency.* Washington, DC: U.S. Government Printing Office.

U.S. Advisory Board on Child Abuse and Neglect (USABCAN). (1993). *Neighbors helping neighbors: A new national strategy for the protection of children.* Washington, DC: U.S. Government Printing Office.

U.S. Advisory Board on Child Abuse and Neglect (USABCAN). (1995). *A nation's shame: Fatal child abuse and neglect in the United States.* Washington, DC: U.S. Government Printing Office.

U.S. Congress, Office of Technology Assessment. (1988, February). *Healthy children: Investing in the future* (OTA-H-345). Washington, DC: U.S. Government Printing Office.

Valenzuela, M. (1990). Attachment in chronically underweight young children. *Child Development, 61,* 1984–1996.

Vasta, R. (1982). Physical child abuse: A dual component analysis. *Developmental Review, 2,* 164–170.

Wekerle, C., & Wolfe, D. A. (1996). Child maltreatment. In E. J. Mash & R. A. Barkley (Eds.), *Child psychopathology* (pp. 492–537). New York: Guilford Press.

Widom, C. S. (1989). Does violence beget violence? A critical examination of the literature. *Psychological Bulletin, 106,* 3–28.

Williamson, J. M., Borduin, C. M., & Howe, B. A. (1991). The ecology of adolescent maltreatment: A multilevel examination of adolescent physical abuse, sexual abuse, and neglect. *Journal of Consulting and Clinical Psychology, 59,* 449–457.

Wodarski, J. S., Kurtz, P. D., Gaudin, J. M., & Howing, P. T. (1990). Maltreatment and the school-aged child: Major academic, socioemotional, and adaptive outcomes. *Social Work, 35,* 506–513.

Wolfe, D. A. (1985). Child abusive parents: An empirical review and analysis. *Psychological Bulletin, 97,* 462–482.

Wolfe, D. A. (1987). *Child abuse: Implications for child development and psychopathology.* Newbury Park, CA: Sage.

Wolfe, D. A. (1988). Child abuse and neglect. In E. J. Mash & L. G. Terdal (Eds.), *Behavioral assessment of childhood disorders* (2nd ed., pp. 627–669). New York: Guilford Press.

Wolfe, D. A. (1991). *Preventing physical and emotional abuse of children.* New York: Guilford Press.

Wolfe, D. A., Fairbank, J., Kelly, J. A., & Bradlyn, A. S. (1983). Child abusive parents' physiological responses to stressful and nonstressful behavior in children. *Behavioral Assessment, 5,* 363–371.

Wolfe, D. A., Grasley, C., & Wekerle, C. (1994). *The Peer Relations Inventory.* (Available from the Youth Relationships Project, Department of Psychology, University of Western Ontario, London, Ontario N6A 5C2, Canada)

Wolfe, D. A., & Jaffe, P. (1991). Child abuse and family violence as determinants of child psychopathology. *Canadian Journal of Behavioural Science, 23,* 282–299.

Wolfe, D. A., Jaffe, P., Wilson, S., & Zak, L. (1985). Children of battered women: The relation of child behavior to family violence and maternal stress. *Journal of Consulting and Clinical Psychology, 53,* 657–664.

Wolfe, D. A., & McGee, R. (1991). Assessment of emotional status among maltreated children. In R. H. Starr, Jr., & D. A. Wolfe (Eds.), *The effects of child abuse and neglect: Issues and research* (pp. 257–277). New York: Guilford Press.

Wolfe, D. A., & McGee, R. (1994). Child maltreatment and adolescent adjustment. *Development and Psychopathology, 6,* 165–181.

Wolfe, D. A., & Mosk, M. D. (1983). Behavioral comparisons of children from abusive and distressed families. *Journal of Consulting and Clinical Psychology, 51,* 702–708.

Wolfe, D. A., Reitzel-Jaffe, D., Gough, R., & Wekerle, C. (1994). *The Conflicts in Relationships Questionnaire: Measuring physical and sexual coercion among youth.* (Available from the Youth Relationships Project, Department of Psychology, University of Western Ontario, London, Ontario N6A 5C2, Canada)

Wolfe, D. A., Sandler, J., & Kaufman, K. (1981). A competency-based parent training program for child abusers. *Journal of Consulting and Clinical Psychology, 49,* 633–640.

Wolfe, D. A., Wekerle, C., & Scott, K. (1997). *Empowering youth to promote nonviolence: Issues and solutions.* Thousand Oaks, CA: Sage.

Wolfe, D. A., Wekerle, C., Reitzel-Jaffe, D., & Lefebvre, L. (in press). Factors associated with abusive relationships among maltreated and non-maltreated youth. *Development and Psychopathology.*

Zahn-Waxler, C., Cole, P. M., Welsh, J. D., & Fox, N. A. (1995). Psychophysiological correlates of empathy and prosocial behaviors in preschool children with behavior problems. *Development and Psychopathology, 7,* 27–48.

Zuravin, S. J. (1988). Fertility patterns: Their relationship to child physical abuse and child neglect. *Journal of Marriage and the Family, 50,* 983–993.

Chapter Twelve

CHILD SEXUAL ABUSE

Vicky Veitch Wolfe
Jo-Ann Birt

The social movement to protect children from sexual abuse has affected child social service delivery systems as no other phenomenon has done in recent years. The growing recognition of the extent of child sexual abuse, and concern about its lifelong effects, have led to significant changes in law, social work, education, and mental health. Most child mental health clinics now devote a significant proportion of their resources to sexual abuse prevention and treatment, which were once relatively ignored by these facilities. Like many other social movements, the movement to protect children from sexual abuse has engendered passionate debate. Stories of ritualistic and Satanic abuse, day care abuse, child pornography, and child prostitution provoke horror and outrage. Nonetheless, the rights of accused perpetrators are vehemently protected, and serious concerns have been voiced about children's suggestibility, children's abilities to testify in criminal trials, and false allegations emanating in the midst of custody and access disputes. Abuse-related stories have saturated our consciousness through coverage in magazines, newspapers, televised news programs, and TV talk shows. A growing backlash against the child protection movement, however, may ultimately undermine many of its recent advances (Myers, 1994).

The professions of psychology and the behavioral sciences have responded to this intense social debate with their strength: empirical, socially relevant research. The past decade has witnessed an astounding growth in the scientific and professional literature devoted to this topic, as evidenced by the dramatic increase in new journals devoted to child maltreatment and sexual abuse. In some areas, seedlings of ideas from the mid-1980s have grown into empirically validated conceptualizations and full-fledged bodies of research, providing the foundations for developing and selecting appropriate assessment strategies for research and practice.

This chapter reviews current issues related to child sexual abuse, with the general assumption that from our core bases of knowledge, behavioral assessment strategies will grow. The chapter consists of three parts: (1) an epidemiological overview of the problem of child sexual abuse, including prevalence and incidence, characteristics of child victims, responses to sexual abuse allegations, and characteristics of offenders and of nonoffending parents (primarily mothers); (2) a conceptual and empirical overview of child sexual abuse sequelae, highlighting symptom profiles specifically associated with sexual abuse, along with factors that attenuate or exacerbate abuse effects; and (3) new developments in investigative interviewing, assessment of abuse-specific sequelae, and assessment of variables thought to mediate these sequelae.

EPIDEMIOLOGICAL OVERVIEW OF THE PROBLEM

Prevalence and Incidence

Prevalence

Epidemiological studies define "sexual abuse" in differing ways, leading to large discrepancies in sexual abuse estimates (Wyatt & Peters, 1986). Prevalence estimates range from 6% to 62% for girls and from 3% to 16% for boys (Finkelhor, 1990). Sexual abuse definitions vary along four dimensions: (1) upper age limit defining childhood; (2) behaviors defined as sexual abuse; (3) criteria for including minors as perpetrators; and (4) criteria for including adolescents as sexual abuse victims. Some studies have included adolescents up to age 18, whereas others have restricted their subjects to those aged 14 or under. Some studies have restricted incidents to those that involved physical contact, whereas others have included sexualized attention, exhibitionism, and invitations to engage in sexual behavior. Many studies have defined sexual abuse as sexual experiences taking place between a child and anyone at least 5 years older. Others have included peers (i.e., individuals less than 5 years older than the victims as perpetrators) when elements of coercion exist. For adolescents, some have limited sexual abuse to situations involving coercion (i.e., abuse of authority or physical force). Children under age 12 are generally considered incapable of providing consent, with coercion implied by the age difference between victim and offender.

At the far extreme, some have argued that sexual abuse estimates should be based on the "social role of victim," including only serious forms of abuse, cases where the victims played a passive or coerced role, and cases resulting in physical harm (Burt & Estep, 1983). Others argue that broader definitions allow greater flexibility in interpreting epidemiological data and allow researchers to examine the impact of sexual abuse according to different definitional criteria. Long and Jackson (1990) used several definitions of sexual abuse in their survey of college students, resulting in large discrepancies in prevalence estimates. However, victims' reports of distress did not differ on the basis of definitional criteria; this finding suggests that broader definitions include more victims affected by their abuse.

Epidemiological studies also differ in the populations sampled. The most sophisticated studies are based upon retrospective accounts of adults randomly contacted via telephone or neighborhood surveys. The most representative U.S. epidemiological study, conducted by the *Los Angeles Times* (Timnick, 1985; Finkelhor, Hotaling, Lewis, & Smith, 1990), included telephone interviews with 2,626 randomly selected adults across the 50 states. Sexual abuse was defined as "attempted or completed sexual intercourse, oral copulation or sodomy with a child, fondling, taking nude photographs, and exhibitionism" (Timmick, 1985, p. 34). Many respondents suggested that this definition should have been broadened to include indecent suggestions. Prevalence was estimated at 27% for females and 16% for men.

Two California-based studies used relatively broad definitions of sexual abuse. Russell's (1983) study included 930 San Francisco women contacted via a random telephone survey. Sexual abuse was defined as unwanted attempted or completed sexual contact by an adult or peer. To assure that respondents fully understood the definition, 14 separate questions about possible sexual contact were asked. When extrafamilial and incestuous abuse were considered together, 38% of Russell's subjects reported such abuse before age 18, and 28% reported such abuse before age 14. Prior to age 18, 16% reported incestuous abuse; prior to age 14, 12% reported such abuse. Prior to age 18, 31% reported extrafamilial abuse; prior to age 14, 20% reported such abuse. When noncontact forms of abuse (e.g., exhibitionism) or nongenital sexual overtures (e.g., kissing or hugging) were included, 54% reported sexual abuse before age 18, and 48% reported sexual abuse before age 14.

Wyatt's (1985) epidemiological study, also conducted in California, included 248 women, aged 18 to 36, matched to regional ethnic populations. Wyatt's definition of child sexual abuse was the most inclusive one employed in the epidemiological studies, in that issues of coercion were not applied to adolescent sexual experiences and victim age was extended to 18; this yielded the highest abuse estimate of all studies, 62%. When definitional restrictions similar to those used by Russell were added to Wyatt's data, estimates of abuse decreased, and the two studies yielded very similar results.

Methodological differences clearly affect abuse estimates. Finkelhor's (1979) survey of 796 college students, a relatively restricted sample, defined sexual abuse as contact or noncontact sexual experiences between a child less than 13 years of age and a "partner" at least 5 years older, or between an adolescent aged 13–16 and a partner at least 10 years older. Sexual abuse was reported by 19% of women and 9% of males; 20% of cases were limited to exhibitionism. The study yielding the lowest incidence rate was based upon a survey mailed to names drawn from a list kept by the Texas driver's license bureau; this survey consisted of one yes–no question about a history of child sexual abuse. With a 50% return rate (1,054 responses), Kercher and McShane (1984) estimated the prevalence of abuse at 12% for women and 3% for men. Martin, Anderson, Romans, Mullen, and O'Shea (1993) contacted New Zealanders via a mailed survey; respondents reporting a history of child sexual abuse were invited for an interview.

During interviews, participants were less likely to report intrafamilial abuse than they did in the postal survey, but were more likely to report extrafamilial and noncontact forms of abuse than they did in the survey. When contact and noncontact forms of abuse prior to age 16 were included, and noncoerced peer sexual contact was excluded, prevalence was estimated at 39%. When noncontact forms of abuse were excluded, prevalence was estimated at 25%. When the definition was narrowed to genital contact, prevalence was calculated at 19.7%.

Epidemiological studies from Canada yield results similar to those from the United States. Badgley (1984) described the results of a stratified, door-to-door sampling across Canada. Approximately 50% of females and 33% of males reported at least one unwanted sexual act during their lifetime, with 80% of assaults occurring during childhood or adolescence. Exhibitionism constituted the largest category of offenses.

Some evidence suggests that sexual abuse may be less prevalent in the United Kingdom than in North America. Baker and Duncan (1985) reported the results of a nationally representative survey, which defined sexual abuse as "a sexually mature" individual's involving a child (anyone under 16 years of age) in any activity that might lead to the "mature" person's sexual arousal, including noncontact sexual acts (such as exposure, showing pornography, or erotic suggestions). Of 2,019 men and women, 12% of females and 8% of males reported a history of sexual abuse.

Incidence

State social service records yield the most conservative estimates of sexual abuse; they also appear to be quite unreliable because of vague definitions, differences in validation procedures, and differences in staff expertise (Muram, Dorko, Brown, & Tolley, 1991). The study conducted by the National Center on Child Abuse and Neglect (NCCAN, 1981) across 26 counties in 10 states is the most comprehensive attempt to date at gathering incidence data across the United States. This study included cases known to child protective service agencies, educators, medical professionals, and other major child-oriented agencies. The yearly incidence of child sexual abuse was estimated by NCCAN at 0.7 cases per 1,000 children. The incidence per 1,000 of other forms of maltreatment was as follows: 3.4 cases of physical assault, 2.2 cases of emotional abuse, 1.7 cases of physical neglect, 2.9 cases of educational neglect, and 1.0

cases of emotional neglect. The American Humane Association (1984) provided a higher incidence estimate for sexual abuse, 1.4 per 1,000. Even though prevalence rates appear to be lower in Great Britain, Mrazek, Lynch, and Bentovim (1983) estimated incidence at 3 per 1,000—more that twice the U.S. estimates.

Victim Characteristics

Relationship to Perpetrator

Researchers have historically distinguished intrafamilial or incestuous abuse from extrafamilial abuse. Roughly one-third to one-half of female victims and one-tenth to one-fifth of male victims are abused by family members; 10–30% are abused by strangers; and approximately 40% are abused by someone known but not related to the victims (Finkelhor, 1994; Timnick, 1985). Approximately 4.5% of girls are abused by a father figure (Russell, 1984). Although biological fathers account for more incestuous abuse than stepfathers, stepfathers are seven times more likely to abuse their stepdaughters (Russell, 1984). Between 90% and 95% of perpetrators are male (Finkelhor, 1994; Timnick, 1985).

Types of Sexual Acts Experienced

Severity

Russell (1983) divided sexually abusive acts into three categories of severity, based on levels of sexual violation: (1) "very serious" sexual abuse (forced, unforced, and attempted vaginal, anal, or oral intercourse); (2) "serious" sexual abuse (forced or unforced digital penetration of the vagina; simulated intercourse; and fondling of genitals or breasts); and (3) "least serious" sexual abuse (forced kissing; touching clothed breasts or genitals; and intentional sexual touching of thighs, legs, buttocks, or other body parts). For incestuous abuse, 23% of cases were classified as very serious, 41% as serious, and 36% as least serious. For extrafamilial abuse, 53% involved very serious abuse, 27% serious abuse, and 20% least serious abuse. The difference in abuse severity between the incestuous and extrafamilial abuse cases may have been due to definitional differences, since Russell limited extrafamilial cases of adolescent sexual abuse to rape or attempted rape. Stepfathers, as compared to biological fathers, were more likely to engage in very serious abuse (47% vs. 26%). Grandfathers and uncles tended to engage in least serious abuse (75% and 54%, respectively). Brothers, cousins, and other male relatives tended to engage in more serious abuse; only 12% of brothers and 19% of cousins committed abuse classified as least serious. The *Los Angeles Times* poll (Timnick, 1985) found that 62% of male victims (9% of all men polled) and 49% of female victims (13% of all women polled) experienced what Russell would have termed very serious abuse, actual or attempted intercourse.

Use of Coercion/Force

The *Los Angeles Times* poll (Finkelhor et al., 1990; Timnick, 1985), defining "coercion" as abuse that involved a weapon or forceful physical restraint, estimated that 15% of male victims and 19% of female victims experienced coercion. In contrast, Russell (1983) found that 41% of incestuous abuse involved force.

Duration/Frequency

Approximately 60% of abuse occurs once (Baker & Duncan, 1985; Finkelhor, 1979); on the other hand, approximately 11% of female and 8% of male abuse victims in the *Los Angeles Times* poll reported abuse that occurred repeatedly over at least 1 year (Timnick, 1985).

Differences between Male and Female Victims

Not surprisingly, girls are at higher risk for sexual abuse than boys, but the discrepancy between boys and girls appears to be smaller than was once thought. Epidemiological research has estimated the ratio of girls to boys at 2.5:1 (Finkelhor & Baron, 1986). However, incidence studies reveal that boys account for fewer than 20% of victims; this suggests that boys are less likely to report their abuse during childhood. Sexual abuse experiences differ for boys and girls (Gordon, 1990; Watkins & Bentovim, 1992). Girls are more likely to be abused by family members over longer periods of time, and report more noncontact abuse (e.g., exhibitionism). Boys are more likely to be abused by someone outside the family, to be abused at a younger age, and to experience force and/or anal–genital or oral–genital contact. Even when severity is controlled for, girls tend to describe their experiences more negatively (Fischer, 1991).

Socioeconomic Status and Racial Background

Population-based prevalence studies reveal no relationship between sexual abuse risk and socio-economic status (SES). However, incidence-based studies show a disproportionate representation of lower-SES children among reported cases of sexual abuse (NCCAN, 1981; Finkelhor, 1990); this suggests that sexual abuse among middle-class and affluent children is less likely to be reported. Several epidemiological studies have examined racial differences in sexual abuse prevalence. Although there appears to be no difference in abuse rates between African-Americans and European-Americans (Wyatt, 1985), some preliminary data suggest that Hispanic females may be more vulnerable to both intrafamilial and extrafamilial sexual abuse (Finkelhor & Baron, 1986).

Who Discloses Sexual Abuse?

The discrepancies between incidence and prevalence studies, noted earlier, highlight the fact that relatively few children disclose their abuse during childhood. In Russell's (1983) epidemiological study, only a few adult survivors of childhood sexual abuse (from 2% of those intrafamilially abused to 6% of those extrafamilially abused) said that they had disclosed their abuse to an official agency during childhood. More recent estimates suggest that higher percentages of children disclose their abuse, perhaps because of greater social awareness and school-based prevention programs. Finkelhor (1994), using prevalence rates, estimated the rate of new abuse cases per year in the United States to be 500,000. With an estimate of 150,000 reported abuse cases per year, he calculated that approximately 30% of sexual abuse is currently disclosed during childhood. Finkelhor's estimate may not be far off the mark. In a recent study, Lamb and Edgar-Smith (1994) found that 36% of their sample of adult abuse survivors said that they had disclosed their abuse prior to age 14.

Several factors influence children's decisions to disclose sexual abuse. In a study of 257 college students, Love, Jackson, and Long (1990) found that 39.6% of victims took active steps to stop their childhood abuse: 20.6% disclosed the abuse, and 19% confronted or resisted the perpetrator. Children who were first abused at an older age, and children who felt abuse-related anger, guilt, or fear, were more likely to terminate the abuse in an active manner. Abuse characteristics did not predict disclosure, suggesting that active termination may have more to do with premorbid child characteristics than with aspects of the abuse. Children's decisions to disclose may hinge on their parents' willingness to accept their stories. Lawson and Chaffin (1992) found that children whose caretakers were willing to accept the possibility of abuse, given a diagnosis of a sexually transmitted disease, were three and a half times more likely to disclose abuse. Unfortunately, children who do not take early steps to stop their abuse are less likely to do so as time passes (Sas, Cunningham, Hurley, Dick, & Farnsworth, 1995; Schultz & Jones, 1983).

Roesler and Wind (1994) interviewed adults about their decisions regarding disclosure during childhood or adolescence. The most commonly reported reasons for not disclosing included fear for personal safety, fear of the effect on the family, fear of blame and punishment, loyalty to the perpetrator, shame, helplessness, and repression of memories. Sas et al. (1995) interviewed children about their thoughts about disclosure following the first episode of abuse: 40% did not realize that the act was wrong; 50% were told by the perpetrator not to tell; and 43% never considered telling about the abuse. Following the first abusive episode, 33% disclosed soon thereafter; 19% did not immediately disclose, but were not abused again; and 44% did not disclose and were repeatedly abused by the same perpetrator. Children who immediately disclosed their abuse reported their reasons as follows: prior education, protection for self and others, retaliation, and a desire to talk about "something unusual that happened." Some children said they spontaneously talked about the abuse without clearly formulating a disclosure plan. Children were less likely to disclose their abuse immediately if the perpetrator was a family member, was an alcoholic, was emotionally close, had "groomed" the child prior to the abuse, or had used force. Older children were more likely to disclose than younger children. Among children who did not disclose immediately, the average delay was 1.5 years. For those abused by a family member, the average delay was 2.6 years. By the time the abuse was either disclosed or discovered, 42% no longer had contact with the perpetrator; 30% were no longer being abused, but continued to be at risk; and 28% continued to be abused. Twenty percent of victims waited a full year after the abuse ended before disclosing. Only 40% disclosed their abuse without a prompt by a concerned adult or friend.

Sauzier (1989) has noted that child sexual abuse often comes to the attention of official agencies through avenues that do not include direct disclosure, such as discovery of the abuse by a third party, medical evidence (e.g., sexually transmitted disease or pregnancy), disclosure of abuse by another child, or behavioral indicators (e.g., sexu-

alized play or excessive masturbation). Mian, Wehrspann, Klajner-Diamond, LeBaron, and Winder (1986), comparing "accidental" with "purposeful" disclosures among cases of child sexual abuse presenting to a hospital-based evaluation team, found that most children disclosed their abuse purposefully (60%); however, older children (as compared to preschool-age children), and children who experienced extrafamilial (as compared to incestuous) abuse, were more likely to provide purposeful disclosures.

Regardless of how sexual abuse comes to light, children often have serious doubts about revealing the "secret." Sorenson and Snow (1991) found high levels of ambivalence in children's disclosures, as evidenced by (1) initial denial of abuse by the victim (75%); (2) vague and vacillating details about the abuse, followed by a more consistent and detailed account (78%); (3) recantation (22%); and (4) reaffirmation of abuse following a recantation (92% of those who recanted eventually reaffirmed the abuse).

Responses to Allegations of Child Sexual Abuse

Professionals' Responses

All states and provinces in North America require professionals to report suspected abuse to official child protection agencies. State and provincial laws vary as to the situations that require reporting (e.g., ongoing abuse, strong potential for abuse, past abuse even when there may be no current risk), the degree of certainty necessary for mandated reporting, and sanctions for failing to report (Walters, 1995). Informant anonymity is protected in some, but not all, jurisdictions. Professionals are protected from criminal and civil liability in all jurisdictions, unless a report is made maliciously or without probable grounds. With the exception of attorney–client privilege, legal and professional confidentiality requirements are suspended when one is reporting suspected abuse. However, professionals who fail to report suspected abuse may be liable for civil damages based upon abuse-related injuries incurred from the point at which the professional failed to take action (*Landeros v. Flood*, 1979).

Despite legal mandates, case law allows that professionals may choose not to report suspected abuse, based upon their own uncertainty about the abuse, belief that someone else will take the responsibility of contacting authorities, or belief that reporting the suspicion would cause more harm than good. One-third of professionals admit that they have suspected abuse but not reported it (Finkelhor, Gomes-Schwartz, & Horowitz, 1984; Kalichman & Craig, 1991), with the primary reason being lack of certainty. Perception of certainty is enhanced when children disclose their abuse directly to the professional (Kalichman, Craig, & Follingstad, 1989), when the children do not recant (Boat & Everson, 1988), and when medical evidence exists (Boat & Everson, 1988). Other reasons for failing to report suspected abuse include lack of confidence in child protective services; concern about negative consequences for the child and family; possible harm to the therapeutic relationship; fear that reporting would disrupt the disclosure process or cause the family to flee from evaluation; vague reporting statutes; concerns about personal liability if the report of abuse is not founded; confidentiality concerns; and ignorance of the legal consequences of failing to report (Walters, 1995). Situational factors may influence professional reporting. Attias and Goodwin (1985) found that female professionals were more likely than males to say they would report suspected abuse even if a child recanted the allegations. Kalichman and Craig (1991) found that professionals were more likely to report abuse of a child than abuse of an adolescent, unless they were concerned that an adolescent's father would not cooperate with their own investigation.

Child Protective Services' Responses

Following a report of suspected sexual abuse, a child protection agency must determine the probability that abuse occurred, assess the risk for further abuse, and select a course of action to protect the child. Often police are involved in the child protective agency's investigation to avoid redundancy. Investigations typically include interviews with the child, the child's parents, and the accused (when this person is not a parent). Interview strategies and interpretation of children's disclosures vary considerably and are the topics of considerable controversy and debate; these are explored more fully later in this chapter.

Given the legal mandate to report any situation in which a child may need protection, it is not surprising that a fairly high percentage of cases prove upon investigation to be unfounded. In fact, Elliott and Briere (1994) found that a relatively high percentage (22%) of "unclear" dispositions following sexual abuse investigations came in cases that had initially been referred by professionals. Jones and McGraw (1987) found that 53% of

sexual abuse allegations investigated by a child protection agency were viewed as reliable and valid (i.e., "founded"). In 24% of the cases, investigators could not come to a reliable conclusion as to whether the abuse occurred; in another 17% of cases, investigators suspected that abuse had occurred, but could not confirm it. Eight percent of allegations were considered fictitious (three-quarters of such allegations originated with an adult rather than a child, often in the midst of custody/access disputes). From a review of five studies, Everson and Boat (1989) concluded that 4–8% of sexual abuse allegations are fabricated, and that the majority of these come from adolescents.

The Jones and McGraw (1987) study highlights the high number of cases in which abuse cannot be confirmed or disconfirmed. This situation leaves victims, families, and the accused in limbo, particularly when an accused perpetrator is a family member or is someone with whom the child may have further contact. Terms such as "confirmed or disconfirmed" or "founded or unfounded" can be imprecise, leading to misinterpretation of investigation results. For instance, if an accusation of sexual abuse made against a father is ruled "unfounded" (even though the agency suspects abuse but feels there is not enough evidence to confirm it), the accused father may feel he has the right to unsupervised access to his child and may use the term "unfounded" in seeking such access. In a follow-up article, Jones and Seig (1988) suggest that investigating agencies use five categories to depict investigation outcomes: "definitely true," "probably true," "possibly false," "probably false," and "definitely false."

In the wake of the realization that some sexual abuse allegations are false, and that some false allegations occur during custody and access disputes, such cases typically receive great scrutiny. Some believe that such allegations are common weapons used to gain advantage in custody disputes; however, recent evidence suggests that only 2% of all custody and access disputes involve allegations of child sexual abuse (Thoennes & Tjaden, 1990). Thoennes and Tjaden (1990) found that approximately half (58%) of all child sexual abuse allegations made in the context of a custody and access dispute are "founded," which is roughly similar to the rate of founded allegations among the general public (Jones & McGraw, 1987). Thirty percent of sexual abuse investigations within the context of custody and access issues were "unfounded" (however, "unfounded" does not necessarily mean "fictitious"). Jones and Seig

(1988) found that 20% of custody and access sexual abuse allegations were fictitious, which is higher than the false-accusation rate for general investigations reported by Jones and McGraw (1987); however, they also found that 70% of the allegations were reliable, which is actually higher than the general rate of affirmation of abuse concerns. In the largest study of sexual abuse forensic evaluations, Elliott and Briere (1994) found no difference in case disposition (i.e., "founded," "unfounded," "unclear") based upon whether or not the case involved a custody dispute. Nevertheless, many professionals believe that high rates of fictitious reports emanate from custody and access disputes. Perhaps because of the serious repercussions of such allegations for custody and access (Sorensen et al., 1995), these cases may go further in the family court system and have higher visibility than other custody disputes, which are often resolved through negotiation or mediation.

Faller (1991) documented several circumstances observed in a sample of custody and access cases involving sexual abuse allegations: (1) Abuse was known to the mother prior to separation and played a role in her decision to separate from the father, but the mother did not reveal the abuse to any public agency until the issue of access arose (8% of cases); (2) the child was abused by the parent prior to the separation, but the child did not disclose this until after the parents separated (19% of cases); (3) abuse began after the separation, related either to the parent's emotional reaction to the separation or the fact that previous barriers preventing abuse were no longer present (39% of cases); (4) false allegations were made after separation because of one parent's overinterpretation of risk, based upon that parent's previous drinking or sexual behavior, the child's reaction to visitation, or misinterpretation of the child's statements about access (e.g., "Daddy hurts me" or "Daddy takes baths with me") (32%); and (5) deliberately fabricated allegations of abuse were brought forth to gain advantage in custody/access proceedings (2%).

Involvement with the Judicial System

Once child protection services or police verify abuse, questions about criminal prosecution arise. Decisions to prosecute vary across jurisdictions. Finkelhor (1983) cited a 43% rate of criminal justice action in Nevada and a 10% rate in Arkansas. Reasons for not pursuing charges include concerns that the process may be detrimental to a victim and family; poor cooperation from the victim and/or the victim's family; beliefs that sexual abuse is a mental disorder and not under the aegis of the criminal justice system; and lack of evidence or concerns about the child's ability to provide testimony (Wolfe & Wolfe, 1988). Despite these complications, criminal action occurs in an average of 24% of reported cases (Finkelhor, 1983). Burgess, Groth, Holmstrom, and Sgroi (1978) reported that the majority of cases they studied resulted in a guilty plea (73.8%), 14.3% resulted in a conviction, and 8.3% resulted in an acquittal. Of those convicted, 12% of the offenders were sent to prison, 13% were ordered into a treatment program, and 75% remained in the community. In a more recent account of judicial actions in Ontario, Sas et al. (1995) found that in 69% of cases where a charge was laid, either a guilty plea or a verdict of guilty was the result; two-thirds of convicted offenders were sentenced to a jail term. Average jail terms were 16 months for adults and 8 months for juveniles.

Only 3–4% of sexually abused children known to official agencies ever testify in criminal trials (Saunders, Kilpatrick, Resnick, Hanson, & Lipovsky, 1992). Even among those cases referred for prosecution, only 11–17% of cases result in a criminal trial in which children testify (Goodman et al., 1992; Lipovsky, Tidwell, Kilpatrick, Saunders, & Dawson, 1991). Nevertheless, up to one-half of children whose cases result in adjudication testify in some other type of proceeding, such as a preliminary hearing (Goodman et al., 1992; Sas, Hurley, Austin, & Wolfe, 1991).

Courtroom testimony can be quite stressful; 74.3% of parents and 63.7% of children who testify in court describe it as a negative experience (Lipovsky et al., 1991). Following children throughout the prosecution process, Sas et al. (1991) reported that 5% dropped out of school, 6% reported suicidal ideation or suicide attempts leading to hospitalization, and 15% reported feeling estranged from extended family members who supported the accused. Prior to testifying, children identify a number of fears, including fears of the testimony itself, the defense attorney, and seeing the defendant; after testifying, children report that the most distressing aspects were seeing the defendant and not having their parents in the courtroom (Goodman et al., 1992). Children also fear retaliation from the defendant and fear that they will not be believed. However, many children feel relieved after testifying in court, showing reductions in anxiety and depressive symptoms (Goodman et al., 1992).

Although children typically find their court experiences stressful, there is little evidence that participating in legal proceedings results in long-term adjustment problems. Adjustment among sexually abused children tends to improve across time, regardless of their court experience, although children who testify may improve at a slower pace (Lipovsky, 1994). Children's adjustment following court proceedings appears to relate to three factors (Goodman et al., 1992; Runyan, Everson, Edelsohn, Hunter, & Coulter, 1988): testifying in multiple, prolonged, or delayed proceedings; harsh direct examination or cross-examination; and maternal support or the lack of it. Nonetheless, children can benefit from participating in the judicial process. Sas et al. (1995) found that 85% of children who provided courtroom testimony were positive about their involvement and reported no regrets; only 9% harbored regrets. Ninety-one percent of victims said they would advise a friend to tell the police if a similar incident occurred; 84% said they would call the police if they were abused again; and 80% said that if they were abused again, they would want the case prosecuted.

Offender Characteristics

Male versus Female Offenders: Similarities and Differences

Females commit 3–13% of all sexual abuse (Kendall-Tackett & Simon, 1987; Schultz & Jones, 1983), accounting for approximately 14% of abuse against males and 6% of abuse against females (Finkelhor & Russell, 1984). In the majority of cases (50–77%), females offend with male partners (Allen, 1991; Kaufman, Wallace, Johnson, & Reeder, 1995). Male and female offenders tend to commit similar types of offenses and use similar tactics to gain compliance and secrecy, with some differences because of differences in anatomy (Allen, 1991; Fischer, 1991; Kaufman et al., 1995; Rudin, Zalewski, & Bodmer-Turner, 1995). Male offenders are more likely to require fellatio and are more likely to commit anal intercourse, whereas female offenders are more likely to use sexual aids (Kaufman et al., 1995). Although both males and females are more likely to offend against girls, female offenders have a higher proportion of male victims (Rudin et al., 1995). Victims (especially male victims) of female offenders, as compared to victims of male offenders, tend to be younger and are less likely to be related to the perpetrators (Fehrenbach & Monastersky, 1988;

Rudin et al., 1995). Female offenders are more likely than males to offend while in a caretaking or babysitting role (Rudin et al., 1995).

Although male and female offenders commit similar acts, the psychological factors leading them to abuse may differ. Allen (1991) found that more female than male offenders reported having negative family relations and experiencing physical or sexual abuse during childhood or adolescence. As adults, female offenders reported more spousal violence and were described as having greater emotional and sexual fulfilment needs than male offenders. In contrast, male offenders had higher rates of alcoholism and antisocial behavior. At least 46% of female perpetrators have a history of sexual abuse themselves (Fehrenbach & Monastersky, 1988; Rudin et al., 1995), whereas approximately 20% of male perpetrators have a history of sexual abuse (Williams & Finkelhor, 1990).

Research with Convicted Male Offenders

Research on male child sexual offenders has typically examined two groups: prison populations and incestuous offenders. The largest and most complex body of research on child sexual offenders has been conducted with prison populations; by and large, these include the most incorrigible and dangerous offenders, typically with multiple convictions for extrafamilial abuse. When intrafamilial offenders are imprisoned, they often have multiple victims, including some victims who were not within the offenders' families. The distinction between prison populations and nonimprisoned incestuous offenders is not that clear, however. When nonimprisoned incestuous offenders are guaranteed confidentiality, 44% of incestuous fathers report molesting other children outside their families (Abel, Becker, Cunningham-Rathner, Mittelman, & Rouleau, 1988). Although some have speculated that incestuous offenders are primarily sexually attracted to adults, Langevin, Handy, Hook, Day, and Russon (1985) point out that a quarter to a third of incestuous offenders have pedophilic erotic preferences.

Most researchers conclude that pedophiles constitute a heterogeneous group requiring further subclassification. Araji and Finkelhor (1986), reviewing prison-based research, highlight four factors thought to motivate pedophilia:

1. *Emotional congruence*. The emotional congruence factor reflects a "fit" between the adult's emotional needs and childlike characteristics. For instance, an emotionally immature pedophile may

find that sexually abusing children promotes feelings of power, omnipotence, or control. Some pedophiles may abuse children in an attempt to master their own childhood sexual trauma (i.e., "identifying with the aggressor"). Feminist theories suggest that male sexual socialization promotes the idea of domination in male–female sexual relationships, and that offenders seek children as "partners" because they are youthful and subservient.

2. *Sexual arousal.* Several studies demonstrate that pedophiles tend to respond more strongly to child than to adult sexual stimuli; they also respond more strongly to child sexual stimuli than do other prisoners and the general population. Many have speculated that pedophiles' sexual responsiveness to children stems from early childhood sexual experiences, particularly among offenders who are "fixated" (i.e., those whose primary source of sexual arousal is children) as compared to either "nonfixated," "regressed," or incestuous offenders (i.e., those whose primary source of sexual arousal is not children). Offenders against male children are particularly likely to have histories of childhood sexual abuse by male offenders with 33–40% of offenders against boys reporting childhood sexual abuse, as compared to 18–24% of offenders against girls (Abel et al., 1988; Gebhard, Gagnon, Pomeroy, & Christensen, 1965).

3. *Blockage.* Blockage theories, and supporting research, suggest that some offenders feel "blocked" from having satisfying sexual relationships with age-appropriate partners, because of either social inadequacy, marital distress, or repressed sexual attitudes; thus, they seek children as substitutes.

4. *Disinhibition.* Disinhibition factors (e.g., poor impulse control, cognitive impairment, or alcohol abuse), though often cited as possible reasons for sexual crimes against children, have not received much empirical support. Gebhard et al. (1965) found that 80% of sexual acts against children were planned, not impulsive. Most molesters are of normal intelligence. Nevertheless, alcohol is involved in 30–40% of cases, and 45–50% of pedophiles have problems with alcohol, particularly incestuous offenders of girls (Aarens et al., 1978).

Research with Incestuous Offenders

There is a growing consensus that incestuous offenders, like extrafamilial offenders, are a heterogeneous group. There is little evidence of blatant psychopathology among incestuous fathers or stepfathers; in fact, the National Committee for the Prevention of Child Abuse (1978) estimated that fewer than 10% of incestuous fathers demonstrated any diagnosable mental illness. Nonetheless, incestuous fathers and stepfathers show evidence of personality problems to a greater extent than do members of the general public. In their literature review, Williams and Finkelhor (1990) found several characteristics distinguishing incestuous from nonincestuous fathers: The former were less involved in child care, less empathic, more passive, more socially isolated, and more paranoid. Smith and Saunders (1995) found that incestuous fathers were characterized as less bold, less radical, less extroverted, less warm, more self-sufficient, and more tense. Incestuous fathers also had more intimacy and trust problems; had poorer social skills; and were more likely to be shy, socially avoidant, and threat-sensitive.

Different dynamics may be in effect when abuse is perpetrated by biological fathers as opposed to stepfathers. In order for a biological father to abuse his daughter, he must break two strong cultural taboos: the taboo against sex with children, and the taboo against incest (Williams & Finkelhor, 1990). Some speculate that early child care inoculates fathers against sexual interest in their daughters; thus, stepfathers, who are less likely to have had contact with their stepdaughters during their early years, have fewer boundaries regarding sexual behavior with their stepdaughters. For fathers to abuse their daughters, other factors may have to be in place before these cultural and familial boundaries are broken. Williams and Finkelhor (1992) found that incestuous fathers were less involved with their daughters prior to the abuse, as compared to nonincestuous biological fathers and their daughters. Gordon (1987) found that incestuous biological fathers were more likely to have financial, marital, and substance use problems than were incestuous stepfathers. However, other research suggests that incestuous stepfathers may be just as psychologically disturbed as incestuous biological fathers, but that the pathology may be expressed differently. Scott and Stone (1986b) found that incestuous biological fathers scored relatively high on the Minnesota Multiphasic Personality Inventory (MMPI) Paranoia and Introversion scales, whereas incestuous stepfathers scored relatively high on the MMPI Depression, Psychasthenia, and Schizophrenia scales. One-third of stepfathers obtained a 49/94 two-point code type—a significantly greater proportion than that found in matched comparison groups. The 49/94 code type suggests deficits in moral conscience, passive–aggressive tendencies, egocentrism, narcissism, unrecognized dependence needs, and rationalization tendencies (Graham, 1990).

In an effort to identify factors associated with "crossing the incest boundary," Williams and Finkelhor (1992) investigated 118 recently identified incestuous biological fathers and compared them to 116 nonabusive fathers. Incestuous fathers more often reported childhood physical, sexual, and emotional abuse, and were more likely to report sexual preoccupation, frequent masturbation, and sexual offenses against others during adolescence. As adults, they reported more anxiety, isolation, and violence, as well as more marital and sexual problems. They did not differ from controls on alcohol abuse, exposure to child pornography, criminal activity, or ability to express empathy.

Despite differences between incestuous and nonincestuous fathers, Williams and Finkelhor (1992) have cautioned that incestuous fathers are quite heterogeneous, and identified five types of incestuous fathers:

1. *Sexually preoccupied*. Many of these men had extensive childhood maltreatment. They were highly sexualized and became sexually interested in their daughters when the girls were quite young. The majority began abusing their daughters prior to age 6, commiting relatively frequent abuse over long durations. These fathers were the incestuous fathers most likely to penetrate their daughters.

2. *Adolescent regressors*. These men recognized sexual interest in their daughters as puberty approached. They appeared "adolescent" and "infatuated" when describing their abusive behavior.

3. *Instrumental sexual gratifiers*. These men abused their daughters sporadically, often fantasizing about other partners. These fathers reported more guilt and remorse than other incestuous fathers did.

4. *Emotionally dependent*. These men used their daughters to satisfy "urgent" needs for closeness and comfort; they often romanticized their relationships with their daughters.

5. *Angry retaliators*. These offenders showed relatively little sexual arousal toward their daughters; their abusive behavior centered around their anger toward their wives (and sometimes their daughters) for perceived neglect, abandonment, or infidelity.

Research with Young Offenders

Increasing attention is being paid to adolescent sex offenders, primarily because of three facts: (1)

Adolescents commit a significant proportion of sexual offenses; (2) many adult sexual offenders began their offending during adolescence; and (3) early intervention might prevent future abusive episodes (Murphy, Haynes, & Page, 1992). Finkelhor's (1979) epidemiological study of college students found that 34% of women and 39% of men reported that they had been involved prior to adulthood with a sexual partner who was at least 5 years older and was between the ages of 10 and 19. Clinic-based studies estimate that approximately half of male child victims and 14–25% of female child victims are abused by adolescents (Farber, Showers, Johnson, Joseph, & Oshins, 1984). Thomas (1982) reported that 46.8% of child victims referred to the Children's Hospital's National Medical Center Program for Sexual Abuse were abused by juveniles. Individuals under age 18 account for 20% of sexual offense arrests in the United States (U.S. Department of Justice, 1977–1980), with the majority of victims being younger children (up to 66%). Well over half (57%) of identified adolescent offenders have had multiple victims prior to being caught (Fehrenbach, Smith, Monastersky, & Deisher, 1986). Adolescents tend to commit serious forms of abuse; approximately 60% of offenders penetrate their victims, and one-third to one-half use or threaten physical force to gain compliance or secrecy (Kaufman, Hilliker, & Daleiden, 1996). Juvenile sex offenders often have additional problems (Becker, 1994), including poor interpersonal skills, depression, learning and academic problems, impulsivity, and other forms of delinquency. Adolescent sex offenders often cannot be distinguished from either violent or nonviolent adolescent nonsexual offenders on the basis of psychological or behavioral factors (Tarter, Hegedus, Alterman, & Katz-Garris, 1983).

Early identification of adolescent offenders has strong prevention potential. Many convicted child molesters report beginning their offending during adolescence, with the modal age of onset being 16 years (Groth, Longo, & McFadin, 1982). Abel et al. (1988) reported that the onset of paraphilic arousal patterns began by age 15 for 42% of offenders, and by age 19 for 57%. Seventy-four percent of offenders who molested young boys reported deviant arousal by age 19.

Strong evidence links a history of victimization to juvenile sexual offending, with 50–80% of juvenile sexual offenders reporting child sexual abuse (Hunter, Goodwin, & Becker, 1994; Ryan, Lane, Davis, & Isaacs, 1987). Sexual abuse history is linked with deviant sexual arousal and having more victims, younger victims, and male victims (Becker, Kaplan, & Tenke, 1992; Hunter et al., 1994; Kaufman et al., 1996). Seriousness of offending has been related to exposure to aggressive role models, having a sexual offender in the extended family, a history of both physical and sexual abuse, and witnessing the abuse of another family member (Hunter & Becker, 1994; Smith, 1988). Fagan and Wexler (1988) found that juvenile sexual offenders, compared to other juvenile offenders, were more likely to come from homes where there was spousal violence and child physical and sexual abuse.

Research with Sibling Offenders

Sibling incest is the most prevalent form of incest, occurring at least five times more often than parent–child abuse (Finkelhor, 1980; Smith & Israel, 1987). Although some consider sibling incest to be within the realm of sexual exploration, there is growing awareness that sibling incest can lead to serious emotional sequelae for victims (Adler & Schutz, 1995). Clinic-based studies of sibling incest reveal that from 46% to 89% of cases involve attempted or completed vaginal or anal penetration, with most victims at least 5 years younger than the offenders. Many offenders have histories of conduct problems and arrests for nonsexual offenses (Adler & Schutz, 1995). Many sibling offenders report having histories of sexual and/or physical abuse themselves (Adler & Schutz, 1995; Smith & Israel, 1987). A maternal history of sexual abuse also appears to be relatively common (Adler & Schutz, 1995; Smith & Israel, 1987).

Some suggest that sibling incest is more likely to occur in either chaotic families or families without a strong parental figure (Smith & Israel, 1987). Incest tends to occur in large families (Finkelhor, 1980; Russell, 1986), particularly if an offending brother has taken on a paternal role. Adler and Schutz (1995) felt that parental minimalization and denial were strong within families with sibling incest. In over half of their small clinic-referred sample of 12, the victims disclosed their abuse to their parents, but the parents failed to take effective action to stop further abuse. As a result, in order for the case to come to the attention of authorities, three-quarters of the victims disclosed their abuse to someone outside the family. In further support of the denial hypothesis, over half of the offenders had past histories indicative of Conduct Disorder, and close to half met diagnostic criteria for Conduct Disorder at the time of referral; however, parental reports of behavioral and emotional problems on the Child Behavior Checklist placed the majority of the offenders in the average range on both the Internalizing and Externalizing broad-band scales.

Based upon a clinical sample of 25 families with sibling incest, Smith and Israel (1987) described three distinctive dynamics in such families: (1) distant, inaccessible parents; (2) parental stimulation of the sexual climate in the home; and (3) family secrets and extrafamilial affairs. Fathers were physically unavailable in 36% of the families, through either death, abandonment, or divorce with no subsequent contact. An additional 24% of fathers were viewed as physically available but emotionally distant; this distance included lack of interest in parenting, lack of bonding between the fathers and children, and difficulty in empathizing with the children's needs. Mothers were physically unavailable in 24% of families through either abandonment or no contact following divorce. Twenty percent of the mothers were considered physically available but emotionally distant, as evident by substance abuse, mental illness, or preoccupation with other siblings. Nearly half of the sibling perpetrators had observed sexual activity between their parents or between one of their parents and another party, ranging from fondling to intercourse. Half of the victims had a history of other intrafamilial or extrafamilial sexual abuse. In 32% of cases, father–daughter incest had preceded the brother's abuse of the same victim. Forty percent of mothers were viewed as "seductive" with their sons, flirting with them, telling them about their sexual exploits, and showing excessive interest in their sexual development and peer sexual relationships. On the other hand, one-third of the mothers were described as overly rigid, puritanical, and noncommunicative about sex. In three-quarters of the families, extrafamilial affairs were in progress at the time of the sibling incest.

Characteristics of Nonoffending Parents

Although mothers rarely commit sexual offenses against their children (Banning, 1989), they have not escaped blame for the problem. Early clinical literature was replete with examples of how mothers of sexually abused children either failed to protect their children from abuse, failed to intercede once abuse was discovered, or colluded either consciously or unconsciously with the offenders (Gomes-Schwartz, Horowitz, & Cardarelli, 1990). Birns and Meyer (1993) attribute this "mother blame" to family systems theories that downplay individual psychopathology and emphasize dysfunctional family dynamics as the etiology of incest. The prevalence of such reasoning is underscored by a survey of social workers (Deitz & Craft, 1980), in which 65%, despite an overwhelming belief that child sexual abuse and spousal abuse often occur in tandem, believed that nonoffending mothers were as much to blame as fathers for the fathers' abusive behavior. In contrast, Herman (1985) argued that mothers should be seen as co-victims rather than colluders, since they are often battered by the same perpetrators. Evidence that incestuously abusive men often begin their abusive behavior during adolescence further weakens theories that dysfunctional family systems constitute the etiology of incestuous abuse (Becker, 1988).

Parental Variables as Risk Factors for Abuse

Epidemiological and clinical studies have identified several parental variables that increase risk of sexual abuse: parental absence (Benedict & Zautra, 1993; Gale, Thompson, Moran, & Sack, 1988; Smith & Israel, 1987), maternal employment (Russell, 1986), maternal youth (Gordon & Creighton, 1988), maternal physical illness (Benedict & Zautra, 1993); a large family (Gale et al., 1988); maternal mental illness and emotional problems (Smith & Saunders, 1995; Williamson, Borduin, & Howe, 1991), and maternal substance use problems (Leifer, Shapiro, & Kassem, 1993).

Maternal emotional problems may play a key role in understanding their ineffectiveness in protecting their children from sexual abuse, particularly in incestuous families. Williamson, Borduin, and Howe (1991) found that different family issues contributed to different forms of child maltreatment: Physical abuse was related to rigid family relationships and poor maternal understanding of child development; neglect was related to extrafamilial difficulties and social isolation; sexual abuse was related to maternal emotional problems. Scott and Stone (1986a) found that mothers of incestuously abused girls had a disproportional percentage of MMPI 34/43 two-point code profiles—a profile type commonly associated with dissociative phenomena. Perhaps some mothers are less protective because of their tendencies to dissociate themselves from familial stressors, and thus to be less sensitive to indicators of sexual abuse.

Emotional problems among mothers of paternally abused children may stem from physical and emotional abuse by their spouses (Herman & Hirschman, 1981; Paveza, 1988; Stark & Fitcraft, 1988). Stark and Fitcraft (1988) found that maternal mental health and substance use problems in families of incestuously abused children appeared to be sequelae to spousal abuse. Several studies have characterized incestuous families as isolated, insular, overly concerned with morality and control, and stifling of self-expression and individuality (Dadds, Smith, Webber, & Robinson, 1991; Saunders, Lipovsky, & Hanson, 1995).

Poor parent–child attachment and relationship patterns also appear to play a role in increasing a child's vulnerability to sexual abuse. Although no studies on attachment have been conducted with sexually abused children per se, maltreated children in general are more prone to attachment disorders (Carlson, Cicchetti, Barnett, & Braunwald, 1989). Insecurely attached children may be more vulnerable to abuse, in that their parents may monitor their activities less closely, may be less sensitive to indicators of sexual abuse, may be less inclined to believe the children's stories of abuse, and may be too preoccupied with their own issues to respond effectively to abuse disclosures. Research by Long and Jackson (1994) supports some of these issues. Using the Family Environment Scale and the Past Experiences Questionnaire with victims of both intra- and extrafamilial forms of sexual abuse, they found that victims were more likely to come from families classified as disorganized, whereas nonvictims were more likely to come from families classified as support-oriented. Family cohesion may also be low, in part, because of few shared cultural, intellectual, or recreational interests or opportunities (Benedict & Zautra, 1993).

Conflict is often high between poorly attached children and their parents (Greenberg, Speltz, & DeKlyen, 1993), and the same is often true of sexually abused children and their families (Benedict & Zautra, 1993; Lipovsky, Saunders, & Hanson, 1992). Parent–child conflict may make it difficult for children to disclose abuse to their parents (Lamb & Edgar-Smith, 1994; Roesler & Wind, 1994). Although some evidence suggests that families of extrafamilially abused children are also chaotic and disorganized (Gruber & Jones, 1981), Edwards and Alexander (1992) have noted that the greatest familial dysfunction is detected in families of the intrafamilially abused.

Poorly attached children may be more vulnerable to abuse, in that they may appreciate the special attention offered by the perpetrators. Insecurely attached children are often socially isolated (Booth, Krasnor, McKinnon, & Rubin, 1994)—a desirable characteristic for many offenders (Elliott,

Browne, & Kilcoyne, 1995). Parker and Parker (1986) suggest that mother–daughter role reversal results in increased father–daughter contact in the absence of the mother, leaving the child vulnerable to abuse. Herman and Hirschman (1981) found that female incest survivors were more likely than controls to report assuming a maternal role within their family during childhood.

Maternal History of Sexual Abuse

Consistent with intergenerational theories of child abuse, a mother's history of child sexual abuse is often thought to increase the risk of abuse for her children, because it affects her ability to serve as a protector and impedes the development of parent–child attachment (Grenspun, 1994). On the whole, there is no evidence to support this notion. Deblinger, Stauffer, and Landsberg (1994) found that maternal reactions to child abuse allegations did not vary as a function of their own history of abuse. Others have speculated that mothers with a history of child sexual abuse may avoid dealing with sexual issues with their children, making them more vulnerable to abuse. Grocke, Smith, and Graham (1995) found the opposite: When children of mothers with and without histories of childhood sexual abuse were compared for their knowledge of sex and sensitivity to sexual abuse issues, children whose mothers had a history of child sexual abuse actually knew *more* about both sexuality and sexual abuse. Wolfe (1991) found that sexual abuse history did not differentiate mothers of sexually abused children from a control group of mothers matched for SES. Furthermore, a history of childhood sexual abuse among mothers of abuse victims did not affect the mothers' belief in their children's stories or their attributions of blame for the abuse. Although the mothers of sexually abused children differed from the controls on psychological symptomatology, comparisons of mothers of abused children based upon maternal history of sexual abuse revealed no differences in psychological symptomatology. Furthermore, though abused children differed from control children on a number of indices of adjustment, child abuse victims did not differ as a function of their mothers' history of child sexual abuse. In contrast, Kelly (1990) found that mothers of children abused in day care settings who reported having a sexual abuse experience during their childhood had higher Symptom Checklist 90 – Revised (SCL-90–R) Global Severity Index scores than did mothers of abused children who did not report a personal sexual abuse experience.

When research samples are differentiated according to incestuous versus nonincestuous abuse, more evidence emerges linking a maternal abuse history to the risk of child sexual abuse. Cole and Woolger (1989) compared adult survivors of incestuous and nonincestuous abuse on attitudes toward their parents and attitudes toward child rearing. Mothers with a history of incestuous abuse scored higher on a scale assessing child indulgence and autonomy promotion, which includes such items as "Most children are toilet-trained by 15 months" and "The earlier a child is weaned from its emotional ties to its parents, the better it will handle its own problems." The authors suggest that mothers with a history of incestuous abuse may have been more parentified in their families of origin, and that this may have affected their ability to make appropriate parenting judgments; such mothers may push their children toward independence too quickly and perhaps abandon their role as protectors prematurely. Cole, Woolger, Power, and Smith (1992) found that incestuously abused mothers were less confident and less emotionally controlled than nonabused control mothers.

Maternal Reactions to Abuse Allegations

Regardless of maternal abuse history, mothers' responses to children's sexual abuse allegations vary considerably. Gomes-Schwartz et al. (1990) described four types of maternal responses to abuse allegations: (1) a decisive, nonambiguous, protective response, with responsibility attributed to the accused; (2) ambivalent loyalties between child and offender, requiring protective services' support to assure adequate child protection; (3) an immobilization response, resulting in a failure to protect the child, but moderate support and no overt blame of the child; and (4) rejection of the child, alignment with the offender, and no child protective action.

Many mothers are decisive, protective, and supportive in response to their children's sexual abuse allegations. However, most studies reveal that some mothers do not support their children's allegations, ranging from 16% (Pierce & Pierce, 1985) to 50% (Tufts New England Medical Center, 1984). Roesler and Wind (1994) found that approximately half of adult sexual abuse survivors who had disclosed their abuse to a parent during their childhood recalled that the parent reacted with anger and/or blame, or simply ignored the situation. In 51% of cases, the abuse continued for at least 1 year following the first disclosure. Sas et al. (1995) found that 16% of their sample felt their mothers did not believe them. Everson, Hunter, Runyon, Edelson, and Coulter (1989) judged 24% of mothers in their sample to be unsupportive of their sexually abused children. Sauzier (1989) reported that 19% of adolescents regretted having disclosed their abuse 18 months later.

In general, the more seriously abuse allegations affect a mother's life style and sense of self, the less likely the mother is to believe the allegations (Elliott & Briere, 1994; Gomes-Schwartz et al., 1990; Lawson & Chaffin, 1992; Sirles & Franke, 1989). Mothers tend to have more difficulty believing allegations against their current partners, particularly when the allegations are made against stepfathers and common-law partners with whom the mothers have either new or intense relationships (Elliott & Briere, 1994; Everson et al., 1989; Faller, 1984; Gomes-Schwartz et al., 1990). Mothers are often faced with the difficult choice between their spouses or their children. Approximately one-fourth of mothers faced with this choice opt to stay with their spouse (Everson et al., 1989; Gomes-Schwartz et al., 1990). In contrast, mothers were often quite supportive when allegations came in the midst of preexisting marital problems or when the spouses had already separated (Faller, 1984; Sirles & Franke, 1989).

Mothers are also less likely to believe their children's allegations when alternative explanations are available (Sirles & Franke, 1989). Young children are perceived as having little sexual knowledge and little motive for making false allegations, and are therefore most often believed by their mothers. As children grow older, mothers are less likely to believe their allegations, particularly when the allegations include very serious forms of abuse or when a child's story indicates that a mother was home when the abuse occurred. Unfortunately, mothers who are not supportive of their children often have children who suffered more episodes of abuse, perhaps because the children were hesitant to disclose the abuse for fear of their mothers' reactions (Elliott & Briere, 1994; Leifer et al., 1993). Mothers also tend to have more difficulty believing their children when their partners have substance use problems or when their partners have also physically abused the children. Apparently, in these circumstances, mothers are more likely to find a reason for the children to lie about the abuse (e.g., retaliation for the physical abuse), or are more accustomed to making excuses for their spouses' inappropriate behavior (Elliott & Briere, 1994). Elliott and Briere (1994) found more recantations among children whose mothers were not supportive.

IMPACT OF SEXUAL ABUSE ON CHILD VICTIMS

In the earlier version of this chapter (Wolfe & Wolfe, 1988), a conceptual model for sexual abuse sequelae was described. The premise behind the model was that children's responses to sexual abuse vary greatly, reflecting individual differences in response to abuse, as well as numerous factors that attenuate or exacerbate sequelae. Some children may present as symptom-free following a sexual abuse experience, whereas others may show serious psychological problems that extend into adulthood. Mediators of impact (abuse variables, child characteristics, family functioning, and community support/stressors) were seen as intertwined with sexual abuse sequelae, evolving across various phases (the abuse itself, the disclosure crisis, and recovery and readjustment phases).

At the time the model was first articulated, very little research was available to confirm its basic premises. However, recent years have seen a great deal of research examining the effects of child sexual abuse and factors thought to mediate abuse-related sequelae. Recent literature reviews suggest three major sets of findings about sexual abuse symptomatology (Kendall-Tackett, Williams, & Finkelhor, 1993; Wolfe & Birt, 1995): (1) Sexually abused children display and report more internalizing and externalizing adjustment problems than their nonabused peers; (2) sexually abused children display a broad range of behavioral and emotional problems, some of which are linked to their sexual abuse experience, while others are linked to familial and environmental circumstances; and (3) two problem areas—Posttraumatic Stress Disorder (PTSD) symptoms and sexuality problems—are disproportionately prevalent among sexually abused children, as compared to their nonabused peers and as compared to appropriate comparison groups (e.g., clinic-referred children). Although sexuality problems are more prevalent among sexually abused children than among children who have experienced other forms of maltreatment, it is unclear whether sexually abused children display more PTSD symptoms than other maltreated children.

Recent evidence supports the Wolfe and Wolfe (1988) model of individual differences in response to sexual abuse. In their review of the literature, Kendall-Tackett et al. (1993) found that 20–50% of children appear to be symptom-free at the time they are assessed. However, at least 30% show clinically significant problems within the first several months following abuse disclosure (Wolfe, Gentile, & Wolfe, 1989). Research has confirmed that abuse, child, family, and community factors all contribute to the type and degree of sequelae documented among child sexual abuse victims (Barnett et al., 1995; Black & DeBlassie, 1993; Caffaro-Ruget, Lang, & van Santen, 1989; Conte & Schuerman, 1987; Elwell & Ephross, 1987; Everson et al., 1989; Herrenkohl, Herrenkohl, Rupert, Egolf, & Lutz, 1995; Livingston, Lawson, & Jones, 1993). Evidence also now documents changing patterns of abuse-related symptoms as children mature and as time since the abuse and time since disclosure passes (Kendall-Tackett et al., 1993).

In this part of the chapter, research on sexual abuse sequelae is reviewed, beginning with a review of research based upon the most commonly used clinical and research tool, the Child Behavior Checklist (CBCL; Achenbach, 1991a). Next, theoretical perspectives and research on PTSD symptoms, other symptoms thought to be related to trauma ("Type II PTSD symptoms"), and sexuality symptoms are reviewed. Abuse-related, child, family, and community factors found to mediate aspects of sexual abuse sequelae are discussed wherever appropriate. The section concludes by examining longitudinal studies of sexual abuse sequelae.

CBCL-Based Research

Research with the CBCL confirms that sexually abused children tend to display relatively high levels of symptoms when compared to normative samples. Not surprisingly, the percentage of cases classified as falling in the clinical range of problems varies, depending upon the sample of sexually abused children. Drawing from a broad sample of children identified by child protective services, Wolfe et al. (1989) found that approximately 30% of victims fell in the clinical range on the broad-band Internalizing, Externalizing, or Social Competence broad-band scales. Other studies based upon clinic referrals have found that approximately 40% of victims fall in the clinical range for at least one of these scales (Friedrich, Urquiza, & Beilke, 1986; Sirles & Smith, 1990). Although sexually abused children tend to display relatively high rates of symptoms as compared to standardization samples, they appear to be *less* symptomatic than other clinical groups on broad-band and narrow-band CBCL scales (Cohen & Mannarino, 1988; Wolfe, 1990a; Wolfe, Michienzi, Sirles, & Evans, 1992). The only narrow-band CBCL scale that differentiates

sexually abused children from nonabused clinic-referred children is the 1991 Sexual Problems scale (Friedrich, Beilke, & Urquiza, 1988a, 1988b). Wolfe et al. (1989) have described a CBCL PTSD scale (described later in this chapter), which discriminates sexually abused, nonabused clinic-referred children, and nonabused standardization sample children (Wolfe et al., 1992).

One of the advantages of the CBCL is that similar versions are available for parents (Achenbach, 1991a), teachers (Achenbach, 1991b), and youths (12–18 years of age; Achenbach, 1991c), thus allowing for cross-informant comparisons. A study by Kiser, Millsap, and Heston (1992) highlights the importance of multiple informants and appropriate comparison groups (e.g., physically abused children) when one is assessing sexual abuse sequelae. Among consecutive admissions to a psychiatric day treatment program for children and youths, sexually abused, physically abused, and physically and sexually abused youths were studied. Mothers and fathers completed the CBCL for these youths, and the young people themselves completed the youth counterpart, the Youth Self-Report (YSR; Achenbach, 1991c). The results were dramatically different, depending on informant and abuse group. Sexually abused patients reported the highest degree of pathology on the YSR, as compared to either the physically abused or the physically and sexually abused groups, with significant differences on the following scales: Internalizing, Depression, Thought Disturbance, Somatic Complaints, and Popularity. For the most part, parental reports on the CBCL did not differentiate sexually abused from physically abused children. Mothers described abused boys as more socially withdrawn and abused girls as more externalizing and less internalizing; fathers of abused boys and girls described them as more hyperactive, more aggressive, and more internalizing, and endorsed more schizoid types of behaviors. These important findings warrant further investigation with a more representative sample.

PTSD Symptoms

The Basic PTSD Model

Wolfe et al. (1989) supported the PTSD formulation of the impact of sexual abuse, based upon three premises: (1) Childhood sexual abuse meets the criteria for "trauma" as defined by the revised third edition of the *Diagnostic and Statistical Manual of Mental Disorders* (DSM-III-R); (2) clinical descriptions of sexually abused children suggest that a substantial number of victims show at least some PTSD symptoms; and (3) preliminary research at that time suggested that individual differences in PTSD symptoms are related to factors known to mediate responses to other forms of trauma (trauma severity, cognitive appraisal of the situation, and social support). The DSM-IV revisions of the diagnostic criteria for PTSD (American Psychiatric Association, 1994) support PTSD as a diagnosis for some child sexual abuse victims. Briefly, these diagnostic criteria include (1) an experience of an event posing serious threat, to which the individual responds with great helplessness, fear, or horror; (2) three sets of symptoms, including reexperiencing aspects of the abuse (e.g., nightmares, intrusive thoughts), avoidance strategies that function as a means of escaping trauma-related stimuli, and persistently increased autonomic arousal; and (3) duration of symptoms for at least 1 month following the traumatic event, and symptoms resulting in clinically meaningful impairment or distress.

The DSM-IV specifically notes that child sexual abuse can be considered traumatic by including in the definition of trauma for children sexual experiences that are inappropriate for their developmental level, even if these do not involve actual injury or violence. The DSM-IV further recognizes that children may manifest their trauma-related symptoms differently from adults. Children's trauma-related dreams may evolve into more general nightmares (e.g., involving monsters, the rescue of others, or threats to themselves or others). Children may not have the sense that they are reliving the past (a common reexperiencing symptom found among adult trauma survivors), but may reexperience the trauma through repeated play. Lessened interest in previously pleasurable events may not be noticed by children, but teachers and parents may note this problem. Children's sense of pessimism about the future may be evidenced by their not including becoming an adult in their view of their future. Children may also display "omen formation," in which they develop a belief that they can foresee negative events. Finally, traumatized children may be particularly prone to develop somatic symptoms, such as headaches and stomachaches.

Broadening the PTSD Perspective

Finkelhor (1990) has criticized the PTSD perspective as too narrow in describing sexual abuse sequelae and as failing to account for cognitive issues resulting from abuse. Along these lines, two recent trauma conceptualizations from Terr (1987) and Janoff-Bulman (1989) provide a basis for expanding the PTSD model to account for other symptoms often noted among sexual abuse victims, such as dissociation, depression and learned helplessness, interpersonal problems, difficulties coping with daily living, and excessive anger and hostility. These problems either have long been recognized as examples of PTSD symptoms (e.g., anger problems may emanate from hyperarousal; dissociation may be an extreme form of avoidance) or have been noted as DSM-defined PTSD-associated symptoms (e.g., depression). However, individual differences related to specific aspects of the trauma have not been fully explored.

Terr (1987) has noted that child sexual abuse differs from other forms of trauma, in that it is often repeated over long periods of time in secret; this requires victims to adapt to their abusive situation via strategies that are either developmentally or psychologically inappropriate or damaging, particularly when these strategies are generalized beyond the abusive situation. Terr includes as examples of these adaptations psychogenic numbing and dissociation, substance use, rage, mistrust and other interpersonal relationship problems, suicidal ideation, and "unremitting sadness." Terr (1987, 1991) has proposed a dual classification for patients suffering from trauma-related disorders: Type I disorders follow exposure to a single traumatic event, whereas Type II disorders result from multiple or long-standing experiences with extreme stress, such as sexual abuse. Although Type I and Type II PTSD patients experience similar symptoms, Type II patients are thought to develop the abnormal coping strategies and psychological symptoms described above, which eventually evolve into these patients' personality style.

Janoff-Bulman (1989) has proposed a cognitive conceptualization for understanding the relationship of trauma to intrusive thoughts and depression. Throughout childhood, a conceptual system develops in regard to expectations about the world and the self. Emotionally healthy individuals develop a system that includes the following concepts: (1) The world is benevolent; (2) the world is meaningful; and (3) the self is worthy. Traumatic events present information contrary to these assumptions; as Piaget's concepts of assimilation and accommodation would suggest, these new experiences require accommodation in the traumatized person's world view. Recurrent, intrusive thoughts emerge, which alternate with denial and avoidance. In support of this theory, Janoff-Bulman

(1989) found that victims differed significantly from nonvictims in terms of attributional style and depression. Silver, Boon, and Stones (1983) have proposed a similar framework for conceptualizing the reexperiencing/avoidance aspects of PTSD. Victims, needing to find meaning in their trauma, experience repetitive, intrusive thoughts about events until they come to some form of understanding or can give "meaning" to what happened to them.

In a more recent study, Kline and Janoff-Bulman (1996) suggest that cognitive adaptations to childhood sexual abuse may result in a deemphasis on the "self." In a study of life narratives, child sexual abuse survivors tended to focus on their past rather than on the present or future, and emphasized others rather than themselves, when compared with a community sample and a sample of adults whose parents had divorced while they were children. Focusing on past events was related to poor adjustment for both child sexual abuse survivors and divorce survivors. Focusing on others was related to poor adjustment only for the sexual abuse group. As descriptions of others (typically their abusers) increased, child sexual abuse survivors referred less to themselves, suggesting that their sense of self was lost or hidden. Others have also conceptualized sexual abuse as affecting the self (Westen, 1994), with the ultimate affect being Dissociative Identity Disorder (previously known as Multiple Personality Disorder; Putnam, 1994), in the form of disruption of memories, distorted sense of personal agency, and depersonalization.

The revised learned helplessness model also addresses alterations in cognitive processes that result from uncontrollable experiences such as sexual abuse. Seligman et al. (1984) established that children attribute causes to events along three dimensions (internal–external, stable–unstable, and global–specific). Although individuals tend to respond to situational factors when making causal attributions, individuals often respond in more ambiguous situations according to their own idiosyncratic style. Peterson et al., (1982) have suggested that a self-enhancing attributional style (similar to the more familiar notion of optimism) is characterized by internal, stable, global attributions about positive events and by external, unstable, specific attributions about negative events; a self-deprecatory attributional style (similar to pessimism) is characterized by external, unstable, specific attributions about positive events and by internal, stable, global attributions about negative events. Those with a self-enhancing attributional style are considered resilient to depression and tend to have positive self-esteem, whereas those with a self-deprecatory attributional style are thought to be depression-prone and tend to have poor self-concepts. Peterson et al. (1982) have further suggested that individual differences in attributional style are both shaped by life events and affect reactions to life events. Children with a positive attributional style are likely to perceive a single sexual abuse experience as caused by external factors that are transient and specific, and are less likely to respond with depressive symptoms or damage to their self-esteem. However, repetitive trauma is likely to cause changes to a child's attributional style, altering his or her belief system so that negative life events are attributed to internal, stable, global causes, and thus making the child more vulnerable to depression and negatively affecting the child's self-esteem.

We and our colleagues (Wolfe & Birt, 1995; Wolfe & Gentile, 1992) have elaborated on these models, using a cognitive–behavioral framework. Whereas severity of abuse (level of sexual intrusiveness, use of coercion/force) is thought to relate to DSM-IV-defined PTSD symptoms, the course of abuse (duration and frequency of abuse, relationship between child and perpetrator) is thought to relate to dysfunctional cognitive processes and dysfunctional coping, as represented by the following: (1) a learned helplessness attributional style and depression; (2) dissociation; (3) excessive emotionality and passivity in coping with day-to-day and trauma-related stressors; and (4) excessive, poorly managed responses to anger-provoking situations.

Research with child sexual abuse victims has documented relatively high rates of PTSD symptoms via a number of assessment strategies, including parent reports (Wells, McCann, Adams, Voris, & Ensign, 1995; Wolfe et al., 1989; Wolfe et al., 1992), child reports (Friedrich, Jaworski, Hexsuchl, & Bengston, 1997; Ligezinska et al., 1995; Pirrelo, 1994; Wolfe et al., 1989; D. A. Wolfe, Sas, & Wekerle, 1994), social worker checklists (Conte & Schuerman, 1987; Mennen & Meadows, 1993), chart reviews (Kiser, Heston, Millsap, & Pruitt, 1991), and professional evaluations (Livingston et al., 1993; McLeer, Deblinger, Atkins, & Ralphe, 1988; McLeer, Deblinger, Henry, & Orvaschel, 1992). In the five studies of PTSD in sexually abused children reviewed by Kendall-Tackett et al. (1993), it was estimated that 53% showed PTSD symptoms. When a sample of ritualistically abused children was removed from the evaluation, it was estimated that 32% of the children showed PTSD symptoms. Recent studies have found that between 49% and 57% of victims meet DSM-III-R or DSM-IV criteria for PTSD (Pirrelo, 1994; D. A. Wolfe et al., 1994). Other studies have demonstrated relatively high levels of PTSD or abuse-related symptoms (e.g., abuse-related fears) in sexually abused children as compared to nonabused peers (Ligezinska et al., 1995; Wells et al., 1995) and to other clinic-referred patients (McLeer et al., 1988; Wolfe et al., 1992). Elliott and Briere (1994) found higher rates of PTSD symptoms among children with confirmed abuse (including those who had and those who had not disclosed) than among children who were referred for evaluation of possible sexual abuse, but for whom abuse was judged not to have happened. However, it is unclear whether sexually abused children display more PTSD symptoms than physically abused children do (Livingston et al., 1993).

Research with adult trauma victims has often linked PTSD symptomatology to trauma severity, familial support, and attributional style (Foy, Sipprelle, Rueger, & Carroll, 1984; Steketee & Foa, 1987). Research with sexually abused children and adult sexual abuse survivors has also found these factors to influence sequelae (Gold, 1986; Silver et al., 1983; Wolfe et al., 1989). Abuse severity (sexual intrusiveness and coercion/force) has been linked with PTSD symptomatology as well, perhaps because this factor has been the most consistently investigated in sexual abuse sequelae research. Severity of sexual abuse has been related to intrusive thoughts, general and abuse-related fears, negative attitudes toward sex, and feelings of vulnerability to further abuse (Wolfe, 1993; Wolfe et al., 1989). Sexually abused children who meet diagnostic criteria for PTSD, as compared to sexually abused children who are not diagnosed as having PTSD, tend to have experienced more severe forms of abuse (Kiser et al., 1991; D. A. Wolfe et al., 1994). Coercion and force have also been related to PTSD symptoms (Basta & Peterson, 1990; Elwell & Ephross, 1987). Children who experience both sexual and physical abuse appear to be at particular risk for PTSD (Kiser et al., 1991).

PTSD is often linked with the availability of social support. Kiser et al. (1991) found that the families of PTSD-positive sexually abused children were more likely than the families of PTSD-negative sexually abused children to be judged by clinicians as dysfunctional. PTSD appears to be more common among incestuously abused children, particularly when the offender was a parental figure (McLeer et al., 1992; Pirrelo, 1994).

Attributional style also appears to be related to PTSD symptoms among sexually abused children. Wolfe and her colleagues (Wolfe, 1993; Wolfe et al., 1989) demonstrated links between general attributional style and abuse-specific attributions and PTSD symptoms following abuse disclosure and at 3- and 9-month follow-ups. Optimism, or positive attributions for positive events, seemed to facilitate resilience, in that PTSD avoidance was less prevalent among more optimistic children. Both general and abuse-specific pessimistic attributions (i.e., internal, global, and specific attributions about negative events; abuse-specific attributions, such as seeing the world as dangerous; feeling vulnerable to further abuse; abuse-related self-blame, guilt, or shame) appear to be associated with PTSD symptoms (Taska & Feiring, 1995; Wolfe et al., 1989).

Some data suggest that younger victims display more PTSD symptoms (Wolfe et al., 1989), particularly sex-related symptomatology, such as sex-related fears. Young children may have more difficulty "making meaning" of their sexual abuse experiences, because of their general lack of knowledge about sexuality (Gordon, Schroeder, & Abrams, 1990).

Type II PTSD Symptoms

Learned Helplessness Attributional Style, Depression, and Suicidal Ideation/Behavior

There is little question that depression and attributional style are related, both in general and clinical populations of children (Joiner & Wagner, 1995) and in sexually abused children (Morrow, 1991; Wolfe et al., 1989; Wolfe, 1990b, 1993). In their meta-analytic review of the relationship between attributional style and childhood depression, Joiner and Wagner (1995) concluded that overall attributional style, attributional style for positive events, and attributional style for negative events were all reliably related to childhood depression, with overall attributional style showing the strongest association with depression. Furthermore, Joiner and Wagner (1995) found evidence that attributional style appears to be more strongly related to depressive symptoms than to other negative affect symptoms (e.g., anxiety) or to behavior problems (e.g., aggression). However, studies have not confirmed a higher predominance of attributional problems among children with a diagnosis of depression than among children who have met criteria for other psychiatric diagnoses. Limited but equivocal research supports the idea that negative life events are related to attributional style and depressive reactions.

It is becoming increasingly clear that a high number of sexually abused children display depressive symptoms. For instance, Koverola, Pound, Heger, and Lytle (1993) found that two-thirds of their clinic-referred sample of latency-age sexually abused children met full criteria for a DSM-III-R diagnosis of Major Depressive Disorder. An additional 10% displayed four of the five diagnostic requirements. Other clinic-based studies have found average scores on depression measures such as the Children's Depression Inventory (CDI; Kovacs, 1983) to fall at or above the 90th percentile (Inderbitzen-Pisaruk, Shawchuck, & Hoier, 1992; Wozencraft, Wagner, & Pellegrin, 1991). A predominance of studies have demonstrated relatively high rates of depressive symptoms among sexually abused children as compared to nonabused, non-clinic-referred children (Cohen & Mannarino, 1988; Inderbitzen-Pisaruk et al., 1992; Ligezinska et al., 1996; Lipovsky, Saunders, & Murphy, 1989; Wolfe, 1993; Wozencraft et al., 1991); however, this finding is not universal (Einbender & Friedrich, 1989). Lanktree, Briere, and Zaidi (1991) found higher rates of depression for clinic-referred sexually abused children than for nonabused clinic-referred children. Even in studies that show relatively high levels of depression as compared to community controls, the average score on measures such as the CDI is often within the average range (Cohen & Mannarino, 1988; Wolfe et al., 1989).

When multidimensional assessment strategies are used in studies involving seriously disturbed clinical populations (psychiatric inpatients, hospitalized substance abusers), depression and suicidal ideation appear to be more prevalent among those with a history of sexual abuse. Using the Diagnostic Interview Schedule for Children (DISC; Costello, Edelbrock, Dukan, & Kalas, 1984), Sansonnet-Hayden, Haley, Marriage, and Fine (1987) found more reports of depression and suicidal ideation/gestures among sexually abused psychiatric inpatients than among nonabused psychiatric inpatients. Edwall, Hoffman, and Harrison (1989), using a clinic-specific semistructured interview, also found greater evidence of suicidal ideation and behavior when sexually abused and nonabused chemically dependent adolescents were compared. Livingston et al. (1993), comparing sexually abused and physically abused clinic-referred children on the DISC, did *not* find group differences on depression; however, they did find other differences, including attentional problems, somatization, ideas of reference, and anxiety.

Wolfe and her colleagues (Wolfe, 1993; Wolfe et al., 1989) also documented a relationship between depression and attributional style among sexually abused children. In addition to the finding that global attributional style was one of the strongest predictors of depression among sexually abused children, sexually abused children were found to be less optimistic and more depressed than nonabused children. Morrow (1991) found a relationship between abuse-specific attributions (e.g., self-blame) and depression and self-esteem. Hazzard, Celano, Gould, Lawry, and Webb (1995) found that children's sense of self-blame and powerlessness regarding their abuse experiences were significantly related to psychiatric evaluations of general adjustment. Three variables were related to children's self-blame regarding their abuse: age (younger children felt more guilty), self-deprecatory general attributional style, and maternal blame of the child. Although Hazzard et al. (1995) found that younger children were more likely to blame themselves for the abuse, other studies have found that older child sexual abuse victims report more depressive symptoms (Birt, 1996; Sas, Hurley, Hatch, Malla, & Dick, 1993).

Several studies support the idea that depressive symptoms are more prevalent among sexually abused children who experience Type II forms of trauma. When abuse-related factors add to prediction of depressive symptoms, duration and frequency of abuse show the strongest relationship to depression. Kiser et al. (1991) and Sas et al. (1993) found that victims of ongoing abuse were more depressed than were victims of a single episode of abuse. Bryant and Range (1996) found that suicidality among college women was related to having experienced sexual abuse along with other forms of maltreatment, as compared to having experienced only one form of abuse or no abuse. Wolfe (1990b) found that severity of abuse was the strongest predictor of PTSD symptoms at disclosure and at a 3-month follow-up. However, no abuse variable predicted PTSD at the 9-month follow-up, in part because many of the PTSD symptoms dissipated over time. In contrast, depression, which had not been predicted by any abuse variable at the initial or 3-month assessments, was predicted at the 9-month assessment by course of abuse.

These findings suggest that PTSD symptoms may be more prominent during the disclosure crisis and may be highly related to the severity of abuse. Depressive symptoms may persist over time for some abused children, particularly those who were abused repeatedly over longer periods of time by someone relatively close to them. Wolfe (1993) found that course of abuse was negatively related to positive attributions about positive events; this suggests that children who have been abused repeatedly, over longer periods of time, by someone emotionally close to them are likely to see positive events in their lives as externally controlled and attributable to specific, unstable causes.

Results from a study by Famularo, Kinscherff, and Fenton (1990) also support Terr's (1987) formulation of sexual abuse sequelae. Using DSM-III PTSD diagnostic criteria, the researchers classified sexually abused children as having either acute PTSD (less than 6 months in duration) or chronic PTSD (more than 6 months in duration). Acute PTSD patients, compared to chronic PTSD patients, showed more difficulties falling asleep, nightmares, hypervigilance, exaggerated startle responses, and generalized anxiety. The chronic PTSD group exhibited a greater prevalence of detachment or estrangement from others, sadness, restricted affect, belief that life would be difficult, and dissociative periods (i.e., depressive types of symptoms). Despite the different patterns of symptoms exhibited by the two groups of children, symptoms evident in the acute PTSD group were also evident in the chronic PTSD group. To support Terr's conceptualization further, children presenting with both acute and chronic PTSD symptoms tended to have histories of repeated traumatization.

Dissociation

Dissociation can be conceptualized as a strategy for coping with overwhelming anxiety in situations of extreme stress (Terr, 1990). Dissociative experiences lie on a continuum from normal everyday dissociative occurrences (e.g., intense thought absorption) to the most extreme form of dissociation, Dissociative Identity Disorder (Ross & Joshi, 1992). The DSM-IV (American Psychiatric Association, 1994) defines the essential feature of dissociative disorders as a disturbance in the typically integrated mental functions of consciousness, identity, memory, and perception. Putnam (1994) has outlined several dissociative dimensions: memory alterations, identity disturbances, passive influence experiences, and trance/absorption phenomena. Memory dysfunctions include deficits in retrieval of information across behavioral states; deficits in autobiographical memory retrieval; difficulties in discerning actual events from events experienced vicariously through dreams, reading, or conversation; and intermittent and disruptive intrusion of traumatic memories into awareness. Disturbances of identity may be manifested as depersonalization and different "personalities," which Putnam (1994) redefines as "narrow ranges of functioning and affect that are best conceptualized as discrete behavioral states" (p. 252). Dissociative patients may feel influenced by forces over which they have little or no control.

Dissociative disorders are closely linked with childhood trauma (Hicks, 1985). Some suspect that children have a greater (or even innate) capacity to dissociate, which dissipates as more effective coping strategies develop. However, when intensely or repeatedly traumatized, young children may use their dissociative capacities to cope, so that dissociative responses are negatively reinforced and therefore maintained as automatic reactions to stressful situations.

Although dissociative tendencies are believed to begin during childhood, most dissociative patients are not diagnosed until they are adults (Putnam, 1985). Dissociative disorders are rarely diagnosed in children, perhaps because of the subtlety of childhood dissociative symptoms (McElroy, 1992) or the ease with which dissociative symptoms can be attributed to other causes. For instance, trance-like behaviors may be misdiagnosed as truancy, conduct problems, or moodiness. Some dissociative symptoms, such as imaginary friends, can be interpreted as normal. Often dissociation goes undiagnosed, either because dissociative symptoms are not evident during assessment or because other diagnoses are given, such as PTSD, depressive disorders, psychotic disorders, or Borderline Personality Disorder (Ogata et al., 1990).

Several studies reveal relatively high rates of parent-reported and child-reported dissociative symptoms among sexually abused children as compared to nonabused, non-clinic-referred children (Birt, DiMito, & Wolfe, 1995; Malinosky-Rummell & Hoier, 1991; Putnam, Helmers, Horowitz, & Trickett, 1995). In contrast, however, Friedrich et al. (in press) found no differences in dissociation between sexually abused and nonabused adolescent psychiatric patients.

Birt et al. (1995) found that children who experienced more serious forms of abuse or more coercion were more likely to report using dissociative coping strategies during their abuse. However, in support of the Type II notion linking dissociation with repetitive abuse, children who

were repeatedly abused displayed more dissociative symptoms on a day-to-day basis. Likewise,
Malinosky-Rummell and Hoier (1991) found that
self-reports and parent reports of dissociative strategies were predicted by the number of sexually
abusive incidents experienced by a child. Friedrich
et al. (1997) also found that both self-reports and
parent reports of dissociation among adolescent
psychiatric patients were positively related to
severity and duration of abuse, as well as to the
victim's age and gender (older girls reported more
dissociative symptoms). In line with the idea that
dissociation is linked to early trauma, Putnam et al.
(1995) found higher levels of dissociation and hypnotizability among those abused at a young age
and those abused by multiple offenders.

Coping Style

"Coping" has generally been defined as "any and
all responses made by an individual who encounters a potentially harmful outcome" (Silver &
Wortman, 1980, p. 281). Generally, coping is
dichotomized into bipolar dimensions, such as
approach versus avoidance or problem-focused
versus emotion-focused coping. No one coping
strategy is effective in all situations, and effective
coping may depend upon selecting the most effective strategies, given the controllability of the
situation. When a stressor is controllable, strategies intended to alter the situation have been associated with lower levels of distress and fewer
negative emotions. However, when a stressor is
uncontrollable, coping strategies that reduce
emotional distress or enable a person to avoid the
stressor appear to be most effective (Band & Weisz,
1988). As noted earlier, children's responses to
abuse situations appear to have more to do with
the children themselves than with anything about
the abuse per se (Love et al., 1990). When confronted with a sexual abuse situation, a child may
perceive the situation as controllable and act to
stop the abuse, either by refusing to participate or
by telling someone about the abuse after the first
episode. However, if the child perceives the situation as uncontrollable, he or she may seek
avenues to reduce distress, such as distancing,
repression, or avoidance. Emotional reactions
such as anger and hostility may be redirected
toward "safer" others, such as peers, siblings, or
nonoffending parents. Once the abuse is disclosed
or terminated, the child may continue to cope with
abuse-related sequelae via avoidant or repressive
strategies. Johnson and Kenkel (1991) found a
significant connection between emotional dis-

tress and two coping strategies among child sexual
abuse victims: wishful thinking and tension reduction (which was defined as responding to stress by
eating, drinking, using drugs, and having sex).
Unfortunately, as is true in much of the coping-
based literature, it is difficult to tell whether high
distress led to use of these strategies, or whether
use of these strategies was partially responsible for
the maintenance of high levels of distress. DiLillo,
Long, and Russell (1994) examined retrospective
reports of childhood coping among survivors of
intra- and extrafamilial sexual abuse. As compared
to extrafamilial victims, intrafamilial victims reported using both more emotion-focused coping
and more problem-focused coping. As in the
Johnson and Kenkel (1991) study, intrafamilial
victims were also more likely to use wishful thinking, as well as self-isolation and self-blame. If it is
assumed that intrafamilial abuse is more stressful
than extrafamilial abuse, this study sheds light on
the chicken–egg question. That is, it appears that
the more stressful the situation, the more likely it
is that victims will employ all forms of coping.

Anger

Anger management problems have historically
been linked to family disruption and discord and
to poor parental child management skills. Anger
problems are also often anecdotally reported by
clinicians working with sexually abused children,
and research has demonstrated relatively high rates
of externalizing behavior problems among such
children as compared to nonclinic control samples. The question thus arises as to whether anger
management problems among sexually abused
children are related to the sexual abuse per se or
to familial factors that occur concomitantly with
sexual abuse, such as family discord and other
forms of maltreatment (e.g., physical and emotional abuse, neglect, or exposure to family violence). We (Birt & Wolfe, 1995) found that parents of sexually abused children reported relatively
high rates of aggressive behaviors. However, in
multiple-regression analyses, it appeared that the
relatively high level of anger found among sexually abused children was more closely related to a
child's perception of family functioning than to
the abuse itself. Nonetheless, abuse-related factors
also contributed to the prediction of various aspects of the anger reported by sexually abused
children. Contrary to the Type II notion that anger
problems may emanate from chronic abuse, the
study found that anger problems may be more
closely linked with Type I symptoms and abuse

severity. Severity of abuse was related to child-reported intensity and duration of physical arousal in response to an anger-provoking situation—symptoms that seem commensurate with the hyperarousal component of PTSD. Sexual abuse victims who also experienced emotional maltreatment reported the highest levels of anger when faced with common childhood stressors. However, sexual abuse victims who also experienced physical abuse were reported by their parents to display the highest levels of aggression.

Sexuality Symptoms

Aside from Freud's early theorizing about sexual development during childhood and adolescence, very little theoretical or empirical research has been devoted to childhood sexuality. Sexual behavior between peers may be more prevalent than the concept of the "latency" stage of sexual development would suggest. Haugaard and Tilley (1988) found that 42% of university students reported having sexual experiences with other children when they were less than 13 years old (the other children being less than 16); however, childhood sexual behavior was generally limited to kissing or exposing of genitals.

The recent upsurge in interest in sexual abuse sequelae has sparked interest in documenting normative levels and types of sexual behavior at various ages. Friedrich, Grambsch, Broughton, Kuiper, and Beilke (1991) established norms for the Child Sexual Behavior Inventory (CSBI; Friedrich, Beilke, & Purcell, n.d.) with a sample of 800 children ages 2 to 12. Although some sexual behaviors were reported relatively frequently (e.g., masturbation), more serious sexual behaviors—such as aggressive sexuality, attempts to engage others in sexual behavior, and behaviors that appeared to be imitations of adult behavior (oral–genital contact, masturbating with objects or inserting objects into genitalia, simulated sexual intercourse)—were rarely reported. Older children were less likely than younger children to display overt sexual behavior. Similar results were found in a Swedish survey of preschool teachers regarding the sexual behavior displayed among their students (Lindblad, Gustafsson, Larsson, & Lundin, 1995). Whereas searching for bodily contact and responding to physical touch were commonly observed "sexual" behaviors, less than 2% of the Swedish sample exhibited more serious forms of sexuality, such as touching an adult's genitals or breasts, using objects to touch their own or another child's genitals or anus, uttering sexual words, masturbating in a manner that either caused pain or was obviously not pleasurable, or engaging in activities that appeared to be imitative of adult sexual activity.

Questions arise as to where to draw the line between normal sexual behavior and sexual behavior that is age-inappropriate, dysfunctional, or coercive. In an attempt to answer this question, Lamb and Coakley (1993) surveyed adults about their sexual play during childhood. Responses to the survey identified five areas of common sexual play: playing "doctor," exposure, experiments in stimulation, kissing games, and fantasy sex play. The more physical the sexual play became, the more likely the respondents were to describe the behavior as abnormal. Perceptions of coercion during sex play were more prevalent among girls who engaged in cross-gender play. Some female respondents described cross-gender involvement that was actually abuse, involving coercion by someone significantly older.

Aside from the traumatic nature of sexual abuse (aspects of abuse that cause fear and overwhelming anxiety), what is it about the sexual aspect of sexual abuse that is harmful to children? Tharinger (1990) has outlined several theoretical perspectives that contribute to the understanding of sexual problems among sexual abuse victims. From a developmental perspective, premature introduction to sexuality may disrupt children's psychosexual development by thrusting them into their phallic stage without prior accomplishment of earlier developmental tasks, which serve as the foundation for understanding and managing the complexity characteristic of interpersonal sexual relationships. Latency-age emphasis on skill building and personal accomplishments may be thwarted by an overwhelming preoccupation with sexuality. Yates (1982) has argued that sexual abuse may prematurely eroticize children, who must then cope with sexual impulses for which they have no appropriate outlet. Eroticized children may confuse sexuality and affection, and may have poor boundaries between acceptable affection and inappropriate sexual overtures. Thus, when eroticized children display sexual behavior, they are likely to be met with punishment and ostracism.

Social learning theorists would suggest that sexually abused children learn their sexual roles and sexual behaviors through the sexually abusive relationship; that is, they learn to use sexuality to gain affection and acceptance, or learn to appease others through sex to avoid other forms of abuse or maltreatment (Tharinger, 1990). Trauma theorists would suggest that sexual trauma may lead children to reenact their sexual experiences through sexual play with either dolls or other children, in an effort to gain mastery over their abuse experience. Likewise, sexually abused children and adolescents may place themselves in vulnerable sexual circumstances, in an unconscious effort to gain mastery over their initial abuse experience (a behavior pattern termed "counterphobic"). Finally, because of the traumatic and exploitative nature of abuse, sexually abused children may develop negative attitudes toward sexuality in general (Tharinger, 1990).

Tharinger (1990), in a literature review, found estimates of sexual problems among sexually abused children ranging from 16% to 41%. In a subsequent review, Kendall-Tackett et al. (1993) concluded that approximately 38% of sexually abused children display sexual behavior problems. Research has demonstrated that parents of sexually abused children report more sexual behaviors, and that such children overtly display more sexual behavior in direct observation situations. Sexually abused children also report more sexual concerns than do several comparison groups: standardization samples and matched community controls (Friedrich et al., 1986, 1992; White, Strom, Santilli, & Halpin, 1986), nonabused clinic-referred children (Friedrich et al., 1988a, 1988b, 1997; Friedrich & Lui, 1985), nonabused hospitalized children (Adams, McClellan, Douglass, McCurry, & Storch, 1995), and physically abused clinic-referred children (Gale et al., 1988; Gomes-Schwartz et al., 1990; Kolko, Moser, & Weldy, 1988).

The high prevalence of sexuality problems among seriously disturbed children and adolescents is surprising, suggesting that sexual problems are often overlooked as a serious issue in pediatric psychiatry. Adams et al. (1995) examined sexual problems among seriously mentally ill children and adolescents treated at a day and residential treatment psychiatric hospital. Of 499 completed chart reviews, 202 patients (40%) exhibited significant sexual problems (the hospital did not specifically specialize or recruit for patients with sexual problems). Three types of sexual problems were identified: (1) hypersexual (overly flirtatious, inappropriate touching); (2) exposing (public masturbation, self-exposing); and (3) victimizing (molestation, incest, rape). Patients with a history of sexual abuse had higher rates of all types of sexual problems than patients without sexual abuse (82% vs. 36%). Patients with exposing and victimizing sexual problems were more likely to have experienced both physical and sexual abuse. In line with the idea that sexually abused children may seek mastery over their sexual experiences by engaging in sexual behavior with peers or by placing themselves in sexually risky situations (counterphobic behavior), females with PTSD were highly represented among the hypersexualized patients.

Sexually abused adolescents are at significant risk for early pregnancy and adolescent prostitution. Contact forms of abuse appear to lead to earlier forays into adolescent sexuality (Wyatt, 1985); more serious forms of abuse appear to lead to earlier consensual sexual intercourse. Two large-scale studies of pregnant and parenting teens found high rates of sexual victimization (61–66%), with particularly high rates of forced sexual intercourse (33–44%; Boyer & Fine, 1991; Gershenson et al., 1989).

Prostitution appears to have its roots in adolescence, with the majority of prostitutes being under age 18 (Fraser, 1985), and the majority of adult prostitutes reporting that they began prostitution as children or adolescents (73%). Most adolescent prostitutes begin soliciting after running away from home (Bagley & Young, 1987), typically in response to sexual, physical, and/or emotional abuse at home. Approximately 60% of prostitutes report a history of childhood sexual abuse, and 70% of prostitutes with a history of childhood sexual abuse feel that their sexual abuse history influenced their entry into prostitution (Bagley & Young, 1987; Silbert & Pines, 1981). Bagley and Young (1987) found that early promiscuity among sexually abused adolescents predicted entry into prostitution. Fifty percent of prostitutes with a sexual abuse history reported having sex as adolescents with at least four males prior to entering prostitution; 29% reported having sex with at least 20 males prior to prostitution.

Longitudinal Studies of Sexual Abuse Sequelae

Most of the published longitudinal studies of sexual abuse sequelae have used global indices of adjustment to assess postabuse adjustment, and have not reported longitudinal changes in PTSD or sexuality symptoms. Kendall-Tackett et al. (1993) reviewed 11 longitudinal studies and concluded that at least 7 studies demonstrated significant abatement of symptoms across time. These studies indicated that 55–65% of sexually abused children showed fewer symptoms at later assessments. A recent study by Oates, O'Toole, Lynch, Stern, and Cooney (1994) similarly found a 2:1 ratio of improvement to deterioration in general adjustment. Despite general improvement in symptoms, between 10% and 33% of sexually abused children showed more symptoms over time, including some children who were symptom-free at the time of the first assessment (Kendall-Tackett et al., 1993; Oates et al., 1994). At an 18-month follow-up, Oates et al. (1994) found that 33% of sexually abused children showed clinical-range depression, 48% displayed significant behavioral problems, and 56% had low self-esteem. One study has reported changes in PTSD across time: Sas et al. (1993) found changes in PTSD symptoms when children were assessed 3 years after participating in criminal proceedings against their offenders. They found that both PTSD symptoms and abuse-related feelings of guilt and self-blame dissipated over time. Children also felt more empowered against the potential for future abuse as time passed.

Several variables appear to exacerbate or attenuate the symptoms displayed by sexually abused children over time. Chronicity of abuse appears to be the only abuse-related variable that consistently relates to duration of symptoms (Famularo et al., 1990; Oates et al., 1994; Wolfe, 1990b). Maternal support appears to be the strongest predictor of symptoms at follow-up points (Everson et al., 1989; Goodman et al., 1992). Oates et al. (1994) found that maternal use of avoidant coping was related to increases in child behavior problems over time. Perhaps mothers who rely on avoidant coping fail to address their children's problem behaviors, and this results in spiraling levels of child difficulties. Sas et al. (1993) found that abuse-related intrusive thoughts, fears, and nightmares at the 3-year follow-up were more prominent among incestuously abused children and among children whose criminal cases resulted in acquittal.

Questions arise as to whether therapy helps children recover from their abuse. When specific symptom areas are assessed and targeted with symptom-specific interventions, therapy appears to result in symptom reduction (Kendall-Tackett et al., 1993). However, being in therapy does not necessarily relate to symptom abatement. Oates et al. (1994) found a positive relationship between depression at the 18-month follow-up and involvement in therapy. Unfortunately, the chicken–egg problem arises again, in that it is difficult to know

whether therapy failed to address depressive symptoms or whether therapy was sought because of persistent depressive symptoms.

Despite evidence of general abatement of symptoms across childhood, there is considerable evidence linking childhood sexual abuse with adult psychological symptomatology. Two recent meta-analyses of studies investigating long-term sequelae of child sexual abuse reveal consistent findings (Jumper, 1995; Neumann, Houskamp, Pollock, & Briere, 1996). A history of childhood sexual abuse is related to a number of individual symptom domains, including anxiety, anger, depression, revictimization, self-mutilation, sexual problems, substance use problems, suicidal ideation/behaviors, impairment of self-concept, interpersonal problems, obsessions and compulsions, dissociation, posttraumatic stress responses, and somatization. The magnitude of the effect of a history of sexual abuse in predicting these symptoms is small to moderate (Neumann et al., 1996), and it is more evident in community and epidemiological studies than in studies of more restricted populations such as college students (Jumper, 1995; Neumann et al., 1996). There appears to be a particularly strong relationship between history of childhood sexual abuse and posttraumatic stress responses and revictimization (Neumann et al., 1996).

BEHAVIORAL ASSESSMENT OF SEXUALLY ABUSED CHILDREN

Inherent in conducting an assessment of sexual abuse sequelae is obtaining accurate information about the sexual abuse experience. Whenever possible, it is wise to solicit historical data and information about the abuse from multiple sources. In most cases, abuse-related information reported by parents, medical personnel, child protective services, and children themselves is consistent and reliable (Kaufman, Jones, Stieglitz, Vitulano, & Mannarino, 1994; McGee, Wolfe, Yuen, Wilson, & Carnochan, 1995). However, Kaufman et al. (1994) found that medical records and parent reports often yielded information about abuse severity and other forms of abuse that was not available in child protective services' files. For example, child protective services' files revealed that 77% of their sample of sexually abused children and adolescents had experienced emotional maltreatment; when medical, parent, and child protective services' records were all surveyed for each case, 98% of cases revealed evidence of emotional maltreatment.

Obtaining Abuse-Related Information from Community Resources

Background information should include the following information: details about all sexual, physical, and emotional maltreatment, as well as history of neglect and exposure to physical violence (Manly, Cicchetti, & Barnett, 1994; Wolfe & Gentile, 1992). Many sexually abused children have complex and chaotic backgrounds that necessitate careful history taking; details about biological parents and stepparents, parental separations, past and current living arrangements, and school placements should all be noted. Details of the disclosure and investigation should also be obtained, along with the legal status of the case regarding prosecution, supervision orders, and foster placement. When one is documenting the various forms of abuse and neglect, the following details are important: types of abusive acts; use of coercion or force; number of perpetrators and relationship of each perpetrator to the victim; time frame for abuse; and estimates of abuse frequency. Specific and detailed questions will yield the most consistent and reliable responses from busy professionals such as caseworkers and police officers, who will in many cases need to comb through agency reports and files to provide specific answers.

The History of Victimization Form (HVF; Wolfe, Gentile, & Bourdeau, 1987) was developed to obtain detailed information from social workers regarding all forms of child maltreatment, and to allow for objective assessment of the severity of various forms of maltreatment. The form has five scales: Sexual Abuse, Physical Abuse, Neglect, Exposure to Family Violence, and Psychological Maltreatment. Each scale contains a Gutman-like checklist of several abusive behaviors, listed in order of escalating severity. Each scale taps issues related to the severity of maltreatment: physical sequelae; relationship of the child to the perpetrator; the emotional closeness between the child and perpetrator; and the time frame, duration, and frequency of the abuse. The Sexual Abuse scale (see Table 12.1 for this portion of the HVF) includes questions about the type and extent of force or coercion used to gain compliance.

The Sexual Abuse scale has undergone two factor analyses, each yielding two factors, Severity of Abuse and Course of Abuse. Course of Abuse includes duration, frequency, and relationship to perpetrator; Severity of Abuse includes type of sexual acts, force or coercion, and number of perpetrators. Duration and frequency appear to relate to relationship to perpetrator, because familial perpetrators have more opportunities to abuse their victims. In a study of the HVF with 48 sexually abused children, Gentile (1988) found that Course of Abuse accounted for 31% of the variance and Severity of Abuse accounted for 34% of the variance. Birt (1996), who studied 62 sexually abused girls, found that Course of Abuse accounted for 20.2% of the variance and Severity of Abuse accounted for 32.4% of the variance.

Investigative Interviewing

Accuracy of Children's Recall

Most researchers agree that children's recall of both stressful and nonstressful events tends to be accurate but incomplete (Goodman, Hirschman, Hepps, & Rudy, 1991; Saywitz, Goodman, Nicholas, & Moan, 1991). As children mature, they typically provide more correct information during free recall (Goodman et al., 1991; Oates & Shrimpton, 1991). However, even children as young as 2 years of age can recall episodes for at least 6 months, and children 3 years of age can provide information about both unique and routine events (Howe & Courage, 1993). Age-related improvements in recall may be attributable to the increasing sophistication of memory retrieval skills. Older children are better than younger children at using retrieval cues and such strategies as rehearsal, monitoring, and spatial categorization (Fivush, 1993). Memory retrieval supports, such as questions or props, can help elicit general as well as event-specific information (Gee & Pipe, 1995; Price & Goodman, 1990). Even young children can accurately recall details about personal experiences over long time periods when provided appropriate cues at recall (Fivush, 1993).

Despite a general consensus that children's free recall is typically accurate, both children's and adults' recollections are subject to distortion—through suggestions by others, through retroactive interference (e.g., memories of a previous abusive situation), through autosuggestion (e.g., previously held beliefs about sexual abuse), or through the confabulation of information to fill memory gaps. There is some evidence that these problems are more prevalent among children (Ceci & Bruck, 1993). Although recent studies have shown that entire events can be implanted and adopted as "real" memories by children (Ceci, Leichtman, & White, in press), Goodman, Bottoms, Shaver, and Qin (1995) have concluded that children are typically remarkably resistant to suggestion follow-

TABLE 12.1. History of Victimization Form (HVF), Sexual Abuse Scale

I. Sexually abusive behaviors:
    1. Invitations for child to engage in sexual behavior.
    2. Exposure of adult genitalia to child.
    3. Child forced to view sexually explicit material.
    4. Child instructed to expose own genitals.
    5. Open-mouthed kissing.
    6. Adult touching of child's clothed body parts with sexual connotation (buttocks, thighs, breasts, genitals).
    7. Adult fondling of child's genitals (under clothing); child instructed to masturbate adult.
    8. Simulated intercourse (adult rubs his/her genitals against child's clothed genital area).
    9. Digital penetration.
    10. Adult oral contact with child's genitals.
    11. Child instructed to have oral contact with adult's genitals.
    12. Vaginal intercourse (include unsuccessful attempts if contact included direct, unclothed contact of adult and child genitals).
    13. Anal intercourse (include unsuccessful attempts if contact included direct, unclothed contact of adult genitals with child's anal area).
    14. Child forced to participate in pornography (photo, film, etc.)
    15. Other (describe): _____

II. Relationship of child to perpetrator:
    1. Stranger
    2. Neighbor, babysitter, acquaintance
    3. Family friend
    4. Relative not living in home
    5. Relative living in home (other than parental figure)
    6. Stepmother
    7. Stepfather
    8. Mother
    9. Father
    10. Foster mother
    11. Foster father
    12. Other: _____

III. Duration and frequency:
    1. Did the abuse occur more than one time? Yes __ No __
    2. If yes, how many times? ____ If exact (or close to exact) number not available, estimate based upon following: Sexual abuse occurred _____ times per (week, month, year) over _____ (weeks, months, years).

IV. Degree of coercion regarding compliance and/or secrecy:
    1. Abuse of authority
    2. Blackmail
    3. Rewards, privileges
    4. Threat of physical coercion or physical harm
    5. Threat to withdraw privileges, affection, etc.
    6. Physical coercion or physical assault
    7. Threats to kill child or someone else special to child
    8. Other: _____

Note. From Wolfe, Gentile, and Bourdeau (1987, pp. 2–4).

ing either neutral or stressful events. Studies suggest that children resist false suggestions that they were undressed, hit, or genitally touched 90–100% of the time. Susceptibility to suggestion appears to occur under fairly specific circumstances (Goodman, Bottoms, et al., 1995): (1) a preschool-age child (3–5 years of age); (2) repeated suggestions from a powerful, intimidating, or authoritative source, such as a parent; (3) suggestions about positive or neutral events rather than about negative events; (4) weak memory about the event or long delay between the event and the recall period; and (5) the child's perception of the plausibility of the suggestion.

Concerns about Children's Suggestibility

Concerns about children's suggestibility during the interview process have focused on two basic issues: types of questions asked (open-ended vs. more specific/leading questions) and the use of props and anatomically correct dolls.

Types of Questions Asked

Although interviewer contamination is minimized when questions are restricted to open-ended questions, younger children tend to reveal more information with more specific and direct forms of questioning (Saywitz et al., 1991). Following open-ended questions with clarifying questions (e.g., "What were you wearing?") and providing prompts for chronological details (e.g., "What happened next?") can enhance the amount of detail provided (White & Edelstein, 1991). It is generally recommended that leading questions be avoided (e.g., asking a child, "What did your daddy do?" prior to the child's indicating that the father did anything to him or her). Coercive or disconfirming interview processes should be avoided (White & Edelstein, 1991). Coercion occurs when a child is pressured to answer in a manner consistent with an interviewer's expectations. Disconfirmation occurs through repeated questioning despite consistent answers from the child; this gives the child the message that his or her responses are unacceptable. Disconfirmation can also occur when a child's answers are followed by questions about the child's understanding of truthfulness (e.g., after a child names an offender, the child may feel intimidated if the interview follows the child's report with a series of questions about whether the child understands the implications of lying).

Use of Dolls and Props

Despite concerns about the potential pitfalls of leading questions, many children do not understand the function of the investigative interview; without specific questions or the availability of anatomically correct dolls or other props, they may reveal very little about specific events, particularly sensitive aspects of events (Goodman, Bottoms, et al., 1995; Saywitz et al., 1991). However, some consider such props to be excitatory, suggestive, and coercive, increasing the probability of incorrect or misleading information (Haugaard & Rap-

pucci, 1988; Yates & Terr, 1988). Anatomically correct dolls are also criticized for promoting evaluator error and misuse (Everson & Boat, 1994) and as not meeting the *Kelley–Frye* scientific criteria for admissibility of evidence in legal proceedings (Fisher & Whiting, in press).[1]

Despite concerns about anatomically correct dolls, the vast majority (92%) of mental health professionals who conduct child abuse investigations use them (Conte, Sorenson, Fogarty, & Rosa, 1991). Close to half (46.4%) of those who used the dolls felt they were useful in most evaluations, and another 28.4% felt the dolls were useful on a case-by-case basis (Oberlander, 1995). Everson and Boat (1994) identified seven functional uses of anatomically correct dolls, based on 20 sets of guidelines for investigative interviews: (1) comforter (child-oriented "play" material helps relax a child); (2) icebreaker (dolls help introduce the sexuality topic in a nonleading, nonthreatening manner); (3) anatomical model (dolls assist in assessing the child's knowledge and terms for sexual parts and functions); (4) demonstration aid (the child can "show" rather than "tell"); (5) memory stimulus (dolls may stimulate memories and spontaneous disclosures of abuse-related details, such as the offender's clothing or body characteristics); (6) diagnostic screen (dolls may prompt the child's disclosure of sexual activity); and (7) diagnostic test (sexual doll play can be interpreted as indicative of abuse; however, no guideline advocates using the dolls in this fashion and most caution against this, although critics of anatomically correct dolls often refer to this issue).

Recent research evidence has quelled many of the concerns about anatomically correct dolls. Dolls do not elicit unfounded reports of sexual behavior or elicit excessive sexual behavior in free-play conditions with nonabused children; they are also useful in discriminating abused from nonabused children in terms of both sexual abuse disclosures and sexual play with the dolls (Everson & Boat, 1990; Goodman & Aman, 1990; White et al., 1986). Dolls are adequately proportional to the human body (Bays, 1990) and have been accepted as appropriate props in some legal jurisdictions (*Kehinde v. Commonwealth*, 1986; *People v. Rich*, 1987).

Saywitz et al. (1991) found dolls to be particularly useful in eliciting sensitive information over and beyond the information provided from simple recall requests, particularly when paired with direct questioning about touching (e.g., pointing to the doll's body parts, including nongenital and genital parts, and asking "Did he touch you there?"). Children 5- and 7-years of age, who had experienced either a genital exam or a scoliosis exam, were asked to recall as much as possible about their visit to the doctor either 1 week or 1 month later. Most of the children in the genital examination condition did not report either vaginal or anal touching during the free-recall condition. When the children were asked to show and tell what happened, using anatomically correct dolls and other props, the children provided approximately twice as much correct information; however, most children continued to leave out information about genital touching. Error rate increased when the dolls and props were added, but none of the errors involved demonstrations of sexually explicit behaviors. Interestingly, children were equally likely to report anal touch during both the free-recall and the doll/prop demonstration conditions (11%), but were less likely to show vaginal contact during the doll/prop demonstration condition than during the free-recall condition (17% vs. 22%). Apparently some children are more likely to reveal sensitive information in free recall than with the dolls/props, whereas others are more likely to reveal such information with dolls/props than in free recall. Several children who had talked about vaginal and/or anal touch during the free-recall phase did not demonstrate those behaviors during the doll/prop demonstration. Other children who had not reported vaginal touch during the free-recall phase demonstrated vaginal touch during the doll/prop demonstration phase; three children who had not reported anal touch during the free-recall phase demonstrated anal touch during the doll/prop demonstration phase.

One of the most interesting aspects of this study was the effect of pairing direct questioning with the doll/prop demonstration. Direct questioning involved 70 yes–no questions, 21 of which were misleading. With the direct questioning, 86% of the children in the genital exam condition reported vaginal touch. However, three children (approximately 8%) in the scoliosis exam condition falsely reported genital or anal touching. Upon further questioning, two of the three children gave no further details about the touching, but one child reported that the touch had tickled and that the doctor had used a long stick; 21% of the children in the genital examination incorrectly reported that the doctor had tapped their spines.

The use of anatomically correct dolls in interviews appears to increase the probability of disclosure among children being evaluated for possible sexual abuse. Leventhal, Hamilton, Rekedal, Tebano-Micci, and Eyster (1989) examined disclosure rates of 60 children under age 7 who were first interviewed without the dolls and then with the dolls. Children were three times more likely to provide a detailed description of sexual abuse and twice as likely to name a suspected perpetrator during the interviews with the dolls. Bybee and Mowbray (1993), in a retrospective analysis of investigative material concerning day care abuse, found that young children (less than 5 years of age) were more likely to make credible, explicit disclosures when interviewed with anatomically correct dolls. Whereas only 30% of those interviewed without the dolls disclosed abuse, 90% made disclosures with the dolls. For those children more than 5 years of age, 58% made disclosures when interviewed with the dolls, whereas 21% of those interviewed without the dolls made disclosures.

The use of anatomically correct dolls with young children (ages 3–4) remains quite controversial. One of the primary reasons for using anatomically correct dolls is to give young children with limited verbal skills a communication tool. However, DeLoache and Marzolf (1995) found that children under 3½ years of age had difficulty using dolls to represent themselves. In fact, young children provided more correct information in direct recall without the dolls than they did when asked to demonstrate the event with dolls. Several studies indicate that the use of anatomically correct dolls with 3-year-olds does not facilitate their ability to respond to questions about medical examinations or doctors' visits (Goodman & Aman, 1990; Ornstein, Follmer, & Gordon, 1995), and may actually increase the probability of their committing errors (Bruck, Ceci, Francoeur, & Renick, 1995; Goodman, Quas, et al., 1995). In contrast, Goodman, Quas, et al. (1995) found that when information about genital touching during a medical procedure was examined separately from other exam-related details, all age groups (3- to 4-year-olds, 5-year-olds, and 7-year-olds) showed a significant increase in correct information during doll use as compared to the free-recall situation. Improvements were particularly pronounced among the 3- to 4-year-olds; 18% of these children reported genital contact during free recall, while 71% reported genital contact during the doll demonstration task.

Guidelines for Investigative Interviewing

Given the widespread but controversial use of anatomically correct dolls, as well as other questions and concerns about conducting investigative interviews with children, various authors and societies have published guidelines for conducting such interviews. Everson and Boat (1994) identified 20 different sets of guidelines established between 1984 and 1991. Although the guidelines vary as to breadth of coverage, they are fairly consistent, with no glaring differences. The most recently established guidelines were published by Lamb (1994), who reported the proceedings from an international meeting of 22 scholars concerned with child sexual abuse investigations. Overall, the group concluded that children's recall of events can be extremely informative and accurate if the interview is free of manipulation. Six recommendations were made for eliciting the most accurate information from children:

1. Interviews should occur as soon after the event as possible.
2. Multiple interviews should be discouraged, particularly if these are conducted by different interviewers.
3. Leading questions should be avoided whenever possible; however, use of leading questions should not automatically be considered reason to disregard a child's recollection of events.
4. With older children, open-ended questions are the best format for eliciting free narrative accounts.
5. For children age 6 or under, who might have difficulty responding to open-ended questions, direct, developmentally sensitive questions can be used with great care to avoid contamination.
6. Every interview should be videotaped, to avoid multiple interviewing and to create a record of how the interview was conducted.

The American Professional Society on the Abuse of Children (APSAC; 1990) guidelines are more specific and address the use of dolls and props, the role of psychological testing, and questions about the presence of others during the process of the child's interview. The APSAC guidelines recommend that tools should be available to assist the child in communicating; these may include drawings, toys, dollhouses, tools, and puppets. The preferred practice for anatomical dolls is to have them available for identification of body parts, clarification of previous statements, or demonstrations by nonverbal or low-verbal children after there has been indication of abuse activity. However, though unusual behavior with dolls may be worthy of note in an evaluation report, such behavior without a direct report of sexual abuse should not be considered conclusive evidence of abuse. Psychological testing may be helpful in understanding the child's developmental and intellectual status and will help in documenting the child's adjustment problems, but, again, such testing should not be used to confirm or disconfirm abuse. The APSAC guidelines suggest that interviews with the child be conducted individually, except when the child refuses to separate from a parent. When a parent is present in the interview, care should be taken that the parent is not in a physical or psychological position to influence the child. Although a joint session with a nonaccused caretaker or a suspected offender may be helpful in evaluating the quality of this person's relationship with the child, such sessions should only be conducted if (1) there is no concern about further trauma to the child; (2) the child is not asked to review the allegations in the presence of the accused; and (3) the child's reaction to the accused during the interview is not used to confirm or disconfirm abuse.

It is important that dolls, like any other assessment tool, be used appropriately. Boat and Everson (1996), who reviewed videotapes of 97 investigative interviews conducted by child protection workers using anatomically correct dolls, documented several categories of questionable practices. In several instances, a doll was initially introduced unclothed, which was potentially suggestive. Some interviewers named the dolls or sex parts for a child. Several interviewers encouraged a child to play with the dolls or told the child to "pretend," giving the impression that the child was free to engage in fantasy-type activities with the dolls. Interviewers sometimes assumed that a child's clothing was off prior to the child's so stating. The most common questionable practices were (1) premature introduction of the dolls and (2) reliance on a doll demonstration in lieu of a verbal report from a child, which often gave the impression that doll demonstrations were preferred over verbal descriptions. In 2 of 14 cases where a child was allowed to play with the dolls, suggestive questions were asked (e.g., when a child put a doll's penis in her mouth, the interviewer said, "Whose wienie have you had in your mouth?").

Recording and Interpreting Investigative Interviews

Not only must the interview be conducted appropriately, but interview data must be coded and interpreted in a reliable, valid manner. Levy, Markovic, Kalinowski, Ahart, and Torres (1995) developed the Anatomical Doll Questionnaire to record and compare interviewers' and observers' observations and perceptions of children's statements and behaviors during interviews featuring anatomically correct dolls. Questions are presented in a dichotomous format and address five areas: (1) statements indicating abusive acts (e.g., "Stated penis placed in mouth"); (2) doll demonstrations following verbal report (e.g., "Demonstrated oral sex by placing doll's penis in another doll's mouth"); (3) child's affect and emotions (e.g., "Child cried during interview"); (4) interview quality (e.g., "Child elaborated on responses regarding abuse"); and (5) other general observations (e.g., "Manipulated doll's genitals before sex abuse discussed"). Interrater agreement was high for children's verbal reports of abusive acts; however, interrater agreement varied considerably for children's demonstrations of sexual behavior. Some demonstrations yielded perfect agreement (demonstrating oral sex with two anatomically correct dolls), while others yielded very poor interrater agreement (touching doll's breast). Interrater agreement for child affective expressions was quite poor.

Wood, Orsak, Murphy, and Cross (1996) describe the use of another investigative interview coding system, the Child Abuse Interview Interaction Coding System (CAIICS; Wood, 1990). Videotapes of investigative interviews are coded in 10-second consecutive intervals for interviewer and child behavior. Interviewer categories include types of questions asked (open-ended, closed, choice, complex), types of support (attention/encouragement, non-disclosure-related praise, disclosure-related praise, physical reassurance, empathy) and type of information provided (instruction about use of props/dolls, instruction on safety skills, explanation of purpose of interview, non-abuse-related information, abuse-related information, commands). Child categories include attention/on-task behaviors (attentive/on-task, attentive/off-task, inattentive/on-task, inattentive/off-task), observed emotion (relaxed/neutral, angry, anxious, sad/hurt, guilt/shame, excited/happy), and type of disclosure (yes–no answer, one- or two-word answer, detailed abuse disclosure, acts out/draws abuse-related events, non-abuse-related narrative, says "I don't know"/"I don't remember"). The CAIICS yielded high interrater reliability for both child and interviewer behaviors, with kappa coefficients ranging from .87 (information provided) to .98 (type of disclosure). Comparisons between the CAIICS and judgments of credibility made by experienced child protection and law enforcement professionals found that child behaviors, but not interviewer behaviors, related to judgments of credibility.

Credibility judgments are often based upon the opinions of those who conduct the investigative interview, not unlike the process described by Wood et al. (1996). However, some efforts have been made to make the process of evaluating credibility more reliable, valid, and criterion-based. Probably the most widely recognized method of assessing disclosure credibility is the Statement Validity Analysis (SVA; Raskin & Yuille, 1989). The SVA consists of three interrelated components: (1) Interview Guidelines, designed to elicit an unstructured narrative of the abuse allegations; (2) Criteria-Based Content Analysis (CBCA), a content analysis of material elicited by the Interview Guidelines, designed to establish whether transcribed statements meet 19 criteria for whether the described event was actually experienced; and (3) a Validity Checklist, which takes into account the specific investigatory context, including the psychological characteristics of the child witness and the adequacy of the interview. The CBCA is the core feature of the SVA, and has thus far been the only component subjected to empirical tests. The 19 CBCA criteria were derived from the Undeutsch hypothesis (Steller, 1989) that the characteristics of statements reflecting actual experience differ from those of statements reflecting imagined experiences. The 19 criteria include general characteristics (e.g., logical structure, quantity of details), specific contents (e.g., contextual embedding, reproduction of conversation), peculiarities of the events (e.g., unusual details, superfluous details), and motivation-related contents (e.g., spontaneous corrections, admitting lack of memory).

Several studies have applied the CBCA to children's real and imagined narratives (Steller, 1989; Yuille, 1988) and to transcripts from confirmed and doubtful cases of child sexual abuse (Esplin, Boychuk, & Raskin, 1988). Esplin et al. (1988) compared 20 confirmed cases of sexual abuse with 20 unconfirmed cases of abuse, and found that 16 of the 19 criteria significantly differentiated the groups. Unfortunately, CBCA interrater agreement is poor (Anson, Golding, & Gully, 1993), probably because of poorly defined criteria and no behavioral anchors.

Assessing Psychological Adjustment

When one is assessing the impact of sexual abuse on a child, a two-pronged approach is recommended (Wolfe & Gentile, 1992): assessment of global adjustment and assessment of abuse-specific symptoms. Global adjustment measures document the magnitude of child adjustment problems, which can be compared to those of nonabused children and other clinic populations. Abuse-specific assessment strategies are needed to tap PTSD and sexuality problems, as well as some of the unique symptom areas related to Type II sexual abuse trauma, such as dissociation and abuse-related attributions. This portion of the chapter focuses on abuse-specific assessment strategies, with a particular emphasis on assessment of PTSD, sexuality, and other trauma-related symptoms, and as well as on family mediators of sexual abuse sequelae. However, research studies have utilized a number of assessment instruments that are beyond the scope of this chapter. The Crime Victims Research and Treatment Center has recently developed a computer program, the Child Abuse and Neglect Database Instrument System (Letourneau & Saunders, 1996), which reviews the majority of assessment instruments used in research with abused and neglected children and adult abuse survivors.

PTSD Symptoms

Compared to other childhood disorders, PTSD has received relatively little attention, particularly in the area of assessment. Nonetheless, increased interest in sexual abuse sequelae, along with concerns about the effects of other forms of trauma (e.g., witnessing domestic violence and living in war-torn areas of the world), have led to considerable advances in PTSD assessment. PTSD assessment strategies include child self-report, parent report, and professional evaluation. Like other psychological symptoms, PTSD can be considered along a continuum of symptomatology and can also be considered a diagnostic entity.

Children's Impact of Traumatic Events Scale—Revised

The Children's Impact of Traumatic Events Scale—Revised (CITES-R; Wolfe & Gentile, 1991) provides a structured format for interviewing children about their perceptions and attributions concerning their sexual abuse. The questionnaire contains 78 statements such as "I try not to think about what happened," to which the child can respond "very true," "somewhat true," or "not true." The original 54 CITES items were based upon three models of sexual abuse sequelae: Finkelhor and Browne's (1985) traumagenic factors model (betrayal, guilt, sexualization, and stig-

matization), the PTSD model (intrusive thoughts and avoidance; Horowitz, Wilner, & Alvarez, 1979), and the eroticization model (Yates, 1982). Wolfe, Gentile, Michienzi, Sas, & Wolfe (1991) found evidence of both convergent and discriminant validity for the original 54-item form. Convergent validity of the CITES was supported by (1) significant correlations between the CITES PTSD scales and other PTSD measures (Sexual Abuse Fear Evaluation, CBCL PTSD scale); and (2) significant correlations between the CITES attributional scales and the Children's Attributional Style Questionnaire (also known as the KASTAN; Kaslow, Rehm, & Siegel, 1984). Correlations among the CITES Eroticization scale, the CBCL Sexual Problems scale, and the CSBI (see "Sexuality Problems," below) were all nonsignificant. Divergent validity was demonstrated by significantly higher correlations among the PTSD scales and among the attributional scales, as compared to correlations between scales that were supposed to measure different constructs (e.g., correlations between the PTSD scales and the CSBI and CBCL Sexual Problems scale, the PTSD scales and the KASTAN, etc.)

The CITES-R is based upon a factor analysis and a multimethod–multitrait analysis of the original 54-item CITES (Wolfe et al., 1991), plus DSM-III-R's refinements in the diagnosis of PTSD with children. The CITES-R yields 11 scale scores, which fall into four areas: PTSD (Intrusive Thoughts, Avoidance, Hyperarousal, and Sexual Anxiety); Attributional Issues (Self-Blame/Guilt, Empowerment, Personal Vulnerability, and Dangerous World); Social Reactions (Negative Reactions from Others, Social Support); and Eroticization. The CITES-R includes items that address all three symptom areas required for a DSM-IV-based diagnosis (reexperiencing, avoidance, hyperarousal). Because the CITES-R was designed specifically for use with sexually abused children, direct comparisons to nonabused children are not possible. Nevertheless, we (Wolfe & Birt, 1994) developed a version of the CITES-R (the Altered Form, or CITES-AF) that is appropriate for use with nonabused children. For the CITES-AF, children respond to questions regarding an event they report as having been stressful. A study is currently underway comparing the CITES-R for sexually abused children and the CITES-AF for nonabused children.

A recent psychometric analysis of the CITES-R with 350 subjects revealed two primary factors: PTSD Symptoms and Mediating Variables (attributions, social reactions). Eroticization items fell into the Mediating Variables factor, in part because of strong correlations between Eroticization and the Self-Blame/Guilt items. Despite the two-factor structure, the 11-scale structure was retained for conceptual and reliability purposes, with some minor revisions to the content of several of the scales. The PTSD broad-band structure was maintained, with narrow-band scale scores for Intrusive Thoughts, Avoidance, Hyperarousal, and Sexual Arousal. However, the broad-band dimensions for Social Reactions and Attributional Issues were not maintained because of poor reliability. Narrow-band scales within these dimensions produced higher, respectable alpha values.

Table 12.2 lists the 11 CITES-R narrow-band scales, with sample items and alpha values for each scale. With the exception of the Personal Vulnerability scale (alpha = .68), alpha values for all of the CITES-R scales are respectable, ranging from .71 (Avoidance) to .89 (Negative Reactions from Others). The broad-band PTSD scale is quite reliable, with an alpha value of .91.

Table 12.3 provides the CITES-R interscale correlations, along with correlations with the CBCL PTSD, Sexual Problems, Internalizing, and Externalizing scales. In general, there is strong overlay among the PTSD and Eroticization scales and the Social Support, Negative Reactions from Others, and Attributional Issues scales, reinforcing the idea that these factors mediate the severity of abuse-related symptoms. The CBCL PTSD scale correlated significantly with each of the CITES-R PTSD scales (r's ranged from .19 to .28). As well, the CBCL Sexual Problems scale correlated significantly with the CITES-R Eroticization scale (r = .17). Supporting the discriminant validity of the PTSD and Eroticization scales, the CBCL Sexual Problems scale did not correlate significantly with any of the CITES-R PTSD scales, and the CBCL PTSD scale did not correlate significantly with the CITES-R Eroticization scale.

Concurrent validity for the CITES-R Attributional Issues scales is supported by a study by Taska and Feiring (1995). Strong relationships were found among all four CITES-R Attributional Issues scales and measures of general, as well as abuse-related, shame. In fact, both shame-related measures were more strongly related to CITES-R Attributional Issues than either depression (CDI scores) or self-esteem.

Trauma Symptom Checklist for Children

The Trauma Symptom Checklist for Children (TSCC; Briere, 1996) is a child version of the

TABLE 12.2. Children's Impact of Traumatic Events Scale—Revised (CITES-R) Narrow-Band Scales, Alpha Values, and Representative Items

Intrusive Thoughts (7 items; alpha = .86)
  7. I have trouble falling asleep because pictures or thoughts of what happened keep popping into my head.
  11. I have dreams or nightmares about what happened.
  23. Pictures of what happened often pop into my mind.

Avoidance (7 items; alpha value = .71)
  3. I try to stay away from things that remind me of what happened.
  32. I try not to think about what happened.
  58. When I'm reminded of what happened, I try to think of something else.

Hyperarousal (6 items; alpha = .73)
  6. I often feel irritable for no reason at all.
  12. I have difficulty concentrating because I often think about what happened.
  18. I am easily startled or surprised.

Sexual Anxiety (5 items; alpha = .86)
  44. I get frightened when I think about sex.
  69. I hope I never have to think about sex again.
  75. I wish there was no such thing as sex.

Social Support (6 items; alpha = .81)
  27. Most people who know what happened are nice and understanding.
  33. Most people believe me when I talk about what happened.
  63. I have someone with whom I feel comfortable talking about the sexual abuse.

Negative Reactions from Others (9 items; alpha = .89)
  4. People who know what happened think bad thoughts about me.
  14. After people learned about what happened, they no longer wanted to spend time with me.
  26. Some kids at school make fun of me because of what happened.

Self Blame/Guilt (13 items; alpha = .84)
  22. This happened to me because I acted in a way that caused it to happen.
  28. I feel I have caused trouble to my family.
  40. I feel guilty about what happened.

Empowerment (6 items; alpha = .83)
  53. If something like this happens again, I think I know what to do to stop it.
  61. I know enough about sexual abuse now that I can protect myself in the future.
  68. My family will protect me from being sexually abused again.

Personal Vulnerability (5 items; alpha = .68)
  15. Something like this might happen to me again.

(continued)

TABLE 12.2. (*continued*)

43. This happened to me because I also have bad luck.
62. I often worry that I will be sexually abused again.

Dangerous World (4 items; alpha = .82)
17. People often take advantage of children.
19. These kinds of things happen to a lot of children.
38. There are many people who do bad things to children.

Eroticization (5 items; alpha = .85)
34. I think about sex even when I don't want to.
46. I have more sexual feelings than my friends.
65. I like to look at naked people in books or on TV.

Note. From Wolfe and Gentile (1991).

---

adult Trauma Symptom Inventory. The 54-item instrument yields six conceptually based sub-scales (Anger, Anxiety, Depression, Dissociation [Overt and Fantasy sub-subscales], Posttraumatic Stress, and Sexual Concerns). Unlike the CITES-R, the TSCC does not orient respondents to their abuse experience and is appropriate for children who have not disclosed abuse, as well as those who have. Reliability and validity studies of the TSCC are based upon a large normative sample of 3,008 nonabused and 508 sexually abused children and adolescents, as well as several stud-ies conducted with smaller samples at various research and clinical centers. Alpha values based upon the normative sample ranged from .58 (Dissociation–Fantasy, three items; however, the combination of Dissociation–Fantasy and Dissociation–Overt results in a respectable alpha value of .83) to .89 (Anger). All TSCC scale scores correlated significantly with each other, as well as with the YSR and parent versions of the CBCL and with a number of scales conceptually related to the individual scales of the TSCC, including the CDI, the Child Dissociative Checklist (CDC), the CITES-R, and the CSBI. All TSCC scale scores were higher among those who had experienced sexual penetration during the abuse. The Anxiety, Posttraumatic Stress, and Sexual Concerns scales were sensitive in detect-ing the effects of a PTSD-specific intervention program.

Elliott and Briere (1994) compared TSCC scores for several groups of children who were referred for evaluation of potential sexual abuse (credible disclosure, partially credible disclosure, recanted disclosure with evidence of abuse, no disclosure with evidence of abuse, and child judged not to have been abused). Significant differences were found on all TSCC scales be-tween children who had disclosed abuse and children who were evaluated for abuse but for whom abuse was not confirmed. TSCC scores were highest for those children who disclosed abuse (credible and partially credible); lowest for children who were believed to have been abused, but either had not disclosed or had re-canted their allegations; and moderate for chil-dren who were judged not to have been abused. Elliott and Briere (1994) suggest that children who do not want to disclose their abuse may at-tempt to hide or repress expression of abuse-related symptoms.

Sexual Abuse Fear Evaluation

Although the DSM-IV criteria emphasize avoid-ance as a PTSD symptom, children often display abuse-related fears prior to developing avoidance strategies. Wolfe (1990b) found that very few chil-dren endorsed avoidance symptoms following disclosure or at the 3-month follow-up; avoidance symptoms were endorsed more often at the 9-month follow-up, suggesting that avoidance symptoms develop over time. In order to assess abuse-related fears, Wolfe and Wolfe (1986) developed the Sexual Abuse Fear Evaluation (SAFE), a 27-item scale embedded into the 80-item Fear Survey Schedule for Children–Revised (FSSC-R; Ollendick, 1983). As on the FSSC-R, children respond to each fear with a 3-point rating ("none," "some," or "a lot"). Factor analysis of the SAFE (Wolfe, Gentile, & Klink, 1988), with a sample of 171 school children and 62 sexually abused children, revealed two factors: Sex-Associated Fears (11 items; alpha = .80) and Interpersonal Discomfort (13 items; alpha = .81). The Sex-Associated Fears scale contains such items as "thinking about sex" and "taking my clothes off." The Interpersonal Discomfort scale includes such items as "people not believing me" and "going to court to talk to a judge." Both sexu-ally abused and nonabused children endorsed SAFE items at relatively high rates (with 11 items, the average Sex-Associated Fear score was 16 for nonabused children and 18 for abused children; with 13 items, the average Interpersonal Discom-fort score was 27 for both sexually abused and nonabused children). Though abused and non-abused children differed only slightly on the Sex-Associated Fears scale, the difference was significant.

TABLE 12.3. Intercorrelations among CITES-R Scales and the CBCL PTSD, Sexual Problems, Internalizing, and Externalizing Scales

CITES-R scales	(1) Intrusive Thoughts	(2) Avoidance	(3) Hyperarousal	(4) Sexual Anxiety	(5) Social Support	(6) Negative Reactions	(7) Self-Blame
1.							
2.	.40**						
3.	.72**	.46**					
4.	.47**	.32**	.29**				
5.	−.02	.40**	−.01	.03			
6.	.39**	.05	.31**	.28**	−.60**		
7.	.37**	−.09	.26**	.36**	−.59**	.79**	
8.	−.11	.31**	−.07	.07	.64**	−.47**	−.47**
9.	.06	.43**	.10	−.10	.61**	−.40**	−.43**
10.	.40**	−.08	.27**	.27**	.44**	.56**	.60**
11.	.37**	−.16*	.25**	.36**	−.56**	.71**	.79**

*$p < .01$. **$p < .001$.

CBCL PTSD Scale

The CBCL (Achenbach, 1991a) was not developed as an assessment instrument specifically for sexually abused children and has not been validated on a sample of children known to have had a sexual abuse experience. Furthermore, because traumatized children were not a specific subsample involved in the validation of the CBCL, factor analyses have not yielded a PTSD type of scale. Nonetheless, examination of CBCL items reveals many PTSD items, which are spread across several Internalizing and Externalizing narrowband scales. Perhaps this explains why the profiles of sexually abused children often show general elevations, but no one broad-band or narrow-band scale has been shown to characterize this population, with the exception of the Sexual Problems scale (Wolfe et al., 1992). In an effort to use the CBCL to document PTSD symptoms via parent report, Wolfe et al. (1989) selected 20 CBCL items that reflected PTSD criteria as defined in the DSM-III-R. Compared to the standardization sample, parents of sexually abused children endorsed PTSD items five times more frequently.

Table 12.4 presents the results of comparisons of individual CBCL items across a sample of 350 sexually abused children and adolescents, 209 nonabused clinic-referred children and adolescents, and the pre-1991 CBCL standardization sample ($n = 1,431$). Nineteen of the 20 CBCL PTSD scale items were endorsed significantly more often for sexually abused children than for the standardization sample (the somatization item "vomiting" did not significantly differentiate the two groups). Thirteen of the 20 items were endorsed significantly more often for the sexually abused sample than for the nonabused clinic-referred sample. Another 22 items differentiated sexually abused children and adolescents from both the standardization sample and the clinic-referred sample. On the basis of these group distinctions and current DSM-IV PTSD diagnostic criteria, several of the original items were deleted from the scale and others were added, resulting in a 23-item scale (alpha for sexual abuse sample = .89), reflecting the three primary symptom domains of PTSD: Reexperiencing ("obsessive thoughts," "daydreams," "nightmares," "confused," "cries a lot," "worries," "self-conscious"); Fears and Avoidance ("clings to adults," "fears animals, situations/places," "fearful/anxious," "secretive," "withdrawn," "nervous, high-strung," "fears doing something bad," "fears going to school"); and Hyperarousal ("argues a lot," "can't concentrate," "stomachaches," "irritable," "moody," "trouble sleeping," "can't sit still," and "impulsive"). The intent of the CBCL PTSD scale is to serve as an adjunct to the regular scoring procedures for the Behavior Problem CBCL form.

Professional and Parent Evaluation and PTSD Diagnosis

Parent report and professional evaluation of PTSD symptoms are particularly important when one is considering the effects of trauma on a very

TABLE 12.3. (*continued*)

(8) Empowerment	(9) Dangerous World	(10) Personal Vulnerability	(11) Eroticization	CBCL PTSD	CBCL Sex. Probs.	CBCL Int.	CBCL Ext.
	.06	.40**	.37**	.28**	.05	.26**	.19*
	.43**	−.08	−.16*	.17*	.05	.13	.21**
	.10	.27**	.25**	.28**	.08	.29**	.21**
	−.10	.27**	.36**	.20*	.03	.16*	.13
	.61**	−.44**	−.56**	.14	.08	.09	.10
	−.40**	.56**	.71**	.18*	.20**	.20*	.26**
	.43**	.60**	.79**	.22**	.20**	.24**	.25**
	.50**	.46**	−.43**	.11	.15*	.08	.11
.50**		−.22**	−.50**	.17*	.02	.18*	.10
−.46**			.59**	.24**	.12	.22**	.24**
−.43**				.10	.43**	.11	.20*

young child, since young children often cannot express the cognitive and emotional states required for DSM-IV diagnoses. Scheerenga, Zeanah, Drell, and Larrieu (1995) noted that eight of the DSM-IV criteria require verbal descriptions from patients regarding their experiences and internal states, and that only 10 of the 19 DSM-IV criteria could be rated by parents of infants and young children with any degree of confidence. Scheerenga et al. (1995) attempted to apply DSM-IV criteria to published reports of children who had experienced trauma (*n* = 20). None of the children met the DSM-IV criteria, primarily because it was difficult to code items that required assessment of a child's response to the traumatic event, avoidance-type symptoms, and symptoms of hyperarousal. However, reexperiencing symptoms were present in 19 of the 20 cases. Scheerenga (1995) developed an alternative 23-item set of PTSD criteria for use with infants and young children, based upon the symptoms described in the published cases of traumatized infants and young children. The 23 items were then used to assess PTSD in 12 unpublished cases of infant trauma; the same cases were also assessed according to DSM-IV criteria. Evaluations using the 23-item alternate criteria yielded moderate interrater agreement (median kappa per item = .83); however, the DSM-IV criteria yielded relatively poor interrater agreement (median kappa per item = .50). Infants and young children who were exposed to extreme trauma were much more likely to receive a diagnosis of PTSD with the new 23-item criteria (8.3 cases

per 12) than with the DSM-IV criteria (1.5 cases per 12). For the new set of diagnostic criteria, the requirement of fear, helplessness, or horror, or the alternative for children of disorganized, agitated behavior, was dropped. The reexperiencing criteria were changed to include the following items: posttraumatic play, play reenactment, recurrent recollections, nightmares, flashback/dissociative episodes, and distress upon exposure to reminders of the trauma. The avoidance criteria were changed to include constriction of play, social withdrawal, restricted range of affect, and loss of developmental skills. The hyperarousal criteria was changed to include night terrors, sleep disturbance, and nighttime awakening, each occurring in the absence of nightmares. Other hyperarousal symptoms included concentration problems and exaggerated startle response. A new diagnostic area was added, new fears and aggression, which included the following: new aggression, new separation anxiety, new fears related to toileting, new fears of darkness, and other new fears.

Other studies have utilized either questionnaire data or information from interviews to document PTSD symptoms and provide DSM-based diagnoses. D. A. Wolfe et al. (1994) used CITES PTSD items to diagnose PTSD according to DSM-III-R criteria, by requiring a minimum of one reexperiencing symptom, three avoidance symptoms, and two arousal items. Diagnoses based upon the CITES items were related to abuse-related fears, anxiety, depression, and feelings of guilt and self-blame. McLeer et al. (1992) devel-

TABLE 12.4. CBCL-PTSD Scale Development: CBCL Item Comparisons among Sexually Abused, Nonabused Clinic-Referred, and Standardization Samples

CBCL items[a]	1. Sexually abused group (n = 350)	2. Clinic-referred group (n = 209)	3. Standardization group (n = 1431)	Group differences
Original CBCL PTSD scale items				
3. Argues a lot	1.23 (.70)	.24 (.55)	.78 (.71)	1 > 2 > 3
8. Can't concentrate	.93 (.77)	.33 (.64)	.37 (.57)	1 > 2 > 3
9. Obsessive thoughts	.62 (.75)	.24 (.49)	.36 (.63)	1 > 2 > 3
11. Clings to adults	.72 (.76)	.29 (.57)	.18 (.46)	1 > 2 > 3
29. Fears certain animals, situations, or places	.52 (.73)	.12 (.41)	.28 (.51)	1 > 3 > 2
34. Feels persecuted[b]	.52 (.68)	.58 (.71)	.09 (.31)	2 > 1 > 3
45. Nervous, high-strung	.789 (.742)	.531 (.707)	.266 (.516)	1 > 2 > 3
47. Nightmares	.62 (.67)	.61 (.71)	.17 (.39)	1 & 2 > 3
50. Fearful/anxious	.47 (.65)	.23 (.50)	.14 (.38)	1 > 2 > 3
52. Feels too guilty	.44 (.65)	.44 (.66)	.06 (.25)	1 & 2 > 3
56b. Headaches[b]	.55 (.69)	.40 (.63)	.17 (.42)	1 & 2 > 3
56c. Nausea[b]	.39 (.63)	.13 (.38)	.05 (.42)	1 > 2 & 3
56f. Stomachaches	.56 (.69)	.20 (.49)	.10 (.32)	1 > 2 & 3
56g. Vomiting[b]	.13 (.40)	.67 (.80)	.02 (.16)	2 > 1 & 3
69. Secretive	.89 (.32)	.27 (.76)	.43 (.14)	1 > 2 & 3
86. Irritable	.99 (.71)	.89 (.78)	.23 (.46)	1 > 3; 2 > 3
87. Moody	.88 (.74)	.69 (.78)	.23 (.46)	1 > 2 > 3
100. Trouble sleeping[b]	.44 (.66)	.85 (.78)	.08 (.29)	2 > 1 > 3
103. Unhappy, sad, depressed[b]	.72 (.67)	.73 (.79)	.10 (.31)	1 & 2 > 3
111. Withdrawn	.41 (.62)	.61 (.79)	.06 (.25)	2 > 1 > 3
Other items significantly higher in sexually abused than in standardization and clinic-referred samples				
1. Acts too young for age	.61 (.72)	.30 (.66)	.30 (.54)	1 > 2 & 3
10. Can't sit still, restless[c]	.75 (.74)	.44 (.73)	.37 (.63)	1 > 2 & 3
12. Complains of loneliness	.597 (.69)	.215 (.54)	.214 (.46)	1 > 2 & 3
13. Confused; seems in a fog[c]	.50 (.65)	.16 (.47)	.07 (.28)	1 > 2 & 3
14. Cries a lot[c]	.58 (.70)	.30 (.61)	.11 (.34)	1 > 2 > 3

(continued)

TABLE 12.4. (*continued*)

16. Cruelty to animals	.47 (.63)	.23 (.53)	.11 (.32)	1 > 2 & 3
17. Daydreams[c]	.74 (.74)	.07 (.35)	.32 (.53)	1 > 3 > 2
19. Demands attention	.97 (.71)	.25 (.56)	.38 (.62)	1 > 2 & 3
22. Disobedient at home	.88 (.67)	.21 (.52)	.34 (.49)	1 > 2 & 3
23. Disobedient at school	.50 (.64)	.16 (.46)	.16 (.39)	1 > 2 & 3
25. Poor peer relations	.55 (.63)	.13 (.43)	.12 (.35)	1 > 2 & 3
26. Not guilty after misbehavior	.62 (.75)	.23 (.55)	.21 (.45)	1 > 2 & 3
27. Jealous	.86 (.72)	.24 (.54)	.40 (.60)	1 > 3 > 2
30. Fears going to school[c]	.24 (.52)	.06 (.31)	.03 (.18)	1 > 2 & 3
31. Fears doing something bad[c]	.39 (.60)	.18 (.53)	.17 (.40)	1 > 2 & 3
38. Teased a lot	.80 (.78)	.38 (.60)	.40 (.62)	1 > 2 & 3
41. Impulsive[c]	.83 (.71)	.56 (.74)	.34 (.53)	1 > 2 > 3
44. Bites fingernails	.71 (.82)	.49 (.72)	.39 (.64)	1 > 2 & 3
61. Poor school work	.60 (.75)	.37 (.62)	.14 (.39)	1 > 2 > 3
71. Self-conscious[c]	.93 (.72)	.67 (.74)	.51 (.63)	1 > 2 & 3
112. Worries[b]	.79 (.71)	.46 (.71)	.26 (.48)	1 > 2 > 3

Note. Overall multivariate analysis of covariance, with age and sex as covariates, significant at .001 level; univariate tests significant for all items at .001 level; post hoc *F* statistics significant at .05 level.
[a]The CBCL items are from Achenbach (1991a, pp. 3–4). Copyright 1991 by Thomas M. Achenbach. Reprinted by permission.
[b]Original items on CBCL PTSD scale that have now been deleted from scale.
[c]CBCL items not on the original CBCL PTSD scale that have been added to the scale, based upon group discrimination and DSM-IV PTSD criteria.

oped a PTSD checklist for use after a structured interview, using DSM-III-R criteria.

Feelings and Emotions Experienced during Sexual Abuse Questionnaire

The DSM-IV PTSD criteria include the stipulation that the individual experienced intense fear, helplessness, or horror during the traumatic event. The Feelings and Emotions Experienced during Sexual Abuse (FEEDSA) questionnaire (Wolfe & Birt, 1993) was developed to assess children's emotional reactions to their sexual abuse experience. The inventory consists of 54 items that reflect negative emotions (e.g., anger, terror), perception that the situation was uncontrollable (e.g., "like I had no control," "like I had to do it"), and dissociation during the event (e.g., "like I disappeared," "like I left my body"). The format is similar to the State portion of the State–Trait Anxiety Scale for Children (Spielberger, 1973), with the response options "none," "some," and "a lot." Factor analysis of an earlier 78-item version of the scale, with 62 girls (Birt, 1996), revealed two subscales: Trauma (48 items; alpha = .95) and Dissociation (6 items; alpha = .80). Items depicting positive reactions to the abuse and control over the abuse situation were rarely endorsed; these were deleted from the item pool, resulting in the present 54-item measure. Birt et al. (1995) found that high FEEDSA Trauma scores predicted dissociation during the abuse.

Sexuality Problems

Childhood sexuality is difficult to assess for two primary reasons (Wolfe & Gentile, 1992): (1) Sexual behavior is generally private and not readily reported by children, and (2) norms for child sexual behavior are not well established. At this point, there are three primary assessment strategies for assessing sexuality with sexually abused children: the CSBI, the Eroticization scale of the CITES-R, and the CBCL Sexual Problems subscale.

Child Sexual Behavior Inventory

The CSBI (see Table 12.5; Friedrich et al., n.d.) is a 35-item, parent report measure designed to assess such child sexual behaviors as self-stimulation, sexual aggression, gender role discrepancies, and personal boundary violations. The CSBI, appropriate for children aged 2–12 years, is rated along a 4-point scale for the previous 6-month period. Factor analyses support a single scale, accounting for 40–53% of the variance in normative and clinical samples. Alpha values for the normative and clinical samples are .82 and .93, respectively. Four-week test–retest reliability for the normative sample was .85. In the normative sample, younger children were rated as displaying more sexual behaviors than older children (Friedrich et al., 1991). Another study found that 26 of the 35 items were endorsed significantly more often for sexually abused children than for the normative sample (Friedrich et al., 1992). The CSBI discriminates sexually abused from nonabused children more reliably than the CBCL Sexual Problems scale, and is more strongly related to sexual abuse characteristics (including type of abuse, number of perpetrators, and use of force). A recent study of a small sample of sexually abused and nonabused inpatient boys, with staff members completing a 43-item version of the CSBI, found modest support for the discriminant validity of the scale ($p = .06$; Wherry, Jolly, Feldman, Adam, & Manjanatha, 1995).

CBCL-Sexual Problems Subscale

The CBCL Sexual Problems subscale consists of six items, which are scored for children ages 4 to 11. The Sexual Problems items contribute to the overall count for the Total Behavior Problems scale, but are not considered as part of either the Internalizing or Externalizing broad-band scores. The six items were endorsed relatively infrequently in the normative sample. Thus, Achenbach (1991a) cautions that the T-scores that are provided should be interpreted in general terms (i.e., scores should be described as falling in the low, moderate, or high range). The items include "acts like opposite sex," "plays with sex parts in public," "plays with sex parts too much," "sexual problems," "wishes to be opposite sex," and "thinks about sex too much." One-week test–retest reliability for the CBCL Sexual Problems scale is .83. Interparent agreement on the scale is poor (.50 for girls and .54 for boys). Alpha values for the Sexual Problems scale are also poor (.56 for boys and .54 for girls), probably because of low endorsement of these items.

CITES-R Eroticization Scale

The CITES-R has a factor-derived Eroticization scale, which consists of four items designed to assess children's sense of heightened sexuality. These items are "I sometimes have sexual feelings when I see people kiss on TV," "I like to look at naked people in books or on TV," "I think about sex even when I don't want to," and "I have more sexual feelings than my friends." Wolfe et al. (1991) failed to find significant correlations between the original CITES Eroticization scale and either the CSBI or the pre-1991 CBCL Sexual Problems subscale (the scale was changed significantly with the 1991 CBCL restandardization). However, more recent psychometric analyses reveal a small but significant correlation between the Eroticization scale and the CBCL Sexual Problems scale (see Table 12.3).

Art and Play Assessments of Sexuality

Less formal assessment strategies (drawings, play observations) have identified sexual behaviors that differentiate sexually abused children from their nonabused peers. Yates, Beutler, and Crago (1985) noted that incest victims tended either to exaggerate or to minimize sexual features in their drawings. Hibbard, Roghmann, and Hoeckelman (1987) found that sexually abused children were more likely to include genital features in their drawings; however, even among sexual abuse victims, the rate of genital features is relatively low (Hibbard & Hartman, 1990). As noted earlier, sexually abused children are more likely to dem-

TABLE 12.5. Child Sexual Behavior Inventory (CSBI) Items and Endorsement Percentages for the Normative Sample (*n* = 880) and a Sexually Abused Sample (*n* = 276)

	Endorsement percentages	
Item	Normative sample	Sexually abused sample
1. Dresses like opposite sex	5.8	6.8
2. Wants to be opposite sex*	4.9	10.2
3. Touches sex parts in public*	19.7	21.8
4. Masturbates with hand*	15.3	28.6
5. Scratches crotch	52.2	45.1
6. Touches breasts	30.7	30.6
7. Masturbates with objects*	0.8	11.2
8. Touches others' sex parts*	6.0	25.7
9. Imitates intercourse*	1.1	14.1
10. Puts mouth on sex parts*	0.1	8.2
11. Touches sex parts at home*	45.8	42.2
12. Uses sexual words*	8.8	30.6
13. Pretends to be opposite sex	13.0	14.1
14. Sexual sounds*	1.4	13.1
15. Asks to engage in sex acts*	0.4	11.6
16. Rubs body against people*	6.7	22.3
17. Inserts objects in vagina/anus*	0.9	11.2
18. Tries to look at people undressing*	28.5	33.5
19. Imitates sexual behavior with dolls*	3.2	17.5
20. Shows sex parts to adults*	16.0	18.0
21. Looks at nude pictures*	15.4	18.4
22. Talks about sexual acts*	5.7	31.6
23. Kisses nonfamily adults	36.2	39.3
24. Undresses in front of others	41.2	42.7
25. Sits with crotch exposed	36.4	36.0
26. Kisses nonfamily children	33.9	29.6
27. Talks flirtatiously*	10.6	15.0
28. Undresses other people*	2.6	18.0
29. Asks to watch explicit TV*	2.7	15.0
30. French kisses*	2.5	13.1
31. Hugs strange adults*	7.3	28.1
32. Shows sex parts to children*	8.1	24.8
33. Overly aggressive; overly passive*	10.4	35.4
34. Interested in the opposite sex*	23.0	33.5
35. Uses opposite-sex toys	53.9	29.1

Note. From Friedrich et al. (1992, p. 307). Copyright 1992 by the American Psychological Association. Reprinted by permission.
*$p < .05$.

onstrate sexual behaviors with anatomically correct dolls (White et al., 1986). However, Everson and Boat (1990) found that nonabused children are also likely to show some level of sexual play with the dolls, with 18% of 5-year-olds displaying intercourse positioning (though not actual intercourse). Friedrich and Lui (1985) reported that sexually abused children demonstrated more interpersonal boundary and sexual behavior problems than did nonabused outpatient referrals during initial interviews by outpatient therapists.

Other Trauma-Related Symptoms: Dissociative Symptoms and Attributational Style

Child Dissociative Checklist

The CDC (Putnam, 1990; see Table 12.6) is a 20-item parent report checklist developed to assess dissociative experiences for children and adolescents aged 6–15 years. Parents report dissociative symptoms displayed by their child over the past 12 months, with the response options "very true," "somewhat or sometimes true," and "not true." Several dissociative symptoms are assessed:

imaginary friends, different identities, moodiness, forgetfulness, thought absorption, and "spaciness." The scale yields one score, with an alpha value of .91 (Putnam, Helmers, & Trickett, 1993), and 1-year test–retest reliability of .84 for sexually abused children and .79 for controls (Putnam, 1990). The CDC discriminates among children with Dissociative Identity Disorder, children with other dissociative disorders, and normal controls. The CDC also discriminates sexually abused from nonabused girls (Putnam et al., 1993).

A child report version of the CDC has been developed (Birt, Lehman, Wolfe, & DiMito, 1992; see Table 12.6). Though it is closely tied to the parent report form, there are some changes. To simplify the questions for children, some CDC items were divided into two or more items. Ten items were added to assess some of the more subtle dissociative experiences, such as derealization

TABLE 12.6. Child Dissociative Checklist (CDC): Parent Report and Child Report Versions

Parent Report Version[a]	Child Report Version[b]
1. Child does not remember or denies traumatic or painful experiences that are known to have occurred.	27. I know I have had very scary, painful, or traumatic experiences, but I cannot remember some things about them.
2. Child goes into a daze or trance-like state at times or often appears "spaced out." Teachers may report that he or she "daydreams" frequently in school.	8. I daydream at school when I should be doing my schoolwork. 15. I sometimes feel "spacey" or in a daze. 24. Teachers say I "daydream" frequently at school. 43. I sometimes enjoy my daydreaming more than what is really going on around me. 28. Others have said I appear to be in a daze or "spaced out."
3. Child shows rapid changes in personality. He or she may go from being shy to being outgoing, from feminine to masculine, from timid to aggressive.	3. I can go quickly from being shy to being outgoing. 5. I can go quickly from feeling fearful to being aggressive. 6. I can go from acting like a boy to acting like a girl.
4. Child is unusually forgetful or confused about things that he or she should know, e.g., may forget the names of friends, teachers, or other important people, loses possessions, or gets lost easily.	4. I forget the names of friends, teachers, or other important people. 18. I lose my things. 34. I get lost easily.
5. Child has a very poor sense of time. He or she loses track of time, may think that it is morning when it is actually afternoon, gets confused about what day it is, or becomes confused about when something happened.	5. I become confused about when things happened. 16. I become confused about what day it is. 22. I may think it is morning, when it is really afternoon.
6. Child shows marked day-to-day or even hour-to-hour variations in his or her skills, knowledge, food preferences, athletic abilities, e.g., changes in handwriting, memory for previously learned information, such as multiplication tables, spelling, use of tools or artistic ability.	10. My handwriting changes from day to day or even hour to hour. 19. From day to day or even hour to hour, my ability to do things like spell words or do multiplication tables changes.
7. Child shows rapid regression in age level of behavior, e.g., a twelve-year-old starts to use baby-talk, sucks thumb, or draws like a four-year-old.	32. I act like I am younger than I am.
8. Child has a difficult time learning from experience, e.g., explanations, normal discipline or punishment do not change his or her behavior.	26. I make the same mistakes over and over again, even though I am corrected or punished for them.

(continued)

TABLE 12.6. (*continued*)

9. Child continues to lie or deny misbehavior even when the evidence is obvious.

7. Others have said they knew I did something wrong, but I didn't remember doing it.

10. Child refers to him or herself in the third person (e.g., as she or her) when talking about self, or at times insists on being called by a different name. He or she may also claim that things he or she did actually happened to another person.

2. At times, I want to be called by names different than my own.

12. People have told me I have done things that I believe someone else did.

11. Child has rapidly changing physical complaints such as a headache or upset stomach. For example, he or she may complain of a headache one minute and seem to forget all about it the next.

23. I get headaches or stomachaches which come and go quickly.

12. Child is unusually sexually precocious and may attempt age-inappropriate sexual behavior with other children or adults.

14. I act in a sexual way toward other children or adults.

13. Child suffers from unexplained injuries or may even deliberately injure self at times.

9. I have had injuries that I could not explain.

21. I have tried to hurt myself on purpose.

14. Child reports hearing voices that talk to him or her. The voices may be friendly or angry and may come from "imaginary companions" or sound like the voices of parents, friends, or teachers.

13. I have heard voices that sounded like of my parents, teachers, or friends.

15. Child has a vivid imaginary companion or companions. Child may insist that the imaginary companion is responsible for things that he or she has done.

1. I have one or more imaginary companions who have done things that others thought I did.

31. I have heard voices from imaginary friends talking to me.

16. Child has intense outbursts of anger, often without apparent cause and may display unusual physical strength during these episodes.

11. When I get angry, I can become very strong.

17. Child sleepwalks frequently.

30. People have told me I walk in my sleep

18. Child has unusual nighttime experiences, e.g., may report seeing "ghosts" or that things happen at night that he or she can't account for (e.g., broken toys, unexplained injuries).

20. Things have happened during the night that I can't explain, like getting hurt or breaking toys.

33. I have seen "ghosts" during the night.

19. Child frequently talks to himself or herself, may use a different voice or argue with self at times.

17. I talk or argue with myself at times and use a different voice.

20. Child has two or more distinct and separate personalities that take control over the child's behavior.

25. At times I feel like I have two or more people inside me that take control over my actions.

Note. New items on the child version that are not represented on the adult form are as follows:
Extreme thought absorption:
    35. Sometimes I realize that my mind is blank, such that I'm not thinking about anything at all.
    42. When I watch television it feels like I'm there with everyone on TV and I'm not really where I am.
    37. When I daydream, it feels more real that what is really going on around me.
Derealization:
    36. Sometimes it feels like my body is not really me and I'm just looking out from inside it.
    38. Sometimes I look around me and it feels like nothing is real.
Dissociative coping:
    39. I like to pretend that I'm different than I really am.
    40. Whenever anything really upsets me, I go off into a daydream.
    41. I like to pretend that my family and friends are different people.
[a]The items in this column are from Putnam (1990, pp. 1–2). Reprinted by permission of the author.
[b]The items in this column (and in the "Note." footnote) are from Birt, Lehman, Wolfe, and DiMito (1992, pp. 1–3).

(feeling that parts of one's external world are unreal) and depersonalization (feeling that parts of oneself are unreal). As with the parent report form, responses are made on a 3-point scale. Birt (1996) reported significant correlations between the parent and child report forms of the CDC (.43 between the two forms for commonly shared items; .34 between the parent report form and the new child report items).

Children's Attributional Style Questionnaire

The KASTAN (Kaslow et al., 1984), is the most widely researched attributional measure for children, is a 48-item questionnaire that assesses a child's tendency to attribute positive events to internal, global, and stable factors and negative events to external, specific, and unstable factors. Each item depicts either a fortunate or an unfortunate event, for which the child selects one of two possible causes. A self-enhancing attributional style is reflected by the difference between the number of internal, stable, and global attributions given for fortunate events, and the number of internal, stable, and global attributions given for unfortunate events. The scale is appropriate for children aged 7–17 years.

Seligman et al. (1984) reported moderate test–retest reliability for the KASTAN over a 6-month period for a sample of 96 elementary school children (fortunate events = .71; unfortunate events = .66). The KASTAN correlates significantly with the CDI in samples of elementary school children (Kaslow et al., 1984; Seligman et al., 1984). Wolfe et al. (1989) found that KASTAN scores predicted several indices of adjustment among sexually abused children, including scores on the CDI, the State–Trait Anxiety Inventory for Children, the CBCL Social Competence scale, and the original CITES Betrayal and Guilt subscales. Taska and Feiring (1995) found that both depression and self-concept were related to KASTAN attributional style in their sample of 83 sexually abused girls.

CITES-R Attributional Issues Scales

In accordance with the revised learned helplessness theory, the CITES-R has four scales that assess abuse-related attributions: Self Blame/Guilt (internal negative), Dangerous World (global negative), Personal Vulnerability (stable negative), and Empowerment (unstable negative). The CITES-R Attributional Issues scales are based upon a factor analysis of a previous version of

the CITES, with some new items added for some of the shorter scales. Previous analyses with the CITES Attributional Issues scales (Wolfe et al., 1989) found that higher stable negative scores (i.e., belief that abuse was caused by stable factors; now divided into the Personal Vulnerability and Empowerment scales) were related to the CBCL Social Competence scale and the CITES Intrusive Thoughts scale. Taska and Feining (1995) found a significant relationship between CITES-R Attributional Issues and CITES-R Avoidance. Birt (1996) found a significant relationship between depression and CITES-R Personal Vulnerability.

Mediators of Sequelae: Family Relations and Social Support

Four areas of family functioning appear to be important mediators of sexual abuse sequelae: caregiver reactions to the abuse, caregiver mental health, warmth of parent–child interactions, and ability to adapt to the changes and stressors resulting from the sexual abuse disclosure.

Caregiver Reactions and Psychological Adjustment

Parent Impact Questionnaire. Researchers who have assessed caregiver reactions to abuse disclosures have typically utilized questionnaires designed specifically for the study; thus, there are no well-established measures to tap this issue. For our research and clinical practice, we developed the Parent Impact Questionnaire (Wolfe, 1988). This questionnaire is typically completed in an interview with the parent, and all response options are objectified through checklists or Likert-type ratings. The Parent Impact Questionnaire has four sections: a brief account of the family-related problems that the parent experienced during childhood and as an adult; the parent's personal history of sexual abuse as a child; the impact of the disclosure on the parent and family; and the parent's beliefs about the child's disclosure, attributions of blame for the abuse, and attitudes regarding community reactions to the abuse disclosure. Impact of disclosure for the parent is assessed via the Impact of Event Scale (IES; Horowitz et al., 1979; see below). Impact of disclosure on the family is assessed via a catalogue of various stressful life events that may accompany abuse disclosures, including arrests of family members; children being taken to shelters; strain on relationships with their children, spouse, extended family, and friends; and involvement with social and mental health services, police, and judicial officials.

Impact of Event Scale. The IES contains 15 items that relate to intrusive thoughts and avoidance regarding a traumatic event. Respondents are oriented to a specific traumatic event and rate the frequency of symptoms along a 4-point scale from "not at all" to "rarely," "sometimes," and "often." Thus, the IES is appropriate for individuals who have identified a traumatic event, but is not suitable for comparisons with nontraumatized controls. Split-half reliability of the IES is .86, and alpha values are .78 for the Intrusive Thoughts scale and .82 for the Avoidance scale. Test–retest reliability for the total scale is .87; it is .80 for the Intrusive Thoughts scale and .79 for the Avoidance scale. Kelly (1990) compared IES scores from mothers and fathers of extrafamilially sexually abused children who either were or were not ritualistically abused. Although the two groups did not differ on either of the two scales, mothers reported more intrusive thoughts than fathers. The Intrusive Thoughts scale was significantly related to the SCL-90-R Global Severity Index.

Parental Reaction to Incest Disclosure Scale. The Parental Reaction to Abuse Disclosure Scale (PRIDS; Everson et al., 1989) is used to document parental reactions and support following disclosure of intrafamilial sexual abuse. Professionals rate three issues along a continuum from +5 ("most supportive") to –5 ("least supportive"), based upon interviews with family members and reports from agency staff members involved with the family: emotional support (e.g., "committed to child and provides meaningful support" to "is threatening or hostile; has abandoned the child psychologically"), belief of the child (e.g., "makes clear, public statement of belief" to "totally denies abuse occurred") and action toward the perpetrator (e.g., "actively demonstrates disapproval of perpetrator's abusive behavior" to "chooses perpetrator over child at child's expense"). Interrater agreement is quite high (.95). In Everson et al.'s (1989) sample of 88 families, 44% of mothers were classified as "supportive" (+3 or greater), 32% as "ambivalent" (+2 to –2), and 24% as "unsupportive" (at or below –3). Maternal support of the PRIDS was significantly related to child distress and psychological adjustment, accounting for more variance than any abuse-related variable. Interestingly, supportive mothers and their children were similar in their reports of child behavioral and emotional adjustment. However, CBCL scores from ambivalent and unsupportive mothers did not correspond to information obtained in clinical interviews with their children.

CITES-R Social Reactions Scales. The CITES-R has two factor-derived Social Reactions scales: Negative Reactions from Others and Social Support. The Negative Reactions from Others scale taps children's perception that others did not believe their disclosure, perception of blame for the abuse or disclosure, and recognition of broken social ties following the disclosure. The Social Support scale taps children's perception that others did believe their disclosure, that they had someone with whom they could discuss their abuse, that family members treated them well following their disclosure, and that professionals and others protected them from further abuse.

Symptom Checklist 90 — Revised. The SCL-90-R (Derogatis, 1977) is a 90-item self-report inventory that assesses nine dimensions of symptomatology: Somatization, Obsessive–Compulsive, Interpersonal Sensitivity, Depression, Anxiety, Hostility, Phobic Anxiety, Paranoid Ideation, and Psychoticism. The inventory also yields three global indices of distress (Global Severity Index, Positive Symptom Total, and Positive Symptom Distress Index). The first of these combines information on numbers of symptoms and intensity of distress, and is considered to be the best single indicator of distress. Each item consists of a symptom, followed by ratings along a 5-point scale ranging from "not at all" to "extremely." Alpha values for nine symptom dimensions range from .77 to .90, and test–retest reliability ranges from .78 to .90. Validity studies demonstrate that the SCL-90-R is sensitive to change and correlates with other well-known measures of psychological functioning such as the MMPI. A briefer, 54-item version of the SCL-90-R is available, the Brief Symptom Inventory (Derogatis & Spencer, 1982).

Kelly (1990) found relatively high SCL-90-R Global Severity Index scores for mothers and fathers of extrafamilially abused children as compared to parents of nonabused children, with 42% of the parents of abused children falling at or above the 90th percentile, or within the clinical range defined by Derogatis (1977). The following scales showed the highest elevations: Depression, Interpersonal Sensitivity, Hostility, Paranoia, and Anxiety. Parents of children who had been ritualistically abused by an extrafamilial perpetrator showed the highest Global Severity Index scores, with 65% falling within the clinical range of symptomatology, as compared to 40% of parents whose children were nonritualistically abused outside the family. Barnett et al. (1995) found a significant correlation between parental symptomatology on the Brief Symptom Inventory and child internalizing symptoms on the CBCL for a sample of sexually abused children and their parents.

Family Interactional Patterns and Adaptability

Family Adaptability and Cohesion Evaluation Scale II. There are a number of self-report family assessment devices available for assessing the families of sexually abused victims. For our research, we have chosen the Family Adaptability and Cohesion Evaluation Scale II (FACES II; Olson, Bell, & Portner, 1982) to assess family functioning, primarily because it assesses two family dimensions we consider important to a child's recovery from abuse experiences: adaptability and cohesion. The FACES II is the result of several factor-analytic studies and was derived from the family system circumplex model of dysfunctional family processes. The FACES II contains 30 family-related statements, which respondents rate on a 5-point scale ("almost never" to "almost always"). Respondents can respond as to how their family truly is and how they wish their family to be. The FACES II has demonstrated adequate test–retest reliability (.80 for Adaptability and .83 for Cohesion over a 4- to 5-week period), internal consistency (overall .90, .78 for Adaptability, and .87 for Cohesion), and construct validity (McCubbin & McCubbin, 1988). Olson et al. (1982) reported evidence that the two scales are indeed orthogonal and that both scales distinguish dysfunctional family from nonproblem families. Olson, Portner, and Lavee (1985) developed a 20-item version of the FACES (FACES III); however, the FACES II appears to have better internal consistency and better concurrent validity (Olson et al., 1982).

Birt (1996) combined child/adolescent and parent FACES II scores with the Harter Social Support Scale for Children (Harter, 1985) to make one factor score. This factor showed a strong inverse relationship with depression. This factor was also positively related to child reports of a positive attributional style, empowerment against further sexual abuse, and use of problem solving and seeking social support when faced with either abuse-related or everyday problems. Alexander and Lupfer (1987) found that both Cohesion and Adaptability discriminated sexually abused from nonabused undergraduate females.

Family Environment Scale. The Family Environment Scale (FES; Moos & Moos, 1986) is a 90-item questionnaire that assesses 10 dimensions of family life: Cohesion, Expressiveness, Conflict, Independence, Achievement Orientation, Moral–Religious Emphasis, Organization, Control, Active–Recreational Orientation, and Intellectual–Cultural Orientation. The FES has good reliability, and has been shown to discriminate victims' from nonvictims' families (Ray, Jackson, & Townsley, 1991). The Cohesion and Organization scales appear to be particularly relevant for families of sexual abuse victims. Studies have shown lower Cohesion scores for the following, as compared to various control groups: mothers of incest victims (Dadds et al., 1991; Saunders et al., 1995), undergraduate females reporting on their families of origin (Long & Jackson, 1994), and mothers of incestuously abused children reporting on their families of origin (Cole et al., 1992). Although some studies have depicted families of sexually abused children as less organized than controls (Long & Jackson, 1994; Cole et al., 1992), other studies have found evidence of higher Organization scores for incestuous families (Dadds et al., 1991; Saunders et al., 1995). Studies using the FES have characterized families of sexually abused children as low on Expressiveness, Independence, and Active–Recreational Orientation (Dadds et al., 1991; Saunders et al., 1995), and high on Moral–Religious Emphasis (Saunders et al., 1995).

Direct Observation of Families. Unfortunately, only one study has used direct observation methodology with sexually abused children and their families (Madonna, Van Scoyk, & Jones, 1991). Observers watched 15-minute segments of videotaped structured family interviews with incestuous and nonincestous clinic-referred families, and rated these on several dimensions of the Beavers–Timberlawn Family Evaluation Scale (Lewis, Beavers, & Gossett, 1976): Family Power Structure (power, coalitions, closeness), Family Mythology, Family Negotiation, Family Autonomy (clarity, responsibility, invasiveness, permeability), and Family Affect (expressiveness, mood, conflict, and empathy). Interrater agreement for the incestuous families ranged from .43 to .83 across the family variables; interrater agreement for control subjects was higher, averaging .94. Unfortunately, observers were aware of the status of the groups because of the nature of the structured interview. Comparisons of incestuous and nonincestous family interactions revealed that the incestuous families were rated as having weaker and less effective parental coalitions and "indistinct" boundaries. The incestuous families were also seen as having "incongruous beliefs" about family functioning, and were rated as having extremely inefficient negotiating and problem-solving styles. Members of incestuous families were rated as unclear in their communications and self-disclosures, and were less likely to accept responsibility for their actions, feelings, and thoughts. Furthermore, incestuous family members were more likely to tell other family members how to act, feel, and think, and were significantly less empathic, open, and responsive in their communications. Range of emotions was likewise more restricted in the incestuous families, with relatively high ratings for avoiding or obscuring conflict. Finally, the incestuous families scored higher on general ratings of dysfunction.

SUMMARY AND CONCLUSIONS

The present chapter provides an overview of the special issues related to childhood sexual abuse, including epidemiological findings, situational correlates of sexual abuse, and the impact of abuse on victims. The chapter provides a framework for conceptualizing the impact of sexual abuse, with consideration of the abuse itself, the child's psychological and developmental state, the family, and the community. Furthermore, the model emphasizes the need to examine the time frame and context in which the assessment takes place. Children's adjustment will vary with regard to time since the abuse and abuse disclosure, as well as with regard to cognitive, social, and sexual development. The numerous factors that affect sexual abuse sequelae highlight the need for multimethod, multibehavior, multi-informant assessment strategies. Parent and child reports of child and family adjustment and functioning often differ substantially, but each viewpoint is important in conceptualizing individual cases. Assessment of PTSD, sexuality, and other trauma-related symptoms provides a rounded view of potential sequelae. Assessment of abuse factors and of family support and functioning is also important for understanding individual differences in abuse-related sequelae. Much of the current literature is based upon either parent or child reports, and very little is based upon direct observation. Nonetheless, studies that have employed direct observation strategies (e.g., observations of play with anatomically correct dolls; observations of incestuous family interactions) have tended to buttress parent and child reports of sexuality problems and family interaction styles.

Recent literature reviews have highlighted PTSD and sexuality problems as abuse-specific sequelae. If PTSD, as defined by the DSM-IV, is to continue as a model for understanding the trau-matic impact of sexual abuse, it will need to evolve to incorporate the complexity of trauma-related symptomatology seen in sexually abused children, particularly variations in sequelae related to severity and course of abuse, family reactions, and child development. Childhood dissociative tendencies and symptoms of depression appear to be related to sexual abuse and PTSD; however, further research is needed to determine whether these symptoms are really best conceptualized as aspects of PTSD or as distinct symptom clusters that have a unique relationship to sexual abuse trauma apart from PTSD. Refinements in assessment strategies is likely to facilitate growth of our understanding of abuse-related PTSD sequelae.

Assessment of sexuality issues also requires further development, particularly with older children and adolescents who are often reluctant to report sexual interests and behaviors, and whose parents are no longer monitoring these areas of privacy. In addition, further refinement is needed in detecting specific types of sexual problems, including sexual anxiety, eroticization, counterphobic behavior, sexual reactivity, and sexual aggression.

NOTE

1. These criteria are derived from the cases of People v. Kelley (1976) and Frye v. United States (1923). Briefly, findings based upon new scientific techniques are admissible as evidence only when it has been demonstrated that the techniques are reliable and have received general acceptance in the scientific community (Elias, 1992).

REFERENCES

Aarens, M., Cameron, T., Roizen, J., Room, R., Schneberk, D., & Wingard, D. (1978). *Alcohol, casualties and crime*. Berkeley, CA: Social Research Group.

Abel, G. G., Becker, J. V., Cunningham-Rathner, J., Mittelman, M. S., & Rouleau, J. L. (1988). Multiple paraphilic diagnoses among sex offenders. *Bulletin of the American Academy of Psychiatry and the Law, 16*, 153–168.

Achenbach, T. M. (1991a). *Manual for the Child Behavior Checklist/4–18 and 1991 Profile*. Burlington: University of Vermont, Department of Psychiatry.

Achenbach, T. M. (1991b). *Manual for the Teacher's Report Form and 1991 Profile*. Burlington: University of Vermont, Department of Psychiatry.

Achenbach, T. M. (1991c). *Manual for the Youth Self-Report and 1991 Profile*. Burlington: University of Vermont, Department of Psychiatry.

Adams, J., McClellan, J., Douglass, D., McCurry, C.,

& Storch, M. (1995). Sexually inappropriate behaviors in seriously mentally ill children and adolescents. *Child Abuse and Neglect, 19*, 555–568.

Adler, N. A., & Schutz, J. (1995). Sibling incest offenders. *Child Abuse and Neglect, 19*, 811–820.

Alexander, P. C., & Lupfer, S. L. (1987). Family characteristics and long-term consequences associated with sexual abuse. *Archives of Sexual Behavior, 16*, 235–245.

Allen, C. M. (1991). *Women and men who sexually abuse children: A comparative analysis*. Orwell, VT: Safer Society.

American Humane Association. (1984). *Highlights of official child neglect and abuse reporting — 1982*. Denver, CO: Author.

American Professional Society on the Abuse of Children (APSAC). (1990). *Guidelines for the psychosocial evaluation of suspected sexual abuse of young children*. Chicago: Author.

American Psychiatric Association. (1994). *Diagnostic and statistical manual of mental disorders* (4th ed.). Washington, DC: Author.

Anson, D. A., Golding, S. L., & Gully, K. J. (1993). Child sexual abuse allegations: Reliability of criteria-based content analysis. *Law and Human Behavior, 17*, 331–341.

Araji, S., & Finkelhor, D. (1986). Abusers: A review of the research. In D. Finkelhor (Ed.), *A sourcebook on child sexual abuse* (pp. 89–118). Beverly Hills, CA: Sage.

Attias, R., & Goodwin, J. (1985). Knowledge and management strategies in incest cases: A survey of physicians, psychologists, and family counselors. *Child Abuse and Neglect, 9*, 165–174.

Badgley, R. F. (1984). *Sexual offenses against children*. Ottawa: Canadian Government Publishing Centre.

Bagley, C., & Young, L. (1987). Juvenile prostitution and child sexual abuse: A controlled study. *Canadian Journal of Community Mental Health, 6*, 5–26.

Baker, A. W., & Duncan, S. P. (1985). Child sexual abuse: A study of prevalence in Great Britain. *Child Abuse and Neglect, 9*, 457–467.

Band, E., & Weisz, J. (1988). How to feel better when it feels bad: Children's perspectives on coping with everyday stress. *Developmental Psychology, 24*, 247–253.

Banning, A. (1989). Mother–son incest: Confronting a prejudice. *Child Abuse and Neglect, 13*, 563–570.

Barnett, D., Glancy, L., Meade, J., Behen, M., Standish, J., Jones, D., & Richardson, K. K. (1995, March). *Factors that mediate the effects of sexual abuse*. Poster presented at the biennial meeting of the Society for Research in Child Development, Indianapolis, IN.

Basta, S., & Peterson, R. (1990). Perpetrator status and the personality characteristics of molested children. *Child Abuse and Neglect, 14*, 555–566.

Bays, J. (1990). Are the genitalia of anatomical dolls distorted? *Child Abuse and Neglect, 14*, 171–175.

Becker, J. V. (1988). The effects of child sexual abuse on adolescent sexual offenders. In G. E. Wyatt & G. J. Powell (Eds.), *Lasting effects of child sexual abuse* (pp. 193–207). Beverly Hills, CA: Sage.

Becker, J. V. (1994). Offenders: Characteristics and treatment. *The Future of Children: Sexual Abuse of Children, 4*, 176–197.

Becker, J. V., Kaplan, M. S., & Tenke, C. E. (1992). The relationship of abuse history, denial, and erectile responses: Profiles of adolescent sexual perpetrators. *Behavior Therapy, 23*, 87–97.

Benedict, L. L. W., & Zautra, A. A. J. (1993). Family environmental characteristics as risk factors for childhood sexual abuse. *Journal of Clinical Child Psychology, 22*, 365–374.

Birns, B., & Meyer, S. L. (1993). Mothers' role in incest: Dysfunctional women or dysfunctional theories? *Journal of Child Sexual Abuse, 2*, 127–135.

Birt, J. (1996). *Abuse-related variables, attributions, coping, and negative sequelae of sexually abused girls*. Unpublished doctoral dissertation, University of Windsor, Windsor, Ontario, Canada.

Birt, J., DiMito, A., & Wolfe, V. V. (1995, March). *Origins of dissociation among sexually abused children*. Poster presented at the biennial meeting of the Society for Research on Child Development, Indianapolis, IN.

Birt, J., Lehman, P., Wolfe, V. V., & DiMito, A. M. (1992). *Child Dissociation Checklist — Child report version*. Unpublished manuscript, London Health Sciences Centre, London, Ontario, Canada.

Birt, J., & Wolfe, V. V. (1995, November). *Relationship between sexual abuse and anger responses in children*. Poster presented at the annual meeting of the Association for Advancement of Behavior Therapy, Washington, DC.

Black, C. A., & DeBlassie, R. R. (1993). Sexual abuse in male children and adolescents: Indicators, effects, and treatments. *Adolescence, 28*, 123–133.

Boat, B. W., & Everson, M. (1988). Use of anatomical dolls among professionals in sexual abuse evaluations. *Child Abuse and Neglect, 12*, 171–179.

Boat, B. W., & Everson, M. (1996). Concerning practices of interviewers when using anatomically correct dolls in child protective services investigations. *Child Maltreatment, 1*, 96–104.

Booth, C., Krasnor, R., McKinnon, J. A., & Rubin, K. (1994). Predicting social adjustment in middle childhood: The role of preschool attachment to security and maternal status. *Social Development, 3*, 189–204.

Boyer, D., & Fine, D. (1991). Sexual abuse as a factor in adolescent pregnancy and child maltreatment. *Family Planning Perspectives, 24*, 4–11.

Briere, J. (1996). *Trauma Symptom Checklist for Children (TSCC): Professional manual*. Odessa, FL: Psychological Assessment Resources.

Bryant, S. L., & Range, L. M. (1996). Suicidality in college women who report multiple versus single types of maltreatment by parents: A brief report. *Journal of Child Sexual Abuse, 4*, 87–94.

Bruck, M., Ceci, S. J., Francoeur, E., & Renick, A. (1995). Anatomically detailed dolls do not facilitate preschoolers' reports of a pediatric examination involving genital touching. *Journal of Experimental Psychology: Applied, 1*, 95–109.

Burgess, A. W., Groth, N., Holmstrom, L., & Sgroi, S. (1978). *Sexual assault of children and adolescents.* Lexington, MA: D.C. Heath.

Burt, M. R., & Estep, R. E. (1983). Who is a victim? Definitional problems in sexual victimization. *Victimology, 6*, 15–28.

Bybee, D., & Mowbray, C. T. (1993). An analysis of allegations of sexual abuse in a multi-victim daycare centre case. *Child Abuse and Neglect, 17*, 767–783.

Caffaro-Rouget, A., Lang, R. A., & van Santen, V. (1989). The impact of child sexual abuse on victims' adjustment. *Annals of Sex Research, 2*, 29–47.

Carlson, V., Cicchetti, D., Barnett, D., & Braunwald, K. (1989). Disorganized/disoriented attachment relationships in maltreated infants. *Developmental Psychology, 25*, 525–531.

Ceci, S. J., & Bruck, M. (1993). Suggestibility of the child witness: A historical review and synthesis. *Psychological Bulletin, 113*, 403–439.

Ceci, S. J., Leichtman, M., & White, T. (in press). Interviewing preschoolers: The remembrance of things planted. In D. Peters (Ed.), *The child witness in cognitive, social, and legal context.* Dordrecht, The Netherlands: Kluwer.

Cohen, J. A., & Mannarino, A. P. (1988). Psychological symptoms in sexually abused girls. *Child Abuse and Neglect, 12*, 571–577.

Cole, P. M., & Woolger, C. (1989). Incest survivors: The relation of their perceptions of their parents and their own parenting behavior. *Child Abuse and Neglect, 13*, 1–8.

Cole, P. M., Woolger, C., Power, T. G., & Smith, K. D. (1992). Parenting difficulties among adult survivors of father–daughter incest. *Child Abuse and Neglect, 16*, 239–249.

Conte, J., & Schuerman, J. (1987). The effects of sexual abuse on children: A multidimensional view. *Journal of Interpersonal Violence, 2*, 380–390.

Conte, J. R., Sorenson, E., Fogarty, L., & Rosa, J. D. (1991). Evaluating children's reports of sexual abuse: Results from a survey of professionals. *American Journal of Orthopsychiatry, 61*, 428–437.

Costello, A., Edelbrock, C., Dukan, M., & Kalas, R. (1984). *Testing of the NIMH Diagnostic Interview Schedule for Children (DISC) in a clinical population.* Pittsburgh, PA: University of Pittsburgh.

Dadds, M., Smith, M., Webber, Y., & Robinson, A. (1991). An exploration of family and individual profiles following father–daughter incest. *Child Abuse and Neglect, 15*, 575–586.

Deblinger, E., Stauffer, L., & Landsberg, C. (1994). The impact of a history of child sexual abuse on maternal response to allegations of sexual abuse concerning her child. *Journal of Child Sexual Abuse, 3*, 67–75.

Deitz, C. A., & Craft, J. L. (1980). Family dynamics of incest: A new perspective. *Social Casework, 61*, 602–609.

DeLoache, J. S., & Marzolf, D. P. (1995). The use of dolls to interview young children: Issues of symbolic representation. *Journal of Experimental Child Psychology, 60*, 1–19.

Derogatis, L. R. (1977). *The SCL-90-R: Administration and scoring procedures manual.* Baltimore: Clinical Psychometric Research.

Derogatis, L. R., & Spencer, M. S. (1982). *Administration and procedures: BSI Manual I.* Baltimore: Clinical Psychometric Research.

DiLillo, D. K., Long, P. J., & Russell, L. M. (1994). Childhood coping strategies of intrafamilial and extrafamilial female sexual abuse victims. *Journal of Child Sexual Abuse, 3*, 45–65.

Edwall, G., Hoffman, A., & Harrison, P. (1989). Psychological correlates of sexual abuse in adolescent girls in chemical dependency treatment. *Adolescence, 24*, 279–289.

Edwards, J. J., & Alexander, P. C. (1992). The contribution of family background to the long-term adjustment of women sexually abused as children. *Journal of Interpersonal Violence, 7*, 306–320.

Einbender, A. J., & Friedrich, W. N. (1989). Psychological functioning and behavior of sexually abused girls. *Journal of Consulting and Clinical Psychology, 57*, 155–157.

Elias, H. M. (1992). Commentary on "Abuse of the child sexual abuse accommodation syndrome." *Journal of Child Sexual Abuse, 1*, 169–171.

Elliott, D. M., & Briere, J. (1994). Forensic sexual abuse evaluations of older children: Disclosures and symptomatology. *Behavioral Sciences and the Law, 12*, 261–277.

Elliott, M., Browne, K., & Kilcoyne, J. (1995). Child sexual abuse prevention: What offenders tell us. *Child Abuse and Neglect, 19*, 579–594.

Elwell, M. E., & Ephross, P. H. (1987). Initial reactions of sexually abused children. *Social Casework, 68*, 109–116.

Esplin, P. W., Boychuk, T., & Raskin, D. C. (1988, June). *A field validity study of criteria-based content analysis of children's statements in sexual abuse cases.* Paper presented at the NATO Advanced Study Institute on Credibility Assessment, Maratea, Italy.

Everson, M. D., & Boat, B. W. (1989). False allegations of sexual abuse of children and adolescents. *Journal of the American Academy of Child and Adolescent Psychiatry, 28*, 230–235.

Everson, M. D., & Boat, B. W. (1990). Sexualized doll play among young children: Implications for the use of anatomical dolls in sexual abuse evaluations. *Journal of the American Academy of Child and Adolescent Psychiatry, 29*, 736–742.

Everson, M. D., & Boat, B. W. (1994). Putting the anatomical doll controversy in perspective: An examination of major doll uses and relative criticisms. *Child Abuse and Neglect, 18,* 113–129.

Everson, M. D., Hunter, W. M., Runyon, D. K., Edelsohn, G. A., & Coulter, M. L. (1989). Maternal support following disclosure of incest. *American Journal of Orthopsychiatry, 59,* 197–207.

Fagan, S., & Wexler, S. (1988). Explanations of sexual assault among violent delinquents. *Journal of Adolescent Research, 3,* 363–385.

Faller, K. C. (1984). Is the child victim of sexual abuse telling the truth? *Child Abuse and Neglect, 8,* 473–481.

Faller, K. C. (1991). What happens to sexually abused children identified in child protective services? *Children and Youth Services Review, 13,* 101–111.

Famularo, R., Kinscherff, R., & Fenton, T. (1990). Symptom differences in acute and chronic presentation of childhood Post-Traumatic Stress Disorder. *Child Abuse and Neglect, 14,* 349–444.

Farber, E., Showers, J., Johnson, C., Joseph, J. A., & Oshins, L. (1984). The sexual abuse of children: A comparison of male and female victims. *Journal of Child Psychology, 13,* 294–297.

Fehrenbach, P. A., & Monastersky, C. (1988). Characteristics of female adolescent sexual offenders. *American Journal of Orthopsychiatry, 58,* 148–151.

Fehrenbach, P. A., Smith, W., Monastersky, C., & Deisher, R. (1986). Adolescent sexual offenders: Offender and offense characteristics. *American Journal of Orthopsychiatry, 56,* 225–233.

Finkelhor, D. (1979). *Sexually victimized children.* New York: Free Press.

Finkelhor, D. (1980). Sex among siblings. *Archives of Sexual Behavior, 9,* 171–194.

Finkelhor, D. (1983). Removing the child—prosecuting the offender in cases of sexual abuse: Evidence from the national reporting system for child abuse and neglect. *Child Abuse and Neglect, 7,* 195–205.

Finkelhor, D. (1990). Early and long-term effects of child sexual abuse: An update. *Professional Psychology: Research and Practice, 21,* 325–330.

Finkelhor, D. (1994). Current information on the scope and nature of child sexual abuse. *The Future of Children: Sexual Abuse of Children, 4,* 31–53.

Finkelhor, D., & Baron, L. (1986). High risk children. In D. Finkelhor, S. Araji, L. Baron, A. Browne, S. Peters, & G. Wyatt (Eds.), *A sourcebook on child sexual abuse* (pp. 60–88). Beverly Hills, CA: Sage.

Finkelhor, D., & Browne, A. (1985). The traumatic impact of child sexual abuse: A conceptualization. *American Journal of Orthopsychiatry, 55,* 530–541.

Finkelhor, D., Gomes-Schwartz, B., & Horowitz, J. (1984). Professionals' responses. In D. Finkelhor (Ed.), *Child sexual abuse: New theory and research.* New York: Free Press.

Finkelhor, D., Hotaling, G. T., Lewis, I. A., & Smith, C. (1990). Sexual abuse in a national survey of adult men and women: Prevalence characteristics and risk factors. *Child Abuse and Neglect, 14,* 19–28.

Finkelhor, D., & Russell, D. E. H. (1984). Women as perpetrators. In D. Finkelhor (Ed.), *Child sexual abuse: New theory and research* (pp. 171–185). New York: Free Press.

Fischer, G. J. (1991). Is lesser severity of child sexual abuse a reason more males report having liked it? *Annals of Sex Research, 4,* 131–139.

Fisher, C. B., & Whiting, K. A. (in press). How valid are child sexual abuse validations? In S.J. Ceci & H. Hembrooke (Eds.), *What can (and should) an expert tell in court?* Washington, DC: American Psychological Association.

Fivush, R. (1993). Developmental perspectives on autobiographical recall. In G. S. Goodman & B. L. Bottoms (Eds.), *Child victims, child witnesses: Understanding and improving testimony* (pp. 1–24). New York: Guilford Press.

Foy, D. W., Sipprelle, R. C., Rueger, D. G., & Carroll, E. M. (1984). Etiology of Posttraumatic Stress Disorder in Vietnam veterans: Analysis of premilitary, military, and combat exposure influences. *Journal of Consulting and Clinical Psychology, 52,* 79–87.

Fraser, P. (1985). *Pornography and prostitution in Canada.* Ottawa: Government of Canada.

Friedrich, W. N., Beilke, R. L., & Purcell, P. (n.d.). *Child Sexual Behavior Inventory.* Unpublished manuscript, Mayo Clinic, Rochester, MN.

Friedrich, W. N., Beilke, R. L., & Urquiza, A. J. (1988a). Behavior problems in young sexually abused boys. *Journal of Interpersonal Violence, 3,* 21–28.

Friedrich, W. N., Beilke, R. L., & Urquiza, A. J. (1988b). Children from sexually abusive families: A behavioral comparison. *Journal of Interpersonal Violence, 2,* 391–402.

Friedrich, W. N., Grambsch, P., Broughton, D., Kuiper, J., & Beilke, R. L. (1991). Normative sexual behaviour in children. *Pediatrics, 88,* 456–464.

Friedrich, W. N., Grambsch, P., Damon, L., Hewitt, S. K., Koverola, C., Lang, R. A., Wolfe, V. V., & Broughton, D. (1992). Child Sexual Behavior Inventory: Normative and clinical comparisons. *Psychological Assessment, 4,* 303–311.

Friedrich, W. N., Jaworski, T. M., Hexsuchl, J. E., & Bengston, B. S. (1997). Dissociative and sexual behaviours in children and adolescents with sexual abuse and psychiatric histories. *Journal of Interpersonal Violence, 12.*

Friedrich, W. N., & Lui, B. (1985). *An observational rating scale for sexually abused children.* Unpublished manuscript, Mayo Clinic, Rochester, MN.

Friedrich, W. N., Urquiza, A. J., & Beilke R. (1986). Behavior problems in sexually abused young children. *Journal of Pediatric Psychology, 11,* 47–57.

Frye v. United States, 293 F. 1023 (1923).

Gale, J., Thompson, R., Moran, T., & Sack, W. (1988). Sexual abuse in young children: Its clinical presentation and characteristic patterns. *Child Abuse and Neglect, 12,* 163–170.

Gebhard, P., Gagnon, J., Pomeroy, W., & Christensen, C. (1965). *Sex offenders.* New York: Harper & Row.

Gee, S., & Pipe, M.E. (1995). Helping children to remember: The influence of object cues on children's accounts of a real event. *Developmental Psychology, 31,* 746–758.

Gentile, C. (1988). *Factors mediating the impact of child sexual abuse: Learned helplessness and severity of abuse.* Unpublished master's thesis, University of Western Ontario.

Gershenson, H., Musick, J., Ruch-Ross, H., Magee, V., Rubino, K., & Rosenberg, D. (1989). The prevalence of coercive sexual experience among teenage mothers. *Journal of Interpersonal Violence, 4,* 204–219.

Gold, E. R. (1986). Long-term effects of sexual victimization in childhood: An attributional approach. *Journal of Consulting and Clinical Psychology, 54,* 471–475.

Gomes-Schwartz, B., Horowitz, J. M., & Cardarelli, A. P. (1990). *Child sexual abuse: The initial effects.* Newbury Park, CA: Sage.

Goodman, G., & Aman, C. (1990). Children's use of anatomically correct dolls to report an event. *Child Development, 61,* 1859–1871.

Goodman, G., Bottoms, B., Shaver, P. R., & Qin, J. (1995, March). *Factors affecting children's susceptibility versus resistance to false memory.* Paper presented at the biennial meeting of the Society for Research in Child Development, Indianapolis, IN.

Goodman, G., Hirschman, J. E., Hepps, D., & Rudy, L. (1991). Children's memory for stressful events. *Merrill–Palmer Quarterly, 37,* 109–158.

Goodman, G., Quas, J. A., Dunn, J., Batterman-Faunce, J., Riddlesberger, M., & Kuhn, G. (1995, March). *On the utility of anatomically detailed dolls when interviewing children.* Paper presented at the biennial meeting of the Society for Research on Child Development, Indianapolis, IN.

Goodman, G., Taub, E., Jones, D., England, P., Port, L. K., Rudy, L., & Prado, L. (1992). Introduction. Testifying in criminal court. *Monographs of the Society for Research in Child Development, 57,* 1–15.

Gordon, B. N., Schroeder, C. S., & Abrams, J. M. (1990). Age differences in children's knowledge of sexuality. *Journal of Clinical Child Psychology, 19,* 33–34.

Gordon, M. (1987). The family environment of sexual abuse: A comparison of natal and stepfather abuse. *Child Abuse and Neglect, 13,* 121–130.

Gordon, M. (1990). Males and females as victims of childhood sexual abuse: An examination of the gender effect. *Journal of Family Violence, 5,* 321–332.

Gordon, M., & Creighton, S. (1988). Natal and non-natal fathers as sexual abusers in the United Kingdom. *Journal of Marriage and Family, 50,* 99–105.

Greenberg, M. T., Speltz, M., & DeKlyen, M. (1993). The role of attachment in the early development of disruptive behavior problems. *Development and Psychopathology, 5,* 191–214.

Grenspun, W. S. (1994). Internal and interpersonal: The family transmission of father–daughter incest. *Journal of Child Sexual Abuse, 3,* 1–14.

Graham, J. R. (1990). *MMPI-2: Assessing personality and psychopathology.* New York: Oxford University Press.

Grocke, M., Smith, M., & Graham, P. (1995). Sexually abused and nonabused mothers' discussions about sex and their children's sexual knowledge. *Child Abuse and Neglect, 19,* 985–996.

Groth, A., Longo, R., & McFadin, J. (1982). Undetected recidivism among rapists and child molesters. *Crime and Delinquency, 28,* 450–458.

Gruber, K. J., & Jones, R. M. (1981). Does sexual abuse lead to delinquent behaviour: A critical look at the evidence. *Victimology: An International Journal, 6,* 85–91.

Harter, S. (1985). *Manual for the Social Support Scale for Children.* Denver, CO: University of Denver.

Haugaard, J. J., & Rappucci, N. D. (1988). *The sexual abuse of children.* San Francisco: Jossey-Bass.

Haugaard, J. J., & Tilley, C. (1988). Characteristics predicting children's responses to sexual encounters with other children. *Child Abuse and Neglect, 12,* 209–218.

Hazzard, A., Celano, M., Gould, J., Lawry, S., & Webb, C. (1995). Predicting symptomatology and self-blame among child sex abuse victims. *Child Abuse and Neglect, 19,* 707–714.

Herman, J. (1985). Father–daughter incest. In A. W. Burgess (Ed.), *Rape and sexual assault.* New York: Garland Press.

Herman, J., & Hirschman, L. (1981). Families at risk for father–daughter incest. *American Journal of Psychiatry, 138,* 967–970.

Herrenkohl, E. C., Herrenkohl, R. C., Rupert, L. J., Egolf, B. P., & Lutz, J. G. (1995). Risk factors for behavioral dysfunction: The relative impact of maltreatment, SES, physical health problems, cognitive ability, and quality of parent–child interaction. *Child Abuse and Neglect, 19,* 191–204.

Hibbard, B., & Hartman, G. (1990). Emotional indicators in human figure drawings of sexually victimized and nonabused children. *Journal of Clinical Psychology, 46,* 211–219.

Hibbard, B., Roghmann, H., & Hoeckelman, R. (1987). Genitalia in children's drawings: An association with sexual abuse. *Pediatrics, 79,* 129–137.

Hicks, R. E. (1985). Discussion: A clinician's perspective. In R. P. Kluft (Ed.), *Childhood antecedents of multiple personality* (pp. 239–258). Washington, DC: American Psychiatric Press.

Horowitz, M. J., Wilner, N., & Alvarez, W. (1979).

Impact of Event Scale: A measure of psychosomatic stress. *Archives of General Psychiatry, 32,* 85–92.

Howe, M. L., & Courage, M. L. (1993). On resolving the enigma of infantile amnesia. *Psychological Bulletin, 113,* 305–326.

Hunter, J. A., & Becker, J. V. (1994). The role of deviant sexual arousal in juvenile sexual offending. *Criminal Justice and Behavior, 21,* 132–149.

Hunter, J. A., Goodwin, D. W., & Becker, J. V. (1994). The relationship between phallometrically measured deviant sexual arousal and clinical characteristics in juvenile sexual offenders. *Behaviour Research and Therapy, 32,* 533–538.

Inderbitzen-Pisaruk, H., Shawchuck, C. R., & Hoier, T. S. (1992). Behavioral characteristics of child victims of sexual abuse: A comparison study. *Journal of Clinical Child Psychology, 21,* 14–19.

Janoff-Bulman, R. (1989). Assumptive worlds and the stress of traumatic events: Applications of the schema construct. *Social Cognition, 7,* 113–136.

Johnson, B. K., & Kenkel, M. B. (1991). Stress, coping, and adjustment in female adolescent incest victims. *Child Abuse and Neglect, 15,* 293–305.

Joiner, T. E., & Wagner, K. D. (1995). Attributional style and depression in children and adolescents: A meta-analytic review. *Clinical Psychology Review,* 777–798.

Jones, D. P. H., & McGraw, J. M. (1987). Reliable and fictitious accounts of sexual abuse of children. *Journal of Interpersonal Violence, 2,* 27–45.

Jones, D. P. H., & Seig, A. (1988). Child sexual abuse allegations in custody or visitation cases: A report of 20 cases. In B. Nicholson & J. Bulkley (Eds.), *Sexual abuse allegations in custody and visitation cases* (pp. 22–36). Washington, DC: American Bar Association.

Jumper, S. A. (1995). A meta-analysis of the relationship of child sexual abuse to adult psychological adjustment. *Child Abuse and Neglect, 19,* 715–728.

Kalichman, S. C., & Craig, M. E. (1991). Professional psychologists' decisions to report suspected child abuse: Clinician and situational influences. *Professional Psychology: Research and Practice, 22,* 84–89.

Kalichman, S. C., Craig, M. E., & Follingstad, D. R. (1989). Factors influencing child sexual abuse reporting: Study of licensed practising psychologists. *Professional Psychology: Research and Practice, 20,* 84–89.

Kaslow, N., Rehm, L., & Siegel, A. (1984). Social-cognitive and cognitive correlates of depression in children. *Journal of Abnormal Child Psychology, 12,* 605–620.

Kaufman, J., Jones, B., Stieglitz, E., Vitulano, L., & Mannarino, A. P. (1994). The use of multiple informants to assess children's maltreatment experiences. *Journal of Family Violence, 9,* 227–248.

Kaufman, K. L., Hilliker, D. R., & Daleiden, E. L. (1996). Subgroup differences in the modus operandi of adolescent sexual offenders. *Child Maltreatment, 1,* 17–24.

Kaufman, K. L., Wallace, A. M., Johnson, C. F., & Reeder, M. L. (1995). Comparing female and male perpetrators' modus operandi: Victims' reports of sexual abuse. *Journal of Interpersonal Violence, 10,* 322–333.

Kehinde v. Commonwealth, 338 S.E.2d 356 (Va. 1986).

Kelly, S. J. (1990). Parental stress response to sexual abuse and ritual abuse of children in day-care centers. *Nursing Research, 39,* 25–29.

Kendall-Tackett, K. A., & Simon, A. F. (1987). Perpetrators and their acts: Data from 365 adults molested as children. *Child Abuse and Neglect, 11,* 237–245.

Kendall-Tackett, K. A., Williams, L. M., & Finkelhor, D. (1993). Impact of sexual abuse on children. A review and synthesis of recent empirical studies. *Psychological Bulletin, 13,* 164–180.

Kercher, G., & McShane, M. (1984). The prevalence of child sexual victimization in an adult sample of Texas residents. *Child Abuse and Neglect, 8,* 495–502.

Kiser, L. J., Heston, J., Millsap, P. A., & Pruitt, D. B. (1991). Physical and sexual abuse in childhood: Relationship with Post-Traumatic Stress Disorder. *Journal of the American Academy of Child and Adolescent Psychiatry, 30,* 776–783.

Kiser, L., Millsap, P., & Heston, J. (1992). A clinical description of victims of physical and sexual abuse in a day treatment population. *International Journal of Partial Hospitalization, 8,* 89–95.

Kline, I., & Janoff-Bulman, R. (1996). Trauma history and personal narratives: Some clues to coping among survivors of child abuse. *Child Abuse and Neglect, 20,* 45–54.

Kolko, D. J., Moser, J. T., & Weldy, S. R. (1988). Behavioral/emotional indicators of sexual abuse in child psychiatric inpatients: A controlled comparison with physical abuse. *Child Abuse and Neglect, 12,* 529–541.

Kovacs, M. (1983). *The Children's Depression Inventory: A self-rated depression scale for school-aged youngsters.* Unpublished manuscript.

Koverola, C., Pound, J., Heger, A., & Lytle, C. (1993). Relationship of child sexual abuse to depression. *Child Abuse and Neglect, 17,* 390–400.

Lamb, M. (1994). *The investigation of child sexual abuse: An interdisciplinary consensus statement.* Bethesda, MD: National Institute of Child Health and Human Development.

Lamb, S., & Coakley, M. (1993). "Normal" childhood sexual play and games: Differentiating play from abuse. *Child Abuse and Neglect, 17,* 515–526.

Lamb, S., & Edgar-Smith, S. (1994). Aspects of disclosure: Mediators of outcome of childhood sexual abuse. *Journal of Interpersonal Violence, 19,* 307–326.

Landeros v. Flood, 17 Cal. 3d 399 (1979).

Langevin, R., Handy, L., Hook, H., Day, D., & Russon, A. (1985). Are incestuous fathers pedophilic and aggressive? In R. Langevin (Ed.),*Erotic preference, gender identity, and aggression* (pp. 161–179). Hillsdale, NJ: Erlbaum.

Lanktree, C. B., Briere, J., & Zaidi, L. Y. (1991). Incidence and impact of sexual abuse in a child outpatient sample: The role of direct inquiry. *Child Abuse and Neglect, 15,* 447–453.

Lawson, L., & Chaffin, M. (1992). False negatives in sexual abuse disclosure interviews: Incidence and influence of caretakers' belief in cases of accidental abuse discovered by diagnosis of STD. *Journal of Interpersonal Violence, 7,* 532–542.

Leifer, M., Shapiro, J. P., & Kassem, L. (1993). The impact of maternal history and behavior upon foster placement and adjustment in sexually abused girls. *Child Abuse and Neglect, 17,* 755–766.

Letourneau, E. J., & Saunders, B. E. (1996). Introduction to CANDIS: A database of standardized measures. *American Professional Society on the Abuse of Children (APSAC) Newsletter, 9,* 12–15.

Leventhal, J. M., Hamilton, J., Rekedal, S., Tebano-Micci, A., & Eyster, C. (1989). Anatomically correct dolls used in interviews of young children suspected of having been sexually abused. *Pediatrics, 84,* 900–906.

Levy, H. B., Markovic, J., Kalinowski, M. N., Ahart, S., & Torres, H. (1995). Child sexual abuse interviews: The use of anatomical dolls and the reliability of information. *Journal of Interpersonal Violence, 10,* 334–353.

Lewis, J. M., Beavers, W. R., & Gossett, J. T. (1976). *No single thread: Psychological health in family systems.* New York: Brunner/Mazel.

Ligezinska, M., Firestone, P., Manion, I. G., McIntyre, J., Ensom, R., & Wells, G. (1995). Children's emotional and behavioral reactions following disclosures of extrafamilial sexual abuse: Initial effects. *Child Abuse and Neglect, 20,* 111–125.

Lindblad, F., Gustafsson, P. A., Larsson, I., & Lundin, B. (1995). Preschoolers' sexual behavior at daycare centers: An epidemiological study. *Child Abuse and Neglect, 19,* 569–577.

Lipovsky, J. A. (1994). The impact of court on children: Research findings and practical recommendations. *Journal of Interpersonal Violence, 9,* 238–257.

Lipovsky, J. A., Saunders, B. E., & Hanson, R. F. (1992). Parent–child relationships of victims and siblings in incest families. *Journal of Child Sexual Abuse, 1,* 35–49.

Lipovsky, J. A., Saunders, B. E., & Murphy, S. M. (1989). Depression, anxiety, and behaviour problems among victims of father–child sexual assault and non-abused siblings. *Journal of Interpersonal Violence, 4,* 452–468.

Lipovsky, J. A., Tidwell, R. P., Kilpatrick, D. G., Saunders, B., & Dawson, V. L. (1991, August). *Children as witnesses in criminal court: Examination of current practices.* Paper presented at the annual meeting of the American Psychological Association, San Francisco.

Livingston, R., Lawson, L., & Jones, J. (1993). Predictors of self-reported psychopathology in children abused repeatedly by a parent. *Journal of the American Academy of Child and Adolescent Psychiatry, 32,* 948–953.

Long, P. J., & Jackson, J. L. (1990, November). *Defining childhood sexual abuse.* Poster presented at the annual meeting of the Association for Advancement of Behavior Therapy, San Francisco.

Long, P. J., & Jackson, J. L. (1994). Childhood sexual abuse: An examination of family functioning.*Journal of Interpersonal Violence, 9,* 270–277.

Love, L. C., Jackson, J. L., & Long, P. J. (1990, November). *Childhood sexual abuse: Correlates of active termination.* Poster presented at the annual meeting of the Association for Advancement of Behaviour Therapy, San Francisco.

Madonna, P. G., Van Scoyk, S., & Jones, D. P. H. (1991). Family interaction within incest and nonincest families. *American Journal of Psychiatry, 148,* 46–49.

Malinosky-Rummell, R. R., & Hoier, T. S. (1991). Validating measures of dissociation in sexually abused and nonabused children. *Behavioral Assessment, 13,* 341–357.

Manly, J. T., Cicchetti, D., & Barnett, D. (1994). The impact of subtype, frequency, chronicity, and severity of child maltreatment on social competence and behavior problems.*Development and Psychopathology, 6,* 121–143.

Martin, K., Anderson, J., Romans, S., Mullen, P., & O'Shea, M. (1993). Asking about child sexual abuse: Methodological implications of a two stage survey. *Child Abuse and Neglect, 17,* 383–392.

McCubbin, H., & McCubbin, M. (1988). Family system assessment in health care. In H. McCubbin & A. Thompson (Eds.), *Family assessment inventories for research and practice* (pp. 57–78). Madison: University of Wisconsin.

McElroy, L. P. (1992). Early indicators of pathological dissociation in sexually abused children.*Child Abuse and Neglect, 16,* 833–846.

McGee, R. A., Wolfe, D. A., Yuen, S. A., Wilson, S. K., & Carnochan, J. (1995). The measurement of maltreatment: A comparison of approaches. *Child Abuse and Neglect, 19,* 233–249.

McLeer, S. V., Deblinger, E., Atkins, M. S., & Ralphe, D. (1988). Post-Traumatic Stress Disorder in sexually abused children. *Journal of the American Academy of Child and Adolescent Psychiatry, 27,* 650–654.

McLeer, S. V., Deblinger, E., Henry, D. & Orvaschel, H. (1992). Sexually abused children at high risk for Post-Traumatic Stress Disorder. *Journal of the American Academy of Child and Adolescent Psychiatry, 31,* 875–879.

Mennen, F. E., & Meadows, D. (1993). The relationship of sexual abuse to symptom levels in emotionally disturbed girls. *Child and Adolescent Social Work Journal, 10,* 319–328.

Mian, M., Wehrspann, W., Klajner-Diamond, H., LeBaron, D., & Winder, C. (1986). Review of 125 children 6 years of age and under who were sexually abused. *Child Abuse and Neglect, 10,* 223–229.

Moos, R. H., & Moos, B. S. (1986). *Family Environment Scale manual.* Palo Alto, CA: Consulting Psychologists Press.

Morrow, K. B. (1991). Attributions of female adolescent incest victims regarding their molestation. *Child Abuse and Neglect, 15,* 477–483.

Mrazek, P. J., Lynch, M. A., & Bentovim, A. (1983). Sexual abuse of children in the United Kingdom. *Child Abuse and Neglect, 7,* 147–153.

Muram, D., Dorko, B., Brown, J. G., & Tolley, E. A. (1991). Child sexual abuse in Shelby County, Tennessee: A new epidemic? *Child Abuse and Neglect, 15,* 523–529.

Murphy, W. D., Haynes, M. R., & Page, I. J. (1992). Adolescent sex offenders. In W. O'Donohue & J. Geer (Eds.), *The sexual abuse of children: Vol. 2. Clinical issues* (pp. 394–429). Hillsdale, NJ: Erlbaum.

Myers, J. E. B. (1994). *The backlash: Child protection under fire.* Thousand Oaks, CA: Sage.

National Committee for the Prevention of Child Abuse. (1978). *Basic facts about sexual child abuse.* Chicago: Author.

National Center on Child Abuse and Neglect (NCCAN). (1981). *Study findings: National study of incidence and severity of child abuse and neglect* (DHHS Publication No. OHDS 81–30325). Washington, DC: U.S. Government Printing Office.

Neumann, D. A., Houskamp, B. M., Pollock, V. E., & Briere, J. (1996). The long-term sequelae of childhood sexual abuse in women: A meta-analytic review. *Child Maltreatment, 1,* 6–16.

Oates, R. K., O'Toole, B. I., Lynch, D. L., Stern, A., & Cooney, G. (1994). Stability and change in outcomes of sexually abused children. *Journal of the American Academy of Child and Adolescent Psychiatry, 33,* 945–952.

Oates, R. K., & Shrimpton, S. (1991). Children's memories for stressful and non-stressful events. *Medical Science Law, 31,* 4–10.

Oberlander, L. B. (1995). Psycholegal issues in child sexual abuse evaluations: A survey of forensic mental health professionals. *Child Abuse and Neglect, 19,* 475–490.

Ogata, S. M., Silk, K. R., Goodrich, S., Lohr, N. E., Westen, D., & Hill, E. (1990). Childhood sexual and physical abuse in adult patients with Borderline Personality Disorder. *American Journal of Psychiatry, 147,* 1008–1013.

Ollendick, T. (1983). Reliability and validity of the Revised Fear Survey Schedule for Children. *Behaviour Research and Therapy, 21,* 685–692.

Olson, D., Bell, R., & Portner, J. (1982). *FACES II: Family Adaptability and Cohesion Evaluation Scales.* St. Paul: Faculty of Social Sciences, University of Minnesota.

Olson, D., Portner, J., & Lavee, Y. (1985). *FACES III.* St. Paul: Faculty of Social Sciences, University of Minnesota.

Ornstein, P. A., Follmer, A., & Gordon, B. N. (1995, April). *The influence of dolls and props on young children's recall of pediatric examinations.* Paper presented at the biennial meeting of the Society for Research in Child Development, Indianapolis, IN.

Parker, H., & Parker, S. (1986). Father–daughter sexual abuse: An emerging perspective. *American Journal of Orthopsychiatry, 56,* 531–549.

Paveza, G. J. (1988). Risk factors in father–daughter child sexual abuse. *Journal of Interpersonal Violence, 3,* 290–306.

People v. Kelley, 17 Cal. 3d 27 (1976).

People v. Rich, 520 N.Y.S.2d 911 (1987).

Peterson, C., Semmel, A., von Baeyer, C., Abramson, A., Metalsky, G., & Seligman, M. (1982). The Attributional Style Questionnaire. *Cognitive Therapy and Research, 6,* 287–299.

Pierce, R., & Pierce, L. H. (1985). The sexually abused child: A comparison of male and female victims. *Child Abuse and Neglect, 9,* 191–199.

Pirrelo, V. E. (1994). *Post-Traumatic Stress Disorder in sexually abused children.* Unpublished master's thesis, North Carolina State University.

Price, D., & Goodman, G. (1990). Visiting the wizard: Children's memory for a recurring event. *Child Development, 61,* 664–680.

Putnam, F. W. (1985). Dissociation as a response to extreme trauma. In R. P. Kluft (Ed.), *Childhood antecedents of multiple personality* (pp. 65–98). Washington: American Psychiatric Press.

Putnam, F. W. (1990). *Child Dissociation Checklist (CDCL).* Unpublished manuscript, National Institute of Mental Health, Bethesda, MD.

Putnam, F. W. (1994). Dissociation and disturbances of self. In D. Cicchetti & S.L. Toth (Eds.), *Disorders and dysfunctions of the self* (pp. 251–266). Rochester, NY: University of Rochester Press.

Putnam, F. W., Helmers, K., Horowitz, L. A., & Trickett, P. K. (1995). Hypnotizability and dissociativity in sexually abused girls. *Child Abuse and Neglect, 19,* 645–656.

Putnam, F. W., Helmers, K., & Trickett, P. K. (1993). Development, reliability, and validity of a child dissociation scale. *Child Abuse and Neglect, 19,* 645–656.

Raskin, D. C., & Yuille, J. C. (1989). Problems in evaluating interviews of children in sexual abuse cases. In S. J. Ceci, M. P. Toglia, & D. F. Ross (Eds.), *New perspectives on the child witness* (pp. 184–207). New York: Springer.

Ray, K. C., Jackson, J. L., & Townsley, R. M. (1991). Family environments of victims of intrafamilial and extrafamilial child sexual abuse. *Journal of Family Violence, 6,* 365–374.

Roesler, T. A., & Wind, T. W. (1994). Telling the secret: Adult women describe their disclosures of incest. *Journal of Interpersonal Violence, 9*, 327–338.

Ross, C. A., & Joshi, S. (1992). Paranormal experiences in the general population. *Journal of Nervous and Mental Disease, 180*, 357–361.

Rudin, M. M., Zalewski, C., & Bodmer-Turner, J. (1995). Characteristics of child sexual abuse victims according to perpetrator gender. *Child Abuse and Neglect, 19*, 963–973.

Runyan, D., Everson, M., Edelsohn, G., Hunter, W., & Coulter, M. (1988). Impact of legal interventions on sexually abused children. *Journal of Pediatrics, 113*, 647–653.

Russell, D. E. H. (1983). The incidence and prevalence of intrafamilial sexual abuse of female children. *Child Abuse and Neglect, 7*, 133–146.

Russell, D. E. H. (1984). The prevalence and seriousness of incestuous abuse: Stepfathers versus biological fathers. *Child Abuse and Neglect, 8*, 15–22.

Russell, D. E. H. (1986). *The secret trauma: Incest in the lives of girls and women*. New York: Basic Books.

Ryan, G., Lane, S., Davis, J., & Isaacs, C. (1987). Juvenile sex offenders: Development and correction. *Child Abuse and Neglect, 11*, 385–395.

Sansonnet-Hayden, H., Haley, G., Marriage, K., & Fine, S. (1987). Sexual abuse and psychopathology in hospitalized adolescents. *Journal of the American Academy of Child and Adolescent Psychiatry, 26*, 753–757.

Sas, L. D., Cunningham, A. H., Hurley, P., Dick, T., & Farnsworth, A. (1995). *Tipping the balance to tell the secret: Public discovery of child sexual abuse*. London, Ontario, Canada: London Family Court Clinic.

Sas, L. D., Hurley, P., Austin, G., & Wolfe, D. A. (1991). *Reducing system-induced trauma for child abuse victims through court preparation, assessment, and follow-up*. London, Ontario, Canada: London Family Court Clinic.

Sas, L. D., Hurley, P., Hatch, A., Malla, S., & Dick, T. (1993). *Three years after the verdict: A longitudinal study of the social and psychological adjustment of child witnesses referred to the Child Witness Project*, London, Ontario, Canada: London Family Court Clinic.

Saunders, B. E., Kilpatrick, D. G., Resnick, H. S., Hanson, R. A., & Lipovsky, J. A. (1992). *Epidemiological characteristics of child sexual abuse: Results from Wave II of the National Women's Study*. Paper presented at the San Diego Conference on Responding to Child Maltreatment, San Diego, CA.

Saunders, B. E., Lipovsky, J. A., & Hanson, R. F. (1995). Couple and familial characteristics of father–child incest families. *Journal of Family Social Work, 1*, 5–25.

Sauzier, M. (1989). Disclosure of child sexual abuse: For better or for worse? *Psychiatric Clinics of North America, 12*, 455–569.

Saywitz, K., Goodman, G., Nicholas, E., & Moan, S. (1991). Children's memories of a physical examination involving genital touch: Implications for reports of child sexual abuse. *Journal of Consulting and Clinical Psychology, 59*, 682–691.

Scheeringa, M. S. (1995, March). *Symptom differences related to types of trauma in children under 48 months of age*. Poster presented at the biennial meeting of the Society for Research on Child Development, Indianapolis, IN.

Scheeringa, M. S., Zeanah, C. H., Drell, M. J., & Larrieu, J. A. (1995). Two approaches to the diagnosis of Posttraumatic Stress Disorder in infancy and early childhood. *Journal of the American Academy of Child and Adolescent Psychiatry, 34*, 191–200.

Schultz, L. G., & Jones, P. (1983). Sexual abuse of children: Issues for social service and health professionals. *Child Welfare, 62*, 99–108.

Scott, R. L., & Stone, D. A. (1986a). MMPI measures of psychological disturbance in adolescent and adult victims of father–daughter incest: *Journal of Clinical Psychology, 42*, 251–259.

Scott, R. L., & Stone, D. A. (1986b). MMPI profile constellations in incest families. *Journal of Consulting and Clinical Psychology, 54*, 364–368.

Seligman, M., Peterson, C., Kaslow, N., Tanenbaum, R., Alloy, L., & Abramson, L. (1984). Attributional style and depressive symptoms among children. *Journal of Abnormal Psychology, 93*, 235–238.

Silbert, M. H., & Pines, A. M. (1981). Child sexual abuse as an antecedent to prostitution. *Child Abuse and Neglect, 5*, 407–411.

Silver, R. L., Boon, C., & Stones, M. H. (1983). Searching for meaning in misfortune: Making sense of incest. *Journal of Social Issues, 39*, 81–102.

Silver, R. L., & Wortman, C. (1980). Coping with undesirable life events. In J. Garber & M. Seligman (Eds.), *Human helplessness: Theory and applications* (pp. 279–340). New York: Academic Press.

Sirles, E. A., & Franke, P. J. (1989). Factors influencing mothers' reactions to intrafamilial sexual abuse. *Child Abuse & Neglect, 13*, 131–139.

Sirles, E. A., & Smith, J. A. (1990, September). *Behavioural profiles of preschool, latency, and teenage female incest victims*. Paper presented at the annual meeting of the International Society for the Prevention of Child Abuse and Neglect, Hamburg, Germany.

Smith, D. W., & Saunders, B. E. (1995). Personality characteristics of father/perpetrators and non-offending mothers in incest families: Individual and dyadic analyses. *Child Abuse and Neglect, 19*, 607–617.

Smith, H., & Israel, E. (1987). Sibling incest: A study of the dynamics of 25 cases. *Child Abuse and Neglect, 11*, 101–108.

Smith, W. K. (1988). Delinquency and abuse among juvenile sexual offenders. *Journal of Interpersonal Violence, 30*, 400–413.

Sorensen, E., Goldman, J., Ward, M., Albanese, I., Graves, L., & Chamberlain, C. (1995). Judicial decision-making in contested custody cases: The influence of reported child abuse, spouse abuse, and parental substance abuse. *Child Abuse and Neglect, 19,* 251–260.

Sorenson, T., & Snow, B. (1991). How children tell: The process of disclosure in child sexual abuse. *Child Welfare, 70,* 3–15.

Spielberger, C. (1973). *Preliminary manual for the State–Trait Anxiety Scale for Children ("How I Feel Questionnaire").* Palo Alto, CA: Consulting Psychologists Press.

Stark, E., & Fitcraft, A. H. (1988). Women and children at risk: A feminist perspective on child abuse. *International Journal of Health Services, 18,* 97–117.

Steketee, G., & Foa, E. B. (1987). Rape victims: PTSD responses and their treatment. A review of the literature. *Journal of Anxiety Disorders, 1,* 69–86.

Steller, M. (1989). Recent developments in statement analysis. In J.C. Yuille (Ed.), *Credibility assessment* (pp. 135–154). Dordrecht, The Netherlands: Kluwer.

Tarter, R. E., Hegedus, A. M., Alterman, A. I., & Katz-Garris, L. (1983). Cognitive capacities of juvenile, violent, nonviolent, and sexual offenders. *Journal of Nervous and Mental Disease, 171,* 564–567.

Taska, L., & Feiring, C. (1995, November). *Children's adaptation to sexual abuse: The role of shame and attribution.* Poster presented at the annual meeting of the Association for Advancement of Behavior Therapy, Washington, DC.

Terr, L. C. (1987, May). *Severe stress and sudden shock: The connection.* Sam Hibbs Award Lecture presented at the annual convention of the American Psychiatric Association, Chicago.

Terr, L. C. (1990). *Too scared to cry: How trauma affects children . . . and ultimately us all.* New York: Basic Books.

Terr, L. C. (1991). Childhood traumas: An outline and overview. *American Journal of Psychiatry, 148,* 10–20.

Tharinger, D. (1990). Impact of child sexual abuse on developing sexuality. *Professional Psychology: Research and Practice, 21,* 331–337.

Thoennes, N., & Tjaden, P. (1990). The extent, nature, and validity of sexual abuse allegations in custody visitation disputes. *Child Abuse and Neglect, 14,* 151–163.

Thomas, J. N. (1982). Juvenile sex offender: Physician and parent communication. *Pediatric Annals, 11,* 807–812.

Timnick, L. (1985, August 25). 22% in survey were child abuse victims. *Los Angeles Times,* pp. 1, 34.

Tufts New England Medical Center, Division of Child Psychiatry. (1984). *Sexually exploited children: Service and research project* (Final report for the Office of Juvenile Justice and Delinquency Prevention). Washington, DC: U.S. Department of Justice.

U.S. Department of Justice. (1977–1980). *Uniform crime reports.* Washington, DC: U.S. Government Printing Office.

Walters, D. (1995). Mandatory reporting of child abuse: Legal, ethical, and clinical implications within a Canadian context. *Canadian Psychology, 36,* 163–182.

Watkins, B., & Bentovim, A. (1992). The sexual abuse of male children and adolescents: A review of current research. *Journal of the American Academy of Child and Adolescent Psychiatry, 33,* 197–248.

Wells, R. D., McCann, J., Adams, J., Voris, J., & Ensign, J. (1995). Emotional, behavioural, and physical symptoms reported by parents of sexually abused, non-abused, and allegedly abused prepubescent females. *Child Abuse and Neglect, 19,* 155–164.

Westen, D. (1994). The impact of sexual abuse on self structure. In D. Cicchetti & S. L. Toth (Eds.), *Disorders and dysfunctions of the self* (pp. 223–250). Rochester, NY: University of Rochester Press.

Wherry, J. N., Jolly, J. B., Feldman, J., Adam, B., & Manjanatha, S. (1995). Child Sexual Behavior Inventory scores for inpatient boys: An exploratory study. *Journal of Child Sexual Abuse, 4,* 95–105.

White, S., & Edelstein, B. (1991). Behavioral assessment and investigatory interviewing. *Behavioral Assessment, 13,* 245–264.

White, S., Strom, G. A., Santilli, G., & Halpin, B. M. (1986). Interviewing young sexual abuse victims with anatomically correct dolls. *Child Abuse and Neglect, 10,* 519–529.

Williams, L., & Finkelhor, D. (1990). The characteristics of incestuous fathers: A review of recent studies. In W. Marshall, D. Laws, & H. Barbaree (Eds.), *Handbook of sexual assault: Issues, theories, and treatment of offenders* (pp. 231–255). New York: Plenum Press.

Williams, L. M., & Finkelhor, D. (1992, July). *The characteristics of incestuous fathers* (Research Report No. CA-90-1377, National Center on Child Abuse and Neglect). (Available from the authors at the Family Research Laboratory, University of New Hampshire, Manchester, NH)

Williamson, J. M., Borduin, C. M., & Howe, B. A. (1991). The ecology of adolescent maltreatment: A multilevel examination of adolescent physical abuse, sexual abuse, and neglect. *Journal of Consulting and Clinical Psychology, 59,* 449–457.

Wolfe, D. A., Sas, L., & Wekerle, C. (1994). Factors associated with the development of Post-Traumatic Stress Disorder among child victims of sexual abuse. *Child Abuse and Neglect, 18,* 37–50.

Wolfe, V. V. (1988). *Parent Impact Questionnaire.* Unpublished manuscript, London Health Sciences Center, London, Ontario, Canada.

Wolfe, V. V. (1990a, February). *Post-Traumatic Stress Disorder among child victims of sexual abuse.* Paper presented at the annual meeting of the Ontario Psychological Association, Toronto.

Wolfe, V. V. (1990b, November). *Type I and Type II PTSD: A conceptual framework for sexual abuse sequelae.* Paper presented at the annual meeting of the Association for Advancement of Behavior Therapy, San Francisco.

Wolfe, V. V. (1991, November). *Does a history of child sexual abuse affect maternal responses to their child's abuse?* Paper presented at the annual meeting of Association for the Advancement of Behavior Therapy, New York.

Wolfe, V. V. (1993, March). *Attributional style and post-traumatic adjustment in sexually abused children*. Paper presented at the biennial meeting of the Society for Research in Child Development, New Orleans.

Wolfe, V. V., & Birt, J. (1993). *The Feelings and Emotions Experienced during Sexual Abuse Scale*. Unpublished manuscript, London Health Sciences Centre, London, Ontario, Canada.

Wolfe, V. V., & Birt, J. (1994). *The Children's Impact of Traumatic Events Scale—Altered Form*. Unpublished manuscript, London Health Sciences Center, London, Ontario, Canada.

Wolfe, V. V., & Birt, J. (1995). The psychological sequelae of child sexual abuse. In T.H. Ollendick & R.J. Prinz (Eds.), *Advances in clinical child psychology* (Vol. 17, pp. 233–263). New York: Plenum Press.

Wolfe, V. V., & Gentile, C. (1991). *The Children's Impact of Traumatic Events Scale—Revised*. Unpublished manuscript, London Health Sciences Centre, London, Ontario, Canada.

Wolfe, V. V., & Gentile, C. (1992). Psychological assessment of sexually abused children. In W. O'Donohue & J. H. Geer (Eds.), *The sexual abuse of children*: Vol. 2, *Clinical issues* (pp. 143–187). Hillsdale, NJ: Erlbaum.

Wolfe, V. V., Gentile, C., & Bourdeau, P. (1987). *History of Victimization Form*. Unpublished assessment instrument, London Health Sciences Centre, London, Ontario, Canada.

Wolfe, V. V., Gentile, C., & Klink, A. (1988). *Psychometric properties of the Sexual Abuse Fear Evaluation Scale (SAFE)*. Unpublished manuscript, London Health Science Centre, London, Ontario, Canada.

Wolfe, V. V., Gentile, C., Michienzi, T., Sas, L., & Wolfe, D. A. (1991). The Children's Impact of Traumatic Events Scale: A measure of post-sexual abuse PTSD symptoms. *Behavioral Assessment, 13*, 359–383.

Wolfe, V. V., Gentile, C., & Wolfe, D. A. (1989). The impact of sexual abuse on children: A PTSD formulation. *Behavior Therapy, 20*, 215–228.

Wolfe, V. V., Michienzi, T., Sirles, E., & Evans, B. (1992, November). *Psychometric properties of the CBCL-PTSD scale*. Poster presented at the annual meeting of the Association for Advancement of Behavior Therapy, New York.

Wolfe, V. V., & Wolfe, D. A. (1986). *The Sexual Abuse Fear Evaluation*. Unpublished manuscript, London Health Sciences Center, London, Ontario, Canada.

Wolfe, V. V., & Wolfe, D. A. (1988). The sexually abused child. In E. J. Mash & L. G. Terdal (Eds.), *Behavioral assessment of childhood disorders* (2nd ed., pp. 670–714). New York: Guilford Press.

Wood, B. (1990). *The Child Abuse Interview Interaction Coding System*. (Available from the author, P.O. Box 33239, Seattle, WA 98133)

Wood, B., Orsak, C., Murphy, M., & Cross, H. J. (1996). Semistructured child sexual abuse interviews: Interview and child characteristics related to credibility of disclosure. *Child Abuse and Neglect, 20*, 81–92.

Wozencraft, T., Wagner, W., & Pellegrin, A. (1991). Depression and suicidal ideation in sexually abused children. *Child Abuse and Neglect, 15*, 505–511.

Wyatt, G. E. (1985). The sexual abuse of Afro-American and white American women in childhood. *Child Abuse and Neglect, 9*, 507–519.

Wyatt, G., & Peters, S. (1986). Methodological considerations in research on the prevalence of child sexual abuse. *Child Abuse and Neglect, 15*, 126–131.

Yates, A. (1982). Children eroticized by incest. *American Journal of Psychiatry, 139*, 482–485.

Yates, A., Beutler, L., & Crago, M. (1985). Drawings by child victims of incest. *Child Abuse and Neglect, 9*, 183–189.

Yates, A., & Terr, L. (1988). Debate forum: Anatomically correct dolls: Should they be used as a basis for expert testimony? *Journal of the American Academy of Child and Adolescent Psychiatry, 27*, 254–257.

Yuille, J. C. (1988). The systematic assessment of children's testimony. *Canadian Psychology, 29*, 247–261.

Part VI

PROBLEMS OF ADOLESCENCE

Chapter Thirteen

FAMILY CONFLICT AND COMMUNICATION IN ADOLESCENCE

Sharon L. Foster
Arthur L. Robin

During adolescence children grow biologically, cognitively, and socially into adulthood. Children develop the capability to think increasingly abstractly (Inhelder & Piaget, 1958), and spend increasing amounts of time in activities and interactions that do not involve the family (Buhrmester & Furman, 1987; Larson & Richards, 1991). Many teens develop romantic interests, begin to date, and establish their sexual orientation (Miller & Dyk, 1993). Not surprisingly, developmental psychologists and family theorists see adolescence as a major stage in family adaptation (e.g., Carter & McGoldrick, 1980; Silverberg, Tennenbaum, & Jacob, 1992), as family members adjust to the changes in the developing adolescent.

Family members must renegotiate their roles during a child's gradual transition from dependent offspring to autonomous adult. Although many families experience some conflict during this process, some encounter more severe distress. We (Foster & Robin, 1989) distinguish "clinically significant" conflict from its more transient cousin via four criteria. Specifically, maladaptive parent–adolescent conflict involves (1) repeated, predominantly verbal disputes, most often about a variety of issues; (2) communication about disagreements that fails to produce satisfactory solutions or resolution of the issues; (3) unpleasant, angry interactions about problem issues; and (4) pervasive negative feelings (e.g., anger, hopelessness, distrust) about other family members, conflictual issues, or family relations. Empirical support for this definition comes from findings that families referred for parent–adolescent interaction problems report discussing more issues and report more anger in their discussions than do nonclinic families (Robin & Foster, 1989), and that observers rate distressed families' discussions of their conflicts as further from resolution and less friendly (Prinz & Kent, 1978). In addition, clinic families typically rate various aspects of family life more negatively than do their nonclinic counterparts (e.g., Epstein, Baldwin, & Bishop, 1983; Prinz, Foster, Kent, & O'Leary, 1979).

We define the term "conflict" as an interaction pattern characterized by mutual disagreement or opposition (Collins & Laursen, 1992; Emery, 1992). Although "clinically significant conflict" is not a psychiatrically defined syndrome, the fourth edition of the *Diagnostic and Statistical Manual of Mental Disorders* (DSM-IV) has introduced a "relational problems" category into which these criteria readily fit. Specifically, the DSM-IV indicates that a Parent–Child Relational Problem exists when "the focus of clinical attention is a pattern of interaction between parent and child (e.g., impaired communication . . .) that is associated with clinically significant impairment in individual or family functioning or the development of clinically significant symptoms in parent or child" (American Psychiatric Association, 1994, p. 681). Although this problem is listed among the V codes, the DSM-IV specifies that it should be coded as an Axis I problem when relationship issues are the primary focus of treatment; otherwise, it is coded on Axis IV. The DSM-IV also provides a proposed Global Assessment of Relational Functioning (GARF) Scale, analogous to the Axis V scale used to quantify individual functioning.

Both the "relational problems" category and the GARF Scale clearly reflect the impact of family-oriented research on the traditionally individually focused diagnostic system reflected in the DSM series. At the same time, the criteria for relational problems lack specificity and are therefore unlikely to be highly reliably used. Family researchers are only beginning to examine whether and how to develop and refine this kind of relationally focused taxonomy that explicitly addresses units such as dyads and triads rather than individuals (Kaslow, 1996).

Several more traditional diagnoses that are applied to the behavior of individuals have been associated with parent–adolescent conflict, although specific conflictual behaviors appear explicitly in only a few diagnostic criteria. The adolescent behavior described by the Oppositional Defiant Disorder (ODD) diagnosis frequently characterizes teens who have conflictual relationships with their parents. Table 13.1 reprints the DSM-IV criteria for ODD.

TABLE 13.1. DSM-IV Criteria for Oppositional Defiant Disorder (ODD)

A. A pattern of negativistic, hostile, and defiant behavior lasting at least 6 months, during which four or more of the following are present:
(1) often loses temper
(2) often argues with adults
(3) often actively defies or refuses to comply with adults' requests or rules
(4) often deliberately annoys other people
(5) often blames others for his or her mistakes or misbehavior
(6) is often touchy or easily annoyed by others
(7) is often angry and resentful
(8) is often spiteful or vindictive

Note: Consider a criterion met only if the behavior occurs more frequently than is typically observed in individuals of comparable age and developmental level.

B. The disturbance in behavior causes clinically significant impairment in social, academic, or occupational functioning.

C. The behaviors do not occur exclusively during the course of a Psychotic or Mood Disorder.

D. Criteria are not met for Conduct Disorder, and, if the individual is age 18 years or older, criteria are not met for Antisocial Personality Disorder.

Note. From American Psychiatric Association (1994, pp. 93–94). Copyright 1994 by the American Psychiatric Association. Reprinted by permission.

Because of the high rates of comorbidity of ODD, Attention-Deficit/Hyperactivity Disorder (ADHD), and Conduct Disorder (CD), families with members with any of these diagnoses would be expected to experience unusually high rates of conflict, and they do. Barkley, Anastopoulos, Guevremont, and Fletcher (1992) compared self-reports and behavioral observations of negative mother–adolescent interactions related to conflict among a group with adolescent ADHD, a group with comorbid ADHD and ODD, and a community control group. The teenagers diagnosed with both ADHD and ODD and their mothers reported significantly more negative, angry interactions and displayed more negative behavior during discussions of neutral issues than did adolescents and mothers in the community sample. Interestingly, fewer differences between the ADHD-only group and the community sample emerged, with only mother report (and not teen report or direct observation) distinguishing this group from the community sample.

Similar connections have been found between aversive interactions and conduct disorder. Data link reports and obervations of negative parent–child interactions with adolescent delinquency (e.g., Alexander, 1973; Hanson, Henggeler, Haefele, & Rodick, 1984), and more recently with CD diagnosed according to DSM criteria. Sanders, Dadds, Johnston, and Cash (1992) and Dadds, Sanders, Morrison, and Rebgetz (1992) compared children (including some young adolescents) formally diagnosed as having either CD, depression, both depression and CD, or no diagnosis. Parent reports of angry discussions significantly differentiated the CD from the non-CD groups (Sanders et al., 1992). In addition, observations indicated that children diagnosed with CD and their mothers displayed less positive solution-oriented behavior and more aversive content in 10-minute discussions of problems in the laboratory (Sanders et al., 1992). Mothers also displayed more aversive behavior during dinnertime observations in the home (Dadds et al., 1992).

Elevated rates of negative interactions also characterize families of teenagers with various other clinically relevant difficulties. Investigations document correlations between self-reports of negative interaction patterns and reported externalizing behavior problems, particularly for boys (DiLalla, Mitchell, Arthur & Pagliocca, 1988; Inoff-Germaine, Nottlemann, Arnold, & Sussman, 1988; Tesser, Forehand, Brody, & Long, 1989), as well as placement in alternative schooling after public school failure (Masselam,

Marcus, & Stunkard, 1990). Observational data indicate that negative interaction patterns correlate with family members' reports of school problems (Simons, Whitbeck, Conger, & Conger, 1991). Furthermore, reports and observations of negative interaction patterns longitudinally predict teacher reports of conduct and anxiety–withdrawal problems (Forehand et al., 1991), teen reports of externalizing problems (Davis, Alpert, Hops, & Andrews, 1995), adolescent self-reported alcohol use (Brody & Forehand, 1993), and diagnosis of schizophrenia or a related disorder (Doane, West, Goldstein, Rodnick, & Jones, 1981).

The relationship between conflict and internalizing problems is less clear-cut. Several investigations report positive correlations between questionnaire indicators of conflict and indicators of internalizing disorders (Feldman, Rubenstein, & Rubin, 1988; Smith & Forehand, 1986; Tesser et al., 1989). As with externalizing problems, however, these results are more consistent for boys than for girls. Inoff-Germaine et al. (1988) also reported that observers' ratings of anger directed by adolescent boys (but not girls) toward their mothers correlated with Internalizing behavior problem scores on the Child Behavior Checklist. In contrast, Sanders et al. (1992) and Dadds et al. (1992) failed to find interaction patterns indicative of angry, hostile conflict in younger depressed children and their families, either in a laboratory setting or during dinnertime observations. Many of these studies (with the exception of those by Sanders et al. and Dadds et al.) failed to control for the possible comorbidity of externalizing and internalizing problems, however. This makes it difficult to ascertain the extent to which conflict is uniquely associated with internalizing problems.

Prevalence rates of negative communication and clinically significant conflict in families with teens characterized by varying diagnostic labels are not available. Nor are there epidemiological data on rates of clinically significant conflict as defined here, either in the population as a whole or in diverse cultural groups. On the basis of questionnaire and interview data from a variety of studies, however, Montemayor (1983) estimated that between 15% and 20% of adolescents experience serious conflicts with their parents. This should be considered a rough estimate at best; rates of conflict in nonclinic families differ markedly, depending upon how conflict is defined and assessed. Vuchinich (1987), for example, reported that families experienced 3.3 conflicts (on average) during each videotaped dinner his observers

coded. On the other hand, Montemayor and Hanson (1985) conducted structured telephone interviews with adolescents, finding that teens reported arguing or quarreling with another family member 0.67 times/day (i.e., twice every 3 days).

ELEMENTS OF CONFLICT

A comprehensive assessment of parent–adolescent conflict requires the clinician to begin with a description of the topics and process of conflictual exchange, and then to provide a viable case conceptualization that points to targets for change and the types of therapeutic efforts that will be used to produce that change. This conceptualization is based upon the clinician's model of those variables that are functionally related to conflict, which should be assessed early in therapy and as treatment progresses. Here we describe elements of conflict that theory and literature suggest to be associated with acrimonious discord between parents and teens, and that may form the pieces of a case conceptualization. We also describe methods for assessing each element, with a particular focus on methods that are compatible with cognitive–behavioral concepts and models; that are widely used or show particular promise for assessing elements of conflict; and that have been sufficiently well examined psychometrically to justify their continued study. Table 13.2 provides an overview of the major domains that should be assessed in order to provide a comprehensive picture of family interactions (particularly as they pertain to conflict); to establish the basis for formulating hypotheses about proximal determinants of maladaptive conflict and proposing a plan for family intervention; and to understand contextual factors that may influence the types of conflicts families present, as well as how the family members interpret and respond to conflict.

We have proposed (Foster & Robin, 1988; Robin & Foster, 1989) that the normative stresses and challenges associated with adolescence provide fertile ground for the development of clinically significant conflict in families with one or more of the following risk factors: (1) poor communication and problem-solving skills, particularly when discussing disagreements; (2) cognitive distortions related to family interaction and family members' behavior; and/or (3) structural patterns such as excessive disengagement, triangulation, and maladaptive coalitions among family members, couple disharmony, and parents' fail-

**TABLE 13.2. Framework for Assessing
Parent–Adolescent Conflict: Assessment Domains**

I. Reasons for referral
   A. Presenting problems
   B. Major and minor conflictual issues

II. Possible determinants of conflict
   A. Microsocial processes
      1. Interaction patterns
      2. Problem-solving skills and deficits
      3. Communication skills and deficits
      4. Belief systems: Irrational assumptions and beliefs
      5. Affect: Experience and expression of negative and positive emotions directed toward others (e.g., anger)
   B. Systemic processes
      1. Structural patterns
         a. Adult (parent or parent surrogate) teamwork
         b. Coalitions and triangulation
         c. Cohesion
      2. Functional patterns: Reinforcing, punishing and avoidance functions of behavior, cognition, affect, structural patterns

III. Contextual factors in which conflictual interactions are embedded
   A. Individual factors
      1. Individual psychopathology
      2. History of deviant behavior
   B. Social/cultural factors
      1. Race/ethnicity and acculturation
      2. Community/neighborhood
      3. Socioeconomic resources and problems
   C. Adolescent peer network
   D. School factors

ure to work well as a team. In addition, evidence now suggests that psychopathology or long-standing subclinical behavior problems on the part of any involved family member is a fourth risk factor for conflict, perhaps because so many forms of psychopathology are correlated with interpersonal interaction difficulties of some sort.

We assume that comprehensive assessment should provide a picture of the family's functioning in each of these areas. In the pages that follow, we overview the first three of these areas,[1] also critically reviewing assessment approaches for each. We make several assumptions in this coverage. First, we assume that clinical assessment should draw from multiple methods and multiple sources. Thus, direct observation, interview, questionnaires completed by family members about

themselves and others, and self-observation all provide potential means for gathering information about families and how they interact. Convergent information provides evidence that the phenomenon being reported or observed is more than an artifact of distorted perception, report, or method variance; contradictory information calls for greater probing and elaboration to determine the reason for discrepancies. Second, we assume that assessment should examine family interactions at both molecular and molar levels of analysis. Thus, the clinician should try to understand the motor, cognitive, and affective behaviors that typify family members' conflictual and nonconflictual exchanges, and what factors support the use of these styles for all involved members. In addition, this analysis should be nested within a more molar-level analysis that asks about the patterning of interactions in the family more generally and over broader time frames, and also asks about the general functions of conflictual interactions within the family system. Finally, at an even more macro level, the clinician's understanding of the family's methods of handling conflict must be embedded in an understanding of cultural and community norms and practices, as well as the challenges or opportunities family members face as a function of socioeconomic status, neighborhood, and the adolescent's school and peer group.

From a behavioral perspective, assessment can have several functions. These can be divided into two general categories: informational functions and therapeutic functions.

Informational functions of assessment involve decision making and description based on the information the assessment process yields. They include the following: (1) defining treatment targets; (2) formulating a coherent conceptualization of family difficulties, strengths, and interaction patterns; (3) conducting functional analyses of specific conflictual issues and communication patterns; (4) providing diagnoses; and (5) establishing a pretreatment baseline against which repeated assessments over time can be compared. Therapists' explicit or implicit theory of factors that promote and maintain parent–adolescent conflict determines what kinds of information they seek and how they combine this information to provide a comprehensive picture of the family and reasonable treatment plan.

Just as important as the informational functions of assessment are its therapeutic functions. Members of a family in distress frequently enter treatment feeling angry and blaming one another for their problems. Rarely do they understand or adopt the interactional–systems view proposed here. This view sees family members as embedded in interlocking patterns of maladaptive communication that are supported by the immediate outcomes these behaviors produce, but that ultimately contribute to escalating, unresolved negative affect. In addition, family members (especially teens and fathers) may feel coerced to participate initially and/or refuse to attend sessions, claiming that they are "not the problem." Teens may discount their externalizaing problems, viewing them as less bothersome than their parents see them (Phares & Danforth, 1994). Early interactions with the family during assessment phases of treatment thus play a key role in laying the groundwork for successful treatment. The key therapeutic functions of assessment include the following: (1) establishing a view of the problem that is shared by the parents, the teen, and the therapist (this generally involves shifting family members' from blaming attributions to interactional attributions—Alexander & Parsons, 1982); (2) engaging reluctant participants in the treatment process; (3) establishing rapport with all involved family members; and (4) establishing explicit treatment goals and, at the end of assessment, a treatment plan or contract. Haley (1976), Alexander and Parsons (1982), and we ourselves (Robin & Foster, 1989) have all described various strategies for accomplishing these therapeutic goals. In addition, many of Jacobson and Margolin's (1979) suggestions for engaging couples in behavioral couple treatment and establishing a collaborative set can also be applied to parents and adolescents entering therapy.

CONFLICT AND CONFLICTUAL ISSUES

Conflict, as mentioned earlier, involves mutual opposition. Assessment of conflict begins by identifying important dimensions of conflict. These include the nature of conflictual topics (i.e., what family members fight about), the frequency of conflictual exchanges, and the intensity or distress associated with these exchanges. Information about conflict frequency and intensity establishes a baseline against which mid- and posttreatment levels can be compared. Information about the issues that provoke disagreements describes the content of family disagreements. In addition, families with excessive conflict often describe these issues as their presenting problems. Assessing conflictual issues thus becomes the starting point

for understanding the family processes that promote and maintain family discord.

Research in developmental and clinical psychology suggests that the arguments of parents and teens often center on mundane, day-to-day issues. Montemayor's (1983) review concluded that over the years, little has changed in this regard: Families over the generations have argued most about chores, the adolescent's room, schoolwork, sibling relations, and activities outside the home (e.g., where the adolescent goes, with whom the adolescent leaves the home, curfew). More recent research (Smetana, 1989; Tesser et al., 1989) corroborated these conclusions with nonclinic families. So did our (Steinfeld, Foster, Prinz, Robin, & Weiss, 1980) findings that distressed mothers and teens, like their less distressed counterparts, argue most often and most angrily about daily events rather than such topics as sexuality, drugs, and alcohol consumption.

Questionnaire Assessment

Formal and informal tools can assist the clinician in pinpointing issues that trouble the family and assessing the frequency with which they occur. Two questionnaires have been used frequently to assess conflict. The first, the Issues Checklist (IC; Prinz et al., 1979; Robin & Foster, 1989) lists 44 issues (e.g., chores, fights with siblings) that can arise between parents and teenagers. Parents and teens complete the IC separately. First, they indicate which issue(s) arose during the last 4 weeks[2] by circling "yes" or "no" for each issue. They then estimate numerically how often they discussed each topic, and how angry the discussions were. The IC yields three scores: (1) the number of issues marked "yes"; (2) an anger intensity score (obtained by summing the anger ratings of each issue marked "yes," then dividing by the total number of "yes" issues); and (3) a frequency × intensity score (calculated by multiplying the frequency score by each associated intensity score, then dividing the sum of these cross-products by the total of all frequency scores). The anger intensity score represents average anger level per *issue*; the frequency × intensity score, anger levels per *discussion*. Holmbeck and colleagues (Fuhrman & Holmbeck, 1995; Holmbeck & Hill, 1991) also report having used a shortened 17-item version of the IC.

As Collins and Laursen (1992) point out, the IC does not explicitly assess disagreement; rather, it asks which topics arose during the rating interval. Thus the IC frequency score assesses frequency of interaction about *potentially* conflictual topics. Nor is the anger intensity score equivalent to conflict; parents and teens could agree on an issue but still have an angry discussion about it (e.g., if an adolescent failed to comply with a parental rule accepted by the family). Similarly, the absence of anger is not synonymous with either mutual opposition or constructive conflict resolution; a topic may have been discussed simply to exchange information, with no mutual opposition between parties. Despite these caveats, numerous developmental and clinical investigations have employed the IC as an indicator of parent–adolescent conflict.

We (Robin & Foster, 1989) reported test–retest reliability scores over a 1- to 2-week interval with a small nondistressed sample. Correlations ranged from .47 to .80, with adolescent scores generally showing less temporal stability than parent scores. Percent agreement regarding occurrence and nonoccurrence of specific issues based on a much larger sample averaged about 68% for both distressed and nondistressed mother–adolescent dyads, but occurrence agreement was lower (44–48%; Robin & Foster, 1989). Correlations between mother and teen reports of occurrence, frequency, and intensity for individual items were even lower (mean = .28), indicating that individual item scores are not psychometrically acceptable, and that mothers and their offspring often do not agree in their reports of what happens at home.

Convergent-validity data for summary scores from the IC are more promising. We (Robin & Foster, 1989) found that intensity scores correlated (on average) –.44 with observations of problem-solving behavior during discussions of conflictual issues. Schreer (1994) also reported significant negative correlations ($-.26 \leq r$'s $\leq -.40$) between mother, father, and teen frequency × intensity scores and ratings of father–adolescent and mother–adolescent communication.

Limited discriminant validity data are available for the IC. Schreer (1994) reported significant correlations (–.29 to –.39) between family members' IC frequency × intensity scores and their scores on the Conventionalization scale of the Parent–Adolescent Relationship Questionnaire (PARQ; Robin, Koepke, & Moye, 1990). (The PARQ is discussed in more detail later.) Because the Conventionalization scale is intended to measure social desirability response biases, these findings raise questions about the accuracy of family members' reports. Schreer also reported that father

and adolescent IC scores did not correlate with family income, but maternal scores did (–.39).

Discriminative validity data indicated that all three scores were significantly higher for clinic samples of mothers, father, and teens than for their nondistressed counterparts (Robin & Foster, 1989). Mothers' scores also discriminated samples with CD and with comorbid CD and depression from depression-only and comparison samples (Sanders et al., 1992). Finally, the anger intensity and frequency × intensity scores were sensitive to change following treatment (Foster, Prinz, & O'Leary, 1983; Robin, 1981).

Another questionnaire that investigators use to assess conflict is the Family Environment Scale (FES; Moos & Moos, 1981). The FES contains 10 subscales, one of which is Conflict. A shorter version of the FES, called the Family Relationship Inventory, contains only three of the FES subscales: Conflict, Expressiveness, and Cohesion. Conflict items assess both frequency of conflict and style of communicating about conflict, and thus confound these two features of disagreements. Internal-consistency estimates have ranged from .75 to .78 (Moos & Moos, 1981; Paikoff, Carlton-Ford, & Brooks-Gunn, 1993), and Moos and Moos (1981) reported test–retest correlations of .85, .66, and .69 over 2-, 4-, and 12-month intervals, respectively.

Paikoff et al. (1993) reported that mother and teenage daughter reports on the FES Conflict subscale correlated .48. Cole and McPherson (1993) reworded items of the Conflict scale to refer to particular dyads in the family; they found that parent–parent and parent–teen agreement on conflict in specific dyads ranged from .27 to .56. Highest correlations were between mothers and fathers (all r's $\geq$ .50).

Cole and McPherson (1993) used a sophisticated multidyad, multisource approach to examine the convergent and discriminant validity of their revised versions of the FES Conflict subscale. Although a confirmatory factor analysis provided substantial evidence of convergent and discriminant validity, inspection of the pattern of correlations suggests that shared method variance may be a problem with adolescent reports of conflict. Paikoff et al.'s (1993) findings also suggest that parent reports have better discriminant validity than those of adolescents. Although the correlation between mother and daughter Conflict scores exceeded the correlation between mothers' Cohesion and Conflict scores, this was not the case with daughters. Other convergent-validity data suggest that scores on the Conflict scale correlate with frequency counts of these events (Anderson, 1984).

Conflict subscale scores also sometimes correlate with various demographic variables, suggesting that these should be controlled or considered in interpreting scores. Two studies found family size to correlate positively with reports of conflict (Boake & Salmon, 1983; Moos & Moos, 1981). Findings have been more variable with regard to parent age, education, and occupation, with Moos and Moos (1981) finding significant relationships, but Paikoff et al. (1993) and Boake and Salmon (1983) failing to replicate these findings. Adolescent age appears unrelated to Conflict scores (Boake & Salmon, 1983; Paikoff et al., 1993).

A number of findings support the construct validity of the FES Conflict subscale, although, like the investigations of convergent validity, most of these rely on questionnaire or self-report information rather than on observational data. Moos and Moos (1981) reported that distressed families scored higher than nondistressed families on the FES Conflict scale. Hibbs, Hamburger, Kruesi, and Lenane (1993) reported similar findings for mothers and fathers who received a psychiatric diagnosis based on a structured diagnostic interview versus those who did not. Adolescent FES Conflict scores also correlated significantly and in predicted directions with self- and parent reports of suicidality on a structured diagnostic interview (Campbell, Milling, Laughlin, & Bush, 1993) and with adolescents' self-reports of general adjustment (Dancy & Handal, 1984). Finally, Hibbs et al. (1993) showed that parents who displayed critical and/or overinvolved styles in a 5-minute oral description of their children also reported higher FES Conflict scores than parents who were low on these dimensions.

Observational Assessment

Observational systems have also been used to assess conflict, principally in audiotaped or videotaped discussions. Some investigators have used frequency of interruptions (or attempted interruptions) as an indicator of conflict (e.g., Jacob, 1974). Others have rightly criticized this practice on the grounds that interruptions per se do not indicate disagreement (Collins & Laursen, 1992; Holmbeck & Hill, 1991). Furthermore, we (Robin & Foster, 1989) and Alexander and Parsons (1973) both reported evidence that nonclinic families interrupted *more* than clinic families. Alexander and Parsons (1973) maintain that interruptions for

clarification are in fact positive communication behaviors, not indicators of disagreement.

Surprisingly few observational systems include categories directly related to conflict as defined here. This may result from the practice of embedding "disagreement" behavior into superordinate observational categories that include other negative communication and problem-solving codes. A few observational systems have specifically targeted mutual-opposition conflicts, however.

In two interesting studies on naturally occurring conflict, Vuchinich (1987) and Vuchinich, Emery, and Cassidy (1988) coded videotapes of family dinners for oppositional initiations and responses, reporting good interobserver agreement (kappas = .75–.81). This system has excellent face validity, and allows the researcher or clinician to isolate mutual-opposition interactions from an ongoing conversational stream. Limited validity data are available for the opposition coding category, however.

Vuchinich, Vuchinich, and Wood (1993) used a different coding system to assess conflict in parent–child problem-solving discussions. Although it was only used to evaluate interparental conflict, the system could easily be adapted for use with teenagers as well. Raters watched a 10-minute videotaped discussion and then rated parental agreement from 1 to 7 on Likert-type scales. Raters used similar scales to assess conflict by rating the extent of disagreement and negative behavior the parents exchanged. Vuchinich et al. (1993) reported interrater agreement correlations of .64–.86 for these ratings. Ratings of agreement and conflict during discussions of a child-selected issue and a parent-selected issue correlated .52–.59. Two-year test–retest correlations for parental agreement and conflict were low to moderate (agreement, $r = .41$; conflict, $r = .35$), but this might be expected, given the length of time between assessments. Mother–father agreement correlated significantly with scores on the Dyadic Adjustment Scale, but conflict scores did not. However, this could have been the case because conflict was assessed in a parent–child discussion. Parents can disagree with each other about child rearing but agree generally about other areas of their relationship (Snyder, Klein, Gdowski, Faulstich, & LaCombe, 1988).

Alternative Assessment Approaches

Daily telephone interviews provide one underutilized alternative to both questionnaire and observational assessment for collecting information on family members' interactions. Montemayor and Hanson (1985) assessed mothers' and adolescents' reports of the frequency and intensity of conflict during that day. Families responded to structured questions by telephone on three randomly selected evenings at approximately 1-week intervals. Coders content-analyzed the telephone conversations to quantify conflict and amount of interaction time teens spent with peers and parents. Reliability averaged 89% on a pretest sample prior to actual data collection.

Similar telephone methods have been used successfully to assess children's behavior problems (Chamberlain & Reid, 1987). In addition, telephone sampling is flexible, is idiographically focused on actual events in the natural environment, has good potential for sampling low-frequency events, and avoids the problems of compliance issues associated with client self-recording in the natural environment. All of these features suggest that this method warrants greater exploration for clinical use.

The clinical interview provides another alternative approach to assessing conflict. Despite the proliferation of structured, well-researched clinical interviews for the purpose of diagnosis, few systematic approaches to interviewing parents and teens about conflictual issues have emerged. In one exception, Smetana and colleagues (Smetana, 1989; Smetana, Yau, Restrepo, & Braeges, 1991a, 1991b) interviewed parents and adolescents separately and asked them to describe topics about which they disagreed. Later questions probed their reasoning about these conflicts. Smetana et al. (1991a) also asked family members to rate the importance, frequency, and severity of each conflict. Coders later categorized the general topic of each discussion, achieving overall interrater agreement kappas of .83–.89 (Smetana, 1989; Smetana et al., 1991a); kappas for individual code categories were not reported. Although Smetana (1989) did not report other formal psychometric analyses of the measure, she did compare how often parents and teens reported different types of issues. Parents reported more issues involving a child's personality or behavioral style than teens, whereas adolescents reported more conflicts involving interpersonal relations and parental regulation than did parents. This may indicate that the interview yields less than perfect agreement on specific issues of dispute, as is the case with the IC. Additional psychometric data are needed to evaluate this approach to assessing conflict more fully.

Less formal assessment approaches can supplement formal tools to assess conflictual areas. In clinical interviews, the therapist can ask family members questions such as "What do you argue most about?", "What makes you really mad?", and "What do you find yourself nagging about a lot?" In-session observations about the topics that provoke arguments or negative affect in sessions also indicate topics that are likely to promote acrimony at home. Finally, family members can be asked to keep logs of conflicts at home, with the proviso that self-observation is often reactive and reduces the occurrence of negative behaviors (Bornstein, Hamilton, & Bornstein, 1986).

CONFLICT AND COMMUNICATION PROCESSES

The fundamental building blocks of effective and ineffective conflict management lie in the interactional processes family members use when disagreements arise. Thus, key steps in assessing parent–adolescent conflict involve pinpointing family members' communication skills and difficulties, particularly in conflictual situations.

Adaptive family interaction requires skills for (1) resolving disputes and (2) sending and receiving messages in clear, accepting, and flexible ways. Although these two sets of behaviors overlap considerably, investigators and clinicians often refer to the first as "problem-solving skills" and the second as "communication skills."

Problem-Solving Skills

"Problem-solving skills" refer to communication behaviors that promote productive solutions to specific conflictual family issues. Most definitions of problem solving involve variations on D'Zurilla and Goldfried's (1971) original formulation of intrapersonal (cognitive) problem solving. As applied to parent–adolescent conflict, problem-solving steps include (1) recognizing and defining the problem to be solved in ways that limit the topic of discussion, promote interaction, and state the key issues that upset the speaker; (2) generating solutions that are future-oriented and pertain to the disagreement; (3) evaluating the solutions in terms of their probable effects if implemented; (4) negotiating and selecting one or more solutions to try; and (5) planning and implementing the solution. We (Robin & Foster, 1989) have added renegotiation as a sixth problem-solving step, because many clinic families report that initial solutions need renegotiation or fine-tuning because they do not work exactly as planned.

Good problem-solving skills allow families to use verbal means to derive solutions to conflictual topics. If the solutions work, the topics that formerly promoted conflicts no longer arise, reducing the antecedents for negative exchanges. Conversely, families who fail to use the behaviors required to reduce their negative exchanges should be at risk for increased conflict.

A number of studies support these contentions. Robin and Weiss (1980), for example, found that mother–adolescent dyads seeking clinical assistance for relationship difficulties showed significantly lower rates of problem specification, positive solutions, evaluation statements, and agreements than nonclinic dyads during discussions of conflictual issues. Similarly, clinic parents and adolescents report poorer problem-solving skills than their nonclinic counterparts do, and reports of poor problem solving correlate highly with reports of general distress and negative interaction in the family (Robin et al., 1990). Observations of family discussions show that indicators of problem solving correlate with other positive and negative communication skills (Forgatch, 1989; Rueter & Conger, 1995a). Furthermore, longitudinal investigations indicate that observations of poor adolescent problem solving predict harsh, inconsistent parenting 2 years later (Rueter & Conger, 1995c).

A number of instruments assess problem solving as defined here, in whole or in part. Table 13.3 provides a descriptive overview of these approaches, with sample items from questionnaires and descriptions of observational categories. In the following pages, we discuss psychometric information about these instruments, organized by the method used to assess problem solving (e.g., questionnaire, observation).

Questionnaire Assessment

Although many questionnaires assess family interaction patterns generally, few focus specifically on the specific steps of problem solving. One exception is the Parent–Adolescent Relationship Questionnaire (PARQ; Robin et al., 1990). The PARQ contains 250 true–false items (284 for teens, who report separately for mothers and fathers on some scales), grouped into numerous subscales based on item content. The Problem-Solving subscale specifically assesses problem-solving behaviors. Robin et al. (1990) reported that the Problem-Solving scale showed good internal consistency

($\geq$.86), and that it discriminated distressed from nondistressed families. Koepke, Robin, Nayar, and Hillman (1987) compared self-reports on the PARQ with ratings on comparable dimensions based on (1) a 45-minute clinical interview and (2) videotaped discussions of a planning task and a conflictual issue. Significant convergent validity correlations indicated low to moderate agreement among methods (r's generally between .30 and .60), but limited discriminant validity with regard to other domains related to conflict. However, this may have been the case because the PARQ Problem-Solving subscale score loads highly (.86–.91) on a higher-order Skill Deficits/Overt Conflict factor, sharing considerable variance with such subscales as Global Distress, Communication, Warmth/Hostility, and Cohesion (Robin et al., 1990). Schreer (1994) reported additional convergent validity data indicating that mother, father, and teen PARQ Problem-Solving scores correlated significantly but moderately (.27 to .52) with global ratings of problem-solving process and outcome in an analogue discussion using the Interaction Behavior Code (IBC; Prinz & Kent, 1978; to be discussed later).

The McMaster Family Assessment Device (Epstein et al., 1983; Miller, Epstein, Bishop, & Keitner, 1985) contains six subscales, one of which is a five-item Problem-Solving subscale. Psychometric properties of this scale have been assessed primarily with adult psychiatric and nonpsychiatric populations, and not specifically with parents and adolescents. Nonetheless, data are promising for such a brief scale: Its internal consistency has been reported to be .74 (Epstein et al., 1983), with a 1-week test–retest correlation of .66 (Miller et al., 1985). Problem-Solving scale scores correlated .53 with clinicians' global ratings of problem solving after a clinical interview, supporting the convergent validity of subscale scores (Miller et al., 1994). These correlations (.42–.65), however, did not generally exceed correlations between the Problem-Solving score and other questionnaires assessing related but allegedly distinct aspects of family interaction (e.g., Perosa & Perosa, 1990a), leading to questions about discriminant validity. On the other hand, Problem-Solving scores failed to correlate significantly with the Marlowe–Crowne Social Desirability Scale (Miller et al., 1985). Supporting the construct validity of the subscale, Problem-Solving scores correlated in expected directions with other questionnaires assessing family adaptability, cohesion, and related constructs (Miller et al., 1985; Perosa & Perosa, 1990a). Finally, the Problem-Solving subscale sig-

TABLE 13.3. Descriptions of Instruments for Assessing Problem Solving

Name	Description	Focus[a]	Sample items or categories	Comments
Parent–Adolescent Relationship Questionnaire (PARQ), Problem-Solving subscale (Robin et al., 1990)	Questionnaire; 15 true–false items (26 for teens)	Individual and dyad	"My mom doesn't ask for my ideas for solving arguments," "My dad always has to win arguments," "My mother and I discuss the pros and cons of our ideas before making decisions," "My dad has some good ideas about how to solve problems."	Part of 250-item (284 for adolescents) questionnaire with additional subscales: Global Distress, Communication, Ruination,[b] Obedience,[b] Perfectionism, Self-Blame,[b] Malicious Intent,[b] Ruination,[c] Autonomy,[c] Approval,[c] Warmth–Hostility, Coalitions, Triangulation, Cohesion, Somatic Concern, Sibling Conflict, School Conflict, Conventionalization
McMaster Family Assessment Device, Problem-Solving subscale (Epstein et al., 1983)	Questionnaire; 5 items rated on 4-point scales	Family	"We usually act on our decisions regarding problems," "After our family tried to solve a problem, we usually discuss whether it worked or not," "We resolve most emotional upsets that come up."	Part of 53-item questionnaire with 6 additional subscales: Communication, Roles, Affective Responsiveness, Affective Involvement, Behavior Control, General Functioning
Depression Observation System, problem-solving categories (Sanders & Dadds, 1989)	Observation; presence–absence of categories scored within 20-second intervals	Individual	Positive solution (constructive proposal for change or compromise)	Contains 3 additional categories: aversive content, angry affect, depressed affect
Modified Marital Interaction Coding System (MICS), problem-solving categories (Robin & Weiss, 1980)	Observation; each utterance coded	Individual	Problem description, positive solution, specification of problem, evaluation, agree, compromise, assent	Contains additional categories (see Table 13.5)
Parent–Adolescent Interaction Coding System (PAICS), problem-solving categories	Observation; each utterance coded	Individual	Agree–assent, appraisal, consequential statements, problem solution, specification of problem	Contains 11 additional categories (see Table 13.5); a shortened version of the PAICS (the PAICS-R) also exists (see text)

636

Solving Problems in Family Interaction II (SPI-FI II; Forgatch & Lathrop, 1995)	Observation with three types of assessment:			
1. Problem-solving categories	1. Each thought unit coded	Individual	Problem description, start solution, stop solution, pro, accept, con, refuse	Contains 11 other categories (see Table 13.5)
2. Coder Impressions II (problem-solving items)	2. Observers rate entire taped interaction on Likert-type scales (12 items)	Family	"How was problem defined?" "What was extent of resolution of problem?" "How well did they stay on topic?"	Includes 68 additional items assessing interpersonal process (see Table 13.5), discipline, monitoring
	3. Family members rate entire interaction on 5-point scales (5 items)	Individual and family	"How well did you understand what the problem was?" "How much did you agree on a solution?" "Do you think you solved this problem during the discussion?"	
Iowa Family Interaction Scales, problem-solving categories (Rueter & Conger, 1995a, 1995b)	Observation: 1. Observers rate entire interaction on 5-point scales	Individual	Constructive problem solving, consisting of facilitative engagement (e.g., describing problem, staying on task, asking for others' views), solution generation (number of solutions, formulation of effective solutions), and interpersonal flexibility (e.g., making concessions, negotiating, acting patient, acting helpful); destructive problem solving, consisting of disruptiveness (e.g., pulling family off task, belittling, withdrawing from discussion), interpersonal insensitivity (e.g., impatience, noncompliance), and denial (avoiding or refusing responsibility for problem, blaming)	Observers rate many other aspects of family interaction, including warmth, listening, angry behavior toward others, threats, intensification of hostility, assertiveness

(continued)

637

TABLE 13.3. (*continued*)

Name	Description	Focus[a]	Sample items or categories	Comments
	2. Family members rate entire interaction on 5-point scales	Family	How well family solved problem; how likely family was to implement the solution(s)	
Unnamed coding system (Vuchinch et al., 1994)	Observation; observers rate entire interaction on 7-point scales	Family	Family problem solving (consisting of ratings of quality of solutions proposed, extent of problem resolution, and overall quality of problem-solving process)	Families also rated on parental warmth and coalitions; individual members' positive and negative behavior rated as well
Interaction Behavior Code (IBC), problem-solving categories (Prinz & Kent, 1978)	Observation; observers rate entire interaction	Family	Outcome (degree of resolution of the problems being discussed); effectiveness at solving problems that came up	Part of larger rating system for assessing communication skills (see Table 13.5)
Community Members' Rating Scale, problem-solving categories (Robin & Canter, 1984)	Observation; observers rate entire interaction on 7-point scales	Dyad or family	Agree, assent, compromise, evaluation, positive solution, problem description, specification of the problem, global problem solving	Contains 16 other categories (see Table 13.5)

[a]Individual = items or categories focus on behavior of individual members; dyad = focus is on twosomes in the family (e.g., mother–father, mother–child); family = focus is on triads or larger family unit as a whole.
[b]Only included for parents.
[c]Only included for adolescents.

nificantly discriminated (1) between families of psychiatric inpatients designated as "healthy" or "unhealthy" on the basis of a clinical interview (Miller et al., 1985), and (2) between heterogeneous samples of clinic and nonclinic families (Epstein et al., 1983).

Observational Assessment

Several observational systems capture aspects of problem solving, many in combination with other communication skills (see Table 13.3). Most are used to code family interaction in analogue tasks designed to capture or prompt conflict. For example, families in research or clinic settings are frequently asked to solve one or more hypothetical or real problems in their family. Some investigators have selected problems for discussion based on parents' and/or teens' reports of angry issues on the IC or a similar instrument (e.g., Forgatch & Stoolmiller, 1994; Robin & Weiss, 1980; Sanders et al., 1992). Others have used revealed- or unrevealed-difference tasks, in which family members complete a questionnaire independently and then are asked to discuss their answers, with disagreements sometimes revealed to them and sometimes not (e.g., Holmbeck & Hill, 1991; Mann, Borduin, Henggeler, & Blaske, 1990). Some investigators have used warm-up tasks prior to collecting an interaction sample, such as interviewing family members separately to clarify and audiotape a statement of their position on the issue, and then playing the tapes to kick off the discussion (Kobak, Cole, Ferenz-Gillies, Fleming, & Gamble, 1993); or asking family members to plan an activity (Forgatch, 1989) or to discuss what they would select if the family could only have one rule (Beaumont, in press). Most investigators include these tasks to accustom the family to interacting in a novel setting, habituate them to the recording equipment, and reduce possible reactivity.

Hypothetical problems and standardized tasks have the advantage of being identical across families, but adolescents and parents may have more difficulty relating to hypothetical than to real-life issues, and this may compromise the generalizability of the interaction sample. On the other hand, using a real problem can create confounds when an investigator compares distressed and nondistressed families. Because distressed families' problems are likely to be more severe than those of nondistressed families, this procedure confounds problem severity with family distress level.[3] In addition, selecting a real problem for discussion before and after therapy in order to evaluate treatment outcome can pose problems if the treatment successfully addresses most but not all of the family's problems. In this case, the most difficult problems are likely to go unsolved and be selected at posttreatment (Robin & Foster, 1989), confounding the pre–post comparison.

Few studies directly address the comparability of communication samples collected with different tasks and instructional sets. The few that do indicate that rates of behavior may differ between tasks designed to elicit more versus less conflict (Gilbert, Christensen, & Margolin, 1984; Henggeler, Borduin, Rodnick, & Tavormina, 1979; Zuckerman & Jacob, 1979). The overall pattern of these findings supports the conclusion that discussions of real problems elicit more frequent engagement and higher rates of negative behavior by individual family members than do discussions of less affectively charged topics, although the exact patterns of differences depend on the coding system.

In addition, other studies provide indirect evidence that researchers and clinicians should consider carefully the kind of situation to which they wish to generalize before selecting a communication task. Barkley, Anastopoulos, et al. (1992), for example, found that ADHD and community comparison groups differed significantly when discussing neutral ("plan a vacation") but not conflictual topics; standard deviations for negative behaviors during the conflictual task showed two to four times the amount of variation found during the neutral discussion. Similarly, Gilbert et al. (1984) showed skewed patterns of couple and parent–child alliances during a family problem-solving task, but not when family members were told to plan an ideal family meal.

Instructions are important, too: Alexander, Waldron, Barton, and Mas (1989) found that mothers and fathers of delinquent adolescents displayed higher proportions of defensive behavior when playing a competitive game than when playing a cooperative game with their teenagers. Stiles and White (1981) indicated that, in comparison to "reach an agreement" instructions, directions to "tell how you feel" produced higher rates of statements intended to disclose or question, and lower rates of advisement and factual statements, in communication between parents and preadolescent children. On the other hand, limited data suggest that discussions of a parent-selected versus a child-selected problem can yield reasonably comparable ratings of problem solving (r's = .68, .71) and parental agreement and disagreement ($.52 \leq r$'s $\leq .59$; Vuchinich et al., 1993).

Another key issue to consider is who should be present for the discussion. Some investigators, for example, include only a mother–teen dyad (e.g., Barkley, Anastopoulos, et al., 1992; Foster et al., 1983). Others include mother, father, and a teenager (e.g., Capaldi, Forgatch, & Crosby, 1994), whereas others include both parents, a teen, and one or more siblings (Rueter & Conger, 1995a, 1995b). Data suggest that this decision may have important consequences for the interaction sample. Gjerde (1986), for example, compared interactions in mother–adolescent, father–adolescent, and mother–father–adolescent discussions. Mothers and fathers of boys (but not girls) showed very different patterns in dyadic than in triadic interactions, with mothers generally seeming more involved and fathers less engaged during triadic than during dyadic interactions. Unfortunately, the topics of dyadic and triadic discussions differed, adding a major confound to these comparisons.

Buhrmester, Camparo, Christensen, Gonzalez, and Hinshaw (1992) corrected this flaw in their study of dyadic versus triadic discussions of conflictual issues in families with 6- to 12-year-old children diagnosed with ADHD and comparison families. They too found differences between dyadic and triadic interactions. Boys showed marginally less involvement with fathers and more resistive behavior in triadic than in dyadic exchanges with their fathers. Observers rated sons as less warm and expressive in triadic than in dyadic discussions. These findings suggest that clinicians or researchers should observe dyads, triads, or larger family units, depending upon the family group or subgroup to whom they wish to generalize, and should not assume that various patterns (with and without the spouse, sibling, etc.) will be comparable.

Regardless of the method used to select a topic for discussion and to choose the participants, a communication sample collected in a research laboratory or clinic may have questionable generalizability to communication at home. Several features of the analogue assessment procedure may differ from those of typical home discussions. First, a family is in a new setting, away from interruptions, and members cannot easily leave the discussion. Second, the physical setting is novel. Third, the researcher or clinician typically gives the family members instructions or goals (e.g., to discuss the problem and come to a solution) that may not be present in their discussions at home. Fourth, family members know they are being observed, leading to possible reactivity to observation procedures. Perhaps because of these factors, 25% of the distressed mothers and 50% of the teens in Foster's (1978) study reported that their pretreatment discussions of problems were "somewhat different" or "very different" from those they had at home. Using a different rating scale with a community sample, Schreer (1994) obtained similar results: 22% of mothers, 17% of fathers, and 41% of adolescents said that their problem-solving interaction was either "not at all," "only slightly," or "a little" like their usual family discussions. Family members' ratings of their anger in the laboratory versus at home supported the hypothesis that analogue discussions reduce the anger associated with conflicts: Only 1 of 189 respondents believed that the taped discussion was more angry than home discussions. Although some (38–43%) believed the level of anger was the same as at home, the largest group (46–53%) rated their anger level as lower in the lab than at home.

Other data also indicate that audiotaped samples of discussions of problems may not tell the whole story of conflictual processes at home. For example, Vuchinich (1987) found that most dinnertime conflicts (in which multiple family members were present) were quite brief—4.6 conflict turns, on average—and ended with standoffs (no resolution; the family moved on to other activities). In contrast, Montemayor and Hanson (1985) interviewed adolescents daily about conflicts with their parents, finding that teens most often reported withdrawal as the method of resolving conflicts at home. The discrepancy between the two studies might be attributable either to different methods of data collection (observation vs. self-report) or to the dinnertime setting in the Vuchinich study. As Vuchinich pointed out, withdrawal from a family dinner can be quite disruptive. Both studies concurred nonetheless that few home conflicts ended with compromise or negotiation.

Despite these findings, few home observations have been conducted with parents and teenagers, possibly because of concerns regarding reactivity and the difficulty of capturing *in vivo* conflictual exchanges without extensive observation time. Jacob, Tennenbaum, Seilhamer, Bargiel, and Sharon (1994) described one interesting exception, however: They placed audiotape recorders in families' homes, and activated these during the dinner hour to record family conversations. Interestingly, Jacob et al.'s comparison of more versus less obtrusive recording revealed little evidence that knowledge of when recording would take place led to different patterns of interaction.

These data highlight the importance of supplementing observations of analogue discussions with additional data related to how the family handles conflicts at home. However, even if discussions in the clinic may not be fully generalizable to those at home, they may be useful for indicating circumstances under which family members do and do not exhibit adaptive problem-solving and communication skills. This in turn may lead to a better understanding of the situations likely to promote better versus worse communication. In addition, communication samples can be used to assess the extent to which family members can demonstrate skills learned during therapy, even if therapists cannot assume that their home performance is similar to that displayed in an analogue task.

Several observation coding schemes can be used to assess problem-solving behavior (see Table 13.3). Sanders et al. (1992) observed families with children (aged 7–14) diagnosed as having CD, depression, comorbid CD and depression, or neither diagnosis. They used a "positive solution" category to code family discussions of issues identified via the IC. Although Sanders et al. (1992) did not report interobserver agreement for this specific category, they indicated that proportions of positive solutions differentiated parents and children in the CD groups from their counterparts in the nonclinical sample.

Sanders et al.'s (1992) code captures only one aspect of problem-solving: generation of positive solutions. Robin's adaptation of the Marital Interaction Coding System (modified MICS; Robin & Foster, 1989) samples the steps of problem solving more completely, with categories that assess the definition, solution generation, and evaluation steps of problem solving (see Table 13.3 for specific categories). Proportions of each problem-solving category can be calculated (to control for total talk time), as can sequential patterns. Although Robin and Weiss (1980) reported across-category interobserver percent agreement averaging 76%, Robin and Canter (1984) reported much lower figures for problem specification, positive solution, and evaluation categories (percent agreement = 39–56%). Interobserver agreement on the agreement (79%) and problem description (89%) categories was much better. In spite of low agreement scores, Robin and Weiss (1980) reported significantly higher percentages of the agree, evaluation, specification of problem, and positive solution categories in nondistressed than in distressed mother–adolescent dyads' discussions of problem issues.

Comparisons of the modified MICS problem-solving categories with global ratings by parents, adolescents, and professionals generally yielded variable agreement on specific categories (Robin & Canter, 1984), although a composite modified MICS score (consisting of some problem-solving and some communication behaviors) correlated .90 with global ratings of problem-solving effectiveness. A similar summary problem-solving communication score also correlated moderately (–.52 and –.44) with family members' reports of communication on the Conflict Behavior Questionnaire (CBQ; Prinz et al., 1979; to be described later in this chapter) and anger levels reported on the IC, respectively (Robin & Foster, 1989).

Two shorter versions of this code, called the Parent–Adolescent Interaction Coding System (PAICS), have also appeared. The PAICS has five problem-solving categories (see Table 13.3), whereas the PAICS-R has two (problem-solves and defines/evaluates) (Barkley, Anastopoulos, et al., 1992). Barkley, Anastopoulos, et al. (1992) reported interobserver percent agreement to be 85% for the first of these categories and 68% for the second. Although Barkley, Guevremont, Anastopoulos, and Fletcher (1992) indicated that the PAICS-R problem solving during conflict discussions did not change following three different treatments (one of which was problem-solving training) with ADHD teens and their parents, Robin (1981) reported that the PAICS problem-solving composite score was significantly higher following problem-solving training than following alternative family therapy or no treatment. Because the PAICS and PAICS-R composites are so similar, it is more likely that Barkley, Guevremont, et al.'s (1992) findings reflected true lack of change than insensitivity of the PAICS-R problem-solving score.

Another comprehensive observational system for assessing problem-solving skills is the Solving Problems in Family Interaction (SPI-FI) system (Forgatch & Lathrop, 1995), now in its second version (SPI-FI II). The SPI-FI II contains 18 categories, 7 of which explicitly relate to the steps of problem solving as defined here (see Table 13.3). As with the modified MICS, proportions or conditional probabilities can be computed from the data. Forgatch and Lathrop (1995) did not report interobserver agreement for specific categories. Instead, they indicated percent agreement of 77–79% and kappas of .74–.75 calculated across all categories of the SPI-FI II.

The SPI-FI II also contains an 80-item observer rating scale, in which observers rate different aspects of family members' problem solving after listening to an audio- or videotaped discussion. Ray

(1995) reported internal consistency and item-to-total correlations for a summary score made up of six of these items, assessing problem definition, variety and quality of solutions, extent of resolution, and likelihood of follow-through. Data from several large samples yielded internal consistencies between .75 and .90 for ratings of parents and children. A total parent–child problem-solving outcome score correlated –.20 to –.27 with measures of child antisocial behavior in various nonclinical samples (but nonsignificantly in a clinical sample). Correlations with measures of good parental discipline were slightly higher (.29–.39). Interestingly, the score did not correlate significantly with assessments of parent monitoring, providing preliminary evidence of discriminant validity.

Another component of the SPI-FI II is a series of five Likert-type scale ratings that family members complete following their discussion. This series provides an "insider" view of the discussion—something other coding systems do not. Unfortunately, limited psychometric data are available for these ratings.

One advantage of employing a multicomponent system like the SPI-FI II is that it can be used to form multimethod, multiagent composites. These reduce some of the difficulties associated with shared method variance in studies of family processes, because constructs or composite scores are formed from data collected by several methods (e.g., observation, parent report, teen self-report) rather than a single method (e.g., teen self-report). For example, Forgatch, Patterson, and Ray (1996) created a problem-solving composite based on observer ratings of the child, observer ratings of the mother, the number of solutions the family proposed, and the conditional probability that the mother would respond with problem solving to any of the child's behaviors. Structural equation models showed that these components loaded on a global problem-solving construct (loadings ranged from .32 to .73). Furthermore, the problem-solving construct significantly predicted indicators of externalizing behavior over a 4-year period in two samples of divorced families.

Two limitations somewhat offset the advantages offered by the breadth, flexibility, and multimethod approach of the SPI-FI II. The first is its length and complexity, particularly if the entire system is used. The second is the need for more information on psychometric properties of the system, particularly intercoder agreement on specific categories, interrater agreement on the global rating scales, and psychometric data on "insider" ratings.

Rueter and Conger (1995a, 1995b) used a different rating system, the Iowa Family Interaction Rating Scales, to assess problem solving. Observers rated 15-minute discussions of family problems on a variety of items, using scales of 1–5 to assess how characteristic each descriptor was of the member or family. They used these ratings to form "constructive" and "destructive" problem-solving categories, made up of ratings that assessed both the steps of problem solving and additional communication behaviors believed to facilitate or disrupt the problem-solving process (see Table 13.3). Because of this, these categories do not perfectly fit the definition of problem solving provided here. Indeed, within the framework of this chapter, the destructive problem-solving category would be conceptualized as assessing negative communication rather than problem solving per se.

Rueter and Conger (1995a, 1995b) reported intraclass correlations between raters ranging from .34 to .82 for the subcategories making up the constructive and destructive problem-solving scores, with most in the .60–.80 range. In addition, items generally showed positive interitem correlations and produced alpha coefficients that exceeded .62. Structural equation modeling indicated that the three components of constructive problem-solving categories loaded positively on a problem-solving construct for adolescent boys and girls, although bivariate correlations among the three categories were variable (r's ranged from .05 to .38). Relationships among problem-solving variables were consistently in predicted directions for parents, as indicated both by construct loadings and by negative correlations between indicators of constructive and destructive problem solving. Support for the concurrent validity of these scores came from findings that constructive mother, father, and daughter problem solving each significantly predicted a composite of mother, father, and offspring ratings of the outcome of the taped discussion, although they accounted for relatively small amounts of total variance (less than 10%). In contrast, boys' constructive problem solving was *negatively* correlated with problem-solving outcome, raising questions about whether the constructive problem-solving categories adequately assess this construct for boys.

The three components of destructive problem solving loaded consistently well on the same construct for boys, girls, mothers, and fathers, and bivariate correlations among the constituent categories ranged from .37 to .64 (Rueter & Conger, 1995b). Ratings of adolescent disruption, denial, and insensitivity also showed positive stability correlations (.27–.46) over a 2-year period (Rueter & Conger, 1995a). Furthermore, the destructive problem-solving construct was significantly linked to family members' ratings of conflict outcome (Rueter & Conger, 1995b), providing evidence of concurrent validity.

One interesting innovation was Rueter and Conger's (1995b) distinction between problem-solving process and problem-solving outcome. They assessed the latter by having each family member rate the problem-solving discussions on two items. One item assessed the member's appraisal of how well the family solved the disagreement, and the second assessed the likelihood of following through on the solutions. Correlations between the two items for different family members ranged from .47 to .61. Correlations among family members' assessment of the same discussion ranged from .22 to .48. As indicated above, the composite effectiveness rating was strongly negatively related to negative behavior, but more weakly and inconsistently related to the constructive problem-solving composite. Correlations between ratings by individual members and individual problem-solving categories showed similar patterns, with strongest and most consistent correlations between outcome ratings and negative behaviors.

These patterns lead to questions about the validity of the constructive problem-solving composite. An alternative possibility, however, is that negative communication is more closely linked to problem-solving outcome than is positive problem-solving behavior (Rueter & Conger, 1995b). This could be the case if positive problem-solving skills are necessary but not sufficient for successful resolution of disagreements. In addition, perhaps problem resolution requires successful use of all of the steps of problem solving, and breakdowns without self-correction at any stage will impede resolution. Resolving these issues will be easier when more data on convergent and discriminant validity are available for Rueter and Conger's constructive problem-solving composite.

Vuchinich, Wood, and Vuchinich (1994) described another problem-solving composite, also composed of observer ratings. Unlike Rueter and Conger's system, Vuchinich et al.'s (1994) raters scored the family as a whole instead of individual members for solution quality, extent of resolution, and overall problem-solving quality (which took into account aspects of communication rather than specific problem-solving steps). Interrater agreement correlations ranged from .76 to .82 for these categories; kappas were also acceptable

(.68–.76). The three-item composite was highly internally consistent (coefficient alpha = .88) and discriminated families referred for behavior problems from at-risk families and a nondistressed comparison sample. The problem-solving composite was negatively associated with parent reports of internalizing ($r = -.41$) and externalizing ($r = -.31$) behaviors on the Child Behavior Checklist. Interestingly, problem solving also correlated significantly and positively with family income, both in the sample as a whole and in the referred group.

All of the observational systems discussed thus far for assessing problem solving involve a single, well-trained observer or rater who evaluates the family discussion. Training such individuals can require a great deal of time. For example, Rueter and Conger (1995a) provided 200 hours of training to coders over a 10-week period, and even then some of their interrater reliability coefficients were inadequate. As an alternative to systems that require such extensive training, some investigators have used global-inferential coding systems in which multiple raters evaluate each communication sample. For example, the McMaster Clinical Rating Scale (Miller et al., 1994) contains an item assessing problem solving based on an in-depth clinical interview; intraclass correlations ranged from .75 to .91.

Most global-inferential systems require only brief observer training. Coders independently evaluate each audiotape or videotape. The average scores of multiple raters are assumed to reflect consensus on the general levels of various communication behaviors or categories. Because the mean of the coders' scores is used in analyses, interobserver agreement statistics are based on these mean scores, which are higher than pairwise agreement scores. If agreement is unsatisfactory, raters can be added to increase the stability of the mean score, just as items can be added to questionnaires to increase internal consistency. The Spearman–Brown prophecy formula (Anastasi, 1988) provides an easy way to estimate the number of raters needed, given knowledge of the average agreement between pairs of raters.

The Interaction Behavior Code (IBC; Prinz & Kent, 1978) relies on four observers' ratings to assess family communication. The bulk of the system assesses positive and negative communication, and is discussed later. The IBC also contains two items specifically related to problem solving: problem-solving effectiveness, and degree of problem resolution during the discussion. Likert-type ratings on both items have proven quite reliable in several studies, with Spearman–Brown estimates of reliability exceeding .82 (Foster, 1978; Prinz & Kent, 1978). In addition, both scores discriminate between distressed and nondistressed mother–adolescent dyads (Prinz & Kent, 1978) and correlate .27–.52 with self-reports of problem-solving behavior on the PARQ (Schreer, 1994).

The Community Members' Rating Scale (Robin & Canter, 1984) is another global-inferential coding system that requires minimal training. Mental health professionals or community members read brief definitions of each coding category; they then evaluate interaction samples, using 21 specific scales derived from the modified MICS. As in the modified MICS, 5 of these relate to problem-solving steps. In addition, observers make global ratings of problem-solving effectiveness.

Robin and Canter (1984) reported that 13 mental health professionals achieved interrater agreement that exceeded .70 on all of the problem-solving categories, with particularly high agreement on the overall problem-solving rating (.96). Mothers, fathers, and teens (groups of 15 each) also agreed well on the problem-solving rating, and on the agree and compromise categories, but their ratings on other categories were highly variable. If scores for only a single rater were used, however, ratings would drop considerably, and most would not be sufficiently reliable for scientific use. For example, the highest professional raters' agreement score (for overall problem solving, .96) was based on an average pairwise correlation of .65 between professional raters.

Convergent validity data for the Community Members' Rating Scale varied, depending on the category. Scores on the problem-solving rating correlated .90 with the modified MICS problem-solving composite score (composed of both problem-solving and communication behaviors). Individual ratings of problem-solving categories did not fare so well when compared with their MICS counterparts, with correlations ranging from –.06 to .68, depending upon the category and the rater group.

Although global-inferential coding systems avoid lengthy training, they do so at a price: Individual categories are rarely reliable enough for use on their own. In addition, the need for multiple raters may offset the practical advantages of minimal training. On the other hand, global-inferential systems may be particularly useful when a researcher or clinician wishes to obtain only a very global rating of communication or problem solving (e.g., to obtain pre- and posttreatment ratings), or when the consensus of untrained raters is important in its own right (e.g., to establish the social validity of behavior change; to compare parents' and clinicians' evaluations of family behavior).

Alternative Approaches

In addition to formal coding systems, clinicians can gain information on family members' problem-solving behavior by asking them whether and how they discuss problems at home. Questions like "Do you ever try to talk about this problem? What happens? How do the discussions typically go?" can elicit family members' descriptions of whether and how they discuss problems with one another. In addition, the clinician can observe impromptu disagreements that arise in a session and note how family members handle them. Issues that require family decisions also sometimes arise in the process of treatment (e.g., when to schedule therapy sessions), and these also provide opportunities to examine whether family members can propose solutions, evaluate different ideas well, and compromise.

Communication Patterns

The skills of clearly and nondefensively sending and receiving messages support problem-solving skills. Accusatory, defensive, or nonresponsive behaviors can derail even the best problem solvers from reaching a solution. Despite the fact that we segregate problem-solving and communication skills in this chapter for conceptual and heuristic reasons, the two sets of behaviors are not empirically independent. Robin et al. (1990) found that family members' reports of problem solving and communication (on PARQ scales based on the model proposed here) loaded on a single higher-order factor, which they called Skills Deficits/Overt Conflict. Observational studies also support linkages between negative communication during discussions of problems and family members' ratings of the quality of their solutions and likelihood of implementation (Rueter & Conger, 1995b). Similarly, observers' ratings of positive communication and problem-solving behaviors correlate highly (.62; Vuchinich et al., 1994).

Clear communication has been operationalized by investigators in varying ways, using global categories labeled with terms such as "supportive communication" (Alexander, 1973; Mann et al., 1990; Rueter & Conger, 1995a, 1995b), "enabling" (Hauser et al., 1987), and "warmth" (Rueter & Conger, 1995a, 1995b; Vuchinich et al., 1994).

In contrast, communication categories capturing problem communication behaviors have included global categories such as "defensive communication" (Alexander, 1973), "conflict/hostility" (Mann et al., 1990), "constraining" (Hauser et al., 1987), and "aversive content" (Sanders et al., 1992). In general, positive communication skills involve behaviors that communicate one's position clearly and nondefensively when a family member is in the speaker role, and demonstrate understanding and perspective taking in the listener role. Negative behaviors express one's opinions in a hostile, attacking, or vague manner, or lead discussions off task. In the listener role, negative behaviors communicate disrespect or disregard for another's statements, express one's own point of view at the expense of listening to others, criticize others in hostile or defensive ways, or withdraw the listener from the interaction.

Investigators have divided superordinate categories into a number of more specific subcategories of positive and negative communication; some of these are described in more detail in the material that follows. Table 13.4 presents a list of negative communication behaviors and positive alternatives to each, devised inductively by reviewing observational codes and clinical experience in working with parent–adolescent conflict.

Behavioral assessment of communication involves two steps. In the first, the clinician ascertains relative strengths and weaknesses in each party's communication, using categories such as those in Table 13.4, and also assesses the situations in which these behaviors occur. In the second step, the clinician examines how these patterns are sequenced over time. Patterns are particularly important to illuminate, as they provide the fundamental building blocks for analyzing the functions of problematic communication (i.e., the important results they produce for all involved family members). Unfortunately, available assessment tools generally capture rates or relative strengths and weaknesses more readily than they do interaction sequences and patterns.

Questionnaire Assessment

Table 13.5 describes a number of questionnaires used to assess family communication patterns. Most provide general indicators of the levels of positivity–negativity that family members perceive in their interactions, rather than profiles of specific strengths and weaknesses in communication. Among the more widely used of these questionnaires are the FES, the Parent–Adolescent Communication Scale (PACS), and the Conflict Behavior Questionnaire (CBQ).

The FES (Moos & Moos, 1981) contains a nine-item Expressiveness subscale, which assesses direct, open communication and expression of feelings. Moos and Moos (1981) reported satisfactory internal consistency (.69) and test–retest stability (.60–.73 over 2- to 12-month intervals), and found that the scale discriminated distressed from nondistressed families. Hibbs et al. (1993), however, did not report significant associations between parents' Expressiveness scores and either (1) parents' negativity or overinvolvement when describing their children, or (2) parental psychiatric diagnosis. Like scores on several other FES subscales, Expressiveness scores correlate consistently with family size, age of the adult respondent (Boake & Salmon, 1983; Moos & Moos, 1981), and sometimes with indicators of socioeconomic status (Moos & Moos, 1981), indicating the need to control for these factors. Factor analyses of the FES showed that parent reports on the Expressiveness scale loaded on a superordinate factor with the Cohesion and Conflict scales (Boake & Salmon, 1983).

Cole and McPherson (1993) assessed the convergent and discriminant validity of three of the FES subscales (Expressiveness, Cohesion, Conflict) by rewording items so that family members reported on different dyads in the family rather than on the family as a whole. Agreement between family members ranged from .04 to .54, with best agreement between mothers and fathers (.36–.54). Although these correlations were not high, they exceeded those found between Cohesion scores in different dyads, providing some support for the discriminant validity of the Expressiveness scale.

The CBQ (Prinz et al., 1979; Robin & Foster, 1989) also assesses general perceptions of communication, although it also contains some items relevant to conflict. The CBQ was originally designed as a 75-item measure (73 items for teenagers) with two subscales: Evaluations of Other and Evaluations of Dyad. Shorter 44-item and 20-item versions yield a single score, each of which correlates above .96 with the original version.

The long version of the CBQ is highly internally consistent (Kuder–Richardson 20s > .90; Robin & Foster, 1989). Test–retest reliability has only been assessed with very small clinic samples, and (with the exception of adolescent appraisal of the mother, which correlated only .37) has ranged from .61 to .85 (depending upon the respondent and the CBQ subscale) over a 6- to 8-week interval (Robin & Foster, 1989). Clinic mothers' and

TABLE 13.4. Common Speaker and Listener Behavior Problems and Alternatives

Problematic behavior	Possible alternative
Speaker behaviors	

Accusatory, blaming, defensive statements
  e.g., "You make me so mad! You don't respect your curfew."
	I-statements ("I feel _____ when _____ happens")
	  e.g., "I get angry when you come in after your curfew."

Putting down, zapping, shaming
  e.g., "You'll never amount to anything."
	Accepting responsibility; I-statements
	  e.g., "I worry about your failing grades."

Interrupting	Listening; raising hand or gesturing when wanting to talk; encouraging speakers to use brief statements

Overgeneralizing; catastrophizing; making extremist, rigid statements
  e.g., "I don't like it that you never help out around here."
	Qualifying; making tentative statements ("sometimes," "maybe"); making accurate quantitative statements
	  e.g., "I don't like it when you don't do your chores."

Lecturing, preaching, moralizing
  e.g., "I need to convince you of the importance of getting along with your sister. Sibling relationships are very important in families, and without a good relationship with your sister, you can't have that. When I was young . . ."
	Making brief, explicit problem statements ("I would like _____")
	  e.g., "I would like you and Susie to fight less."

Talking through a third person
  e.g., "Doctor, I'd like Susie to clean her room."
	Talking directly to another
	  e.g., "Susie, I'd like you to clean your room."

Getting off the topic	Catching self and returning to the problem as defined; putting other problems on a future agenda for discussion

Commanding, ordering
  e.g., "You must be in by 11 on weekends and 9 on weeknights."
	Suggesting alternative solutions
	  e.g., "One idea is for you to come in at 11 on weekends and 9 on weeknights."

Monopolizing the conversation	Taking turns; making brief statements

Dwelling on the past
  e.g., "Last week you didn't do your homework at all." "That's not true! I did my homework on Monday, and didn't have any after that."
	Sticking to the present and future; suggesting changes that will solve the problem in the future
	  e.g., "We need to work out a way for you to get your homework done on time."

Intellectualizing, speaking in abstractions
  e.g., "The problem is your lack of respect for your parents."
	Speaking in simple, clear language that a teenager can understand; talking about the behavior that prompts the abstractions
	  e.g., "I feel hurt and angry when you swear at us when you're angry."

Mind reading
  e.g., "Mom just wants to spoil my fun."
	Reflecting, paraphrasing, validating
	  e.g., "Mom, I feel like you don't want me to have fun. Is that right?"

"Psychologizing"
  e.g., "I think he talks back to us because he is fundamentally insecure about being adopted."
	Inquiring about situations that provoke the behavior and about the consequences of the behavior
	  e.g., "Joe, what situations really make you lose your temper? What bothers you about these things?"

Threatening
  e.g., "If you don't stop lying, I'll send you to live with your father."
	Suggesting alternative solutions
	  e.g., "One solution is to reduce your punishment if you tell the truth."

(continued)

TABLE 13.4. (*continued*)

Problematic behavior	Possible alternative
	Listener behaviors

Mocking, discounting
    e.g., "Getting a maid is a stupid idea."
	Reflecting, validating
	    e.g., "Getting a maid would solve your problem, but I
	    can't afford it."

Talking in a sarcastic tone of voice	Talking in a neutral tone of voice
Avoiding eye contact	Looking at the speaker
Fidgeting, moving restlessly, or gesturing while being spoken to	Sitting in a relaxed fashion; excusing self for being restless
Using words that say one thing, body language that says another	Matching words with feelings; being direct about feelings
Remaining silent, not responding	Reflecting, validating, expressing negative feelings

Note. Adapted from Foster and Robin (1989, pp. 496–497). Copyright 1989 by The Guilford Press. Adapted by permission.

fathers' scores also declined slightly but significantly over the test–retest interval. Agreement between parents and teens on the 22 items the parent and teen long forms share in common is relatively good for nondistressed families (84%), but significantly lower for clinic families (66–68%; Robin & Foster, 1989).

The discriminative validity of CBQ scores is excellent: Scores consistently distinguish clinic from nonclinic families, accounting for 10–50% of the variance in distressed–nondistressed status (depending upon the respondent and the score; Robin & Foster, 1989). In addition, CBQ scores correlate −.52 with observations of problem-solving behavior with the modified MICS (Robin & Foster, 1989). The CBQ has also shown treatment-related changes (Foster et al., 1983; Robin, 1981). Unfortunately, the very limited discriminant validity data on the CBQ are mixed, indicating that adolescent CBQ scores correlated highly (.68–.78) with Marlowe–Crowne Social Desirability scores, although parent CBQ scores were not significantly correlated (Smith & Forehand, 1986).

The PACS (Barnes & Olson, 1985) contains 10 items that assess positive aspects of communication (Open Communication) and 10 that assess problems (Problems in Family Communication). Children evaluate parents, while parents rate their children. Coefficient alphas have exceeded .60 for each of the scales for mothers, fathers, and teens (Barnes & Olson, 1985; Knight, Virdin, & Roosa, 1994; Marett, Sprenkle, & Lewis, 1992; Masselam et al., 1990). Barnes and Olson (1985) reported test–retest correlations of .78 and .77 (interval unspecified). Although Barnes and Olson (1985) reported high factor loadings for items on their respective scales, Knight, Tein, Shell, and Roosa (1992) failed to replicate these findings for the Open Communication scale with samples of Hispanic and Anglo mothers, and with the Problems in Family Communication scale with Hispanic children. Knight et al. (1992) reported low to moderate negative correlations between the two subscales for mothers (−.29 for Anglo mothers, −.42 for Hispanic mothers). Anglo children's reports were uncorrelated, whereas Hispanic children's reports were weakly positively related (.21).

Knight et al. (1992, 1994) also conducted careful analyses of the equivalence of PACS subscales for Hispanic and Anglo samples. Hispanic experts questioned the face validity of 20–30% of the items for Hispanic families (Knight et al., 1992). Despite this, Hispanic and Anglo mothers' reports showed similar patterns of correlations with questionnaire measures of other aspects of family functioning, suggesting that the scales may show functional equivalence in some instances. In contrast, Hispanic and Anglo children's reports on both scales showed different patterns of correlations with other family variables, challenging the cross-ethnic validity of the PACS for children. Neither mother nor child reports correlated with maternal reports of acculturation among Hispanic families (Knight et al., 1994).

Unfortunately, the PACS has not been compared with observations of family interaction. This is unfortunate, because Knight et al.'s (1994) reported patterns of correlations with measures of conduct problems and depression in children

TABLE 13.5. Descriptions of Instruments for Assessing Communication Problems and Skills

Name	Description	Focus[a]	Sample items or categories	Comments
Family Environment Scale (FES), Expressiveness subscale (Moos & Moos, 1981)	Questionnaire; 9 true–false items	Family	"Family members keep their feelings to themselves," "Family members often criticize each other," "We are usually very careful about what we say to each other."	Part of 90-item scale with 9 additional subscales: Cohesion, Conflict, Independence, Achievement Orientation, Intellectual–Cultural Orientation, Active–Recreational Orientation, Moral–Religious Emphasis, Organization, Control; Incongruence score can also be computed
Conflict Behavior Questionnaire (CBQ; Prinz et al., 1979)	Questionnaire; 75 yes–no items (73 for teens); two subscales (Evaluation of Other, Evaluation of Dyad)	Individual and dyad	"My mom doesn't understand me," "We almost never seem to agree," "My child contradicts almost everything I say," "My child seems angry at me."	Shorter 44- and 20-item versions available; content of items assesses conflict and affect as well as communication; teen completes separate questionnaires on mother and father
Parent–Adolescent Communication Scale (PACS; Barnes & Olson, 1985)	Questionnaire; 20 items rated on 5-point Likert-type scales; two subscales (Open Communication, Problems in Family Communication)	Individual	Open Communication: "My child tries to understand my point of view," "My mother is always a good listener," "It is easy for me to express my true feelings to my father." Problems in Family Communication: "My child has a tendency to say things to me which would be better left unsaid," "I don't think I can tell my mother how I really feel about some things."	Child completes one set of 20 items for mother, another 20 for father

Instrument	Method	Level	Categories/Examples	Notes
Parent–Adolescent Relationship Questionnaire (PARQ), Communication subscale (Robin et al., 1990)	Questionnaire; 15 true–false items	Individual and dyad	"My dad almost never understands my side of the argument," "My mom and I try to understand each other's feelings," "My mother nags me a lot," "My teenager listens to me, even when we argue."	Part of 250-item questionnaire with additional subscales (see Table 13.3)
McMaster Family Assessment Device, Communication subscale (Epstein et al., 1983)	Questionnaire; 6 items rated on 4-point scales	Family	"When someone is upset the others know why," "You can't tell how a person is feeling from what they are saying," "We are frank with each other."	Contains 6 other subscales (see Table 13.3)
Modified Marital Interaction Coding System (MICS), communication categories (Robin & Weiss, 1980)	Observation; each utterance coded	Individual	Accept responsibility, approval, command, complain, compliance, disagree, deny responsibility, humor, interrupt, laugh, negative solution, no response, noncompliance, put down, question, talk	Contains 7 additional categories (see Table 13.3)
Parent–Adolescent Interaction Coding System (PAICS), communication categories	Observation; each utterance coded	Individual	Facilitation, humor, command, complain, defensive behavior, interrupt, put-down, no response, talk	Contains additional categories (see Table 13.3); a shortened version of the PAICS (the PAICS-R) also exists (see text)
Solving Problems in Family Interaction II (SPI-FI II; Forgatch & Lathrop, 1995)	Observation:			
1. Communication categories	1. Each thought unit coded	Individual	Nonverbal, positive process, leading question, blame, complain, oppositional, negative evaluation, provide rationale, structuring, unrelated topic, garbage	Contains 7 other categories for problem solving (see Table 13.3)

(continued)

TABLE 13.5. (*continued*)

Name	Description	Focus[a]	Sample items or categories	Comments
2. Coder Impressions II (interpersonal process items)	2. Observers rate entire taped interaction on either 4- or 7-point scales (40 items)	Individual	"Showed empathy, support and genuine concern," "Acted inappropriate/immature during this discussion," "Was critical or blaming toward others not present"	Coder rates mother, father, and adolescent separately; some items assess affect, parenting style, and couple relations; additional 40 coder impression items assess other domains (see Table 13.3)
Defensive/Supportive Behavior Code (Alexander, 1973)	Observation: 5-second observation, 5-second recording system	Individual	Defensive communication (judgmental dogmatism, control and strategy, indifference, superiority), supportive communication (genuine information seeking and giving, spontaneous problem solving, empathic understanding, equality)	
Unnamed observational system (Blaske et al., 1989; Mann et al., 1990)	Observation; some categories involve frequency counts, others involve ratings on Likert-type scales	Individual, dyad, or family, depending on how scores combined	Positive communication (consisting of supportive statements by each family member, explicit information, ratings of dyad affect); supportiveness (consisting of supportive and defensive communication [reverse-scored]); conflict/hostility (consisting of aggressive statements, attempted and successful interruptions, simultaneous speech, rating of dyad conflict)	Family activity category also included
Interaction Behavior Code (IBC), communication categories (Prinz & Kent, 1978)	Observation; observers evaluate presence–absence of 29 behaviors; evaluate 3 others as "no," "a little," or "a lot"; also rate entire interaction for put-downs and friendliness	Individual and family	Negative communication (e.g., negative exaggeration, yelling, ridicule, repeating one's opinion with insistence, making demands, arguing over small points [quibbling]); positive communication (e.g., joking, praising, asking what the other would like, compromise)	Each tape rated by multiple raters (usually four) whose scores are averaged

Measure	Method	Focus[a]	Categories	Notes
Iowa Family Interaction Scales, communication categories (Rueter & Conger, 1995b)	Observation; observers rate entire interaction on 5-point scales	Individual	Hostile interaction style (acting or speaking in hostile fashion, reciprocating hostility, using threats or bullying); warm interaction style (showing concern for other, entering into warm/supportive exchanges)	Rating scale items combined differently in different investigations
Unnamed coding system (Vuchinich et al., 1994)	Observation; observers rate entire interaction on 7-point scales	Individual	Warmth (positive behavior toward another); negative behavior toward another also rated	
Depression Observation System, communication category (Sanders & Dadds, 1989)	Observation; presence–absence of categories scored within 20-second intervals	Individual	Aversive content (consisting of criticize, negative solution, justification, and disagreement)	Also contains 3 other categories (see Table 13.3)
Community Members' Rating Scale, communication categories (Robin & Canter, 1984)	Observation; observers rate entire interaction on 7-point scales	Dyad or family	Accept responsibility, approval, command, complain, disagree, deny responsibility, humor, interrupt, laugh, negative solution, no response, put down, question, talk, global communication rating	Contains 8 additional problem-solving categories (see Table 13.3)

[a] Individual = items or categories focus on behavior of individual members; dyad = focus is on twosomes in the family (e.g., mother–father, mother–child); family = focus is on triads or larger family unit as a whole.

suggest that shared method variance may be a problem in studies that support the validity of the PACS using same-informant questionnaire data. Specifically, Knight et al. (1994) found that maternal PACS scores correlated significantly with their estimates of their children's depression and conduct problems. Child reports on these variables showed similar although less strong relationships. Cross-informant correlations (e.g., between child PACS scores and mother-reported depression and conduct problems, and vice versa) failed to reflect the same relationships, however. Discriminative validity data were more promising: Masselam et al. (1990) reported that mothers', fathers', and teens' scores on both subscales significantly differentiated families with teens who attended an alternative school because of behavioral difficulties from families with teens in public schools.

The PARQ (described earlier) has a Communication subscale that assesses parents' reports of their teens' communication behavior (and vice versa in the adolescent version). The PARQ Communication subscale showed excellent internal consistency (.89 for mothers, fathers, and teens; Robin et al., 1990), and differentiated distressed from nondistressed mothers, fathers, and adolescents (Robin et al., 1990). In addition, Koepke et al. (1987) reported that mothers' and fathers' Communication scores correlated significantly with interview and observation measures of similar content (with teens, scores correlated with interview but not observational data). Unfortunately, PARQ Communication scores also correlated somewhat more strongly with interview categories corresponding to other PARQ subscales than with the specific communication category. This is not entirely surprising, however; as noted earlier, the PARQ Communication subscale loads highly with various other PARQ subscales (e.g., Problem-Solving, Global Distress, Warmth/Hostility, Cohesion) on a single superordinate Skill Deficits/Overt Conflict factor. Nonetheless, whether the Communication subscale shows sufficient discriminant validity to stand on its own warrants further study.

Observational Assessment

A number of formal observation systems assess positive and negative communication. We have described many of these earlier because they contain problem-solving as well as communication categories. Here and in Table 13.5, we describe their communication components.

As they do with problem solving, investigators use different situations to elicit samples of family communication. One common type involves conflict centering around real or hypothetical problems, as described earlier. But some sample other sorts of situations, such as decision making, planning, or everyday conversation in which the situation is not engineered or specifically selected to elicit conflict. Such tasks include planning a vacation with unlimited funds (Barkley, Anastopoulos, et al., 1992); planning a family meal that everyone would enjoy with a limited number of dishes (Gilbert et al., 1984); and solving a puzzle together and discussing family-oriented topics, such as family strengths and what might happen if the mother left for a month (Thomas & Olson, 1993).

The modified MICS (described earlier) contains 16 categories that assess positive and negative aspects of communication not captured in definitions of problem-solving behaviors. Its successors, the PAICS and PAICS-R, contain 10 and 3 communication categories, respectively. Most psychometric data on these systems come from the modified MICS, however.

Satisfactory interobserver agreement on specific categories of these systems can be difficult to establish and maintain, particularly for low-frequency responses. We (Robin & Foster, 1989), for example, reanalyzed data from Robin and Weiss's (1980) study, and reported percent agreement for specific categories of the modified MICS ranging from 0% to 100%. Robin and Canter (1984) also reported variable category agreement (percent agreement from 39% to 92%; average = 73%), with many categories occurring so infrequently that they were never coded during reliability assessments. Barkley, Anastopoulos, et al. (1992) reported somewhat better occurrence agreement figures of .70–.78 for the communication categories of the PAICS-R.

Despite occasionally poor interobserver agreement, however, many categories of the modified MICS significantly distinguish distressed from nondistressed families (Robin & Weiss, 1980). In addition, summary MICS scores have excellent convergent validity, correlating .90 and higher with community members' global ratings of the same discussion (Robin & Canter, 1984). Robin and Canter (1984) also provided data on convergent validity for individual categories. Only a handful correlated above .60 with parents', teens', or professionals' global ratings. This might indicate more about validity problems with global ratings than about such problems with the modified MICS. Nonetheless, these low correlations suggest that even professionals who work with families may not agree with trained observers in how they evaluate the specific components of family interaction.

Other multicategory systems also contain codes relevant to parent–adolescent communication. The SPI-FI II, for example, contains a number of categories related to negative and positive communication, as does Gilbert et al.'s (1984; Gilbert & Christensen, 1988) Family Alliances Coding System. In each of these cases, however, investigators have grouped these individual codes into larger superordinate categories relevant to their investigations. As a result, limited psychometric data on individual codes are available.

All of the systems described thus far require extensive observer training to achieve satisfactory interobserver agreement scores. Because of their fine-grained categories, coding is time-consuming. In addition, many of the codes may occur infrequently in brief discussion samples. These systems do, however, permit sequential analysis of interaction patterns, as well as yielding relative frequencies of each category. Thus they are suitable for analysis of patterns of family interaction at a molecular level.

One solution to the limitations of fine-grained coding systems is to use codes that classify behavior into larger categories. For example, Alexander's (1973) Defensive/Supportive Behavior Code uses a 5-second observation, 5-second recording interval system to code behavior into two broad categories: defensive communication (composed of judgmental dogmatism, control and strategy, indifference, and superiority) and supportive communication (composed of genuine information seeking and giving, spontaneous problem solving, empathic understanding, and equality). Interobserver agreement figures ranged from 65% to 100%, averaging 85% and higher for the broad supportive and defensive categories. Scores on the code categories also did not change significantly for untreated families over a 10- to 12-week interval—a general reflection of test–retest stability (Alexander, 1973). In addition, Alexander (1973) found that defensive communication behaviors occurred significantly more often in families with teenagers referred to juvenile court than in equivalent nonreferred families. Referred children, but not parents, displayed less supportive communication than nonreferred teens. Support for the convergent validity of the categories comes from

findings that families classified by their therapists as most improved after treatment showed higher ratios of supportive to defensive communication at the end of therapy than families classified as less improved (Alexander, Barton, Schiavo, & Parsons, 1976). Observational data also reflected changes as a function of treatment (Alexander & Barton, 1980).

Henggeler, Borduin, and their colleagues (Blaske, Borduin, Henggeler, & Mann, 1989; Mann et al., 1990) have created a similar system that they have used to code taped discussions of families with delinquent teenagers. Observers count the frequency of some codes (e.g., supportive communication, successful interruptions) and assign Likert-type ratings of others (e.g., dyadic affect). These categories combine to form more global categories (verbal activity, supportiveness, conflict/hostility, positive communication). Composition of global categories appears to vary somewhat across studies, as category groupings were based on factor analyses (the results of which differed slightly for different samples). Interobserver agreement figures have generally been good to excellent across codes, regardless of the agreement statistic (percent agreement $\geq 74\%$, correlations $\geq .63$, kappas $\geq .72$; Blaske et al., 1989; Mann et al., 1990). Each of the codes has distinguished families with a teen offender from comparison families, although the specific patterns depend on the type of dyad being assessed (Blaske et al, 1989; Mann et al., 1990). In addition, supportiveness, verbal activity, and conflict/hostility scores have all been sensitive to change as a function of family treatment (Borduin et al., 1995; Mann et al., 1990).

Global-inferential systems (as discussed earlier) provide a second alternative to fine-grained, training-intensive coding systems. The IBC (Prinz & Kent, 1978; Prinz et al., 1979) lists 24 negative and 8 positive behaviors that observers rate on either dichotomous (occurrence–nonoccurrence) or trichotomous ("none," "a little," "a lot") scales. These are summed and divided by the total number of negative or positive behaviors to yield total negative and positive behavior scores. In addition, observers make global ratings of the degree of criticism and friendliness in the discussion, using Likert-type scales of 1–4 or 1–5.

The IBC communication subscales yield interobserver agreement generally above .80, with as little as 2 hours of observer training, when at least four observers code each interaction (e.g., Foster et al., 1983; Prinz & Kent, 1978; Schreer, 1994).

Pairwise agreement on individual items has not been calculated, but would undoubtedly be too low for investigators to use individual positive and negative behavior items on their own (e.g., to select target behaviors). IBC codes correlate .51–.82 with categories of the modified MICS (Robin & Koepke, 1985), and are unrelated to family income (Schreer, 1994).

IBC scores provide only an overview of global aspects of communication and cannot be used to pinpoint communication strengths and weaknesses. In addition, because most categories are dichotomous, the IBC may not be sensitive to changes when negative patterns become less frequent or intense, but still characterize the family member's communication during a discussion.

The Community Members' Rating Scale (Robin & Canter, 1984), described earlier, contains most of the communication categories of the modified MICS. Groups of observers estimate the frequency of each behavior and also provide an overall global rating of the dyad's or family's communication. Interrater agreement correlations based on the mean of groups of 13–15 raters generally exceeded .70, but individual pairwise agreement would not be sufficient to use single raters to evaluate specific categories. As with the problem-solving categories of the Community Members' Rating Scale, correlations between ratings of individual behaviors and the same behaviors coded with the modified MICS yielded variable correlations, with only a few exceeding .50. Composites formed by combining individual categories of the Community Members' Rating Scale fared better psychometrically. The global communication rating correlated .90 with a modified MICS composite score that contained both problem-solving and communication categories. A composite Community Members' Rating Scale score also discriminated distressed from nondistressed dyads, as did a composite of global ratings of conflict, communication, and problem solving.

Other observational systems that use observer ratings have also appeared in the literature. These include the Coder Impressions-II Scale of the SPI-FI II (Forgatch & Lathrop, 1995) and the Iowa Family Interaction Rating Scales (Rueter & Conger, 1995a, 1995b). Both of these comprehensive systems also assess problem solving and were described earlier. In general, the authors of these systems have used individual communication skill categories to assess larger constructs; these constructs have varied from investigation to investigation. Thus, limited psychometric data are available for specific communication components of

these systems, despite their scope and potential utility. In addition, some of the observation codes described elsewhere in this chapter contain one or two global categories that assess positive or negative communication. Table 13.5 provides brief descriptions of some of these.

Alternative Approaches

As it does for observation of problem solving, the clinical interview provides a rich resource for observing family communication. Questions such as "How does your son [daughter] let you know he [she] is angry?", "How do you know when your mom [dad] is really listening to you and when she [he] isn't?", and "What do you like [dislike] most about how you get along together?" can elicit family members' descriptions of their communication at home. Having family members describe a recent argument (or a good talk) is another way to get a picture of how they interact in regard to problem issues.

Observations in the session supplement the content of family members' reports. How do family members behave when they disagree about a fact or an opinion? How does the teen respond to parents' views, attacks, or pronouncements? How do the parents react when the teen voices an opinion or withdraws from the discussion? Comparing the information yielded by observations in a session with family members' oral reports and questionnaire data can also yield important information. We recall vividly one case in which a single mother bemoaned the fact that her teenage son never shared his views or opinions with her, and indicated that she often tried to elicit these opinions, to no avail. Observations in the session revealed that each time he voiced an opinion that disagreed even slightly with her own, she criticized him—a pattern she had never noticed!

COGNITION AND CONFLICT

A key tenet of cognitive–behavioral theories is that interpretations of and cognitive reactions to events can influence subsequent behavior and affect. Irrational-belief models focus on specific types of cognition presumed to promote and maintain conflict. In addition, developmental studies suggest that teens and adults' social reasoning about teen autonomy in decision making may be important in conflict management as well.

We (Robin & Foster, 1989; Foster & Robin, 1988) have proposed that externally oriented irrational beliefs predispose family members to excessive anger and conflict. According to this model, family members who overreact to other members' behavior with one of several types of extreme thinking should be more prone to excessive conflict than those who do not. Specifically, a number of forms of distorted thinking lead to excessive anger, which polarizes and disrupts adaptive problem solving and good communication. Our model includes several externally oriented extreme beliefs for parents[4]:

1. *Ruination*: Distorted appraisal of the consequences of adopting a course of action, usually based on a misappraisal of the probability of a certain outcome or on general catastrophic thinking. For example, parents may fear that adolescents will ruin their future lives (e.g., "If I let her stay out too late, she'll have sex and get AIDS").
2. *Perfectionism*: The assumption that adolescents should instinctively and without instruction know how to behave in accord with parental expectations, even in new situations, and should not make mistakes.
3. *Obedience*: The assumption that adolescents should follow their parents' commands and suggestions without ever questioning their reasons or judgment.
4. *Malicious intent*: The assumption that teens misbehave on purpose to distress or hurt their parents.

Irrational beliefs teens may hold include the following:

1. *Ruination*: As in the parental version, this belief involves the projection of disastrous outcomes from parental rules (e.g., "If you don't let me do what I want, nobody will like me").
2. *Fairness*: The notion that parental rules should always be just and reasonable according to the teen's standards (e.g., "Why can't I stay out until midnight? My brother gets to do that").
3. *Autonomy*: The belief that adolescents are capable of making all of their decisions on their own, and should be given as much freedom as they desire.

Vincent Roehling and Robin (1986) and Robin et al. (1990) provided mixed support for this model. Using different assessment devices, these investigations showed that fathers' endorsement of

beliefs regarding perfectionism, obedience, malicious intent, and ruination discriminated distressed from nondistressed families, as did teens' beliefs regarding ruination. Results for other kinds of beliefs hypothesized to relate to conflict were more inconsistent: Vincent Roehling and Robin (1986) found that adolescent endorsement of beliefs regarding unfairness and autonomy distinguished distressed from nondistressed dyads, but Robin et al. (1990) did not. In addition, whereas Vincent Roehling and Robin reported no significant differences for mothers' endorsement of irrational beliefs, Robin et al. found that distressed mothers endorsed more beliefs related to ruination, obedience, and malicious intent than nondistressed mothers did.

"Malicious intent" refers to one type of parental attribution for child behavior—specifically, a parent's belief that a teenager intentionally behaved negatively to annoy or hurt the parent. Grace, Kelley, and McCain (1993) linked additional aspects of attributional style to parent–adolescent conflict. Mothers and teens each evaluated the probable causes of negative responses by the other member of the dyad in hypothetical conflict situations. For both mother and teen reports, the reported anger intensity of home discussions was significantly related to each party's attributions that the other's negative behavior was internally caused, intentional, selfishly motivated, and blameworthy, and that behavior resulted from a stable, cross-situational (global) cause. Baden and Howe (1992), using a similar scale, also found that mothers of teens with conduct problems rated misbehavior as more global, stable, and intentional than did mothers of a comparison group of teens. The findings of these two studies converge with an extensive body of literature linking negative attributional styles to couple discord, both longitudinally and concurrently (see Bradbury & Fincham, 1990, for a review), and they suggest that negative causal explanations for other family members' behavior are important cognitive components of conflictual processes.

Investigators of each of the types of thoughts described thus far propose that distorted or excessively negative thought content about the other person promotes conflict. Taking a different approach to cognition, social-developmental theorists hypothesize that discrepancies between parents' and teens' views of who "owns" the problem also relate to parent–adolescent conflict. In a series of studies, Smetana and colleagues (Smetana, 1989; Smetana et al., 1991b) explored parents' and teens' views of who should exercise decision-making autonomy over varying aspects of the teens' lives. They speculated that conflict results from renegotiation of family roles as a child moves through adolescence, with primary renegotiations involving "ownership" of decision-making authority in regard to the teen's behavior. As adolescents approach adulthood, teens expect increasing autonomy for their decisions about how to behave. Parents, like their offspring, must shift their views of the balance of parent–teen authority as their adolescents mature.

The reasons or justifications parents and teens provide for their behavioral choices reflect their assumptions and thoughts about parent versus teen authority. Among the nonclinic families studied by Smetana's group, parents and teens had different views. Whether they were asked about their real-life conflicts or provided with hypothetical conflicts, teens justified their positions most often by pointing to reasons related to personal preferences and autonomy. In contrast, parents' reasons regarding the conflictual issue more often involved social-conventional reasons, such as norms, politeness, and responsibility (Smetana, 1989; Smetana et al., 1991b). Teens' reasoning may play different roles for boys and girls: Smetana et al. (1991b) found that male teenagers' personal reasoning correlated positively with ratings of poor communication in parent–teen discussions, and with critical, judgmental parental behaviors. In contrast, girls' personal reasoning was negatively related to parental criticism and positively related to observers' ratings of conflict resolution, humor, and father communication.

These findings suggest that the reasons individuals use to justify their positions in disagreement may be additional important cognitive factors that relate to conflict. These data converge with Robin and colleagues' findings: Recall that clinic parents were particularly likely to endorse obedience beliefs, while their adolescent offspring endorsed autonomy beliefs (Vincent Roehling & Robin, 1986). This suggests that clinic parents and teens may follow the normal reasoning patterns associated with adolescent autonomy seeking, but may endorse exaggerated or excessively rigid positions on issues.

Related developmental research also shows that parents' and teens' views of the legitimacy and source of family rules may be important. These views differ according to the type of issue involved. In nonclinic families, most parents and adolescents viewed parents as having a large role in making rules about moral issues such as lying and stealing, issues involving conventional behavior

(e.g., cursing, manners), and issues involving risk-taking behavior (e.g., drinking alcohol) (Smetana & Asquith, 1994). Views were more discrepant about the legitimacy of parental rules about friendship issues and about issues involving both adolescent personal choice and behavioral conventionality, with parents viewing 82–88% of these issues as subject to parental rules, but teens seeing a smaller proportion (57–64%) as appropriate for parental rules. Teens and parents viewed parental rules as less important or relevant for issues of personal jurisdiction, seeing only 27% and 56–58% of these issues, respectively, as under parental jurisdiction.

Interestingly, parents and teens did not systematically report more discussion or anger intensity about friendship and conventional issues (about which they disagreed in terms of jurisdiction) than about issues for which results were more congruent. This challenges the view that discrepant views of authority promote more frequent or intense conflict. Analyses of discrepancies within families (as opposed to those in the sample as a whole), however, might provide a clearer view of the role of discrepant views in promoting conflict. In a related vein, the degree of discrepancy between parent and teen views of who actually makes decisions in the family predict self-reports of frequency of discussion of potentially conflictual issues, both concurrently and longitudinally (Holmbeck & O'Donnell, 1991). Family members' beliefs about rules, together with congruence in views about rules and decision-making authority, certainly warrant further investigation as potential contributors to maladaptive communication about conflictual issues.

Questionnaire Assessment

Two questionnaire devices, the Family Beliefs Inventory (FBI) and the PARQ, specifically assess irrational beliefs. The FBI (Vincent Roehling & Robin, 1986) consists of 10 vignettes. Each describes a hypothetical parent–teen conflict, followed by a series of specific belief statements tied to the vignette. Respondents use a 7-point scale to rate the extent to which they agree with each of the statements. Scores for each of six belief categories for parents (four for teens) are summed across vignettes to yield one score for each type of irrational belief. Scores can be obtained for Ruination, Obedience, Malicious Intent, Perfectionism, Approval, and Self-Blame for parents. For teens, belief scores include Ruination, Autonomy, Unfairness, and Approval.

Vincent Roehling and Robin (1986) reported internal-consistency statistics for FBI individual belief scores to exceed .65 (with the exception of the Approval scale, which yielded alphas between .46 and .72). Externally oriented belief scales discriminated distressed from nondistressed fathers and teens, but not mothers, leading to questions about the validity of this instrument for assessing mothers' cognitions. Interestingly, the three scales that assessed internally directed beliefs (Approval and Self-Blame for parents, Approval for teens) did not discriminate the two types of families, lending some support to the discriminant validity of the various scales of the instrument. These beliefs would be expected to relate more closely to negative self-directed emotions (e.g., depression and anxiety) than to externalizing problems (e.g., anger and conflict). Correlational analyses suggested that different conflict-enhancing belief subscales were moderately to strongly intercorrelated among mothers, fathers, and teens (*r*'s between .48 and .72), supporting the notion that these may tap a single cognitive response style.

FBI total summary scores failed to correlate consistently with the IC and the CBQ. The total FBI scores, however, include scores for approval and self-blame beliefs as well as the beliefs more strongly tied theoretically to conflict, and this may have attenuated the findings somewhat. Furthermore, Vincent Roehling and Robin (1986) argue that because irrational beliefs are not the only determinant of family conflict, indicators of these beliefs would be expected to show only low to moderate correlations with conflict. These findings indicate the strong need for additional validity data on the FBI.

The PARQ, described earlier (Robin et al., 1990), also assesses irrational beliefs. Subscales for these beliefs include Ruination, Obedience, Malicious Intent, Perfectionism, Approval, and Self-Blame for parents, and Autonomy, Perfectionism (defined here in terms of high expectations for the self rather than the parents), Ruination, Unfairness, and Approval for teens. Each belief scale consists of eight items that are endorsed either "true" or "false." For example, items on the parental Ruination scale include "My adolescent is unable to handle a lot of freedom without getting into trouble" and "If my teenager gets involved with sex, this could ruin his/her life." Robin et al. (1990) reported acceptable internal consistency (i.e., >.60) for most of the external-focus belief scales; internal consistencies for approval, self-blame, and perfectionism were poorer (.38–.58). For parents, factor analyses showed that all of the

belief scales loaded on a higher-order Beliefs factor that correlated only minimally (.11–.13) with the higher-order Skill Deficits/Overt Conflict factor. Interestingly, for adolescents, Ruination, Unfairness, and Autonomy (externally oriented beliefs) loaded on the same higher-order factor as the Problem-Solving and Communication subscales; Perfectionism and Approval (internally directed thoughts) loaded on a separate factor.

Koepke et al. (1987) found that total belief scale scores correlated .27–.40 with a checklist assessing the same domains completed by interviewers after a structured clinical interview. Although these data supported the convergent validity of the belief composite, the composite also correlated just as highly with interview ratings of other dimensions of family interaction as with ratings of beliefs, leading to questions about the discriminant validity of the belief total. Belief scores failed to correlate with direct observational ratings of beliefs as assessed during two 10-minute problem-solving discussions; however, this is not surprising, given that outside observers cannot observe beliefs (which are private events) directly.

The PARQ belief scales provide promising ways of assessing general reports of beliefs, but do not specify the specific situations in which these beliefs are likely to arise. The Mother–Adolescent Attribution Questionnaire (MAAQ) developed by Grace et al. (1993) is more situationally anchored. The MAAQ presents eight hypothetical conflict situations involving such topics as chores, homework completion, and curfew. The adolescent version asks the teen to rate the cause of negative maternal behavior in these situations; mothers rate the cause of negative teen behavior. Each respondent uses 6-point Likert-type scales to rate the extent to which each negative behavior is caused by global, external, and stable factors, and also rates how much he or she believes the behavior to be motivated by selfish reasons, to be intentional, and to merit blame.

Grace et al. (1993) reported that internal consistencies for the attribution scales all exceeded .75. Correlations among attributional dimensions exceeded .50 for teens and .29 for mothers, suggesting that at least some of these dimensions may be part of a general negative attributional style. Each attributional dimension correlated with at least one questionnaire self-report indicator of anger and/or relationship distress. These results, however, could have been the product of shared method variance. When the effects of method variance were eliminated by using parent attributions to predict teen reports of conflict (and vice versa), only attributions of blame significantly predicted negative interaction reported by the other member of the dyad.

Other cognitions that may relate to conflict revolve around parents' and adolescents' views of authority for making rules and justifications for their positions on issues. Smetana and colleagues (Smetana, 1995; Smetana & Asquith, 1994) assessed views on authority for rules with the Parental Authority Questionnaire. This instrument presents hypothetical conflicts of varying sorts (e.g., morality, conventional behavior, etc.); it then asks parents and teenagers to indicate whether parents have the right to make a rule about the issue, whether they are obligated to do so, and (if they make a rule) whether an act is wrong if it violates the rule. Parents and teens then select (from a list of 25 reasons) up to two reasons why behavior suggested in the scenario is right or wrong. Despite the face validity of this instrument, data on reliability and on convergent and discriminant validity are not available. Smetana's (1995) findings that parents who reported authoritative and authoritarian parenting styles viewed more issues as under parental jurisdiction than parents who reported more permissive styles, however, support the discriminative validity of this portion of the scale.

The FBI, the PARQ, the MAAQ, and the Parental Authority Questionnaire are all self-report tasks that involve either reports of general beliefs (the PARQ) or responses to hypothetical conflicts (the FBI, the MAAQ). The extent to which these reports generalize to cognitive reactions during actual conflicts is uncertain. The difficulties of assessing cognition during actual interactions complicates the task of examining this issue empirically. Cognitive events can only be observed by their owners, not by outside observers. Individuals frequently fail to attend their thoughts unless prompted to do so, but self-observing one's thinking in the "heat of battle" is likely to be both extremely difficult and highly reactive. A few alternative assessment methods, however, may come somewhat closer to providing samples of cognition during *in vivo* conflict.

Alternative Approaches

Investigators have described a number of additional methods for examining thoughts. For example, Smetana (1989) interviewed parents and teens about the reasons underlying their points of view about conflictual situations. In this assessment, the interviewer asked each parent and ado-

lescent (1) to identify conflictual issues in their relationship, (2) to describe the reasons why their behavior was right or wrong, and (3) to indicate the other person's viewpoint about the issue. Although reasons could be coded reliability (overall kappas = .93; Smetana, 1989; Smetana et al., 1991a), this method has yet to be subjected to further psychometric scrutiny.

A few investigators have developed other creative methods that provide ways of assessing family members' "on-line" cognition. O'Brien, Margolin, John, and Krueger (1991) played audiotapes of hypothetical interparental and parent–child conflicts for mothers and their 8- to 11-year-old sons. Participants listened to each tape, which was divided into three segments. After each segment, the tape was paused, and participants recorded the thoughts and feelings they had about the tape. Observers later coded these tapes of participants' "articulated thoughts," using categories relevant to the goals of the investigation.

This method carefully controlled the stimuli to which mothers and sons responded, and sampled their reports of thoughts and feelings as the participants experienced them. Nonetheless, participants were explicitly told to assume the role of observers rather than participants in the conflict. Although these data may be representative of their reactions to other family members' conflicts, they may not adequately sample reactions to disagreements in which the respondents participate directly.

Sanders and Dadds (1992) described two alternative ways of assessing cognition that captured this "insider" perspective. They videotaped mothers discussing conflictual issues with their CD or non-CD children (ages 7–14). After the discussion ended, family members separated and completed two kinds of cognitive assessments. In the videotape-mediated recall task, each family member viewed the taped interaction individually. Every 20 seconds, a research assistant stopped the tape for the participant to describe what he or she was thinking at that moment during the discussion. In the thought-listing procedure, mothers and children wrote down each thought they remembered having occurred during the interaction. Coders later categorized whether each thought was positive or negative, and whether the content referred to the family, the self, or something else. Sanders and Dadds (1992) reported overall kappas of .82 and .86 for coding of the videotape-mediated recall and thought-listing data, respectively, but no agreement data for individual categories.

Scores for many categories from the videotape-mediated recall procedure differentiated children with CD and their mothers from comparison children and mothers, supporting the discriminative validity of this procedure. Mothers of CD children recalled more negative and fewer positive thoughts about their families, relative to comparison mothers, and they voiced fewer positive thoughts about themselves. Similarly, the CD children reported more negative thoughts about themselves and fewer positive thoughts about their families during the interaction.[5] Interestingly, although many of the scores from the thought-listing and videotape-mediated recall procedure correlated reasonably well (i.e., 8 of 12 correlations fell between .35 and .57), scores from the thought-listing procedure did not discriminate families with CD children from comparison families, suggesting that the recall procedure is more sensitive than is thought listing for assessing conflict-relevant cognition.

Other results supported the construct validity of thought data produced by the videotape-mediated recall procedure. The percentage of family-related positive thoughts reported by the children correlated negatively ($-.30$) with mothers' reports on the CD scale of the Revised Behavior Problem Checklist. Children's positive thoughts about themselves correlated negatively with mother reports of conduct, attention, motor excess, and anxiety problems ($-.38 < r$'s $< -.29$). Proportions of mothers' negative references to themselves were associated positively with Beck Depression Inventory scores; Beck scores and ratings of marital satisfaction correlated negatively with mothers' reports of positive thoughts about themselves and their families.

Together, these results provide some support for the convergent and discriminant validity of the videotape-mediated recall measure. This procedure has particular promise because it assesses cognition close in time to its occurrence, and thus provides the most direct measure of thoughts used to date with families. The procedure has particular promise for conducting functional analyses of family interactions: Therapists can examine sequential connections among thoughts and behaviors as they occur over time. In addition, scoring parents' and teens' thoughts for the occurrence of the irrational beliefs and intent attributions described earlier would allow investigators to test the hypothesized relationships among these thoughts, negative behavior, and angry affect during interaction processes. Despite the promise of this procedure, however, it has the potential for reactivity, and it will be important to assess the extent to which family members *reconstruct* versus *construct anew* their thoughts as they view the interaction.

Although this question probably cannot be tested directly, indirect support for the former hypothesis comes from Gottman and Levenson's (1985) finding that couples' physiological reactions during a videotape-mediated affect recall task mirrored quite closely their reactions assessed during the task per se; this finding indicated that they might have been "reexperiencing" the conflict as they viewed it on videotape.

Informal methods similar to videotape-mediated recall procedures can be used in clinic settings to sample family members' thoughts. Irrational or anger-producing thoughts are particularly likely when discussions become heated, family members polarize or refuse to negotiate, or one or more members suddenly refuses to participate. Clinicians can ask family members to recount their thoughts at these times (e.g., "What was running through your head just now?" or "You looked like you had a strong reaction to that. What do you think about what your mom just said?"). "Why" questions also can elicit participants' general views on others' behavior (e.g., "Why do you think he does that?" or "Why is this issue so important to you?"). In addition, family members can be asked to note their thoughts during conflicts at home in a conflict log or diary.

Regardless of the method of eliciting thoughts from family members, the information obtained must be interpreted carefully in light of each family's circumstances and culture, particularly when thoughts are labeled "irrational" or "maladaptive." This is especially true with immigrant and first-generation families in the United States and Canada. Many non-European cultures (e.g., Chinese, Mexican, Japanese) strongly emphasize obedience and respect to authority in general and parents in particular. In these cultures, thinking that might be called "rigid" in the U.S. or Canadian majority culture may be more normative. Thus, the roles of beliefs in conflict situations must be carefully appraised when clinicians are dealing with clients from cultures other than those in which the studies cited here were conducted. In these cases, idiographic assessment of the type of cognitions parents hold, the cultural bases for those beliefs, and the role of these beliefs in parent–adolescent conflict must be carried out with particular care and sensitivity. In many cases, ascribing conflict to the clash between the parents' own culturally sanctioned beliefs and those the teen is developing as a result of exposure to the new culture may be a more viable and helpful approach to conceptualizing family acrimony than ascribing conflict to anyone's "irrational beliefs."

In addition, occasionally the so-called "irrational beliefs" and negative attributions described here are rational and realistic. Teenagers who display serious delinquent behavior may be at risk for problems that could ruin their lives. Highly impulsive teenagers may make extremely poor decisions if given too much freedom. On occasion, teenagers will admit that they intentionally act out to get back at a parent for some previous perceived parental misdeed. In these cases, parental concerns may be quite realistic. This again highlights the importance of understanding the role of cognition within the broader context of the nature and scope of the parent–adolescent difficulties. For example, a mother who believes her son will ruin his life with additional freedom may be overreacting if the teenager does reasonably well in school and obeys family rules, but has occasional yelling matches at home over issues such as curfew and chores. The same mother would be reacting quite reasonably if her son were involved in gang activity, were regularly truant from school, and had recently been seen with a gun in his possession. Indeed, a parent who failed to voice serious concerns about the latter teen's future would be thought too cavalier and uninvolved.

AFFECT AND CONFLICT

Investigators have devoted relatively little attention to the role of affect in conflictual parent–adolescent interactions. Nonetheless, clinical anecdotes abound about therapy sessions that are difficult to manage because of explosive affect, and about families whose adaptive problem solving is derailed by excessive anger. On the other hand, families whose members can laugh during discussion of difficult issues frequently seem more able to discuss problems productively than those who cannot.

This clinical lore suggests that expressions of positive affect toward other family members are positively associated with effective interaction, whereas expressions of anger function to disrupt adaptive communication. Data support this: McColloch, Gilbert, and Johnson (1990) indicated that observers rated mothers, fathers, and their aggressive teens as displaying more negative affect in problem-solving discussions than they rated their counterparts in families with nonaggressive teens. These families were also rated as showing less problem focus and poorer listening skills during their discussions. Similarly, Hops, Davis, and Longoria (1995) reported that observ-

ers' codings of teens' aggressive and distressed behavior (codes with specific affective as well as content dimensions) correlated negatively with family members' global ratings of their problem-solving effectiveness during problem-solving discussions. Capaldi et al. (1994) found similar negative correlations between expression of hostile affect and problem-solving outcome.

Assessing affect is complicated by the fact that assessors often fail to agree on what constitutes "emotion." In some cases, assessors include the stimuli or situations that elicit emotion as part of the definition of the emotion, thus confounding the two (e.g., by defining anger as always provoked by frustration; see Rubin, 1986, for a discussion). Finally, some discuss "negative affect" in general terms, failing to distinguish between internalizing negative emotions (anxiety, depression) and externalizing emotions (upset, anger, contempt).

We focus here primarily on negative externalizing affect. We do this because the kinds of problems linked to problem-solving and communication problems most often fall into the externalizing behavior categories, and because families commonly complain of and report anger during their interactions (e.g., Prinz et al., 1979). Furthermore, we follow the "triple-response mode" model of affect commonly used in behavioral assessment. Namely, we view a given "affect" as a construct that can be defined and examined in terms of its motor, physiological, and cognitive components, which may or may not covary (Cone, 1979; Lang, 1971).

Thus, one can assess affect via (1) observations of behavior consensually labeled "emotional," such as shouting, laughing, or talking about feelings ("You're making me really mad"); (2) physiological recording, and (3) self-report of experiences labeled with affective terminology (e.g., answers to the question "How do you feel?"). These responses are distinct from the stimuli or situations that evoke them.

Questionnaire and Verbal Report Assessment

Few assessment approaches specifically target the experience, expression, or physiological dimensions of externalizing negative affect in parent–adolescent interaction. The IC (described earlier) asks respondents to rate how angry the discussions of a series of topics were in the recent past, but does not specify how to interpret the term "angry." Thus, respondents may be labeling their experience of anger, their expression of anger, others' expression of anger, or some combination of these. In addition, many have used this score as an index of conflict rather than of experienced or expressed anger. Nonetheless, as indicated earlier, anger intensity scores on the IC have performed reasonably well psychometrically.

A few additional investigations have more directly examined parent and child reports of affect immediately following conflictual discussions. Sanders et al. (1992) examined family members' reports of others' affect in parent–child discussions by having each parent and child rate how sad, angry, critical, and happy the other seemed during the interaction. Thus, they assessed perception of others' affective behavior rather than one's own affect-related cognition. Parents' (but not children's) single-item ratings of sadness, anger, and happiness distinguished among families of children with depression, CD, comorbid depression and CD, and no diagnosis. Using a similar approach, McColloch et al. (1990) asked family members to rate their own moods after discussing a conflictual topic. Family members with teens characterized as aggressive by their teachers reported more anger and anxiety than did families with nonaggressive teens.

Self-reports have also been used to assess physiological reactions to conflict. O'Brien et al. (1991) asked preadolescent boys and their mothers to report their physiological state while listening to audiotapes of hypothetical marital and mother–son conflicts, using an eight-item rating scale (coefficient alphas = .70 and .80 for sons and mothers, respectively). Boys from homes characterized by marital physical aggression reported more arousal in response to marital conflict than did boys from verbally aggressive homes; with mother–son conflict, the pattern was reversed. Although this study focused primarily on younger children, its findings indicate the need to develop reliable and valid measures that specifically target different responses involving affect during family discussions.

Observational Assessment

Unlike questionnaire and family report measures, direct observation systems clearly assess motor components of emotion. Hops et al. (1995) describe the Living in Family Environments (LIFE) observational system. Although originally designed to assess interactions in families with a depressed member, the LIFE has also been used to code parent–adolescent discussions (Davis et al., 1995). The current version of the code contains 22 content codes and 8 affect codes (e.g., irritable,

happy). Observers code each message for both content and affect, thus permitting sequential analyses. Published reports using the LIFE generally report data on superordinate categories defined by both content and affect, making it difficult to assess the reliability and validity of individual affect codes. Nonetheless, the LIFE system is one of the few used to code parent–child interaction that explicitly includes a variety of affect categories, and it certainly warrants further psychometric scrutiny with parents and teenagers.

Forgatch and Stoolmiller (1994) and Capaldi et al. (1994) used a different observation system, the Specific Affect Coding System (SPAFF; Gottman & Levenson, 1985, 1986), to examine affect in parent–adolescent discussions. The SPAFF is based in part on Ekman and Friesen's (1975) classic Facial Action Coding System for coding affect from facial expression. The SPAFF employs the evaluations of cultural informants (observers judged read affect cues competently within a specific culture) and has been widely used with couples. Observers using the SPAFF classify each speech unit as positive, negative, or neutral, using a variety of verbal and nonverbal cues (including facial expression). They then further subcategorize positive and negative statements into 1 of 11 affect codes, some of which capture externalizing affect (anger, contempt) and some of which relate to more internalizing feelings (anxiety, sadness, whine). Forgatch and Stoolmiller report a percent agreement of 76% and a kappa of .60 across all affect codes. In addition, Capaldi et al. (1994) indicated that externalizing negative affect (anger, contempt) correlated negatively with ratings of the outcome of a problem-solving discussion for mothers (–.40), fathers (–.28) and sons (–.53). Both the SPAFF and the LIFE coding systems provide viable alternatives for coding affective behavior in family interactions.

Alternative Approaches

Most observational assessments related to affect, like those related to behavior and cognition, are based on brief laboratory samples of communication. Larson (1989) describes one fascinating alternative, the Experience Sampling Method, for assessing affect *in vivo*. In Larson's studies (e.g., Larson, 1989; Larson & Richards, 1991), teenagers carried beepers that signaled them at random intervals (about once every 2 waking hours) to record what was happening at the instant the beeper went off. A standard form prompted them to record their activity, location, companions, and affect. To assess affect, participants completed semantic differential scales. The average of three of these (happy–unhappy, cheerful–irritable, friendly–angry) constituted an affect scale.

Correlations between data from youths in grades 5–9 for the first and second half of a week of data collection indicated good temporal stability, ranging from .66 to .71 for the three items making up the affect scale (Larson, 1989). Larson (1989) also reported that a minority of participants (about 8.5%) reported substantially distorting what they reported, with the remainder indicating their reports to be truthful. In addition, Larson (1989) indicated that he had to exclude data from about 7% of the original participants because their reports were either obviously false or too erratic to be useful. Interestingly, compared to participants who supplied better data, these youths were from families of lower socioeconomic status, had lower grade point averages, had higher self-reported depression, and were rated as less mature by teachers. Of the sample that remained, about a fourth of the sample stopped filling out reports before the end of the data collection interval. These findings suggest that additional steps are probably needed to insure that clinic samples comply with data collection and complete home records accurately. Although the Experience Sampling Method has not been used specifically to assess parent–adolescent conflict, it provides interesting possibilities for future research into its use as a method of assessing affect during family interaction in the natural environment.

Family assessors and researchers may also wish to borrow from instruments and approaches used to assess affective responses in couple interaction. For example, Gottman and Levenson (1985, 1986) have asked couples to reconstruct their affect verbally while viewing a tape of their interaction. The fact that partners' physiological reactions closely mirrored those obtained during the interaction per se indirectly supports the premise that these verbal reconstructions also match the original experience of the partners during the interaction, and thus supports their validity as measures of affective experience (Gottman & Levenson, 1985). Methods such as Gottman and Levenson's, which carefully connect different measures of affect during discussion of conflictual topics, show considerable promise for understanding the interplay among the experience of negative affect, the expression of affect, and the physiology of affect. Linking these to measures of other cognitive events (e.g., irrational thoughts) and to the responses of other family members would further expand our

knowledge of how these systems function on a microsocial level.

In addition, informal methods of assessing conflict can be quite useful in clinical practice. Watching family members' reactions in sessions and during family discussions, and then asking them how they felt, helps the therapist learn about the congruence between members' affective expression and affective experience (cognition). Linking these observations with the specific interactional events (antecedents) that provoke anger, and with the effects that expressed affect has on discussion, should provide important clues about the role of affect in family members' discussion. The therapist can assess family members' thoughts with similar questions, providing an efficient way of gathering concurrent information about the connections among behavior, thoughts, and feelings that transpire during family discussions. Home records or diaries that ask family members to record angry exchanges can also be structured to provide the same information about *in vivo* interactions.

SYSTEMIC FACTORS

Our discussion of conflict thus far has focused on the molecular elements of communication and discord. In this section, we examine systemic elements of conflict—that is, the patterning of these molecular behaviors at molar levels of analysis, especially the hierarchical arrangements of interactions among members of the family. Hierarchical arrangements involve patterns of influence and authority within the family (i.e., who makes the decisions and how). Systems-level constructs describe these relationships. Several of these have been proposed as risk factors for excessive conflict between parents and teens, and some have empirical support. These include weak parental teamwork and communication (in two-parent families), triangulation, cross-generational coalitions, and extreme patterns of cohesion–disengagement. In the pages that follow, we first describe and discuss each of these constructs, and then overview approaches for assessing it. Table 13.6 describes each of these instruments and indicates the specific structural construct(s) it purports to assess.

Parental Teamwork

In two-parent families in Western societies, parents are presumed to be at the top of the family hierarchy (they are aided by other adult kinfolk in

TABLE 13.6. Descriptions of Instruments for Assessing Structural Aspects of Parent–Adolescent Interaction

Name	Structural domain	Description	Focus[a]	Sample items or categories	Comments
Marital Satisfaction Inventory (MSI), Conflict Over Childrearing Scale (Snyder, 1979)	Parental teamwork	Questionnaire; 20 true–false items	Individual and dyad	"My spouse and I rarely disagree on how much time to spend with the children," "A large portion of the arguments I have with my spouse are caused by the children," "Sometimes my spouse really spoils the children."	Part of 280-item scale with additional subscales: Global Satisfaction, Conventionalization, Problem-Solving Communication, Sexual Dissatisfaction, Affective Communication, Time Together, Disagreement about Finances, Role Orientation, Family History of Distress, Satisfaction with Childrearing
Parenting Alliance Inventory (PAI; Abidin & Brunner, 1995)	Parental teamwork	Questionnaire; 20 items rated on 5-point scale; two factors	Individual and dyad	Factor 1: "My child's other parent enjoys being alone with our child," "My child's other parent and I communicate well about our child." Factor 2: "My child's other parent believes I am a good parent," "My child's other parent tells me I am a good parent."	
Family Alliances Coding System (Gilbert et al., 1984)	Alliances	Observation; observers code each speech act for affective quality and for content	Individual behavior toward or about second person	Positive alliance (consisting of agree–approve, affection, paraphrase/clarify/reflect, positive appeal, positive coalition, defend/protect); negative alliance (consisting of disagree/disapprove, disaffiliate/sarcasm, attack, opposing question, behavior control, threat, negative appeal, negative coalition)	Also contains three neutral codes (personal statement, structure, guiding question); strength and patterning of different dyadic alliance patterns can be calculated

(continued)

TABLE 13.6. (*continued*)

Name	Structural domain	Description	Focus[a]	Sample items or categories	Comments
Family Adaptiveness and Cohesion Evaluation Scales III (FACES III; Olson et al., 1985)	Cohesion	Questionnaire; 20 items rated on Likert-type scales; two subscales (Adaptability, Cohesion)	Family	Cohesion: "Family members ask each other for help," "We like to do things with just our immediate family," "We approve of each other's friends." Adaptability: "In solving problems, children's suggestions are followed," "Children have a say in their discipline," "Rules change in our family."	Ideal and couple versions available
Family Environment Scale (FES), Cohesion subscale (Moos & Moos, 1981)	Cohesion	Questionnaire; 9 true–false items	Family	"Family members back each other up," "There is plenty of time and attention for everyone in our family," "There is very little group spirit in our family."	Part of 90-item scale with 9 additional subscales (see Table 13.5)
Parent–Adolescent Relationship Questionnaire (PARQ), structural subscales (Robin et al., 1990)	Cohesion	Questionnaire; 15 true–false items	Family	"We are an extremely close-knit family," "There is not much feeling of togetherness in our family," "At home we go out of our way to do things for each other."	Part of 250-item questionnaire with additional subscales (see Table 13.3)
	Coalitions	Questionnaire; 30 true–false items (mother–teen against father, father–teen against mother, parents against teen)	Family	"My mother can get her way by getting my father's help against me," "When mom is critical, my dad sticks up for me," "My mom and I ignore dad's ideas."	
	Triangulation	Questionnaire; 45 true–false items (15 with	Family	"I often feel 'caught in the middle' when my parents	

Instrument	Construct	Method	Focus[a]	Sample items	Notes
		mother in middle, 15 with father in middle, 15 with teen in middle)		disagree," "My mom can make dad and me stop yelling at one another," "My dad doesn't know whose side to take when mom and I disagree."	
Structural Family Interaction Scale—Revised (SFIS-R; Perosa & Perosa, 1993)	Cohesion	Questionnaire; 3 subscales rated on 4-point scales: 1. Enmeshment/Disengagement (11 items) 2. Mother–Child Cohesion/Estrangement (9 items) 3. Father–Child Cohesion/Estrangement (10 items)	Individual, dyad, and family	"When someone in my family gets hurt or upset, we all get involved." "In my family mother and child can talk over differences and settle them fairly." "Father responds when child needs help or support."	Part of 68-item scale with 3 additional subscales: Flexibility/Rigidity, Conflict Avoidance/ Expression, Spouse Conflict Resolved/ Unresolved
	Coalitions/ triangulation	Questionnaire; Cross-Generational Triads/ Parental Coalition subscale (11 items)	Family	"When parents disagree about an issue they sometimes make a child feel 'caught in the middle.'"	
Clinical Rating Scale (Thomas & Olson, 1993)	Cohesion	Observation; observers rate entire family interaction on six 8-point scales, and also make single global rating of cohesion	Family and dyad	Emotional bonding, family involvement, marital relationship, parent–child relationship, internal boundaries, external boundaries	Also includes ratings of communication and adaptability
Unnamed coding system (Vuchinich et al., 1993)	Coalitions, parental teamwork	Observation; observers rate entire interaction on 7-point scale	Dyad	Coalitions: Extent to which mother and father take sides against child Parental conflict: Extent of put-downs, threats, challenges between parents Parental agreement: Positive behavior exchanged between parents	

some cultures). The adults with presumed authority for the children must work together as a team and socialize the children in consistent ways. Failure to work as a team can promote deviant child behavior in various ways. First, it increases the likelihood of inconsistent or inadequate consequences for child behavior. Second, by the time children reach adolescence they can readily learn how to play one parent against the other for their own ends, exacerbating existing behavior problems. Third, adults who communicate poorly expose their children to poor models of problem solving and communication. Finally, exposure to parental conflict has been associated with various externalizing behavior problems in samples composed primarily of preadolescent children (see Davies & Cummings, 1994, and Grych & Fincham, 1990, for excellent reviews).

Parental teamwork problems can be the product of isolated couple discord about child-related problems in the context of an otherwise good relationship. Alternatively, they can be one part of more general communication problems that pervade other aspects of the couple's life. Although neither of these difficulties inevitably accompanies parent–adolescent conflict, each is associated with problems in parent–child communication. Vuchinich et al. (1993) found that Dyadic Adjustment Scale scores (which assess general couple satisfaction) and ratings of parents' agreement during problem-solving discussions with a preadolescent son correlated with ratings of problem-solving effectiveness during the discussion. Furthermore, parents' agreement during a parent–child discussion when the son was in the fourth grade significantly predicted ratings of a similar discussion 2 years later. Similarly, Mann et al. (1990) found that improvements in mother–father supportiveness during a parent–teen discussion significantly predicted reductions in delinquent teens' reported symptomatology following treatment.

Questionnaire Assessment

Assessment of couple teamwork specifically in relation to problems with their teenagers can be accomplished via the Conflict Over Childrearing subscale of Snyder's (1979) Marital Satisfaction Inventory (MSI), a 280-item questionnaire. Untangling specific psychometric data for the Conflict Over Childrearing subscale is sometimes difficult, because published reports on the MSI generally summarize data for the inventory as a whole. Nonetheless, data specific to the Conflict

Over Childrearing subscale indicated that its scores distinguished clinic from nonclinic couples (Scheer & Snyder, 1984); couple reports correlated .74 on the subscale (Snyder, Wills, & Keiser, 1981). In addition, Conflict Over Childrearing scores correlated significantly and positively (r's between .25 and .40) with clinicians' ratings of various aspects of couple interaction about children based on a structured conjoint interview in both clinic (Snyder et al., 1981) and nonclinic (Scheer & Snyder, 1984) samples. Scores also correlated with parent reports of various child behavior problems, with the specific correlates dependent to some extent on the age and gender of the child (Snyder et al., 1988). Less encouraging were findings that reports of child-rearing conflict correlated negatively with interview ratings of husbands' defensiveness (−.33) and couples' reluctance to discuss their marriages (−.27) in clinic samples (Snyder et al., 1981), and with ratings of husbands' unrealistically positive descriptions of their marriages (−.37) and wives' expression of anger toward their mates (.35) in nonclinic samples (Scheer & Snyder, 1984). Although these data suggest that response styles may distort couples' reports, statistically extracting questionnaire indicators of social desirability did not influence the relationship between couples' appraisal of their marriages and reports of child behavior problems (Snyder et al., 1988).

An alternative questionnaire measure of parental teamwork, the Parenting Alliance Inventory (PAI; Abidin & Brunner, 1995), asks each respondent to report his or her views of the other parent's involvement with the child and parenting competence, as well as the degree of agreement–discord between the two parents over child rearing. Factor analyses produced two identical subscales for mothers and fathers: one three-item scale with items pertaining to whether the spouse views the respondent as a "good parent," and the other subscale assessing involvement, agreement, and so forth. Based on a nonclinic sample of parents of preschool children, Abidin and Brunner (1995) reported that (1) overall internal consistency of the scale was .97; (2) spouses' reports correlated .50; (3) a single PAI summary score correlated relatively weakly but significantly with marital satisfaction scores (.20 for mothers, .44 for fathers); (4) the PAI total score showed a greater number of significant correlations with indicators of child adjustment than did more global marital satisfaction scores, although correlations were often low to moderate; and (5) the PAI score failed to correlate significantly with child or parent age, parent education or income, or social desirability scores. PAI items have good face validity, and Abidin and Brunner's (1995) data suggest that further investigation of the PAI would be useful, particularly in relation to observations of parental interactions centering around child-rearing issues.

Observational and Alternative Approaches

Although the technique is not widely used in the literature, an interaction sample in which the parents discuss a problem about their teenager (without the teenager present) also provides a way of gathering information about a couple's problem solving and communication about child-related issues (e.g., Wolfe, 1986). This can be coded with any of the many interaction coding systems mentioned earlier. Parent–parent interaction during a family discussion can also be coded. For example, Gilbert et al. (1984) coded behaviors exchanged between parents, and weighted these for the degree to which they indicated supportiveness of the other (i.e., alliance). Maritally distressed couples with behavior problem children had poorer marital alliance scores than their nondistressed counterparts did. Similarly, Vuchinich et al.'s (1993) raters specifically scored agreements and disagreements (conflict) directed from one parent to another during a problem-solving discussion (with the child present), using Likert-type scales from 1 to 7 (these ratings were described in more detail earlier, in our discussion of the assessment of conflict per se).

The clinical interview with the family can also yield a wealth of data on the couple. Questions such as "How well do the two of you agree on how to handle Lisa when she does _____?", "How are your mom and dad different in how they treat you when you disagree?", "What parts of this situation do the two of you agree about? Disagree about?", and "How does your partner react when you do _____?" can sometimes elicit descriptions of areas in which the parents disagree. Obtaining blow-by-blow descriptions of how each member participates in conflictual interactions, and of how each parent handles situations in which the adolescent disobeys family rules or agreements, can also highlight ways in which (1) the teen manipulates one or both parents, or (2) one parent undermines the other's efforts. Observations in a session of how the parents discuss topics together and handle differing opinions supplement the content of their answers by providing samples of their interactions when discussing their teenager.

In addition to assessing the couple's teamwork, the clinician may wish to appraise the couple's relations generally. A host of instruments assess marital satisfaction, accord, and communication. Among the best-known and researched of questionnaires for assessing couple satisfaction are the Dyadic Adjustment Scale (Spanier, 1976); the Locke–Wallace Marital Adjustment Test (Locke & Wallace, 1959) and its shortened version (Kimmel & Van Der Veen, 1974); and Snyder's MSI (Snyder, 1979), which contains a General Satisfaction subscale, a Conventionalization subscale, and nine additional subscales assessing various aspects of couple interactions and conflict (e.g., Problem-Solving Communication, Sexual Dissatisfaction, Affective Communication). Couple discussions can also be obtained and coded with systems such as the MICS (now in its fourth version; Heyman, Weiss, & Eddy, 1995), which also has a shorter version; the MICS-G, a simplified derivative of the MICS that uses global ratings instead of utterance-by-utterance coding (Weiss & Tolman, 1990); and the Couple Interaction Scoring System (Gottman, 1979). Detailed review of these assessment tools is beyond the scope of this chapter. Weiss and Heyman (1990), Christensen (1987), and Fincham and Bradbury (1987; Bradbury & Fincham, 1987) evaluate many of these instruments and describe general issues in assessing couples' relationships.

Coalitions and Triangulation

It is important to distinguish between strong parental *teamwork* and strong parental *coalitions* held together by mutual parental blame directed at the child. Whereas teamwork should promote child adjustment, blaming coalitions do the opposite. In systems terminology, parental coalitions involving blame are sometimes called "scapegoating" or "detouring," with the latter term also assuming that this pattern helps the parents avoid conflict between themselves by focusing their joint attention on their "bad" teenager. A number of writers suggest that these patterns are maladaptive. Treatment books, for example, frequently advise family therapists to defuse or reframe blaming early in treatment, in order to engage family members in the treatment process (Alexander & Parsons, 1982; Haley, 1976; Robin & Foster, 1989).

Empirical literature supports this clinical advice. Grace et al. (1993) found that rigid, negative maternal attributions regarding a teen's behavior correlated with self-reported conflict. Similarly, Vuchinich et al. (1993, 1994) indicated that ratings of parental coalitions against a son correlated negatively with ratings of problem solving during videotaped discussions.

Poor parental teamwork can set the stage both for cross-generational coalitions and for triangulation. In cross-generational coalitions, one parent and the adolescent side with each other against the other parent. For example, a teenage son may play upon his father's sympathies to get his father to call off the mother's discipline. With triangulation, two conflicting parties each align with a third, who vacillates between the two conflicting parties. For example, a teenage daughter may quarrel with her father over curfew, with the mother interpreting the position of each to the other one. The mother is said to be "triangulated" between the father and the teen.

The literature provides mixed support for role of cross-generational coalitions. Both Schreer (1994) and Vuchinich et al. (1994) found no relationship between cross-generational coalitions (assessed via questionnaire in the former study and observations in the latter) and observers' ratings of communication and problem-solving quality during a family discussion. In contrast, Mann et al. (1990) provided somewhat more support for the role of cross-generational coalitions in family interactions. They videotaped interactions of families with and without delinquent adolescents. Observational data revealed higher proportions of mother–adolescent verbal activity and father–adolescent conflict/hostility in families of delinquent teens than in families of well-adjusted adolescents. Although mother–teen supportiveness and conflict/hostility did not differentiate the groups, Mann et al. (1990) argued that the pattern that did emerge supported systems characterizations of a cross-generational coalition between an overly involved mother and a teen, with a more distant father–teen relationship. Changes in parent–adolescent interactions as a function of therapy, however, failed to predict changes in adolescent symptomatology, again casting doubt on the role of cross-generational coalitions in family interaction processes.

Questionnaire Assessment

Various assessment devices assess coalitions and triangulation in different dyads in the family (see Table 13.6). In addition to scales for Communication, Problem-Solving, and various beliefs, the PARQ (Robin et al., 1990) contains subscales assessing Coalitions and Triangulation. Robin et al. (1990) reported satisfactory internal consistency

(.65–.85) for these subscales. Both scales loaded on a superordinate Family Structure factor for mothers, fathers, and teens. Only teen reports of coalitions, however, distinguished distressed from nondistressed families.

Koepke et al. (1987) reported that Triangulation scores correlated significantly (.51–.53) with interviewers' assessments of triangulation from a clinical interview; scores also correlated .24–.47 with observations during an audiotaped discussion. The Coalitions subscale, however, did not correlate with interview scores, and only correlated with observations weakly in one case (father scores, $r = .29$). This may result, however, from the fact that neither the interview nor the observation was specifically structured to elicit the patterns of behavior that describe these constructs.

Schreer (1994) also found stronger evidence for the validity of the PARQ Triangulation subscale than for that of the Coalition subscale. Adolescents' reports of coalitions between the teen and the mother failed to correlate with either direct observations of communication or IC frequency × intensity scores, with one exception: Teens who reported mother–teen coalitions also reported greater conflict with their fathers ($r = .31$). In addition, family members' reports of coalitions between the same dyads generally failed to correlate significantly, indicating poor cross-informant agreement. In contrast, mothers' reports of triangulation involving fathers in the middle correlated positively with adolescents' reports of problem solving on the PARQ ($r = .38$), and negatively with observers' ratings of mother–teen ($r = -.42$) and father–teen ($r = -.45$) communication.

Another questionnaire, the Structural Family Interaction Scale—Revised (SFIS-R; Perosa & Perosa, 1993), contains seven subscales. One is called Cross-Generational Triads/Parental Coalition and contains 11 items assessing triangulation, parent–child coalitions, and detouring. Perosa and Perosa (1990a) reported an alpha coefficient of .81, and later found that 4-week test–retest correlations with college student respondents exceeded .80 (Perosa & Perosa, 1993). The scale correlated moderately to highly with other subscales of the SFIS-R that assess various structural aspects of family life (e.g., Mother–Child Cohesion/Estrangement, Spouse Conflict Resolved/Unresolved), and with various other questionnaire measures assessing related domains (Perosa & Perosa, 1990a). Many of these correlations were high enough, however, to raise questions about the discriminant validity of the scale; no multimethod studies have as yet examined this issue.

Observational Assessment

A few observational strategies assess patterns of coalitions and triangulation (see Table 13.6). Vuchinich et al. (1994) used observers' ratings to evaluate the extent to which parent–parent and parent–child dyads took sides against each other during triadic problem-solving discussions. Vuchinich et al. (1994) reported interrater correlations of .61–.76. As indicated earlier, correlations between ratings of parental coalitions and related constructs supported the construct validity of the parental coalition ratings. Ratings of cross-generational coalitions, however, failed to correlate either with parents' reports of internalizing or externalizing behaviors on the Child Behavior Checklist, or with observers' ratings of family problem solving. Furthermore, none of the three coalition scores discriminated clinic from nonclinic families. Whether these findings were attributable to problems with measuring cross-generational coalitions during brief interactions, the age of the boys in the study (who were in fourth grade), or faulty theories about the maladaptive function of cross-generational coalitions remains to be tested.

Gilbert et al. (1984) developed the Family Alliances Coding System for assessing alliance patterns in families. Three independent observers code each speech act for affective quality and for content, also noting the person to whom the communication is addressed or to whom it pertains. Codes are weighted, summed, and adjusted for family size and amount of speech to provide indices of alliance for each dyad in the family. Numerical weights ranging from –9.3 to +9.0 are assigned to each code, based on 20 clinical psychology graduate students' ratings of how well the category represents a positive or negative alliance response. Interestingly, Gilbert and Christensen (1988) indicated that code indicators performed equally well without the weightings.

Gilbert et al. (1984) reported that at least two of the three observers who coded each interaction agreed on coding decisions 97% of the time, but provided no specific category agreement information. Discriminative validity data indicated that when individual codes were analyzed, only positive affect scores differentiated families with marital and child behavior problems from nondistressed families. This may have been a result of the limited statistical power imposed by the very small sample (12 families per group), however. In contrast, an overall alliance strength score (formed by summing the weightings for each code, then dividing by the number of times the dyad communicated) between various dyads in the family showed significantly higher alliance scores for almost all dyadic combinations in nondistressed than in distressed families.

As Gilbert and Christensen (1988) point out, this way of scoring data may produce scores that reflect overall positivity and negativity of communication among specific family dyads, rather than their degree of involvement. When Gilbert et al. (1984) examined the relative rank-ordering of alliance patterns among dyads (which were independent of the overall positivity of family communication), differences between distressed and nondistressed families again emerged, with the marital alliance being significantly less salient in distressed than in nondistressed families. In contrast, distressed mothers and target children were more involved in negative exchanges, supporting the notion of skewed alliance patterns in distressed families. Together, these findings provide initial support for the construct validity of this coding system when it is used to assess behavior in problem-solving tasks. Additional data on convergent and discriminant validity are needed, however, particularly to establish whether the structural dimension called "alliance" is substantially different from the constructs of positive and negative communication. In addition, the extent to which this coding system can be used to assess coalitions (as defined here) is unknown.

Cohesion, Disengagement, and Enmeshment

Structural and strategic family therapists describe "cohesion" as a continuum describing the amount of closeness and contact among family members (Aponte & VanDeusen, 1981). Members of "enmeshed" families (at one end of the continuum) have close involvement in the affairs of other members, lack privacy, and emphasize conformity with family norms. These family members state others' positions for them, mind-read, interrupt, invade others' privacy, and provide directives and "shoulds" for how to behave. Certain contingency arrangements are also likely: They may avoid open conflict, and parents may respond negatively to a teen's independence seeking (particularly to activities that take the teen outside the family). On the flip side, family members may richly reinforce adolescent involvement in family problems and activities, and react quickly and strongly to changes in other members' behavior.

At the other end of the cohesion continuum, members of "disengaged" families show a lack of involvement in the lives of other members. They may interact infrequently, and parents may discipline children rarely or erratically. Contingencies for an adolescent's behavior are few and largely ineffective. Acting-out problems reinforced by outcomes outside the household (e.g., peer attention) are likely to be topics of conflict.

Theorists believe that both extremes on the cohesion continuum interfere with successful adolescent development. Enmeshed families punish appropriate independence-seeking behavior, inhibiting the development of adult skills. In contrast, disengaged families fail to regulate teens' transition from childhood to adulthood effectively. As a result, teens are exposed to more challenging and/or riskier situations than they are prepared to handle.

A great deal of controversy surrounds the issue of whether cohesion is truly a curvilinear dimension, with "adaptive" families falling between the extremes of enmeshment and disengagement. Most studies using questionnaires to assess cohesion find a linear, not a curvilinear, relationship between reports of family cohesion and other indicators of child and family adjustment (Perosa & Perosa, 1990b; Prange et al., 1992). These findings clearly support the notion that disengagement is associated with maladaptive outcomes. Furthermore, self-reported disengagement is associated with self-reported family conflict among adolescents with school difficulties (Franklin & Streeter, 1993). Individuals high on self-reported cohesion (the "enmeshed"), however, frequently fail to show elevated individual or family pathology. These findings have led some to criticize the instruments (e.g., Perosa & Perosa, 1990b), and others to conclude that the construct of maladaptive enmeshment may be more a fiction of family systems theorists and therapists than a critical dimension of family functioning (e.g., Cluff & Hicks, 1994).

In addition, factor analyses of cohesion scales on questionnaires consistently show that such scales load on superordinate factors with subscales assessing conflict, communication, and positive feelings toward others in the family (Boake & Salmon, 1983; Gondoli & Jacob, 1993; Robin et al., 1990). This suggests that cohesion as currently operationalized in most inventories is more closely aligned with communication and conflict than with structural aspects of family functioning. Perhaps this is not surprising in light of the fact that the "cohesion" scales of many questionnaires contain a preponderance of items relating to spending time together, supporting one another, or feelings of emotional closeness, with little emphasis on appropriate and inappropriate involvement in the affairs of others. The latter, we would argue, should be more strongly related to structural aspects of family life than the former.

Questionnaire Assessment

The Family Adaptability and Cohesion Evaluation Scales III (FACES III; Olson, Portner, & Lavee, 1985) is the third version of Olson and colleagues' questionnaire designed to measure adaptability and cohesion. In the FACES III, "adaptability" refers to the family's skills at responding to stress and change, while "cohesion" refers to emotional attachment among members.

Olson et al. (1985) based their selection of specific items both on theoretical considerations related to their circumplex model of family functioning and on data on past versions of the instrument. Others have criticized both the content and face validity of the instrument. Perosa and Perosa (1990b), for example, suggest that the FACES III may mix items that assess behaviors with linear and curvilinear relationships to family functioning. Others question whether the FACES III Likert-type scales are the best ways of discriminating enmeshed, disengaged, and "healthy" families (Ben-David & Jurich, 1993; Pratt & Hansen, 1987). Ben-David and Sprenkle (1993) interviewed eight adults about their reactions to Adaptability items of the FACES III. Several respondents found the referents of items unclear. Some respondents indicated they were unsure of what the authors meant by "family." Others had difficulty responding to items such as "In solving problems, children's suggestions are followed," because their behavior varied across situations (e.g., older children in the family were allowed more input than younger ones; children were consulted on issues that involved them but not on issues involving only parents).

Several investigations with parents and adolescents have found that the Cohesion scale has consistently good internal consistency, whereas Adaptability data are more variable (alphas for Adaptability, .58–.83; for Cohesion, .70–.92; Fuhrman & Holmbeck, 1995; Olson et al., 1985; Perosa & Perosa, 1990a, 1990b; Prange et al., 1992; Vandvik & Eckblad, 1993). Although Olson et al. (1985) created the scales to be uncorrelated (and reported an r of .03), others have found correlations between the scales of .19–.42, depending upon the sample and who is doing the reporting (Hampson, Hulgus, & Beavers, 1991; Perosa & Perosa, 1990a; Prange et al., 1992; Vandvik &

Eckblad, 1993). Although Olson et al.'s (1985) original factor analysis revealed two clear factors with no cross-loadings, Vandvik and Eckblad (1993) only partially replicated these results: They reported that some of the Cohesion items loaded on both Adaptability and Cohesion factors with their Norwegian sample.

Although Olson et al. (1985) developed the FACES III with the assumption that abnormally high or low scores on either Cohesion or Adaptability would indicate problematic family relationships, most concur at this point that linear, not curvilinear, relationships characterize the relationships between Adaptability and Cohesion scores and other indicators of adjustment (e.g., Perosa & Perosa, 1990b; Prange et al., 1992). Some (e.g., Ben-David & Sprenkle, 1993) speculate that the fault lies in the way items are worded, not in the constructs; they hypothesize that item wording leads respondents to view the dimensions items assess as linear (i.e., "more is better"). Rewording the Adaptability items to make them more bipolar did not change their linear relationship with other indicators of family functioning, however, although changing the specific response options to capture the extremes more fully made the relationship somewhat more curvilinear (Ben-David & Jurich, 1993). Even with this revision, however, Ben-David and Jurich (1993) found many more "disengaged" than "enmeshed" families. Clearly the FACES III cannot be said to assess maladaptive enmeshment, although it may provide a window into family members' perceptions of disengagement.

Agreement among parent and teen reports has been disappointing, ranging from .18 to .44 for Cohesion and from .13 to .23 for Adaptability (Fuhrman & Holmbeck, 1995; Olson et al., 1985; Prange et al., 1992). Father–mother agreement for Cohesion is somewhat better (.44–.53; Olson et al., 1985; Vandvik & Eckblad, 1993), but is only .25 for Adaptability (Olson et al., 1985). The Cohesion scale has shown good convergent validity with other paper-and-pencil instruments purporting to assess the same construct (Hampson et al., 1991; Perosa & Perosa, 1990a), and also correlates with scores from a family sculpture assessment in which respondents place pieces representing family members on a board, with distances between the pieces used as indicators of perceived emotional distance between family members (Vandvik & Eckblad, 1993). Correlations between the Adaptability scale and other questionnaire measures have been more variable (Perosa & Perosa, 1990a).

Unfortunately, few investigations have compared the FACES III with measures of adaptability and cohesion using methods other than self-reports. This is particularly worrisome in light of discriminant validity data. Perosa and Perosa (1990a) reported that Adaptability scores correlated somewhat but not dramatically less with indicators of cohesion (most r's = .22–.28) than they did with other indicators of adaptability (highest r's = .39–.53). On a more positive note, Olson et al. (1985) reported no correlation between Adaptability and social desirability scores. Cohesion, in contrast, correlated .35 with social desirability; this is substantially less than correlations between Cohesion and other measures of the same construct (.59–.86; Perosa & Perosa, 1990a), however. Correlations between Cohesion and indicators of adaptability do not paint such a rosy picture, with most between .47 and .77 (Perosa & Perosa, 1990a). Prange et al. (1992) reported similar questions about discriminant validity of both the Adaptability and Cohesion scales in their multitrait, multisource (parent, adolescent) approach to examining the two scales of the FACES III.

Various additional data support the construct validity of the two FACES III subscales. Cohesion and Adaptability scores were associated with various other self-reported indicators of general family communication and functioning (Hampson et al., 1991; Perosa & Perosa, 1990b). Low Cohesion was also associated with teen reports of low self-esteem (Franklin & Streeter, 1993) and other internalizing difficulties (Prange et al., 1992), and with parent and teen reports of CD and drug use on the Diagnostic Interview Schedule for Children—Revised (Prange et al., 1992). In contrast, Fuhrman and Holmbeck (1995) found the average of parent and teen Cohesion scores to be unrelated to reports of conflict and to mother and teacher reports of internalizing and externalizing scores on the Child Behavior Checklist. Whether this was the result of sample differences from previous studies (Fuhrman and Holmbeck's sample was 60% African-American) or indicates the need to assess the validity of mother and teen scores separately is not clear. Prange et al. (1992) reported no correlations exceeding .15 between Adaptability and psychological difficulties. Prange et al. (1992) also characterized family types according to Cohesion and Adaptability scores, finding significant differences for clinic and nonclinic parents and teens on Cohesion, but only for parents on Adaptability.

The few studies of the applicability of the FACES III to ethnic and racial groups other than

European-American samples are inconclusive. Although Prange et al. (1992) reported that a clinic sample of parents of white female adolescents reported higher Adaptability scores than parents of their nonwhite counterparts, the mixed ethnicity of the nonwhite group made these data difficult to interpret. Lyon, Henggeler, and Hall (1992) found no difference between Hispanic-American and European-American incarcerated male teens' scores on the FACES III. On an earlier version of the questionnaire (FACES II), however, Knight et al. (1994) found that a nonclinic group of His-panic mothers of 9- to 13-year-old children reported higher Cohesion scores than non-Hispanic moth-ers. Adaptability scores did not differ. Both Adapt-ability and Cohesion correlated positively although relatively weakly (.24, .25) with acculturation scores. These findings, together with criticisms of the con-tent of FACES II for Hispanic families (Knight et al., 1992) suggest that FACES III warrants more investigation before its wholesale adoption for use with Hispanic, African-American, and other non-European-American families.

The FES (Moos & Moos, 1981) also contains a widely used Cohesion subscale, items of which assess "commitment, help, and support family members provide for one another" (Moos & Moos, 1981, p. 2). Unlike the FACES III Cohesion scale, the FES scale has been viewed as assessing cohe-sion in a linear fashion. Internal-consistency esti-mates have ranged from .75 to .88, depending upon the respondent (Moos & Moos, 1981; Paikoff et al., 1993; Perosa & Perosa, 1990a), and Moos and Moos (1981) reported 2-, 4-, and 12-month test–retest reliability correlations of .86, .72, and .63, respectively. Scores on the Cohesion scale also discriminated distressed from nondistressed families (Moos & Moos, 1981) and parents with from parents without a psychiatric diagnosis (Hibbs et al., 1993).

Two studies have applied variations of a multitrait–multimethod approach to examine the convergent and discriminant validity of the FES Cohesion scale. Perosa and Perosa (1990a), who examined several scales assessing cohesion and adaptability, found that the FES Cohesion scale correlated substantially higher with FACES III Cohesion (.86) and other "cohesion" subscales (.61–.89) than with FACES III Adaptability (−.23) or with the FES Control (−.28) subscale. Although correlations with other so-called "adaptability" scales were much higher, this was probably attrib-utable to problems with the discriminant validity of the other scales rather than with the FES Co-hesion scale.

In a similar study, Cole and McPherson (1993) reworded the FES Cohesion items so that moth-ers, fathers, and adolescents reported on cohesion in different dyads in the family. A factor-analytic approach supported the discriminant validity of the Cohesion scale. Inspection of patterns of cor-relations was not as compelling, suggesting that shared method variance may inflate correlations between family members' estimates of cohesion in different family dyads. Correlations between family members on dyadic Cohesion ranged from .31 to .61, with mother–father agreement being the best (.50–.56).

Paikoff et al. (1993) similarly reported that mother–daughter reports on Cohesion correlated .46. Neither mothers' nor adolescent daughters' scores correlated with maternal or child age or with indicators of socioeconomic status (Moos & Moos, 1981; Paikoff et al., 1993), although they were associated with family size (Moos & Moos, 1981).

Other psychometric information indicates that distressed families reported less cohesion on the FES than did nondistressed ones (Moos & Moos, 1981). Hibbs et al. (1993) reported similar find-ings for parents who did and did not qualify for psychiatric diagnoses. Similarly, mothers who showed highly critical or overinvolved styles when describing their children in a brief interview also reported relatively less cohesion than less critical mothers (Hibbs et al., 1993). As indicated earlier, the FES Cohesion, Conflict, and Expressiveness scores all load on the same superordinate factor (Boake & Salmon, 1983).

The PARQ (Robin et al., 1990) contains a Cohesion subscale intended to assess degree of emotional bonding in the family. Internal consis-tency ranged from .79 to .84, and mother, father, and teen reports discriminated distressed from nondistressed groups (Robin et al., 1990). Al-though mother, father, and adolescent responses to the Cohesion scale correlated with scores from a checklist of similar behaviors during a 45-minute family interview, correlations were fairly low (.26–.39) and sometimes failed to exceed correla-tions between Cohesion scores and other interview behaviors, suggesting problems with the discrimi-nant validity of the scale. Observational assess-ments of cohesion during a problem-solving dis-cussion also failed to correlate with reports of cohesion by any of the family members (Koepke et al., 1987). Finally, PARQ Cohesion scores loaded highly on a factor containing Problem-Solving, Communication, and Warmth–Hostility scales (Robin et al., 1990); this suggests that the PARQ Cohesion scale, like the FES Cohesion scale, relates to communication more strongly than to structural dimensions of families. Finally, despite being defined as assessing enmeshment and disengagement, the PARQ Cohesion subscale has been treated as a linear scale in the literature.

Another questionnaire described earlier, the SFIS-R (Perosa & Perosa, 1993), contains three scales related to aspects of enmeshment, disengagement, and cohesion: Enmeshment/Disengagement (which includes perceived support, involvement, and differentiation of boundaries), Mother–Child Cohesion/Estrangement, and Father–Child Cohesion/Estrangement. The latter two subscales assess both parental nurturance and ways of resolving conflicts that encourage closeness; thus, scale content contains elements of conflict resolution as well as cohesion. Coefficient alphas for the three scales were .86, .90, and .91, respectively (Perosa & Perosa, 1990a); Perosa and Perosa (1993) reported that 4-week test–retest correlations exceeded .81. The Mother–Child Cohesion/Estrangement and Father–Child Cohesion/Estrangement scales correlated highly with the Enmeshment/Disengagement score (r's = .61–.66), but not as highly with each other (r's = .28, .41; Perosa & Perosa, 1990a, 1993). All correlated with questionnaires assessing related constructs, such as the FACES III and FES Cohesion scales (Perosa & Perosa, 1990a, 1990b). Correlations with other measures imply that the Enmeshment/Disengagement scale bears a linear, not a curvilinear, relationship to other indicators of adjustment (Perosa & Perosa, 1990a, 1990b, 1993). Data on convergent and discriminant validity with methods other than questionnaires remain to be reported and are particularly warranted, given the relatively high interscale correlations among the subscales of the SFIS-R.

Observational and Alternative Approaches

Few observation systems assess cohesion. One exception is the Clinical Rating Scale (Thomas & Olson, 1993), developed as a companion to the FACES to assess family adaptability, cohesion, and communication. Raters watch a family complete seven interaction tasks that require communication, and then rate the family on a series of 6- or 8-point Likert-type scales. Thomas and Olson (1993) reported that internal consistency of these ratings was quite high (.95 for cohesion) and that two independent raters' scores correlated well (.83). Items also generally loaded on appropriate factors in a factor analysis. Clinic families with teenage sons or daughters were more likely to score

at the extremes on cohesion than nonclinic families, supporting the discriminative validity of the measure and supporting a curvilinear relationship between cohesion and adjustment. Interestingly, disengaged families were far more prevalent than enmeshed ones in the sample.

Despite these promising data, Cluff and Hicks (1994) criticized the Clinical Rating Scale on a number of grounds. These include (1) using rating anchors for the same item that mix domains (i.e., are not on the same continua); (2) using negative labels at both ends of the continuum to force curvilinear findings; and (3) forcing raters to blend constructs in their ratings in ways reflecting a hypothetical construct ("enmeshment") that may actually be composed of multiple behaviors bearing linear relationships to adjustment.

Less formal observational assessment can also be done in the clinical interview. Asking parents how much they are involved in the teen's schooling and academic performance, whether and how they monitor the teen's whereabouts and activities outside the home, and how much they know about the teen's friends may provide clues to disengagement in the family. Questions about parental consequences, explicitness of rules, and consistency in rule enforcement may also provide information about the structure, support, and involvement parents provide for an adolescent. On the other end of the cohesion continuum, interruptions to speak for others, mind-reading communication, behaviors that steer the discussion away from conflictual topics, violations of privacy, and comments that paint the family as ideal and conflict-free may point to inappropriate restrictions on teen autonomy. The latter guidelines, however, should be considered much more tentatively in cultures that emphasize strong family bonds and obligations to the family; greater connection may be normative in these cultural groups. In these cases, the functions of these behaviors must be assessed particularly carefully to see whether within the family's specific milieu these patterns are adaptive, are irrelevant to the problem behavior, or serve to maintain problem interactions.

CLINICAL RECOMMENDATIONS

As this chapter has illustrated, the literature offers a dizzying array of methods for assessing parent–adolescent conflict. To select appropriate assessment tools and approaches requires a general framework for understanding parent–adolescent conflict. The model presented here suggests that this framework should include attention to conflictual issues; interactional processes that surround conflict and conflict resolution; cognitive and affective responses; systemic patterns that characterize conflictual exchanges; and individual psychopathology or problems in the couple relationship.

In addition, a general framework for how to assess families and integrate information can assist the clinician in seeing the larger context of family assessment. Below, we provide a number of general recommendations that emerge from material covered in this chapter and contribute to an overall framework for assessing parent–adolescent conflict:

1. The clinician should assess the dynamics of conflict at molecular and molar levels of analysis. Molecular, minute-by-minute elements of transactions should be considered in terms of the interplay among cognitions, interactional behavior, and affect. The practitioner should look for positive and negative communication behaviors, and examine whether irrational assumptions directed toward others are associated with angry affect and communication breakdowns. More molar systemic patterns should be assessed by looking at parental teamwork, coalitions, disengaged patterns, and triangulation as they relate to issues of conflict and conflictual interactions.

2. The clinician should also consider the broader individual and cultural context in which the family operates. At the individual level, does individual psychopathology play a role in conflict? If so, the literature related to the particular problem should be examined for additional information and approaches to assessment. At a cultural level, the clinician should use prevailing models of family competence cautiously when dealing with individuals from different backgrounds. The relevant literature and cultural informants should be consulted in the formulation of hypotheses.

3. Multimethod assessment should be employed to look for convergent findings. Observations of behavior in sessions, self-reports (interviews, questionnaires), and reports of other family members should be used routinely, and these should be supplemented with methods for collecting data in the natural environment. The clinician should bear in mind, however, that none of these methods is perfect. Observations may be reactive; self- and other-reports may be inaccurate; and observational coding by the clinician may be unreliable, particularly when done informally or by using rating scales. Convergent data enhance confidence in the picture the data paint of family interactions. Discrepant data indicate the need for further assessment to explain the sources of discrepancy, such as self-report biases and reactivity to observation.

4. Dyads and individuals in the family should be considered separately. The clinician should avoid generalizations about "the family," and instead should consider mother–father, mother–teen, and father–teen interactions. Siblings and other family members should be included in the assessment if they are involved in conflict patterns and management. The clinician must remember the lessons of situation specificity: Communication is not necessarily consistent across situations, such the presence or absence of other family members.

5. A functional-analytic approach should be used to formulate hypotheses about factors that maintain conflict at molecular and molar levels. Are there positive payoffs, such as attention and access to preferred activities (i.e., positive reinforcement), following maladaptive behavior? Does a particular type of behavior (e.g., adolescent silence) cause an aversive stimulus (e.g., parental nagging) to cease (i.e., negative reinforcement)? Is adaptive communication ignored (extinction) or criticized (punishment)? Does negative communication prevent something aversive from happening (avoidance)? The clinician should formulate hypotheses in interactional terms: If a mother and son argue frequently, something must reinforce both the son's and the mother's involvement. Often each will unwittingly maintain the other's behavior, as when a mother becomes increasingly nasty until her son complies (the mother's behavior reinforces the son's compliance via cessation of her nastiness; the son's compliance reinforces the mother's escalating negativity).

6. The planned intervention should address the key variables that the hypotheses emphasize and that are necessary to change in order to reduce conflict in the family. The clinician should select variables based on evidence collected during assessment, and should choose an assessment approach to monitor this change systematically over time. Both the maintaining variables targeted for change and the levels of conflict or negative interaction should be assessed. For example, if it appears that a father must reduce his thoughts about malicious intent, and that both the father and his son must improve their communication to reduce conflict, the clinician should assess paternal cognitions, father communication, son communication, and father–son conflict. This approach will allow the clinician both to assess the

effectiveness of the intervention with specific goals (cognition, communication) and on the presenting problem (conflict), and to test hypotheses about the causal relationship among cognition, communication, and conflict.

FUTURE DIRECTIONS

Research on parent–adolescent conflict has increased exponentially since the second edition of this volume. This explosion has had two benefits. First, it has provided a wealth of data directly and indirectly relevant to the model of parent–adolescent conflict used to frame the content of this chapter. These data have both supported and extended the model. Second, this research has provided a number of new instruments for assessing dimensions related to conflict in families. Researchers and clinicians now have a variety of instruments to choose among for assessing communication, cognition, problem solving, and family systems domains.

Despite this proliferation of assessment devices, several nagging problems persist in assessing parent–adolescent conflict, and current research has yet to resolve these adequately. Most observational systems are used to code small samples of family interaction, and we have little idea of whether these brief samples provide an adequate sample of behavior—particularly of low-frequency categories. Even if they do, generalizability to the natural environment is often unaddressed.

Despite a few promising methods for quasi-observational assessment in the natural environment (e.g., daily telephone interviews, home report diaries, hidden microphones activated randomly or at specific times), few investigators have employed these methods, perhaps because they are time- or resource-intensive. If researchers do not use these methods, clinicians are even less likely to do so, given that practitioners have fewer personnel and less time for family assessment than researchers. One needed development that would assist both researchers and clinicians would be to examine which types of tasks and coding schemes provide maximally generalizable data, yet are convenient enough for routine clinical use. In addition, examining which types of families are most reactive to clinic observation and how to predict and assess this reactivity would also help clinicians gauge the quality of the observations they make in analogue discussions and during clinical interviews. Finally, studies examining the various ways that conflict and problem solving arise and end in the natural environment might enable researchers and clinicians to create analogue tasks that mirror more closely the *in vivo* contexts of conflictual family interaction.

Another unfortunate development has been the proliferation of separate observation systems and questionnaires in different laboratories. Often these contain similarly labeled scales or subscales, but closer inspection reveals that similarly named constructs are operationalized quite differently. Assessments of "cohesion" are an excellent example of this, with different questionnaires often showing only minimal content overlap. In addition, content validity of many of these tools is derived from theoretical assumptions about constructs that may or may not hang together in the ways authors propose. Unfortunately, assessments of underlying covariation among behaviors in ways predicted by the instrument often take only the form of internal-consistency statistics, rather than more rigorous examinations of a full range of content relevant to the construct.

Related to this is the need to examine closely the level of analysis an instrument uses to assess a family. Some require ratings or observations of the family as a whole, some of dyads within the family, and some of individual family members. Data suggest that ratings of the family as a whole may at times be too global: Cole and McPherson (1993) found, for example, that correlations among ratings of different dyads using the FES varied considerably. These findings imply that different dyads in the family may have quite different interaction patterns. In addition, Ben-David and Sprenkle (1993) reported that respondents voiced difficulty in deciding how to respond to items of the FACES III that referred to "the family," because their answers would vary according to which family member was involved. Until we understand the role of individual behavior and dyadic exchanges in family relations, instruments that assess individuals and dyads may be more informative than instruments that only assess the family as a whole.

A number of questionnaires can assist clinicians and researchers in obtaining information on family interaction. Many of these, however, lack evidence of discriminant validity, and multimethod approaches have been used to examine the validity of only a handful. Instead, validity data often rely on relationships with other questionnaires. This leads to obvious concerns about the extent to which shared method variance inflates validity correlations between self-report measures. In addition, psychometric properties of each questionnaire subscale must be examined and described for mothers, fathers, and adolescents separately. As indicated previously, the psychometric properties of several questionnaires have been stronger for parent reports than for teen reports.

The applicability of specific instruments and of the general model we propose for families from diverse ethnic and racial groups warrants considerably more than the minimal attention it has received. Knight et al.'s (1992, 1994) data suggest that some of our most widely used instruments may have difficulty passing content validity and other psychometric tests with populations other than those in which European-American families predominate. More importantly, the constructs themselves need close scrutiny for Eurocentrism. Problem solving, with its implicit value on the parents' ceding of authority and power in decision making as teenagers mature, may take different forms in different cultures that stress strong familial ties and obedience. Indeed, more non-Hispanic white teenagers report that their parents display authoritative parenting styles than do Hispanic, Asian-American, and African-American teens (Dornbusch, Ritter, Leiderman, Roberts, & Fraleigh, 1987; Steinberg, Lamborn, Dornbusch, & Darling, 1992). In addition, Steinberg, Lamborn, Darling, Mounts, and Dornbusch (1994) found that adolescents' reports of authoritative and authoritarian parenting bore different relationships to school achievement and self-reported academic competence in European-American, Hispanic, Asian-American, and African-American groups. Although teen reports of parenting styles strong in control/strictness (both authoritative and authoritarian) were negatively related to behavior problems 1 year later, regardless of ethnic group, the use of measures without ethnicity-specific psychometric data makes this conclusion tenuous— especially in light of the fact that the constructs of authoritative and authoritarian parenting were based largely on data from white, middle-class families.

Another assumption that needs close scrutiny is that certain beliefs are "irrational" or "maladaptive" in parent–adolescent relationships. Some of these beliefs may be normative in some cultures (e.g., "obedience" in strongly hierarchical groups), as may strong emotional ties typically seen as indicative of "enmeshment." Until a substantial data base can examine these issues, concepts in this chapter should be cautiously applied to families that differ culturally and demographically from those on which the preponderance of research is based.

With such families, we advise clinicians to be more tentative in their assumptions and more explicit in their hypothesis testing as they assess the family members' difficulties. In addition, a clinician should assess the degree to which many factors—including acculturation of family members; conflicting demands on family members from the culture of origin versus the dominant culture; communication skill in the language used in the family; the extent of affiliation and identification with other members of the culture of origin; and experience of discrimination experiences and stress—may contribute to patterns of family conflict. In addition, different family members and friends may have different roles in child rearing in different ethnic groups (e.g., a grandparent or a boyfriend in a single-parent African-American household), and, ideally, important members should participate in the family assessment.

Finally, research on parent–adolescent conflict could benefit from closer scrutiny of the role of individual psychopathology in the etiology and maintenance of family problems in adolescence. Research to date has emphasized family interaction dynamics. Although this focus is crucial for understanding family processes, examining how these processes relate to individual difficulties such as substance use problems, depression, and ADHD will ultimately contribute to a broader understanding both of individual psychopathology and of how individual and family system processes intertwine and influence each other.

ACKNOWLEDGMENT

We express our appreciation to Monique Mosher for her library assistance.

NOTES

1. Other chapters in this volume provide detailed coverage of ways of assessing other child and parent difficulties.

2. Some versions of the IC ask respondents to indicate conflict during the previous 2 weeks.

3. This can be controlled statistically with covariance strategies in which an indicator of problem intensity is used as the covariate. This strategy has problems, however. Analysis of covariance (ANCOVA) strategies are most interpretable when the covariate and the independent variable are uncorrelated. In quasi-experimental studies (such as comparisons of nondistressed and distressed families), the covariate is sometimes correlated with the independent variable. Because of this, ANCOVA can remove true variance associated with the

independent variable when one is controlling for the covariate. As a consequence, the ANCOVA results are difficult to interpret from a conceptual standpoint (Huitema, 1980).

4. We and our colleagues originally proposed two additional parent beliefs, approval (the parent requires the adolescent's love and unconditional approval of parental actions) and self-blame (the parent is completely at fault for how the teenager turns out); and one additional adolescent belief, approval (the parent must approve of the teenager's behavior). These beliefs, however, are inwardly directed toward the self, not externally directed toward others. This inward direction should produce internalizing, not externalizing, negative affect. In fact, mothers', fathers', and adolescents' endorsement of these internally directed beliefs fail to correlate with dimensions of conflict (Vincent Roehling & Robin, 1986).

5. Sanders et al. (1992) reanalyzed these data with two additional samples: one of mothers and their depressed youngsters, and one of mothers and their children with comorbid diagnoses of depression and CD. The results changed only slightly with the additional samples: Mothers' negative self-directed thoughts no longer differed significantly. Sanders et al. also found that depressed children, like CD children, reported disproportionately high percentages of negative self-directed thoughts and low proportions of positive thoughts about their families. Mothers of depressed children also reported significantly higher proportions of negative thoughts about their families than did comparison mothers. Surprisingly, children with comorbid CD and depression and their mothers did not differ from the comparison group on any of the thought measures.

REFERENCES

Abidin, R. R., & Brunner, J. F. (1995). Development of a Parenting Alliance Inventory. *Journal of Clinical Child Psychology*, 24, 31–40.

Alexander, J. F. (1973). Defensive and supportive communications in normal and deviant families. *Journal of Consulting and Clinical Psychology*, 40, 223–231.

Alexander, J. F., & Barton, C. (1980). Systems–behavioral intervention with delinquent families: Clinical, methodological, and conceptual advances. In J. Vincent (Ed.), *Advances in family intervention, assessment, and theory* (Vol. 1, pp. 53–87). Greenwich, CT: JAI Press.

Alexander, J. F., Barton, C., Schiavo, R. S., & Parsons, B. V. (1976). Systems–behavioral intervention with families of delinquents: Therapist characteristics, family behavior, and outcome. *Journal of Consulting and Clinical Psychology*, 44, 656–664.

Alexander, J. F., & Parsons, B. V. (1973). Short term behavioral intervention with delinquent families: Impact on family process and recidivism. *Journal of Abnormal Psychology*, 81, 219–225.

Alexander, J. F., & Parsons, B. V. (1982). *Functional family therapy*. Monterey, CA: Brooks/Cole.

Alexander, J. F., Waldron, H. B., Barton, C., & Mas, C. H. (1989). The minimizing of blaming attributions and behaviors in delinquent families. *Journal of Consulting and Clinical Psychology*, 57, 19–24.

American Psychiatric Association. (1994). *Diagnostic and statistical manual of mental disorders* (4th ed.). Washington, DC: Author.

Anastasi, A. (1988). *Psychological testing* (6th ed.). New York: Collier/Macmillan.

Anderson, S. A. (1984). The Family Environment Scales (FES): A review and critique. *American Journal of Family Therapy*, 12, 59–62.

Aponte, H. H., & VanDeusen, J. M. (1981). Structural family therapy. In A. S. Gurman & J. P. Kniskern (Eds.), *Handbook of family therapy* (pp. 310–360). New York: Brunner/Mazel.

Baden, A. D., & Howe, G. W. (1992). Mothers' attributions and expectancies regarding their conduct-disordered children. *Journal of Abnormal Child Psychology*, 20, 467–485.

Barkley, R. A., Anastopoulos, A. D., Guevremont, D. C., & Fletcher, K. E. (1992). Adolescents with Attention Deficit Hyperactivity Disorder: Mother–adolescent interactions, family beliefs and conflicts, and maternal psychopathology. *Journal of Abnormal Child Psychology*, 20, 263–288.

Barkley, R. A., Guevremont, D. C., Anastopoulos, A. D., & Fletcher, K. E. (1992). A comparison of three family therapy programs for treating family conflicts in adolescents with Attention Deficit Hyperactivity Disorder. *Journal of Consulting and Clinical Psychology*, 60, 450–462.

Barnes, H. L., & Olson, D. H. (1985). Parent–adolescent communication and the circumplex model. *Child Development*, 56, 438–447.

Beaumont, S. L. (in press). Adolescent girls' conversations with mothers and friends: A matter of style. *Discourse Processes*.

Ben-David, A., & Jurich, J. (1993). A test of adaptability: Examining the curvilinear assumption. *Journal of Family Psychology*, 7, 370–375.

Ben-David, A., & Sprenkle, D. H. (1993). How do they (participants) understand our (researchers [*sic*]) intentions? A qualitative test of the curvilinear assumptions of the adaptability items of the FACES III. *American Journal of Family Therapy*, 21, 17–26.

Blaske, D. M., Borduin, C. M., Henggeler, S. W., & Mann, B. J. (1989). Individual, family, and peer characteristics of adolescent sex offenders and assaultive offenders. *Developmental Psychology*, 25, 846–855.

Boake, C., & Salmon, P. G. (1983). Demographic correlates and factor structure of the Family Environment Scale. *Journal of Clinical Psychology*, 39, 95–100.

Borduin, C. M., Mann, B. J., Cone, L. T., Henggeler, S. W., Fucci, B. R., Blaske, D. M., & Williams, R. A. (1995). Multisystemic treatment of juvenile offenders: Long-term prevention of criminality and violence. *Journal of Consulting and Clinical Psychology, 63*, 569–578.

Bornstein, P. H., Hamilton, S. B., & Bornstein, M. T. (1986). Self-monitoring procedures. In A. R. Ciminero, K. S. Calhoun, & H. E. Adams (Eds.), *Handbook of behavioral assessment* (2nd ed., pp. 176–222). New York: Wiley.

Bradbury, T. N., & Fincham, F. D. (1987). Assessing the effects of behavior marital therapy: Assumptions and measurement strategies. *Clinical Psychology Review, 7*, 525–538.

Bradbury, T. N., & Fincham, F. D. (1990). Attributions in marriage: Review and critique. *Psychological Bulletin, 107*, 3–33.

Brody, G. H., & Forehand, R. (1993). Prospective associations among family form, family processes, and adolescents' alcohol and drug use. *Behaviour Research and Therapy, 31*, 587–593.

Buhrmester, D., Camparo, L., Christensen, A., Gonzalez, A. S., & Hinshaw, S. P. (1992). Mothers and fathers interacting in dyads and triads with normal and hyperactive sons. *Developmental Psychology, 28*, 500–509.

Buhrmester, D., & Furman, W. (1987). The development of companionship and intimacy. *Child Development, 58*, 1101–1113.

Campbell, N. B., Milling, L., Laughlin, A., & Bush, E. (1993). The psychosocial climate of families with suicidal pre-adolescent children. *American Journal of Orthopsychiatry, 63*, 142–145.

Capaldi, D. M., Forgatch, M. S., & Crosby, L. (1994). Affective expression in family problem-solving discussions with adolescent boys. *Journal of Adolescent Research, 9*, 28–49.

Carter, E. A., & McGoldrick, M. (Eds.). (1980). *The family life cycle: A framework for family therapy.* New York: Gardner Press.

Chamberlain, P., & Reid, J. B. (1987). Parent observation and report of child symptoms. *Behavioral Assessment, 9*, 97–109.

Christensen, A. (1987). Assessment of behavior. In K. D. O'Leary (Ed.), *Assessment of marital discord: An integration for research and clinical practice.* Hillsdale, NJ: Erlbaum.

Cluff, R. B., & Hicks, M. W. (1994). Superstition also survives: Seeing is not always believing. *Family Process, 33*, 479–482.

Cole, D. A., & McPherson, A. E. (1993). Relation of family subsystems to adolescent depression: Implementing a new family assessment strategy. *Journal of Family Psychology, 7*, 119–133.

Collins, W. A., & Laursen, B. (1992). Conflict and relationships during adolescence. In C. U. Shantz & W. W. Hartup (Eds.), *Conflict in child and adolescent development* (pp. 216–241). New York: Cambridge University Press.

Cone, J. D. (1979). Confounded comparisons in triple response mode assessment research. *Behavioral Assessment, 1*, 85–95.

Dadds, M. R., Sanders, M. R., Morrison, M., & Rebgetz, M. (1992). Childhood depression and Conduct Disorder: II. An analysis of family interaction patterns in the home. *Journal of Abnormal Psychology, 101*, 505–513.

Dancy, B. L., & Handal, P. J. (1984). Perceived family climate, psychological adjustment, and peer relationship of black adolescents: A function of parental marital status or perceived family conflict? *Journal of Counseling Psychology, 12*, 222–229.

Davies, P. T., & Cummings, E. M. (1994). Marital conflict and child adjustment: An emotional security hypothesis. *Psychological Bulletin, 116*, 387–411.

Davis, B., Alpert, A., Hops, H., & Andrews, J. A. (1995, April). *Triadic family relationships: An investigation of conflict through the use of direct behavioral observation.* Paper presented at the biennial meeting of the Society for Research in Child Development, Indianapolis, IN.

DiLalla, L. F., Mitchell, C. M., Arthur, M. W., & Pagliocca, P. M. (1988). Aggression and delinquency: Family and environmental factors. *Journal of Youth and Adolescence, 17*, 233–246.

Doane, J. A., West, K. L., Goldstein, M. J., Rodnick, E. H., & Jones, J. E. (1981). Parental communication deviance and affective style. *Archives of General Psychiatry, 38*, 679–685.

Dornbusch, S. M., Ritter, P. L., Leiderman, P. H., Roberts, D. F., & Fraleigh, M. J. (1987). The relation of parenting style to adolescent school performance. *Child Development, 58*, 1244–1257.

D'Zurilla, T. J., & Goldfried, M. R. (1971). Problem solving and behavior modification. *Journal of Abnormal Psychology, 78*, 197–226.

Ekman, P. , & Friesen, W. V. (1975). *Unmasking the face.* Englewood Cliffs, NJ: Prentice-Hall.

Emery, R. E. (1992). Family conflicts and their developmental implications: A conceptual analysis of meanings for the structure of relationships. In C. U. Shantz & W. W. Hartup (Eds.), *Conflict in child and adolescent development* (pp. 270–298). New York: Cambridge University Press.

Epstein, N. B., Baldwin, L. M., & Bishop, D. S. (1983). The McMaster Family Assessment Device. *Journal of Marital and Family Therapy, 9*, 171–180.

Feldman, S. S., Rubenstein, J. L., & Rubin, C. (1988). Depressive affect and restraint in early adolescents: Relationships with family structure, family process, and friendship support. *Journal of Early Adolescence, 8*, 279–296.

Fincham, F. D., & Bradbury, T. N. (1987). The assessment of marital quality: A reevaluation. *Journal of Marriage and the Family, 49*, 797–809.

Forehand, R., Wierson, M., Thomas, A. M., Fauber, R., Armistead, L., Kemptom, T., & Long, N. (1991).

A short-term longitudinal examination of young adolescent functioning following divorce: The role of family factors. *Journal of Abnormal Child Psychology, 19*, 97–111.

Forgatch, M. S. (1989). Patterns and outcome in family problem-solving: The disrupting effect of negative emotion. *Journal of Marriage and the Family, 51*, 115–124.

Forgatch, M. S., & Lathrop, M. (1995). *SPI-FI II: The final version*. Unpublished manuscript.

Forgatch, M. S., Patterson, G. R., & Ray, J. A. (1996). Divorce and boys' adjustment problems: Two paths with a single model. In E. M. Hetherington & E. A. Blechman (Eds.), *Stress, coping and resiliency in children and the family*. Hillsdale, NJ: Erlbaum.

Forgatch, M. S., & Stoolmiller, M. (1994). Emotions as contexts for adolescent delinquency. *Journal of Research on Adolescence, 4*, 601–614.

Foster, S. L. (1978). *Family conflict management: Skill training and generalization procedures*. Unpublished doctoral dissertation, State University of New York at Stony Brook.

Foster, S. L., Prinz, R. J., & O'Leary, K. D. (1983). Impact of problem-solving communication training and generalization procedures on family conflict. *Child and Family Behavior Therapy, 5*, 1–23.

Foster, S. L., & Robin, A. L. (1988). Family conflict and communication in adolescence. In E. J. Mash & L. G. Terdal (Eds.), *Behavioral assessment of childhood disorders* (2nd ed., pp. 717–775). New York: Guilford Press.

Foster, S. L., & Robin, A. L. (1989). Parent–adolescent conflict. In E. J. Mash & R. Barkley (Eds.), *Treatment of childhood disorders* (pp. 493–528). New York: Guilford Press.

Franklin, C., & Streeter, C. L. (1993). Validity of the 3–D circumplex model for family assessment. *Social Work Practice, 3*, 258–275.

Fuhrman, T., & Holmbeck, G. N. (1995). A contextual-moderator analysis of emotional autonomy and adjustment in adolescence. *Child Development, 66*, 793–811.

Gilbert, R. K., & Christensen, A. (1988). The assessment of family alliances. In R. J. Prinz (Ed.), *Advances in behavioral assessment of children and families* (Vol. 4, pp. 239–252). Greenwich, CT: JAI Press.

Gilbert, R. K., Christensen, A., & Margolin, G. (1984). Patterns of alliances in nondistressed and multiproblem families. *Family Process, 23*, 75–87.

Gjerde, P. F. (1986). The interpersonal structure of family interaction settings: Parent–adolescent relations in dyads and triads. *Developmental Psychology, 22*, 297–304.

Gondoli, D. M., & Jacob, T. (1993). Factor structure within and across three family-assessment procedures. *Journal of Family Psychology, 6*, 278–289.

Gottman, J. M. (1979). *Marital interactions: Experimental investigations*. New York: Academic Press.

Gottman, J. M., & Levenson, R. W. (1985). A valid measure for assessing self-report of affect in marriage. *Journal of Consulting and Clinical Psychology, 53*, 151–160.

Gottman, J. M., & Levenson, R. W. (1986). Assessing the role of emotion in marriage. *Behavioral Assessment, 8*, 31–48.

Grace, N. C., Kelley, M. L., & McCain, A. P. (1993). Attribution processes in mother–adolescent conflict. *Journal of Abnormal Child Psychology, 21*, 199–211.

Grych, J. H., & Fincham, F. D. (1990). Marital conflict and children's adjustment: A cognitive–contextual framework. *Psychological Bulletin, 108*, 267–290.

Hampson, R. B., Hulgus, Y. F., & Beavers, W. R. (1991). Comparisons of self-report measures of the Beavers system model and Olson's circumplex model. *Journal of Family Psychology, 4*, 326–340.

Haley, J. (1976). *Problem-solving therapy*. San Francisco: Jossey-Bass.

Hanson, C. L., Henggeler, S. W., Haefele, W. F., & Rodick, J. D. (1984). Demographic, individual, and family relationship correlates of serious and repeated crime among adolescents and their siblings. *Journal of Consulting and Clinical Psychology, 52*, 528–538.

Hauser, S. T., Book, B. K., Houlihan, J., Powers, S., Weiss-Perry, B., Follansbee, D., Jacobson, A. M., & Noam, G. G. (1987). Sex differences within the family: Studies of adolescent and parent family interaction. *Journal of Youth and Adolescence, 16*, 119–220.

Henggeler, S. W., Borduin, C. M., Rodick, J. D., & Tavormina, J. D. (1979). Importance of task content for family interaction research. *Developmental Psychology, 15*, 660–661.

Heyman, R. E., Weiss, R. L., & Eddy, J. M. (1995). Marital Interaction Coding System: Revision and empirical evaluation. *Behaviour Research and Therapy, 33*, 737–746.

Hibbs, E. D., Hamburger, S. D., Kruesi, M. J. P., & Lenane, M. (1993). Factors affecting expressed emotion in parents of ill and normal children. *American Journal of Orthopsychiatry, 63*, 103–112.

Holmbeck, G. N., & Hill, J. P. (1991). Conflictive engagement, positive affect, and menarche in families with seventh-grade girls. *Child Development, 62*, 1030–1048.

Holmbeck, G. N., & O'Donnell, K. (1991). Discrepancies between perceptions of decision making and behavioral autonomy. In R. L. Paikoff & W. A. Collins (Eds.), *New directions in child development* (No. 51, pp. 51–69). San Francisco: Jossey-Bass.

Hops, H., Davis, B., & Longoria, N. (1995). Methodological issues in direct observation: Illustrations with the Living in Family Environments (LIFE) coding system. *Journal of Clinical Child Psychology, 24*, 193–203.

Huitema, B. E. (1980). *Analysis of covariance and alternatives*. New York: Wiley.

Inhelder, B., & Piaget, J. (1958). *The growth of logical thinking from childhood to adolescence*. New York: Basic Books.

Inoff-Germaine, G., Nottlemann, E. D., Arnold, G. S., & Sussman, E. J. (1988). Adolescent aggression and parent–adolescent conflict: Relations between observed family interactions and measures of the adolescents' general functioning. *Journal of Early Adolescence, 8*, 17–36.

Jacob, T. (1974). Patterns of family conflict and dominance as a function of child age and social class. *Developmental Psychology, 10*, 1–12.

Jacob, T., Tennenbaum, D., Seilhamer, R. A., Bargiel, K., & Sharon, T. (1994). Reactivity effects during naturalistic observation of distressed and non-distressed families. *Journal of Family Psychology, 8*, 354–363.

Jacobson, N. S., & Margolin, G. (1979). *Marital therapy*. New York: Brunner/Mazel.

Kaslow, F. W. (Ed.). (1996). *Handbook of relational diagnosis*. New York: Wiley.

Kimmel, D., & Van Der Veen, F. (1974). Factors of marital adjustment in Locke's Marital Adjustment Test. *Journal of Marriage and the Family, 36*, 57–63.

Knight, G. P., Tein, J. Y., Shell, R., & Roosa, M. (1992). The cross-ethnic equivalence of parenting and family interaction measures among Hispanic and Anglo-American families. *Child Development, 63*, 1392–1403.

Knight, G. P., Virdin, L. M., & Roosa, M. (1994). Socialization and family correlates of mental health outcomes among Hispanic and Anglo American children: Consideration of cross-ethnic scalar equivalence. *Child Development, 65*, 212–224.

Kobak, R. R., Cole, H. E., Ferenz-Gillies, R., Fleming, W. S., & Gamble, W. (1993). Attachment and emotional regulation during mother–teen problem-solving: A control theory analysis. *Child Development, 64*, 231–245.

Koepke, T., Robin, A. L., Nayar, M. C., & Hillman, S. B. (1987, August). *Construct validation of the Parent Adolescent Relationship Questionnaire*. Paper presented at the meeting of the American Psychological Association, New York.

Lang, P. J. (1971). The application of psychophysiological methods to the study of psychotherapy and behavior modification. In A. E. Bergin & S. L. Garfield (Eds.), *Handbook of psychotherapy and behavior change* (pp. 75–125). New York: Wiley.

Larson, R. (1989). Beeping children and adolescents: A method for studying time use and daily experience. *Journal of Youth and Adolescence, 18*, 511–530.

Larson, R., & Richards, M. H. (1991). Daily companionship in late childhood and early adolescence: Changing developmental contexts. *Child Development, 62*, 284–300.

Locke, H. J., & Wallace, K. M. (1959). Short marital and prediction tests: Their reliability and validity. *Marriage and Family Living, 21*, 251–255.

Lyon, J.-M., Henggeler, S., & Hall, J. A. (1992). The family relations, peer relations, and criminal activities of Caucasian and Hispanic-American gang members. *Journal of Abnormal Child Psychology, 20*, 439–449.

Mann, B. J., Borduin, C. M., Henggeler, S. W., & Blaske, D. M. (1990). An investigation of systemic conceptualizations of parent–child coalitions and symptom change. *Journal of Consulting and Clinical Psychology, 58*, 336–344.

Marett, K. M., Sprenkle, D. H., & Lewis, R. A. (1992). Family members' perceptions of family boundaries and their relationship to family problems. *Family Therapy, 19*, 233–242.

Masselam, V. S., Marcus, R. F., & Stunkard, C. L. (1990). Parent–adolescent communication, family functioning, and school performance. *Adolescence, 25*, 725–737.

McColloch, M. A., Gilbert, D. A., & Johnson, S. (1990). Effects of situational variables on the interpersonal behavior of families with an aggressive adolescent. *Personality and Individual Differences, 11*, 1–11.

Miller, B. C., & Dyk, P. A. H. (1993). Sexuality. In P. H. Tolan & B. J. Cohler (Eds.), *Handbook of clinical research and practice with adolescents* (pp. 95–123). New York: Wiley.

Miller, I. W., Epstein, N. B., Bishop, D. S., & Keitner, G. I. (1985). The McMaster Family Assessment Device: Reliability and validity. *Journal of Marital and Family Therapy, 11*, 345–356.

Miller, I. W., Kabacoff, R. I., Epstein, N. B., Bishop, D. S., Keitner, G. I., Baldwin, L. M., & van der Spuy, H. I. J. (1994). The development of a clinical rating scale for the McMaster model of family functioning. *Family Process, 33*, 53–67.

Montemayor, R. (1983). Parents and adolescents in conflict: All families some of the time and some families most of the time. *Journal of Early Adolescence, 3*, 83–103.

Montemayor, R., & Hanson, E. (1985). A naturalistic view of conflict between adolescents and their parents and siblings. *Journal of Early Adolescence, 5*, 23–30.

Moos, R. H., & Moos, B. S. (1981). *Family Environment Scale manual*. Palo Alto, CA: Consulting Psychologists Press.

O'Brien, M., Margolin, G., John, R. S., & Krueger, L. (1991). Mothers' and sons' cognitive and emotional reactions to simulated marital and family conflict. *Journal of Consulting and Clinical Psychology, 59*, 692–703.

Olson, D. H., Portner, J., & Lavee, Y. (1985). *FACES III*. St. Paul: Faculty of Social Sciences, University of Minnesota.

Paikoff, R. L., Carlton-Ford, S., & Brooks-Gunn, J. (1993). Mother–daughter dyads view the family: Associations between divergent perceptions and daughter well-being. *Journal of Youth and Adolescence, 22,* 473–492.

Perosa, L. M., & Perosa, S. L. (1990a). Convergent and discriminant validity for family self-report measures. *Educational and Psychological Measurement, 50,* 855–868.

Perosa, L. M., & Perosa, S. L. (1990b). The use of a bipolar item format for FACES III: A reconsideration. *Journal of Marital and Family Therapy, 16,* 187–199.

Perosa, S. L., & Perosa, L. M. (1993). Relationships among Minuchin's structural family model, identity achievement, and coping style. *Journal of Counseling Psychology, 40,* 479–489.

Phares, V., & Danforth, J. S. (1994). Adolescents', parents', and teachers' distress over adolescents' behavior. *Journal of Abnormal Child Psychology, 22,* 721–732.

Prange, M. E., Greenbaum, P. E., Silver, S. E., Friedman, R. M., Kutash, K., & Duchnowski, A. J. (1992). Family functioning and psychopathology among adolescents with severe emotional disturbances. *Journal of Abnormal Child Psychology, 20,* 83–102.

Pratt, D. M., & Hansen, J. C. (1987). A test of the curvilinear hypothesis with FACES II and III. *Journal of Marital and Family Therapy, 13,* 387–392.

Prinz, R. J., Foster, S. L., Kent, R. N., & O'Leary, K. D. (1979). Multivariate assessment of conflict in distressed and nondistressed mother–adolescent dyads. *Journal of Applied Behavior Analysis, 12,* 691–700.

Prinz, R. J., & Kent, R. N. (1978). Recording parent–adolescent interactions without the use of frequency or interval-by-interval coding. *Behavior Therapy, 9,* 602–604.

Ray, J. (1995). *Technical report: Problem solving outcome score for two samples across time.* Unpublished manuscript.

Robin, A. L. (1981). A controlled evaluation of problem-solving communication training with parent–adolescent conflict. *Behavior Therapy, 12,* 593–609.

Robin, A. L., & Canter, W. (1984). A comparison of the Marital Interaction Coding System and community ratings for assessing mother–adolescent problem-solving. *Behavioral Assessment, 6,* 303–314.

Robin, A. L., & Foster, S. L. (1989). *Negotiating parent–adolescent conflict: A behavioral–family systems approach.* New York: Guilford Press.

Robin, A. L., & Koepke, T. (1985). *Molecular versus molar observation systems for assessing mother–adolescent problem-solving behavior.* Unpublished manuscript.

Robin, A. L., Koepke, T., & Moye, A. (1990). Multidimensional assessment of parent–adolescent relations. *Psychological Assessment, 2,* 451–459.

Robin, A. L., & Weiss, J. G. (1980). Criterion-related validity of behavioral and self-report measures of problem-solving communication skills in distressed and non-distressed parent–adolescent dyads. *Behavioral Assessment, 2,* 339–352.

Rubin, J. (1986). The emotion of anger: Some conceptual and theoretical issues. *Professional Psychology: Theory, Research, and Practice, 17,* 115–124.

Rueter, M. A., & Conger, R. D. (1995a). Antecedents of parent–adolescent disagreements. *Journal of Marriage and the Family, 57,* 435–448.

Rueter, M. A., & Conger, R. D. (1995b). Interaction style, problem-solving behavior, and family problem-solving effectiveness. *Child Development, 66,* 98–115.

Rueter, M. A., & Conger, R. D. (1995c, March). *The interplay between parenting and adolescent problem-solving behavior: Reciprocal influences.* Paper presented at the biennial meeting of the Society for Research in Child Development, Indianapolis, IN.

Sanders, M. R., & Dadds, M. R. (1992). Children's and parents' cognitions about family interaction: An evaluation of video-mediated recall and thought listing procedures in the assessment of conduct disordered children. *Journal of Clinical Child Psychology, 21,* 371–379.

Sanders, M. R., Dadds, M. R., Johnston, B. M., & Cash, R. (1992). Childhood depression and Conduct Disorder: I. Behavioral, affective, and cognitive aspects of family problem-solving interactions. *Journal of Abnormal Psychology, 101,* 495–504.

Scheer, N. S., & Snyder, D. K. (1984). Empirical validation of the Marital Satisfaction Inventory in a nonclinical sample. *Journal of Consulting and Clinical Psychology, 52,* 88–96.

Schreer, H. E. (1994). *Communication, problem-solving skills, and cross-generational coalitions as predictors of parent–adolescent conflict.* Unpublished doctoral dissertation, California School of Professional Psychology, San Diego.

Silverberg, S. B., Tennenbaum, D. L., & Jacob, T. (1992). Adolescence and family interaction. In V. B. VanHasselt & M. Hersen (Eds.), *Handbook of social development: A lifespan perspective* (pp. 347–370). New York: Plenum Press.

Simons, R. L., Whitbeck, L. B., Conger, R. D., & Conger, K. J. (1991). Parenting factors, social skills, and value commitments as precursors to school failure, involvement with deviant peers, and delinquent behavior. *Journal of Youth and Adolescence, 6,* 645–664.

Smetana, J. G. (1989). Adolescents' and parents' reasoning about actual family conflict. *Child Development, 60,* 1052–1067.

Smetana, J. G. (1995). Parenting styles and conceptions of parental authority during adolescence. *Child Development, 66,* 299–316.

Smetana, J. G., & Asquith, P. (1994). Adolescents' and

parents' conceptions of parental authority and personal autonomy. *Child Development, 65,* 1147–1162.

Smetana, J. G., Yau, J., Restrepo, A., & Braeges, J. L. (1991a). Adolescent–parent conflict in married and divorced families. *Developmental Psychology, 27,* 1000–1010.

Smetana, J. G., Yau, J., Restrepo, A., & Braeges, J. L. (1991b). Conflict and adaptation in adolescence: Adolescent–parent conflict. In M. E. Colten & S. Gore (Eds.), *Adolescent stress: Causes and consequences* (pp. 43–65). New York: Aldine/de Gruyter.

Smith, K. A., & Forehand, R. (1986). Parent–adolescent conflict: Comparison and prediction of the perceptions of mothers, fathers, and daughters. *Journal of Early Adolescence, 6,* 353–367.

Snyder, D. K. (1979). Multidimensional assessment of marital satisfaction. *Journal of Marriage and the Family, 41,* 813–823.

Snyder, D. K., Klein, M. A., Gdowski, C. L., Faulstich, C., & LaCombe, J. (1988). Generalized dysfunction in clinic and nonclinic families: A comparative analysis. *Journal of Abnormal Child Psychology, 16,* 97–109.

Snyder, D. K., Wills, R. M., & Keiser, T. W. (1981). Empirical validation of the Marital Satisfaction Inventory: An actuarial approach. *Journal of Consulting and Clinical Psychology, 49,* 262–268.

Spanier, G. B. (1976). Measuring dyadic adjustment: New scales for assessing the quality of marriage and similar dyads. *Journal of Marriage and the Family, 38,* 15–28.

Steinberg, L., Lamborn, S. D., Darling, N., Mounts, N. S., & Dornbusch, S. M. (1994). Over-time changes in adjustment and competence among adolescents from authoritative, authoritarian, indulgent, and neglectful families. *Child Development, 65,* 754–770.

Steinberg, L., Lamborn, S. D., Dornbusch, S. M., & Darling, N. (1992). Impact of parenting practices on adolescent achievement: Authoritative parenting, school involvement, and encouragement to succeed. *Child Development, 63,* 1266–1281.

Steinfeld, B. I., Foster, S. L., Prinz, R. J., Robin, A. L., & Weiss, J. (1980). *Issues of conflict for mothers and adolescents: A descriptive and developmental analysis.* Unpublished manuscript.

Stiles, W. B., & White, M. L. (1981). Parent–child interaction in the laboratory: Effects of role, task and child behavior pathology on verbal response mode use. *Journal of Abnormal Child Psychology, 9,* 229–241.

Tesser, A., Forehand, R., Brody, G., & Long, N. (1989). Conflict: The role of calm and angry parent–child discussion in adolescent adjustment. *Journal of Social and Clinical Psychology, 8,* 317–330.

Thomas, V., & Olson, D. H. (1993). Problem families and the circumplex model: Observational assessment using the Clinical Rating Scale (CRS). *Journal of Marital and Family Therapy, 19,* 159–175.

Vandvik, I. H., & Eckblad, G. F. (1993). FACES III and the Kvebaek Family Sculpture Technique as measures of cohesion and closeness. *Family Process, 32,* 221–232.

Vincent Roehling, P., & Robin, A. L. (1986). Development and validation of the Family Beliefs Inventory: A measure of unrealistic beliefs among parents and adolescents. *Journal of Consulting and Clinical Psychology, 54,* 693–697.

Vuchinich, S. (1987). Starting and stopping spontaneous family conflicts. *Journal of Marriage and the Family, 49,* 591–601.

Vuchinich, S., Emery, R. E., & Cassidy, J. (1988). Family members as third parties in dyadic family conflict: Strategies, alliances, and outcomes. *Child Development, 59,* 1293–1302.

Vuchinich, S., Vuchinich, R., & Wood, B. (1993). The interparental relationship and family problem solving with preadolescent males. *Child Development, 64,* 1389–1400.

Vuchinich, S., Wood, B., & Vuchinich, R. (1994). Coalitions and family problem solving with preadolescents in referred, at risk, and comparison families. *Family Process, 33,* 409–424.

Weiss, R. L., & Heyman, R. E. (1990). Observation of marital interaction. In F. D. Fincham & T. N. Bradbury (Eds.), *The psychology of marriage: Basic issues and applications* (pp. 87–117). New York: Guilford Press.

Weiss, R. L., & Tolman, A. O. (1990). The Marital Interaction Coding System—Global (MICS-G): A global companion to the MICS. *Behavioral Assessment, 12,* 271–294.

Wolfe, V. V. (1986). *Paternal and marital factors related to child conduct problems.* Unpublished doctoral dissertation, West Virginia University.

Zuckerman, E., & Jacob, T. (1979). Task effects in family interaction. *Family Process, 18,* 47–53.

Chapter Fourteen

ANOREXIA NERVOSA AND BULIMIA NERVOSA

John P. Foreyt
Carmen Mikhail

The Duchess of Windsor is reputed to have said that "no woman can be too rich or too thin." The "too thin" aspect of this adage is emphasized in the eating disorders Anorexia Nervosa and Bulimia Nervosa. Anorexia Nervosa is characterized by a relentless pursuit of thinness, dread of weight gain, food restriction, and overactivity. Bulimia Nervosa, which was originally described in the literature as a symptom of Anorexia Nervosa, involves episodic binge eating of substantial quantities of food followed by purging. As both disorders are complex and multiply determined, their comprehensive assessment is overwhelmingly difficult. Investigators have approached these disorders from individual (behavior, affect, and/or cognition), familial, and cultural theoretical perspectives. Each model of the disorders has specified its own significant constructs to be measured. In the absence of an encompassing theory, assessment procedures and instruments have been developed for limited purposes, and they often measure only a narrow range of behaviors that the creators of these tools deem important. Despite this lack of agreement, it is our intention in this chapter to outline a behavioral approach to the assessment of these disorders.

DEFINITION OF THE DISORDERS

Diagnostic Criteria and Guidelines

Patients with Anorexia Nervosa and Bulimia Nervosa differ in the kind and severity of their symptomatology; this has generated some debate over which characteristics are unique to these disorders. The most widely used criteria for a diagnosis of Anorexia Nervosa are those of the *Diagnostic and Statistical Manual of Mental Disorders*, fourth edition (DSM-IV; American Psychiatric Association, 1994). These are presented in Table 14.1. Like the DSM-III-R criteria set, the DSM-IV version suggests but does not require a minimum body weight for a diagnosis. Halmi (1985) showed that there is no evidence for separating patients into different groups on the basis of weight loss. The DSM-IV criteria are also similar to those of DSM-III-R in the requirements of fear of weight gain and body image disturbance, although we are still not provided with specific standards for their measurement. DSM-IV adds two further requirements: (1) weight and shape as central to the subject's self-evaluation, and (2) denial of the seriousness of the low weight. The DSM-IV criteria also limit the amenorrhea requirement of DSM-III-R to postmenarcheal females. Some researchers (e.g., Schlundt & Johnson, 1990) debate the necessity of including this criterion, as amenorrhea sometimes occurs only as a result of starvation (Henley & Vaitukaitis, 1985).

DSM-IV delineates two subtypes of Anorexia Nervosa. Descriptions of anorexics who strictly limit food intake, as opposed to those who binge and purge, indicate that the groups differ in terms of premorbid adjustment, development of the disorder, and family characteristics (Casper, Eckert, Halmi, Goldberg, & Davis, 1980; Garfinkel, Moldofsky, & Garner, 1980; Strober, 1981b; Strober, Salkin, Burroughs, & Morrell, 1982); these findings highlight the need to distinguish between the two subgroups. Moreover, Anorexia

**TABLE 14.1. DSM-IV Criteria for
Anorexia Nervosa**

A. Refusal to maintain body weight at or above a
   minimally normal weight for age and height
   (e.g., weight loss leading to maintenance of body
   weight less than 85% of that expected; or failure
   to make expected weight gain during periods of
   growth, leading to body weight less than 85% of
   that expected).

B. Intense fear of gaining weight or becoming fat,
   even though underweight.

C. Disturbance in the way in which one's body
   weight or shape is experienced, undue influence
   of body weight or shape on self- evaluation, or
   denial of the seriousness of the current low body
   weight.

D. In postmenarcheal females, amenorrhea, i.e., the
   absence of at least three consecutive menstrual
   cycles. (A woman is considered to have
   amenorrhea if her periods occur only following
   hormone, e.g., estrogen, administration.)

Specify type:

Restricting Type: during the current episode of
   Anorexia Nervosa, the person has not regularly
   engaged in binge-eating or purging behavior
   (i.e., self-induced vomiting or the misuse of
   laxatives, diuretics, or enemas)
Binge-Eating/Purging Type: during the current
   episode of Anorexia Nervosa, the person has
   regularly engaged in binge-eating or purging
   behavior (i.e., self-induced vomiting or the
   misuse of laxatives, diuretics, or enemas)

Note. From American Psychiatric Association (1994, pp. 544–
545). Copyright 1994 by the American Psychiatric Association. Reprinted by permission.

Nervosa is described as a common disorder of
adolescence in DSM-IV, and there are special
considerations in using the criteria for younger
children. Irwin (1981) pointed out that prepubescent girls have a smaller percentage of body fat
than do postpubescent counterparts, and younger
anorexics restrict fluid intake whereas older
anorexics do not. This could affect their fulfilling
the weight criterion, although it must be remembered that the weight criterion is only a suggested
guideline. In DSM-IV the amenorrheal requirements are limited to postmenarcheal females, allowing younger girls to meet the criteria for
Anorexia Nervosa.

Another classification system, which is in close
agreement with that of DSM-IV, is the 10th revision of the *International Classification of Diseases*
(ICD-10; World Health Organization, 1992). Five
disturbances, presented in abbreviated form in
Table 14.2, are necessary for a diagnosis of Anorexia
Nervosa.

Like the DSM-IV, the ICD-10 includes patients
with bulimic episodes in the diagnosis of Anorexia
Nervosa. The ICD-10 also requires a fear of fatness.
Unlike the DSM-IV, the ICD-10 requires the presence of an endocrine disorder. This requirement
may result in more false negatives, as not all
anorexics suffer from an endocrine disorder (Bhanji
& Mattingly, 1988). Furthermore, it is not clear
whether the endocrinological changes are the result of primary hypothalamic disease or are secondary to weight loss alone (Bhanji & Mattingly, 1988).

Still another definition of Anorexia Nervosa has
been provided by Feighner et al. (1972) in their
Research Diagnostic Criteria (RDC). Briefly,
these criteria consist of six main points:

1. Age of onset prior to 25.
2. Weight loss of 25% of original weight.
3. Denial of illness, enjoyment in losing weight,
   a thin ideal body, and unusual hoarding or
   handling of food.

**TABLE 14.2. ICD-10 Diagnostic Guidelines for
Anorexia Nervosa**

1. Body weight is maintained at least 15% below
   that expected, or body mass index (BMI) is 17.5
   or less. Prepubertal patients may fail to make
   expected weight gains.

2. The weight loss is self-induced by avoidance of
   "fattening foods" and by the use of self-induced
   vomiting, self-induced purging, excessive
   exercise, appetite suppressants, and/or diuretics.

3. There is body image distortion whereby a
   dread of fatness persists as an intrusive
   overvalued idea, and the patients impose a low
   weight threshold on themselves.

4. An endocrine disorder involving the
   hypothalamic–pituitary–gonadal axis is
   present, manifested in the female as
   amenorrhea and in the male as loss of sexual
   interest and potency.

5. If onset is prepubertal, the sequence of
   pubertal events is delayed or even arrested. In
   girls, breasts do not develop and there is
   amenorrhea; in boys the genitals remain
   juvenile.

Note. Adapted from World Health Organization (1992,
pp. 176–178). Copyright 1992 by the World Health Organization. Adapted by permission.

4. No known physical illness that could account for anorexia and weight loss.
5. No other known psychiatric disorder.
6. At least two of the following: amenorrhea, lanugo hair, bradycardia, overactivity, bulimia, and/or vomiting.

A weight loss requirement of 25% may exclude patients who might otherwise have been diagnosed positively. Another problem is that persons who were markedly overweight at onset might still be above or near normal weight following a 25% weight loss and could be included. Finally, although the items in the last category are important features of this disorder, there is no logical

connection among them that warrants grouping them together.

The DSM-IV criteria for Bulimia Nervosa are presented in Table 14.3. These differ from those of DSM-III-R in several ways. The amount of food characterizing a "binge" is specified in DSM-IV as being more than most people would eat, given the same period of time and circumstances. In addition, not only the binge eating (as in DSM-III-R) but also the inappropriate compensatory behavior must occur at least twice a week, and last for 3 months. The DSM-IV criteria add the stipulation that these individuals place an excessive emphasis on body shape and weight in their self-evaluation. Other additions are the clarification that the diagnosis not be given when the disturbance occurs only in Anorexia Nervosa, and the inclusion of Purging and Nonpurging subtypes. Diagnosis of Bulimia Nervosa, which is also described as a common disorder of adolescence, will be valid only if subjects acknowledge bingeing and purging behaviors. Because these are usually kept secret and adolescents may fear censure from parents, the behaviors may be difficult to detect. Furthermore, care must be taken to insure that younger adolescents understand the terms "bingeing" and "purging" during the diagnostic interview.

The ICD-10 guidelines (World Health Organization, 1992) for Bulimia Nervosa are given in adapted form in Table 14.4. These guidelines also include the DSM-IV requirements of bingeing and purging. The ICD-10 includes a dread of fatness, whereas DSM-IV lists an overemphasis on body size. In this respect, ICD-10 has satisfied earlier

---

TABLE 14.3. DSM-IV Criteria for Bulimia Nervosa

A. Recurrent episodes of binge eating. An episode of binge eating is characterized by both of the following:
   (1) eating, in a discrete period of time (e.g., within any 2-hour period), an amount of food that is definitely larger than most people would eat during a similar period of time and under similar circumstances
   (2) a sense of lack of control over eating during the episode (e.g., a feeling that one cannot stop eating or control what or how much one is eating)
B. Recurrent inappropriate compensatory behavior in order to prevent weight gain, such as self-induced vomiting; misuse of laxatives, diuretics, enemas, or other medications; fasting; or excessive exercise.
C. The binge eating and inappropriate compensatory behaviors both occur, on average, at least twice a week for 3 months.
D. Self-evaluation is unduly influenced by body shape and weight.
E. The disturbance does not occur exclusively during episodes of Anorexia Nervosa.

Specify type:

Purging Type: during the current episode of Bulimia Nervosa, the person has regularly engaged in self-induced vomiting or the misuse of laxatives, diuretics, or enemas
Nonpurging Type: during the current episode of Bulimia Nervosa, the person has used other inappropriate compensatory behaviors, such as fasting or excessive exercise, but has not regularly engaged in self-induced vomiting or the misuse of laxatives, diuretics, or enemas

Note. From American Psychiatric Association (1994, pp. 549–550). Copyright 1994 by the American Psychiatric Association. Reprinted by permission.

TABLE 14.4. ICD-10 Diagnostic Guidelines for Bulimia Nervosa

1. Patients exhibit a preoccupation with eating and engage in episodes of overeating (large amounts in short period of time).
2. Patients attempt to counteract fattening effects of food by one or more of the following:
   Self-induced vomiting
   Purging
   Starvation
   Use of drugs (appetite suppressants, thyroid pills, diuretics)
   Neglect of insulin treatment (diabetics)
3. There is a morbid dread of fatness; patients set themselves a stringent weight threshold. A history of a previous episode of Anorexia Nervosa is often, but not always, present.

Note. Adapted from World Health Organzation (1992, pp. 178–179). Copyright 1992 by the World Health Organization. Adapted by permission.

criticisms (Russell, 1985; Fairburn & Garner, 1986) of diagnosis placing inadequate emphasis on a patient's fear of fatness. The third guideline of ICD-10 acknowledges this disorder as being related to Anorexia Nervosa and encourages the confirmation of an earlier anorexic episode. The ICD-10 also provides separate diagnostic guidelines for normal-weight bulimia and other eating disorders.

The usefulness of a diagnostic category or label is based, in part, upon its ability to specify homogeneous and distinct disorders. In this respect, Anorexia Nervosa and Bulimia Nervosa are less than desirable diagnostic labels. There is some debate as to whether Bulimia Nervosa is a separate syndrome or merely a manifestation of Anorexia Nervosa. About half of female anorexic patients develop Bulimia Nervosa at a later stage (Casper et al., 1980; Fairburn & Garner, 1986; Garfinkel et al., 1980). Also interesting is the finding of Garner, Garfinkel, and O'Shaughnessy (1985) that bulimics who had never met the weight loss criteria for Anorexia Nervosa were more similar to bingeing anorexics than either group was to restricting anorexics on demographic, clinical, and psychometric variables. If normal-weight bulimics and bingeing anorexics are similar, it might make sense to group these two populations together. Findings regarding the differences between these two populations are reviewed in greater detail later in the chapter.

Differential Diagnosis

Differential diagnosis between Anorexia Nervosa and Bulimia Nervosa is difficult, as the disorders share some common features. Williamson (1990) reported that both groups are similar in their body image distortion and anxiety after eating. Anorexics are 15% or more below normal weight, whereas bulimics are within 10% of normal weight. Anorexics engage in binge eating only occasionally, but bulimics do so frequently. Furthermore, anorexics typically fast and avoid forbidden food, whereas bulimics binge on forbidden food and purge to control weight.

Another important distinction that has been drawn is between normal, weight-preoccupied women and patients with Anorexia Nervosa (the vast majority whom are female; see below). It is assumed that such a contrast should shed light on whether Anorexia Nervosa is a distinct disorder or an extreme example of eating problems that exist on a continuum. Garner, Olmsted, Polivy, and Garfinkel (1984) compared traits of patients with Anorexia Nervosa to those of extremely weight-preoccupied women from large samples of college and ballet students. The nonclinical, weight-preoccupied group was similar to the anorexic group in terms of disturbances in dieting, perfectionism, and attitudes about shape; other disturbances, such as feelings of ineffectiveness, interoceptive unawareness (inability to recognize and discriminate between emotional and physical internal states), and interpersonal distrust, were less common. The authors interpreted these differences as lending support to Bruch's (1962) contention that dieting behavior and weight loss are not *the* distinguishing features of Anorexia Nervosa, and that there exists some other (unique) problem that is responsible for the disorder. A community survey by Cooper, Waterman, and Fairburn (1984) revealed that two-thirds of the women felt "persistently fat" and that some normal-weight women reported being overweight. It seems that weight preoccupation may exist on a continuum, and that Anorexia Nervosa may be a distinct variant or clinical entity. Perhaps the overlap between weight preoccupation and Anorexia Nervosa exists early in the course of the disease; alternatively, as Strober (1986) suggests, Anorexia Nervosa should be viewed "as a final common pathway for diverse causal factors and personality dynamics" (p. 239). For a more theoretical discussion of the conceptualization of Anorexia Nervosa as a syndrome, a symptom (specific and nonspecific), or a normal variant of weight preoccupation, the reader is directed to Garfinkel and Kaplan (1986).

Controversy has also surrounded the relationship between Anorexia Nervosa and obligatory running or exercising and excessive weight loss in athletes (Chipman, Hagan, Edlin, Soll, & Carruth, 1983). Based upon an interview study of a group of 60 male athletes, Yates, Leehey, and Shisslak (1983) claimed that "obligatory runners" resembled anorexic women with respect to family background, socioeconomic class, and such personality characteristics as inhibition of anger, high self-expectations, tolerance of physical discomfort, denial of potentially serious debility, and a tendency toward depression. Blumenthal, O'Toole, and Chang (1984) set out to assess the validity of their claims by comparing 24 anorexics (22 women, 2 men) and 43 "obligatory runners" (22 men, 21 women) on the Minnesota Multiphasic Personality Inventory (MMPI). An Obligatory Runners Questionnaire was developed especially for this investigation in order to classify participants. The items on this scale were chosen to reflect those attitudes described by Yates et al. (1983) as representative of "obligatory runners." The group of runners scored within the normal range on the MMPI, whereas the anorexic group did not. This study suggests that not all "obligatory runners" are necessarily as seriously disturbed as anorexic patients. Owens and Slade (1987) also found that runners do not exhibit nearly the psychopathology of eating-disordered subjects. In another study (Nudelman, Rosen, & Leitenberg, 1988), females with Bulimia Nervosa were more disturbed on all measures of eating than were male high-intensity runners.

Comorbidity of eating disorders with other disorders can lead to misdiagnosis. Obsessional and phobic anxiety symptoms are sometimes so prominent that the features of Anorexia Nervosa are missed (Thompson, 1989). Depression has also been found to be related to both Anorexia Nervosa and Bulimia Nervosa (Prather & Williamson, 1988; Weiss & Ebert, 1983; Williamson, Kelley, Davis, Ruggiero, & Blouin, 1985). In one study (Lee, Rush, & Mitchell, 1985), at least mild depression was found in 77% of bulimics. The two disorders are closely intertwined, as depression may precede or follow binge eating. Obsessive–compulsive features are more common in anorexics than in the general population (Rasmussen & Eisen, 1994), and in one study (Hudson, Pope, Yurgelun-Todd, Jonas, & Frankenburg, 1987), 33% of a bulimic sample met the criteria for Obsessive–Compulsive Disorder at some time in their lives. The diagnostic differentiation between anorexia nervosa and mood disorders, schizophrenia, obsessional disorders, and Conversion Disorder is seen as important (Garfinkel, Kaplan, Garner, & Darby, 1983; Hatsukami, Eckert, Mitchell, & Pyle, 1984; Rasmussen & Eisen, 1994; Walsh, Roose, Glassman, Gladis, & Sadik, 1985).

There has been an increase in the number of studies examining the comorbidity of eating disorders and Axis II personality disorders. In one study (Piran, Lerner, Garfinkel, Kennedy, & Brouillete, 1988), 39.5% of bulimics were diagnosed with Borderline Personality Disorder and 13.1% with Histrionic Personality Disorder, whereas 33% of anorexics were diagnosed with Avoidant Personality Disorder and 10% with Dependent Personality Disorder. Wonderlich and Mitchell (1992) found that from 53% to 93% of individuals with eating disorders displayed at least one personality disorder, and that from 37% to 56% met the criteria for more than one personality disorder. It has been found that those with a concurrent personality disturbance have a greater level of psychopathology (Yates, Sieleni, & Bowers, 1989). As personality disorders may affect treat-

ment, they need to be diagnosed when a diagnosis of an eating disorder is made.

Age of Onset

Anorexia Nervosa

Epidemiological investigations support the belief that Anorexia Nervosa develops in adolescence. Crisp, Hsu, Harding, and Hartshorn's (1980) review of 102 anorexic patients from a London hospital dated onset of illness according to onset of severe dieting, which was at 17.3 (± 4.0) years of age. Martin (1983) described 25 anorexic patients (2 males, 23 females) who averaged 14.9 years of age, with the time between onset of illness and referral being approximately 8 months. In another study (Garfinkel et al., 1983), 20 anorexic patients' age of onset was 16.2 ± 3.4 years. Although these ages can be targeted, there is evidence to suggest that anorexic symptoms develop over time and have a relatively predictable sequence. Beumont, Booth, Abraham, Griffiths, and Turner (1983) have collected data suggesting that there is a temporal sequence to the development of anorexic symptoms. Concern about body weight and engagement in relatively reasonable weight control efforts precede food/weight preoccupation and bizarre methods of weight control, with the latter increasing over time.

Some studies suggest that eating disturbance may develop in preadolescent children. In one study, dieting, fear of fatness, and binge eating were reported by 31–46% of 9-year-old girls and 46–81% of 10-year-old girls, and distortion of body image reached a peak at 11 years old, with a prevalence of 38% (Mellin, Irwin, & Scully, 1992). Koslow (1988) found body size overestimation in 11- and 12-year-old girls, but not in boys. Levels of dietary restraint in 12-year-old girls have been found to be as high as those of older girls and adult women (Wardle & Beales, 1986). A number of reports have described Anorexia Nervosa in young children. Fosson, Knibbs, Bryant-Waugh, and Lask (1987) described 48 children 14 years and younger who met modified diagnostic criteria for Anorexia Nervosa. Another report described 15 children 7 to 14 years old with Anorexia Nervosa (Blitzer, Rollins, & Blackwell, 1961). Russell (1985) and Jacobs and Isaacs (1986) each followed a group of 20 female patients with Anorexia Nervosa that had developed before menarche. In a summary of eating disturbance seen in children 8 to 14 years old (Bryant-Waugh & Kaminski, 1993), the authors described Anorexia Nervosa, food avoidance emotional disorder, food refusal, pervasive refusal, selective eating, Bulimia Nervosa, and appetite loss secondary to depression. Gowers, Crisp, Joughin, and Bhat (1991) utilized a data base of 650 female anorexics to identify 30 girls who developed the disorder before menarche. In a retrospective and longitudinal study of a child psychiatry service, 27 out of 8,051 children met the criteria for Anorexia Nervosa; it was found that early-onset Anorexia Nervosa showed a similar nature, course, and outcome to the adult disease (Higgs, Goodyer, & Birch, 1989).

Bulimia Nervosa and Bulimic Behavior

A survey of 499 bulimic women recruited through a popular women's magazine placed the mean age of onset of Bulimia Nervosa at 18.4 years (Fairburn & Cooper, 1982). In Agras and Kirkley's (1986) sample of 76 bulimic women, the mean age of onset was 19.3 years. Separating the onset of binge eating and of vomiting, Mitchell, Hatsukami, Eckert, and Pyle (1985) found that their sample of 275 bulimic women began bingeing at a mean age of 17.7 years and vomiting at a mean age of 18.8 years. Although the results are not altogether unambiguous, the accumulating evidence seems to suggest that Bulimia Nervosa is a disorder of late adolescence, whereas Anorexia Nervosa is a problem of early adolescence.

Epidemiology

Anorexia Nervosa

A survey of nine girls' schools in England found 1 case of severe Anorexia Nervosa in every 250 girls; in private schools, 1 in 200 girls under the age of 16 and 1 in 100 girls between 16 and 18 years of age had the disorder (Crisp, Palmer, & Kalucy, 1976). Moss, Jennings, McFarland, and Carter (1984) found that 18 of 151 girls in grade 10 scored in a range indicating the presence of anorexic symptoms. Pope, Hudson, and Yurgelun-Todd (1984) surveyed 300 women shoppers. Two, or 0.7%, reported a history of Anorexia Nervosa (according to DSM-III criteria). In a screening study of 1,010 girls aged 14–16 with the Eating Attitudes Test (EAT), a prevalence rate of 0.99% was detected for clinical Anorexia Nervosa and 1.78% for the partial syndrome (Johnson-Sabine, Wood, Patton, Mann, & Wakeling, 1988). In a study of 318 boys and girls in grades 3 through 6, 6.9% scored in the anorexic range on a children's ver-

sion of the EAT (Maloney, McGuire, Daniels, & Specker, 1989).

Bulimia Nervosa and Binge Eating

In a review of 11 studies of high school students (Crowther, Tennenbaum, Hobfoll, & Stephens, 1990), the prevalence rates for DSM-III Bulimia ranged from 1.2% to 16% in girls. (The DSM-III criteria were sometimes modified in these studies.) A country-wide study of U.S. high school students with a large sample size of 5,596 students and a 91% completion rate yielded a prevalence rate for Bulimia of 1.2% for girls and 0.4% for boys (Whitaker et al., 1990). Johnson, Lewis, Love, Lewis, and Stuckey (1984) found that 4.9% of a sample of 1,268 female high school students were engaging in clinically significant levels of bulimic behavior. In order to be included in the study, the women had to meet DSM-III criteria and admit to binge eating at least once per week. Of the sample, 1% binge-ate and purged on a weekly or more frequent basis; 21% reported weekly or more frequent episodes of binge eating. Estimates of the incidence of DSM-III Bulimia in a college population ranged from 4% (Pyle et al., 1983) to 19% (Halmi, Falk, & Schwartz, 1981). The differences in these rates may have been attributable to variation in the populations, discrepancies in self report, or differences in criteria for inclusion. Most worrisome are Hawkins and Clement's (1980, 1984) reports that approximately 66–86% of normal-weight female and 50–67% of normal-weight male undergraduate students admitted to binge eating at least once or twice a month. Unfortunately, the meaning of these admissions is not clear, as "binge eating" was not operationally defined. More interpretable is their finding that 6% of these same students indicated that they vomited after binge eating.

Eating Disorders among Males and in Various Ethnic Groups

Approximately 5–10% of patients with an eating disorder are male (Farrow, 1992). Only 0.2% of male first-year college students meet the requirements for Bulimia Nervosa, compared with 3.8% of female students (Striegel-Moore, Silberstein, Frensch, & Rodin, 1989). Whitaker et al.'s (1990) study of nearly 5,600 students identified only 1 bulimic boy versus 23 bulimic girls. The clinical features and outcome of Anorexia Nervosa and Bulimia Nervosa in males are relatively similar to those in females (Andersen, 1990; Crisp, Burns, & Bhat, 1986; Mitchell & Goff, 1984; Schneider & Agras, 1987), with the obvious exception of amenorrhea. (Because the ratio of male to female patients with these disorders is so low, feminine nouns and pronouns are used in the remainder of this chapter to refer to patients.)

Although originally thought to be confined to upper-middle-class Western society, eating disorders are increasing among all social classes and ethnic groups (Jones, Fox, Babigian, & Hutton, 1980; Yates, 1989). Silber (1986) studied five Hispanic and two African-American adolescents with Anorexia Nervosa, most of whom were the children of professional, achievement-oriented parents. Kope and Sack (1987) reported three cases of Anorexia Nervosa in Vietnamese refugees. In another study (Yates, 1989), Anorexia Nervosa was reported in Navajo girls whose parents had moved away from the reservation. Development of eating disorders in these groups may be the result of adoption of the Western cultural values of slimness, achievement orientation, control, self-discipline, competitiveness, and affiliation with a higher socioeconomic class (Garner & Olmsted, 1983). This idea is supported by Pumariega's (1986) finding of a correlation between disordered eating attitudes and level of acculturation to the U.S. majority culture in Hispanic students. In another study, traditional Kenyan women preferred a larger female figure than did British women, whereas Kenyan immigrants who had been in Britain for at least 4 years were more similar to British women in their body size preferences (Furnham & Alibhai, 1983).

MODELS OF ANOREXIA NERVOSA AND BULIMIA NERVOSA

Relevant dimensions or variables for assessment are chosen on the basis of a theoretical model about the nature of the disorder, the nature of individuals, and the nature of change. Virtually all current models of Anorexia Nervosa and Bulimia Nervosa begin with an explanation of the most salient features of these disorders. With Anorexia Nervosa, these include the time of onset, female gender (in most cases — see above), weight loss, the disturbed body image, the desire to be thin, and the refusal to maintain adequate or moderate/regular dietary intake. The most salient characteristics of Bulimia Nervosa are the binge eating and the purging behaviors. Related features

vary greatly among different orientations. The following discussion reviews several major theoretical orientations and their associated assessment practices.

Biological Models

There are essentially three types of biological models of the eating disorders. One emphasizes the hormonal changes that occur at puberty; another emphasizes statistical relationships between depression and eating disorders, such as incidence of mood disorders in first-degree relatives of eating-disordered patients; and a third emphasizes brain functioning.

The first model suggests that there are abnormalities in hormone output and regulatory mechanisms, such that the changes occurring at puberty in these processes make these abnormalities evident and interfere with normal eating behavior and weight control. However, the endocrine abnormalities that have been found in anorexics seem to be secondary to the starvation process itself, since they can be found in nonanorexic persons who have reached starvation weights (Barbosa-Saldivar & Van Itallie, 1979). The second and most prominent biological model of Anorexia Nervosa and Bulimia Nervosa assumes the existence of a genetic predisposition toward the development of these disorders and links them to affective disorders, including depression (Hudson, Pope, Jonas, & Yurgelun-Todd, 1983). Abnormally high incidences of major affective disorders in first-degree relatives (Fosson et al., 1987; Hudson et al., 1983), and bulimics' response to imipramine treatment (Pope, Hudson, Jonas, & Yurgelun-Todd, 1983), are cited as supporting evidence.

Representing the third type of biological model, Wurtman and Wurtman (1984) have proposed that there may be a disturbance in the feedback mechanism in Bulimia Nervosa, whereby carbohydrate intake registers in the brain in an abnormal fashion. They suggest that the concentration of the neurotransmitter serotonin is abnormal, and that an abnormal craving for carbohydrates is thereby produced. Finally, Rau and Green (1984) have asserted that a small number of bulimics have an epileptic-like, neurologically based disorder of impulse control. They argue that the psychologically based disorder is different and distinguishable from the neurologically based disorder. They claim that in the neurologically based disorder the patients may experience an aura; the patients see binge–purge behavior as inconsistent with their self-image; there is no psychological pattern to the binge eating; postictal phenomena may be present (extended periods of sleeping, unconsciousness, confusion, memory loss or disruption, headaches, or loss of bladder control); and/or the patients may exhibit various neurological "soft signs."

Psychodynamic Models

According to psychodynamic theory, the eating disorders, like any other syndromes or symptom complexes, are the expression of unconscious, internal conflicts that stem from early development. In Anorexia Nervosa and Bulimia Nervosa, these conflicts are thought to involve sexuality, autonomy, and identity. The severe food restriction seen in Anorexia Nervosa patients is considered symbolic of severe sexual conflicts, since the pattern of dieting and self-starvation often begins at the prepubertal period and delays or reverses the development of secondary sexual characteristics. According to Waller, Kaufman, and Deutsch (1940), Anorexia Nervosa is a disorder in which food intake is linked with pregnancy fantasies and the refusal of food serves as a defense against an infantile fantasy of oral impregnation by the father. The fear of anorexic girls that their stomachs are protruding is cited as evidence supporting this hypothesis. The amenorrhea associated with Anorexia Nervosa is seen as both a denial of sexuality (Lorand, 1943) and a symbol of pregnancy (Kaufman & Heiman, 1964).

Selvini Palazzoli (1978), a psychodynamically oriented family theorist, postulates that an anorexic patient has difficulties in the oral incorporative stage, which is crucial to separation and individuation. The anorexic fantasizes the oral incorporation—the devouring—of a maternal, bad, and overcontrolling object. This maternal introject is equated with the anorexic's own body when breasts and secondary sexual characteristics begin to develop. Self-starvation is thus the adolescent's attempt to end the feminization of her body, to minimize her identification with her mother, and to express her anger toward and control over the incorporated bad object (viz., the mother).

Bruch (1973) believes that Anorexia Nervosa stems from core developmental conflicts and deficits relating to autonomy and initiative. She has observed that Anorexia Nervosa patients are typically model children with outstanding performance records who can be considered overly compliant. They subsequently experience themselves as acting only in response to demands coming from others, and not in accordance with their own needs and wants. The illness is an attempt to break away from this dependence on others, a desperate fight against feeling enslaved, and a declaration of ownership and control over their own bodies.

Bulimia Nervosa as a distinct syndrome has not been given wide attention from psychodynamically oriented theorists. Coffman (1984) presents a clinical model of the "binge–purge" syndrome that draws heavily upon Bruch's (1973) discussions of issues of personal authority, effectiveness, and power over a person in authority, such as a parent (or a therapist). In fact, Coffman cautions therapists against focusing exclusively or too heavily on the binge–purge behaviors, because this might be perceived as a demand and thus as a threat to these clients' weak sense of personal control, which might provoke them to maintain or increase the binge eating and purging.

Bruch (1985) doubts the existence of Bulimia Nervosa as a separate clinical entity. She views it as a treatment complication of Anorexia Nervosa (not as the manifestation of a separate disorder), although an increasingly common one. In keeping with this conceptualization, Bruch has identified deficits in self-knowledge and self-definition in bulimics.

From a psychodynamic perspective, then, the assessment of Anorexia Nervosa and Bulimia Nervosa is directed at fundamental ambivalences and conflicts centering around issues of control, personal autonomy, initiative, effectiveness, power, and sexuality. Beyond diagnosis, the psychodynamic approach does not emphasize assessment. Standardized assessment instruments have not been developed to quantify and thereby to validate the presence of these conflicts.

Cognitive-Behavioral Models

Theory

The cognitive-behavioral approach emphasizes the analysis of functional relationships among antecedents, consequences, and individual behaviors as the proper units for studying, eventually understanding, and changing the behaviors of anorexic and bulimic patients. The literature on these disorders has focused on describing the parameters of the maladaptive behaviors and the development of behavioral and cognitive-behavioral treatment programs, rather than specifying the types of pathogenic social learning experiences. Leon (1979, 1980), in contrast, has proposed that extremely negative thoughts and feelings about weight and weight gain become associated with the consumption of food over time, such that it becomes reinforcing to refuse food in order to avoid these negative thoughts and feelings. Crisp (1965, 1980) conceptualizes anorexic patients' symptomatic behavior as an avoidance response whereby psychosexual maturity is avoided or reversed. These patients' behavior not only helps them to avoid negative thoughts, feelings, and fears, but also provides opportunities for much cognitive self-reinforcement through the sense of mastery, virtue, and self-control that it provides (Garner & Bemis, 1982, 1985; Garner, 1986). Thus, contingencies of both positive and negative reinforcement are used to explain the development and the maintenance of Anorexia Nervosa.

Several approaches have been generated within the cognitive-behavioral orientation regarding Bulimia Nervosa and bulimic behavior. Orleans and Barnett (1984) argue that "bulimarexia" (a term used to describe a pattern of behavior that includes binge eating and purging and occurs in normal-weight individuals) is initially acquired as a weight control tactic. They hypothesize that bulimarexia "develops as a faulty weight control practice in an environment where problematic self-control patterns are modeled" (p. 148). Loro's (1984) problem list for binge eaters includes cognitive distortions and irrational beliefs, maladaptive behaviors and faddish dieting practices, deficiencies in emotional expressiveness, and interpersonal issues. Theorists (Hawkins & Clement, 1984; Loro, 1984) have also emphasized the positive, non-eating-related outcomes associated with bingeing and purging. Binge eating provides comfort and distraction from anxiety and depression over interpersonal rejection or academic stress. The binge eater defines her problem as being uncontrolled eating, which is something she can master, if only theoretically. She avoids the more difficult and emotionally challenging interpersonal and academic problems. The binge also provides an opportunity for renewed self-determination, which the binge eater does by making what Hawkins and Clement (1984) call the "purification promise": "If only I could lose 20 pounds, or if only I would never eat any more sweets, then all my problems would be solved" (p. 248). Time-consuming rituals also drive persons who binge and purge into social isolation, which offers similar protection from possible rejection and negative evaluation by others.

In summary, the cognitive-behavioral approach directs its assessment efforts at the individual by delineating the antecedents and consequences (cognitive, behavior, affective, and interpersonal) of the maladaptive behaviors and the associated skills deficits; this delineation is aimed primarily at treatment planning. These approaches have identified areas of difficulties that involve basic knowledge about diet and nutrition, cognitions and emotions (particularly self-evaluative), and interpersonal difficulties.

Research

Researchers from a variety of perspectives have attempted to quantify and empirically investigate the deficits of anorexics and bulimics. Many have tried to do this by using terms that assume the existence of specific traits. Although we prefer not to make such assumptions, we may benefit from the research that has been done in this area. Although we may be more inclined to use concrete descriptors of behavior, or terms such as "assertiveness skills" and "psychosocial competence" rather than "compliance" and "neuroticism," we also recognize that other orientations are frequently describing similar behavioral patterns despite the differences in terminology.

Cognitive dysfunction appears to be a concomitant feature of eating pathology. Strauss and Ryan (1988) found that restricting and bulimic anorexics displayed more catastrophizing than did controls, and that restricting anorexics also displayed more overgeneralization, selective abstraction, and personalization than did controls. Other studies of Anorexia Nervosa (which are unfortunately flawed by a lack of suitable control groups and an overreliance on samples of chronic patients) have reported the presence of neuroticism, obsessionality, and self-doubt, in addition to interpersonal anxiety upon return to normal body weight (Ben-Tovim, Marilov, & Crisp, 1979; Pillay & Crisp, 1977; Smart, Beumont, & George, 1976; Stonehill & Crisp, 1977). Anxiety and obsessive–compulsive traits were found in anorexics as young as 9 to 16 years old (Fosson et al., 1987), and there was a strong association in adolescents between Anorexia Nervosa and premorbid obsessional problems (Rastam, 1992). Strober (1980, 1981a) compared younger Anorexia Nervosa patients with age-matched depressive and personality-disordered controls. The Anorexia Nervosa patients were somewhat obsessional in character, introverted, emotionally reserved and socially insecure, self-denying, deferential to others, given to overcompliance, prone to self-abasement and limited autonomy, and overly rigid and stereotyped in their thinking. After the anorexic patients had recovered their weight, there were few changes, suggesting that the characteristics were not the result of their near-starvation body weights.

As already noted, psychometric studies have also shown that Anorexia Nervosa patients can be meaningfully separated into two groups (Casper et al., 1980; Garfinkel et al., 1980; Strober et al., 1982): those who lose weight by not eating ("restricting anorexics"), and those who binge-eat and purge, usually by vomiting ("bulimic anorexics"). Bulimic anorexics are described as being anxious, unable to identify and articulate internal states, and impulsive—meaning that they sometimes engage in shoplifting, abuse multiple substances, mutilate themselves, and are more sexually active and labile in mood. Bulimic anorexics also have poor interpersonal skills, feel alienated and self-conscious, and have difficulty asserting themselves and expressing strong feelings (Boskind-Lodahl, 1976; Connors, Johnson, & Stuckey, 1984; Johnson, Stuckey, Lewis, & Schwartz, 1982; Norman & Herzog, 1983; Pyle, Mitchell, & Eckert, 1981; Schneider & Agras, 1985).

Casper et al. (1980) found that bingeing anorexics, compared to restricting anorexics, were more extroverted and interested in sex, reported greater incidence of vomiting and compulsive stealing, and had higher degrees of depression and somatization. Of interest is the finding that the bingeing anorexics also had a stronger sense of hunger than did the abstainers, who presumably took pride in their mastery over such bodily sensations. Garfinkel et al. (1980) reported many similar findings and, not surprisingly, found that bingeing anorexics were more likely to abuse laxatives and induce vomiting. Bingeing anorexics also reported a significantly higher premorbid weight, had more obese mothers, did not suffer from low body weight or body image disturbance, and did not deny their illness markedly (Lacey, 1982). Kalucy, Crisp, Lacey, and Harding (1977) had previously found that bulimics had higher premorbid weights. Beumont (1977) found that "vomiters" and "purgers" were more likely to have histrionic personalities (and to have a more chronic course), and that restricters were more likely to exhibit marked obsessionality through self-denial. Restricters were more socially withdrawn than the "vomiters" and "purgers," and were more introverted, anxious, and independent than either the controls or the "vomiters" and "purgers."

Bulimic anorexics also present with complaints of low self-esteem (Connors et al., 1984; Garfinkel & Garner, 1982; Love, Ollendick, Johnson, &

Schlesinger, 1985) and express feelings of inadequacy, helplessness, ineffectiveness, guilt, and self-criticism. Feelings of inadequacy and personal worthlessness were associated with eating disorder symptoms even in sixth- and seventh-grade girls (Killen et al., 1994). It is said that the self-worth of binge eaters frequently depends on the opinions of others, and that they neglect and even fail to recognize their own needs while excessively trying to please others. Furthermore, their initial dieting attempts may have been attempts to increase their self-esteem, which instead led to food-related problems, failures, and ultimately lower self-esteem.

Paradoxically, binge eaters are also described as counterdependent, oppositional, and rebellious (Coffman, 1984; Loro, 1984). For example, it is claimed that they resist taking orders or advice given by authorities (e.g., parents, spouses, or doctors), and are unable to ask for help because they equate dependence with weakness and vulnerability (Johnson & Pure, 1986; Loro, 1984). Clinical evidence also suggests that bulimics are perfectionists, selectively attend to negative evaluations of themselves, and think in dichotomous, all-or-none polarities (Loro, 1984). They further assume that other people are constantly evaluating them and scan other people's behavior for evaluative messages about themselves. Loro (1984) speculates that this style is so disorienting and chaotic that the binge behavior, with its ritualistic and predictable sequence, may serve to reorient bulimics when they begin to feel fragmented and out of control. Alternatively, he suggests that overcontrolled bulimics may use bingeing in order to "let go" and be out of control or impulsive.

ASSESSMENT OF THE EATING-DISORDERED INDIVIDUAL

In the clinical setting, the therapist should be prepared for eating-disordered patients to be very difficult clients to assess. Bulimics tend to be embarrassed and secretive about their unusual eating and purging behaviors, and since the therapist may be the first person they have told about their problems, they may be rebellious or oppositional. Their noncompliance may extend to the assessment procedures. In such cases, the therapist must be skilled in eliciting information.

Anorexics may present a slightly different set of difficulties. Most striking is the denial of their disorder and of their need for treatment. Although a patient's family may be motivated for treatment or symptom relief, the therapist must be careful not to be perceived as siding with the family against the patient. It is crucial for the therapist to establish rapport and a positive relationship with the anorexic patient.

Patients with Anorexia Nervosa and Bulimia Nervosa frequently elicit strong negative feelings in the first interview. When attempts are made to interview and work with these patients, they can be defensive, secretive, disagreeable, and attacking, as noted above. Their behavior may seem so unreasonable and provocative that it is difficult for the interviewer not to become angry. To counteract such negative feelings, it is sometimes helpful for the interviewer to view the symptoms as a reaction to a very disordered environment. The style of interacting may have been very adaptive and self-preserving within the context in which it developed. The interviewer may be seen as trying to dismantle the scheme these patients have developed to preserve themselves, their sense of independence, or their feelings of self-control. Caution should be taken to not label an individual with the eating disorder as *being* "the problem" when the eating disorder might more appropriately be attributed to the social situation or to cultural factors (Strasser & Giles, 1988).

Assessment should cover a wide range of behaviors and problem areas. The manner and sequence in which one approaches a patient should be designed to match the patient's view of the problem, insofar as this is possible. The patient's view of the problem can be solicited upon initial inquiry. This can be adopted, with adjustments, as the rationale or justification for the collection of information that might otherwise be objectionable or provoke noncompliance. If the patient is in an end stage or a physically compromised stage of Anorexia Nervosa, medical considerations must come first and foremost.

Assessment of Medical Symptoms

Anorexia Nervosa and Bulimia Nervosa are medically assessed in terms of endocrinological/metabolic, cardiovascular, renal, gastrointestinal, hematological, and pulmonary dysfunction (for excellent reviews, see Garner, Rockert, Olmsted, Johnson, & Coscina, 1985; Mitchell, 1986a, 1986b). Physical examination, standard laboratory tests, multiple-channel chemistry analysis, complete blood count, and urinalysis should be routine. It is well known that Anorexia Nervosa is a potentially life-threatening disorder; approxi-

mately 10–15% of untreated cases end in death (Schwartz & Thompson, 1981). Medical complications of Bulimia Nervosa and bulimic behavior have also proven fatal. Although these are reviewed below in detail, it is also important to note that the leading cause of death in bingeing anorexics is suicide (Crisp, 1982). There are three observable signs that can alert the clinician to the possibility of Bulimia Nervosa: dental enamel erosion; lesions on the skin over the dorsum of the hand; and hypertrophy of the salivary glands (Mitchell, Pomeroy, & Colon, 1990).

The most dangerous complication of vomiting and purgative (laxative and diuretic) abuse is the depletion of the electrolytes potassium, chloride, and sodium (Garner, Rockert, et al., 1985). The clinician should be alert to complaints of weakness, tiredness, constipation, and depression, which can be produced by electrolyte abnormalities (Webb & Gehi, 1981). Electrolyte abnormalities may result in cardiac arrhythmias and sudden death, or in kidney disturbances (Mitchell et al., 1990; Russell, 1979). Mitchell, Pyle, Eckert, Hatsukami, and Lentz (1983) found electrolyte disturbances in almost 49% of their nonanorexic bulimic patients. Neurological disturbances have also been documented; some have been associated with electrolyte disturbances (Mitchell & Pyle, 1982), whereas others have included muscular spasms and tingling sensations in the extremities (Fairburn, 1982; Russell, 1979) and swollen salivary glands accompanied by facial swelling (Levin, Falko, Dixon, Gallup, & Saunders, 1980; Pyle et al., 1981; Walsh et al., 1981).

Gastrointestinal disturbances associated with Bulimia Nervosa and bulimic behavior include abdominal pain, spontaneous regurgitation of food, extreme dilation of the stomach (leading to rupture and death in some cases), permanent loss of bowel reactivity, and serious tearing of mouth and throat tissue. Gastric acid from self-induced vomiting leads to dental erosion, and loss of enamel causes color changes, caries, and periodontal disease (Brady, 1980; Stege, Visco-Dangler, & Rye, 1982). Edema is common after vomiting and laxative abuse have ceased; many patients notice swelling or "puffiness" caused by excessive water retention. Menstrual irregularities are common among bulimics, even those of normal weight (Pirke, 1990). Johnson, Stuckey, Lewis, and Schwartz (1983) found that 20% of a sample of 50 bulimics had experienced amenorrhea following the onset of eating disorders, and that 50% were experiencing menstrual irregularities at the time of the survey. Needless to say, medical consultation in the assessment of eating disorders is an essential component of professional and ethical practice.

Assessment of Behavior

Weight Regulation

One of the most striking symptoms in both Anorexia Nervosa and Bulimia Nervosa is the preoccupation with weight and thinness. Weight history and preoccupation with weight should be thoroughly assessed. The following should be covered: current weight and height; ideal weight; highest and lowest weight since early adolescence; fluctuations and their relationship to major life events and changes; actual or perceived consequences of weight loss and gain (including occupational and interpersonal); family and peer attitudes toward thinness, dieting, and appearance; and history of weight loss (speed and method). Weight should be taken with the subject dressed in a gown. If anxiety regarding weight is too high, the subject can turn away from the reading on the scale.

More general eating habits are also significant. Food intake, regularity–irregularity of eating habits, nutritional adequacy of intake, purging, and exercise behavior are all likely to play some role in the maintenance or development of an eating disorder. Patients can be asked to explain what calories are, how food is digested, the function of fat, and how most fad diets work, in order that the clinician may assess superstitious and magical thinking associated with food (Garner & Bemis, 1982; Loro, 1984). Johnson (1985) and his colleagues inquire as to whether patients perceive foods as "good" or "bad," and what the effects of ingesting one type or the other are on them. The answer to these questions, as well as information about the onset, precipitants, frequency, duration, and longest asymptomatic period, may help one to discern the functional basis of the disorder. A prolonged period of restrictive eating is the most commonly cited precipitant of binge eating (Johnson et al., 1982; Pyle et al., 1981). Loss or separation from a significant other; interpersonal or job conflict; and difficulty handling sexuality and such emotions as anger, loneliness, and depression are also cited (Johnson et al., 1982).

Important questions regarding dieting include how long the patient has been involved in dieting behavior; when, why, and with whose encouragement the dieting first began; and what role dieting and weight problems played in the patient's family of origin. The extent and function of weigh-

ing and exercise behaviors are also of interest, since they can often become ritualistic and self-defeating. Anorexics have been shown to increase (and decrease) their food intake when given inaccurately low (or high) feedback regarding their body weight, respectively, compared to normal-weight controls (Russell, Campbell, & Slade, 1975). The validity of this finding is limited, in that the anorexic subjects' discharge from the hospital would have been jeopardized by a loss of weight (they had already achieved their "target" weight), whereas there were no similar contingencies for the normal-weight controls. Consequently, they may have modified their eating simply because of their desire to leave the hospital.

Binge Behavior

Assessment of binge behavior includes information about when, where, and with whom it occurs, as well as about its frequency and length. What is consumed (type and quantity), antecedents and consequences of the binge behavior, onset, initial precipitants, associated feelings, and length and circumstances surrounding the longest asymptomatic period are also assessed. A binge–purge diary can be helpful in obtaining some of this information (see Figure 14.1). It has been found that patients with eating disorders who monitor their behavior make better progress than those who do not (Agras, 1987). Self-report methods have been criticized for being too removed from the behavior of interest (Schlundt, 1989). An alternate is the direct measurement of eating during a test meal. In one study, this procedure was used on subjects with Bulimia Nervosa; standard test meals were administered, and subsequent vomiting or purging was prevented (Rosen, Leitenberg, Fondacaro, Gross, & Willmuth, 1985). In this context, Bulimia Nervosa patients showed marked dietary restraint, eating less than did controls.

Most bulimics begin to binge approximately 1½ years after beginning to diet (Garfinkel et al., 1980), and to purge (usually in the form of self-induced vomiting) approximately 1 year after the onset of binge eating (Johnson et al., 1982; Pyle et al., 1981). A group of 40 bulimic patients studied by Mitchell, Pyle, and Eckert (1981) reported a mean of 11.7 binge episodes per week (range of 1–46) averaging 1.18 hours in length (range from 15 minutes to 8 hours). An average of 3,415 calories (range of 1,200–11,500) was consumed, at an average cost of $8.30 per binge (range of $1.00–$55.00). It is common to find that a patient binges

Time of day	Place	With whom	Associated activities	Foods/liquors: Include amounts	Feelings: Before, during, and after eating	Purge yes/no: If yes, vomiting, laxatives, diuretics, etc.	Feelings before, during, and after purge

FIGURE 14.1. Binge–purge diary.

on certain foods and that these foods have acquired a forbidden status, such that the patient perceives that consumption of these foods alone has the power to trigger a binge.

Psychological as well as physical deprivation may trigger binge eating or specific food cravings (Garner, Rockert, et al., 1985; Wardle, 1980; Wardle & Beinart, 1981). Dissatisfaction with body image and poor self-esteem have been shown to be significant predictors of the severity of binge eating (Wolf & Crowther, 1983). Binge eating occurs most often in the afternoon and evening; occurs at times when patients are at home alone; involves foods of which they normally deprive themselves (carbohydrates and sweets); and typically takes place after patients have not eaten during the day. Binge eaters tend to have the most difficulty with unstructured time (Johnson, 1985) and with making transitions between settings (e.g., going from school or work to home; Johnson et al., 1982).

It has been suggested that the phenomenological experience of being out of control, rather than the actual amount of food eaten, is what defines a binge (Johnson, Lewis, & Hagman, 1984). Such a conceptualization emphasizes the role of binge eating in the regulation of affect. The affective states most likely to trigger a binge are boredom, loneliness, anger, and depression (Cooper & Bowskill, 1986; Johnson et al., 1982). How patients perceive themselves and their binge eating is significant. The symptomatic behavior may have relatively unique payoffs or purposes. Some of these may involve cognitive self-statements relating to aggressiveness, self-punishment, eroticism, nurturance, losing control, or acting out.

Purge Behavior

Purge behavior can take many different forms; it ranges from laxative abuse, which is predictive of life impairment (Johnson & Love, 1984), to self-induced vomiting, diuretic abuse, amphetamine abuse, fasting or strict dieting, and excessive exercise. Purging serves to protect the patient against the dreaded weight gain and may also be a way to express anger, to punish oneself, or to regain a sense of control. Initial research by Johnson and Larson (1982) and by Rosen and Leitenberg (1982) suggests that the act of purging may be more tension-regulating than the binge eating, and that although patients may begin to purge so that they can binge-eat, they later binge-eat in order to be able to purge. In the case study reported by Rosen and Leitenberg (1982), the bingeing behavior of one 21-year-old woman dissipated as the purging behavior was prevented, even though the bingeing behavior was never targeted for intervention. Work by Stuart and Davis (1972) and Marks (1978) suggests that purging can be prevented by increasing the interval between the binge and the purge.

Body Image

"Body image" refers to one's physical picture of, as well as emotional feelings and attitudes toward, one's body (Garfinkel & Garner, 1982). Subjects with eating disorders tend to overestimate their own body size. This tendency was originally observed clinically by Bruch (1962) and has since been well documented (e.g., Collins et al., 1987; Cash & Brown, 1987; Garner & Garfinkel, 1981; Rosen, 1990). The utility of the construct is supported by the finding that body image disturbance is related to eating disturbance in adolescents (Attie & Brooks-Gunn, 1989; Fabian & Thompson, 1989; Gross & Rosen, 1988) and is predictive of relapse following treatment (Fairburn, Peveler, Jones, Hope, & Doll, 1993; Rosen, 1990).

Several techniques have been developed to assess body image. In one kind of procedure, subjects estimate various body widths by marking the distance on a sheet of paper (Askevold, 1975), adjusting calipers (Reitman & Cleveland, 1964), or changing the width of a beam of light (Slade & Russell, 1973; Thompson & Spana, 1988). Another kind of procedure involves distorting images of oneself on a mirror (Traub & Orbach, 1964) or video (Allebeck, Hallberg, & Espmark, 1976) to correspond with one's perceived size. A third kind of procedure uses silhouette charts from which subjects select their perceived and ideal sizes (Counts & Adams, 1985; Thompson & Psaltis, 1988). The extent of body size overestimation in subjects with eating disorders varies considerably, in part because of the different size estimation procedures used. In one study (Fichter, Meister, & Koch, 1986), the best discrimination between anorexic and control females was obtained with the lights apparatus, followed by the image-marking procedure and then the video procedure. In another study (Mikhail, Steiger, & Taylor, 1993), anorexic and bulimic women overestimated their sizes using the video, lights, and silhouettes procedures, whereas controls were remarkably accurate. Eating-disordered women overestimated their sizes to the largest extent on the lights apparatus, followed by the silhouettes and then the video. Using silhouettes, they selected slimmer ideal sizes in general and even slimmer ideal sizes for themselves than did controls. Eating-disordered women also retained more concerns about their bodies, as measured by the Body Shape Questionnaire (BSQ; Cooper, Taylor, Cooper, & Fairburn, 1987).

Several questionnaires have been developed to measure different aspects of body image. The Body Cathexis Scale (Secord & Jourard, 1953) is a 40-item measure of satisfaction with one's body. It has been used widely in validating newer measures of body satisfaction or concern. The Eating Disorder Inventory (EDI), discussed in more detail later in this chapter, has a subscale to assess body image concerns. The BSQ (Cooper et al., 1987) is a 34-item self-report instrument assessing concerns with body shape. It discriminates between eating-disordered and non-eating-disordered populations, and is highly correlated with the Body Dissatisfaction subscale of the EDI. On the Body Parts Rating Scale (Berscheid, Walster, & Bohrnstedt, 1973), subjects rate their degree of satisfaction or dissatisfaction with each of 24 body parts. The Body Image Automatic Thoughts Questionnaire (Brown, Johnson, Bergeron, Keeton, & Cash, 1990) measures the frequency of 52 appearance-related cognitions, 37 of which are negative and 15 of which are positive. A similar scale, the Bulimia Cognitive Distortions Scale (Schulman, Kinder, Powers, Prange, & Gleghorn, 1986), also measures cognitive distortions related to physical appearance. One measure, the Body Image Avoidance Questionnaire (Rosen, Srebnik, Saltzberg, & Wendt, 1991), assesses not only attitudes but also behavioral measures associated with a negative body image. The questionnaire has four subscales: Clothing, Social Activities, Eating Restraint, and Grooming and Weighing. Another instrument assessing body image behavior is the Body Dysmorphic Disorder Examination (BDDE; Rosen, Reiter, & Orosan, 1995), a semistructured interview with an administration time of approximately 15–30 minutes. The BDDE measures preoccupation with appearance, self-consciousness, overvalued ideas about the importance of appearance to one's self-worth, and behaviors related to these attitudes. It has good internal consistency and high concurrent validity with other body image measures. A scale that is suitable for use with children as young as 7 years old is the Body-Esteem Scale (Mendelson & White, 1982), a 24-item self-report measure of concerns about one's physical appearance.

Social Skills

A number of writers have discussed the difficulty that anorexics and bulimics seem to have in their interpersonal relationships (Bruch, 1973; Crisp, 1967b; Garfinkel & Garner, 1982). It is informative to assess how symptomatic behaviors may be related to daily activities such as work, school, and play. The symptoms may allow patients to avoid interpersonal relationships without forcing them to confront their own difficulties in that area. They are able to redefine their problem as "uncontrollable overeating" or "overweight appearance," rather than some potentially more personally damaging definition involving interpersonal or academic incompetence. Symptoms may thereby serve a comforting and distracting function (Hawkins & Clement, 1984).

A review of 700 outcome studies of anorexics by Schwartz and Thompson (1981) found that only 47% of anorexics had married or were maintaining active heterosexual lives, although 90% of them worked. Of 102 consecutive anorexic patients seen by Crisp et al. (1980), 23 were excessively shy as children and had serious difficulties in mixing with other children, while 43 had few or no friends during childhood. Warren (1968) found social withdrawal in his entire sample of 10- to 16-year-old anorexics. Compared to a sample from the community, bulimic patients were significantly impaired in their overall adjustment and also in the areas of work, social/leisure, family, and marital adjustment (Johnson & Berndt, 1983). Of the 37 bulimics studied by Leon, Carroll, Chernyk, and Finn (1985), 97% indicated that their problems with eating and weight had interfered "a great deal" with other aspects of their lives (social relationships, 94%; family relationships, 97%; sleep patterns, 97%; and school or job performance, 84%).

Ironically, clinical observation suggests that bulimics tend to take better care of others than they do of themselves. For example, a bulimic may spend time helping a friend complete a school assignment, even if it means that she will not have time to complete her own. Loro (1984) presents a picture of bulimics as nonassertive, socially isolated, counterdependent, and rebellious individuals. These characteristics are seen in their difficulties with saying no to others, setting limits, or standing up for personal rights. Loro suggests that bulimics avoid conflicts because of difficulties in expressing negative emotions, and will give up or give in quickly and "swallow" their anger, disappointment, and frustration. This pattern may be perceived as psychologically adaptive in that they fear that they will lose all control of their emotions should they allow any of them expression. Binge eating is also a way for them to nurture themselves, to lick their wounds. At the same time, they try to deny their sense of helplessness, weakness, and lack of control by refusing to depend upon others

and by actively resisting being under the "control" of others.

Binge eating is also a way to spend time. Binge eaters spend much time alone, in their embarrassment and shame—planning and preparing for binges, actually bingeing, and then recovering from bingeing. The time required to carry out these very private activities keeps them from social activities and results in further social isolation and withdrawal. They become progressively unaccustomed to interacting socially, and this engenders intense feelings of social inadequacy and incompetence. It thus becomes a self-perpetuating cycle.

Like the behaviors of bulimics, anorexics' eating behaviors also become a way to be defiant and to express autonomy and independence. As already discussed, this may be the only area in which these overly compliant, emotionally reserved, dependent, socially insecure people can express strong negative feelings in an overt way, behave independently, and be steadfast and unshakable. The symptomatic behavior may be the expression of positive, adaptive strivings that are either excessive or misguided in the same overdone way as the initial learning and exercise of new, fledgling skills. This fits with Coffman's (1984) treatment model in its emphasis on bulimics' need to experience an increase in their own sense of power, authority, and control (Loro & Orleans, 1981; Seligman, 1975).

Sexual Behavior

The weight loss associated with Anorexia Nervosa has traditionally been viewed as a defense against sexuality, which blossoms with puberty; relatedly, it has been seen as a way to reverse the development of secondary sexual characteristics, including menstruation. Crisp et al.'s (1980) findings lend support to the hypothesis that sexuality may be an area of difficulty for at least some anorexics. They found that 26 of 96 anorexic patients who had reached menarche before the onset of their disorder showed a definite avoidance of heterosexual contacts even before the onset of the illness. Jacobs and Isaacs (1986) found higher levels of sexual anxiety in anorexic than in neurotic prepubertal children. It is well known that libido and sexual behavior decrease in individuals with anorexic weight levels (Keys, Brozek, Henschel, Mickelsen, & Taylor, 1950).

The wide variety of sexual feelings, drives, and experiences among anorexics and bulimics (Abraham & Beumont, 1982; Beumont, Abraham, &

Simson, 1981) suggest that there is probably no one pattern of difficulty, however. Although they do not describe their sexual relationships as pleasant, bulimic anorexics are more sexually active than nonbulimic anorexics (Garfinkel & Garner, 1982). Crisp (1967b) observed that bulimic anorexics "rushed into one relationship after another . . . in the mistaken belief that they would then feel secure and wanted" (p. 128). He noted that their sexual relationships were frequently characterized by fellatio, and that this was followed by vomiting. Garfinkel and Garner (1982) have reported that bulimic anorexics feel misused and unable to enjoy sex, and that feeling sexually out of control exacerbates their bulimia. They suggest that bulimic anorexics do not know "in-betweens" in sexual behavior any more than they do in eating or other areas of self-control. Only 4% of bulimic anorexics and 2.9% of restricting anorexics indicated that they had "frequent and pleasant" sexual intercourse. These observations are consistent with Bruch's (1973) conceptualization of the problems with sexuality in females with eating disorders as reflections of more basic difficulties with autonomy and self-regulation. An inability to self-regulate may be a part of why most bingers think that sex is bad and scary; they see it as "one more way to lose control" (Barnett & Loro, 1981, p. 2). It has also been suggested (Johnson, Lewis, & Hagman, 1984) that binge eating does not carry the same moral, legal, or medical consequences as sexual promiscuity, or the same personal risk of rejection as sexual activity in general.

INSTRUMENTS FOR ASSESSING EATING DISORDERS

There are numerous instruments available for the assessment of disturbed eating attitudes and practices, and these vary widely in aim and scope. As discussed above, food diaries are perhaps the most commonly used. These are generally rather loosely structured; entries are made under several headings and cover what is consumed, in what amount, at what time of the day, where, with whom, and accompanying what activities (sometimes with special attention to mood or affective state).

The Experience Sampling Method, developed by Csikzentmihalyi and Graef (1980) and adopted for use with eating-disordered patients by Larson and Johnson (1981) and Johnson and Larson (1982), is a refined and potentially more revealing method of obtaining information about the actual behaviors of Bulimia Nervosa and Anorexia

Nervosa patients, although it is likely to be utilized more often with the former. This method consists of the use of electronic pagers that emit auditory signals at random intervals during the day. When the signals are heard, subjects complete a self-report diary. The two studies by Johnson and Larson indicated that both anorexics and bulimics spent more time alone, usually in food-related behavior, and experienced more dysphoric and fluctuating moods than normals.

The Diagnostic Survey for Eating Disorders (DSED; Johnson, 1985) can be used as a self-report or standardized interview instrument. It provides information on demographic factors, weight and body image, dieting behavior, binge-eating behavior, purging behavior, exercise and related behavior, sexual functioning, menstrual history, and family history. The DSED itself is extensive rather than intensive, but highlights areas for more intensive probing.

Structured interviews for assessing eating disorders include the Clinical Eating Disorder Rating Instrument (CEDRI; Palmer, Christie, Cordle, Davis, & Kendrick, 1987), the Eating Disorder Examination (EDE; Cooper & Fairburn, 1987), and the Interview for Diagnosis of Eating Disorders (IDED; Williamson, 1990). The CEDRI consists of 35 items that assess behaviors and attitudes common to Anorexia Nervosa and Bulimia Nervosa. The test has high interrater reliability, but its validity has not been adequately assessed. The EDE consists of 62 items that assess current bulimic symptomatology. Cooper and Fairburn (1987) suggest that the interview be used as a measure of treatment outcome rather than for diagnostic purposes. It has high interrater reliability (Rosen, Vara, Wendt, & Leitenberg, 1990; Wilson & Smith, 1989) and established discriminant validity (Cooper, Cooper, & Fairburn, 1989). The EDE is also a sensitive outcome measure in the treatment of Bulimia Nervosa (Garner et al., 1993; Wilson, Eldredge, Smith, & Niles, 1991). The IDED was developed to assist in diagnosing an eating disorder. It assesses the core psychopathology of Anorexia Nervosa, Bulimia Nervosa, compulsive overeating, and obesity. Many of the questions may also be used with family members. These structured interviews should be conducted by trained interviewers and may take up to an hour or more to administer; therefore, they can be time-consuming and costly. However, they do provide a great deal of information in a systematic manner. A less costly method for assessing the essential features of eating disorders is the use of self-report. Self-report measures have been found to be as useful as the EDE in assessment of Bulimia Nervosa, provided that a diagnosis is established and that patients are instructed in the construct of a "binge" (Loeb, Pike, Walsh, & Wilson, 1994).

One of the earliest self-report instruments for assessing eating disorders is the Hunger–Satiety Questionnaire (HSQ; Monello, Seltzer, & Mayer, 1965). The HSQ is a 19-item measure of physical sensations, mood, urge to eat, and preoccupation with thoughts of food. The instrument was developed to characterize the eating patterns of normal and overweight adults and adolescents (Monello & Mayer, 1967; Monello et al., 1965). Subjects specify how they feel immediately upon sitting down to eat, after a few mouthfuls, 2 hours before a typical meal, 30 minutes before a meal, after a few bites, at the end of a meal, and at their hungriest ever. Garfinkel (1974) administered the HSQ to anorexic patients and normal controls. He presented the hunger portion of the questionnaire after a period of fasting, and the satiety or fullness portion after the subjects had eaten a meal. He concluded that anorexic patients were not abnormal in their perception of hunger, but that they associated hunger with negative affect, increased urges to eat, and preoccupation with food. Anorexics differed from controls in their experience of satiety; they reported that they were satiated when they reached a preset goal, rather than when they felt satisfied. Whereas some anorexics endorsed negative affects (nervousness, irritability, etc.) all controls described positive feelings after eating. Bulimics also reported increased preoccupation with food prior to and greater negative affect after eating following a 12-hour fast (Chiodo & Latimer, 1986).

The Psychiatric Rating Scale for Anorexia Nervosa (PRSAN; Goldberg, Halmi, Casper, Eckert, & Davis, 1977) is made up of 14 items, which are rated on a 7-point scale in terms of severity. The items reflect major descriptive and psychopathological features of Anorexia Nervosa, including denial of illness, fear of fat, thin ideal body image, loss of appetite, selective appetite, fear of becoming a compulsive eater, desire for activity, desire to control, manipulativeness, depression, obsessiveness, immaturity, purgative and diuretic abuse, and exaggerated cheerfulness (Slade, 1973). The PRSAN is typically completed by nursing or other professional staff members. Restrictive and bingeing anorexics have been shown to differ on a number of the items, including psychosexual immaturity, fear of fat and of compulsive eating, depressed mood, and use of purgatives and diuretics (Strober, 1981b). Senior ward nurses who made

independent ratings on the PRSAN achieved inter-rater reliabilities of .76 to .90. Unfortunately, it is not clear that other professionals would not differ in their use of the severity ratings, given the ambiguity of such terms as "exaggerated cheerfulness."

The Situational Discomfort Scale (Goldberg et al., 1977) is a 20-item self-report questionnaire relating to food and eating; items are rated according to "bothersomeness" on a 4-point scale. One item is being told to eat everything on the plate, and another describes stomach distension, a consequence of eating. The scale does not predict weight gain during inpatient hospitalization (Goldberg et al., 1977), but bulimics report higher anxiety than do normal controls (Weiss & Ebert, 1983). Validity and reliability evidence are unfortunately lacking, and the findings are thus difficult to interpret.

The Goldberg Anorectic Attitude Scale (Goldberg et al., 1980) assesses attitudes of anorexic patients during hospitalization and does predict weight gain. It has 63 items and a 4-point scale to indicate differing levels of agreement and disagreement. A factor analysis of the scale resulted in the emergence of 13 categories: (1) Staff, (2) Fear of Fat, (3) Parents, (4) Denial, (5) Hunger, (6) Hypothermia, (7) Bloated, (8) Self-Care, (9) Effort for Achievement, (10) Food Is Sickening, (11) Physical versus Mental Problems, (12) Cooking as Hobby, and (13) Heterosexual Disinterest. Weiss and Ebert (1983) found that normal-weight bulimics scored higher than did controls on Fear of Fat, (negative attitudes toward) Parents, Hypothermia, and Food Is Sickening.

The Anorexic Behaviour Scale (Slade, 1973) was designed to assess Anorexia Nervosa patients by means of behavioral observation techniques. It is a checklist of behaviors related to resistance to eating, methods of food disposal, and activity level. It is typically completed by psychiatrists after a brief interview. Differences have been found between 12 Anorexia Nervosa patients and 12 psychiatrically disturbed adolescent controls as observed by senior nurses for 1 month. Goldberg et al. (1977), using this scale, found hyperactivity to be the most characteristic feature of 44 hospitalized anorexics.

The Binge Eating Scale (BES; Gormally, Black, Daston, & Rardin, 1982) is a 16-item scale based upon the DSM-III criteria for Bulimia. The items include behavioral characteristics (e.g., eating quickly, in secret, and large amounts of food) as well as feelings and cognitions (e.g., guilt, fear of being unable to stop eating). Each item consists of three to four statements; the statement that best describes the client is to be endorsed. For example:

1. I don't lose control of my eating when dieting even after periods when I overeat.
2. Sometimes when I eat a "forbidden food" on a diet, I feel like I "blew it" and eat even more.
3. Frequently, I have the habit of saying to myself, "I've blown it now, why not go all the way" when I overeat on a diet. When that happens I eat even more.
4. I have a regular habit of starting strict diets for myself, but I break the diets by going on an eating binge. My life seems to be either a "feast" or "famine." (Gormally et al., 1982, p. 54)

The BES has been shown to discriminate among obese persons judged by trained observers using a structured interview to have either no problem, a moderate problem, or a severe problem with binge eating.

The Binge Scale (Hawkins & Clement, 1980) is a 10-item self-report questionnaire that is used to assess the behavioral parameters of bingeing (frequency, duration). It has been used primarily as a screening device. Hawkins and Clement (1980) reported that the test–retest reliability over a 1-month period was .88, and found that women being treated for binge-eating problems scored higher than did a classroom sample of college students. Katzman and Wolchik (1984) found the Binge Scale to differentiate among bulimic women, binge-eating women, and normal controls. None of these subjects were receiving psychiatric treatment at the time of the study.

The Eating Attitudes Test (EAT; Garner & Garfinkel, 1979), mentioned earlier in the chapter, is a 40-item screening instrument that assesses the symptoms of Anorexia Nervosa. Items are rated on a 6-point ("always–never") scale. A high score may be earned in the absence of sufficient anorexic symptomatology, and thus a high number of false positives may be produced by this instrument. The EAT is not, however, significantly related to measures of dieting, weight fluctuation, or neuroticism (Garner & Garfinkel, 1979). Scores on the EAT correlated significantly with membership in a criterion group of female anorexic patients compared to normal university students (Garner & Garfinkel, 1979), and normal-weight females and obese females scored lower than did anorexic patients. Since clinically recovered anorexics scored in the normal range, the EAT appears to be sensitive to clinical improvement. The EAT was reduced to 26 items after factor analysis, resulting in the EAT-26, and scores on the two scales were significantly correlated (Garner, Olmsted, Bohr, & Garfinkel, 1982). The three factors that emerged upon factor analysis of the EAT-26 were Dieting (defined as pathological avoidance of high-calorie foods), Bingeing and Food Preoccupation, and Self-Control. Not surprisingly, bingeing anorexics scored higher on Bingeing and Food Preoccupation and lower on Self-Control than did restricting anorexics (Garner et al., 1982). A Japanese version of the EAT (Ujiie & Kono, 1994) was useful in detecting Bulimia Nervosa but not Anorexia Nervosa.

The Eating Disorders Inventory (EDI; Garner, Olmsted, & Polivy, 1983), also mentioned earlier, was developed to be more sensitive to the characteristics of both restrictive and bingeing anorexics. The 64-item scale is broken down into eight subscales: (1) Drive for Thinness, (2) Bulimia, (3) Body Dissatisfaction, (4) Ineffectiveness, (5) Perfectionism, (6) Interpersonal Distrust, (7) Interoceptive Awareness, and (8) Maturity Fears. The EDI was validated initially with 117 Anorexia Nervosa patients and 577 normal females. The EDI also distinguished between patients with Anorexia Nervosa and obese and formerly obese individuals. Clinical ratings of experienced clinicians agreed with the EDI scores; it is sensitive to clinical improvement; and differences on subscales have been shown between anorexic and normal-weight bulimics (Garner, Garfinkel, & O'Shaughnessy, 1983). In other studies (Garner, Olmsted, & Polivy, 1983; Gross, Rosen, Leitenberg, & Willmuth, 1986), restricting and bulimic anorexics scored higher than did controls and recovered Anorexia Nervosa patients. The EDI-2, developed by Garner (1991) provides three additional scales: (1) Asceticism, (2) (lack of) Impulse Regulation, and (3) Social Insecurity. It also provides improved norms for subjects as young as 11 years old, although the validity of the three new scales has not been established for children under 12. As the instrument is multidimensional, comparisons can be made prior to and following treatment of specific targeted behaviors or concerns.

The Bulimia Test (BULIT; Smith & Thelen, 1984) was designed to assess symptoms of DSM-III Bulimia, as well as to distinguish bulimic from anorexic patients. The test consists of 32 multiple-choice questions that describe thoughts, feelings, and behaviors associated with Bulimia. It discriminates between bulimics and controls, and between compulsive overeaters and controls (Williamson, Prather, Goreczny, Davis, & McKenzie, 1989). It has good test–retest reliability and internal consistency, and adequate validity. The BULIT-R, updated to accommodate the DSM-III-R criteria for Bulimia Nervosa, has good reliability and good concurrent and criterion-related validity (Welch, Thompson, & Hall, 1993).

The Yale–Brown–Cornell Eating Disorder Scale (Mazure, Halmi, Sunday, Romano, & Einhorn, 1994) consists of eight items assessing severity of illness associated with an individual's unique preoccupations and rituals, and six items assessing motivation for change. Scores on the eight-item scale are highly related with those of other eating disorder indices, and the six items assessing motivation for change are inversely related to diet restriction, drive for thinness, and body dissatisfaction.

Two standardized instruments have been developed to assess eating disorders in younger children. Maloney et al. (1989) designed the chEAT, a children's version of the EAT (Garner & Garfinkel, 1979). Intended for children 8–13 years old, this test consists of 26 items related to weight and dieting concerns. Using this questionnaire on 318 children from grades 3 to 6, Maloney et al. (1989) found that 45% of the children wished to be thinner, 37% had already attempted weight loss, and 6.9% scored in the Anorexia Nervosa range. Of the girls, 8.8% scored in the Anorexia Nervosa range. The authors pointed out that since this frequency approximates that for adolescents and adults, anorexic attitudes may already be set by the preadolescent years. When the chEAT was administered to Israeli school children, 54% of those in grades 3 to 11 wished to lose weight, and 41.6% displayed behaviors aimed toward losing weight (Sasson, Lewin, & Roth, 1995). Of Israeli children in grades 3 to 6, 8.8% had chEAT scores that placed them at risk for Anorexia Nervosa. In grades 7 to 11, only 1.5% of boys versus 16.3% of girls scored in the at-risk range. The chEAT has adequate internal reliability and concurrent validity (Smolak & Levine, 1994). Because the chEAT does not assess fasting or the use of diuretics, diet pills, or laxatives, and because it does not define "binge eating," Childress, Brewerton, Hodges, and Jarrell (1993) developed the Kids' Eating Disorders Survey. Using this instrument to survey 3,175 students in grades 5 to 8, they found that more than 40% of respondents reported feeling fat and/or wishing to lose weight. The frequencies of weight control behavior were 31.4% for dieting, 8.7% for fasting, 2.4% for diet pill use, 4.8% for vomiting, and 1.5% for diuretic use. The frequencies for dieting, fasting, and diet pill use were significantly higher for girls than for boys. Results of these studies indicate that eating disorder symptoms occur in relatively young children and can best be assessed by instruments designed specifically for this population.

Self-report instruments provide a cost-effective means to assess and measure some basic features of eating disorders. However, they are limited in assessing complex features of these disorders, as the questions asked are often rather simple and specific. A subject completing an instrument may not clearly understand terms such as "binge" or "purge." Clearly, a pattern of test scores needs to be used in conjunction with interview data in assessing eating disorders. We need to increase the clinical usefulness of assessment instruments. In particular, we need to refine our understanding of how eating disorder symptoms fluctuate over time and across settings, and how symptoms are related to accompanying thoughts and feelings. For example, we now know that Bulimia Nervosa symptomatology is subject to the seasonal variation often seen in mood disorders (Fornari et al., 1994). We also need assessment instruments that may serve as useful outcome measures. In one follow-up of subjects developing an eating disorder during adolescence (Steinhausen & Seidel, 1993), EAT scores differentiated among three outcome groups, whereas EDI scores did not. Other studies indicate that the EDI and BES can be used to measure treatment effects (Garner et al., 1993).

ASSESSMENT OF THE FAMILY

Systems Theory

Like behavioral theories, systems theory recognizes the influence of the setting. It posits that the functioning of individuals can be properly understood only within their interpersonal and cultural context. Individuals are "arbitrary abstractions" (von Bertalanffy, 1962), and their behaviors are a function of complex, mutually interactive, and interdependent relationships between them and their social and physical environment. In today's culture, the family is the most influential of the various groups that make up the individual's ecosystem. Any maladaptive behavior or symptom exhibited by an individual is considered a link in a chain of nonlinear, circular, and self-regulating interactions among family members. The symptom is seen as a function of the system (the family) and not of the individual, and is assumed to serve a homeostatic, stabilizing role. If the symptom is removed, the entire family must change. Since change is frequently destabilizing, it is resisted by the family. Thus, if the anorexic or bulimic person changes, the entire family will have to change. Any change is likely to elicit homeostasis-directed behavior (behavior aimed at a return to the status quo). Both the symptomatic person and the family can be expected to try to sabotage treatment aimed at change.

Assumptions about Anorexia Nervosa

Theorists and family therapists such as Minuchin, Rosman, and Baker (1978) and Selvini Palazzoli (1978) have sought to understand and intervene at the level of the family in cases of Anorexia Nervosa. They view the family in terms of structure, which includes boundaries, roles, alliances, conflicts (and patterns of conflict resolution), and flexibility. These theorists argue that anorexic behavior serves to keep a child from leaving home and precipitating a restructuring; adds to the blurring of boundaries (justifies the invasion of privacy, forces others to take control of and regulate the intake of another person, etc.); provides a way for parents to express conflict between each other indirectly, and thereby in a way that does not threaten the marriage; and, though not phenomenologically pleasant, gives the child considerable power and influence (the child is elevated to an adult-like status).

The key factor for Minuchin and his associates is that the symptoms also function to alleviate tension between the parents. The three patterns of conflict avoidance, according to Minuchin, are (1) triangulation (parents avoid confronting each other directly by appealing to the child to support their respective positions); (2) parent–child coalition (the child consistently allies with one parent against the other); and (3) detouring (the parents set aside their conflicts and unite at least superficially to protect or blame their sick child—the family's "only problem"). The families of anorexics, and of other young individuals with psychosomatic problems, characteristically engage in five interaction patterns: enmeshment, overprotectiveness, rigidity, lack of conflict resolution, and involvement of a child in parental conflict (Minuchin et al., 1978).

Assumptions about Bulimia Nervosa and Bulimic Behavior

Bulimic behavior, which usually occurs in later adolescence, serves different functions and presents its own challenges. Schwartz, Barrett, and Saba (1985) propose that the symptom is not the result of deep-seated intrapsychic pathology in one or several key family members, but grows out of evolutionary changes. They argue that if one traces the lineage of these patients and families back far enough, one will find a stable kin network—a network in which a close, intimate relationship between parents was not advantageous or adaptive because of the close and high levels of involvement with relatives. In such a context, everyone is involved in everyone else's conflicts, and children never leave the network. Network loyalty is of greatest importance, and children are raised to be obedient rather than personally ambitious and to distrust strangers. In addition, food is the center of most of the interactions and family rituals. These values and structures become problematic only if the family or couple tries to live outside of such a network. The distrust of strangers, the lack of marital closeness, and conflicts between loyalty to the family and the values of the new culture or context result in isolation, overinvolvement of parents with their children, ambivalences about the values of the new context, and a general pattern that represents a less than optimal adaptation. This dysfunctional pattern has been described in detail elsewhere (Johnson & Connors, 1987; Schwartz et al., 1985). The bulimic behavior serves as an adaptive solution in a family whose structure has not fully adapted to its context.

Research

Rakoff (1983) has pointed out that one often sees what one expects to see, and that even if cases exhibit the specific characteristics described by Minuchin, Selvini Palazzoli, and Bruch, the families may have other features that are at least as pathologically significant: "Each case demands that the anorectic symptom be understood and interpreted within the context of the individual family configuration. 'One size' does not fit all" (p. 34). In her work with 25 families, Martin (1983) unexpectedly found that families of anorexics could be classified into two or three types. During the initial interview, Group 1 families denied that they had any problems except those involving the anorexic patients. In these families, the anorexic children were conscientious overachievers. The work with this group was slow and difficult. External psychological precipitants were few in this group, but clustered around entrance into secondary school, departure from secondary school, or leaving home to attend a university. Group 2 families exaggerated their problems and claimed that they were too numerous or too severe to solve. Group 2 families had more external psychological precipitants, and the onset of their symptoms was more closely related to these stresses (deaths, unemployment, illness) and less clustered around school transitions. These children typically began to eat within a few sessions and gained weight rapidly. Treatment tended to be shorter. Treatment was also more focused on the marital couple. These children tended to be younger, in a lower school grade, and from an average social class, with more from working-class backgrounds. Group 3 families—only three families in all—were not enmeshed or overprotective. The families resembled families of children with adolescent behavior disorders. Instead of hiding their weight loss, these children paraded it. Their presentation also followed a period when the subject of Anorexia Nervosa had received publicity in the local news media. This third group of children may be similar to those Bruch (1986) has diagnosed as having "me, too" anorexia, which is stimulated in part by the public attention and inadvertent glamorization of the disorder.

Other research indicates some parental psychopathology and family dysfunction in families of eating-disordered children. In one study (Jaffe & Singer, 1989), marital conflict was found in seven of eight parents of children with eating disorders. Fosson et al. (1987) found overinvolvement of family members in 82% of Anorexia Nervosa cases, failure to resolve conflict in almost 90% of cases, and communication difficulties in 75% of cases. In another study, families of anorexic children were more overinvolved than were those of neurotic children (Jacobs & Isaacs, 1986). Warren (1968) found that 65% of mothers of anorexics were anxious, hypochondriacal, and overprotective.

Standardized Family
Assessment Instruments

Many of the findings discussed as supportive of family hypotheses are anecdotal or focused on family members rather than the family as a unit. It is this line of investigation that has revealed pathological parental personality characteristics. Parents of anorexics have been said to exhibit neurotic constitutions, obsessionality, phobic avoidance, emotional rigidity, and passivity (Beumont, Abraham, Argall, George, & Glaun, 1978; Bliss & Branch, 1960; Kalucy, Crisp, & Harding, 1977). Psychometric studies (Crisp, Harding, & McGuinness, 1974; Strober et al., 1982) have found these parents to be emotionally disturbed. This is ex-

pressed in terms of overcontrolled hostility, social maladjustment, impulsivity, and rigid expectations. Interestingly, parental psychopathology increased as the patients recovered weight (Crisp et al., 1974). It has also been suggested (Johnson et al., 1983) that many eating-disordered patients maintain a certain appearance (thin) to narcissistically gratify the parents, or to achieve at a high level so as to fulfill parents' frustrated or limited opportunities and successes. An excessive interest in food, weight, and activity by all family members has also been identified (Bruch, 1973; Crisp, 1967a; Selvini Palazzoli, 1974). Branch and Eurman (1980) found that at least 50% of a small sample of friends and relatives of patients with Anorexia Nervosa "admired" the patients' appearance and "envied" their "self-control and discipline" in regard to food.

Attention to the marital dyad also revealed that 40% of the parents of 56 anorexic patients had either no sexual activity or only very rare sexual interchanges (Kalucy, Crisp, & Harding, 1977). Using the Short Marital Adjustment Test of Locke and Wallace (1959), Strober (1981b) found that prior to the onset of the subjects' manifest illness, the marriages of parents of bulimic anorexics were more discordant than those of parents of restrictive anorexics, although the mean score of both groups fell within a problematic range.

Strober (1981a) assessed families in a standardized manner, using the Family Environment Scale (FES) developed by Moos (1974). The FES is a 90-item (true–false) instrument that has been designed to assess 10 different dimensions of a family: Cohesion, Expressiveness, Conflict, Independence, Achievement Orientation, Intellectual–Cultural Orientation, Active–Recreational Orientation, Moral–Religious Emphasis, Organization, and Control. Compared to families of bulimic anorexics, families of restricting anorexics demonstrated more support and concern among family members, and had clearer structures, rules, and divisions of responsibilities. Families of bulimic anorexics, in contrast, had higher levels of conflictual interactions and expressions of negativity among members. In another study utilizing the FES (Attie & Brooks-Gunn, 1989), mothers' ratings of the family milieu predicted daughters' eating problems during follow-up testing. These authors found that mothers and daughters had divergent perceptions of family functioning (Attie & Brooks-Gunn, 1990), and that divergence on the FES Cohesion scale was associated with daughters' dieting behaviors (Carlton-Ford, Paikoff, & Brooks-Gunn, 1991). Studies using the FES in families of bulimics indicate that, relative to controls, normal-weight bulimics perceive their families as less expressive and cohesive (Johnson & Flach, 1985; Ordman & Kirschenbaum, 1986; Stern et al., 1989), more conflicted (Humphrey, 1986b; Johnson & Flach, 1985; Ordman & Kirschenbaum, 1986), and more achievement-oriented (Johnson & Flach, 1985; Stern et al., 1989). Using the FES, bulimics' parents rated their families more positively than their daughters did (Humphrey, 1986a; Stern et al., 1989).

Another instrument utilized in family assessment is the Family Adaptability and Cohesion Evaluation Scales III (FACES III; Olson, Portner, & Lavee, 1985), a self-report measure in which members rate their families on adaptability and cohesion, both perceived and ideal. Subjects scoring highly on a self-report measure of bulimic behavior (Coburn & Ganong, 1989) and those meeting DSM-III criteria for Bulimia (Ordman & Kirschenbaum, 1986) had low cohesion scores on the FACES III. Humphrey (1986a) found that five of the eight factors of the FACES III discriminated between families of controls versus normal-weight bulimics and bulimic anorexics. In bulimic and bulimic anorexic families, mothers, fathers, and daughters rated the family members as less involved with one another than did controls, and in bulimic anorexic families all members reported more detachment and isolation than did controls.

The Structural Analysis of Social Behavior (SASB; Benjamin, 1974) is a model of interpersonal and intrapsychic behavior classifying behaviors along 24 behavioral clusters. It can be used with Intrex, a behavioral coding system, to study anorexic and bulimic families. Using the SASB, Humphrey (1986b, 1987, 1988) found that the families of bulimics and bulimic anorexics were more ignoring, blaming, rejecting, and neglectful, as well as less helping, trusting, nurturing, and approaching, than were control families. Restricting anorexics also reported more family distress and hostility than did controls, but perceived their families to be more affectionate than the bulimics did, supporting Humphrey's view of nurturance deficits in families of bulimics. However, no differences were found between anorexics and bulimics on Intrex ratings of parents in another study (Wonderlich & Swift, 1990).

Another approach is that of Eisler, Szmukler, and Dare (1985). Their work suggests that highly abstract clinical descriptions of anorexics and their families (based upon short videotapes of a non-therapeutically oriented lunch session) can be reliably identified and discriminated. The study utilized videotapes of 14 different families, each of which had an anorexic member, and a total of 99 different observers. Clinical observations regarding hypothesized functions of behavior varied in terms of levels of inference or abstraction. Most of the observers were mental health professionals, but fewer than half had more than 3 years of experience in family therapy. Interestingly, these observers were able to match statements to particular families, and their degree of accuracy in doing this did not vary as a function of level of abstraction of the statements or level of experience of the observers. More work along this line is needed to merge clinical insight and systematic observation.

The descriptions above are generally congruent with research findings that families of bulimics are less supportive, orderly, and organized; are less intellectually and recreationally oriented (stranger distrust?); and have high achievement expectations (Garner, Garfinkel, & O'Shaughnessy, 1983; Humphrey, 1986a; Johnson & Flach, 1985; Kay & Leigh, 1954; King, 1963; Ordman & Kirschenbaum, 1986; Strober, 1981b, 1983; Strober et al., 1982).

Nonstandardized Family Assessment Instruments

Many family therapists utilize nonstandardized assessment techniques. These techniques are directed at a family as a whole, including its patterns of interaction, structure, and rigidity. The primary task is to understand the function of the symptom and the patterns of interaction that maintain the symptom. Assessment is typically seen as a continual and recursive process that continues throughout therapy. Selvini Palazzoli (1978) and her colleagues give an example of a father and daughter who were overinvolved with each other, but would have "closed ranks" against the therapist if the therapist had suggested that they decrease their involvement. Instead, the therapist implied that if they were to get close to each other, they would need to change the way they interacted, as they did not really know each other. This suggestion precipitated a discussion between the father and daughter in which they voiced criticism about each other, which implied their differentness.

Family therapists perceive that they are not completely external, objective observers, and that assessment and intervention overlap. In order to affect a system, they believe that they must enter it. In order to enter a system, they must adopt some of its ways of operating, or "join" it. Minuchin et al. (1978) argue that in order to form such a therapeutic system, therapists must respect family hierarchies and values, support family subsystems, and confirm individual members' senses of themselves. The intervention begins with the assessment and directly challenges the family's view of its symptomatic member, its reality. Minuchin and his colleagues conduct a therapy–assessment session in which lunch is served, in order to systematically build a case for the redefinition of the symptomatic member as a "bad" child rather than a "sick" one, while assessing the family at the same time. In the first interview with the family of an anorexic, a therapist adopting Minuchin's approach arranges for lunch to be served and observes the interactions that center around eating. The therapist both observes and attempts to intervene. Reactions to interventions are used in part to assess the rigidity of the symptomatic sequence. A transcript of such a session with the Kaplan family serves to illustrate this approach (Minuchin et al., 1978).

The family was served lunch. After the rest of the family had finished their lunches, the anorexic had only played with her food. Minuchin instructed the parents to make their daughter finish her meal, and he then left the room to watch behind a screen. The mother attempted to plead and reason with the girl and was gentle and comforting. The father behaved as an authority and was demanding and threatening. As the pressure built up, the parents escalated their respective behaviors, and the girl screamed more and more hysterically. Finally and briefly, the mother became more insistent and hysterical, and the father suddenly turned gentle and reasoning. The girl calmed down. But this calm was short-lived, and the father once again resumed his threats and the mother her protective pleading.

This sequence serves to illustrate alliances, triangles, and roles families enact. In this case, the father was a high-status authority, the mother was a high-status friend, and the girl was the low-status subordinate who was caught and oscillated between two sets of directives. The sequence was the result of an aborted transformation; it kept the family from evolving into or beyond the family life cycle stage of the adolescent's departure. In order to interrupt this dysfunctional sequence, Minuchin removed one part at a time from the triangle. He asked that each parent attempt the job alone. Each ended in disaster, the mother wailing that the daughter would kill herself or drive her (the mother) into a mental hospital, and the father smearing a smashed hot dog across the girl's face, attempting to cram it down her throat. Minuchin informed the parents that their daugh-

ter was in a struggle with them, and that she was stronger. He then questioned the girl about why she needed to defeat her parents. The parents' view of the daughter changed from a "sick" child to a "rebellious, bad" child, and they were encouraged to pull together in order to deal with her. In doing this, Minuchin appeared to succeed in breaking a deadly cycle.

Another difference between most individually oriented and family systems theorists is in their orientation toward the symptom. Family systems theorists frequently emphasize the positive or adaptive nature of the symptom, and are thus careful not to advocate change. Instead, they may alternate between restraining and encouraging change even as a part of the assessment. For example, they may ask such questions as this: "Are you sure you are ready to give up this behavior that has been such a large part of your life? I want you to think hard about what might happen if you suddenly let go of this part of you. Perhaps we should work on helping you adjust to it if it is too dangerous to quit." Patients often respond with relief to this type of communication, and these types of questions stimulate the exploration of what the loss of the eating disorder may signify: growing up, getting close to people, upsetting the family, and possibly facing fears about the future and one's competence.

Assessment of rigidity and enmeshment can take many forms. One way to assess them is to offer the family members "a vacation" from their efforts at solving the problem, after tracking these attempts and empathizing with and emphasizing their frustration and ineffectiveness. If they cannot disengage—cannot give up the job to the therapist and medical consultant—this is then considered evidence of their rigidity and enmeshment.

CULTURAL FACTORS

A final, major set of considerations involves those cultural factors that influence the acquisition and maintenance of eating disorders. These are particularly important today, as there appears to be a rise in the eating disorders that may amount to a doubling every decade (Crisp et al., 1976; Halmi et al., 1981; Jones et al., 1980; Nylander, 1971; Theander, 1970). We assume that this rise corresponds to Western culture's increasing preoccupation with food, thinness, and "fat," and the conflicted role pressures being thrust upon contemporary women. A culture-wide intervention or prevention program based upon a thoughtful, thorough assessment may be as powerful as it is ambitious. Schwartz, Thompson, and Johnson (1982) review the systematic efforts to collect information relevant to a sociocultural hypothesis regarding Anorexia Nervosa and Bulimia Nervosa. They note that the selections of 3,500 visitors to Madame Tussaud's London waxworks for the most beautiful woman in the world have slowly shifted from the more ample form of Elizabeth Taylor in 1970 to the anorexic-looking Twiggy. Twiggy first made the top five in 1974 and ranked first by 1976 (Wallechinsky, Wallace, & Wallace, 1977). Garner, Garfinkel, Schwartz, and Thompson (1980) studied *Playboy* magazine's Playmate centerfolds and contestants and winners of the Miss America pageant from 1959 to 1978. These women were thinner than actual norms for comparable women in the population. Weight within these groups also declined across the 20 years, while normative weights increased. Before 1970, Miss America contestants and winners were not different in weight; after 1970, the winners' weights became consistently less than the average weight of all contestants. Kurman (1978), in an analysis of prime-time television programming, found that thin body types predominated (fewer than 2% of actors were obese), and also that youth, female gender, and positive personality attributes were related to thinness.

A thin body shape is considered by women to be the most salient aspect of physical attractiveness (Berscheid et al., 1973), and attractive people are perceived as more popular (Berscheid, Dion, Walster, & Walster, 1971) and more capable (Landy & Sigall, 1974) than are less attractive people. Wooley and Wooley (1980) review research that documents the powerful social stigma against obesity. Not surprisingly, body dissatisfaction in females is high. Only 5% of a sample of college females who were statistically underweight (38% of the sample) perceived themselves to be below average weight (Gray, 1977), and whereas 12% of another sample of college females were actually overweight, over 40% believed that they were overweight (Halmi et al., 1981).

Our culture's preference for thinner females has been related to changing roles for women. Bennett and Gurin (1982) suggest that the thinner shape standard began as an expression of females' liberation from their solely maternal, reproductive role. Weight has also become a symbol for self-control and may be one of the few areas in which competition between women has been encouraged and permitted wholeheartedly (Wooley & Wooley, 1982). To apply the family models of Anorexia

Nervosa and Bulimia Nervosa to the culture, one may hypothesize that women and adolescent girls in the culture today are not given the opportunities for autonomous, self-controlled functioning that men are given. Or, more likely, women are being given conflicting messages. This hypothesis is supported by Heilman and Stopeck's (1985) recent finding that attractiveness had different effects on the degree to which corporate officers' success was attributed to their ability: Males' ability attributions were enhanced by their good looks, and females' ability attributions were detrimentally affected by them. Sex roles also enter into the domain of eating behavior. Women are rated as being more feminine and attractive when judges believe they are eating a small meal, whereas perceptions of males are not influenced by meal size (Chaiken & Pliner, 1987). Furthermore, women have been found to alter their eating behavior when they believe their femininity is being judged by an attractive male (Mori, Chaiken, & Pliner, 1987).

At what age do children assimilate the cultural preference for slimness? Lerner and Gellert (1969) found that of 12 girls in kindergarten, 8 wanted to look like an average-sized peer, 4 desired to look like a thin peer, and none wanted to look like a chubby peer. In another study (Lerner & Schroeder, 1971), kindergarten boys and girls preferred to look like an average figure and demonstrated an aversion to a chubby figure. Lawrence (1990) found that white girls in the third and sixth grades were more concerned about being or becoming overweight than were white boys or black girls and boys. It appears that the sociocultural value of thinness is adopted by kindergarten age, particularly by white girls.

FUTURE DIRECTIONS

With continuing change in the lives of individuals, the family, and the culture, the clinical picture and prevalence of the eating disorders are likely to change. As women adopt—or feel the pressure to adopt—new roles and move into what was formerly a "man's world" with increasing comfort, ease, and regularity, they may begin to develop what have previously been considered "men's problems" (e.g., substance use problems, antisocial/violent behavior), instead of the "womanly" depressive and eating disorders. In both the popular and the professional literature of today, there seems to be some evidence of the beginnings of a movement that is antithetical to the diet industry and the pursuit of thinness. In the popular literature, such books as Orbach's *Fat Is a Feminist Issue* (1978) and *Fat Is a Feminist Issue II* (1982), Chernin's *The Obsession: Reflections on the Tyranny of Slenderness* (1981), and Foreyt and Goodrick's *Living without Dieting* (1994) question the wisdom and meaning of trying to reduce the size of women (both literally and figuratively) by dieting. Meanwhile, in the scholarly literature, Wooley and Wooley (1979, 1983) write about the hazards of dieting and suggest that extremely negative attitudes toward the overweight may be more in need of change than the overweight themselves. Writers today are increasingly challenging the assumptions that "thin" should be "in" and questioning whether the helping professions should legitimize and condone its pursuit. Whether these writers will have a significant impact on the broader culture is open to question. If they do, however, we might expect a decline in the eating disorders as we know them today. We hope that a more moderate view of weight will result in fewer persons' being preoccupied with it. Conceptualizations, assessment procedures, and interventions will have to be adjusted accordingly.

In the meantime, systematic approaches—those that attempt to integrate and assess individuals in behavioral, cognitive, and affective terms, and furthermore to see individuals as developing and interacting within social systems such as families and cultures—provide the framework upon which to build our theoretical and empirical models of the functional bases of the eating disorders.

REFERENCES

Abraham, S., & Beumont, P. J. V. (1982). Varieties of psychosexual experience in patients with Anorexia Nervosa. *International Journal of Eating Disorders, 1*(3), 10–19.

Agras, W. S. (1987). *Eating disorders: Management of obesity, Bulimia, and Anorexia Nervosa.* Oxford: Pergamon Press.

Agras, W. S., & Kirkley, B. G. (1986). Bulimia: Theories of etiology. In K. D. Brownell & J. P. Foreyt (Eds.), *Handbook of eating disorders: Physiology, psychology, and treatment of obesity, Anorexia, and Bulimia* (pp. 367–378). New York: Basic Books.

Allebeck, P., Hallberg, D., & Espmark, S. (1976). Body image—an apparatus for measuring disturbances in estimation of size and shape. *Journal of Psychosomatic Research, 20,* 583–589.

American Psychiatric Association. (1994). *Diagnostic and statistical manual of mental disorders* (4th ed.). Washington, DC: Author.

Andersen, A. E. (1990). *Males with eating disorders.* New York: Brunner/Mazel.

Askevold, F. (1975). Measuring body image. *Psychotherapy and Psychosomatics, 26,* 71–77.

Attie, I., & Brooks-Gunn, J. (1989). Development of eating problems in adolescent girls: A longitudinal study. *Developmental Psychology, 25,* 70–79.

Attie, I., & Brooks-Gunn, J. (1990). Developmental issues in the study of eating problems and disorders. In J. H. Crowther, D. L. Tennenbaum, S. E. Hobfoll, & M. A. P. Stephens (Eds.), *The etiology of Bulimia Nervosa: The individual and familial context* (pp. 35–58). Washington, DC: Hemisphere.

Barbosa-Salvidar, J. L., & Van Itallie, T. B. (1979). Semi-starvation: An overview of an old problem. *Bulletin of the New York Academy of Medicine, 55,* 774–797.

Barnett, L. R., & Loro, A. D. (1981). *Common problems of bulimarexics.* Unpublished manuscript, Duke University Medical Center.

Benjamin, L. (1974). Structural Analysis of Social Behavior. *Psychological Review, 81,* 392–425.

Bennett, W. B., & Gurin, J. (1982). *The dieter's dilemma: Eating less and weighing more.* New York: Basic Books.

Ben-Tovim, D. I., Marilov, V., & Crisp, A. H. (1979). Personality and mental state (P.S.E.) within Anorexia Nervosa. *Journal of Psychosomatic Research, 23,* 321–325.

Berscheid, E., Dion, K., Walster, E., & Walster, G. W. (1971). Physical attractiveness and dating choice: A test of the matching hypothesis. *Journal of Experimental and Social Psychology, 7,* 173–181.

Berscheid, E., Walster, E., & Bohrnstedt, G. (1973, November). The happy American body: A survey report. *Psychology Today,* 119–131.

Beumont, P. J. V. (1977). Further categorization of patients with Anorexia Nervosa. *Australian and New Zealand Journal of Psychiatry, 11,* 223–226.

Beumont, P. J. V., Abraham, S. F., Argall, W. J., George, G. C. W., & Glaun, D. E. (1978). The onset of Anorexia Nervosa. *Australian and New Zealand Journal of Psychiatry, 12,* 145–149.

Beumont, P. J. V., Abraham, S. F., & Simson, K. G. (1981). The psychosexual histories of adolescent girls and young women with Anorexia Nervosa. *Psychological Medicine, 11,* 131–140.

Beumont, P. J. V., Booth, A. L., Abraham, S. F., Griffiths, D. A., & Turner, T. R. (1983). A temporal sequence of symptoms in patients with Anorexia Nervosa: A preliminary report. In P. L. Darby, P. E. Garfinkel, D. M. Garner, & D. V. Coscina (Eds.), *Anorexia nervosa: Recent developments in research* (pp. 129–136). New York: Alan R. Liss.

Bhanji, S., & Mattingly, D. (1988). *Medical aspects of Anorexia Nervosa.* London: Wright.

Bliss, E. L., & Branch, C. H. H. (1960). *Anorexia Nervosa: Its history, psychology and biology.* New York: Hoeber.

Blitzer, J. R., Rollins, N., & Blackwell, A. (1961). Children who starve themselves: Anorexia Nervosa. *Psychosomatic Medicine, 5,* 369–383.

Blumenthal, J. A., O'Toole, L. C., & Chang, J. L. (1984). Is running an analogue of Anorexia Nervosa? An empirical study of obligatory running and Anorexia Nervosa. *Journal of the American Medical Association, 252,* 520–523.

Boskind-Lodahl, M. (1976). Cinderella's stepsisters: A feminist perspective on Anorexia Nervosa and Bulimia. *Signs: Journal of Women in Culture and Society, 2,* 342–356.

Brady, W. F. (1980). The Anorexia Nervosa syndrome. *Oral Surgery, Oral Medicine and Oral Pathology, 50,* 509–516.

Branch, C. H. H., & Eurman, L. J. (1980). Social attitudes towards patients with Anorexia Nervosa. *American Journal of Psychiatry, 137,* 631–632.

Brown, T. A., Johnson, W. G., Bergeron, K. C., Keeton, W. P., & Cash, T. F. (1990). *Assessment of body-related cognitions in Bulimia: The Body Image Automatic Thoughts Questionnaire.* Unpublished manuscript.

Bruch, H. (1962). Perceptual and conceptual disturbances in Anorexia Nervosa. *Psychosomatic Medicine, 24,* 187–194.

Bruch, H. (1973). *Eating disorders: Obesity, Anorexia Nervosa and the person within.* New York: Basic Books.

Bruch, H. (1985). Four decades of eating disorders. In D. M. Garner & P. E. Garfinkel (Eds.), *Handbook of psychotherapy for Anorexia Nervosa and Bulimia* (pp. 7–18). New York: Guilford Press.

Bruch, H. (1986). Anorexia Nervosa: The therapeutic task. In K. D. Brownell & J. P. Foreyt (Eds.), *Handbook of eating disorders: Physiology, psychology, and treatment of obesity, Anorexia and Bulimia* (pp. 328–332). New York: Basic Books.

Bryant-Waugh, R., & Kaminski, Z. (1993). Eating disorders in children: An overview. In B. Lask & R. Bryant-Waugh (Eds.), *Childhood onset Anorexia Nervosa and related eating disorders* (pp. 17–30). Hillsdale, NJ: Erlbaum.

Carlton-Ford, S., Paikoff, R. L., & Brooks-Gunn, J. (1991). Methodological issues in the study of divergent views of the family. *New Directions for Child Development, 51,* 87–102.

Cash, T. F., & Brown, T. A. (1987). Body image in Anorexia Nervosa and Bulimia Nervosa: A review of the literature. *Behavior Modification, 11,* 487–521.

Casper, R. C., Eckert, E. D., Halmi, K. A., Goldberg, S. C., & Davis, J. M. (1980). Bulimia: Its incidence and clinical importance in patients with Anorexia Nervosa. *Archives of General Psychiatry, 37,* 1030–1035.

Chaiken, S., & Pliner, P. (1987). Women, but not men, are what they eat: The effect of meal size and gender on perceived femininity and masculinity. *Personality and Social Psychology Bulletin, 13,* 166–176.

Chernin, K. (1981). *The obsession: Reflections on the tyranny of slenderness.* New York: Harper & Row.

Childress, A. C. Brewerton, T. D., Hodges, E. L., & Jarrell, M. P. (1993). The Kids' Eating Disorders Survey (KEDS): A study of middle school students. *Journal of the American Academy of Child and Adolescent Psychiatry, 32*(4), 843–850.

Chiodo, J., & Latimer, P. R. (1986). Hunger perceptions and satiety responses among normal-weight bulimics and normals to a high-calorie carbohydrate rich food. *Psychological Medicine, 16,* 343–349.

Chipman, J. J., Hagan, R. D., Edlin, J. C., Soll, M. H., & Carruth, B. R. (1983). Excessive weight loss in the athletic adolescent: A diagnostic dilemma. *Journal of Adolescent Health Care, 3*(4), 247–252.

Coburn, J., & Ganong, L. (1989). Bulimic and non-bulimic college females' perceptions of family adaptability and family cohesion. *Journal of Advanced Nursing, 14,* 27–33.

Coffman, D. A. (1984). A clinically derived treatment model for the binge–purge syndrome. In R. C. Hawkins, W. J. Fremouw, & P. F. Clement (Eds.), *The binge–purge syndrome: Diagnosis, treatment, and research* (pp. 211–226). New York: Springer.

Collins, J. K., Beumont, P. J. V., Touyz, S. W., Krass, J., Thompson, P., & Philips, T. (1987). Variability in body shape perception in anorexic, bulimic, obese, and control subjects. *International Journal of Eating Disorders, 6,* 633–638.

Connors, M., Johnson, C., & Stuckey, M. (1984). Treatment of Bulimia with brief psychoeducational group therapy. *American Journal of Psychiatry, 141,* 1512–1516.

Cooper, P. J., & Bowskill, R. (1986). Dysphoric mood and overeating. *British Journal of Clinical Psychology, 25,* 155–157.

Cooper, P. J., Taylor, M. J., Cooper, Z., & Fairburn, C. G. (1987). The development and validation of the Body Shape Questionnaire. *International Journal of Eating Disorders, 6,* 485–494.

Cooper, P. J., Waterman, G. C., & Fairburn, C. G. (1984). Women with eating problems: A community survey. *British Journal of Clinical Psychology, 23,* 45–52.

Cooper, Z., Cooper, P. J., & Fairburn, C. G. (1989). The validity of the Eating Disorder Examination and its subscales. *British Journal of Psychiatry, 154,* 807–812.

Cooper, Z., & Fairburn, C. G. (1987). The Eating Disorder Examination: A semi-structured interview for the assessment of the specific psychopathology of eating disorders. *International Journal of Eating Disorders, 6,* 1–8.

Counts, C. R., & Adams, H. E. (1985). Body image in bulimic, dieting, and normal females. *Journal of Psychopathology and Behavioral Assessment, 7,* 289–301.

Crisp, A. H. (1965). Clinical and therapeutic aspects of Anorexia Nervosa: A study of 30 cases. *Journal of Psychosomatic Research, 9,* 67–78.

Crisp, A. H. (1967a). Anorexia Nervosa: "Feeding disorder," "nervous malnutrition" or "weight phobia"? *Hospital Medicine, 1,* 713–718.

Crisp, A. H. (1967b). The possible significance of some behavioural correlates of weight and carbohydrate intake. *Journal of Psychosomatic Research, 11,* 117–131.

Crisp, A. H. (1980). *Anorexia Nervosa: Let me be.* London: Academic Press.

Crisp, A. H. (1982). Anorexia Nervosa with normal body weight: The abnormal normal weight control syndrome. *International Journal of Psychiatry in Medicine, 11,* 203–233.

Crisp, A. H., Burns, T., & Bhat, A. V. (1986). Primary Anorexia in the male and female: A comparison of clinical features and prognosis. *British Journal of Medical Psychology, 59,* 123–132.

Crisp, A. H., Harding, D., & McGuinness, B. (1974). Anorexia Nervosa: Psychoneurotic characteristics of parents. Relationship to prognosis. *Journal of Psychosomatic Research, 18,* 167–173.

Crisp, A. H., Hsu, L. K., G., Harding, B., & Hartshorn, J. (1980). Clinical features of Anorexia Nervosa: A study of a consecutive series of 102 female patients. *Journal of Psychosomatic Research, 24,* 179–191.

Crisp, A. H., Palmer, R. L., & Kalucy, R. S. (1976). How common is Anorexia Nervosa? A prevalence study. *British Journal of Psychiatry, 128,* 549–554.

Crowther, J. H., Tennenbaum, D. L., Hobfoll, S. E., & Stephens, M. A. P. (Eds.). (1990). *The etiology of Bulimia Nervosa: The individual and familial context.* Washington, DC: Hemisphere.

Csikzentmihalyi, M., & Graef, R. (1980). The experience of freedom in daily experience. *American Journal of Community Psychology, 8,* 404–414.

Eisler, I., Szmukler, G. I., & Dare, C. (1985). Systematic observation and clinical insight—are they compatible? An experiment in recognizing family interactions. *Psychological Medicine, 15,* 173–188.

Fabian, L. J., & Thompson, J. K. (1989). Body image and eating disturbance in young females. *International Journal of Eating Disorders, 8,* 63–74.

Fairburn, C. (1982). *Binge-eating and Bulimia Nervosa* [pamphlet]. Philadelphia: Smith, Kline, and French Laboratories.

Fairburn, C. G., & Cooper, P. J. (1982). Self-induced vomiting and Bulimia Nervosa: An undetected problem. *British Medical Journal, 184,* 1153–1155.

Fairburn, C. G., & Garner, D. M. (1986). The diagnosis of Bulimia Nervosa. *International Journal of Eating Disorders, 5,* 403–419.

Fairburn, C. G., Peveler, R. C., Jones, R., Hope, R. A., & Doll, H. A. (1993). Predictors of 12-month outcome in Bulimia Nervosa and the influence of attitudes to shape and weight. *Journal of Consulting and Clinical Psychology, 61,* 696–698.

Farrow, J. A. (1992). The adolescent male with an eating disorder. *Pediatric Annals, 21,* 769–774.

Feighner, J. P., Robins, E., Guze, S. B., Woodruff, R. A., Jr., Winokur, G., & Munoz, R. (1972). Diagnostic criteria for use in psychiatric research. *Archives of General Psychiatry, 26,* 57–63.

Fichter, M. M., Meister, I., & Koch, H. J. (1986). The measurement of body image disturbance in Anorexia Nervosa: Experimental comparison of different methods. *British Journal of Psychiatry, 148,* 453–461.

Foreyt, J. P., & Goodrick, G. K. (1994). *Living without dieting.* New York: Warner Books.

Fornari, V. M., Braun, D. L., Sunday, S. R., Sandberg, D. E., Matthews, M., Chen, I. L., Mandel, F. S., Halmi, K. A., & Katz, J. L. (1994). Seasonal patterns in eating disorder subgroups. *Comprehensive Psychiatry, 35*(6), 450–456.

Fosson, A., Knibbs, J., Bryant-Waugh, R., & Lask, B. (1987). Early onset Anorexia Nervosa. *Archives of Disease in Childhood, 62,* 114–118.

Furnham, A., & Alibhai, N. (1983). Cross-cultural differences in the perception of female body shapes. *Psychological Medicine, 13,* 829–837.

Garfinkel, P. E. (1974). Perception of hunger and satiety in Anorexia Nervosa. *Psychological Medicine, 4,* 309–315.

Garfinkel, P. E., & Garner, D. M. (1982). *Anorexia Nervosa: A multidimensional perspective.* New York: Brunner/Mazel.

Garfinkel, P. E., & Kaplan, A. S. (1986). Anorexia Nervosa: Diagnostic conceptualizations. In K. D. Brownell & J. P. Foreyt (Eds.), *Handbook of eating disorders: Physiology, psychology, and treatment of obesity, Anorexia, and Bulimia* (pp. 266–282). New York: Basic Books.

Garfinkel, P. E., Kaplan, A. S., Garner, D. M., & Darby, P. L. (1983). The differentiation of vomiting/weight loss as a conversion disorder from Anorexia Nervosa. *American Journal of Psychiatry, 140,* 1019–1022.

Garfinkel, P. E., Moldofsky, H., & Garner, D. M. (1980). The heterogeneity of Anorexia Nervosa. *Archives of General Psychiatry, 37,* 1036–1040.

Garner, D. M. (1986). Cognitive-behavioral therapy for eating disorders. *The Clinical Psychologist, 39,* 36–39.

Garner, D. M. (1991). *The Eating Disorder Inventory—2 professional manuals.* Odessa, FL: Psychological Assessment Resources.

Garner, D. M., & Bemis, K. M. (1982). A cognitive-behavioral approach to Anorexia Nervosa: Bulimia as a distinct subgroup. *Cognitive Therapy and Research, 6,* 123–150.

Garner, D. M., & Bemis, K. M. (1985). Cognitive therapy for Anorexia Nervosa. In D. M. Garner & P. E. Garfinkel (Eds.), *Handbook of psychotherapy for Anorexia Nervosa and Bulimia* (pp. 107–146). New York: Guilford Press.

Garner, D. M., & Garfinkel, P. E. (1979). The Eating Attitudes Test: An index of the symptoms of Anorexia Nervosa. *Psychological Medicine, 9,* 273–279.

Garner, D. M., & Garfinkel, P. E. (1981). Body image in Anorexia Nervosa: Measurement, theory and clinical implications. *International Journal of Psychiatry in Medicine, 11,* 263–284.

Garner, D. M., Garfinkel, P. E., & O'Shaughnessy, M. (1983). Clinical and psychometric comparison between Bulimia in Anorexia Nervosa and Bulimia in normal weight women. In *Understanding Anorexia Nervosa and Bulimia: Report of the Fourth Ross Conference on Medical Research* (pp. 6–14). Columbus, OH: Ross Laboratories.

Garner, D. M., Garfinkel, P. E., & O'Shaughnessy, M. (1985). The validity of the distinction between Bulimia with and without Anorexia Nervosa. *American Journal of Psychiatry, 142,* 581–587.

Garner, D. M., Garfinkel, P. E., Schwartz, D., & Thompson, M. (1980). Cultural expectations of thinness in women. *Psychological Reports, 47,* 483–491.

Garner, D. M., & Olmsted, M. P. (1983). An overview of sociocultural factors in the development of Anorexia Nervosa. In P. L. Darby, P. E. Garfinkel, D. M. Garner, & D. V. Coscina (Eds.), *Anorexia nervosa: Recent developments in research* (pp. 65–82). New York: Alan R. Liss.

Garner, D. M., Olmsted, M. P., Bohr, Y., & Garfinkel, P. E. (1982). The Eating Attitudes Test: Psychometric features and clinical correlates. *Psychological Medicine, 12,* 871–878.

Garner, D. M., Olmsted, M. P., & Polivy, J. (1983). Development and validation of a multidimensional Eating Disorder Inventory for Anorexia Nervosa and Bulimia. *International Journal of Eating Disorders, 2*(2), 15–34.

Garner, D. M., Olmsted, M. P., Polivy, J., & Garfinkel, P. E. (1984). Comparison between weight-preoccupied women and Anorexia Nervosa. *Psychosomatic Medicine, 46,* 255–266.

Garner, D. M., Rockert, W., Davis, R., Garner, M. V., Olmsted, M. P., & Eagle, M. (1993). Comparison between cognitive-behavioral and supportive–expressive therapy for Bulimia Nervosa. *American Journal of Psychiatry, 150,* 37–46.

Garner, D. M., Rockert, W., Olmsted, M. P., Johnson, C., & Coscina, D. V. (1985). Psychoeducational principles in the treatment of Bulimia and Anorexia Nervosa. In D. M. Garner & P. E. Garfinkel (Eds.), *Handbook of psychotherapy for Anorexia Nervosa and Bulimia* (pp. 513–572). New York: Guilford Press.

Goldberg, S. C., Halmi, K. A., Casper, R., Eckert, E., & Davis, J. M. (1977). Pretreatment predictors of weight change in Anorexia Nervosa. In R. A. Vigersky (Ed.), *Anorexia Nervosa* (pp. 31–42). New York: Raven Press.

Goldberg, S. C., Halmi, K. A., Eckert, E. D., Casper, R. C., Davis, J. M., & Roper, M. (1980). Attitudinal dimensions in Anorexia Nervosa. *Journal of Psychiatric Research, 15,* 239–251.

Gormally, J., Black, S., Daston, S., & Rardin, D. (1982). The assessment of binge eating severity among obese persons. *Addictive Behaviors, 7,* 47–55.

Gowers, S., Crisp, A., Joughin, N., & Bhat, A. (1991). Premenarcheal Anorexia Nervosa. *Journal of Child Psychology and Psychiatry, 32,* 515–524.

Gray, S. H. (1977). Social aspects of body image: Perception of normalcy of weight and affect of college undergraduates. *Perceptual and Motor Skills, 45,* 1035–1040.

Gross, J., & Rosen, J. C. (1988). Bulimia in adolescents: Prevalence and psychosocial correlates. *International Journal of Eating Disorders, 7,* 51–61.

Gross, J., Rosen, J. C., Leitenberg, H., & Willmuth, M. E. (1986). Validity of the Eating Attitudes Test and the Eating Disorders Inventory in Bulimia Nervosa. *Journal of Consulting and Clinical Psychology, 54,* 875–876.

Halmi, K. A. (1985). Classification of the eating disorders. *Journal of Psychiatric Research, 19,* 113–119.

Halmi, K. A., Falk, J. R., & Schwartz, E. (1981). Binge eating and vomiting: A survey of a college population. *Psychological Medicine, 11,* 697–706.

Hatsukami, D., Eckert, E., Mitchell, J. E., & Pyle, R. (1984). Affective disorder and substance abuse in women with Bulimia. *Psychological Medicine, 14,* 701–704.

Hawkins, R. C., & Clement, P. F. (1980). Development and construct validation of a self-report measure of binge eating tendencies. *Addictive Behaviors, 5,* 219–226.

Hawkins, R. C., & Clement, P. F. (1984). Binge eating: Measurement problems and a conceptual model. In R. C. Hawkins, W. J. Fremouw, & P. F. Clement (Eds.), *The binge–purge syndrome: Diagnosis, treatment, and research* (pp. 229–251). New York: Springer.

Heilman, M. E., & Stopeck, M. H. (1985). Attractiveness and corporate success: Different causal attributions for males and females. *Journal of Applied Psychology, 70,* 379–388.

Henley, K. M., & Vaitukaitis, J. L. (1985). Hormonal changes associated with changes in body weight. *Clinical Obstetrics and Gynecology, 28,* 615–631.

Higgs, J., Goodyer, I., & Birch, J. (1989). Anorexia nervosa and food avoidance emotional disorder. *Archives of Disease in Childhood, 64,* 346–351.

Hudson, J. I., Pope, H. G., Jonas, J. M., & Yurgelun-Todd, D. (1983). Family history study of Anorexia Nervosa and Bulimia. *British Journal of Psychiatry, 142,* 133–138.

Hudson, J. I., Pope, H. G., Yurgelun-Todd, D., Jonas, J. M., & Frankenburg, F. R. (1987). A controlled study of lifetime prevalence of affective and other psychiatric disorders in bulimic outpatients. *American Journal of Psychiatry, 144,* 1283–1287.

Humphrey, L. (1986a). Family relations in bulimic, anorexic, and nondistressed families. *International Journal of Eating Disorders, 5,* 223–232.

Humphrey, L. (1986b). Structural analysis of parent–child relationships in eating disorders. *Journal of Abnormal Psychology, 95,* 395–402.

Humphrey, L. (1987). Comparison of bulimic–anorexic

and nondistressed families using structural analysis of social behavior. *Journal of the American Academy of Child and Adolescent Psychiatry, 26,* 248–255.

Humphrey, L. (1988). Relationships within subtypes of anorexic, bulimic, and normal families. *Journal of the American Academy of Child and Adolescent Psychiatry, 27,* 544–551.

Irwin, M. (1981). Diagnosis of Anorexia Nervosa in children and the validity of DSM-III. *American Journal of Psychiatry, 138*(10), 1382–1383.

Jacobs, B. W., & Isaacs, S. (1986). Pre-pubertal Anorexia Nervosa: A retrospective controlled study. *Journal of Child Psychology and Psychiatry, 27,* 237–250.

Jaffe, A. C., & Singer, L. T. (1989). Atypical eating disorders in young children. *International Journal of Eating Disorders, 8,* 575–582.

Johnson, C. L. (1985). Initial consultation for patients with Bulimia and Anorexia Nervosa. In D. M. Garner & P. E. Garfinkel (Eds.), *Handbook of psychotherapy for anorexia nervosa and bulimia* (pp. 19–51). New York: Guilford Press.

Johnson, C. L., & Berndt, D. (1983). A preliminary investigation of bulimia and life adjustment. *American Journal of Psychiatry, 140,* 774–777.

Johnson, C. L., & Connors, M. E. (1987). *The etiology and treatment of Bulimia Nervosa.* New York: Basic Books.

Johnson, C. L., & Flach, A. (1985). Family characteristics of 105 patients with Bulimia. *American Journal of Psychiatry, 142,* 1321–1324.

Johnson, C. L., & Larson, R. (1982). Bulimia: An analysis of moods and behavior. *Psychosomatic Medicine, 44,* 341–351.

Johnson, C. L., Lewis, C., & Hagman, J. (1984). The syndrome of Bulimia: Review and synthesis. *Psychiatric Clinics of North America, 7,* 247–273.

Johnson, C. L., Lewis, C., Love, S., Lewis, L., & Stuckey, M. (1984). Incidence and correlates of bulimic behavior in a female high school population. *Journal of Youth and Adolescence, 13,* 15–26.

Johnson, C. L., & Love, S. (1984). *Bulimia: Multivariate predictors of life impairment.* Unpublished manuscript, Northwestern University Medical School.

Johnson, C. L., & Pure, D. L. (1986). Assessment of Bulimia: A multidimensional model. In K. D. Brownell & J. P. Foreyt (Eds.), *Handbook of eating disorders: Physiology, psychology, and treatment of obesity, Anorexia, and Bulimia* (pp. 405–449). New York: Basic Books.

Johnson, C. L., Stuckey, M. K., Lewis, L. D., & Schwartz, D. (1982). Bulimia: A descriptive survey of 316 cases. *International Journal of Eating Disorders, 2*(1), 3–16.

Johnson, C. L., Stuckey, M. K., Lewis, L. D., & Schwartz, D. (1983). A descriptive survey of 509 cases of self-reported Bulimia. In P. L. Darby, P. E. Garfinkel, D. M. Garner, & D. V. Coscina (Eds.), *Anorexia Nervosa: Recent development in research* (pp. 159–171). New York: Alan R. Liss.

Johnson-Sabine, E., Wood, K., Patton, G., Mann, A., & Wakeling, A. (1988). Abnormal eating attitudes in London schoolgirls—a prospective epidemiological study: Factors associated with abnormal response on screening questionnaires. *Psychological Medicine, 18,* 615–622.

Jones, D., Fox, M., Babigian, H., & Hutton, H. (1980). Epidemiology of Anorexia in Monroe County, New York: 1960–1976. *Psychosomatic Medicine, 42,* 551–558.

Kalucy, R. S., Crisp, A. H., & Harding, B. (1977). A study of 56 families with Anorexia Nervosa. *British Journal of Medical Psychology, 50,* 381–395.

Kalucy, R. S., Crisp, A. H., Lacey, J. H., & Harding, B. (1977). Prevalence and prognosis in Anorexia Nervosa. *Australian and New Zealand Journal of Psychiatry, 11,* 251–257.

Katzman, M. A., & Wolchik, S. A. (1984). Bulimia and binge eating in college women: A comparison of personality and behavioral characteristics. *Journal of Consulting and Clinical Psychology, 52,* 423–428.

Kaufman, M. R., & Heiman, M. (Eds.). (1964). *Evolution of psychosomatic concepts: Anorexia Nervosa. A paradigm.* New York: International Universities Press.

Kay, D. W. K., & Leigh, D. (1954). The natural history, treatment, and prognosis of Anorexia Nervosa, based on a study of 38 patients. *Journal of Mental Sciences, 100,* 431–439.

Keys, A., Brozek, J., Henschel, A., Mickelsen, O., & Taylor, H. L. (1950). *The biology of human starvation* (2 vols.). Minneapolis: University of Minnesota Press.

Killen, J. D., Hayward, C., Wilson, D. M., Taylor, C. B., Hammer, L. D., Litt, I., Simmonds, B., & Haydel, F. (1994). Factors associated with eating disorder symptoms in a community sample of 6th and 7th grade girls. *International Journal of Eating Disorders, 15*(4), 357–367.

King, A. (1963). Primary and secondary Anorexia Nervosa syndromes. *British Journal of Psychiatry, 109,* 470–479.

Kope, T. M., & Sack, W. H. (1987). Anorexia Nervosa in southeast Asian refugees: A report on three cases. *Journal of the American Academy of Child and Adolescent Psychiatry, 26*(5), 795–797.

Koslow, R. E. (1988). Differences between personal estimates of body fatness and measures of body fatness in 11 and 12 year old males and females. *Journal of Applied Social Psychology, 18,* 533–535.

Kurman, L. (1978). An analysis of messages concerning food, eating behaviors and ideal body image on prime-time American network television. *Dissertation Abstracts International, 39,* 1907A. (University Microfilms No. 781814)

Lacey, J. H. (1982). The bulimic syndrome at normal body weight: Reflections on pathogenesis and clinical features. *International Journal of Eating Disorders, 2*(1), 59–66.

Landy, D., & Sigall, H. (1974). Beauty is talent: Task evaluation as a function of the performer's physical attractiveness. *Journal of Personality and Social Psychology, 29*, 299–304.

Larson, R., & Johnson, C. (1981). Anorexia Nervosa in the context of daily living. *Journal of Youth and Adolescence, 10*, 455–471.

Lawrence, C. (1990). *Body image, dieting, and self-concept—their relation in young children.* Unpublished master's thesis, University of Missouri.

Lee, N. F., Rush, A. J., & Mitchell, J. E. (1985). Depression and Bulimia. *Journal of Affective Disorders, 9*, 231–238.

Leon, G. R. (1979). Cognitive-behavior therapy for eating disturbances. In P. C. Kendall & S. D. Hollon (Eds.), *Cognitive-behavioral interventions: Theory, research, and procedures* (pp. 357–388). New York: Academic Press.

Leon, G. R. (1980). Is it bad not to be thin? *American Journal of Clinical Nutrition, 33*, 174–176.

Leon, G. R., Carroll, K., Chernyk, B., & Finn, S. (1985). Binge eating and associated habit patterns within college student and identified populations. *International Journal of Eating Disorders, 4*(1), 43–57.

Lerner, R. M., & Gellert, E. (1969). Body build identification, preference, and aversion in children. *Developmental Psychology, 1*, 456–462.

Lerner, R. M., & Schroeder, C. (1971). Physique identification, preference and aversion in kindergarten children. *Developmental Psychology, 5*, 538.

Levin, P. A., Falko, J. M., Dixon, K., Gallup, E. M., & Saunders, W. (1980). Benign parotid enlargement in bulimia. *Annals of Internal Medicine, 93*, 827–829.

Locke, H. J., & Wallace, K. M. (1959). Short marital-adjustment and prediction tests: Their reliability and validity. *Marriage and Family Living, 21*, 251–255.

Loeb, K. L., Pike, K. M., Walsh, B. T., & Wilson, G. T. (1994). Assessment of diagnostic features of Bulimia Nervosa: Interview versus self-report format. *International Journal of Eating Disorders, 16*(1), 75–81.

Lorand, S. (1943). Anorexia Nervosa: Report of a case. *Psychosomatic Medicine, 5*, 282–292.

Loro, A. D. (1984). Binge eating: A cognitive-behavioral treatment approach. In R. C. Hawkins, W. J. Fremouw, & P. F. Clement (Eds.), *The binge–purge syndrome: Diagnosis, treatment, and research* (pp. 183–210). New York: Springer.

Loro, A. D., & Orleans, C. S. (1981). Binge eating in obesity: Preliminary findings and guidelines for behavioral analysis and treatment. *Addictive Behaviors, 6*, 155–166.

Love, S., Ollendick, T., Johnson, C., & Schlesinger, S. (1985). A preliminary report of the prediction of bulimic behaviors: A social learning analysis. *Bulletin of the Society of Psychologists in Addictive Behaviors, 4*, 93–101.

Maloney, M. J., McGuire, J., Daniels, S. R., & Specker, B. (1989). Dieting behavior and eating attitudes in children. *Pediatrics, 84*, 482–489.

Marks, I. M. (1978). Exposure treatments. In S. Agras (Ed.), *Behavior modification* (2nd ed., pp. 163–203). Boston: Little, Brown.

Martin, F. (1983). Subgroups in Anorexia Nervosa: A family systems study. In P. L. Darby, P. E. Garfinkel, D. M. Garner, & D. V. Coscina (Eds.), *Anorexia Nervosa: Recent developments in research* (pp. 57–63). New York: Alan R. Liss.

Mazure, C. M., Halmi, K. A., Sunday, S. R., Romano, S. J., & Einhorn, A. M. (1994). The Yale–Brown–Cornell Eating Disorder Scale: Development, use, reliability and validity. *Journal of Psychiatric Research, 28*(5), 425–445.

Mellin, L. M., Irwin, C., & Scully, S. (1992). Prevalence of disordered eating in girls: A survey of middle class children. *Journal of the American Dietetic Association, 92*, 851–853.

Mendelson, B. K., & White, D. R. (1982). Relation between body-esteem and self-esteem of obese and normal children. *Perceptual and Motor Skills, 54*, 899–905.

Mikhail, C., Steiger, H., & Taylor, D. M. (1993, March). *Body image in anorexic, bulimic, and non-eating-disordered women: Selection of different reference points for normal body concept.* Paper presented at the 14th Annual Scientific Sessions of the Society for Behavioral Medicine, San Francisco.

Minuchin, S., Rosman, B. L., & Baker, L. (1978). *Psychosomatic families: Anorexia Nervosa in context.* Cambridge, MA: Harvard University Press.

Mitchell, J. E. (1986a). Anorexia Nervosa: Medical and physiological aspects. In K. D. Brownell & J. P. Foreyt (Eds.), *Handbook of eating disorders: Physiology, psychology, and treatment of obesity, Anorexia, and Bulimia* (pp. 247–265). New York: Basic Books.

Mitchell, J. E. (1986b). Bulimia: Medical and physiological aspects. In K. D. Brownell & J. P. Foreyt (Eds.), *Handbook of eating disorders: Physiology, psychology, and treatment of obesity, Anorexia, and Bulimia* (pp. 379–388). New York: Basic Books.

Mitchell, J. E., & Goff, G. (1984). A series of twelve adult male patients with Bulimia. *Psychosomatics, 25*, 909–913.

Mitchell, J. E., Hatsukami, D., Eckert, E. D., & Pyle, R. L. (1985). Characteristics of 275 patients with Bulimia. *American Journal of Psychiatry, 142*, 482–485.

Mitchell, J. E., Pomeroy, C., & Colon, E. (1990). Medical complications in Bulimia Nervosa. In M. Fichter (Ed.), *Bulimia nervosa: Basic research, diagnosis, and therapy* (pp. 71–83). New York: Wiley.

Mitchell, J. E., & Pyle, R. L. (1982). The bulimic syndrome in normal weight individuals: A review. *International Journal of Eating Disorders, 1*(2), 61–73.

Mitchell, J. E., Pyle, R. L., & Eckert, E. D. (1981). Frequency and duration of binge-eating episodes in patients with bulimia. *American Journal of Psychiatry, 138,* 835–836.

Mitchell, J. E., Pyle, R. L., Eckert, E. D., Hatsukami, D., & Lentz, R. (1983). Electrolyte and other physiological abnormalities in patients with Bulimia. *Psychological Medicine, 13,* 273–278.

Monello, L. F., & Mayer, J. (1967). Hunger and satiety sensations in men, women, boys, and girls. *American Journal of Clinical Nutrition, 20,* 253–261.

Monello, L. F., Seltzer, C. C., & Mayer, J. (1965). Hunger and satiety sensations in men, women, boys, and girls: A preliminary report. *Annals of the New York Academy of Sciences, 131,* 593–602.

Moos, R. (1974). *Family Environment Scale.* Palo Alto, CA: Consulting Psychologists Press.

Mori, D., Chaiken, S., & Pliner, P. (1987). "Eating lightly" and the self-presentation of femininity. *Journal of Personality and Social Psychology, 53,* 693–702.

Moss, R. A., Jennings, G., McFarland, J. H., & Carter, P. (1984). Binge eating, vomiting, and weight fear in a female high school population. *Journal of Family Practice, 18,* 313–320.

Norman, D. K., & Herzog, D. B. (1983). Bulimia, Anorexia Nervosa, and Anorexia Nervosa with Bulimia: A comparative analysis of MMPI profiles. *International Journal of Eating Disorders, 2*(2), 43–52.

Nudelman, S., Rosen, J. C., & Leitenberg, H. (1988). Dissimilarities in eating attitudes, body image distortion, depression, and self-esteem between high-intensity male runners and women with Bulimia Nervosa. *International Journal of Eating Disorders, 7,* 625–634.

Nylander, I. (1971). The feeling of being fat and dieting in a school population: An epidemiological interview investigation. *Acta Sociomedica Scandinavica, 3,* 17–26.

Olson, D. H., Portner, J., & Lavee, Y. (1985). *FACES III.* St. Paul: Faculty of Social Science, University of Minnesota.

Orbach, S. (1978). *Fat is a feminist issue: The anti-diet guide to permanent weight loss.* New York: Berkeley.

Orbach, S. (1982). *Fat is a feminist issue II: A program to conquer compulsive eating.* New York: Berkeley.

Ordman, A. M., & Kirschenbaum, D. S. (1986). Bulimia: Assessment of eating, psychological adjustment, and familial characteristics. *International Journal of Eating Disorders, 5,* 865–878.

Orleans, C. T., & Barnett, L. R. (1984). Bulimarexia: Guidelines for behavioral assessment and treatment. In R. C. Hawkins, W. J. Fremouw, & P. F. Clement (Eds.), *The binge–purge syndrome: Diagnosis, treatment, and research* (pp. 144–182). New York: Springer.

Owens, R. G., & Slade, P. D. (1987). Running and

Anorexia Nervosa: An empirical study. *International Journal of Eating Disorders, 6,* 771–775.

Palmer, R., Christie, M., Cordle, C., Davis, D., & Kendrick, J. (1987). The Clinical Eating Disorder Rating Instrument (CEDRI): A preliminary description. *International Journal of Eating Disorders, 6,* 9–16.

Pillay, M., & Crisp, A. H. (1977). Some psychological characteristics of patients with Anorexia Nervosa whose weight has been newly restored. *British Journal of Medical Psychology, 50,* 375–380.

Piran, N., Lerner, P., Garfinkel, P. E., Kennedy, S. H., & Brouillete, C. (1988). Personality disorders in anorexic patients. *International Journal of Eating Disorders, 7,* 589–599.

Pirke, K. M. (1990). Menstrual cycle and neuroendocrine disturbances of the gonadal axis in Bulimia (Nervosa). In M. M. Fichter (Ed.), *Bulimia Nervosa: Basic research, diagnosis, and therapy* (pp. 223–234). New York: Wiley.

Pope, H. G., Jr., Hudson, J. I., Jonas, J. M., & Yurgelun-Todd, D. (1983). Bulimia treated with imipramine: A placebo-controlled double-blind study. *American Journal of Psychiatry, 140,* 554–558.

Pope, H. G., Jr., Hudson, J. I., & Yurgelun-Todd, D. (1984). Anorexia Nervosa and Bulimia among 300 suburban women shoppers. *American Journal of Psychiatry, 141,* 292–294.

Prather, R. C., & Williamson, D. A. (1988). Psychopathology associated with Bulimia, binge eating, and obesity. *International Journal of Eating Disorders, 7,* 177–184.

Pumariega, A. J. (1986). Acculturation and eating attitudes in adolescent girls: A comparative and correctional study. *Journal of the American Academy of Child Psychiatry, 25,* 276–279.

Pyle, R. L., Mitchell, J. E., & Eckert, E. D. (1981). Bulimia: A report of 34 cases. *Journal of Clinical Psychiatry, 42,* 60–64.

Pyle, R. L., Mitchell, J. E., Eckert, E. D., Halvorson, P., Neuman, P., & Goff, G. (1983). The incidence of Bulimia in freshmen college students. *International Journal of Eating Disorders, 2*(3), 75–85.

Rakoff, V. (1983). Multiple determinants of family dynamics in Anorexia Nervosa. In P. L. Darby, P. E. Garfinkel, D. M. Garner, & D. V. Coscina (Eds.), *Anorexia Nervosa: Recent developments in research* (pp. 29–40). New York: Alan R Liss.

Rasmussen, S. A., & Eisen, J. L. (1994). The epidemiology and differential diagnosis of Obsessive Compulsive Disorder. *Journal of Clinical Psychiatry, 55,* 5–14.

Rastam, M. (1992). Anorexia Nervosa in 51 Swedish adolescents: Premorbid problems and comorbidity. *Journal of the American Academy of Child and Adolescent Psychiatry, 31,* 819–829.

Rau, J. H., & Green, R. S. (1984). Neurological factors affecting binge eating: Body over mind. In R. C. Hawkins, W. J. Fremouw, & P. F. Clement (Eds.), *The binge–purge syndrome: Diagnosis, treatment and research* (pp. 123–143). New York: Springer.

Reitman, E. E., & Cleveland, S. E. (1964). Changes in body image following sensory deprivation in schizophrenic and control groups. *Journal of Abnormal and Social Psychology, 68,* 168–176.

Rosen, J. C. (1990). Body image disturbances in eating disorders. In T. F. Cash & T. Pruzinsky (Eds.), *Body images: Development, deviance, and change* (pp. 190–214). New York: Guilford Press.

Rosen, J. C., & Leitenberg, H. (1982). Bulimia Nervosa: Treatment with exposure and response prevention. *Behavior Therapy, 13,* 117–124.

Rosen, J. C., Leitenberg, H., Fondacaro, K. M., Gross, J., & Willmuth, M. E. (1985). Standardized test meals in assessment of eating behavior in Bulimia Nervosa: Consumption of feared foods when vomiting is prevented. *International Journal of Eating Disorders, 4,* 59–70.

Rosen, J. C., Reiter, J., & Orosan, P. (1995). Assessment of body image in eating disorders with the Body Dysmorphic Disorder Examination. *Behaviour Research and Therapy, 33,* 77–84.

Rosen, J. C., Srebnik, D., Saltzberg, E., & Wendt, S. (1991). Development of a Body Image Avoidance Questionnaire. *Psychological Assessment: A Journal of Consulting and Clinical Psychology, 3,* 32–37.

Rosen, J. C., Vara, L., Wendt, S., & Leitenberg, H. (1990). Validity studies of the Eating Disorder Examination. *International Journal of Eating Disorders, 9,* 519–528.

Russell, G. F. M. (1979). Bulimia Nervosa: An ominous variant of Anorexia Nervosa. *Psychological Medicine, 9,* 429–448.

Russell, G. F. M. (1985). The changing nature of Anorexia Nervosa: An introduction to the conference. *Journal of Psychiatric Research, 19,* 101–109.

Russell, G. F. M., Campbell, P. G., & Slade, P. D. (1975). Experimental studies on the nature of the psychological disorder in Anorexia Nervosa. *Psychoneuroendocrinology, 1,* 45–56.

Sasson, A., Lewin, C., & Roth, D. (1995). Dieting behavior and eating attitudes in Israeli children. *International Journal of Eating Disorders, 17*(1), 67–72.

Schlundt, D. G. (1989). Assessment of eating behavior in Bulimia Nervosa: The self-monitoring analysis system. In W. G. Johnson (Ed.), *Advances in eating disorders* (Vol. 2, pp. 1–41). Greenwich, CT: JAI Press.

Schlundt, D. G., & Johnson, W. G. (1990). *Eating disorders: Assessment and treatment.* Boston: Allyn & Bacon.

Schneider, J. A., & Agras, W. S. (1985). A cognitive behavioral group treatment of Bulimia. *British Journal of Psychiatry, 146,* 66–69.

Schneider, J. A., & Agras, W. S. (1987). Bulimia in males: A matched comparison with females. *International Journal of Eating Disorders, 6,* 235–242.

Schulman, R. G., Kinder, B. N., Powers, P. S., Prange, M., & Gleghorn, A. A. (1986). The development of a scale to measure cognitive distortions in Bulimia. *Journal of Personality Assessment, 50,* 630–639.

Schwartz, R. C., Barrett, M. J., & Saba, G. (1985). Family therapy for Bulimia. In D. M. Garner & P. E. Garfinkel (Eds.), *Handbook of psychotherapy for Anorexia Nervosa and Bulimia* (pp. 280–307). New York: Guilford Press.

Schwartz, D. M., & Thompson, M. G. (1981). Do anorectics get well?: Current research and future needs. *American Journal of Psychiatry, 138,* 319–323.

Schwartz, D. M., Thompson, M. G., & Johnson, C. L. (1982). Anorexia Nervosa and Bulimia: The sociocultural context. *International Journal of Eating Disorders, 1*(3), 20–36.

Secord, P. F., & Jourard, S. M. (1953). The appraisal of body-cathexis: Body-cathexis and the self. *Journal of Consulting Psychology, 17,* 343–347.

Seligman, M. E. P. (1975). *Helplessness: On depression, development, and death.* San Francisco: W. H. Freeman.

Selvini Palazzoli, M. (1974). *Anorexia Nervosa.* London: Chaucer.

Selvini Palazzoli, M. (1978). *Self-starvation.* New York: Jason Aronson.

Silber, T. J. (1986). Anorexia Nervosa in blacks and Hispanics. *International Journal of Eating Disorders, 5*(1), 121–128.

Slade, P. D. (1973). A short Anorexic Behaviour Scale. *British Journal of Psychiatry, 122,* 83–85

Slade, P. D., & Russell, G. F. M. (1973). Awareness of body dimension in Anorexia Nervosa: Cross sectional and longitudinal studies. *Psychological Medicine, 3,* 188–199.

Smart, D. E., Beumont, P. J. V., & George, G. C. W. (1976). Some personality characteristics of patients with Anorexia Nervosa. *British Journal of Psychiatry, 128,* 57–60.

Smith, M. C., & Thelen, M. H. (1984). Development and validation of a test for Bulimia Nervosa. *Journal of Consulting and Clinical Psychology, 52,* 863–872.

Smolak, L., & Levine, M. P. (1994). Psychometric properties of the Children's Eating Attitudes Test. *International Journal of Eating Disorders, 16*(3), 275–282.

Stege, P., Visco-Dangler, L., & Rye, L. (1982). Anorexia Nervosa: Review including oral and dental manifestations. *Journal of the American Dental Association, 104,* 648–652.

Steinhausen, H. C., & Seidel, R. (1993). Correspondence between the clinical assessment of eating-disordered patients and findings derived from questionnaires at follow-up. *International Journal of Eating Disorders, 14*(3), 367–374.

Stern, S. L., Dixon, K. N., Jones, D., Lake, M., Nemzer, E., & Sansone, R. (1989). Family environment in Anorexia Nervosa and Bulimia. *International Journal of Eating Disorders, 8*, 25–31.

Stonehill, E., & Crisp, A. H. (1977). Psychoneurotic characteristics of patients with Anorexia Nervosa before and after treatment and at follow-up 4–7 years later. *Journal of Psychosomatic Research, 21,* 187–193.

Strasser, M., & Giles, G. (1988). Ethical considerations. In D. Scott (Ed.), *Anorexia and Bulimia Nervosa* (pp. 204–212). London: Croom Helm.

Strauss, J., & Ryan, R. (1988). Cognitive dysfunction in eating disorders. *International Journal of Eating Disorders, 7*(1), 19–27.

Striegel-Moore, R. H., Silberstein, L. R., Frensch, P., & Rodin, J. (1989). A prospective study of disordered eating among college students. *International Journal of Eating Disorders, 8,* 499–509.

Strober, M. (1980). Personality and symptomatological features in young, nonchronic Anorexia Nervosa patients. *Journal of Psychosomatic Research, 24,* 353–359.

Strober, M. (1981a). A comparative analysis of personality organization in juvenile Anorexia Nervosa. *Journal of Youth and Adolescence, 10,* 285–295.

Strober, M. (1981b). The significance of Bulimia in juvenile Anorexia Nervosa: An exploration of possible etiological factors. *International Journal of Eating Disorders, 1*(1), 28–43.

Strober, M. (1983). An empirically derived typology of Anorexia Nervosa. In P. L. Darby, P. E. Garfinkel, D. M. Garner, & D. V. Coscina (Eds.), *Anorexia nervosa: Recent developments in research* (pp. 185–196). New York: Alan R. Liss.

Strober, M. (1986). Anorexia Nervosa: History and psychological concepts. In K. D. Brownell & J. P. Foreyt (Eds.), *Handbook of eating disorders: Physiology, psychology, and treatment of obesity, Anorexia, and Bulimia* (pp. 231–246). New York: Basic Books.

Strober, M., Salkin, B., Burroughs, J., & Morrell, W. (1982). Validity of the bulimia–restricter distinction in Anorexia Nervosa: Parental personality characteristics and family psychiatric morbidity. *Journal of Nervous and Mental Disease, 170,* 345–351.

Stuart, R. G., & Davis, B. (1972). *Slim chance in a fat world: Behavioral control of obesity.* Champaign, IL: Research Press.

Theander, S. (1970). Anorexia Nervosa: A psychiatric investigation of 94 female patients. *Acta Psychiatrica Scandinavica, 214*(Suppl.), 1–194.

Thompson, J. K., & Psaltis, K. (1988). Multiple aspects and correlates of body figure ratings: A replication and extension of Fallon and Rozin (1985). *International Journal of Eating Disorders, 7,* 813–818.

Thompson, J. K., & Spana, R. E. (1988). The adjustable light beam method for the assessment of size estimation accuracy: Description, psychometric, and normative data. *International Journal of Eating Disorders, 4,* 521–526.

Thompson, S. B. N. (1989). Techniques for tackling anxiety. *Therapy Weekly, 15*(49), 6.

Traub, A. C., & Orbach, J. (1964). Psychophysical studies of body image: I. The adjustable body-distorting mirror. *Archives of General Psychiatry, 11,* 53–66.

Ujiie, T., & Kono, M. (1994). Eating Attitudes Test in Japan. *Japanese Journal of Psychiatry and Neurology, 48*(3), 557–565.

von Bertalanffy, L. (1962). General systems theory: A critical review. *General Systems Yearbook, 7,* 1–20.

Wallechinsky, D., Wallace, I., & Wallace, A. (1977). *Book of lists.* New York: Morrow.

Waller, J. V., Kaufman, M. R., & Deutsch, F. (1940). Anorexia Nervosa: A psychosomatic entity. *Psychosomatic Medicine, 2,* 3–16.

Walsh, B. T., Katz, J. L., Levin, J., Kream, J., Fukushimo, D. K., Weiner, H., & Zumoff, B. (1981). The production rate of cortisol declines during recovery from Anorexia Nervosa [Technical note]. *Journal of Clinical Endocrinology and Metabolism, 53,* 203–205.

Walsh, B. T., Roose, S. P., Glassman, A. H., Gladis, M., & Sadik, C. (1985). Bulimia and depression. *Psychosomatic Medicine, 47,* 123–131.

Wardle, I. (1980). Dietary restraint and binge eating. *Behavior Analysis and Modification, 4,* 201–209.

Wardle, J., & Beales, S. (1986). Restraint, body image and food attitudes in children from 12 to 18 years. *Appetite, 7,* 209–217.

Wardle, J., & Beinart, H. (1981). Binge-eating: A theoretical review. *British Journal of Clinical Psychology, 20,* 97–109.

Warren, M. (1968). A study of Anorexia Nervosa in young girls. *Journal of Child Psychology and Psychiatry, 9,* 27–40.

Webb, W. L., & Gehi, M. (1981). Electrolyte and fluid imbalance: Neuropsychiatric manifestations. *Psychosomatics, 22,* 199–203.

Weiss, S. R., & Ebert, M. H. (1983). Psychological and behavioral characteristics of normal-weight bulimics and normal-weight controls. *Psychosomatic Medicine, 45,* 293–303.

Welch, G., Thompson, L., & Hall, A. (1993). The BULIT-R: Its reliability and clinical validity as a screening tool for DSM-III-R Bulimia Nervosa in a female tertiary education population. *International Journal of Eating Disorders, 14*(1), 95–105.

Whitaker, A., Johnson, J., Shaffer, D., Rapoport, J. L., Kalikow, K., Walsh, B. T., Davies, M., Braiman, S., & Dolinsky, A. (1990). Uncommon troubles in young people: Prevalence estimates of selected psychiatric disorders in a non-referred psychiatric population. *Archives of General Psychiatry, 47,* 487–496.

Williamson, D. A. (1990). *Assessment of eating disorders: Obesity, Anorexia, and Bulimia Nervosa.* Elmsford, NY: Pergamon Press.

Williamson, D. A., Kelley, M. L., Davis, C. J., Ruggiero, L., & Blouin, D. C. (1985). Psychopathology of eating disorders: A controlled comparison of bulimic, obese, and normal subjects. *Journal of Consulting and Clinical Psychology, 53,* 161–166.

Williamson, D. A., Prather, R. C., Goreczny, A. J., Davis, C. J., & McKenzie, S. J. (1989). A comprehensive model of Bulimia Nervosa: Empirical evaluation. In W. G. Johnson (Ed.), *Advances in eating disorders* (Vol. 2, pp. 137–156). Greenwich, CT: JAI Press.

Wilson, G. T., Eldredge, K. L., Smith, D., & Niles, B. (1991). Cognitive-behavioural treatment of Bulimia Nervosa: A controlled evaluation. *Behaviour Research and Therapy, 29,* 575–583.

Wilson, G. T., & Smith, D. (1989). Assessment of Bulimia Nervosa and evaluation of the Eating Disorder Examination. *International Journal of Eating Disorders, 8,* 173–180.

Wolf, E. M., & Crowther, J. H. (1983). Personality and eating habit variables as predictors of severity of binge eating and weight. *Addictive Behaviors, 8,* 335–344.

Wonderlich, S. A., & Mitchell, J. E. (1992). The comorbidity of personality disorders and the eating disorders. In J. Yager (Ed.), *Special problems in managing eating disorders* (pp. 51–86). Washington, DC: American Psychiatric Press.

Wonderlich, S. A., & Swift, W. J. (1990). Perceptions of parental relationships in eating disorder subtypes. *Journal of Abnormal Psychology, 99,* 353–360.

Wooley, O. W., & Wooley, S. C. (1982). The Beverly Hills eating disorder: The mass marketing of Anorexia Nervosa [Editorial]. *International Journal of Eating Disorders, 1*(3), 57–69.

Wooley, S. C., & Wooley, O. W. (1979). Obesity and women: I. A closer look at the facts. *Women's Studies International Quarterly, 2,* 69–79.

Wooley, S. C., & Wooley, O. W. (1980). Eating disorders: Obesity and Anorexia. In A. M. Brodsky & R. T. Hare-Mustin (Eds.), *Women and psychotherapy: An assessment of research and practice* (pp. 135–158). New York: Guilford Press.

Wooley, S. C., & Wooley, O. W. (1983). Should obesity be treated at all? *Psychiatric Annals, 13,* 884–888.

World Health Organization. (1992). *International classification of diseases* (10th revision): *Chapter V. Mental and behavioural disorders.* Geneva: Author.

Wurtman, R. J., & Wurtman, J. J. (1984). Nutrients, neurotransmitter synthesis, and the control of food intake. In A. J. Stunkard & E. Stellar (Eds.), *Eating and its disorders* (pp. 77–86). New York: Raven Press.

Yates, A. (1989). Current perspectives on the eating disorders: I. History, psychological and biological aspects. *Journal of the American Academy of Child and Adolescent Psychiatry, 29,* 813–828.

Yates, A., Leehey, K., & Shisslak, C. M. (1983). Running—an analogue of Anorexia? *New England Journal of Medicine, 308,* 251–255.

Yates, W. R., Sieleni, B., & Bowers, W. A. (1989). Clinical correlates of personality disorder in Bulimia Nervosa. *International Journal of Eating Disorders, 8,* 473–477.

Chapter Fifteen

ADOLESCENT SUBSTANCE USE PROBLEMS

Peter W. Vik
Sandra A. Brown
Mark G. Myers

Psychoactive substance use can have a profound impact on adolescent functioning in a variety of psychosocial and physical domains. Teens who misuse addictive substances are at risk of becoming physically and/or psychologically dependent on these drugs. Minor involvement, as well as problematic use of alcohol and drugs, can delay the acquisition of developmentally important social and cognitive skills necessary for academic success and positive peer relations. Heavy substance use can provoke symptoms, behaviors, and complaints that resemble psychiatric disorders, or can complicate the presentation and manifestation of preexisting or independent behavioral and psychiatric conditions. A comprehensive assessment of alcohol and drug consumption is important in order to identify problems resulting from substance involvement, as well as to evaluate alcohol- and drug-related influences on the clinical course of independent problem behaviors.

The extent of detail gathered during an evaluation depends on whether substance use is the primary or a secondary purpose for the assessment. Substance use may be the main focus of an evaluation, such as when a teen enters treatment for dependence on alcohol or other specific drugs. In other circumstances (e.g., a medical examination or an educational assessment), inquiry about substance use may be a secondary issue in the context of a general evaluation. When a clinician detects substance use during a general screening, the teen should receive a thorough evaluation of his or her substance involvement. A detailed assessment determines specific problem areas, iden-

tifies the influences that maintain use, and provides baseline data regarding the severity of substance involvement against which change can be measured. Using this information, a clinician can formulate a treatment plan that is appropriate for the individual adolescent.

When clinicians are assessing substance use problems among adolescents, it is important to recognize the normative context of alcohol and drug use, as well as to consider etiological theories of substance involvement, progression to problem use, and the clinical course of Substance Abuse and Dependence. The purpose of this chapter is to provide clinicians with a general understanding of adolescent substance involvement. We begin by reviewing the clinical background of adolescent substance use, including prevalence estimates, diagnostic criteria, developmental issues, and mechanisms that lead adolescents into and out of problematic involvement with alcohol and drugs. In the second part of this chapter, we review methods of assessment, detail specific psychosocial domains to evaluate in an assessment, and suggest a hypothesis-testing approach to integrate the assessment data.

CLINICAL BACKGROUND

Prevalence

Although it is illegal, use of alcohol and drugs by adolescents is common. Table 15.1 summarizes data from Johnston, O'Malley, & Bachman (1995) describing the proportion of high school seniors in 1995 who had ever tried various substances (lifetime use), who had used them during the past year and month, and who used substances daily. This nationally representative sample of U.S. teenagers indicated that by the senior year of high school most teens (about 81%) had tried alcohol, about 42% had used marijuana, approximately one in five (21.3%) used cocaine or other stimulants, and about 13% had tried hallucinogens (Johnston et al., 1995). Trends among high school seniors from 1975 to 1992 indicate decreases in the use of a number of substances (Johnston, Bachman, & O'Malley, 1993). Specifically, the proportion of teens who reported using marijuana within the past month declined from 32% in 1975 to 12% in 1992; hallucinogen use dropped from 3.4% to 2.3%; use of opiates decreased from 2.2% to 1.5%, and use of both sedatives and tranquilizers dropped from just over 4% to about 1%. Other drugs peaked in popularity during the 1980s, but then declined in use by the 1990s. For example, in 1975, 7.7% of high school seniors reported using stimulants and 2% noted using cocaine during the previous month. In the early 1980s, previous-month stimulant use peaked at about 10–12%, then declined to 2.8% in 1992. Similarly, cocaine use increased to over 6% in 1986, then dropped below 2% by 1990. Unfortunately, use of alcohol, tobacco, and other drugs increased steadily between 1992 and 1994 (Johnson et al., 1995). Annual prevalence of any illicit drug use increased from 27.1% to 39.0% between 1992 and 1994; monthly prevalence went from 14.4% to 23.8%. Monthly prevalence of tobacco use increased from 27.8% to 33.5% over the same time period.

Unpublished data collected from California junior high school students (aged 12–15) revealed that half had tried alcohol at least once (Vik & Brown, 1993). Average age of first drink was 10.4 years, and the beverage typically involved was beer or wine. Furthermore, one-quarter (23%) of students who tried alcohol had become drunk at least once (average age of first drunk episode was 12 years), and 10.5% reported bingeing on alcohol (i.e., consuming five or more drinks at one time). Although from 10% to 21% of the students reported monthly alcohol use, and up to 15% reported weekly use, fewer than 3% drank daily. Windle (1991) reported comparable findings among 8th- and 10th-grade students. He found that 75.9% of 8th-graders and 87.3% of 10th-graders had tried alcohol. Despite frequent alcohol experimentation, Windle noted that only 12% of 8th-graders and 26.8% of 10th-graders reported occasional to frequent alcohol use. Finally, Barnes and Welte (1986) found that 71% of adolescents in 7th to 12th grades had tried alcohol, and that 13% were heavy drinkers.

Similar rates of alcohol and drug use have been found among rural adolescents. Gibbons, Wylie, Echterling, and French (1986) reported that most rural teens (83%) had tried alcohol (average age 16 years); among those who had tried alcohol, 32% had first used before age 10, and over half had tried alcohol by age 12. Among a sample of 12- to 14-year-old rural adolescents, Bloch, Crockett, and Vicary (1991) found that 64% had tried alcohol, and one-third were regular drinkers. In another sample, slightly over 40% of rural teens had used marijuana at some point in their lives, 20% had

TABLE 15.1. Percentages of U.S. High School Seniors Reporting Use of Specific Substances, 1995

Substance	Lifetime use	Past year	Past month	Daily
Alcohol	80.7	73.7	51.3	3.5
Tobacco	64.2	—	33.5	21.6
Any illicit drug	48.4	39.0	23.8	—
Marijuana/hashish	41.7	34.7	21.2	4.6
Inhalants	17.4	8.0	3.2	0.1
Hallucinogens	12.7	9.3	4.4	0.1
LSD	11.7	8.4	4.4	0.1
PCP	2.7	1.8	0.6	0.3
Cocaine	6.0	4.0	1.8	0.2
Stimulants	15.3	9.3	4.0	0.3
Heroin	1.6	1.1	0.6	0.1
Other opiates	7.2	4.7	1.8	0.1
Tranquilizers	7.1	4.4	1.8	<0.05
Barbiturates	7.4	4.7	2.2	<0.05

Note. The data are from Johnston, O'Malley, and Bachman (1995).

tried a stimulant, and 9% had tried cocaine (Donnermeyer, 1992).

Alcohol and other drug involvement varies according to gender and ethnicity. Drinking is more common among boys than girls in early adolescence (12–13 years) and later adolescence (16–18 years); however, equal proportions of males and females (approximately three-fourths) report alcohol use at age 15 (Barnes & Welte, 1986). High school senior boys report more episodes of heavy drinking than girls (Johnston, Bachman, & O'Malley, 1994). Boys are twice as likely as girls to consume five or more drinks per week (18% vs. 8%, on average), particularly from age 15 on (Barnes & Welte, 1986). Similar differences are found among rural girls, who drink less and begin drinking at a later age than rural boys (Gibbons et al., 1986).

Topography of alcohol and drug use also varies among ethnically diverse groups (Allison & Leone, 1994). Tables 15.2 and 15.3 compare white, Hispanic, and black high school seniors according to their lifetime and past-month use of various drugs; the data for these tables are from Johnston et al. (1994). Black students consistently report lower rates of most drug use than white and Hispanic students (Johnston et al., 1994). White and Native American students in 7th to 12th grades show the highest rates of drinking (76% and 73%, respectively) and heavy drinking (16% and 18%, respectively) (Barnes & Welte, 1986). White high school seniors use inhalants, hallucinogens, barbiturates, amphetamines, tranquilizers, alcohol, and tobacco to a greater extent than black and Hispanic teens; however, Hispanic teens report the highest rates of heroin, cocaine, and crack use

(Johnston et al., 1994). Finally, although Asian adolescents display the lowest rates of drinking (approximately 45%), Asian adolescents who drink consume the most alcohol per day, compared to drinkers among other ethnic groups; in particular, male Asian drinkers consume on average five drinks per day (Welte & Barnes, 1987).

Given that dropout rates among black and Hispanic teens are higher than among white teens, the data on ethnic differences in substance use among high school seniors may underestimate use by Hispanic and black teens. Johnston et al. (1994) used conservative procedures to correct for dropouts and student absences, and found minimal changes in overall substance use prevalence. Nevertheless, readers should recognize that these data may not reflect actual ethnic differences.

These surveys suggest that nearly all adolescents will have used alcohol, and that most will have tried some other drug (e.g., tobacco, marijuana, or stimulants), before they graduate from high school. When clinicians evaluate adolescents, they should recognize that minor substance involvement is normative, does not imply a serious behavioral condition, and can probably be resolved with education and advice. Heavy involvement and negative consequences of use, however, are not typical among adolescents and indicate a need for appropriate intervention.

Diagnosis

The *Diagnostic and Statistical Manual of Mental Disorders,* fourth edition (DSM-IV; American Psychiatric Association, 1994) describes a number

TABLE 15.2. Lifetime Use of Substances among U.S. High School Seniors by Ethnic Group, 1993

Substance	White (%)	Hispanic (%)	Black (%)
Alcohol	89.3	87.7	80.7
Been drunk	63.0	61.5	41.6
Tobacco	65.3	63.3	44.4
Marijuana/hashish	35.5	36.8	24.1
Inhalants	19.4	16.2	6.2
Hallucinogens	11.8	9.6	1.1
LSD	11.2	8.8	0.9
Cocaine	6.0	11.1	1.5
Stimulants	16.8	12.3	4.4
Heroin	1.2	1.4	0.5
Other opiates	7.3	4.6	2.0
Tranquilizers	6.9	5.6	2.5
Barbiturates	6.7	4.5	2.1

Note. The data are from Johnston, Bachman, and O'Malley (1994).

TABLE 15.3. Use of Substances during the Past Month among U.S. High School Seniors by Ethnic Group, 1993

Substance	White (%)	Hispanic (%)	Black (%)
Alcohol	55.6	50.5	32.4
Been drunk	33.6	24.8	12.5
Tobacco	33.2	24.2	9.5
Marijuana/hashish	14.9	12.5	8.1
Inhalants	2.6	2.1	1.4
Hallucinogens	2.9	1.7	[a]
LSD	2.6	1.6	[a]
Cocaine	1.2	2.4	[a]
Stimulants	3.7	2.2	1.1
Heroin	0.2	0.4	0.3
Other opiates	1.4	0.9	0.5
Tranquilizers	1.2	0.1	[a]
Barbiturates	1.3	0.8	0.6

Note. The data are from Johnston, Bachman, and O'Malley (1994).
[a]Fewer than 0.05%.

of disorders related to substance use (see Table 15.4). Substance Dependence is defined as the repeated self-administration of a substance, resulting in tolerance, withdrawal, and compulsive drug-taking behavior. To receive a DSM-IV diagnosis of dependence on a specific substance, an individual must evidence at least three of seven specified criteria within a 12-month period (see Table 15.5). The first of these criteria, tolerance, indicates that a given amount of the substance produces less of an effect with continued use, or that an individual uses more of the substance to achieve desired effects. During withdrawal, the second criterion, the individual experiences unpleasant behavioral, physiological, and cognitive symptoms as a result of declining blood and tissue concentrations of the substance (see Table 15.6). Often the person may use the same or a similar substance to avoid withdrawal symptoms. The remaining criteria reflect various behaviors that interfere with and disrupt life functioning and physical health.

Some individuals experience adverse consequences because of their repeated use of psychoactive substances, yet do not evidence tolerance, withdrawal, or compulsive use. Substance Abuse is diagnosed when the Substance Dependence criteria are not met, but the individual encounters hazardous circumstances and/or displays recurrent problems as a consequence of using a psychoactive substance. Poor judgment and irresponsible or dangerous behavior resulting from substance use and leading to significant harmful consequences can lead to a DSM-IV diagnosis of Substance Abuse. Table 15.7 lists the specific criteria used for this diagnosis.

The DSM-IV criteria for Substance Dependence may not reflect the unique features of adolescent substance involvement. Adolescents differ from adults regarding the manner and extent to which substance use affects their life functioning and physical health (Brown, Mott, & Myers, 1990). Detection of withdrawal symptoms may be complicated among adolescents because of the limited duration of their alcohol and drug involvement, as well as the tendency for teens who use substances heavily to use multiple substances. In a study of adolescents hospitalized for Substance Dependence treatment, Stewart and Brown (1995) found that affective symptoms (e.g., depression, anger, and anxiety) were the most common withdrawal symptoms. In addition, though impairment in occupational functioning or romantic relationships is unlikely (given adolescents' developmental status), intensive substance involvement among teens is more likely to result in loss of control over use and reduced involvement in academic and social activities.

Meeting the DSM-IV criteria for Substance Abuse or Substance Dependence offers little guidance for developing appropriate interventions (e.g., Bukstein & Kaminer, 1994). A goal of assessing substance use behavior is to identify personal cues, anticipated effects, and recurrent consequences of drinking and drug involvement, which both maintain the problem use and can be instrumental in changing a teen's substance involvement. As we shall discuss, data for such an evaluation should come from a variety of sources (e.g., the teen, parents, siblings, grandparents, teachers, parole officers), and should include interviews,

TABLE 15.4. DSM-IV Substance-Related Disorders and Their Essential Features

Substance use disorders

Substance Dependence: "a cluster of cognitive, behavioral, and physiological symptoms indicating that the individual continues use of the substance despite significant substance-related problems" (p. 176).

Substance Abuse: "a maladaptive pattern of substance use manifested by recurrent and significant adverse consequences related to the repeated use of substances" (p. 182).

Substance-induced disorders

Substance Intoxication: "the development of a reversible substance-specific syndrome due to the recent ingestion of (or exposure to) a substance" (p. 183).

Substance Withdrawal: "the development of a substance-specific maladaptive behavioral change, with physiological and cognitive concomitants, that is due to the cessation of, or reduction in, heavy and prolonged substance use" (p. 184).

Substance-Induced Delirium: "a disturbance of consciousness that is accompanied by a change in cognition that cannot be better accounted for by a preexisting or evolving dementia. . . . There is evidence from the history, physical examination, or laboratory tests that the delirium is a direct physiological consequence of . . . Substance Intoxication or Withdrawal" (p. 124).

Substance-Induced Persisting Dementia: "the development of multiple cognitive deficits (including memory impairment) that are due to . . . the persisting effects of a substance" (p. 133).

Substance-Induced Persisting Amnestic Disorder: "a disturbance in memory that is . . . due to the persisting effects of a substance" (p. 156); [this disturbance] persists beyond the usual duration of Substance Intoxication or Withdrawal" (p. 161).

Substance-Induced Psychotic Disorder: "prominent hallucinations or delusions . . . that are judged to be due to the direct physiological effects of a substance" (p. 310).

Substance-Induced Mood Disorder: "a prominent and persistent disturbance in mood . . . that is judged to be due to the direct physiological effects of a substance" (p. 370).

Substance-Induced Anxiety Disorder: "prominent anxiety symptoms . . . that are judged to be due to the direct physiological effects of a substance" (p. 439).

Substance-Induced Sexual Dysfunction: "a clinically significant sexual dysfunction that results in marked distress or interpersonal difficulty . . . [and] is judged to be fully explained by the direct physiological effects of a substance" (p. 519).

Substance-Induced Sleep Disorder: "a prominent disturbance in sleep that is sufficiently severe to warrant independent clinical attention . . . and is judged to be due to the direct physiological effects of a substance" (p. 601).

Note. The data are from American Psychiatric Association (1994).

school records, psychological testing, questionnaires, and (whenever possible) direct observation. Occasionally, medical and court records are available and should be incorporated in an assessment. Data from a comprehensive assessment should be considered from the context of normative adolescent substance use and with regard to factors influencing initiation, escalation, and maintenance of substance involvement.

Correlates and Consequences of Adolescent Substance Use Problems

Adolescents typically present for treatment with multiple psychological and behavioral problems; an adolescent substance use assessment must therefore discern to what extent a teen's problems are consequences of, versus antecedents to, substance use. Evaluating the presence of comorbid psychiatric conditions is one of the most important issues to address when assessing adolescent alcohol and drug misuse. Pharmacological properties of different drugs can produce symptoms that are similar across a range of psychiatric diagnoses. For example, alcoholics can appear clinically anxious or depressed, yet their symptoms abate once alcohol use is discontinued for 3–4 weeks (Brown, Inaba, et al., 1995; Brown, Irwin, & Schuckit, 1991; Brown & Schuckit, 1988).

Involvement in substance use places teens at risk for a variety of other psychosocial difficulties.

TABLE 15.5. DSM-IV Criteria for Substance Dependence

A maladaptive pattern of substance use, leading to clinically significant impairment or distress, as manifested by three (or more) of the following, occurring at any time in the same 12-month period:

(1) tolerance,
   (a) a need for markedly increased amounts of the substance to achieve intoxication or desired effect
   (b) markedly diminished effect with continued use of the same amount of the substance

(2) withdrawal,
   (a) the characteristic withdrawal syndrome for the substance . . .
   (b) the same (or a closely related) substance is taken to relieve or avoid withdrawal symptoms

(3) the substance is often taken in larger amounts or over a longer period than was intended

(4) there is a persistent desire or unsuccessful efforts to cut down or control substance use

(5) a great deal of time is spent in activities necessary to obtain the substance (e.g., visiting multiple doctors or driving long distances), use the substance (e.g., chain-smoking), or recover from its effects

(6) important social, occupational, or recreational activities are given up or reduced because of substance use

(7) the substance use is continued despite knowledge of having a persistent or recurrent physical or psychological problem that is likely to have been caused or exacerbated by the substance (e.g., current cocaine use despite recognition of cocaine-induced depression, or continued drinking despite recognition that an ulcer was made worse by alcohol consumption)

Specify if:

   With Physiological Dependence: evidence of tolerance or withdrawal (i.e., either Item 1 or 2 is present)
   Without Physiological Dependence: no evidence of tolerance or withdrawal (i.e., neither Item 1 or 2 is present).

Course specifiers . . . :

   Early Full Remission
   Early Partial Remission
   Sustained Full Remission
   Sustained Partial Remission
   On Agonist Therapy
   In a Controlled Environment

Note. From American Psychiatric Association (1994, p. 181). Copyright 1994 by the American Psychiatric Association. Reprinted by permission.

Behavioral and emotional changes observed among substance-using adolescents can reflect either consequences of substance involvement or symptoms of a co-occurring disorder. As many as three out of four teens with substance use disorders appear to meet criteria for an additional DSM-IV Axis I diagnosis (Bukstein, Brent, & Kaminer, 1989). Common symptoms displayed by teens who misuse alcohol or other drugs include conduct, attentional, and affective problems (Brown, Mott, & Myers, 1990; Tarter, Alterman, & Edwards, 1985), as well as cognitive and academic difficulties (Bennett, Wolin, & Reiss, 1988; Knop, Teasdale, Schulsinger, & Goodwin, 1985).

Conduct disturbance in childhood and early adolescence is consistently associated with risk for later substance use problems during adolescence (Boyle & Offord, 1991; Boyle et al., 1992, 1993; Fergusson, Lynskey, & Horwood, 1993; Windle, 1990). Longitudinal data support the contribution of conduct problems to the etiology of substance involvement (Zucker & Gomberg, 1986), even when prior substance involvement is controlled for (e.g., Windle, 1990). As with all psychiatric symptoms occurring among substance users, the causal relationship between conduct disturbance and substance use in adolescence is bidirectional and reciprocal.

In a study of Conduct Disorder among 166 adolescents in treatment for substance use problems (mean age = 16), Brown, Gleghorn, Schuckit, Myers, and Mott (1996) found that nearly every

TABLE 15.6. Withdrawal Symptoms by Substance

Symptom	Alcohol	Nicotine	Cocaine and amphetamines	Opioids	Sedatives and anxiolytics
Anxiety	X	X			X
Appetite increase		X	X		
Autonomic hyperactivity	X				X
Concentration difficulty		X			
Diarrhea				X	
Dreams (unpleasant/vivid)			X		
Dysphoria/depressed mood		X		X	
Fatigue			X		
Fever				X	
Hallucinations (transitory visual, tactile, auditory)	X				X
Hand tremor	X				X
Heart rate decrease		X			
Hypersomnia			X		
Insomnia	X	X	X	X	X
Irritability		X			
Lacrimation/rhinorrhea				X	
Muscle ache				X	
Nausea/vomiting				X	X
Psychomotor agitation	X		X		X
Psychomotor retardation			X		
Pupilary dilation				X	
Restlessness		X			
Seizure, grand mal	X				X
Weight gain		X			

Note. The data are from American Psychiatric Association (1994).

teen (95%) presenting for treatment appeared to meet the criteria for a Conduct Disorder diagnosis. When these investigators considered only behaviors that occurred in the absence of alcohol and drug intoxication and withdrawal, only half (47%) of the teens continued to meet criteria for an independent diagnosis of Conduct Disorder. Furthermore, engaging in cruel and hostile behaviors (e.g., physical cruelty to people and animals, initiating physical fights, deliberate fire setting, destruction of others' property, and forced sex) differentiated teens with substance-use-independent Conduct Disorder from those whose problematic behavior was a consequence of their substance involvement.

A follow-up of the substance-misusing adolescents studied by Brown, Gleghorn, et al. (1996) revealed that 45% of teens with an independent Conduct Disorder diagnosis progressed to Antisocial Personality Disorder as young adults 4 years later (D. G. Stewart & Brown, 1994). None of the teens whose conduct problems were solely related to their substance use met criteria for Antisocial Personality Disorder in early adulthood. Teens who progressed to a diagnosis of Antisocial Personality Disorder were typically male (74%), had an earlier age of onset for their conduct problems, engaged in more conduct-disordered behavior independent of substance use, and evidenced a more rapid progression from regular drug use to problematic drug use than individuals who did not progress to Antisocial Personality Disorder. Furthermore, the individuals diagnosed with Antisocial Personality Disorder experienced poorer outcomes in regard to substance use, employment, and interpersonal relationships.

In summary, although most substance-misusing teens presenting for treatment exhibit conduct problems, probably only half qualify for an independent Conduct Disorder diagnosis. Of those with independent Conduct Disorder, only half progress to adult Antisocial Personality Disorder. Finally, those with Antisocial Personality Disorder increase their substance involvement and evidence poorer psychosocial functioning 4 years after treatment.

For a time, children with attention deficits were believed to be at greater risk for substance involve-

TABLE 15.7. DSM-IV Criteria for Substance Abuse

A. A maladaptive pattern of substance use leading to clinically significant impairment or distress, as manifested by one (or more) of the following, occurring within a 12-month period:
  (1) recurrent substance use resulting in a failure to fulfill major role obligations at work, school, or home (e.g., repeated absences or poor work performance related to substance use; substance-related absences, suspensions, or expulsions from school; neglect of children of household)
  (2) recurrent substance use in situations in which it is physically hazardous (e.g., driving an automobile or operating a machine when impaired by substance use)
  (3) recurrent substance-related legal problems (e.g., arrests for substance-related disorderly conduct)
  (4) continued substance use despite having persistent or recurrent social or interpersonal problems caused or exacerbated by the effects of the substance (e.g., arguments with spouse about consequences of intoxication, physical fights)

B. The symptoms have never met the criteria for Substance Dependence for this class of substance.

Note. From American Psychiatric Association (1994, pp. 182–183). Copyright 1994 by the American Psychiatric Association. Reprinted by permission.

ment during adolescence (Crowley & Riggs, 1995). For example, Tarter et al. (1985) noted that the difficulty in modulating arousal that is commonly seen in hyperactive children resembled the temperamental characteristics of prealcoholics and persons at high risk for alcoholism, and suggested that these features may share a common underlying neurological mechanism. Recent evidence, however, has demonstrated that any risk for teen substance involvement associated with attentional deficits is best accounted for by the presence of conduct disturbances and aggressive behaviors (Fergusson et al., 1993; Halikas, Meller, Morse, & Lyttle, 1990; Lynskey & Fergusson, 1995). Other findings (Barkley, Fisher, Edelbrock, & Smallish, 1990; Mannuzza et al., 1991) suggest that hyperactivity and conduct problems together may produce the greatest risk for substance use (Crowley & Riggs, 1995).

Negative affect is implicated in a number of theoretical conceptualizations of the etiology of adolescent substance use. It is clear that the use of psychoactive substances can produce dysphoria

(e.g., Brown & Schuckit, 1988; Overall, Reilly, Kelley, & Hollister, 1985), and there is empirical evidence that mood symptoms covary with substance use among adolescents (King, Naylor, Hill, Shain, & Green, 1993; van Hasselt, Null, Kempton, & Bukstein, 1993). Co-occurrence of depressed mood and substance involvement increases the risk for suicidal ideation and attempts among both nonclinical adolescents (Levy & Deykin, 1989) and psychiatric inpatient adolescents (King, Hill, Naylor, Evans, & Shain, 1993; Pfeffer, Newcorn, Kaplan, Mizruchi, & Plutchik, 1988). Thus, teens who misuse substances and evidence negative affect are at risk for suicidal ideation and attempts, and therefore must be identified and monitored carefully.

Cognitive and academic functioning has been studied among adolescents according to their own and their parents' substance use history. Teens who misuse alcohol and drugs have demonstrated mildly lower levels of intellectual and neuropsychological functioning than nonmisusing teens (Moss, Kirisci, Gordon, & Tarter, 1994; Tarter, Mezzich, Hsieh, & Parks, 1995). Although associations between substance misuse and neuropsychological functioning are typically weak and inconsistent, some evidence suggests that adolescents who experience a greater number of alcohol and drug withdrawal symptoms perform more poorly on visual–perceptual, memory, and executive/inhibitory tasks than substance-misusing teens who experience fewer withdrawal symptoms (Tapert & Brown, 1994). This finding suggests that among young alcohol and drug users, neurotoxic effects of substance use that are sufficient to provoke severe withdrawal can have a negative impact on cognitive functioning. Interventions and educational efforts during and immediately following substance withdrawal may therefore have a limited impact because of impaired capacity for cognitive processing.

Substance-misusing teens have demonstrated poorer academic achievement than nonmisusing adolescents (Braggio, Pishkin, Gameros, & Brooks, 1993; Chassin, Mann, & Sher, 1988; Moss et al., 1994). These effects, however, tend to be modest in size. In addition, cognitive and academic difficulties have been found among teens reared by an alcoholic parent (Ervin, Little, Streissguth, & Beck, 1984; Knop et al., 1985; Marcus, 1986; Tarter, Hegedus, Goldstein, Shelly, & Alterman, 1984). Although these studies are limited by their correlational design, the results provoke speculation that the family environments of alcoholic parents may lack stimulation to facilitate academic involvement and achievement. Estimates, however, are that more than half (61%) of teens admitted for inpatient substance use treatment do not attend school prior to treatment. Consequently, the most severely substance-misusing adolescents are not typically represented in school-based studies of substance use and academic achievement. Thus, modest associations between substance use and academic difficulties are likely to underestimate the true effects of substance use on school functioning.

Developmental Issues

Adolescence is a period of rapid biological, social, and cognitive changes (Lerner & Foch, 1987). Hormonal changes provoke physical growth, development of secondary sex characteristics, and fluctuations in emotions. Teens increasingly differentiate themselves from their families, and consequently begin developing independent identities. As part of adolescent individuation and differentiation, peers and peer group affiliations become focal aspects of a teen's identity (Kegan, 1982; Lerner & Foch, 1987). Although abstract reasoning begins to emerge, young adolescents are vulnerable to egocentric thought characteristics (e.g., sense of uniqueness, invulnerability, and central importance to others), which limit their cognitive capacity to reason and to cope with novel situations (Elkind, 1967; Lerner, 1987). All of these changes produce stress for an adolescent and challenge resources for successful adaptation.

As children progress through early adolescence into later adolescence and young adulthood, they experience family, social, and school transitions during which they may be especially vulnerable to initiate or escalate substance use (Petersen, 1987). As a consequence of biological changes, the stress associated with normal adolescent development, and rudimentary or poorly developed social and cognitive resources for coping, teens are vulnerable to affective disturbance and mood swings. Teens exposed to these normative stresses and novel social experiences possess few intrapersonal and interpersonal resources for dealing with these situations. Availability of substances, modeling of use, and preexisting expectations of social skills enhancement or tension-reducing effects from substance use increase the likelihood of a teen's turning to alcohol or drugs in response to stress and challenging new situations.

Given the rapid physical, cognitive, and emotional maturation occurring during adolescence, alcohol and/or drug involvement has tremendous potential to interfere with normal development, and consequently to delay or even prevent the acquisition of cognitive and social skills necessary for successful functioning. Newcomb and Bentler (1988) described the consequences in young adulthood of alcohol and drug use during adolescence. They reported that adolescent alcohol use was related to decreased social conformity, religious commitment, and college involvement, but also to increased perceived social support in young adulthood. Hard drug use during adolescence was related to earlier family formation, elevated family problems, an increased incidence of deviant behavior, less education, earlier entry into the work force, and decreased job stability in young adulthood. From these data, Newcomb and Bentler concluded that alcohol and other drug use diverts teens from accomplishing critical developmental tasks that promote adequate adjustment in young adulthood.

Risk and Protective Factors

The progression of adolescent substance use includes several transitions in consumption patterns. Alcohol and drug involvement progresses from initiation and experimentation to regular use, which then can escalate to Substance Abuse and Dependence (Brown, 1993a). Biological, psychological, and environmental factors contribute differentially to substance use at each progressive phase of involvement. Environmental (e.g., drug availability, drug cost, models of substance misuse) and personal characteristics (e.g., family history, anticipated drug effects) are the primary influences of initial use. Once drug use has begun, the pharmacological properties of substances (e.g., whether they are central nervous system [CNS] depressants or CNS stimulants) contribute to escalated involvement. Subjective experience, pharmacological and anticipated effects, and circumstances of use will combine to determine how often and how much a teen will use. In this section, we review the impact of biological risks, individual or psychological factors, and environmental contexts on adolescent use of alcohol and other drugs.

Biological Risks

It is apparent that biological factors contribute to the development of problematic substance use. After reviewing behavioral genetic research, McGue (1994) concluded that (1) genetic factors exert a moderate influence on male risk for alcoholism, yet only a modest influence among females; (2) common genetic influences can explain, in part, interrelations among a variety of undercontrolled behaviors, including substance misuse; and (3) environmental factors play a significant role in the development of alcoholism, but environmental influence is not necessarily linked to rearing by an alcoholic adult.

Offspring of alcoholics (referred to here as "family-history-positive," or FHP) have been hypothesized to be less sensitive to the physiological and subjective effects of alcohol than individuals with no family history of alcoholism ("family-history-negative," or FHN) (Newlin, 1994; Schuckit, 1984). As a consequence of this "sensitivity" difference, FHP individuals may require larger amounts of alcohol than FHN persons to achieve similar desired effects. Inconsistent empirical data, however, have led Newlin and Thompson (1991) to modify the sensitivity hypothesis. In their "differentiator" model, FHPs are believed to experience exaggerated responses to alcohol during early acute intoxication, when rising blood alcohol levels are associated with positive affect, and diminished responses during later intoxication, when declining blood alcohol levels are associated with negative affect. Enhanced positive affect during drinking, and minimal negative effects from alcohol withdrawal, may function in an instrumental manner to increase alcohol use behavior. In this manner, biological responsivity may contribute to differential alcohol use patterns.

Individual Psychological Factors

A number of personal characteristics have been proposed to explain adolescent substance involvement. Here, we review several psychological variables that have been empirically linked to alcohol and drug use among adolescents.

Expectancies

Alcohol and drug effect expectancies reflect an individual's anticipation of reinforcing effects and consequences from ingestion of various substances (Brown, 1993b). Beliefs about the reinforcement properties of alcohol and drugs are learned via direct and vicarious experiences, including family, peer, and media exposure (Tapert, Stewart, & Brown, in press). Alcohol and drug outcome expectancies are related to the initiation of substance use among adolescents (Brown, 1993b; Mann, Chassin, & Sher, 1987; Sher, 1991; Smith, Goldman, Greenbaum, & Christiansen, 1995) and to relapse drinking among adults (Brown, 1985;

Conners, O'Farrell, & Pelcovits, 1988) and adolescents (Vik, Mott, & Brown, 1996).

Expectancies have been hypothesized to mediate between distal risk factors (e.g., family history) and substance use decisions (Goldman & Rather, 1993; Sher, 1994). Brown (1993b) proposed that children of alcoholics who maintain high reinforcement expectancies may be more vulnerable to early alcohol involvement. Smith et al. (1995) noted that expectancies of increased social facilitation from drinking are particularly effective at predicting future alcohol use among adolescents.

Personality

Both Windle (1990) and Sher (1994) have noted that personality factors may indirectly as well as directly influence teen substance use. Sher has suggested that a family history of alcoholism may provoke character differences that increase the risk of adolescent substance use involvement. Alternatively, personality factors and substance involvement may represent co-occurring manifestations of a common underlying construct of problem behavior (e.g., Donovan & Jessor, 1985). Considerable effort and controversy have surrounded attempts to describe how personality variables contribute to alcohol and drug misuse (Sher, 1994). Efforts to identify premorbid personality characteristics that increase risk for pathological alcohol and drug involvement are confounded by simple models of direct effects, reliance on cross-sectional research designs, and inconsistent definitions and measures of personality variables (Sher, 1994; Windle, 1990).

Undercontrolled behavior represents one domain of personal characteristics that have regularly been associated with alcohol and other drug use (Sher, 1991; Zucker & Gomberg, 1986). Researchers have repeatedly found greater impulsivity, anger, and aggression among FHP than among FHN teens (Forgays, Forgays, Wrzesniewski, & Bonaiuto, 1992; Labouvie & McGee, 1986; Mann et al., 1987; Tomori, 1994). A commonly identified subgroup of alcoholics (typically males), characterized by antisocial behavior, paternal alcoholism, and an early onset of alcohol involvement (Cloninger, 1987), may account for the comorbid Conduct Disorder (Crowley & Riggs, 1995) and Antisocial Personality Disorder observed among some alcoholics. Windle (1990) has cautioned, however, that "undercontrolled behavior" has become an umbrella term encompassing a wide variety of behaviors. A range of behaviors labeled as "undercontrolled" may be poorly correlated and defined, and thus may result in conflicting or inconsistent research findings. Windle has therefore advocated explicit definition of specific under-controlled behaviors associated with teen substance use.

Psychopathology

Externalizing and internalizing problems are among the most consistently agreed-upon classifications of child psychopathology (Cicchetti & Toth, 1991). Externalizing problems are characterized by undercontrolled behavior and are common among male offspring of alcoholics (Sher, Walitzer, Wood, & Brent, 1991). Undercontrolled behavior may reflect a pervasive characterological style (as noted above), or a more severe disorder warranting an independent diagnosis (e.g., Oppositional Defiant Disorder, Conduct Disorder). In either case, externalizing disorders appear to elevate lifetime risk for Substance Dependence (Vaillant, 1983), particularly during adolescence (Donovan, Jessor, & Jessor, 1983). Internalizing problems, such as anxiety, depression, social withdrawal, and somatic complaints, have been observed among children of alcoholics (Chassin, Rogosch, & Barrera, 1991; West & Prinz, 1987) and may be related to the later development of pathological substance involvement (Chassin, Pillow, Curran, Molina, & Barrera, 1993; Sher, 1994).

Self-Efficacy

"Alcohol-specific self-efficacy" is the perceived ability to resist temptations or urges to drink in a high-risk situation. Alcohol-specific self-efficacy has been hypothesized as a major influence in the progression and remission of alcohol problems (Annis & Davis, 1988; Marlatt, 1985). Recent evidence demonstrates that eighth- and ninth-graders distinguish their capacity to resist alcohol in different social situations by reporting lowered self-efficacy in situations involving high pressure to drink (Abrams & Niaura, 1987). Furthermore, adolescents with a family history of alcoholism exhibited lower self-efficacy than teens without a family history of alcoholism (Hays & Ellickson, 1990). Thus, there is theoretical justification and empirical support for the role of self-efficacy in the development of substance use problems.

Self-Esteem

Evidence is mixed regarding the association between global self-esteem and substance use. Among school-based samples, self-esteem shows a modest inverse relationship with current substance use (Dielman, Leech, Lorenger, & Horvath, 1984; Pandina & Schuele, 1983) and future intentions to use drugs and alcohol (Dielman et al., 1984). Similarly, teens in treatment displayed lower self-esteem than the general adolescent population (Ahlgren & Norem-Hebeisen, 1979; Svobodny, 1982), and self-esteem had a modest prospective negative relationship with posttreatment drinking and life problems (Richter, Brown, & Mott, 1991). Thompson (1989), however, found that drinking alcohol increased the self-esteem of students who viewed drinking as sophisticated and worldly prior to alcohol involvement, and Chassin, Tetzloff, and Hersey (1985) found that a positive social image of drinking preceded alcohol use among boys. Finally, Callan and Jackson (1986) found no differences in self-esteem between high-risk (FHP) and low-risk (FHN) children. These findings suggest that self-esteem does not play a simple direct role in adolescent substance use, but that it may combine with other factors (e.g, social image) to influence alcohol use.

Contexts of Use

Teens use drugs in a variety of contexts. Parents' alcohol use, and older siblings' alcohol and drug involvement, increase substance availability and exposure to modeling of use. Peers represent an important socializing factor in teens' lives, and socializing with peers presents a context in which substance use experimentation often occurs. Here, we describe family and peer influences on adolescent substance use.

Family

Problem drinking among parents negatively affects the cohesion and level of affective expression among family members; it also reduces efforts to foster independence, achievement orientation, and participation in intellectual, cultural, and recreational activities among children (Moos & Billings, 1982). A considerable body of research has documented the increased risk of substance misuse, emotional difficulties, and other problem behaviors among children for whom one or both parents have alcohol or drug problems (Bennett et al., 1988; Chassin et al., 1991; Knop et al., 1985; Moos & Billings, 1982; Russell, 1990). Male offspring of an alcoholic parent are estimated to be four to six times more likely than sons of non-alcoholics to develop a substance use problem. Female children of alcoholics are approximately twice as likely as female offspring of nonalcoholics to develop problems with alcohol. Despite this increased risk among children of alcoholics, there is considerable heterogeneity in offspring substance use (McGue, 1994), and children of alcoholics are still more likely not to have a substance use problem than to have one.

Empirical studies have found that children who are raised with an alcohol-misusing parent exhibit poorer emotional, behavioral, and cognitive functioning than offspring of nonalcoholics. Offspring of alcoholics evidence more academic difficulties than children from nonalcoholic households, including lower scores on standardized achievement tests (Bennett et al., 1988; Marcus, 1986), repeating of grades, and referrals to the principal (Knop et al., 1985). Children of alcoholics exhibit more impulsive behaviors and conduct problems (Bennett et al., 1988; Knop et al., 1985), greater temperamental deviations (Tarter et al., 1985), greater self-deprecation (Berkowitz & Perkins, 1988), poorer self-concept (Bennett et al., 1988), and more depression, anxiety, and nightmares (Moos & Billings, 1982) than children of nonalcoholics. Finally, these families display more negative parent–child interactions and poorer problem solving than families without an alcoholic parent (Jacobs & Leonard, 1991).

Parental alcoholism may directly increase the risk for adolescent substance involvement via biological sensitivity to the pharmacological properties of drugs, modeling influences, and increased availability of alcohol and/or other substances (Sher, 1994). McGue (1994) has proposed a diathesis–stress model in which biological and environmental factors combine to determine substance use. According to this model, environmental factors influence substance involvement among individuals with moderate genetic loading, but have little to no impact on individuals with either strong or minimal genetic loading. Genetic factors may also have an indirect impact on use by influencing other risk factors, such as temperament or negative affect. For example, genetic factors may account for temperamental impulsivity. Impulsive individuals, in turn, may be more likely than nonimpulsive teens to use substances without regard for potential negative consequences. Similarly, people with a genetic propensity for negative affect may learn to use substances to soothe themselves and reduce tension.

A more complex genetic model postulates that individuals will seek environments consistent with their genotypes (Scarr & McCartney, 1983). Teens with a temperamental propensity for undercon-

trolled behavior are likely to prefer the company of similarly behaving peers (Bates & Labouvie, 1994). Within this social context, risk of substance use increases due to the greater availability of, experimentation with, and use of alcohol and drugs among impulsive, undercontrolled teens. Evidence suggests that peer relations do in fact mediate the relationship between family history and adolescent substance use (e.g., Chassin et al., 1993; Sher, 1994).

Family history extends beyond genetic transmission to include environmental influences (Cooper, Pierce, & Tidwell, 1995; McGue, 1994; Sher, 1994). Children from alcoholic and/or drug-using families often witness drinking behavior by adults and older siblings, and have ready access to substances (Barnes, 1990; Brown, Mott, & Stewart, 1992; Kandel, 1983). Other aspects of family environment may account for the considerable variability in substance use among children of alcoholics. For example, alcoholic parents appear to monitor their children's behavior less consistently than do nonalcoholic parents, and these unmonitored teens exhibit a greater risk than monitored teens for drug and alcohol involvement (Bates & Labouvie, 1995; Chassin et al., 1993; Dishion & Loeber, 1985). The quality of the relationship between a parent and a child has been linked to adolescent substance use (Hundleby & Mercer, 1987; Kandel, 1978; Needle, Glynn, & Needle, 1983). In particular, teen drinking increases when parent–adolescent conflict is high (Brody & Forehand, 1993). Supportive female caregivers appear to buffer the adverse effects of paternal drinking on their children's alcohol use (Cooper et al., 1995); however, the risk of adolescent drinking is increased among teens reporting a supportive relationship with an alcoholic mother (Cooper et al., 1995). Finally, sibling influences (Barnes, 1990) and family stress (Baer, Garmezy, McLaughlin, Pokorny, & Wernick, 1987) have been linked to elevated adolescent alcohol and drug use.

Peers

As friendships become increasingly important in a child's life (Compas & Wagner, 1991), peers exert a greater influence on the adolescent's identity and socialization process (Kegan, 1982). During early adolescence, social interaction skills with both same-sex and opposite-sex peers are less refined, and there is pressure to conform and be included in social groups. Peer relations play a significant role in the initiation and escalation of adolescent substance use (Bates & Labouvie, 1995; Newcomb & Bentler, 1988; Wagner, 1993), as well as relapse following treatment for adolescent substance misuse (Brown, Mott, & Myers, 1990; Brown, Vik, & Creamer, 1989). As noted previously, peer influences are likely to combine with family factors to determine adolescent substance use (Barnes, 1990). Adolescent problem behavior has been found to increase among teens who are highly invested in friendships with peers who engage in drinking and deviant behavior (Barnes, Farrell, & Banerjee, 1994). We found in our junior high school data that young adolescents who had tried alcohol identified over six times as many close, trusted friends who drank as teens who had not initiated alcohol use reported (Vik & Brown, 1993). Furthermore, the number of close friends who drank increased as the adolescents' frequency of drinking increased.

Social networks may influence both the onset and progression of substance involvement by increasing access to substances, generating stress, and modeling or reinforcing maladaptive coping efforts (Richter et al., 1991). Strained interactions with peers may provoke social anxiety, social pressure to drink, and interpersonal conflict (e.g., Hundleby & Mercer, 1987). For some teens, substance use may provide temporary relief from social stress, or decrease social tension by providing a common behavioral activity. Among adolescents who view substance use as a sign of maturity, alcohol use may enhance self-esteem and improve peer relations in later adolescence, and consequently may facilitate group membership (Thompson, 1989).

Alternative Pathways to Substance Misuse

Biological, psychological, and environmental factors independently account for limited variability in substance use. Conceptual models that incorporate biological, individual, and environmental factors, however, can enhance efforts to explain the etiology, escalation, and maintenance of adolescent alcohol and drug involvement. Recently, Sher (1994) has proposed alternative processes in which mediational chains and moderating factors function as risk mechanisms and protective–vulnerability influences for adolescent substance use. Understanding these alternative processes can enhance a clinical assessment by clarifying the relationship between personal risk and protective influences at an individual level. Conceptual models allow a clinician to utilize an individual's

personal strengths and target specific vulnerabilities to change when developing a comprehensive treatment plan.

Mediational Chains

In a simple mediation model, the association between two variables is explained by the presence of a third variable (the mediator). In complex models, chains of multiple mediational variables explain the relationship between family history risk and pathological substance involvement. Sher (1994) has proposed three prototypic (but not mutually exclusive) pathways to pathological alcohol involvement. In each pathway, important variables are postulated as either proximal or distal mediators of teen alcohol involvement. Similar pathways may account for use of other drugs, as well as alcohol. We review these alternative pathways and the supporting empirical data.

Negative Affect Pathway

Sher (1994) has proposed negative affect as a proximal mechanism linking familial risk to substance use (see Figure 15.1). Family risk is linked to negative affect via two alternative distal mediators: offspring stress and temperament. Chassin and her colleagues (Chassin et al., 1993; Colder & Chassin, 1993) found that a family history of alcoholism increased child stress and temperamental emotionality. Stress and temperament, in turn, resulted in elevated negative affect among adolescents. Negative affect had a mild direct association with teen substance use, but was further mediated by the child's involvement with substance-using peers. In summary, Chassin et al. described a negative affect pathway to teen substance use, demonstrated that this path is accounted for in part by peer use, and identified two mechanisms (stress and emotional temperament) contributing to this pathway.

Roosa, Sandler, Gehring, Beals, and Cappo (1988) found that positive and negative life events predicted depression and anxiety among a nonclinical sample of older (high school) adolescents. Others have shown that negative affect mediates the relationship between stress and substance use among adolescents (Colder & Chassin, 1993), and that involvement with peers who use substances and encourage others to try them explains, in part, the relationship between emotional distress (poor self-esteem, blame/alienation, and anxiety) and adolescent drug involvement (Swaim, Oetting, Edwards, & Beauvais, 1989). These studies pro-

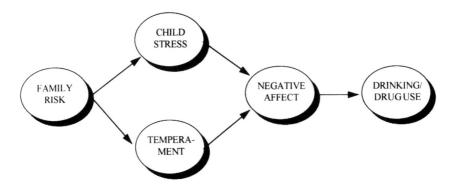

FIGURE 15.1. The negative affect pathway to adolescent substance use.

vide empirical support for a negative affect pathway that includes peer influence as a key mediator between affect and pathological substance involvement. In summary, familial alcoholism increases risk of negative affect in offspring via stress and emotional temperament. Elevated negative affect, in turn, influences teen substance use both directly and indirectly via involvement with substance-using friends.

Deviance Proneness

In the deviance proneness model, Sher (1994) has proposed that deficient parenting increases risk for subsequent temperamental problems, cognitive deficits, and school difficulty and failure (see Figure 15.2). These factors lead teens to associate with substance-using companions. Peer relationships, as noted above, are a proximal determinant of teen alcohol involvement. Dishion and Loeber (1985) found that parental monitoring indirectly influenced teen substance use by predicting friendships with deviant peers. Findings by Chassin et al.

(1993), however, were mixed. The father's monitoring, and, to a lesser extent, the mother's monitoring of a child's behavior mediated between alcoholism in the biological mother and peer group association. In contrast, parental monitoring did not explain the relationship between paternal alcoholism and peer group involvement. This study did not find support for child temperament as a mediator between parental alcoholism and involvement with substance-using peers.

Enhanced Reinforcement

In a third possible pathway to teen substance use, biological variability in alcohol and drug sensitivity produces different reinforcement expectancies from using substances (see Figure 15.3). Sensitivity to the pharmacological effects of alcohol and other drugs, and outcome expectancies associated with alcohol and drug use, mediate between family history and teen substance use (Sher, 1994). Research has demonstrated that the offspring of alcoholics display greater sensitivity to alcohol

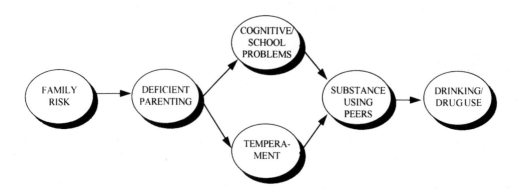

FIGURE 15.2. The deviance proneness model for adolescent substance use.

during early intoxication and endorse stronger belief in the reinforcement properties of alcohol than do children of nonalcoholics (Brown, Creamer, & Stetson, 1987; Mann et al., 1987).

Risk Moderators

Mediational chains posit additional variables as causal mechanisms to explain how a risk factor affects outcome. Additional factors can also moderate associations between risks and outcome by demonstrating that associations have different strengths and/or directions at varying levels of the moderating third variable (Baron & Kenny, 1986; Judd & McClelland, 1989). Moderating variables represent either protective factors that attenuate the impact of a risk mechanism, or vulnerability factors that magnify the effect of a risk (Rogosch, Chassin, & Sher, 1990). Here, we review the moderating influences of self-awareness, social support, and stress and coping.

Self-Awareness

Hull (1987) has proposed that individuals drink alcohol to attenuate painful negative feelings if they are high in dispositional self-awareness (i.e., aware of their negative feelings). Chassin and her colleagues found that family history was unrelated to teen alcohol consumption among adolescents who were self-reflective and introspective (Chassin et al., 1988; Rogosch et al., 1990); however, among less self-aware teens, those with a family history of alcoholism drank more and experienced more alcohol-related negative life consequences than those without a family history risk. These authors suggested that, rather than increasing risk, self-awareness may serve a protective function by allowing teens with alcoholic parents to recognize

potential consequences of alcohol use and therefore minimize their involvement with drinking.

Social Support

Social support is typically conceptualized as a buffer to stress (e.g., Rook & Dooley, 1985) and an aid to coping (Thoits, 1986). Peer relations, however, are among the most consistent and powerful influences of initial substance use (Newcomb & Bentler, 1988), as well as of teen relapse following treatment (Brown et al., 1989; Brown, Mott, & Myers, 1990). Consequently, social support may attenuate risk for substance involvement by providing models for alternative coping efforts, or it may potentiate risks by providing models of substance use for coping, increasing the availability of substances, and generating pressure to use (Vik et al., 1996).

Data collected from teens in treatment for substance use problems highlight the importance of qualitative assessment of social resource networks. Teens who remained abstinent up to 1 year after treatment reported a greater proportion of nonusing supports than did teens who returned to heavy drug use (Richter et al., 1991). Furthermore, teens who perceived themselves as less similar to substance-using supports were unlikely to use alcohol or drugs early following treatment, whereas two-thirds of the teens who felt they were similar to their substance-using supports relapsed early following treatment (Vik, Grizzle, & Brown, 1992). Appraisal of similarity may also underlie teen willingness to engage in abstinence focused activities such as Alcoholics Anonymous (Brown, 1993a).

In summary, teens who remain invested in a substance-using peer group following treatment for substance misuse may find few instrumental and

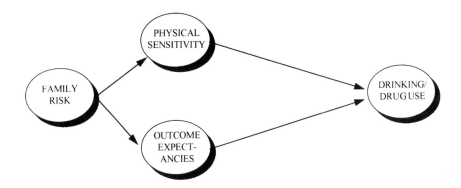

FIGURE 15.3. A biological–cognitive model for adolescent substance use.

emotional support resources for dealing with difficult situations. Given the importance of peer affiliation during this developmental period, it is important for the clinician to assess the quality of social relations and to focus treatment efforts on modifying poor-quality social networks.

Stress and Coping

As noted previously, stress serves a distal causal role in mediational models of adolescent substance involvement. The experience and understanding of stress vary with age and development. Adolescence is a period of rapid growth and maturation, and as such it provokes greater normative stress. At the same time, adolescents may experience events that are common, yet not universal to all adolescents (e.g., parents' divorce, interparental conflict, school changes, family moves); moreover, some teens experience severe uncommon events (e.g., severe illnesses, death of a family member). Appraisal of stressful events is important in most conceptualizations of stress and coping (e.g., Lazarus & Folkman, 1984) and is influenced by cognitive-developmental factors (Burnside, Baer, McLaughlin, & Pokorny, 1986). Developmental changes during adolescence can limit the availability and utilization of effective social and cognitive coping resources. Thus, adolescents can face a wide variety of normative and non-normative stresses during a period when coping appraisal skills and resources are not fully developed.

Stress and coping studies among adults with alcohol and drug problems (e.g., Brown, Vik, et al., 1990; Brown, Vik, Patterson, Grant, & Schuckit, 1995; Cooper, Russell, Skinner, Frone, & Mudar, 1992; Litman, Eiser, Rawson, & Oppenheim, 1979) have supported the moderating or buffering effect of coping on relationships between stress and substance use. Less attention, however, has been given to adolescent coping. Sher (1994) has hypothesized that coping should serve a protective function at two points along the pathway into adolescent substance use: between life stress and emotional distress, and between emotional distress and substance use. In support of this possibility, Wills (1986) reported that alcohol and tobacco use was more common among severely stressed teens possessing few cognitive and behavioral coping skills than among severely stressed teens with adequate coping skills. Wagner (1993) also found that stress, impulsivity, and emotion-focused, relief-oriented coping predicted adolescent substance use. In a series of coping studies using clinical samples of alcohol- and drug-

misusing teens, Myers and Brown (1990; Myers, Brown, & Mott, 1993) found that teens who later returned to substance use were less likely to appraise a high-risk relapse situation as threatening, and identified fewer problem-focused and more wishful-thinking coping skills than teens who subsequently maintained abstinence. Thus, available evidence demonstrates that both cognitive appraisal and coping efforts are associated with adolescent substance involvement.

Pathways Out of Misuse

Just as alternative pathways lead to substance involvement and misuse, youth appear to follow different paths away from substance misuse. Changes in substance involvement can result from treatment, self-help efforts, and natural recovery (Sobell, Cunningham, Sobell, & Toneatto, 1993). Although such diversity in remission has been the focus of much adult research, only recently has it become evident that teens resolve alcohol and drug problems in diverse fashions also. For example, according to a recent study of high-risk teens aged 12–15, over half developed substance use problems following entry into the study, and one-third (34%) of those teens who developed problems resolved their substance use difficulties without specific intervention (Stewart, Vik, Whitteker, & Brown, 1994). Recently, Sobell et al. (1993) explored the factors distinguishing adults who resolved their drinking problems without treatment from a control group of nonresolved problem drinkers who had not sought treatment. Resolved drinkers typically began drinking at an older age, drank more severely, and experienced more consequences of their drinking than did the nonresolved drinkers. Younger individuals (aged 20–35) who stopped using alcohol without treatment drank less prior to changing their use than those who continued drinking. Unfortunately, studies of natural recovery have yet to examine factors that lead adolescents to reduce their substance use.

Brown (1993a) described alternative paths away from substance involvement among a clinical sample of adolescent substance misusers. Involvement in alcohol- or drug-focused self-help groups (e.g., Alcoholics Anonymous, Cocaine Anonymous, Narcotics Anonymous) was the most common precursor of improved substance use outcome among adolescents. Brown, however, identified two alternative avenues to posttreatment success among teens with minimal self-help group participation. In one path, teens utilized family strengths to master lifestyle changes. These teens were typically younger, came from families with little substance use other than alcohol consumption, and reported little exposure to substance use among their closest friends. A second group of teens sustained abstinence with minimal self-help group involvement through participation in structured activities at school or work and recreational opportunities. These teens had parents who misused alcohol and drugs, and they perceived their family as less supportive of their lifestyle change. Thus, in addition to traditional self-help approaches to sustained abstinence for teen substance misusers, alternative avenues to success include greater involvement with a supportive family, and detachment from a nonsupportive family.

Complete abstinence is the most common treatment goal for substance-misusing individuals. It is not clear, however, that viewing abstinence as the only acceptable or successful outcome for substance use problems is realistic or appropriate for adolescents. We have identified five long-term posttreatment patterns of substance use among adolescents who were treated for alcohol and drug problems. Nearly half of the teens (48%) improved during the initial 2 years following treatment (Brown, Myers, Mott, & Vik, 1994). Of these teens who reduced their substance use, 29% remained abstinent the entire 2 years, and 27% continued to use substances at reduced levels and without use-related problems. The remaining 44% used substances heavily during the first 6–12 months after treatment, but by 2 years these teens were either abstinent or using reduced amounts without problems. By 4 years following treatment, one in four teens (25.2%) continued to show improvements in substance use outcome (Brown & Vik, 1994); of the improved teens, 29% were abstaining, 31% using without problems, and 40% slowly improving. An important finding from these studies was that psychosocial problems were more prevalent among teens who were continuing heavy substance use at both the 2- and 4-year follow-up than among teens who had improved (Brown, 1994).

In addition to recognizing precipitants of changes in alcohol and drug use, clinicians should attend to factors that maintain reductions in substance use. Sobell et al. (1993) reported that spousal and friend support, and changes in social activities, physical health, and self-control, were instrumental in helping the youngest cohort in their study (20–35 years old) maintain reduced substance use. Other evidence (Vik et al., 1996) highlights the beneficial impact of social support

and abstinence-focused structured groups, and the deleterious effects of exposure to substance-using peers and family members, on teen substance involvement up to 4 years after treatment for Substance Dependence. These maintenance and risk factors are consistent with the increased family involvement and detachment from family pathways out of substance misuse identified by Brown (1993a).

Adolescent Posttreatment Relapse

Individual, situational, and physiological factors are believed to influence a return to alcohol and drug use among people who have received treatment for substance use problems (Brownell, Marlatt, Lichtenstein, & Wilson, 1986). Considerable attention has been paid to precursors of relapse among adults treated for substance misuse (Marlatt, 1985). Unfortunately, less attention has been given to adolescent relapse, despite important developmental differences and differences in substance use topography, such as social circumstances and locale of use (Brown, Mott, & Myers, 1990). In an effort to clarify features surrounding adolescent relapse, Brown et al. (1989) learned that initial posttreatment use for teens most often occurred in social settings where others were using and few models of abstention were present. Severe relapses (e.g., return to pretreatment levels of substance involvement; problems resulting from substance use) typically occurred within a month of leaving treatment and in the presence of older pretreatment friends, whereas less severe or time-limited relapses were delayed and occurred among same-age new friends.

Others have investigated pretreatment characteristics as predictors of treatment outcome. Teens who fared well following treatment tended to experience few pretreatment legal and substance-related problems, were female, came from broken homes, and had fathers who were not alcoholic (Holsten, 1980). Teens with limited school involvement, males who displayed truant behavior, and females with at least one alcoholic parent fared poorly following treatment (Benson, 1985). High self-esteem and the availability of social support, measured during treatment, was related to alcohol and drug use and psychosocial functioning up to 1 year after treatment (Richter et al., 1991). Given the important influence of social factors on teen relapse (Brown et al., 1989), it is not surprising that teens who seek social support from substance-misusing others display poorer outcomes than those who receive support from people who do not misuse substances (Richter et al., 1991; Vik et al., 1992).

ASSESSMENT METHODS

Assessment Process

Assessment is an evolving process in which continued collection of assessment data can foster refinement of the clinical hypotheses and treatment plan. Figure 15.4 presents a conceptual strategy for conducting an evaluation of teen substance involvement. This process can begin either by screening for teens who are possibly involved in pathological substance use, or with a focused evaluation for teens already identified as problem users. Data from the focused evaluation is used to establish initial hypotheses about use-related contingencies and the functions substance use has in a teen's life. These hypotheses influence initial treatment planning and further collection of assessment data. Additional data, collected during the course of treatment, are used to refine the initial hypotheses and subsequent treatment plan.

Comprehensive assessment of adolescent substance use problems can be an intensive and time-consuming process (Tarter, 1990). Gating strategies can facilitate this process without overwhelming either the client or the clinician. Multiple-gating strategies (e.g., Dishion & Patterson, 1993) involve administering less expensive screening measures to large groups and reserving more expensive measures only for those individuals identified as at risk. An initial screening yields general information, which identifies individuals whose use of alcohol and drugs is hazardous or problematic, and who therefore require comprehensive assessment (Winters & Stinchfield, 1995). For example, use of self-report questionnaires to assess teens' attitudes toward and involvement with alcohol and other drugs, their parents' and friends' attitudes and substance use, and domains of their life that may have been affected by their alcohol and drug use can identify those adolescents possibly engaging in problematic substance use who require further assessment. Table 15.8 summarizes the screening instruments reviewed by Winters and Stinchfield (1995) for which suitable psychometric data were available.

In many cases, alcohol and drug involvement will not be the focus of the initial evaluation. For example, a teen may see a physician for a medical checkup, a school psychologist for academic evaluation, or a counselor for career or vocational planning. During the course of these evaluations, how-

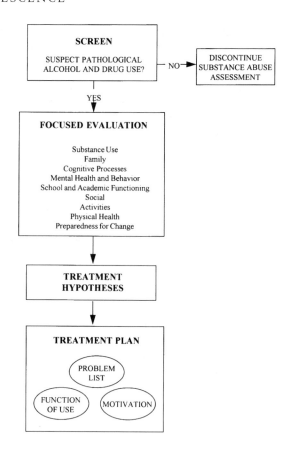

FIGURE 15.4. Conceptual strategy for assessment of adolescent substance involvement.

ever, the professional may become aware of possible substance misuse by the adolescent. The clinician should note any risk factors, such as a family history of substance problems and recent family changes and disruptions. Subtle cues—for instance, an odor of alcohol, tobacco, or marijuana; offhand comments the teen makes about friends' or peers' behaviors; recent changes in the teen's affect, sleep patterns, and academic performance; and engagement in unconventional activities (e.g., staying out late at night, skipping classes, being argumentative)—warrant further inquiry by the professional. Additional probing can clarify the nature of these cues and help a clinician determine whether a thorough evaluation is indicated.

Once evidence suggests that a teen may be misusing substances, a clinician with special training in addictive behaviors can conduct a focused evaluation to assess the extent of the substance use and its impact on psychosocial functioning. Ex-

TABLE 15.8 **Instruments to Screen for Adolescent Substance Involvement**

Instrument	Source	No. of items and type of administration	What is measured
Adolescent Alcohol Involvement Scale (AAIS)	Mayer & Filstead (1979)	14-item self-report questionnaire	Severity of alcohol use problems
Adolescent Drinking Index (ADI)	Harrell & Wirtz (1990)	24-item self-report questionnaire	Loss of control over drinking, and psychological, physical, and social symptoms
Adolescent Drug Involvement Scale (ADIS)	Moberg (1991)	12-item self-report questionnaire; modification of AAIS	Severity of drug use problems
Personal Experience Screening Questionnaire (PESQ)	Winters (1991, 1992)	40-item self-report questionnaire	Presence of substance use problems
Problem Oriented Screening Instrument for Teenagers (POSIT)	Tarter (1990)	139-item "yes–no" self-report questionnaire	Adolescent problems across 10 domains, including substance use and misuse
Rutgers Alcohol Problem Index (RAPI)	White & Labouvie (1989)	23-item self-report questionnaire	Consequences of alcohol use

tensive evaluation should provide sufficient details for developing an individual treatment plan (Donovan, 1988; Tarter, 1990; Winters & Stinchfield, 1995). The first step of the focused assessment is to establish the intended purpose of the assessment. Data from a substance use assessment can help a clinician establish a diagnosis, develop a comprehensive understanding of the client, and formulate treatment decisions (Wagner, Myers, & Brown, 1994). In addition, assessment data can provide baseline information to determine outcome effects, and feedback from an assessment can be used to enhance the teen's motivation and commitment to change addictive behavior (Miller & Rollnick, 1991; Wagner et al., 1995). The second step is to identify specific psychosocial domains affected by the teen's alcohol and drug use. Finally, the clinician must select appropriate measures to gather sufficient data to assess the severity of the problem, identify individual strengths to utilize in formulating a treatment plan, delineate the functions substance use serves for the teen, and provide objective baseline measurements from which to evaluate the efficacy of intervention efforts.

When assessing alcohol and drug use, a clinician forms, tests, and refines hypotheses regarding the contingencies and functions of substance use in the teen's life. The clinician applies his or her knowledge of the course and sequelae of substance involvement to formulate preliminary hypotheses about the antecedents and consequences of the adolescent's substance use. Once the clinician has postulated the association between behaviors and substance use, assessment procedures generate data that the clinician uses to test these hypotheses. From this information, the clinician can (1) conclude that the data are insufficient to validate the hypothesis, and thus that additional data collection is needed; (2) use the data to confirm or disconfirm the hypothesis; or (3) postulate alternative or additional hypotheses (Donovan, 1988). For example, a clinician might initially hypothesize that a teen's depressive symptoms are a consequence of frequent alcohol intoxication. During the course of the evaluation, the clinician collects data in a manner that details the temporal association between depressive symptoms and alcohol use. If the clinician determines that alcohol use has preceded the onset of depression and that the depressive symptoms remit during periods of abstinence (beyond acute withdrawal), then an independent depressive disorder can be ruled out. The clinician continues to observe the teen over time, monitoring depressive symptoms and substance use. If the refined hypothesis is correct, mood symptoms should abate with protracted abstinence (3 to 4 weeks; Brown & Schuckit, 1988), and the revised hypothesis is supported. Below, we review methods to collect assessment data, identify specific domains to evaluate, and present a means for integrating the data into a comprehensive case conceptualization.

Means of Assessment

Substance use assessment employing a clinical hypothesis-testing approach requires a considerable amount of data. Donovan (1988) and Winter and Stinchfield (1995) have advocated a broad-spectrum approach, including multiple assessment methods from a variety of sources that focus on multiple target behaviors. It is important to gather data from multiple sources via several modalities (e.g., self-report forms, toxicology screens), and not to rely on a single source (e.g., the adolescent or parent) for information. Adolescent self-report and parental report can be obtained via structured clinical interviews such as the Diagnostic Interview Schedule for Children (DISC; Fisher, Wicks, Shaffer, Piacentini, & Lapkin, 1992) and responses to standardized psychometric measures (see Table 15.8). The advantage of a clinical interview is that the clinician can probe responses to clarify information about the adolescent's behavior, and can verify that the respondent accurately comprehends the questions being asked. With standardized psychometric instruments, clinicians can obtain valid and reliable estimates of adolescent substance involvement and other problems in a relatively convenient and timely manner. Data from standardized instruments can also be compared against normative samples to determine whether responses reflect normal or atypical functioning. With individuals who know the teen less well (e.g., other relatives, teachers, counselors, physicians, and parole officers), a time-consuming and expensive interview will probably yield limited data. Standardized and well-validated psychometric questionnaires completed by these individuals are more time-efficient than interviews, and they may foster new perspectives and corroborate or disconfirm data obtained from other sources.

Psychometric test data should be gathered and interpreted by a qualified clinical psychologist. Neuropsychological, intellectual, and academic achievement data are especially useful during adolescent substance use assessments. Test results can provide information about general cognitive and personality functioning, can identify learning disabilities and academic delays, and can indicate whether educational compensation or remediation is necessary to overcome deficits and delays.

Direct observation of an adolescent's drinking or drug use is unrealistic. A clinician can, however, observe and rate the adolescent's social behavior. Tarter (1990) suggests simple ratings of eye contact, smiling, duration of verbal responses, verbal elaboration, richness of language content, latency in responding, affect, body gestures, expressions of concern for others, spontaneous communication, and expressions of appreciation. In addition, a clinician can casually observe a teen's level of activity, appropriateness of behavior, and degree of cooperation and conflict with peers and authority figures during school breaks or activities on inpatient drug treatment or residential units. A teacher or teaching aide can be instructed to conduct similar observations in the classroom.

Finally, laboratory measures that detect the presence of drugs in bodily fluids serve the function of determining recent use, but cannot determine the extent of problems, severity of use, or other criteria for Substance Abuse or Dependence. With the exception of marijuana, only very recent use of alcohol (within 24 hours) or other drugs (within several days) can be detected in blood or urine samples (Winters & Stinchfield, 1995). Frequently repeated laboratory measures, however, in conjunction with repeated assessment of psychosocial functioning (e.g., depression, anger, social withdrawal), can verify substance use status and may help clarify temporal relations between substance use and psychosocial functioning. Furthermore, given the variability in content of street drugs, such toxicology screens may identify substances consumed that the teen may have no awareness of.

Domains to Assess

The assessment process should evaluate several domains of functioning (see Table 15.9) that are related to adolescent substance use (Brown, 1993a; Tarter, 1990). Data gathered from these domains can help the clinician formulate an integrated case conceptualization and develop a treatment plan according to key systems of functioning.

Substance Use

Clinicians should consider the intensity, breadth, and consequences of adolescent substance involvement. Both current levels and history of use must be assessed. Intensity of involvement can indicate the presence of physical tolerance to a substance, and can be assessed by type of substance used,

TABLE 15.9. Domains of Functioning to Assess in Conjunction with Adolescent Substance Use

Domains	Issues of importance
Substance use	Type of substances used; intensity (frequency, amount) of use; methods of use (oral, inhalation, injection); contexts of use; history of use.
Family	Substance use and psychiatric history of family members; quality of relationships among family members; parents' parenting abilities.
Cognitive factors	Outcome expectancies; self-efficacy; coping resources; neurocognitive abilities.
Mental health and behavior	Anxiety; depression; anger; suicidality; conduct; thought processes; self-esteem.
School/academic functioning	School attendance; conduct problems; academic achievement.
Social environment	Substance use by peers; types of social activities.
Other activities	Employment; involvement in school activities; recreational interests; hobbies; talents and skills.
Physical health	Quality of nourishment; history of accidents or injuries; nicotine use.
Readiness to change	Has the teen (1) perceived substance use as a problem; (2) considered reducing substance use; (3) taken steps to change use; (4) made a commitment to change?

frequency of substance consumption and intoxication, number of dependence and withdrawal symptoms, and the method of consumption (i.e., oral, inhalation, injection). The quantity of alcohol consumed is easily determined, and this information should be obtained; it is needed to ascertain whether a teen has physical tolerance for alcohol, and it serves as a baseline from which to chart reductions in use. Because of concentration variability in illicit drugs, however, the quantity of such drugs consumed is less specific and should be used only as a gross measure when one is assessing intensity of drug use. Intensity of drug use is more severe among individuals who inject drugs than those who ingest substances orally or by inhalation. In addition, given the typical sequencing of drug experimentation (i.e., alcohol, tobacco, and marijuana use precede experimentation with other substances), use of a given substance may inform the clinician of exposure to other substances.

The breadth of substance involvement refers to the extent and nature of a teen's involvement with different substances. A clinician should ascertain the number of different drugs a teen currently uses and has used in the past, and should determine the intensity of involvement with each substance as described above. A teen's reasons for involvement with or avoidance of a particular substance can provide information about its perceived reinforcement properties, consequences that might

effectively reduce involvement, and the potential for relapsing on a drug other than the teen's drug of preference.

The breadth of substance use is also reflected in the variety of contexts and circumstances where adolescents consume alcohol and drugs. Details about the circumstances of a teen's use inform a clinician about access to and availability of alcohol and other drugs, level of supervision, potential cues to use, and situations that will pose a high relapse risk. The psychoactive properties of a drug, in combination with circumstances and expectancies of use, can inform the clinician of a teen's motivation for use. For example, teens who feel that drug use increases their importance and social appeal may be likely to use multiple types of drugs in social circumstances. Conversely, teens who use CNS depressants (e.g., alcohol, marijuana) alone or in small groups may use these substances to reduce tension or to enhance personal or social pleasure. Teens who progress rapidly from experimentation with alcohol to regular use and use of other drugs evidence a more severe course of Substance Abuse and Dependence than those who progress at a slower rate.

Perhaps the most essential and basic element of adolescent substance use assessment is the client's history of the presenting and related problems. Detailed information regarding age of onset, rate of progression, and negative consequences provides insight into temporal relationships between substance use and other key behaviors. Efforts should be made to determine recency of substance use concurrent with these problems. With this information, a clinician can begin to distinguish problems that are consequent to substance use from those problems that occur independently and may provoke substance use.

The Personal Experience Inventory (Winters & Henly, 1989) is a multidimensional instrument with excellent psychometric properties (Wagner et al., 1995). This instrument measures an adolescent's behavioral involvement with alcohol and other drugs; assesses the teen's use patterns and sequelae of use; evaluates personality characteristics, environmental contexts, and psychosocial stressors; and assists with DSM diagnoses of psychoactive substance use disorders as well as other conditions. The Customary Drinking and Drug Use Record (see Table 15.10) is a structured interview that provides comprehensive quantitative data on consumption, sequencing, consequences, and dependence/withdrawal symptoms associated with use of a variety of substances (Brown, Myers, et al., in press; Lippke et al., 1993). Alternative briefer measures are available (see Wagner et al., 1995) and may be more feasible for screening purposes.

Family

Family structure and the adolescent's role within the family system provide insight into the teen's access to substances and exposure to substance use, the level of support the teen can expect from family members, and the degree of stress the teen will face upon return to the family. Particular attention should be given to the substance use practices of all family members. Age of first involvement, rate of increased involvement, extent of substance use (i.e., number of different substances and frequency of use), and negative consequences of use should be determined for each substance used by each family member, including stepparents and adoptive parents. The clinician should use these data to estimate the extent to which use practices result from exposure to substance-using models, the probability of physiological differences in responding to substance use, and the likelihood of returning to substance use in the family context.

Additional information about biological relatives is useful in understanding the impact of substance involvement. The father's conduct as a child, as well as information about his substance use background, should be noted. Sons of fathers

TABLE 15.10. Features of the Customary Drinking and Drug Use Record

A. Tobacco
   History of use.
      Age first use.
      Age began regular use.
      Daily number of cigarettes during heaviest use period.
      Longest period of smoking abstinence since initiated cigarette use.
   Recent use.
      Cigarettes smoked per day during: the past week; a typical week in the past month.
      Days per month smoked over the past 3 months.
      Time elapsed between waking and first cigarette.

B. Alcohol (questions asked separately for beer, wine, and hard liquor)
   Lifetime use
      Age first use.
      Age began regular use.
      Number of times consumed the beverage.
   Current/recent use (use over the past 3 months).
      Days per month drank the beverage.
      Average number of drinks on drinking days.
      Days since last use and amount consumed.
   Withdrawal symptoms over the past 3 months.

C. Drugs other than alcohol
   Current and lifetime use (inquired for marijuana, amphetamines, barbiturates, hallucinogens, cocaine, inhalants, opiates).
      Age first use.
      Age began regular use.
      Number of time in life used.
      Days per month used over past 3 months.
      Days since last use.
   Withdrawal symptoms over the past 3 months.

D. Topography of use
   Number of times intoxicated.
   Typical location of use.
   Common social circumstances of use.

E. Dependence symptoms
   Criteria assessed for alcohol and three most commonly used drugs.

F. Problems due to substance use (inquired for alcohol and three most common used drugs)
   Relationship breakup.
   Job termination.
   Arrests.
   Health.
   School suspension or expulsion.

who began misusing alcohol and displaying conduct problems during late childhood or early adolescence appear to be at greater biological risk for alcohol and drug problems. In addition, prenatal health care and substance involvement of the biological mothers during pregnancy can indicate risk of teratological influences on adolescent behavior.

Cohesive families, in which members effectively and appropriately express concern and feelings for one another, enhance posttreatment functioning and reduce substance involvement among adolescents (M. A. Stewart & Brown,1994). Families in which alcohol and drugs are readily available provide little support to remain abstinent, and contribute considerable risk and family stress to teens. Teens from such families can receive counseling to identify alternative sources of support, to develop skills to avoid risky circumstances at home, and to cope with negative affect. Several measures, such as the Family Environment Scale (Moos, 1986), the Overt Hostility Scale (O'Leary & Porter, 1987), and the Conflict Tactics Scales (Straus & Gelles, 1990), can provide data regarding family relations.

Cognitive Processes

Cognitive factors will influence a teen's anticipation of reinforcement and consequences from alcohol and drug use, perceptions of personal control over use decisions, and coping repertoire for high-risk situations. Alcohol and other drug expectancies can be assessed via standardized expectancy questionnaires (e.g., Christiansen, Goldman, & Inn, 1982; Goldman, Brown, & Christiansen, 1987; Schafer & Brown, 1990). Similar questionnaires can assess perceived self-efficacy for resisting alcohol or drug use in a variety of contexts (e.g., the Situational Confidence Questionnaire; Annis & Graham, 1988) and specific risks for coping with potential alcohol or drug use situations (the Adolescent Relapse Coping Questionnaire; Myers & Brown, 1996). Finally, during the clinical interview, the clinician can probe a teen's responses to determine his or her capacity for self-reflection, risk appraisal, and introspection. These qualities may serve a protective function (Chassin et al., 1988; Myers & Brown, 1996) among teens who remain with or return to substance-using families during or following treatment.

Mental Health and Behavior

Teens who drink alcohol and use drugs are vulnerable to emotional disturbances, such as affective lability, anxiety, depression, anger, and suicidal ideation. In fact, teens presenting for treatment typically present with multiple emotional and behavioral problems (Tapert et al., in press). In particular, given the affective disruption and behavioral disinhibition consequent to substance use, risk for suicide is high among alcohol- and drug-using teens (King, Hill, et al., 1993; Levy & Deykin, 1989; Pfeffer et al., 1988) and should always be assessed during a mental status evaluation. Excessive substance use can distort thought processes, causing teens to appear psychotic or out of control. Emotional and cognitive changes produced by adolescent alcohol and drug use may be linked to or provoke behavioral problems in a variety of psychosocial realms. Reducing substance use will typically improve functioning in areas negatively affected by excessive substance consumption (Brown et al., 1994).

General measures, such as the Child Behavior Checklist (CBCL; Achenbach, 1991a, 1991b), tap into gross estimates of teen behavior as well as some specific domains of internalizing and externalizing disturbances. Follow-up assessments can provide detailed data in problem areas identified with the CBCL. For example, the Conduct Disorder Questionnaire (Brown, Gleghorn, et al., 1996) is an interview that assesses behavioral disturbances, determines the temporal relation between behavior problems and substance use, and provides sufficient information to diagnose Conduct Disorder.

School and Academic Functioning

Teens with substance use problems are at risk for decreased school attendance and for academic and behavioral problems. Substance use can impair school functioning by interfering with an adolescent's ability to attend to, concentrate on, and process information. As described earlier, teens with academic difficulties may be more likely than teens with no academic problems to associate with deviant peers and subsequently engage in substance misuse (Sher, 1994). Thus, it is again important to establish the temporal relationship between onset of substance involvement and emergence of academic problems. School records can reflect the onset of disciplinary actions, academic difficulties, and attendance problems. Standardized achievement tests (e.g., the Wide Range Achievement Test, the Peabody Individual Achievement Test), in conjunction with intellectual and neuropsychological test data, can help identify teens who are academically delayed, clarify the origin of the difficulties, and indicate appropriate remedial or compensatory strategies. Even in the absence of neuropsychological impairment, academic performance may improve only gradually, given the previous missed learning opportunities common to substance-misusing youths.

Social Environment

It is important to determine the alcohol and drug use characteristics of peers, as well as of family members. As discussed earlier, substance use can dramatically affect the quality of support available from peers. Frequently, it will be necessary for teens to change friends; unfortunately, the process of ceasing contact with substance-using friends can be quite threatening to a teenager, given the developmental significance of peer groups and friendships. Support, encouragement, and guidance will be necessary to facilitate this process, as will training in effective social skills and opportunities to come into contact with peers who are free of substance involvement but have similar interests. The peer network can be assessed by asking about individual friendships and about the teen's perceptions of similarity to peers, level of peer support, and the friends' level of alcohol and drug involvement. The Social Network Evaluation (Schafer, Coyne, & Lazarus, 1981) can facilitate this assessment.

Other Activities

Teens who misuse alcohol and drugs have difficulty maintaining even part-time jobs and frequently decrease their participation in school activities. A clinician should inquire about recreational and school activities in which a teen formerly engaged, and should probe current interests to identify activities that the teen can become involved with. Ideal activities promote social interactions, develop alternative interests, promote self-esteem, and are incompatible with drug and alcohol use.

Physical Health

Adolescents who misuse alcohol and drugs are at elevated risk for accidents, injuries, and malnourishment (Brown et al., 1992). A physical examination should be conducted by a qualified physician to identify any health concerns, particularly those that may be consequent to heavy substance use. A typically unappreciated concern is the prevalent use of tobacco by teens who use other substances. Tobacco use is the best predictor of subsequent health problems and should be addressed in concert with alcohol and other drug use (Myers & Brown, 1994).

Preparedness and Motivation for Change

Recently, theorists (e.g., Miller & Rollnick, 1991; Prochaska, DiClemente, & Norcross, 1992) have abandoned conceptualizations of motivation as a static personality characteristic, and instead have described the motivation to change addictive behaviors as a process. According to this conceptualization, the therapist's interaction with a client is intended to move the client closer to a commitment to change a problem behavior. For example, a teen who does not recognize any negative consequences of substance use may well see no reason to change his or her substance involvement. The therapist needs to provide feedback regarding personal use levels relative to national norms, as well as the impact substance use has had on the teen's life; the goal in this case is to help the teen acknowledge a need to change. A teen who recognizes negative consequences may consider the need to change substance use, but remain cautious about committing to change. For this teen, the therapist's goal is to elicit a commitment from the teen to try to change. Still another adolescent may have committed to change substance use behavior; the therapist's function in this case is to develop strategies with the teen for accomplishing his or her goals for change.

A clinician can determine an adolescent's readiness to change from various factors: what the teen understands to be the reason for the assessment; who brought the teen to the evaluation; whether the teen felt coerced or pressured into coming for the assessment; and how the teen views his or her substance use in relation to personal problems and peers' use. This information is necessary for identifying achievable treatment goals. For example, it is futile to expect commitment to abstinence from a teen who does not consider substance use a problem; however, an appropriate short-term treatment goal is for the teen to recognize how substance use disrupts his or her life.

The clinician is instrumental in moving clients through the process of change. Harsh confrontations will typically evoke denial or resistance, and consequently will hinder progress toward change. Miller and Rollnick (1991) have specified a series of procedures a clinician can utilize to motivate a client to change. These procedures include providing feedback regarding the person's current substance use status relative to national norms, emphasizing personal responsibility for changing substance use, giving clear advice to change substance use practices, offering a menu of alternative strategies for changing substance involvement, responding in an empathic manner, and reinforcing the belief that the person can succeed in changing.

Integration and Case Formulation

The purposes of the case formulation are to summarize the functions that substance use serves in a teen's life, to establish realistic treatment goals, and to develop a plan to accomplish these goals. From the case conceptualization, the therapist can identify factors that promote substance involvement, anticipate impediments to behavior change, and utilize personal strengths that will facilitate reductions in substance involvement and maintain changes. A case formulation should incorporate a comprehensive problem list, the adolescent's motivation to change, common circumstances of use, and personal and social resources for maintaining behavioral change.

The first step is to generate a comprehensive problem list that clarifies the relationship among problems, symptoms, and substance use. The presence of comorbid conditions is a key issue in any assessment of substance use problems. Data collection should permit the clinician to distinguish the course of each potential condition and to evaluate whether certain symptoms are independent of or consequent to the adolescent's substance use. Efforts should be made to establish the temporal relationship between problem behaviors and substance use, and to determine whether any symptoms were evidenced during extended periods of abstinence (e.g., 3 weeks or more). Evidence of an independent condition is present when a problem behavior predates substance use. Problems that emerge following initiation of substance involvement may reflect either an independent condition or consequences of use. Further evidence of a comorbid condition is found if symptoms continue to occur in the absence of substance use.

The second step is for the clinician to evaluate the teen's motivation to reduce substance involvement. Motivation and commitment to change substance use behavior have implications for treatment goals and provide insight into the role of substance use in the teen's life. By considering a teen's motivation to change substance use behavior, a clinician can develop appropriate short-term,

time-limited goals. Exploring a teen's motivation can also provide insight as to how the teen views his or her substance use and what effects of reducing substance involvement the teen anticipates.

Miller and Rollnick (1991) advocate the use of assessment data for increasing motivation to change. Feedback of assessment results, combined with clear advice to reduce substance involvement, is useful for preparing a teen for the intervention and can enhance the efficacy of the treatment plan. As noted earlier, motivation enhancement techniques traditionally include feedback regarding level of substance involvement relative to the general population, physical and emotional health, cognitive functioning, and other negative consequences (Miller, Zweben, DiClemente, & Rychtarik, 1992). The goal is to establish a discrepancy between what an individual desires for himself or herself, and the level at which he or she is currently functioning. For adolescents, it may be beneficial to focus on immediately salient issues (e.g., peer relations), as well as future plans, desires, and goals, and the limited and reduced opportunities self-imposed by excessive substance use. In particular, discrepancies between desired and realized social roles, with an emphasis on potential for improvement, may facilitate adolescents' motivation and preparedness for intervention.

The third step in formulating a case conceptualization is to clarify the contingencies of substance involvement and the functions that substance use serves for a teen. Unconditioned responses to drug use, such as affect and sensation changes, become conditioned responses to previously neutral stimuli (e.g., stressful experiences, parties, gatherings with peers) that have been repeatedly paired with drug use. Hence, certain events can elicit drug desire or craving. Immediately perceived benefits of use (e.g., physical sensations, reduced tension, social facilitation) maintain or escalate the substance use behavior. Eventually, immediate positive reinforcement, rather than delayed and inconsistent negative consequences, leads an individual to engage in compulsive use of the substance. At a cognitive-behavioral level, the clinician can identify typical cognitive, affective, and situational factors that trigger and maintain alcohol and drug use. For example, Brown et al. (1989) found that 90% of teen relapses following inpatient treatment occurred in unsupervised social situations with few models of abstention present. The clinician can clarify the thoughts and feelings associated with these situations, as well as the consequences (positive and negative, immediate and delayed) of alcohol and/or drug use in these circumstances. By establishing this cognitive-behavioral chain, the clinician and teen can identify alternatives to substance use for achieving similar desired effects (e.g., enhancing an activity, reducing negative affect, coping with a difficult situation).

A similar functional assessment can occur at a systems level. The teen's substance use may facilitate avoidance or resolution of an otherwise difficult situation (e.g., learning disability, family conflict). For example, an adolescent's substance involvement may divert attention away from distressing circumstances, maintain barriers in a relationship (e.g., between a stepparent and a child), or allow a teen who feels helpless in regard to important life circumstances the opportunity to demonstrate mastery or control over an aspect of his or her life. System-focused interventions can disrupt maladaptive behavior patterns that maintain substance involvement. For example, altering the structures and roles of relationships among family members can provoke greater attention to and discussion of a teen's substance use, and can facilitate a sense of personal responsibility and efficacy regarding the teen's behavior. Family members may require support and education regarding the process of change. Parents or siblings who do not misuse substances may feel the teen is out of control, and parents may also lack confidence in their parenting abilities. Reestablishing trust can take extended periods of time. Educational interventions directed at all family members can target flawed beliefs about anticipated benefits of use, increase awareness of the negative impact of substance use on multiple life domains, and sensitize individuals to the risk of escalated substance use posed by these maladaptive behavior patterns.

SUMMARY

Alcohol and drug use can damage an adolescent's life in many ways. In this chapter, we have presented theoretical formulations and empirical data explaining the influence of biological, personal, and environmental factors on the initiation and escalation of adolescent substance involvement. Adolescent substance use can have negative effects on family and peer relations, cognitive processes, school and academic functioning, and physical and mental health. We have concluded by proposing an assessment strategy that collects data from several sources via multiple modalities, and recommending a case formulation in which indi-

vidual aspects of substance use are understood to maintain an adolescent's substance involvement. Assessment data and case formulations are used to formulate and test clinical hypotheses, and to provide baseline measures to assess treatment outcome.

REFERENCES

Abrams, D. B., & Niaura, R. S. (1987). Social learning theory. In H.T. Blane & K.E. Leonard (Eds.), *Psychological theories of drinking and alcoholism* (pp. 131–178). New York: Guilford Press.

Achenbach, T. M. (1991a). *Manual for the Child Behavior Checklist/4–18 and 1991 Profile.* Burlington: University of Vermont, Department of Psychiatry.

Achenbach, T. M. (1991b). *Manual for the Teacher's Report Form and 1991 Profile.* Burlington: University of Vermont, Department of Psychiatry.

Ahlgren, A., & Norem-Hebeisen, A. A. (1979). Self-esteem patterns distinctive of groups of drug abusing and other dysfunctional adolescents. *International Journal of the Addictions, 14,* 759–777.

Allison, K., & Leone, P. E. (1994). The dual potentials model: Understanding alcohol and other drug use among ethnically and racially diverse adolescents. In R. L. Peterson & S. Ishii-Jordan (Eds.), *Multicultural issues in the education of behaviorally disordered youth* (pp. 63–77). Cambridge, MA: Brookline Books.

American Psychiatric Association. (1994). *Diagnostic and statistical manual of mental disorders* (4th ed.). Washington, DC: Author.

Annis, H. M., & Davis, C. S. (1988). Self-efficacy and the prevention of alcohol relapse: Initial findings from a treatment trial. In T. B. Baker & D. S. Cannon, (Eds.), *Assessment and treatment of addictive disorders* (pp. 88–112). New York: Praeger.

Annis, H. M., & Graham, J. M. (1988). *Situational Confidence Questionnaire: User's guide.* Toronto: Addiction Research Foundation.

Baer, P. E., Garmezy, L. B., McLaughlin, R. J., Pokorny, A. D., & Wernick, M. J. (1987). Stress, coping, family conflict, and adolescent alcohol use. *Journal of Behavioral Medicine, 10,* 449–466.

Barkley, R. A., Fischer, M., Edelbrock, C. S., & Smallish, L. (1990). The adolescent outcome of hyperactive children diagnosed by research criteria: I. An 8-year prospective follow-up study. *Journal of the American Academy of Child and Adolescent Psychiatry, 29,* 546–557.

Barnes, G. M. (1990). Impact of the family on adolescent drinking patterns. In R. L. Collins, K. E. Leonard, & J. S. Searles (Eds.), *Alcohol and the family: Research and clinical perspectives* (pp. 137–161). New York: Guilford Press.

Barnes, G. M., Farrell, M. P., & Banerjee, S. (1994). Family influence on alcohol abuse and other problem behaviors among black and white adolescents in a general population sample. *Journal of Research on Adolescence, 4*, 183–201.

Barnes, G. M., & Welte, J. W. (1986). Patterns and predictors of alcohol use among 7–12th grade students in New York State. *Journal of Studies on Alcohol, 47*, 53–62.

Baron, R. M., & Kenny, D. A. (1986). The moderator–mediator variable distinction in social psychological research: Conceptual, strategic, and statistical considerations. *Journal of Personality and Social Psychology, 51*, 1173–1182.

Bates, M. E., & Labouvie, E. W. (1994). Familial alcoholism and personality–environment fit: A developmental study of risk in adolescents. *Annals of the New York Academy of Sciences, 708*, 202–213.

Bates, M. E., & Labouvie, E. W. (1995). Personality–environment constellations and alcohol use: A process-oriented study of intraindividual change during adolescence. *Psychology of Addictive Behaviors, 9*, 23–35.

Bennett, L. A., Wolin, S. J., & Reiss, D. (1988). Cognitive, behavioral, and emotional problems among school-age children of alcoholic parents. *American Journal of Psychiatry, 145*, 185–190.

Benson, G. (1985). Course and outcome of drug abuse and medical and social condition in selected young drug abusers. *Acta Psychiatrica Scandinavica, 71*, 48–66.

Berkowitz, A., & Perkins, H. W. (1988). Personality characteristics of children of alcoholics. *Journal of Consulting and Clinical Psychology, 56*, 206–209.

Bloch, L. P., Crockett, L. J., & Vicary, J. R. (1991). Antecedents of rural adolescent alcohol use: A risk factor approach. *Journal of Drug Education, 21*, 361–377.

Boyle, M. H., & Offord, D. R. (1991). Psychiatric disorder and substance use in adolescence. *Canadian Journal of Psychiatry, 36*, 699–705.

Boyle, M. H., Offord, D. R., Racine, Y. A., Fleming, J. E., Szatmari, P., & Links, P. S. (1993). Predicting substance use in early adolescence based on parent and teacher assessments of childhood psychiatric disorder: Results from the Ontario Child Health Study follow-up. *Journal of Child Psychology and Psychiatry, 34*, 535–544.

Boyle, M. H., Offord, D. R., Racine, Y. A., Szatmari, P., Fleming, J. E.,& Links, P. S. (1992). Predicting substance use in late adolescence: Results from the Ontario Child Health Study follow-up. *American Journal of Psychiatry, 149*, 761–767.

Braggio, J. T., Pishkin, V., Gameros, T. A., & Brooks, D. L. (1993). Academic achievement in substance-abusing and conduct-disordered adolescents. *Journal of Clinical Psychology, 49*, 282–291.

Brody, G. H., & Forehand, R. (1993). Prospective associations among family form, family process, and adolescents' alcohol and drug use. *Behaviour Research and Therapy, 31*, 587–593.

Brown, S. A. (1985). Reinforcement expectancies and alcoholism treatment outcome after a one-year follow-up. *Journal of Studies on Alcohol, 46*, 304–308.

Brown, S. A. (1993a). Recovery patterns in adolescent substance abusers. In J. S. Baer, G. A. Marlatt, & R. J. McMahon (Eds.), *Addictive behaviors across the lifespan: Prevention, treatment, and policy issues* (pp. 161–183). Newbury Park, CA: Sage.

Brown, S. A. (1993b). Drug effect expectancies and addictive behavior change. *Experimental and Clinical Psychopharmacology, 1*, 55–67.

Brown, S. A. (1994, August). Recovery patterns of adolescents following alcohol and drug treatment. In S. A. Brown (Chair), *Long-term outcome among adolescents following alcohol and drug treatment.* Symposium presented at the 102nd Annual Convention of the American Psychological Association, Los Angeles.

Brown, S. A., Creamer, V. A., & Stetson, B. A. (1987). Adolescent alcohol expectancies in relation to personal and parental drinking patterns. *Journal of Abnormal Psychology, 96*, 117–121.

Brown, S. A., Gleghorn, A. A., Schuckit, M. A., Myers, M. G., & Mott, M. A. (1996). Conduct Disorder among adolescent substance abusers. *Journal of Studies on Alcohol, 57*, 314–324.

Brown, S. A., Inaba, R. K., Gillin, J. C., Schuckit, M. A., Stewart, M. A., & Irwin, M. R. (1995). Alcoholism and affective disorder: Clinical course of depressive symptoms. *American Journal of Psychiatry, 152*, 45–52.

Brown, S. A., Irwin, M., & Schuckit, M. A. (1991). Changes in anxiety among abstinent male alcoholics. *Journal of Studies on Alcohol, 52*, 55–61.

Brown, S. A., Mott, M. A., & Myers, M. G. (1990). Adolescent alcohol and drug treatment outcome. In R. R. Watson (Ed.), *Drug and alcohol abuse prevention* (pp. 373–403). Clifton, NJ: Humana Press.

Brown, S. A., Mott, M. A., & Stewart, M. A. (1992). Adolescent alcohol and drug abuse. In C. E. Walker & M. C. Roberts (Eds.), *Handbook of clinical child psychology* (2nd ed., pp. 677–693). New York: Wiley.

Brown, S. A., Myers, M. G., Lippke, L. F., Tapert, S. F., Stewart, D. G., & Vik, P. W. (in press). Psychometric evaluation of the Customary Drinking and Drug Use Record (CDDR): A measure of adolescent alcohol and drug involvement. *Journal of Studies on Alcohol.*

Brown, S. A., Myers, M. G., Mott, M. A., & Vik, P. W. (1994). Correlates of success following treatment for adolescent substance abuse. *Applied and Preventive Psychology, 3*, 61–73.

Brown, S. A., & Schuckit, M. A. (1988). Changes in depression among abstinent alcoholics. *Journal of Studies on Alcohol, 49*, 412–417.

Brown, S. A., & Vik, P. W. (1994, August). *Adolescent functioning four years after substance abuse treat ment*. Paper presented at the 102nd Annual Convention of the American Psychological Association, Los Angeles.

Brown, S. A., Vik, P. W., & Creamer, V. A. (1989). Characteristics of relapse following adolescent substance abuse treatment. *Addictive Behaviors, 14*, 291–300.

Brown, S. A., Vik, P. W., McQuaid, J. R., Patterson, T. L., Irwin, M. R., & Grant, I. (1990). Severity of psychosocial stress and outcome of alcoholism treatment. *Journal of Abnormal Psychology, 99*, 344–348.

Brown, S. A., Vik, P. W., Patterson, T. L., Grant, I., & Schuckit, M. A. (1995). Stress, vulnerability and adult alcohol relapse. *Journal of Studies on Alcohol, 56*, 538–545.

Brownell, K. D., Marlatt, G. A., Lichtenstein, E., & Wilson, G. T. (1986). Understanding and preventing relapse. *American Psychologist, 41*, 43–52.

Bukstein, O. G., Brent, L. J., & Kaminer, Y. (1992). Patterns of affective comorbidity in a clinical population of dually diagnosed adolescent substance abusers. *Journal of the American Academy of Child and Adolescent Psychiatry, 31*, 1041–1045.

Bukstein, O. G., & Kaminer, Y. (1994). The nosology of adolescent substance abuse. *American Journal on Addictions, 3*, 1–13.

Burnside, M. A., Baer, P. E., McLaughlin, R. J., & Pokorny, A. D. (1986). Alcohol use by adolescents in disrupted families. *Alcoholism: Clinical and Experimental Research, 10*, 274–278.

Callan, V., & Jackson, D. (1986). Children of alcoholic fathers and recovered alcoholic fathers: Personal and family functioning. *Journal of Studies on Alcohol, 47*, 180–182.

Chassin, L., Mann, L., & Sher, K. (1988). Self-awareness theory, family history of alcoholism, and adolescent alcohol involvement. *Journal of Abnormal Psychology, 97*, 206–217.

Chassin, L., Pillow, D. R., Curran, P. J., Molina, B. S. G., & Barrera, M. (1993). Relation of parental alcoholism to early adolescent substance use: A test of three mediating mechanisms. *Journal of Abnormal Psychology, 102*, 3–19.

Chassin, L., Rogosch, F., & Barrera, M. (1991). Substance use and symptomatology among adolescent children of alcoholics. *Journal of Abnormal Psychology, 100*, 449–463.

Chassin, L., Tetzloff, C., & Hershey, M. (1985). Self-image and social-image factors in adolescent alcohol use. *Journal of Studies on Alcohol, 46*, 39–47.

Christiansen, B. A., Goldman, M. A., & Inn, A. (1982). Development of alcohol-related expectancies in adolescents: Separating pharmacological from social learning influences. *Journal of Consulting and Clinical Psychology, 50*, 336–344.

Cicchetti, D., & Toth, S. L. (1991). A developmental perspective on internalizing and externalizing disorders. In D. Cicchetti & S. L. Toth (Eds.), *Rochester Symposium on Developmental Psychopathology: Vol. 2. Internalizing and externalizing expressions of dysfunction* (pp. 1–19). Hillsdale, NJ: Erlbaum.

Cloninger, C. R. (1987). Neurogenic adaptive mechanisms in alcoholism. *Science, 236*, 410–416.

Colder, C. R., & Chassin, L. (1993). The stress and negative affect model of adolescent alcohol use and the moderating effects of behavioral undercontrol. *Journal of Studies on Alcohol, 54*, 326–333.

Compas, B. E., & Wagner, B. M. (1991). Psychosocial stress during adolescence: Interpersonal and interpersonal processes. In M. E. Colten & S. Gore (Eds.), *Adolescent stress: Causes and consequences* (pp. 67–85). New York: Aldine/de Gruyter.

Conners, G. J., O'Farrell, T., & Pelcovits, M. A. (1988). Drinking outcome expectancies among male alcoholics during relapse situations. *British Journal of Addiction, 83*, 561–566.

Cooper, M. L., Pierce, R. S., & Tidwell, M. O. (1995). Parental drinking problems and adolescent offspring substance use: Moderating effects of demographic and familial factors. *Psychology of Addictive Behaviors, 9*, 36–52.

Cooper, M. L., Russell, M., Skinner, J. B., Frone, M. R., & Mudar, P. (1992). Stress and alcohol use: Moderating effects of gender, coping and alcohol expectancies. *Journal of Abnormal Psychology, 101*, 139–152.

Crowley, T. J., & Riggs, R. D. (1995). Adolescent substance use disorder with Conduct Disorder and comorbid conditions. In E. Rahdert & D. Czechowicz (Eds.), *Adolescent drug abuse: Clinical assessment and therapeutic interventions* (NIDA Research Monograph 156, DHHS Publication No. ADM 95-3908, pp. 49–111). Washington, DC: U.S. Government Printing Office.

Dielman, T. E., Leech, S. L., Lorenger, A. T., & Horvath, W. J. (1984). Health locus of control and self-esteem as related to adolescent health behavior and intentions. *Adolescence, 19*, 935–950.

Dishion, T. J., & Loeber, R. (1985). Adolescent marijuana and alcohol use: The role of parents and peers revisited. *American Journal of Drug and Alcohol Abuse, 11*, 11–25.

Dishion, T. J., & Patterson, G. R. (1993). Antisocial behavior: Using a multiple gating strategy. In M. I. Singer, L. T. Singer, & T. M. Anglin (Eds.), *Handbook for screening adolescents at psychosocial risk* (pp. 375–399). New York: Lexington Books.

Donnermeyer, J. F. (1992). The use of alcohol, marijuana, and hard drugs by rural adolescents: A review of recent research. *Drugs and Society, 7*, 31–75.

Donovan, D. M. (1988). Assessment of addictive behaviors: Implications of an emerging biopsychosocial model. In D. M. Donovan & G. A. Marlatt (Eds.), *Assessment of addictive behaviors* (pp. 3–48). New York: Guilford Press.

Donovan, J. E., & Jessor, R. (1985). Structure of problem behavior in adolescence and young adulthood. *Journal of Consulting and Clinical Psychology*, 53, 890–904.

Donovan, J. E., Jessor, R., & Jessor, L. (1983). Problem drinking in adolescence and young adulthood: A follow-up study. *Journal of Studies on Alcohol*, 44, 109–137.

Elkind, D. (1967). Egocentrism in adolescence. *Child Development*, 38, 1025–1034.

Ervin, C. S., Little, R. E., Streissguth, A. P., & Beck, D. E. (1984). Alcoholic fathering and its relation to child's intellectual development: A pilot investigation. *Alcoholism: Clinical and Experimental Research*, 8, 362–365.

Fergusson, D. M., Lynskey, M. T., & Horwood, L. J. (1993). Conduct problems and attention deficit behavior in middle childhood and cannabis use by age 15. *Australian and New Zealand Journal of Psychiatry*, 27, 673–682.

Fisher, D., Wicks, J., Shaffer, D., Piacentini, J., & Lapkin, J. (1992). *National Institute of Mental Health Diagnostic Interview Schedule for Children: User's manual*. New York: New York State Psychiatric Institute.

Forgays, D. K., Forgays, D. G., Wrzesniewski, K., & Bonaiuto, P. (1992). Alcohol use and personality relationships in US and Polish adolescents. *Journal of Substance Abuse*, 4, 393–402.

Gibbons, S., Wylie, M. L., Echterling, L., & French, J. (1986). Patterns of alcohol use among rural and small-town adolescents. *Adolescence*, 21, 887–900.

Goldman, M. S., Brown, S. A., & Christiansen, B. A. (1987). Expectancy theory: Thinking about drinking. In H. T. Blane & K. E. Leonard (Eds.), *Psychological theories of drinking and alcoholism* (pp. 181–266). New York: Guilford Press.

Goldman, M. S., & Rather, B. C. (1993). Substance use disorders: Cognitive models and architecture. In P. C. Kendall & K. Dobson (Eds.), *Psychopathology and cognition* (pp. 245–292). New York: Academic Press.

Halikas, J. A., Meller, J., Morse, C., & Lyttle, M. D. (1990). Predicting substance abuse in juvenile offenders: Attention Deficit Disorder vs. aggressivity. *Child Psychiatry and Human Development*, 21, 49–55.

Harrell, T. H., & Wirtz, P. W. (1990). *Adolescent Drinking Index*. Odessa, FL: Psychological Assessment Resources.

Hays, R. D., & Ellickson, P. L. (1990). How generalizable are adolescents' beliefs about pro-drug pressures and resistance self-efficacy? *Journal of Applied Social Psychology*, 20, 321–340.

Holsten, F. (1980). Repeat follow-up studies of 100 young Norwegian drug abusers. *Journal of Drug Issues*, 10, 491–504.

Hull, J. G. (1987). Self-awareness model. In H. T. Blane & K. E. Leonard (Eds.), *Psychological theories of drinking and alcoholism* (pp. 272–304). New York: Guilford Press.

Hundleby, J. D., & Mercer, G. W. (1987). Family and friends as social environments and their relationship to young adolescents' use of alcohol, tobacco, and marijuana. *Journal of Marriage and the Family*, 49, 151–164.

Jacobs, T., & Leonard, K. (1991). Parent–child interactions in families with alcoholic fathers. *Journal of Consulting and Clinical Psychology*, 59, 176–181.

Johnston, L. D., Bachman, J. G., & O'Malley, P. M. (1993). *National survey results on drug use from Monitoring the Future Study, 1975–1992: Vol. 1. Secondary school students*. Rockville, MD: U.S. Department of Health and Human Services.

Johnston, L. D., Bachman, J. G., & O'Malley, P. M. (1994). *National survey results on drug use from Monitoring the Future Study, 1975–1993: Vol. 1. Secondary school students*. Rockville, MD: U.S. Department of Health and Human Services.

Johnston, L. D., O'Malley, P. M., & Bachman, J. G. (1995). *National survey results on drug use from Monitoring the Future Study, 1975–1994: Vol. 1. Secondary school students*. Rockville, MD: U.S. Department of Health and Human Services.

Judd, C. M., & McClelland, G. H. (1989). *Data analysis: A model-comparison approach*. San Diego: Harcourt Brace Jovanovich.

Kandel, D. (1978). Convergences in prospective longitudinal surveys of drug use in normal populations. In D. Kandel (Ed.), *Longitudinal research in drug use: Empirical findings and methodological issues* (pp. 3–38). Washington, DC: Hemisphere–Wiley.

Kandel, D. B. (1983). Socialization and adolescent drinking. In O. Jeanneret (Ed.), *Child health and development: Vol 2. Alcohol and youth* (pp. 66–75). Basel: Karger.

Kegan, R. (1982). *The evolving self: Problem and process in human development*. Cambridge, MA: Harvard University Press.

King, C. A., Hill, E. M., Naylor, M. W., Evans, T., & Shain, B. (1993). Alcohol consumption in relation to other predictors of suicidality among adolescent inpatient girls. *Journal of the American Academy of Child and Adolescent Psychiatry*, 32, 82–88.

King, C. A., Naylor, M. W., Hill, E. M., Shain, B., & Green, J. F. (1993). Dysthymia characteristics of heavy alcohol use in depressed adolescents. *Biological Psychiatry*, 33, 210–212.

Knop, J., Teasdale, M. A., Schulsinger, F., & Goodwin, D. W. (1985). A prospective study of young men at high risk for alcoholism: School behavior and achievement. *Journal of Studies on Alcohol*, 46, 273–278.

Labouvie, E. W., & McGee, C. R. (1986). Relation of personality to alcohol and drug use in adolescence. *Journal of Consulting and Clinical Psychology*, 54, 289–293.

Lazarus, R. S., & Folkman, S. (1984). *Stress, appraisal, and coping*. New York: Springer.

Lerner, R. M. (1987). A life-span perspective for early adolescence. In R. M. Lerner & T. T. Foch (Eds.), *Biological–psychosocial interactions in early adolescence* (pp. 9–34). Hillsdale, NJ: Erlbaum.

Lerner, R. M., & Foch, T. T. (1987). Biological–psychosocial interactions in early adolescence: An overview of the issues. In R. M. Lerner & T. T. Foch (Eds.), *Biological–psychosocial interactions in early adolescence* (pp. 1–6). Hillsdale, NJ: Erlbaum.

Levy, J. C., & Deykin, E. V. (1989). Suicidality, depression, and substance abuse in adolescence. *American Journal of Psychiatry, 146*, 1462–1467.

Lippke, L. F., Tammariello, C. F., Brown, S. A., Mott, M. A., Stewart, M. A., & Stewart, D. G. (1993, March). *Toward a comprehensive assessment of teen substance abuse and psychosocial functioning*. Paper presented at the 14th Annual Scientific Sessions of the Society for Behavioral Medicine, San Francisco.

Litman, G. K., Eiser, J. R., Rawson, N. S. B., & Oppenheim, A. N. (1979). Differences in relapse precipitants and coping behaviour between alcohol relapsers and survivors. *Behaviour Research and Therapy, 17*, 89–94.

Lynskey, M. T., & Fergusson, D. M. (1995). Childhood conduct problems, attention deficit behaviors, and adolescent alcohol, tobacco, and illicit drug use. *Journal of Abnormal Child Psychology, 23*, 281–302.

Mann, L. M., Chassin, L., & Sher, K. J. (1987). Alcohol expectancies and the risk for alcoholism. *Journal of Consulting and Clinical Psychology, 55*, 411–417.

Mannuzza, S., Klein, R. G., Bonagura, N., Malloy, P., Giampinl, T. L., & Addalli, K. A. (1991). Hyperactive boys almost grown up. *Archives of General Psychiatry, 48*, 77–83.

Marcus, A. (1986). Academic achievement in elementary school children of alcoholic mothers. *Journal of Clinical Psychology, 42*, 372–376.

Marlatt, G. A. (1985). Relapse prevention: Theoretical rationale and overview of the model. In G. A. Marlatt & J. R. Gordon, (Eds.), *Relapse prevention* (pp. 3–70). New York: Guilford Press.

Mayer, J., & Filstead, W. J. (1979). The Adolescent Alcohol Involvement Scale: An instrument for measuring adolescent use and misuse of alcohol. *Journal of Alcohol Studies, 4*, 291–300.

McGue, M. (1994). Genes, environment, and the etiology of alcoholism. In R. Zucker, G. Boyd, & J. Howard (Eds.), *The development of alcohol problems: Exploring the biopsychosocial matrix of risk* (DHHS Publication No. ADM 94-3495, pp. 1–40). Washington, DC: U.S. Government Printing Office.

Miller, W. R., & Rollnick, S. (1991). *Motivational interviewing: Preparing people to change addictive behavior*. New York: Guilford Press.

Miller, W. R., Zweben, A., DiClemente, C. C., & Rychtarik, R. G. (1992). *Motivational enhancement therapy manual: A clinical research guide for therapists treating individuals with alcohol abuse and dependence* (DHHS Publication No. ADM 92-1894). Washington, DC: U.S. Government Printing Office.

Moberg, D. P. (1991). The Adolescent Drug Involvement Scale. *Journal of Adolescent Chemical Dependency, 2*, 75–88.

Moos, R. H. (1986). *Family Environment Scale* (2nd ed.). Palo Alto, CA: Consulting Psychologists Press.

Moos, R. H., & Billings, A. (1982). Children of alcoholics during the recovery process: Alcoholic and matched control families. *Addictive Behaviors, 7*, 155–163.

Moss, H. B., Kirisci, L., Gordon, H. W., & Tarter, R. E. (1994). A neuropsychologic profile of adolescent alcoholics. *Alcoholism: Clinical and Experimental Research, 18*, 159–163.

Myers, M. G., & Brown, S. A. (1990). Coping and appraisal in potential relapse situations among adolescent substance abusers following treatment. *Journal of Adolescent Chemical Dependency, 1*, 95–115.

Myers, M. G., & Brown, S. A. (1994). Smoking and health in substance-abusing adolescents: A two-year follow-up. *Pediatrics, 93*, 561–566.

Myers, M. G., & Brown, S. A. (1996). The Adolescent Relapse Coping Questionnaire: Psychometric validation. *Journal of Studies on Alcohol, 57*, 40–46.

Myers, M. G., Brown, S. A., & Mott, M. A. (1993). Coping as a predictor of adolescent substance abuse treatment outcome. *Journal of Substance Abuse, 5*, 15–29.

Needle, R. H., Glynn, T. J., & Needle, M. P. (1983). Drug abuse: Adolescent addictions and the family. In C. R. Figley & H. I. McCubbin (Eds.), *Stress and the family: Vol. 2. Coping with catastrophe* (pp. 37–52). New York: Brunner/Mazel.

Newcomb, M. D., & Bentler, P. M. (1988). *Consequences of adolescent drug use*. Newbury Park, CA: Sage.

Newlin, D. B. (1994). Alcohol challenge in high-risk individuals. In R. Zucker, G. Boyd, & J. Howard (Eds.), *The development of alcohol problems: Exploring the biopsychosocial matrix of risk* (DHHS Publication No. ADM 94-3495, pp. 47–68). Washington, DC: U.S. Government Printing Office.

Newlin, D. B., & Thompson, J. B. (1991). Chronic tolerance and sensitization to alcohol in sons of alcoholics. *Alcoholism: Clinical and Experimental Research, 15*, 399–405.

O'Leary, K. D., & Porter, B. (1987). *Overt hostility toward partner*. Stony Brook: Department of Psychology, State University of New York at Stony Brook.

Overall, J. E., Reilly, E. L., Kelley, J. T., & Hollister, L. E. (1985). Persistence of depression in detoxified alcoholics. *Alcoholism: Clinical and Experimental Research, 7,* 188–193.

Pandina, R., & Schuele, J. (1983). Psychosocial correlates of alcohol and drug use of adolescent students and adolescents in treatment. *Journal of Studies on Alcohol, 44,* 950–973.

Petersen, A. C. (1987). The nature of biological–psychosocial interactions: The sample case of early adolescence. In R. M. Lerner & T. T. Foch (Eds.), *Biological–psychosocial interactions in early adolescence* (pp. 35–61). Hillsdale, NJ: Erlbaum.

Pfeffer, C. R., Newcorn, J., Kaplan, G., Mizruchi, M. S., & Plutchik, R. (1988). Suicidal behavior in adolescent psychiatric inpatients. *Journal of the American Academy of Child and Adolescent Psychiatry, 27,* 357–361.

Prochaska, J. O., DiClemente, C. C., & Norcross, J. C. (1992). In search of how people change: Applications to addictive behaviors. *American Psychologist, 47,* 1102–1114.

Richter, S. S., Brown, S. A., & Mott, M. A. (1991). The impact of social support and self-esteem on adolescent substance abuse treatment outcome. *Journal of Substance Abuse, 3,* 371–385.

Rogosch, F., Chassin, L., & Sher, K. J. (1990). Personality variables as mediators and moderators of family history risk for alcoholism: Conceptual and methodological issues. *Journal of Studies on Alcohol, 51,* 310–318.

Rook, K. S., & Dooley, D. (1985). Applying social support research: Theoretical problems and future directions. *Journal of Social Issues, 41,* 5–28.

Roosa, M. W., Sandler, I. N., Gehring, M., Beals, J., & Cappo, L. (1988). The Children of Alcoholics Life-Events Schedule: A stress scale for children of alcohol-abusing parents. *Journal of Studies on Alcohol, 49,* 422–429.

Russell, M. (1990). Prevalence of alcoholism among children of alcoholics. In M. Windle & J. S. Searles (Eds.), *Children of alcoholics: Critical perspectives* (pp. 9–38). New York: Guilford Press.

Scarr, S., & McCartney, K. (1983). How people make their own environments: A theory of genotype–environment effects. *Child Development, 54,* 424–435.

Schafer, C., Coyne, J. C., & Lazarus, A. (1981). The health related functions of social support. *Journal of Behavioral Medicine, 4,* 381–406.

Schafer, J., & Brown, S. A. (1990). Marijuana and cocaine effect expectancies and drug use patterns. *Journal of Consulting and Clinical Psychology, 59,* 558–565.

Schuckit, M. A. (1984). Subjective responses to alcohol in sons of alcoholics and control subjects. *Archives of General Psychiatry, 41,* 879–884.

Sher, K. J. (1991). *Children of alcoholics: A critical appraisal of theory and research.* Chicago: University of Chicago Press.

Sher, K. J. (1994). Individual-level risk factors. In R. Zucker, G. Boyd, & J. Howard (Eds.), *The development of alcohol problems: Exploring the biopsychosocial matrix of risk* (DHHS Publication No. ADM 94-2495 pp. 77–108). Washington, DC: U.S. Government Printing Office.

Sher, K. J., Walitzer, K. S., Wood, P. K., & Brent, E. E. (1991). Characteristics of children of alcoholics: Putative risk factors, substance abuse, and psychopathology. *Journal of Abnormal Psychology, 100,* 427–448.

Smith, G. T., Goldman, M. S., Greenbaum, P. E., & Christiansen, B. A. (1995). Expectancy for social facilitation from drinking: The divergent paths of high-expectancy and low-expectancy adolescents. *Journal of Abnormal Psychology, 104,* 32–40.

Sobell, L. C., Cunningham, J. A., Sobell, M. B., & Toneatto, T. (1993). A life-span perspective on natural recovery (self-change) from alcohol problems. In J. S. Baer, G. A. Marlatt, & R. J. McMahon (Eds.), *Addictive behaviors across the lifespan: Prevention, treatment, and policy issues* (pp. 138–157). Newbury Park, CA: Sage.

Stewart, D. G., & Brown, S. A. (1994, August). Antisocial behavior and long-term outcome of substance abuse treatment. In S. A. Brown (Chair), *Long-term outcome among adolescents following alcohol and drug treatment.* Symposium presented at the annual convention of the American Psychological Association, Los Angeles.

Stewart, D. G., & Brown, S. A. (1995). Withdrawal and dependency symptoms among adolescent alcohol and drug abusers. *Addiction, 90,* 627–635.

Stewart, D. G., Vik, P. W., Whitteker, W. B., & Brown, S. A. (1994, November). *Development and resolution of substance use problems among high risk adolescents.* Paper presented at the annual convention of the Association for Advancement of Behavior Therapy, San Diego.

Stewart, M. A., & Brown, S. A. (1994). Family functioning following adolescent substance abuse treatment. *Journal of Substance Abuse, 5,* 327–339.

Straus, M. A., & Gelles, R. J. (1990). *Physical violence in American families: Risk factors and adaptations to violence in 8,145 families.* New Brunswick, NJ: Transaction.

Svobodny, L. A. (1982). Biographical, self-concept and educational factors among chemically dependent adolescents. *Adolescence, 17,* 847–853.

Swaim, R. C., Oetting, E. R., Edwards, R. W., & Beauvais, F. (1989). Links from emotional distress to adolescent drug use: A path model. *Journal of Consulting and Clinical Psychology, 57,* 227–231.

Tapert, S. F., & Brown, S. A. (1994, August). Neuropsychological correlates of adolescent drug and alcohol abuse. In S. A. Brown (Chair), *Long-term outcome among adolescents following alcohol and drug treatment.* Symposium presented at the annual convention of the American Psychological Association, Los Angeles.

Tapert, S. F., Stewart, D. G., & Brown, S. A. (in press). Drug abuse in adolescence. In A. J. Goreczny & M. Hersen (Eds.), *Handbook of pediatrics: Adolescent health psychology*. Needham Heights, MA: Allyn & Bacon.

Tarter, R. E. (1990). Evaluation and treatment of adolescent substance abuse: A decision tree method. *American Journal of Drug and Alcohol Abuse, 16,* 1–46.

Tarter, R. E., Alterman, A., & Edwards, K. (1985). Vulnerability to alcoholism in men: A behavior-genetic perspective. *Journal of Studies on Alcohol, 46,* 329–356.

Tarter, R. E., Hegedus, A. M., Goldstein, G., Shelly, C., & Alterman, A. I. (1984). Adolescent sons of alcoholics: Neuropsychological and personality characteristics. *Alcoholism: Clinical and Experimental Research, 8,* 216–222.

Tarter, R. E., Mezzich, A. C., Hsieh, Y., & Parks, S. M. (1995). Cognitive capacity in female adolescent substance abusers. *Drug and Alcohol Dependence, 39,* 15–21.

Thoits, P. A. (1986). Social support as coping assistance. *Journal of Counseling and Clinical Psychology, 54,* 416–423.

Thompson, K. M. (1989). Effects of early alcohol use on adolescents' relations with peers and self-esteem: Patterns over time. *Adolescence, 24,* 837–849.

Tomori, M. (1994). Personality characteristics of adolescents with alcoholic parents. *Adolescence, 29,* 949–959.

Vaillant, G. E. (1983). *The natural history of alcoholism*. Cambridge, MA: Harvard University Press.

van Hasselt, V. B., Null, J. A., Kempton, T., & Bukstein, O. G. (1993). Social skills and depression in adolescent substance abusers. *Addictive Behaviors, 18,* 9–18.

Vik, P. W., & Brown, S. A. (1993). *Alcohol and other drug use among junior high school students*. Unpublished manuscript.

Vik, P. W., Mott, M. A., & Brown, S. A. (1996). *Outcome following adolescent alcohol and drug dependence treatment: Test of a model*. Manuscript submitted for publication.

Vik, P. W., Grizzle, K. L., & Brown, S. A. (1992). Social resource characteristics and adolescent substance abuse relapse. *Journal of Adolescent Chemical Dependency, 2,* 59–74.

Wagner, E. F. (1993). Delay of gratification, coping with stress, and substance use in adolescence. *Experimental and Clinical Psychopharmacology, 1,* 27–43.

Wagner, E. F., Myers, M. G., & Brown, S. A. (1994). Adolescent substance abuse treatment. In L. VandeCreek (Ed.), *Innovations in clinical practice: A source book* (Vol. 13, pp. 97–121). Sarasota, FL: Professional Resource Exchange.

Welte, J. W., & Barnes, G. M. (1987). Alcohol use among adolescent minority groups. *Journal of Studies on Alcohol, 48,* 329–336.

West, M. O., & Prinz, R. J. (1987). Parental alcoholism and childhood psychopathology. *Psychological Bulletin, 102,* 204–218.

White, H. R., & Labouvie, E. W. (1989). Towards the assessment of adolescent problem drinking. *Journal of Studies on Alcohol, 50,* 30–37.

Wills, T. A. (1986). Stress and coping in early adolescence: Relationships to substance use in early urban school samples. *Journal of Health Psychology, 5,* 503–529.

Windle, M. (1990). Temperament and personality attributes of children of alcoholics. In M. Windle & J. S. Searles (Eds.), *Children of alcoholics: Critical perspectives* (pp. 129–167). New York: Guilford Press.

Windle, M. (1991). Alcohol use and abuse: Some findings from the National Adolescent Student Health Survey. *Alcohol Health and Research World, 15,* 5–10.

Winters, K. C. (1991). *The Personal Experience Screening Questionnaire and manual*. Los Angeles: Western Psychological Services.

Winters, K. C. (1992). Development of an adolescent alcohol and other drug abuse screening scale: Personal Experience Screening Questionnaire. *Addictive Behaviors, 17,* 479–490.

Winters, K. C., & Henly, G. A. (1989). *The Personal Experience Inventory Test and manual*. Los Angeles: Western Psychological Services.

Winters, K. C., & Stinchfield, R. D. (1995). Current issues and future needs in the assessment of adolescent drug abuse. In E. Rahdert & D. Czechowicz (Eds.), *Adolescent drug abuse: Clinical assessment and therapeutic interventions* (NIDA Research Monograph No. 156, DHHS Publication No. ADM 95-3908, pp. 146–170). Washington, DC: U.S. Government Printing Office.

Zucker, R. A., & Gomberg, E. S. L. (1986). Etiology of alcoholism reconsidered: The case for a biopsychosocial process. *American Psychologist, 41,* 783–793.

AUTHOR INDEX

Note. Italicized numbers represent pages in reference lists.

Aarens, M., 577, *613*
Aasland, O. G., 171, *190*
Abel, G. G., 576, 577, 578, *613*
Abeles, L. A., 257, 259, 272
Abelson, R. P., 20, *59*
Aber, J. L., 528, 532, 555, 556, 560, 567
Abidin, R. R., 38, 48, 110, *115*, 138, 173, 174, 175, *178*, 392, *401*, 435, 448, 547, 551, *560*, 663, 666, 667, 677
Abikoff, H., 32, 48, 106, 112, 113, 115, 116, 133, 135, *178*
Ablon, J. S., *118*
Abraham, S. F., 687, 697, 703, 707
Abrahams, N., 525, *562*
Abramovitch, R., 35, *63*
Abramowitz, R. H., 204, 227
Abrams, D. B., 727, *742*
Abrams, J. M., 586, *617*
Abrams, K., *519*
Abramson, A., *620*
Abramson, L., *621*
Abramson, L. Y., 228
Acevedo, L., 90, *118*
Achenbach, T. M., 5, 6, 8, 12, 14, 15, 16, 17, 18, 20, 23, 24, 28, 32, 36, 39, 40, 41, 48, 53, 73, 92, 93, 97, 100, 106, *116*, 131, 141, 146, 147, 148, 149, 161, 165, 177, *178*, *182*, 187, 198, 199, 200, 206, 207, 208, 213, 221, 222, 223, 224, 225, 226, 232, 263, 350, 353, 359, 376, 396, *401*, 469, 473, 476, 486, 509, 551, 552, 553, 554, *560*, 583, 602, 605, 606, *613*, 739, *742*
Acker, M. M., 166, *178*
Ackerman, A., *448*
Acton, R. G., 175, *178*
Adam, B., 606, *622*
Adams, C. D., 142, 144, *178*
Adams, G. L., 102, *116*
Adams, H. E., 5, 16, 49, 51, 170, 180, 271, 696, 708
Adams, J., 585, 591, *613*, *622*
Adams, W., 386, 388, *406*
Adan, A. M., 219, 224
Addalli, K. A., 746
Addy, C. L., 213, 225
Adelman, H. S., 4, 16, 21, *49*, 51
Adler, A., 540, *562*
Adler, N. A., 579, *614*
Adlestein, D., *183*

Adrian, C., 219, 223, 225
Adrien, J. L., 426, *442*, 443
Affleck, J., 391, *403*
Ager, A., 4, *49*
Ageton, S. S., 152, *182*
Agras, W. S., 239, 251, 263, 688, 689, 692, 694, 707, *714*
Ahart, S., 597, *619*
Ahlgren, A., 727, *742*
Aicardi, J., 417, *446*
Ainsworth, M. D. S., 342, 359, 528, 555, *560*, 562
Akesson, H., 374, *403*
Alain, M., 335, *360*
Albanese, I., *621*
Albert, R., *442*
Albin, R. W., 439, *449*
Aldenkamp, A. P., 462, *476*
Alder, R. J., 133, *188*
Aldous, J., 22, *52*
Aldrich, E. F., *478*
Alessandri, S. M., 553, *560*
Alexander, B., 498, *513*
Alexander, D., *448*
Alexander, J. F., 628, 631, 633, 639, 644, 645, 650, 653, 667, 677
Alexander, J. G., 7, 46, 49
Alexander, P. C., 580, 612, *614*, *615*
Alfaro, J., 527, *560*
Alfeld, C., 499, *517*
Alford, J. B., *511*
Algina, J., 151, *182*
Algozzine, B., 20, 25, 38, *49*, 62
Alibhai, N., 689, *709*
Allan, T. K., 237, 259, 263
Allebeck, P., 696, *707*
Allen, L., 23, *60*
Allen, C. M., 576, *614*
Allen, D. M., 529, 533, 534, *560*
Allen, J., *423*, *443*, 445
Allen, J. P., 171, *178*, 555, *560*
Allen, L., 236, 272
Allen, M., 429, *448*
Allen, R., 77, *126*
Allen, R. E., 530, *560*
Allen, T. W., 75, 78, *126*
Allgood, S. M., 172, *181*
Allison, K., 719, *742*
Alloy, L. B., 4, 66, 228, *621*
Almeida, M. C., 397, *405*
Almond, P. J., 420, 430, 447
Alpern, G., 389, 390, *401*, 429
Alpern, G. D., 258, 278, *442*, 445

Alpern, L., 137, *178*
Alpert, A., 629, 678
Alpherts, W. C. J., 462, *476*
Altepeter, T. S., 76, 77, 85, 99, *116*, 141, 142, 144, 145, 153, 164, 177, 179
Alterman, A. I., 534, 567, 578, 622, 722, 724, 748
Alvarado, L., *563*
Alvarez, W., 599, *617*
Aman, C., 595, 596, *617*
Aman, M., *404*
Aman, M. G., 84, *125*, 394, 395, 396, *401*, 405
Amato, P. R., 137, *178*
Amberson, T. G., 36, *59*
Ambrosini, P. J., 40, *49*, 51, 224, *561*
Ambuel, B., 231, 235, 263, 276, 292
Amen, E. W., 266, 292
American Association on Mental Retardation, 370, 371, 372, 373, 374, 375, 389, *401*, 431
American Humane Association, 571, *614*
American Professional Society on the Abuse of Children, 597, *614*
American Psychiatric Association, 12, 16, 17, *49*, 71, 72, 74, 75, 78, 92, 116, 130, 131, *178*, 199, 200, 201, 202, 223, 231, 232, 260, 263, 328, 335, 359,372, 376, 377, 393, *401*, 408, 410, *442*, 484, 485, 509, 588, *614*, 628, 677, 683, 684, 707, 719, 721, 722, 723, 724, 742
American Psychological Association, 523, *560*
Ames, L. B., 381, 382, *401*
Ammerman, R. T., 4, 56, 531, *561*
Amnell, G., 415, *450*
Amsel, R., 86, 122
Anastasi, A., 8, *49*, 643, 677
Anastopoulos, A. D., 85, 86, 89, 90, 98, 99, 109, 110, 113, *116*, *117*, 628, 639, 640, 641, 677
Ancill, R. J., 4, 49
Anders, T. F., 416, *451*
Andersen, A. E., 689, 707
Anderson, C. A., 4, 13, 56, 76, 116, 130, 134, 184
Anderson, E. A., 172, *185*
Anderson, J., 139, 187, 570, *619*
Anderson, J. C., 238, 263
Anderson, K., 32, 61, 107, *124*

Anderson, L., *444*
Anderson, L. L., 151, *190*
Anderson, S. A., 633, 677
Anderson, V. A., 478
Anderson-Tisdelle, D., 236, 264, 316
Ando, H., 377, *401*, 414, 431, 442
Andrasik, F., 255, 263, 495, 509
Andreasen, N., 258, 267
Andres, J., 516
Andreski, P., 476
Andrews, D. A., 147, 168, *184*
Andrews, D. W., 153, *181*, 339, *361*
Andrews, J. A., 201, 227, 629, 678
Andrews, W., 489, *517*
Angelino, H., 232, 236, 237, 238, 262, 263
Anglin, K., 142, *184*
Angold, A., 198, 202, 220, 221, 223
Annis, H. M., 727, 739, 742
Anson, D. A., 598, *614*
Anthony, J. C., 362
Apollini, T., 391, *402*
Aponte, H. H., 669, 677
Appelbaum, M., 489, *511*
Appelbaum, M. I., 381, *405*
Applegate, B., 92, *116*, 122, *186*
Apter, A., 278
Aradine, C. R., 496, 509
Araji, S., 576, *614*
Aram, D. M., 453, 462, 463, 476
Arana, G. W., 217, 223
Arata, C. L., 258, *271*
Archer, L., *451*
Archer, R. P., 50, 206, 223
Arena, J. G., 255, 263
Argall, W. J., 703, 707
Arick, J., 420, 430, *447*
Arick, J. R., *447*
Arkowitz, H., 16, *49*
Armistead, L., 148, *183*, 678
Armsden, G., 492, *517*
Armstrong, F. D., 268
Armstrong, R., 490, 509
Arnold, E., 394, *401*
Arnold, D. S., 37, *49*, 166, *178*
Arnold, G. S., 628, *680*
Artemyeff, C., 38, *65*
Arthur, J., 57, *185*
Arthur, M. W., 628, 678
Aruffo, J., 262, 270, 321
Asarnow, J. R., 340, 359
Asarnow, R. F., 109, *127*, 429, 442, 456, 476
Asendorpf, J. B., 335, 359, 364
Asher, S. R., 41, *49*, 108, *116*, 328, 329, 331, 333, 335, 338, 339, 344, 345, 346, 347, 354, 356, 357, 359, 361, 362, 363, 365
Ashley, P., *511*
Askevold, F., 696, 707
Asperger, H., 418, *443*
Asquith, P., 656, 658, *681*
Astor, R. A., 533, 554, *561*
Astor-Dubin, L., 44, *56*
Atkeson, B. M., 147, *178*
Atkins, M. S., 90, 97, *116*, 123, 585, 619
Atkinson, S. S., 489, *511*
Attanasio, V., 509
Attar, B. K., 138, *178*
Attermeier, S., 390, *404*
Attias, R., 574, *614*
Attie, I., 696, 703, 707
Attwood, A., 416, 452
August, G. J., 177, *178*, 415, *443*, *451*

Aumiller, K., 329
Austin, G., *621*
Averill, J. R., 251, 263, 537, 538, *561*
AvRuskin, T. W., 503, *510*
Axelrod, S., 438, *443*
Ayllon, T., 256, 263, 270
Ayoub, C., 557, 565
Azar, S. T., 4, 38, *49*, 539, 551, *561*, 566

Babani, L., 492, *518*
Babcock, J., 564
Babigian, H., 35, 52, 328, *361*, 689, 711
Babor, T. F., 171, *190*
Bachman, J. G., 717, 718, 719, 720, 745
Baden, A. D., 137, *178*, 655, 677
Badgley, R.F., 571, *614*
Baer, D. M., 29, 66
Baer, L., 237, 273
Baer, P. E., 728, 732, 742, 744
Bagley, C., 591, *614*
Bagnato, S. J., 272, 319, 379, 383, 384, 385, 388, 390, *401*, 405
Bailey, A., 415, *443*, 450
Bailey, J. S., 438, *449*
Bailey, J. D., 477
Bailey, P. M., 259, 263
Bailey, S. L., 432, 433, *443*
Baird, T. D., 415, *443*
Bakal, D. A., 483, 509
Bakeman, R., 47, 49
Baker, A. W., 571, 572, *614*
Baker, B., 497, *510*
Baker, D. B., 548, *564*
Baker, J. D., 495, *519*
Baker, L., 77, 85, *119*, 198, 224, 416, 434, *444*, 702, 712
Baker, T. B., 6, 67
Baldessarini, R. J., 111, *118*, 217, 223
Baldwin, D. C., 258, 269, 270
Baldwin, D. V., 11, 64, 153, *189*
Baldwin, L. M., 627, 678, 680
Bales v. Clark, 523 R. Supp. 1366, 378, *401*
Ball, J., 427, *445*
Ball, W., 237, 263
Balla, D., 469, 479
Balla, D. A., 100, *127*, 389, *406*, 416, 451
Ballenger, J. C., 231, 235, 263
Baloh, R., 87, *116*
Balthazar, E. E., 389, 390, *401*, 431, 443
Bamber, J. H., 236, 237, 263
Band, E., 589, *614*
Bandura, A., 21, *49*, 230, 232, 242, 256, 263, 299
Banerjee, S., 729, 742
Banis, H., 492, *518*
Bank, L., 4, 14, 19, 30, 63, 134, 140, 142, 157, 158, 162, 171, 177, *178*, 180, *188*, *189*
Bankart, B. B., 231, 263
Bankart, C. P., 231, 263
Banning, A., 579, *614*
Barabas, G., 492, *511*
Barabasz, A., 256, 263
Barahal, R. M., 530, 534, *561*
Barbarin, O., 516
Barber, M. A., 72, *116*
Barber, N. I., 75, *128*
Barbero, G., 492, *513*

Barbosa-Salvidar, J. L., 689, 707
Barbour, L., 392, *404*
Bargiel, K., 640, *680*
Barkley, R. A., 4, 6, 7, 8, 11, 13, 14, 24, 26, 27, 29, 30, 35, 36, 44, 45, 49, 60, 71, 72, 73, 75, 76, 77, 78, 79, 80, 81, 82, 83, 84, 85, 86, 87, 88, 89, 90, 91, 92, 94, 95, 96, 97, 98, 99, 100, 102, 103, 104, 105, 106, 107, 108, 109, 110, 111, 112, 113, *116*, *117*, *118*, *119*, *120*, *121*, *122*, *123*, *124*, *125*, *127*, *128*, 140, 142, 144, *179*, *186*, 344, 359, 394, *401*, 454, 472, 476, 628, 639, 640, 641, 677, 724, 742
Barkovich, A. J., 458, *476*
Barling, J., 5, 49
Barlow, D. H., 4, 13, 14, *49*, 230, 234, 249, 250, 251, 254, 255, 260, 263, 264, 265, 269, 271, 301, 311
Barnard, J., *518*
Barnard, M., 499, *518*, *519*
Barnes, G. M., 718, 719, 728, 729, 742, 743, 748
Barnes, H. L., 647, 648, 677
Barnes, M. A., 454, 459, 469, *476*, 477
Barnett, D., 534, 562, 580, 583, 593, 611, *614*, *615*, *619*
Barnett, L. R., 691, 698, 707, 713
Baron, I. S., 453, 462, 476
Baron, L., 572, *616*
Baron, R. A., 537, *561*
Baron, R. M., 731, 743
Baron-Cohen, S., 411, 412, 423, *443*
Barr, H. M., *127*
Barrera, F. J., *451*
Barrera, M., 727, 744
Barrett, C., 36, 62
Barrett, C. L., 231, 232, 239, 268, 273, 318
Barrett, K., 235, 260, 265, 548, *561*
Barrett, K. C., 260, 261, 265
Barrett, M. J., 702, *714*
Barrett, P., *125*, *510*
Barrett, R. P., 377, 395, *403*, *404*
Barrios, B. A., 23, 31, 39, 41, 42, 43, 49, 140, 153, *179*, 234, 236, 239, 241, 242, 243, 244, 245, 247, 248, 249, 250, 251, 252, 253, 254, 255, 256, 259, 260, 262, 263, 264, 268, 280, 281, 316, 327
Barry, C. T., 461, *480*
Barry, F. D., 523, 565
Bartak, L., 412, 413, 414, 415, 418, *443*, 450
Bartel, N. R., 20, *55*
Barthelemy, C., 442, *443*, 447
Bartholomew, K., 505, *518*
Barton, C., 639, 653, 677
Barton, S., 445
Barton-Henry, M. L., 35, *65*
Bartusch, D. J., *193*
Baskett, L. M., 45, 49
Bass, D., 148, 149, *186*
Basta, S., 586, *614*
Bastien, R., 21, *51*
Bates, J. E., 135, 136, 138, 164, 165, 167, *179*, *181*, *191*, *193*, 342, *361*, 530, 553, *561*, 562
Bates, M. E., 728, 729, 743
Batterman-Faunce, J., *617*

Battle v. Commonwealth of Pennsylvania, 629 F. 2d 269, 378, *401*
Bauer, D. H., 236, 237, *264*
Bauermeister, J. J., 90, *118*
Baum, C. G., 176, *179*
Baum, J., 506, *514*
Bauman, K., 397, *404*
Baumeister, A. A., 370, *401*, 413, *448*
Baumgartel, A., 78, *118*
Baumrind, D., 342, *359*
Bauske, B. W., 44, *67*, 157, *193*
Bavolek, S. J., 551, *561*
Bayles, K., 135, *179*
Bayley, N., 381, 382, 383, *401*, 463, *476*
Bays, J., 595, *614*
Bays, K., *271*
Beach, D. R., 36, *52*
Beales, S., 687, *715*
Beals, J., 729, *747*
Beatty, S. B., 142, *184*
Beauchesne, H. C., *227*
Beaumont, S. L., 639, *677*
Beauvais, F., 729, *747*
Beavers, W. R., 612, 619, 670, *679*
Bechtel, G. C., 15, 29, *63*
Beck, A. T., 38, *49*, 110, *118*, 170, *179*, *186*, 204, 223, 230, 262, *264*, 321, 324, 551, 555, *561*
Beck, D. E., 724, *745*
Beck, M., *510*
Beck, N. C., *226*
Beck, S., 6, *64*, *511*
Beck, S. I., 4, *57*
Becker, D., 498, *511*
Becker, J. V., 576, 578, 579, 580, *613*, *614*, *618*
Becker, L. E., *477*
Becker, M., 505, *514*
Beckman, P. J., 392, *402*
Bedi, G., 76, *122*
Beeghly, M., 530, *561*, *562*
Beery, K. E., 386, *401*
Befera, M., 109, *118*
Begin, G., 345, *360*
Begleiter, M. L., 491, *509*
Begleym, N., 490, *517*
Behar, D., *125*, *402*
Behar, L. B., 351, *359*, *395*
Behen, M., *614*
Beidel, D. C., 230, 234, 235, 236, 248, 250, 254, 262, *264*, 266, 277, 310, 311
Beilke, R. L., 583, 590, *616*
Beinart, H., 695, *715*
Beital, A., 5, *63*
Bekeny, P., 505, 506, *517*
Belar, C. D., 506, *509*
Bell, R., 612, *620*
Bell, R. Q., 22, 37, *49*, *65*
Bell, T., *514*
Bell-Dolan, D. J., 231, 236, 247, *264*, 317, 318, 346, 347, *359*, *361*
Bellack, A. S., 31, *49*, 170, *179*, 234, 235, 277, 279
Bellando, B., *519*
Bellanti, C. J., 342, *364*
Bellefleur, M., *478*
Bellugi, V., 460, *476*
Belsky, J., 5, 8, *50*, 174, *179*, 527, *561*
Belter, R. W., 212, *227*
Bem, D. M., 10, *50*
Bem, D. J., 337, *360*

Bemis, K. M., 691, 694, *709*
Ben-David, A., 670, 671, 675, *677*
Ben-Porath, Y. S., *50*
Bence, R., 421, *449*
Bender, L., 386, 387, *402*, 408, *443*
Bender, M. E., 77, 85, 108, *125*
Benedict, L. L. W., 580, *614*
Bengston, B. S., 585, *616*
Bengston, D., 249, 277, 291
Bengston-Audia, D., 246, 291
Benjamin, L. S., 251, *264*, 704, 707
Benness, B. B., 85, *119*
Bennett, B., 228
Bennett, D., 486, *509*
Bennett, D. S., 135, *179*
Bennett, L. A., 87, *118*, 722, 727, 728, 743
Bennett, W. B., 706, 707
Benoit, D., 529, *561*
Benoit, M., 105, *126*
Benson, D. F., 77, *127*
Benson, G., 137, *193*, 733, *743*
Benson, H., 506, *511*
Benson, J. B., 36, 38, *50*, *60*
Bentler, P. M., 725, 729, 731, *746*
Benton, A., 77, *118*
Bentovim, A., 571, 572, 620, 622, 691, 707
Benz, M., 391, *406*
Berecz, J. M., 231, 235, *264*
Berenbaum, J., 492, *509*
Berg, C. J., 262, *264*, 321
Berg, I., 239, *264*
Bergan, J. R., 255, *264*
Bergeron, G., 348, *363*
Bergeron, K. C., 696, *708*
Bergeron, L., *406*
Berk, L. E., 77, 81, *118*
Berk, R. A., 436, *443*
Berk, S. F., 436, *443*
Berkowitz, A., 728, *743*
Berkowitz, L., 537, 550, *561*
Berler, E. S., 346, *361*
Bernal, M. E., 29, 37, *50*, *65*
Bernardy, N., *515*
Berndt, D., 697, *711*
Berndt, T. J., 339, *359*
Berney, P., 238, *271*
Bernstein, D. A., 242, 243, *264*
Bernstein, G. A., 230, 238, 258, 259, *265*
Bernstein, J. H., 453, 463, 464, 467, 473, *476*
Bersoff, D. N., 34, *50*
Bersoff, D. M., 356, *360*
Berube, H., 393, *406*
Bessler, A., 86, *123*
Bessmer, J. L., 156, *179*, *182*
Best, A., *451*
Beumont, P. J. V., 687, 691, 692, 697, 703, 707, *708*, *714*
Beutler, L., 606, *623*
Beyer, H. A., 378, *402*
Beyer, J. E., 496, *509*
Bhanji, S., 684, *707*
Bhat, A. V., 688, 689, *709*, *710*
Bhate, S. R., 238, *271*
Bhatia, M. S., 78, *118*
Bhavnagri, N., 5, *63*
Bibace, R., 499, *518*
Bidaut-Russell, M., 211, *223*

Biederman, J., 77, 85, 88, 89, 93, 108, 109, 111, *116*, *118*, *120*, 148, 165, *179*, *180*, *186*, 257, *265*
Bielass, M., 505, *517*
Bienenstock, B., 416, *451*
Bierman, K. L., 30, 35, 39, 40, 41, *50*, 143, 165, *179*, 329, 330, 331, 332, 333, 334, 336, 342, 348, 349, 350, 352, 356, 357, 358, 359, 360, 362, 363, 364
Biever, J. L., 249, 268, 304
Biglan, A., 57, *185*
Bihm, E. M., 438, *443*
Bijou, S. W., 8, *50*
Bijur, P. E., 84, *118*, 456, *476*
Billings, A., 727, 728, 746
Billings, A. G., 38, 39, *50*
Binder, A., 530, *563*
Binkoff, J. A., 22, *53*, 414, *444*
Birch, H. G., 135, *192*, 257, 277
Birch, J., 688, *710*
Bird, H., 226, 228, *406*
Bird, H. R., 40, 59, 145, *179*, *190*
Birmingham, B. K., 111, *126*
Birns, B., 579, *614*
Birt, J., 4, 40, 569, 582, 585, 587, 588, 589, 593, 599, 605, 608, 609, 610, *614*, 623
Bishop, D. S., 627, 635, 678, 680
Bjorkvist, K., 343, *363*
Black, C. A., 583, *614*
Black, F. L., 351, *362*
Black, M., 411, *443*
Black, M. M., 530, *563*
Black, S., 699, *710*
Blackwell, A., 687, *708*
Blanchard, E. B., 242, 255, 263, *265*, 509
Blaske, D. M., 553, *561*, 639, 650, 653, *677*, 678, *680*
Blatt, B., 370, *402*
Blatt, S. J., 226
Blechman, E. A., 38, *50*
Blehar, M. C., 342, *359*, *560*
Bleich, A., 278
Blew, P. A., 432, *443*
Bliss, E. L., 703, 707
Bliss, R., *512*
Blitzer, J. R., 687, *708*
Bloch, L. P., 718, *743*
Bloch, S., 506, *514*
Block, G. H., 88, *118*
Block-Pedego, A., 166, *192*
Blondis, T. A., 85, *126*
Bloom, A. S., 429, *443*
Blouin, A. G., 86, *118*
Blouin, D. C., 687, *715*
Blount, R. L., 229, 244, 259, 261, *265*, 293, 497, *509*
Bluebond-Langner, M., 499, *510*
Blum, H. M., *188*
Blumenstein, E., 459, *480*
Blumenthal, J. A., 686, *708*
Blumer, J. L., 263, *292*
Boake, C., 633, 645, 670, 672, *677*
Boat, B. W., 574, 595, 597, 607, *614*, 615
Bobrow, E. S., 503, 504, *510*
Bodmer-Turner, J., 576, *621*
Boer, A. P., 256, *265*
Boggs, S. R., 151, 156, 175, 176, *179*, *182*, 193
Bohan, T. P., 458, 459, *476*, 477, *478*
Bohr, Y., 700, *710*
Bohra, N., 78, *118*

Bohrnstedt, G., 696, 707
Boice, R., 260, 269
Boivin, M., 329, 331, 335, 336, 337, 340, 345, 354, 356, 360
Bolduc, E. A., 265
Boll, R., 493, 517
Boll, T. J., 390, 401, 492, 510
Bolstad, O. D., 42, 58
Bolton, D., 262, 266, 323
Bolton, P., 415, 450
Bonagura, N., 746
Bonaiuto, P., 726, 745
Bond, C. R., 137, 172, 179
Bond, L., 478
Bond, M. H., 343, 363
Bondy, A. S., 242, 276, 283
Boney-McCoy, S., 173, 191
Book, B. K., 679
Boon, C., 585, 621
Boone, L., 87, 124
Booth, A. L., 687, 707
Booth, C., 528, 566, 580, 614
Bootzin, R. R., 242, 243, 273, 301
Borchardt, C. M., 230, 265
Bordeaux, J., 514
Borden, M. C., 416, 443
Bordon, K., 228, 406
Borduin, C. M., 512, 534, 553, 561, 567, 580, 622, 639, 653, 677, 678, 679, 680
Borkovec, T. D., 230, 234, 265
Borkowski, J. G., 472, 476
Borner, H., 87, 123
Borner, S., 493, 510
Bornstein, M. A., 86, 118
Bornstein, M. T., 3, 30, 41, 50, 61, 634, 678
Bornstein, P. H., 3, 9, 11, 30, 41, 50, 61, 265, 285, 297, 313, 634, 678
Borreca, C., 406
Boskind-Lodahl, M., 692, 708
Bott, L., 429, 442
Bottoms, B., 593, 594, 595, 617
Bourdeau, P., 593, 594, 623
Bourgeois, M., 519
Bousha, D. M., 531, 561
Bowers, N. D., 76, 129
Bowers, W. A., 687, 716
Bowskill, R., 695, 708
Boychuk, T., 598, 615
Boyer, D., 591, 614
Boykin, R. A., 41, 63
Boyle, M., 482, 493, 510
Boyle, M. H., 133, 145, 146, 179, 188, 722, 743
Braafladt, N., 219, 225
Bradbury, T. N., 27, 50, 655, 667, 678
Bradford, D. C., 9, 56
Bradley, R., 387, 388, 402
Bradley, R. H., 547, 548, 551, 561
Bradlyn, A. S., 246, 248, 249, 258, 260, 265, 285, 286, 537, 567
Brady, E. V., 206, 220, 223, 238, 265
Brady, W. F., 693, 708
Braeges, J. L., 634, 682
Braggio, J. T., 724, 743
Braiman, S., 715
Branch, C. H. H., 703, 707, 708
Brand, A., 489, 510
Brand, S., 219, 224
Brandt, M., 458, 477
Branston, M., 443

Braswell, L., 112, 122, 123
Brathwaite, J., 533, 562
Braun, D. L., 709
Braunwald, K., 580, 615
Brazelton, B., 387, 388, 402
Bream, L. A., 133, 181
Breaux, A. M., 76, 119, 394, 403
Breen, M., 99, 117
Breen, M. J., 76, 77, 85, 99, 108, 109, 110, 116, 118, 141, 142, 144, 145, 153, 164, 177, 179
Bregman, J. D., 411, 416, 452
Breiner, J., 396, 397, 402
Breiner, J. L., 160, 179
Brener, J., 255, 265
Brent, D., 490, 514
Brent, E. E., 727, 747
Brent, L. J., 722, 744
Breslau, N., 392, 402, 457, 476, 482, 492, 493, 510, 517
Brewerton, T. D., 701, 708
Brewin, C. R., 38, 50
Bricker, W., 363
Brier, N., 397, 402
Briere, J., 574, 575, 582, 586, 587, 592, 600, 601, 614, 615, 619, 620
Brierley, L. M., 409, 411, 452
Briesmeister, J. M., 112, 127
Brigance, A., 390, 391, 402
Briggs, M., 190, 228
Bristol, M. M., 37, 38, 50, 392, 402, 435, 436, 437, 443
Britten, K. R., 412, 436, 447, 451
Brockel, B., 439, 444
Broden, M., 41, 50
Brody, G. H., 8, 33, 38, 47, 50, 54, 172, 183, 628, 629, 678, 682, 728, 743
Brodzinsky, D. M., 103, 124
Broman, S. H., 453, 459, 476
Bromfield, R., 20, 50
Brondino, M. J., 152, 190
Bronfenbrenner, U., 5, 8, 22, 50
Bronowski, J., 79, 81, 82, 118
Bronson, G. W., 237, 265
Brooke, E., 450
Brooks, D. L., 724, 743
Brooks-Gunn, J., 4, 53, 138, 182, 203, 216, 223, 227, 632, 681, 696, 703, 707, 708
Brookshire, B. L., 458, 459, 476, 477, 478
Brophy, C., 105, 123
Brothers, A. M., 415, 450
Broughton, D., 590, 616
Brouhard, B., 481, 518
Brouillete, C., 687, 713
Brouwers, P., 479
Browder, D. M., 431, 451
Brown, B., 264
Brown, B. W., 46, 66
Brown, C. H., 362
Brown, D., 4, 64, 390, 391, 402, 527, 566
Brown, F., 208, 225
Brown, G., 262, 264, 321, 324
Brown, G. G., 476
Brown, H. W., 71, 128
Brown, J. G., 571, 620
Brown, J. M., 497, 510
Brown, L., 389, 390, 402, 428, 431, 432, 443
Brown, M. M., 135, 179, 344, 361
Brown, R. T., 79, 126, 218, 226

Brown, S. A., 4, 171, 717, 718, 720, 721, 722, 723, 724, 725, 726, 727, 728, 729, 731, 732, 733, 735, 736, 738, 739, 740, 741, 743, 744, 745, 746, 747, 748
Brown, S. J., 475, 476
Brown, T. A., 230, 265, 696, 708
Browne, A., 599, 616
Browne, K., 581, 615
Brownell, K. D., 733, 744
Brozek, J., 697, 711
Brubaker, B. H., 272, 319
Bruce, D., 478
Bruce, D. A., 455, 456, 476
Bruch, H., 686, 690, 696, 698, 703, 708
Bruck, M., 593, 596, 615
Bruckel, S., 183
Bruhn, P., 87, 123
Bruininks, R. H., 376, 386, 387, 402, 404, 553, 561
Bruneau, N., 428, 443, 444
Brunner, J. F., 138, 173, 178, 663, 666, 667, 677
Bruschi, C., 364
Bryan, N., 461, 478
Bryant, D. M., 38, 67
Bryant, S. L., 587, 614
Bryant-Waugh, R., 687, 708, 709
Bryson, J. M., 511
Bryson, C. Q., 445
Bryson, S. E., 374, 376, 405, 411, 420, 451, 452
Buchsbaum, H. K., 554, 555, 556, 561
Buchsbaum, K., 355, 361
Bugental, D. B., 21, 38, 41, 50
Buhrmester, D., 40, 41, 54, 77, 122, 128, 331, 354, 362, 553, 554, 555, 556, 561, 627, 640, 678
Buitelaar, J., 452
Bukowski, W. M., 108, 125, 329, 331, 339, 340, 345, 354, 356, 360, 362, 490, 492, 510, 515
Bukstein, O. G., 720, 722, 724, 744, 748
Buktenica, N. A., 386, 387, 402
Bulcroft, R., 185
Bullock, D., 36, 38, 50, 60
Bunney, W. E., Jr., 125
Burbach, D., 517
Burbach, D. J., 4, 64, 495, 512
Burchinal, M., 339, 363, 489, 516
Burge, D., 219, 225, 228
Burge, D. A., 247
Burgess, A. W., 534, 561, 575, 615
Burgess, E. W., 172, 179
Burgess, R. L., 540, 558, 561
Burish, T., 259, 272
Burke, J. C., 437, 447, 451
Burke, J. D., 239, 265
Burke, J. E., 472, 476
Burke, K. C., 239, 265
Burnett, P., 171, 179
Burns, G. L., 150, 151, 152, 161, 179, 191
Burns, T., 689, 709
Burnside, M. A., 732, 744
Burroughs, J., 683, 715
Burry, V. F., 491, 509
Burt, M. R., 570, 615
Burton, J., 429, 446
Burton, R. V., 35, 68
Busby, D. M., 172, 180
Buschke, H., 471, 477

Busemeyer, J. R., 4, 8, *58*
Bush, E., 633, *678*
Bush, J. P., 259, *265*, 497, *510*
Bush, M., 528, *562*
Buss, A. H., *184*, 258, *265*, 268
Busse, R. T., 147, *181*, *182*
Butcher, J. N., 36, *50*, 206, 229
Butler, E. J., 362
Butler, I. J., 453, 472, 474, 478
Butler, R. J., 38, *50*
Buttenwieser, E., 548, *566*
Bybee, D., 596, *615*
Bynum, R., *510*
Byrne, C., *188*
Byrne, T., 87, *127*

Cadman, D., 482, 486, 489, 490, 493, *510*
Cadman, D. T., *188*
Caffaro-Rouget, A., 583, *615*
Cain, L., 390, *404*
Cairns, B. D., 341, 355, 360
Cairns, E., 103, *118*
Cairns, N. U., 491, 492, *510*, *514*
Cairns, R. B., 44, *50*, 341, 355, 360
Caldwell, B., 387, 388, *402*
Caldwell, B. M., 547, 548, 551, *561*
Caldwell, S., 234, 269, 287, 497, *513*
Calhoun, K. S., 5, 16, *49*, *51*, 170, *180*
Caliso, J. A., 557, *561*
Calkins, S. D., 335, 336, 360, *361*, *364*
Callahan, E. J., 242, 256, 272, 283
Callahan, T. D., 454, 478
Callan, V., 727, *744*
Cameron, T., *613*
Camerson, O. G., 239, *277*
Cammock, T., 103, *118*
Camparo, L., 640, *678*
Campbell, D. T., 247, *266*
Campbell, F., 489, *516*
Campbell, I., *403*
Campbell, J. A., 547, *566*
Campbell, J. D., 35, *68*
Campbell, M., 415, *444*, *452*
Campbell, N. B., 633, *678*
Campbell, P. G., 694, *714*
Campbell, R., 489, *517*
Campbell, S. B., 73, 75, 76, 83, 84, 85, 92, 103, *118*, *119*, 131, 133, 136, *180*, 235, *265*
Campbell, V. L., 7, *67*
Campbell, W., 258, 269
Campis, L. K., 169, *180*
Campos, J. J., 36, *55*, 235, 260, 261, *265*, *271*
Canady, A. I., 477
Canino, B., 228,
Canino, G., 190, 226, *406*
Canter, W., 638, 641, 644, 651, 652, 654, *681*
Cantor, N., 9, 28, *50*, *51*
Cantwell, D. P., 77, 85, 86, 88, *119*, *126*, 198, 206, 224, 226, 416, 434, *444*
Capaldi, D. M., 133, 134, 137, 138, 139, 164, 171, 174, *180*, *188*, 640, 660, *678*
Caplan, M., 356, *360*
Cappo, L., 729, *747*
Capuano, F., 271, 305
Caraballo, L., *563*
Carbonell, J. L., 38, *51*

Cardarelli, A. P., 579, *617*
Carek, D. J., 229, 231, 235, *263*
Carey, M., 228
Carey, M. P., 172, *180*
Carlino, C., 505, *514*
Carlson, C., *125*
Carlson, C. I., 46, *51*, 55
Carlson, C. L., 72, 79, *123*
Carlson, G. A., 198, 200, 224, 226
Carlson, J., *181*
Carlson, J. I., *444*
Carlson, V., 532, 555, 560, 567, 580, *615*
Carlson-Green, B., 460, *477*
Carlton-Ford, S., 632, *681*, 703, 708
Carnochan, J., 592, *619*
Carnochan, P., 235, *267*
Caro-Martinez, L., 397, *402*
Caron, C., *51*, 221, 224
Caron, H. S., 503, *510*
Carpenter, P., *516*
Carpentieri, S. C., 429, *444*
Carr, A. C., 4, 5, *49*, *51*
Carr, E., *446*
Carr, E. G., *11*, 22, *51*, 53, 412, 413, 414, 438, 439, 440, 441, *444*, 445
Carr, T., 205, 229
Carroll, E. M., 586, *616*
Carroll, K., 697, *712*
Carroll-Wilson, M., 41, *60*, 205, 227
Carrow-Woolfolk, E., 382, 383, *402*
Carruth, B. R., 686, *708*
Carte, E. T., 36, *57*
Carter, E. A., 627, *678*
Carter, P., 688, *713*
Carter, R., 499, *513*
Carter, R. A., 77, *128*
Carver, R. P., 25, *51*
Casat, C. D., 206, *225*
Casey, K., 525, *562*
Casey, P. H., 548, *561*
Cash, R., 628, *681*
Cash, T. F., 696, *708*
Casper, R. C., 683, 686, 692, 699, *708*, 710
Caspi, A., 135, 139, 140, *180*, *188*, *193*, 337, 360
Cassidy, J., 633, *682*
Castaneda, A., 249, *265*
Castellanos, F. X., 87, *119*
Castelloe, P., 416, 417, *444*
Castenada, A., 41, *51*, 258, 316
Catalano, R. F., 134, *184*
Cataldo, M. F., 133, *190*
Catroppa, C., 478
Cattell, P., 429, *444*
Cattell, R. B., 28, *51*
Caudill, M., 506, *511*
Caul, W. F., 72, *122*
Caulfield, M. B., 47, *67*, 439, *445*
Cautela, J., *51*, 144, *180*
Cautela, J. R., 32, *51*, 144, *180*
Cavell, T. A., 553, *561*
Cecalupo, A., 482, *510*
Ceci, S. J., 593, 596, *615*
Celano, M., 587, *617*
Celebi, S., 156, *180*
Cerezo, M. A., 533, *561*
Cerny, J. A., *63*
Cerreto, M. C., 16, *51*
Certo, N., *443*
Chadwick, M. W., 505, *513*
Chadwick, O., 86, *126*
Chaffin, L., 44, *67*
Chaffin, M., 573, *619*

Chaiken, S., 706, 708, *713*
Chalmers, M., 548, *566*
Chalons, F., *447*
Chamberlain, C., *621*
Chamberlain, P., 133, 140, 162, 177, *180*, 189, 634, *678*
Chamberlin, R. W., 84, *119*
Chambers, W. J., 40, *51*, 208, 209, 210, 224, 227, 247, 275, 555, *561*
Chaney, J., 4, 64, 257, 274, 504, *510*
Chang, J. L., 686, *708*
Chansky, T. E., 270
Chapin, H. N., 239, *263*
Chapman, J., *515*
Chapman, S. B., 454, 477, 478
Charlop, M. H., 413, 432, *444*
Charney, E., 503, *510*
Chasnoff, I. J., 491, *514*
Chassin, L., 235, 249, 278, 309, 724, 726, 727, 728, 729, 730, 731, 739, 744, 746, 747
Chee, P., 76, *119*
Chen, I. L., 709
Chen, L., *118*
Chen, T. C., 87, *125*
Chen, W. J., 120, 165, *180*
Chernin, K., 707, 708
Chernyk, B., 697, *712*
Cherry, T., 498, *515*
Chess, S., 71, *119*, 135, 164, *184*, *191*, 192, 241, 257, 258, 265, 268, 277, 415, *444*
Child Abuse Prevention and Treatment Act of 1974, 524, *562*
Child Abuse Prevention, Adoption and Family Services Act of 1988, 524, 562
Childress, A. C., 701, *708*
Chiodo, J., 699, *708*
Chipman, J. J., 686, *708*
Chlopan, B. E., 38, *51*
Choate, M., 87, *120*
Chow, J., 527, *562*
Christ, M. A. G., 54, 72, *123*, *183*, *184*, 190, 192, 234, 235, 236, *264*
Christen, H. J., 417, *444*
Christensen, A., 41, 56, 148, 164, *180*, 260, 265, 639, 640, 653, 667, 669, *678*, 679
Christensen, C., 172, *180*, 577, *617*
Christiaanse, M., 504, 506, *510*
Christian, D. L., 111, *127*
Christiansen, B. A., 726, 739, 744, *745*, 747
Christie, M., 698, *713*
Christoff, K., 246, *265*, 285
Christopher, J. S., 347, 359, 557, *563*
Chuang, S., 477
Chui, H. C., 415, *444*
Chung, M. C., 435, *451*
Churchill, D. W., 416, *445*
Ciampi, A., 479
Ciaranello, R. D., 416, *451*
Cicchetti, D. V., 4, 6, 8, 10, 23, *51*, 100, *127*, 204, 224, 235, 260, 261, 265, 266, 329, 360, *406*, 411, 416, 418, 420, 431, *451*, 452, 469, 475, 476, 479, 528, 530, 531, 533, 534, 537, 555, 556, 560, *561*, 562, 564, 566, 567, 580, 593, *615*, 619, 727, 744
Cillessen, A. H. N., 334, 360
Ciminero, A. R., 5, 31, 35, *51*, 57, 170, *180*
Cipes, M., 249, 277, 291

Citrin, W. C., 505, *511*
Clark, D. A., 262, 266, 323
Clark, D. B., 249, 262, 266, 303
Clark, G. M., 492, *510*
Clark, J. E., 492, *516*
Clark, L., 351, 353, *360*
Clark, L. A., 206, 213, 220, 228
Clark, P., 429, *444*
Clarke, C., 258, 270
Clarke, D., 37, 62
Clarke, G. N., 208, 224
Clarke, J. C., 249, 273, 313, 314
Clarke, W., 506, *519*
Clarke, W. L., 504, *510*
Clarren, S., 492, *517*
Cleghorn, G., 497, *516*
Clement, P. F., 688, 691, 697, 700,
    710
Clement, P. W., 36, 41, *51*
Clements, S. D., 71, *119*
Cleminshaw, H. K., 38, 55, 169,
    184
Clevanger, T., 245, 266
Cleveland, S. E., 696, *714*
Cloninger, C. R., 726, *744*
Clopper, R., *517*
Close, D., 391, *406*
Cloutier, P. F., 493, *518*
Clucas, T. J., *61*
Cluff, R. B., 670, 673, *678*
Cluss, P. A., 504, *511*
Clyman, R. B., 556, *561*
Coakley, M., 590, *618*
Cobb, I. A., 29, 57
Cobb, J. A., 157, 160, *180*, 189, 537,
    566
Cobb, L., 490, *512*
Coburn, J., 704, *708*
Coburn, P. C., 498, *511*
Cockrell, C. S., 259, 265
Coddington, R. D., 219, 224
Coe, D. A., 419, *451*
Coffman, D. A., 690, 692, 697, *708*
Cohan, J., 246, 277, 291
Cohen, A. S., 230, 263
Cohen, C. I., 540, 562
Cohen, D. J., 4, 8, 23, *51*, 87, 88, *127*,
    278, 411, 415, 448, 449, 452
Cohen, E., 225
Cohen, F. S., 534, 562
Cohen, I. L., 416, *444*
Cohen, J., 177, *189*
Cohen, J. A., 583, 587, *615*
Cohen, N. J., 75, 78, *119*
Cohen, P., 65, 177, *189, 191*, 228
Cohen, R. M., 120, *129*
Cohn, D. A., 137, *181*
Coie, J. D., 21, *51*, 108, *116*, 131, 133,
    134, 135, 138, *180, 181*, 329, 330,
    331, 332, 333, 334, 337, 340, 346,
    350, 352, 355, 357, 358, 359, *360*,
    361, 363, *364*
Colarusso, R., 386, 387, 402
Colbert, K. K., 4, *66*
Colbus, D., 150, *186*, 205, 226
Colder, C. R., 729, *744*
Cole, C. L., 30, *65*
Cole, D. A., 218, 219, 224, 227, 632,
    645, 672, 675, *678*
Cole, H. E., 639, *680*
Cole, P. M., 77, *119*, 524, 568, 581,
    612, *615*
Colegrove, R., 489, 490, *510*
Coleman, C. A., 496, 497, *510*
Coleman, M., 415, *444, 446*

Coles, E. M., 251, 273
Collier, A., 489, *511*
Collins, B. E., 29, *67*
Collins, F. L., 33, *51*
Collins, J. K., 696, *708*
Collins, P., 415, *444*
Collins, W. A., 627, 631, 633, *678*
Colon, E., 693, *712*
Columbus, M., 171, *178*
Colvin, A., 151, 152, *182*
Colvin, G., 161, *192*
Comeau, J., 490, *515*
Compaan, C., 527, 565
Compas, B. E., 4, 16, 21, 41, *51*, *63*,
    197, 198, 203, 206, 208, 215, 216,
    219, 220, 221, 223, 224, 225, 226,
    227, 728, *744*
Compton, P., *517*
Compton, W. M., 223
Conaway, R. L., 557, *563*
Conboy, J., 86, *123*
Condiotte, M., 243, 272
Conduct Problems Prevention
    Research Group, 161, 177, 342,
    364
Cone, J. D., 3, 9, 11, 25, 27, 31, 32,
    33, 42, 43, *51*, 54, 241, 242, 247,
    266, 267, 391, 402, 660, *678*
Cone, L. T., *678*
Conger, K. J., 629, *681*
Conger, R., 558, 559, *561, 562*
Conger, R. D., 43, *52*, 203, 225, 629,
    635, 637, 640, 642, 643, 644, 651,
    654, *681*
Conger, R. E., 142, *189*
Connell, J. P., *14, 52*
Connelly, C. D., 527, *562*
Connelly, J., 348, 353, *361*
Conners, C. K., 23, 36, 48, *52*, 65, 73,
    76, 77, 87, 98, 103, 111, *119, 121*,
    122, 147, 148, 149, *180, 181, 191*,
    199, 206, 223, 224, 228, 394, 395,
    402, 469, *477*
Conners, G. J., 726, *744*
Connolly, A. J., 386, 387, *402*
Connor, J. K., 208, 224, 225, 226
Connors, M., 692, *708*
Connors, M. E., 702, *711*
Connors, R. E., 138, *185*
Conover, N. C., 35, 40, *53*, 143, 149,
    182, 211, 225, 380, *403*
Conrad, J., 333, *362*
Contant, C., *514*
Conte, J., 583, 585, *615*
Conte, J. R., 595, *615*
Conzalez, J. J., 122
Cook, E. H., 88, *119*, 394, *404*
Cook, T., 391, 402, 415
Cook, T. D., 247, *266*
Cooke, E. H., *444*
Cools, J. N., 212, 226
Cooney, G., 592, *620*
Cooper, D. H., *403*
Cooper, J., 266, *321*
Cooper, L., 371, 381, 397, *402*
Cooper, M. L., 728, 732, *744*
Cooper, P. J., 686, 688, 695, 696, 698,
    708, *709*
Cooper, Z., 696, 698, *708*
Coopersmith, S., 41, *52*
Copeland, A. P., 77, *119*
Copeland, D., *516*
Copeland, D. R., 460, *478*
Coplan, R. J., 335, 336, *360, 361*,
    364

Coppotelli, H., 329, *360*
Corbett, J. A., 377, *402*
Corbin, S. M., 265, 497, *509*
Corcoran, C. M., 226
Corcoran, M., 527, *564*
Cordle, C., 698, *713*
Corkum, P. V., 75, 76, 103, *119*
Cormier, W. H., 34, 67, 142, 144, *192*
Cornish-McTighe, D., 231, 235, *263*
Cornsweet, C., 36, *57*
Corter, C., 35, *63*
Coscina, D. V., 693, *710*
Costanzo, P. R., 355, *364*
Costello, A. J., 30, 35, 40, 52, 53, 143,
    145, 148, *182*, 208, 211, 212, 213,
    224, 225, 247, 266, 380, *403*, 587,
    615
Costello, E. J., *181*, 211, 220, 221,
    223, 224
Cotch, P. A., 255, *263*
Cotler, S., 245, 266, 309
Cotterell, J. L., 4, *52*
Cottler, L. B., 223
Coulter, M., 576, *621*
Coulter, M. L., 582, *616*
Coulton, C., 527, *562*
Countermine, T., 20, *49*
Counts, C. R., 696, *708*
Courage, M. L., 593, *618*
Courchesne, E., 415, 429, *444, 448*
Court, J. H., 429, *450*
Cowan, C. P., 137, *181*
Cowan, P. A., 137, *181*
Cowell, C., *477*
Cowen, E. L., 35, 36, *52*, 328, 361,
    362
Cox, A., 412, *443*
Cox, D., 506, *519*
Cox, N. J., *119*
Cox, R., 419, *446*
Coyle, V., 498, *518*
Coyne, J. C., 174, *185*, 212, 213, 224,
    225, 740, *747*
Cradock, C., 245, 266, 309, 310
Craft, J. L., 580, *615*
Crago, M., 606, *623*
Craig, K. D., 497, *510*
Craig, M. E., 574, *618*
Craighead, L. W., 41, 66, 205, 228
Craighead, W. E., 4, 41, 59, 66, 205,
    211, 226, 228
Crane, D. R., 172, *180, 181*
Cranstoun, F., 271, 282, 318
Crawford, J., 439, *444*
Crawford, P., 159, *181*, 493, *511*
Creamer, V. A., 729, 731, 743, *744*
Creer, T., 499, *510*
Creighton, S., 580, *617*
Crick, N. R., 4, 11, *52*, 135, *181*, 330,
    336, 344, 345, *361*
Crider, B., 231, 266
Crimmins, D. B., 413, 438, 439, *445*
Crisp, A. H., 687, 688, 689, 691, 692,
    693, 696, 697, 698, 703, 705, 707,
    708, 709, 710, 711, 713, *715*
Crist, W., 503, *510*
Crittenden, P. M., 528, 529, 530, 531,
    562
Crnic, K. A., 38, *52*, 173, 174, 179,
    181, 392, 399, 402, 403, 435, *446*
Croake, J. W., 236, 237, 240, 266
Crockett, L. J., 718, *743*
Cronbach, L. J., 8, *52*
Crosby, L., 153, *181*, 339, *361*, 640,
    678

Crosby, R. D., 177, *178*
Cross, D. G., 236, 237, 238, 276
Cross, H. J., 598, 623
Crouch, J. L., 524, 532, 562
Crouse-Novack, M. A., *514*
Crowley, T. J., 724, 726, 744
Crowther, J. H., 688, 695, 709, 716
Cruttenden, L., 80, *120*
Csikzentmihalyi, M., 698, 709
Cubic, B. A., 495, *519*
Cuccaro, M. L., 175, *181*
Cuerra, E., 268
Culhane, K. A., *478*
Cull, C. A., 463, 477
Cullinan, D., 377, *403*
Cummings, E. M., 16, 52, 137, *181*, 537, 556, 562, 666, 678
Cummings, J. D., 239, 266
Cummings, M., *517*
Cummings, S. T., 493, *510*
Cunningham, A. H., 573, *621*
Cunningham, C., 76, *117*
Cunningham, C. E., 75, 85, 88, 105, 108, 111, *117*, *119*
Cunningham, J. A., 732, 747
Cunningham, W., 499, *513*
Cunningham-Rathner, J., 576, *613*
Curcio, F., 412, 430, *444*
Curran, P. J., 727, 744
Curtis, G. C., 239, 277
Curtis, S., *118*
Cushing, P. J., 133, *190*
Cuskey, W. R., 499, *514*
Cuthbert, M. I., 251, 271, 288
Cutler, G., 489, *515*
Cutrona, C. E., 540, 562
Cytryn, L., 208, 210, 226, 247, 269

D'Antonio, W. V., 22, 52
D'Zurilla, T. J., 63, 678
Dabbs, J. M., 251, 270
Dadds, M. R., 136, 137, 141, 142, 153, 164, 168, 173, 177, *181*, *190*, 580, 612, *615*, 628, 629, 636, 651, 658, 678, 681
Dahl, R. E., 217
Dahlquist, L., 505, *518*
Dahms, W. T., 492, *513*
Dalby, J. T., 44, *60*
Daleiden, E. L., 578, *618*
Daly, K., 414, *450*
Damasio, A. R., *444*
Damasio, H., 415, *444*
Damon, L., *616*
Dampier, C. D., 496, *518*
Dancy, B. L., 633, 678
Dandes, S. K., 234, *271*, 305, 335, 363
Dandoy, A. C., *270*
Daneman, D., *511*
Danforth, J. S., 77, 111, *119*, 631, 681
Daniele, R., 492, *515*
Daniels, C., 499, *510*
Daniels, S. R., 688, *712*
Darby, B. L., *127*
Darby, P. L., 687, 709
Dare, C., 704, 709
Darling, N., 535, 567, 676, 682
Daro, D. K., 525, 562
Dash, J., 494, *518*
Daston, S., 699, 710
Davey, G. C. L., 261, 266, 269
David, O. J., 87, *119*
Davids, A., 422, *444*

Davidson, K., *478*
Davidson, K. C., 458, 476, 477
Davidson, K. S., 276, 307
Davidson, L. L., 84, *119*
Davidson, P. W., 453, 479
Davidson, R. J., 234, 267
Davies, M., 51, 65, 189, 190, 191, 224, 226, 227, 228, 406, 561, 715
Davies, P., 137, *181*
Davies, P. T., 6, 52, 137, *181*, 666, 678
Davies, W., 490, *515*
Davies, W. H., 492, *510*
Davis, A., *442*
Davis, A. F., 242, 266, 300
Davis, B., 42, 57, 629, 660, 661, 678, 679, 695, 715
Davis, C., 499, *518*
Davis, C. J., 687, 700, *715*, 716
Davis, C. S., 727, 742
Davis, D., 698, 713
Davis, G. E., 220, 224
Davis, J. M., 578, *621*, 699, 708, 710
Davis, M., 199, 204, 205, 505, *511*
Davis, M. S., 503, *510*
Davis, N., 261, 265
Davis, R., 710
Davis, S. C., 683
Davis, S. G., *118*
Davis, W. K., 499, *512*
Dawes, R. D., 5, *56*
Dawson, B., 3, *50*
Dawson, G., 24, 52, *444*
Dawson, V. L., 575, *619*
Day, D., 576, *619*
Day, D. M., 133, *181*
de la Burde, B., 87, *120*
de la Fuente, J. R., 171, *190*
Deal, A. G., 397, 398, 399, 402, 403, 406
DeBaryshe, B., 47, 67
DeBlassie, R. R., 583, *614*
Deblinger, E., 581, 585, *615*, *619*
DeCuir-Whalley, S., 499, *516*
DeFee, J. F., Jr., 259, 266
DeFries, J. C., 88, *121*
DeGiovanni, I. S., 235, 240, 268
DeGroot, A., 199, 224
DeHaan, C., 492, *518*
DeKeseredy, W., 20, *53*
Dekker, M. J. A., 462, 476
DeKlyen, M., 135, 136, 137, *181*, *184*, *191*, 580, *617*
Del Bigio, M. R., 458, 477
Del Dotto, J. E., *476*
Delis, D., 459, *480*
Delis, D. C., 472, 477
DeLoache, J. S., 596, *615*
DeLong, G. R., 417, *444*
DeLoye, G., 499, *510*
Delprato, D. J., 234, 235, 266
Delquadri, J. C., 29, *55*
Deiuty, R. H., 41, 52, 344, *361*
Demaray, M. K., 165, *181*
Demb, H. B., 395, 396, 402
DeMyer, M. K., 411, 414, 416, 422, 435, *444*, *445*, 449
DeMyer, W. E., *445*
Denckla, M. B., 75, 77, *120*, 461, 472, 473, 477, 478
Dennis, M., 453, 454, 458, 459, 460, 469, 476, 477
Denny, C., 111, *126*

Densen-Gerber, J., 534, 562
Denson, R., 87, 88, *120*
Derby, K. M., 7, *52*
Derby, M., 402
Derogatis, L. R., 110, *120*, 258, 266, 550, 551, 555, 562, *615*
DeRosier, M. E., 328, *363*
DesJardins, C., 16, *55*
Despert, J. C., 408, *445*
DeStefano, L., 492, *510*
Deutsch, F., 690, *715*
Devany, J., 414, *450*
deVeber, L. L., 496, *515*
DeVellis, R. F., 414, *450*
DeVito, E., 415, *444*
Dewey, M., *511*
Deykin, E. V., 415, *445*, 724, 739, 746
Diamond, A., 80, *120*
Diamond, R., 77, *121*
Dias, K., 417, *446*
Dibrell, L. L., 262, 266
Dick, T., 573, 587, *621*
Dickson, N., 139, *188*
DiClemente, C. C., 740, 741, 746, 747
Dielman, T. E., 727, 744
Dietiker, K. E., 236, 239, 275, 319, 396, *406*
Dietz, A., 32, *63*
DiLalla, D. L., 419, *445*, 529, 530, 562
DiLalla, L. F., 628, 678
DiLavore, P. C., 426, *445*
DiLillo, D. K., 589, *615*
Diller, L., 492, *515*
Dillon, D., 489, *519*
Dillon, M., 534, *564*
Dimberg, U., 261, 274
Dimino, E., 492, *510*
DiMito, A. M., 588, 608, 609, *614*
DiNardo, P. A., 263
Dion, K., 706, 707
DiRaimondo, C., 499, *510*
Dirlich-Wilhelm, H., *447*
Disbrow, M., 37, 52
Dishion, T. J., 4, 11, 30, 43, 44, 52, 60, 63, 64, 133, 134, 137, 138, 153, 157, *181*, 189, *190*, 329, 331, 339, 341, 342, 355, 358, *361*, 728, 730, 734, 744
Dix, T., 4, 21, 22, 38, 52
Dixon, K. N., 693, 712, 714
Dixon, M. J., *125*
Doane, J. A., 629, 678
Dobkin, P. L., 339, *361*, 364
Doctors, S., 506, *511*
Dodge, K. A., 4, 11, 29, 52, 108, *120*, 131, 133, 134, 135, 138, 161, 165, 167, 180, *181*, 191, 193, 328, 329, 330, 332, 334, 337, 340, 342, 344, 345, 346, 347, 352, 355, 356, 359, 360, *361*, 363, 364, 530, 554, 562
Doerr, H., 37, 52
Doershuk, C. F., 492, *513*
Dokecki, P., 404
Dolan, L. J., 362
Dolgin, M. J., 258, 259, 266, 495, 506, *511*, *516*
Dolinsky, A., *715*
Doll, H. A., 696, 709
Dollinger, S. J., 21, 52, 239, 266
Dollins, J., 232, 263
Donald, W., 493, *518*
Donatelli, L. S., *451*
Donders, J., 477

Dong, Q., 236, 237, 239, 266
Donnellan, A. M., 411, 438, *445*, *449*
Donnermeyer, J. F., 719, *744*
Donovan, A., 392, 402
Donovan, D. M., 744
Donovan, J. E., 266, 726, 727, 735, 736, 745
Dooley, D., 731, 747
Doris, J., 245, 266, 297, 298, 317
Dorkey, M., 266, 292
Dorko, B., 571, 620
Dornbusch, S. M., 535, 567, 676, 678, 682
Dorsey, M., *404*
Dorsey, M. F., 438, 452
Doster, J. A., 16, 49
Dotemoto, S., 29, 67, 111, *128*
Douglas, V. I., 52, 71, 72, 75, 76, 77, 83, 112, *118*, 120, 125, 128, 422, *445*
Douglass, D., 591, *613*
Dow, M. G., 5, 28, 52
Downey, G., 212, 213, 224, 532, 533, 562
Doyle, A., *179*, 348, 353, *361*
Dozois, D. J. A., 3, 27, 30, 60
Drabman, R. S., 4, 7, 25, 31, *51*, 54, 55, 242, 268
Draeger, S., 76, *120*
Drash, A., 498, *511*
Dreger, R. M., 16, 52
Dreher, M., 505, 517
Drell, M. J., 603, 621
Driscoll, J. M., 539, *564*
Droegemueller, W., 523, *564*
Drotar, D., 149, 159, *181*, 456, 469, 474, 479, 486, 490, 492, 493, 506, *511*, *513*, 515, 516, 529, 562
Dryden, M., 136
Dube, W. V., 454, 478
Dubeau, D., 271, 305
duBerger, R., 479
Dubey, D. R., 112, *120*
DuBois, D. L., 219, 224
Dubowitz, H., 530, *563*
Du Bose, R., 381, 402
Duchan, J., 412, *449*
Duchnowski, A. J., 681
Dugas, F., 78, *128*
Dugdale, R. L., 370, 402
DuHaime, A. C., 455, 456, 477
Dukan, M., 587, *615*
Duke, M. P., 41, 63
Dulcan, D., 228, *406*
Dulcan, M., *190*, 226
Dulcan, M. J., 35, 40, 53
Dulcan, M. K., 143, *182*, 208, 211, *224*, 225, 247, 266, 380, 403
Dumas, J. E., 27, 30, 52, 67, 133, 136, 137, 138, 170, 175, *181*, 182, 192, 259, 261, 266, 271, 305, 559, 562
Dunbar, F., 483, *511*
Duncan, G. J., 4, 53, 138, *182*
Duncan, S. P., 571, 572, *614*
Dunlop, G., 236, 266, 447
Dunn, J., 35, 53, *515*, 617
Dunn, L. M., 382, 383, 402
Dunn, N., 493, 517
Dunn, R. M., 469, 477
Dunn, S. M., 499, *511*
Dunne, E. A., 497, *511*
Dunst, C. J., 5, 6, 22, 31, 38, 53, 397, 398, 399, 402, 403, 406
DuPaul, D. G., 100
DuPaul, G., 72, 73, 79, 103, *117*

DuPaul, G. J., 72, 75, 76, 77, 79, 85, 86, 90, 91, 97, 98, 99, 100, 104, 111, 115, *116*, *117*, 120, 126, 495, *511*
DuPaul, G. R., 92, 98, *120*
Durand, V. M., 413, 438, 439, *444*, 445
During, S. M., 175, *178*
Duster, T., 20, 64
Dutton, D. G., 547, *562*
Dwyer, J. T., 417, *444*
Dyer, K., 434, *445*
Dyk, P. A. H., 627, *680*
Dykens, E., 452
Dykman, R. A., 270, 231, 324
Dyson, L. L., 392, 403

Eagle, M., 710
Earls, F., 262, 266
Eaton, I., 377, 392, 403
Eaves, D. M., 416, *445*
Eaves, L. C., 416, *445*
Ebert, M. H., 687, 699, 715
Eccles, J. S., 273, 312
Echterling, L., 718, 745
Eckblad, G. F., 670, 671, 682
Eckburg, P., 119
Eckenrode, J., 533, 535, *562*, 565
Eckert, E. D., 683, 687, 688, 692, 693, 694, 699, 708, 710, 712, 713
Eddy, J. M., 157, *189*, 667, 679
Edelbrock, C. S., 14, 16, 23, 24, 25, 29, 30, 35, 39, 40, 48, 49, 53, 73, 76, 85, 86, 88, 99, 100, 103, *117*, 120, 121, 133, 135, 140, 143, 145, 148, 149, 161, *182*, 189, 207, 208, 211, 212, 213, 223, 224, 225, 247, 266, 380, 403, 587, *615*, 724, 742
Edelsohn, G. A., 362, 576, 582, 616, 621
Edelstein, B., 595, 622
Eder, D., 331, *361*
Edgar, E., 391, 392, 403
Edgar-Smith, S., 572, 580, 618
Edgell, D., 453, 479
Edlin, J. C., 686, 708
Edwall, G., 587, *615*
Edwards, D., *182*
Edwards, J. J., 580, *615*
Edwards, K., 722, 748
Edwards, L. A., 166, 168, *184*
Edwards, R. W., 729, 747
Egeland, B., 20, 53, 173, 174, *189*, 524, 528, 529, 530, 532, *562*, 563
Eggers, C., 418, *445*
Egolf, B. P., 537, *563*, 583, 617
Ehrenreich, N. S., 23, 62
Ehrlich, R. M., 477
Eiben, R., 478
Eidelson, J. I., 264, 324
Einbender, A. J., 530, *563*, 587, *615*
Einfeld, S. L., 395, 396, 403
Einhorn, A. M., 701, 712
Eisen, A. R., 246, 247, 267, 276, 303, 327
Eisen, J. L., 687, 713
Eisenberg, G., 59
Eisenberg, H. M., 456, 473, 477, 478
Eisenberg, L., 241, 267, 409, 445, 450
Eisenstadt, T. H., 148, 150, 151, 156, 175, 176, *182*, 188
Eiser, C., 498, *511*
Eiser, J. R., 732, 746

Eisert, D., 505, 506, *514*
Eisler, I., 704, 709
Ekman, P., 234, 267, 661, 678
Elbert, J. C., 6, 53
Elder, G. H., 203, 225, 337, 360
Eldredge, D., 510
Eldredge, K. L., 698, 716
Eldredge, R., 529, 564
Elfman, M. L., 255, 274
Elias, H. M., 613, *615*
Eliopulos, D., 122
Elkind, D., 725, 745
Elkind, G. S., 75, *128*
Ellenberg, L., 497, *513*
Ellickson, P. L., 727, 745
Elliot, C. H., 497
Elliot, S., 108, 355, *361*
Elliott, A. J., 7, 53
Elliott, C. H., 234, 244, 269, 287, 497, *511*, *513*
Elliott, D. M., 574, 575, 582, 586, 601, *615*
Elliott, D. S., 152, *182*
Elliott, M., 581, *615*
Elliott, S., *121*
Elliott, S. N., 145, 147, *182*, 193, 343, 351, 353, 360, 362, 364
Elliot-Faust, D., 550, *564*
Ellis, C. R., *451*
Ellis, D., 20, 53, 161, *191*
Ellis, R., 350, 364
Elmasian, R., 429, 448
Elmer, E., 528, 563
Elwell, M. E., 583, 586, *615*
Elzey, R., 390, *404*
Emde, R. N., 261, 271, 556, *561*
Eme, R. F., 24, 53, 139, *182*, 236, 239, 262, 267
Emery, G., 170, 179, 230, 264
Emery, R. E., 4, 22, 53, 627, 633, 678, 682
Emmons, L., 503, 506, *511*
Emslie, G. J., 217, 225
Endicott, J., 171, *191*, 204, 228, 258, 267
Endler, N. S., 10, 53
Endriga, M. C., 136, *184*
Engel, M., 23, 64
Engfer, A., 336, 337, *361*
England, P., 617
Enrile, B. G., 459, 480
Ensign, J., 585, 622
Ensom, R., 619
Ephross, P. H., 583, 586, *615*
Epkins, C. C., 267, 322
Epps, J., 149, *186*
Epstein, L. J., 413, *445*
Epstein, L. H., 498, 499, 503, 504, *511*
Epstein, M. H., 377, *403*
Epstein, N., 262, 264, 320
Epstein, N. B., 627, 635, 636, 639, 649, 678, 680
Erbaugh, J., 38, 49, *561*
Erbaugh, J. K., 204, 223
Erhardt, D., 100, *122*
Erickson, M., 529, 563
Erickson, M. F., 532, 563
Erne, D., 4, 55
Ernst, A. R., 496, *516*
Ernst, M., 87, *120*
Eron, L. D., 131, *185*
Ervin, C. S., 724, 745
Eskinazi, B., 87, *121*
Esonis, S., 32, *51*, 144, *180*

Esplin, P. W., 598, *615*
Espmark, S., 696, 707
Estep, R. E., 570, *615*
Estes, A., 6, 24, 106, 108, 153, 158, 159, *188*, *190*, 350, 541
Esveldt-Dawson, K., 26, 59, 150, 152, *186*, 213, 226, 234, 235, 243, 256, 267, 302, 310
Etnyre, G., 503, *512*
Etzwiler, D. D., 498, 505, *511*, *515*
Eurman, L. J., 708
Evans, B., 583, 623
Evans, C., 258, 267, 506, *511*
Evans, E. G., 219, 224
Evans, I. M., 3, 4, 5, 8, 11, 15, 16, 23, 24, 28, 30, 31, 35, 53, 67, 240, 267, 389, *403*
Evans, P. D., 242, 243, 267, 300
Evans, S. W., 109, *120*
Evans, T., 724, *745*
Evans, T. A., 235, 275, 302
Evans-Jones, L. G., 417, *445*
Everson, M. D., 574, 576, 582, 583, 592, 595, 597, 607, 611, *614*, *615*, *616*, 621
Ewigman, B. E., 526, 527, 559, *563*, 567
Ewing, L. J., 76, 92, *118*, *119*, 133, *180*
Ewing-Cobbs, L., 455, 456, 472, 473, *477*, 478
Ey, S., 198, 206, 224, 227
Eyberg, S. M., 107, *126*, 135, 148, 150, 151, 152, 156, 158, 159, 169, 175, 176, 179, 180, 182, 184, 188, 190, 192, 193
Eysenck, H. J., 41, 53
Eyster, C., 596, *619*
Ezekowitz, W., 356, 360
Ezhuthachan, S., 476

Fabian, L. J., 696, 709
Factor, D. C., 435, *445*
Faed, J. M., 87, *127*
Fagan, S., 579, *616*
Fagot, B. I., 167, 168, 177, 182
Fairbank, J., 537, *567*
Fairburn, C. G., 685, 686, 688, 693, 696, 698, 708, 709
Falco, F. L., 47, 67
Faler-Routman, J., 486, 489, *514*
Falk, J. R., 688, *710*
Falko, J. M., 693, *712*
Fallahi, C., 226
Faller, K. C., 575, 582, *616*
Famularo, R., 588, 592, *616*
Faraone, S. V., 77, 88, 93, 109, *118*, *120*, 165, *179*, 180, 265
Farber, E., 578, *616*
Farkas, G., *511*
Farley, A. J., 412, *449*
Farmer, J., 257, 274, 495, *516*
Farnsworth, A., 573, *621*
Farrell, A. D., 5, 28, 53
Farrell, M. P., 729, *742*
Farrington, D. P., 131, 138, 139, 182, *183*, 187
Farris, A. M., *185*
Farrow, J. A., 688, *709*
Fassbender, L. L., 438, *445*
Fauber, R., 33, 38, *54*, 678
Fauber, R. L., 7, 53
Faulstich, C., 633, *682*
Faust, D., 493, *514*

Faust, J., 137, 146, *183*, *186*, 251, 258, 267, 289, 290, 293, 294
Fawcett, N., 268
Fay, G. C., 456, *477*, 478
Fay, W. H., 412, 413, *445*
Feagans, L., 489, *511*
Fechner-Bates, S., 212, *225*
Fee, V. E., 419, *451*
Feehan, M., 92, *124*, 139, *187*, 227
Fehr, F. S., 251, 267
Fehrenbach, P. A., 576, 578, *616*
Feighner, J. P., 684, *709*
Feil, E. G., 177, *192*
Fein, D., 416, 430, *445*
Feinberg, R., *514*
Feingold, B., 87, *121*
Feinstein, C., 395, *403*
Feiring, C., 586, 600, 610, *622*
Feld, S. C., 267
Feldman, E., 29, 52, 108, *120*, 165, *181*, 356, *361*
Feldman, H., 380, 394, 397, *403*
Feldman, J., 606, *622*
Feldman, R., 405
Feldman, R. S., 531, 532, *563*, 566
Feldman, S. S., 629, 678
Felner, R. D., 219, 224
Felton, D. K., 531, *565*
Fennell, E., 453, 476
Fennell, R., *516*
Fenton, T., 588, *616*
Ferenz-Gillies, R., 639, *680*
Ferguson, B., *128*
Ferguson, H. B., 77, 78, *121*, 128
Fergusson, D. M., 87, *121*, 137, *183*, 722, 724, *745*, 746
Fergusson, I. E., 87, *121*
Fermanian, J., *443*
Fernald, C. D., 20, 53
Fernald, W. B., 414, *446*
Fernandez, P., 415, *444*
Ferrari, M., 24, *55*, 235, 267, 491, 492, 493, 494, *511*
Ferster, C. B., 16, 27, 53, 54
Feshbach, N. D., 38, *54*, 556, *563*
Fetrow, R. A., 157, 171, 178, 179, *189*
Feuerstein, M. J., 31, 58
Fichter, M. M., 696, 709
Field, B., 458, 478
Field, T., 170, *183*
Fielding, D., 492, 493, *511*
Fifield, B., 505, 506, *514*
Figuero, J., *511*
Filsinger, E. E., 31, *54*
Filstead, W. J., 735, *746*
Finch, A. J., 41, 63, 206, 212, 220, 225, 227, 228, 229
Fincham, F. D., 27, 50, 267, 312, 655, 666, 667, 678, 679
Finck, D., 29, 67
Fine, D., 591, *614*
Fine, M. A., 7, 65
Fine, S., 218, 225, 587, *621*
Finkelhor, D., 4, *54*, 167, *191*, 569, 570, 571, 572, 574, 575, 576, 577, 578, 579, 582, 584, 599, *614*, *616*, 618, 622
Finkelstein, R., *514*
Finn, S., 697, *712*
Finney, J., 499, *518*
Firestone, P., 75, *121*, 125, *189*, 448, *619*
Fisch, R. O., 497, *512*
Fischel, J. E., 47, 67
Fischer, G. J., 572, 576, *616*

Fischer, K. W., 235, 267
Fischer, M., 73, 75, 76, 85, 86, 88, 90, 96, 99, 100, 108, 109, 110, *117*, *121*, 724, 742
Fiset, L., 239, 273
Fishbein, J., 38, 67
Fishel, P., 492, *516*
Fisher, C. B., 595, *616*
Fisher, D., 736, *745*
Fisher, P., 65, 145, *191*, 228, 258, 276, *406*
Fisher, P. W., *189*, *190*, 211, 225, 226, 227, 228
Fisk, J., 453, *479*
Fisman, S., 420, *451*
Fisman, S. N., 435, *452*
Fitcraft, A. H., 580, *622*
Fitz, C. R., 460, *477*
Fitzgerald, G., 150, *188*
Fitzgerald, G. A., *120*, *129*
Fitzgerald, H. E., 137, 171, *183*, *184*, *185*, 193
Fivush, R., 593, *616*
Flach, A., 704, *711*
Flament, M., 262, 264, 321
Flanagan, R., 4, *54*
Flannery, R., 492, *513*
Fleece, E. L., 234, 273, 288
Fleeson, J., 10, 46, 66, 531, *566*
Fleming, J. E., 179, *188*, 197, 201, 225, *743*
Fleming, W. S., 639, *680*
Flemming, E. L., 52
Fletcher, J. M., 453, 454, 455, 456, 457, 458, 459, 460, 463, 467, 471, 472, 473, 474, 475, 476, 477, 478, 479
Fletcher, K., 75, 86, 113, *117*, *121*
Fletcher, K. E., 394, *404*, 628, 641, 677
Fletcher, K. F., 86, 89, *117*
Flynt, S. W., 392, *403*
Foa, E. B., 586, *622*
Foch, T. T., 725, *746*
Foege, W., 481, *515*
Fogarty, L., 595, *615*
Fogels, H. R., 259, 268
Foley, J. M., 246, 277, 291, 292
Folkman, S., 732, *746*
Follansbee, D. J., 505, *511*, 679
Follette, W. C., 3, 5, 16, *54*, 56
Follingstad, D. R., 574, *618*
Follmer, A., 596, *620*
Folstein, S., 415, *445*
Fombonne, E., *452*
Fondacaro, K. M., 694, *714*
Forbes, L., 249, 269, 307
Ford, J. D., 16, *54*
Ford, M., *493*, *518*
Forehand, R. L., 5, 13, 29, 32, 33, 38, *54*, *61*, 95, 106, 109, 112, 113, *121*, 132, 133, 136, 137, 138, 140, 141, 142, 143, 147, 148, 151, 153, 154, 155, 156, 157, 158, 159, 160, 162, 163, 168, 170, 172, 175, 176, *178*, *179*, *183*, *184*, 188, 189, 190, 193, 257, 260, 267, 273, 397, 402, 559, *563*, 628, 629, 647, 678, 682, 728, *743*
Foreyt, J. P., 683, 707, 709
Forgatch, M. S., 112, *121*, 138, 153, 157, 171, 174, *178*, *183*, 189, 635, 637, 639, 640, 641, 642, 649, 654, 661, 678, 679
Forgays, D., 492, *511*

Forgays, D. G., 726, *745*
Forgays, D. K., 726, *745*
Forman, B. D., 5, 47, *54*
Fornari, V. M., 701, *709*
Forssman, H., 374, *403*
Forster, A. A., 475, *478*
Forsythe, C. J., 220, *224*
Forsythe, W. I., 38, *50*
Fortea Sevilla, M. D., 430, *449*
Fosson, A., 687, 689, 691, 703, *709*
Foster, A. L., *64*
Foster, G. G., 20, *54*
Foster, S., 107, 112, 113, *126*
Foster, S. L., 5, 7, 11, 31, 42, 43, 46,
    47, *51*, *54*, 154, 247, 267, 270, 333,
    346, 347, 348, 350, 359, 361, 362,
    541, 627, 629, 631, 632, 633, 634,
    639, 640, 641, 644, 645, 647, 652,
    653, 654, 667, 679, *681*, *682*
Foster, T., *183*
Foulkes, M. A., *478*
Fowler, M. G., 489, *511*
Fowler, S. A., 29, *66*
Fox, J. E., 234, 244, 245, 249, 250, 254,
    267, 269, 306, 307, 316, 317
Fox, J. J., 29, *67*
Fox, L., 532, *563*
Fox, M., 689, *711*
Fox, N. A., 335, 336, 360, 361, 364,
    524, 568
Foy, D. W., 586, *616*
Fraleigh, M. J., 676, *678*
Frame, C., 393, *404*
Frame, C. L., 148, *183*
Francis, D. J., 471, 476, 477, 478, *479*
Francis, G., 237, 247, 258, 260, 267,
    272, 274, 276
Francis, V., 505, *511*, *514*
Francoeur, E., 596, *615*
Frank, D., *510*
Franke, P. J., 582, *621*
Franke, S., 335, 345, 362
Frankel, F., *183*, 412, 426, *445*
Frankenburg, F.R., 687, *710*
Franklin, C., 670, 671, *679*
Frary, R. B., 232, *274*
Fraser, P., 591, *616*
Fraser, W., 376, *403*
Freeland, C. A. B., 164, *179*
Freeman, B. J., 32, *54*, 267, 286, 411,
    413, 414, 421, 426, 427, 428, 429,
    442, *443*, *445*, *446*, 452
Freeman, J., 527, *565*
Freeman, L., 212, *227*
Freeman, N., 435, *445*
Freeman, N. L., *445*
Freeman, R. J., 218, *225*
Freemon, B., 505, *511*
French, D. C., 134, *181*, 329, 333,
    334, 336, 362
French, J., 429, *446*, 718, *745*
French, J. L., 382, 384, *403*
French, R. deS., 9, 18, *51*, 57
Frensch, P., 688, *715*
Freud, S., 230, 267
Freund, A., 503, 506, *511*, *513*
Freund, R. D., 136, *184*
Frias, D., 533, *561*
Frick, P. J., 3, 26, 36, *54*, 58, 72, *116*,
    122, *123*, 132, 133, 134, 135, 137,
    141, 145, 147, 149, 150, 153, 164,
    165, 167, 171, 177, *183*, *184*, *185*,
    186, *187*, 190, 191, 192, 258, 259,
    267
Friedin, M. R., 77, *127*
Friedland-Bandes, R., 21, *51*

Friedlander, S., 38, *54*
Friedman, A. G., 267, 281, 318, 496,
    510
Friedman, D. H., 4, *62*
Friedman, E., 415, *444*
Friedman, I., 504, *511*
Friedman, L., 57, *185*
Friedman, R., 506, *511*, 540, 558,
    563
Friedman, R. M., *681*
Friedman, S. B., 492, *512*
Friedrich, W. N., 30, *54*, 392, *403*,
    435, *446*, 530, 563, 583, 585, 587,
    589, 590, 591, 606, 607, *615*, *616*
Friedson, E., 20, *64*
Friesen, W. V., 661, *678*
Frith, U., 411, 417, 418, *443*, *446*
Fritz, G., 498, *511*
Frodi, A. M., 530, 534, 537, 563
Frohlke, R., 526, *565*
Frone, M. R., 732, *744*
Frost, A. K., 225
Fry, A. F., 81, *121*
Frye v. United States, 293 F. 1023
    (1923), 613, *616*
Fucci, B. R., *678*
Fuentes, J., 452
Fuhrman, T., 631, 670, 671, *679*
Fujii, K., 78, *122*
Fukushimo, D. K., *715*
Funder, D. C., 10, *50*
Funderburk, B. W., 148, 151, *182*,
    184, 188
Furey, W. M., 137, *183*, *184*
Furlong, J. M., 381, *403*
Furman, W., 25, 40, 41, *54*, 328, 329,
    331, 338, 339, 350, 354, 358, 360,
    362, 627, *678*
Furneaux, B., 413, *446*
Furnham, A., 689, *709*
Fuster, J. M., 77, 81, *121*
Fyans, L. J., 249, 268, 312

Gadow, K., 377, *403*
Gaffney, A., 497, *511*
Gagnon, J., 577, *617*
Gaines, B., 430, 452
Gaines, R. W., 530, *566*
Gajzago, C. C., 409, 423, *449*
Gale, J., 580, 591, *617*
Gallone, A., 206, *226*
Gallup Poll Report, 526, *563*
Gallup, E. M., 693, *712*
Galton, 370, *403*
Gamble, W., 639, *680*
Gambrill, E. D., 241, *267*
Gameros, T. A., 724, *743*
Gammon, G. D., 229
Ganiban, J., 534, *562*
Ganong, L., 704, *708*
Garbarino, J., 538, 539, *563*
Garber, J., 10, 19, *54*, 218, 219,
    225, *226*, 228, 492, 495,
    512, *518*
Garbin, M. G., 110, *118*, 170, *179*
Garcia, K. A., 235, *268*
Garcia, M. R., 217, *225*
Garcia-Coll, C., 258, 267, 270
Gardner, K., 52, *181*
Garfin, D. G., 419, *446*
Garfinkel, B., *116*, *186*
Garfinkel, B. D., 238, 258, 259, *265*
Garfinkel, P. E., 683, 686, 687, 692,
    694, 696, 698, 699, 700, 701, 704,
    706, *709*, *710*, 713

Garland, E. J., 231, 235, 267
Garmezy, L. B., 728, *742*
Garmezy, N., 416, *450*
Garner, A., 498, *512*
Garner, A. M., *515*
Garner, D. M., 683, 685, 686, 687,
    689, 691, 692, 693, 694, 695, 696,
    698, 700, 701, 704, 706, *709*, *710*
Garner, M. V., *710*
Garreau, B., 428, *443*, *444*
Garrison, C. Z., 213, 225, 239, 267
Garson, C., 112, *120*
Garwick, A. W., 489, *515*
Gates, D., 496, *510*
Gatlin, D., 337, *363*
Gatsonis, C., 133, *186*
Gaudet, N., 393, *406*
Gaudin, J. M., 532, 540, 565, 566,
    567
Gaulin-Kremer, E., 246, 259, 277, 291
Gavaghan-Jones, M., 492, *517*
Gavelek, J. R., 556, *564*
Gayton, W. F., 492, 493, *512*
Gdowski, C. L., 36, *54*, 57, 77, *128*,
    633, *682*
Ge, X., 203, 225
Gebhard, P., 577, *617*
Gedaly-Duff, V., 497, *512*
Gee, S., 593, *617*
Geffken, G. R., 431, *450*, 491, 492,
    516
Gehi, M., 693, *715*
Gehring, M., 729, *747*
Gelfand, D. M., 6, *54*
Geller, J., 22, *54*, 137, *184*
Gellert, E., 706, *712*
Gelles, R. J., 526, 527, 538, *563*, 567,
    739, *747*
Gent, C. L., 161, *187*
Gentile, C., 582, 585, 593, 594, 598,
    599, 601, 606, *617*, 623
George, A. E., *444*
George, B., *518*
George, C., 530, *565*
George, G. C. W., 691, 703, 707, *714*
Geraci, R. L., 356, 362
Gerhardt, C., 216, 225
Gerhardt, C. A., 208, *224*, 226
Gershenson, H., 591, *617*
Gerstein, F., 504, *514*
Gersten, J. C., 59
Gersten, M., 265
Gettys, L., 20, *53*
Ghishan, F., *518*
Ghose, L. J., 259, 268
Ghosh, A., 5, *51*
Giaconia, R. M., 203, 225
Giammarino, M., 337, *365*
Giampinl, T. L., *746*
Gianino, A., 15, *66*
Gibaud-Wallston, J., 38, *54*, 169, *184*,
    490, *512*
Gibbons, P., 496, *517*
Gibbons, S., 718, 719, *745*
Giddon, D. B., 259, 268
Giebenhain, J. E., 234, 239, 242, 243,
    244, 245, 248, 249, 250, 251, 254,
    255, 260, 263, 264, 268, 280, 281
Giedd, J. N., *119*
Gifford, E. V., 454, *478*
Gigliotti, F., 453, *479*
Gil, D. G., 538, 563
Gil, K., *517*, *518*
Gilbert, B. O., 245, 246, 268, 286,
    287, 290, 497, 499, 506, *512*
Gilbert, D. A., 660, *680*

Gilbert, R. K., 639, 652, 653, 663, 667, 669, 679
Giles, G., 693, 715
Giles, S., 84, 127
Gilger, J. W., 88, 121
Gilkey, K., 416, 445
Gill, M. J., 446
Gillberg, C., 377, 403, 415, 418, 423, 443, 444, 446
Gillespie, C., 401, 510
Gilliam, J. E., 36, 54
Gillin, J. C., 743
Gioia, P., 189, 227, 228
Girgus, J. S., 202, 219, 227
Giroux, B., 187
Gittelman, R., 32, 48, 87, 113, 116, 121, 124
Gittelman-Klein, R., 86, 106, 116, 123
Giunta, C. T., 219, 224
Gjerde, P. F., 47, 54, 640, 679
Gladis, M., 687, 715
Glancy, L., 614
Glaser, G. H., 534, 565
Glasgow, R. E., 260, 265, 503, 505, 517
Glass, C. R., 249, 250, 268, 270, 304, 305
Glass, R., 445
Glassman, A. H., 687, 715
Glaun, D. E., 703, 707
Gleghorn, A. A., 696, 714, 722, 723, 739, 743
Glennon, B., 234, 235, 243, 244, 248, 268, 297, 298, 317
Gleser, G., 87, 116
Glick, J., 235, 243, 273, 288
Glod, C. A., 75, 128
Glow, P. H., 72, 121, 348, 362
Glow, R. A., 72, 121, 348, 362
Gluck, D. S., 76, 119
Glynn, T. J., 728, 746
Goddard, H. H., 370, 403
Goeke, I. K. E., 273, 299
Goertzel, T., 499, 510
Goff, G., 689, 712, 713
Goffin, B., 189
Gold, E. R., 586, 617
Gold, R., 479
Gold, R. G., 557, 565
Goldberg, S. C., 683, 699, 708, 710
Golden, C. J., 386, 388, 403
Golden, M., 506, 513
Goldenberg, B., 566
Goldfried, M. R., 9, 42, 54, 634, 678
Golding, J., 84, 118, 456, 476
Golding, S. L., 598, 614
Goldman, H. H., 17, 55
Goldman, J., 621
Goldman, M. A., 739, 744
Goldman, M. S., 726, 739, 745, 747
Goldman-Rakic, P. S., 472, 478
Goldsmith, H. H., 36, 55, 135, 184, 257, 260, 265, 268
Goldstein, A. P., 4, 55
Goldstein, G., 30, 55, 430, 447, 724, 748
Goldstein, M., 415, 446
Goldstein, M. J., 629, 678
Goldstein, S., 183
Goldston, D., 514
Gomberg, E. S. L., 722, 726, 748
Gomes-Schwartz, B., 574, 579, 581, 582, 591, 616, 617
Gomez, R., 76, 121
Gonder-Frederick, L., 255, 274

Gondoli, D. M., 670, 679
Gonzales, J. C., 268, 287
Gonzalez, A. S., 640, 678
Goode, S., 404, 448
Goodman, G., 575, 576, 592, 593, 594, 595, 596, 617, 620, 621
Goodman, J. R., 88, 121
Goodman, J. T., 125, 189, 515
Goodman, S., 226
Goodnow, J. J., 21, 65
Goodrich, S., 620
Goodrick, G. K., 707, 709
Goodwin, D. W., 578, 618, 722, 745
Goodwin, J., 574, 614
Goodyear, P., 72, 79, 121
Goodyer, I., 688, 710
Gordon, B. N., 586, 596, 617, 620
Gordon, D., 225
Gordon, D. A., 37, 55
Gordon, H. W., 724, 746
Gordon, J. S., 175, 192
Gordon, M., 90, 103, 104, 118, 121, 124, 572, 577, 580, 617
Gordon, N. J., 399, 403
Gordon, R., 492, 515
Gordon, Y., 211, 226
Goreczny, A. J., 700, 716
Gorfinkle, K., 504, 514
Gorham, K. A., 16, 55
Gormally, J., 699, 700, 710
Gorsuch, R. L., 250, 276
Gortmaker, S. L., 482, 486, 489, 512, 517, 519
Gosling, A., 394, 403
Gossett, J. T., 612, 619
Gotlib, I. H., 6, 26, 60, 204, 213, 214, 215, 216, 225
Gottman, J., 55
Gottman, J. M., 4, 5, 44, 47, 49, 55, 137, 138, 153, 184, 185, 564, 659, 661, 662, 667, 679
Goudreau, D., 452
Gough, R., 568
Gould, J., 393, 407, 409, 411, 416, 452, 587, 617
Gould, M. S., 145, 179
Gowers, S., 688, 710
Goyette, C. H., 73, 121
Gozzi, E. K., 505, 514
Grace, N. C., 655, 657, 667, 679
Grady, K., 5, 56
Graef, R., 698, 709
Graetz, B., 490, 512
Grafman, J., 453, 459, 476
Graham, J. R., 50, 578, 617
Graham, J. M., 739, 742
Graham, P., 237, 240, 268, 275, 346, 348, 353, 362, 376, 406, 581, 617
Graham-Pole, J., 496, 516
Grambsch, P., 590, 616
Grant, I., 732, 744
Grant, K. E., 198, 206, 224, 227
Grant, M., 171, 190
Grant, N. I. R., 188
Grapentine, W. L., 208, 227, 228
Grasley, C., 552, 553, 567
Graves, L., 621
Graves, M. G., 8, 15, 67, 175, 192
Gray, J., 376, 403
Gray, S. H., 706, 710
Graziano, A. M., 235, 240, 245, 257, 268, 281, 282
Graziano, W. G., 137, 183
Green, A. H., 530, 566
Green, B., 41, 66, 87, 116
Green, B. J., 205, 228

Green, C. W., 446
Green, J. A., 44, 50
Green, J. F., 724, 745
Green, L., 81, 121
Green, N., 499, 510
Green, R. S., 689, 713
Green, S., 122, 190
Green, S. M., 72, 100, 123, 177, 186, 187, 192
Greenbaum, P. E., 259, 265, 681, 726, 747
Greenbaum, R., 149, 182
Greenberg, K., 38, 52
Greenberg, L. M., 76, 121
Greenberg, M. T., 135, 136, 173, 174, 181, 184, 191, 342, 362, 393, 403, 435, 446, 580, 617
Greene, E. L., 59
Greene, J. A., 16, 68
Greene, J. W., 487, 488, 492, 495, 518
Greene, R. W., 90, 121
Greene, W. B., 499, 512
Greenfeld, D., 412, 450
Greenhill, L., 116, 186
Greenspan, L., 415, 444
Greenspan, S. I., 19, 39, 55
Greenstein, J., 111, 125
Greenwood, C., 57
Greenwood, C. R., 25, 29, 55
Greger, J., 503, 512
Gregg, G. S., 528, 563
Grenspun, W. S., 581, 617
Gresham, F. M., 108, 121, 147, 182, 351, 353, 360, 362, 371, 404
Grieger, R. M., 34, 50
Griest, D. L., 133, 147, 156, 163, 168, 170, 176, 183, 184, 188, 193, 257, 267, 273, 546, 563
Griffin, W., 172, 181
Griffioen, D., 242, 277
Griffiths, D. A., 687, 707
Grimes, K., 149, 193, 213, 228
Grimm, L. G., 58
Grimwood, K., 461, 478
Grindler, M., 268, 312
Grizzle, K. L., 731, 748
Grocke, M., 581, 617
Grodzinsky, G. M., 72, 73, 77, 79, 90, 103, 104, 117, 121
Gross, A., 535, 563
Gross, A. M., 4, 7, 30, 39, 55, 91, 121, 242, 268, 499, 505, 512
Gross, J., 694, 696, 700, 710, 714
Gross, M. D., 87, 122, 129
Grossman, J., 212, 227
Grossman, J. J., 371, 403
Grossman, R. G., 472, 478
Grotevant, H. D., 46, 51, 55
Groth, A., 578, 617
Groth, N., 575, 615
Grotpeter, J. K., 336, 361
Group for the Advancement of Psychiatry, 17, 55
Grubb, H. J., 258, 272
Gruber, C. P., 36, 59
Gruber, K. J., 580, 617
Gruen, G. E., 256, 274
Gruenewald, L., 443
Grunau, R. V. E., 497, 510
Grusec, E., 242, 263, 299
Grusec, J. E., 21, 37, 38, 52, 55
Grych, J. H., 666, 679
Guare, J. C., 362
Guerra, N. G., 138, 178
Guess, D., 413, 431, 446, 450

Guevremont, D. C., 26, 49, 85, 86, 89, 99, 113, *116, 117,* 628, 641, 677
Guidubaldi, J., 38, 55, 169, *184*
Guite, J., *118*
Gullone, E., 236, 237, 239, 249, 262, 268, *271,* 323
Gully, K. J., 598, *614*
Gunnar, M. R., 497, *512*
Gunnoe, C., *125*
Gunsett, R. P., 414, *446*
Gurin, J., 706, 707
Gurman, A. S., 47, *55*
Guskin, S. L., 20, *55*
Gustafson, K., 492, *518*
Gustafsson, P. A., 590, *619*
Guthrie, D., 412, 426, *445, 446,* 449
Guze, S. B., 709

Haaga, D. A., 170, *184*
Hack, M., 457, 478, 479
Hacker, B., 390, *404*
Hackworth, S. R., 506, *512*
Haddad, C., 417, *449*
Hadjistavropoulos, H. D., 497, *510*
Haefele, W. F., 628, *679*
Haenlein, M., 72, *122*
Hagan, B. J., 5, 47, *54*
Hagan, E. P., 383, 406, 429, *451*
Hagan, R. D., 686, 708
Hagberg, B., 417, *446*
Hagen, E. P., 463, *480*
Hagen, R. L., 38, *51*
Hagerman, R. J., 377, *403*
Haggerty, R. J., 481, 487, *512, 516*
Hagman, E. R., 239, *268*
Hagman, J., 695, 698, *711*
Haigler, E. D., 76, *124*
Haines, J., *401*
Haley, G., 587, *621*
Haley, G. M. T., 218, *225*
Haley, J., 631, 667, *679*
Halikas, J. A., 724, *745*
Hall, D. K., 558, *566*
Hall, A., 701, *715*
Hall, J. A., 672, *680*
Hall, L. J., *404*
Hall, R. V., 29, 41, *50, 55*
Hall, T. W., 245, *268,* 298
Hallberg, D., 696, 707
Hallinan, M. T., 331, *361*
Halmi, K. A., 683, 688, 699, 701, 705, 706, 708, 709, 710, 712
Halper, V., 43, *66*
Halperin, J. M., 76, 103, *122, 124*
Halpern, F., 227
Halpin, B. M., 591, *622*
Halverson, D., *511*
Halvorson, P., *713*
Ham, H. P., 171, *183, 184, 185*
Hamalainen, 139, *184*
Hamburger, A. D., 429, *450*
Hamburger, S. D., 119, *129,* 633, 679
Hamby, D. W., 399, *403*
Hamby, S. L., 167, 173, *191*
Hamdan-Allen, G., 431, *450*
Hameury, I., 428, *443*
Hamilton, J., 596, *619*
Hamilton, S. B., 30, *50,* 634, *678*
Hamlett, K., 210, 226, 492, *518*
Hamlett, K. W., 77, *122,* 263, 292, 491, *512*
Hamm, A. O., 261, *268*

Hammen, C. L., 38, *55,* 170, *186,* 197, 198, 203, 204, 215, 218, 219, 220, 221, 223, 224, 225, 226, 228
Hammer, L. D., *711*
Hammer, M., 532, *563, 566*
Hammill, D., 386, 387, *402*
Hammond, M., 148, 151, 162, 175, 193
Hampe, E., 36, 62, 231, 232, 239, 268, *273,* 318
Hampson, R. B., 670, 671, *679*
Hamre-Nietupski, S., *443*
Han, S. S., 100, *122*
Handal, P. J., 633, *678*
Handelsman, D. J., *511*
Handen, B. L., 380, 394, 397, 402, 403
Handleman, J., 429, *446*
Handy, L., 576, *619*
Hanefeld, F., 417, *444*
Hanf, C., 94, 142, 153, 156, *184*
Hanley, J. H., 152, *190*
Hanlon, C., 227
Hannay, H. J., 472, *478*
Hansen, C., 503, *513*
Hansen, J. C., 670, *681*
Hanson, C. L., 5, *64,* 512, 628, *679*
Hanson, D. J., 550, 551, 557, 558, *563, 565*
Hanson, E., 629, 634, 640, *680*
Hanson, K., *54, 183, 184*
Hanson, R. A., 575, *621*
Hanson, R. F., 580, *619, 621*
Hanson, V., 496, *518*
Harbeck, C., 242, 257, 274, 495, 497, *512, 516*
Hardin, S. B., 239, *267*
Harding, B., 687, 692, 703, 709, *711*
Harding, D., 709
Harding, J., 16, *55,* 402
Hare, R., 36, *54*
Hare, R. D., *183*
Hargreaves, W. A., *68*
Haring, N., *403*
Haring, N. G., 390, 391, *406*
Harkavy, J., 498, 499, 506, *512, 513*
Harmatz, J. S., 111, *118*
Harmon, G., 242, 243, 267, 300
Harnisch, D. L., 249, 268, 312
Harow, E., 258, 266
Harper, D., 490, *512*
Harper, D. C., 496, *516*
Harper, L. V., 22, *49*
Harrell, T. H., 735, *745*
Harrington, D., 530, 548, *563*
Harrington, R., *190*
Harris, A. M., 45, *55*
Harris, B., 230, *268*
Harris, C. V., 246, 265, *285*
Harris, D. B., 41, *64*
Harris, D. J., 491, *509*
Harris, E. L., 461, *478*
Harris, F. C., 247, *268*
Harris, J. C., 414, *446*
Harris, S. L., 4, 7, 12, 16, 24, *55,* 429, 436, 437, 438, *446*
Harrison, D. F., 171, *184*
Harrison, P., 587, *615*
Hart, C. H., 343, *363*
Hart, E. A., *184*
Hart, E. L., 72, 76, *116, 122,* 133, *184, 186*
Hartdagen, S., *123,* 171, *183*
Harter, S., 41, *56,* 218, *225,* 356, 357, 362, 473, 478, 554, 555, *563,* 612, 617

Hartman, C. R., 534, *561*
Hartman, G., 606, *617*
Hartmann, D. P., 5, 6, 9, 23, 25, 31, 33, 39, 41, 42, 43, *54,* 56, 67, 140, 247, 252, 253, 259, 262, 263, 264, 268
Hartshorn, J., 687, 709
Hartsough, C. S., 77, 84, *122*
Hartung, C. M., 75, *124*
Hartup, W. W., 5, 47, *56,* 328, 329, 330, 331, 332, 334, 336, 338, 339, 360, 362, 528, *563*
Harward, H., *478*
Hasazi, J., 492, *511*
Haskett, M. E., 553, 556, *563*
Haslum, M., 84, *118,* 456, 476
Hassanein, R., 491, *514*
Hassibi, M., 241, *265*
Hastings, J., 77, 87, *122*
Hatch, A., 587, *621*
Hatcher, J., 492, *509*
Hatcher, S., 231, 235, *268*
Hatsukami, D., 687, 688, 693, 710, 712, 713
Hattab, Y., *452*
Hatzenbuehler, L. C., 255, *268*
Hauenstein, J., 492, 498, *512*
Haugaard, J. J., 590, 595, *617*
Hauser, S. T., 504, *512,* 644, 645, *679*
Haven, W. G., 20, *68*
Hawes, R., 234, 235, 243, 244, 246, 248, 249, 273, 288, 289
Hawkins, D. R., 483, *512*
Hawkins, G. D., 371, 381, *403*
Hawkins, J. D., 134, *184*
Hawkins, R. C., 688, 691, 697, 700, 710
Hawkins, R. P., 9, 11, 14, 28, 43, *51,* 56
Hawley, B. P., 259, *268*
Hay, D., 88, *123*
Hay, T., 526, *567*
Haydel, F., *711*
Hayden, A., 391, *403*
Hayes, M., 246, 269, 294, 503, 506, 511
Hayes, S., 73, *122*
Hayes, S. C., 3, 5, 16, 31, *54,* 56, 62, 242, 251, 254, 263, 274, 454, *478*
Hayford, J., 498, *509*
Haymes, L. K., 413, *444*
Haynes, M. R., 578, *620*
Haynes, O. M., 38, *59*
Haynes, S. N., 7, 9, 16, 30, 33, 34, 45, *56,* 57, 153, *185,* 247, 251, 269, 558, *564*
Hays, R. D., 727, *745*
Hayvren, M., 347, *362*
Hayward, C., *711*
Hazelrigg, M., 553, *561*
Hazzard, A., 41, *56,* 505, *512,* 587, 617
Healy, B., *183*
Hearn, M. T., 496, *515*
Hebb, D. O., 231, *269*
Heber, R., 371, *403*
Hechtman, L. T., 71, 85, 86, *122,* 128
Hedrick, M., 132, *183*
Heemsbergen, J., *404, 448*
Heflin, A. H., 341, 343, *364*
Hegedus, A. E., 534, *567*
Hegedus, A. M., 578, *622,* 724, *748*
Heger, A., 587, *618*
Heiby, E., 235, 243, 273, 288

Heidish, I. E., 148; *186*
Heilman, K. M., 77, *122*
Heilman, M. E., 706, *710*
Heiman, M., 690, *711*
Hekimian, E., 38, 49, 539, *561*
Helgemo, B., 499, *515*
Heller, K., 547, *566*
Heller, T., 77, 83, *122*, 153, *184*
Helmers, K., 588, 608, *620*
Helsel, W. J., 108, *124*, 232, 351, 363, 377, *404*
Helzer, J. E., 258, *275*
Hemmick, S., 267, *286*
Henderson, A. S., 540, *563*
Henderson, F., 489, *511*
Hendrick, E. B., 132, *183*, 477
Henggeler, S. W., 5, *64*, 152, *190*, 490, 491, 499, *510*, 512, 628, 639, 653, 672, 677, 678, 679, 680
Henker, B., 29, 41, 44, 50, 56, 67, 75, 111, 112, *128*
Henley, K. M., 683, *710*
Henly, G. A., 738, *748*
Henretta, J., 499, *513*
Henriksen, L., 87, *123*
Henry, B., 135, *180*
Henry, D., 585, *619*
Henschel, A., 697, *711*
Henson, R., *511*
Hepps, D., 593, *617*
Herbert, M., 4, *56*
Herbertt, R. M., 237, *269*
Herbsman, C., 77, *122*
Herjanic, B., 40, 56, 145, 146, 208, 225, 247, 258, 262, *269*
Herjanic, M., *184*, 208, 225
Herman, J., 580, 581, *617*
Herman, J. L., 534, *563*
Herman, S., 77, *125*
Hermecz, D. A., 251, 255, 269, 271, 288
Hern, K. L., *122*
Hernandez, M., 540, *563*
Herrenkohl, E. C., 531, 537, 538, 539, 558, 563, *564*, 583, *617*
Herrenkohl, R. C., 531, 537, 538, 539, 558, 563, *564*, 583, *617*
Herrold, A., 506, *513*
Herscovitch, P., *129*
Hersen, J. H., *59*
Hersen, M., 3, 4, 5, 6, 7, 13, 14, 30, 31, 49, 55, 56, 60, 63, 234, 235, 238, 258, 262, 272, 276, 277, 279, 317
Hersh, S., *479*
Hershey, K. L., 135, *190*
Hershey, M., 727, *744*
Herskowitz, R., *512*
Herzberger, S. D., 534, 535, *564*
Herzog, D. B., 225, 692, *713*
Hess, E. 109, *127*
Hess, G. E., 499, *512*
Hessl, D., 24, *52*
Heston, J., 583, 585, *618*
Hetherington, E. M., 4, *56*
Heumann, J. E., 378, *403*
Hewitt, S. K., *616*
Hexsuchl, J. E., 585, *616*
Heyman, R. E., 667, 679, *682*
Hibbard, B., 606, *617*
Hibbs, E. D., 5, 8, *56*, *185*, 633, 645, 672, *679*
Hickman, C., 413, *448*
Hicks, M. W., 670, 673, *678*
Hicks, R. E., 588, *617*

Higgs, J., 688, *710*
Hightower, A. D., 351, 362
Hill, B., 376, *404*
Hill, B. K., *561*
Hill, E., *620*
Hill, E. M., 724, 739, *745*
Hill, J. H., 269, *300*
Hill, J. P., 631, 633, 639, *679*
Hill, K. T., 249, 268, 269, 312
Hilliker, D. R., 578, *618*
Hillman, S. B., 635, *680*
Hilpert, P. L., 258, *271*
Hilsman, R., 218, 219, 226, 228
Himadi, W. G., 260, *269*
Himmelstein, P., 259, 266
Hinchey, F. S., 556, *564*
Hinde, R. A., *184*, 268
Hinden, B., 203, 208, 221, 224, 225, 226
Hingtgen, J. N., 416, *445*
Hinojosa-Rivera, G., 163, *189*
Hinsey, W. C., 30, *63*
Hinshaw, S. P., 4, 13, 36, *56*, 57, 71, 73, 75, 76, 77, 78, 83, 89, 90, 91, 95, 96, 97, 100, 111, 112, 113, *116*, 122, 125, 127, 128, 130, 133, 134, 135, 139, 153, 159, 164, 177, *184*, 344, 362, 640, *678*
Hirano, C., 237, *269*
Hiroto, D., 225
Hirsch, M., *51*, 224, *561*
Hirschman, J. E., 593, *617*
Hirschman, L., 580, 581, *617*
Hirshfeld, D. R., 265
Hiskey, M. S., 383, 385, *404*
Ho, D. V., 343, *362*
Ho, H. H., 416, *445*
Hoag, N. L., 495, *518*
Hoage, C. M., 20, *68*
Hoare, P., 493, *512*
Hobbs, N., 14, 57, 398, *404*
Hobbs, S. A., 4, *57*
Hobfoll, S. E., 688, *709*
Hobson, R. P., 411, *446*
Hoddap, R., 369, 370, 371, 373, 374, 389, *406*
Hodges, E. L., 701, *708*
Hodges, K., 57, 92, *122*, 145, 146, *184*, 247, *269*, 319, 321, 492, 495, *512*, *513*
Hodges, K. H., 40, 208, 210, 211, 212, 226
Hodgson, E. W., 237, 259, 263
Hodgson, R., 262, 269, 275, 323
Hoeckelman, R., 606, *617*
Hoehn-Saric, E., 235, 246, 247, 262, 269, 319, 321, 323
Hoeper, E. W., 226
Hoffman, Λ., 587, *615*
Hoffman, H. J., 460, *477*
Hoffman, R. G., 496, *516*
Hoffman-Plotkin, D., 529, 530, *564*
Hofman, K. J., 461, *478*
Hogan, K. L., 409, 424, *451*
Hogarty, P. S., 381, *405*
Hoge, R. D., 147, 168, *184*
Hoier, T. S., 3, 9, 25, 32, 33, *51*, 587, 588, 589, *618*, 619
Hokoda, A., 267, *312*
Holcomb, C., 57, *185*
Holden, A. E., Jr., 255, 269
Holden, E., 489, *513*
Holden, E. W., 527, *564*
Holden, G. W., 21, 38, 57, 166, 168, *184*

Holdgrafter, M., *447*
Holland, A., 237, 273
Holland, C. J., 34, 57
Holleran, P. A., 136, 168, *184*
Hollingsworth, D. K., 149, *192*
Hollister, L. E., 724, 747
Hollon, S. D., 27, 59, 170, *186*, 216, 228, 259, 272
Holman, A. M., 5, 57
Holmbeck, G. N., 489, *519*, 631, 633, 639, 656, 670, 671, *679*
Holmes, F., 235, 236, 237, 242, 269
Holmes, G. R., 175, *181*
Holmes, J. M., 473, *480*
Holmes, N., 429, *451*
Holmstrom, L., 575, *615*
Holroyd, J., 392, *404*, 435, *446*, 447
Holsten, F., 733, *745*
Holtzman, D., *511*
Holtzworth-Munroe, A., 142, 171, *184*, 554, *564*
Homatidis, S., 435, *447*
Honeybourne, C., 261, *269*
Honig v. Doe, 108 S. Ct. 592, 378, *404*
Honigman, A., 380, *403*
Honjo, S., 237, 269
Honzik, M. P., 23, *60*, 236, 272
Hook, H., 576, *619*
Hooks, M. Y., 416, *452*
Hooven, C., 4, *55*
Hoover, M., 436, *448*
Hoover-Dempsey, K., *404*
Hope, R. A., 696, *709*
Hopkins, J., 86, *128*
Hops, H., 4, 6, 24, 25, 29, 32, 41, 42, 43, 44, 57, 58, 157, 160, *180*, *185*, 192, 201, 208, 224, 227, 629, 660, 661, 678, *679*
Horn, W. F., 247, *269*
Horndasch, R. L., *518*
Horner, R. H., 13, 57, 439, *449*
Horowitz, J., 574, *616*
Horowitz, J. M., 579, *617*
Horowitz, L. M., 18, 57
Horowitz, L. A., 588, *620*
Horowitz, M. J., 599, 610, *617*
Horvath, W. J., 727, *744*
Horwitz, W., 490, *514*
Horwood, L. J., 87, *121*, 137, *183*, 722, *745*
Hoshino, Y., *452*
Hoskins, P. L., *511*
Hosokawa, M. C., 559, *567*
Hotaling G. T., 570, *616*
Houlihan, J., *679*
House, A. E., 32, 67, 107
Houskamp, B. M., 592, *620*
Houston, B. K., 234, 244, 245, 249, 250, 254, 267, 269, 306, 307, 316, 317
Houts, A. C., 22, *53*
Hovanitz, C., 16, 427, *449*
Howe, B. A., 534, 567, 580, *622*
Howe, G. W., 137, 178, 655, *677*
Howe, M. L., 593, *618*
Howell, C. T., 23, 36, 48, 49, 93, 199, 206, 207, 223, 551, *560*
Howell, D. C., 219, 221, 224, 226
Howes, C., 529, *564*
Howing, P. T., 532, *565*, 567
Howitt, J. W., 237, *277*
Howlin, P. A., 412, 413, *447*, *448*
Howrood, L. J., *121*
Hoza, B., *125*, 331, 339, 345, 354, 360, 362

Hre, R. L., 478
Hsieh, Y., 724, 748
Hsu, L. K., 687, 709
Huber, A., 100, 122, 128
Huber, C., 257, 268
Hubert, N. C., 246, 269, 294, 295, 296
Hudson, J. I., 687, 688, 710, 713
Huesmann, L. R., 131, 185
Huffington, C. M., 269, 312
Hufnagle, K. G., 476
Hughes, C. W., 217, 226
Hughes, H. M., 30, 45, 57, 153, 185, 558, 564
Hughes, J. N., 251, 269, 548, 564
Hughes, P., 87, 127
Hughey, J. B., 175, 192
Huitema, B. E., 677, 680
Huizinga, D., 152, 182, 355, 361
Hulbert, T. A., 36, 57
Hulgus, Y. F., 670, 679
Hull, J. G., 731, 745
Humphrey, L., 704, 710, 711
Humphrey, M., 408, 447
Humphreys, L. E., 35, 57
Humphreys, R. P., 477
Humphries, T., 88, 122
Hundleby, J. D., 728, 729, 745
Hunsley, J., 3, 5, 7, 60
Hunter, J. A., 578, 579, 618
Hunter, W., 576, 621
Hunter, W. M., 582, 616
Huntingdon, G. S., 388, 406
Huntzinger, R., 489, 490, 510
Hurley, P., 573, 587, 621
Huron, R., 396, 402
Huser, J., 36, 52
Huszti, H., 515
Hutcherson, S., 234, 273, 288
Hutchinson, S., 505, 512
Huttenlocher, P. R., 404
Hutton, H., 689, 711
Huxtable, K., 492, 519
Hyman, C., 138, 180, 334, 361
Hymel, S, 40, 41, 49, 57, 329, 330, 332, 333, 335, 336, 340, 345, 346, 347, 356, 357, 359, 360, 362, 364
Hynd, G. W., 72, 79, 87, 116, 121, 122, 123, 171, 183, 186

Iacuone, R., 271
Ievers, C. E., 492, 513
Ignasiak, K. D., 257, 268
Iker, H., 510
Ilig, F., 401
Illinois Department of Children and Family Services, 526, 564
Inaba, R. K., 721, 743
Inderbitzen-Pisaruk, H., 587, 618
Ingersoll, G., 506, 513
Inglis, G. B., 276, 294
Ingram, R. E., 170, 186
Inhelder, B., 255, 269, 627, 680
Inn, A., 739, 744
Innes, J. M., 237, 269
Inoff-Germaine, G., 628, 629, 680
Inwald, R. E., 555, 564
Ireton, H., 36, 57
Irwin, C., 687, 712
Irwin, M., 85, 126, 684, 711, 721, 743
Irwin, M. R., 743, 744
Isaacs, C., 61, 578, 621
Isaacs, S., 687, 697, 703, 711
Ismond, D. R., 125

Israel, E., 579, 580, 621
Itard, J. M. G., 408, 447
Ito, Y., 75, 128
Iwata, B. A., 397, 404, 438, 447, 452
Iyengar, S., 514
Izard, C. E., 234, 269
Izzo, L. D., 35, 52, 328, 361

Jacard, J., 357, 364
Jacennik, B., 454, 477
Jacewitz, M. M., 557, 565
Jackson, D., 727, 744
Jackson, J. L., 570, 572, 580, 612, 619, 620
Jackson, K. L., 213, 225
Jackson, R. K., 416, 445
Jackson, Y. K., 137, 183
Jacob, R. G., 29, 57, 105, 106, 122, 266
Jacob, T., 46, 57, 137, 171, 185, 627, 633, 640, 670, 679, 680, 681, 682
Jacobs, B. W., 687, 697, 703, 711
Jacobs, T., 728, 745
Jacobsen, P., 504, 514
Jacobson, A., 512
Jacobson, A. M., 679
Jacobson, J. W., 376, 377, 404
Jacobson, N. S., 42, 57, 142, 171, 172, 185, 186, 538, 547, 564, 631, 680
Jacobson, R. S., 534, 567
Jacobvitz, D., 342, 362
Jaenicke, C., 225
Jaffe, A. C., 231, 235, 276, 703, 711
Jaffe, K. M., 456, 477, 478
Jaffe, P., 535, 547, 567
James, L. D., 265, 509
James, W., 83, 122
Jameson, J. D., 59
Jane, J. A., 478
Janoff-Bulman, R., 584, 585, 618
Janosky, J., 403
Jansen, R. E., 171, 185
Jarcho, H. D., 204, 227
Jarrell, M. P., 701, 708
Jaselskis, C. A., 394, 404
Jason, L. A., 245, 266, 309
Jaworski, T. M., 585, 616
Jay, S. M., 234, 244, 246, 269, 287, 294, 495, 497, 498, 499, 504, 511, 513, 518
Jayaratne, S., 251, 269
Jenike, M. A., 237, 273
Jenkins, C. L., 175, 178
Jenkins, V., 38, 53
Jennett, B., 455, 480
Jennings, G., 688, 713
Jennings, K. D., 138, 185
Jennings, S. J., 444
Jens, K., 390, 404
Jensen, B. I., 30, 34, 57
Jensen, B. J., 56
Jensen, M. P., 242, 270, 497, 513
Jensen, P., 190, 211, 226, 228, 406
Jensen, P. S., 5, 8, 56, 146, 148, 185
Jernigan, T. L., 460, 476
Jersild, A. T., 231, 235, 237, 242, 269
Jessor, L., 727, 745
Jessor, R., 726, 727, 745
Jie, Z., 273, 296
Jimenez, A. L., 90, 118
Joe, V. C., 137, 189
Johansson, S., 37
John, K., 229
John, R. S., 658, 680

Johnson, B., 528, 564
Johnson, B. K., 589, 618
Johnson, C., 578, 616, 692, 693, 708, 710, 712
Johnson, C. L., 688, 692, 693, 694, 695, 697, 698, 702, 703, 704, 706, 711, 714
Johnson, C. F., 576, 618
Johnson, G., 497, 515
Johnson, G. E., 86, 129
Johnson, J., 431, 447, 489, 510, 715
Johnson, J. H., 162, 173, 190, 191, 257, 272, 549, 564
Johnson, K., 491, 513
Johnson, L. C., 251, 269
Johnson, M. P., 489, 511
Johnson, P. L., 32, 58
Johnson, R., 210, 227, 251, 258, 269, 270
Johnson, R. L., 250, 270, 304, 305
Johnson, S., 37, 60, 489, 510, 660, 680
Johnson, S. B., 27, 240, 245, 268, 270, 286, 481, 485, 498, 499, 500, 501, 503, 504, 505, 506, 511, 512, 513, 516, 517
Johnson, S. M., 42, 58, 240, 260, 265, 272, 493, 518
Johnson, T., 270, 309
Johnson, W. B., 385, 386, 407
Johnson, W. G., 505, 512, 683, 696, 708, 714
Johnson-Martin, N., 390, 391, 404
Johnson-Sabine, E., 688, 711
Johnston, B. M., 628, 681
Johnston, C., 5, 19, 20, 22, 38, 46, 47, 54, 58, 61, 77, 85, 88, 108, 109, 110, 122, 124, 137, 138, 168, 169, 174, 184, 185, 187, 490, 513, 558, 565
Johnston, L. D., 717, 718, 719, 720, 745
Johnston, M., 506, 514
Joiner, T. E., 586, 618
Jolly, J. B., 262, 270, 321, 324, 606, 622
Jonas, J. M., 687, 689, 710, 713
Jones, B., 534, 564, 592, 618
Jones, D., 614, 689, 705, 711, 714
Jones, D. P. H., 574, 575, 612, 617, 618, 619
Jones, E., 270, 309
Jones, H. E., 237, 270
Jones, J., 583, 619
Jones, J. E., 629, 678
Jones, M. C., 230, 237, 270
Jones, M. T., 41, 60
Jones, P., 573, 576, 621
Jones, R., 696, 709
Jones, R. H., 37, 55
Jones, R. M., 580, 617
Jones, R. R., 142, 163, 185, 189
Jones, R. T., 249, 270, 277, 284
Jones, S., 406
Jordan, H., 404, 448
Jordan, T. J., 454, 478
Joreskog, K. G., 14, 58
Joseph, J. A., 578, 616
Josephs, A., 271, 282, 318
Joshi, S., 588, 621
Joughin, N., 688, 710
Jourard, S. M., 696, 714
Jouriles, E. N., 38, 58, 137, 138, 173, 185, 547, 564
Jouve, J., 443

Judd, C. M., 731, *745*
Julien, D., 172, *185*
Jumper, S. A., 592, *618*
Jung, K. G., 262, 266
Jurich, J., 670, 671, *677*

Kabacoff, R. I., *680*
Kabela, E., 509
Kadushin, A., 537, *564*
Kaemmer, B., *50*
Kafantaris, V., 225
Kagan, J., 3, 6, 14, 58, 59, 103, 122, 234, 258, 265, 267, 269, 270
Kager, V., 489, *513*
Kalas, R., 35, 40, 53, 143, *182*, 208, 211, 224, 225, 247, 266, 308, *403*, 587, *615*
Kalichman, S. C., 574, *618*
Kalikow, K., *715*
Kalinowski, M. N., 597, *619*
Kalish, B. I., 427, *450*
Kallman, W. M., 31, *58*
Kalucy, R. S., 688, 692, 703, 709, *711*
Kaminer, Y., 395, *403*, 720, 722, *744*
Kaminski, Z., 687, 708
Kamphaus, R. W., 3, 18, 24, 36, 58, 64, 97, 126, 141, 145, 147, 149, 150, 153, 164, 165, 177, *185*, 389, *404*
Kanbayashi, Y., 78, *122*
Kandel, D., 728, *745*
Kandel, D. B., 199, 204, 205, 226, 728, *745*
Kandel, H. J., 256, *270*
Kane, M. T., *270*, 321
Kaneko, W. M., 437, *451*
Kanfer, F. H., 4, 8, 11, 14, 21, 23, 26, 27, 28, 32, 34, *58*, 77, *122*, 259, 270, 282
Kang, T. K., 343, *362*
Kanner, A., 174, *185*
Kanner, L., 240, 241, 270, 408, 409, 413, 422, 434, *445*, *447*
Kaplan, A. S., 686, 687, 709
Kaplan, E., 472, 477
Kaplan, F., 370, *402*
Kaplan, G., 724, *747*
Kaplan, M. S., 579, *614*
Kaplan, R. M., 505, *513*
Kaplan, S., 38, 65, 531, 566
Karlsson, J., 76, 88, 108, *117*, 127
Karoly, P., 4, 27, *58*, 77, *122*, 240, 242, 270, 282, 496, 497, *513*
Karp, M., 498, *513*
Kashani, J. H., 203, 210, 226, 231, 236, 237, 238, 259, 262, 270, 319
Kaslow, F. W., 16, 58, 628, *680*
Kaslow, N. J., 218, 226, 228, 554, *564*, 599, 610, *618*, *621*
Kass, R. E., 32, *63*
Kassem, L., 580, *619*
Kaster-Bundgaard, J., 7, *53*
Kates, N., 4, *58*
Katic, M., 226
Katin-Borland, M., 244, 273, 288
Katsuno, K., 419, *447*
Katz, E., 506, *511*
Katz, E. R., 234, 235, 244, 270, 287, 494, 495, 497, 498, *513*, *518*
Katz, J. L., 709, *715*
Katz, K. S., 491, *512*
Katz, L. F., 4, *55*, 137, 138, *185*
Katz, L. M., *270*
Katz, M., 376, *404*

Katz-Garris, L., 578, *622*
Katzman, M. A., 700, *711*
Kauffman, J. M., 77, *123*
Kaufman, A. F., 469, *478*
Kaufman, A. S., 24, 58, 382, 383, *404*
Kaufman, J., 533, 534, 554, *564*, 592, *618*
Kaufman, K., 551, *568*
Kaufman, K. F., 112, *120*
Kaufman, K. L., 576, 578, 579, *618*
Kaufman, M. R., 690, *711*, *715*
Kaufman, N. L., 58, 382, 383, *404*
Kaukiainen, A., 343, *363*
Kavanagh, K., 24, *58*
Kavanaugh, L., 139, *182*
Kay, D. W. K., 704, *711*
Kaye, K., 10, 47, *58*
Kaysen, D., *119*
Kazak, A., 491, *513*
Kazdin, A. E., 4, 6, 11, 12, 13, 14, 15, 25, 26, 28, 33, 42, 58, 59, 130, 132, 134, 136, 139, 146, 147, 148, 149, 150, 152, 170, 175, 177, *185*, *186*, 205, 206, 213, 214, 218, 226, 234, 235, 238, 247, 258, 262, 263, 267, 270, 272, 276, 317, *511*
Keane, T., 230, *271*
Kearney, C. A., 234, 249, 260, 262, 270, 311, 438, 439, *447*
Kearns, W., 5, *52*
Keating, D. P., 528, *567*
Keenan, K., 88, 93, *118*, *120*, 133, 134, 135, 140, *187*
Keeton, W. P., 696, 708
Kegan, R., 725, 728, *745*
Kehinde v. Commonwealth, 338. S. E. 2d. 356, 595, *618*
Keir, E. H., *478*
Keiser, T. W., 666, *682*
Keith, B., 137, *178*, *517*, *518*
Keitner, G. I., 635, *680*
Kellam, S. G., 161, *193*, 340, *362*
Keller, H., 4, 55, 535, *563*
Keller, J. W., 6, *64*
Kellerman, H., 234, *275*
Kellerman, J., 234, 235, 270, 287, 497, *513*
Kelley, C. K., 242, 243, 248, 270, 282
Kelley, J. E., 242, 266, 300
Kelley, J. T., 724, *747*
Kelley, M. L., 142, *178*, 431, *448*, 553, *561*, 655, 679, 687, *715*
Kelly, J., 227
Kelly, J. A., 4, 59, 533, 537, *564*, 567
Kelly, K. L., 103, 111, *126*
Kelly, M., *513*, 556, 566
Kelly, S. J., 581, 611, *618*
Kelsey, C., 245, 266, 297
Kemp, D. C., *444*
Kemp, C. H., 523, 528, 539, *564*
Kempe, R. S., 528, 539, *564*
Kemptom, T., 148, *183*, 678, 724, *748*
Kendall, P. C., 4, 6, 7, 25, 27, 36, 42, 53, 54, 59, 99, 100, 105, 112, *122*, *123*, 149, 170, *186*, 206, 213, 220, 223, 226, 228, 238, 247, 265, 270, 275, 321, 325
Kendall-Tackett, K. A., 576, 582, 583, 585, 591, 592, *618*
Kendrick, J., 698, *713*
Kendziora, K. T., 136, *186*
Kenkel, M. B., 589, *618*
Kennedy, R. E., 199, 227
Kennedy, S. H., 687, *713*
Kennedy, W. A., 237, *270*

Kenny, D. A., 731, *743*
Kent, R. N., 9, 42, 54, 247, 270, 627, 638, 643, 644, 650, 653, *681*
Keogh, M., 416, *444*
Kerbeshian, J., *452*
Kercher, G., 570, *618*
Kerdyck, L., *186*
Kerdyk, L., *116*
Kermani, E., 489, *513*
Kern, L., 396, *404*
Kern, R. A., 394, *401*
Kerr, A. M., 417, *447*
Kerr, M. M., 340, *364*
Kessler, J. W., 17, *59*
Kestenbaum, C. J., 40, *59*
Keys, A., 697, *711*
Kieffer, J. E., *119*
Kiely, K., *118*
Kienlen, T. L., 438, *443*
Kiesler, C. A., 13, *59*
Kilcoyne, J., 581, *615*
Killen, J. D., 692, *711*
Kilman, B. A., 429, *448*
Kilpatrick, A. C., 540, *566*
Kilpatrick, D. G., 575, *619*, 621
Kim, R., 270
Kimberlin, C. C., 429, *442*, *445*
Kimmel, D. C., 172, *186*, 667, *680*
Kinard, E. M., 531, 533, 534, *564*
Kinder, B. N., 696, *714*
King, A., 704, *711*
King, A. C., *120*, 129
King, A. Y. C., 343, *363*
King, C. A., 724, 739, *745*
King, D., *511*
King, G. A., 551, 559, *564*
King, H. E., 154, *183*
King, J. B., 258, *271*, 285
King, N. J., 31, *59*, 138, *188*, 206, 220, 226, 236, 237, 239, 240, 249, 260, 262, 268, 271, 274, 282, 318, 323
King, S., 490, 509
King, T. R., 245, *266*
Kinney, T., *517*, *518*
Kinsbourne, M., 87, 88, *122*, *123*
Kinscherff, R., 588, *616*
Kinzett, N. G., 87, *121*
Kirchner, G. L., 127
Kirisci, L., 266, 724, *746*
Kirkley, B. G., 688, 707
Kirkpatrick, D. R., 236, 237, 238, 240, *271*
Kirschenbaum, D. S., 704, *713*
Kiser, L. J., 583, 585, 586, 587, *618*
Kistner, J. A., 337, *363*, 499, *515*, 553, 556, *563*
Kita, M., 78, *122*
Kitsuse, J. I., 20, *64*
Kivlahan, C., 526, *563*
Klajner-Diamond, H., 573, *620*
Klaric, S. H., 208, 247, *266*
Klass, E., 381, 383, 399, *405*
Klebanov, P. K., 4, 53, 138, *182*
Klee, S. H., 429, *443*
Klein, D., 106, *116*
Klein, D. F., 32, *48*
Klein, M. A., 633, *682*
Klein, N., 457, *478*, 479
Klein, R., 86, *123*, 498, *511*
Klein, R. G., 39, 59, 133, 135, *178*, *746*
Klein, S., *479*
Klein, S. B., 20, *68*
Klein, S. K., 453, *478*
Klin, A., *452*

Kline, I., 585, *618*
Kline, J., 208, 210, 226, 247, 269, 492, *513*
Kline, R. B., 36, *54*
Kline, W., *452*
Klinedinst, J. H., 259, 277
Klinedinst, J. K., 36, 67, 469, *480*
Klinefelter, D., 206, 223
Klingman, A., 251, 257, 258, 271, *273*, 288, 289
Klink, A., 601, *623*
Klinnert, M. D., 261, *271*
Klonoff, H., 475, *478*
Klorman, R., 87, *123*, 258, 271, 285
Klosko, J. S., 263
Knapp, D., 391, *406*
Knapp, M., 265, 285, 297, 313
Knee, D., 111, *118*
Knibbs, J., 687, *709*
Knight, G. P., 647, 652, 672, 676, *680*
Knights, R. M., 475, *478*
Kniskern, D. P., 47, *55*
Kniskern, J. R., 45, 68, 160, *193*
Knobloch, H., 415, *447*
Knop, J., 722, 724, 727, 728, 745
Knox, D. T., 423, *449*
Knox, F. H., 236, 237, 240, 266
Kobak, R. R., 639, *680*
Kobasa, S. C., 436, *448*
Koch, H. J., 696, *709*
Koegel, R. L., 413, 414, 431, 435, 436, 437, 447, 448, 450, 451
Koenning, G., 505, *518*
Koepke, T., 632, 635, 652, 654, 657, 668, 672, 680, *681*
Koeppl, G. K., 357, 358, 360
Kogan, N., 258, *277*
Kohlenberg, B. S., 412, *451*
Kolb, L. C., 230, *271*
Kolko, D. J., 146, 148, 149, 152, 159, 164, 177, *186*, 496, 497, *513*, 529, 564, 591, *618*
Koller, H., 376, 392, *404*
Kolodny, R., *120*
Kolvin, I., 238, 271, 408, 414, 417, *447*
Kono, M., 700, *715*
Konstantareas, M. M., 435, *447*
Koocher, G. P., 23, *59*
Koontz, K., 490, *515*
Koot, H. M., 199, *224*
Kope, T. M., 689, *711*
Kopp, C. B., 81, *123*
Koppitz, E. M., 386, 387, *404*
Korbin, J., 524, *564*
Korn, S., 415, *444*
Kornhaber, R. C., 242, 243, 249, 271, 300
Korsch, B. M., 505, *511*, *514*
Kortlander, E., *270*
Kosier, T., 86, *123*
Koslow, R. E., 687, *711*
Kotchick, B. A., 5, *54*
Kotsopoulos, S., 44, *59*
Kovacs, M., 32, 40, 41, *59*, 133, *186*, 198, 204, 205, 208, 226, 247, *271*, 490, 493, *514*, 555, 564, 587, *618*
Koverola, C., 550, *564*, 587, *616*, *618*
Kovitz, K., 19, *61*, 169, 187, 558, *565*
Kozak, M. J., 235, *271*
Kozloff, M. A., 430, 436, 437, *447*
Kozlowski, S., 432, 433, *443*
Kraemer, H., *511*
Kraemer, H. C., 416, *451*
Krahn, G. L., 137, 185, 505, 506, *514*
Kramer, J., 75, 104, *124*

Kramer, J. H., 472, *477*
Krasnegor, N. A., 472, *478*
Krasner, L., 8, *66*
Krasnor, L. R., 335, *364*
Krasnor, R., 580, *614*
Krasowski, M. D., *119*
Krass, J., *708*
Kratochwill, T. R., 14, 28, 59, 62, 231, 234, 235, 241, 247, 255, 256, 257, *273*, 275, 325, 395, 396, *405*
Kraus, I., *120*, *179*
Kraus, J. F., 455, *478*
Krauss, D. J., 172, *180*
Kravitz, R. I., 539, *564*
Krawiecki, N., 460, 477, 505, *512*
Kream, J., *715*
Kreiger, R., 531, *566*
Kricheff, I. I., *444*
Krifcher, B., *120*
Krifcher-Lehman, B., *179*
Kron, S., *617*
Kronenberger, W., 492, *514*
Kropp, J. P., 38, *59*, 559, *562*
Krouse, J. P., 77, *123*
Krueger, J., 658, *680*
Kruesi, M. J. P., 633, *679*
Krug, D. A., 420, 421, 430, *447*
Krusei, M. J. P., 76, *129*
Kubany, E. S., 163, *186*
Kubar, W., 496, *516*
Kuczynski, L., 37, 44, *55*, *66*
Kuhn, G., *617*
Kuiper, J., 590, *616*
Kulik, J., 505, *514*
Kulkarni, R., 490, 492, *510*, *515*
Kumar, S., *476*
Kupersmidt, J. B., 329, 330, 333, 337, 339, 350, 360, *361*, *363*
Kurdek, L. A., 40, *59*
Kurita, H., 419, *447*
Kurman, L., 706, *711*
Kuroda, J., *271*, 301
Kurtz, P. D., 532, 533, *565*, *567*
Kury, S. P., 496, *516*
Kurzon, M., 84, *118*
Kusche, C. A., 342, 362
Kusel, S. J., 329, *364*
Kushner, H., 489, *515*
Kusnerik, L., *478*
Kutash, K., *681*
Kutcher, S., 217, *226*
Kwan Tam, K., 526, *567*
Kyle, K. E., 495, *511*
Kyrios, M., 164, *190*

La Taillade, J. J., 142, 171, *186*
Labbe, E. L., 496, *514*
Labouvie, E. W., 726, 728, 729, 735, 743, 745, *748*
Lacey, B. C., 251, *271*
Lacey, J. H., 692, *711*
Lacey, J. I., 251, *271*
Lacey, J. L., 251, *271*
Lachar, D., 36, 54, 57, 59, 67, 77, 97, *123*, 128, 259, 277, 469, 478, *480*
LaCombe, J., 633, *682*
Ladd, G. W., 328, 330, 334, 340, 341, 343, 344, 346, 353, 355, *361*, *363*
Ladish, C., 151, *179*
LaFreniere, P. J., 259, 261, 266, 271, 305
Lagerspetz, K. M., 343, *363*
LaGreca, A. M., 4, 33, *59*, 234, 249, 255, 262, *271*, 335, *363*, 505, *511*

Lahey, B. B., 54, 72, 73, 79, 89, 100, 109, 110, *116*, 122, *123*, 131, 132, 133, 135, 137, 145, 171, 172, 177, *183*, *184*, 186, 187, 190, 192, 226, 228, 247, 268, 305, 406, 559, *562*
Laird, M., 533, *562*
Lake, M., *714*
Lamb, M., 260, 265, 597, *618*
Lamb, M. E., 22, 59, 537, *563*
Lamb, S., 572, 580, 590, *618*
Lambert, D. L., 340, *364*
Lambert, M. J., 5, *63*
Lambert, N., 389, *404*, 431
Lambert, N. M., 77, 78, 84, 122, 123, *447*
Lamborn, S. D., 535, 567, 676, 682
Lamparski, D., 234, 235, 277, 279
Lancy, D., 430, *447*
Land, G., 526, *563*
Landau, S., 32, 62, 103, 105, *124*, 150, *188*, 348, 352, 353, 363
Landeros v. Flood, 17 Cal., 573, *618*
Landesman, S., 357, *364*
Landolf-Fritsche, B., 497, *509*
Landon-Jimenez., 416, *444*
Landrum, T. J., *451*
Landrus, R., 430, *449*
Landry, S. H., 412, *447*, 454, 459, 476, 477, *478*
Landsberg, C., 581, *615*
Landy, D., 706, *712*
Lane, S., 578, *621*
Lang, A. R., 88, *125*, 137, *189*
Lang, P. J., 230, 234, 235, 242, 260, 261, 268, 271, 660, *680*
Lang, R. A., 583, *615*, *616*
Lang, M., 204, *228*
Langer, E. J., 20, *59*
Langer, S. N., 441, *451*
Langevin, R., 576, *619*
Langlois, A., 532, *563*
Langner, T. S., 40, *59*
Lanktree, C. B., 587, *619*
Lann, I., 30, *65*
Lansky, S. B., 491, 492, *510*, *514*
Lantinga, L. J., 172, *180*
LaPadula, M., 86, *123*
Lapey, K., 77, *118*
Lapkin, J., 225, 736, *745*
Lapouse, R., 35, *59*, 236, 237, 238, 262, *271*
Larkin, K. T., 230, *277*
Larmande, C., *447*
Laron, Z., 498, *513*
LaRose, L., 37, *68*
Larrance, D. T., 38, *59*
Larrieu, J. A., 603, *621*
Larry P. v. Riles, 343 F. Supp. 1306, 371, 378, *404*
Larsen, K. H., 249, 268, 304
Larson, J. H., 172, 180, 181, 627
Larson, R., 661, 662, 680, 695, 698, 711, 712
Larsson, I., 590, *619*
Larzelere, R. E., 36, *59*
Lask, B., 687, *709*
Laski, K., *128*
Last, C. G., 4, 39, *59*, 60, 231, 237, 238, 250, 258, 260, 262, 264, 267, 271, 272, 274, 276, 311, 317, 318, 319
Latham, P., 90, 115, *123*
Latham, R., 90, 115, *123*
Lathrop, M., 637, 641, 649, 654, *679*
Latimer, P. R., 483, *514*, 699, *708*
Laudolff, J., *362*

Laughlin, A., 633, *678*
Laurent, J., 234, 235, 272, 324
Laursen, B., 331, 338, 345, 362, 363, 627, 631, 633, *678*
Lautenschlager, G. J., 137, *183*
Lavee, Y., 620, 670, 680, 704, *713*
Lavigne, J. V., 486, 489, 491, 493, 498, 504, 509, *510*, *514*
Lavori, P., *512*
Law, D. B., 272
Law, T. C., 4, 56, 235
Lawrence, C., 706, *712*
Lawry, S., 587, *617*
Lawson, L., 572, 583, *619*
Lawton, J. M., 4, *65*, 177, *190*
Layne, C. C., 41, *60*
Lazarus, A., 740, *747*
Lazarus, R., 174, *185*
Lazarus, R. S., 732, *746*
Lazovik, A. D., 242, *271*
Leadbeater, B. J., 203, 226
Leake, J. L., 258, *278*
Lease, C. A., 237, *276*
LeBaron, D., 573, *620*
LeBaron, S., 235, 244, 246, 248, 272, 287, 288, 496, 497, 498, *514*, *519*
Leblanc, M., *192*
Lebovici, S., *450*
LeBow, J., 13, *60*
LeBuffe, P. A., 18, *62*
Leckliter, I. N., 475, *478*
Leckman, J. F., *452*
LeCouteur, A., 414, 415, 423, 424, 447, 448, *450*
Leddet, I., 422, *447*
Lederer, A. S., 248, 254, 262, 264, 310
Ledingham, J. E., 133, *190*, 192, 335, 346, 348, 356, 363, 364, *365*
LeDrew, L., 381, *403*
Lee, C. M., 6, 26, *60*
Lee, J., 40, 49, 415, *446*
Lee, N. F., 687, *712*
Lee, W. M. L., 256, 272
Leech, S. L., 727, *744*
Leehey, K., 686, *716*
Lefebvre, L., 550, *568*
Lefkowitz, M. M., 131, *185*
Lehman, B., *120*
Lehman, E., 245, 266, 297
Lehman, P., 608, 609, *614*
Lehtinen, L. E., 71, 86, *127*
Leichtman, M., 593, *615*
Leiderman, P. H., 676, *678*
Leifer, M., 580, 582, *619*
Leigh, D., 704, *711*
Leigh, J., 389, 390, *402*
Leitenberg, H., 41, *60*, 205, 218, 227, 229, 242, 251, 256, 263, 272, 283, 687, 694, 695, 698, 700, 710, 713, *714*
Leiter, R. G., 383, 385, *404*, 429, *448*
Leland, H., 389, *404*, 431, *447*
Lelord, G., 426, 428, *442*, 443, *444*, 447
Lemanek, K. L., 4, *59*, 490, *514*
LeMare, L., 336, *364*
Lemley, R. E., 31, *63*
Lenane, M., 235, 275, 633, *679*
Lenkner, D. A., 340, *364*
Lennon, M., 211, 226
Lenox, K. F., 334, *361*
Lentz, R., 693, *713*
Lenz, M. W., *451*
Leon, G. R., 690, 697, *712*
Leonard, B., 492, *515*
Leonard, H., 225

Leonard, H. L., 235, 275
Leonard, K., 137, *185*, 728, *745*
Leone, P. E., 719, *742*
Lerner, C., 504, *510*
Lerner, P., 687, *713*
Lerner, R. M., 4, 5, *50*, 59, 706, 712, 725, *746*
Leske, G., 38, 67, 138, *192*
Leslie, A. M., 411, *443*
Letourneau, E. J., 599, *619*
Leudar, I., 376, *403*
Lev, J., 235, 236, 237, 238, 275
Levenson, R. W., 4, 44, 55, 659, 661, 662, *679*
Leventhal, A., *181*
Leventhal, B. L., 119, 394, *404*
Leventhal, J. M., 491, *516*, 596, *619*
Levin, B., 16, *68*
Levin, D. N., 235, *271*
Levin, H. S., 453, 455, 456, 471, 472, 473, 474, 477, 478
Levin, J., *715*
Levin, L., *444*
Levin, P. A., 693, *712*
Levine, M., 527, *565*
Levine, M. D., 92, *125*
Levine, M. P., 701, *714*
Levine, S., 389, 390, *404*
Leviton, A., *125*
Levy, F., 88, *123*
Levy, H. B., 597, *619*
Levy, J. C., 724, 739, *746*
Levy, R. L., 251, *269*
Lewin, C., 41, 701, *714*
Lewin, L., *57*
Lewinsohn, P. M., 201, 208, 213, 221, 224, 225, 227, 228, 256, 272
Lewis, C., 688, 695, 698, *711*
Lewis, D. O., 534, *565*
Lewis, I. A., 570, *616*
Lewis, J., *267*
Lewis, J. F., 389, 390, *405*
Lewis, J. M., 612, *619*
Lewis, L. D., 688, 692, 693, *711*
Lewis, M., 4, *60*, 149, *191*, 235, 272
Lewis, M. H., 413, *448*
Lewis, P. M., *52*
Lewis, R., *476*
Lewis, R. A., 31, *54*, 647, *680*
Lewis, S., 272, 313
Lewis, T. M., 235, 272
Lewis-Meert, C., 499, *513*
Liao, S., *477*
Lichtenstein, E., 733, *744*
Lick, J. R., 243, *272*
Liebenauer, L. L., 120, *129*
Liebert, D. E., 352, *364*
Liebert, R. M., 269, *300*
Ligezinska, M., 585, 586, 587, *619*
Light, R., 476, 538, *565*
Lighthall, F. F., 276, *307*
Lilienfeld, S. O., 133, *186*
Lilly, M. A., *478*
Lin, T. Y., *450*
Lincoln, A. J., 429, *448*
Lindahl, K. M., 172, *185*
Lindblad, F., 590, *619*
Lindgren, S., 87, *124*
Lindsay, P., 76, *119*
Linehan, M. M., 32, 33, *66*
Links, P. S., 188, *743*
Linscheid, T., 492, *519*
Lipinski, D. P., 41, *63*
Lipman, E. L., *188*
Lipovsky, J. A., 206, 212, 225, 227, 575, 576, 580, 587, *619*, *621*

Lippert, J., *406*
Lippke, L. F., 738, 743, *746*
Lipsedge, M., 239, *264*
Lipsett, L., 536, *565*
Liptak, G., 505, *514*
Litman, G. K., 732, *746*
Litt, I., *511*, *711*
Litt, I. F., 499, *514*
Little, R. E., 724, *745*
Littman, D. C., 136, *184*
Littman, R. A., 30, 63, *363*
Liu, S., *185*
Livingston, R. L., 262, 270, 321, 583, 585, 586, 587, *619*
Lobato, D., 392, *404*, 493, *514*
Lobitz, G. K., 42, 58, 240, 272
Lochman, J. E., 52, 138, 177, *180*, 186, 334, 344, 361, *363*
Locke, H. J., 109, *123*, 172, 179, 187, 667, 680, 703, *712*
Lockyer, L., 412, *450*
Loeb, K. L., 699, *712*
Loeber, R., 4, *54*, 60, 72, 76, 89, 100, 122, 123, 132, 133, 134, 135, 136, 139, 140, 152, 153, 177, *183*, 184, 186, 187, 190, 192, 728, 730, *744*
Logan, G., 76, *119*, 126
Logan, G. D., 73, 75, 79, 104, *126*
Lohr, N. E., *620*
Lollar, D. J., 496, *514*
Loney, J., 32, 62, 78, 85, 86, 103, 105, *123*, 124, 125, 150, *187*
Long, C. G., 492, *514*
Long, G., *61*
Long, J. S., 414, *448*
Long, N., 33, 38, *54*, 132, *183*, 628, 678, *682*
Long, P. J., 234, 235, 236, *264*, 570, 572, 580, 589, 612, 615, *619*
Long, S. H., 532, *563*
Longo, R., 578, *617*
Longoria, N., 660, *679*
Loos, L. M., *447*
Loosen, P. T., 216, *228*
Lopez, R., 88, *123*
Lorand, S., 690, *712*
Lorber, R., 42, *64*, 163, 189, 531, 534, 565, *566*
Lorch, E. P., 75, *124*
Lord, C., 409, 414, 417, 423, 424, 425, 426, 427, 429, 445, 447, 448, *452*
Lord, K., 393, *404*
Lorenger, A. T., 727, *744*
Lorenz, F. O., 203, *225*
Loro, A. D., 691, 692, 694, 697, 698, 707, *712*
Lorsch, N., 413, *448*
Lorys-Vernon, A., *123*
Loss, V., *480*
Lotter, V., 409, 414, 415, 416, *448*
Lotyczewski, B. S., *362*
Lou, H. C., 87, *123*
Lounsbury, M. L., 164, *179*
Lourie, R. S., 19, *55*
Lovaas, I., 88, *128*
Lovaas, O. I., 411, 412, 413, 414, 432, 436, *444*, 445, 448, 450, *451*
Love, L. C., 572, 589, *619*
Love, S. R., 414, 415, *448*, 688, 692, 695, *711*, *712*
Lovejoy, M. C., 168, *187*
Loveland, K. A., 412, 431, *447*, 448, *452*, 489, *514*
Lovitt, T. C., 41, *60*
Lowe, J., 505, *517*

Lowe, K., 503, *514*
Lowe, T. L., 415, *448*
Lowenstein, E., 18, *57*
Lowman, J. T., 491, 499, *514, 517*
Loyd, B. H., 435, *448*
Lubbs, H. A., 373, *404*
Lubin, A., 251, 269
Lucci, D., 416, *445*
Luce, S. C., 432, *443, 445*
Luecke, W. J., 530, *563*
Luerssen, T. G., *478*
Lui, B., 591, 607, *616*
Luiselli, J. K., 256, 272
Luk, S., 75, 76, 88, *123*
Lumley, M. A., 257, 258, 259, 261, 272
Lumley, V., 7, *53*
Lundin, B., 590, *619*
Lundquist, L. M., 557, *563*
Lupatkin, W., 227
Luper, H. L., 15, *67*
Lupfer, S. L., 612, *614*
Lurier, A., 397, *402*
Luscomb, R., 493, *517*
Lushene, R. E., 250, *276*
Lutz, C., 504, *519*
Lutz, J. G., 583, *617*
Lutzker, J. R., 503, *514*
Lynam, D., 140, *180*
Lyman, R. D., 41, 60, 169, *180*
Lynch, D. L., 592, *620*
Lynch, G., 78, *128*
Lynch, M. A., 571, *620*
Lynskey, M. T., 137, *183*, 722, 724, *745, 746*
Lyon, G. R., 166, *187*, 472, *478*
Lyon, J. -M., *672, 680*
Lyons-Ruth, K., 136, 137, *178, 187*
Lytle, C., 587, *618*
Lyttle, M. D., 724, *745*
Lytton, H., 22, *60*

Macchiavello, A., 255, *264*
Maccoby, E. E., 533, *565*
MacDonald, A. W., 177, *178*
MacDonald, M. L., 6, *66*
MacDonald, N., *479*
MacDonald, R. F., 441, *451*
MacDonald, K. B., 5, *63*
Mace, F. C., 11, *60*, 396, *404*
MacFarlane, J. W., 23, *60*, 236, 240, 272
MacKenzie, E. P., 172, *187*
MacLean, D. J., 528, *567*
MacLean, W. E., 377, *404*
MacMahon, B., *445*
MacMillan, D. L., 20, *55*
MacMillan, H. L., *188*
MacMillan, V. M., 550, 551, *565*
MacNaughton, K., *516*
MacPhee, C., 36, 38, *50*
MacPhee, D., *60*
MacWhinney, J. B., *510*
Maddi, S. R., 436, *448*
Madle, R. A., 273, *299*
Madonna, P. G., 612, *619*
Madsen, C. H., 37, *60*
Madsen, C. K., 37, *60*
Magee, V., *617*
Magnusson, D., 10, *53*
Magura, S., 548, 551, *565*
Mahanand, D., 415, *446*
Maher, C., *125*
Mahler, M. S., 408, *448*
Mahoney, A., 173, *185*

Maieron, M. J., 497, *509*
Maiman, L., 505, *514*
Main, M., 136, *187*, 530, *565*
Maisami, M., 235, 262, 269, 319
Makita, K., 408, *448*
Malik, S. C., 78, *118*
Malinosky-Rummell, R. R., 588, 589, *619*
Malkin, A., 226
Malkin, D., 226
Malla, S., 587, *621*
Mallon, J., *517*
Mallory, I., *125, 189*
Malloy, P., 86, *123, 746*
Malone, J., 173, *188*, 245, 268, 286, 503, *513*
Malone, M. A., 76, *123*
Malone, S., 497, *512*
Maloney, M. J., 688, 701, *712*
Maltz, A., 429, *448*
Mandel, F., *566*
Mandel, F. S., *709*
Mandler, G., 255, *272*
Mandler, J. M., 255, *272*
Manion, I. G., 493, *518, 619*
Manjanatha, S., 606, *622*
Manku, M., 84, *125*
Manly, J. T., 533, 567, 593, *619*
Mann, A., 688, *711*
Mann, B. J., 172, *187*, 553, 561, *639, 644, 645, 650, 653, 666, 668, 677, 678, 680*
Mann, L., 724, *744*
Mann, L. M., 726, 731, *746*
Mannarino, A. P., 534, *564*, 583, 587, 592, *615, 618*
Manne, S., 496, 504, *514*
Mannuzza, S., 86, 90, *123*, 724, *746*
Manor, M., 498, *513*
March, C. L., 85, *119*
Marchant, R., 413, *448*
Marcus, A., 724, 728, *746*
Marcus, L., 431, *451*
Marcus, L. M., 436, *448*
Marcus, R. F., *629, 680*
Marder, T., 396, *404*
Marett, K. M., *647, 680*
Margalit, M., 392, *404*
Margolin, G., 20, 41, 46, 47, 56, *60*, 67, 148, *180*, 631, 639, 658, *679, 680*
Maria, B. L., *477*
Mariani, M., 77, *123*
Marilov, V., 691, *707*
Markman, H. J., 46, *60*, 171, 172, *185, 187*
Markovic, J., 597, *619*
Marks, I. M., 231, 234, 235, 239, 261, 264, 272, 695, *712*
Marks, R., 394, *401*
Markwardt, F. C., Jr., 385, 386, *404*, 469, *477*
Marlatt, G. A., 727, 733, *744, 746*
Marmarou, A., *478*
Marold, D. B., 218, *225*
Marr, T. J., 491, *514*
Marriage, K., 218, *225*, 587, *621*
Marrs, A., *118*
Mars, K. T., 346, 353, *363*
Marsh, J., *514*
Marsh, W. L., *119*
Marshall, L. F., *478*
Marshall, R., *122*
Marshburn, E., 395, *404*
Marteau, T., 506, *514*
Martin, B., 539, *565*

Martin, D. A., 498, *518*
Martin, D. C., *127*
Martin, F., 687, 702, *712*
Martin, G., 7, *60*
Martin, H. P., 530, *561*
Martin, I., 251, *272*
Martin, J. A., 36, *59*, 533, 537, 564, 565
Martin, J. E., 75, *121*
Martin, J. L., 414, *446*
Martin, K., 570, *619*
Martin, K. M., 477, *478*
Martin, S., 37, *60*
Martineau, J., *443*
Martinez, C. R., 5, *54*
Marton, P., 112, *120*, 226
Marvinney, D., *561*
Marx, C. M., 263, *292*
Marzolf, D. P., 596, *615*
Mas, C. H., 639, *677*
Masek, B. J., 495, 496, *514, 518*
Mash, E. J., 3, 4, 5, 6, 7, 8, 9, 10, 11, 12, 13, 14, 16, 18, 19, 20, 22, 23, 24, 27, 28, 30, 31, 32, 33, 37, 38, 41, 42, 43, 44, 45, 46, 47, 58, *60*, 61, 65, 85, 88, 90, 107, 108, 109, 110, 124, 137, 169, 167, 185, 187, 247, 261, 272, 453, 478, 490, *513*, 544, 558, 559, 565
Masland, R. H., 373, *404*
Mason, J., 432, *444*
Masse, B., *192*
Masse, L. C., 339, *361, 364*
Masselam, V. S., 628, 647, 652, *680*
Masten, A. S., 12, *61*, 337, 343, 352, 363
Mastenbrook, J., 374, *404*
Masters, J. C., 259, *272*
Masters, K. S., 5, *63*
Matarazzo, J. D., 33, *61*
Matchett, G., 261, *269*
Matese, M., 428, *448*
Mathers, C. D., 458, *478*
Mathews, J., *510*
Matier, K., 76, *122*
Matier-Sharma, K., 103, *124*
Matrin, C. A., 76, *124*
Matson, J. L., 108, *124*, 232, 234, 235, 267, 272, 302, 351, 363, 377, 393, *404*, 414, 415, 419, 448, 451
Mattes, J. A., 77, 87, *124*
Matthews, M., *709*
Matthews, W. S., 492, *511*
Mattingly, D., 684, *707*
Mattison, R. E., 223, 272, 319
Mattsson, A. E., 492, *510*
Maughan, B., *187*
Mauk, J., 396, *404*
Maurer, A., 236, 237, 262, 272
Maurer, R. G., 79, *124, 444*
Mawhood, J., *404*
Mawhood, L., *448*
May, J. G., 376, *405*
Mayer, G. R., 7, *66*
Mayer, J., 699, 713, 735, *746*
Mayer, L. S., *362*
Mazure, C. M., 701, *712*
Mazurick, J. L., 149, *186*
Mazzuca, S., 498, *515*
McAdoo, W. G., 435, *449*
McAffer, V. J., 140, *190*
McAllister, J., 400, 401, *405*
McAllister, J. A., 226
McAuliffe, S., *403*
McBain, M. L., 38, *51*

McBurnett, K., 111, *116*, *123*, *127*, 133, *183*, *186*, *190*, 192
McCain, A. P., 655, 679
McCall, R. B., *184*, 268, 381, *405*
McCallon, D., 419, *446*, 489
McCallum, M., 268, *512*, *513*
McCandless, B. R., 41, *51*, 249, 265, 316
McCann, J., 585, 622
McCarn, J. E., *446*
McCarney, S. B., 98, *124*
McCarthy, D., 382, 283, *405*, 463, 479
McCarthy, E. D., *59*
McCarthy, M., 142, *178*
McCartney, K., 728, *747*
McCarty, J. A., 559, 562
McCathie, H., 237, 239, 254, 262, 272, 276, 318, 319, 325
McCaul, K. D., 503, 505, *517*
McCauley, E., 41, *50*, 356, 357, 360, 489, *515*
McClain, P., 526, 565
McClaskey, C. L., 29, 52, 108, *120*, 165, *181*, 344, 356, *361*
McClearly, C., 476
McClellan, J., 591, *613*
McClelland, G. H., 731, *745*
McClure, F. D., 104, *121*, *124*
McColloch, M. A., 660, 661, *680*
McCollum, A. T., 491, *515*
McConaughy, S. H., 36, 41, 49, 93, *116*, 146, 147, 150, 161, *187*, 207, 223, 551, 560
McConnachie, G., *444*
McConnell, S., 351, 365
McCord, J., 133, *187*
McCorkle, A. D., 259, *268*
McCormack, A., 534, *561*
McCoy, K., 482, *515*
McCubbin, H. I., 46, *61*, 436, *449*, 489, 490, *515*, *516*, 612, 619
McCubbin, M. A., 490, *515*, 612, 619
McCurry, C., 591, *613*
McCutcheon, S. M., 549, *564*
McDermott, P. A., 18, 36, *61*
McDonald, R., 173, *185*
McDonnell, P., *510*
McEachran, A., 40, 523
McElreath, L. H., 150, *182*
McElroy, L. P., 588, *619*
McFadin, J., 578, *617*
McFall, R. M., 4, 11, 20, 25, 30, *61*, 65
McFarland, J. H., 688, *713*
McGaughey, M. C., 175, *178*
McGeary, J., 499, *510*
McGee, C. R., 726, *745*
McGee, G. C., 397, *405*
McGee, R., 78, 92, *124*, 139, *187*, 203, 227, 238, 263, 534, 554, 565, 568
McGee, R. A., 592, *619*
McGee, R. O., 135, *180*
McGhee, D. E., 393, *401*
McGillicuddy-DeLisi, A. V., 21, 35, *61*, 65
McGinnis, J., 481, *515*
McGlynn, F. D., 234, 235, 266
McGoldrick, M., 627, 678
McGrath, P., *125*, *189*
McGrath, P. A., 496, *515*
McGrath, P. J., 497, *515*
McGraw, J. M., 574, 575, *618*
McGregor, P., 7, 67
McGue, M., 725, 728, *746*

McGuinness, B., 703, *709*
McGuire, J., 688, *712*
McGuire, R., 239, *264*
McHale, J. P., 83, *122*, 153, *184*
McHale, S. M., 436, 437, *449*
McIlvane, W. J., 454, 479
McIntyre, A., 245, 266, 297
McIntyre, J., *619*
McIntyre, T. J., 44, *61*
McKendrick, T., *511*
McKenzie, S. J., 700, *716*
McKenzie, T. L., 41, *61*
McKeown, R. E., 213, 225
McKinney, B., 6, *61*, 392, *405*, 492, *515*
McKinnon, J. A., 580, *614*
McKnew, D., 208, 210, 226, 247, 269
McLaren, J., 374, 376, *404*, *405*
McLaughlin, K. J., 249, 270, 284
McLaughlin, R. J., 728, 732, 742, *744*
McLeer, S. V., 149, *186*, 585, 586, 603, *619*
McLennan, J., *447*
McLone, D., 489, *519*
McMahon, R. J., 4, 6, 13, 24, 32, *54*, *61*, 95, 106, 108, 109, 112, 113, *121*, 134, 137, 140, 141, 142, 143, 151, 153, 155, 156, 157, 158, 159, 160, 162, 163, 170, 172, 175, 176, *179*, 183, *184*, *187*, 188, 257, 267, 273, 350, 506, *512*, 541, 559, 563
McManus, S. M., *181*
McMurray, M. B., 72, 75, 76, 77, 79, 85, 99, 100, 103, 104, 111, *117*, *120*
McNabb, N., *510*
McNally, R. J., 261, 273
McNamara, E., 231, 235, 248, 262, 273, 313
McNay, A., 408, *447*
McNeil, C. B., 148, 150, 151, 160, *182*, *188*
McPhee, D., 526, 567
McPherson, A. E., 632, 645, 672, 675, 678
McQuaid, J. R., *744*
McRae, D., 226
McShane, M., 570, *618*
McWatters, M. A., 87, *120*
Meade, J., *614*
Meadow-Orlans, K. P., 38, *61*
Meadows, D., 585, *619*
Mech, E. V., 232, 263
Mee, L. L., 218, 226
Meece, J. L., 249, 273, 277, 312
Meehl, P. H., 28, *62*
Meichenbaum, D., 7, *62*
Meinhold, P., 506, *519*
Meister, I., 696, *709*
Melamed, B. G., 231, 234, 235, 240, 242, 243, 244, 246, 248, 249, 251, 255, 256, 257, 258, 259, 260, 261, 265, 267, 269, 270, 271, 272, 273, 278, 288, 289, 290
Meller, J., 724, *745*
Mellin, L. M., 687, *712*
Mellor, C., 44, *59*
Melnick, S., 77, *122*, 239, 273
Melton, G. B., 23, *62*, 152, *190*, 523, 565
Meminger, S. R., 265
Menard, S., 355, *361*
Mendelson, B. K., 696, *712*
Mendelson, M., 38, *49*, 204, 223, *561*
Mendelsohn, D., *478*

Menkes, J., 454, 455, 458, 460, 462, 479
Menlove, F. L., 232, 242, 263, 299
Mennen, F. E., 585, *619*
Menolascino, F. J., 376, 377, 392, 403, *405*
Menzies, R. G., 249, 273, 313, 314
Mercer, C. D., 20, 49
Mercer, G. W., 728, 729, *745*
Mercer, J. R., 389, 390, *405*
Mercuri-Minich, N., *478*
Merikangas, K. R., 229
Merlo, M., 76, *126*
Merluzzi, T. V., 249, 268, 304
Merry, S., 394, *401*
Mesaros, R. A., 438, *445*
Mesibov, G. B., 408, 417, 430, 435, *449*, *450*, *451*
Messenger, K., 392, 402, 493, *510*
Messer, I., 20, *50*
Messer, S., 103, *124*
Messick, S., 3, *62*
Metalsky, G., 620
Methvin, J., 390, 402
Metz, C., 40, 49
Metzgen, K., *406*
Metzger, R., 230, 265
Metzler, A., 337, *363*
Meyer, E. C., 148, *186*
Meyer, L. H., 4, 53
Meyer, S. L., 579, *614*
Meyer, V., 33, *66*
Meyers, C. E., 20, 62
Meyers, E., 436, *449*
Meyerson, J., 81, *121*
Mezzich, A. C., 724, *748*
Mezzich, J., 9, *51*
Mian, M., 573, 620
Michael, R., 258, *271*
Michaels, R. H., 479
Michalson, L., 235, 272
Michel, M. E., 453, 476
Michelson, L., 41, 62
Michienzi, T., 583, 599, *623*
Michon, J., 81, *124*
Mick, E., *118*
Mickelsen, O., 697, *711*
Middlebrook, J. L., 136, 138, 168, 172, *188*, *190*
Mielke, C., 432, 433, *443*
Mikhail, C., 683, 696, *712*
Milar, C. R., 87, *124*
Milch, A., *518*
Milgrom, P., 239, 273, 296
Milich, R. S., 32, *62*, 72, 75, 78, 87, 99, 103, 104, 105, 106, 112, *116*, *123*, *124*, *125*, 128, 150, *187*, *188*, *189*, 348, *363*, 495
Millard, T., 402
Millberger, S., *118*
Miller, A., 492, *515*
Miller, B. C., 627, *680*
Miller, C. T., 404
Miller, D. J., 249, 274, 290
Miller, G. A., 235, *271*
Miller, G. E., 8, 62, 176, *189*
Miller, H., 37, 62
Miller, I. W., 635, 639, 643, *680*
Miller, J., *406*
Miller, J. F., 380, 381, *405*
Miller, J. Y., 134, *184*
Miller, K. S., 52
Miller, L. C., 36, *62*, 206, 227, 231, 232, 235, 237, 239, 240, 249, 268, 273, 318
Miller, N. E., 481, *515*

Miller, P. M., 256, 273
Miller, S. A., 38, 62
Miller, S. M., 4, 60
Miller, W. R., 735, 740, 741, 746
Milley, J., 512
Milling, L., 633, 678
Mills v. Board of Education, 348 F.
  Supp. 866, 378, 405
Mills, D. L., 437, 451
Mills, E. L., 479
Mills, R. S. L., 261, 275
Millsap, P. A., 583, 585, 618
Milner, J. S., 524, 532, 538, 539, 547,
  551, 557, 561, 562, 565
Milos, M. E., 235, 243, 273, 298, 299
Milroy, T., 86, 128
Miltenberger, R. G., 7, 53, 439, 444
Minde, K., 75, 78, 119
Miner, M. E., 456, 473, 477, 478
Minichiello, W. E., 237, 273
Mink, I. T., 20, 62, 436, 449
Minkunas, D. V., 129
Minuchin, P., 15, 62
Minuchin, S., 702, 704, 705, 712
Mirenda, P. L., 411, 438, 445, 449
Mirsky, A. F., 472, 479
Mischel, W., 9, 10, 20, 27, 30, 62
Mitchell, C. M., 628, 678
Mitchell, E. A., 84, 125
Mitchell, J. E., 687, 688, 689, 692,
  693, 694, 710, 712, 713, 716
Mittelman, M. S., 576, 613
Mitts, B., 41, 50
Miyake, Y., 419, 447
Mize, J., 341, 364
Mizruchi, M. S., 724, 747
Moan, S., 593, 621
Moberg, D. P., 735, 746
Mock, J., 38, 49, 204, 223, 561
Moe, T. L., 451
Moffitt, T. E., 134, 135, 138, 139,
  140, 180, 188, 193
Mokros, H. B., 198, 212, 227
Moldofsky, H., 683, 709
Molina, B. S. G., 339, 362, 727, 744
Molnar, J. M., 4, 62
Monahan, J., 12, 64
Monastersky, C., 576, 578, 616
Monello, L. F., 699, 713
Monk, M. A., 35, 59, 236, 237, 238,
  262, 271
Montagu, J., 105, 125
Montague, J. D., 251, 273
Montemayor, R., 629, 631, 634, 640,
  680
Montgomery, J., 411, 443
Montminy, H. P., 330, 360
Mooney, C., 25, 38, 62
Mooney, K. C., 245, 257, 268, 281, 282
Mooney, K. D., 262, 273, 283
Moore, B., 511
Moore, C., 120
Moore, D., 43, 66
Moore, J. R., 492, 514
Moore, P., 118
Moos, B. S., 20, 32, 62, 436, 437, 449,
  505, 515, 547, 565, 612, 620, 632,
  633, 645, 648, 664, 672, 680
Moos, R., 505, 515, 703, 713
Moos, R. H., 20, 32, 38, 39, 50, 62,
  547, 565, 612, 620, 632, 633, 645,
  648, 664, 672, 680, 727, 728, 739,
  746
Moos, R. J., 436, 437, 449
Moran, P. A. P., 540, 563

Moran, P. B., 535, 565
Moran, T., 580, 617
Moras, K., 230, 265
Moretti, M. M., 218, 225
Morgan, G. A. V., 236, 273
Morgan, S. B., 429, 431, 444, 450,
  491, 516, 517
Morganstern, G., 75, 118
Morgenstern, M., 381, 383, 399, 405
Mori, D., 706, 713
Moroney, R., 404
Morrell, W., 683, 715
Morris, M. J., 505, 511
Morris, R. J., 14, 59, 62, 231, 234,
  235, 241, 247, 255, 256, 257, 273
Morris, R. D., 460, 471, 477, 479
Morris-Yates, A., 213, 215, 227
Morrison, D. C., 36, 57
Morrison, J., 88, 125
Morrison, M., 628, 678
Morrison, P., 337, 343, 352, 363
Morrow, C., 183
Morrow, J., 164, 191
Morrow, K. B., 586, 587, 620
Morse, C., 724, 745
Morse, H. A., 528, 564
Morse, W. C., 23, 64
Mortimer, E. A., 492, 510
Moser, J. T., 591, 618
Moses, B. S., 548, 551, 565
Mosk, M. D., 531, 568
Moskowitz, D. S., 44, 45, 62, 133, 190
Moss, H. A., 454, 479
Moss, H. B., 724, 746
Moss, R. A., 688, 713
Mott, D. E. W., 269, 300
Mott, M. A., 720, 722, 726, 727, 728,
  729, 731, 732, 733, 743, 746, 747,
  748
Mounts, N. S., 535, 567, 676, 682
Mouton, P. Y., 169, 188
Mowbray, C. T., 596, 615
Moye, A., 632, 681
Mrazek, P. J., 529, 565, 571, 620
Mudar, P., 732, 744
Muh, J., 443
Mukai, T., 499, 517
Mulhern, R., 489, 516, 519
Mulhern, R. K., 22, 30, 63
Mulick, J. A., 414, 446
Mullen, E. M., 382, 383, 405
Mullen, P., 570, 619
Mullett, M., 505, 512
Mullins, L., 492, 515
Mulvey, E. P., 12, 64
Mumma, G. H., 331, 364
Mundfrom, D. J., 548, 561
Munn, P., 35, 53
Munoz, R., 709
Munson, S. M., 379, 401
Munster, E., 246, 277, 291
Muram, D., 571, 620
Murase, S., 237, 269
Murphy, C. M., 38, 58, 185, 242, 243,
  273, 301
Murphy, D. A., 111, 125, 150, 189
Murphy, H. A., 77, 122, 123, 150, 189
Murphy, J., 117
Murphy, K. R., 85, 86, 88, 89, 92, 98,
  108, 109, 110, 118, 125
Murphy, M., 598, 623
Murphy, R. R., 332, 355, 361
Murphy, S. M., 587, 619
Murphy, W. D., 578, 620
Murray, P., 259, 277

Mushak, P., 87, 124
Musick, J., 617
Mussen, P. H., 8, 62
Myers, J. E. B., 569, 620
Myers, M. G., 4, 171, 717, 720, 722,
  729, 731, 732, 733, 735, 738, 739,
  740, 743, 746, 748
Myers, P., 506, 511
Myers, P. E., 255, 263

Nadeau, S. E., 77, 122
Nagano-Nakamura, K., 338, 363
Naglieri, J. A., 18, 62
Nakamura, C. Y., 232, 237, 249, 276,
  320
Nakata, Y., 78, 122
Nalven, F. B., 236, 237, 238, 262, 273
Nanson, J. L., 87, 120
Nassau, J., 490, 515
Nathan, P. E., 16, 62
National Centre on Child Abuse and
  Neglect, 525, 526, 527, 565, 571,
  572, 620
National Committee for the Preven-
  tion of Child Abuse, 577, 620
National Institute on Drug Abuse,
  171, 188
National Research Council, 523, 525,
  526, 536, 566
Nawas, M. M., 273
Nay, W. R., 3, 8, 11, 30, 58, 62
Nayar, M. C., 635, 680
Naylor, M. W., 724, 745
Nazarian, L., 505, 514
Neal, A. M., 248, 254, 262, 264, 310
Neale, J. M., 352, 364
Neckerman, H. J., 341, 360
Needle, M. P., 728, 746
Needle, R. H., 728, 746
Needleman, H. L., 87, 125
Needleman, R., 414, 446
Needles, D., 193
Negrete, V. F., 505, 511
Neidig, P. H., 4, 62
Neisworth, J. T., 273, 299, 379, 383,
  384, 385, 388, 390, 391, 401, 405,
  406
Nelles, W. B., 41, 65, 246, 247, 262,
  276, 327
Nelson, K., 499, 510
Nelson, K. B., 453, 457, 479
Nelson, R. O., 3, 5, 7, 8, 9, 16, 23, 24,
  30, 31, 32, 35, 41, 53, 56, 62, 63,
  240, 242, 251, 254, 263, 267, 273,
  274, 276, 283
Nelson, W. M., 41, 63, 228
Nelson-Gray, R. O., 5, 63
Nemzer, E., 714
Ness, M. E., 438, 443
Nesse, R. M., 239, 277
Neuman, P., 713
Neumann, D. A., 592, 620
Newacheck, P., 482, 515
Newberger, C. M., 38, 63
Newberry, M., 490, 515
Newbrough, J., 492, 518
Newby, R., 99, 117
Newcomb, A. F., 108, 125
Newcomb, K., 148, 151, 182, 188
Newcomb, M. D., 725, 729, 731, 746
Newcorn, J., 116, 186, 724, 747
Newcorn, J. H., 76, 103, 122, 124
Newland, T. E., 383, 385, 405
Newlin, D. B., 726, 746

Newman, A., 270, 282
Newsom, C., 409, 412, 413, 414, 427, 438, *444*, 448, 449, 450
Newton, T., 438, *449*
Nezu, A. M., 4, *63*
Nezu, C. M., 4, *63*
Niaura, R. S., 727, 742
Nicholas, E., 593, *621*
Nichols, P. L., 87, *125*
Nici, J., *517*
Niederman, D., 80, *120*
Nielsen, J. B., 87, *123*
Nietzel, M. T., 243, *264*
Nigam, V. R., 78, *118*
Nigg, J., 77, 97, *122*
Nightingale, N. N., 532, *566*
Nihira, K., 20, 62, 389, *404*, 431, 436, *447*, *449*
Niles, B., 698, *716*
Nisbett, R. E., 31, *63*
Nisi, A., 78, *125*
Nitzan, E., 259, *276*
Nixon, S., 21, *52*
Noam, G. G., 149, *193*, 213, 228, 679
Noble, H., 36, *62*, 232, 239, *268*, 273, 318
Noh, S., *452*
Nolan, T., *478*
Nolen-Hoeksema, S., 202, 219, 227
Noll, R., 490, *515*
Noll, R. B., *183*, 492, *510*
Norcross, J. C., 740, *747*
Nordahl, T. E., *129*
Nordquist, V. M., 15, *63*
Nordquist, V. N., 43, *66*
Norem-Hebeisen, A. A., 727, 742
Norman, D. K., *120*, *713*
North, J., 37, *50*
Norwood, W. D., 173, *185*
Notarius, C. I., 46, *60*, 171, *187*
Nottlemann, E. D., 628, *680*
Novak, D., *516*
Novey, E. S., *122*
Nowacek, G., 504, *510*
Nowakowski, M., 555, *563*
Nowicki, S., 37, 41, *55*, *63*
Nucci, L. P., 77, *125*
Nudelman, S., 687, *713*
Null, J. A., 724, *748*
Nunnally, J., 253, 260, *274*
Nunnally, J. C., 8, *63*
Nurcombe, B., 208, 227, 228
Nussbaum, B. R., 150, *179*
Nyhan, W. L., 377, *405*
Nylander, I., 705, *713*

O'Brien, B. S., 133, 134, 165, *183*, *188*
O'Brien, G. T., 250, *271*, 311
O'Brien, M., 174, *188*, 658, 661, *680*
O'Brien, S. F., 329, 331, *363*
O'Brien, W. H., 16, *56*
O'Connor, R. D., 274, 302
O'Connor, T. G., 4, *56*
O'Dell, S. L., 241, 246, 256, 257, 259, 260, *264*, *265*, *268*, *274*, 281, 285
O'Donnell, J. P., 239, 266
O'Donnell, K., 656, *679*
O'Dougherty, M. M., 481, *515*
O'Farrell, T., 726, *744*
O'Keeffe, J., 497, *510*
O'Leary, K. D., 8, 29, 32, 38, 57, 58, *63*, 78, 105, 122, *125*, 138, 172, 173, *188*, *189*, 547, *564*, 627, 632, *679*, *681*, 739, *746*

O'Leary, S. G., 37, *49*, 112, 113, *120*, *125*, 136, 166, *178*, *186*
O'Malley, P. M., 717, 718, 719, 720, *745*
O'Neill, R. E., 161, *192*, 436, 439, *447*, *449*
O'Reilly, C., 391, *406*
O'Shaughnessy, M., 686, 700, 704, *710*
O'Shea, M., 570, *619*
O'Toole, B. I., 592, *620*
O'Toole, L. C., 686, *708*
Oates, R. K., 592, 593, *620*
Ober, B. A., 472, *477*
Oberklaid, F., 135, *190*
Oberlander, L. B., *620*
Obonsawin, M. C., 460, *477*
Obrosky, D., *514*
Ochs, J., 489, *519*
Oetting, E. R., 729, *747*
Offer, D., 204, 227, 482, 493, *510*
Offord, D. R., 111, *119*, 131, 133, *179*, *188*, 197, 201, 225, 722, *743*
Ogata, S. M., 588, *620*
Ogles, B. M., 5, *63*
Ohene-Frempong, K., 490, *514*
Ohman, A., 232, 261, *274*
Ohta, M., 429, *449*
Oldershaw, L., 20, *63*, 558, 559, *564*, *566*
Oliveau, D. C., 239, *263*
Oliver, J. M., 530, *560*
Olkon, D. M., *119*
Ollendick, T. H., 3, 5, 6, 31, 41, *63*, *65*, *116*, 138, *186*, *188*, 206, 226, 232, 236, 237, 239, 240, 247, 249, 256, 260, 262, 266, 267, 270, 271, 274, 281, 284, 318, 416, *443*, 499, *518*, 601, 620, 692, *712*
Ollier, K., 236, 237, 271, *274*
Olmsted, M. P., 686, 689, 693, 700, *710*
Olson, A. E., *181*
Olson, D., 612, *620*
Olson, D. H., 647, 648, 652, 664, 665, 670, 671, 673, 677, 680, 682, 704, *713*
Olson, J., 554, *565*
Olson, R., 267, 293, *515*
Olson, R. A., 269, *287*, 497, *511*
Olson, R. L., 550, *565*
Olweus, D., 24, *63*, 135, *188*, 340, 342, *363*
Oosternink, N., 57, *185*
Oppedisano, G., 224, 226
Oppenheim, A. N., 732, *746*
Opton, E. M., 251, *263*
Orbach, J., 696, *715*
Orbach, S., 707, *713*
Ordman, A. M., 704, *713*
Orleans, C. S., 697, *712*
Orleans, C. T., 691, *713*
Ornitz, E. M., 412, 414, 415, 426, *442*, 445, *449*
Ornstein, M., 217, *223*
Ornstein, P. A., 596, *620*
Orosan, P., 696, *714*
Orr, D., 506, *513*
Orsak, C., 598, *623*
Orton, G. L., 236, 237, *274*
Orvaschel, H., 210, 227, 231, 235, 236, 237, 238, 262, 270, 274, 393, *405*, 585, *619*
Osborne, M., 499, *515*
Oshins, L., 578, *616*
Ost, L. G., 230, 239, 261, *274*

Osteen, V., 57, *185*
Ostermann, K., 343, *363*
Osterweil, Z., 338, *363*
Oswald, D. P., 421, *449*
Ouellette, C., *118*
Ounsted, C., 408, *447*
Overall, J. E., 724, *747*
Overholser, J., 498, *511*
Overlade, D. C., 52
Overweg, J., 462, *476*
Owen, S. M., 151, 152, *179*
Owen, V., 432, 433, *443*
Owens, C., 461, *480*
Owens, R. G., 687, *713*
Ozolins, M., 234, 269, 287, 497, *513*
Ozonoff, S., 429, *449*

Pachman, L., 498, *509*
Paez, P., 51, 224, *561*
Page, I. J., 578, *620*
Page, P., 505, *515*
Page, R., 16, *55*
Pagliocca, P. M., 628, *678*
Paikoff, R. L., 632, 633, 672, *681*, 703, *708*
Pakiz, B., 225
Pal, A., 133, *181*
Palermo, D., 41, *51*, 249, *265*, 316
Palfrey, J. S., 92, *125*
Palkes, H., 88, *128*
Pallmeyer, T. P., 229
Pallotta, G. M., 557, *563*
Palmer, R. L., 688, 698, 709, *713*
Palumbo, D. R., 453, 461, *479*
Palumbo, L. W., 438, *444*
Pancoast, D. L., 206, *223*
Pandey, S., 527, *562*
Pandina, R., 727, *747*
Pannaccione, V. F., 8, *63*
Pappas, B. A., 77, *121*
Parad, H. W., 18, 57, 337, *365*
Park, A., 505, 506, *517*
Parke, R. D., 5, 27, *63*, 328, 330, 341, 355, *363*
Parker, C. M., 150, *179*
Parker, H., 581, *620*
Parker, J. G., 328, 329, 330, 331, 332, 333, 335, 338, 339, 340, 343, 345, 347, 354, 358, 359, *363*
Parker, S., 581, *620*
Parkhurst, J. T., 331, 344, 345, 359, *361*, *363*
Parks, S., 390, 391, *405*
Parks, S. M., 724, *748*
Parrish, R. T., 239, *277*
Parrish, T., 490, *515*
Parry, P. A., 52, 72, 76, 112, *120*, *125*
Parsons, B. V., 7, 46, 49, 631, 633, 653, 667, *677*
Parsons, J. A., 376, *405*
Parsons, M. B., *446*
Parsons, T., 492, *515*
Partridge, F., 227
Partridge, J., 498, *512*
Partridge, J. W., *515*
Pasamanick, B., 415, *447*
Passman, R. H., 22, 30, *63*
Passo, M., 489, *517*
Patenaude, R., 168, *185*
Paternite, C., 85, 86, *125*
Pattee, L., 108, *125*
Patterson, C. J., 339, *363*
Patterson, D. L., 496, *514*
Patterson, D. R., 150, 151, 152, *179*

Patterson, G. R., 4, 8, 11, 14, 15, 19, 23, 26, 29, 30, 35, 37, 38, 40, 43, 52, 60, 63, 64, 66, 107, 112, *121*, *125*, 133, 134, 135, 136, 137, 138, 139, 140, 141, 142, 153, 157, 158, 162, 163, 170, 171, 174, *178*, *180*, *181*, *183*, 188, 189, 342, 363, 364, 537, 540, 559, 566, 642, 679, 744
Patterson, J. M., 436, 449, 489, 492, 493, *515*, *516*
Patterson, T. L., 732, 734, *744*
Patton, G., 688, *711*
Paul, G. L., 242, 244, 245, 264, 274, 309, 310
Paul, R., 449, 452
Paulauskas, S., 133, *186*, 490, *514*
Pauls, D. L., 278, 409, 452
Paveza, G. J., 580, 620
Pear, J., 7, 60
Pearson, D., 394, *405*
Pearson, J. L., 137, *181*
Pederson, A., 35, 52, 328, 361
Pedlow, R., 135, *190*
Peed, S., 154, 156, 183, *189*
Pekarik, E. G., 352, 364
Pelcovits, M. A., 726, *744*
Pelcovitz, D., 531, 535, 566
Pelham, W. E., 77, 85, 88, 90, 97, 98, 99, 108, 109, 111, 113, *116*, *120*, *122*, *123*, *125*, 127, 137, 150, 169, *185*, *189*
Pellegrin, A., 587, 623
Pellegrini, A. D., 8, 50
Pellegrini, D. S., 77, *122*, 352, 363, 491, *512*
Peloquin, L. J., 453, 479
Pelton, L. H., 538, 566
Pennebaker, J. W., 255, 274
Pennington, B. F., 21, *51*, 77, 88, *121*, 128, 429, 449, 453, 463, 464, 468, 472, 473, 475, 479
Pennsylvania Association of Retarded Children, 378, *405*
People v. Kelley, 17. 3d 27 (1976), 613, 620
People v. Rich, 520 N. Y. S. 2d 911, 595, 620
Pepler, D. J., 35, 63
Perachio, N., 103, *124*
Perel, J. M., 210, 227
Peresie, H., *125*
Perez, D., *186*
Perez, J. M., *449*
Peri, J. N., 259, 276
Perkel, D., 499, *510*
Perkins, H. W., 728, *743*
Perkins, M., *448*
Perlberg, A., 259, 276
Perlman, T., 86, *122*, 128
Perlmutter, B. F., 46, 66
Perosa, L. M., 635, 665, 668, 670, 671, 672, 673, *681*
Perosa, S. L., 635, 665, 668, 670, 671, 672, 673, *681*
Perriello, L. M., 100, *120*
Perrin, E., 498, *516*
Perrin, E. C., 149, *181*, 486, 490, 505, 506, *516*
Perrin, J., *120*, *179*
Perrin, J. M., 505, 506, *516*
Perrin, S., 237, 262, 272, 274, 317, 318, 319
Perron, D., *192*
Perrot, A., *443*
Perry, A., 417, 435, 445, 449

Perry, D., 409, *449*
Perry, D. G., 329, 340, 344, 354, 356, 364
Perry, L. C., 329, 340, 344, 354, 356, 364
Perry, R., 4, *444*
Peters, J. E., 71, *119*
Peters, K. G., 72, 75, *120*
Peters, P. L., 140, *190*
Peters, R. DeV., *61*
Peters, S., 569, 623
Petersen, A. C., 4, 63, 197, 199, 200, 201, 202, 203, 204, 205, 216, 223, 227, 725, *747*
Peterson, C., 228, 585, 620, *621*
Peterson, D. R., 19, 36, 64, 147, 148, 149, 150, *189*
Peterson, E. T., 492, *516*
Peterson, L., 4, *64*, 231, 235, 242, 246, 249, 257, 258, 260, 261, 274, 276, 289, 290, 291, 306, 495, 497, 504, 510, 512, 516, 527, 559, 566, 567
Peterson, L. C., 206, 227
Peterson, R., 492, *515*, 586, *614*
Peterson, R. A., 6, *61*, 392, 405
Peterson, R. F., 8, 50
Petrill, S., 461, *480*
Pettis, E., 16, 55
Pettit, G. S., 135, 138, 167, *181*, *191*, *193*, 341, 342, 344, *361*, 364, 530, 562
Peveler, R. C., 696, 709
Peyrot, M., 531, 566
Pfeffer, C. R., 724, 739, 747
Pfeiffer, S. I., 18, 62
Pfiffner, L. J., 113, *125*
Phares, V., 219, 224, 227, 631, *681*
Philips, T., 708
Phillips, J. F., *446*
Phillips, J. S., 21, 26, 58, 259, 270
Phillips, S., 260, 265
Phipps, S., 258, 266, 499, *516*
Piacentini, J. C., 35, *64*, 65, 89, 109, 110, *123*, 145, 147, 177, *189*, *190*, *191*, 225, 226, 227, 228, 258, 276, 406, 736, 745
Piaget, J., 255, 269, 627, 680
Pianta, R. C., 173, 174, *189*, 530, 563
Pickles, A., 131, *190*
Pierce, E. W., 85, *119*
Pierce, G. R., 175, *189*
Pierce, L. H., 581, 620
Pierce, R., 581, 620
Pierce, R. S., 728, *744*
Piers, E. V., 41, 64
Pike, K. M., 699, *712*
Pike, R., 41, 56, 356, 362
Pillay, M., 691, *713*
Pillow, D. R., 727, *744*
Pincus, J. H., 534, 565
Pinderton, P., *511*
Pines, A. M., 591, *621*
Pinter, R., 235, 236, 237, 238, 275
Piotrowski, C., 6, 32, 38, 64
Pipe, M. E., 593, *617*
Piran, N., 687, 713
Pirke, K. M., 693, 713
Pirrelo, V. E., 585, 586, 620
Pishkin, V., 724, 743
Pisterman, S., 112, *125*, 169, *189*, 497, 515
Pistone, L. M., 257, 272
Pizzo, P. A., 479
Plagmann, L., 402
Pless, I. B., 486, 487, *516*

Plienis, A. J., *447*
Pliner, P., 706, 708, 713
Plomin, R., 88, *120*, *184*, 258, 265, 268
Ploof, D., 394, *403*
Plowright, C. M. S., 435, *447*
Plutchik, R., 234, 275, 724, 747
Poindexter, A. R., 438, *443*
Pokorny, A.D., 728, 732, 742, *744*
Polansky, N. A., 540, 547, 548, *566*
Polissar, N. L., 477, 478
Politano, M., 228
Polivy, J., 686, 700, 710
Pollak, T., *513*
Pollard, S., 88, 99, 112, *117*, *125*
Pollock, M., *514*
Pollock, V. E., 592, 620
Pomeroy, C., 693, *712*
Pomeroy, W., 577, *617*
Pontius, W., 416, *445*
Pope, A. W., 331, 334, 364
Pope, H. G., 687, 688, 689, 710, 713
Popovich, D., 391, *405*
Porges, S. W., 55
Porrino, L. J., 75, 76, 104, 105, *125*
Port, L. K., *617*
Porter, B., 138, 172, *189*, 739, 746
Portner, J., 612, 620, 670, 680, 704, 713
Posner, M. I., 135, *190*
Post, D. L., 18, 57
Potter, H. W., 408, *449*
Potts, D. A., 534, *564*
Potts, M. K., 77, 81, *118*
Poulin, J., 335, 360
Pound, J., 587, *618*
Powell, M. B., 137, 173, *181*
Powell, P., 262, 276
Power, T. G., 581, *615*
Powers, M. D., 4, 12, 16, 17, 55, *64*, 436, 437, 438, 446
Powers, P. S., 696, *714*
Powers, S., 679
Powers, S. W., 32, 158, 159, 164, 177, *189*, 244, 261, 265, 293, 497, 509
Powless, D. L., 343, 364
Poznanski, E. O., 198, 212, 227, 237, 275
Prabucki, K., 40, 49
Prado, L., *617*
Prange, M. E., 670, 671, 672, *681*, 696, *714*
Prater, J. M., 265, 509
Prather, R. C., 687, 700, 713, 716
Pratt, D. M., 670, *681*
Pratt, K. C., 236, 237, 238, 275
Pratt, S., 391, *406*
Preator, K., 400, 401, *405*
Prentice-Dunn, S., 169, *180*
Preskorn, S. H., 217, 226
Price, D., 593, 620
Price, J. M., 328, 363
Price-Munn, N., *179*
Prieto, S. L., 218, 227
Prino, C. T., 531, 566
Prins, P. J. M., 234, 250, 275, 296, 314, 315
Prinz, R. J., 8, 62, 176, *189*, 352, 364, 627, 631, 632, 638, 643, 644, 645, 648, 650, 653, 660, 679, 681, 682, 727, 748
Prior, M. R., 76, *120*, 135, 164, *190*, 409, 414, 416, 421, 422, 423, 449
Prizant, B., 412, 413, *449*
Prochaska, J. O., 740, 747

Procidano, M.E., 547, *566*
Proffitt, V., 205, *229*
Prout, H., 395, *406*
Prugh, D. C., 23, *64*
Pruitt, D. B., 585, *618*
Pruitt, S. D., 269, *287*
Prusoff, B. A., *229*
Pruzinsky, T., 35, *65*, 230, *265*
Prystalski, P., 432, 433, *443*
Psaltis, K., 696, *715*
Pueschel, S. M., 393, *405*
Puig-Antich, J., *51*, 208, 209, 210, *224*, 227, 247, *275*, 393, *405*, *561*
Pulkkinen, L., 139, *184*
Pumariega, A. J., *713*
Pumpian, I., *443*
Purcell, P., 590, *616*
Purdon, S. E., 216, *228*
Pure, D.L., 692, *711*
Putallaz, M., 341, 343, 355, 356, *364*
Putnam, F. W., 585, 588, 589, 608, *609, 620*
Pyle, R. L., 687, 688, 692, 693, 694, *710, 712, 713*
Pyles, D. A. M., 438, *449*

Qin, J., 593, *617*
Quas, J. A., 596, *617*
Quay, H. C., 23, 36, 48, *64*, 71, 79, *125*, 147, 148, 149, 150, 172, *189*, 199, 206, 223, 227, 232, *275*
Quinlan, D. M., 203, *226*
Quinn, P. O., 77, *126*
Quinn, S., *509*
Quinton, D., 131, *190*

Rabkin, J. G., 392, *405*
Rachman, S., 5, 53, *64*, 230, 262, 269, *278, 323*
Rachman, S. J., 18, 28, 41, 231, 232, *275*
Racine, Y. A., *179, 188, 743*
Raczynski, J. M., 251, *275*
Radaker, L. D., 255, *275*
Radloff, L. S., 204, *227*
Rae, D. S., 239, *265*
Raimondi, A. J., 458, *479*
Rains, P. M., 20, *64*
Rakoff, V., 702, *713*
Raloff, J., 373, *405*
Ralphe, D., 585, *619*
Ramirez, S. A., 395, 396, *405*
Ramirez, S. Z., 275, *325*
Ramos, O., 417, *446*
Ramsey, B., 490, *516*
Ramsey, E., 161, *192*
Rancurello, M. D., 213, *226*
Range, L. M., 587, *614*
Rapkin, B., *514*
Rapoport, J. L., 76, 77, 87, 105, *119*, *125*, 126, 129, 235, 262, 264, *275*, 321, 412, *450, 715*
Rappaport, J., 36, *52*
Rappaport, M., *278*
Rapport, M. D., 76, 100, 103, 111, *120, 126*
Rappucci, N. D., 595, *617*
Rardin, D., 699, *710*
Raskin, D. C., 598, *615, 620*
Raskin, L. M., 429, *443*
Rasmussen, P., 340, *364*
Rasmussen, S. A., 687, *713*

Rasnake, L., 492, *517*
Rastam, M., 691, *713*
Rather, B. C., 726, *745*
Ratner, J., 258, 271, *285*
Ratzoni, G., *278*
Rau, J. H., 689, *713*
Raven, J., 429, *450*
Rawson, N. S. B., 732, *746*
Ray, J. A., 641, 642, 679, *681*
Ray, K. C., 612, *620*
Ray, R. S., 157, *189*
Ray, W. J., 251, *275*
Rayner, P., 230, *277*
Realmuto, G. M., 177, *178*
Reber, M., 149, *186*
Rebgetz, M., 628, *678*
Rebok, G. W., *362*
Redd, W. H., 504, *514*
Reed, E., *118*
Reed, M. L., 149, 161
Reed, R., *125*
Reeder, M. L., *189*, 576, *618*
Reese, J. H., 20, *54*
Reeves, J. S., 75, *128*
Regier, D. A., *191*, 228, 239, *265*
Regiers, D., *65*
Rehm, L. P., 256, *275*, 599, *618*
Reich, J., 239, *275*
Reich, W., 40, 56, 145, 146, *184, 189*, *223*, 247, 262, 266, 269, 393, *405*, *555, 566*
Reichler, R. J., 414, 416, 430, *450*, *451*
Reid, D. H., *446*
Reid, J., 52, *181*, 490, *514*, 531, *565*
Reid, J. B., 11, 30, 32, 42, 43, 44, 45, 46, *55*, 63, *64*, 67, 133, 137, 142, 153, 157, 158, 159, 162, 163, 177, *180*, *189*, 193, 531, 534, *566*, 634, *678*
Reid, J. C., 210, *226*, 270
Reid, M. P., 52, 357, *364*
Reilly, E. L., 724, *747*
Reimherr, F. W., 86, *128*, 129
Reinherz, H. Z., *225*
Reinhold, D. P., 38, *52*
Reiss, D., 87, *118*, 722, *743*
Reiss, S., 235, 243, 273, 298, 299, *392*, 393, *405*
Reitan, R. M., 386, 388, *405*, 453, 464, 471, *479*
Reiter, J., 696, *714*
Reitman, E. E., 696, *714*
Reitzel-Jaffe, D., 550, 553, *568*
Rejier, D., 228, *406*
Rekedal, S., 596, *619*
Rende, R., 88, *120*
Renick, A., 596, *615*
Renner, B. R., 416, *451*
Renshaw, P. D., 41, 49, 357, *359*
Replogle, W., 236, *264*, 316
Reppucci, N. D., 12, *64*
Reschly, D. J., 381, *405*
Rescorla, L., 416, *450*
Resnick, H. S., 575, *621*
Restrepo, A., 634, *682*
Rettew, D. C., 235, *275*
Rey, J. M., 213, 215, *227*
Reyes, S., *515*
Reynolds, B. S., 412, *450*
Reynolds, C., 97, *126*
Reynolds, C. R., 3, 18, 24, 36, 41, 58, *64*, 249, 258, *275*, 319
Reynolds, L., 503, *516*
Reynolds, L. A., 151, *179*

Reynolds, W. M., 30, 36, 39, 41, *64*, 204, 228, 396, *406*
Reznick, J. S., 258, 265, 267, 270
Rheinscheld, T. L., 395, *406*
Rice, D. G., 234, *271*
Rich, D., 453, *480*
Rich, T. A., 52
Richard, R. C., 36, 41, *51*
Richards, C., 133, *186*
Richards, C. S., 256, *275*
Richards, M., *517*
Richards, M. H., 627, 661, *680*
Richardson, K. K., *614*
Richardson, S., 376, *404*
Richey, V. E., 412, *445*
Richman, G., 397, *404*
Richman, N., 237, *275*
Richmond, B. O., 41, *64*, 249, 258, 275, 319
Richter, S. S., 727, 729, 731, 733, 734, *747*
Richters, J. E., 39, *64*, 137, 148, *185*, *189*, 226
Rickard, H. C., 41, *60*
Rickard-Figueroa, J. L., 496, 497, *513*
Ricks, D. M., 412, *450*
Riddlesberger, M., *617*
Ridge, B., 135, *179, 561*
Ridley-Johnson, R., 249, 274, 290
Rie, É. D., 71, *126*
Rie, H. E., 71, *126*
Riessman, C. K., 490, 493, *517*
Riggs, R. D., 724, 726, *744*
Riikonen, R., 415, *450*
Riley, W., 503, *517*
Rimland, B., 409, 415, 419, 421, *444*, *450*
Rimm, D. C., 259, *272*
Rincover, A., 409, 413, 414, 427, 431, *449, 450*
Ringland, J. T., 47, *55*
Rintelmann, J. W., 217, *225*
Rintoul, B., 218, *229*
Rios, P., *447*
Risi, S., 337, *363*
Riskind, J. H., 264, *324*
Risser, A. H., 453, *479*
Ritchey, W. L., 333, 346, 348, 350, *362*
Ritter, B., 242, *275*, 301
Ritter, P. L., 676, *678*
Ritvo, A., *446*
Ritvo, E., *445, 446*
Ritvo, E. C., 415, *450*
Ritvo, E. R., 414, 415, 426, 427, *445*, *446, 449, 450*
Rivara, J. B., 477, 478, 495, *518*
Rizley, R., 10, *51*, 528, 537, *562*
Roach, M. A., 4, *66*
Robb, J. R., 505, *515*
Robbins, F. R., *447*
Robbins, K., 103, *117*
Robbins, P., 328, 329, 338, 339, *362*
Roberts, D. E., 498, *518*
Roberts, D. F., 676, *678*
Roberts, J., 489, *516*
Roberts, M., 154, *189*, 490, *516*
Roberts, M. A., 76, 77, 106, 112, *126*, 473, *479*
Roberts, M. C., 4, 6, *64*, 67, 261, 265, 491, *516*
Roberts, M. W., 32, *64*, 137, 158, 159, 164, 169, 177, *189*
Roberts, R. D., 71, *126*
Roberts, R. E., 201, 213, 222, 227, 228

Robertson, D. M., *478*
Robertson, K. R., *565*
Robertson, S., *447*
Robin, A. L., 7, 46, 47, 154, 541, 627, 629, 631, 632, 633, 634, 635, 636, 638, 639, 641, 644, 645, 647, 649, 651, 652, 654, 655, 656, 657, 664, 667, 668, 670, 672, 677, 679, 680, *681, 682*
Robin, A. R., 107, 112, 113, *126*
Robin, S. L., *64*
Robins, E., 204, 228, 709
Robins, L. N., 139, 140, *189, 190,* 223, 258, 275
Robinson, A., 580, *615*
Robinson, D. R., 38, 49, 539, *561*
Robinson, E. A., 107, *126,* 150, 151, 152, 156, *182, 190*
Robinson, H. B., 376, 391, *406*
Robinson, N. M., 376, 391, *406*
Robinson, N. S., 218, 219, 228
Robinson, S., 438, *444*
Rockert, W., 693, 695, 710
Rodger, R. S., 420, *452*
Rodgers, A., 150, *186*
Rodgers, T. A., 438, 452
Rodick, J. D., 5, 47, 64, 512, 628, 679
Rodin, J., 688, *715*
Rodnick, E. H., 629, 639, 678
Rodrigue, J. R., 27, 431, *450,* 481, 491, 492, 496, 516
Rodriguez, C. M., 175, *182*
Rodriguez, H., 267, 293
Roesler, T. A., 573, 580, *621*
Roffwarg, H. P., 217, 225
Rogers, A., 205, 226
Rogers, C., 559, 564
Rogers, D., 5, 49
Rogers, D. L., *565*
Rogers, E. D., 38, 67
Rogers, E. S., 138, *192*
Rogers, M., 256, 263
Rogers, S. J., 419, 429, *445, 449*
Rogers, T., 170, *183,* 257, 267
Rogers-Warren, A. K., 428, 431, *450*
Roghmann, H., 606, *617*
Roghmann, K., 487, *516*
Rogosch, F. A., 204, 224, 727, 731, 744, 747
Rohde, P., 201, 221, 227, 228
Rohner, R. P., 547, *566*
Rohrbeck, C. A., 362, 551, 553, *561, 566*
Roid, G. H., 36, 62
Roistacher, R. C., 347, *364*
Roizen, J., *613*
Roizen, N. J., 85, 100, *126*
Rollins, N., 687, 708
Rollnick, S., 735, *740,* 741, *746*
Romanczyk, R. G., 5, 28, 32, 63, *64*
Romano, J., *185*
Romano, S. J., 701, *712*
Romans, S., 570, *619*
Ronan, K. R., 41, 64, 149, *186,* 270, 275, 325
Rook, K. S., 731, 747
Room, R., *613*
Roosa, M. W., 647, 680, 729, 747
Roose, S. P., 687, *715*
Roper, B. L., 9, 56
Roper, M., 148, *185,* 226, 710
Rosa, J. D., 595, *615*
Rosario, M., 532, 563, 566
Rosch, E., *64*
Rosen, D., 499, *517*

Rosen, J. C., 687, 694, 695, 696, 698, 700, 710, 713, *714*
Rosenbaum, J. F., 265
Rosenbaum, M. S., 256, *270*
Rosenbaum, P., 490, *509*
Rosenberg, D., *617*
Rosenberg, R. P., 6, *64*
Rosenberg, T. K., 210, 226
Rosenblad, C., 29, 57, 105, *122*
Rosenblatt, W., 38, 68
Rosenbloom, A., 268, 499, *512, 513*
Rosenbloom, A. L., *513*
Rosenbloom, E. L., *509*
Rosenbloom, L., 417, *445*
Rosenbloom, S., *444*
Rosenblum, N. D., 234, 235, 277, 279
Rosenthal, R. H., 75, 77, 78, *126*
Rosenthal, T. L., 242, 300
Rosman, B. L., 702, 712
Ross, A. O., 7, 16, *65*
Ross, A. W., 150, *182, 190*
Ross, C., 498, 509
Ross, C. A., 588, *621*
Ross, D. M., 71, 75, 78, 84, 88, *126,* 235, 275, 302, 496, 497, *516*
Ross, J., 489, *515*
Ross, S., 505, *517*
Ross, S. A., 71, 75, 78, 84, 88, *126,* 235, 275, 302
Ross, S. M., 496, 497, *516*
Rotatori, A. F., 108, *124,* 351, 363
Roth, D., 701, *714*
Roth, H. P., 503, *510*
Rothbart, M. K., 36, 65, 135, 164, 180, *184, 190,* 268
Rothman, S., 87, *127*
Rouleau, J. L., 576, *613*
Rounds, K., 505, *514*
Rourke, B. P., 453, 459, 463, 464, 465, 468, 470, 471, 475, 476, 477, 479
Rourke, D. A., 438, *452*
Routh, D. K., 71, 77, 105, 106, *126,* 268, 496, *516*
Roux, S., 428, 443, *444*
Rovet, J., 460, *479*
Rowan, A. B., 5, *65*
Rowden, L., 336, *364*
Rowe, E., 533, *562*
Rowe, M., 275, 325
Rowe-Hallbert, A., 137, *189*
Roy, A., 47, 55
Roy, A. K., 153, *184*
Roy, R. R., 267, 286
Royal, G., 490, *516*
Rubenstein, J. L., 79, 629, 678
Rubin, C., 629, 678
Rubin, J., 660, *681*
Rubin, K., 362, 580, *614*
Rubin, K. H., 27, 65, 261, 275, 328, 329, 332, 333, 334, 335, 336, 342, 344, 347, 360, 361, 363, *364*
Rubino, K., *617*
Rubinstein, R. A., *126*
Rubio-Stipec, M., 145, 146, *190,* 226
Ruble, D. N., 21, 22, 38, 52
Ruch-Ross, H., *617*
Ruckstuhl, L. E. Jr., 454, *478*
Rudel, R. G., 75, 77, *120*
Rudin, M. M., 576, *621*
Rudolph, K. D., 197, 203, 204, 219, 225, 228
Rudy, L., 593, *617*
Ruebush, B. K., 249, 276, 307
Rueger, D. G., 586, *616*

Rueter, M. A., 635, 637, 640, 642, 643, 644, 651, 654, *681*
Ruffalo, S. L., *181*
Ruggiero, L., 687, *715*
Rumsey, J., 129, 412, 429, *450*
Runyan, D., 167, *191,* 576, *621,* 582, 616
Rupert, L. J., 583, *617*
Rusby, J. C., 153, 156, 158, 164, *190*
Rush, A. J., 170, *179,* 687, 712
Rush, J., 217, 225
Rush, R. H., 55
Rushall, B. S., 41, *61*
Rushe, R., *564*
Russell, A. B., 525, *566*
Russell, D. E. H., 570, 571, 572, 576, 580, *616, 621*
Russell, G. F. M., 685, 687, 693, 694, 696, *714*
Russell, L. M., 589, *615*
Russell, M., 727, 732, 744, 747
Russell, M. B., 29, 65
Russell, W. R., 456, *479*
Russman, B. S., 453, *479*
Russo, D. C., 133, 140, *190,* 242, 275, 496, *514*
Russo, M., *123*
Russo, M. F., 165, *186, 190,* 192
Russon, A., 576, *619*
Ruttenberg, B. A., 427, *450*
Rutter, M., 8, 15, 26, 30, *51,* 65, 66, 71, 75, 78, 86, *126,* 137, *190,* 202, 221, 223, 224, 239, 275, 346, 348, 353, 362, 376, 392, 404, 406, 408, 409, 411, 412, 413, 414, 415, 416, 417, 419, 424, 426, 429, *443, 444, 445,* 447, 448, *450,* 452, 524, 539, 566
Rutter, R., 131, 138, *190*
Ruzicka, R. L., 235, 276
Ryall, M. R., 236, 239, 275, 319
Ryan, C., 489, 490, *516*
Ryan, G., 578, *621*
Ryan, M., 493, *514*
Ryan, M. R., 396, *406*
Ryan, N. D., 111, *126*
Ryan, R., 691, *715*
Rychtarik, R. G., 741, *746*
Rydell, P. J., 413, *449*
Rye, L., 693, *714*

Saab, P. G., 268
Saba, G., 702, *714*
Sabbeth, B. F., 491, *516*
Sacher, E. J., 227
Sack, W., 580, *617*
Sack, W. H., 689, *711*
Sacks, J., 526, 565
Sadik, C., 687, *715*
Sadoun, R., *450*
Safer, D. J., 77, *126*
Sahler, O., 493, *516*
Saigh, P. A., 247, 251, 262, 275, 276, 319, 326, 327
Sailor, W., *450*
Salisbury, C., 392, *406*
Salkin, B., 683, *715*
Salmon, P. G., 633, 645, 670, 672, 677
Saltoun, M., 246, 269, 294
Saltzberg, E., 696, *714*
Salzberg, A. D., 148, *185*
Salzinger, S., 38, 65, 531, 532, 552, 563, 566

Samit, C., 531, *566*
Sams, S. E., *125*
Samson, G., 499, *512*
Samuelson, G., 503, 506, *516*
Sandberg, D. E., *709*
Sandberg, S., 84, *127*
Sandberg, S. T., 75, 84, *119, 126*
Sanders, F. A., 422, *445*
Sanders, R., Jr., 267, *312*
Sanders, M. R., 4, *65,* 136, 141, 142, 153, 164, 168, 177, *181, 190,* 497, *516,* 628, 629, 636, 639, 641, 645, 651, 658, 661, *678, 681*
Sanders, S., 499, *512*
Sanders, S. H., 497, *510*
Sandgrund, A., 530, *566*
Sandler, H., 490, 498, *516*
Sandler, I. N., 729, *747*
Sandler, J., 540, 551, 563, *568*
Sandman, B. M., *127*
Sandoval, J., 78, *123*
Sanford, M., *179*
Sanford, M. N., *188*
Sanger, M., 498, 499, *516*
Sansbury, L. E., 136, 168, *192*
Sanson, A., 76, *120,* 135, 164, *190*
Sanson, A. V., 76, *121*
Sansone, R., *714*
Sansonnet-Hayden, H., 587, *621*
Santa-Barbara, J., 259, *276*
Santilli, G., 591, *622*
Santilli, L., 490, *516*
Santogrossi, D. A., 32, 63, 255, *271*
Santostefano, S., 23, 31, *65*
Santrock, J. W., 4, *65*
Sanyal, M., 489, *511*
Sappenfield, W., 482, *512*
Sarason, B. R., 175, *189*
Sarason, I. G., 173, 175, *189, 190*
Sarason, S. B., 276, 307, *319*
Sargent, J., 494, *516*
Sarigiani, P. A., 199, *227*
Sarlo-McGarvey, N., 417, *449*
Sarnat, H., 259, *276*
Sas, L. D., 573, 575, 576, 581, 585, 587, 592, 599, *621, 622, 623*
Saslow, G., 34, 58, 259, *270*
Sasson, A., 701, *714*
Sassone, D., 78, *123*
Satterfield, B. T., 86, *126*
Satterfield, J. H., 77, 86, *119, 126*
Satterwhite, B. B., 491, *517*
Sattler, J. M., 3, 6, 16, 24, 30, 33, 34, 39, *65,* 373, 380, 383, 384, 385, 388, 399, 400, *406,* 429, *451,* 463, *480*
Satz, P., 453, 476, *478*
Saunders, B. E., 575, 577, 580, 587, 599, 612, *619, 621*
Saunders, J. D., 171, *190*
Saunders, W., 210, 226, 693, *712*
Sauvage, D., 426, 442, *443, 447*
Sauzier, M., 573, 582, *621*
Savedra, M., 496, 497, *517*
Sawin, D. B., 27, *63*
Saydjari, C., *478*
Saylor, C. F., 220, 221, 228, 229, 262, *276*
Saywitz, K., 593, 595, *621*
Scanlon, E. M., 41, *65*
Scarr, S., 728, *747*
Sceery, W., *125*
Sceery, W. R., 412, *450*
Schachar, R, 76, *119*
Schachar, R. J., 73, 75, 78, 79, 104, *126*

Schaefer, C. E., 112, *127*
Schaefer, E. S., 37, *65*
Schaeffer, C., 174, *185*
Schafer, C., *747*
Schafer, J., 739, 740, *747*
Schafer, L. C., 503, 505, *517*
Schaffer, B., 430, *449*
Schatschneider, C., 453, 457, 461, 467, 468, 469, 475, 478, 479, *480*
Schatz, J., 431, *450*
Schaughency, E. A., *123,* 172, *190*
Schauss, S., 439, *444*
Schechter, N. L., 495, *517*
Scheer, N. S., 666, *681*
Scheeringa, M. S., 603, *621*
Schefft, B. K., 4, 26, 27, *58*
Scheiber, B., 16, *55*
Scheiner, A., *510*
Schellekens, J., 242, *277*
Schepis, M. M., *446*
Scherer, D. G., 152, *190*
Scherer, M. W., 237, 249, 276, *320*
Schiavo, R. S., 653, *677*
Schillinger, J., *515*
Schimmel, L. E., 505, *513*
Schleifer, M., 73, *119*
Schlesinger, S., 692, *712*
Schlundt, D. G., 20, 30, *65,* 683, 694, *714*
Schmaling, K. B., 132, 133, 136, 140, *184, 187*
Schmidt, D., 236, 239, 262, *267*
Schneberk, D., *613*
Schneider, A. M., *183*
Schneider, J. A., 689, 692, *714*
Schneider-Rosen, K., 531, *566*
Schnell, C., 36, *65*
Scholten, C. A., 73, *127*
Schopler, D., *404*
Schopler, E., 408, 409, 411, 414, 416, 418, 419, 429, 430, 435, *448, 449, 450, 451, 452*
Schorr, O., *514*
Schreer, H. E., 632, 635, 640, 644, 653, 668, *681*
Schreibman, D., 137, *193*
Schreibman, L., 411, 412, 432, 436, 437, 438, *444, 447, 448, 451*
Schreiner, B., 481, *518*
Schroeder, C. S., 77, 105, 106, 126, 586, *617,* 706, *712*
Schroeder, H. E., 242, 243, 249, 255, 268, 271, *300*
Schroeder, S. R., 87, *124*
Schroth, P. C., 32, 54, 426, 427, *445, 446*
Schuckit, M. A., 721, 722, 724, 726, 732, 735, 743, 744, *747*
Schuele, J., 727, *747*
Schuerman, J., 583, 585, *615*
Schulenberg, J. E., 204, *227*
Schulman, J. L., 246, 277, 291, *292*
Schulman, R. G., 696, *714*
Schulsinger, F., 722, *745*
Schultheis, K., 249, 274, *290*
Schultz, F., 87, *128*
Schultz, L. G., 573, 576, *621*
Schuster, S., *271*
Schutz, J., 579, *614*
Schwab-Stone, M., *65,* 145, 149, *189, 190, 191, 193,* 211, 213, 226, 227, 228, 258, *276, 406*
Schwartz, D., 692, 693, 706, 710, *711*
Schwartz, D. M., 693, 697, 706, *714*
Schwartz, E., 688, *710*

Schwartz, I. S., 432, 434, *443, 445*
Schwartz, L. A., 39, *50*
Schwartz, R. C., 702, *714*
Schwartzman, A. E., 133, 140, 190, *192,* 335, 346, 348, 363, 364, *365*
Schwarz, J. C., 35, 44, 45, 62, *65*
Schwebel, A. L., 7, *65*
Schwenk, T. L., 212, *225*
Scioli, A., 208, 227, *228*
Scott, K., 552, *568*
Scott, R. L., 577, 580, *621*
Scully, S., 687, *712*
Seagull, E. A. W., 540, *566*
Seashore, M. R., 415, *448*
Seat, P. S., 36, *67*
Seat, P. D., 259, 277, 469, *480*
Secord, P. F., 696, *714*
Secord, W., 384, *406*
Seeley, J. R., 201, 208, 213, 224, 225, 227, *228*
Segal-Andrews, A., 491, *513*
Seidel, R., 701, *714*
Seidman, L. J., *120*
Seidner, A. L., 249, 264, *301*
Seifer, R., 208, 227, *228*
Seig, A., 574, *618*
Seilhamer, R. A., 640, *680*
Seligman, M. E. P., 219, 227, 228, 231, 232, 261, 275, 276, 564, 585, 610, 620, *621, 697, 714*
Seltzer, C. C., 699, *713*
Selvini Palazzoli, M., 690, 703, 704, *714*
Selzer, M. L., 171, *190*
Semel, E., 382, 384, *406*
Semmel, A., *620*
Semple, W. E., *129*
Serbin, L. A., 133, 140, *190,* 335, *364*
Sergeant, J., 71, 73, *127*
Sergis-Deavenport, E., 498, 499, 503, *517*
Serketich, W. J., 137, 170, *182*
Sessa, F. M., *270*
Severson, H., 166, *192*
Severson, H. H., 177, *192*
Sevin, B. A., 419, *451*
Sevin, J., *448*
Sevin, J. A., 419, 420, 428, *451*
Sevitt, M. A., 269, *312*
Sgroi, S., 575, *615*
Shaffer, D., 40, *65,* 86, 116, 126, 145, *186, 189, 190, 191,* 211, 225, 226, 227, 228, 258, 393, *406, 276, 715, 736, 745*
Shah, A., 429, *451*
Shain, B., 724, *745*
Shapiro, A. H., *276*
Shapiro, A. K., 481, 483, *517*
Shapiro, E. S., 30, 41, *65,* 251, *276*
Shapiro, J., 491, *517*
Shapiro, J. P., 580, *619*
Sharabany, R., 354, *364*
Sharma, V., 76, 103, 122, *124*
Sharon, T., 640, *680*
Shaver, P. R., 235, 267, 593, *617*
Shaw, B. F., 170, *179*
Shaw, D. A., 157, *189*
Shaw, K., 234, 271, 305, 335, *363*
Shawchuck, C. R., 587, *618*
Shayne, M., *404*
Shaywitz, B. A., 36, *65,* 87, 88, *127,* 453, 457, *479*
Shaywitz, S. E., 36, *65,* 87, 88, *127*
Shea, C., *227*
Shea, V., 381, *406,* 417, *451*

Shearer, M., 390, *401*
Shedd, C., 236, *263*
Sheeber, L. B., 156, 162, 165, 169, *191, 193*
Shekim, W., 109, *127*
Shell, R., 647, *680*
Shelly, C., 724, *748*
Shelton, K. K., 167, *191*
Shelton, R. C., 216, *228*
Shelton, T. L., 85, 86, 99, *116, 117*
Shepard, M. F., 547, *566*
Shepherd, R. W., 497, *516*
Sher, K. J., 724, 726, 727, 728, 729, 730, 731, 732, 739, *744, 746, 747*
Sheras, P. L., 259, *265*
Sherman, L., 57, *185*
Sheslow, D., 386, 388, *406*
Sheslow, D. V., 242, 243, 276, *283*
Shiere, F. R., 259, *268*
Shifman, L., *268*
Shigetomi, C., 243, 246, 247, 257, 258, 260, 263, 264, 274, 289, 290, 327
Shinn, M. R., 161, *192*
Shisslak, C. M., 686, *716*
Sholevar, E. H., 130, *191*
Sholevar, G. P., 130, *191*
Sholomskas, D., *229*
Short, R. J., 388, *404*
Showers, J., 578, *616*
Shrimpton, S., 593, *620*
Shroff, J. M., *561*
Shrout, P. E., *190*
Shulman, S., 392, *404*
Shurtleff, H. A., 477, *478*
Shute, R., 490, *512*
Siegel, A., 599, *618*
Siegel, B., 416, *451, 452*
Siegel, J. M., 173, *190*
Siegel, L. J., 234, 235, 242, 243, 249, 251, 256, 257, 258, 273, 275, 276, 289, 290
Siegel, L. S., 75, 76, 85, 103, 108, 111, *119*
Siegel, P., *517*
Siegel, S., 506, *511*
Siegel, S. E., 234, 235, 270, 287, 497, *513*
Siegel, T., 148, 150, *186*
Siegel, T. C., 149, *186*
Siegelman, E. Y., 18, *57*
Sieleni, B., 687, *716*
Sigall, H., 706, *712*
Sigel, I., 21, 37, 38, *65*
Sigel, I. E., 8, *50*
Sigelman, C., 490, 499, *517*
Sigman, M., 411, 421, 429, *451, 452*
Sikora, D. M., 347, *359*
Sikora, T., 246, 265, *285*
Silber, T. J., 689, *714*
Silberstein, L. R., 688, *715*
Silbert, M. H., 591, *621*
Silk, K. R., *620*
Siller, J., 503, *510*
Silva, P., 139, *188, 227*
Silva, P. A., 78, 87, 124, *127, 135, 140, 180, 238, 263*
Silver, C., *517*
Silver, H., 523, *564*
Silver, R. L., 585, 586, 589, *621*
Silver, S. E., *681*
Silverberg, J., *226*
Silverberg, S. B., 627, *681*
Silverman, A. B., *225*
Silverman, F., 523, *564*
Silverman, W. K., 34, 41, *65*, 234,

246, 247, 249, 260, 262, 267, 270, 276, 303, 311, 327
Silverstein, A. B., 374, 389, *406*
Silverstein, J., 245, 268, 286, 499, 503, *511, 512, 513, 516*
Silverstein, J. H., 268, *512, 513*
Silverthorn, P., 258, *267*
Simeonsson, R. J., 387, 388, *406, 436, 449*
Siminerio, L., 498, *511*
Simmel, C., 76, 77, *116, 122, 127*
Simmonds, B., *711*
Simmons, J. Q., 412, 414, *445, 448*
Simmons, V., 390, *402*
Simon, A., 238, *276*
Simon, A. F., 576, *618*
Simon, K. M., 414, *449*
Simonds, J. F., 489, *517*
Simonian, S., 505, 506, *517*
Simons, R. L., 203, 225, 629, *681*
Simpson, W. J., 235, *276*
Simson, K. G., 698, *707*
Sines, J. O., 36, *65*
Sines, L. K., 498, *511*
Singer, E., 241, *276*
Singer, L. T., 231, 235, *276*, 703, *711*
Singer, M., 149, *191*
Singh, J., 149, *191*, 438, *451*
Singh, N. N., 395, *401, 451*
Singleton, L. C., 346, *359*
Siperstein, G. N., 371, *404*
Sippola, L. R., 339, *362*
Sipprelle, R. C., 256, *265*, 586, *616*
Siqueland, L., *270*
Sirles, E. A., 582, 583, *621, 623*
Sirois, P., *514*
Sitterle, K. A., 4, *65*
Skelton, J. A., 255, *274*
Skinner, B. F., 27, 54, 73, 77, *127*, 442, *451*
Skinner, E., 218, *228*
Skinner, H. A., 46, *65*, 171, *191*, 259, 276
Skinner, J. B., 732, *744*
Skinner, M. L., 138, *181, 183*, 329, 331, 341, 355, *361*
Skitka, L. J., 30, *66*
Skodal, A. E., 17, *55*
Slabach, E. H., 164, *191*
Slade, P. D., 687, 694, 696, 699, *713, 714*
Slater, E., 238, *276*
Sleator, E. K., 96, 98, *127, 128*
Slee, P. T., 236, 237, 238, *276*
Slentz, K., 391, *406*
Slifer, K., 397, *404*
Slifer, K. J., 397, *404*
Sloan, J., *449*
Sloan, J. L., 431, 436, *449, 451*
Sloggett, B. B., 163, *186*
Slotkin, J., 38, *54*
Small, A. M., *444*
Smallish, L., 73, 75, 85, 86, *117, 121, 724, 742*
Smart, D. E., 691, *714*
Smetana, J., 530, 534, 556, 563, *566*
Smetana, J. G., 631, 634, 655, 656, 658, *681, 682*
Smith, A., 78, 126, 456, *479*
Smith, B., 435, *451*
Smith, C., 499, *512*, 570, *616*
Smith, C. E., *444*
Smith, D., 77, *119*, 256, 263, 698, *716*
Smith, D. H., 231, 235, *267*
Smith, D. A., *185*
Smith, D. W., 577, 580, *621*

Smith, E., 262, *266*
Smith, E. E., 9, *51*
Smith, G. T., 726, *747*
Smith, H., 579, 580, *621*
Smith, I. M., 411, *451*
Smith, J. A., 583, *621*
Smith, K. A., 629, 647, *682*
Smith, K. D., 581, *615*
Smith, L., 127, *517*
Smith, M., 492, *517*, 580, 581, *615, 617*
Smith, M. C., *714*
Smith, R. B., 355, *364*
Smith, S. D., 492, 499, *510, 517*
Smith, W., 578, *616*
Smith, W. K., 579, *621*
Smith, Y. S., 77, *129*
Smits, S. J., 496, *514*
Smolak, L., 701, *714*
Smoot, D. L., 329, 342, *360*
Smucker, M. R., 41, *66*, 205, *228*
Smyth-Staruch, K., 482, *517*
Snell, M. E., 431, *451*
Sneznevskij, A. V., *450*
Snidman, N., 258, *265, 270*
Snow, B., 573, *622*
Snow, M., 149, *192*
Snyder, A. L., 504, *510*
Snyder, D., 416, *445*
Snyder, D. K., 633, 663, 666, *681, 682*
Snyder, J. J., 136, 138, *174, 191*
Sobel, D., 506, *511*
Sobell, L. C., 732, 733, *747*
Sobell, M. B., 732, 733, *747*
Sobesky, W. E., 377, *403*
Sobol, A., 486, *512*
Sohmer, H., 415, *451*
Soll, M. H., 686, *708*
Solomon, A., 170, *184*
Solomon, J., 135, *187*
Soltys, S. M., *270*
Song, A., 389, 390, *406*
Song, L. Y., 149, *191*
Sonnenberg, E., 235, *276*
Sorbom, D., 14, *58*
Sorce, J. F., 261, *271*
Sorensen, E., 575, *621*
Sorensen, E. D., 156, *193*
Sorenson, E., 595, *615*
Sorenson, T., 573, *622*
Sosna, T. D., 151, *179*
Spana, R. E., 696, *715*
Spanier, G. B., 5, 32, 50, *66*, 172, *191*, 547, 566, 667, *682*
Sparrow, S., 469, 473, *479*
Sparrow, S. A., *452*
Sparrow, S. S., 100, *127*, 389, *406*, 416, 431, *451, 452*
Spaulding, B. R., 491, *517*
Specker, B., 688, *712*
Spector, I. P., 172, *180*
Speechley, M., 435, *452*
Speltz, M. L., 135, 136, 156, *184, 191*, 342, 362, 492, 493, *517*, 580, *617*
Spence, S. H., 237, 239, 254, 262, 272, 276, 318, 319, 325
Spencer, C., 489, *517*
Spencer, M. S., 611, *615*
Spencer, T., *118*
Sperling, K. A., 15, *67*
Spevack, M., 503, *517*
Spiegler, B. J., 460, *477*
Spieker, S. J., 528, *566*
Spielberger, C. D., 32, 41, *66*, 249, 250, 258, 276, 320, 555, 566, 605, 622

Spillar, R., 268, *512, 513*
Spinell, A. P., *362*
Spirito, A., 228, 493, *514*
Spitzer, A., 163, *193*
Spitzer, R. L., 171, *191,* 204, 228, 258, 267, 408, *451*
Spock, A., 492, *518*
Spragg, P. A., 393, *406*
Sprague, D. J., 77, *128*
Sprague, J. R., 439, *449*
Sprague, R., 98, *128*
Sprague, R. L., 36, *67,* 395, *406*
Spreen, O., 453, 454, 455, 460, 461, *462, 479*
Sprenkle, D. H., 647, 670, 671, 675, *677, 680*
Sprich, S., *120*
Spyrou, S., 52, *181*
Squire, L. R., 461, *479*
Srebnik, D., 696, *714*
Sroufe, A., 362, 529, *563*
Sroufe, L. A., 8, 10, 20, 46, 53, *66,* 342, 528, 531, *566*
St-Georges, M., 393, *406*
Stabler, B., 489, 490, *517*
Stagg, V., 138, *185,* 340, *364*
Staley, A. A., 239, *266*
Stambaugh, E. E., 32, *67,* 107, *128*
Stancin, T., *479*
Standish, J., *614*
Stanger, C., 149, *191*
Stanley, S. O., 29, *55*
Stanton, W., 139, *188*
Stark, E., 580, *622*
Stark, K. D., 36, *64,* 234, 235, 272, 324
Starnes, A. L., 399, *403*
Starr, R. H., 528, *567*
Staruch, K. S., 492, *510*
Staudenmayer, H., 487, *517*
Stauffer, L., 581, *615*
Steele, B., 523, *564*
Steele, J. J., 231, 235, *263*
Steele, P., 350, *364*
Steele, R., *445*
Steer, R. A., 110, *118,* 170, 179, 262, *264,* 321, *324*
Stege, P., 693, *714*
Stehbens, J., *514*
Steiger, H., 696, *712*
Stein, E., 486, *516*
Stein, M., 85, *126*
Stein, M. A., *119*
Stein, R. E. K., 149, *181,* 490, 493, *517*
Steinberg, L., 535, 567, 676, *682*
Steinberg, T., 490, *514*
Steinfeld, B. I., 631, *682*
Steinhauer, P. D., 259, *276*
Steinhausen, H. C., 493, *510,* 701, *714*
Steinkamp, M. W., 75, *127*
Steinmetz, S., 538, *567*
Steketee, G., 586, *622*
Steller, M., 598, *622*
Stemmler, M., *227*
Stenberg, C., 260, *265*
Stephens, M. A. P., 688, *709*
Stern, A., 592, *620*
Stern, L., 208, 210, 226, 247, *269*
Stern, M., 505, *517*
Stern, R. C., 492, *513*
Stern, S. L., 704, *714*
Sternbach, R. A., 234, *271*
Stetson, B. A., 731, *743*
Stevens-Long, J., 20, *66*

Stevenson, J., 88, *121, 127,* 237, *275*
Stevenson, J. M., 416, *452*
Stevenson, M. B., 4, *66*
Stewart, D. G., 720, 723, 726, 728, *732,* 743, 746, 747, *748*
Stewart, H., 255, *274*
Stewart, J., *514*
Stewart, M., 79, 88, *124, 125, 128*
Stewart, M. A., 77, *84, 127,* 415, *443,* 739, 743, 746, *747*
Stewart, S., 360, 489, 490, *517*
Stewart, S. L., 27, *65,* 333, 334, 335, 336, 342, 347, *361, 364*
Stieglitz, E., 534, 564, 592, *618*
Stiles, W. B., 639, *682*
Still, G. F., 71, 73, *77,* 83, *127*
Stiller, B., *227*
Stinchfield, R. D., 734, 735, 736, *748*
Stokes, G. S., *190*
Stokes, T. F., 29, *66,* 77, *119*
Stone, D. A., 577, 580, *621*
Stone, K., 149, *193,* 213, *228*
Stone, P., *123*
Stone, W. L., 234, 249, 262, *271,* 305, *335,* 363, 409, *424, 451, 452*
Stonehill, E., 691, *715*
Stoneman, Z., 47, *50*
Stoner, G., 76, 90, 91, 97, 100, 111, 115, *120, 126*
Stones, M. H., 585, *621*
Stoolmiller, M., 138, *181,* 639, 661, *679*
Stopeck, M. H., 706, *710*
Stoppani, C., *517*
Storch, M., 591, *614*
Storey, K., 439, *449*
Stormshak, E. A., 337, *342, 364*
Stouthamer-Loeber, M., 54, 100, *123,* 136, 139, 153, 177, *183,* 187, 190, *192, 193,* 342, *364*
Strahan, R. F., 276, *294*
Strain, P. S., 340, 350, 353, *364*
Straker, G., 534, *567*
Strang, J., 453, *479*
Strassberg, Z., 167, *191*
Strasser, M., 693, *715*
Straus, M. A., 46, *66,* 167, 172, 173, *191,* 526, 527, 538, 539, 547, *562,* 567, 739, *747*
Strauss, A. A., 71, *86, 127*
Strauss, C. C., 230, 231, *237, 238,* 264, 267, 276, 317, 318, *321*
Strauss, J., 691, *715*
Strayhorn, J. M., 26, *66,* 166, 167, *191*
Streeter, C. L., 670, 671, *679*
Streiner, D. L., 420, *451*
Streissguth, A. P., 88, *127,* 724, *745*
Streuning, E. L., 392, *405*
Strickland, B. R., 41, *63*
Strickler, E. M., 499, *512*
Strickler, G., 237, *277*
Striegel-Moore, R. H., 688, *715*
Stringfield, S. A., 351, 359, 395, *401*
Strober, M., 683, 686, 691, 692, 699, *703,* 704, *715*
Strohmer, D., 395, *406*
Strom, G. A., 591, *622*
Stroop, J. P., 104, *127*
Strosahl, K. D., 4, 5, 32, 33, *66*
Strzelecki, E., 88, *117*
Stuart, R. G., 695, *715*
Stuchiner, N., 392, *404*
Stuckey, M. K., 688, 692, 693, 708, *711*
Student, M., 415, *451*
Stumbo, P., 87, *128*

Stunkard, A., 503, *517*
Stunkard, C. L., 629, *680*
Sturges, J. W., 244, *265,* 293, 497, *509*
Sturgis, E. T., 156, *183*
Sturm, R., 87, *116*
Sturmey, P., 438, 439, *449, 451*
Stuss, D. T., 77, *127*
Sudhalter, V., 416, *444*
Sugarman, D. B., 173, *191*
Sullaway, M., 148, *180*
Sullivan, H. S., 338, *364*
Sullivan, L. A., *183*
Sullivan, M., 92, *125*
Sulzer-Azaroff, B., 7, *66,* 397, *405*
Sumpter, E. A., *510*
Sunday, S. R., 701, 709, *712*
Sundberg, D., 391, *402*
Sussman, E. J., 628, *680*
Sutarman, M., 251, *277*
Sveen, O. B., 258, *271,* 285
Svejda, M., 261, *271*
Svobodny, L. A., 727, *747*
Swaim, R. C., 729, *747*
Swaiman, K. F., 453, *479*
Swan, G. E., 6, *66*
Swanson, J., 88, 98, *122, 127*
Swanson, J. M., 76, 111, *123, 127*
Swarbrick, L., 105, *125*
Swedo, S. E., 235, *275*
Sweeney, L., 205, *229*
Swenson, C. C., 262, *276*
Swift, W. J., 704, *716*
Szalai, J., *226*
Szapocznik, J., 47, *66*
Szatmari, P., 78, *127,* 179, *188,* 420, 423, 429, 431, 435, *451, 452,* 510, *743*
Szmukler, G. I., 704, *709*
Szumowski, E. K., 76, 85, *119*
Szykula, S., 46, *66*
Szymanski, L., *452*
Szyszko, J., 393, *405*

Tabachnik, N., 4, *66*
Tabrizi, M. A., 51, 210, 224, 227, *561*
Tabrizi, M. D., *227*
Taffel, C., *52*
Tageson, C. W., 218, *227*
Talbot, A., 259, *263*
Tallmadge, J., 88, *127*
Tammariello, C. F., *746*
Tanaka, J. S., 14, *52*
Tanaka, K., 415, *448*
Tanenbaum, R. L., 228, *564, 621*
Tanguay, P. E., 429, 442, *443*
Tannenbaum, L., *184*
Tannock, R., 75, *77, 126, 127*
Tantam, D., 417, *451*
Tapert, S. F., 724, 726, 739, 743, 747, *748*
Taplin, P., 531, *566*
Taplin, P. S., 42, *64*
Tapp, J., 161, *191*
Tarnowski, K., 492, 505, 506, *517*
Tarnowski, K. J., 529, 533, 534, *560*
Tarter, R. E., 534, 567, 578, 622, 722, 724, 728, 734, 735, 736, 746, *748*
Tarver-Behring, S., 108, *127*
Taska, L., 586, 600, 610, *622*
Tattersall, R. B., 505, *517*
Taub, E., *617*
Taubman, M. T., 413, *445*
Tavormina, J., 493, 498, *517*
Tavormina, J. D., 639, *679*

Tavormina, J. F., 492, *512*
Tavormina, J. R., 490, *512*
Tawney, J., 391, *406*
Tay, K. M., 273, *296*
Taylor, C. B., 16, *66*, *711*
Taylor, D. M., 696, *712*
Taylor, E., 75, *126*
Taylor, E. A., 71, 84, *119*, *127*
Taylor, H. L., 697, *711*
Taylor, H. G., 453, 456, 457, 461, 463, 467, 468, 469, 471, 473, 474, 475, 478, 479, 480
Taylor, J., 439, 445, 493, *517*
Taylor, J. A., 258, *277*
Taylor, J. F., 87, *128*
Taylor, L., 4, *49*
Taylor, M.J., 696, *708*
Taylor, P. P., 259, *263*
Taylor, V., 391, *406*
Taylor, W. F., 491, *518*
Teal, M. B., 423, *451*
Teasdale, G., 455, *480*
Teasdale, M. A., 722, *745*
Tebano-Micci, A., 596, *619*
Tebbi, C., 504, 506, *517*
Teegarden, L. A., 151, 161, *191*
Teeter, N. C., 15, *67*
Teicher, M. H., 75, *128*
Tein, J. Y., 647, *680*
Tellegen, A., 50, 220, *228*
Tenke, C. E., 579, *614*
Tennenbaum, D. L., 46, 57, 171, *185*, 627, 640, 680, 681, 688, *709*
Terdal, L. G., 3, 4, 5, 6, 8, 9, 10, 11, 12, 13, 14, 16, 24, 28, 31, 32, 37, 41, 43, *61*, 107, 124, 176, 187, 247, 272, 453, 478, 544
Terr, L. C., 584, 588, 595, 622, 623
Terry, B., 29, 55
Terry, R., 138, *180*, 334, *361*
Tesler, M., 496, *517*
Tesser, A., 628, 631, *682*
Tetzloff, C., 727, *744*
Thach, B. T., 77, *127*
Tharinger, D., 590, 591, *622*
Tharp, R. G., 5, 41, *66*
Theander, S., 705, *715*
Thelan, M. H., 21, *52*
Thelen, E., 413, *451*
Thelen, M. H., *714*
Thibodeaux, S., 52, *181*
Thoennes, N., 574, *622*
Thoits, P. A., 731, *748*
Thomas, A., 135, 164, 184, *191*, *192*, 257, 258, 268, *277*
Thomas, A. M., 257, 274, *678*
Thomas, C., 148, *186*
Thomas, H., *188*
Thomas, J., 503, *511*
Thomas, J. N., 578, *622*
Thomas, M. R., 15, *67*
Thomas, N. R., 235, *276*
Thomas, V., 652, 665, 673, *682*
Thomassin, L., 335, *360*
Thomes, M. M., 172, *179*
Thompson, A. I., 46, *61*
Thompson, C., 498, *512*
Thompson, C. W., *515*
Thompson, J. K., 33, *51*, 696, 709, *715*
Thompson, J. B., 726, *746*
Thompson, K. L., 496, *518*
Thompson, K. M., 727, 729, *748*
Thompson, L., 701, *715*
Thompson, L. A., 88, *120*
Thompson, M., 706, *710*

Thompson, M. G., 693, 697, 706, *714*
Thompson, N. M., 477, *478*
Thompson, P., *708*
Thompson, R., 210, 226, 270, 309, 492, *514*, 580, *617*
Thompson, R. I., 491, 492, *517*, *518*
Thompson, S., 505, *518*
Thompson, S. B. N., 687, *715*
Thompson, S. M., 38, *58*
Thomson, M. L., 251, *277*
Thoresen, C. E., 256, *277*
Thorley, G., 84, 86, *127*, *128*
Thormahlen, P., 390, *404*
Thorndike, R. L., 382, 383, *406*, 429, 451, 463, 480
Thornton, D. H., 5, *52*
Thuline, H. C., 393, *405*
Thurber, S., 149, *192*
Thursby, E., *402*
Thwing, E. J., 36, *57*
Thyer, B. A., 239, *277*
Tidwell, M. O., 728, *744*
Tidwell, R. P., 575, *619*
Tiedemann, G. L., *188*
Tilley, C., 590, *617*
Timm, M. A., 350, *364*
Timnick, L., 570, 571, 572, *622*
Tinkelman, D., 504, *519*
Tinsley, B. R., 346, *359*
Tishelman, A., 347, *359*
Tisher, M., 204, *228*
Titus, J., 492, *515*
Tizard, J., 239, *275*
Tjaden, P., 574, *622*
Tobey, T. S., 256, *277*
Todd, J. B., 276, *294*
Todis, B., 166, *192*
Toedter, L., 531, *564*
Tolan, P. H., 138, *178*
Toler, S. M., 257, 258, *274*
Tolley, E. A., 571, *620*
Tolman, A., *185*
Tolman, A. O., 667, *682*
Tomer, A., 499, 503, *513*
Tomori, M., 726, *748*
Toneatto, T., 732, *747*
Tonge, B. J., 395, 396, *403*
Tonick, I., *446*
Toobert, D., 43, *66*
Torgesen, J. K., 77, *128*
Torres, H., 597, *619*
Toth, S., 528, *562*
Toth, S. L., 204, 224, 533, 556, *561*, 567, 727, 744
Touchette, P. E., 442, *451*
Touliatos, J., 46, *66*
Touyz, S. W., *708*
Towbin, K., *452*
Towle, V. R., 36, *65*
Town, C., 498, *511*
Townsley, R. M., 612, *620*
Tracy, K., 249, 274, *290*
Trainor, C. M., 525, *566*
Traisman, H. S., 491, *514*
Tramontana, M. G., *227*
Traub, A. C., 696, *715*
Travis, L., 481, *518*
Traylor, J., 38, *54*
Treder, R., 357, *364*
Treloar, L., 553, *561*
Tremblay, R. E., 140, *192*, 339, *361*, 364
Trickett, E. J., 20, 62, *66*
Trickett, P. K., 44, *66*, 532, 567, 588, 608, *620*
Trimble, M. R., 463, *477*

Tripp, J., 498, *511*
Trites, R. L., 77, 78, 86, 87, *118*, *128*
Trivette, C. M., 5, 22, 31, 38, 53, 397, 398, 399, 402, 403, *406*
Trocme, N., 526, *567*
Tronick, E., 237, *263*
Tronick, E. Q., 15, *66*
Trost, M. A., 35, 52, 328, *361*
Trueworthy, R. C., 499, *517*
Tryon, W. W., 104, 105, *128*
Tryphonas, H., 77, *128*
Tsai, L., 415, *443*, *451*
Tsai, M. C., 415, *451*
Tsuang, M. T., 88, *118*, *120*, 165, 179, 180
Tucker, F., 492, *512*
Tucker, S., 111, *126*
Tucker, S. B., 76, *126*
Tufts New England Medical Centre, Division of Child Psychiatry, 581, 622
Tuma, A. H., 30, *65*
Tuma, J. M., *51*, 169, *188*
Turbott, S. H., 84, *125*, 394, *401*
Turkat, I. D., 30, 33, *66*
Turner, J., *185*
Turner, J. E., 219, *224*
Turner, S. M., 230, 250, *264*, 266, *277*, 311
Turner, T. R., 687, *707*
Turner, T. M., 333, *362*
Turtle, J. R., *511*
Tuteur, J. M., 551, 555, 559, *567*
Tversky, A., 337, *365*
Twardosz, S., 43, *66*
Twentyman, C. T., 38, 49, 59, 529, 530, 531, 539, 556, *561*, *564*, 566
Tylenda, B., 395, *403*
Tyler, V., 270, *309*

U.S. Advisory Board on Child Abuse and Neglect, 523, 527, *567*
U.S. Congress, Office of Technology Assessment, 527, *567*
U.S. Department of Justice, Federal Bureau of Investigation, 578, *622*
Uauy, R., *517*
Uchigakiuchi, P., 7, 33, *56*
Ujiie, T., 700, *715*
Ullman, D. G., 71, 76, 105, *118*, *128*
Ullmann, L. P., 8, *66*
Ullmann, R., 98, *128*
Ullmann, R. K., 96, *127*
Ulrich, R. F., 73, *121*
Ultee, C. A., 242, *277*
Underwood, L., *517*
Unger, T. E., 243, *272*
Ungerer, J. A., 411, 430, *451*
Unis, A. S., 213, 226, 234, 235, 267, 302
Urbina, S., 8, *49*
Urey, J. R., *512*
Urquiza, A. J., 583, *616*
Uviller, E. T., 255, *272*

Vaal, J. J., 256, *277*
Vaccaro, D., 137, *193*
Vaidya, A. F., *270*
Vaillant, G. E., 727, *748*
Vaitl, D., 261, *268*
Vaitukaitis, J. L., 683, *710*
Vaituzis, C., *119*
Valente, E., 161, *193*
Valente, M., 415, *451*
Valenzuela, M., 529, *567*

Valla, J., 393, *406*
Vallano, G., 109, 111, *120*, *125*
van der Meere, J. J., 73, *127*
van der Spuy, H. I. J., *680*
van der Veen, F., 172, *186*, 667, *680*
Van Goor-Lambo, G., 17, *66*
Van Hasselt, V. B., 7, 14, *56*, 234, 235, 242, 243, 248, 251, 277, 279, 284, 308, 724, *748*
Van Horn, Y., *184*
van Ijzendoorn, H. W., 334, *360*
Van Itallie, T. B., 689, *707*
Van Kammen, W. B., 153, *187*, *192*
van Lieshout, C. F. M., 334, *360*
Van Ostenberg, P., 259, *268*
van Rooijen, L., 171, *190*
van Santen, V., 583, *615*
Van Scoyk, S., 612, *619*
Van Slyke, D.A., 492, *518*
Vance, V. J., 491, *518*
VanDeusen, J. M., 669, *677*
Vandvik, I. H., 670, 671, *682*
Vara, L., 698, *714*
Varni, J. W., 44, *56*, 242, 277, 413, *448*, 492, 494, 495, 496, 498, 499, 503, *513*, *514*, *517*, *518*
Vasey, M. W., 260, *277*
Vasta, R., 537, *567*
Venables, P. H., 251, *272*
Venham, L., 235, 246, 249, 259, 276, 277, *291*
Venter, A., 429, 431, *452*
Verhulst, F. C., 199, 223, *224*
Vermilyea, B. B., *263*
Vernon, D. T. A., 246, 277, 291, *292*
Verstraete, D. G., 505, *515*
Vesey, W., 432, *444*
Vicary, J. R., 718, *743*
Vieyra, M. B., 495, *518*
Vik, P. W., 4, 171, 717, 718, 726, 729, 731, 732, 733, 734, 743, 744, 747, *748*
Vincent Roehling, P., 655, 656, 657, *677*, *682*
Vincent, J. P., 173, *185*
Vincent, T. A., 20, *66*
Vinokur, A., 171, *190*
Virdin, L. M., 647, *680*
Visco-Dangler, L., 693, *714*
Vitaro, F., 335, 339, 360, 361, *364*
Vitulano, L., 534, *564*, 592, *618*
Vivian, D., 78, *125*, 173, *188*
Vodde-Hamilton, M., 111, *125*
Voelker, S. L., 77, *128*
Voeller, K., 453, *476*
Voeller, K. K., 77, *122*
Voeltz, L. M., 11, 15, 28, *67*
Volk, R., *515*
Volkmar, F. R., 408, 411, 413, 415, 416, 418, 420, 421, 431, *449*, *452*
Vollmer, T. R., 438, *447*
Volpe, J. L., 457, *480*
von Baeyer, C., *620*
von Bertalanffy, L., 701, *715*
Voris, J., 585, *622*
Vostanis, P., 435, *451*
Vuchinich, R., 633, 643, *682*
Vuchinich, S., 629, 633, 638, 640, 643, 644, 651, 665, 666, 667, 668, 669, *682*

Waas, G. A., 333, *362*
Waber, D. P., 453, 463, 464, 467, 473, *476*, *480*

Wachs, T. D., 164, *191*
Wachsmuth, R., 76, *119*
Wacker, D. P., 6, 7, *52*, 55, 67, 402, 490, *512*
Wada, K., 78, *122*
Waddell, M., *263*
Wadden, N. P. K., 420, 421, *452*
Wade, S., 231, 235, 276, *479*
Wade, T. C., 6, *67*
Wagner, B. M., 220, 224, 728, 729, 732, 735, 738, *744*
Wagner, E., *362*
Wagner, E. F., *748*
Wagner, K. D., 586, *618*
Wagner, P. E., *566*
Wagner, W., 587, *623*
Wahl, G., 37, *60*
Wahler, R. G., 8, 15, 22, 27, 29, 30, 32, 34, 38, 43, *52*, 63, *67*, 107, 108, 128, 136, 138, 142, 144, 168, 175, 182, *192*
Waite, R. R., 276, *307*
Wakabayashi, S., 431, *442*
Wake, L., 426, *446*
Wakeling, A., 688, *711*
Walco, G. A., 496, *518*
Walder, L. O., 131, *185*
Waldman, I., 116, *186*
Waldman, I. D., 76, *121*, 132, *192*
Waldron, H. B., 639, *677*
Walitzer, K. S., 727, *747*
Walker, C., 6, *67*
Walker, D., 486, 489, *512*, *517*, *519*
Walker, D. K., 92, *125*
Walker, D. L., 338, *359*
Walker, E., 532, 533, *562*
Walker, E. F., 532, *566*
Walker, H. M., 144, 145, 160, 161, 163, 164, 166, 168, 177, *192*, 350, 351, 353, *365*
Walker, J. G., 493, *518*
Walker, J. L., 133, *190*, *192*
Walker, L. S., 487, 488, 492, 493, 495, *512*, *518*
Wall, S., 342, *560*
Wallace, A., 706, *715*
Wallace, A. M., 576, *618*
Wallace, I., 706, *715*
Wallace, K. M., 109, *123*, 172, *187*, 667, *680*, 703, *712*
Wallach, M. A., 258, *277*
Wallander, J., 492, *518*
Wallander, J. L., 491, *516*
Wallechinsky, D., 706, *715*
Waller, D., 489, *517*
Waller, J. L., 213, *225*
Waller, J. V., 690, *715*
Wallis, K. D., 18, *57*
Walsh, B. T., 687, 693, 699, *712*, *715*
Walsh, J. A., 151, *179*
Walsh, M., 499, *518*
Walsh, M. L., 21, *52*
Walster, E., 696, 706, *707*
Walster, G. W., 706, *707*
Walters, D., 573, 574, *622*
Walters, G. C., 558, 559, *564*, *566*
Waltz, J., *564*
Wampold, B. E., 47, *67*
Wandersman, L. P., 38, *54*, 169, *184*, 490, *512*
Wang, L., 239, *267*
Wang, P. O., 460, *476*
Wansley, R. A., 4, *57*
Warbutron, R., *118*
Ward, C. H., 38, 49, 204, 223, *561*

Ward, E. M., 99, *125*
Ward, J., 496, *517*
Ward, L., 238, *276*
Ward, M., *621*
Ward, S. M., 381, *405*
Wardle, I., 695, *715*
Wardle, J., 687, 695, *715*
Ware, W. B., 388, *406*
Wargo, J., 334, *360*
Warner, P., 57, *185*
Warner, V., *229*
Warren, M., 697, 703, *715*
Warshak, R. A., 4, *65*
Warwick, W. J., 489, *516*
Wasik, B. H., 5, 38, 42, *67*
Wasserman, A., 495, *518*
Wasserman, A. A., 218, *229*
Wasserman, R., 492, *511*
Watanabe, H. K., 148, *185*
Waterhouse, L., 416, *445*
Waterman, G. C., 686, *708*
Waterman, J., 530, *561*
Waters, B., 495, *518*
Waters, E., *185*, 342, 359, *560*
Watkins, B., 572, *622*
Watkins, C. E., 7, *67*
Watkins, J. D., 498, *518*
Watson, D., 206, 213, 220, *228*
Watson, J. B., 230, *277*
Watson, S., 146, *186*
Watson, S. M., *512*
Watters, G. V., *479*
Waxman, M., 503, *517*
Waye, M. F., 256, *277*
Wayne, W., 492, *519*
Weatherman, R. F., *561*
Webb, C., 587, *617*
Webb, W. L., 693, *715*
Webber, Y., 580, *615*
Webster, R., 125, *189*
Webster-Stratton, C., 135, 138, 148, 151, 156, 160, 162, 163, 170, 172, 173, 174, 175, 176, *192*, *193*
Wechsler, D., 382, 383, 384, 385, 386, *406*, 429, *452*
Weeks, K., *404*
Wegner, C., 496, *517*
Wehby, J., 161, 164, *191*, *193*
Wehr, J., 491, *514*
Wehrspann, W., 573, *620*
Weidman, C. S., 166, 167, *191*
Weinberg, W. A., 217, *225*
Weiner, H., 183, *715*
Weinrich, M. W., 239, *267*
Weinrich, S., 239, *267*
Weinrott, M. R., 44, 67, 157, *193*
Weinstein, D., 243, 244, 246, 248, 249, 273, 288, *289*
Weinstein, P., 239, *273*
Weinstein, S. R., 149, *193*, 213, 215, *228*
Weintraub, S., 352, *364*
Weiss, B., 135, *193*, 204, 218, 219, 225, 228, *229*
Weiss, D. S., 38, *54*
Weiss, G., 71, 73, 75, 85, 86, *119*, *122*, *128*
Weiss, J., 631, *682*
Weiss, J. G., 635, 636, 639, 641, 649, 652, *681*
Weiss, R. L., 20, 44, 47, *67*, 667, 679, *682*
Weiss, R. V., 18, *61*
Weiss, S. R., 687, 699, *715*
Weiss-Perry, B., *679*
Weissberg, R. P., 356, *360*

Weissman, M. M., 201, 229, 235, 274
Weissman, W., 534, 565
Weist, M., 499, *518*
Weisz, J. R., 20, 50, 205, 218, 228, 229, 234, 235, 243, 244, 248, 268, 297, 298, 317, 589, *614*
Weithorn, L. A., 12, *64*
Weitzman, M., 392, 402, 482, 486, 489, 493, 510, 512, 517, *518*, *519*
Weizman, A., 278
Wekerle, C., 528, 535, 550, 552, 553, 567, 568, 585, 622
Welch, G., 701, *715*
Weldy, S. R., 591, *618*
Wells, G., *619*
Wells, K. C., 133, 147, 156, 163, 170, *183*, *184*, *188*, *193*, 257, 267, 273, 546, *563*
Wells, M. L., 356, *360*
Wells, R. D., 585, 586, 622
Welner, A., 88, *128*
Welner, Z., 88, 128, 145, 146, *189*, *393*, *405*, 555, *566*
Welsh, J. A., 35, 40, 165
Welsh, J. D., 524, *568*
Welsh, M. C., 77, *128*
Welsh, R., 72, *116*
Welte, J. W., 718, 719, 743, 748
Wenar, C., 427, *450*
Wener, A., 86, *128*
Wender, P. H., 71, 86, *128*, *129*
Wendt, S., 696, 698, *714*
Wernick, M. J., 728, 742
Werry, J. S., 36, 67, 71, 75, 76, 128, 452
Werthamer-Larsson, L., 161, *193*, 362
West, K. L., 629, *678*
West, M. O., 727, 748
Westen, D., 585, 620, 622
Westhuis, D. J., 171, *184*
Wetherby, A. M., 430, *452*
Wetzel, R. J., 41, *66*
Wexler, S., 579, *616*
Whalen, C. K., 29, 41, 50, 67, 75, 111, 112, 128
Whaley-Klahn, M. A., 86, *123*
Wheatt, T., 208, *225*
Wheeler, L., 161, *193*, 362
Wheeler, N., 109, *127*
Wheeler, V. A., 333, 335, *359*
Wherry, J. N., 262, 270, 321, 606, 622
Whipple, E. E., 137, 173, 174, *193*
Whitaker, A., 688, *715*
Whitbeck, L. B., 629, *681*
White, B. J., 460, *480*
White, D. R., 696, *712*
White, H. R., 735, 748
White, J. W., 87, *129*
White, J. L., 133, *193*
White, K., 219, *224*
White, M. L., 639, *682*
White, O., 391, *403*
White, O. R., 390, *406*
White, S., 591, 595, 607, 622
White, T., 593, *615*
Whitehurst, G. J., 47, *67*
Whiteside, L., 548, *561*
Whitfield, M. F., 497, *510*
Whiting, K. A., 595, *616*
Whitington, P., 495, *518*
Whitman, P. B., 218, 229
Whitmore, K., 239, *275*
Whitt, J. K., 492, *519*
Whitteker, W. B., 732, 747
Whitten, P., 348, *363*
Wick, P., 234, 271, 305, 335, *363*

Wicks, J., 145, *191*, 258, 276, 736, *745*
Widom, C. S., 528, 539, 567
Wiebe, M. J., 423, *451*
Wiegand, D., 235, 262, 269, 319
Wiener, L., 479
Wierson, M., 148, *183*, *678*
Wigal, T., 111, *127*
Wigfield, A., 269, 273, 277, 312
Wiggins, J. S., 5, *67*
Wiig, E., 382, 384, *406*
Wilcox, K., *518*
Wilcox, L. E., 36, 59, 99, 100, *123*
Wilder, J., 251, 277
Wildman, H. E., 505, *512*
Wilkinson, G. S., 385, 386, *406*, 469, *480*
Willems, E. P., 29, *67*
Willerman, L., 88, *128*
Williams, C. E., 249, 270, 277, 284
Williams, C. L., 50, 206, 229
Williams, D., 548, *566*
Williams, E. E., *451*
Williams, G. A., 345, 359, 365
Williams, J., 489, *519*
Williams, K., 489, *519*
Williams, L., 622
Williams, L. M., 576, 577, 578, 582, *618*, 622
Williams, R. A., 219, 224, 678
Williams, R. L., 41, *67*
Williams, S., 78, 87, *124*, *127*, 139, *187*, 227, 238, 263
Williams, T. F., 498, *518*
Williamson, D. A., 495, 496, *514*, *519*, 686, 687, 700, 713, 715, 716
Williamson, G. G., 38, *68*
Williamson, J. M., 534, 567, 580, 622
Williamson, P., 226
Willis, D. J., 527, *564*
Willis, T. J., 88, *128*
Willmuth, M. E., 694, 700, 710, 714
Willoughby-Herb, S. J., 390, 391, *406*
Wills, K., 489, *519*
Wills, K. E., 453, 458, 459, 473, *480*
Wills, R. M., 666, *682*
Wills, T. A., 137, *193*, 732, 748
Wilner, N., 599, *617*
Wilsher, C., 394, *401*
Wilson, B., 457, 463, 464, 473, *480*
Wilson, C. C., 251, 269
Wilson, D. B., 87, *129*
Wilson, D. M., 711
Wilson, G. T., 698, 699, 712, 716, 733, 744
Wilson, S., 547, 567
Wilson, S. K., 592, *619*
Wind, T. W., 573, 580, *621*
Winder, C., 573, 620
Windle, M., 718, 722, 726, 748
Wine, J. D., 244, 245, 277, 309
Winer, G. A., 258, 277
Wing, L., 394, 407, 409, 411, 412, 413, 415, 416, 417, 418, *450*, *452*
Wingard, D., 613
Winker, J. B., 237, 277
Winn, H. R., 477, 478
Winokur, G., Jr., 709
Winsten, N. E., 534, 567
Winters, K. C., 734, 735, 736, 738, 748
Wirt, R. D., 36, 67, 259, 277, 469, 473, *480*
Wirtz, P. W., 735, *745*
Wish, E., 88, *128*
Wisner, K. L., 234, 235, 267, 302

Witt, J. C., 145, *193*
Witt-Engerstrom, I., 417, *446*
Witteman, J. K., 259, 268
Wodarski, J. S., 532, *565*, 567
Wolchik, S. A., 700, *711*
Wolf, E. G., 427, *450*
Wolf, E. M., 695, *716*
Wolf, L. C., 435, *452*
Wolf, M., 263, 277
Wolf, M. M., 13, 29, 67, 175, *193*
Wolfe, D. A., 4, 26, 37, 40, 68, 523, 525, 528, 531, 533, 534, 535, 536, 537, 538, 539, 540, 541, 544, 547, 550, 551, 552, 553, 554, 556, 557, 558, 563, 564, 565, 567, 568, 575, 582, 583, 585, 586, 592, 599, 601, 603, *619*, 621, 622, 623
Wolfe, V. V., 40, 220, 229, 265, 497, 509, 569, 575, 581, 582, 583, 585, 586, 587, 588, 589, 592, 593, 594, 598, 599, 601, 602, 605, 606, 608, 609, 610, *614*, *616*, 622, 623, 667, 682
Wolfensberger, W., 369, *406*
Wolff, L. S., 166, *178*
Wolfsdort, J., *512*
Wolfson, D., 386, 388, *405*, 453, 464, 471, 479
Wolin, S. J., 87, *118*, 722, 743
Wolpe, I., 10, *68*
Wolpe, J., 230, 278
Wolraich, M., 87, *124*, *128*, *129*
Wolters, P. L., 479
Wonderlich, S. A., 687, 704, 716
Wood, B., 598, 623, 633, 643, 682
Wood, D. D., 247, 268
Wood, D. R., 86, *128*, *129*
Wood, K., 688, *711*
Wood, P. K., 727, 747
Wood, R., 41, *62*
Wood, T. A., 392, 403
Woodcock, R., 385, 386, *407*
Woodcock, R. W., 469, *480*, 561
Woodruff, R. A., 709
Woods, T., 499, *517*
Woodward, C. A., *188*
Woodworth, S., 174, *179*
Woody, D. J., *61*
Woody, P., 497, *511*
Wooley, O. W., 706, 707, 716
Wooley, S. C., 706, 707, 716
Woolford, H., 497, *516*
Woolger, C., 581, *615*
Wootton, J., 167, *191*
Wootton, J. M., 133, *183*
Work, W. C., 362
Workman, E. A., 41, *67*
World Almanac Book of Facts, 415, *452*
World Health Organization, 17, *68*, 199, 229, 410, *452*, 684, 685, 716
Wortman, C., 589, *621*
Wozencraft, T., 587, *623*
Wright, G. Z., 258, 278
Wright, H. H., 175, *181*
Wright, J. C., 18, 57, 337, 341, *365*
Wright, V., 111, *118*
Wruble, M. K., 156, *193*
Wrzesniewski, K., 726, *745*
Wung, P., 187
Wurtman, J. J., 689, 716
Wurtman, R. J., 689, 716
Wyatt, G., 569, *623*
Wyatt, G. E., 570, 572, 591, *623*
Wylie, M. L., 718, *745*
Wysocki, T., 489, 492, 493, 506, *519*

Yamada, E. M., *129*
Yamamoto, K., 262, *266*
Yang, B., 236, *266*
Yang, E., *445*
Yang, R. K., 559, *562*
Yang, Z., 273, *296*
Yanushefski, A. M., 531, *564*
Yarrow, M. R., 35, *68*
Yates, A., 20, 590, 595, 599, 606, *623*, 686, 689, *716*
Yates, B. T., 68, 175, *193*
Yates, W. R., 687, *716*
Yau, J., 634, *682*
Yeates, K., *479*
Yeates, K. O., 459, 472, *480*
Yeates, S. R., 409, 411, *452*
Yirmiya, N., 421, 423, *452*
Yoder, D. E., 411, *449*
Yoder, P., 154, *183*
Yokota, A., 414, 427, *446*
Yoshimura, I., 377, *401*, 414, 431, *442*
Yost, L. W., 41, 60, 205, *227*
Young, D. B., *448*
Young, H. F., *478*
Young, J. G., 87, *127*, 415, *448*
Young, L., 591, *614*
Youngblade, L. M., 540, *561*
Younger, A. J., 346, 353, *365*
Younger, A. S., 348, *363*

Ysseldyke, J. E., 20, *54*
Yuen, S. A., 592, *619*
Yuille, J. C., 598, 620, *623*
Yule, W., 4, 24, 68, 236, 274, 376, *406*, 413, *448*
Yurcheson, R., 234, 273, *288*
Yurgelun-Todd, D., 687, 688, 689, *710*, *713*

Zabin, M. A., 259, *278*
Zachary, R. A., 16, *68*
Zagar, R., 76, *129*
Zahn, T. P., 76, *129*
Zahn-Waxler, C., 24, 68, 77, *119*, 139, *193*, 524, 530, *568*
Zahner, G. E. P., 409, *452*
Zaidi, L. Y., 587, *619*
Zajonc, R. B., 234, *269*
Zak, L., 547, *567*
Zalewski, C., 576, *621*
Zametkin, A. J., 87, 120, *129*
Zanga, J., 489, *517*
Zangwill, W. M., 45, 68, 160, *193*
Zarcone, J. R., 438, 447, *452*
Zatz, S., 235, 249, *278*, *309*
Zaucha, K., 109, *127*, *476*
Zautra, A. A. J., 580, *614*
Zeanah, C. H., 603, *621*

Zeitlin, S., 38, *68*
Zeltzer, L., 235, 244, 246, 248, 258, *266*, 272, 287, 288, 496, 497, 498, *514*, *516*, *519*
Zeman, J., 57, 145, 146, *184*
Zeman, J. L., 495, *512*
Zentall, S. S., 75, 76, 77, *129*, 413, *452*
Zentall, T. R., 413, *452*
Zero to Three/National Center for Clinical Infant Programs, 17, 19, *68*
Zevon, M., *517*
Zhang, Q., *186*
Zigler, E., 369, 370, 371, 373, 374, *389*, *407*, 418, *452*
Zinbarg, R. E., 230, *265*
Zink, M., 495, *516*
Zoccolillo, M., 24, 68, 133, 139, 140, *193*
Zohar, A. H., 262, *278*
Zora, J., 504, *519*
Zucker, R. A., 137, 171, *183*, *184*, *185*, *193*, 722, 726, *748*
Zuckerman, E., *682*
Zukier, H., 31, *63*
Zumoff, B., *715*
Zupan, B. A., 218, *225*
Zuravin, S. J., 527, *568*
Zweben, A., 741, *746*

SUBJECT INDEX

Note. t, table; *f*, figure.

AAIS (Adolescent Alcohol Involvement Scale), 735*t*
AAMD (American Association on Mental Deficiency), 371, 372
AAMR. *See* American Association of Mental Retardation
AAPEP (Adolescent and Adult Psychoeducational Profile), 430
ABC. *See* Aberrant Behavior Checklist; Autism Behavior Checklist
Aberrant Behavior Checklist (ABC), 395, 395*t*, 396
Abusive Behavior Inventory, 547*t*
Academic engaged time, 161
Academic functioning
    assessment
        for ADHD children, 100, 101*t*–102*t*
        in substance use problems, 739–740
        substance use problems and, 724–725
        underachievement, conduct problems and, 134, 144
Academic Performance Rating Scale, 100, 101*t*–102*t*
Achenbach, Conners, and Quay Behavior Checklist (ACQ), 206–207
Achievement tests
    for mental retardation assessment, 385–387, 386*t*
    substance use problems and, 739
ACQ (Achenbach, Conners, and Quay Behavior Checklist), 206–207
Acquired immune deficiency syndrome (AIDS), 489
ACTeRS (ADD-H Comprehensive Teacher Rating Scale), 98
Acting-out behaviors, 130. *See also* Conduct problems
Active behavioral avoidance test, 301*t*
Activity level assessment, of ADHD children, 104–105
Activity Specialist Ratings, 295*t*
Actometers, 104
Acute stress disorder, 233
Adaptive behavior
    in attention-deficit/hyperactivity disorder, 100, 102
    definition of, 100, 389
    in mental retardation, 388–390, 389*t*

Adaptive Behavior Inventory, 389*t*, 390
Adaptive Behavior Inventory for Children, 389*t*, 390
Adaptive Behavior Scale—School, 389–390, 389*t*
Adaptive functioning assessment, in mental retardation, 371–372, 374, 388–390, 389*t*
ADD (attention deficit disorder), 72. *See also* Attention-deficit/hyperactivity disorder
ADDES (Attention Deficit Disorders Evaluation Scale), 98
ADD-H Comprehensive Teacher Rating Scale (ACTeRS), 98
ADHD. *See* Attention-deficit/hyperactivity disorder
ADHD Rating Scale
    in ADHD assessment, 98, 98*t*, 99
    for stimulant drug response evaluation, 111
Adherence, treatment. *See also* Noncompliance
    assessment methods, 499, 501, 503–504, 500*t*–501*t*, 502*f*
    barriers to, 504–506, 506*t*, 507*t*
    conceptualization, 499
ADI (Adolescent Drinking Index), 735*t*
ADI (Autism Diagnostic Interview), 423, 424*t*
ADIS (Adolescent Drug Involvement Scale), 735*t*
Adjustment problems, childhood maltreatment and, 534–536
Adolescent Alcohol Involvement Scale (AAIS), 735*t*
Adolescent and Adult Psychoeducational Profile (AAPEP), 430
Adolescent Behavior Checklist, 395*t*, 396
Adolescent Drinking Index (ADI), 735*t*
Adolescent Drug Involvement Scale (ADIS), 735*t*
Adolescent Interpersonal Competence Questionnaire (AICQ), 553*t*, 554*t*, 555
Adolescent Relapse Coping Questionnaire, 739

Adolescents
    conflict with parent. *See* Conflict, parent–adolescent
    depression in. *See* Depression
    individuation/differentiation, 725
    irrational beliefs of, 655
    maltreatment, 534–536
    as parents, child maltreatment and, 527
    peer relations, normal, 331
    stresses of, normative, 629–630
ADOS. *See* Autism Diagnostic Observation Schedule
Adult psychiatric disorders, childhood social withdrawal and, 335
Affect
    binge eating and, 695
    negative
        depression and, 220–221
        substance use problems and, 724, 729–730, 730*f*
    parent–adolescent conflict and, 660–662
    positive, depression and, 220
    self-regulation, behavioral inhibition and, 80*f*, 81
    triple-response mode model of, 660
AFMI (Attribution for Maltreatment Interview), 554–555, 554*t*
Age
    childhood assessments and, 24
    child physical abuse and, 526
Aggression
    in ADHD subtyping, 78
    age-related changes, 336
    in conduct disorder, 131
    in conduct problems, 133, 135
    parental discipline practices and, 342
    peer rejection and, 333–334
    physical, 352
    relational, 336
    social cognitions and, 344–345
    verbal, 352
Agoraphobia Without History of Panic Disorder, 233
AICQ (Adolescent Interpersonal Competence Questionnaire), 553*t*, 554*t*, 555
AIDS (acquired immune deficiency syndrome), 489
Alabama Parenting Questionnaire (APQ), 167, 168

Alcoholism. *See also* Substance use
  problems
  in ADHD, 86
  family-history-negative, 726
  family-history-positive, 726
  parental, adolescent substance use
    and, 727–728
Alcohol Use Disorders Identification
  Test (AUDIT), 171
Alcohol withdrawal syndrome, 723*t*
Alternative Solutions Test, 356
American Association of Mental
  Retardation (AAMR)
  Adaptive Behavior Scales, 389–390,
    389*t*, 431
  classification of mental retardation,
    372
American Association on Mental
  Deficiency (AAMD), 371, 372
American Professional Society on the
  Abuse of Children (APSAC),
  597
Amnestic Disorder, substance-induced,
  721*t*
Amphetamine withdrawal syndrome,
  723*t*
Analogue Test Taking, 308*t*
Anatomical Doll Questionnaire, 597–
  598
Anger, of sexual abuse victims, 589–
  590
Anger Diary, 551
Anorexia nervosa
  age of onset, 687–688
  assessment, 692
    behavioral, 694–698
    of family, 701–705
    instruments for, 698–701
    of medical symptoms, 693–694
  binge-eating/purging type, 684*t*, 692
  characteristics, 683
  diagnostic criteria, 683–684, 684*t*
  differential diagnosis, 686–687
  epidemiology, 688
  family
    assessment of, 701–705
    assumptions about, 702
  models, 689
    biological, 689–690
    cognitive-behavioral, 690–692
    psychodynamic, 690
  Restricting Type, 684*t*, 692
Anorexic Behaviour Scale, 699
Antisocial behavior
  development, 14
  parental
    assessment of, 170–171
    conduct problems and, 137
Antisocial Behavior Checklist (ASB
  Checklist), 171
Antisocial personality disorder (APD)
  parental, conduct problems and,
    137
  substance use problems and, 723
Anxieties. *See also* Anxiety disorder
  age of acquisition, 239
  age trends, 236–237
  anorexia nervosa and, 687, 691
  assessment instruments
    age-related variations and, 260–
      261
    classification/review of, 241–242
    dispositional variables and, 257–
      258
    evaluation/selection of, 252–255

familial variables and, 258–259
    limitations of, 260
    listing of, 279*t*–327*t*
    mechanical, 251
    observational, 242–247
    self-reports, 247–251
    treatment considerations and,
      255–257
  behavior therapy and, 230
  classification schemes, 231–234,
    241–242
  co-occurrence, 238
  defined, 231, 234
  developmental considerations, 235–
    240
  incidence, 235–236
  individual differences, 237–238
  motoric responses, 234–235, 235*t*
  physiological responses, 234–235,
    235*t*
  problematic, 240–241
  prognosis, 238–239
  as reaction to other problems, 241
  seriousness of, 239–240
  subjective responses, 234–235, 235*t*
  symptoms, 231
  treatment
    alternatives, 241
    assessment and, 255–257
    compound interventions, 257
    contingency management, 256–
      257
    costs of, 241
    decision making for, 240–241
    modeling, 256
    prolonged exposure, 256
    recommendations for, 259–262
    self-management, 257
    systematic desensitization, 255–
      256
  vs. fears, 231
Anxiety disorders, 133, 234, 721*t*
Anxiety Disorders Interview Schedule
  for Children, 246, 248, 327*t*
Anxiolytic withdrawal syndrome, 723*t*
Anxious/depressed syndrome, *vs.*
  depressed mood, 203
APD (Antisocial Personality Disorder),
  137, 723
APQ (Alabama Parenting Question-
  naire), 167, 168
APSAC (American Professional
  Society on the Abuse of
  Children), 597
Arnold–Chiari II brain malformation,
  458
Art assessment methods, for sexuality
  problems, 606–607
Artificial food colorings, ADHD and,
  87
ASB Checklist (Antisocial Behavior
  Checklist), 171
ASIEP (Autism Screening Instrument
  for Educational Planning), 420,
  422, 430
Asperger's disorder, 408–410, 417–418
Asphyxia, perinatal, 457
Assessments, child. *See also specific*
  assessment instruments
  behavioral–systems approach. *See*
    Behavioral-systems assessment
  functional/utilitarian approach, 3
  generalizations, 22–23
  informational organization, 26–27
  need for, 3

normative comparisons in, 25–26
  prevention-oriented, 4
  situations, types of, 24–25
  special considerations in, 23–25
  strategies, development of, 3
Attachment
  disorders, child maltreatment and,
    580
  infant–caregiver, child maltreatment
    and, 528–529
  patterns, conduct problems and,
    135–136
Attention
  in brain injury, 454, 472
  contingency-shaped, 82
  goal-directed persistence, 82–83
  skills assessment of, 472
  substance use problems and, 723–
    724
  sustained, in Attention-Deficit/
    Hyperactivity Disorder, 102–
    103
Attention deficit disorder (ADD), 72.
  See also Attention-deficit/
  hyperactivity disorder
Attention Deficit Disorders Evaluation
  Scale (ADDES), 98
Attention-deficit/hyperactivity disorder
  (ADHD)
  age of onset, 92
  assessment
    adaptive behavior scales/
      inventories for, 100, 102
    child behavior rating scales for,
      97–100, 98*t*, 99*t*
    child interview for, 95–96
    with conduct problems, 159
    direct observational procedures
      for, 105–108
    goals of, 90
    implications for, 89–90
    laboratory tests/measures for, 102–
      105
    observational coding system for, 6
    parental interview for, 91–95, 94*t*,
      95*t*
    parent self-report measures for,
      108–110
    peer relationship measures for, 108
    purposes of, 90–91
    self-report behavior ratings for
      children and, 100
    teacher interview for, 96–97
    theoretical model and, 83–84
  brain abnormalities in, 460
  characteristics, related, 77–78
  chronicity, 89
  comorbid conditions
    conduct disorder, 88–89, 628
    conduct problems, 133, 140, 152,
      159
    mental retardation, 377, 394,
      397
    oppositional defiant disorder, 88–
      89, 628
  conceptualization, changes in, 72
  core deficits, 73
  definition, 73
  developmental course, 84–85
  diagnostic criteria, 71–73, 75, 74*t*,
    92–93
  differential diagnosis, 90
  ethical issues, 114–115
  etiology, 86–89
  historical overview, 71–73

legal issues, 114–115
with or without hyperactivity, 79
outcome predictors, 85–86
parental, 109
predominantly hyperactive–
  impulsive type, 72
prevalence, 78
pure, 85
rule-governed behavior and, 72–73
situational or pervasive, 78
subtyping, 78–79
symptoms, 109
  behavioral inhibition, 115
  cognitive impairments, 77
  inattention, 82–83, 115
  primary, 75–76
  situational/contextual factors and,
    76–77
theoretical model
  assessment and, 83–84
  behavioral inhibition and, 79–82,
    80f
  executive functions and, 79–82,
    80f
treatment, 110–111
  classroom management for, 113
  parent–adolescent intervention
    for, 112–113
  parent training in contingency
    management, 112
  residential, 113–114
  self control strategies for, 112
  stimulant medication for, 111–
    112
Attention span assessment, 102–103
Attribution for Maltreatment Interview
  (AFMI), 554–555, 554t
Attributions Questionnaire, 554t
Audiotape-Aided Thought Recall,
  305t
Audiotape observations, for parent–
  adolescent conflict, 640–641,
  658
AUDIT (Alcohol Use Disorders
  Identification Test), 171
Autism Behavior Checklist (ABC),
  420–421
Autism Diagnostic Interview (ADI),
  423, 424t
Autism Diagnostic Observation
  Schedule (ADOS)
  for autistic disorder, 416–417, 425–
    426, 425t, 427
  for mental retardation, 394
Autism Screening Instrument for
  Educational Planning (ASIEP),
  420, 422, 430
Autistic disorder
  activities/interests patterns, 413
  age of onset, 413–414
  behavior
    management, assessment for,
      438–442, 439t, 440f
    rating scales for, 427–428
    restricted, repetitive and
      stereotypical patterns of, 413
  communication impairment,
    qualitative, 412–413
  diagnosis
    DSM-IV criteria for, 410–413,
      410t
    historical aspects of, 408–409
    Kanner syndrome and, 409, 409t
    pervasive developmental disorders
      and, 410

diagnostic checklists/interviews, 418
  Autism Behavior Checklist, 420–
    421
  Autism Diagnostic Interview, 423,
    424t
  Checklist for Autism in Toddlers,
    423–424
  Childhood Autism Rating Scale,
    418–420
  Diagnostic Checklist for
    Behavior-Disturbed Children,
    421–423
  Parent Interview for Autism, 424–
    425
differential diagnosis, 417–418
effect on family, 435–436
emotional abnormalities in, 414–
  415
etiology, 415–416
family assessments, 434–438
genetic factors in, 415
IQ and, 412, 414
with mental retardation, 377, 393,
  394, 412, 413, 414
neurological abnormalities in, 415–
  416
observational procedures, standardized diagnostic, 425–427, 425t
prevalence, 415
self-injury and, 414
sensory/perceptual abnormalities,
  414
social interaction impairment,
  qualitative, 411
stereotypies, 413
subclassification, 416–417
treatment planning/evaluation
  adaptive behavior scales for, 430–
    431
  echobehavioral assessment for,
    431–432, 434, 433f, 434t
  family assessment for, 436–438
  specialized scales for, 430
  standardized intelligence tests for,
    428–430
Automatic Thoughts Questionnaire,
  218
Autonomic Perception Questionnaire,
  255
Autonomy, parent–adolescent conflict
  and, 655, 656
Avoidant Personality Disorder, 687
Axis I disorders, 17
Axis II disorders, 17, 687
Axis III disorders, 17
Axis IV disorders, 17
Axis V disorders, 17

Bales v. Clark, 378
Balthazar Scales of Adaptive Behavior,
  389t, 390
BASC. *See* Behavioral Assessment
  System for Children
BATs. *See* Behavioral avoidance tests
Battered child syndrome, 523. *See also*
  Child abuse
Battle v. Pennsylvania, 378
Bayley Scales of Infant Development,
  381, 383, 382t, 429
BDDE (Body Dysmorphic Disorder
  Examination), 696
BDI. *See* Beck Depression Inventory
Beavers–Timberlawn Family
  Evaluation Scale, 612

Beck Anxiety Inventory, 321t
Beck Depression Inventory (BDI)
  for childhood depression, 204
  for conduct problems, 167, 170
  for parents
    of ADHD children, 109–110
    of children with conduct
      problems, 170
  with depression, 38–39
Bedtime Illumination Test, 281t
Behavior. *See also specific types of
  behavior*
  assessment
    in anorexia nervosa, 694–698
    in autistic disorder, 438–442,
      439t, 440f
    in bulimia nervosa, 694–698
    of child abuse victims, 551–553,
      553t
    of communication, 645, 646t–
      647t
    definition of, 9
    in depression, 219
    ongoing evaluations, 8
    in substance use problems, 739
  checklists, for depression assessment,
    206–208, 213–216
  disorders, with mental retardation,
    376–377
  hyperactive–impulsive, 75–76, 577
  of maltreated child, during early
    childhood, 529–530
  problems
    behavior–systems assessment and,
      24–25
    coding, 397
    with mental retardation, 376–377,
      377t, 394–396, 395t
  rating scales. *See also specific rating
    scales*
    for attention-deficit/hyperactivity
      disorder, 100
    for autistic disorder, 427–428
    broad-band, 147–150, 148t
    conduct problem-specific, 150–
      153
    rule-governed, ADHD and, 72–73
    situational influences on, 10
Behavioral Approach–Avoidance and
  Distress Scale, 294t–295t
Behavioral Approach Test, 302t
Behavioral Assessment, 304t–305t
Behavioral assessment, of sex abuse
  victims, 592
  background information for, 593
  investigative interviewing for, 593–
    598
Behavioral Assessment System for
  Children (BASC)
  for ADHD assessment, 97
  parent rating scale, 36
  for parents of ADHD children, 112
  peer relationship measures, 108
  teacher form, 113
Behavioral avoidance tests (BATs)
  for blood fears/anxieties, 279t
  characteristics of, 242–243
  for darkness fear, 280t, 282t, 283t
  description of, 326t
  for medical procedure anxiety, 286t
  selection of, 253
  for small animals fear, 299t–300t,
    301t
  for social/stranger interaction
    anxieties, 303t

Behavioral inhibition, in attention-deficit/hyperactivity disorder, 79–82, 80f, 115
Behavioral Interview, 315t
Behavioral Observation Scoring System, 558–559
Behavioral Profile Rating Scale—Revised, 286t
Behavioral Rating Scale, 313t
Behavioral Summarized Evaluation (BSE), 428
Behavioral–systems assessment (BSA)
  of adults, 6
  of childhood disorders, etiological assumptions on, 21–22
  of children, 6
  in classification, 16–19
  components of, 6–7
  conduction of, 6
  definition of, 7–8
  development of, 3–6
  in diagnosis, 16
    categorical, 17
    developmental, 19–20
  dimensions, 22–23
    expanded temporal and contextual base, 30
    multiple targets and, 26–27
    multisituational analysis, 29–30
    normative comparisons and, 25–26
    selection of treatment goals and, 28–29
    special considerations for, 23–25
  exclusion of direct observation and, 7
  in hypothesis testing, 8
  methods, 30–31
    child self-reports, 39–41
    direct observations, 41–42
    family assessment, 46–48
    formal testing with children, 48
    interviews, 33–35
    observational procedures, 43–46
    parent self-ratings, 37–39
    reliability of, 32–33
    selection of, 31–32
    standardization of, 32–33
    structured parental reports, 35–37
    validity of, 32–33
  observational coding system, 11
  ongoing nature of, 4
  outcomes of labeling children and, 20–21
  prototype-based view and, 9–11
  purposes for, 11–14
    design, 13
    diagnosis, 12
    evaluation, 13–14
    prognosis, 12–13
  response classes and, 15
  standardization failure and, 7
  structure/content, 6
  syndromes and, 14–15
  vs. traditional assessment, 9
Behavior Checklist for Infants and Toddlers, 36
Behavior Evaluation Rating Scale, 395, 395t
Behavior Evaluation Scale, 430–431
Behavior observation methods
  in conduct problems, 153–154, 156–164, 155f, 158t
    in clinic, 153–154, 156–159, 155f, 158t
    in home, 159–160

by independent observers, 153–154, 156–161, 155f, 158t
  in school, 160–161
  by significant adults, 161–164
  direct, in ADHD assessment, 105–106
  for illness knowledge assessment, 498–499
  of mentally retarded children, 396–397, 398f
  for treatment adherence, 503
Behavior Observation Scale (BOS), 315t
Behavior Observation System (BOS), 426–427
Behavior Problem Checklist, 36
Behavior Profile Rating Scale, 244, 288t
Behavior Rating Scale, 313t
Behavior Test, 314t–315t
Beliefs, in parent–adolescent conflict, 659–660
Bender Visual Motor Gestalt Test, 380, 386t, 387, 388
BES (Binge Eating Scale), 699–700
Bias
  from diagnostic labels, 20
  direct observations and, 42
Binge eating
  assessment of, 694–695, 695f
  bulimia nervosa and, 688
  triggers/precipitants, 694, 695
Binge Eating Scale (BES), 699–700
Binge–purge behavior, 690
Binge–purge diary, 694, 695f
Binge Scale, The, 700
Biobehavioral systems approach, implementation of, 468–475, 469t, 470t, 474t
Biological factors
  in brain injury, 473–474, 474t
  in depression, 216–218
Biological models, of eating disorders, 689–690
Blacks, substance use prevalence, 719, 719t, 720t
Blind Learning Aptitude Test, 383t, 385
Blockage, pedophilia and, 577
Blood, fear of, 279t
Blood pressure monitoring, with heart rate monitoring, 310t
Body Cathexis Scale, 696
Body Dysmorphic Disorder Examination (BDDE), 696
Body Image Avoidance Questionnaire, 696
Body image disturbance, in eating disorders, 696
Body Shape Questionnaire (BSQ), 696
Body weight regulation, in eating disorders, 694
Borderline Personality Disorder, 687
BOS (Behavior Observation Scale), 315t
BOS (Behavior Observation System), 426–427
Brain
  developmental disorders, mental retardation and, 375t
  injury. See Brain injury
  metabolic activity, in ADHD, 87
  size/density, in ADHD, 87
Brain injury
  in ADHD, 86–87
  assessment, 475–476
    of biological variables, 473–474, 474t

of environmental variables, 474, 474t
    in future, 475–476
    interpretation of, 474–475
    neuropsychological, 463–464, 466, 465t, 466t
  from cerebrovascular disease, 461–462
  from congenital malformations, 454t, 457–459
  from epilepsy, 462–463
  genetic/metabolic/degenerative disorders, 454t, 459–460
  from infectious disorders, 454t, 461
  management, 474–475
  minimal brain damage, 71. See also Brain injury
  neuropsychological assessment, biobehavioral systems approach, 466–468, 467f
  overactivity/distractability and, 71
  from perinatal trauma, 456–457
  research, 453
    advances in, 453
    developmental approaches for, 453–454
  traumatic, 454t, 455–457
  from tumors, 454t, 460–461
Brainstem dysfunction, autistic disorder and, 415
Brain tumors, 460–461
Brazelton Neonatal Behavioral Assessment Scale—Revised, 387t, 388
Brigance Diagnostic Inventory of Early Development, 390, 391t
Bruininks–Oseretsky Test of Motor Proficiency, 386t, 387
BSA. See Behavioral–systems assessment
BSE (Behavioral Summarized Evaluation), 428
BSQ (Body Shape Questionnaire), 696
Bulimarexia, 691
Bulimia Cognitive Distortions Scale, 696
Bulimia nervosa
  age of onset, 688
  assessment, 692–698
    behavioral, 694–698
    of family, 701–705
    instruments for, 698–701
    of medical symptoms, 693–694
  binge eating and, 688
  diagnostic criteria, 685, 685t
  differential diagnosis, 686–687
  family, 701–705, 702
  models, 689
    biological, 689–690
    cognitive-behavioral, 690–692
    psychodynamic, 690
Bulimia Test (BULIT), 700
Bulimia Test—Revised (BULIT-R), 700–701
Bulimic behavior. See also Bulimia nervosa
  age of onset, 688
  family, assumptions about, 702
BULIT (Bulimia Test), 700
BULIT-R (Bulimia Test—Revised), 700–701

CAIICS (Child Abuse Interview Interaction Coding System), 598

California Verbal Learning Test—Children's Version, 471–472
CAMPIS (Child–Adult Medical Procedure Interaction Scale), 497
CAMPIS-R (Child–Adult Medical Procedure Interaction Scale—Revised), 244, 259, 293*t*
CAPI (Child Abuse Potential Inventory), 547*t*, 557
Carolina Curriculum for Infants and Toddlers with Special Needs, 390, 391*t*
Carolina Curriculum for Preschoolers with Special Needs, 390, 391*t*
Carolina Record of Individual Behavior, 387*t*, 388
CARS. *See* Childhood Autism Rating Scale
CAS (Child Assessment Schedule), 40, 210–211, 210*t*
CASQ (Children's Attributional Style Questionnaire), 219, 554*t*
Cattell–Binet Short Form, 429
Cattell Infant Intelligence Scale, 429
CBCA (Criteria-Based Content Analysis), 598
CBCL. *See* Child Behavior Checklist
CBQ (Conflict Behavior Questionnaire), 641, 645, 647, 648*t*
CCI (Child Conflict Index), 163
CD. *See* Conduct disorder
CDC (Child Dissociative Checklist), 607–608, 610, 608*t*–609*t*
CDI. *See* Children's Depression Inventory
CDS (Children's Depression Scale), 204
CEDRI (Clinical Eating Disorder Rating Instrument), 698
CELF-Preschool (Clinical Evaluation of Language Fundamentals—Preschool), 382*t*, 384
CELF-Revised (Clinical Evaluation of Language Fundamentals—Revised), 382*t*, 384
Center for Epidemiologic Studies Depression Scale (CES-D), 204, 212, 215
Cerebellum abnormalities, in autistic disorder, 415
Cerebral palsy, mental retardation and, 375
Cerebrovascular disease, 461–462
CES-D (Center for Epidemiologic Studies Depression Scale), 204, 212, 215
CGPSS (Cleminshaw–Guidubaldi Parent Satisfaction Scale), 169
CHAT (Checklist for Autism in Toddlers), 423–424
chEAT (Eating Attitudes Test—children's version), 701
Checklist for Autism in Toddlers (CHAT), 423–424
Checklists. *See also specific checklists*
child-completed, 41
for depression, 206–208, 213–216
for fears/anxieties, 245–246, 253
for mental retardation, 394–396, 395*t*
CHI (Children's Hostility Inventory), 150, 152
Child abuse
of ADHD child, 114

assessment, 524, 544–545, 559–560
child interviews for, 548–549, 549–550
conceptual model for, 536–541
identifying general problem areas in, 545–549, 546*t*
implications for, 541
of individual strengths/problem areas, 550–556, 551*t*, 553*t*–555*t*
integration with treatment, 559
of maltreated child, 544
of maltreating adult, 543–544
parental interviews for, 545–548, 546*t*, 547*t*, 549
of parent–child relationship, 557–559
purposes of, 542–543, 543*t*
unique aspects of, 541–542
death rates, 526
defined, 524–525
distal events and, 538
in early childhood, 529–531
emotional, 525
experiences, of maltreating parent, 538–539
fatalities, 527
incidence, 525–526
in middle childhood
behavioral dimension of, 531–532
cognitive and social–cognitive dimension of, 532–533
socioemotional dimension of, 533–534
as parental rejection, 534–535
perpetrators, demographic characteristics of, 527
physical, 523
in infancy, 528–529
types of, 525
profile, statistical, 525–526
proximal events and, 537–538
reporting, 114
sexual. *See* Sexual abuse
suspected, 542
victims, behavioral assessment of, 551–553, 553*t*
Child Abuse, Prevention, Adoption and Family Services Act of 1988, 524–525
Child Abuse and Neglect Database Instrument System, 599
Child Abuse Interview Interaction Coding System (CAIICS), 598
Child Abuse Potential Inventory (CAPI), 547*t*, 557
Child Abuse Prevention and Treatment Act, 524
Child adjustment, in Conduct disorders, 168–169
Child–Adult Medical Procedure Interaction Scale (CAMPIS), 497
Child–Adult Medical Procedure Interaction Scale—Revised (CAMPIS-R), 244, 259, 293*t*
Child Assessment Schedule (CAS), 40, 210–211, 210*t*
Child Attention Problems Scale, 98
Child Behavior Checklist (CBCL)
for ages 2–3, 36, 147, 148
for ages 4–18, 18, 36, 147, 148, 148*t*
for attention-deficit/hyperactivity disorder, 97, 99
for child abuse victims, 552, 553*t*

for conduct problems, 147, 149, 153, 165, 177
for depression, 206, 207, 208
direct observation form or DOF, 106, 147, 148, 149, 161
for family conflicts, 629, 643, 668
for fears/anxieties, 290*t*
for parents of ADHD children, 112
peer relationship measures, 108
for psychological adjustment to illness, 486
PTSD scale, 602, 602*t*–605*t*
for sexual abuse victims, 583
sexual problems subscale, 606
social competence ratings, 353
for substance use problems, 739
teacher report form or TRF, 18
for attention-deficit/hyperactivity disorder, 113
for child abuse/neglect, 553*t*
for conduct problems, 147, 148, 148*t*, 149, 160
for depression, 206, 207, 208, 213, 214*t*, 221
description of, 322*t*
for social behavior rating, 350–351
youth self-report form or YSR, 18
for attention-deficit/hyperactivity disorder, 100
for child abuse/neglect, 553*t*
for conduct problems, 147, 148, 148*t*
for depression, 206, 207, 208, 213, 214*t*, 221
Child Behavior Observational Rating, 290*t*
Child behavior rating scales, for ADHD assessment, 97–100, 98*t*, 99*t*
Child Conflict Index (CCI), 163
Child Dental Behavior, 296*t*
Child Development Questionnaire, 259
Child–Directed Interaction, 156, 160
Child Dissociative Checklist (CDC), 607–608, 610, 608*t*–609*t*
Child–family relationship, in behavioral–systems assessment, 4
Childhood Autism Rating Scale (CARS)
comparison with Diagnostic Checklist for Behavior-Disturbed Children and ASIEP, 422
concurrent validity, 419
description of, 416, 418–420
discriminant validity, 419–420
effect of autistic child on family, 435
interrater reliability, 419
Childhood disintegrative disorder, 408–409, 410, 417
Childhood disorders. *See also specific disorders*
dimensional classification of, 17–19
etiology, behavioral–systems assessment of, 21–22
vs. target behaviors, 14–16
Childhood History Questionnaire, 547*t*
Childhood Level of Living Scale (CLLS), 547*t*, 548

Child Protective Service, responses to sexual abuse allegations, 574–575
Child-rearing. *See* Parenting
Child Rearing Disagreements, 173
Child Rearing Practice Questionnaire, 259
Children's Anxiety Evaluation Form, 246, 247–248, 323*t*–324*t*
Children's Attributional Style Questionnaire (CASQ), 219, 554*t*
Children's Attributional Style Questionnaire (KASTAN), 610
Children's Cognitive Assessment Questionnaire, 249, 309*t*
Children's Comprehensive Pain Questionnaire, 496
Children's Depression Inventory (CDI), 204–205, 205*t*, 555*t*, 587, 204–205, 205*t*, 213, 214*t*
Children's Depression Scale (CDS), 204
Children's Fear Survey Schedule
  dental version, 249, 288*t*
  description of, 319*t*
  revised version, 254, 316*t*
Children's Firesetting Interview, 146
Children's Hospital of Eastern Ontario Pain Scale, 497
Children's Hostility Inventory (CHI), 150, 152
Children's Impact of Traumatic Events Scale—Revised (CITES-R)
  attributional issues scales, 610
  description of, 599–600, 600*t*–601*t*, 603
  eroticization scale, 606
  social reactions scales, 611
Children's Manifest Anxiety Scale, 249–250, 254, 316*t*
Children's Manifest Anxiety Scale—Revised, 319*t*
Children's Moral Reasoning Interview, 554*t*
Children's Negative Cognitive Error Questionnaire, 218
Children's Orientation and Amnesia Test (COAT), 456
Children's Posttraumatic Stress Disorder Inventory, 248, 327*t*
Child Self-Control Rating Scale, 553*t*
Child Self-Report, 291*t*
Child Sexual Behavior Inventory (CSBI), 590, 606, 607*t*
Child's Game, 154, 156, 159, 160
Child Well-Being Scales (CWBS), 548
Chromosomal disorders, mental retardation and, 375*t*, 376
Chronic illness
  assessment
    construct independence and, 508–509
    developmental issues in, 508
    disease complexity and, 508
    specificity *vs.* generality of, 508
  health care utilization and, 482
  hypothesis testing, 509
  knowledge
    assessment of, 498–499
    developmental issues and, 499
    need for, 498
  pain of, 494–495
  prevalence, 482, 482*t*

psychological aspects, historical perspective of, 483
theory building, 509
CIC (Community Interaction Checklist), 175
CIRQ (Conflicts in Relationships Questionnaire), 552
CITES-R. *See* Children's Impact of Traumatic Events Scale—Revised
Classical autism (Kanner syndrome), 409, 409*t*, 421, 422
Classroom
  behavioral observations, 45
    in ADHD assessment, 105–106
    in conduct problems assessment, 160–161
  management, for ADHD children, 113
Classroom Environment Scale, 20
Cleminshaw–Guidubaldi Parent Satisfaction Scale (CGPSS), 169
Clinical Eating Disorder Rating Instrument (CEDRI), 698
Clinical Evaluation of Language Fundamentals—Preschool (CELF-Preschool), 382*t*, 384
Clinical Evaluation of Language Fundamentals—Revised (CELF-Revised), 382*t*, 384
Clinical Rating Scale, 665*t*, 673
CLLS (Childhood Level of Living Scale), 547*t*, 548
Close relationships, assessment of, 353–354, 354*t*
Coalitions
  assessment, 667–669
  parent–child, anorexia nervosa and, 702
COAT (Children's Orientation and Amnesia Test), 456
Cocaine withdrawal syndrome, 723*t*
Coercion
  conduct problems and, 138
  model of, 136
  parental, in child maltreatment, 540–541
  in sexual abuse, 572
Cognition
  assessment
    of abused/neglected child, 553–556, 554*t*
    of brain-injured child, 470–473, 470*t*
    in substance use problems, 739
  impairments, in attention-deficit/hyperactivity disorder, 77
  of maltreated child, during early childhood, 530–531
  in parent–adolescent conflict, 654–656
    alternative approaches, 658–660
    questionnaire assessment of, 656–658
Cognitive and Somatic State Anxiety Inventory, 317*t*
Cognitive and Somatic Trait Anxiety Inventory, 316*t*–317*t*
Cognitive Assessment, 311*t*
Cognitive-behavioral theory, 690–691
Cognitive Behavior Questionnaire, 249, 307*t*
Cognitive Bias Questionnaire for Children, 218

Cognitive functioning assessment
  for mental retardation, 381–385, 382*t*–383*t*
  standardized tests for, 381, 383–385, 382*t*–383*t*
Cohesion, assessment, 669–673
COMFORT Scale, 292*t*
Commitment, friendships and, 339
Communication
  in attention-deficit/hyperactivity disorder, 100, 102
  in autistic disorder, 412–413
  defensive, 645
  in parent–adolescent conflict
    alternative assessment approaches for, 644
    patterns in, 644–645, 647, 652–654, 646*t*–651*t*
    problem-solving skills in, 634–635, 639–644, 636*t*–638*t*
  supportive, 644–645
Community Interaction Checklist (CIC), 175
Community Living Assessment and Teaching System, 391, 391*t*
Community Members' Rating Scale, 638*t*, 644, 651*t*, 654
Community resources
  for mentally retarded persons, 397–399, 400
  model, for mental retardation, 398–399, 400
  obtaining abuse-related information from, 593
Compliance. *See also* Noncompliance
  assessment methods, 499, 501, 503–504, 500*t*–501*t*, 502*f*
  barriers to, 504–506, 506*t*
  conceptualization, 499
Compliance Test (CT), 158–159
Compound interventions, for fears/anxieties, 257
Comprehension, in autistic disorder, 412
Compulsive compliance, 529–530
Computers, behavioral–systems assessment and, 4–5
Conceptual models, of depression in young people, 203–204
Conduct disorder (CD)
  adolescent-onset type, 131, 139
  childhood-onset type, 131
  comorbid conditions
    attention-deficit/hyperactivity disorder, 88–89, 109
    conduct problems, 159
  diagnosis, 130
  epidemiology, 130
  essential feature, 131
  severity, 131
  substance use risk and, 722–723
  subtypes, 131
Conduct problems (CP). *See also* Conduct disorder; Oppositional defiant disorder
  assessment, 176–178
    of associated characteristics, 164–166
    behavioral observations for, 153–154, 156–164, 155*f*, 158*t*
    behavioral rating scales for, 147–153, 148*t*
    clinical interviews, 141–145
    of extrafamilial factors, 175
    of familial factors, 166–176

in interactional context, 140–147, 143*t*
mutiple-gating approaches for, 177
structured interviews, 145–147
attention-deficit/hyperactivity disorder and, 133, 140
classification, 131–133
comorbid conditions, 133–134, 176
with depression, 138
development, 134
early-starter pathway of, 134–139
late-starter pathway of, 139
epidemiology, 130–131
girls and, 139–140
observational coding system, 6
overt–covert dimension, 132–133
parenting and, 136
peer rejection and, 334
risk factors, 132–133, 136
types, 130
Conflict, parent–adolescent
affect and, 660–662
assessment
alternative approaches, 633–634
audiotape observations for, 640–641, 658
of family, 629–631, 630*t*
informational functions of, 630–631
observational, 633
questionnaire, 631–633
therapeutic functions of, 631
clinical recommendations, 673–675
cognition, 654–660
alternative assessment approaches for, 658–660
questionnaire assessment of, 656–658
communication patterns, assessment of, 644–645, 647, 652–654, 646*t*–651*t*
observational, 649*t*–651*t*, 652–654
questionnaire, 645, 647, 652, 648*t*–651*t*
defined, 627
dimensions, 631
elements of, 629–631, 630*t*
externalizing problems and, 629
frequency/intensity, 631
future directions, 675–676
internalizing problems and, 629
maladaptive, 627
oppositional defiant disorder and, 90
prevalence of, 629
problem-solving skills, 634–635
alternative assessment approaches for, 644
observational assessment of, 636*t*–638*t*, 639–644
questionnaire assessment of, 635, 639, 636*t*
systemic factors
assessment instruments for, 662, 663*t*–665*t*
coalitions, 667–669
cohesion, 669–673
disengagement, 669–673
enmeshment, 669–673
parental teamwork, 662, 666–667
triangulation, 667–669
Conflict Behavior Questionnaire (CBQ), 641, 645, 647, 648*t*

Conflicts in Relationships Questionnaire (CIRQ), 552, 553*t*
Conflict Tactics Scale (CTS)
for child abuse/neglect, 547, 547*t*
parent version, 167
partner version, 172–173
for substance use problems, 739
Congenital malformations, 454*t*, 457–459
Conners Continuous Performance Test, 103
Conners Rating Scales
for mental retardation, 394–395, 395*t*, 396
for parents, 36
of ADHD children, 98, 99, 104
of conduct problem children, 147, 148, 150
of depressed children, 206
revised version, 112
for teachers
of ADHD students, 98, 99, 104
of conduct problem students, 147, 149, 150
of depressed students, 206
revised version, 113
Contingency management procedures, for fears/anxieties, 256–257
Continuous-performance tests (CPTs), 102–103
Continuous Recognition Memory Test, 472
Contrecoup injury, 455
Coping, substance use problems and, 732
Coping Health Inventory for Parents, 436, 490
Coping styles, of sexual abuse victims, 589
Cornelia de Lange syndrome, 396
Counting tangible products, adherence behavior and, 503–504
Coup injury, 455
CP. *See* Conduct problems
CPTs (continuous-performance tests), 102–103
Criminal behavior, childhood maltreatment and, 534–536
Criminal trials, for sexual abuse, 575–576
Criteria-Based Content Analysis (CBCA), 598
Criterion-based assessment, for mental retardation, 390–391, 391*t*
Cruelty, in Conduct Disorder, 131
CSBI (Child Sexual Behavior Inventory), 590, 606, 607*t*
CT (Compliance Test), 158–159
CTS. *See* Conflict Tactics Scale
Cultural factors
diversity of, 5
in eating disorders, 705–706
peer relations and, 343–344
Custody, of ADHD child, 114
Customary Drinking and Drug Use Record, 738, 738*t*
CWBS (Child Well-Being Scales), 548
Cylert, 111–112
Cystic fibrosis, 482

Daily Diary, 248, 254, 310*t*–311*t*
Daily Discipline Interview (DDI), 162–163
Dandy–Walker syndrome, 458

Darkness, fear of, 280*t*–283*t*
Darkness Tolerance Test, 282*t*, 283*t*
DAS (Dyadic Adjustment Scale), 172, 547, 547*t*, 667
DAST (Drug Abuse Screening Test), 171
DD (dysthymic disorder), 200, 201
DDI (Daily Discipline Interview), 162–163
Death, leading causes of, 481, 481*t*
Deceptiveness, in conduct disorder, 131
Defensiveness, assessment of anxieties/fears and, 258
Defensive/Supportive Behavior Code, 650*t*, 653
Deferred gratification, 83
Degenerative disorders
with brain injury, 454*t*, 459–460
with mental retardation, 375*t*
Deinstitutionalization, 370
Delinquent behavior, in attention-deficit/hyperactivity disorder, 85–86
Delirium, substance-induced, 721*t*
Dementia, substance-induced, 721*t*
Demyelinating disorder, mental retardation and, 375*t*
Dental Fear Survey Schedule—Parent Version, 296*t*
Dental Ratings of Anxiety and Cooperation, 288*t*
Dependent personality disorder, 687
Depressed mood syndromes, 213, 214*t*
Depression
age differences in, 202–203
assessment, 198–200
of behavioral factors, 219
behavior checklists for, 206–208
of biological factors in, 216–218
of comorbid disorders, 220–221
of environmental factors, 219–220
of family factors, 219
implications for, 221–223
instruments for, 221–222
integration of methods for, 212–216, 214*t*
of interpersonal factors, 219
multiple-gating approach for, 222–223
selection of tools for, 221–222
self-report questionnaire, 204–206, 205*t*
sensitivity of, 222
of social-cognitive factors, 218–219
structured diagnostic interviews for, 208–212, 209*t*–211*t*
categorical diagnostic model, 222
classification, 221
comorbid conditions, 197
anorexia nervosa, 687
assessment of, 220–221
assessment tools and, 222
conduct problems, 133, 138
mental retardation, 377
sexual abuse, 586–587
substance use problems, 724
conceptual models, 203–204
constructs, assessment of, 216–221
defined, 199
developmental considerations, 200–203
differential diagnosis, 148
emotional maltreatment and, 534

Depression (*continued*)
  gender differences in, 200–203
  interventions, 221–223
  maternal, conduct problems and, 137
  measurement methods, impediments for, 198
  nature of, 197
  normative considerations, 200–203
  parental
    attention-deficit/hyperactivity disorder and, 109–110
    conduct problems and, 137
  predictors, 197
  prevalence, 197, 201
  symptoms, 198, 199
    adolescent reports, 199
    parent reports, 199
  taxonomy, 198–200
Depression Observation System, 636*t*, 651*t*
Detouring, 667, 702
Development
  changes
    qualitative, 23–24
    rapid/uneven, assessments and, 23–24
  chronic illness knowledge and, 499
  deviation, assessments and, 23–24
  history, in conduct problems, 164
  issues
    in chronic illness, 490, 493, 508
    in substance use problems, 725
  pain/discomfort experience and, 497–498
  treatment adherence and, 506
Developmental Behavior Checklist, 395*t*, 396
Developmental language disorders, 418
Developmental Profile II, 389*t*, 390
Developmental psychopathology, child maltreatment and, 527–536
Developmental quotient (DQ), 381, 383
Developmental Test of Visual–Motor Integration (VMI), 386*t*, 387
Deviance proneness model, 730, 730*f*
Dexamethasone suppression test (DST), 217
Dexedrine, 111–112
Diabetes, life expectancy with, 481–482
Diabetes Daily Record, 501, 502*f*
Diabetes Family Behavior Checklist, 505
Diagnosis. *See also under specific disorders*
  behavioral–systems assessment for, 12
Diagnostic and Statistical Manual of Mental Disorders-II (DSM-II), 72
Diagnostic and Statistical Manual of Mental Disorders-III (DSM-III)
  childhood disorder classifications, 16
  diagnostic criteria
    attention-deficit/hyperactivity disorder, 72
    mental retardation, 393
Diagnostic and Statistical Manual of Mental Disorders-III-R (DSM-III-R), 72

Diagnostic and Statistical Manual of Mental Disorders-IV (DSM-IV)
  childhood disorder classifications, 16
  diagnostic criteria, 17
    anorexia nervosa, 683–684, 684*t*
    Asperger's disorder, 408–409, 410
    attention-deficit/hyperactivity disorder, 72, 73–75, 74*t*, 109
    autistic disorder, 408–409, 410–413, 411*f*
    bulimia nervosa, 685, 685*t*
    childhood disintegrative disorder, 408–409, 410
    disruptive behavior disorders, 131
    dissociative disorders, 588
    dysthymic disorder, 200, 202*t*
    major depressive episode, 200, 201*t*
    oppositional defiant disorder, 628, 628*t*
    parent–child relational problem, 627
    for physically ill children, 484
    posttraumatic stress disorder, 584, 603
    psychological factors affecting medical conditions, 485, 485*t*
    Rett's disorder, 408–409, 410
    substance abuse, 720–721, 721*t*, 724*t*
    substance dependence, 720–721, 721*t*, 722*t*
    substance-related disorders, 720–721, 721*t*
Global Assessment of Relational Functioning Scale, 627–628
Diagnostic Checklist for Behavior—Disturbed Children, 421–423
Diagnostic Interview for Children and Adolescents (DICA)
  in behavioral–systems approach, 40
  for conduct problems, 145, 146
  for fears/anxieties, 258
  Revised Version, 393, 555*t*
Diagnostic Interview Schedule for Children (DISC)
  for attention-deficit/hyperactivity disorder, 92
  for child abuse/neglect, 587
  child version, 145
  for conduct problems, 145
  for depression, 211–212, 211*t*
  parent version, 145
  for substance use problems, 736
  teacher version, 145
  version 2.3, 393
Diagnostic Interview Schedule for Children—Revised, 40
Diagnostic Interview Schedule—Version IIIA, 258
Diagnostic overshadowing, 393
Diagnostic Survey for Eating Disorders (DSED), 698
Diaries, for pain assessment, 496–497
Diet, attention-deficit/hyperactivity disorder and, 87
Digital pulse monitor, 251
Direct Home Observation, 245, 281*t*
Direct observations. *See* Observation, direct
DISC. *See* Diagnostic Interview Schedule for Children
Discipline
  parental self-ratings, 37
  social development and, 341–342

Discomfort, 494. *See also* Pain
Disease status, psychological adjustment to chronic illness and, 486–487
Disengagement, 669–673
Disinhibition
  in attention-deficit/hyperactivity disorder, 75–76
  pedophilia and, 577
Disorganized attachment, conduct problems and, 136
Dispositional variables, in assessment of anxieties/fears, 257–258
Disruptive behavior disorders, 131
Dissociative disorders, of sexual abuse victims, 588–589, 607–608, 610, 608*t*–609*t*
Distortions, direct observations of, 42
Distractibility, 71
Diuretic abuse, 693, 695
Dolls, use in sex abuse investigation interviews, 595–596
Dopamine, autistic disorder and, 415
Down syndrome, 380–381. *See also* Mental retardation
DPICS. *See* Dyadic Parent–Child Interaction Coding System
DQ (developmental quotient), 381, 383
Dreams, trauma-related, 584
Drug Abuse Screening Test (DAST), 171
Drug use. *See under* Substance use problems
DSED (Diagnostic Survey for Eating Disorders), 698
DSM-II (*Diagnostic and Statistical Manual of Mental Disorders*-II), 72
DSM-III. *See Diagnostic and Statistical Manual of Mental Disorders*-III
DSM-III-R *See Diagnostic and Statistical Manual of Mental Disorders*-III-R
DSM-IV. *See Diagnostic and Statistical Manual of Mental Disorders*-IV
DST (dexamethasone suppression test), 217
Dunedin Multidisciplinary Health Study, 139
Dyadic Adjustment Scale (DAS), 172, 547, 547*t*, 667
Dyadic Parent–Child Interaction Coding System (DPICS)
  for home observations, 159
  version II, 153, 156, 158, 177
Dysthymic disorder (DD), 200, 201

Early Independence: A Developmental Curriculum, 391, 391*t*
Early Screening Project, 177
Eating Attitudes Test (EAT), 688, 700, 701
Eating Disorder Examination (EDE), 698
Eating disorders. *See also* Anorexia nervosa; Bulimia nervosa
  assessment, 692–698
    of family, 701–705
    instruments for, 698–701
    in young children, 701
  body image disturbances in, 696

cultural factors, 705–706
in ethnic groups, 688–689
future direction, 706–707
of males, 688–689
models
biological, 689–690
cognitive-behavioral, 690–692
psychodynamic, 690
Eating Disorders Inventory (EDI),
696, 700
ECBI (Eyberg Child Behavior
Inventory), 150–151, 152, 153
Echobehavioral assessment, of autistic
disorder, 431–432, 434, 433f,
434t
Echolalia
delayed, 413
immediate, 412
Ecologically oriented systems model, 5
EDE (Eating Disorder Examination),
698
EDI (Eating Disorder Inventory), 696,
700
Educable mentally retarded (EMR),
372
Education, for mentally retarded
persons, 369, 378
Education for All Handicapped
Children Act of 1975 (P.L. 94–
142), 369, 370, 377–378, 489
Education of the Handicapped Act
Amendments (P.L. 99–457),
369, 370, 378
Electroencephalography (EEG), of
autistic disorder, 415
Electrolyte abnormalities, in eating
disorders, 693
Emotional abnormalities, in autistic
disorder, 414–415
Emotional congruence, pedophilia
and, 576–577
Emotional Disorders Rating Scale,
395, 395t
Emotional Problems Scales: Behavior
Rating Scales, 395, 395t
Employment
of mentally retarded persons, 373
substance use problems and, 740
EMR (educable mentally retarded), 372
Encephalitis, 461
Enhanced reinforcement, adolescent
substance use and, 730–731,
731f
Enmeshment, assessment of, 669–673
Environmental factors
in brain injury, 474, 474t
in depression, 219–220
in mental retardation, 375t, 376
Epilepsy
autistic disorder and, 415
classifications, 462
treatment, 462–463
Ethical issues, in attention-deficit/
hyperactivity disorder, 114–115
Ethnic groups
eating disorders in, 688–689
substance use prevalence in, 719,
719t, 720t
Executive functions
in attention-deficit/hyperactivity
disorder, 77, 79–82, 80f
in brain injury, 472–473
defined, 77
Experience Sampling Method, 661–
662, 701

Eyberg Child Behavior Inventory
(ECBI), 150–151, 152, 153

Faces Affect Scale, 291t
FACES II (Family Adaptability and
Cohesion Evaluation Scales II),
612, 672
FACES III (Family Adaptability and
Cohesion Evaluation Scales
III), 664t, 670–672, 675, 704
Faces—Subjective Units of Disturbance, 285t
Faces Test of Anxiety, 288t
Factitious disorders, 484–485
FAIF (Functional Analysis Interview
Form), 439–442, 440f
Failure-to-thrive (FTT), 529
Fairness, parent–adolescent conflict
and, 655
Family
adaptability, in sexual abuse cases,
612–613
adjustment, in child abuse, 546–547
alcohol misuse in, adolescent
substance use and, 727–728
assessment. See Family assessments
coalitions, 667–669
conflict. See Conflict, parent–
adolescent
dysfunctional, eating-disordered
children and, 703
history/background
in child abuse, 545–546
in parental interviews, 91–92
of substance abuse, 727–728
interaction patterns
in sexual abuse cases, 612–613
in social relationship deficits, 355
maltreating
assessment of, 542
demographic characteristics of,
526–526
of mentally retarded persons, 392,
400–401, 401t
peer relations and, 343–344
contributions, models of, 341–
344
cultural influences on, 343–344
psychological adjustment of child to
chronic illness and, 487, 489
stress, in child abuse, 547–548
structure
changes in, 523
child maltreatment and, 527
support, in child abuse, 547–548
triangulation, assessment, 667–669
variables in assessment of anxieties/
fears, 258–259
Family Adaptability and Cohesion
Evaluation Scales II (FACES
II), 612, 672
Family Adaptability and Cohesion
Evaluation Scales III (FACES
III), 664t, 670–672, 675, 704
Family Alliances Coding System, 653,
663t, 669
Family Assessment Measure-3R, 259
Family assessments
for autistic disorder, 434–438
in behavioral–systems assessment,
46–48
for childhood depression, 219
in chronic illness, 490–494, 491t
of communication patterns

alternative approaches for, 654
observational, 649f-651t, 652–654
questionnaires, 645, 647, 652,
648t–651t
for conduct problems, 166–176
for eating disorders, 701–705
nonstandardized instruments,
704–705
standardized instruments, 703–
704
levels of, 46–47
of mediators of sexual abuse
sequelae, 610–613
for parent–adolescent conflict, 629–
631, 630t
for substance use problems, 738–739
Family Beliefs Inventory (FBI), 656–
657
Family Environment Scale (FES)
in child abuse assessment, 547t
cohesion subscale, 664t
in eating disorders, 703–704
family communication patterns and,
645, 648t
in parent–adolescent conflict, 632–
633, 645, 648t, 672, 675
in sexual abuse, 612
in substance use problems, 739
Family Events List (FEL), 174
Family History Research Diagnostic
Criteria, 258
Family Inventory of Resources for
Management, 490
Family Process Code, 157
Family systems, 5
Family therapy, cognitive-behavioral,
behavioral–systems assessment
and, 7
Fast Track School Observation
Program, 161
Father
alcoholic, ASB Checklist and, 171
incestuous
characteristics of, 576–577
research on, 577–578
of mentally retarded children, 392
FBI (Family Beliefs Inventory), 656–
657
Fear and Avoidance Hierarchy
Ratings, 249, 301t
Fear Frequency and Avoidance Survey
Schedule for Children, 254,
325t
Fear Inventory for Fire Safety, 249,
284t
Fear-related verbalizations, 285t, 297t,
313t
Fears
age of acquisition, 239
age trends, 236–237
assessment instruments
age-related variations and, 260–
261
classification/review of, 241–242
dispositional variables and, 257–
258
evaluation/selection of, 252–255
familial variables in, 258–259
limitations of, 260
listing of, 279t–327t
mechanical methods, 251
observational methods, 242–247
self-report methods, 247–251
treatment considerations and,
255–257

Fears (*continued*)
  behavior therapy and, 230
  classification schemes, 231–234,
    241–242
  clinical. *See* Phobias
  co-occurrence, 238
  defined, 231, 234
  developmental considerations, 235–
    240
  incidence, 235–236
  individual differences, 237–238
  motoric responses, 234–235, 235*t*
  physiological responses, 234–235,
    235*t*
  problematic, 240–241
  prognosis, 238–239
  as reaction to other problems, 241
  seriousness of, 239–240
  subjective responses, 234–235, 235*t*
  symptoms, 231
  treatment
    alternatives, 241
    compound interventions, 257
    contingency management, 256–
      257
    costs of, 241
    decision-making for, 240–241
    modeling, 256
    prolonged exposure, 256
    recommendations for, 259–262
    self-management, 257
    systematic desensitization, 255–
      256
  vs. anxieties, 231
Fear Strength Questionnaire, 245, 282*t*
Fear Survey for Children With and
    Without Mental Retardation,
    325*t*, 395*t*, 396
Fear Survey Schedule for Children
  description of, 249, 320*t*
  revised version, 318*t*–319*t*
  version II, 323*t*
Fear thermometer, 280*t*, 282*t*, 289*t*
Feelings and Emotions Experienced
    during Sexual Abuse
    (FEEDSA), 605–606
FEL (Family Events List), 174
Females
  conduct problems and, 139–140
  sex offenders, 576
FES. *See* Family Environment Scale
Fetal malnutrition, mental retardation
    and, 376
Financial burden, of chronic illness,
    490–491
Finger pulse volume, 279*t*, 308*t*
Fire, fear of, 284*t*
Fire Incident Analysis, 146
Fire Safety/Prevention Knowledge
    Interview, 146
Firesetting History Screen, 146
Firesetting Risk Interview, 146
Flooding, 256
Food additive, attention-deficit/
    hyperactivity disorder and, 87
Forehand observation system
  coding, for home setting, 159
  for conduct problems, 154, 156,
    159, 177
  parent observation procedure for,
    163
Forethought, 81
Formal testing, with children, 48
Fragile X syndrome, 373, 380
Friendship Qualities Scale, 354, 354*t*
Friendship Questionnaire, 357*t*

Friendships
  assessment of, 353–354, 354*t*
  changing, substance use problems
    and, 740
  commitment and, 339
  developmental functions, 338
  reciprocity and, 339
  social needs and, 338
  social relationship deficits and, 338–
    340
  supportive, 345
FTT (failure-to-thrive), 529
Functional Analysis Interview Form
    (FAIF), 439–442, 440*f*
Functional Disability Inventory, 487,
    488*t*

Gastrointestinal disturbances, in
    bulimia nervosa, 693
GCS (Glasgow Coma Scale), 455–456
Gender differences
  in adolescent reasoning, 656
  in childhood assessments, 24
  in conduct problems, 139–140
  in depressive symptoms, 200–203
  in peer relations, 331–332
  of sexual abuse victims, 572
General Anxiety Scale, 319*t*–320*t*
Generalized Anxiety Disorder, 233
Genetic factors
  in attention-deficit/hyperactivity
    disorder, 88
  in autistic disorder, 415
  in brain injury, 454*t*, 459–460
  counseling, for mental retardation,
    376
Gesell Developmental Schedules, 381,
    383, 382*t*
Girls. *See* Females
Glasgow Coma Scale (GCS), 455–456
Global Anxiety Rating, 287*t*, 298*t*
Global-inferential systems, 653
Global Mood Scale, 246, 291*t*
Global ratings
  for fears/anxieties, 246, 248
  for pain assessment, 497
Global Self-Rating, 298*t*
Goldberg Anorectic Attitude Scale,
    699
Gordon Diagnostic System, 103, 104
Gratification, deferred, 83
Guardianship/custody, of ADHD
    child, 114

Halstead–Reitan Neuropsychological
    Test Battery, 464, 465*t*
*Handbook of Family Measurement
    Techniques*, 46
Harter Dimensions of Depression
    Profile for Children and
    Adolescents, 555*t*
Harter Self-Perception Profile for
    Children, 554*t*
Harter Social Support Scale for
    Children, 554*t*
Hawaii Early Learning Profile, 390,
    391*t*
Headaches, 495
Head injury
  mechanical, 457
  mental retardation and, 375*t*
  traumatic, 454*t*, 455–457
    mechanism, 455
    outcome issues, 456

  pathophysiology, 455
  severity, 455–456
Health behaviors, causes of death and,
    481, 481*t*
Health care insurance, 482
Health care provider behavior,
    treatment adherence and, 505–
    506, 506*t*, 507*t*
Health-related disorders. *See also
    specific disorders*
  assessment
    behavioral, 506, 508
    current models of, 483–484, 484*f*
  causes of death and, 481, 481*t*
  chronic illness. *See* Chronic illness
  diagnostic classification, 484–486
  disease-specific functioning, 494
  illness knowledge and, 498–499
  pain/discomfort and, 494–498
  treatment adherence/compliance
    and, 499, 501, 503–506, 500*t*–
    501*t*, 502*f*, 506*t*, 507*t*
  general functioning
    of family, 490–494, 491*t*
    of patient, 486–487, 489–490,
      488*t*
Hearing impairment, in mentally
    retarded patients, 381, 383*t*,
    385
Heart rate monitoring
  with blood pressure monitoring,
    310*t*
  for fears/anxieties assessment, 279*t*,
    280*t*, 284*t*, 289*t*, 294*t*, 296*t*
  for school anxiety, 308*t*, 310*t*
  for social/stranger interaction, 303*t*–
    304*t*
Heights, fear of, 284*t*
Heredity, intelligence and, 370, 376
Herpes simplex encephalitis, 461
HICOMP Preschool Curriculum, 390,
    391*t*
Hindsight, 81
Hiskey–Nebraska Test of Learning
    Aptitude, 383*t*, 385
Hispanics, substance use prevalence,
    719, 719*t*, 720*t*
History of Victimization Form (HVF),
    593, 594*t*
Histrionic personality disorder, 687
Home observation
  in behavioral–systems approach, 45
  in child abuse/neglect, 547*t*, 548
  of conduct problems, 159–160
  of mental retardation, 387*t*, 388,
    396, 397, 398*f*
Home Observation for Measurement
    of the Environment (HOME)
  in child abuse/neglect, 547*t*, 548
  in mental retardation, 387*t*, 388
Home Quality Rating Scale, effect of
    autistic child on family, 436
Home-Related Anxiety, 306*t*
Home Situations Questionnaire
    (HSQ)
  for attention-deficit/hyperactivity
    disorder, 94, 95*t*, 99, 112
  for conduct problems, 142
  for substance use problems, 111
Honig v. Doe, 378
Hospital Fears Rating Scale, 289*t*
Hospital Fears Schedule, 285*t*
Hospital Scenes, 292*t*
Hostility, of abusive parents, 550
HPA axis (hypothalamic–pituitary–
    adrenal axis), 217

HPT axis (hypothalamic–pituitary–thyroid axis), 217
HSQ. *See* Home Situations Questionnaire; Hunger–Satiety Questionnaire
Hunger–Satiety Questionnaire (HSQ), 699
HVF (History of Victimization Form), 593, 594*t*
Hydrocephalus, 415, 458–459
Hyperactive Behavior Code, 105
Hyperactive–impulsive behavior, in attention-deficit/hyperactivity disorder, 75–76
Hyperactivity. *See also* Attention-Deficit/Hyperactivity Disorder
assessment, 104–105
conduct problems and, 135
Hypoconnection syndrome, 375*t*
Hypothalamic–pituitary–adrenal axis (HPA axis), 217
Hypothalamic–pituitary–thyroid axis (HPT axis), 217
Hypothesis testing, 13
Hypoxia, mental retardation and, 376

IAB (*Interview for Antisocial Behavior*), 150, 152
IBC (*Interaction Behavior Code*), 638*t*, 643–644, 650*t*, 653–654
ICD-10. *See International Classification of Diseases*
IC (Issues Checklist), 631–632
IDED (Interview for Diagnosis of Eating Disorders), 698
IEP (Individualized education program), 370, 378
IES (Impact of Event Scale), 610, 611
Illness
chronic. *See* Chronic illness
fear of, 285*t*
Image Clarity Scale, 255
Impact of Event Scale (IES), 610, 611
Impact on Family Scale, 490
Implosion, 256
Impulse control
assessment of, 103–104
poor, 71
Impulsive behavior, 660
Inattention, in attention-deficit/hyperactivity disorder, 71, 75, 115
Inborn error of metabolism, mental retardation and, 375*t*
Incest, offender characteristics, 576–577
Individualized education program (IEP), 370, 378
Individuals with Disabilities in Education Act (P.L. 101–476), 90, 114, 369, 378
Infant–caregiver attachment, child maltreatment during infancy and, 528–529
Infant Characteristics Questionnaire, 164, 553*t*
Infant Mullen Scales of Early Learning, 382*t*, 383
Infants
mentally retarded
assessment of, 381–384, 382–383*t*
interventions for, 378
neuropsychological assessment, 463–464
temperament assessment, 164–165

Infection, mental retardation and, 375*t*, 376
Insecure attachment
conduct problems and, 135–136
infant–caregiver, child maltreatment and, 528–529
Institutions, mental retardation, 369, 370
Insularity, 138
Intelligence, heredity and, 370, 376
Intelligence tests. *See also* IQ tests
autistic disorder and, 428–430
for brain-injured patients, 471
history of, 370
INTER-ACT, 259
Interaction Behavior Code (IBC), 638*t*, 643–644, 650*t*, 653–654
International Classification of Diseases (ICD-10)
diagnostic criteria, autistic disorder, 410–411
diagnostic guidelines
for anorexia nervosa, 684, 684*t*
for bulimia nervosa, 685–686, 685*t*
Interpersonal behavior
assessment
of child abuse victims, 552–553, 553*t*
in depression, 219
problems, in attention-deficit/hyperactivity disorder, 86
Interpersonal Process Code (IPC), 153–154, 156–157, 158*t*, 159
Interpersonal sensitivity, 550
Interpersonal skills, assessment, in ADHD, 100, 102
Interview for Antisocial Behavior (IAB), 150, 152
Interview for Diagnosis of Eating Disorders (IDED), 698
Interviews. *See also specific interviews*
in behavioral–systems assessment, 39–41
of adults, 33–35
generality/flexibility of, 34
purpose of, 34
reliability/validity of, 34–35
child
in abuse/neglect assessment, 548–550, 555*t*
in attention-deficit/hyperactivity disorder, 95–96
in conduct problems, 143–144
semistructured, 40–41
structured, 40–41
unstructured, 39–40
for conduct problem assessment, 141–147
for depression assessment, 213–216
for eating disorders, 693
for fears/anxieties assessment, 246–247
dental fear, 296*t*–297*t*
self-reports, 247–248
for mental retardation diagnosis, 393–394
parental
in ADHD assessment, 91–95, 94*t*, 95*t*
behavioral probes and, 91
in behavioral–systems assessment, 33–35
in child abuse assessment, 549
in child abuse cases, 545–548, 546*t*, 547*t*

in conduct problems assessment, 141–142, 143*f*
demographic data for, 91
developmental issues in, 91
family history in, 91–92
format for, 94*t*
in temperament assessment, 164
for sex abuse investigations, 593–598
accuracy of child's recall and, 593–595
dolls/props usage for, 595–596
guidelines for, 596–597
interpreting, 597–598
recording, 597–598
types of questions for, 595
structured
with children, 40–41
for conduct problems, 145–147
for depression diagnosis, 208–212, 209*t*–211*t*
teacher
for ADHD assessment, 96–97
in conduct problems, 144–145
unstructured, 39–40
Interview Schedule for Children, 40
Intimate Friendship Scale, 354*t*
Intoxication, substance-induced, 721*t*
Intravascular hemorrhage (IVH), 457
IOWA Conners Teacher Rating Scale, 150
Iowa Family Interaction Rating Scales
communication categories, 651*t*
description of, 642–643
problem-solving categories, 637*t*–638*t*
IPC (Interpersonal Process Code), 153–154, 156–157, 158*t*, 159
IQ tests, 374
autistic disorder and, 412, 414
for brain-injured patients, 471
in mental retardation, 381–385, 382*t*
mental retardation and, 371–372, 373, 374, 378–379
in psychiatric disorders, 376–377
Stanford–Binet, 380
Issues Checklist (IC), 631–632
IVH (intravascular hemorrhage), 457

Judicial system, sexual abuse allegations and, 575–576

K-ABC (Kaufman Assessment Battery for Children), 382*t*, 383–384, 388
Kanner syndrome, 409, 409*t*, 421, 422
KASTAN (Children's Attributional Style Questionnaire), 610
Kaufman Assessment Battery for Children (K-ABC), 382*t*, 383–384, 388
Kid's Eating Disorders Survey, 701
Knowledge
chronic illness, assessment of, 498–499
deficit, as treatment adherence barrier, 504
K-SADS. *See* Schedule for Affective Disorders and Schizophrenia for School-Age Children

Labeling, diagnostic, 3, 16, 20–21
Laboratory tests/measures, for ADHD assessment, 102–105

Ladder climb, 284t
Language
  assessment, of mentally retarded
    child, 382t–383t, 384–385
  development, of maltreated
    children, 530–531
  developmental disorders, 418
  metaphorical, of autistic children, 413
  motor control/fluency, behavioral
    inhibition and, 80f, 82
  reconstitution, behavioral inhibition
    and, 80f, 82
  speech internalization, behavioral
    inhibition and, 80f, 81
Larry P. v. Riles 1974, 371
Laxative abuse, 693, 695
Lead poisoning, mental retardation
  and, 373–374, 393
Learned helplessness model, 585, 586
Learning disabilities, 166
Learning problems, behavior-systems
  assessment and, 24–25
Learning skills assessment, of brain-
  injured patients, 471–472
Legal issues
  accountability of ADHD children,
    115
  attention-deficit/hyperactivity
    disorder, 114–115
  of mental retardation, 377–379
Leiter International Performance
  Scale, 383t, 429
Lesch–Nyhan syndrome, 377
LES (Life Experiences Survey), 173–
  174
Leyton Obsessional Inventory—Child
  Version, 321t–322t
Life Events Checklist for Children,
  549
Life Experiences Survey (LES), 173–
  174
Living in Family Environments
  (LIFE), 661
Locke–Wallace Marital Adjustment
  Test, 667
Locomotor activity, mechanical
  recordings of, 105
Loneliness Scale, 357t
Louisville Behavior Checklist, 36, 206
Louisville Fear Survey Schedule, 318t
Luria–Nebraska Neuropsychological
  Battery: Children's Revision,
  386t, 388

MAAQ (Mother–Adolescent Attribu-
  tion Questionnaire), 657–658
McCarthy Scales of Children's
  Abilities, 382t, 383, 388, 463
McMaster Clinical Rating Scale, 643
McMaster Family Assessment Device,
  635, 636t, 649t
MACS (Metro Assessment of Child
  Satisfaction), 506t
Major Depressive Disorder (MDD),
  200, 201
Major Depressive Episode (MDE),
  200, 201t, 203
Maladaptive behaviors, mental
  retardation with, 376–377
Males
  as child abuse perpetrators,
    fatalities, 527
  sex offenders
    convicted, 576–577
    vs. female offenders, 576

Malicious intent, parent–adolescent
  conflict and, 655
Malnutrition, mental retardation and,
  375t
Maltreatment, child, 523. *See also*
  Child abuse; Neglect
  in adolescence, 534–536
  assessment
    conceptual model for, 536–541
    of maltreated child, 544
    of maltreating parent, 543–544
    purposes of, 542–543, 543t
    unique aspects of, 541–542
  behavioral dimension
    in early childhood, 529–530
    in middle childhood, 531–532
  cognitive/social-cognitive dimension
    in early childhood, 530–531
    in middle childhood, 532–533
  demographic characteristics, 526–
    527
  developmental psychopathology
    and, 527–536
  impaired development risk and,
    524–527
  incidence, 525–526
  maltreating parents in, characteris-
    tics of, 538–541
  profile, statistical, 525–526
  proximal events and, 537–538
  socioemotional dimension
    in early childhood, 531
    in middle childhood, 533–534
Manifest disability assessment, 468–
  470, 469t
Marital Adjustment Test (MAT),
  172
Marital relationship, parental
  adjustment
    assessment of, 169–173
    in child abuse, 546–547
    conduct problems of children
      and, 137–138, 169–170
  distress/conflict
    attention-deficit/hyperactivity
      disorder and, 109
    child physical abuse and, 538
    conduct problems of children
      and, 137, 141–142
    impact of child's chronic illness on
      negative, 491–492
      positive, 493–494
Marital Satisfaction Inventory (MSI),
  663t, 666, 667
Marlowe–Crowne Social Desirability
  Scale, 635, 639
MAS (Motivation Assessment Scale),
  438–439, 439t
Mastery, chronic illness and,
  493–494
Matching Familiar Figures Test
  (MFFT), 103, 104
Matching Familiar Figures Test with
  20 stimulus sets (MFFT20),
  103
Maternal Anxiety Rating, 285t
Math Anxiety Questionnaire, 312t
MAT (Marital Adjustment Test), 172
Matson Evaluation of Social Skills
  with Youngsters (MESSY), 108,
  351, 351t
Maudsley Obsessional–Compulsive
  Inventory, 323t
MBD (minimal brain damage), 71
MCIS (Mother–Child Interaction
  Scale), 559

MDD (Major Depressive Disorder),
  200, 201
MDE (Major Depressive Episode),
  200, 201t, 203
Measure of Adolescent Social
  Performance, 553t
Mechanical methods, for fears/
  anxieties assessment, 254–255
Mediational chains, substance use
  problems and, 729–731, 730f
Medicaid, 482
Medical history, in conduct problems,
  164
Medical procedures
  fear of, 285t–297t
  therapeutic, pain associated with, 495
Memory assessment, for brain-injured
  patients, 471–472
Memory for Objects, 255
Meningomyelocele, 458
Menstrual disturbances, with eating
  disorders, 693–694
Mental health, substance use problems
  and, 739
Mental Health Assessment Form for
  School-Age Children, 40
Mental retardation
  assessment, 369, 379–381, 379f
    of academic achievement, 385–
      387, 386t
    of adaptive behavior, 388–390,
      389t
    behavioral observations for, 396–
      397, 398f
    of cognitive functioning, 381–
      385, 382t–383t
    of community resources, 397–
      399, 400
    criterion-based, 390–391, 391t
    disorder-specific knowledge for,
      380
    feedback from, 400
    functional, 397, 398f
    information sources for, 379–380
    of language, 382t–383t, 384–385
    mental *vs.* chronological age in,
      394–395
    of motor impairment, 382t–383t,
      384
    of neuropsychological function-
      ing, 386t–387t, 388
    of perceptual–motor skills, 386t,
      387
    of psychiatric problems in, 392–
      396, 395t
    of psychosocial factors, 391–392
    referral for, 379
    results, integration of, 399–400
    strategies for, 380
    of vision, 383t, 384–385
  causes of, 374–376, 375t
  classifications, 370, 372–374, 373t
    etiological, 373–374, 375t, 376
    mild, 372, 373t, 394
    moderate, 372, 373t, 384, 394
    profound, 372, 373t, 384, 390,
      392, 394
    severe, 372, 373t, 390, 392
  comorbid conditions
    autistic disorder, 412, 413, 414
    psychiatric disorders, 376–377,
      377t
  definition of, 370–372, 374
  differential diagnosis, 417
  education, 369, 378
  historical perspective, 369–370

legal issues, 377–379
legislation, 369
perinatal onset of, 375*t*
postnatal onset of, 375*t*
prevalence, 374
state policies and, 377–379
Merrill–Palmer Scale, for autistic children, 429
MESSY (Matson Evaluation of Social Skills with Youngsters), 108, 351, 351*t*
Metabolic disorders, causing brain injury, 454*t*, 459–460
Metaphorical language, of autistic children, 413
Metro Assessment of Child Satisfaction (MACS), 506*t*
MFFT (Matching Familiar Figures Test), 103, 104
MFFT20 (Matching Familiar Figures Test with 20 stimulus sets), 103
Michigan Alcoholism Screening Test (SMAST), 171
MICS. *See* Modified Marital Interaction Coding System
Middle childhood, peer relations, normal, 330–331
Minimal brain damage (MBD), 71
Minnesota Multiphasic Personality Inventory (MMPI), 170, 206, 577–578
Missouri Children's Behavior Checklist, 36
MMPI (Minnesota Multiphasic Personality Inventory), 170, 206, 577–578
Modeling treatments, for fears/anxieties, 256
Modifiability of children, childhood assessments and, 24
Modified Cognition Checklist, 324*t*
Modified Marital Interaction Coding System (MICS)
communication categories, 649*t*
modified version, 641, 652
problem-solving categories, 636*t*
shortened version, 667
Modified Timed Behavior Checklist, 244, 280*t*
Mood Disorder, substance-induced, 721*t*
Moos Family Environment Scale, 436
Moral development/reasoning, child maltreatment and, 533
Mother
alcohol consumption by
ADHD in children and, 87–88
mental retardation from, 376
blame, in sex abuse cases, 579–580
history of child sexual abuse, 581
of mentally retarded children, 392
of paternally abused children, 580
reaction, to child's sexual abuse allegations, 581–582
Mother–Adolescent Attribution Questionnaire (MAAQ), 657–658
Mother–child interactions, mentally retarded children and, 397
Mother–Child Interaction Scale (MCIS), 559
Motivation Assessment Scale (MAS), 438–439, 439*t*
Motor control/fluency, behavioral inhibition and, 80*f*, 82

Motor-Free Visual Perception Test, 386*t*, 387
Motor skills assessment
for attention-deficit/hyperactivity disorder, 100, 102
for brain-injured patients, 471
MSI (Marital Satisfaction Inventory), 663*t*, 666, 667
Multiple-gating approach, for depression assessment, 222–223
Multiple Option Observation System for Experimental Studies, 161
Multivariate analysis, in behavioral–systems assessment, 18–19
Mutism
functional, 412
selective, 412
My Family and Friends, 357*t*

NABC (Normative Adaptive Behavior Checklist), 102
Narrative story stem technique, 554*t*, 555*t*, 556
National Association for Retarded Citizens, 370
National Center on Child Abuse and Neglect (NCCAN), 571
National Institute of Mental Health Diagnostic Interview Schedule for Children–Version 2.3, 258
Native Americans, substance use prevalence, 719, 719*t*, 720*t*
NCCAN (National Center on Child Abuse and Neglect), 571
Negative Affect Self-Statement Questionnaire, 325*t*–326*t*
Neglect
assessment, 523
conceptual model for, 536–541
implications for, 541
purposes of, 542–543, 543*t*
strategy for, 543*t*
unique aspects of, 541–542
death rates, 526
defined, 524–525
incidence, 525–526
in infancy, 528–529
in middle childhood
behavioral dimension of, 531–532
cognitive and social-cognitive dimension of, 532–533
socioemotional dimension of, 533–534
parental behavior and, 539
profile, statistical, 525–526
Neighborhood, peer relations and, 343–344
Neonatal Facial Coding System, 497
Network of Relationships Inventory, 354, 354*t*
Neural tube defects, 458
Neurofibromatosis
brain injury and, 460–461
mental retardation and, 375–376
Neurological abnormalities, in autistic disorder, 415–416
Neurological factors, in attention-deficit/hyperactivity disorder, 86–87
Neuropsychological assessment
biobehavioral systems approach
description of, 466–468, 467*f*
implementation of, 468–475, 469*t*, 470*t*, 474*t*

of brain injury, 463–464, 466, 465*t*, 466*t*, 475–476
of mental retardation, 386*t*–387*t*, 388
Neuropsychological Evaluation of Older Children, 386*t*, 388
Neurotoxins, attention-deficit/hyperactivity disorder and, 87–88
Nicotine withdrawal syndrome, 723*t*
Nighttime Coping Response Inventory, 283*t*
Nighttime Fear Inventory, 283*t*
Noncompliance
assessment, 140
in conduct problems, 133, 136
parental marital distress and, 172
Nonverbal cues, coding of, 44
Nonverbal learning disability syndrome, 471
Normative Adaptive Behavior Checklist (NABC), 102
Normative information, for childhood assessments, 25–26
Norm-referenced tests, 380, 381, 390
Nurse Ratings, 246, 295*t*

Obedience, parent–adolescent conflict and, 655
Obligatory runners, *vs.* anorexics, 686–687
Observation
of abused/neglected children, 553*t*, 555*t*
audiotape methods, 640–641, 658
in behavioral–systems assessment, 43–46
of brain-injured children, 454
codes
for ADHD assessment, 6, 105–106
category selection, 43–45
for problem-solving behavior assessment, 641
for social behavior assessment, 348, 349*t*
of conduct problems, 153–154, 156–164, 155*f*, 158*t*
costs of, 46
data, using and interpreting, 45–46
direct
for ADHD assessment, 105–108
in behavioral–systems assessment, 41–42
of classroom/playroom behavior, 105–106
exclusion from behavioral–systems assessment, 46
of families of sexually-abused children, 612–613
of fears/anxieties, 252–253
of parent–child interaction, 106–107
of social relationship deficits, 346
of family adaptability, communication and cohesion, 673
of family communication patterns, 649*t*–651*t*, 652–654
for fears/anxieties assessment, 242–247
behavioral avoidance tests, 242–243
checklists, 245–246
global ratings, 246
interviews, 246–247
rating systems, 243–245, 253

Observation (*continued*)
  home
    in behavioral–systems approach, 45
    of child abuse/neglect, 547*t*, 548
    of conduct problems, 159–160
    of mental retardation, 387*t*, 388, 396, 397, 398*f*
  for pain assessment, 497
  of parent–adolescent conflict, 633, 640–641, 658
    affect and, 661
    coalitions/triangulations in, 669
    problem-solving skills in, 636*t*–638*t*, 639–644
    parental teamwork, 667
  of parent–child interaction, in child abuse, 558–559
  settings for, 45
  for social behavior assessment, 348–350, 349*t*
  of socioemotional adjustment, of abused/neglected children, 556
  in substance use problems, 736
Observational Behavior Scale, 285*t*
Observational Scale of Behavioral Distress, 244, 287*t*
Observation of Classroom Behavior, 244, 245, 309*t*
Observation of Separation-Relevant Play, 243, 298*t*
Observation Scale of Behavioral Distress, 497
Observer Impressions Inventory, 157–158
Observer Rating of Anxiety, 287*t*
Observer Rating Scale of Anxiety, 243, 290*t*
Observer Ratings of Anxiety and Cooperation, 289*t*
Obsessive–compulsive disorder, 233, 687, 691
ODD. *See* Oppositional defiant disorder
O'Leary–Porter Scale (OPS), 172
Opioids withdrawal syndrome, 723*t*
Oppositional behaviors, noncompliance; argumentativeness, 130
Oppositional defiant disorder (ODD), 130
  assessment, 145–146, 165
  behaviors, 131
  comorbid conditions, 628
    attention-deficit/hyperactivity disorder, 88–89, 109, 131–132
    conduct problems, 152, 159
  diagnostic criteria, 628, 628*t*
  epidemiology, 130
  essential feature, 131
  family conflict and, 90
  parental, conduct problems and, 137
OPS (O'Leary–Porter Scale), 172
Oregon Project Curriculum for Visually Impaired and Blind Preschool Children, 390, 391*t*
Oregon Social Learning Center, 157–158
Overactivity, 71
Overall Reaction, 314*t*
Overt Hostility Scale, in substance use problems, 739
Oxygen deprivation, brain injury from, 457

PACS (Parent–Adolescent Communication Scale), 647, 648*t*, 652
PAI (Parenting Alliance Inventory), 173, 663*t*, 666–667
PAICS (Parent–Adolescent Interaction Coding System), 636*t*, 641, 649*t*
PAICS-R (Parent–Adolescent Interaction Coding System—Revised), 641
Pain
  assessment methods, 496–497
  chronic, 495–496
  of chronic illness, 494–495
  developmental issues, 497–498
  organic *vs.* psychogenic, 495
  pediatric, description of, 494
Pain Behavior Checklist, 497
Pain disorder, 485
Palmar sweat index, 251, 290*t*
Panic disorders, 233
Pantophobia, 231
Paraliphobia, 231
Parent–Adolescent Communication Scale (PACS), 647, 652, 648*t*
Parent–Adolescent Interaction Coding System (PAICS), 636*t*, 641, 649*t*
Parent–Adolescent Interaction Coding System—Revised (PAICS-R), 641
Parent–adolescent intervention, for attention-deficit/hyperactivity disorder, 112–113
Parent–Adolescent Relationship Questionnaire (PARQ)
  cohesion subscale, 672–673
  conventionalization scale, 632
  family communication patterns and, 649*t*, 652
  for irrational beliefs assessment, 657
  problem-solving subscale, 635, 636*t*
  skills deficits/overt conflict scale, 644
  structural subscales, 664*t*–665*t*
  triangulation subscale, 668
Parental Acceptance and Rejection Questionnaire, 547*t*
Parental Locus of Control Scale (PLOC), 169
Parental Problem-Solving Measure (PPSM), 557–558
Parent Anxiety Rating Scale—General, 317*t*
Parent Anxiety Rating Scale-Separation, 245–246, 297*t*
Parent Attitude Research Instrument, 37
Parent Attitudes Test, 36
Parent Attribution Test, 38
Parent–Child Dyadic Interactions, 553*t*
Parent–child interaction
  in ADHD, 93
  assessment, 8
  in attention-deficit/hyperactivity disorder, 106–107
  in child abuse, 557–559
  in Child's Game, 154, 156
  in conduct problems, 142
  observations, for mentally retarded children, 396
  parental alcohol problems and, 137
  in Parent's Game, 154, 155*f*, 156
  peer relations and, 342–343

sexual abuse and, 580
treatment adherence and, 504–505
Parent Daily Report (PDR), 162
Parent-Directed Interaction, 156, 160
Parent Impact Questionnaire, 610
Parenting
  child abuse/neglect and, 539, 557–558
  childhood fears/anxieties and, 259
  conduct problems and, 136, 166–168
  dysfunctional, adjustment of neglected adolescents and, 535
Parenting Alliance Inventory (PAI), 173, 663*t*, 666–667
Parenting Daily Hassles, 174
Parenting Scale (PS), 166, 167
Parenting Sense of Competence Scale (PSOC), 38, 169, 490
Parenting Stress Index (PSI)
  attention-deficit/hyperactivity disorder assessment and, 110
  autistic disorder assessment and, 435
  child abuse assessment and, 547*t*
  mental retardation assessment and, 392
  purpose of, 38
Parent Interview for Autism, 424–425
Parent management training programs, 37
Parent Observation Record, 497
Parent Opinion Survey, 38
Parent Practices Scale (PPS), 166–167
Parent Problem Checklist, 173
Parent Problem Solving Instrument, 38
Parents. *See also* Father; Mother
  abusive, inaccurate perceptions of children's behavior by, 539–540
  abusive/neglectful, assessment of, 550–556, 551*t*
  of ADHD children, 89, 112
  alcoholic, adolescent substance use and, 727–728
  assessment, of emotional regulation/symptomatology, 550–551
  as child abuse perpetrators, 527
  coalitions, assessment of, 667–669
  of conduct problem children, 136–137, 138
  conflict with adolescent. *See* Conflict, parent–adolescent
  depression, ADHD children and, 109–110
  extreme beliefs of, in parent–adolescent conflict, 655
  insensitivity of, 342
  interviews of. *See* Interviews, parental
  maltreating, 536
    assessment issues for, 543–544
    characteristics of, 538–541
  marital relationship of. *See* Marital relationship, parental
  of mentally retarded children, 392
    assessment feedback for, 400, 401*t*
  nonoffending, characteristics of, 579–582
  personal adjustment, assessment, in conduct problems, 169–170
  personal strain, from child's chronic illness, 492–493
  psychological distress, ADHD children and, 109–110

psychological distress, attention-deficit/hyperactivity disorder and, 109–110
psychopathology of, eating-disordered children and, 703
ratings, of child social behavior, 353
reports
  in attention-deficit/hyperactivity disorder assessment, 97–100, 98t, 99t
  behavioral checklists, parental agreement and, 36
  structured, about child behavior, 35–37
  of target behaviors, 36–37
satisfaction
  with clinic visit, 505, 507t
  with conduct problems treatment, 175–176
self-esteem assessment, in conduct problems, 169
self-reports, for ADHD assessment, 108–110
social cognitions, assessment in conduct problems, 168–169
stress. *See* Stress, parental
teamwork, assessment of, 662–663
  alternative approaches, 667
  observational, 667
  questionnaire, 665–666
training, autistic disorder treatment and, 437
Parent Satisfaction Scale, 38
Parents' Consumer Satisfaction Questionnaire (PCSQ), 176
Parent self-ratings, in behavioral-systems assessment, 37–39
Parent Self-Report, 258
Parent's Game, 154, 155f, 156, 159, 160
Parent training programs, ADHD, 112
PARQ. *See* Parent–Adolescent Relationship Questionnaire
Passive behavioral avoidance test, 301t
PCSQ (Parents' Consumer Satisfaction Questionnaire), 176
PDR (Parent Daily Report), 162
Peabody Individual Achievement Test—Revised (PIAT-R), 385, 386t, 387
Peabody Picture Vocabulary Test—Revised (PPVT-R), 382t, 384
Pediatric Inventory of Neurobehavioral Symptoms, 473
Pediatric Pain Questionnaire, 496
Pediatric Recovery Room Rating Scale, 293t
Pedophiles, characteristics, 576–577
Peer Interaction and Avoidance, 302t–303t
Peer relations
  acceptance, treatment adherence and, 505
  assessment, implications of, 338
  in chronic illness, 490
  close relationships, assessment of, 353–354, 354t
  conduct problems and, 165
  deviant groups, conduct problems and, 138, 139
  dimensions of, 329
  family contributions, models of, 341–344
  friendships, 338–340

group dynamics, 340–341, 354–355
group status, 329
  acceptance, developmental functions of, 338
  alternatives to negative nominations, 347
  friendships and, 339–340
  sociometric nominations and, 346–347
  teacher estimates of, 348
  impaired, 328
  measures, for ADHD assessment, 108
  network characteristics and, 340–341
  normative trends, 330–332
  parent–child relationships and, 342–343
  positive, in promoting adaptive social development, 328, 330
  ratings, of social behavior, 352–353
rejections, 329
  age and, 336–338
  aggression and, 333–334
  assessment of, 346–347
  close friendships and, 339
  consequences of, 340–341
  cultural differences and, 336–338
  gender differences and, 336–338
  social cognitions and, 344–345
  social withdrawal and, 334–336
  vs. neglect, 333
  research, 328–329
  self perceptions, 345
  in social–emotional development, 328–329
  substance use problems and, 728–729, 740
Peer Relations Inventory (PRI), 552–553, 553t
PEI (Pupil Evaluation Inventory), 352
PEP (Psychoeducational Profile), 430
Perceived Competence Scale for Children, 356, 357t
Perceived Social Support Questionnaire, in child abuse assessment, 547t
Perception
  abnormalities, in autistic disorder, 414
  assessment, of brain-injured children, 471
Perceptual–motor tests, 386t, 387
Perfectionism, parent–adolescent conflict and, 655
Perinatal trauma, 456–457
Persistence, goal-directed, 82–83
Personal Experience Inventory, 738
Personal Experience Screening Questionnaire (PESQ), 735t
Personality
  of maltreating parent, 539
  substance use problems and, 726–727
Personality Inventory for Children, 97–98, 259
Personal Report of Confidence as a Speaker, 309t
Pervasive developmental disorders, 410
PESQ (Personal Experience Screening Questionnaire), 735t
Phobias. *See also* Fears
  anorexia nervosa and, 687
  defined, 231
  types of, 231

Phobophobia, 231
Physical abuse, of child. *See* Child abuse
Physical health, substance use problems and, 740
Physiochemical assessment, of pain, 497
PIAT-R (Peabody Individual Achievement Test—Revised), 385, 386t, 387
Pictorial Test of Intelligence, 382t, 384–385, 429
Plasticity, childhood assessments and, 24
Play assessment methods, for sexuality problems, 606–607
Playground Code, 157
Play group observations, 350
Playroom behaviors, direct observation of, 105–106
PLOC (Parental Locus of Control Scale), 169
POSIT (Problem Oriented Screening Instrument for Teenagers), 735t
Posthospital Behavior Questionnaire, 292t
Posttraumatic amnesia (PTA), 456
Posttraumatic stress disorder (PTSD)
  anxiety and, 233
  assessment, CBCL-PTSD Scale, 602, 602t–605t
  child physical abuse and, 535–536
  reexperiencing/avoidance aspects of, 584–585
  symptoms
    assessment of, 599–603, 605–606, 600t–605t, 613
    parental evaluation of, 602–603, 605
    professional evaluation of, 602–603, 605
  in sexual abuse victims, attributional style and, 586
  of sexually abused children, 582, 583
  type I, 584
  type II, 584, 586–590
Poverty, child maltreatment and, 527
PPSM (Parental Problem-Solving Measure), 557–558
PPS (Parent Practices Scale), 166–167
PPVT-R (Peabody Picture Vocabulary Test—Revised), 382t, 384
Prader–Willi syndrome, 393
Pragmatics, in autistic disorder, 412
Predelinquent behavior, in ADHD, 85–86
Preemptive processing, 344
Pregnancy, of sexual abuse victims, 591
Prematurity, mental retardation and, 376
Prenatal infectious disorders, 461
Preschool Behavior Questionnaire, 351, 351t, 395, 395t, 396
Preschool children
  maltreatment of, 529–531
  mentally retarded
    cognitive functioning assessments of, 381–384, 382t–383t
    criterion-based assessments for, 390–391, 391t
    interventions for, 378
    mother–child interactions and, 397

Preschool children (*continued*)
  neuropsychological assessment,
    463–464
  peer relations, normal, 330
Preschool Observational Scale of
    Anxiety, 243, 244–245, 297*t*
Preschool Socioaffective Profile, 305*t*
Prescriptive Behavioral Checklist of
    the Severely and Profoundly
    Retarded, 391, 391*t*
PRI (Peer Relations Inventory), 552–
    553, 553*t*
PRIDS (Parental Reaction to Incest
    Disclosure Scale), 611
Problem Guidesheet, 142, 143*f*
Problem Oriented Screening
    Instrument for Teenagers
    (POSIT), 735*t*
Procedural Behavior Rating Scale, 497
Procedure Behavioral Rating Scale,
    244, 287*t*
Procedure Behavior Checklist, 244,
    287*t*
Prodeclarative pointing, 412
Professionals, responses to sexual
    abuse allegations, 573–574
Professional service model, for mental
    retardation, 398
Prognosis, behavioral-systems
    assessment for, 12–13
Programmed Environments Curricu-
    lum, 391, 391*t*
Prolongation, behavioral inhibition
    and, 80–81, 80*f*
Pronominal reversal, 413
Property destruction, in Conduct
    Disorder, 131
Props, use in sex abuse investigation
    interviews, 595–596
Prostitution, sexual abuse victims and,
    591
Provocative victims, 340
PRSAN (Psychiatric Rating Scale for
    Anorexia Nervosa), 699
PS (Parenting Scale), 166, 167
PSI (Parenting Stress Index), 110,
    174–175, 392
PSOC (Parenting Sense of Compe-
    tence Scale), 169
Psychiatric disorders, with mental
    retardation, 376–377
  assessment of, 392–396, 395*t*
Psychiatric Rating Scale for Anorexia
    Nervosa (PRSAN), 699
Psychoeducational Profile (PEP), 430
Psychological adjustment, to chronic
    illness, 486–487, 488*t*, 489
Psychological factors, health status
    and, 483
Psychological Factors Affecting
    Medical Condition, 485, 485*t*
Psychological Screening Inventory, 40
Psychopathy
  assessment, with conduct problems,
    165–166
  associated/comorbid conditions,
    conduct problems, 134
  substance use problems and, 727
Psychopathy Screening Device, 165
Psychosis, childhood, 408
Psychosocial factors assessment, in
    mental retardation, 391–392
Psychosocial traits assessment, in brain
    injury, 473
Psychosomatic disorders, 483

Psychotic Disorder, substance-
    induced, 721*t*
PTA (posttraumatic amnesia), 456
PTSD. *See* Posttraumatic stress
    disorder
Public Law 94–142 (Education for All
    Handicapped Children Act of
    1975), 369, 370, 377–378, 489
Public Law 99–457 (Education of the
    Handicapped Act Amend-
    ments), 369, 370, 378
Public Law 101–476 (Individuals with
    Disabilities Education Act), 90,
    114, 369, 378
Pupil Evaluation Inventory (PEI),
    352
Purge behavior, assessment, 695–696
Purification promise, 691
Pyramid Scales, 391, 391*t*

QRS (Questionnaire on Resources and
    Stress), 435
Quality of Play Rating, 299*t*
Questionnaire on Resources and Stress
    (QRS), 392, 435
Questionnaires. *See also specific*
    questionnaires
  child-completed, 41
  of cognition, in parent–adolescent
    conflict, 656–658
  of family communication patterns,
    645, 647, 648*t*–651*t*, 652
  of parent–adolescent conflict
    affect and, 660–661
    coalitions/triangulations in, 668
    cohesion, 670–673
  of problem-solving skills, in parent–
    adolescent conflict, 635, 639,
    636*t*
  self-report, for fears/anxieties, 248–
    250
Questions, for sex abuse investiga-
    tional interview, 595

Race
  child physical abuse and, 526–527
  sexual abuse and, 572
  social relations assessment and,
    337–338
RADS (Reynolds Adolescent Depres-
    sion Scale), 204
RAPI (Rutgers Alcohol Problem
    Index), 735
Ratings of Anxiety and Cooperation,
    286*t*
Raven's Coloured Progressive
    Matrices, 429
RBPC (Revised Behavior Problem
    Checklist), 147, 149–150, 206
RCDS (Reynolds Child Depression
    Scale), 204
Real Life Rating Scale (RLRS), 428
Reciprocity, friendships and, 339
Reconstitution, behavioral inhibition
    and, 80*f*, 82
Recreational activities, substance use
    problems and, 740
Rehabilitation Act of 1973, 90, 114
Reitan–Indiana Neuropsychological
    Test Battery for Children, 386*t*,
    388
Reliability, of interviews, in behav-
    ioral–systems assessment, 34–35

Residential treatment, for ADHD,
    113–114
Respiration, 289*t*
Response classes, behavioral-systems
    assessment and, 15
Response-Class Matrix, 107
Reticence, 335
Rett's syndrome
  childhood psychosis and, 408–409,
    410
  differential diagnosis, 417
  stereotyped hand movements and,
    377, 393
Revised Behavior Problem Checklist
    (RBPC), 147, 149–150, 206
Revised Timed Behavior Checklist,
    244, 306*t*
Reye syndrome, 461
Reynolds Adolescent Depression Scale
    (RADS), 204
Reynolds Child Depression Scale
    (RCDS), 204
Risk moderators, adolescent substance
    use and, 731–732
Ritalin, for Attention-Deficit/
    Hyperactivity Disorder, 111–
    112
RLRS (Real Life Rating Scale), 428
Role-Play Assessment, 310*t*
Role-Play Test, 302*t*
Rubella, autistic disorder and, 415
Ruination, 655, 657
Rutgers Alcohol Problem Index
    (RAPI), 735

SAFE (Sexual Abuse Fear Evaluation),
    601
SASB (Structural Analysis of Social
    Behavior), 704
Scapegoating, 667
Schedule for Affective Disorders and
    Schizophrenia for School-Age
    Children (K-SADS)
  child abuse/neglect and, 555*t*
  depression and, 208–210, 209*t*
  development, 40
  mental retardation and, 393
Schizophrenia, 408, 418
School. *See also* Classroom
  adjustment, for chronically ill child,
    489
  anxiety, assessment instruments for,
    306*t*–313*t*
  conduct problems and, 138, 160–
    161
  mentally retarded children in
    behavioral observations of, 396,
    397
    classification of, 373
    diagnosis of, 374
  performance problems, in attention-
    deficit/hyperactivity disorder,
    85
  problems, 628–629
  substance use problems and, 739–
    740, 740
School Absence Questionnaire, 312*t*
School-age children, cognitive
    functioning assessments of,
    382*t*–383*t*, 384
School Archival Records System, 166
School Refusal Assessment Scale, 311*t*
School Situations Questionnaire
    (SSQ), 99, 99*t*, 111, 113, 144

SCICA (Semistructured Clinical Interview for Children and Adolescents), 146
SCRS (Self-Control Rating Scale), 99–100, 113
Sedative withdrawal syndrome, 723*t*
Seizures, 375*t*, 462–463
Self-awareness, substance use problems and, 731
Self-Control Rating Scale (SCRS), 99–100, 113
Self-control strategies, for attention-deficit/hyperactivity disorder, 112
Self-discipline, 83
Self-efficacy, substance use problems and, 727
Self-esteem
  anorexia nervosa and, 692
  depression and, 535
  of maltreated children, 531
  parental, conduct problem children and, 169
  social withdrawal and, 336
  substance use problems and, 727
Self-help groups, for substance use problems, 732–733
Self-help skills assessment, in attention-deficit/hyperactivity disorder, 100, 102
Self-Image Questionnaire for Young Adolescents (SIQYA), 204
Self-injury
  autistic disorder and, 414
  child abuse/neglect and, 534
  mental retardation and, 397, 398*f*
Self-management treatments, for fears/anxieties, 257
Self-Monitoring Log, 248, 313*t*
Self-monitoring procedures
  for abusive parents, 551
  for fears/anxieties, 248
  for treatment adherence, 503
  types of, 41
Self-Perception Profile for Children (SPPC), 218, 473
Self-perceptions, of social distress, 356–357, 357*t*
Self-ratings. *See* Self-reports, ratings
Self-regulation, 77, 80*f*, 81
Self-Report Delinquency Scale (SRD), 152
Self-Report Depression Questionnaire, 396
Self-Reported Antisocial Behavior Scale (SRA), 152–153
Self-reports
  of abused/neglected children, 555*t*
  of adolescent substance use, 734
  of attention-deficit/hyperactivity disorder children, 100
  in behavioral–systems assessment, 39–41
  child, 39–41
  for depression assessment, 204–206, 205*t*, 213–216
  for eating disorders, 701
  for fears/anxieties, 247–251, 253–254
  for mental retardation, 394–396, 395*t*
  for pain assessment, 496
  of parent–adolescent conflict, 661
  parental, for ADHD assessment, 108–110

of parent–child relationship, in child abuse, 557–558
ratings
  for fears/anxieties, 248
  parental, 37–39
Self-starvation, 690
Self-Statement Checklist, 281*t*
Self-Statements Inventory—Revised, 286*t*
Semistructured Clinical Interview for Children and Adolescents (SCICA), 146
Sensation-Seeking Scale for Children (SSSC), 165
Sensory abnormalities, autistic disorder, 414
Separation Anxiety, 299*t*
Separation anxiety assessment
  checklist for, 245–246
  instruments, 297*t*–299*t*
Separation Anxiety Disorder, 232–233
Serotonin, autistic disorder and, 415
SES. *See* Socioeconomic status
SESBI (Sutter–Eyberg Student Behavior Inventory), 150, 151–152, 153
Sexual abuse
  acts
    severity of, 571–572
    types of, 571–572
    use of coercion/force in, 572
  allegations
    child protective services' responses to, 574–575
    involvement with judicial system and, 575–576
    maternal reactions to, 581–582
    professional's responses to, 573–574
  child social service delivery and, 569
  defined, 569–570
  disclosures, 572–573
  dissociative disorders, 588–589
  incidence, 571
  longitudinal studies of, 591–592
  nonoffending parent, characteristics of, 579–582
  offenders/perpetrators
    characteristics of, 576–579
    incestuous, research on, 577–578
    relationship to victim, 571
    sibling, 579
    young, research on, 578–579
  prevalence, 569–571
  PTSD symptoms
    basic model of, 583–584
    broadened perspective of, 584–586
  race and, 572
  reporting, 114
  research, Child Behavior Checklist-based, 583
  risk, parental variables in, 580–581
  sexuality symptoms, 590–591
  sexual problems, 591
  socioeconomic status and, 572
  symptoms, 582
  victims. *See* Sexual abuse victims
Sexual Abuse Fear Evaluation (SAFE), 601
Sexual abuse victims
  behavioral assessment of. *See* Behavioral assessment, of sex abuse victims

characteristics of, 571–573
gender differences of, 572
impact of abuse on, 582–592
recall, accuracy of, 593–595
relationship to perpetrator, 571
suggestibility and, 594, 595–596
testimony in criminal trials, 575
Sexual arousal, pedophilia and, 577
Sexual behavior, assessment, in eating disorders, 697–698
Sexual Congeniality and Compatibility, 172
Sexual dysfunction, substance-induced, 721*t*
Sexuality problems, assessment of, 606–607
Sexually abused children
  with ADHD, 114
  anger of, 589–590
  assessment, 592–613
    of attributional style, 610
    of dissociative symptoms, 607–608, 608*t*–609*t*, 610
    of family relations, 610–613
    of psychological adjustment, 598–599
    of PTSD symptoms, 599–603, 600*t*–605*t*, 605–606, 613
    of sexuality problems, 606–607
    of social support, 610–613
  coping styles, 589
Sexual problems, of sexual abuse victims, 591
SFIS-R (Structural Family Interaction Scale—Revised), 665*t*, 673
Short Marital Adjustment Test, 703
Shyness, peer neglect and, 335
Siblings
  adjustment to child's chronic illness, 493
  anxiety of, 259
  of mentally retarded children, 392
  relationships, effect of autistic child on, 436
  as sex offenders, 579
Sickle cell anemia, 494–495
Side Effects Questionnaire, 111
Similarity model of social judgment, 337
SIQYA (Self-Image Questionnaire for Young Adolescents), 204
Situational Confidence Questionnaire, 739
Situational Discomfort Scale, 699
Skills deficit, as treatment adherence barrier, 504
Skills Test for Insulin Injection, 500*t*
Sleep disorder, substance-induced, 721*t*
Sleep patterns, in depression, 217
Small animals, fear of, 299*t*–301*t*
SMAST (Michigan Alcoholism Screening Test), 171
Smoking, maternal, ADHD in children and, 87–88
Snake Attitude Measure, 300*t*–301*t*
SNAP Checklist (Swanson-Nolan-and-Pelham Checklist), 98
Social Anxiety Scale for Children—Revised, 305*t*–306*t*
Social behavior
  assessment, 348–353, 349*t*
  parents ratings, 353
  peer ratings, 352–353

Social-cognitive skills
  assessment, in depression, 218–219
  deficits, conduct problems and, 135
  developmental assessment, of
    abused/neglected children,
    553–556, 554t
  of maltreated child, during early
    childhood, 530–531
  social relationship deficits and, 355–
    356
Social competence, 332, 343
Social distress feelings, 345
Social environment, substance use
  problems and, 740
Social factors, in attention-deficit/
  hyperactivity disorder, 88–89
Social information processing, 344–
  345
Social interaction
  fear of, assessment instruments for,
    301t–306t
  impairment, qualitative, in autistic
    disorder, 411
  of mentally retarded child, 396–397
  treatment adherence and, 505
Social Interaction Scale, 302t
Social Interaction Self-Statement Test,
  304t
Social needs, friendships and, 338
Social phobia, 233
Social Phobia and Anxiety Inventory
  for Adolescents, 303t
Social referencing theory of emotional
  development, 261
Social relationships
  assessment, 358–359
    conceptual framework for, 330–
      345
    initial considerations, 345–346
    in treatment planning, 357–358
  deficits
    family interaction patterns and,
      355
    friendships and, 338–340
    network affiliations, 354–355
    in peer group contexts, 332–338
    self-perceptions of, 356–357, 357t
    social-cognitive processes and,
      355–356
Social responsibility assessment, 100,
  102
Social Security Act, ADHD children
  and, 114–115
Social skills assessment
  in conduct problems, 165
  in eating disorders, 696–697
Social Skills Rating System, 108
Social support
  of abusive parent, 540
  substance use problems and, 731–
    732
Social validity, 175–176
Social withdrawal
  assessment, 336
  gender differences, 336
  parental discipline practices and,
    342
  peer rejection and, 334–336
  in resolving parent–adolescent
    conflict, 640
Socioeconomic status (SES)
  child maltreatment and, 532–533
  sexual abuse and, 572
Socioemotional development
  of abused/neglected children, 556

family role in, 341
maladaptive, peer rejection and, 329
in middle childhood, maltreatment
  and, 533–534
models, 329–330
normative trends, 330–332
Sociometric method, 332–333
Solving Problems in Family Interaction-I (SPI-FI I), 641
Solving Problems in Family Interac-
  tion-II (SPI-FI II)
  coder impressions-II scale, 654
  communication categories, 649t–
    650t, 653
  description, 637t, 641–642, 653
  problem-solving skills assessment,
    641–642
Somatization Disorder, conduct
  problems and, 133
S-O-R-K-C, 26–27
SPAFF (Specific Affect Coding
  System), 661
Special educational services, for
  ADHD children, 114–115
Specific Affect Coding System
  (SPAFF), 661
Speech delay, in autistic disorder, 412
Speech disturbance, 299t
Speech internalization, behavioral
  inhibition and, 80f, 81
SPI-FI I (Solving Problems in Family
  Interaction-I), 641
SPI-FI II. *See* Solving Problems in
  Family Interaction-II
Spina bifida, 458
Spinal dysraphisms, 459
SPPC (Self-Perception Profile for
  Children), 218, 473
SRA (Self-Reported Antisocial
  Behavior Scale), 152–153
SRD (Self-Report Delinquency Scale),
  152
SSQ (School Situations Question-
  naire), 99, 99t, 111, 113, 144
SSSC (Sensation-Seeking Scale for
  Children), 165
Stability/instability, 10
Standardization
  of behavioral–systems assessment,
    32–33
  of interview format, 34
Stanford–Binet Intelligence Scale,
  429, 463
Stanford–Binet IQ Test, 380, 382t,
  383, 384
State legislation, on mental retarda-
  tion, 377–379
Statement Validity Analysis (SVA),
  598
State–Trait Anxiety Inventory, 258,
  555t
State–Trait Anxiety Inventory for
  Children, 249, 250, 254, 320t–
  321t
Stepfathers, incestuous, 577–578
Stereotypies, of autistic children, 413
Sterilization, of mentally retarded
  patients, 370
Stimulant drugs, for Attention-Deficit/
  Hyperactivity Disorder, 111–
  112
Stranger interaction, fear of, 301t–306t
Stress
  effects, on conduct problem
    children, 138

of mentally retarded persons
  families, 392
parental
  ADHD children and, 89, 110
  assessment of, 173–175
  conduct problem children and,
    138, 173–175
  developmentally delayed children
    and, 6
  substance use problems and, 732
Strokes, 461–462
Stroop Color–Word Association Test,
  104
Structural Analysis of Social Behavior
  (SASB), 704
Structural Family Interaction Scale–
  Revised (SFIS-R), 665t, 668
Structured Clinical Interview, 393–
  394
Substance abuse
  defined, 720
  DSM-IV criteria, 720–721, 721t,
    724t
Substance dependence
  defined, 720
  DSM-IV criteria, 720–721, 721t,
    722t
Substance-induced anxiety disorder,
  234
Substance use problems
  alcohol use
    changes, precipitants of, 733
    developmental issues, 725
    effect expectancies, 726
    maternal, ADHD in children and,
      87–88
    personality and, 726–727
    prevalence, 717–719, 718t–720t
    self-efficacy and, 727
    self-esteem and, 727
  alternative pathways, 729–732, 730f
  assessment, 717
    functional domains in, 736–741,
      737t, 738t
    instruments for, 735t
    integration with treatment, 741–
      742
    means of, 736
    process of, 734–736, 734f, 735t
  associated/comorbid conditions,
    conduct problems, 134
  breadth of usage, 737
  case formulation, 741–742
  change
    motivation for, 741
    preparedness/motivation for, 740–
      741
  contexts of use and, 727–729
  correlates/consequences, 721–725
  developmental issues, 725
  diagnosis, 719–721
  drug use
    changes, precipitants of, 733
    effect expectancies, 726
    personality and, 726–727
    prevalence, 717–719, 718t–720t
    self-esteem and, 727
  health-related disorders and, 484
  interventions, system-focused, 742
  parental
    assessment of, 171
    conduct problems and, 137
  pathways out of misuse, 732–733
  posttreatment patterns, 733
  posttreatment relapse, 733–734

prevalence, 717–719, 718t, 719t
protective factors, 725
risk factors, 725
    biological, 725–726
    psychological, 726–727
risk moderators, 731–732
Sugar consumption, ADHD and, 87
Suicide ideation, substance use
    problems and, 724
Supervision, parental, inadequate,
    conduct problems and, 139
Sutter–Eyberg Student Behavior
    Inventory (SESBI), 150, 151–
    152, 153
SVA (Statement Validity Analysis),
    598
Swanson-Nolan-and-Pelham Checklist
    (SNAP Checklist), 98
Sweat bottle, 294t
Symptom Checklist 90–Revised (SCL-
    90–R)
    for attention-deficit/hyperactivity
        disorder, 110
    for child abuse/neglect, 550
    for fears/anxieties, 258
    in sexual abuse assessment, 611–612
Syndromes, in classification of
    children, 14–15
Systematic desensitization, for treating
    fears/anxieties, 255–256
Systematic Screening for Behavior
    Disorders, 177
Systems theory, 701–702

TAI (Therapy Attitude Inventory),
    176
Target behaviors
    parental reports on, 36–37
    systematic assessments of, 8
    for treatment, selection of, 28–29
    vs. childhood disorders, 14–16
Target Complaint Scale, 279t, 284t,
    308t
Taxonomy of Problem Situations, 356
Taxonomy of Problem Social
    Situations for Children, 108
Taylor Manifest Anxiety Scale, 258
T-CRS (Teacher–Child Rating Scale),
    351, 351t
Teacher–Child Rating Scale (T-CRS),
    351, 351t
Teacher Observation of Classroom—
    Revised Rating Scale, 161
Teacher Rating of Separation Anxiety,
    245, 246, 298t
Teacher Rating of Social Skills—
    Children (TROSS-C), 351,
    351t, 353
Teacher Rating Scale, 307t
Teacher Report Form (TRF). *See
    under* Child Behavior Checklist
Teachers
    of ADHD children, 89–90
        child behavior rating scales for,
            97–100, 98t, 99t
        classroom management training
            for, 113
        interviews for, 96–97
    interviews
        for ADHD assessment, 96–97
        in conduct problems, 144–145
    peer group status estimates of, 348
    ratings, of social behavior, 350–351,
        351t

social cognitions, assessment in
    conduct problems, 168–169
Teachers' Separation Anxiety Scale,
    245, 246, 298t
Temperament
    assessment
        with anxieties/fears, 257–258
        in conduct problems, 135, 164–
            165
    difficult, 135
Test Anxiety Scale for Children, 307t–
    308t
Test Comfort Index, 249, 312t
Test of Auditory Comprehension of
    Language—Revised, 382t, 384
Test of Diabetes Knowledge: General
    Information and Problem
    Solving, 499, 501t
Test of Variables of Attention, 103
Theft/stealing, in Conduct Disorder,
    131
Therapy Attitude Inventory (TAI), 176
Therapy integration, behavioral–
    systems assessment and, 7
Think Aloud Self-Report, 307t
Think-aloud statements, 250, 281t
Thought Checklist for Children, 324t–
    325t
Thought-listing procedures, for fears/
    anxieties assessment, 250
Thyrotropin-releasing hormone
    (TRH), 217
Thyrotropin-stimulating hormone
    (TSH), 217
Timed Behavior Checklist, 244, 245,
    310t
T.M.R. School Competency Scales,
    389t, 390
TMR (trainable mentally retarded),
    372
Tobacco use, health problems and,
    740
Toddler Behavior Checklist, 36
Toddlers. *See* Preschool children
Toxic–metabolic disorder, mental
    retardation and, 375t
Trainable mentally retarded (TMR),
    372
Transactional models of emotional
    disorders, 261
Trauma Symptom Checklist for
    Children (TSCC), 600–601
Treatment. *See also under specific
    disorders*
    compliance/adherence. *See
        Adherence, treatment*
    goals, selection, 28–29
    noncompliance. *See Noncompli-
        ance*
    outcomes, evaluation of, 8
TRF (Teacher Report Form). *See
    under* Child Behavior Checklist
TRH (thyrotropin-releasing hormone),
    217
Triangulation
    anorexia nervosa and, 702
    assessment, 667–669
Tri-Model Imagery Scale, 255
TROSS-C (Teacher Rating of Social
    Skills—Children), 351, 351t,
    353
TSCC (Trauma Symptom Checklist
    for Children), 600–601
TSH (thyrotropin-stimulating
    hormone), 217

Tuberous sclerosis, 415
Tumors, brain, 460–461
Turner syndrome, 459, 460
Twin studies, ADHD, 88

Uniform Performance Assessment
    System, 390–391, 391t
United States
    chronic illness in, prevalence of,
        482, 482t
    deaths in, causes of, 481, 481t
Unnamed coding systems, 638t, 651t,
    665t
Unnamed observational system,
    650t
Unrevealed Differences Task, 490,
    491t
USABCAN (U.S. Advisory Board on
    Child Abuse and Neglect), 523

Validity, of interviews, in behavioral–
    systems assessment, 34–35
Varni–Thompson Pediatric Pain
    Questionnaire, 496
Venham Anxiety-Rating Scale, 246,
    291t
Venham Behavior-Rating Scale, 246,
    291t
Ventricle enlargement, in autistic
    disorder, 415
Verbal report assessment, of parent–
    adolescent conflict, affect and,
    660–661
Victimization, by peers, 340
Videotape assessments
    analogue measures, in conduct
        problems, 168
    of cognition in parent–adolescent
        conflict, 658–659
Vigilance assessment, in ADHD
    children, 102–103
Vineland Adaptive Behavior Inventory,
    100, 102
Vineland Adaptive Behavior Scales,
    389, 389t, 416, 431, 473
Visceral perception test, 255
Vision assessment, in mental
    retardation, 383t, 384–385
Visual analogue scales, for pain
    assessment, 496
Visual Imagery Index, 255
VMI (Developmental Test of Visual–
    Motor Integration), 386t, 387

Walker–McConnell Scale of Social
    Competence and School
    Adjustment, 351, 351t
Walker Problem Behavior Identifica-
    tion Checklist (WPBIC), 350
Water, fear of, 314t–315t
Water Phobia Survey Schedule, 249,
    314t
Wechsler Individual Achievement
    Test, 385, 386t
Wechsler Intelligence Scale for
    Children—Revised (WISC-R),
    429
Wechsler Intelligence Scale for
    Children (WISC-III), 380, 384,
    388
Wechsler Intelligence Test for
    Children, 382t

Wechsler Preschool and Primary Scale
    of Intelligence—Revised
    (WPPSI-R), 382*t*, 383, 384
Wide Range Achievement Test-3
    (WRAT-3), 385, 386*t*, 388
Wide Range Assessment of Memory
    and Learning, 386*t*
Wild Boy of Aveyron, 408
Williams syndrome, 380, 459–460, 467
Will power, 83
WISC-III (Wechsler Intelligence Scale
    for Children), 380, 384, 388
Wisconsin Behavior Rating, 389*t*, 390

WISC-R (Wechsler Intelligence Scale
    for Children—Revised), 429
Withdrawal, substance-induced, 720,
    721*t*, 723*t*
Woodcock–Johnson Psycho-Educa-
    tional Battery—Revised, 385,
    386*t*
Woodcock–Johnson Scales of
    Independent Behavior, 553*t*
Working memory, behavioral
    inhibition and, 80–81, 80*f*
WPBIC (Walker Problem Behavior
    Identification Checklist), 350

WPPSI-R (Wechsler Preschool and
    Primary Scale of
    Intelligence—Revised),
    382*t*, 383, 384
WRAT-3 (Wide Range Achievement
    Test-3), 385, 386*t*, 388

Yale–Brown–Cornell Eating Disorder
    Scale, 701
Yale Children's Inventory, 36
Youth Self-Report (YSR). *See under*
    Child Behavior Checklist